The Financial Analyst's Handbook

Editorial Advisory Board

The Financial Analyst's Handbook

SECOND EDITION

Edited by

SUMNER N. LEVINE

State University of New York
Stony Brook, New York

DOW JONES-IRWIN
Homewood, Illinois 60430

This publication is designed to provide accurate and
authoritative information in regard to the subject matter
covered. It is sold with the understanding that the
publisher is not engaged in rendering legal, accounting, or
other professional service. If legal advice or other expert
assistance is required, the services of a competent
professional person should be sought.

From a Declaration of Principles jointly adopted by a Committee
of the American Bar Association and a Committee of Publishers.

This book was set in Palatino by The William Byrd Press, Inc.
The editors were Richard A. Luecke, Paula M. Buschman, Joan A. Hopkins.
The production manager was Carma W. Fazio.
The drawings were done by Jay Benson, The ArtForce.
The Maple-Vail Book Manufacturing Group was the printer and binder.

ISBN 0-87094-919-5

Library of Congress Catalog Card No. 87–71362

Printed in the United States of America

1 2 3 4 5 6 7 8 9 0 MP 5 4 3 2 1 0 9 8

Introduction

This edition of *The Financial Analyst's Handbook* is intended to be a comprehensive reference for financial analysts, money managers, and financial executives.

Since the publication of the first edition a large number of major developments have occurred in the investment area: Capital markets have become highly internationalized. There has been enormous growth in the trading volume and variety of financial futures and options. A host of new fixed income securities have been introduced into financial markets. In addition, personal computers, now commonplace, have been greatly improved in both power and speed. Access to information has been significantly enhanced by the availability of numerous on-line databases, while the analysis of data has been considerably facilitated by improved spreadsheet and other commercially available programs.

On the more theoretical side, multiple factor models, notably the Arbitrage Pricing Theory (ABT), have received increased attention since the last edition of the Handbook. Consequently, both the ABT and the older Capital Asset Pricing Model are discussed. Material has also been included on the so-called anomalies in risk adjusted returns—notably the small firm and low P/E effects.

The above listing highlights only a few of the many recent developments which have been taken into account in the present edition. In addition, Section II on Economic Analysis has been totally revised to take current developments into account. Section III on Company and Industry Analysis now contains chapters on the computation of cash flow and expanded material on the analysis of industry segments. Section IV on Equity Investments has been enlarged to include substantial material on the analysis of emerging growth companies, takeover situations, foreign equities, and as mentioned above, anomaly investing. Material on Fixed Income Securities, dealt with in Section V, has been enlarged to include zero coupon bonds and the newer mortgage backed securities. Portfolio Theory Practice, discussed in Section VI, has been completely revised and includes extensive discussions on the use of options and futures for hedging and other applications. Quantitative Techniques, Section VII, now includes a new chapter on the use of computers while Section VIII provides an overview of on-line databases, including a discussion of information sources relating to foreign investments. Lastly, Section IX on the important topics of Legal and Ethical Standards has been completely updated to include, among other matters, a discussion of the current status of insider trading issues.

It has been a great pleasure serving as editor of this Handbook. Certainly the task could not have been accomplished without the valuable suggestions and guidance of the Editorial Advisory Board and the splendid cooperation of the many contributors who have shared their expertise and insights with us. Special thanks are due to my wife, Caroline, whose tireless efforts made this edition possible.

Sumner N. Levine

Contributing Authors

W. Scott Bauman, D.B.A., CFA, Chairman and Professor of Finance, Northern Illinois University, De Kalb, Illinois

Nathan Belfer, Ph.D., CFA, Consultant, Wood, Struthers & Winthrop Management Corporation, New York, New York

Leopold A. Bernstein, Ph.D., CPA, Bernard M. Baruch College, The City University of New York, New York, New York

John S. Bildersee, Ph.D., Schools of Business, New York University, New York, New York

Charles P. Bonini, Ph.D., Graduate School of Business, Stanford University, Stanford, California

Jon A. Booker, Ph.D., CPA, Tennessee Technological University, Cookeville, Tennessee

Richard Bookstaber, Ph.D., Principal, Morgan Stanley & Co. Incorporated, New York, New York

Alfred Broaddus, Ph.D., Senior Vice President and Director of Research, Federal Reserve Bank of Richmond, Richmond, Virginia

Robert W. Burke, Senior Vice President, Director—Public Utilities, Moody's Investors Service, New York, New York

Carol S. Carson, Ph.D., Deputy Director, Bureau of Economic Analysis, U.S. Department of Commerce, Washington, D.C.

John P. Cullity, Ph.D., Department of Economics, Newark College of Arts and Sciences, Rutgers University, Newark, New Jersey

Susan S. DiMattia, Business Information Consultant, Stamford, Connecticut

Jeffrey J. Diermeier, CFA, Managing Director, First Chicago Investment Advisors, Chicago, Illinois

Marguerite Durkin, Former Senior Analyst, Merrill Lynch MBS Research, New York, New York

Charles D. Ellis, Ph.D., CFA, Managing Partner, Greenwich Associates, Greenwich, Connecticut

Edwin J. Elton, Ph.D., Nomura Professor of Finance, Graduate School of Business Administration, New York University, New York, New York

Frank J. Fabozzi, Ph.D., CFA, CPA, Visiting Professor, Sloan School of Management, Massachusetts Institute of Technology, Cambridge, Massachusetts

Sylvan G. Feldstein, Ph.D., Vice President and Manager—Municipal Bond Research Department, Merrill Lynch Capital Markets, New York, New York

Thomas G. Fendrich, CFA, Managing Director, Standard & Poor's Corporation, New York, New York

H. Gifford Fong, President, Gifford Fong Associates, Walnut Creek, California

Mario J. Gabelli, CFA, Chairman, Gabelli & Company, Inc. and GAMCO Investors Inc., New York, New York

John G. Gillis, J.D., Partner, Hill & Barlow, Boston, Massachusetts

Stephen W. Glover, Vice President, Smith Barney, Harris Upham International, London, England

Martin J. Gruber, Ph.D., Nomura Professor of Finance, Graduate School of Business Administration, New York University, New York, New York

Peter Hooper, Ph.D., Assistant Director, Division of International Finance, Board of Governors of the Federal Reserve System, Washington, D.C.

Bill D. Jarnagin, Ph.D., CPA, University of Tulsa, Tulsa, Oklahoma

Frank J. Jones, Ph.D., Managing Director, Kidder Peabody & Company, Inc., New York, New York

Roubina Khoylian, Vice President, Venture Economics, Inc., Wellesley Hills, Massachusetts

James L. Kochan, Vice President and Manager, Fixed Income Research, Merrill Lynch Capital Markets, New York, New York

Charles D. Kuehner, Jr., Ph.D., CFA, Vice President, Oppenheimer Industries, Inc., Princeton, New Jersey

Joseph A. Langsam, Ph.D., Vice President, Morgan Stanley & Co. Incorporated, New York, New York

Donald R. Lessard, Ph.D., Sloan School of Management, Massachusetts Institute of Technology, Cambridge, Massachusetts

Sumner N. Levine, Ph.D., State University of New York at Stony Brook, New York

Allan M. Loosigian, President, A. M. Loosigian & Company, Stamford, Connecticut

Steven R. Malin, Ph.D., Senior Economist, The Conference Board, Inc., New York, New York

Meyer Melnikoff, F.S.A., Actuary, Goldman, Sachs & Co., New York, New York

Robert D. Milne, J.D., CFA, President, Duff & Phelps Investment Management Company, Cleveland, Ohio

Franco Modigliani, Ph.D., Sloan School of Management, Massachusetts Institute of Technology, Cambridge, Massachusetts

Maureen Mooney, Assistant Vice President, Fixed Income Research, Merrill Lynch Capital Markets, New York, New York

Geoffrey H. Moore, Ph.D., Graduate School of Business, Columbia University, New York, New York

Alfred C. Morley, CFA, President, Institute of Chartered Financial Analysts, Charlottesville, Virginia; President, Financial Analysts Federation, New York, New York

Lucille Palermo, CFA, Vice President—International Research, Drexel Burnham Lambert Inc., New York, New York

Gerald A. Pogue, Ph.D., Professor of Economics & Finance, Baruch College, City University of New York, New York

Michael E. Porter, Ph.D., Graduate School of Business Administration, Harvard University, Boston, Massachusetts

Richard T. Pratt, Ph.D., Chairman, Merrill Lynch Mortgage Capital, Inc., New York, New York

Stanley E. Pratt, Chairman, Venture Economics, Inc., Wellesley Hills, Massachusetts

Jonathan A. Reiss, CFA, Quantitative Analysis—Fixed Income Investments, Sanford C. Bernstein & Company, Inc., New York, New York

Fred B. Renwick, Ph.D., Graduate School of Business Administration, New York University, New York, New York

William B. Riley, Jr., Ph.D., College of Business and Economics, West Virginia University, Morgantown, West Virginia

Anthony W. Robinson, Vice President, First Chicago Investment Advisors, First Chicago House, London, England

Richard Roll, Ph.D., Allstate Professor of Finance & Insurance, Graduate School of Management, University of California, Los Angeles, California

Stephen A. Ross, Ph.D., Sterling Professor of Economics & Finance, Yale School of Organization and Management, Yale University, New Haven, Connecticut

Alfred S. Rudd, Late of Standard & Poor's Corporation, New York, New York

Harry Sauvain, D.B.A., University Professor Emeritus of Finance, Indiana University, Bloomington, Indiana

John A. Scowcroft, Ph.D., CFA, Vice President and Manager, Merrill Lynch MBS Research, New York, New York

Alan R. Shaw, Senior Vice President, Managing Director, Smith Barney, Harris Upham & Company, Inc., New York, New York

Dennis G. Sherva, CFA, Managing Director, Morgan Stanley & Co. Incorporated, New York, New York

William A. Spurr, Ph.D., Graduate School of Business, Stanford University, Stanford, California

Samuel S. Stewart, Jr., Ph.D., CFA, President, Wasatch Advisors, and College of Business, University of Utah, Salt Lake City, Utah

Francis H. Trainer, Jr., CFA, Manager—Fixed Income Investments, Sanford C. Bernstein & Company, Inc., New York, New York

Rein W. van der Does, Managing Director—International Research, Drexel Burnham Lambert Inc., New York, New York

John R. Walter, Associate Economist, Research Department, Federal Reserve Bank of Richmond, Richmond, Virginia

Roy P. Weinberger, Managing Director, Industrial Corporations, Public Utilities, Standard & Poor's Corporation, New York, New York

Arthur Williams III, CFA, Director, Retirement Plan Investments McKinsey & Company, Inc., New York, New York

Benjamin Wolkowitz, Ph.D., Vice President, Morgan Stanley & Co. Incorporated, New York, New York

Robert A. Young, CFA, Vice President—Convertible Securities Research, Dean Witter Reynolds Incorporated, New York, New York

Contents

PART 1

Background

1

Overview of Financial Analysis

Alfred C. Morley, CFA
President
Institute of Chartered Financial Analysts
President
Financial Analysts Federation

THE FINANCIAL ANALYST AND THE INVESTMENT DECISION-MAKING PROCESS

In the first edition of the *Financial Analyst's Handbook* published in 1975, the initial sentence was: "Financial analysis is an exciting occupation." The author of that statement obviously had keen foresight of the exciting times and challenges for financial analysis which developed during the ensuing years. However, he probably would admit today that the excitement has been far greater and more complex than had been imagined. And with it has come for those practicing in the occupation of financial analysis opportunities, rewards, and, not to be overlooked, frustrations, the levels of which are well in excess of those that might have been forecasted in the mid-1970s. In short, financial analysis has been, is, and undoubtedly will continue to be, a *dynamic* decision-making process which has become broader, deeper, and more complex because of investment *opportunities* and *procedures* having become broader, deeper, and more complex.

Opportunities are evidenced by the increasing number of asset classes and subclasses from which to select investment alternatives individually and in combination. The typical investment portfolio of not too many years ago was composed of stocks, bonds, and cash equivalents (typically, Treasury bills). Today, it is not uncommon for an investment portfolio to include, in addition to those traditional asset classes, such categories as real estate, international stocks and bonds, venture capital commitments, option and futures contracts, and perhaps even exposure to commodities and collectibles. Also, subclasses of traditional and new investment alternatives clearly have been identified; for example, within the common stock classification are those equity groups with, among others, definitive growth, defensive or yield characteristics.

As to investment procedures, the multiplicity of asset classes and subclasses alone has led to the need for more precise portfolio strategy techniques, commonly called the asset allocation process. Within that process, of course, is the requirement for both economic and security evaluation, as well as risk control. Academics and practitioners have developed a number of procedures to contend with asset allocation, valuation, and risk parameters, only a few of which are the capital asset pricing, dividend discount, and multiple economic scenario models; indexing; dedication and immunization; portfolio insurance; and hedging.

The profession and art of financial analysis indeed can be characterized as fascinating and exciting, as it is for those practicing that profession and art, the financial analysts.

The Financial Analyst

At this point in the discussion, the reader can discern that the terms *financial analysis* and *financial analyst* are being applied to security investments and portfolios thereof, and indeed, that is the subject of the remainder of this chapter and of this book. However, before further developing that concept, it should be noted that financial analysis can be defined in much broader terms; for example, to include corporate capital budgeting and long-term business planning.

The primary ingredients of the investment decision-making process are *analysis* and *management*: analysis of individual securities and management of portfolios composed of individual securities. There has been a considerable blurring of these two functions over the years, with many portfolio managers now acting as their own analyst, and conversely, many analysts having been given at least partial responsibility for portfolio management. Thus, the terms *financial analyst* or *investment analyst*, and *investment manager* or *portfolio manager*, are becoming somewhat synonymous. For purposes herein, financial analysis will be considered as relating to the entire function of investment management, and the financial analyst will be viewed within the context of having both analytical and portfolio management responsibilities.

The pool of investment capital has grown rapidly over the past decade, both within and outside of the United States, largely in reflection of strong expansion in employee retirement and profit sharing

The financial analyst/portfolio manager obviously is intimately involved in all aspects of the investment decision-making process. Also intimately involved are the investors, as it is they who own the portfolio and, usually upon advice or counsel of the financial analyst or portfolio manager, determine the content of the portfolio through their expectations and needs. Others who might be, and usually are, involved in the process are suppliers of specialized services. For example, economic consultation will be needed to determine the impact of possible changes in governmental fiscal and monetary policy on financial markets, as well as on particular companies or industries, in order to help develop proper portfolio strategy. Financial analysts on the buy side will utilize analysts from the sell side to assist in identifying positive and negative trends in both general business activity and in specific companies and industries. A wealth of data base, asset allocation programming, and similar services now are available from outside independent vendors to assist the financial analyst/portfolio manager in the investment decision-making process.

The Analytical Process

The following chapters in this book will cover in some detail the approaches and methodologies of analyzing and valuing securities in the various asset classes, as well as the asset allocation and portfolio construction functions. At this point, it is useful to summarize these procedures in the context of the role of the financial analyst.

The financial analyst might carry out the following steps as one approach in the overall analytical and investment decision-making processes.

1. Develop, or acquire from outside sources, a forecast of economic and general business activity over a given time horizon. In actual practice, several such forecasts might be developed, with probabilities attached to each.

2. Determine from the forecast which asset classes and subclasses might benefit from the anticipated trends. That is, within the framework of the economic forecast that seems most appropriate, identify the relative attractiveness of stocks, bonds, real estate, and other major and subasset categories.

3. Within the favored asset classes and subclasses so identified, select those individual or groups of securities which, on an evaluation basis, appear to be particularly attractive relative to market expectations. Stating this another way, and using common stocks as an example, select those industries and specific companies within those industries which meet the valuation criteria.

4. From the list of securities so selected, construct a portfolio

suitable to the needs of the investor as measured by objective, constraints, and risk tolerance.

The foregoing is commonly called the *top-down* approach, but there are many other ways utilized in constructing a portfolio or parts of a portfolio. Among others are:

1. A *screening* process identifying securities meeting preselected criteria. Again using common stocks as an example, such a process might identify all common stocks at or below a given price-earnings multiple or a price-to-book value ratio, or stocks at or above a certain earnings growth rate or dividend yield, and so on.

2. A *technical* approach, which utilizes various relationships of individual securities to the overall market in terms of price movements.

3. A *style* approach, meaning that some financial analysts/portfolio managers are more comfortable emphasizing a particular group of securities; that is, growth stocks, high-yield bonds, and so forth.

Key to the analytical and investment decision-making processes is research and valuation of individual and groups of securities. This methodology attempts to identify change, and of equal importance, change in the rate of change in the numerous variables impacting the market's appraisal of the individual and/or groups of securities. This statement applies to all of the asset classes and subclasses, but for illustrative purposes, the common stock of an individual company will be cited.

A typical analysis of such a stock might begin with an exhaustive review of the company's history, its products and markets, and the earnings, dividends, and financial position on both a current and projected basis. Inherent in this analysis will be an appraisal of management, its decision-making philosophy, and overall, its success on an absolute basis and relative to direct competitors, the industry within which it operates, and to general economic and business activity. This analytical process will develop a wealth of information, much of it quantitative, and derived from a variety of sources, including interviews with officials of the company. The end result of the analysis is a projection of earnings over a given time frame, and this forecast will be compared with expected results of similar companies in order to compare relative attractiveness. The final major step is to determine market valuation; that is, to answer the question as to whether the current price of the stock does or does not discount whatever future expectations that might have been determined.

By way of summary, the profession and art of financial analysis/portfolio management encompasses a variety of disciplines, each interrelated to the other, and requiring the combination of intelligence, creativity, imagination, and experience.

Career Paths of Financial Analysts

As previously stated, there has been a blurring in recent years in the functions of financial analysts and portfolio managers. In effect, this means that financial analysts (research analysts) have been, and continue to be, provided the opportunity of expanding their responsibilities, and thus their career opportunities, by becoming more involved in the investment decision-making process. However, in today's dynamic setting, even greater opportunities for career advancement are developing. For example, investment banking as well as merger and acquisition activity on both the buy and sell sides of the street has increased by considerable magnitude, and with it the need for a greater number of capable people. Almost by definition, the financial analyst can, and often does, play a central role in investment banking and in merger/acquisition endeavors. The ultimate career opportunity, of course, is to become part of management or, indeed, the top official of a firm. Many examples can be cited of financial analysts who have reached this pinnacle over the past several years.

This is not to say that all financial analysts automatically and regularly climb the ladder of success. The pressures on and frustrations of financial analysts pursuing their responsibilities require professional and individual characteristics of the highest order. As in other occupations, all are not suited to the purpose, and it is not uncommon because of pressures, burnout, and inferior performance for some financial analysts to change career paths at varying points in their professional cycle.

PROFESSIONALISM

Those with a commonality of interest typically will join forces for mutual advantage in the performance of their responsibilities and to enhance their status as a professsional group. Financial analysts are no exception, and in fact, it can be clearly stated that the professionalism of financial analysts has been enhanced by collective organizational efforts, primarily through The Financial Analysts Federation and The Institute of Chartered Financial Analysts.

The Financial Analysts Federation

The Financial Analysts Federation (FAF) is a not-for-profit organization with more than 15,500 members in the United States and Canada. Members of the FAF also are members of 55 constituent local societies and chapters, 47 in the United States, 7 in Canada, and 1 international. As to the latter, the International Society of Financial Analysts recently was formed by the FAF to contend with interest in FAF activities by the increasing number of financial analysts working and/or living outside of the United States and Canada.

Members of the FAF include financial analysts, investment counselors, portfolio managers, and pension, endowment, mutual, and other fund managers, who in the aggregate have the responsibility of managing some $2.9 trillion of capital.

The FAF and its constituent societies offer a variety of activities, including information, education, publications, advocacy, and Code of Ethics and Standards of Professional Conduct.

Information. Society meetings, typically on a weekly or monthly basis, and periodic FAF conferences and seminars are the principal public forums at which corporate executives report on the progress of their companies, investment professionals share their concepts and ideas on a variety of matters, public figures address economic and political issues of importance, and so on. During the course of a given year, nearly 1,000 such meetings take place and provide an enormous flow of information valuable to the investment decision-making process.

Education. The Financial Analysts Federation sponsors a number of programs designed to provide continuing education to members. The dynamics of the business alone require that members continuously be updated on new techniques and methodologies, for the benefit of themselves, their firms, and their clients. Among those programs are the annual Financial Analysts Seminar conducted in association with the University of Chicago Graduate School of Business, an Investment Management Workshop held at Princeton University, and a Canadian seminar conducted in association with the University of Western Ontario.

Publications. The FAF publishes six times per year *The Financial Analysts Journal*, considered to be one of the leading professional journals in the field of financial analysis and investment management. The *Journal* typically carries a balance of academic and practitioner literature, all aimed at helping investment professionals to enhance their knowledge and to provide better service to investors.

Advocacy. One of the primary missions of the FAF is to take positions, in behalf of members, on central issues affecting investors and the public at large. For example, the FAF Corporate Information Committee has been effective in encouraging broader and more complete disclosure by corporations as regards both earnings and balance sheet information, and the Financial Accounting Policy Committee has been active and successful in recommending changes in accounting policies to the accounting profession to ensure more accurate measurement of corporate financial information. On its own, and through the constituent societies, the FAF has made important contributions to the determination of governmental fiscal and monetary policy, as well as to the regulatory climate.

Code of ethics/standards of professional conduct. The Federation has taken the lead in developing rigorous standards of professional and ethical conduct and a means to enforce them. Its self-regulatory program recently received presidential recognition for its fairness and firmness. Each member of the FAF is committed to know and follow the Code of Ethics and Standards of Professional Conduct, which are reproduced in their entirety in Appendix A.

The Institute of Chartered Financial Analysts

The Institute of Chartered Financial Analysts (ICFA) was organized in 1959 to enhance the professionalism of those involved in various aspects of the investment decision-making process, and to recognize those who achieve a high level of professionalism by the designation of chartered financial analyst.

The basic missions and purposes of the ICFA are:

1. To develop and keep current a "body of knowledge" applicable to the investment decision-making process. The principal components of this knowledge are financial accounting, economics, quantitative techniques, both fixed-income and equity securities analysis, portfolio management, and ethical and professional standards.
2. To administer a study and examination program for eligible candidates, the primary objectives of which are to assist the candidate in mastering and applying the body of knowledge, and to test the candidate's competency in the knowledge gained.
3. To award the formal designation CFA to those candidates who have passed three levels of examinations, encompassing some 350 hours of study, and a total of 18 hours of testing over a minimum of three years, who meet stipulated standards of professional conduct, and who are otherwise eligible for membership in the Institute.
4. To provide a useful and informative program of continuing education through seminars, publications, and other formats which enable members, candidates and others in the investment constituency to become more aware of and to better utilize the ever-changing and expanding body of knowledge.
5. To sponsor and enforce, in cooperation with The Financial

Analysts Federation, a Code of Ethics and Standards of Professional Conduct, applicable to both candidates and members.

Since the program started, nearly 45,000 examinations have been given and more than 9,000 CFA charters earned and awarded. On June 7, 1986, approximately 5,000 CFA candidates sat for the Level I, II, or III examinations at some 90 test centers in the United States, Canada, Europe, Asia, and the Mideast.

Recent surveys indicate that the growing interest in the CFA program reflects increasing awareness, especially by employers, that the rigorous study and examination program leading to the awarding of the CFA charter is the equivalent of a graduate course in investments, all at relatively nominal cost. There is no other known program designed to provide such a learning/educational/training process to investment professionals, and all that this means in real time, state-of-the-art knowledge. There is growing evidence that those who hold the CFA designation are provided greater opportunities for career advancement, in terms of both responsibilities and financial reward.

APPENDIX A

The Code of Ethics and The Standards of Professional Conduct of the Financial Analysts Federation and The Institute of Chartered Financial Analysts

The Code of Ethics and The Standards of Professional Conduct

Adopted by The Financial Analysts Federation and The Institute of Chartered Financial Analysts. Revised June 17, 1986.

The FAF Resolution

WHEREAS, the profession of financial analysis and investment management has evolved because of the increasing public need for competent, objective, and trustworthy advice with regard to investments and financial management; and

WHEREAS, those engaged in this profession have joined together in an

The ICFA Resolution

WHEREAS, the profession of financial analysis and investment management has evolved because of the increasing public need for competent, objective, and trustworthy advice with regard to investments and financial management; and

WHEREAS, The Institute of Chartered Financial Analysts was orga-

organization known as The Financial Analysts Federation; and

WHEREAS, despite a wide diversity of interest among analysts employed by brokers and securities dealers, investment advisers, banks, insurance companies, investment companies and trusts, pension trusts, and other institutional investors and investment entities, there are nevertheless certain fundamental standards of conduct which should be common to all engaged in the profession of financial analysis and investment management and accepted and maintained by them; and

WHEREAS, the members of The Financial Analysts Federation adopted a Code of Ethics and Standards on May 20, 1962, which have been amended from time to time; and

WHEREAS, The Financial Analysts Federation provides for individual membership in it, requires that all of its member societies adopt its Code of Ethics and Standards of Professional Conduct, and requires that all individual members comply with them;

Now, THEREFORE, the following are the Code of Ethics and Standards of Professional Conduct of The Financial Analysts Federation:

All individual members of The Financial Analysts Federation including fellows, associates, and affiliates are obligated to conduct their professional activities in accordance with the following Code of Ethics and Standards of Professional Conduct. Disciplinary sanctions may be imposed for violations of the Code or Standards.

nized to establish educational standards in the field of financial analysis, to conduct examinations of financial analysts and to award the professional designation of Chartered Financial Analyst, among other objectives; and

WHEREAS, despite a wide diversity of interest among analysts employed by brokers and security dealers, investment advisers, banks, insurance companies, investment companies and trusts, pension trusts, and other institutional investors and investment entities, there are nevertheless certain fundamental standards of conduct which should be common to all engaged in the profession of financial analysis and investment management and accepted and maintained by them; and

WHEREAS, The Institute of Chartered Financial Analysts adopted a Code of Ethics and Standards on March 14, 1964, which have been amended from time to time;

Now, THEREFORE, The Institute of Chartered Financial Analysts hereby adopts the following Code of Ethics and Standards of Professional Conduct:

All members of The Institute of Chartered Financial Analysts and holders of and candidates for the professional designation Chartered Financial Analyst are obligated to conduct their professional activities in accordance with the following Code of Ethics and Standards of Professional Conduct. Disciplinary sanctions may be imposed for violations of the Code or Standards.

The Code of Ethics

A financial analyst should conduct himself[1] with integrity and dignity and act in an ethical manner in his dealings with the public, clients, customers, employers, employees, and fellow analysts.

A financial analyst should conduct himself and should encourage

---

[1] Masculine pronouns, used throughout the Code and Standards, as well as throughout the *Handbook*, to simplify sentence structure, shall apply to all persons, regardless of sex.

others to practice financial analysis in a professional and ethical manner that will reflect credit on himself and his profession.

A financial analyst should act with competence and should strive to maintain and improve his competence and that of others in the profession.

A financial analyst should use proper care and exercise independent professional judgment.

The Standards of Professional Conduct

I.   Obligation to inform employer of Code and Standards

The financial analyst shall inform his employer, through his direct supervisor, that he is obligated to comply with the Code of Ethics and Standards of Professional Conduct, and is subject to disciplinary sanctions for violations thereof. He shall deliver a copy of the Code and Standards to his employer if the employer does not have a copy.

II.   Compliance with governing laws and regulations and the Code and Standards

A.   *Required knowledge and compliance*

The financial analyst shall maintain knowledge of and shall comply with all applicable laws, rules, and regulations of any government, governmental agency, and regulatory organization governing his professional, financial, or business activities, as well as with these Standards of Professional Conduct and the accompanying Code of Ethics.

B.   *Prohibition against assisting legal and ethical violations*

The financial analyst shall not knowingly participate in, or assist, any acts in violation of any applicable law, rule, or regulation of any government, governmental agency, or regulatory organization governing his professional, financial, or business activities, nor any act which would violate any provision of these Standards of Professional Conduct or the accompanying Code of Ethics.

C.   *Prohibition against use of material nonpublic information*

The financial analyst shall comply with all laws and regulations relating to the use of material nonpublic information. (1) If the analyst acquires such information as a result of a special or confidential relationship with the issuer, he shall not communicate the information (other than within the relationship), or take investment action on the basis of such information, if it violates that relationship. (2) If the analyst is not in a special or confidential relationship with the issuer, he shall not communicate or act on material nonpublic information if he knows or should have known that such information was disclosed to him in breach of a duty. If such a breach exists, the analyst shall make reasonable efforts to achieve public dissemination of such information.

D.   Responsibilities of supervisors

A financial analyst with supervisory responsibility shall exercise reasonable supervision over those subordinate employees subject to his control, to prevent any violation by such persons of applicable statutes, regulations, or provisions of the Code of Ethics or Standards of Professional Conduct. In so doing the financial analyst/chartered financial analyst is entitled to rely upon reasonable procedures established by his employer.

III.   Research reports, investment recommendations and actions

A. Reasonable basis and representations

1.   The financial analyst shall exercise diligence and thoroughness in making an investment recommendation to others or in taking an investment action for others.
2.   The financial analyst shall have a reasonable and adequate basis for such recommendations and actions, supported by appropriate research and investigation.
3.   The financial analyst shall make reasonable and diligent efforts to avoid any material misrepresentation in any research report or investment recommendation.
4.   The financial analyst shall maintain appropriate records to support the reasonableness of such recommendations.

B.   Research reports

1.   The financial analyst shall use reasonable judgment as to the inclusion of relevant factors in research reports.
2.   The financial analyst shall distinguish between facts and opinion in research reports.
3.   The financial analyst shall indicate the basic characteristics of the investment involved when preparing for general public distribution a research report that is not directly related to a specific portfolio or client.

C.   Portfolio investment recommendations and actions

The financial analyst shall, when making an investment recommendation or taking an investment action for a specific portfolio or client, consider its appropriateness and suitability for such portfolio or client. In considering such matters, the financial analyst shall take into account (1) the needs and circumstances of the client, (2) the basic characteristics of the investment involved, and (3) the basic characteristics of the total portfolio. The financial analyst shall use reasonable judgment to determine the applicable relevant factors. The financial analyst shall distinguish between facts and opinion in presentation of investment recommendations.

D. Prohibition against plagiarism
The financial analyst shall not, when presenting material to his employer, associates, customers, clients, or the general public, copy or use in substantially the same form, material prepared by other persons without acknowledging its use and identifying the name of the author or publisher of such material. The analyst may, however, use without acknowledgment factual information published by recognized financial and statistical reporting services or similar sources.

E. Prohibition against misrepresentation of services
The financial analyst shall not make any statements, orally or in writing, which materially misrepresent (1) the services that the analyst or his firm is capable of performing for the client, (2) the qualifications of such analyst or his firm, (3) the investment performance that the analyst or his firm has accomplished or can reasonably be expected to achieve for the client, or (4) the expected performance of any investment. The financial analyst shall not make any unsupported oral or written statement that assures or guarantees any investment or its return either explicitly or implicitly.

F. Fair dealing with customers and clients
The financial analyst shall act in a manner consistent with his obligation to deal fairly with all customers and clients when (1) disseminating investment recommendations, (2) disseminating material changes in prior investment advice, and (3) taking investment action.

IV. Priority of transactions
The financial analyst shall conduct himself in such a manner that transactions for his customers, clients, and employer have priority over personal transactions, and so that his personal transactions do not operate adversely to their interests. If a financial analyst decides to make a recommendation about the purchase or sale of a security or other investment, he shall give his customers, clients, and employer adequate opportunity to act on this recommendation before acting on his own behalf.

V. Disclosure of conflicts
The financial analyst, when making investment recommendations, or taking investment actions, shall disclose to his customers and clients any material conflict of interest relating to him and any material beneficial ownership of the securities or other investments involved,

which could reasonably be expected to impair his ability to render unbiased and objective advice.

The financial analyst shall disclose to his employer all matters which could reasonably be expected to interfere with his duty to the employer, or with his ability to render unbiased and objective advice.

The financial analyst shall also comply with all requirements as to disclosure of conflicts of interest imposed by law and by rules and regulations of organizations governing his activities and shall comply with any prohibitions on his activities if a conflict of interest exists.

VI. Compensation

A. *Disclosure of additional compensation arrangements*

The financial analyst shall inform his customers, clients, and employer of compensation arrangements in connection with his services to them which are in addition to compensation from them for such services.

B. *Disclosure of referral fees*

The financial analyst shall make appropriate disclosure to a prospective client or customer of any consideration paid to others for recommending his services to that prospective client or customer.

C. *Duty to employer*

The financial analyst shall not undertake independent practice for compensation in competition with his employer unless he has received written consent from both his employer and the person for whom he undertakes independent employment.

VII. Relationships with others

A. *Preservation of confidentiality*

A financial analyst shall preserve the confidentiality of information communicated by the client concerning matters within the scope of the confidential relationship, unless the financial analyst receives information concerning illegal activities on the part of the client.

B. *Maintenance of independence and objectivity*

The financial analyst, in relationships and contacts with an issuer of securities, whether individually or as a member of a group, shall use particular care and good judgment to achieve and maintain independence and objectivity.

C. *Fiduciary Duties*

The financial analyst, in relationships with clients, shall use particular care in determining applicable fiduciary duty and shall comply with such duty as to those persons and interests to whom it is owed.

VIII.   Use of professional designation

FAF   **ICFA**

The qualified financial analyst may use the professional designation "Fellow of The Financial Analysts Federation," and is encouraged to do so, but only in a dignified and judicious manner. The use of the designation may be accompanied by an accurate explanation (1) of the requirements that have been met to obtain the designation and (2) of The Financial Analysts Federation.

The Chartered Financial Analyst may use the professional designation Chartered Financial Analyst, or the abbreviation CFA, and is encouraged to do so, but only in a dignified and judicious manner. The use of the designation may be accompanied by an accurate explanation (1) of the requirements that have been met to obtain the designation and (2) of The Institute of Chartered Financial Analysts.

IX. Professional Misconduct

The financial analyst shall not (1) commit a criminal act that upon conviction materially reflects adversely on his honesty, trustworthiness, or fitness as a financial analyst in other respects or (2) engage in conduct involving dishonesty, fraud, deceit, or misrepresentation.

APPENDIX B _____
The CFA Candidate Study and Examination Program

Qualifications for the award of the CFA Charter include completion of the three levels of examinations, holding a bachelor's degree or having equivalent work experience, having three years' experience in the investment decision-making process, and having applied for membership in a constituent society of the FAF if one exists within 50 miles of place of residence or work.

The content of the CFA study materials and examinations change over time, in reflection of the dynamics of the business and the resultant ever-changing, ever-expanding body of knowledge. The following information on candidate requirements, study content, and the examinations themselves are those that were applicable in 1986.

SOURCE: © By The Institute of Chartered Financial Analysts.

General Topic Outline, CFA Candidate Study, and Examination Program

Ethical and Professional Standards, Securities Law and Regulations

Candidate Level

I   II   III

Securities Law and Regulations
Nature and applicability of fiduciary standards
Pertinent laws and regulations
Organization and purpose of governing regulatory bodies
Professional Code and Standards
Code of Ethics
Standards of Professional Conduct
Bylaws, Article VIII, Sections 4, 5, and 6
Rules of Procedure
Ethical Standards and Professional Obligations
Public
Customers and clients
Corporate management
Employers
Associates
Other analysts
Insider information
Research reports and investment recommendations
Compensation
Conflicts of interest
Corporate governance/proxy-related issues
Identification and Administration of Ethical Conduct
General business ethical values and obligations
Supervisory responsibilities
The evolution of the Code and the Standards of Professional
   Conduct
Intrafirm relationships
The principles of a professional's code of ethics
Competency and proper care
The concept of self-regulation
Changes in the public's perception of professional ethics
Social responsibility

Financial Accounting

*Not
assigned*

Role and Function of Basic Accounting Statements
Income statement
Statement of financial position
Statement of changes in financial position
Interpretation of Accounting Statements
Definition of asset, liability, revenue and income
Ratio analysis and its limitations
Profitability contrasted with liquidity
Implications of alternative accounting principles

	Candidate Level		
	I	*II*	*III*

Special Topics

Inventory costing
Intercorporate investments
Depreciation methods
Off-balance sheet financing

Pension plans
Discontinued operations and accounting changes
Income taxes
Leases
Business combinations
Accounting for changing prices

Substance versus form in accounting transactions
Implications of efficient markets hypothesis for accounting

Quantitative Analysis

Mathematics of Valuation
Present value
Future value
Rate of return mathematics

Data Analysis
Measures of central tendency
Measures of dispersion
Probability distributions
Hypothesis testing
Regression analysis

Factor Methods
Definition of common factors
Estimation procedures

Risk and Return
Expected return
Standard deviation
Covariance
Systematic and specific risk

Portfolio Construction
Portfolio theory
Optimization

Economics

Focus on Macroeconomics
Concept and measurement of GNP
Business fluctuations and economic forecasting
Inflationary process
Fiscal policy and budget deficits
Money and the federal reserve system

Focus on Microeconomics and Analysis
Consumer behavior and business decision making

Candidate Level

I   II   III

Costs and supply of goods
Business structure and regulation
Capital, interest and profit
Asset class returns
Focus on Analysis, Policy, and Investment Applications
Applications to portfolio management
International economics
Public policy and economic efficiency

Techniques of Analysis—Fixed-Income Securities

Types and Characteristics
Taxable, nontaxable
Type of issuer
Maturities
Indenture provisions
Convertible, nonconvertible

Mathematical Properties
Interest on interest
Determinants of prices and yields
Duration

Credit Evaluation
Ratings and rating services
Earning power
Asset protection
Terms and covenants

Interest Rates
Term structure
Forecasting

Bond Trading
Analysis
Techniques

Risk Management
Futures
Options

New Features
Contingent options and early redemptions
International bond investing

Techniques of Analysis—Equity Securities

Investment Context
Equity instruments (common stocks, convertible and partici-
    pating issues, rights, warrants, options and futures)
Development and application of equity instruments
Characteristics of equity markets: market indexes, relationship
    to economy, comparative risk and returns

Candidate Level

| | I | II | III |

Economic Framework, Industry Analysis, and Evaluation
Identification of company's business(es)
External factors: political, regulatory, social
Demand analysis: end uses, growth (real and nominal), cyclicality
Supply analysis: degree of concentration, ease of entry, capacity
Profitability: demand/supply balance, pricing and costs

Company Analysis and Evaluation
Position(s) within industry(ies)
Sales analysis: growth (real and nominal), cyclicality
Earnings analysis: earnings by business segment, consolidated results, components of return on equity
Flow of funds analysis
Balance sheet analysis
Dividend analysis: payout policy, dividend growth
Management appraisal

Risk Analysis
Qualitative factors: external (political, social, environmental), company business (economic sensitivity, size, growth, financial leverage), stock market (price volatility, share characteristics, market subgroups)
Quantitative measurements: capital asset pricing model (beta, nonsystematic), factor analysis (identification, exposure)

Valuation
Earnings multiples
Dividend discount and other valuation models
Technical analysis
Stock market perceptions
Valuation of equity instruments other than common stocks

Equity Analysis and the Efficient Markets
Weak, semistrong and strong forms of efficient market hypothesis
Implications relative to fundamental and technical analysis

Organization of the Equity Analysis Process
General investment philosophy
Techniques of information collection and processing
Analysts' interaction with other investment professionals
Communication of information inside and outside organization

Equity Analysis Performance Measurement
Criteria
Techniques
Evaluation process

	Candidate Level		
Objective of Analysis—Portfolio Management	*I*	*II*	*III*

Principles of Financial Asset Management
Definition of portfolio management, basic concepts—return, risk, diversification, portfolio efficiency
Evolution of portfolio management—traditional and recent developments

Investor Objectives, Constraints, and Policies
Liquidity requirement
Return requirement
Risk tolerance
Time horizon
Tax considerations
Regulatory and legal considerations
Unique needs, circumstances and preferences
Determination of portfolio policies

Expectational Factors
Social, political and economic
Capital markets
Individual financial assets

Integration of Portfolio Policies and Expectational Factors
Portfolio construction—asset allocation, active/passive strategies
Monitoring portfolio and responding to change—objectives, constraints and policies, expectational factors
Execution—timing, commission costs, price effects

Portfolio Performance Appraisal
Performance criteria—absolute performance, relative to portfolio objectives and risk level, relative to other portfolios with similar objectives
Measurement of performance—valuation of assets, accounting for income, rates of return and volatility
Evaluation of results—relationship to performance criteria, sources of results

Ethical and Professional Standards Requirements

The adoption and enforcement of standards of practice is fundamental for any profession. Knowledge of the applicable laws and regulations that impact a profession is necessary. Ethical and professional standards, however, go beyond the adherence to the letter of the law and involve an attitude of responsibility to the public, clients, employer, and fellow analysts.

Pre-candidate requirements. Candidates are required to show evidence of sound character and to agree, in writing at the time of registration, to abide by the ICFA Code of Ethics, Standards of Professional Conduct, and related rules. Character references are an integral part of the registration requirements. Violation of professional standards may result in suspension from the candidate program or revocation of the Charter.

Candidate level I. The candidate should be familiar with the general purpose and content of the basic securities laws and regulations that pertain to the investment field, including the structure of the principal regulatory bodies (SEC, NASD, NYSE, etc.) that administer these regulations. The candidate should be familiar with the purpose and administrative organization of the ICFA/FAF self-regulation programs. The candidate is expected to be aware of the content of the Code of Ethics, the Standards of Professional Conduct, the Rules of Procedure, and Article VIII (Sections 4, 5, and 6) of the ICFA By-Laws. Candidates must be familiar with the professional obligations and associated sanctions to which members in the ICFA and FAF are subject.

Candidate level II. The candidate should acquire the ability to recognize unprofessional practices and violations of standards in areas where issues are less clear cut, including conflicts of interest, compensation, use of inside information, corporate governance and proxy-related issues, and to understand appropriate responsibilities under the Rules of Procedure.

Candidate level III. The candidate should be able to administer a program of professional and ethical standards within an organization. Emphasis is placed on internal disciplinary controls as well as compliance with securities laws, regulations, and ICFA Standards and Rules. The candidate should demonstrate an awareness of current ethical issues, the importance of the public interest, and the implications of professionalism in financial analysis.

Comments

The sections on ethical and professional standards at the various candidate levels are organized to provide a progression of concepts, each of which builds upon the previous material. Therefore, it is essential for the candidate to review prior subject matter in preparing for more advanced examinations.

It is of critical importance to be thoroughly familiar with not only the securities laws and regulations that pertain to investment work, but also with the Code of Ethics and Standards of Professional Conduct to which the financial analyst subscribes. Furthermore, in order to uphold the integrity of the profession and the reputation of fellow members, the individual CFA has a responsibility to cooperate with the Institute and regulatory agencies in seeing to it that the public interest is respected. In order to discharge these obligations, the CFA must understand ethical and professional standards and, where necessary, know how to interpret and apply these standards in questionable situations.

In summary, these standards obligate the financial analyst to render services to both employer and clients with a high degree of professional and ethical responsibility in the best interests of all concerned—the employer, client, public, and the profession.

Financial Accounting Requirements

The financial analyst works with publicly available financial accounting data. One should be familiar with the form and content of financial statements and also with areas where judgment and alternative accounting principles permit varying treatment of accounting information. A basic objective of investment analysis is comparability among corporate reports for the evaluation of the financial position and the projection of cash flow and earnings. This objective may be accomplished only if the analyst has a sound knowledge of financial accounting principles.

Precandidate requirements. The candidate should understand the principles of accounting equivalent to at least one academic year of accounting as reflected in an elementary college accounting text.

Candidate level I. The candidate should be able to understand accounting principles and techniques. Emphasis is placed on skill in using published accounting data, including corporate financial statements and reports, in a meaningful financial analysis of companies.

Candidate level II. The candidate should gain a sufficiently thorough understanding of financial accounting—including such areas as mergers and acquisitions, inventory and plant valuation, current cost accounting, foreign exchange gains and losses, pensions and leases—to interpret financial statements for the proper evaluation and assessment of company fundamentals. Candidates are expected to be familiar with the statements and interpretations of the Financial Accounting Standards Board and its predecessor, the Accounting Principles Board, as well as the opinions and decisions of regulatory authorities.

Candidate level III. Not assigned.

Comments

The basic sources of corporate financial information are: (1) stockholder annual and quarterly reports and (2) financial statements filed with regulatory agencies, including 10-K's and prospectuses filed with the Securities and Exchange Commission. This information is essential to making the necessary projections as to earnings, cash flow, and capital requirements. The analyst must understand a variety of acceptable accounting methods, some of which can result in alternative ways of reporting specific transactions. For example, relatively technical accounting procedures affect the monetary amounts reported for inventories, leases, intangible assets, pensions, depreciation, and foreign exchange gains and losses. A company's net earnings are derived from the important figure of pretax earnings less the income tax provision, which is affected by such factors as the magnitude and accounting treatment of the investment tax credit, the relative size of foreign income taxes, and the treatment of depreciation and installment receivables.

Furthermore, the net earnings per share may be reported in a number of ways, including (1) primary from continuing operations, (2) primary after extraordinary items, and (3) fully diluted (reflecting potential dilution from securities convertible into common stock, management stock options, and warrants). Financial statement footnotes, reflecting recent SEC directives, have been increased considerably and deserve careful attention.

These and other accounting procedures impact directly upon the financial analyst's work in comparing companies and making projections. One must be able to discern the effects upon a corporation's financial statements of the use of particular accounting procedures and, where necessary, to make adjustments or allowances. In summary, a grasp of financial accounting procedures is fundamental to investment analysis.

Quantitative Analysis Requirements

Financial analysis depends on a sound understanding of quantitative concepts and methods. The financial analyst should understand the quantitative principles that underlie the theory of value for all assets and the tools that are used to measure and forecast value. Increasingly, financial analysis is conducted against a background of scientific techniques which are highly quantitative. The financial analyst should achieve a thorough understanding of these techniques including their merits as well as their limitations.

Precandidate requirements. The candidate should be thoroughly conversant with college-level algebra and have an "intuitive" grasp of differential and integral calculus.

Candidate level I. The candidate should understand the principles of valuation, statistics, and probability theory including hypothesis testing. Emphasis is placed on a conceptual appreciation of these principles.

Candidate level II. The candidate should understand regression analysis including parameter estimation and interpretation and analysis of variance. The candidate should also understand factor methods. Emphasis is placed on conceptual appreciation of these principles.

Candidate level III. The candidate should understand how quantitative methods are applied to financial analysis particularly in such areas as measuring value, portfolio construction, and analysis of risk and return. Emphasis is placed on the application of quantitative principles and methods.

Comments

Quantitative skills are essential for the serious financial analyst. Valuation of assets, for example, depends on the principles of present value. These same principles underlie rate of return mathematics so that even a cursory attempt at performance measurement depends on quantitative skills. Statistics and the theory of probability provide the tools that are necessary to introduce the concept of risk to the valuation problem. Regression analysis allows the financial analyst to measure relationships and to evaluate how financial and economic variables interact with each other. Forecasting, for example, depends importantly on an understanding of regression analysis. Finally, factor methods provide the quantitative framework for analyzing empirical data for the purpose of understanding the systematic factors that influence data such as returns.

These examples merely illustrate the importance of quantitative analysis in the field of finance. Many additional applications exist for the serious financial analyst. The principles and methods as well as the merits and limitations of quantitative analysis should be thoroughly understood.

Economics Requirements

Economic principles provide the theoretical underpinnings for much of modern financial and investment analysis. Assumptions regarding the economy are an integral part of the analysis of companies and industries and investment policy formulation. In addition, the market behavior and motives of companies and their respective industries are generally better understood through the application of economic analysis.

Precandidate requirements.   The candidate should be familiar with the basic principles of microeconomics, macroeconomics, and the monetary system. The candidate should have knowledge at least equivalent to one academic year of principles of economics as reflected in an elementary college textbook. CFA examinations, it should be stressed, emphasize the practical application of economic concepts rather than the abstract theories themselves.

Candidate level I.   The candidate should gain a historical perspective of economic trends; gain an understanding of the structure and operations of money and capital markets; and be able to apply economic reasoning in the investment analysis of the company, its industry, and its investment securities. The emphasis at this level is on macroeconomics.

Candidate level II.   The candidate should have an understanding of the economic dynamics of the business cycle and the fiscal and monetary policy options available to counter adverse cyclical influences. The candidate should also be able to apply and interpret modern techniques used in forecasting economic developments and evaluating their effect on security values.

Candidate level III. The candidate should be able to evaluate current economic conditions in light of the historical record; have a basic understanding of various options in regard to fiscal, monetary, incomes, international, regulatory, and natural resource policies; and formulate investment policy strategies based on a probability assessment of alternative economic scenarios.

Comments

Most domestic corporations are significantly influenced by trends in economic activity in the United States and Canada. The influence is considerable for highly cyclical basic industries and also of consequence to such consumer-oriented groups as drugs or foods. In addition to the direct effects of changes in demand on major industries such as automotive, manufacturing, and building construction, the indirect effects impact the sales and margins of most companies. Where overseas sales and imports are of consequence, corporate operations also reflect economic conditions in foreign countries. The level of demand overseas has often varied from U.S. activity, thus requiring a broader understanding of companies with important foreign markets and/or overseas production.

In summary, the state of the economy affects, in varying degrees, the sales and profit margins of every industry. Thus, the investment analyst needs an understanding of economic forces affecting industries and companies and should be able to apply basic economic analysis to specific investment situations.

Fixed-Income Securities Analysis Requirements

Fixed-income securities represent a significant proportion of the capital structure of an increasing number of corporations and also are an important component of actual or potential portfolios of many institutional and individual investors. These securities include conventional bond and money market instruments, fixed-income securities with convertible or tax-sheltered features, and those that are amortizing in nature. Supply and demand forces in the debt market, investors' expectations, together with economic conditions, affect bond risks, yields and portfolio total returns. As a consequence, a familiarity with the bond market and the analysis and management of fixed-income securities is of growing importance to financial analysts.

Precandidate requirements. The candidate should have the equivalent of two years of college study in business administration—including business finance, corporate financial analysis, and money and banking (or money and capital markets).

Candidate level I. The candidate is expected to understand and be able to analyze the basic characteristics (coupon, maturity, call, conversion, sinking fund, and so on) of fixed-income instruments, including corporate preferreds. The candidate should understand the various contractual forms (mortgage, debenture, pass-through, income bonds, and so forth). The candidate should understand the basic concepts of yield and bond price determination and the price risks attendant on interest rate and purchasing power changes.

Candidate level II. At this level the candidate should have an understanding of the financial and investment implications of the elements and characteristics of fixed-income securities. The candidate should be able to analyze in depth government and corporate issuers and their fixed-income securities. The candidate should understand the implications of the interest rate structure for various types of fixed contracts. Also, the candidate should understand bond trading.

Candidate level III. The candidate should have an understanding of the mechanics of bond management, including analysis of bond swaps and the evaluation of performance. Emphasis at this level is placed on the management of fixed-income securities. The use of risk modifiers, futures and options on fixed-income securities is studied along with new features.

Comments

The analysis of fixed-income securities includes some of the factors covered in equity securities analysis and also some points that are of concern only to the bondholder, including safety of both principal and interest. The typical bond buyer sets standards as to quality rating, recognizing that quality may vary considerably within a particular rating and also that a bond may be downgraded (and in some cases upgraded) by rating services. Traditionally, fixed-income securities have been the responsibility of bond managers and bond traders with many years of specialized experience.

Reflecting the flood of corporate and government financing and decidedly more attractive interest rates, the portfolio managers and the investment analysts in today's market are devoting considerable time to debt securities. This is especially true since many new and creative financing techniques have been introduced into the fixed-income markets.

Equity Securities Analysis Requirements

Equity securities analysis continues as a cornerstone of the CFA program—even with the growing importance of fixed-income analysis and the newer trend toward early specialization in portfolio management and other specific investment fields. Equity securities analysis can be broadly defined as the dynamic process of evaluating industry and company fundamentals within the framework of economic expectations to project income streams and market values. In practice, this begins with the study of past data on industries and companies and an assessment of what factors have impinged on those historical trends. The equity analyst must then attempt to project these factors into the future in order to arrive at an estimate of prospective earnings growth. The process ends with the application of various methods to value those future earnings and an analysis of the associated risks.

Precandidate requirements. The candidate should have the equivalent of two years of college study in business administration—including business finance, corporate financial analysis, and money and banking (or money and capital markets).

Candidate level I. The candidate should be able to approach logically the appraisal of industries and companies from both a quantitative and qualitative point of view. The candidate should be able to understand and interpret financial statements and demonstrate an ability to deal effectively with the important issues of common stock valuation and risk assessment.

Candidate level II. Emphasis is placed on the ability to perform a complete appraisal and evaluation of industries and companies. The current position and outlook for common stocks and other equities as well as the investment implications for different investors are examined. The candidate should be able to apply the techniques of securities analysis, including measures for valuation and risk, to individual companies and also to a group of companies within the same industry.

Candidate level III. Emphasis at this level is placed on the relationship between equity analysis and securities markets. Topics covered include the valuation of international equities, derived securities, and the understanding of the effect of market factors on valuation.

Comments

The number of industries and companies regularly researched by a typical security analyst varies considerably. Thus, some analysts have under their general responsibility a number of industries and many companies while, at the other extreme, some analysts specialize in only one industry or even a segment thereof. As individual corporations have alternative ways of reporting information, some items of which may have a major impact on the size and quality of earnings, a special challenge facing analysts is to appraise on a comparable basis the earnings and performance potential of companies in the same industry.

The work of the typical equity security analyst covers four steps:

1. The collection of all relevant data and facts.
2. The integration of this material into a balanced analysis.

3. The evaluation of the industry, the company, and its equity securities.
4. The dissemination of this material to the employer organization or to clients—with the end result being action relating to the sale, purchase, or retention of specific equity securities.

Portfolio Management Requirements

Essential to portfolio management is the understanding of the principles of financial asset management. These include the basic concepts of risk and return, diversification, and portfolio efficiency. The candidate should be familar with modern portfolio theory and be able to apply it.

Investor objectives, constraints, and policies must be established. Examples would include: return requirements, risk tolerance, liquidity, time horizon, tax considerations, regulatory and legal considerations, plus any unique needs, circumstances, or preferences.

Expectational factors must be included in the process. This involves forecasting, making projections, simulating possible futures, and building investment scenarios. Expectational factors also concern the future circumstances of the investor, as well as changes in societal, political, economic, and market environments domestically and internationally.

Portfolio construction brings together all of the above factors in strategy development, asset allocation, and methods of modifying risk in a multiasset environment.

Execution is the means by which portfolio strategies are implemented.

Anticipating and responding to change is fundamental to portfolio management.

Portfolio performance appraisal includes not only performance measurement, but also relates results to performance criteria and analyzes their sources.

Management skills are necessary for effective investment organizations meeting the needs of clients, employees, and owners.

Precandidate requirements. Because the task of portfolio and investment management involves the integration of economics, financial accounting, fixed-income and equity securities analysis, and ethics, the pre-candidate requirements are the same as for those topic areas.

Candidate level I. The candidate is expected to understand the process and principles of financial asset management, the theory of risk and return, the investment objectives, constraints, and preferences of individual and institutional investors, and be able to formulate investment policy statements for such portfolios.

Candidate level II. At this level, the candidate should be able to formulate portfolio strategies and construct portfolios that reflect investor objectives and constraints, the outlook for the economy, and conditions in the securities markets. This requires an understanding of expected return and risk for individual securities and of how the risks of individual securities and their expected returns combine at the portfolio level.

Candidate level III.   Based on knowledge gained at the preceding levels and in the other topic areas, the candidate is expected to be able to: (1) interrelate economic and market conditions, securities analysis, analysis of the requirements of individual and institutional investors, and efficient portfolio concepts; (2) develop suitable investment policies; (3) construct multiasset portfolios that meet investors' requirements and circumstances; (4) implement strategy; (5) monitor the portfolio and respond to change; and (6) measure and evaluate performance. The candidate is expected to have an understanding of the investment process, including how to organize and implement the portfolio management process and how to evaluate the results.

2

Setting Investment Objectives

Charles D. Ellis, Ph.D., CFA
Managing Partner
Greenwich Associates

"If you don't know where you're going, any road will take you there" is a familiar expression that has all too much application to investment management as it is typically practiced in America today.

There is more than irony in the paradoxical fact that most investment managers devote most of their time, energy, and ability in an apparently futile effort to achieve an objective that appears unattainable and which, even if accomplished, would not be very important compared to a far, far easier task in which most investment managers could consistently achieve the intended objective. Even more significant, this relatively "easy" objective, when achieved, would really matter. Unfortunately, very few investment managers devote any serious time, effort, or talent to attain this objective.

The unimportant and very difficult task to which most investment managers devote most of their time with little or no success is to "beat the market." Realistically, to outperform the equity market by even one half of 1 percent each year would be a great success which few, if any, investment managers have achieved. In fact, during the last several market cycles (the only periods for which we have systematic and reliable measurements of portfolio performance) most major investment organizations have been unable to keep pace with the market averages. Moreover, it appears to be true that their very efforts to beat the market have been a main cause of their own underachievement.

The truly important, but not very difficult task would be to establish sensible investment policies with which to achieve realistic and specified investment objectives. An appropriate change of even quite modest magnitude in the basic asset allocation decision, for example, can capture an improvement in total return that would be significantly greater than the elusive increment sought in the "beat the market" syndrome.

The time-honored term for this important work is *investment counseling*. As Peter Drucker so correctly emphasizes, it's a great deal more important to be working on the really right things than to be doing even the nearly right things unusually well.

In investment management, the real opportunity to achieve superior results is in establishing and adhering to appropriate investment policies over the long term, and this can only be done by setting realistic investment objectives, which is the subject of this chapter.

INVESTMENT COUNSELING

Despite general acknowledgement of the importance of investment counseling in the abstract, the evidence is disturbing and overwhelming that investment counseling is used little, if at all, in practice. Both SEI and Greenwich Associates studies show there is virtually no significant difference in the basic asset allocations of such extraordinarily different kinds of employee benefit funds as defined benefit pension funds and profit sharing funds. Nor does asset mix differ significantly with such theoretically compelling factors as to whether actuarial investment return assumptions are high or low, whether pension benefit obligations are underfunded or fully funded, what fraction of accrued benefit obligations are vested, the average age of the affected work force, or the ratio of active versus retired participants.

The differences between the functions and needs of pension plans and profit sharing plans are profound and allegedly well understood. That their investments are not differentiated leads to the sobering conclusion that while investment counseling may be honored in theory, it is little used in practice.

Whether investment management is primarily an art or a science has long been a favorite topic for informal discussion among professional investors, perhaps because the discussions are typically resolved quite cheerfully by demonstrating that the practice of investment management is clearly not a science, and must therefore be an art. Investment management is neither art nor science. It is instead, a problem in *engineering*. (And quite simple when compared to many of the other engineering problems facing our society such as air traffic control, space probes, or increasing automobile mileage while reducing pollution emissions.) Moreover, recent advances in the availability of data and the important development of modern portfolio theory are providing investment managers—and their more sophisticated clients—with the tools and analytical frame of reference they need to understand the investment problem so it can be solved or managed.

Just as the development of such diagnostic devices as x-ray machines and modern pharmacology made it possible for medical doctors to transform medical practice, it is now possible to transform investment management. When doctors fully understand the causes and pathology of a disease, they usually find the cure usually requires effective impact on only one dominant factor, and is therefore both powerful and cheap. Before the real solution is discovered, doctors attempt to treat the disease with treatments that are not only unproductive, but are also quite costly.

CONTROLLING RISK

Similarly, in investment management it is becoming clear that the crucial factor is not how to increase rates of return, but rather *how to control risk*, and that risk control is not nearly as costly as is the conventional effort to boost rates of return. In fact, the rate of return obtained in an investment portfolio is a derivative of the level of systematic risk (nondiversifiable risk) that is assumed in the portfolio, the consistency with which that risk level is maintained through the market cycle, and the skill with which specific risk (which is disposable through diversification) is eliminated or minimized through portfolio diversification. In formulating policy and strategy in politics, war, business, or investing, the necessary first step is a realistic determination of the true nature of the environment in which operations will be conducted. It is essential that this assessment be very accurate, because no matter how astute the subsequent analysis may be, to the extent that the original assumption or promise is not relevant to the environment, the conclusions will be wrong. The greater the error in the original premise, the greater the error in the ultimate policy and strategy.

There are two quite different kinds of errors in assessment: (1) errors that overstate the importance of minor factors which would cause attention to be devoted to the wrong priorities, and (2) errors that cause misunderstandings of the causal relationships so that efforts to achieve the intended objective will be counterproductive.

What then is a realistic assessment of the rates of return in the equity market? The conventional answer is 9 percent. What an exquisite and extraordinary deception this is. If only it were simply meaningless! Alas, it has, for most investment managers and most of their clients quite considerable meaning. It is the average annual rate of return they expect from investments in common stocks. It is, in fact, the return to which they feel they are entitled in a typical year. However, as everyone knows, the actual experience of equity investors has been nothing like "9 percent compounded" for quite a long time. In fact, for most of the past decade, investors have experienced not gains, but losses. What's wrong? Have equity markets and equity returns somehow changed from a favorable and sublime 9 percent to the violent and adverse? And if so, should the investment objectives of the past be replaced with new objectives? The answer to both questions is "no"—but with one caveat. Inflation—and specifically a change in rate of inflation anticipated in the market—has caused an important change in the nominal rate of return required by equity investors, and this, in turn, has exerted a major effect on the level of stock prices. Simply put, equity investors continue to require about the same rate of return after offsetting inflation as they used to require when rates of inflation were far less. This means that nominal equity returns now must be higher than the nominal returns that were required when the expected rate of inflation was lower (2 percent in the 1950s versus 7 percent in the 1970s).

As a result of the change in the expected rate of inflation, the long-term average rate of return required by equity investors has increased from approximately 9 percent to approximately 14 percent, so the conventional 9 percent expectation is out of date. Even this quite substantial change—from 9 percent to 14 percent is an increase of 56 percent—does not give a realistic measure of normal returns in the stock market because it does not describe the difference or distribution of the year-by-year returns. And as every investor now knows, the differences in year-to-year returns have been considerably more important than the similarities.

Without using statistical terminology, we can now estimate that the returns to the equity investor will—in two-thirds of the years ahead—be within the rather wide range of −9 percent to +37 percent. And we can estimate that in the other one-third of the years, the actual returns will be divided evenly between losses greater than 9 percent and gains greater than 37 percent. And finally, we can say that over the very long term, total rates of return will tend to approximate 14 percent compounded annually. Now it's a vastly different thing to say returns will be "14 percent plus or minus 23 percent two thirds of the time," than to say simply "14 percent" and it matters greatly to those who are trying to specify appropriate investment objectives *or* to examine the feasibility of the investment policies through which the objective is to be achieved *or* to reappraise their established objectives in the light of actual experience *or* to assess the operating performance of an investment manager assigned to achieve the objective.

Instruction in the width of the dispersion of returns—23 percent plus 23 percent equals a "normal" range of 46 percent which is more than three times as large as the average amount of expected return—comes unfortunately for most investment managers in those most distressing circumstances when losses are particularly severe. As the losses are usually unexpected—because they have typically not been discussed in advance—they cause considerable alarm and provoke clients and managers to improvise hastily an ad hoc reappraisal of their investment policies and objectives.

Such reviews can be expected to result all too often in action that is easily described as "the wrong decision at the wrong time for the wrong reasons," and the consequences—typically a substantial shift from equities at currently depressed prices into bonds and other fixed-income investments that will not rise in capital value with the next cycle of the equity market—are predictably harmful to the long-term returns of the portfolio.

Comparable harm is also done when the recently past years' returns have been higher than should be expected, and investment managers and their clients shed the requisite caution and increase the amount of risk assumed in the portfolio. And then, after a few years of adversity of the sort that falls normally within the very wide range of the long-term distribution of annual returns, this extra portfolio risk will magnify the impact of the market's decline, magnify the normal investor anxieties, and lead to the ad hoc revisions that cause investors to "sell low" what they have previously "bought high."

Peter Bernstein has explained this altogether human phenomenon by pointing out that almost everybody dislikes it when stocks go down in price even though it is in their best interest to have stock prices go down—so they can buy more shares with their savings and receive more dividends both now and in the future. As Pogo would say, "we have met the enemy, and he is us."

Since investors and their investment managers are subject to human frailties and foibles, the setting of investment objectives—and the investment policies designed to achieve them—needs to be done with considerable care and extensive analysis of the nature of the investment environment not only so the appropriate objective will be selected, but also so the investors and their managers will be able to hold to that same, still appropriate objective and the still appropriate investment policies when the market has been strongly negative and both objectives and policies look most dubious. A curious idea continues to make the rounds that the investment objective for a particular portfolio should be set in whole or in part according to the funds the investor wants or needs to draw from the portfolio each year. Sometimes this shows up in pension funds where the actuarial rate of return assumption will be put forth as a guide to investment. Sometimes it shows up with college presidents insisting on higher endowment fund returns to make up for operating deficits. And sometimes it arises when personal trust funds are asked to finance a more expensive way of life.

This is nonsense. We now know that the return (per unit of risk) cannot be increased just because an investor wants a higher return with which to finance more spending. Specifically, the spending decisions of the investor cannot contribute to the formulation of sound investment policies and objectives: these must be determined in accordance with the discipline of the investment market. On the contrary, the spending decisions should most definitely be governed by the investment objectives and policies—and results. One qualification of this prescription is worth noting: when spending will exceed current income from dividends and interest, a reserve fund probably should be established and funded with regular percentage withdrawals from the portfolio's long-term invested assets. Otherwise withdrawal of capital will occur in a pattern that would be a harmful reversal of dollar costs averaging; that is, would take a larger percentage of the portfolio's assets at market lows and a smaller percentage at market highs.

Time is the single most important factor that separates the appropriate investment objective of one portfolio from the appropriate objective of another portfolio. Specifically, it is the length of time over which an investor can and will commit the portfolio and evaluate investment results and the investment objectives and policies.

At the extremes, the importance of the investor's time horizon for investment objectives is clear: a one-day or one-week investment in anything but Treasury bills (or the equivalent) would be virtually impossible to justify, and over a half century, it is easy to show that equities are the optimal investment for the entire portfolio.[1] (Note that this self-evident proposition fits with the core assertion that the priority objective in investment management is to control risk, not to maximize returns.)

The governing time horizon for each stratum of the investment portfolio—and it is a remarkably useful exercise to analyze the portfolio of assets in comparison to specified segments of actual or potential obligations as do the banks and insurance companies—will determine the nature of the investments that can and should be made and the investment objectives that should be chosen.

A good example of different time horizons warranting different investment policies will be found in the profit sharing plan of a corporation whose participants have quite different expectations as to how long they will work at the company. An older worker may be quite near retirement, for example, and be particularly interested in preserving accumulated asset values during the last few years of a long career, while a younger worker may be planning to work (and continue investing through the profit sharing plan) for 30 or 40 years into the future. The older worker's time horizon may call for a portfolio 100 percent in short- and intermediate-term fixed-income securities, while the younger worker's time horizon would call for 100 percent equities

---

[1] The question of common stocks versus such other forms of equity investment as real estate will not be analyzed here.

and growth investments. In recognition of these real differences, more and more companies are now providing employees with different time horizons an opportunity to elect different asset allocations and to change the asset allocation as their time horizons change over the years as they approach retirement.

The second major factor that separates investment objectives is the risk tolerance of the investor. As discussed above, the investor who is very well informed about the investment environment will know what to expect, and will be able to take in stride those disruptive experiences that may cause other less informed investors to overreact to either unusually favorable or unusually adverse market experience. Risk tolerance matters only at the market's extremes.

Investment managers and their clients can do a lot to improve portfolio returns by being sure they both are well informed about the realities of the investment environment in which the portfolio will be managed. (The risk tolerance of a corporate pension fund is not just the risk tolerance of the pension staff or even the senior financial officer: it is the risk tolerance of a majority of the board of directors at the moment of most severe market adversity.)

While most observers maintain that the exceptional liquidity of our capital markets is a considerable advantage, it may well be that less liquidity would be beneficial both to the formation of investment objectives and to their faithful implementation in all market conditions. Indeed, in investment management, if it must be done quickly, it is not fiduciary.

The dimensions on which investment objectives are set should always be relative to the market. Where absolute rates of return are appropriate, only fixed-income investments will apply. When investments are made in equities, the objective specified should always be relative to the equity market as a whole or to an agreed-upon sector of the equity market such as large capitalization-growth stocks, utility stocks, or stocks with low price-to-book value ratios. Specifically, an investment manager should not be asked to manage a portfolio of growth stocks and to have as an objective to match or exceed the year-to-year rate of return experienced in the overall stock market.

The level of systematic risk (described as portfolio beta) chosen for a particular portfolio will lead to a specific investment objective specified in terms of a relative-to-market average rate of return over a period of several years, but not in each and every year. In fact, the results achieved by a manager who is achieving superior results over the longer term may appear, in a single period, to be less than the average expected. This is because each manager's actual results (like the market's returns) form a probability distribution with an average return and a range of returns around that average. Consequently, investment objectives should be understood and specified in terms of the mean rate of return and a distribution around that mean.

Fortunately for investment managers and their clients, modern portfolio theory provides the tools with which such probabilistic patterns can be understood conceptually and specified in practice. And this means that the evaluation of the performance of an operating portfolio can be separated from the formulation of investment policies and the determination of investment objectives—with each open for rigorous examination and either modification or reaffirmation.

Such examination should be undertaken at least once each year to determine whether recent experience calls for a change in the long-term assessment of the investment environment or the investor's constraints, and hence in the appropriate investment objective.

Evaluating Policy and Operations

Having established investment objectives that are realistic in the market context and appropriate to the time horizon and risk preferences of the investor, it is appropriate to specify the specific investment policies to be followed by the investment manager in pursuit of the stated objectives. It is in comparison to these investment policies that the operational performance of the investment manager should be measured and evaluated. For example, as noted above, it would be both unfair and misinforming to attempt an evaluation of the operational performance of a portfolio of growth stocks (or utility stocks or foreign stocks or high yield stocks) by comparing its results to the market averages because such a comparison is evaluating both policy and operations which should be examined separately. Specifically, the operational performance of a growth stock portfolio should be critiqued in comparison to an index of growth stocks or portfolios of growth stocks, while the policy of investing in growth stocks would be critiqued by examining the behavior of portfolios of growth stocks in comparison to the behavior of the stock market as a whole.

The separate examination of operations and policy is important. Otherwise, it would not be possible to determine which is contributing to or detracting from investment success. All too often, a portfolio manager has been blamed for the adverse impact of policy over which she or he had no control. And in some cases, the portfolio manager has been credited with good performance when, in fact, his operational performance was a drag on the results that should have devolved from an effective policy.

If the policy is found inappropriate, it should be changed and the new policy made explicit to the portfolio manager. If the operating performance of the portfolio manager does not conform with policy, the manager should be replaced even if such deviation from stated policy resulted in a higher rate of return than would have been earned by following stated policy. (Of course, an incompetent portfolio manager would also be replaced, but this is a different issue.)

An important advantage arising from the separation of investment policy from portfolio operations is the opportunity to control portfolio managers who, because they are human, are tempted to move away from long-term policy—particularly at the high and low points in a market cycle—by reducing portfolio risk at the low point and accepting greater risk at the high point. Segregating responsibility for investment *policy* from responsibility for portfolio *operations* is essential to the work of managing the managers—removing the "what" and obliging them to concentrate entirely on the "how"—so their natural preoccupation with the present will not corrupt the portfolio's long-term policy.

The dimensions along which investment policies can be established include: stock-bond ratios; average maturity and quality ratings—both with high-low ranges—in the bond portfolio; portfolio turnover; whether to keep the equity portfolio fully invested or to engage in market timing;[2] how widely to diversify; what risk level to establish (and whether to vary the risk level, and if so, to what limits); and in what types of stocks to invest.

The tools developed out of modern portfolio theory now make it almost easy to quantify most investment policies and to measure portfolio operation to be sure it is in conformance with policy. This is an extraordinary advantage for the gifted investor and for the serious client. It makes genuine investment counseling possible, and should make it feasible for each portfolio manager to achieve excellent performance—when compared to the realistic investment policies he should be following to achieve the agreed upon objectives of the fund.

---

[2] There is no evidence that market timing works even though most investment managers engage in it. This is a good example of the need to "manage the managers" more fully.

PART 2

Economic Analysis

3

Security Markets and Business Cycles

Geoffrey H. Moore, Ph.D.
Graduate School of Business
Columbia University

John P. Cullity, Ph.D.
Department of Economics
Newark College of Arts and Sciences
Rutgers University

SUMMARY

From 1873 to 1982 the U.S. economy experienced 26 recessions. With rare exceptions, the recessions were accompanied by a decline in stock prices. During the intervening expansions in business activity, stock prices usually rose. Moreover, there have been few sustained or substantial swings in stock prices that have not been closely associated with swings in the business cycle. An understanding of this association, therefore, is clearly of concern to anyone interested in the stock market.

The bond market also is closely attuned to the business cycle. Yields on corporate, municipal, and U.S. government bonds—as well as other interest rates—have nearly always risen during the later stages of upswings in business and fallen during downswings. Bond prices, of course, have moved in the opposite direction. As a rule, prosperity is good for stock prices but bad for bond prices, while depression is bad for stock prices and good for bond prices.

This does not mean, however, that a turn for the worse in business and in stock prices always occurs at the same time. Typically, the turn in stock prices occurs prior to the turn in business activity. Hence stock prices are said to lead the swing in the business cycle, and stock price indexes are "leading indicators." At the peak of the business cycle, it is characteristic that stock prices have already been declining for some months, and at the trough of the business cycle, stock prices usually have already started to rise. Bond yields, on the other hand, frequently continue to decline for some months after a business upswing has begun and occasionally continue to rise after a business recession has begun. Bond yields and other interest rates are generally classified as coincident or lagging indicators.

Business cycles have marked influences on the volume of new issues of stocks and bonds and on the repayment and refunding of bonds. Rising stock prices and falling bond prices tend to encourage the issuance of common stock and to discourage bond financing, so a shift toward stock and away from bonds tends to occur during a business upswing. The opposite movements characterize the contraction phase of the business cycle.

A wide variety of factors, summed up in the term *business cycle*, bring about or are related to these regularities in security market behavior. Among the factors associated with the regularities in the behavior of stock prices during business cycles, probably the most significant are profits and interest rates. Declines in the level or rate of growth of profits or in factors portending such declines—for example, declines in profit margins or in new orders—during the late stage of a business cycle expansion alter appraisals of common stock values and hence tend to produce a decline in stock prices before the downturn of business. At this stage also, a restricted supply of money and credit and the accompanying higher interest rates tend to lower capital values and may cause postponement of plans to exploit potentially profitable investment opportunities, make common stocks a less attractive security to hold, and diminish incentives to borrow for that purpose. Hence, these changes as well as those in profits depress stock prices in the later stages of business expansions. Both sets of factors operate to produce the *lead* in stock prices. Opposite changes occur during business contractions and help to explain the tendency for stock prices to begin to rise while business activity as a whole is still depressed.

But a wide variety of other factors play upon the market—shifts in investor confidence, fears of inflation, prospects for higher taxes or stiffer government regulation, changes in margin requirements, the flow of funds from abroad, a strike in a major industry, the failure of a large enterprise—and these make the underlying regularities more difficult to observe and to predict. Moreover, developments in the securities markets have repercussions of their own. A rise in capital values can lift the propensity of consumers to spend and encourage entrepreneurs to embark on new ventures; a collapse in capital values can do the opposite. Hence there is a feedback from the markets to business.

DEFINITION AND CHARACTERISTICS OF BUSINESS CYCLES

Business cycles, according to a definition formulated in 1946 by Wesley C. Mitchell and Arthur F. Burns, are

> a type of fluctuation found in the aggregate economic activity of nations that organize their work mainly in business enterprises; a cycle consists of expansions which occur at about the same time in many economic activities, followed by similarly general recessions, contractions, and revivals which merge into the expansion phase of the next cycle; this sequence of changes is recurrent but not periodic; in duration business cycles may last from more than one year to ten or twelve years; they are not divisible into shorter cycles of similar character with amplitudes approximating their own.[1]

This definition resulted from extensive observation of economic data for a number of countries over periods ranging back to the late 18th century and up to the 1930s. Studies of more recent data have confirmed the continued existence of business cycles conforming to the definition, and the chronology of cycles has been extended down to date. However, secular shifts in the character of economic activity, such as the shifts toward greater employment in the service industries, including government; the creation of new institutions such as bank deposit insurance and unemployment insurance; and the attention given by government to the use of fiscal and monetary policy to modify the business cycle, particularly to offset any tendency toward recession, have led to long-term changes in the character of the cycle. In general, cyclical fluctuations in recent decades, both in the United States and abroad, have been milder, with the contraction phase often characterized by a reduced rate of growth in aggregate economic activity rather than by an absolute decline. Hence the term *growth cycle* has come to be applied to these milder fluctuations. This shift has generally been accompanied by a higher rate of inflation during the expansion phase of the cycle, often extending into the contraction phase.

Chronologies of business cycles have been constructed for a number of countries. The one in common use for the United States was developed by the National Bureau of Economic Research (NBER). On an annual basis, it extends from 1790 to 1982 and covers 44 expansions and 44 contractions (see Table 1). The monthly and quarterly chronology begins in 1854 and covers 30 cycles. The latest contraction ran from July 1981 to November 1982.

Table 2 gives a record of the chief characteristics of all of the business cycle contractions (recessions) in the United States since 1920. Most of the contractions have lasted about a year. The 43-month contraction during 1929–33 was, of course, substantially longer. The 16-month contractions during 1973–75 and 1981–82 were also somewhat longer

TABLE 1 Business Cycle Expansions and Contractions in the United States, 1790–1982

Dates of Peaks and Troughs						Duration in Months			
By Months		By Quarters		By Calendar Years				Cycle	
Trough	Peak	Trough	Peak	Trough	Peak	Contraction (peak to trough)	Expansion (trough to peak)	Trough to Trough	Peak to Peak
				1790	1796		72		
				1799	1802	36	36	108	72
				1804	1807	24	36	60	60
				1810	1812	36	18	72	54
				1812	1815	6	36	24	42
				1821	1822	72	12	108	84
				1823	1825	12	24	24	36
				1826	1828	12	24	36	36
				1829	1833	12	48	36	60
				1834	1836	12	24	60	36
				1838	1839	24	12	48	36
				1843	1845	48	24	60	72
				1846	1847	12	12	36	24
				1848	1853	12	60	24	72
Dec. 1854	June 1857	1854:4	1857:2	1855	1856	18	30	78	48
Dec. 1858	Oct. 1860	1858:4	1860:3	1858	1860	18	22	48	40
June 1861	Apr. 1865	1861:3	1865:1	1861	1864	8	46	30	54
Dec. 1867	June 1869	1868:1	1869:2	1867	1869	32	18	78	50
Dec. 1870	Oct. 1873	1870:4	1873:3	1870	1873	18	34	36	52
Mar. 1879	Mar. 1882	1879:1	1882:1	1878	1882	65	36	99	101
May 1885	Mar. 1887	1885:2	1887:2	1885	1887	38	22	74	60
Apr. 1888	July 1890	1888:1	1890:3	1888	1890	13	27	35	40
May 1891	Jan. 1893	1891:2	1893:1	1891	1892	10	20	37	30
June 1894	Dec. 1895	1894:2	1895:4	1894	1895	17	18	37	35
June 1897	June 1899	1897:2	1899:3	1896	1899	18	24	36	42
Dec. 1900	Sep. 1902	1900:4	1902:4	1900	1903	18	21	42	39
Aug. 1904	May 1907	1904:3	1907:2	1904	1907	23	33	44	56
June 1908	Jan. 1910	1908:2	1910:1	1908	1910	13	19	46	32
Jan. 1912	Jan. 1913	1911:4	1913:1	1911	1913	24	12	43	36

Business cycle reference dates — Trough			Business cycle reference dates — Peak			Duration in months			
Monthly	Quarterly	Annual	Monthly	Quarterly	Annual	Contraction	Expansion	Cycle (trough–trough)	Cycle (peak–peak)
Dec. 1914	1914:4	1914	Aug. 1918	1918:3	1918	23	44	35	67
Mar. 1919	1919:1	1919	Jan. 1920	1920:1	1920	7	10	51	17
July 1921	1921:3	1921	May 1923	1923:2	1923	18	22	28	40
July 1924	1924:3	1924	Oct. 1926	1926:3	1926	14	27	36	41
Nov. 1927	1927:4	1927	Aug. 1929	1929:3	1929	13	21	40	34
Mar. 1933	1933:1	1933	May 1937	1937:2	1937	43	50	64	93
June 1938	1938:2	1938	Feb. 1945	1945:1	1944	13	80	63	93
Oct. 1945	1945:4	1945	Nov. 1948	1948:4	1948	8	37	88	45
Oct. 1949	1949:4	1949	July 1953	1953:2	1953	11	45	48	56
May 1954	1954:2	1954	Aug. 1957	1957:3	1957	10	39	55	49
Apr. 1958	1958:2	1958	Apr. 1960	1960:2	1960	8	24	47	32
Feb. 1961	1961:1	1961	Dec. 1969	1969:4	1969	10	106	34	116
Nov. 1970	1970:4	1970	Nov. 1973	1973:4	1973	11	36	117	47
Mar. 1975	1975:1	1975	Jan. 1980	1980:1	1979	16	58	52	74
July 1980	1980:3	1980	July 1981	1981:3	1981	6	12	64	18
Nov. 1982	1982:4	1982				16		28	

Averages

	Contraction	Expansion	Cycle (trough–trough)	Cycle (peak–peak)
Annual dates:				
1790–1854, 14 cycles	24	31	55	53
Monthly dates:				
1854–1982, 30 cycles	18	33	51	51
1854–1933, 20 cycles	22	25	47	48
1933–1982, 10 cycles	11	49	60	59
1948–1982, 7 cycles	11	46	57	56
Annual and monthly dates:				
1790–1982, 44 cycles	20	33	52	52

NOTE: The monthly and quarterly dates are based on essentially the same information, with the quarterly dates constrained to fall in the same quarter if the monthly date is in mid-quarter, otherwise in the same or adjacent quarter.

Prior to 1854 the durations are based on calendar year peak and trough dates. For 1812, when there was a brief recession and then a revival, it is assumed that the recession occurred in the first half of the year. For the durations ending in December 1854 and June 1857, it is assumed that the previous annual trough and peak dates were centered on June 1848 and June 1853.

For a basic definition and statement of the method of determining business cycle peaks and troughs, see Arthur F. Burns and Wesley C. Mitchell, *Measuring Business Cycles* (New York: NBER, 1946), chap. 4. Some of the dates shown there (p. 78) have since been revised. The annual chronology has been extended back to 1790 using Willard L. Thorp, *Business Annals* (New York: NBER, 1926), pp. 113–26. See Geoffrey H. Moore and Victor Zarnowitz, "The Development and Role of the National Bureau's Business Cycle Chronologies" (Cambridge, Mass.: NBER, March 1984). For a description of the method used in dating recent cycles, see Geoffrey H. Moore, *Business Cycles, Inflation, and Forecasting* (Cambridge, Mass.: NBER, 1983), chaps. 1 and 2.

TABLE 2 Selected Measures of Duration, Depth, and Diffusion of Business Cycle Contractions (from peak [first date] to trough [second date])

	Jan. 1920 July 1921	May 1923 July 1924	Oct. 1926 Nov. 1927	Aug. 1929 Mar. 1933	May 1937 June 1938	Feb. 1945 Oct. 1945
Duration (months):						
Business cycle (Table 1)	18	14	13	43	13	8
GNP, current dollars	n.a.	6	12	42	9	6
GNP, constant dollars	n.a.	3	3	36	6	n.a.
Industrial production	14	14	8	36	12	27
Nonfarm employment	n.a.	n.a.	n.a.	43	11	22
Depth (percent):[†]						
GNP, current dollars	−23.9	−4.9	−3.0	−49.6	−16.2	−11.9
GNP, constant dollars	−15.8	−4.1	−2.0	−32.6	−18.2	n.a.
Industrial production	−32.4	−17.9	−7.0	−53.4	−32.4	−38.3
Nonfarm employment	−10.5	−2.2	−0.4	−31.6	−10.8	−10.1
Unemployment rate:[‡]						
Maximum	11.9	5.5	4.4	24.9	20.0	4.3
Increase	+10.3	+2.6	+2.4	+21.7	+9.0	+3.4
Diffusion (percent):[§]						
Nonfarm industries, maximum percentage with declining employment, and date when maximum was reached	97	94	71	100	97	n.a.
	Sept. 1920	Apr. 1924	Nov. 1927	June 1933	Dec. 1937	

n.a. = Not available.
* No decline.
[†] Percentage change from the peak month or quarter in the series to the trough month or quarter, over the intervals shown. For the unemployment rate the maximum figure is the highest for any month during the contraction, and the increases are from the lowest month to the highest, in percentage points.
[‡] Since monthly data are not available, annual figures are used from 1920 to 1933.

than the average since 1948. These intervals (the top line of Table 2) represent the consensus among a number of different measures of aggregate economic activity, some of which are shown in this table.

Business contractions vary in depth as well as length. In the Great Depression after 1929, gross national product fell by nearly half and even after allowance for the accompanying fall in the price level, the drop was nearly one third. None of the contractions since the end of World War II have approached this magnitude. The declines in real GNP have ranged from 1 to 4 percent. Similarly, the unemployment rate, which by 1933 had climbed to about 25 percent, has not gone higher than 11 percent in postwar recessions. It is important to note that the maximum level of unemployment reached during a recession does not always give the same reading on its relative severity as the increase in unemployment or the decline in employment or output. The 10.8

3 / SECURITY MARKETS AND BUSINESS CYCLES / 51

Nov. 1948 Oct. 1949	July 1953 May 1954	Aug. 1957 Apr. 1958	Apr. 1960 Feb. 1961	Dec. 1969 Nov. 1970	Nov. 1973 Mar. 1975	Jan. 1980 July 1980	July 1981 Nov. 1982
11	10	8	10	11	16	6	16
12	12	6	3	*	*	3	3
6	12	6	9	6	15	3	6
15	9	13	13	13	9	16	16
13	14	14	10	8	6	4	17
−3.4	−1.9	−2.8	−0.6	*	*	−0.1	−0.4
−1.5	−3.2	−3.3	−1.2	−1.0	−4.9	−2.5	−3.0
−10.1	−9.4	−13.5	−8.6	−6.8	−15.3	−8.6	−12.3
−5.2	−3.5	−4.3	−2.2	−1.5	−2.9	−1.4	−3.1
7.9	6.1	7.5	7.1	6.1	9.0	7.8	10.8
+4.5	+3.6	+3.8	+2.1	+2.7	+4.4	+2.1	+3.6
90	87	88	80	80	88	77	79
Feb. 1949	Mar. 1954	Sept. 1957	Oct. 1960	May 1970	Jan. 1975	Apr. 1980	Aug. 1982

§ Since 1948 based on changes in employment over six-month spans, centered on the fourth month of the span in 30 nonagricultural industries, 1948–59; 172 industries, 1960–1971; 186 industries, 1972–82. Prior to 1948 based on cyclical changes in employment in 41 industries.

SOURCES: U.S. Department of Commerce, U.S. Department of Labor, Board of Governors of the Federal Reserve System, National Bureau of Economic Research. For a fuller version of this table, see Solomon Fabricant, "The Recession of 1969–1970," in The Business Cycle Today, ed. V. Zarnowitz (Cambridge, Mass.: NBER, 1972), pp 100–110.

percent peak in unemployment during 1982 marked that recession as the worst since 1938, but that verdict is not supported by any of the other measures in the table.

Severe business contractions have wide repercussions throughout the economy, affecting not only production and employment, but also commodity prices, profits, interest rates, wages, stock prices, and many other aspects of economic life. Mild contractions are more scattered in their effects. This phenomenon of diffusion is illustrated in the bottom line of Table 2, in terms of the percentage of industries, among those that cover the entire nonfarm sector, in which employment declined. Even in the milder contractions, like those of 1926–27, 1960–61, and 1969–70, the percentage of industries registering declines ranged from 71 to 80. In the severe contractions of 1920–21, 1929–33, and 1937–38, the percentage reached as high as 97 to 100, virtually encompassing all industries. These pervasive movements naturally have a vital bearing on conditions in security markets.

The growth cycle concept referred to above has not yet come into wide use in the United States, but it may do so if recessions continue to become milder and if concern about even the mildest continues to mount. Recent research has identified 10 growth cycles during 1948–86. Six of the periods of slowdown overlapped the business cycle recessions of 1949, 1954, 1958, 1961, 1970, and 1975, while one growth cycle contraction encompassed two recessions: 1980–81 and 1981–82. These seven, of course, were the more serious episodes. Three milder slow-downs occurred in 1951–52, 1962–63, and 1966–67, interrupting the business cycle expansions of 1949–53 and 1961–69.

During the seven slowdowns that overlapped business cycle reces-sions, gross national product in constant dollars declined, though not in every quarter, at average rates of decline ranging from −0.5 percent per year in the mildest to −2.5 percent per year in the sharpest. In the other three slowdowns, real GNP continued to grow in most quarters, at rates that averaged about 2.5 percent per year in 1951–52, 3.5 percent in 1962–63, and 3 percent in 1966–67. During the 9 intervening upswings, on the other hand, growth rates ranged from 4 percent to nearly 12 percent and averaged 6 percent per year. As will be seen, even the milder slowdowns in economic growth have had significant effects on security markets.

STOCK PRICES AND BUSINESS CYCLES

The chronology of business cycles in Table 3 makes it easy to answer the question whether stock prices are higher at the top of a boom than at the bottom of a recession. The answer, surprisingly, is "most of the time but not always." On a number of occasions, most recently in 1953–54, 1960–61, 1980, and 1981–82, Standard & Poor's Index of 500 common stock prices was higher at the bottom of the business cycle contraction than it was when the recession began. The same was true of the Dow-Jones Industrials Index. In most cases, however, as Table 3 shows, the general level of stock prices has been much higher at the top of a boom than at the bottom of a recession. The average of 25 periods of business expansion from 1879 to 1981, shows the index rising 33 percent, or at an annual rate of 11 percent. The average of 26 periods of business contraction shows the index falling 8 percent or at a 2 percent annual rate. Clearly it is of importance from the investor's point of view to know when the turns in the business cycle occur.

The general correspondence between stock prices and business cycles does not mean that knowledge of the business cycle turns would enable one to pick out all the significant declines in stock prices. For example, substantial declines occurred in 1962 and 1966, when no

FIGURE 1   Stock Prices, Profits, Bond Yields, 1948–1985

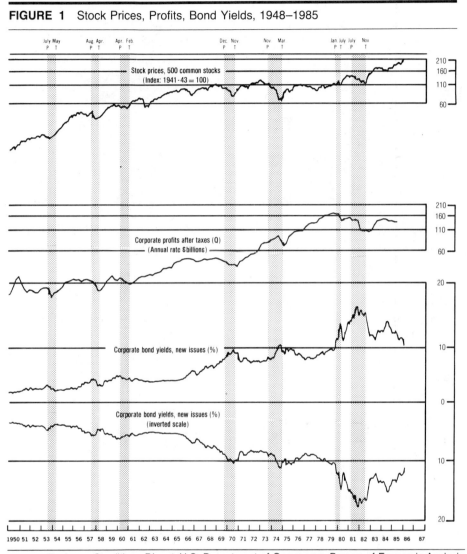

SOURCE: *Business Conditions Digest*, U.S. Department of Commerce, Bureau of Economic Analysis.

business cycle contraction is identified (see Figure 1). In both cases, however, slowdowns in economic growth did occur. The only instances since 1948 of an economic slowdown where there were no substantial declines in stock prices were in 1951–52 and 1980. Apart from these exceptions, the market has reflected all the slowdowns in the economy since 1948, and sustained declines in the market have not occurred at other times.[2]

The reason for most of the exceptions to the rule of higher stock

TABLE 3 Changes in Standard & Poor's Index of Common Stock Prices during Business Cycles, 1873–1982

Business Cycle		Index Standing* (1941–43 = 10) at		Percentage Change during		Length (in months) of		Annual Rate (in percent) of Change during	
Trough	Peak	Trough	Peak	Contraction†	Expansion‡	Contraction†	Expansion‡	Contraction†	Expansion‡
Dec. 1870	Oct. 1873		4.4	−14		65		−3	
Mar. 1879	Mar. 1882	3.8	6.0	−2	58	38	36	−9	16
May 1885	Mar. 1887	4.5	5.9	−10	31	13	22	−9	16
Apr. 1888	July 1890	5.3	5.7	−11	8	10	27	−13	3
May 1891	Jan. 1893	5.1	5.8	−22	14	17	20	−16	8
June 1894	Dec. 1895	4.5	4.6	−4	2	18	18	−3	1
June 1897	June 1899	4.4	6.4	11	45	18	24	7	20
Dec. 1900	Sept. 1902	7.1	9.1	−18	28	23	21	−10	15
Aug. 1904	May 1907	7.5	8.4	−5	12	13	33	−5	4
June 1908	Jan. 1910	8.0	10.4	−9	30	24	19	−5	18
Jan. 1912	Jan. 1913	9.5	9.6	−21	1	23	12	−12	1
Dec. 1914	Aug. 1918	7.6	8.0	8	5	7	44	14	1
Mar. 1919	Jan. 1920	8.6	9.1	−24	6	18	10	17	7
July 1921	May 1923	6.9	9.2	3	33	14	22	3	17
July 1924	Oct. 1926	9.5	13.5	26	42	13	27	24	17
Nov. 1927	Aug. 1929	17.0	28.5	−79	68	43	21	−35	35
Mar. 1933	May 1937	5.9	15.4	−32	161	13	50	−30	26
June 1938	Feb. 1945	10.4	13.8		33		80		4

Trough*		Stock Price Index	Peak*†		Stock Price Index	Percentage Change during		Length (in months) of		Annual Rate (in percent) of Change during	
						Contraction	Expansion	Contraction	Expansion	Contraction	Expansion
Oct.	1945	16.4	Nov.	1948	15.6	19	−5	8	37	30	−2
Oct.	1949	15.8	July	1953	24.2	1	53	11	45	1	12
May	1954	28.4	Aug.	1957	46.1	17	62	10	39	21	16
Apr.	1958	42.7	Apr.	1960	55.3	−7	30	8	24	−10	14
Feb.	1961	62.0	Dec.	1969	92.5	12	49	10	106	15	5
Nov.	1970	86.2	Nov.	1973	102.2	−7	19	11	36	−8	6
Mar.	1975	82.9	Jan.	1980	111.3	−19	34	16	58	−15	6
July	1980	119.3	July	1981	130.3	7	9	6	12	14	6
Nov.	1982	136.7				5		16		4	9

Summary

	Percentage Change during		Length (in months) of		Annual Rate (in percent) of Change during	
	Contraction	Expansion	Contraction	Expansion	Contraction	Expansion
Average, 1873–1982	−8	33	18	34	−2	11
Average, 1873–1948	−12	32	21	29	−3	12
Average, 1948–1982	1	37	11	45	3	10

* Three months average centered on business cycle peak or trough month.
† From peak on preceding line to trough.
‡ From trough to peak.
SOURCE: Standard & Poor's Corporation.

prices at the peak than at the trough of the business cycle is not that stocks were not depressed by the business recession, but rather that they began to decline sooner and to recover earlier than business activity as a whole. For example, in 1981–82, the Standard & Poor's Index reached its highest monthly average (136) in November 1980, eight months before the business cycle peak in July 1981, by which time the index had dropped to 129. The decline in the index continued for a year, reaching bottom in July 1982 at 109. From then on it rose vigorously, so that by the time the November 1982 trough in the business cycle had arrived the index was 138, 7 percent higher than its level at the previous business cycle peak. The December 1980–July 1982 decline in the index was evidently associated with the business recession but occurred much earlier (see Figure 1).

Table 4 shows that this tendency for stock prices to lead the business cycle has persisted for many years. Since 1873, it has happened at 20 of

TABLE 4   Leads and Lags of Common Stock Price Index at Business Cycle Peaks and Troughs, 1873–1982

				Lead (−) or Lag (+) (in months) at	
Peak		Trough		Peak	Trough
Oct.	1873	Mar.	1879	−17	−21
Mar.	1882	May	1885	−9	−4
Mar.	1887	April	1888	+2	+2
July	1890	May	1891	−2	−5
Jan.	1893	June	1894	−5	+9
Dec.	1895	June	1897	−3	−10
June	1899	Dec.	1900	−2	−3
Sept.	1902	Aug.	1904	0	−10
May	1907	June	1908	−8	−7
Jan.	1910	Jan.	1912	−1	−18
Jan.	1913	Dec.	1914	−4	0
Aug.	1918	Mar.	1919	−21	−15
Jan.	1920	July	1921	−6	+1
May	1923	July	1924	−2	−9
Oct.	1926	Nov.	1927	n.s.	n.s.
Aug.	1929	Mar.	1933	+1	−9
May	1937	June	1938	−3	−2
Feb.	1945	Oct.	1945	n.s.	n.s.
Nov.	1948	Oct.	1949	−5	−4
July	1953	May	1954	−6	−7
Aug.	1957	April	1958	−13	−4
April	1960	Feb.	1961	−9	−4
Dec.	1969	Nov.	1970	−12	−5
Nov.	1973	Mar.	1975	−10	−3
Jan.	1980	July	1980	n.s.	n.s.
July	1981	Nov.	1982	−8	−4

TABLE 4 *(concluded)*

Summary

	1873–1982			1873–1945			1948–1982		
	Peak	*Trough*	*Peak & Trough*	*Peak*	*Trough*	*Peak & Trough*	*Peak*	*Trough*	*Peak & Trough*
Median lead, in months	−5	−4	−5	−3	−6	−4	−9	−4	−6
Average lead, in months	−6	−6	−6	−5	−6	−6	−9	−4	−7
Longest lead, in months	−21	−21	−21	−21	−21	−21	−13	−13	−13
Shortest lead or longest lag, in months	+2	+9	+9	+2	+9	+9	−5	−3	−3
Number of: Leads six months or longer	11	9	20	5	8	13	6	1	7
Leads five months or shorter	9	10	19	8	4	12	1	6	7
Exact coincidences	1	1	2	1	1	2	0	0	0
Lags	2	3	5	2	3	5	0	0	0
Percent of timing comparisons that were leads	87	83	85	81	75	78	100	100	100

n.s. = No specific cycle.

SOURCE: Standard & Poor's index of common stock prices: industrials, rails, and utilities. For 1873–1945 leads and lags are from *Business Cycle Indicators*, ed. G. H. Moore. (Princeton, N.J.: Princeton University Press, 1961), pp. 674, 677. For 1948–1982, *Business Conditions Digest*, June 1973; August 1985.

the 26 business cycle peaks and at 19 of the 26 troughs. Since 1948, stock prices led 14 out of 16 business cycle peaks and troughs. The average lead is around five or six months, but there have been wide variations around the average. Table 4 also shows that there have been only three occasions since 1873 when a business recession occurred but no cyclical decline in stock prices was associated with it. One was during the recession that briefly interrupted the boom of the 1920s, in 1926–27; another was in the short "reconversion" recession after World War II, in 1945; the third was during the short recession in the first half of 1980. In all instances, the decline in business activity was relatively mild.

Does the systematic lead in stock prices mean that stock market investors forecast turns in the business cycle, or that they react to other developments that also lead, or that movements in stock prices produce conditions that help to generate the business cycle? Possibly all these factors are at work, but we shall concentrate on two factors that may help to account for the lead: profits and interest rates. Table 5 pulls together some relevant information on profits. Although the turning points in profits and in stock prices do not occur at precisely the same time (the leads would be identical if they did), the tendency is clearly in that direction.[3] It seems reasonable to suppose that promptly available information and astute guesses about profit trends would influence the market and help to account for its propensity to lead the business cycle. Since other leading indicators such as new orders, housing starts, defense contracts, and construction contracts also have a bearing upon profits prospects, they also influence the thinking of investors about the value of equities and contribute to the lead in stock prices.

Although increases in profits are likely to have a favorable effect on stock prices, increases in interest rates are likely to have an unfavorable effect. The higher the discount rate applied to future earnings, the lower the capital value of the equity. The higher the yield on bonds, the more attractive they become as an alternative to holding common stock. Higher interest rates and the accompanying reduced availability of credit may diminish the propensity of investors to borrow in order to buy stocks. Higher interest rates increase the cost of doing business, notably the cost of holding inventory and of accounts receivable, and hence may adversely affect profit margins in certain trades. Thus, increases in interest rates tend to depress stock prices, and the sharper the rise, the greater the effect is likely to be.

Interest rates often do not begin to rise, or do not begin to rise rapidly, for some months after a business upswing gets under way. Often they rise fastest in the late stages of the upswing, as a result of restrictions on the supply of money and credit. Such a development can depress the stock market even though business activity itself is still expanding. If this surge in interest rates is coupled with a profit squeeze

TABLE 5 Leads and Lags of Corporate Profits and Stock Prices at Business Cycle Peaks and Troughs, 1921–1982

Business Cycle		Lead (−) or Lag (+) in Months, at Business Cycle Peaks and Troughs			
		Corporate Profits after Taxes		Stock Price Index Standard & Poor's 500	
Peak	Trough	Peak	Trough	Peak	Trough
	July 1921		−2		+1
May 1923	July 1924	0	+1	−2	−9
Oct. 1926	Nov. 1927	−2	0	n.s.	n.s.
Aug. 1929	Mar. 1933	0	−7	+1	−9
May 1937	June 1938	−6	−1	−3	−2
Feb. 1945	Oct. 1945	−12	+1	n.s.	n.s.
Nov. 1948	Oct. 1949	−6	−5	−5	−4
July 1953	May 1954	−2	−6	−6	−7
Aug. 1957	April 1958	−21	−2	−13	−4
April 1960	Feb. 1961	−11	0	−9	−4
Dec. 1969	Nov. 1970	−13	0	−12	−5
Nov. 1973	Mar 1975	+9	−1	−10	−3
Jan. 1980	July 1980	−5	−2	n.s.	n.s.
July 1981	Nov. 1982	−5	+3	−8	−4

Summary, Peaks and Troughs

	1921–1982		1921–1945		1948–1982	
	Corporate Profits	Stock Prices	Corporate Profits	Stock Prices	Corporate Profits	Stock Prices
Median lead, in months	−2	−5	−1	−2	−5	−6
Average lead, in months	−4	−6	−3	−3	−4	−7
Longest lead, in months	−20	−12	−12	−9	−21	−13
Shortest lead (or longest lag) in months	+9	+1	+1	+1	+9	−3
Number of leads six months or longer	8	9	3	2	5	7
Leads five months or shorter	10	10	3	3	7	7
Exact coincidences	5	0	3	0	2	0
Lags	4	2	2	2	2	0

n.s. = No specific cycle.

SOURCE: For stock prices, see Table 4. For leads and lags in corporate profits after taxes, from 1921 to 1958, see *Business Cycle Indicators*, ed. G. H. Moore (Princeton, N.J.: Princeton University Press, 1961), pp. 674–77. For 1960–1982, see *Handbook of Cyclical Indicators* (Washington, D.C.: U.S. Commerce Department 1984), p. 143.

that also antedates the business downturn, as frequently happens, stock prices can drop sharply even while business is good and getting better.

A similar sequence of events can be described during a business cycle contraction to account for upturns in stock prices prior to the upturn in business. The fall in interest rates helps the market for stocks, and if the customary early upturn in profits also occurs, optimism among investors in common stocks is doubly justified even though business activity is still depressed and sliding downward.

BOND PRICES, INTEREST RATES, AND BUSINESS CYCLES

Among the interrelated factors that pull interest rates and bond yields upward during a business expansion are: (1) the rising demand for business credit, both for operating purposes and for capital investment; (2) the rising demand for mortgage credit, both residential and nonresidential; (3) the rising demand for consumer credit; (4) the widening expectation of an increase in the rate of inflation, which makes lenders reluctant to lend at the same interest rate and borrowers more willing to pay a higher rate; and (5) the sluggish response of the supply of lendable funds. During a business cycle contraction, all or most of these factors operate in reverse and bring interest rates down.

Certain types of interest rates reflect these forces more promptly and in larger degree than other types. Short-term rates on marketable securities such as Treasury bills, federal funds, and commercial paper are the most sensitive. New issue yields on corporate bonds are more sensitive than yields on outstanding issues. Bank rates on business loans, mortgage rates, and rates on consumer loans are relatively sluggish. Not only do they typically move in a narrower range, they usually begin their moves later. As a rule, returns on securities traded in the open market move earlier, more frequently, and by larger amounts than rates on sparsely traded debt instruments.

Table 6 illustrates some of these differences for Treasury bills and corporate bond yields. T bill rates have usually turned a month or two before or after the business cycle peak or trough, while yields on outstanding bonds (high-grade) have usually turned later, especially at troughs. Yields on new issues of corporate bonds (shown in Figure 1) usually turn earlier than those on outstanding issues and hence at about the same time as T bill rates. The basis point change from the peak to the trough of the business cycle has generally been much larger for T bills than for bonds, as the table shows.

Although it is customary to look upon interest rates as being pulled up by a rising demand for funds operating against a sluggish supply during a cyclical expansion and as being pushed down by a declining demand during a contraction, it is also possible to look at them in a

TABLE 6 Leads and Lags and Rates of Change in Treasury Bill Rates and Corporate Bond Yields during Business Cycles, 1920–1982

(1)	(2)	(3)	(4)	(5)	(6)	(7)	(8)	(9)	(10)	(11)	(12)
Business Cycle		Lead (−) or Lag (+), in Months, at Business Cycle				Lead (−) or Lag (+) in Months of Bond Yields versus Bill Rates at		Change in Bill Rates and Bond Yields, in Basis Points per Month, during Business Cycle			
		Trough		Peak		Trough	Peak	Contraction		Expansion	
Trough	Peak	Treasury Bill Rate	Corporate Bond Yield	Treasury Bill Rate	Corporate Bond Yield			Bills	Bonds	Bills	Bonds
March 1919	January 1920		−1	+5	+5		0	2.4	1.8		3.9
July 1921	May 1923	+13	+14	−2	−1	+1	+1	−16.4	−1.5	−4.8	−4.2
July 1924	October 1926	+1		−11				−3.4	−1.7	5.9	−1.0
November 1927	August 1929	−2	+5	−3	+1	+7	+4	−10.7	−0.3	9.3	1.4
March 1933	May 1937	+35*	+46*	−1*	−1*	+11*	0*	−4.6	−0.8	−1.0	−2.6
June 1938	February 1945	+31*	+30*		+35*	−1*		0.0	−0.4	0.4	−0.7
October 1945	November 1948		+6		−9			−0.6	−1.9	2.1	0.0
October 1949	July 1953		+8	−1	−1	+3	0	−13.2	−6.9	2.4	1.5
May 1954	August 1957	+2	+5	−2	0	0	+2	−28.4	−13.9	6.7	5.2
April 1958	April 1960	+2	+2	−4	−3	+27	+1	−8.3	−5.4	8.8	5.4
February 1961	December 1969	−2	+25†	+1	+6	−1	+5	−22.1	2.3	5.0	4.5
November 1970	November 1973	+15	+14	+9	+10	+1	+1	−14.6	9.6	7.2	−2.8
March 1975	January 1980	+21	+22	+2	+2	0	0	−65.2	−1.4	11.2	3.7
July 1980	July 1981	−1	−1	−2	+1	+7	+3	−41.6	−23.6	54.7	34.9
November 1982		−1	+6								
Average, 1920–1982		+5	+9	−1	+1	+5	+2	−16.2	−3.1	8.3	3.5

* Excluded from average.
† This comparison ignores the minor rise in the series from September 1960 to September 1961.

SOURCE: Philip Cagan, "Changes in the Cyclical Behavior of Interest Rates," in *Essays on Interest Rates*, vol. II. ed., Jack M. Guttentag (Cambridge, Mass.: NBER, 1971), pp. 23–32. Bill rates are seasonally adjusted before 1931 and from 1947–61; bond yields are seasonally adjusted 1948–61 only. Unadjusted data, used from 1969, are from *Handbook of Cyclical Indicators* (Washington, D.C.: U.S. Department of Commerce, 1984), p. 101.

different way. Interest payments are a part of the cost of doing business, and an increase in rates can act as a deterrent to new investment. The cost of holding inventories and of account receivables is particularly sensitive to interest changes. High rates may make an industrial or commercial building project look less profitable and cause plans to be cut back or canceled. Tight money and the accompanying high mortgage rates have a particularly prompt and substantial depressing effect on new housing starts. Although high yields on bonds enhance their attractiveness as far as investors are concerned, they have the opposite effect on borrowers, and new issues of bonds may be postponed in the belief that yields will go lower.

From this point of view—that is, looking at the cyclical effects of changes in interest rates rather than their causes—it is useful to compare upturns in rates with subsequent downturns in business and downturns in rates with subsequent upturns in business.

For example, the peak in corporate bond yields in March 1980, which is treated in Table 6 as a lag of two months behind the January 1980 business cycle peak, can also be looked on as a lead of four months before the July 1980 business cycle trough. Since bond prices move inversely to bond yields, this is equivalent to comparing the trough in bond prices with the trough in business. From some viewpoints this is a simpler way to put it, and Table 7 is drawn up on this basis. It shows not only that bond prices lead the business cycle but also that their leads are substantially longer than those of stock prices. Hence bond prices also lead stock prices. The leads vary greatly in length, averaging around a year at peaks and a half year at troughs.[4]

The average sequence during 1920–82 that emerges from the records presented in Tables 6 and 7 is as follows:

	Months
From business cycle trough to bond yield trough (bond price peak)—Table 6, column 4	8
From bond yield trough to stock price peak— Table 7, column 8	13
From stock price peak to business cycle peak— Table 7, column 6	7
From business cycle peak to bond yield peak— Table 6, column 6	1
From bond yield peak to stock price trough— Table 7, column 7	6
From stock price trough to business cycle trough— Table 7, column 4	5

Although the order in which these turning points in financial markets and in business activity have occurred has been followed with considerable fidelity, the length of the intervals has varied enormously.

TABLE 7 Leads and Lags of Corporate Bond Prices and Stock Prices During Business Cycles, 1920–1982

(1) (2) Business Cycle		(3) (4) (5) (6) Lead (−) or Lag (+), in Months, at Business Cycle				(7) (8) Lead (−) or Lag (+) in Months, of Bond Prices versus Stock Prices	
		Trough		Peak			
Trough	Peak	Corporate Bond Prices	Stock Prices	Corporate Bond Prices	Stock Prices	Trough	Peak
Mar. 1919	Jan. 1920			−11	−6		−5
July 1921	May 1923	−13	+1	−8	−2	−14	−6
July 1924	Oct. 1926	−15	−9			−6	
Nov. 1927	Aug. 1929			−16	+1		−17
Mar. 1933	May 1937	−9	−9	−4	−3	0	−1
June 1938	Feb. 1945	−14	−2			−12	
Oct. 1945	Nov. 1948				−5		
Oct. 1949	July 1953		−4	−37	−6		−31
May 1954	Aug. 1957	−10	−7	−35	−13	−3	−22
April 1958	April 1960	−8	−4	−22	−9	−4	−13
Feb. 1961	Dec. 1969	−13	−4	−34	−12	−9	−22
Nov. 1970	Nov. 1973	−5	−5	−22	−10	0	−12
Mar. 1975	Jan. 1980	−6	−3	−37	n.s.	−3	
July 1980	July 1981	−4	n.s.	−13	−8		−5
Nov. 1982		−14	−4			−10	
Average, 1920–1982		−10	−5	−22	−7	−6	−13

SOURCE: Based on Tables 4 and 6. The peaks and troughs in bond prices are taken to be the same as the troughs and peaks in bond yields, respectively.

Hence, the average intervals are of little or no value in pinpointing a future turning point. Moreover, as the blank spaces in the tables indicate, turning points in bond yields, stock prices, and business cycles do not always match, in which case the sequence cannot even be recorded. This means, of course, that many other factors play a part in financial markets. Nevertheless, the sequence has occurred often enough over a long period—it can be traced back to the 1870s—and has survived severe disturbances like the Great Depression of the 1930s and economic controls of World War II. Thus, one can be reasonably confident that it reflects persistent tendencies in the adjustment of financial markets to economic conditions.

THE VOLUME OF STOCK AND BOND FINANCING DURING BUSINESS CYCLES

The most comprehensive study of corporate bond financing during business cycles was conducted during the late 1940s and early 1950s by W. Braddock Hickman for the National Bureau of Economic Research. He covered the period 1900 to 1938 and drew the following conclusion regarding the relationships of bond to stock financing over the various stages of the business cycle:

> While bond extinguishments [repayments plus refundings] usually rise through the expansion phase of the cycle and fall through the contraction phase, bond offerings are usually inverted, rising during most of the contraction phase and falling during most of the expansion. The net change in outstandings—the difference between offerings and extinguishments—consequently shows an inverse relationship to the rise and fall of general business activity. . . .
>
> The conclusion that, on balance, corporations obtain an increasing volume of funds through the bond market during periods of contraction and a decreasing volume during periods of expansion leads to the question, where, then, do corporations obtain funds to meet the increasing monetary requirements of expansion phases? Among the alternative sources of capital funds employed by corporations, a principal one during the period studied was the stock market. The behavior of stock offerings shows that corporations typically obtain an increasing volume of funds in the stock market during expansion stages, when net bond financing declines, and a decreasing amount during contraction stages, when net bond financing expands. Stock and bond financing thus appear to complement each other over the various stages of the cycle. . . . From analysis of the cyclical movements in the net-change series and its components in relation to bond and stock prices, it appears that both the new-money components and total offerings tend to be directly associated with bond prices, while both repayments and total extinguishments are associated with stock prices [and stock offerings]. Since the relation between bond and stock prices during business cycles is complex, and since the price factors do not play with equal strength on the

components of net change in bond financing, no simple formula in terms of bond or stock prices seems adequate to explain the behavior of the net change. In general, however, when the ratio of stock to bond prices turns downward during the contraction stages of the business cycle, corporations tend to shift their financing from the stock to the bond market; and conversely, when the ratio of stock to bond prices turns upward during expansion stages, corporations shift from the bond to the stock market.[5]

In the decades since 1938, where Hickman's study stopped, there has been a vast growth in the volume of stock and bond financing, a sharply rising trend in stock prices and bond yields, and a fall in bond prices. To some extent these trends obscure the cyclical movements, especially because the business cycle contractions have been short. Nevertheless, Table 8 suggests that many of Hickman's conclusions regarding the behavior of the markets before 1938 have remained valid.

Common stock offerings rose during seven of the eight business expansions from 1946 to 1981 and fell in five of the eight contractions (1953–54, 1957–58, 1969–70, 1973–75, and 1981–82). Offerings of preferred stock (which Hickman did not distinguish) have behaved in the manner he described for bonds. They declined in five of the expansions and increased in seven of the contractions, thus conforming inversely to the business cycle. The shift toward common and away from preferred stock financing during the business upswing and the reversal during the downswing appears to reflect cyclical shifts in investor confidence, with prosperity favoring the riskier security and recession favoring the safer.

Bond offerings, on the whole, have not shown as much inverse conformity to the cycle since 1946 as Hickman found for the earlier period. Nevertheless, bond offerings did increase during six of the eight contractions since 1946. Moreover, the ratio of stock to bond offerings usually rose during business expansions and fell during contractions.

In terms of the annual figures used in Table 8, common stock prices rose in seven of the eight business expansions since 1946, while bond prices fell. Hence, the ratio of stock to bond prices conformed positively to the business cycle as a whole.

We end up, then, with a picture resembling Hickman's description, with corporate financing shifting from stocks toward bonds as the price ratio of stocks to bonds becomes less favorable for stocks during the contraction phase of the business cycle and back toward stocks as the price ratio becomes more favorable for stocks during the expansion phase of the cycle. A similar cyclical shift occurs in the relative volume of offerings of common and preferred stock, with preferred stock taking on the character of bonds in this context. It seems fair to say, therefore, that the long record of past experience in security markets during business cycles can serve broadly to illuminate current developments and prospects and can contribute to a better understanding of the factors that have a significant bearing on the outcome of security investments.

TABLE 8 Stock and Bond Prices and the Volume of Offerings during Business Cycles, 1946–1982

Business Cycle		Corporate Securities Offered for Cash ($ millions)						Ratio, Common to Preferred Stock Offerings at		Ratio, Common Stock to Bond Offerings at		Ratio, Preferred Stock to Bond Offerings at	
		Common Stock at		Preferred Stock at		Bonds and Notes at							
T	P	T	P	T	P	T	P	T	P	T	P	T	P
1946	1948	891	614	1,127	492	4,882	5,973	0.79	1.25	0.18	0.10	0.23	0.08
1949	1953	736	1,326	425	489	4,890	7,083	1.73	2.71	0.15	0.19	0.09	0.07
1954	1957	1,213	2,516	816	411	7,488	9,957	1.49	6.12	0.16	0.25	0.11	0.04
1958	1960	1,334	1,664	571	409	9,653	8,081	2.34	4.07	0.14	0.21	0.06	0.05
1961	1969	3,294	7,714	450	682	9,420	18,348	7.32	11.31	0.35	0.42	0.05	0.04
1970	1973	7,037	7,642	1,390	3,371	29,023	20,700	5.06	2.27	0.24	0.37	0.05	0.16
1975	1979	7,414	8,816	3,459	1,964	42,759	26,468	2.14	4.48	0.17	0.33	0.08	0.07
1980	1981	19,282	25,226	3,194	1,696	44,650	38,966	6.04	14.87	0.43	0.65	0.07	0.04
1982		23,197		4,948		44,007		4.69		0.53		0.11	
Average 1946–1981		5,150	6,940	1,429	1,189	19,096	16,947	3.36	5.88	0.23	0.32	0.09	0.07
Conformity Index*		+50		−50		−25		+50		+50		−71	

TABLE 8 *(concluded)*

Business Cycle		Common Stock Price Index (1941–1943 = 10) at		Corporate Bond Yield Moody's AAA (%) at		Corporate Bond Price, S&P's AAA (dollars) at		Ratio, Common Stock Price Index to Bond Price at	
T	P	T	P	T	P	T	P	T	P
1946	1948	17	16	2.53	2.82	123	118	0.14	0.14
1949	1953	15	25	2.66	3.20	121	112	0.12	0.22
1954	1957	30	44	2.90	3.89	117	101	0.26	0.44
1958	1960	46	56	3.79	4.41	103	95	0.45	0.58
1961	1969	66	98	4.35	7.03	95	69	0.69	1.42
1970	1973	83	107	8.04	7.44	62	64	1.34	1.67
1975	1979	86	103	8.83	9.63	56	51	1.54	2.02
1980	1981	119	128	11.94	14.17	41	34	2.90	3.76
1982		120		13.79		36		3.33	
Average 1946–1981		58	72	5.63	6.57	90	81	1.20	1.28
Conformity Index*		+38		+50		−47		+47	

* Number of positively conforming movements minus number of inversely conforming movements divided by the total (16). Positively conforming movements are increases from business trough to following business cycle peak and decreases from peak to following trough. Inversely conforming movements are the opposite. If all movements conform positively the index is +100; if all conform inversely, −100.

SOURCE: Securities and Exchange Commission, Standard & Poor's Corporation, and Moody's Investor Service.

ENDNOTES

1. Wesley C. Mitchell and Arthur F. Burns, *Measuring Business Cycles* (New York: NBER, 1946), p. 3.
2. For further analysis of the relation between stock prices and growth cycles, see Geoffrey H. Moore, "Stock Prices and the Business Cycle," *The Journal of Portfolio Management* 1, no. 3 (Spring 1975), pp. 59–64.
3. The correlation (r) between the length of lead in stock prices and in profits, based on the figures in Table 5, is + .46.
4. The correlation (r) between the length of lead in stock prices and in bond prices, based on the figures in Table 7, is + .56.
5. W. Braddock Hickman, *The Volume of Corporate Bond Financing since 1900* (New York: NBER, 1953), pp. 132–34.

SUGGESTED READINGS

BURNS, ARTHUR F. *Stock Market Cycle Research*. New York: Twentieth Century Fund, Inc., 1930.

CAGAN, PHILLIP. "The Recent Cyclical Movements of Interest Rates in Historical Perspective." *Business Economics*, January 1972.

CONARD, JOSEPH W. *The Behavior of Interest Rates: A Progress Report*. New York: NBER, 1966.

CULLITY, JOHN P. "Signals of Cyclical Movements in Inflation and Interest Rates." Center for International Business Cycle Research, Columbia University, New York, 1986, (*Financial Analysts Journal*, September 1987).

FRIEDMAN, MILTON, and ANNA JACOBSON SCHWARTZ. *A Monetary History of the United States, 1867–1960*. New York: NBER, 1963.

GUTTENTAG, JACK M., and PHILLIP CAGAN, eds. *Essays on Interest Rates, Vol. I*, New York: NBER, 1969.

———. *Essays on Interest Rates, Vol. II*. New York: NBER, 1971.

HAMBURGER, MICHAEL J., and LEVIS A. KOCHIN. "Money and Stock Prices: The Channels of Influence." *Journal of Finance*, May 1972, pp. 231–49.

HICKMAN, W. BRADDOCK. *The Volume of Corporate Bond Financing*. New York: NBER, 1953.

———. *Corporate Bond Quality and Investor Experience*. New York: NBER, 1858.

KERAN, MICHAEL W. "Expectations, Money and the Stock Market," *Federal Reserve Bank of St. Louis Review*, January 1971.

KINDLEBERGER, CHARLES P. *Manias, Panics, and Crashes: A History of Financial Crises*. New York: Basic Books, 1978.

KLEIN, PHILIP A., and GEOFFREY H. MOORE. "Monitoring Profits during Business Cycles." Proceedings of 25th CIRET Conference, Athens, Greece, London: Gowen Publishing, 1981.

MACAULAY, FREDERICK R. *The Movements of Interest Rates, Bond Yields and Stock Prices in the United States since 1856*. New York: NBER, 1938.

MENNIS, EDMUND A. "Security Prices and Business Cycles." *Financial Analysts Journal*, February 1955.

MENNIS, EDMUND A. "Security Prices and Business Cycles." *Financial Analysts Journal*, February 1955.

MILLER, MERTON H. "Discussion." *Journal of Finance*, May 1972, pp. 294–98.

MITCHELL, WESLEY C. "The Prices of American Stocks: 1890–1909." *Journal of Political Economy*, May 1910, pp. 97–113.

————. "Rates of Interest and Prices of Investment Securities: 1890–1909." *Journal of Political Economy*, April 1911, pp. 269–308.

————. *Business Cycles and Their Causes.* Berkeley: University of California Press, 1941.

————. *What Happens during Business Cycles: A Progress Report.* New York: NBER, 1951.

MOORE, GEOFFREY H., ed. *Business Cycle Indicators.* New York: NBER, 1961.

————. "Inflation and Profits." *Business Cycles, Inflation, and Forecasting*, 2d ed. NBER Studies in Business Cycles, No. 24. Cambridge, Mass.: Ballinger, 1983, pp. 281–86.

————. "Why Stock Prices Are a Leading Indicator." *International Economic Scoreboard*, The Conference Board, 10/1982.

MORGENSTERN, OSCAR. *International Financial Transactions and Business Cycles.* New York: NBER, 1959.

POTERBA, JAMES M., and SUMMERS, LAWRENCE H. "The Persistence of Volatility and Stock Market Fluctuations." National Bureau of Economic Research Working Paper 1462, Cambridge, September 1984.

SELDEN, RICHARD T. *Trends and Cycles in the Commercial Paper Market.* New York: NBER, 1963.

SPRINKEL, BERYL W. *Money and Stock Prices.* Homewood, Ill.: Richard D. Irwin, Inc., 1964.

————. *Money and Markets: A Monetarist View.* Homewood, Ill.: Richard D. Irwin, Inc., 1971.

4

Economic Indicators and Their Significance

Nathan Belfer, Ph.D., CFA
Consultant
Wood, Struthers & Winthrop Management Corp.

The analyst is basically concerned with forecasting the prospects of the companies he is interested in. Most, if not all, companies are subject to the vagaries of the business cycle. It is, therefore, important for the security analyst to be acquainted with the details of economic forecasting.

Many indicators of cyclical movements have been developed by the National Bureau of Economic Research, the Federal Reserve Board, and the U.S. Department of Commerce, among others. These are in such areas as money and credit, production, capital spending, employment and unemployment, consumption, income, prices, profits, and costs. The classification of composite indexes is shown in Table 1.

As a result, a vast amount of statistical data relating to the performance of the economy is available. The basic purpose of all these data is to determine where the economy has been, where it is now, and where it is going in the future. In order to simplify the analysis of all this material, economic forecasters have singled out 22 of the most important of the statistical series. These key indicators include 12 leading indicators, 4 coincident indicators, and 6 lagging indicators.

The remainder of this section will be devoted to a discussion of the leading, lagging, and coincident economic indicators. There will be a brief discussion of each, and an attempt will be made to indicate which are the most useful for the security analyst.

Two monthly publications can give the analyst considerable current data on these key economic indicators. These are *Economic Indicators*, published monthly by the Council of Economic Advisors, and *Business*

70

Conditions Digest, a monthly publication of the U.S. Department of Commerce.

LEADING INDICATORS

The leading indicators (Figure 1) are supposed to have forecasting value and should highlight what may happen in the economy six to nine months in the future. These indicators will be discussed briefly.

Average Workweek, Production Workers, Manufacturing

This leading indicator points out the length of the average number of hours worked per week in manufacturing. An increase obviously indicates heightened economic activity in production. Conversely, a downturn is a forecast of declining activity in manufacturing. The workweek changes first because it is a more flexible way to adjust labor input to demand. Some work done at the National Bureau of Economic Research indicates that this index precedes business cycle turning points by about four months. However, the lead period is somewhat longer at peaks than at troughs. It is a useful indicator for the analyst.

Average Weekly Initial Claims for State Unemployment Insurance

This indicator indicates the number of new claims being made each week for unemployment insurance. Its significance lies in the fact that turning points in this index have preceded those in total unemployment. An increase is obviously an unfavorable sign. A decline is an indication that fewer people are being thrown out of work and can be interpreted favorably.

Manufacturers' New Orders (in 1982 dollars), Consumer Goods, and Materials Industries

This is a very significant indicator. An increase is quite bullish, as it shows that manufacturers and retailers are increasing orders in anticipation of favorable business conditions in the future. An increase in activity in the consumer goods and materials industries has a future multiplier effect on the total economy. Conversely, a decline can be interpreted bearishly for the future of the economy. A study made by the National Bureau of Economic Research indicates that this index leads general business conditions by about five months. This indicator is adjusted for inflation by being expressed in 1982 dollars.

TABLE 1 Classification of Composite Index Components by Economic Process

Economic Process / Index	I. Employment and Unemployment	II. Production and Income	III. Consumption, Trade, Orders, and Deliveries	IV. Fixed Capital Investment	V. Inventories and Inventory Investment	VI. Prices, Costs, and Profits	VII. Money and Credit
Leading indicators	1. Average weekly hours of production or nonsupervisory workers, manufacturing 5. Average weekly initial claims for unemployment insurance, state programs		8. Manufacturers' new orders in 1982 dollars, consumer goods and materials industries 32. Vendor performance, percent of companies receiving slower deliveries	12. Index of net business formation 20. Contracts and orders for plant and equipment in 1982 dollars 29. Index of new private housing units authorized by local building permits	36. Change in manufacturing and trade inventories on hand and on order in 1982 dollars, smoothed	99. Change in sensitive materials prices, smoothed 19. Index of stock prices, 500 common stocks	106. Money supply M2 in 1982 dollars 111. Change in business and consumer credit outstanding
Coincident indicators	41. Employees on nonagricul-	51. Personal income less trans-	57. Manufacturing and trade				

	tural pay-rolls	fer pay-ments in 1982 dol-lars	sales in 1982 dol-lars			
		47. Index of industrial production				
Lagging indi-cators	91. Average duration of unemploy-ment in weeks			77. Ratio, manufac-turing and trade in-ventories to sales in 1982 dol-lars	62. Index of labor cost per unit of output, manufac-turing—ac-tual data as a per-cent of trend	109. Aver-age prime rate charged by banks
						101. Com-mercial and indus-trial loans outstand-ing in 1982 dollars
						95. Ratio, consumer installment credit out-standing to personal income

SOURCE: *Handbook of Cyclical Indicators*, Bureau of Economic Analysis, U.S. Department of Commerce, 1984 (updated to reflect adjustments to 1982 dollars).

FIGURE 1 Leading Index Components

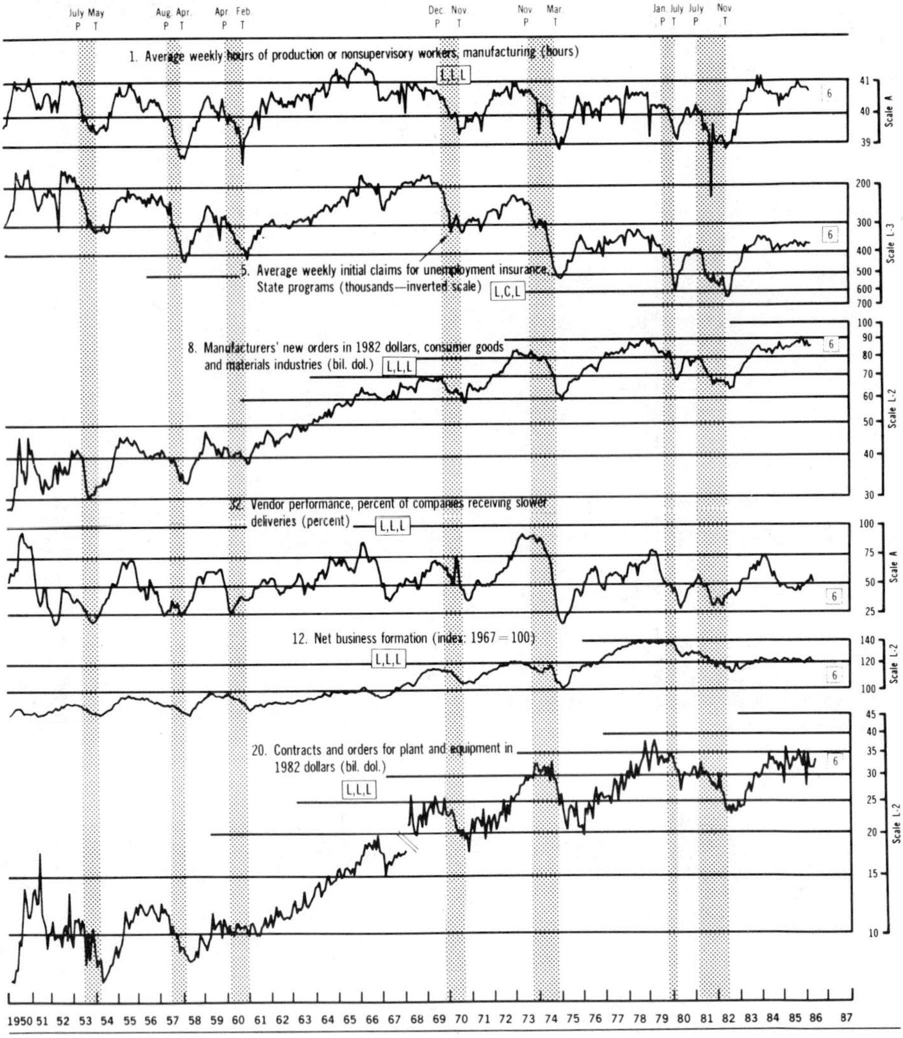

Vendor Performance, Percent of Companies Receiving Slower Deliveries

With an increase in business activity, orders and backlogs will increase. This will result in slower deliveries by suppliers. In a downturn, vendors will be able to fill orders more promptly.

FIGURE 1   *(concluded)*

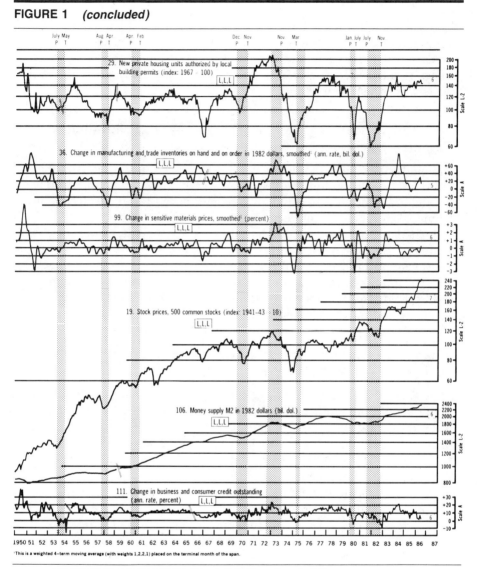

SOURCE: *Business Conditions Digest,* U.S. Department of Commerce.

Index of Net Business Formation

This is a measure of the net number of new businesses formed each month. An increase obviously is a symptom of improved profit opportunities and an indication of heightened business activity in the future. Conversely, a decline is a possible harbinger of lower activity in the future.

Contracts and Orders for Plant and Equipment

This also is a significant indicator. An increase in plant and equipment ordering indicates optimism concerning the future. In addition, increased orders for plant and equipment could have a future multiplier effect on other sectors of the economy. This index is expressed in 1982 dollars to adjust for inflation.

New Private Housing Units Authorized by Local Building Permits

This index measures the number of new private housing units authorized in local communities. An increase in building permits today should result in increased building activity in the future. A decline in permits is an indicator of declining housing activity in the future.

The lag between new building permits and new housing starts is generally several months. However, the lag may be distorted by seasonal weather factors and shortages of building materials and labor.

The figure on new building permits does not include mobile homes. This may diminish somewhat the significance of the index because of the increased importance of mobile home production.

Change in Manufacturing and Trade Inventories on Hand and on Order, Adjusted for Inflation

This index measures the month-to-month change in manufacturing and trade inventories. In a period of rising economic activity, inventories should be increasing. In a period of declining economic expectations, businesses will tend to allow their inventories to decline.

While this has been a fairly reliable leading indicator, it has not behaved normally recently. Increases in consumer spending and in spending on plant and equipment have not always been accompanied by proportionate inventory growth.

Increased inventories result in higher interest and storage expenses. This has raised some questions as to whether businesspeople are changing their attitudes on the ratio of inventories they hold to sales of their products. With more sophisticated computer control of manufacturing and sales activities businesses may be able to reduce the traditional ratio of inventories to sales.

Change in Sensitive Materials Prices

In a period of rising economic activity, sensitive materials prices should rise because of increased demand. The reverse is true in a period of declining business activity. Material prices are especially sensitive to the buildup or depletion of inventories of materials.

Stock Prices, 500 Common Stocks

While this index is an obvious one, it can be a controversial one. The key question is whether or not the stock market anticipates economic activity or is a reflection of the past. It is generally felt today that the stock market does anticipate future economic activity. It is strongly influenced by the outlook for inflation, profits, and interest rates.

A study by Edward A. Mennis found that common stock prices anticipated business cycle movements 80 percent of the time. Unfortunately, however, timing is not so certain. There is no precise figure on the number of months by which stock price movements anticipate business cycle peaks and troughs.

Money Supply M2 in 1982 Dollars

The money supply figures released weekly by the Federal Reserve Board are watched very closely. An expanding money supply may reflect a desire by the Federal Reserve to stimulate future business activity. A tightening generally signals an attempt to reduce inflationary pressure and business expansion. The response by the equity and bond markets to changes in the money supply is usually very rapid.

Change in Business and Consumer Credit Outstanding

This is a closely watched indicator as it highlights purchases by consumers of durable goods such as automobiles, refrigerators, washing machines, and other heavy appliances. Increased purchases by the consumer obviously will result in heightened economic activity. Conversely, a decline in consumer installment debt will be translated ultimately into lower manufacturing activity. The lag between changes in consumer installment debt and manufacturing activity should generally be several months. Increases in debt add to purchasing power and are more sensitive to changes in economic conditions than are changes in income.

Similarly, businesses will increase borrowing for inventories and capital spending if they anticipate a future increase in business activity. A decline in business borrowing will result in a future decline in inventories and manufacturing activity.

COINCIDENT INDICATORS

The four coincident indicators (Figure 2) are of interest, but have only limited forecasting value. They should move directly with the business cycle and show what is happening currently in the economy. They are as follows:

FIGURE 2 Coincident Index Components

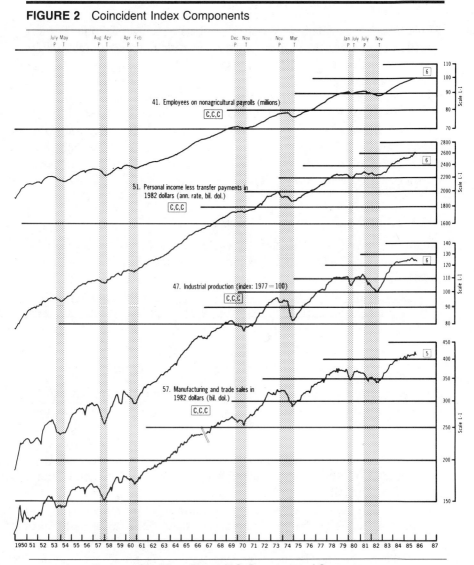

SOURCE: *Business Conditions Digest*, U.S. Department of Commerce.

Employees on Nonagricultural Payrolls

This indicator is simply a measure of the total number of persons employed in the nonagricultural sectors of the economy. An increase goes along with an improvement of business conditions and a reverse in a downturn period. While it is a good measure of short-term current movements in the economy, it has little forecasting significance for the analyst.

Personal Income Less Transfer Payments (in 1982 dollars)

This indicator simply measures the amount of income received by persons in the country. It is obviously directly related to employment, production, and wage rates. It is thus a useful measure of current conditions in business.

Industrial Production

The Federal Reserve index of industrial production is published monthly and is given wide publicity. It is exactly what it states—a measure of industrial production. It is quite useful as a measure of what is going on in the economy currently. However, it is not a gauge of the future.

Manufacturing and Trade Sales

This indicator measures the monthly volume (in 1982 dollars) of sales by manufacturing and wholesale and trade businesses. It simply reflects current events in the economy. Obviously, total sales in manufacturing and trade will move up and down with the business cycle.

LAGGING INDICATORS

Lagging indicators (Figure 3) are only of limited value to the analyst in forecasting the future, but they do reflect imbalances that may build up during a period of prosperity or be corrected during recession. For this reason, the analyst should be acquainted with the following six lagging indicators.

Average Duration of Unemployment

This component indicates the average number of weeks that the unemployed have been out of work. It differs from average weekly claims for unemployment insurance, which is a leading indicator. Its main significance is as a measure of long-term unemployment. When unemployment reaches low levels, it is a sign of shortages developing in the labor market.

Ratio, Manufacturing and Trade Inventories to Sales

This indicator simply measures the stocks on hand at the end of the month in manufacturing and wholesale and retail establishments compared to total sales. The ratio will change in periods of accelerating and declining business activity. The level of inventories, particularly in

FIGURE 3 Lagging Index Components

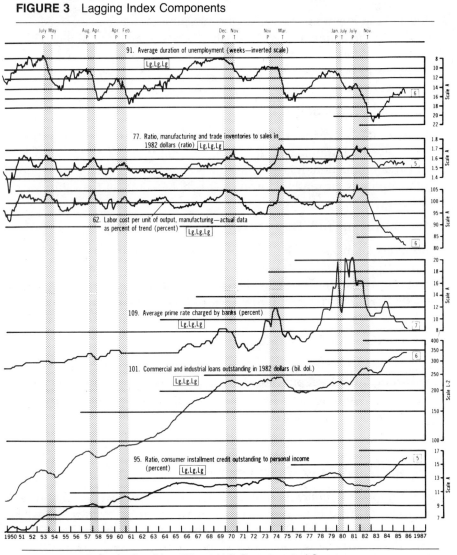

SOURCE: *Business Conditions Digest*, U.S. Department of Commerce.

relation to sales, indicates whether imbalances may be developing or are being adjusted.

Labor Cost per Unit of Output, Manufacturing

This component simply measures the cost of labor involved in manufacturing production. Normally it will increase in an expanding econ-

FIGURE 4 Composite Indexes

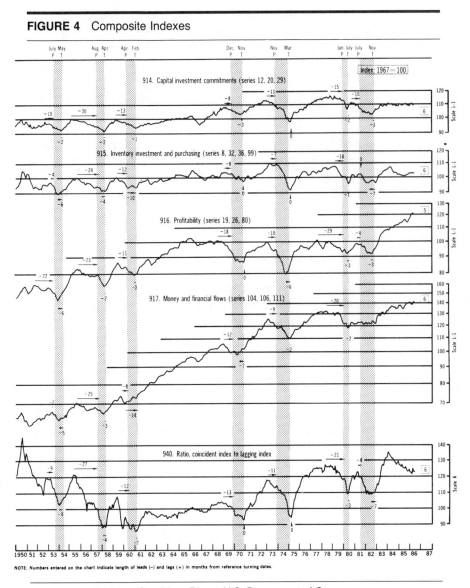

SOURCE: *Business Conditions Digest*, U.S. Department of Commerce.

omy and decline when business is contracting. Changes in unit labor cost are one of the dominant factors influencing profit margins.

Average Prime Rate Charged by Banks

This indicator is the interest rate charged by banks on short-term business loans to their better customers. While it is considered a lagging indicator, sharply rising short-term interest rates may lead to a slow-down in borrowing. This in turn could result in a business turndown in the future. Thus, it has some forecasting potential; for example, rising interest rates generally have a bearish influence on stock prices.

Commercial and Industrial Loans Outstanding (1982 dollars)

This component is simply a measure of borrowing by business and commercial enterprises. The actual level of such loans lags the business cycle. A measure of the rate of change would be more significant for forecasting purposes.

Ratio, Consumer Installment Credit Outstanding to Personal Income

With a decline in economic activity personal income will fall faster than consumer debt. Consumers will have difficulty repaying debt and the ratio will rise. The converse is true when business improves. A more useful measure is the change in business and consumer credit outstanding, which is a leading indicator (discussed previously).

COMPOSITE INDICATORS

The U.S. Department of Commerce summarizes the various indicators into what are known as composite indexes (Figure 4). The 12 leading indicators are lumped together into one series. The same is done for the four coincident indicators and the six lagging indicators. This is a convenient means for the analyst to get a quick summary of the average performance of the various indicators. The charts in Figure 4 show the composite indexes.

APPENDIX 1 _____
Predicting with the Leading Index
Sumner N. Levine

The composite index of leading indicators was designed to forecast swings in the economy. Since it includes the stock market average, the index is not of much value in predicting the market. As a general rule the leading index should rise or fall at least three consecutive months before it can be assumed that the economy is nearing a turning point. Over the postwar period, the leading index began to rise on the average of only three months prior to a recovery. The longest lead time was only about six months. Since many economists prefer to observe a trend in the index for a period of three or four months, it is evident that the leading index is of limited value in predicting an upturn. On the other hand, the leading index foreshadowed the onset of a recession by an average of 10 months which indicates that it is a better prognosticator of a downturn.

False signals are not unknown. For example, in 1950 and 1966 the leading indicator dropped over several months but a slump never developed. Even when the leading index correctly indicates the direction of the economy, there is often little correlation between the magnitude of the change and the vigor of the upturn or downturn. In 1973, before the onset of a major recession, the index fell only 1.7 percent. It was only after the recession was under way did the index take a big drop.

Since the leading index is made up of 12 series, some of which move up and some down, thereby generating conflicting signals, caution must be taken in interpreting small changes. The diffusion index is often used to measure the relative expansion and contraction forces; it is defined as the number of expanding series divided by the total number of series making up the composite index expressed as a percentage. Frequent revision in subsequent months in one or more components making up the leading index adds further elements of uncertainty.

Another index often quoted as a leading indicator is the ratio of the coincident to lagging composite indexes (see Figure 4, lower section). This ratio tends to anticipate a downturn by an average of about 16 months as compared to 10 months for the leading indicator. Unfortunately the ratio index is not much better than the leading index with respect to calling a recovery since it provides only a three-month lead time on the average. It is also of interest that the two indicators do not always move in synchronism. Over the period 1984 to 1986 the leading indicator rose steadily while the ratio indicator declined.

Despite their imperfections and uncertainties, both the leading and ratio indexes are useful tools for forecasting the direction of the economy.

APPENDIX 2
Detailed Definitions of the Leading Indexes

SERIES 1. AVERAGE WEEKLY HOURS OF PRODUCTION OR NONSUPERVISORY WORKERS, MANUFACTURING[1]

(Data contained in this series are seasonally adjusted.)

Data for this series are obtained from the establishment survey conducted each month by the Bureau of Labor Statistics (BLS). An establishment is defined as an economic unit—such as a factory, mine, or store—that produces goods or services. It is generally at a single physical location and is engaged predominantly in one type of economic activity. Where a single physical location encompasses two or more distinct and separate activities, these activities are treated as separate establishments, provided separate payroll records are available.

The data are primarily from payroll records voluntarily reported each month to state employment security agencies by employers in the 50 states and the District of Columbia. These data relate to the payroll period that includes the 12th of the month; however, data for the federal government represent positions occupied on the last day of the calendar month.

Data include full-time, part-time, temporary, and permanent workers. Workers who are on paid leave (such as sick, holiday, or vacation) and persons who worked during a part of the pay period are included. Persons on the payroll of more than one establishment are counted each time they are reported. Persons on a nonpay status for the entire period due to layoff, strike, or leave without pay; the self-employed, unpaid volunteer and family workers; farm and domestic workers; and noncivilian government employees are excluded.

Series 1 measures the average number of hours paid per production or nonsupervisory worker per week in manufacturing industries during the survey week. Unpaid absenteeism, labor turnover, part-time work, and stoppages can cause average weekly hours to be lower than scheduled weekly hours of an establishment; overtime hours can cause average weekly hours to be higher.

---

[1] U.S. Department of Labor, Bureau of Labor Statistics; U.S. Department of Commerce, Bureau of Economic Analysis.

SOURCE: Excerpted from the *Handbook of Cyclical Indicators*, Bureau of Economic Analysis, U.S. Department of Commerce, 1984.

SERIES 5. AVERAGE WEEKLY INITIAL CLAIMS FOR UNEMPLOYMENT INSURANCE, STATE PROGRAMS[2]

(Data contained in this series are seasonally adjusted.)

Insured unemployment measures the number of persons reporting at least one week of unemployment under a state unemployment insurance program in the 50 states and the District of Columbia. It includes some persons who are working part time and would be counted as employed in the payroll and household surveys. It excludes persons who have exhausted their benefit rights and workers who have not earned rights to unemployment insurance.

At present, the state unemployment insurance programs cover approximately 97 percent of wage and salary workers. The self-employed, workers on small farms, and some workers in nonprofit organizations and domestic service are excluded from these programs.

A covered worker, upon becoming unemployed, files an initial claim to establish the starting date for any unemployment compensation that may result from unemployment for one week or longer. The insured unemployment figure is derived by adjusting the data for the number of weeks of unemployment and the time the claim is filed, so that the series refers to the week in which unemployment actually occurred. Monthly totals are computed from weekly data, with split weeks allocated on the basis of a five-day week; these totals are divided by the number of full weeks plus the pertinent fractional portion(s) of split week(s) to secure monthly averages.

Initial claims for unemployment insurance represent first claims filed by workers for unemployment compensation upon becoming newly unemployed or claims for subsequent periods of unemployment in the same benefit year. A benefit year is a 12-month period during which an eligible worker may receive benefits. Since July 1949, transitional claims (claims filed by persons already in a claimant status for determination of benefit rights in a new benefit year) have been excluded.

The data are compiled by the Employment and Training Administration from weekly reports of the employment security agencies in the 50 states, Puerto Rico, the Virgin Islands, and the District of Columbia. (Data for Puerto Rico are omitted from series 5).

Series 5 measures the average number of persons who file first claims for unemployment compensation per week in a given month. The monthly averages of weekly data are adjusted for split weeks as described above. The series is seasonally adjusted by the Bureau of

---

[2] U.S. Department of Labor, Employment and Training Administration; U.S. Department of Commerce, Bureau of Economic Analysis.

Economic Analysis (BEA). It is inversely related to broad movements in aggregate economic activity.

SERIES 8.   MANUFACTURERS' NEW ORDERS IN 1982 DOLLARS, CONSUMER GOODS AND MATERIALS INDUSTRIES[3]

(Data contained in this series are seasonally adjusted; new orders are adjusted also for holiday and working day differences.)

This series is an estimate of manufacturers' new orders based on data collected in the monthly manufacturers' shipments, inventories, and orders survey by the Bureau of the Census. The survey includes most manufacturing companies with 1,000 or more employees and selected smaller companies. Companies with less than 100 employees are not sampled; data for these companies are estimated using overall industry averages. For firms that operate in a single industry category, the reporting unit typically comprises all operations of the company. At the request of the Census Bureau, most larger diversified companies file separate reports for divisions that operate in different industrial areas. The survey methodology assumes that the month-to-month changes in the data from the reporting units classified in each industry category effectively represent the month-to-month movements of the establishments in the Standard Industrial Classification industries that make up the category.

New orders are intents to buy for immediate or future delivery. Only orders supported by binding legal documents, such as signed contracts, letters of intent, or letters of award, are included. The monthly series include new orders received during the month less cancellations. Reporting companies are instructed to include:

1. The sales value of orders for goods to be delivered at some future date.
2. The sales value of orders for immediate delivery that have resulted in sales during the reporting period.
3. The net sales value of contract change documents that increase or decrease the sales value of the orders to which they are related, if the parties are in substantial agreement on the amount involved.

From the total of these items, companies are instructed to deduct the value of partial or complete cancellations of existing orders.

Unfilled orders are orders that have been received but have not yet

---

[3] U.S. Department of Commerce, Bureau of the Census and Bureau of Economic Analysis.

passed through the sales account. Generally, unfilled orders at the end of the reporting period are equal to unfilled orders at the beginning of the period, plus net new orders received during the period, minus net sales.

In many nondurable goods industries and a few durable goods industries, unfilled orders data are not tabulated either because they are not reported by the respondents or because nearly all orders are shipped from inventories or current production. The best estimate of new orders for these industries is the value of current shipments; therefore, these are included in the tabulations.

The constant-dollar new orders series are deflated by the Bureau of Economic Analysis (BEA) using the appropriate producer price indexes. These indexes, which are compiled by the U.S. Department of Labor, Bureau of Labor Statistics (BLS), measure average changes in prices received in primary markets in the United States. They are designed to measure "pure" price changes; that is, price changes not influenced by changes in quality, quantity, shipping terms, or product mix. The deflators are seasonally adjusted either by BLS or by BEA using seasonal adjustment factors supplied by BLS.

Series 8 measures new orders for consumer goods and materials in constant (1982) dollars. These new orders include the durable goods industries other than capital goods and defense producers and the four nondurable goods industries that have unfilled orders: Textile mill products; paper and allied products; printing, publishing, and allied products; and leather and leather products.

For the period prior to 1953 for the durables and prior to 1958 for the nondurables, aggregated totals were deflated using fixed (1958) weights for the components of the producer price indexes. From 1953 to date for the durables and 1958 to date for the nondurables, the deflation was performed separately for each two-digit Standard Industrial Classification industry included in the two totals, and therefore reflects current weights for each of the components.

SERIES 12.   INDEX OF NET BUSINESS FORMATION[4]

(Data contained in this series are seasonally adjusted.)

Series 12 provides a monthly estimate of the net formation of business enterprises. There are no direct measures of the monthly change in the total business population. However, it is believed that this estimate adequately represents the short-term movement of new entries into, and departures from, the total business population.

---

[4] U.S. Department of Commerce, Bureau of Economic Analysis.

The series is a composite index (1967 = 100) computed from the following data:

1. New business incorporations. This series measures the number of domestic stock profit companies receiving charters each month under the general business incorporation laws of the 50 states and the District of Columbia.
2. Number of business failures. A business failure is defined as "a concern that is involved in a court proceeding or a voluntary action that is likely to result in loss to creditors." Firms that are liquidated, merged, sold, or otherwise discontinued without loss to creditors are not considered failures. Data are for the 50 states and the District of Columbia. This component is inverted before inclusion in the index.
3. Confidential data on telephones installed prior to 1979 and confidential public utilities information for 1979 forward.

Data are seasonally adjusted by the Bureau of Economic Analysis (BEA) beginning 1960 and by the National Bureau of Economic Research (NBER) for the period prior to 1960.

SERIES 19.   INDEX OF STOCK PRICES, 500 COMMON STOCKS[5]

(Data contained in this series are not seasonally adjusted.)

Series 19 is an index that measures the average price of stocks listed on the New York Stock Exchange. The basic format of the monthly index was introduced in 1957; it includes 500 stocks and is on a 1941–43 = 10 base. The series is based on daily closing prices for the month. The price of each stock is weighted by the number of shares outstanding. The aggregate current market value is computed and expressed as a relative of the aggregate market value in the base period. The resulting ratios are multiplied by 10. (The base period used results in a price index level that for most purposes can be considered as interchangeable into dollars and cents. The level of the index closely approximates the average price level of all the stocks listed in the New York Stock Exchange.) The index is modified to offset unusual price changes due to issuance of rights, stock dividends, splitups, and mergers.

In July 1976, the index was revised to include some over-the-counter stocks, mainly bank and insurance stocks. Before the revision, three groups were represented: 425 industrials, 60 utilities, and 15 rails. The revised index comprises four groups: 400 industrials, 40 utilities, 20

---

[5] Standard & Poor's Corporation; U.S. Department of Commerce, Bureau of Economic Analysis.

transporation, and 40 financial. Forty-five stocks from the old index also were replaced.

Each stock in the index must represent a viable enterprise typical of the industry group to which it is assigned. Its market price movements must be responsive to changes in the industry. Given a choice among a number of stocks meeting these criteria, preference will be given to the stocks with the largest aggregate market value—usually these are also the more actively traded issues in the industry. Selection of stocks for addition to or removal from the index is the responsibility of the 500 Index Committee at Standard & Poor's.

SERIES 20. CONTRACTS AND ORDERS FOR PLANT AND EQUIPMENT IN 1982 DOLLARS[6]

(Data contained in this series are seasonally adjusted.)

Series 20 measures the value of new contracts awarded to building, public works, and utilities contractors and of new orders for nondefense goods received by manufacturers in capital goods industries. They are the sum of the following series:

1. The value of contracts for commercial and industrial construction about to get under way on commercial buildings (banks, offices and lofts, stores, warehouses, garages, and service stations), and manufacturing buildings (for processing or mechanical usage).
2. The value of contracts for privately owned nonbuilding construction about to get under way on streets and highways, bridges, dams and reservoirs, waterfront developments, sewerage systems, parks and playgrounds, electric light and power systems, gas plants and mains, oil and gas well pipelines, water supply systems, railroads, and airports (excluding buildings).
3. Manufacturers' new orders received by capital goods, nondefense industries (BCD-series 24 for the current-dollar series and series 27 for the constant-dollar series).

The construction contracts data are compiled by the McGraw-Hill Information Systems Company, F. W. Dodge Division. Data cover the value of new construction, additions, and major alterations; maintenance work is excluded. F. W. Dodge construction statistics are based on data obtained from reports to F. W. Dodge supplemented by permit-place reports. The valuation figures approximate actual construction costs exclusive of land, architects' fees, and, in the case of manufactur-

---

[6] McGraw-Hill Information Systems Company, F. W. Dodge Division; U.S. Department of Commerce, Bureau of the Census and Bureau of Economic Analysis.

ing buildings, the cost of equipment that is not an integral part of the structure. Beginning with January 1969, data cover construction in the 50 states and the District of Columbia. In the period 1956–68, data cover the 48 contiguous states and the District of Columbia; prior to 1956, only the 37 states east of the Rocky Mountains and the District of Columbia are included. The F. W. Dodge data are seasonally adjusted by the Bureau of Economic Analysis (BEA).

To obtain the construction contracts data (two of the three components of series 20) in constant (1982) dollars, current-dollar data are deflated by an implicit price deflator obtained by dividing the current-dollar value of nonresidential construction put in place by the 1977 dollar value of nonresidential construction put in place and converting the resulting ratios to an index on a 1982 base. (Values of nonresidential construction—in current and constant dollars—are obtained by subtracting from the total values of new construction the values for private residential buildings and for public housing and redevelopment.)

SERIES 29.   INDEX OF NEW PRIVATE HOUSING UNITS AUTHORIZED BY LOCAL BUILDING PERMITS[7]

(Data contained in this series are seasonally adjusted.)

Series 29 refers to private housing units. A housing unit is defined as a single room or group of rooms intended for occupancy as separate living quarters by a family, by a group of unrelated persons living together, or by a person living alone. Group quarters (such as dormitories, fraternity houses, nurses' homes, and rooming houses) and all transient accommodations are excluded.

Series 29 is an index (1967 = 100) that measures the monthly change in the number of housing units authorized by local permit-issuing places. The data relate to the issuance of permits, not to the start of construction, which frequently occurs several months later. Furthermore, in a small number of cases, permits are not used and are allowed to lapse.

Data for the period 1948–53 are based on estimates of the number of new privately owned dwelling units authorized in urban areas as defined in the 1940 Census of Population. Building permit data from reporting cities, which represent approximately 85 percent of the 1940 urban population, were expanded to represent all urban areas by matching nonreporting to reporting urban places on the basis of city population size and location, and applying trend ratios for reporting places to the matched nonreporting places.

From 1954 to 1958, data are based on reports from approximately

---

[7] U.S. Department of Commerce, Bureau of the Census.

6,600 permit-issuing places, which include practically all large cities; a large proportion of smaller cities; and selected counties, towns, and townships. Data for 1959–62 are based on reports from 10,000 permit-issuing places; for 1963–66, from 12,000 permit-issuing places; for 1967–71, from 13,000 permit-issuing places; for 1972–77, from 14,000 permit-issuing places; and for 1978 to date, from 16,000 permit-issuing places. Permits issued by these 16,000 places account for approximately 88 percent of all new residential construction in the United States. The remaining 12 percent is in areas that do not require building permits.

These periodic changes in the number of permit-issuing places yield data that are not comparable between periods. To achieve comparability for use in *Business Conditions Digest* (BCD), the seasonally adjusted series for the earlier period was adjusted to the level of the current period (16,000 permit-issuing places) and converted to an index, 1967 = 100.

SERIES 32.   VENDOR PERFORMANCE, PERCENT OF COMPANIES RECEIVING SLOWER DELIVERIES[8]

(Data contained in this series are not seasonally adjusted.)

Series 32 measures the percentage of purchasing agents in the Greater Chicago area who experienced slower deliveries in the current month compared with the previous month. It tends to reflect the volume of business being handled by the suppliers of these firms, with slower deliveries usually indicating a higher volume of business.

The survey is conducted monthly among 200 of the approximately 1,000 members of the Purchasing Management Association of Chicago (PMAC). On the basis of information supplied by the Chicago Association of Commerce and Industry, the PMAC sample is selected to represent proportionally the following 15 industries in the Greater Chicago area: Primary metals, 14 percent; food, 12 percent; nonelectrical machinery, 12 percent; electrical machinery, 11 percent; fabricated metal products, 10 percent; printing, 9 percent; chemicals, 8 percent; transportation, 6 percent; apparel and finished textile products, 3 percent; professional and scientific instruments, 2.5 percent; stone, clay, and glass, 2.5 percent; paper and allied products, 2 percent; petroleum and coal, 2 percent; furniture and fixtures, 1.7 percent; and all other, 4.3 percent.

Each month, respondents are asked to report whether deliveries are faster than last month, the same as last month, or slower than last month. PMAC publishes the percentage of respondents reporting in each category.

The series published in *Business Conditions Digest* (BCD) shows the

---

[8] Purchasing Management Association of Chicago.

percentage of companies receiving slower deliveries and is computed by summing the PMAC percentage receiving slower deliveries plus one half of the percentage receiving deliveries unchanged from the previous month.

SERIES 36. CHANGE IN MANUFACTURING AND TRADE INVENTORIES ON HAND AND ON ORDER IN 1982 DOLLARS[9]

(Data contained in this series are seasonally adjusted; sales and shipments are adjusted also for holiday and working day differences.)

This series measures the inventories or sales of manufacturing, merchant wholesalers, and retail establishments. Inventories and sales of agriculture, forestry, and fishing; mining; construction; nonmerchant wholesalers (sales branches of manufacturing companies, agents, brokers, and commission merchants); transportation, communication, electric, gas, and sanitary services; finance, insurance, and real estate; and services are excluded. The series is compiled from data collected each month by the Bureau of the Census in the shipments, inventories, and orders survey and in the merchant wholesalers and retail trade surveys. They are adjusted to benchmarks from the five-year censuses of manufactures, wholesale trade, and retail trade and to interim annual surveys.

The monthly series on manufacturers' inventories and sales have been compiled by the Census Bureau since 1957; prior to that year, the survey was conducted by the Bureau of Economic Analysis (BEA). Merchant wholesalers' inventories and sales and retail sales have been collected and published by the Census Bureau since 1954 and 1951, respectively. Retail inventories have been collected and published by the Census Bureau since January 1979. For prior years, these series were published by BEA from sample data collected by the Census Bureau.

Manufacturers' inventories are book values of stocks-on-hand at the end of the month, and include materials and supplies, work in process, and finished goods. Inventories associated with nonmanufacturing activities of manufacturing companies are excluded. Inventories are valued according to the valuation method used by each company, and the aggregates are a mixture of LIFO (last-in-first-out) and non-LIFO values. Annual information is obtained on the portions of inventories valued by the various accounting methods.

Merchant wholesalers' and retail inventories are also book values of

---

[9] U.S. Department of Commerce, Bureau of the Census and Bureau of Economic Analysis.

merchandise-on-hand at the end of the month. Goods held on consign-ment by wholesalers and retailers are excluded.

Manufacturers' sales are the value of their shipments for domestic use or export. Shipments are measured by receipts, billings, or the value of products shipped (less discounts, returns, and allowances) and generally exclude freight charges and excise taxes. Shipments from one division to another within the same company in the United States and shipments by domestic firms to foreign subsidiaries are included, but shipments by foreign subsidiaries are excluded. For some aircraft and all shipbuilding, the "value of shipments" is the value of the work done during the period covered, rather than the value of the products physically shipped.

Merchant wholesalers' sales include sales of merchandise and receipts from repairs or other services (after deducting discounts, returns, and allowances) and sales of merchandise for others on a commission basis. Sales taxes and federal excise taxes are excluded.

Retail sales include total receipts from customers after deductions of refunds and allowances for merchandise returned. Receipts from rental or leasing of merchandise and from repairs and other services to customers are included also. Since 1967, finance charges, and sales and excise taxes collected from customers and paid to tax agencies by the retailer are excluded.

Manufacturers' inventories and sales of defense products are based on separate reports covering only the defense work of large defense contractors in the ordnance and accessories; communication equipment; aircraft, missiles, and parts; and shipbuilding and tank industries. These defense products cover only work for the U.S. Department of Defense and orders from foreign governments for military goods contracted through the Defense Department.

Series 36 measures the month-to-month amount of change, in constant (1982) dollars, in manufacturing and trade inventories and manufacturers' unfilled orders (excluding unfilled orders for capital goods and defense products). The components of each series are deflated separately and then combined into a total from which monthly changes are computed.

The constant-dollar manufacturing and trade inventories compo-nent is series 70, described above. Manufacturers' unfilled orders measure the end-of-month constant-dollar value of orders that have been received but have not yet passed through the sales accounts. beginning with 1953 for the eight durable-goods industries and begin-ning with 1958 for the four nondurable-goods industries. Prior to these dates, the aggregate durable and nondurable levels were each deflated using fixed-weighted averages (1958 weights) of Producer Price Indexes as deflators.

The series is shown in *Business Conditions Digest* (BCD) as the month-to-month amounts of change and as four-term moving averages of the monthly changes (weighted 1,2,2,1) and placed on the terminal month of the span.

SERIES 99. CHANGE IN SENSITIVE MATERIALS PRICES[10]

(Data contained in this series are seasonally adjusted.)

Series 99 measures the change in a composite index (1967 = 100) based on two sensitive materials price series: "Producer price index, 28 sensitive crude and intermediate materials"[11] (from which series 98 is computed) and "spot market price index, raw industrial materials" (series 23).[12]

Series 99 is shown as percent changes over one-month spans and as four-term moving averages of the monthly changes (weighted 1,2,2,1) and placed on the terminal month of the span.

SERIES 106. MONEY SUPPLY M2 IN 1982 DOLLARS[13]

(Data contained in this series are seasonally adjusted.)

The different money supply measures are popularly known by the abbreviations M1, M2, etc. The money supply series shown in *Business Conditions Digest* are the M1, M2, and total liquid assets versions. M3, which is not shown separately, is included in liquid assets. Deposits held by foreign banks and governments, official institutions, and the U.S. government are excluded from each of the series. Consolidation adjustments have been made in the construction of each series, to avoid

---

[10] U.S. Department of Commerce, Bureau of Economic Analysis; U.S. Department of Labor, Bureau of Labor Statistics; Commodity Research Bureau, Inc.

[11] The index includes prices for the following commodities: Cattle hides; natural rubber; six wastepaper components (No. 1 news, No. 1 mixed, old corrugated boxes, semi-kraft clippings, mixed-kraft clippings, and white news blanks); seven iron and steel scrap components (No. 1 heavy melting; No. 2 heavy melting; No. 1 bundles; No. 2 bundles; melting, railroad No. 1; stainless bundles; and No. 1 cupola cast iron); three nonferrous metal scrap components (copper base scrap; aluminum base scrap; and other nonferrous scrap, n.e.c.); five fibers components (domestic apparel wool, foreign apparel wool, foreign carpet wool, raw cotton, and hard fibers); four lumber and wood components (lumber, millwork, plywood, and other wood products); and sand, gravel, and crushed stone.

[12] The raw industrial materials group consists of burlap, copper scrap, cotton, hides, lead scrap, print cloth, rosin, rubber, steel scrap, tallow, tin, wool tops, and zinc.

[13] Board of Governors of the Federal Reserve System; U.S. Department of Commerce, Bureau of Economic Analysis.

double counting of the public's monetary assets. The major adjustment involves the netting of deposits held by depository institutions with other depository institutions.

The M1 version of the money supply consists of:

1. Currency outside the treasury, the Federal Reserve banks, and the vaults of commercial banks.
2. Outstanding amounts of U.S. dollar-denominated travelers checks of nonbank issuers.
3. Demand deposits at commercial banks and certain foreign-related institutions, less cash items in the process of collection, Federal Reserve float, and foreign demand balances at Federal Reserve banks.
4. Interest-earning checkable deposits consisting of negotiable order of withdrawal (NOW) and automatic transfer service (ATS) accounts at depository institutions other than credit unions, credit union share draft accounts, and demand deposits at thrift institutions.

The consolidation adjustment removes demand deposits held by commercial banks with other commercial banks and the demand deposits held by thrift institutions that are estimated to be used in servicing their checkable deposits.

M2 consists of M1 plus:

1. Money market deposit accounts, savings and small-denomination time deposits (time deposits—including retail repurchase agreements—issued in denominations of less than $100,000) at all depository institutions.
2. Overnight (and continuing contract) repurchase agreements issued by commercial banks and certain overnight Eurodollars (those issued by Caribbean branches of member banks) held by U.S. nonbank residents.
3. Balances in both taxable and tax-exempt general purpose and broker/dealer money market mutual funds (MMMF).

Keogh and individual retirement account balances at depository institutions and in MMMF's are excluded. Consolidation adjustments are made to remove demand deposits held by thrift institutions (not already removed in M1), savings and time deposits held by depository institutions, and assets held by MMMF's.

"Total liquid assets" includes M2 plus:

1. Large-denomination time deposits (issued in denominations of $100,000 or more) at all depository institutions (including negotiable certificates of deposit), term repurchase agreements issued by commercial banks and thrift institutions, and institution-only money market mutual fund shares.

2. Other liquid assets, including nonbank public holdings of U.S. savings bonds, short-term Treasury obligations, bankers acceptances, commercial paper, and term Eurodollars held by U.S. residents.

Consolidation adjustments are made to remove deposits and assets of MMMF's and depository institutions.

Data for M1 and M2 are averages of daily data for member banks and estimates of nonmember bank deposits. Prior to 1980, estimates of nonmember bank deposits were based on quarterly call report data and the relationship of nonmember and small member bank deposits to member bank deposits on those dates; since January 1980, the nonmember component has been derived from a sample of nonmember banks reporting daily data on a weekly basis. Estimates of M1 are available on a monthly and weekly basis; estimates of M2 and liquid assets are available only on a monthly basis.

Series 106 is a measure of real (1982 dollars) money balances based on the M1 and M2 versions of money supply, respectively. The series are deflated by the consumer price index for all urban consumers (CPI-U) compiled by the U.S. Department of Labor, Bureau of Labor Statistics (BLS). The deflator is series 320 converted to a 1982 = 100 base and seasonally adjusted by the Bureau of Economic Analysis using seasonal factors provided by BLS.

SERIES 111. CHANGE IN BUSINESS AND CONSUMER CREDIT OUTSTANDING[14]

(Data contained in this series are seasonally adjusted.)

Series 111, which measures the month-to-month percent change in business and consumer credit outstanding, is compiled by the Bureau of Economic Analysis (BEA) by combining the following series and computing the change:

> *Consumer installment credit* (series 66).
> *Commercial and industrial loans* (series 72).

Real estate loans of weekly reporting large commercial banks. This component measures the amount of outstanding loans, as of the last Wednesday of the month, held by large commercial banks and secured primarily by real estate (as evidenced by mortgages, deeds of trust, land contracts, or other liens on real estate; residential properties that are

---

[14] Board of Governors of the Federal Reserve System; The Federal Reserve Bank of New York; Federal Home Loan Bank Board; U.S. Department of Commerce, Bureau of Economic Analysis.

extended, collected, and serviced by a bank and guaranteed by the Farmers Home Administration; and loans secured primarily by properties guaranteed by government entities in foreign countries). Pooled mortgages against which certificates guaranteed by the Government National Mortgage Association have been issued, loans to real estate companies and mortgage lenders that specialize in mortgage loan originations and that service mortgages for others, mortgage-backed bonds issued by the Federal Home Loan Mortgage Corporation, and notes issued by the Farmers Home Administration are excluded. The data are compiled by the Board of Governors of the Federal Reserve System and are seasonally adjusted by BEA.

The series has a major discontinuity in January 1972. From 1972 to date, the data cover about 170 of the largest commercial banks in the United States, both members and nonmembers of the Federal Reserve System. These banks had assets of $750 million or more in their domestic offices as of December 31, 1977. Prior to January 1972, the data cover about 320 banks with significant changes in the composition of the sample occurring in 1965 and 1959. Effective with data for July 1965, the series reflects banking conditions in (but not outside) the larger cities and includes all branches of reporting banks, regardless of size. The June 1959 revision was instituted to improve bank coverage.

Mortgage loans held by savings and loan associations. This component measures the end-of-month amount of outstanding mortgage loans held by associations affiliated with the U.S. Savings and Loan League. These loans represent over 98 percent of the resources of all operating savings and loan associations. The data are compiled by the Federal Home Loan Bank Board and are seasonally adjusted by BEA.

5

The National Income and Product Accounts

Carol S. Carson, Ph.D.
Deputy Director
Bureau of Economic Analysis
U.S. Department of Commerce

The national income and product accounts (NIPAs) are a system of macroeconomic statistics that display the value of the nation's output, the composition of that output, and the distribution of income generated in its production. They are one of the major branches of national economic accounting—each of which illuminates some aspects of the structure, workings, and performance of the national economy—and are closely related to international economic accounts and regional economic accounts. The NIPAs, as a system, emerged in the 1940s, building on work done in the U.S. Department of Commerce beginning in the 1930s and earlier by private organizations. In the years since, the department's Bureau of Economic Analysis (BEA), formerly the Office of Business Economics, has substantially refined and elaborated the system (1).

AN OVERVIEW

The purpose of the NIPAs, a purpose shared by the other branches of national economic accounting, is to provide a coherent and comprehensive picture of the innumerable economic transactions that occur in an accounting period such as a year. The approach is to provide such a picture through a set of accounts that are aggregations of the accounts belonging to the individual transactors—workers, businesses, and consumers, among others—in the economy, whether or not formal accounting statements exist explicitly for all of them. To set up such a set of accounts, national economic accountants can be viewed as (1) distinguishing groups of economic transactors that engage in the same types of transactions and that are affected by economic developments in the same manner; (2) setting up uniform types of accounts for these groups, called sectors; and (3) showing in these accounts the broad categories of economic transactions in which the sectors engage.[1]

An overview of the resulting system can be obtained from the NIPA five-account summary system, shown in Table 1 . The summary system presents major aggregates of the NIPAs and highlights the interrelations of the sectors.

Account 1, the national income and product account, can be viewed as a consolidation of production accounts for all sectors. Most of the production takes place in businesses—essentially units that produce goods and services for sale at a price intended to at least cover costs of production. However, some production also takes place in the other sectors: Households, government, and the rest of the world. The two sides of this account total to gross national product (GNP), the primary measure of production in the NIPAs. GNP is the market value of goods and services produced by labor and property supplied by residents of the United States. (Definitions of the other items in the five-account summary are provided in the technical note at the end of this chapter.) The two sides of the account show two ways of arriving at this measure.

On the right-hand side, often called the product side, GNP is shown in its most familiar form, as the sum of personal consumption expenditures, gross private domestic investment, net exports of goods and services, and government purchases of goods and services. This sum arrives at the market value of "final" sales of goods and services plus inventory change; purchases by one producing unit from another of intermediate products—that is, products used in further production during the accounting period—are not included because their value is reflected in the value of final sales and inventory change.

On the left-hand side, often called the income side, GNP is shown as the costs incurred and the profits earned in the production of GNP. These charges against GNP can be thought of in two groups. The first of these—compensation of employees, proprietors' income, rental income of persons, corporate profits, and net interest—are factor charges, so-called because they represent income of the factors of production (labor and property). These incomes are recorded in the forms in which they accrue to residents; they are measured before deduction of taxes on

---

[1] For a step-by-step derivation of the national economic accounts from the conventional accounting statements used by businesses and governments and from similar statements that may be assumed to exist for other transactors, see U.S. Department of Commerce (6).

those incomes and after deduction of (i.e., net of) depreciation and other allowances for fixed capital consumed in production. The second group consists of business transfer payments, indirect business taxes, and the current surplus of government enterprises less subsidies. These nonfactor charges plus capital consumption allowances—the latter because GNP is measured before deduction of (i.e., net of) depreciation and other allowances for fixed capital consumed in production—must be added to factor charges to arrive at the required total market value of goods and services. The left-hand side also shows the statistical discrepancy. It reflects measurement error, and it is conventionally entered on the left side to secure balance between estimates of GNP and of the total of factor and nonfactor charges against GNP.

Account 1 shows, in addition to GNP and charges against GNP, two other production aggregates. The first, national income, is an alternative to GNP in that it reflects, rather than the gross market value, the net factor cost of goods and services produced. In other words, it is the income from the production of goods and services measured after depreciation and other allowances for the consumption of fixed capital. The second, charges against net national product, is an alternative in that it reflects the net market value. One further basic distinction can be made in defining the value of production. It is the distinction between national measures and domestic measures. The former delimit production according to the residence of the supplier of the labor and property. For example, as mentioned in defining GNP, GNP is production that is attributed to labor and property supplied by residents of the United States. The latter delimit production according to the location of the labor and property. National measures differ from domestic measures by the net inflow (i.e., the inflow less the outflow) into a nation of labor and property incomes from abroad. Each of the three national measures has a domestic counterpart: Gross domestic product, domestic income, and net domestic product.

The choice of a measure of production from this array depends on the intended use. For example, national income is often used in studies dealing with the allocation of factors of production to various uses. A market price measure is usually preferred for studies of economic behavior and welfare, because the market price is the basis for choice among alternative products. In most other countries, gross domestic product, rather than GNP, is the primary measure, and thus it is often used in international comparisons.

Accounts 2, 3, and 4 are of a different nature than account 1; they record systematically all receipts and the disposition of receipts of "persons," governments, and foreigners, respectively.

The personal income and outlay account, account 2, registers income of persons from all sources and its disposition. Persons in the NIPAs consist not only of individuals but also of several kinds of

TABLE 1 Summary National Income and Product Accounts, 1985

Account 1   National Income and Product Account
($ billions)

Line		
1. Compensation of employees	2,368.2	
2. Wages and salaries	1,965.8	
3. Disbursements (2–7)	1,966.1	
4. Wage accruals less disbursements (3–12) and (5–4)	−.2	
5. Supplements to wages and salaries	402.4	
6. Employer contributions for social insurance (3–20)	205.5	
7. Other labor income (2–8)	196.9	
8. Proprietors' income with inventory valuation and capital consumption adjustments (2–9)	254.4	
9. Rental income of persons with capital consumption adjustment (2–10)	7.6	
10. Corporate profits with inventory valuation and capital consumption adjustments	280.7	
11. Profits before tax	223.2	
12. Profits tax liability (3–17)	91.8	
13. Profits after tax	131.4	
14. Dividends (2–12)	81.6	
15. Undistributed profits (5–6)	49.8	
16. Inventory valuation adjustment (5–7)	−.6	
17. Capital consumption adjustment (5–8)	58.1	
18. Net interest (2–15)	311.4	
19. National income	3,222.3	

Line		
27. Personal consumption expenditures (2–3)	2,600.5	
28. Durable goods	359.3	
29. Nondurable goods	905.1	
30. Services	1,336.1	
31. Gross private domestic investment (5–1)	661.1	
32. Fixed investment	650.0	
33. Nonresidential	458.2	
34. Structures	154.8	
35. Producers' durable equipment	303.4	
36. Residential	191.8	
37. Change in business inventories	11.1	
38. Net exports of goods and services	−78.9	
39. Exports (4–1)	369.8	
40. Imports (4–3)	448.6	
41. Government purchases of goods and services (3–1)	815.4	
42. Federal	354.1	
43. National defense	259.4	
44. Nondefense	94.7	
45. State and local	461.3	

TABLE 1 (continued)

Line

20. Business transfer payments (2–20)	20.9
21. Indirect business tax and nontax liability (3–18)	331.4
22. *Less:* Subsidies less current surplus of government enterprises (3–11)	8.2
23. Charges against net national product	3,566.5
24. Capital consumption allowances with capital consumption adjustment (5–9)	437.2
25. Charges against gross national product	4,003.7
26. Statistical discrepancy (5–12)	–5.5
Gross National Product	**3,998.1**

Line

| | |
| **Gross National Product** | **3,998.1** |

Account 2   Personal Income and Outlay Account
($ billions)

Line

1. Personal tax and nontax payments (3–16)	486.5
2. Personal outlays	2,684.7
3. Personal consumption expenditures (1–27)	2,600.5
4. Interest paid by consumers to business (2–18)	82.6
5. Personal transfer payments to foreigners (net) (4–5)	1.6
6. Personal saving (5–3)	

Line

7. Wage and salary disbursements (1–3)	1,966.1
8. Other labor income (1–7)	196.9
9. Proprietors' income with inventory valuation and capital consumption adjustments (1–8)	254.4
10. Rental income of persons with capital consumption adjustment (1–9)	7.6
11. Personal dividend income	76.4
12. Dividends (1–14)	81.6

13.	Less: Dividends received by government (3–10)	5.2
14.	Personal interest income (1–18)	476.2
15.	Net interest (1–18)	311.4
16.	Interest paid by government to persons and business (3–7)	173.4
17.	Less: Interest received by government (3–9)	91.1
18.	Interest paid by consumers to business (2–4)	82.6
19.	Transfer payments to persons	487.1
20.	From business (1–20)	20.9
21.	From government (3–3)	466.2
22.	Less: Personal contributions for social insurance (3–21)	150.2

Personal income   **3,314.5**

Personal taxes, outlays, and saving   **3,314.5**

Account 3   Government Receipts and Expenditures Account
($ billions)

Line

1.	Purchases of goods and services (1–41)	815.4
2.	Transfer payments	479.5
3.	To persons (2–21)	466.2
4.	To foreigners (net) (4–6)	13.4
5.	Net interest paid	103.6
6.	Interest paid	194.7
7.	To persons and business (2–16)	173.4

Line

16.	Personal tax and nontax payments (2–1)	486.5
17.	Corporate profits tax liability (1–12)	91.8
18.	Indirect business tax and nontax liability (1–21)	331.4
19.	Contributions for social insurance	355.7
20.	Employer (1–6)	205.5
21.	Personal (2–22)	150.2

TABLE 1 *(concluded)*

Line		Government expenditures and surplus			Line		Government receipts
8.	To foreigners (4–7)		21.3				
9.	*Less:* Interest received by government (2–17)		91.1				
10.	*Less:* Dividends received by government (2–13)		5.2				
11.	Subsidies less current surplus of government enterprises (1–22)		8.2				
12.	*Less:* Wage accruals less disbursements (1–4)		–.2				
13.	Surplus or deficit (–), national income and product accounts (5–10)		–198.0				
14.	Federal	–136.3					
15.	State and local	61.7					
	Government expenditures and surplus		**1,265.4**			**Government receipts**	**1,265.4**

Account 4   Foreign Transactions Account
($ billions)

Line			Line		
1.	Exports of goods and services (1–39)	369.8	3.	Imports of goods and services (1–40)	448.6
2.	Capital grants received by the United States (net) (5–11)	0	4.	Transfer payments to foreigners (net)	15.0
			5.	From persons (net) (2–5)	1.6
			6.	From government (net) (3–4)	13.4
			7.	Interest paid by government to foreigners (3–8)	21.3
			8.	Net foreign investment (5–2)	–115.2
	Receipts from foreigners	**369.8**		**Payments to foreigners**	**369.8**

Account 5 Gross Saving and Investment Account
($ billions)

Line		
1.	Gross private domestic investment (1–31)	661.1
2.	Net foreign investment (4–8)	–115.2
	Gross investment	**545.9**

Line		
3.	Personal saving (2–6)	143.3
4.	Wage accruals less disbursements (1–4)	0
5.	Undistributed corporate profits with inventory valuation and capital consumption adjustments	107.3
6.	Undistributed corporate profits (1–15)	49.8
7.	Inventory valuation adjustment (1–16)	–.6
8.	Capital consumption adjustment (1–17)	58.1
9.	Capital consumption allowances with capital consumption adjustment (1–24)	437.2
10.	Government surplus or deficit (–), national income and product account (3–13)	–136.3
11.	Capital grants received by the United States (net) (4–2)	0
12.	Statistical discrepancy (1–26)	–5.5
	Gross saving and statistical discrepancy	**545.9**

NOTE: Numbers in parentheses indicate accounts and items of counterentry in the accounts. For example, the counterentry for wage and salary disbursements (2–7), is in account 2, line 7.

SOURCE: U.S. Department of Commerce, Bureau of Economic Analysis, *Survey of Current Business*, July 1986.

organizations (nonprofit institutions, private noninsured welfare funds, and private trust funds) that are viewed as associations of individuals.

Personal income—the income received by persons from all sources—is sometimes used as a proxy measure of production because it is available not only for the nation as a whole but also for states and smaller areas and because the national measure is available monthly. It differs from production because it excludes some incomes that are earned in production but not distributed to persons—for example, undistributed corporate profits—and includes some incomes that do not represent current production—for example, transfer payments. Because some of these incomes do not follow the course of total production (especially in the short run), the proxy is imperfect. In Chart 1, the production incomes that are not distributed to persons are subtracted, and the incomes that are not from current production are added, in order to derive personal income from national income. Personal income and the measures of its disposition among taxes, outlays, and saving are useful in their own right, especially because persons are the largest among the economic groups that interact to determine the working of the economy: Persons receive most of the income, account for the single largest share of taxes, give rise to the bulk of the demand for GNP, and contribute substantially to the saving that finances investment.

The government receipts and expenditures account, account 3, can be regarded as a budget statement within the framework of the NIPAs. It covers federal and also state and local agencies (except government enterprises). The foreign transactions account, account 4, can be regarded as a summary balance-of-payments statement; it covers the transactions of the rest of the world with the United States. The transactions relate to merchandise trade, and services such as transportation, and income flows.

The gross saving and investment account, account 5, cuts across the sectors and shows the saving and investment of all domestic sectors. The primary elements of saving are personal saving, business saving in the form of undistributed profits and capital consumption allowances, and the government surplus or deficit. Investment includes not only domestic components—investment in structures, equipment, and inventories—but also the net investment outside the United States.

As mentioned at the outset, the five-account summary presents major aggregates of the NIPAs—in addition to GNP, national income, net national product, and personal income—and shows the interrelationships of the sectors. The interrelationships are indicated by the numbers in parentheses following individual items; these numbers give the account and line number where the counterentry occurs, generally in another account. For example, persons pay personal income and other taxes to the government. In account 2, line 1, the "(3-16)" following "personal tax and nontax payments" indicates that account 3,

CHART 1 Major Measures of Production and Income, 1985

- Gross national product: market value of goods and services produced.
- National income: income from the production of goods and services.
- Personal income: income received by persons from all sources.
- Disposable personal income: income remaining to persons after payment of personal taxes.

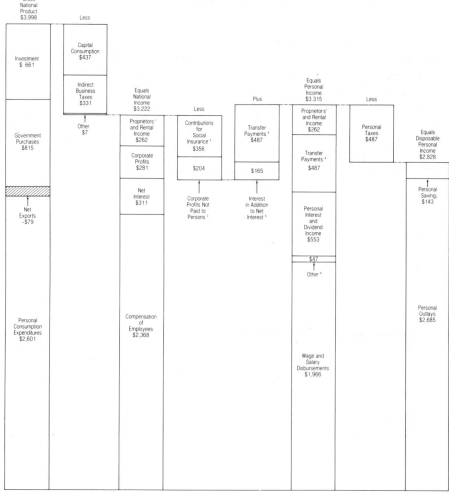

Billion $

1. Business transfer payments and statistical discrepancy, less subsidies less current surplus of government enterprises.
2. Personal and employer contributions, and wage accruals less disbursements.
3. Corporate profits tax liabilities, undistributed corporate profits, and dividends paid to government.
4. Government transfers to persons and business transfer payments.
5. Interest paid by government to persons and business less interest received by government, plus interest paid by consumers.
6. Other labor income less personal contributions for social insurance.

SOURCE: *Survey of Current Business* (July 1986), Tables 1.9 and 2.1.

line 16 shows this item as a receipt of the government sector. Correspondingly, that receipt item is followed by a "(2-1)," referring back to the payment item in the personal account.

NIPA ESTIMATES: THEIR PUBLICATION FORM AND SCHEDULE

The annual estimates presented in Table 1 are only the tip of the iceberg. To begin with, many NIPA estimates are also presented for quarters, and some estimates, for months. The presentation of quarterly estimates shown in the *Survey of Current Business*, the journal of record for the NIPAs, consists of over 50 tables. It shows GNP, the most widely used measure of U.S. production, in current and constant dollars with its associated measures of prices; product component detail in current and constant dollars; national and personal income; corporate profits; and other well-known measures such as inventory stocks, gross domestic product of corporate business, and merchandise trade by end-use commodity category. The estimates usually presented in the July *Survey* (see the description of the publication schedule, which follows), in about 130 tables, show even more detail. For example, annual estimates of personal consumption expenditures are broken down into about 100 different types. Also, several "relationship" tables show the adjustments to source data (such as tax return tabulations) needed to derive NIPA estimates, employment estimates consistent with the income and product measures, and industry breakdowns for GNP and several income components.

Most of the estimates are presented in billions of dollars. Estimates in *current dollars* are valued in the prices of the period in which the transaction takes place. Estimates in *constant dollars* are valued in the prices of a period designated the base period—at present, 1982. For example, if a gallon of grade-A milk was purchased in 1986 for $1.12, it would be entered in current-dollar personal consumption expenditures at $1.12. If it had cost $1.05 in 1982, it would be entered in constant-dollar personal consumption expenditures at $1.05. The designation of 1982 as the base period also means that price levels in 1982 are set equal to 100 in calculating price indexes and implicit price deflators.

For quarters, the estimates (except price indexes) are usually presented as seasonally adjusted annual rates. The seasonal adjustment is done to remove from the time series the variations, due to events such as weather, holidays, and tax payment dates, that normally occur at about the same time and in about the same magnitude each year. The statistical procedures to do this are based on historical experience; the Census Bureau's X-11 program is widely used. After seasonal adjustment, cyclical and other short-term changes in the economy stand out more clearly. Annual rates are the result of putting values for a quarter or a month at their annual equivalent; that is, they are the value that would be registered if the rate of activity were maintained for a full year. For example, if 2 million cars were sold in a quarter, the annual rate of sales for that quarter would be 8 million. Annual rates make it easier to compare values for time periods of different lengths; for example, quarters and years.

A preliminary estimate of GNP is released about 15 days after the end of a given quarter.[2] This estimate is based on source data that are incomplete and subject to revision. Revised estimates (known as 45-day and 75-day estimates) for a quarter are released in the two following months; they incorporate the source data that have subsequently become available. In addition, monthly estimates of personal income and its disposition are released.

Ordinarily, the NIPA estimates for the most recent calendar year and usually the two preceding years are revised each year in July, timed to incorporate annual source data. Comprehensive revisions—often called benchmark revisions—are carried out about every five years, timed to incorporate the quinquennial economic censuses. Conceptual, definitional, or classificational changes made to improve the NIPAs as a tool of economic analysis are usually introduced at the time of the comprehensive revisions. Such a revision was completed in December 1985. Its major features, aside from the introduction of new source data (including BEA's 1977 input-output table), were a shift in the base period from 1972 to 1982, the introduction of improved adjustments (often called the underground economy adjustments) for misreporting of tax return information used to estimate the NIPAs, and a new price index for computers.

USES OF THE NIPAs

NIPA estimates are widely used in analysis of past economic behavior and relationships, in assessments of the current economic conditions, in preparation of forecasts and projections, and in policy formulation and—as it may be called in the private sector—decision making. Looked at another way, NIPA users include business economists, academic researchers, state and local as well as federal government officials, and individual citizens attempting to orient themselves in a fast-changing economy.

The NIPAs can be used in several ways; for example, as time series, for cross-section analysis, or in relation to demographic and other

---

[2] From September 1983 to December 1985, the level and change in four summary figures—current-dollar GNP, constant-dollar GNP, the GNP fixed-weighted price index, and the GNP implicit price deflator—were released as "flash" estimates about 15 days before the end of the quarter.

information. Used in these ways, the NIPAs shed light on a number of aspects of the economy.

Economic growth. Constant-dollar GNP increased at an average annual rate of 2.9 percent from 1929 to 1985, of 3.2 percent from 1948 to 1985, of 3.1 percent from 1959 to 1985, and of 2.7 percent from 1970 to 1985.

Inflation. Prices (as measured by the implicit price deflator for GNP) increased at an average annual rate of 3.7 percent from 1929 to 1985 and of 4.3 percent from 1948–85. For 1959–85 and for 1970–85, prices (as measured by the GNP fixed-weighted price index) increased at an average annual rate of 4.3 percent and 5.9 percent, respectively.

International comparisons. From 1970 to 1985, the average annual rate of growth of U.S. gross domestic product in constant dollars, at 2.8 percent, was in the middle of the range of major industrial countries. Japan and Canada had higher rates (4.8 percent and 3.5 percent, respectively); France had the same rate as the United States; and the United Kingdom, West Germany, and Italy had lower rates (1.8 percent, 2.2 percent, and 2.4 percent, respectively).

Business cycles. Since 1948, constant-dollar GNP has declined two or more quarters six times. The largest drop, 7.0 percent, was in 1957–58; the smallest, 1.5 percent, was in 1969–70. In 1980, a single-quarter decline amounted to 9.1 percent.

Sector and industry origins of GNP. By sector, 85 percent of GNP originated in business in 1985, 10½ percent in government, 3½ percent in households and institutions, and 1 percent in the rest of the world. By industry, the single largest share, 20 percent, originated in manufacturing, followed by wholesale and retail trade (16 percent) and by finance, insurance, and real estate (16 percent).

GNP per employee. On average, each of the 94 million full-time equivalent employees produced about $42,700 of GNP in 1985.

Income distribution. Employee compensation (wages and salaries plus supplemental benefits) accounted for by far the largest share of national income—about 73 percent. Corporate profits accounted for 9 percent; net interest, for 10 percent; proprietors' income, for 8 percent; and rental income of persons, for less than 1 percent, in 1985.

Use of income. For each dollar of personal income received in 1985, persons used about 81 cents to purchase goods and services and for other outlays, paid 15 cents in personal taxes, and saved 4 cents.

Per capita income. On a per capita basis, disposable personal income (i.e., personal income after taxes) was $11,800 in 1985. In constant dollars, per capita income has a little more than doubled since 1948.

Product composition of GNP. In 1985, as has been typical, personal consumption expenditures accounted for almost two thirds of GNP. Nonresidential investment accounted for 11 percent, residential investment for 5 percent, government purchases for 20 percent, and additions to business inventories for a very small amount. Net exports were negative; the United States imported more than it exported.

Comparison of production and demand. Because the United States imported more than it exported in 1985, U.S. demand for goods and services wherever produced increased more than U.S. production; U.S. demand as meaured by constant-dollar gross domestic purchases increased 3.4 percent, and U.S. production as measured by constant-dollar GNP increased 2.7 percent. U.S. demand has increased more than U.S. production each year since 1983.

SOURCES AND METHODS

In addition to the set of definitions introduced in the overview and detailed in the technical note, the tool kit for NIPA users should include basic information about the sources and methods used to prepare the estimates. Because the sources and methods determine the reliability of the estimates, information about them helps the user to assess their reliability in the context in which they will be used.

A Survey of Sources

With few exceptions, the source data are collected not for the purpose of being transformed into income and product estimates, but for other purposes. The source data range widely in terms of collecting agency and primary use, periodicity, statistical techniques, and reliability.

Data collected by federal government agencies—The Census Bureau, Treasury Department, Labor Department, Office of Management and Budget, and Agriculture Department—provide the backbone of the estimates. Government-collected data may be either administrative or nonadministrative. Administrative data are by-products of government functions, such as welfare and social security programs, tax collection, and regulation. Nonadministrative data, sometimes referred to as "general-purpose" or "statistical" data, include the periodic economic and population censuses and sample surveys, such as those that obtain data on manufacturing activity, corporation finance, and households. Most of the relatively few items for which BEA collects data used to estimate the NIPAs refer to international activity, including investment by foreigners in the United States and by U.S. residents abroad. Government data are supplemented by data from trade associations and business, labor organizations, and welfare, education, and religious groups.

The differences in statistical technique and periodicity of collection are factors in determining how and at what stage in the revision schedule a particular data source is used. For benchmarks, use is made of data sources that provide the most complete coverage. Examples are the decennial census of population, the decennial census of housing, the extensive business data collected by the Census Bureau in the quinquennial economic censuses (mainly the censuses of manufactures, wholesale trade, retail trade, service industries, construction industries, agriculture, and mineral industries), the census of governments, data compiled by the Bureau of Labor Statistics on wages and salaries of employees covered by state unemployment insurance, and data related to business income tabulations from tax returns compiled by the Internal Revenue Service and published in its *Statistics of Income* series. The last two sources are available annually and therefore can be used for nonbenchmark as well as benchmark years, although the Internal Revenue Service data are available in complete form only with a lag of several years.

Annual data sources often are based on samples. Among these are the annual surveys by the Census Bureau reported in the *Annual Survey of Manufactures*, the *Annual Retail Trade Report*, the *Annual Wholesale Trade Report*, the *Service Annual Survey*, and *Governmental Finances*.

Quarterly and monthly data sources usually are based on samples. These include the monthly surveys of manufacturing, wholesale trade, and retail trade, which are based on smaller samples than their annual counterparts; the *Quarterly Financial Report*, which is prepared by the Census Bureau and provides financial data for manufacturing, mining, and trade corporations; the monthly surveys of wages and employment by the Bureau of Labor Statistics; and the monthly survey of construction reported by the Census Bureau in *Value of New Construction Put in Place*. One monthly set of data, that reported by the Census Bureau in *Highlights of U.S. Export and Import Trade*, is from documentation intended to cover nearly all goods as they enter and leave the country. Data from the last two sources, although collected monthly, are not replaced by annual data based on a more comprehensive collection system and are used for annual as well as quarterly estimates.

A Survey of Methods

The data pulled together from these diverse sources undergo considerable processing by BEA. In part, this involves adjustment of the data to the stipulated definitions of the economic accounting aggregates. An example is the adjustment of corporate profits as reported by business to the NIPA definition.[3] In addition, gaps in information have to be filled by referring to sources that are themselves incomplete, and conflicting evidence may be received from different sources or for slightly differing periods. The processing is not purely mechanical; judgment necessarily enters, often in subtle ways.

Extrapolation and interpolation are among the generally used methods. They are used to calculate estimates for one or more periods from estimates for other periods for which data are more reliable or more abundant. Extrapolation projects estimates from one period, either forward or backward in time, to other periods; interpolation fills in estimates between two periods. Extrapolations and interpolations may use indicator series or trends. Indicators range from samples of the universe being estimated (e.g., extrapolating dividend payments on the basis of a sample of large, publicly held corporations) to measures only indirectly related to what is being estimated (e.g., extrapolating sales taxes on the basis of retail sales). The results of both procedures become less reliable the longer the period covered by the calculated estimates.

In addition to such general methods, methods specific to various components of the NIPAs are used to piece together the source data. Three of the specific methods, two for product-side components and one related to income-side components, can be used to illustrate several aspects of the estimating work—its complexity, its relationship to business accounting, and the interdependence of the various methods.

The first of these, the commodity-flow method, was developed in its basic form by Simon Kuznets in the 1930s as a way of obtaining the value of consumers' purchases of goods (i.e., commodities) or the value of producers' purchases of durable equipment. A generalization of the commodity-flow method that takes place within an input-output framework is now followed by BEA for benchmark years. The steps outlined below for goods included in personal consumption expenditures do not fully indicate the complexity of commodity-flow methods, but they do provide a notion of what is involved in using them.

1. From among the detailed list of products enumerated in the census of manufactures, those destined for consumer use are segregated. This involves, in addition to the straight selection of products

---

[3] For a description of the steps to derive corporate profits before tax from the item "total receipts less total deductions" in the Internal Revenue Service tabulation, see (5).

destined solely for consumers, an allocation of products whose use is mixed; for example, an estimate of how much flour is purchased by households directly and how much is purchased by bakeries.

2.   Sales by nonmanufacturing producers of commodities destined for consumer use are taken into account. Among these are the products of agriculture, commercial fisheries, and mining, for which the censuses of agriculture and minerals industries provide information.

3.   Transportation charges are added, mainly on the basis of information from the Interstate Commerce Commission, the Department of Transportation, and the Corps of Engineers.

4.   Imports are added, mainly on the basis of Census Bureau data.

5.   Producers' sales to consumers need no further processing. For other sales to consumers, wholesale and retail inventory change and wholesale and retail markups, including sales taxes, are taken into account. Information is mainly from Census Bureau surveys and censuses and the Internal Revenue Service.

Second, the method used to estimate the nonfarm inventory change brings out the relation of the NIPAs to business accounting while, at the same time, illustrating how business accounts must be modified for the NIPAs. Change in business inventories is defined as the change in physical volume of inventories valued at average prices of the period. The basic data available for manufacturing and trade inventories, which make up over 90 percent of the nonfarm total, are book values. These book values (i.e., values as reported by business based on their own accounting system) are derived from Census Bureau censuses or, for noncensus years, sample surveys of wholesalers, retailers, and manufacturers. In general, the change in the book value of inventories does not conform to the NIPA definition, because book values reflect the prices of inventories in the periods in which they were acquired; if prices change, identical physical units in the stock of inventories will generally be valued at different prices. Therefore, adjustments must be made. The adjustments use information on the proportion of inventories reported with different accounting methods (e.g., first-in-first-out and last-in-first-out), the commodity composition and cost of goods held in inventory, and the turnover period. The price information is largely from the producer price indexes; the other information is largely from Census Bureau surveys of manufacturing and trade. The basic steps of the procedure used to derive the NIPA change in business inventories from book values are shown below.

1.   Inventory stocks at book value are separated according to the inventory accounting methods that underlie them. This separation is necessary because the mix of acquisition costs differs according to the several accounting methods.

2.   Prices that correspond to the costs of different commodities in

the stock are selected by reference to turnover periods. In general, the longer the turnover period, the further back in time are the prices that are reflected in these costs.

3. Book-value stocks are divided by indexes based on these prices to convert them into constant-dollar stocks.

4. The differences between the constant-dollar stocks are multiplied by ratios of current prices to constant prices to obtain the NIPA change in business inventories.

The third and last of the specific methods, the perpetual inventory method, is used to derive estimates of the private fixed capital stock. The stock estimates, in turn, form the basis for the estimates of depreciation—the major part of capital consumption allowances—for owner-occupied housing, nonprofit institutions, and farms and for the estimates of the capital consumption adjustment that are shown with proprietors' income, rental income of persons, and corporate profits. The method, an alternative to direct estimates of the capital stock (which are seldom statistically feasible on a comprehensive basis), was described in its classical form by Raymond W. Goldsmith in 1951 and is used in one version or another by economic accountants in most nations. The steps in this method and the information that was used in preparing BEA's most recent estimates of the capital stock (except autos) are summarized below. One of the main advantages of obtaining the stock estimates in this way is that, for the most part, comprehensive, detailed, and relatively reliable estimates of investment flows—with which the method starts—are available within the NIPAs. By using these flows, the resulting stock estimates are consistent conceptually and statistically with the NIPAs.

This method has the additional advantage of yielding alternative valuations of the capital stock. The stock at historical cost (i.e., when an asset is valued in the stock at the price at which it was purchased new) is obtained by cumulating current-dollar investment flows in step 1. The stock at current cost (i.e., when an asset is valued at the price that would have been paid for it had it been purchased in the period to which the stock estimates refer) and the depreciation that is part of the capital consumption allowances are obtained by applying the appropriate price indexes to the constant-cost stock.

Annual Current-Dollar Estimates: Summary for Income and Product

Table 2 shows, in summary form, the sources and methods used to prepare the annual current-dollar estimates of the income and product sides of account 1. The major subcomponents in the table, shown with

Step	*Information Used*
1. Assemble investment flows (supplemented by transfer of used assets) in asset/industry/legal form detail going back far enough in time to account for the stock at a starting date.	Investment flows at the all-industry level for 1929 and later are the NIPA fixed investment series, and those for earlier years are based on a variety of public and private sources.
2. Deflate flows to obtain constant-cost estimates.	Price indexes are those used to derive constant-dollar NIPA fixed investment series: For structures, they are based on various price and cost indexes; for equipment, based on producer price indexes from the Bureau of Labor Statistics and BEA's computer price index.
3. Cumulate the value of the constant-cost investment flows.	. . . .
4. Associate a "life" (i.e., the length of time between the investment and when the asset is retired from the stock) with each asset type in the NIPA fixed investment series to establish when each asset will be retired.	Average service lives are from industry studies in the 1970s by the Treasury Department, "Bulletin F" (1942 ed.) of the Treasury Department, book value data compiled by regulatory agencies, Department of Agriculture data, and trade association data. Distributions of retirements around the average service life are based on a bell-shaped distribution centered on the average (e.g., retirements start at 5 percent of the average life and end at 195 percent for residential structures).
5. Cumulate the value of retirements and subtract these cumulative values from the cumulative value of investment; the result is gross stock at constant prices.	. . . .
6. Calculate the part of each investment flow that is consumed each year.	Straight-line depreciation is applied to the investment flows.
7. Cumulate the value of depreciation and subtract the cumulative value from the gross stock; the result is the net stock at constant cost.	. . . .

TABLE 2 Principal Sources and Methods Used in Preparing Current-Dollar Annual Estimates for the National Income and Product Account

Component*	Subcomponent*	Principal Sources and Method
		Product side (GNP of $3,998.1 billion in 1985)
Personal consumption expenditures ($2,600.5)	Most goods ($1,027.4)	Benchmark years—Commodity flow, starting with Census Bureau manufacturers' shipments, as described in the text. Other years—Retail trade sales from Census Bureau annual survey or, for the most recent year, monthly survey of retailers.
	New and used cars, and trucks ($145.1)	For new vehicles, physical quantity purchased times average retail price: unit sales, information with which to allocate sales among consumers and other purchasers, and average list prices, all from trade sources. For used cars, estimated dealers' margins based on unit sales and change in the consumer net stock of autos at least 1 year old, from trade sources.
	Gasoline and oil ($91.9)	Years except most recent—Physical quantity purchased times average retail price: gallons consumed from the Department of Transportation, information with which to allocate that total among consumers and other purchasers from federal agencies and trade sources, and average retail price by grade from the Bureau of Labor Statistics. Most recent year—Sales from the Census Bureau monthly survey of retailers.
	Rental value of non-farm housing ($378.0)	Benchmark years—Based on data on housing stock and average annual rental from censuses of population and housing. Other years—Based on data on housing stock from the Census Bureau biennial American housing survey or on the number of households from the current population survey and updated average annual rental.
	Auto and other repair; legal services; barbershops, laundries, and other personal services; movie theaters and other recreation;	Benchmark years—Receipts from Census Bureau census of business. Other years— Receipts from Census Bureau service annual survey.

TABLE 2 *(continued)*

Component*	Subcomponent*	Principal Sources and Methods—Product side
	hotels and motels; and commercial education ($195.9)	
	Brokerage, financial services, intercity transportation, and private higher education ($128.8)	For private education, expenses, and for other categories, receipts, from annual reports of government administrative agencies.
	Social welfare activities, elementary and secondary schools, domestic services, and parts of other personal business ($66.2)	Bureau of Labor Statistics tabulations of wages and salaries of employees covered by state unemployment insurance.
	Insurance, hospitals, telephone, electricity, gas, local transport, religious and welfare activities ($364.7)	For insurance, nonprofit hospitals, and part of religious activities, expenses from reports of private organizations; for utilities, receipts from government agencies and trade sources; and for other categories, receipts from reports of private organizations.
	Physicians, dentists, and other medical professional services ($128.9)	Benchmark years—Receipts, adjusted for government payments and prepayment plans, from Census Bureau census of business. Other years—Receipts, adjusted for government payments and prepayment plans, from Census Bureau service annual survey.
Nonresidential structures ($154.8)	New nonfarm buildings ($95.1)	Value of construction put in place from the Census Bureau.
	Public utilities ($28.2)	For telephone and telegraph, same as new nonfarm buildings; for others, federal regulatory data and trade sources.
	Mining exploration,	For petroleum and natural gas, physical quantity times average price: footage drilled and

Component	Source and method
Nonresidential producers' durable equipment ($303.4)	
shafts, and wells ($26.0)	cost per foot from trade sources; for other mining, BEA plant and equipment expenditures survey.
Most equipment ($248.2)	Benchmark years—Commodity flow, starting with manufacturers' shipments from Census Bureau surveys, similar to what was described in the text for personal consumption expenditures. Other years—Abbreviated commodity flow, starting with manufacturers' shipments from the Census Bureau annual survey or, for the most recent year, monthly survey of manufactures.
New and used autos, and trucks ($55.2)	See entry for personal consumption expenditures.
Residential investment ($191.8)	
New permanent-site housing units ($116.2)	For single-family housing, based on phased housing starts and an average construction cost from a Census Bureau survey; for multifamily housing, see entry for nonresidential buildings.
Additions, alterations, and major replacements ($46.8)	Bureau of Labor Statistics consumer expenditure survey.
Brokers' commissions ($16.2)	Physical quantity times price: number of one-family houses sold and mean sales price, from Census Bureau surveys and trade sources.
Producers' durable equipment ($5.5)	See entry for personal consumption expenditures.
Mobile homes ($6.1)	Physical quantity shipped times price: shipments from trade sources and average retail price from Census Bureau survey.
Change in business inventories ($11.1)	
Manufacturing and trade ($6.9)	Benchmark years—Book values from Census Bureau censuses, converted, as described in the text, to NIPA basis. Other years—Mainly book values from Census Bureau surveys, converted, as described in the text, to NIPA basis.
Other nonfarm industries ($5.3)	Mainly book values from Internal Revenue Service tabulations of business tax returns.
Farm (−$1.1)	Physical quantities times current prices, from Department of Agriculture surveys.
Net exports of goods and services (−$78.9)	
Merchandise exports and imports, net (−$122.1)	Import and export documents compiled by the Census Bureau, with adjustments by BEA for coverage and valuation to put them on a balance-of-payments basis.
Receipts and payments of factor in-	For direct investment income, BEA surveys of U.S. companies with affiliates abroad and of U.S. affiliates of foreign companies; for income from securities, Treasury Department sur-

TABLE 2 *(continued)*

Component*	Subcomponent*	Principal Sources and Methods—Income side
	come, net ($41.1)	veys; and for other income, holdings from Treasury Department surveys times appropriate yields or interest rates.
	Receipts and payments for other services, net ($2.0)	For government transactions, reports by federal agencies on their purchases, sales, and loans abroad; for most other categories, quantity measures times average unit values, with most quantity measures (such as number of travelers and freight tonnage) from government agencies and unit values from BEA surveys.
Government purchases of goods and services ($815.4)	Federal ($354.1)	Expenditures from *Treasury Combined Statement of Receipts, Expenditures, and Balances* and *Budget of the United States*, adjusted for timing differences, to exclude (mainly) debt interest, grants-in-aid, transfer payments, subsidies, capital transactions, net expenditures of government enterprises, and foreign currency purchases.
	State and local compensation ($280.1)	Mainly Bureau of Labor Statistics tabulations of wages and salaries of employees covered by state unemployment insurance.
	State and local structures ($53.5)	For highways, expenditures from the Department of Transportation; for other categories, value of construction put in place from the Census Bureau.
	State and local other than compensation and structures ($127.7)	Expenditures reported by these governments to the Census Bureau, adjusted to a calendar-year basis from a fiscal-year basis and adjusted for exclusions and inclusions in a manner similar to that for federal purchases.
		Income side (Charges against GNP)
Compensation of employees ($2,368.2)	Wages and salaries: private plus state and local ($1,836.3)	For most, Bureau of Labor Statistics tabulations of wages and salaries of employees covered by state unemployment insurance; for remainder, wages from a variety of sources (such as Department of Agriculture for farms) and indirect estimation for a very few cases (such as a percentage of revenues for tips not reported as wages).
	Wages and salaries: federal ($129.5)	Wages from the Office of Personnel Management and the *Budget of the United States*.
	Employer contributions for social insur-	Contributions from the Social Security Administration, other agencies administering social insurance, and Census Bureau surveys of state and local government retirement funds.

ance ($205.5)
Other labor income ($196.9)

Contributions from trade sources for life insurance, from Internal Revenue Service tabulations for private pensions, and from Health Care Financing Administration tabulations for health insurance for private industries; contributions from the Office of Personnel Management for life and health insurance for federal government.

Proprietors' income with IVA and CCAdj ($254.4)

Nonfarm income ($193.5)

Years except most recent—Income from Internal Revenue Service tabulations, adjusted for understatement of income on tax returns and for several conceptual differences.

Most recent year—Extrapolations by industry: for construction, trade, and services, by indicators of activity (such as housing put in place); for most others, by past trends.

Nonfarm IVA (−$0.2)
Nonfarm CCAdj ($31.9)

The IVA is described under corporate profits.
The CCAdj is described under capital consumption allowances.

Farm income with IVA ($38.0)

Based on Department of Agriculture data on net income, obtained by deriving gross earnings (cash receipts from marketing, inventory change, government payments, other cash income, and nonmoney income) and subtracting production expenses, adjusted to exclude corporate income based on Internal Revenue Service tabulations.

Farm CCAdj (−$8.8)

The CCAdj is described under capital consumption allowances.

Rent from nonfarm nonresidential properties ($11.2)

Years except the two most recent—Rents paid and received by business and government, adjusted for expenses associated with property (mainly depreciation, taxes, interest, and repairs), from Internal Revenue Service tabulations, Census Bureau surveys, and the *Budget of the United States.*

Two most recent years—Trends.

Rental income of persons with CCAdj ($7.6)

Rent from nonfarm housing ($26.5)

For imputed space rent on owner-occupied housing, as indicated for rental value in personal consumption expenditures, adjusted for expenses from a variety of sources; for rent on tenant-occupied housing, similar sources and methods.

Royalties ($9.6)

Years except most recent—Internal Revenue Service tabulations of royalties.

Most recent year—Trends and related information.

Rent from farms owned by nonoperator landlords ($5.1)

Prepared in conjunction with farm proprietors' income; see that entry.

CCAdj (−$44.8)

The CCAdj is described under capital consumption allowances.

Corporate profits with IVA and CCAdj ($280.7)

Profits: before tax, domestic ($191.3)

Years except the two most recent—Internal Revenue Service tabulations, adjusted to include in profits the depletion allowances on domestic minerals, income of the Federal Reserve and federally sponsored credit agencies, the excess of additions to bad debt

TABLE 2 *(concluded)*

Component*	Subcomponent*	Principal Sources and Methods—Income side
		reserves over losses actually incurred, and an estimate of the amount by which income on tax returns is understated and to exclude capital gains and losses on the sale of property and dividends received from domestic corporations. Two most recent years—Separate extrapolations for about 70 industries based on data from the Census Bureau *Quarterly Financial Report*, regulatory agencies, and compilations of publicly reported company profits.
	Profits: rest of the world ($31.8) IVA (−$0.6)	Net income estimated as part of the balance of payments, based in part on BEA surveys of direct investment. Obtained as the difference between the change in the physical volume of inventories valued in prices of the current period, derived as described in the text, and the change in the book value of inventories reported by business.
Net interest ($311.4)	CCAdj ($58.1) Net interest: domestic monetary ($125.4)	The CCAdj is described under capital consumption allowances. For interest paid and received by business, primarily from Internal Revenue Service tabulations; for other components for all years and for business when these tabulations are not available, interest receipts and payments are from regulatory agencies (such as the Federal Deposit Insurance Corporation), from trade sources, or obtained by applying an interest rate to a stock of assets/liabilities from Federal Reserve Board flow-of-funds accounts.
	Net interest: rest-of-the world monetary ($14.8) Net interest: imputed ($171.1)	Payments and receipts estimated as part of the balance of payments. For financial services furnished without payment by banks and other depository institutions, property income earned on investment of deposits and monetary interest paid (and for mutual depositories, profits) from annual reports of regulatory agencies and the Federal Reserve Board; for financial services furnished without payment by life insurance carriers and private noninsured pension plans, property income earned (and for life insurance carriers, profits) from Internal Revenue Service tabulations and, for the most recent year, from trade sources.
Business transfer		For corporate gifts to nonprofit institutions and bad debts incurred by consumers, Internal

Component	Subcomponent	Source/description
payments ($20.9)		Revenue Service tabulations; for other components (such as liability payments for personal injury), information from other government and trade sources.
Indirect business tax and nontax liability ($331.4)	Federal ($56.1)	For excise taxes and customs duties, collections from the Internal Revenue Service; for nontaxes (such as fines), receipts from the *Budget of the United States.*
	State and local ($275.4)	Census Bureau censuses and surveys of finances.
Subsidies less current surplus of government enterprises ($8.2)	Federal ($20.7)	For subsidies, Treasury Department reports and *Budget of the United States;* for current surpluses, profit and loss statements of enterprises organized as corporations (such as the Tennessee Valley Authority) or financial statements reconstructed from available budgetary data for others.
	State and local (−$12.6)	For subsidies, limited to railroad, data from trade sources; for current surplus, see entry for state and local purchases other than compensation and structures.
Capital consumption allowances with CCAdj ($437.2)	Capital consumption allowances ($467.3)	For depreciation of nonfarm sole proprietorships, partnerships, and corporations, Internal Revenue Service tabulations; for depreciation of farms, nonprofit institutions, tax-exempt cooperatives, and owner-occupied houses, perpetual inventory calculations, as described in the text; for accidental damage to fixed capital, losses reported to insurance companies and government agencies.
	CCAdj ($30.1)	Obtained in two parts: first, the part that places a historical-cost series for capital consumed on a consistent basis with regard to service lives and on a straight-line depreciation pattern is the difference between tax return-based calculations at historical cost and the perpetual-inventory calculations, as described in the text; second, the part that places the historical-cost series on a replacement cost basis is the difference between two perpetual-inventory calculations, one at historical cost and one at replacement cost.

CCAdj = Capital consumption adjustment.
IVA = Inventory valuation adjustment.
* Values shown, in billions of dollars, are for 1985; the subcomponents may not add up to the component totals.

SOURCE: 1985 estimates—*Survey of Current Business,* July 1986.

their 1985 dollar values, are grouped according to the sources and methods used in preparing them.

Table 2's main purpose is to provide a convenient reference. In addition, it provides the basis for several observations about sources and methods (which, in combination, are often referred to as "methodology"). First, on the product side, separate methodologies are often shown for benchmark and other years. In these cases, the sources shown for benchmark years are those that underlie the most recent input-output table (as of 1985, the 1977 table) and the sources shown for other years are used to interpolate and extrapolate from the benchmark years. On the income side, this distinction between benchmark and other years does not appear. For many income-side components, the same methodology is used each year. However, for several, notably corporate profits, the best source data do not become available for several years so that interim methodologies must be used until the best one can be substituted at the time of a July revision. Second, product-side estimates are largely based on nonadministrative data; Census Bureau censuses and surveys dominate. Income-side estimates are largely based on administrative data; tabulations from unemployment insurance programs and tax returns dominate. Third, the product-side estimates provide an illustration of how the estimates reflect the state of development of the underlying statistical system. The goods components are, to a large extent, based on a single basic method: The commodity-flow method is used for benchmark years for most goods in personal consumption expenditures and for producers' durable equipment, and an abbreviated commodity-flow method is used for the latter for other years. Thus, the estimates of these goods are based primarily on the comprehensive data collected in Census Bureau censuses and surveys. In contrast, the services components—in both personal consumption expenditures and net exports—are pieced together from a variety of sources, many of which are less well suited to estimation.

Quarterly Current-Dollar Estimates

The sources and methods used for 15-, 45-, and 75-day estimates differ considerably from those just described for annual estimates. In general, the source data are much less complete and are more subject to revision by the source agency. For example, at the time of the presentation of the estimates 15 days after the end of a quarter, the key data available for personal consumption expenditures are the three months of retail sales (of which two months are subject to revision by the source agency); three months of unit sales of new motor vehicles, one month of information with which to allocate the unit sales among consumers and other purchasers, and two or three months of average list prices (which are subject to modification as information on actual retail prices becomes available); and one or two months of data for services amounting to one half of total services.[4] The estimates for most of the remainder of personal consumption expenditures are extrapolations based either on related indicator series or on past trends. For the 45- and 75-day estimates, revised retail sales, information on sales and inventories of used cars, and more data on selected services (such as electricity) become available.

As suggested by the release of monthly estimates of personal consumption expenditures, source data for this GNP component are more complete or are more reliable extrapolators than are the source data for other components. The change in business inventories and net exports are at the other end of the scale among the product components. For the change in business inventories, book values are limited to those for manufacturing and trade for two months (and data for the second month are subject to revision). For net exports, only merchandise exports and imports (and those only partially for the second month) are available. For both of these components, the difficulty of estimating with only limited data is compounded by their volatility.

Among the income components, source data for wages and salaries are most complete. For almost all private industries, monthly estimates (which are summed to quarterly totals) are prepared by extrapolating annual estimates by the product of total employment, total hours paid, and earnings of production workers from the Bureau of Labor Statistics monthly survey of establishments. Federal civilian wages and salaries are based on monthly data from the Office of Personnel Management, and other government wages and salaries are based on monthly data on employment and BEA estimates of average earnings. Most other income components are prepared by extrapolating annual estimates either by an indicator series (e.g., dividends are extrapolated by reference to dividends paid by a BEA sample of large publicly held corporations) or by past trends. Although dividends paid can be estimated monthly for incorporation in personal income, the corporate profits total, which is estimated largely on the basis of industry extrapolations from the *Quarterly Financial Report*, lags one month (and two months for the fourth quarter). Thus, the preliminary estimate for corporate profits and for the income-side total is released 45 days after the close of a quarter (75 days for the fourth quarter).

---

[4] BEA makes available a table at the time of the 15-day estimates that shows, by month for a given quarter, the key source data available, whether the data are subject to revision or not, and projections by BEA for data that are not available. The table, "Key Source Data and Projections for National Income and Product Estimates," was described in the *Survey of Current Business*, October 1978.

Constant-Dollar Estimates and Associated Price Indexes

To prepare constant-dollar estimates—or, as they are often called, real estimates—for GNP and its product components, in principle each component is valued at its price in a base period. This approach—rather than one of adding together the various physical quantities, which is the approach perhaps suggested by the term *real*—is used because, as the adage says, "you can't add apples and oranges;" dollar values provide the necessary common denominator.

Statistically, most constant-dollar estimates are obtained by dividing the most detailed current-dollar components by appropriate price indexes with 1982, the base period as of 1985, equal to 100. Components of the consumer price index and the producer price indexes, prepared by the Bureau of Labor Statistics, are the principal price indexes used. These indexes are used in preparing constant-dollar estimates of components that account for well over three fourths of GNP. Other price information includes the Census Bureau unit-value indexes for exports and imports and the price index for single-family houses, the Bureau of Labor Statistics export and import price indexes, BEA indexes for defense goods and services and for computers, and indexes prepared by trade sources. For several components, constant-dollar estimates are obtained by extrapolating the current-dollar estimates in 1982 by physical volume measures. For a few components, constant-dollar estimates are directly prepared by multiplying quantities by 1982 prices.

A by-product of the preparation of current- and constant-dollar estimates is the implicit price deflator. It is derived as a current-dollar measure divided by a constant-dollar measure, multiplied by 100. Technically, the implicit price deflator for GNP or a component of GNP is an average of the indexes of prices of all the goods and services that make up GNP or the component, weighted by the composition of GNP or the component in the current period. Thus, changes in the implicit price deflator reflect not only changes in prices but also any shift in composition of GNP or the component.

The implicit price deflator was introduced in 1951, along with the first estimates of constant-dollar GNP. In 1969, BEA introduced fixed-weighted price indexes. The fixed-weighted price indexes are an average of the prices of GNP or the component, weighted by the composition of GNP or the component at a fixed point selected as the base period. Such indexes measure the change in the prices of a fixed market basket; thus, they measure only price change. BEA also introduced chain price indexes, another measure that, from one period to the next, does not reflect shifts in the composition. Since the 1970s, when it became especially useful to distinguish quarter-to-quarter shifts in the composition of GNP from price changes because at times each was large, BEA increasingly featured the GNP fixed-weighted and chain price indexes as appropriate measures of price change.

In recent years, the quantity and quality of the constant-dollar measures (and associated price indexes) have been substantially improved. Several of the major price indexes used as source data have been overhauled by the source agency. In addition, BEA has developed several new sets of price information and improved deflation procedures. For example, beginning in the mid-1970s, BEA (in cooperation with the Department of Defense) developed price indexes at a very detailed level, along with parallel product detail, for defense purchases. Implementation of the standard procedure is especially difficult for defense purchases; some defense spending is for unique products that change rapidly and are otherwise difficult to price. In 1980, BEA introduced improvements in the preparation of constant-dollar estimates of nonfarm inventories. The commodity composition of inventories was estimated in more detail than previously to allow use of more appropriate or detailed indexes of prices (or production costs), and groups of commodities with markedly different turnover periods were delineated to allow use of separate indexes. In 1985, BEA introduced a new price index for computers. The index represents a substantial step in coping with a problem referred to as the "quality change problem," a problem common to many products to one degree or another but particularly pronounced for computer equipment because of rapid technological change. Further, BEA has recently completed a project to improve the constant-dollar estimates for merchandise exports and imports. A major part of this work is the substitution of price indexes developed by the Bureau of Labor Statistics for the Census Bureau unit-value indexes.

THE EVOLUTION OF INCOME AND PRODUCT ACCOUNTS: THE LAST FOUR DECADES

As noted earlier, the NIPAs emerged as a system in the 1940s. The formal presentation was in 1947, when BEA's predecessor agency published a basic revision of the estimates along with a brief description of the new system. The estimates found ready reception; by the mid-1950s, the NIPAs were in wide use in analysis and policy formation. At that time, as shown in the July 1955 *Survey of Current Business*, for example, the NIPAs were presented in 52 tables—41 of annual estimates and 11 of quarterly and monthly estimates. Recent issues of the *Survey* show over 50 tables of quarterly estimates alone, and the July 1986 issue, with about 130 tables, provides even more detail. An impressionistic review of the intervening three decades indicates some of the ways in which the NIPAs were expanded and refined (2).

By the mid-1950s, it was increasingly clear that the usefulness of both the NIPAs and other economic accounting systems would be enhanced if they were integrated definitionally and statistically. BEA continued to develop its regional and international (or balance-of-payments) estimates in this light. In addition, work was begun to integrate the NIPAs and the other branches of national accounts: (1) as a result of a project started in 1959, the 1958 input-output table was integrated with the NIPAs, and currently the product components of GNP are "benchmarked" to the tables; (2) with changes made in the NIPAs in 1965 and in the flow of funds accounts, prepared by the Federal Reserve Board, over the years, the two sets of accounts have moved closer together; and (3) as suggested by the description of the perpetual inventory method earlier, work is well along in developing a set of tangible wealth estimates that are conceptually and statistically integrated with the NIPAs.

By the 1960s, the economic policy focus was on stabilization, mainly based on fiscal policy, and the need for timely NIPA estimates became more urgent. As a result, the 15-day quarterly estimate was provided beginning in 1965, and the number of series provided on a quarterly basis was expanded substantially. As well, the NIPAs had been expanded to include more information on government transactions. For example, estimates by type of function and object breakdown had been developed.

In the late 1960s and in the 1970s, when high rates of inflation became a major concern, BEA began to improve and expand the information on prices associated with the NIPAs. The number of series, including quarterly series, on prices was expanded, and, as described earlier, the fixed-weighted price index was introduced and more appropriate price indexes and procedures for deflation were developed for a number of components.

The NIPAs and associated estimates were expanded along other lines to support research in areas of concern. As interest in the environment came to the fore, estimates of expenditures to abate and control pollution were developed in the NIPA framework. As the accelerated retardation in the growth of productivity emerged in the 1970s, work on depreciation and capital stocks was stepped up. Finally, as concern over the growth of the federal government and federal debt heightened, the cyclically adjusted federal surplus or deficit was refined and related estimates of the federal debt were developed.

In the 1980s, work continued in several directions. Two major improvements—the introduction of improved underground economy adjustments and a new price index for computers—were mentioned earlier in describing the comprehensive revision released in December 1985. Further improvements, as in the past, are likely to include both statistical changes and conceptual changes.

An example of a likely statistical improvement would be the development of constant-dollar measures that are not stated in the prices of a single base year. For many purposes, a base year that is "representative" of the years in which the transactions took place is most appropriate; to continue an earlier example, the purchase of a quart of milk to be included in a constant-dollar measure is best stated in the prices of a year that is representative of the year in which the purchase is actually made. Usually, a representative year is one close chronologically to the year for which the estimate is to be made. Thus, because many constant-dollar NIPA measures extend back to 1929, the use of a single-base year—as of 1985, the base year is 1982—is questionable. It is likely that the present NIPA measures will be supplemented by indexes of GNP and its principal components that are calculated by linking indexes of the components either using each successive year as the base year or using some year within a subperiod, such as a decade, as the base year for that subperiod. Such linked indexes would improve comparisons of business cycles (e.g., a comparison of the strength of the most recent recovery and expansion of real GNP with the strength of those in earlier periods) and the analysis of long-term economic growth.

A research agenda related to the measurement of saving provides examples of conceptual work that could be quite fruitful. To begin with, the NIPA concepts of saving will be reexamined to determine whether the NIPA measure of personal saving—personal income less personal outlays—reflects the changing nature and role of saving in the U.S. economy, particularly as saving may be affected by the development of private and public retirement systems. Several long-standing questions will be examined in the changed context: Should personal income continue to exclude realized capital gains? Should certain items that the employee never sees in his paycheck, such as employer contributions to private pension plans, continue to be included in personal income? Should consumer durables continue to be reflected in personal outlays by the amount of expenditure on them, rather than by the amount of services they provide? Answers different than the ones currently embodied in the NIPAs may lead to the provision of measures of saving that supplement the present one with the goal of enhancing the usefulness of the NIPAs as a tool of economic analysis.

In a number of major respects, the evolution of the NIPAs in the United States has paralleled that of economic accounts in a number of Western developed countries. (The Soviet Union and Eastern European countries developed a system of economic accounts, the material product system, that differs from that used in Western countries; most importantly, the production it covers is limited to goods and services related to production, repair, transportation, and distribution of goods.) At the outset, this parallel development reflected the sharing of information by the relatively few persons who were working in the field in English-speaking countries. In the early 1940s, estimators and users of estimates in the United States were in touch informally with their counterparts in the United Kingdom and Canada as they all sought to develop estimates for use in analysis of productive potential, inflation, and other problems related to the war effort. In 1944, experts of the three countries formalized their consultations to compare conceptual and statistical treatments. After World War II, the experience of these three countries was reflected in the economic accounts put in place in several European countries; these accounts played an important role in framing economic recovery programs.

On a broader scale, the League of Nations, in its annual *World Economic Survey*, in 1939 first published what was then referred to as "national income" estimates. The estimates covered 26 countries—about one third were prepared as "official" estimates—for all or part of the period from 1929 to 1938. Also in 1939, a League committee first considered the problems of international comparability of the estimates. In the mid-1940s, the League convened a group of experts to consider the usefulness of a set of standards to serve as guidelines to nations developing their own estimates and as a vehicle for international reporting. A memorandum prepared by Richard Stone, of the United Kingdom, which served as a basis for the group's discussion, stands as a landmark in the development of the estimates in that it sets out an accounting framework.

Subsequently, the United Nations published its first System of National Accounts (SNA) in 1953. When this system was published, the possibilities of a more comprehensive system were recognized, but it was judged premature to provide guidelines for any part except national income and product in current prices. Thus, the system consisted of 6 accounts and 12 supporting tables designed to present the main flows relating to production, consumption, investment, and international trade.

A revision of the SNA in 1968 reflected the large amount of work in the field in the intervening 15 years: the amount of detail that could be provided by many countries was expanded; attention was being devoted to constant-price measures; and experience had been gained in constructing input-output tables, financial accounts, and, to a lesser extent, balance sheets. In addition, it reflected the expanded use made of disaggregated econometric models.

The revised SNA, more than the earlier version, differs from the accounts in use in the United States. Its primary aggregates are domestic, rather than national, in scope. For example, gross domestic product rather than GNP is the primary measure of production. The SNA is more comprehensive than the NIPAs, incorporating in one system more branches of economic accounting—financial accounts explicitly, input-output tables less directly, and balance sheets in outline form. The SNA system of sectors is more complex; rather than having one set of sectors, the SNA has one set for production accounts and another set for income and outlay and for financial accounts (reflecting the underlying statistical units from which the source data is collected). The latter is more similar to the NIPA sectors and it consists of nonfinancial enterprises, financial institutions, general government, private nonprofit institutions serving households, and households, rather than business, government, persons, and the rest of the world as in the NIPAs. Finally, some definitions differ to varying degrees; for example, investment in the SNA is defined to include government expenditures on capital, rather than being limited to business (and nonprofit institutions) as in the NIPAs.

A number of countries, especially those that have most recently developed a capacity for preparing economic accounts, have put in place national systems along the lines of the SNA. Altogether, roughly 150 countries, including those such as the United States that make conversions from their own systems to the SNA, report at least some national accounts estimates to the United Nations on a comparable basis.

Work toward another revision of the SNA, targeted for 1990, is under way. The goals are clarification of the guidelines and harmonization with other international statistical systems, such as those of the International Monetary Fund for balance of payments and for public sector statistics. These goals are being pursued in light of the expressed need to make the SNA more usable by developing countries and serve better as a framework for coordinating national statistics, including microdata.

This review of the evolution of the NIPAs and of the international systems is of more than historical interest. It highlights an important point. A set of economic accounts must change as the economy it is intended to illuminate changes. It must change as the statistical system on which it is based changes, either in response to changes in the statistical system or because the needs of the accounts help shape those changes. Finally, it must change as the uses and users it serves change. As these sources of change interact, economic accounts will be in a continuing state of evolution to keep their place as a major tool of economic analysis.

TECHNICAL NOTE: DEFINITION OF NIPA COMPONENTS

The definitions of the NIPA components at the level of detail in the five-account summary system are shown below. With the exception of the major aggregates, the components are usually defined in the sequence in which they appear in that summary system. The definition is not repeated when the counterentry appears, but a cross-reference is made to the place of first appearance.

National Income and Product Account: Gross National Product

GNP is the market value of the goods and services produced by labor and property supplied by residents of the United States. It is the sum of purchases of goods and services by persons and government, gross private domestic investment (including the change in business inventories), and net exports (exports less imports). GNP excludes business purchases of goods and services on current account. Its investment component is measured before deduction of charges for consumption of fixed capital.

Personal consumption expenditures (1-27) is goods and services purchased by individuals, operating expenses of nonprofit institutions serving individuals, and the value of food, fuel, clothing, rent of dwellings, and financial services received in kind by individuals. Net purchases of used goods are also included. Purchases of residential structures by individuals and nonprofit institutions serving individuals are classified as gross private domestic investment.

Gross private domestic investment (1-31) is fixed capital goods—structures and equipment—purchased by private business and non-profit institutions, and the value of the change in the physical volume of inventories held by private business. The former includes private purchases of new residential structures purchased for tenant or owner occupancy. Net purchases of used goods are also included.

Net exports of goods and services (1-38) is exports (1-39) less imports (1-40) of goods and services. Imports are deducted because they are included in the expenditure components of GNP, but are not part of national production.

Government purchases of goods and services (1-41) is the compensation of government employees and purchases from business and from abroad. Transfer payments, interest paid by government, and subsidies are excluded. Gross investment by government enterprises is included, but their current outlays are not. Net purchases of used goods are included; sales and purchases of land and financial assets are excluded.

National Income and Product Account: Charges Against Gross National Product and the Statistical Discrepancy.

Charges against GNP is the costs incurred and the profits earned in the production of GNP. Accordingly, it equals GNP, except for the statistical discrepancy. The factor charges—compensation of employees, proprietors' income, rental income of persons, corporate profits, and net interest—represent the incomes of the factors of production (labor and property). The total of these factor incomes is called national income. Three nonfactor charges—business transfer payments, indirect business taxes, and the current surplus of government enterprises less subsidies—are added to national income to yield charges against net national product. Capital consumption is added to charges against net national product to yield charges against GNP.

The aggregates that have been enumerated so far differ from each other because of distinctions that are made between market value and factor cost concepts and between gross and net concepts. GNP is a gross market value measure; national income is a net factor cost measure; and net national product is a net market value measure. One further basic distinction can be made in defining the value of production. This is the distinction between domestic measures and national measures. Domestic measures relate to the physical location of the factors of production; they refer to production attributable to all labor and property located in a country. National measures relate to the ownership of the factors of production; they refer to production attributable to labor and property supplied by residents of a country. The national measures differ from the domestic measures by the net inflow of labor and property incomes from abroad.

In principle, eight measures of production can be derived from these three distinctions; six are shown in this report. GNP has already been defined. Definitions of the other production measures follow: **Gross domestic product** is the gross market value of the goods and services attributable to labor and property located in the United States. **Net national product** is the net market value of the goods and services attributable to labor and property supplied by residents of the United States. **Net domestic product** is the net market value of the goods and services attributable to labor and property located in the United States. **National income**, the income that originates in the production of the goods and services attributable to labor and property supplied by residents of the United States, is a net factor cost measure. Incomes are recorded in the forms in which they accrue to residents and are measured before deduction of taxes on those incomes. **Domestic income** is also a net factor cost measure; it is the income that originates in the production of the goods and services attributable to labor and property located in the United States.

Compensation of employees (1-1) is the income accruing to employees as remuneration for their work. It is the sum of wages and salaries and of supplements to wages and salaries.

Wages and salaries (1-2) consists of the monetary remuneration of employees, including the compensation of corporate officers; commissions, tips, and bonuses; and receipts in kind that represent income to the recipients. It consists of **disbursements** (1-3) and **wage accruals less disbursements** (1-4). Disbursements is wages and salaries as just defined except that retroactive wages are counted when paid rather than when earned.

Supplements to wages and salaries (1-5) consists of employer contributions for social insurance and other labor income. **Employer**

contributions for social insurance (1-6) includes employer payments under the following programs: federal old-age, survivors, disability, and hospital insurance; state and federal unemployment insurance; railroad retirement and unemployment insurance; government employee unemployment insurance and retirement; military medical insurance; and publicly administered workers' compensation. **Other labor income** (1-7) consists primarily of employer contributions to private pension and private welfare funds, including privately administered workers' compensation funds.

Proprietors' income with inventory valuation and capital consumption adjustments (1-8) is the income, including income in kind, of proprietorships and partnerships and of tax-exempt cooperatives. The imputed net rental income of owner-occupants of farm dwellings is included. Dividends and monetary interest received by proprietors of nonfinancial business and rental incomes received by persons not primarily engaged in the real estate business are excluded; these incomes are included in dividends, net interest, and rental income of persons. The inventory valuation adjustment is described following corporate profits, and the capital consumption adjustment is described following capital consumption allowances.

Rental income of persons with capital consumption adjustment (1-9) is the income of persons from the rental of real property, except the income of persons primarily engaged in the real estate business; the imputed net rental income of owner-occupants of nonfarm dwellings; and the royalties received by persons from patents, copyrights, and rights to natural resources. The capital consumption adjustment is described following capital consumption allowances.

Corporate profits with inventory valuation and capital consumption adjustments (1-10) is the income of organizations treated as corporations in the NIPAs. These organizations consist of all entities required to file federal corporate tax returns, including mutual financial institutions and cooperatives subject to federal income tax; private noninsured pension funds; nonprofit organizations that primarily serve business; Federal Reserve banks; and federally sponsored credit agencies. The income is that arising in current production. With several differences, this income is measured as receipts less expenses as defined in federal tax law. Among these differences are: receipts exclude capital gains and dividends received, expenses exclude depletion and capital losses, inventory withdrawals are valued at current replacement cost, and depreciation is on a consistent accounting basis and valued at current replacement cost. Because national income is defined as the income of U.S. residents, its profits component includes income earned abroad by U.S. corporations and excludes income earned in the United States by foreigners. The inventory valuation adjustment is described below, and the capital consumption adjustment is described following capital consumption allowances.

Profits before tax (1-11) is the income of organizations treated as corporations in the NIPAs, as described above, except that it reflects the inventory and depreciation acounting practices used for federal income tax returns. It consists of profits tax liability, dividends, and undistributed corporate profits. This measure is sometimes referred to as book profits.

Profits tax liability (1-12) is the sum of federal, state, and local income taxes on all corporate earnings; these earnings include capital gains and other income excluded from profits before tax. The taxes are measured on an accrual basis, net of applicable tax credits.

Profits after tax (1-13) is profits before tax less profits tax liability. It consists of dividends and undistributed corporate profits. **Dividends** (1-14) is payments in cash or other assets, excluding the corporation's own stock, made by corporations located in the United States and abroad to stockholders who are U.S. residents. The payments are measured net of dividends received by U.S. corporations. Dividends paid to state and local government social insurance funds and general government are included. **Undistributed profits** (1-15) is corporate profits after tax less dividends.

Inventory valuation adjustment (1-16) for corporations is the difference between the cost of inventory withdrawals as valued in determining profits before tax and the cost of withdrawals valued at current replacement cost. A similar adjustment is applied to nonfarm proprietors' income.

Net interest (1-18) is interest paid by business less interest received by business, plus interest received from abroad less interest paid to abroad. Interest payments on mortgage and home improvement loans are counted as interest paid by business, because homeowners are treated as businesses in the NIPAs. In addition to monetary interest, net interest includes imputed interest. The imputed interest payments by financial institutions other than life insurance carriers and private noninsured pension plans to persons, governments, and foreigners have imputed service charges as counterentries in GNP; they are included in personal consumption expenditures, in government purchases, and in exports, respectively.

Business transfer payments (1-20) is payments to persons for which they do not perform current services. Business transfer payments include liability payments for personal injury, corporate gifts to nonprofit institutions, and consumer bad debts; that is, defaults by consumers on debts owed to business.

Indirect business tax and nontax liability (1-21) consists of tax liabilities (except employer contributions for social insurance) that are chargeable to business expense in the calculation of profit-type incomes and of certain other business liabilities to government agencies (except government enterprises) that it is convenient to treat like taxes. Indirect business taxes include sales, excise, and property taxes, and the windfall profit tax on crude oil production. Taxes on corporate incomes are excluded; these taxes cannot be calculated until profits are known, and in that sense are not a business expense. Nontaxes include regulatory and inspection fees, special assessments, fines and penalties, rents and royalties, and donations. Nontaxes generally exclude business purchases from government of goods and services that are similar to business purchases of intermediate products from other businesses. Government receipts from the sale of such products are netted against government purchases so that they do not appear in GNP.

Subsidies less current surplus of government enterprises (1-22). **Subsidies** is the monetary grants paid by government to business, including government enterprises at another level of government. The **current surplus of government enterprises** is their sales receipts and subsidies received from other levels of government less their current expenses. In the calculation of their current surplus, no deduction is made for depreciation charges and net interest paid. Subsidies and current surplus are combined because deficits incurred by government enterprises may result from selling goods to businesses at lower than market prices in lieu of giving them subsidies. For the same reason, the current surplus of government enterprises is not counted as a profit-type income and, accordingly, not as a factor charge.

Capital consumption allowances with capital consumption adjustment (1-24) is capital consumption based on the use of uniform service lives, straight-line depreciation, and replacement cost. For nonprofit institutions serving individuals, it is the value of the current services of the fixed capital assets owned and used by these institutions; it is included in personal consumption expenditures. **Capital consumption allowances** consists of depreciation charges and accidental damage to fixed capital. For nonfarm business and corporate farms, they are as reported on federal income tax returns. For noncorporate farms, nonprofit institutions serving individuals, tax-exempt cooperatives, and owner-occupied houses, they are calculated by BEA based on their expenditures for fixed capital, uniform service lives, straight-line depreciation, and historical cost. **Capital consumption adjustment** (1-17) for corporations is the tax return-based capital consumption allowances less the estimate of capital consumption allowances with capital consumption adjustment. Similar adjustments are calculated for proprietors' income, rental income of persons, and nonprofit institutions serving individuals.

Statistical discrepancy (1-26) is GNP less charges against GNP. It arises because GNP and charges against GNP are estimated independently.

Personal Income and Outlay Account: Personal Income

Personal income is the income received by persons from all sources; that is, from participation in production, from both government and business transfer payments, and from government interest, which is treated like a transfer payment. Persons consist of individuals, nonprofit institutions serving individuals, private noninsured welfare funds, and private trust funds. Proprietors' income is treated in its entirety as received by individuals. Life insurance carriers and private noninsured pension funds are not counted as persons, but their saving is credited to persons. Personal income is the sum of wage and salary disbursements, other labor income, proprietors' income with inventory valuation and capital consumption adjustments, rental income of persons with capital consumption adjustment, personal dividend income, personal interest income, and transfer payments, less personal contributions for social insurance.

Disposable personal income is personal income less personal tax and nontax payments. It is the income available to persons for spending or saving.

Wage and salary disbursements (see 1-3).

Other labor income (see 1-7).

Proprietors' income with inventory valuation and capital consumption adjustments (see 1-8).

Rental income of persons with capital consumption adjustment (see 1-9).

Personal dividend income (2-11) is the dividend income of persons from all sources. It equals dividends (see 1-14) less **dividends received by government** (2-13). Dividends received by government consists of dividends received by state and local government social insurance and other funds.

Personal interest income (2-14) is the interest income of persons from all sources. It equals net interest (see 1-18) plus **interest paid by government to persons and business** (2-16) less **interest received by government** (2-17) plus **interest paid by consumers to business** (2-18). The last item consists only of interest paid by individuals in their capacity as consumers.

Transfer payments to persons (2-19) is income payments to persons, generally in monetary form, for which they do not render current services. It consists of business transfer payments (see 1-20) and **government transfer payments** (2-21). Government transfer payments includes payments under the following programs: federal old-age, survivors, disability, and hospital insurance; supplementary medical insurance; medicaid; state unemployment insurance; railroad retirement and unemployment insurance; government retirement and unemployment insurance; workers' compensation; veterans including veterans' life insurance; food stamps; black lung; supplemental security income; and direct relief. Government payments to nonprofit institutions, other than for work under research and development contracts, are also included.

Personal contributions for social insurance (2-22) includes payments by employees, self-employed, and other individuals who participate in the following programs: federal old-age, survivors, disability, and hospital insurance; supplementary medical insurance; state unemployment insurance; railroad retirement insurance; government retirement; veterans' life insurance; and temporary disability insurance.

Personal Income and Outlay Account: Personal Taxes, Outlays, and Saving

Personal tax and nontax payments (2-1) is tax payments (net of refunds) by persons (except personal contributions for social insurance) that are not chargeable to business expense and certain other personal payments to government agencies (except government enterprises) that it is convenient to treat like taxes. Personal taxes include income, estate and gift, and personal property taxes. Nontaxes include tuitions and fees paid to schools and hospitals operated mainly by government, passport fees, fines and penalties, and donations.

Personal outlays (2-2) is the sum of personal consumption expenditures (see 1-27), interest paid by consumers to business (see 2-18), and **personal transfer payments to foreigners, net** (2-5). The last item is personal remittances in cash and in kind to abroad less such remittances from abroad.

Personal saving (2-6) is personal income less the sum of personal outlays and of personal tax and nontax payments. It is the current saving of individuals (including proprietors), nonprofit institutions serving individuals, private noninsured welfare funds, and private trust funds. Personal saving may also be viewed as the sum of net acquisition of financial assets (such as cash and deposits, securities, and the net equity of individuals in life insurance and in private noninsured pension funds) and of physical assets less the sum of net borrowing and of capital consumption allowances with capital consumption adjustment.

Government Receipts and Expenditures Account: Government Receipts

Personal tax and nontax payments (see 2-1).
Corporate profits tax liability (see 1-12).
Indirect business tax and nontax liability (see 1-21).
Contributions for social insurance (see 1-6 and 2-22).

Government Receipts and Expenditures Account: Government Expenditures

Purchases of goods and services (see 1-41).

Transfer payments (3-2) is transfer payments to persons (see 2-21) and **transfer payments to foreigners, net** (3-4). The latter is U.S. government grants to foreign governments in cash and in kind and U.S. government transfer payments, mainly retirement benefits, to former residents of the United States.

Net interest (3-5) paid by government is interest paid less interest received by government (see 2-17). Interest paid consists of interest paid to persons and business (see 2-16) and **interest paid to foreigners** (3-8). Interest paid to foreigners is interest paid by the U.S. government to foreign businesses, governments, and persons.

Dividends received by government (see 2-13).

Subsidies less current surplus of government enterprises (see 1-22).

Wage accruals less disbursements (see 1-4).

Surplus or deficit $(-)$, **national income and product accounts** (3-13) is the sum of government receipts (lines 16, 17, 18, and 19 of account 3) less the sum of government expenditures (lines 1, 2, 5, 10, 11, and 12 of account 3). It may also be viewed as the net acquisition of financial assets by government and government enterprises, and net government purchases of land and of rights to government-owned land including oil resources.

Foreign Transactions Account: Payments to Foreigners

Imports of goods and services (see 1-40).

Transfer payments to foreigners (see 2-5 and 3-4).

Interest paid by government to foreigners (see 3-8).

Net foreign investment (4-8) is U.S. exports of goods and services and capital grants received by the United States, net (see below), less imports of goods and services by the United States, transfer payments to foreigners (net), and U.S. government interest paid to foreigners. It may also be viewed as the acquisition of foreign assets by U.S. residents less the acquisition of U.S. assets by foreign residents. It includes the statistical discrepancy in the detailed balance-of-payments accounts.

Foreign Transactions Account: Receipts from Foreigners

Exports of goods and services (see 1-39).

Capital grants received by the United States, net (4-2) are mainly the allocation of Special Drawing Rights to the United States.

Gross Saving and Investment Account: Gross Saving and Statistical Discrepancy

Personal saving (see 2-6).

Wage accruals less disbursements (see 1-4).

Undistributed corporate profits with inventory valuation and capital consumption adjustments (see 1-15, 1-16, and 1-17).

Capital consumption allowances with capital consumption adjustment (see 1-24).

Government surplus or deficit (−), national income and product accounts (see 3-13).

Capital grants received by the United States, net (see 4-2).

Statistical discrepancy (see 1-26).

Gross Saving and Investment Account: Gross Investment

Gross private domestic investment (see 1-31).

Net foreign investment (see 4-8).

SELECTED BIBLIOGRAPHY

1. CARSON, CAROL S. "The History and Development of the United States National Income and Product Accounts: The Development of an Analytical Tool." *Review of Income and Wealth* 21 (June 1975), pp. 153–81.

A HISTORY OF THE U.S. ACCOUNTS, INCLUDING REFERENCE TO EARLY PRIVATE ESTIMATES AND PARALLEL DEVELOPMENTS IN OTHER COUNTRIES.

2. ——, AND GEORGE JASZI. *The Use of National Income and Product Accounts for Public Policy: Our Successes and Failures.* BEA Staff Paper 43. Washington, D.C.: U.S. Government Printing Office, January 1986.

AN EVALUATION OF THE USEFULNESS OF THE NATIONAL INCOME AND PRODUCT ACCOUNTS AS TOOLS FOR PUBLIC POLICY BASED ON EXAMINATION OF THE SIZE OF REVISIONS IN GNP ESTIMATES AND BY A REVIEW OF USERS' RECOMMENDATIONS.

3. FOSS, MURRAY F., ed. *The U.S. National Income and Product Accounts: Selected Topics.* Studies in Income and Wealth, vol. 47. Chicago: The University of Chicago Press for the National Bureau of Economic Research, 1983.

PAPERS PRESENTED AT THE CONFERENCE ON RESEARCH IN INCOME AND WEALTH HELD BY THE NATIONAL BUREAU OF ECONOMIC RESEARCH ON MAY 3–4, 1979, DISCUSSING CURRENT ISSUES AFFECTING THE NATIONAL INCOME AND PRODUCT ESTIMATES.

4. KENDRICK, JOHN W. (assisted by CAROL S. CARSON). *Economic Accounts and Their Uses.* New York: McGraw-Hill, 1972.

A BASIC TEXT THAT DESCRIBES THE NATIONAL INCOME AND PRODUCT ACCOUNTS, AS WELL AS OTHER TYPES OF ECONOMIC ACCOUNTS.

5. U.S. DEPARTMENT OF COMMERCE, BUREAU OF ECONOMIC ANALYSIS. *Corporate Profits: Profits before Tax, Profits Tax Liability, and Dividends.* Methodology Paper Series MP-2. Washington, D.C.: U.S. Government Printing Office, May 1985.

A PAPER IN THE SERIES BEING PREPARED BY BEA TO DESCRIBE THE CONCEPTS, SOURCES, AND METHODS OF NIPA COMPONENTS.

6. ———. *An Introduction to National Economic Accounting.* Methodology Paper Series MP-1. Washington, D.C.: U.S. Government Printing Office, March 1985.

AN INTRODUCTION TO THE CONCEPTS OF THE NIPAs, INCLUDING A STEP-BY-STEP DERIVATION OF THE NATIONAL ECONOMIC ACCOUNTS FROM THE CONVENTIONAL ACCOUNTING STATEMENTS USED BY BUSINESSES AND GOVERNMENTS AND FROM SIMILAR STATEMENTS THAT MAY BE ASSUMED TO EXIST FOR OTHER TRANSACTORS. CONTAINS UP-TO-DATE SUGGESTIONS FOR FURTHER READING. (ALSO AVAILABLE IN THE *Survey of Current Business* 65 (March 1985), pp. 59–74 and 76.)

7. ———. *The National Income and Product Accounts of the United States, 1929–82: Statistical Tables.* Washington, D.C.: U.S. Government Printing Office, September 1986.

THE SOURCE FOR THE COMPLETE SET OF ANNUAL, QUARTERLY, AND MONTHLY NIPA ESTIMATES FOR 1929–82. FOR THE COMPLETE SET OF ESTIMATES FOR 1983–85 AND FUTURE YEARS, SEE THE JULY ISSUES OF THE *Survey of Current Business* FOR 1986 AND FUTURE YEARS, RESPECTIVELY. FOR CURRENT QUARTERLY ESTIMATES, SEE THE MONTHLY ISSUES OF THE *Survey.*

6

The Balance of Payments

Peter Hooper, Ph.D.
Assistant Director
Division of International Finance
Board of Governors of the Federal Reserve System

Interactions between the U.S. economy and the rest of the world have grown tremendously in importance over the past two decades. During the first half of the 1980s, the United States experienced an unprecedented net inflow of both goods and capital from abroad, as evidenced in the sharp decline in the U.S. trade balance and the shift in the U.S. status from a net international credit position to a net indebtedness position. Statistical documentation of these developments is found largely in the U.S. international transactions accounts (still commonly referred to as the "balance-of-payments" accounts).

This chapter begins with a definition of the international accounts and accounting procedures. It then describes the several different balances within the accounts that are reported periodically in the press, and outlines how these accounts relate to other U.S. economic accounts, including the gross national product accounts and the U.S. international investment position. The chapter concludes with a brief discussion of concepts of equilibrium in our balance of payments and how the international accounts relate to policymaking.

DEFINITION

The U.S. international transactions accounts are a summary statement of economic transactions between U.S. residents and residents of the rest

The author has benefited from comments and suggestions by Walther Lederer, Jack Bame, Catherine L. Mann, Larry Promisel, and Lois Stekler.

of the world covering a given period of time. Such transactions involve: (1) the purchase or sale of goods, such as food, oil, steel, computers and autos; (2) the payment or receipt of interest and other income derived from real and financial investments held by foreign residents in the United States and by U.S. residents abroad; (3) the purchase or sale of other services, such as those related to tourism, airline transportation, and the transportation services of U.S. and foreign shipping companies; (4) the purchase or sale of fixed assets, such as land, manufacturing plants, and other real property; (5) the purchase or sale of financial assets, such as bank accounts, Treasury bills, stocks, and bonds; and (6) gifts, or the transfer of goods, services, and assets that are not made explicit in exchange for other goods, services, and assets. The parties involved in these transactions, whether residents of the United States or of other countries, include private individuals, corporations, other private institutions, and governments.

ACCOUNTING PRACTICES

In principle, the accounts are constructed on the basis of double-entry bookkeeping, under which each international transaction has a recorded credit entry and a debit entry. Sales of goods, services, and real or financial assets by U.S. residents to foreign residents are counted as credit items in the U.S. accounts—each, in principle involves an inflow of funds received by U.S. residents in payment for those sales. Purchases of goods, services, and assets by U.S. residents from foreign residents are counted as debit items—each in principle involves an outflow of funds paid by U.S. residents in exchange for those purchases.

Under double-entry bookkeeping, every transaction involves both a purchase and a sale, or a debit and a credit that is equal in value. In a simple case of barter, for example, where a U.S. company exchanges wheat for oil from a Saudi Arabian company, the sale (or export) of wheat is a credit item that is balanced against the purchase (or import) of oil, a debit item.

Most transactions involve the exchange of a financial asset on one side of the transaction. Thus, payment for the wheat sold by a U.S. company, might be made in the form of a claim or draft on the Saudi Arabian company's bank. The transaction involving the sale of wheat in exchange for a claim on a bank might also be viewed as the purchase of a claim on a bank in exchange for wheat. In any event, the sale of wheat is counted as a credit item in the U.S. international accounts and the acquisition of the bank claim is counted as a debit item.

How the debit item in this particular transaction is recorded also depends on the location of the bank claim that is transferred. If the Saudi Arabian company pays with a draft on a bank located in Saudi Arabia, the debit item is recorded as an increase in U.S. financial claims on foreigners. But, if the Saudi company pays with a draft on a bank located in the United States, the debit is recorded as a reduction in foreign claims on U.S. residents.

In brief, any transfer of an asset initially owned by a foreign resident to a U.S. resident, which could take the form of either an increase in U.S. claims on foreigners or a reduction in foreign claims on U.S. residents, is counted as a capital outflow, or debit item in the accounts. And, any transfer to a foreigner of an asset initially owned by a U.S. resident, in the form of either an increase in foreign claims on the U.S. residents or a reduction in U.S. claims on foreigners is a capital inflow or credit item in the accounts.

Certain transactions, including gifts, such as the donation of commodities by the U.S. government to a foreign country, and private remittances, such as the transfer of financial assets by U.S. citizens working abroad to their relatives back home, are one-sided transactions. To meet the requirements of double-entry bookkeeping, a second offsetting entry is made in the accounts under the heading of "Unilateral transfers," as either "government grants" or "private remittances." Thus, the gift of a commodity to a foreign country enters (under merchandise exports) as a credit item, and is balanced by an entry for "government grants to foreigners," which is a debit item under unilateral transfers.

MEASUREMENT PROBLEMS

If both sides of each transaction involving the transfer of goods, services, or assets between U.S. residents and foreign residents were recorded accurately, the total of all credits would equal the total of all debits and the accounts would balance. In practice, however, the two sides of most transactions are recorded independently, and the data for the different types of transactions are obtained from different sources or have to be estimated. For many transactions, one or both sides may not be recorded or estimated at all. Data on imports and exports of merchandise are collected at the U.S. port of entry or exit when the goods are cleared through customs. Statistics on many service transactions, such as travel and transportation expenses and income on fixed investments are based on surveys of individuals and corporations. Certain service transactions, such as income earned or paid on stocks, bonds, and bank accounts are estimated by the Department of Commerce. Separate data are reported by U.S. brokers and dealers on transactions in U.S. and foreign securities, and by banks and corporations on changes in outstanding assets abroad and liabilities to foreigners.

The current reporting system does not capture many financial transactions between U.S. individuals and individuals and firms located abroad. Moreover, the existing surveys of service transactions are far from comprehensive. Even the measurement of merchandise trade flows is subject to errors in valuation and coverage (not to mention the potentially sizable flow of goods across the border that bypass legal reporting channels). To offset the net effect of these measurement problems and to ensure that the accounts balance, a "statistical discrepancy" is added to the accounts. When unrecorded transactions and measurement errors are large and predominantly on either the credit or the debit side of the accounts, the statistical discrepancy can be a significant entry.

KEY BALANCES: DEFINITIONS AND RECENT HISTORY

A summary of U.S. international transactions for the years 1980 and 1985 is given in Table 1. As indicated on the bottom line of the table (line 24), the sum of all recorded transactions plus the statistical discrepancy was zero in both years, by definition. The table also shows several intermediate balances that are periodically reported in the press and that play a role in policy issues concerning the U.S. external position.

Trade Balance

The trade balance (or "merchandise trade balance"), shown in line 3, is equal to the value of merchandise exports minus merchandise imports. (By accounting practice, the merchandise balance excludes U.S. net international transactions in military goods.) This balance receives considerable attention in the press partly because it is the only balance that is available on a monthly basis. The collection of data for other items in the accounts (services and capital flows) is more difficult and these data are reported only on a quarterly basis. Even so, the usefulness of the monthly trade balance for policy insight is limited inasmuch as the changes in the monthly data tend to be quite volatile and subject to substantial revision in subsequent months.

Over longer periods of time, the trade balance can provide an indication of shifts in the international competitive performance of the U.S. manufacturing and farm sectors. The balance on U.S. merchandise exports and imports also forms the most important component of broader balances that are of more general policy interest. After having been in surplus for most of the 20th century, the U.S. trade balance fell significantly into deficit during the 1970s. It plummeted to unprecedented levels during the 1980s, as imports of a broad spectrum of goods advanced rapidly and as exports declined somewhat between 1980 and 1985.

TABLE 1   U.S. International Transactions in 1980 and 1985 (billions of dollars)

	1980	1985
Goods:		
1. Merchandise exports, excluding military goods	224	214
2. Merchandise imports, excluding military goods	−250	−339
3. *Trade balance*	−25	−125
Services:		
4. Military sales	8	9
5. Military expenditures	−11	−12
6. Investment income receipts	72	90
7. Investment income payments	−42	−65
8. Other service receipts	38	45
9. Other service payments	−31	−45
10. *Goods and services balance*	9	−103
Unilateral Transfers, net:		
11. U.S. government grants and transfers	−6	−13
12. Private remittances and transfers	−1	−2
13. *Current account balance*	2	−118
Capital Account:		
U.S. assets abroad, net change (increase/capital outflow [−]):		
U.S. government assets:		
14. Official reserve assets*	−7	−4
15. Other	−5	−3
U.S. private assets:		
16. Direct investment abroad	−19	−19
17. Foreign securities (stocks and bonds)	−4	−8
18. Other, including U.S. bank loans abroad	−50	1
Foreign assets in the United States, net change (increase/capital inflow [+]):		
19. Foreign official assets	15	−1
Other foreign assets:		
20. Direct investment in the United States	17	18
21. U.S. securities	8	71
22. Other, including claims on banks in the United States	18	40
23. *Statistical discrepancy* (equals sum of total recorded transactions on goods, services, unilateral transfers, and capital flows listed above, with sign reversed.)	25	23
24. *Overall balance (sum of all items above)*	0	0

NOTE: + Denotes net credit items or net inflow of payments.
   − Denotes net debit items or net outflow of payments.
   Components may not sum to total balances due to rounding.
 * Includes allocations of special drawing rights.
SOURCE: U.S. Department of Commerce, *Survey of Current Business*, June 1986.

Goods and Services Balance

The balance on goods and services (line 10 in Table 1) is equal to the trade balance plus the net of total service transactions, shown on lines 4–9 of the table. Service transactions are defined to include sales and purchases of military equipment, investment income receipts and payments, and other service receipts and payments. Military sales include the transfer of goods and services by U.S. military agencies as well as by U.S. military installations abroad to foreign governments. Military purchases include direct U.S. defense expenditures for military equipment abroad and for the development, maintenance and staffing of U.S. military installations abroad. Investment income receipts include (*a*) the earnings of foreign affiliates of U.S. corporations, and (*b*) earnings derived from stocks, bonds, and other nonbank and bank investments, or loans to foreigners. Investment income payments, similarly, involve the remittance of earnings on assets held by foreign residents in the United States. Other service receipts include: (*a*) the expenditures of foreign tourists in the United States for travel, food, lodging, and so on; (*b*) passenger fares received by U.S. ocean and air carriers from foreign travelers in international travel; (*c*) freight revenue received by U.S. shipping companies from foreigners for shipping U.S. exports and goods between foreign countries; (*d*) port expenditures by foreign shipping companies in the United States; (*e*) fees and royalties paid by foreign residents to U.S. holders of patents, copyrights, and so on; and (*f*) foreign expenditures in the United States for insurance, telecommunications, consulting, and other miscellaneous services.

The balance on goods and services, which is reported quarterly, is of particular interest because it relates directly to the gross national product (GNP) accounts. The goods and services balance measures the contribution of the external sector to total U.S. output of goods and services.

Current Account Balance

The balance on current account (line 13) is equal to the balance on goods and services plus net unilateral transfers. U.S. government grants and transfers include: (*a*) a measure of the total value of goods and services (included elsewhere in the accounts) that are donated to foreign governments and other foreign entities under U.S. foreign assistance programs; (*b*) payments of pensions, annuities, and veterans and other benefits to foreign residents (including Americans) entitled to those benefits; and (*c*) U.S. government contributions for the maintenance of international agencies such as the United Nations, for educational and cultural exchange programs, and for research abroad. Private remittances and transfers is an item that estimates the net transfer of goods, services, and financial assets between U.S. residents and foreign residents that are not made in exchange for other goods, services, and assets. Such transfers may involve gifts, donations, pensions, or inheritances.

In the view of many economists and policymakers, the current account balance is perhaps the most important single indicator of the U.S. international economic position that exists in our international transactions accounts. The economic meaning of the current account balance can be described in terms of the items that lie both above it and below it in the accounts summarized in Table 1. The sum of net transactions in goods, services, and unilateral transfers above the line represents the net inflow or outflow of resources that are either consumed directly or used in the production of goods and services. In this respect, the current account is quite similar to the balance on goods and services. The current account differs conceptually from the goods and services balance in that the latter nets out the value of goods and services that are transferred unilaterally (or the value of goods and services in exchange for which no payments are made).

The items that lie below the current account line include all private and official financial transactions between U.S. and foreign residents, plus the statistical discrepancy. In the absence of measurement errors, the current account balance can also be viewed as the inverse of the capital account balance—the net flow of private and official investment into or out of the United States that finances the current account. The presence of a sizable statistical discrepancy, however, blurs this relationship. While many analysts believe that much of the statistical discrepancy in the U.S. accounts represents unrecorded capital account transactions, the possibility that it also reflects sizable errors in the reporting of current account transactions cannot be ruled out.

The U.S. current account balance showed a small surplus in 1980 (see Table 1). The sizable $25 billion trade deficit, combined with another $7 billion outflow on unilateral transfers, was more than offset by a net surplus on service transactions, particularly income on investments. By 1985, however, the current account position had declined sharply. While this decline was due largely to the fall in the trade balance, a greater net outflow of unilateral transfers and some decline in the surplus on net service transactions also contributed.

The Capital Account

The capital account is broken into changes in U.S. holdings of assets abroad (by the U.S. government and by private U.S. residents), and changes in foreign official and foreign private holdings of assets in the United States. U.S. government holdings of foreign assets (lines 14–15 in Table 1) include: (a) official reserve assets such as gold, special drawing rights, foreign currencies held by U.S. monetary authorities, and the

U.S. reserve position in the International Monetary Fund; (b) U.S. loans to foreign governments and other foreign entities under foreign aid programs; and (c) U.S. government deposits in foreign banks (excluding official reserves) and other loans to foreigners. Changes in U.S. private assets abroad (lines 16–18) include: (a) direct investments (which are defined as flows between U.S. companies and their foreign affiliates in which at least 10 percent of the voting stock of the company is held by the U.S. investor), (b) U.S. net purchases of foreign corporate stocks (where less than 10 percent ownership is held) and bonds, and (c) net changes in U.S. bank claims on foreigners (including their foreign branches) and other U.S. financial and commercial claims on foreigners.

Changes in foreign assets held in the United States, shown in lines 19–22 of the table, are defined similarly. Foreign official assets largely include holdings of U.S. private and government securities by foreign governments. Foreign private assets include: (a) direct investment (transactions with U.S. affiliates that involve at least a 10 percent foreign ownership), (b) other foreign holdings of U.S. corporate stocks and bonds and Treasury securities, and (c) other commercial and financial liabilities of U.S. firms (including banks) to unaffiliated foreigners.

In 1980, notable international capital transactions included large increases in U.S. bank loans to foreigners (reflected in line 18), as well as sizable direct investment abroad (line 16). These net capital outflows were partly offset by sizable capital inflows from abroad in the form of foreign government purchases of U.S. Treasury securities (included in line 19), foreign direct investment in the United States (line 20), and an increase in foreign claims on U.S. banks (line 22). Total net recorded capital flows amounted to an outflow of $27 billion in 1980, compared with a current account inflow of only $2 billion. The statistical discrepancy, at $25 billion, reflected a large net inflow of funds through unrecorded capital account and current account transactions.

By 1985, the composition of the capital account had changed just as dramatically as the size of the current account balance. Net recorded capital flows shifted from a sizable outflow to a large net inflow of $95 billion. The growth in U.S. bank lending to foreigners had all but disappeared by 1985 (as reflected in line 18), due in part to the debt problems facing a number of foreign borrowers among the developing countries. Indeed, U.S. banks were substantially increasing their borrowings from their foreign branches, as reflected in line 22. Even more dramatic was the very large increase in the rate of foreign purchases of U.S. securities, including both Treasury securities and corporate bonds and stocks, shown in line 21. The statistical discrepancy remained little changed between 1980 and 1985, so it is clear that the sharp drop in the U.S. current account position was matched by an equally sharp rise in net foreign capital flowing into the United States. Factors underlying the shift in the current account balance or the overall net capital inflow during this period are discussed below. Shifts in the composition of a given overall net capital inflow among particular categories of assets can be attributed to a variety of factors, such as changes in tax laws and other financial market regulations and innovations. However, changes in broader economic fundamentals that motivate investor preferences, in general, cannot be inferred from such compositional shifts in the capital account.

RELATIONSHIP TO OTHER ECONOMIC ACCOUNTS

Net Goods and Services and the GNP Accounts

The relationship between the international accounts and the GNP accounts can be seen clearly in the standard GNP identity:

$$Y = C + I + G + X - M \tag{1}$$

where:

Y = Total production of goods and services (also equal to total domestic income)
C = Domestic consumption of goods and services
I = Domestic investment expenditures
G = Government expenditures
X = Exports of goods and services
M = Imports of goods and services

In the absence of international trade in goods and services, the country's total output would be equal to its total domestic expenditures ($C + I + G$). In the presence of international trade, the country's current expenditures for consumption, investment and government can exceed its current production if it purchases more from abroad than it sells abroad (i.e., if it runs a deficit on its net goods and services balance). To finance the excess spending on goods from abroad requires a net capital inflow, or an increase in the country's net debt to foreign residents.

International Accounts and the International Investment Position

The U.S. net international investment position is equal to the value of the stock of total U.S. assets abroad net of the stock of total U.S. liabilities to foreign countries. Estimates of these stock positions are based heavily on cumulations of capital flow data from the international accounts.

However, the official U.S. investment position data also incorporate changes in the current market values of (or capital gains and losses on) certain assets and liabilities, which the international accounts data do

TABLE 2 U.S. International Investment Position in 1980 and 1985 (billions of dollars)

	(1)	(2)	(3)	(4)
	End of Year Stocks		Change	Cumulative Capital Flow
	1980	1985	1980–85	1980–85
1. Total U.S. assets abroad	607	952	345	338
U.S. government Assets:				
2. Official reserve assets	27	43	16	18
3. Other	64	87	23	24
U.S. private assets:				
4. Direct Investment Abroad	215	233	18	31
5. Foreign Securities	63	114	51	34
6. Other, including bank loans	239	475	236	231
7. Total Foreign Assets in the U.S.	501	1,060	559	492
8. Foreign official assets	176	202	26	16
Other foreign assets:				
9. Direct investment	83	183	100	94
10. U.S. securities	90	292	202	148
11. Other, including claims on U.S. banks	152	383	231	234
12. Net U.S. position (line 1 minus line 7)	106	−107	−213	−154

NOTE: Components may not sum to totals due to rounding.
SOURCE: U.S. Department of Commerce, *Survey of Current Business,* June 1986.

not. Moreover, the valuation of the stock of U.S. liabilities to foreigners and some of the stock of U.S. claims on foreigners is updated with periodic (though infrequent) benchmark surveys.

The recorded U.S. international investment position in both 1980 and 1985 is summarized in Table 2. Column 3 gives the change in the investment position between 1980 and 1985, and column 4 gives the comparable cumulative net capital flow from the international transactions accounts. Differences between columns 3 and 4 arise largely because column 3 includes estimates of capital gains or losses and other valuation changes not included in column 4. The data in line 12 indicate that the U.S. international investment position changed dramatically from that of a sizable net creditor in 1980 to that of a significant net debtor at the end of 1985; reflecting the cumulative net capital inflows recorded during that period.

The decline in the U.S. position between 1980 and 1985 could well have been understated, inasmuch as the investment position account does not incorporate the statistical discrepancy in the international accounts. The discrepancy was large and consistently positive during this period, suggesting the possibility of large unrecorded net capital inflows. If one were to assume that the discrepancy between 1980 and 1985 reflected only unrecorded capital flows, the decline in the investment position would have been roughly $120 billion greater than shown in the officially recorded data.

BALANCE-OF-PAYMENTS EQUILIBRIUM AND POLICY CONSIDERATIONS

Equilibrium Concepts

The concept of balance-of-payments equilibrium was of considerable interest prior to the shift to generally floating exchange rates that took place in the early 1970s. Interest was sparked again in the mid-1980s as the U.S. trade and current account deficits widened to levels that raised questions about their sustainability in the long run. Under the relatively fixed (or "adjustable peg") exchange rate system of the 1950s and 60s, governments intervened in foreign exchange markets in order to stabilize exchange rates. The intervention took the form of official capital flows that could be viewed as serving to finance potential gaps in net private international transactions at prevailing exchange rates.

Several broad balance concepts were considered during this period. One that received, perhaps, the most attention was the "official settlements balance," or the sum of the current account balance plus all private and government capital flows other than changes in official reserves. (In terms of Table 1, this balance could be derived by summing all the items in the table except lines 14 and 19.) In principle, if the official settlements balance was not in equilibrium (or equal to zero) at prevailing exchange rates, ex ante, governments would have to fill the gap with official financing in order to maintain fixed exchange rates.

During the early 1970s, growing pressures in private international transactions, in the form of large actual and potential capital flows, began to exceed governments' willingness and ability to offset them. After officially pegged exchange rates were adjusted several times, the system of pegged rates against the dollar was abandoned by most industrial countries. Under floating exchange rates, much less immediate importance was attached to balance-of-payments equilibrium concepts. In principle, exchange rates would adjust freely to equate a given country's net excess demands on current account with the willingness of the rest of the world to finance those demands by investing capital in the deficit country. If the ex ante current account deficit exceeded the availability of finance, the country's currency would depreciate. The depreciation, in turn, would tend both to reduce the country's net external demands and to increase the potential capital inflow from abroad. In practice, however, the governments of most of the industrial countries have continued to intervene significantly in foreign exchange markets in an effort to smooth some of the fluctuations of their currencies' exchange rates against the dollar. Even during the floating rate period, net official reserve transactions have been quite large during some years.

With the advent of more flexible exchange rates, many experts assumed that current account balances would tend toward zero in the longer run. This view has been called into question during the early 1980s, especially with the substantial and sustained widening of the U.S. current account deficit, which was matched in part by large and growing surpluses in Germany and especially in Japan. Developments during the 1980s have indicated clearly that it is difficult to define a particular balance-of-payments equilibrium, and that there is good reason to expect the current account to deviate substantially from zero for extended periods of time. To understand the reasons for this it would be helpful to review briefly both the factors that directly influence the current account and how it interacts with the U.S. economy and the rest of the world.

Determination of the Current Account

The direct determinants of the current account are the factors that influence U.S. and foreign demands for each others' goods and services. The two principal factors are: first, the growth of income at home and abroad (which directly affect each region's demand for total goods and services, and therefore its demand for the goods and services of the other region), and second, the relative prices of goods and services produced in the two regions (which in recent years have been most importantly influenced by movements in exchange rates). When either U.S. demand grows faster than demand in the rest of the world, or the relative price of U.S. goods rises as a result of an appreciation of the dollar, the U.S. current account balance will tend, over time, to decline.

A closely related view of current account determination can be derived from the GNP identity discussed earlier. As was shown in equation (1), a deficit on net goods and services (a close relative of the current account) can be viewed as an excess of domestic expenditures over domestic production. Thus, when U.S. domestic expenditures grow faster than total output, the difference will be reflected in a declining current account balance.

Determination of the U.S. current account can also be viewed as the result of the interaction of domestic investment decisions and domestic savings decisions, both at home and abroad. To see this, equation (1) can be rearranged as:

$$Y - C - G = I + X - M \tag{2}$$

where the left-hand side of (2) is equal to total domestic savings, (defined as total income minus private and government consumption expenditures). Government taxes can be added and subtracted from the left-hand side of equation (2) and terms rearranged to obtain:

$$(Y - T - C) + (T - G) = I + X - M \tag{3}$$

which breaks total domestic savings down into private savings (aftertax income minus private consumption) plus government savings (tax revenues minus government spending). It is clear from equation (3) that when the sum of private savings plus government savings (or minus the government deficit) falls short of domestic investment, the gap must be filled by an external deficit (imports must exceed exports), or an inflow of investment from abroad. At the same time, just the opposite must hold abroad—the inflow of investment from abroad can only be accommodated by a net excess of domestic savings over domestic investment in all other countries combined.

In brief, the current account balance is determined by a wide variety of decisions by U.S. and foreign private and government agents that influence total consumption, investment, and saving as well as movements in prices at home and abroad and changes in exchange rates. Developments in the U.S. international accounts during the 1980s provide a good illustration of these various influences.

Recent History: Policy Influences

During the early 1980s an expansionary U.S. fiscal policy resulted in a substantial widening of the U.S. government budget deficit. Concurrently, other industrial countries and developing countries were running relatively contractionary fiscal policies, on average. These policies led to a contraction of total domestic saving relative to investment in the United States (and just the opposite abroad), which in turn led to a widening of the current account deficit. Viewed from another angle, the U.S. tax cut stimulated private domestic expenditures and raised demand for imports, while more contractionary policies abroad meant weaker growth in foreign demand overall and in foreign demand for U.S. exports in particular. At the same time, the U.S. fiscal expansion, in the face of monetary restraint by the Federal Reserve, put upward pressure on U.S. interest rates, increased the relative attractiveness of investing in U.S. assets and caused the dollar to appreciate. The resulting rise in U.S. relative prices further depressed the U.S. trade balance. This effect on the current account was exacerbated by private investment decisions that resulted in a shift in preferences in favor of investment in the United States, strong potential capital inflows and a substantial further appreciation of the dollar.

By mid-1985 the U.S. current account deficit had become a source of major concern to policymakers. The associated weakness in U.S. manufacturing and farm sectors had given rise to significant protectionist pressures which threatened the world trading system. The decline in net exports had also become a significant negative factor in U.S. GNP growth. And, the prospects for substantial further increases in the U.S. net international debt position loomed on the horizon and threatened the possibility of some disruption to financial markets down the road. Partly for these reasons, the United States redoubled its efforts to begin to reduce its large federal government budget deficit. It also began to encourage foreign governments to do more to stimulate their economies, and in cooperation with foreign governments, it took steps to encourage a reduction in the foreign exchange value of the dollar.

SUGGESTED READINGS

A variety of general references on the balance of payments is available. Examples include:

CHACHOLIADES, MILTIADES. *The Principles of International Economics.* New York: McGraw-Hill, 1981.

KINDELBERGER, CHARLES P. AND LINDERT PETER H. *International Economics.* 8th ed. Homewood, Ill.: Richard D. Irwin, 1986.

STERN, ROBERT M. *The Balance of Payments.* Hawthore, N.Y.: Aldine Publishing, 1973.

U.S. OFFICE OF MANAGEMENT AND THE BUDGET. "Report of the Advisory Committee on the Presentation of Balance of Payments Statistics." *Statistical Reporter*, June 1976.

Two textbooks that focus more specifically on the issue of current account determination and the policy aspects of the balance of payments, include:

DORNBUSCH, RUDIGER. *Open Economy Macroeconomics.* New York: Basic Books, 1980.

MEIER, GERALD M. *International Economics, the Theory of Policy.* New York: Oxford University Press, 1980.

A thorough description of the line by line items in the U.S. International Accounts as published by the U.S. Department of Commerce, can be found in:

U.S. DEPARTMENT OF COMMERCE. *Survey of Current Business*, June 1978.

A Primer on the Fed

Alfred Broaddus, Ph.D.
Senior Vice President and Director of Research
Federal Reserve Bank of Richmond

Most Americans have heard of the Federal Reserve System—or, more simply, "the Fed," as the institution is widely known in financial and political circles, or "the System," as it is frequently referred to by its employees and others. Most Americans also know that the Fed is the nation's central bank and that its policies and actions are frequently in the news and the subjects of intense debate. Many citizens, however, have only a vague and imprecise idea of what the System actually does. Ask the man on the street what the Fed does, and he will likely respond that the Fed "controls interest rates," or that it "takes care of the money supply," or that it "watches over banks." When he is pressed, however, to say what interest rates the Fed "controls," or how it exercises this control, or what the money supply is, or exactly what the Fed's responsibilities regarding the banking system are, he will frequently come up short.

The purpose of this article is to answer some of these questions for people who would like to know more about the System, but who do not have the time to study the institution in detail. Particular attention will be paid to the effects of the Fed's actions on the general economy and on banking and other financial markets, but all of its major functions will be discussed. The article is organized as follows. Section 1 describes the

The author wishes to thank Mrs. Sandra D. Baker, Associate Economist at the Richmond Fed, for her assistance in preparing the article. The views expressed in the article are the responsibility of the author and do not necessarily represent the views of the Federal Reserve Bank of Richmond or the Federal Reserve System.

Fed's principal functions and its basic objectives in performing each function. Section 2 outlines the Fed's somewhat complex organizational structure and indicates how this structure developed. Finally, Section 3 discusses Fed monetary policy. Although the Fed has important responsibilities regarding the regulation of financial institutions and the maintenance of the nation's payments mechanism, its preeminent task is to formulate and implement national monetary policy. In addition to outlining some of the mechanical aspects of monetary policy, Section 3 will also attempt to convey some of the flavor of current policy issues.

SECTION 1: SYSTEM FUNCTIONS AND OBJECTIVES

The Fed's principal functions are similar to those performed by most other central banks throughout the world. Specifically, the Fed is responsible for conducting monetary policy, maintaining the liquidity, safety, and soundness of the banking system, and assisting the fiscal authority—in this case the U.S. Treasury—in carrying out some of its duties. In addition, the Fed actively participates in the maintenance and operation of the U.S. payments system and in the continuing effort to increase the efficiency and safety of this system. In recent years Congress has also charged the Fed with promulgating several new laws designed to (a) protect consumers in their transactions with banks and other financial institutions, and (b) promote community development and reinvestment.

Monetary policy. As noted above, the preeminent function of the Fed is the conduct of monetary policy. In its broadest sense, the term *monetary policy* can refer to any action or actions a government or a central bank takes that influence the institutional character of a nation's monetary system or, at a particular time, monetary and financial conditions in the country. In the United States in the 1980s, the term typically refers to Fed actions affecting the growth rate of the nation's money supply, interest rates, and other financial and economic variables, either in the short run or over a longer time.

Although the Fed conducts monetary policy on a day-to-day basis, the basic objectives of policy are mandated by Congress. The initial objective of the System, as seen by the authors of the Federal Reserve Act, was to provide a more elastic currency to reduce the incidence of banking and financial panics, which had plagued the American economy in the 19th and early 20th centuries. As time has passed, however, the mandate has been broadened as monetary policy has rightfully come to be recognized as a central element of overall national economic policy. The most direct statement of the present mandate is given in Section 2A of the Federal Reserve Act, as amended by the Full Employment and Balanced Growth Act (the so-called Humphrey-Hawkins Act) of 1978:

> The Board of Governors of the Federal Reserve System and the Federal Open Market Committee shall maintain long-run growth of the monetary and credit aggregates commensurate with the economy's long-run potential to increase production, so as to promote effectively the goals of maximum employment, stable prices, and moderate long-term interest rates.

Further, in formulating policy in the short run, the System is to take account of ". . . past and prospective developments in employment, unemployment, production, investment, real income, productivity, international trade and payments, and prices. . . ." This mandate is obviously very comprehensive and subject to differing interpretations. In broad terms, however, it is generally understood to mean that the Fed should maintain monetary conditions which encourage real economic growth at a rate consistent with stability in the price level and in financial markets, and balance in international transactions.

Two points should be made about the Fed's monetary policy mandate and the objectives it includes. First, since the broad goals of monetary policy are essentially the same as the longer-run objectives of overall national economic policy, monetary policy should work in concert with the other elements of national policy rather than at cross-purposes with them. It is particularly desirable that monetary policy and fiscal policy (i.e., the federal government's budgetary policy) be mutually supportive in a joint pursuit of the broad goal of sustainable real economic growth with stability of the price level. For example, a highly expansive fiscal policy, as indexed by rapid growth in federal expenditures, might result in political pressure on the Fed to finance the growth in expenditures through monetary expansion, which would risk increasing the rate of inflation. Some economists and others have argued that excessively expansive fiscal policy in the 1980s has put upward pressure on U.S. interest rates and the foreign exchange value of the U.S. dollar, which in turn has produced a more expansive monetary policy than is consistent with longer-run price level stability. Alternatively, an excessively expansive or contractionary monetary policy would obviously disrupt and perhaps defeat the efforts of other arms of the government to promote growth, high employment, and economic stability.

Second, even though the legislative mandate cited above explicitly mentions a large number of economic variables, including production, employment, prices, interest rates, and international trade, experience suggests that it would be unwise, and potentially detrimental to the achievement of the broader goals of national economic policy, to conclude that the Fed can "fine tune" the economy with monetary policy. During the 1960s, some economists and policymakers believed it was possible to determine empirically the trade-offs between certain important economic variables, such as employment and the rate of inflation, and subsequently to achieve rather precisely specified combinations of economic results via the adroit manipulation of monetary and fiscal policy instruments. Disappointment with the actual results of this approach to policy has produced a greater awareness of the limitations of macroeconomic policy in general and monetary policy in particular. Specifically, the research of Milton Friedman and others indicated that the Fed's monetary policy actions affect the economy with lags or delays that are both long and difficult to predict.[1] As a result of these lags and their variability, efforts to manipulate the economy via monetary policy may be destabilizing. Further, the "rational expectations" school of monetary economics, which developed in the 1970s, has emphasized how the public's tendency to anticipate Fed policy actions reduces or eliminates the effect of these actions on real variables such as employment and output.[2] Against this background, some students of monetary policy have suggested that the Fed's policy mandate be narrowed to emphasize and give priority to the System's responsibility to maintain price stability on the grounds that price stability is the only feasible objective of monetary policy.[3]

Liquidity and stability of financial markets. Closely related to the monetary policy responsibilities just outlined is the Fed's responsibility to maintain the liquidity and stability of banking and other financial markets. At the time the System was created, in 1913, commercial banks were the dominant financial institutions. Therefore, maintenance of the liquidity and stability of the financial system amounted largely to maintenance of the liquidity and stability of the commercial banking system. The principal tool available to the Fed for this purpose is the so-called discount window, through which the Fed is able to loan reserve funds to banks and other depository institutions under certain specific conditions. Most such loans are very short term and are made to enable borrowers to cover unanticipated deposit outflows, temporary difficulties in obtaining funds from other sources and similar contingencies. Longer-term loans—referred to as "extended credit"—are also available to deal with seasonal liquidity problems and certain other circumstances. Prior to 1980, only commercial banks that were members of the System had regular access to the discount window. The Monetary Control Act of 1980 extended access to all institutions having deposits subject to the System's reserve requirements, which, in addition to commerical banks, includes savings banks, savings and loan associations, credit unions, and U.S. branches and agencies of foreign banks. This extension of access to the window was

---

[1] See Friedman [11].

[2] For an excellent nontechnical discussion of rational expectations, see McCallum [16].

[3] See Black [2].

appropriate in view of the increasing importance of nonbank financial institutions in the American financial system.

It should be emphasized that the Fed's responsibility to ensure the liquidity of the financial system is indeed a responsibility to the *system* rather than to individual institutions. The purpose of the Fed's lending activities is to prevent liquidity problems at a single institution or a small number of institutions from spreading and disrupting the financial system as a whole. Therefore, in managing the discount window and establishing operational policies for the window, the Fed is guided by concern for the financial system. Also, the Fed strongly encourages institutions to seek funds from other sources before coming to the window. In its role as guardian of the liquidity of the financial system, the Fed is sometimes referred to as the "lender of last resort."

In addition to the discount window, the Securities and Exchange Act of 1934 required the Fed to regulate extensions of credit by securities brokers, banks, and other lenders for the purpose of buying or carrying specified securities—primarily stocks and related instruments. The purpose of these so-called margin requirements, which the System administers under its Regulations T, U, G, and X, is to limit potentially destabilizing fluctuations in financial asset prices that might result from excessively leveraged financial transactions.

Regulation and supervision of banks and other financial institutions. In addition to its desire for a more elastic currency, Congress also intended, in creating the Fed, to improve the regulation and supervision of commercial banks as another way of reducing the incidence of bank failures and resulting financial panics. To this end, the Fed has a number of regulatory and supervisory duties aimed at ensuring the safety and soundness of the banking system and the efficiency of its operations. Many of these responsibilities were specified in the original Federal Reserve Act; others have been added by amendments to that Act and other legislation. The System shares these responsibilities with other federal financial regulatory agencies and with state regulatory agencies in accordance with applicable federal and state laws.

The terms *regulation* and *supervision* are often used loosely as synonymous, but they actually refer to distinct Fed duties. Regulations are rules that the System establishes and administers in conformance with federal law, such as the various regulations aimed at maintaining a competitive banking market structure. Supervision, in contrast, refers to the System's oversight—largely through on-site examinations—of individual banks, bank holding companies, and certain other institutions to ensure that they are being operated and managed in a safe and sound manner. In addition to regulating and supervising the domestic activities of U.S. banks and bank holding companies, the Fed now regulates and supervises the activities of foreign banking organizations in the United States and many of the activities of U.S. banking organizations in foreign countries. These internationally oriented duties have assumed increased importance in recent years due to the dramatic increase in international banking activities.

There have been substantial changes in both the form and content of the Fed's regulatory duties in the 1980s, due partly to the landmark Depository Institutions Deregulation and Monetary Control Act of 1980 (DIDMCA). Before 1980, the Fed's reserve requirements (to be discussed in greater detail in Section 3 of this article) applied only to commercial banks that were members of the System. The DIDMCA extended these requirements to nonmember banks and other depository institutions. While expanding the scope of the Fed's regulatory authority in this respect, the Act reduced it in several other areas. Especially important were (1) the phased elimination of interest rate ceilings on time deposits, which the Fed had regulated for many years under its Regulation Q, and (2) the authorization, effective at the beginning of 1981, of interest-bearing NOW (for negotiable order of withdrawal) accounts nationwide. The combined effect of these two changes was to eliminate, by the end of the phase-out period in early 1986, all interest ceilings on all deposits except ordinary demand deposits for which the prohibition of the payment of interest remains in effect. Since NOW accounts are functionally equivalent to demand deposits, however, interest can now be paid on transactions accounts, and the rate is not subject to a ceiling. These changes are what most people have in mind when they speak of the "banking deregulation" of the 1980s. By increasing the cost of many sources of funds, the changes have had a substantial impact on the day-to-day management and operations of depository institutions. They have also affected the way the public manages its money balances and other liquid assets. Consequently, while deregulation has reduced the Fed's regulatory duties in a formal way, it has presented new challenges during the transition in both the supervisory area and in the conduct of monetary policy.[4]

In addition to the effect of deregulation, the economic turbulence of the early 1980s has strongly challenged the Fed's supervisory resources as well as those of other federal supervisory agencies and state agencies. The severe recession in 1981 and 1982, the decline in agricultural land values and farm income that accompanied the recession and persisted after it ended, and the sharp drop in petroleum prices and some other commodity prices in 1985 and 1986 reduced the quality of some assets held by individual banks and led to a significant increase in the rate of individual bank failures. Faced with these problems, the Fed took steps

---

[4] For a survey of these developments, see Broaddus [6].

in late 1985 to strengthen its supervision of state member banks and bank holding companies.

Although the Fed has only limited formal regulatory and supervisory duties outside the commercial banking sector, it is increasingly recognized that the System's overall responsibility for the health and stability of the financial system requires it to assist in dealing with specific problems in other financial sectors and markets. Specifically, the Fed played an active role in containing certain short-run disruptions that arose in the largely unregulated government securities markets in the 1980s. This role was a natural one since, as discussed in Section 3, the Fed participates actively in this market in the course of conducting its daily operations implementing monetary policy. Also, the System played an important behind-the-scenes role in efforts to resolve serious problems that affected certain state-insured thrift institutions in Ohio and Maryland in 1985. This activity was also appropriate since the DIDMCA extended both Fed reserve requirements and access to the discount window to thrifts.

Consumer and community affairs. Congress has given increased attention to the welfare of consumers and the condition of local communities in the 1970s and 1980s, as evidenced by the passage of a number of laws designed to protect consumers in their business dealings and to promote local economic development. The Fed has been given the responsibility to write regulations implementing many of the laws that govern consumer credit and other consumer financial transactions and community reinvestment and development. In doing so, the System seeks to ensure that the objectives of each law are fully and efficiently met.

Among the most important statutes covering consumer financial transactions are the Truth in Lending Act, the Fair Credit Billing Act, the Equal Credit Opportunity Act, the Fair Credit Reporting Act, the Consumer Leasing Act, the Real Estate Settlement Procedures Act, and the Electronic Fund Transfer Act. In general, all these laws attempt to ensure that consumers are given adequate information to make informed and intelligent financial decisions, and that they are treated fairly by the institutions they do business with. As an example, the Equal Credit Opportunity Act prohibits financial institutions from discriminating in granting credit on the basis of sex, race, religion, marital status, and other similar criteria. The Fed's Regulation B sets out specific procedures to implement this prohibition, such as a requirement that applicants who have been denied credit be notified of the reasons for the denial. In the case of some of the laws, the Fed and other regulatory authorities conduct periodic examinations to determine whether financial institutions are complying with the requirements of the laws. The System is advised by a Consumer Advisory Council in carrying out all of its consumer-related regulatory responsibilities. The council, which meets several times each year, has 30 members representing consumer interests, lending institutions, and other sectors.

The principal statutes governing community reinvestment and development are the Home Mortgage Disclosure Act and the Community Reinvestment Act. The Home Mortgage Disclosure Act requires depository institutions to disclose where their mortgage and home improvement loans have been made so that depositors, potential depositors, and others can make informed judgments regarding whether or not specific institutions are meeting the needs of the local community for housing-related credit. The Community Reinvestment Act (CRA) encourages banks and other institutions to help meet the housing and other credit needs in their respective communities, including needs in low- and moderate-income areas, provided such credit is consistent with the safety and soundness of the lenders. Compliance with this law is evaluated during bank examinations, and the extent of compliance is taken into account by the System when it considers certain applications for branches, bank mergers and bank holding company formations and acquisitions.

The Fed has developed an extensive internal mechanism to discharge its responsibilities under the CRA. In particular, a community affairs officer has been appointed at each of the 12 Federal Reserve banks. Among other things, these officers and their staffs provide information to depository institutions regarding private and public resources available to assist in community development. They also attempt to facilitate communication between borrowers, lending institutions, local government agencies, and others in matters relating to the financing of community development initiatives. Under current procedures, community and neighborhood groups can protest bank merger applications and bank holding company applications in cases where they believe the institutions involved are not complying with the requirements of the CRA. The community affairs officers play a leading role in efforts to resolve the issues underlying these protests.

Relationships with the U.S. Treasury and services to it. The central bank has a close relationship with the fiscal authority in virtually all countries, and in some countries the central bank is actually under the direct control of the fiscal authority. Whatever the formal relationship, the actual working relationship in practice determines the extent to which the central bank can exert an independent influence on the economy through monetary policy. In the United States, the Fed works closely with the U.S. Treasury both in the larger task of formulating and implementing national economic policy and in the day-to-day accomplishment of routine fiscal operations. The System is independent of the Treasury, however, both in a legal sense and, since the celebrated

"Accord" between the Fed and Treasury in 1951, in the sense of its ability to formulate and carry out monetary policy free of any immediate and direct constraint imposed by the Treasury.

At an operational level, the Fed performs a variety of relatively routine fiscal tasks for the Treasury as its "fiscal agent."[5] The Fed is essentially the Treasury's banker since it maintains an account at the Fed and makes most of its payments—both for purchases of goods and services and transfers such as social security disbursements—from this account. The majority of these payments are made by Treasury checks, which are cleared and paid by the Fed. A minority of repetitive payments, such as for some government employee salaries, are made through automated clearinghouses, most of which are operated by the Fed.

The Fed also carries out, on behalf of the Treasury, the routine operations related to issuing, servicing, and redeeming Treasury securities, such as accepting tenders from individuals and institutions that wish to purchase securities, collecting payments, and paying interest coupons. Most Treasury securities are no longer issued in the form of physical certificates. Instead, they are simply recorded in "book entry" form at the Fed for the account of depository institutions, which may, in turn, be holding some of the securities for the accounts of customers.

Apart from coordinating with the Treasury on the broader questions of monetary and fiscal policy, the Fed works closely with the Treasury on a daily operational basis in actually implementing monetary policy. As noted in Section 3, the Treasury's disbursements and receipts affect the volume of reserves available to the banking system. Since the reserve position of the banking system is a central instrument the Fed uses in conducting monetary policy operations, the Treasury informs the Fed early each business day of its projected expenditures and receipts, which enables the Fed to take offsetting actions.

Services to depository institutions. In addition to the fiscal services it provides to the Treasury, the Fed offers a number of services to depository institutions and, through these institutions, to the general public. These services are actually provided by the 12 Federal Reserve banks discussed in Section 2, and most of them are related to the operation of the nation's payments mechanism. One of the principal reasons the Fed was created was to provide a safe and efficient system for transferring funds, especially between different localities, to supplant the slow and inefficient mechanism that existed at the time. Against this background, a major underlying reason for the Fed's

---

[5] More precisely, the 12 Federal Reserve banks discussed in Section 2 of this article serve as the Treasury's fiscal agents.

participation in the payments mechanism, both in the past and at present, has been to increase the system's efficiency and to assist it in advancing technologically as well as to provide a source for specific services. This broader mandate was renewed by Congress in 1980 in the DIDMCA. The DIDMCA also substantially altered the terms under which the Fed provides services. Prior to the act's passage, the System offered these services without charge, but only to member banks. The act extended direct access to the services to all depository institutions, but it required the Fed to charge fees that cover their full cost over the longer run, including the taxes and capital costs the Fed would incur if it were a private firm. The purpose of the fees is to encourage efficient use of the services and to enable private institutions to compete in their provision where appropriate.

Among the most important of the Fed's payments services are (1) the distribution, through depository institutions, of coin and currency to the public in accordance with its needs, and (2) the clearing and settlement of checks. The introduction of service fees initially reduced the number of checks presented to the Fed for processing. In 1985, however, the number increased 4.8 percent to approximately 15.5 billion. The System also provides several electronic payments services including wire transfers of funds and automated clearinghouse (ACH) services. The FedWire electronic transfer network enables depository institutions to transfer large amounts of funds nationwide with great speed. Such transfers can be used, among other things, to settle transactions in Federal funds, Treasury securities, and other securities, and therefore contribute substantially to the breadth, efficiency, and liquidity of the nation's money and capital markets. During 1983, approximately 38 million individual transfers valued at about $84 trillion were executed over FedWire. ACHs use magnetic tapes to effect recurring transfers, such as salary payments, payment of regular insurance payments, and the like. Since ACHs eliminate paper checks, it is widely believed that they can significantly increase the speed with which routine payments are made as well as reduce their cost and risk. To date, however, the public's use of ACH facilities has been surprisingly limited.

In addition to the services already described, the Fed also provides net settlement services which private wire transfer services, ACHs, and other facilities can use to effect final net payment among their respective users on the books of the Fed. The System also provides certain nonpayments services including (1) the safekeeping and transfer of U.S. government and agency securities and state and local government securities, and (2) so-called noncash collection services where the System collects payments for certain specified noncash items including maturing state and local government securities and bankers acceptances.

SECTION 2: STRUCTURE AND ORGANIZATION OF THE FED

The structure of the Federal Reserve is a complex mixture of (*a*) private and public elements and (*b*) centralized authority and decentralized authority. Further, the institutional position of the Fed within the overall structure of the federal government is distinctive and unusual. These structural characteristics reflect both the longer-run history of central banking in the United States and the political compromise that surrounded passage of the Federal Reserve Act in 1913. Specifically, both the public and private sectors of the economy have participated in U.S. central banking activities from the earliest days of the Republic. The First Bank of the United States, established in 1791, performed a mixture of central and private banking functions, and its capital was provided by both the federal government and private individuals. This same mingling of private and public elements also characterized the much larger Second Bank of the United States, which operated between 1816 and 1836, and the national banking system created by the National Banking Act of 1863. When a new central bank was proposed in the early 1900s, a debate arose between (*a*) banking and financial interests in the large cities of the Northeast, which favored a highly centralized institution dominated by private bankers, and (*b*) agrarians, populists, and others in the South and West, who preferred a less centralized structure, but one in which the public sector would play a considerable role. The Federal Reserve Act and the central banking structure it established constitute the compromise that arose out of this conflict. The present structure, of course, also reflects broad financial and political trends over the period since 1913.

A. Internal Structure

Figure 1 depicts the internal organizational structure of the Fed. The following paragraphs describe the powers and responsibilities of each of the principal elements of the organization in turn.

Board of Governors. The Board of Governors is the central governing body in the System. It is an agency of the federal government and consists of seven members appointed by the President of the United States with the advice and consent of the Senate. The full term of a member of the Board is 14 years, with one member's term expiring every even-numbered year. The purpose of this long term of office is to insulate members from routine day to day political pressures. A member who has served a full term may not be reappointed, although members who have served part of an unexpired term may be reappointed to a full term. The President appoints one of the members Chairman and

FIGURE 1 Organization of the Federal Reserve System

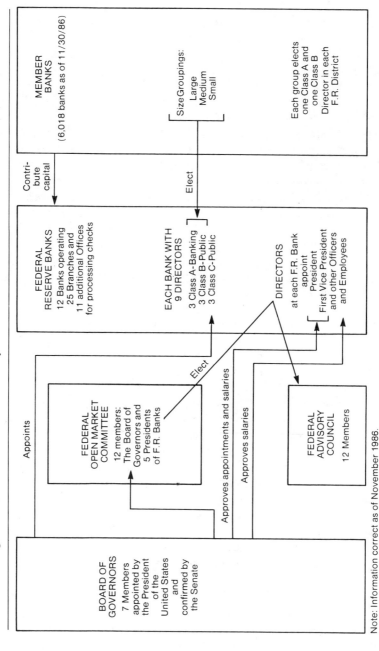

Note: Information correct as of November 1986.

SOURCE: Board of Governors of the Federal Reserve System.

another Vice Chairman for four-year terms, again with the advice and consent of the Senate. The Chairman of the Board is the dominant figure in the System and is typically regarded by the general public as one of the most influential individuals in the government.

The Board of Governors has general cognizance over all of the System's activities described in Section 1 of this article. Its principal responsibility is the formulation and implementation of monetary policy and its role in this function is preeminent within the Fed. As Figure 1 indicates, the members of the Board comprise a majority of the voting members of the Federal Open Market Committee, which directs the Fed's open market operations (i.e., the System's purchases and sales of U.S. Treasury securities and other securities in the open financial markets) and oversees the general conduct of monetary policy.[6] The Board also reviews and approves all discount rate actions taken by the Federal Reserve banks, and it has the authority to alter the reserve requirements of depository institutions within certain limits specified by law. Outside the area of monetary policy, the Board has final responsibility for all of the regulatory and supervisory activities, margin requirement responsibilities, and consumer protection and community affairs activities described in Section 1. It also has a specific mandate to assist in the maintenance and further development of a safe and efficient national payments mechanism. In addition to these duties, the Board exercises general supervisory authority over the activities of the Federal Reserve banks. As noted in Figure 1, the Board appoints three of the nine members of the board of directors of each bank, and it must approve the appointment of each bank's president and first vice president. The Board also examines the banks annually and approves their annual operating budgets and any major construction expenditures.

The Board is directly responsible to Congress. It reports to Congress and congressional committees on its activities on a continuing basis through testimony and other means. It also makes a variety of statistical and other information related to its activities available to Congress and the public in its annual report, a monthly *Federal Reserve Bulletin,* and other publications. The Board funds its expenditures through assessments on the Federal Reserve banks rather than via congressional appropriations. Its financial accounts are audited annually by a public accounting firm, and these accounts are also subject to audit by the General Accounting Office.

Federal Open Market Committee.   As noted above, the Federal Open Market Committee directs the Fed's domestic open market operations, which are the principal mechanism used to carry out monetary

---

[6] The Federal Open Market Committee, open market operations, and the other tools of monetary policy are discussed in greater detail in Section 3.

policy actions on a day-to-day basis. It also oversees the System's activities in foreign exchange markets. The Chairman of the Board of Governors is traditionally Chairman of the Committee. In addition to the seven members of the Board of Governors, the Committee at any point in time includes five of the Reserve bank presidents as voting members. The president of the Federal Reserve Bank of New York is a permanent voting member and traditionally Vice Chairman of the Committee in recognition of the important role this bank plays in actually carrying out open market operations. The other 11 Reserve bank presidents share the four remaining voting memberships on a rotating basis. In recent years the Committee has held eight regular meetings per year in Washington. It also meets via telephone conference from time to time when circumstances warrant.

The role of the Federal Open Market Committee in the Fed's monetary policymaking process will be discussed in greater detail in Section 3. The important point to note about the Committee from an organizational standpoint is its inclusion of Reserve bank presidents as voting members. It is true that the members of the Board of Governors constitute a majority of the voting members of the Committee. Nonetheless, the presidents add an important dimension to the Committee's deliberations since they do not reside in Washington, and they are in direct contact with leading business people and others in their respective districts. This partially decentralized feature of the Committee's organizational structure is consistent with the intent of the authors of the Federal Reserve Act to preserve a degree of regional autonomy in the Fed's overall structure. Because the presidents are not appointed by the President of the United States or confirmed by the Senate, several lawsuits in recent years have challenged the constitutionality of their role in the Committee. None of these suits has been successful to date.

Federal Reserve banks. There are 12 Federal Reserve banks whose head offices are located in the following cities: Boston, New York, Philadelphia, Cleveland, Richmond, Atlanta, Chicago, St. Louis, Minneapolis, Kansas City, Dallas, and San Francisco. Each of these banks serves a particular, numbered geographic Federal Reserve district as shown by the map in Figure 2. There are also Federal Reserve bank branches in 25 other cities as well as facilities that provide particular operational services in several additional cities.

As suggested earlier, the Federal Reserve banks represent the more decentralized and private elements of the Fed's overall structure. The corporate structure of the Reserve banks is similar to that of private commercial banks. Like private banks, each Reserve bank has a board of directors consisting of private individuals, which elects the bank's officers and oversees the general operations of the bank. The banks also issue capital stock, and their officers carry titles similar to those used in

FIGURE 2 Boundaries of Federal Reserve Districts and Their Branch
Territories

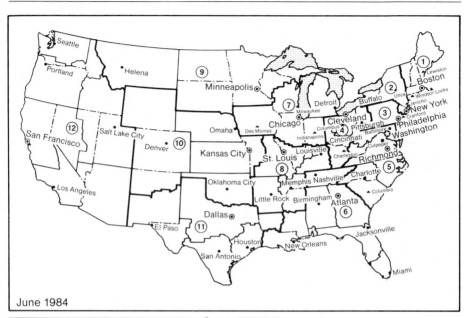

June 1984

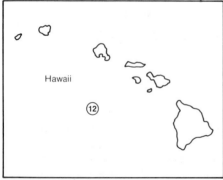

LEGEND:

—— Boundaries of Federal Reserve Districts
——— Boundaries of Federal Reserve Branch Territories
✪ Board of Governors of the Federal Reserve System
◉ Federal Reserve Bank Cities
• Federal Reserve Branch Cities
■ Federal Reserve Bank Facility
▲ Regional Check Processing Office

SOURCE: Board of Governors of the Federal Reserve System.

most private financial institutions. While similar to private companies in these respects, however, the Reserve banks are different in many other, fundamental respects. First, because the banks' principal general responsibility is to promote the public interest rather than the narrower interests of their stockholders, profit considerations do not play a dominant role in determining the banks' actions, even though the banks earn substantial profits as a by-product of their routine operations. As noted earlier, the Board of Governors has general supervisory authority over the banks, and for this reason the powers and privileges of the banks' stockholders are more limited than in most private corporations. Second, in the unlikely event that any of the banks was ever liquidated, any assets remaining after the stock was redeemed at face value would be transferred to the federal government.

Each of the Reserve bank boards of directors has nine members structured to be broadly representative of both the bank's stockholders and the public served by the bank. Specifically, each board has three Class A directors, three Class B directors, and three Class C directors. The Class A directors are usually commercial bankers. They represent banks that are members of the Federal Reserve System, since these banks are the Reserve bank stockholders. Class B directors represent the public and are drawn from diverse sectors, including agriculture, business, and labor. They may not be officers, directors, or employees of any bank. As indicated in Figure 1, the Class A and B directors of each Reserve bank are elected from that bank's district by the member banks in the district. The Class C directors also represent the public and are appointed by the Board of Governors. The Board of Governors also appoints one of the Class C directors chairman of the board and another deputy chairman. In addition to the 12 Reserve bank boards, each Reserve bank branch has a board consisting of either five or seven members, a majority of whom are appointed by the respective bank boards.

The Reserve bank boards have several important responsibilities. First, they oversee the management and operation of their respective banks, subject to the general supervision of the Board of Governors. Second, they establish the discount rates that the banks charge on loans to depository institutions in their districts, subject to the approval of the Board of Governors. Third, they appoint the president and first vice president of their respective banks, subject again to the approval of the Board of Governors. Finally, the members of each bank and branch board provide the System with regular information on business and financial conditions in specific industries, sectors, and geographic regions. Although several of the specific actions of the Reserve bank boards must be approved by the Board of Governors, these boards are highly influential within the Fed because of the caliber, experience, and diversity of individual members. The information they provide on business conditions, in particular, often provides an early warning of emerging developments in the economy, in financial markets, and in banking and financial institutions. Further, the directors' participation in setting the discount rate gives them a specific role in the monetary policymaking process, since—as discussed in more detail in Section 3— the discount rate is one of the instruments of monetary policy.

Each Reserve bank currently derives approximately 95 percent of its earnings from its proportionate share of the interest on the System's portfolio of domestic securities acquired in the course of conducting monetary policy. Practically all the remainder is derived from its share of the interest earned on the System's holdings of foreign currencies, the interest from its loans to depository institutions, profits from the sale of securities and foreign exchange, and the fees for its services to depository institutions. Each bank's earnings are allocated first to (1) the payment of the bank's expenses, (2) an assessment to cover its proportionate share of the expenses of the Board of Governors, (3) the payment of a statutory 6 percent dividend to the bank's stockholders, and (4) any addition to the bank's surplus needed to maintain surplus equal to paid-in capital. Remaining earnings are then transferred to the U.S. Treasury. In 1985, the total current income plus additions of the 12 Reserve banks was approximately $19.4 billion, and the amount transferred to the Treasury was approximately $17.8 billion.

Several informal bodies exist within the Fed to facilitate communication among the Reserve banks and between the Reserve banks and the Board of Governors on issues of mutual concern. A Conference of Chairmen of the Federal Reserve Banks meets at the Board of Governors offices in Washington twice a year. In addition, a Conference of Presidents of the Reserve Banks meets several times each year at one of the Federal Reserve offices and maintains close contact with the Board of Governors. There is also a Conference of First Vice Presidents. While these conferences were not formally established by the Federal Reserve Act as were the Federal Open Market Committee and the Reserve bank boards, in practice they are important forums for the discussion and resolution of high-priority issues and problems.

Member banks.   At the end of 1985, about 6,000 of the approximately 14,000 commercial banks in the United States were members of the Federal Reserve System. All national banks are required to be members, and state-chartered banks may voluntarily become members if they meet the requirements for membership established by the Board of Governors. As suggested earlier, membership carries both responsibilities and privileges. For example, member banks are required to subscribe to the stock of their respective Reserve banks, and they are supervised and examined by the Reserve banks, but they elect six of the nine members of the Reserve bank boards, and they receive the annual 6 percent dividend on Reserve bank stock.

Prior to 1980, the duties and privileges of member banks delineated them more sharply from nonmember institutions than presently, because only members were subject to Fed's reserve requirements, and only members had access to the Fed's payments and other operational services, which were provided without charge. Also, only member banks had access to the Fed's discount window. As pointed out in Section 1, the Depository Institutions Deregulation and Monetary Control Act of 1980 subjected all depository institutions to Fed reserve requirements, although some smaller institutions do not actually hold required reserves because their reservable liabilities are below an exempted amount.[7] At the same time, the Act extended access to the discount window to all nonmember depository institutions with deposit liabilities subject to Fed reserve requirements. It also extended access to the Fed's operational services to all depository institutions that are eligible for federal deposit insurance and required the Fed to charge all institutions explicit fees for these services.

Advisory committees. In addition to the principal arms of the Fed discussed above, there are a number of advisory councils and committees in the System that exist for specific purposes. The Federal Advisory Council, which is shown in Figure 1, has 12 members—one elected annually by each of the 12 Reserve bank boards. The members are typically prominent commercial bankers. The council meets at least four times a year with the Board of Governors to discuss current issues related to Fed monetary and regulatory policies and other relevant matters. Other advisory groups include the Consumer Advisory Council, made up of 30 members with an interest in consumer affairs, and the Thrift Institutions Advisory Council, which comprises representatives of savings and loan associations, savings banks, and credit unions. The Consumer Advisory Council keeps the System informed of major consumer issues in view of the Fed's statutory responsibilities in this area discussed in Section 1. The establishment of the Thrift Institutions Advisory Council in the early 1980s reflected the extension of Fed reserve requirements and access to the discount window and Fed operational services to thrifts by the DIDMCA. In the mid-1980s, each Reserve bank established a Small Business and Agricultural Advisory Committee to provide a channel for direct communication with the Fed to representatives of these two sectors from all regions of the country.

---

[7] A central purpose of the DIDMCA was to resolve the problem created by the accelerated attrition of member banks during the late 1970s that had resulted from the steep rise in interest rates during that period. This increase in rates significantly increased the opportunity costs of holding required reserves.

Several members of each of these committees meet as a group with the Board of Governors each year.

B. Position of the Fed within the Overall Structure of the Government

One of the most frequently misunderstood aspects of the Fed is its institutional position within the federal government. There have been numerous instances throughout recorded history where the centers of political power within governments—monarchs or prime ministers or legislative bodies—have abused the power to control the monetary system. The framers of the Federal Reserve Act were aware of this risk and sought to insulate the Fed to some extent from routine political pressures through various provisions of the Act. For this reason, the Fed is often described as "independent."

It is true that the Fed has somewhat greater freedom to act than some other government entities, since its actions do not have to be formally ratified by the President, its expenses are funded from its own earnings rather than through the regular congressional appropriations process, and the full terms of members of the Board of Governors are lengthy. The System is not independent of the rest of the government, however, in any general sense, either as an institutional matter or in practice. In particular, it is not a separate branch of the government protected by the Constitution like the judicial system. It is, instead, essentially a creature of Congress. It exists by virtue of an act of Congress, and it could be significantly altered or even abolished at any time Congress wished to do so. Further, while the Fed does not report directly to the President or any other arm of the Executive Branch, it is a generally accepted principal that Fed monetary policy should complement the fiscal and other economic policies and programs of the administration wherever possible in seeking to attain the longer-run national economic goals of high employment and stability in the price level. It would be difficult if not impossible for the Fed to follow a policy substantially at odds with the policies favored by a clear majority of the rest of the government.

The close working relationship between the Fed and other federal entities is manifested in a variety of ways. The Chairman of the Board of Governors and other Board members testify frequently before congressional committees on the state of the economy and monetary policy, domestic and international financial developments, regulatory matters, and a variety of other issues. Since monetary policy and many of the other policy areas in which the Fed is active are inherently controversial, these congressional hearings are sometimes contentious, and the Fed's representatives are typically required to explain and defend the System's actions in depth. In addition to its relations with Congress, the

Fed is in close contact with the Executive Branch and other government agencies. The Chairman of the Board of Governors meets with the President from time to time and has regular consultations with the Secretary of the Treasury and other high officials on a variety of issues. There are also frequent contacts between members of the Fed's permanent staff and their counterparts in other agencies, particularly the Treasury. In short, through a variety of formal and informal contacts, the Fed is kept fully apprised of the views of other officials and agencies on issues of mutual concern, and it has ample opportunity to communicate its own views on these matters.

SECTION 3: THE FED AT WORK: THE IMPLEMENTATION OF MONETARY POLICY

This section describes Fed monetary policy in the context of events and major policy developments in the late 1970s and early 1980s. As noted in the introduction to this article, monetary policy is the preeminent responsibility of the Fed, and the special attention given to this particular Fed function in this section reflects its importance. Monetary policy is a complex field, and it is the subject of an extensive technical literature. The purpose of what follows is to provide a reasonably thorough nontechnical overview of the topic along with some of the flavor of major recent developments and policy issues.

A. Strategy, Procedures and Mechanics of Monetary Policy

Overview. The term *monetary policy*, again, refers to the actions the Fed takes to influence national and international monetary and financial conditions with a view to helping achieve the nation's basic economic objectives of price level stability, high employment, and reasonable balance and stability in its trade and payments relations with other nations. This conception of monetary policy implies certain relationships. First, the Fed must be able to influence monetary and financial conditions. Second, monetary and financial conditions must have some impact on at least some of the objectives—or, to employ the jargon of economists, the "goal variables"—of economic policy such as stability in the price level.

It is generally recognized that the Fed, like other central banks, can influence domestic monetary and financial conditions. It is also agreed that the Fed can influence international monetary conditions, given the importance of the U.S. monetary system and financial markets in the world economy. It should be understood, however, that the System's influence over most financial variables is indirect. Everyone who works in a policymaking capacity at the Fed for any length of time is eventually asked what the Fed plans to "do" to interest rates and the money supply at some point in the future. The System has direct administrative control over only one interest rate, however, the discount rate, and it has no direct control over the several aggregations of currency, bank deposits, and other liquid assets that comprise the various measures of the national money supply. What the Fed can influence directly is the volume and growth of reserves held by private commercial banks and other depository institutions—that is, balances held by depository institutions at Federal Reserve banks.[8] Through this influence on bank reserves, the Fed can indirectly affect interest rates and the growth of money and credit. For example, if the public's demand for money and credit is substantial, due, perhaps, to strong growth in the general economy, a restrictive approach to the provision of reserves by the Fed tends to put immediate upward pressure on the Federal funds rate, which is the short-term interest rate charged for the use of reserves when they are sold (lent) and bought (borrowed) in the so-called Federal funds market. The rise in the Federal funds rate, in turn, causes other interest rates to rise, which acts to reduce both the supply and demand for money and credit and hence their growth. Conversely, if the Fed supplies reserves generously in relation to the demand for money and credit, interest rates will come under downward pressure, and the growth of money and credit will tend to increase.

The second basis for the conduct of monetary policy is the presumption that relationships exist between the monetary and financial variables that the Fed can influence, on the one hand, and the goal variables of economic policy on the other. The nature of these relationships and their empirical characteristics have been the subject of extensive research and analysis by monetary economists for many years. Despite its extent, the results of this research are still not fully conclusive, and much disagreement remains on particular points. Most economists agree that a stable and predictable positive relationship exists over the long run between the rate of growth of the money supply and the rate of inflation: specifically, a sustained rise in the growth rate of the money supply is followed eventually by a rise in the trend rate of inflation. Some economists also believe that short-run relationships exist between (1) changes in the growth rates of monetary variables, and (2) real economic variables such as the rates of growth of production and

---

[8] These reserves totaled a little over $28.5 billion at the end of 1985. The use of the word *influence* rather than *control* in this sentence was deliberate. The Fed cannot control total reserves precisely in the short run under present institutional arrangements, because total reserves include reserves borrowed from the discount window, and depository institutions play a significant role in determining the level of borrowing in the short run. The Fed can, however, control nonborrowed reserves with considerable precision in the short run.

employment. As suggested in Section 1, however, views regarding the nature of these short-run relationships and their usefulness as a basis for monetary policy have changed substantially over the last two decades. In particular, the research of the rational expectations school of economists has produced a growing consensus that the only changes in the growth rate of the money supply that affect real economic variables are those that are not anticipated by the public. Since the public's anticipations are difficult to observe and quantify accurately on a current basis, this view implies that these short-run relationships cannot be predicted reliably, and for that reason the Fed cannot exploit them to fine tune the economy. As pointed out in Section 1, this attitude toward what can be achieved through monetary policy is considerably less ambitious than the view held by many economists and policymakers in the 1960s.

The strategy of monetary policy and monetary targeting. This evolution of prevailing views regarding the nature of the relationships between monetary and other economic variables has had a substantial impact on the strategy of monetary policy over time: that is, on the procedures that Fed employs to achieve its longer-run objectives. It is probably fair to say that the Fed did not have a clear and well-articulated, longer-run strategy for monetary policy prior to the 1970s. The rising inflation and other dislocations in that decade, however, forced the System to lengthen its horizon in formulating policy. Further, the growing influence of monetarist doctrine in the economics profession, among policymakers, and in some quarters of the Congress probably caused the Fed to give greater—although by no means exclusive—attention to the behavior of monetary aggregates in conducting policy. These developments culminated in 1975 in the passage of House Concurrent Resolution 133 in which Congress expressed its sense that the Fed should manage the longer-run growth of monetary and credit aggregates and keep that growth consistent with the nation's broad economic goals.[9] The System had been setting internal monetary growth targets for several years before the passage of this resolution. Following the passage of the resolution, however, it began to report the targets to the Congress in public testimony. In 1978, the Full Employment and Balanced Growth Act (the Humphrey-Hawkins Act) made the requirements of the resolution law.

In accordance with the terms of the Humphrey-Hawkins Act, the Fed has developed a formal procedure for establishing targets for the growth of various monetary and credit aggregates and reporting these targets to Congress. Under the present procedure, the Federal Open

---

[9] The language of the resolution's reference to monetary and credit aggregates is identical to that in the Humphrey-Hawkins Act of 1978 quoted in Section 1 of this chapter.

TABLE 1 Target Ranges for Monetary Growth, 1984
(Measured from fourth quarter 1983 to fourth quarter 1984)

	Percent
M2	6–9
M3	6–9
M1	4–8
Total domestic nonfinancial debt	8–11

SOURCE: Board of Governors of the Federal Reserve System.

Market Committee typically sets target ranges for three monetary aggregates, M1, M2, and M3, and a monitoring range for one credit aggregate, Domestic Nonfinancial Debt Outstanding, at its meeting in February of each year for the period running from the fourth quarter of the preceding year to the fourth quarter of the current year. The base for each target range is the actual level of the relevant aggregate in the fourth quarter of the preceding year, calculated as an average of daily data over the quarter. The upper and lower endpoints of each range are quarterly average levels in the fourth quarter of the current year. Although it would be possible to discuss the targets in terms of dollar levels, they are normally discussed in terms of growth rates, and the widths of the ranges are always established in terms of so many percentage points difference between the growth rate implied by the top of a range and the growth rate implied by the bottom of a range. The ranges have typically been 3 or 4 percentage points wide, but they have sometimes been wider.

As an example, Table 1 shows the target ranges established by the Committee for 1984 at the beginning of that year. As the table shows, the range for M1 in 1984 had a 4 percentage point spread, while the ranges for the other aggregates had three point spreads. The target ranges are frequently depicted graphically both in official publications and the financial press. Figure 3 depicts the M1 range for 1984 in terms of the traditional target "cone," along with the actual growth path during that year. Because the width of the cone (in terms of dollar levels) is much narrower at the beginning of a target period than at the end, its usefulness for monitoring progress toward achieving the target during the early quarters of the period is limited. For this reason, the Fed began to supplement the cone in 1985 for so-called parallel bands of constant (dollar level) width throughout the period, as shown in Figure 4. This chart shows the target range for 1985 for M2. As the chart shows, the actual level of M2 was above the top of the cone throughout much of this target period, but it was always at or below the top parallel band, and it finished the year within the range.

FIGURE 3   Target Range for M1, 1984

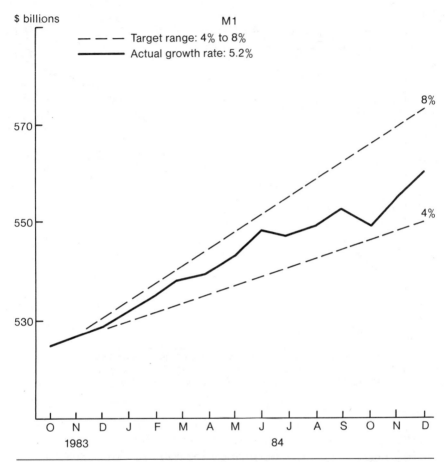

SOURCE: Board of Governors of the Federal Reserve System, "Monetary Policy Objectives for 1985," Summary of Report to the Congress on Monetary Policy pursuant to the Full Employment and Balanced Growth Act of 1978, February 20, 1985, p. 6.

As noted above, the Fed typically sets ranges for three monetary aggregates and one credit aggregate. Table 2 lists the principal components of the monetary measures.[10] M1 is the narrowest of these aggregates and attempts to measure the public's transactions balances. M2 includes M1 and several other categories of liquid assets. M3 includes M2 and still other categories of relatively liquid assets. The

[10] More precise and detailed definitions of these aggregates are provided in the footnotes to Table 1.10 of the monthly *Federal Reserve Bulletin*.

FIGURE 4   Target Range for M2, 1985

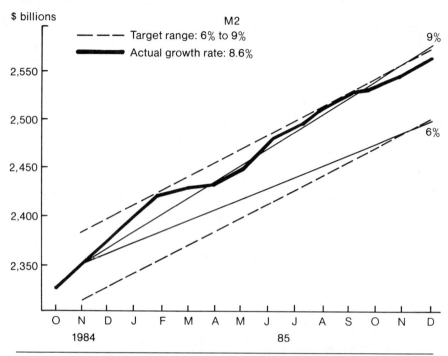

SOURCE: Board of Governors of the Federal Reserve System. "Monetary Policy Objectives for 1986," Summary of Report to the Congress on Monetary Policy pursuant to the Full Employment and Balanced Growth Act of 1978, February 19, 1986, p. 6.

credit aggregate, referred to as Domestic Nonfinancial Debt Outstanding, is essentially the total debt outstanding in U.S. credit markets less borrowings by foreigners and financial institutions.[11] The latter elements are excluded because, unlike other components of total debt, they are not closely related to U.S. economic activity. Ranges have been established for M1, M2, and M3 since the formal targeting procedure was initiated in 1975. A range has been set for domestic nonfinancial debt only since 1983.

In addition to the target-setting at the beginning of the year, the Federal Open Market Committee reevaluates all of the targets at its meeting in July to determine whether or not they are still appropriate in the light of economic and financial developments since the initial setting. The Committee has made several changes in specific targets at its

---

[11] See Board of Governors of the Federal Reserve System [5; Table 2.2, pp. 24–25].

TABLE 2   Components of M1, M2, and M3, March 1984
(Billions of dollars, seasonally adjusted except as noted)

Aggregate and Component	Amount
M1	535.3
Currency	150.9
Travelers checks of nonbank issuers	5.0
Demand deposits	244.0
Other checkable deposits at all depository institutions	135.4
M2*	2,230.0
M1	535.3
Overnight RPs issued by commercial banks[†]	47.0
Overnight Eurodollars held by U.S. residents at overseas branches of U.S. banks[†]	11.3
Money market mutual fund shares (general-purpose and broker/dealer, taxable and nontaxable)[†]	144.8
Savings deposits at all depository institutions	305.5
Money market deposit accounts at all depository institutions[†]	392.5
Small-denomination time deposits at all depository institutions[‡]	803.4
M3*	2,767.8
M2	2,230.0
Large time deposits at all depository institutions[§]	347.9
Money market mutual funds (institution-only)[†]	45.0
Term RPs at all depository institutions[†,ǁ]	55.9
Term Eurodollars held by U.S. residents[†]	93.9

---

   * M2 and M3 both differ from the sums of their components because of consolidation adjustments and the seasonal adjustment technique. The consolidation adjustment for M2 represents the amount of demand deposits and vault cash at commercial banks owned by thrift institutions that is estimated to be used in servicing their time and savings deposits. The consolidation adjustment for M3 is the estimated amount of overnight repurchase agreements and overnight Eurodollars held by institution-only money market mutual funds. The nontransaction component in M2 and the nontransaction component in M3 alone are seasonally adjusted only as aggregates. The individual seasonally adjusted series included in these nontransaction components in the table are not used in calculating seasonally adjusted M2 or M3.
   † Not seasonally adjusted.
   ‡ Time deposits in amounts of less than $100,000; includes retail repurchase agreements.
   § Time deposits in amounts of $100,000 or more.
   ǁ Excludes retail repurchase agreements.
   SOURCE: Board of Governors of the Federal Reserve System, *The Federal Reserve System: Purposes and Functions.* 1984, pp. 22–23.

July meeting over the years. These changes have taken the form both of changes in the percentage growth rates and changes in the base period for the target. Changes in the base (referred to as "rebasing") have usually involved moving the base period forward from the fourth quarter of the preceding year to the second quarter of the current year. For example, at its meeting in July 1985, the Committee moved the base for the M1 target forward to the second quarter of that year. Also, the growth rate range for M1 was widened from the 4 to 7 percent range established at the February meeting to 3 to 8 percent.

To fulfill the reporting requirements of the Humphrey-Hawkins Act, the Fed chairman reports the results of the Committee's target-settings in congressional testimony shortly after the February and July meetings. These appearances have become focal points for the public discussion of monetary policy in recent years, and they therefore receive substantial attention in the media and elsewhere.

Several comments regarding this strategy and procedure are in order. First, although the Humphrey-Hawkins Act required the Fed to report its intentions regarding the growth of money and credit, neither the letter nor the spirit of the law required the Fed to make the target ranges the exclusive basis for the conduct of monetary policy, and the Fed has not done so. The Fed has consciously allowed the actual growth of particular aggregates to deviate from their ranges on a number of occasions, especially in the early- and mid-1980s, when it felt that the actions it would have had to take to bring growth back within the ranges might have damaged the economy. It has also given substantial attention to other economic and financial variables in formulating and implementing policy such as interest rates, foreign exchange rates, and various measures of overall economic activity, such as the gross national product. Further, as indicated in greater detail in Section 3B, it has frequently changed the weights it has attached both to the monetary and credit aggregates it explicitly targets and the other financial and economic variables it monitors. For example, it has explicitly reduced the weight given to M1 on several occasions in the 1980s due to the unusual behavior of the velocity of M1 in this period; that is, the reduced predictability of the empirical relationship between M1 and GNP.

This generally flexible and discretionary approach to the conduct of monetary policy has many defenders among professional economists and others, both inside and outside the Fed. Those who favor this approach point out that flexibility is particularly necessary in a period of rapid institutional change, such as the extensive deregulation in banking and financial markets in the 1980s. Others, however, especially monetarist economists and adherents to the rational expectations school, believe that a highly descretionary policy may tend to destabilize the economy rather than stabilize it over the longer run. These economists generally favor a monetary policy strategy where the Fed's reaction to emerging economic and monetary developments would be determined to a greater extent than at present by preannounced rules and would therefore be easier for the general public and financial market participants to anticipate. The full range of this debate is beyond the scope of this article. With respect to the Fed's monetary targeting strategy, those who favor a greater reliance on rules have criticized several features of the procedures outlined above. First, they have pointed out that targeting several measures of the money supply and shifting the emphasis among them reduces the potentially healthy discipline that targeting imposes on the Fed itself. Since the growth rates of the various aggregates the Fed targets frequently diverge in the short run, the Fed may at times avoid reacting to the aberrant behavior of one aggregate by transferring its attention to another. Although such shifts in emphasis may be justifiable in some cases, they may not be desirable in others. Also, the shifting reduces the usefulness of the targets as statements of the System's policy intentions to the public. Second, those who favor rules have criticized the practice of using the *actual* level of an aggregate in the fourth quarter of the preceding year as the base for the target in the current year on the grounds that doing so leads to the automatic ratification of any deviation from the preceding year's target, regardless of whether the deviation was desirable for economic reasons or not.[12]

Whether or not the Fed's monetary targeting strategy has actually improved the conduct of monetary policy over the years it has been used is still an open question. The growth of the M1 aggregate exceeded the top of its range significantly in both 1977 and 1978, and some economists believe that the rapid growth occasioned by these averages and the accompanying upward "base drift" contributed to the high inflation and resulting financial turmoil in 1979, 1980, and 1981. In short, the targeting procedure does not appear to have been very useful in assisting the Fed to achieve price level and financial stability in this period. On the other hand, the existence of the targeting strategy has probably served as a useful and continuous reminder to the public, Congress, and the Fed itself of the longer-run goals of monetary policy. The strategy will probably continue to be useful in the future, although modifications may be required in the light of the watershed financial deregulation of the 1980s.[13]

The tactics of monetary policy: instruments. It is not enough for the Fed to have a longer-run strategy in conducting monetary policy. Like other institutions, it lives in the short run, and it must respond to an endless series of economic and financial disturbances—some of which can be anticipated, but most of which cannot—in implementing

---

[12] This phenomenon has come to be known as "base drift." For a discussion of the problems posed by base drift, see Broaddus and Goodfriend [8]. For a more sympathetic view of the phenomenon, see Walsh [23].

[13] For a useful nontechnical discussion of some of the broader current issues surrounding the Fed's monetary targeting strategy, see Federal Reserve Bank of Minneapolis [10]. See also McCallum [16].

policy. For this reason, the Fed uses a set of tactical procedures to assist in implementing the longer-run strategy outlined above and in attaining its strategic objectives. This subsection and the next two describe the three principal elements of this tactical apparatus: the instruments or tools of monetary policy, the tactical operating procedures, and the policymaking process in the short run.

The Fed uses three principal instruments in conducting monetary policy on a day-to-day basis: open market operations, the discount rate, and reserve requirements.[14] Of these, open market operations are the most important. The following paragraphs briefly describe the mechanical aspects of these instruments. The next subsection describes how the System welds the specific actions it takes with these various instruments into a coordinated tactical procedure.

As the name implies, *open market operations* are simply purchases and sales of securities by the Fed in the open money and bond markets. The purpose of these purchases and sales is to affect the aggregate reserve position of depository institutions; that is, the level and growth of the noninterest-bearing reserve deposits these institutions hold, in the aggregate, at Federal Reserve banks.[15] The basic mechanics of these operations are quite simple. If the Fed wishes to increase the level of reserves, it purchases securities in the open market. It ultimately pays for the purchase by crediting the reserve account of some depository institution for the amount purchased, which increases the level of aggregate reserves by that amount. Conversely, if the Fed wants to reduce the level of reserves, (Or, more importantly in practice, if it wishes to reduce the rate of growth of reserves, it buys securities at a less rapid pace.) it sells securities in the market. Payment for the sales is eventually effected by reducing some depository institution's reserve account for the amount of the sale, which reduces the aggregate level of reserves. This description of the mechanics of open market operations focuses on individual transactions in isolation. In reality, of course, such individual transactions are part of a continuous stream of transactions involving the public and other institutions in addition to the Fed. Therefore, it is not generally useful in practice to think of Fed open

---

[14] The Fed has used other tools in the past, notably direct credit controls and interest rate ceilings, although many economists do not regard these tools as appropriate instruments of monetary policy. The Fed's power, noted in Section 1, to set margin requirements on certain classes of securities is sometimes regarded as an instrument of monetary policy, but it is not regarded as an important tool in practice under the Fed's present operating procedures.

[15] In addition to affecting reserves themselves, these operations also affect the Federal funds rate, which is the interest rate charged for the use of reserve funds in the open market. The Federal funds rate has played a key role in the implementation of monetary policy in the 1970s and 1980s as indicated in subsequent sections of this chapter.

market operations in terms of the isolated effect of particular purchases and sales. Instead, the focus is on the broader effects of operations on the growth of reserves over time: purchases tend to increase growth; sales reduce it.

The Fed's open market operations are controlled and supervised by the Federal Open Market Committee. They are executed in the market, under the Committee's direction, by the Federal Reserve Bank of New York acting as the Committee's agent. A department at the New York bank, known popularly as the "Trading Desk," or simply the "Desk," actually carries out the operations. A manager for domestic operations, who is a senior officer of the New York bank, supervises the Trading Desk. The manager has direct day-to-day control of open market operations. He reports directly to the committee and receives his instructions from the committee.

Although in principle the Fed could conduct open market operations using any public or private securities, it is restricted by law to the use of U.S. government (i.e., U.S. Treasury) securities, obligations issued or guaranteed by agencies of the United States, and a few short-term securities. In practice, the vast majority of operations are carried out using Treasury securities, and they would undoubtedly be concentrated in Treasuries even in the absence of legal restrictions. To be effective in an economy and financial system as large as that of the United States, it is essential that the Fed be able to conduct large purchases and sales flexibly without unduly disrupting the market. The market for U.S government securities is extremely broad and active, and is therefore ideal for open market operations.

The Fed's open market operations are an important factor affecting the aggregate volume of reserves available to depository institutions, but by no means the only factor. Independent actions on the part of the general public and the U.S. Treasury also have important effects on reserves. When the public's demand for currency increases, for example, as it typically does before important holidays, depository institutions obtain the currency from the Fed. They pay for it through reductions in their reserve balances at the Fed, which reduce aggregate reserves. Conversely, a reduction in the public's desire for currency increases reserves. As pointed out in Section 1, the Treasury maintains an account on the books of the Fed and uses this account to make routine payments for the federal government's purchases of goods and services and in connection with transfers such as medicare disbursements. When the Treasury makes such a payment, the Treasury account at the Fed is drawn down, and the funds flow into the reserve account of some depository institution, which increases aggregate reserves. The reverse occurs when the public makes payments to the Treasury, such as tax payments. These examples cover just a few of the myriad factors other than the Fed's open market operations that continuously influence the aggregate reserve position of depository institutions.[16] In order to manage the reserve position the Fed must neutralize these other factors. It does this on a continuous basis through so-called defensive open market operations, which constitute the majority of its operations. Indeed, as can be seen in Table 3, the total dollar volume of Fed open market transactions in a given year typically exceeds the net change in the System's portfolio of securities by a substantial amount.

Against this background, the Fed's open market operations can be divided into two broad categories: (1) outright, permanent purchases or sales and (2) temporary purchases or sales in the form of "repurchase agreements" (for temporary purchases), or "matched sale-purchase transactions" (for temporary sales). Outright transactions are most likely to be used when the Fed wants the operation to have a lasting effect on reserves. Outright purchases might be used in the autumn months, for example, to offset the persistent seasonal drain of reserves caused by the buildup of currency in the hands of the public prior to Christmas. Repurchase agreements and matched sale-transactions agreements are used when the Fed expects to want to reverse the effect of an operation on reserves within a few days or weeks. Under a repurchase agreement, the Fed buys securities from a dealer who agrees to repurchase them by a specified date at a specified price, which increases reserves over the duration of the agreement. Matched sale-purchase transactions involve an immediate sale of securities to a dealer matched by an agreement for the Fed to repurchase the securities by a specified date at a specified price. In this case, reserves are reduced over the duration of the agreement. Repurchase agreements or matched sale-purchase transactions might be used, for example, to offset anticipated temporary effects of fluctuations in the Treasury's balance at the Fed on reserves.

The Fed carries out the majority of its operations in the market with 40 so-called primary securities dealers, about a third of which are departments of large money center banks and the remainder securities brokerage houses. All of these dealers make regular markets in Treasury and federal agency securities, and are therefore prepared at all times to quote prices at which they will buy securities and prices at which they will sell them. The Fed executes most of its transactions, both outright and temporary, using an auctionlike procedure, where it announces what securities it wishes to buy or sell and in what amounts, receives price or interest rate proposals from the various primary dealers for the transaction, and accepts the proposals most favorable to the Fed up to the dollar amount of the operation.

Although the majority of its operations are carried out with primary dealers, the Fed can also affect reserves via its financial dealings with

---

[16] For a detailed treatment of all factors affecting reserves, see Board of Governors of the Federal Reserve System [5; Appendix to Chapter 3, pp. 45–56].

TABLE 3 Federal Reserve Open Market Transactions, 1985

Type of Transaction	Millions of dollars
U.S. Government Securities:	
Outright transactions (excluding matched transactions):	
Treasury bills	
Gross purchases	22,214
Gross sales	4,118
Exchange	0
Redemptions	3,500
Others within 1 year:	
Gross purchases	1,349
Gross sales	0
Maturity shift	19,763
Exchange	−17,717
Redemptions	0
1 to 5 years:	
Gross purchases	2,185
Gross sales	0
Maturity shift	−17,459
Exchange	13,853
5 to 10 years:	
Gross purchases	458
Gross sales	100
Maturity shift	−1,857
Exchange	2,184
More than 10 years:	
Gross purchases	293
Gross sales	0
Maturity shift	−447
Exchange	1,679
All maturities:	
Gross purchases	26,499
Gross sales	4,218
Redemptions	3,500
Matched transactions:	
Gross sales	866,175
Gross purchases	865,968
Repurchase agreements:	
Gross purchases	134,253
Gross sales	132,351
Net change in U.S. government securities	20,477
Federal Agency Obligations:	
Outright transactions:	
Gross purchases	0
Gross sales	0
Redemptions	162
Repurchase agreements:	
Gross purchases	22,183
Gross sales	20,877
Net change in federal agency obligations	1,144
Bankers Acceptances:	
Repurchase agreements, net	0
Total net change in System Open Market Account	21,621

NOTE: Sales, redemptions, and negative figures reduce holdings of the System Open Market Account; all other figures increase such holdings. Details may not add to totals because of rounding.
    SOURCE: Board of Governors of the Federal Reserve System. *Annual Report.* 1985, pp. 208–9.

foreign central banks and other foreign official institutions. On any given day, the Fed has orders from some of these "customers" to invest funds overnight. In this situation the Fed has a choice: it can either temporarily sell securities to these institutions from its own account, which reduces reserves, or it can pass the orders through to private dealers, in which case reserves are not affected. The choice on a particular day reflects the overall objectives of the Fed's operations on that day.

Table 3 summarizes the Fed's open market transactions in 1985 and illustrates some of the points made above. As already noted, the table shows that the total volume of transactions in 1985 greatly exceeded the net change in the System's portfolio of approximately $21.6 billion. The table also indicates that the volume of repurchase agreements and matched sale-purchase transactions was much larger than the volume of outright purchases and sales. Finally, the table shows that the vast majority of operations are carried out using U.S. Treasury securities. Further, since most repurchase agreements and matched sale-purchase transactions are conducted with short-term Treasury bills and, as the table indicates, a sizable portion of outright transactions are done with bills, it is clear that a majority of the Fed's total operations are conducted using bills. The liquidity of bills makes them especially suitable for open market operations.[17]

The second instrument or tool of monetary policy is the *discount rate*. As pointed out in Section 1, all depository institutions with reservable deposits may borrow reserves from the Fed's discount window for short-term adjustment purposes and a limited number of other reasons, subject to certain administrative restrictions contained in the System's Regulation A. The discount rate is the interest rate charged on these loans. As a technical matter, a depository institution can borrow from the window in two ways: (1) by "discounting," that is, selling loans or other assets carrying its endorsement to the Fed, or (2) through an advance, which is a loan from the Fed to the institution on the institution's note, which must be secured by acceptable collateral. At present, nearly all borrowing at the window is via advances because of their greater convenience. In the early days of the System, however, discounting was the more common procedure, and this historical legacy is the origin of the terms *discount window* and *discount rate*. Most borrowing at the window is at the basic discount rate. Higher rates are charged for certain categories of extended credit.

Each of the 12 Federal Reserve banks has a discount window managed by a discount officer, and the boards of directors of the banks set the rates for their respective banks subject to the approval of the

---

[17] For an excellent nontechnical description of open market operations, see Meek [18]. See also Partlan, Hamdani, and Camilli [20].

Board of Governors. When the System was created, it was anticipated that discount rates would vary from one bank to another in recognition of differing economic conditions across Federal Reserve districts. At present, the discount rates are generally uniform across the country except for brief transitional differences when the rate is being adjusted either upward or downward.

As noted in Section 1, providing loans through the discount window is one of the Fed's most important functions in the context of its broad responsibility for the liquidity and stability of U.S. financial markets. The focus of the present discussion, however, is on the role of the discount rate as an instrument of monetary policy. Essentially, the Fed uses the discount rate to reinforce its efforts to manage reserves through open market operations. Although many depository institutions are reluctant to borrow from the window, and all institutions are subject to various rules and administrative constraints when they do borrow, a discount rate that is low in relation to other short-term rates tends to encourage borrowing, and, conversely, a high discount rate in relation to other rates tends to discourage borrowing. Therefore, if the Fed, for example, were trying to restrain the growth of reserves, and this restraint were putting upward pressure on the Federal funds rate and other market rates, the maintenance of an unchanged discount rate might tend to raise the aggregate level of borrowing at the window at least temporarily, which would work against the thrust of open market operations. In this situation, the Fed might raise the discount rate to reinforce its open market operations. In addition to its direct impact on borrowing, the announcement of the discount rate increase would be a strong signal of the direction of Fed policy to both the financial markets and the general public, because such changes are highly visible and receive considerable attention from the news media.[18] Similarly, if the Fed were trying to stimulate reserve growth through open market operations, it might reduce the discount rate at some point.[19]

While it can be broadly said that the Fed reinforces its open market operations with changes in the discount rate, in general this reinforcement is highly discretionary and judgmental with respect to both the magnitude and timing of discount rate changes. Stated differently, there are no specific rules or formulas controlling the manner in which the Fed

---

[18] For a detailed analysis of the effects of discount rate announcements, see Cook and Hahn [9].

[19] In addition to changing the basic discount rate, on some occasions in the recent past the Fed has added surcharges to the basic rate as a means of reinforcing restrictive open market operations. For example, in 1980 and 1981 the System added a 2 to 4 percentage point surcharge to adjustment borrowing by larger institutions that borrowed in two successive weeks or in more than 4 weeks in a 13-week period.

manages the discount rate in conjunction with its other policy actions, and the timing and magnitude of changes in the rate in particular instances reflect a variety of external factors including the strength of the monetary or economic trends the Fed may be reacting to and its perception of expectations in the financial markets. At the same time, the short-run impact of discount rate changes on market interest rates depends to some extent on the particular short-run operating procedures the Fed is using in implementing policy, and the Fed has to take these relationships into account in deciding on discount rate actions in particular circumstances. Specifically, changes in the discount rate have generally stronger and more immediate effects on market rates under the operating procedures the Fed has used in the 1980s.[20]

Although the Board of Governors exercises final control over the discount rate, the participation of the Reserve bank boards of directors in the process of setting the rate has considerable practical importance. Specifically, when a Reserve bank board proposes a change in the rate, the Board of Governors must consider the proposal and make an explicit decision to approve it, disapprove it, or table it for later consideration. In this way, the Board is made aware of the thinking of a cross section of well-informed citizens from a variety of backgrounds and regions regarding the appropriate level of the rate and, more generally, the appropriate direction of monetary policy as a whole.

The third major instrument or tool of monetary policy are *reserve requirements*. Under current law, all depository institutions operating in the United States (including not only domestic commercial banks but also savings banks, savings and loan associations, credit unions, Edge Act and agreement corporations, and U.S. branches and agencies of foreign banks) must hold required reserves against their (1) net transactions accounts, (2) nonpersonal time deposits, and (3) Eurocurrency liabilities.[21] These required reserves must be held in the form either of vault cash or deposits at a Federal Reserve bank. The Board of Governors of the Fed establishes these requirements in terms of percentages of particular categories of reservable liabilities. The panel on the right-hand side of Table 4 shows the reserve requirements in effect in June 1986. As the table indicates, at that time depository institutions had to hold reserves equal to 12 percent of their net transactions accounts in excess of $31.7 million, and so forth. Under the law, the Board sets the requirements within specific ranges for each category of reservable liabilities. The range for net transactions deposits (in excess of an initial tier, which was $31.7 billion in June 1986) is 8 to 14 percent, and the range for nonpersonal time deposits is 0 to 9 percent. There are no limits

---

[20] See Broaddus and Cook [7].

[21] In this context, the term Eurocurrency liabilities refers to funds that U.S. depository institutions raise abroad for use in the United States.

TABLE 4 Reserve Requirements of Depository Institutions
(Percent of deposits)

	Member Bank Requirements before Implementation of the Monetary Control Act			Depository Institution Requirements after Implementation of the Monetary Control Act[6]	
Type of Deposit, and Deposit Interval[2]	Percent	Effective Date	Type of Deposit, and Deposit Interval[5]	Percent	Effective Date
Net demand:[2]			Net transaction accounts:[7,8]		
$0 million–$2 million	7	12/30/76	$0–$31.7 million	3	12/31/85
$2 million–$10 million	9½	12/30/76	Over $31.7 million	12	12/31/85
$10 million–$100 million	11¾	12/30/76			
$100 million–$400 million	12¾	12/30/76	Nonpersonal time deposits:[9]		
Over $400 million	16¼	12/30/76	By original maturity:		
			Less than 1½ years	3	10/6/83
Time and savings:[2,3]			1½ years or more	0	10/6/83
Savings	3	3/16/67			
			Eurocurrency liabilities:		
Time:[4]			All types	3	11/13/80
$0 million–$5 million, by maturity:					
30–179 days	3	3/16/67			
180 days to 4 years	2½	1/8/76			
4 years or more	1	10/30/75			
Over $5 million, by maturity:					
30–179 days	6	12/12/74			
180 days to 4 years	2½	1/8/76			
4 years or more	1	10/30/75			

NOTE: This table shows percentage reserve requirements as of June 1986 without important supplemental information. This information is provided in the detailed footnotes to the table showing reserve requirements in the monthly *Federal Reserve Bulletin*. See, for example, Table 1.15 on page A7 of the *Federal Reserve Bulletin* for June 1986.

SOURCE: Board of Governors of the Federal Reserve System.

on the requirements that can be established for Eurocurrency liabilities. In addition to the regular requirements shown on the right-hand side of Table 4, the Board can also place a supplemental requirement of up to 4 percentage points on net transactions accounts, and, for periods up to 180 days, it can establish requirements outside the regular ranges and on other liabilities. When it imposes these supplemental requirements and extensions, however, the Board must follow certain procedures prescribed by law.

With regard to monetary policy and monetary control, reserve requirements affect the quantitative relationship between the aggregate reserves held by depository institutions and the various monetary aggregates the Fed seeks to influence, all of which include some reservable liabilities. More precisely, reserve requirements put limits on the volume of reservable deposits and other liabilities that can be supported by any given volume of aggregate reserves. Therefore, the Fed could, if it chose to, manipulate reserve requirements to reinforce its other policy actions. For example, if it had adopted a generally restrictive posture, it might raise reserve requirements, and vice versa. In practice, the Fed rarely uses reserve requirements in this way. Frequent changes in the requirements would obviously be a substantial administrative burden on both the Fed itself and the institutions subject to the requirements. Further, even relatively small changes in reserve requirements can have a sizable impact on the availability and cost of reserves and are therefore not appropriate for effecting the generally incremental changes in reserve conditions the Fed is usually trying to achieve on a day-to-day basis. For this reason, the System tends to focus on reserve requirements as a central element of the institutional apparatus linking reserves quantitatively to the monetary aggregates rather than as an instrument to be manipulated. In this light, a topic of continuing interest is how the structure and coverage of the requirements might be changed to make the quantitative relationship between reserves and the monetary aggregates more predictable.

The structure and coverage of reserve requirements has in fact been changed in important ways in recent years. As noted earlier, the Depository Institutions Deregulation and Monetary Control Act of 1980 extended reserve requirements to all depository institutions. Prior to the passage of this act, the requirements had applied only to member banks and a few other categories of institutions. The Act also simplified the structure of the requirements by making them more uniform within particular deposit categories and eliminating the requirements against personal savings and time deposits. (The left panel of Table 4 shows the structure of the requirements prior to 1980, which can be compared to the present structure shown on the right.) Both of these changes were consistent with making the structure of the requirements potentially more efficient for controlling the monetary aggregates, especially the narrow M1 aggregate. Specifically, the extended coverage makes all of the deposits included in M1 reservable, while reducing the coverage of assets not in M1. The greater simplicity of the requirement structure can increase the predictability of the quantitative relationship between reserves and the monetary aggregates by reducing the impact on this relationship of changes in the distribution of deposits across different deposit categories and different size classifications of depository institutions.

In addition to these changes in structure and coverage, one other recent change in reserve requirements potentially relevant to monetary control should be pointed out. Prior to 1984, all reserve requirements were lagged: reserves were held in a given week against reservable liabilities held two weeks earlier. Since 1984, the requirements against net transactions accounts have been nearly contemporaneous. Specifically, depository institutions must maintain some average level of reserves (determined by the percentage requirement) over a two-week "maintenance period" ending on a Wednesday against the average level of net transactions deposits held over a two-week "computation period" ending on the Monday two days earlier. Depository institutions may adjust their balance sheet positions more rapidly in response to Fed actions affecting reserves under this new contemporaneous accounting procedure than under the former fully lagged system. If so, these more rapid adjustments might facilitate the control of M1.[22]

Although reserve requirements are a potentially important element in the Fed's strategy of controlling monetary aggregates, it should be noted that this potential importance varies with the particular tactical procedures the Fed employs.[23] The structure of reserve requirements would be highly significant in a regime where the Fed was controlling the monetary aggregates using total reserves as the control instrument, since the empirical relationship between reserves and the aggregates and the predictability of this relationship would be critically important in such a regime. Reserve requirements play a less important role in other operating regimes.[24]

---

[22] The adjustment-forcing character of contemporaneous accounting is reduced to some extent by carry-over privileges, which allow institutions to carry a reserve deficiency of up to 2 percent of requirements forward to the next maintenance period. (Excess reserves up to 2 percent of requirements can also be carried forward.) In addition to the carry-over allowance, the existence of the discount window, where, under current procedures, the discount rate is typically below the Federal funds rate, also reduces the incentive for rapid adjustment, which has led some economists to suggest that the discount rate be set at a penalty level above the Federal funds rate. For a thorough analysis of the ramifications of contemporaneous reserve accounting, see Goodfriend [14].

[23] These procedures are discussed further in the next subsection.

[24] In a detailed study, Goodfriend and Hargraves [15] argue that reserve

The tactics of monetary policy: operating procedures. This subsection describes the Fed's tactical operating procedures; that is, the procedures the System uses in conducting monetary policy over a short-run horizon of several weeks. The purpose of the procedures is to link the Fed's day-to-day open market operations with its longer-run strategic objectives. In essence, the operating procedures guide open market operations with a view to making them as consistent as feasible at any point in time with the System's longer-run strategy.

Because the Fed's strategy since the mid-1970s has been to pursue the nation's basic economic goals by controlling monetary aggregates, the System's operating procedures in recent years have aimed at facilitating monetary control. In general, there are two kinds of short-run procedures that the Fed (or any other central bank, for that matter) can use to control the monetary aggregates. One approach is to control them from the supply side by controlling total reserves. The other is to control them from the demand side by controlling conditions in the money markets as indexed by some short-term interest rate or some other money market variable.

Each of these two broad categories of control procedures requires further explanation. In a regime in which total reserves was the control variable, the Fed would use its target ranges for the growth of the monetary aggregates to construct a desired path for the growth of total reserves. This path would take account of both the necessary growth of required reserves, given the monetary targets and the level of reserve requirements, and any excess reserves depository institutions might be likely to hold above required reserves. The Fed would then conduct open market operations in such a way as to make the actual growth of total reserves conform as closely as feasible to the desired path. In doing so, of course, it would continuously update the desired path on the basis of new information bearing on the relationship between the growth of total reserves and the monetary aggregates.

In practice the Fed has never used a total reserve control procedure because it has not been able to control total reserves closely in the short run under either past or present institutional arrangements. While the System can control *nonborrowed* reserves through open market operations, it cannot control *total* reserves, because the level of borrowing at the discount window is determined in the short run by the preferences of depository institutions. In order to control total reserves, it would be necessary for the System to make institutional changes that would allow it to determine the level of borrowing at the same time it is independently determining the level of nonborrowed reserves. Two alternative institutional changes that would have this effect would be: (1) to make

requirements have played only a minor role in the conduct of monetary policy in the United States historically.

the discount rate a continuous penalty rate, or (2) to control the total level of borrowing closely by administrative fiat.

The other broad approach to controlling the monetary aggregates is from the demand side via control of a short-term interest rate or some other variable that is a good barometer of short-term money market conditions. There is wide agreement among economists that the public's demand for money balances is strongly influenced by the behavior of short-term interest rates. The reason for this relationship is as follows. Two of the most important components of any definition of money are currency and demand deposits, neither of which pay explicit interest. Therefore, a change in market rates affects the opportunity cost of holding money balances, as an alternative to interest-bearing nonmoney assets, and hence the public's money demand. For example, an increase in market rates increases the opportunity cost and therefore reduces the demand for money. Similarly, a reduction in rates reduces the opportunity cost and increases demand. Hence, the Fed could work to restrain money growth by acting to make money market conditions tighter, which would put upward pressure on short-term interest rates, and vice versa. Obviously, this procedure in principle would be more appropriate for controlling the narrow M1 measure of money than the broader aggregates, such as M2 and M3, since noninterest-bearing currency and demand deposits are a larger proportion of M1 than of M2 or M3. Whether or not this approach to monetary control is effective in practice, of course, depends on the predictability of the empirical relationship between the particular money market variable selected and the monetary aggregates.

The Fed had used three variants of the latter, money market conditions approach to monetary control between the mid-1970s, when it first began to announce target ranges for the aggregates, and the mid-1980s.[25] Prior to October 1979, the System attempted to estimate the level of the Federal funds rate—the overnight interest rate on reserve funds in the open money market—consistent with the rate at which it wanted M1 and the other monetary aggregates to grow. It then used open market operations to hold the Federal funds rate within a narrow range around that level in the short run. An important disadvantage of this approach in practice was that when the public became fully aware that the Fed was using the Federal funds rate in this way, financial markets became very sensitive in the short run to even small changes in the rate, and small adjustments in the rate sometimes produced strong political reactions. Both conditions made it difficult for the Fed to adjust the rates as frequently as necessary for effective control of the monetary aggregates.

---

[25] For a more detailed account of what follows, see Wallich [22].

Against this background, in October 1979, the Fed stopped using the Federal funds rate as its direct control instrument and began to focus on various reserve measures in order to improve its monetary control performance. Even though there has been a general shift of focus toward reserves, however, it is important to distinguish these recent control procedures from controlling the aggregates by controlling total reserves. From October 1979 until late 1982, the Fed used nonborrowed reserves as its instrument. In this regime, the System set a path for nonborrowed reserves that it believed was consistent with the desired paths of the monetary aggregates. With nonborrowed reserves thus predetermined, any change in depository institution demand for total reserves occasioned by a deviation of the monetary aggregates from their desired paths had to be accommodated by a corresponding change in the level of borrowing at the discount window, either upward or downward. This change in borrowing, in turn, affected the Federal funds rate and other short-term interest rates and hence the demand for money.[26] For example, if the growth of the monetary aggregates began to exceed the desired paths, the demand of depository institutions for total reserves would rise, which would cause the level of borrowing at the window to increase. The increased borrowing would then put upward pressure on the Federal funds rate and other market rates, given the general reluctance to borrow and the Fed's administrative restrictions on borrowing. The rise in rates, finally, would reduce the demand for money and the growth of the monetary aggregates.

In many ways the nonborrowed reserves procedure was potentially the strongest monetary control procedure the Fed has employed in practice, because when followed strictly, it generated an automatic response of reserve market conditions and interest rates to deviations of the monetary aggregates from their paths. For various reasons explained further in Section 3B below, the Fed dropped this approach in the fall of 1982 and began to use the level of borrowing as its instrument. In this regime the System aims at maintaining the level of borrowing in some relatively narrow desired range and then accommodates changes in depository institution demand for reserves by adjusting nonborrowed reserves through open market operations. This post-1982 approach is similar in essence to the pre-October 1979 procedure of controlling the Federal funds rate, because in this regime, as in the pre-October 1979 regime, the Fed influences the growth of the aggregates by affecting the level of the Federal funds rate and other market rates. The difference is that instead of controlling the Federal funds directly and tightly, in the

---

[26] At a technical level, the relationship between borrowing at the window and short-term market rates was the central relationship in the nonborrowed reserve regime. See Goodfriend [12] for a thorough analysis of the nonborrowed reserves operating procedure.

borrowed reserve regime the System influences the rate indirectly, and it does not generally attempt to control it as tightly.

This description of the three operating regimes the Fed has used in recent years requires two rather detailed but important and related qualifications—or at least clarifications. First, although some economists regard the nonborrowed reserve procedure used between October 1979 and the fall of 1982 as intermediate between the total reserve and money market condition classes of operating procedures delineated above, a case can be made that in its implementation the nonborrowed reserve procedure belonged to the class of money market condition procedures. Although market forces played a larger role in determining the level of the Federal funds rate in the short run in the nonborrowed reserve regime than in the other two regimes, the average level of the funds rate was still a central indicator of the Fed's operating stance in the short run. Second, the nonborrowed reserves procedure was not always followed slavishly in the 1979–82 period. Specifically, the nonborrowed reserve path was sometimes altered to accommodate at least part of the impact of unanticipated movements in the monetary aggregates on required reserves. To the extent that such alterations were made, the changes in required reserves did not have to be accommodated at the discount window, and they did not affect the Federal funds rate and other money market conditions. In short, in practice the differences between the 1979–82 regime and the other two regimes were not as great as the description above might suggest.

Two final points regarding the Fed's tactical procedures should be made. First, under all of the approaches that have been used—especially the pre-October 1979 approach and the post-1982 borrowed reserve procedure—it is possible to "look through" the monetary aggregates to the final goal variables of policy. In this way, one can think of the process as running directly from the Fed's influence on money market conditions to broader credit market conditions and long-term interest rates, and then to such goal variables as aggregate spending, income, and employment. It is probable that many individual policymakers who have a generally neo-Keynesian view of the monetary policy transmission mechanism regard the process in this manner. Further, this view of the process probably became more widespread in the 1980s due to the unusual and unpredictable behavior of monetary velocity that accompanied the extensive financial deregulation in this period.

Second, as suggested in the discussion of the discount rate in the preceding subsection, the role of the discount rate has been enhanced to some degree by the nonborrowed reserve and borrowed reserve control procedures of the 1980s. In both of these regimes, where the Federal funds rate tends to vary somewhat more flexibly than in the pre-October 1979 regime, and the aggregate level of borrowing tends to be somewhat less flexible, changes in the discount rate are often followed by roughly equal changes in the Federal funds rate in the same direction. This occurs because the level of borrowing in the short run is strongly influenced by the width of the (typically positive) spread between the Federal funds rate and the discount rate. With borrowing relatively constant in the short run under these regimes, a change in the discount rate requires a corresponding change in the Federal funds rate to maintain a relatively constant spread.

The policymaking process. The process by which specific decisions are made within the strategic and tactical framework outlined in the preceding subsections is of considerable interest to participants in financial markets, because many market professionals believe that knowledge of the process may be helpful in anticipating the timing of the Fed's major policy actions and may therefore be profitable. The process centers around two events: (1) meetings of the Federal Open Market Committee (FOMC), and (2) the establishment of the discount rate by the boards of the Reserve banks with the concurrence of the Board of Governors.

At present the FOMC has eight regular meetings each year, all of which are held at the offices of the Board of Governors.[27] The nonvoting Reserve bank presidents as well as the voting presidents attend each meeting and participate fully in the discussion. Senior members of the Board of Governors staff also attend, and each Reserve bank president is accompanied by one member of his staff, usually the director of his bank's research department. Prior to the meeting, all participants will have received and studied a considerable volume of documentation prepared by the staffs of the Board of Governors and the Trading Desk at the Federal Reserve Bank of New York. The most important documents are the so-called Greenbook and the Bluebook. The Greenbook contains comprehensive macroeconomic and financial projections for several quarters in the future. The staff uses a large structural model of the economy in preparing these forecasts, but the model output is modified extensively by judgmental adjustments in developing the final projections. The Bluebook summarizes recent financial and monetary data and presents a set of two or three alternative specifications for the short-run operating instructions to be included in the "directive" to the manager for domestic operations. These alternatives are based on a combination of econometric and judgmental estimates of the short-run relationship between (1) the operating instrument the FOMC is using (the level of borrowing at the discount window in late 1986), and (2) the monetary aggregates. Further, if the FOMC is considering the longer-

[27] The structure and composition of the FOMC is discussed in Section 2. The frequency of FOMC meetings has varied historically. Through much of the 1970s, for example, meetings were held each month.

run target ranges for the monetary aggregates at a particular meeting, the Bluebook presents alternative sets of ranges, sometimes with projections of important economic variables, such as the growth of real GNP and the implicit GNP price deflator, thought to be consistent with each alternative. All FOMC participants are briefed on the content of these documents by their respective staffs, since much of the discussion at the meeting itself begins with the projections and policy alternatives presented in these materials.

The agenda for FOMC meetings in recent years has been fairly standard. The meetings typically begin with a report of the Manager for Foreign Operations at the Federal Reserve Bank of New York, who conducts foreign currency operations as agent for both the FOMC and the Treasury.[28] His report is usually followed by a discussion of international financial and monetary developments. The Manager for Domestic Operations (i.e., the Manager of the Trading Desk) then reports on domestic open market operations during the period since the last FOMC meeting. The burden of this report is to show that the Desk's actions were consistent with the directive given him by the FOMC at the last meeting.[29]

Following consideration and acceptance of the domestic manager's report, the Committee discusses current economic conditions and the economic outlook in detail as background for the deliberation on monetary policy that follows. This portion of the meeting begins with a presentation by the director of the Division of Research and Statistics at the Board of Governors which summarizes and explains the economic projections in the Greenbook. Each of the participants then has an opportunity (which he usually takes) to state his individual view of the economy. These statements typically include the speaker's reactions to the projections in the Greenbook—particularly points of disagreement regarding either the broad profile of the forecasts or detailed parts of it. The Reserve bank presidents may present projections that have been developed independently by their own research staffs, and they often provide information regarding regional conditions in their districts that might have a bearing on the national outlook. Many of the participants also relay anecdotal information to supplement the formal statistical information provided in the Greenbook.[30]

After the economic go-round is completed, the Committee turns its

---

[28] The international dimensions of Fed monetary policy are discussed in the next subsection.

[29] The content of the directive is discussed below.

[30] Prior to each FOMC meeting, each of the Reserve banks sends a report on conditions in its district to the Board of Governors. These reports are compiled in a so-called Beigebook that is distributed to all FOMC participants and also transmitted to Congress.

attention to monetary policy. The staff director for monetary and economic policy of the Board of Governors staff summarizes the various short-run policy alternatives presented in the Bluebook. The Committee discusses these options—usually in a "go-round" in which all participants indicate their preferences—and decides on the particular positions it wishes to adopt, which may or may not coincide with one of the alternatives in the Bluebook. It then considers and votes on a written short-run directive to be issued to the manager of the Desk to guide open market operations over the period to the next FOMC meeting. At its meetings in February and July, the Committee also considers and sets (or reaffirms) long-run ranges for the monetary aggregates. In doing so, it follows the targeting procedure outlined earlier in this article. The discussion of the long-run ranges at these meetings occupies a separate position on the agenda from the discussion of the short-run situation, and the Committee's decision on the ranges is arrived at through a separate vote. Also, as pointed out earlier, the Fed chairman publicly announces decisions on the long-run ranges in congressional testimony shortly after these meetings in accordance with the requirements of the Humphrey-Hawkins Act.

The short-run directive is very important because, in addition to instructing the manager, it provides a relatively precise public record of the substantive short-run actions taken by the FOMC at a particular meeting. In order to interpret the directive, however, it is necessary to understand its structure.[31] The directive is usually about six paragraphs long. The first several paragraphs provide background information on domestic economic and financial developments and conditions in foreign exchange markets. A later paragraph states or restates the Committee's long-run target ranges for the monetary and credit aggregates and any special circumstances relevant to these ranges. The final paragraph is the key paragraph. It contains the detailed short-run operational instructions to the manager.

The structure of the operational paragraph evolves slowly over time in accordance with changes in the FOMC's tactical operating procedures and other developments, but financial market professionals are usually aware of the structure at any given time and hence are able to interpret the meaning of relatively small changes in language and other nuances. As an example, Figure 5 shows the operational paragraph of the directive issued at the FOMC meeting on September 23, 1986, when, as

---

[31] Under the procedures in effect in late 1986, the directive issued at an FOMC meeting is included in the "Record of Policy Actions" for the meeting, which is released to the public shortly after the *next* meeting of the Committee. In this way, the public is never informed of the directive currently in effect. The desirability of this practice has become a matter of considerable debate. See Goodfriend [13].

FIGURE 5

Operational Paragraph of Directive Issued at FOMC Meeting on
September 23, 1986

In the implementation of policy for the immediate future, the Committee seeks to
maintain the existing degree of pressure on reserve positions. This action is expected
to be consistent with growth in M2 and M3 over the period from August to December
at annual rates of 7 to 9 percent. While growth in M1 is expected to moderate from
the exceptionally large increase during the past several months, that growth will
continue to be judged in the light of the behavior of M2 and M3 and other factors.
Slightly greater reserve restraint *would,* or slightly lesser reserve restraint *might,* be
acceptable depending on the behavior of the aggregates, taking into account the
strength of the business expansion, developments in foreign exchange markets,
progress against inflation, and conditions in domestic and international credit
markets. The Chairman may call for Committee consultation if it appears to the
Manager for Domestic Operations that reserve conditions during the period before
the next meeting are likely to be associated with a federal funds rate persistently
outside a range of 4 to 8 percent.

Votes for this action: Messrs. Volcker, Corrigan, Angell, Guffey, Heller, Mrs. Horn, Messrs.
Johnson, Melzer, Morris, Rice, and Ms. Seger. Vote against this action: Mr. Wallich.

NOTE: Emphasis added.
SOURCE: Board of Governors of the Federal Reserve System.

noted in the preceding subsection, the Committee was using borrowed
reserves as its operating instrument. Experienced market observers
interpreted this particular directive as follows. The first sentence said in
effect that for the period immediately following the meeting, the
objective for borrowed reserves had not been changed. The phrase
"degree of pressure on reserve positions" was understood to refer to the
borrowing objective, and the word "maintain" indicated that the objective had been left unchanged. The second and third sentences discussed
the short-run behavior of the monetary aggregates believed to be
consistent with an unchanged borrowing objective. At the time of this
meeting, the Committee was giving somewhat less attention, in relative
terms, to the behavior of the narrow M1 measure of money than to the
broader M2 and M3 measures because of the unusual behavior of the
velocity of M1 at the time.[32] This ordering was indicated by: (1) the
statement of the expected short-run M2 and M3 growth rates before the
reference to M1, and (2) the absence of an explicit expected growth rate
for M1. The fourth sentence indicated how the manager should adjust
the borrowing objective in the light of new information regarding the
aggregates and economic and financial developments. The key words in

[32] The behavior of the monetary aggregates in this period is discussed
further in Section 3B.

this sentence were "would" and "might." Because *would* is a somewhat stronger term than *might*, the sentence suggested that the Committee was somewhat more inclined to raise the borrowing objective—that is, "tighten" its short-run policy position—in the light of emerging developments than to ease its position.

To summarize, the directive shown in Figure 5 instructed the manager (1) to maintain the existing short-run policy stance initially, and (2) to move somewhat more aggressively to tighten policy than to ease it if conditions changed in one direction or the other. Market analysts interpreted these instructions as constituting a very slight "snugging" or tightening of the FOMC's overall posture compared with the directive it had issued at its preceding meeting on August 19. At that meeting, the Committee had voted to "decrease slightly" the pressure on reserve positions. As Figure 5 shows, one member of the Committee voted against the action taken at the September 1986 meeting. Such dissents are fairly frequent, since the FOMC must often make its policy decisions in the face of substantial uncertainties. The Record of Policy Actions that includes a particular directive also includes a brief statement of the reasons for any dissenting votes.

The other principal element of the policymaking process is the setting of the discount rate. The boards of directors of the Reserve banks (or the executive committees thereof) are required by law to consider and set the basic discount rate and related rates at least every 14 days. Before making its decisions on the rate, the boards are briefed in detail on recent national economic and financial developments by the research staffs at the banks. The focus on national considerations is appropriate because, as indicated above, the discount rate is uniform across all Reserve banks except for brief transition periods when the rate is being changed. Therefore, if the Board of Governors approves a change at one bank, the change will quickly be followed at all banks. All Reserve bank actions on the discount rate, including renewals as well as changes, are transmitted immediately to the Board of Governors, which considers them and either approves, disapproves, or tables them. If the Board approves a change in the rate, the change is announced publicly on the same day. Such announcements are usually made late in the afternoon after U.S. financial markets have closed in order to avoid disrupting the markets. A summary of the Board's discount rate actions is published each year in the Board's *Annual Report*.

As suggested earlier, the significance of the role of the Reserve bank boards in setting the discount rate should not be underestimated even though the Board of Governors must approve all actions on the rate. The members of the Reserve bank boards are knowledgeable citizens from a wide variety of backgrounds. If several of the boards are simultaneously recommending a change in the rate in the same direction, the Board of Governors will naturally give this circumstance considerable weight in deciding whether or not to approve the proposal. Also, under current procedures, the boards of the banks routinely convey the reasons for their actions to the Board of Governors, which then takes these reasons into account in reaching its final decisions.

In the period prior to October 1979, when the FOMC was using the Federal funds rather than borrowed reserves as its operating instrument, there was a looser short-run relationship between the Federal funds rate and the discount rate than in the 1980s. Therefore, there was less reason before 1980 than subsequently to coordinate discount rate changes with the FOMC's actions affecting open market operations and the Federal funds rate. As already noted, discount rate actions have a direct and relatively predictable short-run impact on the Federal funds rate in the nonborrowed reserve and borrowed reserve regimes of the 1980s. For this reason, somewhat greater attention has been given to the need to coordinate discount rate actions and open market operations at FOMC meetings in the 1980s than earlier.

International dimensions of monetary policy. Up to this point the discussion has focused on the domestic aspects of Fed monetary policy. Fed policy has an increasingly important international dimension, however, because of the dramatic growth of U.S. trade and financial relationships with other countries in recent years. Financial markets are now highly integrated throughout the industrial world. As a result, the Fed's monetary policies can have significant impacts, especially in the short run, on economic and financial developments in other countries, and, conversely, the monetary policy actions of central banks in other developed countries can influence events in the United States. For this reason, the Fed necessarily takes account of international economic and financial conditions in pursuing its domestic economic objectives, and it communicates regularly with other central banks around the world to facilitate attainment of the shared goal of stability in international product and financial markets. It should be noted that this need to take account of international factors in conducting monetary policy continues to exist in the present regime of floating exchange rates. In principle, such a regime can insulate the economies of individual countries from the effects of the monetary policy actions of other countries. In reality, however, lags in the adjustment of exchange rates to the policy actions of particular countries allow the impacts of such changes to cross borders. More importantly, the current regime is not a "pure" float in which exchange rates are determined entirely by private market conditions. Instead, central banks intervene in the exchange markets individually and jointly from time to time to achieve specific exchange rate objectives.

As an example of circumstances where the Fed might allow international conditions to influence its policy actions, consider a hypothetical situation where the U.S. economy had been growing at a persistently slow pace and the current rate of domestic inflation was relatively low. Under these conditions, the Fed might want to consider easing its short-run policy stance somewhat to include, perhaps, a reduction in the discount rate. If the dollar were coming under strong downward pressure in the exchange markets for some reason, however, the Fed might delay taking such action in order to avoid weakening the dollar further, particularly if it seemed likely that monetary policy might also be eased in one or more other important countries in the near future. It should be emphasized here that although the Fed gives continuous attention to international developments in deciding on particular policy actions, the domestic objectives of policy remain paramount. Therefore, as in this example, international considerations are more likely to affect the timing of the Fed's actions than the longer-run substance of policy in most cases.

In addition to taking account of international events and conditions in conducting domestic monetary policy, on occasion the Fed also carries out certain foreign currency operations that can directly affect exchange rates in the short run. These operations are actually conducted by a Manager for Foreign Operations at the Federal Reserve Bank of New York under (1) an Authorization for Foreign Currency Operations and (2) a Foreign Currency Directive established by the Federal Open Market Committee (FOMC). These operations are approached in a very different manner, however, from the domestic open market operations discussed earlier. Specifically, whereas the directive for domestic open market operations is typically adjusted each month in accordance with emerging economic and financial developments, the Foreign Currency Directive is not usually changed. In general, the latter directive instructs the Manager for Foreign Operations to make purchases and sales in foreign exchange markets (i.e., to "intervene" in these markets) as appropriate to counter any disorderly conditions that may arise in the current floating rate regime. The manager reports his actions at each FOMC meeting, and the Committee must ratify them as a way of ensuring they have been consistent with the continuing directive. It is important to point out here that the Fed conducts its foreign currency operations in close coordination and cooperation with the U.S. Treasury, which is responsible for managing the nation's overall reserve position. It should also be noted that the potential effect of both the Fed's foreign currency operations and those of other central banks on the reserve position of U.S. depository institutions is routinely "sterilized" or offset in the course of domestic open market operations. In other words, neither the Fed's interventions in foreign exchange markets nor those of other central banks are allowed to affect U.S. money market conditions.

Although the principal purpose of foreign currency operations in the floating rate regime of the 1970s and 1980s has been to counter disorderly exchange market conditions, in recent years the System has intervened on some occasions to achieve broader goals, as illustrated particularly by events in the second half of 1985. The U.S. dollar appreciated sharply against other major currencies in the early 1980s, probably largely as a result of fiscal policy initiatives in this period that increased the real after-tax rate of return to capital investment in the United States. This appreciation had a severely depressing effect on many U.S. business firms that export or that compete with imported goods in U.S. markets. Against this background, a depreciation of the dollar that began in February 1985 was greeted with considerable relief. In August and September of that year, however, the dollar reversed course and began to appreciate sharply, which intensified growing demands in Congress for protectionist legislation. In this situation, representatives of the G-5 countries met in New York in late September, and following this meeting these countries intervened actively and concertedly in the exchanges to encourage the appreciation of nondollar currencies. From the time of this meeting through November, the Fed and the Treasury together sold approximately $3.3 billion, and the other G-5 countries sold about $9.7 billion. Following these operations, the dollar turned back down and declined another 12 percent over the remainder of the year.

The foreign currency operations of both the Fed and other major central banks have been greatly facilitated in recent years by the existence of a so-called "swap" network of reciprocal currency exchange arrangements. Under these arrangements the Fed can acquire foreign currencies from its counterparts abroad when needed to support the dollar in the foreign exchange market, and foreign central banks can acquire dollars from the Fed to support their respective currencies. As of January 31, 1986, the Fed had swap arrangements with 14 foreign central banks and the Bank for International Settlements. The total amount of these facilities on that date was $30.1 billion.

An individual currency swap involves a *spot* transaction and a simultaneous *forward* transaction. In the spot transaction the Fed swaps (i.e., exchanges) dollars for a foreign currency with another central bank. In the forward transaction the two banks agree to reverse the swap three months later. The bank that initiates the swap is said to make a swap "drawing" and is typically thought of as the "borrower" in the transaction. As an example, the Fed might obtain German marks for the purpose of supporting the dollar by drawing on its swap arrangement with the German Bundesbank. In the spot transaction the Fed would exchange dollars for marks, which it would then use to purchase dollars in the open market. At the same time it would make a forward commitment to reverse the exchange three months later. At the end of the three months, the Fed would have to reacquire the marks—which it would typically do in the market—to meet its forward obligation.

Both the Fed and its partner central banks in the swap network have used the arrangements actively at various times since the network came into being in the early 1960s. The Fed, for example, used the network to acquire substantial amounts of several foreign currencies for intervention operations when the dollar was under sharp downward pressure in the late 1970s. More recently, the central bank of Mexico made sizable drawings of dollars through the facility during the liquidity crisis in that country in 1982.

B. Some Major Recent Developments and Issues in Monetary Policy

This section will present a brief and highly selective overview of the recent history of Fed monetary policy and certain key current issues regarding policy. In general the focus will be on the period from approximately 1973, when the first of the two oil price "shocks" of the 1970s occurred, and the end of 1985. Although this 12-year period is relatively brief in the context of history of Fed policy, it has been a period of rapid and dramatic change in both the actual conduct of policy and the economic analysis of policy. In particular, the U.S. economy in this period has gone through a transition from a situation in the late 1970s where the inflation rate was rising steadily and alarmingly to a sustained condition of significantly lower and more stable inflation in the mid-1980s. The following discussion attempts to illuminate the role Fed policy played in this transition and to extract any lessons these events may contain regarding the overall conduct of policy.[33]

The acceleration of inflation after 1965. The period from the end of the Korean War inflation in 1953 to 1965 was distinguished by remarkable price stability in the United States by historical standards. The average annual inflation rate during this 12-year span as measured by the implicit GNP deflator was 2.3 percent. Further, the annual rates ranged narrowly between a high rate of 4.0 percent in 1956 and a low rate of 1.2 percent in 1963.[34]

This tranquil price behavior ended in the late 1960s due at least in part to the concurrent initiation of major new federal social programs and the military buildup in Vietnam. The inflation rate rose from 3.0 percent in 1965 to 5.8 percent in 1968 and then held at 5.5 percent in 1969

---

[33] For a more complete summary of this period, see Axilrod [1]. See also Wallich [22].

[34] The inflation and money supply growth data referred to in this section are summarized in Table 5.

TABLE 5 Inflation and M1 Growth Rates
(Fourth quarter to fourth quarter)

Year	Inflation Rate*	M1 Growth Rate**
1950	4.7%	—%
1951	2.9	—
1952	2.8	—
1953	−0.4	—
1954	2.7	—
1955	3.4	—
1956	4.0	—
1957	2.8	—
1958	2.0	—
1959	2.3	—
1960	1.3	0.5
1961	1.3	2.9
1962	2.5	1.8
1963	1.2	4.0
1964	1.5	4.4
1965	3.0	4.4
1966	4.1	2.8
1967	2.5	6.4
1968	5.8	7.3
1969	5.5	3.9
1970	5.2	5.0
1971	6.1	6.7
1972	4.4	8.4
1973	8.2	5.8
1974	10.0	4.8
1975	8.3	5.0
1976	5.7	6.2
1977	6.8	8.1
1978	8.0	8.2
1979	8.9	7.5
1980	9.9	7.3
1981	8.7	5.1
1982	5.2	8.7
1983	3.6	10.4
1984	3.6	5.4
1985	3.3	11.9

* Inflation measured by the increase in the gross national product implicit price deflator.

** Comparable data for 1950–1959 are not available. The definition of M1 has been revised, and published historical data begins in January 1959.

SOURCE: U.S. Department of Commerce, Bureau of Economic Analysis and the Board of Governors of the Federal Reserve System.

and 5.2 percent in 1970 despite a downturn in the economy. Although a 5.2 percent inflation rate may seem moderate when viewed from the perspective of the mid-1980s, it was almost universally regarded as unsatisfactory in 1971 and presented a major political problem to the Administration and Congress. Consequently, President Nixon announced a comprehensive wage and price control program on August 15, 1971, that endured in various forms until early 1974. This program may have temporarily restrained price increases in its early phases, since the inflation rate declined from 6.1 percent in 1971 to 4.4 percent in 1972. Any such effect, however, was short-lived, as the rate climbed back to 8.2 percent in 1973 and rose further to 10.0 percent in 1974. At a superficial level, this sharp acceleration of inflation in the mid-1970s reflected the progressive dismantling of the price control program. More fundamentally, it almost certainly reflected (1) a significant acceleration in the growth of M1 in 1971 and 1972 and, (2) after 1973, the impact of the OPEC petroleum embargo and the first oil price shock.

Probably as a result in part of the restrictive actions taken by the Fed in 1973 and 1974 to contain the inflation, the economy passed through a prolonged and severe recession between the fourth quarter of 1973 and the first quarter of 1975. After growing at an average annual rate of 5.0 percent in 1972 and 5.2 percent in 1973, real (i.e., inflation-adjusted) GNP declined 0.5 percent rate in 1974 and 1.3 percent in 1975. The weakness in the economy reduced the upward pressure on prices temporarily, but to a much smaller degree than in the years immediately following other postwar downturns. From its 10.0 percent peak in 1974, the rate declined to 8.3 percent in 1975 and 5.7 percent in 1976. It then turned back up and rose persistently to 6.8 percent in 1977, 8.0 percent in 1978, and 8.9 percent in 1979 before peaking at 9.9 percent in 1980.

Economists and others have given considerable attention to the reasons for this sharp and sustained rise in inflation in the late 1970s and early 1980s. Part of the increase probably reflected the lingering impact of the first oil price shock and subsequent dislocations in other commodity markets. Further, the second oil price shock in 1979 following the revolution in Iran was very likely a factor in the rise in the price level in that year and in 1980. Beyond their direct effects, these highly visible increases in the prices of key commodities, in conjunction with the observed persistent increase in the general price level, created an atmosphere in which the public began to expect a sustained rise in inflation, and as time passed these inflationary expectations, in turn, helped fuel further increases in wages and prices.

In addition to these pressures from particular commodity markets, however, many if not most economists now believe that fiscal and monetary policy played an important role in the inflationary process. After rising to a then record level of $70.5 billion in fiscal year 1976 as a result of the 1974–75 recession, the federal budget deficit declined only moderately to the $50–55 billion range in fiscal years 1977 and 1978. Some economists believe these high deficits contributed to the acceleration of inflation. Others focus more attention on monetary developments. The growth rate of M1 rose sharply in the late 1970s and exceeded 8 percent in both 1977 and 1978. Moreover, the growth of M1 frequently exceeded the tops of its annual targets during this period,[35] which very probably reduced the credibility in the eyes of the public of the Fed's announced strategy of controlling the growth of the money supply in order to reduce inflation. Any loss of credibility that occurred would have tended to heighten inflationary expectations and thereby fuel the rise in inflation.

October 6, 1979 to late 1982: the turn to disinflation. Whatever its causes, by the second half of 1979 the acceleration of inflation and the accompanying intensification of inflationary expectations had created a precarious and potentially unstable condition in the U.S. economy. In particular, there was a clear risk that the public's fear of still further increases in inflation would lead to speculative excesses in commodity markets and other markets. Indeed, there was evidence of speculative pressures in the markets for precious metals in the late summer of 1979. More disturbingly, the U.S. dollar, which had declined dramatically in the foreign exchange markets in late 1978, came under renewed downward pressure in September 1979, which suggested that the reduction in the credibility of the Fed's anti-inflationary stance had become international in scope.

In these circumstances the Federal Open Market Committee decided at an extraordinary Saturday meeting on October 6, 1979, to make a more determined effort to control the growth of the monetary aggregates in order to enhance the credibility of its effort to restore price stability. Specifically, as noted earlier, the Committee shifted its operational focus from the Federal funds rate to nonborrowed reserves as the principal operating variable for controlling the aggregates. As Chairman Volcker put it in Congressional testimony:

> Consequently, we are now placing more emphasis on controlling the provision of reserves to the banking system—which ultimately governs the supply of deposits and money—to keep monetary growth within our established targets. In changing that emphasis, we necessarily must be less concerned with day-to-day or week-to-week fluctuations in interest rates because those interest rates will respond to shifts in demand for money and

---

[35] Between 1975, when the longer-run target ranges were first used, and the end of 1978, a four-quarter-ahead target was set in each quarter of the year. In 1978, the current practice of setting only one target for any given calendar year was instituted in accordance with the terms of the Humphrey-Hawkins Act.

reserves. . . . . What is involved is a tactical change in the approach to control of the money stock.[36]

Much has been written and said about the FOMC's October 6, 1979 action, especially in the light of subsequent events. As noted in the general discussion of the Fed's operating procedures in Section 3A, the nonborrowed reserve targeting procedure adopted in October 1979 was not equivalent to targeting total reserves as advocated by some monetarist economists. It was, however, a significant change. In particular, by ceasing its attempt to control the highly visible (and politically sensitive) Federal funds rate tightly in the very short run, it was believed that the Committee would be able to move more boldly and promptly in the future to take the operational actions necessary to hold the monetary aggregates under control.

An interesting and important issue here is the extent to which the October 6 change in procedure, per se, contributed to the longer-run decline in inflation in 1982. It is quite possible that the shift in operational focus and the publicity it received helped, in the months immediately following the action, to relax some of the more extreme inflationary pressures that had been building in some markets. The growth rate of M1, which had reached 10.0 percent in the second quarter of 1979 and 10.4 percent in the third quarter declined to 4.3 percent in the fourth quarter and 5.7 percent in the first quarter of 1980. Further, in keeping with Chairman Volcker's reference to interest rates in the quotation above, the Federal funds rate was allowed to fluctuate considerably more widely in the days and weeks immediately following the action than before the action. These developments may well have persuaded financial market participants and others that the action constituted an important and substantive change in the Fed's behavior, and this perception, in turn, may have reduced inflationary expectations to some degree.

It is less clear, however, that the change in operating procedures in October 1979 as such was the dominant factor leading to the broad and sustained reduction in inflation after 1981. Because of a variety of technical complexities, comparing the actual growth of the monetary aggregates with their target ranges after the fact is not as straightforward as one might expect. Table 6 shows the results of one attempt to do so.[37]

---

[36] The quotation is from Chairman Volcker's statement to the Subcommittees on Domestic Monetary Policy and on International Trade, Investment and Monetary Policy of the House Committee on Banking, Finance, and Urban Affairs, November 13, 1979. See *Federal Reserve Bulletin*, December 1979, pp. 958–62, for the full statement.

[37] Table 6 reproduces Table II in an article by Broaddus and Goodfriend [8]. The text of this article discusses the construction of the data in the table in detail. In particular, the data are adjusted for certain shifts between different types of

TABLE 6 Expressed or Implied Annual Target Ranges for Effective M1 and Corresponding Actual Effective M1 Growth, 1975–1984

Target Period	Target Range	Midpoint of Target Range	Actual
4Q75–4Q76	4.5–7.5	6.0	5.8
4Q76–4Q77	4.5–6.5	5.5	7.9
4Q77–4Q78	4.0–6.5	5.25	7.2
4Q78–4Q79	4.5–7.5	6.0	6.8
4Q79–4Q80	4.0–6.5	5.25	6.9
4Q80–4Q81	3.5–6.0	4.75	2.4
4Q81–4Q82	2.5–5.5	4.0	9.0
4Q82–4Q83	4.0–8.0	6.0	10.3
2Q83–4Q83	5.0–9.0	7.0	7.4
4Q83–4Q84	4.0–8.0	6.0	5.2

NOTES: (1) The ranges in this table are the same as, or were derived from, the target ranges that were announced by the Federal Reserve at the beginning of the year to which the target applied. For 1979 and subsequent target years announcements have been contained in the Federal Reserve's annual Monetary Policy Report to Congress, which is usually published in the March issue of the *Federal Reserve Bulletin.* For 1976, 1977, and 1978, the announcements are contained in Burns (1976), Burns (1977), and Miller (1978), respectively. (2) The target ranges for 1979 and 1981 are adjusted for anticipated shifts into or out of NOW accounts or similar accounts as explained in the text. The ranges for the periods 4Q79–4Q80 and 4Q80–4Q81 are the ranges that were set for what was then referred to as M-1B.

SOURCE: Alfred Broaddus and Marvin Goodfriend, "Base Drift and the Longer Run Growth of M1: Experience from a Decade of Monetary Targeting," *Economic Review,* Federal Reserve Bank of Richmond (November–December 1984), p. 7.

These data indicate that the "effective"[38] growth of M1 exceeded the top of its target range in 1980, the first full year following the October 1979 change. In 1981, the effective growth rate fell below the bottom of the target range for that year. Finally, in 1982, the growth rate exceeded the top of the range by a substantial amount.[39] To be sure, several unanticipated events occurred during this period that may account for part of

deposits during the period covered that occurred as a result of interest rate deregulation and the introduction of new types of deposit accounts such as NOW (negotiable order of withdrawal) accounts. It should be emphasized that the data are the responsibility of the authors of this article. They are not official Federal Reserve statistics.

[38] See [8], pp. 5–8, for a detailed elaboration of the meaning of the term "effective" in this context.

[39] It should be noted that the nonborrowed reserve procedure was essentially dropped well before the end of 1982.

these deviations of actual growth from the targets. For example, the sharp acceleration of M1 in the second half of 1980 may have been due in part to the end of the special credit control program in effect in the spring of that year. Nevertheless, the persistent deviations of actual M1 growth from its target ranges during the period of nonborrowed reserve targeting indicated in Table 6 suggest that the move to nonborrowed reserve targeting in October 1979 did not in itself improve monetary control significantly. For this reason, although the change may have enhanced the credibility of the Fed's anti-inflationary program to some extent—or at least prevented a further significant erosion of credibility—it does not appear that the change played a decisive role in bringing about the later sustained reduction in inflation and inflationary expectations.[40]

If the October 1979 change in operating procedures was not a dominant factor in the later decline in inflation, what factors were important? The data in Table 6 suggest a plausible hypothesis: specifically, that the sharp decline in effective M1 growth in 1981, as distinct from the change in operating procedures in 1979, was the dominant event. As the table shows, after rising for four consecutive years at rates near or in excess of 7 percent, the actual effective growth rate of M1 dropped sharply to 2.4 percent in 1981. This decline followed a period in late 1980 and early 1981 when market interest rates had risen sharply, as indexed by increases in the daily average Federal funds rate to close to 20 percent and yields on longer-term Treasury securities just under 13 percent. Probably as a result of these monetary and financial developments, the economy sank into a deep recession in the third quarter of 1981 that lasted through the fourth quarter of 1982, during which the unemployment rate rose to a postwar record high of 10.7 percent. Few observers would argue that the Fed deliberately engineered the recession to reduce inflation. The Fed's willingness to allow this painful disinflation process, however, rather than easing policy aggressively to end it, almost certainly raised the public's awareness not only of the Fed's concern with the long-term risks posed by high and rising inflation and inflationary expectations but also its determination to bring both under control. If this hypothesis is valid, it is consistent with the generally accepted view that the credibility of the Fed's stance against inflation increased in the early 1980s. An increase in credibility based on a perceived willingness to tolerate the temporarily painful disinflation process and allow it to gain momentum, however, is not necessarily equivalent to credibility based on the perception of improved monetary control due to the change in operating procedures.

---

[40] For a somewhat different view see Axilrod [1], p. 18.

Late 1982–1986: problems with monetary targeting. As already indicated, the period of nonborrowed reserve targeting ended in late 1982. The nonborrowed reserve procedure was dropped at the same time that M1 was deemphasized in relation to the other monetary aggregates as an intermediate target of monetary policy. The discussion of the Fed's monetary targeting strategy in Section 3A pointed out that the strategy is based on the assumption of a steady and predictable relationship in practice between the monetary aggregates and broader measures of aggregate economic activity. M1 was deemphasized as a monetary target in the fall of 1982 because there was a growing concern at the time that the predictability of the relation between M1 and the economy was breaking down, at least temporarily. More precisely, there was a growing concern that the public's demand for the assets included in M1, given the aggregate level of national income, was becoming unpredictable.

There were several reasons for this concern.[41] First, a substantial volume of the temporarily authorized "all-savers" certificates were scheduled to mature in October 1982. Since most certificate holders could not reinvest in the certificates, a sizable share of the proceeds were expected to be placed in transactions accounts included in M1 for some uncertain time period until more permanent substitute investments could be found. These temporary flows of funds were expected to produce a temporary acceleration of M1 growth of some unknown magnitude that it would be inappropriate to resist with monetary policy, because the increase would not be due to basic economic trends. Further, the scheduled authorization of money market deposit accounts at depository institutions later in the year was expected to further disrupt the relationship between M1 and the economy. Beyond these relatively short-run dislocations, however, there was a belief that the public's longer-run demand for M1 balances, given the level of income, might be changing in ways that were not yet clear. In particular, the newly authorized interest-bearing transactions accounts such as NOW accounts, which by late 1982 were included in the M1 aggregate, were growing very rapidly. There was reason to believe that the public's demand for balances in this type of account responded differently to changes in market interest rates from the demand for ordinary demand deposits. Moreover, to the extent that the public used these interest-bearing accounts as a vehicle for savings as well as transactions, the long-term relationship between an M1 that included a large proportion of these accounts and the economy might differ significantly from historical relationships. These concerns were reinforced at an empirical

---

[41] For a fuller statement of these reasons, see Axilrod [1], pp. 18–19.

level by the behavior of the velocity of M1 in the early 1980s.[42] After rising fairly smoothly at an average annual rate of 3.1 percent through most of the postwar period, M1 velocity slowed noticeably in 1980 and declined in 1982.

In these circumstances, the FOMC decided formally to de-emphasize M1 at its meeting in October 1982. At the same time, it replaced the nonborrowed reserve operating procedure with the borrowed reserve operating procedure discussed in Section 3A. As indicated there, the borrowed reserve target is similar in important respects to the pre-October 1979 operating procedure when the monetary aggregates were controlled via direct control of the federal funds rate. Under the borrowed reserve procedure, the funds rate is influenced indirectly through the level of borrowing rather than directly.

From the vantage point of late 1986, it appears that the decision to de-emphasize M1 as a monetary target was appropriate. M1 grew 11.9 percent between the second quarter of 1982 and the second quarter of 1983. In the past, such sharp accelerations in money growth have often been followed by rising inflation and strengthened inflationary expectations. The 1982–1983 acceleration, however, was not followed by a significant rise in inflation either immediately or with a lag, and the sustained decline in nominal interest rates in the period suggests diminished rather than strengthened inflationary expectations.

During the second half of 1983 and in 1984, M1 velocity stopped declining and appeared to be resuming its upward trend. As a result, it seemed possible that it might be feasible to return to a firmer monetary targeting strategy. Although the nonborrowed reserve operating procedure was not reinstituted, the FOMC did formally restore M1 to a position of equal weight with the other monetary aggregates at its meeting in July 1984.

In 1985 and 1986, however, M1 velocity dropped sharply again. The decline appeared to be related in part to the substantial decline in nominal interest rates during the period, in an environment in which restrictions on the interest depository institutions could pay on most types of deposit accounts were being progressively dismantled.[43] In this

---

[42] The velocity of M1 is the ratio of the level of GNP in current dollars to the dollar level of M1 and can be thought of roughly as the number of times an average dollar is spent in a year. Rapid growth in velocity implies that GNP is growing rapidly in relation to the growth of the money stock, which in turn implies that the public's demand for money is low in relation to the growth of income. Conversely, slow growth in velocity implies that money is growing rapidly in relation to GNP and hence that the demand for money is high in relation to income.

[43] All interest restrictions on all types of accounts except demand deposits were phased out by March 31, 1986.

situation, the opportunity costs of holding the interest-bearing transactions accounts included in M1 became progressively lower until, by the second half of 1986, they had virtually disappeared. This steady reduction in opportunity costs, in turn, probably contributed to a significant increase in the demand for M1 and hence to very rapid growth in M1 in both 1985 and 1986.

As a result of these developments, by late 1986 the Fed's monetary targeting strategy had been significantly diluted. The measured growth rate of M1 was nearly 15 percent from the fourth quarter of 1985 to the fourth quarter of 1986, 7 percentage points above the upper limit of the 4 to 8 percent target range set for the period. In view of the decline in velocity, however, the FOMC did not attempt to bring the growth rate down to the target range—or, for that matter, to reduce the growth rate significantly at all. In effect, the Committee simply monitored the growth of M1 in the context of the behavior of velocity.[44] Some weight was given to the behavior of the broader M2 and M3 aggregates in this period, but it is probably fair to say that in practice at least equal weight was given to the current state of the general economy and the near-term outlook for the economy. In short, in late 1986 the strategy of monetary policy was essentially to react in a discretionary manner to the signals provided not only by the monetary aggregates but a number of other economic and financial variables as well.

There are legitimate grounds for debate regarding whether the Fed's present discretionary approach to the conduct of monetary policy is justified by the technical difficulties described above. It is certainly true that a reasonable case can be made that such an approach is in fact justified, especially when institutional and political considerations as well as purely economic factors are taken into account. Many economists would argue, however, that the Fed would risk losing the credibility as an inflation-fighter it earned in the late 1970s and early 1980s if it attempted to pursue a highly discretionary and judgmental policy indefinitely, since the credibility of policy in a discretionary regime is entirely dependent on the public's confidence in the determination of the Fed's current leadership at a particular time. The existence of objective longer-term criteria for policy helps the Fed maintain credibility. For this reason, some observers hoped that the System would be able to return to a firmer monetary targeting strategy once the disruptive impact of recent deregulatory actions on the relationship between the monetary aggregates and the economy has diminished.

One final point is worth making here. Although the elimination of many interest rate regulations in the early 1980s almost certainly

---

[44] The real growth of the economy in 1986 was relatively sluggish throughout most of the year.

contributed to the unpredictable behavior of the velocity of the monetary aggregates in this period, the reduction in inflation that followed the sharp tightening of monetary policy in 1981 also probably played an important role. This disinflation was unusually pronounced by peacetime standards, and its speed and extent were probably largely unanticipated. In these circumstances, it should perhaps not be surprising that the public's demand for money balances and therefore monetary velocity behaved unpredictably. If the price level remains relatively stable, however, the disruption of the behavior of velocity from this source should diminish, which would tend to favor a firmer monetary targeting strategy.

SECTION 4: CONCLUSION

This article has reviewed the Fed's principal functions and responsibilities, described its structure, and discussed both the mechanics of conducting monetary policy and major current policy issues. Since considerable ground has been covered, it may be useful to summarize briefly some of the article's major points.

1. The Fed has a wide variety of responsibilities in the areas of monetary policy, the maintenance of liquidity and stability in financial markets, the regulation of depository institutions, the provision of services to the Treasury and depository institutions, the maintenance of an efficient national payments mechanism, and the promotion of community development and redevelopment. While these responsibilities may appear diverse at first glance, they are all essential aspects of the Fed's general mandate to maintain a stable and efficient national monetary system.

2. With regard to monetary policy specifically, the Federal Reserve Act as amended requires the Fed to conduct policy with a view to achieving certain objectives involving a number of macroeconomic variables including production, employment, the price level, interest rates, and international trade. It is not clear, however, that it is feasible for the Fed to pursue all of these objectives simultaneously. In particular, some economists believe that the only feasible objective for the Fed over the long run is price stability.

3. An important and somewhat unique feature of the organizational structure of the Fed is the participation of the regional Federal Reserve banks in the conduct of monetary policy. Although the Board of Governors is the dominant governing body in the System, both the boards of directors and the senior officers of the Reserve banks have a voice in the formulation of policy, and in practice their views can have a substantive effect on policy decisions.

4. The current longer-run strategy of Fed monetary policy is to control the growth of certain monetary aggregates over time in order to foster stability in the price level and stable longer-run economic growth. The strategy is implemented by establishing annual target ranges for the growth of the various aggregates.

5. The Fed has used three short-run operating procedures for controlling the growth of the monetary aggregates since the longer-run targeting strategy was formally instituted in 1975. From 1975 to 1979, the Fed sought to influence the aggregates by tightly controlling the Federal funds rate. Between late 1979 and late 1982, the System used nonborrowed reserves as its operating instrument. Although this procedure was not equivalent to controlling the monetary aggregates by controlling total reserves as advocated by some monetarist economists, it was potentially a strong monetary control procedure because if followed closely it produced a relatively automatic response of reserve and money market conditions to deviations of the monetary aggregates from their target ranges. Since late 1982 the System has used borrowed reserves as its operating instrument, which is similar in important respects to the pre-October 1979 Federal funds rate regime.

6. At a mechanical level, the Fed uses three tools in conducting monetary policy on a day-to-day basis: open market operations, the power to change the discount rate, and reserve requirements. Of these, open market operations and the discount rate are the two actively used tools. The role of the discount rate has been more important in the post-1979 nonborrowed and borrowed reserve operating regimes than in the earlier Federal funds rate regime.

7. A major event in the recent history of monetary policy was the actions the Fed took in the 1979–1982 period, which have been followed by a sustained reduction in both inflation and inflationary expectations. Although the FOMC's change to a nonborrowed reserve operating procedure on October 6, 1979, probably contributed to the reduced inflation and the accompanying rise in the credibility of the Fed's anti-inflationary program, this article took the position that the sharp reduction in the effective growth of M1 in 1981, as distinct from the change in operating procedure, and the recession in 1981 and 1982 were probably the dominant factors.

8. The role of monetary targeting in the conduct of monetary policy was diminished in practice in the mid-1980s because of the disruptive impact of interest rate deregulation on the predictability of the relationship between the monetary aggregates and economic activity. As of late 1986, the Fed was following a discretionary and judgmental approach to policy that probably gave as much weight to current general economic conditions as to the behavior of the monetary aggregates. Some observers are concerned that the credibility of the Fed's

longer-run stance against inflation might be impaired if it followed this discretionary approach to policy for too long a time.

REFERENCES

1. AXILROD, STEPHEN H. "U.S. Monetary Policy in Recent Years: An Overview." *Federal Reserve Bulletin* 71 (January 1985), pp. 14–24.

2. BLACK, ROBERT P. "A Proposal to Clarify the Fed's Mandate." *CATO Journal*, 5 (Winter 1986), pp. 787–95.

3. BOARD OF GOVERNORS OF THE FEDERAL RESERVE SYSTEM. *Annual Report.* Various issues.

4. ———. *Federal Reserve Bulletin.* Various issues.

5. ———. *The Federal Reserve System: Purposes and Functions.* 7th ed. Washington, D.C., 1984.

6. BROADDUS, ALFRED. "Financial Innovation in the United States: Background, Current Status and Prospects." Federal Reserve Bank of Richmond, *Economic Review* (January–February 1985), pp. 2–22.

7. BROADDUS, ALFRED, and TIMOTHY COOK. "The Relationship between the Discount Rate and the Federal Funds Rate under the Federal Reserve's Post-October 6, 1979 Operating Procedure." Federal Reserve Bank of Richmond, *Economic Review* (January–February 1983), pp. 12–15.

8. BROADDUS, ALFRED, and MARVIN GOODFRIEND. "Base Drift and the Longer Run Growth of M1: Experience from a Decade of Monetary Targeting." Federal Reserve Bank of Richmond, *Economic Review* (November–December 1984), pp. 3–14.

9. COOK, TIMOTHY, and THOMAS HAHN. "The Information Content of Discount Rate Announcements and Their Effect on Market Interest Rates." Federal Reserve Bank of Richmond Working Paper 86–5, September 30, 1986.

10. FEDERAL RESERVE BANK OF MINNEAPOLIS. "The Fed's Money Supply Ranges: Still Useful after All These Years." Federal Reserve Bank of Minneapolis *Annual Report.* 1985.

11. FRIEDMAN, MILTON. "The Lag in Effect of Monetary Policy." *Journal of Political Economy* 79 (October 1961), pp. 447–66.

12. GOODFRIEND, MARVIN. "Discount Window Borrowing, Monetary Policy, and the Post–October 6, 1979 Federal Reserve Operating Procedure." *Journal of Monetary Economics* 12 (September 1983), pp. 343–56.

13. ———. "Monetary Mystique: Secrecy and Central Banking." *Journal of Monetary Economics* 17 (January 1986), pp. 63–92.

14. ———. "The Promises and Pitfalls of Contemporaneous Reserve Requirements for the Implementation of Monetary Policy." Federal Reserve Bank of Richmond, *Economic Review* (May–June 1984), pp. 3–12.

15. GOODFRIEND, MARVIN, and MONICA HARGRAVES. "A Historical Assessment of the Rationales and Functions of Reserve Requirements." Federal Reserve Bank of Richmond, *Economic Review* (March–April 1983), pp. 3–21.

16. McCALLUM, BENNETT T. "On Consequences and Criticisms of Monetary Targeting." *Journal of Money, Credit and Banking* 17 (November 1985), pp. 570–97.

17. ———. "Significance of Rational Expectations Theory." *Challenge*, January–February 1980, pp. 37–43.

18. MEEK, PAUL. *Open Market Operations.* 5th ed. New York: Federal Reserve Bank of New York, 1985.

19. MENGLE, DAVID. "The Discount Window." Federal Reserve Bank of Richmond, *Economic Review* (May–June 1986), pp. 2–10.

20. PARTLAN, JOHN C., KAUSER HAMDANI, and KATHLEEN M. CAMILLI. "Reserves Forecasting for Open Market Operations." Federal Reserve Bank of New York, *Quarterly Review* (Spring 1986), pp. 19–33.

21. ROTH, HOWARD. "Effects of Financial Deregulation on Monetary Policy." Federal Reserve Bank of Kansas City, *Economic Review* (March 1985), pp. 17–29.

22. WALLICH, HENRY C. "Recent Techniques of Monetary Policy." Federal Reserve Bank of Kansas City, *Economic Review* (May 1984), pp. 21–30.

23. WALSH, CARL E. "In Defense of Base Drift." *American Economic Review* 76 (September 1986), pp. 692–700.

8

How to Interpret the Weekly Federal Reserve Data

John R. Walter
Associate Economist
Research Department
Federal Reserve Bank of Richmond

The Federal Reserve System (Fed) regularly releases data gathered in the performance of its bank regulation and monetary policy responsibilities. *The Wall Street Journal* publishes "Federal Reserve Data," a table including some of the data items the Fed releases. This table is normally found in the second section of *The Wall Street Journal* on Friday and includes data for: Monetary Aggregates, Key Assets and Liabilities of the 10 Leading New York Banks, Commercial Paper Outstanding, Member Bank Reserve Changes, and Reserve Aggregates.

The figures published in "Federal Reserve Data" are closely watched by individuals interested in the financial markets and in the performance of the economy for two reasons. First, much of the data in this table can be useful in determining what the Fed has recently done and what it is likely to be doing during the next few weeks. Knowing this is valuable because Fed actions affect interest rates, financial markets, and the performance of the economy. This source of information is important because the Fed does not normally explain recent actions or divulge its plans for the future. These figures, therefore, provide an up-to-date indicator of what the Fed may be doing. Second, some individuals believe that a few of the items in "Federal Reserve Data" provide

This chapter benefited from helpful comments by Timothy Q. Cook and David L. Mengle.

FEDERAL RESERVE DATA

MONETARY AGGREGATES
(daily average in billions)

	One week ended:	
	Dec. 1	Nov. 24
Money supply (M1) sa	721.4	711.5
Money supply (M1) nsa	724.9	705.4

	Four weeks ended:	
	Dec. 1	Nov. 3
Money supply (M1) sa	714.6	701.4
Money supply (M1) nsa	716.1	698.8

	Month	
	Nov.	Oct.
Money supply (M1) sa	713.4	701.2
Money supply (M2) sa	2780.1	2764.9
Money supply (M3) sa	3460.6	3444.5

nsa-Not seasonally adjusted. sa-Seasonally adjusted.

KEY ASSETS AND LIABILITIES
OF THE 10 LEADING NEW YORK BANKS
(in millions of dollars)

		Change from
ASSETS:	Dec. 3, 1986	Nov. 26, 1986
Total loans, leases and investments, adjusted	200,796	− 2,380
Commercial and industrial loans	61,331	+ 649
Loans to depository and financial institutions	18,683	− 1,225
Loans to individuals	19,996	+ 78
Real estate loans	35,407	+ 242
U.S. government securities	14,172	+ 64
Other securities including municipal issues	16,213	− 48
Municipal securities	14,174	− 63
LIABILITIES:		
Demand deposits	63,957	+ 1,683
Other transaction deposits including NOW accounts	6,800	+ 205
Savings and other nontransaction deposits	85,537	− 486
Includes large time deposits of $100,000 or more	34,390	+ 263

COMMERCIAL PAPER OUTSTANDING
(in millions of dollars)

All issuers	326,471	− 4,600
Financial companies	243,207	− 2,583
Nonfinancial companies	83,264	− 2,017

MEMBER BANK RESERVE CHANGES

Changes in weekly averages of reserves and related items during the week and year ended December 10, 1986 were as follows (in millions of dollars)

		Chg fm	wk end
	Dec. 10	Dec. 8	Dec. 11
Reserve bank credit:	1986	1986	1985
U.S. Gov't securities:			
Bought outright	198,033 +	4,250	+21,459
Held under repurch agreemt	602 −	1,129	+ 391
Federal agency issues:			
Bought outright	7,829	....	− 398
Held under repurch agreemt	41 −	314	− 42
Acceptances—bought outright			
Held under repurch agreemt	....	....	....
Borrowings from Fed	383 −	198	− 298
Seasonal borrowings	33 −	23	− 18
Extended credit	306 −	4	− 212
Float	879 −	411	− 657
Other Federal Reserve Assets	15,742 −	127	+ 1,599
Total Reserve Bank Credit	223,510 +	2,072	+22,056
Gold Stock	11,084	....	− 6
SDR certificates	5,018	....	+ 300
Treasury currency outstanding	17,554 +	10	+ 526
Total	257,167 +	2,082	+22,877
Currency in circulation	207,921 +	759	+13,332
Treasury cash holdings	459	....	− 97
Treasury dpts with F.R. Bnks	2,794 +	188	+ 229
Foreign dpts with F.R. Bnks	205 −	50	− 40
Other dpts with F.R. Bnks	425 −	119	− 13
Service related balances, adj	2,194 −	185	+ 384
Other F.R. liabilities & capital	6,337 −	91	− 189
Total	220,334 +	501	+13,605

RESERVE AGGREGATES
(daily average in millions)

	Two weeks ended:	
	Dec. 3	Nov. 19
Total Reserves (sa)	54,412	53,727
Nonborrowed Reserves (sa)	53,802	52,916
Required Reserves (sa)	53,228	52,802
Excess Reserves (nsa)	1,184	925
Borrowings from Fed (nsa)-a	242	374
Free Reserves (nsa)	942	551
Monetary Base (sa)	236,889	235,705

a-Excluding extended credit. nsa-Not seasonally adjusted. sa-Seasonally adjusted.

CHART 1 M1 Growth Compared to Target Range, 1986

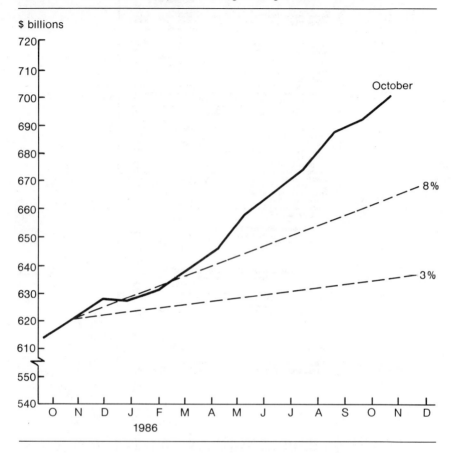

$ billions

information that can help them recognize when there are changes taking place in the level of economic activity.

MONETARY AGGREGATES

In 1975, the Fed began announcing in yearly congressional testimony its proposed target ranges for the growth of the monetary aggregates, the Fed's measures of the money supply. These target ranges give maximum and minimum growth rates for certain monetary aggregates. The Fed is now required, by the Humphrey-Hawkins Act of 1978, to set annual target ranges for the growth of the monetary aggregates. The 1986 target ranges, or cones, for the monetary aggregates M1, M2, and M3 are shown in Charts 1–3, respectively. In order to keep money growing at a rate that holds the monetary aggregates' levels within their

CHART 2   M2 Growth Compared to Target Range, 1986

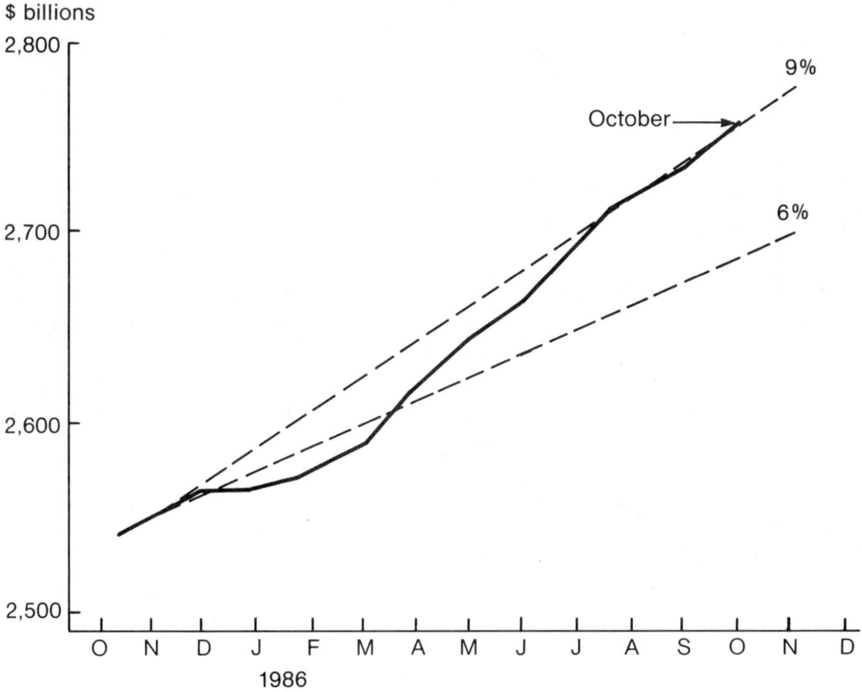

specified cones, the Fed puts either upward or downward pressure on the Fed funds rate through open-market operations or changes in the discount rate. The Fed funds rate is the interest rate depository institutions pay to borrow Federal funds from one another. Federal funds are short-term loans made through despository institutions' reserve accounts held at the Fed. The level of the Fed funds rate is determined by depository institutions' supply of, and demand for, funds. The discount rate is the rate depository institutions pay to borrow from the Fed.

To slow the growth rate of money the Fed puts upward pressure on the Fed funds rate and to speed it up it puts downward pressure on the Fed funds rate. Because the cones specify a range within which the monetary aggregates can grow, several weeks of fairly high- or low-money supply growth are required to put the aggregate outside of its range. The Fed, therefore, does not automatically react to one week's high- or low-money supply figure. Several such figures are required to elicit action by the Fed to put pressure on the Fed funds rate. Further, the Fed often allows the monetary aggregates' growth to deviate from

CHART 3 M3 Growth Compared to Target Range, 1986

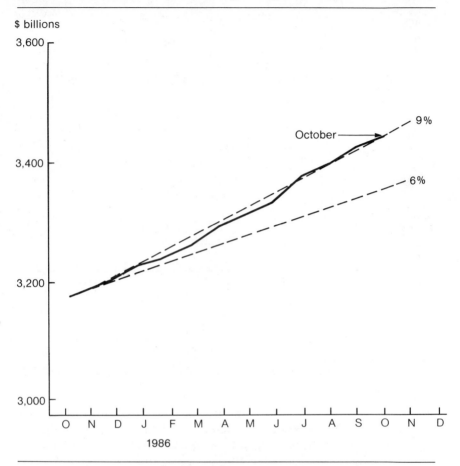

these growth ranges when, according to its perception, such a policy will be beneficial.

When the market believes that the Fed is attempting to maintain control of money supply growth, interest rates react to the weekly release of the money supply figures. When a higher than expected M1 figure is announced by the Fed on Thursday afternoon, the market increases its estimate of the probability that the Fed will put upward pressure on the Fed funds rate at some time in the future. An increase in the Fed funds rate generally produces increases in other interest rates. Therefore the market bids up interest rates in anticipation of this now more likely future event. If the money supply comes in lower than expected the market increases its estimate of the probability that the Fed will put downward pressure on the Fed funds rate at some time in the future and it therefore bids down interest rates. If the market believes the Fed is not emphasizing the control of money growth it does not react to high- or low-money supply figures.

The "Monetary Aggregates" section of *The Wall Street Journal* table includes the money supply data made available by the Board of Governors of the Federal Reserve System each Thursday at 4:30 P.M. in its H.6 release. This section of the table uses the following terms:

1. **Monetary aggregates.** Estimates of the monetary aggregates are derived by summing (*a*) the deposits of all depository institutions, that is, banks, thrifts, and credit unions, that report figures weekly to the Fed, with (*b*) estimated amounts for those depository institutions that do not report to the Fed weekly, plus (*c*) estimates of items included in the different measures of money that are not deposits of depository institutions (currency and money market fund balances, for example). Due to errors, the numbers that result from this process are subject to large revisions.

2. **Daily average.** For the period in question the Fed sums the daily figures and divides by the number of days.

3. **sa** is seasonally adjusted. Seasonal adjustment is the method of compensating for the fact that some data move up and down depending upon the week, month, or season in the year. There are definite seasonal patterns to money growth. Since seasonal increases or decreases in money growth do not affect economic variables such as GNP or inflation, the Fed adjusts the monetary aggregate measures so that seasonal variations are eliminated.

4. **nsa** is not seasonally adjusted. These are simply the raw data as aggregated and estimated by the Fed.

5. **M1** currently includes currency held by the nonbank public, traveler's checks of nonbank issuers, demand deposits net of cash items in process of collection and interbank balances, NOW accounts, ATS accounts, and credit union share draft balances.

6. **M2** is M1 plus overnight repurchase agreements (RPs) and overnight Eurodollars, general-purpose and broker/dealer money market mutual fund balances, money market deposit account balances, savings deposits, and small time deposits.

7. **M3** is M2 plus large time deposits, term RPs, term Eurodollars, and institution-only money market mutual fund balances.

KEY ASSETS AND LIABILITIES OF THE 10 LEADING NEW YORK BANKS

These data are released by the New York Federal Reserve Bank at 4:15 P.M. on each Thursday. The figures reported are the aggregation of the amounts outstanding of certain asset and liability items for 10 large New

York banks as of the Wednesday eight days earlier, and the change in these figures from the previous week. The figures include assets and liabilities of domestic offices only and are not seasonally adjusted.

Analysts view a change in the ratio of commercial and industrial loans to the sum of the deposit items (demand deposits; other transaction deposits including NOW accounts; and savings and other nontransaction deposits) as an indication of a possible change in firms' commercial activity. If the ratio rises analysts might interpret this as resulting from increased commercial activity. A falling ratio may be the result of slowed commercial activity. There are, of course, many other factors which can affect this ratio, but it does provide analysts with information which they believe is helpful in determining the direction of commercial activity. Because the data are only slightly more than a week old they are among the most current available for determining the direction of the economy.

The following items in the "Key Assets and Liabilities of the 10 Leading New York Banks" section of the table are therefore of prime interest to analysts:

1. **Commercial and industrial loans.** These are loans made by the 10 banks to sole proprietorships, partnerships, corporations, and other business enterprises for commercial or industrial purposes, plus loans made to individuals for commercial, industrial, or professional purposes. Loans secured by real estate, banker's acceptances, and commercial paper are excluded.
2. **Demand deposits.** These are the noninterest-bearing checkable deposits of the banks.
3. **Other transaction deposits including NOW accounts.** These are transactions balances other than demand deposits. They include NOW accounts, Super NOW accounts, and savings accounts allowing telephone and preauthorized transfers.
4. **Savings and other nontransaction deposits held by individuals, partnerships, and corporations.** These include money market deposit accounts, interest-bearing and noninterest-bearing savings deposits, and time deposits with original maturities of seven days or more.

COMMERCIAL PAPER OUTSTANDING

The "Commercial Paper Outstanding" data provide a measure of debt entered into by corporations directly rather than through a bank. Commercial paper is a short-term unsecured promissory note of a corporation. The figures included in this section of the table are released on each Thursday afternoon by the New York Federal Reserve Bank and are not seasonally adjusted. The total commercial paper figure, *all issuers,* is the amount of outstanding commercial paper sold by compapanies reporting to the Fed. This figure is separated into the commercial paper of financial companies and that of nonfinancial companies.

Along with commercial and industrial loans from the previous section of the table, commercial paper outstanding provides a measure of credit growth and thereby may give some indication of the direction of the economy. For example, if the commercial paper figure, is growing, while the 10 New York Banks' commercial and industrial loans to deposits ratio is growing, analysts view this as evidence that the economy may be strengthening. A decline in commercial paper and in the commercial and industrial loans to deposits ratio may indicate a slowing economy.

Commercial paper may be increasing while the commercial and industrial loans figure is shrinking relative to deposits, indicating that corporations are raising funds through commercial paper sales rather than borrowing from banks. Such a result would not necessarily indicate growth in the economy. Rather, it could simply show the extent to which corporations are bypassing commercial banks for funds.

MEMBER BANK RESERVE CHANGES

The "Member Bank Reserve Changes" section of this table is a restatement of the consolidated balance sheet of the Federal Reserve banks plus the monetary accounts of the U.S. Treasury. The figures given in this section of the table are the average of the daily amounts outstanding for the week ending on the most current Wednesday, the changes from the previous week, and the changes from the same week one year ago. The figures come from the H.4.1 release made by the Board of Governors on each Thursday afternoon and are not seasonally adjusted.

Depository institutions are required by law to maintain, as reserves, deposits with Federal Reserve banks or vault cash in proportion to some of their liabilities. When there are changes in the Federal Reserve Banks' assets and liabilities, when the Reserve banks make any purchases, sales, loans, collections, or payments, or when there are changes in the monetary accounts of the Treasury, reserves are necessarily provided to, or removed from, depository institutions. Changes in the Fed's balance sheet and in the monetary accounts of the Treasury therefore produce changes in depository institutions' reserves. In order to offset these changes to keep reserve provision stable, the Fed buys and sells securities, either outright or under repurchase agreements, from securities dealers. When it buys securities it provides bank reserves, when it sells them it absorbs bank reserves. Because items on the Fed's balance sheet and in the Treasury's monetary accounts change on a daily basis, the Fed buys and sells securities on a daily basis. The buying and selling of securities by the Fed is known as open-market operations.

To predict and interpret Fed open-market operations requires the replication of the Fed's decision to add or subtract reserves. This depends most importantly on movements in the numbers given in the "Member Bank Reserve Changes" section of the table. By making daily forecasts of what these numbers will be and then determining how the Fed is likely to respond to such numbers, analysts attempt to predict the volume of Fed purchases and sales of securities on any given day.

Accuracy in such a prediction requires a broad and detailed understanding of what causes changes in the Fed balance sheet and the monetary accounts of the Treasury and how the Fed generally responds to all of the different possible changes. This type of knowledge comes only with experience and through the investment of resources in data gathering. The data provided in this section of the "Federal Reserve Data" table are the most up-to-date statement available of the Fed's balance sheet and the monetary accounts and therefore provide some of the most important data for the analyst's forecast of the day-to-day open-market operations of the Fed.

Analysts make forecasts of Fed open-market actions for two reasons. First, analysts believe that deviations from forecasted purchases and sales by the Fed may provide some limited evidence of a shift in Fed monetary policy. For example, suppose analysts believe the Fed is going to withdraw reserves through an open-market sale of securities to offset an increase in float. But instead the Fed makes a large purchase of securities. Then analysts may, under certain circumstances, interpret this as evidence that the Fed is loosening monetary policy. Second, since the Fed is a large participant in the securities market, information on whether the Fed will be buying or selling and what it will be buying or selling on any given day may help in the prediction of movements in prices or rates paid on those securities being bought or sold by the Fed. Analysts believe that forecasting Fed open-market operations helps them forecast the movements of prices and rates on these securities.

When the Fed wishes to stabilize, increase, or decrease reserves it increases or decreases it holdings of the first four items in this section of *The Wall Street Journal* table through open-market purchases or sales. These four items are:

1. **U.S. government securities—Bought outright.** This is the average amount of U.S. government securities held by the 12 Federal Reserve banks for the week ended on the specified date.
2. **U.S. government securities—Held under repurchase agreements.** This is the average of the Fed's holding of U.S. government securities purchased with the stipulation that they will be resold to the seller at some agreed-upon future date, normally less than 15 days from the data of purchase. Purchases of securities held under repurchase agreements are, therefore, temporary injections of reserves which will be withdrawn later.

3. **Federal agency issues—Bought outright.**   See (4).
4. **Federal agency issues—Held under repurchase agreements.**
   Federal agency issues are debt obligations of federal agencies,
   such as the Federal National Mortgage Association, Federal
   Home Loan Banks, or the Federal Land Banks.

RESERVE AGGREGATES

This last section of the "Federal Reserve Data" table comes from data
released by the Board of Governors each Thursday afternoon in the H.3
release. The figures given in this section of the table are averages of the
daily amounts outstanding for the two weeks ending on the specified
Wednesdays. The figures are for two weeks because depository institutions' reserve maintenance period is two weeks long. The reserve
maintenance period is the length of time over which depository institutions must hold reserves to satisfy their reserve requirements. These
figures are carefully watched for the information they may provide
about the Fed's current monetary policy. While the H.3 is released
weekly, other than revisions, new figures are only provided every two
weeks.

Total reserves are the reserves of the banking system and are the
deposits of all depository institutions with the Fed and the vault cash of
these institutions. These can be classified into those reserves that are
borrowed from the Fed and those that are not, *nonborrowed reserves*. Total
reserves can also be classified into two categories: *required reserves*, which
are held by banks to meet reserve requirements, and *excess reserves*,
which are any reserves held in addition to required reserves.
Nonborrowed reserves of depository institutions are affected when the
Fed buys and sells securities in the open market. When the Fed
purchases securities in the market nonborrowed reserves are increased;
when it sells securities in the market nonborrowed reserves are decreased.

Free reserves are *excess reserves* minus *borrowings from Fed*. While at
one time the Fed used this as a target in monetary policy it no longer
does so. Some analysts view growth in this figure as an indication of less
reserve restraint by the Fed.

Monetary base is made up of total reserve deposits with the Fed plus
currency in circulation.

Borrowings from the Fed, in this section of *The Wall Street Journal*
table, is the average amount of adjustment and seasonal credit discount
window loans outstanding for the two-week period. Discount window
loans are those loans made by the Fed to depository institutions. The
Fed makes three types of discount window loans: adjustment credit
loans; seasonal credit loans; and extended credit loans.

Adjustment credit loans are made by the Fed to depository institutions to allow them to meet their temporary reserve deficiencies or to provide for other temporary funds demands. Seasonal credit loans are made generally to rural depository institutions to help them meet their seasonal reserve needs. Extended credit loans are made by the Fed to depository institutions facing sustained liquidity pressures.

All depository institutions' reserves originate with the Fed. Those reserves that the Fed does not provide by purchases of securities, must be borrowed at the discount window. A significant change in borrowings from the Fed is therefore viewed by many Fed watchers as evidence that the Fed may have changed its provision of nonborrowed reserves through open-market operations; that is, that it may have loosened or tightened monetary policy. An increase in borrowings from the Fed may lead analysts to conclude that the Fed has provided fewer reserves, while a decline in borrowings from the Fed may cause analysts to conclude that the Fed has provided more reserves. (Changes in extended credit are treated by the Federal Reserve as changes in nonborrowed reserves so that analysts are little concerned with movements in extended credit.)

Analysts are cautious in their conclusions based on changes in borrowings from the Fed because a change in borrowings for any given two week period may be the result of the Fed's misforecasts of the levels of one or more of the items in the "Member Bank Reserve Changes" section of the table. If this is the case the level of borrowings should soon be returned to its previous level, demonstrating that the Fed has not changed monetary policy. As an example, such an event may occur when the Fed misforecasts excess reserves for a week or for several weeks. Suppose banks suddenly decide to hold $100 million more excess reserves. If the Fed supplies nonborrowed reserves under the assumption that excess reserves are going to be $800 million during the period but instead they come in at $900 million, banks would have to increase their borrowings from the Fed to provide themselves with the extra $100 million in reserves. Borrowings from the Fed would therefore increase by $100 million. During the following weeks, however, the Fed would inject enough reserves through open market operations to provide for this higher level of excess reserves. The increase in borrowings in this case was not the result of a change in Fed monetary policy but simply the result of a misforecast of excess reserve demand.

As discussed before, the H.3 release contains new figures only every other Thursday. Analysts seeking to track adjustment plus seasonal credit on a weekly basis must gather information in the off weeks from the figures on discount window loans given in the "Member Bank Reserve Changes" section of *The Wall Street Journal* table. This section provides a figure for total discount window loans including adjustment credit, seasonal credit, and extended credit, and calls the total *borrowings from Fed* also. In addition, the "Member Bank Reserve Changes" section provides seasonal and extended credit figures separately. The analyst can determine adjustment credit by subtracting *seasonal borrowings* and *extended credit* from the *borrowings from Fed* figure.

SELECTED REFERENCES

BROADDUS, ALFRED. "Aggregating the Monetary Aggregates: Concepts and Issues." Federal Reserve Bank of Richmond, *Economic Review* 61 (November/December 1975).

FEDERAL FINANCIAL INSTITUTIONS EXAMINATION COUNCIL. "Instructions— Reports of Condition and Income." Board of Governors of the Federal Reserve System, Federal Deposit Insurance Corporation, Office of the Comptroller of the Currency, FFIEC 031, December 1984, p. RC–19.

LOEYS, JAN G. "Market Views of Monetary Policy and Reactions to M1 Announcements." Federal Reserve Bank of Philadelphia, *Business Review* (March/April 1984), pp. 9–17.

McCARTHY, F. WARD, AND RAYMOND W. STONE. "Basics of Fed Watching." *The Handbook of Treasury Securities*. Ed. Frank J. Fabozzi. Chicago: Probus, 1987.

MENGLE, DAVID L. "The Discount Window." Federal Reserve Bank of Richmond, *Economic Review* 72 (May/June 1986), pp. 2–10.

SAMANSKY, ARTHUR M. *Statfacts: Understanding Federal Reserve Statistical Reports.* Federal Reserve Bank of New York, 1981.

——————————— 9 ———————————

Monetary Policy and Financial Markets

Steven R. Malin, Ph.D.
Senior Economist
The Conference Board, Inc.

DEVELOPING MONETARY POLICY TOOLS

Throughout the first half of the 1980s, economic policymakers confronted a powerful and sometimes perplexing mix of financial, economic, and political changes. Major and deeply entrenched trends in the economy and financial markets reversed dramatically and long-established relationships among nominal and real variables weakened or collapsed. In just five years, a bewildering set of new relationships formed that strained economic theory and tested the imagination of financial market participants. At the heart of these changes were dramatic shifts in monetary and fiscal policy priorities in a rapidly changing financial environment. The focus of these changes was financial market deregulation, which inspired innovations in financial services, new financial management techniques by businesses and households, and globalization of world financial and economic markets. Under these conditions, domestic financial markets were bound to experience unprecendented volatility in both trading volumes and securities prices.

Money in Monetary Policy

Between the mid-1960s and the mid-1980s, financial market participants looked increasingly toward the Federal Reserve for policy adjustments

---

Note: The reader is referred to the appendixes for basic concepts and definitions (the Editor).

having the strongest and most immediate impact on performance in economic, money, and capital markets. During the early 1960s, monetary policy objectives were commonly expressed in such general terms as "the smooth and efficient operation of money markets." While money supply aggregates, as either money market indicators or explicit policy targets, generally received no mention in the FOMC's (Federal Open Market Committee) operating directive (instructions given to the FOMC account manager for open-market operations), they were monitored by the Fed to determine their broader effects on the economy. In 1966, the FOMC began to supplement its operating directives with a "proviso clause" that included a broad reference to either bank credit or the money supply. A typical proviso clause would instruct the account manager to carry out the FOMC's directive as written "providing that bank credit does not deviate significantly from the current projections or liquidity pressures do not develop." For three years, proviso clauses offered only formal recognition of monetary aggregates as indicators of money market conditions.

Toward the end of the 1960s, the Fed began to consider new ways to improve its instructions to the Open Market Trading Desk.[1] Much of the impetus for change came from monetarists who blamed excessive monetary growth and credit expansion in 1968 on the FOMC's use of directives phrased in terms of money market conditions. Consequently, considerable support developed within the Federal Reserve System and in the private sector for a more precise quantitative policymaking strategy.

In 1970, the FOMC began to adopt specific short-run growth targets for several money supply aggregates. (This move was hailed widely by economists as the most significant development in monetary policy since the 1950s.) For the first time, growth in the monetary aggregates was specified as a *target* for open-market operations, rather than as a *consequence*. For example, the policy directive issued on March 10, 1970 stated the FOMC's intention to "see moderate growth in money and bank credit over the months ahead" by conducting open-market operations "with a view to maintaining money market conditions consistent with that objective."[2]

Each quarter, the FOMC established money supply goals expressed quantitatively and reviewed as the quarter progressed. For the federal funds rate, the narrowly defined M1 and the more broadly defined M2 money supply aggregates, the FOMC set two-month moving tolerance ranges (January–February, February–March, and so on), usually 3 percentage points in width. At each meeting, the FOMC established an initial federal funds rate level thought to be consistent with the short-run tolerance ranges for the money supply aggregates. Whenever the growth of the monetary aggregates deviated from their respective tolerance ranges, the Fed adjusted the federal funds rate within its target range—or else changed the federal funds rate target range. This adjustment process resulted in a change in the supply of bank reserves and the demand for money, as well as an ultimate return of monetary aggregates to their target ranges. However, whenever the performance of the federal funds rate and the monetary aggregates diverged from their respective target ranges, the federal funds rate received primary attention.

A troublesome combination of accelerating inflation and deepening recession in 1973–74 prompted Congress to monitor Federal Reserve policies more closely. In March 1975, Congress passed House Concurrent Resolution 133 requiring the Federal Reserve's Board of Governors to report semiannually on monetary policy objectives to the House Banking, Currency and Housing Committee and the Senate Banking, Housing and Urban Affairs Committee. This report was to include ranges of growth or diminution of monetary and credit aggregates in the upcoming 12 months.[3] The Federal Reserve responded by setting annual targets (as well as two-month tolerance ranges) for several monetary aggregates.

Between 1975 and 1979, the FOMC revised its yearly targets each quarter, using actual money supply levels of the previous quarter as the base. Under this procedure, known as base drift, any quarterly overshoot or shortfall in money supply growth was embedded in the next quarterly base (i.e., it raised or lowered the base from which the FOMC specified the next yearly objectives). Consequently, when persistent misses occurred in one direction, the procedure tended to have a cumulative impact on the longer-run monetary growth trend. Since the Fed's continued emphasis on federal funds rate targeting typically tended to generate *cumulative* excesses (rather than *self-reversing* misses), base drift tended to build self-reinforcing monetary growth acceleration into the economy.

In 1978, passage of the Full-Employment and Balanced Growth Act of 1978 (the Humphrey-Hawkins Act) incorporated provisions to eliminate the money supply growth biases arising from base drift. The act requires the Board of Governors of the Federal Reserve System to establish annual money and credit expansion objectives for the period from the fourth quarter of the previous year to the fourth quarter of the current year. Before February 20 of each year, the Board of Governors must report to Congress growth targets for several money supply aggregates; before July 20, it must report progress toward reaching the money growth targets and state preliminary money growth objectives for the following year. (Monetary policy objectives stated every February and July are supposed to be consistent with the goals of full employment and price stability set forth in the most recent *Economic Report of the President*.) Although the Board of Governors may adjust annual monetary growth targets at any time, the base period must not change.

During 1979, excessive credit expansion, sharply rising interest rates, and accelerating inflation forced the Federal Reserve to consider new, more direct means of controlling monetary growth. On October 6, 1979, the Fed adopted a new operating procedure described at the time as "placing greater emphasis in day-to-day operations on the supply of bank reserves and less on fluctuations in the federal funds rate."[4] The 1979 procedures were designed to maintain growth in a "family of reserve aggregates" (total reserves, nonborrowed reserves, and the monetary base) consistent with achieving the Fed's announced monetary growth targets. Under this procedure, the Fed would adjust the level of nonborrowed reserves (the only reserve aggregate directly under the Fed's control) with sufficient open-market sales or purchases to return the monetary aggregate to its desired growth path whenever monetary growth deviated from its target range because of a temporary or cyclical change in the demand for money. The Fed hoped that the new procedure would increase confidence in its ability to decelerate monetary growth steadily in order to wind down inflation—even at the price of wider short-term swings in interest rates and greater intrayear volatility of money supply growth rates than before. In the words of Federal Reserve Board Governor Henry C. Wallich, "Under the old procedures watching the Federal Funds rate was the proper way to watch what the Federal Reserve was doing. Under the new procedures, it is the money supply that needs to be watched for such signals."[5] (See Exhibit 1.)

When strictly adhered to, the operating procedures introduced in 1979 improved the Fed's effectiveness in achieving its policy objectives. However, when domestic or international conditions warranted it, the Fed abandoned its emphasis on achieving the announced growth target for one or the other of the monetary aggregates. By abandoning rules and applying discretion, the Fed intermittently focused on interest rates or exchange rates whenever adjustments in their respective levels were considered necessary in order to alleviate acute economic or financial distresses. As long as inflation remained under control in the 1980s, the Fed was willing to "fight the fires of the moment." For the financial markets, this "rules tempered by discretion" approach spawned greater confidence in Federal Reserve policies and laid the groundwork for the great "bull markets" of the mid-1980s.

Beginning in the autumn of 1982, the Federal Reserve modified its operating procedure to target directly on the level of borrowing at the discount window. Under the modified procedure, the Fed fixes the level of borrowed reserves in the period between FOMC meetings, and accommodates changes in demand for reserves by adjusting the level of nonborrowed reserves. Accordingly, the Fed *eases* monetary policy by

EXHIBIT 1   Federal Reserve Policy: Responses to a Temporary or Cyclical Decline In the Demand for Money

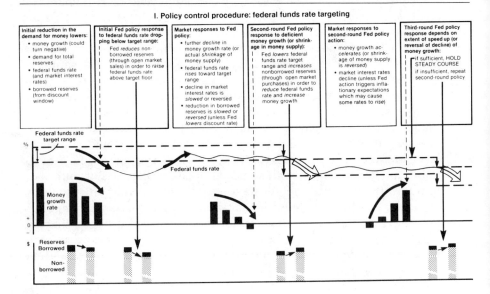

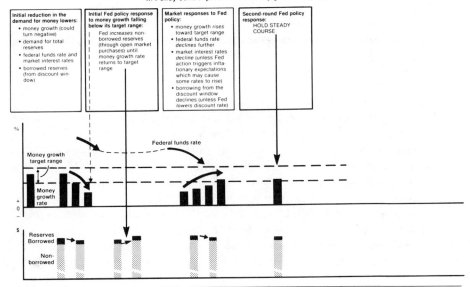

SOURCE: The Conference Board, Inc.

EXHIBIT 1 Federal Reserve Policy: Responses to a Temporary or Cyclical Increase in the Demand for Money

I. Policy control procedure: federal funds rate targeting

Initial increase in the demand for money raises:	Initial Fed policy response to federal funds rate exceeding its target range:	Market responses to Fed policy:	Second-round Fed policy response to excessive money growth:	Market responses to second-round Fed policy action:	Third-round Fed policy response depends on extent of slowdown of money growth:
• money growth • demand for total reserves • federal funds rate and market interest rates • borrowed reserves (from discount window)	Fed increases *non-borrowed* reserves (through open market purchases) in order to *reduce* federal funds rate below target ceiling	• further *rise* in money growth rate • federal funds rate *declines* toward target range • market interest rates *decline* (unless Fed action triggers inflationary expectations which may cause rates to *rise*)	Fed *reduces* non-borrowed reserves (through open market sales) in order to *raise* the federal funds rate to a *new higher* target range	• money growth rate *slows down* • borrowing from Fed *increases* (unless Fed raises discount rate) • market interest rates *rise* (unless Fed action reduces inflationary expectations which may cause some rates to *decline*)	• if sufficient, HOLD STEADY COURSE • if insufficient, repeat second-round policy

II. Policy control procedure: money growth targeting

Initial increase in the demand for money raises:	Initial Fed policy response to money growth exceeding its target range:	Market responses to Fed policy:	Second-round Fed policy response:
• money growth • demand for total reserves • federal funds rate (and other market interest rates) • borrowed reserves (from discount window)	Fed *reduces* non-borrowed reserves (through open market sales) until money growth rate returns to target range	• money growth *slows down* toward target range • federal funds rate *rises* • market interest rates rise (unless Fed action reduces inflationary expectations which may cause some rates to *decline*) • borrowing from the discount window increases (unless Fed *raises* discount rate)	HOLD STEADY COURSE

injecting nonborrowed reserves into the banking system and reducing the target level of borrowed reserves; a move toward *restraint* is executed by withdrawing nonborrowed reserves and raising the borrowed reserves target.

For observers of monetary policy, the borrowed reserves targeting procedure complicates interpretation of the Fed's open-market operations. Before 1979, the federal funds rate level at which the manager of the Open Market Trading Desk bought or sold securities in the open market provided clues about the direction for monetary policy. However, according to Federal Reserve Governor Henry Wallich, the federal funds rate level at which the Desk now enters the market "is not indicative of any particular rate desired by the [System Open Market] Desk. It is simply the rate that happens to prevail on a day when the manager believes that reserves should be added or drained in order to achieve the desired level of discount-window borrowing, on average, for the reserve-maintenance period." Thus, as long as the Fed does not encourage a change in the level of discount-window borrowing, "there is little reason to expect the funds rate to move strongly, at least for longer than transitory periods."[6]

Economic Relationships Begin to Break Down

Changes in Federal Reserve operating procedures and intensified world-wide focus on U.S. monetary policy coincided with the apparent breakdown of many long-established relationships between measures of money and performance in real, financial, and foreign exchange markets.[7] Although the proximate causes for these breakdowns may never be determined conclusively, regulatory and institutional changes in banking and financial markets, as well as increasingly sophisticated cash management practices by businesses and households, probably played a major role. For more than four decades (beginning in the early 1930s), preoccupation with preserving the viability of individual banks had dominated regulatory philosophy. Thus, some bank regulations—particularly the prohibition of interest payments on demand deposits and limitations on interest payments for savings deposits—were designed to encourage competition among financial institutions. However, historically high-interest rates between 1974 and 1982, as well as evolving foreign and nonbank competition for money market funds, forced changes in bank regulatory philosophy and a revamping of the banking and financial markets.

Beginning around 1970, major regulatory and institutional changes led to the development of new transactions-oriented accounts, to increased liquidity of savings accounts, to new liquid deposits and nondeposit alternatives, and to changes in liquidity and maturity of time accounts.[8] New money substitutes permitted individuals and businesses to hold funds in relatively liquid forms that earn positive interest yields not available on conventional demand deposits or cash balances. These developments encouraged competition, but began to blur the distinctions between deposits at commercial banks, thrift institutions, and other financial institutions. Changes in bank holding company laws, liberalization of regulations governing thrift institutions, and a more competitive international banking environment reinforced the move to more intensive competition and more daring innovations.

Intensified use of these innovative alternatives to cash was a rational response by businesses and households to the general increase in interest rates in 1973–74, 1978–79, and 1980–81. During each of these periods, nominal short-term interest rates broke through their previous record levels by wide margins. These record-high rates sensitized virtually everybody to the advantages of economizing on their holdings of cash and noninterest-bearing demand deposits. Business managers intensified their use of a variety of cash management techniques that improve information about near-term cash flows and minimize their cash balances.

On February 7, 1980, the Federal Reserve issued a revised set of monetary definitions that took into account the many financial and regulatory changes of the 1960s and 1970s.[9] The Fed had long recognized that movements in the money supply, especially the narrowly defined M1 money supply, were increasingly difficult to predict with conventional money demand equations and other economic measures. Faced with uncertainty about macroeconomic relationships involving money (particularly M1), achievement of policy goals set in terms of money supply growth targets became less assured. Consequently, a redefinition of the monetary aggregates was needed.

In general, the revised money supply definitions adopted in 1980 regroup money into two broad divisions: funds used to conduct transactions and funds held for a longer period of time (principally as a store of wealth.) On the whole, each successively broader measure incorporates assets less liquid than those in the aggregates preceding it. Assets that serve similar functions—and presumably are close substitutes in the eyes of the public—are grouped together irrespective of the financial institution at which they are held.

Barely seven weeks after the Fed announced the revised money supply aggregates, Congress passed new legislation that provided fresh impetus to reexamination of the relationship between conventional transactions balances and new financial assets. On March 31, 1980, Congress approved the Depository Institutions Deregulation and Monetary Control Act of 1980 (P.L. 96-211), the most comprehensive banking legislation since the passage of the Federal Reserve Act in 1913.[10] The act was designed to enhance the Fed's ability to implement monetary policy, apply operating requirements more uniformly to all depository

institutions, allow small savers a market rate of return, remove impediments to competition between depository institutions and other financial institutions, and increase the availability of financial services to the
public. The act also authorized nationwide introduction to NOW accounts by all depository institutions beginning in January 1981 and
stipulated that interest rate ceilings on all time and savings deposits be
phased out by 1986.

Yet instead of facilitating the monitoring and execution of monetary
policy, the 1980 legislation made the Fed's task more difficult. Phasing
out of interest rate controls, as well as the proliferation of NOW
accounts and "other checkable deposits," resulted in shifts of funds
between M1- and M2-type accounts. To the extent that some fraction of
funds shifted into NOW accounts and other interest-bearing transactions accounts, the reliability of relationships became less assured
between the narrowly defined monetary aggregate, real economic
activity, and inflation. Among money-watchers, doubts intensified
about the reliability of the revised money supply aggregates as indicators of economic performance or the Fed's policy stance.

Growing strength of money market mutual funds (MMMFs) offered
by nonbank financial institutions during the 1970s also forced major
adjustments in the menu of financial instruments offered by depository
institutions. In order to remain competitive, banks and thrifts introduced an array of financial instruments that bear money market rates of
interest, beginning in the late 1970s. (By 1982, about two thirds of the
non-M1 component of M2 bore market rates of return, compared to only
5 percent in 1978.) For money-watchers, these complicated further the
interpretation of fluctuations in the monetary aggregates. During periods of sharply changing interest rates, changes in accrued interest
earnings, as well as deliberate adjustments in the level of deposits held
by depositors, altered the relative growth rates of M1 and M2.[11] During
1981, for example, unprecedented high-interest rates contributed to
sharp increases in MMMF assets and to the growth of M2 in excess of its
target limit; over the same period, growth in M1 was modest. For banks,
relatively high yields offered by MMMFs from 1978 through 1982
resulted in declines in average balances in conventional checking
accounts and induced higher yields on short-term CDs.[12]

The Garn-St Germain Depository Institutions Act of 1982 cleared the
way for the Depository Institutions Deregulation Committee to issue
rules governing a so-called super-NOW account to be offered after
January 4, 1983.[13] (Super-NOW accounts offer unlimited checking or
third-party transfers and, unlike conventional NOW accounts, an unrestricted interest rate.) On balance, the volume of transactions balances
included in M1 probably have not increased dramatically as a result of
the introduction of super-NOW accounts. Nevertheless, as funds in
super-NOWs promised to become a larger share of household transac-

tions balances, and as cash managers became less sensitive to the opportunity cost of holding transactions balances, the behavior of M1 relative to other economic variables threatened to deviate even more widely from past historical experience.

Perhaps nowhere has the breakdown in long-established relationships among economic and financial measures been more acute than in the 1980s growth pattern of M1 velocity—the ratio of current dollar GNP to the M1 money supply.[14] (M1 velocity represents the number of times the money supply must turn over per year in order to validate the transactions involved in creating nominal GNP.) During most of the 20th century, nominal GNP increased by about 3 percentage points more per year than did M1, so velocity tended to increase at a steady and relatively predictable pace. Moreover, policymakers and money market observers could rely on a relatively stable and long-established positive relationship between velocity and nominal interest rates. In the 1920s, for example, both interest rates and velocity fluctuated little; during the 1930s, they both generally declined. In the three decades beginning in 1950, interest rates and velocity both rose steadily, except during 1950–51, 1971–72, and 1975–76 (when interest rates declined in association with Nixon administration wage-price controls and a major onetime shift in demand for M1, respectively). In the mid-1980s, changes in interest rates and velocity coincided closely (with a one-quarter lag in velocity), with declines in the inflation rate clearly the dominant factor explaining velocity changes. (See Exhibit 2.)

According to standard bodies of economic theory, increases in inflation and nominal interest rates tend to determine the long-run pattern of velocity, while changes in real interest rates tend normally to determine the short-run, or business cycle, pattern of velocity.[15] In most of the post-World War II period, the generally rising inflation trend did, in fact, dominate the steady upward velocity trend. However, between 1982 and 1985, money supply increased by about 1 *percentage point a year more* than GNP, instead of the customary 3 *percentage points a year less*. Consequently, over the short run, M1 put less than usual upward pressure on GNP; over the long run, this unusual pattern contributed to an easing of inflation.[16]

ESTABLISHING FEDERAL RESERVE CREDIBILITY

Despite attenuation of long-established relationships among economic and financial measures, financial market participants reacted more rapidly and strenuously in the 1970s and early 1980s to monetary policy adjustments than ever before. In the equity markets, broad movements in stock indexes increasingly reflected anticipations by institutional investors about potential changes in monetary policy, interest rates, and corporate earnings. On individual days, large changes in broad stock

EXHIBIT 2   Velocity and Interest Rates

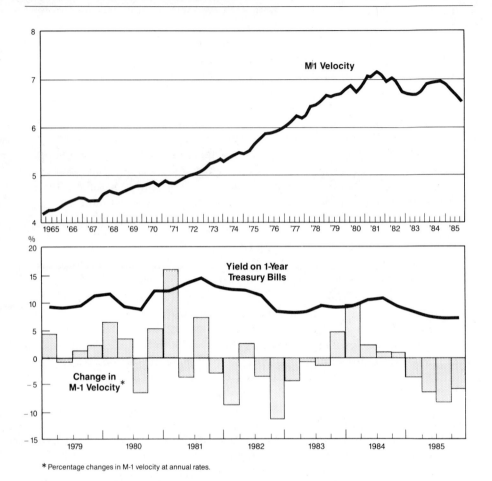

* Percentage changes in M-1 velocity at annual rates.

SOURCES: Federal Reserve; The Conference Board.

indexes began to reflect anticipated changes in monetary policy that would either confirm or contradict expectations. Under these conditions, equity markets came to "double discount" monetary policy adjustments: once when the policy change became widely anticipated, and again when the change was consummated. With market participants increasingly sensitized, every Federal Reserve pronouncement came under scrutiny and each action became a window to the Fed's credibility.

Eroding Credibility: The Period before October 1979

Throughout most of the 1970s, members of the Federal Reserve Board acknowledged publicly that controlling inflation deserved the top priority of monetary and fiscal policy. Moreover, beginning with the chairmanship of Arthur F. Burns, Federal Reserve chairmen and a majority of board members endorsed repeatedly the view that a *gradual and persistent* reduction of the average growth rate of the money supply is a necessary condition for winding down the rate of inflation. However, during most of the 1970s, the Federal Reserve's performance fell far short of its intent. In 1977 and 1978, growth in the narrowly defined M1 money supply accelerated to a pace of more than 8 percent a year, after growing an average 5.5 percent annually over the previous two years. Not only did this acceleration itself appear to signal that the policy was becoming more expansionary, but also the credibility of the Fed's policy pronouncements was eroded by the consistency with which actual M1 growth came in above adopted target ranges. The negative psychological impact of this performance on the financial markets was reinforced by widespread mistrust of the Fed's own federal funds rate target operating procedure. Consequently, most economists and the financial community generally hailed the Fed's 1979 decision to revise its operating procedure, target directly on money supply growth, and fulfill the promise of gradual reductions in the rate of inflation.

Monetary Growth Targeting: The First Year

The experience with money growth targeting from October 1979 through late 1980 provides the backdrop for analysis of monetary policy execution throughout the first half of the 1980s—and financial market responses to it. In brief, a profile of monetary growth targeting in its first year indicates the major swings in money growth rates broadly coincided with swings in interest rates—and that both mirrored sharp fluctuations in real economic growth. This not unexpected pattern supported the widely held view that changes in *demand for money* dominated the intrayear volatility of money and interest rates. Yet in the process, it was the Fed's inability—or unwillingness—to control the growth rate and volatility of *the supply of money* that had the most meaningful impact on interest rates, the equity markets, and the value of the dollar in foreign exchange. With money supply growth seemingly out of control during much of 1980, the Fed's credibility as a determined inflation fighter with clout was undermined severely. In the process, interest rates reached all-time record highs, the stock market continued a long retreat, and confidence in the Fed's policy execution was largely shattered. By late in 1980, some members of the Federal Reserve Board acknowledged that timely actions to reverse money supply growth excesses earlier that year could have helped to reestablish the credibility of the Fed's policy pronouncements and to reduce the risk and inflationary expectation premiums built into interest rates.

The 1981 Downward Bias in Monetary Policy

Drastic actions to rapidly and severely curtail money supply growth during the final quarter of 1980 set the tone for monetary policy through mid-1982 and provided the opening round in a series of policy confrontations between the Federal Reserve, the Congress, and the newly elected Reagan administration.[17] By early 1981, private economists, as well as those at the Fed, recognized that the President Reagan's Program for Economic Recovery placed an excessive burden on the Federal Reserve as the sole short-term inflation fighter. Proposals for sharp increases in defense spending and huge multiyear "supply-side" tax cuts created an expansionary thrust that was not likely to be offset fully by cuts in civilian programs. Most experts outside the government expected larger budget deficits, higher interest rates, and less real growth than had been projected officially. Such skepticism tended to raise risk premiums in financial markets—particularly on long-term interest rates—and complicated the task of monetary restraint.

Aware of these problems, the Federal Reserve favored some modifications of the proposed fiscal program—particularly delays and a scaling down of the large supply-side tax cuts—in order to make the task of monetary restraint less burdensome and more manageable. As President Reagan's fiscal program achieved one success after another in its struggle through Congress, the Fed was bound to become more concerned with the dangers of exceeding its money growth target ranges than with the risks of monetary shortfalls. With the lesson of the 1980 overshooting fresh in mind, the fiscal program for 1982 moving through Congress victoriously, and the 1982 election year on the horizon, the Fed's policy deliberations appear to have developed a downward bias for monetary policy that was welcomed by many outside experts. Throughout the first three quarters of 1981, the Fed maintained an exceedingly tight monetary policy that drove most short-term interest rates to historically high levels and virtually shut off the growth in the narrowly defined M1 money supply. By the fall, this policy strained interest rate sensitive sectors of the economy and laid the foundations for a severe and protracted recession. In the process, overall inflation rates began to decline and a new era of long-term disinflation commenced.

This cautious approach may have been induced, or reinforced, by confusing and conflicting growth patterns of the narrow and broader monetary aggregates. For most of the year, the narrow M1B aggregate (now M1) tracked well below its lower target limit while the broader M2 aggregate remained around the upper limit of its target range. Hence, while shortfalls of M1B indicated a need for greater ease, brisk growth in M2 provided support for a more cautious policy of continued restraint. Given the Fed's 1981 policy bias in favor of restraint, the Federal Open Market Committee decided to make M1B growth contingent upon containment of M2 within its target range. This approach to monetary restraint proved to be self-reinforcing. To the extent that slow growth in M1B gave an upward bias to interest rates, interest-sensitive components of M2 (especially money market mutual funds) were enlarged at the expense of M1B growth. Thus, the more rapid expansion in M1B depended on slower growth in M2; slower growth in M2 depended on lower short-term interest rates that would result from more rapid expansion in M1B. As long as the economic indicators signaled modest real growth in the economy, the Fed seemed unwilling to break this circle.

As 1982 got under way, Chairman Volcker expressed his concern over another potentially severe conflict in the financial markets between tight money and large budget deficits. In Mr. Volcker's own words:

> Even with inflation subsiding, the threat of prolonged large Federal deficits as the economy recovers points to a more imminent concern—direct Government competition for a limited supply of savings and loanable funds. The clear implication is greater pressure on interest rates, than otherwise, with those interest rates serving to "crowd out" other borrowers. The most vulnerable, of course, are home buyers and others particularly dependent on credit. But the consequences for business investment generally are adverse as well.[18]

Accordingly, both monetary restraint and lower budget deficits seemed essential in order to move the economy toward sustained recovery without inflation. But excessive zeal in getting money growth and inflation down threatened to be counterproductive in terms of its costs in high short-term interest rates, lost real output, and irreconcilable conflicts between monetary and fiscal policy targets.

Monetary Policy in 1982: From Monetary Dogmatism to Pragmatic Monetarism

By the spring of 1982, signs of economic weakness had become discouraging, and the debilitating influence of continued minimal reserve provision and extremely high real interest rates was increasingly recognized.[19] In the process of reestablishing its credibility as an inflation fighter, reducing volatility in money and financial markets, and countering the potentially inflationary stimulation of President Reagan's Program for Economic Recovery, the Fed's high-interest rates policy was a major cause of mounting business failures and near depression levels of activity in such major sectors as housing, automobiles, and steel. Recovery and its sustainability remained contingent upon reductions in *real* interest rates and the ability of the corporate and financial sectors to restructure their balance sheets. Yet with inflation rates rapidly falling to about 4 percent, most nominal interest rates above 13 percent, and a flat or negatively sloping yield curve most of the time, real interest rates rose to double digits and funding of short-term debt became unattractive—if not prohibitive.

Despite extensive inventory liquidations early in 1982, the failure of the bond market to open up for sustained periods of time, and a severe cash squeeze created by high-interest rates and dismal profits, prevented demand for short-term credit from moderating. A further portion of this heightened credit demand stemmed from distress borrowing and high debt-servicing needs that exhausted nearly half of all internal cash flow. Continued expansion of short-term borrowing raised the ratio of short term to total credit market debt to more than 42 percent, a post-World War II record. However, the heavy volume of short-term borrowing kept upward pressure on M1 and encouraged the Fed to withdraw reserves from the banking system. Consequently, by June 1982, short-term interest rates remained in the 13 to 15 percent range, and, with inflation moderating, perpetuated a flat to negative yield curve that impeded corporate reliquefication. In the context of a deepening recession, slowing inflation, and record numbers of business failures and bailouts, including several large financial institutions (such as Drysdale Government Securities, Penn Square Bank, and Seafirst Corporation), many observers had expected the Fed to begin more aggressive easing. Instead, Chairman Volcker reiterated the Fed's longstanding position that it would be shortsighted to abandon a strong sense of discipline in monetary policy in an attempt to bring down interest rates.

Yet by midsummer, the confluence of domestic and international financial strains and economic distress made a move toward aggressive easing both necessary and desirable. Serious international pressures, particularly the near bankruptcy of the Mexican government, provided the critical final impetus for a change in the monetary policy course. Domestically, continued credit stringency plus projected large structural federal budget deficits for years to come and a cyclical deficit becoming more and more bloated, threatened to create a credit crunch whenever the economy finally revived. Meanwhile, cash-short companies facing heavy short-term credit burdens and a virtually closed bond market remained in a precarious financial condition. Amid growing domestic and international pressures, some members of Congress threatened to introduce new legislation to make the Federal Reserve more accountable for its policies to the Congress.

In July 1982, the execution of monetary policy took dramatic shift toward reflation—a substantial acceleration in the growth of money and credit over an extended period of time. For the first time in more than a year and a half, the Fed initiated a concerted series of actions designed to reduce interest rates and stimulate money supply growth, even though M1 was near—and to broader M2 aggregate was above—its upper target growth limit. By mid-July 1982, the Fed's new "pragmatic monetarism" and simultaneous weakening of demand for credit brought down most short-term interest rates almost 200 basis points from their June 1982 levels. On July 19, the Fed lowered the discount rate from 12 to 11.5 percent. Still, the Fed explained the discount rate reduction (the first of seven one-half percentage point reductions between July and December 1982) as necessary to realign its lending rate with other, already lower, short-term money market rates. Money supply growth reaccelerated, and M1 again exceeded its upper target growth limit by mid-August 1982. Monetary growth excesses continued to accumulate through year-end 1982.

Financial markets responded almost immediately with favor to the Fed's initial midyear 1982 easing moves. With inflation rates in single digits throughout 1982 and fears allayed that the Fed might try once again to reduce M1 within its target growth range, interest rate declines accelerated. Soon thereafter, the federal funds rate dipped below 10 percent, other short-term interest rates sank below prior resistance levels, and the yield curve finally turned sharply positive. Yet despite this credit-market rally, the corporate financial structure remained strained. Widening yield differentials between relatively safe Treasury bills and less safe money market instruments reflected investors' concern and their flight to quality issues.

In mid-August 1982, a series of events provided new impetus to the credit market rally and touched off a dramatic surge in the equity markets. On August 13, 1982, the Fed reduced the discount rate for the third time in less than a month, confirming to credit market skeptics that the trend toward lower interest rates would continue. Financial market participants interpreted passage of the Tax Equity and Fiscal Responsibility Act of 1982—which raised taxes in a recession and election year—as an encouraging sign that future federal budget deficits might be brought under control. Two influential Wall Street economists—who earlier had predicted new record-high interest rates—reversed their forecasts and predicted still lower interest rates.[20] Despite the beginnings of new inflationary expectations and fears among some Fed watchers that a new round of tightening might be imminent, the Fed decided at its October 5, 1982 meeting not to roll back the summertime monetary growth surge. In early October 1982, the equity markets

EXHIBIT 3   Money, Interest Rates, and Stock Market Performance

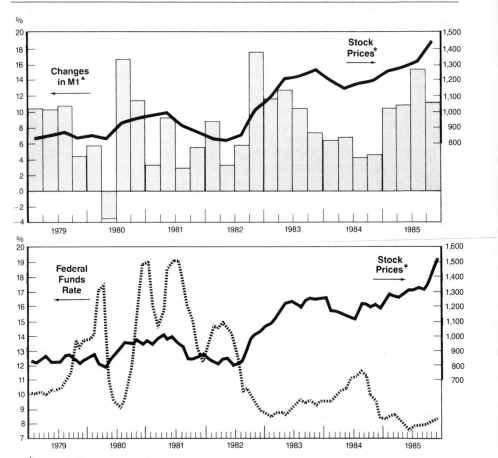

* Mean level of Dow Jones Industrial Average.

▲ Percentage changes at annual rates.

SOURCES: Federal Reserve; Dow Jones; The Conference Board.

ratified the Fed's decisions with an upward explosion of stock prices and new record trading volumes. (See Exhibit 3.)

As 1982 drew to a close, most economic forecasters anticipated a modest recovery with moderate inflation rates. In this environment, the Fed would have to continue a relatively loose monetary policy designed to bring down real as well as nominal interest rates and accommodate faster growth that would not only be preinflationary, but would also result later in drastic braking actions that would drive up interest rates and end the economic recovery prematurely.

Policy Rules Tempered by Discretion in 1983

Despite greater flexibility in the execution of monetary policy in 1983—or, perhaps, because of it—the Federal Reserve was confronted with its most complicated task since 1979: to successfully hold down the rate of inflation, support economic recovery at home and financial stability abroad, and neutralize a huge federal budget deficit—all at once.[21] In early 1983, monetary policy priorities shifted from an aggressive assault on inflation through severe monetary stringency to defense of disinflation and the fledgling economic recovery. With inflation under control and monetary growth targeting suspect, control over interest rates—particulary the federal funds rate—once again became the fulcrum of monetary policy (as had been the case prior to October 1979).

Throughout 1983, the Fed encouraged interest rate stability. For the first time in more than a decade, the Fed kept the discount rate unchanged for an entire calendar year. In the financial markets, both short- and long-term interest rates fluctuated by no more than 100 to 150 basic points over the course of the year. By comparison, most short-term interest rates experienced great volatility and large intrayear swings between 1980 and 1982, when the Fed was more willing to tolerate interest rate instability in order to contain money supply growth and wind down the rate of inflation.

With monetary policy guided more by Federal Reserve discretion and less by rules than at any time since 1979, the Fed could take advantage of soaring dollar exchange values and massive inflows of capital from abroad to provide increased flexibility in the execution of domestic monetary policy. Competition from relatively cheaper foreign imports contributed to reinforcement of disinflationary momentum and allowed the Fed to expand the money supply more rapidly early in 1983 than would otherwise have been consistent with price stability. Purchases of Treasury securities by foreigners facilitated the financing of the federal debt without monetization by the Fed or significant increases in interest rates. This was particularly timely in 1983 when normal cyclical forces, associated with the first year of an economic recovery, typically increase total demand for credit and the proportion of funds borrowed by the government sector (as a percentage of total credit market demand). With the personal savings rate in 1983 near its lowest level in 33 years and federal budget deficits comprising an unprecedented share of GNP for years to come, typical cyclical financial patterns threatened to put upward pressure on interest rates that could "crowd out" vital private sector borrowers.

Despite this relative ease of Treasury financing, financial market participants and Federal Reserve officials warned that large federal budget deficits could put the sustainability of the economic recovery at risk before long. In his July 1983 congressional testimony, Chairman Volcker warned:

> . . .[T]he government will be financed, but others will be squeezed out in the process. While that threat has been widely recognized, there has been a comfortable assumption that the problem would not become urgent until 1985 or beyond. That might be true in the context of a slowly growing economy. But the speed of the current economic advance certainly brings the day of reckoning in financial markets earlier.[22]

With a presidential election year ahead in 1984, the window of opportunity for meaningful resolution of these imbalances before long began to close. In the financial markets, growing near-term pessimism was measured in the failure of the broad stock market indexes to advance for months at a time. Monetary policy at year-end 1983 broadly confronted the same array of complex domestic and international issues as it had a year prior. However, intensifying cyclical pressures on prices and credit markets and greater uncertainty as to the continued strength of the economic expansion, put a premium on timely policy adjustment. The Fed was expected to continue its approach to monetary policy which implied relative interest rate stability—but without dramatic easing. Extreme or long-delayed policy adjustments that could seriously upset price and interest rate stability were likely to be avoided. In the context of this largely defensive policy stance, the Fed would have welcomed gradual reductions in interest rates if they reflected a weakening in economic growth to a more sustainable pace, rather than monetary accommodation. Moreover, as in 1983, the Fed seemed willing to risk higher interest rates for brief periods in order to slow down unsustainable surges in real economic growth or to combat flare-ups in inflationary expectations. However, significant and sustained increases in interest rates in the 1984 election year would subject the Fed to strong criticisms from Congress and the administration. These criticisms would then be amplified by protests from exporters and foreign governments, as well as from bankers concerned over the fragile Third World debt structure.

Toward Stability in 1984 and 1985: Reaching the Cherished Goal

In 1984 for the second consecutive year, the Fed took its cues for changes in monetary policy primarily from changes in domestic economic conditions and financial markets, rather than from money growth rates (as had been the case from October 1979 through October 1982).[23] However, in 1984 (unlike as in 1983), the Fed tolerated wide swings in interest rates. As the year wore on, a difficult policy decision confronted and split the FOMC: should greater restraint be applied in order to slow down economic growth, credit expansion, and incipient inflationary expectations, or was less restraint called for in order to prevent already high-interest rates from choking off economic activity, raising the foreign exchange value of the dollar further, and widening the trade deficit?

During most of 1984, downward revisions in inflationary expectations were reflected in a steep decline in yields on long-term corporate and government bonds throughout the summer months and a flattening in the yield curve. In midsummer, the Fed began to sharply increase provision of nonborrowed reserves to the banking system. The Fed's revised policy stance came amid mounting criticisms from within the Reagan administration and by some members of Congress that flat money supply growth between June and August would lead eventually to a dramatic economic slowdown, if not a recession, in late 1984 or early 1985. By Labor Day, the spread between yields on 1-year Treasury bills and 30-year Treasury bonds was reduced to only 70 basis points (compared to 190 basis points in February and 175 basis points in April). Confirmation of the Fed's intention to ease was contained in the policy directive of the October 2, 1984 FOMC meeting. The directive gave clear authority for further ease—". . . [I]n the event of significantly slower growth in the monetary aggregates, evaluated in relation to the strength of the business expansion and inflationary pressures, domestic and international financial market conditions, and the rate of credit growth."[24]

During the final four months of 1984, the Fed reduced the target level of borrowed reserves on three different occasions and kicked off a round of interest rate declines that affected all portions of the maturity spectrum, especially short- and medium-term interest rates. Yield spreads between short- and long-term Treasury issues widened to more than 200 basis points in December and 225 basis points in early January 1985, levels experienced only once in the previous seven years (in January 1983). The M1 money supply, which declined at a 0.2 percent annual rate between June and October 1984, increased in November and December at an average annual rate of 10.1 percent; M2 increased at a 16 percent annual rate in November and December.

As in 1983, the strong dollar and massive inflows of foreign capital increased the options for domestic monetary policy. The strong dollar, through relatively inexpensive foreign imports, helped hold down the U.S. inflation rate and, hence, allowed the Fed to expand the money supply more rapidly early in 1984 than would otherwise have been consistent with the Fed's commitment to disinflation. Purchases of Treasury securities by foreigners facilitated the financing of the large federal budget deficits without excessive monetization by the Fed. Moreover, foreign capital inflows, by augmenting the pool of domestic savings in the United States, helped avoid the "crowding out" of vital domestic investment that had to compete with the federal deficits in the U.S. financial markets.

Large inflows of foreign capital notwithstanding, the huge volume of Treasury financing in 1984 continued to intrude heavily on the financial markets. Although the federal government's share of total credit decreased to an estimated 25 percent in 1984, from an average 36 percent in 1983, Treasury borrowing remained well above $150 billion. (During the six previous economic expansions, the federal government's share of total credit in the second recovery year averaged about 5 percent, and typically it declined relative to private sector borrowing.) However, unlike in 1982 and 1983, when commercial banks and nonbank institutions acquired the bulk of new Treasury issues, households and foreigners provided the majority of federal deficit financing in 1984. In this environment, accelerating private sector demand for credit on top of large Treasury financing emerged as the major source of concern to the financial markets in 1984. One important factor affecting the acceleration in loan demand was the hectic pace of mergers and acquisitions, particularly leveraged buyouts.

For Fed watchers, Chairman Volcker's late-1984 expressions of optimism about U.S. inflation provided a refreshing injection of candor. After five years of cautionary rhetoric about inflation, Chairman Volcker declared on November 29, 1984 that "the inflationary dragon is on the defensive."[25] Less than two months later, on January 9, 1985 the chairman told a group that "there are some reasons to believe . . . that we're beginning to build into the economy a trend toward more stability of prices."[26]

By the fourth quarter of 1984, most private sector economists, several prominent members of the Reagan adminstration, and even some members of the Federal Reserve Board (notably Vice Chairman Preston Martin and Martha Seeger) had already expressed optimism that the consumer price index would increase by less than 5 percent in 1985 and 1986. Yet, a major rally in the equity markets awaited confirmation that Chairman Volcker had finally joined the legion of inflation optimists. In the two trading sessions following Chairman Volcker's January 9, 1985 statement, the equity markets posted their sharpest advances in more than five months.

With the Fed willing to acknowledge major progress against inflation, 1985 monetary policy focused more intently on conditions for extending the two-year-old economic recovery. Monetary policy in 1985 stressed sustainable economic growth and "orderliness" in the financial and foreign exchange markets. At the heart of this Federal Reserve strategy was continued encouragement of gradual reductions in interest rates associated with noninflationary ease in the financial markets. However, the Fed also wanted to avoid rapid and drastic interest rate declines that might have to be reversed before long and that would increase volatility in domestic and international financial markets. Within the Federal Reserve, many economists feared that indications of significant economic weakness could dampen the appetite of foreigners for U.S. investments, set off a major decline in the value of the dollar, and add new inflationary pressure. Moreover, as long as inflation and inflationary expectations remained under control, the Fed could take further timely easing actions to reverse any excessive economic weakness.

Orderly declines in both interest rates and the exchange value of the dollar were widely thought to require not only steady and sustainable real economic growth and modest inflation, but also a modicum of continued good fortune. A major shock in domestic or world financial markets—such as the bankruptcy of a major financial institution, or a flare-up in the LDC debt problem—could have upset orderly progress in 1985. Moreover, the large federal budget deficits continued to worry the Fed. In the July 1984 words of Paul Volcker: "The Treasury is going to get the funds it needs to cover the federal deficit. The question is whether other sectors will get enough funds, at reasonable interest rates, to support the balanced, higher investment, economic expansion we want."[27]

In short, monetary policy in 1985 was executed in an unaccustomed milieu. For the first time in five years, the Fed had acknowledged that sustained economic growth and decline in both interest rates and the exchange value of the dollar supplanted inflation fighting as the number one concern of monetary policy. Yet the transition in the goals required an accompanying transition in styles if the Fed's new monetary policy was to succeed. Wide fluctuations in both interest rates and real economic growth rates that were associated with the Fed's five-year anti-inflationary commitment had to be replaced by greater stability and orderliness in the economy and in financial markets. Without it, the major structural imbalances in the economy and financial system could be transformed from merely unsustainable to downright debilitating to long-term prospects for prosperity.

INTERNATIONAL INFLUENCES ON MONETARY POLICY: TOWARD GREATER POLICY COORDINATION

Throughout the first half of the 1980s, achievement of stable and orderly markets required monetary policy execution with an unaccustomed eye on level and volatility of currency exchange rates and pressures on the economic and financial viability of debtor nations. Although the relative weight of these considerations in policy design varied from period to period, the Fed regularly pronounced concern about international considerations in its policy deliberations. As international considerations became more prominent in monetary policy formulation, financial market participants increasingly embraced Chairman Volcker as the most powerful and effective policymaker in the world. Not coincidentally Paul Volcker's appointment by President Carter in 1979 reflected the administration's concern about the deteriorating exchange value of the dollar and the need to reestablish worldwide confidence in U.S. economic policy.

Chairman Volcker's international reputation as a shrewd central banker and a committed inflation fighter facilitated the Fed's transition from federal funds rate targeting to direct money growth targeting only two months after his August 1979 appointment to the Fed chairmanship. Ironically, however, international considerations carried little weight in the formulation of monetary policy during Volcker's first two years in office. Instead, the Fed focused on controlling money supply growth and counteracting the potentially inflationary influence of President Reagan's Program for Economic Recovery.

It was not until 1982 that the Fed made changes not only in its pronouncements, but in its policies to account more directly for relationships between financial and monetary conditions domestically and a number of deepening international financial and economic strains.[28] In the first instance, these strains reflected the impact of the Fed's tight money high-interest rate policy on the economies and financial stability of other industrial trading partners and, in turn, on the debt repayment problems of LDC's and other debtor nations (most notably Mexico). With the world economy in 1982 deep in recession, the dollar gaining strength rapidly against major foreign currencies, and several large debtor nations approaching bankruptcy, pressure built on the Fed to ease money supply growth rates and reduce domestic interest rates. However, the Fed generally resisted foreign appeals for lower interest rates until there was convincing evidence that inflation was under control and that meaningful attempts to reduce interest rates would not reignite inflationary expectations.

By autumn 1982, financial difficulties in Brazil captured the attention of the international financial community. The Fed responded to the Brazilian situation in particular, and to international financial fragility in general, by lowering the discount rate by one-half percentage point on December 14, 1982. This response capped a string of related U.S. actions over several weeks that included President Reagan's trip to Brazil (and the subsequent granting of $1.23 billion in short-term credits to that country), and participation by Chairman Volcker in a meeting of European finance ministers that produced $1.5 billion in additional loans from the United States, West Germany, Great Britain, and France.

After mid-1982, complex relationships among domestic interest rates, the exchange value of the dollar, and international financial conditions limited the Fed's choices of politically acceptable alternatives. Pressures on the Fed came from foreign central banks forced repeatedly to raise their own domestic interest rates in defense of their currencies; from 1980 through 1983 especially, these actions constrained economic growth in industrialized countries and intensified financial strains in developing and debtor countries. Domestically, exporters complained that the sharp run-up in the value of the dollar damaged the competitiveness of U.S. merchandise abroad, encouraged imports, constrained necessary price increases, and stimulated protectionist sentiments in many industries. Moreover, some members of the financial community expressed concern that large purchases of Treasury securities by foreigners the uncertainty of future Treasury financings at stable interest rates. In the words of Chairman Volcker:

> The picture of the largest and strongest economy in the world relying, in a capital-short world, on large inflows of funds to finance directly or indirectly, internal budget deficits, is not an inviting one for the future. The implication would be a persistently weak trade position, instability in the international financial system and exchange rates, and a lack of balance in our recovery.[29]

With international financial pressures mounting throughout the early 1980s and the trade deficit at record levels, the Fed needed to *at least appear* receptive to pleas for lower interest rates and a decline in the exchange value of the dollar. (For the first time since October 1982, the Fed intervened in currency exchange markets in July 1983 in a symbolic effort to carry out its promise to calm currency markets when they become "disorderly.") Yet the Fed felt compelled to avoid excessive monetary ease that would temporarily depress short-term interest rates, but at the risk of destabilizing currency exchange markets by raising inflationary expectations and long-term interest rates. Instead, the Fed kept interest rates stable, repeated its appeal for budgetary compromise, and urged Congress to increase support for international lending facilities such as the IMF. (See Exhibit 4.) By the end of 1983, the imminent danger of a loan default by a developing country had abated—at least temporarily—and worldwide economic growth began to accelerate (albeit unevenly among countries). However, the problems of an *overvalued* dollar and large trade deficits remained unresolved.

Despite these intensifying domestic and international concerns over the soaring value of the dollar during the 1983–85 period, the United States typically refused to intervene in, or tamper with, "market forces." Former Treasury Secretary Donald Regan told a September 24, 1984 meeting of the International Monetary Fund: "I don't think the dollar can be driven down through intervention."[30] However, at a January 17, 1985 meeting of top economic officials from industrial countries, the former Treasury secretary appeared to ease the conditions under which the United States would intervene in foreign exchange markets. He indicated that the United States would consider future intervention

EXHIBIT 4 Interest Rates and Exchange Rates

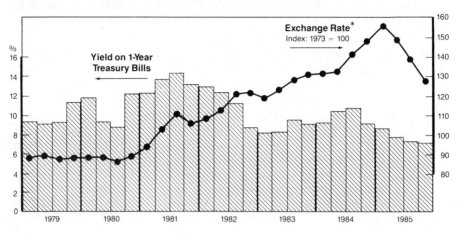

* Index of weighted-average exchange value of the U.S. dollar against currencies of other G-10 countries plus Switzerland.

SOURCES: Federal Reserve; The Conference Board.

either when the currency markets are "disorderly," or if U.S. intervention "would be helpful."[31]

In February 1985, the seemingly inexorable rise in the value of the dollar began to slow up and reverse. Between February and September 1985, the dollar lost more than 9 percent of its value relative to the yen and 14 percent against the deutsche mark. Reversals in the exchange value of the dollar reflected primarily a growing sense among worldwide currency traders that U.S. economic expansion had slowed and that a recession was imminent; severe narrowing of interest rate differentials as both short- and long-term U.S. interest rates plunged to their lowest levels in half a decade; and general pessimism over the prospects for meaningful reductions in the federal budget deficit. In the equity markets, however, the reversal of dollar appreciation was greeted with little response. During most of the first three quarters of 1985, the stock market drifted upward irregularly.

During the fourth quarter of 1985, the stock and bond markets rallied behind two separate events: (1) a September meeting of finance ministers and central bankers of five industrialized countries, where they agreed to intervene simultaneously and forcefully to stabilize currency markets; and (2) the November and December 1985 shattering of OPEC pricing policies that promised to reduce the per-barrel price of crude oil to its lowest level since the mid-1970s. In the wake of these announcements, investors repeatedly pushed the broad stock averages to new record highs. As 1986 began, many financial market experts predicted that the Dow Jones Industrial Average would exceed 2,000 before the end of the year. In the capital markets, long-term corporate bond yields dropped below 10 percent for the first time in more than seven years.

INTERNATIONALIZED MONETARY POLICY AND THE STOCK MARKET

Stock market performance in the 1980s reminds us once again that monetary policy makes a difference through its impact on interest rates and economic conditions conducive to economic growth or contraction. During the 1960s and 1970s, relatively accommodative monetary policy, accelerating inflation, and sharp cyclical swings in the economy coincided with wildly fluctuating share prices and disappointing returns to stock market investors. The inflation-adjusted value of the Standard & Poor's 400 declined by about 50 percent between 1966 and year-end 1981. While earnings per share for the Standard & Poor's 400 increased at a 7.5 percent annual rate between 1966 and 1981, the average price-earnings (P/E) ratio was roughly halved. (It had roughly doubled from 1945 to 1965.) Increases in the inflation rate loomed as the most significant contributor to declines in P/E ratios over this period.[32] For companies, the general inability to adjust prices fully and promptly for cost shocks resulted in declines in both real and nominal profit levels. Stock investors, in turn, demanded an additional return on investment assets to compensate for the erosion of their own purchasing power. These two influences were manifest in the form of lower P/Es for common stocks. Consequently, many investors shied away from common stocks, seeking the more secure and higher returns offered by money market investments and fixed-income securities. Other investors turned to real estate, precious metals, and "collectibles" in order to offset erosion of real wealth by inflation. Corporations reluctant to raise capital via stock issues at the depressed prices relied increasingly on debt financing, raising debt ratios, and making capital structures riskier. Stock investors, in turn, demanded even higher premiums for owning stocks, thereby exerting further downward pressure on P/E ratios.

The stock market rally that began in August 1982 reflected primarily a widespread expansion in P/E ratios associated with the process of disinflation and its sanguine effects on corporate earnings.[33] (See Exhibit 5.) Throughout the 1982 to 1985 period, moderation in the inflation rate and prospects for long-term, satisfactory inflation performance meant that the Fed could continue to follow an easy monetary policy consistent with economic growth and stable to falling interest rates. This percep-

---

EXHIBIT 5 Stock Prices, Earnings, and the Real Economy

Dates	Stock Prices[1]	Corporate Profits[2] (billions of dollars)	Real Economic Growth[3] (% annual rates)	Inflation Rate[4]
1982 Q3	855.9	$ 78.8	−3.2%	7.3%
1982 Q4	1016.5	75.2	0.6	1.5
1983 Q1	1093.8	80.7	4.0	0.4
1983 Q2	1200.9	96.6	8.9	4.4
1983 Q3	1213.4	108.4	5.5	4.2
1983 Q4	1253.3	110.1	6.7	4.2
1984 Q1	1195.1	114.9	11.5	5.1
1984 Q2	1139.1	117.3	5.1	3.7
1984 Q3	1179.9	107.1	2.1	3.7
1984 Q4	1199.9	108.0	0.6	3.6
1985 Q1	1263.4	105.3	3.7	3.2
1985 Q2	1286.6	104.8	1.1	4.2
1985 Q3	1319.4	110.9	3.0	2.4
1985 Q4	1433.9	112.1	0.8	4.2

[1] Quarterly mean of the Dow Jones Industrial Average.
[2] Corporate profits, after taxes, domestic total.
[3] Percentage changes in real GNP at annual rates.
[4] Percentage changes in CPI-U at annual rates.
SOURCES: Dow Jones; Department of Commerce; Bureau of Labor Statistics; The Conference Board.

---

tion was generally reinforced by the strength of the U.S. dollar in foreign exchange, which increased import competition, but helped to keep inflation under control. In 1984 and 1985 especially, a widespread perception that the Fed would take steps to *reverse* the long-term uptrend in the value of the dollar encouraged the equity markets by auguring still lower interest rates and, perhaps, less import competition and potentially stronger competitiveness. With the dollar relatively strong, foreign competition still intrusive, and upward price spiraling no longer a viable means of raising profit levels, companies were constrained to seek profit increases by improving productive efficiency, by moving into new industries, and by merging with other companies. Consequently, labor's share of income suffered, costs were greatly reduced in many industries, and profitability of nonfinancial companies exceeded its post-World War II average at each relative phase of the business cycle. Shifts in the industrial base toward services and high-tech manufacturing better positioned companies for long-term growth. Thus, the lower inflation environment encouraged by relatively tight monetary policies from 1980 to 1982 provided the leeway in subsequent policy to encourage lower interest rates and renewed interest in stock market investments.

PROVING THE MONEY/STOCK-PRICE RELATIONSHIP: AN UNRESOLVED CONTROVERSY

Despite the apparently close association between renewed monetary policy ease and bullish stock market performance in the mid-1980s, the theoretical roots of the money/stock price relationship remain controversial. For nearly 30 years, some economists have maintained that movements in aggregate indexes of common stock prices can be predicted from prior changes in the money supply.[34] This belief has been supported by numerous statistical studies that purport to show that changes in the quantity of money have an important and explicit influence on movements in equity prices. However, underlying doubts about the analytical underpinnings of the linkages, as well as the statistical methodologies used to support them, have cast doubt on the usefulness of money supply changes as a predictor or leading indicator of stock prices.

At the heart of the controversy is the monetarist thesis which describes a powerful, though indirect, transmission of lagged money supply growth rates to common stock price indexes. One of the first studies to attract attention to this relationship was conducted by Beryl Sprinkel in 1964.[35] From casual observation, Sprinkel concluded that "All cyclically related price movements since at least 1918, as well as most intermediate movements, have been closely associated with monetary change. Similarly, changes in monetary growth are associated with changes in the rate of change in corporate profits before taxes, with the money supply usually shortly in the lead." Since Sprinkel maintains that "the price of stock is equal to the discounted value of expected earnings," it follows that "The major factors determining the value of the stock are expected earnings and the interest rate." In this context, money supply affects stock prices indirectly by influencing income creation, or business activity, and by influencing the level and structure of interest rates. Moreover, changes in the money supply influence the willingness of asset-holders to buy or sell common stocks as they respond to changing liquidity pressures (i.e., higher rates of monetary growth raises liquidity and hence the demand for stocks). The substitution of money balances for other financial assets, in turn, generates pressures leading to changes in prices of stocks.[36]

Sprinkel's thesis rests heavily on the so-called present value approach, which states that the value of stocks can be expected to increase directly with the expected rate of earnings growth and to decrease with interest rates on competing investments such as bonds. If inflation expectations raise costs more than prices, real interest rates may increase by more than real expected earnings. Hence, in the early phase of a developing inflation, stock prices may respond favorably as expected earnings rise more than interest rates. Later, however, perhaps after monetary restraint is applied and interest rates rise, it becomes more difficult to raise prices, and costs continue their upward movement. Thus, rising inflation expectations depress stock prices because they raise interest rates at a time of flat or declining real earnings. Conversely, declining inflation expectations have a favorable impact on stock prices through both lower interest rates and more favorable cost patterns consistent with the more stable price trend. Sprinkel observed that changes in the money supply have a longer lead time over business cycle turning points than over stock price changes. Based on visual examination of data, he concluded that "changes in monetary growth lead changes in stock prices by an average of about 15 months prior to a bear market and by about 2 months prior to bull markets."[37]

Yet Sprinkel's conclusion has been questioned repeatedly by other researchers concerned about the methodology employed in his study. These researchers point out that any lead-lag statistical relationship runs the risk of improperly identifying the direction of causality unless careful (and still sometimes imprecise) statistical testing is carried out.[38] Sprinkel and many others who attempted to model the money supply/stock price relationship failed to carry out statistical tests that would verify that the direction of causality runs from money supply to stock prices instead of the other way around—from changes in stock prices to future changes in the money supply.

This latter sequence is embodied in a widely accepted view regarding the determination of stock prices known as the efficient market hypothesis.[39] According to this hypothesis, the stock market is said to be efficient in that stock prices are determined by market participants on the basis of all available information at a rate so rapid as to be treated as almost instantaneous. Thus, if the public expects a change in the money supply to occur that would ultimately affect that overall price level, corporate profits, and other real economic conditions, stock market participants would immediately buy and sell stocks at prices that take account of these expected effects. In other words, expected changes in money supply would be discounted immediately into the prices of stocks.[40] Consequently, if subsequent changes in money were to occur as expected, stock prices would change before, rather than after, changes in money supply. If a change in the money supply is unexpected, stock market participants will discount this information immediately into stock prices. Hence, an unexpected money supply change would produce a synchronous relationship, or at most, a very short lag, between money supply changes and stock prices.

In a widely cited 1974 study covering the 1947 to 1970 period, Richard V. L. Cooper related stock yields (a measure that combines the percentage change in the price of a stock with its dividend yields) to the current percentage change in money supply, past percentage changes in money supply for up to 12 months, and to future percentage changes in money for up to 6 months.[41] Cooper's distributed lag regression found a weak relationship between stock yields and rates of change of the money supply. Moreover, the money supply variable in the current period was found to be not statistically significant in explaining stock yields. This result tended to contradict the efficient market hypothesis which holds that a synchronous adjustment of stock yields should occur if the market is efficient. Cooper also found only one of the lagged money supply variables, and only two of the future money supply variables, to be statistically significant in explaining stock yields. On the basis of these inconclusive results, Cooper concluded that it was difficult to assess the significant lead and lag relationships from regression analysis.

Richard Auerbach of the Federal Reserve Bank of Kansas City modified Cooper's approach in order to test again for the lead-lag relationship between stock yields and the rate of change of the money supply.[42] Auerbach adjusted money supply and stock price data to remove the effects of cyclicality and trend, and computed correlation statistics between the current stock yield and the money supply variable in the current month and each of the prior 60 months. In order to test whether stock yields lead money supply growth, the variables were reversed and correlations were computed between the current money variable and the stock yield in the current month and each of the 60 prior months. Results of Auerbach's tests support the following conclusions:

- Rates of change in the money supply are not related to future changes in the money.
- Stock yields are related to synchronous and future rates of change in the money supply.
- The relation between stock yields and synchronous and future rates of change in the money supply is weak, with stock yields associated with only about 9 percent of the variation in the money supply.

Theoretically, these findings are consistent with the efficient market hypothesis and the belief that the public is knowledgeable about a relationship between money and other variables, such as the price level—as Cooper suggested. The public tends to anticipate some money supply changes and discounts this information into stock prices one or two months before the money supply changes. Unanticipated money supply changes are discounted into stock prices in the same month as the monetary change occurs. Auerbach cautions, however, that these conclusions maybe have been affected by his statistical procedure, which removed trends and periodicities from the data. Under these conditions, prior values of the money supply series can provide no useful information for this forecast. Since it is questionable that the public has the ability to predict changes in the money supply accurately, other explanations may underlie this result.

CONCLUSION: LEGACIES OF DEREGULATION AND INNOVATION IN FINANCIAL MARKETS

Experiences with both monetary policy and financial market performance since 1979 point to the constancy of change that disrupts past relationships among economic and financial variables and reestablishes new ones. With each passing year, financial innovations, structural changes in the economy, and the increasing vulnerability of the domestic economic and financial systems to external shocks weaken the usefulness of past relationships as guides to policy and market performance. In a rapidly changing environment, monetary policy rules made flexible by discretionary actions are needed to "fight the fires of the moment." For Fed watchers, it becomes increasingly difficult to anticipate the timing as well as the magnitude of interim adjustments in monetary policy. Consequently, financial market participants tend to discount changes in monetary policy not once, but twice: first, when a change in policy is anticipated, and again after the change is made.

The financial revolution of the 1970s and 1980s and the changing structure of domestic and international markets mean that interest rates and stock market performance will be shaped for years to come by unaccustomed factors.[43] Here are six:

1. Exceedingly rapid credit growth. In the period from the beginning of the 1982 cyclical recovery through March 1986, debt in the domestic nonfinancial sector increased at the most rapid rate since World War II for the first 40 months of a cyclical recovery. Yet even this record growth pace may have been understated if the effects of new financing techniques, a lack of encompassing accounting requirements, and international transactions not recorded in credit compilations are accounted for in the total. Financial innovations and deregulation, loosening of credit standards, and occasional bailouts of a few large institutions, spurred the massive credit-creation process. *Securitization of debt* has become a new byword in the financial markets as the debt of weaker borrowers reaches the open market through guarantees, credit insurance, and the allure of supposed marketability. However, in the event of credit stringency, there is an inherent danger of a flaring of interest rates and of much wider credit quality spreads. In the past, when credit tightened, marginal borrowers sought refuge in the banking system. Nowadays, marginal U.S. borrowers have greater access to the open credit market, either directly or through innovative financing techniques.

2. Short-term rates have become the key financing rates for private borrowers. In the past, corporate financing during the second and third years of business expansions was dominated by long-term borrowing. Now, however, short-term corporate borrowing and both variable-rate and medium maturity financing are increasingly important; hence traditional long-term corporate borrowings are becoming relatively small. Households are now financing homes primarily through adjustable rate mortgages linked to fluctuations in different types of interest rates.

The key role of short-term interest rates has several ramifications for financial markets and for interest rates generally. For the Fed, short-term rates have increasingly become the instrument of monetary stimulation or restraint. When interest rates rose in the past, variable-rate financing was either not available, or was unacceptable to private sector borrowers who were thereby locked into long-term financing by standards, convention, or financial conservatism. Under the recent system of finance, several new rules seem to prevail:

- Small and consistent increases in short-term rates do not hamper risk taking, arbitraging, and hedging, and thus do not restrain borrowing.
- Small and consistent increases in short-term rates tend to be accompanied by parallel movements in long-term interest rates. The long-term market now functions more for speculation than for financing.
- Large increases in short-term rates over short-time periods restrain economic activity eventually by raising the private cost of borrowing.
- Only sizable increases in short-term rates produce a negative yield curve, because the relatively more speculative long-term, fixed-rate market begins to anticipate changes in the direction of interest rate movements.

The economy is probably not as responsive to a rise in short-term interest rates as it is to a decline in short-term rates. Higher debt-servicing burdens imposed by sharp increases in short-term rates hit borrowers with a lag, and restrain only when these costs are rising more rapidly than profits and income. For a rise in short-term rates to restrain economic activity, borrowers must perceive it to be lasting.

3. Real interest rates are much higher than ever before. The restrictive force of high real interest rates in the 1980s has been overcome by offsetting benefits, such as large increases in income and profits and a tax structure that reduces net borrowing costs. Financing either short-term or at floating interest rates avoids the interest rate lock-in effect when borrowers finance long-term at fixed rates. Moreover, real rates are lower at the short end of the yield curve as long as the yield curve is positively sloped, further reducing the obstacle caused by high real rates of interest. In the early 1980s, high real interest rates were being perceived as transitory, and by concentrating on short and floating-rate financing, borrowers regarded these financing costs as temporary.

4. Disintermediation has become embedded in the financial system. Since the early 1980s, households tend increasingly to invest their funds directly in credit market obligations, rather than placing them with financial institutions. In the past, alternating swings of intermediation and disintermediation were helpful benchmarks in timing interest rate fluctuations. When disintermediation set in, interest rates were sure to rise, and when funds flowed rapidly into financial institutions, interest rates fell. With virtually all legal interest rate restrictions now virtually removed, this relationship no longer holds. The absence of disintermediation ensures increased competition for funds, as interest rates rise cyclically. With many institutions now paying market interest rates on their liabilities, they are also under pressure to pursue aggressive lending and investing policies to offset these costs, and thus run the risk of additional credit quality problems in the future. Nowadays, market bidding for funds involves not only depository institutions, but also contractual savings institutions, such as insurance companies, where liability maturity has been shortened dramatically by new market interest-sensitive services.

5. Never before in the post–World War II economic recoveries has the federal deficit been such a large proportion of economic activity. In the absence of so large a budget deficit, interest rates in the early 1980s would have been significantly lower. (In the recession, the deficit kept rates from falling further; in the recovery, it pushed them higher than they otherwise would have been.) Moreover, the huge deficit accelerated the emergence of a huge financial futures market in U.S. government securities and improves market making and distribution in them as well. At the same time, the enormous issuance of intermediate-and long-term government securities probably induced private borrowers to crowd into the short-maturity range.

6. The dollar shifted from relentless strengthening during the 1980–85 period to a rapid decline in value during 1985–86. Ironically, the intensifying strength of the dollar early in the cyclical recovery that began in December 1982 contrasts with the first few years of past recoveries, when the dollar typically weakened. This time around, dollar strength from 1980–85 helped keep inflation under control, permitted a looser monetary policy that provided liquidity for both interest rate declines and stock market advances, and attracted foreign funds into the United States that supplemented the shortfall in savings and helped finance the large federal budget weakness. However, dollar weakness beginning in 1985 could be expected (with a lag) to encourage withdrawals of foreign funds.

For financial market participants, the unaccustomed factors that will shape future money, capital, and equity market performance present new challenges and offer fresh opportunities to profit. Policymakers, financial market participants, and financial innovators will continue to devise new products, services, and strategies intended to take fuller advantage of the increasingly deregulated international financial marketplace. In this environment, previous relationships between monetary policy and financial market performance will remain useful guides to savers and investors, borrowers and lenders, policymakers and the constituencies they serve. No matter how attenuated previous relationships become, flexible and vigilant money-watchers will continue to search for and find clues to financial market performance in the decisions of policymakers. For these risk takers, the search will enhance prospects for financial market success.

ENDNOTES

1. For a complete discussion of changes in instructions to the Open Market Trading Desk, see Michael E. Levy and Steven R. Malin, "Monetary Policy in Transition: Sorting out the Confusion," *Economic Policy Issues* 1 (The Conference Board, 1981), pp. 3–6.

2. See "Record of Policy Actions of the Federal Open Market Committee," meeting held on March 10, 1970, *Federal Reserve Bulletin*, June 1970, pp. 507–16.

3. Developments leading to passage of House Concurrent Resolution 133 are described in Robert D. Auerbach, *Money, Banking, and Financial Markets*, 2d ed. (New York: Macmillan, 1985), pp. 587–88.

4. Reasons for adopting the money growth targeting procedures are presented in "Statement by Paul A. Volcker, Chairman, Board of Governors of the Federal Reserve System," before the Joint Economic Committee of Congress, October 17, 1979, *Federal Reserve Bulletin*, November 1979, pp. 888–90.

5. Statement from discussion between Henry C. Wallich and Michael E. Levy, Director, Economic Policy Analysis, The Conference Board.

6. From Henry C. Wallich, "Recent Techniques of Monetary Policy," remarks to the meeting of the Midwest Finance Association, Chicago, April 5, 1984.

7. For a complete discussion of the breakdown of long-established economic and financial relationships, see Steven R. Malin, "Monetary Aggregates," in *The Handbook of Economic and Financial Measures*, ed. Frank J. Fabozzi and Harry I. Greenfield (Homewood, Ill.: Dow Jones-Irwin, 1984), pp. 243–63.

8. A chronicle of regulatory changes and financial innovations of the 1960s and 1970s is

found in Anne Marie Laporte, "Proposed Redefinition of the Money Stock Measures," Federal Reserve Bank of Chicago *Economic Perspectives*, March/April 1979, pp. 7–13. For a summary of cash management procedures designed to minimize holdings of noninterest-earning accounts, see Marvin Goodfriend, James Parthemos, and Bruce Summers, "Recent Financial Innovations: Causes, and Implications for Monetary Control," Federal Reserve Bank of Richmond *Economic Review*, March/April 1980, pp. 14–27.

9. Concise discussions of the motives for redefinition of money supply aggregates are found in Steven R. Malin, "Monetary Aggregates," *Across the Board*, September 1980, pp. 57–64; Marie L. Gonczy, "Monetary Aggregates Redefined," Federal Reserve Bank of Chicago *Economic Perspectives*, March/April 1980, pp. 11–18; and Daniel J. Larkins, "The Monetary Aggregates: An Introduction to Definitional Issues," *Survey of Current Business*, January 1983, pp. 34–46.

10. Provisions of the Depository Institutions Deregulation and Monetary Control Act of 1980 are listed in Levy and Malin, "Monetary Policy in Transition," pp. 10–12.

11. More than 90 percent of the increase in M2 during 1982 was attributable to interest earned on money market mutual funds.

12. An excellent discussion of the characteristics and expected behavior of money market deposit accounts and super-NOWs is found in John A. Tatom, "Money Market Deposit Accounts, Super-NOWs and Monetary Policy," Federal Reserve Bank of St. Louis *Review*, March 1983, pp. 5–16. For the Fed's own expectations about the characteristics of MMDAs and super-NOWs, see Frederick T. Furlong, "New Deposit Instruments," *Federal Reserve Bulletin*, May 1983, pp. 319–21.

13. U.S. Congress, Garn-St Germain Depository Institutions Act of 1982, 97th Congress, 2d session, September 8, 1982.

14. See George Garvy and Martin R. Blyn, *The Velocity of Money* (New York: Federal Reserve Bank of New York, 1977); also Daniel L. Thornton, "Why Does Velocity Matter?" Federal Reserve Bank of St. Louis *Review*, December 1983, pp. 5–13.

15. For excellent discussions of the inflation/velocity relationship, see M. A. Akhtar, "Why Gradualism in Monetary Policy Will Not Cure the Current Inflation Problem?" Federal Reserve Bank of New York, Research Paper no. 8109, May 1981; also Paul A. Reardon, "Velocity: Another Variable for Monetary Policy," American Council of Life Insurance *Economic Perspectives*, July 1983.

16. A historical perspective on new velocity relationships is provided by Lawrence J. Radecki and John Wenninger, "Recent Instability of M1's Velocity," Federal Reserve Bank of New York *Quarterly Review*, Autumn 1985, pp. 16–22.

17. See Steven R. Malin, "Controlling Money Growth: Safety Rules for Collision Courses," *Economic Policy Issues* 1 (The Conference Board, 1982), pp. 1–15.

18. "Monetary Policy Report to the Congress," submitted February 10, 1982, *Federal Reserve Bulletin*, March 1982, pp. 125–34.

19. For a review of 1982 monetary policy, see Steven R. Malin, "Changing Designs in Monetary Policy: Toward a New Pragmatism?" *Economic Policy Issues* 1 (The Conference Board, 1983), pp. 1–15.

20. Throughout 1982, the business media closely followed and evaluated the forecasts of Henry Kaufman of Salomon Brothers and Albert Wojnilower of First Boston. Given their close and extensive following, reversals of their respective positions on the outlook for interest rates were bound to evoke broad reactions in the financial markets.

21. The Fed's 1983–84 policy dilemma is discussed in Steven R. Malin, "Monetary Policy in 1984: Reading the Fed's Cues," *Economic Policy Issues* 1 (The Conference Board, 1984), pp. 5–15.

22. See "Monetary Policy Report to the Congress," submitted July 20, 1983, *Federal Reserve Bulletin*, August 1983, pp. 579–90.

23. See Steven R. Malin, "Monetary Policy in 1985: Extending the 1984 Criteria," *Economic Policy Issues* 1 (The Conference Board, 1985), pp. 5–15.

24. "Record of Policy Actions of the Federal Open Market Committee," meeting held on October 2, 1984, *Federal Reserve Bulletin*, January 1985, pp. 33–37.

25. See Laurie McGinley, "Money, Liquidity Will Be Adequate," *The Wall Street Journal*, November 30, 1984, p. 3.

26. Laurie McGinley, "Volcker Voices Optimism about Inflation But Renews Warnings on Budget Deficit," *The Wall Street Journal*, January 11, 1985, p. 3.

27. "Monetary Policy Report to the Congress," submitted July 25, 1984, *Federal Reserve Bulletin*, August 1984, pp. 609–22.

28. Deepening international financial and economic strains are discussed in Steven R. Malin, *Economic Policy Issues* 1 (1984 and 1985).

29. "Monetary Policy Report to the Congress," July 20, 1983.

30. See Stephen Grover, "Dollar Survives Further Action to Prop Mark," *The Wall Street Journal*, September 25, 1984, p. 3.

31. Reported in Art Pine, "U.S. Says It Is Willing to Intervene More to Curb Speculation on Currency Market," *The Wall Street Journal*, January 18, 1985, p. 27.

32. Relationships between P/E ratios and share prices are discussed in John W. Peavy, III and David A. Goodman, "How Inflation, Risk and Corporate Profitability Affect Common Stock Returns," *Financial Analysts Journal*, September–October 1985, pp. 59–65; and Eugene H. Hawkins et al., "Earnings Expectations and Security Prices," *Financial Analysts Journal*, September–October 1984, pp. 24–38.

33. Some analysts attribute the 1982 stock market resurgence, at least in part, to a recurrent election-year phenomenon. For fuller discussions, see Roger D. Huang, "Common Stock Returns and Presidential Elections," *Financial Analysts Journal*, March–April 1985; also, Anthony F. Herbst and Craig W. Slinkman, "Political-Economic Cycles in the U.S. Stock Market," *Financial Analysts Journal*, March–April 1984, pp. 38–44.

34. For an excellent critique of money/stock price models, see Robert D. Auerbach, *Money, Banking, and Financial Markets*, 2d ed. (New York: Macmillan, 1985), pp. 237–51.

35. Beryl W. Sprinkel, *Money and Stock Prices* (Homewood, Ill.: Richard D. Irwin, 1964); also see "Monetary Growth as a Cyclical Indicator," *Journal of Finance*, September 1956, pp. 333–46.

36. See Beryl W. Sprinkel, "Monetary Policy and Financial Markets," in *Financial Analyst's Handbook* ed. Sumner N. Levine (Homewood, Ill.: Dow Jones-Irwin, 1975), pp. 800–17.

37. Sprinkel, "Monetary Policy and Financial Markets," pp. 812–16.

38. These tests are described in Robert D. Auerbach, "Money and Stock Prices," Federal Reserve Bank of Kansas City *Monthly Review*, October 1976, pp. 3–11.

39. For a review of the efficient markets hypothesis, see Eugene F. Fama, "Efficient Capital Markets: A Review of Theory and Empirical Work," *Papers and proceedings of the Twenty-Eighth Annual Meeting of the American Finance Association, Journal of the American Finance Association*, May 1970, pp. 383–416; also see Donald J. Mullineaux, "Efficient Markets, Interest Rates, and Monetary Policy," in *Financial Institutions and Markets in a Changing World*, ed. Donald R. Fraser and Peter S. Rose (Plano, Tex.: Business Publications, Inc., 1984), pp. 667–91.

40. See Douglas K. Pearce", The Impact of Inflation on Stock Prices," in *Financial Institutions and Markets in a Changing World*, pp. 251–70.

41. Richard V. L. Cooper, "Efficient Capital Markets and the Quantity Theory of Money," *Journal of Finance*, June 1974, pp. 887–908.

42. See Robert D. Auerbach, June 1974.

43. Several of these factors are discussed in Henry Kaufman, "The Significance of Heightened Market Responsiveness in 1986," a talk before the 58th Annual Investment Seminar—Mid-winter Meeting of the New York State Bankers Association, New York, January 30, 1986. Also see Thomas D. Simpson and Patrick M. Parkinson, *Some Implications of Financial Innovations in the United States* (Washington, D.C.: Board of Governors of the Federal Reserve System, September 1984).

APPENDIX 1 _____

Sumner N. Levine

We recall that the gross national product, defined as all *final* goods and services *produced* in the United States, is given by the expression

$$GNP = I + C + G + (X - M)$$

where G = Government expenditures
C = Consumer goods expenditure
I = Private investment (plant, equipment, housing, and so on)
X = Exports
M = Imports

The value of GNP is in current dollars (i.e., unadjusted for inflation).

How are the GNP and the financial markets affected by changes in the money supply (M)? From the expression for monetary velocity (V)

$$MV = GNP$$

it is evident that if V is not significantly decreased by an increase in M then GNP must increase with M. However, even without this assumption, it follows that an increase in M must increase GNP, particularly during a slack economy. When the Fed increases the money supply, interest rates (i) and credit restrictions ease. The lower rates and anticipated economic upturn cause bond prices (B), and stock prices (S) to increase. At the same time, investment (I) and consumer demand (C) increase, resulting in an increase in GNP. This sequence can be represented by

$$M\uparrow \rightarrow i\downarrow \rightarrow \begin{bmatrix} C\uparrow & I\uparrow \\ B\uparrow & S\uparrow \end{bmatrix} \rightarrow GNP\uparrow$$

Monetary contraction, particularly when the economy is overheated, results in an increase in interest rates and a tightening of credit. The sequence is the reverse of the above.

$$M\downarrow \rightarrow i\uparrow \rightarrow \begin{bmatrix} C\downarrow & I\downarrow \\ B\downarrow & S\downarrow \end{bmatrix} \rightarrow GNP\downarrow$$

While the above discussion oversimplifies matters, it does provide a helpful framework for viewing monetary influences.

APPENDIX 2
Glossary of Monetary Terms

Bankers Acceptance. Bankers acceptances are negotiable time drafts, or bills of exchange, that have been accepted by a bank which, by accepting, assumes the obligation to pay the holder of the draft the face amount of the instrument on the maturity date specified. They are used primarily to finance the export, import, shipment, or storage of goods.

Book-Entry. One form in which Treasury and certain government agency securities are held. Book-entry form consists of an entry on the records of the U.S. Treasury Department, a Federal Reserve Bank, or a financial institution.

Certificate of Deposit (CD). A form of time deposit at a bank or savings institution; a time deposit cannot be withdrawn before a specified maturity date without being subject to an interest penalty for early withdrawal. Small-denomination CDs are often purchased by individuals. Large CDs of $100,000 or more are often in negotiable form, meaning they can be sold or transferred among holders before maturity.

Demand Deposit. A deposit payable on demand, or a time deposit with a maturity period or required notice period of less than 14 days, on which the depository institution does not reserve the right to require at least 14 days written notice of intended withdrawal. Commonly takes the form of a checking account.

Deposit Ceiling Rates of Interest. Maximum interest rates that can be paid on savings and time deposits at federally insured commercial banks, mutual savings banks, savings and loan associations, and credit unions. Ceilings on credit union deposits are established by the National Credit Union Administration. Ceilings on deposits held by the other depository institutions are established by the Depository Institutions Deregulation Committee (DIDC). Under current law, deposit interest rate ceilings are being phased out over a six-year period, ending in 1986 under the oversight of the DIDC.

Discount Rate. The interest rate at which eligible depository institutions may borrow funds, usually for short periods, directly from the Federal Reserve Banks. The law requires the board of directors of each Reserve Bank to establish the discount rate every 14 days subject to the approval of the Board of Governors.

Discount Window. Figurative expression for Federal Reserve facility for extending credit directly to eligible depository institutions (those with transaction accounts or nonpersonal time deposits).

Federal Funds. Reserve balances that depository institutions lend each other, usually on an overnight basis. In addition, Federal funds include certain other kinds of borrowings by depository institutions from each other and from federal agencies.

SOURCE: *Federal Reserve Glossary*, Board of Governors of the Federal Reserve System, 1985.

Federal Open Market Committee (FOMC). A 12-member committee consisting of the seven members of the Federal Reserve Board and 5 of the 12 Federal Reserve Bank presidents. The president of the Federal Reserve Bank of New York is a permanent member while the other Federal Reserve presidents serve on a rotating basis. The committee sets objectives for the growth of money and credit that are implemented through purchases and sales of U.S. government securities in the open market. The FOMC also establishes policy relating to System operations in the foreign exchange markets.

Federal Reserve Notes. Nearly all of the nation's circulating paper currency consists of Federal Reserve notes printed by the Bureau of Engraving and Printing and issued to the Federal Reserve Banks which put them into circulation through commercial banks and other depository institutions. Federal Reserve notes are obligations of the U.S. government.

Fiscal Agency Services. Services performed by the Federal Reserve Banks for the U.S. government. These include maintaining deposit accounts for the Treasury Department, paying U.S. government checks drawn on the Treasury, and issuing and redeeming savings bonds and other government securities.

Fiscal Policy. Government policy regarding taxation and spending. Fiscal policy is made by Congress and the administration.

Gross National Product (GNP). Total value of goods and services produced in the economy.

Inflation. A rise, over time, in the average level of prices.

Lender of Last Resort. As the nation's central bank, the Federal Reserve has the authority and financial resources to act as "lender of last resort" by extending credit to depository institutions or to other entities in unusual circumstances involving a national or regional emergency, where failure to obtain credit would have a severe adverse impact on the economy.

Matched Sale-Purchase Agreements. When the Federal Reserve makes a matched sale-purchase agreement, it sells a security outright for immediate delivery to a dealer or foreign central bank, with an agreement to buy the security back on a specific date (usually within seven days) at the same price. Matched sale-purchase agreements are the reverse of repurchase agreements and allow the Federal Reserve to withdraw reserves on a temporary basis.

Money. Anything that serves as a generally accepted medium of exchange, a standard of value, and a means to save or store purchasing power. In the United States, paper currency (nearly all of which consists of Federal Reserve notes), coin and funds in checking and similar accounts at depository institutions are examples of money.

Money Market Certificate. A certificate of deposit in a minimum denomination of $10,000 with a maturity of six months. The interest rate on money market certificates is related to the yield on six-month Treasury bills, in accordance with regulations issued by the Depository Institutions Deregulation Committee.

Monetary Policy. Federal Reserve actions to influence the availability and cost of money and credit, as a means of helping to promote high employment, economic growth, price stability, and a sustainable pattern of international transactions. Tools of monetary policy include open-market operations, discount policy, and reserve requirements.

Money Stock.   M1   The sum of currency held by the public, plus travelers' checks, plus demand deposits, plus other checkable deposits (i.e., negotiable order of withdrawal [NOW] accounts, and automatic transfer service [ATS] accounts, and credit union share drafts.)

M2 — M1 plus savings accounts and small-denomination time deposits, plus shares in money market mutual funds (other than those restricted to institutional investors), plus overnight Eurodollars and repurchase agreements.

M3 — M2 plus large-denomination time deposits at all depository institutions, large denomination term repurchase agreements, and shares in money market mutual funds restricted to institutional investors.

Negotiable Order of Withdrawal (NOW) Account.   An interest earning account on which checks may be drawn. Withdrawals from NOW accounts may be subject to a 14-day or more notice requirement although such is rarely imposed. NOW accounts may be offered by commercial banks, mutual savings banks, and savings and loan associations and may be owned only by individuals and certain nonprofit organizations and governmental units.

Open-Market Operations.   Purchases and sales of government and certain other securities in the open market by the New York Federal Reserve Bank as directed by the FOMC in order to influence the volume of money and credit in the economy. Purchases inject reserves into the depository system and foster expansion in money and credit; sales have the opposite effect. Open-market operations are the Federal Reserve's most important and most flexible monetary policy tool. They are used to promote either higher or lower growth in money and credit and to offset undesired changes in reserve positions of depository institutions stemming from movements in currency, float, Treasury deposits, and other factors.

Productivity.   The amount of physical output for each unit of productive input.

Recession.   A significant decline in general economic activity extending over a period of time.

Repurchase Agreements.   When the Federal Reserve makes a repurchase agreement with a government securities dealer, it buys a security for immediate delivery with an agreement to sell the security back at the same price by a specific date (usually within 15 days) and receives interest at a specific rate. This arrangement allows the Federal Reserve to inject reserves into the banking system on a temporary basis to meet a temporary need and to withdraw these reserves as soon as that need has passed.

Reserves.   Funds set aside by depository institutions to meet reserve requirements. For member banks, reserve requirements are satisfied with holdings of vault cash and/or balances at the Federal Reserve Banks. Depository institutions that are not members of the Federal Reserve System may hold their reserves in the same manner, or they may pass the reserve balances through a correspondent institution to the Federal Reserve Banks.

Reserve Requirements.   Reserves that must be held against customer deposits of banks and other depository institutions. The reserve requirement ratio affects the expansion of deposits that can be supported by each additional dollar of reserves. The Board of Governors sets reserve requirements within limits specified by law for all depository institutions (including commercial banks, savings banks, savings and loan associations, credit unions, some industrial loan banks, and U.S. agencies and branches of foreign banks) that have transaction accounts or nonpersonal time deposits. A lower reserve requirement allows more deposit and loan expansion and a higher reserve ratio permits less expansion.

Small Saver Certificate.   A certificate of deposit with a minimum maturity of 2½ years offered by banks and thrift institutions to individuals. The interest rate on these certificates is related to the average yield on 2½-year Treasury securities, in accordance with regulations issued by the Depository Institutions Deregulation Committee. There is no minimum denomination required on these certificates.

The Desk.   The trading desk at the New York Federal Reserve Bank, through which open-market purchases and sales of government and federal agency securities are made. The desk maintains direct telephone communication with major government securities dealers. A "foreign desk" at the New York Federal Reserve Bank conducts transactions in the foreign exchange market.

Transaction Account.   A checking account or similar account from which transfers can be made to third parties. Demand deposit accounts, negotiable order of withdrawal (NOW) accounts, automatic transfer service (ATS) accounts, and credit union share draft accounts are examples of transaction accounts at banks and other depository institutions.

Treasury Bills.   Short-term U.S. Treasury securities issued in minimum denominations of $10,000 and usually having original maturities of 3, 6, or 12 months. Investors purchase bills at prices lower than the face value of the bills; the return to the investors is the difference between the price paid for the bills and the amount received when the bills are sold or when they mature. Treasury bills are the type of security used most frequently in open-market operations.

Treasury Bonds.   Long-term U.S. Treasury securities usually having initial maturities of more than 10 years and issued in denominations of $1,000 or more, depending on the specific issue. Bonds pay interest semiannually, with principal payable at maturity.

Treasury Notes.   Intermediate-term coupon-bearing U.S. Treasury securities having initial maturities from 1 to 10 years and issued in denominations of $1,000 or more, depending on the maturity of the issue. Notes pay interest semiannually, and the principal is payable at maturity.

Treasury Securities.   Interest-bearing obligations of the U.S. government issued by the Treasury as a means of borrowing money to meet government expenditures not covered by tax revenues. Marketable Treasury securities fall into three categories—bills, notes, and bonds. The Federal Reserve System holds more than $125 billion of these obligations, acquired through open-market operations. Marketable Treasury obligations are currently issued in book-entry form only; that is, the purchaser receives a statement, rather than an engraved certificate.

Velocity. The rate at which money balances turn over in a period for expenditures on goods and services (often measured as the ratio of GNP to the money stock). A larger velocity means that a given quantity of money is associated with a greater dollar volume of transactions.

10

The Determinants of Interest Rates on Fixed-Income Securities

Frank J. Jones, Ph.D.
Managing Director
Kidder, Peabody & Company, Inc.

Benjamin Wolkowitz, Ph.D.
Vice President
Morgan Stanley & Co.

This chapter discusses the determination of interest rates on fixed-income securities. In discussing the determination of interest rates, first the general level of interest rates at a specific time, and then the factors that cause differences in interest rates at a specific time are considered. The interest rates on securities issued by the U.S. Department of the Treasury (hereafter Treasury) are commonly accepted as the benchmark interest rates in the U.S. economy and, typically, in the world. The interest rates on Treasury securities are commonly accepted as being reflective of the general level of interest rates because there are more Treasury securities outstanding than of any other marketable securities in the world, the Treasury issues securities of every maturity spectrum on a regular basis, and Treasury securities have virtually no credit risk.

The discussion of interest rate determination is structured so that the conceptual analysis is followed by applications of the conceptual conclusions. Most of these applications use Treasury securities as the basis for comparison. The first part of this discussion considers the

SOURCE: Adapted from *The Handbook of Fixed Income Securities*, 2nd edition, (1987) edited by Frank J. Fabozzi and Irving M. Pollack, Dow Jones-Irwin.

determination of the general level of interest rates, which can be considered "the" interest rate, or, alternatively, the general level of interest rates, for which a Treasury security interest rate (either a 91-day Treasury bill rate or a long-term Treasury bond rate) is the benchmark. The three major rationales or theories for interest-rate determination—liquidity preference, loanable funds, and inflation and the real rate of interest—are discussed. A synthesis of these approaches is also provided. A fourth rationale, the "tone of the market," is also reviewed and shown to have an impact on interest rates in the short term.

The second part of the discussion on interest-rate determination discusses the factors that cause differences among interest rates at a specific time; that is, why all interest rates are not equal to the general level of interest rates, or alternatively, why, at any time, a variety of levels of interest rates coexist. This discussion relates to the rationales for structures of interest rates. There are three such factors or reasons for differences among interest rates. The first factor is maturity. The impact of maturity on a security's interest rate is considered in the context of three hypotheses: the liquidity hypothesis, the expectations hypothesis, and the segmentation hypothesis.

Second, differences among interest rates on securities at a time also occur due to differences in credit risk. Investors respond to a risk-return trade-off in that the greater the risk associated with a particular security, that is, the less creditworthy the issuer, the greater the required return. This concept of credit risk is explained and illustrated with a number of actual market examples.

A third important reason for differences among interest rates on securities is taxability, with regard to the tax exemption on coupons for municipal securities, the difference in tax treatment between coupon return and capital appreciation, and flower bonds. The subject of taxability and its impact on interest rates is also discussed.

The chapter concludes with an overview of interest-rate determination, which combines all the concepts introduced and demonstrates how they interact to determine market interest rates.[1] This synthesis of

---

[1] This chapter discusses interest rates as though the interest rates on securities were directly comparable. Interest rates on all securities, however, are not, without adjustment, directly comparable. Typically, market makers refer to the value of securities in terms of their prices, not their interest rates. The interest rates on the securities are then calculated from their prices. Interest rates are important because they provide a common basis for comparing the returns on securities of different maturities and of different principal values. For these reasons, interest rates are always calculated on an annual basis, typically for $100 of maturity value. However, in calculating interest rates from prices, different assumptions are used for different securities. Thus, within the general term *interest rate* are included the returns on several types of securities that are calculated according to different assumptions and are called, alternatively,

theory and actual experience, relying on Treasury issues as a basis for comparison, provides a comprehensive overview of interest-rate determination.

RATIONALE FOR INTEREST RATE DETERMINATION

In a broad sense the economy can be conceived of as being composed of two sectors—the real sector and the financial sector. The real sector is involved with the production of goods and services with physical resources—labor and capital. Important examples of components of the real sector include automobile production, steel production, and housing construction. The financial sector is concerned with the transfer of funds from lenders to borrowers. Important examples of components of the financial sector include commercial banks, insurance companies, and securities dealers.

In the financial sector equilibrium is attained when the demand for borrowed funds equals the supply of loanable funds, as discussed below. The interest rate is the variable that causes this equality or equilibrium.

To an individual deciding whether to currently consume an amount of funds or abstain from consumption and supply the funds to the financial sector (i.e., save) the interest rate can be viewed as compensation for abstaining from current consumption. For example, an individual with $100 of disposable income when the interest rate is 10 percent must decide between consuming the $100 today or saving it for one year, after which the individual would have $110 to consume. The $10 of added consumption is in effect a reward for abstaining from current consumption. The greater the reward, that is, the higher the interest rate, the more a saver should be willing to supply loanable funds. In the aggregate, the supply of loanable funds is directly related to the interest rates, which are reflected in the upward sloping supply curve of Exhibit 1.

The steepness of this curve depends on the saver's preference for future consumption relative to present consumption. The greater this preference for savings, the flatter the supply curve—the more willing a saver is to save. In this case there is a greater increase in savings for a given increase in interest rates.

---

discount return, yield, bond equivalent yield, repo equivalent yield, and other measures of return. Thus, in comparing interest rates on different securities, adjustments must often be made so that the interest rates compared are calculated on the basis of the same assumptions. However, the magnitudes of the differences among interest rates calculated on the basis of different assumptions are in most cases small. This chapter ignores the effect of different assumptions used in calculating interest rates and uses the term *interest rate* as though the returns on all securities were comparable.

EXHIBIT 1 The Supply and Demand of Loanable Funds

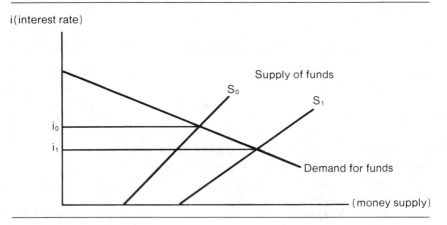

i(interest rate)

Supply of funds

S_0

S_1

i_0

i_1

Demand for funds

(money supply)

To a borrower of funds, the interest rate represents a cost. In the context of the preceding example, at an interest rate of 10 percent, borrowing $100 for one year will cost the borrower $10 in interest. To a business borrower, this $10 interest expense is the cost of borrowing to improve capital plant and equipment. If a business borrower can make operations sufficiently more efficient and consequently more profitable as a result of becoming more capital intensive, then borrowing should occur. The higher the interest rate, however, the greater must be the profitability associated with an investment for it to pay off. Since more investments will pay off at low interest rates than at high interest rates, the demand for funds by borrowers will decline as interest rates rise. For this reason, the demand for funds curve in Exhibit 1 is downward sloping.

The catalyst for achieving equality between the aggregate supply of funds and the aggregate demand for funds in the financial system is the interest rate. The financial sector is not, however, one uniform, homogenous market. Rather, the financial sector is composed of a number of financial institutions and markets that, although distinct, are interrelated. Each of these specific components of the financial sector is specialized, attracting funds from specific types of savers and making funds available to specific types of borrowers. There is, however, some substitution in which savers and/or borrowers who usually borrow or lend in one part of the financial sector may switch to a different part because of a change in relative interest rates.

Interest rates bring the supply and demand for funds into equality in each part of the financial system and operate in the same way to bring the total or aggregate supply and demand for funds in the financial system into equality.

Interest rates are not constant, rather they vary over time. Understanding what affects interest rates and why they are variable is key to understanding the operations of the financial sector. The determination of the general level and variability of interest rates is explainable by several different theories or frameworks. The three major theories, liquidity preference, loanable funds, and inflation and the real rate of interest, are described below. In addition to a general conceptual discussion of the theories, a discussion of how these theories can be used in practice is provided. The focus in this section is on the general level of interest rates, not on any particular interest rate.

Liquidity preference. "Liquidity preference" is synonymous with the "demand for money." And, as is the case with the demand for other financial assets and liabilities, the demand for money is dependent on the level of interest rates.

The relationship between the demand for money and interest rates can be explained in two ways. The first relies on a Keynesian construction called the speculative demand for money. In this approach, it is assumed that the investor has as investment alternatives either holding cash, which has a zero return and no risk, or holding a bond that has two forms of return, a coupon return and a potential capital gain or loss. If the capital loss on bonds is large enough to exceed the coupon return, the total return on bonds will be negative, and holding money, even at a zero return, would be preferable.

Since the prices of and interest rates on fixed-income securities move inversely, bonds incur a capital loss when interest rates rise and a capital gain when interest rates fall. Thus, when interest rates are low, there will typically be an expectation that they will rise, thus resulting in a capital loss on bonds. In anticipation of such a capital loss, holding cash is preferable. Conversely, if interest rates are presently high, they will typically be expected to decline, so that a capital gain on bonds is anticipated and holding bonds is preferable.

Interest rates affect the relative demand for money and bonds as illustrated by a downward sloping demand curve shown in Exhibit 2. The demand for money increases as the current interest rate decreases because the lower the present interest rate is, the more it is expected to rise, and thus the greater the expected capital loss is and the more investors are inclined to hold money. With respect to Exhibit 2, as the interest rate rises from i_2 to i_1, the quantity of money demanded decreases from Q_2 to Q_1.

A second way to explain the relationship between interest rates and the demand for money is to conceive of the interest rate as the foregone return for holding money instead of an interest-bearing asset. Consequently, the higher the rate of interest, the greater is the return foregone by holding money, and the less money is held. In other words,

EXHIBIT 2 The Supply and Demand of Money

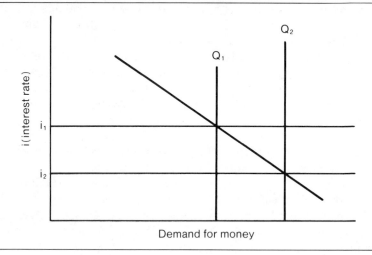

Demand for money

according to Exhibit 2 as interest rates rise, the cost of holding money rather than an interest-earning asset rises. Consequently, as interest rates rise a smaller amount of money is held.

According to either explanation, the liquidity preference theory of interest rates explains the level of the interest rate in terms of the supply and demand for money. Thus, if the Fed increases (decreases) the supply of money and there is no change in the demand relationship, the interest rate will decrease (increase). Again referring to Exhibit 2, increasing the supply of money from Q_1 to Q_2 while leaving the demand relationship unchanged results in a lower equilibrium interest rate. In general, an increase in the supply or a decrease in the demand for money will cause interest rates to decline, whereas a decrease in supply or an increase in demand will cause interest rates to rise.

The liquidity preference theory of interest rate determination can be used for determining both short-term and long-term changes in interest rates.

A partial, short-term analysis of interest rate determination is based solely on tracking and analyzing short-term movements in the money supply. Since the Fed has the primary responsibility for determining the money supply, there has developed a school of interest rate analysts commonly known as Fed watchers who continually monitor and interpret the Fed's activities to infer from these activities the Fed's intentions regarding future activities that will affect the money supply and, consequently, interest rates. The weekly money supply statistics announced by the Fed on Friday afternoons and widely disseminated by the financial press are carefully examined for indications of changes in

Fed policy that could affect interest rates. Exhibit 3 provides a weekly table of Federal Reserve money supply statistics. An additional discussion of how the Fed's money supply data are interpreted is provided below.

In addition to watching and interpreting the market money supply data, the Fed's open-market operations and their effect on the federal funds rate are continuously monitored. As an example, the following discussion appeared in *The Wall Street Journal* (January 20, 1982):

> Some specialists said the recent rise in the funds rate reflected an apparently tougher stance adopted by the Fed late last month in supplying reserves to the banking system. And many contend the recent surge in the money supply will force the Fed to get even tougher.

A longer-term application of the liquidity preference theory is based on the relationship between the money supply and the level of gross national product (GNP). This relationship is formally expressed by the equation: $M \times V = P \times Y$ (called the quantity theory of money), where V is the velocity of money, P is the price level, and Y is real gross national product. The product of P and Y, $P \times Y$, is nominal GNP, referred to simply as GNP.

According to this theory, if the level of the money supply over some future time period is less (greater) than the actual amount needed to support the expected level of GNP, then the level of interest rates is likely to rise (fall). It is due to this relationship that economic forecasters go through the complex exercise of predicting GNP and the money supply and their interrelationship in order to provide forecasts of interest rates.

Predicting GNP and money supply relationships is usually conducted in the context of large econometric models of the U.S. economy. These multiequation models attempt to capture the complex interactions in the economy that result in the determination of interest rates, GNP, and money supply. The results of such models are frequently the basis for long-range financial planning by corporations and others.

Loanable funds. The loanable funds theory of interest rate determination is based on the reasoning related to the supply and demand for loanable funds provided at the beginning of this section. This theory of interest rate determination depends on the supply of funds available for lending by savers and the demand for such loanable funds by borrowers. As indicated above, as the return to lending rises (as interest rates rise), the supply of loanable funds increases. Conversely, when interest rates decline, the return to lenders declines; thus so does the supply of such funds.

Since interest rates represent a cost to borrowers, the opposite relationship applies to borrowers: As interest rates rise, borrowers'

EXHIBIT 3 Weekly Federal Reserve Money Supply Statistics (December 27, 1986)

Federal Reserve
All data in millions of dollars

	Latest Week	Previous Week	Year Ago
Monetary Aggregates			
M-1* as of Dec 15	n.a.	$720,700	622,600
Adj. Mon. Base (St. Louis Fed) *(12/17)	254,300	254,900	235,100

Reserve Position, Eight New York Banks Daily averages for two weeks ended Dec 17

	Latest Week	Previous Week	Year Ago
Excess (Deficit) Reserves (Incl. carryover)	R 34	(12)	4
Borrowings at Federal Reserve	57	0	0
Net Federal Funds Purchases	R 29,495	28,518	8,268
Basic Reserve Surplus (Deficit)	R (29,518)	(28,530)	(8,264)

Federal Reserve Credit Daily averages, week ended Dec 24

	Latest Week	Previous Week	Year Ago
Gov'ts. and Agencies Held Outright	204,898	205,341	186,114
Gov'ts. and Agencies Under Repurchase	3,806	1,283	1,500
Float	1,482	R 1,094	1,347
Other Assets	16,407	16,113	14,667

Other Factors Affecting Reserves Daily averages, week ended Dec. 24

	Latest Week	Previous Week	Year Ago
Gold STock	11,084	11,084	11,090
Special Drawing Rights	5,018	5,018	4,718
Currency in Circulation	209,785	208,369	195,964
Treasury Deposits	3,391	3,524	3,577

Other Items

	Latest Week	Previous Week	Year Ago
Gov't. Securieis Held by Fed for Foreign accounts as of Dec. 24	163,173	164,764	125,161
Business Loans, National**, Dec 10	263,574	R 263,868	251,974
Commercial Paper, National, Dec 17	325,562	324,974	293,161

Ten New York Banks, Balance Sheet Items Wednesday, Dec 17

	Latest Week	Previous Week	Year Ago
Loans and Leases, Adjusted	169,029	R 168,789	159,014
Business Loans**	62,323	R 61,764	58,927
Treasury and Agency Securities	13,580	13,809	14,047
Tax-Exempt Securities	14,176	14,162	11,544
Demand Deposits	65,129	R 63,874	57,844
Nontransaction Balances	95,895	R 95,238	88,622
Time Deposits Larger than $100,000	34,093	34,229	34,440

R Revised.* Seasonally adjusted.** Excluding acceptances. n.a. Not available.

EXHIBIT 4 The Supply and Demand of Loanable Funds

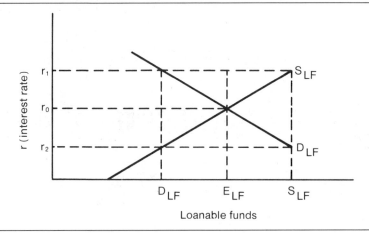

demand for funds decreases, and as interest rates decline, borrowers' demand for funds increases. These relationships are illustrated by Exhibit 4.

In Exhibit 4 the equilibrium level of interest rates is r_0, and the quantity of funds lent and borrowed at that rate is E_{LF}. If the interest rate were initially higher than r_0, for example r_1, then the supply of funds, S_{LF}, would exceed the demand, D_{LF}, at that rate. This excess supply of funds would exert downward pressure on interest rates, causing them to decrease to r_0, the point at which supply and demand would be in equilibrium. Alternately, if rates were below the equilibrium level, for example at r_2, then the demand would exceed the supply. The effect of market pressures in this case would be to cause interest rates to increase again to the equilibrium level, r_0.

The loanable funds theory of interest rate determination applies to aggregate borrowing and lending in the economy. If, at a given interest rate, intended aggregate borrowing is greater than intended aggregate lending, then interest rates will rise. Then the actual measured levels of borrowing and lending at the higher level of interest rates will be equal. If intended aggregate borrowing is less than intended aggregate lending, interest rates will decline until the actual measured levels of borrowing and lending will be equal at the lower level of interest rates.

To apply the loanable funds theory, aggregate borrowing and lending is typically divided into its components or sectors, as illustrated in Exhibit 5. Even though some borrowers and lenders can shift among types and maturities of sources and uses of funds and some cannot, a structure or taxonomy such as shown in Exhibit 5 can be used in either case for determining aggregate borrowing and lending. This structure is

EXHIBIT 5 Summary of Supply and Demand for Credit ($ billions)

	1979	1980	1981	1982	1983	1984E	1985P	Amt. Out. 31 Dec 84E	Table Refer.
Net Demand:									
Privately held mortgages	$113.1	$84.2	$73.7	$15.9	$83.7	$148.5	$136.4	$1,485.5	2
Corporate and foreign bonds	35.7	40.2	34.9	39.1	37.9	50.5	45.3	656.9	3
Total long-term private	148.8	124.3	108.6	54.9	121.7	199.0	181.7	2,142.4	
Short-term business borrowing	98.0	67.1	117.3	47.5	60.1	141.6	153.2	1,006.7	8
Short-term other borrowing	49.3	11.2	37.7	27.7	60.5	97.9	120.7	695.5	8
Total short-term private	147.2	78.3	155.0	75.2	120.6	239.5	273.9	1,702.2	
Privately held federal debt	76.2	118.7	123.0	214.1	241.0	257.3	277.9	1,728.1	6
Tax-exempt notes and bonds	27.8	31.9	29.5	63.9	54.3	66.5	63.2	542.8	4
Total government debt	104.0	150.6	152.4	278.0	295.3	323.8	341.1	2,270.9	
Total Net Demand for Credit	$400.0	$353.3	$416.0	$408.1	$537.6	$762.4	$796.7	$6,115.6	▶
Net Supply*:									
Thrift institutions	$56.5	$54.5	$27.8	$31.3	$136.8	$155.8	$171.7	$1,117.1	9
Insurance, pensions, endowments	77.9	88.2	89.2	107.1	96.1	105.3	105.4	1,190.2	9
Investment companies	29.3	15.9	72.4	52.4	6.0	49.9	58.0	261.3	9
Other nonbank finance	27.8	13.1	28.8	4.9	12.0	50.6	41.3	307.8	9
Total nonbank finance	191.4	171.7	218.1	195.6	250.9	361.5	376.5	2,876.3	
Commercial banks	122.2	101.4	107.6	107.2	140.2	169.0	164.8	1,761.6	
Nonfinancial corporations	7.0	1.8	18.4	13.6	22.8	12.6	23.1	160.6	10
State and local governments	7.1	0.6	2.0	10.3	17.2	11.0	9.7	93.6	11
Foreign investors	-4.6	23.2	16.3	18.1	28.5	30.7	30.8	283.2	11
Subtotal	323.1	298.7	362.4	344.8	459.5	584.8	604.8	5,175.3	
Residual: households direct	76.9	54.6	53.7	63.3	78.1	177.6	191.9	940.4	12
Total Net Supply of Credit	$400.0	$353.3	$416.0	$408.1	$537.6	$762.4	796.7	$6,115.6	◀
Memo:									
Net issuance corporate stock	$-1.9	$18.2	$11.9	$19.5	$27.8	$-89.1	$-26.8	$2,030.0	
Total credit and stock	398.1	371.5	427.9	427.6	565.3	673.3	769.9	8,145.6	
Percentage of Total Absorbed by:									
Households	56.2%	42.9%	40.1%	28.8%	40.6%	45.8%	44.3%		
Nonfinancial business	24.3	25.3	25.1	18.5	15.0	9.6	15.2		
Financial institutions	7.3	10.1	11.8	4.4	8.4	-2.7	5.1		
Government	7.9	15.6	17.6	45.7	33.5	46.4	34.2		
Foreigners	4.3	6.1	5.4	2.6	2.5	0.9	1.2		

* Excludes funds for equities and other demands not tabulated above.
SOURCE: "1985 Prospects for Financial Markets," (Salomon Brothers Inc, Dec. 11, 1984) p. 26.

useful for summarizing actual, measured aggregate borrowing and lending for past years, as done for 1979–84 in Exhibit 5; as indicated above, borrowing and lending must be equal.

The structure is also useful for forecasting interest rates. For this purpose, an estimate is developed of the expected or intended levels of borrowing and lending of each type shown in Exhibit 5 over a period of time. Then the sum of all types of borrowing (aggregate borrowing) is compared with the sum of all types of lending (aggregate lending). If the former is greater than the latter, interest rates are forecast to increase. And due to the increase in interest rates, actual borrowing would be less than expected borrowing and actual lending would be greater than expected lending. Then, ex post, actual measured borrowing and lending would be equal. For example, the data in Exhibit 5 provide estimates of the actual measured sources and uses of funds in 1985 after interest rates changed to their equilibrium levels.

Often, instead of developing as complete a taxonomy of borrowing and lending as described above, analysts focus on only the major types of borrowing and lending, such as federal government borrowing, business borrowing, and mortgage borrowing. Then by forecasting increases or decreases in these types of borrowing, analysts assess whether there will be upward or downward pressures on the interest rate.

A popularization of the application of the loanable funds theory on a sectoral basis is referred to as "crowding out." Large federal deficits require the U.S. Department of the Treasury to increase the amount of debt it has outstanding; and the issue of Treasury debt is alleged to compete with private-sector borrowing, assuming a fixed supply of available credit. Thus an increase in the demand for funds by the Treasury causes interest rates to increase and forces out the private-sector issues. An example of the crowding out application of the loanable funds theory appeared in *The Wall Street Journal* (1981):

> Many dealers said they continue to be concerned about the size of the Treasury's financing needs. Traders also expressed nervousness over recent increases in short-term interest rates. But many said they remain confident that bond prices will rebound early next year, mainly because they anticipate further evidence of erosion in the economy.

And another example appeared in a *New York Times* story (1981):

> Unusually heavy year-end Government borrowings continued to weigh on the money market last week, raising short-term rates a point on average and reducing prices of longer-term coupon securities as much as two points, or $20 for each $1,000 of face value.

Thus the crowding-out concept derives for the loanable funds theory but focuses only on Treasury borrowing. Most applications of loanable funds use an intermediate approach between a complete taxonomy of sources and uses of funds and only a single use of funds; they consider a few major uses of funds and perhaps changes in the aggregate supply of funds.

Inflation and the real rate of interest.   Interest rates represent a rate of return for lenders and a cost to borrowers. To be a meaningful representation of cost or return, however, interest rates should be related to the rate of change of prices. The significance of this relationship can be considered by the following example. Consider a saver who has placed $5,000 in a money market fund earning a return of 12 percent per year. At the end of a year the saver has $5,600, a 12 percent increase in purchasing power. If, however, the price level had increased by 10 percent per year, then the net increase in purchasing power of the savings would be only 2 percent.

The 12 percent return on the savings is referred to as the nominal rate of interest, since it measures the percent increase in the nominal number of dollars earned or paid over a period of time. The measure of change in purchasing power of 2 percent is referred to as the real rate of interest since it measures the real change in purchasing power. The difference between these two rates is the rate of inflation. Thus the real rate of interest (IR) equals the nominal rate of interest (IN) minus the rate of inflation (DP): $IR = IN - DP$.

From the lender's perspective, the real rate of interest represents the increase in real purchasing power resulting from foregone consumption—savings. From the borrower's perspective, the real rate of interest represents the real cost of borrowing. The inflation component of the nominal rate of interest the borrower pays on the borrowed funds represents a deterioration of the principal of the loan (often described as paying back in cheap dollars), not a real cost of borrowed funds. A business should as a rule continue to borrow and invest until the real rate of return on investments equals the real rate of interest paid on borrowing.

Thus there are two major determinants of the real rate of interest. The first is the return on investment—the return to capital. If a business can improve its efficiency of operations and earn a higher rate of return from investment, it will be inclined to pay a higher real rate of return on borrowed funds. The other influence is the preference of consumers. The more consumers want to consume currently rather than forego consumption, the higher the real rate of return will have to be to induce them to alter their plans and save.

Then the real rate of interest and the rate of inflation jointly determine the nominal rate of interest. The effect of the rate of inflation on the nominal rate of interest is to cause the nominal rate to change so that the real rate is unaffected by the rate of inflation. Lenders, unless subject to a "dollar illusion," are concerned with the return of the real purchasing power on their savings rather than the nominal return. Such concern causes consumers to negotiate for nominal rates that keep their real rate of return at least constant. Thus, to the extent their savings are sensitive to the real rate of interest, an increase in inflation without a corresponding increase in the real rate of interest will cause a decrease in savings. Consequently, there is upward pressure on the nominal rate of interest during periods of inflation, which prevents the real rate of interest from decreasing below its original level. To prevent savings from decreasing requires an increase in the nominal rate equal to the increase in the rate of inflation.

Inflation has a somewhat similar effect on the willingness of borrowers to pay a higher nominal rate of interest for funds. Inflation affects the return on investment by affecting the prices of goods and services produced. An investment earning a given amount net of the interest on borrowings will earn a higher nominal amount after inflation because the value of the goods and services produced by the investment have been inflated. If the interest payments on the borrowings do not increase as well, then the real rate of return on investment will also increase. Presumably, under such circumstances borrowers will continue to increase their demand for funds until the nominal cost of borrowing has increased such that the real cost is at its preinflation level.

Over time, however, the real rate of interest may change for two reasons. First, the real rate of interest, since it is the real return on capital, may decrease during recessions because of a substantial amount of unused capital and a low return to the used capital. Similarly, it may increase during periods of economic growth because all capital is productively employed.

The second reason for changes in the real rate relates to *unexpected* changes in the rate of inflation. The nominal interest rate on a security at any time should reflect the *expected* average rate of inflation over the maturity of the security. If the financial markets *expect* a higher rate of inflation in the future, nominal interest rates should increase to reflect these expectations. However, if inflation changes unexpectedly, the initial nominal rate of interest will not correctly reflect the change, and the actual real rate of interest over the period will be different from the normal level of the real rate in the opposite direction of the unexpected change in the rate of inflation.

Consider the following example. Between times T_0 and T_1 the nominal rate of interest is 8 percent, the rate of inflation is 5 percent, and the real rate of interest is 3 percent. Assume these are the normal levels.

Assume that at T_1 the rate of inflation *unexpectedly* increases to 6 percent. Since the change is unexpected, the nominal rate does not change, and thus the real rate of interest decreases to 2 percent. Assume that by T_2 the financial markets recognize the change in the rate of inflation and the nominal rate of interest increases to 9 percent, restoring the real rate of interest to 3 percent.

At T_3 the rate of inflation *unexpectedly* decreases to its original level of 5 percent. Because the change is unexpected, the nominal rate remains at 9 percent, so the real rate increases to 4 percent. By T_4 the financial market recognizes the change in the rate of inflation, the nominal rate of interest decreases to 8 percent, and the real rate of interest decreases to its original normal level of 3 percent. Thus, although expected changes in the rate of inflation should have no effect on the real rate of interest, unexpected changes in inflation will cause the real rate of interest to change in the opposite direction.

Typically, interest rates are referred to in nominal terms. Similarly, interest rate determination models relate to the nominal rate of interest. As discussed above, the nominal rate of interest and the rate of inflation are directly related. Since the nominal rate of interest is, by definition, equal to the real rate of interest plus the rate of inflation, the rate of inflation is a major component of the level of the nominal rates of interest. In fact, given the levels of inflation and interest rates that have been observed during the last decade, changes in the nominal rate of interest have been due in greater measure to changes in inflation than to changes in the real rate of interest.

Exhibit 6 provides a plot of the real rate of interest from 1965 until recently. Calculations of the real rate of interest can be made from different measures of the rate of inflation and different interest rates, although in concept the measure of the inflation rate used should be the expected inflation rate over the maturity of the security whose interest rate is used. The interest rate can be either a short-term or a long-term interest rate. Very often the inflation rate used is based on an average over several previous periods or a projection of the trend of the past inflation rate into the future. The real rate of interest in the plot in Exhibit 6 equals the average prime rate charged by banks minus the contemporaneous change in the consumer price index (CPI). Alternatively, the real rate plotted could have been the long-term Treasury bond rate minus an expected long-term rate of inflation.

Exhibit 6 shows that there has been considerable variation in the real rate of interest, the difference between the interest rate and the inflation rate. These changes in the real rate have been due both to changes in the strength of the economy and errors in inflationary expectations.[2] Although the correlation is less than perfect, the real rate of interest tends

---

[2] Some observers claim that the real rate of interest has been high in recent years because the real rate contains a risk premium to account for the increased volatility of interest rates since October 1979, when the Fed announced that it would devote more attention to controlling the money supply and less to controlling the interest rate.

EXHIBIT 6   The Real Rate of Interest

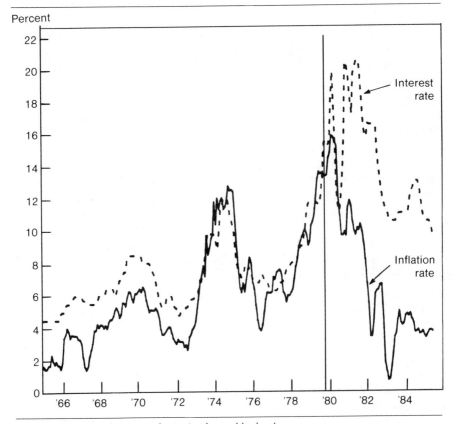

* Interest rate: Average prime rate charged by banks.
† Inflation rate: Consumer price movement, six-month spans (annual rate).
SOURCE: U.S. Commerce Department.

to be low during recessions and high during periods of economic strength.

To summarize, in models of the determination of the nominal rate of interest, the factors that affect the rate of inflation and the real rate of interest should be considered separately. Since there has been even greater volatility in the rate of inflation than in the real rate of interest, an accurate determination of the rate of inflation is an important part of an accurate determination of the nominal rate of interest.

Synthesis.   The three different theories or rationales of the level of interest rates that were described in this section are not exclusive but, rather, are compatible and complementary ways of considering interest-rate determination. The liquidity preference theory, which considers the supply and demand for money, and the loanable funds theory, which considers the supply of and demand for loanable funds, are equivalent ways of considering interest rate determination. A model that included both money and loanable funds would show that these two theories would determine the same interest rate. The impact of the inflation and the real rate of interest theory on the level of interest rates is complementary to the other two explanations by introducing the effect of inflation to either. Thus the three theories described in this section should be viewed as a unified approach to interest rate determination.

Tone of the market. The factors discussed above that affect interest rates—the supply and demand for money, the supply and demand for funds, and the inflation rate—are objective in nature. These fundamental factors undoubtedly determine the level of interest rates after some lag. But there is another type of influence on interest rates that responds very quickly—within hours, or even minutes, and at times includes subjective as well as objective factors—this type of influence is called the tone of the market.

The tone of the market determines the very short-run direction and volatility of interest rates and is due to actions by professionals in the interest rate markets, mainly dealers in government securities, corporate bonds, and municipal bonds, and also large institutional investors in these securities. The professionals continually monitor the nation's and the world's economic, political, and social condition and quickly assess their likely impacts on interest rates. In particular, they watch for changes in the condition of the nation's economic goals, inflation, unemployment, economic growth, and balance of payments and watch for changes in economic policies, monetary policy, and fiscal policy. Even more specifically, they monitor the volume of new issues of Treasury, corporate, and municipal debt that will be brought to the market in the next few days and weeks, and Fed open-market operations and monetary policy.

By monitoring and quickly assessing the likely impact of these factors on interest rates, the professionals are able to rapidly alter their portfolio strategies in view of new information. If dealers and portfolio managers expect interest rates to increase, they reduce the size of their portfolio to avoid losses, thus lowering the demand for securities and increasing interest rates. In response to the same expectations, they may reduce their holdings of long-term securities but increase their holdings of short-term securities, thus increasing long-term rates relative to short-term rates, a normal phenomenon during times of rising interest rates. Through these portfolio activities, the expectation that interest rates will rise actually causes interest rates to rise, at least for a short period of time. If interest rates are expected to decrease, the opposite will occur.

At times professionals may respond not only to recent information but to expectations or anticipations of future information. Operating on the basis of future information is more subjective than operating after the release of new information. And at times the psychology of the market may be counter to the fundamental factors: Professionals may expect future information that will reverse interest rate trends based on recently available data.

The tone of the market, whether determined by objective (fundamental) or subjective (psychological) factors, affects interest rates very quickly. And activities by professionals that set the tone of the market by quickly translating new information or expectations of future information into present interest rate changes add to the efficiency of the financial markets. In this regard, the size of government bond dealers' inventories, particularly just before and after large Treasury auctions, are important. If dealers have large amounts of securities on their shelves, they are more likely to be aggressive sellers and less likely to be aggressive bidders at subsequent auctions, thus providing a bearish influence to the market. Dealer inventories of corporate bonds similarly affect this market. At times, the sizes of dealer and other professional open interest in the Treasury futures markets may have similar effects. For example, if dealers have substantial short positions in the Treasury bill, note, or bond futures markets prior to a Treasury auction to hedge their takedowns, a bullish event may prompt them to liquidate these short positions, which will exaggerate the price increase.

The following quote from *The Wall Street Journal* indicates the nature and importance of the tone of the market:

> Bond prices swung widely as speculators stepped up their involvement in the credit markets.
>
> The Treasury recently offered 8⅜ percent bonds of 2008, for example opened at 99²²⁄₃₂ bid, 99²⁴⁄₃₂ asked, traded as high as 100 bid, 100⅛⁄₃₂ asked only to finish the session at their opening levels.
>
> The earlier firming came as dealers purchased inventory for possible markups in any subsequent resumption of the strong price rally of the past two weeks.

INTERNATIONAL EFFECTS ON INTEREST RATES

International influences on U.S. interest rates have been important for decades. For example, there have often been substantial international flows of "hot money"; that is, money invested in short-term, liquid, low credit risk investments in search of high yields. Because these flows of hot money were mainly in response to interest rates they, to some extent, stabilized international interest rate differentials. That is, countries which tried to increase their interest rates for stabilization purposes attracted foreign funds which, in turn, limited the increase in interest rates.

International influences on interest rates, however, have become much more important in recent years, mainly because the very large federal deficits in the early and mid-1980s have been financed by foreign, mainly initially Mideast and, later, Japanese, funds. These U.S. investments were possible because of the large balance-of-payment surpluses of these countries. An important recent difference in international effects on interest rates has resulted from the fact that Japanese investors have not invested in short-term hot money investments, but instead in long-term Treasury bonds. And this has caused some changes in the way international factors affect interest rates. International interest rate differentials continue to affect the degree of international inflows of funds, but recently it has been international bond yields; for example, the differential between Japanese and U.S. bond yields, rather than international short-term yields that affect international funds flows. The domestic return to Japanese investors, however, depends not only on the level of U.S. interest rates but also changes in the dollar-yen exchange rate. For example, a weakening of the U.S. dollar relative to the yen during the holding period of the Treasury bond reduces the Japanese return. Thus, an expected weakening of the dollar will reduce the degree of foreign investment in the United States, thus tending to increase U.S. interest rates.

The large U.S. domestic deficits and the significant purchases of Treasury debt by foreigners have also affected the flexibility of the Fed's implementation of monetary policy. For example, during 1986 the U.S. economy was weak and the Fed considered loosening monetary policy by decreasing the discount rate in order to strengthen the economy. Lower interest rates would, however, have weakened the dollar which would have worsened the U.S. trade deficit as well as reduced the Japanese purchases of the large issues of Treasury debt. For this reason, decreases in the discount rate were curtailed.

Overall, international effects are important determinants of interest rates, both due to Fed policy and financial market forces.

THE STRUCTURES OF INTEREST RATES

It is often asked what determines or affects "the" interest rate as if there were a single interest rate. However, from the financial markets it is obvious that there is not one but several interest rates. And although these interest rates may move, in general, in the same direction at the same time, the amounts of their movements and at times even the direction of their movements may differ substantially. Thus the spreads, or differences, between interest rates vary. These observations are illustrated by Exhibit 7.

This section discusses the factors that tend to make interest rates differ among themselves. These factors are often the basis for the "structures" of interest rates. There are three different structures of interest rates, and even if securities are identical in every other respect, their interest rates may differ because of maturity, credit risk, and taxability. These three structures of interest rates are discussed below.

Maturity structure (term structure) of interest rates. This section considers the relationship between a security's interest rate and its term to maturity. This relationship is usually referred to as the maturity structure or term structure of interest rates. A common analytical construct in this context is the yield curve (or term-structure curve), which is a curve illustrating the relationship between the interest rate and the maturity of securities that are identical in every way other than maturity.

There are three distinct explanations of the relationship between the maturities of securities and their interest rates.

Liquidity hypothesis. Although there are several aspects to a security's liquidity, the major aspect is the security's potential for capital gain or loss, often called market risk. The major determinant of a security's market risk is its maturity, since the longer the security's maturity, the greater the price change for a given change in its interest rate. For example, the prices of Treasury bonds are more volatile than the prices of Treasury bills.

Since there is a trade-off between the risk and the return on a security, investors typically require a higher return to invest in a security with higher risk. Because a security with a longer maturity has greater market risk and, for this reason, less liquidity, interest rates should increase with maturity as a compensation to investors. This relationship between the level of interest rates and the maturity of a security is called the liquidity preference hypothesis and is illustrated in Exhibit 8. This hypothesis does not purport to be a complete explanation of the term structure of interest rates, but only a complement to the other explanations described below.

Expectations hypothesis. The expectations hypothesis begins with a premise considered in a preceding section, that lenders desire to maximize their return from providing funds and borrowers desire to minimize their cost of borrowing funds. However, unlike the preceding discussion, the expectations hypothesis explicitly considers how lenders and borrowers attain their objectives over a period of time rather than just at any moment in time.

EXHIBIT 7 Plot of Interest Rates

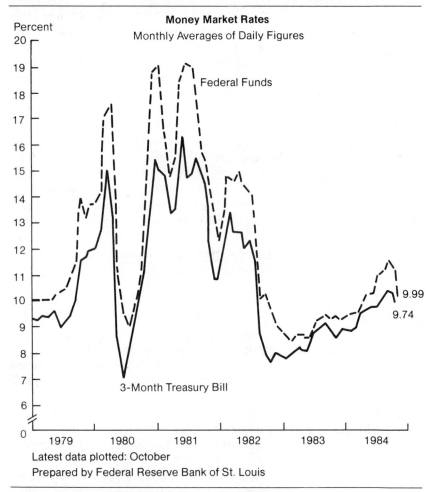

Latest data plotted: October
Prepared by Federal Reserve Bank of St. Louis

SOURCE: *Monetary Trends*, Federal Reserve Bank of St. Louis.

To consider the temporal aspect of maximizing investment return and minimizing borrowing cost and how these decisions affect the relationship between interest rates and maturities, consider a two-period planning horizon. Consider each period to be one year, although it could be any other discrete period of time. A lender considering strategy over this two-period planning horizon has two alternatives—either to purchase a security with a maturity equal to the two periods or

EXHIBIT 7 *(concluded)*

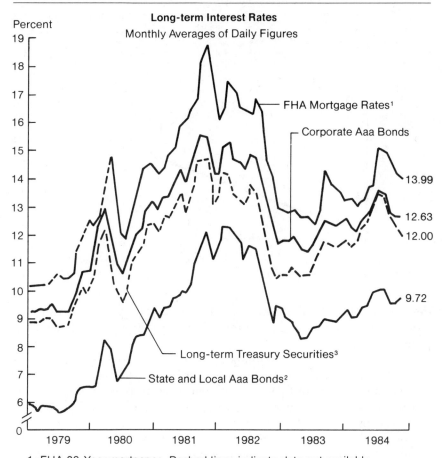

1. FHA 30-Year mortgages. Dashed lines indicate data not available.
2. Monthly averages of Thursday figures.
3. Average of yields on coupon issues due or
   callable in ten years or more.

   Excluding issues with Federal Estate Tax privileges. Yields are
   computed by this bank.

   Latest data plotted: October

   Prepared by Federal Reserve Bank of St. Louis

purchase a security with a one-period maturity with the intention of reinvesting for an additional period at the end of the first period. The lender's decision will depend on a comparison of the currently available two-period interest rate with the average of the currently available

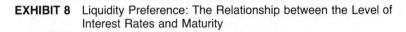

EXHIBIT 8 Liquidity Preference: The Relationship between the Level of Interest Rates and Maturity

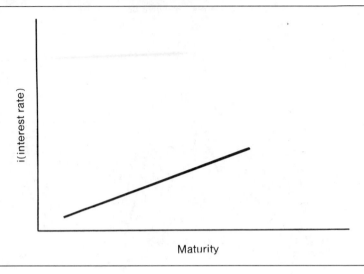

one-period rate and the expected one-period rate, one period hence. Obviously, the lender will select the strategy with the higher anticipated return.

The borrower who is planning over the same two-period horizon is also faced with two alternatives—either to issue a security with a two-period maturity or to issue a one-period security with the intention of issuing another one-period security, one period hence. The borrower's decision will be based on the total cost of funds over the two periods. If the two-period interest rate is less than the average of the current one-period rate and the one-period rate expected one period hence, then the borrower will issue a two-period security. Otherwise, the borrower will sequentially issue two, one-period securities.

The decisions made separately by lenders and borrowers will affect the relative interest rates over the two-period horizon. For example, if the two-period interest rate exceeds the average of the one-period rate and the expected one-period rate one period hence, then all lenders would choose to invest for two periods and all borrowers would sequentially issue two, one-period securities. As a consequence, there would be an excess supply of funds in the two-period market, causing the two-period interest rate to decrease, and an excess demand for funds in the one-period market, causing the one-period interest rate to increase. According to the expectations hypothesis, the interest rates will continue to change until the current two-period rate equals the effective rate for two sequential one-period securities. Under this circumstance, both borrowers and lenders will be indifferent between a single two-period transaction and two sequential one-period transactions, and thus interest rates will be in equilibrium.

The expectations hypothesis is also applicable to a larger number of periods. However, the basic conclusion that the current long-term rate should equal the average of the current and expected future short-term rates remains the same. As a result, borrowers and lenders will be indifferent between relying on a long-term security or a series of short-term securities.

The expectations hypothesis does not imply that all interest rates will be equal, only that the average of the observed and anticipated short-term rates will equal the long-term rate. If interest rates are expected to remain stable, however, so that future short-term rates are expected to equal the currently observed short-term rate, then current interest rates across all maturities will be equal, as illustrated by the yield curve shown in Exhibit 9. This is a "flat" yield curve.

If rates are expected to increase, the shape of the yield curve will be different. With an anticipated increase in interest rates, lenders will purchase short-term securities so that they can earn the higher anticipated rate after their initial short-term-maturity security matures and they subsequently reinvest in another short-term security at a higher rate, and also so that they avoid the capital losses that longer-term securities would incur when interest rates rise. Borrowers, on the other hand, would be induced to issue long-term securities in order to lock in

EXHIBIT 9   Flat Yield Curve

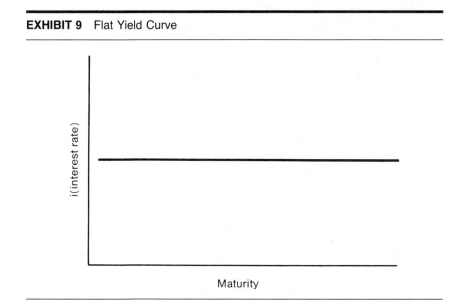

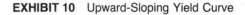

EXHIBIT 10 Upward-Sloping Yield Curve

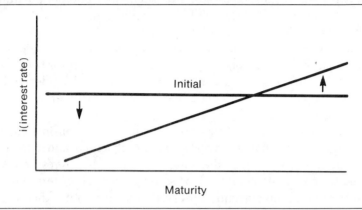

the currently low rates for a long period of time, thereby eliminating the need for issuing new securities at the higher rates. These actions of lenders and borrowers would result in an excess supply of short-term funds, causing short-term rates to decrease, and an excess demand for long-term funds, causing short-term rates to increase. These pressures on short- and long-term interest rates would produce an upward-sloping yield curve as illustrated in Exhibit 10.

According to the expectations hypothesis, these pressures on interest rates will continue until, again, the current long-term interest rate equals the average of the current and expected short-term rates. For example, if the current one-year rate is 12 percent, the expected one-year rate one year hence is 13 percent, and the expected one-year rate two years hence is 14 percent, then the current two-year rate would be 12.5 percent, and the current three-year rate should be the average of these three one-year rates, 13 percent.[3] Thus the yield curve based on the current one-year, two-year, and three-year rates would be upward sloping.

The explanation is similar if interest rates are expected to decrease in the future. In this case, lenders would purchase only long-term securities in an attempt to lock in currently high interest rates before rates decrease and to reap the capital gain that would result from the decrease in interest rates. Borrowers, on the other hand, would issue only short-term securities, thereby paying currently high rates for a short period of time with the expectation of subsequently issuing longer term securities when rates decrease. Consequently, there would be an excess

---

[3] This example ignores the effect of compound interest.

EXHIBIT 11 Downward-Sloping Yield Curve

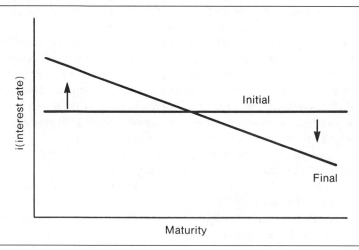

supply of funds in the long-term market and an excess demand for funds in the short-term market, which would cause long-term interest rates to decrease and short-term interest rates to increase. These pressures on interest rates would result in a downward-sloping, or inverted, yield curve as illustrated in Exhibit 11.

As indicated above, the liquidity hypothesis is not intended to be a complete explanation of the term structure of interest rates. Rather it is intended to supplement the expectations hypothesis. The combined effects of the liquidity hypothesis and the expectations hypothesis are shown in Exhibit 12.

The expectations hypothesis produces a horizontal yield curve when interest rates are normal, an upward-sloping yield curve when interest rates are low, and a downward-sloping yield curve when interest rates are high. Supplementing the expectations hypothesis with the liquidity hypothesis, which always predicts an upward-sloping yield curve, provides an upward bias to a yield curve based only on the expectations hypothesis. Indeed, upward-sloping yield curves have historically been the most frequently observed, and for this reason upward-sloping yield curves are frequently referred to as normal yield curves. During recessionary periods, when interest rates are low and are expected to increase, the yield curve has a steep upward slope. When the economy is strong, credit is tight, and interest rates are high, however, downward-sloping yield curves are observed. Both observations are consistent with the expectations hypothesis.

Segmentation hypothesis. The basis for the segmentation hypo-thesis is the antithesis of the basis for the expectations hypothesis. Whereas the expectations hypothesis assumes that both borrowers and lenders are able to alter the maturity structure of their portfolios, each group shifting among the maturities of their respective borrowings or investments, the segmentation hypothesis assumes that both borrowers and lenders are constrained to particular segments of the maturity spectrum for institutional and legal reasons. For such market partici-pants, shifting among maturities is not feasible, and therefore various maturity securities are not considered to be substitutes for one another, independent of the levels of the various interest rates.

In practice, there are numerous financial market participants whose borrowings or investments are, for a variety of reasons, constrained to only one portion of the maturity spectrum. For example, pension fund managers and insurance companies have a relatively small amount of their investments in short-maturity securities, whereas commercial banks and thrifts have a relatively small amount of their investments in long-term bonds.

If indeed the market is segmented so that borrowers and lenders active in the market for one maturity are unlikely to be active in the market for any other maturity, then the interest rate associated with a particular maturity would have to be the result of the supply and demand pressures for only that maturity. Consequently, a change in supply and demand factors in one maturity will affect the interest rate

EXHIBIT 12   Expectations Hypothesis plus Liquidity Hypothesis

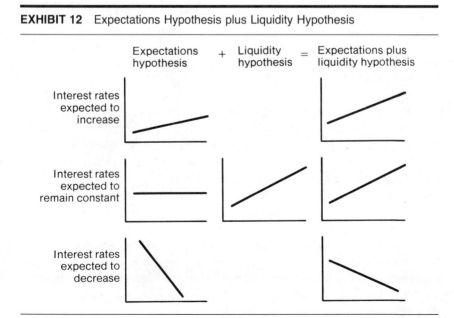

for only that maturity and have no impact on the interest rate for any other maturity.

The segmentation hypothesis and the expectations hypothesis are competing, incompatible explanations of the relationship between interest rates and maturities on securities. For technical reasons, resolving which is the more correct explanation of the relationship is an intractable problem. In reality there are probably some elements of both theories that are correct while neither one is completely correct in explaining the relationship. In particular, it is unlikely that all borrowers and lenders are locked into one portion of the available maturity structure and unable to switch to another when interest rates dictate. Alternatively, there are undoubtedly some market participants who are restricted to particular segments of the maturity structure.

Either hypothesis could provide correct conclusions without the hypothesis holding in its extreme version. For example, for the expectations hypothesis to apply, not all borrowers and lenders have to be able to shift among maturities on the basis of relative interest rates, only enough to affect the relative interest rates. Similarly, for the segmentation hypothesis to apply, not all borrowers and lenders have to be restricted to particular segments of the maturity range, only enough so that the interest rates associated with each maturity segment are influenced by different supply-and-demand considerations. Observers of debt markets have noted characteristics supportive of both hypotheses in their less-than-extreme versions. However, most observers tend to support the expectations hypothesis complemented by the liquidity hypothesis as the dominant explanation for the observed relationship between interest rates and maturity.

The combined expectations-hypothesis/liquidity-hypothesis description of the maturity structure of interest rates can be applied to the actual behavior of the financial markets. The conclusions that can be drawn from a combination of the expectations hypothesis and the liquidity-preference hypothesis are that when the level of interest rates is normal the yield curve will have a slight upward slope—the long-term rates will be slightly greater than short-term rates. When the general level of interest rates is low, the term structure will have a steeper upward slope. Finally, when the level of interest rates is high, the term structure will have a downward slope. Pragmatically, the segmentation hypothesis adds nothing that either contradicts or supports this observation.

Empirical observations support conclusions derived from the expectations and the liquidity hypotheses. Exhibits 13, 14, and 15 show yield curves on different dates with various slopes. Note that the general level of interest rates is higher for the downward-sloping yield curve.

A recent, pragmatic explanation of the term *structure of interest rates* is based on identifying the different factors which affect short-term and

EXHIBIT 13   Yield Curve—November 29, 1984

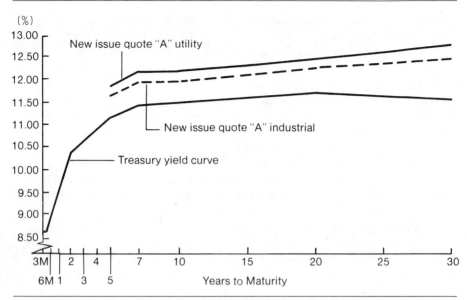

SOURCE: The yield curve graphs are furnished courtesy of Paine, Webber Fixed Income Research.

EXHIBIT 14   Yield Curve—September 3, 1981

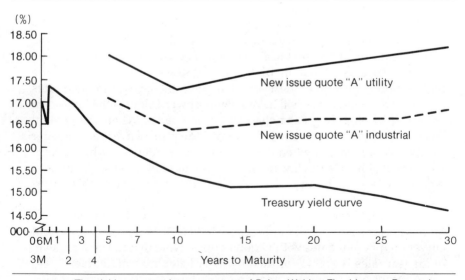

SOURCE: The yield curve graphs are courtesy of Paine, Webber Fixed Income Research.

EXHIBIT 15 Yield Curve—August 5, 1982

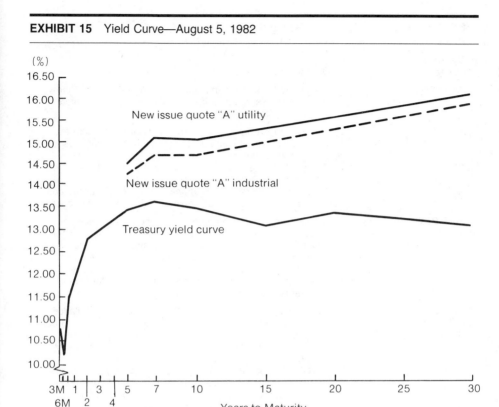

SOURCE: The yield curve graphs are furnished courtesy of Paine, Webber Fixed Income Research.

long-term interest rates. According to this version, short-term interest rates are determined mainly by Fed policy such as setting the discount rate, lending funds to commercial banks and savings institutions at the discount window and increases in bank reserves via open-market operations. Long-term interest rates, on the other hand, are determined by inflationary expectations, as indicated by changes in the GNP deflator, the CPI, the rate of growth of GNP, and other indicators of the rate of economic growth. This explanation could be viewed as an alternative, pragmatic version of the segmentation hypothesis.

Credit risk. The two major characteristics of a security are return and risk. In turn, there are two major types of risk, market risk and credit risk. Market risk refers to the volatility of the price of a security due to changes in the general level of interest rates. The market risk of a security is thus determined primarily by its maturity, since the longer

EXHIBIT 16 Corporate Bond Rating Categories*

Standard & Poor's Rating Categories†	Description
AAA (Aaa)	Bonds rated AAA have the highest rating assigned by Standard & Poor's to a debt obligation. Capacity to pay interest and repay principal is extremely strong.
AA (Aa)	Bonds rated AA have a very strong capacity to pay interest and repay principal and differ from the highest rated issues only in small degree.
A (A)	Bonds rated A have a strong capacity to pay interest and repay principal, although they are somewhat more susceptible to the adverse effects of changes in circumstances and economic conditions than bonds in higher rated categories.
BBB (Baa)	Bonds rated BBB are regarded as having an adequate capacity to pay interest and pay principal. Whereas they normally exhibit adequate protection parameters, adverse economic conditions or changing circumstances are more likely to lead to a weakened capacity to pay interest and repay principal for bonds in this category than for bonds in higher rated categories.
BB (Ba) B (B) CCC (CCa) CC (Ca)	Bonds rated BB, B, CCC, and CC are regarded, on balance, as predominantly speculative with respect to capacity to pay interest and repay principal in accordance with the terms of the obligation. BB indicates the lowest degree of speculation and CC the highest degree of speculation. While such bonds will likely have some quality and protective characteristics, these are outweighed by large uncertainties or major risk exposures to adverse conditions.
C	The rating C is reserved for income bonds on which no interest is being paid.
D	Bonds rated D are in default, and payment of interest and/or payment of principal is in arrears.
Plus(+) or minus(−):	The ratings from "AA" to "B" may be modified by the addition of a plus or minus sign to show relative standing within the major rating categories.

* These Standard & Poor's corporate bond rating categories also apply to municipal bonds.

† The ratings in parentheses refer to the corresponding ratings of Moody's Investors Service, Inc.

SOURCE: Standard & Poor's Corporation Bond Guide.

the maturity, the greater the price change of the security for a given magnitude of interest rate change in the opposite direction. Thus, the term *structure of interest rates* relates to the market risk of a security. This section considers the other type of risk, credit risk.

The credit risk of a security is a measure of the likelihood that the issuer of the security, the borrower, will be unable to pay the interest or principal on the security when due. Credit risk is thus a measure of the creditworthiness of the issuer of the security. Federal securities, that is, issues of the U.S. Department of the Treasury, have the lowest credit risk. Federal agencies are perceived to have the next lowest credit risk because they are backed by the federal government. Corporate securities are rated lower than federal agencies with respect to credit risk. The relative credit risks of long-term corporate securities are rated by several private financial corporations. Exhibit 16 describes the rating categories of the two major ones—Moody's and Standard & Poor's.

Although the creditworthiness of different issuers of bonds affect the bonds' credit risk, even different bonds of the same issuer can have different credit risk depending on the characteristics of the specific bond. For example, a debenture, an unsecured bond, may have a higher credit risk than a bond that is collateralized by real or financial assets or a sinking-fund bond of the same issuer.

Some money market instruments are also rated by private financial corporations. Both Standard & Poor's and Moody's rate commercial paper issues. For example, the grades usually acceptable to commercial paper investors are Standard & Poor's A–1, A–2, and A–3 and Moody's Prime–1, Prime–2, and Prime–3. Exhibit 17 provides descriptions of the Standard & Poor's commercial paper rating categories. However, other

---

EXHIBIT 17   Standard & Poor's Commercial Paper Rating Definitions

Rating Category	Description
A	Issues assigned this highest rating are regarded as having the greatest capacity for timely payment. Issues in this category are delineated with the numbers 1, 2, and 3 to indicate the relative degree of safety.
A-1	This designation indicates that the degree of safety regarding timely payment is either overwhelming or very strong. Those issues determined to possess overwhelming safety characteristics will be denoted with a plus (+) sign designation.
A-2	Capacity for timely payment on issues with this designation is strong. However, the relative degree of safety is not as high as for issues designated "A-1."
A-3	Issues carrying this designation have a satisfactory capacity for timely payment. They are, however, somewhat more vulnerable to the adverse effects of changes in circumstances than obligations carrying the higher designations.
B	Issues rated "B" are regarded as having only an adequate capacity for timely payment. However, such capacity may be damaged by changing conditions or short-term adversities.
C	This rating is assigned to short-term debt obligations with a doubtful capacity for payment.
D	This rating indicates that the issue is either in default or is expected to be in default upon maturity.

SOURCE: Standard & Poor's Corporation Bond Guide.

money market instruments, such as domestic bank negotiable certificates of deposit (CDs), are not rated by these agencies.

Interest rates are higher for securities with greater credit risk, since investors have to be compensated for the additional risk. Consequently, the interest rate on a Treasury security is less than that on an AAA corporate security, which is in turn less than that on an A corporate security, all with the same maturity. These spreads tend to widen when interest rates are high and to narrow when interest rates are low. This is consistent with a "flight to quality," an increased preference by investors for low credit-risk instruments when interest rates are high and investors perceive low credit-risk borrowers as vulnerable. Money market spreads similarly show a widening when interest rates are high and a narrowing when interest rates are low; that is, a flight to quality at high interest rates.

The credit-risk structure of interest rates explains variations in the interest rates on various securities of the same maturity due to differences in the credit risk of the issuers and issues. In addition, the size of the spreads between securities with high credit risk and low credit risk varies with the level of interest rates.

Taxability structure.   There are three aspects of taxability that cause interest rates on different securities to differ at a specific time.

Tax-exempt municipals.   The coupon payments on Treasury and corporate bonds are subject to federal income tax. Consequently, the aftertax yield on Treasury and corporate bonds is less than the coupon yield by an amount determined by the bondholder's tax bracket. The federal government does not tax the coupon payment on state and local securities.[4] Since municipal securities are tax exempt, their aftertax yield is the same as their pretax yield. Because investors are concerned with aftertax rather than pretax yields, municipal securities can be issued with lower coupons than the coupons on similar Treasury or corporate securities. For example, to an investor in the 30 percent tax bracket, a 7 percent municipal security selling at par has the same aftertax yield as a 10 percent Treasury or corporate security.

Thus, municipal bond interest rates differ from the interest rates on Treasury and corporate bonds because of the difference in taxability. The yield spread is always positive; that is, the yield on Treasury bonds is higher than the yield on municipal bonds.

The magnitude of the spread changes over the interest-rate cycle for

---

[4] State and local governments cannot tax the coupon payments of federal securities, but this exemption is not as important as the federal exemption on state and local government securities because the income tax rates of state and local governments are lower than federal income tax rates.

two reasons. First, municipal bonds have a higher credit risk than Treasury bonds, and the phenomenon related to the flight to quality discussed in the last section is applicable. Here the flight to quality is from municipals to Treasuries when interest rates are high. In this case, however, since the rate on Treasury bonds is higher than the rate on municipal bonds, the flight to Treasury bonds during times of high interest rates tends to narrow the spread.

In addition, the spread between Treasury and municipal bond yields changes over the interest rate cycle for reasons of taxability. The spread is the absolute difference between the Treasury and the municipal bond interest rates. However, the tax rate as it is applied to the coupon on Treasury securities has a relative or proportional effect. Thus, for example, to an investor in the 50 percent tax bracket a 4 percent municipal security has the same aftertax yield as an 8 percent Treasury security, for a spread of 4 percent. However, a 6 percent municipal security has the same aftertax yield as a 12 percent Treasury security, for a spread of 6 percent. Similarly, an 8 percent municipal security has the same aftertax yield as a 16 percent Treasury security, for a spread of 8 percent. Thus, because of the proportional nature of the federal income tax structure, the absolute spread between Treasury and municipal bonds varies over the interest rate cycle, being larger when interest rates are high and smaller when interest rates are low.

Overall, since due to the flight to quality the spread between Treasury and municipal bonds narrows when interest rates are high, and due to the proportional nature of the income tax, the spread widens when interest rates are high. Thus the two effects are countervailing. Based on the historical Treasury bond/municipal bond interest rate spreads, the latter effect of interest rates on the spread dominates the former effect.

The spread between municipal and Treasury bonds may also vary structurally due to changes in tax legislation that affect the level of the personal income tax and the attractiveness of other tax shelters that compete with municipal securities as tax-reducing investments.

Level of coupon. A second aspect of taxability also causes interest rates among different securities, even of the same issuer and maturity, to differ *for bonds issued on or before July 18, 1984.* This aspect is the magnitude of the coupon of the security.

Although coupon payments on Treasury and corporate bonds are taxed at the ordinary income tax rate, capital gains are taxed at a preferential tax rate. If a bond is acquired after July 22, 1984 and held for more than six months, the long-term capital gains tax, which is 40 percent of the personal income tax rate, will apply. The holding period to qualify for a long-term capital gain for a bond purchased on or before July 22, 1984 is more than one year. For a bond issued on or before July

18, 1984 and held to maturity, therefore, the aftertax value of 1 percent of pretax coupon return is less to an investor than the aftertax value of 1 percent of pretax capital gains. This does not apply to bonds issued after July 18, 1984 that are held to maturity.[5]

The yield-to-maturity of a bond, as it is commonly calculated, includes both the coupon return and the return due to capital gain or loss (the difference between the current market price and the par value of the bond) on an annual basis as if the security were held to maturity. If, for example, a 30-year security with an $80 coupon is selling for $1,000, its 8 percent yield-to-maturity is entirely due to the coupon return. If another 30-year security with a $60 coupon issued on or before July 18, 1984, is initially selling for $773.77 for an 8 percent yield-to-maturity, its yield-to-maturity consists of a 7.75 percent coupon return, and the remainder is due to the capital gain over the 30-year life. Since this low-coupon "discount security" (a security selling for less than its maturity value of $1,000) has a portion of its return due to capital gains, which is taxed at a lower rate, the aftertax return on the low-coupon discount bond is greater than that of the high-coupon bond selling at "par" (its maturity value of $1,000). Therefore, the price of the discount bond will be bid up, and thus the yield-to-maturity at its new actual trading price will be somewhat less than the 8 percent yield on the par bond. The lower yield on the discount bond will compensate for its more favorable tax treatment.[6] Thus, low-coupon discount bonds normally sell at a yield somewhat lower than high-coupon bonds selling at par or at a premium (at a price greater than its maturity value) or even at a smaller discount because of this tax advantage. The yield spread, almost without exception, is positive (the yield on the high-coupon bond is greater than the yield on the low-coupon bond).

Flower bonds. Several Treasury bonds issued during the 1950s and early 1960s exhibit another type of taxability. These bonds, known as flower bonds, are acceptable *at par* in payment of federal estate taxes when owned by the decedent at death. These bonds were issued with low coupons. Due to their tax advantages, the (pretax) yields on these bonds is lower than on other Treasury bonds without the estate tax eligibility provision.

---

[5] The rules concerning capital gain treatment briefly discussed here do not apply to original issue discount bonds.

[6] If the bond had been issued after July 22, 1984, the entire appreciation realized at maturity would be treated as ordinary income. Also note that at the time of this writing, Congress is considering the elimination of the favorable capital gains tax treatment.

Interest rate structure: A summary. Factors that affect interest rates tend to affect all interest rates in generally the same way. For this reason, discussions of the determinants of interest rates often seem as if there were a single interest rate. This section provides the transition from the consideration of a single interest rate to the actual multiplicity of interest rates observed in the financial world.

There are three major structures of interest rates that contribute to the multiplicity of interest rates observed: the maturity structure, the credit-risk structure, and the taxability structure. There are, in addition, other factors that cause differences in interest rates. One such factor is the liquidity of the security, often measured by the size of the bid/ask spread (the smaller the spread, the more liquid the security). The liquidity of a security may depend on the size of the original issue or the time since the original issue. Securities tend to be less liquid if the original-issue size was small and as the time since original issue increases. These aspects of liquidity supplement the market-risk aspect discussed above.

The fundamental factors that affect these three structures, and changes in the relationships among interest rates on the basis of these structures over the interest-rate cycle, are discussed in this section.

OVERVIEW OF INTEREST-RATE DETERMINATION

Four potentially exclusive rationales for determining the level of "the" interest rate: liquidity preference, loanable funds, inflation and the real rate of interest, and the tone of the market have been discussed. The perspective was on the factors that affect the general level of interest rates at a specific time, not on the differences among various interest rates at a specific time. We then discussed the structures of interest rates, the factors that tend to, given the general level of interest rates, affect the differences among specific interest rates at a specific time. As discussed, the three major factors are the maturity, the credit risk, and the taxability of the specific security. Now we shall integrate these various perspectives on interest rate determination.

Most models of interest rate behavior, whether used for explaining past interest rate behavior or forecasting future interest rate behavior, and whether they are judgmental or econometric models, incorporate elements of the liquidity preference, loanable funds, and inflation and the real rate of interest rationales. Thus these three rationales are viewed as complementary rather than competitive as explanations for interest rate behavior. There are, however, some differences in the applicability of these three rationales and also the tone of the market rationale depending on whether the short-run or long-run responses of interest rates are being considered and whether short-term or long-term interest rates are being considered.

Liquidity preference is an important explanation of very short-run changes in interest rates, particularly changes in short-term interest rates in response to changes in the money supply. Money supply announcements made by the Federal Reserve Bank of New York every week are closely watched, and the financial markets respond quickly to them.

The nature of the response of interest rates, particularly short-term interest rates, to money supply announcements has changed significantly during the last decade. If it was announced a decade ago that money supply had increased significantly, interest rates declined and vice versa, as expected by the liquidity preference rationale. However, today when an announcement is made that money supply has increased significantly, interest rates usually increase rather than decrease, and vice versa. There are two reasons for this change in response.

First, since the mid-1970s the Federal Reserve System has, as an important part of its implementation of monetary policy, set ranges for future money-supply growth. It then conducts monetary policy so that the actual money-supply growth fits within these ranges. Thus, an announcement of a large increase in the money supply is now interpreted by the markets as requiring the Federal Reserve System to subsequently tighten money-supply growth to keep the money-supply growth within the announced ranges. The markets, thus anticipating a subsequent decline in money-supply growth, respond by making interest rates increase in response to the expected tightening. Here again the liquidity preference rationale is operable, but now the market responds to expectations of subsequent money-supply growth rather than to the announcement of the past money-supply growth.

The second reason for the change in response is that inflation has become a more important force in determining interest rates. In view of the quantity theory of money, there is an important relationship between money supply and inflation. Thus an announcement of a high growth in the money supply often causes market participants to conclude that inflation will accelerate, at least if this money-supply growth rate continues, thus causing interest rates to increase due to the inflation and real rate of interest rationale. For both of these reasons, interest rates now often increase rather than decrease when there is an announcement of an increase in the money supply.

Essentially, all explanations of the level of interest rates include some measure of the money supply as a determinant, particularly for short-term interest rates, and particularly for short-run changes. The liquidity preference rationale, however, is also used for determining the level of interest rates on a longer term basis. This use is implemented, as discussed above, in the context of the quantity theory of money: $M \times V = P \times Y$. By forecasting a likely growth in the money supply, M, and a likely range of increases in real GNP, Y, an assumption about the likely range of inflation, P, can be made from the quantity theory. From this rate of inflation and an assumption about the real rate of interest, the nominal rate of interest can be determined. This conceptual construction obviously relies jointly on the liquidity preference and the inflation and real rate of interest rationales of interest-rate determination.

The loanable funds rationale is typically used to explain and forecast interest rates on a long-term basis and applies, in general, to both long- and short-term interest rates. By developing a taxonomy of the likely sources and uses of funds over a period of time, as provided above, and including an assumption about changes in the money supply, a forecast of potential imbalances between the supply and demand for funds can be made. Projected imbalances of supply over demand are then used as the basis for forecasting a decrease in interest rates and of demand over supply for forecasting an increase in interest rates.

It is in this context that crowding out (borrowing by the federal government sector, which makes borrowing by the private sector more expensive or impossible) is considered. In addition, increased borrowing by the business or consumer sectors put upward pressures on interest rates, and vice versa. In the loanable funds context, short- and long-term sources and uses of funds are typically aggregated, thus implicitly assuming substitutability among securities of various maturities.

With the higher levels of inflation seen in the late 1970s and early 1980s, the inflation and real rate of interest rationale has become very important in explaining the nominal level of interest rates. As discussed, although they are attributable both to variations in inflation and variations in the real rate of interest, variations in the nominal rate of interest are more attributable to the former than the latter. Thus the real rate of interest might vary over a range of from −1 percent to 4 percent, and inflation might vary over a range of 5 percent to 15 percent. Therefore, including a measure of inflation in an explanation for the general level of interest rates is essential.

However, it is more difficult to include an accurate measure of the determinants of the real rate of interest. In general, the real rate of interest tends to vary over the business cycle, being high during periods of prosperity and low during periods of recession. Most explanations of the general level of interest rates include inflation explicitly but do not consider the real rate of interest explicitly.

Thus, most explanations of the general level of interest rates include elements of the liquidity preference, loanable funds, and the inflation and real rate of interest rationales, although there are some differences in emphasis depending on whether short-term or long-term interest rates and whether short-term changes or long-term changes in the rates are being considered. The "tone of the market" rationale should also be

---

EXHIBIT 18 Interest Rate Variability by Maturity

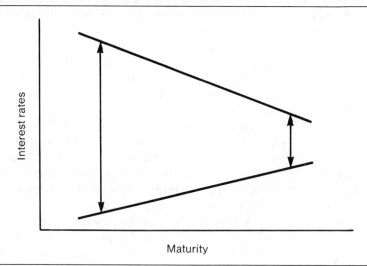

considered in determining interest rates, although typically only for very short run changes and mainly in the short-term interest rates. Therefore, models that forecast quarterly interest rates often do not include the tone of the market.

Having determined the general level of interest rates, or "the" interest rate, by the methods summarized above, consideration can be given to determining specific interest rates on specific securities. To make this determination, given the general level of interest rates, the maturity, the identity of the issuer, and the taxability of the specific security must be considered—that is, the interest rate on the specific security must be considered with respect to the three structures of interest rates discussed above. In relating a specific interest rate to the general level of interest rates, two issues must be considered: (1) the normal spread between the specific interest rate and an interest rate reflective of the general level of interest rates, such as the 91-day Treasury bill rate or the long-term Treasury bond rate, and (2) variations in the magnitude in this spread over the interest-rate cycle.

The conclusions of the three maturity structures of interest rates are as follows. When the level of interest rates is low, interest rates increase with maturity (the term structure of interest rate curve has a positive slope). And when the level of interest rates is high, interest rates decrease with maturity (the term structure of interest rate curve has a negative slope). Thus, short-term interest rates vary through a much wider range than the long-term interest rates, as illustrated in Exhibit 18.

And thus the spread between short-term and long-term interest rates (long term minus short term) varies considerably over the interest-rate cycle and becomes less positive (or more negative) as interest rates increase.

With respect to the identity of the issuer, the greater the credit risk of the issuer, the higher the interest rate on the security. It is in this regard that Treasury securities are the benchmark for interest rates. The Treasury has the lowest credit risk of any issuer, and thus Treasury securities have the lowest adjustment for credit risk. Different issues of the same issuer may also have different credit risks due to the nature of the securities. The spread between high credit-risk interest rates and low credit-risk interest rates (high credit risk minus low credit risk) increases with the level of interest rates, due to a "flight to quality" when interest rates are high.

Finally, the taxability of the issue must be considered. The most important aspect of taxability relates to municipal securities whose coupons are exempt from the federal income tax. Due to this tax exemption, actual pretax interest rates on municipals are lower than on Treasury and corporate securities. Because taxes are on a relative or proportionate basis, the spread between Treasury and municipal securities (Treasury rate minus municipal rate) widens (narrows) as the level of interest rates increases (decreases).

Another aspect of taxability relates to the magnitude of the coupon, which determines the degree of the discount or the premium of a security, since coupon income is taxed as personal income and capital appreciation as capital gains. Thus the higher the coupon on a security, the higher will be its interest rate to compensate for the greater tax liability. Finally, flower bonds have lower yields due to their estate tax advantages.

Overall, the determination of interest rates occurs in two steps. First, the general level of interest rates is determined by the eclectic combination of the methods described above. Second, the appropriate spread between the interest rate on the specific security being considered and the general level of interest rates is determined by considering the factors that affect the structures of interest rates. The benchmark interest rate used in such spread analysis is typically the interest rate on a U.S. Treasury debt security.

11

Market Timing and Technical Analysis

Alan R. Shaw
Senior Vice President
Managing Director
Smith Barney, Harris Upham & Co. Inc.

THE HISTORY AND EVOLUTION OF TECHNICAL SECURITY ANALYSIS

Over recent years, the use of technical analysis in the investment decision-making process has become more commonplace. Today's more sophisticated investor generally has some type of technical application at hand, whether it be a simple chart package, or a sophisticated computer program.

Yet, for some reason, there is still some misunderstanding about the technician's craft. Some critics still flaunt technical analysis as being akin to astrology, or worse.

As we are updating this contribution to the *Handbook,* the stock market as measured by the Dow Jones Industrial Average has just suffered its greatest one-day *point* drop in history, dropping 61.87 points. The financial press was abundant with reasons for the decline, but emphasis has been placed on the "cautious words" having recently been pronounced by a number of stock market technicians. This theory, in turn, resulted in a feature story on the first page of the second section of *The Wall Street Journal.* The headline: "Stock Market's Technical Analysts Get New Respect after Price Drop." While the article does afford a somewhat credible review of some of the negative technical factors that led some analysts to offer words of warning, we suppose to "balance" the story it was necessary to offer a few words of criticism regarding the technical approach. Reading the views of some well-known, but obviously straight-on-fundamentally oriented portfolio managers, we had a feeling of déjà vu. Said one, "These analysts [technicians] might as well look at random numbers and try to predict the next one." Another manager noted, "In the long run, you could do as well with Ouiji boards or tarot cards." An academic input was interesting as well: "These people make a lot of predictions, and occasionally one of them will come right. But listening to them regularly can be hazardous to your wealth."

We sense that more thoughtful students are finally realizing that *all forms* of market analysis have their own particular shortcomings. Random walk is being debunked by the same theoreticians that first supported it. Modern portfolio theory (MPT) has lost many of its original followers. Fundamental earnings estimates are often far off target, and economic forecasts can often turn out to be ill founded, or vary greatly from one economist to another. All forms of analysis are really exercises in educated guess work. Technical methods are no different.

One reason we suspect the technical approach has had more than its share of critics is because there haven't been all that many textbooks available on the subject. Yet many authoritative works on the approach can be found with copyrights dating from the turn of the century, if not earlier. Books on fundamental analysis became greater in number *after* the passage of the Securities and Exchange Commission Acts of 1932, and 1933. To wit, the so-called bible of fundamental analysis, *Security Analysis,* by Graham and Dodd, was first in print as of 1934.

Our research indicates technical analysis is the *oldest* form of security analysis known to man. We believe charts were first used in Japan in the 17th century to plot the price of rice, possibly representing the earliest application of trend analysis disciplines. Technical analysis is a common investment tool in Japan today. The Japanese stock market is the second largest capitalized formal trading market in the world (after the NYSE), and many Japanese technicians use methods more specialized to their market's trends. In the United States, technical applications can be traced back over 100 years when financial statements were *not readily available* for any type of quantitative analysis. In the late 1800s and early 1900s, if a "researcher" visited the corporate offices of a major concern and asked, "How's the business?" he was no doubt politely told, "It is none of yours!"

Over the years we have learned to look at our role of a technician as being close in kind to that of a navigator. We think of our clients as the "pilots," entrusted with the decision-making role in guiding their personal or professional accounts. Technical studies of the market, group behavior, or stock trends can determine evidence of shifting demand/supply activity which can easily be likened to the navigator warning the pilot of a storm ahead. Like the navigator, the technician will not always be correct in his readings, or a change in "patterns" could easily develop rendering the original interpretation invalid. But whatever the outcome, we sure wouldn't want to fly with a pilot that constantly ignores his navigator. Of course, a record of the navigator's "calls" should be maintained as well.

Success in the stock market comes by minimizing risk. But, unfortunately, many look at the market from the viewpoint of reward only, sometimes taking unnecessary risk to achieve it. Buying a stock with apparent strong fundamentals and little regard for the stock's technical position can easily result in a quick loss. Many stocks can "top-out" when, as the saying goes, "business couldn't be better." On the other hand, undue risk is also taken when making a commitment strictly on technical grounds. Many good-looking stocks have fallen out of so-called base formations due to an unexpected poor earnings report. Therefore it seems logical that a combination of both types of securities analysis should result in better decision making and the results that follow. Since technical analysis is primarily a timing tool, it could be said that fundamental analysis represents the "what" input, while technical analysis is the "when."

Cutting losses short is crucial for long-term investment success. We have often referred to a simple philosophy whereby we look at our decision making as an exercise that can result in only one of five eventual outcomes. We can experience an unchanged position, a large profit, large loss, small profit, or a small loss. If we can possibly eliminate one of these outcomes, obviously the large loss, then we are merely left with the other four. Over a number of years the small profits, losses and unchanged positions will "offset" each other. Therefore we are left with the enjoyment of occasionally booking the large profit. Many technical methods can be employed as long-term disciplines to guard against the large loss. We are sure that other analytical inputs can be loss-inhibiting procedures as well, but the author believes the technical approach seems to lend itself quite readily to such an application.

Technical analysis is applicable to all price trends that are founded upon a fairly efficient marketplace where buyers meet sellers in an auction process. As such, applications are not limited to only stocks and stock markets, domestic or international. Indeed, technical analysis can be profitably utilized for bonds, or fixed-income markets, groups or sectors within the stock market, foreign stock markets, currencies and obviously not to be overlooked, commodities. In fact, there are probably more technical methods around today for the growing futures derivatives than any other application. The growth of the personal computer has led to a proliferation of technical software for both stocks and commodities, with the latter really possessing an inordinate number of packages, many sophisticated, but a good number not worth a small fraction of their cost.

Within the space of this chapter, we shall attempt to explore the more standard technical approaches as well as highlight some of the widely followed market indicators with a brief discourse on some personal computer applications.

BASIC TECHNICAL ASSUMPTIONS—NECESSARY LOGICAL THOUGHTS SUPPORTING THE APPROACH

Before embarking into any area of study there is usually a set of rules or assumptions that probably should first be explored. As previously mentioned, technical analysis is based upon the study of supply and demand, or the *price* movements within the general stock (or other) market's framework. It is what the movements themselves mean over the short to longer term, that the technician is concerned with. A well-rounded security analyst who utilizes all inputs available must be a very inquisitive person; he will always be anxious to know "why" a stock is moving up or down. And, in this regard, it has often been said that a good technician has to be an even better fundamentalist.

It is known that the stock market is one of a number of leading economic indicators as compiled by different sources. Although the market is, of course, concerned with day-to-day business developments and worldwide news events, it is *primarily* concerned with future expectations. In this regard, the market is therefore looked at as more of a barometer than a thermometer. Specifically, it has not been uncommon to witness a stock rising in a viable uptrend when *current* news concerning the company is not all that positive. By the same token, one can witness a stock initiate a major downtrend while earnings are most favorable. To carry our thesis a step further, it would be most uncommon to witness a stock begin a major upside trend just *before* earnings start to deteriorate. The reverse oddity would occur if a stock commenced a major downtrend just before earnings began to show substantial recovery.

Let us review what we consider to be the three basic and necessary assumptions regarding technical analysis before we embark on the actual methods themselves.

Assumption 1.   As said, the market and/or an individual stock acts like a barometer rather than a thermometer. Events are usually discounted in advance with movements likely the result of "informed"[1] buyers and sellers at work. We should never forget, as we explore the technical implications of market analysis, that the price formations or patterns (as they are called by some) that evolve due to supply/demand

---

[1] Not to be confused with an insider.

FIGURE 1 Major Trend References

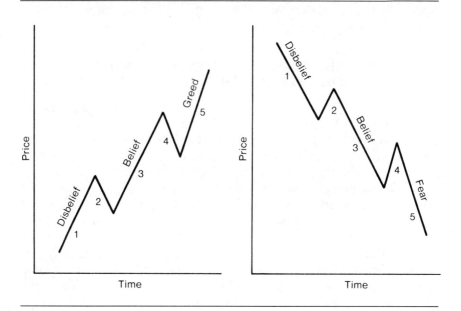

behavior are, for the most part, the result of fundamentalists, speculators, technicians, or whomever, putting their money to work based
upon their established convictions. The market is a *discounting* mechanism.

Market (and stock) trends tend to move to extremes in a psychological sense. On one end you have "greed," which is normally associated
with a top (nobody left to buy), while on the other extreme you have
"fear" (nobody left to sell).

One technical theory that we have supported concerns the "five-
leg" pattern associated with a major trend, up or down. As the
discounting mechanism matures, and more believers emerge to support
a major trend, eventually the above extremes are reached. Figure 1
attempts to portray the discounting scheme. At first, as the stock begins
to climb, the advance is fraught with skeptics abounding. We call this
the disbelief phase (Leg 1). Profit taking develops (Leg 2), which in turn
is followed by another upturn (Leg 3). By now future fundamental
improvement may be more widely accepted (function of stock price?).
We call this the belief leg. Another correction occurs (Leg 4) which is
then followed by the "everyone's-got-to-own-it" stage (greed—Leg 5).
A major bear trend develops most often with the opposite psychological
implications. The stock tops out when the fundamentals look good, and
begins a serious break which is not recognized by most as a new bear

market (disbelief). After a brief rally, a renewed trend of deterioration commences, breaking the prior lows, and possibly accompanied by the first tangible signs of fundamental (earnings) deterioration (belief). After another interim rally, the stock breaks down again, instituting the fear syndrome (Leg 5).

Assumption 2.   This assumption should not be too difficult to understand or accept as it deals with basic stock market dynamics or the law of supply and demand. First, we should define the terms that are used.

We know there is a buyer for every seller of stock. But one of these forces is usually stronger or more influential—especially in the long run. For instance, if 50,000 shares of stock were to change hands on a downtick trade, especially with a concession representing a large spread from the last sale, we would consider that the seller was a stronger influence than the buyer. For, if a buyer (or buyers) were all that anxious to purchase the stock, it would be logical to expect that the trade would have taken place with little or no concession of price at all. In periods of a more vibrant market atmosphere, a trade would, in all likelihood, occur on an uptick. A major concession in price on a large block trade is usually looked upon as evidence of *distribution*, and it can be a sign of the stock moving from strong to weak hands.

Accumulation by definition occurs when a stock moves from weak to strong hands or, more importantly when supply is *eliminated* from the marketplace. Such a trade could take place on an uptick in price.

Our second assumption reads: Before a stock experiences a markup phase, whether it be minor or major, a period of accumulation usually will take place. Conversely, before a stock enters into a major or minor downtrend, a period of distribution usually will be the preliminary occurrence. Accumulation or distribution can occur within neutral trading trends. Accumulation is often referred to as the building of a "base," while a trend of distribution is also called a "top." Obviously an uptrend in prices denotes on-balance buying, while a downtrend is indicative of extreme supply. The ability to analyze accumulation or distribution within neutral price patterns will be discussed later. Such analysis is a prime technical challenge. It can allow the technician to anticipate a move, rather than wait to react to a "breakout."

Assumption 3.   This third assumption is tied into the first two discussed. It is an observation that can be readily made by any student willing to expend the time and effort. It deals with the scope and extent of market movements in relation to each other. As an example, in most cases, a short phase of stock price consolidation—or backing and filling—will be followed by a relative short-term movement, up or down, in the stock's price. On the other hand, a larger consolidation

FIGURE 2

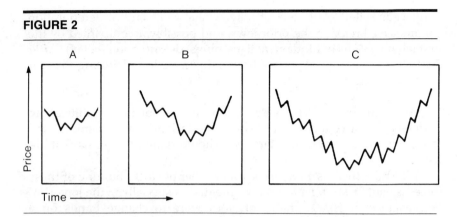

phase can lead to a greater potential stock price move. Figure 2 should aid in the understanding of this assumption.

In Example A, the minor downward movement in price was followed by a short-term consolidation phase before the stock began to move up once again. In Example B, however, the downside adjustment was somewhat more severe than in the former case and thus the consolidation pattern was slightly longer in perspective. Example C is an extreme, reflecting a major downward trend. Simply stated, when the bulldozer, crane, steel ball, and wrecker visited this scene, it took longer for the masons, plumbers, carpenters, and electricians to accomplish their rebuilding process; the consolidation pattern was of longer duration.

Assumption 3 therefore states: *Usually*, movements in the market tend to have a relationship to each other.

These are the three basic assumptions. They are simple and we hope logical to understand. They provide the basis for many technical disciplines, some of which we shall now study.

BASIC TECHNICAL METHODS—CHART UTILIZATION, TYPES, THEIR CONSTRUCTION, AND SERVICES AVAILABLE

Despite the growth of a number of mechanical and/or automated stock market techniques, the basic tool of most technically oriented market students is still the chart. The growth of personal computer use, along with packaged software programs, has led to a more automated approach, but charts are still very often hand drawn. Through the years, three basic types of charting techniques have been developed with perhaps one, the bar graph, enjoying greater popularity.

FIGURE 3

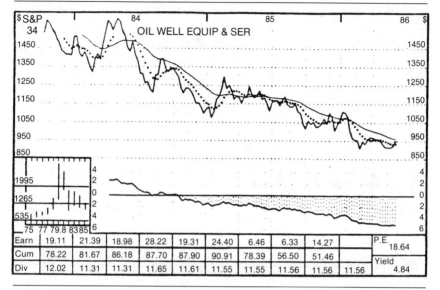

Basic Chart Types

The three standard types of charts are the line, bar, and point and figure. In each case the type of chart chosen to record price activity is determined by the amount of information available, and the purpose of the study.

A *line chart,* as illustrated in Figure 3, is used to denote the trend of a *single* statistic. As an example, the daily closing price of a stock; a weekly group statistic; or a monthly economic figure would most often be plotted on a line chart basis. Figure 3 illustrates a group statistic plotted weekly. In addition, the illustration also contains moving averages (running through the price curve), as well as a relative strength line denoted at the graph's bottom.

The *bar chart* is the most commonly used technical tool. It is simple to construct as it portrays the high, low, and closing prices of a particular stock or stock market average, for a particular time period chosen. In the latter regard, bar charts are kept either on a daily, weekly, or monthly basis. The type of bar chart will, of course, be predicated upon the time horizon of the investor. The *short-term trader* would most likely find the *daily* bar chart of help while the *longer-term investor* would most likely utilize the *weekly* or *monthly* bar chart. In addition to price action, a bar chart also contains a volume histogram (see Figure 4), especially the daily and weekly varieties. Most often the monthly bar chart simply reveals price action. The daily and weekly commercial chart services

FIGURE 4

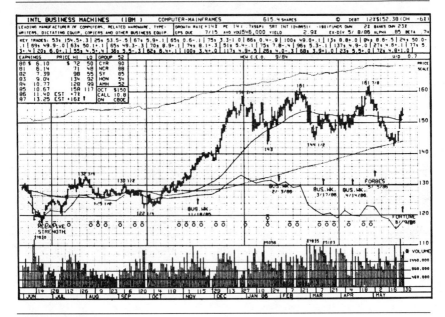

DAILY BAR CHART

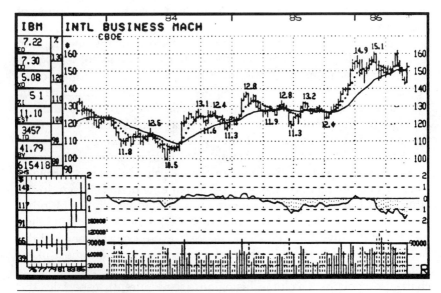

WEEKLY BAR CHART

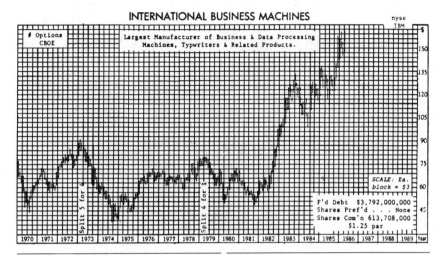

INTERNATIONAL BUSINESS MACHINES

MONTHLY BAR CHART
SOURCE: M.C. Horsey & Co., Inc., Salisbury, MD 21801.

illustrated also include moving averages and relative strength plots (discussed later).

The two types of charting techniques reviewed above can be portrayed on graph paper utilizing one of two types of scales—the arithmetic or semilog delineation. Again, the utilization of the type of scale depends greatly upon the desires of the chartist. There are those who wish to analyze stock price movements on a percentage basis and therefore their graphs would be kept on a semilog basis. Long-term trend analysis is often more useful on a semilog (geometrical) price scale. On the other hand, simple short-term trend analysis, or stock price movement in terms of points rather than percentages, is desired by others. Thus, for them, a straight arithmetic scale suffices. Figure 5 illustrates a bar chart plotted with a semilog scale and an arithmetic scale for about the same time period. There are positive and negative factors for each approach, most often hinging on the price level of the stock and the amount of price history under study.

The *point and figure* method represents the third technique. To many, the point and figure approach is a bit more mysterious, and indeed to some, the mastering of the technique of maintaining a point and figure (P&F) chart is a cumbersome chore. Unlike the bar chart, the basic difference in a point and figure graph is that there is no element of time, and therefore no distinct depiction of volume trends. But, it can be argued that volume to a certain degree is incorporated in a point and figure chart in a relative sense. On a P&F graph one does not put in a figure (the use of an *x* is most commonly practiced) until the stock moves up or down one full point or more (thus the name). Therefore, it stands to reason that more figures will be plotted for an active stock than for an

FIGURE 5

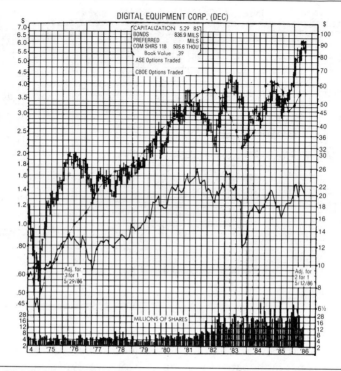

SEMILOG MONTHLY BAR CHART

SOURCE: Securities Research Company, A Division of United Business Service Company, 208 Newbury Street, Boston, MA 02116.

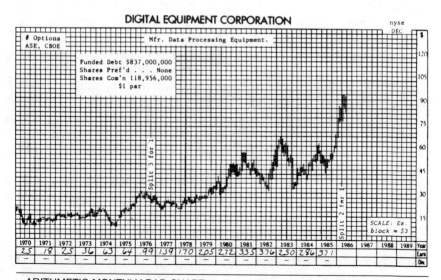

ARITHMETIC MONTHLY BAR CHART

SOURCE: M. C. Horsey & Company., Inc., Salisbury, MD 21801.

inactive one; volume will create price reversals. Remembering that a plot is only made when a full-point movement is experienced, the next factor to keep in mind is that each column on a point and figure chart must represent a *trend* or a direction in price. Remembering these two inputs should add greatly in the understanding of point and figure chart construction.

Like the bar chart, there are a number of different types of point and figure graphs utilized—again, depending upon the investor's time horizon or investment philosphy. The one-point reversal, which as mentioned, illustrates movements of one point or more in each direction, is the most popular point and figure approach. But, if a more intermediate to longer-term trend analysis of a particular equity is desired, no doubt a *three-point* or *five-point reversal* chart will be utilized. In the latter two cases, each column on the graph illustrates movements of a minimum of three or five points in each direction, respectively. In some cases, to further facilitate longer-term stock price movement analysis, point and figure charts are kept on a *unit* basis. Put simply, a reversal chart of more than one point, such as a three- or five-point reversal, condenses the horizontal axis of the graph, while the use of a unit scale reduces the vertical axis. A chart on a stock like IBM would, no doubt, also be kept on three- or five-point reversals, as well as on a unit basis. In fact, a combination of all can be utilized. Versatility is a great asset of the P&F approach. Figure 6 illustrates the IBM example. We have highlighted the time factor on each graph within the same designated space.

Let us be more specific regarding the construction technique for a point and figure graph. Whereas a bar chart depicts a daily, weekly, or monthly specific price range, a point and figure chart illustrates trades only as they occur, *and in their sequence.* Figure 7 provides a theoretical illustration of a week's price movement in a particular stock. The first set of statistics indicates the initial day's opening (O), high (H), low (L), and close (C), with an accompanying illustration showing how these statistics would be produced on a daily bar chart. Volume is added below. The second set of statistics, however, actually shows the sequence of trades with the fractions eliminated from each day's stock price movement. Or, put another way, the second set of data outline each day's high and low differential, but with a sense of the intraday trend.

To construct a point and figure chart, a starting point must be realized. This is illustrated by the darkened square at the price of 47. Monday's trading reveals that the first full one-point move occurred as a decline to 46, before an intraday move up to 47. Remembering that each column on a point and figure chart must represent a "trend," it is therefore mandatory that column 1 cannot contain one "fill-in" by itself. Thus, to start our chart, the first *x* is placed at the 46 line representing Monday's first full-point move. Because the column now contains a

FIGURE 6

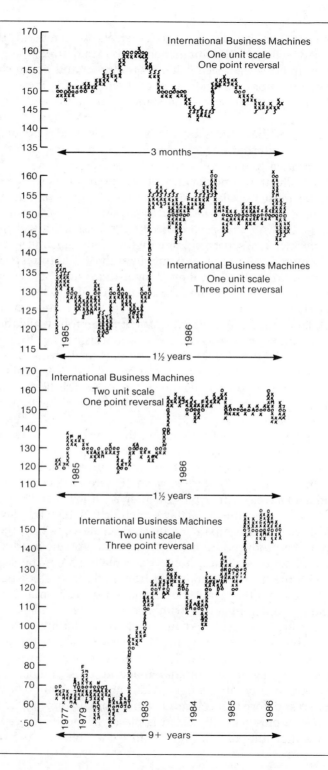

FIGURE 7

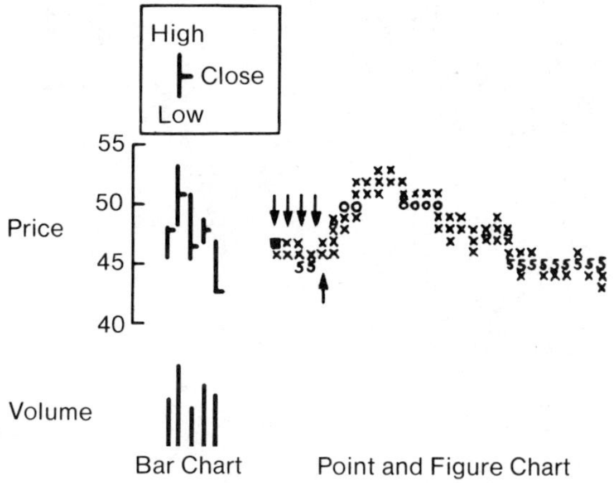

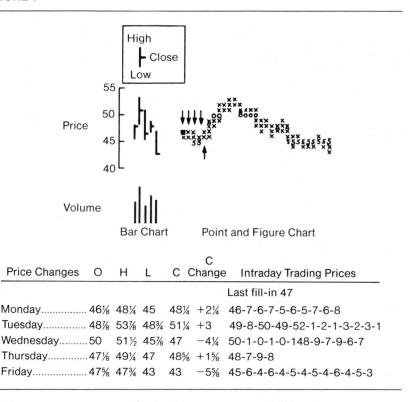

Price Changes	O	H	L	C	C Change	Intraday Trading Prices
						Last fill-in 47
Monday	46⅛	48¼	45	48¼	+2¼	46-7-6-7-5-6-5-7-6-8
Tuesday	48⅞	53⅞	48¾	51¼	+3	49-8-50-49-52-1-2-1-3-2-3-1
Wednesday	50	51½	45⅞	47	−4¼	50-1-0-1-0-148-9-7-9-6-7
Thursday	47⅛	49¼	47	48⅝	+1⅝	48-7-9-8
Friday	47⅝	47¾	43	43	−5⅝	45-6-4-6-4-5-4-5-4-6-4-5-3

movement in sequence from 47 to 46, it can be classified as a "down" column (see arrow). This means that from this point on, if there were never to be an up move of one point or more over a period of one day, week, two weeks, and so on, we would continuously plot the down moves of the stock in the first column of the grid. However, we note that following the initial 46 entry, the stock does move up to 47. Therefore, to record the 47 price, we must move one column to the right, up one box, and place an *x* in the 47 slot. The next intraday move is back down to a full number price of 46, thus we move a box below the last 47 fill-in as, once again, the chart cannot have a "trendless" column. Completing this maneuver, we would now have two down columns in succession. According to the statistics, we note that the next reversal is back up to 47. Thus, we move a column to the right and repeat the procedure to record the 47 move. The next illustrated trade again reveals some intraday pressure taking the stock to the low of the day or a price of 45. To record this movement and reach the 45 level, an *x* must be placed in the 46 box, and then a fill-in is made at 45. (Note: On the 45 line, instead

FIGURE 8

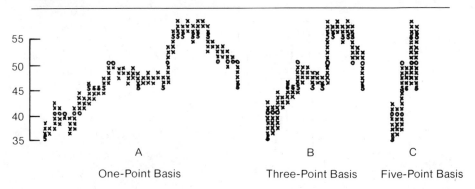

of an x, the digit 5 is used. Similarly, with prices ending in a zero, a 0 is used. The use of fives and zeros simply helps break up the monotony of a concentrated group of xs and makes the "chart reading" easier.

From 45, the stock rallies briefly to 46 before once again reacting to 45. This sequence of reversals is plotted next. Then a strong rally to 47 occurs. In order to move to 47, from the last fill-in at 45, a fill-in is required in the 46 slot. (There is no such thing as a "gap" on a P&F chart.) As you will note, this is the first up column we have recorded in the brief pattern. From 47, a reaction to 46 takes place necessitating a move to the next column and down one box. The stock then closes on a firm note necessitating fill-ins to 48. As the first line of the statistic indicates, the close was actually 48¼, but a full number 48 was the last reversal we will plot on the point and figure graph. Only if the stock had managed to reach 49 would an extra box have been added to the chart. The reader can study the following days' price reversals and how they are plotted on the graph. It is advisable for those who wish to pursue the construction technique in greater detail to make a practice example using the price reversals as set forth and then compare their chart to the one illustrated in final form in Figure 7.

As mentioned earlier, the one-point reversal chart is the most commonly kept point and figure graph. But, if one wishes to condense the one-point chart so that a longer-term analysis can be accomplished, the three-point reversal or five-point reversal approach is advised. The three-point reversal, as the title indicates, simply reveals all movements of three points or more in each direction and eliminates the minor fluctuations. Figure 8A is a one-point chart and has been condensed in Figure 8B to a three-point basis. A close study of the chart will reveal the technique described. The five-point reversal chart is shown in Figure 8C, and illustrates an even greater condensation of the original one-point chart. It is obvious, that a three- or five-point reversal chart will only be necessary if many columns of price reversals on a one-point graph are to be condensed. Some astute short-term traders maintain their point and figure charts on a half-point basis. This necessitates a lot more work and is probably only useful for stocks selling at very low quotes.

Because it is necessary to maintain a point and figure chart with accurate statistics, and because the point and figure chart does reveal *intraday movements in their sequence* of trading, a newspaper will not normally suffice as a source of data. This is especially true regarding higher priced stocks where intraday price reversals can be quite numerous. Some point and figure chartists used to maintain their P&F graphs by utilizing the "Fitch Sheets," a service published by Francis Emery Fitch and most often found in the back office section of brokerage firms. The service included the daily price movements, in their sequence, for all listed stocks from the opening to the close. Students interested in maintaining their own point and figure charts can secure a service, "The MFS Report," published by Mellon Financial Services. This outfit publishes a computerized price change service designed specifically for point and figure chartists. The computer eliminates fractions and, supplies daily price reversals in alphabetical order by symbol (see Figure 9).

A common query is, "Well, what type of chart should I maintain?" Or, "Why a bar chart instead of a point and figure chart?" These are questions difficult to answer because the investment objectives of the different practitioners must first be understood. Bar charts have certain advantages over point and figure charts. They are often favored by short-term traders. On the other hand, point and figure charts have a certain advantage over bar charts, particularly on an intermediate to longer-term basis. Ideally, both approaches should be used hand in hand when analyzing any particular stock. In the discussion that follows, perhaps the reader can distinguish the advantages most pertinent to his needs. Figure 10 lists a number of the more popular commercial technical chart services that may be purchased for both the bar and point and figure approaches. As noted, many of the commercial services also contain studies on general stock market indicators, group profiles, and so on.

BASIC TECHNICAL METHODS (CONTINUED)—ANALYSIS OF SUPPORT AND SUPPLY LEVELS

One of the most important aspects of technical analysis, the type of chart technique notwithstanding, involves the judgment of so-called support and resistance levels. Schematics are shown in Figure 11. Often one reads about a stock that is selling, let us say, at 36, having support at

FIGURE 9

```
POINT AND FIGURE PRICE CHANGES        SECTION  1  DAILY SERVICE    PAGE   1
                    MELLON FINANCIAL SERVICES
              161 WILLIAM ST., NYC 10038
                    TEL  212-766-2700
        THE MFS REPORT            SHOWING ALL ONE POINT EVEN DOLLAR PRICE
CHANGES FOR ALL COMMON STOCKS LISTED ON THE NEW YORK STOCK EXCHANGE
                          01-06-87                        ISSUE 2196
```

AGS	31	AVT	27	CAO	36	DSN	29	FHP	48
AMP	38	AYD	26	CRS	32	DEX	23	FHP	49
AZP	30	AYD	27	CRN	37	DIG	23	FHP	47
AFP	76	AYD	26	CAR	79	DEC	108	BEN	36
AFP	77	BLL	37	CAR	78	DEC	110	BEN	37
AFP.WI	38	ONE	24	CGC	17	DEC	109	BEN	36
ABF	31	BCM	39	CNT	58	DIS	48	FQA	25
APD	37	BCM	41	CNT	57	DIS	49	GMT	35
ABS	44	BT	49	CV	29	DIS	48	GTE	60
AL	30	BNR	22	CRT	33	DOV	47	GEC	105
ASN	43	BCS	30	CMB	38	DOV	46	GCI	37
AAL	25	B	32	CHL	44	DJ	42	GMI	13
ALX	42	BBF	34	CB	63	DJ	41	GDV	19
AT	41	BAX	21	CC	31	DSL	22	GD	73
AT	42	BAY	27	CIR	19	DRY	33	GRL	20
AT	41	BGC	24	CLE	10	DRY	34	GIS	46
AT	42	BI	22	CGP	38	DUK	48	GRX	17
AMB	45	BLC	52	CGP	39	DNB	111	GSX	46
AC	90	BLC	53	CCE	15	DNB	110	GRN	58
AC	88	BMS	33	PMA	59	DNB	111	GRN	60
ACA	23	BMS	32	CSP	33	DD	89	GP	40
ACY	81	BS	08	CSP	32	ESY	32	GEB	42
AEP	29	BIP	26	CDO	17	EPI	39	GRB	19
AXP	61	BA	52	CWE	36	EFU	29	GTY	22
AFL	28	BA	51	CES	41	ETN	77	GOT	21
AGC.WS	18	BCC	65	CMY	32	EBS	35	GRA	51
AHP	79	BBN	43	CPQ	21	AGE	29	GRA	52
AIT	137	BBN	44	CPQ	22	EME	11	GNN	70
AIG	63	BDS	15	CA	29	EGN	21	GNT	25
AIG	66	BSE	27	CA	30	ENE	41	G	33
AIG	64	BMY	85	CTG	21	ESC	19	GFD	26
AIG	65	BTY	32	CNC	13	EFG	08	GW	66
AST	44	BRK	23	CIC	48	ESB	33	GW	67
ASC	58	BG	37	CTB	27	FEN	12	GW	66
ASC	57	BNS	21	GLW	57	FCI	09	HAL	26
AWK	43	BUR	43	CBL	35	FFF	42	JHI	25
AHR	11	BNI	59	CBL	34	FMO	42	HBJ	29
ADD	23	BNI	58	CYR	86	FNM	42	HSC	27
APC	21	BDC	14	CYR	87	FNM	41	HMX	29
BUD	28	CBS	135	CYR	86	FBO	30	HMX	28
ARS	19	CBS	136	CUM	69	FDS	87	HPC	53
ACK	31	CBS	135	CW	55	FDS	88	HPC	55
ARM	15	CAF	56	DMN	15	FIN	09	HPC	54
ATA	27	CZM	44	DHR	14	FIR	28	HSY	26
ASH	58	CIW	12	DAY	30	FBS	27	HLT	70
ARC	62	CPB	59	DAY	31	FNB	31	HIT	68
AUG	17	CCB	276	DH	44	I	56	HIA	72
AUG	18	CCB	275	DF	29	FVB	30	HIA	73
AUS	20	CCB	276	DE	24	FW	39	HLY	101
AUD	37	CCB	275	DAL	50	FLE	27	HLY	100
AUD	38	CCB	276	DLX	39	FLA	48	HLY	101
AVE	29	CPH	34	DLX	38	F	61	HMC	85

SOURCE: The Mellon Financial Services, "The MFS Report," January 6, 1987.

28–30, with potential overhead resistance at 43–45. Just what is the writer talking about?

Let us assume that you have been following the price movement of a certain stock that has been trading for a period of time in a neutral fashion—or fluctuating between the levels of 26 and 30. Obviously, during this neutral price movement the forces of supply and demand

FIGURE 10

Service	Publisher and Location	Type	Markets	Averages, a; Groups, b; Indicators, c
Chartcraft	Chartcraft, Inc. Larchmont, N.Y.	P&F—monthly x3	NYSE AMEX OTC Options	a,b,c
		P&F—quarterly x3	NYSE	a
		P&F—weekly x3	AMEX Options	a
Market Charts	Market Charts, Inc. New York, N.Y.	P&F x1,x3	AMEX NYSE	a,b,c
Cycli-Graphs Security Charts	Securities Research Boston, Mass.	Bar—monthly	AMEX	a,c
		Bar—weekly	NYSE	a,b,c
		Bar—35 year (Semi-log)		a,b
Daily Graphs	William O'Neil & Co. Inc. Los Angeles, Cal.	Bar—daily (Arithmetic)	AMEX NYSE	a,c
Horsey—The Stock Picture 25-Year Picture	M. C. Horsey & Co. Salisbury, Md.	Bar—monthly (Arithmetic)	NYSE,AMEX (1900 stock total)	a,b
Mansfield	R. W. Mansfield Jersey City, N.J.	Bar—weekly (Arithmetic)	AMEX,NYSE, OTC	a,b,c
Trendline	Trendline Div. New York, N.Y. Standard & Poor's	Bar—daily (Arithmetic)	NYSE AMEX (Total-728 stocks)	a,c

FIGURE 11

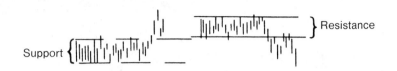

have been fairly equal. Ultimately the stock will break out of this consolidation pattern in either an upward or downward direction. If the direction is upward, thus indicating a surge of demand, a distinctive clue would be given that the on-balance activity that most likely occurred during the consolidation phase was accumulation rather than distribution (review Assumption 2). Let us assume you made a commitment in the stock in the 26–30 zone prior to the upside breakout.

Often, an investment "story" is not bought by all on the first go-round. Some extra convincing is necessary. Such convincing can be accomplished by the mere price performance of the stock itself. In our illustration, the stock has just moved up in price as profiled by the breakout from the consolidation phase. Let us assume that some adverse external news comes to the fore, and the stock experiences some minor selling pressure, falling back to the area of the original price consolidation. Chances are quite good that those who purchased shares initially would *not* now be sellers of the stock. In fact, they may even be inclined to buy more. And, of added importance, investors who did not purchase the shares initially may now seize upon this *second* opportunity to make a commitment. The motivations just discussed are primarily predicated upon (1) the recent price activity in the stock, during which it was just selling at a higher price after breaking out of the consolidation trend and (2) a feeling of confidence, to a degree based on this price action, that the stock will eventually resume its upward trend. It is mainly because of these psychological factors that market analysts would anticipate that the stock in question should find support between 26 and 30. At least initially, there is a good chance of the stock bouncing back up.

Thus, by definition, a support level is a phase of price consolidation—or congestion—*below* the current quotation of a stock. Utilizing Assumption 3 for a minute, the extent of the lateral consolidation often has a bearing on the validity of the support. Minor consolidation suggests a minor support level, where a more elongated congestion zone would suggest major support.

It should now be simple to explain resistance (or supply). Let us say your investment made between 26–30 turns out to have been an error in judgment. Instead of the stock moving up, it breaks down out of the congestion pattern, reaching a level of 20. Mass psychology now begins to work quite differently. Rather than taking the opportunity to buy more shares at the current cheaper price, many investors will simply bemoan their mistake and hope for a chance to break even. This psychological behavior suggests that on any strength back into the overhead consolidation area, the stock will meet supply, or sellers will dominate. Whereas in the first example you did not buy the stock to break even, in the latter case you are hoping that a break-even position can be attained. Thus, by definition, a resistance zone is an area of price activity *above* a stock's current quotation. The influence of the resistance may well depend upon the duration of the consolidation pattern.

Support and supply levels in individual stocks are real, as people are actively buying and selling the specific equities. But, it is important to recognize that when talking about support and supply levels for market averages, they are more psychological than real; one does not buy and sell the averages directly. Furthermore, using the Dow Jones Industrial Average as an example, when the Dow was "first" at 1100 (before moving to 1300), the prices of its 30 stocks were more or less quite different than the "second" time the Dow came back to "support" at 1100.

Knowing the type of security being analyzed also aids in deciding the extent of support or supply validity. Digital Equipment possesses different market characteristics than American Telephone. Where one issue may attract trading money, the other may enjoy a greater "investment" stature. Thus, if we were analyzing a supply area of three previous years for both stocks, our respect for the Telephone configuration might be much greater than for Digital.

Trend Analysis

Many users of technical analysis do not wish to get too involved in all the possible applications. In fact, they could use their market charts as nothing more than a road map is used to travel across the country. Trend analysis of stock price movements, as an example, aids the investor to at least examine where on the route he will be making a commitment. The simple observation of a stock's chart can reveal to the portfolio manager the precise point in trend where a particular issue is currently being recommended. The stock may have already moved up in price from $30 to $85 per share. He can therefore ask an analyst making a presentation, "Where have you been with your story before visiting me?" And perhaps, more importantly, he may add, "Where do you still have to go when you leave here?" The portfolio manager's observation of the chart pattern reveals the stock's price performance and certainly indicates that he is not the first to hear the bullish tale and, more importantly, he had better not be the last.

As simple as it is, a trendline can be a powerful technical tool to the novice and professional alike. "The trend is your friend," is the positive cliché to the old "Don't fight the trend" slogan. Trendlines give guidance to the short-term trader and the investor. The trader can use trend progressions for the establishment of "stop-loss" disciplines while the investor can "let his profits run" using the elementary trendline approach. Trendlines can also keep the "bottom fisher" from entering too early and getting caught in the final declining phase (often the most dramatic) of the given stock's bear market. A stock can't go up until it stops going down, and the breaking of down trendlines will be the first clue that negative momentum is waning.

Stock (and market) trends often tend to accelerate at or near the end of a move. On the upside, the acceleration of demand can be likened to the "everyone's got to own 'em" stage. On the downside, the familiar climactic "washout" occurs. These respective trends we also refer to as the greed and fear stages.

It should be remembered that the mere violation of a trendline is not the sole reason a technician becomes concerned. It's the implied change in the supply/demand trend behind the shift that is meaningful. An uptrend, by definition, is a series of higher lows followed by higher highs, in that sequence. A downtrend is, of course, the opposite progression. Sticking with the uptrend, let's more fully define the higher low, higher high progression in terms of supply/demand. Who creates the higher low? The higher high?

It is simple logic that a buyer, or demand, is the force creating the higher lows in an uptrend. And the persistence of demand, over time, is what creates the higher low pattern. On the supply side, the seller(s) is actually profiling a *bullish* bent. How? Because he is selling at progressively higher levels. So, an uptrend is not just a series of higher lows and higher highs but actually the portrayal, over time, of bullish signs of demand and supply. Once these forces begin to change their style (for whatever reason), the technician will be alerted by trend violations. Uptrend violations will most often be spotted by the demand factor first giving a clue of change. The higher lows will not follow through. Then the technician will look for signs of a change in the supply side, which will manifest itself by a change in the progression of the higher highs. Lower highs, followed by lower lows, will be the complete evidence of a trend change from positive to negative. We cover this a bit more later.

Figure 12 contains six charts from the long-term, monthly *Securities Research Cycli-Graph*. Technical theory suggests that semilog scales are quite helpful for long-term trend analysis. These charts would seem to support that view. Armco's major trend is still negative, but you can note the intermediate-term trends that developed within the longer-term progression. The chart of Great Western Financial continues to display positive supply/demand characteristics while Marion Laboratories certainly exemplifies "the trend is your friend" at work. Note, however, that Marion uptrends are developing a more accelerated profile, thus possibly indicating the stock may be nearing an "exhaustion" phase. The trader would be more conscious of the Marion uptrend in place since late 1985 while the investor, immediate or long term, may place more emphasis on the longer-term uptrends back to 1984 or 1981. Morse Shoe displays "fanning" tendencies and the last two rallies halted under the price uptrend—not necessarily a long-term positive. Diebold terminated a major uptrend in early 1984, then violated "support" at roughly 46, and currently profiles a negative trend progression. Smith International is the mirror image of Marion Laboratories. Smith represents a good example of the hazards of "bottom fishing" over the past four years. As the stock approached "ultimate support," a climactic decline was experienced.

We try to remember that stocks often look "expensive" in bull markets, yet they can continue to climb. Stocks often look "cheap" in major bear trends, and they can get "cheaper." Trend analysis, while very simple, provides an important discipline for "letting profits run," and "cutting losses short."

Moving Averages

In addition to the above-stated approach to trend analysis, market students also may follow *moving averages* of a stock's price trend. A moving average is really a *mathematical* trendline. Moving averages can be calculated for different time periods such as a 10-day moving average for the short term, a 50-day moving average for the intermediate term, or a 200-day moving average for longer-term analysis.

There are three types of moving averages used by technicians. These are: (1) simple; (2) weighted; and (3) exponential. A simple moving average is calculated merely by adding the closing prices of the number of days under question and dividing by the number of days. A 200-day moving average would be the sum of the closes for the previous 200 market days divided by 200. The simple moving average treats all the entries equally.

The weighted and exponential moving averages will place more emphasis on the more recent price activity. Many market students take the time (or use their computers) to calculate the weighted or exponential varieties as they feel the more recent price action is indeed more important than the price of 25, 50, or 200 days ago.

The weighted moving average is really simple to calculate, but time consuming. For a 10-day weighted moving average, we would take the

FIGURE 12

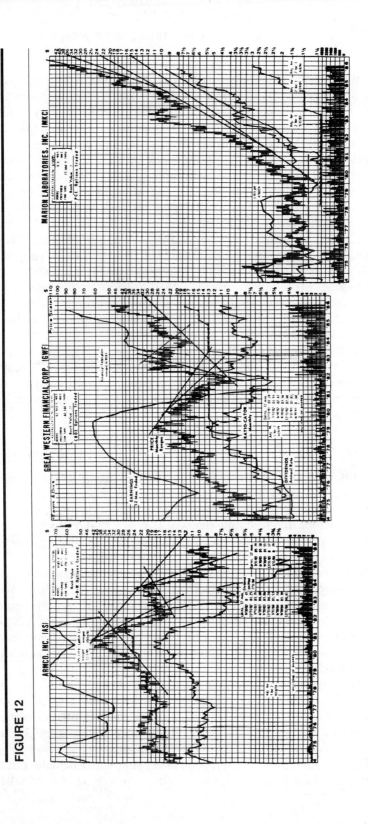

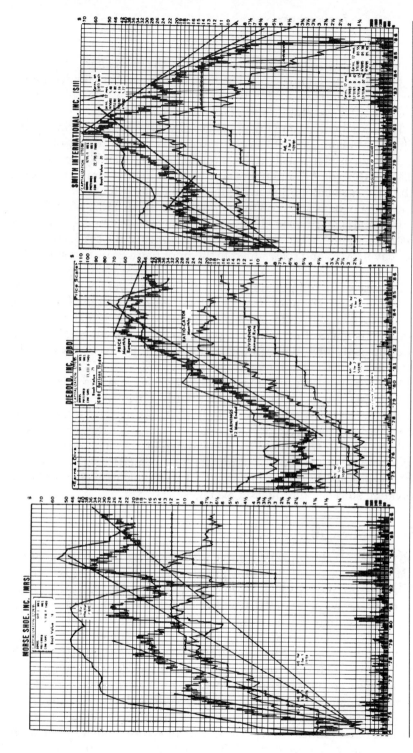

SOURCE: Securities Research Company, A Division of United Business Service Company, 208 Newbury St., Boston, Mass. 02116.

current day and multiply the price times 10, the day before times 9, the day before times 8, and so on. The final number is then divided by the sum of the multipliers for the 10-day period which would be x divided by 55.

The exponential moving average (EMA) which is akin to the weighted version, is even more simple to calculate in that only two numbers are used in a daily calculation, today's price and the prior day's EMA are utilized. A "smoothing constant" is first determined to use in each day's calculation. Simply defined, divide the number 2 by 1 plus the number of days you wish to smooth. For a 10-day EMA—2 is divided by 10 + 1 (11) and equals 0.18, which is the smoothing constant. The constant is multiplied by each day's closing price of the stock minus the prior day's EMA, and then added to the prior day's EMA to result in the new EMA.

Because of its computation, a moving average will always lag stock price movement. The movement of a stock below an uptrending moving average is considered to be a sign of impending weakness. More important is that as the moving average itself flattens out and begins to trend down, it often will confirm that a shift in the basic trend in the stock has occurred.

While most of the popular commercial chart services carry 50- or 200-day simple moving averages, it's fairly obvious that a constant moving average is probably not applicable to each and every stock. Individual equities have their own particular market characteristics or volatility factors that should dictate different moving average time periods to track their individual trends. New computer software allows the technician to *optimize* or find the most applicable moving average for individual stocks and/or market averages.

Relative Strength

One of the oldest approaches of technical analysis, and still one of the most widely used is relative strength. As the term signifies, action of a stock or a group of stocks is often compared to the market as a whole, so that it can be determined whether or not the stock is acting better than or worse than the market.

Making money in a bull market is not a difficult task. If the general trend is up, we agree that a "dart" thrown at the stock table should result in the "choice" of a winner. In these days of competitive performance on the professional level, relative performance has taken on an even more important aspect. Professional portfolio managers must show the ability to outperform the market or else funds can be invested in an "index fund" that is guaranteed to emulate the market with little or no management fee. Such "passive" portfolio management has grown extensively in recent years for at least a portion of pension assets. Some academic studies have supported a difficulty in outper-forming the market on a consistent basis.

Technicians often apply relative strength analysis first to the market's groups, believing that a strong group is a prerequisite to picking a strong stock. Our research supports this view. While one can, of course, pick a good-acting stock from a broad relative strength stock screen, it's a lot easier if the tide of the group's behavior is supportive.

Many different mathematical computations may be used to calculate relative strength, but the simplest (and most common) is when the daily (or weekly) close of a stock (or group) is divided by a market average or index, most often the S&P 500. The result can be related to a specific time period to result in a *ratio*. If this ratio moves up or down over a period of time, it will indicate whether or not the stock is acting better than or worse than the general market trend. A stock that is moving laterally while the market is trending lower will possess a strong relative strength curve. A stock that is moving laterally as the market moves laterally will possess flat relative strength, indicating that the issue is acting in line with the general market trend.

Relative strength is an important technical tool but must be used properly. As an example, it should be noted that, without utilizing any other technical discipline, one could find a stock "topping" out while maintaining a strong relative strength curve—or it could bottom out while relative strength appears poor. Thus, it is inadvisable to utilize relative strength as a sole technical tool.

Many times the technician will use relative strength to determine future market leadership, or the pending loss of same. Groups that act well in the tail end of a bear market, often emerge as the new bull market's leaders. Leaders in a bull market may show signs of losing that status if relative strength "divergence" begins to profile a mature trend. Simply said, if the absolute price index of a group goes on to make a bull trend high without the relative numbers confirming, a change in the group's trend may not be far off.

TECHNICAL ANALYSIS OF INDIVIDUAL STOCKS

Bar Chart Analysis

At this stage we will briefly explain some of the basic tenets of technical analysis, now that the construction of charts and some of the routine technical methodologies have been reviewed. In particular, the ability to distinguish major trend reversals in a stock's performance is important. It is in this regard that a great deal of the mystery regarding technical analysis comes to the fore. Perhaps the terminology itself is at fault. Our purpose is to be brief and not to get too deeply involved in semantics or esoteric technical definitions.

One of the common reversal patterns that occurs on the different charts of stock price movement is called a *head and shoulders* configuration. We suppose that some observer came up with this descriptive name many decades ago simply because the pattern does profile those parts of the human anatomy for which it is named. The head and shoulders reversal pattern is really nothing more than the indication of a stock moving from an uptrend to a downtrend, or vice versa (see Figure 13).

While observing such a reversal phase, it is important to note volume trends. As an example, if a head and shoulders top is being formed, volume on each of the rally phases within the top formation usually decreases. On the other hand, if it is a head and shoulders bottom that is being observed, volume should show an increase on each of the rally phases within the reversal pattern. The completion of a head and shoulders top or bottom is not considered final until the penetration of a so-called neckline. In a top formation, this neckline is really nothing more than a support line. Put another way, the penetration of such a support line usually coincides with the initiation of the new trend; it will represent a new reaction low.

Variations of the above-mentioned reversal formations are great in number. The so-called double and triple top and bottom classifications are but two (see Figure 14).

Often, stocks may also display very unusual price and/or volume activity while coming to a peak or a trough in their major trends. Such action may be followed by consolidation at either a lower (in the case of a top) or higher (in the case of a bottom) trading range than where the extreme high or low level was first registered. Many times, such unusual price and/or volume action is caused by external news coming to the fore, and the trend in force is accentuated and an extreme level in stock prices is at least temporarily reached.

While talking about reversal formations in particular, there are some easy rules that can be followed to aid the technical student in his judgment. Strangely enough, a good deal of analytical frustration materializes simply by the lack of logical reasoning. A beginning technical practitioner may find himself reading more into stock price behavior than, in fact, exists. We have prepared the "seven question" discipline, and the queries tend to occur in the offered sequence. A "floater" is added for additional reference. An illustration (Figure 15) is offered to enhance the presentation.

First of all, when analyzing a stock for a potential reversal in trend, a simple but most important question must be asked. *"Does the stock have a move of substance to reverse?"* A major reversal formation certainly would not be looked for in a stock that has only moved from 20 to 26, but if a move from 20 to 60 had been experienced, any reversal in trend could be major.

FIGURE 13

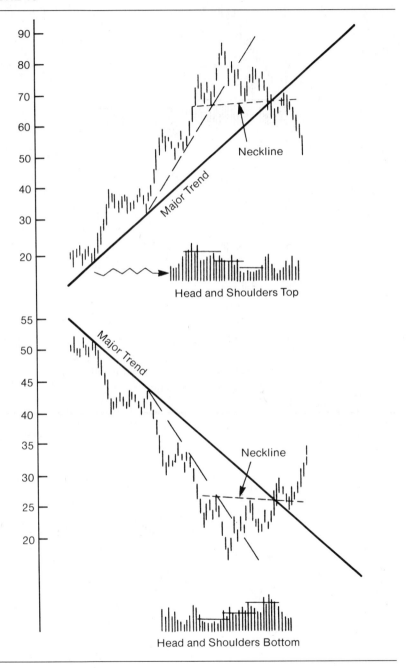

Neckline

Major Trend

Head and Shoulders Top

Major Trend

Neckline

Head and Shoulders Bottom

FIGURE 14

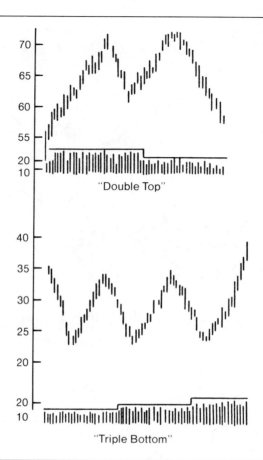

"Double Top"

"Triple Bottom"

FIGURE 15

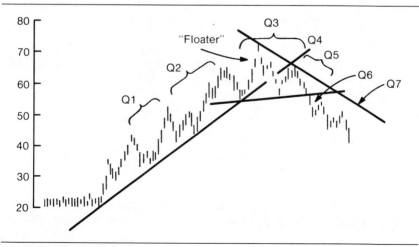

THE SEVEN QUESTIONS (WITH A "FLOATER")

If the first question is answered yes, we then ask *"Has the stock fulfilled readable price objectives?"* As mentioned earlier, technical analysis does afford the occasional opportunity to calculate price objectives. Various methods can be employed, and we shall be more explicit in the discussion regarding point and figure charting.

If the answer to question 2 is yes, we can then move to question 3, *"Has the stock violated its trends?"* If a trend violation does occur, it could be the forerunner or an early warning for a reversal in the major direction of the stock's price movement.

Question 4 then asks, *"Are there signs of distribution (or accumulation) evident?"* Evidence of distribution can take on many forms. Bar charts display certain patterns (head and shoulders, as an example), and point and figure charts display others. This question does pivot off our second basic assumption as reviewed earlier.

"If distribution (or accumulation) is evident, is it significant enough to imply that a more than minor movement in price could be in the offing?" This fifth question is in reference to our basic assumption number three.

If we have answered the first five questions in an affirmative manner, Question 6 asks, *"Has the stock violated a readable support (or resistance) level?"* A yes answer here takes us to the last question (7) in the sequence, which the market technician of experience should not have to reach; and that is, *"Has the stock initiated a downward (or an upward) trend?"*

The floater question, which can be inserted in between any of the above seven, asks, *"Is there any evidence of unusual price and/or volume action?"* Sharp upward or downward runs following a major move can often be an indication of a "climactic" phase of market action, especially if accompanied by a bulge in turnover.

All analysis should be practiced with the thought of anticipating and not reacting. A good fundamental analyst should be anticipating trends of earnings, product development, and so on; a good technician attempts to anticipate stock price trends. Thus, an astute technician should be turning bearish during a stock's top formation rather than afterward, or turning bullish during a bottom pattern rather than during the following upward trend. But reacting to a change is certainly not a crime.

Although the head and shoulders reversal pattern, as well as the double and the triple tops, can be observed on both bar charts and point and figure charts, there are certain price configurations more easily identified on bar charts; point and figure charts have a number of peculiar patterns of their own.

Although primarily continuation patterns, the *triangles* (Figure 16) are an example of a formation more readily apparent on a bar chart than on a point and figure. The three types of triangles that are most often found are the symmetrical, the ascending, and the descending. Two of

FIGURE 16 Triangles

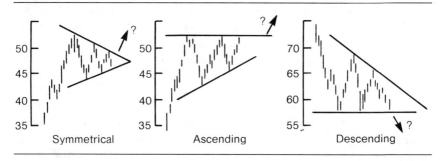

the triangle patterns have some predictive value; namely, the ascending and descending. These two configurations reveal a positive force of market action versus a neutral force. The ascending triangle, for example, illustrates a positive force of buying (higher lows) versus the neutral force of selling (the flat top). In most cases, the positive force will eventually win out, indicating that the ascending triangle is a consolidation phase most often found in an uptrend. Conversely, the descending triangle has the same qualifications; an aggressive force of selling (the descending highs) against a neutral force of buying (the flat bottoms). The descending version is, therefore, most often found within a major downtrend.

The symmetrical triangle, as illustrated, is made up of two positive forces—the buying side (the ascending bottoms) and the selling side (the descending tops). Although such a triangle is often completed with a move in the direction from which the stock came, we caution that there have been times when a symmetrical triangle has also been a reversal pattern. By using trendlines and following closely a stock's movement within the neutral trend, a hint is often given as to the possible direction of the impending move. Volume trends and relative strength analysis can often be additional aids toward determining the eventual direction of the *breakout*.

Aside from the triangles, there are a number of other technical configurations that qualify as consolidation patterns. In particular, there is a pattern called the *wedge* and then there are two short-term configurations that go by the names of *flag* and *pennant*. The wedge, as a consolidation configuration, is illustrated in Figure 17. The pattern is somewhat similar to the triangular variety except that the trendlines move in the same direction. The *falling* wedge usually occurs in a major uptrend pattern. The slope of the trendlines indicates that the sellers may be aggressive but the buyers are relatively less timid. This is indicated by the fact that the slope of the underlying trendline is not as great as the slope of the overhead downtrend line. In addition, as this

FIGURE 17

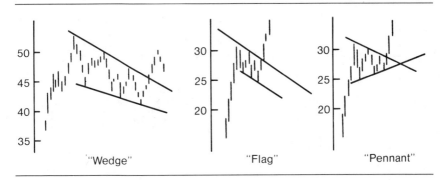

short-term phase of profit-taking occurs, volume usually shows a marked decrease.

The flag and pennant formations are very short term in nature and indicative of a spritely market for the stock under observation. These patterns will most often occur early in an upward or downward trend. The flag is illustrated in Figure 17. As you can see, it is made up of a few quick days of sharp moves which are then followed by a short-term phase of profit-taking. The stock will usually resume its upward trend. The pennant is nothing more than a small symmetrical triangle attached to a staff. It again is most often an illustration of short-term consolidation before a resumption of the underlying trend.

An explanation of bar chart analysis would not be complete without some explanation of the technical configuration known as a *gap*. Although there are a number of gaps readily formed within the marketplace, there are only three that the market technician is concerned with. These are the *breakaway gap*, the *runaway gap*, and the *exhaustion gap*.

Let us first point out that there is an old market legend that states: since nature abhors a vacuum, so does the stock market. Therefore, as the theory goes, a gap must be "filled." This is not necessarily true. By definition, a gap is a void of price action, only to be found on a bar chart, where a stock has opened at a level higher than the previous day's intraday high, and either maintains that opening level or, in fact, moves up and closes higher during the day's trading. Although some gaps are often filled and perhaps quickly so, one should not be wedded to the old belief that this will always occur.

The breakaway gap, by definition, is a void in price that occurs after a phase of consolidation. A stock will break away vibrantly from the consolidation zone and leave a gap in its wake. If, in fact, it is a true breakaway gap, it will *not* be immediately filled.

The runaway gap most often occurs within the framework of a trend

FIGURE 18

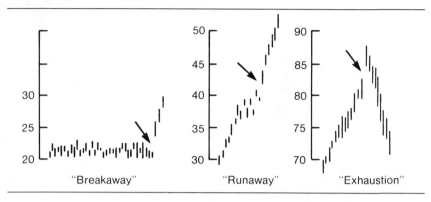

in force. In an upward pattern, a runaway gap simply confirms that heavy demand for the shares continues.

The exhaustion gap carries such a connotation because it usually occurs in the terminal phases of a stock's upward (or downward) trend. The exhaustion gap will be quickly filled by subsequent price action thus indicating a marked reduction in the momentum of the stock's trend. Figure 18 illustrates the three gaps discussed.

We have reviewed a number of the basic tenets surrounding bar chart analysis. Space has precluded an in-depth description as well as an examination of a number of other bar chart configurations. But, of those described herein, let us try to draw a chart of a stock's major trend (Figure 19), and insert within that trend where the patterns reviewed most often occur.

The initial phase of consolidation is our point of departure. The stock breaks out and, in doing so, creates a breakaway gap. As the stock is in what could be called the discovery stage, demand for the shares is brisk, thus two, three, or four days of a rapid price advance occurs. Short-term profit-taking appears and the stock spurts upward again. It is in this phase of the stock's upward trend that a flag and/or a pennant formation will most often develop. Oftentimes, the initial trend of a stock is too steep to be sustainable. Therefore, as more serious profit-taking occurs along in the trend, the slope will obviously become less pronounced. That phase of profit-taking, which results in a more gradual trend, could take on the form of a wedge. Following the confirmation of a new recovery high, the next form of consolidation may well be that of a triangle. Obviously, as the stock moves up further in price, its trend is becoming more mature. Thus, any consolidation phase will tend to be longer in nature. Finally, as the markup phase completes

FIGURE 19

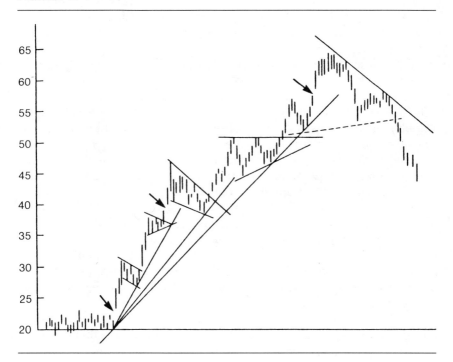

itself and the major trend draws to an end, a major reversal pattern becomes obvious.

Point and Figure Analysis

In a number of ways, point and figure chart analysis differs markedly from bar chart analysis. As mentioned earlier, because a point and figure chart only indicates price movement of a certain magnitude, and only when such a move occurs is it plotted, there is no element of time or volume included on the graph. A one-point reversal chart of IBM on a full sheet of point and figure chart paper could represent only a few months of price activity, while for an issue like American Telephone & Telegraph, the same space could represent almost 10 years. The *volatility* and the *price level* of the stock will have a great bearing on the number of price reversals that are most apt to occur within a given time period.

In our view, the two most important functions of point and figure charting is that the experienced practitioner is afforded the opportunity to analyze from time to time—perhaps more discernable than on a bar chart—(1) whether or not a stock is undergoing a phase of distribution or accumulation while in fact the basic price trend is neutral, and (2) by utilizing the point and figure "count" theory, a determination can often be made as to the extent of a price movement in either an upward or downward direction. One cannot always project a time parameter for an impending move.

Like bar charts, point and figure charting affords the opportunity to analyze stock price *trends,* as well as *support* and *resistance* levels. In addition, there are certain technical price configurations such as the head and shoulders reversal, a rounding top or bottom, a V pattern, or a double or triple top that can be observed on a point and figure graph as well as on a bar chart. But as the bar chart has a number of its own peculiar formations such as the triangles, wedge, pennant, flag, and gap, so does the point and figure graph display its own peculiar patterns. Figure 20 illustrates some of these pattern formations by name.

When a stock is moving upward or downward, one need not be a technician to determine that the stock is being accumulated or distributed, respectively. On the other hand, when a stock is in fact going through a neutral phase, with neither an upward nor downward bias evident, it would be most helpful to arrive at some determination as to the direction of the next move. Point and figure charting lends itself to this type of analysis.

Figure 21 illustrates a typical consolidation phase as it might appear on a point and figure graph. You will note in our example that there are nine columns of the down variety and four columns of the up variety. Stated another way, this neutral configuration of price consolidation illustrates there are nine *failures* for the stock to go lower against only four failures on upside attempts. A failure to move lower indicates that demand at least equaled, if not exceeded, supply at that point, while a failure to move higher is indicative of supply at least equaling if not exceeding demand. Thus, in our illustration, demand appears to be the more prominent characteristic. Therefore, we sense evidence of accumulation rather than distribution. Explained another way, within a point and figure price consolidation pattern, price reversals that occur in the lower portion of the congestion phase are looked upon as representing accumulation activity while price reversals in the upper portion are usually representative of distribution. If this analysis of detecting accumulation proves correct, the stock should eventually move upward instead of downward out of the congestion phase.

Of course, the technician will probably have much more price data to work with than we illustrated in Figure 21. As an example, Figure 22 reveals that the stock was in a significant downward move prior to entering into the consolidation segment illustrated in Figure 21. Often the previous pattern of the stock can further enhance the analysis of a congestion phase. In other words, the mere inability of the stock to move lower following a prolonged downtrend implies basic accumula-

FIGURE 20

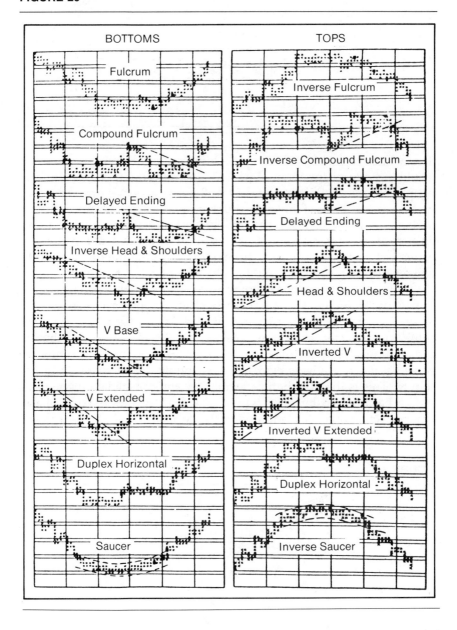

FIGURE 21

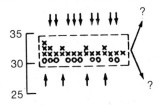

tion, while the inability to continue higher after a significant uptrend would indicate distribution. Figure 23 illustrates the type of point and figure configuration that could very well follow a stock's upward trend. In this regard, you will note the number of excessive failures in the up portion of the congestion pattern versus the reversals in the lower portion. This consolidation phase is in all likelihood a top reversal pattern. The resulting move from such a configuration should be downward.

Within the confines of a major uptrend, consolidation phases will, of course, occur. Figure 24 is a typical consolidation pattern in an upward trend. The trading range between 51 and 58 is considered to be the entire consolidation zone. But note the distinct phases of distribution and accumulation in the illustration. At the 58 level, the stock refuses to move higher, thus giving evidence of encountering either resistance or supply. This is the distribution segment of the consolidation zone and should be followed by some type of a setback or profit-taking phase. This correction occurs as indicated by the decline to 51. But note how the

FIGURE 22

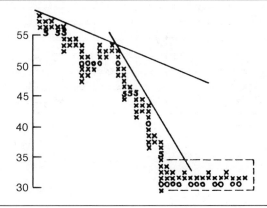

FIGURE 23

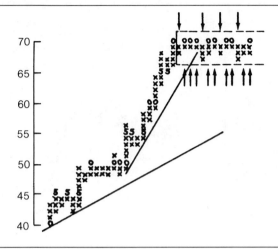

issue ceases to decline any further at the 51–53 level. Evidence of demand equaling, if not exceeding supply, is again at hand as the stock *refuses to move lower*. A new upside move commences resulting in a breakout, and the consolidation pattern has been completed. Such a consolidation zone in a downtrend would appear something like Figure 25. In this case accumulation activity precedes distribution of the shares—just the opposite of the foregoing example.

The discussion above concerning the accumulation and distribution patterns obviously draws heavily upon our Assumption 2. The forthcoming dissertation is concerned with Assumption 3, as previously explained.

FIGURE 24

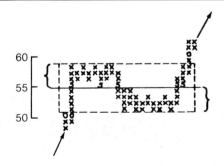

FIGURE 25

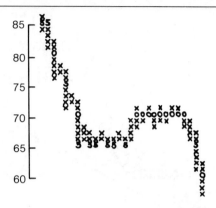

It stands to reason that the more supply that is eliminated from the marketplace (accumulation), the greater the impact should be on the following move (upward). Therein lies the logic or rationale behind the so-called point and figure *objective theory* (sometimes called the *count*). Once a consolidation pattern has been determined to be either distribution or accumulation, the mere extent of that lateral consolidation usually will have a bearing upon the extent of the ultimate move. The bigger the base, the bigger the upward move; the larger the top, the greater the downside adjustment.

According to one approach, a point and figure count is accomplished by merely counting the number of boxes within the consolidation phase, placing emphasis on the price level with the greater fill-ins. In Figure 26 this would be a count across the 36 price line; the example shows the greater number of *x*s falling on this level. In addition, the 36 line also indicates the initiation point of the new upward trend phase (arrow). In our illustration, a count of 21 points results, which added to the price level of 36 offers an upside price target of approximately 57.

FIGURE 26

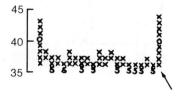

Application of the point and figure count should, of course, be done with great caution and only after much experience. A stock's volatility or popularity in the marketplace can have an influence on an objective's validity. For instance, a glamour stock in vogue at the time may tend to exceed projected price targets as market enthusiasm leads to greater extremes. On the other hand, to utilize the count theory for a utility stock could be foolhardy, as objectives of great magnitude can result from consolidation phases.

The point and figure objective theory is simply another tool. Obviously, the type of market background will play a great role in the validity in the projected targets. A bull market will enhance upward objectives, and a bear market will usually be marked by a number of downside calculations. The count approach can also be used on the other reversal charts. On a three-point reversal chart, as an example, the number of lateral boxes in a consolidation phase would be multiplied by three to achieve an upside or downside objective potential. We caution, however, that objectives calculated off the three-point reversal chart should not be used as a primary input, but more or less as a confirmation to the one-point calculation. Figures 27A and 27B afford good examples of the count technique as it could have been applied to Bausch & Lomb in 1973, a year that fundamentals were little changed.

In 1980, we participated in the Fifth Annual Market Technicians Association's seminar sharing some thoughts on the point and figure approach. Some of the above points were explained and a number of "past" illustrations were used. At the close of our presentation we felt it could be of interest to leave the audience with an illustration for the "future," since most of the discussion had been academic. We used the attached charts of Marion Labs (Figure 28) showing what appeared to be a major base on both the one-point and three-point reversal graphs. Take your own counts off the charts. Where would you have been a buyer? Where was the breakout? Marion has split 2 for 1 three times since 1980 making the original $14 price about 1¾. Said another way, with Marion recently trading around 45 per share, adjusted for the three splits, that would work to 360 for the original 14 stock. Our "count," taken across the entire width of the base using the 13 or 14 price line would have been about 95 points to "only" 109.

Our description of bar chart and point and figure chart utilization has primarily focused on the more common aspects. By no means could a complete dissertation be accomplished in our allocated space. Technical students of the market will need to experiment for themselves with each of the two charting techniques to discover which one they would feel most comfortable with. Obviously, the use of both approaches would be most ideal for both short- and long-term stock analysis.

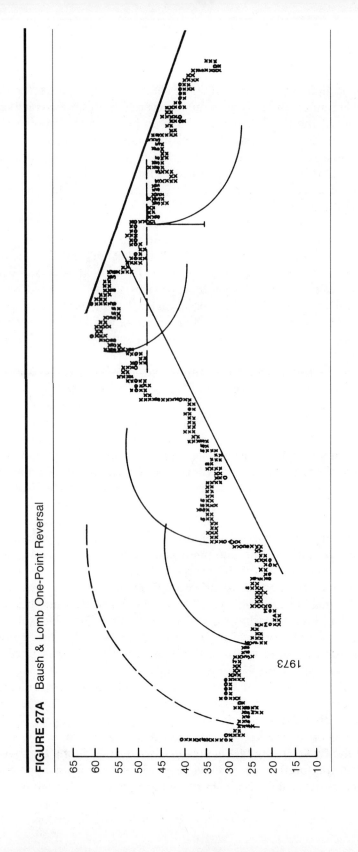

FIGURE 27A Baush & Lomb One-Point Reversal

FIGURE 27B   Baush & Lomb Three-Point Reversal

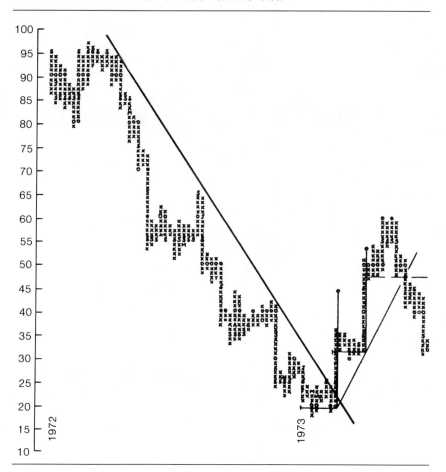

Group or Sector Analysis

The final result of a totally integrated analysis will more than likely be the purchase or sale of an individual stock. More often, the casual technician's style will be more oriented to the use of methods already discussed to follow the trends of individual issues. The more complex or integrated approach will include some type of technical analysis of the market's many sectors or groups. Fortunately, there are a number of readily available data sources to support group analysis, with the more popular being the Barron's groups published each week in the named-for magazine, and the weekly Standard & Poor's group statistics that must be subscribed to at a more expensive monetary outlay. We have

FIGURE 28

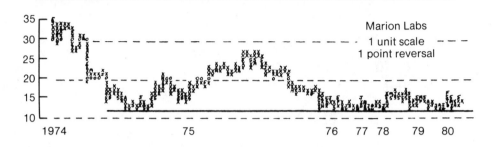

Marion Labs
1 unit scale — — —
1 point reversal

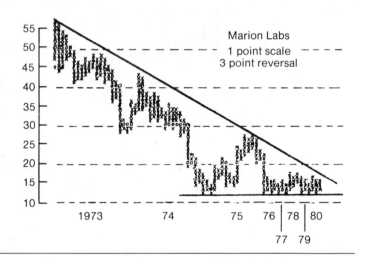

Marion Labs
1 point scale — — — —
3 point reversal

personally followed the Standard & Poor's (S&P) data over the years as there is a great deal more history to deal with, and we have found that the majority of the professional world relates more so to the S&P definitions.

Group analysis should be practiced, if time permits. Finding a strong group can be a great shortcut in finding strong stocks. Equally important is that the trend of the group can have a strong tidal influence on the success of your individual stock commitment. Buying a seemingly strong stock within a poor-acting group may be akin to "fighting the tape." A good overview of the market's group activity can also allow "theme" investing to be a part of your portfolio decision making. If the foods look good, so may the soft drinks or the soaps. A consumer stock orientation could lead to better performance in certain market cycles, while a more economically sensitive portolio would be the better choice in other market environments.

There are a number of technical methods that can be used for group analysis. Tracking the trend of the absolute price is obviously quite simple, and standard technical disciplines like support/resistance, trendlines and moving averages lend credibility to the study. Many technicians find momentum input (price rate-of-change) a helpful tool to gauge acceleration or deceleration of price movement.

In our view, the most important tool in group analysis is relative strength. While many individual investors may tend not to compare their investment performance to the market, as we noted earlier, professional portfolio managers are closely judged on their ability to outperform the S&P 500. Relative strength leads to "portfolio weighting." If, for example, your individual technical analysis reveals that most of the components within the group have supportive promise, then you must overweight the group to accomplish the outperformance, and you will stay overweighted until your technical input dictates a change in relative trend is under way. S&P publishes the market weights for all their industry categories or you could do it yourself at any time providing you have a computer at hand. In recent years, the food group has had an S&P weight of over 3.0 percent as a percent of the total 500 Index's makeup. So if you felt strongly about outperformance, you may have had about 10 percent or so of your portfolio invested in this area. And as Figure 29 reveals, you would have significantly outperformed the market, which itself was experiencing a major bull trend. On the other hand, even though the domestic oil group (Figure 30) was nearing past historic highs, the relative strength was negatively diverging and showing weakness. Your portfolio should have been underweighted as a result.

Stock Market Analysis

The final input to the totally integrated technical effort is to study the market itself. Contrary to most beliefs, to be able to "call" the direction of the general market does not necessarily mean positive investment performance will result. One way to explain this is to scheme the total technical approach as a triangle (see Figure 31). We'll put overview or general stock market analysis at the top apex, group analysis on the lower left, and individual stock input on the lower right. Indeed, a correct stock market forecast based on extensive analysis could lead one to the proper group, but this is doubtful. Infrequently, if at all, will a stock market overview correctly direct the analyst to the right stock. Group work can lead to a market forecast as well as the right direction

FIGURE 29

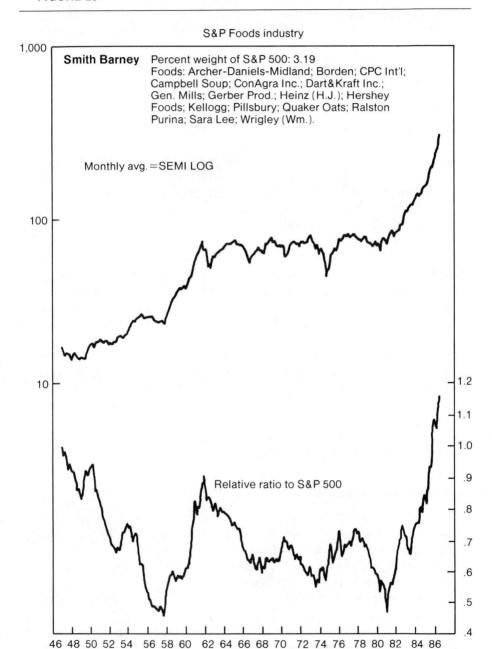

S&P Foods industry

Smith Barney Percent weight of S&P 500: 3.19
Foods: Archer-Daniels-Midland; Borden; CPC Int'l;
Campbell Soup; ConAgra Inc.; Dart&Kraft Inc.;
Gen. Mills; Gerber Prod.; Heinz (H.J.); Hershey
Foods; Kellogg; Pillsbury; Quaker Oats; Ralston
Purina; Sara Lee; Wrigley (Wm.).

Monthly avg. =SEMI LOG

Relative ratio to S&P 500

FIGURE 30

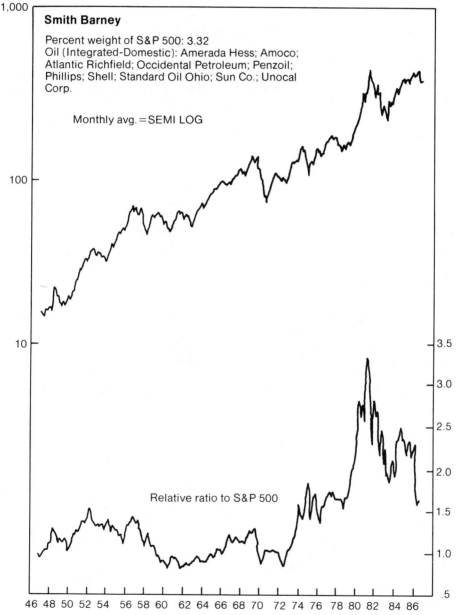

S&P Integrated domestic oil industry

Smith Barney

Percent weight of S&P 500: 3.32
Oil (Integrated-Domestic): Amerada Hess; Amoco;
Atlantic Richfield; Occidental Petroleum; Penzoil;
Phillips; Shell; Standard Oil Ohio; Sun Co.; Unocal
Corp.

Monthly avg. = SEMI LOG

Relative ratio to S&P 500

FIGURE 31

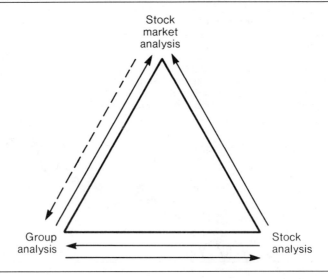

to stock picking. Correct stock picking may well lead one to the right groups and may remotely result in a correct market forecast.

But forecasting the direction of the stock market will always be a prime obsession of the technician. And with the growing number of derivatives, futures, options, and options on the futures, a correct market outlook can have more direct portfolio implications than ever before.

A review of general stock market technical approaches and indicators could, without difficulty, be a book in itself. We shall only highlight some of the more popular techniques practiced by most stock market technicians.

To analyze the "market," one first has to have a good grasp of what the "market" is. Is it an average of 30 stocks, an index of 500 issues, a cumulative number of daily advances versus declines, an unweighted index of 1,700 issues? We remember overhearing a stockbroker telling his client that the Dow Jones Industrial Average was making new highs, climbing through 1200, and thus the investor should be joyful of his newfound wealth. Our broker friend was quickly, but politely informed by his client, "That's your Dow, sonny, mine's at 850!" Investors make the quick mistake that the averages *are* the market. Of course, yardsticks are necessary to evaluate performance, but they may not be totally indicative of individual or even institutional portfolio performance.

Understanding the makeup and the calculation of the leading stock market indexes goes a long way toward successful forecasting, or just better comprehension of "what's goin' on." We are sometimes amazed at stock market predictions that seem to ignore the basic construction of the index that's being forecast. Back in 1973, we read a famous adviser's annual forecast that the popular Dow Jones Industrial Average would climb to over 1500 by Easter! The Dow was just a bit under 1000 at the time. According to our calculations, by looking carefully at the prices of each of the 30 component stocks and understanding their different "price weights" within the index, the adviser was really forecasting that a significant economic boom would hit the country in less than five months. While 5 of the 30 stocks were trading at all-time highs at the time of the forecast, to reach 1500 we figured that no fewer than 10 others would probably have to accomplish the same feat, and for some of them this meant a move over 100 percent. Possible, but not probable. We confronted our adviser friend with this input and, after some thought, he recognized the folly of his forecast. He simply had not thoroughly thought out the mathematical ramifications.

The Dow is a simple mathematical average, but highly distorted in its makeup. The divisor was never 30 (due to reconstruction through the years), but if you were to start your own Dow today, you would do so by picking 30 stocks, adding up the closing prices, and dividing by 30. The Dow's divisor has been reduced through the years due to substitutions and/or stock splits. The divisor today has actually fallen under 1.00 to become a "multiplier." Each move of a point in each stock now translates into a greater than one point move in the average. If each of the 30 stocks were to close the day up one point, using the current divisor of .889, the Dow would end up the day 35.75 points.

The weight of a stock in the Dow Jones averages (transportation and utility alike) is simply determined by the current price of the stock. Study Figure 32 for a quick review. IBM is the highest priced stock and thus is the heaviest weighted, while Navistar, being the lowest priced component, has the smallest influence. If, let's say, each of the above components worked hard to double its earnings in an effort to double their share price, while both companies would be congratulated for their efforts, the effect of the double for IBM on the DJIA would be almost 20 times the effect of Navistar. Fair? Not really, but that's the inherent problem with the Dow, and when a stock splits 2:1, it immediately loses a great deal of its clout on the average's performance.

The Dow Jones Utility Average is followed by many market students as a so-called interest rate sensitive barometer. It is thus perceived as being a leading indicator for the general market. While we would generally subscribe to this view, we also realize that the DJUA is not made up entirely of electric utility stocks—there are four natural gas components. At one time these four energy-related issues commanded about 65 percent of the weight of the DJUA and were almost directly responsible for the average's movements. Yet we would read in the

---

FIGURE 32 Dow Jones Industrial Average Components Ranked by Price*

DJIA Component	Price	Percent Weight
International Business Machines	138	8.3%
Merck	114	6.8
Minnesota Mining & Manufacturing	113	6.8
American Can Co.	89	5.3
DuPont	81	5.0
Procter & Gamble	78	4.7
Phillip Morris	76	4.6
General Electric	75	4.5
General Motors	73	4.4
International Paper	67	4.0
McDonald's	65	3.9
Exxon	65	3.9
American Express	64	3.8
Westinghouse	58	3.5
Eastman Kodak	56	3.4
Sears	47	2.8
United Technologies	44	2.6
Owens Illinois	43	2.6
Woolworth	43	2.6
Chevron	43	2.6
Allied Signal Inc.	42	2.5
Aluminum Co. of America	36	2.2
Goodyear Tire & Rubber	34	2.0
Texaco Inc.	31	1.9
American Telephone & Telegraph	23	1.3
Union Carbide	22	1.3
USX Corp.	19	1.1
Inco Ltd.	12	.7
Bethlehem Steel	8	.5
Navistar	7	.4
	1666	100%

Total ÷ by current divisor of .889 =   1874 − DJIA level

* Prices as of 8/21/86.

press that the drop in the utilities could be forecasting higher interest rates. As you can see on Figure 33, recent component weights again favor the electrics. But this is another example of knowing the makeup of an index before reading too much into its performance.

The Standard & Poor's indexes are also weighted with price and shares outstanding (capitalization) used in the calculation. As a result, unlike the Dow, a stock split in the S&P 500 will make no difference in the index's final calculation. Because of its broadness and diversification, the S&P 500 is more often considered the "market," and the benchmark to which most professional money managers' performance is compared.

FIGURE 33 Dow Jones Utility Average Components Ranked by Price*

DJUA Component	Price	Percent Weight
Consolidated Edison	52	10.6%
Public Service Electric & Gas	47	9.5
Panhandle Eastern†	44	8.9
Columbia Gas†	41	8.3
Southern California Edison	38	7.7
Houston Ind.	36	7.3
Commonwealth Edison	33	6.7
American Electric Power	31	6.2
Consolidated Natural Gas†	30	6.0
Pacific Gas & Electric Co.	27	5.5
Centerior Energy	26	5.3
Niagra Mohawk Power	24	4.9
People's Energy†	23	4.7
Philadelphia Electric	23	4.7
Detroit Edison	18	3.7
	493	100%

Total ÷ by current divisor of 2.277 =   217 – DJUA

* Prices as of 8/21/86.

† Four natural gas components equal 28 percent.

An issue like IBM, where both a high price and a large capitalization are present, will tend to exert the greatest influence on the S&P's movement. Figure 34 is a computer run ranking the percentage weight of the first 40 most influential component stocks as of June 10, 1986. As you can see, the first 10 names equaled 18.35 percent of the Standard & Poor's 500 weight, the first 25, 30.15 percent. In other words, only 5 percent of the index's components exert almost one third the influence on the indicator's behavior.

Other broad-based market indicators that are of a weighted nature include the New York Stock Exchange Common Stock Index, the American Stock Exchange Market Value Index, and the NASDAQ Index. One quick word regarding the AMEX Market Value Index. The worth of the entire American Stock Exchange approximates the capitalization of "only" IBM. Furthermore, as you can see on Figure 35, the top 10 weighted stocks on the Amex represent about one third the weight of the entire exchange.

The Value Line Investment Survey publishes an index that is *unweighted* in its makeup. This geometric compilation truly reflects the price movement of the majority of stocks, as each component issue carries the same weight, regardless of its price or capitalization. The recent population of the Value Line included 1,665 stocks; about 1,250 from the NYSE, 110 from the AMEX, 285 from OTC, and 20 from

FIGURE 34

Jun 10, 1986	Stock	% Mkt Wt	Mkt Value (Millions)
1	INTERNATIONAL BUS MACH	5.38	91339.6
2	EXXON CORP	2.51	42711.8
3	GENERAL ELEC CO	2.15	36478.1
4	AMERICAN TEL&TELEG CO	1.53	26064.9
5	GENERAL MTRS CORP	1.43	24318.4
6	ROYAL DUTCH PETE CO	1.23	20873.4
7	DU PONT E I DE NEMOURS	1.20	20322.3
8	BELLSOUTH CORP	1.00	16904.1
9	SEARS ROEBUCK & CO	0.99	16748.8
10	PHILLIP MORRIS COS INC	0.93	15814.0
11	AMOCO CORP	0.92	15653.0
12	FORD MTR CO DEL	0.86	14655.4
13	COCA COLA CO	0.86	14538.7
14	CHEVRON CORPORATION	0.80	13641.6
15	WAL MART STORES INC	0.80	13560.4
16	MERCK & CO INC	0.80	13508.3
17	EASTMAN KODAK CO	0.79	13412.8
18	BELL ATLANTIC CORP	0.78	13233.2
19	AMERICAN EXPRESS CO	0.77	13131.1
20	NYNEX CORP	0.75	12711.2
21	PROCTER & GAMBLE CO	0.74	12652.6
22	AMERICAN HOME PRODS CP	0.74	12561.5
23	MOBIL CORP	0.74	12556.8
24	JOHNSON & JOHNSON	0.73	12423.6
25	MINNESOTA MNG & MFG CO	0.72	12239.9
26	RJR NABISCO INC	0.71	12089.8
27	AMERICAN INFORM TECH	0.71	12023.0
28	BRISTOL MYERS CO	0.67	11350.4
29	ABBOTT LABS	0.66	11152.2
30	HEWLETT PACKARD CO	0.65	10983.1
31	PACIFIC TELESIS GROUP	0.64	10815.8
32	DOW CHEM CO	0.64	10791.6
33	GTE CORP	0.63	10618.5
34	LILLY ELI & CO	0.62	10514.7
35	STANDARD OIL CO OHIO	0.61	10349.7
36	PFIZER INC	0.61	10343.2
37	DIGITAL EQUIP CORP	0.60	10260.0
38	ATLANTIC RICHFIELD CO	0.57	9710.2
39	U S WEST INC	0.57	9611.4
40	SOUTHWESTERN BELL CORP	0.56	9513.7

FIGURE 35   MARKET VALUE RANKING OF AMEX STOCKS AS OF 8/21/86

		Mkt Value	Weight	Cum Wt
1	B A T INDS LTD	9174.4	11.11	11.11
2	IMPERIAL OIL LTD	4905.4	5.94	17.06
3	IMPERIAL GROUP PLC	3828.3	4.64	21.70
4	NEW YORK TIMES CO	2878.1	3.49	25.18
5	TEXACO CDA INC	2385.2	2.89	28.07
6	WANG LABS INC	2029.9	2.46	30.53
7	WASHINGTON POST CO	1999.9	2.42	32.95
8	I C H CORP	1476.2	1.79	34.74
9	COURTAULDS PLC	1422.4	1.72	36.47
10	HASBRO INC	1372.7	1.66	38.13
11	AFFILIATED PUBNS INC	1145.2	1.39	39.52
12	DILLARD DEPT STORES	1111.4	1.35	40.86
13	BRASCAN LTD	1082.7	1.31	42.17
14	PALL CORP	1039.3	1.26	43.43
15	GIANT FOOD INC	952.8	1.15	44.59
16	HOME GROUP INC	933.5	1.13	45.72
17	PLACER DEV LTD	908.4	1.10	46.82
18	DOMTAR INC	893.8	1.08	47.90
19	WICKES COS INC NEW	882.7	1.07	48.97
20	AMDAHL CORP	842.9	1.02	49.99
544	WICHITA INDS INC	3.6	0.00	99.95
545	BETHLEHEM CORP	3.5	0.00	99.96
546	WESPERCORP	3.1	0.00	99.96
547	ANGLO ENERGY LTD	3.0	0.00	99.96
548	ICO INC	3.0	0.00	99.97
549	GENERAL EMPLOYMENT ENT	2.9	0.00	99.97
550	DIGICON INC	2.8	0.00	99.97
551	ENERSERV PRODS INC	2.8	0.00	99.98
552	PLYMOUTH RUBR INC	2.8	0.00	99.98
553	SFM CORP	2.7	0.00	99.98
554	LA POINTE INDS INC	2.7	0.00	99.99
555	AUDIOTRONICS CORP	2.7	0.00	99.99
556	CUSTOM ENERGY SVCS INC	2.4	0.00	99.99
557	USR INDS INC	2.3	0.00	100.00
558	PREMIER RES LTD COLO	1.9	0.00	100.00
559	ORMAND INDS INC	1.2	0.00	100.00
560	CASTLE INDS INC	0.9	0.00	100.00
561	IMPERIAL INDS INC	0.6	0.00	100.00
562	U N A CORP	0.6	0.00	100.00
563	BELTRAN CORP	0.0	0.00	100.00
TOTAL MARKET VALUE		82543.8		

FIGURE 36

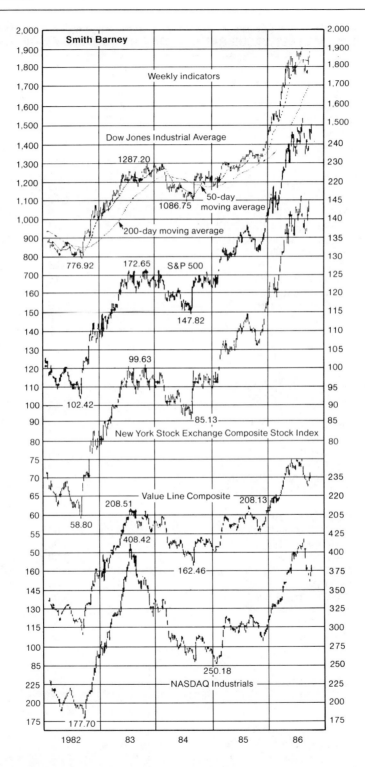

Canada. A comparison of the Value Line to the S&P will illustrate small stock-big stock relative performance. Figure 36 illustrates the above-mentioned indexes, and you can perhaps note some different patterns.

Aside from the price averages and indexes, there are a vast number of other indicators that technicians use to judge the "health" of the market. Perhaps the most popular stock market indicator is the advance/decline (A/D) statistic. A/D data are followed to measure the market's "breadth" or the range of stock participation. Our research indicates that the A/D statistics were first compiled and plotted back in the mid-1920s and prior to the use of broad-based averages.

The A/D data are readily available in any newspaper that has a half way decent business section. The presentation usually includes the number of issues that traded on the exchanges (NYSE, AMEX, and OTC) along with the number that advanced, declined, and were unchanged. The easiest and most popular breadth indicator is the advance/decline line in which the daily difference between the advancing and declining issues is accumulated. Some technicians may ratio the data or create a more complex index, but our findings suggest the simple way is sufficient.

The theory behind the A/D data is also quite simple. As long as the "army" (breadth) stays in step with the "generals" (e.g., DJIA), then the trend, by definition, is healthy and should sustain. It's when the army starts to show signs of retreating, or not keeping pace with the generals, that the technician becomes concerned about the viability of the underlying trend. Lagging breadth is empirical evidence of a growing selectivity in the market, a good sign that the market averages may be nearing a point of correction or consolidation. Such behavior carries the technical label "negative breadth divergence." We don't have the space to fully explain the intricacies of breadth analysis, but you can observe the outlined trends on Figure 37 to gain a quick insight to the points described above.

Another simple way to keep tabs on the health of the market is by tracking the number of stocks that are hitting new 12-month highs and lows each day (week). The more common calculation involves a 10-day (week) smooth of the high-low data. An expansion of the indicator in a rising market provides a strong confirmation of the trend. If the averages were to rise without such a high-low expansion, a sign of narrowness would be flashed which could be a negative omen.

You often hear of the market being *overbought*, or *oversold*. These are often misused terms in the statistical sense and often merely reflect some observer's feeling for the day. Technicians have statistical methods for determining an overbought state (or oversold), but even here, sometimes we sense a misinterpretation of the data. Actually, in our view, the ability of the market to register an overbought condition during an advance is not a negative, but a positive sign of the vitality of

FIGURE 37

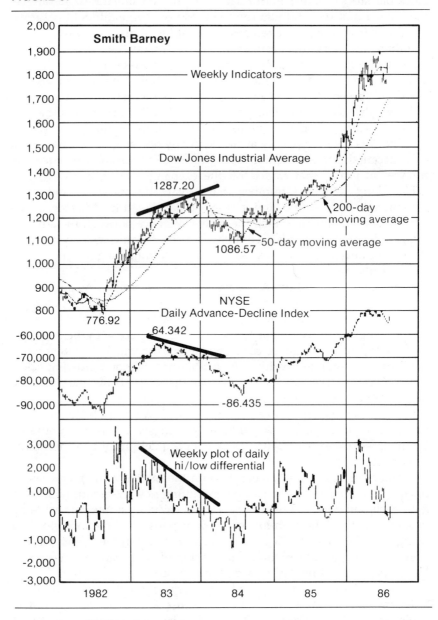

the advance. The lack of an overbought reading during an advance in the averages often indicates the weakness of the rally, thus making it suspicious.

The most common OB/OS calculation is again, the easiest to maintain. Using the aforementioned A/D data, a simple 10-day accumulation of the A/D differential creates the indicator. While the thresholds of importance may vary, our approach has been to appreciate a reading of +1600 as indicating an overbought, with −1600 the level of an oversold. The market student may find a further refinement of the calculation also helpful (e.g., extreme overbought).

To try and understand the implications of an overbought market consider the following example. The hot dog vendor on the corner is setting up his stand about 11 A.M., still some time before the lunch hour crowds. An early line of customers begins to form (demand), and the vendor assesses his inventory of weiners (supply), and sets a price of $1.00 for the product (quote). A number of things begin to happen. The price must be right as the line begins to lengthen; the demand makes itself felt as the vendor looks into his pot and notes a rapidly dwindling supply. He raises the price again. There's still a good line. He raises the price again. The line now starts to shorten, but not entirely due to his higher price. After all, the demand or appetite for the product is being satisfied as well. Somewhere the combination of higher price, demand satisfaction (if not supply depletion), for the time being, will result in an "overbought" condition for the vendor. A new demand factor, renewed supply, and possibly a lower price may be needed to start the procedure over again. Maybe not the best explanation, but it's kind of what happens in the equity market over and over again.

Volume data are just as important in overview work as in individual stock analyses. Expanding volume in a rising trend tells us that the bull is putting one of his most important tools to work. Volume can be tracked a number of ways. A simple histogram, a running total, or a comparison of daily up-volume to down-volume can be helpful.

We have only touched the tip of the technical iceberg in our indicator discussion. The following bibliography has been carefully put together for your use assuming we have sufficiently whetted your appetite to further explore the world of technical analysis. There are literally hundreds of stock market indicators that can be followed. Some are good, and some are bad. Over recent years the growth of the derivatives (options, futures, and so on) has reduced the importance of a number of heretofore potent and reliable statistics. The monthly short interest, margin debt, odd-lot trading are but three of the more popular series that have been affected by the derivatives. New indicators, particularly on the sentiment front, have evolved thanks to the derivatives. The Put/Call ratio, spread of futures to spot markets are a couple that have a wide following.

All in all, time is the greatest ingredient needed for technical stock market analysis. The average investor will no doubt only be able to follow some of the easiest indicators as he tries to keep tabs on his portfolio as well. Furthermore, technical analysis doesn't stop with the stock market. Technical work can be extremely useful for the bond market (interest rates), commodities, as well as for tracking foreign stock

FIGURE 38

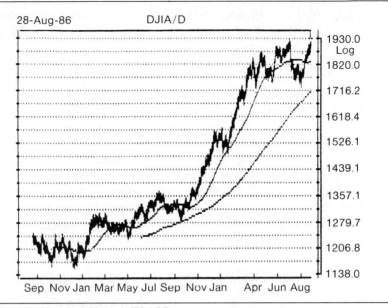

28-Aug-86   DJIA/D

1930.0
Log
1820.0
1716.2
1618.4
1526.1
1439.1
1357.1
1279.7
1206.8
1138.0

Sep Nov Jan Mar May Jul Sep Nov Jan   Apr Jun Aug

DOW JONES INDUSTRIAL AVERAGE—
DAILY BAR CHART WITH 50-
DAY AND 200-DAY MOVING AVERAGES

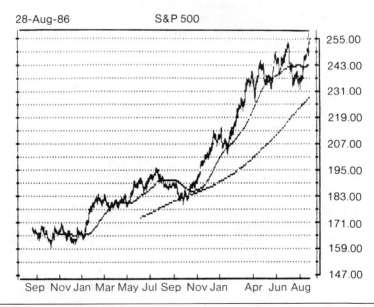

28-Aug-86   S&P 500

255.00
243.00
231.00
219.00
207.00
195.00
183.00
171.00
159.00
147.00

Sep Nov Jan Mar May Jul Sep Nov Jan   Apr Jun Aug

S&P 500 COMPANY INDEX—
DAILY BAR CHART WITH 50-
DAY AND 200-DAY MOVING AVERAGES

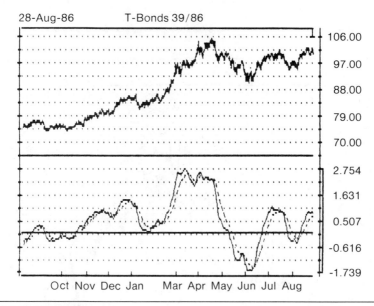

T-BOND FUTURES—
PERPETUAL CALCULATION—
DAILY BAR CHART WITH
AN EXPONENTIAL MOVING AVERAGE

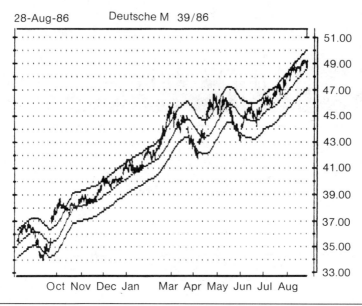

DEUTSCHE MARK FUTURES—
PERPETUAL CALCULATION
DAILY BAR CHART WITH
ENVELOPE BANDS

FIGURE 39

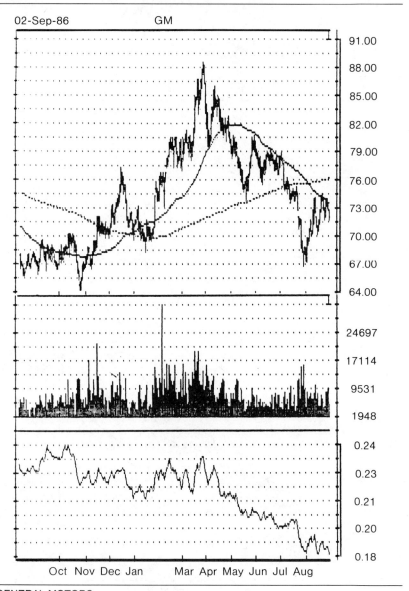

GENERAL MOTORS—
DAILY BAR CHART
50- AND 200-DAY MOVING AVERAGES
VOLUME HISTOGRAM
RELATIVE STRENGTH TO S&P 500

FIGURE 39 (*Concluded*)

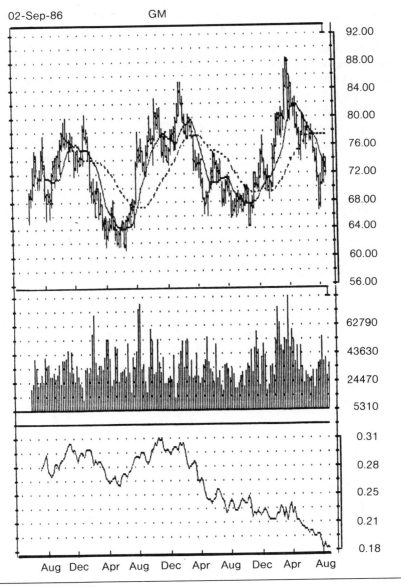

02-Sep-86 GM

92.00
88.00
84.00
80.00
76.00
72.00
68.00
64.00
60.00
56.00

62790
43630
24470
5310

0.31
0.28
0.25
0.21
0.18

Aug Dec Apr Aug Dec Apr Aug Dec Apr Aug

GENERAL MOTORS—
WEEKLY BAR CHART
10- AND 30-WEEK MOVING AVERAGES
VOLUME HISTOGRAM
RELATIVE STRENGTH TO S&P 500

markets and currencies. As one of my colleagues used to say, "if it moves, we chart it."

The personal computer is becoming a mandatory tool for the average technician or investor to excel. For over two decades the large IBM-type mainframe has provided support for stock screening, indicator testing and computation, and so on. The personal computer allows quick and automated daily, weekly, and monthly reviews. There's a lot of software out there to choose from. Our staff had the pleasure (and sometimes chore) of reviewing over 50 technically oriented software packages recently over a 12-month period. The findings were published in *PC Magazine,* April 15, 1986. We found some very good programs and some that were so bad there wasn't even sufficient documentation. We advise technical students to request samples, demo disks, or whatever before shelling out hundreds of dollars for something that won't do the job. Of the better software packages, we have found the Compu-Trac system a very helpful and complete technical software package. We close the chapter with a number of computer drawn studies with appropriate labels affixed where necessary (see Figures 38 and 39).

Remember, you needn't buy a stock at the bottom, or sell it at the top to experience profitable stock market transactions. To catch and ride the intervening trends should be sufficient for handsome profits. Investing requires the maintenance of disciplines. And technical analysis, the oldest form of stock market analysis, contains the rigors needed for much of that discipline.

BIBLIOGRAPHY

EDWARDS, ROBERT D., and JOHN MAGEE. *Technical Analysis of Stock Trends.* 5th ed. Springfield, Mass.: John Magee, 1984.

FOSBACK, NORMAN G. *Stock Market Logic.* Fort Lauderdale, Fla.: The Institute for Economic Research, 1976.

GORDON, WILLIAM. *The Stock Market Indicators.* Palisades Park, N.J.: Investors Press, 1968.

GRANVILLE, JOSEPH E. *A Strategy of Daily Stock Market Timing for Maximum Profit.* Englewood Cliffs, N.J.: Prentice-Hall, 1960.

JILER, WILLIAM L. *How Charts Can Help You in the Stock Market.* New York: Commodity Research Publishing Corp., 1962.

MURPHY, JOHN J. *Technical Analysis of the Futures Markets.* New York: New York Institute of Finance, 1986.

PRING, MARTIN J. *Technical Analysis Explained.* 2d ed. New York: McGraw-Hill, 1985.

WHEELEN, ALEXANDER H. *Study Helps and Point and Figure Technique.* N.J.: Morgan, Rogers and Roberts, 1971.

ZWEIG, MARTIN E. *Winning on Wall Street.* New York: Warner Books, 1986.

PART 3

Company and Industry Analysis

12

How to Conduct an Industry Analysis

Michael E. Porter, Ph.D.
Graduate School of Business Administration
Harvard University

How should one go about analyzing an industry and competitors? What types of data does one look for and how can they be organized? Where does one look for these data? This chapter deals with these questions and some of the other practical problems involved in conducting an industry analysis. There are basically two types of data about industries: published data and those gathered from interviews with industry participants and observers (field data). The bulk of discussion in this chapter will center on identifying the important sources of published and field data, their strengths and weaknesses, and strategies for approaching them most effectively and in the right sequence.

A full-blown industry analysis is a massive task, and one that can consume months if one is starting from scratch. In beginning an industry analysis there is a tendency to dive in and collect a mass of detailed information, with little in the way of a general framework or approach in which to fit this information. This lack of method leads to frustration at best, and confusion and wasted effort at worst. Thus before considering specific sources, it is important to consider an overall strategy for conducting the industry study and the critical first steps in initiating it.

SOURCE: Reprinted with permission of The Free Press, a division of Macmillan, Inc. from *Competitive Strategy: Techniques for Analyzing Industries and Competitors*, by Michael E. Porter. Copyright © 1980 by The Free Press.

INDUSTRY ANALYSIS STRATEGY

There are two important aspects in developing a strategy for analyzing an industry. The first is to determine just what it is one is looking for. "Anything about the industry" is much too broad to serve as an effective guide for research. Although the full list of specific issues that need to be addressed in an industry analysis depends on the particular industry under study, it is possible to generalize about what important information and raw data the researcher should look for. A simple but exhaustive set of areas under which to collect raw data is given in Figure 1. The researcher who can fully describe each of these areas should be in a position to develop a comprehensive picture of industry structure and competitors' profiles.

With a framework for assembling data, the second major strategy question is how sequentially to develop data in each area. There are a number of alternatives, ranging from taking one item at a time to proceeding randomly. As hinted earlier, however, there are important benefits in getting a general *overview* of the industry first, and only then focusing on the specifics. Experience has shown that a broad understanding can help the researcher more effectively spot important items of data when studying sources and organize data more effectively as they are collected.

A number of steps can be useful in obtaining this overview:

1. Who is in the industry. It is wise to develop a rough list of industry participants right away, especially the leading firms. A list of key competitors is helpful for quickly finding other articles and company documents (some of the sources discussed later will aid in this process). An entering wedge for many of these sources is the industry's *Standard Industrial Classification* (SIC) code, which can be determined from the Census Bureau's *Standard Industrial Classification Manual.* The SIC system classifies industries on a variety of levels of breadth, with two-digit industries overly broad for most purposes, five-digit industries often too narrow, and four-digit industries usually about right.

2. Industry studies. If one is lucky, there may be a relatively comprehensive industry study available or a number of broadly based articles. Reading these can be a quick way of developing an overview. (Sources of industry studies are discussed later.)

3. Annual reports. If there are any publicly held firms in the industry, annual reports should be consulted early. A single annual report may contain only modest amounts of disclosure. However, a quick review of the annual reports for a number of major companies over a 10- or 15-year period is an excellent way to begin to understand the industry. Most aspects of the business will be discussed at one time or another. The most enlightening part of an annual report for an overview is often the president's letter. The researcher should look for

---

FIGURE 1 Raw Data Categories for Industry Analysis

Data Categories	*Compilation*
Product lines	By company
Buyers and their behavior	By year
Complementary products	By functional area
Substitute products	

Growth
  Rate
  Pattern (seasonal, cyclical)
  Determinants

Technology of production
  and distribution
  Cost structure
  Economies of scale
  Value added
  Logistics
  Labor

Marketing and Selling
  Market segmentation
  Marketing practices

Suppliers

Distribution channels (if indirect)

Innovation
  Types
  Sources
  Rate
  Economies of scale

Competitors—strategy, goals, strengths and weaknesses, assumptions

Social, political, legal environment

Macroeconomic environment

---

the rationales given for both good and bad financial results; these should expose some of the critical success factors in the industry. It also is important to note what the company seems to be proud of in its annual report, what it seems to be worried about, and what key changes have been made. It is also possible to gain some insights into how companies are organized, the flow of production, and numerous other factors from reading between the lines in a series of annual reports from the same company.

The researcher will generally want to come back to annual reports and other company documents later in the study. The initial early reading will fail to uncover many nuances that become apparent once the knowledge of the industry and the competitor is more complete.

Get into the Field Early

If there is any common problem in getting industry analyses underway, it is that researchers tend to spend too much time looking for published sources and using the library before they begin to tap field sources. As will be discussed later, published sources have a variety of limitations: timeliness, level of aggregation, depth, and so on. Although it is important to gain some basic understanding of the industry to maximize the value of field interviews, the researcher should not exhaust all published sources *before* getting into the field. On the contrary, clinical and library research should proceed simultaneously. They tend to feed on each other, especially if the researcher is aggressive in asking every field source to suggest published material about the industry. Field sources tend to be more efficient because they get to the issues, without the wasted time of reading useless documents. Interviews also sometimes help the researcher identify the issues. This help may come, to some extent, at the expense of objectivity.

Get over the Hump

Experience shows that the morale of researchers in an industry study often goes through a U-shaped cycle as the study proceeds. An initial period of euphoria gives way to confusion and even panic as the complexity of the industry becomes apparent and mounds of information accumulate. Sometime later in the study, it all begins to come together. This pattern appears to be so common as to serve as a useful thing for researchers to remember.

PUBLISHED SOURCES FOR ANALYSIS OF INDUSTRY AND COMPETITORS

The amount of published information available varies widely by industry. The larger the industry, the older it is, and the slower the rate of technological change, the better the available published information tends to be. Unfortunately for the researcher, many interesting industries do not meet these criteria, and there may be little published information available. However, it is *always* possible to gain some important information about an industry from published sources, and these sources should be aggressively pursued. Generally, the problem the researcher will face in using published data for analyzing an economically meaningful industry is that they are *too broad*, or too aggregated, to fit the industry. If a researcher starts searching for data with this reality in mind, the usefulness of broad data will be better recognized and the tendency to give up too easily will be avoided.

Two important principles can greatly facilitate the development of references to published materials. First, every published source should be combed tenaciously for references to other sources, both other published sources and sources for field interviews. Often articles will cite individuals (industry executives, security analysts, and so on) who usually do not appear by accident; they tend to be either well-informed or particularly vocal industry observers, and they make excellent leads.

The second principle is to keep a thorough bibliography of everything that is uncovered. Although it is painful at the time, taking down the full citation of the source not only saves time in compiling the bibliography at the end of the study but also guards against wasteful duplication of efforts by members of research teams and the agony of not being able to remember where some critical piece of information came from. Summary notes on sources or Xerox copies of useful ones are also useful. They minimize the need for rereading and can facilitate communication within a research team.

Although the types of published sources are potentially numerous, they can be divided into a number of general categories, which are discussed briefly below.[1]

Industry Studies

Studies that provide a general overview of some industries come in two general varieties. First are book-length studies of the industry, often (but not exclusively) written by economists. These can usually best be found in library card catalogs and by cross-checking references given in other sources. Participants in or observers of an industry will almost always know of such industry studies when they exist, and they should be questioned about them as the study proceeds.

The second broad category is the typically shorter, more focused studies conducted by securities or consulting firms, such as Frost and Sullivan, Arthur D. Little, Stanford Research Institute, and all the Wall

---

[1] L. Daniels (1985) is an excellent general source of business information. There are also a number of computerized abstract services for references and articles available at major business libraries, which can speed the task of finding articles and sorting the useful ones from those that are not so useful. [See Chapter 52 for further references.]

Street research houses. Sometimes specialized consulting firms collect data on particular industries, such as SMART, Inc., in the ski industry and IDC in the computer industry. Often access to these studies involves a fee. Unfortunately, although there are a number of published directories of market research studies, there is no one place where they are all compiled, and the best way to learn about them is through industry observers or participants.

Trade Associations

Many industries have trade associations, which serve as clearinghouses for industry data and sometimes publish detailed industry statistics.[2] Trade associations differ greatly in their willingness to give data to researchers. Usually, however, an introduction from a member of the association is helpful in gaining the cooperation of staff in sending data.

Whether or not the association is a source of data, members of the staff are extremely useful in alerting the researcher to any published information about the industry that exists, identifying the key participants and discussing their general impressions of how the industry functions, its key factors for company success, and important industry trends. Once contact with a trade association staff member has been made, this person can in turn be a useful source of referrals to industry participants and can identify participants who represent a range of viewpoints.

Trade Magazines

Most industries have one or more trade magazines which cover industry events on a regular (sometimes even daily) basis. A small industry may be covered as part of a broader-based trade publication. Trade journals in customer, distributor, or supplier industries are often useful sources as well.

Reading through trade magazines over a long period of time is an extremely useful way to understand the competitive dynamics and important changes in an industry, as well as to diagnose its norms and attitudes.

Business Press

A wide variety of business publications cover companies and industries on an intermittent basis. To obtain references, there are a number of standard bibliographies, including the *Business Periodicals*

---

[2] There are a number of published directories of trade associations.

Index, The Wall Street Journal Index, and the *F&S Index,* United States (and companions for Europe and International).

Company Directories and Statistical Data

There are a variety of directories of both public and private U.S. firms, some of which give a limited amount of data. Many directories list firms by SIC code, and thus they provide a way to build a complete list of industry participants. Comprehensive directories include *Thomas Register of American Manufacturers,* the Dun and Bradstreet *Million Dollar Directory* and *Middle Market Directory, Standard and Poor's Register of Corporations, Directors and Executives,* and the various *Moody's* publications. Another broad list of companies classified by industry is the Newsfront *30,000 Leading U.S. Corporations,* which give some limited financial information as well. In addition to these general directories, other potential sources of broad company lists are financial magazines (*Fortune, Forbes*) and buyers guides.

Dun and Bradstreet compiles credit reports on all companies of significant size, whether they be public or private. These reports are not available to any library and provided only to subscribing companies who pay a high fixed cost for the service plus a small fee for individual reports. Dun and Bradstreet reports are valuable as sources about private companies, but since data provided by the companies are not audited, it must be used with caution; many users have reported errors in the information.

There are also many statistical sources of such data as advertising spending and stock market performance.

Company Documents

Most companies publish a variety of documents about themselves, particularly if they are publicly traded. In addition to annual reports, SEC form 10-K's, proxy statements, prospectuses, and other government filings can be useful. Also useful are speeches or testimony by firm executives, press releases, product literature, manuals, published company histories, transcripts of annual meetings, want ads, patents, and even advertising.

Major Government Sources

The Internal Revenue Service provides in the *IRS Corporation Source Book of Statistics of Income* extensive annual financial information on industries (by size of organizations within the industry) based on corporate tax returns. A less detailed, printed version of the data is in the IRS's *Statistics of Income.* The main drawback of this source is that the financial data for an entire company are allocated to that company's principle industry, thereby introducing biases in industries in which many participants are highly diversified. However, the IRS data are available annually back to the 1940s, and it is the only source that gives financial data covering all firms in the industry.

Another source of government statistics is the Bureau of the Census. The most frequently used volumes are *Census of Manufacturers, Census of Retail Trade,* and *Census of the Mineral Industries,* which are available quite far back in time. As with the IRS data, the census does not refer to specific companies but rather breaks down statistics by SIC code. Census material also has considerable regional data for industries. Unlike IRS data, census data are based on aggregates of data from establishments within corporations, such as plant sites and warehouses, rather than corporations as a whole. Therefore, the data are not biased by company diversification. One feature of the *Census of Manufacturers* that can be particularly useful is the special report, *Concentration Ratios in Manufacturing Industry.* This section gives the percentages of industry sales of the largest 4, 8, 20, and 50 firms in the industry for each SIC four-digit manufacturing industry in the economy. Another useful government source for price level changes in industries is the Bureau of Labor Statistics, *Wholesale Price Index.*[3]

Leads on further government information can be obtained through the various indexes of government publications, as well as by contacting the U.S. Department of Commerce and the libraries of other government agencies. Other government sources include regulatory agency filings, congressional hearings, and patent office statistics.

Other Sources

Some other potentially fruitful published sources include the following:

- Antitrust records.
- Local newspapers in which a competitor's facilities or headquarters are located.
- Local tax records.

GATHERING FIELD DATA FOR INDUSTRY ANALYSIS

In gathering field data it is important to have a framework for identifying possible sources, determining what their attitude toward cooperation with the research is likely to be, and developing an approach to them. Figure 2 gives a schematic diagram of the most important sources

---

[3] Currently referred to as producer price index (PPI)—The Editor.

FIGURE 2 Sources of Field Data for Industry Analysis

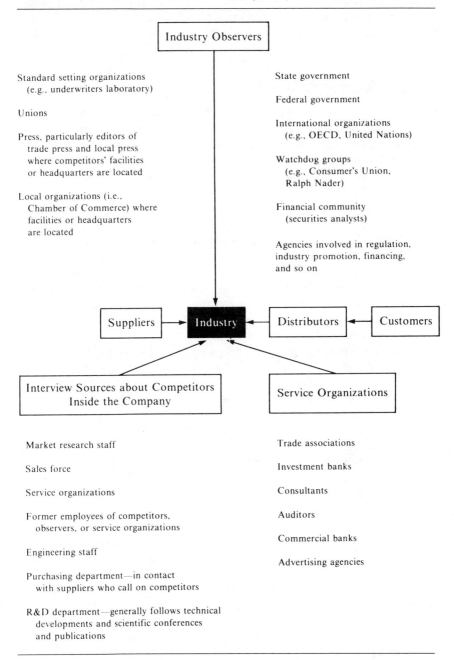

of field data, which are participants in the industry itself, firms and individuals in adjacent businesses to the industry (suppliers, distributors, customers), service organizations that have contact with the industry (including trade associations), and industry observers (including the financial community, regulators, etc.). Each of these sources has somewhat differing characteristics, which are useful to identify explicitly.

Characteristics of Field Sources

Industry competitors will perhaps be the most uncertain about cooperating with researchers, because the data they release have a real potential of causing them economic harm. Approaching sources in the industry requires the greatest degree of care (some guidelines will be discussed later). Sometimes they will not cooperate at all.

The next most sensitive sources are service organizations, such as consultants, auditors, bankers, and trade association personnel, who operate under a tradition of confidentiality about individual clients, though usually not about general industry background information. Most of the other sources are not threatened directly by industry research, and in fact they often perceive it as a help. The most perceptive outside observers of the industry are often suppliers' or customers' executives who have taken an active interest in the whole range of industry participants over a long period of time. Retailers and wholesalers are often excellent sources as well.

The researcher should attempt to speak with individuals in all of the major groups since each of them can supply important data and provide useful cross-checks. Because of their differing perspectives, the researcher should *not* be surprised if they make conflicting and even directly contradictory statements. One of the arts of interviewing is cross-checking and verifying data from different sources.

The researcher can make the initial field contact at any point shown in Figure 2. Initially, to gather background, it is best to make contact with someone who is knowledgeable about the industry *but who does not have a competitive or direct economic stake in it.* Such interested third parties are usually more open and provide the best way of gaining an unbiased overview of the industry and of the key actors involved, which is important early in the research. When the researcher is in a position to ask more perceptive and discriminating questions, direct industry participants can be tackled. However, to maximize the chances of success in any interview, it is important to have a personal introduction, no matter how indirect. This consideration may dictate the choice of where to begin. Field research always involves an element of opportunism, and following a method of analysis should not deter the researcher from pursuing good leads.

It is important to remember that many participants in an industry or observers of it know each other personally. Industries are not faceless; they are composed of people. Thus one source will lead to another if the researcher is adept at his task. Particularly receptive subjects for field interviews are often individuals who have been quoted in articles. Another good method to develop interviews is to attend industry conventions to meet people informally and generate contacts.

Field Interviews

Effective field interviewing is a time-consuming and subtle process, but one that will amass the bulk of critical information for many industry studies. Although each interviewer will have his or her own style, a few simple points may be useful.

Contacts. It is generally most productive to make contacts with potential sources by telephone, rather than by letter, or by a telephone call following up a letter. People are apt to put a letter aside and avoid a decision about whether to cooperate. A telephone call forces the issue, and people are more likely to cooperate with an articulate and well-informed verbal request than they are with a letter.

Lead time. Researchers should begin to arrange interviews as early as possible, since lead times may be long and travel schedules difficult to coordinate; it may take months to arrange and complete them. Although at least a week is necessary lead time for most interviews, often the researcher can get an interview on very short notice as peoples' schedules change. It is desirable to have identified a number of alternative sources for any interview trip; if time becomes available they just might be willing to meet on short notice.

Quid pro quo. When arranging an interview, one should have something to offer the interviewee in return for his or her time. This can range from an offer to discuss (selectively of course) some of the researcher's observations based on the study, to thoughtful feedback on the interviewees' comments, to summaries of results or extracts of the study itself when feasible.

Affiliation. An interviewer must be prepared to give his or her affiliation and make some statement about the identity or (at least) the nature of his or her client if the study is being conducted for another organization. There is a moral obligation to alert an interviewee if information may be used to his or her detriment. If the identity of the interviewer's firm or client cannot be disclosed, some general statement must be made regarding the economic stake of the firm or client in the business being studied. Otherwise interviewees generally will not (and should not) grant an interview. Failure to disclose the identity of the firm or client will often limit (though not necessarily destroy) the usefulness of the interview.

Perseverance. No matter how skillful the interviewer, scheduling interviews is invariably a frustrating process; many times an interview is declined or the interviewee is openly unenthusiastic about it. This is in the nature of the problem and must not deter the interviewer. Often an interviewee is much more enthusiastic once a meeting has commenced and the relationship between interviewer and interviewee has become more personal.

Credibility. Interviewers greatly build credibility in arranging interviews and conducting them by having some knowledge of the business. This knowledge should be displayed early both in initial contacts and in interviews themselves. It makes the interview more interesting and potentially useful for the subject.

Teamwork. Interviewing is a tiring job and should ideally be done in teams of two if resources permit. While one member asks a question, the other can be taking notes and thinking up the next round of questions. It also allows one interviewer to maintain eye contact while the other takes notes. Teamwork also allows for a debriefing session immediately after the interview or at the end of the day, which is extremely useful in reviewing and clarifying notes, checking for consistent impressions, analyzing the interview, and synthesizing findings. Often much creative work in industry research is done in such sessions. A solo interviewer should leave time for such activity as well.

Questions. Gathering accurate data depends on asking unbiased questions, which do not prejudge or limit the answer nor expose the interviewer's own leanings. The interviewer must also be sensitive not to signal with his or her behavior, tone of voice, or expression what the "desired" answer is. Most people like to be cooperative and agreeable, and such signaling may bias the answer.

Notes. In addition to taking notes, the researcher can benefit from writing down observations about the interview itself. What publications does the individual use? What books are on the shelves? How are the offices decorated? Are they plush or sparse? Does the interviewee have any sample products in the office? This type of information often provides useful clues in interpreting the verbal data that result from the interview and also provides leads for additional sources.

Relationships. It is important to recognize that the subject is human, has never met the researcher before, has his or her own set of personal characteristics, and may be quite uncertain about what to say or not say. The style and vocabulary of the subject, his or her posture and attitude, body language, and so on give important clues and should be diagnosed quickly. A good interviewer is usually adept at quickly building a relationship with the subject. Making an effort to adapt to the style of the interviewee, to lower the level of uncertainty, and to make the interaction personal rather than keeping it on an abstract business level will pay off in the quality and candor of the information received.

Formal versus informal. Much interesting information often comes after the formal interview is over. For example, if the researcher can get a plant tour, the interviewee may become much more open as the setting becomes removed from the more formal setting of the office. The researcher should attempt to engineer interviews so that the inherent formality of the situation is overcome. This may be done by meeting on neutral ground, getting a tour, having lunch, or discovering and discussing other topics of common interest besides the industry in question.

Sensitive data. It will generally be most productive to start an interview with nonthreatening general questions rather than asking for specific numbers or other potentially sensitive data. In situations in which concern over sensitive data may be likely, it is usually best to state explicitly at the beginning of an interview that the researcher is not asking for proprietary data but rather impressions about the industry. Often individuals will be willing to provide data in the form of ranges, "ball park" figures, or "round numbers" that can be extremely useful to the inteviewer. Questions should be structured as follows: "Is the number of salespersons you have closer to 100 or 500?"

Pursuing leads. A researcher should always devote some time in interviews to asking questions such as the following: Whom else should we speak to? What publications should we be familiar with? Are there any conventions going on that might be useful to attend? (A large number of industries have conventions taking place in January and February.) Are there any books that might be enlightening? The way to maximize the use of interviews is to gain further leads from each one. If an interviewee is willing to provide a personal reference to another individual, the offer should always be taken. It will greatly facilitate the arrangement of further interviews.

Phone interviews. Phone interviews can be quite productive relatively late in a study when questions can be highly focused. Phone interviews work best with suppliers, customers, distributors, and other third-party sources.

FOR FURTHER INFORMATION

Some very helpful publications of interest to industry and company researchers are given below:

1. Lorna Daniells, "Business Information Sources", University of California Press, Berkeley, California (1985).
2. Leonard M. Fuld, "Competitor Intelligence", John Wiley & Sons, New York, New York (1985).
3. James Way, "Encyclopedia of Business Information Sources", Gale Research Company, Detroit, Michigan (1986), 6th edition.
4. Washington Researchers Staff, "How to Find Information About Companies", Washington Researchers Publishing Company, Washington, DC (1985), 4th edition.

The Editor

13

Analysis of Financial Statements: Conventional and Modern

Fred B. Renwick, Ph.D.
Graduate School of Business Administration
New York University

SECTION 1:
Conventional Analysis of Financial Statements

BACKGROUND: INFORMATION FROM FINANCIAL STATEMENTS

Traditionally, *financial analysis* consists of investigating a business organization (or industry group) to determine the current economic conditions of the enterprise. Financial statements, prepared and certified by professional accountants, constitute the main focus of conventional financial analysis. Information concerning the current *profitability*, *growth*, and *risk* (or *uncertainty*) of the business or industry is received via financial statements, and analysts traditionally use this information to form opinions or judgments concerning whether to recommend purchase or sale of credit or equity instruments issued by the business.

Nowadays, ever since the mid-1960s when the efficient market hypothesis (EMH) became popular, many financial analysts view the traditional investigation of accounting statements as a waste of time. The rationale for ignoring financial statements is as follows: Since markets are informationally efficient, security prices already reflect whatever information is contained in the accounting statements; therefore (modern) financial analysis consists of investigating relationships and interactions among security prices and rates of return. The *beta*, *alpha*, and *diversifiable risk* of the stock—in the framework of modern financial analysis—are used to form recommendations concerning whether to purchase or sell securities issued by the business. For true believers in the EMH, no need exists to go near the accounting statements.

The dichotomy or division between the two views can be illustrated simply by noting:

a. Traditional financial analysts believe accounting statements contain much valuable information concerning whether to recommend purchase or sale of the firm's securities, and the "analysis" consists of interpreting this financial statement information.
b. Modern financial analysts believe accounting statements contain no valuable information concerning whether to purchase or sell the firm's securities, so the "analysis" consists of collecting and interpreting capital market data.

Which view is correct? No one knows for sure. Since uncertainty exists concerning whether security prices are informationally efficient, this author recommends that financial analysts ignore neither the traditional nor the modern view. Do both. The immediately following sections of this chapter explain and illustrate methods and procedures for conventional financial analysis. The concluding sections illustrate modern financial analysis.

THE PROBLEM

Given: Conventional financial statements (balance sheet, consolidated income statement, statement of accumulated retained earnings, and statement of source and application of funds) for Universal Manufacturing Corporation (UMC). Typical statements are shown in Exhibits 1, 2, and 3, respectively.

The reader is assumed to understand each line item and know how to calculate relevant ratios from each statement. The job here is to go one step further and interpret the economic significance of the ratios and render an opinion or judgment concerning whether to invest money in UMC. In short, in light of the given financial statements, what do you— the reader—think of Universal Manufacturing Corporation as a possible investment?

The answer depends upon whether UMC as a business has relatively low risk and is growing profitably. Ideally, all three characteristics are necessary for a favorable recommendation: (1) relatively low credit and business risk, (2) increasing physical capacity to produce goods and services for the marketplace, and (3) relatively high or uptrending profitability as a business. At the opposite extreme, a clear signal to sell results if all three factors are opposite from the buy signal; namely, (1) relatively high risk, (2) declining or shrinking physical capacity to

EXHIBIT 1

UNIVERSAL MANUFACTURING CORPORATION
Balance Sheet
December 31, 1988

Assets	1988	1987
Current assets:		
Cash	$ 350,000	$ 250,000
Marketable securities at cost		
(market value: 1988, $2,980,000;		
1987, $1,900,000)	2,850,000	1,830,000
Accounts receivable		
Less: Allowance for bad debt:		
1988, $24,000; 1987, $21,000	4,800,000	4,370,000
Inventories	5,600,000	4,950,000
Total current assets	$13,600,000	$11,400,000
Fixed assets (property, plant, and equipment):		
Land	$ 734,000	$ 661,000
Building	5,762,000	5,258,000
Machinery	11,435,000	10,011,000
Office equipment	614,000	561,000
	18,545,000	16,491,000
Less: Accumulated depreciation	6,435,000	5,671,000
Net fixed assets	12,110,000	10,820,000
Prepayments and deferred charges	90,000	61,600
Intangibles (goodwill, patent, trademarks)	200,000	200,000
Total assets	$26,000,000	$22,481,600

Liabilities	1988	1987
Current liabilities:		
Accounts payable	$ 2,910,000	$ 2,300,000
Notes payable	1,420,000	730,000
Accrued expenses payable	430,000	350,000
Federal income taxes payable	1,240,000	1,320,000
Total current liabilities	$ 6,000,000	$ 4,700,000
Long-term liabilities:		
First mortgage bonds, 8% interest, due 2008	$ 2,000,000	$ 2,000,000
Total liabilities	$ 8,000,000	$ 6,700,000

Stockholders' Equity

	1988	1987
Capital stock:		
Preferred stock, 6% cumulative, $100		
par value each; authorized, issued,		
and outstanding 13,600 shares	1,360,000	1,360,000
Common stock, 30 cents par value each;		
authorized, issued, and		
outstanding 760,000 shares	228,000	228,000
Capital surplus	1,112,000	1,112,000
Accumulated retained earnings	15,300,000	13,081,600
Total stockholders' equity	$18,000,000	$15,781,600
Total liabilities and stockholders' equity	$26,000,000	$22,481,600

EXHIBIT 2

UNIVERSAL MANUFACTURING CORPORATION
Consolidated Income Statement
December 31, 1988 and 1987

	1988	1987
Net sales	$23,850,000	$19,810,000
Cost of sales and operating expenses		
Cost of goods sold	8,940,000	7,209,000
Depreciation	800,000	750,000
Selling and administrating expenses	8,232,000	6,814,000
Operating profit	$ 5,878,000	$ 5,037,000
Other income		
Dividends and interest	342,000	183,000
Total income	$ 6,220,000	$ 5,220,000
Less: Interest on bonds	160,000	160,000
Income before provision for federal income tax	$ 6,060,000	$ 5,060,000
Provision for federal income tax	2,240,000	1,980,000
Net profit for year	$ 3,820,000	$ 3,080,000
Common shares outstanding	760,000	760,000
Net earnings per share	$ 4.92	$ 3.95

Statement of Accumulated Retained Earnings	1988	1987
Balance January 1	$13,081,600	$11,413,200
Net profit for year	3,820,000	3,080,000
Total	$16,901,600	$14,493,200
Less: Dividends paid on		
Preferred stock	81,600	81,600
Common stock	1,520,000	1,330,000
Balance December 31	$15,300,000	$13,081,600

produce products, and (3) relatively low or downtrending profitability. Unfortunately, many companies in real life will be neither a clear-cut buy nor a clear-cut sell. In cases where companies have either one or two of the three factors trending in the desired direction, but not all three, the financial analyst must exercise judgment in forming a buy or sell opinion. The following sections explain and illustrate the critical elements in formulating that judgment.

PROFITABILITY OF BUSINESS ENTERPRISE

How profitable is UMC? A quick glance at UMC's consolidated income statement (see Exhibit 2) shows the following key accounting measures of profitability:

EXHIBIT 3

UNIVERSAL MANUFACTURING CORPORATION
Statement of Source and Application of Funds
December 31, 1988

	1988	
Funds were provided by		
Net income	$3,820,000	
Depreciation	800,000	
Total		$4,620,000
Funds were used for		
Dividends on preferred stock	$ 81,600	
Dividends on common stock	1,520,000	
Plant and equipment	1,720,300	
Sundry assets	398,100	
Total		$3,720,000
Increase in Working Capital		$ 900,000
Analysis of changes in working capital—1988:		
Changes in current assets:		
Cash	$ 100,000	
Marketable securities	1,020,000	
Accounts receivable	430,000	
Inventories	650,000	
Total		$2,200,000
Changes in current liabilities:		
Accounts payable	$ 610,000	
Notes payable	690,000	
Accrued expenses payable	80,000	
Federal income tax payable	(80,000)	
Total		$1,300,000

1. Total net operating profit (before both interest and tax); $6,220,000.
2. Total net operating profit (after taxes, but before interest): $3,980,000.

Where:

Total income	$6,220,000
Less: Provision for total taxes	2,240,000
After tax total income	$3,980,000

3. Total taxable income (profit, as legally defined in the Internal Revenue Service Tax Code). For financial analytic purposes, we can use: net operating income minus total interest paid

($6,060,000), implying an average tax rate of 36.96 percent for UMC.

$$(\$6,220,000 - \$160,000)T = \$2,240,000$$

$$T = \frac{\$2,240,000}{(\$6,220,000 - \$160,000)} = 0.3696$$

4. Total net income (available for distribution to common shareowners): $3,738,400.

Net profit for the year	$3,820,000
Less: Dividend requirements on preferred stock	81,600
Earnings available for common stock	$3,738,400
Preferred stock, 6% cumulative, $100 par value each; authorized, issued, and outstanding 13,600 shares	$81,600

5. Cash flow, which equals net income plus depreciation: $4,620,000.

$$\$3,820,000 + \$800,000 = \$4,620,000$$

6. Net earnings per share: $4.92.
7. Total dividends paid to common stockholders: $1,520,000.

The profitability analysis starts by relating the above-listed accounting figures to the relevant capital employed to generate that income. That is, how much capital was used to produce the stated amounts of income?

RETURN ON ASSETS AND RETURN ON CAPITAL

From UMC's balance sheet, the following total assets and capital were at management's disposal for operating the business:

1. Total assets: $26,000,000.
2. Total capitalization: $19,800,000.

Total assets	$26,000,000	
Less: Intangibles	$ 200,000	
Less: Total current liabilities	$ 6,000,000	
Total capitalization	$19,800,000	100.00%

Economist's View of Profitability

From an economic view, profitability is capital's contributive or remunerative proportionate share of total income, so we get:

1. Before-tax return on total assets: 23.92 percent.

$$\frac{\$6,220,000}{\$26,000,000} = 0.2392$$

2. After-tax return on total assets: 15.31 percent.

$$\frac{\$3,980,000}{\$26,000,000} = 0.1531$$

3. Before-tax return on total capitalization: 31.41 percent.

$$\frac{\$6,220,000}{\$19,800,000} = 0.3141$$

4. After-tax return on total capitalization: 20.10 percent.

$$\frac{\$3,980,000}{\$19,800,000} = 0.2010$$

Investor's View of Profitability

From an investor's view, profitability is the rate of capitalization which equates the future income stream to the present value of capital used to generate the income; so assuming the above-stated income amounts will continue periodically in perpetuity, we get:

1. Before-tax return on total assets: 27.67 percent.

$$\frac{\text{Total income}}{\text{Last year's total assets}} = \frac{\$6,220,000}{\$22,481,600} = 0.2767$$

2. After-tax return on total assets: 17.70 percent.

$$\frac{\text{Total income after tax but before interest}}{\text{Last year's total assets}} = \frac{\$3,980,000}{\$22,481,600} = 0.1770$$

3. Before-tax return on total capitalization: 35.38 percent.

$$\frac{\$6,220,000}{\$17,581,600} = 0.3538$$

where last year's total capitalization:

Total assets	$22,481,600
Less: intangibles	200,000
Less: total current liabilities	4,700,000
Total capitalization	$17,581,600

4. After-tax return on total capitalization: 22.64 percent.

$$\frac{\$3,980,000}{\$17,581,600} = 0.2264$$

Conclusion

The above rates of return can be used by the analyst to compare opportunity rates if the total capital and assets were to be employed elsewhere other than UMC. For example, less profitable corporations would realize less than $6,220,000 (before tax) on total assets of $26,000,000. A 10 percent return would generate only $2,600,000, or $3,620,000 less than UMC produced. By this standard we can say that UMC is relatively profitable as a business enterprise.

RETURN ON EQUITY

Total net income available for distribution to common shareowners, as shown on UMC's income statement, is generated by the stockowners' total investment. The return on equity ratio, from the investor's viewpoint of profitability (discounted cash flow units) is 25.92 percent.

$$\frac{\text{Income available for distribution to common stockholders}}{\text{Last year's total equity of common stockholders}} = \frac{\$3,738,400}{\$14,421,600}$$

where:

Last year's total stockholder equity	$15,781,600
Less: Preferred stock value	1,360,000
Last year's common stock equity	$14,421,600

Using current ratio (economic viewpoint) units, the return on equity is 22.47 percent.

$$\frac{\$3,738,400}{\$16,640,000} = 0.2247$$

where:

Current year's total stockholder equity	$18,000,000
Less: preferred stock value	1,360,000
Current year's common stock equity	$16,640,000

Income becomes available for distribution to common stockowners after bondholders and total taxes are paid; so variability in total net operating income is transmitted to equity owners. In other words, equity ownership is more risky than making a contractual loan to UMC.

Further, since income available for distribution to common shareowners is divided between retained earnings and total dividends paid, the following dividend ratios can be useful:

1. Discounted cash flow units (dividend yield): 10.54 percent.

$$\frac{\text{Total dividends paid to common stockholders}}{\text{Last year's total equity of common stockholders}}$$

$$= \frac{\$1,520,000}{\$14,421,600} = 0.1054$$

2. Current ratio units (dividend yield): 9.13 percent.

$$\frac{\text{Total dividends paid to common stockholders}}{\text{Current year's total equity of common stock owners}}$$

$$= \frac{\$1,520,000}{\$16,640,000} = 0.0913$$

A NOTE ON EARNINGS PER SHARE AS A MEASURE OF PROFITABILITY

Earnings per share (earnings available for distribution to common shareholders, divided by the total number of common shares outstanding), $4.92, is used by some financial analysts as a measure of business profitability. However, as noted above, using either an economist's or an investor's view, "profitability" implies employing physical or financial capital in the process of producing income. Consequently, the size or amount of income generated is correctly assessed in light of the size or amount of capital—not the number of shares of common stock— employed in the production process.

PROFIT MARGIN

Profit margin—the ratio of total profit to total income (profit per dollar, or per physical unit of sales)—is another way of expressing the economic concept that profit is the proportionate share of aggregate income contributed by capital. Since total sales revenue is related—via unit selling prices, physical quantity of goods produced and sold, and productivity of capital or total physical output per unit of capital input— to total assets, the financial analyst can develop and show relationships between the various profit margin ratios and both return on assets and return on equity. From UMC's consolidated income statement, we get:

1. Operating margin of profit: 24.65 percent.

$$\frac{\text{Operating profit}}{\text{Net Sales}} = \frac{\$5,878,000}{\$23,850,000} = 24.65\%$$

Previous year:

$$= \frac{\$5,037,000}{\$19,810,000} = 25.43\%$$

2. Operating cost ratio: 75.35 percent.

	Amount	Ratio
Net sales	$23,850,000	100.00%
Operating cost	17,972,000	75.35
Operating profit	$ 5,878,000	24.65%

3. Net profit ratio: 16.02 percent.

$$\frac{\text{Net profit for the year}}{\text{Net sales}} = \frac{\$3,820,000}{\$23,850,000} = 16.02\%$$

Previous year: 15.55 percent.

$$= \frac{\$3,080,000}{\$19,810,000} = 15.55\%$$

Further Analysis

At this point, to complete the connections, a serious analyst will seek additional information from management—information usually not reported in financial statements—concerning each of the five following variables:

p = Average price per unit of goods sold. Price depends upon product demand and market structure, together with managerial pricing policies.

c = Average cost per unit of goods sold. Unit cost depends upon labor and capital expense and raw materials and overhead.

Q_{sales} = Physical quantity of goods sold. Unit price and quantity of goods sold usually interact via product demand.

$Q_{produced}$ = Physical quantity of good produced. Goods produced but not sold remain in inventories. The change in the physical stock of inventories equals $Q_{produced}$ minus Q_{sales}.

λ_k = Productivity of capital, or the ratio of $Q_{produced}$ to total assets, where $Q_{produced}$ equals λ_k multiplied by total assets. Productivity of capital is the link between the corporation's physical assets and total quantity of real output produced.

Suppose, after discussions with corporate management, we discover that the average unit cost equals $3 and average unit selling price is $5. We can compute:

1. Ratio of price-to-cost = $\frac{\$5}{\$3}$ = 1.66. If the ratio of price-to-cost falls below (or to) 1.00, the business is headed for financial disaster because losses will be incurred on each unit sold. If the ratio of price-to-cost rises very high, competitors will be attracted by the relatively large margins of profit.
2. Difference between price and cost = ($5 − $3) = $2 per unit, which is an alternative way to state profit margin.
3. Operating profit = $(p - c)\ Q_{sales}$ = $5,878,000; which implies 2,939,000 physical units sold.

$$Q_{sales} = \frac{\$5,878,000}{\$2} = 2,939,000 \text{ units}$$

From UMC's balance sheet, inventories changed by $650,000 ($5,600,000 − $4,950,000 = $650,000). If we learn from management that inventories are priced at cost, then we can compute:

1. Change in the physical stock of inventories: 216,666 units. Note: financial analysts must confront and deal with a variety of policies and practices concerning inventory accounting (first-in, first-out; last-in, first-out, inflation, and the like). Ideally, a physical count and inspection of the inventory will occur, but often a physical count is impractical. Consequently we proceed using estimates.

$$Q_{produced} - Q_{sales} = \frac{\$650,000}{\$3} = 216,666 \text{ units}$$

2. Total physical quantity produced: 3,155,666 units.

$$Q_{produced} = 2,939,000 + 216,666 = 3,155,666 \text{ units}$$

3. Output per unit of capital input (productivity of capital): 12.14 percent.

$$\lambda_k = \frac{3,155,666 \text{ units}}{\$26,000,000} = 0.1214 \text{ or } 12.14\%$$

UMC produces 12.14 physical units of output per $100 of total assets.

4. Operating profit per unit produced: $1.86.

$$\frac{\$5,878,000}{3,155,666 \text{ units}} = \$1.86 \text{ per unit}$$

5. Operating profit per unit sold: $2.00.

$$\frac{\$5,878,000}{2,939,000 \text{ units}} = \$2.00 \text{ per unit}$$

6. Operating cost per unit produced: $5.70.

$$\frac{\$17,972,000}{3,155,666 \text{ units}} = \$5.70 \text{ per unit}$$

7. Operating cost per unit sold: $6.12.

$$\frac{\$17,972,000}{2,939,000 \text{ units}} = \$6.12 \text{ per unit}$$

8. Net income per unit produced: $1.21.

$$\frac{\$3,820,000}{3,155,666 \text{ units}} = \$1.21 \text{ per unit}$$

9. Net income per unit sold: $1.30.

$$\frac{\$3,820,000}{2,939,000 \text{ units}} = \$1.30 \text{ per unit}$$

We turn next to considerations of sources of growth.

GROWTH RATES OF INCOME

Where is UMC's apparent growth coming from? The analysis is straight-forward. One can start with dividends and work upward toward total assets, or start with total assets and work downward ending with dividends. In either case, we work with the understanding that "growth" implies change. The change can be in either quantity, quality, or variety of product; but we shall consider only quantity changes.

Dividend changes result from changes in either total net income or total retained earnings, or both. Ideally, dividend increases should result from increases in total net income, not from decreases in retained earnings. From the statement of accumulated retained earnings, we compute dividend growth of 14.29 percent.

$$\frac{\$1,520,000 - \$1,330,000}{\$1,330,000} = 0.1429$$

Net income changes result from changes in either (*a*) total net operating income, (*b*) total interest paid, or (*c*) total taxes paid, or a combination thereof. Ideally, net income growth should result from growth in total net operating income. From UMC's income statement, we compute net income growth of 24.03 percent.

$$\frac{\$3,820,000 - \$3,080,000}{\$3,080,000} = 0.2403$$

Total net operating income changes result from changes in either:

a. The operating margin of profit, together with the total physical quantity of goods and services sold.

b. The return on total assets, together with total assets.

From UMC's income statement, we compute total operating income growth of 19.16 percent.

$$\frac{\$6,220,000 - \$5,220,000}{\$5,220,000} = 0.1916$$

Net sales revenue changes result from changes in either unit selling price (inflationary growth) or from changes in the physical quantity of goods sold (real growth), or both. Ideally, growth in sales should result in increases in total physical quantity of goods and services produced and sold, not simply from price increases. From UMC's income statement, we compute growth of net sales to be 20.39 percent.

$$\frac{\$23,850,000 - \$19,810,000}{\$19,810,000} = 0.2039$$

Common stock equity changes result from changes in either external (new) equity offerings or internal (retained earnings) accumulations, or both. Since UMC's balance sheet shows no change in the number of common shares outstanding (760,000), the growth in equity is entirely via retained earnings. From our calculations above concerning return on equity, we calculate the growth in equity to be 15.38 percent.

$$\frac{\$16,640,000 - \$14,421,600}{\$14,421,600} = 0.1538$$

Total asset changes result from changes in either or both total liabilities and total stockholders' equity. From UMC's balance sheet, we calculate growth in total assets to be 15.65 percent.

$$\frac{\$26,000,000 - \$22,481,600}{\$22,481,600} = 0.1565$$

An additional way to view changes in total assets is to compute changes in the fractions of various categories of assets. From UMC's balance sheet, we get:

	Current Year		Previous Year	
Total current assets	$\dfrac{\$13,600,000}{\$26,000,000} =$	52.31%	$\dfrac{\$11,400,000}{\$22,481,600} =$	50.71%
Net fixed assets	$\dfrac{\$12,110,000}{\$26,000,000} =$	46.58%	$\dfrac{\$10,820,000}{\$22,481,600} =$	48.13%
Other assets	$\dfrac{\$\ \ \ 290,000}{\$26,000,000} =$	1.11%	$\dfrac{\$\ \ \ 261,600}{\$22,481,600} =$	1.16%
Total assets	$\dfrac{\$26,000,000}{\$26,000,000} =$	100.00%	$\dfrac{\$22,481,600}{\$22,481,600} =$	100.00%

The liabilities side of the balance sheet shows a small redistribution of total liabilities among long-term and short-term liabilities:

	Current Year	Previous Year
Total current liabilities	$\dfrac{\$6,000,000}{\$8,000,000} = 75\%$	$\dfrac{\$4,700,000}{\$6,700,000} = 70\%$
Long-term liabilities	$\dfrac{\$2,000,000}{\$8,000,000} = 25\%$	$\dfrac{\$2,000,000}{\$6,700,000} = 30\%$
Total liabilities	$\dfrac{\$8,000,000}{\$8,000,000} = 100\%$	$\dfrac{\$6,700,000}{\$6,700,000} = 100\%$

Long-term trendline growth rates can be computed if data concerning each of the above-listed variables are available for, say, 5 to 10 years. Note, however, long-term trendlines have no economic explanatory power. One objective of financial analysis is to explain the causes of change in trend or to set forth probable causes of future change in trend, so naïve trendline computations and analyses are omitted.

We turn next to considerations of risk of UMC.

FINANCIAL RISK AND UNCERTAINTY ASSESSMENT OF BUSINESS ENTERPRISE

Risk, as generally used in financial analysis, implies volatility (dispersion or variance) about the expected profit or sensitivity to changes in market factors (beta risk). Default (likelihood of loss) is a special case of volatility risk and information concerning UMC's ability to service its fixed expenses can be obtained from the *coverage ratios*[1] computed from UMC's income statement.

---

[1] Defined as:

$$\text{Interest coverage:} \quad \frac{\text{Net operating income before interest and taxes}}{\text{Interest charges on bonds}}$$

or

$$\text{Cash flow coverage:} \quad \frac{\text{Annual cash flow before interest and taxes}}{\text{Interest on bonds plus principal repayments}/(1 - \text{Tax rate})}$$

EXHIBIT 4

UNIVERSAL MANUFACTURING CORPORATION
Ten-Year Financial Summary

	1988	1987	1986	1985	1984	1983	1982	1981	1980	1979
Net sales	$23,850,000	$19,810,000	$17,240,000	$15,610,000	$14,020,000	$12,604,000	$11,040,000	$9,426,000	$8,324,000	$7,611,000
Total net operating income	6,220,000	5,220,000	4,678,000	4,300,000	3,907,000	3,740,000	3,300,000	2,840,000	2,600,000	2,360,000
Net profit for the year	3,820,000	3,080,000	2,775,000	2,555,000	2,288,000	2,105,000	1,827,000	1,512,000	1,314,000	1,179,000
Earnings per share	4.92	3.95	3.56	3.28	2.94	2.71	2.36	1.95	1.70	1.53
Dividends per share	2.00	1.75	1.55	1.43	1.40	1.40	1.24	1.12	1.10	1.03
Net working capital	7,600,000	6,700,000	6,300,000	5,500,000	5,023,000	3,596,000	3,424,000	2,964,000	2,604,000	2,261,000
Total assets	26,000,000	22,481,600	19,934,000	17,594,000	15,390,000	12,433,000	9,890,000	8,348,000	7,365,000	6,643,000
Net plant and equipment	12,110,000	10,820,000	9,918,000	8,747,000	6,743,000	4,740,000	3,635,000	3,150,000	2,830,000	2,479,000
Long-term debt	2,000,000	2,000,000	2,000,000	2,000,000	2,000,000	2,000,000	2,000,000	1,000,000	1,000,000	1,000,000
Preferred stock	1,360,000	1,360,000	1,360,000	1,360,000	1,360,000	1,360,000	1,360,000	1,360,000	1,360,000	1,360,000
Common stock and surplus	1,340,000	1,340,000	1,340,000	1,340,000	1,340,000	1,340,000	1,340,000	1,340,000	1,340,000	1,340,000
Book value per share	21.63									

For additional assessment of uncertainty and risk concerning Universal Manufacturing Corporation—beyond the conventional coverage ratios—we need financial statement data to compute each of the following:

1. *Variance* and *coefficient of variation*[2] of sales, net operating income, net income and dividends over the past nine or more years.
2. The *"earnings beta,"* which is the slope coefficient of the regression of UMC's net income (normalized by the preceding period's stock value) on the average normalized earnings for an entire sample of corporations.
3. The *"asset beta,"* which is the slope coefficient of a regression of UMC's percentage change in sales on the contemporaneous percentage change in gross national product.

Part of the data necessary to investigate risk of UMC is usually stated in the corporate annual report. A typical 10-year financial summary is shown on Exhibit 4 which states net sales, total net operating income, net profit for the year, earnings per share, and other relevant data. From the data on Exhibit 4, we can compute for net operating income a coefficient of variation of 0.3122, which implies a standard deviation of 31.22 percent of the mean over the 10-year time span.

$$\text{Mean} = \mu_{NOI} = \frac{1}{10} \sum_{t=1}^{10} (NOI)_t = \$3{,}916{,}500$$

$$\text{Sample standard deviation} = \left[\frac{1}{(10-1)} \sum_{t=1}^{10} ((NOI)_t - \mu_{NOI})^2 \right]^{1/2}$$

$$= \$1{,}222{,}847.79$$

$$\text{Coefficient of variation (NOI)} = \frac{\$1{,}222{,}847.79}{\$3{,}916{,}500} = 0.3122$$

Additional data which the analyst must get from other sources include: price per common share of UMC, price-earnings ratios of UMC's industry group, and the aggregate gross national product (GNP).

Armed with the above data, the analyst can compute the above-stated risk measures; namely, variance, coefficient of variation, average

---

[2] The coefficient of variation is the standard deviation divided by the mean (average).

EXHIBIT 5 A Summary of Selected Results from the Analyses

Company (Universal Manufacturing Corporation)			Common Stock (Stock 2 in Section 2)		
Profitability (Percent; Current Ratio Units)	Growth (Percent; Annual Change)	Risk (Uncertainty, Safety; Stability)	Alpha	Beta	Diversifiable Risk
1. Return on Assets: 23.92	1. $g_{Dividends}$: 14.29	1. Coefficient of Variation of Net Operating Income: 0.3122	+2.0456	+0.14	0.41
2. Return on Capital: 31.41	2. $g_{Net\ Income}$: 24.03	2. Asset Beta			
3. Return on Equity: 22.47	3. g_{NOI}: 19.16	3. Earnings Beta			
4. Operating Margin of Profit: 24.65	4. $g_{Net\ Sales}$: 20.39	4. Interest Coverage			
5. Dividend Yield: 9.13	5. g_{Assets}: 15.65	5. Cash-Flow Coverage			
	6. g_{Equity}: 15.38				

deviation about the trendline, standard deviation, earnings beta, and asset beta.[3]

CONCLUSION

We have investigated Universal Manufacturing Corporation as a business enterprise using conventional analysis of financial statements, supplemented with discussions with corporate management concerning selected critical variables. The profitability, growth, and risk of the business were the main variables for analysis. Selected results from these analyses are summarized on Exhibit 5, along with additional conclusions from modern security analysis as explained in greater detail below in Section 2.

On balance, we found the enterprise to be relatively profitable, experiencing growth for the right reasons, and exhibiting relatively stable trends. UMC rates a "buy" recommendation using the above criteria. The reasons are: UMC's economic value is increasing because of its relatively stable, profitable expansion of capacity to produce goods and services. Some analysts would withhold a "buy" recommendation until receiving knowledge that the stock can be purchased cheaply (low price relative to earnings per share of $4.92). Other analysts would "buy" economic value at current market prices, and not go bargain hunting. Of course, if economic value can be found at bargain prices, then "buy" with enthusiasm.

In the following section, we shall see that financial statements and discussions with management can have nothing to do with the "buy-sell" recommendation.

REFERENCES

BERNSTEIN, L. *Financial Statement Analysis.* 3d ed. Homewood, Ill.: Richard D. Irwin, 1983.

FOSTER, G. *Financial Statement Analysis.* Englewood Cliffs, N.J.: Prentice-Hall, 1986.

HAWKINS, D. F. *Corporate Financial Reporting and Analysis.* 3d. ed. Homewood, Ill.: Richard D. Irwin, 1986.

---

[3] See Chapter 48 for specifics concerning the calculation of these statistical quantities.

SECTION 2:
Modern Security Analysis

Modern security analysis differs significantly from traditional or conventional fundamental and technical analysis. In a world wherein information is used as a scarce economic good, rarely or never to be wasted, prices of every security fully reflect all knowledge possessed by potential as well as actual participants in the marketplace. In such a world, the only reasons underlying systematic changes in price (or returns) are: *(a)* new information heretofore unavailable, or *(b)* changes in personal beliefs or expectations regarding future events or factors which affect security prices and returns. All other changes in price (or return) are of a "nonsystematic" nature, which implies temporary deviations or movements from equilibrium, and are due to no special causes. Modern security analysis therefore focuses on systematic or identifiable causes of change in equilibrium prices of risky financial claims.

If securities markets and prices are informationally efficient (and we presume they are), then the analyst's job simplifies to estimating three (and only three) parameters for every marketable security; namely:

a. The expected systematic risk over the future holding period or *beta*, of the security.
b. The diversifiable or nonmarket component of total expected risk of the security.
c. The risk-adjusted expected return, or *alpha*, of the security.

Beta measures the change or responsiveness of the security's excess return when the market's excess return changes by a small amount. Beta is the appropriate measure of risk of an individual security. The term *excess return* is used extensively in modern security analysis, and refers to the premium or remuneration paid or received for risk bearing. Excess return, as explained below in greater detail on Table 3, is the difference between the risky expected return and the alternative risk-free, or guaranteed return.

The nonmarket-related risk, together with the systematic or market-related risk, equals the total risk or volatility of the security. If markets and prices are informationally efficient, then investors will hold well-diversified portfolios; so no extra remuneration will be paid or expected for bearing risk not related to the market. But if the portfolio is small, with less than 15 or 20 securities, then the nonmarket-related risk is incompletely diversified away, and becomes an important consideration for the analyst.

Alpha measures the expected deviation or difference between the stock's expected excess return, from its equilibrium value, over the future holding period. Equilibrium implies no cause for change, or no motivation to exchange or trade one security for another. In equilibrium, alpha for a security equals zero. If the stock offers more excess return than is warranted by its systematic risk, then alpha for that stock is positive. Positive alpha stocks therefore represent "buy" situations because rational investors always prefer returns which are larger than smaller alternative returns which are justified by the associated risks. Similarly, if the stock offers less excess return than is warranted by its systematic risk, then alpha for the stock is negative. Negative alpha stocks therefore represent "sell" situations.

To summarize, modern security analysis consists of estimating three and only three parameters which identify or characterize every security; namely: *(a)* the expected riskiness or beta of the security, *(b)* the diversifiable or nonmarket-related risk of the security, and *(c)* the expected risk premium or excess return, alpha, of the security.

The following sections explain and illustrate, using three stocks, the complete basis for rendering buy-hold-sell recommendations as an efficient market analyst. We shall show what to do, what data are necessary, how to analyze the data, how to interpret results from the analysis, and how to translate conclusions from the analysis into specific stock recommendations.

Security, Market Portfolio and Risk-Free Return Data

The problem is as follows. Assume that three risky securities from one of the stock exchanges or over-the-counter are identified. Your job is to analyze all three, with the objective of formulating a buy, hold, or sell recommendation. You, the analyst, must know how to proceed; what to do. What data and information are necessary for modern security analysis?

The answer is: only money and capital market data are necessary. No need exists to collect and analyze financial statements, talk with top management, chart historical price trends and cycles, and the like; all because, if markets are perfectly efficient, then current price will already fully reflect whatever knowledge may be obtained from these traditional sources.

At the outset, three following considerations are necessary:

a. The time interval of the future holding period return, which is a subjectively chosen time span, such as monthly, quarterly, or annually.

b. The number of historical holding period returns to analyze, which also is a subjectively chosen number, such as 30, 100, or 3,000 holding period returns.

TABLE 1 Input Data: Security, Market and Risk-Free Historical Returns

(1)	(2)	(3)	(4)	(5)	(6)
		Total Rate of Return, Annualized			
Time Period	Stock 1	Stock 2	Stock 3	Market Portfolio	R_F
0	9.5	10.1	9.5	10.0	8.0
−1	20.5	11.5	24.0	20.5	8.5
−2	5.0	11.0	1.5	7.0	9.0
−3	13.0	11.5	23.0	16.5	8.5
−4	−0.5	9.0	−5.1	1.5	7.5
−5	8.0	9.5	15.5	11.0	7.0
−6	12.5	11.5	26.5	17.5	7.5
−7	7.5	9.8	11.0	7.0	8.0
−8	6.5	10.0	6.0	5.0	9.0
−9	14.6	12.0	16.0	14.5	8.5
Arithmetic average return	9.66	10.59	12.79	11.05	8.15

c. The return on investment, which must be the total rate of return (dividend yield plus capital change) realized historically from each security.

These input data, together with information regarding the market portfolio and risk-free returns, are set forth in Table 1.

Historical versus future returns. Note what at first glance might appear to be a paradox. The analyst needs critical decision variables—risks and expected returns—pertaining to future time and events, but we almost always start the analysis from historical experience. One reason is, historical experience usually is useful for aiding judgment and beliefs concerning future events. Another reason is, correct analysis of the sample will enable us to make inferences, within well-defined limits of betting odds, regarding possible outcomes over the next future time interval under consideration.

What ought to be the time interval or span over which to calculate returns on investment in securities? The future holding period time interval, as noted above, is a subjective or personal choice. Typical holding periods and time intervals, are daily, weekly, monthly, quarterly, annual, or longer. The speed of adjustment to equilibrium is important when considering short future holding period time intervals, such as daily or weekly. Since modern security analysis assumes equilibrium, and also assumes that observed returns tend to move, for economic reasons, toward equilibrium, the question becomes: How fast or rapid is the equilibrating process? Many studies show the process to be quite rapid, almost instantaneous. We, therefore, can think in terms of equilibrium returns daily, weekly, monthly, quarterly, annually, or for other time periods.

One guideline or suggestion for selecting a time interval is to follow customer preferences. If the customer plans, for example, on quarterly progress reviews and thinks in terms of quarterly returns, then the historical observations also should be quarterly—not monthly or annual or some other—returns. Since betas (and other statistics we will be using) calculated using quarterly time intervals are not directly comparable with betas calculated using some alternative time interval (i.e., daily, monthly, or annual), investment advice on quarterly returns should be based on quarterly input data. In other words, monthly betas match monthly returns, annual betas match annual returns. The same time interval should be used for both the expected future holding period and the historical observations. Cross matching introduces unwanted biases and errors. For this study, assume that the time interval as shown in Table 1 is quarterly.

How many historical periods are necessary or sufficient for analysis? Table 1 shows 10 time periods, from 0 (present) back to −9 (9 periods ago). In practice, the objective is to select a sufficiently "large-size" sample so that correct inferences can be made, based on the sample observations. Standard statistical estimates and regressions, such as we are using, generally require a sample size of not less than 30 observations. Consequently, for monthly holding periods, a little more than two years of data are necessary. For quarterly holding periods, a minimum of seven and a half years of data are necessary. Typically, 15 or 20 years (60 or 80 quarters) of data are used. Note the problem encountered in getting a large-size sample if annual returns are used. The markets and economic conditions 30 or 60 years ago might have been quite different from current markets and economic conditions. For this study, solely to shorten the calculations, suppose 10 (instead of 60 or 80) quarterly observations are sufficient.

For the holding period return, total rate of return—dividend yield plus capital change—is required for every security. Some investors, for personal, tax, or other reasons, may emphasize income (dividend yield or interest income) more than capital gains, or capital gains more than current income. But using either component, dividend yield or capital change, without the other is a mistake. Rational investors always prefer larger to smaller total rates of return. On Table 2, for example, some investors may incorrectly prefer security or portfolio 1 because of the "high" income component (15 percent as compared with 1 percent).

The fact is, the owner of security or portfolio 2 ends with more money (38 percent as compared with 13 percent). All rational investors, given a choice, prefer 38 percent instead of 13 percent. Moreover, as we shall see later, if securities (or portfolios) 1 and 2 have equal risks, then

TABLE 2 Components of Expected Return

	Security or Portfolio (percent)	
	1	2
Income	15%	1%
Capital gain	−2%	37%
Total rate of return	13%	38%

rational investors will borrow (go short) at 13 percent from security 1 and lend (go long) at 38 percent to security 2 to profit the difference or spread of 25 percent. At 25 percent compounded, money doubles in 3.1 periods.

Both components, income plus capital change are necessary for calculating total rate of return. After-tax total rates of return typically are used. However, tax effects on dividend (or interest) income and capital gains often are ignored in the analysis. For this study, imagine the total rates of return quarterly (stated as annualized equivalent rates), on each of the three securities are all after tax and are as listed in columns 2, 3, and 4 in Table 1.

Columns 5 and 6 in Table 1 pertain to returns from the market portfolio together with returns from risk-free securities.

The market portfolio and market risk premiums play a critically important role in modern security analysis. Ideally, the market portfolio contains an appropriate fraction of every marketable security, from every market, everywhere. As a practical matter, we must select and use a proxy for "the market portfolio." Typical proxies of "the market" include indexes maintained and published by Standard & Poor's Corporation, Value Line, Dow Jones & Company, Wilshire Associates, the New York Stock Exchange, and the American Stock Exchange. Other proxies also exist, or can be computed by the analyst, using a computerized data base such as CRSP or Compustat. After a proxy is selected, an alternative proxy should never be used either during or after the analysis because betas (and other relevant statistics) which are calculated using one proxy for the market portfolio are not directly comparable with betas (for the same stock) which are calculated using a different proxy. Stay with whichever proxy you selected for the market portfolio. For this example, assume that the market portfolio's total rates of return, dividend yield plus capital change (stated as annualized equivalents of quarterly rates) are as listed in column 5 in Table 1.

Finally, a risk-free rate of return must be considered. In practice, the term *risk-free* in fact implies default-free, insured, or guaranteed rate of return over the future expected holding period. Uncertainty never can be associated with the risk-free rate. Typically, U.S. Treasury bill or bond rates are used in the calculations. The U.S. government, presumably, always is both able and willing to pay its money and debt obligations as promised. Note that the risk-free rate does not mean constant or unchanging over all future time. The risk-free rate must be constant only for the next forthcoming holding period. After the next holding period expires, a new risk-free rate may exist, thereby reflecting new or different investment opportunities.

We need to note and compare the time interval covered by the risk-free rate and the corresponding time interval covered by the risky returns. The two time intervals must be identical; otherwise an unwanted bias gets into the analysis. For example, if an annual return on a stock (or the market) is compared with a three-month return on Treasury bills, then the analyst is implicitly assuming something which ought to be stated explicitly regarding nine-month, risk-free returns available upon expiration of the three-month T bill. The time interval for the guaranteed rate should coincide with the time interval for all four risky rates listed in Table 1.

The next step involves calculating excess returns for each of the securities, and for the market portfolio.

Market Risk Data/Beta and Market Return

The first computations involve subtracting the risk-free rate from each of the four risky returns, listed on Table 1, to get the excess returns. The excess returns, also called risk premiums, are listed on Table 3.

Excess returns, from an economic point of view, represent extra payment or money earned for bearing risk in excess of the guaranteed or insured alternative investment. For example, if an insured account

TABLE 3 Excess Returns, Historically (risky minus risk-free returns)

(1) Time Period	(2) Stock 1	(3) Stock 2	(4) Stock 3	(5) Market
0	1.5	2.1	1.5	2.0
−1	12.0	3.0	15.5	12.0
−2	−4.0	2.0	−7.5	−2.0
−3	4.5	3.0	14.5	8.0
−4	−8.0	1.5	−12.6	−6.0
−5	1.0	2.5	8.5	4.0
−6	5.0	4.0	19.0	10.0
−7	−0.5	1.8	3.0	−1.0
−8	−2.5	1.0	−3.0	−4.0
−9	6.1	3.5	7.5	6.0
Arithmetic average excess return	1.51	2.44	4.64	2.90

guarantees 5 percent, then all rational investors will require or expect more than 5 percent from a risky security where no guarantees are given. Excess returns, in equilibrium, should never be neither zero nor negative; they should always be positive in equilibrium. The size or amount by which the premium must be positive is a personal or subjective preference, and depends on how averse the investor is to risk bearing. More averse investors will require larger excess returns or premiums than will other investors who are less averse to risk bearing. For example, if a risky security promises, 9 percent, when the T bill rate is 6 percent, then one rational risk-averse investor might subjectively accept the 3 percent premium, or excess return, as satisfactory remuneration for choosing the risky over the risk-free security. Some alternative investor with a greater aversion to risk bearing, might rationally reject the 3 percent excess return as insufficient or unsatisfactory remuneration, and will therefore subjectively prefer, or be happier with, the guaranteed 6 percent T bill rate than with the risky 9 percent.

Note from the discussion in the preceding paragraph how changes over time in the risk-free rate can cause changes in investment decisions and in the allocation of capital to competing securities. For example, if that same risky security (discussed above) promises 9 percent return when the T bill rate has shifted up to 15 percent, then no rational investor will forego a guaranteed 15 percent to get into a risky 9 percent return, which is equivalent to paying (not receiving) 6 percent for the privilege of investing. All rational investors, under these conditions, will prefer the 15 percent T bill rate over the 9 percent risky return.

Negative excess returns can and do materialize after the fact—after the final closing prices and dividend receipts become known. But ex ante, before the fact, no rational investor will prefer negative expected excess returns.

In one sense, the above discussion illustrates the nature of risk; namely, exposure of capital to possible (alternative opportunity) losses (after the fact) in exchange for a chance (before the fact) at an extra return. On balance, in equilibrium, the expected extra return must compensate and pay adequately to compensate for the extra risk. Negative expected excess returns or risk premiums imply willingness by investors to pay (the amount of the negative premium) for risk bearing, which is perverse behavior for business investors.

We see from Table 3 that over the time periods observed, the market offered a premium (or excess return) which fluctuated, mostly positive but sometimes negative, and averaged 2.90 percent for the 10 time intervals under analysis. Stocks 1 and 2 offered a lower average excess return, 1.51 and 2.44 percent, respectively. Stock 3 offered 4.64 percent, a larger average excess return than the market. The question now is: To what extent does variability or fluctuation, or risk in the market explain or impact the excess returns on our three stocks? For an answer, we must calculate two numbers; namely: *(a)* the variance, volatility, or total risk of the market portfolio, and *(b)* the beta for each of the three securities.

Characteristic lines for risky securities. To help visualize and better understand the calculations we are about to do, take the data from Table 3 and plot all the points as shown on Chart 1, where the stock excess returns are plotted along the vertical axis and the market excess returns are plotted along the horizontal axis.

What we are doing on Chart 1 is known formally as plotting and calculating the characteristic line for our three securities. The characteristic line is the focal point of modern security analysis because its complete specification identifies the three parameters we identified at the outset, in our opening paragraphs; namely:

CHART 1

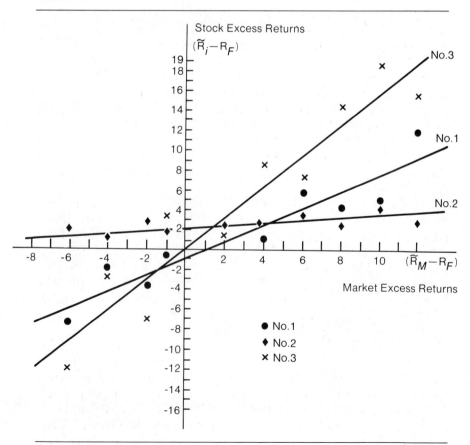

a. *Beta*, which is the slope of the characteristic line. The slope of the line determines the expected difference on stock excess returns when market excess returns differ by one unit.
b. The *nonmarket-related risk* of the security, which is the scatter or average deviation of the observed points about the characteristic line. The nonmarket-related risk is that component or part of a security's total risk which can be diversified arbitrarily close to zero if portfolios are sufficiently large in size.
c. *Alpha*, which is the vertical axis intercept point on the characteristic line. The intercept identifies the stock's excess return when the market's excess return equals zero.

Every security has a characteristic line. The three key measures from the characteristic line (alpha, beta, and nonmarket risk) summarize a security's prospects if markets are efficient. Estimation of these variables is the responsibility of the security analyst.

Market risk calculations. Analysis of our transformed input data from Table 3 can start with considerations of riskiness of the market's excess returns. Market excess returns are critically important because modern security analysis rests on evidence that: *(a)* excess returns for individual securities, in equilibrium, are determined to a large extent by excess returns available in the market generally, and *(b)* risk of individual securities, in equilibrium, is determined to a large extent by risk in the market generally.

How risky was the market over the time periods observed? The answer involves calculating the variance or standard deviation (sometimes called volatility) of the excess returns on the market. Variance, as the name suggests, simply measures the average variability of the individual returns about their long-term, or arithmetic, average. More precisely, variance, as illustrated on Table 4, is the average of the squared deviations (or differences) between *(a)* the 10 observed excess returns on the market (column 2 in Table 4), and *(b)* the average excess return on the market (2.9 percent), which for our example at the bottom of column 4 in Table 4, works out to 33.69.

The risk of the market's excess return is the standard deviation, which is calculated by taking the square root of the variance, which, for our example, works out to the square root of 33.69, or approximately 5.80 percent.

To summarize, the market's excess return, over the period analyzed, averaged 2.90 percent, ranged from a high of plus 12.0 percent to a low of −6.0 percent, and has a standard deviation (average difference either side of the 2.90 percent mean) of 5.80 percent.

The next step in the analysis involves estimating how responsive each of our three securities was to the fluctuations just analyzed for the

TABLE 4   Market Risk Data

(1) Time Period	(2) Market Excess Return	(3) Deviation from Average Excess Return	(4) Squared Deviation
0	2.0	(2.0 − 2.9)	0.81
−1	12.0	(12.0 − 2.9)	82.81
−2	−2.0	(−2.0 − 2.9)	24.01
−3	8.0	(8.0 − 2.9)	26.01
−4	−6.0	(−6.0 − 2.9)	79.21
−5	4.0	(4.0 − 2.9)	1.21
−6	10.0	(10.0 − 2.9)	50.41
−7	−1.0	(−1.0 − 2.9)	15.21
−8	−4.0	(−4.0 − 2.9)	47.61
−9	6.0	(6.0 − 2.9)	9.61

Total = 336.90
Divide the total by 10 to get the average = 33.69

market's excess returns. In other words, we must calculate beta for each of our three stocks.

Beta calculations.   Beta, as we noted, is the slope of the characteristic lines plotted on Chart 1, and as such can be computed using methods similar to how we analyzed market risk data in Table 4. That is to say, for each stock (1, 2, and 3) from Table 3, we calculate and list in column 2, Table 5, the deviation of each of the 10 observations about the average excess return for that stock.

Second, for the market risk from Table 3, we calculate and list in column 3, Table 5, the deviation of each of the 10 observations about the average excess return, 2.90 percent.

Third, we multiply column 2 for each of the three stocks by column 3, the market, and tabulate the products in columns 4, 5, and 6 on Table 5. Beta, then, is simply the average value of columns 4, 5, and 6, divided by 33.69, the market risk or average from Table 4.

To summarize, we get the following results from Table 5:

$$\beta \text{ (stock 1)} = (29.631/33.69) = 0.88$$
$$\beta \text{ (stock 2)} = (4.564/33.69) = 0.14$$
$$\beta \text{ (stock 3)} = (53.904/33.69) = 1.60$$

A beta of unity implies that the stock's excess returns vary identically with the market's excess returns; the stock excess return will change by the same amount as a given change in the market excess return. A beta greater (or less) than unity implies that the stock's excess returns vary more (or less) than a given change in the market's excess return. That is to say, a beta less than unity (stocks 1 and 2) implies the

TABLE 5 Security Risk Data: Calculating Stock Betas

(1)	(2)	(3)	(4)	(5)	(6)
	Deviation from Average Excess Return		Product: Column 2 Multiplied by Column 3		
Time Period	Stock 1	Market	Stock 1	Stock 2	Stock 3
0	(1.5 − 1.51)	(2.0 − 2.9)	0.009	0.306	2.826
−1	(12.0 − 1.51)	(12.0 − 2.9)	95.459	5.096	98.826
−2	(−4.0 − 1.51)	(−2.0 − 2.9)	26.999	2.156	59.486
−3	(4.5 − 1.51)	(8.0 − 2.9)	15.249	2.856	50.286
−4	(−8.0 − 1.51)	(−6.0 − 2.9)	84.639	8.366	153.436
−5	(1.0 − 1.51)	(4.0 − 2.9)	−0.561	0.066	4.246
−6	(5.0 − 1.51)	(10.0 − 2.9)	24.779	11.076	101.956
−7	(−0.5 − 1.51)	(−1.0 − 2.9)	7.839	2.496	6.396
−8	(−2.5 − 1.51)	(−4.0 − 2.9)	27.669	9.936	52.716
−9	(6.1 − 1.51)	(6.0 − 2.9)	14.229	3.286	8.866
		Total	296.310	45.640	539.04
Divide the total by 10 to get the average			29.631	4.564	53.904
Divide the average by 33.69, market risk from table 4, to get *beta*			0.88	0.14	1.60

stock return will change by a fraction of a given change in the market returns. A beta greater than unity (stock 3) implies that the stock return will change by a greater amount than a given change in the market return, for the market proxy used in the analysis. A zero beta implies independence from the market's returns—a risk-free security. A negative beta implies the stock's excess return moves in the opposite direction from the market's excess return.

Betas from returns versus betas from excess returns. It is important to note that some analysts use short-cut procedures for calculating betas. Data are often taken from Table 1 instead of from Table 3 to plot Chart 1 and to calculate the listings on both Tables 4 and 5. In our particular case at hand, the final answers come out close to the original answers; namely:

$$\beta' \text{ (stock 1)} = (30.002/33.4225) = 0.90$$
$$\beta' \text{ (stock 2)} = (4.5155/33.4225) = 0.14$$
$$\beta' \text{ (stock 3)} = (52.9305/33.4225) = 1.58$$

In our particular case, the differences between β and β' for our three stocks are small because of our relatively small observed variations in the risk-free rate. From Table 1, our mean risk-free rate is 8.15, with a range between 9 and 7. In practice generally, the risk-free rate often moves from single- to double-digit numbers, and back again; so equilibrium relationships (i.e., excess returns from Table 3) should be used instead of the simpler comovement relationships (total returns from Table 1) between market and security returns.

Nonmarket Risk of the Securities/Alpha and Excess Returns

Alpha calculations. Alpha, as we noted, is the vertical axis intercept of the characteristic line, and as such can be calculated as shown on Table 6.

In the first row of Table 6, we list (from Table 3), the stock's average excess return. Then we multiply the stock's beta from the above calculations (row 2 in Table 6) by 2.90, the market's average excess return (from Table 3), to get the results on row 3, Table 6. Finally, alpha equals the difference between row 1 and row 3 on Table 6. To summarize, from Table 6 we get the following results:

$$\alpha \text{ (stock 1)} = 1.51 - 0.880 \text{ (2.90)} = -1.042$$
$$\alpha \text{ (stock 2)} = 2.44 - 0.136 \text{ (2.90)} = 2.0456$$
$$\alpha \text{ (stock 3)} = 4.64 - 1.60 \quad \text{(2.90)} = 0.000$$

Alpha, in equilibrium, must equal zero, otherwise the stock would be a buy (if alpha is positive), because positive excess returns on stocks are preferred if market excess returns are zero, or a sell (if alpha is negative), because negative excess returns on stocks are *not* preferred if market excess returns are zero.

For our particular example at hand, an alpha less than zero (negative alpha, stock 1) implies negative or less excess return expected on the security than explained or predicted by the market excess return. An alpha greater than zero (stock 2) implies positive or more excess return expected on the security than explained or predicted by the market excess return. An alpha equal to zero (stock 3) implies that the stock expected excess return equals that predicted by the beta risk of the security.

TABLE 6 Calculations of Alpha

		Stock 1	Stock 2	Stock 3
(1)	Stock average excess return	1.51	2.44	4.64
(2)	Beta	0.88	0.14	1.60
(3)	Beta multiplied by 2.90, market average excess return	2.55	0.41	4.64
(4)	Difference: Row 1 minus Row 3 equals Alpha	−1.04	+2.03	0.00

TABLE 7 Expected Excess Returns Calculations

(1)	(2)	(3)	(4)	(5)	(6)	(7)
			Stock 1		*Stock 2*	*Stock 3*
Time Period	*Market Excess Return*	*Beta, 0.88, Multiplied by Col. (2)*	*Alpha, −1.04 Plus Col. (3)*	*Beta, 0.14, Multiplied by Col. (2)*	*Alpha, 2.04, Plus Col. (5)*	*Beta, 1.60, Multiplied by Col. (2)*
0	2.0	1.76	0.72	0.28	2.32	3.20
−1	12.0	10.56	9.52	1.68	3.72	19.20
−2	−2.0	−1.76	−2.80	−0.28	1.76	−3.20
−3	8.0	7.04	6.00	1.12	3.16	12.80
−4	−6.0	−5.28	−6.32	−0.84	1.20	−9.60
−5	4.0	3.52	2.48	0.56	2.60	6.40
−6	10.0	8.80	7.76	1.40	3.44	16.00
−7	−1.0	−0.88	−1.92	−0.14	1.90	−1.60
−8	−4.0	−3.52	−4.56	−0.56	1.48	−6.40
−9	6.0	5.28	4.24	0.84	2.88	9.60
Average	2.90	2.55	1.51	0.40	2.44	4.64

Nonmarket risk of the securities. Nonmarket-related risk is that part or component of total risk of a security which: (a) remains unexplained by market variations, and/or (b) can be diversified arbitrarily close to zero if a sufficiently large number of securities are added to the portfolio. The calculation or estimation of nonmarket risk is best done in two steps as follows, and as illustrated on both Tables 7 and 8.

Step 1 involves calculating the expected excess return for each time period, for each stock, as predicted by the stock's characteristic line on Chart 1. These calculations are set forth in Table 7, where column 2 is the market's excess return from Table 3, and is the common factor causing change in excess return for every security in the marketplace.

The predicted excess return for our three stocks (columns 4, 6 and 7 on Table 7) is calculated by first multiplying the stock's beta by the market's excess return (columns 3, 5, and 7 in Table 7), and then adding alpha for the stock.

Step 2 involves calculating the difference between (a) the observed or realized excess return on each stock (columns 2, 6, and 10 in Table 8; taken from columns 2, 3, and 4, respectively, in Table 3); and (b) the calculated or predicted excess return (columns 3, 7, and 11 of Table 8; taken from columns 4, 6, and 7 respectively, from Table 7).

The differences between actual or observed and calculated or predicted excess returns (columns 4, 8, and 12 in Table 8) are first squared and then averaged (columns 5, 9, and 13 in Table 8). The nonmarket-related risk, finally is the square root of the average squared

TABLE 8 Nonmarket-Related Risk Calculations

(1)	(2)	(3)	(4)	(5)	(6)	(7)	(8)	(9)	(10)	(11)	(12)	(13)
		Stock 1				Stock 2				Stock 3		
Time Period	Realized Excess Return	Calculated Excess Return	Difference Col. (2) – Col. (3)	Square of Difference	Realized Excess Return	Calculated Excess Return	Difference Col. (2) – Col. (3)	Square of Difference	Realized Excess Return	Calculated Excess Return	Difference Col. (2) – Col. (3)	Square of Difference
0	1.5	0.72	0.78	0.6084	2.1	2.32	−0.22	0.0484	1.5	3.20	−1.70	2.89
−1	12.0	9.52	2.48	6.1504	3.0	3.72	−0.72	0.5184	15.5	19.20	−3.70	13.69
−2	−4.0	−2.80	−1.20	1.4400	2.0	1.76	0.24	0.0576	−7.5	−3.20	−4.30	18.49
−3	4.5	6.00	−1.50	2.2500	3.0	3.16	−0.16	0.0256	14.5	12.80	1.70	2.89
−4	−8.0	−6.32	−1.68	2.8224	1.5	1.20	0.30	0.0900	−12.6	−9.60	−3.00	9.00
−5	1.0	2.48	−1.48	2.1904	2.5	2.60	−0.10	0.0100	8.5	6.40	2.10	4.41
−6	5.0	7.76	−2.76	7.6176	4.0	3.44	0.56	0.3136	19.0	16.00	3.00	9.00
−7	−0.5	−1.92	1.42	2.0164	1.8	1.90	−0.10	0.0100	3.0	−1.60	4.60	21.16
−8	−2.5	−4.56	2.06	4.2436	1.0	1.48	−0.48	0.2304	−3.0	−6.40	3.40	11.56
−9	6.1	4.24	1.86	3.4596	3.5	2.88	0.62	0.3844	7.5	9.60	−2.10	4.41
	1.51	1.51	0.00	0.0000	2.44	2.44	0.00	0.00	4.64	4.64	0.00	0.00
	Sum			32.80				1.69				97.50
	Average			3.28				0.17				9.75
	Square root			1.81				0.41				3.12

TABLE 9 Summary of Characteristic Line Calculations (Alpha, Beta, and Nonmarket-Related Risk; Three Securities)

	Actual Excess Return	Predicted Excess Return (characteristic line)	Nonmarket-Related Risk
Stock 1	$(\bar{R}_i - R_F)$	$-1.042 + 0.880\,(\bar{R}_M - R_F)$	1.81
Stock 2	$(\bar{R}_i - R_F)$	$2.046 + 0.136\,(\bar{R}_M - R_F)$	0.41
Stock 3	$(\bar{R}_i - R_F)$	$1.60\,(R_M - R_F)$	3.12

deviation between actual and predicted excess returns. Our results from the bottom line of columns 5, 9, and 13 of Table 8 are:

$$\text{Nonmarket risk (stock 1)} = 1.81$$
$$\text{Nonmarket risk (stock 2)} = 0.41$$
$$\text{Nonmarket risk (stock 3)} = 3.12$$

The nonmarket-related risk measures the average scatter or dispersion about the stock's characteristic line. A small scatter, such as stocks 1 and 2 implies a tighter fit; a better prediction of the actual realized excess return. A large scatter, such as stock 3 implies a loose fit or a not so good prediction of the actual realized excess return. A zero scatter implies a perfect fit—a perfect prediction of realized excess return—which would be rare of any individual security in the marketplace, but which can be achieved in a portfolio context by adding more individual securities to the portfolio.

To summarize, nonmarket risk of a security is that part or component of total risk which remains unexplained after accounting for market effects. Nonmarket risk is important for characterizing individual securities; but if a portfolio contains more than 15 or 20 stocks, then the nonmarket risk of individual securities becomes an unimportant consideration.

Calculated excess returns. An overall summary of our scatter plots on Chart 1 and calculations from Tables 4 through 8 can be set forth succinctly as shown in Table 9.

We shall turn next to another way of looking at what we did in Chart 1 and Table 9; namely, instead of plotting the stock's excess return on the vertical axis and the market's excess return on the horizontal axis as we did on Chart 1, we can plot the stock expected total return (not excess return) on the vertical axis and the stock's beta on the horizontal axis to get the scatter about the security market line.

Security market line. The security market line (SML) is one of the most important tools for modern analysts. The SML is a straight line

CHART 2 Security Market Line

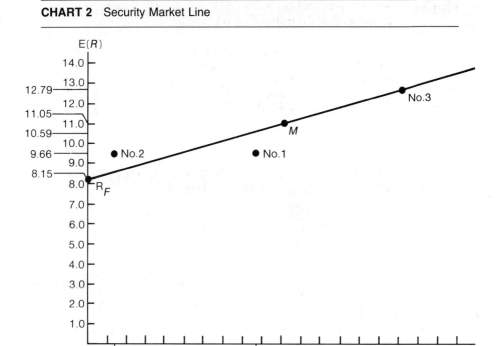

along which all returns, in equilibrium, must lie; otherwise disequilibrium and opportunities for arbitrage will exist. The security market line can be calculated using input data from Table 1.

Since beta for the market portfolio always equals unity (by definition, regardless of which proxy is subjectively selected for the market portfolio), and since beta for the risk-free return always equals zero, the two points determine a straight line, as drawn on Chart 2.

The equation for our security market line is:

$$E(R_i) = R_F + [E(R_M) - R_F]\beta_i$$
$$= 8.15 + [11.05 - 8.15]\beta_i$$
$$= 8.15 + 2.9\ \beta_i$$

The three securities can be plotted relative to the line. Security 1 plots below the line. Security 2 plots above the line. Security 3 plots approximately on the line.

The computations using historical data now are completed. We turn next to an interpretation of our results and to considerations regarding expectations over the forthcoming future holding period.

Interpretation of Results

Based on our above calculations of both the three characteristic lines and the security market line, we now are prepared to formulate buy, hold, sell recommendations regarding the three securities. To do this, we must consider future, as compared with observed historical, values of the three parameters. Our computations are correct and accurate over recently experienced history; but what about the forthcoming holding period? The answer, once again, rests on the analyst's subjective judgment and beliefs because no one knows the future for sure.

Current: Undervalued and overvalued stocks. "No change" is one widely used belief. That is, one possibility is the analyst believes and is willing to bet that the next holding period in the sequence will not differ significantly from the distribution experienced over the past 60 or more observations; so the calculations plotted on Charts 1 and 2 are used as is, as a proxy for the "true" values next period. Under these conditions, the recommendations are: Sell stock 1, Buy stock 2, and Hold stock 3.

Stock 1 is a sell because, for any level of market excess return, from Chart 1, some alternative security with the same beta (but with zero instead of negative alpha) will offer a larger expected excess return and, for a given level of risk, larger expected returns always are preferred over smaller ones.

Stock 2 is a buy because, from Chart 1, for any level of market excess return, some correctly priced alternative security with the same beta (but with zero instead of positive alpha) will offer a smaller expected excess return.

Stock 3 is a hold because it plots directly on the security market line, implying that its expected excess return is commensurate with its beta risk.

Future: Timing purchases. Expected market premiums next period are important for the recommendation. If alternative securities are ruled out and the choices limited to the three securities under analysis, then the recommendations depend upon the expected market premium next period, or what the market is expected to do. If market premiums are expected to be high next period (anything larger than approximately 1.5 on Chart 1), then high beta stock 3 is the place to be. If market premiums are expected to be low next period (anything below approximately 1.5 on Chart 1), then low beta stock 2 is the place to be. Stock 1 remains out of the buy picture, but remains a good candidate for selling or shorting, since, for any level of market expected return, we will be in either stock 3 or stock 2. In all cases, the nonmarket-related risk can be diversified away if we are trading from a large-size portfolio.

Past: Alphas and betas. Movement or change toward market averages is another widely used belief for both alpha and beta. An alternative possibility therefore is that either or both alpha and beta will change toward market averages over the forthcoming holding period.

Alphas, in equilibrium, tend toward zero. For stock 1, alpha moving from minus one to zero implies rising expected returns, falling prices; and remains on the sell or short list. For stock 2, alpha moving from plus two to zero implies decreasing expected return, rising price; and remains on the buy list. Stock 3 remains a hold because its alpha already is at the equilibrium point of zero.

Betas, over time, tend to regress toward unity, and tend to vary from one time span to another; that is, betas are nonstationary. Consequently, an analyst might reasonably believe that the beta for stocks 1 and 2 will increase (toward unity), and the beta for stock 3 will decrease (toward unity). These beliefs, together with the outlook for market premiums next period, will guide the recommendation regarding where to be, or what to hold.

To summarize, high alpha stocks are buy candidates; low or negative alpha stocks are sell candidates. If market premiums are expected to be large, then high beta stocks go on the buy list. If market premiums are expected to be small or negative, then low beta stocks go on the buy list.

We turn next to a discussion of our recommendations.

Discussion

We need critical discussion of what we just finished doing. Is the security market line, in practice, satisfactory or adequate for assessing performance of all individual securities? Are markets, in practice, really efficient? Does there remain a place for fundamental analysis, in light of informational efficiency of markets? What about technical analysis of securities?

The security market line criterion. Does security market line analysis, as we explained, and did, in the preceding paragraphs, always work in practice? How did the stock perform? Was performance outstanding, average or poor? Did performance exceed expectations or not. Can performance of individual securities always be assessed using the security market line as the criterion? Does the security market line tell the whole story?

The answer, provided we obey the restrictions set forth above in the opening parts of our analysis, is yes. Specifically, beta is *not* a universal constant which uniquely characterizes every security. Beta, as we noted earlier, depends upon:

1. Which particular index is used as the market proxy. Everyone must agree on which index to use as a market proxy. The beta (and therefore the security market line criterion) for a given stock will differ depending on whether beta is calculated using say, the S&P 500 or the NYSE Composite Index.
2. The time interval over which the returns are calculated. Everyone must also agree on the time interval for calculating the returns. The beta (and therefore the security market line criterion) for a given stock will differ depending on whether beta is calculated using daily or quarterly or annual returns.
3. The size of sample or number of returns used in the calculation. The beta (and therefore the security market line criterion) for a given stock will differ depending on whether beta is calculated using a sample size of 50 or 60, as compared with 300 or 400, preceding returns; and may differ between bull and bear markets.
4. The duration of the stock or bond.

Impediments to informational efficiency. Are markets really efficient? Do prices always fully reflect all information available to actual and potential participants in the market? The answer is, no one knows, for sure. It has been argued persuasively that the efficient market's theory never can be tested; therefore can be neither accepted nor rejected absolutely. Nevertheless, we can gain more understanding of the analysis by discussing some of the major causes or sources of inefficiency. Why might markets be inefficient? Some critical reasons are:

-   *Costly information.* In reality, information—investment research—is an economic commodity, not a free good. Investment results depend upon both quantity and quality of (expensive) information.
-   *Human emotions and psychology.* In reality, investors may "over" or "under" react to new information, or may choose securities on some noneconomic basis (e.g., morals, ethics, social concerns, and the like).
-   *Size of transaction.* Efficiency assumes perfectly competitive markets where investors can buy or sell any desired quantity at the quoted price. In practice, the price quote for a hundred shares of IBM or Du Pont might differ significantly from the price quote for a hundred thousand shares.
-   *Infrequent trades.* Datawise, "no change" in price can arise from either no trade or successive trades at the same price. Zeros can introduce ambiguity into a data base.
-   *Institutional practices.* This is a "catchall" which includes real-

world phenomena such as margin requirements, regulation of short sales, commissions, taxes, inflation and the like.

Fundamental security analysis and beta analysis.   Does modern security analysis render traditional fundamental analysis useless or obsolete? The answer, for the following reasons, is no.

Fundamental analysts typically spend time and energy investigating financial statements, interviewing management, and studying product, factor, and financial markets—all with the objective of estimating business profitability, risk, growth, and future returns to investors in the individual company, industry, or aggregate corporate sector.

However, stock betas, as shown by many studies, are relatively efficient in that beta coefficients capture or contain much of the information uncovered by fundamental analysts. For example, stock betas reflect fundamentals, such as changes in financial leverage of the corporation, earnings cyclicity and variability, dividend payout, and growth rates of output.

On the other hand, stock betas are not omnipotent. Stock betas typically fail to capture or transmit early warning signals regarding particular types of information easily obtained by a fundamental analyst sitting, talking, and receiving personal subjective impressions from top management. Betas often fail to signal relevant events, such as possible fraud, likelihood of either a forthcoming lawsuit or bankruptcy, and the like.

Beta analysis therefore can be viewed as a supplement to—not a replacement of—classical fundamental security analysis. Modern security analysis—beta analysis—sharpens the questions fundamental analysts should ask, and requires conventional fundamental analysts to improve the economic use of information and the rationality of expectations.

Fundamental analysts believe and bet that financial statements, interviews with management, and other public information will enable them to uncover superior returns.

Information efficiency requires that all publicly available information is known and acted upon by all market participants; therefore, the odds are against any one analyst discovering information overlooked by all other analysts. On balance, if markets are fully efficient then the best use of the analyst's time involves: (a) investigating factors which are common to all security returns (e.g., the market), and (b) studying comovements among returns on securities.

Technical analysis, timing and efficient market prices.   Does modern security analysis render conventional technical analysis impotent or sterile? The answer, for the following reasons, is: most likely.

At one extreme, market technicians spend time and energy analyzing trends, cycles, and seasonal patterns in prices. The belief or bet by technicians is that: (1) trends exist and once started, tend to persist until some indicator points to the contrary; hence, technicians believe that what appear to be trends can be safely extrapolated; (2) cycles exist and repeat themselves over the years, and each specific cycle, though different from specific previous cycles, contains elements common to all other cycles, hence, current cycles can be compare profitably with previous cycles; and (3) seasonal fluctuations in price give rise to profitable investment or trading opportunities.

At the opposite extreme, the unpredictability—the random walk hypothesis—of stock market prices is a powerful contender. The following paragraphs discuss the pros and cons of both sides.

Do ex ante trends in price really exist? The answer, if markets are efficient, is no. Over the short run—that is, day to day—if investors *know* tomorrow's price will be higher (or lower) than today's price, then buying (or selling) will create demand (or absence thereof), thereby causing no difference, in equilibrium, between today's and tomorrow's price. The best expectation of tomorrow's price is today's price (less one day's risk-free interest); price movements in what appear to be trends should not be extrapolated. Over the longer run—for instance, year to year—the situation might be as follows. Suppose that investors *know* next year's stock price will be $120 plus an $8 dividend. If the risk-free, one-year rate is 15 percent, then today's price must be $111.30, ($120 + $8)/1.15).

An alternative view of the same situation is as follows. If investors *believe*, but do not *know*, that next year's price will be $129, and a risk premium of $9 is required to compensate for the uncertainty associated with the $129, then today's futures price will be $120; that is, the expected spot at settlement less the risk premium ($129 − $9 = $120). Our conclusion is, viewed either way, short or long term, if fully informed rational investors *know* or believe that future price (less a risk premium) will be higher or lower than today's price, then buying or selling will instantaneously restore equilibrium; so that what might appear to be a profitable trend might in fact be an illusion. Extrapolating what appears to be a trend can cause much grief.

Do cycles and seasonals really exist? The answer has little or nothing to do with whether markets are efficient, but the answer is more disturbing than if we did invoke assumptions regarding efficiency. For more than 80 years, econometricians have known that a summation of random causes will result in cycles and patterns which are indistinguishable from observed economic and stock price series. If, therefore, a randomly generated series is an indistinguishable substitute for an observed series, then "analyzing" the observed series is the same as "analyzing" the randomly generated series. Analyzing a sequence of chance, or randomly generated numbers, appears alien to scientific security analysis.

To summarize, informational efficiency requires that today's price equals expected price tomorrow, otherwise a buy or sell will be executed until equilibrium is restored between today's price and tomorrow's expected price. Trends and cycles can be nothing other than random or chance variations because the current price reflects all information contained in the historical time series of price.

SECURITY SELECTION IN PORTFOLIO CONSTRUCTION

Can modern security analysis be used to improve portfolio selection? The answer, as illustrated below, is yes. Modern security analysis can play a significant role in portfolio construction and revision.

Security Selection—Recommendations

Suppose, with the aid of a computer, that you have now analyzed every stock on the New York Stock Exchange, the American Stock Exchange, the Regional Exchanges, and most of the Over-the-Counter and foreign securities, and have computed alpha, beta, and nonmarket-related risk for every security—all several thousand securities. You now are ready to serve as consultant to portfolio managers. What do you do? The answer is, you set forth recommendations and opinion to the portfolio managers, who will be either passive or active in the management of portfolios.

Diversifiable risks and portfolio beta—passive management. Passively managed portfolios never attempt to "beat the market." Passive managers acknowledge and accept the fact that the market is a formidable opponent to beat; therefore, the objective of passively managed portfolios is to seek expected returns commensurate with a subjectively chosen beta risk. The two following steps therefore can be taken by the security analyst.

First, work with "correctly" priced securities whose expected returns lie along the security market line, and recommend eliminating all nonmarket-related risk in the portfolio. This can be achieved by adding more securities (selected by simple random sampling from the entire universe of securities) to the portfolio. Intuitively, as the number of securities in a portfolio increases from two to three to six to n, the total risk of the portfolio decreases toward only the market-related risk. The nonmarket component reduces arbitrarily close to zero. In the limit, as n increases indefinitely, the portfolio in fact becomes the market portfolio. How many securities are necessary to achieve the objective of eliminating all or most of the diversifiable risk? The answer is, approximately 15 to 20. One inference is that a portfolio containing 50 or 100 (simple randomly selected) stocks is no better diversified than an alternative smaller portfolio containing 20 (simple randomly selected) stocks.

Second, the owner of the portfolio must stipulate or specify an allowable or permissible sensitivity of portfolio expected returns to changes in market returns. If the owner is able and willing to tolerate a change of ½ if the market changes by 1, then the portfolio requires a beta of 0.50. The total money is allocated or distributed over the 15 or 20 selected stocks in such a way so that the weighted individual stock betas sum to 0.50. For example, using only two stocks to illustrate the point, consider stock 3 (beta equals 1.60) from Chart 2, together with Treasury bills (beta equals 0.00). If x stands for the fraction of money allocated to one security and $(1 - x)$ stands for the fraction of money allocated to the second security, then we can write the following equation:

$$\beta_{\text{portfolio}} = x\beta_1 + (1 - x)\beta_2 = 0.50$$

Substituting the values for the betas, we get:

$$\beta_{\text{portfolio}} = x(0.00) + (1 - x)\,(1.60) = 0.50$$

Solving for x, we get $x = 68.75$ percent of total money in Treasury bills, together with $(1 - x)$ equals 31.25 percent of total money in stock 3. The expected return on the portfolio is 9.6 percent, calculated as follows:

$$
\begin{aligned}
E(R_p) &= xR_F + (1 - x)E(R_i) \\
&= (0.6875)(8.15)+(0.3125)(12.79) \\
&= 9.6\%
\end{aligned}
$$

The same answer can be obtained from the security market line.

$$
\begin{aligned}
E(R_{p)} &= R_F + [E(R_M) - R_F]\beta_p \\
&= 8.15 + (11.05 - 8.15)(0.50) \\
&= 9.6\%
\end{aligned}
$$

Note that an equivalent portfolio can be constructed using any two other securities on the line. For example, consider "correctly priced" securities having betas of 0.88 and 0.14, respectively. Then the required portfolio is:

$$\beta_{\text{portfolio}} = x(0.88) + (1 - x)(0.14) = 0.50$$

Solving for x, we get x equals 48.65 percent in the 0.88 beta stock and $(1 - x)$ equals 51.35 percent in the 0.14 beta stock. The expected return on the portfolio is 9.6 percent.

$$
\begin{aligned}
E(R_p) &= x\,E(R_1) + (1 - x)E(R_2) \\
&= (0.4865)[8.15 + 2.9(0.88)]+(0.5135)[8.15+2.9(0.14)] \\
&= 0.4865(10.702) + (0.5135)(8.556) \\
&= 9.6\%
\end{aligned}
$$

The moral of the story is that *any* correctly priced security (high-flyer, blue chip or T bill) can be used to construct a desired beta portfolio.

Note how far we have come away from the original Prudent Man Rule, where every stock in a portfolio was required to stand alone, ignoring the interaction and covariation of returns among other stocks within the portfolio. Nowadays, we recognize and admit that a portfolio, because of covariance and interaction among returns, is different from the individual separate stocks being held.

Size of the portfolio is important to discuss. Holding a minimum of 15 to 20 stocks, we noted, eliminates most of the diversifiable risk, which is good. But the price we pay, via diversification, for avoiding possible disaster, is to limit possible spectacular gains (and the transactions costs are high). For example, suppose that we hold an equal fraction of money in each of 20 stocks. No one stock—even a financial disaster stock—will do significant damage to the overall portfolio because only one twentieth of the total money was allocated to it. But by the same token, the year's winning stock also will contribute little to the overall portfolio because only one twentieth of the total money was allocated to it. In other words, holding only market risk sort of guarantees realizing only market returns.

Size of the investment portfolio also limits the universe of potential stocks. Consider, for example, the plight of a large size institutional investor with $30 or $40 billion in common stock. If a policy decision is made to invest no less than 1 percent in any particular stock, then the minimum-sized purchase (or sale) of a stock will be $300 million or $400 million. A *small* company whose total capitalization is *only* $300 million or $400 million will be excluded from consideration. The game is one where only the big folks can play. To summarize, since modern portfolios usually are selected on the basis of their sensitivity or responsiveness to market fluctuations (i.e., the beta risk of the portfolio), and since a desired beta usually can be realized from a linear combination of two given betas, it follows that any security can contribute in some way to portfolio construction. Every security offers some return (either too high, too low, or correct) and, therefore, can potentially contribute to a desired portfolio. The question becomes not "which security" but whether to go long (buy) or short (sell), together with "how much"?

Contribution to excess returns—active management. Active portfolio management requires: (1) tactical decisions (stock picking, the search for overvalued and undervalued stocks, arbitrage opportunities); (2) strategic decisions (altering the structure of the portfolio, anticipating changes in interest rates or anticipating shifts in the valuation of major categories of stocks); and (3) philosophic decisions (enduring investment commitments—through good times and bad—to which a manager adheres with persistence and fidelity). Actively managed portfolios *do* attempt to beat the market, but by using sound economic reasoning, not chance alone. The risks are calculated, for which extra rewards are expected to be forthcoming. The security analyst can contribute to actively managed portfolios in the following ways.

Stock pricing and tactical decisions. Regarding *stock picking* and tactical decisions, reconsider low and high alpha stocks (1 and 2, respectively) from Chart 2. For their estimated betas, correctly priced securities will offer expected returns of:

$$E(R_1) = 8.15 + 2.9(0.88) = 10.70\%$$
$$E(R_2) = 8.15 + 2.9(0.14) = 8.56\%$$

If the analyst can find correctly priced securities someplace in the market, then two arbitrages can be executed by either:

a. Selling (borrowing from) stock 1 at 9.66 percent and simultaneously buying (lending to) the correctly priced stock at 10.70 percent, thereby profiting the difference; or
b. Buying (lending to) stock 2 at 10.59 percent and simultaneously selling (borrowing from) the correctly priced stock at 8.56 percent, thereby profiting the difference of 2.03 percent.

Alternatively, if the analyst is unable to locate correctly priced stocks someplace in the market, then equivalent correctly priced stocks can be created in the following way by diversifying correctly between the market portfolio and Treasury bills:

$$E(R_{1\ portfolio}) = xR_F + (1 - x)E(R_M) = 10.70\%$$
$$= x(8.15) + (1 - x)(11.05) = 10.70\%$$

If $x = 12$ percent of the portfolio in T bills, then the correct return of 10.70 percent is obtained as follows:

$$E(R_{1\ portfolio}) = (0.12)(8.15) + (0.88)(11.05) = 10.70\%$$

Similarly, for the second portfolio:

$$E(R_{2\ portfolio}) = x\ R_F + (1 - x)E(RM) = 8.56\%$$
$$= x(8.15) + (1 - x)(11.05) = 8.56\%$$

If $x = 85.86$ percent of the portfolio in T bills, then

$$E(R_{2\ portfolio}) = (0.8586)(8.15) + (0.1414)(11.05) = 8.56\%$$

The two recommendations therefore are:

• For security 1: sell (short) the overpriced security 1 at expected return of 9.66 percent and, for the same risk, simultaneously buy (go long) the correctly priced portfolio 1 at 10.70 percent, thereby locking in the difference or spread of 1.04 percent. The security analyst or portfolio manager, using actual numbers from live securities and portfolios can decide subjectively whether the size of the expected spread is worth executing.

- For security 2: sell (short) the correctly priced portfolio 2 at 8.56 percent and, for the same risk, simultaneously buy (go long) the underpriced security 2 at expected return of 10.59 percent, locking in the difference or spread of 2.03 percent.

Finally, regarding our recommendation that stock 1 is a *sell* candidate and stock 2 is a *buy* candidate, more can be said if the portfolio is of large size (more than 15 or 20 stocks) where only beta risk matters. For example, given the 2,000 or more stocks analyzed by our computer, why not rank the entire population of stocks on the basis of alpha and buy (go long) every stock in the high alpha decile and simultaneously sell (go short) every stock in the low or negative alpha decile? In this way, simultaneous profit advantage can be taken from both the underpriced (large or positive alpha) and overpriced small or negative alpha) stocks. If short sales from the portfolio are prohibited for legal or other reasons, then only one side—the buy side—of the transaction can be executed.

Timing and strategic decisions. Regarding *timing* and strategic decisions, modern security analysts will recommend, as previously noted, concentration in high beta stocks if future market excess returns are expected to be large, and switching to concentration in low beta stocks if future market excess returns are expected to be small. But guessing the market *can* be tricky. One key factor in contributing positively to long-term average performance of portfolios is avoiding accidents by way of realizing negative returns. For example, to break even after having lost 30 percent of the portfolio during one period, the return during the second period must exceed 40 percent.

$$(1 - .30)(1 + x) = 1.00$$
$$x = 42.86 \text{ percent}$$

If a competing portfolio manager was investing over both periods in T bills at 10 percent, then our "active" manager, after losing 30 percent during period one, must realize more than 72 percent next period.

$$(1 - .30)(1 + x) = (1.10)^2$$
$$x = 72.86\%$$

Large returns are nice to take, but negative returns are difficult to overcome.

Is active management worthwhile; Is it worth the expense? Many practicing analysts believe, yes; but consider the following requirement.

Suppose, as an "active" manager, your goal is to outperform "the market" by 25 percent per annum, net of expenses. What must be your gross performance? Let:

- $E(R_M)$ = 15 percent
- Average turnover = 0.40 percent per annum
- Average costs (dealer spreads plus commissions) = 3 percent
- Management and custody fees = 0.20 percent per annum

Then, to outperform the market by 25 percent, net, we must gross 42.33 percent more than the market return.

$$15(1 + x) - [0.40(3 + 3)] - (0.20) = 15(1.25)$$

$$x = \left(\frac{2.4 + 0.20 + 18.75}{15}\right) - 1 = 42.33\%$$

To break even with the market (assuming you already hold a market portfolio and do no trading), the active manager must gross 17.33 percent more than the S&P 500.

$$15(1 + x) - [0.40(3 + 3)] - (0.20) = 15$$

$$x = \left(\frac{2.4 + 0.20 + 15}{15}\right) - 1 = 17.33\%$$

As we said previously, the market is a formidable opponent to beat.

Regarding holding unique *diversifiable risks*, modern security analysts will recommend against the practice, unless evidence shows that on average over the long term, markets in fact do remunerate investors for bearing nonmarket-related risks. This would be a contradiction of the model, but it does happen. For example, those few analysts who concentrated 80 to 90 percent of their holdings in gold mining stocks in the late 1960s, or in oil and energy stocks in the early 1970s reaped spectacular returns. In terms of market efficiency, these few analysts obtained and exploited information not yet recognized or acted upon by their fellow analysts.

Some Anomalies or Exceptions to the Market Rules[4]

Are markets always efficient? Our previous answer, based on testability of the hypothesis, was that no one knows, for sure. Here, we turn to a

---

[4] See also Chapter 24.

different type of evidence; namely, several well-known deviations from the rules or anomalies to security market line pricing.

Abnormal excess returns. Low P/E ratio and small capitalization stocks are the two most extensively studied anomalies to security market line pricing. The experiments can be described as follows.

Visualize all the stocks (NYSE, AMEX, O.T.C., Regionals, and so on) being ranked, for each time period, by either (or both) price-earnings ratio or size of the company. The high P/Es or large-size companies will rank, for every time period, in the top decile while the low P/Es or small companies will rank correspondingly in the bottom decile. When viewed in light of the security market line (as we did previously for stocks 1, 2, and 3), the small capitalization and low P/E stocks on average tend to provide larger excess returns than predicted by the model.

One conjecture is that possible correlation exists between P/E ratio and size; so that one (not two) separate effects exist. One belief is that the effect is one of size, not P/E (i.e., size is a proxy for P/E; not the other way around). But the P/E believers point to flaws in the design of the size experiments. On balance, whether one or two effects exists remains unsettled.

What's the cause of the anomalies? The presumption is that a sufficiently large number of informed investors roam the marketplace such that well-known inefficiencies cannot persist for long time periods of maybe 20 or 30 years. That leaves the security market line model itself, which may possess one or more missing factors. Some other conjectures are that low (P/E) and/or small capitalization stocks are in fact assets which are significantly different from high (P/E) and/or large capitalization stocks. Supporting this latter conjecture is evidence, such as frequency of trading, required margin, supply and dissemination of public information, and the like. On balance, we must conclude as before: no one knows, for sure. The SML may have an omitted factor; but the now well-known "factor analytic" models appear also unable to explain the anomalies. In any case, small or low (P/E) stocks behave inconsistently with the basic model of efficient market returns.

Zero beta securities. Gold bullion and gold mining stocks in general, over long time spans, tend to produce betas which are not significantly different from zero. Of course, the precise beta depends upon which index is selected as the market proxy, together with the time span over which the betas are calculated. Sampling variation exists. But, as we said, gold and gold stock betas in general tend to be close to zero.

The anomaly is the expected return. Returns from both gold bullion and gold mining stocks (zero beta assets) significantly exceed returns from U.S. Treasury bills (another zero beta asset). The theory presumes that arbitrage should occur between the alternative zero beta assets until, in equilibrium no difference is expected between the three returns. But no such arbitrage has driven the rates to equality. Why? That is, why do gold stocks yield returns greater than Treasury bill rates, though the market risk is similarly low (i.e., beta of 0.0). No one knows, for sure.

Is beta dead? Have the anomalies, together with other things, blasted beta analysis out of the water? Is beta dead?

Many practicing analysts never knew beta ever was alive. Some analysts ignore beta. Nevertheless, we can point to the following significant (and probably lasting) contributions of beta analysis.

- *Portfolio*, rather than individual security, risks and returns are important, indeed critical for prudent investment management.
- *Overall market effects* are critical to monitor. Much money can be lost in great stocks if the entire market moves downward.
- *Positive premiums* are required for risk bearing. If the federal government pays 15 percent, stocks are unattractive at anything equal to or less than 15 percent.
- Total risk of every individual stock can be viewed as a sum of common (or market-related) plus idiosyncratic (or nonmarket-related) components. Only the market-related part of total risk is consistently or predictably important.

Summary

Security analysis has come a long way since the early days of estimating multiples and earnings; and of charting price changes. The situation is not significantly different from comparisons between modern space vehicles and the early airplanes at Kittyhawk. The methods and procedures nowadays are far more powerful and efficient; but human judgment remains a critical factor for success.

What principles did we learn? We should have learned the relationships between risk and equilibrium expected returns in markets which are informationally efficient. Also, we should have learned how to analyze informationally efficient securities. Specifically:

a. Two critical variables, risk and expected return (over the future holding period), determine whether a security is a "buy," "hold," or "sell" candidate.
b. Regarding risk, the systematic component, beta, of total risk (variance) of a security's expected return is the enduring (and often the sole) source of extra remuneration because (i) the nonmarket-related risk can be diversified away and therefore merits no premium in the portfolio and thus in the marketplace,

if such portfolio holdings are dominant; and (*ii*) beta determines the rate of change in portfolio variance of return as the quantity of investment changes for a particular security.

c. Regarding alpha, for a given systematic risk (beta), the expected value of alpha must equal zero; otherwise the security is a "buy" (for positive or large alpha) or "sell" (for negative or small alpha).

d. Expected return from any security, in equilibrium, depends linearly on its beta risk.

e. A desired portfolio beta can be realized from a linear combination of betas from individual securities.

f. All other considerations, in principle, are redundant or cost ineffective, or both.

Applications. The methods and procedures above explained and illustrated are applicable to all marketable securities. A stock is a stock is a stock! Utilities, transportations, industrials, energy stocks, hi-tech, and all others are subjected to the calculations which result in the three parameters: beta, alpha and nonmarket-related risk; no special methodologies are necessary (or desirable) for different industry clusters.

Limitations. Three significant limitations of modern security analysis are:

a. The requirement that either the distribution of returns is normal or investors choose among risky alternatives on the basis solely of mean and variance. Both assumptions may be violated in practice; so the predictions of the theory become subject to large error. Specifically, some investors may choose to maximize long-term terminal wealth instead of minimize one period portfolio risk. Some investors may be influenced by moral, ethical, cultural, social, or other personal considerations when choosing among alternative securities; and not by mean-variance alone.

b. The ability of the analysis to explain the serious anomalies discussed above. The exceptions to the principles may not loom large but if they sum to 15 percent, they cannot be ignored. An identical investment in debt markets or real assets will involve a majority of exceptions to the rules.

c. The relatively large, minimum size of a "well-diversified" portfolio. Fifteen to twenty stocks, (at $50 per share, times 100 shares each) amounts to $75,000 and $100,000 minimum-sized portfolio. For the small investor with $1,000 or $2,000, modern security analysts can only recommend purchase of shares in a mutual fund.

Note that portfolio analysis must include nonsecurity type financial assets (many of which, such as municipal bonds or commercial paper, have clearly imperfect markets), plus holdings of nonfinancial assets (such as housing, fine art, and diamonds whose markets are even less perfect).

Conclusions

What does all this mean? It means, of course, the theory of efficient markets is far from perfect. Few theories are perfect. Anomalies exist. Some important factors may be omitted. Some of the underlying assumptions may differ from real-world investor behavior and motivations. But any analyst who chooses to ignore the theory does so at his or her own peril.

Finally, we note the important services of active securities analysis for portfolio construction.

REFERENCES

ELTON, E. J., AND M. GRUBER. *Modern Portfolio Theory and Investment Analysis*. 3rd ed. New York: John Wiley & Sons, 1987.

HAGIN, R. L. *The Dow Jones-Irwin Guide to Modern Portfolio Theory*. Homewood, Ill.: Dow Jones-Irwin, 1979.

HAUGEN, R. A. *Modern Investment Theory*. Englewood Cliffs, N.J.: Prentice-Hall, 1986.

LEVY, H., AND M. SARNAT. *Portfolio Investment Selection: Theory and Practice*. Englewood Cliffs, N.J., 1984.

MALKIEL, B. G. *Random Walk down Wall Street*. 4th ed. New York: W. W. Norton, 1985.

SHARPE, W. F. *Investments*. 3rd ed. Englewood Cliffs, N.J.: Prentice-Hall, 1985.

TINIC, S. M. AND R. R. WEST. *Investing in Securities: An Efficient Market Approach*. Reading, Mass.: Addison-Wesley Publishing, 1979.

14

10-K and Other SEC Reports

DISCLOSURE STATUTE

A basic purpose of the Federal securities laws is to provide disclosure of material financial and other information on companies seeking to raise capital through the public offering of their securities, as well as companies whose securities are already publicly held. This aims at enabling investors to evaluate the securities of these companies on an informed and realistic basis.

The Securities Act of 1933 is a *disclosure* statute. It generally requires that, before securities may be offered to the public, a registration statement must be filed with the Commission disclosing prescribed categories of information. Before the sale of securities can begin, the registration statement must become "effective," and investors must be furnished a prospectus containing the most significant information in the registration statement.

The Securities Act of 1934 deals in large part with securities already outstanding and requires the registration of securities listed on a national securities exchange, as well as "Over-the-Counter" securities in which there is a substantial public interest. Issuers of registered securities must file annual and other periodic reports designed to provide a public file of current material information. The Exchange Act also requires disclosure of material information to holders of registered securities in solicitations of proxies for the election of directors or approval of corporate action at a stockholder's meeting, or in attempts to acquire control of a company through a tender offer or other planned stock acquisition. It provides that insiders of companies whose equity

SOURCE: *A Guide to SEC Corporate Filings*, © 1985 Disclosure Information Group, 5161 River Road, Bethesda, MD 20816

securities are registered must report their holdings and transactions in all equity securities of their companies.

Effective December 15, 1980, the Securities and Exchange Commission adopted and proposed major changes in its disclosure systems under the Securities Act of 1933 and the Securities Exchange Act of 1934. These changes were intended to reinforce the concept of an integrated disclosure system.

The changes that were adopted include amendments to Form 10-K, amendments to the Proxy rules, expansion of amendments to Regulation S-K (which governs nonfinancial statement disclosure rules), uniform financial statement instructions, a general revision of Regulation S-X (which governs the form, content and requirements of financial statements), as well as a new simplified optional form for the registration of securities issued in certain business combinations.

The integrated disclosure system is based on the belief that investors expect to be furnished the same basic information package, both to support current information requirements of an active trading market and to provide information in connection with the sale of newly issued securities under the Securities Act.

The program is intended to:

- Improve disclosure to investors and other users of financial information
- Achieve a single disclosure system at reduced cost
- Reduce current impediments to combining shareholder communications with official SEC filings

---

10-K (MUST BE FILED 90 DAYS AFTER CLOSE OF FISCAL YEAR)

ITEMS REPORTED

Form 10-K—Part I

1. **Business.** Identifies principal products and services of the company, principal markets and methods of distribution and, if "material," competitive factors, backlog and expectation of fulfillment, availability of raw materials, importance of patents, licenses, and franchises, estimated cost of research, number of employees, and effects of compliance with ecological laws.

    If there is more than one line of business, for each of the last three fiscal years a statement of total sales and net income for each line which during either of the last two fiscal years, accounted for 10 percent or more of total sales or pretax income.

2. **Properties.** Location and character of principal plants, mines, and other important properties and if held in fee or leased.

3. **Legal Proceedings.** Brief description of material legal proceedings pending; when civil rights or ecological statutes are involved, proceedings must be disclosed.

4. **Principal Security Holders and Security Holdings of Management.** Identification of owners of 10 percent or more of any class of securities and of securities held by directors and officers according to amount and percent of each class

Form 10-K—Part II

5. **Market for the Registrants' Common Stock and Related Security Holder Matters.** Includes principal market in which voting securities are traded with high and low sales prices (in the absence thereof, the range of bid and asked quotations for each quarterly period during the past two years) and the dividends paid during the past two years. In addition to the frequency and amount of dividends paid, this item contains a discussion concerning future dividends.

6. **Selected Financial Data.** These are five-year selected data including net sales and operating revenue; income or loss from continuing operations, both total and per common share; total assets; long-term obligations including redeemable preferred stock; cash dividends declared per common share. Also, additional items that could enhance understanding and trends in financial condition and results of operations. Further, the effects of inflation and changing prices should be reflected in the five-year summary.

7. **Management's Discussion and Analysis of Financial Condition and Results of Operations.** Under broad guidelines, this includes: liquidity, capital resources and results of operations; trends that are favorable or unfavorable as well as significant events or uncertainties; causes of any material changes in the financial statements as a whole; limited data concerning subsidiaries; discussion of effects of inflation and changing prices. Projections or other forward-looking information may or may not be included.

8. **Financial Statements and Supplementary Data.** Two-year audited balance sheets as well as three-year audited statements of income and changes in financial condition.

Form 10-K—Part III

9. **Directors and Executive Officers of the Registrant.** Name, office, term of office, and specific background data on each.
10. **Remuneration of Directors and Officers.** List of each director and three highest paid officers with aggregate annual remuneration exceeding $40,000 and total paid all officers and directors.

Form 10-K—Part IV

11. **Exhibits, Financial Statement Schedules and Reports on Form 8-K.** Complete, audited annual financial information, and a list of exhibits filed. Also, any unscheduled material events or corporate changes filed in an 8-K during the year.

Form 10-K—Schedules

I. Marketable securities. Other security investments
II. Amounts due from directors, officers, and principal holders of equity securities other than affiliates
III. Investments in securities of affiliates
IV. Indebtedness of affiliates (not current)
V. Property, plant, and equipment
VI. Reserves for depreciation, depletion, and amortization of property, plant and equipment
VII. Intangible assets
VIII. Reserves for depreciation and amortization of intangible assets
IX. Bonds, mortgages, and similar debt
X. Indebtedness to affiliates (not current)
XI. Guarantees of securities of other issuers
XII. Reserves
XIII. Capital shares
XIV. Warrants or rights
XV. Other securities
XVI. Supplementary profit and loss information
XVII. Income from dividends (equity in net profit and loss of affiliates)

18-K (MUST BE FILED 9 MONTHS AFTER CLOSE OF FISCAL YEAR)

Annual report for foreign governments and political subdivisions thereof.

20-F (MUST BE FILED 6 MONTHS AFTER CLOSE OF FISCAL YEAR)

Annual report filed by certain foreign issuers of securities trading in the United States.

Item 1. Business
Item 2. Management Discussion & Analysis of the Statements of Income
Item 3. Property
Item 4. Control of Registrant
Item 6. Remuneration of Directors and Officers
Item 7. Options to Purchase Securities from Registrant or Subsidiaries
Item 8. Pending Legal Proceedings
Item 9. Nature of Trading Market
Item 10. Capital Stock to be Registered
Item 11. Debt Securities to be Registered
Item 12. Other Securities to be Registered
Item 13. Exchange Controls and other Limitations Affecting Security Holders
Item 14. Taxation
Item 15. Changes in Securities and Changes in Security for Registered Securities
Item 16. Defaults upon Senior Securities
Item 17. Interest of Management in Certain Transactions
Item 18. Financial Statements and Exhibits

10-Q (MUST BE FILED 45 DAYS AFTER CLOSE OF FISCAL QUARTER)

This is the quarterly financial report filed by most companies, which, although unaudited, provides a continuing view of a company's financial position during the year.

ITEMS REPORTED

Form 10-Q—Part I—Financial Statements

1. Income statement
2. Balance sheet
3. Statement of source and application of funds
4. A narrative analysis of material changes in the amount of

revenue and expense items in relation to previous quarters, including the effect of any changes in accounting principals.

Form 10-Q—Part II

1. **Legal Proceedings.** Brief description of material legal proceedings pending; when civil rights or ecological statutes are involved, proceedings must be disclosed.
2. **Changes in Securities.** Material changes in the rights of holders of any class of registered security.
3. **Changes in Security for Registered Securities.** Material withdrawal or substitution of assets securing any class of registered securities of the registrant.
4. **Defaults upon Senior Securities.** Material defaults in the payment if principal, interest, sinking fund or purchase fund installment, dividend, or other material default not cured within 30 days.
5. **Increase in Amount Outstanding of Securities or Indebtedness.** Amounts of new issues, continuing issues or reissues of any class of security or indebtedness with a reasonable statement of the purposes for which the proceeds will be used.
6. **Decreases in Amount Outstanding of Securities or Indebtedness.** Amounts of decreases, through one or more transactions, in any class of outstanding securities or indebtedness.
7. **Submission of Matters to a Vote of Security Holders.** Information relating to the convening of a meeting of shareholders, whether annual or special, and the matters voted upon, with particular emphasis on the election of directors.
8. **Other Materially Important Events.** Information on any other item of interest to shareholders not already provided for in this form.

8-K (CORPORATE CHANGES 1-6 MUST BE FILED 15 DAYS AFTER THE EVENT. 7 HAS NO MANDATORY FILING TIME)

This is a report of unscheduled material events or corporate changes deemed of importance to the shareholders or to the SEC.

1. Changes in control of registrant.
2. Acquisition or disposition of assets.
3. Bankruptcy or receivership.
4. Changes in registrant's certifying accountant.
5. Financial statements and exhibits.

6. Resignations of registrant's Directors.
7. Other materially important events.

10-C (MUST BE FILED 10 DAYS AFTER CHANGE)

"Over-the-Counter" companies use this form to report changes in name and amount of NASDAQ-listed securities. It is similar in purpose to the 8-K.

13-F (MUST BE FILED 45 DAYS AFTER CLOSE OF FISCAL QUARTER)

A quarterly report of equity holdings required of all institutions with equity assets of $100 million or more. This includes banks, insurance companies, investment companies, investment advisers and large internally managed endowments, foundations and pension funds.

PROXY STATEMENT

A proxy statement provides notification to designated classes of stockholders of matters to be brought to a vote at a shareholders' meeting. Proxy votes may be solicited for changing the company officers, or many other matters. Disclosures normally made via a proxy statement may in some cases be made using Form 10-K (Part III).

REGISTRATION STATEMENTS

Registration statements are of two principal types: (1) "offering" registrations filed under the 1933 Securities Act, and (2) "trading" registrations filed under the 1934 Securities Exchange Act.

"Offering" registrations are used to register securities before they may be offered to investors. Part I of the registration, a preliminary prospectus or "red herring," is promotional in tone; it carries all the sales features that will be contained in the final prospectus. Part II of the registration contains detailed information about marketing agreements, expenses of issuance and distribution, relationship of the company with experts named in the registration, sales to special parties, recent sales of unregistered securities, subsidiaries of registrant, franchises and concessions, indemnification of directors and officers, treatment of proceeds from stock being registered, and financial statements and exhibits.

"Offering" registration statements vary in purpose and content according to the type of organization issuing stock:

S-1	Companies reporting under the '34 Act for less than three years. Permits no incorporation by reference and requires complete disclosure in the prospectus.
S-2	Companies reporting under the '34 Act for three years or more but do not meet the minimum voting stock requirement. Reference of '34 Act reports permits incorporation and presentation of financial information in the prospectus or in an annual report to shareholders delivered with the prospectus.
S-3	Companies reporting under the '34 Act for three or more years and having at least $150 million of voting stock held by nonaffiliates, or as an alternative test, $100 million of voting stock coupled with an annual trading volume of 3 million shares. Requires minimal disclosure in the prospectus and allows maximum incorporation by reference of '34 Act reports.
S-4	Registration used in certain business combinations or registrations. Replaces S-14, S-15, 7/85.
N-1A	Used by open-end management investment companies other than separate accounts of insurance companies.
N-2	(Formerly S-4) Used by closed-end investment companies.
N-5	Registration of small business investment companies.
N-SAR	Replaces form N-1R, N-30A-2, N-30A-3, N-5R, 2-MD.
S-6	Used by unit investment trusts registered under the Investment Act of 1940 on Form N-8B-2.
S-8	Used to register securities to be offered to employees under stock option and various other benefit plans.
S-11	Used by real estate companies, primarily limited partnerships and investment trusts.
S-18	Short form registration up to $7.5 million.
SE	Nonelectronic exhibits of registrants filing with the EDGAR PILOT PROJECT.
F-1	Registration of securities by foreign private issuers eligible to use Form 20-F, for which no other form is prescribed.
F-2	Registration of securities of foreign private issuers meeting certain 34 act filing requirements.
F-3	Registration of securities of foreign issuers offered pursuant to certain types of transactions.
F-6	Registration of depository shares evidenced by American depository receipts.

CHART A   Quick Reference Chart to Contents of SEC Filings

Report contents	10-K	19-K 20-F	10-Q	8-K	10-C	6-K	Proxy statement	Prospectus	'34 Act F-10 8-A 8-B	'33 Act "S" Type	ARS	Listing application	N-SAR
Auditor													
□ Name	A	A	■				■	A	A	A	A	■	A
□ Opinion	A	A						■	A		A		A
□ Changes				A				■					
Compensation plans													
□ Equity	■		■				F	F	A	F		■	
□ Monetary	■							F	A	F		■	
Company information													
□ Nature of business	A	A				F		A	A	A			
□ History	F	A						A	A		■		
□ Organization and change	F	F		A		F	■	A	F	A			
Debt structure	A					F		A	A	A	A		A
Depreciation & other schedules	A	A				F		A	A	A			
Dilution factors	A	A		F		F		A	A	A	A		
Directors, officers, insiders													
□ Identification	F	A				F	A	A	A	A	F		
□ Background	■	A				F	F	A	■	A	■		
□ Holdings	■	A		■			A	A	A	A			
□ Compensation		A					A	A	A	A			
Earnings per share	A	A	A			F			A		A		A
Financial information													
□ Annual audited	A	A							A		A		A
□ Interim audited		A					■	■					
□ Interim unaudited	■		A	■		F		F		F	F		
Foreign operations	A						■	A	A	A		F	
Labor contracts		■		■					F	F			
Legal agreements	F	■		■					F	F		■	
Legal counsel								A		A		■	
Loan agreements	F		F	■					F	F		■	■
Plants and properties	A	F		■				F	A	F		■	
Portfolio operations													
□ Content (listing of securities)													A
□ Management													A
Product-line breakout	A							A		A			
Securities structure	A	A			■			A	A	A			
Subsidiaries	A	A					■	A	A	A		■	
Underwriting				■				A	A	A			
Unregistered securities	■						■	F		F			
Block movements				F			■		A			■	

Legend

A - always included-included-if occured or significant

F - frequently included

■ Special circumstances only

Tender offer/acquisition reports	13D	13G	14D-1	14D-9	13E-3	13E-4
Name of issuer (subject company)	A	A	A	A	A	A
Filing person (or company)	A	A	A	A	A	A
Amount of shares owned	A	A				
Percent of class outstanding	A	A				
Financial statements of bidders			F		F	F
Purpose of tender offer			A	A	A	A
Source and amount of funds	A		A		A	
Identity and background information			A	A	A	
Persons retained, employed or to be compensated			A	A	A	A
Exhibits	F		F	F	F	F

"Trading" registrations are filed to permit trading among investors on a securities exchange or in the over-the-counter market. Registration statements which serve to register securities for trading fall into three categories:

1. **Form 10** is used by companies during the first two years they are subject to the 1934 Act filing requirements. It is a combination registration statement and annual report with information content similar to that of SEC required annual reports.
2. **Form 8-A** is used by 1934 Act registrants wishing to register *additional* securities for trading.
3. **Form 8-B** is used by "successor issuers" (usually companies which have changed their name or state of incorporation) as notification that previously registered securities are to be traded under a new corporate identification.

PROSPECTUS

When the sale of securities as proposed in an "offering" registration statement is approved by the SEC, any changes required by the SEC are incorporated into the prospectus. This document must be made available to investors before the sale of the security is initiated. It also contains the actual offering price, which may have been changed after the registration statement was approved.

ANNUAL REPORT TO SHAREHOLDERS

The Annual Report is the principal document used by most major companies to communicate directly with shareholders. Since it is not a required, official SEC filing, companies have considerable discretion in determining what types of information this report will contain and how it is to be presented.

Recent changes (effective December 15, 1980) required by the SEC were made to standardize the presentation of disclosure items in annual reports to make them consistent with similar requirements in SEC filings. For example, selected financial data relating to a registrant's financial condition and results of continuing operations will be presented in the Annual Report in the same manner as in the 10-K.

In addition to financial information, the Annual Report to Shareholders often provides non-financial details of the business which are not reported elsewhere. These may include marketing plans and forecasts of future programs and plans.

FORM 8 (AMENDMENT)

Form 8 is used to amend or supplement filings previously submitted. 1933 Act registration statements are amended by filing an amended registration statement (pre-effective amendment) or by the prospectus itself, as previously noted.

LISTING APPLICATION

Like the ARS, a listing application is not an official SEC filing. It is filed by the company with the NYSE, AMEX, or other stock exchange to document proposed new listings. Usually a Form 8-A registration is filed with the SEC at about the same time.

N-SAR

This report is the equivalent of the 10-K for registered management-investment firms. In addition to annual financial statements, this report shows diversification of assets, portfolio turnover activity, and capital gains experience.

TENDER OFFERS/ACQUISITION REPORTS

13-G (MUST BE FILED 45 DAYS AFTER END OF EACH CALENDAR YEAR)

An annual report (short form of 13D) which must be filed by all reporting persons (primarily institutions) meeting the 5 percent equity ownership rule within 45 days after the end of each calendar year.

1. Name of issuer.
2. Name of person filing.
3. 13D-1 or 13D-2 applicability.
4. Amount of shares benefically owned:
   a. Percent of class outstanding.
   b. Sole or shared power to vote.
   c. Sole or shared power to dispose.
5. Ownership of 5 percent or less of a class of stock.
6. Ownership of more than 5 percent on behalf of another person.
7. Identification of subsidiary which acquired the security being reported on by the parent holding company (if applicable).

8. Identification and classification of members of the group (if applicable).
9. Notice of dissolution of the group (if applicable).

13-D (MUST BE FILED WITHIN 10 DAYS OF THE ACQUISITION DATE)

Similar information of 5 percent equity ownership in connection with a tender offer filed within 10 days of the acquisition date—

1. Security and issuer.
2. Identity and background of person filing the statement.
3. Source and amount of funds or other consideration.
4. Purpose of the transaction.
5. Interest in securities of the issuer.
6. Contracts, arrangements or relationships with respect to securities of the issuer.
7. Material to be filed as exhibits which may include but are not limited to:
   a. Letter agreements between the parties.
   b. Formal offer to purchase.

14D-1

Tender offer filing made with the SEC at time offer is made to holders of equity securities of target company, if acceptance of offer would give the offerer over 5 percent ownership of the subject securities—

1. Security and subject company.
2. Identity and background information.
3. Past contacts, transactions, or negotiations with subject company.
4. Source and amount of funds or other consideration.
5. Purpose of the tender offer and plans or proposals of the bidder.
6. Interest in securities of the subject company.
7. Contracts, arrangements or relationships with respect to the subject company's securities.
8. Persons retained, employed, or to be compensated.
9. Financial statements of certain bidders.
10. Additional information.
11. Material to be filed as exhibits which may include but are not limited to:
    a. The actual offer to purchase.

b. The letter to shareholders.

c. The letter of transmittal with notice of guaranteed delivery.

d. The press release.

e. The summary publication in business newspapers or magazines.

f. The summary advertisement to appear in business newspapers or magazines.

14D-9 (MUST BE FILED 10 DAYS AFTER MAKING THE TENDER OFFER)

A solicitation/recommendation statement that must be submitted to equity holders and filed at the SEC by the management of a firm subject to a tender offer within ten days of the making of the tender offer—

1. Security and subject company.
2. Tender offer of the bidder.
3. Identify and background.
4. The solicitation or recommendation.
5. Persons retained, employed, or to be compensated.
6. Recent transactions and intent with respect to securities.
7. Certain negotiations and transactions by the subject company.
8. Additional information.
9. Material to be filed as exhibits.

13E-4

Issuer tender offer statement pursuant to the Securities Exchange Act of 1934—

1. Security and issuer.
2. Source and amount of funds.
3. Purpose of the tender offer and plans or proposals of the issuer or affiliates.
4. Interest in securities of the issuer.
5. Contracts, arrangements or relationships with respect to the issuer's securities.
6. Person retained, employed or to be compensated.
7. Financial information.
8. Additional information.
9. Material to be filed as exhibits which may include but are not limited to:
   The offer to purchase which is being sent to the shareholders to whom the tender offer is being made.

13E-3

Transaction statement pursuant to the Securities Exchange Act of 1934 with respect to a public company or affiliate going private—

1. Issuer and class of security subject to the transaction.
2. Identity and background of the individuals.
3. Past contracts, transactions, or negotiations.
4. Terms of the transaction.
5. Plans or proposals of the issuer or affiliate.
6. Source and amount of funds or other considerations.
7. Purpose, alternatives, reasons and effects.
8. Fairness of the transaction.
9. Reports, opinions, appraisals and certain negotiations.
10. Interest in securities of the issuer.
11. Contracts, arrangements or relationships with respect to the issuer's securities.
12. Present intention and recommendation of certain persons with regard to the transaction.
13. Other provisions of the transaction.
14. Financial information.
15. Persons and assets employed, retained or utilized.
16. Additional information.
17. Material to be filed as exhibits.

15

Site Visits

Alfred S. Rudd
Late of Standard & Poor's Corporation

Site visits are invaluable to the financial analyst as a means to clarify and to supplement the information which is available from published sources on a company. The focus of the site visit is, of course, an interview with an officer or officers of the company under investigation. Frequently, it is possible, and may be desirable, to supplement the interview with an inspection of the subject company's operating facilities. To arrange for the interview, the analyst should contact the company by letter or telephone, preferably the former, asking for an appointment and outlining his business affiliation and the nature of his interest in the company. In making the contact, the analyst probably would be well advised to address his inquiry to the company's chief financial officer or, possibly, its president. Large corporations, however, usually have a designated spokesman to the financial community and, in such cases, the inquiry would be referred to that person. In any event, the analyst should approach the interview with the primary objective of obtaining answers to the questions which have arisen during his initial investigation. The purpose of the site visit should not be for news gathering.

Before making a site visit, it is essential that the analyst examine thoroughly and analyze carefully all available published information on the subject company. Its annual and interim reports to stockholders for, perhaps, the latest five years should be reviewed in detail, as well as any other releases to stockholders and the press. Its 10-K and other reports to the SEC, and its proxy statements, should be read carefully. In addition, it is advisable to seek any additional information on the company or its industry which is available in publications of the

452

financial statistical services, in reports by industry associations, various trade publications, and by appropriate government agencies.

The analyst should obtain a good working knowledge of the company, its products, its markets, its place in industry, its financial history, and possibly the nature of its competition and of its problems, as well as its aims. At the same time, the analyst will have developed many questions as to "why" certain things have happened, and "why" the company's financial record and present financial standing is what it is. To obtain optimum results from his site visit, the analyst should make a complete listing of all inquiries to be made and organize those inquiries in logical sequence to cover each area of interest and to expedite his investigation. A carefully organized interview featuring precisely worded questions and a minimum of generalizations, stands the best chance of eliciting the full cooperation of the person or persons being interviewed, because it is the hallmark of the analyst who has "done his homework."

With adequate preparation, the analyst has an opportunity through a site visit to round out his knowledge and understanding of a company in several ways. He should be able to obtain a more precise understanding of the interplay of various economic (and sociopolitical) forces as they affect the company in determining (a) the demand for its products or services; (b) the prices received for those products or services; (c) the direct and indirect costs of providing them; and (d) the requirements and means available to finance its operations. A more accurate, or even precise, identification probably can be made of the nature and intensity of the company's direct and indirect competition. A clearer picture may be obtained of the manner in which the company's product mix, operating procedures, and financial policies resemble, as well as differ from, those of its competitors and why. From this, it may be possible to ascertain, and then to discuss, the company's apparent particular strengths and weaknesses. Some questioning is appropriate with respect to the company's operating and financial controls, for subsequent evaluation. If the site visit also includes an inspection of the company's operating facilities, possibly there will be some opportunity to observe if those operating policies and controls are being implemented, as intended.

The site visit also provides an opportunity to canvass at first hand some of the fundamental aspects of the company, such as its broad business policies and its operating and financial philosophies. It is usually pertinent to discuss the company's long-range planning and the direction of its research and development work, if that is important. Also, inquiry can be made about technological, market, or other developments, present and potential, which may have significant influence on demand for the company's products or services, or on their prices and/or costs. Finally, it is conceivable that from his site visit the analyst can begin to obtain some basis for evaluating the calibre of the company's management.

If the site visit extends beyond an interview to an inspection of the company's operating facilities, the analyst should find it valuable to communicate, if the opportunity is presented, with as many as possible of the company's personnel, representing various phases of its activities. Through that communication, he may be able, for example, to broaden his understanding of the company's operating procedures, sales policies and methods, and employee relations. Specific questions with respect to certain products or production methods frequently find their best answers in the plant.

At the conclusion of the site visit, and to supplement his findings, the analyst may find it helpful to discuss some of his questions on the subject company's products or services, and markets, with some of its competitors, suppliers, and customers. Those conversations could provide somewhat better perspective for the answers to those questions. However, the analyst never is justified in discussing with those sources the results of his findings on the site visit. On broader topics, such as industry problems, the analyst may find it advisable to check his conclusions by ascertaining the views held by appropriate industry associations, government departments, and the trade press. Those views may warrant some shading of the emphasis placed on certain problems, or conceivably bring out an entirely different viewpoint.

In evaluating the information obtained from a site visit, and from any subsequent investigation, the analyst should take care to check and recheck for possible errors or misunderstandings if his findings appear to contradict published financial data. If such discrepancies appear, it is more than possible that the analyst's recollections or notes may be at fault. Obviously, all such discrepancies must be reconciled, or the analyst is not warranted in using the information. There is a tendency, all too frequently, for a judgment to be colored by "first impressions," favorable or unfavorable. The analyst is cautioned to beware of any such tendency, insofar as it is possible, and to make his judgments objectively and only after careful consideration. Finally, having weighed all of his findings and drawn his conclusions, the analyst would be well advised to discuss frankly with the company's management the essence of his conclusions and his reasoning in arriving at those conclusions. Management usually welcomes an independent and carefully reasoned assessment.

At all times during his investigation, and particularly at the site visit, the analyst must be constantly aware of his obligation, under the regulations governing transactions in securities, to avoid obtaining any information of a material nature which might be considered "inside information." If, as might happen, any inkling is given at any time to what seems to be significant new information about the subject company (or another), management should be so informed, with the suggestion that the information be made public. Until the latter has been done, the analyst is obligated not to use such information, directly or by implication, either privately or publicly.

16

Earnings per Share[1]

Bill D. Jarnagin, Ph.D., CPA
University of Tulsa

Jon A. Booker, Ph.D., CPA
Tennessee Technological University

APPROACH TO CALCULATING EARNINGS PER SHARE

APB Opinion No. 15 provides guidelines for the calculation of earnings per share (EPS). At first reading, the Opinion appears to be rather general, and not overly difficult to apply. However, a more careful reading reveals a myriad of complex rules. Some are relatively easy to apply, while others are not. Overall, the Opinion is quite complex. In attempting to explain and analyze the Opinion, the basic problem is one

APB Opinion No. 15 (May 1969)
Earnings Per Share
SFAS No. 55 (February 1982)

and

SFAS No. 85 (March 1985)

[1] SFAS No. 21 states that nonpublic enterprises are not required to present earnings per share information (see Topic 2 for a complete discussion of SFAS No. 21).

Source: Bill D. Jarnagin and Jon A. Booker, *Financial Accounting Standards* (Chicago, Ill.: Commerce Clearing House, 1985).

of approach. The authors have elected to use a building block approach to the calculation of EPS. Each component part of the calculation will be broken down into its essential features and these features will be analyzed in detail. Once the reader comprehends a particular feature of the calculation, additional features will be added. The end product of this type of analysis is the ability to attack each important area of the earnings per share calculation and put the various pieces together into a complete computation of EPS. Much of what has been written about EPS has been either too general to be of any practical use or too detailed to apply to a wide variety of situations. The discussion and related example material should provide the reader with an in-depth understanding of the EPS calculation.

Flowcharts, diagrams, and other materials will be provided for each section of the EPS calculation. An overall flowchart of the entire EPS process is too difficult to follow, and often is more confusing than helpful. Several flowcharts and diagrams relating to a specific area of interest are more meaningful and useful to the reader.

THE CORPORATE CAPITAL STRUCTURE AND ITS IMPORTANCE IN THE EPS CALCULATION

An excellent beginning for the discussion of EPS is identification of the type of capital structure the corporation has and, therefore, of the required EPS computations. The Opinion identifies two types of capital structures that are of importance to the computation of EPS. One type is referred to as a "simple" capital structure, and the other is known as a "complex" capital structure. The identification of a given capital structure as simple or complex depends upon the makeup of the equity securities on the right-hand side of the balance sheet.

Flowchart 1 shows the decision process required for proper classification of the capital structure of a corporation. The flowchart introduces several new terms which will be defined. The reader may not fully appreciate the meaning of these terms at this stage of the discussion, but the terms will become familiar through use.

If the equity securities of a corporation consist only of common stock (Block 1), the capital structure will be classified as simple, and will lead to one type of EPS calculation. However, if the equity securities consist of common stock and "common stock equivalents," the capital structure may be either simple or complex (Block 2). A common stock equivalent is a security that gives the holder the right, through conversion or exercise, to obtain shares of common stock. These securities *are not* shares of common stock. They are rights to obtain stock if certain specified conditions are met. For example, stock options, warrants or their equivalent always are viewed as common stock equivalents, because they give the holder the right to obtain common shares.

FLOWCHART 1

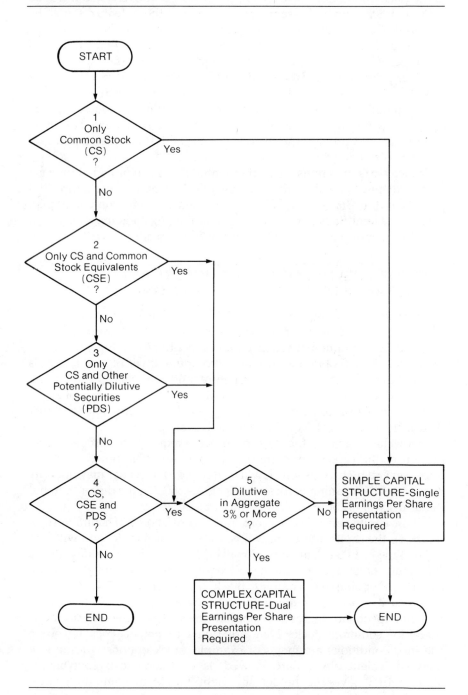

Convertible debt securities and convertible preferred stocks may be common stock equivalents if they meet certain tests that will be discussed later.

Another capital structure might consist only of common stock and "potentially dilutive securities"; that is, the capital structure would have no common stock equivalents. The capital structure of this corporation could *not* contain options, warrants, or their equivalent, because these securities always are considered common stock equivalents. Recall from the above discussion that convertible debt or preferred stock may or may not be common stock equivalents. If a corporation has convertible debt or preferred stock that *fails* to meet the tests for classification as common stock equivalents, these securities become known as "potentially dilutive securities." A key part of the phrase used is "dilutive." For any security to be considered dilutive, it must have the effect of decreasing earnings per share (or increasing a loss per share). That is to say that dilutive securities would reduce EPS below what would have been reported if the securities were not issued. The fact that the securities are referred to as "potentially" dilutive means that it is not known at this stage whether or not the securities *are* dilutive. That is something that will be determined in the process of computing EPS. If a corporation's capital structure is made up of common stock and potentially dilutive securities, it may be either a simple or a complex structure for purposes of APB Opinion No. 15 (Block 3).

Finally, a capital structure may contain common stock, common stock equivalents *and* potentially dilutive securities (Block 4). This is merely a combination of the elements described above. Again, such a capital structure may be either simple or complex.

The final test for the last three capital structures deals with the dilutive effect of the common stock equivalents and the potentially dilutive securities. For the capital structure to be classified as complex, the dilutive effect of these securities must be 3 percent or more of EPS in the aggregate (Block 5). That is, the presence of common stock equivalents and potentially dilutive securities must reduce EPS (or increase a loss per share) by at least three percent. If EPS is diluted by 3 percent or more, the capital structure is complex; and if the dilutive effect is less that 3 percent, the structure is classified as simple.

Before proceeding to the required reporting of EPS under a simple or complex capital structure, it is important to clear up some common misconceptions about the classification of a capital structure. First, many people believe that, if a corporation has common stock equivalents or potentially dilutive securities, the capital structure is complex. This is not true. The mere presence of these types of securities does not mean that the capital structure is complex; rather, it is the *dilutive* effect of these securities that leads to the proper classification. Another common error is to confuse nonconvertible debt and preferred stock with convertible debt and convertible preferred. Nonconvertible senior securities have nothing to do with the classification of the capital structure. A corporation may have many types of sophisticated nonconvertible senior securities and still have a "simple" capital structure for purposes of calculating EPS. The term *complex*, as used in APB Opinion No. 15, has special meaning and is defined by reference to Blocks 2 through 5 on Flowchart 1.

An enterprise with a simple capital structure, as defined above, is required to report only *one* earnings per share calculation. The Opinion (Paragraph 14) suggests that this calculation be referred to as "Earnings Per Common Share." If an enterprise has a complex capital structure, a *dual* presentation of earnings per share is required. If the capital structure contains common stock equivalents that are dilutive, the Opinion (Paragraph 15) suggests that one computation of earnings per share should be referred to as "Primary Earnings Per Share," and the second computation should be labeled "Fully Diluted Earnings Per Share." But if the complex capital structure contains no common stock equivalents *or* common stock equivalents that are not dilutive, the Opinion (Paragraph 16) suggests that the first computation of earnings per share should be entitled "Earnings Per Common Share—assuming no dilution," and the second computation should be referred to as "Earnings Per Common Share—assuming full dilution." The remainder of the discussion will focus on how to calculate the various amounts indicated above.

UNADJUSTED EARNINGS PER SHARE—A STARTING POINT

The basic formula for the calculation of earnings per share is net income, divided by number of common shares outstanding. This is a very simplistic notion of the concept of earnings per share, but is a helpful way to begin the analysis of unadjusted earnings per share.

For purposes of the following discussion, unadjusted earnings per share is defined as the computation of earnings per share, ignoring *all* common stock equivalents (options, warrants and their equivalent, and convertible securities classified as CSE) and potentially dilutive securities (convertible debt and preferred that fail the tests necessary to be classified as common stock equivalents). From this point forward, options, warrants, convertible debt, convertible preferred stock, and so on will be referred to as "contingent equity issues." This is done to eliminate much of the description that would be needed in the absence of some shorthand term. By ignoring *all* contingent equity issues, much of the problem of computing earnings per share has been assumed away. However, it is necessary to do so at this point in order to begin the

---

EXHIBIT 1 Weighted Average Shares—General Example

---

1. Book-It, Inc. had 2,400,000 common shares outstanding on January 1, 198A and 3,000,000 shares outstanding on December 31, 198A (the end of the fiscal year).
2. Of these amounts, 2,300,000 common shares were outstanding during the entire year.
3. 600,000 shares were sold on June 1, 198A.
4. 100,000 shares were sold on July 1, 198A.
5. 100,000 shares were repurchased on October 1, 198A, to be held in the treasury. The repurchased shares were from the shares outstanding at the beginning of the year.

---

process of examining the components of earnings per share. Of course, all of the contingent equity issues will be discussed later in this section.

Unadjusted earnings per share (EPSU) is equal to net income available to common shareholders, divided by the weighted average number of common shares outstanding. Both the numerator and denominator of this equation are different from the basic formula given above, and therefore need to be analyzed in detail.

Calculation of Weighted Average Number of Shares— The Denominator

The first step in the calculation of EPSU is to compute the weighted average number of common shares outstanding for the period. Each share of common stock must be weighted for the portion of time it is outstanding during the period. Some shares of common stock may be outstanding for the entire year, and other shares may be outstanding for only a few months. The use of a weighted average takes this fact into consideration, whereas a simple average would ignore it. In the illustration below, it is crucial to remember the EPSU ignores all contingent equity issues.

To show the computation of the weighted average number of common shares outstanding during a time period, assume the facts listed in Exhibit 1.

Table 1 on page 462 represents the computation of the weighted average number of common shares outstanding for 198A, based upon these assumptions.

The actual number of shares outstanding at the end of 198A is 3,000,000, compared with a weighted average number of shares outstanding of 2,775,000. The 100,000 shares of Treasury stock repurchased were outstanding from January 1 through October 1 (nine months), and were weighted accordingly. The 2,400,000 shares outstanding at the beginning of the year were reduced by the number of Treasury shares

TABLE 1 Computation of Weighted Average Number of Shares Outstanding

	(1)	(2)	(3)	(1 × 3)
Assumption from Exhibit 1	Number of Shares	Months Outstanding	Fraction of Year	Weighted Average Shares
2	2,300,000	12	12/12	2,300,000
3	600,000	6	6/12	350,000
4	100,000	7	7/12	50,000
5	100,000	9	9/12	75,000
Weighted average shares outstanding				2,775,000

purchased to arrive at the 2,300,000 shares that were outstanding for the entire period. The shares issued during the period were weighted for the number of months each issue actually was outstanding during 198A.

An alternative approach to the weighting of the shares outstanding at the *beginning* of the year would have been to weight the 2,400,000 for the nine months all shares were outstanding, and then weight 2,300,000 (2,400,000 – 100,000 Treasury shares) for the remaining three months of the year. If this approach were used, the following results would be obtained:

$$2,400,000 \times 9/12 = 1,800,000$$
$$2,300,000 \times 3/12 = \underline{575,000}$$
$$2,375,000$$

The total weighted average shares of 2,375,000 are identical to combining assumptions 2 and 5 (2,300,000 + 75,000) from Table 1. Regardless of the technique, the results will be the same.

Flowchart 2 identifies some additional adjustments that may be required in the calculation of the weighted average number of shares outstanding.

If, during the period under consideration, a business combination, accounted for as a pooling of interests, is consummated, the weighted average number of shares outstanding will have to be adjusted to give effect to the number of shares issued (Block 1). (See APB Opinion No. 16, "Business Combinations," in Topic 13 for a detailed analysis of accounting for business combinations accounted for as purchases and pooling of interests.) Appropriate weighting is required for the following items in connection with a pooling of interests:

1. Shares issued in the pooling are weighted from the date of acquisition to the balance sheet date.
2. Shares eliminated in the pooling are weighted from the beginning of the accounting period (or later, if issued later) to the

FLOWCHART 2

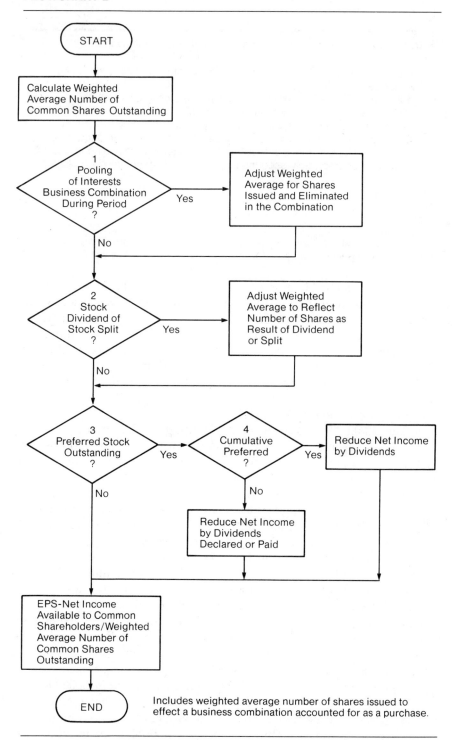

START

Calculate Weighted Average Number of Common Shares Outstanding

1 Pooling of Interests Business Combination During Period ?

Yes → Adjust Weighted Average for Shares Issued and Eliminated in the Combination

No

2 Stock Dividend of Stock Split ?

Yes → Adjust Weighted Average to Reflect Number of Shares as Result of Dividend or Split

No

3 Preferred Stock Outstanding ?

Yes → 4 Cumulative Preferred ?

Yes → Reduce Net Income by Dividends

No → Reduce Net Income by Dividends Declared or Paid

No

EPS-Net Income Available to Common Shareholders/Weighted Average Number of Common Shares Outstanding

END

Includes weighted average number of shares issued to effect a business combination accounted for as a purchase.

EXHIBIT 2 Weighted Average Shares—Business Combination

---

1. Jar, Inc., had 3,000,000 shares of common stock outstanding during the entire year of 198A.
2. 400,000 additional common shares were sold on April 1, 198A.
3. 300,000 shares of common stock of Jar, Inc., were used to effect a business combination appropriately treated as a purchase on July 1, 198A.
4. 570,000 shares of common stock of Jar, Inc. were used to acquire 95 percent of Book-It, Inc.'s 300,000 common shares outstanding in a 2-for-1 exchange appropriately accounted for as a pooling of interest on October 1, 198A.

---

acquisition date, after being restated in terms of the acquiring enterprise's stock.

If the business combination was effected by a purchase, and common stock was issued in part or full consideration, the shares issued would be weighted from the date of acquisition to the balance sheet date.

To illustrate the proper accounting for weighted average number of shares outstanding when a business combination has occurred during the accounting period, assume the facts in Exhibit 2.

Table 2 presents the computations of the weighted average number of common shares outstanding to 198A for Jar, Inc. based on the assumptions established in Exhibit 2.

The 3,000,000 shares were outstanding for 12 months and the 400,000 shares sold in April 1 were outstanding for nine months, and both were weighted accordingly. Jar, Inc. issued 300,000 shares to effect a purchase business combination. These shares should be weighted from the date of acquisition to the balance sheet date, or six months. The reason for this weighting is that, in a purchase combination, income of the acquired company prior to the date of combination is not incorporated with the income of the acquiring company.

The shares issued to effect the pooling of interests require a more complex weighting. Jar, Inc. issued 570,000 of its common shares to effect the combination on October 1. These 570,000 shares were outstanding for three months and should be weighted accordingly. Jar, Inc. acquired 285,000 (300,000 × 95%) of the shares of the combining company. These shares had been outstanding on the books of the combining company from the beginning of the year until the date of combination. Because Jar, Inc. issued two of its shares for each share of the combining company, the 285,000 shares represent 570,000 (285,000 × 2) shares of Jar, Inc. stock. The 570,000 equivalent shares of Jar, Inc. stock should be weighted for the nine months prior to the combination. The reason for this weighting is that, in a pooling of interests, the

TABLE 2 Computation of Weighted Average Number of Shares
Outstanding—Business Combination

	(1)	(2)	(3)	(1 × 3)
Assumptions from Exhibit 2	Number of Shares	Months Outstand-ing	Fraction of Year	Weighted Average Shares
1	3,000,000	12	12/12	3,000,000
2	400,000	9	9/12	300,000
3	300,000	6	6/12	150,000
4(a)	570,000	3	3/12	142,500
4(b)	570,000	9	9/12	427,500
Weighted average shares outstanding				4,020,000

income of the combining company is incorporated with the income of the combined company as if the combination took place at the beginning of the period. Therefore, the shares of Jar, Inc. are considered to be outstanding for the entire period (142,500 + 427,500 = 570,000).

The last adjustment to the denominator in the EPSU calculation is required when there has been a stock dividend or a stock split distributed during the period (Block 3). When the number of common shares outstanding changes as a result of splits or stock dividends, the weighted average number of shares should be adjusted to reflect the change. The adjustment should be on a retroactive basis for all periods presented. If the stock dividend or stock split occurs after the balance sheet date, but before the financial statements are issued, the adjustment still is required on a retroactive basis. The effects of stock dividends and stock splits and the computation of weighted average number of shares outstanding is illustrated, using the assumptions listed in Exhibit 3. Table 3 presents the computations of the weighted average number of common shares outstanding for 198C and 198B, based on the assumptions presented in Exhibit 3.

The computation of the weighted average number of shares *prior* to the stock dividend and split have been discussed at length in previous examples. By referring back to Exhibit 3, recall that the stock dividend was distributed after the sale of additional shares was completed. The dividend will be paid on these additional shares. Therefore, the number of *weighted* shares issued in connection with the dividend is equal to 10 percent of the total weighted average number of shares (1,825,000) prior to the dividend. The dividend percentage would not apply to any increases or decreases in the number of shares *after* the date of record of the dividend. This requires an additional step in the calculation of the weighted average number of shares outstanding; that is, the weighted average number of shares outstanding at the date of record for the stock dividend.

EXHIBIT 3 Assumptions for Weighted Average Shares—Splits and Dividends

---

1. Book-It, Inc. had 1,500,000 common shares outstanding during the entire year of 198C.
2. 300,000 additional common shares were sold on April 1, 198C.
3. 200,000 shares were sold on July 1, 198C.
4. Book-It, Inc. declared and paid a 10 percent stock dividend on September 1, 198C.
5. A 2-for-1 stock split occurred on January 15, 198D. The year end for Book-It is December 31, and the financial statements were not released until March 3, 198D.
6. The weighted average number of shares calculated for 198B, before considering any stock splits or dividends, was 1,200,000. Book-It is presenting comparative statements for 198C and 198B.

In this example, the stock split occurred after the end of the year, but prior to the financial statement release date. When this occurs, the weighted average shares must give recognition to the split *as if* the split had occurred in the period under consideration, in this case, 198C. The 2-for-1 split results in a doubling of the previously calculated weighted average number of shares outstanding of 2,007,500. The final total

---

TABLE 3 Weighted Average Number of Shares Outstanding for 198C and 198B—Dividends and Splits

---

1. Computation of weighted average shares for 198C:

Assumptions from Exhibit 3	(1) Number of Shares	(2) Months Outstanding	(3) Fraction of Year	(1 × 3) Weighted Average Shares
1.	1,500,000	12	12/12	1,500,000
2.	300,000	9	9/12	225,000
3.	200,000	6	6/12	100,000
Total weighted average shares before dividend and split				1,825,000
4. 10% stock dividend (1,825,000 shares × 10%)				182,500
Total weighted average shares before stock split				2,007,500
5. 2-for-1 stock split				2,007,500
Total weighted average shares outstanding				4,015,000

2. Computation of weighted average shares for 198B:

Weighted average shares outstanding for 198B (Assumptions)	1,200,000
10 percent stock dividend (1,200,000 × 10%)	120,000
Weighted average shares before split	1,320,000
2-for-1 stock split	1,320,000
Weighted average shares outstanding, retroactively restated for 198B	2,640,000

weighted average number of shares outstanding then is equal to 4,015,000. This number will be used as the denominator of the EPSU calculation.

Because Book-It, Inc. plans to present comparative financial statements for the years 198C and 198B, a restatement of the weighted average number of shares outstanding in 198B is required to reflect the distribution of the stock dividend and the stock split. The determination of the new weighted average number of shares for 198B will be made as if the dividend and split occurred at the end of 198B. At the end of 198B, Book-It, Inc. calculated the weighted average number of shares to be 1,200,000 for purposes of computing EPSU. Because the stock dividend occurred prior to the split, it must be considered first. The 10 percent stock dividend will add an additional 120,000 *weighted* shares to the previous total of 1,200,000. The stock split then is applied to this new total of 1,320,000, to give a total weighted average number of shares in 198B of 2,640,000. This is the value of the denominator that will be used to calculate EPSU for 198B.

This completes the discussion of items affecting the denominator in the unadjusted earnings per share computation. Remember that consideration has not been given to any contingent equity issues in the above examples. Attention now is directed to items that affect the numerator in the EPSU calculation.

CALCULATION OF NET INCOME AVAILABLE TO COMMON SHAREHOLDERS—THE NUMERATOR

The numerator of the equation for the calculation of EPSU may require adjustment for certain senior securities. The effects of debt securities already have been included in the numerator; that is, interest expense has been deducted to arrive at the net income figure. However, there will be an adjustment necessary if the company has preferred stock outstanding (Block 3). Dividends on preferred stock are not shown on the income statement as a reduction in income, because such dividends are considered as distributions to equity holders. However, the earnings per share computation is based upon the *common* shares outstanding, and must be based upon income available to the common shareholders. Therefore, it is necessary to reduce reported net income by an amount equal to dividends on preferred stock. If the preferred stock is cumulative (Block 4), net income is to be reduced by dividends indicated. If the preferred is noncumulative, net income will be reduced by dividends paid or declared. Remember that the discussion is about preferred dividends; cash dividends on common stock *are not* deducted from income in the computation of EPS.

To illustrate the adjustments to the numerator required for preferred stock outstanding, assume that Jar, Inc., had net income of $5,000,000

EXHIBIT 4 Assumptions for Unadjusted EPS Calculation

---

1. Jar, Inc. had 5,000,000 shares of common stock outstanding during the entire year of 198A.
2. 500,000 shares of common stock were issued on July 1, 198A.
3. 400,000 shares of common stock were issued on October 1, 198A.
4. Jar, Inc. had 200,000 shares of 10 percent, $50 par cumulative preferred stock. All dividends have been paid, including the dividends for 198A.
5. Net income for the Company in 198A was $6,000,000.

---

for the year 198C. The company has 100,000 shares of 8 percent, $100 par value cumulative preferred stock outstanding during the year. Dividends have not been paid in 198C. The adjustment to reported net income is computed below:

Reported net income before adjustment	$5,000,000
Adjustment for dividends ($100 par × 8% × 100,000 shares)	800,000
Net income for EPSU computation	$4,200,000

If the preferred stock had been noncumulative, there would be no adjustment to net income for purposes of the computation.

The example in Exhibit 4 is used to illustrate the complete calculation of EPSU by including items that affect both the numerator and the denominator.

Table 4 shows the adjustments necessary to arrive at net income available for common shareholders and weighted average number of common shares outstanding for 198A.

Unadjusted earnings per share is computed by dividing net income

---

TABLE 4 Computation of Numerator, Denominator for Unadjusted EPS

---

1. Computation of numerator:

Net income	$6,000,000
Preferred dividends paid ($50 par × 10% × 200,000 shares)	1,000,000
Net income available to common shareholders	$5,000,000

2. Computation of denominator:

Assumptions from Exhibit 4	(1) Number of Shares	(2) Months Outstanding	(3) Fraction of Year	(1 × 3) Weighted Average Shares
1	5,000,000	12	12/12	5,000,000
2	500,000	6	6/12	250,000
3	400,000	3	3/12	100,000
Weighted average shares outstanding				5,350,000

---

available to common shareholders by the weighted average number of common shares outstanding during the period. The computation is shown below:

$$EPSU = \frac{\$5,000,000}{5,350,000} = \$.935$$

With the calculation of unadjusted earnings per share, the first major building block in the process of computing earnings per share, in accordance with the provisions of APB Opinion No. 15, has been completed. The goal of this section has been to provide the reader with some essential background information that is necessary to proceed to the next section, which deals with contingent equity issues. Consideration of contingent equity issues will further complicate the determination of the numerator and denominator, as discussed above.

CONTINGENT EQUITY SECURITIES

For purposes of the following discussion, contingent equity securities are divided into three major categories: (1) options, warrants, and their equivalent; (2) convertible securities; and (3) contingent agreements. Consideration first will be given to options, warrants, and their equivalent. Since these securities may have a dilutive effect on EPS, the discussion below assumes that a dual presentation of EPS will be required. Whether a dual presentation will, in fact, be required is not known; however, making that assumption will aid in organizing the presentation. Further assume that the dual presentation required will include "Primary earnings per share" and "Fully diluted earnings per share." The discussion of options, warrants, and their equivalent will be centered around their effect upon both primary and fully diluted EPS.

Options, Warrants, and Their Equivalent—General Considerations

Options and warrants are securities that allow the holder to purchase shares of common stock for a specified price. The number of shares that may be purchased depends upon the terms of the option or warrant. Options, warrants, and their equivalent are collectively referred to as common stock equivalents.

Paragraph 37 of the Opinion identifies some securities that are to be treated as warrants, and some special types of warrants. These securities, which are viewed as warrants, include:

1. Convertible securities *requiring* a cash payment at the date of conversion.

2. Convertible securities that *allow* a cash payment at the date of conversion.
3. Warrants specifying that the proceeds from exercise *must* be used to retire debt or other securities.
4. Warrants that *require* that debt of the issuing entity, instead of cash, be tendered as part or all of the total exercise price.
5. Warrants that *permit* the holder to tender cash or debt or other securities of the issuing entity in payment of the exercise price.

The unique feature of items 1 and 2 above is that the convertible security permits or requires the payment of cash upon conversion. Normally, convertible securities do not require the payment of cash, but merely require that the security be surrendered. If cash in not permitted or required upon conversion, the security will not be included in items 1 and 2. Similarly, the unique feature of the *warrants* listed above relates to the method of payment of the exercise price, or the restricted use of the proceeds received upon exercise. While these securities are considered to be warrants, there are other items that are considered to be the equivalent of options or warrants. Securities considered to be the equivalent of options or warrants include (FASB, *Accounting Standards Original Pronouncements Issued Through June, 1983,* "Unofficial Accounting Interpretations of APB Opinion No. 15," 1983, p. 579):

1. Stock purchase agreements.
2. Unpaid stock subscriptions.
3. Deferred compensation plans requiring common stock issuance.
4. Stock appreciation rights and other variable stock options or awards payable in stock.[2]

Common stock equivalents give the holder the right to become a common shareholder and, therefore, these securities represent an equivalent number of common shares that may be issued if the holder exercises his right. If certain tests are met, earnings per share is calculated on the *assumption* that the common stock equivalents are converted into actual common shares. The actual exchange into com-

---

[2] FASB Interpretation No. 28 specifies that such stock appreciation rights and other variable stock option plan awards are considered to be common stock equivalents in the computation of earnings per share. When applying the treasury stock method, the "proceeds" are equal to the sum of the amount the employee must pay, the amount of compensation attributable to future services that has not been charged to expense, and any tax benefit that will be credited to capital. FASB Interpretation No. 31 modified FASB Interpretation No. 28 by requiring that the rights or awards that are payable in stock or *cash* be determined as common stock equivalents according to the terms most likely to be elected, based on the current fact situation existing at the end of the period. If the election appears to favor the payment of cash, the rights or awards are not considered common stock equivalents.

mon shares has not taken place, but it is assumed that it has. Providing the tests are met, the holders of common stock equivalents are treated like common shareholders for purposes of the earnings per share computation.

Flowchart 3 outlines the major tests and related procedures to be followed to determine if common stock equivalents will be treated as if they were exercised for common stock, for purposes of the EPS calculation.

To begin the process, all options, warrants, and their equivalent must be identified. Once identified, all common stock equivalents are handled on an "assumed exercise" basis for the first major test. The assumed exercise method assumes that common stock equivalents *are exercised* and the applicable number of common shares are issued, either at the beginning of the accounting period or later if the common stock equivalents were issued later. After applying the assumed exercise method, the total number of common shares that would have to be issued if all common stock equivalents were exercised is known. The number of shares determined by the assumed exercise method are compared with the total number of shares outstanding at the end of the period. If the number of shares issuable under the various common stock equivalent agreements exceeds 20 percent of the total outstanding common shares (Block 1), the *modified* treasury stock method will be used to handle the shares. If the number of issuable shares does not exceed 20 percent of the outstanding common shares, the treasury stock method will be used to handle the shares. The modified treasury stock method is illustrated on the left side of Flowchart 3, and the treasury stock is shown on the right side.

When the "20 percent test" *is* met and the modified treasury stock method is used, all common stock equivalents are handled on an aggregate basis; that is, analysis of individual options, warrants, and their equivalent is not required. The number of common shares issuable to replace the common stock equivalents already is known. The first step in the modified treasury stock method is to determine the aggregate proceeds that will be received from the assumed exercise of the common stock equivalents. The aggregate proceeds, it is assumed, will be used to buy back as many shares of common stock as possible, but not more than 20 percent of the outstanding shares at the balance sheet date, at a price equal to the average market price for the period. The difference between the number of shares issuable under the common stock equivalents agreements and the number of shares assumed to have been repurchased with the proceeds is the increment to be used in calculating the weighted average number of common shares outstanding for the period.

If there are any proceeds left after the assumed repurchase of 20 percent of the stock outstanding, these proceeds should be assumed to

FLOWCHART 3

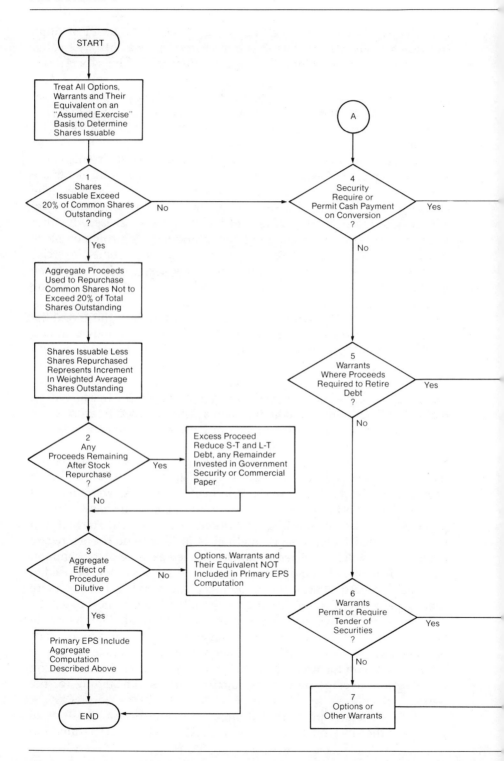

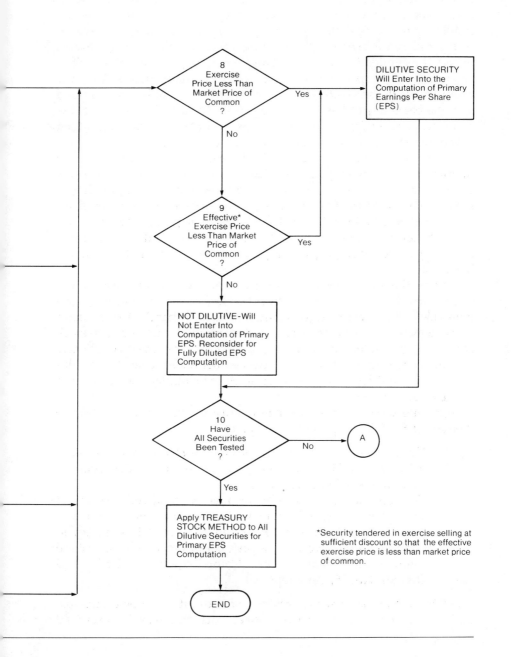

8
Exercise Price Less Than Market Price of Common ?

Yes → DILUTIVE SECURITY Will Enter Into the Computation of Primary Earnings Per Share (EPS)

No ↓

9
Effective* Exercise Price Less Than Market Price of Common ?

Yes

No ↓

NOT DILUTIVE - Will Not Enter Into Computation of Primary EPS. Reconsider for Fully Diluted EPS Computation

10
Have All Securities Been Tested ?

No → A

Yes ↓

Apply TREASURY STOCK METHOD to All Dilutive Securities for Primary EPS Computation

END

*Security tendered in exercise selling at sufficient discount so that the effective exercise price is less than market price of common.

first eliminate short-term and long-term debt, and any remaining proceeds are assumed to be invested in government securities or commercial paper (Block 2). (In many cases it may not be possible to buy back 20 percent of the common stock outstanding, because the exercise price may be less than the average market price. If the exercise price is less than the average market price, there may be more than 20 percent of the shares outstanding represented by common stock equivalents; yet it still may not be possible to repurchase 20 percent of the stock, because of the difference between the exercise price and the average market price.) The elimination of debt and investment in government securities or commercial paper would be assumed to have occurred at the beginning of the accounting period, or later if the debt had been issued after the beginning of the accounting period. The after-tax interest of the assumed debt elimination or government securities purchased is added to the numerator in the primary earnings computation.

If the application of the modified treasury stock method has a dilutive effect upon earnings per share, all common stock equivalents will be included in the calculation of *primary* earnings per share (EPSP). If the effects of the method are anti-dilutive, none of the common stock equivalents will be included in the calculation of primary earnings per share. When the "20 percent test" is met, the modified treasury stock method requires an *aggregate* computation for common stock equivalents.

When the shares issued, upon assumed exercise of the common stock equivalent, represent 20 percent or less of the outstanding common stock, the treasury stock method is used to handle the common stock equivalents. Under the treasury stock method, each common stock equivalent is handled on an individual basis to determine if it will enter into the computation of primary earnings per share. Only those common stock equivalents that are determined to be dilutive are considered in the EPSP computation.

Options, warrants, and their equivalent are considered to be dilutive if either of the following conditions is met:

1. The average market price exceeds the exercise price for substantially all (an 11-week period) of the three months prior to computation of EPS (Block 8);
2. "The security which may be (or must be) tendered is selling at a price below that which it may be tendered under the option or warrant agreement and the resulting discount is sufficient to establish an effective exercise price below the market price of the common stock that can be obtained upon exercise." (APB Opinion No. 15, Paragraph 37)

(The Opinion *implies* that the options and warrants must be exercisable within five years of the balance sheet date and may be exercised currently if the holder desires.) If a common stock equivalent is found to be dilutive, it will be included in the calculation of EPSP; if it is not dilutive, it will be ignored.

The treasury stock method assumes that all dilutive common stock equivalents are exercised at the beginning of the period, or later if issued after the beginning of the period. The proceeds received, in excess of any required use of those proceeds, such as the retirement of debt, are assumed to be used to repurchase shares of common stock at the average market price for the period. The difference between the shares issuable under the common stock equivalents agreements and the number of shares repurchased with the proceeds represents the incremental number of shares in the determination of the weighted average shares outstanding.

If options, warrants, and their equivalent *do not* meet the test for inclusion in the calculation of primary earnings per share, they still must be considered for the calculation of fully diluted earnings per share (EPSFD). Generally, if common stock equivalents are not included in the primary earnings per share computation, they will not be included in the fully diluted calculation. However, exceptions to this general rule do exist. When common stock equivalents *are included* in the EPSP computation, they must be reconsidered for the EPSFD computation. Recall that, for the EPSP computation, the exercise price of the common stock equivalents was compared with the *average* market price to determine if the security was dilutive. If the end of period market price is greater than the average market price, additional incremental shares will result. These incremental shares will be included in the calculation of EPSFD. If the average price is greater than the end of period price, no new computation is necessary and the same number of incremental shares will be used in both the primary and fully diluted EPS computations. The fully diluted computation is based upon a comparison of the end of period price with the exercise price, so as to obtain the maximum possible dilutive effect of the common stock equivalent.

Common Stock Equivalents—Effects on Primary EPS

The discussion above may have been difficult to follow, because of the technical nature of the treatment of common stock equivalents. The examples that follow will define more clearly any areas that proved hard to follow.

The impact of common stock equivalents on primary earnings per share and fully diluted earnings per share have been isolated in order to make the problem more manageable. To illustrate the effects of common stock equivalents on the computation of primary earnings per share, assume the facts listed in Exhibit 5 prevail.

In reviewing these assumptions, notice that none of the options or

---

EXHIBIT 5 Options and Warrants—Example 1

1. Jar, Inc. has a December 31 year end. Earnings per share are to be calculated for the year ended December 31, 198C.
2. 1,500,000 common shares were outstanding for the entire year.
3. 50,000 warrants previously had been issued in 198A, with the holder receiving the right to purchase 50,000 common shares, at a price of $20 per share, any time after December 31, 198B.
4. The company granted 200,000 stock options to a limited number of key employees on April 1, 198C. The options gave the holders the right to purchase 200,000 common shares, at a price of $22 per share, at any time after the date of grant.
5. The market price of Jar, Inc.'s common stock was above $22 per share for substantially all of 198C. Important average stock prices and the ending market price are presented below:

Average for the Year 198C	$24 per share
Average for April 1 to December 31, 198C	$25 per share
December 31, 198C ending market price	$30 per share

6. Jar, Inc. reported net income of $5,000,000 for the year ended December 31, 198C.

---

warrants permits or requires the tendering of debt or other securities. Therefore, it will not be necessary to determine the "effective" exercise price. The total number of shares of common stock to be issued upon conversion of all options and warrants is 250,000 shares (50,000 under warrants, and 200,000 under the option agreement). The 250,000 shares that could be issued total less than 20 percent of all common shares outstanding at the end of the period (250,000/1,500,000 = 16.67 percent). The common stock equivalents do not meet the "20 percent test," and the treasury stock method will be used to determine any incremental shares.

Since the treasury stock method is to be used, each common stock equivalent must be tested separately to determine if it is dilutive. The average market price of the stock for 198C was $24 per share, which exceeded the $20 per share exercise price of the warrants. In addition, the market price of the stock was in excess of $22 per share for substantially all of 198C. Based upon these facts, the warrants are considered to be dilutive, and will enter into the calculation of EPSP. The next step is to determine the number of incremental shares resulting from the application of the treasury stock method. The following formula provides a short-cut approach to the calculation of the incremental shares:

$$S = \frac{MP - EP}{MP} \times NS$$

Where

    S = Incremental shares.

    MP = Average market price (or the greater of average or ending market price for fully diluted EPS).

    EP = Exercise price of the option or warrant.

    NS = Number of shares issuable upon exercise of the option or warrant.

This equation can be used only when the treasury stock method is applicable. It cannot be used if the options and warrants are anti-dilutive, or if the total number of issuable shares exceeds 20 percent of the outstanding common shares.

Based upon the information given in the example problem, the formula will provide the following results for the warrants:

$$S = \frac{\$24 - \$20}{\$24} \times 50,000 = 8,333$$

Therefore, 8,333 incremental shares will be added to the weighted average number of shares outstanding for the company.

The 200,000 options will be considered next. The average market price per share applicable to the options is $25, which is the average price for the period of time the options were outstanding. The appropriate average market price exceeds the option price of $22 per share; and, therefore, the options also are considered to be dilutive for purposes of computing EPSP. The assumption is made, under the treasury stock method, that the options were exercised during the year, and that the proceeds from the exercise were used to repurchase common stock. The number of incremental shares to be added to the weighted average number of shares can be determined by using the formula given above. The results of the formula, when applied to the options, would be:

$$S = \frac{\$25 - \$22}{\$25} \times 200,000 = 24,000$$

Since the options were issued after the beginning of the year, they must be weighted for the appropriate period of time they have been outstanding. In this case the options were issued on April 1, 198C, and were outstanding for nine months during the period. The *weighted* incremental shares would be determined as follows:

$$24,000 \times \tfrac{9}{12} = 18,000$$

The 18,000 weighted shares will be added to the weighted average number of common shares outstanding during 198C.

All contingent equity issues in this example have been considered. The final step in the determination of the denominator for EPSP is to calculate the weighted average common shares outstanding during 198C. Since there were no new issues of common stock or purchases of treasury stock, the 1,500,000 common shares were outstanding all year.

The total weighted average number of common shares outstanding would be determined as follows:

Weighted average common shares	1,500,000
Incremental shares from warrants	8,333
Weighted incremental shares from options	18,000
Total weighted average shares outstanding	1,526,333

Because there is no preferred stock outstanding, the numerator of the EPSP will not be adjusted. The final step is to calculate EPSP. The calculation is shown below:

$$EPSP = \frac{\$5,000,000}{1,526,333} = \$3.28$$

Common Stock Equivalents—Effects on Fully Diluted EPS

Once primary earnings per share has been calculated, it is necessary to reconsider all options and warrants that were used or omitted from the primary calculation in the computation of fully diluted earnings per share. In the example problem given, all options and warrants were considered dilutive for the primary earnings per share computation. Therefore, any incremental shares used in the primary computation also will be used in the fully diluted computation. For purposes of fully diluted earnings per share, the exercise price of the warrants and options must be compared with the market price at the end of the period to determine if any additional incremental shares will be added to the fully diluted computation. Of course, if the average market price exceeds the end of period price, the average will be used, and no additional computations will be necessary.

By referring back to Exhibit 5, notice that the December 31 market price is $30 per share, which is greater than the average market price of $24 per share for the warrants and $25 per share for the options. As a result, there will be some additional incremental shares for purposes of calculating fully diluted earnings per share. By using the equation given above, the following results are obtained for the warrants:

$$S = \frac{\$30 - \$20}{\$30} \times 50,000 = 16,667$$

For fully diluted earnings per share, there are 16,667 incremental shares as a result of the dilutive warrants. Since some incremental shares already are included in the primary calculation, only the additional incremental shares will be added. The additional incremental shares would be determined as follows:

Incremental shares using December 31 market price	16,667
Incremental shares using average market price	8,333
Additional incremental shares to be added	8,334

The results for the options are shown below:

$$S = \frac{\$30 - \$22}{\$30} \times 200,000 = 53,333$$

The incremental shares using the year-end market price must be weighted for the nine months that the options were outstanding. Therefore, the weighted incremental shares would be 40,000 (53,333 × $\frac{9}{12}$).

Incremental shares using December 31 market price	40,000
Incremental shares using average market price	18,000
Additional incremental shares to be added	22,000

Based upon these computations, the total weighted average number of common shares outstanding for purposes of calculating fully diluted earnings per share would be determined as follows:

Number of shares used for primary EPS computation	1,526,333
Additional incremental shares for warrants	8,334
Additional incremental shares for options	22,000
Total weighted average shares for fully diluted EPS computation	1,556,667

Since there will be no change in the numerator, the computation of fully diluted earnings per share for Example 1 would be determined as follows:

$$EPSFD = \frac{\$5,000,000}{1,556,667} = \$3.21$$

Before a final determination can be made as to the proper presentation of EPS, it is necessary to see if the dilutive effect is 3 percent or more of unadjusted earnings per share (EPSU). If the dilutive effect is 3 percent or more, a dual presentation is required; if it is less than 3 percent, only unadjusted earnings per share will be reported.

To determine if the EPS calculations are dilutive by 3 percent or more, the fully diluted earnings per share (EPSFD) must be compared with unadjusted earnings per share; that is, with earnings per share before consideration of any contingent equity issues. There is no preferred stock, so the numerator of EPSU will be equal to the reported net income of $5,000,000. There were no security issues or repurchase of treasury shares during the period, so the denominator of the EPSU equation will be the weighted average number of common shares outstanding of 1,500,000. Unadjusted earnings per share would be calculated as follows:

$$EPSU = \frac{\$5,000,000}{1,500,000} = \$3.33$$

The following equation can be used to determine the dilutive effect of the computations made above:

$$ADR = \frac{EPSFD}{EPSU}$$

Where

ADR = Aggregate dilution reciprocal.
EPSFD = Fully diluted earnings per share.
EPSU = Unadjusted earnings per share.

The formula provides the following recipirocal for the information in Example 1:

$$ADR = \frac{\$3.21}{\$3.33} = 96.4 \text{ percent}$$

Since 96.4 percent is less than 97 percent, a dual presentation of earnings per share is required. EPSP will be reported at $3.28, and EPSFD will be reported at $3.21.

The approach taken to the solution of the Example 1 problem was to determine common stock equivalents on an incremental basis. The example that follows utilizes the gross approach in the computation of fully diluted earnings per share.

Common Stock Equivalents—Effects on Primary EPS

The example just completed was relatively straightforward, although it did introduce several new concepts. To illustrate a more complex situation, the assumptions listed in Exhibit 6 will be used.

The analysis begins, as before, with a determination of the number of shares that would be issued if all options and warrants outstanding were exercised. The warrants identified in Assumption 3 of Exhibit 6 would require the issuance of 100,000 shares of common stock. The options in Assumption 4 were exercised in 198D and are part of the common stock outstanding, and thus no longer would represent a contingent equity security. The warrants identified in Assumption 5 also represent the exercise of a former contingent equity security and do not

---

EXHIBIT 6   Options and Warrants—Example 2

---

1. Book-It, Inc. has a December 31 year end. The period under consideration is January 1, 198D to December 31, 198D.
2. 2,000,000 common shares were outstanding on January 1, 198D.
3. 100,000 warrants were issued in 198B with the right to purchase 100,000 shares of common stock at a price of $30 per share any time after December 31, 198C. The warrants expire on December 31, 198E. The proceeds from the exercise of the warrants must be used to retire an eight percent, $2,500,025 note, payable on December 31, 198E. Book-It has a 50 percent tax rate.
4. 100,000 options were exercised on October 1, 198D. The options had been granted to a limited number of employees on April 1, 198C, with the right to purchase 100,000 shares of stock at a price of $28 per share.
5. 20,000 warrants that were issued in 198A were exercised on July 1, 198D for 20,000 shares of common stock. The warrants had an exercise price of $35 per share.
6. The market price was above $31 for all of 198D. The averages and period-end market prices for the time periods indicated below are:

Average for 198D	$35
Average from January 1 to October 1, 198D	$37
Average from January 1 to July 1, 198D	$34
July 1, 198D market price	$34
October 1, 198D market price	$36
December 31, 198D market price	$38

7. Net income for Book-It for 198D was $10,000,000.

---

represent any issuable shares. Therefore, the shares that would be issued if all options and warrants were exercised amount to the 100,000 common shares from Assumption 3. This total must be compared with the total number of shares outstanding at the end of 198D for purposes of the "20 percent test." The number of shares outstanding on December 31, 198D is shown below:

Shares outstanding at the beginning of 198D	2,000,000
Issued upon the exercise of options on October 1	100,000
Issued upon the exercise of warrants on July 1	20,000
Total shares outstanding at December 31, 198D	2,120,000

The relationship between the number of shares issuable upon the exercise of all of the outstanding warrants and the total number of shares outstanding at the end of 198D is shown below:

$$\text{Percentage relationship} = \frac{100{,}000}{2{,}120{,}000} = 4.7 \text{ percent}$$

The issuable shares represent 4.7 percent of the total number of shares outstanding. This is less than the 20 percent required to meet the "20 percent test"; therefore, the treasury stock method is applicable to the handling of the warrants for purposes of computing primary earnings per share.

The warrants are the only common stock equivalent outstanding at the end of the period. If they are to be included in EPSP they must be dilutive. To be dilutive, the exercise price—either actual or effective—must be less than the market price of the common stock for substantially all of the three-month period preceding the calculation of EPSP. The average market price of the common stock was $35 per share for 198D, and the exercise price of the 100,000 warrants is $30 per share. Therefore, the warrants are considered to be dilutive and will be used in the EPSP computation.

The proceeds received from the exercise of the warrants must be used to retire the 8 percent, $2,500,025 note payable. Any proceeds in excess of $2,500,025 will be used to repurchase common stock at the average market price. The proceeds of $3,000,000 (100,000 warrants × $30 per share) will be used to retire the $2,500,025 debt, and the excess proceeds of $499,975 ($3,000,000 – $2,500,025) are assumed to be used to repurchase common stock at the average market price of $35 per share. The number of shares that can be repurchased with the excess proceeds is shown below:

$$\text{Number of shares repurchased} = \frac{\$499,975}{\$35} = 14,285$$

The difference between the number of shares issuable (100,000) and the number of shares that could be repurchased with the excess proceeds (14,285) represents the incremental number of shares that will be added to the weighted average number of shares in the denominator of the equation to calculate EPSP. The number of incremental shares to be added is equal to 85,715.

However, the assumed exercise of the warrants affects both the denominator *and* the numerator of the equation. Remember the assumption was that the 8 percent debt would be retired with the proceeds from the exercise, and that the retirement would be treated as if it occurred at the beginning of 198D. Therefore, the interest expense in connection with the retired debt must be removed from the numerator of the equation. If the assumption is made that the debt is retired, then it is impossible to have any interest from the debt included in income.

The interest expense recorded in 198D for the debt assumed to be retired was $200,002 ($2,500,025 × 8%). This must be removed from the reported income for 198D. Interest is deductible for income tax purposes, and the fact that the company had interest expense reduced its tax liability. Therefore, it is necessary to remove the aftertax effect of the

$200,002 interest expense. The aftertax interest is computed using the following formula:

$$AI = I\,(1 - T)$$

Where:

AI = Adjusted aftertax income
I = Period interest expense
T = Tax rate

Based upon the information developed above, the formula provides the following results:

$$AI = \$200,002\,(1 - .50) = \$100,001$$

So $100,001 must be *added* to net income in an adjustment to the numerator of the EPSP equation.

The next problem to be addressed is the treatment given to the options that were exercised on October 1, 198D. At the end of the year, all the options were exercised and had to be included in the computation of the weighted average number of shares outstanding during 198D. However, the options were a contingent equity issue for part of 198D and had to be treated as such for the partial period. The options were outstanding for nine months in 198D, and the first step is to determine if they were dilutive during this period of time. The average market price for the partial period (January 1 through October 1) was $37 per share, and the exercise price of the options was $28 per share. Since the average market price was greater than the exercise price, the options were dilutive for the partial period and will enter into the calculation of EPSP. To determine the incremental shares to be added to the denominator, the following formula can be used:

$$S = \left(\frac{MP - EP}{MP} \times NS\right) \times PT$$

Where:

S = Incremental shares.
MP = Average market price per share.
EP = Exercise price per share of options or warrants.
NS = Number of shares issuable upon exercise.
PT = Partial time period.

Application of the formula to the information given provides the following incremental shares:

$$S = \left(\frac{\$37 - \$28}{\$37} \times 100,000\right) \times 9/12 = 18,243$$

These 18,243 incremental shares will be added to the number of weighted average shares represented by the exercised options.

The options were exercised on October 1, 198D, and were considered as common stock outstanding for three months of 198D. The options resulted in a total of 100,000 common shares being issued. This represents 25,000 weighted common shares (100,000 × 3/12). The 25,000 shares just determined will be added to the 18,243 incremental shares, to equal a total of 43,243 shares, which represents the common share effect of the options identified in Assumption 4. There is no adjustment to the numerator of the EPSP equation as a result of the exercise of the options.

The final contingent issue to be considered is the warrants identified in Assumption 5 of the problem. The treatment of the warrants is similar to the treatment given the options above. The average market price for the partial period (January 1 through July 1, 198D) was $34 per share, and the exercise price was $35 per share. Because the exercise price exceeded the average market price, the warrants are considered to be anti-dilutive during the partial period. The warrants will not be considered in the calculation of EPSP. This is a very unusual situation and was developed for illustrative purposes only.

The warrants were exercised on July 1, 198D for 20,000 common shares. The common shares were outstanding for six months and represent 10,000 weighted shares (20,000 × 6/12).

The analysis of the options and warrants now has been completed, and it is helpful to recap the results of the preceding computations to show their effect on the computation of EPSP.

	Increase (Decrease) In:	
	Numerator (Income)	Denominator (Shares)
Proceeds to retire debt	$100,001	85,715
100,000 options exercised	none	43,243
20,000 warrants exercised	none	10,000
Total	$100,001	138,958

The addition of the $100,001 to the $10,000,000 of reported net income gives a final numerator for primary earnings per share of $10,100,001. Since there were no issues or repurchases of common stock during the period, the denominator of the equation consists of the 138,958 shares from above, and the 2,000,000 shares that were outstanding all year, for a total of 2,138,958. The computation of EPSP is shown below:

$$\text{EPSP} = \frac{\$10,100,001}{2,138,958} = \$4.722$$

This same information now will be used to compute fully diluted earnings per share.

Common Stock Equivalents—Effects upon Fully Diluted EPS

After primary earnings per share have been calculated, it is necessary to reconsider all options and warrants for the fully diluted earnings per share computation. If the end of period market price per share of the common stock is greater than the average market price per share, additional common shares will be added to the denominator of the EPSP equation. If the average market price per share is greater than the end of period market price, the incremental shares used in the EPSP computation will also be used in the EPSFD computation.

First consider the 100,000 warrants issued that required that the proceeds from exercise be used to retire the $2,500,025, 8 percent note payable. With an exercise price of $30 per share, the total proceeds from the exercise of all warrants would be $3,000,000. As computed in the EPSP calculation, the excess proceeds would amount to $499,975. The ending market price per share of common stock was $38, while the average for the year was $35 per share. Since the end of period market price is greater than the average price during the period, the ending price will be used to determine the number of shares that could be repurchased with the excess proceeds. This is done in order to obtain the maximum possible dilution resulting from the issue of the warrants. The computation of the shares repurchased is shown below:

$$\text{Number of shares repurchased} = \frac{\$499,975}{\$38} = 13,157$$

The difference between the number of shares (100,000) issued upon exercise of the warrants and the number of shares (13,157) that could be repurchased with the excess proceeds is equal to the number of shares that will be included in the denominator of the EPSFD computation, along with the weighted average number of common shares. In this case, 86,843 shares will be added to the denominator of the EPSFD equation for the warrants.

The next item to be reconsidered is the 100,000 options that were exercised on October 1, 198D. The market price of the common stock was $36 per share on October 1 (the end of the period for the options), and the average market price of common shares for the period January 1 through October 1 was $37 per share. Because the end of period price was less than the average market price, no additional consideration is needed for the options. The 18,243 incremental shares calculated for the primary earnings per share computation also will be used in the fully diluted computation. The optioned common shares that were outstanding from October 1 through December 31, 198D, have a weighted number of shares equal to 25,000. The total number of shares included in the denominator from the options is 43,243 (25,000 + 18,243), which is the same total used in the primary earnings per share computation.

The final item to be reconsidered is the issue of 20,000 warrants that were exercised on July 1, 198D. There were no incremental shares from the partial period included in the primary earnings per share computation, because the exercise price of $35 per share was greater than the average market price of $34 per share. The conclusion was that the warrants were anti-dilutive.

When warrants or options are exercised during the year, they are included in the calculation of fully diluted earnings per share, even though they are anti-dilutive. The market price on the *date of exercise* is used to determine the number of shares that could have been purchased with the proceeds. The proceeds from the exercise of the 20,000 warrants was $700,000 (20,000 × $35 per share). The $700,000 proceeds could have been used to repurchase 20,588 ($700,000/$34 market price per share) common shares on the exercise date. The difference between the 20,588 shares repurchased and the 20,000 shares issued represents 588 incremental shares that are anti-dilutive and that must be *deducted* from the weighted average shares outstanding.

From the EPSP computation, it was determined that the weighted shares represented by the exercise of the warrants was 10,000 (20,000 × 6/12). Therefore, the number of shares to be included from the exercise of the warrants in the fully diluted earnings per share computation is 9,706 (10,000 − (588 × 6/12)).

All options and warrants now have been reconsidered, and the recap below summarizes the results of the calculations to this point.

	Increase (Decrease) In:	
	Numerator (Income)	Denominator (Shares)
Warrants to retire debt	$100,001	86,843
100,000 options exercised	none	43,243
20,000 warrants exercised	none	9,706
Total	$100,001	139,792

The numerator of the fully diluted earnings per share equation will be the same as that used in the primary earnings per share computation—$10,100,001. The 139,792 shares shown above will be added to the 2,000,000 weighted average number of common shares outstanding to yield a denominator for the equation of 2,139,792. Fully diluted earnings per share is calculated below:

$$\text{EPSFD} = \frac{\$10,100,001}{2,139,792} = \$4.72$$

After completing all of the previous calculations, it is now time to determine if the common stock equivalents used in the computations are, in the aggregate, dilutive by 3 percent or more. If they are not dilutive by 3 percent or more, none of the above calculation will be used, and only one earnings per share presentation is required.

The extent of the dilution is measured by the relationship between the fully diluted earnings per share and the unadjusted earnings per share. Unadjusted earnings per share do not include any contingent equity issues. The weighted average number of common shares outstanding for purposes of computing the unadjusted earnings per share is determined as follows:

Shares outstanding entire year	2,000,000
Weighted shares from exercise of options	25,000
Weighted shares from exercise of warrants	10,000
Total weighted average shares outstanding	2,035,000

Since there were no senior nonconvertible securities outstanding, there would be no adjustment to the reported net income of $10,000,000. The computation of the unadjusted earnings per share is shown below:

$$\text{EPSU} = \frac{\$10,000,000}{2,035,000} = \$4.91$$

Finally, the fully diluted earnings per share of $4.718 is divided by the unadjusted earnings per share of $4.91 to determine the aggregate dilution reciprocal (ADR). The computation is shown below:

$$\text{ADR} = \frac{\$4.72}{\$4.91} = 96.1 \text{ percent}$$

Since the aggregate dilution reciprocal is below 97 percent, the common stock equivalents are, in the aggregate, dilutive by three percent or more. Therefore, a dual presentation of earnings per share is required as follows:

Primary earnings per share	$4.722
Fully diluted earnings per share	$4.72

OPTIONS, WARRANTS, AND THEIR EQUIVALENT— THE "20 PERCENT" RULE

In the two examples given above, the treasury stock method was used to handle options, warrants, and their equivalent, because the number

---

EXHIBIT 7 Options, Warrants and the "20 Percent" Rule

---

1. Book-It, Inc. has a December 31 year end and is preparing to calculate earnings per share for the year ended December 31, 198D.
2. 1,000,000 shares of common stock were outstanding during all of 198D.
3. 300,000 warrants were issued in 198A, giving the holders the right to purchase 300,000 shares of common stock, at a price of $50 per share, any time after December 31, 198B.
4. 25,000 warrants were issued on 198C, giving the holders the right to purchase 25,000 shares of common stock, at a price of $58 per share, any time after December 31, 198C.
5. The market price of the stock was above $51 per share for all of 198D. The average market price and the year-end market price of the common stock were equal to $53 per share.
6. Book-It, Inc. has $2,000,000 of 8 percent short-term notes payable and $5,000,000 of 7 percent long-term bonds payable. There is no other short- or long-term debt.
7. Book-It reported net income for 198D of $8,500,000. The tax rate applicable to the company is 50 percent.

---

of shares that could be repurchased with the proceeds from the exercise of these items was less than 20 percent of the outstanding common stock. The assumptions listed in Exhibit 7 provide an example where the "20 percent" test is met, and the modified treasury stock method must be used. Primary and fully diluted earnings per share will be discussed together, instead of being separated as in the previous examples. By now the reader should be familiar with the procedure required to handle contingent equity issues in the primary and fully diluted computations, and separate discussion is not necessary.

As with the two previous examples, the first step is to determine the number of issuable shares relating to the options and warrants. In this example, 325,000 common shares would be issued if the warrants and options all were exercised (300,000 from the 198A warrants and 25,000 from the 198C warrants). This total must be compared with the total number of common shares outstanding at the end of the period. The issuable shares represent 32.5 percent of the total shares outstanding (325,000/1,000,000 = 32.5 percent); therefore, the common stock equiv- alents meet the "20 percent" rule, and the modified treasury stock method will be used. Under the modified treasury stock method, all common stock equivalents are considered in the aggregate, rather than individually, to determine if they are dilutive.

Like the treasury stock method, the modified treasury stock method assumes that the proceeds from the exercise of the warrants will be used to repurchase shares of common stock at the average market price during the period. However, the number of common shares assumed to be repurchased must not exceed 20 percent of the total outstanding common stock at the end of the period. In this example, there were

1,000,000 common shares outstanding on December 31, 198D; therefore, no more than 200,000 (1,000,000 × 20%) shares may be treated as repurchased. If there are proceeds remaining after the repurchase of 20 percent of the shares outstanding, they will be assumed to be used to retire short-term debt of the company; if all the short-term debt is retired with the proceeds, the remainder will be used to retire long-term debt. Finally, if proceeds still remain after all short- and long-term debt has been retired, they will be invested in government securities or commercial paper.

The proceeds from the assumed exercise of the warrants is determined as follows:

300,000 warrants × $50 per share price	$15,000,000
25,000 warrants × $58 per share price	1,450,000
Total proceeds from exercise of warrants	$16,450,000

With proceeds of $16,450,000, the company could repurchase 310,377 common shares at the average market price of $53 per share ($16,450,000/$53). However, under the modified treasury stock method, the company is limited to the repurchase of 200,000 common shares, i.e., 20 percent of the common shares outstanding. Given this limitation, the following computation is necessary:

Total proceeds from exercise of warrants	$16,450,000
Repurchase of 200,000 shares (200,000 × $53)	(10,600,000)
Excess proceeds from exercise	$ 5,850,000

The excess proceeds will be used to eliminate the short-term debt first. Book-It, Inc. has $2,000,000 of short-term notes payable that will be eliminated by the excess proceeds. After this has been done, the remaining proceeds amount to $3,850,000 ($5,850,000 − $2,000,000). The $3,850,000 remaining proceeds will be used to reduce the long-term debt of $5,000,000. The long-term debt assumed to be remaining after the reduction is equal to $1,150,000 ($5,000,000 − $3,850,000). There are no proceeds available to be invested in government securities or commercial paper, because the entire amount of the long-term debt was not eliminated.

The modified treasury stock method assumes that the debt is retired at the beginning of the year (or later if issued after the beginning of the year). If the debt is to be eliminated, the interest associated with the debt also must be eliminated. The following computation shows the interest expense associated with the debt assumed to be retired:

Short-term debt ($2,000,000 × 8%)	$160,000
Long-term debt ($3,850,000 × 7%)	269,500
Pretax interest to be eliminated	$429,500

Since net income is reported on an aftertax basis, and the interest in this calculation is on a pretax basis, it is necessary to adjust the interest to an aftertax basis. The tax rate applicable to Book-It was given as 50 percent. By using the formula discussed earlier, the following aftertax adjustment is necessary:

$$\text{Aftertax interest} = \$429,500 \ (1 - .50) = \$214,750$$

The $214,750 will be added to the numerator for the earnings per share computation.

The adjustment required to the denominator of the equation is based upon the incremental shares resulting from the assumed exercise of the warrants. If all the warrants were to be exercised, 325,000 common shares would be issued. However, the proceeds from the exercise could be used to repurchase 200,000 common shares (due to the limitation), so there would be 125,000 incremental shares as a result of using the modified treasury stock method. These incremental shares will be added to the denominator of the earnings per share equation.

For purposes of the "20 percent" rule, the numerator of the earnings per share equation would be $8,714,750 ($8,500,000 net income + $214,750 interest adjustment), and the denominator would be 1,125,000 shares (1,000,000 shares outstanding the entire year + 125,000 incremental shares). Therefore, earnings per share under the "20 percent" rule would be computed as follows:

$$\text{EPS} = \frac{\$8,714,750}{1,125,000} = \$7.75$$

The last step is to determine if the earnings per share just calculated is dilutive, when compared to the unadjusted earnings per share. For purposes of calculating EPSU, there are no adjustments necessary to either the numerator or the denominator. This is true because no new shares were issued during the period and no treasury shares were acquired, and there is no preferred stock outstanding. The computation of EPSU is shown below:

$$\text{EPSU} = \frac{\$8,500,000}{1,000,000} = \$8.50$$

Because the earnings per share calculated under the modified treasury stock method is less than the EPSU, the warrants are considered to be dilutive in the aggregate. However, some of the common stock equivalents used may be anti-dilutive. An examination of the 25,000 warrants issued in 198C indicate that they are anti-dilutive, since the exercise price of $58 per share is greater than the average market price of $53 per share. The modified treasury stock method requires that all contingent equity issues be handled in the aggregate; and, obviously, the impact of the other warrants offset the anti-dilutive effect of the warrants issued in 198C.

Since the average market price per share is equal to the end of period market price, there would be no additional incremental shares for the fully diluted earnings per share computation. The $7.75 per share calculated above is both the fully diluted and primary earnings per share amount.

To determine the proper presentation of earnings per share, the aggregate dilution reciprocal must be computed. This computation is shown below:

$$\text{ADR} = \frac{\$7.75}{\$8.50} = 91.2 \text{ percent}$$

Since the ADR is below 97 percent, the common stock equivalents are, in the aggregate, dilutive by 3 percent or more, and a dual presentation of earnings per share is required. The following presentation would be appropriate for this example:

Primary earnings per share	$7.75
Fully diluted earnings per share	$7.75

Had there been a difference between the average market price per share and the end of period market price per share, there might have been some additional incremental shares to be considered in the fully diluted earnings per share computation. However, this point has been covered in the two previous examples and was intentionally omitted from the example just concluded.

Options, Warrants, and Their Equivalent—Variations in Stock Prices

One assumption made in all of the previous examples was that the average market price exceeded the exercise price for substantially all of the year. This avoided the problem of handling common stock equivalents in a situation where the value of the common stock varied widely from one time period to the next. In reality, the incremental number of shares resulting from the assumed exercise of common stock equivalents probably will be calculated on a quarter-by-quarter basis. In fact, if the average market price does not exceed the exercise price for substantially all of each of the four *quarters* of the year, the weighted average computation must be made on a quarter-by-quarter basis.

The assumptions listed in Exhibit 8 are designed to illustrate the computation of incremental shares from options and warrants on the quarter-by-quarter method.

Because the shares issuable upon exercise of the warrants do not

---

EXHIBIT 8 Options and Warrants in a Quarterly Computation

1. 200,000 warrants were issued prior to the current year, giving the holders
   the right to purchase 200,000 shares of common stock at $25 per share.
2. The following average market price and ending market price information is
   provided for each quarter of the current year:

Quarter	Average Market Price	Ending Market Price
1	$28	$30
2	$23	$26
3	$24	$23
4	$29	$28

3. The 200,000 shares issuable upon exercise of the warrants do not
   represent more than 20 percent of the outstanding common stock at the end
   of the year.

---

exceed 20 percent of the common shares outstanding, the treasury stock
method of handling the warrants is appropriate. For purposes of
computing primary earnings per share, the warrants will be considered
to be dilutive if the average market price per share during the quarter is
greater than the exercise price. If the warrants are not dilutive in any
quarter, they will not be considered in the primary earnings per share
computation. The equation for determining the number of incremental
shares was given earlier, but will be repeated for convenience.

$$S = \frac{MP - EP}{MP} \times NS$$

Where:

S = Incremental shares.
MP = Average market price (or the greater of average or ending
     market price for fully diluted EPS).
EP = Exercise price of options or warrants.
NS = Number of shares issuable upon exercise.

Table 5 shows the determination of whether the warrants are
dilutive in a given quarter and, if dilutive, the number of incremental
shares the warrants would represent. The computations in Table 5 apply
only to the computation of primary earnings per share.

The average market price in the second quarter was $23 per share,
which was less than the exercise price of $25 per share; thus, the
warrants cannot be considered to be dilutive. In the third quarter, the
average market price was $24 per share, which still is less than the
exercise price, so the warrants also were excluded in this quarter.

When an option or warrant is found to be dilutive, the formula given

TABLE 5 Incremental Shares for Primary EPS

Quarter	Are Warrants Dilutive	Computation	Incremental Shares
1	Yes	$\dfrac{\$28 - \$25}{\$28} \times 200{,}000 = 21{,}429 \times 3/12$	5,357
2	No	None	-0-
3	No	None	-0-
4	Yes	$\dfrac{\$29 - \$25}{\$29} \times 200{,}000 = 27{,}586 \times 3/12$	6,897
Total incremental shares			12,254

yields the incremental shares for the entire year; the incremental shares must be weighted for the three-month period under consideration. The total incremental shares (12,254) will be added to the weighted average number of common shares outstanding, and this total will be used in the denominator of the primary earnings per share equation.

Once the number of incremental shares has been determined for the calculation of primary earnings per share, it is necessary to reconsider all of them for the fully diluted earnings per share computation. The number of incremental shares used in the EPSFD computation is based upon the end of period market price per share, rather than on the average price. However, if the average market price per share is greater than the end of period price, the average price will be used in the calculation of EPSFD. During the first and second quarters of the year, the ending market price is greater than the average price; and, therefore, the end of period price will be used to determine the number of incremental shares for the first two quarters. In the third quarter, both the average market price per share and the end of period price are less than the exercise price, so the warrants are considered anti-dilutive in the third quarter. In the fourth quarter, the average market price is greater than the end of period price, so the average market price will be used, rather than the ending market price. Table 6 summarizes the computation of incremental shares for the fully diluted earnings per share calculation.

The 17,153 incremental shares computed in Table 6 must be compared to the 27,586 incremental shares computed using the end of period market price (end of quarter 4 market price of $29), and the larger number selected for use in the earnings per share computation.

The total incremental shares to be added to the weighted average common shares outstanding for the computation of fully diluted earn-

---

TABLE 6 Incremental Shares for Fully Diluted EPS

Quarter	Are Warrants Dilutive	Computation	Incremental Shares
1	Yes	$\dfrac{\$30 - \$25}{\$30} \times 200{,}000 = 33{,}333 \times 3/12$	8,333
2	Yes	$\dfrac{\$26 - \$25}{\$26} \times 200{,}000 = 7{,}692 \times 3/12$	1,923
3	No	None	-0-
4	Yes	$\dfrac{\$29 - \$25}{\$29} \times 200{,}000 = 27{,}586 \times 3/12$	6,897
Total incremental shares			17,153

---

ings per share is 27,586. This is 15,332 (27,586 − 12,254) more shares than was used in the primary earnings per share computation.

This completes the discussion of material relating to the effect of options, warrants, and their equivalent on the computation of earnings per share. The next section will deal with the effects of convertible securities on the EPS calculation.

FLOWCHART AND GENERAL DISCUSSION— CONVERTIBLE SECURITIES

Convertible securities are securities that may be exchanged for common stock, based upon some predetermined agreement. The most common types of convertible securities are convertible debt and convertible preferred stock. The issuing company uses the conversion privilege to make the security offering more attractive to the investor. The holder of the convertible security may become a common shareholder by "trading in" the debt or preferred stock for a specified number of common shares. These types of securities could have a dilutive effect upon earnings per share if converted. This is the reason they must be considered in the computation of earnings per share.

Flowchart 4 depicts the classification and accounting process for convertible securities. A convertible security may be considered a common stock equivalent and included in the calculation of primary earnings per share, or it may fail the tests necessary to become a common stock equivalent and only be considered in the process of computing fully diluted earnings per share. For a convertible security to be classified as a common stock equivalent, it must be convertible currently or within five years from the balance sheet date (Block 1), and meet the "effective yield" test (Block 2). The effective yield test specifies

FLOWCHART 4

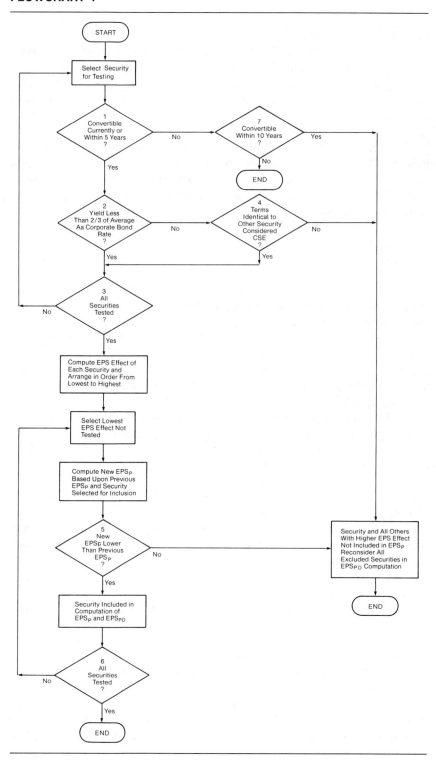

that, for a convertible security to be classified as a common stock equivalent, its effective yield must be less than two thirds of the average Aa corporate bond yield at the date of *issuance*. The effective yield of a security is "based on the security's stated annual interest or dividend payments, any original issuance premium or discount, and any call premium or discount and shall be the lowest of the yield to maturity and the yields to all call dates" (Paragraph 3 of SFAS No. 85).

The effective yield test is performed on the date the security is issued. Once the security has been classified as a common stock equivalent, its status does not change. A security that previously has not been classified as a common stock equivalent later may become a common stock equivalent if another convertible issue (with identical provisions to the excluded security) is classified as a common stock equivalent on the date of issue (Block 4). If two securities have identical provisions, it would not be appropriate to classify one issue and not the other as a common stock equivalent.

If a convertible security fails to meet the effective yield test, and is not classified as a common stock equivalent, it will not be included in the computation of primary earnings per share. However, it may be considered again during the computation of fully diluted earnings per share. Be careful not to confuse convertible securities with convertible securities that permit or require a cash payment upon conversion. The latter are considered to be the equivalent of warrants for the purpose of calculating EPS.

For a convertible security classified as a common stock equivalent to enter into the calculation of primary earnings per share, it must be dilutive. Convertible securities are the last items considered in the EPS computation. Options and warrants and contingent agreements already would have been considered prior to consideration of the convertible securities. (The effects of contingent agreements will be discussed in the next section. While they are important to the computation of earnings per share, *warrants, options,* and *convertible securities* are of primary importance at this stage of the discussion.) The convertible securities must be dilutive in relation to the previous calculation of primary earnings per share. To be dilutive, the earnings per share effect of the convertible security must be less than the previously calculated primary earnings per share amount (Block 5). The earnings per share effect of a convertible security is determined by dividing the number of shares obtainable upon conversion into the annual dividend or aftertax interest associated with the security. If there is more than one convertible security, the earnings per share effect of each must be determined separately, and the test for dilution will begin with the security that has the lowest earnings per share. A new primary earnings per share will be computed, using the previous EPSP and the earnings per share effect determined to be the lowest. Each successive convertible security will be compared to the new primary earnings per share amount to determine if it is dilutive. The process continues on an individual security basis until all securities have been tested (Block 6).

When convertible debt is found to be a common stock equivalent that has a dilutive effect upon earnings per share, the number of shares issuable upon conversion are included in the denominator of the EPSP computation, using the "if converted" method. "If converted" method assumes that the debt was converted at the beginning of the year (or later if issued after the beginning of the year), and it is necessary to adjust the numerator of the equation for the aftertax effect of the interest expense recorded during the period. If there is a discount or premium associated with the convertible debt, it must be taken into consideration in the determination of interest expense and the aftertax effect of the expense.

It also is assumed that convertible preferred stock that is classified as a common stock equivalent and is dilutive was converted at the beginning of the period (or later if issued later). The number of common shares issuable upon conversion should be included in the denominator of the EPSP equation. There may be an adjustment necessary for the preferred dividend declared, paid or in arrears. In an earlier discussion, preferred dividends were deducted from net income to arrive at net income available for common shareholders. If the assumption is made that the preferred stock is converted into common shares, this deduction is not appropriate, and the preferred dividends must be added back to net income. If preferred dividends were not previously deducted from net income, no adjustment is required.

If a convertible security is used in the EPSP computation, it also will be used in the fully diluted calculation. Convertible securities that were not included in the EPSP computation must be reconsidered for the EPSFD computation. If the security is convertible within 10 years of the balance sheet date (Block 7) and is dilutive, using the same procedures described for the primary earnings per share computation, it will enter into the EPSFD computation. The adjustments necessary to the numerator and denominator for EPSFD would be determined in the same manner as would the adjustment for the EPSP computation.

Convertible Securities—Effects on Earnings Per Share

To illustrate the effects of convertible securities on the calculation of primary and fully diluted earnings per share, the assumptions listed in Exhibit 9 will be used.

A review of the convertible securities indicates that all issues are convertible currently and therefore may be included in the effective yield test. Before the effective yield test can be applied, the effective yield for each security must be computed. For purposes of this example, the

---

EXHIBIT 9 Convertible Securities—Example 1

---

1. Book-It, Inc. has a December 31 year end and is preparing to calculate earnings per share for the year ended December 31, 198E.
2. There were 4,000,000 shares of common stock outstanding during the entire year.
3. On July 1, 198C, Book-It sold $1,000,000 of 8 percent convertible bonds at par. Each $1,000 bond is convertible into 100 shares of common stock at any time after December 31, 198C.
4. On January 15, 198D, the company sold $500,000 of 7 percent convertible debt at par. The debt is convertible into 125,000 shares of common stock any time after July 1, 198D.
5. On January 1, 198E, the company sold 25,000 shares of 8 percent, $50 par value, noncumulative convertible preferred stock at $40 per share. Each share of preferred stock is convertible into four common shares any time after January 1, 198E. No dividends have been declared or paid during 198E.
6. Book-It, Inc. reported net income of $10,000,000 for the year ended December 31, 198E. The company's tax rate is 50 percent.
7. The average Aa corporate bond yield on certain key dates is shown below:

	Percent
July 1, 198C	13%
January 15, 198D	12
January 1, 198E	11

8. The effective yield for the bonds and preferred stock is as follows:

		Percent
8% bonds	—	8%
7% debt	—	7
8% preferred	—	10

---

effective yield for each security is provided and computed as the interest rate that equates the present value of the future cash payments (both principal and interest in the case of debt) with the selling price of the security.

For the 8 percent bonds and the 7 percent debt, the selling price is equal to the par value. For this reason, the effective yield will be equal to the stated yield. The 8 percent preferred effective yield is based upon the selling price of $40 per share, rather than upon the par value of $50 per share and is 10 percent effective. The cash yield of each security must be compared to the average Aa corporate bond yield on the date the security was sold. If the effective yield is less than two thirds of the average Aa corporate bond yield, the convertible security will be considered to be a common stock equivalent. Table 7 shows the determination of common stock equivalency for each security.

TABLE 7 Classification of Convertible Securities

Security	Average Aa Corporate Bond Yield*	Two Thirds of Average Aa Corporate Bond Yield	Effective Yield	Common Stock Equivalent
8% Bonds	13%	8.67%	8%	Yes
7% Debt	12%	8.00%	7%	Yes
8% Preferred	11%	7.33%	10%	No

* At date of sale of security.

Only the 8 percent bonds and the 7 percent debt meet the effective yield test and may be considered in the computation of EPSP. The 8 percent preferred will be reconsidered in the computation of EPSFD.

The two securities that qualified as common stock equivalents must be dilutive before they will enter into the computation of primary earnings per share. Because there is more than one security, the dilutive effect of each security must be determined individually. The earnings per share effect of each convertible security must be determined. The earnings per share effect for debt is calculated by dividing the number of shares issuable upon conversion into the aftertax interest expense adjustment. Table 8 shows the calculation of the earnings per share effect for the two securities.

The convertible security with the lowest earnings per share effect must be considered first; therefore, an analysis of the 7 percent debt is required. To determine whether the 7 percent debt is dilutive, primary earnings per share calculated prior to the inclusion must be compared with the primary earnings per share that will result from including the 7 percent debt. If the latter EPSP is lower than the former, the debt is considered to be dilutive and is included in the primary earnings per share calculation.

Convertible securities are the last items to be considered in the earnings per share computation. Primary earnings per share after considering options, warrants, and contingent agreements would be used as the initial value for comparison. Because there are no options, warrants or contingent agreements in this example, the initial primary earnings per share to be used would be the unadjusted earnings per share.

Since the preferred stock is noncumulative, and no dividends have been declared or paid in 198E, there will be no adjustment necessary to the reported earnings of $10,000,000. No additional common stock was sold or repurchased during 198E; thus, the weighted average number of

---

TABLE 8 Earnings Per Share Effect

Security	Aftertax Interest	Number of Shares Issued on Conversion	Earnings Per Share Effect*
8% Bonds	$40,000[†]	100,000[‡]	$.40
7% Debt	$17,500[§]	125,000	$.14

* Aftertax interest/number of shares issued on conversion.
[†] $80,000 interest expense × (1 − .50) = $40,000.
[‡] $1,000,000/$1,000 = 1,000 bonds × 100 shares per bond = 100,000 shares.
[§] $35,000 interest expense × (1 − .50) = $17,500.

---

common shares for the EPSU computation would be 4,000,000. The calculation of EPSU is shown below:

$$EPSU = \frac{\$10,000,000}{4,000,000} = \$2.50$$

The earnings per share effect of the 7 percent debt is $0.14, which is less than the EPSU of $2.50; therefore, the 7 percent debt is dilutive and will be considered in the primary earnings per share computation. The 7 percent debt now is treated on an "if converted" basis, and a new primary earnings per share is calculated. The numerator of the new EPSP will be equal to $10,017,500 ($10,000,000 + $17,500 aftertax interest adjustment). The denominator of the equation will be increased by the number of shares issuable upon conversion and will be equal to 4,125,000 shares (4,000,000 + 125,000 issuable shares). The new primary earnings per share is computed below:

$$EPSP = \frac{\$10,017,500}{4,125,000} = \$2.43$$

This new primary earnings per share amount will be used as the basis of the next comparison to determine the dilutive effect of the 8 percent bonds.

The $0.40 earnings per share effect of the 8 percent bonds is less than the $2.43 new primary earnings per share, so the bonds are considered to be dilutive and will be included in the EPSP computation. The numerator of the EPSP equation is adjusted for the aftertax interest associated with the bonds and is equal to $10,055,200 ($10,017,500 + $40,000). The denominator is increased by the number of shares issuable upon conversion and is equal to 4,225,000 shares (4,125,000 + 100,000). The new primary earnings per share is calculated below:

$$EPSP = \frac{\$10,057,500}{4,225,000} = \$2.38$$

Since there are no more convertible securities to be considered in the EPSP calculation, the $2.38 is equal to the primary earnings per share.

Had there been additional convertible securities, the $2.38 would have served as the basis for the next comparison.

The final step in the process is to compute fully diluted earnings per share. All convertible securities included in the EPSP amount will be included in the EPSFD computation. The starting point for the computation of EPSFD is to use the numerator of $10,057,500 and the denominator of 4,225,000 shares from the EPSP computation.

The only convertible security that needs to be reconsidered for the EPSFD computation is the 8 percent preferred stock. If the preferred stock is dilutive, it will enter into the computation of EPSFD. To determine if the issue is dilutive, the earnings per share effect must be calculated, and compared to the EPSP amount. The annual dividend per share on the preferred stock is $4 ($50 par value × 8%). Each share of preferred stock may be converted into four shares of common stock, so the earnings per share effect on the preferred stock is $1 ($4 dividends/4 shares issuable stock upon conversion). The $1 earnings per share effect of the preferred stock is less than the $2.38 primary earnings per share; therefore, the issue is dilutive and will enter into the EPSFD computation on an "if converted" basis.

No dividends were declared or paid in 198E, and the preferred stock is not cumulative. There is no adjustment to the numerator of the equation for EPSFD. The 25,000 preferred shares may be converted into 100,000 common shares (25,000 × 4 common shares for each preferred share). The denominator of the EPSFD equation must be increased by the 100,000 issuable shares. The denominator will be equal to 4,325,000 after the adjustment (4,225,000 + 100,000). The computation of fully diluted earnings per share is shown below:

$$\text{EPSFD} = \frac{\$10,057,500}{4,325,000} = \$2.325$$

The aggregate dilution reciprocal is equal to 93 percent ($2.325 EPSFD/$2.50 EPSU), which means that the aggregate dilution is more than 3 percent and that a dual presentation of earnings per share is required.

The example just completed was designed to introduce the reader to the handling of convertible securities in the calculation of earnings per share. To illustrate a more complex situation, the assumptions in Exhibit 10 will be used.

All of the convertible securities are convertible currently or within five years of the balance sheet date and will enter into the effective yield test to determine if they represent common stock equivalents. The annual cash outflows associated with each of the convertible securities is shown in Table 9 on page 503.

The effective yield is computed as the rate that equates the present value of the annual cash outflow and the present value of the principal

---

EXHIBIT 10 Convertible Securities—Example 2

---

1. Jar, Inc. has a December 31 year end, and is preparing to calculate earnings per share for the year ended December 31, 198F.
2. There were 6,000,000 shares of common stock outstanding during all of 198F.
3. On January 1, 198A, Jar, Inc. sold $500,000 of a 9 percent, six-year convertible debt at par. Each $1,000 bond is convertible into 100 shares of common stock any time after January 1, 198A.
4. On July 15, 198C, the company sold a package of $1,000,000, 8 percent $100 par value convertible preferred stock and 75,000 shares of common stock, for a total amount of $1,900,000. The estimated fair value of the preferred stock at the date of sale was $1,020,000, and the fair value of the common stock was $980,000. The preferred stock is convertible into 80,000 shares of common stock any time after December 31, 198D. The preferred stock's effective yield is 8.3 percent.
5. On August 15, 198E, Jar, Inc. sold $500,000 of 9 percent, four-year convertible debt for $500,000. Each $1,000 bond is convertible into 100 shares of common stock any time after August 15, 198E.
6. On January 1, 198F, the company sold $300,000 face value 6 percent, five-year convertible bonds for $287,701. The bonds were priced to yield 7 percent. Each $1,000 bond is convertible into 50 common shares any time after January 31, 198F.
7. On July 1, 198F, $800,000 of 5 percent convertible debt outstanding was converted into 10,000 shares of common stock.
8. Jar, Inc. reported net income of $6,080,000 for the year ended December 31, 198F. The company's tax rate is 50 percent. Preferred dividends of $80,000 were paid during the year.
9. The average Aa corporate bond yield on certain key dates is shown below:

January 1, 198A	14%
July 15, 198C	11%
August 15, 198E	10%
January 1, 198F	11%

---

repayment with the selling price of the security. The principal repayment amounts are provided in Exhibit 10. Notice that the effective yield for the preferred stock is given in Exhibit 10, Item 4 as 8.3 percent. For a detailed computation of effective yield for securities, see APB Opinion No. 21 in Topic 7 and APB Opinion No. 14 in Topic 8.

Table 10 shows the computation of the effective yield for all of the convertible securities.

Next, the effective yield must be compared to two thirds of the average Aa corporate bond yield in effect on the date the securities were sold. Table 11 provides the comparison and the determination of the common stock equivalency of each security.

Table 11 indicates that the 9 percent debt issued on January 1, 198A, and the 6 percent bonds qualify as common stock equivalents, because their effective yield was less than two thirds of the average Aa corporate

TABLE 9 Cash Outflows

Security	Par or Face of Security	Interest Rate	Annual Cash Outflow*
9% Debt—1/1/198A	$ 500,000	9%	$45,000
8% Preferred	$1,000,000	8%	$80,000
9% Debt—8/15/198E	$ 500,000	9%	$45,000
6% Bonds	$ 300,000	6%	$18,000

* Cash outflow = Par or face of security × interest rate.

bond yield at the date of issue. However, take a minute to review and compare the 9 percent debt securities issued on January 1, 198A, with the 9 percent securities issued on August 15, 198E. Notice that the two issues have identical provisions. One qualified as a common stock equivalent, and the other did not. In this situation, both issues should be treated as common stock equivalents. So the 9 percent debt issued on August 15, 198E, also will qualify as a common stock equivalent.

Before any of these securities can be used in the computation of primary earnings per share, they must be dilutive on an individual basis. The earnings per share effect of each issue must be calculated. The preferred stock does not qualify as a common stock equivalent, so the earnings per share effect for each security in this example is determined by dividing the aftertax interest by the number of common shares issuable upon conversion.

Table 12 summarizes the computation of the aftertax interest for each issue.

One unusual item on Table 12 is the amortization of the discount associated with the 6 percent bonds. The bonds have a face value of $300,000, but were sold for $287,701, so as to yield an effective interest rate of 7 percent to the investor. The discount amortized during the

TABLE 10 Computation of Effective Yield

Security	Annual Cash Outflow	Principal Repayment	Sales Price	Effective Yield*
9% Debt—1/1/198A	$45,000	$ 500,000	$500,000	9%
8% Preferred	—	$1,000,000	—	8.3%[†]
9% Debt—8/15/198E	$45,000	$ 500,000	$500,000	9%
6% Bonds	$18,000	$ 300,000	$287,701	7%

* Effective yield = Rate that equates the present value of the annual cash outflow and the present value of the principal repayment with the selling price of the security.
[†] Given in Exhibit 10, Item 4.

TABLE 11 Determination of Common Stock Equivalents

Security	Average Aa Corporate Bond Yield	Two Thirds of Average Aa Corporate Bond Yield	Effective Yield	Common Stock Equivalent
9% Debt—				
1/1/198A	14%	9.3%	9.0%	Yes
8% Preferred	11%	7.3%	8.3%	No
9% Debt—				
8/15/198E	10%	6.7%	9.0%	No
6% Bonds	11%	7.3%	7%	Yes

period raised the interest expense and must be included in the aftertax interest computation.

In addition to the three securities specifically identified as common stock equivalents, consideration must be given to the $800,000 of 5 percent convertible debt that was converted during 198F. In a case where convertible securities are converted during the year, the "if converted" method is applied to the partial period when the securities were still outstanding. The "if converted" method is used in the primary earnings per share calculation only if the securities are dilutive. The aftertax interest relating to this issue for the six months ended June 30, 198F (the day of conversion) is $10,000 ($800,000 × .05 = $40,000 × ½ = $20,000 × (1 − .50) = $10,000). The weighted number of shares issuable upon conversion are 5,000 (10,000 × 6/12). Now that we have developed this information, Table 13 shows the computation of the earnings per share effect of the securities.

The securities are arranged in order of their earnings per share effect, from the lowest ($0.45) to the highest ($2.00). Now each security will be compared with the previous primary earnings per share to determine if it is dilutive. Since convertible securities are considered last

TABLE 12 Computation of Aftertax Interest

Security	Annual Cash Outflow	Adjust. for Discount Amortization	Expense	(1 − Tax Rate)	Aftertax Interest*
9% Debt—1/1/198A	$45,000	-0-	$45,000	.50	$22,500
9% Debt—8/15/198E	$45,000	-0-	$45,000	.50	$22,500
6% Bonds	$18,000	$2,139†	$20,139	.50	$10,070

* Aftertax Interest = Expense × (1 − Tax rate).
† $287,701 × 7% effective interest rate = $20,139 − $18,000 = $2,139.

TABLE 13 Computation of Earnings Per Share Effect

Security	Aftertax Interest	Number of Shares Issued on Conversion	Earnings Per Share Effect*
9% Debt—1/1/198A	$22,500	50,000[†]	$0.45
9% Debt—8/15/198E	$22,500	50,000	$0.45
6% Bonds	$10,070	15,000[‡]	$0.67
5% Partial Period	$10,000	5,000	$2.00

* EPS Effect = Aftertax interest/number of shares issuable on conversion.
[†] $500,000/$1,000 = 500 bonds × 100 shares per bond = 50,000 shares.
[‡] $300,000/$1,000 = 300 bonds × 50 shares per bond = 15,000 shares.

in the earnings per share calculation, options, warrants and contingent agreements already will have been considered in the calculation of primary earnings per share. In the example, however, there were no options, warrants or contingent agreements, so all comparisons will be made on the basis of unadjusted earnings per share.

For purposes of calculating EPSU, all contingent equity issues are ignored. Reported net income of $6,080,000 must be reduced by the preferred dividends paid during the year. The numerator of the EPSU equation would be $6,000,000 ($6,080,000 − $80,000 preferred dividends). Through the conversion of the 5 percent debt, 10,000 additional common shares were issued on July 1, 198F. These shares are to be weighted for the period of time outstanding and added to the weighted average number of common shares. The conversion represents 5,000 weighted shares (10,000 × 6/12). The only other common shares outstanding during the year were the 6,000,000 shares. Thus, the denominator of the EPSU equation would be 6,005,000 shares. Unadjusted earnings per share is computed below:

$$\text{EPSU} = \frac{\$6,000,000}{6,005,000} = \$0.999$$

The analysis of the earnings per share effect of the convertible securities classified as common stock equivalents begins with the 9 percent debt issued on January 1, 198A. The earnings per share effect of $0.45 is less than the EPSU of $0.999; therefore, the securities are dilutive and will enter into the computation of primary earnings per share. Once this has been determined, a new EPSP must be calculated to include the convertible debt with the lowest earnings per share effect (the 9 percent debt issued on January 1, 198A). The numerator of the EPSU equation will be increased by the aftertax interest of the debt, and the denominator will be increased by the number of shares issuable upon conversion. This is done because the assumption is made that the debt was converted at the beginning of the year. The computation of the new EPSP is shown below:

$$EPSP = \frac{\$6,000,000 + \$22,500}{6,005,000 + 50,000} = \frac{\$6,022,500}{6,055,000} = \$0.995$$

The new EPSP includes the 9 percent debt on an "if converted" basis, and will serve as the basis for determining if the other securities are dilutive.

The next security to consider is the 9 percent debt issued on August 15, 198E. The adjustment to the numerator of the new EPSP equation would be the same as that made for the 9 percent debt issued earlier. The second computation of EPSP is shown below:

$$EPSP = \frac{\$6,022,500 + \$22,500}{6,055,000 + 50,000} = \frac{\$6,045,000}{6,105,000} = \$.990$$

The second issue of 9 percent debt was included in the EPSP calculation because its earnings per share effect of $0.45 was less than the new EPSP of $0.995.

The next convertible security to be considered is the 6 percent bond issue. Its earnings per share effect of $0.67 is less than the new EPSP, just calculated to be $0.990; therefore, it will be included in the determination of primary earnings per share. Still another EPSP computation is required to reflect the inclusion of the 6 percent debt. The computation is based upon the last EPSP calculation, and is shown below:

$$EPSP = \frac{\$6,045,000 + \$10,070}{6,105,000 + 15,000} = \frac{\$6,055,070}{6,120,000} = \$0.989$$

The newest EPSP amount includes the 9 percent debt issues of January 1, 198A, and August 15, 198E, and the 6 percent bonds on an "if converted" basis. The last security to be analyzed is the 5 percent debt that was converted during the current period. The earnings per share effect of the 5 percent debt is $2.00 (Table 13), which is greater than the latest EPSP amount of $0.989; therefore, the 5 percent debt is not dilutive and will not be included in the calculation of primary earnings per share.

All convertible securities now have been considered for the calculation of primary earnings per share. The next step is to calculate fully diluted earnings per share. Remember that, if a convertible security is used in the EPSP computation, it will be carried forward and used in the fully diluted computation. The calculation of fully diluted earnings per share starts with a numerator of $6,055,070 and a denominator of 6,120,000 shares.

For purposes of computing fully diluted earnings per share, the 8 percent preferred stock issue must be reconsidered, along with the 5 percent debt that was converted during the year. The 8 percent preferred failed the effective yield test, and therefore was excluded from primary earnings per share, because it was not a common stock equivalent. The issue will be included in the calculation of fully diluted earnings per share if it is dilutive; that is, if its earning per share effect is less than the EPSP amount of $0.989. The preferred issue pays an annual dividend of $80,000 ($1,000,000 × 8%). Each share of preferred is convertible into eight shares of common stock, and there are 80,000 common shares issuable upon conversion of the preferred. The earnings per share effect of the preferred issue is $1.00 ($80,000/80,000 common shares). The $1 per share effect is greater than the EPSP amount, previously determined to be $0.989. For this reason, the preferred issue is anti-dilutive and will not be included in the computation of fully diluted earnings per share.

The last item to be considered is the 5 percent debt issue that was converted on July 1, 198F. The issue was not included in the primary earnings per share calculation because it was found to be anti-dilutive. However, for the computation of fully diluted earnings per share, any convertible security that was converted during the period and required a partial period adjustment is considered in the computation, whether dilutive or not. Table 13 indicates the aftertax interest and the number of shares issuable, properly weighted for the partial period of six months. The numerator of the fully diluted earnings per share equation will be increased by the $10,000 aftertax interest, and the denominator will be increased by the 5,000 weighted shares issuable upon conversion. The computation of fully diluted earnings per share is shown below:

$$\text{EPSFD} = \frac{\$6,055,070 + \$10,000}{6,120,000 + 5,000} = \frac{\$6,065,070}{6,125,000} = \$0.99$$

The inclusion of the anti-dilutive 5 percent debt issue increases the earnings per share from $0.989 to $0.99.

To complete the example, it is necessary to determine if, in the aggregate, the contingent equity issues are dilutive by 3 percent or more. This is determined by comparing the fully diluted earnings per share to the unadjusted earnings per share. The calculation of the aggregate dilution reciprocal is shown below:

$$\text{ADR} = \frac{\$0.99}{\$0.999} = 99 \text{ percent}$$

This means that the aggregate dilution of the convertible securities is only 1 percent $(1 - 0.99)$; therefore, the company is considered to have a simple capital structure, and only a single earnings per share presentation is required. In the example, earnings per share will be reported at the unadjusted amount of $0.999.

The purpose of this second example is twofold: first, to introduce several new concepts in the calculation of earnings per share when a company has convertible equity securities; and, second, to illustrate that, even if a company has a complicated capital structure, a dual presentation of earnings per share is not always required. The dual presentation is not a function of the number or variety of the convertible securities, but rather of their *dilutive* effect.

The final item to be covered deals with contingent agreements. When computing earnings per share, consideration must be given to warrants, options, and their equivalent *and* contingent agreements, before an analysis of convertible securities is begun. However, because of the complexity of the computations required for options, warrants and convertible securities, the authors moved the discussion of contingent agreements to the end of the section. Remember that the effects of contingent agreements must be determined before starting into convertible securities.

CONTINGENT AGREEMENTS

[Paragraphs 88-92 of the AICPA Accounting Interpretation of APB Opinion No. 15 provides additional information about contingent agreements.]

For any one of several reasons, an enterprise may enter into an agreement that requires the issuance of shares of common stock if some future condition is realized. These types of agreements are referred to as contingent agreements because the consideration involved will be paid if some future event takes place; that is, the consideration is contingent upon the future event. When the contingent agreement involves the issuance of common stock, it will affect the computation of earnings per share.

The shares of stock that are contingently issuable normally are classified as common stock equivalents and enter into the computation of primary earnings per share. The arrangement for distributing the stock generally does not affect the status of common stock equivalency. For example, the agreement may state that the stock will be issued only if the future condition is met, or it may require that the stock be placed in escrow and issued if the contingency is met (or returned to the company if the contingency is not met), or the stock may be issued with the stipulation that it be returned to the company if the future condition is not met. Regardless of the method of distribution, common stock involved in a contingent agreement generally will be considered to be common stock equivalents for purposes of calculating earnings per share.

There is an infinite variety of contingent agreements possible; and, obviously, the discussion cannot cover all types of contingent agreements. Three basic types of agreements will be discussed in this section. The first basic type of agreement requires that shares of common stock will be issued after the passage of a given time period. A second type of agreement specifies that shares of common stock will be issued, provided a certain level of earnings is achieved and maintained. The third basic type of agreement specifies that shares of common stock will be issued, depending upon the future market price of the stock. Each of these agreements will be discussed.

Contingent Agreements Involving the Passage of Time

If the contingent agreement specifies that a certain number of common shares will be issued after a given time period has elapsed, the contingent shares will be included in the computations of both primary and fully diluted earnings per share. The denominator of both equations will be increased by the number of common shares contingently issuable. There would be no adjustment to the numerator of either equation.

Contingent Agreements Involving Future Earnings

A contingent agreement of this type usually is involved in a business combination accounted for as a purchase. The acquiring company may specify that additional shares of stock will be issued if the acquired company maintains a certain earnings level or achieves a level of earnings higher than current earnings.

If the specified earnings level currently is being met, the contingently issuable shares will be included in both the primary and fully diluted earnings per share computations. The shares to be issued will be added to the denominator of each equation, and no adjustment will be required in the numerator of either equation. If the earnings level is not currently being met, the contingently issuable shares will not enter into the computations of primary earnings per share. However, the shares may enter into the computation of fully diluted earnings per share if their issuance would have a dilutive effect.

To illustrate the treatment of contingently issuable shares in an agreement specifying a certain earnings level, the assumptions listed in Exhibit 11 will be used.

The shares are not issuable to the prior owners of the acquired company until December 31, 198D, but the $180,000 current earnings level of the acquired company is greater than the $150,000 required level. The earnings condition is met in 198C, and the contingently issuable shares will be included in the computations of both primary and fully diluted earnings per share. The 50,000 contingent shares are added to the 300,000 common shares outstanding during the entire year, to give a denominator of 350,000 shares for both primary and fully diluted earnings per share. There is no adjustment required to the

---

EXHIBIT 11   Contingent Agreement Involving Future Earnings

---

1. Book-It, Inc. reported net income of $1,500,000 for the year ended December 31, 198C and had 300,000 common shares outstanding during the entire year.
2. On January 1, 198C, Book-It acquired a wholly owned subsidiary in a business combination, properly accounted for as a purchase. As part of the agreement to combine, Book-It agreed to issue an additional 50,000 shares to the previous owners of the acquired company on December 31, 198D, if the acquired company's earnings exceeded $150,000 for each of the years 198C and 198D.
3. Book-It is preparing to compute earnings per share for 198C, and has determined that the earnings of the acquired company are $180,000 for the year ended December 31, 198C.

---

numerator, so it will be equal to the $1,500,000 reported income of Book-It, Inc. The computation of primary earnings per share is shown below:

$$EPSP = \frac{\$1,500,000}{350,000} = \$4.29$$

Fully diluted earnings per share also are equal to $4.29.

If the reported income of the acquired company was $120,000, the earnings condition would not have been met, and the contingently issuable shares would not enter into the computation of primary earnings per share. Assuming the company reported income of $120,000, the calculation of primary earnings per share will be as follows:

$$EPSP = \frac{\$1,500,000}{300,000} = \$5.00$$

Using the same assumed earnings level, the contingently issuable shares will be included in the computation of fully diluted earnings per share. The 50,000 contingent shares will be added to the denominator as before, but, in this case, an adjustment to the numerator also is required. The adjustment is equal to the difference between the *required* earnings level and the current reported earnings level. This amount is determined below and will be added to the numerator of the fully diluted earnings per share computation.

Required level of earnings	$150,000
Reported earnings	120,000
Adjustment to numerator	$ 30,000

After the adjustment, the numerator of the equation is equal to $1,530,000 ($1,500,000 earnings of Book-It + $30,000 adjustment). The

---

EXHIBIT 12 Contingent Agreement Involving Market Price of Stock

---

1. Jar, Inc. reported income of $2,000,000 for the year ended December 31, 198B, and is preparing to calculate earnings per share.
2. On January 1, 198B, Jar, Inc. acquired a company through a business combination, properly accounted for as a purchase. As part of the agreement to combine, Jar, Inc. agreed to issue an additional 75,000 shares to the previous owners of the acquired company on December 31, 198C, if the market value of Jar, Inc. common stock fell below $45 per share.
3. Jar, Inc. had 500,000 shares of common stock outstanding during the entire year of 198B. The market price per share on December 31, 198B was $43.

---

calculation of fully diluted earnings per share is as follows:

$$\text{EPSFD} = \frac{\$1,530,000}{350,000} = \$4.37$$

For the contingently issuable shares to be included in the fully diluted earnings per share amount, they must have a dilutive effect. In this example, primary earnings per share are $5.00, and fully diluted earnings per share are $4.37; thus, the contingent shares are dilutive and will be included in fully diluted earnings per share.

Since primary earnings per share are equal to unadjusted earnings per share in this example, the aggregate dilution reciprocal is equal to 87.4 percent ($4.37/$5.00), and a dual presentation of earnings per share is required.

Contingent Agreements Involving the Market Price of Stock

Contingent agreements may involve consideration based upon the future market price of common stock. A company might guarantee that the market price of its stock will reach a certain level by some future date, or it may guarantee that the market price of its stock will not fall below a certain level. If the guaranteed price is not realized, the company will issue additional shares of common stock.

To determine if the contingently issuable shares will be included in primary and fully diluted earnings per share, the end of period market price of the stock must be compared to the guaranteed value of the stock as specified in the agreement. If the comparison indicates that the guaranteed market price currently is not being met, the contingently issuable shares will be included in the denominator of both the primary and fully diluted earnings per share computations. If the guaranteed market value currently is being obtained, the contingently issuable shares will not be considered in the earnings per share computation.

To illustrate the treatment afforded contingent shares involved in an agreement concerning market price, the assumptions in Exhibit 12 will be used.

Since the end of period market price of $43 is less than the guaranteed price of $45 per share, the contingently issuable shares will be included in the denominator of both the primary and fully diluted earnings per share computations. No adjustment to the numerator is required. The computation of primary earnings per share is shown below:

$$EPSP = \frac{\$2,000,000}{500,000 + 75,000} = \frac{\$2,000,000}{575,000} = \$3.48$$

In this example, fully diluted earnings per share would be the same as primary earnings per share.

This completes the discussion of contingent agreements. The next section identifies the required disclosures relating to earnings per share and provides illustrations of the disclosures.

DISCLOSURES

The disclosures required by APB Opinion No. 15 are listed in AICPA Accounting Interpretation Number 100. The reader should consult this list, since it is comprehensive and concise.

The presentation of earnings per share by LaMaur, Inc., Mapco, Inc. and Brunswick Corporation for 1979, 1980 and 1981 are shown below in Exhibits 13–15. La Maur, Inc. was required to report a single earnings per share amount. Note A to the Financial Statements of the company discusses the computation of the weighted average number of shares

---

EXHIBIT 13 La Maur, Inc. (Dec.)

	1981	1980	1979
Earnings per share (based on average shares outstanding)			
Earnings before extraordinary item	$1.46	$.83	$.56
Extraordinary loss	—	—	.11
Net earnings	$1.46	$.83	$.45

Notes to Consolidated Financial Statements
Note A (in part): Summary of Significant Accounting Policies
7. Earnings per share
   Net earnings per share of common stock are based on the weighted average number of shares outstanding, which were 1,719,000, 1,683,000, and 1,658,000 for the years ended December 31, 1981, 1980 and 1979, respectively. These shares give effect to the 20 percent stock dividend paid in the second quarter of 1981. Shares issuable upon the exercise of stock options are excluded from the computation since the effect on earnings per share would be insignificant.

SOURCE: Reprinted from *Accounting Trends and Techniques*, Copyright © 1982 by the American Institute of Certified Public Accountants, Inc., p. 286.

EXHIBIT 14 Mapco, Inc. (Dec.)

	1981	1980	1979
Primary earnings per common share (Note 11)	$3.51	$4.48	$3.28
Average common shares outstanding	27,607,221	27,261,339	27,021,928
Fully diluted earnings per common share (Note 11)	$3.41	$4.35	$3.28
Assumed common shares outstanding	30,667,330	29,144,483	27,021,928

Note 11: Earnings per Share

Primary earnings per common share were based on the weighted average number of common shares and common share equivalents outstanding during the year as retroactively adjusted for the ERC 20 percent stock dividend declared June 23, 1980. Equivalent shares consist of those shares issuable upon the assumed exercise of ERC stock options and a warrant, calculated under the treasury stock method.

Fully diluted earnings per share were computed on the same basis as above with the additional assumption that all of the 10 percent Convertible Subordinated Debentures were converted into common stock at the date of issuance and that the related interest expense, net of statutory income taxes, was restored to net income.

The following table summarizes the average number of common shares and equivalents used in the calculation of primary and fully diluted earnings per share:

	1981	1980	1979
Primary:			
Weighted average common shares	27,607,221	26,949,779	26,734,303
Stock options and warrants	—	311,560	287,625
Average common shares outstanding	27,607,221	27,261,339	27,021,928
Fully diluted:			
Average common shares outstanding	27,607,221	27,261,339	27,021,928
Convertible subordinated debentures	3,060,109	1,883,144	—
Assumed common shares outstanding	30,667,330	29,144,483	27,021,928

SOURCE: Reprinted from *Accounting Trends and Techniques*, Copyright © 1982 by the American Institute of Certified Public Accountants, Inc., p. 289.

outstanding, which includes a 20 percent stock dividend. Both Mapco and Brunswick Corporation have complex capital structures, and are required to disclose both primary and fully diluted earnings per share for 1979–81. The footnotes relating to the computation of earnings per share show the determination of the weighted average number of shares used for the primary and fully diluted earnings per share denominators.

EXHIBIT 15 Brunswick Corporation (Dec.)

	1981	1980	1979
Earnings per common share:			
Primary:			
Continuing operations	$1.88	$ .13	$1.66
Discontinued operations	1.13	.88	.73
Net earnings	$3.01	$1.01	$2.39
Fully diluted:			
Continuing operations	$1.82	$ .12	$1.62
Discontinued operations	1.01	.88	.64
Net earnings	$2.83	$1.00	$2.26

Notes to Consolidated Financial Statements
December 31, 1981, 1980 and 1979
Note 3: Earnings per common share
    Net earnings and the number of common shares used in the computation of earnings per share were determined as follows:

	1981		1980		1979	
	Primary	Fully diluted	Primary	Fully diluted	Primary	Fully diluted
(in thousands, except per share data)						
Adjusted net earnings						
Earnings from continuing operations	$42,540	$42,540	$ 6,104	$ 6,104	$36,903	$36,903
Deduct: preferred dividends	(3,576)	—	(3,587)	(3,587)	(3,587)	—
Add back: interest expense, net of income taxes, on debentures due						
2006	1,068	1,068	—	—	—	—
1987	—	260	—	†	—	†
1981	—	—	—	†	—	230
Adjusted earnings from continuing operations	40,032	43,868	2,517	2,517	33,316	37,133
Earnings from discontinued operations	24,217	24,217	17,824	17,824	14,522	14,522
Adjusted net earnings	$64,249	$68,085	$20,341	$20,341	$47,838	$51,655

EXHIBIT 15 *(concluded)*

Adjusted number of common shares						
Average shares outstanding	20,269	20,269	20,168	20,168	20,051	20,051
Incremental shares for exercise of stock options	93	93	*	79	*	50
Shares issuable upon conversion						
Preferred stock	—	2,566	—	†	—	2,571
Debentures due						
2006	1,009	1,009	—	—	—	—
1987	—	101	—	†	—	†
1981	—	—	—	†	—	233
Adjusted number of common shares	21,371	24,038	20,168	20,247	20,051	22,905
Earnings per common share						
Continuing operations	$ 1.88	$ 1.82	$ .13	$ .12	$ 1.66	$ 1.62
Discontinued operations	1.13	1.01	.88	.88	.73	.64
Net earnings	$ 3.01	$ 2.83	$ 1.01	$ 1.00	$ 2.39	$ 2.26

* Not included in calculation as dilution was not significant.
† Not included in calculation as effect of conversion would be anti-dilutive.

SOURCE: Reprinted from *Accounting Trends and Techniques*, Copyright © 1982 by the American Institute of Certified Public Accountants, Inc., pp. 287 and 288.

17

Cash Flow—Computation and Interpretation

Leopold A. Bernstein, Ph.D., CPA
Bernard M. Baruch College
The City University of New York

Few analytical terms are more widely used and, at the same time, more poorly understood than that term *cash flow*. It is the purpose of this chapter to define the concept of cash flow, to illustrate the computation of its important components, and to discuss the analytical uses to which it can be put.

WHAT IS CASH FLOW?

Standing alone and unqualified, the term *cash flow* is, in its literal sense, meaningless. A company can experience cash *inflows*, that is, cash receipts, and it can experience cash *outflows*; that is, cash disbursements. Moreover these cash inflows or outflows can relate to a variety of activities; for example, the profit-directed activities which we will refer to as "operations," or to financing activities, or to investing activities. We can also identify the difference between the inflows and outflows of cash for any of these activities separately and for all activities of the enterprise combined. These then can best be referred to as net inflows or net outflows of cash. Thus a net inflow of cash will reconcile to an *increase* in the cash balance for the period while a net outflow will correspond to a *decrease* of the cash balance during the period. To avoid confusion it is best to describe specifically what type of cash flow is referred to. Is it, for any given period, the net change in the cash balance? The difference between the cash inflows and outflows related to operations? What other specified type of cash flow? Most, but by no means all, writers when referring to cash flow mean cash generated by operations. The problem, from an analyst's point of view, is that the computation of this figure can range from the simplistic to the incorrect and misleading. Later on we shall illustrate the proper computation of cash flow from operations (CFFO) as well as the erroneous versions of it.

THE SIGNIFICANCE OF CASH FLOW

Cash is universally acknowledged to be the most liquid of assets, one that affords an enterprise the greatest degree of liquidity and flexibility of choice. It is thus not surprising that cash represents the beginning as well as the end of the accounting cycle. The profit-directed activities of an enterprise (e.g., operations) require that cash be converted into a variety of assets (e.g., inventories of all kinds), which in turn are converted into receivables as part of the sales process. Operating results are finally and definitively realized when the collection process returns the cash stream to the entity so that a new cycle, expected to have profitable potential at the time, can begin.

Analysts of financial statements and other users have long recognized that the increasing intricacy of the accrual accounting system masks real cash flows from operations and widens their divergence from reported net income. Not only do they point to net operating cash inflows as ultimate validators of profitability, they also emphasize that it is cash, and not "net income," that must be used to repay loans, to replace and expand the stock of plant and equipment in use, and to pay dividends.

The valid measurement of an enterprise's cash inflows and outflows from various sources is, thus, an important analytical tool in the assessment of short-term liquidity, long-term solvency, and operating performance.

Accountants have recognized the importance of cash flow as a major analytical measure. According to Statement of Financial Accounting Concepts No. 1, a basic objective of financial reporting is to facilitate prediction of the amount, timing, and uncertainty of future cash flows to the business entity, so that the amount, timing, and uncertainty of future cash flows to investors and creditors may be predicted. Recently attempts have been made to shift the statement of changes in financial position (SCFP) from the widely used working capital focus to a cash focus. A 1981 Financial Accounting Standards Board (FASB) exposure draft on "Reporting Income, Cash Flows and Financial Position of Business Enterprises" recommends the adoption of the cash flow concept for the funds statement. That same year, the SEC issued a release on the "Staff's Assessment of Disclosures under [the] New Management Discussion and Analysis Format."[1] The release states that "cash flow from operations is an especially helpful indicator, and the staff encourages its display as a three-year trend." Also in 1981, the Financial Executives Institute issued a call to its members "to develop a more meaningful and informative funds statement that will emphasize cash flows."[2] There has, in fact, been a significant shift from a working capital to a cash focus in the SCFP included in published financial statements. Such a shift may lead one to expect that, at long last, analysts will find in the financial statements that sought-after and analytically significant cash flow from operations (CFFO) figure. However, a review of published financial statements reveals that there exist such wide variations in the practice of reporting CFFO as to make direct comparisons impossible and to render conclusions based on *reported* amounts often downright misleading.

Currently, the FASB is actively considering the issuance of guidelines for classifying cash flow statements by operating, investing, and financing activities. New guidelines are planned to be issued in 1987. However, with past experience as a guide we must conclude that the current lack of consistency of definition and presentation of published cash flow figures cannot be relied upon to simply vanish. Consequently credit and equity analysts must approach the analysis of financial statements armed with an independent, competent understanding of the meaning and significance of the various cash flow measures and how they are computed and interpreted.

COMPUTATION OF CASH FLOWS

The analyst who wants to compute and analyze any aspect of an enterprise's cash flows must start with the published financial statements. The financial statement most directly informative in this respect is the SCFP which may or may not focus on cash or the forthcoming statement of Cash Flows which will focus on the change in cash. Working with this statement requires a basic understanding of how it is prepared.

The analytical focus is most often on CFFO and most references to cash flow are really intended to refer to the net cash inflows or outflows from operations.

CFFO represents the *net* inflow (or outflow) of *cash* during a period resulting from the profit-directed activities of the enterprise. The term *profit-directed activities* is a deliberate expansion of the term *operations* that emphasizes the inclusion of sources and uses of funds needed to *support* such activities. For example, an increase in receivables as a result of sales, while increasing working capital, does not increase cash; it represents net income that has not yet been realized in cash. Conversely, a decrease in receivables indicates cash inflows in excess of the amount shown as the sales that are a part of net income (e.g., operations) for the relevant period. Similarly, changes in other working

---

EXHIBIT 1 Format for Presenting a Statement of Sources and Uses of Cash

---

Net income

Add back—depreciation

Subtotal (A)

Add back—other expenses not using working capital (e.g., deferred taxes, goodwill amortization)

Deduct—revenues and credits not providing working capital (e.g., undistributed equity in income of investees, reversals of deferred taxes)

Equals—Working capital provided by operations (WCFO) (B)

To convert WCFO to CFFO add or deduct changes in working capital accounts (other than cash) *that relate to operations* (C)—thus:

Add:

    Decreases in trade accounts and note receivable.
    Decreases in inventory.
    Decreases in prepaid expenses.
    Increases in trade accounts and notes payable.
    Increases in accrued liabilities.

Subtract:

    Increases in trade accounts and notes receivable.
    Increases in inventory.
    Increases in prepaid expenses.
    Decreases in trade accounts and notes payable.
    Decreases in accrued liabilities.

Equals—Cash flow from operations (CFFO) (D)

If we add to CFFO—other cash inflows: (e.g., the detail of all nonoperating *sources* of cash)

and deduct—other cash outflows: (e.g., the detail of all nonoperating *uses* of cash)

We obtain—the net change of cash for the period (E)

NOTES:

A. This is the crude "cash flow" measure so often referred to. It does not represent cash flow of any kind and is at best only part of CFFO and may understate or overstate the actual CFFO by a significant amount.

B. This number is found in many SCFP and may, alternatively, be used as the starting point of this computation.

C. Changes in other current accounts relate to other than operating activities; for example, changes in bank loans or in current portion of long-term debt relate to financing activities, and changes in dividends payable relate to capital transactions.

D. Can be positive (net inflow) or negative (net outflow).

E. Corresponds to the change in the cash and cash equivalents accounts for the period.

capital accounts that relate to profit-directed activities, such as inventories, prepayments, accruals, and accounts payable, must be considered in arriving at the CFFO figure. In short, by these adjustments we convert an accrual-based net income, a measure of operating performance, to cash flow from operations, a measure of the cash consequences of the profit-directed activities of the enterprise.

The published SCFP may focus on changes in working capital or it may focus on changes in cash. Some even focus on management's own concept of funds. So far, in actual practice many published SCFP, regardless of their focus, will not necessarily disclose the CFFO or, if they do, they may disclose an incorrect figure or one which management wants the reader to accept.[3] While a standard proposed to be issued in 1987 is intended to limit such abuses the analyst must be equipped to evaluate whether this objective has, in any given situation, been actually realized.

The analyst needs a framework which will enable him or her to convert the amounts found in the published financial statements to a valid CFFO amount. With it, regardless of the location of specific amounts in the SCFP or elsewhere they can be rearranged in such a way as to yield the desired amount of CFFO for any given period.

A framework which we will refer to, as the "net" method of computing cash from operations, and which can be expanded to add other sources and uses of cash as well, is illustrated in the schematic tabulation in Exhibit 1. The full reconciliation of the change in cash is an optional reassuring step and represents a computation in which CFFO is an intermediate subtotal. As indicated in Exhibit 1 we can start our computation with "net income" or with "working capital provided by operations" (if disclosed in the SCFP).

ILLUSTRATION OF THE COMPUTATION OF CFFO

To illustrate the computation of CFFO and the reconciliation of all other sources and uses of cash to the net change in the cash balance for the period we shall use the financial statements found in the 1985 annual report of Sperry Corporation. The consolidated statements of changes in financial position are shown in Exhibit 2.

Please note that Sperry's SCFP is prepared on a cash focus basis. We know this because the difference between "Source of funds" and "Application of funds" is a (decrease) increase in cash; that is, the change in cash for the year. However, even though the SCFP is on a cash focus basis it does not give us CFFO. Instead the "Funds provided from continuing operations" are in fact working capital rather than cash. Thus, Sperry provides a good example of the widespread inconsistencies and shortcomings found in practice—in this case a cash focus SCFP

EXHIBIT 2

SPERRY CORPORATION
Consolidated Statements of Changes
in Financial Position
Years ended March 31
(in millions)

	1985	*1984*	*1983*
Source of funds:			
Income from continuing operations.....	$ 286.7	$200.0	$122.3
Add income charges not affecting funds:			
Depreciation, amortization and obsolescence:			
Rental machines	118.2	114.1	119.0
Property, plant, and equipment....	104.0	89.6	79.4
Write-down of security investment ...	33.4	—	—
	255.6	203.7	198.4
Deduct income credits not affecting funds:			
Deferred income taxes	154.7	8.5	11.1
Share of undistributed earnings of companies accounted for by the equity method..................	24.3	23.4	41.9
	179.0	31.9	53.0
Funds provided from continuing operations	363.3	371.8	267.7
Issuance of common stock	81.9	306.8	61.7
Decrease (increase) in long-term receivables	420.7	113.8	(89.1)
Decrease (increase) in other assets ...	22.1	(111.9)	(25.7)
Increase (decrease) in bank and other loans...........................	13.4	(272.1)	(142.8)
Increase in accounts payable and other payables and accruals	57.4	181.2	65.2
Increase (decrease) in long-term debt .	179.3	(147.3)	141.1
Income (loss) from discontinued operations	—	16.2	(4.2)
Decrease in net assets of discontinued operations	—	235.1	80.9
	1,138.1	693.6	354.8
Application of funds:			
Additions to rental machines, net of sales, and retirements: 1985, $70.2; 1984, $39.7; 1983, $89.1	108.4	120.1	124.5
Additions to property, plant and equipment, net of sales and retirements: 1985, $19.8; 1984, $31.5; 1983, $42.1................	171.2	119.2	118.8

EXHIBIT 2 (*concluded*)

Cash dividends declared	107.4	102.5	86.1
Increase in short-term accounts receivable	281.2	112.2	64.4
Increase (decrease) in inventories	386.9	172.3	(164.0)
Decrease (increase) in accrued federal and foreign income taxes	9.5	(59.5)	56.8
Decrease (increase) in current maturities of long-term debt	14.3	(1.7)	19.8
Accumulated translation adjustment. . . .	63.0	16.5	79.2
Other, net	25.7	10.4	(29.2)
	1,167.6	592.0	356.4
(Decrease) increase in cash	(29.5)	101.6	(1.6)
Cash, beginning of year	166.8	65.2	66.8
Cash, end of year	$ 137.3	$166.8	$ 65.2

showing, however, funds provided by operations on a working capital basis rather than on cash basis as consistency would require.

In many cases all the information needed to prepare a cash statement (including its subset, CFFO) is found in the SCFP. In other cases additional information must be obtained from other financial statements (e.g., comparative balance sheets) and footnotes and this is the case with Sperry. Consequently Exhibit 3 presents the consolidated balance sheets and Exhibit 4 are pertinent footnotes from Sperry's financial statements.

Using this information we can now prepare the 1985 statement of sources and uses of cash (or cash statement) of Sperry as shown in Exhibit 5.

As the statement indicates, CFFO was $131.9 million in 1985 which contrasts with $363.3 source of "funds" (in actuality working capital) as reported in this cash focused SCFP by Sperry.

INTERPRETATION OF CASH FLOW NUMBERS

A consideration of the analytical meaning of CFFO must be based, in the first instance, on an understanding of what such a statement portrays and what it does not portray.

So far we have considered three statements (or portions of statements) that deal with operations: (1) income statement, (2) working capital from operations (WCFO), and (3) cash flow from operations (CFFO).

There seems to be endless confusion, among users of financial statements, about the concept of "operations" and about the different aspects of operations that these three statements are designed to portray.

EXHIBIT 3

SPERRY CORPORATION
Consolidated Balance Sheets
At March 31
(in millions)

	1985	1984
Assets		
Current assets:		
Cash, including interest-bearing deposits: 1985, $98.4; 1984, $155.1..........................	$ 137.3	$ 166.8
Accounts and notes receivable:		
U.S. government contracts, direct and indirect .	135.4	103.3
Sales-type leases, less allowance for unearned income: 1985, $120.1; 1984, $173.8	368.2	438.3
Commercial, less allowance for doubtful accounts: 1985, $24.1; 1984, $26.3.........	549.0	415.0
Due from wholly owned finance company......	428.8	243.6
	1,481.4	1,200.2
Inventories (note 6)	1,567.1	1,180.2
Prepaid expenses	123.8	91.9
Total current assets....................	3,309.6	2,639.1
Long-Term Receivables (note 7):		
Sales-type leases, less allowance for unearned income: 1985, $138.4; 1984, $226.0	816.1	1,225.5
Due from wholly owned finance company........	110.0	110.0
Other, less allowance for doubtful accounts: 1985, $1.6; 1984, $1.7...........................	69.0	80.3
	995.1	1,415.8
Investments at equity (note 9):		
Wholly owned finance and insurance companies .	364.4	345.6
Other companies	82.1	81.8
Rental machines, at cost:......................	664.0	682.4
Less allowance for depreciation and obsolescence	459.4	468.0
	204.6	214.4
Property, plant and equipment, at cost (note 8):	1,270.8	1,128.2
Less allowance for depreciation and amortization.	577.0	501.6
	693.8	626.6
Other assets	123.8	179.3
	$5,773.4	$5,502.6
Liabilities		
Current liabilities:		
Bank and other loans (note 10)................	$ 125.2	$ 111.8
Accounts payable............................	274.6	240.1
Other payables and accruals (note 13)	895.7	872.8
Accrued federal and foreign income taxes	260.5	270.0
Current maturities of long-term debt............	20.9	35.2

EXHIBIT 3 (*concluded*)

Dividend payable	27.2	26.2
Total current liabilities	1,604.1	1,556.1
Long-term debt (note 11)	889.0	709.7
Deferred income taxes	279.2	433.9

Stockholders' Equity

Capital stock:
Series preferred stock, no par value:
  Authorized and unissued—5,000,000 shares
Common stock, $.50 par value (note 14):
  Authorized: 100,000,000 shares
  Outstanding shares: 1985, 56,747,939; 1984,

54,347,911	28.4	27.2
Additional paid-in capital (note 14)	987.9	907.2
Retained earnings (note 15)	2,279.1	2,099.8
Accumulated Translation Adjustment (note 16) . . .	(294.3)	(231.3)
Total stockholders' equity	3,001.1	2,802.9
	$5,773.4	$5,502.6

The function of the *income statement* is to measure the *profitability* of the enterprise for a given period. This is presently done by relating, as well as is possible, expenses and revenues to a period regardless of when these are actually paid or received. While no other statement measures profitability as well as the income statement, it does not show the *timing* of cash flows and the effect of operations on liquidity and solvency. Consequently, other specialized statements are needed to focus on the latter, which are different dimensions of earnings-related activities.

Working capital from operations (WCFO) is a specialized operations concept. It is first and foremost a *definitional* concept depending, as it does, on the accountant's definition of working capital.[4]

EXHIBIT 4 Sperry Corporation (note to financial statements)

7. Long-Term Receivables and Operating Leases

At March 31, 1985 long-term receivables under sales-type leases before allowance for unearned income were collectible by fiscal years as follows: 1987, $404.5 million; 1988, $290.7 million; 1989, $173.4 million; 1990, $71.0 million; thereafter, $14.9 million. Interest rates on all long-term receivables ranged from 8 percent to 23 percent per annum.

Rental income to be received under noncancellable operating leases was as follows: 1986, $105.8 million; 1987, $57.1 million; 1988, $36.7 million; 1989, $19.6 million; 1990, $5.0 million.

EXHIBIT 5

SPERRY CORPORATION
Statement of Sources and Uses of Cash*
Year ended March 31, 1985

	($ millions)
Sources of cash:	
Income from continuing operations	286.7
+ Expense (− revenue) not affecting working capital:	
Depreciation, amortization and obsolescence (118.2 + 104.0)	222.2
Write-down of security investments.	33.4
Deferred income taxes.	(154.7)
Undistributed earnings of equity accounted investees.	(24.3)
= Working capital from continuing operations[†]	363.3
+(−) Changes in current assets and current liabilities related to operations:	
(I) D in receivables–current.	(281.2)
(I) D in inventories.	(386.9)
(I) D in prepaid expenses[‡].	(31.9)
I (D) in accounts and accruals payable.	57.4
I (D) in taxes payable	(9.5)
Decrease in long-term receivables[§].	420.7
= Cash flow from operations (CFFO).	131.9
Long-term borrowing.	179.3
Issuance of common stock	81.9
Decrease in other assets.	22.1
Bank and other loans.	13.4
Total sources	428.6
Uses of cash:	
Additions to rental machines.	108.4
Additions to property, plant, and equipment	171.2
Decrease in current maturities of long-term debt	14.3
Cash dividends	107.4
Accumulated translation adjustment[‖]	63.0
Other—net[‡]	(6.2)
	458.1
Increase (decrease) in cash (cash equivalents)	(29.5)

* All the amounts required for the preparation of this statement were taken from Sperry's Consolidated SCFP with the exception of items discussed in footnotes ‡ and § below.

† Working capital from continuing operations (designated as funds by Sperry) is shown in the SCFP and could also have provided the starting point of this cash statement.

‡ Sperry does not disclose the change in prepaid expenses in the SCFP but carries it instead in the "Other—net" category. Only a review of the balance sheet (Exhibit 3) reveals this. Consequently we extract the change from "Other—net" shown as use of 25.7 in the SCFP − less source of 31.9, representing prepaid expenses, resulting in "Other—net" of 6.2 (source).

§ The nature of changes in long-term receivables must always be carefully scrutinized in order to determine that they do in fact relate to operations. Note 7 to Sperry's financials (Exhibit 4) clarifies the relationship of these receivables to operations.

‖ This account is just one example of the limitations of a cash statement prepared on the basis of aggregate information and data supplied. One can doubt that the entire translation adjustment shown is a cash outflow. In any event, any resulting inaccuracies should be relatively minor and should not invalidate the analytical conclusions derived from the cash statement taken as a whole.

WCFO excludes from the measurement of operations those items of revenue and expense that do not affect current assets or current liabilities, as defined. Thus, it is a very specialized notion of operating results and certainly does not measure profitability. It does attempt to measure the amount of working capital provided by operations and as such is designed to supply significant information to those who view working capital as a significant measure of liquidity.[5] In most cases, this amount will exceed net income because it excludes such important and substantial costs as depreciation, depletion, amortization of intangibles, and deferred income taxes. The financial community's frequent reference to this measure of cash flow is, as we have seen, both superficial and uninformed.

Cash flow from operations encompasses the broadest concept of operations of these three measures. Here we encompass all earning-related activities of the enterprise. As the earlier discussion made clear, here we are not concerned only with costs and revenues but also with the cash demands of these activities, such as investments in customer receivables and in inventories as well as the financing provided by suppliers of goods and services used in operations.

Like WCFO, CFFO focuses on the liquidity aspect of operations and is *not* a measure of profitability because it does not include important items of cost such as the use of long-lived assets in operations or revenue items, such as the equity in the undistributed earnings of nonconsolidated subsidiaries or affiliates.

Importance of the Components of CFFO

It must be born in mind that a *net* figure, as such, be it net income, WCFO, or CFFO, is of very limited analytical value. Whether the purpose of the analyst is the evaluation of past performance or the prediction of future performance or conditions, the key to such analytical procedures is information about the *components* of such measures.

The analyst, in the evaluation of operating performance and in the determination of present or future earning power, focuses not on net income but rather on the components that make up that number. Similarly the evaluation of past cash flows and their analysis as a basis for the projection of future CFFO must be based on the components of that number rather than on the net amount.

Because WCFO and CFFO, as measures of performance, are less subject to distortion than is the net income figure, the analysis of the trend of the former, over time, can provide valuable analytical insights. Divergences in trends among these performance measures can also provide significant analytical clues.

The SCFP—cash focus, or its subset CFFO, is particularly well suited to the evaluation of current liquidity and the projection of short-term cash position.

The analyst obtains details about the components of CFFO in one of two formats.

1. The format shown in Exhibit 5 which, in arriving at CFFO, merely lists the changes in operating current assets and liabilities without associating them with specific revenue or costs. This format, known as the net or indirect approach, concentrates on producing a correct net figure for CFFO.

2. There is, however, another format which focuses on the revenue inflow and the cost outflow *components* of CFFO, adjusted by the related current account changes (e.g., sales adjusted by the change in receivables, and so on). This format, known as the direct, or more descriptively, the inflow-outflow approach is analytically more significant and valuable because it gives the analyst a feel of actual cash flows through the enterprise. Even though some inflows require related outflows, this format nevertheless enables the analyst to judge the degree of discretion that management has over the size and directions of its cash flows. Moreover, for purposes of short-term forecasting, this format is a more meaningful tool because it contains details about the financing options available to management.

In order to compute CFFO under this, second, format we must use the revenue, cost, and expense details provided in the income statement. For this purpose we use Sperry Corporation's consolidated statements of income and retained earnings presented in Exhibit 6.

Using the data in Exhibit 6 we can now present Sperry's CFFO on the inflow-outflow basis as shown in Exhibit 7.

The CFFO as well as the WCFO concepts are subject to the limitation that they *exclude*, by definition, those elements of revenue and expense that do not affect current accounts. That, as we saw, means that they exclude from consideration such important costs as those associated with the operating use of long-lived assets. No comprehensive, longer-term analysis of operations can, of course, be undertaken without a consideration of all elements of costs and expenses.

Accounting is a complex measurement system governed by many conventions and specialized definitions. The special-purpose statements that we have examined here, the income statement and those that measure WCFO and CFFO, have been developed to fill specialized needs by the use of specific and sometimes narrow perspectives. The valid analytical use of these statements requires that the analyst bear firmly in mind these specialized definitions as well as their inherent limitations.[6]

EXHIBIT 6

SPERRY CORPORATION
Consolidated Statements of Income
and Retained Earnings
Years ended March 31
(in millions)

	1985	1984	1983
Revenue:			
Net sales of products	$4,159.3	$3,368.7	$3,243.9
Rentals and services.	1,527.9	1,545.3	1,419.7
Total.	5,687.2	4,914.0	4,663.6
Other income (Note 2)	7.4	36.0	65.4
	5,694.6	4,950.0	4,729.0
Costs and expenses:			
Cost of sales of products . . .	2,906.6	2,248.4	2,136.4
Cost of rentals and services	760.5	805.7	750.4
Selling, general and administrative expenses	1,098.5	1,015.4	1,063.2
Research and development	460.7	410.4	375.7
Interest (Note 3).	174.4	166.6	228.9
	5,400.7	4,646.5	4,554.6
Income from continuing operations before taxes on income	293.9	303.5	174.4
Provision for taxes on income (Note 5)	7.2	103.5	52.1
Income from continuing operations	286.7	200.0	122.3
Income (loss) from discontinued operations, net of income taxes (Note 4)	—	16.2	(4.2)
Net income	286.7	216.2	118.1
Retained earnings, beginning of year.	2,099.8	1,986.1	1,954.1
Cash dividends declared	(107.4)	(102.5)	(86.1)
Retained earnings, end of year	$2,279.1	$2,099.8	$1,986.1
Net income (loss) per share:			
Continuing operations	$5.15	$3.86	$2.74
Discontinued operations	—	.31	(.09)
Total	$5.15	$4.17	$2.65
Weighted average number of shares outstanding	55,712,567	51,817,534	44,602,332
Cash dividends declared per share	$1.92	$1.92	$1.92

EXHIBIT 7

SPERRY CORPORATION
Operating Cash Receipts and Disbursements
For year ended March 31, 1985
(in millions)

Cash receipts from operations:

Net sales of products.......................................	$4,159.3
Rentals and services	1,527.9
Other income..	7.4
	5,694.6
(I) D in current receivables	(281.2)
(I) D in long-term receivables.............................	420.7
= Cash receipts from customers..........................	5,834.1

Cash disbursements for operations:

Total costs and expenses (5,400.7 + 7.2)...................	5,407.9
− Depreciation, amortization and obsolescence	(222.2)
+ or − Noncurrent deferred income taxes (here add back)	154.7
− Write-down of security investments	(33.4)
I (D) in inventories	386.9
I (D) in prepaid expenses	31.9
(I) D in accounts and accruals payable	(57.4)
(I) D in taxes payable......................................	9.5
= Cash disbursements for operations	5,677.9
− Undistributed equity in income of investees	(24.3)
Cash flow from operations	131.9

Further Implications for Analysis

The balance sheet portrays the variety of assets held by an entity at a given moment in time and the manner in which those assets are financed. The income statement portrays the results of operations for a specific fiscal period. Income results in increases of a variety of kinds of assets, some cash, some current, and some noncurrent. Expenses result in the consumption of different kinds of assets (or the incurrence of liabilities)—some cash, some of a current and some of a noncurrent nature. Thus, net income cannot be equated with an increment in liquid resources. It is quite conceivable that a very profitable enterprise may find it difficult to meet its current obligations and to lack funds for further expansion. The very fact that a business is successful in expanding sales may bring along with it a worsening of liquidity and the tying up of its funds in assets that cannot be liquidated in time to meet maturing obligations.

Clear thinking and analysis demands that we separate issues of operating performance and profitability from those concerned with the financing of the enterprise. Both are vital; they are interconnected, but they are not identical, and confusing the two can lead to fuzzy analysis.

The SCFP sheds light on the effects of earning activities on liquid resources and focuses on such matters as what became of net income during the period, and on what assets were acquired and how they were financed. It can highlight more clearly the distinction between net income and funds provided by operations.

The disparity between net income and WCFO, on one hand, and CFFO on the other, can also be very significant. An interesting study[7] of the behavior of a variety of analytical measures of W. T. Grant Company, prior to its bankruptcy, highlighted its inability to generate any meaningful cash from operations even though it was, for many years prior to its bankruptcy, able to report relatively steady net income and WCFO amounts.

The ability of an enterprise to generate cash from operations on a consistent basis is an important indicator of financial health. Analysts must, however, guard against too simplistic an interpretation of CFFO figures and trends.

Prosperous as well as failing entities may find themselves unable to generate cash from operations at any given time—but for different reasons. The entity caught in the "prosperity squeeze" of having to invest its cash in receivables and inventories in order to meet ever-increasing customer demand will often find that its profitability will facilitate financing by equity as well as by debt. That same profitability should ultimately turn CFFO into a positive figure. The unsuccessful firm, on the other hand, will find its cash drained by slowdowns in receivable and inventory turnovers, by operating losses, or by a combination of these factors. These conditions usually contain the seeds of further losses and cash drains and may also lead to the drying up of trade credit. In such cases, a lack of CFFO has different implications. Even if the unsuccessful firm manages to borrow, that will only magnify the ultimate drains of its cash. Thus, profitability is a key consideration, and while it does not ensure CFFO in the short run, it is essential to a healthy financial condition in the long run.

The unsuccessful or financially pressed firm can increase its CFFO by reducing accounts receivable and inventories, but usually this is done at the expense of future profitability. It should be readily apparent that the evaluation of CFFO must be done with great care and with a consideration of all surrounding circumstances.

A number of academic studies[8] have been undertaken with the objective of testing, on a statistical basis, whether CFFO numbers can predict insolvency. The basic test in such studies is whether the behavior of CFFO numbers, per se, prior to the insolvency or bankruptcy event, have predictive value.

Although these studies are serious and commendable efforts, the problem with them and with the conclusions derived from them is that, in actual analysis for any serious purpose, we do not use such numbers per se but only in conjunction with an examination of the detailed factors which comprise them as well as all the surrounding and attending circumstances. Broad statistical studies do not focus on the components of CFFO nor do they, or can they, capture or incorporate the varied and ever-changing attending circumstances which every serious analysis must consider.

In conclusion, the best defense that can be used by credit and equity analysts against the inaccurate and misleading presentations of CFFO discussed above, is to approach the analysis of financial statements independently and armed with a clear understanding of what CFFO is and how it is computed. At present, an analyst who accepts a published figure designated as CFFO or by similar terminology runs the risk of working with inaccurate and misleading measures. A working knowledge of how CFFO is computed will enable the analyst to assess the validity of the figure disclosed and, if need be, to adjust it to the correct amount.

ENDNOTES

1. Release No. 33-6349 (ASR No. 299).
2. Financial Executives Institute, "Alert," December 14, 1981.
3. For examples, see L. A. Bernstein and M. M. Maksy, "Again Now: How Do We Measure Cash Flow from Operations?" *Financial Analysts Journal*, July–August 1985.
4. It is also subject to the weaknesses of the accounting model. Thus, working capital with inventories valued on the LIFO basis is different from working capital with inventories valued on the FIFO basis.
5. In the U.S. the accounting profession is now moving away from according working capital importance as a measure of liquidity.
6. A further and more extensive discussion of these issues can be found in Leopold Bernstein's *Financial Statement Analysis: Theory, Application, and Interpretation*, 3d ed. (Homewood, Ill.: Richard D. Irwin, 1983).
7. J. A. Largay and C. P. Stickney, *"Cash Flows, Ratio Analysis and the W. T. Grant Company Bankruptcy,"* The *Financial Analysts Journal*, July–August 1980.
8. See, for example, C. J. Casey and N. J. Bartczak, "Cash Flow—It's Not the Bottom Line," *Harvard Business Review*, July–August 1984, and letters to the editor in subsequent issues.

18

Forecasting Corporate Earnings*

Samuel S. Stewart, Jr., Ph.D., CFA
President
Wasatch Advisors
and
College of Business
University of Utah

In keeping with the practical and results-oriented thrust of this *Handbook*, the basic purpose of this chapter is to enable the reader to make an earnings forecast. This chapter will also review studies concerning the accuracy and value of earnings forecasts. The author's viewpoint is that the primary benefit of forecasts lies in their function as an instrumental variable in predicting stock returns. Thus, instead of being concerned with the interplay of only two variables, the forecast and the actual earnings, this chapter will be concerned with three variables: the forecast, the actual earnings, and the corresponding stock returns.

When the first edition of the *Financial Analyst's Handbook* appeared just over a decade ago, research on how to forecast corporate earnings was in its infancy. Early findings on the value of forecasting were, in fact, rather pessimistic. Forecasting was not viewed as particularly accurate. Furthermore, the information upon which the forecast was based was deemed to be already reflected in stock prices. Forecasts thus seemed to offer little ability to increase an investor's return.

During the past decade, a large number of both academic and professional studies of forecasting have appeared. Their main findings counter the pessimism of the early researchers. Not only is the contemporary assessment of accuracy more optimistic, but, at least to some

---

* The author acknowledges the assistance of Venice Edwards with the research and final preparation of this chapter.

degree, a forecast—and particularly a forecast revision—is seen as providing new information, different from that already reflected in the market.

The large number of studies precludes a thorough review in this chapter, but a brief overview of the major findings will be helpful. The articles cited are intended as examples only. Those interested in a more comprehensive research survey should turn to Brown, Foster, and Noreen's excellent monograph "Security Analyst Multi-Year Earnings Forecasts and the Capital Market" published by the American Accounting Association in 1985.

RESEARCH REVIEW: EARNINGS FORECASTS AND STOCK RETURNS

Due to our interest in forecasts as an instrumental variable for predicting stock returns, we will organize this research review around three relationships: (1) earnings and stock prices, (2) forecasts and earnings, and (3) forecasts and stock prices. The growing optimism concerning both forecast accuracy and value is reflected in all three areas.

Both academics and professionals have long agreed on the strong relationship between earnings and stock prices. Recent studies confirm that a perfectly accurate forecast of earnings could produce superior investment performance.

Two factors account for the more favorable recent assessment of the relationship between forecasts and earnings. The first is a more careful selection of the appropriate benchmarks for measuring accuracy. The second is improved statistical methodology: larger, more systematic forecast samples and better techniques. One technique that has become standard is to focus on excess returns above those available from an alternative investment entailing a similar degree of risk. Another possibility is an actual improvement in forecasts due to, among other things, improved access to computers.

The most surprising finding about forecasts and stock prices is the implicit evidence of market inefficiency. Forecasts appear to have the ability to capture information not reflected in market prices. Some students of the market have suggested that this fact indicates deteriorating efficiency. A more accurate explanation is that better techniques and greater access to data and computer power have created the technological capacity to analyze the actual degree of market efficiency.

Earnings and Stock Prices

The strong theoretical relationship between earnings and stock prices has received steady support from empirical data. While the discounted dividend model posits dividends, not earnings, as the source of stock

EXHIBIT 1   S&P 400 Stock Price and Earnings, 1947–1985

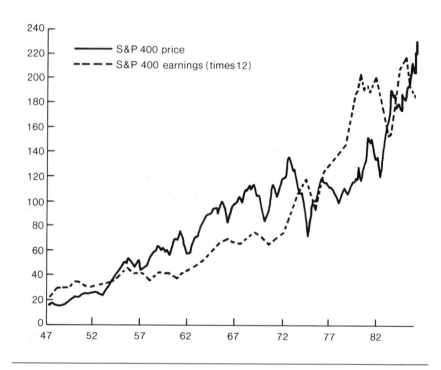

value, both theory and evidence document the close association between earnings and dividends. In practice, earnings are viewed as the
primary economic influence on stock prices, possibly due to management's ability to manipulate dividends in the short run.

Exhibit 1 presents graphic evidence of the close relationship between earnings and price for the S&P 400 Stock Price Index during the
post-World War II period.

Formal studies detail this correlation. Early research such as that by
Murphy (1968) and Niederhoffer and Regan (1972) arrayed stocks both
by earnings changes and price changes for various periods of time. They
found a close association between the ranking of stocks in each array.
The strength of the relationship increased as the time period lengthened.

More recent research focuses on the value of perfect information.
This value depends on the rates of return earned if actual earnings had
been known at the beginning of the period. Arnott (1985), Kerrigan
(1984), and Elton, Gruber, and Gultekin (1981) have all shown that a
perfect forecast could result in substantial excess returns.

All evidence suggests that earnings account for the major portion of stock returns.

Forecasts and Earnings

Most recent studies show that earnings can be forecast with reasonable accuracy, a change from earlier studies which emphasized the impossibility of accurate earnings forecasts. The reasons for this shift in consensus are most likely different statistical methodology and improved forecasting ability. Yet, the fit between an earnings forecast and the subsequent earnings is not as good as the fit between earnings and stock returns.

Assessing forecast accuracy.   Determining whether a forecast is accurate is not as easy as it might seem. A major complicating factor is identifying the appropriate "loss function." This function determines the significance of various degrees of inaccuracy. For example, when an analyst is using earnings as an instrumental variable for stock returns, it's not particularly important if the earnings forecast is not correct. What really matters is the failure of an earnings forecast to identify stock returns.

Another loss function issue is how to weigh errors of different size. Should small errors and large errors be given equal weight? Or should large errors be given a larger penalty—as is often the case in statistics? Should positive errors be offset with negative errors—again, following normal statistical methodology? Or should positive errors be ignored— because investors are likely pleased if earnings are above forecast? There are no generally right answers to these questions, only answers that are correct in specific situations. Yet the answers do affect the assessment of forecast accuracy.

A second major complication in assessing accuracy is selecting a benchmark to provide a point of comparison when analysts try to answer the question: Accurate compared to what? Most researchers use a comparative benchmark rather than just expressing error as a percent of actual earnings.

A variety of benchmarks have been used. Early studies tended to use naïve models. Such models would forecast next-period earnings as equal to last-period earnings. Or they would forecast the change in next-period earnings as equal to the change in last-period earnings. Later studies have used more sophisticated statistical models as benchmarks for assessing analyst forecasts or have used analyst forecasts as a benchmark for assessing sophisticated model forecasts. Another option has been comparing management forecasts against analyst forecasts and vice versa to determine relative accuracy.

No general-purpose benchmark has been agreed upon and it is

probably not realistic to expect one. This is because the appropriate benchmark depends upon the specific purpose of the study. Moreover, all assessments depend on specific benchmarks. Such assessments must, by their very nature, be relative rather than absolute.

Horizon, bias, and industry considerations. Many studies have found evidence of horizon, bias, and industry impacts on forecast accuracy. Not surprisingly, the further into the future the forecast attempts to peer, the less accurate the forecast. Some of the initial research examined the accuracy of five-year growth rate forecasts. As a result, Cragg and Malkiel (1968) concluded almost two decades ago that analysts had little forecasting ability. However, recent studies that have examined accuracy for shorter periods (years and quarters) have concluded that analyst forecasts are reasonably accurate. The most comprehensive study was done by Brown, Foster, and Noreen (1985). They found quarter-by-quarter improvement in forecast accuracy over two-year periods. Exhibit 2 depicts the improvement in forecast accuracy over time. It plots levels of decile accuracy as the futurity of the earnings forecasts for 500 securities decreases.

Researchers have generally concluded that analyst forecasts have an optimistic bias. However, the bias is not large. Brown, Foster, and Noreen (1985) note that the available data are really too skimpy—forecasts have been formally issued and assembled for only a few years—to reach solid conclusions concerning bias. Although their study confirmed an optimistic bias, more forecasts were pessimistic than optimistic. In this case the bias resulted from a few large, too-optimistic forecasts.

Several studies have found that forecast accuracy depends on the industry in which a firm operates. Not surprisingly, earnings for firms in the more stable consumer goods industries can be forecast with relative accuracy. Earnings for firms in the more cyclical capital goods industries can be forecast less accurately. The general assessment of forecast accuracy depends on the mix of consumer goods and capital goods firms in the sample.

Exhibit 3, which compares the forecast accuracy of four analytical groups and one naïve model, demonstrates the dependence of forecast accuracy on the type of business operation. For example, firms in industries with reasonably stable demand, such as drugs, food products, and oil, are relatively easy to forecast in comparison to firms in industries with fluctuating demand, such as aerospace, automobiles, and steel. However, it should be noted that in spite of improved analyst accuracy in near-term forecasts of stable demand industries, the accuracy of such forecasts is not markedly different from those generated by a naïve model. In fact, there is some evidence indicating that analysts enjoy the greatest superiority in forecasting long-term results of firms in

EXHIBIT 2   Distribution Statistics for [(Actual EPS−Forecast EPS)/Security Price at End of Forecast Month] × 100

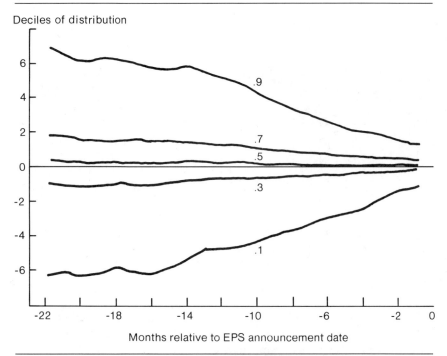

Deciles of distribution

Months relative to EPS announcement date

Data Base.   Institutional Brokers Estimate System at monthly intervals for the period January 1976 to December 1980 containing consensus security analyst earnings per share forecast information for 500 securities for each year of a two-year forecast horizon.

SOURCE: Philip Brown, George Foster, and Eric Noreen, "Security Analyst Multi-Year Earnings Forecasts and the Capital Market," *Studies in Accounting Research #21*, 1985, p. 45.

variable demand industries. This finding should not be surprising due to the importance of nonquantifiable, judgment-type factors in such situations.

Statistical forecasts versus judgmental forecasts.   Some forecasts are generated by explicit statistical models while others incorporate human judgment. Studies of forecast accuracy have often focused on the comparative quality of statistical and judgmental forecasts. (See the sections on statistical forecasts and judgmental forecasts.)

While early studies generally concluded that there was little difference in the accuracy of statistical and judgmental forecasts, later studies generally concede that judgmental forecasts are more accurate. As noted, the apparent relative improvement in judgmental forecasts is

EXHIBIT 3 Mean Percent Error of the Analytical Groups by Industry

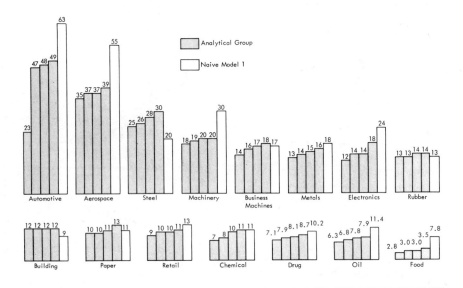

probably only partly real and probably partly due to the application of different statistical methodology. No published research has appeared which studies the possible improvement in accuracy over time.

Analyst forecasts. To many, *earnings forecast* means an earnings forecast issued by a sell-side Wall Street security analyst for the good reason that most earnings forecasts are of this type. Forecasts with the greatest publicity certainly are. Such forecasts are an important element in the securities business. In fact, those skeptical of the value of forecasts in increasing investor returns explain the persistence of forecasting by noting the use of forecasts as a marketing tool.

Sell-side forecasts are made by analysts employed by about 70 major brokerage firms. Typically, they project yearly earnings for one to three years and quarterly earnings for up to two years. Often a "long-term" (usually understood as about five years) growth rate is estimated.

These forecasts are issued and revised periodically. Some revisions would certainly be spurred by new developments while others are mandated reassessments which must occur at regular calendar intervals. Although both initial forecasts and revisions are ultimately issued in printed form, important clients get the "first call" over the telephone. Note that this type of information release can bias the results of studies which take the publication date to be the date of the forecast.

In recent years, issuing and revising forecasts has become more standardized, thanks to the increasing popularity of services which collect analyst forecasts from various brokerage firms and assemble them in a common format published at regular intervals. The leading service is the Institutional Brokers Estimate System (I/B/E/S) produced by Lynch, Jones and Ryan. Two other services are *Icarus* published by Zacks Investment Research and *The Earnings Forecaster* published by Standard & Poor's. Exhibit 4 shows the type of information available from I/B/E/S.

The recent proliferation of research on analyst forecasts is largely due to the growth of these collection services which make a variety of forecasts readily available. They have also helped make forecast revision periodic rather than sporadic. Exhibit 5 gives an indication of the pattern of forecast revision for several security analysts. The 1971 earnings estimates for Abbott Labs were generally lowered as the year progressed. Analyst E tended to be early in recognizing the earnings decline while analyst J tended to be late.

Another widely available source of analyst estimates is *The Value Line Investment Survey.* These estimates, all produced by Value Line analysts, are published and revised according to a quarterly update schedule. The unique feature of the Value Line service is that it is a stand-alone source of research, readily available for purchase by the general public.

The accuracy of analyst forecasts has generated considerable controversy. The early research, such as that by Cragg and Malkiel (1968) and Elton and Gruber (1972), concluded that analyst forecasts were no more accurate than those produced by simple statistical models. More recent research, including studies by Brown and Rozeff (1978) and Fried and Givoly (1982), concludes that analyst forecasts are actually more accurate.

Among the reasons for the disparate findings are: assessing accuracy over different horizons, a different industry mix of sampled firms, different benchmarks, different statistical measures—and a possible increase in accuracy over time due to better forecasting methods.

Management forecasts. Management forecasts are earnings forecasts issued by management. Exhibit 6 presents an example of such a forecast. In principle, the accuracy of management forecasts ought to be superior to analyst forecasts because management forecasts can reflect inside information. In contrast, analyst forecasts are presumably based on information already in the public domain. Most studies, including those by Jaggi (1980) and Ruland (1978), confirm the superior accuracy of management forecasts.

In the early 1970s, the Securities and Exchange Commission consid-

EXHIBIT 4 I/B/E/S Monthly Summary Data Definitions (company data by sector and industry)

Price: Price as of the day prior to date of report; shown in eighths.

Actual—Fiscal Year and EPS:
Earnings per share for the most recently reported fiscal year end. Industry and sector aggregates are computed by share-weighting the EPS of each constituent company.

Estimates—Fiscal Year 1 and Fiscal Year 2:
Mean—Average of all available estimates. Aggregates are share weighted.

Percent Change—Actual—Percent change of mean estimate from last year's actual EPS.

Relative—Percent change of mean estimate from last year's actual EPS relative to the average change for all I/B/E/S Summary Data companies (unweighted).

6 mo.— Percent change of mean estimate from its level six months ago.

Revisions—% up—Percent of estimates revised up since last month.

% down—Percent of estimates revised down since last month.

Coefficient of Variation—Coefficient of variation—Industry and sector aggregates are net income weighted; that is, individual company coefficients of variation are weighted by their shares times their mean estimate.

Sector/Industry/Company	Price	Fiscal Year	Actual	Estimates—Fiscal Year 1							Estimates Fiscal Year 2							Estimated 5-Year Growth Rate	
					Percent Change			Revisions		Coefficient of Variation		Percent Change			Revisions		Coefficient of Variation		
			EPS	Mean	Actual	Relative	6 Mo.	% Up	% Down		Mean	Actual	Relative	6 Mo.	% Up	% Down		Median	S.D.
Financial Services	6-6	12/85	2.62	3.56	36.0	0.99	-1.2	10	10	7.5	4.56	67.8	1.04	-12.9	6	7	7.8	12	4
Finance and loan	25-7	12/85	3.19	3.86	20.9	0.88	-10.4	8	8	7.9	4.83	49.1	0.92	NA			2.4	12	10
Commercial Credit			0.99	1.44	44.7	1.05	-3.7		13	47.1	1.07	NM	NM	NA			9.8	9	8
Foothill Group			-0.69D	0.52	NM	NM	-43.8		17	14.8	1.07	NM	NM	NA			9.8	20	3
Leucadia National			2.73	2.35	-13.8	0.62	14.2			54.2								7	10
Personal Loans	54-4	12/85	3.71	4.43	19.4	0.87	-10.8	11	6	4.9	5.27	42.1	0.88	NA			2.2	12	11
Beneficial			3.82	5.02	31.3	0.95	-9.4			1.9	6.50	70.2	1.05	NA			0.0	12	9
Household International Corp	44-3	12/85	3.45D	4.12	19.3	0.86	-11.7	22	11	6.9	4.63	33.9	0.83	NA			3.8	12	8

SOURCE: Institutional Brokers Estimate System (I/B/E/S), a service of Lynch, Jones & Ryan, members New York Stock Exchange, Inc., and other principal exchanges.

EXHIBIT 5 Improvements in Forecast Accuracy over Time: Catallactics Casper—Broker Forecasts, Abbott Labs (calendar 1971 EPS analysis from 1/01/71 to 12/31/71)

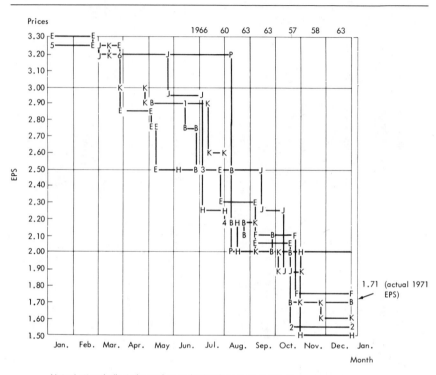

Note: Letters indicate issue date and value forecasts of Abbott Laboratories 1971 EPS for different analysts.

ered requiring disclosure of management forecasts as a part of the normal reporting procedure for public companies. The SEC ultimately backed away from this proposal due to difficulties in standardizing the process for the wide variety of public companies.

Lender forecasts. Lending institutions generate a large number of forecasts related to credit worthiness, usually estimating earnings as an incidental part of the process. These forecasts rarely become public information except indirectly as bond ratings are issued and changes in those ratings result.

Presumably the accuracy of these forecasts is not substantially different from the accuracy of analyst forecasts. The default of several highly rated bonds offers indication of at least some forecast error.

EXHIBIT 6

Five-Year Forecast

We have included a sales forecast for each of our major product lines and operating groups for 1988.

While we recognize that long-term forecasts are subject to many variables and uncertainties, our experience has been that our success is determined more by our own activities than by the performance of any industry or the economy in general.

In addition, the balance and diversity of our products and markets have been such that a shortfall in expected performance in one area has been largely offset by higher than anticipated growth in another.

Although variations may occur in the forecast for any individual product line, we have a relatively high level of confidence that our overall five-year growth forecast is achievable.

Assumptions Used In Forecast

- Average 2-3 percent annual real growth in GNP.
- Average inflation 5-7 percent.
- Present tax structure to continue.
- No change in currency exchange rates.
- No acquisitions.
- No additional financing.
- Dividend payout ratio 20 percent.
- Four percent after-tax return on investment of excess cash.
- No exercise of stock options.

5-Year Cash Flow Forecast, 1984-1988

	(In Thousands)
Net Income	$770,000
Depreciation	110,000
	880,000
Working Capital	(160,000)
Note Payments	(280,000)
Capital Expenditures	(150,000)
Equity Income	(70,000)
Dividends	(150,000)
Net Cash Change	70,000
Beginning Cash, 1-1-84	160,000
Cash, 12-31-88	$ 230,000

Sales Growth — Five-Year Forecast

	SALES FORECAST			ACTUAL SALES (In Thousands)		
	5-YEAR GROWTH RATE 1984-1988	1988		5-YEAR GROWTH RATE 1979-83	1983	1978
PRODUCTS FOR THE HOME AND FAMILY						
Building and Home Improvement Products:						
Faucets	15%	$ 490,000		9%	$ 243,000	$155,000
Other Building Products	14%	510,000		30%	261,000	71,000
	15%	1,000,000		17%	504,000	226,000
Other Products for the Home and Family:						
Personal Communications	1%	60,000		4%	56,000	46,000
Recreational Accessories	12%	50,000		1%	28,000	26,000
Other Specialty Products	18%	115,000		38%	50,000	10,000
	11%	225,000		10%	134,000	82,000
Total Products for the Home and Family	14%	$1,225,000		16%	$ 638,000	$308,000
PRODUCTS FOR INDUSTRY[A]						
Oil-Field and Related Products	—	—		21%	$ 104,000	$ 40,000
Specialty Industrial Products:						
Cold Extrusions	—	—		5%	88,000	70,000
Specialty Valves and Closures	—	—		21%	85,000	33,000
Other Industrial Products	—	—		1%	144,000	135,000
	—	—		6%	317,000	238,000
Total Products for Industry	—	—		9%	$ 421,000	$278,000
Total Masco Sales	14%	$1,225,000		13%	$1,059,000	$586,000

Sales Growth By Specific Markets And Products[1][2]

	FORECAST			ACTUAL (In Thousands)		
	5-YEAR GROWTH RATE 1984-1988	1988		5-YEAR GROWTH RATE 1979-83	1983	1978
Masco Faucet Sales[1]	15%	$490,000		9%	$243,000	$155,000
Faucet Industry Sales—Units	7%	35,000		(5)%	25,000	32,000
Masco Market Share—Units	2%	38%		5 %	34%	27%
Housing Completions	4%	1,700		(4)%	1,400	1,700

(1) Excludes foreign sales. (2) Industry data Masco estimates. (3) Includes foreign sales.

(A) As of July 2, 1984, the Industrial and Energy-Related operations of Masco Corporation were transferred to Masco Industries, Inc.   October 1984

SOURCE: Excerpt from 1985 Masco Corporation Annual Report.

Forecasts and Stock Prices

Given our interest in predicting stock returns, even highly accurate forecasts may be of little value if the information from which they are derived is already reflected in stock prices. The central issue of market efficiency is how fast information is captured by stock prices. Investors can presumably interpret information as quickly and as astutely as forecasters. If so, even though highly accurate, how useful can an explicit forecast in predicting stock prices be?

In the past decade, researchers have become much less uniformly convinced that markets are highly efficient. It seems apparent from the evidence that there is a clear relationship between forecasts of superior (inferior) earnings and the subsequent realization of superior (inferior) stock market returns. However, while recent research tends to support a more moderate degree of market efficiency than early research, most studies suggest that forecasts, though accurate, offer little additional value. Most of the information is already reflected in prices.

The most intriguing research has studied the relationship between forecast revision and error and subsequent stock market return. Niederhoffer and Regan (1972) noted, but did not statistically confirm, a relationship between forecast error and return. Earnings greater than forecast were associated with high returns. Earnings below forecast led to low returns.

Since 1972, their observation has been documented by a series of studies. For example, see Brown and Kennelly (1972); Latane and Jones (1977); Joy, Litzenberger, and McEnally (1977); and Jones, Rendleman, and Latane (1985). These studies have analyzed standardized unexpected earnings (SUE)—earnings which differ from forecast earnings (often generated by a naïve model) by large amounts. Such studies find that SUE are associated with both immediate and continuing excess returns. If the surprise is favorable, the returns are positive and vice versa.

That unexpected earnings lead to immediate returns confirms the concept of market efficiency. Expectations are reflected in prices. However, an efficient market should respond immediately and completely to the failure of those expectations. The fact that excess returns continue indicates, of course, less than perfect market efficiency. It suggests that not only does the failure of a forecast provide information but it takes time for investors to gauge the precise impact of the new information.

The forecast revision evidence is similar to the SUE evidence. Forecast revisions are associated with immediate market reactions in the expected direction, suggesting that the information upon which the initial forecast was based was indeed reflected in market prices. The new information ought to lead to both altered forecasts and stock prices. However, as with SUE, the revised forecast also leads to continuing excess returns. If the revision was positive, the returns are also. If the revision was negative, the returns are negative. Givoly and Lakonishok (1979, 1980); Hawkins, Chamberlin, and Daniel (1984), and others have all confirmed this effect.

Coupling these findings with those concerning the value of perfect information suggests that there is little value in generating "me too" forecasts. However, superior forecasts, including superior revision of consensus forecasts, seem to offer substantial value.

FORECASTING EARNINGS

Before it is possible to talk about how to generate a forecast, it is necessary to understand two major issues. The first issue concerns the degree to which the forecast will be statistical or judgmental. The second issue concerns the degree to which the forecast will depend on top-down or bottom-up variables.

Statistical forecasts versus judgmental forecasts. Statistical forecasts are those in which the earnings forecast is the dependent variable in an explicit mathematical model. The earnings forecast may be obtained as a direct result of combining the parameters of the model with estimates of the independent variables. In the simplest cases, the independent variables are known. For example, earnings may be forecast as a multiple of earnings in the previous period.

In contrast, judgmental forecasts are obtained without reference to an explicit forecasting model. Analysts' earnings forecasts are often judgmental, while management forecasts are almost always judgmental. In many cases, judgmental forecasts stem from statistical forecasts, possibly supplemented by a "fudge factor." In almost all cases, a statistical model would play at least an implicit role in preparing a judgmental forecast. In any case, the distinguishing feature of a judgmental forecast is that it ultimately depends on human judgment.

The difference between statistical and judgmental forecasts tends to be one of degree rather than one of kind. The best forecasts are apt to combine elements of both techniques. Statistical models are very good at capturing the more scientific, logical "if . . . then . . . " aspects of a forecast. The more artistic aspects, including the relevance of particular if . . . statements require human judgment.

As noted, some researchers have concluded that statistical and judgmental forecasts are equally accurate. Others have found that judgmental forecasts have superior accuracy. To some extent, evaluating statistical and judgmental forecasts is itself a subjective process—a matter of taste—that reveals a possibly unconscious preference for either statistical or judgmental approaches.

EXHIBIT 7

Top-Down Forecasts

1. Estimate sensitivity of earnings to economic and industry variables (GNP, interest rates, etc.).
2. Measure (forecast) economic and industry variables.
3. Combine estimated sensitivities with forecasted variables.

Bottom-Up Forecasts

1. Estimate sensitivity of earnings to other firm variables (sales, margins, etc.).
2. Measure (forecast) firm variables.
3. Combine estimated sensitivities with forecasted variables.

Bottom-up versus top-down forecasts. Many factors influence a company's earnings. Some factors, such as rising interest rates, impact most of the firms in the economy. Other factors, such as falling oil prices, affect most of the firms in a particular industry. Still other factors, such as a management change, influence only a single firm. Forecasts that emerge from an analysis of the relationship of economy and industry factors to firm earnings are termed *top-down* forecasts. In contrast, forecasts which begin with an assessment of factors unique to a specific firm are called *bottom-up* forecasts.

Top-down and bottom-up forecasts need not be mutually exclusive. However, analysts do tend to adopt one of these two approaches. Exhibit 7 illustrates the basic steps necessary for making either a top-down or a bottom-up forecast.

The critical elements of bottom-up forecasts are estimates of the sensitivity of earnings to other firm-specific variables. Historical relationships offer some evidence, but management decisions can and do alter these relationships. For example, management decisions can alter income statement variables (such as margin) and balance sheet variables (such as asset intensity). A bottom-up forecast usually depends on a forecast of sales.

The critical elements of top-down forecasts are estimates of the sensitivity of earnings to economy and industry variables. An analyst usually identifies such sensitivities by looking at historical relationships. Statistical techniques such as regression analysis are useful in obtaining numerical estimates of earnings sensitivity. A top-down earnings forecast also requires forecasting the relevant economy and industry variables. Such forecasts can either be generated by the analyst or obtained from a number of public and private sources. A top-down forecast is made by combining the forecasted variables with the estimated sensitivities.

Academic studies provide mixed evidence about the relative merits of top-down and bottom-up forecasts. Researchers (including Brown and Ball, 1967) have found that economy and industry variables explain more than half of the earnings variability of a typical firm. Not surprisingly, studies (e.g., King, 1966) also show that such factors explain more than half of the rate of return on a firm's stock. Nevertheless, Elton, Gruber, and Gultekin (1984) found that the firm-specific component of earnings is the source of most forecast error.

Statistical/Mechanical Earnings Models

The simplest type of earnings forecast is generated mechanically with the aid of a statistical model. Once the model has been created—statistically estimated—the analyst can readily produce the forecast by combining the parameters of the model with actual or estimated values of the independent variables. For example, if a company has very stable earnings growing at 10 percent a year, next year's earnings might be estimated by adding 10 percent to this year's earnings.

Usually statistical earnings models are more complex than this example. A useful model must usually consist of variables and parameters. In an earnings model, the dependent variable is earnings. The independent variables are those elements used to forecast the dependent variable. The parameters of the model describe how the dependent variable is related to the independent variables. As the independent variables of the model change, the forecasted dependent variable changes. The parameters of the model remain constant. The parameters of the model are statistically estimated from the historical relationship between the independent variables and the dependent variable.

While operating a model is simple, creating it can be quite complex. It can require a good deal of skill. It can also require a high degree of judgment. A necessary decision, requiring both skill and judgment, is determining what independent variables to use. Another is what statistical technique to use in estimating the parameters of the model—the relationship between the independent variables and the dependent variable. A third decision is what historical time period to use in estimating the parameters.

Not surprisingly, many statistical earnings models are the result of academic research. Some of the earliest were created merely to serve as benchmarks in assessing the accuracy of analysts' forecasts. Later, analysts became interested in the mechanical forecast itself. Increasingly sophisticated statistical methods were applied to estimating earnings models.

In recent years, Wall Street analysts have become more deeply involved in creating statistical models, probably the result of an increasingly quantitative business school curriculum coupled with widely available computing ability. Sometimes the analyst uses these earnings models in preparing a forecast. Increasingly, earnings models are becoming part of a more general quantitative approach to investing.

Time-series properties of earnings. A number of studies have investigated the time-series properties of earnings. These studies typically create earnings models which have a single independent variable: historical earnings. These studies investigate the time-series properties of both earnings levels and earnings trends. An important issue is whether changes in earnings levels tend to be permanent or whether there is a reversion to previous earnings levels.

The general finding of these studies is that randomness is *not* one of the time-series properties of earnings. Both successive earnings levels and successive earnings trends are clearly and systematically related. Consequently, there is fundamental statistical justification for the construction of earnings models.

Another uniform finding is that the predictability of earnings depends on the industry. Earnings for firms in more cyclical capital goods industries reflect greater randomness and are more difficult to forecast. Earnings for firms in more stable consumer goods industries reflect less randomness and are easier to predict.

This finding is particularly important because many studies do not accommodate these differences in industry. Instead, their statistical results are implicitly extended to all firms. However, such findings simply may not be applicable to specific firms in specific industries.

Another consistent finding is that quarterly earnings have a seasonal component. Obviously caution is needed in applying this finding. The seasonality factor for a toy company is much different from that for a toothpaste company.

The most successful statistical technique seems to contain some element of exponential smoothing that recognizes and accommodates such variables. It is perhaps the subconscious recognition that such accommodations need to be made that makes many analysts uncomfortable with a strictly mechanical approach.

Judgmental Forecasts

Judgmental earnings forecasts may, and probably do, use statistical information and models, but the ultimate decisions are made by human judgment. Most Wall Street forecasts are of the judgmental type— "touched by human hands."

The primary advantage of a judgmental forecast over a statistical forecast is that the human brain can easily take account of a wide variety of factors while a statistical forecast can only consider the factors included in the explicit model. If additional factors are to be included, the model must be reestimated. Rebuilding a statistical model can be an expensive and time-consuming process.

The difference between judgmental and statistical models may be likened to the difference between structural and reduced-form econometric models. The simpler reduced-form model is adequate for generating forecasts when nothing in the basic economic structure has changed. However, when the structure changes, the reduced-form model is no longer adequate.

We can infer from the previous discussion of forecast accuracy that judgmental forecasts are apt to be somewhat more accurate than statistical forecasts. This is true, but the assertion is still somewhat misleading. Statistical models almost certainly play some role in the preparation of these more accurate forecasts, just as human judgment plays a role in creating the statistical model. Clearly, debating the relative merits of either system is an exercise in futility. A good forecast is likely to reflect both statistical models and human judgment.

The disadvantage of relying exclusively on judgmental forecasts is that they are hard to troubleshoot. It is difficult to find the source of error. In contrast, when statistical forecasts are wrong, it is easy to find the error because the forecasting model is explicit. Each step can be checked. The source of trouble can be quickly located. Not so for judgmental forecasts. When an analyst grows "cold," his forecasts are of little use.

Joe Granville offers a good example of this. In the mid- to late 1970s, his stock market calls were right on target. He appeared on many talk shows. His picture was on the cover of *Time*. But he grew cold in the early 1980s. He persistently forecast a major market decline and, when the market continued to advance, Granville was dismissed as a fallen prophet. Even with hindsight, it is hard to tell why Joe's judgmental forecasts were right in the 1970s and wrong in the 1980s.

Short-term versus long-term forecasts. The longer the forecast period, the greater the need for a judgmental forecast. The reason is simply because the longer the period, the greater the number of factors that can affect earnings. Next quarter's earnings are not likely to be affected by changes in inflation and interest rates, but next year's are. Next year's earnings are not likely to be affected by a product innovation, but the long-term growth rate will be.

A convenient division of labor used by many analysts is suggested by these relationships. Short-term forecasts are prepared with heavy reliance on statistical models. Fudge factors play only a minor role, if that, in modifying the statistical forecast. In contrast, analysts produce long-term forecasts, especially forecasts of long-term growth rates, with a heavy reliance upon human judgment. Statistical models play little, if any, role in their preparation.

The role of judgment in top-down forecasts. Judgment generally plays a greater role in preparing a top-down forecast than it does in preparing a bottom-up forecast. This is because top-down forecasting models tend to be either implicit or reduced form. In contrast, bottom-up forecasting models tend to be explicit and structural.

Top-down models require judgment because they tend to be inherently more complex. It is difficult to define the precise structural relationship of earnings to the numerous factors in the macroeconomy. Even if a statistical—reduced form—association is estimated, the relationship is not likely to be stable.

Assessing competitive factors. It takes judgment to estimate the impact of competition on a firm's earnings. Effective competition implies a changing industry structure. Market share is gained and lost as rivals shift competitive tactics. Statistical models can't easily capture the effects of competitive interplay.

The developmental stage an industry finds itself in has a major impact on the nature of competition within an industry. (See the discussion of evolutionary stages below.) It tends to determine whether competition will be primarily on the basis of price or on the basis of quality—product features and service. The stage of industry evolution also determines whether the toughest competitors are likely to be large firms or small firms.

As a rule of thumb, price is apt to be an effective competitive weapon for firms with low-cost production selling commodity products, but the identification of such firms involves a rather sophisticated process. Judgment is required to determine to what extent a firm is selling commodity products, which firm is the low-cost producer, and which competitive tactics are most likely.

A good example of the role of judgment in such decisions is the evolving perception of the chemical industry. In the 1950s and early 1960s, chemical firms compiled impressive growth rates due to strong economic growth nationally and the exploitation of technology developed during World War II. As a result, many investors perceived chemical companies as growth stocks. However, more astute analysts recognized that commodity products and large fixed costs would likely result in price becoming an important competitive tactic. As a result, they correctly recognized that the historical growth of the industry was not likely to be carried over into the 1970s.

Quality—product features and service—is always an effective competitive weapon, provided it can be delivered at a reasonable price. Determining what constitutes a reasonable price requires judgment. Firms and even industries have been built on a correct assessment of what customers are willing to pay for. One of the most notable examples is the air express industry. The founders of Federal Express perceived that customers desired and were willing to pay for door-to-door rather than city-to-city delivery service. Its impressive profits are based on its ability to provide that service.

Judgment and accounting credibility. Judgment also plays an important role in the correct assessment of accounting numbers. Most of the time, the numbers contained in financial statements may be taken at face value. However, on some occasions, they can't. Astute analysts have made handsome returns by judging correctly between these occasions.

Perhaps the most infamous example of "cooked books" was the Equity Funding scandal. Ray Dirks, an analyst who followed the company, was able to combine his knowledge of the accounting practices of the firm with a tip from a disgruntled former employee to get his clients to bail out of the stock.

Commercial services attempt to judge accounting credibility. One of the best known is Thornton "Ted" O'Glove's *Quality of Earnings Report.* This publication identifies firms which O'Glove feels are taking accounting shortcuts, boosting short-term earnings at the expense of long-term earnings.

In summary, judgment can play an important role in the preparation of an earnings forecast, particularly true if the forecast is a long-run, top-down forecast for a firm operating in a highly competitive industry.

Bottom-Up Earnings Forecasts

Bottom-up earnings forecasts rely on firm-oriented variables and relationships. While bottom-up forecasts may be based on implicit, more judgmental models, they tend to be based on explicit, more statistical models. This is because the bottom-up variables which determine earnings are limited in number and easy to identify.

Perhaps the most widely used bottom-up models are pro forma income statements. Exhibit 8 presents an example of such an earnings model. A pro forma income statement forecasts sales, expenses, and earnings based on historical levels and trends. If necessary, these historic relationships may be modified to reflect changing conditions.

Another type of bottom-up earnings model attempts to combine income statement and balance sheet relationships. Du Pont originally used an abbreviated version of this model for financial analysis. However, the model has been expanded and modified by several researchers including Stewart (1975) and Babcock (1980). A typical example of such a model appears in Exhibit 9. Exhibit 10 presents a similar model.

At the heart of this combination model is an equation which explains earnings as the product of levels of equity investment and profitability. Thus, earnings changes are explained either by investment changes or

EXHIBIT 8

CORDURA CORPORATION
Pro Forma Income Statement

	1980	1981	1982	1983	1984	1985	5-Year Growth (%)	Estimates			3-Year Growth (%)
								1986	1987	1988	
Publishing:											
Sales ($M)	19.6	22.6	25.6	30.3	33.6	36.5	13.2	41.5	47.0	53.0	13
Profits ($M)	4.22	5.12	6.81	7.9	9.8	10.7	20.5	12.2	14.1	15.9	14
Margins (%)	21.5	22.7	26.6	26.1	29.2	29.3		29.5	30.0	30.0	
Employee benefits:											
Sales ($M)	7.3	7.8	8.1	8.5	8.8	10.4	7.3	11.8	13.2	14.9	13
Profits ($M)	1.69	1.41	1.07	1.49	1.43	1.68	-0.1	1.9	2.1	2.3	11
Margins (%)	23.2	18.1	13.2	17.5	16.2	16.2		15.9	15.7	15.5	
Mitchellmatix:											
Sales ($M)			2.3	1.9	4.5	6.5	NMF	11.0	17.0	25.0	57
Profits ($M)			0	0	-0.2	0.6	NMF	1.2	2.9	5.5	109
Margins (%)			0.0	0.0	-4.4	9.2		11.0	17.0	22.0	
Total operating income (before investment income):											
Sales ($M)	26.9	30.4	36.0	40.7	46.9	53.4	14.7	64.3	77.2	92.9	20
Profits ($M)	5.91	6.53	7.88	9.39	11.09	12.98	17.0	15.3	19.1	23.7	22
(−) Corporate expense ($M)	2.09	2.21	1.65	2.08	2.63	2.99	7.4	3.3	3.6	4.0	10

Pretax operating income ($M)	3.82	4.32	6.23	7.31	8.46	9.99	21.2	12.0	15.5	19.8	26
(−) Operating taxes ($M)	1.77	1.86	2.83	3.41	3.96	4.46	20.2	5.4	7.0	8.9	26
After-tax operating income ($M)	2.05	2.46	3.40	3.90	4.50	5.53	22.0	6.6	8.5	10.9	25
Operating tax rate (%) (before investment effect)	46.4	43.0	45.5	46.7	46.8	44.6		45	45	45	
Net income (including investment income): After-tax operating income ($M)	2.05	2.46	3.40	3.90	4.50	5.53	22.0	6.6	8.5	10.9	25
After-tax investment income ($M)	2.05	2.39	2.50	3.62	4.21	3.80	13.1	4.1	4.4	4.6	7
Net income ($M)	4.10	4.85	5.90	7.52	8.71	9.33	17.9	10.8	12.9	15.5	18
E.P.S. ($)	0.90	1.06	1.26	1.44	1.52	1.62	12.5	1.85	2.20	2.61	17
Shares out (M)	4.42	4.59	4.69	5.24	5.74	5.77		5.82	5.87	5.92	
Income mix: Publishing (%)	35.7	39.8	49.7	43.6	45.7	48.9		49.1	48.7	47.1	
Employee benefits (%)	14.3	11.0	7.8	8.2	6.7	7.7		7.5	7.2	6.8	
Mitchellmatix (%)	0.0	0.0	0.0	0.0	−0.9	2.7		4.9	10.0	16.3	
Investment income (%)	50.1	49.2	42.5	48.2	48.3	40.7		38.5	34.1	29.7	

NOTE: The company does not break out Mitchellmatix from the total publishing segment. All Mitchellmatix numbers are PaineWebber estimates.
SOURCE: Jeff Adams, PaineWebber, May 9, 1986.

EXHIBIT 9 How Is Share Price Determined?

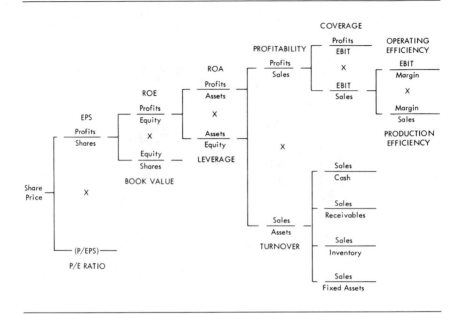

by profitability changes. Profitability, in turn, is seen as the product of leverage and asset profitability. Asset profitability is seen as the product of margin and asset intensity. If desired, the variables in the model can be decomposed into subvariables which provide greater levels of detail.

Sales growth. Several methods can be used to generate a bottom-up sales forecast. One is to extrapolate the historical sales trend. This extrapolation can be done with the aid of various statistical techniques, depending upon the desired degree of sophistication. An analyst needs to be careful in extrapolating sales. Unless underlying environmental factors in the economy are reasonably stable, forecasting by extrapolation can lead to serious error. For example, during the mid-1980s, growth in auto sales surged. However, extrapolation of this trend would have produced a bad forecast. Auto sales tend to follow a cycle, with years of surging demand giving way to seasons of declining sales. Another method of forecasting sales is to estimate sales per unit and then multiply by the number of units. This method is particularly appropriate if the primary means of growth is unit expansion. For example, the sales of each unit of a chain restaurant such as McDonald's tend to follow a stable growth pattern. The primary source of growth is the addition of new units.

This method can also be applied to forecasting the sales of a multiproduct company. The analyst estimates the sales for each product, then estimates total sales by adding up all products. This method can be applied to the auto industry. It is particularly appropriate if mix changes are anticipated due to rising sales of some products and sagging sales of other products. Exhibit 11 presents a sales forecast for Collins Foods which combines the unit and product line methods.

Margin growth. Margin growth is an important element of a bottom-up earnings forecast. Very few firms have stable margins over time and over differing sales levels, because the factors which affect margin tend to be volatile. The amount of price markup over cost is an important competitive weapon. The degree of fixed costs likewise exerts a big impact on margins.

If a firm sells a commoditylike product, pricing policy is an important method of competition. For example, gas stations and grocery stores often use price wars. If a firm initiates a price cut or responds to one by a competitor, its gross margin will suffer. A margin forecast must allow for such a possibility.

Nearly all firms experience fluctuating margins due to fixed costs. Ideally, the fluctuations will be upward as sales increases combine with fixed costs. However, firms with cyclical sales or facing severe competitive pressures can experience margin declines due to the combination of falling sales and fixed costs. The auto industry offers a good example of wide fluctuations in margin due to the combination of cyclical sales and relatively high fixed costs.

Consistent margin growth usually comes from one of two sources. One is spreading overhead/economies of scale. If some costs can be fixed over a wide range of production, then margin growth can continue throughout that range. The second source of continuing growth is due to more efficient production as a result of the learning curve. This concept states that learning effects permit each additional unit to be produced slightly more cheaply than the last. As cumulative production increases, unit costs decline. As a result, margins tend to increase, as long as the price is not cut.

Capital growth. Bottom-up earnings forecasts are also affected by capital requirements. If additional sales require additional capital investment, the resulting costs must be considered when forecasting earnings. Capital costs can either be interest costs (if debt is issued) or dilution costs (if equity is issued).

Perhaps the best example of the impact of capital costs is offered by the utility industry during the 1970s. Strong economic growth produced strong growth in electric power sales. As a result of inflation, the revenue growth of utilities was especially strong. However, earnings

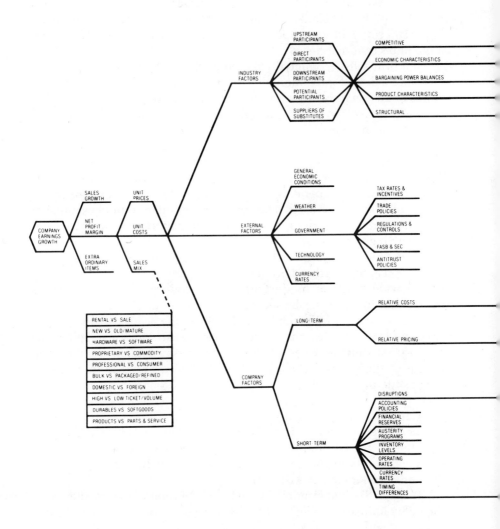

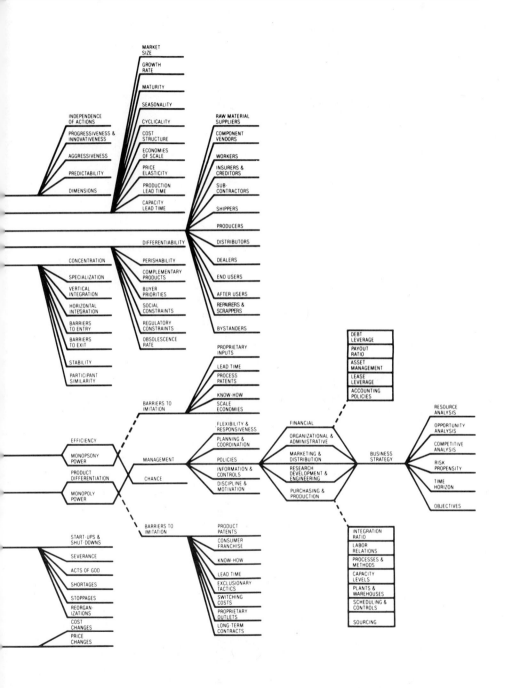

EXHIBIT 11 Sales Forecast for Collins Foods

	1981	1982	1983	1984	1985E	1986E	1987E	Growth 3 Year	Growth 1986–87
Sales/unit (000s):									
Kentucky Fried Chicken	391.24	432.82	503.84	461.45	550.00	594.00	641.52	11.61	8.00
Owned Sizzler	686.69	785.71	835.94	1,071.00	1,129.91	1,192.05	1,257.61	5.50	5.50
Franchised Sizzler	26.97	28.67	30.87	31.27	32.99	34.80	36.72	5.50	5.50
Food Service	11.88	13.72	16.85	23.18	27.82	33.38	38.39	18.31	15.00
Total	370.57	431.85	507.60	580.03	661.93	711.68	754.39	9.16	6.00
Units:									
Kentucky Fried Chicken	231	236	189	249	250	260	270	2.74	3.85
Owned Sizzler	137	133	142	139	143	153	164	5.61	7.00
Franchised Sizzler	341	315	302	312	321	353	387	7.44	9.63
Food Service	6	6	6	6	6	6	6	0.00	0.00
Total	715	690	639	706	720	772	827	5.40	7.09
Sales (millions):									
Kentucky Fried Chicken	90.38	102.15	95.23	114.90	137.50	154.44	173.21	14.66	12.15
Owned Sizzler	94.08	104.50	118.70	145.74	161.58	182.40	205.90	12.21	12.88
Franchised Sizzler	9.20	9.03	9.32	9.76	10.59	12.29	14.21	13.35	15.66
Food Service	71.30	82.30	101.10	139.10	166.92	200.30	230.35	18.31	15.00
Total	264.95	297.98	324.36	409.50	476.59	549.43	623.67	15.05	13.51

SOURCE: Jeff Cardon, Wasatch Advisors, March 1984.

did not keep pace with sales. In some cases, they experienced no growth at all. This is because new plants were required to meet the additional demand for electricity. New capital was required to build the new plants. Because capital was particularly expensive during this period, its costs negated the increase in sales.

As hinted at in the example, capital market conditions play an important role in determining capital costs. These costs are determined by both the general level of interest rates and the specific level of a firm's stock price in relation to its earnings or book value.

In the current economic environment, restructuring has come to play an important role in determining capital costs. Debt-financed stock repurchase clearly affects capital costs. Even asset restructuring usually involves some change in a firm's capital structure and capital costs.

Top-Down Analysis

Top-down analysis should begin at the international level. National factors should then be considered. Industry conditions should be thoroughly analyzed, including the industry stage.

International factors. In today's increasingly international economy top-down analysis should begin at the international level. The volume of world trade is growing. In some cases, foreign competition poses a greater threat than local, regional, or national competition. Global political and financial considerations can have a significant impact on domestic conditions.

Traditionally, the great advantage foreign competition has is low-cost labor. Its greatest disadvantages have been lack of technical skills and high transportation costs. As a result, foreign competition has been keenest in simple products which require a high degree of labor to produce and have a relatively high price-to-weight ratio; that is, shoes, for instance.

While these traditional factors remain largely intact, the growing technical skills of foreign competitors broaden the competitive arena. For example, the consumer electronics industry in general and the production of VCRs in particular have become based in the Pacific Basin.

International political and financial developments can exert an important influence on the degree of competition. For example, the United States may offer to permit free trade in shoes in return for a voluntary quota on a product more critical to the domestic economy.

Widely fluctuating exchange rates may provide the greatest competitive and analytical challenge. In recent years, the dollar has fallen, risen, and fallen relative to the yen. The magnitude of the fluctuations is beyond the ability of many competitors to offset by a competitive pricing policy. Instead, such extreme currency movements can effectively open up a market, close it, and then open it again.

Of course, international considerations loom largest for firms operating directly in the global arena. Their normal operations are directly affected by these international factors. For example, we have just lived through a period in which a strong dollar became a severe drag on the profitability of such multinational firms.

National considerations. The most obvious national influence on the operations of most firms is the condition of the national economy. During boom periods, the sales of all firms tend to increase. During recession periods, the sales of all firms tend to weaken. Several studies have found that national economic conditions explain nearly half of the earnings fluctuations of a typical firm.

Of course, some firms are more sensitive than others to fluctuations in the national economy. The degree of sensitivity is an important analytical consideration. Top-down analysis often combines this sensitivity estimate with a forecast of the national economy to produce an earnings forecast.

Another important national factor is interest rates. As with the general level of economic activity, firms respond with varying degrees of sensitivity to interest rate levels and movements. This sensitivity is also an important analytical factor. For example, interest rates are an important cost for a firm with a large amount of debt. Changes in rates can provide significant cost advantages or disadvantages.

Another national factor is inflation. While inflation exerts its impact through specific costs and prices, many believe that inflation results from national fiscal and monetary policies. Again, firms respond with varying sensitivities to inflation. And the degree of sensitivity is an important analytical factor.

Finally, the general legal and institutional framework, including the tax code, exerts a large impact on most firms. For example, the energy crisis led to the imposition of mileage standards for cars. The desire for clean air and water resulted in numerous antipollution laws. Proposed changes in the tax code may affect the real estate industry.

Industry considerations. Factors unique to a specific industry can exert an important influence on earnings. Possibly the most significant of those factors, as discussed in the section on judgmental considerations, is competition. Other important industry influences stem from similarities among firms in their sensitivity to national economic events. Researchers have found that these industry similarities account for a portion of earnings beyond that explained by national economic factors.

An important consideration in industry analysis is the developmental stage of the industry which can, in itself, account for many of the characteristics of a particular industry. The earliest stage of industry evolution is extractive. This stage includes mining (including oil production) and agriculture. The resulting products tend to be the necessary commodities of life. These industries face a relatively inelastic demand. As a result, even small shifts in supply can lead to large price fluctuations. Due to the commodity nature of the products, competitive advantage tends to depend on low-cost production capability. Firms tend to be large in order to reap scale economies.

Manufacturing is the next evolutionary stage. Two important differences separate manufacturing industries from extractive industries. One is that the manufactured products tend to be neither as necessary nor as commoditylike as extractive products. The other is that labor, including labor embodied in machinery, tends to be a more important factor of production for manufacturing firms.

Because manufactured products are less necessary, demand tends to fluctuate more. If costs are fixed—as they often are in manufacturing industries due to high reliance on capital goods—earnings can be rather volatile.

Service industries are the next stage of evolution. As their name suggests, service industries provide services rather than goods. Often, the service is rendered to supplement the extractive or manufacturing process, such as providing distribution of the goods produced by these industries. Labor is an ever more important factor of production. In fact, human capital is often an important element in rendering a service. This is clearly evident in a service business such as advertising. A creative writer has unique skills. These skills are not interchangeable with those of another writer, as the skills of a steelworker might be.

Earnings variability in the service industry tends to be the result of competition between firms in the industry. In contrast, causes of variability in the extractive and manufacturing industries tend to be due to factors outside of the industry.

The information industry seems to be the final stage of evolution. Because it is the final stage, it is difficult to define with any precision. Most likely it requires only human capital and produces information rather than data. The distinction between the information and service industries likely depends on the degree of convenience involved. Service industries provide convenience. Information industries provide services which could not be self-provided. For example, a diaper cleaning service provides convenience. A law firm provides "information."

In summary, knowledge of the stage of industry evolution helps the analyst focus on the most likely sources of earnings variability.

Summary

Preparation of an earnings forecast is a complex task. The nature of the forecast depends on the relative mix of statistics and judgment in its preparation. It also depends on whether the forecast is top-down or bottom-up.

BIBLIOGRAPHY

ABDEL-KHALIK, A. RASHAD, and JOSE ESPEJO. "Expectations Data and the Predictive Value of Interim Reporting." *Journal of Accounting Research*, Spring 1978, pp. 1–13.

ALBRECHT, STEVE W.; LARRY L. LOOKABILL; and JAMES C. McKeown. "The Time-Series Properties of Annual Earnings." *Journal of Accounting Research*, Autumn 1977, pp. 226–44.

ARNOTT, ROBERT D. "The Use and Misuse of Consensus Earnings." *The Journal of Portfolio Management*, Spring 1985, pp. 18–27.

_____, and WILLIAM A. COPELAND. "The Business Cycle and Security Selection." *Financial Analysts Journal*, March–April 1985, pp. 26–32.

BABCOCK, GUILFORD C. "The Roots of Risk and Return." *Financial Analysts Journal*, January–February 1980, pp. 56–63.

BASI, BART A.; KENNETH J. CAREY; and RICHARD D. TWARK. "A Comparison of the Accuracy of Corporate and Security Analysts' Forecasts of Earnings." *The Accounting Review*, April 1976, pp. 244–54.

BROWN, LARRY D., and M. S. ROZEFF. "The Superiority of Analysts Forecasts as Measures of Expectations: Evidence from Earnings." *The Journal of Finance*, May 1978, pp. 1–16.

BROWN, LARRY D., and M. S. ROZEFF. "Univariate Time Series Models of Quarterly Accounting Earnings per Share: A Proposed Model." *Journal of Accounting Research*, Spring 1979, pp. 179–89.

BROWN, LARRY D., and M. S. ROZEFF. "The Predictive Value of Interim Reports for Improving Forecasts of Future Quarterly Earnings." *The Accounting Review*, July 1979, pp. 585–91.

BROWN, LARRY D., and M. S. ROZEFF. "Adaptive Expectations, Time Series Models and Analyst Forecasts Revision." *Journal of Accounting Research*, Autumn 1979, pp. 341–51.

BROWN, P., and R. BALL. "Some Preliminary Findings on the Association between the Earnings of a Firm, Its Industry, and the Economy." *The Journal of Accounting Research: Empirical Research in Accounting: Selected Studies*, 1967, pp 55–85.

BROWN, PHILIP; GEORGE FOSTER; and ERIC NOREEN. "Security Analyst Multi-Year Earnings Forecasts and the Capital Market." *Studies in Accounting Research #21*, 1985.

_____, and J. KENNELLY. "The Information Content of Quarterly Earnings: An Extension and Some Further Evidence." *The Journal of Business*, July 1972, pp. 403–15.

_____, and V. NIEDERHOFFER. "The Predictive Content of Quarterly Earnings." *Journal of Business*, October 1968, pp. 488–97.

BUCHENROTH, S., and R. JENNINGS. "A Descriptive Analysis of the Time-Series Behavior of Financial Analyst Earnings Forecasts." Working paper, Indiana University, Bloomington, Ind., 1984.

CHUGH, LAL C., and JOSEPH W. MEADOR. "The Stock Valuation Process: The Analysts' View." *Financial Analysts Journal*, November–December 1984, pp. 41–48.

COLLINS, W. A., and W. S. HOPWOOD. "A Multivariate Analysis of Annual Earnings Forecasts Generated from Quarterly Forecasts of Financial Analysts and Univariate Time Series Models." *Journal of Accounting Research*, Autumn 1980, pp. 390–406.

COPELAND, R., and R. J. MARIONI. "Executives' Forecasts of Earnings per Share versus Forecasts of Naïve Models." *The Journal of Business,* October 1972, pp. 497–512.

CRAGG, J. G., and B. G. MALKIEL. "The Consensus and Accuracy of Some Prediction of the Growth of Corporate Earnings." *The Journal of Finance,* March 1968, pp. 67–84.

CRICHFIELD, T.; T. DYCKMAN; and J. LAKONISHOK. "An Evaluation of Security Analysts' Forecasts." *Accounting Review,* July 1978, pp. 651–68.

ECKEL, NORM. "An EPS Forecasting Model Utilizing Macroeconomic Performance Expectations." *Financial Analysts Journal,* May–June 1982, pp. 68–77.

ELTON, E. J., and M. J. GRUBER. "Earnings Expectations and the Accuracy of Expectational Data." *Management Science,* April 1972, pp. 409–24.

————; M. J. GRUBER; and M. GULTEKIN. "Expectations and Share Prices." *Management Science,* September 1981, pp. 975–87.

————. "Professional Expectations: Accuracy and Diagnosis of Errors." *Journal of Financial and Quantitative Analysis,* December 1984, pp. 351–63.

FOSTER, GEORGE. "Quarterly Accounting Data: Time-Series Properties and Predictive Ability Results." *The Accounting Review,* January 1977, pp. 1–21.

FRIED, D., and D. GIVOLY. "Financial Analysts' Forecasts of Earnings: A Better Surrogate for Earnings Expectations." *Journal of Accounting and Economics,* October 1982, pp. 85–107.

FULLER, RUSSELL J., and RICHARD W. METCALF. "Management Disclosures: Analysts Prefer Facts to Management's Predictions." *Financial Analysts Journal,* March–April 1978, pp. 55–57.

GIVOLY, DAN, and JOSEF LAKONISHOK. "The Information Content of Financial Analysts' Forecasts of Earnings." *Journal of Accounting and Economics,* Winter 1979, pp. 165–85.

————. "Financial Analysts' Forecasts of Earnings: Their Value to Investors." *Journal of Banking and Finance,* September 1980, pp. 221–33.

————. "The Quality of Analysts' Forecasts of Earnings." *Financial Analysts Journal,* September–October 1984, pp. 40–47.

GREEN, DAVID, JR., and JOEL SEGALL. "The Predictive Power of First Quarter Earnings Reports." *Journal of Business,* January 1967, pp. 44–55.

GRIFFIN, PAUL A. "The Time Series Properties of Quarterly Earnings: Preliminary Evidence." *Journal of Accounting Research,* Spring 1977, pp. 71–83.

HAWKINS, EUGENE H.; STANLEY C. CHAMBERLIN; and WAYNE E. DANIEL. "Earnings Expectations and Security Prices." *Financial Analysts Journal,* September–October 1984, pp. 24–38.

HITSCHLER, W. ANTHONY. "To Know What We Don't Know or the Caribou Weren't In the Estimates." *Financial Analysts Journal,* January–February 1980, pp. 28–32.

JAGGI, BIKKI. "Further Evidence on the Accuracy of Management Forecasts vis-à-vis Analysts' Forecasts." *The Accounting Review,* January 1980, pp. 96–101.

JOHNSON, TIMOTHY E., and THOMAS G. SCHMITT. "Effectiveness of Earnings per Share Forecasts." *Financial Management,* Summer 1974, pp. 64–72.

JONES, CHARLES P.; RICHARD J. RENDELMAN, JR.; and HENRY A. LATANE. "Stock Returns and SUEs during the 1970s." *The Journal of Portfolio Management,* Winter 1984, pp. 18–22.

————. "Earnings Announcements: Pre- and Post-Responses." *The Journal of Portfolio Management,* Spring 1985, pp. 28–32.

JOY, O. M.; R. L. LITZENBERGER; and R. W. McENALLY. "The Adjustment of Stock Prices to Announcements of Unanticipated Changes in Quarterly Earnings." *Journal of Accounting Research,* Autumn 1977, pp. 207–25.

KERRIGAN, THOMAS J. "When Forecasting Earnings, It Pays to Watch Forecasts." *The Journal of Portfolio Management,* Summer 1984, pp. 19–26.

KING, BENJAMIN F. "Market and Industry Factors in Stock Price Behavior." *Journal of Business* 39, 2, January 1966, pp. 139–90.

KLEMKOSKY, ROBERT C., and WILLIAM P. MILLER. "When Forecasting Earnings, It Pays to Be Right!" *The Journal of Portfolio Management*, Summer 1984, pp. 13–18.

LARSEN, ROBERT A., and JOSEPH E. MURPHY, JR. "New Insight into Changes in Earnings per Share." *Financial Analysts Journal*, March–April 1975, pp. 77–83.

LATANE, HENRY A., and CHARLES P. JONES. "Standardized Unexpected Earnings—A Progress Report." *The Journal of Finance*, December 1977, pp. 1457–465.

LEV, B. "Some Economic Determinants of Time-Series Properties of Earnings." *Journal of Accounting and Economics*, April 1983, pp. 31–48.

LOREK, K. S.; C. L. McDONALD; and D. PATZ. "A Comparative Examination of Management Forecasts and Box-Jenkins Forecasts of Earnings." *The Accounting Review*, April 1976, pp. 321–30.

LOREK, KENNETH S. "Predicting Annual Net Earnings with Quarterly Earnings Time Series Models." *Journal of Accounting Research*, Spring 1979, pp. 190–204.

MAGEE, R. P. "Industry-Wide Commonalities in Earnings." *Journal of Accounting Research*, Autumn 1974, pp. 270–87.

MANEGOLD, J. G. "Time-Series Properties of Earnings: A Comparison of Extrapolative and Component Models." *Journal of Accounting Research*, Autumn 1981, pp. 360–73.

McDONALD, C. "An Empirical Examination of the Reliability of Published Predictions of Future Earnings." *The Accounting Review*, July 1973, pp. 502–10.

MURPHY, J. E. "Earnings Growth and Price Change in the Same Period." *Financial Analysts Journal*, January/February 1968, pp. 97–99.

NELSON, C. F. "Rational Expectations and the Predictive Efficiency of Models." *The Journal of Business*, July 1975, pp. 331–34.

NIEDERHOFFER, V., and P. J. REGAN. "Earnings Changes, Analysts' Forecasts, and Stock Prices." *Financial Analysts Journal*, May/June 1972, pp. 65–71.

RULAND, WILLIAM. "The Accuracy of Forecasts by Management and Financial Analysts." *The Accounting Review*, April 1978, pp. 439–47.

STEWART, SAMUEL S., JR. "Corporate Forecasting." *Financial Analyst's Handbook.* Homewood, Ill.: Dow Jones-Irwin, 1975, pp. 907–27.

TRUEMAN, BRETT. "Why Do Managers Voluntarily Release Earnings Forecasts?" *Journal of Accounting and Economics*, 1986, pp. 53–71.

WAYMIRE, G. "Earnings Volatility and Voluntary Management Forecast Disclosure." *Journal of Accounting Research*, Spring 1985, pp. 268–95.

ZACKS, LEONARD. "EPS Forecasts—Accuracy Is Not Enough." *Financial Analysts Journal*, March–April 1979, pp. 53–55.

PART 4

Equity Investment Analysis

19

Analysis of Common Stocks

Harry Sauvain, D.B.A.
University Professor Emeritus of Finance
Indiana University

Studying common stocks is one of the most interesting things anyone can do—anyone, that is, who enjoys working with accounting data, learning how companies operate, observing what goes on in industries, and trying to interpret changes in the entire economic system. With ingenuity and diligence one can examine data that others have neglected and perhaps draw inferences that they have not been smart enough to infer. There is competition in this kind of activity and a kind of excitement that comes from knowing that your conclusions may be very profitably right or very expensively wrong. But it is a difficult kind of study because so many kinds of change affect the size of returns from common stocks and because the size of returns from one period to another vary widely.

THE LEGAL POSITION OF COMMON STOCKS

Common stockholders own the equity in a business corporation. The equity in accounting terms is total assets minus all liabilities and minus the right to assets of any preferred stock. Preferred stock is an equity-type security, but its owners are limited in their right to assets in liquidation. Common stockholders own what is left.

The chief legal right of common stockholders is the right to receive dividends when, as and if declared by the directors of their company.

The author wishes to acknowledge the valuable comments of Professor Mark Foster, Professor Emeritus of the University of Virginia.

But they stand last in line after payments are made to all other classes of securities. The compensation for this absence of preference is the absence of limitation upon the amount of dividends they may receive. When a company prospers over a period of time, dividends to common stockholders may double and quadruple. And with any pronounced increase in earnings and dividends per share, the market price per share may appreciate to provide sizable capital gains.

The other principal legal right of common stockholders is to vote at annual and special meetings of stockholders, usually on the basis of one vote per share. To the mine run of stockholders, this right isn't worth much. The ordinary stockholder signs a proxy authorizing one or more persons identified with management to vote his or her stock. Thus management is able to go to stockholders' meetings with proxies for enough stock to decide the actions to be taken at the meetings. However, this isn't always true. A stockholder who owns a sufficiently large portion of the outstanding stock may elect himself/herself to the board of directors under the system of cumulative voting. And one who owns a sufficient majority of the stock may control a company.

Some companies have outstanding two classes of common stock usually denominated Class A and Class B. The usual difference between the two is that one class is entitled to vote and the other is not. The purpose of this arrangement is to reduce the amount of money required to control a company. A variation of this two-class arrangement provides one vote per share for one class of stock and only a fraction of a vote per share to the other class.

Not long ago a leading company, General Motors, came up with the greatest innovation in common stock financing in the memory of the oldest analyst. In addition to its regular common stock, it issued a class of common stock identified as Class E stock with different rights than its regular common. This stock was issued in connection with the acquisition of another company. What is remarkable about it is that it does not share equally with the regular common either in right to dividends or right to vote. Instead, owners of Class E stock are entitled to dividends based on earnings of the acquired company which continues to operate as a wholly owned subsidiary. Subsequently, this leading company issued another special class of common stock denominated Class H stock to finance acquisition of still another company. Some assets of the parent company were transferred to this wholly owned subsidiary and the Class H stock is entitled to dividends based on earnings of the expanded wholly owned company.

THE PROBLEM OF STOCK SELECTION

First, let's define the problem. It is to estimate the most probable rate of return from owning a stock over a period of time such as one year and to estimate the risk assumed in such an investment. Total rate of return is dividends expected to be received plus or minus gain or loss of principal from change in market prices divided by cost of investment. Thus, if a stock may be purchased at $40, with an expected dividend of $2 during a year, and an expected market price of $42 at end of period, the total rate of return is $4 divided by 40, which is a rate of 10 percent.

The uncertainties of stock ownership being as they are, it is unlikely that even the smartest analyst can estimate the total rate of return for a year at a specified percentage and be right. It is better to estimate a distribution of rates of return with probabilities assigned to each rate and to take as the expected rate of return the rate that has the greatest probability of being realized in the estimation of the analyst. Rates with a probability of .05, which is 1 in 20, may be taken as the upper and lower ranges of the distribution and greater probabilities assigned to other rates in the distribution. For example:

Rate	Probability
8%	.05
9	.2
10	.5
11	.2
12	.05

Here the range of rates with a probability of .05 or more covers only 4 percentage points and the most probable rate is 10 percent. But the range of rates may be as broad as one thinks it should be. It might begin at 2 percent and increase by 2 percentage points to 16 percent with probabilities assigned to each rate. And the rate with the greatest probability may not be at the midpoint of the distribution, but may be whatever rate is considered most likely.

The range of rates is very important, because it indicates degree, or level, of risk. In the first distribution above the range of rates is only 4 percentage points. In the second illustration it would be from 2 to 16 points. Clearly the second stock is more risky.

Both the risk and return are subjective judgments based on study of the historical record of a company's earnings, dividends, and financial strength plus estimates of the effect on prices of developments in the economy that affect stock prices. The quantification of risk and return, however, should not be permitted to give an impression of mathematical precision. Such are the vagaries of the stock market that they may prove far from accurate. The way to improve accuracy is to review and possibly change estimates as new information becomes available.

Estimates of risk and return on stocks are relative. The analyst's task is to find the more favorable relationships of risk and return among some number of stocks that are considered the universe from which selection may be made. The problem may take the form of defining a level of risk and then seeking the one or more that seem likely to provide the highest rates of return. Or, it could take the form of defining a desired rate of return and seeking among the stocks that appear to offer that rate the one or more with the least risk.

THE EFFICIENT MARKET CONCEPT

Academic theorists have advanced a concept that, if valid, makes the estimation of risk and returns from stocks a mission impossible. Briefly, the idea is that the market price of a stock at any particular moment is a result of all information available about the stock up to that moment and its evaluation by sophisticated investors. The next change in price will be a result of new information, but no one knows what the new information will be. It may cause the price to rise or to decline. Therefore, future prices for stocks cannot be predicted with better than random chance that a prediction will be correct.

The efficient market concept assumes that there is a continuous flow of information to the public relevant to the value of stocks, that there are numerous investors alert to new information, able to evaluate it quickly and capable of prompt action according to their evaluations. This includes not only information about companies, but about industries, changes in the national economy and even in the political climate.

There is, indeed, a continuous flow of information to the public about all of these possible influences on the value of stocks. The federal securities laws require full disclosure of information about their businesses by companies that have publicly distributed securities beginning with the registration statement required by the Securities Act to the publication of annual reports, quarterly earnings statements, and the public announcement of significant events in their operations. Information about industries is available in all sorts of periodicals as well as in the publications of government agencies. Newspapers report information on changes in the national economy by publishing statistical data as well as interpretation of the data by economists and business leaders. .

But this flow of information is not perfect. There are time lags between events and public information about them. Frequently information is not as complete as stock analysts would like it to be. There are also lags in the interpretation of information by investors. Some are timid and not willing to act until additional information seems to confirm the initial bit of information. Some have to wait for approval by higher authorities in investing institutions before they can act. Thus the full effect of information may not be felt until some time after it is published and in the meantime other information may have influenced stock prices.

Probably the greatest defect in the system of publicizing information affecting stock prices is that some individuals have information about companies that is not public; it is called inside information. Company executives know a great deal more about what is going on in their companies than is revealed to the public. They know corporate plans for the future development of their businesses and of problems that are not evident to the public. They also know prospects for mergers or acquisitions before any public announcement is made about such things. Some inside information is known also to people in the lower ranks of the corporate hierarchy, such as the secretary to the president, or the head of the shipping department, or the engineer engaged in developing a new product. The federal securities laws try to discourage trading in stocks on the basis of nonpublic information by making it illegal, but the effort is not completely successful. There are always some people who have nonpublic information and some of them try to use it to make profits in the stock market.

A second assumption of the efficient market concept is that security markets function with such a high degree of efficiency that there are no impediments to transactions that give effect to changes in supply and demand following publication of new information. The markets are open to anyone who has money to buy or securities to sell. The cost of transactions is usually small relative to the value of transactions so investors are not deterred by transaction costs. There is such intensity of competition among middlemen in the markets that none can influence market prices by manipulating price quotations.

There is no doubt that there has been marked improvement in the operational efficiency of the security markets over a long period of years. In 1975, the Securities and Exchange Commission abolished the fixed schedule of commissions charged for services as brokers by members of the organized stock exchanges and there is now vigorous price competition for brokerage commissions. Members of the New York Stock Exchange may now go "off Board" to execute transactions in listed stocks when they can get a better price in another market. The over-the-counter market has been competing vigorously with the organized exchanges and with considerable success. The machinery for transmission and execution of orders has been greatly improved by electronic equipment.

It seems fair to say that the operational efficiency of the security markets is good, but not perfect. Efficiency is greatest for the stocks of large companies with large numbers of shares outstanding. These are the stocks that are watched most carefully and traded most actively with low transactions costs. However, there are thousands of companies with relatively small common stock capitalizations whose stocks are traded much less actively and with greater transactions costs.

This efficient market thesis is not capable of precise empirical verification. It may be almost literally true of short-term price changes, but not of changes over periods of months or years. There is a momentum in the affairs of business corporations that tends to continue into the future. A business is a combination of products or services, capital, management, and employees. It tends to continue in a given pattern of profitability until some strong force causes change. When such a pattern is defined, it is reasonable to estimate future prices within some moderate range of accuracy.

Eugene Fama, probably the greatest authority on the pricing efficiency of markets, says that, "The definitional statement that in an efficient market prices 'fully reflect' available information is so general that it has no empirically testable implications."[1]

Richard West concludes that even in efficient markets, investors need to know how to analyze risk levels and to understand the alternatives facing them.[2]

CAUSES OF UNCERTAINTY OF RETURNS

The term *risk* is commonly used in the singular, but uncertainty of future rates of return is a product of several different influences. These influences are sometimes called types of risk, but this is more for convenience than precise definition. In fact several different influences affect stock prices all the time and the effect of one cannot be distinguished clearly from the effect of another.

A principal influence on rate of return is the uncertainty of companies' earnings, dividends, and financial ability to meet their obligations. This is sometimes called *financial risk* and it is the chief occupation of stock analysts to estimate this influence on uncertainty of returns. Classifications of stocks as to riskiness by the rating agencies are ratings chiefly in terms of financial risk.

A powerful influence upon stock prices, particularly in recent years, is changes in market rates of interest. A rise in interest rates exerts a downward influence upon stock prices because higher interest rates make fixed-income obligations with little financial risk more attractive to investors. A decline in interest rates has the opposite effect. This influence is termed *interest rate risk*.

---

[1] Eugene F. Fama, "Efficient Capital Markets: A Review of Theory and Empirical Work," *The Journal of Finance*, May 1970, pp. 383–417.

[2] Richard R. West, "The Efficiency of Securities Markets," *Handbook of Financial Markets*, ed. Frank J. Fabozzi and Frank G. Zarb, 2nd ed. (Homewood, Ill.: Dow Jones-Irwin, 1986), p. 33.

Investors generally have an aversion to risk, but that aversion is not constant. Sometimes when the economy is expanding and stock prices are rising, their aversion becomes less and investment in stocks becomes more attractive to them. The fact that stock prices have been rising makes them seem less risky. There is also the opposite phase of aversion to risk. It comes during periods of recession and declining stock prices. They see prices of their stocks decline and their aversion to risk increases. This influence upon stock prices may be termed the *risk aversion risk.*

In virtually all investments there is the risk that the purchasing power of returns from investment will be reduced by price inflation. If the amount of return in dollars does not increase in a period when prices for goods and services generally are increasing, the purchasing power of the constant amounts in dollars decreases. However, if investment returns increase in dollar amounts, the increase reduces or eliminates the loss of purchasing power. There have been periods in our history when returns from common stock have increased proportionally more than the rise in the price level and provided a gain in purchasing power. This uncertainty of the purchasing power of future returns is called *purchasing power risk.*

Changes in the political climate may affect future returns from securities. Generally a shift in control of the federal government from liberal to conservative has a favorable effect upon stock prices because it implies a lessening of government regulation of business and greater freedom in the marketplace. Conversely, a shift from conservative to liberal has an opposite effect. This kind of change may be called *political risk.*

Financial risk is often termed *unsystematic risk* because it is peculiar to individual companies and their stocks. The other types of risk are called systematic risks because they are caused by changes in our whole economic system. Theoretically unsystematic risk can be reduced greatly by diversification among stocks of many companies whose earnings are affected by their different fortunes within the economic system. The idea is that losses or small returns on some will be offset by larger gains on others. However, it must be added that stocks at different levels of financial risk are affected differently by systematic risks. Therefore, financial risk is the logical starting point for estimating rates of return on stocks.

FINANCIAL RISK

The study of financial risk begins with earnings per share. Earnings are the source from which dividends are paid and changes in earnings are the basis for changes in amounts of dividends. Different companies follow different policies as to the proportion of earnings paid out as dividends, but study of the record of earnings and dividends provides a basis for estimating future dividends. Earnings are also a principal influence upon market prices. In the absence of strong systematic influences, changes in price tend to follow changes in earnings.

It is entirely reasonable to estimate risk and return on common stocks from historical information about companies and the economic environment in which they operate. Well-established companies with long records of operation have established patterns of change in earnings and dividends that may be assumed to continue into the future in at least an approximate manner. A company is an aggregation of capital, management and labor that does not change radically in any short time period. Patterns do change, but it is the business of analysts to anticipate changes, or at least to recognize them as soon as they appear.

The use of past patterns of change is well illustrated by the common practice of grouping companies according to their records and of referring to groups with similar patterns by some descriptive term. Thus, we often hear of blue chip stocks. They are stocks of large companies with broad lines of products and relatively stable patterns of increase in earnings per share at a moderate rate. A quite different group is called growth stocks. They are characterized by a relatively high rate of earnings growth for at least a few years past. Defensive, or income, stocks have a record of unusual stability in earnings and dividends through the business cycle. The opposite of income stocks is cyclical stocks that experience relatively wide swings in earnings that follow the business cycle. There are no precise standards for classifying stocks in this manner. What is one person's blue chip stock may be another's income stock.

HOW MUCH ARE EARNINGS PER SHARE?

Earnings per share are, of course, the net income after all expenses, interest, and taxes divided by the average number of shares outstanding during a year or a quarter of a year. But it isn't always that simple. Sometimes a company has outstanding bonds or preferred stock convertible into common stock at the option of security holders. Sometimes there are warrants or rights to buy stock. Some income statements give effect to extraordinary debits or credits to income and there may be tax loss carryforwards that affect the statement of earnings. It is the purpose of the common stock analyst to establish a record of earnings per share that shows as nearly as possible the regular, recurring earnings from operations. Sometimes this requires selection from among several versions of per share earnings the one that indicates most nearly the earning power of a company.

When convertible securities are converted, they increase the number of shares among which earnings must be divided and thus "dilute" earnings per share. The Financial Standards Accounting Board, which establishes rules followed by most public accounting firms, has ruled that per share earnings must be stated in such a manner as to give effect to conversion of some or all of the convertible securities outstanding. When convertible securities have been sold on a cash yield basis at less than two thirds of banks' prime lending rate at time of issue, they must be assumed to have been converted and the resulting amount of earnings per share is called primary diluted earnings. When these and all other convertible securities are assumed to have been converted, the per share earnings are said to be fully diluted. Thus an analyst may have to decide whether to use the per share figure without dilution, with primary dilution or with full dilution. The choice may be affected by an estimate of the likelihood of conversion within the time period of the analyst's estimate of risk and return.

Some companies issue warrants, or rights to purchase their stock, to buyers of their bonds or preferred stock at time of issue. Or they may be issued to executives of a company under incentive compensation systems. However they come about, they must be recognized as a possible cause of dilution of earnings per share and taken into account in determining diluted earnings per share.

Companies often make extraordinary charges against income in an accounting period by reason of large downward valuation of assets, or sale of fixed assets at a loss. There may also be extraordinary credits by reason of sale of fixed assets at a profit. Such debits and credits are not recurring and there is a question whether an analyst should recognize them in his determination of the most suitable version of earnings per share for the purpose of estimating future earnings. In any particular instance, the decision may be influenced by its surrounding circumstances.

The same sort of question arises when a company carries forward a tax loss from an earlier period and applies it to a current period, thus reducing its taxes for a current period and improving its statement of earnings. Large investment tax credits may also reduce taxes sufficiently to improve earnings for an accounting period. How much weight should be given to effects on earnings that are a result of our system of taxing corporations?

Mergers and acquisitions compound the problem of developing a series of annual per share earnings as a basis for estimating risk and return. Earnings after a merger are not comparable to those before, but prior years earnings for both companies can be reconstructed to create an historical record that is helpful. There is the same problem when a company sells an important product division or subsidiary company. If earnings of the portion of a business sold can be ascertained, the historical record may be revised by deducting its earnings from previously reported earnings. In any event, corporate financial statements for the period in which the sale occurs, report "income from continuing operations" as well as the regular statement of earnings. The record of earnings per share can be reconstructed in an approximate fashion by using the relationship between these two figures.

There are a couple of other circumstances that require adjustment of historical earnings per share, but they are easier to accomplish. Frequently, companies split their stock by issuing to shareholders more than one share for each share presently owned. Commonly stock is "split" by issuing two shares for one, but any ratio that provides more than one for one may be used. In order to make per share earnings before a split comparable to those after, earnings for earlier years must be divided by the ratio of new shares to old shares. Thus, a two for one split would require dividing earnings per share for previous years by two.

It is no small task to put together a series of earnings per share figures for 5 to 10 years past that are reasonably comparable and represent the basic earning power of a company. Whether some adjustments are made for unusual credits or debits to earnings is a matter of judgment, but at the very least, one should not be influenced in appraisal of the record by large variations in per share earnings that do not come from the regular operations of a company.

The Wall Street Journal reported on January 31, 1986, that, "A security analyst at a Xerox presentation yesterday, taking note of the number of special items, jocularly suggested that those present should vote on what Xerox's earnings actually were."

Table 1 shows the lower part of the income statement of a company and the manner in which the several different versions of per share earnings were presented.

THE VARIATION IN EARNINGS PER SHARE

Since earnings per share are the base for dividend payments and a principal influence upon market price, variations in earnings over time are a historical measure of financial risk. A decline in earnings may lead directors to lower dividends per share and an increase implies the opposite. Market prices tend to change as earnings change except as they are affected by systematic risk. Thus, the size of variations in earnings per share from year to year is a good measure of financial risk.

If per share earnings over a period of years fluctuated in a horizontal zone with no visible trend, one could take an arithmetic average of annual data and compare each year's amount with the average by expressing it as a percent of the average. Then the size of the percentage variation would be an indicator of financial risk. The greater the size, the greater the risk.

TABLE 1

XYZ COMPANY
Income Statement
Several Versions of
Earnings per Share
(in millions)

	1984	1983	1982
Earnings before extraordinary item.......	$68,083	$37,650	$26,425
Extraordinary item—benefit from use of tax loss carryforward	7,946	24,900	22,600
Net earnings	76,029	62,550	49,025
Earnings per share of stock:			
Primary:			
Before extraordinary item	$1.71	$1.48	$1.27
Extraordinary item	0.26	1.18	1.15
Net earnings	1.97	2.66	2.42
Fully diluted:			
Earnings before extraordinary item...	1.58	1.34	1.20
Extraordinary item	0.24	0.96	1.04
Net earnings	1.82	2.30	2.24
Shares of stock used in computing per share amounts:			
Primary (000s)	30,822	21,196	19,948
Fully diluted (000s)................	33,818	25,947	21,962

SOURCE: From annual report of a NYSE listed corporation.

But in fact there is almost always some trend in periodic earnings per share over a time period. The trend is usually upward, because most companies pay only part of their earnings as dividends and retain the other part to finance growth of the business. The portion retained adds to the amount of capital represented by common stock. Thus, with no great change in profitability, earnings per share increase because the amount of capital per share increases. However, the trend could be downward when profitability declines.

Then a measure of the instability of earnings per share is the average of the differences between trend values of earnings per share and reported earnings per share expressed as a percentage of trend values. This requires, first, computation of trend values for a period of years. With a computer, or a pocket calculator, this computation can be made readily using the least squares procedure to determine trend values. These trend values minimize the sum of the squared differences between per share earnings and their corresponding trend values. Then the difference for each year may be expressed as a percentage of trend

TABLE 2 Calculation of Trend Values of Earnings per Share

Year	Y	X	$Y(X - \bar{X})$	X^2	$A + B(X - \bar{X})$		-Y-trend
1	$ 1.80	-2	-3.60	4	$2.00	-.38	$1.62
2	1.60	-1	-1.60	1	2.00	-.19	1.81
3	2.00	0	0	0	2.00	0	2.00
4	2.10	+1	+2.10	1	2.00	+.19	2.19
5	2.50	+2	+5.00	4	2.00	+.38	2.38
	10.00		1.90	10			

$$A = \frac{10.00}{5} = \$2.00 \qquad B = \frac{\$1.90}{10} = 0.19$$

value and these percentages averaged to provide a statistical measure of the instability of annual earnings relative to the trend of earnings.

The least squares equation is Y-trend = $A + B (X - \bar{X})$. Y is annual earnings per share. Y-trend is trend values of Y. X is the numbers of the years in the series of per share earnings. Then A is the sum of Y divided by the number of years in the series; that is, the average of per share earnings. B is the sum of Y times (it's X value minus the average of the X values) divided by the sum of squared values of $(X - \text{average } X)$. This procedure is illustrated in Table 2.

The difference between Y and Y-trend may then be calculated as a percent of Y-trend for each year and these percentages averaged. The average of percentage differences is a measure of instability of earnings and may be compared with percentage differences calculated in the same way for other stocks. Table 3 illustrates this calculation for the data in Table 2. Figure 1 shows the Y and Y-trend data graphically.

The rate of increase in EPS trend in year i (represented by Y_i') can be estimated by applying the least squares technique to the expression

$$\log Y_i' = A + X_i \log B$$

Using the numerical values in Table 2, the annual rate of increase is 10 percent. Estimates of future earnings, dividends, and market price should be in percentage terms so that they will be proportionate to the past. For example, an increase in an amount from $1.00 to $1.10 is an increase of 10 cents and an increase of 10 percent. But an increase of 10 percent from $4.00 requires an additional 40 cents in earnings.

You can get a mathematically better measure of the variation in

TABLE 3 Percentage Differences between Y and Y-Trend

Year	Y	Y-trend	Y − Y-trend	| Y − Y-trend |
1	$1.80	$1.62	+$0.18	11.1%
2	1.60	1.81	−0.21	11.6
3	2.00	2.00	0	0
4	2.10	2.19	+0.09	4.1
5	2.50	2.38	+0.12	5.0
				31.8 ÷ 5 = 6.36%

periodic amounts from their trend values by calculating the coefficient of determination between per share amounts and trend values. This coefficient is the sum of the squared differences between Y and $\overline{Y}$ divided into the sum of the squared differences between Y estimate and Y. The higher the resulting percentage the greater is the stability of earnings. Table 4 illustrates this calculation for the data in Table 2.

The coefficient of determination is the best single quantitative measure of financial risk provided by historical accounting data. One can go on with such data and estimate a rate of total return for the next

FIGURE 1 The Variations of Annual Earnings per Share Relative to Trend Values of Annual Earnings (dollars per share)

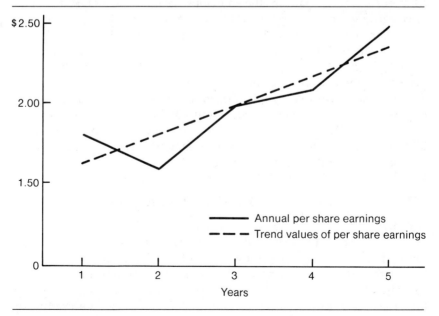

Annual per share earnings
Trend values of per share earnings

Years

TABLE 4 The Coefficient of Determination

		Total Variation				Explained Variation		
Year	Y	$\overline{Y}$	$(Y - \overline{Y})$	$(Y-\overline{Y})_2$	Y est.	Y	Y est. $-\overline{Y}$	(Y est. $-\overline{Y})_2$
1	$1.80	2.00	−0.20	0.0400	$ 1.63	$2.00	−0.37	0.1369
2	1.60	2.00	−0.40	0.1600	1.80	2.00	−0.20	0.0400
3	2.00	2.00	—	—	1.98	2.00	−0.02	0.0004
4	2.10	2.00	+0.10	0.0100	2.19	2.00	+0.19	0.0361
5	2.50	2.00	+0.50	0.2500	2.39	2.00	+0.39	0.1521
		10.00		0.4600	10.00			+0.3655

Coefficient of determination:

$$\frac{\text{Explained variation}}{\text{Total variation}} \quad \frac{0.3655}{0.4600} = +0.7946$$

NOTE: The slight differences between Y est in Table 2 and in Table 4 are due to differences in methods of calculation and to rounding of amounts.

year by extrapolating the data. For example, in the illustration above the trend value of earnings per share in the fifth year was $2.39, the dividend payment was $1.19 and the market price was 28½. These last two amounts are assumed. The rate of growth in earnings for the five years was 10 percent.

Now the sixth year's earnings may be projected for the next year at 10 percent more than in the previous year, which is $2.62. The price-earnings ratio is presently 12, so the market price at end of the sixth year will be about $31½. The dividend will be 50 percent of sixth year per share earnings, which is $1.31. Now the total return is $3 of capital gain plus $1.31 of dividends which is $4.31. The total return is 15 percent on the current price of 28½.

This way of calculating total rate of return is entirely quantitative; it requires no subjective judgments about conditions that will influence earnings, dividends, and market price in the future. It simply assumes that the future will be like the past. The element of risk is assumed to be the same in the future as in the past.

THE PROBLEM OF ESTIMATING FUTURE EARNINGS

Not many people who consider themselves knowledgeable about investment in common stocks are satisfied with an estimate of risk and return based entirely on extrapolation of the historical record. They believe that earnings, dividends, and market prices can be forecast more accurately than that. This need is evidenced by the fact that they pay for investment services of several kinds that periodically forecast future change in average stock prices and offer advice on which stocks to buy for maximum returns. Most stock brokerage firms do the same thing for their customers with periodic written and oral communications to their customers. Institutional investors employ analysts to seek out stocks with better than average risk-return relationships. So, as a matter of fact, demand induces supply and there are a great many people engaged professionally in common stock analysis and many professionals command good salaries.

The term *professionals* is used deliberately to suggest that common stock analysis is a difficult task requiring a broad knowledge of economics and finance because there are so many kinds of change that affect earnings and prices, and different kinds of change affect different kinds of stocks differently. Analysts must ascertain what kinds of change particularly affect different stocks and in the end evaluate the magnitude of their effect upon earnings.

Business corporations do business in an economic and political system that is worldwide. Most of our larger industrial companies sell some significant portion of their products in foreign markets where conditions are different than domestic markets. The domestic market is very much affected by the business cycle and estimates of earnings for the next year or two may be heavily weighted by an expected rise or decline in the cycle. Some industries or product categories are affected more than others by these periodic expansions and contractions in the national economy. In addition, there are long-term changes in the structure of the economy that increase the demand for some products and services and reduce it for others.

Corporate managements work constantly to adapt their business to these changing conditions. They modify their product lines from time to time as demand changes, they work constantly at sales promotion and new product development, and at the same time try to reduce costs and improve profit margins.

The complexity of the problem of estimating risk and rate of return virtually requires analysts to specialize in stocks of one or a few major industries. By specialization they learn which of all these conditions affecting earnings are most important for those companies. Frequently, their appraisals of stocks turn on only a few major influences upon corporate earnings. By working at it full time, expert analysts come to know the prospects for companies almost as well as the managements of those companies.

ASSEMBLY OF INFORMATION

The financial statements published by all companies with publicly traded stock are the core of the wide range of data required to appraise their stocks. The usual practice is to arrange income statements for recent years on a comparative basis so that changes from year to year can be observed. It is very helpful to calculate each item as a percentage of sales so that a change in relative size can be observed. Much the same may be done with balance sheets except that some kinds of assets and liabilities can be condensed and some ratios of balance sheet items can be added.

Many statistical series published by government departments and agencies are useful in interpreting changes in financial statements. Retail and wholesale price indexes for industries or groups of products make possible inferences about price changes affecting the products of a company. There is an index of industrial production with subdivisions for groups of industries and kinds of products. Data on gross national product and income show classifications by segments of the economy.

Corporate annual reports to shareholders generally try to present companies in the best possible light, but the law requires some disclosures that are useful to a stock analyst. There is always a management discussion of the results of operations in the year of a report and there are notes to consolidated financial statements that not only explain accounting policies but also provide additional information on particulars of the business operation. And in the full text of the annual report, managements discuss major changes in conditions affecting the company and often indicate business policies. For analysts who want to delve deeper, there is the 10-K report that companies are required to file annually with the Securities Exchange Commission. It provides a great deal of detailed and technical data that is of interest to stock analysts.

In the pages following, we will discuss the principal kinds of developments that affect the financial statements of industrial companies and illustrate their application to the Procter & Gamble Company. This discussion is all too limited. The kind of information used and its interpretation is different for public utility companies, merchandising companies and financial institutions. But the way of going about it is much the same for business corporations generally.

ESTIMATE OF SALES

The beginning point is sales because it is sales that bring in the money to pay operating expenses, interest, taxes and other charges, and leave a balance that is earnings on the common stock. Generally, fluctuations in dollar amounts of sales have a strong influence year by year on earnings for the common, because some kinds of expenses are more or less fixed and this permits some portion of an increase in sales to be carried down to the bottom line. Conversely, reduction of sales may have a disproportionately adverse effect on earnings.

The first step, of course, is to learn what kinds of products a company sells. This permits classification of products by industry and by the broader divisions of capital goods, consumers' durable goods and consumers' nondurable goods.

The economic environment affects sales.   The most important of environmental influences upon sales is, of course, the business cycle. Sales of capital goods are most affected by the ups and downs of the cycle because purchases can be deferred in the downward phase of the cycle and purchased in the expansion phase. Similarly, consumers' durable goods (automobiles, refrigerators) can be postponed and purchased when times are better. Nondurable consumers' goods are least affected by the cycle. Goods in this category are used up in a relatively short time and the demand for them is inelastic.

More fundamental for many companies over periods of several years are changes in the structure of the economy that affect the demand for goods of all kinds. The demand for all sorts of products is in a constant process of change as new products are developed, as the distribution of population by geographical areas changes, as the age distribution of consumers changes and as living standards improve. Think of the kinds of goods on which your grandparents spent their money and compare that with the kinds of goods on which you spend your money.

One of the more revolutionary changes in the past several decades is the great increase in the number of women in the labor force and in the number of two-income families. Women who are single and employed have different needs for goods and services than homemakers. Women who are married and employed have different family needs and two-income families have increased family income as well as greater discretionary income. The increased prevalence of two-income families affects in some degree the demand for all consumer durable and nondurable goods.

Demographic changes affect the demand for different kinds of goods and services. Population has become more concentrated in urban areas, particularly in suburban areas, while towns and rural communities have declined and even disappeared. Thus the neighborhood grocery has been supplanted by chain supermarket grocery stores offering a wide range of products. Population has also shifted among geographical areas with major trends to the south and southwest, but some countertrend to the northeast where development of high-tech industries has provided good employment opportunities.

Another kind of demographic change that has broad implications for many kinds of goods and services is the increase in longevity of the population. There are more older people (senior citizens) than used to be and the proportion of the population in the upper age brackets is expected to increase at an increasing rate. Moreover, a larger proportion of these older people are fairly well off financially by reason of employers' retirement income, social security, and income from their own accumulations of assets. Older people are demanding more modern and more convenient housing, more personal services, leisure time facilities, and medical services.

Markets outside the United States present a different problem of appraisal and a more difficult problem because conditions affecting demand for goods from the United States vary from country to country. Economies of other countries have different rates of growth and different business cycles. In some foreign markets, competition from their domestic producers is intense and more difficult to face by reason of government subsidies in one form or another. Tariffs, import quotas, and exchange rates for the dollar change over time periods. The rise in the value of the dollar in the 1980s seriously impeded American exports. Sometimes changes in the political climate in other countries affects ability of U.S. companies to do business in their markets.

Company policy affects sales. Table 5 shows sales data for Procter & Gamble and sales by categories of products. It is immediately apparent that this company is engaged almost entirely in manufacturing and selling consumers' nondurable goods. Some principal products are soaps, detergents, diapers, feminine protection products, coffee, baking mix, orange juice, cookies, and proprietary medicines. These products are consumed in relatively short-time periods and repurchased.

The stability of sales has been little affected by the business cycle in recent years. Neither is there evidence that sales are affected by changes in the structure of the economy, except that the annual rate of increase in sales has been slightly lower than the annual rate of increase in total personal consumption expenditures for the entire economy. The data on sales by categories of products shows a distinct decline in laundry and cleaning products relative to total sales and an increase in food and beverage relative to total sales. The percentage of sales in foreign markets shows a significant decline.

These relatively small changes in dollar amounts of sales fail to show that the company has engaged in a major restructuring of its product line in recent years. Beginning in 1981, the company introduced a series of new and technically improved products. They include Citrus Hill orange juice, a new series of products for feminine protection, a line of chocolate chip cookies, Ivory Shampoo and Ivory Conditioner, a new kind of laundry detergent, an improved brand of toothpaste, decaffeinated coffee, and a new brand of potato chips. It also acquired a pharmaceutical company that produces a new brand of analgesic for arthritis. Management reports that it is now competing in categories that represent 16 percent of total retail sales through food, drug, and mass merchandising stores and that the company has virtually doubled the size of the markets in which it competes.

TABLE 5 Sales Data for Procter & Gamble (dollars in millions)

	1982	1983	1984	1985
Net sales ($)	$11,994	$12,452	$12,946	$13,557
Sales by categories of products:				
Laundry and cleaning	4,736	4,756	4,715	4,886
Personal care products	4,450	4,780	4,930	5,107
Food and beverage	2,192	2,249	2,461	2,815
Other products	962	1,079	1,309	1,237
Corporate	(346)	(412)	(465)	(491)
Sales by geographical areas:				
United States	8,610	9,074	9,554	10,243
International	3,737	3,685	3,737	3,625
Corporate	(353)	(307)	(345)	(316)
Net sales (%)	100.0%	100.0%	100.0%	100.0%
Sales by categories of products:				
Laundry and cleaning	39.5	38.2	36.4	36.0
Personal care products	37.7	38.4	38.1	37.7
Food and beverage	18.3	18.1	19.0	20.8
Other products	8.0	8.7	10.1	9.1
Corporate	(2.9)	(3.3)	(3.6)	(3.6)
Sales by geographical areas:				
United States	71.8	72.9	73.8	75.6
International	31.2	29.6	28.9	26.7
Corporate	(2.9)	(2.5)	(2.7)	(2.3)

SOURCE: Annual reports of the Procter & Gamble Co., Inc.

This aggressive policy of new product development does not show up very distinctly in the distribution of sales among product groups as shown in Table 5, because new products are well distributed over the product categories. However, it is worth noting that sales of laundry and cleaning products have declined 3.5 percentage points relative to total sales and that the food and beverage category has increased 2.5 percentage points.

Sales in foreign (international) markets have become a smaller percentage of total sales in recent years. This is attributed in part to the high rates for the dollar relative to principal foreign currencies, but it might be inferred that management has been very much absorbed with new product development.

Thus we have identified clearly a development that will have a very important influence on future earnings—the restructuring of the product line.

Product Diversification

Broad diversification of products is generally considered desirable because the diversity of products distributes the risk of decline and failure of one or more lines of products. However, good diversification is more than just having a miscellaneous lot of products; it requires distribution of sales as nearly as practical over products that are subject to different risks. Even then, it must be kept in mind that all products are subject to changes brought about in some degree by developments in the national and sometimes the international economy.

In recent years there has been a distinct tendency for major industrial companies to broaden their product offerings. There has been a large number of corporate "takeovers" in recent years that have extended some companies into different manufacturing industries and even into service industries. Some companies have bought product divisions of other companies especially divisions manufacturing and selling nondurable consumer goods.

However, there is a different view of product diversification. It often dilutes earnings by averaging the more profitable lines with the less profitable lines. Many companies have achieved unusual prosperity by focusing management effort on a few products where it has some advantage such as patent protection over other companies. Highly profitable lines can often be kept so by continued technological improvements.

Company policy.   It has been established that Procter & Gamble has adopted a policy of greatly increasing the number of products it sells. But has this policy affected very much the level of risk in its product lines? The new products are in very much the same category of consumers' nondurable goods marketed through retail stores. It has not changed the stability of sales in the business cycle, but it may have improved the sales position relative to some structural changes in the economy. The two-income family, for instance, may use less soap and detergents and more orange juice and personal care products. But the company experiences strong competition in the market for the new products and has not reduced the riskiness of its entire product line. The new products must prove profitable if the restructuring is to benefit the company. Thus another important influence on future earnings has been identified.

Advertising and Sales Promotion

A company must sell its products in competition with other companies that sell much the same thing and accordingly amounts of sales are affected by the effectiveness of its advertising and sales promotion.

There are many methods of sales promotion and they may be used by a company in greater or less degree and with more or less effectiveness.

Companies that manufacture capital goods do not sell to the general public, but to other manufacturers. They would largely waste their money on newspaper advertising. They must rely chiefly on salespersons who call on customers. Banks use newspaper advertising, but it is largely institutional advertising designed to enhance the public's view of their reputability. Some companies sell entirely by mail-order catalogs and the quality of the catalogs directly affects their sales volume. Companies offering highly specialized products may find that trade journals are the most effective sales medium. Pharmaceutical companies rely on "detail men" who call on physicians and try to persuade them of the merits of their prescription medicines. Some companies provide direct telephone lines to their principal customers and promote sales by the convenience of ordering.

Consumer goods retailed to the general public require large-scale advertising in all the news media—newspapers, magazines, radio, and television. For companies in the automobile industry, large-scale advertising is essential and the same is true of companies selling soap and toothpaste. This kind of advertising must be done very skillfully to be effective and there is always some uncertainty about how effective a given advertising program will be. Sales promotion may take many different forms. The distribution of free samples is often used to introduce new products and discount coupons are often provided in newspapers.

Company policy.   You don't have to go very far to learn that the Procter & Gamble Company is a large advertiser in the news media and that generally its advertising has been successful. Some of its principal brand names are virtually household words established over a long period of years. Additionally, it uses whatever sales promotion methods are likely to be successful. At one time it packed diamonds, sapphires, emeralds, and garnets into all packages of several of its brand name products. The company has reported large outlays for advertising in support of the new products in its restructuring program. This advertising must be successful if the restructuring program is to sell in large volume the new products introduced in the last few years. There is some risk in this area.

New and Improved Products

In this age of rapid advances in all sorts of technologies, an important element in sales growth is improvement of established products and development of entirely new products. This is especially important in the so-called high-tech industries. Hardly a month goes by without a company in the computer industry bringing out a new model that is said to be smaller, faster, and cheaper than those of its competitors. The office equipment industry has been virtually revolutionized by introduction of electronic devices to speed references to company data and communication with other persons in the same organization. In the pharmaceutical industry there is great competition among companies to develop new products by laboratory research, and automobile companies are trying almost frantically to improve the performance of the century-old internal combustion engine.

The constant improvement in existing products may be as important as new product development for many kinds of companies. The packaged food industry has responded strongly to public demand for products preferred by today's nutrition-conscious consumers. The caffeine is taken out of coffee and cholesterol from margarine. Fly casting rods are now made of synthetic materials instead of bamboo.

Company policy. Intermingled with the product restructuring program of Procter & Gamble is a strong element of product improvement. Its new cookies are made by a patented process which uses one kind of dough for the inside and another kind for the outside. This increases their shelf life and improves taste. Their new line of diapers is an old one completely redesigned and manufactured in a different way. The new shampoo is a development of a brand of soap that has one of the best known brand names in the retail business and the new brand of toothpaste is an improvement on a previous formulation of that product.

The company's record of new product development and product improvement is one of the best of all companies providing consumer nondurable goods. Assuming that its sales promotion efforts are successful, its achievements in product development provides a base for a higher rate of growth in sales in future years.

Government Regulation

The time was when government regulation was associated principally with railroads and public utility companies, but that time has passed. In fact, government rules and requirements affect in some degree almost all companies whose stocks are publicly traded. Government agencies regulate everything from the use of publicly owned land in western states to the requirement that cigarette companies print on each package a warning that "Smoking by Pregnant Women May Result in Fetal Injury, Premature Birth, and Low Birth Weight." Manufacturers of packaged foods are required to print on packages detailed information about the ingredients and number of calories per serving. Drug companies must obtain approval of a government agency before they may publicly distribute new prescription products. Employers of any sizable number of employees are required to comply with standards for safety and health of employees established by a government agency. In recent history, government prescribed routes that airlines could use in carrying passengers and operations of trucking companies were affected by a number of rules concerning routes and the maximum number of successive hours drivers could drive.

In some lines of business, government regulation served to limit competition and to support rates and prices with significant benefit to regulated companies. This side of government regulation appeared conspicuously a few years ago when regulation was relaxed and the passenger airlines rushed to acquire new routes and competition brought something like chaos to the structure of airline fares.

The company.   Procter & Gamble is in a business less affected by government regulation than most companies. It must comply with rules of the federal Food and Drug Administration in labeling its food products and must have approval before offering new drug products to the public. But of all the conditions affecting sales, government regulation is least important.

The Quality of Management

Almost everyone who talks or writes about security analysis says that the quality of management of companies is the most important influence upon earnings. But the big question is: How do you appaise the quality of management? Some say that you appraise quality by the bottom line of the income statement; that is, by earnings per share on the common stock. If the record is good, the management is good. However, professional analysts generally want to know more about the upper echelon executives before coming to conclusions.

It is a common practice for analysts to visit the offices of companies in which they specialize, talk to officers, hear their plans for the future, and get personal impressions of the characteristics of management. Most companies welcome analysts from brokerage firms and large institutional investors because analysts' recommendations affect market prices for their stock. Company officers may not disclose material information that has not been made public, but they can discuss freely their hopes and aspirations. Then an experienced analyst who already has about all the information that has been made public may obtain impressions and draw inferences by discussions with company executives. They can also formulate their own estimates of the abilities of those to whom they talk.

For the purpose of estimating the success of a company over a period of several years, a major question is how management personnel is likely to change. Who will be the next chief executive officer? Sometimes the answer is obvious: there is a crown prince and everyone knows who he is. When an operating company is controlled by a holding company, the holding company generally determines the next chief executive and a visit to the holding company may enable one to sense which way the wind is blowing. If a company is controlled by a family, family considerations influence the choice. In most companies, though, there is a sort of hierarchy of top officers and a process of self-selection of the next CEO from among this group. In the course of several visits, an alert analyst may be able to estimate with a good chance of being right how the executive alignment will develop when the current CEO retires. In any event, he will have an appraisal of the abilities of the principal officers.

The company. Without attempting to appraise the quality of the management of Procter & Gamble, it may be noted that the policy of restructuring its line of products was adopted following the retirement of the chairman and CEO and the appointment of a new chairman. In fact, there has been a major change in the group of officers at the higher level. A new president was named, two new vice chairmen were appointed, there appeared a new executive vice president, and a number of new vice presidents. Apparently these new officers have taken a long view of the future and moved to adapt the company to that view.

ESTIMATING OPERATING PROFIT

In conventional income statements there is a listing of operating expenses following the statement of sales. Sales minus total operating expenses is operating profit. Operating profit divided by sales is the operating profit ratio. This ratio is the most important measure of changes in the profitability of a company from year to year, and an estimate of how it is likely to change in the future is a primary basis for estimating changes in earnings per share.

Interpreting past changes in the operating profit ratio is a particularly difficult task because it is subject to so many interrelated changes in the operation of businesses. An increase in unit sales volume tends to improve the profit margin because some operating expenses are relatively fixed, but this relationship varies with the nature of a business.

All of the kinds of changes considered in estimating sales must be taken into account in interpreting changes in operating expenses. Thus, change in product diversification may have an influence because some products normally provide larger profit margins than others. New product introduction with attendent sales promotion tends initially to reduce profit margin.

Among companies engaged principally in manufacturing, changes in production facilities continuously affect operating expenses. Plants grow old and obsolete with time and their per unit production costs increase. In the course of time, large companies with multiple production facilities reduce operations in less efficient plants or close them entirely. They build new plants with improved technologies and sometimes in new locations that afford cost advantages. Even relatively modern plants are improved by increased automation and changes in production processes to lower costs.

The cost and effectiveness of sales promotion and changes in policies of management in this area obviously have an effect. Government regulation may add to costs of doing business, or affect rates or prices, and certainly the quality of management affects efficiency of operations.

The efforts of common stock analysts to interpret changes in the principal influences upon the operating ratio and to estimate future changes are handicapped by lack of all the information they may desire. Many companies in their annual reports list only two or three items of operating expenses, which means that there may be many different influences upon a single item of expense. However, additional information is often provided in the text of annual reports and in the notes to financial statements. Companies like to publicize the construction of new plants and there are often news reports of important advances in automation. In the sections of annual reports under the heading of management's discussion of operations, there may be significant information about changes in a system of manufacturing facilities. Visits by analysts to company managements may enable one to draw inferences about the direction in which a company is moving. And visits to competitors may provide some critical comment on what a company is doing or not doing.

The company. Table 6 shows operating expenses and some supplementary data relative to sales for Proctor & Gamble.

Even to an unpracticed eye, a scrutiny of Table 6 shows that something was going wrong in the operations of this company in the four years for which data are presented. Although sales continued to increase at about 4 percent a year, operating expenses increased at a greater rate and the operating profit ratio decreased from 12.3 percent in the fiscal year ended June 30, 1983, to 7.3 percent in 1985.

Only two items of operating expense are shown in the consolidated income statement, but it is evident that the decline in the operating ratio was due largely to the increase in marketing, administrative, and other expenses, which rose from 22 percent of sales in the first year of the period to 25.7 percent in the last year. The cost of products sold as a percentage of sales has no distinct trend.

TABLE 6 Sales, Operating Expenses and Supplementary Data

	1982	1983	1984	1985
In millions of dollars				
Net sales	$11,994	$12,452	$12,946	$13,552
Cost of products sold	7,990	8,020	8,533	9,099
Marketing, administrative and other	2,639	2,903	3,026	3,477
Total operating expenses	10,629	10,923	11,579	13,576
Operating profit	1,365	1,529	1,387	976
Supplementary data:				
Depreciation	$ 267	311	330	367
Capital expenditures	625	604	906	1,122
Research and development costs	286	327	369	400
In percent of net sales				
Net sales	100.0%	100.0%	100.0%	100.0%
Cost of products sold	66.6	64.4	66.1	67.1
Marketing, administrative and other	22.0	23.3	23.3	25.7
Total operating expenses	88.6	87.7	89.4	92.8
Operating profit	11.4	12.3	10.6	7.2
Supplementary data:				
Depreciation	2.2	2.5	2.5	2.7
Capital expenditures	5.2	4.9	7.0	9.0
Research and development costs	2.4	2.6	2.8	3.0

NOTE: The company's fiscal year ends June 30.

The supplementary data contribute a little to understanding of the change in profit margin ratio. Depreciation, which is included in cost of goods sold, increased slightly and may account for the slight increase in that item of expense. Capital expenditures, which are not an operating expense, increased. This does not affect operating profit but it does suggest improvements in plant and equipment that may bring economies in cost of goods sold. Research and development expenses are relatively small in amount, but increased sufficiently to suggest greater effort in product development.

Information in the company's annual reports make clear that the restructuring of the product line that began in 1983 required the increase in advertising and sales promotion expense relative to amounts of sales. The introduction of several new major brands of products had to be supported by such expenditures on a large scale.

Earnings by Product Categories

Just how this policy of product restructuring has worked out by product categories is shown in Table 7. The data include a small amount of other income and other expense in addition to operating profit.

TABLE 7 Earnings before Income Taxes by Product Categories (dollars in millions)

Product Category	1982		1983		1984		1985	
	Amount	Percent	Amount	Percent	Amount	Percent	Amount	Percent
Laundry and cleaning products	$ 660	47.2	$ 725	46.8	$ 740	51.9	$ 691	68.8
Personal care products	550	39.3	694	44.8	689	48.3	332	33.1
Food and beverage	133	9.5	117	7.5	(91)	(6.3)	(110)	(11.0)
Other products	53	3.8	29	1.9	96	6.7	104	10.4
Corporate	3	0.0	(15)	0.0	(7)	(0.0)	(13)	(1.3)
Total earnings	$1,399	100.0	$1,550	100.0	$1,427	100.0	$1,004	100.0

NOTE: Discrepancies in total percentages due to rounding.

What stands out in the distribution of earnings by product categories is the severe decline in the profitability of the food and beverage category. In the last two years this division operated at a loss. Although there is no information about the distribution of advertising and sales promotion expenses by product categories, it is a reasonable inference that a large portion of these expenses were allocated to foods and beverages. Many of the new and improved products fall in this category and these are the products for which the company made the greatest sales promotion effort. Earnings of the personal care products division were substantially reduced in the last year of the series and this, too, is probably due to heavy advertising of new products.

The laundry and cleaning products, long the mainstay of the company's earnings, increased in amounts and in proportion to total earnings until 1985. Then the dollar amount declined, but the percentage of total increased by reason of decline in total earnings. Other products, which include cellulose pulp, chemicals, and animal food ingredients, prospered in these years and became a more important segment of the company's earnings.

This analysis supports strongly the conclusion that the decline in earnings in the past few years is attributable chiefly to the very large expenditures for promotion of new and improved products. It indicates that among all of the influences upon earnings in the future by far the most important is the success of the policy of product restructuring combined with reduction in expensive sales promotion.

THE EARNINGS SECTION OF THE INCOME STATEMENT

In the usual arrangement of the income statement there is first sales and then operating expenses. Deduction of operating expenses from sales gives operating profit. Generally there are some items of income from sources other than operating profit and there may be some expenses not considered operating expense. Other income is added to operating profit and other expense is deducted to yield total income. Then interest on debt is subtracted and the balance is net income before taxes. Sometimes this amount is reduced by tax losses carried forward. Deduction of taxes gives net earnings for the common stock. This "bottom line" is the one that tells the story for common stockholders. It is usually converted to earnings per share by dividing the total by the average number of shares outstanding during the period of the earnings statement.

It is helpful to develop some supplementary data from the income statement such as the effective income tax rate on taxable income, the rate of earnings on total common equity, the percentage of net earnings distributed as dividends, the book value per share, and the average number of shares outstanding.

Changes in all of these items following the statement of operating profit deserve examination because there may be changes in amounts from year to year that affect significantly earnings for the common stock. *Other income* may change as a result of change in relationships with affiliated companies, or in amount of income from affiliated but unconsolidated companies, or in amount of income from securities owned for investment. Extraordinary gains on sale of capital assets may appear under this heading. Similarly, there are often *other expenses* not considered to be operating expenses and in this category there may be unusual charges for write-down of assets or for loss on capital assets sold. Tax losses carried forward may substantially reduce taxes in one year and not appear in another. The net of other income and other expenses is added to, or deducted from operating profit to arrive at total income before interest expense. The balance after interest is net earnings subject to tax.

There are several statistical series that may be calculated using the earnings data. One is the effective income tax rate which is amount of income tax divided by net earnings subject to tax. This rate evidences tax advantages gained by investment credits, tax losses carried forward and other "tax breaks." It is helpful to know the rate of earnings after taxes on the common stock equity. A financially successful company shows a rate on common equity in the range of 10 to 20 percent. Then the proportion of earnings paid as dividends is important because retained earnings are added to equity capital and increase book value per share. Book value may be included in supplementary data for ready observation of its growth from year to year. The average number of shares outstanding period by period may be observed to see the effect of any dilution by conversion of securities or sale of stock at less than book value. Sometimes there is an increase in book value per share by repurchase of stock by the company.

The Company

Table 8 shows the earnings section of the income statement of the Procter & Gamble Company.

The most striking changes evidenced by Table 8 are the decline in earnings per share in 1985, the first in some 20 years, and the continued increase in amount of annual dividends per share throughout the period. The increase in dividends in 1985, in face of a sharp drop in earnings, may be taken as evidence that management considers the earnings shrinkage to be temporary and expects full recovery within a year or two.

There are no very unusual changes in the other items in the earnings section—no convertible securities, no tax loss carryforwards and no extraordinary credits or charges to income. However, the shrinkage in

TABLE 8

PROCTER & GAMBLE COMPANY
Income Statement—The Earnings Section
(dollars in millions except per share data)

	1982	1983	1984	1985
Operating profit	$1,365	$1,529	$1,387	$ 976
Other income	129	129	179	193
Total income	1,494	1,658	1,566	1,169
Less: interest expense....	95	108	139	165
Income before taxes......	1,399	1,550	1,427	1,004
Less: income taxes.......	622	684	537	369
Net earnings	777	866	890	635
Earnings per share.......	$ 4.69	$ 5.22	$ 5.35	$ 3.80
Dividends per share	2.05	2.25	2.40	2.60
Retained earnings per share................	2.64	2.97	2.95	1.20
Supplementary data:				
Effective income tax rate	44.5%	44.1%	37.6%	36.8%
Rate of earnings on common equity	28.7%	18.8%	17.5%	12.0%
Dividends as percentage of earnings	43.7%	43.1%	44.9%	68.4%
Book value per share...	$ 25.14	$ 27.73	$ 30.53	$ 31.53
Average shares outstanding (in millions)............	165.6	165.9	166.4	167.2

earnings in 1985 was cushioned to some extent by an increase in other income, an increase in interest expense, which is tax deductible, and a decline in the effective tax rate. These changes enabled the company to report an increase in earnings per share in 1984, despite a decrease in operating profit in that year. The supplementary data show a sharp decline in the rate of earnings on equity capital in 1985. With the unusually large percentage of earnings paid as dividends, there was a relatively small increase in book value per share. Continued retention of a relatively small portion of earnings would reduce the importance of retained earnings a source of equity capital. The average number of shares of common outstanding has increased only slightly in recent years.

STRENGTH OF THE BALANCE SHEET

When financial analysts discuss a company which they regard with favor, they almost always remark at some point, "And it also has a strong balance sheet." The point is important. Many a company with a good record of earnings and apparently excellent prospects for the future has experienced some degree of calamity because it had a weak balance sheet. Often it has tried to do too much business with too little capital or too much borrowed capital. Conversely, a weak company that has been struggling to establish a relatively new line of products may succeed because it had a strong balance sheet; which is to say that it had the capital to get its products established in the market. With a strong balance sheet, a company can finance new product development, improve the technology of production, expand its distribution system, and spend the money necessary for advertising and sales promotion.

Many financial analysts devote a great deal of attention to the current assets and current liabilities section of the balance sheet. There are usually four or five items on each side of the current section and each of them can be scrutinized in some detail, but often a review of total current assets and liabilities is sufficient to indicate distinct weakness or strength. The dollar amount of net working capital (current assets minus current liabilities) compared year by year shows whether working capital is growing more or less consistently with the growth of sales. If so, there is little cause for concern.

Table 9 shows a summary of the working capital position of the Procter & Gamble Company.

Writers on analysis of financial statements often place great emphasis on the current ratio; for example, current assets divided by current liabilities, and textbooks often say that the ratio should be at least 2 to 1. Actually, the current ratio cannot be appraised intelligently unless one goes on to study the conditions that affect the level of that ratio, such as the terms of sale, inventory turnover, terms of purchase, and the amount of bank loans and other liabilities due within one year. When there are indications of weakness in the current position, study of these conditions is clearly indicated. Procter & Gamble has gotten along very well with a current ratio of about 1.6 to 1.8. The other part of the balance sheet where analysts look for strength or weakness is in the capitaliza-

---

TABLE 9

PROCTER & GAMBLE COMPANY
The Working Capital Position
(in millions)

	1982	1983	1984	1985
Current assets	$ 3,113	$ 3,468	$ 3,656	$ 3,816
Current liabilities............	1,912	2,078	2,374	2,078
Working capital.........	1,201	1,390	1,282	1,738
Current ratio	1.63	1.67	1.54	1.84
Sales.....................	$11,994	$12,452	$12,946	$13,552

tion section. Capitalization consists of bonds, preferred stocks, and the common equity. The main point is that too much debt is a potential source of trouble; interest must be paid in full when due or the bankruptcy court looms ahead. On the other hand a moderate amount of debt on the balance sheet of a profitable company contributes to earnings because its cost, after adjustment for the tax deductibility of interest, is low. If a company can borrow at a low rate and earn a higher rate, the excess belongs to the common stockholders. Debt leverages earnings upward. The governing factor in judging the strength of capitalization is the record of stability of earnings. Companies with particularly stable earnings can afford a relatively high percentage of debt in total capitalization and the contrary is true.

The Procter & Gamble Company had long-term debt at the end of fiscal 1985 equal to 13.6 percent of total capitalization. In view of the long record of relatively stable earnings, the modest debt ratio contributes to the stability of the balance sheet and provides modest leverage for net earnings. The conclusion is that the company has a strong balance sheet.

SUBJECTIVE ESTIMATES OF RISK AND RETURN

A thorough and thoughtful study of a company over a period of years ought to provide a better estimate of risk and return than an extrapolation of the pattern and trend of earnings and dividends per share. Such a study reveals the principal influences upon earnings and enables an analyst to base estimates of the future upon the chief causes of change rather than upon a multitude of conditions that might affect earnings to some extent.

Thus, in the case of Procter & Gamble, it is clear that its fortunes depend very largely upon the success of its restructuring of product lines and that this depends in considerable part upon success of its advertising and sales promotion efforts. Capital outlays have improved some production facilities and there is likely to be little increase in cost of products sold. Marketing, administrative, and other expenses were at a high level in 1985, by reason of a full-scale sales promotion program. In 1986, there may be some increase, but not very much. These observations suggest an increase in operating profit of between 2 and 3 percentage points. There is nothing to suggest change in other income or in interest expense. If these estimates are about right, taxes will increase about 1½ times and net earnings will be $780 million, which is $4.64 per share in 1986 as compared with $3.80 in 1985.

About the first of October 1985, the stock of the company was selling at about 56½, which is 14.9 times 1985 earnings. Assuming no change in systematic risk, the price-earnings ratio on October 1, 1986, is estimated at 16 times 1986 earnings, which indicates a market price of 74¼ . It is unlikely that the amount of annual dividend will change from the 1985 figure of $2.60, until there has been a greater recovery in per share earnings.

The total rate of return, then, is a dividend of $2.60 plus a capital gain of $17.75, which is $20.35. On an initial investment of 56½, the total rate of return is about 36 percent.

These conclusions have been reached with too much confidence; it is time to pause and consider the chances, that they are wrong and perhaps wrong by a large margin. The probability of realizing other rates of return must be considered in order to estimate the riskiness of a purchase at 56¼. The dividend history of the company indicates that management is very unlikely to reduce the dividend barring some financial catastrophe, and is unlikely to raise it until pre-1985 levels of earnings have been attained. The great uncertainty is market price. Failure of earnings to recover in 1986 would reduce the price-earnings ratio and perhaps reduce market price below 56½ percent. There is some chance of a negative rate of return. There is a greater probability that earnings will not recover in 1986, to the estimated amount. This would mean a smaller amount of earnings per share and a lower price earnings ratio. On the other side, there is some chance of earnings in 1986 increasing to a larger amount than $4.64, and for the market price on October 1, 1986, to be considerably larger than 74¼.

Here is a subjective probability distribution of total rates of return on Procter & Gamble stock for the year ended October 1, 1986:

Rate	Probability
Loss	.05
10%	.10
20	.25
36	.40
40	.15
45	.05
	1.00

Note that this distribution is skewed toward lower rates of return; the estimator thinks that the chance of a lower future rate is greater than the chance of a higher rate.

PRESENT VALUE CONCEPT

This calculation of the rate of total return on the stock of Procter & Gamble Company takes no account of the present value of money. One could discount future dollars at a rate of return considered appropriate to the degree of risk and add the sum of present values to arrive at the worth of the stock today.

TABLE 10 Present Value of a Series of Amounts to Be Received

At End of Year	Amount of Dividend	Discount Factor	Present Value
1	$ 1.000	.909	$ 0.909
2	1.060	.826	0.876
3	1.123	.751	0.843
4	1.191	.683	0.813
5	1.262	.621	0.784
6	1.338	.564	0.755
7	1.419	.513	0.728
8	1.504	.467	0.702
9	1.594	.424	0.676
10	1.689	.385	0.650
Principal	33.780	.385	13.010
Total present value			$20.75

The present value calculation is often used to discount at a suitable rate a series of future payments increasing at an assumed rate per period. Assume that a dividend on a stock is expected to be $1.00 at the end of the first year and to increase at a constant rate of 6 percent per annum for 10 years. These projected dividends are to be discounted at the rate of 10 percent and a principal amount equal to 20 times the dividend in the 10th year is to be received at the end of the 10th year. Table 10 illustrates the procedure. Tables of compound interest and discount may be used to extrapolate the amounts of dividends and their present values.

When the rate of increase and the rate of discount are constant for the time period in which amounts are to be received, the calculation may be shortened by discounting amounts by the percentage by which the rate of discount exceeds the rate of increase, except that the amount of principal to be recovered at end of period must be discounted at the full discount rate.

SYSTEMATIC RISK

If estimation of risk and future rates of return on individual common stocks in terms of financial risk seems a complex procedure, the estimation of total risk is more so. It must also take into account changes in rates of return on stocks caused by systematic risk. We have previously defined systematic risk as the uncertainty of future influences on total rates of return due to changes in the total economic environment. The most important of these risks is that of changes in open-market rates of interest on obligations free of financial risk, but they also include changes in investors' aversion to risk, price inflation, and changes in the political climate. Unfortunately, the precise effect of these changes on stock prices cannot be measured separately. We can only observe changes in stock prices and changes in the different kinds of systematic risk and draw inferences about the cause and effect relationship.

Historically, changes in interest rates have had the greatest effect on stock prices of all the systematic risks. Interest rates on long-term government bonds reached a very low level in the early 1950s, and crept gradually upward until the latter 1960s when they stood at about 5½ to 6 percent. Then yields rose steeply to a peak of about 15 percent in 1981. Meanwhile, average annual earnings per share on S&P's 500 stocks increased from about $5.00 in the late 1960s to about $15.00 in 1981. The tripling of earnings would ordinarily be the basis for a corresponding rise in average stock prices, but it did not follow. In fact, the depressing effect of rising interest rates permitted a rise of less than 50 percent in average stock prices to 1981.

In the early 1980s the power of interest rate changes was demonstrated even more impressively. Interest rates on long-term government bonds fell dramatically from the lofty level of 15 percent to about half that rate in 1986. The result was a strong rise in average stock prices. Prices increased 2½ times from 1980 to 1986. This boom in stock prices gained only small support from the moderate improvement in average earnings per share. The relationship of stock prices, interest rates and average annual earnings per share for Standard & Poor's 500 Stock Index from 1979 through 1985 is shown in Figure 2.

In the latter part of the bull market of the 1980s, there was undoubtedly a decline in investors' aversion to risk. The period was one of good feeling and increasing confidence in the growth of the American economy. A sustained rise in stock prices always generates greater confidence that prices will continue to rise. As the market goes up, the aversion to risk in common stocks goes down.

In this period the political scene shifted in a manner to encourage investor confidence. The president was popular with the people and the government was conservative with a trend increasingly toward a free market economy.

Price inflation has played a considerable role in the markets of the last two decades, but its influence on stock prices was exerted chiefly by its effect on market rates of interest. The annual rate of increase in consumer prices rose from about 3 percent in 1967 to a peak of more than 13 percent in 1979. High rates of inflation were a principal cause of the rise in interest rates during the same period. As a general rule, investors demand rates of interest that are sufficiently greater than the rate of price inflation to leave a balance as real return on investment after

FIGURE 2 Interest Rates, Earnings per Share and Stock Prices for Standard
& Poor's 500 Stock Index (the vertical scale measures percentage
changes)

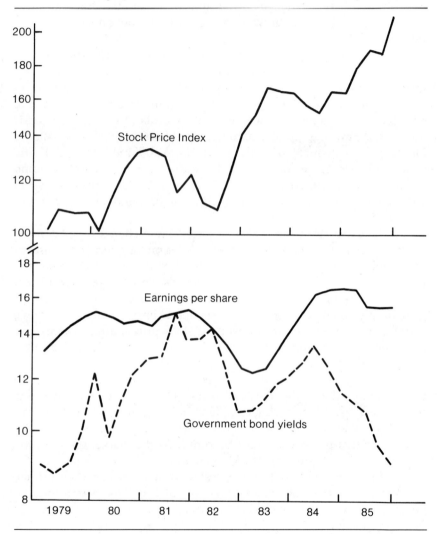

deduction of the rate of price inflation. When average annual rates of
price inflation became smaller interest rates declined accordingly.

It has sometimes been said that common stocks are a good inflation
hedge; that is, that returns on stocks increase sufficiently as the price
level rises to compensate for decrease in purchasing power of the dollar.
This has not worked out very well in the recent period of pronounced

TABLE 11 Instability of Annual Rates of Total Return for Standard & Poor's 500 Stock Index

Year	Y	Y-trend	Y − Y-trend	$\dfrac{\mid Y - Y\text{-}trend \mid}{Y\text{-}trend}$
1979	11.9%	13.28	−1.38	10.4%
1980	31.3	14.45	16.85	116.6
1981	−4.8	15.63	−20.43	130.7
1982	20.3	16.80	3.50	20.3
1983	22.2	17.08	4.22	23.5
1984	5.9	19.15	−13.25	69.2
1985	30.8	20.33	10.47	51.5
Total				422.2%
Average				60.3%

price inflation, but over relatively long periods in the past average annual rates of return on large numbers of stocks have exceeded comparable average annual rates of return on high-grade bonds. Thus they have provided better returns in constant dollars than bonds.

SYSTEMATIC RISK AND TOTAL RATES OF RETURN

The wide fluctuations in average stock prices over periods of years indicates clearly that systematic risk is a major influence upon rates of total return on common stocks. Thus, total risk in terms of the instability of annual rates is greater than financial risk. Total risk can be measured by the same statistical methods used in measuring the instability of earnings per share; that is, by taking differences between annual total rates of return and the trend values of those rates and then expressing their magnitudes as percentages of trend values. The average of annual percentages for a period of years is a quantitative measure of total risk and such averages may be used to compare risk in one stock with risk in another. Table 11 shows variations in annual total rates of return (Y) on Standard & Poor's 500 Stock Index for the period 1979–85.

Data for this broad average of stocks may be used as a basis for comparison with individual stocks. Table 12 shows the same calculations for the Procter & Gamble stock.

ON FINANCIAL RISK AND SYSTEMATIC RISK

Financial risk is a basic element in estimation of total rates of return. It is the kind of risk that must first be determined before systematic risks can be considered. Different grades of stocks in terms of financial risk are differently affected by systematic risk. Thus income stocks with

TABLE 12 Instability of Annual Rates of Total Return for Procter & Gamble Stock

Year	Y	Y-trend	Y − Y-trend	$\frac{Y - Y\text{-}trend}{Y\text{-}trend}$
1979	−13.3%	10.35%	−23.65	228.5%
1980	−2.3	11.20	−13.50	120.5
1981	22.2	12.05	+10.15	84.2
1982	52.2	12.90	+39.30	304.7
1983	0	13.75	−13.75	100.0
1984	4.0	14.60	−10.60	72.6
1985	27.5	15.55	+11.95	76.8
Total				987.3
Average				141.0%

relatively small financial risk are most affected by changes in interest rates. They are bought for income rather than for price appreciation and the dividend yield is what makes them attractive. They compete more directly with bonds than do stocks of other general categories in financial risk, so when yields on bonds change yields on income stocks change in the same direction. Conversely, speculative growth stocks are least affected by systematic risk, prospective appreciation in price is the objective of investors, and bond yields do not compete with the prospect of large capital gains. Blue chip stocks are less affected by changes in bond yields than income stocks, but more affected than speculative stocks. Cyclical stocks may be helped by cyclical decline in interest rates in the latter part of a business recession.

Similarly, the more risky stocks in terms of financial risk are more influenced by changes in investors' aversion to risk than income stocks. Growth stocks flourish in the market when aversion to risk is relatively low, and conversely. Blue chip stocks are sensitive to changes in the political scene.

Clearly, investment in common stocks is no child's play. Useful estimates of risk and probable return in terms of financial risk require careful, thorough, and continuous consideration of the almost innumerable influences that constantly affect the size of dividends and the level of market prices. But constant study of how changes in the economy, in industries and in individual companies enable common stock analysts to identify the principal influences on individual stocks and to focus on them in estimating financial risk. Consideration of systematic risk requires further study of changes in the entire economic system that also influence stock prices.

20

A Review of Preferred Stock

John S. Bildersee, Ph.D.
Schools of Business
New York University

Preferred stocks offer investors an expected return commensurate with the risk accepted by those investors like any other efficiently priced investment. However, it has been said that a traditional preferred stock combines the worst features of common stock, such as a subordinated position relative to debt, with the worst features of bonds, such as a fixed return even if a firm is highly profitable. This type of thinking has dominated the market for traditional preferred stocks for the past two decades. As a result, except for the utilities industry, there have been very few new issues of traditional preferreds during this period. For example, utility issues accounted for 90.4 percent of the gross proceeds from corporate preferred stock offerings in 1970 and 72.9 percent in 1975. Even in 1980, during what was then the busiest year for new manufacturing company issues in about 20 years, utilities accounted for 48.2 percent of gross proceeds, almost twice that of the manufacturing firms.

Despite the traditionally negative view of preferred stocks, they have enjoyed a comeback during the past three years. This new popularity has been driven mainly by the distribution of many new specialized issues. These issues have been distributed primarily by financial corporations. These companies obtained only 7.6 percent of the gross proceeds of new issues in 1981. However, their share of the new issues market rose to 40.3 percent, 42.5 percent, 47.8 percent, and 57.2 percent during the 1982 through 1985 period as the new type of preferred stock became more popular. These typical new preferreds are issued by financial corporations and some other corporations. They are, effectively, a different type of security from the traditional preferred stock as they emphasize a different combination of expected return and risk than do traditional preferreds. Whereas traditional preferreds emphasize a constant dollar return per period at the expense of variations in the stock price, the common characteristic for issues of the new type of preferred stock is an approximately constant stock price at the expense of a fixed dollar dividend. Both types of preferred stocks will be discussed here.

TRADITIONAL PREFERRED STOCKS

A traditional preferred stock has some features in common with common stocks and some features in common with corporate debt. Features similar to common stock features include voting rights, dividend distribution, tax benefits for corporate investors, and the lack of a maturity date. Features similar to debt features include a fixed dollar return under normal circumstances and preference in asset claims relative to common stocks.

As a permanent, fixed dollar return security, the typical preferred is priced by $P = D/r$ where P is the price, D is the constant dividend, and r is the market interest rate. This formulation shows the sensitivity of preferred stocks to market rates. The price of a preferred stock rises as the market rate falls and falls as the market rate rises. Alternatively, the market return (or current yield) on the preferred is calculated as $r = D/P$.

Dividends are permanently fixed for traditional preferreds. Sometimes this is stated as a percent of par value instead of a fixed dollar amount. Although nonpayment of the dividend does not constitute default, dividends must be paid to preferred stockholders before any dividends may be paid to common stockholders.

If the preferred stock is a cumulative preferred, any dividends not paid to preferred stockholders are still due them. The resulting arrearage must be paid in full before any dividends may be paid to common stockholders. However, if a preferred is noncumulative, an undistributed dividend does not create a corporate dividend obligation to preferred stockholders. In some cases, a series of missed dividends leads to an increase in the voting power of the preferred stockholders.

Taxable corporate investors may exclude 80 percent of their dividend income obtained from investments in most preferred stocks issued by taxable corporations. The exceptions were generally issued before October 1, 1942. These preferred stocks offer a deduction of approximately 60 percent. This tax advantage encourages corporate investors to exert a major influence in the preferred stock market as, for a corporate tax rate of 34 percent, the effective tax rate is 6.8 percent ($0.34 \cdot 0.20$).

Although preferred stocks are permanent securities, management may feel that it does not want the preferred stock to be a permanent part of the firm's capital structure. In this case, the firm can include one or more features enabling it to eliminate the stock in the future. These features include call, convertibility, and sinking fund provisions.

A call provision enables the firm to retire the entire preferred stock issue at any time within a prespecified period. The period when a call can be made usually begins several years after the security has been issued. This assures the investors that they can, at least, own the preferred stock for those several years. The call price is greater than the security's issue price. The premium above the issue price usually disappears in several steps during the first 20 years of the security's life.

While enabling the company to retire the preferred stock if market rates fall, this provision can be very costly to investors. Since the firm can retire the stock at the predetermined price at any time, the market price of the security will not rise above that price even if the market rate falls sufficiently to push the price of an identical, but not callable, preferred stock above the call price. Investors require some compensation for allowing the issuer to limit their potential return. This means that the issuer has to pay a somewhat higher dividend yield to investors in return for the option to call the security at a later time.

Some preferred stocks are convertible. This means that, at some time after the issue of the security, investors may unilaterally convert their preferred stock into common stock. Unlike the call feature, the convertibility feature benefits the investor. As a result, the investor pays for this option by reducing the dividends they require the issuer to pay on the preferred while accepting a conversion price that is normally greater than the current price of the firm's common stock.

A convertible preferred stock is valued at the maximum of its value as a fixed-income security and its value as an common stock. In the former case, the fixed dividend provides an interest-like flow typically associated with debt. As long as the dividend return is the dominant aspect of the total return to investors in the convertible preferred stock, the security behaves like a typical preferred stock. Since the investor can convert his preferred stock into common stock at a fixed rate irrespective of the common stock's price, the investor also has a participation in the firm's profits and growth. If the value of a convertible preferred is greater when converted to common stock than it would be based solely on its fixed dividend rate, then the preferred behaves like the firm's common stock except for participating directly in common stock dividend flows. This dual nature makes the convertible preferred unstable as its character may change from time to time.

The sinking fund provision creates one maturity date or a sequence of maturity dates for the security and may lead to the retirement of the entire issue. The usual sinking fund provision requires that the firm either make open-market purchases or tender offers for a fixed number of preferred shares periodically. In this case, the yield on an investment is probabilistic as a portion of the preferred issue may be called at a fixed price at any time. The lowest yield on an investment that will eventually be called completely includes the current dividend and accrual from the current price to the sinking fund call price. If the current price of a preferred stock is 88¾, it has a $7 coupon and a $100 sinking fund call price that will be exercised within the next 30 years; then, using present value analysis, the minimum yield will be 8 percent. However, the current yield is $7/$88.75 or 7.89 percent.

Some traditional nonconvertible preferreds appear to behave like common stock while others appear to behave like bonds. The similarity of any particular preferred to common stock or debt depends on its combination of features and the fundamental business risks accepted by the firm issuing the security. Preferreds rated as high-quality preferreds by rating agencies such as Standard & Poor's and Moody's generally act in a market rate sensitive manner like bonds. However, low rated preferred stocks often act like common stocks due to continued uncertainty about the firm's ability to cover its dividend obligations.

NEW PREFERRED STOCKS

New preferred stocks are similar to traditional preferreds in level of preference. However, new preferreds have many features that distinguish them from traditional preferreds. Although there are many variations in terms, the primary innovation is the variable dividend. The dividend is reset periodically to the new market rate so that the price of the underlying preferred stock never varies significantly from par value.

This combination of a varying dividend rate and an approximately fixed price is in distinct contrast to the traditional fixed dividend, market rate sensitive preferred. Investors in new preferred stocks give up their claim to a fixed dividend and, in return, can invest in an equity security with little or no short-term risk of capital. Moreover, corporate investors in these securities retain the advantage of the 80 percent dividend exclusion for tax purposes. As a result, these preferreds, which have been issued primarily by financial services firms and manufacturing firms, are a competitive investment for corporations wanting to invest their funds without great capital risk while wanting a higher rate of return than that available from debt securities.

This form of preferred stock is still developing and changing. As a result, each preferred may have features that make it behave uniquely and serve special purposes such as capital preservation or the need for equity securities in a corporate buyout. Two major types of new preferreds are adjustable rate preferreds and money market preferreds.

Adjustable rate preferred stocks were marketed first. The first adjustable rate preferred stocks had dividend "collars." A collar sets a minimum and a maximum allowable dividend rate for the security. If the market rate remains in this range, then the dividend rate on the security is set by a predetermined formula. For example, the Citicorp adjustable rate preferred 2d series dividend rate is determined by the maximum of the three-month U.S. Treasury bill rate, the 10-year U.S. Treasury rate and the 20-year U.S. Treasury rate less 4.125 percent.

The dividend rate on this Citicorp preferred cannot move outside of the 6 percent to 12 percent per year range. If the market rate leaves this range, then the dividend rate is restricted by the collar. While the minimum rate provides dividend protection to investors and the maximum rate provides dividend protection to the issuer, it also creates a hybrid security. For example, if the market rate rises above the collar and so that the dividend becomes fixed, then the new preferred acts like a traditional preferred and its price falls with additional increases in the market rate. In this case, invested capital is at risk. In response to this price risk, the more recently issued Citicorp adjustable rate preferred 4th series has no collar.

The convertible feature is enjoying a new popularity as one feature of adjustable rate preferreds. This feature is now being used, at times, in conjunction with an exchangeability option. This combination is popular today among firms that are currently suffering losses, but want to retain low costs of capital. While convertibility gives investors the right to obtain common stock, exchangeability allows the firm to replace the preferred with another security at its option. The typical exchange can take place several years after the issue of the security and may be for a subordinated convertible debenture issued by the company or some other acceptable security.

Money market preferred stocks were developed, in part, to respond to the limited ability of adjustable rate preferred stocks with collars to protect investor's capital in a market with highly variable market rates. Money market preferred have usually been issued by financial services companies or special subsidiaries of these companies. They typically have their yields or prices reset every seven weeks through auctions, thereby keeping their yields current, keeping their prices at or near par, and maintaining their 85 percent dividend deductibility for corporate investors. At each auction after the initial auction, the current holders of the securities may typically hold the security, hold it only if the dividend rate meets or exceeds the holder's bid, or sell the security.

As an example, International Paper issued three series of Dutch Auction Rate preferred stocks under an SEC Rule 415 shelf registration in late 1985 with initial dividend rates to be reset at auction every seven weeks. As is frequently the case, these issues of money market preferreds were in large units. Each issue included 750 units priced initially at $100,000 per unit.

Development of new preferred stocks has not ended. For example, BCI Holdings Corporation, with privately held common stock, recently issued a cumulative exchangeable preferred stock as part of a buyout of previously publicly traded Beatrice Companies common stock. However, dividends for the first six years may, at the company's option, be paid in terms of extra shares thereby conserving cash to cover the debt obligations associated with the buyout. This stock was exchanged for debt several months after its issue.

An additional recent development is planned by Texas Instruments. They intend to issue an auction rate convertible preferred stock. Since the convertibility is equivalent to a call on the underlying common stock, they expect the dividend rate to be lower than that on conventional auction rate preferred stocks and that the rate will fall as the value of underlying common stock rises.

Unlike the popular image of preferreds as a dying, unpopular type of security, these new types of preferreds have injected a new excitement into the market. However, with this new popularity has come an increased variety of securities so that there really is no longer a typical preferred stock. Instead, each preferred stock has to be analyzed on its merits, features, and risks.

REFERENCES

Standard & Poor's Stock Guide

This monthly publication contains information on most preferred stocks.

Standard & Poor's Bond Guide

A monthly publication containing information on convertible preferred stocks.

Moody's Bond Record

A monthly publication containing information on preferred stock and other fixed-income instruments.

The Wall Street Journal

A daily publication containing information on new financing.

21

Venture Capital Investment

Stanley E. Pratt
Chairman

Roubina Khoylian
Vice President
Venture Economics, Inc.

INTRODUCTION

Equity and equity-related investment in growth companies that are privately held is a very different world from traditional marketable investments. Rather than investment, the dominant influence in venture capital is really that it is "the business of developing businesses." As such, this type of investing encompasses a broad spectrum of financing from early stage investments to leveraged buyouts.

Three key attributes characterize venture capital investment:

- It involves some potential equity participation for the venture capitalist either through direct purchase of stock, or through warrants, options, or convertible securities.
- Venture capitalists have active, ongoing involvement in their portfolio companies, often through participation on the board of directors, allowing them to add value to their investments.
- It is a long-term investment discipline that often requires a period of 5 to 10 years for investments to provide a significant return.

Venture capital generally involves situations in which more conventional sources of financing (e.g., public markets, commercial banks, and insurance companies) are not accessible. Venture capital opportunities are thus influenced to some extent by the receptivity of public markets toward new issues and the availability of funds from credit-oriented institutions. For example, during the period of tight credit and virtually nonexistent new issue activity in the mid-1970s, venture capital groups which raised capital in the late 1960s and early 1970s were in a position to provide financing to many dynamic, new businesses including Cray Research, Federal Express, Paradyne Corporation, Prime Computer, and Tandem Computers.

The closing off of more conventional funding sources not only leads new entrepreneurs to the venture capitalists' doors, it also tends to produce more financing opportunities for later stage expansions. Venture capital funds that operate with capital committed for up to 10 years are protected to some degree during periods of tight capital. When the public market and other sources of financing are not accessible over a long period of time the venture capitalist's portfolio companies' ongoing need for funds can become both a major problem and a significant investment opportunity.

Each financing has its own special characteristics and the analytical requirements, terms, pricing, and monitoring for each can differ quite drastically. In one short chapter on the subject of venture capital it is not possible to cover the differing complexities of all types of transactions. However, the key elements of venture transactions will be described with some reference made to differences between the various aspects of venture capital financing.

DESCRIPTION OF THE VENTURE CAPITAL INDUSTRY

As a reference point, it is important to understand the current structure and composition of the venture capital industry. The profession, those groups dedicated to the ongoing practice of venture capital investment, presently consists of approximately 550 firms.[1] There are many other groups, including corporations, banks, pension funds, and individuals, that invest in venture capital situations, but generally they are not investors specializing in ongoing venture capital investment. Many startup ventures, for example, are financed by friends, relatives, suppliers, customers, and others who have special relationships with the entrepreneur. Such investors certainly play a significant role in the creation and financing of new and young companies, but they are not part of the professional venture capital community.

The total capital of the industry was close to $20 billion, as of year-end 1985, and venture capital firms have been investing $2.5 to $3.0 billion annually over the last three years. The U.S. venture capital

---

[1] *Pratt's Guide to Venture Capital Sources* (Wellesley Hills, Mass.: Venture Economics), updated annually, provides a directory of venture capital firms with detailed investment preferences.

industry consists of four main groups of venture capital firms. These are private venture capital firms, small business investment companies including minority enterprise small business investment companies, subsidiaries of financial corporations, and subsidiaries of nonfinancial corporations.

Private venture capital firms.   Private venture capital firms are the dominant institutionalized source of venture capital. This group includes family firms and institutionally funded independent private partnerships. As of year-end 1985, there were 285 private firms accounting for $14.2 billion of the industry's capital. Several early private firms were started by families such as the Rockefellers (Venrock), the Phipps (Bessemer Securities), and the Whitneys (J. H. Whitney & Company). Operating in the 1940s and 1950s, such groups were the precursors of the venture capital industry. Other families such as the Colliers (Collier Enterprises), the Hillmans (Hillman Ventures), and the Watsons (Greylock) were later additions to this group. While the majority of capital now comes into the venture capital industry through private partnerships, these family firms remain among the most experienced, influential, and sophisticated investors.

Institutionally funded private firms are generally organized as limited partnerships. Limited partnerships are structured such that the general partners (venture capitalists) are responsible for management of the partnership, which is financed primarily through capital commitments from limited partners (investors). The general partners receive an annual management fee—often 2 percent to 3 percent of the capital committed—as compensation for their management. They also receive a percentage of the net long-term capital gain—their carried interest which is generally 20 percent of the profits. The limited partnership structure differs from the corporate one in that:

- The partnership itself is not taxed.
- The partnership's life is fixed at the time of formation, and is fitted to the duration of investment holding periods.
- The limited partners' liability is limited to their interest in the partnership.

In the late 1960s and early 1970s, investment banking firms including Donaldson, Lufkin & Jenrette; Hambrecht & Quist; Oppenheimer; PaineWebber; Smith Barney; and Tucker Anthony were most active in organizing venture capital funds. More recently, partnerships organized by professional venture capitalists have become the most common type of firm. There are presently over 250 such firms in the United States. These firms are funded by insurance companies, endowment funds, pension funds, corporations, wealthy individuals, and foreign investors.

Small business investment companies (SBICs). There are now approximately 390 private and public firms licensed as SBICs by the federal government. These firms are structured in accordance with the Small Business Investment Company Act of 1958. They must have a minimum equity capital of $1 million and have access to government loans to achieve three to one or four to one leveraging of the private committed capital.

Of the several different kinds of SBICs, a major distinction exists between those that are: (1) lending oriented (some 170 firms primarily placing loans with local businesses), and (2) equity oriented (some 220 firms primarily involved in venture capital investments). This latter group generally includes large SBICs with $2 million or more in private capital which, due to their qualification as "venture capital-oriented," can be leveraged with governmental loans at a 4:1 ratio.

The equity-oriented SBICs, which accounted for $2.0 billion of the total capital pool in 1985, include: (1) bank-related SBICs; (2) corporate-owned SBICs; (3) subsidiaries of private venture capital partnerships; and (4) SBICs funded by individuals.

Venture capital subsidiaries of financial corporations. A number of commercial bank holding and insurance companies have established venture capital subsidiaries to provide financing for the high-risk/high-potential situations that do not meet their usual loan criteria. At year-end 1985, there were roughly 50 venture capital subsidiaries of financial corporations managing $1.8 billion, excluding the capital managed by their SBIC subsidiaries.

Since many types of financial institutions now supply the majority of new venture capital commitments to private venture capital partnerships, one might expect to see substantial forward integration into venture capital with more direct investing by financial institution venture subsidiaries. To date, however, this has not happened to a great degree because of the very specialized skills required of venture capitalists. Indeed, many financial institutions attempting to form captive venture subsidiaries have subsequently pulled back upon discovering they could not easily convert their credit analysts and lending officers into venture capitalists.

Further, there is some evidence of commercial banks moving away from captive subsidiaries. In 1980, Bank of America, for example, spun off its venture subsidiary to become the sole limited partner in a private venture partnership. More recently, the trend has been for banks to join with other investors to fund independent venture capital partnerships.

Venture capital subsidiaries of nonfinancial corporations.
Approximately 60 large industrial corporations, including General Electric, W. R. Grace, and Xerox, have venture capital divisions accounting for $1.7 billion of the capital pool. Also, more than 50 other major corporations have invested in independent partnerships or made occasional venture capital investments on a direct basis. These investments are most often in situations in which the product, market, or technology are related to the parent corporation's operations or where the business is of interest as a diversification opportunity.

Foreign corporations such as Elf Aquitaine, Olivetti, Inco, and Northern Telecom have also made direct venture investments in the United States. In addition to Canadian and European involvement in U.S. venture capital, there has been increasing Japanese interest.

VENTURE CAPITAL INVESTMENT CRITERIA

The single most important factor behind a venture capitalist's investment decision is judgment of the character and quality of the management team that intends to develop the new business. It is often said that real estate investors concentrate upon three factors: location, location, and location. Venture capitalists, in much the same way, look for a solid management team as indicated by these five investment criteria:

1. Management.
2. Management.
3. Management.
4. Market niche.
5. Product or service.

Most successful entrepreneurs have some background of management experience, often at the divisional or departmental level of a larger corporation. It is important that they understand how to commercialize a product or service in order to build a new business. As General Georges Doriot, the founding father of the U.S. venture capital industry observed, "We can back a first rate management team with a second rate product and have success; but if we back a first rate product with a second rate management team we can seldom achieve our objectives."

The competence of the management team is judged by their capability of defining a clear market opportunity and how their product or service will be sold within that market. A new business must address a clear market need that is too small to be of interest to major potential competitors, a niche that will enable the company to survive its initial development. This niche, however, must be in a market area that promises exceptional growth within three to five years so that the new business can establish itself as a significant factor within that time period. Within five to seven years the market must be potentially large enough so that reasonable market penetration could lead to enough interest for a possible public stock offering or for acquisition by a larger corporation. Venture capitalists must have an exit vehicle for realizing a gain on their investment. While the initial objective may be an independent publicly traded company, the market growth must be at least great enough to stimulate the acquisition interests of large corporations.

While the particular product or service is important, this factor is often overemphasized by entrepreneurs seeking financing. Venture capitalists avoid products in search of a market; they seek markets in search of a product. A proprietary position in a rapidly growing market can offset errors in judgment of the original management team since the expanding demand for the products or services will attract new managers capable of carrying out the business plan. The product must have a sufficient gross profit margin to provide initial cash flow before the entry of major competitors into the market. Adequate profit margins must be maintained even after aggressive competitor pricing enters into the picture. A high gross margin is a reflection of the value added to the product or service offered for which the customers are willing to pay.

Since venture capitalists know that most of their investments will not meet their return objectives, they seek opportunities with exceptionally high return potential. The broad rule of thumb is to foresee the possibility of at least 10 times their money in five years. They will seek greater potential return in early stage companies that will require five to seven years to develop, but also often invest for comparable rates of return in three- to five-year expansion opportunities. The following chart shows the relationships of targets to annual rates of return:

Profit Targets of Venture Capitalists	Compounded Annual Rates of Return (pretax)
Triple their money in three years	44%
Triple their money in five years	25
Four times their money in four years	41
Five times their money in three years	71
Five times their money in five years	38
Seven times their money in three years	91
Seven times their money in five years	48
Ten times their money in three years	115
Ten times their money in five years	58

TYPES OF INVESTMENTS FINANCED BY VENTURE CAPITALISTS

Stage of Development

Venture capitalists invest in companies at different stages of their business development, from seed and startup through expansion steps to acquisition of existing business through management leveraged buyouts (LBOs). Factors such as the availability of capital, the existing portfolio companies' need for capital, opportunities for new investment, and the IPO (initial public offering) market can influence whether investments are made in new startups or in follow-on rounds of financing for existing companies. During the mid-1970s when the new issues market collapsed, venture capitalists concentrated their time and money on companies already in their portfolios rather than to new opportunities. By comparison, the abundance of new investment opportunities in the early 1980s, in conjunction with the high levels of capital flowing into the industry, brought about an increase in startup activity. Later stage, follow-on rounds of financing have become more significant in the last two years as the prior startups have begun to develop, requiring expansion financing. LBO/acquisition activities are greatly influenced by interest rates and the desires of large corporations to spin out divisions or subsidiaries.

Venture capital assumes quite different roles in a business depending on the stage of development of a portfolio company and the purpose for which the funds are provided. Table 1 details 1984 and 1985 investments by stages. Definitions of the stage categories follow.

Seed stage investment generally involves a relatively small amount of capital provided to an investor or entrepreneur to prove a concept. It may involve product development, but rarely involves any marketing.

Startups involve either companies in the process of being organized or those that have been in business a short time (one year or less) but have not sold their product commercially. Generally, such firms would have selected the key officers, prepared a business plan, and made market studies.

First-stage financing involves companies that have expanded their initial capital (often developing a prototype) and require funds to initiate commercial manufacturing and sales.

Second-stage financing describes an investment in a company that is producing and shipping with growing accounts receivable and inventories building up. At this stage, the company needs working capital for its initial expansion. Although it has clearly made progress, it may still be operating at a loss.

TABLE 1 Venture Capital Investments by Financing Stage (percent)

	Percent of Number of Companies Financed		Percent of Dollar Amount Invested	
	1985	1984	1985	1984
Seed	6%	7%	2%	3%
Startup	13	15	11	12
First stage	17	21	12	18
Total early stage	36%	43%	25%	33%
Second stage	30	28	33	31
Third stage/bridge	24	19	30	23
Total expansion	54%	47%	63%	54%
LBO/acquisition	5	5	8	9
Other	5	5	4	4
Total other	10%	10%	12%	13%
Total	100%	100%	100%	100%

SOURCE: *Venture Capital Yearbook 1986* (Wellesley Hills, Mass.: Venture Economics, 1986), p. 33.

Third-stage financing is provided for the major growth expansion of companies whose sales volume is increasing and which are breaking even or making a profit. Funds may be utilized for further plant expansion, marketing, working capital, or development of new or improved products.

Bridge financing describes the situation where a company is expecting to go public within six months to a year. Often bridge financing is structured so that it can be repaid from proceeds of the public underwriting.

Management / leveraged buyouts involve financing provided to enable operating management to acquire a product line or business (which may be at any stage of development). This usually involves revitalization of the operation with entrepreneurial management acquiring a significant equity interest.

Industry Preferences

Historically, venture capital investments have been focused on computer- and electronics-related areas. Venture capitalists, however, will generally consider any investment opportunity which offers the potential for superior returns. The level of investments in various industry sectors is shown in Table 2.

Although many view capitalists as "high-technology" investors, the

TABLE 2 Venture Capital Investments by Industry Category (percent)

	Percent of Number of Companies Financed		Percent of Dollar Amount Invested	
	1985	*1984*	*1985*	*1984*
Commercial communications	4%	3%	4%	4%
Telephone and data communications	10	10	12	11
Computer hardware and systems	20	22	25	29
Software and services	15	14	10	11
Other electronics	13	13	14	13
Genetics engineering	3	3	5	2
Medical/health care related	11	11	10	8
Energy related	2	2	1	2
Industrial automation	4	3	4	3
Industrial products and machinery	4	4	2	3
Consumer related	8	7	7	7
Other products and services	6	8	6	7
	100%	100%	100%	100%

SOURCE: *Venture Capital Yearbook 1986* (Wellesley Hills, Mass.: Venture Economics, 1986), p. 28.

real emphasis of venture capital investment is on the application of technology developments to productivity improvement and commercially viable markets, and not for the support of new scientific and technological breakthroughs.

SPECIALIZED SKILLS AND DISCIPLINES OF VENTURE CAPITAL INVESTING

The most important characteristic that differentiates venture capitalists from other investors is their long-term, ongoing involvement with the managements of firms receiving capital. Apart from financing, the venture capitalist's supportive role includes:

 a. Providing assistance in finding and selecting key management team members.
 b. Making customer and supplier introductions.
 c. Providing assistance with long-range planning, financing, and marketing.
 d. Providing a young company increased credibility with potential customers, suppliers, and bankers.

Given the potential value of a venture capitalist's nonmonetary contributions, many successful entrepreneurs emphasize the importance of who is providing the funding, rather than how much capital and at what price.

Venture capitalists often provide entrepreneurs with a critical intangible—supportive peer relationships. Being an entrepreneur can be a lonely task and a respected peer, independent of the operating management team, with whom to discuss business problems can be an invaluable tool. Experienced venture capitalists have seen and dealt with many problems inherent in new business development. They can be particularly supportive with problems (e.g., how to meet next month's payroll) which are too sensitive for direct discussion with subordinates.

Venture capitalists often develop specialized skills which become key elements of the strategies of different venture investment firms. Venture capitalists who are experienced in working with entrepreneurs in early stage business development often become more comfortable and proficient in this area than with larger stage expansion situations. Management leveraged buyouts require different analysis, structuring and monitoring than other types of deals, and specialists have evolved in this area. The understanding of current and future technology developments is important for related investments and some venture capitalists develop such expertise. Venture capitalists can often make important contributions to the formulation of marketing strategies for targeted specialized niches.

In the early attempt to institutionalize venture capital investment in the 1950s and early 1960s, many investors (especially financial institutions) perceived venture investing as merely an extension of traditional finance and investment activity. As a result, they incorrectly assumed that the traditional skills of passive financial analysis were sufficient for successful venture investing. It has since been recognized that (1) even superior passive analytical skills are not enough, (2) the broad range of skills required are not easily taught and are learned only through experience, and (3) the critical long-term orientation is a difficult discipline to adopt and maintain, especially in the current quantitative performance-oriented environment.

HOW VENTURE CAPITALISTS DIFFER FROM TRADITIONAL SECURITY ANALYSTS

When venture-backed companies succeed, the venture capital investment process seems very simple. Often forgotten is the fact that it takes years of specialized training and disciplined investment skills to achieve such success.

Venture capital investment is, at its core, a long-term, hands-on process requiring patience and involvement on the part of investors. These disciplines are what most clearly distinguish venture capitalists from security analysts.

Investing in private companies, venture capitalists must wait until a portfolio company develops to the stage of going public or being acquired in order to realize a return on investment. To reach that stage the role of the venture capitalist involves more than merely financing. While security analysts invest, venture capitalists become participants in their portfolio companies, helping them to develop and hopefully to prosper.

A venture capitalist's process of investigating and evaluating companies differs markedly from a security analyst's. The venture capitalist generally begins an investigation with a detailed business plan from the company that is predominantly based upon future expectations. The security analyst, however, relies principally upon analysis of past performance.

Since venture capitalists are making long-term commitments, they must engage in a detailed investigation of the management team that will be responsible for the company's development. It requires strong entrepreneurial skills to build a small company into a viable growth company—skills very different from those required to run an established publicly held company.

The partnership concept between the venture capitalist and entrepreneur carries a marked difference from that of the objective security analyst. The venture capitalist is often a director of the company, actively involved with the problems of the business and helping to make critical decisions. The venture capitalist often plays a role in setting internal budgets and financial planning procedures, assists the company in obtaining loans, and helps arrange for the initial public offering.

The security analyst is therefore at a disadvantage in attempting to engage in venture capital investing directly. Venture capital investing on a part-time basis has proven to be particularly treacherous, being too demanding and time consuming to be conducted successfully on a less than full-time basis. The myriad problems of developing businesses are often all consuming and the lack of liquidity in private investing removes the option of selling one position to move to another.

Security analysts, however, have certain critical skills and expertise often not shared by venture capitalists. They can be in a far better position to know when it is time to sell a maturing investment and when the market for a company's shares is far too overpriced. In addition, they have the broader perspective to judge the merits and potential of the venture-backed company compared to other companies in the same field. The differing disciplines can be complementary. A relationship with an established venture capitalist can combine the best of both skills—the venture capitalist's ability to spot and negotiate a solid opportunity and then work to make sure it succeeds as anticipated, and the security analyst's ability to sense market conditions and security values in terms of when to sell. An often viable alternative is to participate with venture capitalists as part of their investment syndicates, joining in later stage follow-on financings.

THE VENTURE CAPITAL PROCESS

Screening

Venture capital firms receive hundreds of financing proposals each year, only 2 percent to 3 percent of which are eventually funded. Many proposals are sent in cold, while others are referred by a wide variety of sources including other venture firms, investment bankers, consultants, attorneys, and business acquaintances. Referrals from knowledgeable and proven contacts, such as other venture capital firms or key bankers and entrepreneurs, have the greatest potential for serious consideration and subsequent funding.

The starting point for a venture capitalist's evaluation is a written business plan. The business plan, together with the management's discussion of it, enables potential investors to focus upon management's planning skills and experience. It must be a product of the principal managers, rather than a polished exposition by outside consultants, since it documents management knowledge and expertise in the disciplines necessary for independent business development. It should combine a historical, factual review with careful research and understanding to produce a realistic future plan. It is not a selling document, but shows the anticipated developments and the structures necessary to enable financing the proposal. Finally, it provides a mechanism for measuring potential and actual progress. Most business plans presented are far too optimistic, but those that are too conservative will not attract an investor's attention. It is thus important to present reasonable expectations that both the management and the venture capitalist can accept as achievable.

Perhaps the most important part of the business plan and its presentation is the clear identification of the existing and future market needs as well as the niche that will allow a new or smaller growing business to exist and successfully expand. Too often, entrepreneurs are enthusiastic about a marvelous product and they expect the potential investor to recognize the product's need without documentation as to why or how the customer will purchase the product.

If presentations are made with adequate homework, facts are presented to avoid unpleasant surprises, and a natural and realistic exposition is made; the proper chemistry may be developed with venture capitalists to bring about a remarkable amount of assistance even prior to any final decision. While there are no fixed industry standards for such a presentation, a serious business plan should contain the following:[2]

    I.   A brief summary (one to three pages).

   II.   Description of the business and the industry.
          1.   The company (products/services, customers, history, roles of principals, market penetration, financial performance, past problems).
          2.   The industry (nature, current status and prospects; principal participants; growth in sales and profits; recent trends).

   III.   Features and advantages of products and services.
          1.   Description.
          2.   Proprietary position.
          3.   Potential.

   IV.   Market research and analysis.
          1.   Customers.
          2.   Market size and trends.
          3.   Competition.

   V.   Estimated market share and sales.
          1.   Marketing plan and strategy.
          2.   Pricing.
          3.   Sales tactics.
          4.   Service and warranty policies.
          5.   Advertising, public relations, and promotion.

   VI.   Design and development plans.
          1.   Development status and tasks.
          2.   Difficulties and risks.
          3.   Costs.

   VII.   Operations plan.
          1.   Geographic location.
          2.   Facilities and improvements.
          3.   Strategy and plans.
          4.   Labor force.
          5.   Management team (describing duties and responsibilities with complete résumés).
          6.   Organization.
          7.   Management compensation and ownership.
          8.   Board of directors.
          9.   Management assistance and training needs.
         10.   Supporting professional services.

   VIII.   Overall schedule.

---

[2] Brian Haslett and Leonard E. Smollen, "Preparing a Business Plan," *Pratt's Guide to Venture Capital Sources* (Wellesley Hills, Mass.: Venture Economics, 1986).

IX. Critical risks and problems.
X. The financial plan.
    1. Profit and loss forecast.
    2. Cash flow forecast.
    3. Balance sheet forecasts.
    4. Cost and cash flow control.
    5. Proposed offering.
    6. Desired financing.
    7. Capitalization.
    8. Use of funds.

Investigation

Perhaps the most frustrating aspect of the venture capitalist's investigation process is the time required during the period from original introduction to the closing of an investment. Realistic planning should allow for at least three to six months for contact, courtship, and investigation. When a business needs funds yesterday, the process is even more problematic than usual and only the most intuitive venture capitalists will respond. Adequate investigation and familiarization takes time, and venture capitalists are just as busy and jealous of time as operating managements. Time frames should be discussed initially and reasonable schedules should be set up and maintained.

After an initial meeting, the responsible venture capital firm will indicate within a week or two whether it is interested in seriously considering a proposal. If so, the investigation begins in earnest with extensive checking of the management, an analysis of product, technical and marketing considerations, and financial analysis. While these studies require a great deal of time and effort on the part of both parties, they are necessary to establish the understanding required for long-term involvement.

At the same time, the entrepreneur should be conducting an investigation and analysis of the venture capital firm. Some investors can offer a great deal more than others, especially in specific industries or in particular stages of business development. The experience and expertise of the investor should be carefully reviewed. Perhaps the best way to check on venture capitalists is to contact the managements of other companies in which the venture capitalist has invested. This should include successful businesses, as well as disappointing experiences and outright failures, to determine how a potential investor will react to both good and bad developments. The nature and frequency of communications between the venture capitalist and the managements of portfolio companies should be noted. In general, the entrepreneur should seek strong rather than relatively passive investors, much the same as venture investors desire to back strong management teams. It is critical to determine each side's capacities to establish mutual trust and working relationships.

Negotiations and Pricing

Once the investigations have been completed, the final details of the investment are subject to the give and take of direct negotiation. Usually the negotiations are handled by the chief executive officer of the operating management team and the venture capitalist. Advisers, such as attorneys and accountants, can be helpful, but decisions cannot be delegated since management must live with final determinations during the difficult times of building a business. Generally, compromise is necessary for both parties and it is important that both sides feel that a fair deal has been reached. Each side must leave a little bit at the table and not burden the relationship with unrealistic projections or expectations. If unrealistic expectations are created initially, the entrepreneur will be suffering from a credibility gap right from the start. An open and honest relationship will reduce the number of surprises later.

Too often, entrepreneurs confuse ownership with control. Management controls a business and the venture capitalist's role is generally supportive—enabling greater growth than might have been accomplished without such involvement. If a business fails to develop in accordance with planned expectations, venture capitalists as stockholders may push for changes through the board of directors. Directors may seek changes in the controlling management of the business, but ownership positions in developing businesses are seldom responsible for such restructuring. Most often, venture capitalists operate through persuasion in the expectation that their original decision to back a particular management team was correct.

The structure of a financing determined in these negotiations must be clearly understood by all parties. The amount of capital investment is usually determined with the expectation that additional funds will be made available in a series of steps that are dependent on the development of the business. The use of debt and equity is structured in accordance with the requirements and capabilities of the business as well as the objectives and needs of the investor.

Depending upon the stage of development of the business being financed, the venture capitalist seeks a potential return of 5 to 10 times the investment and a means of assuring future liquidity. Factors relating to these liquidity requirements are a part of the venture capitalist's negotiating objectives.

The pricing of a venture capital investment can be the most subjective and sensitive aspect of the negotiating process. Pricing involves the valuation of a company before and after the financing based upon an analysis of the risk versus the potential return. The venture capitalists' expected return on investment (ROI) will vary. As a general rule, venture capitalists financing higher risk seed or startup companies will look for compounded annual returns on the order of 50 percent or more. With second-stage financings, venture capitalists may be satisfied with an annual return of 30 percent to 40 percent, while later stage investors may only expect returns in the range of 25 percent to 30 percent.

In assessing risk, venture capitalists will specifically consider three aspects: (1) product risk, that is, the viability of the product or service concept; (2) market risk; and (3) management risk. Venture capitalists do use analytic tools in assessing risk and future potential, but in dealing with the unknown, the final valuation will be a judgment call based on the knowledge, experience, and intuition of the individual investor. Certain factors will be of primary consideration:

- Upside versus downside potential of the venture.
- The accuracy and credibility of financial projections.
- Time required to achieve profitability.
- Future dilution based on anticipated additional rounds of financing.
- Capital gains versus current income.
- The potential for exiting either through an eventual public offering of stock or through acquisition or merger of the company.

Evaluation of the management team, however, is the principal factor in determining whether to make an investment and how to set the pricing. Generally, the more relevant the accomplishments of the management team, the higher the valuation of the company. The qualifications, track record, competence, and commitment of the management team will be judged carefully.

Exiting

The realization of a return for venture capital investors requires a mechanism for eventually cashing in and exiting from an investment. The two major vehicles for successfully exiting from an investment in a privately held company are: (1) a public offering of the company's stock; and (2) acquisition of the company by another corporation. While we often hear more about the successful developments that have gone public, most venture capital exits are from mergers or acquisitions.

The public route is often limited by the market's receptivity to new issues. In addition, an initial public offering does not generally provide venture capital investors with immediate liquidity for their shares purchased through private placement.

The Securities and Exchange Commission (SEC) has relaxed a

number of its regulations governing the sale of restricted securities over the past several years. These revisions have helped the entrepreneurial process by making it easier for small businesses to raise capital. Furthermore, these changes have benefited venture capitalists directly by making it easier for them to sell shares and thus realize capital appreciation on their investments.

The SEC requires that a registration statement be filed before securities are offered for sale to the public. The registration consists of the prospectus and supplemental information. Certain small and private offerings of stock are exempted from this costly registration procedure. In 1982, the SEC issued changes to these rules. The new provisions, known as Regulation D, did the following:

- Raised to $500,000 from the original $100,000 the amount of unregistered securities a company could sell.
- Eliminated the ceiling of 100 individual buyers of unregistered securities.
- Raised to $5 million from $2 million the amount of securities eligible to be sold to so-called accredited investors and extended the time limit from six months to one year.
- Redefined an "accredited investor" to widen private individual participation in stock flotation not requiring disclosure documentation.

Many venture investors realize gains through acquisition by or a merger with a larger corporation. For the period 1984 through 1985, acquisitions of venture-backed companies were at almost twice the level of initial public offerings. In such transactions, venture capital investors may receive cash, shares of the acquiring company's stock, or some combination of the two. If shares of the acquirer are received, this does not generally involve any limitations in the selling of these shares as the venture capitalist is not likely to own more than a minor percentage of the larger corporation's outstanding stock.

CLOSING COMMENTS

After such a lengthy and often tiresome investment process, what type of return can a venture capitalist hope to realize? Typically, venture investors seek to realize 10 times their investment within a five- to seven-year time frame for early stage deals or three to five times their investment over a three- to five-year period in expansion financings. The real winners, however, will dramatically exceed these objectives— as much as 20 or more times the investment—while losses are limited to the capital employed. This open-ended upside potential with limited downside risk is the sine qua non driving all venture capitalists. Most successful venture investors recognize that they will have losers, that few investments will be major winners, and that most will fall between major successes or total failure.

SELECTED REFERENCES

GLADSTONE, DAVID J.   *Venture Capital Handbook.* Reston, Va.: Reston Publishing Co., 1983.

LEE, STEVEN J., and ROBERT D. COLMAN.   *Handbook of Mergers, Acquisitions, and Buyouts.* Englewood Cliffs, N.J.: Prentice-Hall, 1981.

LEVINE, SUMNER.   *Investment Managers Handbook.* Homewood, Ill.: Dow Jones-Irwin, 1980.

————.   *Investing in Venture Capital and Buyouts.* Homewood, Ill.: Dow Jones-Irwin, 1985.

LIPPER, ARTHUR.   *Investing in Private Companies.* Homewood, Ill.: Dow Jones-Irwin, 1984.

PRATT, SHANNON.   *Valuing a Business.* Homewood, Ill.: Dow Jones-Irwin, 1981.

PRATT, STANLEY E.   *How to Raise Venture Capital.* New York, N.Y.: Charles Scribner's Sons, 1981.

————, and JANE K. MORRIS.   *Pratt's Guide to Venture Capital Sources.* Wellesley Hills, Mass.: Venture Economics, 1987.

WALLNER, NICHOLAS, and J. TERRENCE GREVE.   *How to Do Leveraged Buyouts or Acquisitions.* San Diego, Calif.: Buyout Publications, 1982.

Among the special periodicals of interest are the following:

Venture Capital Journal, Venture Economics, Inc.; Wellesley Hills, Mass.

Mergers and Acquisitions, Mergers and Acquisitions; Philadelphia, Pa.

Venture, Venture Magazine Inc.; New York, N.Y.

Private Placements, Dealers Digest; New York, N.Y.

Dow Jones-Irwin Business and Investment Almanac, Dow Jones-Irwin; Homewood, Ill.

22

Analysis of Leveraged Buyouts, Takeovers, and Asset Value Investments

Mario J. Gabelli, CFA
Chairman
Gabelli & Company, Inc.
and
GAMCO Investors, Inc.

PORTFOLIO MANAGEMENT TECHNIQUES

Before I detail our analytical methodology, allow me to briefly describe our basic philosophy, goals, research procedures, and portfolio management techniques. We invest primarily in common stocks selling at a significant discount to the underlying company's private market value. We define private market value (PMV) as the price an informed industrialist would be likely to pay to acquire the company's assets. Simply stated, our philosophy is that assets purchased in the stock market at 50–60 cents on the dollar can eventually be sold to other investors for a significantly higher price. In many instances, these "other investors" will be leveraged buyout (LBO) specialists or corporate acquirers who use the same criteria we do in evaluating an investment.

To limit the time horizon in which private market values are likely to be realized, we look for situations in which a catalyst is working to help surface value and attract investment attention. Catalysts include: (1) changes in a regulatory environment; (2) increasing merger and acquisition activity within an industry; (3) management succession questions such as the death of a founder; (4) share repurchases and other restructuring activities such as the sale of a division; and (5) substantial stock purchases by outside interests. Acknowledging that even with catalysts present it can take time for private market values to be realized, we favor companies whose values will grow at least at the rate of inflation.

We invest in a stock only if we see the realistic potential for 50 percent appreciation within two years irrespective of the broad stock market environment. We maintain an awareness of the economic, political, and psychological factors that impact the market; however, under normal circumstances, the direction of the broad market should not be the dominant influence on our stock's appreciation potential. Our goal is to consistently achieve an annual 10 percent real rate of return (after tax and in excess of the prevailing inflation rate). This goal appears modest, and, in fact, we've comfortably exceeded this objective every year we've been in business. Over the longer term, however, achieving this goal will mean superior investment performance.

In tandem, Gabelli & Company, Inc. and GAMCO Investors, Inc. form an independent research organization. Other than broad-based economic and industry studies, we do not use outside sources for ideas or analysis. We subject each and every investment candidate to intensive analysis, applying our own asset-oriented criteria to identify opportunities. Once a stock has passed a rigorous examination and is included in a portfolio, it is monitored daily and held only as long as it continues to represent value by our standards. When a stock becomes fully priced relative to our private market value estimates, it is liquidated and replaced by another qualifying equity.

Our strategy is to be 100 percent invested at all times with the exception of periods in which we cannot find stocks that offer value. We are willing to take very substantial positions in stocks we favor because in buying one share we are expressing our belief that our clients would be well served by owning the entire company. We view stocks as pieces of a company and are willing to buy as many pieces at the right price as is feasible. In addition, I believe large positions are often more liquid than smaller positions when there may be a leveraged buyout specialist or corporate acquirer seeking a large block of stock.

I've described our basic philosophy and how we work. Now, I'll detail the conceptual and fundamental cornerstones of private market value investing. There are four exogeneous methods for private market values to be realized: leveraged buyouts; takeovers; liquidations; and corporate restructurings. Perhaps the best way to illustrate private market value analysis is to describe our experiences with some of the stocks we have recommended and owned whose PMV has surfaced via these four methods.

IDENTIFYING LEVERAGED BUYOUT CANDIDATES

Let's start with the leveraged buyout, a transaction which is still not thoroughly understood by many sophisticated investors. The term *leveraged buyout* (LBO) generally refers to the acquisition of an existing company or a division of a company by a new corporation formed by the acquirer for that sole purpose and funded simultaneously with substantial amounts of institutional debt relative to contributed equity. The amount of leverage employed depends upon the nature of the business acquired and the level of confidence the acquirer and the lending institutions have in the cash-generating capability of the target company. The benefits to the acquiring group, which almost always consists of the financial partners and company management, are as follows:

1. The company becomes owned by management and a limited number of sophisticated and supportive investors with common goals and objectives.
2. Management has strong additional incentives through meaningful equity participation.
3. Dividends subject to double taxation are converted into tax-deductible interest payments.
4. Through partnerships or S corporations the investors can take advantage of noncash tax benefits created through stepped-up depreciation and other techniques.
5. If successful, the investors in the new company achieve a rate of return that is substantially greater than that which can be earned from most other alternative investments.

Leveraged buyout opportunities in publicly held companies are created when the stock market fails to accurately appraise the productive value of assets. Many public companies are managed for short-term earnings-per-share results rather than long-term return-on-capital, cash flow, and return-on-asset goals. The securities markets tend to penalize companies that operate to achieve these longer-term objectives and thus undervalue these companies on a long-term fundamental basis. An LBO generally provides the public shareholders of the company with a cash price for their shares at a substantial premium over the public market and more closely in line with the real or private market value of their security holdings.

Thinking like a leveraged buyout specialist, we try to locate undervalued stocks of companies that qualify on most, but not necessarily all, of the following criteria:

- Cash flow in excess of debt service, capital, improvements, and working capital requirements (free cash flow).

- A history of profitable operations.
- A committed and conservative management team, with depth and stability.
- Relatively low cyclicality.
- Moderate unit growth.
- A high current asset base and inventory values in excess of book value.
- Undervalued and salable nonoperating assets.
- Off-balance-sheet assets.
- An efficient, modern asset base which is not single-purpose equipment.
- Products and processes that are not subject to replacement due to technological changes.
- A relatively low debt level.
- An excessive cash position.
- Limited off-balance-sheet liabilities.

Growth companies rarely meet these qualifications. In most instances, prospective LBO targets have passed their growth phase and are well along in what could be described as their golden years. These are not the kind of companies that excite earnings growth-oriented investors and consequently the stock market pays them little tribute. Yet, these are established, profitable enterprises with management in place, a predictable income stream, and minimal capital needs. By recasting the balance sheet via a leveraged buyout and using operating income to service debt rather than pay dividends and taxes, the LBO partners controlling a small, highly leveraged equity base can get an exceptional return on their investment. So, too, can the public shareholder who is bought out at a price usually significantly higher than the public market value of the shares. In the cradle-to-grave life cycle of a public company, LBO candidates are closer to the grave. As is illustrated in Exhibit 1, we try to buy them just before the leveraged buyout specialists begin to prepare the plot.

LBO CRITERIA

The key fundamental criteria in evaluating an LBO candidate is free cash flow, which we define as pretax, preinterest, predepreciation, operating income minus debt service, and any capital expenditures needed to sustain operating income. Since the price an LBO specialist will be willing to pay to take a company private will largely be determined by how much cash the company can generate to service debt, free cash flow is generally the most important consideration in our private market

---

EXHIBIT 1

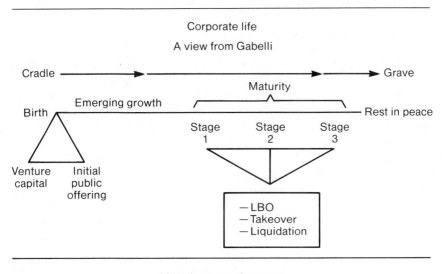

Corporate life

A view from Gabelli

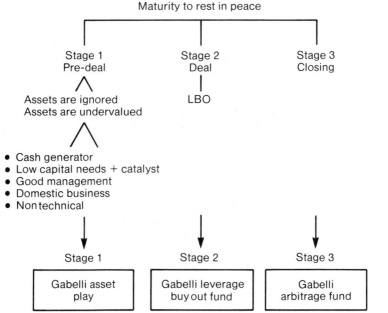

Maturity to rest in peace

value estimates. Consequently, to a large extent private market value (PMV) analysis is free cash flow analysis. In making our PMV estimates, we are also cognizant of other cash-generating factors such as the prospective sale of marginally profitable businesses or other passive assets, cash on the balance sheet producing investment income, and/or any marketable securities that could be sold to produce cash. Of course, the cost of debt must also be factored into the PMV equation.

EXAMPLES OF PRIVATE MARKET VALUE ANALYSIS

I've given you the theory. Not let me give you a few real-life examples of how our private market value analysis has identified leveraged buyout situations. I'll begin by reviewing our experience with Houdaille Industries, Inc., a company I first wrote up while still employed as an analyst with William D. Witter, Inc., and on which I continued to report after founding Gabelli & Company, Inc., in 1977.

Houdaille was a diversified manufacturer of industrial goods, auto parts, machine tools, and construction materials; in short, a somewhat boring company in somewhat mundane industries. Coupled with its lack of "sex appeal" was a lackluster earnings record that turned off most investors. I was attracted to Houdaille because of its steady growth in book value, large cash position, stable revenue stream, declining capital expenditures, and accelerating free cash flow. At the time, I was confident management would be able to translate these asset-oriented strengths into increasing profitability. I believed institutional investors would appreciate it. Over the three-year period I recommended the stock, earnings did not develop as I anticipated. I stuck with it, however, because free cash flow and book value were still accelerating and I remained convinced that sooner or later either earnings would follow suit or another corporate entity would spot the big discrepancy between stock price and asset value and buy the company. In my final (October 20, 1978) research report on Houdaille, I concluded, " . . . $35–$40 per share is the price any eventual suitor would pay to own this company."

In early 1979, a unique investment partnership, Kohlberg Kravis Roberts & Co. (KKR) took Houdaille private at approximately $40 per share via a still somewhat novel transaction, the leveraged buyout. When I looked at the deal closely, I realized that not only did my clients (the shareholders) make money, but KKR and Houdaille management also did very well. I reasoned that since the economics of LBOs made dollars and sense, there would be many more in the future. I wanted to recommend and own the stocks of companies likely to be targets. Thus, private market value investing became my primary focus.

Since Houdaille, we have recommended and owned positions in more than a dozen companies that have been LBO'd. Our research on these companies provides excellent examples of private market value analysis at work. The following is a Gabelli & Company research report on Cowles Broadcasting, Inc., a stock our GAMCO clients inherited with the liquidation of its parent, Cowles Communications.

GABELLI & COMPANY, INC.

Asset Play No. 12   December 28, 1982

Cowles Broadcasting, Inc.

Current Price: 16
(CWL–NYSE)

The Company

Cowles Broadcasting was spawned from the liquidation of Cowles Communications, our first Asset Play. In addition to other assets, each former shareholder of Cowles Communications will receive one share of Cowles Broadcasting, with such shares distributed on or about January 14, 1983. As background, we initially recommended Cowles Communications on April 5, 1977, at $14. Since then, we re-recommended it in seven separate Abstracts. Its last trade on the NYSE was $51.00 on December 16, 1982.

We refer to the new company as the "son of" (daughter if you prefer) of Cowles. It has two main assets: two television stations—WESH-TV, the NBC affiliate in Daytona–Orlando, Florida, and KCCI–TV, the CBS affiliate in Des Moines, Iowa—and about $4 million in cash with no debt. We place the private market value of CWL *today* at around $22.50–$26.25 per share. We believe these values will rise over time. We believe accumulation of the shares at current levels is timely for investors seeking long-term capital gains.

Private Market Value of Cowles—Our Assumptions

Our assumptions for the private market value of CWL are as follows:

- Rule of 7 (currently the FCC restricts TV station ownership to seven stations) is modified, permitting group operators with more mature properties to bid on CWL.
- Revenue for CWL's stations over the next five years should grow as follows:

	Spot		
	National	*Local*	
Des Moines	10%	8%	
Daytona	11	13	
Total			10.8%

- Private market value in 1985 would be derived as follows: The broadcast properties:

	Operating Profit ($ million)	Multiple Cash Flow	Private Value ($ million)
Des Moines	$ 4.0	9–10	$ 36–40
Daytona-Orlando	6.0	11–13	66–78
Total	$10.0		$102–118
Per shares			$25.75–$30.00

Cash, which we estimate will be roughly $4.0 million at the end of 1982, will be close to $10 million or $2.50 per share at the end of 1985.

- This would place total private market value at $28–$33 per share then.
- No shares are repurchased, though we would suggest that management pursue "aggressive cap shrink" now that the company is no longer hobbled by Investment Company Act considerations.
- License renewal question will be out of the way by June 1983.

Our Rate of Return Model

If we are correct, a total return to investors who bought the stock at various prices might be determined from the following matrix:

If CWL's Purchase Price	and Realized Value*		Annual Rate of Return (percent)	
	18 Months	3 Years	18-Month Workout	3-Year Workout
$12	$26.00	$34.00	77.8%	61.1%
14	26.00	34.00	57.1	47.6
16	26.00	34.00	41.7	37.5
18	26.00	34.00	29.6	29.0
20	26.00	34.00	20.0	23.3

* We are assuming payout ratio of 50 percent, or an average of about $0.50 per share over the next three years. Sale of assets completed by either July 1984 at $25.00 (18-month workout) or December 1985 at $32.50 per share (three-year workout).

SOURCE: Gabelli & Company, Inc., calculations.

In sum, we believe that long-term equity-oriented investors should purchase Cowles' Broadcasting. If a deal is completed within 18 months from today, the annualized rate of return would be over 40 percent. If the time frame is stretched out because litigation proves sticky, which we do not believe will be the case, we believe values will continue to grow, providing a still attractive 37.5 percent return in a three-year workout.

You will note that Cowles's TV stations are appraised at different multiples of operating cash flow.

The Des Moines station, located in a slower growth market, is valued at 9–10 times cash flow and the Orlando station, in the fast-growing Florida market, is appraised at 11–13 times cash flow. The compounded annualized growth rate of a broadcast property, or any franchise-type business, is an important consideration in determining the cash flow multiple used to determine PMV.

As the box (below) and Table 1 prepared by GAMCO Vice President Douglas Jamieson reveal, there is a wide swing in the compounded annualized growth rate of broadcast properties in different markets.

CASES A THROUGH F

Assumption

The television station in our model has $20 million in revenues and $10 million in operating expenses, generating operating income of $10 million.

The Cases

- **Case A: Toledo-type market.** Case A could be a station in a low-growth market, where revenues and costs grow in line at 8.0 percent. The result is an 8 percent compounded annual growth rate in operating income.
- **Cases B–E: Atlanta-type market.** In Cases B through E, we assume growth rates in revenues at incrementally higher levels, from 10 to 16 percent. Costs are assumed to grow at a slower pace than revenues, from 9 to 12 percent. The results are compound annual growth rates ranging from 11.0 percent to 19.4 percent.
- **Case F: Phoenix-, Orlando-, Tampa-type market.** Case F would be a typical Sunbelt station, where revenue growth is at 20 percent while the costs are growing at 14 percent. The resulting annualized compounded growth rate is 24.8 percent.

The moral of the story is that analysts must consider compound growth in formulating a value model based on a multiple to operating cash flow. Cowles Broadcasting's Des Moines station located in a Case B 10–16% annual operating cash flow growth market is not worth as much as its Orlando station in a Case F 20% plus annual operating cash flow growth market.

TABLE 1 Growth in Operating Income: Six Scenarios (A–F)

	0	1	2	3	4	5	6	Compound Growth Rate (percent)
Case A:								
Revenue growth = 8%	$20.00	$21.60	$23.33	$25.19	$27.21	$29.39	$31.74	
Cost growth = 8%	10.00	10.80	11.66	12.60	13.60	14.69	15.87	
Operating profit	$10.00	$10.80	$11.66	$12.60	$13.60	$14.69	$15.87	8.0%
Case B:								
Revenue growth = 10%	$20.00	$22.00	$24.20	$26.62	$29.28	$32.21	$35.43	
Cost growth = 9%	10.00	10.90	11.88	12.95	14.12	15.39	16.77	
Operating profit	$10.00	$11.10	$12.32	$13.67	$15.17	$16.82	$18.66	11.0
Case C:								
Revenue growth = 12%	$20.00	$22.40	$25.09	$28.10	$31.47	$35.25	$39.48	
Cost growth = 10%	10.00	11.00	12.10	13.31	14.64	16.11	17.72	
Operating profit	$10.00	$11.40	$12.99	$14.79	$16.83	$19.14	$21.76	13.8
Case D:								
Revenue growth = 14%	$20.00	$22.80	$25.99	$29.63	$33.78	$38.51	$43.90	
Cost growth = 11%	10.00	11.10	12.32	13.68	15.18	16.85	18.70	
Operating profit	$10.00	$11.70	$13.67	$15.95	$18.60	$21.66	$25.20	16.7
Case E:								
Revenue growth = 16%	$20.00	$23.20	$26.91	$31.22	$36.21	$42.01	$48.73	
Cost growth = 12%	10.00	11.20	12.54	14.05	15.74	17.62	19.74	
Operating profit	$10.00	$12.80	$14.37	$17.17	$20.48	$24.38	$28.99	19.4
Case F:								
Revenue growth = 20%	$20.00	$24.00	$28.80	$34.56	$41.47	$49.77	$59.72	
Cost growth = 14%	10.00	11.40	13.00	14.82	16.89	19.25	21.95	
Operating Profit	$10.00	$12.60	$15.80	$19.74	$24.58	$30.51	$37.77	24.8

In updates on Cowles Broadcasting, we raised our PMV estimates from the initial $22.50–$26.25 figure to north of $40 per share. In January 1985, Cowles Broadcasting went private via a leveraged buyout at $46.05 per share returning almost 300 percent on our investment in less than three years.

Wometco Cable TV, Inc.

For another example of our private market value analysis leading us to an LBO, I've included the following Gabelli & Company report on Wometco Cable Television, Inc., a spinoff from Wometco Enterprises, at one time one of our largest portfolio holdings. I've chosen Wometco Cable TV because it is an excellent example of both free cash flow analysis and the effect of catalysts in surfacing private market value.

WOMETCO CABLE TV, INC.	
	March 1983
Current Price:	
(WCTV–OTC)	17 bid
1983 Price Range	18–13
Operating Income per Share:	
1984P	$4.00
1983E	3.30
1982A	2.42
Private Market Value per Share:	
1985P	$38.00
1984P	30.80
1983E	25.50

The Company

Wometco Cable TV, Inc. (WCTV-17-OTC) was spawned from Wometco Enterprises, Inc. (WOM-32-NYSE) when, in a public underwriting led by Drexel Burnham Lambert and E. F. Hutton & Company, Inc., in May 1981, 1,170,000 shares of new stock were sold to the public at $16.00 per share. About $17 million was raised for WCTV. Today, based on its roughly 240,000 basic subscribers at April 30, 1983, Wometco ranks as the 22nd largest MSO (or multiple system cable TV operator).

Wometco Cable Internal Attributes

- All of its 240,000 basic subscribers are served by 20 or more channel systems.

- **Growth prospects,** based on the geographic location of its systems, are *favorable*. Even if no new franchises are acquired, we project 330,000 basic subscribers by the end of 1985:

	1980	1981	1982	1983E	1984P	1985P
Number of basics (000)	142	195	229	265	300	330

- **Capital expenditures are trending down**

	1980	1981	1982	1983E	1984P	1985P
Outlays ($ million)	$23.5	$33.7	$29.3	$23.0	$18.0	$18.0

- **Operating margins are exploding upwards**

	1 Qtr.	2 Qtr.	3 Qtr.	4 Qtr.	Year
1981	31.3%	31.6%	30.5%	31.8%	31.4%
1982	33.8	36.0	38.5	40.4	37.6
1983	41.3	—	—	—	41.0E

- **Private market values are now $25–$30 per share and rising rapidly**

	1983E	1984P	1985P	1986P
PMV/share	$22.50	$30.80	$38.00	$45.00

The Assets

As of January 1, 1983, Wometco had 46 cable TV systems located in eight states. Certain industry trends should influence the value of cable systems. In turn, they provide an underpinning to the growth in the private market of WCTV we envision. Thus, even if the two-year time frame we allow for surfacing of values in our asset play is stretched out, we think investors will be compensated by a commensurate increase in the private market value of WCTV. These factors include:

Improving government regulation, notably S. 66. This bill provides assurances that a cable operator who lives up to his franchise agreement can expect a renewal of his franchise. The bill would curtail state and local authority to regulate cable television. The measure also grants cable systems full control over the rates they charge subscribers for basic service in large markets, calls for timely consideration of a cable system's renewal application, and establishes a renewal test that prevents cities from arbitrarily refusing franchise renewal.

- Investors will refocus on the free and clear cash flow that will be generated by companies such as Wometco one year hence.
- Industry fundamentals will be aided by addressable two-way converters and pay per view.

The Catalyst

Wometco Enterprises, Inc., the parent of Wometco Cable, Inc., is now controlled by the children of its founder, Mitchell Wolfson. We were particularly privileged to have known Mr. Wolfson for close to 14 years. He was a terrific patriarch. When he died on January 28, 1983, we believe a series of opportunities for the existing shareholders were set in motion. Simply stated, we believe that Wometco, which we have been recommending for the past 18 months and which we also believe is a superb asset play, will be the envy of many corporate types. Corporate America is casting about for cash generating entities, of which Wometco Enterprises has three: (1) broadcasting, (2) coke bottling, and (3) cable TV.

- **Legislation is increasingly favorable** for stepped-up merger activity in the broadcasting area.
- **New entrants are appearing in broadcasting,** notably, Kohlberg Kravis Roberts & Co. (New York), Rockefeller (Outlet), and Forstmann-Little.
- **New financial techniques are surfacing,** in particular, the purchase of Ziff Davis TV stations by the management through a leveraged buyout accomplished through a "retail syndicate."

Value Matrix

Without trying to be precise in an accounting sense, we believe the data in Table 2 should help investors relate to such questions as:

- What happens if average revenues rise $1 per subscriber per month?
- What if 10,000 more basic subscribers are added?
- What if the operating margin changed by 1 percent?

How Do These Values Surface?—Several Alternatives

There are many ways for investors to realize both the present and future values that we see in Wometco Cable TV. Among the possibilities are:

- **Growth in cash flow and higher multiple of cash flow.** The higher cash flow would stem from the internal analysis we did on

TABLE 2 Value Matrix

	10,000 Basic Subscribers	$1.00 Monthly Basic Charge	$1.00 Monthly Pay Charge	1% Margin
Operating Cash Flow/Share	$0.13	$0.40	$0.20	$0.08
PMV/Share	$1.30	$4.00	$2.00	$0.80

SOURCE: Gabelli & Company, Inc., estimates.

Wometco. The higher valuation is likely as investors focus attention on the industry's rising "free and clear" cash flow. Also favorable legislation would bring more corporate buyers, particularly coincident with the passage of legislation with language similar to S. 66. Thus, the company has to do nothing but continue to manage its affairs as well as it has done in the past and we should make our investment hurdle rates.

- **Swap of Wometco for Wometco Cable TV.** Wometco might offer to its shareholders the right to receive two shares of WCTV for each of its own shares. This would result in approximately 3.5 million shares of Wometco common being exchanged for Wometco Cable. This would give a broader market to WCTV and allow it to pursue its own destiny or, in turn, to be pursued more freely by outside entities. From Wometco's point of view, this action would help improve its own private market value, simplify its asset base, and make itself easier to acquire.

Wometco Parent	Shares o/s	WOM PMV*
Before swap	17.5 million	$45
After swap	14.0 million	$48

* Private market value of Wometco Enterprises based on Gabelli & Company, Inc., estimates.

- **Wometco Enterprises might consider repurchasing outstanding shares of WCTV.** The reasons that Wometco spun off the WCTV in the past no longer seem necessary. Perhaps a purchase price of $25 in cash might be forthcoming. This would represent a slight discount from our perceived private market value, but the "cleanness and quickness" of the deal would support this discount. It would cost cash generating Wometco only $30 million to pursue this option.
- **Sale of Wometco Cable to another entity.** Obviously, this is the

easiest of all alternatives and would be part of a larger program within the arena of Wometco Enterprises that would surface.

We don't care to place probabilities as to which alternative will be the one to surface the values.

In this situation there were two powerful catalysts at work: the unfortunate death of founder Mitchell Wolfson and government Regulation S. 66 which freed the cable TV industry from pricing restraints and arbitrary license renewal standards which clouded the future of all cable TV enterprises.

On March 1, 1984, Wometco Cable TV was merged into Wometco Cable Acquisition Corp., a private company controlled by preeminent leveraged buyout specialists Kohlberg Kravis Roberts & Co. (KKR). WCTV shareholders received $29.50 per share, slightly less than my 1984 private market value estimate of $30.80 per share, but significantly more than KKR's initial $25.00 bid. The dissolution of WCTV within less than a year of our recommendation and at a price approximating our PMV estimate teaches two lessons. First, when powerful catalysts are at work, private market values surface rapidly. Second, investors should not automatically accept the first buyout bid. If enough investors know what the fair price of the stock is and stick to their guns, the bid is likely to increase.

Storer Broadcasting, Inc.

In the case of Storer Broadcasting (later Storer Communications), our private market analysis put us into a profitable leveraged buyout and a unique opportunity to participate in the equity portion of the deal. We first recommended Storer at $22 per share in March 1978. In our initial Storer report, I estimated the company's PMV at approximately $65 per share. I continued to recommend and to buy the stock through 1985 even though the stock had climbed significantly and exceeded my initial private market value estimate. The reason? Due to accelerating operating cash flow from the company's broadcast properties and cable TV operations, our PMV estimate rose even more dramatically than Storer's stock price. Following is a private market value model we did on Storer in early 1983 (Table 3).

Basing value on 10 times Storer's broadcasting operating earnings (operating cash flow) plus $1,000 per cable subscriber minus declining debt paid by excess cash flow divided by the outstanding shares, I saw Storer's per share private market value growing from $72 in 1983 to $167 in 1988. Kohlberg Kravis Roberts & Co. bought us out of Storer at $91 cash per share and a warrant to buy a share of SCI Holdings, the new private company, in January 1986. I was pleased to see that KKR shared my opinion of Storer's true worth—on a cash basis they paid $1 less than

TABLE 3 Storer Communications—Estimated Private Market Value

	Broad-casting Operating Earnings ($ million)	Prevailing Acquisition Price (10 × cash flow) ($ million)	Cable Subscribers (million)	Prevailing Acquisition Price ($1,000/subscriber) ($ billion)	Outstanding Debt ($ million)	Shares Outstanding (million)	Estimated Private Market Value (per share)
1988	$89.0	$890.0	1.9	$1,900	—	21.2	$167.00
1987	81.0	810.0	1.8	1,800	$ 75.0	21.2	146.00
1986	74.0	740.0	1.6	1,600	400.0	21.2	110.00
1985	67.0	670.0	1.5	1,500	530.0	21.2	92.00
1984	61.0	610.0	1.5	1,500	666.0	21.2	80.00
1983	53.2	532.0	1.4	1,400	628.0	21.2	72.00

my $92 PMV estimate—and I was also happy to receive my SCI Holdings warrant, the subject of the following Gabelli & Company report.

SPECIAL SITUATION

SCI Holdings, Inc.   New Warrants   Trading When Issued   11/21/85

Son of Storer. Storer Communications, a long-standing favorite of ours, and still the largest investment position for our clients, has scheduled a special shareholders' meeting for this Friday, November 22, 1985. At that time, shareholders will approve a merger with a newly organized company created by the preeminent leveraged buyout specialist, Kohlberg Kravis Roberts & Co. The transaction calls for payment to each shareholder of $91 cash and a warrant to purchase one share of stock in the new privately owned company, SCI Holdings, Inc.

The Concept

The ownership of Storer warrants represents the first opportunity for the public investor to participate in the equity of a deal created by Kohlberg Kravis Roberts & Co. Stated another way, ownership of the warrant represents a call on KKR's exit strategy. Since KKR makes money only when they realize profits on their carry in private deals (bah!), the public shareholders may make money because KKR has motivation to sell the assets in SCI at a financially opportune time.

The Time Frame

The shareholders are scheduled to approve a merger on Friday, November 22nd. The FCC has yet to approve the license transfers, but, in light of recent decisions, notably Murdoch/Metromedia, ABC/CapCities, we do not anticipate any insurmountable structural barriers. However, a minor glitch may unfold. A gadfly, named Traylor, may attempt to disrupt the transfer. He is the same individual who attempted to interfere in the sale of Wometco to KKR. While the functionings of due process may delay the closing, we assume that the transaction will close by mid-December/early January. Thus, a purchase of Storer common today at $92 will create the new Storer warrant for $1 plus cost to carry the investment for 45 days.

Why Storer?

Why are we interested in Storer? Obviously, not solely because of KKR. The new Storer will emerge almost as a pure play in cable. For example, we estimate that by 1988, roughly three quarters of Storer's operating cash flow will be generated by its cable operations. Moreover, we anticipate that KKR might capitalize on the current voracious appetite for broadcast properties by selling off one or several television stations to increase the return on their investment, as well as provide greater financial flexibility. This would make it even more of a cable play.

THE MATH—WHAT WILL THE PRIVATE MARKET VALUE OF SCI HOLDINGS BE IN 1995?

In Exhibit 2, we depict the financing of the merger. In this regard, we wish to note the initial capitalization.

EXHIBIT 2

FINANCING THE MERGER

The Financing

General. SCI Holdings has entered into agreements with the banks and expects to enter into agreements with the partnership and two limited partnerships of which KKR Associates is the general partner, with the Management Investors and with the purchasers of the Debt Securities, and Scipsco expects to enter into agreements with the purchasers of the Preferred Stock, to provide the Financing in the approximate amount of $2.48 billion. The sources and applications of the funds constituting the Financing are estimated to be as follows:

Source of funds:	
Bank debt (7 ½ year senior revolving credit)	$ 740,000,000
Working capital line of credit	50,000,000
Issuance of the notes	600,000,000
Issuance of the senior subordinated debentures	600,000,000
Issuance of the preferred stock	261,100,000
Issuance of holdings common stock	227,264,000
Issuance of the warrants	5,000,000
Total	$2,483,364,000
Application of funds:	
Payment of cash for shares of Storer common stock	1,929,200,000
Available for payment of fees and expenses incurred in connection with the consummation of the merger, repayment of certain indebtedness of Storer and for working capital	554,164,000
Total	$2,483,364,000

SOURCE: Storer Communications, Inc., October 23, 1985, p. 26.

In Exhibit 3, we track the pro forma ownership of the new company. Yes, there will be 212 million shares outstanding.

Finally, in Exhibit 4, we find management's projected operating data through 1990.

In analyzing the data, we concluded that the operating numbers are achievable.

- Cash flow from cable will represent 80 percent of the 1990 money.
- We are optimistic with cable reflecting industry dynamics, and the maturity of Storer Systems.
- The franchised nature of the business and the discreet nature permits a series of "mini-exit" windows.

THE RATE OF RETURN—OUR NUMBERS— OUR METHODOLOGY

In Table 4, we unfold our approach both as to arriving at a private market value for Storer in 1995 and a value for the warrant at that time.

In Table 5, we walk you through our model regarding cash flow and its impact on debt. The driving force to calculating the 1990 and 1995 values of the merger warrants is estimating the private market value (PMV) of SCI Holdings, Inc., by those dates.

Assumptions underlying our projections are:

- Operating cash flow to 1990 is projected by management to increase 15 percent per annum, a projection with which we agree.
- Operating cash flow from 1990 to 1995 increases at 10 percent per annum.
- PMV valuation of 10X operating cash flow.
- Debt reduction as scheduled by SCI Holdings in proxy material and our data.

Table 6 is our "workout matrix" of the merger warrants' value to 1995, given the above assumptions. In looking at the numbers, we point out that our projections do not include any "time value" premium which might build up in the warrants. In addition, they do not reflect an "earlier exit strategy" by KKR, which would likely enhance the return.

When looking at the numbers, they should be viewed not for their "accounting" precision, but rather as a springboard for reflection on various price/time purchase points. For example, if one were to purchase a warrant for $3 in December 1985, the internal rate of return would be 21.8 percent to 1995. If one were to purchase the warrant at $4 per share, the rate of return would be 18.4 percent.

In sum, the combination of purchasing Storer warrants to achieve a 20 percent compounded rate of return, which on its own is attractive, coupled with an opportunity to participate in KKR's LBO make us

EXHIBIT 3 Ownership of SCI Holdings Common Stock after the Effective Time

After completion of the Financing and consummation of the Merger, SCI Holdings Common Stock is expected to be beneficially owned as follows:

Name and Address	Number of Shares	Percent	Fully Diluted (1)	
			Number of Shares	Percent
KKR Associates (2) 9 West 57th St., Suite 4170 New York, NY 10019	107,696,000	97.2%	107,696,000	50.3%
SCI Partners (2) 9 West 57th St., Suite 4170 New York, NY 10019	—	—	67,340,000	32.0
Management Investors (3) (approximately 25 persons) c/o Storer Communications, Inc. 12000 Biscayne Boulevard Miami, FL 33131	3,052,300	2.3	15,264,000	7.2
Storer common stockholders (4)	—	—	21,200,000	10.0
	110,743,300	100.0	212,000,000	100.0

EXHIBIT 4

SCI HOLDINGS
Six-Year Consolidated Operating Projection 1985–1990
(in thousands)

	Actual		Projected				
	1984	1985	1986	1987	1988	1989	1990
Net revenues.	$536,324	$602,793	$661,796	$743,259	$823,190	$907,420	$999,625
Expenses, including depreciation	468,354	496,662	514,536	547,215	586,805	629,009	672,727
Operating income	67,970	106,131	147,260	196,044	236,385	278,411	326,898
Income (loss) before extraordinary items	(16,742)	1,459	78,600	83,760	113,507	145,418	179,937
Extraordinary items: Tax benefit of net operating loss carryforward	0	6,092	10,145	0	0	0	0
Net income (loss)	$ (16,742)	$ 7,551	$ 88,745	$ 83,760	$113,507	$145,418	$179,937

SOURCE: Storer Proxy, p. 42.

TABLE 4 Storer LBO Analysis—Merger Warrant Valuation, 1986 Estimated–1995 Projected

($ million)	1986E	1987P	1988P	1989P	1990P	1991P	1992P	1993P	1994P	1995P
Operating cash flow	$ 262.0	$ 312.0	$ 356.0	$ 405.0	$ 458.0	$ 503.8	$ 544.2	$ 609.6	$ 670.6	$ 737.6*
Valuation multiple	10X	10X	10X	10X	10X	10X	10X	10X	10X	10X
Total	$2,620.0	$3,120.0	$3,560.0	$4,050.0	$4,580.0	$5,038.0	$5,542.0	$6,096.0	$6,706.0	$7,376.0
Less: (LTD + Preferred stock)	(2,339.1)	(2,443.3)	(2,540.0)	(2,614.0)	(2,527.9)	(2,540.8)	(2,273.8)	(2,061.0)	(2,061.0)	(2,061.0)
Plus: Warrant exercise†	—	—	—	—	—	—	—	—	—	$ 265.0†
Estimated PMV	$ 280.9	$ 676.7	$1,020.0	$1,436.0	$2,052.1	$2,497.8	$3,268.2	$4,035.0	$4,645.0	$5,580.0
Shares o/s (million)	212.0	212.0	212.0	212.0	212.0	212.0	212.0	212.0	212.0	212.0
PMV per share	$1.30	$3.20	$4.80	$6.80	$9.70	$11.80	$15.40	$19.03	$21.91	$26.30
Less: Warrant exercise price	(4.72)	(4.72)	(4.72)	(4.72)	(4.72)	(4.72)	(4.72)	(4.72)	(4.72)	(4.72)
Est. warrant value	—	—	$0.10	$2.10	$5.00	$7.10	$10.70	$14.90	$19.40	$21.60

* Internal projections are about 5 percent lower.
† Includes merger warrants and warrants held by Drexel Burnham and Storer management group.
SOURCE: Storer Communication Inc., Proxy, October 23, 1985 and Gabelli & Company, Inc. estimates.

TABLE 5 SCI Holdings, Inc.—LTD Schedule ($ million)

	1985	1986	1987	1988	1989	1990	1991	1992	1993	1994	1995
Bank debt	$ 740.0	$ 715.0	$ 615.0	$ 490.0	$ 365.0	$ 200.0	$ 120.0	$ 40.0	—	—	—
Zero notes	600.0	685.0	783.0	894.0	1,022.2	1,017.8	1,012.9	757.0	$465.0	$131.0	—
Senior subordinated debentures (at face value)	600.0	600.0	600.0	600.0	600.0	600.0	600.0	600.0	600.0	600.0	$ 400.0
Storer 10% Subordinated debentures due 2003 (at face value)	138.0	138.0	138.0	138.0	138.0	138.0	138.0	138.0	127.7	117.3	107.0
Preferred stock	261.1	305.4	357.3	418.0	489.0	572.1	669.3	738.8	742.0	742.0	742.0
New financing required (balance)	—	—	—	—	—	—	—	—	126.3	470.7	812.0
Total LTD and preferred	$2,339.1	$2,443.4	$2,493.3	$2,540.0	$2,614.2	$2,527.9	$2,540.2	$2,273.8	$2,061.0	$2,061.0	$2,061.0

SOURCE: Storer Communications Inc., Proxy; 1984 Annual Report; Gabelli & Company, Inc., projections.

TABLE 6 Storer Merger Warrants—Annualized Return on Investment to 1995 (1995 warrant value = $21.60)

Workout Matrix Warrant Price	12/31/85	6/30/86	12/31/86	6/30/87	12/31/87	6/30/88	12/31/88
$2.00	26.90%	28.50%	30.30%	32.30%	34.60%	37.30%	40.50%
2.50	24.10	25.50	27.10	28.90	30.90	33.30	36.10
3.00	21.80	23.10	24.50	26.10	28.00	30.10	32.60
3.50	20.00	21.10	22.40	23.90	25.50	27.50	29.70
4.00	18.40	19.40	20.60	21.90	23.50	25.20	27.20
5.00	15.80	16.70	17.70	18.80	20.10	21.50	23.20
6.00	13.70	14.40	15.30	16.30	17.40	18.60	20.10
7.00	11.90	12.60	13.30	14.20	15.10	16.20	17.50
8.00	10.40	11.00	11.70	12.40	13.20	14.20	15.20

SOURCE: Gabelli & Company, Inc., calculations.

recommend this highly speculative and somewhat unique financial instrument.

It's too early to tell whether our SCI Holdings warrants recommendation will bear fruit long term. As of this writing, the warrants are selling at 3½ bid, 3⅝ ask. My confidence in the idea is reflected in the fact that GAMCO clients still own all the warrants received from the Storer buyout. Our continuing faith in what we've nicknamed Son of Storer reflects our characteristic willingness to hold onto stocks as long as they remain private market value bargains. I am a postage stamp investor. I stick to stocks as long as I believe they can deliver profits.

Our "Rest in Peace" List

Three of the four examples I've presented have been broadcast and/or cable TV companies. Although these industries do lend themselves to private market value analysis, they are not the only industries in which we've owned and recommended stocks that have been retired from public life—some by LBO transactions. As Exhibit 5, showing a list of transition of major GAMCO client holdings, indicates, we've identified LBO candidates in a range of industries.

In today's market, leveraged buyouts no longer seem to be limited in scope or size. Kohlberg Kravis Roberts & Co.'s recent leveraged buyout of Beatrice, a $6.2 billion deal, indicates there is virtually no company too big to be LBO'd provided it qualifies via the criteria I listed earlier. With the federal government and the Federal Reserve contemplating and enacting regulations regarding the financing of leveraged buyouts, one must concede that LBO activity is likely to slow. However, as long as the stock market undervalues public companies' assets and as long as capital remains free to seek its highest rate of return, leveraged buyout transactions will take place. Analysts who learn to spot the qualifiers will continue to be rewarded.

IDENTIFYING TAKEOVER CANDIDATES

The corporate takeover is the best known and most frequent method for private market values to be realized. We have owned many more stocks which have been taken over than have been LBO'd, but I prefer to analyze a company from the perspective of a leveraged buyout specialist rather than a potential corporate acquirer. LBOs are usually achieved at lower premiums to public market prices than takeovers because the value of the target's assets alone determines the economics of the deal. Corporate acquirers have additional resources such as stock and/or cash to finance a takeover. Since we don't always know who a prospective corporate acquirer may be, it is often difficult to factor in the impact of these resources on a company's private market value or likely takeover

EXHIBIT 5 Transition of Major Holdings (1977–1984)

Investment	Name of Company	Acquiring Concern
Broadcasting & CATV	Combined Communications	Gannett
	Cowles Broadcasting	H & C Communications
	Cox Communications	*Private firm*
	Gross	*Going private*
	Kingstrip	Lin Broadcasting
	Metromedia	*Private firm*
	Outlet	Rockefeller Center
	Rust Craft	*Private firm*
	Sonderling Broadcasting	Viacom
	Starr Broadcasting	*Private group*
	Storer Communications	*Private firm*
	Teleprompter	Westinghouse
	Wometco	*Private firm*
	+Various CATV & Newspapers	
Motion pictures	Columbia Pictures	Coca-Cola
	Twentieth Century Fox	*Private firm*
Service companies	Avis	Norton Simon
	Baker Industries	Borg-Warner
	Brinks	Pittston
	Burns Int'l	Borg-Warner
	International Courier	Gelco
	Loomis	Mayne Nickless
	Pacific Holdings	*Private firm*
Other	ACF	Carl Icahn
	Cadence	*Private firm*
	Esquire	Gulf & Western
	Stokely-Van Camp	Quaker Oats
Auto parts: Distribution	APS	Gulf & Western
	Curtiss-Noll	Congoleum
	General Automotive	Genuine Parts
	Whitlock	LCP Holdings
Manufacturing	Altamil	*Private firm*
	American Mfg.	Allied
	Anderson Co.	Champion Spark Plug
	Bendix	Allied
	Budd Co.	Thyssen
	CR Industries	IFI
	Globe-Union	Johnson Controls
	Houdaille	*Private group*
	Maremont	Alusuisse
	McCord	Ex-cello
	Monroe Auto	Tenneco
	Moog	IFI
	Norris Industries	*Private group*
	Raybestos (partial)	Echlin
	STP	Esmark
	Texstar	Hillman
	Weatherhead	Dana
	Wix	Dana

price. By using the more conservative PMV estimate derived from a leveraged buyout perspective, I feel more secure. The financial considerations such as cash, free cash flow, and salable assets are similar for LBOs and takeovers. So, if you buy a stock on the basis of its value to a leveraged buyout specialist, the higher premium you receive from a takeover is pure gravy.

Having said this, I will mention that in the analysis of takeovers, an investor does benefit from several sources of information frequently not present in a prospective LBO situation. The most obvious is the ability to monitor significant corporate purchases of the stock. I receive a service that alerts me to all 13d filings. A 13d is required by the SEC whenever any investor purchases more than 5 percent of a publicly owned company. An amendment must be filed any time there is a material change in this position, which is defined as a change exceeding 1 percent.

When I come upon an intriguing 13d filing, I try to answer numerous questions. Why is one corporation investing in the stock of another? Will the businesses complement each other? Might the acquirer be looking for entry into a business which is cheaper to buy than to build? Does it need a cash cow to support its other businesses? The next step is to determine how difficult and expensive an acquisition would be. How much stock does the management of the target company own? Is management in the mood to "make love" or will it respond to an offer by putting up the obstacles to a takeover bid? Can the prospective acquirer afford to pay a fair price for the target company? If adding substantial debt is necessary to make an acquisition, what will the capital costs be? Are there any potential regulatory problems? Finally, how is the 13d filer accumulating the stock? Is it being purchased patiently and consistently on the bid side of the market or aggressively in large blocks on the offering side? If I can come up with logical answers to these questions and if the target company qualifies as a true private market value by our standards, I may buy a stock as a pure takeover play.

In industries which are already experiencing increased merger and acquisition activity, the analyst benefits from prevailing takeover formulas such as multiples of revenues, earnings, or cash flow. You should be aware, however, that these formulas are not static. They will vary with supply and demand as is the case with what I refer to as a buffalo group like the cable TV and group broadcasters in the last several years. For example, when Taft Broadcasting acquired Gulf Broadcast in one of the first shots fired in the group broadcaster takeover wars, it paid approximately 12 times calender 1985 cash flow. In some of the ensuing deals for Cox Communications' broadcast properties, hungry acquirers bid the multiple to cash flow price up to 15.

Economic forces may also impact prevailing merger and acquisition formulas. For example, today the multiple to cash flow equation for broadcast acquisitions may be coming down due to weakening of the broadcast advertising market. We own Taft Broadcasting because it is selling at a deep discount to our private market value estimate of $137 per share. As the PMV model in Table 7 indicates, we are valuing Taft's TV stations, most of which are in the top 40 growth markets, at just 10 times cash flow even though there is some takeover flavor (via San

TABLE 7 Private Market Value Model

	Prepared March 1984		Updated August 1985
	Fiscal 1984	PMV	Fiscal 1986
Broadcasting:			
TV station at 10 × Cash flow	$613(*)		$770
Radio station at 8 × Cash flow	72		96
	$685		$866
5 TV stations	-0-		750
Total TV		$685	$1,616
Taft Entertainment Co.:			
Hanna Barbera			
Cy Fisher			
World Vision			
Miscellaneous	$125–$150		$150–$200
Miscellaneous assets:			
Equity in Kings Ent. Co. (1/3 ownership)	$ 10		$ 15
Equity in CATV with T COMA	20		40
Philadelphia Phillies at cost	15		15
R. E. in King Island	20		20
Golf Course			
Kings Diner			
Winter Wonderland (Toronto, Can.)	50		70
Other	20		20
		$135	$ 180
		970	1,946
Less: Debt		45	700
By 9.1 shares o/s		$925	$1,246
PMV per share		$100(†)	$137

*TV station now (10 × CF before); Radio now at 8 (6 × CF before).
COMMENTS: † Based on 9.2 shares outstanding.
PREPARED BY: Mario J. Gabelli, 8/27/85.

Francisco Partners, Robert Bass of the infamous Bass Brothers owns 11 percent of Taft stock), and recent takeovers in the industry have been at higher multiples to cash flow.

The Crayon Explosion

Another thing to consider in analyzing takeover candidates is that what didn't happen yesterday may still happen tomorrow. Consider our experience with Binney & Smith. As the following report indicates, we viewed Binney & Smith as a demographic play with some takeover flavor.

Demographic Play No. 1   Update No. 4
    Binney & Smith, Inc.—(BYS-24-NYSE)—AGGRESSIVE BUY

Year	EPS	P/E		Current
1982P	$3.10	7.7	Dividend: $1.04	Return: 4.3%
1981E	$2.40	10.0	3,532,000 shares	
1980	$1.68	14.3	Range (1980–81):	29-19

The Company

Binney & Smith, a small but highly profitable company with estimated revenues of $118 million in 1981, is best known for its Crayola brand of crayons, a market which it dominates. In our last published report (Abstract—November 29, 1979—For Sale), we indicated that "accounts that were willing to speculate on a change in management's position toward making love" should retain positions. All others should sell. We now recommend aggressive purchase. To review the fundamentals on which we base our recommendation:

- *Demographics*
    We have written about the trends in live births in previous reports and recent developments continue to unfold favorably for the company.
    Again, our case is that there will be a 2 percent per annum gain in children in the three-to-nine-year-old age bracket in the early 1980s versus a decline for most of the past 15 years. (Incidentally, from our own observations in the Gabelli household, we have concluded that children consume—not use—crayons at an age earlier than three, and that parents are a prime market for the "survival" kits that Binney is now marketing).

- *Management Change*

    Jack K. Kofoed (age 54) assumed the role of chief executive officer on January 1, 1981. While he is not new to the company, events since he has assumed the helm have pointed to a more aggressive pursuit of both revenues growth and profit improvement:

    Price increases have been accelerated.

    Low growth product lines are being weeded out.

    Crayola brand awareness is being capitalized on.

    Crayola markers are finally profitable.

    Marketing channels are being broadened.

    New product development is acclerating.

- *Earnings Breakout*

    Refer to Table 8.

    Revenues and earnings appear to be in a breakout phase which we believe is sustainable.

    For 1981 we are projecting revenues of $118 million, up 25 percent over the $94 million reported for 1980 and earnings of $2.40–$2.50 per share, up nearly 50 percent from the depressed $1.68 per share earned in 1980.

    Beyond this year, we project revenues growth in excess of 14 percent from internal sources. Table 8 depicts our growth model for revenues through 1985. Reflecting better operating efficiency, declining financial costs, and lower tax rates, earnings gains should approach 20 percent per annum. However, we note that earnings will remain seasonal and quarterly results somewhat erratic on a year-to-year basis.

- *Financial Position Is Excellent:*

    Long-term debt of $10.5 million represented only 16 percent of total capitalization at September 30, 1981.

    Book value is estimated at $15.50 per share at December 31, 1981.

    Future growth financed internally.

- *Sell-Out Always Possible:*

    In this regard, a little history might prove helpful. It was on September 7, 1979, that the Kellogg Company offered to acquire BYS for $36 per share for 45 percent of the stock and 1.75 shares of Kellogg for the balance. While the board of directors rejected that offer, perhaps the board is reexamining its fiduciary duty to provide public (i.e., nonfamily) shareholders the option of accepting a premium bid. At the time Kellogg's offer was made, we observed that it was at 3 times book value and 18 times our earnings estimate.

    New lower long-term capital gains tax rate, high (versus inflation) reinvestment rates, and new estate tax laws might

TABLE 8 Binney & Smith Inc.—Sales by Product, 1974–1983P

Area of Activity	1974	1975	1976	1977	1978	1979	1980	1981P	1982P	1983P	Percent of Total 1981P	Expected Growth 1981–1985P	Total Expected Growth 1981–1985P
Artists' materials:													
Crayons and chalks	$27.1	$30.8	$33.5	$35.4	$38.3	$40.1	$47.0	$ 59.0	$ 67.0	$ 77.0	50.0%	13.0%	6.5%
Paints, brushes, and other	20.0	21.0	21.5	23.3	27.0	26.8	31.0	36.0	40.0	47.0	30.5	12.0	3.6
Activities	3.0	3.4	4.8	8.0	9.8	11.0	16.0	23.0	30.0	36.0	19.5	20.0	3.9
Other:													
Total revenues	$50.1	$56.0	$59.8	$66.7	$75.0	$78.7	$94.0	$118.0	$137.0	$160.0	100.0%		14.0%
Percent change	12.5%	11.9%	6.7%	11.5%	12.4%	4.9%	19.4%	26.7%	16.1%	16.8%			

SOURCE: Gabelli & Company, Inc., estimates.

combine to spark renewed merger fever from major family holders who own 1,284,542 shares of common stock, or 36.9 percent of the total. (In addition, another 10 percent is closely held.) Externally, interest in the company could be whetted again by declining cost of capital and perceived brighter dynamics.

The fact that no one appeared willing to follow up on Kellogg's original takeover bid eliminated Binney & Smith as a takeover candidate in the minds of most investors. We stuck with the stock because it continued to qualify as a decent private market value discount, earnings prospects were favorable, and there was a hunger developing in consumer nondurable industries for brand names. Our patience paid off when Binney & Smith was acquired by Hallmark for $56 per share in August 1984.

The Thunderbolt Stock Story

Occasionally, we've been taken out of portfolio companies which we couldn't honestly qualify as well-documented takeover candidates. I always have a list and in some cases positions in what I call thunderbolt stocks. These are undermanaged companies which have failed to properly utilize assets to create good operating results, and thus sell at significant discounts to PMV. There are no catalysts present to give me any great faith that private market value is likely to surface in the foreseeable future. The hope is that someone or something will appear like a thunderbolt and either turn these companies around or take them over.

Transway International Corp. was one thunderbolt stock that did get hit by lightning. The following comments made in a June 1984 Stock Market Innovators interview illustrated my thoughts on Transway.

Innovators: Anything interesting at the moment?

Gabelli: I've always got some stocks. Let me give you situations that I didn't develop in my recent *Barrons* interview. The first is Transway Int'l (NYSE, TNW). At $30⅞ per share, Transway is currently selling at about its accounting book value. Private market value is much higher. For your $30⅞ you get Great Dane, the largest manufacturer of refrigerated trailers in the U.S. Good market niche, efficient manufacturer . . . Great Dane was the only player in the game which remained profitable at the bottom of the last business cycle. I see a few good years ahead. Cash flow should be $45 million next year. I think this business alone is worth the full price of Transway stock.

On top of Great Dane, you get a propane distribution business which should produce a cash flow of $10–15 million next year. I figure this is worth another $16 per share. Add $5 per share of cash, and you get a private market value somewhere in the $50 per share range. This isn't even counting Transway's other two divisions, a transportation company and a freight forwarding business. You could liquidate these businesses and wipe out all of Transway's $68 million debt.

So far no catalyst has surfaced. However, I would mention that management owns very little stock and doesn't appear to be the kind of folks who would stand in the way of their shareholders making some money. I'm buying the stock right now.

Transway was acquired by International Controls for cash and stock valued at $48.15 per share in December 1985.

IDENTIFYING LIQUIDATION CANDIDATES

The most straightforward way for private market values to be realized is a pure liquidation of a public company. Since a liquidation involves disposing of assets usually in the private market, our brand of analysis lends itself to identifying liquidation candidates. In fact, Gabelli & Company's first official asset play, Cowles Communications, also became the first stock we recommended and owned which was liquidated. The following Gabelli & Company research report tells the story.

Gabelli & Company, Inc.   April 15, 1977
Asset Play No. 1
Cowles Communications, Inc.
Current Price: 14
(CWL-NYSE)

We recommend Cowles on the basis of:

- *Dividends.* The present $0.16 per share quarterly rate is likely to jump to $0.20 per share during the second half of this year. We envisage annual dividends growth of 10 percent beyond.
- *Assets.* The stock is selling at over a 30 percent discount from the $20 per share valuation we place on the company's assets.

	Private Market Value per Share
Cash at year-end	$ 1.30
Two TV stations (our estimate)	7.50
Ownership of 23% of *The New York Times* ($17-ASE)	11.20
	$20.00

- No long-term debt on the balance sheet at year-end.

We believe that Cowles's assets are of above-average interest. First, the company's two TV stations are in rapidly growing markets, are handily capable of enjoying revenues growth of 8–10 percent and pretax profits growth of 12 percent, and generate what we describe as "free and clear" cash flow, which is "domestic" in nature. Second, while we don't hold ourselves out as experts on *The New York Times*, our examination of the just released 1976 annual report points to an improving financial posture there. This could lead to higher dividends, and just as important, "inflation indexed" growth in asset value for *The Times*.

The question arises, "What will Cowles do with itself?" To understand all the alternatives we must first discuss what we perceive to be the main obstacle to some form of "surfacing" of the assets. This involves continued legal jousting over the license renewal of Cowles's Florida TV station. Almost seven years ago, a challenge against WESH-TV was initiated by a group seeking the license. The issue centered on whether the station's studio was out of the "city of license." The FCC, in a 4-1 decision, voted to renew the license on January 5, 1977. However, the challenger applicant has filed an appeal with the U.S. Court of Appeals. We doubt any actions regarding the disposition of corporate assets will be pursued until this issue is resolved. Based on our observation of somewhat similar proceedings (e.g., *Carter* v. *Maxwell*), we conclude it is reasonable to expect resolution of this within the next 12 months.

The Company

We do not wish to repeat history here. Let it suffice to say that since October 1971, Cowles has operated as a closed-end, nondiversified management investment company. From 1971 to the present, the company has been pruning its corporate base to where it presently has only two assets: two television stations and the stock position in *The New York Times*.

The TV Stations

In Table 9 we depict financial highlights of the two markets. Note the growth rate versus the national average.

In 1975 Orlando enjoyed a 14.4 percent growth in National Spot, while Des Moines was up 18.2 percent—both above the national average. While FCC data is not available, we expect 1976 results were good.

In Table 10 we depict the stations' recent operating performance and our projections. We also depict our approach at arriving at approximate market values for the properties.

Precise split-up of revenues for each of the Cowles properties is not available, but we suspect that WESH-TV generates significantly more profits than does KCCI-TV for Cowles.

Since Cowles charges all management's salaries against its operating

TABLE 9

Market	Ranking—1975* By Revenues	By Profit
Orlando-Daytona, Florida	47	45
Des Moines-Ames, Iowa	66	67

Market Growth—
Five-Year Compound Growth 1969–1974, Spot Advertising

	National	Local	Total
Orlando-Daytona	9.3%	8.2%	8.9%
Des Moines-Ames	14.8	18.2	16.5
Industry total—U.S.	3.6	13.1	7.1

* Latest available data.
SOURCE: FCC.

properties (such costs were $507,218 in 1976), the use of the industry's historical rule of thumb of valuing a station (8 to 10 times operating profits) appears to provide conservative values for the two stations. Also, we observe that the expected prices paid for TV stations are likely to climb in light of Combined Communications' recent proposed purchase of WMAL-TV in Washington, D.C.

The License Challenge

The renewal application of Cowles Florida Broadcasting, Inc., for the license to operate WESH-TV is still being contested. On December 7, 1973, Federal Communications Commission Administrative Judge Chester F. Naumowicz, Jr., released an initial decision in which he granted renewal of the license. This decision was appealed to the FCC and oral arguments were heard in November 1974.

TABLE 10   TV Operating Performance ($ million)

	1974	1975	1976	1977E	1980E
Revenues—net	7.7	8.5	10.8	12.3	16.5
Operating profit	1.1	1.8	2.6	3.4	5.0
Station value ($ million):					
At 8 × Operating profit	$ 8.8	$14.4	$20.8	$27.2	$40.0
At 10 × Operating profit	11.0	18.0	26.0	34.0	50.0

Regarding KCCI-TV, the FCC released a memorandum opinion and order granting the motion of the company to dismiss the petition to deny the renewal of the license on January 26, 1976, filed by the U.S. Department of Justice. The FCC unanimously granted the renewal application for KCCI-TV subject to whatever action the FCC may deem appropriate as a result of the matters pending involving the renewal application of WESH-TV. The FCC found on review of the application of KCCI-TV that the company is legally, technically, financially, and otherwise qualified to remain an FCC licensee. The most recent license renewal application for KCCI-TV for a three-year period beginning February 1, 1977, and ending January 31, 1980, was granted by the commission on January 20, 1977.

On July 2, 1976, the FCC announced a decision granting the renewal of the license application of Cowles Broadcasting, Inc., the licensee of WESH-TV. Three of the seven commissioners dissented from the decision by the majority of the commission granting the renewal. *However, after reconsideration, on January 5, 1977, the commission clarified its earlier decision and after such clarification the final vote of the commission was 4-1 in favor of renewal.*

The challenger-applicant, which had applied for a construction permit to operate WESH-TV, has filed an appeal with the U.S. Court of Appeals for the District of Columbia and proceedings attendant to this matter may continue for an indefinite period.

If we were to assume an end to the legal imbroglio over the licenses, then we would speculate that Cowles:

- Could buy more TV stations.
- Spin-off the extant stations to its shareholders.
- Sell the stations and pay a tax on the profit.
- Keep the stations in Cowles and sell off or spin off the other assets to its shareholders.
- Sell off the entire company or merge into *The New York Times.*

We believe that the last option is the most probable alternative. If we were to speculate that the license challenge were terminated, which might take one year, and that a merger would be pursued, we have calculated that *The New York Times* could pay $25 per share in cash for Cowles, finance the $100 million purchase at 10 percent, and enjoy an enlargement of its earnings base.

Other Comments

Finally, we observe that earnings for the first quarter of 1977 from the TV stations may be flat year to year. This is traceable to strong political advertising in 1976's first quarter in Florida, which is absent this year.

The New York Times (ASE-NYT.A-$17)

Market Value. Cowles owns 2.6 million shares of *The New York Times* Class A stock, or 23 percent. Thus, for each share of Cowles an investor indirectly obtains approximately .66 shares of *the New York Times*.

Market Value	
If Price of N.Y. Times	Then Value/Share of CWL
$14	$ 9.25
16	10.85
18	11.85
20	13.20
22	14.50

Dividends. *The New York Times* pays a $0.60 per share dividend. Under present tax law 85 percent of dividends received by one corporation from another corporation are excludable from taxable income. Thus, Cowles only pays a 7.2 percent tax on such dividends received from *The Times*. Assume that:

If annual dividends—N.Y.T.	$0.60	$0.80	$1.00
Total cash received on 2.6 million shares	$1,560,000	$2,080,000	$2,600,000
Less taxes at 7.2%	112,000	150,000	187,000
Net available cash	$1,448,000	$1,930,000	$2,413,000
Available/CWL share	$0.37	$0.49	$0.60

Thus, if *The Times* were to increase its dividend rate, as some have speculated, we would expect Cowles to pass through this dividend increase to its shareholders, particularly as it has no debt, extra cash, and a large untapped "borrowing power."

In Sum

We believe that Cowles represents a sound investment on the basis of rising dividends and a sizable discount from replacement cost of its assets. If we were to assume no change in price in *The New York Times* from the current $17.00 per share price, an end to the legal hassle at WESH-TV, a liquidation of the company, the return to Cowles' shareholders over the next three years could be derived as follows:

	1977	1978	1979	Total
Expected dividends	$0.72	$0.82	$0.96	$ 2.50
Expected value of assets				22.00
				$24.50

If CWL Bought at	Annual Return Would Be
$12	35%
13	29
14	25
15	21
16	17

Cowles Communications took much longer to work out than we first anticipated. We owned and continued to recommend Cowles Communications through December 16, 1982, at which time it was formally liquidated. In mid-January 1983, Cowles shareholders received $2.25 in cash, two thirds of a share of *The New York Times* stock which after a 3-for-1 split effectively became two shares, and one share of a new company, Cowles Broadcasting which traded initially at 16. Add it all up and it was a $64 value for a stock we first bought at about $14 per share, or about 4½ times our original investment over 5¾ years. We are satisfied with that rate of return.

REALIZING PRIVATE MARKET VALUES THROUGH CORPORATE RESTRUCTURING

A prevailing misconception about asset value investing is that you only make money when the stocks are taken over, LBO'd, or liquidated. This is hardly the case. There are numerous examples of private market value discounts we have owned and recommended that have survived and prospered because assets have been redeployed to produce greater profitability or to fund restructuring and/or substantial share repurchases. The moral of the story is that undervalued assets can be and often are used to benefit shareholders.

Our recent experience with GenCorp, the former General Tire, is a good example. Our firm has been following GenCorp for quite a while. It was managed, or I should say undermanaged, by the founding O'Neil family for as long as we've known it. GenCorp had been in decent businesses, but was never able to produce profits comparable to the quality competition, or in some cases even the industry average. The company was characterized by a lot of excess fat in its operating divisions, participation in many marginal businesses, and family management too stubborn or lethargic to change anything. We had never owned GenCorp stock, but it had long been on my thunderbolt list. I became an active buyer last year when a catalyst emerged in the form of new CEO Bill Reynolds. I was familiar with Mr. Reynolds from his management role at TRW and felt he was a guy who could change GenCorp's destiny and surface its $110–$120 private market value. The change in the FCC Rule of 7 which allowed broadcast companies to own more than seven TV stations was another catalyst. GenCorp's RKO division owned TV stations in New York and LA, two flagship markets. The stations had miserable operating records, but were worth a great deal of money to any group broadcaster looking for an entry into these heretofore closed markets.

I began accumulating GenCorp stock in the mid-30s per share in the fall of 1984. Mr. Reynolds did not disappoint. He dumped Frontier Airlines, a consistent money loser; closed the Akron, Ohio, tire plant; and eliminated half the capacity of the big Waco, Texas, plant. He also put the LA and New York television stations up for bid. Both are in the process of being sold for a combined total of almost $600 million, part of which we believe will be used for a major share repurchase program. In the process of Reynolds's restructuring, GenCorp stock has climbed to the mid-70s as I write.

In an October 14th interview in *Barron's*, I portrayed GenCorp as a likely takeover or leveraged buyout candidate. With the stock now in the mid-70s versus 47 at the time of this interview, the prospects for an exogenous event have narrowed along with the spread between stock price and private market value. I now view a major share repurchase program and rapidly rising earnings as the primary factors that will push GenCorp stock significantly higher. Am I disappointed it wasn't taken over or LBO'd? No, we've already doubled our money from our initial investment in GenCorp and expect to make even more money in the future on the basis of the cap shrink and continuing redeployment of assets.

Q: . . . What else do you like, Mario?

A: The other great value that should not be ignored is General Tire, now known as GenCorp. GenCorp is an outstanding takeover play. If I were going to spot one for you and be a bird dog on it, and one that I want to hammer away on because of its broadcast assets, I would pick on Gencorp. I think the investors should own GenCorp.

Q: Why should they own GenCorp?

A: There are 23 million shares of stock. We think that their non-RKO assets— that is, their tire business, their aerojet business, and their industrial products business, minus all the liabilities, plus some minor other assets— is worth about $45 a share. Then, the investor picks up through RKO, which is 100 percent owned by GenCorp, a bottling business—Pepsi Cola Bottling—which is worth about $13–$14 a share.

Q: You got hit by lightning on that offer for Frontier, which Gencorp owns a piece of.

A: No, no. We were always of the opinion that the company would sell out their investment in Frontier. It took longer than we thought, true. They had a great problem getting $17–$20, and now apparently—whatever the reasons—they are going to get $24 a share. So it is an extra $5 times 5 million shares—it is $25 million. That is only $1 per share incrementally of GenCorp—that extra $5. But what it does is all of a sudden it tells the world: "My God, look they are getting $125 million in cash." And that buys a lot of chopped liver.

Q: And the rye bread to put it on.

A: They have got three or four other cash assets that are worth another $25. In addition to that, the company has a television license in New York—WOR—and in L.A.—KHJ—and one in Memphis, and some radio stations. They are No. 1 in the radio market in New York. And I think those broadcast properties are worth another $40 a share. So an investor today is getting New York and L.A. for nothing. The O'Neils have moved on. They are retiring. They have professional management. Bill Reynolds has moved in, and he is doing a marvelous job.

Q: Is that hassle with the government over?

A: No. But it is not with the government these days. A bunch of people in L.A. decided that the company did a no no back about 10 years ago, and they pooled their resources, and challenged the license. I believe that this company committed major violations of the rules and their character was impuned; however, I believe the shareholders suffered a penalty—the loss of their license in Boston. I think they took their punishment for the violations. I think that any standards of fair play for the shareholders will indicate that, yes, there were problems, and yes, they got caught and were guilty, and yes, they took a penalty. And I believe that when this comes under examination again by the full Federal Communications Commission that the shareholders will not lose more value. The stock is worth $110–$120 a share.

Q: You're talking about it as an asset play.

A: Well, that is all that counts. But earnings are going to improve dramatically. You have terrific management. Book value on a historical basis is nothing but accounting. And that is not an important number. But I am mentioning it: It is close to $50. They are going to earn $5 for the year ending Nov. 30.

Q: So the only thing that is hanging over the company is this dispute.

A: No, there are lots of little glitches in every story. But I think that those glitches should not be focused on. The entire forest of the company, the value, the virtues of the company, should be focused on. And I think that at $47, GenCorp offers outstanding value for the patient investor, and particularly in this environment. You have a management change. The O'Neils are all retiring. The company is improving internally, dramatically. I think the shareholders of GenCorp who have been frustrated for a long time, are now going to enjoy a major upside opportunity.

Q: But just what, Mario, if we dare ask, will make the stock go higher?

A: It could happen one of several ways. They could buy back their own shares, which they should. They could do a leveraged buyout. They could be taken over in a hostile way. I mean why shouldn't Carl Icahn, after doing Uniroyal, focus on this one, because he understands the tire business now.[1]

EXPERT ANALYSIS

I've provided numerous examples of our private market value analysis including free cash flow value models, and reflections on many of the conceptual considerations we employ in our asset-oriented stock picking process. I haven't yet mentioned the role that outside experts play in our evaluation methodology. I'm not referring to investment experts, but to the true experts in any business—the brilliant people working in the industries we follow. I would be remiss if I didn't credit these experts with some of our success. Through my years in the investment business, I've become an expert at knowing the real experts in a variety of industries. Today, I can call up a half dozen of the people I know in a particular industry, list the assets of a competitor, and ask what they would pay for them in a sealed bid, winner-take-all auction. I usually get some interesting answers and novel perspectives which help me accurately evaluate an investment candidate's private market value. Analysts shouldn't be shy about consulting with industry professionals who often have a better feel for what's happening within their industry than do the people on Wall Street.

---

[1] Reprinted by courtesy of *Barron's National Business and Financial Weekly*.

23

Investing in Emerging Growth Stocks

Dennis G. Sherva, CFA
Managing Director
Morgan Stanley & Co. Incorporated

INTRODUCTION

Investing in small, rapidly growing companies can be one of the most rewarding sectors of the stock market for professional money managers as well as individual investors. There are several factors that make emerging growth stocks appealing investments. It is often easier for companies with a small sales base to grow rapidly and earn superior financial returns than it is for large enterprises with a billion or more dollars in revenue. Small or emerging growth companies can focus on specific industry, market, or product niches, allowing the investor an undiluted participation in an attractive business. In addition, with more than 25,000 publically traded small companies in the United States and frequent new issues being offered, many of the stocks are not widely followed in the investment community and, at times, can be inefficiently priced.

The attractive characteristics of emerging growth stocks that provide the opportunity to capture superior investment returns are accompanied by business and market risks that are substantially higher than equities in general. It is the management of these risks that determines how much of the potential return in the emerging growth sector will actually be realized. A disciplined approach to stock selection accompanied by an equally rigorous approach to valuation can provide the portfolio manager with the tools that minimize risk while seeking the long-term capital appreciation potential of emerging growth stock investing. Because of the risks inherent in rapidly growing small companies, mistakes cannot be completely avoided and employing appropriate

CHART 1 Life Cycle of a Company

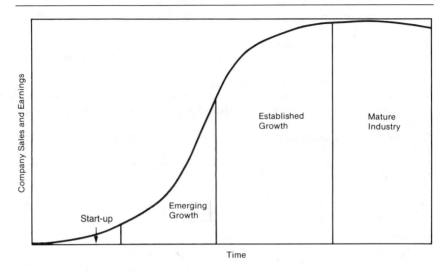

Time

selling disciplines is equally important to having effective buying strategies. Finally, appropriate diversification is necessary in constructing and managing stock portfolios to further control risk.

CRITERIA FOR STOCK SELECTION

All companies and industries go through a life cycle with several stages of development. In the idealized evolution of a company, as illustrated in Chart 1, the second, or emerging growth, phase (shaded area) is usually the most dynamic period in a firm's history and is the time that can yield the greatest returns to investors. The initial stage is the startup and very early building of a company when products or services are developed, manufacturing and marketing operations put in place, and the business begins to generate revenues. Companies typically lose money until late in the first stage. Venture capital plays an important role in starting and nurturing companies through this early phase. The third, or established growth, phase is associated with companies that continue to grow for many years after they have become large. While the annual growth rate is rarely in excess of 20 percent, companies such as IBM, Merck, McDonald's, and Dun & Bradstreet have maintained a growth pattern for decades and reached billions of dollars in revenues. The fundamental business risks of the established growth companies are typically less than for those enterprises at an earlier and more rapid growth stage. Most companies and industries eventually enter a mature

---

TABLE 1 Emerging Growth Companies—Criteria for Stock Selection

---

1. Earnings per share growth rate of at least 20 percent per annum over the next five years.
2. High operating or pretax profit margins.
3. High return on shareholders' equity so that as much growth is internally financed as possible.
4. Clean balance sheet with little or no debt.
5. Conservative accounting practices.
6. Leadership position (number one or two) in the industry, product, or market served.
7. Exceptional management to handle sustained, rapid growth.
8. Annual sales of $10 to $100 million.

---

phase characterized by negligible unit growth, increased cyclicality, and where investors seek higher dividend returns. Most automobile, steel, and electric utility companies among others are in this stage.

Identifying the best companies in the second or emerging growth stage of their development is the key to realizing the potentially high-investment returns. Successful emerging growth companies exhibit a set of attributes that are helpful in screening the numerous candidates. By making sure that all portfolio holdings meet the specific criteria, many mistakes can be avoided and the percentage of winners increased. There are eight primary criteria that are particularly important. Additionally, there are a number of secondary characteristics that have been found to be useful and should further improve the selection process.

Primary Criteria

The criteria listed in Table 1 are straightforward, but need further discussion to narrow the range of interpretation. In the first criterion, earnings per share expansion of at least a 20 percent annual rate is used as the benchmark for growth, but there should also be a reasonably close parallel with sales increases. Profit margin improvement can cause earnings to expand faster than sales for a time, but sales ultimately must keep pace. During the period of high inflation in the late 1970s and early 1980s, the minimum earnings per share growth rate was raised from 15 percent per year to 20 percent. With inflation at lower levels, a 15 percent growth rate hurdle could again be used. The growth rate criterion is based on projected results during the next five years, not on historical data. While past results may be a guide to the future, it is the company's performance in the upcoming quarters and years that is most important. Moreover, a number of small growth companies are recent startups with no significant record of sustained performance to serve as a guide. Others are going through the transition from explosive early growth that is clearly unsustainable to a more moderate rate as the sales base increases. A period of five years is chosen because there is a reasonable chance of correctly estimating the size of a market, market share, pricing, the competitive environment, and the numerous other factors that go into making growth rate projections. Rarely is there truly long-term visibility in the sense of forecasting 10 or 15 years into the future. The key is to keep rolling the projections ahead five years on an annual basis and challenging the underlying assumptions in the forecast model. The average annual earnings growth rate of the companies in a portfolio of emerging growth stocks will typically be between 20 percent and 30 percent.

One of the best guides to separating the outstanding companies from the mediocre ones is how profitable they are and how sustainable is the profitability. Generally, the higher the profit margin, the stronger the company's competitive position. Pricing flexibility is one of the key factors that enables companies to achieve and maintain high profit margins. The ability of a company to pass on cost increases and be more in control of pricing than competitors is an important attribute of a successful business. The absolute level of profit margins must be analyzed in the context of the company's industry and competition. An 11 percent pretax profit margin would be considered excellent for many retail trade or distribution businesses, but would be unsatisfactory for most high-quality manufacturing or service operations where pretax margins of 20 percent or higher are not unusual. A well-diversified portfolio of emerging growth companies should have an average pretax profit margin near 20 percent. If interest income is a significant contributor to pretax earnings then the operating profit margin will be a better indicator of the profitability of the company's basic business. While numerous companies have had sustained pretax margins of 20 percent to 30 percent or even higher for many years, unusually high margins can be a risk and must be scrutinized carefully to see if they can be maintained. For example, companies with a single "fad" product that are the first to enter a market can initially produce high profit margins, but they are not sustainable as competition enters that market or the fad fades.

The third criterion of having a high return on shareholders' equity is a key measure of the health of a business whether the company is small or large. A company with a 20 percent sales and earnings growth rate and no debt on its balance sheet should have at least a 20 percent return on average equity over a complete economic cycle to fund growth internally. With no debt, the return on total capital would also be 20 percent. Companies with a growth rate of 25 percent, 30 percent, or more often cannot generate a high enough return on equity to finance all of the growth internally and must raise capital from external sources such as by selling more common stock. Because of capital-raising efforts or high-internal cash generation, companies can accumulate excess cash which can mask the underlying returns on the operations of the business. By subtracting the excess cash equivalents from shareholders' equity and deducting the related interest income from earnings, one can calculate the return on "operating" equity to assess the trends in the basic business. While the level of the return on equity is important, so is the year-to-year trend, which can signal changes in the business. It is not uncommon for a portfolio of emerging growth companies to have a return on shareholders' equity that averages in the 18 percent to 25 percent range.

Because there is so much business and operating risk in rapidly growing small companies, it is prudent to minimize financial risk. Companies should therefore, as a fourth criterion, have little or no short- or long-term debt and where external financing is needed to fund growth, issuance of additional equity is preferred over debt securities. An exception to an unleveraged balance sheet may be the capitalized lease obligations that are frequently part of the liabilities of specialty retailers and restaurant companies. In general, emerging growth companies should be aggressive in their research and development, marketing, and expansion plans but conservative in their financial structure. The debt to total capitalization typically averages less than 12 percent in a portfolio of small-growth companies.

The accounting practices and policies used by emerging growth companies must also be conservative. Since the Financial Accounting Standards Board has clarified practices in several areas in recent years, one area where there is still a lot of management discretion and therefore deserves particularly close examination is revenue recognition policies, which can vary greatly from company to company, even in the same industry. Whether the sale of a computer is booked as revenue at the time of shipment from the factory, when it is installed, or when it is accepted by the customer can greatly affect the quality of reported revenues and earnings. Are long-term service or maintenance contracts booked as revenue when the contract is signed or prorated as the service is performed? The more conservative the accounting, the less chance there is for investors to encounter negative surprises.

If there were one criterion that could be viewed as more sacrosanct than the others, it would be the sixth, which is the requirement for a company to be number one or a close number two in its industry, product, or market niche. One of the most common mistakes investors in emerging growth stocks can make is to identify an attractive area of business, but instead of investing in the leader, buy the shares of the lesser participants in the industry because they may look cheaper than the leader.

As an example of the risks, in the early 1970s investors looked at the minicomputer industry, which was growing at a 40 percent annual rate, and decided they should participate. But as is often the case, the leader, Digital Equipment, was selling at a high price/earnings ratio whereas other industry participants such as Microdata, General Automation, Modular Computer, and Computer Automation were also growing fast, but their stocks were selling cheaper. When the industry shakeout came, as it inevitably does, Digital Equipment prospered while all of the other companies mentioned floundered and investors were badly hurt. The same scenario was replayed in the CAD/CAM market in the late 1970s, the personal computer business in the early 1980s, and the warehouse club retail chains in the mid-1980s. This pattern is not confined to technology companies, but can be seen in health care, retailing, and even some services.

Leaders tend to remain leaders in their businesses, which is not surprising, since they produce the largest volume of goods or services, should have the lowest unit costs, and can invest more in research, production, marketing, financial strength, and management controls, in order to stay in front. There is often room for a company in second place to do well, such as Data General in the minicomputer example, but the error is to go down to the third, fifth, or even lower ranked companies in the industry. The mistake an investor can make is to be drawn by the lower valuation of the lesser companies. If the leading company looks too expensive, the investor should wait for a correction in the market and then buy at a more reasonable price. Buying nonleadership companies when the strong ones are too expensive usually results in a portfolio replete with low-quality companies near the top of a market—a formula for real disaster in emerging growth stocks.

The definition of a leadership position generally means the largest share of the relevant market. The defined market is usually obvious but some analytical judgment is necessary. For example, Cray Research is not the world's largest computer company, but in large-scale scientific computers, the company has over 80 percent of the market and earns the high returns and has the pricing control that are characteristic of an industry leader. The market niche definition can, however, be taken too far. Just because a company is the leader in, say, half-height 5¼-inch computer disk drives does not meet the test because the market definition is too narrow and, in that case, the product not sufficiently differentiable from full-height 5¼-inch drives or even 3½-inch drives. In some businesses, such as retailing or restaurants, the relevant market may be geographic and more than one company can prosper with a specific merchandising format if they compete in different areas of the nation. However, as these retail chains grow and enter each other's territories, shakeouts occur and even here one or two leaders eventually emerge. This occurred in the discount store business in the 1970s.

Since companies growing at 20 percent to 50 percent annual rates double in size every two to four years, the seventh criterion takes on immense importance because it takes a talented and dedicated management team to keep the business on track. Judging management capability correctly is a difficult, subjective, and imprecise process, but generally the more experience an investor accumulates in meeting and appraising different management teams, the easier it will be to see the differences between weak and strong management groups. With the advent of turnkey computer accounting and material reporting and planning systems, the likelihood of poor financial controls has been reduced in recent years. However, a vitally important function of management that often does not get enough investor scrutiny is marketing and sales. Most publically traded emerging growth companies have already developed their products, established a manufacturing capability, and have financial controls. At that point, an important part of the future success will be the strength of the marketing and sales organization. In the race for industry leadership, it is often the company with the best marketing, sales, and distribution that will grab and hold the lead.

Another facet of judging the quality of management is to appraise the turnover of key employees. In successful small-growth companies, there is typically little management turnover. This is not surprising since profitable, rapidly growing companies are a good place to work. They are able to pay people competitively, provide significant advancement opportunities, and stock option incentive awards typically reach down several layers into the organization. If a pattern of key people leaving a company begins to develop, the investor must question what could be going wrong. It may be an early tip-off of troubles ahead.

Size per se is not a criterion because it is all of the other characteristics that are most important. However, most small-growth companies typically will have sales between $10 million to $100 million at the time the initial investment is made. When a company reaches $400 million or more in revenue, it may still be attractive but is getting beyond the emerging stage of development. What is important is not to set an arbitrary threshold of size before a company will be considered for investment. For example, not buying shares in a company until its sales or market value reaches $100 million only cuts off the investor from some of the early appreciation potential. Similarly, companies with $150 to $250 million in sales are not too big to be included in an emerging growth stock portfolio.

Secondary Characteristics

The difference between the primary criteria for stock selection and the secondary characteristics is that each stock in the portfolio should meet all of the primary criteria whereas there will be exceptions to the secondary characteristics. For example, one secondary characteristic is that emerging growth stocks should have few years, if any, in which earnings decline from the previous year. However, there are exceptions since some companies are more affected by the economic cycle and may encounter periodic recession-related earnings setbacks. To eliminate all companies that have experienced a decline in earnings would preclude participating in the dynamic upside of cyclical growth stocks or those undergoing a reacceleration in their business following a temporary setback.

Another attractive secondary characteristic is to invest in companies with a high proportion of recurring revenues, repeat customer sales, or a product that is consumable or disposable and must be repurchased. Service companies frequently have recurring revenues related to long- or short-term contracts with high-renewal rates. Other companies that choose to rent or lease their products rather than sell them outright can build significant recurring revenue streams. Some products such as filters or personal checks must be frequently replaced or are consumed when used resulting in stable demand trends. Businesses with these characteristics generally have above-average visibility in sales and earnings and fewer interruptions in the growth pattern.

It is also worthwhile to look for companies that sell products or services to many customers in many different markets. Dependence on one, or two, or three important customers can be extremely risky if contracts are canceled or the customer fails to perform in its own business, leading to order cutbacks. No single customer should account for more than 10 percent of a company's business and the proportion should decline significantly as one goes down the customer list. An exception may be the Department of Defense as a single customer for military suppliers, but even here a company's business should be spread over many defense programs to minimize the risk of cancellations.

There is also less risk in a business where the average selling price of the product or service is low. Big ticket sales items usually have narrow customer bases, long procurement approval processes, lengthy installation cycles, and are more subject to downturns in poor economic periods. Products such as manufacturing capital equipment for the semiconductor industry or business jet aircraft have erratic sales and earnings patterns that make long-term investing difficult. However, there are occasional exceptions; Cray Research, selling only a few $10 to $20 million supercomputers each year, has compiled an extraordinary record of consistent, rapid growth. Nonetheless, products requiring very large expenditures by the customer generally are riskier companies in which to invest and the successful exceptions are rare.

Good emerging growth companies should also have barriers to entry into their business and relatively few competitors. Only infrequently are companies protected by patents. More often, the company has managed to do some things far better than its competitors such as to develop a technologically difficult product, a strong distribution organization, or a superior level of customer service. Virtually every business will have some competition, but a company's competitive advantage should be strong enough to maintain a leading market share and to discourage numerous new entrants. A plethora of competitors in an industry may make the business so difficult that even the leading companies cannot do well. This happened in the computer disk drive market in the early 1980s when over 100 companies were competing for the market and pricing became so competitive that no one was a long-term winner.

Where to Find Emerging Growth Stocks

Most emerging growth company candidates are concentrated in four to five industries including electronic technology, health care, consumer, and the services sector of the economy. Occasionally, companies that meet the criteria can be found in the general industrial category, such as office supplies and specialized machinery. The industry groups noted here are broadly defined with several submarkets in each one. For example, electronic technology includes components and semiconductors, computer systems, computer peripherals, computer software, defense electronics, telecommunications and data communications equipment, and instrumentation as important categories, while the consumer area includes specialty retailers, restaurant chains, and consumer products such as cosmetics and apparel.

A large number of standard industrial categories are not represented in emerging growth stocks. There are few, if any, rapidly growing, small aluminum, automobile, steel, paper, or utility companies. Most of these businesses are in older, mature industries—generally not fruitful areas for entrepreneurial growth. Consequently, emerging growth portfolios are concentrated in fewer industries than traditional large company portfolios.

Finding emerging growth stocks that meet the specified criteria is more of a company-by-company analytical process than a numerical screening endeavor. There is no computerized data base of information on all small companies that would lend itself to formal computational screening. Rather, the process is one of gathering information on individual companies including prospectuses, annual and quarterly reports, product literature, and Securities and Exchange Commission Form 10-K and 10-Q filings, then studying the material to determine if the established criteria are met. Subsequent meetings with management as well as talking with customers, competitors, and suppliers of the company are important to substantiate the analysis of published information.

Initial public offerings (IPOs) are a prolific area for finding emerging growth stocks since many of the companies are still small. However, only a few of the numerous offerings are companies that meet the criteria and they must also be carefully analyzed. One of the dangers of IPOs is that as an industry gains popularity with investors, valuations increase and nonleading companies go public riding on the valuations of the industry leaders. Disciplined application of the criteria is as much needed to screen IPOs as it is for existing publically traded stocks.

Things to Avoid

There is nothing particularly unique about the set of criteria and characteristics recommended for screening for high-quality emerging growth companies. It is useful, however, to turn the coin over and look at some of the things that should be avoided. Since the objective is to invest in growing businesses, small companies that are asset valuation plays, liquidation candidates, potential turnarounds, or possible take-over or merger speculations are not within the scope of emerging growth stocks. While such approaches to investing are perfectly valid and can generate significant returns if correctly implemented, they are best left to specialists in those areas and should not find their way into emerging growth portfolios.

One of the more difficult things to avoid is the "fad" or "concept" stocks that frequently appear and masquerade as emerging growth companies. They can be tempting because, on the surface, they may seem to have the right attributes and meet the established criteria. Moreover, such stocks can capture investor interest and be spectacular market performers—for a short time. They are like defective rockets in that they soar explosively, peak out quickly, and fall back down in ashes. The temptation is to believe one can consistently get in early before the sharp run-up, recognize the top before others, and get out before the crash. It is likely that few investors, if any, who trade in fad or concept stocks realize outstanding long-term results.

Over the years, there have been enumerable fad or concept stocks including hand-held calculators, smoke detectors, gambling enterprises, solar energy, robotics, and such consumer products as slow cookers, running shoes, and hand soap in a pump bottle. The latter is a good example of a defective rocket. In 1979, a small over-the-counter company, Minnetonka Laboratories, developed Softsoap, a liquid handsoap in a convenient container with a pump nozzle. The product was well received by consumers, the company's sales and earnings began to rise dramatically, and the stock price rose nearly ninefold in less than two years. Superficially, Minnetonka Laboratories may have looked like it met the emerging growth criteria since it was growing fast, was achieving a high profit margin and return on equity, had little debt, was the leader in its market, had credible management, was small in size, and even had a consumable, repeat sale product. Analyzed more closely, however, it could be seen that the company's product was not unique, proprietary, or highly differentiable and that it was a business with low barriers to entry and many strong personal care product companies as potential competitors. As competition increased, market share and pricing flexibility was lost and the high-operating profitability disappeared. In less than a year, the stock price declined 90 percent.

While there are pure concept stocks with no real business underpinnings, many of the fad stocks are not just in passing, fad businesses. Hand-held calculators, smoke detectors, as well as SoftSoap are real products in everyday use. The problem is that the early leaders become investment fads, get overvalued, but have businesses where either market saturation or increased competition (or both) preclude sustained long-term profitable growth. Consumer products (particularly durables) are most subject to market saturation problems and low barriers to entry. Separating the real from the masquerading emerging growth companies will do much to enhance portfolio returns and minimize the exposure to catastrophic 90 percent stock price declines.

AN EXAMPLE OF AN EMERGING GROWTH STOCK: SHARED MEDICAL SYSTEMS

A good example of an emerging growth company that has provided outstanding returns to investors is Shared Medical Systems Corporation (SMS), headquartered outside of Philadelphia, Pennsylvania. SMS is the leading worldwide provider of computer-based information systems and associated services to the health care industry. The company provides hospitals, clinics, and physician groups with integrated financial, administrative, and patient management software systems that use diverse computing and networking technologies.

The company was founded in 1968 by former IBM employees, became profitable in 1972, and went public with an initial common stock offering in 1976. As shown in Chart 2, the share price has risen dramatically during SMS's first decade as a public company. Adjusted for stock splits, the share price has risen from an initial offering price of $2.50 in 1976 to $40.00, 10 years later, or a 32 percent compound annual rate of price appreciation. In addition, the company paid its first dividend in 1977 and has increased the cash distribution each year at a rate faster than earnings growth.

SMS's share price appreciation has primarily been the result of substantial growth in revenues and earnings. Table 2 lists the company's revenue, pretax earnings, pretax profit margin, tax rate, return on average shareholders' equity, and per share earnings and dividend each year from 1971 through 1985. Since 1972, the first year of profits,

CHART 2

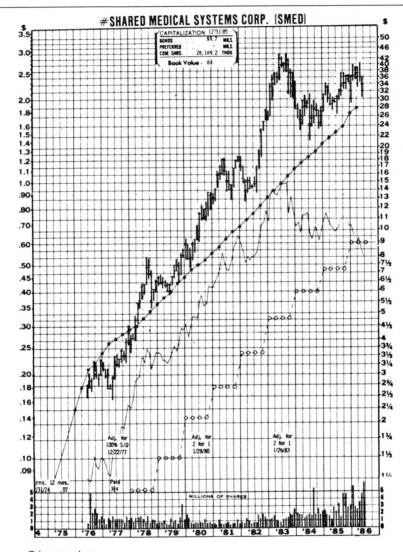

SHARED MEDICAL SYSTEMS CORP. (SMED)

CAPITALIZATION 12/31/85
BONDS . . . $9.7 MILS.
PREFERRED . . . - MILS.
COM. SHRS. 26,169.2 THOU.

Book Value . 6½

Adj. for
100% S/D
12/22/77

Adj. for
2 for 1
1/28/80

Adj. for
2 for 1
1/26/83

Erns. 12 mos.
12/31/74 .07

Paid
3½¢

MILLIONS OF SHARES

——— Price per share
● ● ● Earnings per share
o o o Dividends
Left scale Earnings and dividends
Right scale Price

SOURCE: Securities Research Company. A division of United Business Service Company, 208 Newbury Street, Boston, MA. 02116.

TABLE 2 Emerging Growth Stocks—Shared Medical Systems—Historical Growth and Returns ($000s except EPS)

Year	Revenue	Pretax Earnings	Pretax Margin	Tax Rate	Return on Average Equity	Per Share	
						Earnings	Dividends
1985	$312,207	$74,332	23.8%	43.8%	29.3%	$1.66	$0.51
1984	256,753	62,637	24.4	46.1	29.9	1.37	0.42
1983	210,814	51,424	24.4	47.0	30.3	1.11	0.34
1982	165,772	41,024	24.7	47.9	29.7	0.88	0.26
1981	131,616	32,950	25.0	49.6	28.8	0.69	0.20
1980	106,581	26,216	24.6	49.3	28.8	0.55	0.15
1979	82,803	21,566	26.0	50.1	29.2	0.45	0.11
1978	63,051	18,028	28.6	52.3	29.7	0.36	0.08
1977	45,686	13,268	29.1	48.8	29.9	0.29	0.06
1976	35,468	9,274	26.2	43.4	35.2	0.23	—
1975	22,563	4,654	20.6	40.3	35.8	0.15	—
1974	13,248	2,301	17.4	46.8	25.6	0.07	—
1973	9,516	1,615	17.0	52.8	24.0	0.04	—
1972	6,116	864	14.1	52.6	20.0	0.02	—
1971	3,495	(687)	—	—	—	(0.07)	—
Compound annual growth rate, 1972–1985	35%	41%				40%	

revenues, pretax earnings, and earnings per share have risen at compound annual rates of 35 percent, 41 percent, and 40 percent, respectively. Moreover, the company's operating results have been highly consistent with no year-to-year (or even quarterly) declines in sales or earnings. Pretax profit margins have been relatively stable at a high level in the 24 percent to 29 percent range since the company went public. Significantly, SMS's return on equity has also been high and remarkably consistent in the 29 percent to 30 percent area during the past decade. The sustained high level of return on equity indicates that the company has been able to invest additional capital in its business at the same incremental return as it has historically.

SMS has met all of the primary criteria for selecting emerging growth stocks as well as having many of the attractive secondary characteristics. The company's sales and earnings growth has consistently exceeded the 20 percent minimum rate, profit margins have been far above average, and the return on shareholders' equity has been high enough to internally finance rapid growth. SMS's capitalization has never been comprised of more than 10 percent debt and in recent years the company has been able to generate excess cash. Accounting practices have also been conservative as indicated by perpetual software license fees being recognized over the installation period rather than as an immediate sale. Early in its development, SMS became the leader in providing data processing services to hospitals and has maintained that leadership position despite a number of competitors. Shortly after the company went public in 1976, the company was servicing an estimated 94,000 hospital beds or 12 percent of the defined market, compared with 81,000 beds or 10 percent of the market for its closest competitor. The company widened its market share lead over its nearest competitors in subsequent years. Management has been comprised of a group of dedicated professionals strong on marketing as well as technology, and with a turnover of key people that has been low. In the year of the initial public offering, the company's sales were $35 million, well within the $10 to $100 million range typical of small-growth company candidates.

There are other positive attributes of SMS's business that made the investment opportunity attractive and reduced risks. One of the best features has been a recurring revenue stream based on long-term contracts with hospitals generally ranging from one to seven years. Revenues from services provided under the contracts are billed monthly on a transaction basis. The stability of the monthly billings together with the recession-resistant nature of health care has produced a highly visible pattern of growth with no earnings disappointments. In addition, because SMS has contracts with several hundred medical facilities, no single customer accounted for more than 5 percent of revenues in any year and the cancellation of any contract is not significant enough to adversely affect results. Indeed, there have been relatively few contract cancellations because once the company's systems are installed and become an integrated part of the customers daily operations, there is considerable reluctance to change vendors. While data processing activities are important to a hospital or clinic and the sales cycle for new contracts can be long, the annual cost is a small part of the hospital's total operating budget. Moreover, since SMS is selling a service, not computer equipment, there is no large, single capital investment required of the customer that could be a barrier to sale. Shared Medical Systems has been an outstanding emerging growth stock and serves as a good benchmark for judging other candidates.

VALUATION OF EMERGING GROWTH STOCKS

High Betas Require Use of Valuation Disciplines

In order to realize the superior returns that are available through investments in emerging growth stocks, there are two parts to the decision-making process that must be correctly implemented. Identifying the most attractive small-growth companies using a set of criteria is one half of the process. It is not enough, however, just to have a portfolio of outstanding emerging growth companies like Shared Medical Systems if the stocks are selling at such high valuations as to make them unattractive investments on an absolute or a relative return basis. Selecting the right stocks to buy must be coupled with reasonable valuation and is the other important part of successfully investing in emerging growth stocks.

A strategy of simply buying and holding emerging growth stocks in a portfolio that is always fully invested is unlikely to achieve the returns that a more actively managed portfolio will produce by adjusting the level of equity exposure when valuations of the group are excessively high or low. For example, the compound annual rate of return of the T. Rowe Price New Horizons Fund[1] was 11.4 percent during the 1960–86 period. While outperforming the 9.8 percent rate of appreciation of the Standard & Poor's 500 Index during the same interval, the rate of return is low considering the opportunities stemming from the well-above-average rate of earnings growth for the small companies held by the Fund and the stock price appreciation achieved during long periods of superb upside performance, such as occurred in 1974–80 when the compound annual return of the Fund was 32 percent over the six-year period.

It is not that the New Horizons Fund has been poorly managed; indeed its long-term record is among the best of the aggressive growth mutual funds and the stock selection has been excellent. The moderating factor in the fund's performance is that it has (as is appropriate, given its charter) remained nearly fully invested at all times, with a cash position rarely in excess of 15 percent or below 5 percent. The problem is that emerging growth stocks are extremely volatile with betas of between 1.5 and 2.5 for a diversified portfolio. The result of this volatility is that while price appreciation is outstanding in bull markets, so much is given back in severe market downturns that the rate of return

---

[1] A valid long-term index of emerging growth stocks as defined in this article does not exist so the T. Rowe Price New Horizons Fund, an open-end mutual fund managed by T. Rowe Price Associates in Baltimore, Maryland, is widely used as a proxy for such an index. It is a good window on this sector of the stock market, because it is large ($1.5 billion) and its assets are invested in about 200 stocks, making the portfolio statistically representative. Investments are confined to shares of small, high-quality growth companies that generally match the criteria described herein. In addition, the fund is well diversified, with 24 percent of the portfolio in consumer stocks, 30 percent in the service sector of the economy, 32 percent in electronic technology, and 14 percent in other areas. Probably of greatest value is the relatively long record of the fund, which stretches back to its inception in 1960. The 26-year time span covers several major market tops and bottoms, periods of high and low inflation, and years of economic calm as well as turbulence.

in a constantly, fully invested portfolio is only modestly better than the general market. In the bear markets of 1962, 1969–70, 1973–74, and 1981–82, the net asset value declines registered by the New Horizons Fund were 43 percent, 47 percent, 71 percent, and 52 percent, respectively, which erased a great deal of the prior appreciation and diminished the long-term rate of return to investors. The risks are clear when one considers that in an emerging growth portfolio with a beta of 2.0 and a 50 percent cash position, the stocks would still decline as much as the overall market in a downturn. Without any cash reserve, steep market declines are obviously devastating.

The high beta of emerging growth stocks is due, in part, to the higher perceived business risks inherent in rapidly growing small companies. There are also market-related factors including the relatively thin trading liquidity of the shares that results from the small-market capitalizations and often reduced floating supply of stock in companies heavily owned by insiders. There is also a more limited universe of investors in small companies that can make trading difficult, particularly under adverse market conditions. Because of the share price vulnerability in bear markets, it is just as important to be cautious and reduce equity exposure by raising cash in periods when valuations and risks are high as it is to be aggressive when valuations are attractive and the risk reward is favorable. In order to maximize long-term investment returns in emerging growth stocks, it is imperative to avoid as much of the major market downturns as possible. Most investors do well in a bull market; it is in bear markets that portfolio managers have the greatest opportunity to develop records vastly superior to those of their competitors by doing a better job of protecting assets.

Valuation Tools

Managing emerging growth stock portfolios to minimize the exposure to major declines need not depend solely on an ephemeral ability to predict bull and bear markets. Rather, by focusing on the absolute and relative valuation level of the emerging growth sector of the market, the investor can avoid stocks when valuations and price risk are high and increase holdings at times when valuations and price risk are low. There are several valuation tools that can be helpful in determining whether small-growth stocks as a group are attractive. None of the tools are "black box" answers, but taken together can be helpful in identifying valuation extremes.

Tracking the share performance of the emerging growth group is imprecise because of the absence of a recognized published index. However, there are substitutes that reasonably approximate the sector including the T. Rowe Price New Horizons Fund, the NASDAQ Industrial Average, and the Lipper Analytical Services Small Growth

CHART 3   Morgan Stanley Emerging Growth Stock Index, 1/1/78 = 100

Company Mutual Fund Index. The Morgan Stanley Emerging Growth Stock Index started in 1978 is also a good proxy. It is a capitalization weighted index of 100 companies that is periodically updated with new names to keep it representative of the area over time. The 1978 to 1986 performance of the Morgan Stanley index is shown in Chart 3. The rising secular trend of emerging growth stock prices since the end of 1977 can be clearly seen, as well as the sharp price swings around the trend, particularly the 1982–83 price explosion and subsequent downturn. Keeping watch on stock price movements of the emerging growth group with one of the indexes is helpful in alerting investors to valuation extremes. A further refinement on analyzing raw stock price indexes is to look at their price momentum, such as the year-to-year percentage change in prices. Such an "oscillator" on the Morgan Stanley Emerging Growth Stock Index is depicted in Chart 4. At the market tops in 1981 and 1983, small-growth company share prices reached a peak year-to-year rate of gain of 100 percent and 150 percent, respectively. At major market bottoms such as 1982 and 1984, the rate of gain, after having fallen steadily for many months, got down to the −25 percent to −35 percent level. While not a valuation technique itself, the price momentum oscillator places emerging growth stock prices in perspective and is one of several factual indicators that help to confirm valuation extremes.

Discount models are broadly used valuation tools and have proven

CHART 4 Morgan Stanley Emerging Growth Stock Index Year-to-Year Percent Change

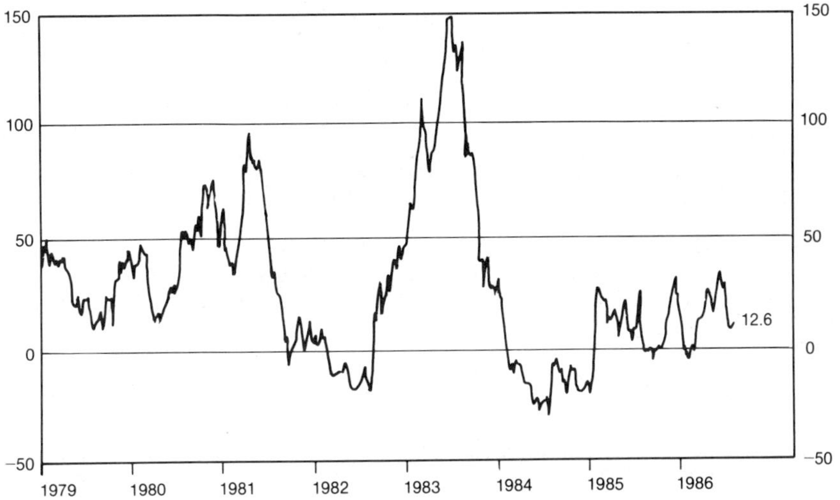

valuable in appraising the emerging growth sector of the market. In the parlance of the academicians, emerging growth stocks are "long-duration" investments and are also highly sensitive to the level of inflation and interest rates. Lower inflation means declining interest rates, reduced discount rates applied to common stock valuation, and rising price/earnings ratios, particularly for rapid growth companies. In the dividend/earnings discount models, companies growing at 20 percent, 30 percent, or faster annual rates theoretically have very large earnings in distant years. When those large profits are discounted back at say, a 20 percent rate, the present value is fairly small, but at a discount rate of 9 percent, the present value rises dramatically. Chart 5 shows the pattern of emerging growth share prices in relation to their intrinsic value during the 1980s as calculated using a discount model. At the market peak for small-growth stocks in 1981 and 1983, share prices rose to 80 percent to 100 percent premiums above intrinsic value (the discounted future stream of earnings). When share prices have declined to or below intrinsic value, such as during 1980, 1982, and 1984, it has signaled an attractive buying opportunity.

Price/earnings (P/E) ratios are the most frequently used valuation tool, but have the greatest relevance when placed in the context of inflation and interest rate levels and the multiple accorded the overall market. The longest available P/E history of emerging growth stocks is the data from the T. Rowe Price New Horizons Fund. As shown in Chart

CHART 5 Morgan Stanley Emerging Growth Stock Discount Model

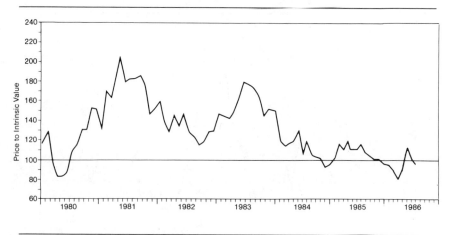

SOURCE: Morgan Stanley Research.

CHART 6 New Horizons Fund Price/Earnings Ratio

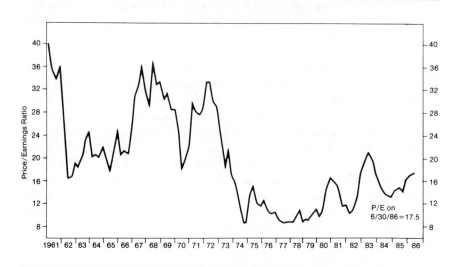

NOTE: This chart is intended to track the average price/earnings ratio of New Horizons portfolio companies, based on earnings per share estimates issued by the Fund's investment advisor for 12 months ahead from each quarter-end.

SOURCE: T. Rowe Price Associates.

CHART 7   New Horizons Fund P/E Relative to S&P 500

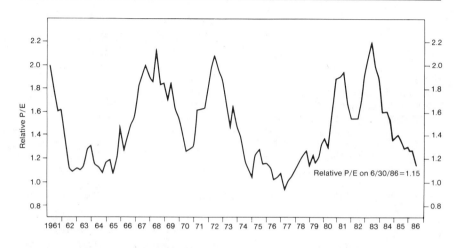

Relative P/E on 6/30/86 = 1.15

NOTE: This chart is intended to track the average price/earnings ratio of New Horizons portfolio companies, with the Standard & Poor's 500 Index as of each quarter-end, with earnings per share estimates issued by the fund's investment advisor for 12 months ahead from each quarter-end.

SOURCE: T. Rowe Price Associates.

6, the P/E of the small growth companies in the New Horizons Fund (consistently based on estimated earnings one year forward) has ranged from a high of 40 in 1961 to a low of 9 in the mid-1970s. The declining trend of P/Es that began in the late 1960s, and which continued through most of the 1970s resulted from the rising level of inflation and interest (discount) rates during that period. Since growth stock valuations are highly sensitive to changes in discount rates, the declining pattern of multiples is understandable. With the break in oil prices and the disinflationary trend that began in the early 1980s, P/E ratios appear to be trending upward once again and are far below the high levels reached in the preinflationary 1960s.

One of the best and most reliable indicators of valuation levels in emerging growth stocks is the price/earnings ratio in relation to the multiple for the general market. The P/E of the New Horizons Fund relative to the multiple of the Standard & Poor's 500 Index is shown in Chart 7. During the past two and one-half decades, the relative P/E has ranged from 2.2 at market highs to near 1.0 at the extreme lows. Each time small-growth stocks have risen in price to where they are selling at twice the market multiple, it has signaled a major selling opportunity. In fact, this indicator has called every major market top in emerging growth stocks for over 25 years, without failure and without exception.

TABLE 3 Emerging Growth Stocks—New Horizons Fund Relative P/E Based
on Fundamentals

	New Horizons Fund Equities	S&P 500	Relative
Projected 5-year earnings growth rate	24%	7%	3.4
Return on equity	18	13	1.4
Pretax profit margin	18	8	2.3
Equity to total capital	89	68	1.3
Average relative fundamentals			2.1

SOURCE: T. Rowe Price Associates, Standard & Poor's *Analyst's Handbook*, and Morgan Stanley & Co. estimates.

The 1961, 1968, 1972, 1981, and 1983 peaks were all followed by substantial share price declines ranging from 35 percent to 75 percent. Conversely, when the relative P/E has fallen below the midpoint of 1.6 and reached the 1.4 level, it has paid to reinvest and reduce cash positions in anticipation of long-term share price appreciation.

The excellent record of the relative P/E of the New Horizons Fund at indicating valuation extremes (particularly tops) is so good that it invites suspicion. However, the historical ceiling at the 2.0 to 2.2 relative P/E level is not arbitrary; it relates to the fact that the underlying fundamentals of the small-growth companies in the portfolio are about twice as good as those of the typical company in the S&P 500 Index. The data in Table 3 shows the earnings growth rate, return on equity, operating profit margin, and balance sheet strength of emerging growth companies in comparison to the S&P 500. The fundamentals of the companies in the fund exceed those of the S&P 500 on every measure and, on average, are about twice as attractive. Consequently, when in a rising, confident, ebullient stock market emerging growth share prices appreciate to a relative P/E level of about 2.0–2.2, at which point they fully reflect or discount their superior characteristics, there is no fundamental reason for valuations to rise substantially higher. It is conceivable that unbridled enthusiasm and a consequent supply/demand imbalance of small growth company shares in the marketplace could temporarily push valuations still higher, but such a move would come under the heading of greater fool and is unlikely to be sustained. Unless the relative fundamentals dramatically change over time (which is improbable for a broad list of emerging growth stocks), the historical range of relative P/Es should continue to be a valid indicator of valuation extremes.

There are additional but more subjective tools that can also be used to assess the risk conditions in emerging growth stocks. The level of

CHART 8 Aggressive Growth Mutual Funds Net Purchases and Redemptions

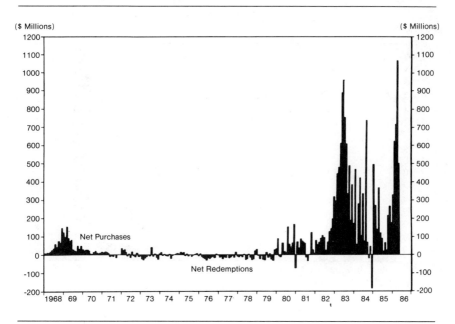

SOURCE: Investment Company Institute.

investor interest in small growth stocks and speculative activities in the market can be used to confirm more fundamentally based indicators at valuation extremes. While there is a lot of anecdotal evidence about the level of investor enthusiasm for emerging growth stocks, one of the best windows on what specific actions investors are taking is the data on net purchases and redemptions of the aggressive growth mutual funds. These funds typically have a charter requiring them to invest in emerging growth-type equities. Moreover, pension and other institutional investors as well as individuals are substantial holders of these mutual funds so the data is a good reflection of investor sentiment generally toward small growth stock investments. Chart 8 shows the monthly net purchases and redemptions of the aggressive growth mutual funds since 1968.

As can be seen in Chart 8 there were net redemptions of aggressive growth mutual funds virtually every month during the 1974–79 interval when emerging growth stock valuations were at historically low levels and about to embark on a long period of enormous price appreciation. At the other extreme, in 1983, when valuations reached peak levels, net purchases were unprecedented in scope. The bottom in small growth

CHART 9   Volume of Initial Public Offerings*

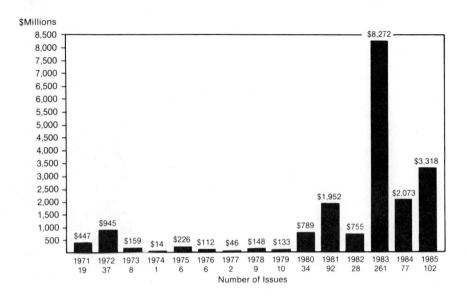

*Includes all nonfinancial initial public offerings $10 million or larger.

stocks in late 1984 was also confirmed by the largest amount of net redemptions ever recorded in a single month. While individual retirement account (IRA) inflows in the first four months of each year and the renewed growth of the mutual fund industry in general require using the net purchase and redemption data with some care, there is the unmistakable pattern of most investors buying when they should be selling, and selling when they should be buying. Awareness of this tendency has proven valuable in providing confirmation as to the attractiveness of small growth stocks.

A similar measure of investor enthusiasm for higher risk equities is the level of initial public offerings (IPOs) of common stock. When share prices and valuations are low, the number and value of IPOs is small, but supply of new issues rises dramatically after a period of stock price increases and consequent higher valuations. As indicated by the yearly volume of initial public offerings shown in Chart 9, there was very little IPO activity during the 1974–79 period when small growth company valuations were low. As emerging growth share price performance began to improve, the volume of IPOs rose and reached a peak of blowoff proportions in 1983 at the same time that small-growth stock valuations crested. Speculative excesses in the IPO market are a warning of danger to emerging growth stock investors.

PORTFOLIO CONSIDERATIONS

Time Horizon

Investing in emerging growth stocks is not conducive to short-term trading. For institutional portfolios of $50 million or more, the relative illiquidity of most small-growth stocks and the attendent high transactions costs preclude aggressive in-and-out trading. On the other hand, the visibility in any individual company is rarely so good that a stock can be bought with the preset policy of not selling it for 10 or 20 years. "One decision" investing is not appropriate to emerging growth stocks. A reasonable time horizon on which to base investment decisions is to look ahead one and one-half to two years and to keep rolling the horizon forward as time passes. The typical holding period may average 3 to 4 years, with some particularly successful investments held for as long as 10 years and others that run into trouble may be sold in less than a year. It is unusual for a stock to be held for more than a decade, because it will either become too large to be classified as an emerging company or the fundamentals of the business, such as the growth rate, will fall below the minimum criteria. Most successful emerging growth stock investing results from owning a growing enterprise that increases in market value over several years.

Diversification

Because the specific business and market risks are high in rapidly growing, small companies, portfolio diversification is of prime importance. Indeed, an emerging growth portfolio should be diversified in three ways; (1) by the number of positions held, (2) in different industries, and (3) according to the risk profile of a company's business.

Even in small portfolios or in the emerging growth segment of larger portfolios, there should be no fewer than 12 to 15 separate holdings. Two, three, or four holdings in the sector as "exposure" to the area are not sufficient diversification and do not give adequate recognition to the risks involved. In portfolios with more assets, individual positions that each represent 3 percent to 5 percent of the total portfolio or 20 to 33 companies is reasonable in that each holding is large enough that successful investments will have a materially positive effect on performance and the losers are not so outsized as to preclude the overall portfolio from doing well. In particularly large portfolios of $300 million or more, the list of holdings will have to be greater, but at any point in time there are a limited number of truly outstanding emerging growth candidates so there is a risk of lowering the average quality of the stocks in a portfolio as assets increase. The median capitalization of emerging growth stocks varies with market levels but is generally in a range of

---

TABLE 4 Emerging Growth Stocks—
Asset Allocation Ranges

	Asset Allocation Range (percent)
Electronic technology	15%–40%
Consumer	15 –35
Services	20 –30
Health care	10 –20
General industrial	5 –10

$100 to $200 million. If the portfolio guidelines are to keep each holding at no more than 5 percent of a company's outstanding shares, it means that the median maximum position size will be $5 to $10 million. The largest emerging growth stock portfolio is the $1.5 billion T. Rowe Price New Horizons Fund with 200 companies and an average position size of $7.5 million.

It is also important to diversify emerging growth portfolios among different industries and business niches. Economic and market developments can alter the factors that make a particular industry attractive and overconcentration on one or two areas can increase the risk of missing significant changes in the investment landscape. In the late 1970s, it was popular for some small-growth stock investors to focus exclusively on technology and/or energy. But with the break in oil prices in the early 1980s and the peaking of technology shares in 1983, investment interest shifted to the consumer, health care, and service sectors of the economy and the undiversified portfolios performed poorly. Well-diversified portfolios may miss part of the extraordinary performance that accrues to portfolios that are concentrated in areas that are temporarily most in favor, but unless the focused holdings are radically altered on a timely basis, they will underperform as new sectors of the market blossom. The most consistent long-term returns can be achieved by having portfolio investments represented in different industries and business niches at all times. Table 4 indicates some suggested asset allocation ranges for the major industries where emerging growth stocks are typically found. The small-growth stock sector is much like the general market in that different groups rotate in and out of favor and shifting portfolio weightings within the asset allocation ranges as economic and market factors dictate can significantly improve portfolio returns.

Another, more subtle, type of diversification is accomplished according to the risk inherent in a company's business. Single-product companies pioneering a new business and trying to grow at very rapid annual rates of 40 percent or more are incurring a high risk in comparison to more established companies growing at 20 percent rates with a recurring revenue stream and not on the leading edge of technology. For example, the risk in owning a small, fast-growing company, such as Applied Biosystems, Stratus Computer, or Ryan's Family Steak Houses is much higher than in more proven, slower growing companies, such as Sigma-Aldrich, John H. Harland, or IMS International. A portfolio that only owns the first type of company is exposed totally to the highest business and market risk within the emerging growth sector. By diversifying risky companies with less risky holdings, portfolios will participate in the substantial potential rewards of the high-risk companies but, as a whole, are better able to withstand the greater number of disappointments that normally will occur in the high-risk group.

Selling Tactics and Observations

The concept of analyzing each portfolio holding by its level of risk can be combined with valuation disciplines to provide portfolio managers with a framework in which to implement decision making at the turning points of valuation extremes. Organizing stocks in a portfolio according to risk category can be more useful than the standard breakdown by industry. Because the criteria that have been established for emerging growth stocks screen out financial (balance sheet) risk, each holding can be assigned a rating based on the two other major risk parameters, business and market risk. Business risk is defined as fundamental risk due to the economic cycle, technology changes, competition and management control, among other factors. Market risk is associated with the beta or share price volatility, which is particularly important for stocks with high price/earnings ratios.

As illustrated in Chart 10, portfolio holdings can be arrayed into one of three designated categories based on the perceived degree of business and market risk. When the various valuation tools indicate that the risk/reward for emerging growth stocks is unfavorable and equity exposure should be reduced, selling should begin with the highest risk (Group III) companies and continue into the Group II and Group I categories until the desired amount of cash is raised. Group I companies should have fewer fundamental disappointments and earnings surprises as well as less price volatility than the average emerging growth stock. They will not be unscathed, but will be better holdings than the high-risk issues in a market downturn. Few, if any, portfolios will reach 100 percent cash positions since there is rarely the visibility or confidence to be completely out of the market. However, by riding through a market decline with cash reserves and the remainder of the portfolio in the more risk adverse group of stocks, some insulation from the worst effects of major market declines can be achieved.

CHART 10 Emerging Growth Stocks—Managing Portfolio Risk

	Examples		*Business Risk*	*Market Risk*	
Group I	John H. Harland		Low	Low	
	Luby's Cafeterias				
	Sigma-Aldrich				
		RAISE CASH			*REINVEST*
Group II	Community Psychiatric Centers		Medium	Medium	
	Paychex				
	Shared Medical Systems				
Group III	Applied Biosystems		High	High	
	Ryan's Family Steak Houses				
	Stratus Computer				

The risk categorization is a useful format for making major valuation and market-driven portfolio changes, but there are also some observations that can be applied to individual stock selling decisions. While there are emerging growth companies that have become large enterprises by keeping their sales and earnings expanding for many years, the number of such legendary investments are, in reality, only a small proportion of the universe of companies that, at one time or another, were considered to be emerging growth issues. Because the risks are high, many emerging growth companies stumble and never reach their full potential. Consequently, investors should have the mental set that rather than assuming they own the next great Digital Equipment, McDonald's, or Wal-Mart Stores, that instead they hold the next Computervision, Datapoint, or Levitz Furniture, which after a few years of success ran into significant problems and subsequent investor disappointment. The recurring experience is that most emerging growth companies that encounter a serious break in their growth and profitability pattern from factors other than the economic cycle do not get their business back on track.

The significance of the high casualty rate in emerging growth stocks is that when something first begins to go wrong at a company, investors should not give the company the benefit of the doubt, but rather sell the shares promptly and reassess the situation from the sidelines. This is often counterintuitive and may seem too abrupt to those aware of the widely publicized glamorous emerging growth successes, but the probabilities favor selling. From a practical portfolio management viewpoint, it is wise to take the position that there is no such thing as one bad quarter, even though there are always many reasons to explain away the shortfall and assure investors that steps have been taken to recover momentum in the next quarter. Similarly, the first earnings estimate cut is rarely the last and profit forecasts often follow the stock down. In emerging growth stocks, there are usually a sufficient number of attractive alternatives in which to invest so that flows of new money into a stock which has had a serious fundamental disappointment will be curtailed and the shares will significantly underperform the group.

Keeping Portfolios Fresh

Being in the right areas and stocks is important in any portfolio, but keeping the list of holdings "fresh" is particularly important in emerging growth stocks. Indeed, the evolving nature of small-growth companies coupled with the application of selling disciplines will force actions that should prevent a portfolio from getting outdated. Looking back at the history of many small growth company investment portfolios and observing the behavior of emerging growth equities over several market cycles, it is clear that roughly 70 percent of the emerging growth stocks that really do well in a bull market are new, fresh names. Only about 30 percent are repeaters from the last market cycle and, importantly, there are a great many nonrepeaters. That many of the names change from stock market cycle to cycle is not surprising since some companies grow large and can no longer be considered "emerging," others fail fundamentally and are no longer of interest, and many attractive new candidates appear from the IPO markets or are existing companies that have developed gradually into dynamic businesses. As a general rule, approximately four out of five holdings in a well-managed emerging growth portfolio should be different every five years.

What are the characteristics of emerging growth stocks that have excellent market performance in one cycle and then repeat by fully participating in the next major upswing in small-growth stocks? The key characteristic is that the companies that are repeaters are those that continue to meet the specified criteria, in particular, those that maintain an acceptable earnings growth rate. Companies should come through the testing period of a bear market with their earnings momentum unscathed, but if they have a profit shortfall, it should be an economic cycle problem, and not a permanent fundamental management, product, or competitive dislocation. For example, Shared Medical Systems's earnings growth was untouched by the 1982 recession, but the stock price nonetheless declined by 32 percent during the 1981–82 bear market. Because the company continued to meet the established criteria and the stock was reasonably valued, the shares participated in the 1982–83 bull market by rising 245 percent in price in 10 months. On the other hand, companies that have economy-related earnings setbacks can also be repeaters. For example, the stock price of Best Products, a catalog showroom merchandising company, went from $0.33 per share to $15 in the 1970–72 bull market but then declined from $15 to $0.50 in the 1973–74 bear market, as earnings fell because of the recession. However, there was nothing wrong with the catalog merchandising business at that time, and Best Products' internal fundamentals remained strong. The Company's profits recovered sharply with the economy, and the stock price proceeded to advance from $0.50 at the low in 1974 to $22 at the new peak in 1978—clearly a repeater.

It is particularly important for portfolios not to be stuck in the "nonrepeaters." Many investors come out of a bear market carrying deadweight from the last market cycle. For a lot of small growth companies, the souffle really does rise only once. The nonrepeaters can be identified as those stocks that had enormous price appreciation in the previous bull market, gained widespread recognition, and became broadly owned. But these things are not enough to make a bad stock; one other ingredient is necessary, and that is a serious, internal, fundamental failure that cannot be blamed solely on the economy. Examples include Computervision in the 1983–84 market decline, Datapoint in the 1981–82 bear market, Levitz Furniture in the early 1970s, Mohawk Data in the cycle before that, and Transition Electronics in the early 1960s. The pattern of these situations is that the stocks have a bounce off the bottom when the first leg up in the new bull market occurs, but then they go dead. When so many investors are disappointed so badly, it takes a long time to heal the scars and the offending stocks typically do not perform well in the next market cycle. It is better to take the money out of these kinds of situations and reinvest it in the repeaters and the new, fresh candidates. Those portfolios carrying the least deadweight left over from the last market cycle and having the most exposure to the new, fresh opportunities will be in the top of the performance ratings in the next bull market.

24

Anomaly Investing

Meyer Melnikoff, F.S.A.
Actuary
Goldman, Sachs & Co.

Anomaly investing, or attribute investing, are terms which have recently entered the vocabulary of investment. Essentially, the terms refer to a style of investing which seems to provide above-average risk-adjusted returns, over the long run. The style selects stocks for purchase by reference to one or more common characteristics of the stocks rather than by the traditional methods, which require a thorough analysis of the prospects of each stock, recognizing all known facts, as well as the implications of expected future trends. The characteristics by which stocks are selected in anomaly investing include many which are employed to evaluate stocks in the traditional manner, such as price-earnings ratio, price-to-book value ratio, and total capitalization. Furthermore, although it is not *necessarily* a feature of anomaly investing, the characteristics by which selection is made are generally limited to known information, based on past history, excluding all factors which attempt to forecast the future.

The term *attribute* investing is obviously used to refer to the characteristic(s) by which the stocks are selected. The term *anomaly* investing has a less obvious meaning: the performance of stocks so selected, in successful applications, is an anomaly in modern portfolio theory and capital asset pricing theory. In other words, the concepts seem to work in practice, but not in theory!

Although the classic works on investment, such as *Security Analysis* by Graham, Dodd, and Cottle, (16) refer to many of the characteristics which are used in anomaly investing, they are there used as one of several tools by which each stock is evaluated on its own, rather than as a tool to be used to select stocks for investment. As common stock investing is surely an application of risk theory, another application of risk theory provides an analogy which seems particularly apt to this author; namely, life insurance underwriting. In traditional underwriting, each individual seeking insurance is separately examined medically, and separately evaluated as to his prospects for longevity. By contrast, in some of the newer approaches to life insurance underwriting, such as are used in group insurance, so long as (1) the group to be insured has a sufficiently large number of members, (2) the group is selected in accordance with an appropriate set of basic rules (such as, for example, all the employees actively at work for a single employer), and (3) the amounts of insurance on each life are determined in a manner to preclude individual selection (as by basing the amount of insurance on an objective characteristic such as compensation, instead of letting each individual choose his own amount of insurance), then the traditional medical examination can be dispensed with, as well as all other elements of individual underwriting. In the same way, for attribute or anomaly investing, the stocks to be purchased are selected by the characteristics they have in common, and without consideration of the characteristics in which they differ. Accordingly, another term which may be used to describe this style of investment is *set* investing, applying "set" in the mathematical sense to mean "the universe of stocks that have preselected characteristics." Set investing would be investing in the *set* of all stocks which have a selected *attribute* (or attribute combination), and which provide investment performance which is an *anomaly* in modern portfolio theory.

As is generally true of most new ideas, the concepts of anomaly investing evolved over many years, during which many individuals contributed to its development. Among the contributors are many of the prominent names in recent American investment history. The subject may be divided, although somewhat arbitrarily, into four segments, according to the attribute(s) employed.

LOW PRICE-EARNINGS RATIO (LOW P-E)

More has been written about this attribute than any other. The first published article identified by this author to point in the direction of anomaly investing was written by S. Francis Nicholson. Entitled "Price Earnings Ratios," it appeared in the July–August 1960 issue of the *Financial Analysts Journal*. (28) He began this brief article by expressing a simple question he had (in 1960) posed to sophisticated financial analysts and businessmen: "Within three to ten years, will the better price performance be in common stocks with the current price-earnings multiples of over 25 times, or in those under 12 times?" The answers he had received were nearly 10 to 1 in favor of high multiples, which he explained: "It is assumed they are bought for growth, and the low multiples only for income."

He undertook two studies which (although they did not recognize transaction costs or taxes) produced results that indicated a contrary conclusion: "that on the average the purchase of stocks with low price-earnings multiples will result in greater appreciation in addition to the higher income provided."

Study no. 1 covered 100 stocks, "predominantly industrial issues of trust investment quality and including many of the largest companies," for the 20 years 1939–59, and observed the results over various periods of 5, 10, 15, and 20 years. (See Table 1.)

Study no. 2 covered 29 chemical companies for the 17 years 1937–54, and observed the results over various periods of 3, 6, and 10 years. (See Table 2.)

In his general conclusions, Nicholson suggested that: "High price-earnings multiples typically reflect investor satisfaction with companies of high quality, or with those which have experienced several years of expansion and rising earnings. In such cases, prices have often risen faster than earnings. A resultant increase in price-earnings ratios may be justified in individual instances, but under the impact of public approval or even glamour, it often runs to extremes. When this occurs, upward price trends are eventually subject to slow-down or reversal. High multiple stocks then develop trends which *on the average* compare unfavorably with low multiple stocks which have not yet been bid up to vulnerable price levels." (28)

In the May–June 1966 issue of the *Financial Analysts Journal*, there appeared an article entitled "Prices, Earnings and P-E Ratios" by James D. McWilliams. (21) Using a sample of 390 stocks, divided into P-E ratio deciles at the beginning of each year of measuring performance, McWilliams analyzed the resulting performance over the 12 years 1952–64. In each year, he determined the results for each decile of P-E ratios. His findings were that: (1) Over the entire period of measurement, although not in each year, the performance of low P-E stocks was substantially better than that of high P-E stocks, but the relative results were not perfectly monotonic by P-E ratio. (2) The variability of performance of individual stocks in each year, about the mean of the decile in which they were located, did not show any discernable pattern by P-E ratio. (3) The best performing individual stocks in each year could be found in any P-E decile; that is, they were not necessarily to be found in a low P-E decile.

The September 20, 1966, issue of *The Commercial and Financial Chronicle* contained an article entitled "Price Performance Outlook for High and Low P-E Stocks," by Paul F. Miller, Jr. and Ernest R. Widmann. (24) Covering the period 1948 through 1964, they selected from the "Compustat" tapes all companies with annual sales exceeding

TABLE 1 Results of Study No. 1—100 Stocks (price appreciation in each period according to price-earnings groups)

	1939–1944	1939–1949	1939–1954	1939–1959	1944–1949	1944–1954	1944–1959	1949–1954	1949–1959	1954–1959	1957–1959
Price-earnings ratios at beginning of each period:											
Lowest 20 P-E ratios	48%	102%	444%	1,175%	56%	307%	691%	188%	470%	123%	56%
Next lowest 20 ratios	16	76	237	524	37	238	540	91	273	95	42
Middle 20 P-E ratios	−5	25	114	329	36	152	570	122	328	88	40
Next highest 20 ratios	−4	18	140	378	26	100	305	84	291	79	26
Highest 20 P-E ratios	5	43	206	542	33	156	508	51	273	115	39
Lowest 40 P-E ratios	32	89	340	850	46	272	615	140	372	109	49
Middle 20 P-E ratios	−5	25	114	329	36	152	570	122	328	88	40
Highest 40 P-E ratios	1	29	169	457	30	128	406	68	282	97	33
Average for 100 stocks	12	53	228	589	38	191	523	107	327	100	40

NOTE: An inconsequential adjustment in the foregoing table was made in the periods beginning 1939, to omit four companies which had deficits or only nominal earnings.

SOURCE: S. Francis Nicholson, "Price-Earnings Ratios," *Financial Analysts Journal*, January–February 1960, pp. 43–45.

TABLE 2   Results of Study No. 2—29 Chemical Stocks

At the Beginning of Each 3-, 6-, or 10-Year Period	3-Year Average Appreciation from Each Year 1937–1954, Inclusive	6-Year Average Appreciation from Each Year 1937–1951, Inclusive	10-Year Average Appreciation from Each Year 1937–1947, Inclusive
5 stocks with highest P/E ratios	21%	50%	116%
5 stocks with lowest P/E ratios	56%	101%	191%
Highest 50% P/E ratios	24%	54%	109%
Lowest 50% P/E ratios	40%	89%	153%
Total number of years covered	18	15	11
Number of years in which average appreciation was higher:			
In the highest 50% ratios	2	3	3
In the lowest 50% ratios	16	12	8

SOURCE: S. Francis Nicholson, "Price-Earnings Ratios," *Financial Analysts Journal*, January–February 1960, pp. 43–45.

$150 million, and with fiscal years ending between September 30 and January 31, but excluding any showing no earnings or registering deficits. They grouped the stocks into five P-E classes, using year-end prices and fiscal year earnings, and derived an average price performance for each P-E quintile. The authors concluded that "the low price-earnings group has consistently outperformed the high price-earnings group. In fact, there is a distinct tendency for the groups to fall in a pattern of inverse rank correlation with the height of the P-E ratio." They also examined the statistical distribution of stock price performance in the lowest and highest P-E quintiles, and found them almost identical.

Nicholas Molodovsky, in an article in the May–June 1967 issue of the *Financial Analysts Journal*, entitled "Recent Studies of P-E Ratios," (25) raised questions about the methodology which had been employed in some P-E studies, including both studies mentioned above, by Nicholson and McWilliams. Most interesting are quotes from correspondence which Molodovsky (25) had recently received from Paul F. Miller, Jr., from which the following are excerpted:

> In observing the significance of data in this report, as in previous price-earnings studies, attention is called to the need for analytical judgments on

factors other than earnings ratios; and the preference for good earnings in relation to prices should not lead to using price-earnings ratios as an all-conclusive formula for sound investment.

Please don't misunderstand our emphasis on these studies. We have never claimed that selection by P-E ratios is a substitute for earnings growth in determining investment success. In fact, several studies which we have conducted prove conclusively *that there is no substitute for earnings growth in successful investment selection.* However, *I am somewhat wary of earnings projections and even short-term earnings estimates.* I think you will agree that even one-year estimates of earnings can be woefully inadequate and inaccurate. . . . You will notice in our more recent studies that we have shown that the market tends to be correct in appraising high price-earnings ratio and low price-earnings ratio stocks *as groups;* that is, the high P-E stocks do indeed tend to have better earnings growth over a period of time than do the low P-E stocks. Quantifying this very roughly, it appears that *approximately 65% of the issues in the high P-E categories do turn out to have superior trends; likewise, 65% of the stocks in the low P-E categories tend to have drab or declining earnings trends. It is the balance of 35% that makes the difference in the average price performances of the two groups. In the high P-E ratio group, 35% of the issues proved to be disappointments, and evidently record substantial losses. In the low P-E ratio group, 35% of the issues turned out to have very good earnings trends, and, of course, record substantial investment profits.* Of the 65% of the issues in the high P-E group that turn out well from an earnings standpoint, profits are normally realized at an above-average rate; and in the 65% of the low P-E stocks that experienced drab or declining earnings, the market results are below average, although not, as a rule, very heavily in the negative column. . . . It is evidently the *penalty concept* as it applies to the *high P-E stocks,* and the *reward concept* applied to the *low P-E stocks,* both in those cases where surprises occur that causes the advantage on average to be in favor of the low P-E ratio issues. . . . We have never said that the odds favor investment in any one low P-E stock versus any one high P-E stock or even a select group of low P-E stocks versus high P-E stocks. All we have commented on is the action of *relatively large groups of stocks in these P-E ratio categories.* [Italics supplied by author.]

In the same issue of the *Financial Analysts Journal,* Paul F. Miller, Jr. and Thomas E. Beach contributed a brief, but very pithy article entitled "Recent Studies of P-E Ratios—A Reply," (23) which includes Table 3. Other quotes from Miller and Beach in this article are:

The success of the low P-E approach over an interval of several years is particularly interesting. Early critics had believed that longer time periods would provide an opportunity for the earnings growth of high P-E stocks to make itself felt enough in their stock prices to outperform the low P-E group. We believe these results . . . provide reasonably good evidence that, on average, a group of low P-E stocks is apt to outperform a group of high P-E stocks. . . . Our evidence indicates that the low P-E concept works not so much because the preponderance of stocks in the high P-E group is "weak," but because the minority, which indeed does prove disappointing

TABLE 3 Performance of Stocks Ranked in Quintiles by P-E at Each Year-End, 1948–1964

P-E Quintile	Performance during Subsequent *One-Year* Periods Number of Years in Which Price Performance Ranked				
	First	*Second*	*Third*	*Fourth*	*Fifth*
First (high P-E)	1	3	2	3	8
Second	1	1	2	11	2
Third	1	5	7	1	3
Fourth	2	7	4	2	2
Fifth (low P-E)	12	1	2	0	2

P-E Quintile	Performance during Subsequent *Three-Year* Periods Number of Periods in Which Price Performance Ranked				
	First	*Second*	*Third*	*Fourth*	*Fifth*
First (high P-E)	2	1	1	2	9
Second	0	1	0	10	4
Third	1	3	8	2	1
Fourth	2	8	3	1	1
Fifth (low P-E)	10	2	3	0	0

SOURCE: Paul F. Miller, Jr. and Thomas E. Beach, "Recent Studies of P-E Ratios—A Reply," *Financial Analysts Journal*, May–June 1967, pp. 109–10.

from the standpoint of earnings growth, is severely penalized. . . . These disappointments in the high P-E group typically suffer such precipitous price declines that the entire group's performance is materially affected. An opposite situation characteristically occurrs in the low P-E group. . . . The major practical application of the low P-E concept, in our opinion, is as one tool available to a research director in determining how research time can best be spent. Our studies of high and low P-E stocks indicate that the market's appraisal of industries with apparent lackluster earnings prospects is sometimes in error, and that low multiple stocks in these industries may turn out to be the future market leaders. Research undertaken with the objective of finding these industries is both more positive and apt to yield better results than that aimed at making sure that the growth prospects of high multiple stocks have not changed.

An interesting insight into the significance, or perhaps the lack of significance, of the price-earnings ratio is provided by "Price-Earnings

TABLE 4 Annual Earnings Related to Mean Prices

Grouped According to Quintiles in Each Year 1937–1962, Inclusive	Average Price Appreciation Percentage						
	After:						
	1 Yr. %	2 Yr. %	3 Yr. %	4 Yr. %	5 Yr. %	6 Yr. %	7 Yr. %
A. Lowest price-earnings ratios	16	34	55	76	98	125	149
B. Next higher	9	22	34	48	65	82	100
C. Next higher	7	18	30	43	60	77	96
D. Next higher	6	14	24	35	50	65	83
E. Highest price-earnings ratios	3	11	21	31	46	65	84

SOURCE: S. Francis Nicholson, "Price Ratios in Relation to Investment Results," *Financial Analysts Journal*, January–February 1968, pp. 105–9.

Ratios and Future Growth of Earnings and Dividends" by Joseph E. Murphy, Jr. and Harold W. Stevenson, which appeared in the *Financial Analysts Journal* of November–December, 1967. (27) The study examined the results of about 200 stocks, during the period 1950–64. Their conclusion was that the P-E ratio is an "unreliable judge of which companies would record superior growth of earnings per share. . . . A high P-E ratio is not a prophecy of superior earnings growth, nor is a low P-E ratio a portent of inferior earnings growth. This lack of systemic relationship characterizes all eleven industries studied and persists in all of the periods studied."

S. Francis Nicholson made another contribution to this field with his article "Price Ratios in Relation to Investment Results," which appeared in the *Financial Analysts Journal* for January–February 1968. (29) Dealing with 189 companies in 18 industries, over the 25-year period 1937–62, he studied the performance of stocks chosen by the ratios of prices to: (1) earnings; (2) depreciation charges; (3) sales; and (4) book value. Among his findings were:

> The tabulations of average price changes generally show the more favorable results at most times in categories based on the higher amounts of earnings, depreciation charges, sales and book value as they are related to market prices. . . . Within the separate industry groups, a preponderance of favorable relative price performance could be observed in the categories reflecting greater rather than lesser amounts of earnings, depreciation, sales and book value. . . .

The following comments and Table 4 are part of his paper.
Nicholson's comments include:

With the large number of items and periods averaged above, the pattern of price changes seems remarkably consistent. . . .

The performance of the A group after 4 years was best in 22 out of 23 years. The worst performance after 4 years occurred in the E group in 13 years and in the D group in 6 years.

William Breen, in an article entitled "Low Price-Earnings Ratios and Industry Relatives," published in the July–August 1968 issue of the *Financial Analysts Journal*, (7) tested whether a low price-earnings multiple is more properly an industry-relative concept or a market-relative concept. Using several statistical tests on portfolios consisting solely of securities which had shown an average annual compounded growth in earnings over the five years preceding the selection year of at least 10 percent, Breen reached the following conclusions:

First, low price-earnings multiples, measured either relative to the whole population, or to industry classification, when combined with a control on average past growth in earnings, give portfolio performance which in most years is superior to the performance of randomly selected securities.

Second, the evidence seems to (weakly) support the hypothesis that the relevant measure of low price-earnings is a comparison based on the whole market, rather than on an industry basis. . . .

. . . these results give some credence to the assertion that in the future, industry specialists will be less important than "characteristics" specialists in the analytical assessment of common stocks.

In the November 1, 1968 issue of the Marine Midland Investment Research publication *The Investment Strategist*, entitled "The Price-Earnings Ratio and the Strategy Stimulator," (30) D. Peterson examined the performance of low P-E and high P-E stocks in periods of market advances and market declines. Studying 900 stocks over the period 1948–67, he selected a stock for purchase at the end of a year if it fell into one of two groups: (1) low P-E—if its P-E ratio at the end of the year was lower than the lowest *market* P-E ratio during that year; (2) high P-E—if its P-E ratio at the end of the year was higher than the highest *market* P-E ratio during that year. On this basis his results were as shown in Tables 5 and 6.

Peterson concludes that "Assuming (1) the only factor known to an investor is the P-E ratio of a stock and (2) that past investment behavior is a guide to future investment behavior, the stocks with a relatively low P-E ratio should be selected for capital appreciation . . . [although] low P-E stocks have generally outperformed high P-E stocks during market advances, they do not suggest any superior defensive strategy during market declines."

In 1970, Ernest Widmann (36) reported, in an article entitled "Low Multiple Stocks: A Key to Value?" published in *Probes Into Investment Techniques* (a service of Drexel Harriman Ripley), an update of many previous Drexel studies measuring price performance of stocks grouped

TABLE 5 Analysis of Performance of Low and High P-E Stocks during
Market Advances

Year	S&P 425	Low P-E Stocks	High P-E Stocks
1954	49.7%	56.6%	43.0%
1958	37.6	58.8	68.2
1961	23.1	36.1	22.1
1963	20.1	19.8	19.7
1967	23.3	51.7	46.7
5-year average	30.8%	44.6%	39.9%

SOURCE: D. Peterson, "The Price-Earnings Ratio and the Strategy Stimulator," Marine Midland Investment Research, *The Investment Strategist*, November 1, 1968.

by price-earnings ratios. Considering solely the 30 stocks in the Dow Jones Industrial Average, over the 34-year period 1936–69, dividing the stocks into three groups by P-E ratio, at the beginning of each year (low 10, middle 10, and high 10), and designating the price performance of each P-E rank, into performance ranks (first, second, and third), the summary of the performance rankings for each P-E rank is shown in Table 7.

Widmann cited Table 7 as well as a comparable table for the nine years 1961–69 as further evidence that the low-multiple group usually outperforms the high-multiple group. He also probed into the eight years when the low-multiple group did not rank first, and discovered that inferior performance occurred only in weak markets. Although acknowledging that there was no conclusive evidence why this perverse relationship existed in periods of market weakness, he suggested that negative earnings surprises among low-multiple stocks in such periods might be the explanation.

TABLE 6 Analysis of Performance of Low and High P-E Stocks during
Market Declines

Year	S&P 425	Low P-E Stocks	High P-E Stocks
1953	−7.5%	−1.9%	−0.4%
1957	−14.4	−14.7	−15.8
1960	−4.7	4.7	5.8
1962	−12.8	−17.4	−22.0
1966	−13.4	−10.6	−8.3
5-year average	−10.6%	−8.0%	−8.1%

SOURCE: D. Peterson, "The Price-Earnings Ratio and the Strategy Stimulator," Marine Midland Investment Research, *The Investment Strategist*, November 1, 1968.

TABLE 7 Summary of Performance Rankings, 1936–1969

Performance Rank	DJIA Stocks Grouped by P-E's		
	Low 10	Middle 10	High 10
First	26	4	4
Second	3	23	8
Third	5	7	22

SOURCE: Ernest R. Widmann, "Low Multiple Stocks: A Key to Value?" Drexel Harriman Ripley, *Probes Into Investment Techniques*, June 1970.

Sanjoy Basu, in several articles (2, 3, 4) published over a period of years, beginning in 1975 and concluding after his death in 1983, considered the investment performance of common stocks in relation to their price-earnings ratios as well as their total market capitalization. In an article entitled "The Information Content of Price-Earnings Ratios," published in *Financial Management*, Summer 1975, (2) he made a significant contribution to the question of whether the market capitalizes earnings of firms in an unbiased manner. He undertook to empirically examine the market reaction, in the months following the announcement of annual income reports, to securities trading at different multiples of earnings.

Studying about 500 securities trading on the New York Stock Exchange, over 14 periods of 18 months beginning with years 1956–69, he allocated each security to one of five portfolios, according to its P-E ratio at the beginning of each year, from A-highest P-E, to E-lowest P-E.

He then determined the resulting *abnormal* return (which may be considered a measure of "risk-adjusted" performance) for each of the five portfolios: (*a*) for each of the first 18 months following the income report as well as (*b*) for the accumulated period to the end of each of the first 18 months following the report (2). His findings included the following statements:

1. In general, there was a persistent *upward* drift in the abnormal performance for Portfolios E and D, beginning about three months after the announcement, and continuing for about 12–14 months, reaching a return by month 12 of *3.5 percent to 2 percent per year more* than implied by their level of risk; conversely, there was a generally *downward* drift in the abnormal performance for Portfolios A and B, reaching a return by month 12 of *2.2 percent to 1.6 percent per year less* than implied by their level of risk.

2. The findings in (1) appeared to be relatively stable by year of experience, with Portfolios E and D showing *positive* abnormal returns in 11 out of 14 years, and portfolios A and B showing

negative abnormal returns in 10 out of 14 years. Clearly, however, these abnormal returns did not occur in every year.
3. The market's reaction to *individual* securities, as distinguished from P-E ranked portfolios, was quite diverse; in effect each P-E ranked portfolio consisted of securities that may be considered "winners" or "losers" on a risk-adjusted return basis.

He concluded that "tax-exempt as well as tax-paying investors, who entered the securities markets with the objective of rebalancing their portfolios annually, could have taken advantage of the market disequilibria by acquiring low P-E stocks." From the point of view of those investors, a "market inefficiency seems to have existed." However, he added that, "while there is no evidence to indicate this period was atypical, the extent to which the results can be generalized to other periods is unclear."

In an article published in the *Journal of Finance* in 1977, Basu (3) considered the excess, risk-adjusted rates of return shown by low P-E stocks as a test of the efficient market hypothesis, and reached the following conclusion (using the expression "price-ratio hypothesis" to mean the thesis that low P-E stocks outperform high P-E stocks):

> . . . the behavior of security prices over the 14-year period studied is, perhaps, not completely described by the efficient market hypothesis. To the extent low P-E portfolios did earn superior returns on a risk-adjusted basis, the propositions of the price-ratio hypothesis on the relationship between investment performance of equity securities and their P-E ratios seem to be valid. Contrary to the growing belief that publicly available information is instantaneously impounded in security prices, there seem to be lags and frictions in the adjustment process. As a result, publicly available P-E ratios seem to possess "information content" and may warrant an investor's attention at the time of portfolio formation or revision. (3)

David Dreman has written about low P-E stocks in several publications. In *Barron's*, dated February 28, 1977, his article, "Watch Those Multiples: Low Price-Earnings Ratios Yield the Best Investment Results," (10) reported on work he had completed with William Avera and Cliff Atherton. Using all stocks listed on the New York Stock Exchange with 20 contiguous quarters of earnings, dividends, and price information between the second quarter of 1967 and the second quarter of 1976, the resulting sample included about 70 percent of the common stocks on the NYSE. The results of this analysis appear in Table 8.

Dreman made the following general recommendations about low P-E investing in his *Barron's* article (10):

1. Invest in large companies.
2. Maintain adequate diversification.
3. Adopt and adhere to a mechanical formula for buying and selling.

TABLE 8   P-E: More Is Less?—The Ups and Downs of Average Total Returns (annualized) (from mid-1967 through mid-1976)

Stocks Grouped by Multiples		Quarter	With Portfolio Switching after Each			Holding Original Portfolio for 9 Years
			1-Year Period	2-Year Period	3-Year Period	
Highest P-E decile	(1)	1.6%	1.1%	0.0%	1.1%	1.4%
	(2)	2.0	3.4	2.6	−0.7	3.2
	(3)	2.3	3.0	1.8	−0.5	5.4
	(4)	2.8	2.8	1.9	−2.4	5.9
	(5)	4.8	5.4	5.6	2.2	5.8
	(6)	5.1	7.1	6.7	2.3	4.5
	(7)	9.4	7.5	7.4	3.0	6.9
	(8)	11.8	8.4	8.7	4.1	8.4
	(9)	11.8	9.6	11.4	5.1	7.0
Lowest P-E decile	(10)	19.4	10.2	11.4	8.9	8.9

SOURCE: David Dreman, "Watch Those Multiples: Low Price-Earnings Ratios Yield the Best Investment Results," *Barron's Business and Financial Weekly*, February 28, 1977, p. 11.

He has developed these and other ideas at greater length in his two books, *Psychology and the Stock Market* and *Contrarian Investment Strategy* (11, 12).

In an article by Rose Darby (9) in *Pensions and Investment Age*, dated April 28, 1986, entitled "Low P-E Effect Is Valid for Overseas Equities," Sandor Cseh was reported to have carried out a study of the P-E effect in overseas stocks, considering the experience from 1978 through 1985 of 1,500 stocks in six markets: Japan, United Kingdom, Germany, The Netherlands, Switzerland, and France. According to Cseh, these six markets represent almost 90 percent of the world's stock market capitalizations outside the United States. "Although the low P-E approach did not work in individual years, the study found a clear relationship between P-E ratios and returns," he said.

TOTAL MARKET CAPITALIZATION ("SMALL CAP" OR "SMALL FIRM SIZE")

Rolf W. Banz in an article published in the *Journal of Financial Economics* in 1981, entitled "The Relationship between Return and Market Value of Common Stocks," (1) found that the stocks of smaller firms had higher risk-adjusted returns, on average, than the stocks of larger firms, over a 40-year period, 1926–75. He also found that the effect is most pronounced for the stocks of the smallest firms, and it is not very stable over time.

Banz added that he knew of no theoretical foundation for such an effect, and did not know whether the basic factor was firm size itself, or whether firm size was just a proxy for unknown factors correlated with size. He offered, as purely a conjecture, a possible explanation as follows: less information is generally available about small firms, and therefore many investors may not desire to hold such stocks. Accordingly, there are fewer potential buyers, and this leads to higher returns.

In the same issue of the *Journal of Financial Economics*, Marc R. Reinganum, in an article entitled "Misspecification of Capital Asset Pricing—Empirical Anomalies Based on Earnings' Yields and Market Values," (31) studied the effects of both firm size and low P-E (or its reciprocal, high E-P, known as earnings yield). He concluded that portfolios based on both attributes experience average returns systematically greater, on a risk-adjusted basis, than those predicted by the capital asset pricing model. Furthermore, these "abnormal" returns persist for at least two years after a portfolio selected by the attributes is established (without periodic realignment according to the attribute). He concluded, however, that the low P-E (or high E-P) effect is subsumed by the small firm-size effect, which appeared to him to be the more fundamental attribute, for which low P-E is a form of proxy.

Richard Roll, in "A Possible Explanation of the Small Firm Effect," published in the *Journal of Finance*, September 1981, (34) suggested that the riskiness of small firms had been understated, in portfolio returns, due to their infrequent trading, and therefore the abnormal returns which some studies have attributed to small firm stocks may be spurious.

Marc Reinganum, (32) in an article in the *Journal of Finance* of March 1982 entitled "A Direct Test of Roll's Conjecture on the Firm Size Effect," described the results of studies which determined that, although there had been some bias toward underestimating the riskiness of small firm stocks, the bias was too small to explain the small firm effect.

Sanjoy Basu, in an article in the *Journal of Financial Economics* of 1983 entitled "The Relationship between Earnings' Yield, Market Value and Return for NYSE Common Stocks—Further Evidence,"(4) examined in some detail both high E-P (low P-E) stocks and small firm stocks. He found portfolios constructed by each attribute provided abnormally high risk-adjusted returns, and that the effect of each attribute on expected returns was considerably more complicated than previously documented in the literature. Even when experimental control was exercised over firm size, stocks of high E-P firms, on average, earned higher risk adjusted returns than stocks of low E-P firms.

In a paper entitled "Portfolio Strategies Based on Market Capitalization," which appeared in the Winter 1983 issue of the *Journal of*

TABLE 9 Investment Characteristics of the 10 Market Value Portfolios

Portfolio	Average Annual Return*	Average Percent on AMEX[†]	Average Median Value[‡]	Median Share Price[§]	Estimated Portfolio Beta[‖]
MV1	32.77	92.19	4.6	5.24	1.58
MV2	23.51	77.33	10.8	9.52	1.57
MV3	22.98	52.09	19.3	12.89	1.50
MV4	20.24	34.05	30.7	16.19	1.46
MV5	19.08	21.33	47.2	19.22	1.43
MV6	18.30	12.73	74.2	22.59	1.36
MV7	15.64	8.37	119.1	26.44	1.28
MV8	14.24	4.73	209.7	30.83	1.22
MV9	13.00	3.39	434.6	34.43	1.11
MV10	9.47	2.25	1,102.6	44.94	.96

* In a given year, a portfolio return is calculated by averaging the one-year holding period returns of the securities within the portfolio. The portfolio returns are averaged over the 18 years of the study from 1963 through 1980. Returns are reported in percentages.
[†] The percentage of firms within each portfolio that are listed on the American Stock Exchange averaged over the 18 years of the study.
[‡] The median value of the common stock (in millions of dollars) for firms within each portfolio averaged over the 18 years of the study.
[§] The median share price in dollars at the time of the portfolio formation (end of December) of securities within each portfolio averaged over the 18 formation periods.
[‖] Betas are calculated using the CRSP value-weighted NYSE-AMEX market index and Dimson's aggregated coefficients estimator. The aggregated coefficients estimate is computed with a contemporaneous, 20 lagged, and 5 leading market returns.
SOURCE: Marc Reinganum, "Portfolio Strategies Based on Market Capitalization," *Journal of Portfolio Management*, Winter 1983, pp. 29–36.

Portfolio Management, (33) Marc Reinganum provided further measures of the extent of the abnormally high rates of return from small firm stocks, including Table 9. It represents the investment characteristics of 10 market value portfolios, for the 18 years 1963–80. Each portfolio is composed of 10 percent of the number of stocks traded on the New York and American Stock Exchanges at the end of each year, classified by total market capitalization with MV1 designating the smallest stocks and MV10 the largest.

OTHER ATTRIBUTES

A number of other attributes have been studied.

1. High Dividend Yield

Litzenberger and Ramaswamy (19) found that yield had a strong positive effect on risk-adjusted returns. However, Morgan (26) found only a weak effect; Black and Scholes (6) found no significant effect whatsoever; and Long (20) found a negative effect.

2. Low Price to Book Value Ratio (Low P-BV)

Dennis Stattman (35) found a significant positive relationship between a low P-BV and excess returns; but he also reported that the low price to book value relationship was just a proxy for the small firm size effect.

3. High Earnings Growth (High Earnings Momentum)

4. High Relative Price Strength (High Price Momentum)

Attributes 3 and 4 were discussed by Robert A. Levy and Spero L. Kripotos in an article in the November–December 1969 issue of the *Financial Analysts Journal*, entitled "Earnings Growth, P-E's and Relative Price Strength." (18) This study of 227 actively traded and widely held securities, over the eight years 1957–64, considered all possible two-way combinations of the three characteristics indicated in the title. Measuring performance in 26-week periods, it concluded that high earnings growth, low P-E, and high relative price strength, were all effective in the test period, and in order of best performance first, they appeared to be high earnings growth, high relative price strength and low P-E.

5. Low Earnings Relatives (Low Earnings Momentum)

Alex Gould and Maurice Buchsbaum discussed this attribute in an article in the same issue of *The Financial Analysts Journal* entitled "A Filter Approach Using Earnings Relatives." (15) This study of 200 stocks over the 20-year period 1948–67 suggested that low-earnings growth relatives may be predictive of turnaround situations. However, as the authors pointed out, the limitations of the data did not permit the inclusion of companies which subsequently went into bankruptcy, a likely result of sustained low-earnings growth relatives.

6. High Residual (Nonmarket) Risk

Cooperman, Einhorn, and Shangkuan have studied this attribute in their publications described in the next section.

ATTRIBUTE COMBINATIONS

1. Low P-E Historical Relative, Low P-E Market Relative, High Earnings Momentum, and High Price Momentum

In a letter to the editor of *The Financial Analysts Journal*, published in the September–October 1973 issue with the title "Yes, Virginia, There Is

Hope: Tests of the Value Line Ranking System," (5) Fischer Black reported on an analysis which Value Line had carried out with his assistance. The Value Line investment survey, which contained information on about 1,400 stocks, provided, among other items, a ranking of each stock from 1 to 5, designed to predict the performance of each stock over the next 12 months. The rankings, although subject to some degree of subjective judgment to reduce the magnitude and frequency of rating changes, were based essentially on a weighting of a measure of three attributes: (1) price-earnings ratios, relative to historical norms as well as to market ratios; (2) earnings momentum; and (3) price momentum; with each based almost entirely on published information. For a period of five years, beginning April 1965, five portfolios were created, each consisting of equal weights of each stock with the same ranking, with the portfolios realigned each month. The resulting portfolios had about the same risk and were each well diversified. Tests not recognizing the cost of transactions indicated that the success of the rankings was very consistent over time. Furthermore, when transaction costs of 2 percent or less in and out were recognized, the strategy continued to be successful, but at a lower level of significance.

2. Low P-E Historical Relative, Low P-E Industry Relative, and Small Firm Size

In *Hyper-Profits*, published in 1985, David A. Goodman and John W. Peavy III (14) explored a system to invest in stocks that combined three "attributes":

a. A low P-E industry relative—that is, a low P-E ratio by comparison *with other stocks in its industry.*
b. A low P-E historical relative—that is, a low P-E ratio by reference *to its own historical P-E.*
c. Small firm size, by reference to its total market capitalization.

This book contains many examples of the effectiveness of these three attributes, especially when combined.

3. Small Firm Size and Low P-E

4. Low P-BV and Low P-E

5. High Dividend Yield and Low P-E

Leon G. Cooperman, Steven G. Einhorn, and Patricia C. Shangkuan (8) have discussed many aspects of anomaly investing in their Goldman Sachs Portfolio Strategy publications. Combinations 3, 4, and 5 were studied in the July 11, 1986 "Risk, Return and Equity Valuation," (13) by Einhorn and Shangkuan, which contained the following discussion on anomaly investing:

> We have spent considerable time in previous publications identifying attributes historically associated with outperforming stocks. Such attributes include low P-E, low price/book value (P-BV), high dividend yield, smaller capitalization, and above-average nonmarket risk. It is appropriate to update the performance of these approaches. Table 10 details the investment return based on the anomalies noted. As indicated, stock portfolios based on these attributes have rather consistently outperformed the S&P 500. One would think that the excess returns associated with these anomalies would be recognized by investors and arbitraged away. That these excess returns have not been arbitraged away suggests an inefficiency in the market that investors can seize.
>
> Focusing on 1986 year-to-date performance: Portfolios based on low P-E and smaller capitalization stocks have outperformed the S&P 500. Portfolios based on high residual (nonmarket) risk have performed in line with the market. Portfolios based on low P-BV and high dividend yield have underperformed the market. The anomalies noted can be combined and, to the extent that there is a low correlation between the different anomalies, portfolios based on a combination may do better than portfolios constructed from one anomaly. Table 11 shows this by means of three portfolios. The first is constructed by identifying the smallest 100 companies in the S&P 500 by capitalization, and then selecting the 50 lowest P-E companies from this sample. The second is based on identifying the 100 companies in the S&P 500 with the lowest P-BV ratio, then selecting from this sample the 50 lowest P-E companies. The third is constructed by identifying the 100 companies in the S&P 500 with the highest dividend yield, then selecting the 50 lowest P-E companies from this sample.
>
> A comparison of Tables 10 and 11 shows the following: (1) The portfolio consisting of only the bottom 20 percent by market capitalization (Table 10) outperformed the combination portfolio #1 based on small size and low P-E (Table 11). In only 6 of 18 years (1974, 1975, 1976, 1981, 1984, and 1985) did the combination portfolio outperform the portfolio of only small capitalization companies. (2) The portfolio consisting of only the bottom 20 percent of companies by P-E (Table 10) underperformed the combination portfolio #1 of small size and low P-E (Table 11). In 16 of 18 years (the exceptions being 1970 and 1984), the combination portfolio of small size and low P-E outperformed low P-E. (3) The portfolio consisting of only the bottom 20 percent of companies by P-E (Table 10) outperformed the combination portfolio #2 based on low P-E and low P-BV in 10 to 18 years. (4) The portfolio consisting of only the bottom 20 percent of companies by low P-BV (Table 10) outperformed the combination of low P-BV and low P-E in 8 of 18 years. (5) In 10 of 18 years, the portfolio consisting of only the bottom 20 percent of companies by P-E (Table 10) outperformed the combination portfolio #3 based on low P-E and high dividend yield. (6) In 12 of 18 years, portfolio #3 (based on low P-E and high dividend yield) outperformed the portfolio consisting of high dividend yield issues.

TABLE 10 Anomaly Investing, Total Return, 1968–1986

| | | | S&P 500 | | | | | | |
| | | | Bottom 20% by* | | | Top 20% by* | | | |
	S&P 500†	S&P 500*	Size	P/E	Price-to-Book	Residual Risk	Dividend Yield	T-Bills	Long-Term Government Bonds
1968	10.8	29.3	74.2	30.5	37.3	NA	26.5	5.2	(0.3)
1969	(8.3)	(8.1)	(8.2)	(17.5)	(20.5)	NA	(15.6)	6.6	(5.1)
1970	3.5	2.3	3.8	7.8	4.3	NA	11.7	6.5	12.1
1971	14.1	27.7	48.3	19.0	19.9	31.7	12.5	4.4	13.2
1972	18.7	18.1	21.3	14.8	14.3	12.5	13.0	3.8	5.7
1973	(14.5)	(16.7)	(13.2)	(17.7)	(10.6)	(15.8)	(10.9)	6.9	(1.1)
1974	(26.0)	(23.9)	(18.6)	(12.8)	(12.1)	(28.9)	(10.8)	8.0	4.4
1975	36.9	61.8	98.7	83.3	94.8	94.1	65.4	5.8	9.2
1976	23.6	36.0	61.9	50.3	57.3	47.1	44.6	5.1	16.8
1977	(7.2)	1.8	27.0	11.0	8.4	14.2	4.1	5.1	(0.7)
1978	6.4	12.2	26.1	13.1	7.5	23.7	1.6	7.2	(1.2)
1979	18.2	31.6	53.5	26.3	30.5	57.9	19.5	10.4	(1.2)
1980	31.5	34.4	43.9	26.4	18.5	65.3	17.6	11.2	(4.0)
1981	(4.9)	4.3	20.0	15.1	13.5	(0.9)	17.1	14.7	1.9
1982	20.4	33.8	62.5	30.9	37.0	51.0	29.4	11.4	40.3
1983	22.3	29.4	46.4	24.4	41.2	38.6	28.2	8.8	0.0
1984	6.0	0.6	(3.1)	14.3	1.0	(8.4)	10.2	10.0	15.5
1985	31.0	29.9	21.4	28.4	19.1	20.5	29.5	7.9	32.0
1986‡	18.7	20.3	22.9	22.1	12.9	18.6	14.4	2.9	13.3
1968–1972§	7.3	12.9	24.5	9.7	9.3	NA	8.7	5.3	4.9
1973–1980§	6.4	13.8	29.8	18.8	20.1	25.9	13.9	7.4	2.6
1981–1985§	14.2	18.7	27.4	22.4	21.4	18.0	22.6	10.5	16.9
1968–1985§	8.8	14.9	27.6	17.2	17.4	NA	14.7	8.0	7.0

* Equal-weighted. No rebalancing in given year.
† Capitalization-weighted.
‡ As of May 30, 1986.
§Compound annualized return.
SOURCE: Steven Einhorn and Patricia Shangkuan, "Risk, Return and Equity Valuation," Goldman Sachs Portfolio Strategy publications, July 11, 1986.

TABLE 11   Anomaly Combinations, Total Return, 1968–1986

	S&P 500[a]	S&P 500[b]	Combination #1[b,c]	Combination #2[b,d]	Combination #3[b,e]
1968	10.8%	29.3%	54.2%	28.8%	26.7%
1969	(8.3)	(8.1)	(17.3)	(16.6)	(16.1)
1970	3.5	2.3	3.6	1.2	12.2
1971	14.1	27.7	43.2	16.9	9.1
1972	18.7	18.1	19.2	15.4	13.1
1973	(14.5)	(16.7)	(17.4)	(11.5)	(15.5)
1974	(26.0)	(23.9)	(12.2)	(4.4)	(6.7)
1975	36.9	61.8	105.2	93.4	69.5
1976	23.6	36.0	67.4	61.8	51.0
1977	(7.2)	1.8	26.1	10.3	8.2
1978	6.4	12.2	18.0	9.5	3.4
1979	18.2	31.6	40.9	24.8	24.2
1980	31.5	34.4	30.8	24.0	21.6
1981	(4.9)	4.3	26.6	19.8	19.7
1982	20.4	33.8	58.7	29.3	23.0
1983	22.3	29.4	40.0	36.1	24.5
1984	6.0	0.6	9.7	13.8	18.4
1985	31.0	29.9	33.5	26.8	29.0
1986[f]	18.7	20.3	28.2	17.8	18.3
1968–1972[g]	7.3	12.9	17.7	8.0	8.0
1973–1980[g]	6.4	13.8	27.2	14.2	16.6
1981–1985[g]	14.2	18.7	32.7	24.9	22.9
1968–1985[g]	8.8	14.9	25.9	15.3	15.8

[a] Capitalization-weighted.

[b] Equal-weighted. No rebalancing in given year.

[c] Smallest (by capitalization) 20 percent of companies in S&P 500. Of these smallest companies, portfolio shown is the 50 lowest P/E companies. In effect, this portfolio is a combination of the two anomalies of small size and low P/E.

[d] Bottom 20 percent of companies in S&P 500 by price/book value ratio. Of these low price/book companies, portfolio shown is the 50 lowest P/E ones. In effect, this portfolio is a combination of the two anomalies of low price/book and low P/E.

[e] Top 20 percent companies in S&P 500 by dividend yield. Of these high yield companies, portfolio shown is the 50 lowest P/E companies. In effect, this portfolio is a combination of the two anomalies of high dividend yield and low P/E.

[f] As of May 30, 1986.

[g] Compound annualized return.

SOURCE: Steven Einhorn and Patricia Shangkuan, "Risk, Return and Equity Valuation," Goldman Sachs Portfolio Strategy publications, July 11, 1986.

Tables 10 and 11 from the recent publication of Einhorn and Shangkuan provide a comprehensive wrapup of the results observed of different varieties of anomaly investing, in a uniform format.

Several of the papers cited above included statements cautioning that the superior results experienced in the past by particular forms of anomaly investing might not necessarily be indicative of their performance in the future. This is undoubtedly true, but more needs to be said.

In the first place, it is always possible that any single study could have design flaws which are not apparent to anyone, and which thereby lead to unwarranted and unsupportable conclusions. This risk is reduced when multiple studies by different individuals are able to reach comparable conclusions, especially when great care is used to ensure that no bias or hindsight enters into the studies.

Another concern may be derived from "data mining" or overworking the data applicable to a limited period, and which thereby reaches conclusions that may be particularly reflective of the characteristics of the period studied, and, to that extent, possibly not applicable to other periods. This risk is reduced as the duration of the studies is extended to longer periods of time.

More fundamental is the general question of the predictive value of past experiences, especially as they relate to matters of likelihood rather than determination. This is a subject within the domain of an actuary. In dealing with idealized subjects, such as the toss in a vacuum of a perfectly weighted two-headed coin, or the selection of cards from a perfect deck of 52, it is possible, on a combinatorial set-theoretic basis (a rigorous mathematical discipline), to compute the theoretical likelihood of particular events. Even when such ideal probabilities are determined, their predictive value applies not to each event, but to the likelihood of events over a large number of trials. Such calculations can be extended to fairly complex, but still relatively idealized, subjects. How can we estimate the likelihood of events in the real world, when idealization is not possible? For example, in estimating the mortality rates which can be expected of human beings, there is no alternative but to analyze past experience as carefully as possible, and to make such assumptions as to future trends as seem reasonable. Similarly, estimating the future results of common stock investing involves so many unknown factors that no theoretical a priori calculation can be carried out to predict future results. And yet, in the real world, actions must be taken in the full knowledge of many uncertainties—or how else could insurance companies, or investment managers, conduct their affairs. All that is possible is to follow a course similar to that applicable to mortality, and estimate future likelihoods based on past experience, taking into account any assumptions as to future trends that seem reasonable. In both areas, mortality and investment, it is possible that the future may differ widely, and unpredictably, from the past. Will women continue to have lighter mortality, on average, than men? Will low P-E stocks continue to have better performance, on average, than high P-E stocks? Future changes in the environment could well affect both relationships; and this author cannot be certain of either—but, for the foreseeable future, I believe both are more likely than not—not for every individual (person or stock), in every quarter, or in every year, but on the average, over the long term.

One further thought is relevant. It is contributory to the credibility of the inference for the future that can be drawn from past events, if there is a plausible rationality for the experience. Any attempt to link common stock performance to the stars, or the tides, might therefore be considered with much skepticism. But such considerations must be restrained. In modern science, especially quantum theory and particle physics, many important recent discoveries defy "common sense" and rationality. Increasingly the men at the leading edge in such fields say the role of science is not to answer the question of "Why?" so much as to answer the question of "Under what conditions?" And there may be benefit to such an attitude in areas of complex uncertainties, such as common stock investing.

REFERENCES

1. BANZ, ROLF W. "The Relationship Between Return and Market Value of Common Stocks." *Journal of Financial Economics* 9 (1981), pp. 3–18.

2. BASU, SANJOY. "The Information Content of Price-Earnings Ratios." *Financial Management* 4, no. 2 (Summer 1975), pp. 53–64.

3. ———. "Investment Performance of Common Stocks in Relation to Their Price-Earnings Ratios: A Test of the Efficient Market Hypothesis." *The Journal of Finance* 32, no. 3 (June 1977), pp. 663–81.

4. ———. "The Relationship Between Earnings' Yield, Market Value and Return for NYSE Common Stocks—Further Evidence." *Journal of Financial Economics* 12 (1983), pp. 129–86.

5. BLACK, FISCHER. "Yes, Virginia, There Is Hope: Tests of the Value Line Ranking System." *Financial Analysts Journal*, September–October 1973, pp. 10–14.

6. BLACK, FISCHER, and MYRON S. SCHOLES. "The Effects of Dividend Yield and Dividend Policy on Common Stock Prices and Returns." *Journal of Financial Economics* 1 (May 1974), pp. 1–22.

7. BREEN, WILLIAM. "Low Price-Earnings Ratios and Industry Relatives." *Financial Analysts Journal*, July–August 1968, pp. 125–27.

8. COOPERMAN, LEON G., STEVEN G EINHORN, and PATRICIA C. SHANGKUAN. Goldman Sachs Portfolio Strategy Publications: April 1985; November–December 1985; January 1986; July 1986.

9. CSEH, SANDOR, quoted by ROSE DARBY in "Low P-E Effect Is Valid for Overseas Equities." *Pensions and Investment Age*, April 28, 1986, p. 32.

10. DREMAN, DAVID. "Watch Those Multiples: Low Price-Earnings Ratios Yield the Best Investment Results." *Barron's*, February 28, 1977, p. 11.

11. ———. *Psychology and the Stock Market*. New York: Amacom, 1977.

12. ———. *Contrarian Investment Strategy*. New York: Random House, 1979.

13. EINHORN, STEVEN G., and PATRICIA C. SHANGKUAN. "Risk, Return, and Equity Valuation," Goldman Sachs Portfolio Strategy Publications, July 11, 1986.

14. GOODMAN, DAVID A., and JOHN W. PEAVY, III. *Hyper-Profits*. Garden City, N.Y.: Doubleday Publishing, 1985.

15. GOULD, ALEX, and MAURICE BUCHSBAUM. "A Filter Approach Using Earnings Relatives." *Financial Analysts Journal*, November–December 1969, pp. 61–64.

16. GRAHAM, BENJAMIN, DAVID L. DODD, AND SIDNEY COTTLE. *Security Analysis* 4th Edition. New York: McGraw-Hill, 1962.

17. KRAUS, ALAN, and ROBERT H. LITZENBERGER. "Skewness Preference and the Valuation of Risk Assets." *The Journal of Finance*, September, 1976, pp. 1085–1100.

18. LEVY, ROBERT A., and SPERO L. KRIPOTOS. "Earnings Growth, P-E's and Relative Price Strength." *Financial Analysts Journal*, November–December 1969, pp. 60–67.

19. LITZENBERGER, ROBERT H., AND KRISHNA RAMASWAMY. "The Effect of Personal Taxes and Dividends on Capital Asset Prices: Theory and Empirical Evidence." *Journal of Financial Economics* 7 (June 1979), pp. 163–95.

20. LONG, JOHN B., JR. "The Market Valuation of Cash Dividends: A Case to Consider." *Journal of Financial Economics* 6 (June–September 1978), pp. 235–64.

21. McWILLIAMS, JAMES D. "Prices, Earnings and P-E Ratios." *Financial Analysts Journal*, May–June 1966, pp. 137–42.

22. MILLER, PAUL F., JR. "A Basic Research Study Examining the Relationship between Price-Earnings Ratios and Subsequent Price and Earnings Performance." Drexel Harriman Ripley Institutional Research, October 1966.

23. MILLER, PAUL F., JR., and THOMAS E. BEACH. "Recent Studies of P-E Ratios—A Reply." *Financial Analysts Journal*, May–June 1967, pp. 109–10.

24. MILLER, PAUL F., JR., and ERNEST R. WIDMANN. "Price Performance Outlook for High and Low P-E Stocks." *The Commercial and Financial Chronicle*, September 20, 1966, pp. 13–14.

25. MOLODOVSKY, NICHOLAS. "Recent Studies of P-E Ratios." *The Financial Analysts Journal*, May–June 1967, pp. 101–8.

26. MORGAN, I. G. "Dividends and Capital Asset Prices." School of Business, Queen's University, Kingston, Ontario, Canada, June 1980.

27. MURPHY, JOSEPH E., JR., and HAROLD W. STEVENSON. "Price-Earnings Ratios and Future Growth of Earnings and Dividends." *Financial Analysts Journal*, November–December 1967, pp. 111–14.

28. NICHOLSON, S. FRANCIS. "Price-Earnings Ratios." *The Financial Analysts Journal*, July–August 1960, pp. 43–45.

29. _____. "Price Ratios in Relation to Investment Results." *Financial Analysts Journal*, January–February 1968, pp. 105–9.

30. PETERSON, D. "The Price-Earnings Ratio and the Strategy Stimulator." *The Investment Strategist*, Marine Midland Investment Research, November 1, 1968.

31. REINGANUM, MARC R. "Misspecification of Capital Asset Pricing: Empirical Anomalies Based on Earnings' Yields and Market Values." *The Journal of Financial Economics* 9 (1981), pp. 19–46.

32. _____. "A Direct Test of Roll's Conjecture on the Firm Size Effect." *Journal of Finance* 37, no. 1 (March 1982), pp. 27–35.

33. _____. "Portfolio Strategies Based on Market Capitalization." *Journal of Portfolio Management*, Winter 1983, pp. 29–36.

34. ROLL, RICHARD. "A Possible Explanation of the Small Firm Effect." *The Journal of Finance* 36, no. 4 (September 1981), pp. 879–88.

35. STATTMAN, DENNIS. "Book Values and Expected Stock Returns." Unpublished M.B.A. Honors Paper, The University of Chicago, 1980.

36. WIDMANN, ERNEST R. "Low Multiple Stocks: A Key to Value?" Drexel Harriman Ripley, *Probes Into Investment Techniques*, June 1970.

25

Investing in Foreign Securities

Rein W. van der Does
Managing Director—International Research
Drexel Burnham Lambert Inc.

Lucille Palermo, CFA
Vice President—International Research
Drexel Burnham Lambert Inc.

SUMMARY

Investors through the ages have understood that the risk of investing capital could be reduced by means of diversification among uncorrelated investments. Generally speaking, however, investors did not diversify outside their own countries. This is particularly true of U.S. investors, whose own markets are by far the broadest, most liquid in the world (although U.S. corporations have led the way to international diversification of their own operations and in so doing earned the designation *multinational*). Increasingly, however, investors are realizing that not only does the internationally diversified portfolio hold out the probabilities of significant risk reduction (because stock markets around the world rarely move in unison), it also holds out the possibilities of greater reward. In order to reduce risk, portfolio managers diversify into many different positions within various industries. Why would they not diversify into a variety of equity markets and different currencies? Moreover, many foreign economies are less mature and have the potential to expand faster than that of the United States. Combined with the development of efficient telecommunications systems that have facilitated transnational exchanges of information and trading and the growing internationalization of business in general, this factor has sparked an ever-greater awareness of the potentials offered by international investing.

In this chapter, we discuss the topics of *why* an investor should diversify internationally or globally (twice the market capitalization from which to choose, potentially higher returns, reduced risks) (Section 1); *how* to go about choosing and effecting a non-U.S. investment (Section 2); and the *possible drawbacks* of "going global," which include varying and often less stringent accounting standards than prevail in the United States, less liquid markets, and limited information flows (Section 3). We would note from the beginning, however, that, while the differences in accounting standards and securities regulation are an important area for analysis, a trend is developing for major companies abroad to present their accounts on a basis consistent with U.S. standards. Attracted by the size and the competitiveness of the U.S. capital market, it appears reasonable to assume that many foreign enterprises will list their securities on U.S. stock exchanges and adhere to SEC regulations. For this reason we discuss the advantages/disadvantages of American Depositary Receipts (ADRs). We also include in Section 4 brief comments on the characteristics of major world markets. These comments were kindly provided by local banks or brokers, to whom we are grateful.

SECTION 1—THE RATIONALE FOR "GOING GLOBAL"

Although managers were initially slow to broaden their investment horizons in the years immediately following the enactment of the 1974 Employee Retirement Income Security Act (ERISA), the pace of international investing has clearly quickened in recent years. There can be no doubt that "going global" is an idea whose time has come. Information provided by Intersec Research Corporation and by our estimates indicates that the portion of total ERISA funds committed to markets outside the United States has increased from 1.3 percent at year-end 1981 to 3.6 percent at the end of 1986. Moreover, not only has the piece of the pie dedicated abroad increased, but the size of the pie itself has grown appreciably. Consequently, from approximately $5.2 billion at the end of 1981, the absolute value of ERISA money invested abroad will have risen to an estimated $44 billion by year-end 1986. (See Tables 1 through 3B.)

The obvious question that arises is "Why?," or even, "Why bother?" The obvious answer is that there are recognizable and quantifiable advantages in doing so. These advantages include *(a)* a greater selection, in fact a doubling of the size of the market capitalization from which to choose securities; *(b)* potentially greater returns considering the degree to which many foreign markets have outperformed the U.S. equity market over the past 10–15 years; and *(c)* the lower risk that results from carrying the diversification process one step further.

TABLE 1 ERISA Assets Invested Overseas

	Year-End 1981	Year-End 1982	Year-End 1983	Year-End 1984	Year-End 1985E	Projected* 1986	Projected* 1990
Total overseas ($ billion)	$5.2	$7.0	$11.7	$15.0	$27.0	$44.0	$120.0
As percent of ERISA	1.3%	1.4%	1.8%	2.2%	2.7%	3.6%	6.9%

* Estimates by Drexel Burnham Lambert.
SOURCE: Intersec Research Corporation, Stamford, Conn.

TABLE 2 Net Purchases of Foreign Stocks in All Countries by U.S. Investors (in millions)

	First Quarter	Second Quarter	Third Quarter	Fourth Quarter
1979	$ 4	$ -62	$ 538	$ 411
1980	658	427	801	293
1981	134	164	-242	17
1982	-231	99	109	1,320
1983	994	1,837	626	207
1984	-354	-6	729	715
1985	1,869	219	987	786

SOURCES: U.S. Treasury; Securities Industry Association.

The United States Is Only Half the Story

Despite its considerable size, the capitalization of the U.S. stock market, as measured by the S&P 500 Stock Index, represents less than half the capitalization of the total world "stock market" as measured by share indexes in the 20 largest (including the United States) stock markets around the globe. As shown in Table 4, the market cap of all issues included in the S&P 500 totaled $2.2 trillion, or 45 percent of the world market capitalization. What is more, the market cap of the local share markets often represents 50 percent or less of GNP, indicating rather underdeveloped stock markets.

Asking a money manager competing in the performance arena to limit himself to American equities is a little like sending a boxer into the arena with one hand tied behind his back. And it is not just a question of size—it can also mean missed opportunities. To exclude Japanese equities from your prescribed list of investments is to eliminate the chance to invest in some of the most successful consumer electronics and automobile concerns in the world. Likewise, to forego Australian investments precludes the shares of companies with some of the world's richest natural resource bases. Europe boasts world-class pharmaceutical and chemical firms, and since the development of North Sea oil, energy companies as well. France has a line of specialty-situation companies such as Moet Hennessey, Skis Rossignol, Club Mediterranee, and L'Oreal. Moreover, some of these overseas companies are selling at valuations well below those of their American counterparts—Swiss and Australian banks, Dutch insurers, and Belgian utilities, for example. Reasons for the price disparities vary; sometimes they stem from the greater inefficiencies of overseas markets, sometimes from local investors' preferences.

TABLE 3A Gross Purchases of Foreign Stocks by U.S. Investors (in millions)

	1979	1980	1981	1982	1983	1984	1985
Europe	$ 3,369	$ 6,779	$ 5,710	$ 6,541	$13,633	$13,509	$21,039
France	650	1,136	823	801	1,440	1,013	1,219
Netherlands	231	521	251	433	1,154	1,306	1,899
Switzerland	613	1,526	933	707	1,778	1,321	1,619
United Kingdom	1,443	745	2,908	3,618	6,483	7,925	12,907
Canada	4,510	6,682	4,885	2,939	4,970	4,427	6,824
Asia	1,657	3,254	6,557	5,121	9,397	10,742	14,178
Japan	1,404	2,701	5,398	4,331	7,974	9,099	11,771
Others	480	1,144	1,598	1,066	2,327	2,043	3,882
Total	$10,016	$17,859	$18,750	$15,667	$30,327	$30,721	$45,923

SOURCES: U.S. Treasury; Securities Industry Association.

TABLE 3B Net Purchases of Foreign Stocks by U.S. Investors (in millions)

	1979	1980	1981	1982	1983	1984	1985
Europe	$ -137	$ 459	$ 316	$ 799	$ 2,211	$ 923	$ 1,751
France	4	206	69	215	392	123	301
Netherlands	81	255	39	115	228	-106	-31
Switzerland	-63	26	33	75	84	79	279
United Kingdom	-171	-17	-38	218	1,125	627	617
Canada	912	642	-583	-53	464	-175	1,220
Asia	-27	886	243	491	1,207	-38	690
Japan	-24	841	252	479	880	-383	129
Others	38	102	212	106	-117	379	244
Total	$ 786	$ 2,089	$ 188	$ 1,343	$ 3,765	$ 1,089	$ 3,905

SOURCES: U.S. Treasury; Securities Industry Association.

TABLE 4 Country Ranking

	By Market Capitalization[a]			By GNP[b]			Market Cap as Percent of GNP
	End 1985 ($ billions)	As Percent of Total[d,h]	Rank	1985E[b,c] ($ billions)	As Percent of Total[d,h]	Rank	
United States	$2,209.1	45.3%	1	$3,916	40.7%	1	56.4%
Japan	1,270.2	26.0	2	1,796	18.7	2	70.7
United Kingdom	396.8	8.1	3	525	5.5	5	75.6
Germany	202.4	4.1	4	792	8.2	3	25.5
Canada	152.8	3.1	5	328	3.4	7	46.6
France	115.3	2.4	6	632	6.6	4	18.3
Italy	103.9	2.1	7	411	4.3	6	25.3
Switzerland	102.0	2.1	8	116	1.2	11	87.7
Australia	65.6	1.3	9	155	1.6	10	42.3
Netherlands	57.7	1.2	10	157	1.6	9	36.7
Sweden[f]	37.5	0.8	11	104	1.1	12	35.9
Hong Kong	35.9	0.7	12	36	0.4	20	99.7
Spain[f]	31.2	0.6	13	176	1.8	8	17.8
Belgium[f]	26.6	0.5	14	93	1.0	13	28.6
Singapore/Malaysia[e]	23.8	0.5	15	50	0.5	19	47.6
South Africa[g]	18.1	0.4	16	57	0.6	18	32.0
Denmark	15.3	0.3	17	68	0.7	15	22.6
Norway	9.3	0.2	18	63	0.7	16	14.7
Austria	4.2	0.1	19	87	0.9	14	4.8
Mexico[f]	3.7	0.1	20	61	0.6	17	6.1
	$4,881.4	100.0%		$9,623	100.0%		50.7%

[a] SOURCE: Morgan Stanley Capital International. Figures may not agree with those cited in comments on individual national markets in Section 4, due to a different composition of the local stock market index.

[b] Based on exchange rates of March 31, 1986, and latest available GNP/GDP figures or estimates.

[c] SOURCE: IMF, "International Financial Statistics," April 1986; Drexel Burnham Lambert estimates.

[d] As percent of only those countries included in this table.

[e] Malaysia—$33.1 billion; Singapore—$17.3 billion.

[f] Based on 1984 GDP.

[g] Gold shares only.

[h] Numbers may not add due to rounding.

International Diversification Can Enhance Returns Also

Table 5 clearly shows the superior performance of some foreign equity markets over the past 15 years or so (since the breakdown of Bretton Woods and the abolition of fixed exchange rates) relative to returns realized in the United States.

Why does a market outperform the U.S. market? The most obvious

TABLE 5 Performance of the International Equity Markets (in local currency and currency adjusted)

	Year-End 1971–1984			1985			Year-End 1985–5/31/86		
	Stock Market Index	National Currency Parity v. U.S.$	Combined Change	Stock Market Index	National Currency Parity v. U.S.$	Combined Change	Stock Market Index	National Currency Parity v. U.S.$	Combined Change
DJIA	36.10%	—	36.10%	27.66%	—	27.66%	21.3%	—	21.3%
S&P 500	63.82	—	63.82	26.33	—	26.33	17.1	—	17.1
Australia	113.06	−30.88%	47.27	38.23	−17.34%	14.27	23.2	4.7%	29.4
Belgium	63.47	−29.38	15.45	34.58	25.90	69.43	22.9	6.1	30.3
Canada	142.32	−24.10	83.93	20.84	−5.51	14.19	7.6	1.3	9.1
France	143.52	−45.89	31.78	45.72	28.30	86.96	33.4	1.4	35.2
Germany	70.81	3.69	77.12	76.14	28.88	127.01	0.9	5.2	6.1
Netherlands	88.69	−8.58	72.50	40.52	29.08	81.39	13.1	5.5	19.4
Hong Kong	251.65	−27.33	155.54	45.99	0.16	46.22	2.0	0.0	2.0
Italy	106.83	−69.85	−37.65	98.45	16.10	130.39	71.3	4.7	−9.4
Japan	325.34	24.31	428.75	13.61	25.61	42.70	26.8	14.8	45.6
Singapore	308.98	32.26	440.92	−23.70	3.46	−21.06	5.8	6.1	0.6
South Africa (Ind)	387.84	−61.71	86.79	23.52	−47.86	−35.61	10.0	−4.3	5.3
Sweden	351.49	−45.87	144.38	28.29	18.83	52.45	36.6	2.3	39.8
Switzerland	0.60	50.35	51.25	52.46	26.38	92.69	−2.9	6.5	3.5
United Kingdom (Ind)	99.85	−54.59	−9.24	18.81	24.67	48.12	16.8	2.1	19.2
Gold Bullion	610.34	—	610.34	6.47	—	6.47	4.3	—	4.3
Indexes South Africa	1154.22	−61.71	380.23	21.68	−47.86	−34.97	−2.7	−4.3	−6.9
United Kingdom	879.35	−54.59	344.76	−47.84	24.67	−34.97	−13.9	2.1	−12.1

SOURCE: Drexel Burnham Lambert International Research Department.

TABLE 6A Annual Growth of Real GNP (percent change)

	1980	1981	1982	1983	1984	1985	1986P‡	1987P‡
Australia*	2.2%	4.0%	3.0%	(2.0)%	5.7%	4.8%	3.5%	2.0%
Belgium	1.0	(1.9)	(0.5)	0.5	1.5	0.9	2.5	2.5
Canada	0.1	3.0	(4.4)	3.0	5.0	4.5	3.0	3.0
France	1.3	0.7	1.8	0.9	1.6	1.3	3.0	2.5
Germany	1.8	(0.2)	(1.1)	1.3	2.7	2.5	3.5	3.0
Netherlands	0.5	(0.7)	(1.6)	1.3	1.7	2.0	3.0	3.0
Hong Kong	11.0	8.0	2.4	5.7	9.6	1.0	4.0	4.5
Italy	3.8	(0.2)	(0.3)	(1.5)	2.8	2.3	3.0	3.0
Japan†	4.0	3.3	3.2	3.7	5.0	4.5E	3.0	3.0
Singapore	10.3	10.0	6.3	7.9	8.2	(1.8)	(1.5)	0.0
Switzerland	4.2	2.5	(1.1)	1.0	2.6	3.2	3.0	3.0
United Kingdom	(1.9)	(2.8)	0.9	3.0	2.5	3.5	3.0	3.5
United States	(0.2)	1.9	(2.5)	3.4	6.6	2.3	2.6	4.0

* Fiscal year ending June.
† Fiscal year ending March of the following year.
‡ Estimates by Drexel Burnham Lambert International Research Department.

TABLE 6B Consumer Price Index (percent change)

	1980	1981	1982	1983	1984	1985	1986P‡	1987P‡
Australia*	10.2%	10.1%	10.7%	11.2%	4.5%	6.7%	8.0%	7.0%
Belgium	6.8	7.6	8.7	7.7	6.3	4.9	2.0	1.5
Canada	10.2	12.5	10.8	5.8	4.4	4.0	3.5	3.5
France	13.6	13.4	11.8	9.3	6.7	4.7	3.0	3.0
Germany	5.5	5.9	5.3	3.3	2.4	2.0	0.5	0.5
Netherlands	6.5	6.7	6.0	2.8	3.3	2.2	0.0	0.0
Hong Kong	15.5	14.0	10.6	10.0	8.1	3.2	4.0	4.0
Italy	21.2	18.7	16.3	14.7	10.8	8.6	6.0	5.0
Japan†	7.8	4.0	2.4	1.9	2.2	1.9	0.5–1.0	0.5
Singapore	8.5	8.3	3.8	1.2	2.6	1.9	0.0	1.0
Switzerland	4.0	6.5	5.7	2.9	2.9	3.4	1.5	1.5
United Kingdom	18.0	11.0	8.6	4.6	4.6	5.5	4.0	4.0
United States	13.5	10.2	6.0	3.2	4.3	3.5	1.9	2.7

* Fiscal year ending June.
† Fiscal year ending March of the following year.
‡ Estimates by Drexel Burnham Lambert International Research Department.

factor is a better economic outlook—faster GNP, and/or corporate profit growth, lower inflation, favorable terms of trade, and so on. As reflected in Table 6, rates of growth have varied widely between the United States and its trading partners, and even among those trading partners.

Relative over- or underperformance can also be caused by events in the local marketplace such as national elections or by technical factors such as creation of IRA-type accounts, and corporate tax-paying season. Therefore, the ongoing process of internationalization of commerce and trade may have led to greater interdependence among the nations of the world, but that situation does not, of course, mean that all economies and stock markets will henceforth move in tandem. Opportunities still exist for enhancing returns by including non-U.S. markets in one's investment perspective.

International Diversification Reduces Risk

Modern portfolio theory stresses diversification as a means to reduce risk. Investing internationally is a natural extension of that process. Regardless of extensive industry and company diversification, an entire portfolio will, to some degree, be influenced by national economic and political developments in its home market, so long as it is limited to that one market. The only way to reduce this systemic risk, however small, is to take positions in markets that are not directly exposed to these same influences.

These intuitive conclusions are borne out by studies conducted by Quantec Limited on the performance of the major national equity markets around the world. Using a running five-year history, Quantec has developed matrixes showing the correlation of price movements of these markets to each other. A correlation coefficient equal to 1.0 would indicate perfect correlation, suggesting the two markets were driven by the same forces. Conversely, a coefficient of 0 suggests there is no relationship whatsoever and a coefficient of -1.0 would imply they moved in opposite directions in response to the same forces or were driven by exactly opposing forces. As can be seen in Table 7, the highest correlation achieved between two markets (assuming perfect currency hedging) according to the Quantec research is 0.74 (between the United States and Canada), and 0.56 and 0.54 (between the United States and Switzerland and the Netherlands, respectively). Correlations between the United States and Canada and the Netherlands do not change significantly when returns in U.S. dollars are studied. (See Table 8.) As can be expected, the correlation between Germany and Switzerland in U.S. dollars is relatively high at 0.72, but we are surprised at the lack of correlation between the Hong Kong and Singapore markets.

Interestingly, although the growing internationalization of industries and stock markets would lead us to suspect increasing correlation

TABLE 7 Correlation Matrix of Markets with Perfect Currency Hedging, April 1986

	Hong Kong	Singapore	Japan	Australia	U.S.A	U.K.	Canada	Switzerland	Netherlands	Germany	France	Belgium	Norway	Denmark	Sweden	Italy	Spain	
Hong Kong	1.00	0.14	0.24	0.27	0.17	0.43	0.26	0.37	0.45	0.36	0.13	0.09	0.39	0.18	0.26	0.29	0.20	Hong Kong
Singapore	0.14	1.00	0.13	0.30	0.23	0.16	0.18	0.08	0.19	0.11	-0.11	0.16	0.17	0.27	0.20	-0.05	-0.01	Singapore
Japan	0.24	0.13	1.00	0.32	0.41	0.53	0.34	0.37	0.46	0.41	0.34	0.30	0.15	0.21	0.23	0.35	0.26	Japan
Australia	0.27	0.30	0.32	1.00	0.38	0.41	0.55	0.33	0.37	0.17	0.21	0.15	0.39	0.27	0.22	0.26	0.09	Australia
United States	0.17	0.23	0.41	0.38	1.00	0.50	0.74	0.56	0.54	0.30	0.41	0.25	0.39	0.34	0.40	0.29	0.13	United States
United Kingdom	0.43	0.16	0.53	0.41	0.50	1.00	0.54	0.46	0.63	0.37	0.40	0.40	0.37	0.21	0.35	0.43	0.22	United Kingdom
Canada	0.26	0.18	0.34	0.55	0.74	0.54	1.00	0.62	0.57	0.24	0.31	0.16	0.38	0.30	0.44	0.40	0.12	Canada
Switzerland	0.37	0.08	0.37	0.33	0.56	0.46	0.62	1.00	0.58	0.62	0.43	0.26	0.39	0.28	0.37	0.29	0.14	Switzerland
Netherlands	0.45	0.19	0.46	0.37	0.54	0.63	0.57	0.58	1.00	0.50	0.41	0.32	0.46	0.38	0.32	0.37	0.17	Netherlands
Germany	0.36	0.11	0.41	0.17	0.30	0.37	0.24	0.62	0.50	1.00	0.32	0.26	0.20	0.22	0.19	0.23	0.15	Germany
France	0.13	-0.11	0.34	0.21	0.41	0.40	0.31	0.43	0.41	0.32	1.00	0.35	0.42	0.06	0.09	0.35	0.26	France
Belgium	0.09	0.16	0.30	0.15	0.25	0.40	0.16	0.26	0.32	0.26	0.35	1.00	0.29	0.22	0.04	0.24	0.06	Belgium
Norway	0.39	0.17	0.15	0.39	0.36	0.37	0.38	0.39	0.46	0.20	0.42	0.29	1.00	0.34	0.32	0.11	0.08	Norway
Denmark	0.18	0.27	0.21	0.27	0.34	0.21	0.30	0.28	0.38	0.22	0.06	0.22	0.34	1.00	0.33	0.18	-0.01	Denmark
Sweden	0.26	0.20	0.23	0.22	0.40	0.35	0.44	0.37	0.32	0.19	0.09	0.04	0.32	0.33	1.00	0.27	0.22	Sweden
Italy	0.29	-0.05	0.35	0.26	0.29	0.43	0.40	0.29	0.37	0.23	0.35	0.24	0.11	0.18	0.27	1.00	0.37	Italy
Spain	0.20	-0.01	0.26	0.09	0.13	0.22	0.12	0.14	0.17	0.15	0.26	0.06	0.08	-0.01	0.22	0.37	1.00	Spain
Serial correlation	0.15	0.16	0.04	0.08	0.10	-0.21	0.20	0.15	-0.09	-0.06	0.18	0.19	0.04	0.04	0.21	0.23	0.22	Serial correlation

NOTES: This matrix shows the correlations between pairs of foreign markets in their local currencies and is equivalent to the assumption that the currency risk has been perfectly hedged. (This is not, of course, possible in practice.)

Most of the main blocs are still in evidence, although the Pacific Basin bloc is now even less cohesive. Continental Europe has also become somewhat less cohesive, reflecting the absence of the constraints imposed by E.M.S.

The Core Global bloc, on the other hand, is still very significant.

SOURCE: Quantec Limited, *World Market Research Quarterly*, second quarter 1986.

TABLE 8 Correlation Matrix of Markets in U.S. Dollars, April 1986

	Hong Kong	Singapore	Japan	Australia	U.S.A	U.K.	Canada	Switzerland	Netherlands	Germany	France	Belgium	Norway	Denmark	Sweden	Italy	Spain
Hong Kong	1.00	0.13	0.25	0.23	0.14	0.34	0.21	0.24	0.36	0.28	0.09	0.09	0.32	0.11	0.37	0.27	0.17
Singapore	0.13	1.00	0.23	0.26	0.21	0.13	0.20	0.17	0.19	0.15	-0.04	0.20	0.22	0.31	0.17	-0.03	-0.01
Japan	0.25	0.23	1.00	0.45	0.39	0.50	0.37	0.49	0.50	0.51	0.45	0.46	0.27	0.32	0.41	0.49	0.34
Australia	0.23	0.26	0.45	1.00	0.31	0.47	0.52	0.37	0.33	0.17	0.24	0.21	0.43	0.28	0.33	0.26	0.22
United States	0.14	0.21	0.39	0.31	1.00	0.46	0.72	0.47	0.58	0.32	0.38	0.33	0.35	0.39	0.36	0.30	0.16
United Kingdom	0.34	0.13	0.50	0.47	0.46	1.00	0.58	0.52	0.62	0.40	0.45	0.48	0.44	0.31	0.46	0.46	0.33
Canada	0.21	0.20	0.37	0.52	0.72	0.58	1.00	0.52	0.58	0.23	0.29	0.23	0.37	0.37	0.42	0.40	0.13
Switzerland	0.24	0.17	0.49	0.37	0.47	0.52	0.52	1.00	0.67	0.72	0.54	0.49	0.47	0.49	0.40	0.37	0.27
Netherlands	0.36	0.19	0.50	0.33	0.58	0.62	0.58	0.67	1.00	0.60	0.51	0.45	0.53	0.48	0.40	0.42	0.24
Germany	0.28	0.15	0.51	0.17	0.32	0.40	0.23	0.72	0.60	1.00	0.50	0.44	0.32	0.40	0.35	0.38	0.27
France	0.09	-0.04	0.45	0.24	0.38	0.45	0.29	0.54	0.51	0.50	1.00	0.52	0.53	0.25	0.25	0.49	0.44
Belgium	0.09	0.20	0.46	0.21	0.33	0.48	0.23	0.49	0.45	0.44	0.52	1.00	0.45	0.40	0.23	0.24	0.23
Norway	0.32	0.22	0.27	0.43	0.35	0.44	0.37	0.47	0.53	0.32	0.53	0.45	1.00	0.41	0.41	0.29	0.12
Denmark	0.11	0.31	0.32	0.28	0.39	0.31	0.37	0.49	0.48	0.40	0.25	0.40	0.41	1.00	0.38	0.29	0.12
Sweden	0.37	0.17	0.41	0.33	0.36	0.46	0.42	0.40	0.40	0.35	0.25	0.41	0.41	0.38	1.00	0.41	0.30
Italy	0.27	-0.03	0.49	0.26	0.30	0.46	0.40	0.37	0.42	0.38	0.49	0.24	0.29	0.29	0.41	1.00	0.45
Spain	0.17	-0.01	0.34	0.22	0.16	0.33	0.13	0.27	0.24	0.27	0.44	0.23	0.12	0.12	0.30	0.45	1.00
Serial correlation	0.15	0.16	0.04	0.08	0.10	-0.21	0.20	0.15	-0.09	-0.06	0.18	0.19	0.04	0.04	0.21	0.23	0.22

NOTE: In this correlation matrix the countries have been arranged so as to highlight blocs of markets that tend to move together. There are four main blocs to be seen, which to some extent overlap with each other:

Continental Europe	Core Global	English-Speaking	Pacific Basin
Switzerland	Switzerland	Australia	Australia
Netherlands	Netherlands	Canada	Japan
Germany	Canada	U.S.A.	Singapore
France	U.S.A.	U.K.	Hong Kong
Belgium	U.K.		
Norway			

These blocs have been determined by finding groups of correlations that are relatively high, and that have significantly lower correlations around them.

The blocs are by no means absolute classifications; nevertheless, they do seem to be relatively stable over time, although not all the groupings are equally significant.

For example, the Pacific Basin bloc, intuitively appealing though it may be, is by far the least cohesive of the four blocs, while Belgium and Norway probably appear in the Continental European bloc more by force of circumstance than by any particular significance of their own.

SOURCE: Quantec Limited, *World Market Research Quarterly*, second quarter 1986.

TABLE 9 Foreign Equities on the NYSE and Dates Listed (as of April 1, 1986)

Company	Industry (Country)	American Depositary Receipts (ADRs)	Date Listed
ASA Limited	Investment company (South Africa)		12/8/58
Banco Central, S.A.	Banking (Spain)	X	7/20/83
Benguet Corporation	Mining (Philippines)		6/27/49
British Petroleum Company Ltd.	Holding company—petroleum (United Kingdom)	X	3/23/70
British Telecommunications plc	Telecommunications (United Kingdom)	X	12/3/84
Club Med, Inc.	Resort management (British West Indies)		9/25/84
Elscint Ltd.	Medical technology (Israel)		9/20/84
Erbamont N.V.	Pharmaceutical (Netherlands Antilles)		6/21/83
Hitachi, Ltd.	Diversified manufacturing (Japan)	X	4/14/82
Honda Motor Co., Ltd.	Motorcycles, automobiles (Japan)	X	2/11/77
Imperial Chemical Industries plc	Chemicals (United Kingdom)	X	11/1/83
KLM Royal Dutch Airlines	Airline (Netherlands)		5/22/57
Kubota, Ltd.	Agricultural machinery, pipe (Japan)	X	11/9/76
Kyocera Corporation	Ceramic products (Japan)	X	5/23/80
Matsushita Electric Industrial Co., Ltd.	Electronic products (Japan)	X	12/13/71
Novo Industrial A/S	Pharmaceutical (Denmark)	X	7/9/81
Pioneer Electronic Corporation	High fidelity stereo; audio (Japan)	X	12/13/76
Plessey Company Ltd.	Electronic equipment systems (United Kingdom)	X	7/20/70
Royal Dutch Petroleum Co.	Petroleum (Netherlands)	*	7/20/54
Schlumberger, N.V.	Petroleum (Netherlands Antilles)		2/2/62
"Shell" Transport and Trading Co., Ltd.	Petroleum (United Kingdom)	X[†]	3/13/57
Sony Corporation	Radios, records, televisions (Japan)	X	9/17/70

TABLE 9 (*concluded*)

Company	Industry (Country)	American Depositary Receipts (ADRs)	Date Listed
TDK Corporation	Electronics (Japan)	X	5/15/82
Tricentrol Limited	Oil and gas; car dealerships (United Kingdom)	X	7/15/80
Unilever plc	Foods, commodities (United Kingdom)	X	12/12/61
Unilever, N.V.	Foods, commodities (Netherlands)		12/12/61
Universal Matchbox Group Ltd.	Toy manufacturer (Hong Kong)		3/24/86

* 10 guilder shares.
† New York shares.
SOURCE: New York Stock Exchange.

among different markets, in fact the correlation coefficients were lower at the end of March 1986 than they were one year before!

SECTION 2—THE MECHANICS OF FOREIGN SECURITIES INVESTMENT

As indicated in Section 1 of this chapter, "ERISA" pension progress toward internationalization should continue to show dramatic growth during the next few years. After making the decision to invest abroad, an investor is faced with the simple question, How? The answer is not so simple, as it involves matters of strategy one must assume (i.e., active versus passive, top-down versus bottom-up, individual positions versus mutual funds) and the mechanics of buying and selling (registered shares versus ADRs, varying settlement practices, and so on). We will discuss these issues.

Listing of Foreign Securities

The principal market for individual foreign securities is generally their home countries. Exceptions occur from time to time, however. Examples: London has been an active market for South African gold mining stocks and a number of Australian securities; New York for the shares of Unilever N.V., Philips N.V., Royal Dutch, KLM Royal Dutch Airlines, Sony Corporation, Novo, Hitachi, Ericsson, B.A.T. Industries, Jaguar, and some South African gold mining stocks.

TABLE 10 Issues of Foreign Corporations (Other Than Canadian) Dealt in on the American Stock Exchange (as of 1/2/86)

	Organized under Laws of
Stocks:	
Alliance Tire and Rubber Company Ltd. (Class A)	Israel
American Israeli Paper Mills Ltd. (Ordinary)	Israel
Anglo Energy Ltd. (Class A)	Bahama Islands
Atlas Consolidated Mining & Development Corp. (Class B)	Philippines
Ausimont Compo N.V. (Common)	Netherlands
B.A.T. Industries Ltd. (ADRs for Ordinary Shares)	Great Britain
Courtaulds Ltd. (ADRs for Ordinary Shares)	Great Britain
ETZ Lavud Ltd. (Ordinary)	Israel
Imperial Group Ltd. (The) (ADRs for Ordinary Shares)	Great Britain
Laser Industries Ltd. (Ordinary)	Israel
O'Okiep Copper Co. Ltd. (American Shares)	South Africa
Philippine Long Distance Telephone Co. (Common)	Philippines
San Carlos Milling Co., Inc. (Capital)	Philippines
Tubos de Acero de Mexico, S.A. (ADRs for Common Stock)	Mexico
WTC International N.V. (Common)	Netherlands Antilles
Bonds:	
American Israeli Paper Mills Limited (11¾% Debentures)	Israel
Anglo Company, Inc. (11⅞% Debentures due 1998)	Bahama Islands
Ito-Yokado Co., Ltd. (5¾% Debentures due 1993)	Japan
Komatsu Ltd. (7¼% Debentures due 1990)	Japan

SOURCE: American Stock Exchange.

As detailed in Tables 9 and 10, a small number of foreign companies have listed their shares or ADRs on the New York Stock Exchange (27) or the American Stock Exchange (18, excluding Canadian companies). A much larger number of foreign enterprises have a "sponsored" listing on NASDAQ (167) or are "unsponsored" and traded over-the-counter.

What is an American Depositary Receipt (ADR)? An American Depositary Receipt (ADR) provides an efficient means for investors to purchase and/or sell foreign securities. The ADR is a *surrogate* for the underlying share; that is, it is eligible for cash and stock dividends. The advantages of holding ADRs are:

- International clearing and settlement is simplified (with the transaction not much different from that for domestically traded securities).

- ADRs trade freely in the United States (depending on the level of activity and interest) and are quoted in U.S. dollars (reflecting daily exchange rate fluctuations).
- ADR holders receive all dividends in U.S. dollars as well as documentation for withholding tax credits, offset against U.S. income taxes under double taxation agreements.

A potential disadvantage is that foreign companies often have rights issues. Due to legal restrictions, the rights generally must be sold by the U.S. depositary bank *with proceeds credited to the ADR holder* (thus, a dilution of a U.S. holder's equity may occur).

How are ADRs created? In instances where foreign stocks are popular in the United States, an "unsponsored" ADR program is typically set up by a U.S. depositary bank, usually at the request of U.S. market makers. A "sponsored" ADR, on the other hand, is requested by the foreign company itself. Most ADRs are unsponsored and the holder is assessed a nominal fee applying to the issuance or cancellation of the ADRs.

With sponsored ADRs, the company, rather than the shareholders, picks up the tab for dividend distribution by paying a fee to the depositary bank, and the bank automatically mails annual reports and other relevant information to shareholders. Shareholders of unsponsored ADRs must specifically request this information.

How are ADRs bought and sold?

1. An investor places an order for ADRs (here we assume an ADR program already exists).
2. ADRs can generally be obtained quickly and easily in the United States. If not:
3. The trader buys underlying shares in the foreign market, which are then deposited into the local custodian bank of the U.S. depositary bank.
4. The U.S. depositary bank issues the ADRs, which are credited to the brokerage firm for final delivery to the investor.
5. ADRs can be sold either to another buyer in the United States or through the above process in reverse (with the local custodian bank delivering the foreign shares to the appropriate designee).

The advantages of ADRs for the foreign company. What investors should realize is that ADR creation itself is strictly a mechanical process. It is the increased interest in foreign investments, resulting from expanded research coverage or a more visible company profile—a form of advertisement for the company's products—that can "internationalize" a foreign stock. Hence, the stock's valuation may eventually be judged by standards prevailing elsewhere or, increasingly, on a global basis. It is in this way that significant multiple expansion can occur in combination with rising foreign ownership of the shares.

Moreover, a foreign company might have other reasons—quite apart from access to the U.S. capital market—for wanting to set up an ADR program. ADRs can, for example, be used as a vehicle for U.S. acquisitions, or as a means of compensating U.S. management with stock options.

Finally, as international financial markets become increasingly global and liquid, arbitrage (involving price, exchange rates, and net U.S. foreign buying and selling) will ensure that prices are kept relatively equal across markets.

The Active/Passive Approach

Passive. The frequently used "passive" method of investment can be applied to overseas investment in many different ways. Cost considerations may make it comparatively attractive to obtain global exposure while avoiding much of the burden of a full-fledged international research effort. A frequently used "passive" method involves a two-step approach: allocating a comparatively modest portion of a portfolio's assets to non-U.S. securities, then weighting it on the basis of each country's market capitalization or GNP (Table 4).

However, a *wholly* passive approach is not feasible in international markets. *In practice, any international investment manager must take into account the practical limitations of size and liquidity within each market. Therefore, subjective, active decisions will have to be made,* for example with respect to (1) the number of *countries* involved; (2) the number of *companies* in each country; and (3) the *size* of the average position in each company.

Active. Active international investment managers aim to outperform passively achieved results by proper evaluation of foreign exchange trends, correct monitoring of the particular timing forces that tend to move individual markets, and selection of specific groups and candidates within each country.

Mutual Funds

Many investors have avoided foreign investing—even when they recognized its potential profitability—because it has been costly and complicated. It has meant finding a broker capable of making the purchase, getting up-to-date information on the stock and on the market in which it is traded, converting the value of the stock into dollars to track its progress, and knowing when and how to sell.

A mutual fund investment avoids many of these problems. With a single purchase, you invest in a diversified foreign investment portfolio with professional management that can learn about foreign market activities quickly and accurately—usually far faster than an individual investor.

Mutual funds can be distinguished between (1) international (non-U.S.) versus global (including U.S.); (2) closed- and open-ended; and (3) load and no-load.

Table 11, provided by Lipper Analytical Services, Inc., tabulates *open*-ended global (U.S. and foreign) and international (only foreign securities) mutual funds by total assets as of December 31, 1985.

Table 12, tabulates *closed*-end funds, operative in one or more countries. These country-specific funds are traded on the NYSE or ASE, and typically sell at a discount or a premium to net asset value. As these funds are becoming very popular, we have also included the latest introduced funds, which are not yet being traded.

SECTION 3—THE POTENTIAL DRAWBACKS

Investments in foreign securities involve certain risks or difficulties not directly assumed when investing within one's own borders. By far the greatest risks are *(a)* the possibility of unfavorable currency swings; *(b)* varying accounting and reporting standards in different countries, which make comparative valuation difficult; *(c)* the less-developed public relations efforts at most foreign organizations compared to U.S. firms and therefore the lack of comparable investment information flows country by country; and *(d)* the tendency for most countries to withhold taxes on dividends and/or interest payments (the withholdings can often be credited against U.S. taxes, however). These problems we will discuss below.

Other concerns include sovereign risks (such as that of expropriation), a changing fiscal regime, and greater economic or social instability than enjoyed in the United States, problems that require individual studies of each particular circumstance.

Finally, technical and/or trading factors may vary significantly in each market; for example, settlement practices, liquidity, withholding taxes, and so on. Non-U.S. securities markets, while growing in volume, have, for the most part, substantially less volume than U.S. markets, and securities of many foreign companies are less liquid and their prices more volatile than securities of comparable U.S. companies. Transaction costs on non-U.S. securities markets are generally higher than in the United States. There is generally less government supervision and regulation of exchanges, brokers, and issuers than there is in

TABLE 11 Open-Ended International and Global Funds

	Total Assets in Millions		
	12/31/85	9/30/85	12/31/84
INTERNATIONAL FUNDS:			
Range of assets ($0.1 to $25.0 million):			
GT Japan Growth	$ 0.5 NL	$ 0.3	$ *
Newport Far East	1.4 NL	1.2	1.3
GAM International	14.4 NL	8.9	0.1
Nomura Pacific Basin	22.2 NL	15.6	*
Financial Port-Pacific	1.8 NL	2.5	0.8
GT International Growth	1.8 NL	0.9	*
GT Europe Growth	1.3 NL	0.5	*
Sigma World	1.9	0.6	*
U.S. Boston-Intl	1.8 NL	1.1	*
Canadian Fund	22.9	22.4	22.2
	$ 69.9	$ 54.0	$ 24.4
Range of assets ($25.0 to $100.0 million):			
Transatlantic Fund	$ 41.3 NL	$ 33.7	$ 28.1
GT Pacific Growth FD	42.1 NL	43.2	45.9
FT International	40.3 NL	24.5	11.3
IDS International	78.2	39.4	3.7
Europacific Growth	70.7	47.4	20.2
Kemper International FD	70.0	50.3	40.6
Keystone International R	39.0 NL	31.4	26.3
	$ 381.6	$ 269.9	$ 176.1
Range of assets ($100.0 million and higher):			
Fidelity Overseas	$ 174.2	$ 78.4	$ 0.4
Merrill Lynch Pacific	151.4	139.8	105.3
Vanguard World-Intl Gro	139.9 NL	77.0	*
T. Rowe Price Intl Fund	376.8 NL	285.3	180.8
Alliance International	103.2	77.4	61.9
Trustees Commingled Intl	581.6 NL	551.3	314.5
Scudder International	427.4 NL	323.1	183.8
Templeton Foreign	117.8	95.1	69.2
	$2,069.3	$1,627.4	$ 915.9
International total	$2,520.9	$1,951.3	$1,116.4
GLOBAL FUNDS:			
Range of assets ($0.1 to $100.0 million):			
Pru-Bache Global FD	$ 88.8 NL	$ 49.8	$ 9.5
Putnam Intl Equities	90.4	64.9	47.3
Principal World	2.5	2.0	1.5
World Trends	12.2	*	*

TABLE 11 (*concluded*)

	Total Assets in Millions		
	12/31/85	9/30/85	12/31/84
First Inv International	30.4	30.7	30.8
Mass Finl Intl Tr-Bond	6.1	59.2	34.3
Alliance Global	0.3	*	*
J. Hancock Global	6.1	2.2	*
	$ 236.8	$ 208.8	$ 123.4
Range of assets ($100.0 million and higher):			
Oppenheimer A I M	$ 280.6	$ 232.1	$ 215.5
Paine Webber Atlas	118.9	90.9	75.0
Shearson Global	153.6	94.8	39.6
United Intl Growth	140.5	117.8	102.2
Merrill Lynch Intl Hldgs	218.4	198.2	202.5
Dean Witter World Wide R	131.4 NL	104.2	99.1
Templeton Growth	1,353.5	1,170.6	942.8
Templeton World	2,470.6	2,276.4	1,727.8
Templeton Global II	355.7	293.2	190.4
Templeton Global I	277.8	258.5	233.0
New Perspective Fund	777.2	673.1	621.1
	$6,278.2	$5,509.8	$4,449.0
Global total	$6,515.0	$5,718.6	$4,572.4

* Not in existence.
NL = No load.
SOURCE: Lipper Analytical Services, Inc.

the United States. An investor might have greater difficulty taking appropriate legal action in non-U.S. courts. These variances will be discussed briefly in the comments about the individual national stock market sections in Section 4 of this chapter.

Impact of Currency Movements

There are two ways in which changes in exchange rates can affect the value of a foreign holding. The most obvious is in the valuation of the security price itself. For example, assume you bought a German equity, which, of course, is denominated in deutsche marks, when the exchange rate was U.S.$1.00 = DM3. The stock price at the time of purchase was DM150; therefore, you paid U.S.$50 (forgetting commissions and other transaction costs). Assuming the share price rose to DM200 and the exchange rate did not change, you made a profit of DM50 or U.S.$16.67, equal to 33 ⅓ percent both in deutsche marks and U.S. dollars. Now assume the share price rose to DM200, but the value

TABLE 12 Closed End Specialized Country Funds

Name	Listing	Initial Offering Price	When Issued	No. of Shares Outstanding	52 Weeks Price Range High	52 Weeks Price Range Low	Price 7/14/86	NAV	Premium (discount)
France Fund	NYSE-FRN	$12	5/30/86	7,500,000	$12⅛	$10¼	$10½	$11.85	(11.5)%
Italy Fund	NYSE-ITA	$12	2/25/86	6,325,000	17⅞	10⅞	10⅞	12.65	(14.0)
First Australia Fund	ASE-IAF	$10	12/12/85	5,800,000	12⅜	8	8	9.07	(11.8)
First Australia Prime Income Fund	ASE-FAI		4/17/86	85,500,000	11¾	8⅛	8½	8.60	(1.2)
Korea Fund	NYSE-KF	1) $10 2) $32¼	8/22/84 5/22/86	5,000,000 1,240,000	36	16½	33½	22.97	+45.8
Mexico Fund	NYSE-MXF	1) $12 2) $2.80	6/11/81 11/17/83	10,000,000 9,990,908	3½	2	2½	3.78	(33.9)
Scandinavia Fund	ASE-SCF	$10	6/17/86	6,500,000	9⅝	7⅞	7⅞	9.11	(13.6)
Japan Fund	NYSE-JPN	NA	1963	23,184,043	18¾	10⅞	16	20.80	(23.1)
ASA Ltd.	NYSE-ASA	NA	1959	9,600,000	51	33	30⅜	44.19	(31.3)
The Nordic Fund*		$12		6,250,000					
Germany Fund*	NYSE-GER	$10		10,000,000					
India Fund*									

*Not yet traded.

SOURCE: Drexel Burnham Lambert Incorporated.

TABLE 13 Example of Effect of Currency on Foreign Security Purchases

Purchase Price	Exchange Rate	Purchase Price
DM150	U.S.$1.00 = DM3	U.S.$50

Upon sale:

Case A. No change in exchange rate; German currency stock price advances 33⅓ percent.

		Sale Price in	Gain/Loss in	
Sale Price	Exchange Rate	U.S.$	DM	U.S.$
DM200	U.S.$1.00 = DM3	U.S.$66.67	+33⅓%	+33⅓%

Case B. Value of the deutsche mark depreciates 33⅓ percent; German currency stock price advances 33⅓ percent.

		Sale Price in	Gain/Loss in	
Sale Price	Exchange Rate	U.S.$	DM	U.S.$
DM200	U.S.$1.00 = DM4	U.S.$50.00	+33⅓%	0%

Case C. Value of deutsche mark appreciates 50 percent; German currency stock price advances 33⅓ percent.

		Sale Price in	Gain/Loss in	
Sale Price	Exchange Rate	U.S.$	DM	U.S.$
DM200	U.S.$1.00 = DM2	U.S.$100.00	+33⅓%	+100.0%

of the deutsche mark fell to just 25 cents, or U.S.$1.00 = DM4. The DM200 at this exchange rate equals U.S.$50, so, despite a 33 ⅓ percent gain in the German currency price of the stock, in U.S. dollars the price is flat. (If the deutsche mark had declined to U.S.$1.00 = DM5, your stock would have been worth U.S.$40. You would have lost $10 or 20 percent!) Of course, the reverse also applies. If the value of the deutsche mark had risen to 50 cents, equal to U.S.$1.00 = DM2, your DM200 stock would have gotten you U.S.$100—a 100 percent profit. That is because the currency effect is a compounding one, not additive. The 33 ⅓ percent increase in the German price, compounded by the 50 percent advance of the German currency, results in a 100 percent gain. (See Table 13.)

A more subtle effect of currency fluctuations is the impact they can have on a company's operations. For example, a decline in the U.S. dollar favorably impacts margins for companies importing goods (e.g., machinery and equipment) denominated in U.S. dollars, but conversely, reduces local currency revenues (and so margins) for companies selling products denominated in U.S. dollars, for example, oil, gold, and other commodities. Moreover, just as the advance in the dollar from 1981 through 1984 benefited the margins and competitiveness of foreign companies exporting their products to the United States, so has the dollar decline begun in February 1985 adversely affected foreign-based exporters to the United States.

What makes exchange rates fluctuate?   Foreign exchange rates change (1) in relation to the perception of a country's economic outlook (inflation, and its effects on purchasing power parities; balance of payments positions; output; money supply; and so on) or of its political environment; or (2) in reaction to interest rate differentials, where high returns in one country will attract capital flows away from other areas, and therefore create demand for the currency of the higher return country (see Table 14); or (3) in reaction to technical factors such as seasonal influences (Canadians heading south for vacations in winter).

Exchange rate volatility has increased in recent years, accentuating both the chance for enhanced returns and the risk of losses. In fact, the currency risk is perhaps the greatest one an investor assumes when he commits U.S. dollars abroad. An overvalued dollar makes foreign purchases relatively less expensive at time of purchase—be they French wines, Riviera vacations, Japanese autos, or foreign securities. But exchange markets are dynamic and eventually an overvalued currency will be depreciated. For an investor, therefore, unlike a vacationer or wine connoisseur, the key issue is not so much where the exchange rate stands at the time of purchase, but where it is going!

Tables 15 and 16 show quarter-end exchange rates since 1984, and monthly average exchange rates from 1981 (expressed in U.S. cents per foreign currency unit) for the currencies of some of the United States' major trading partners.

Disparate Accounting Standards

A company's financial reports may be clear and complete, there may be adequate research coverage of the situation and its investor relations effort may be optimum. But how can you value its stock against that of a competitor in a different country if Company A in Germany can set aside earnings in special reserves, or reports on a full replacement cost accounting basis, while Company B in the United States or Japan does not? Clearly, disparate accounting principles can severely distort the picture.

Generally speaking, accounting principles in Canada and the United Kingdom are close to those in the United States. Additionally, some overseas firms report also on U.S. or U.K. standards, particularly those whose shares or ADRs are traded in the United States or London.

TABLE 14 Comparative International Rates of Return—Nominal and Real, May 30, 1986

		Nominal Yield			Pretax Real Rates of Return			
	Inflation 1986E[a]	Stock Market[b]	90-Day T-bills[c]	Long-Term Government Bonds[d]	Stock Market	90-Day T-bills	Long-Term Government Bonds	Yield Gap Stocks/Bonds[e]
United States	1.90%	3.20%	6.24%	7.88%	1.30%	4.34%	5.98%	(4.68)
Belgium	2.00	3.70	7.31	8.50	1.70	5.31	6.50	(4.80)
Canada	3.50	2.90	8.33	9.50	(0.60)	4.83	6.00	(6.60)
France	3.00	2.10	7.25	7.80	(0.90)	4.25	4.80	(5.70)
Germany	0.50	1.70	4.50	5.70	1.20	4.00	5.20	(4.00)
Netherlands	0.00	3.40	5.88	6.40	3.40	5.88	6.40	(3.00)
Italy	6.00	1.40	11.75	11.08	(4.60)	5.75	11.08	(11.10)
Japan	0.75	0.70	4.66	5.00	(0.05)	3.91	4.25	(4.30)
Switzerland	1.50	1.90	4.44	4.30	0.40	2.94	2.80	(2.40)
United Kingdom	4.00	4.50	9.50	9.00	0.50	5.50	5.80	(4.30)

[a] Estimates by International Research Department of Drexel Burnham Lambert, except for the United States, where estimates are by Richard B. Hoey, chief economist at Drexel Burnham Lambert.
[b] Drexel Burnham Lambert estimates of current yields.
[c] *Financial Times of London*, June 2, 1986.
[d] Drexel Burnham Lambert International Research.
[e] Gap in percentage points.

TABLE 15 Quarter-End Exchange Rates (U.S. cents per unit of foreign currency)

	First Quarter	Percent Change versus Previous Quarter	Second Quarter	Percent Change versus Previous Quarter	Third Quarter	Percent Change versus Previous Quarter	Fourth Quarter	Percent Change versus Previous Quarter	Annual Percent Change
1984:									
Australian dollar	93.68	4.1%	86.30	-7.9%	83.05	-3.8%	82.60	-0.5%	-8.2%
Brazilian cruzeiro	0.076	-29.6%	0.059	-22.4	0.045	-23.7	0.032	-28.9	-70.4
British pound	143.90	-0.9%	135.70	-5.7	123.45	-9.0	115.92	-6.1	-20.2
Canadian dollar	78.35	-2.5%	75.80	-3.3	75.88	0.1	75.76	-0.2	-5.7
French franc	12.53	4.4%	11.72	-6.5	10.64	-9.2	10.39	-2.3	-13.4
German mark	38.58	5.0%	35.96	-6.8	32.59	-9.4	31.75	-2.6	-13.6
Italian lira	0.0619	2.5%	0.0585	-5.5	0.0527	-9.9	0.0517	-1.9	-14.4
Japanese yen	0.4466	3.4%	0.4213	-5.7	0.4053	-3.8	0.3978	-1.9	-7.9
Mexican peso	0.575	-3.2%	0.498	-13.4	0.503	1.0	0.446	-11.3	-24.9
Netherlands guilder	34.19	4.6%	31.91	-6.7	29.03	-9.0	28.13	-3.1	-13.9
Swiss franc	46.52	1.4%	42.92	-7.7	39.57	-7.8	38.46	-2.8	-16.2
1985:									
Australian dollar	70.35	-14.8%	67.00	-4.8%	70.20	4.8%	68.25	-2.8%	-17.4%
Brazilian cruzeiro	0.023	-28.1	0.017	-26.1	0.013	-23.5	0.011	-15.4	-65.6
British pound	124.00	7.0	130.95	5.6	140.75	7.5	144.52	2.7	24.7
Canadian dollar	73.21	-3.4	73.59	0.5	72.79	-1.1	71.53	-1.7	-5.6
French franc	10.64	2.4	10.83	1.8	12.25	13.1	13.33	8.8	28.3
German mark	32.52	2.4	32.99	1.4	37.26	12.9	40.90	9.8	28.8
Italian lira	0.0509	-1.5	0.0517	1.6	0.0549	6.2	0.0601	9.5	16.2
Japanese yen	0.3992	0.4	0.4027	0.9	0.4626	14.9	0.4996	8.0	25.6
Mexican peso	0.412	-7.6	0.315	-23.5	0.271	-14.0	0.227	-16.2	-49.1
Netherlands guilder	28.90	2.7	29.34	1.5	33.14	13.0	36.31	9.6	29.1
Swiss franc	38.68	0.6	39.45	2.0	45.52	15.4	48.59	6.7	26.3

1986:

		4.8%	-May 30-	-0.1%	4.7%
Australian dollar	71.50		71.45		
Brazilian cruzeiro	0.0073	−34.0	0.0072	−0.6	−34.4
British pound	148.20	2.5	147.50	−0.5	2.1
Canadian dollar	71.58	0.1	72.49	1.3	1.3
French franc	13.89	4.2	13.51	−2.7	1.4
German mark	42.64	4.3	43.02	0.9	5.2
Italian lira	0.0629	4.6	0.0629	0.1	4.6
Japanese yen	0.5629	12.7	0.5737	1.9	14.8
Mexican peso	0.207	−9.0	0.182	−11.8	−19.8
Netherlands guilder	38.17	5.1	38.31	0.4	5.5
Swiss franc	51.31	5.6	51.76	0.9	6.5

TABLE 16 Monthly Average Exchange Rates (U.S. cents per unit of foreign currency)

	Jan.	Feb.	March	April	May	June	July	Aug.	Sept.	Oct.	Nov.	Dec.
Australian dollar:												
1981	118.19	116.26	116.29	115.32	114.06	114.07	114.27	113.99	114.86	114.32	114.55	113.39
% Change	6.5%	5.3%	6.7%	5.7%	0.9%	-1.1%	-1.4%	-1.5%	-1.8%	-2.6%	-1.9%	-2.9%
1982	111.41	108.5	106.03	105.15	105.94	103.23	101.09	97.83	95.82	94.35	94.27	96.82
% Change	-5.7%	-6.7%	-8.8%	-8.8%	-7.1%	-9.5%	-11.5%	-14.2%	-16.6%	-17.5%	-17.7%	-14.6%
1983	98.26	96.62	88.39	86.76	87.85	87.72	87.54	87.93	88.77	91.37	91.59	90.04
% Change	-11.8%	-10.9%	-16.6%	-17.5%	-17.1%	-15.0%	-13.4%	-10.1%	-7.4%	-3.2%	-2.8%	-7.0%
1984	90.60	93.48	95.13	92.31	90.61	88.26	83.42	84.73	83.08	83.64	85.88	84.00
% Change	-7.8%	-3.2%	7.6%	6.4%	3.1%	0.6%	-4.7%	-3.6%	-6.4%	-8.5%	-6.2%	-6.7%
1985	81.51	73.75	69.70	65.84	67.68	66.51	69.95	70.70	68.96	70.25	67.74	68.11
% Change	-10.0%	-21.1%	-26.7%	-28.7%	-25.3%	-24.6%	-16.1%	-16.6%	-17.0%	-16.0%	-21.2%	-18.9%
								Using May 30, 1986 exchange rate				
1986	70.00	69.93	70.79	72.28	72.70E	71.45	71.45	71.45	71.45	71.45	71.45	71.45
% Change	-14.1%	-5.2%	1.6%	9.8%	7.4%	7.4%	2.1%	1.1%	3.6%	1.7%	5.5%	4.9%
Brazilian cruzeiro:												
1981	1.555	1.421	1.351	1.308	1.192	1.127	1.064	1.011	0.968	0.906	0.858	0.812
1982	0.768	0.725	0.694	0.662	0.629	0.596	0.562	0.531	0.496	0.464	0.438	0.409
% Change	-50.6%	-49.0%	-48.6%	-49.4%	-47.2%	-47.1%	-47.2%	-47.5%	-48.8%	-48.8%	-49.0%	-49.6%
1983	0.381	0.324	0.249	0.231	0.215	0.193	0.175	0.155	0.143	0.127	0.115	0.106
% Change	-50.4%	-55.3%	-64.1%	-65.1%	-65.8%	-67.6%	-68.9%	-70.8%	-71.2%	-72.6%	-73.7%	-74.1%
1984	0.098	0.088	0.079	0.072	0.067	0.061	0.055	0.051	0.045	0.041	0.037	0.033
% Change	-74.3%	-72.8%	-68.3%	-68.8%	-68.8%	-68.4%	-68.6%	-67.1%	-68.5%	-67.7%	-67.8%	-68.9%
1985	0.031	0.027	0.024	0.022	0.019	0.017	0.016	0.015	0.013	0.012	0.011	0.008
% Change	-68.4%	-69.3%	-69.6%	-69.4%	-71.6%	-72.1%	-70.9%	-70.6%	-71.1%	-70.7%	-70.3%	-75.8%
								Using May 30, 1986 exchange rate				
1986	0.0088	0.0077	0.0072	0.0072	0.0072E	0.0072	0.0072	0.0072	0.0072	0.0072	0.0072	0.0072
% Change	-71.6%	-71.6%	-69.9%	-67.2%	-62.0%	-57.6%	-54.9%	-51.9%	-44.5%	-39.9%	-34.4%	-9.8%

British pound:

	1	2	3	4	5	6	7	8	9	10	11	12
1981	240.29	229.41	223.19	217.53	208.84	197.38	187.37	182.03	181.46	184.07	190.25	190.33
% Change	6.1%	0.2%	1.2%	−1.5%	−9.3%	−15.5%	−21.1%	−23.2%	−24.4%	−23.8%	−20.5%	−18.9%
1982	188.60	184.70	180.53	177.20	181.03	175.63	173.54	172.50	171.20	169.62	163.21	161.60
% Change	−21.5%	−19.5%	−19.1%	−18.5%	−13.3%	−11.0%	−7.4%	−5.2%	−5.7%	−7.9%	−14.2%	−15.1%
1983	157.56	153.29	149.00	153.61	157.22	154.80	152.73	150.26	149.86	149.69	147.66	143.38
% Change	−16.5%	−17.0%	−17.5%	−13.3%	−13.2%	−11.9%	−12.0%	−12.9%	−12.5%	−11.7%	−9.5%	−11.3%
1984	140.76	144.17	145.57	142.10	138.94	137.70	132.00	131.32	125.63	121.96	123.92	118.61
% Change	−10.7%	−5.9%	−2.3%	−7.5%	−11.6%	−11.0%	−13.6%	−12.6%	−16.2%	−18.5%	−16.1%	−17.3%
1985	112.71	109.31	112.53	123.77	124.83	128.08	138.07	138.40	136.42	142.15	143.96	144.47
% Change	−19.9%	−24.2%	−22.7%	−12.9%	−10.2%	−7.0%	4.6%	5.4%	8.6%	16.6%	16.2%	21.8%
1986	142.44	142.97	146.74	149.85	151.09E	147.50	147.50	147.50	147.50	147.50	147.50	147.50
% Change	26.4%	30.8%	30.4%	21.1%	21.0%	15.2%	6.8%	6.6%	8.1%	3.8%	2.5%	2.1%

—Using May 30, 1986 exchange rate—

Canadian dollar:

	1	2	3	4	5	6	7	8	9	10	11	12
1981	83.97	83.44	83.94	83.97	83.26	83.05	82.60	81.77	83.28	83.14	84.23	84.38
% Change	−2.3%	−3.6%	−1.5%	−0.4%	−2.3%	−4.4%	−4.8%	−5.2%	−4.1%	−2.8%	−0.1%	−1.0%
1982	83.85	82.37	81.92	81.62	81.06	78.39	78.75	80.31	80.98	81.29	81.55	80.74
% Change	−0.1%	−1.3%	−2.4%	−2.8%	−2.6%	−5.6%	−4.7%	−1.8%	−2.8%	−2.2%	−3.2%	−4.3%
1983	81.38	81.45	81.55	81.14	81.35	81.15	81.15	81.05	81.13	81.17	80.86	80.20
% Change	−2.9%	−1.1%	−0.5%	−0.6%	0.4%	3.5%	3.0%	0.9%	0.2%	−0.1%	−0.8%	−0.7%
1984	75.53	80.13	78.76	78.15	77.26	76.69	75.54	76.72	76.07	75.82	75.94	75.75
% Change	−7.2%	−1.6%	−3.4%	−3.7%	−5.0%	−5.5%	−6.9%	−5.3%	−6.2%	−6.6%	−6.1%	−5.5%
1985	75.53	73.82	72.25	73.22	72.70	73.12	73.93	73.66	72.98	73.17	72.65	71.66
% Change	0.0%	−7.9%	−8.3%	−6.3%	−5.9%	−4.7%	−2.1%	−4.0%	−4.1%	−3.5%	−4.3%	−5.4%
1986	71.07	71.21	71.38	72.05	72.67E	72.49	72.49	72.49	72.49	72.49	72.49	72.49
% Change	−5.9%	−3.5%	−1.2%	−1.6%	0.0%	−0.9%	−1.9%	−1.6%	−0.7%	−0.9%	−0.2%	1.2%

—Using May 30, 1986 exchange rate—

TABLE 16 (continued)

	Jan.	Feb.	March	April	May	June	July	Aug.	Sept.	Oct.	Nov.	Dec.
French franc:												
1981	21.54	20.14	20.15	19.55	18.23	17.68	17.25	16.72	17.77	17.76	17.78	17.50
% Change	−13.0%	−17.5%	−13.1%	−14.9%	−23.8%	−27.3%	−30.0%	−30.7%	−26.1%	−24.4%	−21.1%	−20.2%
1982	17.15	16.62	16.28	16.01	16.60	15.20	14.59	14.43	14.15	13.97	13.86	14.59
% Change	−20.4%	−17.5%	−19.2%	−18.1%	−8.9%	−14.0%	−15.4%	−13.7%	−20.4%	−21.3%	−22.0%	−16.6%
1983	14.77	14.52	14.24	13.67	13.48	13.05	12.84	12.43	12.41	12.57	12.25	11.93
% Change	−13.9%	−12.6%	−12.5%	−14.6%	−18.8%	−14.1%	−12.0%	−13.9%	−12.3%	−10.0%	−11.6%	−18.2%
1984	11.63	12.04	12.50	12.28	11.84	11.88	11.44	11.29	10.75	10.63	10.87	10.52
% Change	−21.3%	−17.1%	−12.2%	−10.2%	−12.2%	−9.0%	−10.9%	−9.2%	−13.4%	−15.4%	−11.3%	−12.8%
1985	10.31	9.91	9.92	10.59	10.55	10.71	11.30	11.72	11.55	12.40	12.64	13.01
% Change	−11.3%	−17.7%	−20.6%	−13.8%	−10.9%	−9.8%	−1.2%	3.8%	7.4%	16.7%	16.3%	23.7%
								Using May 30, 1986 exchange rate				
1986	13.37	13.97	14.29	13.88	14.02E	13.51	13.51	13.51	13.51	13.51	13.51	13.51
% Change	29.7%	41.0%	44.1%	31.0%	32.9%	26.1%	19.6%	15.3%	17.0%	9.0%	6.9%	3.8%
German mark:												
1981	49.77	46.76	47.50	46.22	43.60	42.05	40.98	39.99	42.55	44.37	44.86	44.29
% Change	−14.2%	−18.3%	−12.1%	−13.3%	−21.9%	−25.7%	−28.4%	−28.4%	−23.9%	−18.3%	−13.9%	−12.8%
1981	43.59	42.27	42.02	41.72	43.24	41.17	40.55	40.30	39.91	39.49	39.15	41.33
% Change	−12.4%	−9.6%	−11.5%	−9.7%	−0.8%	−2.1%	−1.0%	0.8%	−6.2%	−11.0%	−12.7%	−6.7%
1983	41.85	41.19	41.48	40.99	40.54	39.23	38.59	37.40	37.48	38.41	37.25	36.36
% Change	−4.0%	−2.6%	−1.3%	−1.7%	−6.2%	−4.7%	−4.8%	−7.2%	−6.1%	−2.7%	−4.9%	−12.0%
1984	35.57	37.06	38.50	37.77	36.38	36.50	35.10	34.65	32.99	32.60	33.35	32.21
% Change	−15.0%	−10.0%	−7.2%	−7.9%	−10.3%	−7.0%	−9.0%	−7.4%	−12.0%	−15.1%	−10.5%	−11.4%
1985	31.54	30.28	30.32	32.31	32.16	32.64	34.38	35.79	35.23	37.81	38.53	39.81
% Change	−11.3%	−18.3%	−21.2%	−14.5%	−11.6%	−10.6%	−2.1%	3.3%	6.8%	16.0%	15.5%	23.6%
								Using May 30, 1986 exchange rate				
1986	41.01	42.89	43.95	43.99	44.64E	43.02	43.02	43.02	43.02	43.02	43.02	43.02
% Change	30.0%	41.6%	45.0%	36.2%	38.8%	31.8%	25.1%	20.2%	22.1%	13.8%	11.7%	8.1%

Italian lira:

1981	0.1048	0.0981	0.0971	0.0928	0.0877	0.0824	0.0823	0.0804	0.0842	0.0837	0.0839	0.0829
% Change	−15.1%	−20.6%	−16.5%	−18.7%	−26.1%	−31.2%	−31.6%	−31.9%	−28.3%	−26.8%	−23.8%	−22.6%
1982	0.0814	0.0792	0.0773	0.0757	0.0779	0.0736	0.0723	0.0718	0.0709	0.0694	0.0681	0.0715
% Change	−22.3%	−19.3%	−20.4%	−18.4%	−11.2%	−10.7%	−12.2%	−10.7%	−15.8%	−17.1%	−18.8%	−13.8%
1983	0.0728	0.0714	0.0699	0.0689	0.0681	0.0662	0.0654	0.0629	0.0624	0.0632	0.0615	0.0599
% Change	−10.6%	−9.8%	−9.6%	−9.0%	−12.6%	−10.1%	−9.5%	−12.4%	−12.0%	−8.9%	−9.7%	−16.2%
1984	0.0586	0.0601	0.0619	0.0611	0.0589	0.0591	0.0571	0.0562	0.0527	0.0534	0.0537	0.0523
% Change	−19.5%	−15.8%	−11.4%	−11.3%	−13.5%	−10.7%	−12.7%	−10.7%	−15.5%	−15.5%	−12.7%	−12.7%
1985	0.0513	0.0489	0.0481	0.0506	0.0504	0.0512	0.0526	0.0534	0.0525	0.0561	0.0571	0.0584
% Change	−12.5%	−18.6%	−22.3%	−17.2%	−14.4%	−13.4%	−7.9%	−5.0%	−0.4%	5.1%	6.3%	11.7%
								Using May 30, 1986 exchange rate				
1986	0.0601	0.0630	0.0646	0.0641	0.0652E	0.0629	0.0629	0.0629	0.0629	0.0629	0.0629	0.0629
% Change	17.2%	28.8%	34.3%	26.7%	29.4%	22.8%	19.6%	17.8%	19.8%	12.1%	10.1%	7.7%

Japanese yen:

1981	0.4942	0.4862	0.4791	0.4652	0.4533	0.4462	0.4305	0.4288	0.4358	0.4321	0.4484	0.4568
% Change	17.6%	18.8%	19.0%	16.4%	3.6%	−2.8%	−4.8%	−4.0%	−6.6%	−9.6%	−4.5%	−4.3%
1982	0.4448	0.4251	0.4145	0.4097	0.4221	0.3981	0.3921	0.3861	0.3798	0.3682	0.3787	0.4133
% Change	−10.0%	−12.6%	−13.5%	−11.9%	−6.9%	−10.8%	−8.9%	−10.0%	−12.8%	−14.8%	−15.5%	−9.5%
1983	0.4297	0.4235	0.4197	0.4206	0.4259	0.4166	0.4158	0.4091	0.4126	0.4294	0.4255	0.4265
% Change	−3.4%	−0.4%	1.3%	2.7%	0.9%	4.6%	6.0%	6.0%	8.6%	16.6%	12.4%	3.2%
1984	0.4277	0.4281	0.4439	0.4441	0.4339	0.4281	0.4114	0.4128	0.4074	0.4053	0.4105	0.4033
% Change	−0.5%	1.1%	5.8%	5.6%	1.9%	2.8%	−1.1%	0.9%	−1.3%	−5.6%	−3.5%	−5.4%
1985	0.3934	0.3839	0.3877	0.3971	0.3972	0.4019	0.4147	0.4211	0.4228	0.4658	0.4901	0.4931
% Change	−8.0%	−10.3%	−12.7%	−10.6%	−8.5%	−6.1%	0.8%	2.0%	3.8%	14.9%	19.4%	22.3%
								Using May 30, 1986 exchange rate				
1986	0.5003	0.5410	0.5596	0.5711	0.5942E	0.5737	0.5737	0.5737	0.5737	0.5737	0.5737	0.5737
% Change	27.2%	40.9%	44.3%	43.8%	49.6%	42.7%	38.3%	36.2%	35.7%	23.2%	17.2%	16.3%

TABLE 16 *(continued)*

	Jan.	Feb.	March	April	May	June	July	Aug.	Sept.	Oct.	Nov.	Dec.
Mexican peso:												
1981	4.279	4.254	4.223	4.188	4.151	4.106	4.065	4.031	3.986	3.937	3.888	3.836
% Change	−2.4%	−2.8%	−3.5%	−4.3%	−5.1%	−6.0%	−6.6%	−7.1%	−8.2%	−9.1%	−9.9%	−10.9%
1982*	3.778	3.151	2.204	2.167	2.132	2.096	2.058	1.109	1.429	1.429	1.429	0.679
% Change	−11.7%	−25.9%	−47.8%	−48.3%	−48.6%	−49.0%	−49.4%	−72.5%	−64.1%	−63.7%	−63.2%	−82.3%
1983	0.663	0.634	0.618	0.651	0.665	0.671	0.669	0.659	0.657	0.636	0.616	0.607
% Change	−82.5%	−79.9%	−72.0%	−70.0%	−68.8%	−68.0%	−67.5%	−40.6%	−54.0%	−55.5%	−56.9%	−10.6%
1984	0.601	0.594	0.578	0.558	0.504	0.509	0.509	0.508	0.506	0.492	0.474	0.455
% Change	−9.4%	−6.3%	−6.5%	−14.3%	−24.2%	−24.1%	−23.9%	−22.9%	−23.0%	−22.6%	−23.1%	−25.0%
1985	0.439	0.424	0.406	0.406	0.392	0.339	0.288	0.294	0.268	0.245	0.251	0.225
% Change	−27.0%	−28.6%	−29.8%	−27.2%	−22.2%	−33.4%	−43.4%	−42.1%	−47.0%	−50.2%	−47.0%	−50.5%
1986	0.223	0.208	0.204	0.198	0.188E	0.182	0.182	0.182	0.182	0.182	0.182	0.182
% Change	−49.2%	−50.9%	−49.7%	−51.2%	−52.1%	−46.3%	−36.8%	−38.0%	−32.0%	−25.7%	−27.4%	−19.0%
Netherlands guilder:												
1981	45.81	42.87	42.91	41.66	39.22	37.82	36.83	36.01	38.33	40.15	40.91	40.43
% Change	−12.8%	−17.4%	−12.9%	−14.2%	−22.6%	−26.7%	−29.6%	−29.8%	−25.4%	−19.8%	−15.0%	−13.5%
1982	39.77	38.54	38.19	37.60	38.90	37.25	36.71	36.64	36.44	36.22	35.89	37.46
% Change	−13.2%	−10.1%	−11.0%	−9.7%	−0.8%	−1.5%	−0.3%	1.7%	−4.9%	−9.8%	−12.3%	−7.3%
1983	38.01	37.34	37.27	36.38	36.05	35.02	34.50	33.43	33.51	34.24	33.25	32.41
% Change	−4.4%	−3.1%	−2.4%	−3.2%	−7.3%	−6.0%	−6.0%	−8.8%	−8.0%	−5.5%	−7.4%	−13.5%
1984	31.64	32.84	34.10	33.49	32.34	32.38	31.10	30.73	29.25	28.90	29.57	28.54
% Change	−16.8%	−12.1%	−8.5%	−7.9%	−10.3%	−7.5%	−9.9%	−8.1%	−12.7%	−15.6%	−11.1%	−11.9%
1985	27.92	26.75	26.82	28.59	28.49	28.96	30.55	31.82	31.33	33.54	34.21	35.34
% Change	−11.8%	−18.5%	−21.3%	−14.6%	−11.9%	−10.6%	−1.8%	3.5%	7.1%	16.1%	15.7%	23.8%
									Using May 30, 1986 exchange rate			
1986	36.38	37.96	38.94	39.02	39.73E	38.31	38.31	38.31	38.31	38.31	38.31	38.31
% Change	30.3%	41.9%	45.2%	36.5%	39.4%	32.3%	25.4%	20.4%	22.3%	14.2%	12.0%	8.4%

Swiss franc:

1981	54.91	51.50	52.04	50.67	48.40	48.23	47.68	46.09	49.51	53.08	56.00	55.10
% Change	-12.4%	-15.5%	-8.2%	-10.9%	-19.5%	-21.2%	-23.3%	-23.9%	-18.9%	-11.8%	-3.4%	-1.6%
1982	54.22	52.88	52.95	50.96	51.28	48.10	47.71	47.35	46.69	46.01	45.60	48.57
% Change	-1.3%	2.7%	1.7%	0.6%	6.0%	-0.3%	0.1%	2.7%	-5.7%	-13.3%	-18.6%	-11.9%
1983	50.82	49.55	48.40	48.57	48.61	47.34	47.21	46.23	46.25	47.34	46.08	45.49
% Change	-6.3%	-6.3%	-8.6%	-4.7%	-5.2%	-1.6%	-1.0%	-2.4%	-0.9%	2.9%	1.1%	-6.3%
1984	44.68	45.35	46.53	45.64	44.09	43.80	41.47	41.41	39.92	39.61	40.49	39.06
% Change	-12.1%	-8.5%	-3.9%	-6.0%	-9.3%	-7.5%	-12.2%	-10.4%	-13.7%	-16.3%	-12.1%	-14.1%
1985	37.61	35.66	35.67	38.54	38.24	38.88	41.56	43.55	42.11	46.10	46.94	47.52
% Change	-15.8%	-21.4%	-23.3%	-15.6%	-13.3%	-11.2%	0.2%	5.2%	5.5%	16.4%	15.9%	21.7%
1986	48.40	51.16	52.22	52.59	53.62E	51.76	51.76	51.76	51.76	51.76	51.76	51.76
% Change	28.7%	43.5%	46.4%	36.4%	40.2%	33.1%	24.5%	18.9%	22.9%	12.3%	10.3%	8.9%

Using May 30, 1986 exchange rate

* Official rate of 70 pesos to the U.S. dollar used from September through November, 1982.

Currency and interest rate differentials, as well as the growing internationalization of many companies' businesses, have often behooved managements to seek financing in markets outside their own. If companies wish foreigners (particularly Americans) to invest in them, they clearly have to provide their accounts in a manner to which those foreigners can relate.

The number of practices that differ country to country is quite large; fortunately, most of them are nonmaterial. Several, however, can have considerable impact in determining a company's income or its balance sheet valuations. These typically relate to accounting for goodwill, depreciation, discretionary reserves, inflation, currency translations, consolidated subsidiaries, and taxes. Also, in Japan and Europe, companies report on a "parent-company" basis, not consolidated, and also can make large allocations to reserves to shelter income. Swedish companies, for example, are not allowed to use accelerated depreciation for income tax purposes—clearly increasing their income tax liability. However, they can allocate portions of revenues into certain "untaxed" reserves; that is, these allocations are deductible for income tax purposes, thereby diminishing income tax liability. Are these reserves to be considered a future liability akin to deferred taxes? (They become taxable only when reduced from one accounting period to another.) Or are they a "somewhat restricted" portion of stockholders' equity? Are earnings to be considered after these reserve allocations are deducted or before?

Similarly, Heineken in the Netherlands uses replacement cost accounting for reporting purposes. In the United States, the reporting guidelines of the Financial Accounting Standards Board (FASB) require only cost of sales, depreciation, and amortization expenses to be adjusted in the determination of the difference between net income based on GAAP (accounting based on historical cost) or current cost accounting. Considerable flexibility is allowed in the methods used to measure current cost. With an annual inventory turnover of about $22 \times$ at Anheuser-Busch (only $7 \times$ at Heineken), we feel the major difference between replacement and GAAP accounting is determined by the level of depreciation charges. According to Anheuser-Busch's 1984 annual report, the depreciation charge in 1984 was about 31 percent higher under replacement cost accounting than under GAAP ($266.4 million against reported $203.4 million). Heineken's earnings in the 1980–83 period could have been understated by at least 40 percent after adjusting for Generally Accepted Accounting Principles in the United States, and about 25 percent in 1984 and 1985.

Although a detailed discussion of all differences is not within the scope of this work, Table 17, included in an article written by Frederick D. S. Chois and Vinod B. Bavishi, and printed in the August 1982 edition of *Financial Executive*, provides a sketch of the differences alluded to herein.

TABLE 17 Synthesis of Accounting Differences

Accounting Principles	U.S.	Australia	Canada	France	Germany	Japan	Neth.	Sweden	Switz.	U.K.
1. Marketable securities recorded at the lower of cost or market?	Yes	Yes	Yes	Yes	Yes	Yes	Yes	Yes	Yes	Yes
2. Provision for uncollectible accounts made?	Yes	Yes	Yes	No	Yes	Yes	Yes	Yes	Yes	Yes
3. Inventory costed using FIFO?	Mixed	Yes	Mixed	Mixed	Yes	Mixed	Mixed	Yes	Yes	Yes
4. Manufacturing overhead allocated to year-end inventory?	Yes	Yes	Yes	Yes	Yes	Yes	Yes	Yes	No	Yes
5. Inventory valued at the lower of cost or market?	Yes	Yes	Yes	Yes	Yes	Yes	Yes	Yes	Yes	Yes
6. Accounting for long-term investments: less than 20 percent ownership: cost method.	Yes	Yes	Yes	Yes*	Yes	Yes	No(K)	Yes	Yes	Yes
7. Accounting for long-term investments: 21–50 percent ownership: equity method.	Yes	No(G)	Yes	Yes*	No(B)	No(B)	Yes	No(B)	No(B)	Yes
8. Accounting for long-term investments: more than 50 percent ownership: full consolidation.	Yes	Yes	Yes	Yes*	Yes	Yes	Yes	Yes	Yes	Yes
9. Both domestic and foreign subsidiaries consolidated?	Yes	Yes	Yes	Yes	No**	Yes	Yes	Yes	Yes	Yes

TABLE 17 *(continued)*

Accounting Principles	U.S.	Australia	Canada	France	Germany	Japan	Neth.	Sweden	Switz.	U.K.
10. Acquisitions accounted for under the pooling of interest method?	Yes	No(C)	No(C)	No(C)	No(C)	No(C)	No(C)	No(C)	No(C)	No(C)
11. Intangible assets: goodwill amortized?	Yes	Yes	Yes	Yes	No	Yes	Mixed	Yes	No**	No**
12. Intangible assets: other than goodwill amortized?	Yes	Yes	Yes	Yes	Yes	Yes	Yes	Yes	No**	No**
13. Long-term debt includes maturities longer than one year?	Yes	Yes	Yes	Yes	No(D)	Yes	Yes	Yes	Yes	Yes
14. Discount/premium on long-term debt amortized?	Yes	Yes	Yes	No	No	Yes	Yes	No	No	No
15. Deferred taxes recorded when accounting income is not equal to taxable income?	Yes	Yes	Yes	Yes	Yes	Yes	Yes	No	No	Yes
16. Financial leases (long-term) capitalized?	Yes	No	Yes	No	No	No	No	No	No	No
17. Company pension fund contribution provided regularly?	Yes	Yes	Yes	Yes	Yes	Yes	Yes	Yes	Yes	Yes
18. Total pension fund assets and liabilities excluded from company's financial statement?	Yes	Yes	Yes	Yes	No	Yes	Yes	Yes	Yes	Yes

19.	Research and development expensed?	Yes	Yes	Yes	Yes	Yes	Yes	Yes	Yes	Yes	Yes	Yes
20.	Treasury stock deducted from owner's equity?	Yes	NF	Yes	Yes	No	Yes	Yes	Mixed	NF	NF	NF
21.	Gains or losses on treasury stock taken to owner's equity?	Yes	NF	Yes	Yes	No	No**	No	Mixed	NF	NF	NF
22.	No general purpose (purely discretionary) reserves allowed?	Yes	Yes	No	No	No	No	No	No	No	No	Yes
23.	Dismissal indemnities accounted for on a pay-as-you-go basis?	Yes	Yes	Yes	Yes	Yes	Yes	Yes	NF	Yes	NF	Yes
24.	Minority interest excluded from consolidated income?	Yes	Yes	Yes	No	No	Yes	Yes	Yes	Yes	No	Yes
25.	Minority interest excluded from consolidated owner's equity?	Yes	Yes	Yes	No	No	Yes	Yes	Yes	Yes	No	Yes
26.	Are intercompany sales/profits eliminated upon consolidation?	Yes	Yes	Yes	Yes	Yes	Yes	Yes	Yes	Yes	Yes	Yes
27.	Basic financial statements reflect a historical cost valuation (no price level adjustment)?	Yes	No	Yes	Yes	Yes	No**	Yes	No**	No	No	No

TABLE 17 *(concluded)*

Accounting Principles	U.S.	Australia	Canada	France	Germany	Japan	Neth.	Sweden	Switz.	U.K.
28. Supplementary inflation-adjusted financial statements provided?	Yes	No**	No**	No	No	No	No**	No	No**	Yes
29. Straight-line depreciation adhered to?	Yes	Yes	Yes	Mixed	Mixed	Mixed	Yes	Yes	Yes	Yes
30. No excess depreciation permitted?	Yes	No	Yes	No	Yes	Yes	No	No	No	No
31. Temporal method of foreign currency translation employed?	Yes	Mixed	Yes	No(E)	No(E)	Mixed	No(E)	No(L)	No(E)	No(E)
32. Currency translation gains or losses reflected in current income?	Yes	Mixed	Yes	Mixed	Mixed	Mixed	No(J)	Mixed	No(H)	No

KEY: Yes—Predominant practice.
Yes*—Minor modifications, but still predominant practice.
No**—Minority practice.
No—Accounting principle in question not adhered to.
NF—Not found.
Mixed—Alternative practices followed with no majority.
B—Cost method is used.
C—Purchase method is used.
D—Long-term debt includes maturities longer than four years.

E—Current rate method of foreign currency translation.
F—Weighted average is used.
G—Cost or equity.
H—Translation gains and losses are deferred.
I—Market is used.
J—Owners' equity.
K—Equity.
L—Monetary/nonmonetary.

SOURCE: Used by permission from Frederick D.S. Chois and Vinod B. Bavishi, "Diversity in Multinational Accounting," *Financial Executive*, August 1982. © 1982 by Financial Executive Institute.

The Lack of Information Abroad

There is often less publicly available information about a foreign company than on one in the United States, and foreign companies are often not subject to accounting, auditing, and financial reporting standards and requirements comparable to or as uniform as those of U.S. companies. There is generally less government supervision and regulation of exchanges, brokers, and issuers than there is in the United States.

The frequency of financial reports also varies. Some large enterprises that have adopted accounting standards similar to those in the United States publish quarterly statements; some companies in the United Kingdom and Japan publish financial statements semiannually; and others publish annually. For instance, many Swiss and German companies only supply six-months revenue figures (no earnings), and once a year these companies disclose the prior-year earnings results. However, the frequency and the depth of reporting for most foreign companies is improving rapidly. Nevertheless, U.S. portfolio managers, having had the luxury of quarterly earnings reports, may find the lack of available information disheartening.

Dividend Withholding Taxes

In most foreign countries, taxes are withheld at the source on dividend payments. The taxes withheld can be claimed, under certain conditions, as a credit against U.S. tax liabilities.

Foreign issuers pay their dividends in their national currencies. For American shares, the dividend is paid by the company's agent in the United States in dollars representing the conversion of the foreign currency at the then current rates of exchange. For ADRs, the dividends are paid by the company to the bank, the holder of record of the underlying shares. The ADR issuer converts the dividend received into U.S. dollars and distributes the proceeds to the ADR holders after deducting handling charges; such handling charges typically amount to $0.01 per share per dividend payment.

Dividend withholding tax rates vary from country to country. The rates at which taxes are withheld from dividend payments to U.S. persons are influenced by the bilateral tax agreements between the foreign country involved and the United States. Due to these tax agreements, withholding tax on *dividends* is often reduced from a maximum of 30 percent to 15 percent, and on *interest* from 30 percent to 15 percent or even 0 percent.

SECTION 4—THE FRAMEWORK FOR 13 FOREIGN STOCK MARKETS

Investment in foreign securities involves a number of factors which affect the underlying business. The principal stock exchanges are those of the leading industrialized nations. The following text, provided by local banks or brokers, attempts to provide a framework of the key factors as they affect some of the leading stock markets.

THE AUSTRALIAN STOCK MARKET[1]

For the 12 months to March 31, 1986, the Australian stock market had an average daily trading volume of 68 million shares valued at U.S.$76 million (at the exchange rate of U.S.$0.735 to A$1.00). The total market capitalization of the 1,127 companies quoted on the Australian Stock Exchange was U.S.$85 billion as of March 31, 1986.

All domestic capital transactions, including those for portfolio share investments, are free of exchange control restrictions with the exception of interest-bearing investments in Australia by foreign governments, their agencies such as central banks not akin to private sector entities, and intergovernmental organizations. Procedural requirements apply in respect to certain offshore foreign exchange payments in accordance with certain government taxation screening arrangements.

Taxation

Interest withholding tax. The withholding tax on interest payments to nonresidents is a flat 10 percent. However, where double taxation agreements exist, the Australian Taxation Office will consider applications for exemption from withholding tax by overseas investors who enjoy exemption in their country of domicile. Written application must be made to obtain this exemption and must be accompanied by evidence of tax-free status in the country of domicile.

Dividend withholding tax. Dividend income for nonresident investors is subject to withholding tax at a rate of 30 percent. However, Australia has reciprocal taxation agreements with the United States and other countries, and in these cases the rate is reduced to 15 percent.

Brokerage charges. Rates of brokerage commissions on stock exchange transactions are deregulated; for investment institutions commissions are negotiable. The Australian Fixed Interest Market is quoted

---

[1] Provided by Potter Partners, Melbourne, Australia.

on and trades on a net yield to redemption basis and transactions to clients are on a net price basis inclusive of charges.

Stamp duties on market transactions. A rate of A$0.30 for every A$100.00 or part thereof applies to transactions in listed marketable securities by member firms on the Australian Associated Stock Exchanges. The rate is payable by both buyers and sellers. An exemption is made for transactions in commonwealth, semigovernment, and corporate fixed interest securities, on which no stamp duty is payable.

Trading sessions. There are two trading sessions per day in Australia five days a week, with trading hours between 10:00 A.M. and 12:15 P.M. and again between 2:00 P.M. and 3:15 P.M.

After the market is officially closed, brokers may transact "off-room" sales which must immediately be reported to the exchange. Similarly, any business that involves the matching of a buyer and seller of Australian securities by an Australian broker outside Australia must be reported to the stock exchange as an overseas sale. A list of overseas sales, or overnight sales, is published by the exchange during the morning trading session following the trade.

THE BELGIAN STOCK MARKET[2]

Market Characteristics

At the end of 1985, some 195 domestic companies were listed on the Brussels Stock Exchange, Belgium's most important stock exchange, representing a total market value of BF1,051 billion (U.S.$20.9 billion at the year-end 1985 exchange rate). As a result, Brussels ranked 13th on the world list of stock exchanges (8th in Europe), while the ratio of stock market capitalization/GNP reached 21.9 percent. Over the whole year 10.6 percent of the market value changed ownership; this put the daily trading volume (only of the official market) at half a billion Belgian francs (U.S.$10 million). Stock market performance is measured mainly by two indexes, a return index and a price index, both comprising all listed Belgian stocks and with the base January 1, 1980 = 1,000 points. It should also be noted that all quoted stocks are in the form of "bearer shares."

The most important stocks are petroleum producer and distributor Petrofina, which represents more than 10 percent of the stock market capitalization; three utilities: EBES, INTERCOM, and UNERG (together are 18 percent of the market); three holding companies: Société Générale de Belgique, Groupe Bruxelles Lambert, and COBEPA (12 percent);

---

[2] Provided by Banque Bruxelles Lambert, S.A., Brussels, Belgium.

three banks: Générale de Banque, Banque Bruxelles Lambert, and Kredietbank (7.5 percent); energy-trust Tractebel (4.5 percent); chemical company Solvay (4 percent); and two insurers: Royale Belge and AG.

Ordinary Shares and AFVs

With Belgian equities a distinction is to be made between ordinary shares and AFV shares. This last category enjoys certain advantages. For example, the issuing company may distribute to the holders of its shares a tax-free portion of realized earnings (the superdividend). Consequently, their total dividend usually exceeds that of ordinary shares. Moreover, there are other advantages from which only Belgians can benefit; for example, a lower withholding tax (20 percent instead of 25 percent). However, between 1992 and 1994, these special advantages will be phased out.

Trading

As far as transactions are concerned, it should be noted that only brokers are allowed to carry out orders on the stock market floor. These orders may, however, also be accepted by banks, which in turn will call upon a number of brokers for their execution and will ensure that the necessary requirements are met. This last method could certainly be advantageous to foreign investors.

Transactions take place on the official stock exchange floor or on the so-called over-the-counter market. In this "dealer market," large orders can be handled at any time of the day and brokerage fees as well as settlement dates are often negotiable. Primarily institutional investors are active in this market, which is organized by banks and the major brokers. The official market offers two different transaction possibilities:

- First, the cash market (one third of transactions), where settlement is the next day, trading volume is usually small, and daily price movements can be limited to 5 percent.
- Second, the forward market (two thirds of transactions), where most of the major stocks are listed, except for the banks and insurance companies. Here, settlement is twice monthly.

Taxes

In Belgium, capital gains from shares are not taxed, unless realized by companies incorporated in Belgium. Dividend withholding tax amounts to 25 percent for ordinary shares and 20 percent for AFV shares. Belgium has tax agreements with several foreign countries. U.S. investors, for instance, pay only 15 percent tax on the dividends of Belgian shares.

Transaction Costs

On trades executed on the dealer market, brokerage fees are negotiable. On trades conducted on the stock exchange floor, transaction fee schedules apply as follows:

Cash Market

1. Brokerage fees:
   a. Variable part:

Transaction Size	Fee
Up to BF2 million	1.00%
BF2 to 5 million	0.90
BF5 to 10 million	0.80
Above BF10 million	0.60

If the stock price is lower than BF600, the following fee scale is applicable for the portion up to BF2 million:

Stock Price	Fee
BF 1 to 15	10%
BF 16 to 100	BF 1.50 p.s.
BF101 to 200	BF 2.00 p.s.
BF201 to 400	BF 4.00 p.s.
BF401 to 600	BF 6.00 p.s.

   b. Fixed part: BF100
   The total brokerage fee may not be higher than 6 percent of the transaction (10 percent if stock price is below BF600) and certainly not lower than BF40.
2. Complementary charges:
   a. 0.04 percent for handling orders.
   b. 0.025 percent for acceptance of orders.
3. Taxes: 0.35 percent.

Forward Market

1. Brokerage fee:

Transaction Size	Fee
Up to BF5 million	0.80%
BF5 to 10 million	0.60
Above BF10 million	0.50

2. Complementary charges:
   a. 0.040 percent: execution.
   b. 0.025 percent: acceptance.
3. Taxes: 0.17 percent.

THE CANADIAN STOCK MARKET[3]

Canada has five different stock exchanges, which together handled trades valued at Can$57.8 billion (U.S.$41.3 billion at the year-end 1985 exchange rate) in 1985, up 60 percent from 1984 levels of trading. By volume, 6.9 billion shares changed hands in 1985, 40 percent more than in the prior year. As shown in the following table, over 75 percent of the volume as measured in Canadian dollars and nearly half of the number of shares were traded on the Toronto Stock Exchange (TSE), the country's largest.

Trading Distribution on the Five Canadian Stock Exchanges

Exchange	By Canadian Dollar Value (billions)				
	1985	Percent	1984	Percent	1985 v. 1984, % Change
Toronto	$44.2	76.5%	$26.7	73.8%	+65.6%
Montreal	10.6	18.3	7.0	19.4	+50.5
Vancouver	2.7	4.7	2.2	6.2	+21.8
Alberta	0.3	0.5	2.1	0.6	+41.2
Winnipeg	*	*	0.2	*	−52.1
Total	$57.8	100.0%	$36.1	100.0%	+59.8%

Exchange	Volume by Number of Shares				
	1985	Percent	1984	Percent	1985 v. 1984, % Change
Toronto	3,298,482,113	47.6%	2,124,026,184	42.6%	+55.3
Montreal	643,265,072	9.3	400,900,618	8.0	+60.5
Vancouver	2,752,966,088	39.8	2,260,273,571	45.3	+21.8
Alberta	229,372,061	3.3	202,473,571	4.1	+13.3
Winnipeg	1,862,121	*	2,342,622	*	−20.5
Total	6,925,947,455	100.0%	4,990,016,566	100.0%	+38.8

* Less than 0.1%.

---

[3] Provided by Davidson Partners, Toronto, Canada.

Daily TSE trading in 1985 averaged Can$175.4 million on 13.1 million shares exchanged in 12,508 transactions. (The all-time high daily trading record for market value was set on August 17, 1985, at Can $860.8 million.) The 10 most actively traded company issues in 1985 were Canadian Pacific Ltd., Dome Petroleum, Bell Enterprises, Nova Alberta A (nonvoting), Bank of Nova Scotia, Gulf Canada, Canadian Tire A (nonvoting), Alcan Aluminum, Ranger Oil and Laidlaw B (nonvoting).

At year-end 1985, the quoted market value of all issues listed on the TSE totaled Can$585.2 billion (U.S.$418.6 billion). An important characteristic of the TSE is the high proportion of foreign incorporated firms listed on it—of the total market cap cited above, 62.4 percent (Can$365.2 billion) represented foreign-based firms. The total number of equity securities listed on the TSE at year-end 1985 was 1,438, comprised of 989 industrial issues and 449 mining and energy issues. Another important characteristic is the somewhat heavy weighting of resource-related shares, as measured by the market capitalization of the TSE 300 Composite Share Index. However, the bias toward resource-oriented shares in the TSE 300 has diminished in recent years. Metals and minerals accounted for 9.5 percent of its weighting at year-end 1985 (versus 12.9 percent at year-end 1982), oil and gas 12.0 percent (13.8 percent at year-end 1982), and paper products another 1.8 percent (1.5 percent at year-end 1982). In total, resources companies at year-end 1985 represented 27.0 percent of the index total market capitalization, versus 32.3 percent at year-end 1982.

Commissions

Beginning May 1984, structured commission schedules on equity trades were eliminated and brokers now negotiate their fees with clients.

Dividend Withholding Taxes

Dividends paid to foreign holders of Canadian equities are subject to 25 percent withholding tax; however, depending on reciprocal tax treaties signed with different countries, this rate may be reduced. For example, U.S. investors pay 15 percent withholding, creditable against U.S. taxes and, in some cases, refundable upon filing required applications for tax-exempt status.

THE AMSTERDAM STOCK EXCHANGE (ASE)[4]

In the 19th century, the Amsterdam Stock Exchange (ASE) played an important role in financing the construction of North American railroads. Other American companies also made use of the facilities offered

---

[4] Provided by Pierson, Heldring & Pierson, Amsterdam, The Netherlands.

Toronto Stock Exchange 300 Composite Index—Breakdown by Industry Sector
According to Market Capitalization at December 31, 1985

Industry Sector	Percentage of Total
Metals and minerals	9.5%
Golds	3.7
Oil and gas	12.0
Paper and forest products	1.8
All resources	27.0%
Consumer products	9.9
Industrial products	11.0
Real estate and construction	1.7
Transportation	0.9
Pipelines	2.9
Utilities	12.5
Communications and media	3.9
Merchandising	4.8
Financial services	16.6
Management companies	8.8
Total	100.0%

by Dutch merchant banks. As a result, Amsterdam developed into the most important market outside of the United States for American securities. The international flavor of the ASE is particularly reflected in the number of foreign shares, 276, listed on the Amsterdam Stock Exchange versus the number of shares of Dutch companies: 207. Of the foreign shares the major portion are U.S. based.

Characteristics

Total market capitalization at year-end 1985 was approximately fl 145 billion (U.S.$58 billion), versus just fl 57 billion at year-end 1982. A rather limited number of shares dominate this number: Royal Dutch, currently valued at 35 percent of the total; Unilever and Philips each close to 10 percent; three large insurance companies together 11 percent; two banks more than 6 percent; and Akzo and Heineken, respectively, 4.7 percent and 3.2 percent. The 10 largest companies thus represent 80 percent of share market capitalization.

Amsterdam has participated in the world's bull markets, taking off in early 1983; the ANP-CBS General (Composite) Index at year-end 1982 stood at 100 and had moved up to 265 by the end of April 1986. Trading volume has also shown strong growth: fl 27 billion in 1982, fl 60 billion in 1983, fl 81 billion in 1984, and fl 115 billion in 1985.

Trading System

The Amsterdam Stock Exchange is open Monday through Friday from 10:00 A.M. to 4:30 P.M. About 30 very active shares, representing approximately 92 percent of share market capitalization, trade during the full stock exchange session. Also most bonds and shares under the ASA's system (see below) and on the Parallel Market are traded from 10:00 A.M. to 4:30 P.M. All other securities are traded from 11:30 A.M. to 4:30 P.M. The system of continuous trading is now applied to all trades.

The Official List comprises approximately 2,000 securities, about 70 percent of which are domestic and foreign bonds and the remaining 30 percent represent Dutch and foreign securities.

Transaction Costs

Commissions are charged by members according to a fixed-rate schedule. However, since 1984 members are allowed to grant discounts on sizable transactions.

The commission rate schedule pertaining to shares is as follows:

	Commission	
Value of Transaction	Percent	fl
Up to and including fl 5,000	1.5	7.50
Over fl 5,000 up to and including fl 20,000	1.0	32.50
Over fl 20,000 up to and including fl 1,000,000	0.7	92.50
Over fl 1,000,000	0.7	7.50

The following discounts on commissions, calculated according to the above schedule, may be applied.

Value of Transaction	Percentage Discount (percent)
Over fl 1,000,000	15%
Over fl 2,500,000	30
Over fl 5,000,000	45
Over fl 10,000,000	50
Over fl 15,000,000	65

Furthermore, a stamp duty of 0.12 percent on the value of the transaction is charged. However, foreign professional intermediaries (members of stock exchanges, licensed dealers) dealing with members of the ASE on a negotiated (net) basis are exempt from stamp duty.

On May 5, 1986, trading under the Amsterdam Interprofessional

Market System (AIM) was initiated: on a transaction in shares with a value over fl 1,000,000 and in bonds with a value over fl 2,500,000, commissions can be negotiated and contracts can be made on a net basis. These transactions can be done bypassing the intermediary of the "hoekman." However, the "hoekman" remains the intermediary in case of dealings between ASE members.

Taxes

A 25 percent withholding tax is applicable to dividends paid to residents as well as to nonresidents. Dependent on double-tax agreements, foreign holders of shares may be able to recover part of the tax withheld, either by tax credit or by rebate. There is no withholding tax on interest on (convertible) bonds.

Parallel Market

This market, established in 1982 by the Amsterdam Stock Exchange and under its supervision, offers small- and medium-sized companies the advantages of a regulated secondary market. Listing requirements are less stringent than those of the Official Market.

European Options Exchange (EOE)

Established in Amsterdam in the 1970s, the EOE has grown into an important participant on the ASE. Volume in options on a number of Dutch stocks has grown dramatically. Currently, options can be traded on 15 Dutch stocks and about 10 Dutch government bonds. Furthermore, currency, gold, and silver options are listed.

ASAS

In September 1980 the Amsterdam Stock Exchange introduced trading in original American shares under the ASA system (Amsterdam security account system). No physical handling of share certificates in Amsterdam is involved: all settlements are done by book entry only. Settlement procedures are those of the home market.

THE FRENCH STOCK MARKET[5]

Domestic and foreign shares in France are traded on the Paris Bourse and on six regional stock exchanges located in Bordeaux, Lille, Lyons,

---

[5] Provided by Jean-Pierre Pinatton, Agents de Change, Paris, France.

Marseille, Nancy, and Nantes. Trading takes place on the Official List (the Forward market and the Cash market) and on the Second Marché. The Second Marché was created in February 1983 and is mainly intended for medium-sized firms.

Market Characteristics

At the end of 1985, some 966 companies were listed on the French stock market. This figure includes 769 domestic firms and 197 foreign companies. As of December 31, 1985, the market capitalization of French stocks amounted to FF675.3 billion, of which FF649.6 billion represented stocks listed in Paris. Total annual trading volume in French shares reached FF146.8 billion (FF142 billion of that traded on the Paris Stock Exchange); that is, 21.7 percent of the whole market capitalization. In 1985, the average market yield was 3.7 percent.

The stock market performance is measured by the CAC Index, equal to 100 on December 31, 1981. The Second Marché has had its own index since the end of 1984, equal to 100 on December 31, 1984.

In 1985, the 15 most active stocks on the forward market, as measured by average daily trading volume, were:

- *From FF10 bn to FF16 bn:* Michelin (tires), Thomson-CSF (electrical and electronics), BSN (food), Peugeot (automotive), Campagnie du Midi (diversified holdings), Moet-Hennessy (beverages), Lefarge-Coppee (cement/building materials), and Carrefour (retail trade).
- *From FF6 bn to FF10 bn:* Air Liquide (gas chemicals), Elf-Aquitaine (oil), Total (oil), Club Méditerranée (leisure), Générale des Eaux (utilities), Pernod Ricard (beverages), and Source Perrier (beverages).

Trading

Agents de Change (stockbrokers) are granted by law the monopoly for the negotiation of all securities in France. All *Agents de Change* are members of the Compagnie des Agents de Change (National Broker's Association), and have joint, several, and unlimited liability for the due completion of the trades and the deposits of securities and cash on their books. Trading on the forward market and the other markets presents two basic differences. On the Forward Market, trading is done in lots, with settlement on the last day of the month. On the cash market and the Second Marché, however, any quantity may be negotiated for settlement the next day.

Transaction Costs

Charges for transactions include:

- *Brokerage fee.* The rate of commission is fixed by the Minister of Finance on an official sliding scale and decreases as the size of transactions increases.

Transaction Size	Paris Bourse (percent)	Regionals (percent)
FF1 to 600,000	0.650%	0.750%
FF600,000 to 1,100,000	0.430	0.500
FF1,100,000 to 2,200,000	0.325	0.375
above FF2,200,000	0.215	0.250

In addition, a stamp tax of 0.30 percent for trades under FF1,000,000 and 0.15 percent for trades above FF1,000,000 is charged.

Finally, a value-added tax of 18.6 percent of commissions (not applicable to foreign investors) is also imposed.

THE GERMAN STOCK MARKET[6]

Because of the federal nature of the country, Germany has eight stock exchanges. In order of importance they are located in Frankfurt, Dusseldorf, Hamburg, Munich, Berlin, Hannover, Stuttgart, and Bremen.

By the end of 1985, shares of 451 domestic companies were listed on at least one of the various exchanges. Total market capitalization of all classes of stocks of these companies amounted to DM438 billion (U.S.$179 billion) based on year-end 1985 prices. This compares with 471 companies and DM134 billion at the end of 1975.

Turnover on stock exchange floors in domestic German shares expanded from DM13.2 billion in 1974 to DM210.7 billion in 1985, when daily trading averaged DM843 million. (See Table 18.) During the first two months of 1986, trading totaled DM67 billion, one third of the entire 1985 volume in deutsche marks. (However, an increasing volume of trading is being transacted both before and after trading hours in and outside of Germany, on which there are no statistics recorded.)

The following statistics (Table 19) concerning the activity of international investment comprises all dealings by foreigners in the German stock market both on and off the exchanges. They are therefore not

---

[6] Provided by Sal. Oppenheim, Cologne, Germany.

TABLE 18   Trading Activity in German Shares

Turnover Domestic Shares (until 1984 except Berlin)		German Shares Ranked by Turnover in 1985 (based on dealings in Frankfurt, Dusseldorf, Hamburg, and Munich)			
Year	DM billion	Company	Number of Shares Traded (millions)	Average Price 1985 (DM)	Total Value (DM millions)
1974	13.2				
1975	27.5				
1976	24.9	Siemens	31.93	568	18,136
1977	27.6	Deutsche Bank	24.29	540	13,117
1978	34.1	VW	36.08	288	10,391
1979	25.7	BASF	46.43	221	10,265
1980	27.7	Bayer	38.97	222	8,651
1981	30.9	Dresden Bank	29.79	251	7,477
1982	35.2	Daimler	7.83	855	6,695
1983	84.1	Thyssen	53.36	122	6,510
1984	84.7	Hoechst	28.75	222	6,383
1985	210.7	Commerzbank	30.18	208	6,277

readily comparable with the figures given above which are based on the "floor dealings" only.

Taxes

There are two main kinds of taxes levied upon German common stock investors: a 25.0 percent withholding tax on dividends and interest on convertible bonds and a 0.25 percent capital turnover tax (reduced to 0.125 percent provided the order originates from abroad). Banks and authorized dealers are exempt.

TABLE 19   Foreign Investors Trading Volume in German Stock Exchanges

	DM Billion
1979	9.6
1980	12.4
1981	15.5
1982	15.2
1983	34.3
1984	35.2
1985	104.9
1986/1	21.3
1986/2	15.3

Commissions

Customarily, German private clients pay a commission of 1 percent of turnover. This rate is reduced to 0.5 percent for institutions in most cases. However, there is no fixed commission system; therefore, special negotiated commission rates and/or net trading does occur in exceptional cases. In all dealings done through the exchanges, a jobbing fee of 0.08 percent has to be paid and is charged on top of the bank commission and the capital turnover tax wherever applicable.

In April 1986 the boards of German stock exchanges agreed to create a new organization to implement stock market reform. Among the main points under discussion are:

- Longer settlement periods.
- Prolonged trading hours (currently from 11:30 A.M. to 1:30 P.M. only).
- Improved electronic links among the different floors.

THE HONG KONG STOCK MARKET[7]

Size of Daily Trading Volume in Number of Shares and Values

From the inception of the newly unified stock exchange at the beginning of April 1986 through April 18, 1986, the value of daily turnover of the 251 company issues listed on the Hong Kong Exchange averaged HK$419.8 million and the number of shares 99.5 million. Market capitalization of all companies listed was HK$275 billion (U.S.$35.1 billion) on April 18, 1986.

Commission Structure and Stamp Taxes

On both purchases and sales of any securities on a Hong Kong register an ad valorem duty of HK$6 per HK$1,000 is charged on trades in Hong Kong registered securities anywhere in the world. On transactions originating from Hong Kong, the normal minimum brokerage fee is 0.5 percent on consideration, payable by both buyer and seller. On transactions originating from London or elsewhere, commission fees are usually 1 percent.

Recent Changes

A new unified stock exchange called The Stock Exchange of Hong Kong Limited has been in operation since April 2, 1986. This stock exchange,

---

[7] Provided by HongKong & Shanghai Banking Corporation, Hong Kong.

situated in Exchange Square, replaced four earlier stock exchanges—the Hong Kong Stock Exchange, the Far East Exchange, the Kam Ngan, and the Kowloon Exchanges—which are no longer in operation.

Trading Information

The predominant feature of trading on the Hong Kong stock market is that business has to be settled by making delivery of shares in "good delivery" against payment before 1:00 P.M. on the next working day following the transaction. By "good delivery," it is meant that each share certificate must be accompanied by a matching stamped transfer deed signed by the registered shareholder so that it is fully negotiable. Shares are traded in "board lots," each of which is composed of a certain number of shares (which varies for different issues). Trading not done in a "board lot" is usually conducted on unfavorable terms.

Despite the fact that most registers in Hong Kong are computerized, registration is still a lengthy process and can take three weeks or more. During this time, the registered owner is unable to sell the stock. Therefore, individuals normally only register if there is a dividend to be paid or if there is a rights or bonus issue. The Stock Exchange also fixes the spread and variances between prices of shares. The stipulated spreads are as follows:

Spread Table

From	$ .01	to	$ .25 -	$0.001
Over	.25	to	.50 -	0.005
Over	.50	to	2.00 -	0.010
Over	2.00	to	5.00 -	0.025
Over	5.00	to	10.00 -	0.05
Over	10.00	to	30.00 -	0.10
Over	30.00	to	50.00 -	0.25
Over	50.00	to	100.00 -	0.50
Over	100.00	to	200.00 -	1.00
Over	200.00	to	500.00 -	2.00
Over	500.00	to	1,000.00 -	2.50
Over	1,000.00	to	9,995.00 -	5.00

Dividend Withholding Tax

There is no tax on dividends, but a 17 percent interest is levied as a withholding tax on loan stock, at source. Dividends are paid to shareholders registered on the date on which the share register of the company closes ("books close"), but are only paid after the books reopen again, usually 10 to 20 days after they are closed.

THE ITALIAN STOCK EXCHANGE[8]

The most important stock exchange in Italy is the Milan Borsa, established in 1800, which covers over 90 percent of total volume of equities and 80 percent of the bonds traded.

The Milan Borsa, which until the end of the 1970s was a very small market dominated by wealthy Italian families, has become in recent years one of the most active European centers, because of the impressive growth of the domestic mutual funds, introduced in 1983, and the better economic and political climate.

The numbers reported below give an idea of the market's development:

Milan Stock Market at a Glance

Year-End	Number of Listed		Capitalization		Trading Volume	
					Total	Daily Avg.
	Companies	Issues	L/bn	$/bn	(billion lire)	
1976	155	178	6,994	8.0	1,092	4
1977	144	168	5,371	6.2	754	3
1978	143	165	8,145	9.8	1,635	7
1979	139	164	10,339	12.8	2,875	11
1980	134	174	23,543	25.3	7,343	29
1981	132	178	28,749	23.9	12,334	49
1982	138	190	27,299	19.9	3,770	15
1983	139	201	34,698	20.9	5,880	23
1984	143	213	49,793	25.7	7,143	28
1985	147	214	98,195	56.5	26,315	104
1986 (3/31)	150	222	157,600	99.7	16,697	269

Dealing System

Mercato and Tormino (forward market). The market operates on a "monthly account" basis, by means of a callover system similar to the French one. It opens at 10:00 A.M. local time and the trading lasts until the fixing of all listed shares has taken place (1:30 P.M. to 2:30 P.M.).

Chiusura (fixing). Each day all listed shares are called out for the fixing, always following the same order established by the Stock Exchange Stockholders' Committee, starting at 10:00 A.M. All buying and selling orders are matched at the fixing price, and the fixing lasts until all the orders are executed. When the fixing differs more than 20 percent from the previous day, the fixing is temporarily suspended and

---

[8] Provided by Banca Manusardi E.C., Milan, Italy.

delayed to the end of the session, in order to allow brokers to advise their clients and get new instructions for the second call. The fixing is the most significant indication of the day, as most trades are concentrated on that specific moment.

Durante (before or after fixing). Sometimes, especially when the market is very active, and mainly on the most marketable shares, it is possible to deal in the so-called *durante,* which is a bid-and-offer price usually done for limited amounts of shares, before or after the fixing. No stockbroker or bank is obliged to quote price "durante" in the sense that dealing is possible only when a counterparty is available.

Block trading. It is quite difficult and can take place only for shares of large marketability, and it usually bears a premium (for purchase) or discount (for sales) on market prices.

Mercati Ristretti (restricted local markets). Those are cash markets with a very small number of stocks listed, primarily local popular banks and smaller companies, and take place *once a week* in the principal Italian bourses. The Milan "Mercato Ristretto" is done on Wednesdays at 3:30 P.M., and it is the most important one.

Terzo mercato (gray or OTC market). This is a sort of OTC market, and allows unofficial trading in nonlisted stocks or in new issues, before they get the official listing. It operates on a bid/offer basis and the volumes are in most cases irrelevant. Dealing in "terzo mercato" stocks must be treated very carefully.

Fixed Commissions and Expenses on Equities

On forward settlement trades (between 11 and 45 business days). Commissions are fixed at 0.35 percent for the stockbroker and 0.35 percent for the bank. A 0.1125 percent stamp duty also applies. On block trading, it is possible to negotiate commissions.

On Cash settlement trades (up to 10 working days). Cash settlement is unusual, but whenever it occurs, brokers include in the price the interest between the cash value date and the settlement date on the forward market. Stamp duties on cash settlement are 0.075 percent.

Settlement Procedures

The Italian settlement system still works on the basis of "physical" delivery of shares: the stocks bought/sold on the stock market are received/delivered from/to the so-called "Stanza di Compensazione," the domestic clearinghouse under the management of the Bank of Italy.

Shares in Italy are in *Registered Form,* which means that the name of the registered holder must be typewritten on the mantel of the certificate.

Due to the sharp increase in trading volumes over the last two years, the "Stanza di Compensazione" releases the shares with four to five weeks delay, and it takes an additional four to six weeks for the brokers to register the stocks, swap instructions with the custodian banks for the clients, and finally deliver the certificates to the custodian's premises.

At present there is a bill under discussion in Parliament to utilize for settlement a computerized "book entry" clearinghouse, in order to abolish physical deliveries (so-called "Monte Titoli").

100% margin requirements on purchases. According to the rule *n,* 929 issued by Consob (the Italian SEC) on July 3, 1981, all individuals and nonbanking institutions buying shares on Italian stock markets must deposit a cash margin ahead of settlement, as a guarantee against speculation. This margin was originally 30 percent, but it has been progressively increased to 100 percent throughout the last few years. Banks and brokers, whenever operating on client's behalf, are not subject to the margin requirements.

Withholding Tax on Dividends

Foreign residents are subject to a 30 percent withholding tax on dividends paid on Italian shares. (In 1982, 1983, and 1984, this tax was temporarily increased to 32.4 percent.) Under reciprocal tax agreements, the rate is reduced to 15 percent for residents of most of the developed countries. Savings shares (which are in bearer form) pay only a 15 percent withholding tax (16.2 percent in 1982, 1983, and 1984).

The Italian Mutual Funds

Domestic funds. Authorized in 1983 after a long discussion in Parliament, domestic investment funds started raising money in July 1984. By the first quarter of 1986, there were 43 open-end funds and their sales had experienced rapid growth, due to extremely favorable tax treatment and to the bearer form. Their assets are primarily bond oriented, but equity exposure more than doubled in the 12 months to March 31, 1986: from 15.4 percent in March 1985, to 34.3 percent in March 1986.

The Italian mutual funds can invest up to 10 percent of their total assets (as of three months before) in foreign securities with exemption

Net Assets of Italian Funds (in billion lire)

	Income Funds		Balanced Funds		Equity Funds		Total	
		%		%		%		%
12/31/84	701	60.2	225	19.3	239	20.5	1,164	100.0
12/31/85	6,873	34.7	7,122	36.0	5,789	29.3	19,784	100.0
3/31/86	8,824	23.9	15,471	41.8	12,685	34.3	36,980	100.0

from the 25 percent cash deposit at the Bank of Italy in a noninterest-bearing account.

THE JAPANESE STOCK MARKET[9]

Japan has stock exchanges in eight of its major cities, but the Tokyo Stock Exchange (TSE) accounts for 83 percent of Japan's total transactions. With the steady development of the Japanese economy, the number of TSE listed companies increased to 1,476 at year-end 1985 (from 485 in 1949) and the total market capitalization to ¥190,127 billion (from ¥153 billion), a size second in the world only to the New York Stock Exchange. The TSE has two two-hour sessions: a morning session from 9:00 A.M. to 11:00 A.M. and an afternoon session from 1:00 P.M. to 3:00 P.M. There is only a morning session on Saturdays, the first business day of the year (January 4), and the last business day of the year (December 28). It is closed on Sundays, national holidays, and the second Saturday of the month. Settlement is made on the fourth business day (excluding Saturdays) after a trade. The minimum trading unit is 1,000 shares except for 45 companies for which it is 100 shares, one company for which it is 2,000 shares, and another, 3,000 shares. Volume in 1985 totaled 121.9 billion shares or ¥78.7 trillion (equivalent to daily volume of 428 million shares and ¥276 billion). The turnover ratio in that year was 48 percent.

Of the total transactions on the first section processed through the top 12 securities firms in 1985 (excluding those on a dealer basis which account for 25 percent of the total), individuals accounted for 50.3 percent; foreigners 16.0 percent; banks 10.5 percent; business corporations 10.0 percent; investment trusts 5.6 percent; life and nonlife insurance companies 1.1 percent; and others 6.7 percent. As of the end of March 1986, TSE listed shares were held 36 percent by financial institutions, 29.5 percent by business corporations, 23 percent by individuals, and 7.4 percent by foreigners. Investing by individuals

---

[9] Provided by Nomura Research Institute, Tokyo, Japan.

declined to a nine-year low, while that of financial institutions rose further. Trading is characterized by the high proportion (nearly 20 percent) of margin transactions permitted on TSE first section issues.

Japanese companies have to meet strict disclosure requirements. Papers they have to submit to the regulatory authorities include audited financial statements for each fiscal year, a semiannual report (due within three months following the end of every half-year term), and consolidated financial statements that cover important subsidiaries, if any (which are due within four months following the end of each fiscal year).

Individual investors' capital gains are exempt from taxes in principle. However, if trading is done on fewer than 50 days a year and fewer than 200,000 shares or fewer than 200,000 shares per issue, institutional transactions are all subject to taxes.

Withholding tax on foreign investors is 20 percent, but differs for the countries that have tax treaties with Japan. The tax is 15 percent for the United States, the United Kingdom, and West Germany and 10 percent for Poland and the Philippines.

Securities transactions tax is 0.55 percent of the selling price. Commissions are not negotiable and are fixed as follows:

Commissions	Transactions
¥2,500	¥200,000 or under
1.25%	¥200,000–¥1 million
1.05% plus ¥2,000	¥1–¥3 million
0.95% plus ¥5,000	¥3–¥5 million
0.85% plus ¥10,000	¥5–¥10 million
0.25% plus ¥1.25 million	¥100 million or over

THE JOHANNESBURG STOCK EXCHANGE (JSE)[10]

The Johannesburg Stock Exchange is the only stock market trading in the Republic of South Africa. At year-end 1985, 664 companies were listed on the exchange, with a further 163 preference share issues listed; 156 constituted mining or mining finance shares, 124 were financial shares, and the remainder were industrial companies. The JSE also provides a floor for the trading of fixed interest-bearing South African government and municipal stocks (765 securities listed). Corporate debentures, notes, and loan stocks are also traded and 153 such securities were listed at the end of 1985.

The total market capitalization of the JSE at the end of December 1985 amounted to R187.3 billion at the December 31, 1985, exchange rate. Ordinary shares made up 83.3 percent of this total (R156.0 billion—

---

[10] Provided by Davis Borkum Hare & Co., Johannesburg, South Africa.

U.S.$71.9 billion) and fixed interest stocks 16.1 percent (R30.2 billion— U.S.$13.9 billion).

A sliding scale brokers commission structure is applicable for the purchase or sale of securities, declining from 1.2 percent brokerage for transactions up to R5,000 (U.S.$2,300) to 0.2 percent for single transactions in excess of R1,500,000 (U.S.$692,250). In the case of fixed interest-bearing government and municipal stocks, a different brokerage scale is applicable, sliding from 0.05 percent for transactions up to R20,000 (U.S.$9,230) to 0.01 percent for transactions in excess of R500,000 (U.S.$230,750). However, many foreign transactions are conducted on a net basis.

A marketable securities tax (MST), at the rate of 1.5 percent, is chargeable on the purchase of all classes of shares and options, but is not chargeable on sales. Where MST has been paid, the transfer of shares is exempt from stamp duty on registration, but all arbitrage/nonresident transactions are exempt from stamp duty. No MST or stamp duties are payable on transactions in fixed interest government and municipal stocks. A 15 percent nonresident shareholders tax is levied on all dividends paid to foreign holders of South African equities (10 percent on interest payments).

Foreign transactions in listed South African securities are effected through an investment currency—the financial rand. Financial rands are created by the sale of listed South African securities owned by foreigners and are freely transferable between nonresidents, but currently may only be used for investment in locally quoted securities. All interest and dividends accruing to nonresidents are paid out in the normal currency—the commercial rand. The financial rand trades at a significant discount to the commercial rand; accordingly, nonresidents receive an effective premium on dividends and interest.

According to research undertaken by JSE stockbrokers Davis Borkum Hare & Co., close to 27 percent of the issued share capital of South African mining shares is held by foreign investors. Foreign holdings of South African industrial, financial, and fixed interest stocks are minimal.

THE SWEDISH STOCK MARKET[11]

The Swedish stock market has attracted attention during the 1980s with an extraordinary performance. Following the introduction of a tax-incentive program for household equity investments and a turnaround in corporate profits, the market took off in 1981. Between 1980 and 1983 share prices quintupled and the trading volume increased 10-fold. Since

---

[11] Provided by Skandinaviska Enskilda Banken, Stockholm, Sweden.

then, sustained liquidity in the market has placed Sweden among the 10 largest international markets based on trading volume.

The Stockholm Stock Exchange

Year	Turnover SKr (billion)	Market Value SKr (billion)	Turnover Ratio* (percent)	Net Export SKr (billion)
1980	7.6	56.5	13.3	−0.232
1981	18.6	95.3	19.4	0.345
1982	29.1	136.3	21.3	1.369
1983	75.6	245.3	30.8	6.111
1984	70.3	230.7	30.5	1.487
1985	83.4	286.8	29.1	4.804

* Annual turnover as percent of market value.

Trading at the Stockholm Stock Exchange—the only exchange in Sweden—is dominated by the companies on a special list of the 16 most traded companies. These are generally export-oriented engineering companies also accounting for a dominant share of Sweden's exports of high-quality goods (50 percent of Sweden's industrial production is sold abroad).

Registered Shares

The Swedish share handling system is based on registered shares instead of bearer shares. Each sale or purchase will include the cancellation of an old certificate and the issuance of a new one. Settlement takes place five banking days after the transaction day. On that day the seller will be paid and the buyer can collect his shares. However, sellers are obliged to surrender their shares on the transaction day.

An independent company, Vardepapperscentralen (VPC), handles the computer records for all companies, issues and cancels share certificates, and makes dividend payments. Dividends, bonus shares, scrip rights, and so on, are directed to the registered holder.

An investor may choose to register his shares via a nominee, normally his ordinary bank or broker. In such cases, the name of the investor will not be known to the company or to Swedish authorities. The nominee will forward dividends, and so forth, to the investors.

The Stock Exchange

The Stockholm Stock Exchange is the only authorized market in Sweden. The market is a callover—auction—market followed by a free "after market" among the floor traders. Only members of the Stock Exchange are allowed on the floor; at present 12 commercial banks and 14 independent broker firms are members. A few more are recognized by the Bank Inspection Board for brokering outside the stock exchange.

Trading starts at 10 A.M. local time and commences with the 16 most traded companies. After a short intermission, other industrial stocks, banks, insurance, and holding companies on the A1 list will follow. After the callover of companies on the A2 list, the auction will finish with convertible bonds and debentures with warrants. A total of about 170 companies are listed.

The free after market in each share will commence as soon as the last deal for that company has been closed in the callover market. Trading on the Stock Exchange will cease by 2:30 P.M. local time, but brokers may trade from their portfolio after that. Such contracts are reported to the exchange prior to the opening of the market the next day. Prices and volumes for all contracts concluded by authorized brokers must be reported to the exchange.

Commissions and Trust Fees

Swedish brokers charge the following commissions, with slight variations, for contracts covering listed equities: 0.45 percent for the first SKr 500,000 of each contract note and 0.30 percent for amounts exceeding SKr500,000 of each contract. A minimum commission per contract of SKr200 applies.

Trust fees are based on the market value of the securities in trust, the number of different types of securities in the portfolio and the number of transactions during the period. Charges may differ between the trust banks and other agents since they are free to set their prices independently.

Foreign Exchange Regulations and Taxes

Sweden still maintains *foreign exchange regulations* affecting portfolio investments in Swedish equities. Through decisive efforts from the Bank of Sweden during the 1980s about SKr25 billion worth of investment currency has been created for equities.

THE SWISS STOCK MARKET[12]

With a December 31, 1985, market value of SwF169.6 billion (U.S.$82.4 billion), the Swiss stock market is among the largest in the world. By industry group, that value was broken down at that date as follows:

---

[12] Provided by Bank J. Vontobel & Co., Zurich, Switzerland.

Listing by Industry Groups

Industry	Market Value (SwF million)	In Percent of Total
Banks	SwF 59,779	35.3%
Insurance	19,842	11.7
Chemicals/pharmaceuticals	30,842	18.2
Mechanical engineering	8,825	5.2
Light electronics	1,525	0.9
Building	2,922	1.7
Metals/steels	1,192	0.7
Industrial holding companies	7,401	4.4
Electric light and power	5,046	3.0
Food manufacturing	24,979	14.7
Food retailing	548	0.3
Department stores	2,455	1.4
Airlines	2,687	1.6
Packaging and paper	428	0.3
Breweries	1,093	0.6
Total Swiss market	SwF 169,564	100.0%

All told 2,577 securities were listed on the Zurich Exchange at year-end 1985, representing over 800 issuers. The lion's share of these securities are bonds; only 205 were actually Swiss equities, as shown below.

Securities Listed on the Zurich Stock Exchange

	Securities	Issuers
Swiss bonds	1,406	267
Foreign bonds	776	332
Swiss stocks	205	131
Foreign stocks	190	184
Total bonds	2,182	511
Total stocks	395	315
Total bonds and stocks	2,577	826

Trading Information

Daily trading data are not made public; however, annual volume in 1984 and 1985 totaled SwF308.3 and SwF451.7 billion, respectively. The 10 most actively traded Swiss shares in 1985 were Ciba-Geigy, Nestle, Oerlikon-Buhrle, Alusuisse, Jacobs Suchard, BBC Brown Boveri, Sandoz, Schweizerischer Bankverein, Schweizerische Bankgesellschaft, and Swissair.

Stock issues often consist of both bearer and registered form. Usually, only bearer form is available to nonresidents. Dividends are usually paid annually. There are currently no preferred shares.

Bonds are usually issued in bearer form. Interest is paid annually; some denominations are as low as SwF1,000. Maturities are up to 25 years. Some are convertible and some issued with options to buy shares. There are also a larger number of foreign currency issues.

Rights, also called share subscription rights, are issued to current shareholders and are usually good for a couple of weeks.

Warrants, usually issued with bonds, may be good for up to several years. They usually state whether they are good for bearer or registered stocks.

Certificates of participation are, in effect, nonvoting shares.

Dividend Withholding Taxes

Through a tax treaty with the United States, withholding for U.S. citizens on Swiss securities is reduced to 5 percent on interest and 15 percent on dividends. As with most foreign withholding, however, one must apply for the reduction; otherwise it is 35 percent. Capital gains from Swiss securities are taxable only in the United States.

Commission Structure

Bank charges in Switzerland for execution of trades currently apply as follows:

---

1. Brokerage

a. Transactions on Swiss stock exchanges:

Domestic shares and other equities:	%	SwF bonds:	%
up to SwF 50000.—	0.8	up to SwF 50000.—	0.6
for the next SwF 50000.—	0.7	for the next SwF 50000.—	0.4
for the next SwF 50000.—	0.6	for the next SwF 200000.—	0.3
for the next SwF 150000.—	0.5	for the next SwF 700000.—	0.2
for the next SwF 300000.—	0.4	for the next SwF 1 million	0.1
for the next SwF 400000.—	0.3	amounts in excess of	
for the next SwF 1 million	0.2	SwF 2 million	on enquiry
amounts in excess of			
SwF 2 million	on enquiry		

Foreign shares and other equities:	%	Foreign currency bonds:	%
up to SwF 50000.—	1.0	up to SwF 50000.—	0.6
for the next SwF 50000.—	0.9	for the next SwF 50000.—	0.5

for the next SwF 50000.—	0.7	for the next SwF 50000.—	0.4
for the next SwF 150000.—	0.5	for the next SwF 150000.—	0.3
for the next SwF 300000.—	0.4	for the next SwF 700000.—	0.2
for the next SwF 400000.—	0.3	SwF 1 million upwards	
for the next SwF 1 million	0.2	(freely negotiable)	on enquiry
amounts in excess of			
SwF 2 million	on enquiry		

b. For gross trades executed on foreign exchanges the following global rates apply, based on the gross value of the trade (foreign commission included):

Equities:	up to SwF 50000.—	for the next SwF 50000.—	for the next SwF 150000.—
United States	2.5%	1.5%	1.0%
Federal Republic of Germany	1.4%	1.3%	1.2%
United Kingdom	2.7%	1.7%	1.3%
Canada	2.7%	1.7%	1.3%

Bonds:	up to SwF 50000.—	for the next SwF 200000.—
All countries	1.5%	0.8%

THE UNITED KINGDOM STOCK MARKET[13]

The U.K. stock market is the world's third largest market, after the United States and Japan, with a capitalization of $365 billion as of February 28, 1986. There are around 2,100 U.K. registered companies, 500 overseas registered, and 72 Republic of Ireland registered. Of the U.K. registered, by far the largest number (over 1,350) fall into the broad subsector, commercial and industrial. By market value terms, the largest stock exchange groupings are utilities (which includes British Telecom, the largest quoted company), oil and gas, electronics, and electricals. The £ interest market comprises around 20 percent of the total market capitalization.

Alternative Markets

There are two other markets in the United Kingdom that deal in company shares: these are the unlisted securities market (the USM) and the over-the-counter market (OTC). Shares on the USM are equivalent to shares in the full market, in that there is a particular pitch for them on the exchange trading floor and the market is also subject to regulation by the exchange. The main difference lies in the less stringent requirements for listing. There are 339 companies currently listed on the USM; the market capitalization is around £2.4 billion. The OTC, on the other hand, is not regulated by the stock exchange and is therefore a little more speculative. Companies tend to be much smaller and do not

---

[13] Provided by Savory Milln, London, United Kingdom.

necessarily have much history—the market makers in the stocks are independent companies and are usually contacted directly when a client wishes to deal.

Turnover

As the stock exchange still relies very much on verbal trading, it is not as yet possible to record the exact number of trades made in a day. This will be possible once automated quotations are introduced (see below). However, the stock exchange does produce turnover figures. March 1986 was a record month, with total turnover of £50.9 billion, £16.2 billion of which was in equities and the remainder in gilt-edged transactions. Total turnover for 1985 was £390.5 billion, with 6,709,465 transactions recorded. Of these, 83% were in ordinary shares, but this represented only 27 percent by value. The turnover in March on the USM was over £220 billion by value, with 38,368 trades transacted.

Commissions

The existing system is one of fixed commissions in most areas with some parts of the market already operating under negotiated commissions. Rates for shares (registered and bearer) are as follows:

1.65%	on the first	£7,000 consideration
1.25%	on the next	£8,000
0.9%	on the next	£10,000
0.75%	on the next	£25,000
0.625%	on the next	£80,000
0.55%	on the next	£170,000
0.4%	on the next	£600,000
0.27%	on the next	£1,100,000
0.17%	on the excess	

Different rates apply for government bonds; short-lived British Funds, Eurocurrency bonds and overseas securities are subject to negotiated commissions. Beginning October 27, 1986, all commissions will be negotiated.

Settlement Periods

Settlement of equity deals is organized into periods called accounts, generally lasting two weeks except when interrupted by public Mondays. All trades that are transacted within an account are matched up within the central office at the stock exchange and someone who buys and sells a stock within an account is never actually registered as owning the stock.

Once the account period is over, all investors' net positions are worked out and payments are made on settlement day, which is generally the second Monday after the end of the account. Company registrars are also informed of any changes of ownership and share certificates returned and sent out. This has eliminated the need for each equity trade to be matched against another. Gilts continue to be settled on the day following the execution of the trade.

Other Dealing Costs

Stamp duty is payable on sales of shares and totals 1 percent of the consideration. The CSI Levy is payable on all deals over £5,000 and totals 60p. Value-added tax (VAT) of 15 percent of the commission is also payable by investors that are liable to pay VAT.

Income Tax

Dividends on U.K. companies are generally paid net of the rate of income tax (currently 29 percent). Overseas investors can claim exemption from this by sending the appropriate form to the Inland Revenue.

"Big Bang"

The U.K. stock market stands on the brink of the most fundamental change that it has ever faced. On October 27, 1986, the so-called day of "Big Bang," the system of fixed commissions will be abolished along with single capacity. The new automated dealing system (SEAQ) will commence full-time operation on that day.

The current structure of the stock exchange does not allow a market maker, or "jobber," in securities to deal directly with the public. Neither can a broker buy shares to hold onto his own account. This is the essence of the single capacity system—this will also disappear on October 27, 1986.

It was realized that brokers would lack the necessary capital to become market makers at the same time that increasing technology requirements also began to make demands on the limited cash resources of member firms. Consequently, the exclusivity of the exchange had to end and outside firms, mainly the major financial conglomerates, were allowed to take stakes in member firms. Many of these deals are now finalized, with the member firms being 100 percent owned.

This has led to teaming up of some of the major names on the London market, with jobbers and brokers joining together with the clearing banks or merchant banks to provide services to clients in all areas. Smaller brokers may decide to move into market making only in a small way, for example only in specialized areas.

APPENDIX
Sources of Information

Large amounts of information can be gathered on the economic, corporate, and financial fronts in the individual countries. The quality of the underlying information varies widely depending on the country and the source. Some of the sources of information are listed below and are meant to serve only as a broad guide.

In each country, a substantial amount of information, economic data, and industrial statistics are published by: (1) the government and its agencies, (2) the central bank, (3) the manufacturers' association or industry groups, (4) the commercial banks, and (5) the brokerage firms. In addition, a number of research-oriented firms publish material on a large number of international securities.

A. General Economic Information

International Financial Statistics
  (monthly and yearbook)
  International Monetary Fund
  700 19th Street, N.W.
  Washington D.C. 20431

Direction of Trade Statistics
  (annual and updates)
  International Monetary Fund
  Same address as above.

OECD Main Economic Indicators
  (monthly)
  OECD Publications &
  Information Centre
  Suite 1207
  1750 Pennsylvania Avenue,
  N.W.
  Washington D.C. 20006-4582

OECD Economic Outlook
  (biannual)
  OECD Publications &
  Information Centre
  Same address as above.

OECD Quarterly National Accounts Bulletin
  (quarterly)
  OECD Publications &
  Information Centre
  Same address as above.

OECD Observer
  (monthly)
  OECD Publications &
  Information Centre
  Same address as above.

OECD Economic Surveys
  (country analysis)
  OECD Publications &
  Information Centre
  Same address as above.

Monthly Bulletin of Statistics
  (monthly)
  United Nations
  Sales Section
  New York, N.Y. 10017

Morgan Stanley Capital
International Perspective
  (monthly and quarterly)
  Morgan Stanley
  1633 Broadway
  New York, N.Y. 10019

The Federal Reserve Bank of St.
Louis Review
  (monthly)
  The Federal Reserve Bank of
  St. Louis
  P.O. Box 442
  St. Louis, Missouri 63166

International Economic Conditions
  (monthly)
  The Federal Reserve Bank of
  St. Louis
  Same address as above.

Monetary Trends
  (biweekly)
  The Federal Reserve Bank of
  St. Louis
  Same address as above.

World Financial Markets
  (monthly)
  Morgan Guaranty Trust Co. of
  New York
  23 Wall Street
  New York, N.Y. 10015

Bank for International Settlements
  Buchdruckerei, Basel
  Switzerland

B. Weekly Business Publications (Local)

Canadian Business Magazine
  CB Media Ltd.
  70 the Esplanade, 2d floor
  Toronto, Ontario M5E, 1R2
  Canada

German Business Weekly
  German-American Chamber of
  Commerce
  666 Fifth Avenue
  New York, N.Y. 10103

Far Eastern Economic Review
  Centre Point
  181 Glouchester Road
  Hong Kong

Japan Economic Journal
  Tokyo International
  P.O. Box 5004
  Tokyo, Japan

Beleggers Belanger
  P.O. Box 152
  Amsterdam 1000, AD
  The Netherlands

Financial Mail
  171 Main Street
  2001 Johannesburg
  South Africa

Sweden Business Report
  Affarsvalden, Box 1234
  S-111 82
  Stockholm, Sweden

Finanz und Wirtschaft
  CH-8021
  Zurich
  Switzerland

The Economist
  54 St. James Street
  London SW 1A 1PJ
  England

The Investor's Chronicle
  30 Finsbury Square
  London EC 4P 4B4
  England

Business Week
  McGraw-Hill, Inc.
  1221 Avenue of the Americas
  New York, N.Y. 10020

Forbes
  Forbes Inc.
  60 Fifth Avenue
  New York, N.Y. 10011

C. Monthly Business Publications (Local)

L'Opinion Vie Français
  67 Avenue Franklin D.
  Roosevelt
  75381 Paris
  Cedex 08
  France

Asian Business Information
  G.P.O. Box 12507
  Hong Kong

Asian Finance
  Suite 9D Hyde Center
  223 Glouchester Road
  Causeway Bay
  Hong Kong

Asian Business
  Far Eastern Trade Press Ltd.
  15 C Lockheart Centre
  301 Lockheart Road
  Hong Kong

Hong Kong Business Today
  1181 Hong Kong Plaza
  186-191 Connaught, West
  Hong Kong

Toyokeizai Tokei Geppo
  OCS America, Inc.
  27-08 42nd Road
  Long Island City, N.Y. 11101

Kikai Tokei Geppo
  OCS America, Inc.
  Same address as above.

Sweden Now
  M. Oskogsgrand 11
  Box 27315, S-102 54
  Stockholm, Sweden

Euromoney
  Euromoney Publications
  Nestor House
  Playhouse Yard
  London EC4V 5EX
  England

Business
  Business People Publications
  234 King's Road
  London SW3 5UA
  England

Institutional Investor
  488 Madison Avenue
  New York, N.Y. 10022

D. Local Newspapers

The Financial Post
  MacLean Hunter Building
  777 Bay Street
  Toronto, Ontario M5W 1A7
  Canada

Globe & Mail Report on Business
  444 Front Street W
  Toronto, Ontario M5V 2S9
  Canada

Toronto Star
  1 Yonge Street
  Toronto, Ontario M5E 1E6
  Canada

AGEFI
  108 rue de Richelieu
  Paris 75002
  France

Handelsblatt
  GLP International
  21 Smith St.
  P.O. Box 9868
  Englewood, N.J. 07631

Asian Wall Street Journal
  G.P.O. Box 9825
  Hong Kong

Denpa Shinbun
  OCS America, Inc.
  27-08 42nd Road
  Long Island City, N.Y. 11101

Nihon Shoken Shinbun
  OCS America, Inc.
  Same address as above.

Nikkei Sangyo Shinbun
  OCS America, Inc.
  Same address as above.

Nikkei Shinbun
  OCS America, Inc.
  Same address as above.

Het Financieele Dagblad
  Gebouw 'Metropool'
  Weesperstraat 85-87
  Postbus 216
  Amsterdam 1000 AE
  The Netherlands

The Financial Times of London
  14 East 60th St.
  New York, N.Y. 10022

E. Local Statistical Sources

ANZ Bank Quarterly Survey
  (Australian quarterly)
  ANZ Bank
  355 Collins St.
  Melbourne 3000
  Australia

Canadian Statistical Review
  (monthly)
  STATISTICS CANADA
  Ottawa K1A 0Z8
  Canada

DAFSA
  (monthly)
  Société de Documentation et
  d'Analyses Financières
  125 rue Montmarte
  Paris, 2
  France

Monthly Reports of the Deutsche Bundesbank
  (monthly)
  Deutsche Bundesbank
  P.O. Box 10 06 02
  D-6000 Frankfurt 1
  West Germany

Hoppenstedt Borsenfuehrer
  (quarterly)
  Verlag Hoppenstedt & Co.
  Postfach 4006
  D-6100 Darmstadt 1
  West Germany

Hong Kong Government Information Services
  (monthly and quarterly)
  Beaconsfield House, 4th Floor
  4 Queen's Road
  Central, Victoria
  Hong Kong

La Borsa Valori
(monthly)
Sede Palazzo della Borsa
Piazza degli Affari, 6
20123 Milano, Italy

Review of Economic Conditions in Italy
(quarterly)
Banco di Roma
Viale U. Tupini, 180
00144 Rome
Italy

Balance of Payments Monthly
The Bank of Japan
2-1, 2-chome,
Hongokucho, Nihonbashi
Chuo-ku, Tokyo
Postal Code 103
Japan

Monthly Finance Review
Institute of Fiscal and
Monetary Policy
Ministry of Finance
Tokyo, Japan

Tokyo Stock Exchange Monthly
(monthly)
2-1-1 Nihombashi-Kayaba-Cho,
Chuo-ku, Tokyo 103
Japan

Economic Statistics Monthly
(monthly)
Research and Statistics
Department
The Bank of Japan
2-1, 2-chome,
Hongokucho, Nihonbashi
Chuo-ku, Tokyo
Postal Code 103
Japan

Svenska Aktiebolag
(monthly)
Kungl. Boktryckeriet P.A.
Norstedt & Soner
Box 2030 S103-12
Stockholm, Sweden

Schweizerische Nationalbank Monatsbericht
(monthly)
Orell Fussli Graphische
Betriebe
8036 Zurich 3
Switzerland

Agence Economique et Financière
4 rue Montblanc
Geneva
Switzerland

National Institute Economic Review
(monthly)
National Institute for Economic
& Social Research
2 Dean Trench Street
Smith Square
London SW1P 3HE
England

Bank of England Quarterly
(quarterly)
Economics Division, Bank of
England
London EC2R 8AH
England

Extel Statistical Services, Ltd.
(weekly, monthly, quarterly,
and annual service)
37/45 Paul Street
London EC2A 4PB
England

Moody's Services Ltd.
(monthly)
6–8 Bonhill Street
London EC 2A 4BU
England

F. Market Handbooks

China Handbook
Synergy Publishing Inc.
Suite 603
New York, N.Y. 10013

French Company Handbook
1 rue Bourdaloue
Paris 75009
France

Japan Company Handbook
Wako Securities Co., Ltd.
3 Kitahama 3-chome,
Higashi-ku
Osaka
Japan

Van Oss' Effectenboek
J. H. DeBussy
Amsterdam 1000
The Netherland

*South African Stock Exchange
Handbook*
Flesch Financial Publications
(Pty) Ltd.
P.O. Box 3473
Cape Town 8000
South Africa

*Handbuch der Schweizerischen
Anlagewerte*
Editions Cosmos S.A.
Bern, Switzerland

26

International Diversification

Donald R. Lessard, Ph.D.
Sloan School of Management
Massachusetts Institute of Technology

INTRODUCTION

In contrast to many innovations in investment management, international diversification has appeal to individuals with a wide range of investment perspectives. To disciples of modern portfolio theory, it is a logical extension of the arguments made at the domestic level for holding passive, well-diversified portfolios. To active managers, who seek to outguess other market participants, it is a new frontier, where insightful analysis is likely to result in superior performance.

The potential advantage of international diversification is a better ratio of reward to risk than that obtainable with a purely domestic portfolio—a higher expected return for a given level of risk or a lower level of risk for a given return. While it is possible that this advantage can be gained by consistently investing in one or a few foreign markets which outperform the U.S. market on a risk-adjusted basis, it is more likely to follow from the fact that returns from common stocks in various countries do not move in lockstep and thus the risk-return combinations available with an internationally diversified portfolio are likely to be superior to those of the individual stock markets.

There is now extensive evidence that the comovement of returns across countries is low enough that international diversification results in a considerably improved risk-return mix, and internationally diversified funds consistently rank near the top in this regard. The question is no longer whether investors should commit a substantial proportion of their assets abroad, but whether this commitment should remain in the

5 to 15 percent range or should approach the 50 percent implied by market capitalizations.

While most outright obstacles to international investment have diminished in recent years, there remain several reasons why investors may be justified in maintaining some degree of "home country bias" in their portfolio holdings. The traditional perceived obstacles to international investment include concern over currency risks and political risks; perceived limitations on the size, depth, and efficiency of foreign markets and difficulties in obtaining information regarding foreign securities.

Financial theory and investor experience show that currency risk should not be an obstacle to foreign investment, but at most a reason for hedging. Questions regarding the size, depth, or efficiency of foreign markets tend to affect both foreign and domestic investors, and the boom in international money managers suggest that information is available to all comers at a competitive price. However, domestic investors often face more favorable tax treatment on distributed income, especially when domestic and cross-border withholding taxes are taken into account.

This chapter first reviews the evidence regarding the advantages of international diversification. It then examines the various perceived drawbacks to foreign investment.

THE POTENTIAL ADVANTAGES OF INTERNATIONAL DIVERSIFICATION

The concept underlying international diversification is the same one applying to diversification along any other dimension—whenever the returns of different assets are not subject to exactly the same risks, the risk of a diversified portfolio of these assets will be lower than the risk of the typical individual security.

The proportion of the risk of individual investments that is diversifiable depends on the degree of correlation among the returns on these assets. Within the United States, the degree of synchronization or correlation between returns on shares of individual firms and a broad-based market index typically is around .5. This means that on average, the undiversifiable or systematic risk of a security is 50 percent of its total risk. Figures for countries other than the United States are typically even higher, ranging up to 70 percent.

In general, the proportion of risk of securities which is systematic in other countries is higher than in the United States. This reflects the fact that these countries typically have a less diverse industrial base than the United States and, in some cases, a more volatile political environment. This is particularly true for less developed countries where there is much less room for risk reduction through domestic diversification.

FIGURE 1   Risk Reduction through National and International Diversification

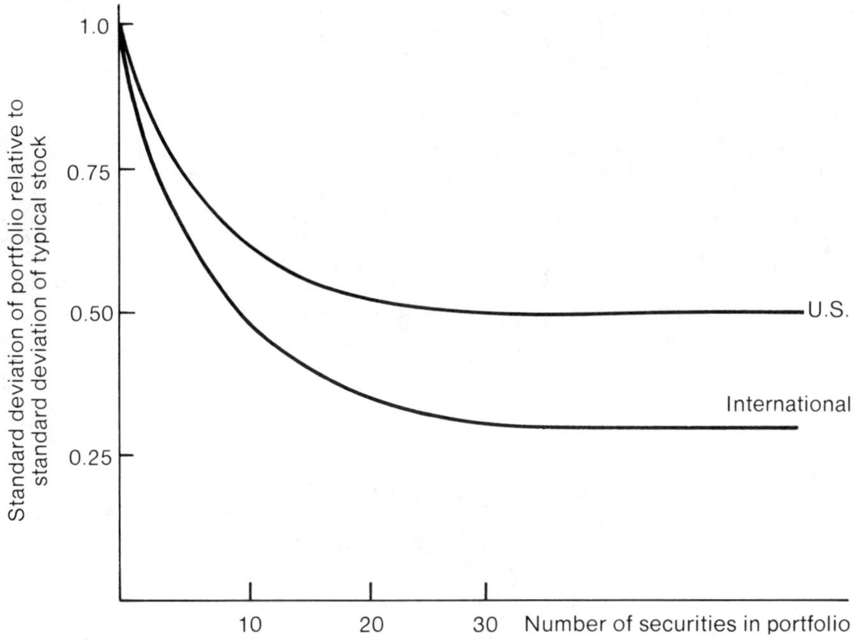

SOURCE: B. H. Solnik, "Why Not Diversify Internationally Rather Than Domestically?" *The Financial Analysts Journal* (July–August 1974), pp. 48–54.

When diversification is extended across national boundaries, a substantial proportion of the risk which is systematic within each country can be eliminated. Figure 1 shows this, comparing the risk reduction obtainable through diversification within the United States to that obtainable through international diversification. In the international case, portfolio risk drops to 33 percent of that of the typical stock, one-third less than the U.S. figure.

The reason for this additional diversification is that returns on diversified single-country portfolios display considerable independence. Many of the factors affecting share values are essentially domestic in nature. Differences among nations in tax laws, monetary policies, and general political climate are illustrative. Even factors that influence the world economy, such as the oil shocks of 1973, 1978, and 1985, can affect individual economies differently. This can be seen by examining the correlations between returns on the stock markets of six major countries and the United States for different periods of time through 1985 (Table 1).

TABLE 1 Correlations of Major World Equity Markets with the United States*

Country	1959–63	1964–68	1969–73	1973–74	1975–79	1980–85
France	.45	.02	.20	.37	.32	.45
Germany	.48	.12	.41	.52	.38	.35
Japan	.02	.07	.42	.39	.36	.26
Netherlands	.67	.60	.54	.37	.50	.33
Switzerland	.52	.35	.49	.49	.45	.47
United Kingdom	.29	.19	.41	.08	.34	.34

*All returns measured in U.S. dollars, based on stock market data reported by *Capital International Perspective*, Capital International S.A., Geneva, Switzerland.

Are correlations increasing? Since low correlations among countries are key to diversification gains, an important question is whether markets are moving more closely together over time. It is well recognized that in recent years, the major nations of the world have become both politically and economically more interdependent. In the mid-1970s it appeared that correlations between the United States and other major stock markets were rising as well, but the subsequent pattern is one of considerable variation from period to period with no discernable trend. For the period 1978–83, for example, correlations between the United States and other major markets were roughly at the same level as in the early 1960s, although cross-correlations among markets within the European and Asian blocs have increased substantially. Perhaps most striking from a U.S. investor's perspective is that the correlation of Japan with the United States remains quite low, despite that country's increased financial and industrial integration into the world economy.

While there are strong international economic influences at work, there also are powerful political factors that are largely domestic in nature. Internal disruption, or even disagreement over economic growth versus income distribution, can cause returns in a particular country to fall out of synchronization with the rest of the world. Nevertheless, even during the periods of highest market correlation, international diversification still would have reduced portfolio risk substantially.

Expected Returns and Gains from International Diversification

Although the degree of correlation indicates the extent to which risk can be reduced through international diversification, it does not provide a complete view of the advantages of international diversification, since it does not reveal exactly how domestic and internationally diversified portfolios will compare in terms of risk-adjusted returns. This comparison requires knowledge about the expected returns in each market as well as the correlations.

However, because of the risk-reduction resulting from relatively low correlations, even relatively low expected returns on foreign markets would result in superior risk-adjusted performance by an internationally diversified portfolio compared to the U.S. market. This is best illustrated by example.

Minimum expected returns that justify international investment. The appropriate measure of the risk to a U.S. investor of a foreign holding is its contribution to the risk of one's total portfolio. Assuming that the domestic portfolio is well diversified, the contribution to the portfolio risk of the foreign investment is its β (beta)

TABLE 2 Risk and Required Return Measures for Foreign Market Portfolios (estimated from data for 1980–1985)

Country	Annualized Standard Deviation of Returns (measured in U.S. dollars)	Correlation with U.S. Market (S & P 500)	Market Risk (beta) from U.S. Perspective	Minimum Risk Premium from U.S. Perspective
France	26.6	.41	.76	4.5
Germany	20.1	.35	.49	2.9
Japan	19.4	.26	.35	2.1
Netherlands	32.9	.33	.75	4.5
Switzerland	19.2	.47	.63	3.8
United Kingdom	21.7	.34	.51	3.1
United States	14.4	1.00	1.00	6.0

SOURCE: Author's computations using Capital International data.

coefficient, technically the covariance of the security in question with the base portfolio divided by the variance of the base portfolio.

Taking the German market portfolio as a representative foreign holding, we note that it has an annual standard deviation of return of 20.1 percent compared to 14.4 percent for the United States and a correlation of .35 with the U.S. market. Thus the German stock market has a beta relative to the U.S. market portfolio of .47. As a result, a U.S. investor could consider the German market as attractive as the U.S. market if the expected return in excess of the risk-free interest rate was as little as one half the excess return expected from the U.S. market. Table 2 presents the results of similar calculations for the major foreign markets based on correlations and standard deviations measured over the 1980–85 period, and on the assumption that the U.S. investor demands (expects) a risk premium of 6.0 percent on the U.S. market portfolio that has a beta of 1.

Realized and expected returns. The past performance of foreign markets suggests the best of both worlds—lower risk and higher returns. Table 3 shows that realized total returns on most foreign markets have outstripped U.S. returns over most recent time periods. However, research findings for the United States and other markets show that past returns (unless perhaps for very long periods) provide little information regarding future returns. Further, at least part of the performance of foreign markets can be traced to circumstances that are unlikely to be repeated—the postwar economic recovery of Europe, its subsequent boom resulting from the common market, and the economic phenomenon of Japan propelled in part by a major increase in the

TABLE 3 Realized Total Rates of Return in U.S. Dollars (percent per year compounded)

1959–78			1959–84
		Japan	15.6
Japan	17.0	Hong Kong* (20 years, 5 mos)	17.3
Austria	11.1	Sweden	10.9
Germany	11.5	Singapore† (18.5 years)	15.0
Switzerland	12.4	Norway	10.1
Denmark	8.4	United Kingdom	9.9
Belgium	8.3	Switzerland	9.4
South African Gold Shares	12.5	Netherlands	9.2
Norway	8.4	Germany	8.6
Netherlands	8.5	Australia	8.6
France	5.8	United States	8.2
Sweden	9.4	Denmark	8.2
United Kingdom	9.3	Canada	7.8
Canada	6.5	Austria	7.0
United States (S&P 500)	6.5	Belguim	7.0
Spain	7.8	Spain	6.3
Australia	8.3	France	5.2
Italy	−.2	Italy	1.9

Note: With certain noted exceptions, index data are from *Capital International Perspective*, Geneva, Switzerland. All returns include reinvestment of estimated dividends and are adjusted to U.S. dollars at current exchange rates. Source withholding taxes on dividends for a U.S.-domiciled investor have been deducted. For most markets, this tax rate is about 15 percent.

*Hang Seng Index—base 1964 = 100.
†Straits Time Industrial Index—base 1966 = 100.

SOURCES: 1959–78, author's computations reported in previous edition. 1959–84, G. L. Bergstrom, D. R. Lessard, J. K. Koeneman, and M. J. Siegel, "International Securities Markets," in *Handbook of Financial Markets* 2nd ed., ed. F. J. Fabozzi and F. G. Zarb (Homewood, Ill.: Dow Jones-Irwin, 1986).

degree of world economic integration. Structural shifts of this magnitude are unlikely to recur in the near future for mature industrialized countries, although Singapore and Hong Kong provided similar returns in the late 1970s and other emerging markets may do so in the 1980s.

Nonetheless, analysis of fundamental economic conditions in various countries does provide a helpful point of departure in considering the growth of overall activity, corporate profits, and hence, share values. Savings rates and rates of capital formation in many countries, for example, continue to outstrip those of the United States. The key question from an investor perspective, though, is the extent to which these anticipated outcomes are capitalized in share values and the rate at which they are capitalized; that is, the expected rate of return given normal expectations of future economic outcomes. Some insight is

---

TABLE 4 Price-Cash Earnings Ratios for Major World Stock Markets

---

Country	Average each year-end 1974–1978	December 1985
Singapore	10.0	12.3
Hong Kong	8.8	15.4
Italy	6.5	5.5
Japan	6.6	9.0
Australia	5.5	7.2
Canada	5.0	7.0
United Kingdom	4.6	6.8
United States	5.9	6.9
Belgium	4.1	3.8
Austria	4.2	16.0
Germany	3.8	6.0
Spain	6.2	2.9
Sweden	3.1	6.0
Denmark	3.4	6.5
France	2.8	4.3
Netherlands	3.1	3.3
Norway	3.8	3.7

SOURCE: *Capital International Perspective*, January 1975–January 1979, January 1986. Geneva, Switzerland.

provided by the current price-cash earnings multiplier—a crude measure of the market capitalization rate.[1] These ratios, shown in Table 4, suggest that unless investors in general expect poorer economic performance from countries other than the United States, expected returns abroad are as high or higher than those for the United States.

An alternative approach to estimating expected returns is to consider the implications of varying assumptions regarding domestic and international capital market equilibrium. The primary issue here is whether national markets are viewed as part of an integrated global market or as separate, segmented markets.

Capital market equilibrium and expected returns. If various national markets are completely isolated from each other, returns will be based solely on a domestic risk-return trade-off that reflects the total riskiness of a national portfolio and the risk preferences of domestic investors. In contrast, if capital markets are integrated into a single market, all securities will be priced in terms of their undiversifiable risk

---

[1] Cash earnings are defined by Capital International as reported earnings plus depreciation.

TABLE 5 Required Returns Implied by Alternative Views of World Market
Integration—Based on 1960–1980

| | | Segmented Model | | Integrated Model | |
Country	Realized Compound Return	Standard Deviation	Implied Premium	Beta (World)	Implied Premium
Austria	9.10	16.90	5.63	0.01	0.05
Belgium	9.20	13.80	4.60	0.45	2.46
Denmark	9.50	24.20	8.07	0.60	3.28
France	6.20	21.40	7.13	0.50	2.73
Germany	8.30	19.90	6.63	0.45	2.46
Italy	2.40	27.20	9.07	0.41	2.24
Netherlands	9.30	17.80	5.93	0.90	4.92
Norway	10.30	49.00	16.33	−0.27	−1.48
Spain	8.40	19.80	6.60	0.04	0.22
Sweden	8.40	16.70	5.57	0.51	2.79
Switzerland	10.20	12.50	4.17	0.87	4.75
United Kingdom	10.00	33.60	11.20	1.47	8.03
Hong Kong	24.60	61.30	20.43	2.81	15.35
Japan	15.60	31.40	10.47	0.81	4.43
Singapore	23.20	66.10	22.03	2.59	14.15
Australia	9.80	22.80	7.60	1.02	5.57
Canada	10.70	17.50	5.83	0.77	4.21
United States	10.70	17.70	5.90	1.08	5.90

SOURCE: Computations following approach outlined in Lessard [1976] based on return
and covariance data reported by Ibbotsen, Carr, and Robinson [1982].

from a world perspective. If the capital asset pricing model applies in
this world market, then investors presumably should hold the world
market portfolio. A portfolio restricted to the U.S. market would not
provide the maximum return for a given level of risk, since it implies
bearing diversifiable, and hence uncompensated, risk.

A rough test of the desirability of international diversification under
either extreme scenario—complete segmentation or complete integration—is possible if certain simplifying assumptions are made about the
risk premiums that investors demand per unit of portfolio standard
deviation. In the case of segmented markets, assume that investors in
each country demand the same ratio of risk premium to total standard
deviation (total risk). Table 5 provides estimates of risk premia that
would be required on various national market portfolios under these
two extreme assumptions regarding world capital market equilibrium.
These illustrations are based on standard deviations for the 1960-1980
period, and a risk premium of 5.90 percent is assumed for the United

States. This risk premium corresponds to .5 percent per unit standard deviation, roughly the realized level over long periods of time.

In the case of Germany, for example, with segmented markets the market risk premium needs to be greater than that for the United States (6.63 percent compared with 5.90 percent). This larger premium is necessary to provide the same risk-return ratio as demanded for the United States, since the standard deviation of the German market is greater than that of the U.S. market.[2]

The German risk-return situation changes significantly under the scenario of complete integration. In an integrated world setting, the risk premium for the German market is lower for two reasons. First, the standard deviation of the world market portfolio is less than that for the U.S. market; accordingly, its risk premium must be less (5.46 percent compared with 5.90 percent under our assumptions).[3] Second, the German beta in terms of the world market portfolio is .45. Accordingly, the risk premium is 2.5 percent, $(.45 \times 5.46)$ which is well below the 6.63 percent risk premium under the assumption of complete segmentation.

To contrast the segmentation and integration views, the results can be interpreted as follows. If national stock markets are segmented, an international portfolio will have superior risk-adjusted performance because securities are priced in terms of their domestic systematic risk, some of which is diversifiable. If national markets are integrated, holding a solely domestic portfolio will imply inferior risk-adjusted performance because the securities are priced to reflect only their global systematic risk. Thus, the purely domestic component of risk which is not diversified away will not be offset by any risk premium.

It is unlikely that principal national markets (and major stocks) are either completely segmented or integrated. There are substantial international investment flows and many shares are cross-listed on various exchanges. This fact would appear to ensure that comparative valuation is in terms of both national and international perspectives. Yet total integration does not appear to be the case given the home country bias in the portfolio holdings of virtually all investors. It is most likely that prices are determined in a relatively complex fashion because of the obstacles to international capital flows and because of differences in

---

[2] On the basis of the standard deviation figures from Table 2, the risk premium for the German market based on its total risk would be 6.63 percent.

$$6.63 = \frac{19.9}{17.7} \times 5.9\%$$

[3] The U.S. beta is 1.08 in terms of the world market. Accordingly, the risk premium for the world market is less than that assumed for the U.S. market.

$$\frac{5.90\%}{1.08} = 5.46\%$$

preferences and perceptions by domestic and international investors toward what to them are either local or foreign securities.

OBSTACLES TO INTERNATIONAL INVESTMENT

Currency Risk

The prime motivation for diversifying a portfolio internationally is to improve the reward-to-risk trade-off by taking advantage of the relatively low correlation among returns on assets of different countries. However, since international investment implies investing in assets which provide returns in a variety of currencies whose relative values may fluctuate, it involves taking foreign exchange risks. A key question facing the investor, then, is whether these exchange risks are so large as to offset the benefits of international diversification. A related question is what, if any, special strategies should be followed to reduce the impact of foreign exchange risk. In dealing with these two questions, it is useful to consider why foreign exchange risk is singled out from the host of risks an investor takes when investing internationally.

The first response is simply that it is a new type of risk, at least for most U.S. investors, and therefore deserves special consideration. While undoubtedly true, this response provides little basis for action other than to call for investor education.

A more basic reason is that foreign exchange risk is perceived as a special type of risk which affects some investors but not others and hence does not fit into a normal reward to risk framework. It is a common perception that foreign exchange risks of investing, say, in the United Kingdom, affect U.S. but not U.K., investors. As a result, in contrast to the market risks of securities from a domestic perspective, it may be perceived that these risks will not be accompanied by a commensurate risk premium. If this is true, it has two important implications for passive international investment strategies: (1) investors will want to hedge some or all of the foreign exchange risks implicit in their foreign equity holdings; and (2) investors also may want to shift the weighting of their risky equity asset holdings toward a higher proportion of domestic shares and away from the world market portfolio. If, in contrast, exchange risk affects all investors equally, it will have no special implications for passive portfolio investment strategies.

With active strategies, of course, the existence of fluctuations in exchange rates means that the exchange dimension is a relevant one for making speculative bets. Whether these operations will be limited to outright currency speculation or will involve shifting equity portfolio weights across or within countries will depend on expected relationships between exchange rate and stock price movements.

The appropriate treatment of exchange risk depends on its nature—

FIGURE 2   Inflation, Interest Rates, Premiums, and Exchange Rates

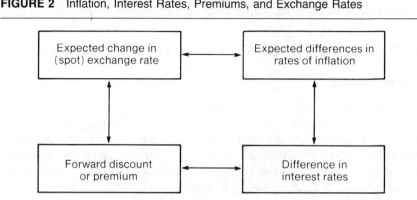

---

whether it is a risk which affects all investors equally or only certain investors—and its magnitude compared to other equity market risks. To understand the nature and importance of currency risk, it is necessary to take into account how exchange rates are related to returns on securities in relatively efficient markets. If security markets function reasonably well, anticipated future trends in exchange rates will be reflected in both interest rates and security prices. There will be uncertainty about these future currency values, but this uncertainty can, to a large extent, be avoided by hedging; that is, borrowing or entering into forward currency contracts. Even if this uncertainty is not hedged, in most cases it will not increase significantly the volatility of foreign common stock returns from the standpoint of a U.S. investor relative to that of a local investor and, in the long run, will not cause the average returns from the two perspectives, if measured in real terms, to diverge.

Linkage between exchange rates, interest rates, and price levels.   The key relationships to be considered are those among expected differences in inflation, differences in interest rates, expected changes in exchange rates, and forward rates. Four key relationships are illustrated in Figure 2. Since these interrelationships are consistent, any three of them determine the fourth. Similarly, if any one of them is violated, at least one other must be violated. Each of these linkages is reviewed below.

Expected changes in (spot) exchange rates and expected differences in rates of inflation.   Theory and empirical evidence suggest that, over time, exchange rates do adjust to reflect relative rates of inflation. Therefore, in an efficient market, anticipations of relative inflation will lead to anticipation of corresponding changes in exchange rates.

Interest rates and expected rates of inflation. This linkage derives from the Fisher effect, which implies that nominal rates of interest in each country adjust to reflect anticipated inflation. As a result, the differences in interest rates will reflect the differences in expected rates of inflation.

Interest rates and the forward premium or discount. For most currencies there are two types of exchange rates: spot rates, which are rates that apply to current transactions; and forward rates, which apply to exchange transactions at a particular point in the future. The foward discount or premium is the percentage difference between the current exchange rate and the forward rate, a rate at which future exchange transactions can be "locked in." The relationship between interest rates and the forward discount or premium rate is very powerful, since it is based on arbitrage. It must match exactly the difference in interest rates or investors will be able to profit without bearing any risk by borrowing in the country with the relatively low-interest rate (including the cost of forward cover), investing in the money market in the country with the high rate, and removing exchange risk by covering in the forward market.

Anticipated exchange rates and forward rates. If forward rates differ from anticipated exchange rates, market participants will be induced to speculate on the difference between them, tending to move the forward rate toward the expected future spot rate.

Implications for the relevance of foreign exchange risks. With all these channels, there is little question that expected changes in exchange rates should be incorporated in interest rates and stock prices in a well-functioning market. In fact, if all these relationships were to hold exactly, anticipated currency fluctuations would be irrelevant for international investment strategies.

Of course, even if anticipated exchange rate changes are fully reflected in interest rates and stock prices, after-the-fact deviations from anticipated rates may have a significant impact on the relative performance of national stock markets.[4] Table 6 illustrates the relative importance of anticipated and realized exchange rate changes and stock market returns in local currency during 1978, a relatively typical year.

---

[4] Of the equilibrium tendencies discussed above, only that between interest rates and forward rates holds ex post. All others are ex ante relationships and realized outcomes are likely to deviate from them even in efficient markets.

TABLE 6 Stock Market Returns and Exchange Rate Changes for 1978 (in percent per year)

Country	Stock Market Return in Local Currency	Anticipated Change in Exchange Rate	Realized Change in Exchange Rate	Total Return in U.S. Dollars
Canada	+24.8	0.0	−7.7	+15.3
France	+44.7	−6.6	+12.7	+63.1
Germany	+4.6	+4.6	+15.8	+21.1
Italy	+34.4	−10.0	+5.1	+41.2
Japan	+21.6	+3.9	+23.5	+50.1
Netherlands	−2.3	+1.0	+15.4	+12.7
Switzerland	−4.3	+5.3	+23.6	+18.3
United Kingdom	+1.6	+0.5	+6.9	+8.6
United States	+0.4	—	—	+0.4

SOURCES: Market returns and realized exchange rate changes from December 31, 1977 to December 31, 1978 as reported in *Capital International Perspective*. Anticipated exchange rate changes are forward premiums/discounts as of January 3, 1978 from Citibank, *Foreign Exchange and International Money Markets*.

Realized exchange rate changes are large relative both to anticipated changes and stock market returns.

The effect of these changes on the relative performance of stock market investments in different countries from the perspective of U.S. investors diversifying abroad and foreign investors purchasing shares in the United States, however, are symmetrical. In 1978, for example, the year-end value of a U.S. investor's holdings of Swiss shares (assuming he or she bought the "market") relative to the amount invested at the start of the year would have been 1.178 times that for the investor's U.S. holdings.[5] But from the Swiss investor's perspective, the relative per-

---

[5] The formula for computing the relative performance of U.S. and Swiss holdings for the U.S. investor is

$$\frac{1 + \$R_{sw}}{1 + \$R_{us}} = \frac{(1 + SfR_{sw})(1 + e)}{1 + \$R_{us}}$$

where $\$R_{sw}$ and $\$R_{us}$ are the U.S. dollar percentage total returns (dividend plus capital gain) on the Swiss and U.S. markets respectively, SfR_{sw} is the total return on the Swiss market in Swiss francs and e is the percentage charge in the value of Swiss francs in terms of U.S. dollars.

$$\frac{.957 \times 1.236}{1.004} = 1.178$$

From a Swiss investors perspective, the formula is restated as

$$\frac{1 + SfR_{sw}}{1 + SfR_{us}} = \frac{1 + SfR_{sw}}{(1 + \$R_{us})(1 + e)}$$

TABLE 7 Stock Market Returns and Exchange Rate Changes for 1985 (in percent per year)

Country	Stock Market Return in Local Currency	Anticipated Change in Exchange Rate	Realized Change in Exchange Rate	Total Return in U.S. Dollars
Canada	19.0	−0.6	−5.7	+12.2
France	39.9	−1.4	+27.6	+78.5
Germany	80.9	+4.0	+27.9	+135.0
Japan	13.4	+3.5	+25.1	+70.2
Netherlands	20.3	+3.7	+28.3	+54.3
Switzerland	61.6	+4.9	+25.3	+100.3
United Kingdom	17.6	−.3	+24.4	+46.3
United States	27.2	—	—	27.2

SOURCES: Market returns and realized exchange rate changes from December 31, 1981 to December 31, 1985 as reported in *Capital International Perspective*. Anticipated exchange rate changes estimated from 12-month Eurodeposits as reported by Morgan Guaranty, *World Financial Markets*.

formance of the two markets would have been the same. With hindsight, both would have preferred Swiss shares. It is precisely this uncertainty about the relative returns in various markets that can be reduced by diversifying across countries.

1985 was an unusual year in this regard as shown in Table 7. The dollar fell drastically while virtually all equity markets were strong. Thus, currency and equity returns were compounded from a U.S. investor's perspective.

Whether the interaction of stock prices and exchange rate changes magnifies the variability of relative returns across countries or not depends on the correlation between exchange rates and stock prices. These correlations in turn depend on a variety of factors including the nature of the currency movement—whether it was anticipated and whether it was in line with realized rates of inflation. They also include the circumstances of the firm in question—its distribution of net monetary balances denominated in various currencies and the exposure of its operating margins to changes in exchange rates. The only case in which

where e is now the percentage change in the value of the U.S. dollar in terms of Swiss francs,

$$\frac{1}{1.236} - 1 \text{ or } -.191$$

$$\frac{.957}{(1.004)(.8091)} = 1.178$$

the U.S. dollar price of foreign shares will move one for one with the value of foreign currencies is when share prices in those currencies are independent from exchange rate changes. This appears unlikely for individual firms, but may be approximately true for an entire stock market.

Managing currency risks. If a manager decides against bearing the risks of fluctuations in a particular currency, several routes are open. It is possible to hedge by borrowing in the currency in question in the same amount as the market value of the equity investment at that time or by entering into forward contracts for an equal amount. Either of these steps will offset the majority of the currency exposure of the equity portfolio.

The expected cost of hedging in the case of borrowing is the difference between the interest differential of the two currencies and the expected percentage change in the exchange rate. The cost of hedging through forward contracts is the difference between the forward discount or premium and the expected percentage change in the exchange rate. Barring controls on capital flows or on access to forward markets, these two costs will be identical through the interest rate parity relationship.

The cost of hedging is often incorrectly defined as the interest differential itself or the forward discount or premium, with no consideration of the expected change in exchange rates. This incorrect definition often leads to statements that hedging is "prohibitively expensive" and rests on the implicit assumption that foreign exchange markets are inefficient and do not reflect anticipations regarding a currency's future. Hedging occasionally is expensive, but substantial research shows that its cost ranges from 0.5 percent to 0.7 percent per year for most major countries.

In addition to hedging currency risks, an active manager may occasionally wish to take a position in a currency to take advantage of a forecast of currency movements that differs from the general market expectation. Again, the alternatives include taking a money market position; that is, borrowing or lending, buying or selling forward exchange, or buying or selling stock. It should be clear, however, that buying shares in a particular country to take advantage of an expected currency appreciation involves assuming substantial additional uncertainty because equity returns are even more volatile than currency changes. If the forecast is limited solely to a currency movement, taking an equity position is an unreasonable strategy. By the same logic, selling equities to avoid a currency risk is also an unreasonable strategy. Forward contracts or borrowing and lending allow the manager to deal with exchange risk much more specifically.

Political or Sovereign Risk

Political or sovereign risk is viewed by many as a major obstacle to international investment. Clearly, political factors are a major determinant of the attractiveness for investment in any country. Countries viewed as likely candidates for internal political upheaval or with a pronounced trend toward elimination of the private capital sector will be unattractive to all investors, foreign and domestic alike; as a result, securities of these countries should be priced accordingly, and little new private real investment will take place. The general question of the impact of political risk on international investment strategies can be broken down into three specific questions: (1) Are political risks properly reflected in securities prices? (2) Do they differ from the perspectives of foreign and domestic investors and, (3) If so, what does this imply about international investment strategies? There is little research relating to any of these questions. Most research on political or sovereign risk focuses on the conflict between host governments and firms with direct investment or on the risk associated with bank loans to developing countries. Little has been directed at portfolio investment.

In judging whether political risks are properly reflected in prices, the only evidence is that relating to the overall efficiency of markets. The evidence suggests that information is reflected rapidly in major markets, and that realized returns, in general, bear a reasonable relationship to the risks taken.

The key consideration is that local investors as well as foreign investors typically are affected by these risks. There is no reason to believe that local investors will be systematically optimistic regarding their country's future. When political risks increase significantly, such investors will attempt to diversify out of the home market as rapidly as will foreigners. As a result, prices will fall until someone will be satisfied to hold the securities of a risky country.

Political risks are principally domestic phenomena that can be substantially diversified away internationally. As a result they will loom much larger to the domestic investor whose portfolio is concentrated in home assets. Accordingly, domestic shares might well be more attractive to foreign than domestic investors in periods of high perceived political risk.

Limited Size and Depth of Foreign Markets

A recurrent objection to international diversification is that the practical scope for foreign investing is limited. Many markets are perceived to be small, less liquid, and less efficient than those of the United States. Some investors question whether foreign markets are large enough and active enough to allow them to accumulate meaningful positions and realize

FIGURE 3 Percentage Breakdown of World Stock Market Capitalization

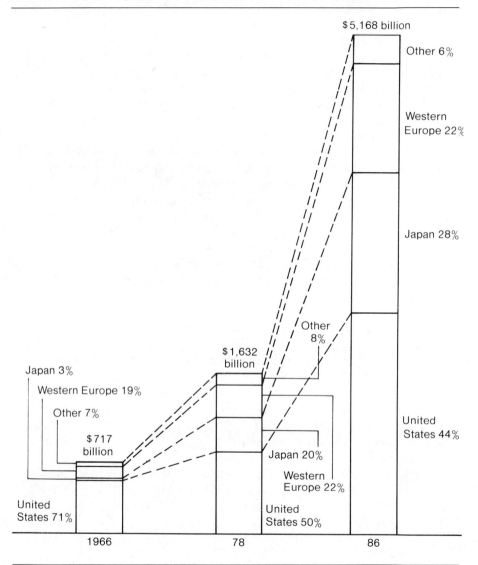

SOURCE: *Capital International Perspective*, March 1976, March 1979, July 1986.

profits from them. The fact is that foreign markets have come of age.
Figures 3 and 4 illustrate the growth of these markets since 1966 in terms
of capitalization and turnover. The growth of the capitalization of
foreign markets is especially striking—increasing from 24 percent of the
world total in 1966 to 56 percent in 1985.

FIGURE 4   Percentage Breakdown of World Share Turnover

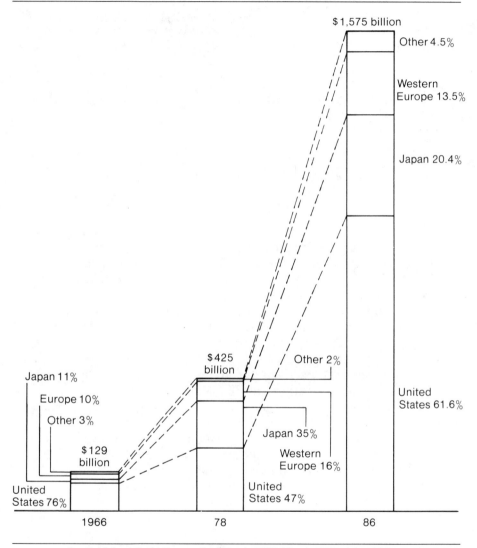

SOURCE: *Capital International Perspective*, March 1976, March 1979, July 1986.

Undoubtedly, there are many foreign stocks whose total capitalization and turnover are too limited for them to be of interest to most U.S. institutional investors. Further, in many markets—particularly the Japanese and German—market capitalizations are often misleading indicators of an issue's marketability because a large proportion of the shares may be owned by banks, holding companies, or other concerns.

TABLE 8 Stock Market Concentration Ratios (1984)

Exchange	Percentage of Total Equity Capitalization Accounted for by 10 Largest Stocks
Amsterdam	77.4
Brussels	50.7
London	26.4
Milan	48.0
Paris	21.2
Germany (all exchanges)	37.8
Zurich	76.0
Japan	17.0
New York	23.9

SOURCE: *Capital International Perspective*, May 1984.

However, these considerations do not imply that these markets are less attractive to foreign institutional investors than to local investors. In fact, just the opposite may be the case. Domestic investors who depend primarily on their own market for liquidity and diversification are likely to be more constrained by these limitations than international investors who, through diversification, can virtually eliminate the nonmarket risk unique to individual companies even if they hold only a small number of shares in each market. They also do not have to rely on any single market for liquidity and, as a result, can take a longer view in regard to each market and security, even though they will wish to realize profits within a reasonable period in each market and currency.

The constraints on diversification within a single market become apparent when one considers the degree of concentration within various markets. As shown in Table 8, a small number of shares account for a major proportion of the value of all shares in most smaller markets, such as Belgium, Netherlands, and Switzerland, as well as in Germany.

Considering that 30 or more issues in about equal proportions are necessary to diversify away most of the specific (nonmarket) risk within a single national market, even a moderate sized domestic fund will find it difficult to achieve a high degree of diversification. This fact implies that domestic investors in such markets will want to hold foreign assets and that a substantial proportion of the shares of the dominant companies should be held by foreigners even if the systematic risk component of returns in the local economy is closely related to the world market index.

Since all shares must be held by someone, investors must be induced to accept the limitations imposed by the thinness and concentration of particular markets. It would appear that many of these limitations will be more severe for domestic than for international investors. As a result, the fact that certain markets are narrow may be a motivation for, rather than an obstacle to, international investment.

Relative Efficiency of Foreign Markets

A closely related concern is that of market efficiency. Although less efficiency may be desirable from an active investment manager's perspective because it implies that superior performance is possible, it may well put the international investor at a disadvantage relative to the domestic investor who has greater knowledge and better information.

The evidence on market efficiency is of three types: (1) direct tests of the randomness of stock price changes, (2) analyses of the relationship between realized returns and risk, and (3) tests of the actual performance achieved by professional managers.

Tests of the random walk hypothesis. Most empirical research has focused on testing for the weak form of efficiency—whether sequences of price changes are related. Researchers have performed extensive tests of the major European markets, and recently these same tests have been extended to the major Asian markets. The studies find that price changes show greater serial correlation in foreign markets than in the U.S. market. However, the magnitude of these departures from randomness typically is not sufficient to yield gains from trading strategies based on past prices.

Tests of the risk return trade-off. Two types of risk-return tests provide some basis for inferring the efficiency of stock markets. One is a test of the extent to which returns on various securities move together and how stable relationships among them are over time. The other is a test as to whether realized returns confirm that over the long run riskier securities provide higher returns.

The stability of betas for individual stocks is a test of the stability of the price relationship between individual issues and the stock market. Studies have found that betas for individual French and German securities were as stable as those for individual U.S. securities.

Regarding the relationship of realized returns to market risks, extensive tests for individual markets show that riskier securities, have in, fact provided higher realized returns. Further, the relationships between risk and return are more consistent when the international systematic risk as well as the purely domestic risk is taken into account. On balance, the risk-return trade-offs appear consistent with modern capital market theory and thus indicate relatively well-functioning markets.

Tests for superior performance. For the most part, performance measurement abroad is substantially less advanced than in the
United States. In part, this is attributable to the difficulty of defining
superior performance in the international context in which most European managers operate.

To be valid, tests of performance must compare portfolio results
with benchmark results for the same universe of securities. If a study
shows that domestically managed funds outperform the market index,
care must be taken to ensure that their performance does not reflect
foreign holdings or domestic securities not included in the benchmark
index. Taking this into account, there appear to be no credible studies
which show consistently superior performance by managed funds in
any major foreign market. Since many European funds contain shares
listed outside of the base country, foreign shares listed on the local
exchange, and bonds, tests of efficiency for any single market are
extremely difficult.

In summary, studies of foreign markets suggest that they generally
can be considered to be efficient in the sense that prices adjust rapidly to
new information and relationships between risk and return are consistent with those predicted by capital market theory. Whether they are
efficient to the extent that most professional managers are unable to
consistently outperform appropriate market benchmarks remains an
open question. However, the results available suggest that the ability to
consistently outperform the market is, at best, uncommon.

Taxes, Restrictions on Ownership, and Other Institutional Obstacles

From time to time there have been several institutional obstacles that
may make international investing costly, undesirable, or, in some cases,
impossible. They include formal barriers to international transactions
such as exchange controls that do not allow investors in one country to
invest overseas or limit overseas investment to a fixed pool, such as
those that were imposed in the United Kingdom through 1981, double
taxation of portfolio income for certain investors in particular countries,[6]
and restrictions on ownership of securities according to the nationality
of the investor. These obstacles also include informal barriers such as the
difficulty of obtaining information about a market, differences in reporting practices that make international comparisons difficult, and, perhaps
most important, subtle impediments to foreign investment based on

---

[6] U.S. pension funds, for example, may have to pay a withholding tax on
income from some foreign countries but have no U.S. tax against which it can be
credited.

traditional practice. Most formal barriers have been relaxed, but tax factors and tradition remain as obstacles.

Many managers resist stepping into uncharted territory and may thus overestimate the risks associated with foreign investment. This resistance is reinforced by the fear that governmental rules (such as ERISA) will penalize managers for investing abroad if things go poorly, simply because such investments represent a departure from traditional practice.

Little research has been conducted on the impact of these institutional and governmental obstacles on either appropriate investment strategies or portfolio performance. One study of U.K. investment trusts found that they benefited little from international diversification and attributed this to the costs imposed by the U.K. foreign investment controls. Whether these costs were necessary or whether they reflected unnecessary trading remains an open question.[7] The U.S. interest equalization tax clearly hindered overseas investment by U.S. individual and institutional investors and, undoubtedly, the difficulty of buying into the Japanese market in the mid-1960s meant that its subsequent performance was academic to most U.S. investors.

A major implication of the existence of such obstacles is that even if one assumes an integrated, efficient world capital market, investors with different legal domiciles or tax situations may want to hold different portfolios. However, it is difficult to determine by how much such optimal portfolios should differ from the world market portfolio. This would depend on the balancing of the effect of the obstacles against the gains from more complete diversification. Several theoretical studies have introduced obstacles into models of capital market equilibrium under restrictive assumptions and shows that investors will not hold the world market portfolio.[8] Instead, investors will hold relatively high proportions of their home market portfolios and will weigh their holdings of foreign assets equally rather than by market values. More research, both in terms of quantifying specific obstacles and ascertaining their impact on capital market equilibrium, is required before optimum international portfolios can be specified for particular investors.

Conclusions Regarding Obstacles to International Investment

When examined closely, many of the obstacles to international investment are less serious than commonly thought. This does not mean that

---

[7] J. R. F. Guy, "An Examination of the Effects of International Diversification from the British Viewpoint on Both Hypothetical and Real Portfolios," *Journal of Finance* (December 1978).

[8] See references to Black (1974), Errunza and Losq (1985) and Stulz (1981a; 1981b; 1985).

there are no difficulties, but it does appear that the advantages of diversification, when properly pursued, outweigh the drawbacks.

Regarding the major specific areas of concern, currency risks do not appear to reduce significantly the gains from broadly based diversification. There is little reason to believe that political risks are systematically ignored by local investors or that they weigh more heavily on foreign investors. Finally, major foreign markets are not as narrow or inefficient as generally may be perceived.

REFERENCES (BY TOPIC)

Correlations of Returns and Gains from International Diversification

BERGSTROM, G. L. "A New Route to Higher Returns and Lower Risk." *Journal of Portfolio Management*, Fall 1975.

———; D. R. LESSARD; J. K. KOENEMAN; and M. J. SIEGEL. "International Securities Markets." In *Handbook of Financial Markets*, ed. F. J. Fabozzi and F. G. Zarb. 2nd ed. Homewood, Ill.: Dow Jones-Irwin, 1986.

CHOLERTON, K., P. PIERAERTS; and B. SOLNIK. "Why Invest in Foreign Currency Bonds?" *Journal of Portfolio Management*, Summer 1986.

EUN, E., and B. RESNICK. "Estimating the Correlation Structure of International Share Prices." *Journal of Finance*, December 1984.

GRUBEL, H. G. "Internationally Diversified Portfolios: Welfare Gains and Capital Flows." *American Economic Review*, December 1968.

LESSARD, D. R. "World, Country, and Industry Relationships in Equity Returns: Implications for Risk Reduction through International Diversification." *The Financial Analysts Journal*, January-February 1976.

LEVY, H., and M. SARNAT. "International Diversification of Investment Portfolios." *American Economic Review*, September 1970.

MALDONADO, R., and A. SAUNDERS. "International Portfolio Diversification and the Inter-temporal Stability of International Stock Market Relationships." *Financial Management* 10 (Autumn 1981).

RIPLEY, D. M. "Systematic Elements in the Linkage of National Stock Market Indices." *Review of Economics and Statistics*, September 1973.

SOLNIK, B. H. "Why Not Diversify Internationally Rather Than Domestically?" *The Financial Analysts Journal*, July-August 1974.

———, and B. NOETZLIN. "Optimal International Asset Allocation." *Journal of Portfolio Management*, Fall 1982.

Pricing of Securities in an International Context

ADLER, M., and B. DUMAS. "International Portfolio Choice and Corporate Finance: A Synthesis." *Journal of Finance*, June 1983.

BLACK, F. "International Capital Market Equilibrium with Investment Barriers." *Journal of Financial Economics* 1, 1974.

ERRUNZA, V., and E. LOSQ. "International Asset Pricing under Mild Segmentation: Theory and Test." *Journal of Finance*, March 1985.

SOLNIK, B. "Equilibrium in an International Capital Market under Uncertainty." *Journal of Economic Theory* 8 (1974).

STULZ, R. M. "On the Effects of Barriers to International Investment." *Journal of Finance*, September 1981a, pp. 923–34.

———. "A Model of International Asset Pricing." *Journal of Financial Economics*, December 1981b, pp. 383–406.

———. "Pricing Capital Assets in an International Setting: An Introduction." In *International Financial Management*, ed. D. Lessard. New York: John Wiley & Sons, 1985.

On Currency Risks

ADLER, M., and B. DUMAS. "International Portfolio Choice and Corporate Finance: A Synthesis." *Journal of Finance*, June 1983.

——— and D. SIMON. "Exchange Risk Surprises in International Portfolios." *Journal of Portfolio Management*, Winter 1986.

CHOLERTON, K., P. PIERAERTS, and B. SOLNIK. "Why Invest in Foreign Currency Bonds?" *Journal of Portfolio Management*, Summer 1986.

CORNELL, B. "Spot Rates, Forward Rates and Exchange Market Efficiency. *Journal of Financial Economics*, December 1977.

GIDDY, I. "An Integrated Theory of Exchange Rate Equilibrium." *Journal of Financial and Quantitative Analysis*, November 1976.

KOHLHAGEN, S. *The Behavior of Foreign Exchange Markets—A Critical Survey of the Empirical Literature*. Monograph no. 3 of the Salomon Brothers Center for Study of Financial Institutions. New York: New York University, 1978.

LEVICH, R. N. "On the Efficiency of Foreign Exchange Markets: Review and Extension." In *International Financial Management*, ed. D. R. Lessard. Boston: Warren, Gorham, and Lamont, 1979.

OLDFIELD, G. C., and D. E. LOGUE. "What's So Special about the Foreign Exchange Market?" *Journal of Portfolio Management*, Spring 1977.

SOLNIK, B. H., and B. NOETZLIN. "Optimal International Asset Allocation." *Journal of Portfolio Management*, Fall 1982.

The Efficiency of Foreign Markets

GUY, J. R. F. "The German Stock Exchange." *Journal of Banking and Finance*, June 1977.

———. "The Performance of the British Investment Trust Industry." *Journal of Finance*, May 1978.

HAWAWINI, G. A. *European Equity Markets: Price Behavior and Efficiency*. Monograph of the Salomon Brothers Center for Study of Financial Institutions. New York: New York University, 1984.

LAU, S. L.; S. T. QUAY; and C. M. RAMSEY. "The Tokyo Stock Exchange and the Capital Asset Pricing Model." *Journal of Finance*, May 1974.

SOLNIK, B. H. "A Note on the Validity of the Random Walk for European Stock Prices." *Journal of Finance*, December 1973.

On the Performance of Internationally-Diversified Portfolios

BRINSON, G. P., and N. FACHLER. "Measuring Non-U.S. Equity Portfolio Performance," *Journal of Portfolio Management*, Spring 1985.

CORNER, D. C., and D. C. STAFFORD. *Open-End Investment Funds in the EEC and Switzerland*. Boulder, Colo.: Westview Press, 1977.

FARBER, A. L. "Performance of Internationally Diversified Mutual Funds." In *International Capital Markets*, ed. E. J. Elton and M. H. Gruber. New York: American Elsevier, 1975.

GUY, J. R. F. "An Examination of the Effects of International Diversification from the British Viewpoint on Both Hypothetical and Real Portfolios." *Journal of Finance*, December 1978.

McDONALD, J. B. "French Mutual Fund Performance: Evaluation of Internationally Diversified Portfolios." *Journal of Finance*, December 1973.

PART 5

Fixed Income Investing

27

Industrial Bond Analysis

Roy P. Weinberger
Managing Director
Industrial Corporations
Public Utilities
Standard & Poor's Corporation

Credit analysis of industrial corporations has always been challenging to practitioners, importantly reflecting the diversity of industries represented in this classification, plus the widely different operational and financial profiles of participants even in the same industry. Instability wrought by the rapid internationalization of an increasing number of industrial markets, by the unexpected and substantial easing of inflationary pressures, and by widespread management concern that shareholders receive "value" for their investments has made this test of analytical acumen even more difficult.

Debt ratings have over the years achieved wide investor acceptance as easily usable tools with which to differentiate credit quality and make investment decisions. In order to retain that utility in an environment of seemingly constant change and where bond portfolios are increasingly under active management, debt rating organizations have supplemented their traditional rating symbols with watch lists and rating outlook commentaries. (See Chapter 35 for rating definitions, watch list criteria, and rating outlook explanation.)

The quality of opinions contained in these informational enhancements are only as good as the methods and processes in place to handle

The author wishes to acknowledge the contributions made to this article by members of Standard & Poor's industrial debt rating group: Joe Hynes and Bill Wetreich for their respective work on paper producers and packaged food companies, and Mark Bachmann for his work on cash flow analysis.

TABLE 1 Rating Methodology Profile

Business Risk	Financial Risk
Industry characteristics	Financial characteristics
Issuer position:	
For example:	
Technology	Financial policy
Marketing	Profitability
Efficiency	Capital structure
Management	Cash flow protection
Composite: Competitive	
position	Financial flexibility

---

information and convert it into analytical judgments. Credibility of ratings, in the minds of users of that analysis, is fundamentally tied to the accuracy, consistency, and timeliness of those judgments. Rating firms can address the first two of these critical issues by establishing and enforcing an appropriate framework for analysis. Timeliness of action and communication can also be encouraged by systems and structures, but success in this area is ultimately reliant on organizational values and strategies.

At Standard & Poor's the analytical framework is embodied in a tool labeled the rating methodology profile (RAMP). As shown in Table 1, the RAMP is divided into two parts—business risk and financial risk. In reality though there is no real separability of the RAMP's variables; they are all interdependent. It is critical to understand that the rating process is not limited to the examination of various financial measures. Proper assessment of current and future debt protection levels requires that financial statement analysis be performed within a broader framework. This involves a thorough review of the industries or business segments in which a company participates, a judgment as to the company's competitive position within that industry, and an evaluation of management.

INDUSTRY CHARACTERISTICS

Industries are analyzed with respect to the following factors:

1. Profitability—growth and stability.
2. Ability to control investment in the asset base.
3. Nature and mix of assets.
4. Protective structural considerations.

(Refer to Appendix 1 for a more detailed outline.)

TABLE 2 Industry Characteristics

Risk Scale:
  Much worse than average.
  Somewhat worse than average.
  Average.
  Somewhat better than average.
  Much better than average.
Packaged food and beverage:
  Overall assessment—much better than average risk:
    Recession-resistant.
    Mature.
    Highly predictable earnings and cash flow.
    Highly competitive.
    Favorable cost structure.
    Modest capital requirements.
Pulp and paper:
  Overall assessment—average to somewhat better than average risk:
    Long-term demand growth.
    Mature.
    Cyclical earnings and cash flows.
    Defensible international competitive position.
    Limited vulnerability to technological change.
    High operating leverage/capital intensity.

Table 2 illustrates the conclusions drawn from this analysis for two industries—packaged food and beverage, and pulp and paper.

One goal of this analysis is to establish financial performance expectations for industry participants at various rating levels. For industries with no significant degree of earnings cyclicality, the expectations deal with a pattern of performance over a period of time. For industries in which earnings are expected to be cyclical or volatile, an attempt is made to identify ratios (i.e., debt to capital) which should remain relatively less volatile.

It is also important to establish what the key ratios are for each industry in determining the performance expectations, with particular emphasis on those which may be "leading indicators" of changes in credit quality.

Industry analysis is performed by appropriate groups of analysts on a periodic basis (i.e., once or twice a year) independent of actual rating assignments.

ISSUER POSITION

For each industry, analysts determine the key factors to be analyzed in evaluating industry participants. These factors are identified and peri-

TABLE 3 Key Rating Factors for Packaged Food and Beverage Companies

Product portfolio:
  Brand franchise strength.
  Maturity.
  Value added content.
  Competitive environment.
  Diversification.
Marketing capability:
  New product program/R&D capability.
  Marketing and advertising effort.
  Critical mass.
	Cost efficiency:
	  Raw material sourcing.
	  Modern plant and adequate capacity.
	  Efficient distribution and sales channels.
	Strategic management:
	  Growth objectives.
	  Commitments and results.
	Nonfood and international:
	  Foreign risk v. returns.
	  Issuer position and industry.
	  Characteristics of nonfood business.

odically confirmed as part of the industry analysis process outlined above. The factors include the "keys to success" for participants in the industry, as well as important "areas of vulnerability."

In performing rating analysis on any company, the analyst evaluates the company on each of the keys to success and areas of vulnerability which have been identified for that industry. The evaluation is done within the context of the particular industry.

In addition, for any particular company, the list of key factors may include one or more factors of special significance for that particular company, even if that factor(s) is not common to the industry. For example, the fact that a company had only one major production facility should certainly be included as an area of vulnerability, even if that was not a key factor for the industry as a whole.

Tables 3 and 4 illustrate the key rating factors established for two major industries, packaged food and beverage companies and pulp and paper producers. While some overlap exists, it should be clear that the industry analysts have expended considerable efforts to tailor the analytical framework and focus the competitive evaluation on the issues that matter.

To summarize, as displayed in Table 5, we now have the structural characteristics, which tell us something about the competitive environment of the industry we're looking at. We've also gained insights as to what factors to stress in analyzing a participant in that industry. Putting these together we should have the ability to make a judgment about the business risk a company faces. As with the evaluation of industry characteristics each company's business risk can be qualitatively evalu-

TABLE 4 Key Rating Factors for Pulp and Paper Producers

The weighted importance of these variables is determined by predominant product lines.
Cost position:
  Low-cost status:
    Operating margins.
    Return on assets.
    Mill margins.
    Mill cash cost/ton.
    Mill cost/ton.
    Labor-hours/ton.
  Modern efficient asset base:
    Capital expenditures percent of net fixed assets over last 10 years.
    Repair and maintenance expenditures as percent of net fixed assets over
      last 10 years.
    Capex/inflation adjusted depreciation.
    Are facilities "built-out"—is there room for additions?
    Are facilities integrated (on-site pulping)?
    Are machines new, in good running order?
    Mill site configuration and layout.
    Process control and computer utilization.
  Mill location:
    Closeness to growth/Sun Belt markets.
    Closeness to major metropolitan regions.
    Closeness to deep seaports for export.
    Freight advantages.
    Harvest costs.
  Labor relations:
    Union versus nonunion mills.
    History of labor disruptions.
    Advantageous wage rates and work rule flexibility.
    Union contracts on the horizon and how contracts are spread out.
Customer satisfaction:
  Quality, service, customer loyalty:
    Brightness, opacity, strength, runability, printability.
    Independent surveys.
    Evaluations by commercial printers and publishers, and customers.
    Capacity utilization. (Although not a pure indicator of quality, service, or
      customer loyalty, it does provide some directional insight.)
Product mix:
  Value-added versus commodity grades.
  Sales revenue/ton.
  Diversity of mix.
  Breadth of products, full-line, one-source supplier.
  Consumer versus nonconsumer end markets.
  Relative pricing sensitivity in key grades.
Self-sufficiency:
  Fiber self-sufficiency and long-term adequacy:
    Fiber sources— internal sources versus long-term private cutting contracts
      versus government contracts versus outside/market purchases.

TABLE 4 *(concluded)*

Fiber mix—softwood versus hardwood versus recycled paper.
Reforestation programs.
Energy mix and self-sufficiency:
  Fuel mix—internal sources versus oil versus coal versus gas.
  Cogeneration, hydropower.
  Ability to quickly convert or swing to alternative energy source

Marketing prowess:
  Gain or loss of market share.
  Distribution channels.
  Advertising cost/sales.
  New product introductions.
  Degree of influence on pricing.
  Forward integration:
  Percent of in-house paper used by converting facilities.
  Wholesale and retail distribution centers.

Management strategy/execution:
  Senior management leadership and vision.
  Planning skills.
  Quality of operating managers, ability to implement plans.
  Skill at acquiring, or building capacity, at an advantageous level of investment.

---

ated as being much worse than average, somewhat worse than average, average, somewhat better than average, or much better than average.

Finally, based on the level and nature of business risk faced by a company, and with the basic financial characteristics normally displayed by a company in its industry as a reference point, we form the last link in the chain, our financial expectations. This represents the financial

---

TABLE 5

Industry: Structural Considerations

Competitive Environment

Company's Situation

Financial Expectations

TABLE 6 Food and Beverage Industry: Financial Analysis—General Guidelines for Debt Leverage Ratios*

Rating Category	Well-Above Average	Above Average	Average	Industrial Medians
	Business Risk Profile†			
BBB	60%	55%	50%	45%
A	50	45	40	30
AA	40	35	30	25
AAA	30	25	n.a.	15

Note: Debt leverage = Total debt as percent of capitalization.
n.a. = Not applicable.
* For major industry participants.
† Designations refer to peer comparisons.

position and performance we will expect from the company in order to rate its debt at any particular level.

Returning to the industry examples we have been using, and referring to Table 6, we can see where our business risk evaluation process has led us. Focusing for simplicity on just one, but very important, financial measure we can observe that expectations regarding appropriate debt leverage are considerably less stringent at all rating levels for major participants in industries such as packaged food and beverage, viewed as having much better than average industry characteristics. Pulp and paper producers evaluated as having average business risk profiles would, by comparison, be expected to maintain debt leverage much closer to the industrial ratio medians in order to achieve the same rating.

MANAGEMENT

Assessment of a company's management focuses on:

1. The financial record as a reflection of management's success or failure.
2. Conservatism or aggressiveness with respect to financial risk.
3. Organizational considerations.

According to many annual reports, corporate managements are innocent victims of "depressed" market conditions, "volatile" interest rates, or "irresponsible" competition. Yet in the final analysis management can and should be held fully responsible for the corporation's results. This is because at some point management made all the basic decisions as to what business to be in, chose competitive strategies, and determined how the business should be financed. Successful companies are constantly rethinking these issues. So an important focus of S&P's evaluation is an assessment of management's sensitivity and responsiveness to change.

In the short run, of course, it is important to know whether to attribute specific results—both financial and qualitative—to management. S&P must decide to what extent they are the result of good management, devoid of management influence, or achieved despite management.

As a corollary, one of the basic principles of S&P's management evaluation is that stated intentions can rarely substitute for past performance. It is not unusual when even the most sophisticated and well-thought-out plans are not executed successfully.

S&P's evaluation is sensitive to various potentials for problems. These include situations where:

1. There is substantial organizational reliance on an individual chief executive or financial officer, especially one who may be close to retirement.
2. The finance function and finance considerations do not receive high organizational recognition.
3. The transition of management to professional and organizational from entrepreneurial or family-bound remains to be accomplished.
4. A relatively large number of changes occur in a short time.
5. The relationship between organizational structure and management strategy is unclear.
6. A substantial presence by one or a few shareholders exists, providing stability of ownership or constraints on management prerogatives. Depending on circumstances, this could have either positive or negative implications.

ACCOUNTING QUALITY

A rating is not an audit, and the rating process does not entail auditing a company's financial records. Ratings are based on audited data, generally for a five-year period. Analysis of the audited financials begins by reviewing the accounting quality to determine whether ratios and statistics derived from financial statements can be accurately used to measure a company's performance and position relative to both its competition and the larger universe of industrial companies. The rating business is very much one of comparisons, so it is important to have a common frame of reference.

Accounting policies reviewed include, among other things:
1. Consolidation basis.
2. Income recognition (for example, successful efforts versus full

cost in the oil industry and percentage of completion versus completed contract in the construction industry).
3. Depreciation methods and asset lives.
4. Inventory pricing methods.
5. Amortization of intangibles.
6. Employee benefits.

Although it is not always possible to recast a company's financial statements to best reflect reality—or even to be totally comparable—it is useful to have some notion of the extent to which performance is overstated or understated. At the very least, the choice of accounting alternatives can be characterized as generally conservative or liberal.

PROFITABILITY

This category actually encompasses two analytical areas. First, a company's earning power is, in the long run, the most important determinant of credit protection, and history provides some insight into potential performance under varying conditions. Second, earnings are viewed in relation to a company's burden of fixed charges. Strong performers can score poorly in this latter evaluation through aggressive debt financing, and the opposite is also true. In both respects, S&P appraises how financially healthy the company is from an operating viewpoint, inasmuch as a corporation is viewed as an ongoing enterprise rather than as one being liquidated.

The more significant measures of profitability that S&P uses are:
1. Returns on capital.
2. Profit margins.
3. Earnings on assets/business segments.
4. Inflation-adjusted earnings.
   (Refer to Appendix 2 for a glossary and formulas for basic ratios.)

Pretax return on average invested capital and operating income as a percentage of sales are ratios that indicate a company's financial health regardless of how it is capitalized. Obviously, all else being equal, a company that generates higher operating margins and returns on capital has a greater ability to generate equity capital internally, attract capital externally, and withstand business adversity. Earnings power, ultimately, is what attests to the value of the firm's assets.

While the absolute levels of the ratios are important, it is equally important to focus on trends and the comparison of a ratio to that of competitors. Various industries follow different cycles and have different earnings characteristics. Therefore, what may be considered favorable for one business may be relatively poor for another. For example, the drug industry usually generates high-operating margins and high returns on capital. The construction industry generates low-operating margins and high returns on capital. The pipeline industry has high-operating margins and low returns on capital. Comparisons to a company's peers will influence S&P's perception of a firm's competitive strengths and pricing leadership/flexibility.

There are several fixed charge coverage ratios that S&P evaluates, but the two primary ones are pretax interest coverage and pretax coverage of interest and total rents. If preferred stock is outstanding and material, fixed charges are adjusted to include preferred dividends. To reflect more accurately the ongoing earnings available to pay fixed charges, the reported figures are typically adjusted. The effect of unremitted equity is excluded, as well as those of nonrecurring or extraordinary gains and losses. Similarly, S&P is interested in coverage of interest incurred, and adjustments are made where interest has been capitalized.

The analysis of earnings protection and the other financial categories evaluates both historical and projected performance. Because ratings are an assessment of the likelihood of timely payment of interest and future repayment of principal, the evaluation emphasizes future performance. The rating analysis does not attempt to forecast performance precisely by making extremely specific economic assumptions. Rather, the forecast analysis emphasizes the variability of expected future performance based on a range of economic scenarios.

Particularly important are management expectations for sources of future earnings growth. S&P evaluates whether existing businesses can provide satisfactory growth, particularly in a less inflationary environment, and to what extent acquisitions or divestitures may be necessary to achieve corporate goals. S&P assumes a corporation's central focus is to augment shareholder values over the long run. Thus, a lack of indicated earnings growth over a long period, rather than on a year-to-year basis, is considered a weakness. On its own, this may hinder a company's ability to attract financial and human resources. Equally important, limited earnings growth opportunities may lead management to seek them externally, leading to additional business and financial risks. Thus, demonstrated success in managing earnings growth through internal and external sources is viewed as a credit strength.

CAPITAL STRUCTURE

Financial leverage, simply put, is the extent to which a firm uses other parties' funds or capital to finance itself. It directly reflects the relation of liabilities to equity. As an indicator of financial risk, the general concept is straightforward: the more leveraged a company is, the less able it is to pay off its borrowed funds. This is because it is less able to withstand diminution in asset values or cash flows than a company with lower leverage. In a sense, the notion of leverage is used to indicate the burden of fixed charges a company must service.

In another vein, the concept of asset protection refers to measurement of the relative amount of equity supporting the asset base. A variation on this theme is asset protection relative to outstanding debt. Here focus tends more toward viewing the company on a liquidating basis rather than as an ongoing concern. Since ratings address primarily the risk of default and only secondarily whether or not a creditor ultimately will be paid off, S&P's view of leverage is principally of it being a proxy for the level of fixed charges that must be serviced rather than as a measure of asset protection provided. Nonetheless, the nature of the assets is a critical determinant of the appropriate leverage for a given level of risk. Assets with stable values that are liquid justify greater use of debt financing than those with clouded marketability. In this context, trade receivables, grain and tobacco inventory, proven oil reserves and even stand-alone business entities would be viewed positively relative to assets that might be concentrated in, say, fixed plant and equipment.

Several ratios are used by S&P to capture the degree of leverage utilized by a company. They include:

1. Long-term debt/capitalization.
2. Total debt/capitalization + short-term debt.
3. Total debt + off-balance-sheet liabilities/capitalization + short-term debt + off-balance-sheet liabilities.

The traditional measure of long-term debt/capitalization is losing its significance as a measure of permanent debt leverage, as companies rely increasingly on short-term borrowings. It is now common to find permanent layers of short-term debt, which finance not only seasonal working capital but an ongoing portion of the asset base. Off-balance-sheet items that are factored into the leverage analysis include:

1. Operating leases.
2. Debt of joint ventures and unconsolidated subsidiaries.
3. Guarantees.
4. Take-or-pay contracts and obligations under throughput and deficiency agreements.
5. Receivables that have been factored or transferred.

S&P uses various methodologies to determine the proper capitalized value for each of the off-balance-sheet items. In general, the relevance of the activity financed to the mainstream business of the organization and the likelihood of its need for financial support are key considerations. Thus, debt of joint ventures which are sound, stand-alone credits may be viewed as a much less onerous liability than capitalized operating rents.

The key to meaningful analytical results is, of course, knowing the true values to assign a company's assets, hence its equity base. Yet, S&P does not purport to perform asset appraisals as the basis for its ratings. S&P's analysis of asset protection attempts to highlight materially undervalued or overvalued assets relative to book value so that leverage can be viewed in an alternate light. Examples include inventories, natural resource assets, and intangible assets. When intangible assets are material in size, S&P assesses whether earnings support the value of this goodwill before determining whether to regard it at full value. In fact, the value of all corporate assets is ultimately measured by their long-term earnings power.

Beyond numerical analysis, S&P emphasizes the importance of examining management's philosophies and intentions toward leverage. Although it might appear that each corporation has set goals in this area, that is not the case. A surprising number of companies have not given this question serious thought, much less reached firm conclusions. And some of those that have set goals do not have the wherewithal, discipline, or management commitment to achieve them. A company's leverage goals, then, need to be viewed in the context of past performance, the financial dynamics affecting the business, its current leverage position, and management's commitment. For example, if a management states that its goal is to operate at 35 percent debt to capital, S&P factors that into its analysis to the extent it appears plausible, attainable, and supported by the record. However, if a company has aggressive spending plans, mediocre profitability and faint hope of selling equity, that 35 percent would carry little weight.

CASH FLOW PROTECTION

Earnings may be the best long-term determinant of creditworthiness, but when an interest or principal payment date arrives, earnings is not what matters. Because the obligation can't be serviced out of earnings, the payment has to be made with cash. Thus, cash flow analysis is critical in all credit-rating decisions, and has taken on added importance as the debt market has been increasingly populated by highly leveraged, speculative grade issues. Companies with investment grade ratings generally have ready access to external cash to cover temporary shortfalls. Junk bond issuers lack this degree of flexibility and have fewer alternatives to internally generated cash for servicing debt.

Although there is usually a strong relationship between cash flow and reported earnings, many transactions and accounting entries affect one and not the other. Hence, analysis of cash flow patterns can reveal

TABLE 7 Cash Flow Summary Analysis: Palm Beach, Inc. (in $ millions)

	1984	1983	1982	1981	1980
Working capital from operations (FFO)	18.58	22.34	16.78	21.68	19.10
Decrease (increase) in noncash current assets	(33.12)	1.05	25.13	(23.07)	(41.68)
Increase (decrease) in nondebt current liabilities	15.07	(12.61)	(10.49)	4.12	11.13
Net decrease (increase) in working capital	(18.05)	(11.56)	14.64	(18.95)	(30.55)
Operating cash flow	0.53	10.78	31.42	2.73	(11.45)
Capital expenditures	(11.06)	(9.74)	(6.18)	(7.41)	(8.58)
Free operating cash flow	(10.53)	1.04	25.24	(4.68)	(20.03)
Cash dividends	(4.45)	(5.14)	(5.56)	(5.56)	(5.56)
Discretionary cash flow	(14.98)	(4.10)	19.68	(10.24)	(25.59)
Acquisitions	0.00	0.00	0.00	0.00	0.00
Asset disposals	0.73	0.23	0.00	0.00	0.00
Net other sources (uses) of cash	(0.44)	(0.09)	1.11	0.62	0.88
Prefinancing cash flow	(14.69)	(3.96)	20.79	(9.62)	(24.71)
Increase (decrease) in short-term debt	3.00	0.00	(44.00)	14.60	25.40
Increase (decrease) in long-term debt	6.12	13.02	31.05	(1.13)	(0.82)
Net sale (repurchase) of equity	0.32	(7.07)	(5.52)	0.00	0.00
Decrease (increase) in cash and securities	5.25	(1.99)	(2.32)	(3.85)	0.13

a level of debt-servicing capability that is either stronger or weaker than might be apparent from earnings.

How cash flow data are interpreted depends on a company's asset mix, growth rate, strategic policies, and other factors. There is no simple correlation between creditworthiness and the level of current cash flow. A company serving a low-growth or declining market may exhibit relatively strong cash flow due to minimal fixed and working capital needs. Growth companies, in comparison, often exhibit thin or even negative cash flow because of investments to support growth. For the low-growth company, credit analysis weighs the positives of strong current cash flow against the danger that this high level of protection might not be sustainable. For the high-growth company, the problem is just the opposite: weighing the negatives of a current cash deficit against prospects of enhanced protection once current investment begins yielding cash benefits.

In the case of Palm Beach Inc., an apparel company with subordinated debt rated B− (see Table 7), profitability has been solid during the past five years, but operating cash flow has been thin and, in 1984, barely above breakeven. The key problem has been steadily increasing investment in working capital, a major cash consumer. Subtracting capital expenditures, the level of free operating cash flow has been negative in three of the last five years and sharply negative in 1984. This pattern is of concern because the company's sales volume has declined annually since 1981. The combination of negative cash flow and declining sales could indicate the company's inability to control cash costs being capitalized in inventory. The apparently adequate level of reported earnings might simply reflect accrual accounting "magic" that masks inability to generate cash or cover debt service obligations without increased reliance on debt.

S&P's analysis puts more emphasis on speculative grade credits' short-term cash flow prospects than on those of stronger companies. Weaker companies often face volatile business environments and have a greater tendency toward major asset shifts and financial restructuring. Hence, their financial records rarely are reliable indicators of the future. Evaluation of cash flow capability must rely more heavily than usual on subjective judgments about near-term market conditions, capital spending plans, cost-cutting programs, and other factors affecting the cash budget.

Financial disclosure guidelines governing cash flow reporting are too broad to force a clear presentation of the data. The statement of changes in financial position, or "funds flow" statement, addresses the cash flow issue, but is an awkward tool. Not only do companies use a variety of conflicting formats, but many reports reconcile to working capital rather than cash. Nonetheless, by examining this statement and the balance sheet, it is possible to construct an approximation of the major elements of a company's cash flow picture that also facilitates comparative analysis among companies.

Table 7 illustrates the cash flow analysis format used by S&P. At the top is the item from the funds flow statement usually labeled *funds from operations* or *working capital from operations*. This quantity is net income adjusted for depreciation and other noncash debits and credits that have been factored into it. Subtract the net increase in working capital investment to arrive at *operating cash flow*. Next, *capital expenditures* and *cash dividends*, respectively, are backed out to arrive at *free operating cash flow* and *discretionary cash flow*. Finally, the cost of acquisitions is subtracted from the running total, proceeds from asset disposals added, and other miscellaneous sources and uses of cash netted together. *Prefinancing cash flow* is the end result of these computations, which represents the extent to which the company's cash flow from all internal sources has been sufficient to cover all of its internal needs.

The bottom part of the table reconciles prefinancing cash flow to the various categories of external financing and to changes in the company's own cash balance. In the example, Palm Beach experienced a $14.7 million cash shortfall in 1984, which had to be met with a combination of additional borrowings and a drawdown of its own cash.

FINANCIAL FLEXIBILITY

This category may be defined as an evaluation of a company's financing needs, plans and alternatives, and its flexibility to accomplish its business objectives without damaging creditworthiness. It addresses a company's potential sources and uses of funds, such as divestitures and acquisitions beyond what is generated from, or employed in, ongoing operations. Also, this category recognizes a company's relative vulnerability to the vagaries of the capital markets. Benefits or detriments derived from a company's affiliation with other entities—for example, a parent company—are considered at this point as well.

Volatile financial markets in recent years have prompted many previously infrequent borrowers to divide their financing needs into several pieces and accept the average cost. It is risky for a growing company to hold out for the absolutely lowest interest rate. Likewise, prefinancing is viewed more favorably than gambling on the price and availability of funds during the quarter when they will be required. Financial flexibility may be seriously jeopardized when a firm accumulates bank borrowings and commercial paper with the hope of funding out when market conditions improve.

A firm's access to various capital markets can augment financial flexibility. A company's experience with different financial instruments and capital markets gives management alternatives if conditions in a particular financial market suddenly turn sour. The size of a company and its financing needs can play a role in whether it can raise funds in the public debt markets.

Access to the common stock market is primarily a question of management's willingness to accept dilution of earnings per share, rather than whether funds are available. When a new common stock offering is projected as part of a company's financing plan, S&P tries to measure management's commitment to this financing vehicle, even at unattractive prices. The judgment is based on past financing practices and S&P's understanding of management's operating and financial strategies. A history of equity offerings and a favorable stock price trend lend credibility to a projected stock sale.

Regardless of a company's degree of financial leverage, an imbalance within the debt or equity components can detract from financial flexibility. Reliance on short-term money or interest-sensitive, longer maturity funds creates obvious risks. However, the use of short-term borrowing to finance a seasonal bulge in receivables or inventory or to finance foreign operations in a local currency for which no long-term funds are available would not be viewed unfavorably. An imbalanced capital structure might also be caused by an unusually short maturity schedule for long-term debt and limited-life preferred stock. Of course, there is no problem if maturing obligations—and all other cash requirements—clearly will be financed with internally generated funds. But a growing business typically refunds maturing long-term debt with new long-term debt. S&P generally assumes that limited-life preferred stock also will be refunded with long-term debt rather than new preferred, unless there is reason to believe that the company's aftertax cost of preferred stock always will be no more expensive than debt.

A company's ability to generate cash through asset disposals may enhance its financial flexibility. Potential asset disposals will be considered to provide added flexibility only if S&P believes they can be accomplished under terms acceptable to the company. Management's stated intention to sell certain assets is not enough. S&P must be mindful of market conditions as well. All firms are viewed as going concerns and S&P does not normally expect a company to repay debt by liquidating operations. It is not considered a strength if a company proposes to sell a business integral to its other operations. There is little benefit in selling natural resource properties or excess manufacturing facilities if these must be replaced in a few years.

A firm's financial flexibility may be considered impaired by the expectation that the company will make a sizable acquisition requiring external financing. Management's stated acquisition goals and past bids that were not consummated provide clues for estimating future actions. Additionally, management's growth objectives, the likelihood that existing operations will meet those objectives and the company's debt leverage tolerance level are analyzed.

S&P's standard ratios of financial leverage and asset protection incorporate certain off-balance sheet liabilities, such as lease commitments and production payments, which can be readily measured. There are other potential liabilities, however, that cannot easily be quantified but which may profoundly affect many aspects of a company's operations and finances. Pension obligations and serious legal problems are two of the most prominent and slippery risk areas that the analyst confronts.

Apart from the question of how to value unfunded pension obligations on a company's balance sheet, there are other immediate implications. One occurs when a pension burden hinders a company's ability to sell assets because a potential buyer is reluctant to assume the liability. This off-balance sheet item also has played a pivotal role in discouraging some managements from closing excess, inefficient, and costly manufacturing facilities. Such a closing may require the immediate recognition of future pension obligations and result in a substantial charge to equity. Despite what management does in this situation, the firm's financial flexibility is impaired.

A company's expected earnings protection and cash flow adequacy can be adjusted for the cash costs of resolving a major lawsuit against the firm. A complex web of suits, countersuits, and insurance protection, as well as the uncertainty inherent in all litigation, often requires the analyst to use a range of estimated costs. The intangible costs, however, must also be reflected qualitatively in S&P's assessment of a firm's financial flexibility. Disputes with suppliers or customers can have a long-term effect on a company's competitive position. Similarly, a well-publicized product failure may cost a company far more in lost sales than the payment to the injured individual. A potential liability so large that it seems to threaten a firm's solvency—such as recently faced by Texaco—often will limit the company's access to capital, at least temporarily.

INDENTURE PROVISIONS AND LOAN COVENANTS

The indenture spells out in rather lengthy detail the rights and obligations of the lender and borrower. In many instances, it restricts the borrower from paying dividends or incurring certain types of borrowings unless specified levels of retained earnings, working capital, or debt in relation to assets are maintained. In reality the typical industrial indenture provides extremely limited protection to creditors, inasmuch as short-term borrowings are usually not restricted, and creative financial management will inevitably find a "solution" to an indenture problem. Therefore, a pragmatic approach should be taken when analyzing the value of indenture provisions. The key question is how likely is it that the borrower will be able or willing to operate within the constraints of the indenture? Indentures or loan covenants which are so tight that they are likely to be violated with the slightest of deviations from expectations are no source of comfort. To avoid violation, management may well be forced operate the business in a manner which hurts its long-term competitiveness. If covenants are breached, control over key decisions may effectively be transferred to the lender group, a development which typically bodes ill for a corporation's viability.

APPENDIX 1 _____

Profitability

Demand

1. Nature of markets.
2. Impact of economy—key indicators.
3. Size of market.
4. Growth.
5. Cyclicality.
6. Price sensitivity.
7. Importance of contracts.
8. Regional or international factors.
9. Current status and one- to two-year outlook.
10. Longer range outlook.

Supply

1. Nature of products—commodity or differentiated.
2. Nature of industry—concentrated or fragmented, current players, nonprofit motivated, or government-supported competition.
3. Industry capacity—utilization, growth prospects.
4. Ease of entry and exit—basis for entry, frequency of new entrants, legislative or regulatory barriers, potential new entrants.
5. Basis of competition—price, marketing, company size, new product introductions, R&D, product performance, low cost.
6. Reserve base.
7. Access to raw materials, energy, labor.
8. Political risk—domestic or foreign.
9. Import competition or barriers.
10. Current status and one- to two-year outlook.
11. Longer-range outlook.

Prices

1. Basis of pricing—commodity, product performance, differentiation, price leadership, marketing network, contract.
2. Impact of cartels, controls, supports, regulation.
3. Domestic or international pricing basis.
4. Volatility.
5. Current status and near-term outlook.
6. Longer-range outlook.

Costs

1. Fixed versus variable cost concentration—sensitivity to volume.

2. Labor—union, nonunion, contracts, pensions.
3. Raw materials—availability, contracts, project financings.
4. Energy.
5. Quality of reserves.
6. Age of facilities.
7. Efficiency of operation—ability to control costs.
8. Transportation—closeness to markets.
9. Regulation, legislation.
10. Taxes.
11. Current status and near-term outlook.
12. Longer-range outlook.

Ability to Control Investment in Asset Base

1. Fixed versus working capital intensity.
2. Capital spending requirements—growth, maintenance, flexibility in timing, environmental and safety requirements, new technology, impact of inflation, ease of starting and stopping, ability to delay.
3. Ability/need to shut down facilities—age of facilities, relative profitability, labor cost impact.
4. Potential for fixed asset-based financing—recourse, nonrecourse.
5. Ability to control growth in inventories and receivables—turnover analysis, use of captive finance company, sales to dealers, ability/willingness of customers, dealers and distributors to self-finance purchases or to carry inventories.
6. Seasonal patterns.
7. Potential for working capital asset-based financing and/or third-party sales agreements.

Nature and Mix of Assets

1. Market value versus book value.
2. Asset classes.
3. Working capital turnover.
4. Marketability.
5. Liquidity.

Protective Structural Considerations

1. Regulation.
2. Monopolistic—oligopolistic conditions.
3. Profit motive.

APPENDIX 2

Glossary

Balances for Pretax Returns & Coverages. Net income from continuing operations before (1) special items, (2) minority interest, (3) gains on reacquisition of debt, plus income taxes plus interest expense.

Equity. Shareholders' equity, plus minority interest, plus deferred investment tax credits.

Gross Interest. Gross interest accrued before (1) capitalized interest, and (2) interest income.

Gross Rent Expense. Gross operating rents paid before sublease income.

Long-Term Debt. As reported, including capitalized lease obligations on the balance sheet.

Operating Income. Sales minus cost of goods manufactured (before depreciation), selling, general and administrative, and research and development costs.

Total Debt. Long-term, current maturities, commercial paper, and other short-term borrowings.

Formulas for Basic Ratios

$$\text{Pretax fixed charge coverage} = \frac{\text{Balances for pretax returns and coverages}}{\text{Gross interest}}$$

$$\text{Pretax fixed charge coverage including rents} = \frac{\text{Balances for pretax returns and coverages} + \text{gross rents}}{\text{Gross interest} + \text{gross rents}}$$

$$\text{Funds from operations as percent of long-term debt} = \frac{\text{Working capital from operations}}{\text{Long-term debt}}$$

$$\text{Operating income as a percent of sales} = \frac{\text{Operating income}}{\text{Sales}}$$

Pretax return on permanent capital =

$$\frac{\text{Balances for pretax returns and coverages}}{\text{Sum of (1) the average of the beginning of year and end-of-year current maturities, long-term debt, noncurrent deferred taxes, minority interest, and stockholders' equity, and (2) average short-term borrowings during year per footnotes to financial statements.}}$$

$$\text{Long-term debt as percent of capitalization} = \frac{\text{Long-term debt}}{\text{Long-term debt} + \text{equity}}$$

$$\text{Total debt as a percent of capitalization} + \text{short-term debt} = \frac{\text{Total debt}}{\text{Total debt} + \text{equity}}$$

SUGGESTED READINGS

FABOZZI, F., and I. POLLACK. *Handbook of Fixed Income Securities.* 2d. ed. Homewood, Ill.: Dow Jones-Irwin, 1986.

―――. *Standard & Poor's Rating Guide.* New York: McGraw-Hill, 1979.

MAGINN, J., and M. D. ANDERSEN. "Fixed Income Analysis Process: Return and Risk Analysis." In *Managing Investment Portfolios, 1986–1986 Update,* ed. J. Maginn and D. L. Tuttle. Boston: Warren, Gorham and Lamont, 1985.

―――. *Standard & Poor's Debt Rating Criteria, Industrial Overview.* New York: Standard & Poor's Corporation, 1986.

28

Utility Bond Analysis

Robert W. Burke
Senior Vice President
Director—Public Utilities
Moody's Investors Service

INTRODUCTION

Electric, gas, and telephone utilities historically have been among the most highly regulated industries in the United States. Indeed, in Europe and most of the rest of the world, utilities generally are owned by the state. This stems from the perception, here and abroad, that utilities are "natural monopolies."

Utility companies are capital intensive, since a significant portion of their cost of service stems from investments in generating stations, gas pipelines, and telephone switches. Utility investments, unlike ships or planes, cannot be moved to provide service in another area. And, unlike factories and commercial buildings, they cannot be remodeled to make different products or provide new services. Moreover, technological advances traditionally have enhanced economies of scale in the utility business.

Utilities also are considered to be natural monopolies from the consumer's standpoint. Compared to food, clothing, housing, automobiles, and other consumer goods, a utility's product, such as electricity, is generally uniform and indistinguishable. And, although consumers' purchases of goods and services normally show wide variance, everyone in an industrial society demands access to adequate utility service.

In the writing of this chapter I owe special thanks to Associate Directors, Jeffrey deL. Evans, Fred Price, John T. Spellman, and their staffs.

We at Moody's hope that this chapter will help guide analysts of regulated utilities through the maze of financial, economic, and regulatory issues that confront these industries. Our focus here is on those segments of companies in the electric, gas, and telephone industries that remain regulated—even though there is a general trend toward deregulation, and substantial portions of the gas and telephone industries, having already gone through this process, are no longer "regulated" in the traditional sense.

First, we outline the regulated industries' general characteristics, including their present status (subject to change) as so-called natural monopolies. We give a brief history of the structural changes affecting these industries: the onset of technological change, increasing competition, and the corporate form the utilities are taking now and prospectively. We next present fundamentals of utility analysis. These encompass service territory, characteristics from a credit perspective, the demand for utility service and growth therein, their assets, and construction issues. We examine operating costs and their implications for the bond rating process.

We describe and examine the regulatory process, pinpointing key items when analyzing rate orders from a credit perspective, then the competitive forces that are increasingly coming into play. We describe regulated companies' financial statements before delving into the credit ramifications of each element in a company's financial presentation of itself—both historical and projected. And finally, we examine certain accounting issues that have long-term implications for regulated industries.

Regulation—Legal Basis

Despite the moves in recent years to deregulate key sectors of the American economy—such as banking, transportation, and oil and gas production—virtually all businesses remain subject to some degree of government regulation. This ranges from local zoning ordinances to federal rules on testing and selling pharmaceuticals, airline safety, and equal employment opportunity. Regulations like these set general parameters on competition between private employers so that the broader public interest is not impaired.

More stringent government regulations, applicable to particular sectors of the economy, such as transportation and finance, typically have served to limit who is eligible to compete in a market and what they may charge for a service or product. In general, regulations that pertain to individual industries are designed to maximize the social benefits of free enterprise, while minimizing potential damage to the public welfare from unchanneled competition. And, since competition is effectively limited, supplemental regulations are required to prevent the protected industry from garnering excess profits. Nonetheless, individual companies still have a chance to excel, owing to the oportunity to earn above-industry-average profits from superior management and better products and services.

In exchange for a monopoly franchise, which typically includes a grant of the public right of eminent domain, it is the responsibility of utilities' management to provide service on demand to everyone who can pay. And, to protect both investors and consumers, utility companies are required to charge "just and reasonable" rates. Overall, utilities are entitled to rates sufficient to allow them to compete with other industries in raising needed capital on reasonable terms. This means that utilities are entitled to charge customers for all operating and capital costs that are prudently incurred. Capital costs consist of depreciation charges (the mechanism by which investors recoup their original investment) and financing costs, which provide investors with a return on their investment while it is being utilized. Financing costs include fixed obligations, such as interest payments and preferred stock dividends, as well as a fair return for common stockholders.

Deregulation of Regulated Utilities

Telephone. Until 1984, approximately 80 percent of telephone service in the United States was provided by the American Telephone & Telegraph Company. Five large non-Bell holding companies served approximately 15 percent of all customers, and about 1,400 companies served the remaining 5 percent of the market. Intrastate long-distance service was provided by the local Bell operating companies with some participation by others, while interstate service was managed by the AT&T Long Lines Department with facilities owned primarily by the Bell operating companies and AT&T. Beginning in the late 1970s, other long-distance carriers began to compete in the interstate long-distance market. In settlement of an antitrust suit brought by the U.S. Department of Justice, AT&T agreed in 1982 to divest itself of local telephone operations. In exchange, the consent decree permitted the company to enter the field of computer-based information transfers, from which it was previously excluded. As a result, seven regional holding companies now own the 22 operating companies that previously constituted the Bell System.

Natural gas. The natural gas industry historically has been segmented in three major categories: the producers, which include major companies also involved in oil-drilling activities; the federally regulated interstate natural gas pipeline companies; and the state-regulated distribution utilities. Many pipelines and some distributors have diversified

TABLE 1 Electric Generating Capacity (Megawatts)

Year	Total	Privately Owned	Cooperatives	Publically Owned
1975	508,414	399,036	9,136	100,242
1976	531,449	415,828	9,946	105,675
1977	560,338	438,385	10,866	111,087
1978	579,312	453,647	11,635	114,030
1979	598,443	464,144	13,837	120,462
1980	613,695	477,083	15,422	121,190
1981	634,808	490,767	18,406	125,635
1982	650,104	499,111	21,463	129,530
1983	658,182	505,487	22,202	130,493
1984	672,463	514,863	24,738	132,862
1985	688,733	530,405	24,574	133,754

SOURCE: Edison Electric Institute.

into nonregulated upstream activities, such as oil and gas exploration and production as well as drilling services. Additionally, there are several large companies with major operations in all three segments of the industry. But, typically, the degree of vertical integration is not significant, and companies tend to focus their major business functions on either interstate pipeline transmission or local distribution.

Evolving federal efforts to deregulate interstate transmission companies are changing the role of some pipeline companies from their typical merchant activities to transporters of natural gas that is owned by third parties. Therefore, these companies are slowly becoming subject to increased competitive pressures.

Electric. Investor-owned electric utilities are responsible for most of the generation, transmission, and distribution of electricity in the United States (see Table 1). Although a few electric companies have significantly diversified into nonregulated activities, the industry remains heavily regulated. These companies normally are vertically integrated and regulated by state public service commissions. However, there are also municipally owned electric systems and, in more rural areas, electric cooperatives that are owned by their customers. In addition, the U.S. government owns production agencies such as the Tennessee Valley Authority and Bonneville Power Administration. Some combination utility companies sell electricity and also serve as the local natural gas distributor.

Evolution toward Competitive Markets

In recent years, economic and technological changes have culminated in efforts to deregulate some areas of utility service in the United States and to provide more opportunities for competition. This has been particularly apparent in the telephone and gas industries.

Under the direction of the Federal Communications Commission, competitive entry was permitted in specialized segments of the long-distance telephone market beginning in 1968. Through judicial intervention, long-distance competition across the full spectrum of services was permitted in 1978. The FCC fully opened the terminal equipment market in 1982, nearly a quarter century after approving the first competitive entry into this business. The divestiture of the Bell operating companies greatly accelerated competition in the marketplace with the creation of seven new, independent organizations to enter the terminal equipment market and an independent AT&T Communications to offer users alternatives to some of the local operating companies' services.

The three segments of the natural gas industry have experienced widely differing degrees of competition. Historically, the gas producers have been subject to the most intense competition, which has been reflected by the extreme volatility of earnings and cash flow. Partial decontrol of gas wellhead prices, beginning in 1978, resulted in a myriad of prices based on various gas vintages. Those pipelines with access to high volumes of low-cost gas had clear advantages over their less fortunate peers. This set the stage for competition among pipeline companies, which subsequently intensified in an environment featuring concurrent conditions of oversupply and decreased demand. Recent decisions by the federal courts and the Federal Energy Regulatory Commission have added impetus to competition among pipelines, stripping them of much of the regulatory protection they had enjoyed for decades.

Gas distribution companies have not totally escaped exposure to competition, principally in the threat of bypass from pipelines connecting directly with industrial end users and from fuel switching by those industrial customers capable of using residential oil as an alternate fuel. However, with the aid of state regulators determined to limit this risk, distribution companies are expected to preserve their basic customer base.

Efforts to redefine the electric utility franchise and to separate generation from transmission and distribution services are becoming more common. However, the prospects for significant change in the fundamental structure of the electric utility industry remain uncertain; to a large extent, attempts to redefine the franchise may have zero-sum results because potential near-term benefits to certain companies or classes of customers may be at the expense of other utilities or customers. Also, it is unclear to what extent such fundamental changes can provide real gains over the longer term without technological developments that significantly alter the economics of the electric utility business.

Developments in Corporate Structure

The telephone industry is already dominated by large holding companies. While numerous unaffiliated operating companies provide local telephone service, they represent only a modest portion of the market. The trend toward the formation of holding companies outside the bounds of the 1935 Holding Company Act accelerated in the mid-1980s in the electric utility industry. Typically, electric utilities that most recently became wholly owned subsidiaries of a holding company have completed major construction programs and have sufficient generating capacity for many years into the future. With healthy cash flow, but low capital requirements, these utilities seek alternative investments in order to maintain and improve shareholder returns. Therefore, the formation of holding companies among electric utilities generally is tied to efforts to diversify into other businesses.

To be sure, the formation of a holding company is not required for diversification. An electric utility can create its own wholly owned subsidiaries to enter new fields. Nonetheless, the holding company format helps to segregate the earnings derived from regulated utility operations from the profits derived from nonregulated activities. This is important because nonregulated businesses often are more risky and, if they are successful, the investment returns can be significantly higher. However, if regulators include the profits from nonregulated activities in calculating the utility's revenue needs, the benefits essentially flow through to ratepayers instead of the company's investors. If this occurs, investors are placed in the position of absorbing extra risk without the prospect of proportional returns. Analysts should therefore focus on regulators' willingness to respect management prerogatives in the conduct of nonregulated businesses.

FUNDAMENTALS OF UTILITY ANALYSIS

Service Territory

Analysis of the service territory focuses on many economic, political, and demographic factors which shape demand. A knowledge of economic and political factors provide the analyst with an indication of the degree of support that can be expected from regulators. The analyst should pay particular attention to principal industries within a service area, population growth trends, and unemployment and per capita income figures.

The economic base of the service territory dictates the mix of sales to each class of service (residential, industrial, and commercial for electrics and gas distributors; business and residential for telephones). The type of service provided by telephone companies (local, long-distance, and interexchange access) is also significant. Since each class and type of service is priced differently, it is important for the analyst to understand their potential sensitivity to economic cycles. In addition, each customer class presents a different usage pattern to which the utility adapts its system. Overdependence on a particular customer or customer class could cause swings in revenue flows and cause volatility in debt protection measurements.

Economic activity has a direct bearing on revenues. For electric and gas utilities, industrial load is quickly affected by economic recessions or by large industrial users going out of business. For telephone companies, high service sector employment provides opportunity for high customer usage.

The degree to which an area is rural or urban will have a direct effect on the cost of providing service. The rate of customer growth and the mobility of the population, especially business customers, will affect revenues and operating costs dramatically. Rapid customer growth may lead to the construction of costly new facilities.

In summation, a service territory analysis will give the analyst a strong indication of the support the company can expect from its regulators and of what revenue streams might be subject to economic fluctuation. Finally, a service territory analysis will indicate how a utility must manage its resources if it is to meet the demand for its services and contain its operating costs.

Demand for Utility Services

Stable growth of demand for services is an important consideration in assessing the credit quality of a utility. Stability permits management to plan for the future with a high degree of certainty that the future demand will justify the deployment of plant and equipment. Fluctuating or erratic demand may result in situations where the level of demand will cause less than optimal utilization of plant and equipment. Lower than expected demand levels can impair profitability because the depreciation and capital costs, as well as some operating costs for the plant and equipment, do not decline in proportion to the lower demand level. Alternatively, higher rates may not be achievable or may simply weaken the company's competitive position.

In a capital-intensive business, growth in demand volumes will support stronger profitability as more revenue is generated through increased asset utilization. Profitability is improved because there is more revenue to recover the high fixed costs.

Moderate demand growth helps reduce the need for rate relief. Typically, as demand increases, profitability is enhanced. Rates authorized by the public service commission that are designed to achieve a certain rate of return assume a certain level of demand. If demand exceeds the assumed level, revenues will increase while costs remain relatively fixed. The profits resulting from the demand increase enable the company to improve earnings without obtaining a rate increase from the regulators. The delays, expense, and risk involved in applying for a rate increase are thereby avoided, assuming demand trends are not creating a need for large capital programs.

Heavy demand volumes, however, may encourage the growth of competition. Currently, this is more true for gas and telephone utilities, but is becoming a factor in the electric utility industry as well. The utility may not be able to fully satisfy the demand from all customers. Competitors may be able to gain market share by meeting some of this demand; they may gain customers whose service requirements are either specialized or not being met at an acceptable price by the existing utility.

Heavy increases of demand volume over a lengthy period also may cause financial strain by requiring a large commitment to plant expansion, as noted above. Outlays for large generating units or expansion of the local telephone network can be greater than will be supported by the existing capital base. Difficulty in making necessary capital investment can lead to weakened service quality, which often causes less than satisfactory regulatory response to requests for rate increases. Service quality considerations most often occur in the telephone industry, because weakened distribution network facilities cause more immediate service quality problems, while electric utilities usually can buy power if generation capability is lacking.

Electric Demand Analysis

Electric kilowatt-hour sales increases should ultimately translate into higher revenues and earnings for the electric utility. A positively sloped electric sales trend is often indicative that revenues and profits are growing. These higher revenues, if reflected in earned returns, permit a utility to remain financially viable and healthy.

An electric utility provides services to several classes of customers—residential, commercial, industrial, and resale (wholesale customers). (See Table 2.) Revenues from the residential ratepayers are most secure, although conservation has tended to slow sales growth in recent years. Revenue from the commercial sector is the next most stable, and revenues from industrial customers are the least stable because many industries are sensitive to economic cycles. Based on market conditions, wholesale revenues may vary widely. It is important for the analyst to consider a utility's transmission access and costs of power production relative to its neighbors when gauging off-system sales potential.

When customer and population growth are sufficient to outweigh conservation, the increased electric sales that result boost revenues and

TABLE 2 Electric Utility Industry

Electric Revenues (in billions)

	1985	1984	1983	1982	1981	1980
Residential	$ 58,602	$ 55,636	$ 51,261	$ 47,123	$42,824	$37,587
Commercial	44,163	40,931	37,090	34,031	31,325	27,370
Industrial	40,882	40,576	36,526	35,829	33,030	27,317
Other	5,245	5,058	4,630	4,362	3,837	3,188
	$148,892	$142,201	$129,507	$121,345	$111,016	$95,462

Electric Sales (million kilowatt-hours)

	1985	1984	1983	1982	1981	1980
Residential	794,404	777,421	750,850	732,678	730,479	734,411
Commercial	613,155	578,163	546,252	516,959	521,698	524,122
Industrial	821,661	837,661	780,020	770,398	819,641	793,812
Other	89,253	86,679	80,476	79,707	78,866	73,749
	2,318,473	2,279,924	2,157,598	2,099,742	2,150,684	2,126,094

	Residential		Commercial		Industrial	
	% Total Sales	% Total Revenues	% Total Sales	% Total Revenues	% Total Sales	% Total Revenues
1985	34.3	39.4	26.4	29.7	35.4	27.5
1984	34.1	39.1	25.4	28.8	36.7	28.5
1983	34.8	39.6	25.3	28.6	36.2	28.2
1982	34.9	38.8	24.6	28.0	36.7	29.5
1981	34.0	38.6	24.3	28.2	38.1	29.8
1980	34.5	39.4	24.7	28.7	37.3	28.6

SOURCE: Edison Electric Institute.

increase capacity usage. But growth in customers and increased demand will eventually compel a utility to acquire long-term power supplies from other utilities and/or build new power stations.

Electric sales can be extremely sensitive to weather conditions. In connection with this, the analyst examines whether electricity is used for space heating (as in the Pacific Northwest), as well as whether air conditioning load plays a major role.

Electric utilities may be combination utilities; that is, provide both electricity and gas to their customers. As with electricity, gas sales and revenues are influenced to a major degree by weather conditions, the level of industrial activity, the cost of competing energy sources, and customer growth.

The characteristics of capacity demand (load) are also a concern in electric utility analysis. To determine how load is spread out over a period of time, a utility calculates the load factor; that is, the average load at a particular point in time as a percentage of peak load (highest capacity demand). A utility service area containing large industrial users of electricity will generally have a high load factor because industrial power demand is continuous over a longer period of time. By contrast, an electric company with a large residential class will generally have a lower load factor because power demand from these customers tends to fluctuate.

To increase load factor, electric utilities have implemented load management programs. Time-of-day rates, appliance control, and interruptible industrial tariffs all act to increase load factor.

Natural Gas Demand Analysis

Natural gas sales to all classes of customers peaked in 1972. (See Table 3.) The decline in gas sales since then reflects the gas shortage in the 1970s and rising gas prices in the late 1970s and early 1980s; these factors forced into being an era of conservation that still exists. Industrial sales during this time declined faster than total sales, reflecting not only the effects of prices and conservation, but also the structural changes that have been occurring in basic industries, which are heavy users of gas. In the mid-1980s, new laws and regulations encouraged gas production, and a surplus of natural gas developed. This "bubble" has lasted for several years. Ironically, the present excess supply of and lower demand for gas could lead to shortages in the long term as producers cut back exploratory budgets. Supply and demand for gas are rarely in balance, since market responses are slow.

Residential and commercial customers form the base of a local gas distribution company's business, providing a fairly stable, but weather-sensitive, source of revenues. The industrial load and electric generation load of a gas company can be very important, providing revenues

TABLE 3 Gas Utility Industry Sales, by Class of Service, 1960–1985* (trillions of Btus)

Year	Total	Residential	Commercial	Industrial[†]	Other[†]
1960	9,287.7	3,188.1	919.8	4,709.4	470.4
1961	9,589.0	3,321.0	988.1	4,785.6	494.3
1962	10,234.8	3,536.9	1,092.9	5,100.1	504.9
1963	10,766.3	3,668.0	1,136.6	5,438.1	523.6
1964	11,591.2	3,869.7	1,273.5	5,912.0	536.0
1965	11,980.3	3,999.0	1,344.8	6,146.5	490.0
1966	12,859.1	4,175.4	1,462.8	6,653.3	567.6
1967	13,488.3	4,365.3	1,577.6	7,014.3	531.1
1968	14,472.4	4,552.7	1,704.9	7,595.1	619.7
1969	15,391.6	4,820.4	1,878.1	8,135.8	557.3
1970	16,043.5	4,923.7	2,006.6	8,439.2	674.0
1971	16,685.7	5,040.1	2,155.5	8,645.5	844.7
1972	17,082.1	5,141.8	2,275.7	8,775.7	888.8
1973	16,479.9	4,993.6	2,280.8	8,370.8	834.7
1974	16,000.3	4,864.8	2,293.4	8,153.2	689.0
1975	14,862.9	4,991.0	2,386.8	6,837.1	648.0
1976	14,813.5	5,014.2	2,422.6	7,192.0	184.6
1977	14,340.9	4,946.3	2,409.4	6,796.4	188.9
1978	14,748.4	5,106.7	2,499.5	6,931.5	210.7
1979	15,440.3	5,083.1	2,485.8	7,641.4	230.0
1980	15,413.2	4,826.1	2,453.3	7,956.6	177.2
1981	15,374.8	4,609.7	2,375.4	8,239.3	150.4
1982	14,182.7	4,769.8	2,471.3	6,794.3	147.3
1983[‡]	12,857.5	4,449.6	2,298.2	5,969.4	140.2
1984R	13,161.7	4,628.3	2,396.0	5,991.0	146.4
1985	12,615.5	4,513.0	2,338.1	5,634.9	129.5

* Excludes data for Alaska prior to 1961.
† Prior to 1976, "Other" electric generation is included in the "Other" class of service. For 1976 and beyond all electric generation is included in the Industrial category.
‡ Revised.
SOURCE: American Gas Association, *Gas Facts* (1985).

during nonheating months, when there is a low demand for gas. During the gas shortages of the 1970s, many industrial and electric-generation customers invested in equipment with fuel-switching capability. At times when natural gas competes with other, more competitively priced fuels, gas distribution companies with heavy industrial load to customers with fuel-switching capability are vulnerable to significant load loss. To combat this, the gas companies have been forced to develop new pricing structures, with the approval of state regulators, to retain important loads and also to expand into new markets. Because many gas companies already have high heating saturation loads, customer additions are therefore tied to the economic growth of the service territory.

(See Table 4.) On the other hand, companies in the New England and Middle Atlantic areas, which have low saturation levels, have the potential to add new customers. But even with customer growth, capital investment dollars for the average gas distribution company are small compared with the large capital programs of electric companies.

Telephone Demand Analysis

Demand for telephone services is measured in numerous ways, reflecting the different types of service offered. The most fundamental measurement of demand is the number of lines in service. (See Table 5.). An economically robust service territory for a telephone company will generate high growth rates for lines in service. Lines in service is essentially a measure of the number of customers a company has.

Toll minutes-of-use reflects the amount of long-distance calling within local access and transport area (LATA) and is an important measure of demand, because this demand generates more revenue as usage increases. The company typically charges the customer for toll usage according to the length of the call (minutes-of-use), the distance of the call, and the time of day and day of the week the call is made.

Intrastate access minutes-of-use is an additional measure of demand—the amount of long distance calling between LATAs within a state. Growth of access minutes enhances profitability because each minute generates revenues, and access rates are priced well above the direct cost of providing the service.

Interstate access minutes-of-use measures the amount of long-distance calling between customers in the company's service territory and out-of-state locations. Strong growth of interstate calling can provide considerable support to earnings because the profit associated with these calls is generally higher than found in local services.

Local messages represent an additional measure of the volume of demand—the number of telephone calls within the company's local calling area. While these calls generally do not produce additional revenues because of the widespread use of local flat-rate tariff structures, implementation of local measure service permits revenue growth as local message volume increases.

Instead of measuring simply the absolute number of minutes-of-use or messages, it is useful to measure the intensity of demand by comparing volumes of messages or minutes-of-use against the number of access lines in service. If local messages per access line are high relative to other telephone companies', this may benefit the company, depending on whether usage-sensitive pricing is in effect. If usage-sensitive pricing is in effect, the company will receive more revenue as local usage increases. If flat-rate pricing is in effect, customers only pay a flat rate for local service no matter how many local calls they make. Toll

TABLE 4 Gas Utility Industry Househeating Customers, by State—Yearly Average for 1970–1985 (000's)

Division and State	1970	1975	1980	1984	1985 Number	1985 Saturation*
United States	**31,208.7**	**34,371.4**	**38,162.6**	**40,037.0**	**40,781.5**	**88.8**
New England	**778.8**	**857.1**	**1,008.8**	**1,113.2**	**1,138.3**	**67.6**
Connecticut	181.0	195.8	216.3	256.4	254.1	64.5
Maine	5.7	4.8	6.7	9.4	9.2	75.4
Massachusetts	443.3	531.5	635.6	677.4	698.1	67.0
New Hampshire	24.2	28.0	36.0	38.3	40.3	80.5
Rhode Island	116.0	86.3	103.0	119.0	123.1	72.2
Vermont	8.6	10.7	11.2	12.1	13.5	86.7
Middle Atlantic	**3,827.2**	**4,127.7**	**4,516.6**	**4,909.5**	**5,011.2**	**64.8**
New Jersey	713.7	793.4	942.6	1,105.3	1,156.7	65.7
New York	1,536.7	1,686.2	1,797.0	1,915.3	1,951.4	52.0
Pennsylvania	1,576.8	1,648.1	1,775.0	1,874.4	1,903.1	85.6
East North Central	**7,527.9**	**8,432.0**	**9,166.2**	**9,583.5**	**9,671.3**	**94.4**
Illinois	2,107.4	2,390.9	2,616.6	2,734.3	2,758.1	89.5
Indiana	813.0	947.6	1,049.9	1,144.6	1,158.4	96.8
Michigan	1,647.3	1,901.2	2,162.0	2,278.6	2,302.9	97.1
Ohio	2,379.2	2,482.0	2,507.3	2,520.8	2,534.1	98.0
Wisconsin	581.0	710.3	830.4	905.2	917.8	90.8
West North Central	**2,915.5**	**3,260.7**	**3,589.9**	**3,720.4**	**3,753.0**	**95.3**
Iowa	515.8	572.9	632.9	653.4	657.9	96.6
Kansas	563.4	595.4	649.6	648.3	649.5	92.5
Minnesota	513.1	598.3	690.9	768.9	783.7	95.1
Missouri	915.6	1,022.8	1,082.8	1,080.0	1,090.1	95.2
Nebraska	298.4	336.2	375.1	397.1	397.3	98.2
North Dakota	41.8	56.5	70.6	78.2	78.9	94.9
South Dakota	67.4	78.6	88.0	94.5	95.6	97.7
South Atlantic	**2,599.2**	**2,969.9**	**3,312.7**	**3,587.9**	**3,625.9**	**90.1**
Delaware	42.5	46.6	51.9	53.9	55.4	69.7
District of Columbia	83.2	86.1	92.0	97.1	98.3	75.2
Florida	247.9	261.7	368.3	411.1	370.8	88.0
Georgia	718.9	810.7	946.0	1,028.2	1,066.7	96.7
Maryland	443.3	528.8	550.2	588.7	594.9	79.8

TABLE 4 *(continued)*

					1985	
Division and State	*1970*	*1975*	*1980*	*1984*	*Number*	*Saturation**
North Carolina	209.6	274.4	288.2	363.2	380.0	96.8
South Carolina	179.7	226.9	257.1	254.3	260.1	90.9
Virginia	339.0	378.3	402.8	439.5	450.2	87.9
West Virginia	335.1	356.4	356.2	351.9	349.5	98.3
East South Central	**1,695.1**	**1,868.0**	**1,965.4**	**2,001.9**	**2,008.2**	**97.6**
Alabama	539.2	579.9	625.3	620.3	623.0	98.1
Kentucky	490.1	538.0	562.3	567.9	561.2	96.1
Mississippi	311.0	341.8	356.1	357.7	358.6	98.8
Tennessee	354.8	408.3	421.7	456.0	465.4	97.8
West South Central	**4,278.3**	**4,496.0**	**4,997.8**	**5,107.2**	**4,982.8**	**93.4**
Arkansas	371.0	405.8	433.9	463.2	379.1	80.8
Louisiana	737.3	859.3	931.3	924.6	894.8	96.4
Oklahoma	628.3	665.7	731.8	803.7	782.4	96.1
Texas	2,541.7	2,565.2	2,900.8	2,915.7	2,926.5	93.7
Mountain	**1,646.2**	**2,040.4**	**2,406.4**	**2,661.5**	**2,649.2**	**96.2**
Arizona	390.0	492.4	509.1	546.6	475.0	86.5
Colorado	508.7	610.9	759.1	854.3	903.8	100.0
Idaho	65.9	91.4	82.2	97.3	99.0	98.8
Montana	126.9	147.1	161.8	166.9	167.0	99.6
Nevada	65.9	100.7	155.3	175.9	162.3	87.8
New Mexico	203.4	239.4	291.6	320.4	330.0	100.0
Utah	217.6	272.6	338.3	386.5	398.8	98.9
Wyoming	67.8	85.9	109.0	113.6	113.3	99.5
Pacific	**5,940.5**	**6,319.6**	**7,200.8**	**7,351.9**	**7,941.6**	**97.4**
Alaska	14.4	24.0	36.2	57.2	61.9	100.0
California	5,506.9	5,794.5	6,618.4	6,715.0	7,288.5	97.9
Hawaii	0.0	0.0	0.0	0.0	0.0	0.0
Oregon	166.3	206.7	224.9	243.0	245.2	92.6
Washington	252.9	294.4	321.3	336.7	346.0	98.4

* Percentages refer to proportion of residential gas customers using gas for heating.

SOURCE: American Gas Association, *Gas Househeating Survey.* Data represent average number of customers developed from number of year-end customers as shown in survey. ©, American Gas Association, *Gas Facts* (1985).

TABLE 5 Access Lines

Year	Bell Operating Companies	Annual Increase (percent)	Independent	Annual Increase (percent)	Total	Annual Increase (percent)
1986	95,900	2.1	25,500	4.8	121,400	2.6
1985	93,945	2.9	24,330	5.7	118,275	3.4
1984	91,329	2.6	23,020	3.1	114,349	2.7
1983	89,042	2.4	22,331	3.0	111,373	2.6
1982	86,921	1.1	21,672	1.1	108,593	1.1
1981	85,987	2.5	21,429	3.0	107,416	2.6
1980	83,884	3.1	20,808	3.6	104,692	3.2
1975	69,880	—	16,855	—	86,735	—

SOURCE: United States Telephone Association (Estimated).

minutes-of-use per access line is an important measure of demand because charges for toll calls are usage based. Thus, revenue to the company will increase as toll usage increases. The same principle holds true for interLATA minutes-of-use per access line.

Given the magnitude of the company's investment in plant and equipment, it is in the company's interest to generate high usage of its facilities. High demand for telephone service will help the company achieve the high asset turnover necessary to get optimal return on its capital investment.

The underlying strength and composition of the economy in the company's service territory determine the nature and strength of demand for telecommunications service. A strong, growing local economy will generate strong demand for telecommunications services. In a healthy economy, individuals and businesses are more inclined to spend more for telecommunications. Further, an economy composed of information-intensive businesses will typically generate stronger demand for telecommunications. Businesses such as banking, brokerage houses, insurance companies, real estate and governmental institutions represent an important source of demand. More affluent communities are also typically an important source of demand for both basic telephone service, enhanced calling features, and long distance calling.

Asset Base

The composition of the company's assets is reviewed as part of the analytical process. Because of the capital-intensive nature of a regulated industry, this review by its very nature requires a concentration on the technology that the investment has purchased. As its goal, the analysis focuses on providing the analyst with information on the company's ability to meet customer demand, not only today but in the future. The ability to meet demand and assure a constant revenue stream is not a question of technology alone but also a function of operational efficiencies and the resulting level of costs that are built into the company's price structure.

Electric Utility Asset Analysis

Capability and reserve margins.   The asset base consists of the utility's electric generating plants and transmission and distribution facilities. The most basic question to be answered is whether the company's generating capacity is sufficient to meet its electric load requirements and provide an adequate reserve margin. The reserve margin is simply the difference between the peak demand on the company's system and the total capability (in megawatts) of generating plants available (owned plant plus firm contracts) to meet the demand, expressed as a percentage of peak demand. When this difference is measured on the basis of the company's owned generating capability, the measure is known as the capacity margin and is obviously always smaller than the reserve margin. Reserve capacity is necessary since peak demand cannot be perfectly predicted, and generating plants are subject to both scheduled and unscheduled outages. While there is no "correct" reserve margin, the industry generally considers 15 percent–20 percent to be adequate.

The appropriate reserve margin may differ from utility to utility, depending on the type and age of its plants, the demand patterns in its service territory, and the company's ability to purchase power from other utilities. In the case of a utility with a large proportion of hydroelectric power, energy availability rather than analysis of plant capacity is a more important consideration. The analyst should evaluate projected reserve margins in light of their implications for the company's construction and financing program.

A utility may purchase power from other utilities. Most utilities are members of regional power pools that enable them to join forces to provide adequate power for an entire region, buy and sell power among themselves on an economy basis, or meet unexpected demand on any particular company's system. These power pools usually require their members to maintain a specific reserve margin.

An electric utility's generating assets consist of base-load plants, which are generally large (500–1,200 mw), high in capital costs, and low in fuel costs. They are meant to be run for extended periods of time. Utilities also maintain peaking units, which are much smaller (20–100 mw) and less expensive to build but which often incur higher fuel costs. These units are meant to be activated for very short periods of time during periods of high demand on the system or during unscheduled outages of base-load plants. Cycling units are intermediate in size and are generally used to meet weekly and seasonal fluctuations in demand.

Base-load plants are generally coal-fired or nuclear. Gas and oil-fired units have, in large part, been relegated to cycling duty. For each type of plant, the analyst will consider the fuel cost and supply outlook. Fuel diversification among a utility's base-load plants provides diversity of production, which reduces operating risk. Each type of plant may, however, be vulnerable to particular problems. Coal plants, for example, must meet exacting environmental standards and may need to be modified as these standards change. Nuclear plant technology has proven to be very demanding, and generic problems such as corrosion of the steam generator tubes have developed. The credit analyst should determine whether such problems exist and what their implications might be in terms of cost or potential plant outages.

Asset concentration has become increasingly important in analyzing electric utilities. This term refers to the degree to which a utility's plant is made up of relatively few generating units, or to the circumstance where a single plant represents a disproportionately high percentage of the company's total plant investment, in dollar terms. The concept is particularly important with regard to investment in nuclear power because of the vulnerability of nuclear plants to shutdown due to safety-related problems. In general, a utility whose total base-load capacity includes only two base-load generating units of the same size has a higher degree of asset concentration than one with six units. The first utility risks losing half its generating capacity in the event of an unscheduled plant outage, while the second utility would lose a much smaller portion of its capacity.

Asset concentration is also evaluated in terms of dollar investment in the plant relative to a number of measures, including capitalization, common equity, and rate base. These measures are important because they help the analyst determine the financial impact that impairment of the asset would have on the company. For example, if a plant must be removed from rate base, the analyst needs to determine what the associated decline in the company's income would be. Obviously, the larger the plant investment relative to total rate base, the greater is the financial impact if a company's regulatory commission determines that it may no longer earn on the asset.

Similarly, if an asset becomes permanently impaired and there is a substantial undepreciated investment which must be written off, the balance sheet impact—a reduction in retained earnings and common equity—may have significant implications for credit quality.

Plant performance. The performance record of an electric utility's generating plants is an important determinant of its ability to control and recover costs. One measure of performance is a generating unit's availability factor—the percentage of time that the unit is available for use. Another measure is the capacity factor, which is the average load on the unit expressed as a percentage of rated capacity. High availability and capacity factors contribute to the company's ability to control costs and, ultimately, rate levels. Analysts also look at heat rate, a measure of the Btus needed to generate a given unit of electricity. The lower the heat rate, the more cost-efficient the generating facility.

Utilities maintain insurance on their generating plants to provide a degree of financial protection in the event of damage at a plant. Nuclear plants in particular are generally covered by both property and liability insurance in the maximum amounts available under federal law.

In the event of an extended outage at a generating facility, a company may be forced to rely on purchased power to meet its load, sometimes for a considerable period. Consequently, the number and quality of a company's interconnections with other utilities are important in providing the utility with access to reasonably priced purchased power.

An electric utility cannot escape the scrutiny of its state regulatory commission even in the area of plant operations. Regulators may have the authority to remove units from a company's rate base in the event they undergo severe damage, such as occurred in the nuclear accident at General Public Utilities' Three-Mile Island plant in 1979. Even a less severe plant outage, which may entail significant purchased power costs for the utility, may have negative financial repercussions if a commission determines that some or all of those costs may not be passed along to the ratepayer. Similarly, regulators have begun to impose relatively strict operating criteria on new nuclear plants, with earnings penalties imposed when the plants do not meet the standards.

Transmission and distribution facilities. The above discussion has centered on electric utilities' asset base in terms of generating plant. Also important, of course, are its transmission and distribution facilities, although clearly generating plants usually make up a higher percentage of a company's total assets and rate base. Transmission facilities provide for the movement of bulk power over high-voltage lines from the generating plant to various substations. Here the power is sent out over lower-voltage distribution lines, first to service lines and then to the customer. A company's quality of service and reliability may be affected by how modern and well maintained its transmission and distribution system is. In addition, capital spending to maintain or improve a utility's transmission and distribution facilities can sometimes become a significant component of the company's construction budget.

Assets under construction. The nature of a utility's construction program is an extremely important determinant of a company's credit quality (see Table 6). The type of technology used for new generating plants has important implications for cost, scheduling, licensing, environmental impact, and fuel supply issues.

The major types of technologies used in the recent past for most base-load plant additions are traditional coal-fired plants and nuclear power plants. In a very few instances, pumped storage (a type of hydroelectric project) facilities have been built to meet peak requirements. Oil and gas-fired base-load generating facilities, while technologically feasible, were generally unattractive in the 1970s and early 1980s, largely because of fuel supply and cost issues.

The type of technology chosen will be a major determinant of a new unit's cost per kilowatt, which is a standard method of evaluating the cost of plants of differing sizes and fuel sources. Clearly a relatively low cost per kilowatt is positive from the standpoint of the company's

TABLE 6 Construction Expenditures in the Electric Utility Industry (in millions)

	Generating Plant	Transmission Plant	Distribution Plant	Other	Total
1986	$19,762	$2,401	$6,915	$2,440	$31,518
1985	23,498	2,409	6,314	2,044	34,265
1984	27,608	3,101	6,088	1,782	38,579
1983	29,922	3,200	5,381	1,601	40,104
1982	29,836	3,497	5,228	1,654	40,215
1981	27,209	3,169	4,950	1,882	37,210
1980	25,688	3,280	5,307	1,650	35,925
1979	22,673	3,384	5,329	1,666	33,052
1978	19,817	2,736	5,347	1,216	29,116
1977	19,095	3,106	4,522	988	27,711
1976	16,612	2,945	4,548	1,084	25,189
1975	12,724	2,279	4,071	981	20,055
1974	12,504	2,451	4,577	1,024	20,556
1973	10,924	2,450	4,434	915	18,723
1972	9,700	2,134	3,989	777	16,600
1971	8,522	2,164	3,346	690	14,722
1970	6,837	2,109	3,081	511	12,538

SOURCE: *Electrical World Prospective*, Edison Electric Institute.

financing requirements, ability to fully recover costs through the regulatory process, and ability to keep rates competitive.

Nuclear facilities have been the most expensive to build, although when recently completed nuclear plants were conceived, cost projections were far lower than actual costs. The cost of nuclear plants completed in 1985 averaged about $2,400 per kilowatt, which is two and one-half times the average cost of coal plants completed at about the same time.

Strict safety and licensing standards required by the Nuclear Regulatory Commission, particularly since the 1979 Three-Mile Island accident, have been a major cause of the high cost of nuclear plants. Nuclear technology has proven to be far more complicated and demanding from an engineering and contruction standpoint than fossil fuel technology. In addition, since nuclear plants take far longer to build (as long as 10 to 15 years), the financing costs are far higher than for plants with shorter construction periods.

Nuclear plants have environmental considerations which are unique to the technology. For example, since the water discharged from these plants is generally warmer than from other types of plants, elaborate cooling systems are necessary to meet water discharge temperature standards. Also, widespread concerns about nuclear plant safety have frequently led to opposition to nuclear plants from environmentalists and other antinuclear groups. In the future, analysts will need to focus on decommissioning/decontamination of nuclear plants retired from service. No one really knows the costs involved, and present-day estimates will probably come up short.

In terms of fuel supply, it is generally thought that there is an ample supply of uranium concentrate to fuel today's nuclear reactors for a long time to come.

Coal plants, while far cheaper than nuclear plants, are still relatively expensive, having become so in recent years largely due to the necessity of meeting stricter air quality standards. Federal and state emission standards, which limit the amount of sulfur dioxide and other gases and particulates that can be released, have resulted in the need for scrubbers and precipitators to remove these pollutants. Switching from the burning of high-sulfur coal to low-sulfur coal has been one way that some companies in the industry have attempted to deal with these concerns without retrofitting older coal plants with pollution control equipment. Also, federal legislation dealing with "acid rain" is likely and may lead to considerable capital spending by utilities, with corresponding pressure on electric rates. This could result in higher capital needs, which the analyst must evaluate in terms of impact on future earnings.

Gas-fired plants have traditionally been less expensive to build than nuclear or coal, but concern about natural gas supplies prompted the federal government to impose limitations on its usage for boiler fuel (these were in effect during the late 1970s and early 1980s). A major effort is currently underway to repeal the Fuel Use Act, allowing the construction of new gas-fired plants. Today, gas-fired technology is primarily used for peaking units.

The concept of asset concentration is also very important when analyzing a utility's construction program from a credit risk standpoint. During the late 1970s and early 1980s, the industry experienced a large number of cancellations of nuclear plants under construction, mainly due to the tremendous escalation in nuclear plant cost projections. In the event of plant cancellation, the credit impact is chiefly a function of how much has been invested in the plant relative to capitalization, common equity, and rate base and whether regulators allow recovery from ratepayers of that canceled plant investment.

Finally, a utility's construction program is designed to augment its generating capacity and its reserve margin. Adding capacity in large increments (e.g., a 1,000-mw coal or nuclear plant) may lead to a large reserve margin, particularly for a relatively small utility or in cases where anticipated load growth has not materialized. While large rate base additions may often be the most cost-effective way of providing new capacity in the long run, they have given rise in recent years to punitive regulatory actions concerning excess capacity. Consequently, a utility whose construction program adds capacity in small increments are frequently better positioned to secure adequate rate base treatment for their new plants.

Telephone Utility Asset Analysis

Net telephone plant accounts represent almost 90 percent of total assets for an operating telephone company. Examples are land and buildings, which might contain the corporate headquarters building; station equipment, which would account for the investment in telephone sets and computer terminals; and vehicles and work equipment, which would contain trucks and trenching equipment. For analytical purposes, however, attention is focused on the two main activities of the telephone company; that is, switching and transmission of telephone messages. The switching assets are designated central office equipment and the transmission assets are contained in the outside plant category. Together these two accounts represent in excess of 70 percent of a telephone company's net plant account. The distribution of investment between these two accounts is purely a function of the physical characteristics of a company's networks. For example, a company serving a very concentrated service territory with many large cities would most probably have a majority of its investments in central office equipment. Conversely, a company serving a geographically dispersed population would have the majority of its investment in outside plant.

A number of generalities concerning the cost functions of switching systems are important. Electronic switches are less costly than electromechanical switches to maintain, require less investment in terms of land or buildings, and can be easily adapted to new service offerings simply by changing software instructions. Compared with analog electronic switches, digital electronic switches require less physical space, contain a greater degree of functionality, and foster a reduced capital investment in other network components. Also, capacity additions to digital facilities can be accomplished in much smaller increments, thus assuring more efficient use of capital.

While the introduction of digital technology into the local switching plant is a relatively new phenomenon, digital technology has been incorporated into the transmission function since the 1960s. The advantages in these applications are increased capacity, improved quality of transmission, reduced capital cost, and new service offerings.

Technology in the local loop covers every medium from twisted copper in the subscriber loop to microwave radio systems and fiber optic applications. As with switching facilities, digital is the technology of choice as it permits high-speed, high-capacity services to be offered. Capacity can be added through engineering techniques without incurring the expense for additional cable or conduit.

Historically, each succeeding generation of technology has been added to, rather than replaced, existing telephone plant. The application of the digital medium to analog plant is expected to result in a mix of technologies for many years to come. Nonetheless, the vast majority of all incremental growth should be met by the application of a digital medium. Thus fiber optic technology, digital radio, T-1 carrier, and subscriber line carrier sytems should all play a prominent role in a company's construction budget. Should they not be in evidence, the company's ability to serve future demand and develop new product offerings should be seriously questioned.

The movement to a completely digital network not only has begun but has received greater emphasis since the breakup of the Bell system in 1984. The network of the future, referred to as Integrated Services Digital Network (ISDN), is intended to bring to the subscriber a wide range of services (voice, data, text, or video) over the same network facilities, allowing the use of a wide variety of terminal equipment. While field trials are scheduled for 1987 and 1988, much work is still to be done in the standards areas before the full promise of digital technology can be passed along to the subscriber.

Adequate capital recovery for the telecommunications industry has become increasingly important. This problem arises when new, modern equipment is deployed to replace not-yet-fully-depreciated, inferior equipment, because of the vast improvement in technology and its related maintenance cost savings. Like most utility plants, telephone equipment has been historically depreciated over very long lives. But because of the need to meet sophisticated customers' requirements, companies are increasingly installing new, advanced plant. The risk is that write-offs or underdepreciated plant could occur.

Gas Distribution Industry Asset Analysis

Net plant assets of undiversified gas distribution companies represent about 60 percent of total company assets, the remainder being primarily current assets. Current assets include a substantial amount of accounts receivable, as well as gas in storage. Net plant is approximately equal to total capitalization for gas distribution companies, similar to the relationship in electric utilities. The absolute value of net plant, however, is substantially smaller than that for the average electric utility. Total net plant of the U.S. gas distribution industry, as compiled by the American Gas Association, is approximately $7 billion. In comparison, figures compiled by Edison Electric Institute for the electric industry indicate a total of approximately $100 billion. There are a few electric utility companies with a total net plant exceeding that of the entire gas distribution industry.

Technologically, gas plant has not changed significantly, and consists primarily of underground mains and distribution lines. Some systems in older cities still have substantial amounts of older cast iron pipe in their systems which, although serviceable, is being gradually replaced with steel pipe or relined with plastic liners.

Gas distribution systems are expanding, but only at moderate rates, and thus do not budget a high amount of capital expenditures. This is an important factor in the analysis of prospective debt protection measurements. Many distribution companies have propane distribution subsidiaries in contiguous areas. When the area's population expands, natural gas mains are extended, increasing capital needs.

OPERATING COST ANALYSIS

As important as the new technologies are for the protection of the revenue base and the generation of incremental growth, they are equally important in the control of expense growth and reduction in expense levels. The new technologies, through their incorporation of computerized software control, provide for increasing productivity. This productivity results in reduced revenue requirements and lower operating costs. Thus, on the one hand, strong control over the level of operating expenses reduces the need for rate relief and permits a company to earn the allowed levels of return. On the other hand, it permits the company to introduce a level of pricing that will keep its service offerings price competitive.

Electric Utility Industry Operating Cost Analysis

Fuel cost. Fuel costs make up the largest proportion of an electric utility's operating costs. The major types of fuel used for electric generation include coal, oil, natural gas, nuclear, and hydroelectric power (see Tables 7 and 8). The most obvious shifts during this period are the rebound in coal, the declining role of natural gas, the growing contribution of nuclear, and the growth and subsequent decline in the use of oil.

From an analytical standpoint, total dependence on a single fuel source is generally viewed as a negative. Such a company is much more vulnerable in the event of external shocks that can affect a fuel's availability or price. The credit analyst should look favorably on a balanced fuel mix, which includes two or more fuel sources (see Exhibit 1).

Coal continues to be the dominant fuel in the U.S. electric industry. While the cost of coal has risen over time, it remains the cheapest of the fossil fuels (coal, oil, and natural gas). To the price of coal at the mine mouth must be added transportation charges, which can add significantly to the ultimate cost of the fuel.

Another way in which coal varies is in its sulfur content. The coal with the lowest sulfur content is generally found in the West. Most eastern coal is fairly high in sulfur content. Environmental standards

TABLE 7 Sources of Energy for Electric Generation Total Electric Utility Industry* (by year and energy source kilowatt-hours in millions)

Year	Total Generation	Coal	Fuel Oil	Gas	Nuclear	Hydro	Other†
1985	2,469,841	1,402,128	100,202	291,946	383,691	281,149	10,724
1984	2,416,305	1,341,681	119,808	297,394	327,634	321,150	8,638
1983	2,310,285	1,259,424	144,499	274,098	293,677	332,130	6,456
1982	2,241,211	1,192,379	146,423	305,260	282,773	309,213	5,164
1981	2,294,812	1,203,554	206,070	345,777	272,674	260,684	6,054
1980	2,286,414	1,161,969	245,547	346,233	251,121	276,039	5,506
1979	2,247,359	1,075,595	302,948	329,486	255,155	279,790	4,387
1978	2,206,313	976,618	364,153	305,392	276,403	280,432	3,315
1977	2,124,166	985,465	357,866	305,444	250,882	220,446	4,063
1976	2,037,674	944,562	319,779	294,610	191,107	283,734	3,883
1975	1,917,619	852,972	288,873	299,766	172,506	300,065	3,437
1974	1,866,436	829,842	299,306	319,931	113,727	300,928	2,703
1973	1,856,216	845,704	312,805	340,449	83,334	271,634	2,290
1972	1,749,637	772,871	272,530	375,735	54,092	272,626	1,783
1971	1,612,589	714,676	218,608	374,026	38,106	266,314	859
1970	1,531,609	706,102	182,488	372,884	21,797	247,456	882
1969	1,442,182	706,001	137,847	333,279	13,928	250,193	934
1968	1,329,443	684,905	104,276	304,433	12,528	222,491	810
1967	1,214,365	630,483	89,271	264,806	7,655	221,518	632
1966	1,144,350	613,475	78,926	251,151	5,520	194,756	522
1965	1,055,252	570,926	64,801	221,559	3,657	193,851	458
1964	983,990	526,230	56,954	220,038	3,343	177,073	352

Note: Total may not equal sum of components due to independent rounding.
* Generation by petroleum coke included in fuel oil from 1954 to 1980, and 1983 to 1984. In 1981 and 1982 petroleum coke included in coal.
† Includes generation by geothermal, wood, waste, wind, and solar.
SOURCE: U.S. Department of Energy. Energy Information Administration. *Monthly Power Plant Report* (EIA-759).

TABLE 8 Sources of Energy for Electric Generation in Percent of Total—Total Electric Utility Industry (by year and energy source)

Year	Coal	Fuel Oil	Gas	Nuclear	Hydro	Other
1985	**56.8%**	**4.1%**	**11.8%**	**15.5%**	**11.4%**	**0.4%**
1984	55.5	5.0	12.3	13.6	13.3	0.4
1983	54.5	6.3	11.9	12.7	14.4	0.3
1982	53.2	6.5	13.6	12.6	13.8	0.2
1981	52.4	9.0	15.1	11.9	11.4	0.3
1980	50.8	10.7	15.1	11.0	12.1	0.2
1979	47.9	13.5	14.7	11.4	12.4	0.2
1978	44.3	16.5	13.8	12.5	12.7	0.2
1977	46.4	16.8	14.4	11.8	10.4	0.2
1976	46.4	15.7	14.5	9.4	13.9	0.2
1975	44.5	15.1	15.6	9.0	15.6	0.2
1974	44.5	16.0	17.1	6.1	16.1	0.1
1973	45.6	16.9	18.3	4.5	14.6	0.1
1972	44.2	15.6	21.5	3.1	15.6	0.1
1971	44.3	13.6	23.2	2.4	16.5	0.1
1970	46.1	11.9	24.3	1.4	16.2	0.1
1969	49.0	9.6	23.1	1.0	17.3	0.1
1968	51.5	7.8	22.9	0.9	16.7	0.1
1967	51.9	7.4	21.8	0.6	18.2	0.1
1966	53.6	6.9	21.9	0.5	17.0	*
1965	54.1	6.1	21.0	0.3	18.4	*

Note: Total may not equal sum of components due to independent rounding.
* Less than one tenth of one percent.
Based on Table 7
SOURCE: Edison Electric Institute, *Statistical Fact Book.*

currently limit the emission of sulfur products into the air. There is growing concern that the problem of "acid rain" is caused or at least worsened by power plant emissions; Federal legislation has been repeatedly proposed which would require dramatic reductions in such emissions. If such environmental legislation is adopted, many coal-burning utilities would be faced with the need to invest large amounts of capital to put scrubbers on their coal-fired generating units. Many new coal plants today already have such scrubbers, but much of the older coal-fired capacity would have to be retrofitted. The operating costs for a scrubbed coal unit are also significantly higher than for nonscrubbed units. The credit analyst must assess the impact of compliance with potential new environmental legislation on a company's capital and rate increase requirements. While expenditures of this type are clearly recoverable from ratepayers in theory, their magnitude may make it difficult in practice, or may limit regulators' willingness to allow rates to fully compensate the company for these expenditures.

EXHIBIT 1 Fuel Mix

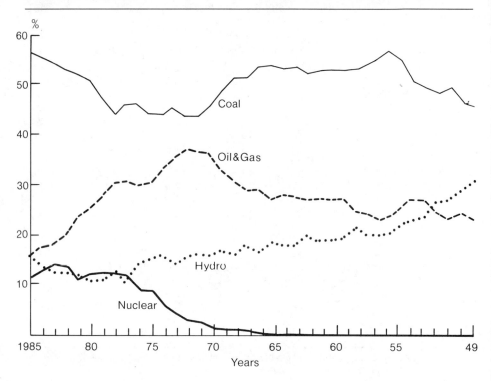

SOURCE: Edison Electric Institute, *Statistical Year Book*.

Coal costs can vary significantly depending on the supplier. Long-term coal contracts can be attractive from a security-of-supply perspective. Also, if coal prices tend to be rising, long-term contracts can provide a degree of protection from price escalation as well. However, there are also risks inherent in these arrangements. If prices are falling, a utility which is locked into a high-cost contract risks the wrath of regulators who may question the prudency of the utility management's judgment in entering into that contract, and may even disallow a portion of fuel costs from rates. Alternatively, if a utility attempts to get out of a high-cost, long-term contract, it may risk a "breach of contract" lawsuit by the coal supplier. Another risk inherent in being too dependent on coal is the possibility of a long, nationwide coal strike. However, most coal-fired utilities stockpile sufficient quantities of coal to see them through perhaps 75–100 days of coal needs.

Oil as a fuel source has been subject to dramatic price fluctuations over the past 15 years. Much of the oil used by U.S. utilities is imported from foreign sources. The Arab oil embargo of 1973 and the resulting soaring oil prices reminded U.S. utilities of the danger of being too dependent on foreign oil as a generating fuel. Generally, utilities in the eastern United States were hardest hit by the high cost of oil. Consequently, many of these utilities began programs to switch from oil to coal. The increased capital costs necessary to do so were thought to be prudent by managements as well as regulators. As late as 1985, some eastern utilities were still pursuing plans for such oil-to-coal conversions. However, the dramatic decline in oil prices in 1985–86 and the high capital costs of building coal units caused some regulators to turn down such conversion programs.

From an analytical standpoint, oil dependence should be viewed negatively. The potential for dramatic price increases and even shortages or curtailed supplies is a matter of concern from a credit standpoint.

Natural gas as boiler fuel supplied nearly one quarter of the nation's fuel mix in 1970. However, a natural gas shortage was perceived later in that decade, culminating in the passage of the Fuel Use Act of 1978. The act prohibited the use of natural gas for new generating units. Gas prices were rising considerably during this period as well, reflecting the perceived shortage. The Natural Gas Policy Act was also passed, deregulating the price of certain types of gas and providing for further price deregulation over time. The act was designed to provide incentives for gas exploration and development in light of the shortage situation.

But the gas shortage was relatively short lived. By the early 1980s, a gas "bubble" developed, and gas prices softened to reflect these newfound supplies as well as the competition provided by falling oil prices. Natural gas is a relatively clean fuel. The role it will play in the future generating mix of the industry will likely depend upon the federal legislation governing its use. Repeal or modification of the Fuel Use Act could lead to the construction of new gas-fired units.

Nuclear fuel remains one of the cheapest fuels available. The development of nuclear power was driven in part by this very fact. During the 1960s, nuclear power was heralded as the cheap, clean, efficient technology of the future. Also, the dislocation in fossil fuel prices in the late 1960s and early 1970s influenced many utility managements to strive for fuel diversity. However, nuclear power proved to be much more expensive than originally expected. As capital costs soared and regulatory problems multiplied, nuclear plant costs far exceeded the cost of nuclear fuel as an analytic consideration. Nevertheless, once completed a nuclear plant offers a company a very low marginal cost of production, which may maintain industrial load or provide a basis for effective off-system competition with other electricity providers.

Hydroelectric power is an extremely economical source of power. Since there are no true fuel costs, the operating costs of a hydro facility are very low. However, variability of rainfall and river flow make hydro a somewhat unreliable generating source. In periods of favorable hydro conditions, the increased availability of hydropower can be used to displace more expensive energy and keep rates down.

Since most of the good hydropower dam sites are already taken, hydropower has been declining in terms of its overall contribution to the industry's generating mix. New hydro projects are rare, but the upgrading of existing sites, or even the development of very small new projects has become more economical in light of rising fossil fuel costs.

An important aspect of a utility's ability to control its operating costs is the efficiency of its generating units. The measure of a plant's fuel efficiency is heat rate—the energy, measured in British thermal units, required to produce one kilowatt-hour of electricity. Consequently, the lower the heat rate, the less fuel is needed to produce a given amount of electricity, and the better able a company is to control its fuel costs. The analyst will look at a company's heat rate and its trend over time as an indicator of the company's generating efficiency, especially as it compares with the industry average.

If efficiency indicators are significantly below average, regulatory penalties may occur. The analyst will look for management's ability to successfully implement efficiency and productivity programs, since regulators will frequently compare one company's operating costs and productivity measures to those of other utilities.

Telephone Industry Operating Cost Analysis

Many manufacturers produce technologies that can be used to duplicate the services offered by the local telephone companies. The expansion of technology and the realization that regulation is a risk as well as a blessing has driven managements to place a greater degree of emphasis on expense control than ever before. Because of the increasingly competitive nature of the industry, costs can no longer be assumed to be passed through to the subscriber. Managements believe that protection of the revenue base can be most effectively assured by becoming the low-cost provider of their services.

The largest single cost to a telephone company is labor, and technology is viewed as an effective means of reducing the labor component. The control of this factor of production can most accurately be tracked through the ratio measuring the number of access lines per employee in the organization. As much as possible, this ratio should be normalized for nonrecurring shifts of employees between various subsidiaries of the same organization.

Another ratio which has proved to be particularly helpful in determining a company's effectiveness in controlling its cost is controllable cost per access line. Essentially, this ratio focuses on the level of operating costs that are subject to the decision of operating managers in the field. All expenses associated with the financial decisions of the corporation (interest expense, depreciation expense, and taxes) are excluded from consideration. Definitionally, controllable expenses are net operating expenses less depreciation. In some cases it may prove helpful to further divide controllable expense into the individual expense lines. Should this detail be available, then maintenance expenses, network expenses, or any other operating expense could be subject to the same type of analysis.

Significantly, the control of operating expenses must be viewed in light of the quality of service that is being provided. Ultimately, the local exchange companies are service providers, and regulators spend a good deal of time listening to the ratepayer about the quality of service. Should this be forgotten by management, a regulator is in a position to reduce the company's revenue requirement request or to reduce the level of allowable earnings during the next rate case proceedings. While such actions by regulators are unusual, they do occur; an analyst should be concerned with the quality of service being provided, as it ultimately affects the company's financial statements. Fortunately, many companies believe that investment in high-quality service pays significant dividends in terms of expense reduction. To this end, the industry has developed a series of measurements designed to place quality of service before its operating management.

Statistics are available on all operational functions in the network. Switching and trunking activities are studied as closely as transmission and operator services. Additionally, operational statistics are available by service offering (e.g., business, residence, and public). While many of these statistics are helpful in managing the business, two are particularly helpful in providing an overview of the service quality provided by the organization. These are a measurement of customer trouble reports and the amount of unfilled orders. The first measures the experience of active service users, while the latter measures the timeliness of the company's service. Generally speaking, these two measurements are the most significant in terms of regulatory oversight.

Gas Distribution Industry Operating Cost Analysis

State regulators judge the reasonableness of operating costs of gas distribution companies. The major component of distribution company operating costs, however, is the cost of natural gas purchased from others. This component amounts to approximately 75 percent of total revenues for the average gas distribution company.

The cost of gas purchased from transmission company suppliers is adjusted frequently (usually every six months) to respond to variable prices paid to gas producers. In general, state regulatory treatment of these cost changes is an automatic pass-through (Purchased Gas Adjustment). Thus, this item is usually not specifically reviewed in the company's rate cases.

In the current shift to deregulation in gas transmission, however, distribution companies are being given the option to purchase their own gas at the wellhead and have it transported. State regulators recognize the supply and price risk in this option and are limiting, either explicitly or implicitly, the amount purchased on a spot basis. In addition, many distribution companies are not sufficiently large to economically operate a gas-purchasing operation covering a wide geographical area. While currently low spot prices makes spot purchases attractive, the potential for price increases in the spot market results in higher risk for those companies relying on a spot strategy. Because they are not large, other operating expenses for gas distribution companies tend to receive less regulatory and analytical scrutiny.

REGULATION

In exchange for an exclusive franchise to serve a territory, telephone, electric, and gas companies are regulated to prevent abuses of monopoly power. The purpose of the regulatory process is to assure the utility a fair rate of return on its investment and the recovery of its expenses, while also implementing public policy goals (such as universal service for telephones). Such regulatory overview comes from many different groups, including state and federal commissions and agencies, as well as legislative and judicial bodies. These monitor a variety of areas, such as expenses, earnings, tariff structure, and construction programs.

The intrastate operations of a utility are regulated by the public service commission in each state of operation, while interstate operations are regulated by one or more industry-specific federal agencies. In the latter case, the Federal Communications Commission (FCC) supervises the telephone industry and the Federal Energy Regulatory Commission (FERC) regulates electric and gas companies. In addition, the Nuclear Regulatory Commission (NRC) oversees the construction and operation of nuclear power plants. Any decision by these various regulators can be appealed to the judicial system, at either the state or federal level, as appropriate. Federal and state legislative bodies play roles in the regulatory process to the extent that they change the rules to reflect such factors as more/less regulation, new accounting/tax procedures, and economic development.

State Regulatory Environment

Virtually all states and the District of Columbia have regulatory commissions, which operate as agencies of state government and have jurisdiction to regulate telephone, electric, and gas companies. The regulatory powers of the commissions may vary somewhat, but the determination of utilities' rates is clearly the most important. In this area, state regulatory commissions wield tremendous power over utilities' financial health. More than three fourths of the state commissions also have the authority to regulate the issuance of securities by the utilities under their jurisdiction.

Most state or territorial commissions are made up of either three or five commissioners, although there is one state with a single commissioner and a handful which have seven commissioners. Some states require the commissions to have representation from both major political parties. Commissioners may be either appointed by the governor (38 commissions), popularly elected (13 commissions), or (in the case of 2 commissions) chosen by the state legislature. New Mexico and Texas maintain two separate commissions, between which the responsibility for the various regulated industries is divided. The District of Columbia also maintains a public service commission.

States may have widely varying legal qualifications for service on a utility commission, but generally commissioners must be U.S. citizens, qualified electors, and importantly, without financial interests in the industries regulated. Commissioners' backgrounds tend to be law, business, engineering, or economics, although only eight states have specific statutory professional requirements. In practice, new commissioners seldom have much familiarity with regulatory methods, and the analyst must be concerned over rate decisions that arise from a commissioner's inexperience. A commissioner's term of office is determined by state law and generally ranges from 3 to 10 years, with 4- or 6-year terms the most common. Reappointment or reelection is possible, although more often a commissioner will serve only a single term or even less.

The commissioners themselves are supported by a staff that, in terms of size, varies greatly from state to state. For example, Delaware and Hawaii have very small staffs, while the staff of the California Public Utilities Commission has about 1,000 positions. The expertise and effectiveness of commission staffs also vary from state to state and are no doubt influenced by the financial resources of the commissions and their ability to pay competitive salaries to staff professionals. Many commission staffs tend to suffer from high turnover rates. In some states, such as Missouri, the staff's function is to represent the customer's interest, versus the commissioners' role of balancing the interests of the consumer and the utility investor.

The organizational structure of state commissions often follows functional lines, with separate divisions for rates, accounting, or legal affairs. Commissions may also be organized according to industries regulated.

Commission appointments, elections, and sometimes staff appointments are subject to political considerations. Often these positions are attained in part because the political views of the commissioner or staff member coincide with the governor's opinions or particularly favor consumers' interests. Political influence over regulation varies from state to state and may, of course, change over time.

There can be many participants in a utility rate case, including intervenors, who generally represent very narrow interests. Consumer groups frequently are very involved in the regulatory process. Increasingly, these consumer interests are represented by a Citizens Utility Board (CUB). A CUB will generally participate in a rate case with the intent of keeping residential rates as low as possible. Intervenors representing industrial customers sometimes participate in rate hearings. Other forms of consumer organizations, including environmental groups, may also present testimony during rate cases.

Analysis of Rate Orders

In a proceeding before a state public service commission (PSC), the Federal Energy Regulatory Commission (FERC), or the Federal Communications Commission (FCC) to determine "just and reasonable" rates, parties to the case seek to accurately measure the utility's "rate base," its cost of capital, and its revenues and expenses in the "test period." (Rate base is the value established by the regulatory commission upon which a utility is permitted to earn a specified rate of return. Usually, this represents the amount of utility property used and useful in public service, and in some jurisdictions it may include the value of a portion of construction work in progress or CWIP.) However, each of these concepts is subject to differences in interpretation and implementation, and the analysis of a rate order must focus on the overall impact that the order will have on the utility's financial position. In this regard, it is important to note that a rate decision which is founded on principles appropriate for a financially healthy electric utility may exacerbate the position of a utility that is already in financial distress. Moreover, a commission generally retains considerable discretion in shaping the final rate award, even considering legal restraints on ratemaking practices in its particular jurisdiction. Analysis of rate orders often provides important clues about changes taking place in the local regulatory and political environment.

The test period in a rate case is normally 12 months long, but it need not be a calendar year. If the test period precedes the date on which the rate case is filed, it is considered to be fully historical. However, the test period may include some historical information and some projected data. The test period is generally called forecasted if it is entirely in the future at the time of filing. Nonetheless, regulatory authorities typically are permitted 6 to 12 months to make a decision in a case, and it is possible for a forecasted test year to be completely historical by the time new rates are approved. Therefore, a "fully forecasted" test year takes in the 12-month period immediately following the date that new rates take effect.

The time frame for the test period is especially important if the rate of inflation is high and/or the utility has a major plant entering commercial service. To the extent that a rate boost is insufficient to cover increases in actual operating expenses, the utility will not have a reasonable opportunity to earn the return on its capital investment that regulators have deemed to be fair. To ameliorate this problem, particularly in jurisdictions where a forecasted test period is forbidden, some state regulators are permitted to consider "known and measurable" changes in revenues and expenses occurring within 12 months of the end of the test year. In jurisdictions where this option is also forbidden, regulators are sometimes allowed to "annualize" data recorded near the end of the test period.

Even when a historical test year is utilized, regulators have wide latitude in determining the revenues and expenses that they will "allow." For example, they may decide that salary levels were too high or that the utility employed too many people. They may determine that the utility was at fault in a plant outage and not reimburse the company for higher-cost purchased power. In a case with a forecasted test period, regulators may opt for a more optimistic sales projection, thereby mitigating the need for higher rates. Therefore, the type of test year is important, but it is only one aspect of the analysis of a rate order's adequacy.

After assessing the elements of revenue and expense that determine the utility's operating income, the regulators must decide if it provides a sufficient return on the company's invested capital. The rate base, which is the measure of invested capital, always includes plant-in-service. The rate base can be measured at the end of the test period, or it may be an average value. If the test year is fully forecasted, an average rate base is often considered the best measure of the utility's investment. When the test period is historical at the time new rates become effective, a year-end rate base may be considered most appropriate.

In some jurisdictions, regulators are permitted to include a utility's investment in unfinished projects, called construction work in progress (CWIP), in rate base. However, many jurisdictions require that investments be "used and useful" in order to merit rate base treatment. A return on CWIP-in-rate-base is much more favorable to a utility's financial well-being.

Having decided on the size of the utility's rate base, regulators must look at its cost of capital in order to assess the adequacy of operating income. The overall cost of capital depends on the proportion of debt, preferred stock, and common equity in the capital structure, as well as the cost of each financing source. But, like the test period and the rate base, a utility's cost of capital can be measured in different ways. Capitalization ratios may be based on actual test period data, or they may be calculated pro forma for subsequent securities sales or anticipated financings. In some cases, where the commission disagrees with a utility's financing policies, capitalization ratios may be based on what the regulators deem most appropriate. This occurs most often when the commission believes that a company has too much common equity, the most expensive form of financing.

In regulating subsidiaries of holding companies, regulators often use a "double leverage" approach, whereby the subsidiaries' capital structure for ratemaking purposes is recast to reflect the fact that an equity infusion by the parent actually is composed of both debt and equity. The effect of using a "double leverage" approach is to lower the allowed dollar return on equity (since debt costs less than equity) and, thus, lower the total revenue requirements.

The cost of debt and preferred stock generally is based on embedded costs, pro forma for financings outside the test period, if this is commission policy. Alternatively, embedded costs can be annualized, like operating expenses, to reflect rates at the end of the test period. The return allowed on common equity (ROE) is often the key variable in determining the overall cost of capital, since commissions have considerable latitude in arriving at their equity return findings. (ROE is defined as net income available for common equity divided by average common equity for a given period.) However, the approved equity return (if the utility has been provided with a reasonable opportunity to earn it) should be considered adequate if it allows the company to sell common stock at least at book value.

When a utility cannot obtain adequate rate relief, it will often appeal the commission decision through the state court system. The judicial process is lengthy, politically sensitive, and highly unpredictable from an investor's standpoint. In some highly political regulatory jurisdictions, more constructive rate treatment is obtained in the judicial system.

Legislation often limits the scope and discretion of the state regulators. Statutory guidelines differ considerably from state to state. Some laws provide state regulators with flexibility, while others prescribe detailed regulatory policies. Laws providing an electric utility a cash return on construction work in progress is constructive from an investor's viewpoint, since cash flow is enhanced and external financing reduced. But if this is prohibited or legislation is enacted to disallow investments in an abandoned plant project, a commission may be unable to prevent severe financial trouble.

Selected Electric Industry Regulatory Issues

Fuel expenses represent a substantial portion of an electric utility's overall business expense. Fuel prices often change suddenly and drastically. To prevent the need for frequent, full-scale rate hearings every time fuel prices fluctuate, most state regulatory agencies have adopted the use of fuel adjustment clauses, which primarily reflect the changes in fuel costs that are passed on to ratepayers. Even so, fuel adjustment clauses are not timely, and the recovery of fuel expenses generally lag a short period of time. Nevertheless, the fuel adjustment clauses help stabilize financial results from month to month.

A ratemaking practice for electric utilities that has increased in prevalence is the phasing in of the revenue requirement of newly completed plants. This phenomenon has developed primarily because many recent plant additions have become very expensive relative to the existing rate base. Consequently, under the traditional ratemaking approach, the rate increase required to reflect the new asset in rates (assuming little or no CWIP was previously included in the rate base and allowed to earn a return) becomes very large (20 percent–50 percent). Political concerns about ratepayers' ability to absorb these large rate increases ("rate shock"), as well as the effects of price elasticity on demand, have prompted regulators to adopt various types of phase-in rate approaches, which raise rates gradually over a period of several years.

Virtually all phase-in plans are negative from the investor's standpoint, in that they delay the cash flow and earnings-quality improvement that the utility would experience under traditional ratemaking treatment. However, these plans may vary greatly in design and timing of increases and, as a result, each phase-in rate order must be analyzed case by case to determine the ultimate financial impact on the utility. In general, the shorter the phase-in period and the larger the first-year rate increase, the better off will be the credit position of the company. A real concern surrounding phase-in rate orders is the question of whether the rate increases promised to be implemented in subsequent years will be upheld if the makeup of the state regulatory commission changes before that time.

Most state regulators permit the utilities to recover canceled plant investments over a period of several years, but often without a return on the unamortized balance. Larger canceled plant investments with longer recovery periods slow the utilities' financial improvement and reduces investor confidence in the affected electric utility. Some state regulators have been more punitive, disallowing certain costs and therefore permitting only partial recovery of investments. This outcome can leave companies under severe financial strain for a long period of time.

Often, these disallowances of plant investment arise from prudency audits. In practice, a full-blown prudency hearing provides a commission carte blanche to disallow plant investment, thereby reducing rate allowances. Under this scenario, the utility may have to take a write-off against earnings. If this write-off is sizable, the company may be left with a vastly reduced equity account and a corresponding inability to earn enough of a rate base return to be able to pay a common stock dividend, thereby sharply limiting its access to capital markets. Some companies may even have to omit preferred dividend payments. Even the threat of sizable write-offs is often sufficient to trigger bond and preferred stock rating downgrades.

Since 1973, load growth has slowed considerably. Some electric utilities, while in the midst of major capacity construction, have found their capacity needs to be adequate without the new plant. In response, some state regulatory commissions have imposed severe excess capacity penalties on the basis that the new plant is not used and useful. For example, the Pennsylvania Public Utility Commission (PUC) penalized Pennsylvania Power and Light Company for alleged excess capacity concerning its Susquehanna nuclear units. When Unit 1 at Susquehanna was completed and placed in service, the PUC considered Pennsylvania Power and Light's reserve margins to be excessively high and as a result denied a return on 12.6 percent (945 mw) of the company's total system generating capacity mix. When Susquehanna Unit 2 was put into commercial operation, the PUC took a slightly different approach. It denied a return on the common equity portion of the investment in Unit 2. The conflict between the short-term political realities that guide commissions and the long-term power planning of an electric utility can find its expression in financial distress.

Selected Telephone Industry Regulatory Issues

The issue of cost-based pricing is of particular concern for telephone companies and regulators. Historically, regulators have sought to keep the price of basic local telephone service at affordable levels. Prices for other services, especially long-distance toll calls, were kept high to make up for the revenue shortfall resulting from pricing basic local service below cost. With deregulation, the artificially high prices for toll service provide an opportunity for new firms to enter the long-distance business and gain market share by offering long-distance service at an attractive price below the artificially high price levels of the existing telephone company. To prevent serious erosion of their long-distance market share, telephone companies have pressed regulators to allow rate increases on basic service and rate decreases on toll service. This adjustment would result in prices that more closely reflected the cost of providing the service.

The cost methodology used by the regulators has important pricing implications and, therefore, deserves the analyst's attention. For competitive services, pricing based on the incremental cost of providing the service will allow the company to compete effectively. In general, the company will press regulators to move rates closer to the costs of providing the service. In the past, as noted, regulators typically priced toll service well above the actual cost of that service. High prices on toll services provide a subsidy that allows the company to keep local service rates low. But competitive forces are making it uneconomical to continue this subsidy. Thus, companies and regulators need to find ways to move rates closer to costs. The removal of subsidy flows from intraLATA toll rates and both intra- and interstate interexchange access charges is one of the most important problems facing the telephone regulators. While significant reductions in interexchange carrier access charges have occurred since their inception in June 1984, a continuing downward trend is important if the local exchange companies are to retain the largest customers' access business over the long run.

Increasingly, customers are calling on telephone companies to provide specialized services and facilities that are not covered under existing standard tariffs. In a competitive environment, the telephone company needs the freedom to respond to these customer requests. If the company is unable to respond, it will run the risk of losing the customer and the revenue contribution from that customer. State regulators can provide the necessary flexibility by authorizing the company to meet customers' specialized needs under contract pricing arrangements or special assembly tariffs.

Capital recovery is another issue that affects a telephone company's ability to respond effectively to competition. Depreciation expense allows the company to recover the cost of its investment in plant and equipment. Historically, the anticipated useful lives of telephone plant and equipment for depreciation purposes were relatively long. However, technological advances in telephone switching and transmission equipment have resulted in an economic need to replace older equipment before it is fully depreciated. Modern equipment will often be more efficient, less labor intensive, and less costly to operate, with greater capacity and more of the features required by the more sophisticated customers. In fact, many local exchange companies will come under increased competitive pressure to install newer equipment that will meet the demand for advanced telecommunications services. The company will need to accelerate the depreciation rates on its existing investment in older, obsolete equipment to recover the capital investment in that equipment. This accelerated depreciation will reflect the shortened economic lives of the technologically obsolete equipment, even though this plant and equipment may still have relatively long useful lives. The company will look to the state public service commission, in conjunction with the Federal Communications Commission (FCC), to get approval for higher rates to cover the increased depreciation expense.

The local exchange telephone company charges the customer for local service essentially according to two pricing schemes: a flat rate for all local calls; or measurement of local service use, known as local measured service. The telephone company will want to get regulatory authorization for the local measured service option, because this will allow the company to charge the customer for the number of phone calls and the length of each call and to charge based on time of day and day of week. As a result of this procedure, the telephone company will benefit because revenue will increase as usage increases. Under flat rate pricing, there is no revenue increase as local usage increases.

Tariff structure is important because of the signals it sends to the marketplace. A local measured usage pricing system tells the customer that each call has a cost, and the customer should make a judgment about how much telephone service he or she really needs. A flat rate pricing sytem, on the other hand, tells the customer that the cost for local usage will basically remain constant; that is, an additional phone call will not cost more. Charging separately for a dial tone line, with a separate, additional charge for usage, communicates to the customer that there is a cost simply to have access to a telephone line with a dial tone.

Companies providing long-distance telephone service (or "interexchange" carriers) need access to the local network in order to complete the call. The local exchange carrier, the owner of the local network, imposes a fee, or an access charge, on each long-distance telephone call. The access charges for interstate long-distance calls are determined by the FCC. The access charges for intrastate, interLATA long-distance calls are determined by the state commissions.

Access charges include several elements, the two most important being traffic-sensitive costs and allocated nontraffic-sensitive costs. The inclusion of nontraffic-sensitive costs, which are recovered on a traffic-sensitive basis, means that large users are paying for their local distribution plant many times over. This uneconomic pricing creates a great incentive for these large customers to use alternative connections to long-distance service providers, or in other words, to "bypass" the local telephone company. Efforts to reduce the amount of nontraffic-sensitive costs included in interexchange carrier access charges are important to reducing competitive revenue losses. The analyst should look favorably on commission actions that reduce coverage of nontraffic-sensitive cost revenue requirements through traffic-sensitive, long-distance pricing schemes.

Selected Natural Gas Industry Regulatory Issues

The Natural Gas Act (NGA) of 1983 gave the Federal Power Commission (FPC), the predecessor of the Federal Energy Regulatory Commission (FERC), authority to regulate interstate pipeline rates, terms, and conditions of natural gas sales. Although production of natural gas was not regulated by the NGA, the Supreme Court had decided in 1954, in *Phillips Petroleum Company* v. *Wisconsin*, that the FPC should regulate natural gas wellhead prices. Passage of the Natural Gas Policy Act (NGPA) of 1978 finally eased the controls over the natural gas industry, providing for phased decontrol of most wellhead prices.

The NGPA pricing mechanism was based on an expected slow rise in crude oil prices, but worldwide problems disrupted this scenario. Crude oil prices rose sharply and gas prices moved up, so that by 1983, ceiling prices of new unregulated gas exceeded market clearing prices. With pipeline companies finding it difficult to market gas at uncompetitive levels and demand down, they turned to special marketing programs and FERC-approved blanket certificate transportation for low priority end users. But on May 10, 1985, the U.S. Court of Appeals (D.C. Circuit) found these programs unduly discriminatory to "core markets" or captive customers (largely residential and commercial). In response to this decision, FERC issued Order No. 436, which promotes transportation options for all transmission company customers. This order allows faster entry into and exit from the market and generally provides for increased competition and more flexible pricing.

Also in Order 436, the local gas distributors were given the opportunity to reduce contract demands with suppliers, diversify their source of supplies, and lower their cost of gas. But this was at the price of shifting direct sales to industrial customers to transportation revenues, as some industrial customers want directly to producers for gas. The attitude of state regulators to distribution company transportation tariffs and risks encountered in reducing firm supplier purchases raises questions of the abilities of gas distributors to respond to changing market conditions. Overall, gas distribution companies have been fairly treated by state regulators, who have permitted flexible-rate tariffs, allowing natural gas to compete with residual fuel oil for those industrial customers with fuel-switching capability. While these sales generally are not much above breakeven, they do permit gas utilities to spread their fixed costs, thus limiting rates charged to noninterruptible customers. With reasonable regulation, the average distribution company, with its good cash flow and modest capital requirements, should be able to sustain a sound capital structure.

COMPETITION

Regulation, as a substitute for free market forces, works to provide the least cost to the ratepayer when true monopoly conditions exist. But monopoly conditions, across a wide spectrum of currently regulated services, do not exist today; competition is a fact of life. Alternative providers of services, whether telecommunications or energy, exist today and are expected to multiply in the future. This is not to say that each market served by a regulated utility is subject to competition, but merely that revenue streams that were once fully protected from competitive influences are no longer protected. In this changed environment, business risk has increased dramatically. Revenue flows are subject to the pressures not only of the marketplace, but of regulatory decisions which must balance economics and social policy. Achieving an equitable balance between these two forces could prove to be the greatest challenge to regulators in the years to come and a critical factor in utility company analysis and credit ratings.

Competition in the Electric Utility Industry

During the first 70 years of this century, technology made quantum leaps in efficiency, yet the concept of central station power generation, and the transmission and distribution of electricity within a designated service territory, were tenets that were not questioned. Electric utilities were viewed as homogeneous entities that responded in kind to similar industry challenges. During this era, rate regulation was often a perfunctory exercise, since increasing economies of scale resulted in a periodic lowering of rates to customers as more widespread use of electric power became prevalent.

Beginning in the late 1960s and early 1970s, electric utilities' economic fundamentals began to change and competition began to emerge. Inflation took its toll on earnings, and with electric generation efficiencies on a plateau, the need for rate increases became more prevalent. Companies with high sales growth levels saw their production costs escalate more rapidly than their slower growing neighbors'. Electric utilities began to be differentiated from one another. The energy crisis of 1973–74, the growing expense of nuclear power, and the need to comply with ever-changing environmental regulations caused rate levels charged to customers to escalate dramatically in the 1970s. The Public Utility Regulatory Pricing Act of 1978 (PURPA) was legislated in response to calls for greater price competition in the electric industry, against a backdrop of skyrocketing electric rates. This act mandated a market for electricity generated by a nonutility entity, with subsequent sale to a utility at an avoided cost rate—that rate at which a utility would add the least efficient unit to its system and still have a profit. Practically, the law's effect was to open the floodgates to alternative power producers.

Aside from PURPA-induced competition, electric utilities are competing with each other to a greater extent than 10 years ago. Price-level variations between neighboring companies and an abundance of excess capacity are forcing the relaxation of traditional regulatory policies. Electric companies operating in a low-cost environment would be well situated to supply new energy needs in an adjacent company's territory, if franchise rights were to be relaxed and transmission facilities arranged. Recent examples include an attempt by Pennsylvania Power & Light to serve a steel mill in Philadelphia Electric's territory. While regulatory approval in this circumstance was denied, other attempts are in progress. As utilities vie with one another for lucrative industrial plant sitings, many of them are offering attractive electricity rates to fend off competition. Recently, Japanese automobile makers establishing a U.S. manufacturing facility were courted by utilities in Michigan, Illinois, Ohio, and Kentucky. This type of competition by individual companies may intensify over the next decade.

Those companies enduring financial hardships are finding their competitive positions impaired. They could be forced into a defensive situation, such as a merger with another company. The recent Cleveland Electric Illuminating Company combination with Toledo Edison is one example. The creation of wholesale power producers is another competitive development. Alamito Company only wholesales power, and as a result it is not subject to state jurisdictional regulation, but rather to regulation by FERC. Its risk as a company is directly tied to its ability to sell a product (electricity) in a rapidly changing marketplace.

Regulatory policies are under scrutiny. Several developments in the regulatory arena suggest the outlines of a less restrictive future environment. An interesting market experiment is under way in the Southwest, where FERC allows six electric utilities to buy and sell power competitively. The arrangement is designed to allow pricing flexibility in bulk power sales while permitting the retention of 25 percent of the profits so derived. As a precondition, the participants have agreed to wheel power for one another, even though an individual company may be hurting its own sales. FERC is attempting to eliminate inequities in the supply and demand situation on a regional basis. However, high-cost producers could be at a competitive disadvantage.

Other less dramatic regulatory mandates include requiring least-cost dispatch of electricity by all electric utilities within a state jurisdiction. While this employs a particular state's facilities more productively, it could cause some financial complications to high-cost producers and, if the utilities were members of different power pooling arrangements, could upset dispatch capabilities of the various pools.

Traditionally, transmission facilities were employed to give an electric utility the option to draw on its neighbor in times of emergency (such as a major unit outage from an accident or storm damage) and to allow power transmission during the time in which a new generating unit was under construction. Then major holding companies optimized bulk transmission power among operating affiliates. Today, American Electric Power Company, Middle South Utilities, and Southern Company increase operating efficiency through optimal dispatch of electricity from a large number of generating units. Lately, the importance of adequate transmission paths has grown as utilities with excess capacity desire to sell electricity off system. Finally, state regulators are looking at mandatory wheeling of power by an "outside utility" over jurisdictional companies' lines if lower rates will result. In Texas, for example, Houston Lighting and Power has been required to transmit power from a cogenerator to Texas Utilities. This open-access concept of transmission, somewhat analogous to the interstate highway system, could bring together any producer and customer in what would amount to a nationwide market of the transmission grid from select utilities, with a user fee charged to either the buyer or seller of energy.

Competition in the Telephone Industry

Competition for users' telecommunication dollars has existed for many years. However, it was usually limited to competition among the industry's various product offerings. For example, Centrex services, which provide telephone call switching services of the telephone company central office for large customers, have competed with Private Branch Exchange (PBX) services provided by switching equipment on the customer's premises. In addition, private line services have competed with the public switch network, and Wide-Area Telephone Service (WATS) has competed with Message Telephone Service (MTS). What differentiates competition today is the number of unregulated alternative-service providers. These providers have very little interest in being all things to all people. They are interested in selling their product, whether piecemeal or in entire networks, to those individuals or companies that can afford to pay for an alternative communications network. It is "bypass" of the public switch network which is at the heart of the competitive concerns expressed by both operating company managements and regulators alike.

From a user's perspective, alternatives to the offerings of the local exchange companies are sought when the price of existing services becomes too expensive or if desired service offerings are not available. Analytically, it would appear that pricing considerations are the most pressing problem today. For many years, regulation has attempted to assure that there is a telephone in each household in America, the so-called universal service concept. To accomplish this, regulation has held the price of local telephone service artificially low while raising the prices of other services well above cost so as to provide an appropriate return for shareholders. This cross-subsidy presents a challenge to regulators and operating management. Subsidies have been established not only between interstate and intrastate services, but also among various intrastate services themselves. Pricing services above the cost of providing services or above what the market place is willing to pay leaves the door open for alternative providers of services to enter.

Adding to the effects of technology advances and price and cost imbalances was the signing of the Modification of Final Judgment in 1982. By this decree, the former affiliates of the Bell System divided into two mutually exclusive industries. The parent, American Telephone and Telegraph Company, was separated from the operating companies. Most important, the transmission of long-distance service was separated from local distribution, breaking the built-in incentive of the dominant long-distance provider to subsidize local distribution. Additionally, lines of business were swapped between the groups to create totally regulated companies and totally unregulated companies. Since January 1, 1984, these two groups of companies have been not only each other's customers but also each other's competitors. For the local exchange companies, the activities of AT&T present the greatest financial threat.

Quantifying the financial impact of competition and bypass is difficult for company managements in the regulatory process. Quantifying the potential impact on a company's financial performance is even more difficult for the analyst. The question often becomes one of determining, not so much if bypass is occurring or will occur, but rather when does the revenue effect become material.

It is possible to establish an economic profile of those institutions that could benefit most from instituting a telecommunications bypass alternative. Thus, those local exchange companies having a larger portion of potential bypassers in their service territory may be considered to have a larger potential bypass risk than other companies. Also, companies having large geographic concentrations of those customers are more likely to face competition.

An initial starting point may be size. Because of the expense and expertise required to run a telecommunications network, it is reasonable to expect larger corporations to have the investment and expertise available to operate their own telecommunications network. In addition, even if investment in fixed asssets is precluded, the same organization may have the expertise to, at least, choose between other service providers to the local exchange company. Thus local exchange companies whose territory includes a high percentage of Fortune 500 corporate headquarters probably have greater bypass risks than others.

Other institutions that could have a high interest in bypassing the local exchange companies include those with a large branch office network or manufacturing facilities at distributed locations. State governments appear to be particularly active in considering bypass alternatives, as do banking institutions incorporated in states that permit statewide banking.

Other services of the local exchange company subject to potential bypass are central office services or Centrex. Users of these services may be inclined to seek alternatives because of additional features not available on Centrex. In particular, those organizations with large data needs may consider a PBX alternative. An example of these are large universities that are attempting to integrate their voice and data requirements and provide their students with direct access into university data bases from computer terminals.

With all the potential for bypass and revenue diversion due to competition, a review of the local exchange companies' financial statements in the past few years shows a strengthening of financial position rather than a weakening. Industry participants have been successful in limiting the actual number of firms engaged in bypass. A review of these telephone companies' activities provides a sound basis for an analyst to judge the degree of a firm's success in controlling its bypass risk.

Along with divestiture came a new structure of industry pricing—the so-called access charge system. It replaced the former separations and settlements agreements. A major objective of the access charge pricing system is the elimination of the subsidy between interstate and intrastate services. The most direct method developed for removing non traffic-sensitive expenses from the charges of the interexchange carriers was the customer access line charge (CALC). This charge advanced to $2 per access line in 1986, and any additional increase would reduce per-minute charges by local companies to interexchange carriers, thus permitting further reductions in the price of long-distance service. Hence, large users of interexchange services would be inclined to remain on the facilities of the public switched network. In addition, restructuring of access charges paid by interexchange carriers which act to reduce the sensitivity of incremental calling to access cost should reduce the incentive of interexchange carriers to actively promote bypass.

Local regulatory decisions are as important as federal regulatory decisions to the financial health of the industry. Local regulators have had a social goal of fostering universal service by maintaining low basic exchange rates, but bypass may be encouraged unless local exchange rates bear more of the costs of services and other services are reduced in price. Particularly sensitive are toll rate levels, which for years have been kept high to support the low level of basic exchange rates. Regulatory decisions that reduce the amount of subsidy in "competitive services" and increase the price of basic exchange services help to combat the bypass danger.

Marketing and customer responsiveness have also greatly aided the companies in reducing the number of potential bypassers. Companies with active marketing programs designed to meet the needs of their customer base are more likely to avoid bypass. These programs may include timely service and support the development of new product offerings, or merely more frequent contact with the customer base to assure high quality of service.

Another development with great potential for combating bypass is legislation that either gives the local regulators increasing pricing flexibility or redefines the services of the local exchange company into regulated and competitive categories. In the latter case, many of these services would be either tariffed or removed from regulation entirely. Those local exchange companies with a larger percentage of their revenue base either detariffed or unregulated should provide the investor with a reduced degree of bypass risk, compared with those organizations remaining entirely subject to regulation.

While the financial threat of bypass is a real concern to the analyst in relation to the level of future earnings streams, to date the industry has been very successful in limiting its impact. Those organizations which develop a sophisticated marketing culture, are actively involved in the political arena, and are working with their regulators to reduce the amount of subsidy in price levels should be the most successful in combating the threat of bypass and establishing a reduced level of financial risk for the investor.

Competition in the Gas Distribution Industry

Gas distribution companies face competition from several directions. Large interruptible industrial customers can often shift from gas to oil, depending on price and supply considerations. Gas distributors will structure contracts with such customers in ways designed to minimize the profit impact of these shifting customer requirements. Another source of competition arises from competing energy sources in the residential gas market although in general, gas currently has a price advantage. Here, the price of oil or electricity relative to gas plays a major role. The analyst should identify long-term energy price trends to help determine the dimension of the market for gas at the retail level.

FINANCIAL ANALYSIS

In essence, a company's financial statements consolidate into one reasonably comparable presentation the results of operational and financial management decisions. Using a variety of methods, the analyst extracts from the financial statements information that will help assess the future financial strength of the company and helps the analyst to discern the degree of stability and variability of that future financial strength. It is essential in the process to evaluate the extent to which management derives flexibility in decision making from the ability of the company's finances to support business expansion or absorb business reversals.

Financial analysis, however, goes beyond simply a review of the financial statements, to incorporate an understanding of management's financial goals and objectives and its plans for achieving these goals. Financial analysis requires a full understanding of a company's operations in order to determine the degree of management's flexibility to attain its financial goals. All this assumes that, for the utility company, regulation remains supportive of management's prerogatives. With their much improved balance between cash generation and capital expenditures, electric and telephone utility managements are increasingly able to actively manage their financial measures and thereby determine, to a significant degree, the level of credit quality they wish to provide to fixed-income investors. Assuming supportive regulation, understanding management's orientation then becomes central to the determination of proper credit ratings.

Financial Statement Presentation

The organization of a utility's balance sheet differs from that of a nonregulated company and is indicative of the capital-intensive nature of the industry. For this reason, utility plant, a noncurrent asset, is listed first. In contrast, nonregulated companies list assets in order of decreasing liquidity, with current assets shown first. The four major asset classifications of a utility balance sheet, listed in order of statement presentation are: utility plant, other investments, current assets, and deferred charges. (See Table 9.)

An important sub-account in the utility plant section of the balance sheet for certain utilities is construction work in progress (CWIP). CWIP represents utility plant in the process of construction. Although CWIP cannot be depreciated, certain regulators permit a cash return on a percentage of CWIP, which improves the company's ability to generate cash and fund construction and helps avoid consumer rate shock. The analyst should regard favorably jurisdictions which permit a cash return on CWIP in rate base.

On the owner's equity/liability side of the balance sheet, capitalization is listed first, primarily because of the importance attached to a utility's ability to access capital markets in order to fund the replacement of old facilities and build new plant. By contrast, a non-regulated company would list current liabilities first—emphasizing near-term liquidity. The other major classifications for this side of a utility balance sheet (listed in order of statement presentation) are current liabilities, deferred credits, and commitments and contingencies.

The four major classifications of a utility income statement are operating revenues, operating expenses, other income and deductions, and interest charges (Table 10). The netting of these four major classifications will result in net income. If preferred and/or preference stock is outstanding, the subtraction of preferred and/or preference dividends results in the balance available for common stock. Ongoing utility operations are separated from other items on the income statement. The netting of operating revenues with operating expenses yields the operating income line. The term "above-the-line" indicates elements of net income which are directly related to utility operations. Above-the-line items include only those expenses that are considered in operating expenses when determining rates. Below-the-line expenses, excluding direct financing costs, are those which are not recovered directly through rates. Operating revenues specified by regulators usually allow investors to earn a return on common equity, preferred stock, and debt securities. These allowed returns are, in theory, to be used to pay common and preferred dividends as well as to service debt. This indirect recovery accounts for the listing of dividends and interest expense as "below-the-line" items.

When utilities are not allowed to earn a return to cover their construction financing costs during the construction period, they are allowed to capitalize financing costs for future recovery. Electric utilities are permitted to capitalize the cost of both equity and debt capital through a noncash income addition and an interest charge offset, which are the two components of "allowance for funds used during construction" (AFUDC). These capitalized amounts are added to utility plant under construction (i.e., CWIP) and ultimately included in rate base as plant in service, earning a return and being recovered through depreciation. But, with regulators becoming increasingly reluctant to reflect all the costs of major new plant in rate base, analysts should be skeptical of large amounts of AFUD in a company's income statement. Telephone companies traditionally capitalize the cost of debt in an income statement account called Interest During Construction.

The major asset-acquisition and financing activities of a utility are highlighted by the statement of changes in financial position, which for utility reporting purposes is often called a statement of sources and uses of funds or a "funds statement." Funds can be defined as working capital, cash, or even construction expenditures, as is the case with some telecommunications concerns.

Sources of funds are typically segregated into two broad groups: internally generated and external financing. The extent to which these funds are derived from operations is a primary measure of financial flexibility. The sources and uses statement is particularly important

TABLE 9 Investor-Owned Electric Utilities Combined Balance Sheets

Year ended December 31 (millions of dollars)	1985	1984	1983	1982	1981
Assets					
Utility plant:					
Electric	397,870	372,516	343,600	319,723	290,723
Accumulated provision for depreciation and amortization......	81,420	77,938	70,527	64,552	58,783
Net electric utility plant	316,450	294,578	273,073	255,171	231,940
Nuclear fuel	13,480	11,587	9,421	8,056	7,449
Accumulated depreciation...........	4,910	4,219	3,755	3,591	3,324
Net nuclear fuel...................	8,570	7,368	5,666	4,465	4,125
Net total electric utility plant	325,020	30,946	278,739	259,636	236,065
Other..............................	19,000	18,567	20,058	17,084	16,241
Accumulated depreciation...........	6,520	6,368	6,546	5,462	4,959
Net other utility plant	12,480	12,199	13,512	11,622	11,282
Total utility plant including nuclear fuel.	430,350	402,670	373,078	344,862	314,413
Accumulated depreciation...........	92,850.	88,525	80,828	73,605	67,066
Net total utility plant including nuclear fuel	337,500	314,145	292,250	271,258	247,347
Other property and investment	9,960	9,359	8,367	6,656	5,737
Total current and accrued assets	39,150	37,823	33,196	31,799	28,100
Total deferred debits	19,940	18,065	12,001	7,486	6,532
Total assets......................	406,550	379,392	345,814	317.198	287,716

Liabilities

Common capital stock	51,660	47,842	44,742	40,491	35,406
Other paid-in capital†	36,650	33,886	31,580	27,305	23,838
Retained earnings	45,360	40,423	35,369	30,984	27,511
Total common capital stock equity	133,670	121,151	111,691	98,779	86,755
Preferred stock	29,550	29,882	29,479	28,616	26,817
Mortgage bonds	112,910	108,997	104,244	98,998	93,783
Other long-term debt	37,000	32,696	28,034	24,694	20,780
Total long-term debt	149,910	141,693	132,278	123,692	114,563
Total capitalization	313,130	293,727	273,448	251,088	228,135
Total current and accrued liabilities	37,160	36,996	33,898	33,356	32,395
Accumulated deferred income taxes	31,830	26,438	21,075	3,909	2,869
Accumulated deferred investment tax credits	15,290	14,136	12,059	127	115
Other deferred credits and operating reserves	9,140	8,096	5,334	18,310	15,931
Total liabilities	406,550	37,392	345,814	317,198	287,716

* Estimated—based on data from third quarter 1985, and do not reflect fourth quarter plant write-offs.
† Includes premium on common and preferred stock.
SOURCE: Edison Electric Institute, estimated for 1985.

TABLE 10 Investor-Owned Electric Utility Income

(millions of dollars)	1985	1984	1983	1982	1981
Total electric revenue...........	125,770	120,090	109,446	101,693	94,270
Operating expenses...........	69,750	67,338	62,892	61,243	58,842
Depreciation...........	10,150	9,106	8,370	7,588	6,893
Total expenses	79,900	76,444	71,262	68,831	65,735
Electric operating income before taxes...........	45,870	43,646	38,184	32,862	28,535
Taxes...........	21,710	20,850	17,523	14,604	12,189
Electric operating income after taxes	24,160	22,796	20,661	18,258	16,347
Other income*	8,970	8,670	7,807	6,833	5,703
Total income before interest charges	33,130	31,464	28,468	25,091	22,050
Interest charges†	12,750	11,771	10,649	10,066	9,421
Net income before extraordinary items	20,380	19,693	17,819	15,025	12,629
Extraordinary items...........	—‡	—‡	(228)	121	28
Net income after extraordinary items	20,380	19,693	17,591	15,146	12,656
Dividends	14,910	13,905	13,021	11,470	9,838
Retained earnings...........	5,470	5,788	4,570	3,676	2,818

The above figures for all United States including Alaska and Hawaii. 1985 figures are based on data from 3rd quarter 1985, and do not reflect 4th quarter plant write-offs.

SOURCE: Edison Electric Institute, estimated for 1985.
* Figures include allowance for other funds during construction (previously included with AFUDC).
† Amortization, interest on long-term debt, allowance for borrowed funds used during construction-credit, etc.
‡ Not meaningful.

because it highlights changes in cash flow and the impact of these changes on external financing requirements. Analysts should also pay special attention to extraordinary items, such as the effects of electric plant phase-ins and abandonments, which may be material in terms of reducing earnings in future periods, even though they do not provide or consume funds.

Capital Requirements

Because of the utilities' capital-intensive nature, financial analyses focuses on cash capital requirements and a company's ability to meet those requirements through internal versus external sources. Construction expenditures typically account for the largest component of capital requirements. When analyzing construction expenditures, capitalized interest (or AFUDC) should be eliminated so that only cash construction expenditures are included.

Projected construction expenditures typically embodied in five-year financial plans should be examined in light of realistic demand-growth assumptions based upon the economic outlook for the service territory. Extensive dependence on a single economic sector or industry or single customer could expose the utility to revenue and demand-growth fluctuations. In any case, higher-cost nuclear generation projects under construction should be viewed as more risky than other types of units, since nuclear construction cost estimates are notoriously unreliable. In addition, these plants have become subject to frequent delays, and outright cancellations can occur at any point in the construction licensing process.

Other factors affecting the level of construction expenditures include regulation and CWIP policies. All else being equal, permitting a return on CWIP in rate base eases the financial strain on a company involved in accessing external capital markets. If a company is in a cash squeeze because of a heavy construction program, and has no CWIP earning a rate base return, routine plant maintenance is often the first item to be neglected and/or deferred.

When analyzing working capital requirements, the individual components should be examined. Current maturities of long-term debt, as well as short-term debt maturities, should be excluded and listed with debt maturities and retirements to avoid double counting. Heavy reliance on short-term debt (except for very small utilities, which may run up to about 10 percent of capitalization) could indicate an inability to fully access one or more capital markets within a short period of time.

Internal Cash Generation

A utility's ability to meet cash capital requirements (including debt maturities and sinking fund payments) through internal cash generation is a key measure of financial strength. Sources of internal funds include: net income less preferred and common stock dividends, capitalized financing costs, and equity income of nonconsolidated subsidiaries plus depreciation and amortization accruals; deferred income taxes and investment tax credits; and other sources. The analyst should note that capitalized financing cost (or AFUDC) is deducted from net income in this calculation. A cash return on CWIP in rate base during periods of construction serves to improve cash flow.

The internal cash calculation should subtract noncash contributions from subsidiaries. Cash from operations should be the focus of primary liquidity analysis. All extraordinary items should be excluded from internal cash flow when calculating debt protection measures. In diversified utilities, the upstreaming of dividends from subsidiaries (given the subsidiaries' ability to do so) should be viewed with certain considerations in mind. First, the degree of control the parent company has over subsidiary dividends should be examined. It is not unusual to find dividend restrictions in company charters or debt indentures. Second, given this degree of parental control, the percentage of subsidiary earnings actually upstreamed should be scrutinized.

Finally, depreciation expense usually reflects a company's optimistic view that all rate relief requested is received. If a material plant investment is assumed to have near total cost recovery in financial projections, the analyst should calculate incremental depreciation recovery under a variety of regulatory scenarios.

Rate relief assumptions used in financial projections should be examined for reasonableness. Utility commissions are political, and if the service territory's economic prospects are substandard or the utility's rate needs in support of internal cash are large, regulators can find a way to temper any final rate order.

External Financing

Capital requirements which cannot be financed through internal cash flow must be financed externally through the issuance of debt, preferred stock, or common stock. For analytical purposes, it is important to know the aggregate amount of securities to be issued. Also, knowing the type of security and the timing of its issuance will enable an analyst to better estimate interest cost and capitalization structure. Finally, it is important to know if there are any internal or external restrictions that would preclude or limit the issuance of debt or preferred stock.

The amount of the external financing program has a direct relationship to the pressure which will be put on a utility's debt protection. The size of external financing requirements relative to capital expenditures in a given year is a key analytical relationship which helps determine the extent of financial strain. Relating the amount of internally generated funds to total capital requirements (construction commitments, debt maturities, and sinking fund requirements) shows the entire amount of external financing that will be necessary, and an estimate of the associated cost. Comparing external financing requirements to the size of a utility's capitalization at the beginning of the financing period measures the percentage growth in capitalization necessary to support the capital expenditures. This provides guidance as to how much pressure financing may put on profitability and interest coverage. A high amount of external financing may translate to financing costs that increase faster than revenues. If revenues derived from the ratemaking process and sales growth are insufficient to make up for higher operating and interest expenses, a utility will have difficulty maintaining its profitability and interest coverage.

As long as a utility has financing flexibility, it can issue any type of security for new money or refunding purpose in any amount appropriate to its size. However, bond indentures and preferred stock charters have provisions which limit the sales of securities if certain criteria such as earnings coverage and bondable property tests are not met or which limit the preferred and common stock dividend payout if the payout would lower the common equity percentage below a certain point. A cut in common stock dividends generally inhibits further issuance of common stock, thereby forcing even greater reliance on debt and further unbalancing the capital structure.

For indenture or charter restrictions to take effect, a company's credit protection usually will already be significantly strained. Financing flexibility for companies with financial or operational problems could also be curtailed if financing approvals are not received from public utility commissions. Many utilities must receive approvals for each financing from their regulators, whether state or federal. Although the restrictions on the issuance of new securities are designed to protect existing security holders, credit ratings may be negatively impacted if, for example, a company must run up its short-term, variable-rate borrowings to levels that cannot be funded out on a timely basis.

Capitalization

The credit analysis of utilities puts great emphasis on the strength of a company's balance sheet, particularly its capital structure. Because utilities are regulated, the accepted view is that utilities can traditionally support a much more highly leveraged capital structure than most industrial concerns. The latter are viewed as riskier because of the competitive nature of their businesses. Traditionally, utilities have relied heavily on debt financing—the cheapest method of raising capital. Many utilities (most electrics and some telephone and gas companies) maintain a layer of preferred stock in their capital structure. Common equity makes up the balance of the utility's capital structure. A credit analyst will view the common equity component largely as a cushion for the holders of bonds and preferred stock. The greater the proportion of total equity in a utility's capital structure, the more protection there is for senior security holders.

The capital structure must also be viewed in light of off-balance-sheet obligations that, in reality, reflect strong debt characteristics. Utilities often have off-balance-sheet fuel financing activities, and lease obligations are increasingly in evidence. Long-term purchased power and fuel contracts can be viewed as being debt-like obligations, depending on the nature of the contract.

When analyzing an individual company, the credit analyst should consider the company's current capitalization ratios as well as their trend over time, both historical and projected—although with more emphasis on the projected trend. The ratios will be compared with industry averages and evaluated against the degree of operating and business risk facing the particular utility in question. Because the business or competitive risk of all the utility industries has increased in recent years, credit analysts view the decline in leverage and strengthening of equity that has occurred as a major positive and something that utilities should strive to continue. In particular, electric utilities with a large nuclear exposure are viewed as having a large, specific operating risk that should be offset by a strong capital structure.

Because common equity is the most expensive component of the cost of capital, some regulatory commissions have begun to impose caps on a utility's common equity ratio for ratemaking purposes. This phenomenon has occurred at common equity levels of more than 50 percent for some electric companies. While some utilities have addressed this development through buybacks of their own common stock, others have taken equity on which they cannot earn a regulated return and put it to work in passive investments in preferred stock, leveraged leases, and so forth. Still others have diversified into nonregulated businesses.

The rise in common equity ratios may have implications for the return on equity allowed by regulators as well. Clearly, a given return level will require higher revenues to the extent that the equity base is higher. Also, regulators will likely perceive a conservatively leveraged company to be less risky. Consequently, returns on equity allowed by regulators may be expected to drop (regardless of any changes in general interest rates) for such companies. But whether the inroads of competition and market forces will permit this remains to be seen.

TABLE 11 Weighted Average of Yields on Newly Issued Domestic Bonds and Preferred Stocks, 1965–1985

Year	Utility Bonds			Industrial Bonds	Pre-ferred Stock
	Electric and Gas	Telephone	All Utilities		All Utilities
1985	11.83%	11.54%	11.78%	11.64%	10.08%
1984	14.25	12.73	13.33	12.58	13.16
1983	12.70	11.72	12.53	11.50	12.06
1982	14.93	14.23	14.56	13.65	14.42
1981	16.31	15.45	16.30	15.16	15.11
1980	13.46	12.59	13.09	11.66	12.28
1979	10.85	10.29	10.64	9.49	9.76
1978	9.30	9.07	9.22	8.98	9.03
1977	8.43	8.21	8.38	8.15	8.43
1976	8.92	8.41	8.80	8.61	9.12
1975	9.97	9.27	9.76	9.12	10.63
1974	9.59	9.22	9.21	8.87	9.95
1973	7.91	7.87	7.88	7.86	7.50
1972	7.50	7.36	7.46	7.51	7.53
1971	7.72	7.58	7.71	7.80	7.74
1970	8.79	8.75	8.85	8.86	9.01
1969	7.98	8.00	7.99	7.84	7.75
1968	6.80	6.55	6.72	6.64	6.44
1967	6.07	5.77	6.01	5.79	6.03
1966	5.53	5.51	5.61	5.52	5.37
1965	4.61	4.61	4.68	4.80	—

SOURCE: *Moody's Investors Service.*

Reflecting the high level of financing during the 1970s and early 1980s (much of it when interest rates were at record highs), the utility industry's embedded cost of capital has been trending significantly upward. (See Table 11.) The higher a company's embedded cost of debt, the greater earnings must be to produce a given level of interest coverage. As interest rates have fallen, beginning in 1984, many utilities have reduced the high-cost debt in their capital structures through refundings, debt calls, and tender offers. The interest-cost savings can sometimes have a meaningful positive effect on coverage ratios and, to the extent internal funds are used to retire debt, on leverage as well.

Not to be forgotten in the analysis of a utility company's debt structure is the maturity schedule of that debt. Maturities should be managed to avoid having large amounts coming due in a short period. This could result in difficulty should general markets be unreceptive at a given time or should the company's own financial condition restrict its access to markets.

Profitability

Another area in financial analysis concerns profitability. A number of considerations are important in analyzing this area. An understanding of the utility's revenue growth and customer mix, along with its costs and tax structures, is critical to analyzing internal cash generation (as discussed earlier) and interest coverage (to be looked at in the following section).

The revenue growth of a utility company is a function of demand growth in the service territory, rate case filings, new service offerings, and revenue mix. In the case of gas distribution companies, however, the influence of purchased gas costs on revenues may cause revenues to decrease, because of declining gas costs, even while the financial health of the enterprise is improving. In areas where economic activity is particularly strong or the weather is extreme (either very hot or very cold), usage of some utility services will be high and will support enhanced revenues. Likewise, as expenses rise, in part because of inflation or fuel cost increases, rate cases are filed to recover the higher cost of business. Revenue mix, either between intrastate and interstate jurisdictions or by type of service, can determine whether a company will achieve revenue growth matching demand and indicate the potential variability in the revenue growth. Concentrations of revenue geographically and by customer indicate a potential for competitive entry.

A company's controllable costs (defined as total operating expenses less depreciation) as a percentage of total operating revenue—the controllable ratio—is a tool for analyzing the company's cost structure relative to its industry. "Cost structure" encompasses many items and cannot be analyzed separately from the service territory. Such factors as rural/urban service territory, affluent/less affluent customer base, modern/less modern network, and fast/slow demand growth will determine cost structure. For example, a more rural utility will have a lower customer density and, because of larger distances for repairmen to travel and cable or pipe to install, will sustain higher costs to serve those customers. In addition, the utility could have less need to modernize its plant because of few large customers, and therefore have higher maintenance expenses. But the absolute level of the controllable ratio is of less importance than the changes in the ratio over time. A declining controllable ratio shows that revenues are growing faster than expenses, either through higher demand growth or expense control.

Depreciation rates are reviewed to determine the growth of this expense in relation to operating revenues. Since depreciation expense is flowed through to the ratepayer in the form of higher rates, regulated companies have historically only been able to depreciate high-technology equipment over a long period (i.e., 25 years). In the case of the telecommunications industry, which is in the process of being deregulated, regulators are beginning to shorten the allowed life span of the equipment in order to more appropriately reflect its technological life, with resulting increases in rates. However, a full increase in rates may not occur due to an increase in cost cutting by the utility. Higher depreciation expense with no increase in rates has also been approved by commissions in order to reduce earnings when a utility is earning over its allowed rate of return. Thus, depreciation expense for many telephone companies is growing faster than revenues, and will continue to do so in the near term.

It is interesting to note that, as depreciation rates increase and construction programs decline, depreciation expense may exceed new plant additions. The declining asset base will lead to a decline in revenues, all other things being equal.

Pretax operating margin—defined as total operating revenues less total operating expenses and general taxes divided by total operating revenues—is a key profitability measure used in financial analysis. This ratio shows how many cents are available per dollar of revenue to pay income taxes and fixed charges—defined as interest expense and preferred stock dividends. If a company limits growth in operating expenses relative to revenues, as can be seen when analyzing the controllable ratio and depreciation rates, the pretax operating margin will rise.

A company's income tax rates, on both the state and federal levels, are critical in analyzing interest coverage. Regulators determine rate base and the overall allowed return on assets. A lower tax rate results in less pretax income needed to produce the same net income as a high tax rate would. Lower pretax income means lower interest coverage, even though net income is the same.

Return on equity (ROE)—net income available for common equity divided by average common equity for a period—combines all the profitability concepts discussed in this section. ROE measures earnings achieved per dollar of common equity capital. If ROE declines, net income is not rising as fast as the common equity base. Also, because ROE is the key factor in regulatory determination of the allowed rate base return level, and the cost of debt and preferred stock is generally a cost pass-through to the ratepayer, ROE is a key measure of financial performance for rate base-regulated companies.

Earnings Coverages

Coverages of interest obligations by earnings is a critical element in credit analysis because timely payment of interest is a key determinant of credit quality. Pretax interest coverage measures how well earnings before income taxes cover the issuer's interest payments. Utility analysts use two primary methods to calculate coverage ratios: (1) including allowance for capitalized construction funds and (2) on the basis of cash earnings only. In addition to interest coverage, fixed charge protection measurements often include coverage of other fixed obligations such as lease payments and preferred stock dividends. Greater emphasis is placed upon coverage calculations excluding capitalized costs, because interest must be paid in cash whether or not capitalized for financial reporting purposes.

The level of interest coverage is determined by the interrelationship between the cost of debt, capital structure, and level of profitability. A substantial equity component of capitalization earning a high level of ROE relative to the industry spells high interest coverage on a pretax basis. However, the quality of a utility's earnings may be adversely affected by major construction that is reflected in growing levels of AFUDC on the income statement. Because AFUDC accounts for capitalized interest on a plant investment that may not be included in rate base by regulators, the analyst should generally be critical of pretax interest coverage calculated using AFUDC. A calculation of interest coverage that excludes AFUDC often comes closer to describing interest protection afforded the bondholder. This assumes that large plant investments may be phased into rates only gradually or, in extreme cases, disallowed by regulators from earning any return at all. In this latter case, a utility has no incentive to build additional plant, and investors should consider the prudence of further investment in such jurisdictions.

The rapid rise of borrowing costs in the late 1970s and early 1980s coincided with a period of heavy construction—and debt financing—for many electric utilities. Since return on CWIP was typically disallowed at that time, interest expense soared while utility earnings failed to keep pace. Interest coverage calculated without AFUDC then fell sharply for many electrics, as did bond ratings. Utilities at or near the end of their construction programs are receiving only gradual rate recognition of their considerable investment in new plant from their respective commissions. As a result, coverage protection is improving only modestly. But, as interest rates drop, utilities may be able to reduce their high embedded costs of debt and improve coverage protection by refunding high-coupon debt, thereby improving credit quality without resorting to regulatory relief.

Accounting Practices

GAAP and FASB 71 versus utility accounting. In December 1982, the Financial Accounting Standards Board (FASB) issued Statement of Financial Accounting Standards 71, "Accounting for the Effects of Certain Types of Regulation." Utility financial reporting was strengthened by FASB in two ways. First, the type of regulation required for a departure from generally accepted accounting principles was identified. Second, an indication of when rate decisions require different accounting treatments was provided. Even with these clarifications, there is still room for accounting judgment in the application of FASB 71.

The following criteria are prerequisite for the application of FASB 71 for companies with regulated operations:

- If rates for regulated services or products provided to customers are established by, or are subject to, approval by an independent third-party regulator or by the company's own governing board empowered by statute or contract to established rates that bind customers.
- The regulated rates are designed to recover the specific enterprise's costs of providing regulated services or products.

In view of the demand for the regulated services or products and the level of competition, direct and indirect, it is reasonable to assume that rates set at levels which will recover the enterprise's costs can be charged to and collected from customers.

When analyzing capitalized or deferred expenses, the analyst should be aware that before such costs (which would otherwise be expensed) can be capitalized or deferred, the regulatory intent to allow the specific future recovery of such costs must be clear and probable.

Recently enacted changes to FASB 71, known as FASB 90, involve the accounting treatment of disallowed plant costs and abandoned plant. The new accounting standards will have a material impact on the financial position of many companies with canceled plant or with large, recently completed construction projects for which regulators have not permitted full recovery.

The remainder of this section consists of a topical discussion intended to highlight items whose nature and/or calculation is peculiar to regulated industry.

Flow-through versus normalized tax methods. Utility taxes can be grouped into two broad categories for ratemaking purposes: general taxes and income taxes.

General taxes are all taxes, including property, sales, and franchise taxes, that are paid to local taxing authorities. Often, a public utility is the single largest local taxpayer. This is a manifestation of the political philosophy that a utility is a conduit by which ratepayers can be taxed by municipalities. These taxes are nearly always recoverable through rates.

Federal, state, and even local governments can levy income taxes on utilities. Taxes paid are generally recoverable through rates; however, there can be differences in the amount of taxes paid and the amount of taxes allowed for ratemaking purposes. Two alternative methods have evolved which allow utilities to match tax expenses with revenues during periods of benefit for tax preference items.

1. "Flow-through" accounting assumes that reduced income taxes from preference items are tax savings which should accrue to the ratepayer by reducing the revenue requirement.
2. "Normalized" accounting recognizes reduced income taxes as a deferral. Here, a deferred-tax account is established and rates are not adjusted, and it may be argued that benefits accrue to the shareholder.

From an analytical viewpoint, normalization allows the utility greater cash flow. Companies, especially those with large construction requirements, tend to benefit if their commissions allow normalization. The 1969 tax law allows for adoption of normalized accounting on a prospective basis.

Accelerated depreciation methods are exceptionally beneficial to capital-intensive companies, when investment is recovered more quickly in the earlier years of an asset's life. Over the years, changes in the Internal Revenue Code have benefited utilities. The Tax Reform Act of 1969 permitted liberalized depreciation by allowing the utility to elect accelerated methods with normalization. The Economic Recovery Tax Act of 1981 (ERTA) was enacted with the intent of stimulating capital formation. ERTA established on accelerated cost recovery system (ACRS), which introduced the concept of a "recovery period" for certain classes of assets rather than focusing on the useful life on a depreciable asset. However, the Tax Reform Act of 1986 was generally negative for utilities. Among other things, the law eliminated the investment tax credit, modified ACRS to require generally longer tax depreciation lives, and postponed certain tax deductions, all of which serve to reduce cash flow.

Depreciation. Depreciation is recorded in order to match a portion of the original cost of an asset with the revenue generated during a given period. Book depreciation, tax depreciation, and depreciation allowed recovery by regulators, although conceptually the same, may all be mechanically different. Accelerated methods are generally not available to utilities for book or ratemaking purposes, but are for tax purposes (this tax preference item can be accounted for by the normalized or the flow-through method, as per our previous discussion). When analyzing phase-in of the costs of high-cost plants, regulators may make what appear to be arbitrary adjustments to plant cost or depreciation charges that effect recoverability of plant investment during the phase-in period.

Fuel clauses. A fuel adjustment clause (a deferred charge) is a ratemaking mechanism that permits a utility to recover deferred fuel costs (for fuel actually consumed) from customers in the future. If fuel costs decline, this clause may serve to actually lower rates as the utility "over-collects." The analyst should be sensitive to the fuel mix of an electric utility (e.g., dependence on oil) when assessing the potential impact of fuel clause adjustments.

Pension funds. Pension liabilities of public utilities are usually fully funded because pension expense is also usually recoverable.

AFUDC. Ongoing construction expenditures need to be either funded internally or financed externally via an equity or debt offering. When utilities are not allowed to earn a return to cover their construction financing costs during the construction period, they are allowed to capitalize financing costs for future recovery through a noncash credit to income known as AFUDC (allowance for funds used during construction). As discussed in the Financial Statement Presentation section, AFUDC has two components on the income statement—the equity portion is recorded as a credit to other income, while the debt component is recorded as reduction of gross interest expense. On the balance sheet, these amounts are capitalized and added to the basis of utility plant under construction (i.e., CWIP) and ultimately included in rate base as plant in service, earning a return and being recovered through depreciation.

SELECTED REFERENCES

EDISON ELECTRIC INSTITUTE. *Statistical Year Book of the Electric Utility Industry.* Washington, D.C.: Edison Electric Institute, various years.

———. *Year-End Electric Power Survey.* Washington, D.C.: Edison Electric Institute, various years.

———. *EEI Pocketbook of Electric Utility Industry Statistics.* Washington, D.C.: Edison Electric Institute, various years.

GRAHAM, BENJAMIN; DAVID J. DODD; and SIDNEY COTTLE, with CHARLES TATHAM. *Security Analysis.* New York: McGraw-Hill, 1962.

HYMAN, LEONARD S. *America's Electric Utilities: Past, Present and Future.* Arlington, Va.: Public Utilities Reports, Inc., 1985.

JOSKOW, PAUL L., and RICHARD SCHMALENSEE. *Markets for Power: An Analysis of Electric Utility Deregulation.* Cambridge, Mass.: The MIT Press, 1983.

KAHN, ALFRED E. *The Economics of Regulation.* New York: John Wiley & Sons, 1970–71.

Moody's Public Utilities Manual. New York: Moody's Investors Service, various dates.

PACIFIC GAS AND ELECTRIC, *Resource: An Encyclopedia of Utility Industry Terms.* San Francisco: Pacific G&E, 1984.

PHILLIPS, CHARLES F., JR. *The Regulation of Public Utilities: Theory and Practice.* Arlington, Va.: Public Utilities Reports, 1984.

U.S. DEPARTMENT OF ENERGY, ENERGY INFORMATION ADMINISTRATION. *Statistics of Privately Owned Electric Utilities in the United States.* Washington, D.C.: U.S. Government Printing Office, various years.

Electric Power Monthly (various issues).

Monthly Energy Review (various issues).

U.S. FEDERAL POWER COMMISSION. *Statistics of Privately Owned Electric Utilities in the United States.* Washington, D.C.: U.S. Government Printing Office, various years.

YOUNG, HAROLD H. *Forty Years of Public Utility Finance.* Charlottesville, Va.: The University of Virginia, 1965.

29

Municipal Bonds

Sylvan G. Feldstein, Ph.D.
*Vice President and Manager—Municipal Bond
Research Department
Merrill Lynch Capital Markets*

Frank J. Fabozzi, Ph.D., CFA, CPA
*Visiting Professor
Sloan School of Management
Massachusetts Institute of Technology*

Municipal bonds are securities issued by state and local governments and their creations such as "authorities" and special districts. Most recent available information indicates that approximately 37,000 different states, counties, school districts, special districts, towns, and other public issuing bodies have issued municipal bonds. Although some investors buy municipal bonds as a way of supporting public improvements such as schools, playgrounds, and parks, the vast majority buy them because interest income from such bonds generally is exempt from federal income taxes. Consequently, municipal bonds are purchased by those who are in high marginal tax brackets, because on an aftertax basis they offer a yield that is greater than comparable bonds that are fully taxable.

Municipal bonds come in a variety of types, with different redemption features, credit risks, and marketability. Consequently, the holder of municipal bonds is exposed to the same risks as the holder of corporate and Treasury bonds: interest rate risk, reinvestment risk, and call risk. Moreover, the holder of a municipal bond, like the holder of a corporate bond, faces credit risk.

In this chapter we describe the basic characteristics of municipal bonds as well as the municipal bond industry.

TYPES OF MUNICIPAL OBLIGATIONS

Bonds

In terms of municipal bond security structures, there are basically two different types. The first type is the general obligation bond, and the second is the revenue bond.

General obligation bonds are debt instruments issued by states, counties, special districts, cities, towns, and school districts. They are secured by the issuer's general taxing powers. Usually, a general obligation bond is secured by the issuer's unlimited taxing power. For smaller governmental jurisdictions such as school districts and towns, the only available unlimited taxing power is on property. For larger general obligation bond issuers such as states and big cities, the tax revenues are more diverse and may include corporate and individual income taxes, sales taxes, and property taxes. The security pledges for these larger issuers such as states are sometimes referred to as being *full faith and credit obligations*.

Additionally, certain general obligation bonds are secured not only by the issuer's general taxing powers to create monies accumulated in the general fund but also from certain identified fees, grants, and special charges, which provide additional revenues from outside the general fund. Such bonds are known as being *double-barreled* in security because of the dual nature of the revenue sources.

Also, not all general obligation bonds are secured by unlimited taxing powers. Some have pledged taxes that are limited as to revenue sources and maximum property tax millage amounts. Such bonds are known as *limited-tax general obligation bonds*.

The second basic type of security structure is found in a revenue bond. Such bonds are issued for either project or enterprise financings in which the bond issuers pledge to the bondholders the revenues generated by the operating projects financed. Below are examples of the specific types of revenue bonds that have been issued over the years.

Airport revenue bonds.   The revenues securing airport revenue bonds usually come from either traffic-generated sources—such as landing fees, concession fees, and airline apron-use and fueling fees—or lease revenues from one or more airlines for the use of a specific facility such as a terminal or hangar.

College and university revenue bonds.   The revenues securing college and university revenue bonds usually include dormitory room rental fees, tuition payments, and sometimes the general assets of the college or university as well.

Hospital revenue bonds. The security for hospital revenue bonds is usually dependent on federal and state reimbursement programs (such as Medicaid and Medicare), third-party commercial payers (such as Blue Cross and private insurance), and individual patient payments.

Single-family mortgage revenue bonds. Single-family mortgage revenue bonds are usually secured by the mortgages and mortgage loan repayments on single-family homes. Security features vary but can include Federal Housing Administration (FHA), Veterans Administration (VA), or private mortgage insurance.

Multifamily revenue bonds. These revenue bonds are usually issued for multifamily housing projects for senior citizens and low-income families. Some housing revenue bonds are usually secured by mortgages that are federally insured; others receive federal government operating subsidies, such as under section 8, or interest-cost subsidies, such as under section 236; and still others receive only local property tax reductions as subsidies.

Industrial development and pollution control revenue bonds. Bonds have been issued for a variety of industrial and commercial activities that range from manufacturing plants to shopping centers. They are usually secured by payments to be made by the corporations or businesses that use the facilities.

Public power revenue bonds. Public power revenue bonds are secured by revenues to be produced from electrical operating plants. Some bonds are for a single issuer, who constructs and operates power plants and then sells the electricity. Other public power revenue bonds are issued by groups of public and private investor-owned utilities for the joint financing of the construction of one or more power plants. This last arrangement is known as a *joint power* financing structure.

Resource recovery revenue bonds. A resource recovery facility converts refuse (solid waste) into commercially salable energy, recoverable products, and a residue to be landfilled. The major revenues for a resource recovery revenue bond usually are (1) the "tipping fees" per ton paid by those who deliver the garbage to the facility for disposal; (2) revenues from steam, electricity, or refuse-derived fuel sold to either an electric power company or another energy user; and (3) revenues from the sale of recoverable materials such as aluminum and steel scrap.

Seaport revenue bonds. The security for seaport revenue bonds can include specific lease agreements with the benefiting companies or pledged marine terminal and cargo tonnage fees.

Sewer revenue bonds. Revenues for sewer revenue bonds come from hookup fees and user charges. For many older sewer bond issuers, substantial portions of their construction budgets have been financed with federal grants.

Sports complex and convention center revenue bonds. Sports complex and convention center revenue bonds usually receive revenues from sporting or convention events held at the facilities and, in some instances, from earmarked outside revenues such as local motel and hotel room taxes.

Student loan revenue bonds. Student loan repayments under student loan revenue bond programs are sometimes 100 percent guaranteed either directly by the federal government—under the Federal Insured Student Loan program (FISL) for 100 percent of bond principal and interest—or by a state guaranty agency under a more recent federal insurance program, the Federal Guaranteed Student Loan program (GSL). In addition to these two federally backed programs, student loan bonds are also sometimes secured by the general revenues of the specific colleges involved.

Toll road and gas tax revenue bonds. There are generally two types of highway revenue bonds. The bond proceeds of the first type are used to build such specific revenue-producing facilities as toll roads, bridges, and tunnels. For these pure enterprise-type revenue bonds, the pledged revenues usually are the monies collected through the tolls. The second type of highway bond is one in which the bondholders are paid by earmarked revenues outside of toll collections, such as gasoline taxes, automobile registration payments, and driver's license fees.

Water revenue bonds. Water revenue bonds are issued to finance the construction of water treatment plants, pumping stations, collection facilities, and distribution systems. Revenues usually come from connection fees and charges paid by the users of the water systems.

Hybrid and Special Bond Securities

Though having certain characteristics of general obligation and revenue bonds, there are some municipal bonds that have more unique security structures as well. They include the following:

Federal Savings and Loan Insurance Corporation-backed bonds. In this security structure, the proceeds of a bond sale were deposited in a savings and loan association that, in turn, issued a certificate of deposit (CD). The CD was insured by the Federal Savings and Loan Insurance Corporation (FSLIC) up to a limit of $100,000 of combined principal and interest for each bondholder. The savings and loan association used the money to finance low- and moderate-income rental housing developments. While these bonds are no longer issued, there are billions of dollars of these bonds in the secondary market.

Insured bonds. These are bonds that, in addition to being secured by the issuer's revenues, also are backed by insurance policies written by commercial insurance companies. The insurance, usually structured as a surety type insurance policy, is supposed to provide prompt payment to the bondholders if a default should occur.

Lease-backed bonds. Lease-backed bonds are usually structured as revenue-type bonds with annual rent payments. In some instances the rental payments may only come from earmarked tax revenues, student tuition payments, or patient fees. In other instances the underlying lessee governmental unit is required to make annual appropriations from its general fund.

Letter of credit-backed bonds. Some municipal bonds, in addition to being secured by the issuer's cash flow revenues, also are backed by commercial bank letters of credit. In some instances the letters of credit are irrevocable and, if necessary, can be used to pay the bondholders. In other instances the issuers are required to maintain investment quality worthiness before the letters of credit can be drawn upon.

Life care residence revenue bonds. Life care residence bonds are issued to construct long-term residential facilities for older citizens. Revenues are usually derived from initial lump-sum payments made by the residents.

Moral obligation bonds. A moral obligation bond is a security structure for state-issued bonds that indicates that if revenues are needed for paying bondholders, the state legislature involved is legally authorized, though not required, to make an appropriation out of general state tax revenues.

Municipal utility district revenue bonds. These are bonds that are usually issued to finance the construction of water and sewer systems as well as roadways in undeveloped areas. The security is usually dependent on the commercial success of the specific development project involved, which can range from the sale of new homes to the renting of space in shopping centers and office buildings.

New housing authority bonds.   These bonds are secured by a contractual pledge of annual contributions from HUD. Monies from Washington are paid directly to the paying agent for the bonds, and the bondholders are given specific legal rights to enforce the pledge. These bonds can no longer be issued.

Tax allocation bonds.   These bonds are usually issued to finance the construction of office buildings and other new buildings in formerly blighted areas. They are secured by property taxes collected on the improved real estate.

"Territorial" bonds.   These are bonds issued by U.S. territorial possessions such as Puerto Rico, the Virgin Islands, and Guam. The bonds are tax exempt throughout most of the country. Also, the economies of these issuers are influenced by positive special features of the U.S. corporate tax codes that are not available to the states.

"Troubled city" bailout bonds.   There are certain bonds that are structured to appear as pure revenue bonds but in essence are not. Revenues come from general-purpose taxes and revenues that otherwise would have gone to a state's or city's general fund. Their bond structures were created to bail out underlying general obligation bond issuers from severe budget deficits. Examples are the New York State *Municipal Assistance Corporation for the City of New York Bonds (MAC)* and the State of Illinois *Chicago School Finance Authority Bonds.*

Refunded bonds.   These are bonds that originally may have been issued as general obligation or revenue bonds but are now secured by an "escrow fund" consisting entirely of direct U.S. government obligations that are sufficient for paying the bondholders. *They are among the safest of all municipal bonds if the escrow is properly structured.*

Notes

Tax-exempt debt issued for periods ranging not beyond three years is usually considered to be short term in nature. Below are descriptions of some of these debt instruments.

Tax, revenue, grant, and bond anticipation notes: TANs, RANs, GANs, and BANs.   These are temporary borrowings by states, local governments, and special jurisdictions. Usually, notes are issued for a period of 12 months, though it is not uncommon for notes to be issued for periods of as short as three months and for as long as three years. TANs and RANs (also known as TRANs) are issued in anticipation of the collection of taxes or other expected revenues. These are borrowings to even out the cash flows caused by the irregular flows of income into the treasuries of the states and local units of government. BANs are issued in anticipation of the sale of long-term bonds.

Construction loan notes: CLNs. CLNs are usually issued for periods up to three years to provide short-term construction financing for multifamily housing projects. The CLNs generally are repaid by the proceeds of long-term bonds, which are provided after the housing projects are completed.

Tax-exempt commercial paper. This short-term borrowing instrument is issued for periods ranging from 30 to 270 days. Generally the tax-exempt commercial paper has backstop commercial bank agreements, which can include an irrevocable letter of credit, a revolving credit agreement, or a line of credit.

In this chapter we shall refer to both municipal bonds and municipal notes as simply municipal bonds.

Newer Market-Sensitive Debt Instruments

Municipal bonds are usually issued with one of two debt retirement structures or a combination of both. Either a bond has a "serial" maturity structure (wherein a portion of the loan is retired each year), or a bond has a "term" maturity (wherein the loan is repaid on a final date). Usually term bonds have maturities ranging from 20 to 40 years and retirement schedules (which are known as sinking funds) that begin 5 to 10 years before the final term maturity.

Because of the sharply upward-sloping yield curve that existed in the municipal bond market between 1979 and 1986, many investment bankers introduced innovative financing instruments priced at short or intermediate yield levels. These debt instruments are intended to raise money for long-term capital projects at reduced interest rates. Below are descriptions of some of these more innovative debt structures.

Put or option tender bonds. A "put" or "option tender" bond is one in which the bondholder has the right to return the bond at a price of par to the bond trustee prior to its stated long-term maturity. The put period can be as short as one day or as long as 10 years. Usually, put bonds are backed by either commercial bank letters of credit in addition to the issuer's cash flow revenues or entirely by the cash flow revenues of the issuer.

Super sinkers. A "super sinker" is a specifically identified maturity for a single-family housing revenue bond issue to which all funds from early mortgage prepayments are used to retire bonds. A super sinker has a long stated maturity but a shorter, albeit unknown, actual life. Because of this unique characteristic, investors have the opportunity to realize an attractive return when the municipal yield curve is upward sloping on a bond that is priced as if it had a maturity considerably longer than its anticipated life.

Variable-rate notes. Variable-rate notes have coupon rates that change. When a variable-rate note has a put feature it is called a *variable-rate demand obligation* which may be puttable after one day, seven days, quarterly, semiannually, annually, or longer. The coupon rate is tied to one of various indexes. Specific examples include percents of the prime rate, the J. J. Kenney Municipal Index, the Merrill Lynch Index, or a percent of the 90-day Treasury bill rate. A bank letter of credit is usually required as liquidity backup for variable-rate demand obligations.

A variation of variable-rate obligations is one in which the investor in advance selects the interest rate and interest payment date from 1 up to 90 or 180 days. The security may have a nominal 30-year maturity. Such a bond has a put feature of a variable-rate demand obligation and the maturity flexibility of tax-exempt commercial paper. One version of this new investment vehicle is called UPDATES (Unit Priced Demand Adjustable Tax-Exempt Securities).

Zero-coupon bonds. A zero-coupon bond is one in which no coupon interest payments are paid to the bondholder. Instead, the bond is purchased at a very deep discount and matures at par. The difference between the original-issue discount price and par represents a specified compounded annual yield. In the municipal bond market there is also a variant of the zero-coupon bond called a "municipal multiplier" or "compound interest bond." It is a bond that is issued at par and *does* actually have interest payments. However, the interest payments are not distributed to the holder of the bond until maturity. Rather, the issuer agrees to reinvest the undistributed interest payments at the bond's yield to maturity when it was issued. For example, suppose that a 10 percent, 10-year bond with a par value of $5,000 is sold at par to yield 10 percent. Every six months, the maturity value of the bond is increased by 5 percent of the maturity value of the previous six months. So at the end of 10 years, the maturity value of the bond will be equal to

$13,267 [= \$5,000 \times (1.05)^{20}]$. In the case of a 10-year zero-coupon bond priced to yield 10 percent, the bond would have a maturity value of $5,000 but sell for $1,884 when it is issued.[1]

THE LEGAL OPINION

Municipal bonds have legal opinions. The relationship of the legal opinion to the safety of municipal bonds for both general obligation and revenue bonds is threefold. First, bond counsel should check to determine if the issuer is indeed legally able to issue the bonds. Second, bond counsel is to see that the issuer has properly prepared for the bond sale by having enacted the various required ordinances, resolutions, and trust indentures and without violating any other laws and regulations. This preparation is particularly important in the highly technical areas of determining whether the bond issue is qualified for tax exemption under federal law and whether the issue has not been structured in such a way as to violate federal arbitrage regulations. Third, bond counsel is to certify that the security safeguards and remedies provided for the bondholders and pledged either by the bond issuer or by third parties, such as banks with letter-of-credit agreements, are actually supported by federal, state, and local government laws and regulations.

The popular notion is that much of the legal work done in a bond issue is boilerplate in nature, but from the bondholder's point of view the legal opinions and document reviews should be the ultimate security provisions. This is because if all else fails, the bondholder may have to go to court to enforce his or her security rights. Therefore, the integrity and competency of the lawyers who review the documents and write the legal opinions that usually are summarized and stated in the official statements are very important.[2]

THE COMMERCIAL CREDIT-RATING OF MUNICIPAL BONDS

Of the municipal bonds that were rated by a commercial rating company in 1929 and plunged into default in 1932, 78 percent had been rated double-A or better, and 48 percent had been rated triple-A. Since then,

---

[1] Variations on the zero-coupon bond were introduced to allow municipal issuers to circumvent restrictions on the amount of par value that they were legally permitted to issue.

[2] For specific studies on recent problems with legal opinions, see Chapter 11 on contemporary defaults and related problems in Sylvan G. Feldstein and Frank J. Fabozzi, *Dow Jones-Irwin Guide to Municipal Bonds* (Homewood, Ill.: Dow Jones-Irwin, 1987).

the ability of rating agencies to assess the credit worthiness of municipal obligations has evolved to a level of general industry acceptance and respectability. In most instances, they adequately describe the financial conditions of the issuers and identify the credit-risk factors. However, a small but significant number of recent instances have caused market participants to reexamine their reliance on the opinions of the rating agencies.

As an example, the troubled bonds of the Washington Public Power Supply System (WPPSS) should be mentioned. Two major commercial rating companies—Moody's and Standard & Poor's—gave their highest ratings to these bonds in the early 1980s. Moody's gave the WPPSS Projects 1, 2, and 3 bonds its very highest credit rating of Aaa and the Projects 4 and 5 bonds its rating of A1. This latter investment-grade rating is defined as having the strongest investment attributes within the upper medium grade of creditworthiness. Standard & Poor's also had given the WPPSS Projects 1, 2, and 3 bonds its highest rating of AAA and Projects 4 and 5 bonds its rating of A+. While these high-quality ratings were in effect, WPPSS sold over $8 billion in long-term bonds. By 1986, over $2 billion of these bonds were in default.

In fact, since 1975 all of the major municipal defaults in the industry initially had been given investment-grade ratings by these two commercial rating companies. Of course, it should be noted that in the majority of instances, ratings of the commercial rating companies adequately reflect the condition of the credit. However, unlike 25 years ago when the commercial rating companies would not rate many kinds of revenue bond issues, today they seem to view themselves as assisting in the capital formation process.[3] The commercial rating companies now receive fairly substantial fees from issuers for their ratings, and they are part of large, growth-oriented conglomerates. Moody's is an operating unit of the Dun & Bradstreet Corporation and Standard & Poor's is part of the McGraw-Hill Corporation.

Today, many institutional investors, underwriters, and traders rely on their own in-house municipal credit analysts for determining the credit worthiness of municipal bonds. However, other investors do not perform their own credit-risk analysis, but, instead, rely upon credit-risk ratings by Moody's and Standard & Poor's. In this section, we discuss the rating categories of these two commercial rating companies.

---

[3] See Victor F. Zonana and Daniel Hertzberg, "Moody's Dominance in Municipals Market Is Slowly Being Eroded," *The Wall Street Journal*, November 1, 1981, pp. 1 and 23; and Peter Brimelow, "Shock Waves from Whoops Roll East," *Fortune*, July 25, 1983, pp. 46–48.

Moody's Investors Service

The municipal bond rating system used by Moody's grades the investment quality of municipal bonds in a nine-symbol system that ranges from the highest investment quality, which is Aaa, to the lowest credit rating, which is C. The respective nine alphabetical ratings and their definitions are the following:

Moody's Municipal Bond Ratings

Rating	Definition
Aaa	Best quality; carries the smallest degree of investment risk.
Aa	High quality; margins of protection not quite as large as the Aaa bonds.
A	Upper medium grade; security adequate but could be susceptible to impairment.
Baa	Medium grade; neither highly protected nor poorly secured—lacks outstanding investment characteristics and is sensitive to changes in economic circumstances.
Ba	Speculative; protection is very moderate.
B	Not desirable investment; sensitive to day-to-day economic circumstances.
Caa	Poor standing; may be in default but with a workout plan.
Ca	Highly speculative; may be in default with nominal workout plan.
C	Hopelessly in default.

Municipal bonds in the top four categories (Aaa, Aa, and A, and Baa) are considered to be of investment-grade quality. Additionally, bonds in the Aa through B categories that Moody's concludes have the strongest investment features within the respective categories are designated by the symbols Aa1, A1, Baa1, Ba1, and B1, respectively. Moody's also may use the prefix *Con.* before a credit rating to indicate that the bond security is dependent on (1) the completion of a construction project, (2) earnings of a project with little operating experience, (3) rentals being paid once the facility is constructed, or (4) some other limiting condition.[4]

The municipal note rating system used by Moody's is designated by four investment-grade categories of Moody's Investment Grade (MIG):

---

[4] It should also be noted that, as of 1984, Moody's applies numerical modifiers 1, 2, and 3 in each generic rating classification from Aa through B to municipal bonds that are issued for industrial development and pollution control. The modifier 1 indicates that the security ranks in the higher end of its generic rating category; the modifier 2 indicates a midrange ranking, and the modifier 3 indicates that the bond ranks in the lower end of its generic rating category.

Moody's Municipal Note Ratings	
Rating	*Definition*
MIG 1	Best quality
MIG 2	High quality
MIG 3	Favorable quality
MIG 4	Adequate quality

A short-term issue having a "demand" feature (i.e., payment relying on external liquidity and usually payable upon demand rather than fixed maturity dates) is differentiated by Moody's with the use of the symbols VMIG1 through VMIG4.

Moody's also provides credit ratings for tax-exempt commercial paper. These are promissory obligations (1) not having an original maturity in excess of nine months, and (2) backed by commercial banks. Moody's uses three designations, all considered to be of investment grade, for indicating the relative repayment capacity of the rated issues:

Moody's Tax-Exempt Commercial Paper Ratings	
Rating	*Definition*
Prime 1 (P-1)	Superior capacity for repayment
Prime 2 (P-2)	Strong capacity for repayment
Prime 3 (P-3)	Acceptable capacity for repayment

Standard & Poor's

The municipal bond rating system used by Standard & Poor's grades the investment quality of municipal bonds in a 10-symbol system that ranges from the highest investment quality, which is AAA, to the lowest credit rating, which is D. Bonds within the top four categories (AAA, AA, A, and BBB) are considered by Standard & Poor's as being of investment-grade quality. The respective 10 alphabetical ratings and definitions are the following:

Standard & Poor's Municipal Bond Ratings	
Rating	*Definition*
AAA	Highest rating; extremely strong security.
AA	Very strong security; differs from AAA in only a small degree.
A	Strong capacity but more susceptible to adverse economic effects than two above categories.
BBB	Adequate capacity but adverse economic conditions more likely to weaken capacity.
BB	Lowest degree of speculation; risk exposure.
B	Speculative; risk exposure.
CCC	Speculative; major risk exposure
CC	Highest degree of speculation; major risk exposure.
C	No interest is being paid.
D	Bonds in default with interest and/or repayment of principal in arrears.

Standard & Poor's also uses a plus (+) or minus (−) sign to show relative standing within the rating categories ranging from AA to BB. Additionally, Standard & Poor's uses the letter p to indicate a provisional rating that is intended to be removed upon the successful and timely completion of the construction project. A double dagger (‡) on a mortgage-backed revenue bond rating indicates that the rating is contingent upon receipt by Standard & Poor's of closing documentation confirming investments and cash flows. An asterisk (*) following a credit rating indicates that the continuation of the rating is contingent upon receipt of an executed copy of the escrow agreement.

The municipal note-rating system used by Standard & Poor's grades the investment quality of municipal notes in a four-symbol system that ranges from highest investment quality, SP−1+, to the lowest credit rating, SP−3. Notes within the top three categories (i.e., SP−1+, SP−1, and SP−2) are considered by Standard & Poor's as being of investment-grade quality. The respective ratings and summarized definitions are:

Standard & Poor's Municipal Note Ratings

Rating	Definition
SP–1	Very strong or strong capacity to pay principal and interest. Those issues determined to possess overwhelming safety characteristics will be given a plus (+) designation.
SP–2	Satisfactory capacity to pay principal and interest.
SP–3	Speculative capacity to pay principal and interest.

Standard & Poor's also rates tax-exempt commercial paper in the same four categories as taxable commercial paper. The four tax-exempt commercial paper rating categories are:

Standard & Poor's Tax-Exempt Commercial Paper Rating

Rating	Definition
A–1+	Highest degree of safety.
A–1	Very strong degree of safety.
A–2	Strong degree of safety.
A–3	Satisfactory degree of safety.

How the Rating Agencies Differ

Although there are many similarities in how Moody's and Standard & Poor's approach credit ratings, there are certain differences in their respective approaches as well. As examples we shall present below some of the differences in approach between Moody's and Standard & Poor's when they assign credit ratings to general obligation bonds.

The credit analysis of general obligation bonds issued by states, counties, school districts, and municipalities initially requires the collection and assessment of information in four basic categories. The first category includes obtaining information on the issuer's debt structure so that the overall debt burden can be determined. The debt burden usually is composed of (1) the respective direct and overlapping debts per capita as well as (2) the respective direct and overlapping debts as percentages of real estate valuations and personal incomes. The second category of needed information relates to the issuer's ability and political discipline for maintaining sound budgetary operations. The focus of attention here is usually on the issuer's general operating funds and whether or not it has maintained at least balanced budgets over the previous three to five years. The third category involves determining the specific local taxes and intergovernmental revenues available to the issuer, as well as obtaining historical information on both tax collection rates, which are important when looking at property tax levies, and on the dependency of local budgets on specific revenue sources, which is important when looking at the impact of federal revenue sharing monies. The fourth and last general category of information necessary to the credit analysis is an assessment of the issuer's overall socioeconomic environment. Questions that have to be answered here include determining the local employment distribution and composition, population growth, and real estate property valuation and personal income trends, among other economic indexes.

Although Moody's and Standard & Poor's rely on these same four informational categories in arriving at their respective credit ratings of general obligation bonds, what they emphasize among the categories can result at times in dramatically different credit ratings for the same issuer's bonds.

There are major differences between Moody's and Standard & Poor's in their respective approaches toward these four categories, and there are other differences in conceptual factors the two rating agencies bring to bear before assigning their respective general obligation credit ratings. There are very important differences between the rating agencies, and although there are some zigs and zags in their respective rating policies, there are also clear patterns of analysis that exist and that have resulted in split credit ratings for a given issuer. The objective here is to outline what these differences between Moody's and Standard & Poor's actually are. Furthermore, although the rating agencies have stated in their publications what criteria guide their respective credit-rating approaches, the conclusions here about how they go about rating general obligation bonds are not only derived from these sources, but also from reviewing their credit reports and rating decisions on individual bond issues.

How do Moody's and Standard & Poor's differ in evaluating the four basic informational categories? Simply stated, Moody's tends to focus on the debt burden and budgetary operations of the issuer, and Standard & Poor's considers the issuer's economic environment as the most important element in its analysis. Although in most instances these differences of emphasis do not result in dramatically split credit ratings for a given issuer, there are at least two recent instances in which major differences in ratings on general obligation bonds have occurred.

The general obligation bonds of the Chicago School Finance Authority are rated only Baa1 by Moody's, but Standard & Poor's rates the same bonds AA−. In assigning the credit rating of Baa1, Moody's bases its rating on the following debt- and budget-related factors: (1) The deficit funding bonds are to be retired over a 30-year period, an unusually long time for such an obligation; (2) the overall debt burden is high; and (3) the school board faces long-term difficulties in balancing its operating budget because of reduced operating taxes, desegregation program requirements, and uncertain public employee union relations.

Standard & Poor's credit rating of AA− appears to be based primarily upon the following two factors: (1) Although Chicago's economy has been sluggish, it is still well diversified and fundamentally sound; and (2) the unique security provisions for the bonds in the opinion of the bond counsel insulate the pledged property taxes from the school board's creditors in the event of a school-system bankruptcy.

Another general obligation bond wherein split ratings have occurred is the bond issue of Allegheny County, Pennsylvania. Moody's rates the bonds A, whereas the Standard & Poor's rating is AA.

Moody's A credit rating is based primarily upon four budget-related factors: (1) above-average debt load with more bonds expected to be issued for transportation related projects and for the building of a new hospital, (2) continued unfunded pension liabilities, (3) past unorthodox budgetary practices of shifting tax revenues from the county tax levy to the county institution district levy, and (4) an archaic real estate property assessment system, which is in the process of being corrected.

Standard & Poor's higher credit rating of AA also appears to be based upon four factors: (1) an affluent, diverse, and stable economy with wealth variables above the national medians, (2) a good industrial mix with decreasing dependence on steel production, (3) improved budget operations having accounting procedures developed to conform to generally acepted accounting principles, and (4) a rapid debt retirement schedule that essentially matches anticipated future bond sales.

Are state general obligation bonds fundamentally different from local government general obligation bonds? There is also another difference between the credit rating agencies in how they apply their analytical tools to the rating of state general obligation bonds and local government general obligation bonds. Moody's basically believes that the state and local bonds are not fundamentally different. Moody's applies the same debt- and budget-related concerns to state general obligation bonds as they do to general obligation bonds issued by counties, school districts, towns, and cities. Moody's has even assigned ratings below A to state general obligation bonds. When the state of Delaware was having serious budgetary problems in the period beginning in 1975 and extending through 1978, Moody's gradually downgraded its general obligation bonds from Aa to Baa1. It should be noted that when Moody's downgraded Delaware general obligation bonds to Baa1 and highlighted its budgetary problems, the state government promptly began to address its budgetary problems. By 1982 the bond rating was up to Aa. In May of 1982, Moody's downgraded the state of Michigan's general obligation bonds from A to Baa1 on the basis of a weak local economy and the state's budgetary problems. Another example of Moody's maintaining a state credit rating below A was in Alaska, where until 1974 the state general obligation bonds were rated Baa1. Here, Moody's cited the heavy debt load as a major reason for the rating.

Unlike Moody's, Standard & Poor's seems to make a distinction between state and local government general obligation bonds. Because states have broader legal powers in the areas of taxation and policy making that do not require home-rule approvals, broader revenue bases, and more diversified economies, Standard & Poor's seems to view state general obligation bonds as being significantly stronger than those of their respective underlying jurisdictions. Standard & Poor's has never given ratings below A to a state. Additionally, of the 38 state general obligation bonds that both Moody's and Standard & Poor's rated in mid-1986, the latter agency had given ratings of AA or better to 34 states and ratings of A to only four states. On the other hand, Moody's had given ratings of Aa or better to only 30 states, and ratings in the A range to eight states. On the whole for reasons just outlined, it seems that Standard & Poor's tends to have a higher credit assessment of state general obligation bonds than does Moody's. Furthermore, it should be noted that Moody's views these broader revenue resources as making states more vulnerable in difficult economic times to demands by local governments for increased financial aid.

How do the credit-rating agencies differ in assessing the moral obligation bonds? In more than 20 states, state agencies have issued housing revenue bonds that carry a potential state liability for making up deficiencies in their one-year debt service reserve funds (backup funds), should any occur. In most cases if a drawdown of the debt reserve occurs, the state agency must report the amount used to its governor and the state budget director. The state legislature, in turn, may appropriate the requested amount, though there is no legally enforceable obligation to do so. Bonds with this makeup provision are the so-called moral obligation bonds.

Below is an example of the legal language in the bond indenture that explains this procedure.

In order to further assure the maintenance of each such debt service reserve fund, there shall be annually apportioned and paid to the agency for deposit in each debt service reserve fund such sum, if any, as shall be certified by the chairman of the agency to the governor and director of the budget as necessary to restore such fund to an amount equal to the fund requirement. The chairman of the agency shall annually, on or before December first, make and deliver to the governor and director of the budget his certificate stating the sum or sums, if any, required to restore each such debt service reserve fund to the amount aforesaid, and the sum so certified, if any, shall be apportioned and paid to the agency during the then current state fiscal year.

Moody's views the moral obligation feature as being more literary than legal when applied to legislatively permissive debt service reserve makeup provisions. Therefore, it does not consider this procedure a credit strength. Standard & Poor's, to the contrary, does. It views moral obligation bonds as being no lower than one rating category below a state's own general obligation bonds. Its rationale is based upon the implied state support for the bonds and the market implications for that state's own general obligation bonds should it ever fail to honor its moral obligation.

As for the result of these two different opinions of the moral obligation, there are several municipal bonds that have split ratings. As examples, in mid-1986 the Nonprofit Housing Project Bonds of the New York State Housing Finance Agency, the General Purpose Bonds of the New York State Urban Development Corporation, and the Series A Bonds of the Battery Park City Authority have the Moody's credit rating of Ba, which is a speculative investment category. Standard & Poor's, because of the moral obligation pledge of the state of New York, gives the same bonds a credit rating of BBB+, which is an investment-grade category.

How do the credit-rating agencies differ in assessing the importance of withholding state aid to pay debt service? Still another difference between Moody's and Standard & Poor's involves their respective attitudes toward state-aid security-related mechanisms. Since 1974 it has been the policy of Standard & Poor's to view as a very positive credit feature the automatic withholding and use of state aid to pay defaulted debt service on local government general obligation bonds. Usually the mechanism requires the respective state treasurer to pay debt service directly to the bondholder from monies due the local issuer from the state. Seven states have enacted security mechanisms that in one way or another allow certain local government general obligation bondholders to be paid debt service from the state-aid appropriations, if necessary. In most instances the state-aid withholding provisions apply to general obligation bonds issued by school districts.[5]

---

[5] The states involved are Indiana, Kentucky, New Jersey, New York, Pennsylvania, South Carolina, and West Virginia.

Although Standard & Poor's does review the budgetary operations of the local government issuer to be sure there are no serious budgetary problems, the assigned rating reflects the general obligation credit rating of the state involved, the legal base of the withholding mechanism, the historical background and long-term state legislature support for the pledged state aid program, and the specified coverage of the state aid monies available to maximum debt-service requirements on the local general obligation bonds. Normally, Standard & Poor's applies a blanket rating to all local general obligation bonds covered by the specific state-aid withholding mechanism. The rating is one or two notches below the rating of that particular state's general obligation bonds. Whether the rating is either one notch below or two notches below depends on the coverage figures, the legal security, and the legislative history and political durability of the pledged state-aid monies involved. It should also be noted that, although Standard & Poor's stated policy is to give blanket ratings, a specified rating is only granted when an issuer or bondholder applies for it.

Although Moody's recognizes the state-aid withholding mechanisms in its credit reviews, it believes that its assigned rating must in the first instance reflect the underlying ability of the issuer to make timely debt-service payments. Standard & Poor's, to the contrary, considers a state-aid withholding mechanism that provides for the payment of debt service equally as important a credit factor as the underlying budget, economic, and debt-related characteristics of the bond issuer.

What is the difference in attitudes toward accounting records? Another area of difference between Moody's and Standard & Poor's concerns their respective attitudes toward the accounting records kept by general obligation bond issuers. In May 1980 Standard & Poor's stated that if the bond issuer's financial reports are not prepared in accordance with generally accepted accounting principles (GAAP) it will consider this a "negative factor" in its rating process. Standard & Poor's has not indicated how negative a factor it is in terms of credit rating changes but has indicated that issuers will not be rated at all if either the financial report is not timely (i.e., available no later than six months after the fiscal year-end) or is substantially deficient in terms of reporting. Moody's policy here is quite different. Because Moody's reviews the historical performance of an issuer over a three- to five-year period, requiring GAAP reporting is not necessary from Moody's point of view, although the timeliness of financial reports is of importance.

MUNICIPAL BOND INSURANCE

Municipal bond insurance is a contractual commitment by an insurance company to pay the bondholder any bond principal and/or coupon interest that is due on a stated maturity date, but has not been paid by the bond issuer. Once issued, this municipal bond default insurance usually extends for the term of the bond issue.

The bondholder or trustee who has not received payments for bond principal and/or coupon interest on the stated due dates for the insured bonds must notify the insurance company and surrender to it the unpaid bonds and coupons. Under the terms of the policy, the insurance company is usually obligated to pay the paying agent sufficient monies for the bondholders. These monies must be enough to cover the face value of the insured principal and coupon interest that was due but not paid. Once the insurance company pays the monies, the company becomes the owner of the surrendered bonds and coupons and can begin legal proceedings to recover the monies that are now due it from the bond issuer.

The Insurers

Municipal bond insurance has been available since 1971. Some of the largest and financially strongest insurance companies in the United States are participants in this industry, as well as smaller monoline insurance companies. By mid-1986, approximately 25 percent of all new municipals were insured. The following companies are some of the major municipal bond insurers as of 1986:

> American Municipal Bond Assurance Corporation (AMBAC)
> Bond Investors Guaranty Insurance Company (BIG)
> Financial Guaranty Insurance Corporation (FGIC)
> Municipal Bond Insurance Association (MBIA)

Market Pricing of Insured Municipal Bonds

In general, although insured municipal bonds sell at yields lower than they would without the insurance, they tend to have yields substantially higher than Aaa/AAA-rated noninsured municipal bonds.

EQUIVALENT TAXABLE YIELD

An investor interested in purchasing a municipal bond must be able to compare the promised yield on a municipal bond with that of a comparable taxable bond. The following general formula is used to approximate the equivalent taxable yield for a tax-exempt bond:[6]

$$\text{Equivalent taxable yield} = \frac{\text{Tax-exempt yield}}{(1 - \text{marginal tax rate})}$$

---

[6] For a more precise procedure for determining the equivalent taxable yield see Martin L. Leibowitz, "Total Aftertax Bond Performance and Yield Measures for Tax-Exempt Bonds Held in Taxable Portfolios," in *The Municipal Bond Handbook*, Vol. I., eds. Frank J. Fabozzi, Sylvan G. Feldstein, Irving M. Pollack, and Frank G. Zarb (Homewood, Ill.: Dow Jones-Irwin, 1983), Chapter 32.

For example, suppose an investor in the 28 percent marginal tax bracket is considering the acquisition of a tax-exempt bond that offers a tax-exempt yield of 8 percent. The equivalent taxable yield is 11.11 percent, as shown below.

$$\text{Equivalent taxable yield} = \frac{.08}{(1 - .28)} = .1111$$

When computing the equivalent taxable yield, the traditionally computed yield-to-maturity is not the tax-exempt yield if the issue is selling below par (i.e., selling at a discount) because only the coupon interest is exempt from federal income taxes.[7] Instead, the yield-to-maturity after an assumed tax on the capital gain is computed and used in the numerator of the formula. The yield-to-maturity after an assumed tax on the capital gain is calculated in the same manner as the traditional yield-to-maturity. However, instead of using the redemption value in the calculation, the net proceeds after an assumed tax on the capital gain is used.

There is a major drawback in employing the equivalent taxable yield formula to compare the relative investment merits of a taxable and tax-exempt bond. The yield-to-maturity measure assumes that the entire coupon interest can be reinvested at the computed yield. Consequently, taxable bonds with the same yield-to-maturity cannot be compared because the total dollar returns may differ from the computed yield. The same problem arises when attempting to compare taxable and tax-exempt bonds, especially since only a portion of the coupon interest on taxable bonds can be reinvested, although the entire coupon payment is available for reinvestment in the case of municipal bonds.

STATE AND LOCAL TAX TREATMENT[8]

The tax treatment of municipal bonds varies by state. There are three types of tax that can be imposed: (1) an income tax on coupon income, (2) a tax on realized capital gains, and (3) a personal property tax.

There are 43 states that levy an individual income tax, as does the District of Columbia. Six of these states exempt coupon interest on *all* municipal bonds, whether the issue is in state or out of state. Coupon interest from obligations by in-state issuers is exempt from state indi-

---

[7] An investor who purchases a tax-exempt bond at a premium will not be entitled to a capital loss if the bond is held to maturity because the premium must be amortized.

[8] The source of information for this section is from Steven J. Hueglin, "State and Local Tax Treatment of Municipal Bonds," in *The Municipal Bond Handbook*, Vol. I, eds. Frank J. Fabozzi, Sylvan G. Feldstein, Irving M. Pollack, and Frank G. Zarb (Homewood, Ill.: Dow Jones-Irwin, 1983), Chapter 4.

vidual income taxes in 32 states. Five states levy individual income taxes on coupon interest whether the issuer is in state or out of state.

State taxation of realized capital gains is often ignored by investors when making investment decisions. In 42 states, a tax is levied on a base that includes income from capital transactions (i.e., capital gains or losses). In many states where coupon interest is exempt if the issuer is in state, the same exemption will not apply to capital gains involving municipal bonds.

There are 20 states that levy a personal property tax. Of these 20 states, only 11 apply this tax to municipal bonds. The tax resembles more of an income tax than a personal property tax. For example, in several states, personal property taxes are measured on the annual income generated by a bond.

In determining the effective tax rate imposed by a particular state, an investor must consider the impact of the deductibility of state taxes on federal income taxes. Moreover, in 13 states, *federal* taxes are deductible in determining state income taxes.

THE PRIMARY AND SECONDARY MARKETS

The Primary Market

A substantial number of municipal obligations are brought to market each week. A state or local government can market its new issue by offering them publicly to the investing community or by placing them privately with a small group of investors. When a public offering is selected, the issue is usually underwritten by investment bankers and municipal bond departments of commercial banks. Public offerings may be marketed by either competitive bidding or direct negotiations with underwriters. When an issue is marketed via competitive bidding, the issue is awarded to the bidder submitting the lowest best bid.

Most states mandate that general obligation issues be marketed via competitive bidding; however, this is generally not required for revenue bonds. Usually state and local governments require that a competitive sale be announced in a recognized financial publication, such as *The Bond Buyer*, which is the trade publication of the municipal bond industry. *The Bond Buyer* also provides information on upcoming competitive sales and most negotiated sales as well as the results of the sales of previous weeks.

When an underwriter purchases a new bond issue, it relieves the issuer of two obligations. First, the underwriter is responsible for the distribution of the issue. Second, the underwriter accepts the risk that investors might fail to purchase the issue at the expected prices within the planned time period. The second risk exists because the underwriter may have incorrectly priced the issue and/or because interest rates rise, resulting in a decline in the value of unsold issues held in inventory. The underwriter spread (that is, the difference between the price it paid the issuer for the issue and the price it reoffered the issue to the public) is the underwriter's compensation for undertaking these risks as well as for other services it may have provided the issuer.[9]

An official statement describing the issue and issuer is prepared for new offerings.

The Secondary Market

Although municipal bonds are not listed and traded in formal institutions, as are certain common stocks and corporate bonds on the New York and American stock exchanges, there are very strong and active billion-dollar secondary markets for municipals that are supported by hundreds of municipal bond dealers across the country. Markets are maintained on local credits by regional brokerage firms, local banks, and by some of the larger Wall Street firms. General market names are supported by the larger brokerage firms and banks, many of whom have investment banking relationships with the issuers. Buying and selling decisions are often made over the phone and through municipal bond brokers. For a small fee these brokers serve as intermediaries in the sale of large blocks of municipal bonds among dealers and large institutional investors. These brokers are primarily located in New York City and include Chapdelaine & Company, Drake & Company, the J. J. Kenny Company, and Titus & Donnelly, Inc., among others.

In addition to these brokers and the daily offerings sent out over *The Bond Buyer*'s "munifacts" teletype system, many dealers advertise their municipal bond offerings for the retail market in what is known as *The Blue List*. This is a 100+ -page booklet which is published every weekday by the Standard & Poor's Corporation. In it are listed state municipal bond and note offerings and prices.

In the municipal bond market, an odd lot of bonds is $25,000 (five bonds) or less in par value for retail investors. For institutions, anything below $100,000 in par value is considered an odd lot. Dealer spreads—the difference between the dealer's bid and ask prices—depend on several factors. For the retail investor, the dealer spread can range from as low as one quarter of one point ($12.50 per $5,000 of par value) on large blocks of actively traded bonds to four points ($200 per $5,000 of par value) for odd lot sales of an inactive issue. The average spread for retail investors seems to be around two points ($100 per $5,000 of par value). For institutional investors, the dealer spread rarely exceeds one half of one point ($25 per $5,000 of par value).

---

[9] For example, in the case of negotiated offerings there is the value of the origination services provided by the underwriter. Origination services represent the structuring of the issue and planning activities surrounding the offering.

REGULATION OF THE MUNICIPAL SECURITIES MARKET[10]

As an outgrowth of abusive stock market practices, Congress passed the Securities Act of 1933 and the Securities Exchange Act of 1934. The 1934 act created the Securities and Exchange Commission (SEC), granting it regulatory authority over the issuance and trading of *corporate* securities. Congress specifically exempted municipal securities from both the registration requirements of the 1933 act and the periodic reporting requirements of the 1934 act. However, antifraud provisions did apply to offerings of or dealings in municipal securities.

The reasons for the exemption afforded municipal securities appear to have been due to (1) the desire for governmental comity, (2) the absence of recurrent abuses in transactions involving municipal securities, (3) the greater level of sophistication of investors in this segment of the securities markets (that is, institutional investors dominated the market), and (4) the fact that there were few defaults by municipal issuers. Consequently, from the enactment of the two federal securities acts in the early 1930s to the early 1970s, the municipal securities market can be characterized as relatively free from federal regulation.

In the early 1970s, however, circumstances changed. As incomes rose, individuals participated in the municipal securities market to a much greater extent. As a result, public concern over selling practices occurred with greater frequency. For example, in the early 1970s, the SEC obtained seven injunctions against 72 defendants for fraudulent municipal trading practices. According to the SEC, the abusive practices involved both disregard by the defendants as to whether the particular municipal bond offered to individuals were in fact appropriate investment vehicles for the individuals to whom they were offered and misrepresentation or failure to disclose information necessary for individuals to assess the credit risk of the municipal user, especially in the case of revenue bonds. Moreover, the financial problems of some municipal users, notably New York City, made market participants aware that municipal users have the potential to experience severe and bankruptcy-type financial difficulties.

Congress passed the Securities Act Amendment of 1975 to broaden federal regulation in the municipals market. The legislation brought brokers and dealers in the municipal securities market, including banks that underwrite and trade municipal securities, within the regulatory scheme of the Securities Exchange Act of 1934. In addition, the legislation mandated that the SEC establish a 15-member Municipal Securities

---

[10] This discussion is drawn from Thomas F. Mitchell, "Disclosure and the Municipal Bond Industry," Chapter 40 and Nancy H. Wojtas, "The SEC and Investor Safeguards," Chapter 42 in *The Municipal Bond Handbook*, Vol. I, eds. Frank J. Fabozzi et al.

Rule Making Board (MSRB) as an independent, self-regulatory agency, whose primary responsibility is to develop rules governing the activities of banks, brokers, and dealers in municipal securities.[11] Rules adopted by the MSRB must be approved by the SEC. The MSRB has no enforcement or inspection authority. This authority is vested with the SEC, the National Association of Securities Dealers, and certain regulatory banking agencies such as the Federal Reserve Bank.

The Securities Act Amendment of 1975 does *not* require that municipal issuers comply with the registration requirement of the 1933 act or the periodic-reporting requirement of the 1934 act. There have been, however, several legislative proposals to mandate financial disclosure. Although none has been passed, there is clearly pressure to improve disclosure. Even in the absence of federal legislation dealing with the regulation of financial disclosure, underwriters began insisting upon greater disclosure as it became apparent that the SEC was exercising stricter application of the antifraud provisions. Moreover, underwriters recognized the need for improved disclosure to sell municipal securities to an investing public that has become much more concerned about credit risk by municipal issuers. Thus it is in the best interest of all parties—the issuer, the underwriter, and the investor—that meaningful disclosure requirements be established.

THE CHANGING NATURE OF THE MUNICIPAL BOND INDUSTRY

By the mid-1980s there were three characteristics of the municipal bond industry that distinguished it from what it was in 1960, 1970, and even as recently as 1980. First, municipal bond and note volume increased along with the volatility of interest rates—regardless of the maturity, credit quality, or type of financing structure involved. Second, new financing techniques emerged resulting in more diverse, complex, and changing bond and note security structures. Third, there was growing reliance on retail investors and on those institutional buyers such as bond funds which catered primarily to individuals.

Increased Volume and Interest-Rate Volatility

A characteristic of the municipal bond industry by the mid-1980s was that it had become a major capital market. As an example, according to *The Bond Buyer* tax-exempt state and local government long-term debt outstanding by year-end 1960 was only $66 billion, whereas by year-end

---

[11] For a detailed discussion of the MSRB, see Frieda K. Wallison, "Self-Regulation of the Municipal Securities Industry," Chapter 41 in *The Municipal Bond Handbook*, Vol. I, eds. Frank Fabozzi, et al.

1985 it was over $700 billion.[12] This represented a 1,060 percent increase over 25 years. During this same period outstanding U.S. government direct and guaranteed debt increased from $237 billion in 1960 to $1,858 billion by year-end 1985, an increase of 784 percent.[13]

With this increased volume also has come a further expansion of the municipal bond industry. Numerous brokerage firms and commercial banks—both national and regional in scope—have entered the municipal bond business. By the 1980s many had extensive municipal securities trading and syndicate departments, public finance, and new business specialists, as well as institutional and retail salesmen and credit analysts. Even the traditional institutional buyers of municipal bonds, such as property and casualty insurance companies, had begun to maintain quasi-trading positions in municipals. An increasing number of investors also began to "buy and trade" municipals, discarding the traditional "buy and hold" investment strategy.

One corollary of this broadening base of market participation was that there were more transitory and speculative forces in the marketplace than in the past. These forces may help explain the volatility of interest rates that characterize the municipal bond and note markets almost on a daily basis as well as the relative lack of sustained trading patterns in many sectors of the market. It should also be noted that the dramatic moves in the business cycle and changing Federal Reserve Board monetary strategies have also been overall contributing factors.

New Financing Techniques

Along with the increased municipal bond volume, issuers and investment bankers have been using new financing techniques and security structures. Additionally, as inflation and U.S. government borrowing increased in the early 1980s, many traditional private sector borrowers began to look to tax-exempt securities—and particularly revenue bonds—as more economical financing vehicles. For instance, in 1970 only 33.5 percent, or $5.959 billion, of the total amount of municipal bonds issued in that year were revenue bonds; in the first 11 months of 1984, 70.3 percent, or $56.859 billion, of all municipals issued were revenue bonds.[14] By 1984, revenue bonds were being used to raise capital for hospitals, major corporations with pollution control projects, airports, seaports, single-family home mortgage lenders, electric utilities, and builders of multifamily housing, among others. Revenue bonds

---

[12] These data were derived from *The Bond Buyer*.

[13] These data were prepared by the Merrill Lynch Securities Research Division.

[14] Data were derived from *The Bond Buyer*, December 6, 1984, p. 17.

have also been used to provide capital for loans to students and small businesses.

Because of the availability of various federal aid and taxation benefits, many municipal revenue bonds have elaborate bond security structures which could be subject to future adverse congressional actions and IRS interpretations.[15] Housing bonds backed by future federal "Section 8" appropriations and leveraged lease resource recovery revenue bonds incorporating certain tax benefits for the plant vendors are but two examples. Additionally, because of the dramatic changes that occurred in the early 1980s in the U.S. tax code and in specific federal aid programs as the results of Reaganomics, the "state of the art" in structuring revenue bonds has been undergoing constant change. Even state and local government general obligation bond issuers, because of their dependency on numerous intergovernmental aid and revenue sharing programs, developed more complex financial structures.

In addition to the greater reliance on revenue bonds, it should also be noted that investor fears of inflation have eroded confidence in long 20- to 30-year municipals regardless of the particular security structure used. Unlike the U.S. Treasury market where an inverted yield curve existed for much of the late 1970s and early 1980s, the municipal bond market was characterized by having a very steep yield curve—where the yield differential between 1-year notes and 30-year bonds of equal creditworthiness were at times as wide as 500 basis points.

Because of the widespread investor resistance to buying long municipals, investment bankers introduced several new financing techniques. These included "put" bonds, variable coupon rate bonds, "super sinkers," and "zero" coupon bonds, all described earlier in this chapter. Commercial banks used tax-exempt commercial paper, lines of credit, and letters of credit in structuring new municipal bond and note financings. Government bond dealers and investment bankers incorporated "collateralized" repurchase agreements (repos) into several bond and note security structures. The goal of these various innovative structures was either to attract investors to long-term municipal debt instruments and/or to reduce the financing costs for the borrowers.

---

[15] As an example of the potential role of the IRS, in June of 1980 the Battery Park City Authority sold $97.315 million in construction loan notes which at the time received legal comfort from bond counsel that interest on the notes were exempt from federal income taxation. In November of 1980, however, the IRS held that interest on such notes was not exempt. The issue was not resolved until September 1981 when the Authority and the IRS signed a formal agreement by which the Authority agreed to pay annually to the IRS the arbitrage gains and the IRS, in turn, agreed that the interest paid on the notes was not taxable.

Increased Importance of the Retail Investor

With the growth of confiscatory federal, state and local government taxes on personal incomes in the 1960s and 1970s, individuals—particularly upper-income as well as middle-income wage earners—looked to municipal securities as a convenient way to shelter nonearned incomes. The increased bond volume and reduced commercial bank and casualty insurance company earnings which decreased their traditional robust appetites for tax-exempt bonds made municipal yields very attractive for retail investors. As an example, in September of 1982 short-term ready-access municipal note funds offered investors federal tax-free yields of over 6.5 percent compared to 5.5 percent in taxable passbook savings accounts.

Because of the strong demand by retail investors for tax-exemption, certain anomalies in yield relationships began to occur by the early 1980s. During one week in the spring of 1982, Dade County, Florida, sold general obligation bonds due in 25 years at a yield of 14 percent. The bonds were rated A-1 by Moody's and A by Standard & Poor's. During the same week New York City sold 25-year general obligations as well. Its bonds—at the time rated Ba-1 by Moody's and BBB by Standard—sold at a yield of only 14½ percent. This narrow yield spread of 50 basis points resulted from the higher tax burden on individuals in New York. High personal income taxes created strong demands for local municipal bonds which are tax-exempt from state of New York, New York City, and federal income taxes.

Municipal bond funds—which sell primarily to individuals—also became major institutional forces in the marketplace. These institutional buyers, unlike many insurance companies and banks, were "yield" buyers who bought long-term A-rated revenue bonds for their relatively high yields. This preference by the bond funds for A-rated paper along with the weaker market for the high grades, i.e., AA- and AAA-rated bonds, brought about some other very unusual yield relationships. As an example, in 1982 the state of Florida sold 20-year high investment grade, AA-rated general obligations at a yield of 13.90 percent. At the same time the North Carolina Eastern Municipal Power Agency sold 20-year A-rated revenue bonds at a yield of 13¼ percent. As the result of the increased role of retail buyers and the weaker demand by banks and insurance companies for high grades, by the 1980s the market at times priced retail-type weaker credit quality bonds at comparable or lower yields than it did higher quality bonds.

30

U.S. Government and Agency Securities

Thomas G. Fendrich, CFA
Managing Director
Standard & Poor's Corporation

The role of the U.S. government in the credit market is a huge and increasing one and any analysis of U.S. Treasury and agency securities should begin within the context of this fact. Of the $7.6 trillion of total nonfinancial debt outstanding in the United States at the end of 1986, close to $1.6 trillion represented privately held Treasury securities, both the marketable and nonmarketable type. (See Table 1.) In addition, however, U.S. government-guaranteed or direct loans plus debt guaranteed indirectly through government-sponsored financial intermediaries totaled $1.0 trillion. Finally, the U.S. government insures over $2 trillion of deposits at commercial banks, thrift institutions, and credit unions. While the orientation of the government has been to increasingly contain or limit the government's role in the credit markets, the 1980s realities of continuing sizable deficits and the increasing volatility of deregulated financial markets suggest that federal and related securities will occupy center stage of the credit markets for decades to come. In fact, it is possible their attractiveness as preservation-of-capital vehicles may increase over time as nonfederal credit securities tend toward higher yielding risk vehicles and as corporate creditworthiness continues to deteriorate.

U.S. TREASURY DEBT

U.S. Treasury debt represents a direct obligation of the U.S. Treasury and its safety rests on the taxing power and monetary creation and

TABLE 1 U.S. Treasury Debt (annual net increases in amounts outstanding, dollars in billions)

	1981	1982	1983	1984	1985	1986E	Amt.Out.31 Dec 86E
Outstanding Marketables							
Bills	$28.9	$66.8	$ 32.0	$ 30.6	$ 25.5	$ 29.8	$ 429.7
Notes	53.7	89.7	108.3	131.7	107.4	114.4	926.9
Bonds	14.5	4.7	29.1	34.2	43.1	38.6	249.7
Nonmarketables: Government account series	11.6	8.8	26.5	54.3	46.0	51.7	383.9
State and local series	−0.9	2.7	11.1	7.7	43.1	20.2	107.7
Foreign government series (U.S.$)	−2.7	−2.0	−2.5	−1.3	−1.6	−3.9	3.6
Foreign public series (non-U.S.$)	−2.4	−2.3	−1.7	0.0	0.1	0.0	0.0
Savings bonds	−4.4	−0.1	2.7	2.6	4.5	13.2	91.2
Guaranteed and noninterest-bearing	0.1	0.0	8.1	−8.2	0.9	0.1	2.8
Total public and guaranteed debt	98.5	168.2	213.5	251.5	269.0	264.1	2,195.6
Less trust fund holdings	10.8	6.1	26.9	53.3	59.3	52.0	400.9
Less agency holdings	0.2	1.5	−0.8	0.4	1.2	−0.1	4.0
Less federal reserve holdings	9.6	8.4	12.6	8.9	20.5	18.0	199.3
Privately held treasury debt	$77.8	$152.3	$174.8	$188.9	$188.1	$194.2	$1,591.3
Ownership: Thrifts	$−3.7	$ 8.5	$ 20.9	$ 10.7	$ −9.2	$ 7.4	$ 50.7
Insurance and pensions	17.8	20.2	28.0	50.5	41.8	51.0	281.5
Investment companies	19.0	23.4	−19.2	8.9	52.1	52.4	141.9
Other nonbank finance	−0.6	0.4	−12.4	1.0	3.6	3.6	0.6
Total nonbank finance	32.6	52.5	17.3	71.1	88.3	114.4	474.7
Commercial banks	1.8	19.4	47.8	1.9	12.1	16.3	214.5
Nonfinancial corporations	−1.0	5.2	8.0	7.3	−3.0	8.3	41.8
State and local governments	−0.9	5.7	16.1	13.2	50.2	23.9	125.2
Foreign investors	6.7	12.6	16.4	25.4	20.2	60.4	266.2
Residual households direct	38.6	56.9	62.2	70.1	20.4	−29.1	469.0
Total ownership	$77.8	$152.3	$174.8	$188.9	$188.1	$194.2	$1,591.3

SOURCE: Salomon Brothers Inc. Prospects for Financial Markets in 1987.

FIGURE 1 Debt of All Nonfinancial Sectors as Percent of GNP

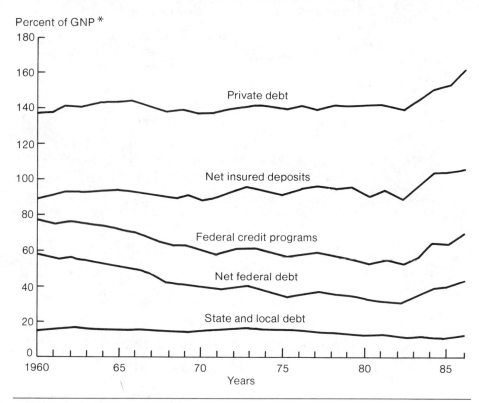

Percent of GNP *

* Debt at end of fiscal year as percent of GNP for fiscal year.
source: Council of Economic Advisers, based on data from various government agencies.

control powers of the U.S. government. A default on U.S. Treasury debt is essentially unimaginable under most scenarios, as long as U.S. dollar-denominated debt held by foreigners (external debt) is on a net basis nominal or rising gradually. Any questions of confidence related to the U.S. economy would first reflect themselves largely in either interest rate adjustments or the value of the dollar.

Direct annual federal debt issuance is related to federal deficit financing needs. It has been suggested that federal debt (see Figure 1) has not increased substantially relative to GNP. While this is true, the substantially increased levels of the federal deficit since 1982, averaging $185 billion annually versus $60 billion annually in the previous five-year period, have served to limit the growth in the nation's gross savings available for investment (see Table 2). Expectations of continuing large federal deficits impact on the type of securities the Treasury

TABLE 2 Federal Receipts, Outlays, Surplus or Deficit, and Debt Selected
Fiscal Years 1929–1987 (in billions of dollars, fiscal years)

Calendar Year or Quarter	Receipts	Outlays	Surplus or Deficit (−)
1929	3.9	3.1	0.7
1933	2.0	4.6	−2.6
1939	6.3	9.1	−2.8
1940	6.5	9.5	−2.9
1941	8.7	13.7	−4.9
1942	14.6	35.1	−20.5
1943	24.0	78.6	−54.6
1944	43.7	91.3	−47.6
1945	45.2	92.7	−47.6
1946	39.3	55.2	−15.9
1947	38.5	34.5	4.0
1948	41.6	29.8	11.8
1949	39.4	38.8	.6
1950	39.4	42.6	−3.1
1951	51.6	45.5	6.1
1952	66.2	67.7	−6.5
1953	69.6	76.1	−6.5
1954	69.7	70.9	−1.2
1955	65.5	68.4	−3.0
1956	74.6	70.6	3.9
1957	80.0	76.6	3.4
1958	79.6	82.4	−2.8
1959	79.2	92.1	−12.8
1960	92.5	92.2	.3
1961	94.4	97.7	−3.3
1962	99.7	106.8	−7.1
1963	106.6	111.3	−4.8
1964	112.6	118.5	−5.9
1965	116.8	118.2	−1.4
1966	130.8	134.5	−3.7
1967	148.8	157.5	−8.6
1968	153.0	178.1	−25.2
1969	186.9	183.6	3.2
1970	192.8	195.6	−2.8
1971	187.1	210.2	−23.0
1972	207.3	230.7	−23.4
1973	230.8	245.7	−14.9
1974	263.2	269.4	−6.1
1975	279.1	332.3	−53.2
1976	298.1	371.8	−73.7

TABLE 2 *(concluded)*

Calendar Year or Quarter	Receipts	Outlays	Surplus or Deficit (–)
Transition quarter	81.2	96.0	–14.7
1977	355.6	409.2	–53.6
1978	399.6	458.7	–59.2
1979	463.3	503.5	–40.2
1980	517.1	590.9	–73.8
1981	599.3	678.2	–78.9
1982	617.8	745.7	–127.9
1983	600.6	808.3	–207.8
1984	666.5	851.8	–185.3
1985	734.1	946.3	–212.3
1986	769.1	989.8	–220.7
1987 (est)	842.4	1,015.6	–173.2

Note: Federal grants-in-aid to state and local governments are reflected in federal expenditures and state and local receipts. Total government receipts and expenditures have been adjusted to eliminate this duplication.

SOURCE: Department of the Treasury, Office of Management and Budget, and Department of Commerce, Bureau of Economic Analysis.

issues and the approaches the administration takes toward agency, insured, and related indirect obligations, will be discussed below.

Marketable Treasury securities are of three types: bills, notes, and bonds. The interest return is fully exempt from state and local taxes.

Treasury bills, or T-bills, are negotiable, noninterest-bearing securities issued at auction on a discounted price basis for original maturities of 3, 6, or 12 months in denominations ranging from $10,000 to $1 million.

T-bills represent the most liquid and highest quality short-term marketable security available. Amounts outstanding had risen by the mid-1970s to over half of the privately held Treasury debt as the yield curve rose sharply on long-term issues and the Treasury strove to finance at the lower cost short end of the market. Since then, net new issuances of T-bills have risen less sharply than longer-term Treasury notes and bonds. The decline in inflation and interest rates and the flattening of the yield curve in the mid-1980s facilitated this movement. (See Figure 2.) Another factor was the need to fund lending through the Federal Financing Bank, which heightened the Treasury's direct market presence.

Treasury notes are coupon securities, with semiannual interest payments issued for periods of 1 to 10 years. Treasury notes are not callable,

FIGURE 2 Yields of Treasury Securities, March 31, 1986 (based on closing bid quotations)

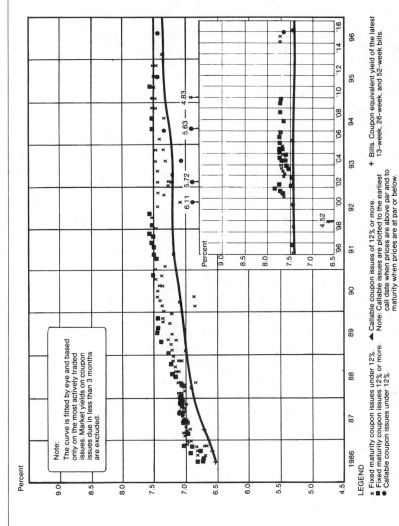

Percent

Note:
The curve is fitted by eye and based only on the most actively traded issues. Market yields on coupon issues due in less than 3 months are excluded.

LEGEND

x Fixed maturity coupon issues under 12%
■ Fixed maturity coupon issues 12% or more.
● Callable coupon issues under 12%.

▲ Callable coupon issues of 12% or more.
Note: Callable issues are plotted to the earliest call date when prices are above par and to maturity when prices are at par or below.

+ Bills. Coupon equivalent yield of the latest 13-week, 26-week, and 52-week bills.

SOURCE: Treasury Bulletin U.S. Department of the Treasury

and as bonds mentioned below are issued at auction in essentially a wholesale market. *Treasury bonds* are issues with maturities exceeding 10 years. The yields to maturity for Treasury securities form the primary yield curve indicating at any point in time the term structure of interest rates at a risk-free rate by maturity. Comparative yields are shown in Table 3.

The significance of the yield curve rests on it being the sum total of market expectations for future interest rate levels and most fixed-income portfolio management strategies look to it as a starting point for observation and analysis.

Normally, the yield curve will turn upward to reflect greater uncertainties regarding interest rates in the long term. An *inverted* yield curve, with short-term rates higher than long-term rates, generally reflects expectations that short-term interest rates will fall or strong confidence in low or declining inflation in the long run.

Treasury securities offer investors practically no credit risk coupled with outstanding liquidity. They should thus always remain the fixed-income securities against which most other fixed-income securities would be priced. In favorable markets, raising substantial sums of Treasury securities is, by definition, not a financing issue for the Treasury. In unfavorable markets, Treasury financing access is unlikely to be a problem because any illiquidity would be extremely serious. Instead adverse financial effects could quickly ripple through to less creditworthy securities and less liquid markets.

During 1986, long-term Treasury securities benefitted materially relative to corporate securities from their call protection features. The large declines in long-term interest rates led to a broad universe of taxable securities being subject to call risk, or in the case of mortgages, prepayment risk. Called bonds and refundings exceeded $35 billion in 1986 for corporate bonds, versus less than $10 billion in 1985, and investor preferences shifted in favor of noncallable Treasuries.

With future large increases in Treasury debt levels in prospect, the Treasury will likely take approaches to financing that will minimize effects on the capital and money markets and minimize costs at the same time. The primary approaches relied upon to date have been to increase the predictability and regularity of financing auctions and maintain the simplicity of the issues. The primary concession to innovative financing has been to facilitate the issuance of stripped Treasuries or zero coupon Treasuries so as to capitalize on the portion of the investment market seeking to lock in reinvestment rates.

Ownership of Treasury securities has increased on most fronts, with financial institutions, individuals, foreign investors, life insurers, and pension funds showing relatively large percentage increases in their holdings. In 1986, foreign investors stepped up their purchases dramatically, to 30% of net new issues from 10% in prior years. Some observers

TABLE 3 Bond Yields and Interest Rates, 1929—1986 (percent per annum)

| Year and Month | U. S. Treasury Securities | | | | Triple A Corporate Bonds | High-Grade Municipal Bonds (Standard & Poor's) |
| | Bills (New Issues) | | Constant Maturities | | | |
	3-month	6-month	3-year	10-year		
1929					4.73	4.27
1933	0.515				4.49	4.71
1939	0.023				3.01	2.76
1940	0.014				2.84	2.50
1941	0.103				2.77	2.10
1942	0.326				2.83	2.36
1943	0.373				2.73	2.06
1944	0.375				2.72	1.86
1945	0.375				2.62	1.67
1946	0.375				2.53	1.64
1947	0.594				2.61	2.01
1948	1.040				2.82	2.40
1949	1.102				2.66	2.21
1950	1.218				2.62	1.98
1951	1.552				2.86	2.00
1952	1.766				2.96	2.19
1953	1.931		2.47	2.85	3.20	2.72
1954	0.953		1.63	2.40	2.90	2.37
1955	1.753		2.47	2.82	3.06	2.53
1956	2.658		3.19	3.18	3.36	2.93
1957	3.267		3.98	3.65	3.89	3.60
1958	1.839		2.84	3.32	3.79	3.56
1959	3.405	3.832	4.46	4.33	4.38	3.95
1960	2.928	3.247	3.98	4.12	4.41	3.73
1961	2.378	2.605	3.54	3.88	4.35	3.46
1962	2.778	2.908	3.47	3.95	4.33	3.18
1963	3.157	3.253	3.67	4.00	4.26	3.23
1964	3.549	3.686	4.03	4.19	4.40	3.22
1965	3.954	4.055	4.22	4.28	4.49	3.27
1966	4.881	5.082	5.23	4.92	5.13	3.82
1967	4.321	4.630	5.03	5.07	5.51	3.98
1968	5.339	5.470	5.68	5.65	6.18	4.51
1969	6.677	6.853	7.02	6.67	7.03	5.81
1970	6.458	6.562	7.29	7.35	8.04	6.51
1971	4.348	4.511	5.65	6.16	7.39	5.70
1972	4.071	4.466	5.72	6.21	7.21	5.27
1973	7.041	7.178	6.95	6.84	7.44	5.18
1974	7.886	7.926	7.82	7.56	8.57	6.09
1975	5.838	6.122	7.49	7.99	8.83	6.89
1976	4.989	5.266	6.77	7.61	8.43	6.49
1977	5.265	5.510	6.69	7.42	8.02	5.56
1978	7.221	7.572	8.29	8.41	8.73	5.90
1979	10.041	10.017	9.71	9.44	9.63	6.39

TABLE 3 *(concluded)*

| Year and Month | U. S. Treasury Securities | | | | Triple A Corporate Bonds | High-Grade Municipal Bonds (Standard & Poor's) |
| | Bills (New Issues) | | Constant Maturities | | | |
	3-month	6-month	3-year	10-year		
1980	11.506	11.374	11.55	11.46	11.94	8.51
1981	14.029	13.776	14.44	13.91	14.17	11.23
1982	10.686	11.084	12.92	13.00	13.79	11.57
1983	8.63	8.75	10.45	11.10	12.04	9.47
1984	9.58	9.80	11.89	12.44	12.71	10.15
1985	7.48	7.66	9.64	10.62	11.37	9.18
1986	5.98	6.03	7.06	7.68	9.02	7.38
Dec. '86	5.49	5.53	6.43	7.11	8.49	6.93

SOURCE: *Economic Report of the President*, February 1987. Data resources.

speculate that future ownership trends are likely to be more volatile and uncertain. On the other hand, most of the above parties will increasingly be seeking ways to maximize yields for performance reasons. In addition, foreign investors could be influenced by currency trends or economic trends to materially reduce purchases at any point in time. This could lead to increases in short- and long-term yields and smaller spreads vis-à-vis high-quality corporates. However, at the point where financial market trends affect or coincide with negative economic effects, one could see a rush to quality, and by definition, into Treasury securities for safety and liquidity.

Even with huge regular offerings, Treasury offerings do differ materially in liquidity, largely reflecting the relative success and nature of specific offerings. The result is a yield curve that is not a smooth curve throughout its length. Instead, the yield curve will reflect the ownership and liquidity characteristics of each issuance. Traders and experienced market participants use their knowledge of the specific trading patterns which tends to institutionalize the yield relationships along the yield curve as it adjusts to changing interest rates.

STRIPS AND FORWARD CONTRACTS

Important additions to the government securities market during the first half of the 1980s were stripped Treasury certificates, options, and futures. The stripped Treasuries enable the sale of essentially zero coupon Treasuries, which for an investor covers the primary, important risk of reinvestment at possibly future lower rates. This is quite useful for establishing dedicated portfolios designed to meet a return target. The advantage/disadvantage of zero coupon securities is that it provides much greater price volatility. Options and futures provide hedging and speculating capabilities for investors and portfolio managers so as to reduce or to take advantage of systematic risk.

Stripped Treasury securities were first introduced as trademarked investment banking firm products such as TIGRs—treasury investment growth receipts by Merrill Lynch or certificates of accrual on Treasury securities (CATS) by Salomon Brothers. Irrevocable trusts are credited in a custodian bank which issues zero coupon receipts representing a share in the trust where the securities are held as collateral. The Treasury's own STRIPS program, separate trading of registered interest and principal of securities, was launched in 1984.

Futures contracts on U.S. governments consist of a Treasury bond contract (8 percent and at least 15 years to maturity or first call) and a Treasury note contract (8% and 6½–10-year maturity) traded on the Chicago Board of Trade or T-bill contract on the International Monetary Market and a Ginnie Mae Collateralized Deposit Receipt (CDR) contract offering a mortgage-related security for hedging purposes.

The Ginnie Mae contract does not function as a perfect hedging vehicle, however, because above par value, homeowners begin to increase prepayments, thus partially performing the function of a call. Thus, futures on high coupon Ginnie Maes tend to anticipate this and trade in a nonparallel relationship as interest rates decline.

Also available on the Chicago Board of Trade are options, both puts and calls, on Treasury bonds and notes. The Treasury bond futures contract and options are the highest volume contracts, thus offering the most liquidity.

The availability of forward contracts has enabled a broad and growing class of investors to shift their attention from betting on future interest rate trends to betting on spread relationships either of a timing nature or relative to a specific portfolio of securities. The ability to lock in an interest rate conveniently has additional appeal in these times when interest rate volatility is high and where corporate finance transactions are becoming highly trade and position oriented. Finally, the ability to take a position in Treasuries through the cash market, on options or futures, has dramatically widened possibilities for taking on larger levels of risk with smaller levels of capital.

FEDERALLY SPONSORED AGENCY AND CORPORATION SECURITIES

Federal agency securities have their origins in a public interest that sufficient credit be made available to particular sectors of the economy, either at times of credit unavailability, a recession, or as a matter of national interest or secular characteristics not easily remedied by the private markets. This public interest manifested itself in congressional legislation authorizing a government agency or federally sponsored corporation to perform that function with a specific charter, powers, credit access, and line of responsibility. The magnitude and growth of agency debt are shown in Tables 4 and 5.

This federal agency approach has been enormously effective in directing credit to the targeted markets and parties, reflecting the ability to raise low-cost capital with presumably de facto support from the federal government.

Until 1974, most all agencies issued their own securities, rather than borrow from the Treasury and thereby increase the national debt. A major objective of the agency concept as it is practiced in the United States is that each agency or corporation is intended to operate on an economically sound, self-sustaining basis. In this manner, the agency debt would not be viewed as adding to the "obligations" of the federal government, but instead as self-supporting debt. This factor and the tripartite system of government are regarded as the main reasons for the absence of formal backing of such agency debt. In fact, in the United States, written or verbal expressions of federal support are generally absent, except for a rare comment such as appeared in the *1985 Economic Report to the President*. This situation is in contrast to many foreign government agency relationships, where even in the absence of formal guarantees, there may be substantial written and oral indications of support related to that government's willingness and ability to provide financial support in the form of liquidity, subsidies, or capital.

The question then is asked: Will the federal government provide financial support to a federally sponsored agency or corporation so as to enable them to pay their debt obligations if needed? The conclusion made almost invariably by most market participants is yes. After all, federal agency financing is accomplished for what has been officially deemed to be the public interest. Investors purchase these obligations under rights reserved specifically for Treasury and agency issues, such as an absence from registration requirements. Finally, and most compellingly, the reality of the Treasury not paying on any obligation of one agency would have major negative consequences on financing costs of all agency-sponsored securities while creating losses for financial institution holders which might seriously deplete their capital positions and thus impair the smooth functioning of the financial system. In other words, it is perceived that there would be a very high, and likely, an unacceptable cost associated with a lack of federal government support for federal agency and sponsored corporation securities.

Instead, the primary risks of agency securities would relate to overall lesser liquidity and to market price exposures during times of

TABLE 4 Federal and Federally Sponsored Credit Agencies—Debt Outstanding (in millions, end of period)

Agency	1982	1983	1984	1985	Sept. 86
Federal and federally sponsored agencies	$237,787	$240,068	$271,220	$293,905	n.a.
Federal agencies	33,055	33,940	35,145	36,390	36,473
Defense	354	243	142	71	37
Export-Import Bank	14,218	14,853	15,882	15,678	14,274
Federal Housing Administration	288	194	133	115	117
Government National Mortgage Association participation certificates	2,165	2,165	2,165	2,165	2,165
Postal Service	1,471	1,404	1,337	1,940	3,104
Tennessee Valley Authority	14,365	14,970	15,435	16,347	16,702
United States Railway Association	194	111	51	74	74
Federally sponsored agencies	204,732	206,128	236,075	257,515	n.a.
Federal Home Loan Banks	55,967	48,930	65,085	74,447	87,133
Federal Home Loan Mortgage Corporation	4,524	6,793	10,270	11,926	n.a.
Federal National Mortage Association	70,052	74,594	83,720	93,896	91,629
Farm Credit Banks	73,004	72,816	71,193	68,851	63,073
Student Loan Marketing Association	2,293	3,402	5,745	8,395	10,555
Federal Financing Bank debt	$126,424	$135,791	$145,217	$153,373	156,871
Lending to federal and federally sponsored agencies:					
Export-Import Bank	14,177	14,789	15,852	15,670	14,268
Postal Service	1,221	1,154	1,087	1,690	2,854
Student Loan Marketing Association	5,000	5,000	5,000	5,000	4,978
Tennessee Valley Authority	12,640	13,245	13,710	14,622	15,077
United States Railway Association	194	111	51	74	74
Other lending:					
Farmers Home Administration	53,261	55,266	58,971	64,234	65,374
Rural Electrification Administration	17,157	19,766	20,693	20,654	21,460
Other	22,774	26,460	29,853	31,429	32,786

SOURCE: *Federal Reserve Bulletin*, January 1987.

TABLE 5 Federal Agency Debt (annual net increases in amounts outstanding, billions)

	1981	1982	1983	1984	1985	1986E	Amt Out. 31 Dec 86E
Outstanding budgeted and federally sponsored agencies:							
Federal Home Loan Banks	$ 17.8	$ 0.6	$ -7.0	$ 18.4	$ 4.9	$ 13.1	$ 89.1
FNMA and other housing credit	4.3	10.3	3.9	7.4	5.7	1.8	90.5
Total Farm Credit	8.4	0.5	0.5	-1.2	-2.9	-7.8	60.5
Other agencies	-0.2	0.9	1.3	0.6	0.2	8.7	13.5
Total budgeted and sponsored	30.4	12.4	-1.3	25.2	7.9	15.8	253.7
Mortgage pool securities guaranteed by:							
GNMA	11.9	13.2	40.9	20.1	32.2	53.0	258.3
FHLMC	2.7	22.9	14.8	12.8	29.4	57.0	165.2
FNMA	0.7	13.7	10.7	11.1	18.8	30.0	85.0
Farmers Home Administration	-0.3	-0.2	0.0	0.5	-0.5	3.4	3.7
Collateralized Mortgage Obligations	0.2	0.2	1.7	2.6	3.1	1.8	10.6
Total Mortgage Pools	15.2	49.8	68.1	47.1	82.9	145.2	522.9
Total agency debt	45.6	62.1	66.8	72.3	90.9	161.0	$ 776.6
Less trust fund holdings	0.0	0.0	0.0	0.0	0.0	0.0	00.0
Less agency holdings	0.2	-0.1	-0.4	0.2	0.1	-0.4	0.4
Less federal reserve holdings	0.1	0.1	-0.7	-0.1	1.1	-1.8	8.1
Privately held federal agency debt	$ 45.3	$ 62.1	$ 67.9	$ 72.1	$ 89.6	$163.2	$ 768.0
Ownership:							
Thrifts	$ 8.3	$ 31.4	$ 35.7	$ 17.6	$ 1.2	$ 31.0	$ 186.5
Insurance and pensions	21.0	20.5	26.7	12.6	22.5	31.0	190.9
Investment companies	5.6	1.6	1.4	9.6	10.0	15.0	47.9
Other nonbank finance	0.0	0.0	0.0	2.9	3.2	4.0	10.1
Total nonbank finance	34.9	53.9	63.8	42.7	36.8	81.0	$ 435.4
Commercial banks	9.8	7.3	0.7	-1.3	-2.4	9.0	84.4
Nonfinancial corporations	0.0	0.1	-0.0	-0.1	-0.1	1.2	2.8
State and Local governments	-5.4	1.7	10.2	10.1	8.1	15.0	75.9
Foreign investors	0.3	0.2	0.5	1.2	4.6	8.0	15.2
Residual households direct $	5.7	-0.7	-7.2	19.5	42.7	48.9	154.3
Total ownership	45.3	$ 62.1	$ 67.9	$ 72.1	$ 89.6	163.2	$ 768.0

TABLE 5 *(concluded)*

	1981	1982	1983	1984	1985	1986E	Amt. Out. 31 Dec 86E
Summary of privately held federal debt							
Privately held treasury debt	$ 77.8	$152.3	$174.8	$188.9	$188.1	$194.2	$1,591.3
Privately held fed. agency debt	45.3	62.1	67.9	72.1	89.6	163.2	768.0
Privately held federal debt	$123.2	$214.3	$242.7	$261.1	$277.7	$357.4	$2,359.3

SOURCE: Salomon Brothers Inc: *Prospects for Financial Markets in 1987.*

serious stress for the institution. The two most prominent examples were Fannie Mae in the early 1980s and Farm Credit System in 1985–86.

In Fannie Mae's case, yields spiked up during a period of poor financial results and high interest rates, which rendered the nation's largest savings and loan association in earnings difficulty, and its capital have weakened in market value terms. For Farm Credit System, accelerated losses, write-offs, capital and earnings power questions and unclear lines of access to support led to a market confidence crisis during which long-term yields spiked up as much as 200 basis points, and short-term rates rose materially as well.

The December 1985 passage of new legislation for regulating the Farm Credit Administration and for providing access to Treasury borrowings was an important air-clearing step, although subsequent financial problems have continued to unsettle the market from time to time.

Federal administration policies toward the agencies during the 1970s stressed efforts to minimize the effects and costs of agency financing on the federal government and on Treasury issuances. Establishment of the Federal Financing Bank (FFB) enabled the small- and moderate-sized agencies to borrow from the FFB, which in turn borrows from the Treasury.

FEDERAL HOME LOAN BANKS

The Federal Home Loan Bank system, a U.S. government system created under the Federal Home Loan Bank Act of 1936, performs a "central banker" function for the nation's savings and loans and thrift institutions. Some 3,400 thrift institutions are members of the system and thereby are required to own capital stock in one of 12 regional district Federal Home Loan banks. The system is supervised and regulated by the Federal Home Loan Bank Board, an independent federal agency, whose three board members are appointed by the president of the United States. The bank board is the governing body for all member institutions and state chartered institutions insured by the Federal Savings and Loan Insurance Corporation (FSLIC). The Bank Board oversees FSLIC and the Federal Home Loan Mortgage Corporation, and through its collective powers has primary authority for the institutions that are the main providers of private financing for residential real estate.

The FHL banks lend to S&Ls in a similar way to the Federal Reserve lending to commercial banks. While the Fed can lend to banks by monetizing the debt, the FHL banks have to borrow, which function is accomplished through consolidated debt obligations that are joint and several obligations of the 12 FHL banks, but not backed by the full faith and credit of the U.S. government.

It is in reality almost inconceivable to most informed observers that the U.S. government would allow a default on FHLB securities. Nevertheless, analysts have been increasingly concerned with the health of the thrift industry in times of high interest rates, and the relative inadequacies of the FSLIC funds which insure a major portion of the nation's deposits and which are being depleted through thrift insolvencies. A 1986–87 perspective indicated activity toward an FSLIC recapitalization plan which could detract from FHLB overall capital strength. Other proposed solutions, such as risk-adjusted deposit insurance for thrifts providing increased funding for the FSLIC fund are imperfect and the long-term outlook suggests that the question of investor confidence may well arise from time to time. FHLB notes and bonds totaled $89 billion at year-end 1986 with borrowings of $13 billion during the year.

FEDERAL NATIONAL MORTGAGE ASSOCIATION (FANNIE MAE)

Fannie Mae was established by Congress in 1938, and in 1968 was divided into Fannie Mae (a privately owned corporation) and the Government National Mortgage Association. Its purpose has been to help maintain an active market in mortgages insured or guaranteed by the Federal Housing Administration, the Veterans Administration and the Farm Home Administration, and in 1970 it was given authority to include conventional mortgages. Fannie Mae is subject to regulation by the Secretary of Housing and Urban Development and the Secretary of the Treasury.

Fannie Mae purchases mortgage loans using specific industry standards and private mortgage insurance for conventional mortgages. In 1981, it began insuring mortgage-backed securities. Debt financing is done through the issuance of debentures, short-term notes and an increasing number of innovative financing devices.

Fannie Mae's stock is traded on the New York Stock Exchange and has tended to mirror the risks and opportunities related to the thrift industry, particularly related to substantial interest rate risk. This tends on occasion to have a rub-off effect on investor confidence in the debt securities, which are not backed by the federal government and whose interest income is subject to full state and local taxation.

Fannie Mae also tends to be a subject of controversy, partly related to its dual profit-making and public policy mandates. In the late 1970s, Fannie Mae was under particular pressure to finance inner-city housing. In the 1980s, with the growth of mortgage securitization, the lowering of restrictions on interstate banking and the growth of private firms in the secondary mortgage market, the administration had been increasingly questioning Fannie Mae's continuing relationship with the federal government and urging full privatization.

At year-end 1986, Fannie Mae had outstanding about $90 billion of debentures and notes and $85 billion of mortgage-backed securities. Fannie Mae has an extensive involvement in innovative financing stemming from its need for profitability, on its own merits and so as to build a competitive capital base. The profit orientation encourages it to tap as wide an investor base as possible at a minimum low cost. The high leverage of the capital base tends to impact the profitability materially.

GOVERNMENT NATIONAL MORTGAGE ASSOCIATION (GINNIE MAE)

Ginnie Mae is a wholly owned government corporation within the Department of Housing and Urban Development that is responsible for management, liquidity, and special assistance functions related to residential mortgages. Ginnie Mae's special assistance is to a large extent in the form of financing of mortgage or mortgage purchase commitments which are resold at market prices to investors. Ginnie Mae pass-through certificates are created when private mortgage investors put together pools of mortgages acquired through Ginnie Mae and sell them to investors. Ginnie Mae certificates are guaranteed and carry a full faith and credit backing by the U.S. government.

FEDERAL HOME LOAN MORTGAGE CORPORATION (FREDDIE MAC)

Freddie Mac was established by Congress in 1970 to enhance the growth of a secondary market in residential mortgages. Mortgages are purchased from members of the FHLB system or other authorized financial institutions. The capital stock is owned by the Bank System and its members and the board of directors are the same as for the FHLB board. If needed, Freddie Mac may borrow from the bank board.

Freddie Mac is the leading seller of conventional mortgage securities, including participation certificates (PCs) and collateralized mortgage obligations (CMOs). Freddie Mac's activities are similar to Fannie Mae's, but its operations differ. It takes little to no interest rate risk and it can only purchase mortgages from regulated institutions (thereby streamlining operating costs and procedures).

Freddie Mac securities are taxable at the state and local level. At year-end 1986, $165 billion of PCs, CMOs, and notes and debentures were outstanding.

FARM CREDIT SYSTEM

The Farm Credit System operates under the Farm Credit Act of 1971, and importantly, the Farm Credit Amendments Act of 1985. It consists of Federal Land Banks, Federal Intermediate Credit Banks, Banks for Cooperatives, and the Farm Credit System Capital Corporation; operations are divided into 12 districts. The system's purpose is to function as a cooperatively owned network of borrower-owned banks to support the supply of dependable credit to farmers, rural homeowners, and businesses engaged in agricultural activity.

Reflecting the development and accentuation of serious agricultural loan loss, delinquency, and related problems in 1985, new legislation strengthened the Farm Credit Administration's role as an arm's-length regulator of the system, while providing mechanisms to reallocate system resources among institutions and authorizing the U.S. Treasury to make funds available to the system through the Capital Corporation subject to congressional appropriation.

The Farm Credit System finances its activities largely through the role of consolidated systemwide bonds and notes which are joint and several obligations of the Farm Credit Banks. Regulations had limited Bank Group borrowing to 20 times capital and surplus, although new regulations will supersede these. Farm Credit System debt averaged $60 billion at year-end 1986.

The Farm Credit System attracted the most investor concern of any federally sponsored intermediary in 1985 as reports of the worsening loan problems and the system's request for assistance led to a spiral of increasing spreads on Farm Credit System's obligations to Treasury securities. Some securities traded at rates of 100–200 basis points more than Treasuries, and were competitive with A- and BBB-rated corporate bonds or lower-rated commercial paper. Standard & Poor's Corporation placed under review the continued eligibility of Farm Credit System securities as acceptable collateral in AAA-rated financings. Investor confidence was not materially restored until the new federal legislation was enacted (at which time S&P reaffirmed eligibility). Farm Credit System securities continued subsequently to trade at historically higher yield spreads to Treasuries and this condition may continue or flare up in the future depending on the extent to which loan losses persist.

From a long-term perspective, knowledgeable investors are cognizant of the trends toward a secular decline in the role of agriculture in the U.S. economy, the inherent weakness in Farm Credit System's capital base related to the fact that borrowers must take on equity when they take on a loan, the lack of earning power, and of the departure of the healthier borrowers to other sources. They are also aware that the Farm Credit System supplies two thirds of agricultural credit, has performed a "lender of last resort" function here, of the political and economic significance of farming to the United States, and finally the potential for political gamesmanship.

The realistic result is that investors need to consider the potential for higher market price risk and lesser liquidity in Farm Credit System securities as a trade-off against more advantageous yields. Investors who believe that the system's securities will regain substantial market strength take comfort from the reforms planned and their expectation that, at worst, Treasury infusions would strengthen a system that should not remain in disequilibrium over the long term.

STUDENT LOAN MARKETING ASSOCIATION (SALLIE MAE)

Sallie Mae, established in 1965, has issued nonvoting stock, which began trading in 1983, and its function is to facilitate a secondary market for Federally Guaranteed Student Loans. The board is partially appointed by the president and a $1 billion line of credit exists at the Secretary of the Treasury's discretion. Sallie Mae has had an excellent profitability record and a mandate directed to student lending. Sallie Mae has been a leader in innovative financing and benefited from such leadership.

Primary long-term issues relate to administration desires to fully privatize Sallie Mae and the corporation's profit growth objectives. For holders of its senior securities, this creates some long-term uncertainty, although there is little doubt Sallie Mae has managed its growth to date conservatively and successfully.

MORTGAGE-RELATED SECURITIES

Mortgage-related securities of Ginnie Mae, Fannie Mae, and Freddie Mac are, for the most part, not included in the debt statistics related to the above entities, but nevertheless represent a significant and growing segment of the federally sponsored capital markets. Mortgage securities are largely viewed on a stand-alone basis backed mainly by residential mortgage assets underwritten with generally accepted credit standards. The mortgage-related securities trade in a different market environment than do Treasuries and direct federally sponsored agency debt securities, so that an astute investor's knowledge about each of these markets can result in arbitrage strategies. Key considerations here would include techniques to deal with the variable prepayment rates on mortgages, that depend on the type of mortgages in a pool, and assumptions regarding future interest rates and prepayment rates.

The controversy regarding the administration's efforts to gradually privatize much agency and credit-intermediary financing is a relatively important one for investors holding long-term securities because it could eventually affect future liquidity and market prices of the securities. The administration's position is that the federal relationship implicitly supports these financings. This creates an off-balance-sheet subsidy in the form of lower interest rates paid for by the general public that builds up the capital and surplus of the agency or corporation enabling it to continue and build activities that could and perhaps should be accomplished by the private sector. Proponents of agency financing point to its success in directing credit to public interest needs in a highly efficient manner with minimum actual financial support from the government. This school of thought sees agency financing as having had important and favorable effects on economic activity, and that in times of weak economic activity or tight credit these vehicles provide a particularly effective safety valve to prevent sharp contractions in credit flows and resultant economic activity. Finally, they wonder whether the subsidy effect or agency financing is material in the context of the larger issue of the total federal deficit and its effect on the federal government's financing needs.

REFERENCES

FABOZZI, FRANK J. AND IRVING R. POLLACK, *The Handbook of Fixed Income Securities* (Homewood, Illinois: Dow-Jones-Irwin, 1987)

KAUFMAN, HENRY, *Prospects for Financial Markets* (New York: Salomon Brothers, 1987)

OLIVA, WILLIAM C. AND DAVID M. HEAD, *Structure and Operations of Selected Federal Agencies and International Organization* (New York: Salomon Brothers, December, 1985)

STIGUM, MARCIA, *The Money Market*, revised edition (Homewood, Illinois: Dow-Jones-Irwin, 1983)

Economic Report to the President: 1985 and 1986. U.S. Government Printing Office.

31

Mortgage Backed Securities

Richard T. Pratt
Chairman
Merrill Lynch Mortgage Capital, Inc.

John A. Scowcroft
Vice President and Manager
Merrill Lynch MBS Research

Marguerite Durkin*

The mortgage market is the largest domestic debt market. At year-end 1985, total mortgage debt outstanding was $2.27 trillion—16 percent larger than U.S. Treasury and agency securities outstanding, 300 percent larger than U.S. corporate bonds outstanding, and 340 percent larger than all state, local, and municipal debt outstanding. Almost two thirds of this debt—$1.5 trillion—was secured by mortgages on one-to-four family residences (see Figure 1). Residential mortgage debt also accounts for a major share of all new funds raised each year in the domestic markets. Between 1975 and 1985, for example, net new residential mortgage debt was 20 percent of total domestic new debt issuance.

Despite its huge size, the residential mortgage market operated somewhat independently of other domestic debt markets up until the early 1970s. Since then, a volatile economy, increased borrower sophistication and deliberate federal policy have helped integrate the mortgage market with other domestic and worldwide capital markets. This chapter gives an overview of how this integration came about, and of how

---

* This chapter was written in collaboration with Marguerite Durkin, formerly a Senior Analyst at Merrill Lynch MBS Research.

FIGURE 1   Total Domestic Debt Outstanding, Year-End 1985

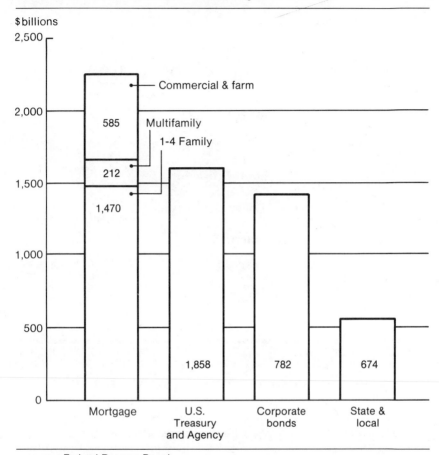

SOURCE: Federal Reserve Board.

the mortgage market operates currently. Divided into three sections, it discusses:

1. The historical development of the modern mortgage market.
2. The valuation and performance of mortgage securities.
3. Widely traded mortgage securities, particularly the pass-through securities issued or guaranteed by the Government National Mortgage Association (GNMA), the Federal National Mortgage Association (FNMA), and the Federal Home Loan Mortgage Corporation (FHLMC).

SECTION 1: DEVELOPMENT OF THE RESIDENTIAL MORTGAGE MARKET

BASIC MARKET STRUCTURE

The modern residential mortgage market has two, interrelated sectors. These are: (1) the primary mortgage market; and (2) the secondary mortgage market.

Primary Mortgage Market

The primary mortgage market includes all transactions that occur between a mortgage borrower and a direct (i.e., primary) lender. Individual households are the dominant borrower type, assuming more than 99 percent of new debt during 1985. Primary lenders are predominantly thrift institutions, which originate loans for their own investment portfolios or for resale, and mortgage banks, which originate and pool loans for resale into the secondary market (see Table 1).

Secondary Mortgage Market

The secondary mortgage market includes all transactions that involve at least one party who is not a direct mortgage borrower or lender. Secondary market transactions include the sale of mortgages by a mortgage originator to a pension fund, mortgage pool, or federal agency. Other common secondary market transactions include the sale

---

TABLE 1   Net New Residential Mortgage Debt, by Borrower and Lender Type (in billions)

	1977	1979	1981	1983	1985
Net borrowers:					
Households	$89.7	$117.6	$75.0	$110.2	$154.7
Other	3.6	(1.0)	(2.8)	6.8	0.6
	$93.3	$116.6	$72.2	$117.0	$155.3
Net lenders:					
Savings institutions	$52.1	$ 42.8	$16.6	$ 27.5	$ 32.9
Mortgage pools	15.7	21.8	14.3	65.2	78.7
Federal agencies	0.5	9.2	5.1	9.4	11.7
Other	25.0	42.8	36.2	14.9	32.0
	$93.3	$116.6	$72.2	$117.0	$155.3

SOURCE: Federal Reserve Board, *Quarterly Flow of Funds Report.*

of mortgages by one portfolio investor to a second investor or the sale of mortgages into a financing subsidiary to collateralize a debt offering.

Secondary mortgage market activity is dominated by *securitized loan* transactions. A securitized loan is a mortgage loan that has been pooled with other loans into a *mortgage-related security*. Mortgage securities are simply legal structures that add credit guarantees and legal enhancements to packages of individual loans that make it easier to trade the loans in a secondary market. Almost $700 billion worth of mortgages had been packaged into mortgage-related securities by year-end 1986. This volume will grow as both new and currently outstanding mortgage loans are securitized. Thrift institutions, mortgage bankers, federal agencies, Wall Street broker/dealers, and large institutional investors, such as pension funds, insurance companies, and fixed-income mutual funds are the largest purchasers and sellers of mortgage-related securities.

EVOLUTION OF THE MORTGAGE MARKET

Early History

The easiest way to understand the current mortgage market is to trace its historical development. Prior to the Great Depression, most residential mortgage loans were short-term, nonamortizing instruments. That is, a borrower would pay interest only on his or her loan, and refinance or pay the loan in full at the end of the loan period (typically five years). Two consequences of the deflation that characterized the Great Depression were wage cuts and falling real estate values. Homeowners could not afford to refinance their mortgage loans when they came due and widespread loan default contributed to the failure of more than 9,000 financial institutions between 1930 and 1933. Faced with a collapsing financial system, the federal government took a number of initiatives to stabilize the system overall, and the market for mortgage credit specifically. For the mortgage market, the most important of these actions were the Federal Home Loan Bank Act of 1932, the Homeowners Loan Act of 1933, and the National Housing Act of 1934.

The *Bank Act of 1932* created the Federal Home Loan Bank (FHLB) system to act as lender of last resort to thrifts suffering temporary liquidity shortages. When liquidity dried up, thrifts could pledge mortgage assets as collateral for borrowings (called *advances*) from their district banks. The bank system would fund these advances by issuing short-term government debt. In return for cheap funding (and later, for federal deposit insurance and special tax benefits), thrifts agreed to submit to regulation by the Federal Home Loan Bank Board (FHLBB). Initially, bank board regulation was heavy. Thrifts were limited to investment in "eligible mortgage assets," defined by the board to be long-term, fixed-rate loans. The bank board also regulated thrift liability structure, encouraging thrifts to finance their mortgage assets primarily through short-term consumer savings deposits. In the late 1970s, the FHLBB responded to changing market and economic conditions and reversed much of its early regulatory position to one that allowed thrifts wider asset and liability selection. This new policy focus was intended to give thrifts the flexibility to deal with volatile interest rates. The FHLBB remains an important mortgage market institution. As the primary regulator of federally chartered savings associations, which owned 36 percent of the nation's residential mortgage loan balances at year-end 1985, the board continues to play a major role in both primary and secondary mortgage market product design and funding.

The *Homeowner's Loan Act of 1933* and the *National Housing Act of 1934* created two entities that, like the FHLBB, also have become important mortgage market institutions. In 1934, Congress authorized the Federal Housing Administration (FHA) to issue government-guaranteed mortgage insurance on privately funded mortgage debt. This shifted a portion of the credit risk of residential mortgages—particularly of low down payment mortgages—from private lenders to the federal government and thereby made mortgage loans more attractive to potential investors. In 1933, Congress created the Federal National Mortgage Association (FNMA). In 1938, Congress authorized FNMA to purchase FHA-insured loans from private lenders. By funding these mortgage purchases with cash that it raised in the short-term government securities market, FNMA brought additional funds into the mortgage market. Like the FHLBB, FNMA and the FHA grew to become major mortgage market institutions. At year-end 1984, for example, 20 percent of total residential loan balances outstanding were FHA insured (or guaranteed by the Veterans Administration under similar programs). At year-end 1985, FNMA directly held or guaranteed 9 percent of all residential mortgage debt outstanding.

Primary mortgage market institutions created during the New Deal were relatively unchanged into the late 1960s. Aided by the FHLBB, the thrift industry became the dominant supplier of residential mortgage credit, as well as the financial services industry sector most dependent on the mortgage market. The mortgage market was relatively self-contained, as thrifts raised almost all of their liabilities from household savers and made almost all of their loans to household borrowers. Because the spread between long-term mortgage yields and short-term deposit costs was positive and stable for long periods of time, thrift institutions could operate profitably in this closed system, without needing to access institutional debt markets.

Because primary market lenders had little need to buy or sell mortgage assets, the secondary mortgage market was fairly inactive until the late 1960s. The activity that did occur focused on correcting regional imbalances of funds as thrifts in high-growth areas of the country sold their mortgages to thrifts with an excess of investable deposits. There also was a limited degree of specialization within the market as mortgage bankers originated loans for sale to thrift investors. Because the transaction costs associated with a loan sale were very high, purchases and sales tended to occur among an informal "old boys" network of buyers and sellers who dealt with each other regularly, or else were limited to the small number of institutions that could handle transactions large enough to justify heavy fixed information and transaction costs.

Unstable economic conditions during the late 1960s profoundly altered the secondary mortgage market. Rising interest rates squeezed thrift profit margins, as the cost of household deposits increased while the yield on long-term, fixed-rate mortgage assets remained low. Low earnings meant that the thrift industry could not generate the new capital necessary to support additional loan volume, particularly the new credit demanded by a population that needed to house a baby boom generation entering its adolescence. Seeking to increase the supply of mortgage credit, the federal government took a number of actions designed to strengthen the secondary mortgage market. The most important of these actions was the National Housing Act of 1968.

Creation of GNMA, FNMA, and FHLMC

The National Housing Act of 1968 split FNMA into two new entities—the Government National Mortgage Association (GNMA) and the Federal National Mortgage Association (FNMA). GNMA remained a wholly owned corporation of the U.S. government with a legislative mandate to guarantee or purchase below-market rate special assistance housing loans, and to guarantee privately issued securities backed by market rate FHA/VA residential loans. FNMA was chartered as a privately capitalized, shareholder-owned corporation, authorized to purchase market rate FHA/VA loans. In return for limiting its activities to mortgage finance and submitting to limited management oversight by the federal government, FNMA was given a $2.25 billion credit line with the U.S. Treasury.

The privatization of FNMA in 1968 did not immediately generate an active, private secondary mortgage market, as had been intended. Still faced with the need to attract new, private capital to the mortgage market, GNMA introduced a new type of security in 1970. This new security—the *GNMA Pass-Through*—was designed to make mortgages easier to trade, and therefore more attractive to nontraditional mortgage investors who would bring additional funds into the market.

Under the GNMA pass-through structure, a thrift or mortgage

banker sold a group of newly originated loans to a trust. Simultaneous with the sale of mortgages to the trust, the GNMA issuer sold investors certificates evidencing a pro rata, undivided ownership interest in the mortgages backing the trust. An independent custodian took physical possession of all mortgage documents as trustee for the security owners. The original issuer or its designate collected monthly payments on the pooled mortgages and performed other administrative tasks, passing through all payments made on the pooled mortgages (less a small servicing fee) to the trust owners. If a mortgagor did not make his or her loan payment, the GNMA pass-through structure required that the issuer continue to make payments out of its own funds (for which the issuer eventually would be compensated upon collecting mortgage insurance proceeds from the FHA or VA). If a servicer defaulted on a payment, GNMA guaranteed that it would make "full and timely payment" of all principal and interest due to the pool investors.

The GNMA structure addressed the following difficulties associated with unsecuritized mortgage transactions:

1. **Credit Risk.** The GNMA guarantee made the security a direct obligation of the U.S. government rather than of the individual mortgagor or security issuer. This cut the time and expense associated with credit evaluation of individual mortgagors and loan servicers.
2. **Ease of Transfer.** All mortgage loan documents were held by a pool trustee. Ownership could be perfected by registering and taking possession of a single certificate of ownership in a trust rather than of a large number of individual mortgages and mortgage notes.
3. **Low Valuation Costs.** GNMA required that all loans accepted for pooling have common origination dates, coupons, and maturities. In addition, underwriting and documentation standards had to be met. Investors, therefore, could value a GNMA pool using easily accessible, publicly available data. This allowed the pools to be traded quickly and inexpensively.
4. **Inexpensive Diversification.** By buying shares in a mortgage pool, investors could achieve diversification with a smaller investment than if they were buying individual mortgage loans. This expanded the universe of potential investors, increasing mortgage market liquidity.

As part of the 1970 legislation that authorized GNMA to guarantee loan pools, FNMA was allowed to purchase conventional mortgage loans (loans not insured by a government entity). In addition, the Emergency Home Finance Act of 1970 established the Federal Home Loan Mortgage Corporation (FHLMC) as a corporation wholly owned by the 12 Federal Home Loan district banks. FHLMC was authorized to purchase conventional mortgage loans and non-GNMA conforming FHA/VA loans. To fund its loan purchases, FHLMC issued its first participation certificate (PC) in 1973. FHLMC PCs were mortgage pass-through securities structured similarly to the GNMA pass-through, backed by pools of conventional or FHA/VA mortgage loans.

Expansion of the Secondary Mortgage Market

At first, the new GNMA and FHLMC pass-through securities were only moderately successful at bringing new capital into the mortgage market. Between 1970 and 1981, GNMA and FHLMC had issued only $150 billion in pass-throughs. Thrift institutions remained the single largest group of pass-through investors, as nontraditional mortgage investors, such as pension funds, insurance companies, and individuals, continued to resist the mortgage market because of the uncertain cash flows and specialized bookkeeping and valuation models associated with residential mortgage investments.

By the late 1970s, however, thrift institutions faced a serious liquidity crisis once again. As the yield on 90-day Treasury bills rose from 4 percent to 16 percent between 1977 and 1980 (see Figure 2), billions of dollars of deposits fixed by law at artificially low yields moved out of thrifts and into short-term, market rate instruments such as money market share accounts. Between 1977 and 1981, for example, the share of new household financial assets invested in thrift institution savings deposits fell from 28 percent to 7 percent while the percentage of new household savings invested in money market share accounts went from 0 percent to 32 percent.

The loss of funds available to make new mortgages caused by the massive disintermediation of deposits was intensified when the yield curve inverted. As Figure 2 shows, short-term rates exceeded long-term rates for most of the period between 1979 and 1981. During 1981 alone, as thrifts were forced to fund low-yielding mortgages booked in the 1960s and 1970s with short-term deposits and advances costing up to 18 percent, the industry as a whole lost $5 billion out of a total net worth of $33 billion. Assuming a 5 percent capital requirement, this capital loss cut funds available for mortgage investment by an additional $100 billion.

Faced with an industry incapable of funding existing assets profitably and unable to raise new long-term money at rates affordable to most home buyers, the federal mortgage agencies took several steps to increase the flow of funds into the mortgage market. In 1981, at the height of the thrift funding crisis, FHLMC established its *PC Guarantor* (or *Swap*) program. Under this program, thrifts sold their below-market rate mortgages to FHLMC. FHLMC paid for these mortgages with participation certificates backed by the same mortgages that it had just

FIGURE 2 90-Day Treasury Bill versus 10-Year Treasury Note (monthly average yield, bond equivalent)

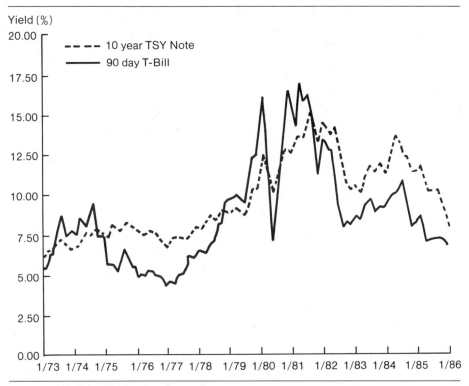

SOURCE: Merrill Lynch Mortgage Research.

purchased from the thrift. Because the transaction involved swapping one asset for an equivalent asset of equal value, capital starved thrifts did not have to take an accounting loss on the transaction. The transaction did have real economic value for the thrifts, however, because unlike the whole loans that the thrift was swapping, PCs were acceptable collateral for low-cost liabilities such as reverse repurchase agreements or medium-term note issues. As thrift institutions swapped their inventory of old, low-yielding mortgage product into pass-through securities, the volume of outstanding FNMAs and FHLMCs increased dramatically (see Table 2).

Loans securitized under FNMA's and FHLMC's swap programs helped to create the modern mortgage market. As the face value of securitized loans outstanding increased to $500 billion by 1986, major Wall Street broker/dealers and institutional investors saw enough profit potential to invest in the analytical tools and market education necessary

TABLE 2 New Pass-Through Issuance, by Year (in millions)

	GNMA	FHLMC	FNMA	Total
1970	$ 452			$ 452
1971	2,702			2,702
1972	2,662			2,662
1973	2,953	$ 322		3,275
1974	4,553	45		4,598
1975	7,447	450		7,897
1976	13,764	960		14,724
1977	17,440	4,057		21,497
1978	15,358	5,712		21,070
1979	24,940	3,796		28,736
1980	20,647	2,526		23,173
1981	14,257	3,529	$ 717	18,503
1982	**16,011**	**24,169***	**13,970**	**54,150**
1983	50,496	19,691	13,340	83,527
1984	27,857	18,684	13,546	60,087
1985	45,868	38,829	23,649	108,346
1986	86,045	83,479	54,823	224,347
Total	$353,452	$206,249	$120,045	$679,746

* Beginning of the FHLMC swap program.
SOURCE: GNMA, FNMA, FHLMC.

to create a market in the pass-through securities. FHLMC estimates that 1985 annual trading volume of all GNMA, FNMA, and FHLMC pass-throughs exceeded $1 trillion, up from $160 billion in 1981.

THE CURRENT MARKET

Current mortgage market conditions are best understood by looking at how the market has changed since 1981. The most important of these changes can be summarized as follows:

Primary Market Changes

In 1981, the predominant mortgage instrument offered by primary market lenders was the long term, fixed rate mortgage. Borrowers who wanted short term funds (e.g., those who knew that they would be moving in a short period of time or who were willing to bear interest rate risk) still had to pay for fixed rate, long term debt. Lenders, on the other hand, were forced to bear all interest rate risk. Because financial institutions were not particularly efficient issuers of long term debt, this meant that lenders had to finance long term assets with short term debt (i.e., consumer savings deposits). When an inverted yield curve pointed out the enormous risk inherent in this strategy, industry executives and federal regulators moved to broaden industry and lending powers to allow for a more flexible management of interest rate risk. In 1981, for example, the FHLBB permitted federally chartered savings associations to invest in adjustable rate mortgage loans (ARMS). A typical adjustable rate mortgage had short repricing periods, allowing earnings to rise and fall as the thrift's cost of funds rose and fell. Thrifts could price the new ARMs attractively, particularly when long term, fixed rate money was expensive. As borrower understanding and acceptance of the product grew, ARMs became an important share of new loan origination (see Figure 3).

The 1981 funding crisis brought thrifts greater liability as well as greater investment powers. In 1981, the Depository Institutions Decontrol Act (DIDCA) gradually lifted rate ceilings on thrift deposit accounts.

FIGURE 3 ARMs as a Percent of New Mortgage Originations

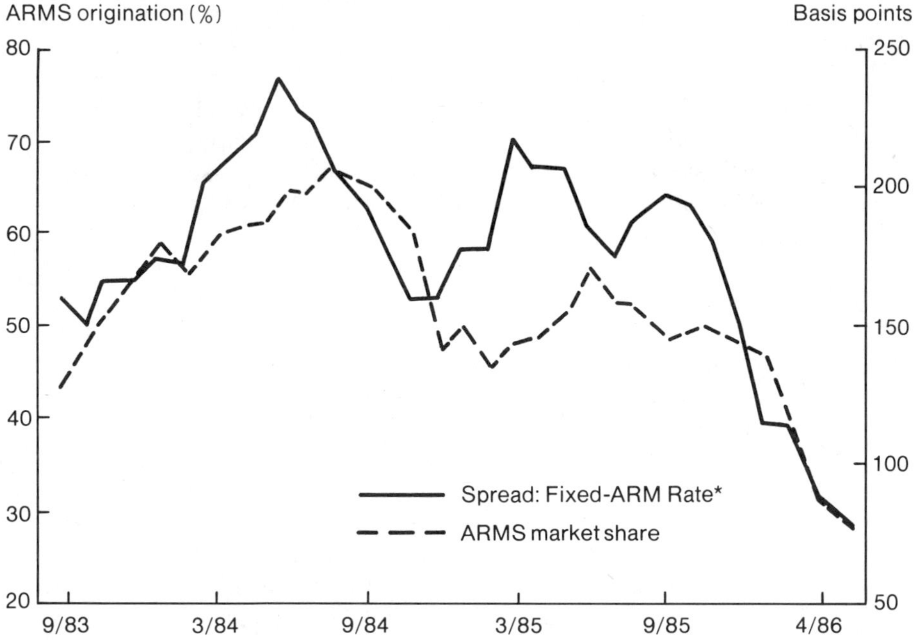

*Fixed Rate: FHLBB Contract Interest Rate for Fixed Rate 90% LTV Loans
Adjustable Rate: FHLBB Contract Interest Rate for Limited
Rate Change ARMS, 90% LTV

SOURCE: HUD, FHLBB

Between 1981 and 1986, thrifts regained most of the market share of new consumer assets lost to non-mortgage market borrowers. Thrifts also were allowed to issue intermediate and longer term liabilities such as mortgage bonds.

Together, expanded thrift lending and funding powers have brought about a wider diversity of mortgage loan products offered in the primary markets, and therefore, a wider diversity of secondary market securities. Primary lenders increasingly can design mortgage products to take advantage of funds availability in different debt markets, and residential mortgage borrowers now compete on a much more equal basis with all other debt issuers in the domestic, and even the world-wide, capital markets. As of 1986, the thrift industry's primary role has shifted from that of intermediary between the short term saver and the long term borrower to that of intermediary between the household mortgage borrower and the institutional capital markets.

Secondary Market Changes

At the same time that new thrift borrowing and lending powers were affecting the cost and supply of residential mortgage loans, developments in the secondary mortgage markets also were affecting the cost and supply of mortgage credit. The development of highly creditworthy, highly liquid mortgage pass through securities helped increase the number and type of secondary mortgage market investors. Between 1983 and 1985, for example, non-thrift investors increased their ownership share of pass through securities at the expense of traditional thrift lenders (see Table 3). Assuming that this ownership represented capital that otherwise would not have been invested in residential mortgages, the creation of agency guaranteed pass throughs may have brought at least $25 billion of new funds into the market since 1983 alone.

The new mortgage market investors were primarily institutions, which typically were far more sensitive to general credit market conditions than traditional mortgage lenders. Unlike thrifts or mortgage bankers who had fixed costs that limited their ability to move into and out of different debt markets, the new pass through investors evaluated mortgages as just another investment alternative. Mortgage borrowers, therefore, had to pay market rates for their new loans. In return, however, they were assured access to huge institutional debt markets as long as they could pay competitive rates.

In addition to expanding the range of investors who held mortgages directly, pass throughs also increased the flow of indirect investment into the market. In 1979, thrifts had access to two funding sources: short term consumer savings deposits and short term agency debt (via FHLB

TABLE 3   GNMA, FNMA, and FHLMC Ownership by Investor Type (in billions)

	1983*		1985†		
Thrift institutions	$ 99.0	36%	$122.6	30%	(thrift
Insurance companies	8.2	3			ownership)
Pension funds	6.4	2			
Bank trust departments	6.9	3	291.3	70	(total nonthrift
Securities broker/dealers	20.6	8			ownership)
Nominees	89.0	32			
Others	44.0	16			
Total	$274.1	100%	$413.9	100%	

* Ownership as of: December 30, 1983 (GNMA and FHLMC); December 31, 1983 (FNMA).
† Estimated ownership as of December 31, 1985.
SOURCE: GNMA, FNMA, and FHLMC.

advances and FNMA loan purchase activity). Although savings deposits and FHLB advances still accounted for 88% of thrift liabilities at year end 1985, thrifts had tripled their use of "Other Borrowings" (see Table 4). These "Other Borrowings"—structured debt transactions, collateralized commercial paper and money market preferred stock, reverse repurchase agreements, domestic and Euronote issues, and interest rate

TABLE 4

ALL FSLIC-INSURED INSTITUTIONS
Comparative Balance Sheets
(in billions)

	1978 (year end)		1985 (year end)	
Assets				
Mortgage loans and pools	$439.6	86.1%	$ 760.6	71.2%
Other loans	11.5	2.2	45.3	4.2
Cash and government securities. . .	43.3	8.5	55.2	5.1
Other	16.3	3.2	208.4	19.5
Total assets.	$510.7	100.0%	$1,069.5	100.0%
Liabilities				
Savings deposits	$420.4	82.3%	$ 844.0	79.0%
FHLB advances	31.6	6.2	84.4	7.8
Other borrowings	10.3	2.0	72.2	6.7
All other liabilities.	20.3	4.0	22.1	2.1
Net worth.	28.1	5.5	46.8	4.4
Total liabilities and net worth. .	$510.7	100.0%	$1,069.5	100.0%

SOURCE: FHLBB.

swaps—were new funding sources issued primarily in institutional debt markets. Because many thrifts were considered weak or unknown credits, they gained access to these institutional debt markets only because they could use their highly liquid, highly creditworthy pass through securities as collateral.

The Future?

Late 1986 marked another important transitional period in the mortgage market. Three aspects of the market saw dramatic changes: (1) the mix between government and private influence on market operations; (2) the development of derivative mortgage products; and (3) the scope of the market itself.

The "Private/Public" Partnership

As has been pointed out so far, the current mortgage market is a mix of private and public activity. While the federal government makes no direct financial contribution to the market (GNMA guarantee and FHA insurance programs are self supporting), the market operates with high liquidity because of the existence of direct or presumed federal government credit guarantees on a large portion of its outstanding securities. Without limits on future growth, the federal government or federally sponsored credit agencies eventually could own or guarantee a large percentage of the nation's $1.5 trillion residential mortgage debt. Concern over this has prompted federal officials to suggest policy changes ranging from imposing "user" fees on GNMA, FNMA, and FHLMC pass through securities that would eliminate the value of any implicit government credit guarantees on the securities, to a limitation on mortgage agency purchase programs, to the complete privatization of FHLMC. These proposals could have profound impact on both current and future market operations. Because each proposal has strong supporters and opponents, however, it is difficult to predict what, if any, legislative action will be taken in the near future.

As federal withdrawal from the market is debated, however, a number of private corporations are increasing their market involvement. The standardized documentation, underwriting, appraisal and loan servicing procedures developed by GNMA, FNMA, and FHLMC for their own operations have been adopted by non-federal agency market participants. Several large Wall Street broker/dealers as well as a number of large insurance companies and consumer finance companies (e.g., GMAC and GECC) have entered both the primary and secondary markets. These firms have the financial resources, access to worldwide capital markets and capital depth to compete with FNMA and FHLMC, effectively decreasing federal presence in the residential mortgage markets whether or not any legislative changes are enacted.

Product Design: Derivative Mortgage Securities

Section 3 of this chapter discusses mortgage products in detail. In the context of future developments in the market, however, it should be noted that an important new tax reporting entity—the Real Estate Mortgage Investment Conduit (REMIC)—was created as part of the Tax Reform Act of 1986. This new tax entity will allow cash flows from a single pool of mortgage assets to be restructured into a wide variety of securities with different performance characteristics. By creating securities that appeal to different investor groups, issuers can further widen the funds available for investment in the mortgage market. In mid-1986, FNMA responded to market demand for alternative mortgage products with the introduction of a multi-class pass through security called the stripped MBS. In the form that was most popular as of late 1986, this security divided the cash flows on a single pool of mortgage assets into a "principal only" portion (PO security) and an "interest only" portion (IO security). These two securities have very different performance characteristics than the mortgage cash flows from which they are created. Between introduction of the security in mid-1986 and March 1987, FNMA had issued more than $5 billion of stripped MBS. Collateralized mortgage obligations—another type of derivative mortgage product—have grown into an $80 billion market in the three years between 1983 and 1986.

If derivative mortgage products remain popular, the effect on the market could be profound. Some analysts fear that the market will become fragmented and illiquid as billions of dollars of new and existing pass through securities are removed from active trading and "locked up" as the raw material for a large number of complex, non-standard derivative products. Other analysts look to derivative products as a welcome innovation that will add further liquidity and efficiency to the market.

Scope of the Market

The final development that could profoundly affect the residential mortgage market is a predicted explosion in the securitization of all financial assets—not just of mortgages. In 1986, *securitized assets* as diverse as automobile loans and consumer credit card receivables were well received by the market.

Because the securitization of these assets is similar to the securitization of residential mortgage loans, they have been packaged and traded by mortgage market professionals. The market for all securitized assets could develop parallel to the mortgage market by the 1990s, or the mortgage market could become just one segment of a larger, securitized debt market.

SECTION 2: EVALUATING A MORTGAGE SECURITY

Two methods commonly are used to value a mortgage security: (1) yield-to-maturity (or yield to a prespecified investment horizon); and (2) total return. *Yield-to-maturity* is the discount rate, or internal rate of return, that makes the present value of a security's cash flows equal to its price. *Total rate of return* is the cash inflow from a security, expressed as a percentage of the cash outflow on the security. Because both valuation methods require that an investor make assumptions about the amount and timing of a security's cash flows, the estimation of these cash flows is a crucial part of the valuation of a mortgage security.

ESTIMATING MORTGAGE CASH FLOWS

As with any fixed-income security, a mortgage security's cash flows consist of (1) coupon interest; (2) return of principal; and (3) reinvestment income on principal and interest payments. Mortgage cash flows, however, are timed slightly differently from the cash flows typical of other fixed-income securities. The most important of these cash flow timing differences are:

1. Monthly payment of interest.
2. Monthly amortization of principal.
3. Unscheduled principal prepayments.

Monthly Payment of Interest

Most mortgages require monthly rather than semiannual payment of interest. Assuming that these monthly interest payments can be reinvested at a positive rate, a mortgage security with 12 monthly payments (reinvestment periods) will always have a higher effective yield than an equal coupon security with only two, semiannual payments. Table 5 shows the basis point difference between *mortgage yield* (12 monthly interest payments) and *corporate bond equivalent yield* (2 semiannual payments). Note that the difference between the two types of yields increases as the mortgage coupon increases. This yield difference makes it important to know whether a yield quote is mortgage yield or bond equivalent yield.

TABLE 5 Mortgage Yield to Bond Yield Conversion Table

Mortgage Coupon	Corporate Bond Equivalent Yield	Difference
4%	4.03%	0.03%
8	8.14	0.14
12	12.30	0.30
16	16.54	0.54

Monthly Amortization of Principal

The second important difference between mortgage cash flows and the cash flows on a typical corporate bond is that most corporate and Treasury securities pay only interest until bond maturity, at which time all principal is returned in a lump sum. Mortgage loans, in contrast, usually are *self-amortizing* instruments. That is, each monthly payment consists of both interest and principal. These payments are scheduled so that the loan balance is paid down fully by the last payment on the loan, usually without any single loan payment being significantly larger than any other loan payment. Most residential mortgages offered in today's primary market pay principal based on one of three basic amortization plans: (1) level payment, fixed-rate; (2) graduated payment; or (3) adjustable rate.

Fixed-Rate, Level Payment Loan

The most common type of residential mortgage loan outstanding is the fixed-rate, level payment loan. This mortgage has equal payments over a fixed term, with each payment a mix of interest and principal. As the principal portion of the payment is applied to the loan balance each period, the required interest due the next period falls. As an increasingly large amount of principal is paid down each period, the loan completely amortizes over its term without any additional lump sum payments required. Amortization patterns on a level payment, fixed-rate loan are a function of loan coupon, payment amount, and loan term. A lower coupon loan will amortize more quickly than a higher coupon loan, holding payment amount constant. A long-term loan requires a smaller monthly payment to amortize fully than a short-term loan with the same interest rate. Figure 4 shows the amortization pattern of a 12 percent, fixed-rate, level payment loan with 30 annual payments. Amortization is slow at first, but increases rapidly over the latter years of the mortgage (e.g., 25 percent of the loan balance pays down over the final three years of the loan).

FIGURE 4 Annual Cash Flows: Fixed-Rate, Level Payment Mortgage (12 percent coupon; 30 payments; $100,000 mortgage)

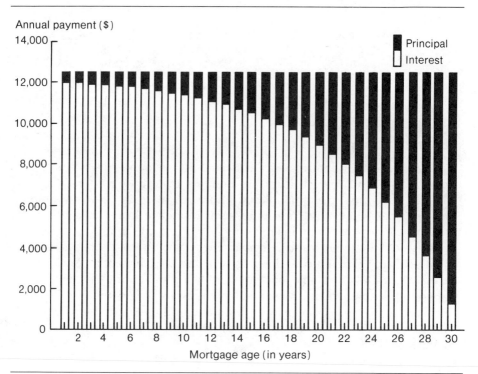

Graduated Payment Loan

The typical graduated payment loan (GPM) bears a fixed interest rate and term. Payments, however, vary over the life of the loan. One of the most common GPM plans—FHA Plan III—has payments that increase 7.5 percent each year for five years. Payments then are level over the remaining term of the loan. The GPM lender accrues interest on the loan at the coupon rate. If the loan payment is not large enough to cover contractual interest, the shortfall is capitalized and added to the loan balance as additional principal, called *negative amortization*. At year six, the outstanding loan balance begins to amortize just like a fixed-rate, level payment loan. Figure 5 shows the cash flow pattern of a 12 percent, Plan III GPM with a 30-year term. Initial payments on the GPM are lower than payments on the equivalent, level payment mortgage. Later payments are higher, however, reflecting the higher principal balance on the GPM.

FIGURE 5 Annual Cash Flows: GPM Mortgage (12 percent coupon; 30 payments; $100,000 mortgage; 7.5 percent annual increase for five years)

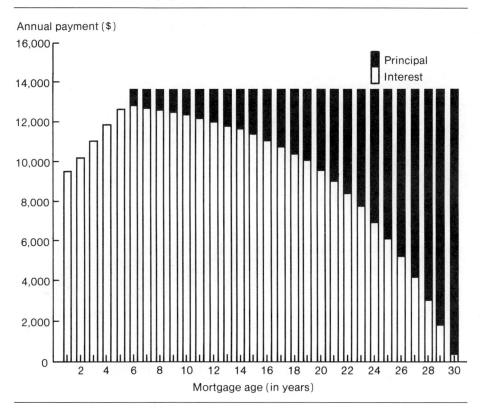

Adjustable Rate Loans

An adjustable rate mortgage (ARM) usually carries a fixed term and a rate that adjusts periodically. There are a wide variety of adjustable rate mortgage plans on the market. The most popular have the following characteristics: a fixed term; a specified adjustment formula, such as a rate set equal to an index value plus a margin; and minimum and maximum rate or payment change allowed each period and over the life of the loan.

Figure 6 shows the amortization pattern of a 30-year loan with annual rate adjustments, a 2 percent periodic and a 5 percent lifetime cap on rate changes, and no negative amortization. Assuming an initial loan coupon of 12 percent and the index rate values shown in Table 6, the loan will amortize as shown in Figure 6.

FIGURE 6   Annual Cash Flows: Simple Adjustable Rate Mortgage (12 percent coupon; 30 payments; $100,000 mortgage; 2 percent/5 percent periodic/lifetime cap)

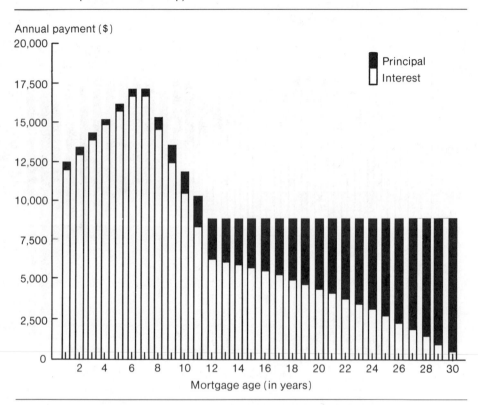

TABLE 6   Changes in the Mortgage Index Rate

Change Date	Index Value	Mortgage Coupon
0	12%	12%
1	13	13
2	14	14
3	15	15
4	16	16
5	19	17
6	18	17
7	14	15
8	10	13
9	9	11
10	8	9
11	7	7

TABLE 7 Yield to Maturity* as a Function of Prepayment Assumption

	Estimated Prepayment Rate			
Price[†]	0%	6%	12%	30%
90	13.85%	14.53%	15.28%	17.92%
95	13.04	13.36	13.71	14.95
99.5	12.38	12.41	12.44	12.56
105	11.63	11.35	11.04	9.93
110	11.01	10.48	9.89	7.80

* Bond equivalent yield.
[†] 12 percent mortgage; 360-month remaining term; 30-day delay; no servicing fee.

Unscheduled Principal Prepayments

The third, and most important difference between mortgage cash flows and the cash flows on a (noncallable) corporate bond or Treasury security is that the typical residential mortgage is prepaid at some time in its life. Most residential mortgages carry an unlimited call option, allowing the borrower to prepay his or her mortgage at any time without penalty. Depending on whether the mortgage carries a discount, premium, or current coupon, this prepayment option can have a significant effect on security yield. Table 7 shows the effect of using different prepayment rates to estimate the yield on a fixed rate, 12 percent mortgage with a remaining maturity of 360 months. Priced at 95, the security yields 13.04 percent at a zero prepayment rate estimate. Yield increases to 13.36 percent when the security is assumed to prepay at 6 percent per year. The yield on a discount security increases when prepayment rates increase because the faster return of principal implied by the higher prepayment rate shortens the discount accretion period. The effect of prepayments on the yield estimate for a premium bond is opposite the effect on a discount bond. Estimated yield on a premium security decreases when estimated prepayments increase because the early payment of principal shortens the premium amortization period. Finally, notice that estimated yield on the near par security (priced at 99.5) is relatively insensitive to the prepayment estimate used. This is because the bond discount is very small and changes in its accretion period have very small yield impacts.

MEASURING MORTGAGE PREPAYMENTS

Table 7 demonstrates that an accurate prepayment estimate is crucial if the expected yield on a mortgage security is to approximate the yield that actually will be realized from holding the security. The mortgage market, therefore, has developed a number of analytical techniques to measure and estimate mortgage prepayment rates. These models include: (1) fixed life; (2) FHA experience; (3) conditional prepayment rate (CPR); and (4) PSA standard prepayment (PSA).

Fixed Life

The *fixed life* prepayment model is the oldest mortgage prepayment model, and the model least used in the market. Fixed life assumes that a mortgage borrower pays principal as scheduled to some date, at which time the borrower prepays his or her loan balance in full. The market convention is that a 30-year mortgage prepays in full at the end of 12 years (see Figure 7). This convention is called the *12-year life assumption* or *30/12* (pronounced "thirty-to-a-twelve"). Fifteen-year mortgages are quoted on a "fifteen-to-a-seven" year prepayment convention.

Yields calculated based on the 30/12 fixed life convention are called *quoted yield*. While the balloon prepayment pattern assumed by the fixed

---

FIGURE 7   Annual Cash Flows: 12-year Fixed Life Assumption (12 percent coupon; 30 payments; $1 million pool)

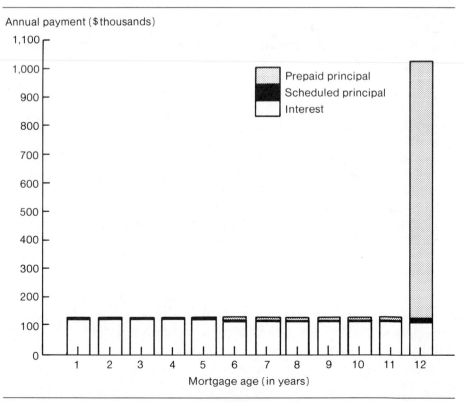

life convention may be a fair reflection of the prepayment characteristics of an individual mortgage, it is unrealistic to assume that all mortgages that make up a mortgage pool will prepay in one lump sum at exactly the same time. Several prepayment models more suitable for measuring prepayments on a pool of mortgages have replaced quoted yield. These include the FHA, CPR, and PSA models. Yields calculated using these prepayment models are called *cash flow yields*.

FHA Experience

The Federal Housing Administration keeps detailed statistics on the number of loans that terminate (i.e., pay in full, default, or terminate insurance coverage) at each year of policy coverage. FHA Experience is the number of loans that remained insured at the end of each policy year, expressed as a fraction (or *factor*) of all loans initially in the population. These experience factors often are interpreted as the probability that a mortgage loan (or percentage of mortgage principal in a pool) will survive to a given mortgage age (see Figure 8).

FIGURE 8   FHA Experience Factors: Equivalent CPRs

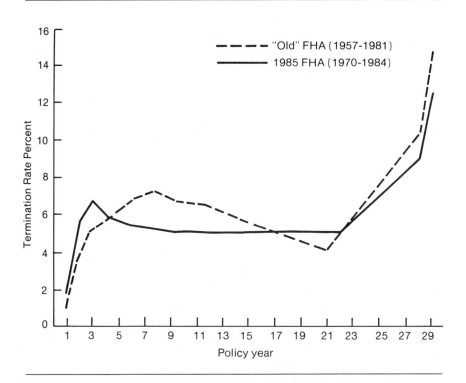

FHA Experience is a better prepayment model than fixed life in that it is based on the actual prepayment behavior of a large number of loans. FHA Experience often is misused, however. FHA Experience represents the prepayment experience of a specific loan type: loans insured under section 203 of the National Housing Act. These loans have certain characteristics such as maximum size, minimum down payment, and loan assumability that cause them to prepay differently from other loan types. FHA Experience, therefore, is most useful when used to estimate the prepayment behavior of the FHA/VA loans backing GNMA pools; it may not reflect the prepayment experience of FHLMC or FNMA pools backed by mortgage loans that are not government insured.

FHA Experience is of limited use even for predicting GNMA pool prepayments, however. Because FHA Experience documents loan prepayment behavior as a function of only one loan characteristic—loan age—the effect of loan coupon and historic interest rate conditions on termination rates is not captured in the experience factors. If, for example, the current differences between loan coupon and market rate for a group of loans are not the same as the average difference between coupon and market rates that had existed when all of the loans in the FHA population were the same age as the loans being valued, FHA termination rates may not be a useful prepayment rate estimator.

A final criticism of FHA Experience is that it is difficult to use. First, because FHA is updated periodically, the market must be aware of subtle differences that may exist among different annual series. Second, it is difficult to interpret prepayment speeds that differ from "100 percent of FHA" (i.e., prepayment at other than the FHA termination rate for a given policy year). By market convention, prepayments at rates other than 100 percent of FHA are expressed as exponential rather than as simple linear multiples of "100 percent of FHA Experience." For example, if "100 percent of FHA Experience" implies that a given loan pool will prepay at a 6 percent rate, 200 percent FHA implies that the pool will prepay at a 12.36 percent rate,[1] and not at a 12 percent rate. As a final difficulty, FHA factors are reported on an annual basis; there is no market convention for the conversion of annual FHA rates to monthly equivalents.

Conditional Prepayment Rates

The conditional prepayment rate (CPR) model is the simplest prepayment model, and the model most commonly used in the market. A conditional prepayment rate reflects the dollar amount of all unscheduled principal payments made on a loan between two dates.

---

[1] $100 \times [1.06^2 - 1]$. Prepayment at "50 percent FHA" would be prepayment at a 2.96 percent rate—at $100 \times [1.06^{.5} - 1]$.

This paydown is expressed as an annualized percentage of the loan balance outstanding at the first date. The following formulas show the calculation of *One Months' CPR*:

$$CPR = [(1 + SMM/100)^{12} - 1] \times 100$$

where: SMM = Single monthly mortality

$$SMM = [1 - (PF_t/R_t) / (PF_{t-1}/R_{t-1})] \times 100$$

where: PF_t = Outstanding loan balance at end of month t, as a fraction of the original loan balance

R_t = Fraction of loan balance scheduled to be outstanding at the end of time t if no prepayments had occurred during month t.

Any prepayment model can be expressed in a CPR format. For example, FHA termination rates often are converted to a set of CPR equivalents (see Figure 8). Also, a number of different types of CPR are quoted in the market. These include: historical CPR; projected CPR; and break-even CPR (BEPR).

Historical CPR

Historical CPR is the CPR actually experienced by a loan pool over a specified period of time. Historical factors (outstanding pool balances expressed as a fraction of original pool balances) for GNMA, FNMA, and FHLMC pools are reported monthly by *The Bond Buyer* under contract with GNMA, FNMA, and FHLMC. Wall Street broker/dealers and electronic information services use these factors to calculate historical CPRs.

Historical CPRs are appropriate prepayment estimators for investors who expect that future economic conditions will remain stable. During much of 1984, for example, seasonally adjusted One Months', Two Months', and Twelve Months' CPRs were relatively constant. At that time, historical CPRs would have been a good estimator of future prepayment rates.

Historical CPRs may not be appropriate prepayment estimators for long-term investment horizons, or during periods of economic volatility. The CPR model assumes that a loan prepays at a constant rate over its remaining maturity. That is, a new loan with a 6 percent annual prepayment rate is assumed to prepay approximately 0.5 percent of its principal balance each month for the remaining 360 months of its maturity (see Figure 9). Strong empirical evidence implies, however, that a security's CPR changes over time as the security ages and as economic and interest rate conditions change.

FIGURE 9 Annual Cash Flows: 6 Percent CPR Assumption (12 percent coupon; 30 payments; $1 million pool)

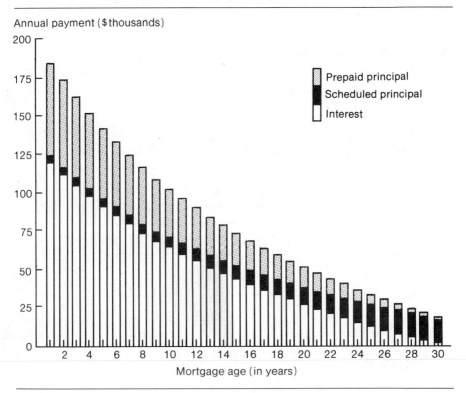

Projected CPR

Projected CPR is an application of the basic CPR model. A projected CPR is simply the single CPR implied by the price and yield associated with a set of non-CPR-type cash flows. Projected CPRs can be derived from cash flows generated by sophisticated econometric models, historical prepayments, or simple rules of thumb.

Break-Even Prepayment Rate (BEPR)

A BEPR is the single prepayment rate implied by the current market price of a security and the yield on the current coupon mortgage security (i.e., the security priced closest to, but not more than par). A security's BEPR can be interpreted as the market consensus prepayment estimate for the security. Investors use BEPRs to determine whether a security is

FIGURE 10 PSA Prepayment Model

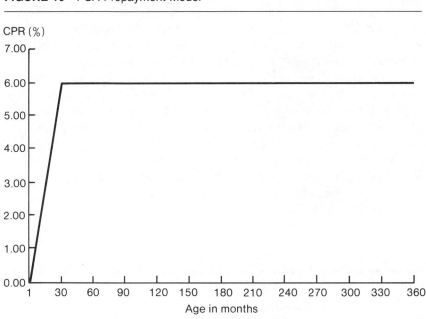

over- or undervalued based on the investor's personal prepayment estimate and yield relative to current coupon yield.

PSA Standard Prepayment Model (PSA)

The PSA Standard Prepayment Model is the most recent prepayment model to gain wide market use. Adopted in July 1985 by major Wall Street broker/dealers as the standard prepayment model for the CMO market, PSA combines the aging effect displayed by the FHA experience model with the simplicity of the straight-line CPR model (see Figure 10).

The PSA model assumes that a security prepays at a 0.2 percent annual rate at its first payment. This rate increases by 0.2 percent at each payment until payment 30. At payment 30, a security is assumed to prepay at a constant 6 percent annual rate over its remaining term. To compute 200 percent PSA, simply double each CPR. PSA is widely used in the CMO market and other mortgage markets.

FACTORS THAT INFLUENCE PREPAYMENT RATES

The following factors have been identified as important influences on mortgage prepayment rates:

Mortgage Coupon

A mortgage's coupon—or, more precisely, the difference between a mortgage's coupon and current market rates—is probably the single most important factor affecting a mortgage's prepayment behavior. Figure 11 graphs prepayment rates as a function of pool coupon. Note that prepayment rates are lowest on pools with coupons lower than 10 percent (i.e., for pools backed by mortgages with rates less than market rates at the time the chart was constructed). For pools with coupons above 10 percent, prepayments increase rapidly as coupon rates increase. This is because a borrower with a below market rate mortgage has no financial incentive to pay off his or her mortgage early, as compared to borrowers with above-market rate mortgages who can significantly reduce their mortgage payments by refinancing to a lower rate loan.

FIGURE 11   CPR as a Function of Security Coupon

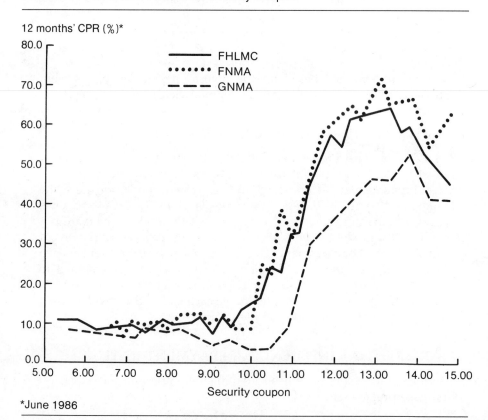

12 months' CPR (%)*

FHLMC
FNMA
GNMA

Security coupon

*June 1986

Mortgage Age

The likelihood that a given mortgage will prepay is affected by its age as well as by its coupon. Figure 8 shows the prepayment experience for two populations of FHA-insured loans. Both populations of loans show a distinct aging pattern, which is interesting given that each population includes a wide range of loan coupons and loans with different origination dates.

The prepayment patterns shown in Figure 8 are consistent with the economic life cycle of the typical mortgage borrower (or, more precisely, the population of mortgage borrowers). Low termination rates during the early mortgage years reflect low borrower mobility: borrowers are least likely to sell or refinance their home immediately after purchasing or refinancing it once already. Both curves in Figure 8 also show prepayment rates that increase as the mortgage population ages. This increase probably reflects the more mobile portion of the population that moves by age four or five of their mortgage to a larger house, a new job, or ends a household through divorce or for other reasons. Stable prepayment rates after years four to five probably reflect the relatively homogeneous population that is left in the population after the more mobile group drops out. This homogeneous population seems to prepay its mortgages at a relatively uniform rate until about mortgage age 20, at which time a large number of mortgagors seem to pay off their mortgages in full.

General Economic Conditions

While prepayments on a mortgage security are affected by the age of the mortgages backing the security, interest rates (and the associated economic environment) are also important determinants of prepayments. Figure 12 shows prepayments over time for all GNMA 8 percent pools issued during 1978; this sample contains mortgages with the same coupon and originated at approximately the same date. According to the figure, prepayment rates are highly correlated with changes in the general level of interest rates. One obvious explanation of this phenomenon is that worker mobility and borrower wealth increase as economic activity increases (and interest rates decrease). Workers move to new jobs in new geographic locations; home buyers have heightened income expectations and move to larger housing units. The same forces work in reverse during periods of economic decline, causing prepayment rates to slow.

Seasonality

Figure 12 also shows that there is distinct seasonality in prepayment rates over all interest rate environments. Rates peak in spring and

FIGURE 12 Security CPR versus Market Interest Rate

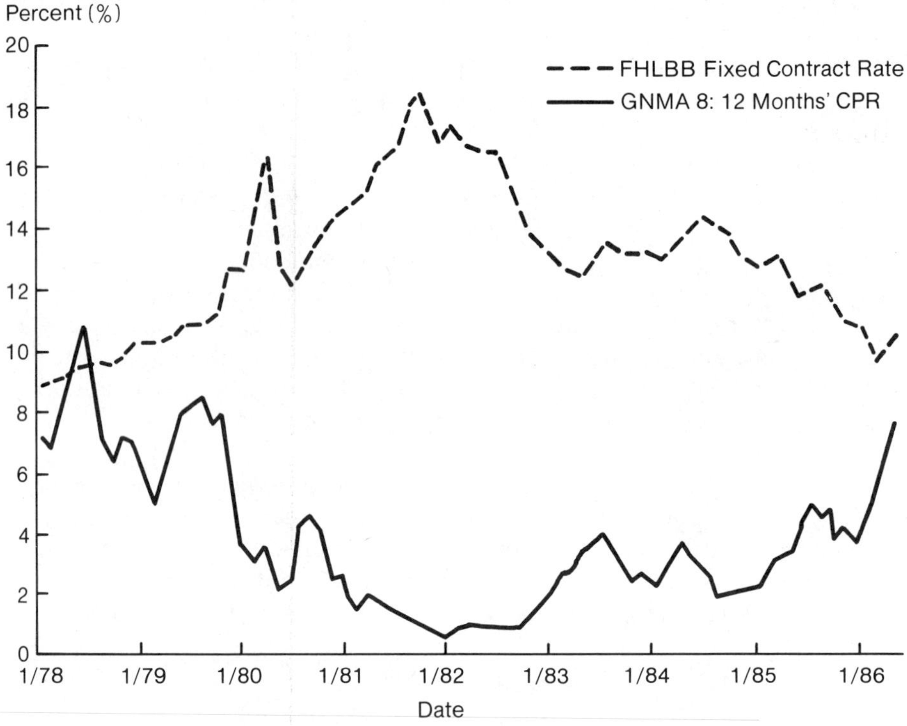
Percent (%)
20
18
16
14
12
10
8
6
4
2
0
FHLBB Fixed Contract Rate
GNMA 8: 12 Months' CPR
1/78
1/79
1/80
1/81
1/82
1/83
1/84
1/85
1/86
Date

summer, as home buyers take advantage of good weather and school vacations to move.

Security Specific Characteristics

A final factor affecting security prepayment behavior is the security type being examined. Figure 11 shows prepayments as a function of security coupons for GNMAs, FNMAs, and FHLMCs. GNMA prepayments are noticeably lower than FNMA and FHLMC prepayments across all coupons. This systematic prepayment difference probably is a result of differences between the mortgage collateral backing GNMA pools versus those backing FNMA and FHLMC pools.

One important factor affecting prepayment rate differences among GNMA loan pools and FNMA and FHLMC pools is that GNMA pools consist of FHA/VA mortgages only. By law, these mortgages are assumable. Most FNMA and FHLMC pools, on the other hand, are backed by pools of conventional loans, which may or may not be assumable. Prepayments on below market rate loans that are assumable should be lower than prepayment rates on similar loans that are not assumable. FNMA and FHLMC pool collateral differs from GNMA collateral in ways other than loan assumability that also can explain the higher prepayments observed on FNMA and FHLMC pools. First, FNMA and FHLMC pools allow a wider mortgage coupon range than do GNMA pools. This means that a FNMA or FHLMC pool can include mortgages with higher coupons than allowed in a GNMA pool. That portion of the FNMA or FHLMC pool carrying higher coupons than the GNMA pool increases the FNMA/FHLMC prepayment speeds versus GNMA speeds. A final reason why FNMA and FHLMC prepayment speeds are higher than GNMA speeds might be that almost all new FHA/VA mortgages are securitized, giving the population of all GNMA pools a fairly wide geographic distribution. FNMA and FHLMC, on the other hand, traditionally purchase mortgages from high-growth, capital deficit areas of the country such as California and Florida. FNMA and FHLMC prepayments might be systematically higher than GNMA prepayments if these regions have higher prepayment rates than the country as a whole.

ADDITIONAL FACTORS THAT AFFECT MORTGAGE CASH FLOW ESTIMATES

As Figures 4 through 12 show, monthly coupon payments, scheduled principal amortization, and early principal prepayments are the primary determinants of a mortgage security's cash flows. There are several additional factors, however, that make estimation of the amount and timing of a mortgage security's cash flows different from cash flow estimation for other types of fixed-income securities. These cash flow differences, which occur because of the securitization process and are not inherent to the cash flows on the mortgages underlying a security, are: (1) payment delay; (2) servicing fees; and (3) pool homogeneity.

Payment Delay

Most mortgages pay interest at the end of the month based on the principal outstanding on the loan at the beginning of the month. The investor does not receive any reinvestment income on this interest payment, meaning that payments are received subject to a 30-day *delay*. Most mortgage securities add additional delay days to the 30-day payment delay standard on most mortgages. These additional delay days give the pool servicer time to collect payments on the mortgages, complete pool accounting, and pass payments on to the mortgage pool investors. Note that there may also be a difference between actual and stated delay days. Table 8 shows the effect of payment delay on different

TABLE 8 Effect of Delay Days on Yield to Maturity* (in percent)

Mortgage Rate	Stated Number of Delay Days					
	0	30	45	50	55	75
4%	4.08%	4.03%	4.01%	4.00%	4.00%	3.97%
8%	8.25	8.14	8.08	8.06	8.05	7.98
12%	12.51	12.30	12.21	12.17	12.17	12.02
16%	16.87	16.54	16.39	16.34	16.29	16.09

* Bond equivalent yield; price at 100; 360 payments remaining; no servicing fee; 6 percent CPR

security coupons under different prepayment rate assumptions. Note that the yield decrease due to delay increases as the mortgage rate increases.

Servicing Fees

Most loans sold in the secondary market are sold on a servicing retained basis. That is, the original seller of the loan retains the right to service the loan, collecting a small fee for the performance of its duties as servicer. The coupon on a mortgage security, therefore, is not necessarily the same as the coupon on the loans backing the security. Servicing fees usually are a percentage of the outstanding balance of the loan, typically between 25 and 50 basis points for a residential mortgage loan.

Servicing fees are important to the calculation of mortgage yield. Because principal payments on the loan are determined by the coupons on the underlying loans, and not by the security coupon, investors must know the underlying loan coupons to estimate the security cash flows.

Pool Homogeneity

The final factor affecting security cash flow estimation is the coupon and maturity ranges allowed on the loans backing a security. FNMA pools, for example, can include mortgages with coupons 50 to 250 basis points higher than the security coupon. Cash flow estimates, however, are based on the assumption that the security is a single mortgage with a coupon equal to the most recently reported weighted average coupon (WAC) of the mortgages in the pool. A security's WAC usually does not remain constant over time, because higher coupon mortgages in the pool tend to prepay more quickly than lower coupon mortgages. Unfortunately, an updated WAC usually is not reported each month and must be estimated. The same estimation problem exists for pool maturity. If a pool weighted average remaining maturity (WAM) is not reported, it is assumed to be equal to the remaining maturity of the security itself (usually the maturity at time of securitization of the loan in the pool with the longest remaining maturity). Fortunately, most pass-through securities are structured to minimize the yield understatement that can result from using generic, worst case WAC or WAM assumptions. Yield understatement tends to be trivial for most securities and coupons, on the order of 1 to 5 basis points. Worst case assumptions, however, can cause yield understatements on high coupon securities (approximately 14 percent and above) of as much as 20 to 25 basis points.

HISTORICAL PERFORMANCE OF MORTGAGE PASS-THROUGH SECURITIES

The key thing to understand about mortgage securities is that they are just another type of fixed-income security. Security characteristics such as payment delay and servicing fees that at first seem complicated are easily accommodated by most fixed-income valuation models. There is only one important difference between mortgage securities and most other fixed-income securities. This is prepayment risk—the risk that the security will be called away if mortgage borrowers exercise their call option and prepay their mortgages. Fortunately, analytical techniques and security structures have been developed to measure and control this prepayment risk. The following section looks at mortgage market performance over time, showing how prepayment risk affects mortgage performance. This section also will show that, historically, mortgage investors have received attractive yield premiums for bearing prepayment risk.

Mortgage Yield Spreads Over Time

Historical yield calculations do not eliminate the need to estimate a prepayment rate as part of the yield calculation. For a mortgage security that has not yet reached maturity, the only certain cash flows are those that have already occurred, such as price. The amount and timing of the principal and interest payments that remain until the security's maturity date remain uncertain.

Because a mortgage security's maturity can be highly sensitive to changes in interest and prepayment rates, it is difficult to calculate meaningful historical yield spreads. Yield spread changes between two points in time may reflect changes in the relative yield curve positions of two securities rather than a fundamental change in the yield spread between the two securities. Figure 13 shows the sensitivity of mortgage

FIGURE 13   Amortization under Different CPR Assumptions (12 percent coupon; 360 payments; $1 million pool)

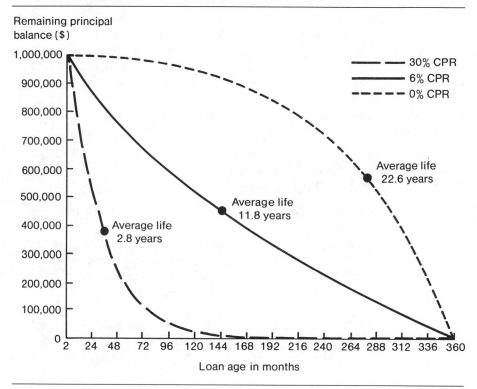

average life[2] to prepayment estimate. Figure 14 shows how mortgage yield spreads can vary as a function of maturity.

The sensitivity of yield spreads to changing interest and prepayment rates can be minimized by comparing the yield on the current coupon GNMA against the yield on the 10-year Treasury security. This method allows the historic yield spread to reflect the yield on an intermediate maturity mortgage pass-through versus the yield on a comparable maturity Treasury security. Figure 15 traces historical yields between the

---

[2] *Average life*, a common maturity measure for mortgage backed securities, is the average number of years that a dollar of principal remains outstanding. It is calculated as follows:

$$\text{Average life} = [P_1 T_1 + P_2 T_2 + \ldots + P_N T_N]/(P_1 + P_2 + \ldots + P_N)$$

where P_i = All principal paid down during period i.
T_i = The period in which the principal payment occurs.

FIGURE 14 Mortgage Yield Curve

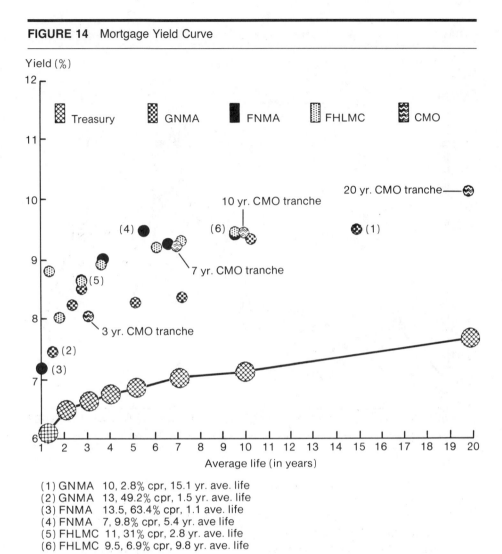

(1) GNMA 10, 2.8% cpr, 15.1 yr. ave. life
(2) GNMA 13, 49.2% cpr, 1.5 yr. ave. life
(3) FNMA 13.5, 63.4% cpr, 1.1 ave. life
(4) FNMA 7, 9.8% cpr, 5.4 yr. ave life
(5) FHLMC 11, 31% cpr, 2.8 yr. ave. life
(6) FHLMC 9.5, 6.9% cpr, 9.8 yr. ave. life

* July 17, 1986 Prices; July 1986 3 Months CPR.

current coupon GNMA SF30 pass-through and the current 10-year Treasury note. Over the period shown, GNMA to 10-year Treasury yield spreads averaged 117 basis points, with a standard deviation of 49 basis points. High spread for the period was 244 basis points; low spread was 42 basis points. Notice that, since 1982, yield spreads have varied inversely with the direction of interest rate changes. For example, between January 1982 and January 1983, yield spreads widened as

FIGURE 15 Current Coupon GNMA versus 10-year Treasury (monthly average yield, bond equivalent)

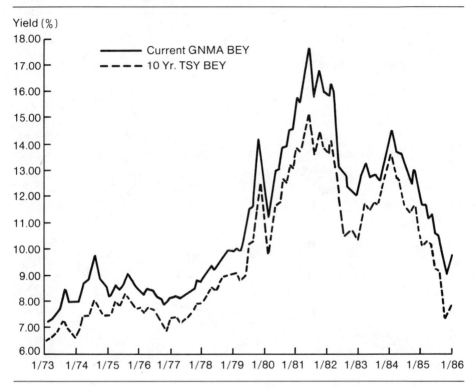

interest rates fell. Between January 1983 and March 1984, on the other hand, yield spreads tightened as interest rates rose. Finally, between March 1984 and July 1986, yield spreads widened again, as the 10-year Treasury rate fell 500 basis points in just 16 months.

Option theory can help explain the shifting yield spreads observed in Figure 15. Owning a mortgage is equivalent to owning a non-callable bond and selling short a call option on the bond. As market volatility changes, the value of the call option changes, causing mortgage versus Treasury yield spreads to change. Historically, the market seemed to assume, in a falling rate market, that further rate decreases were more likely than stable or rising rates. Fear of falling rates and the increased probability that the prepayment option would be exercised caused MBS/Treasury yield spreads to widen as rates fell. The opposite effect was observed in rising rate markets.

Over the second half of 1986, however, the historic relationship between changes in rate levels and MBS/Treasury yield spreads was not observed. Over this period, yield spreads actually tightened as rates fell.

FIGURE 16   Total Rate of Return (by quarters)

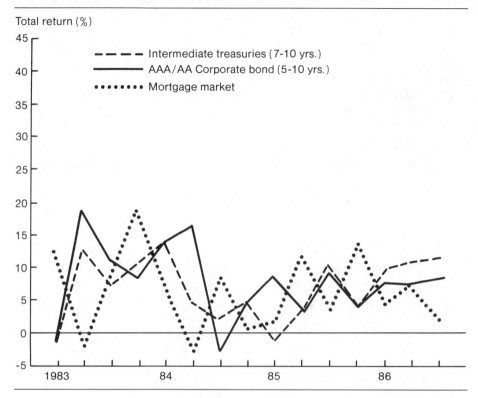

The most likely explanation for this behavior is, that as the market developed a deeper understanding of MBS price behavior it realized that MBS prices should reflect changes in interest rate volatility and that changes in the direction of the absolute rate level were not the same as volatility changes.

Historic Rates of Return

Total returns can be more useful than yield comparisons in that they reflect the actual returns realized on a security over a given holding period (i.e., they do not incorporate any prepayment estimate). Figure 16 graphs mortgage market total returns against comparable Treasury and corporate returns. Notice that mortgages consistently underperformed Treasury and corporate securities in bull markets and outperformed them in bear markets. This performance pattern is explained by *par compression*. Par compression is simply the tendency for the prices of mortgage securities to trade near par as interest rates fall and the securities become premium coupons. Investors tend not to pay much more than par for premium coupon mortgage securities because of the high probability that borrowers may exercise their call options and refinance at lower rates. Par compression means that premium mortgages tend to underperform noncallable Treasury or corporate securities, which experience full price appreciation as interest rates fall. In bear markets, on the other hand, mortgage returns historically have exceeded Treasury and corporate returns. Because par-compressed mortgage prices were insensitive to interest rate drops, they also were relatively insensitive to rising interest rates.

SECTION 3: TYPES OF MORTGAGE-RELATED SECURITIES

Mortgages are traded in three basic forms: (1) as *pass-through securities*; (2) as *pay-through bonds*; and (3) in *whole loan form*.

THE PASS-THROUGH MARKET

Mortgage pass-through securities, also called *mortgage-backed securities* or *MBS*, are certificates evidencing an undivided, pro rata, beneficial ownership interest in a group of specific mortgage loans held in trust. Certificate holders own the mortgages and are entitled to all cash flows in direct proportion to their ownership interest.

Pass-through securities often are credit enhanced. That is, the pool issuer adds its own or a third-party guarantee to the security payments. GNMA and FNMA, for example, guarantee that they will make "full and timely" payment of all principal and interest due on their securities if, for some reason, mortgage borrowers or pool servicers do not make a required payment. A pass-through security does not necessarily have to carry any credit enhancement. Different pass-through structures subject investors to different levels of default risk.

GNMA, FNMA, and FHLMC pass-throughs are referred to collectively as *agency* pass-throughs. The agency pass-through market is highly liquid. With more than $500 billion in volume outstanding at year-end 1986 and a $1 trillion 1985 trading volume, the agency pass-through market is the fastest growing sector in the fixed income market.

It is important to note that GNMA securities are the only agency pass-throughs backed by the full faith and credit of the U.S. government. FNMA and FHLMC are privately owned corporations; guarantees on their securities are backed by FNMA and FHLMC corporate assets and not by the federal government. Although the U.S. government has no legal obligation to honor FNMA or FHLMC corporate guarantees, FNMA and FHLMC pass-throughs trade in the market as if they were federal agency obligations. This is because of the very close ties that

FNMA and FHLMC have with the federal government. FNMA, for example, is classified as a *federally sponsored credit agency* in government budget documents. Its debt operations are subject to approval by the U.S. Treasury and FNMA is subject to federal audit and management control. In addition, the Secretary of the Treasury is enabled (but not obligated) to extend FNMA up to $2.25 billion in credit. FHLMC has no direct credit line with the U.S. Treasury. It is wholly owned, however, by the FHLB system which, like FNMA, is a privately owned corporation classified by the government as a federally sponsored credit agency, and which has its own $4 billion credit line with the Treasury. FHLMC directors are presidential appointees. Any major change in FHLMC operations must be approved by act of Congress.

GNMA GUARANTEED PASS-THROUGH SECURITIES

The GNMA market is the oldest and largest mortgage pass-through market. As of June 30, 1986, $233 billion of GNMA pass-through volume was outstanding in 120,000 pools. This volume was almost 50 percent of total mortgage-related security volume outstanding.

GNMA guarantees loan pools under two programs: GNMA I and GNMA II. The GNMA II security was designed to be an improvement on the GNMA I pass-through structure. GNMA II has not superseded GNMA I as had been hoped, however. Only 8 percent of the size of the GNMA I market, the GNMA II market is far less liquid. There are a number of differences between the GNMA I and GNMA II programs. First, GNMA II security payments are made through a central paying agent, meaning that the investor receives a single check each month covering all GNMA II pools owned. GNMA I investors receive separate checks from each GNMA I issuer. Second, GNMA II payments carry a 50-day payment delay versus the 45-day delay on GNMA I pools. Finally, GNMA II pools can include loans with a wider range of mortgage coupons than GNMA I pools. Table 9 lists the most important differences between the GNMA I and GNMA II programs.

Creation of a GNMA Pool

GNMA does not issue securities itself. GNMA guarantees securities that are issued by private corporations. A package of mortgage loans is converted to a GNMA pool by the following process:

1. A private issuer applies to GNMA for a commitment to guarantee a security. Simultaneous with applying for this commitment, the lender (a) assembles a pool of mortgages; (b) arranges with an independent custodian to take physical possession of the mortgage documents and pool custodial accounts; and (c) makes

TABLE 9 Comparison of GNMA I and GNMA II Programs

	GNMA I	GNMA II
Issuers	Single issuer	Single or multiple issuers
Underlying mortgage types	Fixed-rate level pay (SF) Buydown loan (SF buydown) Graduated payment (GPM) Growing equity (GEM) Mobile home (MH) Construction loan (CL) Project loan (PL)	Fixed-rate level pay (SF) Graduated payment (GPM) Growing equity (GEM) Mobile home (MH) Adjustable payment (APM)
Interest rate range:	Single coupon per pool (except mobile home pools)	100 basis points
Minimum servicing fee	50 basis points (except MH, PL, CL pools)	50 basis points (except MH pools)
Delay days	45	50
Paying and transfer agent	Issuers	Chemical Bank
Minimum pool size	12 loans $1 million (SF pools) $500,000 (other pools)	12 loans $1 million (SF pools) $500,000 (non-SF pools) $350,000 (MH pools)
Number of pools outstanding (6/30/86)	113,644	6,577
Amount outstanding (6/30/86)	$214.0 billion	$16.5 billion

arrangements to market the security, usually through a forward sale to a GNMA broker/dealer.

2. Once the issuer has assembled the loan pool, it submits all pool documents to GNMA. Within 20 days, GNMA delivers to the issuer certificates evidencing ownership in the pool. The issuer delivers these certificates to its broker or other purchasers.

3. Once the issuer has sold its certificates, it is responsible for (a) collecting all mortgage payments, including insurance proceeds on foreclosed mortgages, and passing these proceeds through to investors on a timely basis; (b) accounting for and administering the pool; and (c) maintaining accurate ownership registration books. For these services, the pool servicer is entitled to a 50 basis point annual fee, assessed against the outstanding principal balance of the pool at the beginning of each month. The pool issuer must also pay GNMA a 6 basis point annual guarantee fee.

General GNMA Pool Requirements

Except where specifically noted, each mortgage in a GNMA pool must:

1. Carry FHA, FmHA, or VA mortgage insurance.
2. Have a first scheduled payment date no earlier than 12 months prior to the date on which GNMA issues its commitment to guarantee the security, and no later than 1 month after the security issue date.
3. Have an original balance of not more than $135,000, unless written on a property located in a HUD-designated high-cost housing region.

Each GNMA pool also must conform to the following structure:

- *Pool Collateral Mix.*   Each pool must contain a single-loan type (e.g., a GPM pool must contain only GPM loans). The only exception to this is that GNMA II SF pools can contain buydown loans.
- *Pool Size.*   At time of issue, each pool must contain at least 12 loans with a total outstanding principal balance of at least $1 million (SF pools), or at least $500,000 (all other pools). No single-loan balance can be more than 10 percent of the sum of all of the original balances of the pooled loans.
- *Mortgage Rates Allowable in Pool.*   Under the GNMA I program, all of the mortgages in a single pool must have the same coupon rate. Under the GNMA II program, underlying mortgages may have different rates, except that the highest and lowest rate coupons in the pool must be within 100 basis points of each other. Under both programs, the pool coupon must be 50 basis points less than the rate on the lowest coupon mortgage in the pool.
- *Maturity.*   At least 90 percent of the principal balance of each pool must consist of mortgages with original maturities of at least 20 years. GNMA will guarantee pools with original maturities not meeting this requirement (e.g., 15-year pools) if: (*a*) no loan in the pool has an original maturity of 20 years or longer; (*b*) at least 90 percent of the pool principal is in mortgages with the same original term and that term is the stated maturity of the pool; and (*c*) the pool maturity is noted prominently on the pool certificate.
- *Payments of Principal and Interest.*   Principal and interest payments on a GNMA pool are passed through to certificate holders on the 15th (GNMA I) or 20th (GNMA II) day of each month. Interest is paid each month at the specified security coupon rate, based on the outstanding principal balance of the security on the first day of the previous month. Principal paid each month is the

scheduled principal payment due on the pooled mortgages on the first day of the payment month. For example, the May 15 GNMA I principal payment is the principal that mortgagors are scheduled to pay on May 1. All unscheduled principal payments received during the month preceding the payment month also are passed through to the investor. For example, all unscheduled principal payments made during April are passed through to the investor on May 15. Payments are made to owners of record as of the last business of the day of the month preceding the payment month.

- *Minimum Denomination.* GNMA certificates of ownership are issued in $25,000 minimum denominations, and $5,000 multiples thereof.
- *Registration and Transfer.* GNMA I pool ownership was evidenced in certificate or book form until early 1987, at which time all newly issued GNMA I's were registered in book entry form, and the process began to convert all existing certificated GNMA I's to book entry ownership. GNMA II ownership and transfer is in book entry form only.

Descriptions of GNMA Pass-Throughs Outstanding

In addition to the general pool requirements set out above, each GNMA pool must meet the requirements of its specific pool type.

GNMA Single-Family (SF) Pool. Each GNMA SF pool consists of fixed-rate, level payment, fully amortizing loans secured by liens on one- to four-unit residential properties. No buydown loans (loans where a portion of each monthly payment comes from an escrow account, deposited by a home builder, for example) are permitted in GNMA I pools unless the entire pool consists of buydown loans and the pool certificates are labeled as buydown securities. GNMA II SF pools can include buydown loans.

The GNMA SF market is the largest and most liquid GNMA market, accounting for 40 percent of all mortgage securities outstanding as of June 30, 1986. At that time, there were 102,000 GNMA SF pools outstanding, with balances totaling $190 billion. Approximately $8 billion of this volume was 15-year pools. Coupons on 30-year pools ranged from 5.25 percent to 17 percent. Coupons on 15-year pools ("Midgets") ranged from 9 percent to 13.5 percent.

GNMA Graduated Payment Mortgage (GPM) Pool. Each GPM pool consists of fixed-rate, fully amortizing loans, secured by liens on one-to-four unit residential properties. Loans must have one of the following nonlevel payment plans: *Type GP*, which allows up to 5 annual increases in monthly payments; or *Type GD*, which allows up to 10 annual increases in monthly payments.

GPM pools may include buydown loans. Negative amortization on the securities is allowed during the graduated payment period. At the end of the graduated payment period, the loan payments must fully amortize the remaining loan balance in equal monthly payments.

GPM loans were extremely popular in the late 1970s and early 1980s. As a result, GPM pools are concentrated in the 11 percent to 13 percent coupon range. As of June 30, 1986, outstanding GPM pool volume was $14 billion in 9,300 pools. Approximately 99 percent of outstanding GPM balances—all but 60 pools—were Type GP pools.

GNMA Growing Equity Mortgage (GEM) Pool.

Each GEM pool consists of fixed-rate, fully amortizing loans secured by liens on one- to four-unit residential properties. All loans must have one of the following, nonlevel payment plans: *Type GA*, which allows 4 percent annual increases in monthly payments over the entire term of the loan; or *Type GD*, which allows any type of increasing payment plan approved by the FHA, FmHA, or VA.

GEM loans are exempt from the general GNMA pool maturity requirements because the growing payment feature means that loans will amortize more quickly than 20 years. GEM pools can include buydown loans. GEM loans have yet to become popular with mortgage borrowers. At June 30, 1985, there were only 60 GEM pools outstanding, with balances of $59 million.

GNMA Manufactured Housing (MF) Pool.

Each MH pool consists of level payment, fixed-rate loans secured by liens on manufactured housing units. Loans must meet the following requirements:

Maturity. Any single pool can contain loans with different maturites, except that at least 50 percent of the principal balance of the pool must consist of mortgages with original terms equal to the term of the longest maturity loan in the pool. All loan maturities must be within five years of each other. *Type A* loans have 12-year original terms; *Type B* loans have 15-year original terms; and *Type C* loans have 18-year original terms. *Type D* loans have original terms of up to 20 years.

Coupon range. The face interest rate on all loans in a pool must be within 150 basis points of the rate on all other loans in the pool. The coupon rate on the security is between 225 and 475 basis points less than the rate on the lowest rate mortgage in the pool. With only $3 billion in 5,500 pools outstanding as of June 30, 1986, the MH market is relatively illiquid. Pool coupons range between

9.5 percent and 13.25 percent. Almost 90 percent of MH pool balances outstanding as of June 30, 1986 were Type B pools.

GNMA Adjustable Payment Mortgage (APM) Pool. Each APM pool consists of loans secured by liens on one- to four-family residential properties. Loans must have a nonlevel payment plan that is not allowed under any of the pool types listed above. Pools are guaranteed under the GNMA II program only and are of two types. *Type AR (adjustable rate)* pools consists of mortgages with rates that adjust annually based on the weekly average constant maturity one-year Treasury rate index. Rates may not change more than 1 percent annually or more than 5 percent over the life of the loan. *Type AZ (adjustable payment)* pools consist of mortgages with payments that adjust on some basis other than mortgage rate.

Type AR pools are the only type of APM pool issued as of June 30, 1986. Because the 1 percent/5 percent rate adjustment caps were too restrictive for most primary market lenders when the program was instituted in 1984, initial security volume was low. In late 1985, however, the yield curve flattened and the 1 percent/5 percent ARM became popular in the market. As of June 30, 1986, GNMA AR volume outstanding was $1 billion in 75 pools. Coupons ranged from 7 percent to 11 percent, reflecting the relatively limited time period over which most of the pools were originated.

GNMA Project Loan (PL) Pool. Project loan pools are backed by a single, FHA-insured mortgage on a completed project (e.g., multifamily residential building, nursing home, or hospital). The outstanding principal balance of the mortgage at the issue date of the pool must be at least $500,000. The security coupon is either 25 or 45 basis points below the mortgage coupon. Loans are not required to begin amortization on the first loan payment, and nonlevel payment schedules are allowed.

GNMA project loan pools are issued under the GNMA I program only. As of June 30, 1986, 923 pools were outstanding with balances of $5 billion. Pool coupons ranged from 5.65 percent to 17.25 percent.

GNMA Construction Loan (CL) Pool. Construction loan pools are backed by a single FHA insured mortgage on an FHA project under construction. If a project is not completed at loan maturity, investors have the option of extending the loan term or of receiving full principal payment from the issuer in cash.

GNMA CL pools are issued under the GNMA I program only. As of June 30, 1986, only 32 pools were outstanding, with balances of $360 million. Pool coupons ranged from 8.05 percent to 14.05 percent.

GNMA Mortgage Backed Serial Notes (SN). Mortgage backed serial notes are a series of 200 consecutively numbered units backed by a single pool of mortgage loans. Pooled loans must meet GNMA SF pool requirements. Each note issue must be at least $5 million; each note unit must have a beginning balance of at least $25,000.

Interest is paid monthly to all unit owners at the unit coupon rates. Principal payments are made when sufficient funds have been received by the issuer to retire the outstanding unit with the lowest sequence number. A unit's stated maturity is the latest possible date that the unit principal will be paid, based on the pool amortization schedule. A unit's actual maturity depends on how quickly any principal prepayments are made on the loans in the pool. Mortgage serial note holders hold an undivided ownership interest in the entire mortgage pool backing the note series. Note certificates carry the regular GNMA credit guarantee.

GNMA serial notes are multiclass pass-through securities. Although note holders as a group own the mortgages backing the security, different unit holders have different claims on the pool cash flows. Tax law changes in 1983 made the multiclass pass-through structure unworkable. Only $185 million of serial notes, backed by 68 pools were outstanding at June 30, 1986. The restrictions on multiclass pass-throughs were eased in early 1986, meaning that the serial note structure may be revived.

Table 10 lists the characteristics of the major GNMA programs.

FHLMC ISSUED PASS-THROUGH SECURITIES

The Federal Home Loan Mortgage Corporation (Freddie Mac) is a corporate instrumentality of the United States, wholly owned by the 12 FHLB system banks. FHLMC's primary activity is to purchase mortgages on residential properties, thereby expanding the size and stability of the secondary market for residential mortgage loans.

FHLMC operates principally as a loan conduit. That is, FHLMC purchases loans and loan participations, which it resells to investors in the form of guaranteed mortgage securities. FHLMC is both the security issuer and guarantor.

Creation of a FHLMC Pool

Each day, FHLMC posts net required yields for the different types of mortgage product that it will purchase. FHLMC purchases primarily fixed-rate, level payment, fully amortizing loans secured by first liens on one- to four-family residential properties. FHLMC also purchases FHA or VA loans not eligible for GNMA pooling; flexible payment loans (GPMs); and multifamily conventional loans on a negotiated basis. Because it is subject to default risk on the loans that it purchases and

TABLE 10 Comparison of Selected GNMA Programs

	Single Family	GPM	Manufactured Housing	ARM	Project
Mortgage type	Level pay; buydown	Graduated payment	Level pay	Adjustable rate	Level or nonlevel pay
Maximum term	Either greater than or less than 20 years	At least 20 years	12 to 20 years	At least 20 years	Up to 40 years
Servicing fee	50 bp	50 bp	225–475 bp	50 bp	25 or 45 bp
Guarantee fee	6 bp	6 bp	6 bp	6 pb	Varies
Minimum pool size	$1 million	$500,000	$500,000 (I) $350,000 (II)	$500,000	$500,000
Pools outstanding (6/30/86)	102,168	10,209	5,416	75	923
Balance outstanding (6/30/86)	$197.7 billion	$13.9 billion	$3.1 billion	$1.0 billion	$5.0 billion
Coupon range	5¼–17%	8.5–17.5%	6–17.5%	7–11%	5.65–17.25%
Program	GNMA I and II	GNMA I and II	GNMA I and II	GNMA II	GNMA I

repackages into guaranteed mortgage securities, FHLMC requires that each loan that it purchases meet minimum credit, loan-to-value and other underwriting standards.

More than 90 percent of FHLMC loan purchases are financed through the sale of pass-through securities. FHLMC issues two types of pass-through securities: (1) the cash (standard) participation certificate; and (2) the guarantor (swap) participation certificate.

FHLMC distributes its securities in periodic auctions to a 19-member dealer group, directly to investors as private placements or through underwritten public offerings. Loan sellers usually are responsible for pool servicing, for which they receive a fee. FHLMC earns a separate guarantee and administrative fee based on the spread between the participation certificate (PC) coupon rate and the net required yields on the loans backing the PC, usually in a 20 to 25 basis point annual range.

FHLMC guarantees the full and timely payment of all interest due on a PC and the full payment of principal as it is collected by FHLMC. FHLMC PCs are not guaranteed by the U.S. government, or by any agency of the United States.

FHLMC Guaranteed Cash PCs: General Pool Requirements

FHLMC Cash PCs represent undivided ownership interests in specific fixed-rate, first lien residential mortgages or participations therein purchased by FHLMC for cash. FHLMC Cash PCs must have the following characteristics at time of issuance.

- *Pool Size.* FHLMC Cash PC pools must have original principal balances of at least $50 million. They normally consist of at least 500 mortgages.
- *Mortgage Rates Allowed in Pool.* Cash pools have no coupon range restrictions. FHLMC purchases whole loans at a price (not to exceed par) that will generate the required net yield to FHLMC plus a 37.5 basis point minimum servicing fee to the loan seller. The only restriction on Cash PC coupons is that the net required yield on all whole mortgages in a pool must be equal to or greater than the PC coupon. This means that the PC coupon may be higher than the rate on a mortgage or mortgage participation backing the PC.
- *Payments of Principal and Interest.* The first principal and interest payment due to a PC purchaser will be made by the 15th day of the second month following the settlement month. For example, the first payment on a PC with May settlement will be made on July 15. Payments will be made by the 15th of each following month and for one month following sale of the PC. Interest is paid monthly at the PC coupon rate, based on the loan

principal estimated to be outstanding at the beginning of the second month prior to the payment month. For example, the May 15 interest payment is based on the March 1 estimated pool balance. Monthly principal payments are the difference between the principal balance of the pool at the beginning and end of the second month prior to the payment month. For example, the May 15 principal payment represents all scheduled and unscheduled principal paid on the pool during the month of March. Notice that the balances at the beginning of each month are estimates. This is because the FHLMC accounting cycle ends on the 15th of the month and beginning month balances are unknown. Payments are due to owners of record as of the last business day of the second month previous to the payment month. For example, ownership of record on March 31 entitles the investor to the May 15 payment.

- *Registration and Transfer.* Participation certificates are registered and transferred in book entry form only.
- *Minimum Denominations.* FHLMC PCs are sold in minimum denominations of $25,000 and increments of $1.

Types of FHLMC Cash PC Outstanding

FHLMC issues a number of different types of Cash PCs. The three most actively traded types are:

FHLMC 30-Year Conventional Cash PC (Series 16 and 17).

These pools consist of fixed-rate, level payment, fully amortizing loans secured by first liens on one- to four-unit residential properties. Loans cannot carry any type of government mortgage insurance and must have an original term of between 10 and 30 years. (FHLMC estimates, but does not guarantee that most loans in a pool have original terms of between 26 and 30 years.) Loans originated after October 15, 1982 cannot be assumable. Loans may be any age at time of pooling. Up to 5 percent of the pool balance may be multifamily loans. Up to 2.5 percent of the pool balance may consist of flexible payment loans.

The 30-Year Cash PC market is the fourth largest agency pass-through market. As of June 30, 1986, $26.6 billion of 30-Year Conventional Cash PCs were outstanding, backed by 270 pools. Coupons range from 6.375 percent to 16.75 percent.

FHLMC 15-Year Conventional Cash PC (Series 20).

These pools consist of conventional loans with original terms of between 10 and 15 years. Loans must have been originated after October 15, 1982, and are not assumable.

As of June 30, 1986, $8.7 billion of 15-Year Cash PCs (also called "non-Gnomes") were outstanding in 40 different pools. Because all volume had been issued since 1982, coupon range was narrow, with 50 percent of volume concentrated in three coupons: the 8.5s, the 9.5s, and the 10.5s.

Multifamily Cash Plan B PC (Series 22). Multifamily Plan B PCs consist of fixed-rate loans or loan participations secured by first liens on five or more unit residential properties. Mortgages can amortize on 15- to 30-year schedules; loan terms, however, must be between 10 and 15 years. Loans must prohibit prepayment over some portion of their term. As of June 30, 1986, only three Multifamily Plan B pools had been issued; issue volume, however, was $1.7 billion (or almost $600 million per pool).

FHLMC Guarantor PCs: General Pool Requirements

FHLMC issues Guarantor PCs (also called "Swap" PCs) by purchasing mortgages from a single seller and paying for the mortgages with PC's equal to the face value of the purchased mortgages. The seller can keep the PCs as a portfolio investment or resell them in the secondary market. Guarantor PCs are structured like Cash PCs, with the following exceptions:

- *Collateral Mix.* The loans in a Guarantor pool are purchased from a single seller. Loans in a Cash pool usually are purchased from a number of sellers.
- *Minimum Pool Size.* Guarantor pools must be at least $1 million at issue, versus $50 million for Cash pools. This size difference, and the purchase of mortgages from a single issuer versus multiple issuers, means that Guarantor PCs may be less geographically diverse than Cash PCs.
- *Mortgage Rates Allowable in Pool.* All mortgage rates must be within 2 percent of all other mortgage rates in the pool. The pool coupon must be at least 37.5 basis points less than the lowest coupon mortgage in the pool.
- *Maturity.* Mortgages in Guarantor pools may be any age at time of purchase by FHLMC. FHLMC prepares an offering circular that reports the weighted average remaining maturity (WAM) and weighted average coupon (WAC) of each Guarantor pool at the time of pool formation (for pools issued as of July 1983).
- *Minimum Denomination.* Guarantor pools are issued in $1000 minimum denominations and $1 multiples thereof.

FHLMC Guarantor PCs Outstanding

FHLMC issues a number of types of Guarantor PCs.

30-Year Guarantor PC (Series 18, 25 and 27). These pools consist of conventional loans with original terms of between 10 and 30 years. The 30-Year Guarantor PC market is the second largest agency pass-through market. As of June 30, 1986, $75.5 billion in balances were outstanding in over 26,200 pools. Coupons ranged from 3.5 percent to 18 percent, reflecting the wide age range of mortgages swapped into the securities.

15-Year Guarantor PC (Series 21). These pools—also called "Gnomes"—consist of loans with original maturities of no more than 15 years. Loans must have been originated after October 15, 1982 and cannot be assumable.

As of June 30, 1986, $4.4 billion of Gnomes were outstanding. Coupons ranged from 6.25 percent to 14 percent. Over 50 percent of outstanding volume was in three coupons—the 9s, the 10s, and the 10.5s.

FHA/VA Guarantor PC (Series 14). These pools consist of level payment, fixed-rate, fully amortizing loans or loan participations secured by first liens on one- to four-unit residential properties. Loans must carry FHA or VA mortgage insurance and must have been originated more than 12 months prior to delivery to FHLMC. Loan terms cannot exceed 30 years.

As of June 30, 1986, $2.1 billion of FHA/VA Guarantor pools were outstanding. Coupons ranged from 4 percent to 15 percent. Over 80 percent of this volume was in pools with coupons of 9 percent or less, reflecting the age of these loans at the time that they were swapped into securities.

Multifamily Plan A Guarantor PC (Series 23 and 24). Plan A Multifamily pools consist of fixed-rate, conventional loans, or loan participations secured by conventional mortgages on five or more unit residential properties. Loans can be level payment (Series 23) or nonlevel payment (Series 24). Original term must be between 10 and 30 years. Prepayments are allowed, subject to prepayment fees.

As of June 30, 1986, there were approximately $330 million of Series 23 pools outstanding. Pool coupons ranged from 5.5 percent to 12.25 percent.

Table 11 summarizes differences between Cash and Guarantor PC pools.

FNMA GUARANTEED MORTGAGE BACKED SECURITIES (MBS)

The Federal National Mortgage Association (Fannie Mae) is a federally chartered, privately owned corporation. FNMA's primary function is to

---

TABLE 11   FHLMC Program Descriptions

	Cash	*Guarantor*
Sellers	Multiple	Single seller
Mortgage type	Level-pay conventional; Multifamily Plan B; ARMs	Level-pay convention-al; Level-pay FHA/VA Multifamily Plan A
Mortgage rate range	No range restriction	200 bp range Pass-through coupon is at least 37.5 basis points less than low-est mortgage rate in pool
Minimum pool size	$50 milllion	$1 million
Loan original terms	8 to 30 years	8 to 30 years
Pools outstanding*	300	26,200
Balance outstand-ing* (6/30/86)	$37 billion	$82 billion

* Estimated, as of June 30, 1986.

---

provide credit to the mortgage market by purchasing loans from primary market lenders.

Like FHLMC, FNMA directly issues its own mortgage pass-through securities. Unlike either GNMA or FHLMC, FNMA also purchases mortgages for its own portfolio. At year-end 1985, FNMA held $93 billion in mortgage assets, making it the second largest U.S. financial institution. FNMA funds its mortgage portfolio through the issuance of discount notes and debentures, making it the single largest user of the U.S. debt markets after the U.S. Treasury. FNMA also issues mortgage pass-through securities called *FNMA Guaranteed Mortgage Pass-Through Certificates (FNMA MBS)*.

Creation of a FNMA MBS

FNMA purchases a wide variety of loan products both for portfolio investment and for conversion into FNMA Guaranteed MBS. Loans backing MBS may be sold out of FNMA's portfolio, or may be purchased specifically for pooling pursuant to a pool purchase contract with an approved FNMA lender. FNMA purchases loans for cash, or with MBS certificates evidencing an ownership interest in the specific loans that back the certificates.

FNMA is the direct issuer of FNMA MBS pools. FNMA is entitled to the difference between the MBS coupon and the mortgage rate on all pooled loans as compensation for servicing and guaranteeing the pools. Typically, FNMA contracts with the original loan seller to service the pooled loans, sharing a portion of its fee with the servicer. FNMA distributes MBS through a dealer group, through direct private placement with investors, and through underwritten issues. FNMA unconditionally guarantees the full and timely payment of all principal and interest due to the investor on a FNMA Guaranteed MBS.

FNMA Guaranteed MBS: General Pool Characteristics

Except where noted, FNMA MBS pools have the following characteristics:

- *Mortgage Collateral.* FNMA purchases a wide variety of mortgage products for both portfolio investment and for resale into MBS pools. FNMA's primary purchase programs, however, are for fixed-rate, level payment, self-amortizing conventional mortgage loans secured by liens on one- to four-unit residential properties. Loans may be any age at time of purchase by FNMA, but cannot have original maturities longer than 30 years. Prior to April 15, 1986, FNMA also purchased FHA insured or VA guaranteed loans with origination dates more than one year prior to the date of purchase by FNMA. As of April 15, 1986, FNMA also purchased newly originated FHA/VA loans for inclusion in MBS pools. Because FNMA is subject to default risk, loans that it purchases must conform to FNMA underwriting standards and loan to value ratios.
- *Pool Size.* Pools must have an unpaid principal balance of at least $1 million at time of securitization.
- *Payments of Principal and Interest.* Principal and interest is paid to pool certificate holders on the 25th of each month. Interest is paid monthly at the security coupon rate, based on the pool balance on the first day of the previous month. Monthly principal payments consist of all principal scheduled to be made by the mortgagor on the first day of the month in which the payment to the issuer is made. Unscheduled principal payments consist of all prepayments made between the second day of the previous month and the first day of the payment month. For example, the May 25 principal payment consists of principal scheduled to be made by the mortgagor on May 1 and all unscheduled prepayments received between April 2 and May 1. Payments are made to the owner of record as of the last business day of the month preceding the month in which payment is made.
- *Mortgage Rates Allowable in Pool.* The MBS coupon must be less than the lowest mortgage rate in the pool, net of FNMA's 50 basis point minimum servicing fee.

- *Allowable Maturities.* FNMA expects that the majority of loans in a pool will have original terms of between 20 and 30 years (Type CL and GL) or of between 8 and 15 years (Type CI), but does not guarantee this. FNMA VRM pools can consist of loans with maturities of up to 40 years. Loans may be any age at the time of pooling, except that FHA/VA loans must be at least one year old.
- *Minimum Denomination.* Certificates are sold in minimum denominations of $25,000 and $1 increments thereof.
- *Transfer and Registration.* FNMA MBS are sold in book registration form only.

FNMA Guaranteed MBS Outstanding

FNMA issues a wide variety of pass-through securities. Many of these securities have large outstanding volumes (e.g., FNMA VRMs at $6 billion) but were issued as private placement swaps with the mortgage sellers and have yet to be traded as standardized securities. The following FNMA MBS are those that are traded most actively:

FNMA Conventional Long-Term (CL) MBS. Pools consist of fixed-rate, level payment, fully amortizing conventional loans secured by first liens on one- to four-unit residential properties. Loans must have original terms of between 16 to 30 years. The FNMA CL market is the second largest pass-through market. At June 30, 1986, 15,800 pools and $44.2 billion in principal were outstanding.

FNMA Conventional Intermediate (CI) MBS. Each pool consists of conventional, fixed-rate, level payment loans with original maturities of between 8 and 15 years. FNMA CI MBS had 3,500 pools and $4.6 billion in principal outstanding as of June 30, 1986. Half of this volume was in two coupons: the 10.5s and the 11s.

FNMA Government Long-Term (GL) MBS. FNMA GL pools consist of FHA insured or VA-guaranteed fixed-rate, level payment loans secured by first liens on one- to four-unit residential properties. All loans in pools issued prior to April 15, 1986, must have a first payment date more than one year prior to purchase by FNMA. As of June 30, 1986, there were 279 FNMA GL pools outstanding, with principal balances totaling $3.0 billion. Coupon distribution was fairly wide—6.25 percent to 15.75 percent—reflecting the wide age range of mortgages purchased by FNMA. FNMA, however, announced plans to securitize $10 billion of FHA/VA portfolio holdings, beginning during the summer of 1986. Over time, these sales are expected to triple GL trading volume.

FNMA Stripped MBS (SMBS). "Strip" MBS are multi-class pass-through securities backed by a single pool of FNMA MBS certificates. SMBS differ from non-strip MBS in the following ways:

Security Structure. SMBS divide the cash flows from a pool of mortgage assets into two security classes—a "principal only" (PO) class, and an "interest only"(IO) class. Owners of each class hold an undivided, pro rata ownership interest in the cash flows allocated to their particular class of certificates.

Principal and Interest Payments. SMBS certificate owners receive payments on the 25th of each month, similar to the payment schedule on MBS certificates. FNMA guarantees the full and timely payment of all cash flows due to the investor. Principal only certificate owners receive all principal payments due on the MBS certificates that make up the SMBS pool. Interest only certificate holders receive interest at the SMBS pass through rate on the principal balance ("notional principal amount") of the underlying MBS certificates as of the first day of the month preceding the payment month.

Mortgage Collateral. As of February 1987, SMBS are backed by pools of FNMA MBS certificates, which in turn are backed by pools of fixed-rate, level payment mortgages on single family residences. Substantially all loans in the pools have original maturities between 20 and 30 years.

Mortgage Rates Allowable in Pool. The weighted average coupon (WAC) of any MBS certificate (as of its issue date) included in the SMBS pool cannot be more than 150 basis points higher than the SMBS pass through rate (Individual mortgage loans backing the SMBS, therefore, could possibly carry rates in excess of 150 basis points of the SMBS rate, although it is unlikely.)

Maturity Range of Loans in Pool. The weighted average maturity (WAM) of any MBS certificate (as of its issue date, less the number of months since its issuance) included in the SMBS pool must be within two years of the WAM of any other MBS certificate included in the SMBS pool.

Minimum Pool Size. SMBS pools must have outstanding principal balances of at least $200 million as of pool issue date.

Minimum Denomination. SMBS certificates are issued in $1,000 minimum denominations and $1 increments thereof.

Registration and Transfer. SMBS certificates are registered and transferred in book entry form only.

SMBS were first issued in mid-1986, after changes in IRS regulations allowed the issuance of multi-class pass throughs. Because PO and IO securities have performance characteristics different from their underlying mortgages that make them attractive hedges of many types of mortgage or fixed income portfolios, SMBS have become immediately popular with investors. Between mid-1986 and March 1987, more than $5 billion of SMBS securities had been issued. During early 1987, in fact, a substantial portion of new MBS issuance was immediately swapped into SMBS by major Wall Street broker/dealers.

Table 12 summarizes the major features of GNMA, FNMA, and FHLMC pool structures.

PRIVATELY ISSUED PASS-THROUGH SECURITIES

Private sector institutions including large commercial banks, Wall Street broker/dealers and large mortgage bankers have issued pass-through securities similar to the agency pass-throughs described above. These are often referred to as conventional pass-through securities, private pass-throughs or Connie Mae's. The conventional pass-through market is extremely small, estimated to be approximately 2 percent of the size of the agency pass-through market.

Most private pass-through securities have some type of credit enhancement. Typically, private mortgage insurance or some type of junior/senior subordinated ownership structure protects investors against principal losses up to some percentage of the outstanding balance of the pool (e.g., 5 percent or 10 percent). The conventional pass-through market is relatively small because the credit enhancement necessary to give the structure a AAA or AA rating makes the structure less attractive to issuers than selling loans to one of the federal agencies or in whole loan form. Most private pass-through issues, therefore, are backed by *nonconforming* loans. That is, they consist of loans that are not eligible for inclusion in a GNMA, FNMA, or FHLMC pool, usually because the loan balances exceed agency maximums. The Bank of America issued the first publicly offered nonagency pass-through security in 1977. Approximately $11 billion of private pass-throughs had been issued as of year-end 1986.

MORTGAGE-RELATED BONDS

There are two basic types of mortgage-related bonds. These are the *mortgage-backed bond* and the *mortgage pay-through bond*.

TABLE 12 Comparison of Major Pass-Through Programs

	GNMA I SF 30	FHLMC Guarantor 30-Year	FNMA CL MBS
Issuer	Private lender	FHLMC	FNMA
Mortgage type	Level payment FHA/VA	Level payment conventional	Level payment conventional
Original term	90% of pool balance must be at least 20 years	10 to 30 years	20 to 30 years
Allowable mortgage age at pool issuance	1 year or less	Any age	Any age
Allowable mortgage coupon range in pool	All loans must have same rate	200 bp	200 bp
Minimum servicing and guarantee fees	50 bp servicing, 6 bp guarantee	37.5 bp servicing	30 bp servicing, 20 bp guarantee
Stated delay	45 days	75 days	55 days
Minimum pool size	$1 million	$1 million	$1 million
Distribution of loans in pool	Regional	Regional	National or regional
Pools outstanding*	102,000	26,200	15,846
Balance outstanding* (6/30/86)	$191.0 billion	$75.5 billion	$44.2 billion
Coupon range	5.25–17%	3.5–18%	6.5–16%
Credit guarantee	Full and timely payment of principal and interest	Full and timely payment of interest. Ultimate payment of principal	Full and timely payment of principal and interest

* Estimated, as of June 30, 1986.

Mortgage-Backed Bonds

Mortgage-backed bonds (MBBs) are corporate bonds that are collateralized by mortgages or mortgage pass-through securities. Typical MBB structures pay interest semiannually and principal at bond maturity. Investors have no ownership interest in the mortgage collateral; they own the bond only.

To the investor, MBBs are simply a standard corporate bond. Mortgage-backed bonds are considered mortgage-related securities, however, because they are collateralized by a pool of mortgages or mortgage-related securities. Most MBB structures require that the issuer pledge a pool of high-quality mortgage assets such as GNMA pass-throughs to secure bond payments. These assets are marked to market monthly. If the collateral value falls below a minimum value, the issuer must add additional collateral, or the bond trustee will liquidate existing collateral in favor of the bondholders. The bond collateralization feature means that the credit quality of the bond is based on the quality of the bond collateral rather than on the creditworthiness of the issuer. By extensively overcollaterizing a bond, a weak issuer can raise funds in the AAA debt markets.

Approximately $7 billion of mortgage-backed bonds had been issued by mid-1986, mostly by thrift institutions and home builders. Issue volume fell in the mid-1980s, however, as more efficient debt securities were introduced into the market.

Mortgage Pay-Through Bonds

Mortgage pay-through bonds are securities that resemble both mortgage-backed bonds and mortgage pass-through securities. Like a corporate bond, a pay-through bond usually pays interest semiannually rather than monthly and is a general obligation of the bond issuer (investors do not own the mortgage assets that collateralize the bond). As are cash flows on a pass-through security, cash flows on a pay-through bond are determined by the cash flows on the specific pool of mortgage assets that collateralize the bond. Typically, a pay-through bond pays principal semiannually, based on the actual payments received on the mortgage securities backing the bond.

The pay-through bond is attractive to nontraditional mortgage investors because it does not require monthly accounting and management yet still has some of the performance characteristics of a pass-through security. The pay-through structure is attractive to the issuer versus a pass-through structure because the issuer retains ownership of the bond collateral. Also, because the principal payments on a pay-through bond match the cash flows on its underlying mortgage collateral, the issuer is less subject to reinvestment and price risk, and therefore can achieve a AAA rating with less overcollateralization than required by the mortgage-backed bond structure. This means that the issuer can raise more funds per dollar of collateral.

The pay-through bond market is dominated by the *collateralized mortgage obligation (CMO)*. Created in 1983, the CMO market grew to $77 billion by year-end 1986.

Collateralized Mortgage Obligations

A collateralized mortgage obligation (CMO) is a series of bonds backed by a single pool of specific mortgage assets (e.g., a number of GNMA pass-through certificates or a pool of whole loans). Because of dramatic changes in the CMO market in late 1986, it is difficult to characterize a "typical CMO". Prior to November 1986, when the first "floater" CMO was issued, the typical CMO consisted of four or more classes of fixed-rate bonds with different maturities, with one or more of the bond classes an accrual bond over some portion of its life. Interest was paid or accrued semi-annually or quarterly on each bond class, while all principal payments on the collateral were used to retire the bonds sequentially, in order of their maturity (that is, no principal payments were made on a bond until all earlier maturity bonds had been retired). This structure became known as the "fixed-rate" CMO structure, to distinguish it from the "floater" structure. CMO "floaters" were first introduced in November 1986 and quickly came to dominate the market. CMO floaters consist of two or more classes of bonds, with at least one class of bonds carrying a floating interest rate. The most typical floaters carry interest rates at some spread to LIBOR. These classes are combined with "inverse floaters"—bonds that carry coupons that float in the opposite direction to the LIBOR floaters—or discount coupon bonds. Floater CMOs tend to be combined with other fixed and floating rate bond classes. Some classes may be sequential pay, while others may pay pro-rata. The distinguishing characteristic of all of the bonds is that they restructure the cash flows on mortgage assets to create an arbitrage between the mortgage market and some other debt market. Fixed rate CMO bonds are priced at a spread to the comparable average life Treasury security; floater bonds at LIBOR plus a fixed spread.

The CMO structure is attractive to both issuers and investors. Issuers take advantage of a positively sloped yield curve or supply and demand conditions in different debt markets to finance a single pool of mortgage assets at a lower average cost than that available if the mortgages were financed with a single class of debt. In fact, as of late 1986, the CMO market was dominated by "arbitrage" issues. Arbitrage CMOs are simply bonds issued by special financing subsidiaries set up by major Wall Street investment houses to arbitrage among different debt markets (prior to the rise of the arbitrage CMO, the securities were issued primarily by homebuilders, who used the structure to provide financing to purchasers of their homes while capturing the benefits of the installment sale tax treatment, since eliminated, and portfolio investors such as thrifts or FHLMC, who used the structure to lock in a positive spread on their mortgage assets that was relatively insensitive to interest rate risk).

The CMO is attractive to mortgage investors as well as to issuers. Because their cash flows are determined by the cash flows on the pass-through securities that collateralize them, the CMO bonds are still subject to prepayment risk and offer high yields relative to alternative instruments. Because of the sequential pay structure, however, where earlier classes must be paid down prior to any principal payments on the later classes, holders of longer maturity classes are offered some level of call protection not available on similar maturity mortgage pass-throughs. Most important, however, the division of mortgage cash flows offers investors access to a much wider variety of mortgage instruments than available in the pass-through market. For example, thrift institutions, which are very efficient issuers of short-term funds, can shorten their asset maturity by purchasing short maturity CMO bonds with average lives in the two-to-five year range rather than intermediate maturity mortgage pass-throughs. Insurance companies, on the other hand, can purchase longer maturity pieces in the twenty-year range, which match their liabilities better than shorter average life pass-through securities. Finally, floater bonds appeal to European and Japanese investors, who otherwise would not invest in any type of residential pass-through security.

CMO residuals

CMO residuals are excess cash flows that arise because of requirements imposed on CMO issuers by national rating agencies for the CMO to receive a AAA rating, and by federal tax authorities for the transaction to be classified as a financing rather than as a sale of assets subject to recognition of taxable gain or loss on the sale of the assets collateralizing the bonds. These cash flows arise because the prepayment estimates and reinvestment rates required by the rating agencies for pricing purposes understate the cash flows that actually occur under most market conditions and because the IRS requires a minimum cash investment by the issuer for the issuer to be considered to retain an ownership interest in the assets. Originally, these cash flows were "passed forward" to the investors as a return of principal. As the security was refined, however, these residual cash flows almost always were retained by ("passed back" to) the issuer, who could sell them in the market depending on the legal structure of the entity issuing the CMO.

Residual cash flows are highly attractive to many investors. Because their cash flows are extremely sensitive to prepayment rates, residuals carry a relatively high yield. In stable markets, they therefore represent an extremely attractive investment. More important, however, is that certain types of residuals increase in value as interest rates increase, making them extremely attractive hedges for non-callable fixed income portfolios. Unlike other hedge instruments, which have a negative yield in stable rate markets, CMO residuals provide a high positive yield in stable rate environments, while offsetting losses on fixed income portfolios in rising rate markets.

More than $73 billion of CMOs had been issued as of year-end 1986, with almost $60 billion of this volume issued during 1986 alone. Certain technical amendments and the creation of a new tax reporting entity called a "REMIC" as part of the Tax Reform Act of 1986 have made CMOs an even more attractive security structure for both issuers and investors. As the final IRS regulations are drafted, volume may increase to even higher levels, limited only by the availability of pass-through securities eligible for collateralization.

WHOLE LOANS

Traditionally, whole loans have been defined to be unsecuritized mortgage loans. That is, they were individual mortgage loans not packaged into some type of mortgage security. There are two basic transaction structures in the whole loan market. These are: (1) the sale of loans in whole loan form; and (2) the sale of loan participations. In addition, as FNMA and FHLMC have begun to issue a wide variety of relatively nonstandardized pass-through securities (e.g., FNMA VRMs and GNMA, FNMA and FHLMC ARMs), the scope of the whole loan desk at many institutions has been expanded to include the purchase and sale of any type of mortgage product—securitized as well as unsecuritized—that requires the specialized legal, analytical, and marketing skills required to trade individual loan packages.

When a loan is sold in whole loan form, all documents associated with the mortgage are shipped from the seller to the purchaser, and a change of ownership must be recorded in the county seat where the property securing the loan is located. This is because possession of the documents and recordation of the loan sale are necessary to safeguard the new owner's security interest in the loan. As a result, whole loan sales can be expensive and time consuming to transact. Participation sales involve the retention of some ownership interest in the loan by the seller. In this structure, loan documents do not change hands.

The whole loan market has been influenced heavily by the agency pass-through market. Whole loan packages typically are sold subject to many of the same documentation standards, servicing requirements and warranties associated with sale of mortgages to one of the federal agencies. For example, many large traders use standard documentation for all of their transactions that allows them to execute sales relatively quickly among parties familiar with the documentation.

Whole loan market activity is difficult to measure. At year-end 1985, there were approximately $1.4 trillion of residential mortgage loans outstanding that had not been converted into mortgage securities. It is unknown, however, how often these loans changed hands in the market. FHLMC, for example, estimates that whole loan transactions during 1985 were approximately $200 billion. This compares with a $1 trillion trading volume in the agency pass-through markets over the same period.

SUMMARY

This chapter tries to make two important points. The first point is that the mortgage market is relatively new. During its earliest years of operation, activity focused on the creation of basic market structures: security design; market creation; education of issuers and investors; and the development of rudimentary tools to measure market risks. These activities are still continuing, with the development of more sophisticated derivative mortgage products and prepayment and options pricing models.

The second point to take away is the interconnection between the primary and secondary mortgage markets. Given the emphasis that the U.S. political system places on widespread home ownership and the characteristics of the typical residential borrower, it is likely that: 1) the residential mortgage market will continue as one of the largest, if not ultimately the largest, U.S. debt market; and 2) that the market will always have to deal in some way with the mortgage prepayment option. Households probably always will have less flexibility to alter their financial characteristics to satisfy capital market preferences than large institutional investors will have to alter their risk return profiles to capitalize on the risks and returns inherent in the mortgage market. For this reason, the trends observed in late 1986 are likely to define the market over the next several years. It therefore is more likely that new secondary market product developments such as derivative mortgage securities and more efficient prepayment and option pricing models will be developed to understand and control prepayment risk than that prepayment risk will be eliminated through innovations in primary market product design.

Convertible Securities: Definitions, Analytical Tools, and Practical Investment Strategies

Robert A. Young, CFA
Vice President
Convertible Securities Research
Dean Witter Reynolds Inc.

INTRODUCTION

A convertible security has attributes of both bonds and common stocks. As such, convertibles can be used to enhance the performance of a broad range of investment accounts. However, convertibles are only poorly understood because their terminology and analytical tools are different from mainstream investing in either equity or fixed-income investments. Most investors view convertibles as simple extensions of their common stocks, but fail to consider the specific investment characteristics of convertibles that can cause converts to act very differently from their commons. An important reason for this limited understanding is the general scarcity of convertible research information available, in marked contrast to the virtual flood of investment research information on equity and fixed-income securities. For example, in mid-1986, there were just two sources of continuous analysis and recommendations on the IBM convertible debentures,[1] while in marked contrast, 39 analysts were following IBM, according to IBES.[2] Furthermore, much of the convertible research that is available is either little more than statistical reports without analysis and recommendation, or so theoretical in nature so as to preclude easy practical application.

Colleagues and customers ask many questions about convertibles, with virtually all of them dealing with definitions and terminology; only a small proportion concern investment strategies and recommendations. This suggests two things: that there is great interest in convertibles among institutional investors as well as great misunderstanding. It seems as if every investor has heard that "convertible securities are the best of both worlds," which has the unstated implication that convertibles will consistently provide superior results relative to their underlying commons. This is simply not the case. The very existence of a convertible, however, means the potential exists to improve the risk-adjusted return for a given attractive equity as compared to either a buy-and-hold strategy or an unhedged investment program. Part of the reason is that convertible securities can be viewed as a relatively inefficient segment of the financial marketplace. Investors of most persuasions—fundamental, technical, and modern portfolio theorists—can agree that inefficiency and profit potential often go hand in hand.

The objective of this chapter is to fill a small portion of that research gap, a gap that is filled by plentiful investment research for equities and fixed-income investments. We will begin with key definitions and then graphically "build" a convertible framework, one attribute at a time, drawing on real data for actual convertible securities. We will then develop and explain with specific examples, the primary analytical tool—conversion premium. Particular attention will be paid to the investment performance consequences of call features. Key attributes of convertibles will be demonstrated with actual examples. And finally, we will suggest practical convertible strategies with full explanation of analytical techniques and real-life examples.

WHAT IS A CONVERTIBLE?

A convertible security is simply either a debenture or a preferred stock that can be converted into a specified number of shares of common stock. As such, the convert derives part of its value from its underlying common stock. This means that when the common goes up in price, the convertible will also go up. In contrast, an increase in the price of the common stock of a company would not ordinarily translate into an increase in the price of its bonds. For purposes of most of our discussion, the terms *bond, debenture, debt,* or *fixed income,* will also implicitly include *preferred stocks.* Although there are differences, bonds and preferred stocks have similar characteristics: both have a fixed-income payment—a coupon in the case of a bond, and a dividend in the case of a preferred stock—and both are senior securities to common stocks. Differences between convertible debentures and preferreds will be discussed in a later section.

Investors seem to view convertible securities as a blend of common stock and debenture. The word *hybrid* better describes how a convertible acts and what it can do for us as investors. As a hybrid, a convertible has attributes of both stocks and bonds. That is, it has the fixed, assured income payment associated with fixed-income instruments, but also allows the convertible investor to participate in the growth of the common stock through the conversion feature.

That is why most investors seem to view convertibles as the "best of both worlds" because compared to stocks, converts provide a higher, more secure income stream, and yet have less risk than common stocks. Compared to bonds, converts offer participation in the appreciation of the underlying common stock and still provide a good current return. Just as a hybrid of wheat or corn is bred to have certain desirable traits, convertibles would seem to have the best attributes of both common stocks and bonds: high current income plus equity participation.

Who Benefits from Converts, the Company or the Investor?

But, there is a flip side to the convertible story—if convertibles are so good for investors, then why do companies issue them? The answer is very simple, because convertibles are good for corporations, too. Because of the conversion feature, investors will accept a lower yield than on straight debt that does not have the conversion feature. This means the issuing company has to pay less interest expense than if it issued straight debt. Also, the price at which the convertible issue can be converted into common stock is generally 15 percent to 25 percent higher than the price of the common at the time the convertible bonds are issued. When a company issues convertible securities, it is essentially issuing equity because the determination of whether or not the security will be converted is largely up to the exogenous factors of the financial markets and at the option of the holder. However, because of the conversion premium at issue, the company is issuing about 20 percent less equity than if it sold common stock. It seems that convertibles can also be the best of both worlds for companies.

Well, who does benefit more from converts, the investor or the company? The answer is "it depends"; it depends upon what happens to the value of the common and other factors. Some years ago, one investor wrote that converts were "the worst of both worlds,"[3] because a convertible offers a lower interest payment than straight debt and the investor has a claim on fewer shares of common stock than if be bought the common outright. In this view, a convertible was viewed as the undesirable combination of a discount bond and a diluted equity interest. That conclusion seems a bit harsh. I prefer to apply the comment by the economist, Milton Friedman, that "there is no free lunch." By this Friedman means that for every benefit, there is a cost: the conversion feature is an attractive benefit, but the price we "pay" for this feature is the combination of lower interest income, the premium of the conversion price over the current stock price, and possibly lower liquidity. These factors could result in lagging investment performance.

Convertible analysis is the identification, analysis, and evaluation of costs versus benefits. The results of the analysis will vary with the investment environment. A hybrid of corn that was developed to prosper in well-irrigated and well-fertilized midwestern fields may not do so well in arid untended environments. What is an asset in one environment can well be a liability in a different environment. The same is true with our "hybrid-securities," convertibles: convertibles will flourish in some investment environments and languish in others. Convertibles are not securities investments for all seasons. Because of their specific attributes, there are periods of time when they will provide superior returns compared to their underlying common stocks, and times when they will underperform. I believe it is possible to identify periods of potential superior and inferior performance relative to the common. It is also important to understand that investors pay for the conversion feature, it is not free. The key issue, then, is to evaluate the cost versus the benefits, to see if the conversion feature is worth it. Many times it is and many times it is not.

CONVERTIBLE TERMINOLOGY: THE LANGUAGE OF CONVERTIBLES, DEFINITIONS WITH NUMERIC EXAMPLES

As is the case with any other speciality, convertible securities have their own special terminology. We will assume that the reader is familiar with general investment terms pertaining to equity and fixed-income securities. In order to provide the clearest definitions, complete arithmetic examples are provided so you will be able to perform the calculations for yourself. You may wish to set up these terms in a convertible file if you have a personal computer. For our example, we will use the currently popular IBM convertible debenture priced as of September 12, 1986.

As you go through these examples, please remember that it is much more important to understand the concepts of these terms rather than get bogged down in the arithmetic.

IBM 7.875 PERCENT CONVERTIBLE DEBENTURES DUE NOVEMBER 21, 2004

Terms	Convertible	Common
Conversion:		
Price	$153.66	
Shs/Conv.	.651 shares	
Current price	$118.50	$137.38
Coupon	7.875%	
Dividend	NM	$4.40
Current yield	6.6%	3.2%

Conversion price. The conversion price is the price of the common stock at which the convertible can be converted. The conversion price is generally expressed as a percentage premium to the common price existent when the convertible is issued. Most convertibles are issued after the close of trading, generally in midweek, and with the conversion price generally a 15 percent to 30 percent premium to the closing price of the underlying common. The conversion price for the IBM converts in our example is $153.66.

Conversion ratio. The conversion price is the price of the convertible bond divided by the number of shares into which the bond can be converted. This is the conversion ratio. Most debentures have face values of $1,000, but trade on a price basis that is expressed as a percent of par. In our example, the IBM convert has a par value of $1,000. At its current price of $118.50, each debenture has a market value of $1,185.00. When reviewing a number of convertibles, particularly when accessing a financial data base for pricing, it may be useful to evaluate them on a price basis, as we have done in our example. The conversion ratio is 0.651 shares of IBM common for each debenture on a $100 price basis. In order to calculate the number of shares available on a $1,000 face value basis, just multiply this conversion ratio by 10.

CONVERSION VALUE

The conversion value = the number of common shares per convertible × the current common stock price.

.651	shares per convert
$137.38	times common price
$89.40	equals conversion value

The **conversion value** is simply the value of the shares of common stock that would be received if the convertible security were converted into its underlying common stock. When a convertible is issued, the indenture specifies exactly how many common shares can be received for each debenture generally by specifying the conversion price and frequently publishing the conversion ratio. The conversion value is calculated by multiplying the number of common shares that would be received times the current price of the common.

The **conversion premium** is just the difference between the current price of the convertible and the value of the common stock that can be acquired upon conversion. It is expressed both as a dollar premium and as a percentage premium over conversion value. However, it is necessary to calculate both the percentage and dollar conversion premiums,

CONVERSION PREMIUM

The difference between the conversion value and the price of the convertible, expressed as the percentage premium of the convertible price over the conversion value. In terms of evaluation, it is a "cost."

Dollar		*Percent*	
$118.50	Convert price	$29.10	$ conversion premium
$89.40	minus conversion value	$89.40	divided by the conversion value
$29.10	equals $ conversion premium	32.5%	equals conversion premium (percent)

as will shortly be evident. The conversion premium is a measure of the dilution of an investor's equity interest compared to outright purchase of the common. Therefore, it is appropriate to view the conversion premium as a "cost" factor. The percentage conversion premium is the *primary analytical tool* for convertibles, so it is important that this concept be understood.

INCOME ADVANTAGE

The extra annual income from the convert compared to the common stock for *equal dollar investments*. In terms of evaluation, it is a "benefit."

Common Equivalent Income for Equal Dollar Investment:
$118.50	convertible price
$137.38	divided by common price
.863 =	number common shares that equals value of one convert
$4.40	times common dividend
$3.80 =	common equivalent income for equal dollar investments.

Income Advantage ($):
$7.88	convertible annual income
$−3.80	less: common equivalent income
$4.08 =	income advantage of the convertible.

The primary reason for owning a convertible is that it provides a higher and more secure stream of current income than the underlying common stock. It is important to compare the convertible to the common for equal dollar investments.

BREAK-EVEN PERIOD

The dollar conversion premium divided by the dollar income advantage for equal dollar investments; a cash payback analysis.

$29.10	Dollar conversion premium
	divided by
$4.08	income advantage
	equals break-even period
7.1	years

The concept of the **break-even period** is an important secondary tool for measuring the "benefit" (the income advantage) versus the "cost" (the conversion premium), by determining how long it takes for the additional income to offset the premium. The IBM example illustrates that it would require over seven years for the higher income to offset the 32.5 percent conversion premium. It is important to calculate the common equivalent income on an equal dollar investment basis so that the break-even analysis of the convert versus the common is on an apples-to-apples basis.

A popular but incorrect method of calculating the break-even period is to divide the percentage conversion premium by the difference between the percentage yields of the convert and its common. This method is incorrect because the conversion premium percentage is expressed as a percentage of the conversion value, while the current yields for both the convert and the common are expressed as percentages of their respective market values. In order for this method to be arithmetically correct, the dollar conversion premium would also have to be expressed as a percentage of market value, as a percentage of the convertible price, not of the conversion value. Some investors calculate breakevens based on equal share investments. Such an analysis is not appropriate for most investment purposes because the comparison deals with unequal dollar-value investments.

Call provisions. Call provisions were inherited from fixed-income securities. The call price is the price, usually in the 105–110 range, at which the company can redeem or buy back the debentures, usually after a protected period of two to four years, which is the period of call protection. Companies call or redeem bonds for two reasons, most commonly to force conversion into the underlying common stock and occasionally to redeem the issue for cash. In the former circumstance, the company's cash expenditure is reduced while the latter avoids equity dilution. It is important for convertible investors to be aware of call features because convertibles with call protection behave differently than convertibles without call protection.

Conversion terms summary.   These are the general definitions of terms for convertible securities. However, each convertible is specifically governed by the terms of its indenture which should be reviewed. Accordingly, some convertibles will have unusual or even unique terms.

THE CONVERSION PREMIUM—THE PRIMARY ANALYTICAL TOOL

Chart 1 shows the inverse relationship between the conversion premium, expressed as a percent, and the price of the convertible issue. The important observation is that as the price of the convertible rises, the conversion premium declines; or, conversely, as the convertible declines, the premium widens, cushioning the fall in value of the convertible investment. This is *the most important attribute of a convertible, its*

CHART 1   Conversion Premiums versus Convert Price

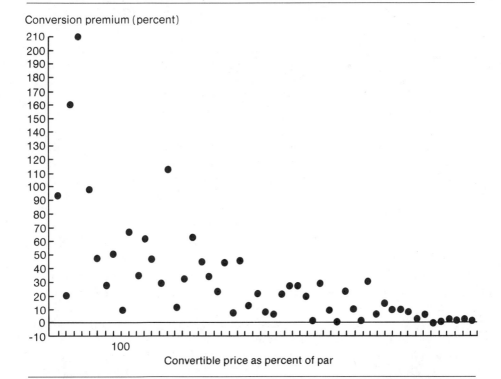

Conversion premium (percent)

Convertible price as percent of par

CHART 2 Building a Convertible—I

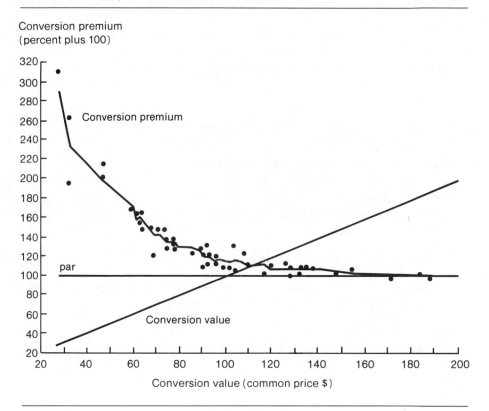

Conversion premium
(percent plus 100)

Conversion value (common price $)

ability to cushion unanticipated price declines in the common stock. As a point of interest, this and most other charts in this work were derived from the convertible debentures and preferreds continuously followed in the *Convertible Issues Review*, which is a monthly publication of PNC Financial. These charts represent real issues and real prices as determined by the financial markets.

Chart 2 is similar to the previous chart except it plots the percentage conversion premium (scatter plot) versus the conversion value. The irregular solid line is a moving average of the scatter-plot points. The upward sloping line is the conversion value, which is directly proportional to the common stock price. Notice that there is a more discernable relationship between the premium and the conversion value than the premium and convertible price in Chart 1, although the nature of the relationship is essentially the same. The horizontal line is at 100, which is the par value of most debentures on a price basis. The preferreds have been adjusted to a par of 100. As the conversion value rises, the conversion premium declines. As the conversion premium moves above par (100), the conversion premium declines toward zero.

As indicated above, convertibles with call protection act differently than convertibles without call protection. Since there are more convertibles without call protection than with, we have deleted the call protected issues from our sample in Chart 3. The key difference between Charts 2 and 3 is that the latter shows that the conversion premium for noncall protected convertibles declines more rapidly than for the total population, and therefore for call-protected convertibles, particularly as the conversion value approaches par.

In the absence of call protection, the convertible is more likely to be called, which reduces the benefit of a convertible. Accordingly, there is a commensurate reduction in the cost associated with that benefit, the conversion premium. Unfortunately, our limited sample has a gap in issues for study. However, other cross-sectional snapshots of the same population at different times suggest that the trend of conversion

CHART 3 Building a Convertible—IA (call-protected issues deleted)

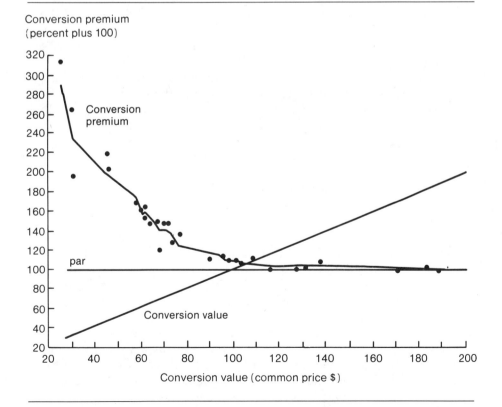

Conversion premium (percent plus 100)

premiums indicated by the jagged line accurately reflects the structure of conversion premiums.

Therefore, the conversion premium is inversely related to the conversion value, which is directly proportional to the stock price. As the stock price rises, the conversion premium declines.

A measure of relative performance. The conversion premium is the key analytical tool in evaluating the attractiveness of a convertible. It is also a graphic representation of the relative price performance of a convertible relative to its underlying common stock. Relative price is a common tool utilized for comparative performance evaluation of a common stock versus an index, such as the Standard & Poor's 400 Industrial Index. The relative price is calculated by dividing the price of the common by the value of the index. This ratio is plotted over time. When the relative price line is rising, the stock is outperforming the index, and vice versa.

The conversion premium is calculated by dividing the convertible price by the conversion value, and adjusting that ratio to a percentage. (While this procedure differs from the example presented above, both methods are arithmetically equivalent.) Therefore, the conversion premium line is also an indicator of the relative price performance of the convertible.

There is an important conclusion here that does not appear to be widely appreciated. That is when the common rises, the convert will tend to underperform on a price basis. The more rapid the rise of the common, the greater the underperformance of the convert. This relationship should cause investors who subscribe to the "best of both worlds" viewpoint to reexamine their assumptions. Underperformance in a bull market is not generally considered a positive attribute. In general terms, investors expecting a rapid rise in the common would be well advised to purchase the common and avoid the convert. However, purchase of a convertible to reduce the risk (volatility) of a position or to hedge timing and value factors would be perfectly appropriate.

The average conversion premium. Chart 4 plots the average conversion premiums for the convertible debentures included in our monthly publication. For an 18-month period, the average moved around the 27 percent level. In mid-1985, convertible issues gained in popularity and new mutual funds dedicated to convertibles were created. As a result, conversion premiums in general expanded. As indicated in previous charts, premiums tend to decline as stocks rise. However, during the first half of 1985, premiums rose with an advancing market. When the stock market surged later in the year, the inevitable happened and conversion premiums declined which indicated that convertibles were underperforming a rapidly rising market.

CHART 4 Conversion Premiums and the Market

Conversion premium (percent)

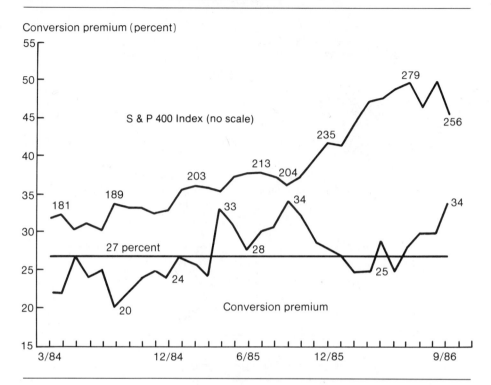

There are few indexes of convertible performance because many convertibles are such short-lived instruments making it difficult to construct an index. We selected this particular sample because it tends to reflect trends of conversion premiums in the new issue market. It will have to be revised periodically. While the average conversion premium of a sample of convertibles can be calculated, the average for an individual issue over time is a meaningless concept as indicated by Charts 1, 2, and 3.

BUILDING A CONVERTIBLE

We have already begun to build a convertible structure utilizing cross-sectional data from a sample of existing convertible debentures with Charts 2 and 3. Charts 5 and 6 show the distribution of convertible prices versus the conversion value; Chart 5 presents the total population and Chart 6 excludes call-protected issues. As the convertible price rises above par, it moves closer to the conversion price line. In the left third

CHART 5 Building a Convertible—II

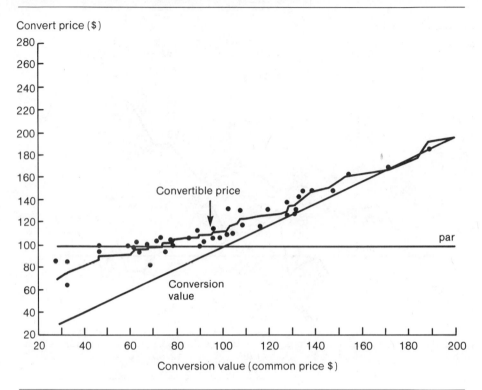

Convert price ($)

Conversion value (common price $)

of the chart, the convertible is acting more like a fixed-income item; in the right third, the convertible is almost a perfect common substitute; while in the middle, the convertible is in transition from mostly a fixed-income instrument to primarily an equity instrument.

It is important to note in Chart 6 that when the convertible price just exceeds par, it tends to flatten as the conversion value (stock price) continues to rise for noncall protected convertibles.

In Chart 7, which is the sum of Charts 3 and 6, we begin to see how convertibles work, the changing pace of convertible response to common stock price changes, with the varying movement in the conversion premium.

In Chart 8, we eliminated the scatter plots and added the bond or investment value, the lower horizontal line, which is the value of a convertible as a nonconvertible fixed-income issue. Since a convertible has a lower coupon than straight debt, it is valued as a discount instrument. The investment value tends to serve as a floor on the value

CHART 6 Building a Convertible—IIA (call-protected issues deleted)

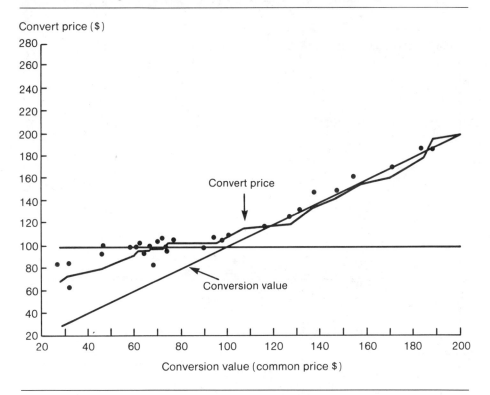

Convert price ($)

Conversion value (common price $)

of a convert, which is a primary source of a convertible's ability to moderate the downside risk of a common stock.

Chart 9 is the most important chart in this chapter, for it summarizes the performance of convertibles relative to their underlying common stocks. In Chart 9, we have converted data to proportional (logarithmic) scales in order to facilitate performance comparisons. Comparison of the slopes of the lines of the convertible price to the debenture price reflects relative price change. Also, changes in the distance between these lines reflect differential price performance.

Starting at the left side of the chart, as the conversion value or stock price rises from left to right, the debenture price rises slowly, as indicated by its flat slope. The convertible's underperformance is also indicated by the narrowing distance between the convertible price line and the conversion value line. This is because the conversion premium is so large that a declining premium absorbs much of the common stock price rise. For a while, the convertible price is caught at a price just

---

CHART 7 Building a Convertible—III (call-protected issues deleted)

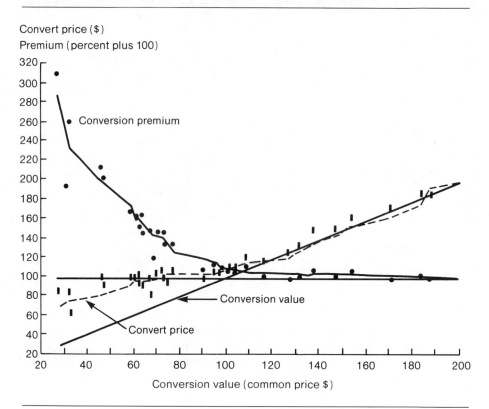

Convert price ($)
Premium (percent plus 100)

Conversion value (common price $)

---

above par even as the common stock price rises. This is because the risk of call causes the premium to erode to a low level.

This is a period of substantial underperformance of a convertible versus its underlying common stock. It has been my experience that this phenomenon is not widely understood even though the underperformance can be so significant that we instituted a special investment rating for convertibles to indicate that the call price may restrict convertible price appreciation. Far more convertible investors are concerned about the risk of call, even though the evidence shows that the relative underperformance of a convertible is greater *before* the convert is called, not when the convert is called.

After the premium has fallen to the 0 percent to 10 percent range, the debenture price line begins to rise at a faster rate, which means it is acting more like a common stock. In the right portion of the chart, the convertible is virtually a perfect common stock equivalent that has little

CHART 8   Building a Convertible—IV (call-protected issues deleted)

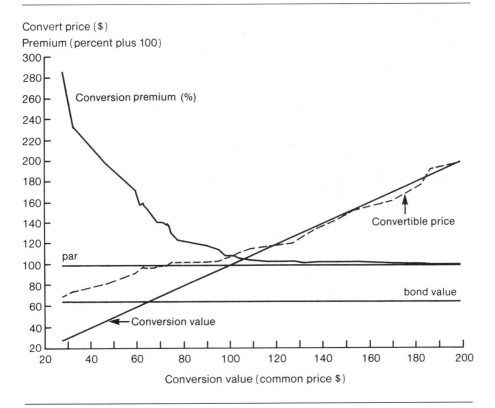

Convert price ($)
Premium (percent plus 100)

underperformance risk relative to the common, because the conversion premium has eroded to low levels. Some convertibles sell at modest discounts to conversion value because they are subject to call, and on call, accrued interest on convertible debentures would be lost. When the debenture price is well above 110, the premium is low, so the debenture is performing more like its common stock than as a bond. At such levels, the convertible provides little downside protection.

Remember that the conversion premium line is a relative strength indicator for convertibles. The consistently declining conversion premium indicates that a convertible generally underperforms a rising common.

Reading Chart 9 from right to left illustrates how convertible securities reduce downside risk when a common stock is declining. Initially, the convertible will decline about as rapidly as its common, because it is a good common stock substitute and offers no particular

CHART 9 Building a Convertible—V (proportional scale)

Convert price ($)
Premium (percent plus 100)

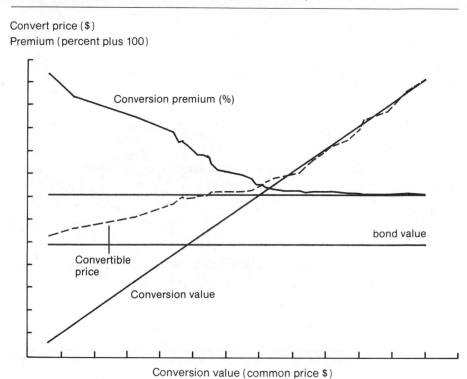

Conversion premium (%)

bond value

Convertible
price

Conversion value

Conversion value (common price $)
————— Rising common stock price —————▶

defensive advantage. However, as the debenture price falls below the 105–110 level, moving from right to left in the chart, the premium begins to rise because the risk of call is diminished. For a time, the convertible may decline at just a modest rate even though the common continues to decline. After a while, the convertible begins to decline more rapidly, but as indicated by both the lower slope of the convertible line and the widening gap between the convertible price line and the conversion value, the convertible is outperforming a declining common stock. Since the conversion premium line is a relative strength line, its upward trend, as we read from right to left, shows that the convertible is outperforming. Whenever the premium is rising, the debenture is performing better than its underlying common stock; in this chart, it means the debenture is declining less than the common. This chart clearly illustrates the ability to reduce risk in down markets; the expansion of the conversion premium reduces the rate of decline.

CALL PROTECTION—PROTECTOR OF THE CONVERSION PREMIUM

So far, we have merely stated that convertibles with call protection have different investment characteristics than convertibles without call protection. Now we will show you. Chart 10 was constructed in the same manner as the previous series of charts, except that it includes only those issues with significant call protection remaining. It is immediately obvious that Chart 10 is quite different from Chart 9, particularly in the center portion where the convertible price is at or just above par. The prices of convertibles with call protection participate more fully in common stock appreciation (Chart 10), as compared to a convertible price stagnated by the call price (Chart 9). This means the conversion premium declines more slowly for call-protected convertibles and, since the conversion premium is an indicator of the relative price performance of the convertible versus its common, call-protected convertibles have better relative price performance at and above par than noncall-protected convertibles.

Clearly then, call protection protects the conversion premium, protects part of the value of a convertible security. Therefore, call features must be examined carefully. Two years of call protection are

CHART 10 Building a Convertible—VI (issues with call protection)

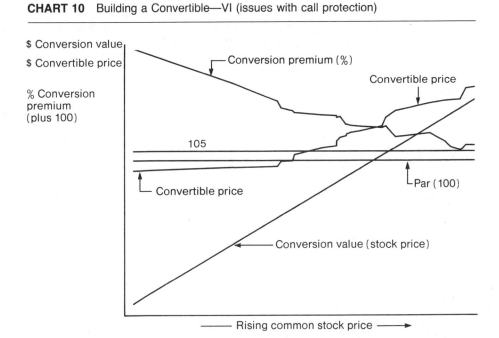

most common, with three years frequently available from lesser quality or out-of-favor issuers. Our research indicates that the most severe premium erosion (convertible relative price underperformance) tends to occur during the last year or so of call protection. Therefore, two years of call protection is in reality one year of effective call protection. An issue with three years of call protection has approximately twice as much effective call protection as an issue with two years of initial protection. The conversion premium will decline during effective call protection as the common stock rises, but at a lesser rate than if there was no call protection. The faster the common stock rise, the greater the rate of conversion premium erosion, the greater the relative price underperformance.

Convertibles issued as part of mergers or acquisitions tend to have longer call protection periods. For example, the IBM 7.875% debentures had four years of call protection and the Burroughs $3.75 preferred A had three years of protection. These convertibles were issued for the acquisition of ROLM Corp. and Sperry Corp., respectively.

CALL PRICE—A HIDDEN CONSIFICATOR OF RELATIVE VALUE

Examination of the center portion of Chart 9 illustrates the effect of call price on the return from a convertible security. As the convertible price approaches call price (above par but below the call price), there is a period when the *convertible price substantially underperforms the common price, which results in a significant, hidden loss of relative value.* The degree of the loss is a function of the conversion premium; when the convertible price exceeds the call price, the greater the conversion premium, the greater the relative loss versus investment in the rising underlying common. In some instances, this hidden loss can equal as much as 10 percent to 20 percent or more, and frequently within a relatively short time period. The convertible price is stable, even though the conversion value (stock price) continues to rise, as we read the chart from left to right. This period of substantial underperformance of the convertible versus the underlying common stock is reflected by the decline of the conversion premium line, which is an indicator of relative convertible price performance versus the underlying common stock. This is true for convertibles where call protection has expired. The call price line in Chart 10 is drawn at 105, which is the average call price of our sample. Each convertible security has specific call terms included in its indenture.

The key observation here is that convertibles can significantly underperform their rising commons as the debenture price approaches call price of unprotected issues. The investor can easily avoid this problem by simply not participating in noncall-protected convertibles that are approaching call price. However, most investors are not aware that a convertible can significantly underperform a common stock, as we have just demonstrated is the case when the convertible price is approaching its call price.

HOW CONVERTIBLES WORK

The Essence of Convertible Investing: Improving the Risk/Reward Ratio

Charts 9 and 10 are the most important charts because they illustrate *how, where,* and *why* convertible securities perform, that convertibles can reduce the risk of unanticipated stock price declines. These charts also show that convertibles tend to underperform on a price basis when commons are rising. They also show that relatively high-yield convertibles, which often have relatively high conversion premiums associated with the left side of the chart, do in fact enjoy some equity participation in a rising common, despite reasonably large conversion premiums.

Charts 9 and 10 show that convertibles are neither the best nor the worst of both worlds; convertibles provide superior performance in environments (declining interest rates and stock prices) that take advantage of their assets, and poorly in environments (rising interest rates and stock prices) that do not.

HOW CONVERTIBLES ARE VIEWED BY MOST INVESTORS

Chart 11 illustrates how most investors view convertible securities. Whereas Charts 9 and 10 reflect convertibles without and with call protection, respectively, Chart 11 was derived from our total sample. In a sense, Chart 11 depicts the "average convertible." Most investors know the story about the economist that drowned while fording a river that was on average three-feet deep. There must be many convertible investors that endured significantly different relative performance than could be expected from the mythical average convertible.

Beginning at the left side of Chart 11, the price track of the convertible approaches its investment value when the common price is well below the conversion price. In the leftmost portion of the chart, the convert acts largely like a discount fixed-income security. We have little disagreement with this view, except to note that the convertible market appears to be relatively inefficient in general, and particularly so in the left portion of the charts.

As the common (conversion value) rises, from left to right, the conversion price smoothly approaches the conversion value line, as the upward push of the conversion value causes the convertible to act more

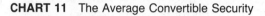

CHART 11   The Average Convertible Security

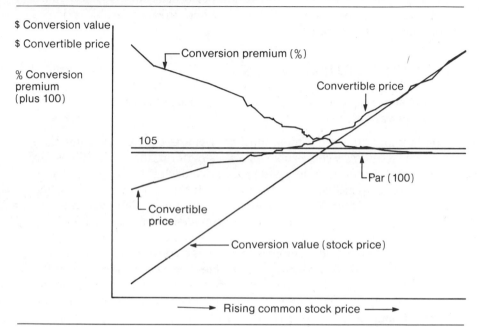

like its common stock. The portion of the convertible price curve close to par (the center portion of the charts) is where the notion of the average convertible will cost investors the most. In the case of noncall-protected issues, the "average" overstates the conversion premium and convertible price relative to what the market will bear. Investors could overpay for such issues and incur significant opportunity losses in the form of hidden significant relative price underperformance versus a rising common stock.

Conversely, the "average" understates the fair conversion premium and convertible price for well-protected issues, which can cause opportunity losses as investors mistakenly avoid attractive convertibles. The rate of conversion premium erosion (underperformance relative to the underlying common) will actually be less than indicated by the average.

As the common continues to rise, forcing the conversion value above par (the right portion of the charts), the convertible price approaches the conversion value until it is acting essentially like its underlying common. This relationship is essentially correct, although convertible debentures subject to call may sell below conversion value by the amount of accrued interest, as previously discussed.

In most cases where a chart of convertible price performance is presented, it looks much like Chart 11. However, most of the observed charts are stylized, approaching asymptotically the investment value on the left and the conversion value on the right. This is true in both theoretically and practically oriented works. In discussing how convertibles act with sophisticated researchers and convertible traders, it is clear that every source I have ever met views convertible price action in accordance with Chart 11.

There is just one problem with this state of affairs, it is incorrect. Chart 11 and its stylized counterparts are smooth and clean in comparison to the irregular fact of the real world as presented in Charts 9 and 10. Remember, Charts 9 and 10 were built step by step from data on existing convertibles. The biggest difference is that our charts take into account the existence of call provisions, while Chart 11 seemingly does not. Chart 11 is not so much wrong as incomplete; it reflects the general price track of convertibles that have call protection, although it also somewhat oversimplifies the evenness of transition from part bond, part stock to largely common stock.

Convertibles with Call Protection Act Differently Than Convertibles without Call Protection

In our view, what is needed are two price track charts, one for convertibles without call protection (Chart 9) and one with call protection (Chart 10). This is not done to confuse matters or to encourage you to purchase our service, but this is how the financial markets treat the two different types of convertibles, those with and those without call protection.

The simple fact of the matter is that the existence of the call feature affects the convertible price in an uneven manner. When the convertible price approaches the call price, the risk of call increases. When a convertible is called, the primary benefit, incremental current income versus the common stock, will cease to exist, so the convertible has less value. As a result, the "cost" (the conversion premium) of this disappearing "benefit" (the incremental income), must be reduced. This is what does occur in the financial marketplace, notwithstanding the widespread ignorance of this phenomenon.

Charts 12 and 13 will illustrate how the market treats convertibles without and with call protection. Chart 12A portrays the key parameters of the K mart 6.0 percent convertible debenture due July 15, 1999, using monthly data from late 1979 through September 1986. This debenture was callable throughout the period presented. Please focus on the period beginning late 1982 when the common stock price turned up, coincident with the birth of a bull stock market. The debenture price also turned up. As the debenture price approached par, the conversion premium began to erode quickly. For two years, the debenture price oscillated around par, causing the conversion premium to oscillate in

CHART 12A   K mart 6.0 Percent Convertible Debenture

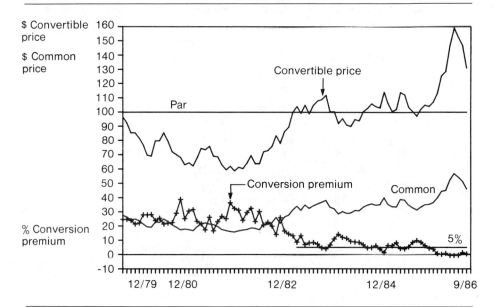

about a 0 percent to 10 percent range. With the debenture price near par, the premium had fallen significantly from the 20 percent to 40 percent level experienced previously, because the propinquity to call price caused the premium to decline. Finally, early in 1986, the bull stock market drove K mart stock to higher ground, which caused the debenture price to significantly exceed both par and the call price. At this point, with call likely, the premium fell to zero percent.

Chart 12A clearly shows that the K mart convertible debenture acted in accordance with tendencies of noncall protected convertibles as portrayed in Charts 10 and 11, but Chart 12A doesn't look like the other two. Chart 12B presents the same data as in Chart 12A, but it is presented on a proportional (logarithmic) scale basis, the same manner of presentation utilized in Charts 9 and 10. Focusing on the debenture price as it approaches par and the call price, the conversion premium declines rather dramatically, and falls to zero when the convertible price and conversion value exceed the call price. This action is similar to the action in Charts 9 and 10, and quite different from the gradual premium erosion implied in Chart 11. This chart is different in appearance than Charts 9 and 10 because this debenture had a relatively low coupon during this period (because it was issued when interest rates were lower), and therefore traded at a lower premium than more current issues with more current (higher) coupons.

CHART 12B K mart 6 Percent Convertible Debenture Proportional Scale

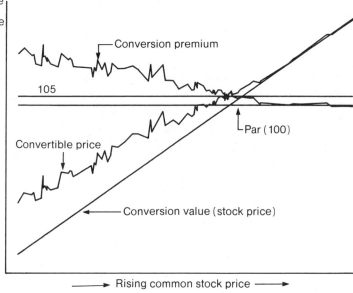

$ Convertible price

$ Conversion value

% Conversion premium (plus 100)

105

Conversion premium

Par (100)

Convertible price

Conversion value (stock price)

⟶ Rising common stock price ⟶

Charts 13A and 13B will illustrate how call protection reduces the rate of premium erosion as the convertible approaches call price. Chart 13A presents virtually the full price history of the Westinghouse Electric 9.0 percent convertible debenture due August 15, 2009. Because of WX stock price movement, the debenture sold above par from issue, but maintained a 20 percent to 30 percent conversion premium for some time because of call protection. Late in 1984, the stock spurted enough to lift the conversion value to near par, which is also near the call price. As the conversion value approached par, the conversion premium began to erode; the convertible price gradually approached the conversion value and the conversion premium gradually approached zero. This metamorphisis is more obvious in Chart 13B, which presents the data on proportional scales. Chart 13B is similar in structure to Chart 10.

Notice that for a given conversion value, the conversion premium is higher for the Westinghouse debenture than for the K mart debenture. Much of the difference in convertible price action is due to the difference in call protection, particularly in the center portion of the charts.

Therefore, in order to develop a good, useful understanding of convertibles, an investor should understand how the conversion pre-

CHART 13A   Westinghouse Electric 9.0 Percent Convertible Debenture

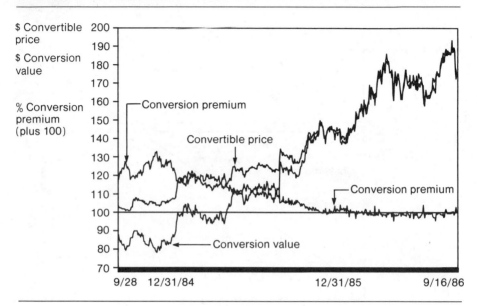

CHART 13B   Westinghouse Electric 9.0 Percent Convertible Debenture
Proportional Scale

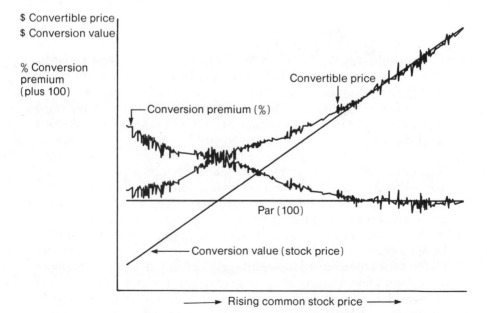

mium changes in response to common stock price (conversion value) for convertibles with and without call protection. In other words, review and understand Charts 9 and 10.

WHEN A CONVERTIBLE IS CALLED

When a convertible is called, it is worth the higher of the call price or the conversion value. Companies call or redeem convertibles for two reasons. The most common is to force conversion into the underlying common stock. Forced conversion usually reduces the company's cash expenditure as the dividends paid on the new common stock is typically less than the aftertax interest on convertible debentures or the convertible preferred dividend.

In order to force conversion, the conversion value must exceed the call price. Typically, companies wait until the conversion value exceeds the call price by 10 percent to 25 percent to ensure that the convertible issues will in fact be converted and the company will not have to redeem the issue for cash. Any conversion premium that exists will evaporate when the issue is called, and represents potential loss. Typically, under these circumstances, neither accrued income nor the final coupon/dividend are paid, although the indenture must be reviewed to be certain. The point is that calls to force conversion generally involve some loss of income. With two potential sources of loss, it is important for investors to be aware of call provisions.

Companies also may call a convertible for cash redemption. The convertible would generally be selling above the call price, but the conversion value would be less than the call price. Cash redemption means that common stock will not be issued when the convertible is retired, which reduces equity dilution. If the convertible price is greater than the call price, then this excess is at risk. Calls for redemption generally include accrued income through the call/redemption date.

Most issues are called to force conversion. This reflects two factors, the long-term trend of rising stock prices and the long-term trend of rising bond yields. In order to call for cash, the convertible price has to rise from issue, but the common stock must not rise enough to push the conversion value above the call price. In order for the convertible price to rise under these circumstances, fixed-income yields must fall. As indicated in Chart 14, interest rates rose from the late 1940s through the 1981–82 peak, with only cyclical rate declines. This means that bond prices were declining throughout this period. Because bond prices were declining, there were few opportunities when corporations could call convertibles for cash redemption. Only cyclical opportunities were available and they would have been limited by the period of call protection.

However, the trend of interest rates apparently reversed in the

CHART 14

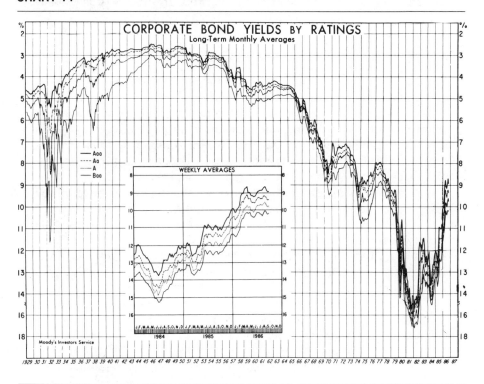

CORPORATE BOND YIELDS BY RATINGS
Long-Term Monthly Averages

SOURCE: Moody's Investors Service.

1981–82 period as a result of disinflationary economic forces. There has been an increase in the frequency of convertibles called for cash in the 1985–86 period because some companies now have the opportunity to call for cash because of the apparent reversal of a 35-year trend of rising interest rates. In addition, the first half of the 1980s has been characterized by leveraged buyouts and management interest in "increasing shareholder value." Both factors usually involved the purchase of common stock. This attitude reinforces the desire to call convertibles for cash redemption as a means of reducing the number of outstanding common shares. Therefore, because of an apparent reversal in the long-term interest rate trend and a different management attitude toward share repurchase, there could a larger proportion of convertibles redeemed for cash in the 1980s than has historically been the case.

It is important for convertible investors to be aware of call features because convertibles with call protection behave differently than convertibles without call protection.

Conditional call. In recent years, increasing numbers of convertible indentures contained conditional or provisional call provisions. Under these provisions, a convertible can be called if the *common stock* trades at a specified premium, typically 40 percent to 50 percent, above the conversion price for a specified period of time, typically at least 20 days out of a 30-consecutive trading day period. With the typical conversion premium for institutional quality issues in the 20 percent to 25 percent range, this feature comes into play when the common has advanced 75 percent to 85 percent from the level at issue. When invoked, the convertible can be called *even within the initial period of call protection.* Such strong common price gains means the convert will advance smartly as well. It also means that the conversion premium must decline to zero. Therefore the convert will underperform the common by the amount of the conversion premium, less any incremental income.

Chart 15 illustrates the effect of the conditional call feature on convertible performance. The Digital Equipment 8.0 percent convertible debenture was called pursuant to its conditional call feature. For some time, the conversion premium remained intact, until the common price soared above the conversion price. As the common price approached the conditional call price, the conversion premium eroded at a rapid pace, which indicated significant price underperformance compared to

CHART 15 Digital Equipment 8.0 Percent Convertible Debenture

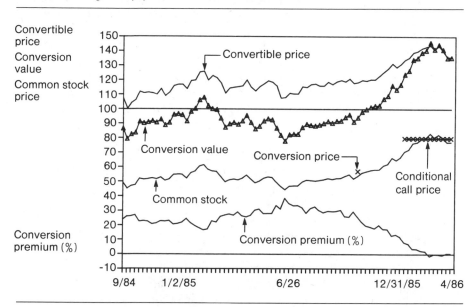

its common stock. It is important to note that the relative price relationship between the convertible and its common changes rather significantly as the conditional call price is approached.

The point is, as the likelihood of call increases, the more rapidly the conversion premium erodes, whether call protection is approaching expiration or as the conditional call feature comes into play. As call becomes more likely, the pace of erosion of any conversion premium accelerates.

WHY ARE CONVERTIBLES SO POORLY UNDERSTOOD?

Convertibles are poorly understood by most investors, even those who can be considered to be fairly sophisticated in other areas of investments. I believe there are two primary reasons for this misunderstanding, or perhaps more correctly, incomplete understanding of convertible securities. The first reason is the terminology; convertible terminology is so different from either traditional equity or fixed-income analysis that most investors are so preoccupied with understanding the terminology that they are unable to progress through it to analysis and investment strategies for convertibles. Most of the convertible questions I receive are about terminology; few are about investment strategies. Second, there is a shortage of convertible research sources to aid the typical investor, and those sources seem to be incomplete. As discussed above, most convertible services are little more than statistical compilations. The few services that rate convertibles do so inconsistently and almost universally embrace the "average convertible" methodology, which we have demonstrated as incomplete, particularly with regard to noncall protected issues.

In addition, there are those seemingly ubiquitous convertible phrases, ". . . the best of both worlds" and ". . . get paid while you wait." Both phrases, the former in particular, imply that convertibles will provide consistently superior returns in all market environments. Both are half-truths. The simple fact of the matter is that no single investment or type of investment can provide superior returns in all markets.

For these reasons, we encourage convertible investors to understand the concept of conversion premium, which has the dual role of the primary analytical tool for convertibles and as the indicator of convertible price performance relative to its underlying common stock. Then look at Charts 9 and 10, to see how convertibles actually perform. If necessary, go through each stage of the convertible-building cycle to understand how the basic components work.

An unanswered question remains, Why have most analysts used an incomplete view of convertible price action? The answer is a simple one, we believe, they probably did not look for better answers. We must remember that widespread availability of computer power is a relatively recent phenomenon. Convertibles require substantial quantities of number crunching and access to a broad data base. Until recently, those two factors meant mainframe computers and access to one of the few limited data bases or construction of a custom data base. More succinctly, in order to analyze convertibles, one needed a lot of money and expensive facilities. In the absence of money, analysts and academics probably hypothesized how convertibles would act and then searched for available data that supported the hypothesis. Since this is a relatively inefficient sector of the financial markets where the short lives of many convertibles prevented adequate time-series analysis, the investigators were able to find data to support the hypothesis of the convertible price line as presented in Chart 11. As is the case with other complex phenomena (financial markets, weather, politics, and history) where solid knowledge is small in relation to the sea of available data, and where the number of defined and precisely measurable variables is similarly small, it is often possible to find "evidence" to support more than one hypothesis. In a phrase, the hypothesis dominated the result. Since some people are lazy by nature, most convertible analysts and traders adopted this "theoretical view of a convertible."

INVESTMENT VALUE REVISITED

Referring to Chart 9, it should be noted that the investment or bond value, which is the theoretical value of a convertible excluding its conversion priviledge, is not a constant, stable number. The investment value will fluctuate according to interest rate trends in the fixed-income marketplace. Referring to Chart 14, we see that with yields rising from the late 1940s through the 1981–82 peak, that the effect of this trend would be to lower investment values of existing convertible securities. With the investment value falling, the downside protection of a convertible is eroded. In contrast, when interest rates fall, as has been the case from the 1981–82 interest rate peak through 1986, the investment value is rising which improves the defensive character of convertibles by raising the investment value floor.

SUMMARY OF ATTRIBUTES AND ANALYTICAL TOOLS

The most important characteristic of a convertible security is its ability to have less downside risk than its underlying common, which can shield the investor from unanticipated stock price declines. The downside protection feature derives from the convertible terms, primarily its relatively high-current yield, which means convertibles have less volatility than their commons. In general, convertibles seem to reflect about half of the price movement of their commons, although there is substantial variability among convertible issues. "Busted converts," issues that are selling primarily on a yield basis because the common stock declined substantially from the price when the convertible was issued, have low sensitivity to common price changes. Conversely, recently issued convertibles can reflect 60 percent to 80 percent of common stock appreciation but participate in just 25 percent to 40 percent of any unanticipated common stock declines, subject to specific terms. When appreciated substantially from its level at the time of issue of the convertible, the conversion premium has shrunk toward 0 percent and the current yield is much reduced from issue, the convertible approaches the state of being a perfect equity substitute. However, such convertibles have minimal defensive characteristics.

The key analytical tools of convertible analysis are, in order of importance, the conversion premium, call features, and breakeven. The conversion premium is also an indicator of the relative price performance of the convert versus its common. Rather than seek "low" conversion premiums, investors should identify "appropriate" conversion premiums relative to terms and price level. Investor expectations for the common stock also impact convertible terms, particularly the premium.

As discussed above, call features are critical to effective convertible analysis because the call option potentially limits convertible performance. Call protection enhances convertible performance by reducing the rate of erosion of the conversion premium when the underlying common stock is advancing. This, of course, improves the relative price performance of the convertible.

Breakeven is the most misunderstood of the convertible terms and analytical tools. Fortunately, it is not the most important tool. Breakeven analysis is most appropriate for "total return" accounts that are indifferent to return whether it be from current income or price change. Furthermore, such accounts must have explicit return targets and be essentially risk averse, so they will be tolerant of inferior total returns relative to the common should the common stock advance strongly. In my experience, there are few true total return accounts.

CONVERTIBLE INVESTMENT STRATEGIES

The attributes of convertibles make them appropriate for a wide range of investment objectives. The greatest value added of a convertible is its ability to decline less than its underlying common stock. In addition, convertibles generally provide more stable returns and have higher current yields than their commons.

The first law of convertible analysis is that the single most important determinant of the performance of a convertible is the performance of its underlying common stock. Therefore, it is imperative that an investor have a constructive outlook for the common before even considering the convertible.

RISK CONTROL STRATEGY—FOR CONSERVATIVE AND AGGRESSIVE ACCOUNTS

Convertibles are particularly useful in shielding investors from unanticipated common stock price declines. If an equity investment does not perform as expected, the loss can be reduced by the convert's premium expansion, because most convertibles will decline less than the common. This may be the most useful of convertible securities attributes. This strategy applies to both conservative and aggressive investors alike. Chart 16 presents the first two years of the IBM 7.875 percent convertible debenture, which represents the first half of the call protection period. From early 1986 through October 1986, the IBM stock declined approximately 25 percent. The convertible debenture declined about half that rate, as the conversion premium expanded from 20 percent to 40 percent. Although no investor intends to lose money, it is better to lose less. Part of this superior relative performance is attributable to the superior call protection. Conversely, the convertible substantially underperformed the common late in 1985 when the common advanced strongly.

The availability of convertibles can also broaden the effective investment horizon of more conservative or income-oriented accounts. For example, Digital Equipment may not be considered an appropriate

CHART 16 IBM 7.875 Percent Convertible Debenture

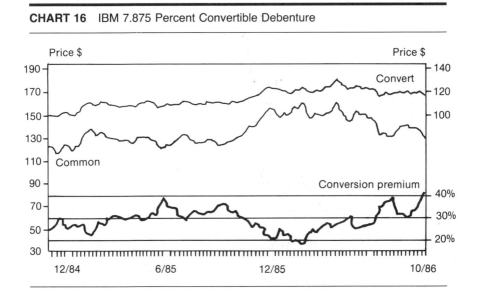

investment for many accounts because it pays no dividend as a matter of policy, or because of perceived volatility. Its 8.0 percent debenture due September 10, 2009, dealt with both problems and allowed participation in substantial price appreciation, as is reflected in Chart 15.

The Chi-Chi's 9.0 percent debenture due October 15, 2009, hit an "air pocket" late in 1984 when a rare management presentation was viewed negatively. The stock quickly declined 25 percent. However, the 9.0 percent convertible debentures declined just 9 percent as the conversion premium doubled, absorbing most of the shock. The protective power of convertibles was more dramatically displayed during the next two years when the stock fell by 50 percent, while the convertible debenture declined just 13 percent.

The Chi-Chi's example illustrates that convertibles can significantly reduce the downside risk associated with higher-P/E and higher-risk common stocks. It should be no'ed, however, that the performance of the debenture benefited fiom a rignificant decline in interest rates which raised the investment vɛ ue floor.

It appears that the greater the potential risk of a common stock, the greater the ability of the convertible to shield the investor from most of that risk. There is one notable exception—high relative price-earnings ratio stocks. The more popular a stock, the higher its relative price-earnings valuation, and, unfortunately, the less attractive the convertible from a defensive point of view, because the issuer will be able to command a higher conversion premium, a lower coupon, a shorter initial call protection period, or a combination. To the extent that a high multiple contributes to the risk of a common, it also reduces the defensive character of the convertible.

INCOME ACCOUNT STRATEGY

Investing in convertibles for income is probably the most traditional investment strategy because of the higher current yield from the convertible compared to the underlying common stock, while still getting some equity participation via the conversion privilege. The income account strategy is consistent with the "best of both worlds" concept. However, just buying and holding convertibles can involve significant opportunity losses at specific convertible price levels. We would encourage income investors to carefully scrutinize call features, being particularly sensitive to near-term expiration of call protection. There are numerous examples of convertibles selling above the call price with call protection about to expire. When a convertible is called, there is a potential loss of value, as described earlier. The greater potential loss for income-oriented investors, however, is the hidden loss of value due to the absence of call protection, which also was described above.

In some instances, convertibles may offer effective equity participation and/or diversification potential to investors with relatively high-current income requirements.

Incremental Income Convertibles. There are a few convertible debentures that offer incremental income relative to the common that are unlikely to be called. For example, the K mart 6.0 percent debentures are unlikely to be called even though the debenture is selling well above its call price and call protection has expired. It will not be called because the aftertax interest expense on the debenture is less than the cash dividends that would be paid on the common that would be issued on conversion. In 1986, the 4.2 percent current yield on the debenture is significantly above the 3.0 percent current yield on the common. So, if the convertible can be purchased close to its conversion value, the convertible is like a special class of common with a modestly higher yield. I call these "found-money convertibles." It is important to note that such issues are effective equity substitutes, which means they do not have the defensive characteristics typically associated with convertibles; they will not meaningfully shield investors from downside equity participation.

TOTAL RETURN STRATEGY

Total return is defined as price appreciation (growth) plus yield. The long-term average total return from equities is approximately 9 percent. A convertible's yield pickup can help meet or exceed the average return by purchasing a high-yielding convert that also has reasonable upside equity participation potential. For example, in March 1985, the Texas Industries 9.0 percent convertible debenture had a 9.7 percent current yield on its $93 price. Although the conversion premium was modestly above-average at 35 percent, the large income advantage (9.7 percent versus 2.8 percent for the common) resulted in a below-average 3.8 year break-even period. The convert was expected to capture about half the price appreciation of the common stock, which plus the good current yield could provide an attractive total return. As of October 1986, the common declined one point, which when combined with the only average yield, resulted in a well-below average return. The debenture actually appreciated 7.5 percent to par, courtesy of the general decline in interest rates and provided almost a 7 percentage point higher yield than the common. On balance, the debenture provided a good total return compared to historical averages. However, total return investing requires a disciplined explicitness of return requirements.

COMMON-CONVERTIBLE SWAP PROGRAM

The existence of convertibles and the awareness of price, conversion premium and call feature relationships suggest potential profit through an arbitrate program between the common and its convertible. Assuming the common stock has attraction, the swap out of the common into the convertible when the convertible is likely to capture most of the common's upside potential but is shielded from most of the downside potential because of likely conversion premium expansion, could enhance the overall return from investment in the particular equity. The history of the IBM 7.875 percent convertible debenture in Chart 16 provides an excellent example of the potential from this technique. Sale of the convertible for purchase of the common in mid-1985 set the stage for superior returns from the common through year-end. A reversal of this position, sale of the common for purchase of the convert when the conversion premium was a relatively low 20 percent set the stage for superior performance when the common declined subsequently.

There is always risk when positions are established, but use of the convertible, when and if appropriate, would minimize exposure to losses and provide at least partial appreciation during any stock advances, versus an unhedged investment program in just the common. We should note that going forward from current relationships, the swap potential of the IBM debenture will erode because half of the call protection period is over.

SUMMARY

Convertible securities are neither the best nor the worst of both worlds. Rather, each convertible is a hybrid, part common stock, part discount debenture, with specific performance attributes that will be determined by the performance of its underlying common stock and its specific terms. The most significant attribute of convertible securities in general is their ability to reduce risk, to provide less volatile returns than their underlying common stocks. Because of this, convertible securities have potentially broad application in investment portfolios.

As is the case with any investment, valuation parameters must be monitored closely to allow for improved returns and in order to avoid losses, both nominal and relative to the underlying common. Of particular importance is the call feature, which can produce losses including potentially significant hidden opportunity losses. The primary analytic tools are the conversion premium (which is also an indicator of relative price performance), call features and breakeven.

Convertible securities are another tool that can contribute to your investment success by increasing the total return from your portfolio and reducing your risk exposure. But like any tool, they must be used in the right way and in the right circumstances. For example, purchase of a convert with a high conversion premium will probably not provide rapid price appreciation; and the purchase of a convertible debenture at a price of 150 will not provide much less risk than the common.

◢ ENDNOTES

1. The two known sources are the *Value Line Convertibles* service and the *Convertible Issues Review* published by PNC Financial and prepared by the author.
2. Institutional Brokers Estimate System, July 17, 1986, p. 25.
3. Author and source unknown, except that it was probably a financial publication in the early 1970s.

SUGGESTED REFERENCES

Noddings, T. C. *Dow Jones—Irwin Guide to Convertible Securities.* Homewood, Ill.: Dow Jones-Irwin, 1973.

Lyons, A. S. editor, *Convertible Securities and Warrants.* New York, NY: Value Line, 1970.

Ritchie, Jr., J. C. "Convertible Securities and Warrants." In Handbook of Fixed Income Securities, eds. F. J. Fabozzi and I. M. Pollock. 2nd ed. Homewood, Ill.: Dow Jones-Irwin, 1986.

33

Zero Coupon Bonds

James L. Kochan
Vice President and Manager

Maureen Mooney
Assistant Vice President
Fixed Income Research
Merrill Lynch Capital Markets

Few recent financial innovations have had an impact upon the markets as great as that from the introduction in 1982 of zero coupon Treasury issues. In only four years, these securities have become staples of both actively and passively managed portfolios. They have also become key components of virtually every type of structured investment product and they have helped spawn a host of complex hybrid investment products and strategies. Hardly a month goes by without the discovery of yet another use for these instruments by investment bankers or portfolio managers.

Initially, Treasury zeros were offered as a solution to a serious problem with the concept of yield-to-maturity, a problem that took on greater importance with the emergence during the 1970s of unusually high bond yields and an unprecedented degree of interest rate volatility. Prior to 1970, with bond yields relatively low and stable, the yield-to-maturity (YTM) was an acceptable approximation of the total return one could expect from a note or bond.

Since 1970, however, the yield-to-maturity of a bond at the date of purchase has been far less helpful in predicting the actual return from

SOURCE: Adapted from *The Handbook of Treasury Securities*, ed. Frank Fabozzi, Probus Publishers, Chicago: 1986.

owning the security over a long holding period. In order for the realized total return from a bond to equal the time-of-purchase quoted YTM, each of the semiannual coupon payments must be reinvested at that purchase-date yield. When bond yields reached the 14 percent to 17 percent range, the YTM lost much of its earlier meaning. Investors recognized that achieving such exalted reinvestment rates on a consistent basis would be virtually impossible and that realized returns would be lower than the YTM. They began to search for alternative investments that promised true returns closer to prevailing (generous) market yields; that is, investments with little or no reinvestment risk.

Zero coupon notes and bonds were ideally suited to this problem because they do not make coupon payments but instead are sold at a deep discount to their face value. At maturity the zeros are redeemed at face value.[1] This aspect of zeros results in its price being more volatile than coupon issues of the same maturity. The introduction of TIGRs by Merrill Lynch in August 1982 was a major step forward in the evolution of this investment product, as they allowed a portfolio manager to eliminate both reinvestment risk and credit risk. While no investment vehicle entirely eliminates market risk, for a portfolio manager seeking to fund a well-defined earnings objective, the TIGRs were near perfect. Consequently, they were received enthusiastically and multiplied far beyond original expectations.[2] It should be noted that zero coupon bonds are also issued by corporations and municipalities. The latter are the so-called tax-free zero bonds. However, the U.S. Treasury zeros have the advantage over other zero issues in that they are also free of default and call risks.

THE TREASURY STRIPS

The introduction in early 1985 of the Treasury's book-entry zeros, or STRIPS (separate trading of registered interest and principal of securities), was a second milestone in the evolution of the market for zero coupon instruments. Producing the earlier Treasury-related zeros entailed costs such as custodial, legal, and insurance fees, which served to

---

[1] For example, a $1,000 face value zero coupon bond with a 10-year maturity priced to yield 10 percent would be sold at $376.89, as shown by the discount calculation given below, which assumes a semiannual payout:

$$P = \frac{\$1,000}{(1.05)^{20}} = \$376.89$$

[2] Over the years a variety of features have been added to zero bonds. Some corporate zeros provide for conversion of the bonds into common stock. Municipal zeros may permit conversion into tax-free coupon issues. Put features may be present, obligating the issuer to redeem the zero issue within a specified time.

limit the number of institutions creating these products. The Treasury's innovation allowed STRIPS to be created more efficiently which, in theory, expands the list of producers of Treasury zeros. Most of the primary dealers soon began to create and make markets in the STRIPS.

The Treasury facilitated the creation of this new product when it decided to allow trading, via the Federal Reserve's book entry system, of the individual interest and principal payments of some of its securities. The Treasury now conducts conventional auctions of notes and bonds that have the special feature of allowing the separate trading of each of the coupon payments and the corpus (principal). The successful bidders in the auctions of these designated issues can exchange the coupon issues for the component parts (which will be in registered form) and reoffer to investors each of the separate interest payments and the corpus. These reoffered instruments are, of course, zero coupon securities and are called STRIPS by market participants.

PORTFOLIO STRATEGIES

Because the accrued value of the Treasury zeros is taxable, these notes are usually employed in pension, IRA, and other tax-deferred accounts.[3] Portfolio applications of the Treasury zeros range from the most aggressive arbitrage strategies designed to profit from small fluctuations in yield spreads to holding the issues to maturity as part of a structured portfolio. In general, however, these applications may be grouped into three categories:

1. Active trading in response to variations in yield spreads.
2. Adjusting portfolio duration quickly and efficiently using zeros.
3. Structured portfolios.

ACTIVE TRADING OF STRIPS AND TIGRs

The bond market volatility of the past 10 years has created substantial opportunities to profit from short-term swings in market yield spreads. This has sparked the formation of a host of so-called arbitrage accounts that seek trading opportunities across a wide range of markets and sectors. Many specialize in the Treasury market, employing strategies such as yield curve arbitrage and/or trading the sector spreads. The latter would include active trading between Treasury zeros and coupon issues of the same maturity or duration.

As the charts of yield spread history show quite forcefully, there have been considerable opportunities to trade these spreads in the past year. Spreads between issues of comparable maturities have fluctuated

---

[3] For taxable investment accounts tax-free (municipal) zero bonds may be appropriate.

TABLE 1 Durations on Treasuries and STRIPS

Treasury Issue	Duration	STRIPS	Duration
6 ⅝s '88	1.89	8/15/88	2.02
6 ⅝s '89	2.79	5/15/89	2.77
7 ¼s '90	3.44	8/15/90	4.02
7 ½s '91	4.24	8/15/91	5.02
7 ¼s '93	5.54	8/15/93	7.02
7 ⅜s '96	7.01	5/15/96	9.02
7 ¼s '96	12.11	2/15/16	29.53

over wide ranges. While these variations suggest the potential for profitable trades, the investor must remember that in most instances, zeros and coupon issues of the same maturity are not comparable securities. These securities will often have substantially different durations, and the duration statistic is the more relevant measure of term to maturity.[4]

Table 1 shows the durations of coupons and STRIPS of similar maturities. A very useful attribute of duration is that it describes the relative price volatility of a set of securities. For example, durations of 30 years for the STRIPS of February 15, 2016 and 12.11 years for the Treasury 7 ¼ of May 15, 2011 imply that the price response of the STRIPS (to equal changes in yields) will be 29.53/12.11 = 2.44 times greater than on the Treasury bond.

Table 2 and spread charts (Figures 1–3) demonstrate that the

TABLE 2 Yield Spread Comparisons between Treasuries and STRIPS (from 7/85 through 7/86)

Treasury Issue	Maturity-Matched Spreads			Duration-Matched Spreads		
	Avg.	High	Low	Avg.	High	Low
2-year	2	22	−30	2	22	−30
3-year	15	30	−9	4	33	−16
5-year	25	43	−3	10	31	−10
7-year	22	40	−10	−5	26	−34
10-year	29	52	1	6	34	−22
20-year	30	57	−24	−8	20	−30
30-year	−20	30	−87	24	110	−14

[4] The standard term to maturity concept treats all cash flows equally. Duration expresses maturity as a weighted average of the present value of each of the cash flows of a bond. The duration of a zero coupon bond is always the time remaining to maturity as discussed in Chapter 41.

FIGURE 1 Spreads between Five-Year Treasury and STRIPS of the Same Maturity and Duration

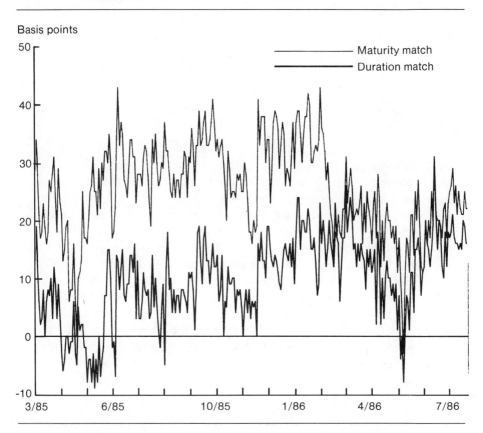

duration-matched spreads are considerably tighter than maturity-matched spreads. If the five-year Treasury notes are matched against zeros of similar duration (4.5 to 5 years) the average zero/coupon spread over the past 12 months has been approximately 10 basis points, whereas the five-year maturity-matched zero/coupon spread averaged 25 basis points.

The 10-year Treasury notes should be paired with zeros maturing in seven years. The average zero/coupon spread in these sectors has been approximately 5 basis points, with a range of −22 to 34 basis points. Thirty-year bonds should be paired with zeros maturing in the 11- to 12-year range. The average STRIPS-to-Treasury spread has been roughly 24 basis points, with a range of −14 to 110 basis points.

Variations in yield spreads between zeros and coupons of the same duration may arise because of a major change in the shape of the

FIGURE 2 Spreads between 10-Year Treasury and STRIPS of the Same
Maturity and Duration

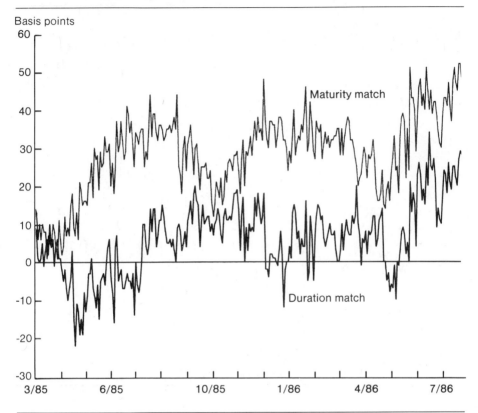

Treasury yield curve or because of unusual supply/demand shifts. A
theoretical equilibrium may be defined between a zero curve and the
coupon curve. The theoretical spot rate curve is used to represent that
relationship.

The theoretical spot rate curve derives an implied yield curve for
zero coupons from the Treasury yield curve. The starting points for the
theoretical curve are the two active Treasury zeros—the six-month and
one-year bills. Using these issues and coupon issues, it is possible to
define the implied yield of an 18-month zero, and then use that yield to
find the implied yield for a 24-month zero and so on along the full
maturity schedule. The cash flows from a note due in 1½ years can be
duplicated by using a six-month T-bill, a year bill, and a zero coupon
due in 1½ years, with par amounts equaling the coupon and principal
payments. The present values of a current 1½ year note and a synthetic

FIGURE 3 Spreads between 30-Year Treasury and the STRIPS of the Same Maturity and Duration

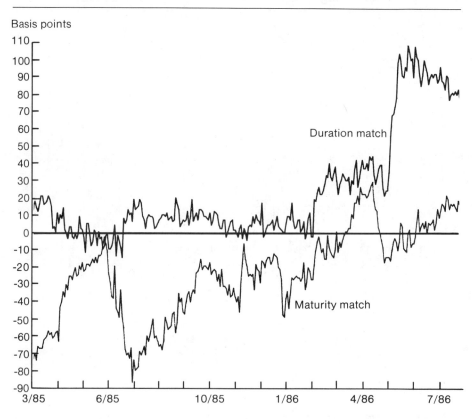

note should be identical. That value is the sum of the prices of the 6-month, 12-month and 18-month components. As the first two components are known, a unique solution for the price of the final component is possible. The discount rate that produces that solution is the theoretical spot rate for an 18-month zero. The example below illustrates this procedure. The unknown term X is the theoretical spot rate for a 1½-year maturity. The present value formulas for the synthetic note and the 8 percent note are also listed below. Because these two formulas are equal, it is possible to solve for X which in this case is 6.02 percent. This 18-month discount rate can then be used in conjunction with the 6- and 12-month rates to produce a solution for the two-year spot rate.

6 month T-bill	5.50%
1 year T-bill	5.60%
8% 1½-year note	6.00% (102.8286 price)

Present Value of Note   *Present Value of Synthetic*

$$\text{Price} = 1{,}028.286 = \frac{40}{(1.03)} + \frac{40}{(1.03)^2} + \frac{1{,}040}{(1.03)^3} = \frac{40}{(1.0275)} + \frac{40}{(1.028)^2} + \frac{1{,}040}{(1 + x/2)^3}$$

The theoretical spot rate curve may be viewed as defining an equilibrium between yields on zeros and Treasury notes and bonds. (See Figure 4.) Consequently, variations in zero yields away from the spot rate curve would generally signal trading or investment opportunities in the zeros or the equivalent coupons. These should be superior decision rules than those that rely solely upon historical spread relationships

FIGURE 4 Comparative Yields: TIGRs versus Treasuries, August 4, 1986

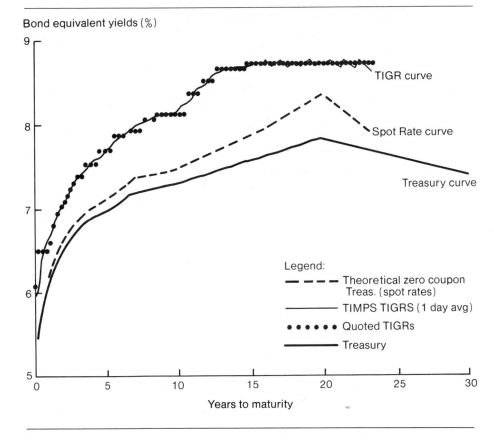

Bond equivalent yields (%)

TIGR curve

Spot Rate curve

Treasury curve

Legend:
- - - - Theoretical zero coupon Treas. (spot rates)
——— TIMPS TIGRS (1 day avg)
● ● ● ● ● Quoted TIGRs
——— Treasury

Years to maturity

between zeros and comparable coupons, as these historical relationships may become irrelevant if the yield curve changes abruptly. For example, a yield curve that is very steep between one and seven years produces a spot rate curve that rises even more rapidly than the coupon curve and rather wide equilibrium yield spreads between TIGRs and coupons in the two- to seven-year maturities. In contrast, zero-to-coupon yield spreads would be expected to be quite narrow if the yield curve were flat or inverted. In that instance, the theoretical spot curve would be very close to or even below the Treasury curve.

To be sure, yields on zeros have deviated from those implied by the spot rate curve, particularly when market yields are unusually high or low or when the yield curve has had a strange configuration. During the summer of 1984, yields on two- to seven-year zeros were consistently 10 to 30 basis points *below* the levels suggested by the spot curve. During that period, the relatively high level of yields prompted strong demand for zeros because of their inherent absence of reinvestment risk. In 1986, yields on zeros were much *higher* than suggested by the spot rate curve. Market yields had declined to the lowest levels in a decade, so the absence of reinvestment risk was apparently not of great value to investors. Consequently, zeros became very cheap to Treasury coupons.

Also in 1986, a combination of factors including strong foreign demand for the active Treasury notes and bonds created very wide spreads between these issues and virtually every other market. Active Treasuries became expensive relative to corporates, agencies, and municipals. The active Treasuries were also expensive relative to zeros. In the zero market, a very light supply of new issues, particularly in the longest maturities, also contributed to a sharper increase in yield spreads than would have been suggested by the theoretical spot curve. In fact, during most of 1986, it was profitable to convert STRIPS back into coupon issues while it was unprofitable for dealers to create STRIPS from most notes and bonds.

While the events of 1986 created unusually generous yield spreads, marking zeros as good values to long-term investors, the emergence of such unprecedented spreads made short-term trading between zeros and coupons unusually treacherous. The lesson to be gained from this experience is that in volatile markets, active trading between these instruments can be quite risky.

In an era of extraordinary volatility in market interest rates, intermediate and long zeros are not well suited for portfolios with short investment horizons. However, short-term zeros may be suitable for these investors.

ENHANCING PORTFOLIO RETURNS

Two strategies that have been employed by portfolio managers with longer investment horizons are creating combinations of zeros and coupons to enhance yield and using zeros to adjust the duration of the portfolio. Whenever zeros are unusually cheap relative to coupon issues, it often becomes possible to combine a zero with short to intermediate notes to replicate the duration of an active Treasury note. For example, an investor may be interested in purchasing the five-year Treasury note, which in August of 1986 had a duration of 4.24 years and a yield of 7.10 percent. By purchasing a combination of four-year notes and five-year zeros, the investor would have matched the duration of the five-year Treasury but captured a yield to maturity of around 7.25 percent. Thus the portfolio manager could have increased the yield on the portfolio without incurring more market risk than if he or she had purchased the five-year note. This type of transaction is best suited for investors who do not plan to trade the securities actively. Transactions costs would be greater than if only the five-year were purchased. Therefore, these costs would erode the yield advantage if the holding period were relatively short.

Zeros have also been used to adjust the duration of a portfolio with a minimum of transactions costs. A manager of a large portfolio has several options he may employ to lengthen the average duration of the portfolio in anticipation of a favorable interest rate outlook. He may sell several blocks of shorter maturities and purchase an equivalent amount of longer issues. At the minimum, he would incur considerable transactions costs. If he were dealing with corporate issues, he might also incur additional credit risk in the new portfolio. Another option would be to use fixed income options or perhaps futures contracts to adjust the portfolio duration. However, those products may not be available or appropriate to many portfolios. A third option would be to purchase a moderate amount of long-term zeros whose relatively long durations would significantly boost that of the entire portfolio. In addition, the eventual reversal of this position would also be relatively easier and less costly than if a substantial number of disparate issues had to be traded.

Finally, zeros can be used to adjust the price performance characteristics (the convexity) of a portfolio. A portfolio of mortgage-backed securities or callable corporate bonds may not perform well if interest rates were to decline sharply because prices of these issues may not rise very much. Adding long zeros to this type of portfolio would improve the price performance by introducing greater positive convexity into the portfolio.

ZEROS AND PASSIVE PORTFOLIO MANAGEMENT

Because they have no coupons to reinvest, zeros are particularly well suited for most passive portfolio management applications. Zeros have a locked-in rate of return to their maturity date compared with coupon issues where the return will vary depending on the available reinvestment rate for the coupons. This property of zeros can be used to offset a liability due in several years or to target an amount of money for some future date by acquiring a zero with a maturity date or duration equal to the target date.

IMMUNIZATION

In the case of any zero coupon bond, the duration is always equal to the time left to maturity. For coupon bonds, duration is a function of the coupon, maturity, and price. Duration is the time-weighted average of the present value of the future cash flows divided by the present value, expressed in years. In other words, it is the average life weighted by the present value of the future cash flows. Immunization is a technique that makes a portfolio behave as a single, zero coupon bond. It locks in a rate of return, although with a lesser degree of certainty than the zero coupon, and there is only one payment made which is at the target date (or maturity date). All coupon payments are put back into the portfolio. To immunize, the portfolio must have a market-weighted average duration equal to the target date. As long as the portfolio has an average duration equal to the time left to the target date, the portfolio will closely maintain its original yield. This calls for periodic adjusting in the portfolio because its duration will not move linearly toward its target date. Zeros in an immunized portfolio can minimize the amount of adjusting that is needed and thereby add stability to the portfolio.

In addition, zeros can extend the length of time that a portfolio can be immunized. In today's market, the longest duration on a coupon bond is between 7 and 10 years, which limits immunized portfolios to that horizon. Zeros, on the other hand, have durations beyond 20 years. They can be incorporated into a portfolio to extend the average duration and thereby extend the time the portfolio can be immunized. A simple way to immunize is to use only a zero and achieve a guaranteed yield with no adjusting necessary. However, an immunized portfolio that includes zeros, Treasuries, agencies, and corporates will be more diversified and can have whatever quality rating the investor seeks.

DEDICATION

Zeros are also effective in another passive management strategy, dedication. A dedicated portfolio is one in which the cash outflows from the portfolio (coupon and principal payments) are matched to a stream of liability payments. Most commonly, this stream is the retired lives portion of a pension fund. The benefit of a dedication program to the company is the difference between the cost of the portfolio and the present value of the future liabilities using an actuary's conservative discount rate (which is usually well below today's yields). This difference can reduce the contribution the company must make into the fund. As the outflows from the portfolio must be predictable, low coupon and noncallable bonds are frequently used. There is a scarcity of these types of issues with maturities in 1997–2005. Zeros, because they are available in a wide range of maturities, can fill this gap. The more closely the timing of the cash flows is matched to the liabilities, the less reliance upon an uncertain reinvestment rate and the more efficient the portfolio becomes. Zeros can also be used to offset a balloon payment in a dedicated portfolio or to dedicate an increasing liability stream, since they have no coupon payments to impact the earlier years.

DEFEASANCE

Defeasance is a specialized dedicated portfolio that is used to retire outstanding debt. This is accomplished by creating a portfolio of Treasury notes and bonds (or their equivalent such as STRIPS or TIGRs) in which the cash flows match those of the outstanding debt. These securities are then placed in an irrevocable trust. They allow the client to remove the debt from their books for financial reporting purposes and thus improve their debt-related ratios. Often, the cost of assembling the portfolio is likely to be below the par value of bonds being retired, so the issuer can realize a one-time increase in reported earnings. It is difficult to match the coupon and principal payments of a discount bond using current-coupon Treasuries. Zeros can facilitate this process and, in some cases, at a higher yield.

LOW-COST SYNTHETIC NOTES

Zero coupons can be used to create a synthetic Treasury note or bond, sometimes at a lower cost than actually buying the equivalent Treasury note. To create the synthetic note, the cash flows of the note must be duplicated with a series of zero coupons. For example, the cash flows of $1 million of the Treasury 8s of February 15, 1989 are listed in Table 3 along with a schedule of matching zeros. The amount of the coupon and principal received from the Treasury note becomes the par value of the zero coupon.

The $1 million of the Treasury 8s of February 15, 1989 at a price of 103.28125 (6.55 percent YTM) would cost $1,033,682. The zero portfolio, with the same cash flows, would cost $1,027,388, a savings of $6,294,

TABLE 3 Creation of a Synthetic Treasury 8% 1989 with a Par Value of $1 Million (yields as of 8/12/86)

Par	TIGR Price	TIGR Yield	Cost
40,000 2/15/87	97.080	6.10%	$ 38,832
40,000 8/15/87	94.139	6.20	37,656
40,000 2/15/88	90.849	6.55	36,339
40,000 8/15/88	87.714	6.70	35,086
40,000 2/15/89	84.565	6.85	33,826
1,000,000 2/15/89	84.565	6.85	845,649
Total			$1,027,388

	Cost	Yield
	$1,027,388	6.82%
	1,033,682	6.55
Cost/yield advantage of the synthetic	$ 6,294	+27 basis points

roughly ⅝ of a point or 27 basis points. While there is a savings in this example, this is not always the case. The yield spread between the Treasury note and the zero coupon of the same maturity influences the profitability of creating a synthetic Treasury. Another factor is the steepness of the zero yield curve in the shorter maturities. A steeper curve in those maturities will result in a lower profit than will a flatter curve. If the zero yield curve becomes inverted, creating a synthetic note with zeros could become very profitable. Investors should be prepared to take advantage of any anomalies in the zero-to-coupon yield spreads and enhance yield by replacing Treasuries with zeros.

34

International Fixed-Income Markets and Securities

Anthony W. Robinson
Vice President
First Chicago Investment Advisors
London, England

Stephen W. Glover
Vice President
Smith Barney, Harris Upham International
London, England

INTRODUCTION

In the last five years there has been a tremendous growth in both the number and complexity of fixed-income-related securities available to bond investors around the world. Interest rate swaps, Euro-commercial paper, options and futures on foreign bond markets and currencies, currency swaps, bonds denominated in synthetic currencies, such as the European Currency Unit, could all legitimately be dealt with in a chapter on global fixed-income markets. Needless to say such a relatively short chapter as this cannot hope to cover such a wide range of topics in anything resembling adequate detail.

We have decided to approach the subject of global fixed-income markets from the perspective of the U.S. institutional investor. Rather than concentrate on extensive descriptions of the types of assets available, we have instead focused exclusively on straight debt issued in the international capital markets and the effect the purchase of such debt has on U.S. institutional portfolios. In this chapter we consider the attraction of international bonds and their role in asset allocation for the U.S. institutional investor. We identify the two major asset classes which comprise international bonds, namely, international dollar and nondollar bonds, describe the characteristics of each and advance arguments in both cases for their inclusion in U.S. domestic investment portfolios. We necessarily devote greater attention to nondollar fixed income as it is much the larger, as well as the more complex and esoteric, of the two asset classes.

In our treatment of nondollar bonds we look at four principal aspects. We consider the *size* of the bond market outside the United States and suggest it is too large to be ignored. An analysis of historic *returns* is presented in which it becomes clear that considerable timing opportunities have existed between foreign bond markets and the U.S. market, and among the markets themselves. We look at the individual *risk* of each of the markets and of the asset class as a whole. Finally, we consider the intermarket *correlations* and advance the case that the inclusion of nondollar bonds improves the risk/return trade-off in both domestic bond and multiasset portfolios.

In the case of international dollar bonds we draw attention to the lower volatility such securities exhibit versus domestic bonds of like quality and duration. A chart is included to show the historical yield spread between international and domestic dollar bonds which shows that opportunities for yield enhancement have frequently been available. We also show that the correlation between the same two asset classes, while being expectedly high, is sufficiently less than perfect as to suggest diversification benefits in this area as well.

In the final section we discuss the components of return and propose a method for managing a nondollar bond portfolio, covering the four main areas of decision making: market allocation, duration decision (to reflect expected interest rate movements), maturity, and issue selection. We conclude with a presentation of the practical and administrative considerations of international fixed-income investment.

DEFINITIONS

One of the most confusing aspects of this subject to those who have little experience with international fixed-income markets is the nomenclature. To many, the terms *foreign bond, international bond, nondollar-denominated bond,* and even *Eurobond* are interchangeable. However, in practice, each has a very specific meaning. Rather than try to strictly define these terms, we describe below the meanings ascribed to them by practitioners—that is, the dealing community and investment professionals.

International Bonds

Throughout this chapter we refer to international bonds as being a fixed-income instrument which is either dollar or nondollar denominated, but where the original issuer is a non-U.S. organization, and/or the end buyer is a non-U.S. resident and/or the bond is distributed mainly outside the United States. In short, the term international bond is the generic name of the asset class. It *includes* dollar-denominated foreign bonds, Eurobonds (whether dollar denominated or not), and non-U.S. dollar-denominated bonds.

Nondollar-Denominated Bonds

As implied by the title, this group includes all bonds denominated in currencies other than U.S. dollars.

Foreign Bonds

These may be dollar or nondollar denominated. Their distinguishing feature is that they are issued by organizations/governments resident outside the country where they are sold and in whose currency they are denominated. For example, if the kingdom of Sweden were to issue, as it has done, U.S. dollar-denominated bonds in New York, register those bonds with the U.S. authorities, and sell them primarily to U.S. residents, those bonds would be foreign bonds, or, in this instance, more colloquially called Yankee bonds. Similar bonds issued in Tokyo and London, but denominated in yen and sterling, respectively, and registered with the relevant authorities, are called Samurais and Bull-dogs.

Eurobonds

Again, these may be denominated in any currency, but they are not registered with the authorities of the country in whose currency they are denominated, nor are they sold primarily to residents of that country. Thus, continuing with the above example, if the kingdom of Sweden issued a U.S. dollar-denominated bond, which was not registered with the U.S. authorities, in this case the Securities and Exchange Commission, and was initially distributed outside the United States, that bond would be a Eurobond. Similarly, if a U.S. corporation issued a dollar-denominated bond outside the United States without registering it with the SEC, that bond would also be a Eurobond. A schematic representation of these various types of bonds is shown in Figure 1.

CHARACTERISTICS OF THE NONDOLLAR FIXED-INCOME MARKETS

In this section we describe the size, return, and risk characteristics of the nondollar fixed-income markets, both individually and as a whole.

FIGURE 1

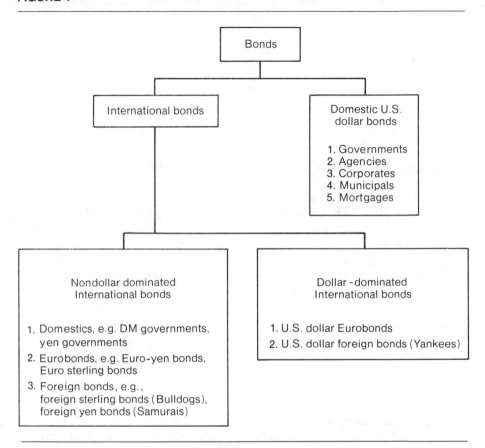

Size

The first consideration to bear in mind is the sheer size of the asset class. As of the end of 1985 the nominal value outstanding of the major world bond markets was $5.933 billion (see Figure 2), about 47 percent of which was represented by bond markets outside the United States. The largest non-U.S. bond market is Japan, which accounted for more than 18 percent of the world total, although all these foreign markets are large enough to warrant attention and close monitoring.

Figure 3 shows the investable capital market at the same date. This represents the total set of investment opportunities to the U.S. institutional investor. It comprises all the asset classes available, the proportions of which have been adjusted to exclude securities which are unlikely to be held for legal, trading, cost, or other reasons. Nondollar

FIGURE 2 Major World Bond Markets Nominal Value Outstanding (as of December 31, 1985—$5,933 billion)

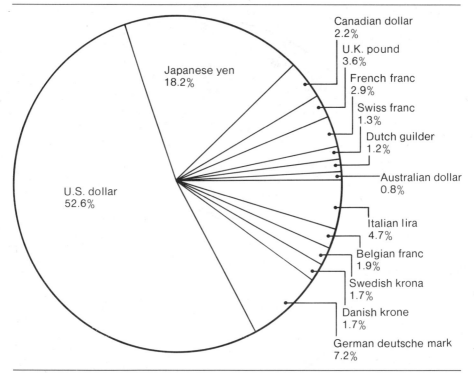

SOURCE: Salomon Brothers Inc.

bonds account for a huge 24 percent of this universe, the largest asset class of all. We shall give reasons why this proportion does not represent an optimal holding in institutional portfolios, but we shall suggest that this is far too large an asset class to be ignored.

It applies, ex ante, that the larger the opportunity set of investable asset classes (or of distinct markets and instruments within asset classes) the greater the number of investment options and, therefore, the greater the ability of the sophisticated investment manager or group of specialist managers to add value to securities portfolios. This does not mean that managers are not liable to make bad (or suboptimal) decisions which negatively impact performance, but that the *potential* for higher reward increases with the greater number of investment opportunities available.

In the extreme case where investments were confined to a single asset class there would be only two real decisions available to the manager: the choice of which securities to hold as against a specified

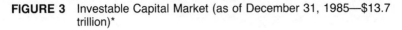

FIGURE 3 Investable Capital Market (as of December 31, 1985—$13.7 trillion)*

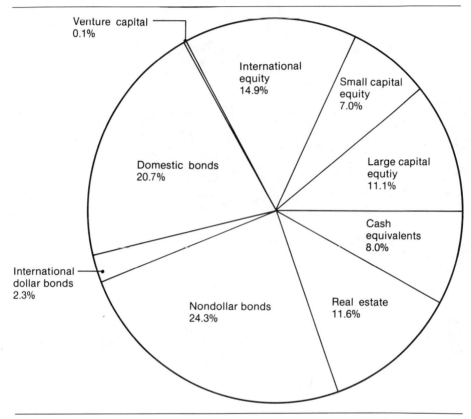

* Preliminary estimate.
SOURCE: First Chicago Investment Advisors.

index and the securities/cash mix. The existence of other asset classes displaying different return and (as we shall see) risk characteristics would severely restrict the ability of this manager to compete with his or her peers with wider discretion in asset allocation.

A number of institutional investors and their investment advisers, for example, perceived the U.S. dollar to be significantly overvalued against foreign currencies toward the end of 1984, which led to a substantial increase in the size and number of nondollar fixed-income portfolios as the vehicle best suited to exploit this opportunity. The reward was a return from nondollar bonds during 1985 of 37.6 percent compared to a return from domestic bonds of 21.3 percent and from domestic equities of 32.2 percent. Although we cite these data with the benefit of hindsight, most investment managers and economists would have agreed beforehand that a significant downward correction in the external value of the U.S. dollar was inevitable. The only point we wish to emphasize is not that investment managers are able to predict the future, but that in the absence of discretion to invest in foreign fixed-income markets these opportunities would have been unavailable.

Return—Historic

Table 1 shows the annual returns in both local currency and dollar terms of the major world bond markets over the period 1978–85. Although Japan was the only market to outperform the United States in dollar terms over the whole period, nonetheless in only one of the eight years, 1984, was the United States the best performing market. Furthermore, the range of dollar-adjusted returns, as seen in the final column, has been consistently large and has averaged 32 percent for the period, suggesting a very large scope for active market allocation decisions.

Return—Expected

Although Table 1 shows clearly that there have been frequent opportunities to increase the return of an otherwise all-dollar bond portfolio by using, on occasion, certain nondollar bond markets, it is not possible to argue that any single bond market, whether United States or non-United States, will produce a persistently higher rate of return in the long term after foreign exchange movements have been taken into account. The subject of forecasting the returns from nondollar bond markets over shorter time periods is dealt with in some depth later in this chapter. But, in the long term, it is the inflation rate which determines the bond yields in any country. However, relative inflation rates also determine, in the long term, the rate of exchange between one currency and another. Thus an economy with a low rate of inflation, for example, Germany, and consequently a comparatively low bond yield, will also have, by definition, a relatively strong currency. The return from the German bond market over the long term should equate to the returns from higher yield markets which have had correspondingly weaker currencies. Figure 4 supports this hypothesis. There have been periods when nondollar bonds have outperformed their domestic counterparts and vice versa. But over a longer time span the returns from both asset classes tend to equality.

This is in complete contrast to the likely future returns from non-U.S. equity markets as compared to the U.S. equity market. If we accept that equity prices are a function in the long term of corporate profits, then a less mature economy which generates a high rate of economic growth and, therefore higher levels of corporate profits, will

TABLE 1 Percent Returns from World Bond Markets, 1978–1985 (annualized)

	United States	Canada		Germany		Japan		United Kingdom		Switzerland		Netherlands		France		Non-dollar bonds	Percent range in US$ Terms
		L.C.	US$	L.C.	US$	L.C.	US$	L.C.	US$	L.C.	US$	L.C.	US$	L.C.	US$		
1978	-0.1	2.2	-5.5	1.1	16.2	7.3	31.8	-2.7	3.2	10.3	34.7	6.4	22.1	17.0	31.1	18.5	40.2
1979	1.9	-1.7	-0.6	1.6	7.3	-3.3	-21.5	3.2	12.4	-2.4	-0.6	2.8	6.8	-3.5	0.1	-5.0	33.9
1980	-0.8	3.7	1.7	1.8	-10.6	4.4	22.9	19.7	28.9	0.8	-9.6	5.6	-5.8	3.7	-8.1	13.7	39.5
1981	4.0	-3.0	-2.4	5.1	-8.4	14.3	5.5	1.6	-18.9	-0.3	-1.6	6.4	-8.5	6.0	-16.0	-4.6	24.4
1982	31.3	41.4	35.8	20.8	14.2	10.4	3.3	49.3	26.4	12.4	1.2	23.2	15.8	20.2	1.9	11.9	34.6
1983	4.1	10.4	9.5	5.5	-7.7	10.9	12.6	12.6	1.1	3.4	-4.8	6.4	-8.6	19.8	-2.8	4.4	21.2
1984	14.3	15.2	8.8	14.7	-1.0	11.5	2.7	8.9	-13.1	2.4	-14.6	13.2	-2.6	18.0	1.5	-2.0	28.9
1985	28.5	24.8	17.5	10.9	43.4	9.1	37.3	12.5	40.6	5.8	34.3	10.2	42.7	18.2	52.8	37.2	35.3
1978–1985	9.8	10.8	7.4	7.4	5.4	7.9	10.4	12.2	8.3	3.9	3.5	9.1	6.5	12.1	5.7	8.5	32.3 (avg.)

SOURCE: Salomon Brothers Inc.

FIGURE 4   Domestic and Nondollar Bonds

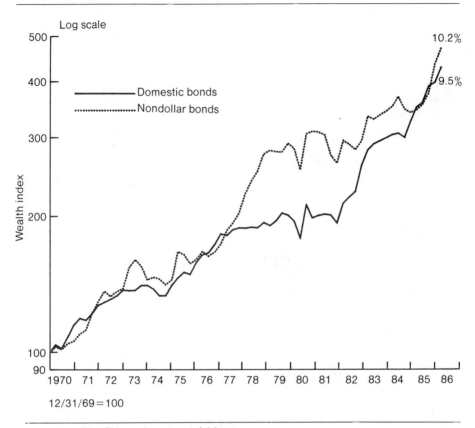

SOURCE: First Chicago Investment Advisors.

generate higher equity returns than a more mature economy, where
economic growth has stabilized at a somewhat lower level.

An analysis of the longer term equity returns from the Far Eastern
markets compared to the U.S. and Continental European equity markets
supports this general statement.

In order to argue that one bond market will, over the long term,
outperform another, one has to demonstrate that there are higher,
sustainable, *real* interest rates in that economy. Given the free movement of capital between the major Western economies, it is reasonable
to suppose that any structural differences in real interest rates will be of
a temporary nature, due to the force of arbitrage. We cannot, therefore,
argue for the *permanent* inclusion of nondollar bonds in a U.S. portfolio
on the basis of return alone.

Risk

Risk as we define it here is not that normally associated with fixed-income investments: that is, default risk, reinvestment risk, and, in the case of international securities, sovereign risk as well. (We deal with default and sovereign risk in some detail later.) Where these risks are perceived they affect levels of yield in a positive manner and are indeed largely avoidable by adherence to high-quality ratings and the use of zero coupon bonds and modern immunization techniques. In other words they are risks which have been absorbed in the marketplace and translated into levels of certain returns. The risk which is more difficult to avoid is that of uncertainty, and involves fluctuations in security values which are unanticipated and difficult to forecast due to the lack of privileged information. Speculators gamble on it with the odds stacked against them. Prudent asset allocation does not, but strives to diversify its impact to the greatest extent possible.

The risk of uncertainty is statistically quantifiable in terms of volatility or standard deviation. The principal forces which govern it are short-term changes in interest rates, duration, and the dynamics of the foreign exchange markets.

Duration measures the sensitivity of the price of a bond to a given change in yield. It is a better indicator of potential bond volatility than is maturity as it takes into account the level of coupon payment as well as the term outstanding. Briefly put, a bond with the same maturity but a higher coupon than another will exhibit lower price sensitivity if other things remain equal. Duration, however, does not account properly for very large shifts in yields or for *non*parallel movements in the yield curve. Nor is it an adequate measure of relative risk except when interest rate changes are the same across markets, a clearly unacceptable assumption. In the extreme case where interest rates, and consequently prices, were stable, a higher duration would fail to denote higher volatility.

Duration, therefore, is somewhat less than half the story in the determination of risk. Standard deviation, on the other hand, will capture the risk inherent in yield movements and their throughput effect on prices via duration. Standard deviation measures the probability of return expectations being realized. The greater the standard deviation of a securities market the greater the chance of unexpected surprises to the investor.

Table 2 shows the standard deviations of total return for the major world bond markets over the period 1975 to 1985 in local currency and U.S. dollar terms. It will be seen that all the nondollar bond markets except Canada and the United Kingdom have proved themselves less risky than the U.S. Treasury market when measured in local currencies. However, they are all more risky than the United States when the

TABLE 2 Major World Bond Market Risk Statistics, 1975–1985*

	Annualized	
Country	Standard Deviation Local Currency Terms	Standard Deviation U.S. Dollar Terms
Canada	11.70%	13.79%
France	8.05	14.51
Germany	5.07	14.27
Japan	4.68	14.07
Netherlands	6.06	13.97
Switzerland	5.70	15.91
United Kingdom	11.72	18.35
Nondollar bonds		11.90
United States		8.02

* 132 monthly observations from December 31, 1974 to December 31, 1985. All returns dollar adjusted.

SOURCE: First Chicago Investment Advisors.

returns are dollar adjusted. The reason is simple: foreign exchange volatility compounds the risk of the local market to the domestic investor. It is principally the risk of foreign exchange which has deterred so many U.S. institutions from investing abroad. Much of the reason for this has been lack of knowledge and understanding of the currency markets and their perception as an esoteric and, consequently, dangerous area. Furthermore the sheer size, diversity, and growth of the U.S. economy have in the past led to perceptions that adequate return opportunities were available at home. However, certain factors have led to an increasing awareness, in particular the greater dependence of the U.S. economy on international trade, the detrimental effects on the balance of payments which have resulted from an overvalued dollar, and the importance of foreign investment in funding a large domestic budget deficit. Figure 5 shows the extent to which the return from nondollar bonds has been a function of foreign exchange. What emerges is that over short, specific time periods the proportion of return due to foreign currency movements has been considerable, which is both a risk and an opportunity, but that over the longer term currency tends to have a much lesser significance.

One final point before we leave this section is that the standard deviations shown in Table 2 are very period specific. Figure 6 shows the trailing 24-month standard deviations for the nondollar bond market as a whole in U.S. dollar terms. In other words the standard deviations have been calculated over every 24-month subperiod over the period 1977 to 1985. It may seem somewhat obtuse to talk about the "risk of the risks," or gamma, but this figure clearly demonstrates that the risk itself

FIGURE 5   Currency Effects on Nondollar Bonds: Nondollar Bonds in Local
Currency and Dollar-Adjusted Terms

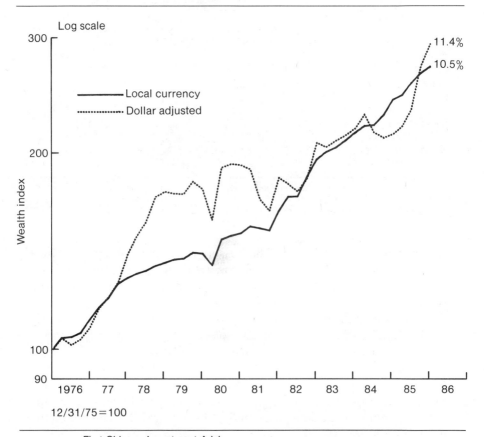

SOURCE: First Chicago Investment Advisors.

has been unstable. We must therefore be very careful when defining the
risk of nondollar bonds as being a specific number.

THE ROLE OF NONDOLLAR BONDS IN INSTITUTIONAL PORTFOLIOS

The return and risk criteria which we dealt with in the two preceding
sections can be viewed as opposite sides of the same coin. As a general
statement, greater return cannot be achieved without the acceptance of
higher risk. This would seem to imply that nondollar bonds are
unattractive to the U.S. investor in the longer term, owing to the fact
that they exhibit higher risk for no greater expected return. Indeed, in

FIGURE 6   24-Month Trailing Standard Deviation for Nondollar Bonds

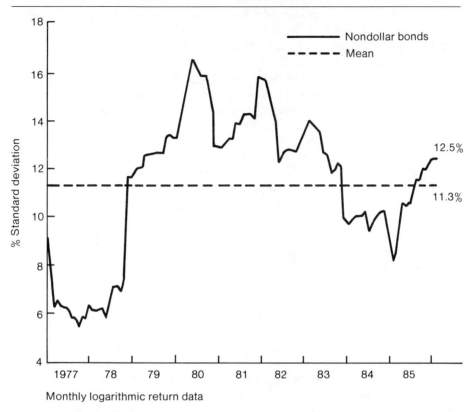

SOURCE: First Chicago Investment Advisors.

the case of direct and sole investment in nondollar bonds this would be true. What we now seek to show is that when nondollar bonds are *combined* with other asset classes a superior trade-off between risk and return is achievable for the overall portfolio. In other words, if we can demonstrate that the inclusion of nondollar bonds in a dollar-based portfolio reduces overall portfolio risk per unit of return (which is the same as increasing return per unit of risk), we can establish a case for a permanent *normal* allocation to the asset class.

The *normal* portfolio is that combination of assets or asset classes which the investor should hold when his or her forecast returns do not differ from those implied by the market; that is, when he or she believes all assets to be fairly priced.

The normal portfolio for any particular investor should comprise assets held in proportions which maximize returns for a chosen level of risk. Investors vary in the degree of risk they are able to tolerate, and should therefore differ in their choice of normal portfolio. In practice, of course, many investors use established passive indexes as proxies for their normal portfolios, as these represent convenient and accepted yardsticks of performance. This concept of the normal portfolio can be applied at any level of portfolio construction. It can be used to specify the policy weights for asset classes in an overall asset allocation context or for markets within asset classes, or for securities within markets. The return generated by the normal portfolio is the one the investor will obtain in the absence of any active decisions.

There is one force which operates in the opposite direction and serves to *reduce* risk in multiasset portfolios: imperfect correlation. Although markets fluctuate, they do not do so in perfect harmony. Consequently, the risk of allocating funds to a particular investment is not the total risk of that investment weighted by the proportion it represents in the overall portfolio, but the *marginal* risk it contributes to the portfolio given both its innate risk and the lack of correspondence of its performance with that of other assets held.

The correlations of bond markets including the United States over the period 1975 to 1985 are contained in Table 3. The numbers for nondollar markets against the United States are considerably less than unity. Furthermore the correlation for nondollar bonds as a whole is lower when including foreign exchange than in local currency terms, as shown in Table 4. The significance of these correlation data is shown in Figures 7 to 9. Figure 7 shows various combinations of U.S. and nondollar bonds in terms of risk and return over the period 1974 to 1985. Although over this specific period nondollar bonds outperformed domestic bonds, the key point is that by adding increments of nondollar bonds to a domestic bond portfolio, *the risk per unit of return* on the resulting portfolio was initially reduced.

Asset allocation research suggests that the larger the number of distinct investable asset classes used in a "normal" portfolio, the lower the level of risk achievable over time for each unit of return. (Brinson, Diermeier, and Schlarbaum, 1986). Applying this observation to the conclusions drawn from Figure 7 implies that there should be a normal allocation of around 25 percent to non-U.S. bonds within an otherwise domestic bond portfolio. This percentage is significantly less than that suggested by size alone but still represents a normal commitment to foreign fixed-income investment considerably in excess of the current allocation among institutional investors in the United States.

The reason these two proportions differ markedly is that there continues to exist a high degree of segmentation among the major world bond markets. If we could envision a single world bond market, by contrast, and if we were to assume a single currency and no restriction on capital movements, then we could conceive of a normal world bond

TABLE 3 Major Bond Market Correlation Matrix, 1975–1985* (based on logarithms of monthly returns)

	Canada	France	Germany	Japan	Netherlands	Switzerland	United Kindgom	Nondollar Bond	United States
Canada	1.000								
France	0.369	1.000							
Germany	0.460	0.774	1.000						
Japan	0.282	0.509	0.564	1.000					
Netherlands	0.460	0.795	0.934	0.544	1.000				
Switzerland	0.454	0.713	0.858	0.579	0.832	1.000			
United Kingdom	0.389	0.367	0.435	0.357	0.454	0.434	1.000		
Nondollar bond	0.484	0.670	0.786	0.865	0.777	0.760	0.700	1.000	
United States	0.766	0.262	0.377	0.263	0.414	0.377	0.313	0.420	1.000

* 132 monthly observations from December 31, 1974 to December 31, 1985. All returns dollar adjusted.

SOURCE: First Chicago Investment Advisors.

TABLE 4 Historical Performance—Correlation Matrix (monthly returns, December 31, 1974–December 31, 1985)

	Nondollar Bonds/$	Nondollar Bonds/LC	U.S. Bonds
Nondollar bonds/dollars	1.000		
Nondollar bonds/local currency	0.668	1.000	
U.S. bonds	0.420	0.590	1.000

SOURCE: First Chicago Investment Advisors.

FIGURE 7 Risk and Return—U.S. and Nondollar Bonds

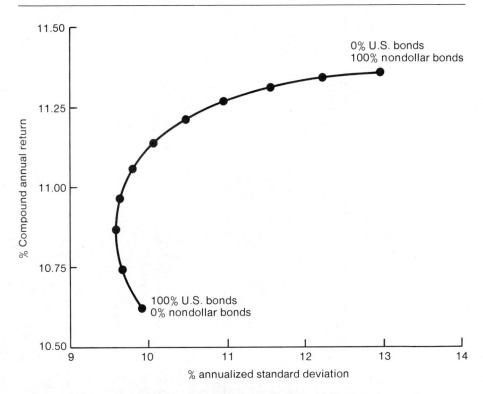

Based on 44 quarterly observations: 12/31/74 — 12/31/85

SOURCE: First Chicago Investment Advisors.

FIGURE 8 Risk and Return—60/40 Stock/Bond Mix and Nondollar Bonds

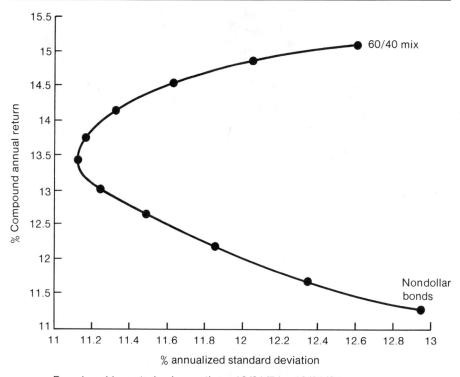

Based on 44 quarterly observations: 12/31/74 — 12/31/85

SOURCE: First Chicago Investment Advisors.

portfolio as being composed of all significant bond markets in the world in proportion to their market value. A significant home bias would, in this idealistic state, add to the risk of such a portfolio and limit its return potential. Not many people would argue in favor of Virginians solely buying bonds issued in Virginia. And in an integrated world bond market Americans would be ill-advised to restrict their fixed-income investments to the United States.

The lower the degree of integration, however, the greater will be the home bias. We must reemphasize at this point that we are discussing the normal portfolio—that collection of fixed-income investments that should be held in the absence of any specific return assumptions or other value judgments. Our argument is that given that world bond markets are neither totally integrated (suggesting a market capitalization weighted global bond portfolio) nor totally segmented (suggesting a 100

FIGURE 9   Risk and Return—Median Large-Plan and Nondollar Bonds

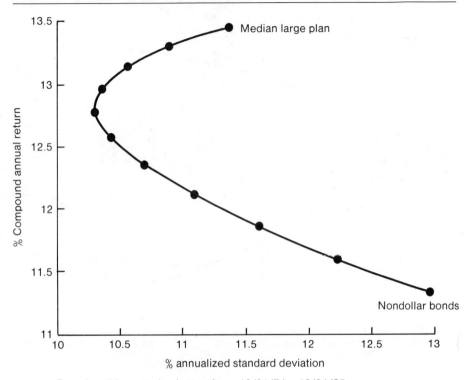

Based on 44 quarterly observations: 12/31/74 — 12/31/85

percent home bias) the normal allocation to nondollar bonds ought to be a proportion greater than zero, but less than the 47 percent suggested by size alone. In other words, the degree of integration is not sufficiently low as to justify the excessive degree of home bias currently observable.

In the past, assets of the typical U.S. pension plan were largely restricted to domestic equities and bonds in roughly a 60/40 percent proportion. Figure 8 shows the effect, given historic returns, volatility, and correlations, of adding increments of nondollar bonds to such a dollar portfolio over the same time period as Figure 7. Although, in this case, the return from nondollar bonds was lower than a straightforward 60/40 equity/bond portfolio, the low correlation between the two asset classes ensured that the risk per unit of return again declined initially as a result of the inclusion of nondollar bonds.

We can pursue this argument further. If we add increments of nondollar bonds over the same period to the median performing large domestic pension plan (Figure 9) we see that, again, nondollar bonds reduce the risk per unit of return of the whole portfolio. This is because the other asset classes in which the median large U.S. pension plan has invested have different risk/return characteristics. We cannot argue that nondollar bonds will increase the return on a portfolio—that depends on the specific historic time period chosen—but we can say that nondollar bonds have in the past *reduced the risk per unit of return*. By so doing the use of nondollar bonds allows the investor to pursue higher return opportunities elsewhere.

As long as returns from different assets are not subject to exactly the same risks, the overall risk of an efficient portfolio of these assets will tend to be lower than the risk of an individual component. Only when either the specific risk of an asset class is too high and/or its correlation with other asset classes too great will there be little opportunity of reducing overall portfolio risk by its inclusion.

On this last point Figure 6 shows that although the specific risk of nondollar bonds has varied considerably in the past, it has shown no sign of a sustained increase over time. Similarly, Figure 10 shows the stability of the correlation between nondollar and domestic U.S. bonds. The same technique of plotting the correlation between the two asset classes over every 24 months within the period 1972–85 is used. Again, although the correlation has fluctuated sharply, it has always been low and shows no sign of any recent increase.

THE ROLE OF INTERNATIONAL DOLLAR BONDS IN INSTITUTIONAL PORTFOLIOS

Most of our discussion of the arguments for using international bonds has centered on nondollar bonds because the case for these is more complex and therefore worthy of deeper analysis. The rationale for considering international dollar bonds, that is, dollar-denominated Eurobonds and foreign bonds (Yankees), in U.S. institutional portfolios is more straightforward.

Figure 11 shows the size of the Eurodollar and Yankee bond markets as of December 3, 1984. Although they represent only 10.9 percent of the total dollar bond market they are nevertheless of substantial absolute size, totaling some $340 billion. The liquidity of both Euros and Yankees is not therefore a constraint. As with nondollar markets, the mere size of the international dollar fixed-income securities outstanding should be sufficient reason to prompt U.S. investors to consider them as a longer term medium of investment.

Figure 12 shows the cumulative return from international dollar bonds compared to domestic bonds. Over time, Eurodollar and Yankee bonds have tended to outperform domestic fixed-income securities. This

FIGURE 10 24-Month Trailing Correlation—Domestic Bonds and Nondollar Bonds

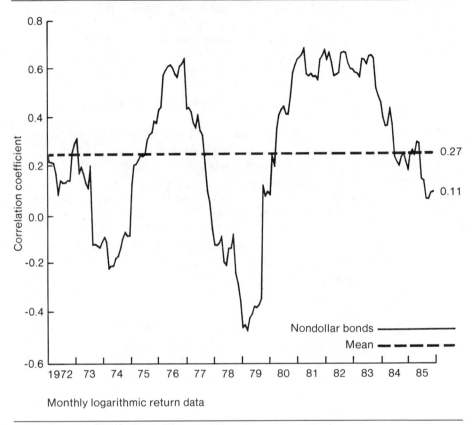

Monthly logarithmic return data

SOURCE: First Chicago Investment Advisors.

outperformance has not been due to differences in duration. The Eurodollar bond market as a whole has a shorter maturity than the domestic U.S. market, but this is offset by the inclusion of the returns from Yankee bonds (which have a duration of 6.4 years against 3.9 years on Eurodollar bonds as of March 1986) in our computation of international dollar bond returns in Figure 12.

One possible reason for this higher return could be due to the different type of default risk inherent in international dollar bonds. Both domestic and international dollar bond issuers sometimes default on their fixed-income obligations because of their financial problems. However, there is a further default risk associated with international dollar bonds in that otherwise financially healthy borrowers in these markets may be prevented from making coupon and capital payments

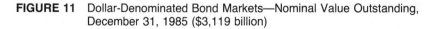

FIGURE 11   Dollar-Denominated Bond Markets—Nominal Value Outstanding, December 31, 1985 ($3,119 billion)

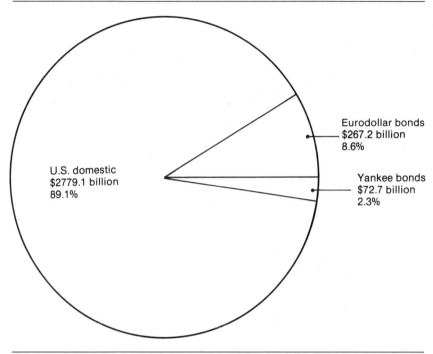

Eurodollar bonds
$267.2 billion
8.6%

U.S. domestic
$2779.1 billion
89.1%

Yankee bonds
$72.7 billion
2.3%

SOURCE: Salomon Brothers Inc.

by the governments of the countries in which the borrowers are resident. This second type of default risk is known as sovereign risk and it is absent from the domestic U.S. bond markets. If investors in Eurodollar and Yankee bonds are rational, and we must assume they are, they will demand a higher return from these bonds to compensate them for their greater default risk. Whether the extra return is *sufficient* compensation for the extra default risk is for the investor to decide. In the opinion of the authors, prudent quality constraints on bonds purchased in the international dollar bond markets can reduce sovereign risk to a negligible level.

Figure 13 shows the historical yield spread between Eurodollar and domestic bonds. Although the yield spread has been volatile, it has tended to favor Euros, as is indicated by the higher returns from international dollar bonds in Figure 12. This volatility in the yield spread is another way of saying that there is an imperfect correlation between the international and domestic bond markets. Table 5 shows these correlations. As one would expect, the coefficients are high, but they are

FIGURE 12   Dollar-Denominated Bonds

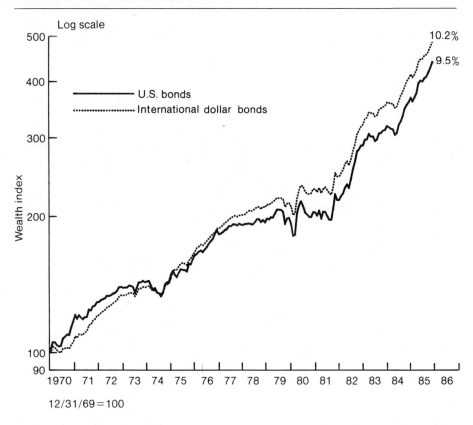

SOURCE: First Chicago Investment Advisors.

sufficiently less than perfect as to suggest that investors may profit from switching opportunities between the two markets *and* some diversification benefit if both domestic and international dollar bonds are held in a combined portfolio.

Finally Table 6 shows the standard deviations of the same two asset classes. It can be seen that the volatility of international dollar bonds is much lower than for domestics. There is at least one good reason for this. Many holders of such bonds are foreigners whose base currency is not dollars. There tends to be a positive relationship between U.S. dollar strength and interest rates. For example, in times of rising domestic interest rates U.S. financial assets become relatively more attractive to foreigners, who consequently purchase dollars to take advantage of the opportunity. Hence for, say, a German investor a rise in U.S. interest rates will negatively impact the valuation of his international dollar bond

FIGURE 13 Yield Spread—Global-Euro Bond Index—Domestic Bond Index

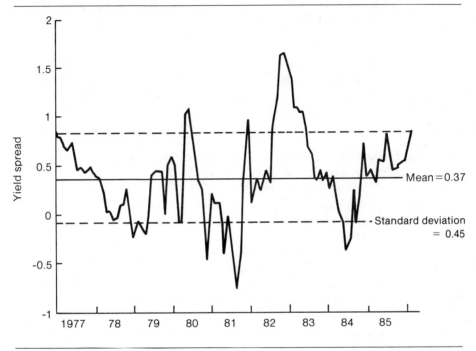

SOURCE: First Chicago Investment Advisors.

portfolio but this will tend to be offset by a currency gain. As a result, he will be less likely to trade his portfolio than the domestic investor.

International dollar bonds should therefore be a permanent part of dollar bond portfolios. In the longer term, their return is greater than domestic bonds, and they offer diversification benefits. Portfolio managers should overweight Eurobonds above this permanent normal

TABLE 5 Historical Performance—Correlation Matrix (monthly returns, December 31, 1977–December 31, 1985)

	Eurodollar Bonds	Foreign U.S. Bonds	Domestic U.S. Bonds
Eurodollar bonds	1.000		
Foreign U.S. bonds	0.900	1.000	
Domestic U.S. bonds	0.902	0.949	1.000

SOURCE: Salomon Brothers Inc.

TABLE 6 International Dollar Bond Risk Statistics, December 31, 1969–
December 31, 1985

	Standard Deviations (percent)
International dollar bonds	7.0%
U.S. domestic bonds	8.8

SOURCE: First Chicago Investment Advisors.

---

weighting when the expected returns from international dollar bonds
are greater than those from domestic bonds, and underweight them
when their expected returns are lower.

In this section we have presented the reader with data and analysis of
the historic returns, risks, and diversification benefits of both dollar- and
nondollar-denominated international bonds. We have advanced what
we hope is a persuasive case for their use both as an integral part of a
normal U.S. institutional portfolio *and* as a vehicle for pursuing abnormal return opportunities when these are perceived. We now shift our
emphasis to the practical aspects of managing an international *nondollar*
bond portfolio. We could, of course, do this for international dollar
bonds as well but this would lead to unnecessary repetition and
confusion. We consider the principal components of return, the decisions facing the portfolio manager, the indexes available for performance measurement purposes and the day-to-day realities of trading in
foreign bond markets.

REQUIRED AND EXPECTED RETURNS

Although we argued in a previous section that in the *longer term* all bond
markets will produce similar returns if those returns are measured in a
single currency, it is nevertheless possible to construct a framework for
assessing the strategic attractiveness of one bond market against another. In this section we present such a framework. We discuss first the
subject of required return; that is, that return a U.S. investor should
require in order to induce him or her to invest in a bond market, and go
on to deal with the components of expected return from nondollar bond
markets. Finally, we combine the two to suggest a measure of the
short-term attraction of one market against another.

Required Return

Before an investor attempts to forecast a return from any asset class, in
this case bonds, it is first useful to consider what minimum level of

return that investor should demand. In other words, it is useful to establish a hurdle rate against which to compare forecast return in order to arrive at a judgment of how much to invest in a particular area. It has become a widespread approach in capital market practice to determine the level of return available at no risk and then to assess any possibilities of higher return in the light of the extra risk that these incur. This is the methodology we shall employ here. The risk-free rate to the U.S. investor is commonly defined as that obtainable on Treasury bills. If we buy longer bonds the investor requires a higher return than that available on cash equivalents in order to compensate him for the higher level of risk inherent in those securities. If interest rates rise, long bond prices will fall entailing capital losses for investors, and vice versa. An analysis of historical bond returns in the United States (Ibbotson Associates, 1985) shows that bonds have indeed produced a higher return than cash over time. This higher return is known as the maturity premium on bonds. It is that return demanded by investors over and above the return on risk-free assets; that is, Treasury bills. The most satisfactory empirical method of estimating this maturity premium is to analyze time series data on inflation and money market rates and returns from longer bonds over as long a period as possible and determine what the historical differential has been. It is then possible to make some estimate of the future real returns investors are likely to demand.

We have already suggested that longer-term returns from fixed-income markets tend to equality when measured in a common currency. If so, it follows that maturity premiums will tend to be similar across markets. Consequently, the return which the U.S. investor requires on domestic bonds is a good proxy for the return required from other bond markets. Thus:

Required return = U.S. inflation + Bond maturity premium

Expected Return

The most obvious breakdown of expected return from nondollar bond markets is between foreign exchange movements and the return generated by the securities themselves in local currency terms.

Foreign Exchange

In an actively managed portfolio of nondollar fixed-income securities an assessment must be made of the likely return from movements in the dollar against foreign currencies. We do not attempt to provide an exhaustive summary of the various theories purporting to explain foreign exchange rate movements, although a broad understanding of the alternative approaches is certainly useful. We approach the problem from the viewpoint of the portfolio manager who is faced with the practical decision of making an active forecast of foreign exchange.

Purchasing Power Parity

In Figures 14 to 16 we show the dollar/sterling, deutsche mark/dollar and yen/dollar exchange rates plotted against the rate implied by the inflation differences between the respective economies. Thus, in Figure 16, the dotted line represents how the yen/dollar exchange rate *would* have moved purely on the basis of differences between the Japanese and U.S. wholesale price indexes (WPI) from 1973 to the present. This trend estimates the purchasing power parity (PPP) rate which is that rate which would equalize the price of goods between the two countries concerned. As can be seen there is a significant long-term relationship

---

FIGURE 14 Sterling and Purchasing Power Parity

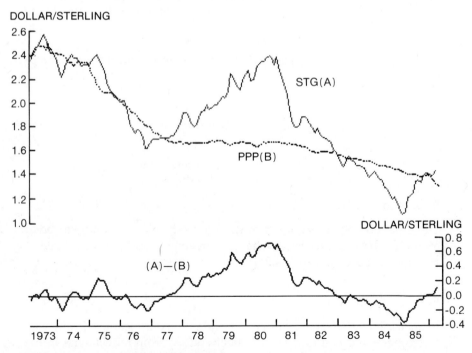

PPP: Purchasing power parity (WPI basis)

SOURCE: Nomura Research Institute.

FIGURE 15 Deutsche Mark and Purchasing Power Parity

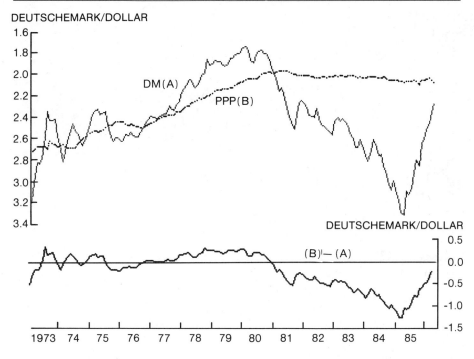

PPP: Purchasing power parity (WPI basis)

SOURCE: Nomura Research Institute.

between movements in this PPP rate and the actual spot rate, although at any given time there can be a wide deviation. Nevertheless it can be argued that an analysis of PPP rates gives the portfolio manager an indication of the fundamental value of one currency against another.

This approach is perhaps the simplest analytical tool available to a portfolio manager faced with the problem of forecasting exchange rates. However, there are problems associated with it. The PPP exchange rate, as defined above, takes no account of the differences in the real cost of production between countries or the comparative advantage one country may have in producing certain goods. It assumes that all economies can produce all goods equally efficiently.

In addition, structural shifts in trade flows can affect exchange rates a great deal, an excellent example being the United Kingdom and North Sea oil. Oil has certainly raised the value of sterling during the late 1970s and early 1980s relative to its likely trend without oil, largely due to the

FIGURE 16 Yen and Purchasing Power Parity

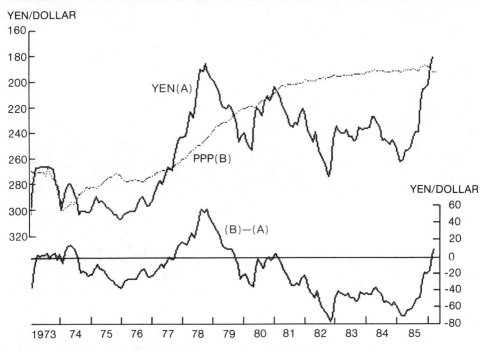

PPP: Purchasing power parity (WPI basis)

SOURCE: Nomura Research Institute.

beneficial impact on current account. The sterling/dollar rate which produces PPP, balances the trade account, and balances the current account may well be three different rates (Morrison, 1985).

Equilibrium in *financial* markets, as well as in the markets for goods and services, is also important, on the basis that funds may flow across borders for reasons other than to balance trade flowing in the opposite direction. In 1985, for example, it was estimated that the volume of speculative capital flows approached $50,000 billion per annum, as compared to world trade of only $2,000 billion. Using PPP to forecast exchange rates can therefore be argued to confuse cause and effect. Since capital flows are now 25 times greater than trade flows, one could suggest that exchange rates determine current account balances rather than the other way round.

Despite these defects, we believe that an analysis of exchange rates based on PPP, produces at least some useful insights for the portfolio manager. At the very least it provides a benchmark against which to compare the market, or spot, exchange rate at any given time. The spot rate may differ from the PPP rate for various reasons, indeed we have suggested some above, but Figures 14 to 16 show that the spot rate has at least moved in a range, albeit a wide one, around the PPP rate in the past. In short, PPP-derived exchange rates provide the portfolio manager with an idea of the fundamental value of a currency. They alert him to the fact that exchange rate movements have produced pricing anomalies in the goods, as opposed to the capital markets, and that when these anomalies have become extreme in the past they have normally been corrected by a reversal of the original exchange rate movement.

Technical Analysis

Technical analysis, which purports to forecast future price movements from an analysis of past price changes, is predicated on the assumption that the price being analyzed moves in some form of discernible cycle. In recent years the proponents of this technique, who are commonly called chartists, have developed their skills far beyond the drawing of simple trend lines on price charts. Sophisticated computer models are now frequently used to generate support points, momentum indicators and trend lines, and to develop an understanding of exceptions to these signals.

The proponents of technical analysis argue in its favor on two counts:

1. At the very least, technical analysis describes the current flow of demand and supply of a particular currency. Since foreign exchange markets are the closest actual example of the theoretical economist's ideal of perfect competition, chartists argue that fundamental analysis is of little use in making short-term predictions of price movements. As nobody within the foreign exchange market has "superior knowledge" and all information is immediately disseminated (two of the conditions of perfect competition) it is by definition not possible to make predictions on the basis of economic data since all such data are already discounted by the market. Chartists argue that the best guide to the next foreign exchange rate set by the market is the last rate set by the market. This is because trends in investor behavior are readily apparent, and that once these trends have been isolated, predictions can be made on the basis of them.
2. It is sufficient for technical analysis to be successful if enough investors *believe* it to be successful. In other words, if enough market participants believe technical analysis to be a useful

TABLE 7 Durations—Government Bond Markets

	Duration (years)
Japan	5.4
Germany	5.5
United Kingdom	6.9
Netherlands	4.5
France	5.1
Switzerland	5.8
Canada	6.9
Australia	5.1
United States	7.1

Note: These indexes exclude bonds of less than five years to maturity.
SOURCE: Salomon Bros., *International Bond Indices*, March 31, 1986.

predictor, then they will act on that basis, and by these actions bring about the exchange rate movement originally forecast.

The authors view these two arguments with skepticism. The implicit philosophy of technical analysis is that, because something happened in the past, it is likely to happen in the future. To our minds this is an abuse of the use of statistics. Pure projection of a past trend without a theoretical basis for that projection is in our view unsound. Many chartists are beginning to share this view, and are combining elements of fundamental analysis with the technical approach. Euromoney (August 1985) gives a good descriptive overview of currency forecasting services based on this overall approach.

Local Currency Returns

The local currency return from nondollar-denominated bond markets is a function of the income yield on that market plus or minus changes in the capital value. Clearly, the latter is determined by the duration of each particular market and the degree of interest rate movements within that market. Duration, as we have mentioned, measures the price sensitivity of a bond to fluctuations in its yield to maturity. It is computed from the three principal specifications of a bond: maturity, coupon, and yield to maturity. Clearly the duration of each individual bond within a particular market will be different from the durations of others. Nevertheless it is possible to make an estimate of a market's duration by using average statistics for each of the above variables. Table 7 shows the durations of the eight non-U.S. government bond indexes published by Salomon Brothers, as of March 31, 1986. These indexes

FIGURE 17 Bond Yields and CPI (Germany)

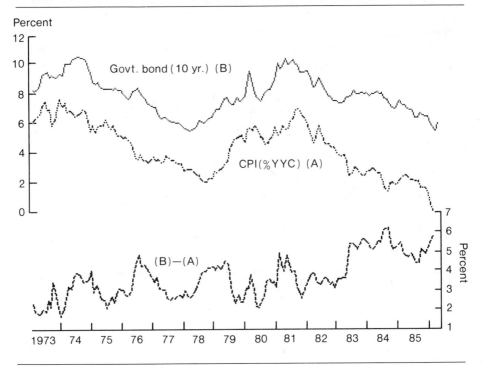

SOURCE: Nomura Research Institute.

specifically exclude bonds with less than five years to maturity and therefore their durations are somewhat longer than the markets they represent. However, they are published monthly, and are easily obtainable. They are thus useful, if not perfect, tools for the portfolio manager.

Returning to the two components of local currency return, the income yield is observable at any time in the market, but prospective capital changes are more difficult to forecast. For example, Figures 17 and 18 show inflation and bond yields in Germany and Japan. Although there is clearly a long-term relationship, substantial fluctuations are apparent in the short term. This is because bond market prices are driven by expectations about future inflation rather than by current inflation rates. However, one interesting point that these histories do show is that in periods of rising inflation, bond yields also rise, but to a much lesser extent, and in periods of falling inflation, bond yields fall, but again to a lesser extent. Identifying a relationship between bond yields and inflation, no matter how close does little to help the international fixed-income manager in a practical sense. It merely creates the additional problem of how to forecast inflation rates accurately, something which has eluded economists for centuries. It is beyond the scope of this chapter to describe alternative methods of forecasting inflation. Suffice to point out that economic theory and empirical evidence would support the view that it is the prospective rate of inflation within each economy which is the biggest single influence on bond yields. Once the foreign exchange and local currency returns have been forecast individually, the U.S. dollar return from each non-U.S. bond market can be calculated as follows:

Expected U.S.$ return = FX change × (Income yield + Price change)

Assume that over the next year we forecast a fall in yield levels on German government bonds with more than five years to maturity from 5.5 percent to 4.5 percent. Assume also that we forecast an appreciation of the DM against the U.S. dollar of 5 percent over the same period.

FIGURE 18   Bond Yields and CPI (Japan)

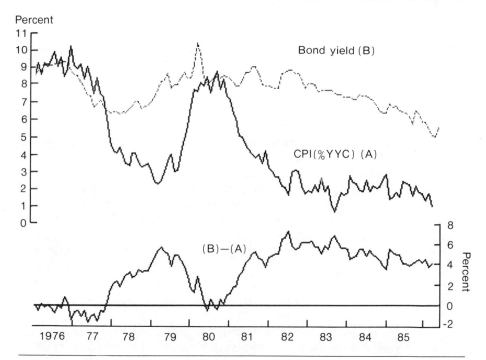

SOURCE: Nomura Research Institute.

With the single additional assumption that we buy current coupon bonds in that market, that is, the income yield approximates to the yield to maturity, the expected percentage return from the German government bond market over the next year is:

$$1 - (1 + 0.05)(1 + 0.055 + 0.055) = 16.55\%$$

Note that the income yield and capital gain (calculated from the duration of the German government bond market listed in Table 7 of 5.5 years) are *added* together, but this combined local currency return is *multiplied* by the forecast foreign exchange return.

Excess Return

Securities portfolios can only outperform their passive benchmarks, or normal portfolios, if they are invested in assets which generate a higher return than the average. If an investor perceives no opportunities for excess return he should invest in the normal portfolio. We can define excess return in terms of the concepts already established in this section.

Excess return = Expected return − Required return

If the investor can identify mispriced securities or markets, he may be able to construct a superior active portfolio. In terms of the above equation, this involves weighting such a portfolio toward those assets for which a positive excess return is forecast, and away from those for which the excess return is negative.

Applying this methodology to a nondollar bond portfolio, we can use the concept of excess return to measure the relative attraction of individual markets. It is to active portfolio construction that we now turn.

PORTFOLIO CONSTRUCTION

Having discussed the principal components of return from nondollar bonds, we are now in a position to suggest a framework within which the investment manager can construct a portfolio.

Market Allocation

The single most important decision in managing a multicurrency fixed-income portfolio is the market allocation decision; that is, the proportion to be invested in each market. A brief survey of the various U.S. dollar returns from the major bond markets during 1985, shown in Table 1, has illustrated the divergence which can take place in a typical year.

Although the U.S. dollar was particularly weak against the yen, sterling, and the continental European currencies which means the U.S. dollar returns from these bond markets were excellent, it appreciated against the Australian and Canadian dollars. Active allocation to these two markets, and particularly the Australian dollar market, would have had a far greater impact on performance than the overall duration or maturity structure of the portfolio.

In arriving at normal market allocation weights, it is necessary to consider the portfolio's investment objectives. These may be various.

The most common is to set a passive index as a performance benchmark. Three international fixed-income indexes are currently published, all measuring the performance of the major non-U.S. bond markets in dollar terms, individually and collectively. These indexes are produced by Salomon Brothers, Intersec Research Corp., whose indexes are published monthly in *Institutional Investor Magazine,* and Lombard Odier & Cie, Geneva, a Swiss private bank. Each index is calculated differently and has its own individual characteristics. Most importantly, the weights attached to individual markets within each index are different. If any of these indexes is selected as a performance benchmark, then the market weights within that index are a useful starting point in portfolio construction. For example, if the manager were totally neutral about the outlook for currency and interest rate movements, he should invest his portfolio in line with the chosen index. Once he had formulated views about which markets offered higher excess returns he would adjust his market allocation relative to his benchmark index.

It should be noted that the normal set of market weights as suggested by a benchmark index is unlikely to represent the minimum risk portfolio. If the latter were the desired objective, an analysis of historic returns, risks, and correlations of the nondollar bond markets would generate a second possible normal position. Further, if the principal requirement from a nondollar bond portfolio were the minimization of risk in a *combined* portfolio of nondollar bonds and other asset classes, a third set of portfolio weights could be generated. Hence, the starting position for any portfolio of multicurrency bonds will very much depend upon the return requirements and the degree of risk aversion of a particular investor.

The basic point of this section is to emphasize that the market allocation decision should be taken with reference to some normal position, defined, in this case, as that allocation which the portfolio manager would adopt were he to believe that all nondollar bond markets were in equilibrium. Assuming that a portfolio manager's objective were to produce a return superior to the Salomon Brothers Non-U.S. Bond Index, his normal position would be defined by the market allocation of that index, namely:

	Index Weighting* (percent)
Japan	45.9%
United Kingdom	20.0
Germany	12.6
Switzerland	3.0
Canada	5.8
France	5.1
Netherlands	4.6
Australia	2.5
European currency unit	0.4
	100.0

* As of December 31, 1985.

The next step is for the portfolio manager to calculate his excess U.S. dollar return for each market, as described previously. Although it is possible to make market allocation decisions on the basis of excess dollar returns only, if the portfolio manager wishes to capture any of the diversification/risk reduction benefits described in the second and third sections of this chapter, he will set a range for each market which will be a function of both its size and its correlation with other markets, within which that market's weighting within his portfolio will always fall. Given his excess dollar returns, the portfolio manager is now able to allocate his portfolio between markets relative to his normal position. Once he has done this, the remaining decisions facing the international bond portfolio manager are no different from those of the domestic manager.

Duration Decision

Once the multicurrency bond portfolio has been allocated between markets, the next decision is to decide upon the duration within each market. Clearly this will be a function of the manager's interest rate outlook for that country. If he were to be optimistic that interest rates would fall, he would buy bonds with a longer duration than that of the market. Conversely if he forecast that interest rates will rise, his bond holdings within that market will have lower duration than the market as a whole. One possible method is a "trigger" system. For a forecast change in yield of ±50 basis points within a market, the average duration of bonds within that market might be equal to the market duration. For a forecast yield change of ±100 basis points, the duration might be 0.90 or 1.1 times the market duration. For a forecast yield change of ±150 basis points, the duration might be 0.85 or 1.15 times the market, and so on. The position and magnitude of these "trigger points" is somewhat arbitrary, but should be related to the confidence the portfolio manager has in his interest rate forecasts, and in the degree of risk tolerance of the client.

Maturity Decision

Once a duration target has been set for each market, the portfolio manager must decide on the best combination of maturities that will produce that duration. This will, to a large extent, depend upon the shape of that market's yield curve and the portfolio manager's forecast change in that curve. For example, assume a market with a duration of 4.0 years. Assume also that a general rise in yield levels is forecast over the next year such as to induce the portfolio manager to adopt a duration strategy equal to only 0.7 of that of the market. This target duration of 2.8 years can be achieved by either:

1. Buying bonds with a duration grouped around 2.8 years.
2. Buying a mixture of bonds, some with a longer duration, some with a shorter duration.
3. Buying only a few very long-dated, high-duration bonds, and retaining the rest of the portfolio's exposure to that market in cash.

If the portfolio manager forecasts no change in the shape of the yield curve he would probably opt for (1). If there is a kink in the yield curve such that bonds in a particular area yield less than those of slightly longer maturities, the portfolio manager may well achieve a slightly higher return by "bar-belling" his maturity distribution somewhat. In that case, option (2) above would be appropriate. If the yield curve were positively sloped and the rise in yield levels was expected to result in a flattening of the curve, long maturities may well outperform shorter dated securities *even in a period of rising interest rates*. Strategy (3) above would then be appropriate.

Issue Selection

Finally, after the portfolio manager has decided upon his market allocation and duration and maturity strategies within each market, he must choose individual bond issues which meet these criteria. In terms of enhancing the total return of a multicurrency fixed-income portfolio it has been the experience of the authors that little value can be added by the manager in this area. In the U.S. bond market there is a wide spread in yield between similar maturity bonds depending upon the credit quality of the issuer. U.S. Treasuries obviously represent the best quality credit, and as credit quality decreases, yields rise. Indeed the "junk" bond market in the U.S. has flourished in recent years as many investors have decided that the higher yields on these securities are more than adequate compensation for the greater credit risk. Outside the U.S. yield differences between good and poor quality credits are much less extreme. In the domestic German bond market, for example, admittedly good quality corporate bonds have been issued on a yield basis below that of similarly dated German governments. However good the quality of the corporate credit, this is clearly inappropriate. In the other two large non-U.S. domestic bond markets, Japan and the United Kingdom, this rarely happens, but anomalous yield differences have frequently existed between Eurobonds and similarly dated governments denominated in the same currency. In the past this has been due in large part to the existence of withholding taxes. Investors have been willing to forgo higher yields on better quality bond issues in return for receiving their coupon payments with no taxes withheld. Following the abolition of withholding taxes on domestically issued bonds in the United States, Germany, and France, this negative yield difference between Eurobonds and governments in the same currency has become much rarer. Withholding taxes are discussed in some detail below.

Even if investors were offered a higher yield for buying poorer quality bonds in the international fixed-income markets, the portfolio manager is faced with the task of determining whether the higher yield is sufficient compensation. In other words, he must form an opinion as to the credit rating of the poorer quality bond. The two major domestic rating agencies, Moody's and Standard & Poor's, now publish credit ratings for many non-U.S. borrowers and these are very useful. However, many international borrowers are not rated by either these or any other rating agency. In these cases the portfolio manager must resort to the borrower's financial statements. However, given the paucity of financial information published by many non-U.S. corporations and, indeed, many other foreign borrowers, credit analysis is generally both difficult and hazardous. For this reason the authors would recommend a policy of buying only those bonds given a rating of A or better by either Moody's or Standard & Poor's. In practice, the portfolio manager will find the yield pickup on non-U.S. corporates, provincial governments and government agencies in nondollar bond markets is rarely sufficient to induce him to invest in anything other than governments. By confining a nondollar bond portfolio to government issues alone, it is possible to have a portfolio which is rated AAA.

PRACTICAL/ADMINISTRATIVE CONSIDERATIONS

Commissions/Dealing Costs

It is now possible to deal on a net price basis in all major non-U.S. bond markets. These include:

Japan	Canada
United Kingdom	Netherlands
Germany	France
Switzerland	Australia

There are no dealing taxes in any Euro or foreign bond market, but in the domestic markets in the United Kingdom there is a flat rate stamp tax of £0.60 on all government bond trades. In France, there are commission charges on all bond trades executed on the Paris Bourse but the rate depends upon the size of the transaction and the maturity of the bond concerned. For most transactions commission rates vary between 0.125 percent and 0.0625 percent but most major French banks will quote potential investors a net price. There are no stamp taxes in France, or any commission charges or stamp taxes in any other domestic fixed-income market. Total consideration is therefore calculated as:

Price × Nominal ± Commission charges and stamp taxes (if any) + Accrued interest

Spreads between bid and offer prices vary between markets and frequently between individual issues within markets. It is difficult to give precise details by market since spreads are also, to a certain extent, a function of turnover levels. As a general rule, the greater the turnover in a particular bond or market, the smaller will be the spread. Suffice to say it is unusual to find spreads greater than 0.75 percent or smaller than 0.125 percent. The important point is that dealing costs are significantly higher in nondollar denominated bond markets than in the U.S. Treasury market. Portfolio managers must therefore take this into account when considering their investment strategies.

Withholding Taxes

Table 8 shows the current rates of withholding tax in the major international bond markets, together with the amounts reclaimable by U.S. residents. It must be stressed, however, that these rates are only applicable if the bonds to which they pertain are held over a coupon date. In all of the markets where withholding taxes are levied, it is possible for U.S. investors to sell their bonds for delivery before the coupon becomes payable (i.e., the coupon payment dates in Japan and the ex-dividend dates in the United Kingdom and Australia) and simultaneously enter into a repurchase agreement, at albeit a slightly higher price for settlement on or after the coupon payment or ex-dividend date. The coupon is therefore taken in the form of accrued interest and is included in the sale proceeds. The repurchase cost will be lower than the sale proceeds by the extent of the accrued interest received and any difference in dealing prices. These sale and repurchase

TABLE 8 Withholding Taxes to U.S. Residents on Domestically Issued Bonds

	Percent of Coupon Payment	Percent Reclaimable	Net* Percent of Coupon
Japan	10%	0	10%
United Kingdom[†]	30	30% reclaimable by U.S. tax-exempt funds	0 or 30
Germany	0	—	—
Netherlands	0	—	—
Switzerland	35	30% reclaimable	5
France	0	—	—
Canada	0	—	—
Australia	10	10% reclaimable by U.S. tax-exempt funds	0 or 10

* In some cases, U.S. residents may be able to offset these net foreign withholding taxes against their federal U.S. income taxes.

[†] Certain government bonds issued in the United Kingdom are free of withholding taxes to non-U.K. residents, irrespective of the investor's domestic tax status in his own country.

agreements are now a very commonplace event in the three countries where they are applicable, and have led to calls for the withholding taxes in these countries to be abolished altogether.

Custody/Settlement

Table 9 lists the normal settlement periods for all the main international bond markets, together with the *usual* place of settlement. In any over-the-counter market it is always possible to arrange specific settlement requirements, such as a different settlement date or physical delivery, but deviations from the norm may result in further charges being levied by the broker/counterparty.

Rather than arrange for settlement on an ad hoc basis, institutional U.S. investors would be well advised to appoint an international custodian bank, which, on receipt of instructions from its client or client's investment manager, would settle all trades in any international fixed-income market, arrange payment/receipt in the currency specified, maintain full financial accounts, and provide portfolio valuations as and when required (normally monthly). The settlement of international fixed-income transactions is a complex process where the services of experts are normally essential.

More detailed information on the specific types of fixed-income instruments available in the major non-U.S. bond markets, the calculation of accrued interest and yields to maturity, coupon payment dates, and methods and dealing practices are beyond the scope of this chapter.

TABLE 9 *Normal* Settlement Details for International Bond Markets

	Settlement Period	Place of Settlement
United States:		
Eurodollar bonds	7 calendar days	Euroclear/Cedel
U.S. foreign bonds (Yankees)		
German:		
Governments	3/5 working days	Settlement Bank
Euro/foreign bonds	7 calendar days	Euroclear/Cedel
United Kingdom:		
Governments	Next working day	Settlement Bank
Euro/foreign bonds	7 calendar days	Euroclear/Cedel
Japan:		
Governments	Negotiable	Settlement Bank
Euro/foreign bonds	7 calendar days	Euroclear/Cedel
France:		
Governments	2 working days	Settlement Bank
Euro/foreign bonds	7 calendar days	Euroclear/Cedel
Netherlands:		
Governments	2 working days (flexible)	Settlement Bank
Euro/foreign bonds	7 calendar days	Euroclear/Cedel
Switzerland:		
Governments	3 working days	Settlement Bank
Euro/foreign bonds	7 calendar days	Euroclear/Cedel
Canada:		
Governments	5 working days	Settlement Bank
Euro/foreign bonds	7 calendar days	Euroclear/Cedel
Australia:		
Governments	7 calendar days (normally flexible)	Settlement Bank
Euro/foreign bonds	7 calendar days	Euroclear/Cedel

Practical information of this kind can be obtained directly from the major market makers/brokers in each market. Salomon Brothers and Merrill Lynch have both published guides to domestic bond markets in Europe and Japan specifically aimed at the U.S. investor.

CONCLUSION

We believe nondollar bonds are a unique asset class which portfolio managers can no longer afford to ignore. There will be periods when they significantly outperform domestic securities, and for this reason alone U.S. investors should be prepared to invest in the asset class on an opportunistic basis. More importantly, however, a permanent normal allocation to nondollar bonds will reduce the risk of the total portfolio. The significance of this point is that a lower risk portfolio enables the portfolio manager to pursue higher return opportunities elsewhere, especially in areas which might before have been considered "too risky."

International dollar bonds offer U.S. investors yield pick-up and risk reduction opportunities. They should be viewed as a straightforward alternative to domestic bonds and bought when their forecast excess return is deemed to be more attractive.

BIBLIOGRAPHY

BERNSTEIN, PETER L. "Winning Big by Playing Safe." *Institutional Investor*, January 1983.

BOND MARKET RESEARCH. *International Bond and Money Market Performance, 1978–1983.* New York: Salomon Brothers Inc, May 1984.

———*International Bond Manuals.* New York: Salomon Brothers Inc.
Periodic booklets describing individual bond market characteristics.

BRINSON, GARY P.; JEFFREY J. DIERMEIER; and GARY G. SCHLARBAUM. "A Composite Portfolio Benchmark for Pension Plans." *The Financial Analysts Journal*, March/April 1986.

DIERMEIER, J. J. "Asset Allocation Strategies." In *Financial Analyst's Handbook*, ed. Sumner N. Levine. 2nd ed. Homewood, Ill.: Dow Jones-Irwin, 1987.

IBBOTSON ASSOCIATES. *Stocks, Bonds, Bills, and Inflation: 1985 Yearbook.* Ibbotson Associates: Chicago, 1985.

IBBOTSON, ROGER G.; RICHARD C. CARR; and ANTHONY W. ROBINSON. "International Equity and Bond Returns." *The Financial Analysts Journal*, July/August 1982.

LESSARD, DONALD R. "International Diversification." In *The Investment Manager's Handbook*, ed. Sumner N. Levine. Homewood, Ill.: Dow Jones-Irwin, 1980.

MORRISON, DAVID. "They Overshoot Currencies Don't They?" *The Economics Analyst*. London: Simon & Coates, 1985.

ROSENBERG, MICHAEL R. "Structuring the Investment Process." In *Global Bond Portfolio Management, Special Report No. 6.* New York: Merrill Lynch Pierce Fenner & Smith, 1985.

SHARPE, WILLIAM F. *Investments.* 3rd ed. Englewood Cliffs, N.J.: Prentice-Hall, 1985.

35

Bond Ratings

STANDARD & POOR'S

RATING DEFINITIONS

Debt

A Standard & Poor's corporate or municipal debt rating is a current assessment of the creditworthiness of an obligor with respect to a specific obligation. This assessment may take into consideration obligors such as guarantors, insurers, or lessees.

The debt rating is not a recommendation to purchase, sell or hold a security, inasmuch as it does not comment as to market price or suitability for a particular investor.

The ratings are based on current information furnished by the issuer or obtained by Standard & Poor's from other sources it considers reliable. Standard & Poor's does not perform any audit in connection with any rating and may, on occasion, rely on unaudited financial information. The ratings may be changed, suspended or withdrawn as a result of changes in, or unavailability of, such information, or for other circumstances.

The ratings are based, in varying degrees, on the following considerations:

1. Likelihood of default-capacity and willingness of the obligor as to the timely payment of interest and repayment of principal in accordance with the terms of the obligation;
2. Nature of and provisions of the obligation;
3. Protection afforded by, and relative position of, the obligation in

---

SOURCE: Standard & Poor's Corporation, 25 Broadway, New York, New York 10004.

the event of bankruptcy, reorganization or other arrangement under the laws of bankruptcy and other laws affecting creditors' rights.

AAA. Debt rated AAA has the highest rating assigned by Standard & Poor's. Capacity to pay interest and repay principal is extremely strong.

AA. Debt rated AA has a very strong capacity to pay interest and repay principal and differs from the higher rated issues only in small degree.

A. Debt rated A has a strong capacity to pay interest and repay principal although it is somewhat more susceptible to the adverse effects of changes in circumstances and economic conditions than debt in higher rated categories.

BBB. Debt rated BBB is regarded as having an adequate capacity to pay interest and repay principal. Whereas it normally exhibits adequate protection parameters, adverse economic conditions or changing circumstances are more likely to lead to a weakened capacity to pay interest and repay principal for debt in this category than in higher rated categories.

BB, B, CCC, CC, C. Debt rated BB, B, CCC, CC and C is regarded, on balance, as predominantly speculative with respect to capacity to pay interest and repay principal in accordance with the terms of the obligation. BB indicates the lowest degree of speculation and C the highest degree of speculation. While such debt will likely have some quality and protective characteristics, these are outweighed by large uncertainties or major risk exposures to adverse conditions.

BB. Debt rated BB has less near term vulnerability to default than other speculative issues. However, it faces major ongoing uncertainties or exposure to adverse business, financial or economic conditions which could lead to inadequate capacity to meet timely interest and principal payments.

B. Debt rated B has a greater vulnerability to default but presently has adequate capacity to meet interest payments and principal repayments. Adverse business, financial or economic conditions will likely impair capacity or willingness to pay interest and repay principal.

CCC. Debt rated CCC has a currrently identifiable vulnerability to default, and is dependent upon favorable business, financial and economic conditions to meet timely payment of interest and repayment of principal. In the event of adverse business, financial or economic conditions, it is not likely to have the capacity to pay interest and repay principal.

CC. The rating CC is typically applied to debt subordinated to senior debt which is assigned an actual or implied CCC rating.

C. The rating C is typically applied to debt subordinated to senior debt which is assigned an actual or implied CCC-debt rating.

CI. The rating CI is reserved for income bonds on which no interest is being paid.

D. Debt rated D is in default, and payment of interest and/or repayment of principal is in arrears.

Plus (+) or minus (−). The ratings from "AA" to "CCC" may be modified by the addition of a plus or minus sign to show relative standing within the major rating categories.

Provisional ratings. The letter "p" indicates that the rating is provisional. A provisional rating assumes the successful completion of the project being financed by the debt being rated and indicates that payment of debt service requirements is largely or entirely dependent upon the successful and timely completion of the project. This rating, however, while addressing credit quality subsequent to completion of the project, makes no comment on the likelihood of, or the risk of default upon failure of such completion. The investor should exercise his own judgment with respect to such likelihood and risk.

L. The letter "L" indicates that the rating pertains to the principal amount of those bonds where the underlying deposit collateral is fully insured by the Federal Savings & Loan Insurance Corp. or the Federal Deposit Insurance Corp.

Continuance of the rating is contingent upon S&P's receipt of an executed copy of the escrow agreement or closing documentation confirming investments and cash flows.

NR. This indicates that no rating has been requested, that there is insufficient information on which to base a rating, or that S&P does not rate a particular type of obligation as a matter of policy.

Debt obligations of issuers outside the United States and its territories are rated on the same basis as domestic corporate and municipal issues. The ratings measure the creditworthiness of the obligor but do not take into account currency exchange and related uncertainties.

Bond investment quality standards. Under present commercial bank regulation issued by the Comptroller of the Currency, bonds rated in the top four categories (AAA, AA, A, BBB, commonly known as "Investment Grade" ratings) are generally regarded as eligible for bank investment. In addition, the Legal Investment Laws of various states may impose certain rating or other standards for obligations eligible for investment by savings banks, trust companies, insurance companies and fiduciaries generally.

CreditWatch. CreditWatch highlights potential changes in ratings of bonds and other fixed income securities. It focuses on events and trends that place companies and government units under special surveillance by S&P's analytical staff. These may include mergers, voter referendums, actions by regulatory authorities, or developments gleaned from analytical reviews. Unless otherwise noted, a rating decision will be made within 90 days. Issues appear on CreditWatch where an event, situation, or deviation from trend has occurred and needs to be evaluated as to its impact on credit ratings. A listing, however, does not mean a rating change is inevitable. Since S&P continuously monitors all of its ratings, CreditWatch is not intended to include all issues under review. Thus, rating changes will occur without issues appearing on CreditWatch.

Rating "outlook." To highlight rating direction, credit analyses include an "outlook" covering a three-year period. There are four designations: *positive* indicates the rating may be raised; *negative*, it may be lowered; *stable*, it is not likely to change; and *developing* means the rating may be raised or lowered. The outlook focuses on alternatives that could result in a change. Rating actions may differ from the outlook based on unexpected events.

Commercial Paper

A Standard & Poor's commercial paper rating is a current assessment of the likelihood of timely payment of debt having an original maturity of no more than 365 days. Ratings are graded into four categories, ranging from "A" for the highest quality obligations to "D" for the lowest. The four categories are as follows:

A. Issues assigned this highest rating are regarded as having the greatest capacity for timely payment. Issues in this category are delineated with the numbers 1, 2 and 3 to indicate the relative degree of safety.

A-1. This designation indicates that the degree of safety regarding timely payment is either overwhelming or very strong. Those issues determined to possess overwhelming safety characteristics are denoted with a plus (+) sign designation.

A-2. Capacity for timely payment on issues with this designation is strong. However, the relative degree of safety is not as high as for issues designated "A-1".

A-3. Issues carrying this designation have a satisfactory capacity for timely payment. They are, however, somewhat more vulnerable to the adverse effects of changes in circumstances than obligations carrying the higher designations.

B. Issues rated "B" are regarded as having only an adequate capacity for timely payment. However, such capacity may be damaged by changing conditions or short-term adversities.

C. This rating is assigned to short-term debt obligations with a doubtful capacity for payment.

D. This rating indicates that the issue is either in default or is expected to be in default upon maturity.

The commercial paper rating is not a recommendation to purchase or sell a security. The ratings are based on current information furnished to Standard & Poor's by the issuer or obtained from other sources it considers reliable. The ratings may be changed, suspended, or withdrawn as a result of changes in or unavailability of such information.

Municipal Notes

A Standard & Poor's note rating reflects the liquidity concerns and market access risks unique to notes. Notes due in 3 years or less will likely receive a note rating. Notes maturing beyond 3 years will most likely receive a long-term debt rating. The following criteria will be used in making that assessment.

- Amortization schedule (the larger the final maturity relative to other maturities the more likely it will be treated as a note).
- Source of Payment (the more dependent the issue is on the market for its refinancing, the more likely it will be treated as a note).

Note rating symbols are as follows:

SP-1   Very strong or strong capacity to pay principal and interest. Those issues determined to possess overwhelming safety characteristics will be given a plus (+) designation.

SP-2   Satisfactory capacity to pay principal and interest.

SP-3   Speculative capacity to pay principal and interest.

Tax-Exempt Demand Bonds

Standard & Poor's assigns "dual" ratings to all long-term debt issues that have as part of their provisions a demand or double feature.

The first rating addresses the likelihood of repayment of principal and interest as due, and the second rating addresses only the demand feature. The long-term debt rating symbols are used for bonds to denote the long-term maturity and the commercial paper rating symbols are used to denote the put option (for example, "AAA/A-1+"). For the newer "demand notes," S&P's note rating symbols, combined with the commercial paper symbols, are used (for example, "SP-1+/A-1+").

MOODY'S

RATING DEFINITIONS

Short-Term Debt Ratings

Moody's short-term debt ratings are opinions of the ability of issuers to repay punctually senior debt obligations which have an original maturity not exceeding one year.

Among the obligations covered are commercial paper, Eurocommercial paper, bank deposits, bankers' acceptances and obligations to deliver foreign exchange. Obligations relying upon support mechanisms such as letters-of-credit and bonds of indemnity are excluded unless explicitly rated.

Moody's employs the following three designations, all judged to be investment grade, to indicate the relative repayment ability of rated issuers:

- Issuers rated **Prime-1** (or supporting institutions) have a superior ability for repayment of senior short-term debt obligations. Prime-1 repayment ability will often be evidenced by many of the following characteristics:

SOURCE: Moody's Investors Service Publishing and Executive Offices, 99 Church Street, New York, New York 10007.

> Leading market positions in well-established industries.
> High rates of return on funds employed.
> Conservative capitalization structure with moderate reliance on debt and ample asset protection.
> Broad margins in earnings coverage of fixed financial charges and high internal cash generation.
> Well-established access to a range of financial markets and assured sources of alternate liquidity.

- Issuers rated **Prime-2** (or supporting institutions) have a strong ability for repayment of senior short-term debt obligations. This will normally be evidenced by many of the characteristics cited above but to a lesser degree. Earnings trends and coverage ratios, while sound, may be more subject to variation. Capitalization characteristics, while still appropriate, may be more affected by external conditions. Ample alternate liquidity is maintained.
- Issuers rated **Prime-3** (or supporting institutions) have an acceptable ability for repayment of senior short-term obligations. The effect of industry characteristics and market compositions may be more pronounced. Variability in earnings and profitability may result in changes in the level of debt protection measurements and may require relatively high financial leverage. Adequate alternate liquidity is maintained.
- Issuers rated **Not Prime** do not fall within any of the Prime rating categories.

Obligations of a branch of a bank are considered to be domiciled in the country in which the branch is located. Unless noted as an exception, Moody's rating on a bank's ability to repay senior obligations extends only to branches located in countries which carry a Moody's sovereign rating. Such branch obligations are rated at the lower of the bank's rating or Moody's sovereign rating for bank deposits for the country in which the bank is located.

When the currency in which an obligation is denominated is not the same as the currency of the country in which the obligation is domiciled, Moody's ratings do not incorporate an opinion as to whether payment of the obligation will be affected by actions of the government controlling the currency of denomination. In addition, risks associated with bilateral conflicts between an investor's home country and either the issuer's home country or the country where an issuer's branch is located are not incorporated into Moody's short-term debt ratings.

Moody's makes no representation that the rated obligations are exempt from the registration under the U. S. Securities Act of 1933 or issued in comformity with any other applicable law or regulation. Nor does Moody's represent that any specific obligation is legally enforceable or a valid senior obligation of a rated issuer.

If an issuer represents to Moody's that its short-term debt obligations are supported by the credit of another entity or entities, then the name or names of such supporting entities or entities are listed within the parenthesis beneath the name of the issuer, or there is a footnote referring the reader to another page for the name or names of the supporting entity or entities. In assigning ratings to such issuers, Moody's evaluates the financial strength of the affiliated corporations, commercial banks, insurance companies, foreign governments or other entities, but only as one factor in the total rating assessment. Moody's makes no representation and gives no opinion on legal validity or enforceability of any support arrangement.

Moody's ratings are opinions, not recommendations to buy or sell, and their accuracy is not guaranteed. A rating should be weighed solely as one factor in an investment decision and you should make your own study and evaluation of any issuer whose securities or debt obligations you consider buying or selling.

Note: Moody's ratings are subject to change. Because of the possible time lapse between Moody's assignment or change of a rating and your use of this publication, we suggest you verify the current rating of any security or issuer in which you are interested.

Long-Term Debt Ratings*

Aaa. Bonds which are rated Aaa are judged to be of the best quality. They carry the smallest degree of investment risk and are generally referred to as "gilt edged." Interest payments are protected by a large or by an exceptionally stable margin and principal is secure. While the various protective elements are likely to change, such changes as can be visualized are most unlikely to impair the fundamentally strong position of such issues.

Aa. Bonds which are rated Aa are judged to be of high quality by all standards. Together with the Aaa group they comprise what are generally known as high-grade bonds. They are rated lower than the best bonds because margins of protection may not be as large as in Aaa securities or fluctuation of protective elements may be of greater amplitude or there may be other elements present which make the long-term risk appear somewhat larger than the Aaa securities.

---

* Preferred stock ratings are the same as long-term debt but lowercase with quotation marks.

A. Bonds which are rated A possess many favorable investment attributes and are to be considered as upper-medium-grade obligations. Factors giving security to principal and interest are considered adequate, but elements may be present which suggest a susceptibility to impairment some time in the future.

Baa. Bonds which are rated Baa are considered as medium-grade obligations (i.e., they are neither highly protected nor poorly secured). Interest payments and principal security appear adequate for the present but certain protective elements may be lacking or may be characteristically unreliable over any great length of time. Such bonds lack outstanding investment characteristics and in fact have speculative characteristics as well.

Ba. Bonds which are rated Ba are judged to have speculative elements; their future cannot be considered as well-assured. Often the protection of interest and principal payments may be very moderate, and thereby not well safeguarded during both good and bad times over the future. Uncertainty of position characterizes bonds in this class.

B. Bonds which are rated B generally lack characteristics of the desirable investment. Assurance of interest and principal payments or of maintenance of other terms of the contract over any long period of time may be small.

Caa. Bonds which are rated Caa are of poor standing. Such issues may be in default or they may be present elements of danger with respect to principal or interest.

Ca. Bonds which are rated Ca represent obligations which are speculative in a high degree. Such issues are often in default or have other marked shortcomings.

C. Bonds whch are rated C are the lowest rated class of bonds, and issues so rated can be regarded as having extremely poor prospects of ever attaining any real investment standing.

Note: Moody's applies numerical modifiers, 1, 2, and 3 in each generic rating classification from Aa through B in its corporate bond rating system. The modifier 1 indicates that the security ranks in the higher end of its generic rating category; the modifier 2 indicates a mid-range ranking; and the modifier 3 indicates that the issue ranks in the lower end of its generic rating category.

Moody's bond ratings, where specified, are applied to senior bank obligations with an original maturity in excess of one year. Among the bank obligations covered are bank deposits and obligations to deliver foreign exchange. Obligations relying upon support mechanisms such as letters-of-credit are excluded unless explicitly rated.

Obligations of a branch of a bank are considered to be domiciled in the country in which the branch is located. Unless noted as an exception, Moody's rating on a bank's ability to repay senior obligations extends only to branches located in countries which carry a Moody's sovereign rating. Such branch obligations are rated at the lower of the bank's rating or Moody's sovereign rating for the bank deposits for the country in which the branch is located. When the currency in which the obligation is denominated is not the same as the currency of the country in which the obligation is domiciled, Moody's ratings do not incorporate an opinion as to whether payment of the obligation will be affected by the actions of the government controlling the currency of denomination. In addition, risk associated with bilateral conflicts between an investor's home country and either the issuer's home country or the country where an issuer branch is located are not incorporated into Moody's ratings.

Moody's makes no representation that rated bank obligations are exempt from registration under the U.S. Securities Act of 1933 or issued in conformity with any other applicable law or regulation. Nor does Moody's represent any specific bank obligation is legally enforceable or a valid senior obligation of a rated issuer.

Long-Term Municipal Ratings

Moody's ratings represent the opinion of Moody's Investors Service as to the relative investment classification of bonds. As such, they should be used in conjunction with the description and statistics appearing in Moody's Municipal & Government Manual and Municipal Credit Reports. Reference should be made to those for information regarding the issuer.

Aaa. Bonds which are rated Aaa are judged to be of the best quality. They carry the smallest degree of investment risk and are generally referred to as "gilt edge." Interest payments are protected by a large or by an exceptionally stable margin and principal is secure. While the various protective elements are likely to change, such changes as can be visualized are most unlikely to impair the fundamentally strong position of such issues.

Aa. Bonds which are rated Aa are judged to be of high quality by all standards. Together with the Aaa group they comprise what are generally known as high grade bonds. They are rated lower than the best bonds because margins of protection may not be as large as in Aaa securities or fluctuation of protective elements may be of greater amplitude or there may be other elements present which make the long-term risks appear somewhat larger than in Aaa securities.

A. Bonds which are rated A possess many favorable investment attributes and are to be considered as upper medium grade obligations. Factors giving security to principal and interest are considered adequate, but elements may be present which suggest a susceptibility to impairment sometime in the future.

Baa. Bonds which are rated Baa are considered as medium grade obligations; i.e., they are neither highly protected nor poorly secured. Interest payments and principal security appear adequate for the present, but certain protective elements may be lacking or may be characteristically unreliable over any great length of time. Such bonds lack outstanding investment characteristics and in fact have speculative characteristics as well.

Ba. Bonds which are rated Ba are judged to have speculative elements, their future cannot be considered as well assured. Often the protection of interest and principal payments may be very moderate, and thereby not well safeguarded during both good and bad times over the future. Uncertainty of position characterizes bonds in this class.

B. Bonds which are rated B generally lack characteristics of the desirable investment. Assurance of interest and principal payments or of maintenance of other terms of the contract over any long period of time may be small.

Caa. Bonds which are rated Caa are of poor standing. Such issues may be in default or there may be present elements of danger with respect to principal or interest.

Ca. Bonds which are rated Ca represent obligations which are speculative in a high degree. Such issues are often in default or have other marked shortcomings.

C. Bonds which are rated C are the lowest rated class of bonds, and issues so rated can be regarded as having extremely poor prospects of ever attaining any real investment standing.

Con. (. . .). Bonds for which the security depends upon the completion of some act or the fulfillment of some condition are rated conditionally. These are bonds secured by (a) earnings of projects under construction, (b) earnings of projects unseasoned in operation experience, (c) rentals which begin when facilities are completed, or (d) payments to which some other limiting condition attaches. Parenthetical rating denotes probable credit stature upon completion of construction or elimination of basis of condition.

Note: Those bonds in the Aa, A, Baa, Ba and B groups which Moody's believes possess the strongest investment attributes are designated by the symbols Aa 1, A 1, Baa 1, and B 1.

Short-Term Municipal Loan Ratings

Ratings: Moody's ratings for state and municipal short-term obligations will be designated Moody's Investment Grade or **(MIG)**. Such ratings recognize the differences between short-term credit risk and long-term risk. Factors affecting the liquidity of the borrower and short-term cyclical elements are critical in short-term ratings, while other factors of major importance in bond risk, long-term secular trends for example, may be less important over the short run.

A short-term rating may also be assigned on an issue having a demand feature–variable rate demand obligation (VRDO). Such ratings will be designated as **VMIG** or, if the demand feature is not rated, as **NR**. Short-term ratings on issues with demand features are differentiated by the use of the **VMIG** symbol to reflect such characteristics as payment upon periodic demand rather than fixed maturity dates and payment relying on external liquidity. Additionally, investors should be alert to the fact that the source of payment may be limited to the external liquidity with no or limited legal recourse to the issuer in the event the demand is not met.

A VMIG rating may also be assigned to commercial paper programs. Such programs are characterized as having variable short-term maturities but having neither a variable rate nor demand feature.

Definitions: Moody's short-term ratings are designated Moody's Investment Grade as **MIG 1** or **VMIG 1** through **MIG 4** or **VMIG 4**. As the name implies, when Moody's assigns a **MIG** or **VMIG** rating, all categories define an investment grade situation.

The purpose of the **MIG** or **VMIG** ratings is to provide investors with a simple system by which the relative investment qualities of short-term obligations may be evaluated.

Gradations of investment quality are indicated by rating symbols, with each symbol representing a group in which the quality characteristics are broadly the same.

Changes in Rating: A change in rating may occur at any time in the case of an individual issue. Such a rating occurs because Moody's observed some alteration in the investment risks of the short-term obligation or because the previous rating does not fully reflect the quality as now seen. Such rating changes may include the suspension or withdrawal of a rating.

Limitations to Uses of Ratings: Short-term obligations carrying the same rating are not claimed to be of absolutely equal quality. In a broad sense they are alike in position, but since there are only four rating levels used in grading thousands of short-term obligations, the symbols cannot reflect fine shadings of risks. Therefore, it should be evident to the user of ratings that two short-term obligations identically rated are unlikely to be precisely the same in investment quality.

As ratings are designed exclusively for the purpose of grading short-term obligations according to their investment qualities, they should not be used alone as a basis for investment decisions. For example, they have limited value in forecasting the direction of future trends of market price. Market price movements are influenced not only by the quality of individual issues but also by length of maturity. During its life even the best quality short-term obligation may have wide price movements, while its investment status remains unchanged.

The matter of market price has no bearing whatsoever on the determination of ratings, which are not to be construed as recommendations with respect to attractiveness. The attractiveness of a given short-term obligation will depend on its yield, its maturity date and other factors as well as on its investment quality, the only characteristic to which the rating refers.

Since ratings involve judgments about the future, an effort is made when assigning ratings to look at worst potentialities in the visible future, rather than solely at the past record and current status. Therefore, investors should be aware that a rating includes the recognition of many non-statistical factors.

Moody's ratings represent the opinion of Moody's Investors Service as to the relative investment classification of short-term obligations. As such, they should be used in conjunction with the information on the issuer appearing in Moody's Municipal & Government Manual and Municipal Credit Reports. Reference should be made to these for information regarding the issuer.

Absence of Rating: Should no rating be assigned, among other reasons, it may be for one of the following:

1. An application for rating was not received or accepted.
2. The issue or issuer belongs to a group of securities that are not rated as a matter of policy.
3. There is a lack of essential data pertaining to the issue or issuer.

4. The issue was privately placed, in which case the rating is not published in Moody's publications.
5. The issue was judged not to be of investment grade.

Where no rating has been assigned or where a rating has been suspended or withdrawn, it may be for reasons unrelated to the quality of the issue. When no rating is applied to either the long- or short-term aspect of the VRDO, it will be designated **NR**.

Because of the generally short-term nature of these obligations, the user of these ratings should monitor them closely in case any change in investment status may occur.

Short-Term Municipal Loan Ratings

MIG 1/VMIG 1. This designation denotes best quality. There is present strong protection by established cash flows, superior liquidity support or demonstrated broad-based access to the market for refinancing.

MIG 2/VMIG 2. This designation denotes high quality. Margins of protection are ample although not so large as in the preceding group.

MIG 3/VMIG 3. This designation denotes favorable quality. All security elements are accounted for but there is lacking the undeniable strength of the preceding grades. Liquidity and cash flow protection may be narrow and market access for refinancing is likely to be less well established.

MIG 4/VMIG 4. This designation denotes adequate quality. Protection commonly regarded as required of an investment security is present and although not distinctly or predominantly speculative, there is specific risk.

Issues or the features associated with **MIG** or **VMIG** ratings are identified by date of issue, date of maturity or maturities or rating expiration date and description to distinguish each rating from other ratings. Each rating designation is unique with no implication as to any other similar issue of the same obligor. **MIG** ratings terminate at the retirement of the obligation while **VMIG** rating expiration will be a function of each issue's specific structural or credit features.

Note: Moody's ratings are subject to change. Because of the possible time lapse between Moody's assignment or change of a rating and your use of this publication, we suggest you verify the current rating of any security or issuer in which you are interested.

36

Bond Rating Outlines

INDUSTRIAL COMPANY RATING METHODOLOGY PROFILE

I. **Industry risk:** Defined as the strength of the industry within the economy and relative to economic trends. This also includes the ease or difficulty of entering this industry, the importance of any diversity of the earnings base and the role of regulation and legislation.
   A. Importance in the economic cycle.
   B. Business cyclicality; earnings volatility, lead-lag and duration, diversity of earnings base, predictability and stability of revenues and earnings.
   C. Economic forces impacts; high inflation, energy costs and availability, international competitive position, social-political forces.
   D. Demand factors; real growth projections relative to GNP and basis for projections, maturity of markets.
   E. Basic financial characteristics of the business: fixed or working capital intensive; importance of credit as a sales tool.
   F. Supply factors: raw materials, labor, over/under utilized plant capacity.
   G. Federal, state, foreign regulation.
   H. Potential legislation.
   I. Fragmented or concentrated business.
   J. Barriers to entry/ease of entry.

II. **Issuer's industry position—market position:** The company's sales position in its major fields and its historical protection of its position and projected ability for the future.
   A. Ability to generate sales.
   B. Dominant and stable market shares.
   C. Marketing/distributing requirements of business— strengths, weaknesses, national, international, regional.
   D. R&D—degree of importance—degree of obsolescence—short or long product life.
   E. Support/service organization.
   F. Dependence on major customers/diversity of major customers.
   G. Long-term sales contracts/ visibility of revenues/backlogs/prepayments (*e.g.*, subscriptions).
   H. Product diversity.

SOURCE: *Credit Overview*, Standard & Poor's Corporation, 25 Broadway, New York, New York 10004.

III. **Issuer's industry position—operating efficiency:** This covers the issuer's historical operating margins and assesses its ability to maintain or improve them based upon pricing or cost advantages.
   A. Ability to maintain or improve margins.
   B. Pricing leadership.
   C. Integration of manufacturing operations.
   D. Plant and equipment: modern and efficient or old and obsolete. Low or high cost producer.
   E. Supply of raw material.
   F. Level of capital and employee productivity.
   G. Labor; availability, cost, union relations.
   H. Pollution control requirements and impact on operating costs.
   I. Energy costs.

IV. **Management evaluation:**
   A. The record of achievement in operations and financial results.
   B. Planning—extent, integration and relationship to accomplishments. Both strategic and financial. Plan for growth—both internal and external.
   C. Controls—management, financial and internal auditing.
   D. Financing policies and practices.
   E. Commitment, consistency and credibility.
   F. Overall quality of management; line of succession—strength of middle management.
   G. Merger and acquisition considerations.
   H. Performance vs. peers.

V. **Accounting quality:** Overall accounting evaluation of the methods employed and the extent to which they overstate or understate financial performance and position.
   A. Auditor's qualifications.
   B. LIFO vs. FIFO inventory method.
   C. Goodwill and intangible assets.
   D. Recording of revenues.
   E. Depreciation policies.
   F. Nonconsolidated subsidiaries.
   G. Method of accounting and funding for pension liabilities. Basic posture of the pension plan assumptions.
   H. Undervalued assets such as LIFO reserve.

VI. **Earnings protection:** Key measurements indicating the basic long-term earnings power of the company including:
   A. Returns on capital.
   B. Pretax coverage ratios.
   C. Profit margins.
   D. Earnings on asset/business segments.
   E. Sources of future earnings growth.
   F. Pension service coverage.
   G. Ability to finance growth internally.
   H. Inflation-adjusted earnings capacity.

VII. **Financial leverage and asset protection:** Relative usage of debt, with due allowance for differences in debt usage appropriate to different types of businesses.

A. Long-term debt and total debt to capital.
B. Total liabilities to net tangible stockholders' equity.
C. Preferred stock/capitalization.
D. Leverage implicit in off-balance sheet financing arrangements, production payments, operating rentals of property, plant and equipment, nonconsolidated subsidiaries, unfunded pension liabilities, etc.
E. Nature of assets.
F. Working capital management—accounts receivable, inventory, and accounts payable turnover.
G. Level, nature and value of intangible assets.
H. Off-balance sheet assets such as undervalued natural resources or LIFO reserve.

VIII. **Cash flow adequacy:** Relationship of cash flow to leverage and ability to internally meet all business cash needs.
A. Evaluation of size and scope of total capital requirements and capital spending flexibility.
B. Evaluation of variability of future cash flow.
C. Cash flow to fixed and working capital requirements.
D. Cash flow to debt.
E. Free cash flow to short-term debt and total debt.

IX. **Financial flexibility:** Evaluation of the company's financial needs, plans, and alternatives and its flexibility to accomplish its financing program under stress without damaging creditworthiness.
A. Relative financing needs.
B. Projected financing plan.
C. Financing alternatives under stress—ability to attract capital.
D. Capital spending flexibility.
E. Asset redeployment potentials—nature of assets and undervalued liabilities.
F. Nature and level of off-balance sheet assets or liabilities. This would include unfunded vested pension benefits and LIFO reserves.
G. High level of short-term debt/high level of floating rate debt.
H. Heavy or unwieldy debt service schedule (bullet maturities in future)—either of debt or sinking fund preferred stock.
I. Heavy percentage of preferred stock as a percentage of total capital.
J. Overall assessment of near-term sources of funds as compared to requirements for funds/internal financial self-sufficiency/need for external financing.
K. Ownership/affiliation.

RETAIL COMPANY RATING METHODOLOGY PROFILE

I. **Industry risk:** Defined as the strength of the industry or segment within the economy and relative to economic trends. This also includes the ease or difficulty of entering this industry, the importance of any diversity of the earnings base and the role of regulation and legislation.
A. Industry overview and economic environment.
    1. Necessity of a particular segment of the trade
    2. Character of goods sold (luxuries or necessities, durables or

consumables, big ticket or small ticket, staple or fashion, level of volume, unit profitability, relative breadth and depth of lines, lead times)
B. Short- and long-term outlook
C. Relative sensitivity of this segment to changes in:
   1. Inventories
   2. Receivables
   3. Leases vs. owned property
D. Population factors:
   1. Rate of growth: absolute, by region
   2. Trend in real DPI per capita
   3. Savings rates
   4. Effect of demographics on
      a. Age brackets
      b. Household formations
E. Effect of economy on performance:
   1. Sensitivity to recession
   2. Lags or leads other segments
F. Impact of:
   1. Legislation
   2. Regulation
   3. Controls
G. Ease of entry
H. Susceptibility to changes in the state of the art and to new formats

II. **Trade position—revenues:** The company's historical, current, and anticipated sales position in its major fields.
   A. Relative position in market; price leadership
   B. Attractiveness of geographical territory and site selections therein
   C. Customer franchise:
      1. Customer recognition
      2. Image
      3. Customer loyalty
   D. Diversity of mix: breakdown of sales
   E. Merchandising skills
   F. Promotional and advertising effectiveness

III. **Trade position—operating efficiency:** An assessment of the firm's historical operating margins and its ability to maintain or improve them based upon pricing or cost advantages.
   A. Condition of physical plant:
      1. Degree of modernity of stores, distribution centers, manufacturing facilities
      2. Productivity of physical plant
      3. Degree of computerization and automation
   B. Economies of scale:
      1. Extent of vertical integration
      2. Bulk buying
      3. Optimal use of facilities
      4. Clustering of stores (advertising, distribution, supervision)
   C. Gross profit margin factors:
      1. Markdown experience and policy
      2. Shrinkage rates

      3. Branded vs. private label products
      4. Imports vs. domestic goods
  D. Relative exposure to energy costs and availability
  E. Relative vulnerability to contingent rents
  F. Labor—labor intensiveness of operations, cost, availability, productivity, turnover, and stoppage experience
  G. Margins:
      1. Ability to maintain or improve margins
      2. Relative to peers
      3. Track record and stability
  H. Size of administrative overhead
  I. Capital efficiency trends

IV. **Management evaluation:**
  A. The record of achievement in operations and financial results
  B. Planning—extent, integration and relationship to accomplishments. Both strategic and financial
  C. Controls—management, financial and internal auditing
  D. Financing policies and practices
  E. Commitment to stated plans and credibility
  F. Overall quality of management, line of succession—strength of middle management
  G. Merger and acquisition considerations
  H. Performance vs. peers
  I. Other

V. **Accounting quality:** Overall accounting evaluation of the methods employed and the extent to which they overstate or understate financial performance and position.
  A. Auditor's qualifications
  B. LIFO vs. FIFO inventory method
  C. Goodwill and intangible assets
  D. Depreciation policies
  E. Nonconsolidated subsidiaries
  F. Method of accounting and funding for pension liabilities. Basic posture of the pension plan assumptions
  G. Undervalued assets such as LIFO reserve and owned properties
  H. Reserving policy
  I. Contingent rentals, sub-lease income

VI. **Earnings protection:** Key measurements indicating the basic long-term earnings power of the company including:
  A. Returns on assets
  B. Pretax fixed charge coverage with rent expense
  C. Profit margins
  D. Earnings stability and growth
  E. Return and earnings assessed on an inflation-adjusted basis

VII. **Financial leverage and asset protection:** Relative usage of debt, with due allowance for differences in debt usage appropriate to different types of businesses.

A. Total debt/total equity
B. Total liabilities/total equity
C. Total debt/total capitalization plus capitalized rents
D. Total equity/total capitalization plus capitalized rents
E. Preferred stock/total capitalization
F. Salability of assets
G. High level of short-term or floating rate debt
H. Off-balance sheet assets and contingent liabilities
I. Level and pattern of store closing reserves
J. Leverage implicit in off-balance sheet financing arrangements, operating rentals of property, plant and equipment, nonconsolidated subsidiaries, unfunded pension liabilities, etc.
K. Nature of assets.
L. Working capital management—accounts receivable, inventory, and accounts payable turnover. Seasonal borrowing patterns.
M. Level, nature and value of intangible assts

VIII. **Cash flow adequacy:** Relationship of cash flow to leverage and ability to meet all business cash needs.
A. Measured against total debt and annual debt servicing requirements
B. Consistency and predictability of cash flow; level of depreciation component
C. Cash flow to cash requirements
D. Cash flow measurements as adjusted to reflect working capital requirements and inflation-adjusted fixed capital requirements

IX. **Financial flexibility:** Evaluation of the company's financing needs, plans, and alternatives and its flexibility to accomplish its financing program under stress without damaging creditworthiness.
A. Relative financing needs
B. Projected financing plan
C. Financing alternatives—ability to attract capital
D. Capital spending flexibility
E. Asset redeployment potentials—nature of assets and undervalued liabilities
F. Nature and level of off-balance sheet assets or liabilities. This would include unfunded vested pension benefits and LIFO reserve
G. Bank lines:
   1. Magnitude
   2. Strength and diversity of lenders
   3. Terms: compensating balances or fees; price of lines
H. Comparative liquidity: availability of receivables for sale; short-term investments
I. High level of short-term debt or high level of floating rate debt
J. Heavy or unwieldy debt service schedule (bullet maturities in future)—either of debt or sinking fund preferred stock
K. Heavy percentage of preferred stock as a percentage of total capital
L. Overall assessment of near-term sources of funds as compared to requirements for funds/internal financial self-sufficiency/need for external financing
M. Ownership/affiliation
N. Restrictive loan covenants; capacity for sales/leasebacks; debt capacity

BANK HOLDING COMPANY RATING METHODOLOGY PROFILE

I. **Company characteristics:** Definition of the type of holding company, description of the operating subs, and evaluation of scope of operations, importance in markets and competition.
   A. Holding company type, bank only or bank and non-banks, multi-bank vs. unit bank
   B. Operating entities description, areas of location of business, international vs. domestic, commercial banking vs. consumer banking
   C. Regulated by whom, subject to what state laws, usury ceilings, unusual tax situations
   D. Primary competition, critical mass for market leadership, unusual areas of expertise or strength
   E. Company diversification by lines and types of business
   F. Diversification of funding sources, stability and strength of local funding sources, access to national market sources
   G. Concentrations of lending risk, by industry, by country and type of borrower (public vs. private), by product line

II. **Asset quality:** Determination of the credit quality of fund uses.
   A. Comparison of historical charge-off record to industry and peer norms
   B. Historical non-performing assets to industry peers
   C. Conservatism of management, reserving policy, recovery rate, recent gross charge-offs
   D. Analysis of non-performers and charge-offs by type, indication of reasons for problems, geographic, industry concentration, lending aggressiveness, lack of controls
   E. Analysis of current loan portfolio condition, nonperformer breakout, appraisal of current condition
   F. Assessment of potential areas of problems
   G. Investment portfolio credit quality
   H. Earnings coverage of potential problems

III. **Asset/liability management:** To what degree is management able to measure and react to interest rate environment changes.
   A. General evaluation of company's measurement abilities
   B. Ability to measure short-term position taking and strategic positions
   C. Analysis of shifts in position over the past few years, rationale behind changes
   D. Ability of the company to shift positions, how flexible is the balance sheet
   E. Management's expressed philosophy regarding position taking
   F. Susceptibility to structural changes in the banking industry

IV. **Liquidity:** Potential liability loss and diversity of funding sources.
   A. Individual bank characteristics that promote liquidity, upstream and/or downstream correspondents, government underwriting bank
   B. Asset sources of liquidity, net liability sensitivity
   C. Diversification of funding sources, access to funding sources, stability, importance in individual liability markets
   D. Use of the discount window, access to the Federal Reserve

V. **Capital adequacy:** Equity cushion available to support operating deficiencies.
   A. Capital ratio comparison with peers

B. Off-balance sheet risk assessment
C. Relationship of asset quality to capital
D. Investment portfolio depreciation to capital
E. Dividend payout ratio/internal growth rate of equity
F. Ability to tap outside sources of equity, market to book of equity
G. Capital composition analysis, preferred stock, convertibles, common

VI. **Profitability:** Earnings protection and ability to form capital to promote growth.
   A. Margin trends, net interest income trends, ability to maintain volume
   B. Other income analysis, breakdown, variability or consistency of other income categories, ability to grow non-interest income
   C. Operating expense ratios, composition of overhead, ability to cover overhead growth, level and trend of overhead ratios
   D. Impact of loss provisions, current level, past volatility, relationship of provisions to maintenance of adequate reserves
   E. Tax payment position and cushion, lines of business and strategies that impact on tax cushion, consequences of asset decisions and interest rate levels on cushion
   F. Net operating income analysis, peer relationships
   G. Impact of securities gains or losses and other unusual gains or extraordinary losses
   H. General opinion of quality and consistency of earnings and profitability

VII. **Capitalization breakdown/ holding company vs. operating subs:** Analysis of liability structure and cash flow at the parent level.
   A. Debt capital composition, maturity breakdown
   B. Non-restricted sources of funds, dividend capacity of nonbank subs
   C. Net asset liquidity at the parent level
   D. Double leverage ratios, composition of double leverage
   E. Present subsidiary payout policy, extra or reserve bank dividend ability
   F. Financing philosophies, acquisition and expansion plans
   G. Projected cash flow adequacy of the parent

VIII. **Recent earnings and future developments:** Near-term operating results and known future developments impacting operating results.
   A. Impact of interest environment on recent results
   B. Near-term earnings prospects based on interest rate scenario and economic environment
   C. Recent unusual income or cost streams
   D. Impact of branch, building, or acquisition expansion on projections
   E. Management's competence at forward planning, how realistic

Summary:

The ability of the company to sustain or improve upon the key characteristics outlined above including both quantitative and subjective appraisals

---

THRIFT INSTITUTION RATING METHODOLOGY PROFILE
I. **Market position and area:**
   A. Absolute size

    B. Relative size and competitive position
    C. Geographical scope and penetration
    D. Economic base
    E. Political and regulatory environment

 II. **Profitability:**
    A. Level and trend of historical earnings
    B. Quality of earnings
    C. Overhead control
    D. Interest spread analysis
    E. Earnings outlook

III. **Asset liability management:**
    A. Exposure to interest rate risk
    B. Lending and investment strategy
    C. Liability management

IV. **Liquidity:**
    A. Level of liquid assets
    B. Historical deposit flows
    C. Liability breakdown
    D. Commitment position
    E. Borrowing flexibility
    F. Liquidity outlook

 V. **Asset quality:**
    A. Level and trend of non-performing assets
    B. Current asset mix—risk evaluation
    C. Construction loan exposure and risk
    D. Loan underwriting standards
    E. Asset quality outlook

VI. **Financial leverage:**
    A. Level and trend of capital ratio
    B. Dividend policy (if applicable)
    C. Capital outlook

VII. **Management**

FINANCE COMPANY RATING METHODOLOGY PROFILE

 I. **Industry risk:** The relationship of the industry to the economy and the possible impact of various economic scenarios. This section also covers the ramifications of legislation.
    A. Importance of the industry within the economy

    B. Influence of inflation

    C. Need for capital

    D. Legislation and regulation

II. **Asset portfolio evaluation—qualitative analysis:** An analysis of the com-

position of the portfolio with respect to type, mix, and diversity of receivables and evaluation of growth prospects.
A. Basic characteristics
1. Consumer vs. commercial
2. Secured vs. unsecured
3. Size: absolute and relative
B. Diversity
1. Geographic
2. Customer
3. Type of product, manufacturer, supplier
4. Internal guidelines limiting concentrations
C. Lending criteria
D. Growth
1. Relative to peer group
2. Fundamental portfolio characteristics during periods of either rapid growth or decline

III. **Asset portfolio evaluation—quantitative analysis:** Performance of the portfolio with respect to a quantitative assessment of the credit quality.
A. Credit quality
1. Delinquencies
2. Charge-offs
3. Recoveries
4. Policies with respect to payment definition, charge-offs, extensions and business rewritten
B. Reserve adequacy
1. Coverage levels, trends relative to peers and portfolio characteristics
2. Methodology for establishing reserves
3. Adjustments reflecting changes in the portfolio and the economic environment
C. Liquidity
1. Salability of receivables: time frame, market size, discounting
2. Realizable value of owned equipment and property

IV. **Non-finance activities:** An evaluation of non-finance related businesses
A. Characteristics of activity
1. Risk vs. return
2. Management involvement
3. Prospects
B. Does it provide dividends or require capital?
C. Is the activity appropriately capitalized? Is there double leverage?
D. Plans for future diversification
1. Acquisitions or start-up?
2. Divestitures?

V. **Capitalization:** Analysis of capital leverage, debt maturity, financing requirements.
A. Appropriateness of total leverage in relation to peer group
B. Mix of fund sources
C. Debt servicing capacity
D. Use of "bullet" debt or preferred stock; preferred stock/capitalization
E. Equity quality

      1. Goodwill and intangibles
      2. Equity investments
      3. Excess or inadequate loss reserves
      4. Understated assets and off-balance sheet liabilities.
   F. Financing needs and plans
      1. Short- and long-term financing requirements
      2. Growth flexibility
      3. Projected changes in leverage

VI. **Asset and liability management:** An examination of the company's funding of its assets. This section examines the company's management of assets and liabilities with regard to maturity and interest rate sensitivity. What is the company's philosophy toward matching interest sensitive liabilities with interest sensitive assets and what has been the performance?
   A. Interest rate sensitivity: assets vs. liabilities
      1. Percentage of floating rate assets and liabilities; management philosophy toward interest sensitive assets and liabilities on the balance sheet
      2. Percentage of assets where the interest rate can be fixed at specific levels
   B. Company policy regarding the matching of interest sensitive assets and liabilities; what is the degree of tolerance for mismatching between its assets and liabilities?
   C. Maturity structure assets and liabilities
      1. Nominal and average life
      2. Actual experience

VII. **Earnings protection:** Review of the company's performance, based on profitability measures.
   A. Trend of key profitability measures—growth, yields, spreads, returns, both absolute and relative to peers
   B. Level and volatility of interest coverage
   C. Expectations regarding future operating results
      1. In relation to past performance
      2. In relation to peers

VIII. **Ownership/affiliation:** Discussion of the degree of strength derived from parental support.
   A. Nature of relationship
      1. Legal
      2. Financial
      3. Management
   B. Past support and ability and willingness of owner/affiliate to provide added protection in the future
   C. Does the ownership/affiliation either strengthen or weaken the owner's creditworthiness?

IX. **Management:** Evaluation of management's performance, policies, controls, planning, and depth.
   A. Planning and controls
   B. Response of management to changing conditions

C. Depth and capability of middle management
D. Management credibility
E. Management philosophy towards acquisitions, diversification, portfolio risk and leverage

X. **Accounting:** Analysis of accounting methods and comparison with industry practices.
   A. Auditor's report
   B. Conservative vs. liberal accounting practices
   C. Treatment of investment tax credit
   D. Write off method and reserves for losses
   E. Treatment of intangible assets
   F. Accounting practices of non-finance activities
   G. Off-balance sheet liabilities and understated assets

INSURANCE COMPANY RATING METHODOLOGY PROFILE

I. **Industry risk:** A determination of the inherent risk in the type of insurance business being underwritten.
   A. Relative pricing stability and the nature of competition from within and outside the industry.
   B. Nature of tail in claims reporting or settlement.
   C. Real or potential regulatory or legislative strengths or problems.
   D. Sensitivity to inflation and changing economic scenarios.
   E. Relative growth potential of the market.

II. **Company characteristics:** An assessment of the structure of the company, its market position and its diversification.
   A. Mix of insurance business: life vs. health vs. property-casualty, etc.
   B. If property-casualty, nature of tail: long or short.
   C. Risk diversification: geographically and by product line.
   D. Market factors: niches, competition, distribution system, major sources of business (either broker or customer).
   E. Organizational factors: holding vs. operating company, ownership of non-insurance activities, cash generators/users, level and use of debt.
   F. Size and age of company: on an absolute and relative basis.

III. **Underwriting performance:** Evaluation of the company's ability to grow the underwriting business and maintain profitability, as well as the quality of those earnings.
   A. Growth of business: past and prospective for types of policies being written, assets and earnings—on an absolute and relative basis.
   B. Sources, stability and quality of underwriting earnings: profits by underwriting segments, effect of reinsurance and reserve changes, inflation and cyclical sensitivity.
   C. Return on assets, profit margins: on an absolute and relative basis.
   D. Adequacy of reserves: development of reserves on prior year's books of business, Schedule P analysis, etc.

IV. **Investment activities:** An assessment of the performance and risk characteristics of the investment portfolio.
   A. Portfolio composition: breakdown by type of investment and policy
   regarding new investments.
   B. Portfolio quality: average ratings for bonds, nature of common stock
   investments, investments in parents, subsidiaries and affiliates, and
   policy regarding quality of new investments.
   C. Concentrations: by issuer, industry and geographically (for mortgage and
   real estate investments).
   D. Maturity structure and liquidity considerations: average maturity of bond
   portfolio, amount of investments maturing within one year, publicly traded
   bonds versus private placements, total cash flow expected from portfolio
   in next year, percentage of overall cash flow (including from operations)
   committed, and policy regarding lending and investment commitments.
   E. Performance: current yield and trend in yield relative to peer group,
   delinquency and default rates on bond and mortgage portfolio—currently
   and in the past, performance and quality of equity investments.

V. **Non-insurance activities:** An analysis of investments in non-insurance
related subsidiaries that the issuer currently owns, as well as the track record
of past ventures.
   A. Appropriateness of activity: tie-in to insurance, risk, return and/or prospects.
   B. Is activity appropriately capitalized currently and will outside capital be
   required in the future?
   C. Acquisitions, divestitures and future diversification.

VI. **Earnings protection:**
   A. Fixed charge coverage, debt servicing capability.
   B. Profit margins.
   C. Return on assets for consolidated entity.
   D. Earnings mix, stability and growth.

VII. **Leverage:** An evaluation of the adequacy of the surplus to cover the risks
inherent in the underwriting business and the investment portfolio, internal
growth, and the quality of any excess surplus. The appropriateness of the
current and projected levels of debt.
   A. Historical and projected operating leverage: primarily, the premiums
   written to statutory surplus for a property-casualty insurer and the
   liabilities to statutory surplus plus mandatory security valuation reserves
   for a life insurance company.
   B. Sufficiency of capital for future growth.
   C. Surplus quality: vulnerability to downturn in equity markets (common
   stocks to statutory surplus), adequacy of reserves, intangible assets,
   double leverage and investments in parents, subsidiaries and affiliates.
   D. Debt leverage: current and forecasted level, usage of short-term debt.
   E. Shareholder dividend policy.

VIII. **Financial flexibility:** An assessment of the ability to raise funds and/or
increase liquidity quickly.
   A. Position and visibility of the company within its own and other markets.
   B. Restrictions on cash flows and/or dividends by regulations, indentures,
   etc.

    C. Diversification of cash flows and/or dividend streams.
    D. Ability of the company and industry to attract equity capital.

IX. **Management evaluation:**
    A. Extent of planning and forecasting and quality of previous projections.
    B. Record of achievement.
    C. Philosophy regarding acquisitions or expansion, operating and financial leverage.
    D. Responsiveness to changing market, economic, regulatory and/or legislative conditions.
    E. Depth and experience of middle management.
    F. Controls: internal auditing, investment committee practices.

Addendum

I. **Industry risk:**
    A. Life companies are viewed as having lower business risk than health and property-casualty insurers as the revenue and earnings streams usually are more predictable, less volatile, and show year to year growth. Also, life insurance loss reserving is much more a science that health and property-casualty reserving. Health insurers are next in line in terms of earnings stability and reserving methods, but closer to the volatile property-casualty insurers than the stable life companies. Of course a health or property-casualty company can structure its business or carve out a good niche that will offset initial concerns.
    B. The tail of a property-casualty business refers to the length of time between putting a policy on the books and paying on the last claim. Long-tail business is viewed as less desirable for three reasons: inflation plays havoc with reserves; the adequacy of reserves remains questionable longer; and since reserves/ surplus is much higher for a long-tail company, reserve adequacy is much more important.

II. **Underwriting performance:**
    A. In assessing reserve adequacy for a property-casualty insurer, emphasis is placed on reserve development, which shows how much a company has added to reserves one year and then two years after the original reserve had been established on past years' books of business. Also used are prospective methods, which project ultimate losses on a book of business based on trends of paid losses on past years' books. The results of reserve adequacy tests cannot be heavily weighted as there are flaws in each approach.

PUBLIC UTILITY RATING METHODOLOGY PROFILE
Non-financial criteria
  I. **Market or service territory**
    A. General:
      1. Size & growth rate of market
      2. Economic trends
      3. Diversity of customer base
      4. Demand components
      5. Dependencies

      6. Per capita income

      7. Area ratings

      8. Customer growth

      9. Other

   B. For telephone utilities:

      1. Toll growth and the intercity common carriers

II. Fuel-power supply

   A. For electric utilities:

      1. Fuel mix

      2. Fuel contracts

      3. Reserve margin

      4. Reliability

      5. Environmental factors

      6. Transmission capability

      7. Power purchases/power sales

      8. Other

   B. For gas pipelines and distributors:

      1. Long-term supply adequacy

      2. Non-traditional sources such as LNG

      3. Reserve life indices

      4. Gas supply diversification

III. Operating efficiency

   A. For electric utilities:

      1. Peak load and capacity factors

      2. Environmental problems

      3. Generating plant availability

      4. Plant outages

      5. KWH pricing

   B. For gas pipelines and distributors:

      1. Plant utilization

      2. Storage adequacy

      3. Lost and unaccounted gas

      4. Non-gas operating costs

   C. For telephone utilities:

      1. Central office modernization

      2. Maintenance costs

      3. Trouble reports

      4. Public service commission complaints

      5. Held orders and service levels

IV. Regulatory treatment

   A. Earnable returns on equity

   B. Regulatory quality

      1. Quality of earnings

      2. Aids to cash flow

   C. Regulatory timing

      1. Earnings stabilization techniques

      2. 'Make-whole' processes

      3. Forecasted test years and rate bases

V. Management
A. Results and commitments, including to credit quality
B. Strategic & financial planning
C. Public and private priorities
D. Effective communication with the public, regulatory bodies, and the financial community
E. Financial policies and controls
F. Business philosophy
G. Other

VI. Competition/monopoly balance
A. Relative exposure to competition
B. Gas utilities and alternate fuel costs
C. Telephone utilities and other common carriers and equipment suppliers
D. Electric utilities and competitive energy sources
E. Move to diversify
F. Diversification risks and compensatory financial policies

Financial criteria
I. Construction/asset concentration risk
A. Nature and breakdown of projected expenditures
B. Projected cancellations
C. Post completion risks
D. Construction expenditures to capitalization
E. Construction work in progress to capitalization and common equity

II. Earnings protection
A. Pretax coverages including and excluding AFDC for debt and senior equities
B. Returns on equity
C. Overall returns on capital
D. Risk-adjusted benchmarks

III. Debt leverage
A. Capital ratios
B. Funding ratios
C. Short-term debt/capitalization
D. Off-balance sheet commitments and liabilities
E. Inflated or undervalued assets
F. Risk-adjusted benchmarks

IV. Cash flow adequacy
A. Capital spending needs
B. Net (of common dividends) cash flow ex AFDC/capital outlays
C. Net cash flow/capitalization
D. Refunding requirements
E. Gross cash flow service of gas company debt

V. Financial flexibility/capital attraction
A. Cash flow—capital requirement deficiencies
B. Need and ability to sell common equity

    C. Market/book value
    D. Indenture and charter tests
    E. Preferred stock ratio
    F. Short-term debt usage
    G. Non-traditional financing resources

VI. **Accounting quality**
    A. Overlaps other criteria areas
    B. Regulatory treatment
        1. 'Flow thru' versus normalization
        2. Depreciation rates
        3. Balancing accounts
    C. Management treatment
        1. Unbilled revenues
        2. Off-balance sheet financings
    D. Current costs versus historic costs

SOVEREIGN GOVERNMENT RATING
METHODOLOGY PROFILE

Political risk

I. **Characteristics of political system**
    A. Type of government
    B. Process and frequency of political succession
    C. Degree of public participation
    D. Degree of centralization in decision-making process

II. **Executive leadership**
    A. Relationship with supporting government institutions
    B. Relationship with supporting political coalitions

III. **Government institutions**
    A. Responsiveness and access to executive leadership
    B. Effectiveness and efficiency
    C. Policy responsibilities

IV. **Social coalitions**
    A. Major socio-economic and cultural groups (*i.e.*, church, military, landowners, management, labor, ethnic groups, etc.)
    B. Political parties and their constituencies

V. **Social indicators**
    A. Level and growth of per capita income, and other measures of the standard of living
    B. Distribution of wealth and income
    C. Regional disparities
    D. Homogeneity of the populace

VI. **External relations**
    A. Relationship with major trading partners
    B. Relationship with neighboring countries
    C. Participation in international organizations

Economic risk
  I. **Demographic characteristics**
    A. Level and growth of population
    B. Age distribution
    C. Urbanization trends

 II. **Structure of the economy**
    A. Extent and quality of infrastructure
      1. Transportation and communications
      2. Utilities
      3. Housing
      4. Education
      5. Health services
    B. Natural resource endowment
      1. Agriculture, forestry, fishing
      2. Non-energy minerals
      3. Energy resources
    C. Distribution of productive activities
      1. Agriculture and livestock
        a. Land tenure system
        b. Degree of mechanization
        c. Principal crops
        d. Markets
      2. Forestry and fishing
      3. Mining
      4. Construction
        a. Residential
        b. Non-residential
      5. Manufacturing
        a. Concentration and size of manufacturers
        b. Product types (*i.e.*, consumer, intermediate and capital goods)
        c. Markets
      6. Services—financial/non-financial, public/private
    D. Public sector participation in productive activities

III. **Recent economic trends**
    A. Composition and growth of aggregate demand (nominal and real terms)
      1. Consumption
        a. Private sector
        b. Public sector
      2. Investment
        a. Private sector
        b. Public sector
      3. External savings (*i.e.*, exports—imports)
    B. Domestic economy
      1. Total production (*i.e.*, GDP)
      2. Prodution by sector
        a. Agriculture, forestry and fishing
        b. Mining
        c. Construction
        d. Manufacturing
        e. Utilities
        f. Services

3. Prime movements and major determinants
   a. External factors
   b. Wages
   c. Public sector deficit financing
   d. Private sector credit expansion
   e. Supply bottlenecks
4. Employment trends
   a. Level of growth of employment and labor force
   b. Labor participation rates
   c. Unemployment rate and structure
   d. Sectoral trends
   e. Regional trends
   f. Composition of employment: public vs. private
C. External sector
   1. Current account balance
      a. Export growth and composition
         i. Agricultural commodities
         ii. Minerals
         iii. Manufactured goods
      b. Destination of exports (*i.e.*, markets)
      c. Price and income elasticity of exports
      d. Import growth and composition
         i. Food
         ii. Other consumer goods
         iii. Energy
         iv. Other intermediate goods
         v. Capital goods
      e. Price and income elasticity of imports
      f. Geographic origin of imports
      g. Terms of trade
      h. Services account
         i. Interest payments and receipts
         ii. Transportation
         iii. Other
      i. Transfers
   2. Capital account balance
      a. Direct investment
      b. Long-term capital flows
         i. Private sector
         ii. Public sector
      c. Short-term capital flows
      d. Access to capital markets
         i. Types of instruments used
         ii. Types of borrowers & lenders
   3. International reserves
      a. Level
      b. Composition (*i.e.*, gold, foreign exchange)
      c. Secondary reserves
   4. External debt
      a. Amount outstanding
      b. Composition by borrower
         i. Central government
         ii. Other public sector

        iii. Publicly guaranteed
        iv. Private
    c. Composition by lender
        i. Bilateral
        ii. Multilateral
        iii. Private financial institutions
        iv. Suppliers credits
    d. Maturity structure
    e. Currency composition
    f. Growth rate
    g. Comparison with export earnings and GDP
    h. Debt service payments
        i. Amortization
        ii. Interest
        iii. Comparison to export earnings
        iv. Future debt service schedule

IV. **Economic policy**
   A. Price and wage policies
     1. Wage settlement process
        a. Trade union activity
        b. Management groups
        c. Role and influence of government
     2. Degree of wage indexation
     3. Productivity trends
     4. Non-wage benefits and unemployment insurance
     5. Direct price controls
        a. Public sector tariffs
        b. Private sector pricing
     6. Price subsidies (agricultural, industrial, etc.)
   B. Monetary policy
     1. Level of development of financial system
        a. Types of financial institutions
        b. Types of financial instruments
        c. Role of government in credit allocation
        d. Foreign participation
     2. Trends for monetary aggregates
        a. Money supply growth targets and actual experience
        b. Domestic credit expansion
           i. Public sector
           ii. Private sector
        c. Velocity (national income/money supply)
        d. Changes in international reserves
     3. Monetary policy instruments
        a. Reserve requirements
        b. Open market operations
        c. Credit controls
        d. Interest rate regulations
        e. Ability to sterilize international reserve flows
        f. Controls on foreign borrowing and lending
        g. Rediscount facilities
   C. Fiscal policy

1. Structure of the public sector
   a. Central government
   b. Social security system
   c. State agencies and enterprises
   d. Regional and local governments
2. Budgetary process
   a. Executive branch
   b. Legislative branch
   c. Major constituencies (business, labor, etc.)
3. Revenues
   a. Composition
      i. Direct taxes—personal income, corporate income, property, others
      ii. Indirect taxes—value added, sales, export & import duties, others
      iii. Service charges and public sector tariffs
   b. Income elasticity of revenues
   c. Distribution of tax burden by income groups
   d. Overall tax burden (% of GDP)
   e. Tax collection and evasion
   f. Tax incentives (*i.e.*, investment, export, employment)
4. Expenditures
   a. Current expenditures
      i. Distribution by expenditure category
      ii. Transfers to households
      iii. Transfers to other levels of government
   b. Capital expenditures
5. Current operating balance (absolute level and relative to GDP)
6. Gross financing requirements (*i.e.*, operating balance plus net capital expenditures)
   a. Trend relative to GDP
   b. Means of financing
      i. Domestic money creation
      ii. Domestic borrowing
      iii. External borrowing
7. Public sector debt: domestic and external
   a. Size (direct and guaranteed)
   b. Debt service requirement
   c. Debt management
D. External policies
   1. Exchange rate policy
   2. International reserve management
   3. Export promotion measures
   4. Import substitution/trade protectionist measures
E. Long-term planning and special programs
   1. Energy
   2. Industrial development/ restructuring
   3. Employment creation
   4. Others

PART 6

Portfolio Theory and Practice

37

Risk, Return, and CAPM: Concepts and Evidence

Franco Modigliani, Ph.D.
Sloan School of Management
Massachusetts Institute of Technology

Gerald A. Pogue, Ph.D.
Baruch College
City University of New York

1. INTRODUCTION

Portfolio theory deals with the selection of optimal portfolios by rational risk-averse investors; that is, by investors who attempt to maximize their expected portfolio returns consistent with individually acceptable levels of portfolio risk. Capital markets theory deals with the implications for security prices of the decisions made by these investors; that is, what relationship should exist between security returns and risk if investors behave in this optimal fashion. Together, portfolio and capital markets theories provide a framework for the specification and measurement of investment risk, for developing relationships between expected security return and risk, and for measuring the performance of managed portfolios such as mutual funds and pension funds.

The purpose of this article is to present a nontechnical introduction to portfolio and capital markets theories. Our hope is to provide a wide class of readers with an understanding of the foundation upon which

SOURCE: This chapter is an expansion and update of the original article which appeared in two parts in the March/April 1974 and May/June 1974 issues of the *Financial Analysts Journal*.

the modern risk and performance measures are based by presenting the main elements of the theory along with the results of some of the more important empirical tests. We are attempting to present not an exhaustive survey of the theoretical and empirical literature but, rather, the main thread of the subject leading the reader from the most basic concepts to the more sophisticated but practically useful results of the theory.

2. INVESTMENT RETURN

Measuring historical rates of return is a relatively straightforward matter. We will begin by showing how investment return during a single interval can be measured and then present three commonly used measures of average return over a series of such intervals.

The return on an investor's portfolio during a given interval is equal to the change in value of the portfolio plus any distributions received from the portfolio expressed as a fraction of the initial portfolio value. It is important that any capital or income distributions made to the investor be included, or else the measure of return will be deficient. Equivalently, the return can be thought of as the amount (expressed as a fraction of the initial portfolio value) that can be withdrawn at the end of the interval while maintaining the principal intact. The return on the investor's portfolio, designed R_P, is given by

$$R_P = \frac{V_1 - V_0 + D_1}{V_0} \tag{1a}$$

where

V_1 = the portfolio market value at the end of the interval
V_0 = the portfolio market value at the beginning of the interval
D_1 = cash distributions to the investor during the interval

The calculation assumes that any interest or dividend income received on the portfolio securities and not distributed to the investor is reinvested in the portfolio (and thus reflected in V_1). Furthermore, the calculation assumes that any distributions occur at the end of the interval or are held in the form of cash until the end of the interval. If the distributions were reinvested prior to the end of the interval, the calculation would have to be modified to consider the gains or losses on the amount reinvested. The formula also assumes no capital inflows during the interval. Otherwise, the calculation would have to be modified to reflect the increased investment base. Capital inflows at the end of the interval, however, can be treated as just the reverse of distributions in the return calculation.

Thus, given the beginning and ending portfolio values, plus any contributions from or distributions to the investor (assumed to occur at the end of the interval), we can compute the investor's return using Equation (1a). For example, if the XYZ pension fund had a market value of $100,000 at the end of June, capital contributions of $10,000, benefit payments of $5,000 (both at the end of July), and an end-of-July market value of $95,000, the return for the month is a loss of 10 percent.

The arithmetic average return is an unweighted average of the returns achieved during a series of such measurement intervals. For example, if the portfolio returns [as measured by Equation (1a)] were −10 percent, 20 percent, and 5 percent in July, August, and September, respectively, the average monthly return is 5 percent. The general formula is

$$R_A = \frac{R_{P1} + R_{P2} + \ldots + R_{PN}}{N} \tag{1b}$$

where

R_A = the arithmetic average return
R_{PK} = the portfolio return in interval k, k=1, . . . , N
N = the number of intervals in the performance-evaluation period

The arithmetic average can be thought of as the mean value of the withdrawals (expressed as a fraction of the initial portfolio value) that can be made at the end of each interval while maintaining the principal intact. In the above example, the investor must add 10 percent of the principal at the end of the first interval and can withdraw 20 percent and 5 percent at the end of the second and third for a mean withdrawal of 5 percent of the initial value per period.

The time-weighted return measures the compound rate of growth of the initial portfolio during the performance-evaluation period, assuming that all cash distributions are reinvested in the portfolio. It is also commonly referred to as the "geometric" rate of return. It is computed by taking the geometric average of the portfolio returns computed from Equation (1a). For example, let us assume the portfolio returns were −10 percent, 20 percent, and 5 percent in July, August, and September, as in the example above. The time-weighted rate of return is 4.3 percent per month. Thus, one dollar invested in the portfolio at the end of June would have grown at a rate of 4.3 percent per month during the three-month period. The general formula is

$$R_T = [(1 + R_{p1})(1 + R_{p2}) \ldots (1 + R_{PN})]^{1/N} - 1 \tag{1c}$$

where

R_T = the time-weighted rate of return
R_{PK} = the portfolio return during the interval k, k=1, . . . , N
N = the number of intervals in the performance-evaluation period

In general, the arithmetic and time-weighted average returns do not coincide. This is because in computing the arithmetic average, the amount invested is assumed to be maintained (through additions or withdrawals) at its initial value. The time-weighted return, on the other hand, is the return on a portfolio that varies in size because of the assumption that all proceeds are reinvested. The failure of the two averages to coincide is illustrated in the following example: Consider a portfolio with a $100 market value at the end of 1972, a $200 value at the end of 1973, and a $100 value at the end of 1974. The annual returns are 100 percent and −50 percent. The arithmetic and time-weighted average returns are 25 percent and zero percent, respectively. The arithmetic average return consists of the average of $100 withdrawn at the end of Period 1 and $50 replaced at the end of Period 2. The compound rate of return is clearly zero, the 100 percent return in the first period being exactly offset by the 50 percent loss in the second period on the larger asset base. In this example, the arithmetic average exceeded the time-weighted average return. This always proves to be true, except in the special situation where the returns in each interval are the same, in which case the averages are identical.

The dollar-weighted return measures the average rate of growth of all funds invested in the portfolio during the performance-evaluation period—that is, the initial value plus any contributions less any distributions. As such, the rate is influenced by the timing and magnitude of the contributions and distributions to and from the portfolio. The measure is also commonly referred to as the "internal rate of return." It is important to corporations, for example, for comparison with the actuarial rates of portfolio growth assumed when funding their employee pension plans.

The dollar-weighted return is computed in exactly the same way that the yield to maturity on a bond is determined. For example, consider a portfolio with market value of $100,000 at the end of 1973 (V_0), capital withdrawals of $5,000 at the end of 1974, 1975, and 1976 (C_1, C_2, and C_3), and a market value of $110,000 at the end of 1976 (V_3). Using compound interest tables, the dollar-weighted rate of return is found by trial and error to be 8.1 percent per year during the three-year period. Thus, each dollar in the fund grew at an average rate of 8.1 percent per year. The formula used is

$$V_0 = \frac{C_1}{(1 + R_D)} + \frac{C_2}{(1 + R_D)^2} + \frac{C_3}{(1 + R_D)^3} + \frac{V_3}{(1 + R_D)^3}$$

(1d)

where

R_D = the dollar-weighted rate of return

What is the relationship between the dollar-weighted return (internal rate of return) and the previously defined time-weighted rate of return? It is easy to show that under certain special conditions both rates of return are the same. Consider, for example, a portfolio with initial total value V_0. No further additions or withdrawals occur and all dividends are reinvested. Under these special circumstances all of the C's in Equation (1d) are zero so that

$$V_0 = \frac{V_0(1 + R_{P1})(1 + R_{P2})(1 + R_{P3})}{(1 + R_D)^3}$$

where R_P's are the single-period returns. The numerator of the expression on the right is just the value of the initial investment at the end of the three periods (V_3). Solving for R_D we find

$$R = [(1 + R_{P1})(1 + R_{P2})(1 + R_{P3})]^{1/3} - 1$$

which is the same as the time-weighted rate of return R_T given by Equation (1c). However, when contributions or withdrawals to the portfolio occur, the two rates of return are not the same. Because the dollar-weighted return (unlike the time-weighted return) is affected by the magnitude and timing of portfolio contributions and distributions (which are typically beyond the portfolio manager's control), it is not useful for measuring the investment performance of the manager. For example, consider two identical portfolios (designated A and B) with year-end 1973 market values of $100,000. During 1974 each portfolio has a 20 percent return. At the end of 1974, portfolio A has a capital contribution of $50,000 and portfolio B a withdrawal of $50,000. During 1975 both portfolios suffer a 10 percent loss resulting in year-end market values of $153,000 and $63,000, respectively. Now both portfolio managers performed equally well, earning 20 percent in 1974 and -10 percent in 1975, for a time-weighted average return of 3.9 percent per year. The dollar-weighted returns are not the same, however, due to the different asset bases for 1975, equaling 1.2 percent and 8.2 percent for portfolios A and B, respectively. The owners of portfolio B, unlike those of A, made a fortuitous decision to reduce their investment prior to the 1975 decline.

In the remainder of this article, when we mention rate of return, we will generally be referring to the single interval measure given by Equation (1a). However, from time to time we will refer to the arithmetic and geometric averages of these returns.

3. PORTFOLIO RISK

The definition of investment risk leads us into much less well explored territory. Not everyone agrees on how to define risk, let alone how to measure it. Nevertheless, there are some attributes of risk which are reasonably well accepted.

If an investor holds a portfolio of treasury bonds, he faces no uncertainty about monetary outcome. The value of the portfolio at maturity of the notes will be identical with the predicted value. In this case the investor bears no monetary risk. However, if he has a portfolio composed of common stocks, it will be impossible to exactly predict the value of the portfolio as of any future date. The best he can do is to make a best guess or most likely estimate, qualified by statements about the range and likelihood of other values. In this case, the investor does bear risk.

One measure of risk is the extent to which the *future* portfolio values are likely to diverge from the expected or predicted value. More specifically, risk for most investors is related to the chance that future portfolio values will be less than expected. Thus, if the investor's portfolio has a current value of $100,000 and an expected value of $110,000 at the end of the next year, he will be concerned about the probability of achieving values less than $110,000.

Before proceeding to the quantification of risk, it is convenient to shift our attention from the terminal value of the portfolio to the portfolio rate of return, R_p, since the increase in portfolio value is directly related to R_p.[1]

A particularly useful way to quantify the uncertainty about the portfolio return is to specify the probability associated with each of the possible future returns. Assume, for example, that an investor has identified five possible outcomes for his portfolio return during the next year. Associated with each return is a subjectively determined probability, or relative chance of occurrence. The five possible outcomes are:

Possible Return	Subjective Probability
50%	0.1
30	0.2
10	0.4
−10	0.2
−30	0.1
	1.00

---

[1] Footnotes appear at end of article.

Note that the probabilities sum to 1.00 so that the actual portfolio return is confined to take one of the five possible values. Given this probability distribution, we can measure the expected return and risk for the portfolio.

The expected return is simply the weighted average of possible outcomes, where the weights are the relative chances of occurrence. The expected return on the portfolio is 10 percent, given by

$$E(R_p) = \sum_{j=1}^{5} P_j \, R_j$$

$$= 0.1(50.0) + 0.2(30.0) + 0.4(10.0) \qquad (2)$$
$$+ \ 0.2(-10.0) + 0.1(-30.0)$$

$$= 10\%$$

where the R_j's are the possible returns and the P_j's the associated probabilities.

If risk is defined as the chance of achieving returns less than expected, it would seem to be logical to measure risk by the dispersion of the possible returns below the expected value. However, risk measures based on below-the-mean variability are difficult to work with and are actually unnecessary as long as the distribution of future return is reasonably symmetric about the expected value.[2] Exhibit 1 shows three probability distributions: the first symmetric, the second skewed to the left, and the third skewed to the right. For a symmetric distribution, the dispersion of returns on one side of the expected return is the same as the dispersion on the other side.

Empirical studies of realized rates of return on diversified portfolios show that skewness is not a significant problem.[3] If future distributions are shaped like historical distributions, then it makes little difference whether we measure variability of returns on one or both sides of the expected return. If the probability distribution is symmetric, measures of the total variability of return will be twice as large as measures of the portfolio's variability below the expected return. Thus, if total variability is used as a risk surrogate, the risk rankings for a group of portfolios will be the same as when variability below the expected return is used. It is for this reason that total variability of returns has been so widely used as a surrogate for risk.

It now remains to choose a specific measure of total variability of returns. The measures most commonly used are the variance and standard deviation of returns.

The variance of return is a weighted sum of the squared deviations from the expected return. Squaring the deviations ensures that deviations above and below the expected value contribute equally to the

EXHIBIT 1 Possible Shapes for Probability Distributions

Symmetric Probability Distribution

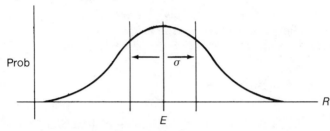

Probability Distribution Skewed to Left

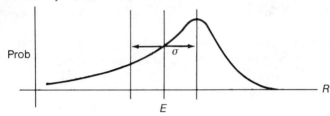

Probability Distribution Skewed to Right

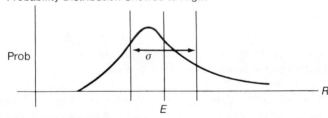

measure of variability, regardless of sign. The variance, designated (σ_p^2) for the portfolio in the previous example is given by

$$
\begin{aligned}
\sigma_p^2 &= \sum_{j=1}^{5} P_j (R_j - E(R_p))^2 \\
&= 0.1(50.0 - 10.0)^2 + 0.2(30.0 - 10.0)^2 \\
&\quad + 0.4(10.0 - 10.0)^2 + 0.2(-10.0 - 10.0)^2 \\
&\quad + 0.1(-30.0 - 10.0)^2 \\
&= 480 \text{ percent squared}
\end{aligned}
\tag{3}
$$

The standard deviation (σ_p) is defined as the square root of the variance. It is equal to 22 percent. The larger the variance or standard deviation, the greater the possible dispersion of future realized values around the expected value and the larger the investor's uncertainty. As a rule of thumb for symmetric distributions, it is often suggested that roughly two thirds of the possible returns will lie within one standard deviation either side of the expected value and that 95 percent will be within two standard deviations.

Exhibit 2 shows the historical return distributions for a diversified portfolio. The portfolio is composed of approximately 100 securities, with each security having equal weight. The month-by-month returns cover the period from January 1945 to June 1970. Note that the distribution is approximately, but not perfectly, symmetric. The arithmetic average return for the 306-month period is 0.91 percent per month. The standard deviation about this average is 4.45 percent per month.

Exhibit 3 gives the same data for a single security, National Department Stores. Note that the distribution is highly skewed. The arithmetic average return is 0.81 percent per month over the 306-month period. The most interesting aspect, however, is the standard deviation of month-by-month returns—9.02 percent per month, more than double that for the diversified portfolio. This result will be discussed further in the next section.

Thus far our discussion of portfolio risk has been confined to a single-period investment horizon such as the next year; that is, the portfolio is held unchanged and evaluated at the end of the year. An obvious question relates to the effect of holding the portfolio for several periods—say for the next 20 years: Will the one-year risks tend to cancel out over time? Given the random-walk nature of security prices, the answer to this question is no. If the risk level (standard deviation) is maintained during each year, the portfolio risk for longer horizons will increase with the horizon length. The standard deviation of possible terminal portfolio values after N years is equal to $\sqrt{N}$ times the standard deviation after one year.[4] Thus the investor cannot rely on the "long run" to reduce his risk of loss.

A final remark should be made before leaving portfolio risk measures. We have implicitly assumed that investors are risk averse, i.e., that they seek to minimize risk for a given level of return. This assumption appears to be valid for most investors in most situations. The entire theory of portfolio selection and capital asset pricing is based on the belief that investors *on the average* are risk averse.

4. DIVERSIFICATION

When one compares the distribution of historical returns for the 100-stock portfolio (Exhibit 2) with the distribution for National Department

	Range		Freq	1│││5│││10│││15│││20│││25│││30│││35│││40│││45│││50│
1	-13.6210	-12.2685	1	*
2	-12.2685	-10.9160	2	**
3	-10.9160	-9.5635	2	**
4	-9.5635	-8.2110	3	***
5	-8.2110	-6.8585	8	********
6	-6.8585	-5.5060	9	*********
7	-5.5060	-4.1535	17	*****************
8	-4.1535	-2.8010	18	******************
9	-2.8010	-1.4485	27	***************************
10	-1.4485	-0.0960	28	****************************
11	-0.0960	1.2565	30	******************************
12	1.2565	2.6090	50	**
13	2.6090	3.9615	35	***********************************
14	3.9615	5.3140	33	*********************************
15	5.3140	6.6665	18	******************
16	6.6665	8.0190	14	**************
17	8.0190	9.3715	4	****
18	9.3715	10.7240	2	**
19	10.7240	12.0765	2	**
20	12.0765	13.4290	3	***

Average return = 0.91% per month.
Standard deviation = 4.45% per month.
Number of observations = 306.

EXHIBIT 3 Rate of Return Distribution for National Department Stores (January 1945–June 1970)

	Range		Freq	1|||5|||10|||15|||20|||25|||30|||35|||40|||45|||50
1	−32.3670	−29.4168	1	*
2	−29.4168	−26.4666	0	
3	−26.4666	−23.5163	0	
4	−23.5163	−20.5661	1	*
5	−20.5661	−17.6159	1	*
6	−17.6159	−14.6657	3	***
7	−14.6657	−11.7155	13	*************
8	−11.7155	−8.7653	11	***********
9	−8.7653	−5.8151	39	***************************************
10	−5.8151	−2.8649	47	***
11	−2.8649	0.0853	45	***
12	0.0853	3.0365	34	**********************************
13	3.0365	5.9857	28	****************************
14	5.9857	8.9359	25	*************************
15	8.9359	11.8861	17	*****************
16	11.8861	14.8363	17	*****************
17	14.8363	17.7865	9	*********
18	17.7865	20.7366	8	********
19	20.7366	23.6868	5	*****
20	23.6868	26.6370	2	**

Average return = 0.81% per month.
Standard deviation = 9.02% per month.
Number of observations = 306.

Stores (Exhibit 3), he discovers a curious relationship. While the standard deviation of returns for the security is double that of the portfolio, its average return is less. Is the market so imperfect that over a long period of time (25 years) it rewarded substantially higher risk with lower average return?

Not so. As we shall now show, not all of the security's risk is relevant. Much of the total risk (standard deviation of return) of National Department Stores was diversifiable. That is, if it had been combined with other securities, a portion of the variation in its returns could have been smoothed out or cancelled by complementary variation in the other securities. The same portfolio diversification effect accounts for the low standard deviation of return for the 100-stock portfolio. In fact, the portfolio standard deviation was less than that of the typical security in the portfolio. Much of the total risk of the component securities had been eliminated by diversification. Since much of the total risk could be eliminated simply by holding a stock in a portfolio, there was no economic requirement for the return earned to be in line with the total risk. Instead, we should expect realized returns to be related to that portion of security risk which cannot be eliminated by portfolio combination.

Diversification results from combining securities having less than perfect correlation (dependence) among their returns in order to reduce portfolio risk. The portfolio return, being simply a weighted average of the individual security returns, is not diminished by diversification. In general, the lower the correlation among security returns, the greater the impact of diversification. This is true regardless of how risky the securities of the portfolio are when considered in isolation.

Ideally, if we could find sufficient securities with uncorrelated returns, we could completely eliminate portfolio risk. This situation is unfortunately not typical in real securities markets where returns are positively correlated to a considerable degree. Thus, while portfolio risk can be substantially reduced by diversification, it cannot be entirely eliminated. This can be demonstrated very clearly by measuring the standard deviations of randomly selected portfolios containing various numbers of securities.

In a study of the impact of portfolio diversification on risk, Wagner and Lau [27]* divided a sample of 200 NYSE stocks into six subgroups based on the Standard & Poor's Stock Quality Ratings as of June 1960. The highest quality ratings (A+) formed the first group, the second highest ratings (A) the next group, and so on. Randomly selected portfolios were formed from each of the subgroups, containing from 1 to 20 securities. The month-by-month portfolio returns for the 10-year

---

* References appear at end of article.

TABLE 1   Risk versus Diversification for Randomly Selected Portfolios of A+
Quality Securities (June 1960–May 1970)

Number of Securities in Portfolio	Average Return (Percent/Month)	Std. Deviation of Return (Percent/Month)	Correlation with Market	
			R	R²
1	0.88%	7.0%	0.54	0.29
2	0.69	5.0	0.63	0.40
3	0.74	4.8	0.75	0.56
4	0.65	4.6	0.77	0.59
5	0.71	4.6	0.79	0.62
10	0.68	4.2	0.85	0.72
15	0.69	4.0	0.88	0.77
20	0.67	3.9	0.89	0.80

SOURCE: Wagner and Lau [27], Table C, p. 53.

period through May 1970 were then computed for each portfolio (portfolio composition remaining unchanged). The exercise was repeated 10 times to reduce the dependence on single samples, and the values for the 10 trials were then averaged.

Table 1 shows the average return and standard deviation for portfolios from the first subgroup (A+ quality stocks). The average return is unrelated to the number of issues in the portfolio. On the other hand, the standard deviation of return declines as the number of holdings increases. On the average, approximately 40 percent of the single security risk is eliminated by forming randomly selected portfolios of 20 stocks. However, it is also evident that additional diversification yields rapidly diminishing reduction in risk. The improvement is slight when the number of securities held is increased beyond, say, 10. Exhibit 4 shows the results for all six quality groups. The figure shows the rapid decline in total portfolio risk as the portfolios are expanded from 1 to 10 securities.

Returning to Table 1, we note from the next to last column in the table that the return on a diversified portfolio follows the market very closely. The degree of association is measured by the correlation coefficient (R) of each portfolio with an unweighted index of all NYSE stocks (perfect positive correlation results in a correlation coefficient of 1.0).[5] The 20-security portfolio has a correlation of 0.89 with the market. The implication is that the risk remaining in the 20-stock portfolio is predominantly a reflection of uncertainty about the performance of the stock market in general. Exhibit 5 shows the results for the six quality groups.

Correlation in Exhibit 5 is represented by the correlation coefficient squared, R^2 (possible values range from 0 to 1.0). The R^2 coefficient has a useful interpretation: it measures the proportion of variability in

EXHIBIT 4 Standard Deviation versus Number of Issues in Portfolio

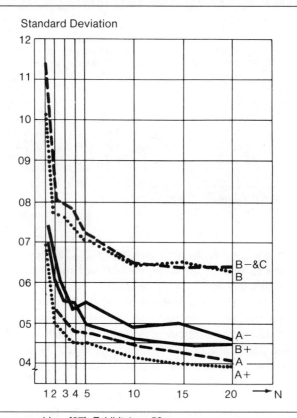

SOURCE: Wagner and Lau [27], Exhibit 1, p. 50.

portfolio return that is attributable to variability in market returns. The remaining variability is risk, which is unique to the portfolio and, as Exhibit 4 shows, can be eliminated by proper diversification of the portfolio. Thus, R^2 measures the degree of portfolio diversification. A poorly diversified portfolio will have a small R^2 (0.30–0.40). A well diversified portfolio will have a much higher R^2 (0.85–0.95). A perfectly diversified portfolio will have an R^2 of 1.0; that is, all the risk in such a portfolio is a reflection of market risk. Exhibit 5 shows the rapid gain in diversification as the portfolio is expanded from 1 to 2 securities and up to 10 securities. Beyond 10 securities the gains tend to be smaller. Note that increasing the number of issues tends to be less efficient at achieving diversification for the highest quality A+ issues. Apparently the companies comprising this group are more homogeneous than the companies grouped under the other quality codes.

EXHIBIT 5 Correlation versus Number of Issues in Portfolio

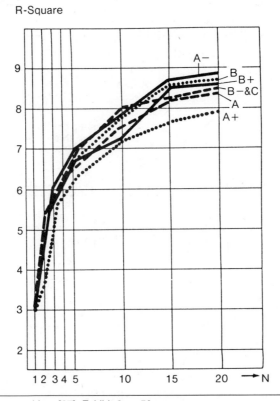

SOURCE: Wagner and Lau [27], Exhibit 2, p. 50.

The results show that while some risks can be eliminated via diversification, others cannot. Thus, we are led to distinguish between a security's "unsystematic" risk, which can be washed away by mixing the security with other securities in a diversified portfolio, and its "systematic" risk, which cannot be eliminated by diversification. This proposition is illustrated in Exhibit 6. It shows total portfolio risk declining as the number of holdings increases. Increasing diversification gradually tends to eliminate the unsystematic risk, leaving only systematic, i.e., market-related risk. The remaining variability results from the fact that the return on nearly every security depends to some degree on the overall performance of the market. Consequently, the return on a well diversified portfolio is highly correlated with the market, and its variability or uncertainty is basically the uncertainty of the market as a whole. Investors are exposed to market uncertainty no matter how many stocks they hold.

EXHIBIT 6 Systematic and Unsystematic Risk

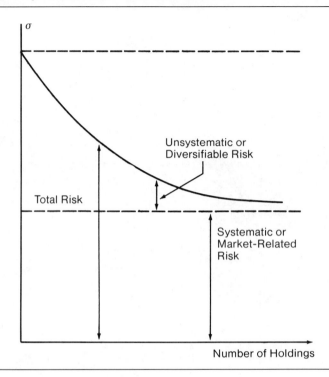

5. THE RISK OF INDIVIDUAL SECURITIES

In the previous section we concluded that the systematic risk of an individual security is that portion of its total risk (standard deviation of return) which cannot be eliminated by combining it with other securities in a well diversified portfolio. We now need a way of quantifying the systematic risk of a security and relating the systematic risk of a portfolio to that of its component securities. This can be accomplished by dividing security return into two parts: one dependent (i.e., perfectly correlated) and a second independent (i.e., uncorrelated) of market return. The first component of return is usually referred to as "systematic," the second as "unsystematic" return. Thus, we have

$$\text{Security return} = \text{Systematic return} + \text{Unsystematic return} \quad (4)$$

Since the systematic return is perfectly correlated with the market return, it can be expressed as a factor, designated beta (β), times the market return, R_m. The beta factor is a market sensitivity index indicating how sensitive the security return is to changes in the market level.

The unsystematic return, which is independent of market returns, is usually represented by a factor epsilon (ϵ'). Thus, the security return, R, may be expressed

$$R=\beta R_m + \epsilon' \tag{5}$$

For example, if a security had a β factor of 2.0 (e.g., an airline stock), then a 10 percent market return would generate a systematic return for the stock of 20 percent. The security return for the period would be the 20 percent plus the unsystematic component. The unsystematic component depends on factors unique to the company such as labor difficulties, higher than expected sales, etc.

The security returns model given by Equation (5) is usually written in a way such that the average value of the residual term, ϵ', is zero. This is accomplished by adding a factor, alpha (α), to the model to represent the average value of the unsystematic returns over time. That is, we set $\epsilon'=\alpha + \epsilon$ so that

$$R=\alpha + \beta R_m + \epsilon \tag{6}$$

where the average ϵ over time is equal to zero.

The model for security returns given by Equation (6) is usually referred to as the "market model." Graphically, the model can be depicted as a line fitted to a plot of security returns against rates of return on the market index. This is shown in Exhibit 7 for a hypothetical security.

The beta factor can be thought of as the slope of the line. It gives the expected increase in security return for a 1 percent increase in market return. In Exhibit 7, the security has a beta of 1.0. Thus, a 10 percent market return will result, on the average, in a 10 percent security return. The market-weighted average beta for all stocks is 1.0 by definition.

The alpha factor is represented by the intercept of the line on the vertical security return axis. It is equal to the average value over time of the unsystematic returns (ϵ') on the stock. For most stocks, the alpha factor tends to be small and unstable. (We shall return to alpha later.)

Using the definition of security return given by the market model, the specification of systematic and unsystematic risk is straightforward—they are simply the standard deviations of the two return components.[6]

The systematic risk of a security is equal to β times the standard deviation of the market return:

$$\text{Systematic risk} = \beta\sigma_m \tag{7}$$

The unsystematic risk equals the standard deviation of the residual return factor ϵ:

$$\text{Unsystematic risk} = \sigma_\epsilon \tag{8}$$

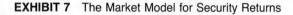

EXHIBIT 7 The Market Model for Security Returns

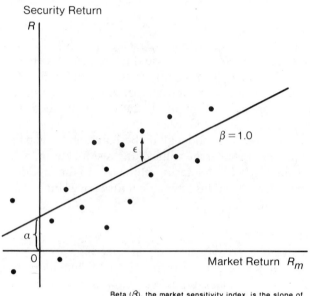

Beta (β), the market sensitivity index, is the slope of the line.

Alpha (α), the average of the residual returns, is the intercept of the line on the security axis.

Epsilon (ϵ), the residual returns, are the perpendicular distances of the points from the line.

Given measures of individual security systematic risk, we can now compute the systematic risk of portfolio. It is equal to the beta factor for the portfolio, β_p, times the risk of the market index, σ_m:

$$\text{Portfolio systematic risk} = \beta_p \sigma_m \qquad (9)$$

The portfolio beta factor in turn can be shown to be simply an average of the individual security betas, weighted by the proportion of each security in the portfolio, or

$$\beta_p = \sum_{j=1}^{N} X_j \beta_j \qquad (10)$$

where

X_j = the proportion of portfolio market value represented by security j

N = the number of securities

Thus the systematic risk of the portfolio is simply a weighted average of the systematic risk of the individual securities. If the portfolio is composed of an equal dollar investment in each stock (as was the case for the 100-security portfolio of Exhibit 2), the β_p is simply an unweighted average of the component security betas.

The unsystematic risk of the portfolio is also a function of the unsystematic security risks, but the form is more complex.[7] The important point is that with increasing diversification this risk can be reduced toward zero.

With these results for portfolio risk, it is useful to return to Exhibit 4. The figure shows the decline in portfolio risk with increasing diversification for each of the six quality groups. However, the portfolio standard deviations for each of the six groups are decreasing toward different limits because the average risks (β) of the groups differ.

Table 2 shows a comparison of the standard deviations for the 20-stock portfolios with the predicted lower limits based on average security systematic risks. The lower limit is equal to the average beta for the quality group ($\bar{\beta}$) times the standard deviation of the market return (σ_m). The standard deviations in all cases are close to the predicted values. These results support the contention that portfolio systematic risk equals the average systematic risks of the component securities.

The main results of this section can be summarized as follows: First, as seen from Exhibit 4, roughly 40 to 50 percent of total security risk can be eliminated by diversification. Second, the remaining systematic risk is equal to the security β times market risk. Third, portfolio systematic risk is a weighted average of security systematic risks.

The implications of these results are substantial. First, we would expect realized rates of return over substantial periods of time to be

TABLE 2 Standard Deviations of 20-Stock Portfolios and Predicted Lower Limits (June 1960–May 1970)

(1) Stock Quality Group	(2) Standard Deviation of 20-Stock Portfolios $\sigma \cdot$ Percent/Month	(3) Average Beta Value for Quality Group $\bar{\beta}$	(4) Lower Limit* $\bar{\beta} \cdot \sigma_m$ Percent/Month
A+	3.94%	0.74	3.51%
A	4.17	0.80	3.80
A−	4.52	0.89	4.22
B+	4.45	0.87	4.13
B	6.27	1.24	5.89
B− & C	6.32	1.23	5.84

* σ_m = 4.75% per month.
SOURCE: Wagner and Lau [27], p. 52, and Table C, p. 53.

related to the systematic as opposed to total risk of securities. Since the unsystematic risk is relatively easily eliminated, we should not expect the market to offer a risk premium for bearing it. Second, since security systematic risk is equal to the security beta times σ_m (which is common to all securities), beta is useful as a *relative* risk measure. The β gives the systematic risk of a security (or portfolio) relative to the risk of the market index. Thus, it is often convenient to speak of systematic risk in relative terms (i.e., in terms of beta rather than beta times σ_m).

6. THE RELATIONSHIP BETWEEN EXPECTED RETURN AND RISK: THE CAPITAL ASSET PRICING MODEL

The first part of this article developed two measures of risk: one is a measure of total risk (standard deviation), the other a relative index of systematic or nondiversifiable risk (beta). The beta measure would appear to be the more relevant for the pricing of securities. Returns expected by investors should logically be related to systematic as opposed to total risk. Securities with higher systematic risk should have higher expected returns.[8]

The question to be considered now is the form of the relationship between risk and return. In this section we describe a relationship called the Capital Asset Pricing Model (CAPM), which is based on elementary logic and simple economic principles. The basic postulate underlying finance theory is that assets with the same risk should have the same expected rate of return. That is, the prices of assets in the capital markets should adjust until equivalent risk assets have identical expected returns.

To see the implications of this postulate, let us consider an investor who holds a risky portfolio[9] with the same risk as the market portfolio (beta equal to 1.0). What return should he expect? Logically, he should expect the same return as that of the market portfolio.

Let us consider another investor who holds a riskless portfolio (beta equal to zero). The investor in this case should expect to earn the rate of return on riskless assets such as treasury bills. By taking no risk, he earns the riskless rate of return.

Now let us consider the case of an investor who holds a mixture of these two portfolios. Assuming he invests a proportion X of his money in the risky portfolio and $(1-X)$ in the riskless portfolio, what risk does he bear and what return should he expect? The risk of the composite portfolio is easily computed when we recall that the beta of a portfolio is simply a weighted average of the component security betas, where the weights are the portfolio proportions. Thus, the portfolio beta, β_p, is a weighted average of the beta of the market portfolio and the beta of the risk-free rate. However, the market beta is 1.0, and that of the risk-free rate is zero. Therefore,

$$\beta_p = (1 - X) \cdot 0 + X \cdot 1 \tag{11}$$
$$= X$$

Thus, β_p is equal to the fraction of his money invested in the risky portfolio. If 100 percent or less of the investor's funds is invested in the risky portfolio, his portfolio beta will be between zero and 1.0. If he borrows at the risk-free rate and invests the proceeds in the risky portfolio, his portfolio beta will be greater than 1.0.

The expected return of the composite portfolio is also a weighted average of the expected returns on the two-component portfolios; that is,

$$E(R_p) = (1 - X) \cdot R_F + X \cdot E(R_m) \tag{12}$$

where $E(R_p)$, $E(R_m)$, and R_F are the expected returns on the portfolio, the market index, and the risk-free rate. Now, from Equation (11) we know that X is equal to β_p. Substituting into Equation (12), we have

$$E(R_p) = (1 - \beta_p) \cdot R_F + \beta_p \cdot E(R_m)$$

or

$$E(R_p) = R_F + \beta_p \cdot (E(R_m) - R_F) \tag{13}$$

Equation (13) is the Capital Asset Pricing Model (CAPM), an extremely important theoretical result. It says that the expected return on a portfolio should exceed the riskless rate of return by an amount which is proportional to the portfolio beta. That is, the relationship between return and risk should be linear.

The model is often stated in "risk-premium" form. Risk premiums are obtained by subtracting the risk-free rate from the rates of return. The expected portfolio and market risk premiums—designated $E(r_p)$ and $E(r_m)$, respectively—are given by

$$E(r_p) = E(R_p) - R_F \tag{14a}$$

and

$$E(r_m) = E(R_M) - R_F \tag{14b}$$

Substituting these risk premiums into Equation (13), we obtain

$$E(r_p) = \beta_p \cdot E(r_m) \tag{15}$$

In this form, the CAPM states that the expected risk premium for the investor's portfolio is equal to its beta value times the expected market risk premium.

We can illustrate the model by assuming that the short-term

(risk-free) interest rate is 6 percent and the expected return on the market is 10 percent. The expected risk premium for holding the market portfolio is just the difference between the 10 percent and the short-term interest rate of 6 percent, or 4 percent. Investors who hold the market portfolio expect to earn 10 percent, which is 4 percent greater than they could earn on a short-term market instrument for certain. In order to satisfy Equation (13), the expected return on securities or portfolios with different levels of risk must be:

Expected Return for Different Levels of Portfolio Beta

Beta	Expected Return
0.0	6%
0.5	8
1.0	10
1.5	12
2.0	14

The predictions of the model are inherently sensible. For safe investments ($\beta = 0$), the model predicts that investors would expect to earn the risk-free rate of interest. For a risky investment ($\beta > 0$) investors would expect a rate of return proportional to the market sensitivity (β) of the investment. Thus, stocks with lower-than-average market sensitivities (such as most utilities) would offer expected returns less than the expected market return. Stocks with above-average values of beta (such as most airline securities) would offer expected returns in excess of the market.

In our development of CAPM we have made a number of assumptions that are required if the model is to be established on a rigorous basis. These assumptions involve investor behavior and conditions in the capital markets. The following is a set of assumptions that will allow a simple derivation of the model.

a. The market is composed of risk-averse investors who measure risk in terms of standard deviation of portfolio return. This assumption provides a basis for the use of beta-type risk measures.

b. All investors have a common time horizon for investment decision making (e.g., one month, one year, etc.). This assumption allows us to measure investor expectations over some common interval, thus making comparisons meaningful.

c. All investors are assumed to have the same expectations about future security returns and risks. Without this assumption, the analysis would become much more complicated.

d. Capital markets are perfect in the sense that all assets are completely divisible, there are no transactions costs or differential taxes, and borrowing and lending rates are equal to each other and the same for all investors. Without these conditions, frictional barriers would exist to the equilibrium conditions on which the model is based.

While these assumptions are sufficient to derive the model, it is not clear that all are necessary in their current form. It may well be that several of the assumptions can be substantially relaxed without major change in the form of the model. A good deal of research is currently being conducted toward this end.

While the CAPM is indeed simple and elegant, these qualities do not in themselves guarantee that it will be useful in explaining observed risk-return patterns. In Section 8 we will review the empirical literature on attempts to verify the model.

7. MEASUREMENT OF SECURITY AND PORTFOLIO BETA VALUES

The basic data for estimating betas are past rates of return earned over a series of relatively short intervals—usually days, weeks, or months. For example, in Tables 3 and 4 we present calculations based on month-by-month rates of return for the periods January 1945 to June 1970 (security betas) and January 1960 to December 1971 (mutual fund betas). The returns were calculated using Equation (1a).

Description of Columns in Tables 3 and 4

Column Number	Symbol	Description
1	NOBS	Number of monthly returns
2	ALPHA	The estimated alpha value
3	SE.A	Standard error of alpha
4	BETA	Estimated beta coefficient
5	SE.B	Standard error of beta
6	SE.R	Standard error of the regression— an estimate of the unsystematic risk
7	R**2	R^2 expressed in percentage terms
8	ARPJ	Arithmetic average of monthly risk premiums
9	SD.R	Standard deviation of monthly risk premiums
10	CRPJ	Geometric (time-weighted) average of monthly risk premiums

TABLE 3 Regression Statistics for 30 Randomly Selected Securities* (January 1945–June 1970)

Security	(1) NOBS	(2) ALPH	(3) SE.A	(4) BETA	(5) SE.B	(6) SE.R	(7) R**2	(8) ARPJ	(9) SD.R	(10) CRPJ
1 City Investing Co.	306.00	0.30	0.53	1.67	0.14	9.20	31.43	1.45	11.09	0.87
2 Foster Wheeler	306.00	-0.12	0.49	1.57	0.13	8.36	32.98	0.96	10.20	0.46
3 Pennsylvania Dixie	306.00	-0.20	0.47	1.40	0.12	8.15	29.33	0.77	9.67	0.33
4 National Gypsum Co.	306.00	-0.18	0.32	1.38	0.08	5.45	47.29	0.77	7.49	0.50
5 Radio Corp. of America	306.00	0.02	0.38	1.35	0.10	6.60	37.02	0.95	8.30	0.62
6 Fox Film Corp.	306.00	-0.04	0.53	1.31	0.14	9.15	22.35	0.87	10.36	0.38
7 Intercontinental Rubber	306.00	0.69	0.64	1.28	0.17	10.95	16.13	1.58	11.94	0.92
8 National Department	306.00	-0.05	0.45	1.26	0.12	7.73	27.05	0.81	9.04	0.41
9 Phillips Jones Corp.	306.00	0.36	0.44	1.25	0.12	7.54	27.89	1.22	8.86	0.85
10 Chrysler Corp.	306.00	-0.26	0.37	1.21	0.10	6.29	34.12	0.58	7.73	0.28
11 American Hide & Leather	306.00	0.55	0.66	1.16	0.17	11.36	12.78	1.35	12.14	0.67
12 Adams Express	306.00	0.11	0.23	1.16	0.06	3.93	54.87	0.91	5.84	0.75
13 Caterpillar Tractor	306.00	0.43	0.32	1.14	0.08	5.45	38.09	1.22	6.92	0.99
14 Continental Steel Co.	306.00	0.21	0.36	1.12	0.10	6.22	31.31	0.99	7.50	0.72
15 Marland Oil Co.	306.00	0.06	0.29	1.11	0.08	4.99	40.69	0.82	6.47	0.62
16 Air Reduction Co.	306.00	-0.59	0.29	1.08	0.08	4.98	39.73	0.16	6.41	-0.05

17 National Aviation	306.00	0.22	0.39	1.04	0.10	6.71	25.15	0.94	7.74	0.65
18 NA Tomas Co.	306.00	0.28	0.63	1.01	0.17	10.88	10.72	0.98	11.50	0.37
19 NYSE Index	306.00	0.0	0.0	1.00	0.0	0.0	0.0	0.69	3.73	0.62
20 American Ship Building	306.00	0.31	0.52	0.99	0.14	9.01	14.53	0.99	9.73	0.54
21 James Talcott	306.00	0.33	0.42	0.98	0.11	7.23	20.43	1.01	8.09	0.68
22 Jewel Tea Co. Inc.	306.00	0.21	0.32	0.95	0.08	5.42	30.14	0.87	6.47	0.66
23 International Carrier	306.00	0.34	0.26	0.93	0.07	4.39	38.41	0.98	5.58	0.83
24 Keystone Steel & Wire	306.00	0.18	0.30	0.84	0.08	5.19	26.90	0.76	6.05	0.58
25 Swift & Co.	306.00	−0.09	0.30	0.81	0.08	5.08	26.08	0.47	5.89	0.30
26 Southern California	306.00	0.00	0.22	0.77	0.06	3.77	36.60	0.53	4.72	0.42
27 Bayuk Cigars	306.00	−0.04	0.39	0.71	0.10	6.76	13.49	0.45	7.26	0.19
28 First National Store	306.00	−0.08	0.31	0.67	0.08	5.33	18.01	0.38	5.88	0.21
29 National Linen Service	306.00	0.61	0.33	0.63	0.09	5.75	14.50	1.04	6.20	0.86
30 American Snuff	306.00	0.17	0.25	0.54	0.07	4.33	17.74	0.54	4.77	0.43
31 Homestake Mining Co.	306.00	0.16	0.38	0.24	0.10	6.60	1.77	0.33	6.65	0.11
32 Commercial Paper	306.00	0.0	0.0	0.0	0.0	0.0	0.0	0.28	0.17	0.28
Mean sec. values	306.00	0.13	0.39	1.05	0.10	6.76	27.25	0.86	7.88	0.54
Standard deviations	0.0	0.28	0.12	0.31	0.03	2.10	11.85	0.33	2.13	0.26

* Based on monthly data, regression results sorted by beta (column 4).

TABLE 4 Regression Statistics for 49 Mutual Funds* (January 1960–December 1971)

Security	(1) NOBS	(2) ALPH	(3) SE.A	(4) BETA	(5) SE.B	(6) SE.R	(7) R**2	(8) ARPJ	(9) SD.R	(10) CRPJ
1 McDonnell Fund	144.00	0.58	0.82	1.50	0.22	9.76	25.18	1.13	11.24	0.67
2 Value Line Spec. Sit.	144.00	0.02	0.40	1.48	0.11	4.78	57.62	0.57	7.32	0.30
3 Keystone S-4	144.00	0.03	0.28	1.43	0.08	3.38	71.77	0.55	6.34	0.35
4 Chase Fund of Boston	144.00	0.11	0.33	1.42	0.09	3.94	64.78	0.63	6.61	0.41
5 Equity Progress	144.00	-0.54	0.41	1.26	0.11	4.85	48.89	-0.08	6.77	-0.31
6 Oppenheimer Fund	144.00	0.42	0.24	1.23	0.06	2.89	72.16	0.88	5.46	0.73
7 Fidelity Trend Fund	144.00	0.79	0.29	1.23	0.08	3.52	63.39	1.24	5.80	1.07
8 Fidelity Capital	144.00	0.41	0.24	1.20	0.06	2.81	72.17	0.85	5.31	0.71
9 Keystone K-2	144.00	0.08	0.22	1.17	0.06	2.63	73.90	0.51	5.13	0.38
10 Delaware Fund	144.00	0.18	0.19	1.15	0.05	2.32	77.62	0.60	4.90	0.48
11 Keystone S-3	144.00	0.18	0.19	1.14	0.05	2.32	77.50	0.60	4.88	0.48
12 Putnam Growth Fund	144.00	0.21	0.19	1.13	0.05	2.25	78.19	0.62	4.80	0.51
13 Scudder Special Fund	144.00	0.39	0.28	1.12	0.07	3.33	61.93	0.80	5.37	0.66
14 Energy Fund	144.00	0.06	0.18	1.10	0.05	2.18	78.39	0.46	4.67	0.35
15 One William Street	144.00	0.13	0.22	1.06	0.06	2.66	69.33	0.52	4.78	0.41
16 The Dreyfus Fund	144.00	0.17	0.14	1.04	0.04	1.69	84.40	0.55	4.26	0.46
17 Mass. Investors Gr. Stk.	144.00	0.15	0.16	1.03	0.04	1.96	79.65	0.52	4.34	0.43
18 Windsor Fund	144.00	0.18	0.16	1.03	0.04	1.95	79.87	0.56	4.33	0.47
19 Axe-Houghton Stock	144.00	0.39	0.30	1.02	0.08	3.62	52.96	0.76	5.26	0.62
20 S&P 500 Stock Index	144.00	0.0	0.0	1.00	0.0	0.0	0.0	0.37	3.76	0.30
21 T. Rowe Price Gr. Stk.	144.00	0.05	0.14	0.98	0.04	1.72	82.08	0.41	4.06	0.32
22 Mass. Investors Trust	144.00	-0.02	0.14	0.97	0.04	1.72	82.07	0.34	4.04	0.26
23 Bullock Fund	144.00	0.09	0.19	0.96	0.05	2.32	71.10	0.44	4.29	0.35
24 Keystone S-2	144.00	0.04	0.12	0.96	0.03	1.45	86.12	0.39	3.89	0.31
25 Eaton & Howard Stock	144.00	-0.05	0.13	0.95	0.03	1.52	84.75	0.30	3.89	0.23

#	Fund										
26	The Colonial Fund	144.00	0.06	0.19	0.95	0.05	2.27	71.24	0.41	4.23	0.32
27	Fidelity Fund	144.00	0.15	0.11	0.95	0.03	1.31	88.08	0.50	3.79	0.43
28	Invest. Co. of America	144.00	0.26	0.20	0.95	0.05	2.40	68.79	0.61	4.29	0.51
29	Hamilton Funds—HDA	144.00	-0.12	0.23	0.93	0.06	2.73	62.55	0.22	4.44	0.12
30	Affiliated Fund	144.00	0.08	0.10	0.90	0.03	1.22	88.55	0.41	3.59	0.34
31	Keystone S-1	144.00	0.03	0.10	0.88	0.03	1.21	88.18	0.35	3.51	0.29
32	Axe-Houghton Fund B	144.00	0.01	0.20	0.86	0.05	2.44	63.68	0.32	4.03	0.24
33	American Mutual Fund	144.00	0.20	0.20	0.85	0.05	2.38	64.35	0.51	3.97	0.43
34	Pioneer Fund	144.00	0.24	0.16	0.84	0.04	1.88	73.85	0.55	3.67	0.48
35	Chemical Fund	144.00	0.57	0.25	0.83	0.07	3.03	51.50	0.88	4.33	0.79
36	Stein R&F Balanced Fd.	144.00	0.06	0.10	0.79	0.03	1.21	86.05	0.35	3.22	0.30
37	Puritan Fund	144.00	0.19	0.15	0.78	0.04	1.79	72.89	0.48	3.43	0.42
38	Value Line Income Fd.	144.00	0.07	0.17	0.78	0.04	2.01	67.96	0.36	3.54	0.29
39	Geo. Putnam Fd. Boston	144.00	0.07	0.10	0.77	0.03	1.18	85.75	0.35	3.12	0.30
40	Anchor Income	144.00	-0.03	0.13	0.74	0.04	1.60	75.24	0.24	3.21	0.19
41	Loomis-Sayles Mutual	144.00	0.05	0.10	0.74	0.03	1.22	83.96	0.32	3.04	0.27
42	Wellington Fund	144.00	-0.12	0.13	0.72	0.03	1.54	75.60	0.14	3.11	0.09
43	Massachusetts Fund	144.00	0.04	0.11	0.72	0.03	1.26	82.16	0.30	2.98	0.26
44	Nation-Wide Sec.	144.00	-0.32	0.15	0.67	0.04	1.78	66.45	-0.08	3.07	-0.12
45	Eaton & Howard Bal. Fd.	144.00	-0.07	0.12	0.62	0.03	1.46	71.62	0.16	2.74	0.12
46	American Business Shares	144.00	0.12	0.09	0.53	0.02	1.10	76.96	0.31	2.28	0.29
47	Keystone K-1	144.00	0.01	0.11	0.53	0.03	1.32	69.59	0.21	2.39	0.18
48	Keystone B-4	144.00	0.12	0.13	0.30	0.03	1.51	35.82	0.23	1.88	0.21
49	Keystone B-2	144.00	0.05	0.10	0.16	0.03	1.16	22.03	0.11	1.31	0.10
50	Keystone B-1	144.00	-0.08	0.10	0.07	0.03	1.21	4.43	-0.06	1.23	-0.07
51	30-Day Treasury Bills	144.00	0.0	0.0	0.0	0.0	0.0	0.0	0.34	0.12	0.34
	Mean sec. values	144.00	0.12	0.19	0.93	0.05	2.32	69.25	0.46	4.25	0.36
	Standard deviations	0.0	0.22	0.12	0.30	0.03	1.42	17.50	0.27	1.64	0.23

* Based on monthly data, regression results sorted by beta (column 4).

It is customary to convert the observed rates of return to risk premiums. Section 6 showed that risk premiums are obtained by subtracting the rates of return that could have been achieved by investing in short-maturity risk-free assets, such as treasury bills or prime commercial paper. This removes a source of "noise" from the data. The noise stems from the fact that observed returns may be higher in some years simply because risk-free rates of interest are higher. Thus, an observed rate of return of 8 percent might be regarded as satisfactory if it occurred in 1960 but regarded as a relatively low rate of return when interest rates were high in 1969. Rates of return expressed as risk premiums will be denoted by small r's.

The market model of Equation (6), when expressed in risk-premium form, is the basic equation used to estimate beta. The market model in risk-premium form is given by

$$r = \alpha + \beta r_m + \epsilon \qquad (16a)$$

The use of risk premiums instead of returns as in Equation (6) simply changes the interpretation of alpha, leaving beta unchanged. In the return form, the expected value of alpha as given by the CAPM is $R_F(1 = B_p)$ [compare Equations (6) and (13)]. In the risk-premium form, the expected value of alpha is zero [compare Equations (15) and (16a)]. In the latter case, measured values of alpha different from zero can thus be interpreted as an *excess return* earned by a stock or portfolio beyond the return predicted by the CAPM on the basis of the asset's beta value. (More on the interpretation of alpha in Section 9).

Beta for a security is calculated by regressing the observed security risk premiums, r, on the observed risk premiums on the market, r_m. By this procedure we are, in effect, estimating the parameters of the market model of Equation (16a). The equation of the fitted line is

$$r = \hat{\alpha} + \hat{\beta} r_m + \hat{\epsilon} \qquad (16b)$$

where $\hat{\alpha}$ is the intercept of the fitted line and $\hat{\beta}$ represents the stock's systematic risk. The $\hat{\epsilon}$ term represents variation about the line resulting from the unsystematic component of return. We have put hats (ˆ) over the α, β, and ϵ terms to indicate that these are estimated values. It is important to remember that these estimated values may differ substantially from the true values because of statistical measurement difficulties. However, the extent of possible error can be measured, and we can indicate a range within which the true value is almost certain to lie.

Exhibit 8 shows a risk-premium plot and fitted line for National Department Stores. The market is represented by a weighted index of all NYSE securities. The plot is based on monthly data during the period January 1945 to June 1970.

The estimated beta is 1.26, indicating above-average systematic risk. The estimated alpha is −0.05 percent per month, indicating that the

EXHIBIT 8   Returns on National Department Stores versus NYSE Index
(percent per month) (January 1945–June 1970)

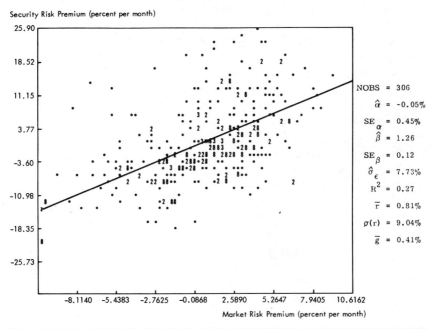

Security Risk Premium (percent per month)

NOBS = 306

$\hat{\alpha}$ = -0.05%

SE$_{\alpha}$ = 0.45%

$\hat{\beta}$ = 1.26

SE$_{\beta}$ = 0.12

$\hat{\sigma}_{\epsilon}$ = 7.73%

R^2 = 0.27

$\bar{r}$ = 0.81%

$\sigma(r)$ = 9.04%

$\bar{g}$ = 0.41%

Market Risk Premium (percent per month)

excess return on the security averaged −0.60 percent per year over the 25-year period. The correlation coefficient is 0.52; thus, 27 percent of the variance of security returns resulted from market movements. The remainder was due to factors unique to the company.

Our interpretation of the estimated alpha and beta values must be conditioned by the degree of possible measurement error. The measurement error is estimated by "standard error" coefficients associated with alpha and beta.

For example, the standard error of beta is 0.12. Thus, the probability is about 66 percent that the true beta will lie between 1.26 ± 0.12 and about 95 percent that it will lie between 1.26 ± 0.24 (i.e., plus or minus two times the standard error). Thus, we can say with high confidence that National Department Stores has above-average risk (i.e., true beta greater than 1.0).

The standard error for alpha is 0.45, which is large compared with the estimated value of −0.05. Thus, we cannot conclude that the true alpha is different from zero, since zero lies well within the range of estimated alpha plus or minus one standard error (i.e., −0.05 ± 0.45).

Table 4 presents the same type of regression results for a random collection of 30 NYSE stocks.[10] The table contains the following items: Column (1) gives the number of monthly observations; columns (2) and (3), the estimated alpha ($\hat{\alpha}$) and its standard error; columns (4) and (5), the estimated beta ($\hat{\beta}$) and its standard error; column (6), the unsystematic risk $\hat{\sigma}_\epsilon$, column (7), the R^2 in percentage terms; columns (8) and (9), the arithmetic average of monthly risk premiums and the standard deviation; and column (10), the geometric mean risk premium. The results are ranked in terms of descending values of estimated beta. The table includes summary results for the NYSE market index and the prime commercial paper risk-free rate.[11] The last two rows of the table give average values and standard deviations for the sample. The average beta, for example, is 1.05, slightly higher than the average of all NYSE stocks.

The beta value for a portfolio can be estimated in two ways. One method is to compute the beta of all portfolio holdings and weight the results by portfolio representation. However, this method has the disadvantage of requiring beta calculations for each individual portfolio asset. The second method is to use the same computation procedures used for stocks but to apply them to the portfolio returns. In this way we can obtain estimates of portfolio betas without explicit consideration of the portfolio securities. We have used this approach to compute portfolio and mutual fund beta values.

Exhibit 9 shows the plot of the monthly risk premiums on the 100-stock portfolio against the NYSE index for the same 1945–1970 period. As in the case of National Department Stores, the best-fit line has been put through the points using regression analysis. The slope of the line ($\hat{\beta}$) is equal to 1.10, with a standard error of 0.03. Note the substantial reduction in the standard error term compared to the security examples. The estimated alpha is 0.14, with a standard error of 0.10. Again, we cannot conclude that the true alpha is different from zero. Note that the points group much closer to the line than in the National Department Store plot. This results, of course, from the fact that much of the unsystematic risk causing the points to be scattered around the regression line in Exhibit 8 has been eliminated. The reduction is evidenced by the R^2 measure of 0.87 (versus 0.27 for National Department Stores). Thus, the market explains more than three times as much of the return variation of the portfolio than for the stock.

Table 5 gives regression results for a sample of 49 mutual funds. The calculations are based on monthly risk premiums for the period January 1960 to December 1971. The market is represented by the Standard & Poor's 500 Stock Index. Average values and standard deviations for the 49 funds in the sample are shown in the last two rows of the table. The average beta value for the group is 0.93—indicating, on the average, that the funds were less risky than the market index. Note the relatively low

EXHIBIT 9   Returns on 100 Stock Portfolio versus NYSE Index (percent per month) (January 1945–June 1970)

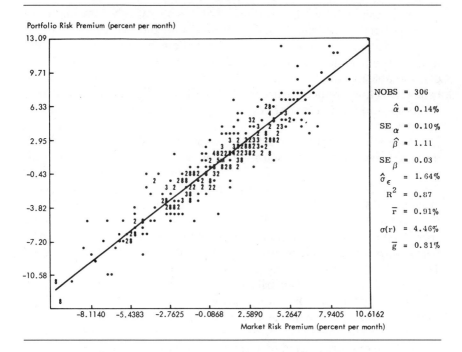

TABLE 5   Correlation of 52-Week Beta Forecasts with Measured Values for Portfolios of N Securities (1962–1970)

Forecast for 52 Weeks Ended	Product Moment Correlations: N=				
	1	5	10	25	50
12/28/62	.385	.711	.803	.933	.988
12/27/63	.492	.806	.866	.931	.963
12/25/64	.430	.715	.825	.945	.970
12/24/65	.451	.730	.809	.936	.977
12/23/66	.548	.803	.869	.952	.974
12/22/67	.474	.759	.830	.900	.940
12/20/68	.455	.732	.857	.945	.977
12/19/69	.556	.844	.922	.965	.973
12/18/70	.551	.804	.888	.943	.985
Quadratic mean	.486	.769	.853	.939	.972

SOURCE: Robert A. Levy [13], Table 2, p. 57.

beta values of the balanced and bond funds, in particular the Keystone B1, B2, and B4 bond funds. This result is due to the low systematic risk of the bond portfolios.

Up to this point we have shown that it is a relatively easy matter to estimate beta values for stocks, portfolios, and mutual funds. Now, if the beta values are to be useful for investment decision making, they must be predictable. Beta values based on historical data should provide considerable information about future beta values if past measures are to be useful. How predictable are the betas estimated for stocks, portfolios of stocks, and mutual funds? Fortunately, we have empirical evidence at each level.

Robert A. Levy [13] has conducted tests of the short-run predictability (also referred to as stationarity) of beta coefficients for securities and unmanaged portfolios of securities. Levy's results are based on weekly returns for 500 NYSE stocks for the period December 30, 1960, through December 18, 1970 (520 weeks). Betas were developed for each security for 10 nonoverlapping 52-week periods. To measure stationarity, Levy correlated the 500 security betas from each 52-week period (the historical betas) with the 52-week betas in the following period (the future betas). Thus, nine correlation studies were performed for the 10 periods.

To compare the stationarity of security and portfolio betas, Levy constructed portfolios of 5, 10, 25, and 50 securities and repeated the same correlation analysis for the historical portfolio betas and future beta values for the same portfolios in the subsequent period. The portfolios were constructed by ranking security betas in each period and partitioning the list into portfolios containing 5, 10, 25, and 50 securities. Each portfolio contained an equal investment in each security.

The results of Levy's 52-week correlation studies are presented in Table 5. The average values of the correlation coefficients from the nine trials were 0.486, 0.769, 0.853, 0.939, and 0.972 for portfolios of 1, 5, 10, 25, and 50 stocks, respectively. Correspondingly, the average percentages of the variation in future betas explained by the historical betas are 23.6, 59.1, 72.8, 88.2, and 94.5.

The results show the beta coefficients to be very predictable for large portfolios and progressively less predictable for smaller portfolios and individual securities. These conclusions are not affected by changes in market performance. Of the nine correlation studies, five covered forecast periods during which the market performance was the reverse of the preceding period (61–62, 62–63, 65–66, 66–67, and 68–69). Notably, the betas were approximately as predictable over these five reversal periods as over the remaining four intervals.[12]

The question of the stability of mutual fund beta values is more complicated. Even if, as seen above, the betas of large unmanaged portfolios are very predictable, there is no a priori need for mutual fund betas to be comparatively stable. Indeed, the betas of mutual fund portfolios may change substantially over time by design. For example, a portfolio manager may tend to reduce the risk exposure of his fund prior to an expected market decline and raise it prior to an expected market upswing. However, the range of possible values for beta will tend to be restricted, at least in the longer run, by the fund's investment objective. Thus, while one does not expect the same standard of predictability as for large unmanaged portfolios, it may nevertheless be interesting to examine the extent to which fund betas are predictable.

Pogue and Conway [21] have conducted tests for a sample of 90 mutual funds. The beta values for the period January 1969 through May 1970 were correlated with values from the subsequent period from June 1970 through October 1971. To test the sensitivity of the results to changes in the return measurement interval, the betas for each subperiod were measured for daily, weekly, and monthly returns. The betas were thus based on very different numbers of observations, namely 357, 74, and 17, respectively. The resulting correlation coefficients were 0.915, 0.895, and 0.703 for daily, weekly, and monthly betas. Correspondingly, the average percentages of variation in second-period betas explained by first-period values are 84, 81, and 49, respectively. The results support the contention that historical betas contain useful information about future values. However, the degree of predictability depends on the extent to which measurement errors have been eliminated from beta estimates. In the Pogue-Conway study, the shift from monthly to daily returns reduced the average standard error of the estimated beta values from 0.11 to 0.03, a 75 percent reduction. The more accurate daily estimates resulted in a much higher degree of beta predictability, the correlation between subperiod betas increasing from 0.703 to 0.915.[13]

Exhibit 10 shows a Pogue-Conway plot of the first-period versus second-period betas based on daily returns. The figure illustrates the high degree of correlation between first- and second-period betas.

In summary, we can conclude that estimated individual security betas are not highly predictable. Levy's tests indicated that an average of 24 percent of the variation in second-period betas is explained by historical values. The betas of his portfolios, on the other hand, were much more predictable, the degree of predictability increasing with portfolio diversification. The results of the Pogue and Conway study and others show that fund betas, not unexpectedly, are not as stable as those for unmanaged portfolios. Nonetheless, two thirds to three quarters of the variation in fund betas can be explained by historical values.

The reader should remember that a significant portion of the measured changes in estimated beta values may not be due to changes in the true values but, rather, to measurement errors. This observation

EXHIBIT 10   Interperiod Beta Comparison: Daily Data for 90 Mutual Funds

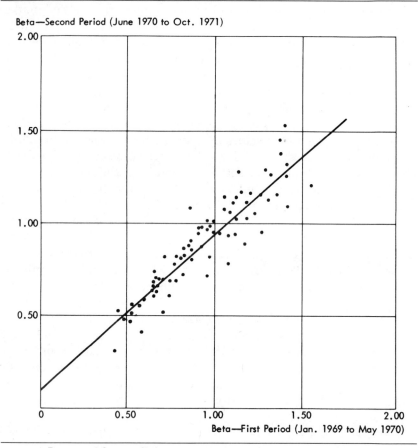

Beta—Second Period (June 1970 to Oct. 1971)

Beta—First Period (Jan. 1969 to May 1970)

SOURCE: Pogue and Conway [21].

is particularly applicable to individual security betas where the standard errors tend to be large.

8. TESTS OF THE CAPITAL ASSET PRICING MODEL

When we wrote the first version of this paper in the early 1970s, the question of the empirical validity of the CAPM seemed well on the way to a satisfactory if not perfect conclusion. The empirical tests seemed to a large extent to be consistent with the predictions of the model. However, in 1977 Richard Roll published an extensive paper [37] which severely criticized these empirical tests. While Roll did not attack the CAPM theory itself, he raised the possibility that, due to our inability to observe the rates of return on the true market index, the model might not be testable at all.

This section is divided into three parts. The first part summarizes three of the main studies conducted in the traditional manner, prior to the criticism by Richard Roll of the methodology used. In the second section, Roll's criticism of these tests is summarized. Finally, in the third section, we will summarize some of the tests conducted after Roll's criticisms which purport to be improvements over the previous studies.

Traditional Tests of the Capital Asset Pricing Model

The major difficulty in testing the CAPM is that the model is stated in terms of investors' expectations and not in terms of realized returns. The fact that expectations are not always realized introduces an error term, which from a statistical point of view should be zero *on the average* but not necessarily zero for any single stock or single period of time. After the fact, we would expect to observe

$$R_j = R_f + \beta_j(R_m - R_f) + \epsilon_j \qquad (17a)$$

where R_j, R_m, and R_f are the realized returns on stock j, the market index, and the riskless asset; and ϵ_j is the residual term.

If we observe the realized returns over a series of periods, the average security return would be given by

$$\overline{R}_j = \overline{R}_F + \beta_j(\overline{R}_M - \overline{R}_F) + \overline{\epsilon}_j \qquad (17b)$$

where $\overline{R}_j$, $\overline{R}_M$, and $\overline{R}_F$ are the average realized returns on the stock, the market, and the risk-free rate. If the CAPM is correct, the average residual term, $\overline{\epsilon}_j$, should approach zero as the number of periods used to compute the average becomes large. To test this hypothesis, we can regress the average returns, $\overline{R}_j$, for a series of stocks ($j = 1, \ldots, N$) on the stocks' estimated beta values, $\hat{\beta}_j$, during the period studied. The equation of the fitted line is given by

$$\overline{R}_j = \gamma_0 + \gamma_1\hat{\beta}_j + \mu_j \qquad (18a)$$

where γ_0 and γ_1 are the intercept and slope of the line and μ_j is the deviation of stock j from the line. By comparing Equations (17b) and (18a), we infer that if the CAPM hypothesis is valid, μ_j should equal $\overline{\epsilon}_j$ and hence should be small. Furthermore, it should be uncorrelated with $\hat{\beta}_j$, and hence we can also infer that γ_0 and γ_1 should equal $\overline{R}_F$ and $\overline{R}_M - \overline{R}_F$ respectively.

The hypothesis is illustrated in Exhibit 11. Each plotted point represents one stock's realized return versus the stock's beta. The vertical distances of the points from the CAPM theoretical line (also called the market line) represent the mean residual returns, $\overline{\epsilon}_j$. Assuming the CAPM to be correct, the $\overline{\epsilon}_j$ should be uncorrelated with the $\hat{\beta}_j$,

EXHIBIT 11 Relationship between Average Return ($\tilde{R}_j$) and Security Risk (β_j)

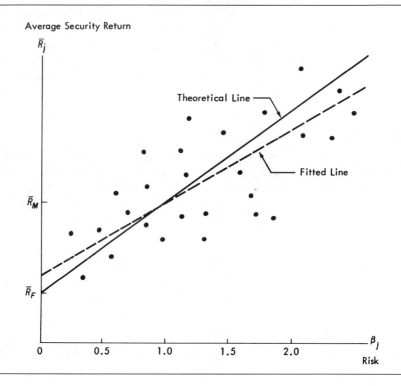

and thus the regression equation fitted to these points should be (1) linear, (2) upward sloping with slope equal to $\overline{R}_M - \overline{R}_F$, and (3) should pass through the vertical axis at the risk-free rate.

Expressed in risk-premium form, the equation of the fitted line is

$$\bar{r}_j = \gamma_0 + \gamma_1 \hat{\beta}_j + \mu_j \tag{18b}$$

where $\bar{r}_j$ is the average realized risk premium for stock j. Comparing Equation (18b) to the CAPM in risk-premium form, Equation (15), the predicted values for γ_0 and γ_1 are 0 and $\bar{r}_m$, the mean market risk premium ($\overline{R}_M - \overline{R}_F$). Thus, shifting to risk premiums changes the predicted value only for γ_0 but not for γ_1.

Other Measures of Risk

The hypothesis just described is only true if beta is a complete measure of a stock's risk. Various alternative risk measures have been proposed, however. The most common alternative hypothesis states that expected return is related to the standard deviation of return—that is, to a stock's total risk, which includes both systematic and unsystematic components.

Which is more important in explaining average observed returns on securities, systematic or unsystematic risk? The way to find out is to fit an expanded equation to the data:

$$R_j = \gamma_0 + \gamma_1 \hat{\beta}_j + \gamma_2 (S\hat{E}_j) + \mu_j \qquad (19)$$

Here $\hat{\beta}_j$ is a measure of systematic risk and $S\hat{E}_j$ a measure of unsystematic risk.[14] Of course, if the CAPM is exactly true, then γ_2 will be zero—that is, $S\hat{E}_j$ will contribute nothing to the explanation of observed security returns.

Empirical Tests of the Capital Asset Pricing Model

If the CAPM is right, empirical tests would show the following:

1. On the average, and over long periods of time, the securities with high systematic risk should have high rates of return.
2. On the average, there should be a linear relationship between systematic risk and return.
3. The slope of the relationship (γ_1) should be equal to the mean market risk premium ($\overline{R}_M - \overline{R}_F$) during the period used.
4. The constant term (γ_0) should be equal to the mean risk-free rate (R_F).
5. Unsystematic risk, as measured by $S\hat{E}_j$, should play no significant role in explaining differences in security returns.

These predictions were tested in a number of statistical studies. The first studies, including those by Jacob [9] and Miller and Scholes [19], were based on individual securities. These studies looked at the relationship between average realized security returns and their estimated risk (beta) levels during various historical time periods. These studies by and large found positive correlations between average security returns and risk levels. However, the strength of the relationship, as measured by the slope of the risk-return regression line, was typically far less than predicted by the theory.

While tests based directly on securities provide some overall support for the CAPM theory, they are inefficient from a statistical viewpoint for two reasons.

The first problem is well known to economists. It is called errors in variables bias and results from the fact that beta, the independent variable in the test, is typically measured with some error. These errors are random in their effect—that is, some stocks' betas are overestimated and some are underestimated. Nevertheless, when these estimated beta values are used in the test, the measurement errors tend to attenuate the relationship between mean return and risk.

By carefully grouping the securities into portfolios, much of this measurement error problem can be eliminated. The errors in individual stocks' betas cancel out so that the portfolio beta can be measured with much greater precision. This, in turn, means that tests based on portfolio returns will be more efficient than tests based on security returns.

The second problem relates to the obscuring effect of residual variation. Realized security returns have a large random component, which typically accounts for about 70 percent of the variation of return. (This is the diversifiable or unsystematic risk of the stock.) By grouping securities into portfolios, we can eliminate much of this "noise" and thereby get a much clearer view of the relationship between return and systematic risk.

It should be noted that grouping does not distort the underlying risk-return relationship. The relationship that exists for individual securities is exactly the same for portfolios of securities.

Friend and Blume studies. Professors Friend and Blume [3, 8] have conducted two interrelated risk-return studies. The first examines the relationship between long-run rates of return and various risk measures. The second is a direct test of the CAPM.

In the first study [8], Friend and Blume constructed portfolios of NYSE common stocks at the beginning of three different holding periods. The periods began at the ends of 1929, 1948, and 1956. All stocks for which monthly rate-of-return data could be obtained for at least four years preceding the test period were divided into 10 portfolios. The securities were assigned on the basis of their betas during the preceding four years—the 10 percent of securities with the lowest betas to the first portfolio, the group with the next lowest betas to the second portfolio, and so on.

After the start of the test periods, the securities were reassigned annually. That is, each stock's estimated beta was recomputed at the end of each successive year, the stocks were ranked again on the basis of their betas, and new portfolios were formed. This procedure kept the portfolio betas reasonably stable over time.

The performance of these portfolios is summarized in Table 6. The table gives the arithmetic mean monthly returns and average beta values for each of the 10 portfolios and for each test period.

For the 1929–69 period, the results indicate a strong positive association between return and beta. For the 1948–69 period, while higher beta portfolios had higher returns than portfolios with lower betas, there was little difference in return among portfolios with betas greater than 1.0. The 1956–69 period results do not show a clear relationship between

TABLE 6   Results of Friend-Blume Study (returns from a yearly revision policy
for stocks classified by beta for various periods)

| | Holding Period | | | | | |
| | 1929–1969 | | 1948–1969 | | 1956–1969 | |
Portfolio No.	Beta	Mean Return (Percent)	Beta	Mean Return (Percent)	Beta	Mean Return (Percent)
1	0.19	0.79%	0.45	0.99%	0.28	0.95%
2	0.49	1.00	0.64	1.01	0.51	0.98
3	0.67	1.10	0.76	1.25	0.66	1.12
4	0.81	1.28	0.85	1.30	0.80	1.18
5	0.92	1.26	0.94	1.35	0.91	1.17
6	1.02	1.34	1.03	1.37	1.03	1.14
7	1.15	1.42	1.12	1.32	1.16	1.10
8	1.29	1.53	1.23	1.33	1.30	1.18
9	1.49	1.55	1.36	1.39	1.48	1.15
10	2.02	1.59	1.67	1.36	1.92	1.10

Monthly arithmetic mean returns.
SOURCE: Friend and Blume [8], Table 4, p. 10.

beta and return. On the basis of these and other tests, the authors
conclude that NYSE stocks with above-average risk have higher returns
than those with below-average risk but that there is little payoff for
assuming additional risk within the group of stocks with above-average
betas.

In their second study [3], Blume and Friend used monthly portfolio
returns during the 1955–68 period to test the CAPM. Their tests involved
fitting the coefficients of Equation (18a) for three sequential periods:
1955–59, 1960–64, and 1965–68. The authors also added a factor to the
regression equation to test for the linearity of the risk-return relationship.[15]

The values obtained for γ_0 and γ_1 are not in line with the Capital
Asset Pricing Model's predictions, however. In the first two periods, γ_0
is substantially larger than the theoretical value. In the third period, the
reverse situation exists, with γ_0 substantially less than predicted. These
results imply that γ_1, the slope of the fitted line, is less than predicted in
the first two periods and greater in the third.[16] Friend and Blume
conclude that "the comparisons as a whole suggest that a linear model
is a tenable approximation of the empirical relationship between return
and risk for NYSE stocks over the three periods covered."[17]

Black, Jensen, and Scholes.   This study [1] is a careful attempt
to reduce measurement errors that would bias the regression results. For

TABLE 7 Results of Black-Jensen-Scholes Study

$$R_p = \gamma_o + \gamma_1 \hat{\beta}_p + \mu_p$$

1931–1965
Tests Based on 10 Portfolios
(averaging 75 stocks per portfolio)

Regression Results[a]			Theoretical Values	
$\hat{\gamma}_o$	$\hat{\gamma}_1$	R^2	$\gamma_o = \overline{R}_F$	$\gamma_1 = \overline{R}_M - \overline{R}_F$
0.519	1.08	0.90	0.16	1.42
(0.05)[b]	(0.05)			

[a] Units of coefficients: percent per month.
[b] Standard error.
SOURCE: Black, Jensen, and Scholes [1], Table 4, p. 98, and Figure 7, p. 104.

each year from 1931 to 1965, the authors grouped all NYSE stocks into 10 portfolios. The number of securities in each portfolio increased over the 35-year period from a low of 58 securities per portfolio in 1931 to a high of 110 in 1965.

Month-by-month returns for the portfolios were computed from January 1931 to December 1965. Average portfolio returns and portfolio betas were computed for the 35-year period and for a variety of subperiods. The results for the complete period are shown in Table 7. The average monthly portfolio returns and beta values for the 10 portfolios are plotted in Exhibit 12. The results indicate that over the complete 35-year period, average return increased by approximately 1.08 percent per month (13 percent per year) for a one-unit increase in beta. This is about three quarters of the amount predicted by the CAPM. As Exhibit 12 shows, there appears to be little reason to question the linearity of the relationship over the 35-year period.

Black, Jensen, and Scholes also estimated the risk-return trade-off for a number of subperiods.[18] The slopes of the regression lines tend in most periods to understate the theoretical values but are generally of the correct sign. Also the subperiod relationships appear to be linear.

This paper provides substantial support for the hypothesis that realized returns are a linear function of systematic risk values. Moreover, it shows that the relationship is significantly positive over long periods of time.

Fama and MacBeth. Fama and MacBeth [6] have extended the Black-Jensen-Scholes tests to include two additional factors. The first is an average of the β_j^2 for all individual securities in portfolio p, designated $\hat{\beta}_p^2$. The second is a similar average of the residual standard

EXHIBIT 12   Results of Black, Jensen, and Scholes Study (1931–1965)

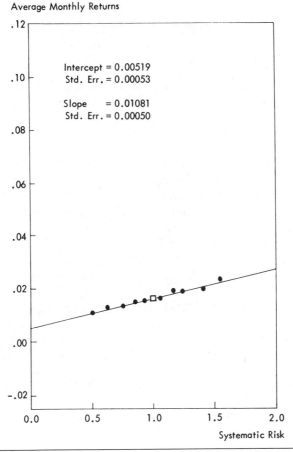

Average monthly returns versus systematic risk for the 35-year period 1931–1965 for 10 portfolios and the market portfolio.

source: Black, Jensen, and Scholes [1], Figure 7, p. 104.

deviations, $\hat{SE}_j$, for all stocks in portfolio p, designated $\hat{SE}_p$. The first term tests for nonlinearities in the risk-return relationship; the second, for the impact of residual variation.

The equation of the fitted line for the Fama-MacBeth study is given by

$$\bar{R}_p = \gamma_0 + \gamma_1\hat{\beta}_p + \gamma_2\hat{\beta}_p^2 + \gamma_3\hat{SE}_p + \mu_p \qquad (20)$$

where, according to the CAPM, we should expect γ_2 and γ_3 to have zero values.

The results of the Fama-MacBeth tests show that while estimated values of γ_2 and γ_3 are not equal to zero for each interval examined, their average values tend to be insignificantly different from zero. Fama and MacBeth also confirm the Black-Jensen-Scholes result that the realized values of γ_0 are not equal to $\bar{R}_f$, as predicted by the CAPM.

Summary of Test Results

Based on the empirical test results available when we wrote the original version of this article in 1974, we drew the following three specific conclusions and an overall conclusion regarding the empirical validity of the CAPM:

1. The evidence shows a significant positive relationship between realized returns and systematic risk. However, the slope of the relationship (γ_1) is usually less than predicted by the CAPM.
2. The relationship between risk and return appears to be linear. The studies give no evidence of significant curvature in the risk-return relationship.
3. Tests that attempt to discriminate between the effects of systematic and unsystematic risk do not yield definitive results. Both kinds of risk appear to be positively related to security returns. However, there is substantial support for the proposition that the relationship between return and unsystematic risk is at least partly spurious—that is, it partly reflects statistical problems rather than the true nature of capital markets.

Obviously, we cannot claim that the CAPM is absolutely right. On the other hand, the empirical tests do support the view that beta is a useful risk measure and that high beta stocks tend to be priced so as to yield correspondingly high rates of return.

More than a decade later we have to concede that much of the earlier testing was inadequate. Much of the credit for pointing this out belongs to Richard Roll.

Roll's Critique of Tests of the Capital Asset Pricing Model

In 1977 Richard Roll published a paper [37] which criticized the previously published tests of the CAPM. Roll argued that while the CAPM is testable in principle, no correct test of the theory had yet been presented. He also argued that there was practically no possibility that a correct test would ever be accomplished in the future.

The reasoning behind Roll's assertions revolves around the fact that there is only one potentially testable hypothesis associated with the CAPM, namely, that the true market portfolio is mean-variance efficient. Furthermore, since the true market portfolio must contain all worldwide assets, the value of most of which cannot be observed (e.g., human capital), the hypothesis is in all probability untestable.

The hypothesis tested in the traditional tests of the CAPM, namely, that there is a linear relationship between average security returns and beta values, sheds no light on the question whatsoever. This follows since an approximately linear relation between the risk and return would be achieved in tests involving large, well diversified common stock portfolios irrespective of whether securities were priced according to the CAPM or some totally different model. The result is tautological. The fact that a positive relationship between realized returns and betas was typically found simply indicates that the returns on the proxy indexes used for the true market portfolio were larger than the average return to the global minimum variance portfolio.

Post-Roll Tests of the CAPM

Since 1977 there have been a number of studies which purport to either support or reject the CAPM. These tests have attempted to examine implications of the CAPM other than the linearity of the risk-return relation as the basis of their methodology. Unfortunately, none provides a definitive test, and most are subject to substantial criticism. We shall mention three studies which will give the reader a flavor of the post-Roll tests.

The Cheng and Grauer test [29]. In 1980 Cheng and Grauer published the results of a test of the CAPM which they claimed to be "free from the ambiguity imbedded in past tests" (p. 660). In this test they assumed that the joint distribution of security returns is stationary and that the CAPM is valid. These assumptions permit a test of the CAPM which circumvents the need to identify the "true" market portfolio. The authors show that the above assumptions imply that the equilibrium value of any firm must move in lockstep with the value of other firms. This property, referred to by the authors as the "invariance law of prices," extends to portfolio values as well as firm values. The authors test whether the predicted relationship holds among portfolio market values over various historical periods. The advantage of this approach is that the market portfolio is not required and betas do not have to be estimated.

The results of their tests are inconclusive. Some results favor the CAPM; others reject it. The authors conclude that on balance their results provide evidence against the CAPM. The study, however, has been criticized on the basis that the two main assumptions are mutually inconsistent. Also, and as admitted by the authors, their test is a joint test of the CAPM and the stationarity of the return distributions. The test cannot reject the possibility that the CAPM holds and the return distributions are nonstationary.

The Gibbons test [34]. In 1982 Gibbons developed an alternative methodology for testing the CAPM that focused on the link between the market model and the CAPM. If the CAPM is valid, the estimated value of the intercept term in the market model should equal the product of the risk-free rate and one minus the portfolio beta. Similarly extended versions of the CAPM, which limit the ability of investors to borrow at the riskless rate, can be tested by replacing the risk-free rate by the return on the portfolio with the smallest standard deviation that is uncorrelated with the market index (the zero-beta portfolio). Based on his tests, Gibbons concluded that to the extent his market index was an adequate proxy, the data were inconsistent with both the risk-free and zero-beta versions of CAPM. The author's procedures, however, are still subject to the Roll criticism. Since a proxy index of unknown efficiency was used to compute the test beta values, the estimates may be unrepresentative of the true values, leading to a false rejection of the CAPM. Based on these tests, we still do not know if the CAPM is actually valid and Gibbons simply used a poor proxy or if the CAPM is simply an invalid model.

The Stambough test [43]. In 1982 Stambough conducted a sensitivity analysis to determine whether changing the nature of the market proxy has a significant impact on the results of tests of the CAPM. He expanded the types of investments included in his proxy from stocks on the NYSE to corporate and government bonds to real estate to durable goods such as house furnishings and automobiles. His results indicate that the nature of the conclusions aren't materially affected as one expands the composition of the proxy for the market portfolio.

These results at first appear to be comforting until one realizes that even in the broadest indexes examined, many investments were not included at the domestic level, including human capital. More importantly, the market portfolio should be internationally diversified, and the total invested capital of the United States is only a small fraction of invested capital worldwide. Moreover, many of these investments can be expected to exhibit a low degree of correlation with returns on investments in the United States. Stambough's results tell us only that when we move from using a market proxy that represents a very small fraction of the market portfolio to a proxy that represents a larger but still only a very small fraction, empirical results don't tend to change much.

Summary

To test the CAPM, one must directly test whether the market portfolio is a member of the mean-variance efficient set. None of post-Roll tests have been able to accomplish this. And in line with Roll's criticism, such tests are not likely to appear anytime soon. The problem facing researchers is that the CAPM market portfolio contains every single capital asset in the economic system. There is no possible way to determine whether such a portfolio is efficient relative to the minimum variance set for the entire capital-asset population. The observable market portfolio is only a tiny fraction of the true market portfolio. Moreover, even if the true market portfolio is efficient with respect to the total population, there is no reason to believe that a submarket portfolio is going to be efficient with respect to a subpopulation of assets even though the subpopulation is a very large fraction of the total. Because of this, the testing of the central hypothesis of the CAPM will remain an elusive goal.

This is not to say that the CAPM is defective on a theoretical level. The model follows logically from its assumptions, and it comes to a conclusion that is intuitively appealing. It makes sense that investors will price securities according to the contribution that each makes to the risk of their overall portfolios. Thirty years ago we believed that the risk of an individual security could be measured on the basis of the standard deviation of its rate-of-return distribution without regard to its relationships with other securities. The insight provided by the CAPM was a major step forward in our understanding of the way securities are priced in the marketplace. In fact, it may be possible that the CAPM may be the true underlying structure for security prices, but we are simply having a difficult time proving it.

It is also true that the CAPM is an accepted model in the securities industry. It is used by firms to make capital budgeting and other decisions. It is used by some regulatory authorities to regulate utility rates. It is used by rating agencies to measure the performance of investment managers. It would not be so widely used if it were not regarded as an extremely useful benchmark. It is, therefore, extremely important to understand the model in terms of both its strengths and weaknesses.

Work on deriving alternatives to the CAPM is underway. The arbitrage pricing theory is an alternative that captures the appealing intuition of the CAPM while purporting, at least by some, to be testable at the empirical level. We will examine this model in the next section.

9. THE ARBITRAGE PRICING THEORY

The Arbitrage Pricing Theory (APT) was first introduced by Stephen Ross [41] in 1976. It was developed as a generalization of the CAPM, permitting expected security returns to be influenced by a variety of risk factors as opposed to the single market index of the CAPM. Supporters of the APT argue that it has two major advantages over the CAPM. First, it makes less restrictive assumptions about investor preferences toward risk and return. The CAPM theory assumes investors trade off between risk and return solely on the basis of the expected returns and standard deviations of prospective investments. The APT, on the other hand, simply requires some rather unobtrusive bounds be placed on potential investor utility functions. Second, since the APT does not rely on the identification of the true market index, the theory is potentially testable.

The fundamental assumption of the APT is that security returns are generated by a series of indexes or factors. It is assumed the covariances between security returns are attributed to the common reliance of the securities on some or all of the same factors. The APT does not specify what these factors are, but it is assumed that the relationship between security returns and the factors is linear. The rate of return on security j in time period t is given by:

$$R_{jt} = E(R_{jt}) + B_{j1} f_{1t} + \ldots + B_{jn} f_{nt} + e_{jt} \tag{20}$$

where $f_{1t}, \ldots, f_{nt}$ represent the unanticipated returns on factors 1 through n in period t, $B_{j1}, \ldots, B_{jn}$ represent the sensitivity of the return on security j to variation in the factors, and e_{jt} is the unique risk of security j in period t.

Assuming that sufficient securities are available to ensure the residual risk of all securities can be completely diversified away (in effect, an infinite number of securities), then the expected rate of return on security j is given by:

$$E(R_{jt}) = A_o + B_{j1} A_{1t} + \ldots + B_{jn} A_{nt} \tag{21}$$

where A_o is the risk-free rate in period t, and A_{it} is the price per unit of factor risk i in period t.

The price of risk for each factor is found by forming a well diversified portfolio with zero risk on all factors except the one of interest with a risk level (B_{jl}) equal to 1.0. The expected return on this portfolio is equal to the price per unit of risk for that factor. However, as with the CAPM, this is not easy to measure because expected security returns are not directly observable. This leads to the use of historical data to estimate expected returns and to many of the same estimation problems that plague the CAPM.

The fact that the APT model employs multiple factors does not imply that it is mutually exclusive to the CAPM. Indeed, the expected rates of return on securities in the CAPM could well be explained by their relationship to a number of market factors. Suppose, for example, that the covariance among all securities can be fully explained by three portfolios which serve as indexes or factors. When aggregated, the weights for the individual securities in the three portfolios sum to the weights in the overall market portfolio. The expected return on any security would then be explained in terms of its beta value relative to each of the three factors and the expected risk premiums of the factors. This is precisely the form of the prediction of the multifactor APT model as shown in Equation (22). Under the CAPM, however, the market-weighted sum of the risk premiums on the three factors would equal the risk premium on the market index, and the weighted sum of the three factor betas would equal the CAPM beta.

The distinctive advantage of the APT model is that it permits investors to specifically tailor their portfolios to their tastes and circumstances by adjusting the exposure to the individual factor risks. Thus, several investors could have portfolios with the same CAPM beta but have quite different exposures across the various factor risks.

To date, the attempts to empirically test the APT have been inconclusive. (See, for example, references [31], [32], [40], and [42].) Indeed, due to the inability to find a set of factors that consistently explain security returns, the issue has been raised whether the APT is testable at all. The APT gives no direction as to the choice of the factors themselves or even how many factors might be required. (However, Richard Roll and Stephen Ross have suggested a set of four plausible factors in Chapter 38 of this book.) The APT has replaced the problem with the market portfolio in the CAPM with the uncertainty over the choice and measurement of the underlying factors.

All things considered, we feel that both models provide interesting conceptual insights into the issues of the pricing of risk and portfolio selection in securities markets. Neither can be said to dominate the other in terms of theoretical content or the simplicity of empirical testing. Only the future will decide which has the best claim to the ultimate truth. Indeed, on this question, both will probably make valuable contributions to the development on the next generation of equilibrium models.

10. MEASUREMENT OF INVESTMENT PERFORMANCE

The basic concept underlying investment performance measurement follows directly from the risk-return theory. The return on managed portfolios, such as mutual funds, can be judged relative to the returns on unmanaged portfolios at the same degree of investment risk. If the return exceeds the standard, the portfolio manager has performed in a superior way, and vice versa. Given this, it remains to select a set of "benchmark" portfolios against which the performance of managed portfolios can be evaluated.

Performance Measures Developed from the Capital Asset Pricing Model

The CAPM provides a convenient and familiar standard for performance measurement; the benchmark portfolios are simply combinations of the riskless asset and the market index. The return standard for a mutual fund, for example, with beta equal to β_p, is equal to the risk-free rate

($\overline{R}_F$) plus β_p times the average realized risk premium on the market ($\overline{R}_M - \overline{R}_F$). Thus, the return on the performance standard ($\overline{R}_S$) is given by

$$\overline{R}_S = \overline{R}_F + \beta_P(\overline{R}_M - \overline{R}_F) \tag{21}$$

where $\overline{R}_M$ and $\overline{R}_F$ are the arithmetic average returns on the market index and riskless asset during the evaluation period. The performance measure, designated α_p, is equal to the difference in average returns between the fund and its standard; that is,

$$\alpha_p = \overline{R}_P - \overline{R}_S \tag{22}$$

where $\overline{R}_P$ is the arithmetic average return on the fund. Under the CAPM assumption, the expected values of $\overline{R}_P$ and $\overline{R}_S$ are the same; therefore, the expected value for the performance measure α_p is zero. Managed portfolios with positive estimated values for α_p have thus outperformed the standard, and vice versa. Estimated values of alpha ($\hat{\alpha}_p$) are determined by regressing the portfolio risk premiums on the corresponding market risk premiums.

The interpretation of the estimated alpha must take into consideration possible statistical measurement errors. As we discussed in Section 7, the standard error of alpha (SE_α) is an indication of the extent of the possible measurement error. The larger the standard error, the less certain we can be that measured alpha is a close approximation of the true value.[19]

A measure of the degree of statistical significance of the estimated alpha value is given by the ratio of the estimated alpha to its standard error. The ratio, designated as t_α, is given by

$$t_\alpha = \hat{\alpha}_p/SE_\alpha \tag{23}$$

The statistic t_α gives a measure of the extent to which the true value of alpha can be considered to be different from zero. If the absolute value of t_α is large, then we have more confidence that the true value of alpha is different from zero. Absolute values of t_α in excess of 2.0 indicate a probability of less than about 2.5 percent that the true value of alpha is zero.

These methods of performance measurement were originally devised by Michael Jensen [10, 11] and have been widely used in many studies of investment performance, including that of the recent SEC Institutional Investor Study [22].

A performance measure closely related to the Jensen alpha measure was developed by Jack L. Treynor [25]. The Treynor performance measure (designated TI)[20] is given by

$$TI = \alpha/\beta \tag{24}$$

The difference between the α and TI performance measures is simply that the fund alpha value has been divided by its estimated beta. The effect, however, is significant, eliminating a so-called leverage bias from the Jensen alpha measures. This is illustrated in Exhibit 13.

Funds A and B in Exhibit 13 have the same alpha values. (The alphas are equal to the vertical distance on the diagram between the funds and the market line.) By combining portfolio B with the riskless rate (that is, by borrowing or lending at R_F), any return-risk combination along line Y can be obtained. But such points are clearly dominated by combinations along line X—attainable by borrowing or lending combined with fund A. As Exhibit 13 shows, the alpha for fund A, when levered to the same beta as fund B (Point A'), dominates the latter's alpha value.

EXHIBIT 13 Relationship between the Jensen and Treynor Measures of Investment Performance

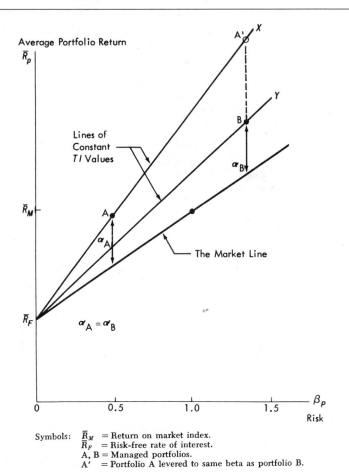

Symbols: $\bar{R}_M$ = Return on market index.
$\bar{R}_F$ = Risk-free rate of interest.
A, B = Managed portfolios.
A' = Portfolio A levered to same beta as portfolio B.

The Treynor measure eliminates this leverage effect. All funds which lie along a line (such as X or Y) have the same TI value; therefore, borrowing or lending combined with any fund outcome will not increase (or decrease) its performance measure. The Treynor measure thus permits direct performance comparisons among funds with differing beta values.

Problems with the Market Line Standard

The risk-adjusted performance measures described above are based on the CAPM. And given our inability to observe the true market index and thus test the model, we are confronted with problems on several levels in applying these measures in practice.

The first problem relates to the lack of conclusive empirical testing of the CAPM. One could take the position that since the model is really untested, the performance measures based on it are suspect and should be ignored. We feel that this is neither a sensible nor a practical position to take.

If one accepts the CAPM as a useful even if not perfect theoretical framework, then the second problem relates to how one measures portfolio risk and the risk-return market line. As Roll [38] has shown, if the proxy used for the true market index is unrepresentative of the complete asset opportunity set (i.e., inefficient), then the performance measures will be more related to the character of the proxy index than the quality of the performance being measured.

Those applying the CAPM-based performance standards in practice typically assume (usually implicitly) that, first, the CAPM is a reasonably valid representation of how securities are priced and that, second, the proxy index is sufficiently correlated with the true index to avoid serious biases in the estimated performance measures. However, even this act of faith faces a further empirical challenge. The traditional tests of the CAPM summarized in Section 8 show that the observed risk-return lines are typically flatter than predicted by the CAPM. This result tends to bias the performance measures in favor of low-risk portfolios and against high-risk funds. This problem can be corrected if the security market line is replaced by an "empirical" risk-return line. This line would pass through the return on the proxy market index and have an intercept equal to the return on the zero beta portfolio instead of the risk-free rate. The return on the zero-beta portfolio can be estimated using the procedures developed by Black, Jensen, and Scholes [1].

A comparison of these standards is illustrated in Exhibit 14. The market line performance measure (designated as α_1 in Exhibit 14) is equal to the vertical distance from the portfolio to the market line. The empirical line measure (designated α_2) is the vertical distance from the

EXHIBIT 14 Measurement of Investment Performance: Market Line versus Empirical Standard

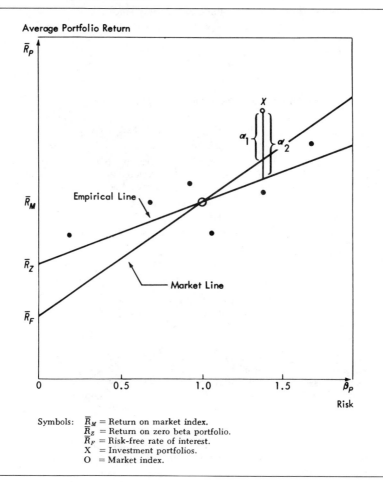

Average Portfolio Return

Symbols: $\bar{R}_M$ = Return on market index.
$\bar{R}_Z$ = Return on zero beta portfolio.
$\bar{R}_F$ = Risk-free rate of interest.
X = Investment portfolios.
O = Market index.

portfolio to the empirical line. Since ideally all the stocks used to develop the empirical line are contained in the market index, the empirical line, like the market line, would be expected to have a return equal to market return, $\bar{R}_M$, for beta equal to 1.0. The intercepts on the return axis, however, are typically different for the two lines. The market line intercept, by definition, is equal to the average risk-free rate. The empirical line intersects the return axis at a point different from $\bar{R}_F$, and typically above it. This intercept equals the average return on a portfolio with "zero beta," designated $\bar{R}_Z$.

ENDNOTES

1. The transformation changes nothing of substance since

$$\widetilde{M}_T = (1 + \widetilde{R}_p) M_0$$

$$= M_0 + M_0\widetilde{R}_P$$

where

$\widetilde{M}_T$ = terminal portfolio value
$\widetilde{R}_P$ = portfolio return

Since $\widetilde{M}_T$ is a linear function of $\widetilde{R}_P$, any risk measures developed for the portfolio return will apply equally to the terminal market value.

2. Risk measures based on below-the-average variation are analytically difficult to deal with. H. Markowitz, in Chapter 9 of [18], develops a semivariance statistic which measures variability below the mean and compares it with the more commonly used variance calculation.

3. See, for example, M. E. Blume [2].

4. This result can be illustrated as follows: The portfolio market value after N years, $\widetilde{M}_N$, is equal to

$$\widetilde{M}_N = M_0[(1 + \widetilde{R}_{P1})(1 + \widetilde{R}_{P2}) \ldots (1 + \widetilde{R}_{PN})]$$

where M_0 is the initial value and $\widetilde{R}_{pt}$ (t = 1, . . . , N) is the return during year t [as given by Equation (1a)]. For reasonably small values of the annual returns, the above expression can be approximated by

$$\widetilde{M}_N = M_0[1 + \widetilde{R}_{P1} + \widetilde{R}_{P2} + \ldots + \widetilde{R}_{PN}]$$

Now if the annual returns, $\widetilde{R}_{pt}$, are independently and identically distributed with variance σ^2, the variance of $\widetilde{M}_N$ will equal $(M_0)^2 N\sigma^2$, or N times the variance after one year. Therefore, the standard deviation of the terminal value will equal $\sqrt{N}$ times the standard deviation after one year. The key assumption of independence of portfolio returns over time is realistic, since security returns appear to follow a random walk through time.

A similar result could be obtained without the restriction on the size of the $\widetilde{R}_{pt}$ if we had dealt with continuously, as opposed to annually, compounded rates of return. However, the analysis would be more complicated.

5. Two securities with perfectly correlated return patterns will have a correlation coefficient of 1.0. Conversely, if the return patterns are perfectly negative correlated, the correlation coefficient will equal -1. Two securities with uncorrelated (i.e., statistically unrelated) returns will have a correlation coefficient of zero. The average correlation coefficient between returns for NYSE securities and the S&P 500 Stock Index during the 1945–1970 period was approximately 0.5.

6. The relationship between the risk components is given by

$$\sigma^2 = \beta^2\sigma_m^2 + \sigma_{\epsilon'}^2$$

This follows directly from Equation (5) and the assumption of statistical independence of R_m and ϵ'. The R^2 term previously discussed is the ratio of systematic to total risk (both measured in terms of variance):

$$R^2 = \frac{\beta^2 \sigma_m^2}{\sigma^2}$$

Note also that the R^2 is the square of the correlation coefficient between security and market returns.

7. Assuming the unsystematic returns (ϵ'_j) of securities to be uncorrelated (reasonably true in practice), the unsystematic portfolio risk is given by

$$\sigma^2(\varepsilon'_p) = \sum_{j=1}^{N} X_j^2 \, \sigma^2(\varepsilon'_j)$$

where $\sigma^2(\epsilon'_j)$ is the unsystematic risk for stock j. Assume the portfolio is made up of equal investment in each security and $\bar{\sigma}^2(\epsilon')$ is the average value of the $\sigma^2(\epsilon'j)$. Then, $X_j = 1/N$ and

$$\sigma^2(\varepsilon'_p) = \frac{1}{N} \, \bar{\sigma}^2(\varepsilon')$$

which, assuming $\bar{\sigma}^2(\epsilon')$ is finite, obviously approaches zero as the number of issues in the portfolio increases.

8. From this point on, systematic risk will be referred to simply as risk. Total risk will be referred to as total risk.

9. We use the term *portfolio* in a general sense, including the case where the investor holds only one security. Since portfolio return and (systematic) risk are simply weighted averages of security values, risk-return relationships which hold for securities must also be true for portfolios, and vice versa.

10. The sample was picked to give the broadest possible range of security beta values. This was accomplished by ranking all NYSE securities with complete data from 1945 to 1970 by their estimated beta values during this period. We then selected every 25th stock from the ordered list. The data was obtained from the University of Chicago CRSP (Center for Research in Security Prices) tape.

11. The commercial paper results in Table 3 are rates of return, not risk premiums. The risk premiums would equal zero by definition.

12. Correlation studies of this type tend to produce a conservative picture of the degree of beta coefficient stationarity. This results from the fact that it is not possible to correlate the true beta values but only estimates which contain varying degrees of measurement error. Measurement error would reduce the correlation coefficient even though the underlying beta values were unchanged from period to period.

13. These results are consistent with those found by N. Mains in a later study [16]. Mains correlated adjacent calendar-year betas for a sample of 99 funds for the period 1960 through 1971. The betas were based on weekly returns. The average correlation coefficient for 11 tests was 0.788, with individual values ranging from a low of 0.614 to a high of 0.871.

14. SE_j is an estimate of the standard error of the residual term in Equation (17a). Thus, it is the estimated value for $\sigma(\epsilon_j)$, the unsystematic risk term defined in Equation (8). See column (6) of Tables 3 and 4 for typical values for securities and mutual funds.

15. Their expanded test equation is

$$\widetilde{R}_j = \gamma_0 + \gamma_1 \hat{\beta}_j + \gamma_2(\hat{\beta}_j)^2$$

where, according to the CAPM, the expected value of γ_2 is zero.

16. Table 1, p. 25, of Blume and Friend [3] presents period-by-period regression results.

17. Blume and Friend [3], p. 26.

18. Figure 6 of Black, Jensen, and Scholes [1], pp. 101–3, shows average monthly returns versus systematic risk for 17 nonoverlapping two-year periods from 1932 to 1965.

19. See columns 2 and 3 of Table 4 for typical mutual fund $\hat{\alpha}$ and SE_α values.

20. Treynor's work preceded that of Jensen. In a discussion of Jensen's performance measure [26], Treynor showed that his measure (as originally presented in [25]) was equivalent to

$$TI = R_F - \alpha/\beta$$

Since R_F is a constant, the TI index for ranking purposes is equivalent to that given in Equation (24).

REFERENCES

[1] BLACK, FISCHER, MICHAEL C. JENSEN, and MYRON S. SCHOLES. "The Capital Asset Pricing Model: Some Empirical Tests." In *Studies in the Theory of Capital Markets,* ed. Michael Jensen. New York: Praeger Publishers, 1972, pp. 79–121.

[2] BLUME, MARSHALL E. "Portfolio Theory: A Step toward Its Practical Application." *Journal of Business* 43 (April 1970), pp. 152–173.

[3] _____, and IRWIN FRIEND. "A New Look at the Capital Asset Pricing Model." *Journal of Finance,* XXVIII (March 1973), pp. 19–33.

[4] BREALEY, RICHARD A. *An Introduction to Risk and Return from Common Stocks.* Cambridge, Mass.: MIT Press, 1969.

[5] FAMA, EUGENE F. "Components of Investment Performance." *The Journal of Finance* XXVII (June 1972), pp. 551–67.

[6] _____, and JAMES D. MACBETH. "Risk, Return and Equilibrium: Empirical Tests." Working paper no. 7237, University of Chicago, Graduate School of Business, August 1972.

[7] FRANCIS, JACK C. *Investment Analysis and Management.* New York: McGraw-Hill, 1972.

[8] FRIEND, IRWIN, and MARSHALL E. BLUME. "Risk and the Long Run Rate of Return on NYSE Common Stocks." Working paper no. 18–72, Wharton School of Commerce and Finance, Rodney L. White Center for Financial Research.

[9] JACOB, NANCY. "The Measurement of Systematic Risk for Securities and Portfolios: Some Empirical Results." *Journal of Financial and Quantitative Analysis* VI (March 1971), pp. 815–34.

[10] JENSEN, MICHAEL C. "The Performance of Mutual Funds in the Period 1945–1964," *Journal of Finance* XXIII (May 1968), pp. 389–416.

[11] _____. "Risk, the Pricing of Capital Assets, and the Evaluation of Investment Portfolios." *Journal of Business* 42 (April 1969), pp. 167–247.

[12] _____. "Capital Markets: Theory and Evidence." *The Bell Journal of Economics and Management Science* 3 (Autumn 1972), pp. 357–98.

[13] LEVY, ROBERT A. "On the Short Term Stationarity of Beta Coefficients." *Financial Analysts Journal* 27 (November–December 1971), pp. 55–62.

[14] LINTNER, JOHN. "The Valuation of Risk Assets and the Selection of Risky Investments in Stock Portfolios and Capital Budgets." *Review of Economics and Statistics* XLVII (February 1965), pp. 13–37.

[15] _____. "Security Prices, Risk, and Maximal Gains from Diversification." *Journal of Finance* XX (December 1965), pp. 587–616.

[16] MAINS, NORMAN E. "Are Mutual Fund Beta Coefficients Stationary?" Working paper, Investment Company Institute, Washington, D.C., October 1972.

[17] MARKOWITZ, HARRY M. "Portfolio Selection." *Journal of Finance* VII (March 1952), pp. 77–91.

[18] _____. *Portfolio Selection: Efficient Diversification of Investments.* New York: John Wiley & Sons, 1959.

[19] MILLER, MERTON H., and MYRON S. SCHOLES. "Rates of Returns in Relation to Risk:

A Reexamination of Recent Findings." In *Studies in the Theory of Capital Markets*, ed. Michael Jensen. New York: Praeger Publishers, 1972, pp. 47–78.

[20] MODIGLIANI, FRANCO, and GERALD A. POGUE. *A Study of Investment Performance Fees.* Lexington, Mass.: Heath-Lexington Books, 1974.

[21] POGUE, GERALD A., and WALTER CONWAY. "On the Stability of Mutual Fund Beta Values." Working paper, MIT, Sloan School of Management, June 1972.

[22] SECURITIES AND EXCHANGE COMMISSION. "Investment Advisory Complexes." *Institutional Investor Study Report of the Securities and Exchange Commission.* Washington, D.C.: U.S. Government Printing Office, 1971, chap. 4, pp. 325–47.

[23] SHARPE, WILLIAM F. "Capital Asset Prices: A Theory of Market Equilibrium under Conditions of Risk." *Journal of Finance* XIX (September 1964), pp. 425–42.

[24] _____. *Portfolio Theory and Capital Markets.* New York: McGraw-Hill, 1970.

[25] TREYNOR, JACK L. "How to Rate the Management of Investment Funds." *Harvard Business Review* XLIII (January–February 1965), pp. 63–75.

[26] _____."The Performance of Mutual Funds in the Period 1945–1964: Discussion." *Journal of Finance* XXIII (May 1968), pp. 418–19.

[27] WAGNER, WAYNE H., and SHEILA LAU. "The Effect of Diversification on Risk." *Financial Analysts Journal* 26 (November/December 1971), pp. 48–53.

[28] ALEXANDER, G. J., and J. C. FRANCIS. *Portfolio Analysis.* 3rd ed. Englewood Cliffs, N.J.: Prentice-Hall, 1986.

[29] CHENG, PAO L., and ROBERT R. GRAUER. "An Alternative Test of the Capital Asset Pricing Model." *American Economic Review* 70, no. 4 (September 1980), pp. 660–71.

[30] _____. "An Alternative Test of the Capital Asset Pricing Model: Reply." *American Economic Review* 72, no. 5 (December 1982), pp. 1201–7.

[31] DHRYMES, PHOEBUS J., IRWIN FRIEND, and N. BULENT GULTEKIN. "A Critical Reexamination of the Empirical Evidence on the Arbitrage Pricing Theory." *Journal of Finance* 39, no. 2 (June 1984), pp. 323–46.

[32] _____, IRWIN FRIEND, MUSTAFA N. GULTEKIN, and N. BULENT GULTEKIN. "New Tests of the APT and Their Implications." *Journal of Finance* 40, no. 3 (July 1985), pp. 659–74.

[33] DYBVIG, PHILIP H., and STEPHEN A. ROSS. "Yes, the APT Is Testable." *Journal of Finance* 40, no. 4 (September 1985c), pp. 1173–88.

[34] GIBBONS, MICHAEL R. "Multivariate Tests of Financial Models: A New Approach." *Journal of Financial Economics* 10, no. 1 (March 1982), pp. 3–27.

[35] HAUGEN, R. A. *Modern Investment Theory.* Englewood Cliffs, N.J.: Prentice-Hall, 1986.

[36] JACOB, N. L., and R. R. PETTIT. *Investments.* Homewood, Ill.: Richard D. Irwin, 1984.

[37] ROLL, RICHARD. "A Critique of the Asset Pricing Theory's Tests Part I. On Past and Potential Testability of the Theory." *Journal of Financial Economics* 4, no. 2 (March 1977), pp. 129–76.

[38] _____. "Ambiguity When Performance Is Measured by the Security Market Line." *Journal of Finance* 33, no. 4 (September 1978), pp. 1051–69.

[39] _____, and STEPHEN A. ROSS. "An Empirical Investigation of the Arbitrage Pricing Theory." *Journal of Finance* 35, no. 5 (December 1980), pp. 1073–1103.

[40] _____, STEPHEN A. ROSS. "A Critical Reexamination of the Empirical Evidence on the Arbitrage Pricing Theory: A Reply." *Journal of Finance* 39, no. 2 (June 1984b), pp. 347–50.

[41] ROSS, STEPHEN A. "The Arbitrage Theory of Capital Asset Pricing." *Journal of Economic Theory* 13, no. 3 (December 1976), pp. 341–60.

[42] SHANKEN, JAY. "The Arbitrage Pricing Theory: Is It Testable?" *Journal of Finance* 37, no. 5 (December 1982), pp. 1129–40.

[43] STAMBOUGH, ROBERT F. "On the Exclusion of Assets from Tests of the Two-Parameter Model: A Sensitivity Analysis." *Journal of Financial Economics* 10, no. 3 (November 1982), pp. 237–68.

38

The Arbitrage Pricing
Theory Approach to Strategic
Portfolio Planning

Richard Roll, Ph.D.
Allstate Professor of Finance and Insurance
Graduate School of Management
University of California, Los Angeles

Stephen A. Ross, Ph.D.
Sterling Professor of Economics and Finance
School of Organization and Management
Yale University

ABSTRACT

Arbitrage Pricing Theory (APT) asserts that an asset's riskiness, hence its average long-term return, is directly related to its sensitivities to unanticipated changes in basic economic variables. Empirical work has identified the following four as critical: (1) inflation, (2) industrial production, (3) risk premia, and (4) the term structure of interest rates. The central focus of portfolio strategy is, thus, choosing an appropriate pattern of sensitivities. This choice will depend upon the economic characteristics of the beneficiaries of the portfolio's income and upon whether they are more or less concerned with the economic factor risks than the average investor.

This chapter is an extension and update of an article of the same title published in the *Financial Analysts Journal*, May/June 1984.

Introduction

The Arbitrage Pricing theory (APT) has now survived several years of fairly intense scrutiny.[1] Most of the explanations and examinations have taken place on an advanced mathematical and econometric level, which means that few persons outside academia have had the time to read them.[2] Nevertheless, APT has gained the notice of the investment community, and their curiosity will no doubt grow considerably during the next few years as the logical appeal and, more importantly, the practical implications of APT become apparent. This chapter aims to accelerate the process by providing an intuitive description of APT and by discussing its merits for portfolio management.

The Intuition

At the core of APT is the recognition that only a few systematic factors affect the long-term average returns of financial assets. APT does not deny the myriad factors that influence the daily price variability of individual stocks and bonds, but it focuses on the major forces that move aggregates of assets in large portfolios. By identifying these forces, we can gain an intuitive appreciation of their influence on portfolio returns. The ultimate goal is to acquire a better understanding of portfolio structuring and evaluation and thereby to improve overall portfolio design and performance.

The Influence of Systematic Factors

The total return on an individual stock in, say, the coming year will depend on a variety of anticipated and unanticipated events. Anticipated events will be incorporated by investors into their expectations of returns on individual stocks and thus will be incorporated into market prices. Generally, however, most of the return ultimately realized will be the result of unanticipated events. Of course, change itself is anticipated, and investors know that the most unlikely occurrence of all would be the exact realization of even the most probable future scenario. But even though we realize that unforeseen events will occur, by their very nature we cannot know either their direction or their magnitude. What we can know is the sensitivity of asset returns to these events.

Asset returns are also affected by influences that are not systematic to the economy as a whole, influences that impinge upon individual firms or particular industries but are not directly related to overall economic conditions. Such forces are called idiosyncratic to distinguish them from the systematic factors that describe the major movements in market returns. Because, through the process of diversification, idiosyncratic returns on individual assets cancel out, returns on large portfolios are influenced mainly by the systematic factors alone.

Systematic factors are the major sources of risk in portfolio returns. Actual portfolio returns depend upon the same set of common factors, but this does not mean that all large portfolios perform identically. Different portfolios have different sensitivities to these factors. A portfolio that is so hedged as to be insensitive to these factors, and that is sufficiently large and well proportioned that idiosyncratic risk is diversified away, is essentially riskless.

Because the systematic factors are the primary sources of risk, it follows that they are the principal determinants of the expected, as well as the actual, returns on portfolios. The logic behind this view is not simply the usual economic argument that more return can be obtained only by bearing more risk. While this line of reasoning certainly contains a great truth, its appeal comes more from Calvin than from Adam Smith. There is a far simpler reason why the expected return on a portfolio is related to its sensitivity to factor movements.

The logic is the same as that which leads to the conclusion that two three-month Treasury bills or two shares of GM must sell for the same price. Two assets that are very close substitutes must sell for about the same price, and nowhere in the entire economy are there any closer substitutes than two financial assets that offer the same return. Two portfolios with the same sensitivities to each of the systematic factors are very close substitutes. In effect, they differ only in the limited amount of idiosyncratic or residual risk they might still bear. Consequently, they must offer the investor the same expected return, just as the two Treasury bills or the two shares of the same stock offer the same expected return.

At this point, a bit of mathematics is probably desirable, if not inevitable. What we have said so far can be understood by breaking down the actual return, R, on any asset—be it a stock, bond, or portfolio—into three constituent parts as follows:

$$R = E + bf + e \tag{1}$$

where

E = the expected return on the asset
b = the asset's sensitivity to a change in the systematic factor
f = the actual return on the systematic factor
e = the return on the unsystematic, idiosyncratic factors

Equation (1) merely says that the actual return equals the expected return plus factor sensitivity times factor movement plus residual risk.

As we have noted, however, there is more than one systematic factor. There are several important ones, and if all of them are not represented, then our understanding of how the capital market works is inadequate. Our basic equation, then, must be expanded to incorporate multiple systematic factors.

Empirical work suggests that a four-factor model adequately, if not completely, captures the influence of systematic factors on stock market returns. Equation (1) may thus be expanded to:

$$R = E + (b1)(f1) + (b2)(f2) +$$
$$(b3)(f3) + (b4)(f4) + e \qquad (2)$$

Each of the four middle terms in Equation (2) is the product of the returns on a particular economic factor and the given asset's sensitivity to that factor.

What are these factors? They are the underlying economic forces that are the primary influences on the stock market. Our research has suggested that the most important factors are (1) unanticipated inflation, (2) changes in the expected level of industrial production, (3) unanticipated shifts in risk premia, and (4) unanticipated movements in the shape of the term structure of interest rates. We will elaborate on this choice of the factors in more detail below. Right now, our task is to show that there is a simple relation between the factor sensitivities of an asset—b1, b2, b3, and b4—and the asset's expected return, E.

Factor Sensitivity and Asset Returns

Figure A shows a hypothetical plot of Equation (2) using the third factor as an example and holding factors one, two, and four at zero. The figure shows the straight-line relation between actual realized returns and movements in factor three for a particular asset. A more sensitive asset—i.e., one with a larger value for b—would have a steeper line, indicating that factor three has a greater influence on its return. Conversely, the plot for an asset with a lower b would be closer to the horizontal; its return would be less affected by movements of the third factor. There is, in fact, nothing to prevent a sensitivity from being negative. If this were the case, then a rise in the factor would cause this asset's price to fall.

Notice that a factor return of zero ($f = 0$) does not mean the actual return on the asset will be zero. It just means that, in this case, the actual return will equal the expected return, E. The factor movements represented by f are unanticipated. Any anticipated changes have already been incorporated into the expected return on the portfolio, E. Thus, f stands for the deviation of the actual factor return from its expected return. When it is zero, actual factor movements have been just as was expected, and actual portfolio returns will be just what investors had expected. Put simply, if there are no surprises in factor movements, then there can be no surprises in portfolio returns.

FIGURE A Returns and Factor Three

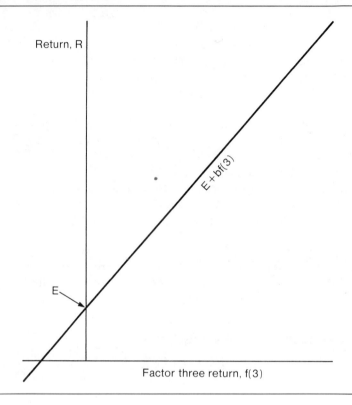

Figure B illustrates the relation that must hold between expected return, E, and sensitivity, b. Here point A represents a riskless asset, perhaps a short-maturity bond, with an expected return, r, of 15 percent. Points B and C represent two stocks with, respectively, expected returns of 20 and 35 percent and sensitivities of one and two.

A portfolio that is evenly divided between the bond A and stock C will have a return that is a simple average of the returns of the two constituent assets:

$$E = \tfrac{1}{2} \times 15\% + \tfrac{1}{2} \times 35\%$$

$$= 25\%$$

The sensitivity of this portfolio will also be halfway between the sensitivities of bond A and stock C:

$$b(3) = \tfrac{1}{2} \times 0 + \tfrac{1}{2} \times 2$$

$$= 1$$

FIGURE B Expected Return and Exposure

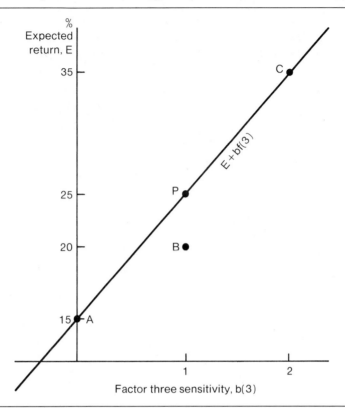

This portfolio is plotted as point P in Figure B.

Notice that P lies directly above stock B. Consider what this means. A portfolio of bond A and the higher risk stock C has the same sensitivity to systematic factor risk as stock B. But although the portfolio has the same sensitivity as stock B, it has a higher expected return—25 percent versus an expected return of only 20 percent for stock B.

More importantly, no matter what value factor three happens to take, the portfolio's return will dominate that of stock B. Figure C displays the actual returns on the portfolio P and on stock B in relation to the factor three return. Regardless of the outcome (and remember that the actual outcomes are not known in advance), portfolio P does 5 percent better than stock B. The situation presented is the very same sort of arbitrage opportunity that would occur in the bond market if two Treasury bills with the same maturity sold at different yields. It is the same sort of situation that foreign exchange traders exploit when they

FIGURE C Actual Returns: Stock B versus Portfolio P

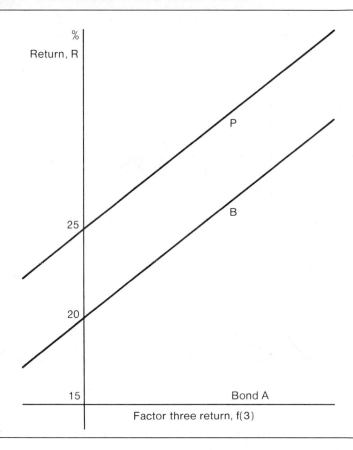

discover discrepancies in exchange rates across different currencies. In well functioning capital markets, such opportunities exist only momentarily, until they are closed by traders whose reward comes from eliminating such gaps.

When this arbitrage takes place, with investors reducing their holdings of stock B and covering themselves by purchasing portfolio P, the price of stock B falls and that of stock C rises. At the lower price, stock B becomes more attractive relative to stock C. This process terminates only when portfolio P and stock B offer the same expected return. In fact, as in the foreign exchange market or in the bond market, the process works sufficiently rapidly that a gap would probably be too fleeting for an outside investor even to notice.

The arbitrage opportunity is eliminated only when all three assets in Figure B lie on the same line; in any other case, there will always be

FIGURE D   Equilibrium Expected Returns

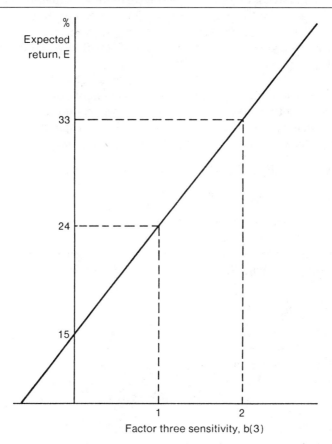

another portfolio that beats (or is beaten by) one of the assets, no matter what unanticipated developments come to pass.

Figure D plots the line on which all three assets must fall. As we have drawn it, there is a direct positive relation between the expected return, E, on any portfolio or individual asset and its risk sensitivity, b(3). The slope of this line measures the market price of this type of risk.

In Figure D, the price of risk for factor three is displayed as the difference between the expected return at a sensitivity of one and the riskless return. As the riskless rate is 15 percent and assets with a factor three sensitivity of one have a 24 percent return, the market price of this risk is 9 percent (24%–15%). This means that any asset with a b(3) of one—i.e., any asset whose return rises or falls by 1 percent whenever the third factor rises or falls by 1 percent—will have an expected return

9 percent above the riskless return of 15 percent. An asset that is more sensitive will have a higher expected return; for example, the return for an asset with a b of two is 33 percent (15% + 2 × 9%). In others words, the price of risk for factor three of 9 percent is the rate at which the investor is rewarded for assuming a unit of sensitivity to movements in this factor.

In summary, the expected return on any asset is directly related to that asset's sensitivity to unanticipated movements in major economic factors. If we let E3 stand for the return on a portfolio with a sensitivity of one to factor three (E3 equals 24 percent in the example of Figure D), then the total expected return (E) on the portfolio may be computed as:

$$E = r + (E1 - r)(b1) + (E2 - r)(b2)$$
$$+ (E3 - r)(b3) + (E4 - r)(b4) \tag{3}$$

This equation simply states algebraically the relation we have proved: the expected return on any asset, E, exceeds the riskless return, r, by an amount equal to the sum of the products of the market prices of risk, Ef − r, and the sensitivities of the asset to each of the respective factors.

Examining the Factors

We have defined sensitivities as the responses of asset return to unanticipated movements in economic factors. But what are these factors? If we knew them, we could measure directly the sensitivities of individual stocks to each. We could, for example, attribute a particular fraction of the observed price movements in a given stock to movements in the economic factor.

Unfortunately, this is much more difficult than it sounds. To begin with, any one stock is so influenced by idiosyncratic forces that it is very difficult to determine the precise relation between its return and a given factor. At a more practical level, we have so much more data available on individual stock returns than we have on broad economic factors that this approach would be very inefficient. Imagine, for example, attempting to see what happens to the yield on a Phoenix Power and Light bond when the money supply changes. A much better approach would be first to determine the impact of an index of municipal bond yields on the Phoenix bond; this can be done with considerable accuracy. We can then see how sensitive bond yields as a whole are to money supply changes. The sensitivity of the Phoenix bond to the money supply can then be determined as the product of these two sensitivities, each of which can be measured with some precision.

The biggest problem in the measurement of sensitivities, however, is separating unanticipated from anticipated factor movements. The b's measure the sensitivity of returns to unanticipated movements in the factors. By just looking at how a given asset relates to movements in the money supply, we would be including the influence of both anticipated and unanticipated changes, when only the latter are relevant. Anticipated changes are expected and have already been incorporated into expected returns. The unanticipated returns are what determine the b's, and their measurement is one of the more important components of the APT approach.

What economic factors relate to unanticipated returns on large portfolios? As noted above, empirical research indicated that the following four economic factors are relevant:[3]

1. Unanticipated changes in industrial production, MP.
2. Unanticipated changes in risk premia (as measured by the spread between low-grade and high-grade bonds), UPR.
3. Unanticipated changes in interest rates and, in particular, in the slope of the term structure of interest rates, UTS. (Notice that much of the impact of changes in the level of interest rates is captured by inflation variables.)
4. Unanticipated changes in inflation, DEI and UI.

It is possible, of course, to think of many other potential systematic factors, but our research has found that many of them influence returns only through their impact on the above four factors. The money supply, for example, is an important variable, but it is not as good a yardstick against which to measure sensitivities because most of the influence of unpredicted money supply changes is captured by the other variables. For instance, the change in interest rates on a Friday (from before the money supply announcement to after) is an adequate measure of the surprise in the announcement.

It should also be pointed out that the listing of the factors is less a listing of specific variables and more a listing of categories of variables. Inflation, for example, comes in at least two separable and distinct forms. An unexpected change in the price level, UI, caused, perhaps, by a sudden shock to energy or commodity prices has a quite different impact on stocks than a change in the rate of inflation, DEI, caused, perhaps, by a change in Federal Reserve policy. To make this concrete, a sudden drop in oil prices by $5 a barrel could occur simultaneously with an increase in the rate of growth in the money supply and, therefore, in the expected rate of inflation. Since these two effects are distinguishable and since different stocks react differently to them, we distinguish between them in our empirical work. This will be demonstrated in the next section.

It's hardly surprising that the variables listed above were found to be important determinants of market returns; they appear in the traditional discounted cash flow (DCF) valuation formula. If c denotes the dividend stream of the stock, then quite generally the price, p, of a stock equals the expected discounted dividends,

$$p = E(c)/k \qquad (4)$$

where k is the cost of capital or capitalization rate for the stock minus the dividend growth rate. It follows from this formula that changes in stock prices occur because of changes in either expected cash flows or in the risk adjusted discount rate, k.

Two of the factors—changes in industrial production and unanticipated inflation—are related to the numerator in the DCF formula, i.e., to the expected cash flows themselves. Expected industrial production is a proxy for the real value of future cash flows. Inflation enters because assets are not neutral; their nominal cash flow growth rates do not always match expected inflation rates. The other two variables would seem intuitively to be more related to the denominator in the DCF formula, i.e., to the risk-adjusted discount rate. The risk premium measure is an amalgam of investor attitudes toward risk bearing and perceptions about the general level of uncertainty. The term structure of interest rates enters because most assets have multiple-year cash flows and, for reasons relating to risk and time preferences, the discount rate that applies to distant flows is not the same as the rate that applies to flows in the near future.

These variables make intuitive sense, and it also makes sense that they are indeed "systematic." Every asset's value changes when one of these variables changes in an unanticipated way. Thus, investors who hold portfolios that are more exposed to such changes, i.e., portfolios that contain assets whose b's are higher on average, will find that their portfolios' market values fluctuate with greater amplitude over time. Furthermore, insofar as the market is averse to such risks, they will be compensated by a higher total return in the long run. But of course, generally they will have to bear up under more severe reactions to bear markets.

A Catalog of Asset Sensitivities

Individual stocks vary widely in their sensitivities to the economic factors. Even within the same industry two stocks can have quite different patterns of sensitivities. Furthermore, over time, a company can change its basic character through acquisitions and purposeful strategic choices as well as by changes in the markets in which it operates. These changes will result in changes in its exposure to the underlying economic factors.

To see how different industrial groupings respond to the different economic factors, turn to Table 1. The table lists the major industrial groupings and their average sensitivities to the economic factors in the period from 1958 through 1977. The table was constructed by grouping firms by SIC codes, forming equally weighted portfolios of all of the firms within each SIC group, and then regressing time series of the monthly returns of these industry portfolios on time series of the macroeconomic factors. Keep in mind that while a firm may be squarely in a particular grouping, firms in the same grouping can behave quite differently. For example, two oil companies with different reserve positions can respond quite differently to unanticipated changes in the price level. At a practical level this means that the portfolio manager who thinks of the energy stocks, for example, as being a homogeneous group with common sensitivities could be in for quite a surprise when oil prices rise unexpectedly and the particular oil stocks he is holding do not.

The first row in the table reports on the characteristics, i.e., the sensitivities or b's for the value weighted market portfolio. Somewhat surprisingly, the market reacts negatively to monthly production, MP, with a coefficient of about $-.076$. This is to be interpreted as saying that over this period a monthly increase in production of 1 percent lowered the return on the market by about 8 basis points. This is surprising, but a look down the table reveals that about half of the industries respond positively and about half respond negatively. Also, it should be noted that no attempt was made to filter out the expected and the unexpected components of the growth in production other than simply lagging the series forward by one month. For example, the stock return for April was compared with the future change in industrial production from April to May.

The change in the risk premium, UPR, is measured as the difference between the returns on a low-grade bond portfolio (under Baa) and on a high-grade (Aaa) government portfolio. This is empirically a very significant variable, and as the table reveals, not only is the market portfolio positively related to UPR so, too, is every industry grouping. This means that when low-grade bond returns exceed high-grade returns, the yield spread declines and stocks rise. Since stocks are riskier instruments than high-grade bonds, this is as we would expect, but the uniformity of the results across industries is very encouraging.

The third variable is UTS, and this is the return on a portfolio of long government bonds minus the current T-bill rate. As the positive coefficients indicate, the bond market and the stock market were positively related over this period, and a rise in yields adversely affected stocks as well as bonds. Notice that this result is a *partial* result. In other words, this occurs when the inflation variables, DEI and UI, are held constant so that it corresponds to an increase in real rates.

The impact of the inflation variables by themselves is uniformly

TABLE 1 Industry Sensitivities (December 1957–November 1977)

Industry Market	Number of Companies	MP	UPR	UTS	DEI	UI	Constant
Metal mining	10	−0.076	1.11	0.485	−11.6	−3.67	0.73
Bituminous coal and lignite	3	0.333	1.12	−0.056	−35.1	−1.32	1.36
Oil and gas extraction	4	−0.035	2.40	0.390	−25.8	−8.17	1.53
Nonmetallic minerals, excluding fuels	2	−0.266	1.16	0.524	−2.30	−3.00	1.12
Building contractors	2	0.261	1.43	0.114	−29.7	−1.31	0.97
Food and kindred products	2	−0.204	1.95	0.525	−33.1	−2.53	1.61
Tobacco manufactures	40	−0.059	1.09	0.462	−12.8	−3.72	1.11
Textile mill products	8	−0.076	0.78	0.308	−13.9	−4.05	1.16
Apparel and other textiles	15	0.147	1.13	0.351	−10.1	−5.20	1.07
Lumber and wood products	6	0.187	1.18	0.582	−22.0	−7.02	1.20
Furniture and fixtures	4	0.111	1.28	0.830	−13.3	−6.92	1.35
Paper and allied products	2	0.217	1.08	0.307	−20.1	−3.69	0.66
Printing and publishing	15	0.079	1.14	0.426	−9.62	−2.70	0.87
Chemicals and allied products	2	0.072	1.06	0.311	−6.61	−5.93	0.94
Petroleum and coal products	41	−0.063	1.35	0.367	−14.2	−5.21	1.18
Rubber and miscellaneous plastics	22	−0.109	1.02	0.447	−7.98	−2.36	1.09
Leather and leather products	9	0.097	1.31	0.497	−8.32	−5.47	0.79
Stone, clay, and glass products	5	0.067	1.18	0.548	−22.1	−6.97	1.21
Primary metal industries	19	0.067	1.20	0.623	−10.1	−5.70	0.75
Fabricated metal products	41	0.087	1.31	0.361	−8.82	−4.91	0.92
Electric and electronic equipment	15	−0.002	1.25	0.435	−10.3	−4.62	1.12
	24	−0.043	1.56	0.438	−17.7	−6.61	1.25

Transportation equipment	45	0.102	1.37	0.403	−15.0	−5.88	1.08
Miscellaneous manufacturing industries	5	−0.105	1.43	0.496	−17.8	−7.94	1.15
Railroad transportation	12	−0.112	1.48	0.488	−8.74	−5.96	1.06
Local and interurban highway transportation	3	0.089	1.14	0.614	−15.0	−3.26	1.05
Water transportation	2	0.115	1.77	0.685	−26.6	−5.64	1.12
Air transportation	11	0.145	1.87	0.755	−32.1	−9.29	1.25
Transportation services	3	−0.080	1.08	0.297	−11.3	−4.83	1.16
Communication	6	0.023	0.97	0.651	−11.9	−4.82	0.98
Utilities	93	−0.048	0.65	0.832	−5.44	−3.55	0.84
Wholesale trade—durables	6	−0.022	1.38	0.557	−17.4	−4.88	1.38
General merchandise stores	13	−0.119	1.19	0.470	−16.3	−5.70	1.24
Food stores	8	0.017	1.10	0.317	−25.5	−4.66	0.73
Auto dealers and service stations	1	0.033	1.44	0.307	−13.7	−3.36	1.07
Apparel and accessory stores	4	−0.025	1.26	0.480	−11.7	−6.93	1.37
Furniture and home furnishing stores	2	−0.051	1.27	0.240	−15.0	−4.24	1.28
Eating and drinking places	1	0.084	1.40	0.626	−28.2	−3.48	1.46
Miscellaneous retail	5	0.207	1.13	0.256	−34.7	−6.07	0.95
Credit agencies except banks	7	0.045	0.82	1.10	−12.3	−4.87	0.76
Real estate	4	0.263	1.00	0.399	−5.40	−3.33	1.30
Holding and other investments	17	−0.029	1.26	0.451	−9.66	−4.47	0.85
Hotels and lodging places	1	−0.327	1.79	0.388	−20.0	−7.59	1.95
Personal services	1	−0.219	1.12	0.339	−16.3	−6.72	1.25
Motion pictures	6	0.000	1.94	0.549	−33.3	−6.78	1.56

MP: Monthly growth rate in industrial production.
UPR: Unanticipated change in risk premium ("under Baa" return—Aaa bond return).
UTS: Unanticipated change in the term structure (long-term government bond return—Treasury bill rate).
DEI: Change in expected inflation.
UI: Unanticipated inflation.

negative. The change in the expected inflation is given by DEI, and the actual unanticipated inflation, UI, was measured by the difference between actual inflation during a month and the inflation that was expected to prevail at the beginning of the month. (The expected inflation was measured by a statistical regression on past T-bill rates and inflation rates.) The message is clear that over this period unanticipated increases in inflation, both the level and the rate, adversely affected stocks, and, again, the result is surprisingly uniform across industries.

It would be wrong, though, to place too much weight on these results; while UPR and UTS are strongly significant variables, the individual significance of the production and inflation variables was much weaker. This is due in part to the difficulty of measuring such macroeconomic variables in the absence of markets that regularly report on their values.

Beyond the broad impact of the macrovariables, Table 1 substantiates many of the intuitive views held by analysts of the impact of the economy on different industries. The utility sector, for example, is highly interest sensitive with a coefficient on UTS of .83 as compared with .48 for the market as a whole. Similarly, credit agencies other than banks with a coefficient of 1.1 on UTS do extremely well when long-term yields decline. The strong positive showing of the retail sector on the production variable, with a coefficient of .21 on MP, is also not unexpected. However, the negative partial impact of MP on the oil and gas industry is somewhat surprising. Since these are partial effects, though, they are most meaningful not as absolute numbers but rather in terms of their relative effects across industries.

The oil and gas extraction companies, for example, have a negative coefficient on the inflation variables, but their coefficient of -2.3 on the rate of change, DEI, is the smallest negative response of any sector. Similarly, their coefficient of -3.0 on UI is also quite small. While the rise in inflation in this period negatively impacted on all sectors, it clearly impacted this sector the least. Subsequent studies of the effect of inflation on this sector beyond 1977 further strengthens these results.

Obviously, there is not space to discuss all of the findings in Table 1, but the interested reader will find some surprises along with confirmation of many common views. As we shall see, the sensitivities of the sectors to the macrovariables is a basic building block in the construction and planning of portfolios.

Strategic Portfolio Planning

No "off-the-shelf" approach to strategic planning is appropriate for all investment funds any more than one size of suit fits all customers. Below, we outline some general considerations that figure into the determination of investment goals.

The Structuring Decision

Traditionally, portfolio strategy; i.e., the portfolio allocation decision, is perceived as the choice of the proper mix of stocks and bonds (with real estate and other assets occasionally included). Every portfolio has its own pattern of sensitivities to the systematic economic factors. Stocks as a group and bonds as another group have different sensitivities to systematic risks; hence the traditional approach may offer a rough solution to the choice of the optimal pattern of risk exposure. But the results can be improved significantly by examining the sensitivity of each asset to systematic risks.[4]

The principal problem facing the architect of the fund's investment strategy is *not* that of deciding on the allocation of funds to assets but, rather, is that of determining the most desirable exposure to systematic economic risks. Altering the mix of stocks and bonds in the portfolio will certainly affect the amount and type of risk exposure, but so will nearly every other purchase and sale decision. The strategist must first choose the desired level of exposure, then appropriate transactions can move the fund toward that desired position.

For example, assume that two of the empirically relevant exposures—to the general level of risk tolerance and to the term structure of interest rates—are held constant and that we are interested in the choice of exposure to inflation risk and to industrial production risk. In Figure E the horizontal axis depicts the sensitivity, or "exposure," of a portfolio to inflation risk. The vertical axis plots the same portfolio's exposure to production risk. From now on we will refer to these sensitivities as the inflation and productivity betas, respectively.

As was discussed for individual assets, the betas measure the average response of a portfolio or of an asset to unanticipated changes in the respective economic factors. For example, a portfolio with an inflation beta of 1 will tend to move up and down by 1 percent in response to a 1 percent unanticipated change in inflation. A beta greater than 1, say an inflation beta of 1.5, means that the portfolio's returns are magnified by inflation, with a 1 percent unanticipated inflation leading to a 1.5 percent additional return on the portfolio. Similarly, if beta is less than 1, unanticipated inflation has a less than proportional impact on the portfolio's returns. A portfolio with a beta of 0.5 will show a 0.5 percent increase in return for every 1 percent unexpected inflation. And a portfolio with a beta of zero will, on average, be unaffected by unanticipated inflation. Of course, many assets actually have negative betas and tend to do worse than expected when inflation is greater than expected. A utility stock with an inflation beta of −0.3 loses 0.3 percent of return for each 1 percent unanticipated inflation.

In Figure E, point A depicts a large investment fund with an inflation sensitivity of about 0.7 and a production sensitivity of 0.4. Is

FIGURE E Sensitivities to Productivity and Inflation Risks

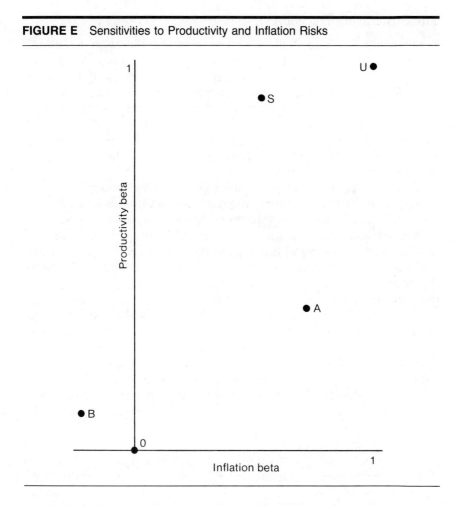

this a usual or an unusual pattern of sensitivities? There is no way to answer this question without referring to some landmarks.

One obvious landmark is the origin, 0—the point at which both betas are zero. A portfolio at this point would be affected by neither unanticipated inflation nor by changes in expected industrial production. This may seem to be desirable, but it is not necessarily so. For one thing, such a portfolio offers no insurance against unexpected inflation risk; when inflation is greater than anticipated, this portfolio will, on average, not respond. Perhaps more importantly, there is a trade-off between return and risk exposure. Moving a portfolio to 0, where it will not respond to changes in inflation or to productivity, will have an impact on average return.

Point U represents unit sensitivity to both economic factors. A portfolio located at U will increase in value by 1 percent with either a 1 percent unexpected inflation or a 1 percent unexpected increase in industrial production. The expenditures of an investment portfolio such as a pension fund are probably exposed to the risk of inflation in an adverse way; unanticipated increases in inflation will, on average, increase expenditures. The inflation sensitivity of a portfolio at U will help to offset this. Industrial production, however, could tell a different story. Declines in industrial production will generally be associated with increases in unemployment, which, in turn, will place greater economic burdens on individuals and corporations. In addition, productivity changes will be associated with changes in the relative prices of the goods and services purchased by the plan sponsor and its beneficiaries, and these may also be adverse. But rather than helping the fund to insure against these risks, a portfolio with a productivity beta of 1 actually magnifies them. When industrial production turns down, so too does the return on the portfolio. Whether or not point U is attractive depends upon the particular situation of the fund.

Point B represents the typical pattern of sensitivities for a portfolio of long-term government bonds. Notice that it has a negative beta with inflation and a slightly positive beta with productivity. Investments in bonds are subject to significant adverse inflation effects and are also somewhat sensitive to productivity (although to a far lesser extent than equities). Productivity sensitivity is larger for corporate bonds than for governments, for obvious reasons.

Point S is the location of a broad-based market index of large, listed stocks. Although this is a useful reference point, it would be wrong to ascribe too much importance to it. The right choice of a pattern of sensitivities for a given fund depends upon a variety of considerations unique to that fund and to the markets in which its beneficiary is a buyer, and these will not generally result in choosing the market index of stocks. The market index should not be ignored, but neither should it be worshipped. It is simply a useful landmark on the horizon, a signpost that is a guide in unfamiliar territory.

APT and the CAPM

We now have the necessary apparatus to relate the well known Capital Asset Pricing Model (CAPM) to APT. The CAPM asserts that only a single number—the CAPM beta against a market index—is required to measure risk. As Figure F illustrates, the CAPM beta measures the distance along a ray from the origin through S, where a broad-based market index is located. We assume that portfolio S is the market index used in computing CAPM betas; it could be any of the commonly used indexes, such as the S&P 500.

Portfolio S has a CAPM beta of 1.0 (by construction). Another

FIGURE F CAPM and APT Betas

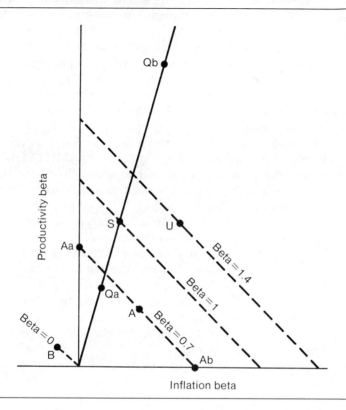

portfolio, such as Qa, which is located halfway along the ray between O and S, has a CAPM beta of 1/2. Similarly, Qb has a CAPM beta of 2, because it is twice as far from the origin as S itself. Note that the CAPM beta of any portfolio can be measured by its distance along the ray relative to the market index S. The CAPM beta is a relative risk measure.

But there are many portfolios that are not on the ray OS. For instance, portfolios such as B, A, and U, all of which have certain desirable properties, are located in the productivity-inflation space off the CAPM ray. What are their CAPM betas? It turns out that there are entire families of portfolios with a particular value of the CAPM beta whose members are not on the ray. The dashed lines in Figure F show some of these families. For example, portfolio A is in the family whose CAPM beta is 0.7; but so are all the portfolios along the dashed line that passes through A. There are portfolios in this family that have no inflation risk (such as Aa), and there are portfolios with no productivity risk (such as Ab). All of them have CAPM betas of 0.7. We doubt very much, however, that most investment managers and clients would regard them as equally desirable.

If S happens to be a mean-variance efficient portfolio, a so-called optimized portfolio, then all portfolios whose CAPM betas are the same will have equal returns on average over time. In this sense, the CAPM beta measures the overall desirability of an asset as perceived by the average investor in the marketplace. Even in this case, however, it is not necessarily true that a particular individual or client will consider all portfolios with the same expected return equally desirable. For example, portfolios Aa and Ab in Figure F might have the same long-term expected return, but they are exposed to far different types of risk and neither is preferable for all funds.

Finally, there is usually no reason to think that a particular portfolio such as S, even though it is a broad index such as the S&P 500, is itself optimized. If it is not optimized, then portfolios A, Aa, and Ab will not have equal expected returns even though they do have equal CAPM betas. Recent empirical evidence has shown unequivocally that most of the commonly used market indexes are not optimized portfolios. Under this condition, the CAPM beta is not even a reliable indicator of expected return, and as we have already seen, it is virtually worthless as a measure of the type of risk to which the portfolio is exposed.

Now consider fund A, located on the exposure terrain with an inflation sensitivity of 0.7 and a productivity sensitivity of 0.4. What should be the strategy for fund A? How should it go about making its strategic investment decision? To put the question another way, where should the fund go to in Figure E? Should it move closer to S, the stock market index? Should it be somewhere between B and S, divided between bonds and stocks? Just choosing between bonds and stocks limits the fund to a position along a line between B and S. The strategic decision is clearly broader than this.

The appropriate choice of risk exposure depends upon the uses to which the income generated by the fund is to be put. Just as different individuals choose to live in different places, different investment funds will choose different patterns of risk exposure.

Analyzing Portfolio Strategy

To choose the optimal pattern of risk sensitivities and move to the best position in Figure E, we must examine the economic situation of the sponsors and the beneficiaries of the fund. To argue that there is one best strategy for everyone—such as "buying the market"—is simply wrong. In the case of pension systems, we might assume that the principal goal is to serve the interests of the beneficiaries by meeting the promised pension benefits with a minimum of additional taxes (if the plan is public) or of corporate contributions (if it is private), but this goal structure may not be appropriate in all cases (for example, for a nonprofit institution such as a university).

The economic situations confronting the sponsor and the beneficiaries are determined by the markets within which they operate and by the uses to which they put funds. The sensitivity of prices in these markets to overall inflation, for example, is an important determinant of the proper investment policy. The location of the organization is important as well. A company that employs blue-collar workers in the Los Angeles area has a different pattern of expenditures than a white-collar service firm located in New York.

Although organizations do not constitute a homogeneous group, they all share broad economic concerns. The key questions involve (*a*) their patterns of expenditures, (*b*) their other sources of income, and (*c*) the economic conditions they will face. These questions can be answered by detailed economic study. In the case of a company, for example, central questions would be: What are its products, its costs, and its prospects? How sensitive is it to the business cycle? In the case of a museum, the study might begin with an examination of the markets for antiquities. How have these markets behaved, and what plans does the museum have for new acquisitions? Also of great importance is the need to meet current and forecast expenditures of a more prosaic sort, such as those related to maintenance and security. Such a study must be continually updated if the fund is to respond to changes in the economic environment and to changes in the goals and operations of the organization. But even before the initial study is concluded, it will have important implications for strategic portfolio decisions.

Given an economic profile of the organization, one can begin to structure the overall risk exposure of the portfolio. Expenditures on major commodity groups—on salaries and materials, say—should be compared with the general expenditure pattern in the country as a whole. For example, suppose that the organization spends less on food and relatively more on travel than the average investor. The higher expenditure on travel would render it more vulnerable to energy costs than the typical investor, whereas the lower expenditures on foodstuffs would make it less exposed to food prices.

At the strategic level, these considerations will influence the optimal pattern of risk exposure. To the extent that food prices coincide with general inflation, for example, the optimal portfolio could be less hedged against inflation—i.e., it could have a lower inflation beta than a broad-based market average. Similarly, to the extent that food prices tend to be somewhat independent of productivity risk, the organization could accept a higher sensitivity to productivity risk than is contained in a broad-based average such as a value-weighted index. By bearing more risk in this dimension, the portfolio could expect a higher return.

The influence of these kinds of considerations on the idiosyncratic risk of specific industry groupings has tactical implications. If the organization is unconcerned about inflation in agricultural prices, it would also wish to skew its portfolio holdings out of this sector. Similarly, a sensitivity to energy costs might lead it to skew its portfolio holdings in the direction of the energy sector. An organization will wish to hold a pattern of investments tailored to its own needs. Its optimal portfolio will, therefore, have a pattern of investments that is modestly skewed from the broad-based market index owned by the average investor.

It should be emphasized that tactical portfolio adjustments can be accomplished without reducing the average return on the portfolio. The strategic decisions determining the level of exposure to systematic economic factors influence the average return, but the tactical decisions can be made without any sacrifice of portfolio return because they deal merely with idiosyncratic risk.

Implementing the Strategy

To implement the chosen strategy, the fund may direct the investments itself, or it may select investment managers who will follow established investment policy guidelines. The adoption of the APT approach to strategy has implications for the choice and the evaluation of investment managers. If the strategy dictates that investments should be made in particular sectors, then it would be natural to look for managers who specialize in these sectors.

More generally, managers implicitly tend to choose portfolios that have particular patterns of sensitivities to the economic factors. One manager might, for example, focus on high price-earnings ratio companies so that his portfolio has a characteristic pattern of sensitivities. Another might be heavily invested in utilities, and this would result in a different pattern of sensitivities. The investment strategy for the portfolio as a whole may be implemented by choosing a portfolio of managers in such a way that pooling them together results in the desired pattern of sensitivities. If, for example, manager A's portfolio typically has an inflation beta of 2 and manager B's portfolio has an inflation beta of 1, then a desired inflation of beta 1.4 for the overall strategy could be achieved by placing 40 cents with manager A for every 60 cents given to manager B.

Of course, the complete manager evaluation issue is more complicated than this. Given that a manager has a certain pattern of risk exposures, we also want to know whether he or she accomplishes this in the least costly fashion and with the least amount of idiosyncratic risk. This is the subject of performance evaluation, which is well developed in the APT framework but is beyond the scope of this article.

Finally, a fund's choice of investments will generally be constrained by legal and other considerations. Typical of such constraints is the requirement that all investments be of a certain grade or from an approved list or that the investments include bonds or equities from a particular issuer. Because of its flexibility, the APT approach to strategy is particularly well suited to these situations, and it can be adapted to special situations when many traditional approaches cannot.

For example, suppose that the portfolio is constrained to hold a significant portion of its investments in the equities of the bonds of a particular company or government agency. For two related reasons it will generally be the case that this constraint is binding in the sense that the fund would rather reduce its holdings of this security. First, the large holding subjects the fund to a substantial amount of idiosyncratic risk, and second, the fund may already be implicitly subject to much of the risk associated with the issuer.

The total risk of this security, however, can be substantially mitigated if the remainder of the portfolio is explicitly selected to offset its influence. If the security in question has a lower than desired sensitivity to inflation risk—e.g., a beta of 0.6 when the desired beta is 0.9—then the influence of the holding on the inflation exposure of the portfolio may be countered by choosing alternative investments with inflation betas in excess of 0.9. As a result, however, the fund may be subjected to idiosyncratic risk, which would not be a problem if the constraints were absent.[5]

SUMMARY

The well-known Capital Asset Pricing Model asserts that only a single number—an asset's beta against the market index—is required to measure risk. Arbitrage Pricing Theory asserts that an asset's riskiness, hence its average long-term return, is directly related to its sensitivities to unanticipated changes in basic economic variables or factors. Empirical work has identified the following four factors as critical: (1) inflation, (2) industrial production, (3) risk premiums, and (4) the term structure of interest rates. Assets, even if they have the same CAPM beta, will have different patterns of sensitivities to these systematic factors.

The central focus of portfolio strategy is the choice of an appropriate pattern of sensitivities. This choice will depend upon the economic characteristics of the beneficiary of the portfolio's income—in particular, upon whether the beneficiary is more or less concerned with the economic factor risks than the broad average of investors. An organization, for example, may expect to spend less on food than the average investor. To the extent that food prices coincide with general inflation and are somewhat independent of productivity risk, the organization's optimal portfolio could have a lower inflation beta and a higher productivity beta than the broad-based average.

Such concerns also have tactical implications. The organization unconcerned about inflation in agricultural prices would also wish to skew its portfolio holdings out of this sector. Conversely, a sensitivity to energy costs might lead it to skew its holdings in the direction of the energy sector. Implementation of the chosen strategy can be carried out directly by the fund itself, or it may be delegated to select investment managers who follow established investment policy guidelines.

ENDNOTES

1. Arbitrage Pricing Theory was originated by Stephen A. Ross in "The Arbitrage Theory of Capital Asset Pricing," *Journal of Economic Theory*, December 1976, pp. 341–60. Theoretical refinements have been made by the following: Gregory Connor, "A Factor Pricing Theory for Capital Assets" (Working paper, Northwestern University, 1981); Gur Huberman, "A Simple Approach to Arbitrage Pricing Theory," *Journal of Economic Theory*, October 1982, pp. 183–91; Nai-fu Chen and Jonathan E. Ingersoll, Jr., "Exact Pricing in Linear Factor Models with Finitely Many Assets: A Note," *Journal of Finance*, June 1983, pp. 985–88; Philip H. Dybvig, "An Explicit Bound on Deviations from APT Pricing in a Finite Economy," *Journal of Financial Economics*, December 1983, pp. 483–96; Mark Grinblatt and Sheridan Titman, "Factor Pricing in a Finite Economy," *Journal of Financial Economics*, December 1983, pp. 497–507; Robert Stambaugh, "Arbitrage Pricing with Information," *Journal of Financial Economics*, November 1983, pp. 357–59; Gary Chamberlain and Michael Rothschild, "Arbitrage and Mean/Variance Analysis on Large Markets," *Econometrica*, September 1983, pp. 1281–1304; and Jonathan E. Ingersoll, Jr., "Some Results in the Theory of Arbitrage Pricing," *Journal of Finance*, September 1984, pp. 1021–39; Nai-fu Chen, Richard Roll, and Stephen A. Ross, "Economic Forces and the Stock Market: Testing the APT and Alternative Asset Pricing Theories," *Journal of Business*, July 1986, pp. 383–403.

2. Empirical testing with equities is described in the following: Richard Roll and Stephen A. Ross, "An Empirical Investigation of the Arbitrage Pricing Theory," *Journal of Finance*, December 1980, pp. 1073–1194; Nai-fu Chen, "Arbitrage Asset Pricing: Theory and Evidence" (Dissertation, Graduate School of Management, University of California at Los Angeles, 1981); Mark R. Reinganum, "The Arbitrage Pricing Theory: Some Empirical Results," *Journal of Finance*, May 1981, pp. 313–21; Patricia Hughes, "A Test of the Arbitrage Pricing Theory" (Working paper, University of British Columbia, August 1981); Lawrence Kryzanowski and Minh Chan To, "General Factor Models and the Structure of Security Returns," *Journal of Financial and Quantitative Analysis*, March 1983, pp. 31–52; and Stephen J. Brown and Mark I. Weinstein, "A New Approach to Testing Asset Pricing Models: The Bilinear Paradigm," *Journal of Finance*, June 1983, pp. 711–43. Tests with Treasury bills are presented in George Oldfield, Jr., and Richard J. Rogalski, "Treasury Bill Factors and Common Stock Returns," *Journal of Finance*, May 1981, pp. 337–50. Issues of testability are discussed by Jay Shanken, "The Arbitrage Pricing Theory: Is It Testable?" *Journal of Finance*, December 1982, pp. 1129–40; Philip H. Dybvig and Stephen A. Ross, "Yes, the APT Is Testable," *Journal of Finance*, September 1985, pp. 1173–88; and Gunter Franke, "On Tests of the Arbitrage Pricing Theory" (Working paper, Universitat Giessen, 1983).

3. See Chen, Roll, and Ross, "Economic Forces and the Stock Market."

4. The systematic, and idiosyncratic, risks at the heart of the APT approach to investment strategy have been identified in technical econometric work. For assets on which data are available, the pattern of exposure of each asset is known.

5. In some countries other than the United States, constraints on investments are so stiff as to preclude achievement of the desired overall pattern of systematic risk exposure.

39

Comments on the Efficient Market–Random Walk Hypothesis

Charles D. Kuehner, Ph.D., CFA
Vice President
Oppenheimer Industries, Inc.

Fred B. Renwick, Ph.D.
Graduate School of Business Administration
New York University

INTRODUCTION

In recent years, no single issue has split both the academic world and the financial community as much as has the efficient market–random walk debate. Since the mid-1960s, both groups have focused a great deal of attention on the *efficiency* of the securities markets. By efficiency they did not mean how efficiently stock certificates were moved from seller to buyer or how promptly customers' bills were collected. Rather, they meant how efficient stock prices are in reflecting value.

> Efficiency in this context means the ability of the capital markets to function so that prices of securities react rapidly to new information. Such efficiency will produce prices that are "appropriate" in terms of current knowledge, and investors will be less likely to make unwise investments. A corollary is that investors will also be likely to discover great bargains and thereby earn extraordinary high rates of return.[1]

---

[1] James H. Lorie, *Public Policy for American Capital Markets* (Washington, D.C.: U.S. Dept. of Treasury, 1974), p. 3. Also, for several alternative interpretations of "efficiency," see Mark E. Rubenstein, "Securities Market Efficiency in an Arrow-Debreu Economy," *American Economic Review*, December 1975, pp. 812–24.

The idea that market prices embody what is knowable and relevant for judging securities and adjust rapidly to such information "was considered bizarre in 1960 but by 1970 was very generally accepted by academicians and by many important financial institutions.[2] The practical significance of the efficient market hypothesis to investors is simply this: To do unusually well in selecting investments, one must have superior insight and abilities to see into the murky future better than other investors.

As the efficient market concept has developed, there has been a noticeable movement of the academicians into the fold, the so-called true believers. Paul Samuelson seems to reflect the general academic point of view. He did admit that certain institutional investors did perform better in certain years "and there were other years when they didn't."[3] He also noted that when investigators seek to identify either the portfolio managers or methods "endowed with superior investment prowess, they are unable to find them." Samuelson challenged those who doubt the random walk concept to "dispose of it by producing brute evidence to the contrary." To be sure, there were a number of exceptions in the academic community. For example, Downes and Dyckman stated that several studies exist "whose results are not consistent with the efficient markets hypothesis in, at most, its semistrong form. Unfortunately, these studies have been largely ignored by summarizers of the efficient markets literature."[4] In the main, practicing security analysts and portfolio managers, the "nonbelievers," have been seemingly unconvinced of the merits of the efficient market hypothesis. Even Ben Graham, one of the pioneers of fundamental security analysis, raised the caveat, "It may be that the professionally managed funds are too large a part of the total picture to be able to outperform the market as a whole."[5]

---

[2] James H. Lorie and Richard Brealey, *Modern Developments in Investment Management* (New York: Praeger Publishers, 1972) p. 101.

[3] Paul A. Samuelson, "Where Are the People Who Are Beating the Market?" *Institutional Investor*, November 1975, pp. 83–88.

[4] David Downes and Thomas R. Dyckman, "A Critical Look at the Efficient Market Empirical Research Literature as It Relates to Accounting Information," *The Accounting Review*, April 1973, pp. 300–317. One significant exception to this general lack of recognition is the "Symposium on Some Anomalous Evidence Regarding Market Efficiency" published as a special issue of the *Journal of Financial Economics* 6 (June–September 1978), pp. 93–330.

[5] Benjamin Graham, quoted in Leopold A. Bernstein, "In Defense of Fundamental Investment Analysis," *Financial Analysts Journal*, January/February 1975, p. 58.

REQUIREMENTS FOR AN EFFICIENT MARKET

Kenneth Arrow, Fischer Black, Harold Demsetz, Eugene Fama, James Lorie, and others have set forth the following various requirements for an efficient market.

1. Effective Information Flow

This means that news is disseminated quickly and freely across the entire spectrum of actual and potential investors. Thus, investors can react rapidly and appropriately as new information develops. Requirements from the Securities and Exchange Commission (SEC) and other regulatory bodies concerning full disclosure of material information are embodied in this concept.

2. Fully Rational Investors

This embodies the three following requirements from investors:

1. *Rational choice* among risky ventures and in risk-taking situations. Rational investors must have "attitudes of risk aversion," which means preference for certainty and liquidity, unless a sweetner—additional return—is promised and expected as compensation for bearing additional risk.[6]
2. *Rational expectations* regarding future returns. Expectations are "rational" in that they "are essentially the same as the predictions of the relevant economic theory."[7]
3. *Rational beliefs* regarding expected returns and risks associated with the proposed investment. This means putting your money where your mouth is: willingness and ability to act upon personal assessments of the situation at hand. For a rational person—"*all* uncertainties can be reduced to *risk*,"[8] and all rational persons have a rate of substitution between belief and money.[9]

---

[6] Kenneth Arrow, "The Role of Securities in the Optimal Allocation of Risk Bearing," *Review of Economic Studies*, April 1964, p. 91. Reprinted as chapter four in Kenneth J. Arrow, *Essays in the Theory of Risk-Bearing* (Amsterdam: North Holland Publishing Company, 1976), pp. 121–33.

[7] John Muth, "Rational Expectations and the Theory of Price Movements," *Econometrica*, July 1961, p. 315.

[8] Daniel Ellsberg, "Risk, Ambiguity and the Savage Axioms," *The Quarterly Journal of Economics*, November 1961, p. 645.

[9] Leonard J. Savage, "Elicitation of Personal Probability and Expectations," *Journal of the American Statistical Association*, December 1971, p. 784.

3. Rapid Price Change to New Information

Prices change in response to new information: "All the information needed to predict the expected value of the next price level is reflected in the current price."[10] "Such changes are sometimes considered to constitute excessive volatility . . . when price changes are in response to new information, public policy should facilitate, rather than impede them."[11] "It is worth emphasizing again that price continuity or stability is not in itself a desirable characteristic of an efficient market. It is both undesirable and unprofitable for a specialist or market maker to resist changes in the price of a stock."[12]

Demsetz sets forth a *comparative institutional* approach—an alternative to the majority view that economic efficiency requires an ideal norm: flexible pricing in free and perfectly competitive markets. Demsetz notes that real-world institutional arrangements are not necessarily inefficient solely because of discernable deviations or discrepancies from the ideal, but, rather, "Users of the comparative institution approach attempt to assess which alternative real institutional arrangement seems best able to cope with the economic problem; practitioners of this approach may use an ideal norm to provide standards from which divergences are assessed for all practical alternatives of interest and select as efficient that alternative which seems most likely to minimize the divergence."[13] Achieving economic efficiency through choice of appropriate institutional arrangement, according to Demsetz, includes granting of monopoly and tariff privileges by governments, which seems best able to cope with the economic problem at hand. Demsetz's approach, the *comparative institutional* approach to market efficiency, uses "an ideal norm to provide standards from which divergences are assessed for all practical alternatives of interest"; then that alternative is selected and declared efficient if it seems most likely to minimize the divergence or comes closest to the ideal. Demsetz's view is that real-world institutional arrangements and markets are not necessarily inefficient solely because they might be imperfect.

---

[10] Stephen F. LeRoy, "Efficient Capital Markets: Comments," *The Journal of Finance*, March 1976, pp. 139–41.

[11] Lorie, "Public Policy," p. 3.

[12] Fischer Black, "Toward a Fully Automated Stock Exchange," *Financial Analysts Journal*, July/August 1971, p. 35.

[13] Harold Demsetz, "Information and Efficiency: Another Viewpoint," *The Journal of Law and Economics*, April 1969, pp. 1–20.

4. Low Transaction Cost

Sales commissions and taxes on securities should be low enough so as not to impede either potential buyers or sellers from implementing their investment decisions.

5. Continuous Trading

The investor who desires to buy or sell can do so immediately. This focuses on the viability of the market and the close proximity of "bid" and "ask" prices. Consequently, the execution of a small trade should not ordinarily change prices significantly, if at all.

Black holds that the market should be structured in a way that large investors are not disadvantaged in dealing with many small investors. Specifically, he opines that the trading cost to the large investor should be the same for a given size transaction, whether he is trading with one large investor or many small investors. Admittedly the cost of handling the latter would be higher. However, Black contends that the extra cost of handling many small orders should be borne by the small investors who are responsible for such costs.

In commenting on some of the preconditions for efficiency. Fama notes that these "are not descriptive of markets met in practice," but "these conditions, while sufficient for market efficiency, are not necessary." For example, he states that as long as transactions take account of all available information, even large costs do not necessarily mean that when transactions do occur, prices will not fully reflect available information. Also, "even disagreement among investors as to the significance of given information does not imply market inefficiency unless some investors are consistently able to make better evaluation of such information than is implicit in market prices."[14]

Finally, Sullivan underscores Arrow's original proposition that efficient markets can—but not necessarily must—imply optimal allocations of economic goods and services. By optimal allocations we mean that resources are allocated in such a way that no other choice will make every individual better off.

Sullivan, after investigating stock price behavior of corporations possessing considerable market power, questioned the exact meaning of the term *efficient capital market* and concluded: "even if the capital market is efficient in that it correctly values shares based on all available information, . . . it does not imply that the existence of an efficient capital market is a sufficient condition for the overall optimum perfor-

---

[14] Eugene F. Fama, "Efficient Capital Markets: A Review of Theory and Empirical Work," *Journal of Finance*, May 1970, pp. 383–417; and *Foundations of Finance* (New York: Basic Books, 1976), pp. 133–68.

mance of the economy or even for the optimum allocation of capital within the economy." Therefore, the Capital Asset Pricing Model views the capital market as efficient in that it values the firm given all available information; it is not efficient in that it necessarily allocates capital to firms which will employ it in the socially optimum manner.[15]

SITUATION PRIOR TO EMERGENCE OF THE EFFICIENT MARKET CONCEPT

It would be helpful, before proceeding with a review of empirical research on the question of the efficient market hypothesis, to delineate it from the two basically different schools of stock price evaluation into which random walk emerged in the early 1960s.

Technical Analysis

Technical analysis is *internally* oriented. In this, technicians endeavor to predict future price levels of stocks by examining one or many series of past data *from the market itself*.

> The basic assumption of all the chartist or technical theories is that history tends to repeat itself, i.e., past patterns of price behavior in individual securities will tend to recur in the future. Thus, the way to predict stock prices (and, of course, increase one's potential gains) is to develop a familiarity with past patterns of price behavior in order to recognize situations of likely recurrence.
> The techniques of the chartist have always been surrounded by a certain degree of mysticism, however, and as a result most market professionals have found them suspect. Thus, it is probably safe to say that the pure chartist is relatively rare among stock market analysts.[16]

Pinches states that technical analysts "believe that the value of a stock depends primarily on supply and demand and may have very little relationship to any intrinsic value."[17] He summarizes a general statement of technical analysis, including:

1. Market prices are determined by supply and demand.
2. At any moment, supply and demand reflect hundreds of rational and irrational considerations: facts, opinions, moods, and guesses about the future.

---

[15] Timothy G. Sullivan, "A Note on Market Power and Returns to Stockholders," *The Review of Economics and Statistics*, February 1977, pp. 108–13.

[16] Eugene F. Fama, "Random Walks in Stock Market Prices," *Financial Analysts Journal*, September/October 1965, pp. 55–59.

[17] George E. Pinches, "The Random Walk Hypothesis and Technical Analysis," *Financial Analysts Journal*, March/April 1970, pp. 104–10.

3. Disregarding minor fluctuations, market prices move in trends which persist over an appreciable length of time.
4. Changes in trend represent a shift in balance between supply and demand. However caused, these shifts are detectable "sooner or later in the action of the market itself."

As we will see below, chartists assume that successive price changes in individual securities are *dependent*. This means that future stock prices are importantly dependent upon patterns of past price changes reflecting the shift between supply and demand. Among the many techniques used by technical analysts are:

1. Charting—past prices, e.g., Dow theory.
2. Determining—major trends (the tides), intermediate corrections (the waves), and minor fluctuations (ripples).
3. Share volume trends—rising, falling, and so on.
4. Combined volume and price charts.
5. Point and figure charts—channels, wedges, head and shoulders, triple tops, triple bottoms, and so on.
6. Support areas versus resistance levels.
7. Breadth of market—advance-decline lines.
8. Odd lots—purchases versus sales.
9. Odd-lot volume related to round-lot volume.
10. Odd-lot short sales.

Charles Jones, Donald Tuttle, and Cherrill Heaton concluded:

> Many of the technical indicators . . . are intuitively appealing. They all have followers who claim to have used them successfully. Yet they do not stand up well when subjected to rigorous, unemotional testing. In brief, we could not recommend investing a nickel on the basis of any single technical indicator or combination of indicators.[18]

Jerome Cohen, Edward Zinbarg, and Arthur Zeikel stated:

> We can understand the characterization of technical analysis as "crystal ball gazing." But we consider this characterization to be rather unfortunate, for it casts aside the good with the bad. The more scholarly and sophisticated technical analyst uses his tools with a proper sense of proportion . . . if a stock looks attractive to him on technical grounds he probes into its fundamental . . . he is certainly not unmindful of earnings growth, of values, or of the impact of business cycles.[19]

---

[18] Charles P. Jones, Donald L. Tuttle and Cherrill P. Heaton, *Essentials of Modern Investments* (New York: The Ronald Press, 1977), p. 279.

[19] Jerome B. Cohen, Edward D. Zinbarg, and Arthur Zeikel, *Investment Analysis and Portfolio Management* (Homewood, Ill.: Richard D. Irwin, 1977), p. 586. (See also the 4th edition, 1982.)

The broad consensus of several different technical indicators may be helpful in understanding market psychology for whatever value that nebulous term might have. Roberts states:

> Perhaps no one in the financial world completely ignores technical analysis—indeed, its terminology is ingrained in market reporting—and some rely intensively on it. Technical analysis includes many approaches, most requiring a good deal of subjective judgment in applications. In part these approaches are purely empirical; in part they are based on analogy with physical processes, such as tides and waves.[20]

Fundamental Analysis

Fundamental analysis is *externally* oriented. "The fundamentalist never measures the attractiveness of a stock by the fickle standards of the marketplace but, rather, determines the price at which one is willing to invest and then turns to the marketplace to see if the stock is selling at the required price."[21] The fundamental analyst focuses on the intrinsic value of a stock.

> The assumption of the fundamental analysis approach is that at any point in time, an individual security has an intrinsic value (or in the terms of the economist, an equilibrium price) which depends on the earnings potential of the security. The earnings potential of the security depends in turn on such fundamental factors as quality of management, outlook for the industry and the economy, etc.
>
> Through a careful study of these fundamental factors the analyst should, in principle, be able to determine whether the actual price of a security is above or below its intrinsic value. If actual prices tend to move toward intrinsic values, then attempting to determine the intrinsic value of a security is equivalent to making a prediction of its future price; and this is the essence of the predictive procedure implicit in fundamental analysis.[22]

Fundamental analysis embraces many facets of a company in developing an evaluation of intrinsic value. Among the factors considered are:

1. Growth: revenues, expenses, net income, earnings per share, assets.
2. Management: record, innovation, motivation, plans, long-range objectives, philosophy.
3. Earnings rates: on total capital, on equity capital, objectives.

---

[20] Harry V. Roberts, "Stock Market Patterns and Financial Analysis: Methodological Suggestion," *Journal of Finance*, March 1959, pp. 1–10.

[21] Frank E. Block, "The Place of Book Value in Stock Evaluation," *Financial Analysts Journal*, March/April 1964, p. 29.

[22] Fama, "Random Walks," pp. 56–57.

4. Capital structure: policy, credit ratings, debt ratio objectives, fixed charge coverage.
5. Dividends: payment policy, past growth, percent payout.
6. Accounting policies: reserves, inventory policies, depreciation policies, tax normalization versus flow through.
7. Ratios: acid test ratio, quick ratio, current assets to current liabilities.
8. Marketing: market share, short- and long-term strategy, competition.
9. Labor: labor relations policies and environment, labor cost trends, labor intensity.
10. Economic environment: inflation, sensitivity to business cycles, long-term trends of industry, raw materials situation.
11. Technology: research and development, plant obsolescence, patent protection, productivity.
12. Social and political environment: government regulatory environment, tax situation, geographic decentralization.
13. Earnings per share: growth rates, stability, outlook.
14. Market price per share: growth, volatility, price-earnings multiple.
15. Per share: cash flow, book value, intrinsic value.
16. Risk: subjective evaluation.

THREE FORMS OF THE EFFICIENT MARKET–RANDOM WALK HYPOTHESIS

We have already touched upon the efficient market concept and its preconditions, i.e., the requirements for its efficiency. In its present stage of development, the efficient market hypothesis takes three different forms: weak, semistrong, and strong. Each form stems from a different level of information or knowledge concerning a stock.

1. The Weak Form

This is the oldest statement of the hypothesis. It holds that present stock market prices reflect all known information with respect to past stock prices, trends, and volumes. Weak form tests analyze whether trading rules based only on historical price and volume data can lead to unusual profits. It is asserted such past data cannot be used to predict future stock prices.

Reflecting the historical development of this form, which focused on various statistical tests for random movement of successive stock prices, it has also been characterized as the *random walk hypothesis*. The weak form implies that knowledge of the past patterns of stock prices does not aid investors to attain improved performance. Random walk theorists view stock prices as moving randomly about a trend line which is based on rational expectations regarding fundamental factors.[23] Hence, they contend that (1) analyzing past data does not permit the technician to forecast the movement of prices about the trend line and (2) new information affecting stock prices enters the market in random fashion, i.e., tomorrow's news cannot be predicted nor can future stock price movements be attributable to that news.

In its present context, the weak form of the efficient market hypothesis is a direct challenge to the chartist or technician. It was the earliest focus of interest and has received by far the greatest attention in the literature.

past & current

2. The Semistrong Form

This form holds that current market prices *instantaneously* reflect all publicly known information. The semistrong form is the position most widely held by scholars. Semistrong form tests analyze whether all publicly available information and announcements (quarterly financial reports, public disclosures, and the like) are quickly and fully reflected in market prices. The semistrong form holds that such data cannot be analyzed successfully to achieve superior investment results.

This form of the efficient market hypothesis reflects a substantially greater level of knowledge and market efficiency than the weak form. The second stage, or level, of information content includes all knowledge which is available from such publications as annual reports, quarterly reports, press releases, and news flashes on "the broad tape," i.e., the Dow Jones news wire service. The semistrong form holds that since such public information is already embedded, i.e., fully discounted, in current stock prices, analyzing such data cannot produce superior investment performance.

The shift from the weak, i.e., random walk, form to the semistrong form of the efficient market hypothesis represented a quantum jump.

> This stronger assertion has proved to be especially unacceptable and unpalatable to the financial community, since it suggests the fruitlessness of efforts to earn superior rates of return by the analysis of all public information. Although some members of the financial community were willing to accept the implications of the weaker assertion about the randomness of price changes and thereby to give up technical analysis, almost no members of the community were too willing to accept the implications of the stronger form and thereby to give up fundamental analysis.[24]

---

[23] Sidney Robbins, *The Securities Markets* (New York: Free Press, 1966), pp. 44–47.

[24] James H. Lorie and Mary T. Hamilton, *The Stock Market—Theories and Evidence* (Homewood, Ill.: Richard D. Irwin, 1973), p. 81. © 1973 by Richard D. Irwin, Inc.

It is crystal clear that the semistrong form represents a direct challenge to traditional financial analysis based on the evaluation of publicly available data.

3. The Strong Form

This form holds that present market prices reflect all information that is *knowable* about a company, including all relevant information that might be developed by exhaustive study, including interviews with corporate managements, by numerous fully competent institutional security analysts.

Strong form tests investigate whether professional traders, insiders, or professional forecasting services can develop unique insights or privileged information which can be used for earning significantly large profits. The strong form holds that consistently superior investment performance is not possible.

The strong form ratcheted the efficient market hypothesis up to a still higher level of information and knowledge. In large measure, the strong form reflects the intense competition that exists among the nation's leading financial institutions. These institutions have staffs of security analysts who are top graduates of the nation's leading business schools, are highly motivated, and are held to high standards of professional performance. Security analysts who can outperform their peers in this environment move to higher positions in the investment analysis and management hierarchy. Those who fail to meet these lofty standards tend to move to other pursuits.

> . . . even if half of the professional money managers outperform the market as a whole, the market conforms to the strong form of efficiency as long as they do not generate superior results consistently. That is, in a strong form market, up to half of the time money managers could outperform the market as a whole, if only during the remainder of the time their performance was inferior to the general market.[25]

The strong form of the random walk hypothesis constitutes a direct challenge to the most knowledgeable segment of the investment community: the institutional investor.

This concludes our capsule review of the efficient market–random walk hypothesis. Its significance to the practicing security analysts is pointed up in the words of James Lorie and Richard Brealey, two founding fathers of the efficient market hypothesis, who summarize their views in these words:

> It is extremely unlikely, in principle, that the efficient market hypothesis is strictly true, particularly in its strongest form. For example, as long as

---

[25] See Dan Dorfman, "Why Can't Research Directors Hold Their Jobs?" *Institutional Investor*, October 1973, pp. 48–50 ff.

information is not wholly free, one might expect investors to require some offsetting gain before they are willing to purchase it. Nor does the empirical evidence justify unqualified acceptance of the efficient market hypothesis even in its weakest form. The important question, therefore, is not whether the theory is universally true but whether it is sufficiently correct to provide useful insights into market behavior. There is now overwhelming evidence to suggest that the random walk hypothesis is such a close approximation to reality that technical analysis cannot provide any guidance to the investment manager. When one turns to the stronger forms of the hypothesis, the evidence becomes less voluminous and the correspondence between theory and reality less exact. Nevertheless, the overriding impression is that of a highly competitive and efficient marketplace in which the opportunities for superior performance are rare.[26]

RECENT DEVELOPMENTS

As indicated above, most academics tend to adhere to the semistrong hypothesis. However, because of various anomalies (see chapter 24) which have become evident in recent years, a number of scholars now tend to the view that the market is largely efficient in the semistrong sense though it is not entirely so. There may exist, often for short periods, pockets of inefficiency (for example, with small or out-of-favor companies) which can be exploited.[27,28]

Yale Professor Malkiel states his reservations thus: " . . . while I may be excommunicated from some academic sects because of my only lukewarm endorsement of the semistrong and particularly the strong form of efficient theory, I make no effort to disguise my heresy."[29]

William Sharpe of Stanford University notes that while the market appears to conform quite well to the weak form of efficiency, it conforms less well to semistrong efficiency. Sharpe also takes the position, along with many others, that the market is not efficient in the strong sense.[30]

Perhaps the most extreme position is that of the former efficient market advocate Professor Barr Rosenberg of the University of California at Berkeley who now flatly states that stock prices are inefficient.[31]

In summary, it is evident that to succeed, security analysts face a doubly difficult task. Not only must they uncover promising situations

---

[26] Lorie and Brealey, *Modern Developments*, p. 102.

[27] George Anders, "Some Efficient Market Scholars Decide It's Possible to Beat the Market After All," *The Wall Street Journal*, (December 31, 1985).

[28] Julie Romer, "Ferment in Academia," *Institutional Investor*, (July 1985).

[29] Burton Malkiel, *Random Walk Down Wall Street*, 4th ed. (New York: W. W. Norton, 1985).

[30] William Sharpe, *Investments*, 3rd ed. (Englewood Cliffs, N.J.: Prentice-Hall, 1985).

[31] Floyd Norris, "Better Mousetrap," *Barron's* (December 16, 1985).

but they must do so before the opportunity is recognized by others. According to the efficient market hypothesis, this poses a particular challenge because of the rapidity with which publicly available information is assimilated by the market. However, the feeling persists that while this is difficult, it is not impossible.

It is appropriate to conclude with an anecdote attributed to Malkiel about a hard-line efficient market professor and one with a less rigid, more modern view. The former advises a student who sees a $20 bill on the sidewalk not to pick it up because if it were a real $20 bill someone would have already picked it up. The more modern professor tells his student to pick it up—but to be quick about it.

40

Asset Allocation Strategies

Jeffrey J. Diermeier, CFA
Managing Director
First Chicago Investment Advisors

I. INTRODUCTION

It is often said that there are only two things certain in life: death and taxes. For the investor one more certainty can be added: asset allocation. In one form or another there is no way of avoiding judgment regarding the allocation of investment capital across available asset classes.

Asset allocation lies at the heart of total portfolio management whenever more than one asset class is involved. Since at the most aggregate level portfolios are rarely invested solely in one asset class, asset allocation is a major issue for almost all investors. In fact, it is widely becoming commonly accepted that successful allocation across asset class boundaries can be the single largest determinant in meeting the investor's goals and objectives.

This chapter will deal with the breadth of issues that fall under the asset allocation umbrella in the following order. Asset allocation using derivative securities of financial futures and options will be covered within the policy and strategic asset allocation sections:

- Asset Allocation Defined.
- The Importance of Asset Allocation.
- Asset Allocation Performance.
- Policy Asset Allocation.
- Strategic Asset Allocation.
- Time Horizon.

II. ASSET ALLOCATION DEFINED

Any time current wealth and income are not consumed, the individual or corporation becomes by definition a saver and an investor and faces the following general set of questions:

What asset classes to include or exclude from investment consideration.

How to weight the asset classes to be allowed into the investor's portfolio.

How to invest in sectors within, or possibly across, the asset classes.

What specific securities to hold within each asset class and/or sector.

The first two decisions are issues of asset allocation. As opposed to security selection these are issues of market selection. The first decision refers to the types of assets that the investor allows to enter his portfolio. This decision is typically made at the asset class or investment market level, with the term *asset class* referring to individual securities that are of a common financial form, i.e., common stocks, bonds, real estate, commodities, Treasury bills, and so on. Because substantial empirical evidence has demonstrated that securities of a common financial form perform in a significantly similar fashion, it is logical in a decision hierarchy to group such securities together for purposes of convenience. At issue in the first instance of asset allocation decision making is what financial forms are worthy of investment.

The second decision involves the weighting of the individual asset classes. It can be broken down into two components. The first views the weighting decision from a policy level. This might be appropriate when there is a division of responsibility or labor or when a philosophical attitude exists whereby a default, neutral, or normal[1] portfolio weighting scheme is of interest. For example, in the management of the typical U.S. pension fund, there is often a clear division of labor between those ultimately responsible for the well-being of plan assets, usually a retirement subcommittee acting on behalf of the company's board of directors, and the day-to-day operators or managers of the assets. Another example would involve the wealthy individual investor who hires investment management expertise for the daily oversight of accumulated wealth.

In both cases it is valuable, for purposes of planning and control, for the owners of the assets to determine how they would like to see their assets allocated across the allowed investment markets on average under typical market conditions. Even when the owners of the assets oversee the day-to-day management of the assets, they may prefer to establish default asset allocations for periods when market insight is lacking. The resulting policy or normal portfolio weighting scheme has the added advantage of being a useful benchmark by which to gauge the performance results of activist asset allocation decisions.

The second type of portfolio weighting decision across asset classes involves active or strategic asset allocation. This refers to the strategic over- or underweighting of the asset classes, relative to their policy weights, to take advantage of some perceived temporary opportunity across the investment markets. When applied in the two-asset class case of U.S. common stocks and bonds, it is commonly referred to as market timing.[2] Strategic asset allocation here is used in the broader sense to include any number of potential asset classes.

For purposes of clarification, it should be noted that no one named convention dominates the descriptions provided above. The convention to be used here is that of policy and strategic asset allocation. Another often used convention uses the terms *strategic*, in lieu of policy, and *tactical*, in place of strategic, resulting in a strategic/tactical convention. The policy/strategic convention is preferred here as it saves the word *tactical* for use in tertiary maneuverings in the implementation of basic strategy.

III. THE IMPORTANCE OF ASSET ALLOCATION

To empirically assess the importance of asset allocation, a schematic was put together as in Chart 1. The schematic addresses issues of policy asset allocation, strategic asset allocation (timing), and security selection. It does not address sector allocation within or across asset classes due to limitations of empirical data. All sector allocation results will be unidentified and buried within the security selection analysis.

In the schematic a square is divided into four quadrants. In the lower right hand Quadrant I you'll find a representation of the investor's policy portfolio return. This quadrant reflects the investor's decision of what asset classes to include in the portfolio and at what normal weights.

Moving to the upper right hand corner, the return effects of policy plus timing are recorded in Quadrant II. The purpose of timing is to achieve incremental returns relative to the policy return. Quadrant III, the lower left hand corner, reports returns due to policy and security selection. Security selection is the active selection of investments within an asset class; it is the actual asset class return in excess of the asset class passive benchmark, weighted by its normal total fund position. Finally, in Quadrant IV, the upper left hand corner, the actual return to the total portfolio is reported. This is the result of the interaction of the actual portfolio segment weights and actual segment returns.

In a paper by Brinson, Hood, and Beebower[3] an attempt was made to attribute the aggregate pension plan's portfolio variance to decisions of asset class policy, asset class timing, and security selection. The

CHART 1 A Simplified Framework for Return Accountability

		Selection	
		Actual	Passive
Timing	Actual	Actual portfolio return (IV)	Policy and timing return (II)
	Passive	Policy and security selection return (III)	Policy return (passive portfolio benchmark) (I)

Active returns due to:

	Quadrant
Timing	II − I
Selection	III − I
Other	IV − III − II − I
Total	IV − I

SOURCES: First Chicago Investment Advisors and SEI Corporation.

analysis could not directly estimate the percentage of portfolio variance explained by policy level decisions because a good policy database does not exist. As a proxy for pension plan asset allocation policy, the average stock/bond/cash weights of 91 individual pension plans were used. These are all of the plans in the SEI large plan universe of plans over $100 million market value, where asset class weight and return data exist for a 10-year quarterly history ending December 31, 1983. Chart 2 shows the average weights of the plans over the history and the existence of a catchall "other" category. That category was ignored for purposes of this analysis.

Chart 3 indicates how returns were calculated each quarter for each quadrant for each of the 91 plans in the database. For each plan, three hypothetical strings and one actual return string of 40 quarters' length were put together. From that three least squares regressions were run

CHART 2 Large Pension Plan Investments (distribution of investment weights,* 1974–1983)

	Stocks	Bonds	Cash Equivalents	Other
Actual:				
Mean	57.5%	21.4%	12.4%	8.6%
Minimum	32.3	0.0	1.8	0.0
Maximum	86.5	43.0	33.1	53.5
Standard deviation	10.9	9.0	5.0	8.3
Normalized:[†]				
Mean	62.9%	23.4%	13.6%	
Minimum	37.9	0.0	2.0	
Maximum	89.3	51.3	35.0	
Standard deviation	10.6	9.4	5.2	

* Based on SEI large plan universe; 91 pension plans.
  [†] Other data removed from weights and allocated proportionately to stocks, bonds, and cash equivalents.
  SOURCES: First Chicago Investment Advisors and SEI Corporation.

regressing the policy series, the policy plus timing series, and the policy plus selection series against the dependent variable series of actual plan returns.

The average total variance of the 91 plans was 204 units annualized. As Chart 4 shows, of that total, 93.6 percent, on average, was explained by the proxy policy portfolios rebalanced quarterly and invested in passive portfolios of the S&P 500, the Shearson Lehman Government/ Corporate Index, and 30-day Treasury bills. On average, 95.3 percent can be explained by portfolios constructed using the actual beginning-of-quarter mix, rebalanced quarterly, and the passive stock/bond/cash return series. Also, 97.8 percent can be explained, on average, by hypothetical portfolios using the average plan mix, rebalanced quarterly, and the actual active stock/bond/cash return series.

This analysis clearly suggests that, at the least, large institutional portfolio owners focus their attention on the difficult decisions of what asset classes to include in their portfolios and at what normal weights. It also suggests that for all the Wall Street discussion of market timing, little material shifting of asset class weights has been evident in terms of aggregate institutional portfolios.

IV. ASSET ALLOCATION PERFORMANCE

The above analysis can be followed up with an analysis of performance attributable to the policy, timing, and selection decisions covering those same 91 pension plans. The most difficult part of this analysis is to determine the attribution to the policy decision. Policy returns for the

CHART 3 Computational Requirements for Return Accountability (quarterly calculations)

Selection

		Actual	Passive
Timing	Actual	$\Sigma_I(\text{WAI} \times \text{RAI})^*$ (IV)	$\Sigma_I(\text{WAI} \times \text{RPI})$ (II)
	Passive	$\Sigma_I(\text{WPI} \times \text{RAI})$ (III)	$\Sigma_I(\text{WPI} \times \text{RPI})$ (I)

Where

WPI = policy (passive) weight for asset class I
WAI = actual weight for asset class I
RPI = passive return for asset class I[†]
RAI = active return for asset class I

---

* Study used actual returns.
† S&P 500, Shearson Lehman Government/Corporate Bond Index, and 30-day Treasury bills.
SOURCES: First Chicago Investment Advisors and SEI Corporation.

pension plans were individually calculated using their average historic stock/bond/cash weights, quarterly rebalancing, and passive component returns. The issue is to what to compare those returns. What is needed is some natural default policy weighting scheme that could be applied by the plan-sponsor community.

One method, and a popular one in the literature, would be to define a natural default policy portfolio as a market-weighted basket of all available and utilized asset classes. For purposes of this paper the primary wealth-generating asset classes of domestic stocks, bonds, real estate, venture capital, and cash equivalents, as well as international stocks and bonds, were selected. Chart 5 from Brinson and Diermeier[4]

CHART 4 Percent of Total Return Variation Explained by Investment Activity (average of 91 plans, 1974–1983)

Selection

	Actual	Passive
Actual	100.0% (IV)	95.3% (II)
Passive	97.8% (III)	93.6% (I)

Timing

Variance explained:

	Average	Minimum	Maximum	Standard Deviation
Policy	93.6%	75.5%	98.6%	4.4%
Policy and timing	95.3	78.7	98.7	2.9
Policy and selection	97.8	80.6	99.8	3.1

SOURCES: First Chicago Investment Advisors and SEI Corporation.

reveals the estimated market proportions for this aggregate investable capital market. These end-of-year capitalization weightings have been estimated, annually, back to the end of 1959. Hence, a hypothetical portfolio return series was constructed, weighted by the new beginning-of-year weights, each year. This serves as one natural default policy portfolio alternative.

A second alternative is similarly defined but excludes international securities on the presumption that a U.S.-only capital market portfolio would be of interest. The current U.S.-only weights are exhibited in Chart 6.

If there is a flaw in the capitalization weighted scheme, it is that there is no way to ensure that the risk of these aggregate portfolios resembles that of the typical pension plan. To avoid this "apples and oranges" problem, First Chicago Investment Advisors (FCIA) created

CHART 5 Investable Capital Market, December 31, 1984 ($10.7 trillion)

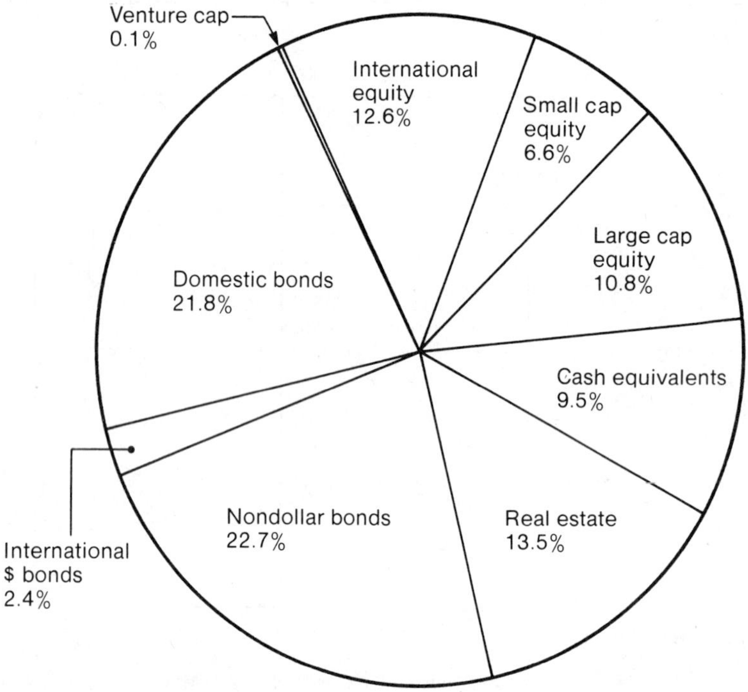

Venture cap
0.1%

International
equity
12.6%

Small cap
equity
6.6%

Large cap
equity
10.8%

Domestic bonds
21.8%

Cash equivalents
9.5%

International
$ bonds
2.4%

Nondollar bonds
22.7%

Real estate
13.5%

SOURCE: First Chicago Investment Advisors.

the Multiple Markets Index (MMI),[5] which uses the assets of the investable capital market but weights the assets in a manner so as to produce a risk profile similar to that estimated for the typical pension plan. The weights are derived from a Markowitz[6] optimization scheme using FCIA's equilibrium risk and return estimates. The MMI's weights are displayed in Chart 7.

Chart 8 shows the results of the plan sponsor performance attribution. The lower right hand box shows the decade's results of the three default policy portfolios. The investable capital market with and without foreign securities provided annual returns of 9.7 percent and 9.8 percent, respectively, with volatility near that of the U.S. bond market. The Multiple Markets Index, with its weights calibrated to raise the level of risk to that accepted by the typical pension plan, provided a much healthier return of 12.8 percent.

The upper left hand box in the exhibit shows that despite the assumption of greater risk than each proxy policy portfolio, the average return payoff for the 91 plans was less. For greater risk, the typical plan

CHART 6   U.S. Investable Capital Market, December 31, 1984 ($6.7 trillion)

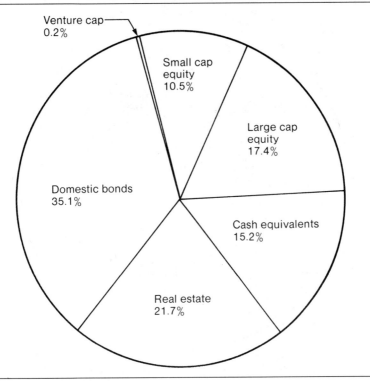

SOURCE: First Chicago Investment Advisors.

underperformed the total capital market by 70 to 380 basis points per annum, depending on the proxy.

Where did the shortfall occur? First a look at results from average asset allocation. The passive timing/passive selection quadrant shows the average annualized return of the portfolios invested at their average quarterly weights, using passive components. These portfolios did provide a slightly higher return than the investable capital market, with and without foreign securities. Relative to the MMI, where the risk is more comparable, the return of the average allocation series was 270 basis points per annum less.

The active timing/passive selection box reveals that by allowing the sample pension plans the right to deviate from the average weights (the asset class timing proxy) the cost was about 67 basis points per annum (9.44–10.11).

The passive timing/active selection box indicates that allowing the pension plans to actively manage the component assets cost the plans

CHART 7 Multiple Markets Index, First Chicago Investment Advisors

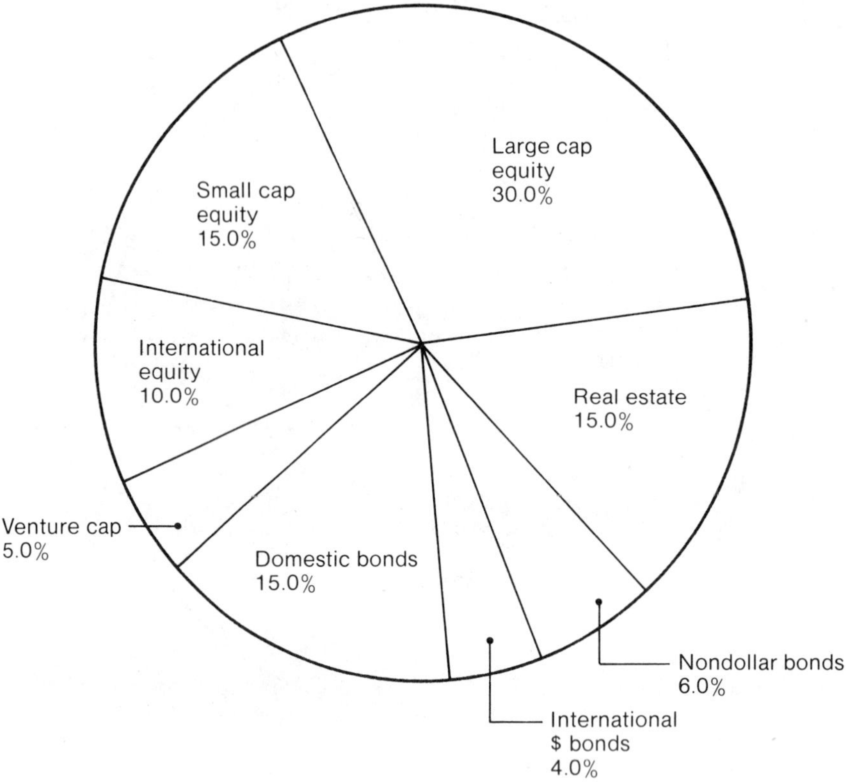

SOURCE: First Chicago Investment Advisors.

on average another 36 basis points (9.75–10.11) per annum. The two active management losses, 67 basis points from timing and 36 basis points from security selection, sum to 103 basis points. This sum approximates the difference between the total plan results and the passive timing/passive selection portfolio. As noted in the chart, the return loss is further heightened by the absorption of the risk associated with active portfolio management. As Chart 9 indicates, the above results in the cross-sectional test yield significantly negative results for both asset class timing and total active results.

The negative strategic asset allocation results agree with the preponderance of prior empirical attempts at measuring strategic asset allocation performance. In a seminal article in 1975 Sharpe set the tone for subsequent studies by demonstrating, with conventional assumptions concerning transaction costs, that a manager had to be able to predict

CHART 8   Average Large Plan Investment Performance Results* (1974–1983)

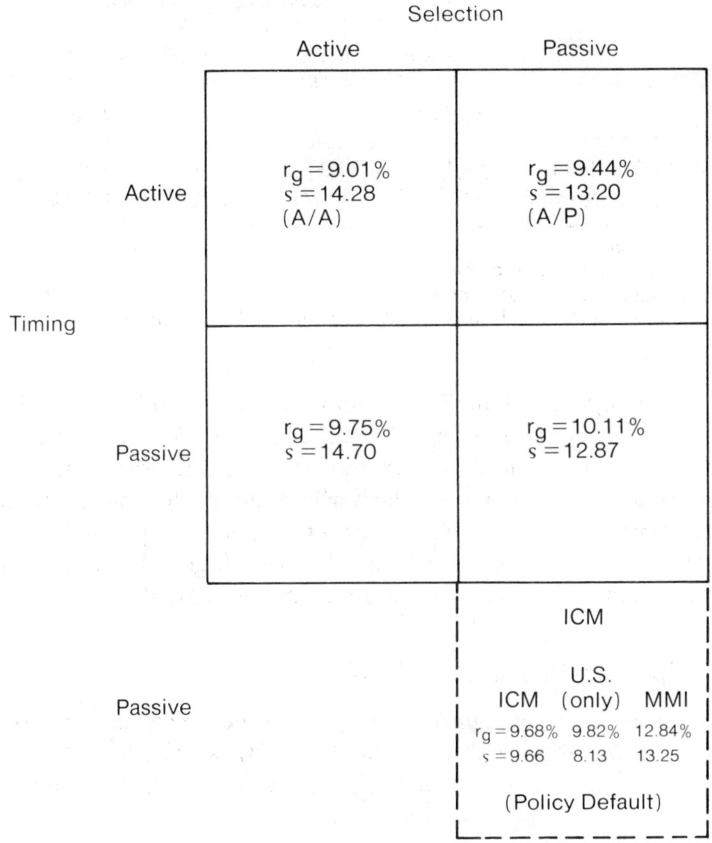

Selection

	Active	Passive
Active	$r_g = 9.01\%$ $s = 14.28$ (A/A)	$r_g = 9.44\%$ $s = 13.20$ (A/P)
Passive	$r_g = 9.75\%$ $s = 14.70$	$r_g = 10.11\%$ $s = 12.87$

Timing

Passive

ICM

	ICM	U.S. (only)	MMI
$r_g =$	9.68%	9.82%	12.84%
$s =$	9.66	8.13	13.25

(Policy Default)

Key:
r_g = average of the 91 geometric annual returns
s = average of the 91 annualized quarterly standard deviations

* 91 large pension plans (SEI Corp.). Data are calculated quarterly.
SOURCES: First Chicago Investment Advisors and SEI Corporation.

the stock market's direction each year with 70 percent accuracy just to be break even.[7] Studies by Jensen,[8] Kon,[9] Henriksson,[10] and Chang and Lewellen[11] have attempted to measure the market timing performance of the mutual fund industry. All studies found a lack of skillful market timing on the part of the mutual fund industry.

Recently, however, partly as a result of the development of the financial futures and options markets, which reduce transaction costs of market timing, and partly due to good performance from strategic asset

CHART 9 Average Large Plan Active Results

Active Returns	Compound Annual Returns				
	Average Return	Minimum Return	Maximum Return	Standard Deviation	t-Statistic
Timing only	−0.66%	−2.68%	0.25%	0.49%	−4.26[†]
Security selection only	−0.36	−2.90	3.60	1.36	−0.84
Other (cross product)	−0.07	−1.17	2.57	0.45	−0.51
Total active return	−1.10%*	−4.17%*	3.69%*	1.45%*	−2.41*[‡]

* Not additive.
[†] Significant at the 99.9 percent level.
[‡] Significant at the 95 percent level.
SOURCES: First Chicago Investment Advisors and SEI Corporation.

allocators using disciplined and quantitative methods, strategic asset allocation is enjoying a revival. Recent articles by Vandell and Kester[12] and Grauer and Hakansson,[13] demonstrating that excess profits were achievable in the past from simple market timing rules, have fanned that revival. Growing recognition that large pension plans with huge amounts of capital are forced by size toward bigger ideas, like strategic asset allocation, has further promoted this movement.

V. POLICY ASSET ALLOCATION

The performance results described in the preceding section call attention to the need for improved asset allocation. The attribution of returns to policy decisions, weight variation, and security selection reveals the importance of the asset allocation policy decision.

Asset Allocation Criteria

The first asset allocation policy decision is that of selecting a set of asset classes for inclusion. This requires a set of criteria which can be used to distinguish the worthy from the unworthy asset classes. These criteria should be uniformly applied to all asset classes under consideration. An example of a set of criteria is found in Chart 10.

The goal of this screening process is to select asset classes from which the investor could obtain satisfactory returns for the risk involved. Satisfactory return could result because of the nature of the asset class to provide, on average, a fair rent for capital invested, or it could result from extraordinary skill in a generally poor yielding market. Most investors should prefer asset classes of the former rather than the latter type.

For our purposes we will assume that the primary asset classes

---

CHART 10   Suitability Criteria

- Analytical
    Adequate control and regulation
    Marketability and liquidity
    Meaningful impact
    Nonredundant
    Manageable estimation risk
    Earning after cost investments
    Covariance with other assets
- Legal
- Talent availability

---

currently used by institutional plan sponsors pass this screening process. Broadly speaking those asset classes include domestic stocks, bonds, real estate, venture capital, and cash equivalents as well as foreign stocks and bonds, both dollar and nondollar denominated.

Policy Weights

The second asset allocation policy decision involves the assignment of normal weights to the asset classes selected for inclusion in the portfolio, absent any specific insights about short-term asset class performance.

Three separate approaches for determining investment policy weights are suggested. The first approach determines the market value weights of all the investable asset classes and uses these as the investment policy weights. The second uses information about the investor's unique circumstances. The third approach is more quantitative but probably not any more precise. It uses risk/return optimization to determine an appropriate set of investment policy weights.

Market value approach.   A logical starting point in the determination of investment policy weights is to estimate the proportions of the total market portfolio made up of the individual asset classes (refer back to Chart 5). The assumptions underlying the development of the capital asset pricing model lead to the prescription of market value weights.[14] Every investor, under these assumptions, would hold the market portfolio. Commonsense considerations also suggest market value weights for a relatively uninformed investor.

The investable capital market portfolio has some interesting properties. The fact that it is sufficiently diversified to own all available capital assets in the world suggests that its growth over time would reflect the growth of the global economy.[15] Reasons why its growth might not reflect growth in total output would be:

CHART 11 Investable Capital Market versus Industrial Country Gross Domestic Product

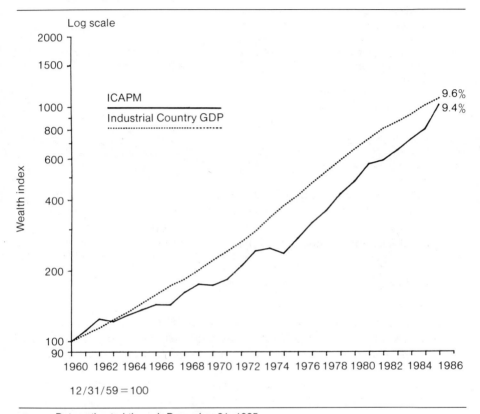

NOTE: Data estimated through December 31, 1985.
SOURCE: First Chicago Investment Advisors.

- Wealth transfers from investment to human capital.
- Increased taxation of gains from investment capital and redistribution of proceeds to noninvestment areas.
- Reduced expectations of future output.

As Charts 11 and 12 illustrate, the actual growth in the size of the investable capital market has mirrored growth in industrial country aggregate gross domestic product over the longest time period of available data: 1960 through 1985. Similarly, the U.S.-only portion of the investable capital market has grown at a comparable rate to U.S. gross national product from 1948 through 1985. This evidence strongly suggests that a portfolio built to mimic the world's capital market portfolio would grow in line with gross output. Ultimate return would be a function of reinvesting the yield from the capital market back into new

CHART 12   U.S. Investable Capital Market versus U.S. Gross National Product

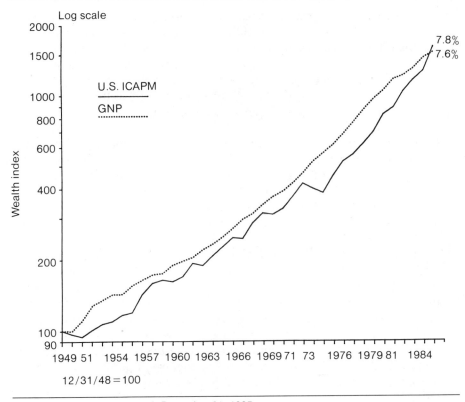

NOTE: Data estimated through December 31, 1985.
SOURCE: First Chicago Investment Advisors.

issues and secondary offerings of capital assets, which are an important element of capital market growth. Over the last two decades estimates of the yield of the U.S. capital market and the amount of new capital raised suggests that net yield (gross yield − new issues) has been fairly close to zero, so that capital market returns performed at the rate of the U.S. GNP.

Customized policy approach.   A second approach to policy allocation follows the New Equilibrium Theory (NET) construct that investors are heterogeneous, having different tax situations, institutional constraints, and time horizons.[16] As Sharpe stated:

> One should hardly conclude that every investor should hold a market-value balanced portfolio. Cash requirements, tax situations, legal and institutional restrictions, investment horizons and predictions differ. But divergences

from the standard mix of bonds and stocks should be justifiable in terms of these differences.[17]

Under this approach the investor must do a good bit of self-analysis and soul-searching to determine if he has any unique characteristics. At the institutional plan management level major efforts are often undertaken so as to understand the organization's attitude toward: (a) risk, (b) the future liabilities of the retirement plans that the investment funds are meant to cover, and (c) the potential integration of the investment plan assets with the organization's other assets.

For example, regarding risk, an organization with greater risk tolerance typically will be willing to load up, as a matter of policy, with investments of a higher risk nature. As to liabilities, some firms put great efforts into estimating future cash outflows so as to buy investment assets that literally match the character of the liabilities. An obligation to a pension fund retiree due in five years might be matched with an equal size zero-coupon bond of five-year maturity. Many variations on this theme exist today in the institutional environment.

Regarding integration, this is best explained by a simple example. A real estate construction company may want to avoid real estate since it is already exposed to this industry. If the real estate industry collapses, not only would the basic business suffer but so would the pension plan, at what could be precisely the wrong time. Many variations on this theme can be found in current practice and theory.

Related issues of the importance of time horizon in determining the investor's attitude toward risk, as well as the use of portfolio insurance tools, are sufficiently interesting that they will be dealt with later in this chapter.

Risk/return optimization.   A third approach that can be used to obtain investment policy weights is portfolio optimization. Optimization is used to construct a frontier of policy portfolios offering a varying array of return/risk possibilities with no one portfolio dominating any other.

Typically called mean-variance optimization (see Appendix for a brief description), this technique is a quantitative approach to the problem, and it produces answers that are apparently very precise. However, the results are quite sensitive to changes in the inputs and the form of the inputs themselves.

As an example of a mean-variance application, the Multiple Markets Index (MMI) was developed using the set of inputs described in Charts 13 and 14. The only constraints placed on the optimization were that all weights must be nonnegative and the maximum weight for venture capital is 5 percent to allow for its aggregate size limitations. The mean-variance efficient portfolio with estimated risk equal to that of the typical pension fund was selected as the MMI.

CHART 13 Long-Term Optimization Inputs

	Risk* Premia† (Percent)	Less- Passive‡ Fee‡ (Percent)	Realizable Risk Premia* (Percent)	Risk* (Standard Deviation)
Large capital	5.80%	.10%	5.70%	16.50%
Small capital	7.55	.20	7.35	22.00
International stocks	6.35	.25	6.10	20.50
Venture capital	15.00	2.00	13.00	40.00
Domestic bonds	2.30	.10	2.20	8.50
Dollar bonds	2.25	.10	2.15	8.00
Nondollar bonds	2.30	.15	2.15	11.00
Real estate	4.80	.80	4.00	14.00
T-bills	0.00	.00	0.00	1.50

* Optimization Inputs.
† The difference between the required rate of return and the rate of a riskless asset.
‡ These are the annual costs (expressed as a percentage) required to carry the investment; for real estate it includes property taxes, management fees, insurance and so forth; for an equity portfolio it includes the costs charged by fund management.
SOURCE: First Chicago Investment Advisors.

The returns, standard deviations, and correlation coefficients used in the optimization process are long-term estimates. Long-term estimates are used because the policy-setting process by nature requires some continuity over time. It should not be upset by short-term fluctuations in the capital markets.

Assessments of long-term equilibrium rates of return were obtained by separately estimating a risk-free real rate of return, an inflation premium, and a risk premium and adding them together.[18] The inflation premium and the real rate of return are assumed to be the same for each

CHART 14 Long-Term Asset Class Correlation Forecasts

		1	2	3	4	5	6	7	8	9
1.	Large capital equity	1.00								
2.	Small capital equity	.85	1.00							
3.	International equity	.55	.55	1.00						
4.	Venture capital	.40	.45	.55	1.00					
5.	Domestic bonds	.45	.40	.30	.15	1.00				
6.	International dollar bonds	.45	.40	.35	.20	.90	1.00			
7.	Nondollar fixed income	.15	.20	.65	.20	.25	.30	1.00		
8.	Real estate	.50	.55	.50	.45	.30	.35	.20	1.00	
9.	Cash equivalents	.00	.00	.00	.00	.00	.00	.00	.00	1.00

SOURCE: First Chicago Investment Advisors.

CHART 15 Long-Term Asset Class Risk Premiums (segmented markets approach)

Asset Class	Risk	Risk Premiums*
Large capital equity	16.50%	6.60%
Small capital equity	22.00	8.80
International equity[†]	17.80	7.12
Venture capital	40.00	16.00
Domestic bonds	8.50	3.40
International dollar bonds	8.00	3.20
Nondollar bonds[†]	7.25	2.90
Real estate	14.00	5.60
Cash equivalents	1.50	0.60

* Price of risk assumed to be 40 basis points per unit of risk.
† Risk in local currency terms.
SOURCE: First Chicago Investment Advisors.

asset class. Only the risk premiums vary across the asset classes, and as a result, only the risk premiums need enter the optimization process.

In a world of risk-averse investors, it is clear that risk premiums should be positively related to risk. The procedure for estimating risk premiums involves estimating measures of risk for the asset classes and estimating the relationship between risk and expected return. It requires that the various estimates entering the optimization process be consistent with one another.

Two measures of risk were estimated: (1) the standard deviation of returns from each asset class and (2) the beta coefficient, which measures the sensitivity of the returns in each asset class to returns on the aggregate investable capital market portfolio. The beta estimates reflect the correlation of the asset class with the investable capital market as defined above.

We assume that risk premiums could be set in two extreme states of the world. Our intuition is that in reality risk premiums are established in the marketplace somewhere between the two extremes after proper consideration for taxes.

In the one extreme, investors set asset class risk premiums with a relatively narrow view of the world. Risk (measured by the variance, the square of the standard deviation) is perceived to be that of each asset class in isolation. This might result from the tendency of investors to specialize in one market. Chart 15 shows a set of risk estimates for the investable asset classes. From this viewpoint, where all asset classes are perceived to be segmented from one another, it is, nevertheless, suggested that an invisible hand assures that all risk expectations demand the same proportional risk premium. The table indicates what a set of resultant risk premiums might look like in a "segmented" world.

CHART 16 Long-Term Asset Class Risk Premiums (integrated markets approach)

Asset Class	Beta	Risk Premiums*
Large capital equity	1.31	4.74%
Small capital equity	1.81	6.55
International equity†	0.46	1.94
Venture capital	2.44	8.83
Domestic bonds	0.59	2.14
International dollar bonds	0.56	2.03
Nondollar bonds†	0.20	0.87
Real estate	1.02	3.69
Cash equivalents	0.00	0.00

* Assumes risk premiums to the investable capital market portfolio in local currency terms of 3.6 percent.
† Beta in local currency terms.
SOURCE: First Chicago Investment Advisors.

At the other extreme, it is assumed that all asset class markets are perfectly intergrated. In this case the risk of each asset class is only the incremental risk that the individual asset class brings to the total portfolio. In this case the covariance matrix of class return expectations is given full credit. Here the beta of the individual asset class to the investable capital market stands as the more appropriate risk measure. Chart 16 indicates a sample of risk premiums so derived. The optimization inputs discussed earlier lie between the two boundary conditions.

As you might infer, it would be wealth maximizing for the investment community to move from a state of segmentation to one of integration. An integrated society would, on average, perceive less total risk than a segmented society. This is important as it would tend to lower society's cost of capital and encourage greater risk taking. Greater societal wealth would result.

The notion of segmented and integrated pricing bounds is not new to the literature. Lessard used this concept in his discussion of international security pricing.[19] He concluded it is unlikely that principal national markets are either completely segmented or integrated. He does note that in either of the extreme scenarios, international diversification is desirable. In the case of segmented markets, an internationally diversified portfolio will provide superior risk-adjusted performance. Conversely, if markets are completely integrated, a portfolio that is not internationally diversified will yield inferior risk-adjusted performance.

Chart 17 illustrates the risk/return frontiers generated from the prior inputs for two lists of assets. The lower line is what would be available from all combinations of stock/bond portfolio mixes. The upper line

CHART 17 Attainable Efficient Frontiers

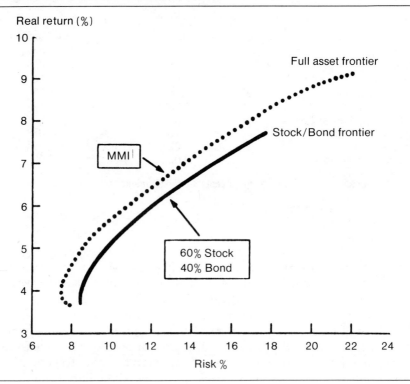

SOURCE: First Chicago Investment Advisors.

reflects the return and risk combinations available from the full list of available assets. Two observations immediately come to mind. First, the full asset frontier unambiguously offers more return per unit of risk than the limited stock/bond frontier. Second, the full asset frontier gives a wider range of options with regard to risk and prospective return. These are two logically correct and powerful arguments for investing in the totality of the global capital markets.

The MMI was constructed to be risk neutral relative to the typical pension plan, which for forecasting purposes was proxied by a 60/40 stock/bond mix. Overall the MMI holds, as a matter of policy, 45 percent in domestic stocks, 19 percent in dollar-denominated fixed income, 15 percent in U.S. real estate, 5 percent in U.S. venture capital, 10 percent in foreign stocks, and 6 percent in foreign bonds. These weights agree with the attitudes of the typical pension plan under the customized policy approach discussed earlier.

The selection of the proper portfolio off of the frontier requires some knowledge of the investor's attitude for trading risk vis-à-vis return. The MMI's level of risk acceptance was set to equal that of the so-called typical institutional investor. Any individual investor may likewise want to develop his estimate of his risk acceptance by comparing it to some benchmark group.

More formally the risk tolerance approach requires the identification of the rate at which the investor is willing to trade off or is indifferent to marginal expected return and risk. There is no requirement that this optimal trade-off be static for the investor. It can vary as his wealth, circumstances, and expectations vary. Nevertheless, oftentimes a simplifying assumption is made involving constant proportional risk tolerance, at least over the region of likely outcomes and alternative interesting investment portfolios. Assuming constant proportional risk tolerance, we can put forth a utility function in the form as follows which is unrelated to investor wealth:

$$E(U_{pi}) = E(R_p) - (1/T_i) \cdot E(V(R_p))$$
$$\text{Utility} \quad \text{Return} \quad \text{Risk penalty}$$

where

$E(U_{pi})$ = the expected excess utility of the portfolio for the investor over the risk-free rate

$E(R_p)$ = the expected excess return of the portfolio over the risk-free rate

T_i = the investor's risk tolerance

$E(V(R_p))$ = the expected variance of the portfolio

The investor's utility would be equivalent to a fully risk adjusted rate of return or certainty equivalent return if the risk tolerance function were linear as assumed in Chart 18. The risk tolerance parameter (T) acts to identify the rate at which the investor demands to be compensated for each additional unit of undiversifiable risk. In the case of the MMI the implied risk tolerance parameter is 73, so that the implied preferred payoff rate is 1.4 basis points of return for each additional unit of variance (1/73).

This can be implied because a risk tolerance parameter of 73 provides the highest level of utility from the range of portfolios that make up the attainable frontier. Chart 19 illustrates this point. The chart shows the utility calculation from several portfolios lifted off of various points on the frontier. As you can see, at a risk tolerance parameter of 73, the MMI policy portfolio is optimal in that it has the highest utility for the hypothetical typical pension investor. A different risk tolerance parameter would produce maximum utility in another portfolio elsewhere on the frontier.

In this framework it is incumbent on the investor to arrive at his own estimate of his risk tolerance function. Although difficult to intuit and

CHART 18 The Risk Tolerance Function

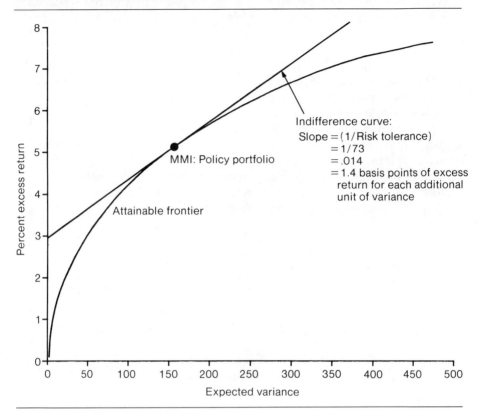

CHART 19 Frontier Portfolio Utility

			Risk		
	Low	Low-Mid	Mid*	Mid-High	High
Excess return	3.42%	4.42%	5.22%	6.00%	6.93%
Standard deviation	8.05	10.54	12.78	15.14	18.23
Variance	64.80	111.09	163.33	229.22	332.33
Optimal risk tolerance	73	73	73	73	73
Utility (at given risk tolerance)	2.53%	2.90%	2.98%	2.86%	2.38%

* MMI.

CHART 20   Pattern of Returns from a Call Option and Cash

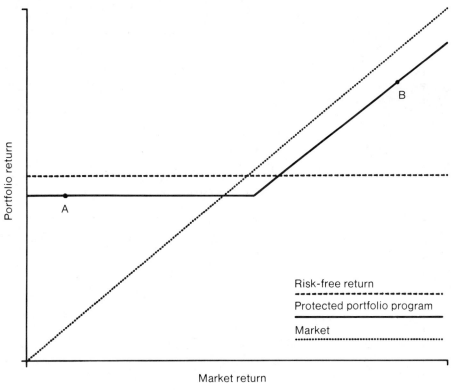

Risk-free return

Protected portfolio program

Market

analyze, the asset allocator who has a good sense of his willingness to trade risk for reward is at a great advantage over the typical investor.

Policy Allocation Using Futures and Options

Futures and options can alter the distribution of forecast returns created by the policy allocation process in an infinite number of ways. Such alterations are clearly a matter of policy if permanent alteration is desired to more closely fit the portfolio to the investor's tolerance for certain kinds of potential outcomes. To understand this capability, a basic review of derivative instruments (futures and options) is required.

Chart 20 indicates the basic payoff pattern of purchasing a call option on a market index with a portion of the portfolio's assets and putting the remainder in cash equivalents, vis-à-vis the payoff pattern of the underlying market. The call option allows the investor to buy the underlying market at a predetermined (strike) price for a specified

CHART 21 Pattern of Returns from a Put Option and Cash

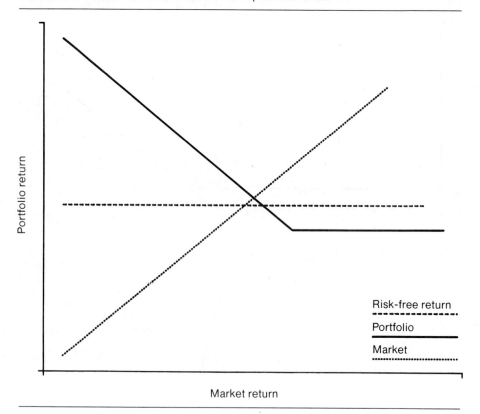

Risk-free return

Portfolio

Market

period of time in the future. The kink in the payoff line occurs at the strike price. As the market's price exceeds the strike price, the value of the call increases. The value of the call will not decrease below zero so that the portfolio's value will not drop below the value of the risk-free rate less the cost of the call option.

A put option gives the investor the right to sell or put the security of interest to the seller of the put at a predetermined price. The payoff pattern of a put and cash equivalent portfolio is described as in Chart 21 with the kink in the line again occurring at the strike price. As the security drops in price the put becomes more valuable because the holder of the put has a guaranteed sales price. As the security rises the put declines in value. The put/cash equivalent portfolio will not decline in value below the value of the cash equivalent portion of the portfolio less the cost of the put option. This occurs only when the underlying security finishes the option period above the strike price.

Portfolio insurance, or, as it is often called, dynamic asset allocation,

CHART 22 Portfolio Distributions

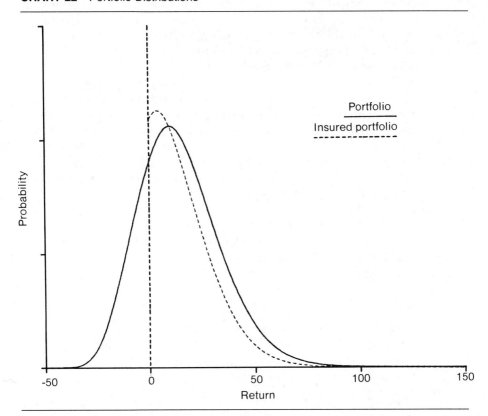

occurs when the investor who already owns a risky asset portfolio buys an actual or synthetic put option on the portfolio. This produces the same payoff pattern as owning a call option. It is accomplished by summing the payoff patterns of the market line and the portfolio line in Chart 21. The two lines offset each other to the left of the kink and rise at the market to the right of the kink, as in the call option diagram.

As a result the portfolio is insured or, more appropriately, assured that losses will not occur below the predetermined strike price. This allows the investor to effectively truncate the distribution of potential return outcomes on the portfolio. He can do so at any level below the level of the risk-free investment rate for the appropriate time horizon as in Chart 22. This suggests that the investor could, as some have, create a portfolio that is protected from ever providing a negative rate of return over the period of interest. Note that dynamic approaches using cash and the underlying security and/or futures can alter return distributions in many ways beyond simple truncation. Scaled and partial participation of market movements in a wide variety are available.

There are several ways to implement portfolio insurance. The two most straightforward are the methodologies just examined: (1) buying calls plus holding cash and (2) buying puts plus holding stock. Other approaches use a combination of stock and cash or stock and futures to replicate the outcomes which the put and call approaches yield. For example, the price sensitivity of the insured portfolio using puts to the price movement of the underlying risky portfolio can be accurately estimated using option theory. If the portfolio was at point A in Chart 20, the total portfolio would be insensitive to a small price movement in the underlying portfolio. To replicate this strategy using stock and cash, nearly 100 percent must be invested in cash. If, however, the portfolio was at point B, the total portfolio would be very sensitive to any movement in the underlying portfolio. To replicate this position the portfolio should be close to 100 percent invested in the underlying portfolio. The exact proportions between the risky portfolio and cash are determined by the following factors which are the bases of option pricing theory:[20]

1. The strike price.
2. Time remaining in the option period.
3. Expected volatility of the risky portfolio.
4. Return of the risky portfolio relative to the floor return (i.e., the price of the risky portfolio relative to the strike price).
5. Short-term interest rate.

In lieu of using cash, futures can be used to hedge the risky portfolio. The advantage of using futures is to reduce transaction costs, potentially by a factor of five or more. On the negative side, hedging with futures introduces two types of tracking error.

First, futures contracts exist for certain standard investment indexes such as the S&P 500, Value Line Composite, and the NYSE Index, among others, as well as for Treasury bonds, notes, and bills. It may be that the investor's underlying portfolio does not perfectly conform to one of or a combination of existing futures contracts. This introduces an element of tracking error which is surely an uncompensated risk.

Second, various factors cause futures and option contracts to trade at prices that differ slightly from perceived theoretical value. As a result risk is introduced because the derivative instrument does not perfectly mimic its underlying progenitor.

Portfolio insurance can be used for policy asset allocation to the degree the investor desires a permanent alternative to the portfolio's underlying return distribution. Once the investor is aware that portfolio insurance can be incorporated into his asset allocation policy, a number of questions arise:

1. How should the risk/reward trade-off of portfolio insurance be evaluated?
2. If portfolio insurance is chosen:
   a. What assets should be covered?
   b. At what level should the floor return be set?
   c. At what length should the time horizon be set?

The distribution of an insured portfolio is typically skewed (Chart 22). Shorthand descriptions of return distributions, (i.e., expected return and standard deviation used in mean-variance optimizations) are inadequate to properly analyze the merits of the protective put. The full portfolio distribution must be analyzed.

Overlaying a generalized utility function on the return distribution is one way to account for both risk and return in an appropriate fashion. When the utility function is quadratic, expected utility can be defined in terms of mean and variance, as we did in the policy optimization process.[21] When a mean-variance description of the distribution is inadequate, a more generalized utility function can be used to translate potential outcomes, as defined by the end-period wealth of the investor, into units of utility. Therefore, by taking a portfolio's distribution of potential returns, translating returns into wealth relatives, and translating wealth relatives into units of utility, the utilities can be multiplied by the probability of occurrence to derive an expected utility of the portfolio's return distribution. Ranking of policy portfolio utilities allows the investor to choose rationally between portfolios of very different risk/return characteristics. More formally:

$$E(U_{pi}) = \Sigma\ U(W)\ P(W)$$

where

$E(U_{pi})$ = as previously defined
$U(W)$ = the utility of a given level of wealth
$P(W)$ = the probability of the wealth outcome
W = wealth

As a result of simulations of portfolio return distributions and utility functions, some general statements can be made. An investor who has any of the following characteristics should consider using a protective put strategy in asset allocation policy.

- Where risk aversion decreases more rapidly than the average investor's as the value of the portfolio increases.
- Where there is greater sensitivity concerning downside risk than the average investor's.
- Where there is a belief in trends.
- Where there is prohibition from diversifying out of risky assets

but a desire exists to manage risk beyond that capability within the risky set.
• Where a guarantee is desired that returns will be some minimum (e.g., zero) but where a participation in upside returns is of interest.

VI. STRATEGIC ASSET ALLOCATION

In the investor's portfolio the opportunity exists to shift the existing asset class mix away from policy to take advantage of short-term opportunities in the marketplace. These opportunities might arise from relative mispricings in the broad capital market or from shifting equilibrium conditions. Effective strategic asset allocation requires a careful coordination and integration of the policy assumptions into the strategic framework. This is because the definition of strategic asset allocation is done in reference to policy norms. It is when the current outlook differs from the basic policy assumptions that a need arises to alter the portfolio strategically.

Strategic asset allocation is not only conducted in reference to the portfolio's policy norms, but most practitioners put boundaries on the maximum and minimum positions that can be held within an asset class.

Range Setting

The setting of the ranges themselves is actually a matter of policy. It involves analysis of the opportunities presented by shifts in the capital markets, assumptions as to the ability of the investor to capture that potential after transaction and other costs are deducted, and predetermination of how the portfolio should be altered from the policy norms to profit from those opportunities. This latter step is usually carried out through the use of computer simulation.

The steps to be followed in the setting of strategic asset allocation ranges are as follows:

1. Identify abnormal opportunity per asset class.
2. Estimate forecasting ability per asset class (i.e., the correlation between forecast abnormal and actual return).
3. Determine transaction costs (round-trip).
4. Identify the investor's risk tolerance.
5. Run reoptimizations with bullish and bearish abnormal returns per asset class.
6. For each reoptimization check the portfolio weight of the asset class under analysis at the investor's risk tolerance.

For example, the investor may review a chart of historical inflation-adjusted returns over holding periods of interest to him to identify

CHART 23 Non-U.S. Equities—Inflation Adjusted Five-Year Compound Annualized
Returns

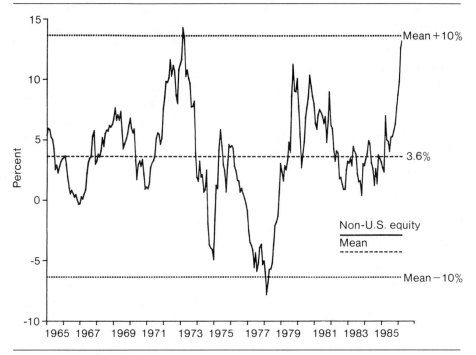

NOTES: Deflated by P.C.E. deflator.
Data estimated through March 31, 1986.

potential opportunity. Chart 23 shows five year holding period real
returns for non-U.S. equities in dollars. As compared with a mean
annual holding period return of 3.6 percent, the chart indicates that over
the past 25 years abnormal opportunities of a magnitude of ±10 percent
per annum have arisen. If the investor had perfect foresight he could
have anticipated these extraordinary returns and heavily skewed his
portfolio to take advantage of the opportunity.

Man is not endowed with the characteristic of perfect foresight.
Therefore, potential opportunities must be tempered by an assessment
of the ability to identify opportunity. To do this an information coefficient,[22] which is akin to a forward looking correlation between the
investor's ability to forecast returns and actual returns, is utilized. A
perfect forecaster would have a correlation of 1.0, and all perceived
opportunities would be as good as money in the bank. A correlation of
0.0 suggests no forecasting ability and clearly is not a sufficient basis
with which to engage in strategic asset allocation.

CHART 24 Range Setting—Non-U.S. Stocks

		Extraordinary Return
Opportunity (annual)	10%	
Information coefficient	.12	
Capturable opportunity (annual)		1.2%
Transaction cost (round-trip)	4.0%	
Amortization period	5 years	
Transaction cost (annual)		0.8%
Expected abnormal performance		0.4%

In our example an information coefficient of 0.12 is utilized so that the pretransaction cost capturable opportunity is defined as 1.2 percent per annum for the five-year potential holding period. (See Chart 24.)

Transaction costs, if set high enough, would become a formidable barrier to any revision of the portfolio. In our example we assume 2 percent one-way transaction costs for non-U.S. stocks, or 4 percent round-trip. Round-trip costs are of relevance under the assumption that after the opportunity has been fully exploited the investor would return to his policy portfolio. The transaction costs are amortized over the life of the holding period. As Chart 24 indicates this still provides an expected abnormal performance of 0.4 percent per annum so that some portfolio shift should be desired given such an opportunity. Note that any perceived opportunity of 6.7 percent or less would suggest no portfolio revision as the cost of the transaction would equal or exceed the capturable opportunity (6.7 × .12 = 0.8 percent).

The next step in determining the proper width of the strategic ranges is to identify the investor's risk tolerance so that the appropriate portfolio strategy can be anticipated under positive and negative market conditions. This is derived from the prior policy work.

With that information, reoptimizations using the Markowitz procedure can be run for all interesting asset classes. In the non-U.S. stock market case, the 1.2 percent pretransaction cost capturable opportunity can be added to or subtracted from the equilibrium return and reoptimizations run using round-trip transaction costs. Frontiers of optimal portfolios under the input conditions will be generated, with the risk tolerance parameter helping to select the portfolio of interest from the frontier.

In the non-U.S. stock example the appropriate weights of non-U.S. stocks at the predetermined MMI risk tolerance level are 15 percent and 5 percent for the positive and negative scenarios, respectively. As a result when future strategic investment opportunities arise, in magnitude to those anticipated by this exercise, the investor will have already identified the proper investment posture for the portfolio. This can be done to determine ranges for all asset classes.

Strategic Techniques

Institutional investors go about strategically allocating assets in several ways. Each technique has its own supporters and its own underlying rationale. Generally they can be broken down into four categories:

- Comparative valuation.
- Business cycle anticipation.
- Liquidity/flow of funds approaches.
- Technical analysis.

Comparative Valuation

The challenge of the comparative valuation approach is to be able to objectively compare asset class expectations relative to each other and to their policy norm assumptions on a consistent basis. The language of finance is most useful in achieving comparability. This is particularly true if mean-variance analysis was used to help generate the normal policy weights. The returns of that policy analysis can be used as hurdle rates by which to judge the current attractiveness of the individual asset classes.

It is important that valuation models, such as the ones used to generate expected return or other comparative techniques, are consistent in the macroeconomic assumptions employed. Key macrovariables of economic growth, income shares, inflation, and business and interest rate risk should be held constant across all asset classes and inconsistencies monitored and corrected. In the strategic multiasset setting, for example, one has to be careful that bond market valuation does not assume a 5 percent inflation expectation while the real estate rent increase assumptions imbed a 10 percent inflation expectation. Chart 25 shows how strategic decisions could be structured. As stated before, the investor's equilibrium expectations are used for policy purposes. For strategic purposes those same expectations can be compared to strategic expectations over a shorter time horizon to stimulate portfolio revisions. The difference between the two—loosely called asset class alphas—can be combined with tactical judgment for reoptimization and ultimate portfolio revision.

Typically, strategic asset allocators will use some form of John Burr Williams's discount model[23] to put into present value the cash flows eminating from the asset class. An example of such a model is given below. It includes a currency adjustment factor which kicks in when non-U.S. assets are utilized. This particular model assumes a purchasing power parity currency adjustment. The model inputs require:

CHART 25 Asset Class Timing Decisions

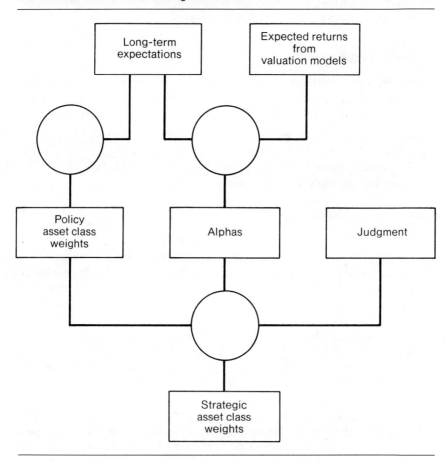

- A current value of the market in question.
- Forecasts of cash flows translated to dollars for the next five years.
- An equilibrium discount rate, a cash flow growth rate, and an exchange rate growth rate for the period after the first five years.
- A method such as the Gordon-Shapiro model to value the asset class to perpetuity five years from the present.

The model for a five-year horizon is:

$$V_0 = \sum_{i=1}^{5} \frac{CF_T(\$/Fx)_T}{(1 + R)^T} + \frac{V_5(\$/Fx)_5}{(1 + R)^5}$$

CHART 26 Expected Asset Class Returns—Five-year Horizon Annualized

	Policy Return	Strategic Return	Alpha	Risk
30-day T-bill (bond equivalent)	6.5%	6.6%	0.1%	1.5%
Salomon Brothers bonds	8.8	8.7	−0.1	8.5
Long-term government bonds	9.5	9.2	−0.3	12.0
Domestic equities:				
S&P 500	12.5	8.5	−4.0	16.9
Small capital	14.0	10.2	−3.8	22.0
Real estate	11.3	10.5	−0.8	14.0
International:				
Equities	12.9	9.9	−3.0	20.5
Dollar bonds	8.7	9.0	0.3	8.0
Nondollar bonds	8.8	9.3	0.5	11.0
Venture capital	21.5	20.5	−1.0	40.0
Aggregates:				
Investable capital market	10.3	9.1	−1.2	9.0
Multiple markets index	12.1	9.9	−2.2	12.9

NOTE: Assumes 5 percent inflation.
SOURCE: First Chicago Investment Advisors.

---

where
  V_o = present value of asset
  $(CF)_T$ = annual cash flow provided by asset (interest, dividends, rent, and so forth) in local currency at time T
  V_T = cash (local currency) received on sale of asset at year five
  R = internal rate of return
  $/FX = factor to convert local currency to dollars

Chart 26 provides a sample output from such a series of models as well as aggregations of abnormal return for the investable capital market as a whole and a particular benchmark portfolio of interest—in this case the MMI. The alphas or abnormal opportunities in the table can thus be scaled down by appropriate information coefficients and fed into the computer for reoptimization mean-variance analysis and eventual strategic revision.

Business Cycle Anticipation

The second commonly used strategic asset allocation technique, business cycle anticipation, tries to forecast the investment market's anticipation of business cycle recoveries and recessions. It assumes, first, that there is some sense of a business cycle to the economy whereby economic expansion is followed by economic slowdown followed by economic contraction followed by recovery and expansion and so on. Its

CHART 27 U.S. Stock Price Index (Total Return) at Signal Dates Based on Inverted Lagging Index

Inverted Lagging Index Signals (+1 Month)		Stock Price Index (Total Return) at		Percent Change in Stock Price Index		Interval in Months		Percent Change in Stock Price Index, Annual Rate	
P1 + 1	T1 + 1	P1 + 1 (Sell)	T1 + 1 (Buy)	T1 + 1 to P1 + 1 (Hold Stock)	P1 + 1 to T1 + 1 (No Stock)	T1 + 1 to P1 + 1	P1 + 1 to T1 + 1	T1 + 1 to P1 + 1	P1 + 1 to T1 + 1
10/50	6/49	5.949	3.919	51.8	43.5	16	20	36.8	24.2
12/52	6/52*	9.336	8.536	9.4	5.5	6	14	19.7	4.7
9/55	2/54	17.618	9.848	78.9	11.3	19	19	44.4	7.0
9/57	4/57	18.516	19.614	-5.6	1.4	5	6	-12.9	2.8
6/59	3/58	27.213	18.767	45.0	-4.6	15	15	34.6	-3.7
	9/60		25.968						

7/62	8/62*	29.891	30.512	15.1	2.1	22	1	8.0	28.3
9/63	3/67	38.318	53.967	25.6	40.8	13	42	23.4	10.3
1/69	5/70	65.193	50.837	20.8	−22.0	22	16	10.9	−17.0
5/73	3/74	76.538	70.453	50.6	−8.0	36	10	14.6	−9.5
9/77	7/80	84.186	123.248	19.5	46.4	42	34	5.2	14.4
8/81*	12/81	131.462	133.615	6.7	1.6	13	4	6.2	4.9
5/84	9/85	185.137	238.197	38.6	28.7	29	16	16.5	20.8
Total or average				1,790.1%	221.9%	238	197	16.0%	7.4%
				5,978.0%		435		12.0%	
Standard deviation				15.2				15.0	12.9

* P2 or T2 signal, since they preceded P1 or T1.

SOURCE: Center for International Business Cycle Research, Columbia Business School, September 1986.

strategic thesis is that at various points in the cycle corporate profits and interest rates will behave in a way that will stimulate or depress stocks, bonds, real estate, and other financial instruments. If the investor could anticipate expanding output, profits, rents, and interest rates, he could predict the direction and potential magnitude of shifts in the capital markets.

One of the more difficult aspects of this approach revolves around the fact that in the United States the stock market itself is considered to be the best leading indicator of the economy.[24] What is needed is a leading indicator of the best leading indicator that the Bureau of Economic Analysis (BEA) has uncovered over many years of research. This assumes, of course, that it is obvious that an indicator that moves coincidently with the investment markets should be of little help in making superior market forecasts.

Moore in 1975[25] and more recently in 1984[26] attempted to link the stock market and bond market to measurements in the BEA's cadre of economic indicators. Because of the leading nature of stock prices, Moore used lagging indicators of economic activity (inverted) to forecast the best leading indicator, common stocks. This is a technique common to many business cycle tools that forecast stock prices—the use of lagging indicators reconfigured to lead the next cycle. As a result economic indicators such as rising unemployment can become a bullish indicator for the stock market. Clearly such techniques work best in a very smooth and uninterrupted business cycle format. To the degree that the business cycle lacks substance or consistent form, so will this approach.

Chart 27 shows that Moore had some success using his inverted lagging signals over past historic periods. Historically his indicators would have had the investor in the stock market when on average it provided 16.0 percent total returns per annum and out of the market when it provided a 7.4 percent annual return. Although some separation is noted, the returns of 7.4 percent achieved when out of the market compare unfavorably to post-war Treasury bill returns of 4.5 percent.

Regarding U.S. bonds, Moore found that the best leading indicators of bond market peaks and troughs were the Center for Business Cycle Research's leading inflation indicators.[27] Chart 28 indicates the peak and trough predictions put out by this indicator and subsequent bond returns. In this case good separation is found, and down market forecasts provide returns below that of Treasury bills.

Both indicators, however, suffer from a lack of real-time experience. Numerous economic series have in the past found to "anticipate" capital market movements only to fail in that task in succeeding years.

CHART 28 Inflation Signal System: Total Return on Long-Term Bonds

Inflation Signals		Total Return Index at		Percent Change in Total Return Index from		Total Return Index at		Percent Change in Total Return Index from	
T2 (L>+1, ΔR>0)	P2 (L<−1, ΔR<0)	T2	P2	P2 to T2 (Percent)	T2 to P2 (Percent)	T2	P2	P2 to T2 (Percent)	T2 to P2 (Percent)
2/50		3.145				2.680			
	5/51		3.107		−1%		2.611		−3%
7/52		3.189		+3%		2.657		+2%	
	11/53		3.226		+1		2.657		0
11/54		3.505		+9		2.888		+9	
	8/56		3.388		−3		2.775		−4
1/59		3.484		+3		2.711		−2	
	1/60		3.498		0		2.701		0
9/61		3.906		+12		3.091		+14	
	6/66		4.491		+15		3.390		+10
8/67		4.485		0		3.397		0	
	3/70		4.291		−4		3.235		−5
6/71		4.889		+14		3.593		+11	
	4/74		5.430		+11		3.829		+7
11/75		6.200		+14		4.485		+17	
	4/80		7.388		+19		5.200		+16
5/81		7.051		−5		5.016		−4	
	10/81		6.767		−4		4.873		−3
4/83		11.370		+68		7.557		+55	
	11/84		12.584		+11		8.347		+10
12/85		16.549		+32		11.027		+32	
Cumulated percent change, total return				+255	+51			+217%	+29
Cumulated rate of return per year				+9.5	+1.9			+8.6	+1.2

SOURCE: Center for International Business Cycle Research, Columbia Business School, September 1986.

Liquidity/Flow of Funds Approaches

A third approach at anticipating capital market movements is the liquidity or flow of funds approach. In essence, this method argues that when money (i.e., liquidity) is flooded into the system via the Federal Reserve or from overseas investment, financial assets rise in value. Some view this effect as being automatic and are unsure what transmission process might exist between rising money supply and rising market prices. Others, such as Sprinkel and Genetski[28] believe that by altering interest rates, changes in money supply have an immediate and direct influence on the value of financial assets. Furthermore, they argue that once the effect of excess money is absorbed into the economic system, business activity begins to increase, which increases the demand for credit, which also influences the prices of financial assets. Eventually, an overly excessive expansion of money supply will lead to higher levels of inflation which also has an influence on the pricing of financial assets.

Fama[29] and Geske and Roll,[30] among others, have amply demonstrated the negative relationship between inflation and stock prices.

Fama suggests that lower anticipated growth rates of real economic activity are associated with higher inflation rates. Lower activity decreases the need for money balances, and therefore, with a fixed or rising supply of money, only inflation can clear money supply and demand. The lower real activity leads to lower stock prices and property rents.

Geske and Roll argue that a reduction in economic activity leads to a reduction in government revenues. This will cause increased government borrowing, an increased budget deficit, and rising fears of inflation as well as potentially causing higher real interest rates. High real rates squeeze corporate margins and dissuade new capital investment, hence leading to lower stock prices.

As the above suggest, the timing of the causal factors and reactions to changing money supply are crucial to understanding the linkages between markets and money. In a world of perfect knowledge and instantaneous adjustments, an extraordinary increase in the money supply would immediately raise the prices of all other items and deflate the value of money and potentially have little effect on the real economy. Since inflation is generally believed to occur with a near two year lag to unusual money growth, and real activity typically rises approximately six months after accelerating money supply, it is clear historically that we do not live in that perfect world. As a result those who anticipate shifts in money growth, which is no mean feat, or believe that the lags following money changes are sufficiently long and stable have used this approach to strategic asset allocation.

Chart 29 illustrates the liquidity approach to stock market anticipation in its simplest form. Money balances, defined as money (M1)

CHART 29 Money balances and the S&P 500

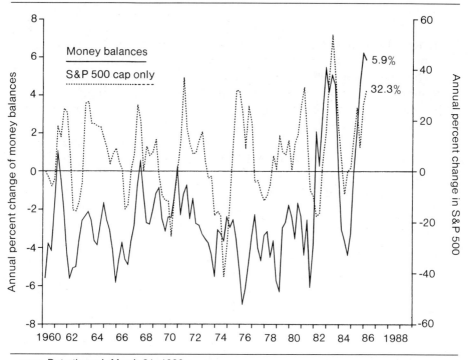

NOTE: Data through March 31, 1986.

divided by gross national product, indicate the degree of excess liquidity sloshing around the system, forcing adaptable financial instruments to adjust quickly while the real economy responds with a lag. Although many variants on this theme exist, most are attempts to better define the money/liquidity variable and the leads or lags associated with movements in the capital market. Note that the BEA[24] found money supply to be the second best leading indicator of the economy, after stock prices, in their 1975 study.

Technical Analysis

The last of the major approaches to strategic asset allocation falls under the broad umbrella of technical analysis. This approach is applied by a rather larger constituency to both individual security price changes and broader market movements as well. The application to broad markets, primarily domestic and international stock, bond, and short-term fixed income markets, is of interest to some strategic asset allocators.

According to Edwards and Magee, "Technical analysis is the science of recording, usually in graphic form, the actual history of trading (price changes, volume of transactions, etc.) in a certain stock or in 'averages' and then deducing from the pictured history the probable future trend."[31] Pring goes further to suggest, "the stock market moves in trends which are determined by the changing attitudes of investors to a variety of economic, monetary, political and psychological forces. . . . Technical analysis is therefore based on the assumption that people will continue to make the same mistakes that they have made in the past . . . the recurrence of similar characteristics is sufficient to permit the technicians to identify major juncture points."[32]

For technical analysis to be successful would be a gross violation of the Efficient Market Hypothesis (EMH). The violation would be so gross that tests of technical strategies are called weak form tests of the hypothesis. Tests of technical strategies have thus far refuted the tested strategies as not being profitable with any statistical reliability. But technicians counter that: (a) the investment world operates in an environment where decisions must, per force, be made with reliability that may be less than statistically significant (as defined by the life sciences industry) and (b) tests of technical decision rules are by nature applied to only the simplest of rules and that many more complex rules have never been tested. Unfortunately, practitioners of the trade do not see it in their interest to seriously test and publish their findings.

The tool kit of the technician includes analysis of price patterns, trendlines, moving averages, momentum, price/volume, advance/decline, and so on. An example of a strategic asset allocation application of technical analysis is the Dow Theory,[33] the oldest of the well-known methods for identifying major U.S. stock market trends. Developed by Charles Dow in the early 1900s, the object of the theory is to determine changes in the primary direction of the market. Once established, a primary trend is assumed to exist until it is reversed. A fairly elaborate set of tests is established so as to avoid mistaking a correction or minor reversal for a reversal of the primary trend.

Several rationales exist for the persistence of technical analysis in the face of the empirical evidence gathered thus far.

Nonhomogeneous flow of information. Standard EMH, in its simplified form, assumes that investors have homogeneous beliefs given identical sets of information. Should information or its synthesis leak out to some investors first and other investors later, a pattern could evolve with respect to the relevant investment price. Treynor and Ferguson suggest, "past prices when combined with other valuable information can indeed be helpful in achieving unusual profit. However, it is the non-price information that creates the opportunity. The past prices serve only to permit its efficient exploitation."[34]

Autocorrelation in underlying processes. If you make the assumption that security prices are not wholly set by expectations which provide for random deviations around the expectational set, the opportunity arises for price patterns due to trends in underlying economic processes. For example, an oftmade assumption is that the Federal Reserve controls short-term interest rates, which in turn maintain a systematic influence on long-term rates. If the Federal Reserve, due to uncertainty in interpreting the economic landscape, reacts to fundamental shocks to the money/credit demand function by taking a small step-wise approach to achieving desired policy, trends in short rates can develop. Another example exists in the inflation generating process, which may shift as a result of slowly evolving macro- and micro-economic events. To the degree the market has not learned to anticipate the length and magnitude of the underlying inflation shaping forces, it will systematically be surprised by the persistence of the trend as long as it exists. In hindsight, this is what many believe caused the long trend shown in Chart 30 to persist.

Barriers to arbitrage. A third explanation for the persistence of market trends is the existence of trading and other costs which serve to prevent optimal use of information. The higher the trading costs for a given market, the greater the likelihood that market prices could move explosively, as opposed to countercyclically. In essence, information which could serve to subvert and arbitrage trends away (such as knowledge of trends themselves) could be effectively barred, at least temporarily, from voting in the marketplace. This argument is self-defeating to the asset allocator who cannot profit from identification of market price patterns due to high transaction costs. It may not be self-defeating, however, to the low cost trader.

Cognitive psychology. Much work has been published on the manner in which humans form judgments. This research has shown that individuals, even experts, make systematic errors in the way they make decisions in certain situations.[35] The EMH assumes that investors behave in a rational manner. This research on information processing and decision theory strongly suggests that individuals behave irrationally in certain circumstances.

These biases, if applied on a grander scale to the marketplace, are thought to be involved in the great historic manias of tulip bulbs, Florida real estate, and other such super trends.[36]

CHART 30 Long-Term Government Bond Yields

NOTE: Data through December 31, 1985.

Strategic Allocation Using Futures and Options

The most popular use for financial futures of the stock index and fixed income variety is to alter the portfolio's exposure to broad market moves. Through selling of stock index futures the investor can quickly and relatively inexpensively reduce his exposure to the index, being left with a cash equivalent-like return in its place. Conversely, buying such a contract can increase market exposure with great alacrity. Financial future instruments which can be used for strategic asset allocation purposes are:

In addition to the above are currency contracts and non-U.S. equity and fixed income contracts, primarily for Canada, the United Kingdom, Japan, Australia, and Hong Kong. Options can also be used to create a synthetic future by buying a call and selling a put of the same strike price. The S&P 100 (OEX), a composite index composed of 100 of the

---

Description of Underlying Index

Equities:

S&P 500	500 companies, mostly industrial, capitalization weighted.
Major Market Index	20 blue chip stocks, price weighted.
Value Line	Equal weighted, geometrically averaged index of 1,700 stocks.
NYSE	Over 1,500 stocks on the NYSE, capitalization weighted.
SPOC	250 of the largest OTC stocks.

Fixed income:

Treasury bonds	Based on an 8 percent coupon bond with 16 years to maturity.
Treasury notes	Based on an 8 percent coupon note with 4–6 years to maturity.
Treasury bills	Based on a 90-day Treasury bill.
Municipal Bond Index	Based on 40 municipal bonds.

---

large optionable stocks value weighted, is a likely candidate for this transformation due to its high liquidity.

The expected return from a portfolio hedged against an underlying long market position is equal to the following:

$$r_h = r_f + a_s + a_f - t_f \pm e$$

where

r_h = return to the hedged portfolio

r_f = short-term interest rate

a_s = alpha of the hedged securities

a_f = alpha of the futures

t_f = transaction costs of the futures trade

e = tracking error of the future underlying securities relative to the hedged securities

As a benchmark, the hedged strategy should be compared against selling the security and investing in short-term cash. The return from this strategy is equal to the following:

$$r_c = r_f - t_s$$

where

r_c = return to cash portfolio

r_f = short-term interest rate

t_s = transaction costs of the underlying security book

Financial futures should be used to hedge the assets as opposed to direct selling of the underlying securities if the following statement is true:

$$r_f + a_s + a_f - t_f \pm e > r_f - t_s$$

and it follows:

$$a_s + a_f + (t_s - t_f) \pm e > 0$$

The alpha of the futures contract can be accurately estimated using the following formulas:

$$a_f = p_t - f_f$$

and

$$f_f = v_s + r_f - y$$

where

p_t = actual futures price
f_f = fair futures price
v_s = value of the underlying security
r_f = risk-free interest
y = income earned on the security (e.g., dividend or coupon)

This alpha can be positive or negative but will usually be relatively small. If it wasn't small, arbitrageurs would attempt to correct the imbalance.

Transaction costs are almost always lower in the futures market than in the underlying market. To the extent that they are lower depends on the underlying market and the expected holding period of the futures contract. For short holding periods in the equity market, transaction costs are lower than in the spot market by a factor of five or more.

The tracking error can be positive or negative. Its size can be reduced by optimally selecting a combination of futures whose characteristics most closely match those of the portfolio to be hedged.

To this point our discussion on hedging has focused on what is called short hedging, that is, having a long position in the actual market and selling futures against those assets. Long hedging is also used in the financial futures market. A long hedge is undertaken by a prospective purchaser of the underlying market. This hedge may also be called security substitution or an anticipatory hedge.

Strategic Asset Allocation Concluded

Once asset allocation policy is put in place whereby both asset class norms and strategic ranges are established, the issue of strategic asset allocation or market timing can be addressed. The many different ways of attacking strategic asset allocation can, for the most part, be catego-

CHART 31   Annual Extra Return—Typical Timing Manager

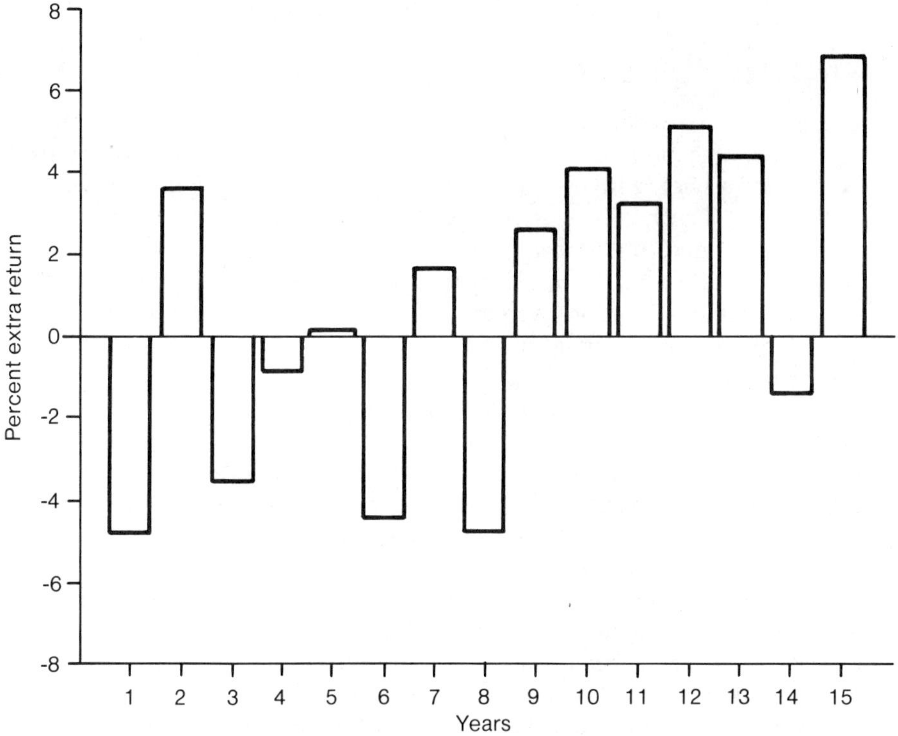

rized into one or more of four different styles: (1) comparative valuation, (2) business cycle analysis, (3) liquidity/flow of funds approaches, and (4) technical analysis. Furthermore, strategic allocation can be enhanced by the use of relatively low transaction cost derivative instruments.

These approaches are used in the hopes of providing incremental portfolio returns. Interpreting ongoing performance results for any one asset allocator can be a difficult task. Despite the chatty mythology that the market gives the investor daily feedback, it can take a long period of time for a truly valuable strategic asset allocation process to rear its head. For example, a simple experiment was conducted for a hypothetical nine asset class portfolio. We assumed that over 15 periods a strategic asset allocator, using market portfolios within each of the asset classes, has an active return distribution with a mean of plus 1 percent and a standard deviation of 5 percent. Despite this clearly valuable process, poor short-term period results can occur. A representative series of outcomes reveals that the successful strategic allocator in Chart 31 may not survive the firing squad in periods 1 through 8. It is clear that short-term performance alone cannot provide much information to the intelligent investor.

VII. TIME HORIZON

There are two widely divergent views on the question of how the investor's time horizon should affect portfolio policy. Those offering "practical" advice to investors are generally in agreement with Ellis who states: "The length of time investments will be held, the period of time over which investment results will be measured and judged, is the single most powerful factor in any investment program.[37] Advocates of "dynamic asset allocation" agree that time horizon is a very important consideration as the initial proportions are affected by the length of the portfolio protection period.

In contrast, many students of time horizon have concluded that the investor's time horizon is not a very important variable when determining portfolio policy. This view is captured by the following statements by Fischer and Pennacchi: "Early analysis of portfolios held for the short and long term focused on the effects of changes in the investor's horizon on the optimal portfolio. No systematic effects of the investment horizon on the optimal portfolio were found."[38] Fischer and Pennacchi go on to note that for the most widely accepted class of utility functions—the hyperbolic absolute risk aversion class—optimal portfolios are invariant to the length of the horizon when asset returns are identically and independently distributed over time and the "holding period" or revision horizon is given. Interestingly, however, optimal portfolios are not invariant to the length of the revision horizon in this setting.

Time Horizon and the Revision Horizon

Time horizon is an elusive concept and there are undoubtedly many different uses of the term. The revision horizon is a distinct concept, and understanding the relationship between these two horizons is critical.

The time horizon can be thought of as a planning horizon. For an investor who is concerned solely with the distribution of wealth at some future date, T, date T is the horizon date, and the time horizon is of length T. The notion of the time horizon loses some of its crispness when there are intermediate withdrawals from or contributions to the portfolio. Date T is the horizon date in the sense that the investor looks no further ahead than T.

The investor's revision horizon is the interval of time between successive portfolio actions. The revision horizon could, in principle, vary between some arbitrarily short interval of time and the investor's time horizon. Individuals on average revise their portfolios less frequently than do institutions, but a revision horizon of more than one year is unusual. Pension plan portfolios are typically managed by professional investment managers who provide continuous portfolio monitoring and, at least in principle, the possibility of perpetual revisions. Even a pension portfolio being managed in a passive mode is likely to be rebalanced on at least a quarterly basis.

Traditional View

The traditional view is that the investor's time horizon is critically important in setting portfolio policy. There seems to be wide agreement among consultants and money managers on the importance of the investor's time horizon. The importance of time horizon is certainly accepted by the authors (most of whom are consultants or money managers) of the chapters in the Maginn and Tuttle book that is used in the Institute of Chartered Financial Analyst's portfolio management curriculum.[39] Every chapter on portfolio construction has at least a short section on the impact of the time horizon. And as McEnally notes, if saying something often enough will make it so, it must be that "time diversification is indeed the surest route to lower risk—for this has certainly been the message of a number of articles in this publication [*The Journal of Portfolio Management*] in recent years."[40]

The normative advice provided by those who hold the traditional view is that investors with longer time horizons should invest more in riskier assets than investors with shorter time horizons. It is not clear why the normative advice takes the form it does. The cited readings typically provide no formal model. This makes it difficult to know for sure what rationale underlies the normative advice. It is, however, possible to infer some plausible explanations.

The three most likely explanations include: (1) the investor's aversion to risk is systematically affected by his time horizon; (2) the available trade-off between risk and return is systematically affected by the length of the investor's time horizon even when return distributions are assumed stationary and independent across time; and (3) investors attempt to match assets and liabilities in order to minimize risk.

The first question is whether time horizon has an impact on risk aversion that is independent of the impact of wealth. In the usual formal model of the multiperiod portfolio problem, utility is a function of wealth, and portfolio decisions are affected by the amount of wealth possessed by the investor. To the extent it is assumed that the level of wealth and the time horizon of the investor are closely (and inversely) related, some statements about the relationship between the investor's time horizon and his portfolio are better understood as statements relating wealth levels and portfolio decisions. However, there is not necessarily a relationship between time horizon and wealth. An investor with a high level of wealth may have a long time horizon, just as an investor with little wealth may have a very short time horizon. Mossin, in his classic article on the multiperiod portfolio problem, addresses the question of "time effect" directly.[41] He specifically asks: "With a given wealth and a given yield (return) distribution for the immediate period, how does the optimal investment depend upon the number of periods left before the horizon?"

Mossin concludes that the time effect for each investor is dependent on how relative-risk-aversion changes for that investor as wealth changes. It can be positive, negative, or zero. There is no reason to conclude that investors with shorter horizons should always invest less in risky assets. In fact, it is likely that in many cases writers who say that time horizon is the crucial consideration are really thinking of wealth and complicitly assuming a relationship between wealth and the time horizon.

The second notion that risk is actually reduced or the risk-return trade-off is favorably altered when the time horizon is extended are undoubtedly what most writers have in mind when they assert there is a direct relationship between the length of the time horizon and the appropriate risk level for the portfolio.

Consider the claim that time diversification reduces risk. Assume that returns are lognormally distributed, stationary, and independent across time. Assume, further, that revision horizons (holding periods) are equal in length. Finally, assume there are no impediments to trading so that continuous portfolio revision is possible if desired.

McEnally[40] provides a careful analysis of the claim that time diversification reduces risk. He concludes that, under most reasonable definitions, risk increases rather than decreases with the time horizon. The belief that longer horizons imply less risk is the result of focusing on the standard deviation of average annualized rates of return over single-year and multiple-year horizons, which does decline as the time horizon is lengthened. McEnally concludes, ". . . a comparison of variation in annualized returns over horizons of different length is a classic example of comparing things that are not comparable and is an inappropriate application of a single-period risk measure in a multiple-period investment context."

Some analysis does not make the mistake of drawing conclusions on the basis of the standard deviation of average annualized returns. For example, the standard deviation of terminal wealth increases with the square root of time while return increases proportionately with time. As a result, the risk-return trade-off is apparently more favorable if one has a longer time horizon, as both do not increase proportionately. Unfortunately, the variance of terminal wealth increases proportionately with time just as expected return does. When mean-variance analysis is appropriate for choosing a portfolio, the choice between a risky asset and a risk-free asset is dependent on the variance of return and not on the standard deviation. Proportionate changes in expected return and variance will have no effect on the choice.

The third explanation for the conventional wisdom is the notion that asset-liability matching underlies the basic recommendation that investors with longer horizons should hold portfolios that are more risky. The idea is one of minimizing risk rather than trading off risk and return.

The use of immunized and dedicated bond portfolios is consistent with the notion of risk minimization. It is important to note that the low risk alternative for an investor will depend upon the time horizon so that the shortest maturity investments are not necessarily the lowest risk investments. Very short maturity investments are risk free only to those investors with very short liabilities. The investor with a 10-year planning horizon will realize that a 10-year zero coupon bond is a less risky investment alternative than a policy of rolling T-bills, particularly if the investor's liabilities are nominal in nature. Risk minimization is, of course, a nondominated and, hence, a defensible strategy. It does provide a rationale for tying portfolio decisions to the investor's time horizon. Still, risk minimization is not likely to be an optimal strategy for many investors.

The Academic View

The multiperiod portfolio problem has received a great deal of attention in the academic literature. Examinations of the effects of the investor's time horizon on optimal portfolio composition have been conducted by Hakansson,[42,43] Leland,[44] Merton and Samuelson,[45] and Ross.[46] Two basic questions were addressed in this research: (1) Do all investors tend to hold the same portfolio as the horizon is lengthened? and (2) Should or might one want to maximize the expected growth rate of the portfolio?

Closely related research on myopia in portfolio choice by Mossin,[41] Hakannsson,[47] and Samuelson[48] considered the circumstances under which optimal portfolio composition is, for a given revision horizon, independent of the time horizon. (Myopia is a desirable property because of the complexity of the multiperiod problem which is a complex dynamic programming problem.) The investor's optimal portfolio composition is independent of time horizon when the investor's utility function exhibits constant relative risk aversion. Investors with constant absolute risk aversion utility functions are effected by the time horizon. Even in this case, however, complete myopia is nearly optimal when the horizon is a long way off. So in many cases, investors with constant absolute risk aversion can also ignore time horizon in making portfolio decisions.

The available empirical evidence is consistent with investors having constant relative risk aversion over wide ranges of wealth.[49] This fact and the analytical results on myopia have led to a lessened interest in the time horizon issue in the academic literature. The emphasis has shifted from the effect of the time horizon on optimal portfolio composition to the effect of the revision period.

Goldman[50] showed that changes in the revision horizon have systematic effects on portfolio composition in cases where asset returns are serially uncorrelated. He provides a proof showing that portfolios tend systematically to become less diversified as the revision horizon lengthens, assuming utility functions characterized by constant relative risk aversion and asset returns generated by diffusion processes. Goldman's article shows that the key consideration from the time dimension is the revision horizon and not the time horizon.

Fischer[51] and Fischer and Pennacchi[38] analyze the same problem as Goldman in the case where asset returns are serially correlated. Changes in the revision horizon result in changes in the relative risk of assets in the presence of serial correlation. Portfolio composition is affected by these changes, tending to reduce the weight in positively serially correlated assets. The net change in portfolio composition resulting from a change in the revision horizon depends on the relative strengths of the Goldman effect and the risk-aversion effect. Estimates of stochastic processes and assumptions about relative risk aversion are necessary to determine the impact of the revision horizon on portfolio composition.

Fischer estimates stochastic processes generating asset returns for common stocks and T-bills. He presents two major conclusions: (1) The differential dynamics of asset returns do not cause optimal portfolios to change dramatically with the length of the revision horizon. Fischer's favored method of estimating stochastic processes indicates that the portfolio moves, if at all, toward stocks as the revision horizon lengthens. (Most of the time the portfolio does not change.) (2) For specified utility functions, and given the historical behavior of stock and bill returns, portfolios should be heavily invested in the riskier asset class.

Fischer and Pennacchi do a more extensive analysis using different methods to estimate stochastic processes for stock and bill returns, and they do the analysis in both nominal and real returns. In their words, "The most striking result was how little the portfolio proportions changed as the period lengthened."

Zero-Coupon Bonds in the Policy-Setting Framework

The advent of zero-coupon bonds has drawn attention to the time horizon issue. The mere existence of these bonds leads quite naturally to focusing on the questions: (1) What is the risk-free asset? and (2) Is it the same for investors with different time horizons? Zero-coupon bonds do provide a way of obtaining a risk-free return over a defined time interval for an investor with nominal liabilities. They provide a convenient alternative to an immunized bond portfolio over a defined interval. Furthermore, they provide a means of matching assets and liabilities directly for investors who are truly interested in risk minimization for a part or all of their assets.

Zero-coupon bonds that are longer in duration do not, of course, provide a risk-free real rate of return. Inflation is uncertain, and as a result, a risk-free nominal return is not a risk-free real return. Most investors are interested in real returns.

Consider, however, the investor who is interested in nominal returns. Should such an investor with horizon T pay particular attention to zero-coupon bonds which pay off at time T? There is no question about the fact that he should be aware of them as they provide one possible strategy for investing his portfolio from the present to the horizon. They are a risk-free investment for such an investor and are preferred to alternative strategies with lower expected returns.

However, the investor with time horizon T is not limited to a revision period of that length. He has many opportunities to revise his portfolios prior to time T. In looking forward, the presumption is that he will maximize the expected utility of wealth at time T; he will select the strategy that provides the maximum expected utility today. All available assets are candidates for inclusion in the portfolio. There is, however, no guarantee the selected portfolio will involve positive investment in the zero-coupon bond that matches his time horizon.

Summary: Portfolio Composition and Time

The analysis leads to the conclusion that time may not be a very important consideration in the setting of asset allocation policy but that ultimately the investor's desires, preferences, and even biases will win out. Time horizon is irrelevant for all investors exhibiting constant proportional risk aversion. It is safely ignored by investors exhibiting constant absolute risk aversion as long as the horizon is "distant." Most investors need pay little attention to their time horizons in the setting of policy.

The revision horizon is potentially important even for investors with constant proportional risk aversion. However, as a practical matter, it is not important for either institutional investors or individual investors. Time horizon may be important for investors with very clearly specified liabilities in the future but only under the potentially irrational desire to match a portion of their current wealth to the future liability. Matching, a form of risk minimization, is quite defensible as an asset allocation strategy when it is broadly applied. It is when the investor engages in some risk minimization and some wealth maximization, simultaneously, that a natural conflict arises.

VIII. SYNOPSIS

Asset allocation policy, for most investors, will be the dominating factor in their overall investment success or failure. As a result, a fair share of investor resources should be devoted to the pursuit of an optimal policy, designed to personally suit the goals, aspirations, and fears of the investor. Clearly, the more the investor knows and is able to articulate about his objectives and investment characteristics, the better able he and his advisors will be to blend those characteristics with that of the marketplace. An often-used investor characteristic, time horizon, may however, not be as important as many practitioners would suggest.

Strategic allocation, which more ambitiously involves the pursuit of excess profit by attempting to time market swings, has had a checkered career when viewed broadly. By definition it is a zero sum game before trading costs; the only issue is whether some strategic asset allocators can extract economic value from other allocators or from those who do not attempt to strategically allocate. Various methods of strategic asset allocation are currently in use, each with some level of appeal depending on your prior experience. Recent success in fostering a strategic asset allocation revival has centered around more quantitative, consistently applied theories of present value and capital asset pricing.

To both areas of policy and strategic asset allocation has come a new generation of tools and implements. Futures, options, and synthetic options have given investors the capability to alter portfolio return distributions reliably as well as change the exposure to domestic stock, bond, and cash equivalent asset classes quickly and inexpensively. As time evolves and foreign market trading costs are competed to lower levels and as foreign derivative instruments develop, these new tools will take on larger roles in global asset allocation.

ENDNOTES

1. A. Rudd and H. K. Clasing, Jr., *Modern Portfolio Theory* (Homewood, Ill.: Dow Jones-Irwin, 1982).
2. R. C. Merton, "On Market Timing and Investment Performance. I. An Equilibrium Theory of Value for Market Forecasts," *Journal of Business* 54, no. 3 (1981).
3. G. P. Brinson, L. R. Hood, and L. G. Beebower, "The Determinants of Portfolio Performance," *Financial Analysts Journal*, July/August 1986.
4. G. P. Brinson, and J. J. Diermeier, "Investable Capital World Wealth: 1959–1984" (First Chicago Investment Advisors, 1986, Mimeographed).
5. G. P. Brinson, J. J. Diermeier, and G. G. Schlarbaum, "A Composite Portfolio Benchmark for Pension Plan Sponsors," *Financial Analysts Journal*, March/April 1986.
6. H. M. Markowitz, "Portfolio Selection," *Journal of Finance*, March 1952; and *Portfolio Selection* (New York: John Wiley & Sons, 1959).
7. W. F. Sharpe, "Likely Gains from Market Timing," *Financial Analysts Journal*, March/April 1975.

8. Michael C. Jensen, "The Performance of Mutual Funds in the Period 1945–1964," *Journal of Finance*, May 23, 1968, pp. 389–416.

9. S. J. Kon, "The Market-Timing Performance of Mutual Fund Managers," *Journal of Business* 56, no. 3 (1983).

10. Roy D. Henriksson, "Market Timing and Mutual Fund Performance: An Empirical Investigation," *Journal of Business* 57, no. 1 (1984).

11. E. G. Chang and W. G. Lewellen, "Market Timing and Mutual Fund Investment Performance," *Journal of Business* 57, no. 1 (1984).

12. Robert F. Vandell and George W. Kester, *A History of Risk-Premia Estimates for Equities: 1944 to 1978* (Charlottesville, Va.: The Financial Analysts Research Foundation, 1983).

13. Robert R. Grauer and Nils H. Hakansson, "Returns on Levered Actively Managed Long-Run Portfolios of Stocks, Bonds and Bills, 1934–1983," *Financial Analysts Journal*, September/October 1985.

14. William F. Sharpe, "Capital Asset Prices: A Theory of Market Equilibrium under Conditions of Risk," *Journal of Finance*, September 1964; J. Lintner, "The Valuation of Risk Assets and the Selection of Risky Investments in Stock Portfolios and Capital Budgets," *Review of Economics and Statistics*, February 1965; and J. Mossin, "Equilibrium in a Capital Asset Market," *Econometrica*, October 1966.

15. J. J. Diermeier, R. G. Ibbotson, and L. B. Siegel, "The Supply of Capital Market Returns," *Financial Analysts Journal*, March/April 1984.

16. R. G. Ibbotson, J. J. Diermier, and L. B. Seigel, "The Demand for Capital Market Returns: A New Equilibrium Theory," *Financial Analysts Journal*, January/February 1984.

17. William F. Sharpe, "Bonds vs. Stocks: Some Lessons from Capital Market Theory," *Financial Analysts Journal*, November/December 1973.

18. This basic framework is attributed to Irving Fisher, *The Theory of Interest* (New York: Macmillan, 1930). The exact relationship between nominal returns and real returns is multiplicative. However, the common rule of thumb is to ignore the cross product, and we follow this convention.

19. D. R. Lessard, "International Diversification," in *Investment Managers' Handbook*, ed. S. N. Levine (Homewood, Ill.: Dow Jones-Irwin, 1980).

20. Fischer Black and Myron Scholes, "The Pricing of Options and Corporate Liabilities," *The Journal of Political Economy*, May–June 1973, pp. 637–54.

21. E. J. Elton and M. J. Gruber, *Modern Portfolio Theory and Investment Analysis* (New York: John Wiley & Sons, 1981).

22. K. Ambachtsheer and J. L. Farrell, Jr., "Can Active Management Add Value?" *Financial Analysts Journal*, November/December 1979.

23. J. B. Williams, *The Theory of Investment Value* (Cambridge, Mass.: Harvard University Press, 1938).

24. V. Zarnowitz and C. Boschan, "Cyclical Indicators: An Evaluation of New Leading Indexes," *Business Conditions Digest*, May 1975.

25. G. H. Moore, "Stock Prices and the Business Cycle, *The Journal of Portfolio Management*, Spring 1975.

26. G. H. Moore, "Sequential Signals and Financial Markets" (Unpublished, Center for International Business Cycle Research, Columbia Business School, January 1985).

27. G. H. Moore, "A New Inflation Barometer," *The Morgan Guaranty Survey*, July 1983.

28. B. W. Sprinkel and R. J. Genetski, *Winning with Money: A Guide for Your Future* (Homewood, Ill.: Dow Jones-Irwin, 1977).

29. E. Fama, "Stock Returns, Real Activity, Inflation and Money," *American Economic Review*, September 1981.

30. R. Geske and R. Roll, "The Fiscal and Monetary Linkage between Stock Returns and Inflation," *Journal of Finance*, March 1983.

31. R. D. Edwards and J. Magee, *Technical Analysis of Stock Trends* (Boston, Mass.: John Magee Inc., 1966).

32. M. J. Pring, *Technical Analysis Explained* (New York: McGraw-Hill, 1980).

33. G. W. Bishop, Jr., "Evolution of Dow Theory," *Financial Analysts Journal* 17 (1961).

34. J. L. Treynor and R. Ferguson, "In Defense of Technical Analysis," *Journal of Finance* (Papers and proceedings, July 1985).

35. (a) Baruch Fischhoff, "Hindsight = Foresight: The Effect of Outcome Knowledge on Judgment under Uncertainty," *Journal of Experimental Psychology: Human Perception and Performance*, 1975. (b) Hersh Shefrin and Meir Statman, "The Disposition to Sell Winners Too Early and Ride Losers Too Long: Theory and Evidence," *The Journal of Finance* 40 (July 1985), pp. 777–90. (c) Hersh Shefrin and Meir Statman, "Explaining Investor Preference for Cash Dividends," *Journal of Financial Economics* 13 (June 1984), pp. 253–82. (d) Paul Slovic, "Psychological Study of Human Judgment: Implications for Investment Decision Making," *Journal of Finance* 27 (September 1972), pp. 779–99.

36. G. LeBon, *The Crowd: A Study of Popular Mind* (New York: Viking Press, 1960).

37. C. D. Ellis, *Investment Policy* (Homewood, Ill.: Dow Jones-Irwin, 1985).

38. S. Fischer and G. Pennacchi, "Serial Correlation of Asset Returns and Optimal Portfolios for the Long and Short Term "(NBER working paper no. 1625, June 1985).

39. J. L. Maginn and D. L. Tuttle, eds., *Managing Investment Portfolios* (Boston: Warren, Gorham & Lamont, 1983).

40. R. W. McEnally, "Time Diversification: The Surest Route to Lower Risk?" *The Journal of Portfolio Management*, Summer 1985.

41. J. Mossin, "Optimal Multiperiod Portfolio Policies," *Journal of Business*, April 1968.

42. N. H. Hakansson, "Multi-Period Mean-Variance Analysis: Toward a General Theory of Portfolio Choice," *Journal of Finance*, September 1971.

43. N. H. Hakansson, "Convergence to Isoelastic Utility and Policy in Multiperiod Portfolio Choice," *Journal of Financial Economics*, September 1974.

44. H. Leland, "On Turnpike Portfolios," in *Mathematical Methods in Investment and Finance*, ed. Karl Shell and G. P. Szego (Amsterdam: North Holland, 1972).

45. R. C. Merton and P. A. Samuelson, "Fallacy of the Log-Normal Approximation to Optimal Portfolio Decision Making over Many Periods," *Journal of Financial Economics*, May 1974.

46. S. A. Ross, "Portfolio Turnpike Theorums for Constant Policies," *Journal of Financial Economics*, August 1974.

47. N. H. Hakansson, "Optimal Investment and Consumption Stategies under Risk for a Class of Utility Functions," *Econometrica*, September 1970.

48. P. A. Samuelson, "Portfolio Selection by Dynamic Stochastic Programming," *Review of Economics and Statistics*, August 1969, pp. 239–46.

49. I. Friend and M. E. Blume, "The Demand for Risky Assets," *American Economic Review*, December 1985; and R. A. Morin and A. F. Suarez, "Risk Aversion Revisited," *Journal of Finance*, September 1983.

50. M. B. Goldman, "Anti-Diversification on Optimal Programs for Infrequently Revised Portfolios," *Journal of Finance*, May 1979.

51. S. Fischer, "Investing for the Short and the Long-Term," in *Financial Aspects of the United States Pension System*, ed. Z. Bodic and S. B. Shoven (Chicago: The University of Chicago Press, 1982).

APPENDIX
The Returns-Risk Optimization Model
Sumner N. Levine

We consider a portfolio made up of n different classes of assets (domestic and foreign stocks, bonds, money market investments, and so forth) each with an *expected* return, r_i, and a standard deviation of the return given by σ_i. We also assume that the covariances, between the ith asset (say, stocks) and the jth asset (for example, bonds) are known.

Given the above, we wish to construct a portfolio consisting of such proportions, x_i, of the ith asset so as to maximize the quantity

$$Z = \bar{r}_p - A \sigma^2 (r_p) \qquad (1)$$

where $\bar{r}_p$ is the expected return of the portfolio given by

$$\bar{r}_p = \sum_{i=1}^{n} x_i r_i \qquad (2)$$

and $\sigma^2 (r_p)$ is the variance (risk) of the portfolio consisting of the n assets. The variance is given by

$$\sigma^2 (r_p) = \sum_{i}^{n} x_i^2 \sigma_i^2 + \sum_{i,j(i \neq j)}^{n} x_i x_j \sigma_{ij} \qquad (3)$$

The quantity A is the marginal rate of substitution of variance for expected return.

We also require

$$\sum_{i}^{n} x_i = 1 \qquad (4)$$

The last condition gives rise to the LaGrangian expression:

$$L = r_p - A \sigma^2 (r_p) + \lambda (1 - \sum^{n} x_i) \qquad (5)$$

The LaGrangian may be maximized by setting the partial derivatives with respect to each x_i and λ equal to zero. The resulting n + 1 equations are then solved for x_i's and λ.

As a notational point, it should be noted that the covariance is often expressed in terms of the correlation coefficient (ρ) and the standard deviations (σ):

$$\sigma_{ij} = \rho_{ij} \, \sigma_i \, \sigma_i \qquad (6)$$

41

Immunization and Other Passive Strategies for Fixed-Income Portfolios

H. Gifford Fong
President
Gifford Fong Associates

INTRODUCTION

Bond portfolio management strategies may be categorized according to the schematic diagram shown in Figure 1. Three main elements are identified including active management, passive management, and immunization. Active management may be exemplified by rate anticipation and/or sector valuation. Rate anticipation, in turn, depends on maturity (or duration) control of the portfolio, and sector valuation is concerned with anticipating spread relationship changes. Passive management can be represented by either indexing or a buy-and-hold strategy. Buy-and-hold strategies essentially direct cash flow to the then highest yielding securities which are, in turn, held to maturity, while indexing seeks a portfolio with the characteristics of an index. Immunization refers to the class of strategies which may include cash flow matching as a special case of immunization where the objective is to fund a series of liabilities (dedication).

Each of the above can be differentiated by the amount of expectational input required. The more the expectational input, the more active the strategy. What emerges is a continuum of expectational input from none required for passive strategies to an expectations-driven strategy of active management. The more the reliance on expectations, the greater the return potential but also the greater the associ-

---

FIGURE 1   Fixed-Income Management

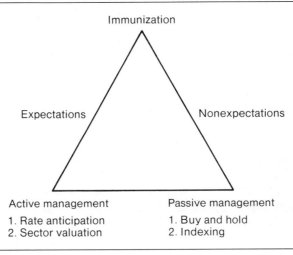

Immunization

Expectations

Nonexpectations

Active management
1. Rate anticipation
2. Sector valuation

Passive management
1. Buy and hold
2. Indexing

---

ated risk. In this context immunization may be considered a hybrid where expectations may or may not be used.

The emphasis in this chapter will be on the nonexpectational approaches to immunization and other passive strategies. As such, risk minimization will be the key objective. This orientation will provide a framework for understanding the basic nature of each of these strategies. Incorporation of the use of expectations can be considered a source of management differentiation once the basic framework is understood and in place. However, as will be seen, there are still return enhancement techniques which are available. Expectational inputs will be kept to a minimum resulting in, perhaps, a lower expected return but also a lower expected uncertainty (standard deviation) of return.

Dedication strategies will be covered first, followed by a discussion of indexing as a form of passive management. The theory of each strategy will be followed by an example of application.

DEDICATION STRATEGIES

Dedication for fixed-income portfolios includes both immunization as well as cash-flow-matching approaches. In a generic sense, dedication refers to the allocation of a portfolio for the purposes of funding a schedule of liabilities. However, there are important differences between the two alternatives. After a review of each strategy, a comparison between them will be made.

IMMUNIZATION

Immunization, a hybrid strategy having both active and passive elements, is a strategy that was originally formulated a number of years ago by Macaulay [1983] and Reddington [1952]. A number of advances extending their analysis will be discussed.

Investors who require a high degree of assurance of compound return over the time horizon may use this bond management approach. By accepting a more modest return than the highest that can be expected, they achieve a greater likelihood of realizing the desired return. This is another example of the classic trade-off between return and risk. More recent work has extended the concept of immunization to explicit risk measures and multiperiod analysis. (See, for example, Fong and Vasicek [1980].)

Classical immunization can be defined as the process by which a fixed-income portfolio is created having an assured return for a specified time horizon irrespective of interest rate change. In a more concise form, the following are the important characteristics:

1. Specified time horizon.
2. Assured rate of return during holding period to a fixed horizon date.
3. Insulation from the effects of potential adverse interest rate change on portfolio value at the horizon date.

Potential users include life insurance companies, some pension funds, and some banks for their own investment portfolios. Life insurance companies can use immunization to invest the proceeds from their guaranteed investment contracts (GICs) and fixed annuities. GICs provide for a lump-sum payment at a prespecified time in the future at some rate of return guaranteed by the insurance company. Annuities provide for a series of payments for a predetermined time frame (sometimes to death). In both contracts the specific terms are important, especially the premature redemption and reinvestment terms. These are investment vehicles that have a specified required payment at some defined future date. The difference between the promised return on the contract or annuity and the realized return would be revenue available for expenses and profit. It is the ability to fund specified liabilities on a timely basis that makes immunization attractive. Pension funds seeking to fund the retired lives liability or seeking an alternative to a GIC vehicle for the funding of such liabilities have also used immunization strategies. This latter application represents a customized asset alternative that can fill an investment need customized for the fund sponsor. Use among banks and other savings institutions involves structuring the assets of the investment portfolio to match the liabilities of the balance sheet.

The fundamental mechanism underlying immunization is a portfolio structure that balances the portfolio capital changes (from interest rate changes) with the return from reinvestment of portfolio cash flows (coupon payments and maturing securities). In other words, if rates rise, the higher reinvestment return will offset the decrease in portfolio value caused by such a rise; conversely, as rates decline, the increase in portfolio value will offset a lower reinvestment return. To accomplish this balance matching the duration of assets and liabilities is required.

Duration can be defined as a measure of the time required to receive the cash flows from the security where each of the cash flows is weighted by a discount factor—usually the security's yield to maturity (see the appendix to this chapter). By maintaining the duration of assets the same as the duration of liabilities, the balance between changes in portfolio prices and reinvestment return would be maintained.

Based upon the beginning of the time horizon, the term structure of interest rates or yield curve will determine the assured rate of return. It is the total return of the portfolio assuming no change in the term structure. This will always differ from the portfolio's present yield to maturity unless the term structure is described by a flat line, since by virtue of the passage of time there will be a return effect as the portfolio moves (matures) along the yield curve. Therefore, if there is an upward sloping yield curve, the yield to maturity will tend to overstate the target return; and conversely, with a downward sloping yield curve, the yield to maturity will tend to understate the target rate of return. Proxies for the target rate of return include the internal rate of return of the portfolio and the duration weighted yield to maturity (where each security's yield to maturity would be weighted by its duration as well as concentration in the portfolio). The most precise target rate of return would be estimated by simulating the management of the portfolio over the time horizon, taking into account transaction costs and assuming no change in the term structure. From a practical standpoint, the internal rate of return is the best choice followed by the duration yield to maturity.

The time horizon limiting factor is the ability to match the investor's desired time horizon with the weighted average duration of the portfolio. The most typical immunized time horizon is five years; it is a common planning period for GICs, and it allows flexibility in security selection since there is a fairly large population of eligible securities. With the introduction of zero-coupon securities (whose duration equals their maturity), longer duration portfolios are possible. However, beyond the duration range afforded by coupon securities, there generally is a paucity of availability and a tendency for what is available to be priced relatively expensively. In addition, the type of security in the portfolio should be limited to high quality, very liquid instruments since portfolio rebalancing is required to keep the portfolio duration synchronized with the horizon date.

Since a critical requirement is the matching of asset duration to the liability duration, estimation of individual security duration is important (the portfolio duration being a weighted average of the individual security durations). Therefore, use of securities with uncertain future cash flows may pose a problem. For example, callable bonds and mortgage-backed securities which have prepayment and/or refunding provisions make the calculation of duration difficult. In periods of volatile interest rates (especially declining rates), significant errors in duration estimation may arise resulting in severe mismatching of asset and liability durations. While there is a potential for higher return from these securities under appropriate assumptions, these assumptions require expectational input. This is another example of return enhancement by virtue of additional risk in the form of necessary expectations required.

Perhaps the most critical assumption of classical immunization techniques concerns the type of interest rate change anticipated. Specifically, the yield curve is assumed always to move in a one-time parallel fashion during the portfolio time horizon, i.e., interest rates either move up or down by the same amount for all maturities. This would appear to be an unrealistic assumption, since such behavior is rarely, if ever, experienced in reality. According to the theory, if there is a change in interest rates that does not correspond to this shape-preserving shift, matching the duration of the investor's desired time horizon no longer assures immunization. For a more complete discussion of these issues, see Cox, Ingersol, and Ross [1979].

Figure 2 illustrates the nature of portfolio value given an immunized portfolio and parallel shifts in rates. The curve ab represents the behavior of the portfolio value for various changes in rates, ranging from a decline to an increase as shown on the horizontal axis. Point V_0 (on line tt') is the level of portfolio value assuming no change in rates. It can be seen that an immunized portfolio subjected to parallel shifts in the yield curve will actually provide a greater portfolio value than the assured target value, which, therefore, becomes the portfolio's minimum value.

Figure 3 illustrates the relationship when interest rates do not shift in a parallel fashion and indicates the possibility of a portfolio value less than the target. Depending upon the shape of the nonparallel shift, either the A or the B relationship will occur. The important point is that merely matching the duration of the portfolio with the portfolio time horizon as the condition for immunization may not prevent significant deviations from the target rate of return.

To handle this problem, the concept of maturity variance has been introduced by Fong and Vasicek [1980]. The greater the dispersion of cash flows about the liabilities being funded, the greater the risk. Risk is defined as the potential dispersion of return (standard deviation) around the target return. In the special case of choosing from a universe

FIGURE 2 Portfolio Value for Various Changes in Rates

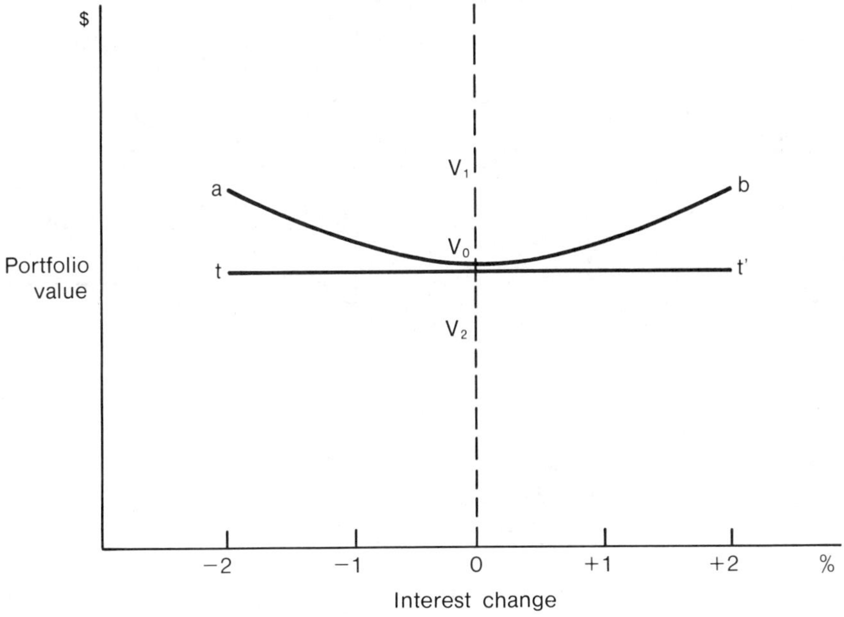

of pure discount securities, holding securities with the same maturities as the liabilities would result in no immunization risk. At the other extreme, high coupon securities that are "laddered" over the portfolio time horizon would result in very high immunization risk. A laddered portfolio is one constructed with securities having regularly spaced maturities (the steps of the ladder being each maturity). This type of portfolio would have a part of the portfolio regularly maturing and subject to reinvestment. But because of the representation of many maturities and frequent principal reinvestment requirements, there is high exposure to reinvestment risk and, therefore, high immunization risk exposure. Such a portfolio would have high sensitivity to nonparallel (as well as parallel) changes in rates. Therefore, for a single-period liability, such as one represented by a GIC, the best minimum risk portfolio would be one holding securities that best resembles a portfolio of pure discount securities.

Where there are a number of liabilities to fund, a dedicated portfolio approach may be appropriate. This is a portfolio with a structure designed to fund a schedule of liabilities from portfolio return and asset value, with the portfolio's value diminishing to zero after payment of the last liability. Two approaches to a dedicated portfolio are available.

FIGURE 3 Immunization

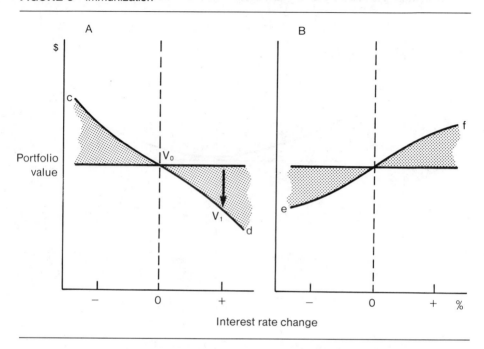

The first uses an immunization approach. For a multiperiod situation, where there is a series of liabilities over the portfolio time horizon, the following two conditions must exist: (1) the (composite) duration of the portfolio assets equals the (composite) duration of the liabilities and (2) the distribution of durations of individual portfolio assets has a wider range than the distribution of durations of the liabilities.

The first condition is straightforward; the second requires that the portfolio payments received be more dispersed in time than the liabilities. That is, there must be an asset with a duration equal to or less than the duration of the shortest duration liability in order to have funds to pay the liability when it is due. And there must be an asset with a duration equal to or greater than the longest duration liability in order to avoid the reinvestment rate risk that might jeopardize payment of the longest duration liability. This bracketing of shortest and longest duration liabilities with a shorter and a longer duration asset ensures the balancing of changes in portfolio value with changes in reinvestment return. Finally, there is still the concern for excessive asset dispersion relative to the profile of liability cash flows. Hence, minimizing the maturity variance as was previously discussed remains important. If all of these conditions are met, then the portfolio can be structured to generate the necessary cash flows on a timely basis at minimum immunization risk. For a more complete discussion of these sophisticated immunization techniques, see Fong and Vasicek [1980].

CASH FLOW MATCHING

A procedure called cash flow matching is an alternative to multiple-period (liability) immunization. This method can be intuitively described as follows. A bond is selected with a maturity that matches the last liability. An amount of principal equal to the amount of the last liability is then invested in this bond. The remaining elements of the liability stream are then reduced by the coupon payments on this bond, and another bond is chosen for the new, reduced amount of the next-to-last liability. Going backward in time, this is continued until all liabilities have been matched by the payments on the securities in the portfolio.

Table 1 displays a portfolio chosen to match a sequence of liability payments shown in the second-to-last column of Table 2. Table 1 also includes a number of descriptive statistics of the individual securities held and the portfolio as a whole. Table 2 provides a cash flow analysis of sources and applications of funds. The last column in the table shows the excess funds remaining at each time period that are reinvested at the assumed 6 percent reinvestment rate supplied by the user.

To the extent such matching is possible, it would indeed produce a portfolio similar to an immunized portfolio, since interest rate changes would not affect a portfolio whose payments match exactly in timing and amount the liabilities to be paid. However, given typical liability schedules and bonds available for cash flow matching, perfect matching is unlikely. Under such conditions a minimum immunization risk approach would probably be at least equal to cash flow matching and would probably be better, since an immunization strategy would require less money to fund liabilities. This is due to the higher reinvestment risk of cash flow matching as discussed in Gifford Fong Associates [1981].

One of the key inputs to the analysis of cash flow matching is the reinvestment rate assumption. This is the rate used to estimate the return on excess cash balances. Since this rate is subject to a high degree of uncertainty over time, it should be approached conservatively, resulting in most estimates being lower than the existing short-term rate. As compared to the internal rate of return of the portfolio, this reinvestment rate acts as a drag on overall returns. This can be contrasted to immunization where excess cash balances tend to be less since cash outflows are taken care of by rebalancing the portfolio to provide the necessary funds. That is, even with the use of linear programming optimization techniques where optimal combinations of bonds are created, cash flow matching may be technically inferior to immunization.

TABLE 1 Characteristics of a Sample Universe for Cash Flow Matching (evaluation date December 31, 1981)

Price Scan

Bond No.	Par Value (Dollars)	Percent of Total	CUSIP	Issuer Name	Coupon (Percent)	Effective Maturity Date	Price (Dollars)	YTM (Percent)	Duration (Years)
15	$ 517	2.2%	888888AA	Cash	0.000%	1/1/82	$100.000	0.0%	0.00
14	233	0.9	313388FB	Federal Home Ln. Bks.	7.850	8/27/84	86.000	14.36	2.36
13	1,199	4.6	912827KT	United States Treas. Nts.	9.625	8/15/85	88.125	13.89	2.99
12	1,215	3.8	812404AD	Sears Roebuck Accep. Corp.	8.375	12/31/86	75.500	15.61	4.04
11	2,353	7.6	901178BY	Twelve Fed. Ld. Bks.	7.600	4/20/87	75.625	14.30	4.23
10	2,474	10.0	667332AF	Northwest Bancorporation	15.350	5/1/89	94.750	16.60	4.46
9	4,080	18.1	313311FX	Federal Farm Cr. Bks.	14.700	7/22/91	100.000	14.69	5.10
8	1,382	4.5	912810CJ	United States Treas. Bds.	10.125	11/15/94	77.438	13.94	6.63
7	6,021	21.7	912810CR	United States Treas. Bds.	11.500	11/15/95	84.938	13.98	6.61
6	1,402	3.7	149123AK	Caterpillar Tractor Co.	8.750	11/1/99	61.125	15.08	7.02
5	1,357	3.7	302292AC	Exxon Pipeline Co.	8.875	10/15/00	63.750	14.55	7.17
4	1,294	5.4	912810CW	United States Treas. Bds.	13.375	8/15/01	95.344	14.07	6.77
3	2,649	6.7	880370AK	Tenneco Inc.	8.375	4/1/02	58.500	14.91	7.12
2	1,206	3.2	370424BW	General Mtrs. Accep. Corp.	9.400	7/15/04	59.875	16.04	6.41
1	1,228	4.0	749285AF	RCA Corp.	12.250	5/1/05	76.000	16.24	6.46

Portfolio Totals

Average duration (years)	5.563
Average yield (percent)	14.440
Duration weighted average yield (percent)	14.715
Average effective maturity	1-5-94
Total par value ($000)	28610.000
Total market value ($000)	24001.990
Number of issues	15

SOURCE: Gifford Fong Associates.

TABLE 2 Cash Flow Analysis of a Sample Universe for Cash Flow Matching: Reinvestment Rate—6 Percent (evaluation date December 31, 1981) (in dollars)

Date	Previous Cash Balance +	Interest on Balance +	Principal Payments +	Coupon Payments +	Reinvestment of Payments −	Liability Due =	New Cash Balance
12-31-82	$ 0	$ 0	$ 517	$3,128	$125	$3,770	$ 0
12-31-83	0	0	0	3,128	93	3,104	117
12-31-84	117	7	233	3,128	98	3,584	0
12-31-85	0	0	1,199	3,110	120	4,428	0
12-31-86	0	0	1,215	2,994	88	4,298	0
12-31-87	0	0	2,353	2,803	185	4,170	1,171
12-31-88	1,171	71	0	2,714	82	4,038	0
12-31-89	0	0	2,474	2,524	180	3,900	1,278
12-31-90	1,278	78	0	2,334	72	3,762	0
12-31-91	0	0	4,080	2,334	181	3,624	2,971
12-31-92	2,971	181	0	1,734	47	3,474	1,460
12-31-93	1,460	89	0	1,734	47	3,330	0
12-31-94	0	0	1,382	1,734	57	3,174	0
12-31-95	0	0	6,021	1,594	89	3,012	4,692
12-31-96	4,692	286	0	902	28	2,850	3,059
12-31-97	3,059	186	0	902	28	2,682	1,493
12-31-98	1,493	91	0	902	28	2,514	0
12-31-99	0	0	1,402	902	42	2,346	0
12-31-00	0	0	1,357	779	42	2,178	0
12-31-01	0	0	1,294	659	51	2,004	0
12-31-02	0	0	2,649	375	134	1,836	1,321
12-31-03	1,321	80	0	264	9	1,674	0
12-31-04	0	0	1,206	264	42	1,512	0
12-31-05	0	0	1,228	75	53	1,356	0

SOURCE: Gifford Fong Associates.

TABLE 3 Strategy Comparison

Immunization	Cash Flow Matching
Rebalancing required	Buy and hold
Duration matching	No duration requirement
Minimum cost	Intuitive appeal

Using cost of the initial portfolio as an evaluation measure, the author has found that cash-flow-matched portfolios can cost from 3 to 7 percent more, in dollars, than immunized portfolios using a typical corporate universe. However, cash flow matching is easier to understand, and this has occasionally led to its suboptimal selection over an immunization strategy for dedication problems. Cash flow matching has the advantage of being intuitively understandable.

Value Enhancement

Basic to immunization are the assumptions that the securities utilized will be default free, their cash flows known with certainty (for calculating duration) and liquid. For cash flow matching, the default-free and cash-flow-certainty condition is necessary, and the liquidity assumption is not as necessary once the position is taken. It is possible to relax these assumptions by introducing expectations by management and potentially adding value (return) in the process.

Using callable bonds, mortgage-backed securities, corporate bonds, and other security types goes beyond the basic assumptions of the analysis and, hence, is the means of return enhancement with an associated risk. Private placement securities, while not liquid for rebalancing purposes, are candidates for a core portion of portfolio holdings which may also offer a source of incremental return.

Finally, ongoing monitoring of potential swap candidates can be a regular source of value enhancement. This transforms the need of rebalancing to a desired opportunity.

Strategy Comparison: Immunization and Cash Flow Matching

Table 3 summarizes a comparison of immunization and cash flow matching. The first item refers to the need for rebalancing the immunized portfolio. Since duration changes at a different rate than time, even if interest rates did not move there would be a rebalancing requirement to maintain the duration of assets equaling the duration of liabilities. In a multiple-liability situation, each cash outflow would also require a rebalancing to generate the necessary cash. This can be compared to cash flow matching which theoretically does not require rebalancing. However, to the extent non-Treasury securities are used, ongoing credit analysis can be important. Moreover, value enhancement provides an incentive to rebalancing.

Immunization does require that the duration of assets and liabilities be matched while cash flow matching does not consider duration at all. In the case of a typical cash-flow-matched portfolio, the duration of assets will be less than the duration of liabilities. This is the case since cash must be available at the time a liability arises. To the extent there is not perfect matching, cash is generated ahead of time, which reduces the overall duration. Consequently, in an upward sloping yield curve environment, the estimated yield of the cash-flow-matched portfolio will be less than an immunized portfolio.

The last comparison is the most compelling. Immunization does provide a least-cost solution; however, it is a more complicated strategy. Cash flow matching is costlier yet is intuitively understandable and therefore an easier strategy to accept.

PASSIVE STRATEGIES

A buy-and-hold strategy essentially means purchasing and holding a security to maturity or redemption (e.g., by the issuer via a call provision) and then reinvesting cash proceeds in similar securities. Ongoing cash inflows, as well as outflows, are generally present via coupon income being received and reinvested. The emphasis is on minimizing the expectational inputs, i.e., the assumptions about the future level and direction of interest rates. By holding securities to maturity, any capital change resulting from interest rate change is neutralized or ignored (by holding to maturity, the par amount of the bond will be received). Portfolio return, therefore, is controlled by coupon payments and reinvestment proceeds. While interest rate forecasting is largely ignored, analysis is still important to minimize the risk of default on the securities held.

The passive or buy-and-hold strategy is used primarily by income-maximizing investors who are interested in the largest coupon income over a desired horizon. These types of investors include endowment funds, bond mutual funds, insurance companies that are seeking the maximum yield over an extended period of time, or other large pools of money where the size of the fund and large cash inflow make portfolio turnover difficult because of possible market impact. The buy-and-hold strategy was justifiable for many investors because fixed-income securities were traditionally characterized as safe assets with predictable cash flows and low price volatility. By assuming a long-term perspective, a return in excess of inflation with interest rate risk minimized is the objective. This is a classic example of seeking less than maximum return to avoid the inherent risk associated with the highest return strategy and, in turn, should be dictated by the investment objectives, constraints, and attendant policies of the investor.

INDEXING

Another technique for a passive strategy is an index fund. Index funds basically provide diversification along with minimum transaction costs. Moreover, a return tied to a recognized bogey has an appeal.

The objective of indexing is to replicate the characteristics of a given index with an actual bond portfolio. The choice of the index is a nontrivial task. A number of alternative indexes are available from many dealers such as Shearson Lehman, Salomon Brothers, and Merrill Lynch. Which index is most appropriate should be directly related to the investment objectives of the investor. Suffice it to say there is quite a range of alternatives which have differing return and risk characteristics. The focus here will be on the methodology of creating and maintaining a portfolio with index characteristics once the index is chosen.

If it were possible to buy the whole universe of bonds that was used in the calculation of the index, in amounts proportional to the amount outstanding of each bond, then the performance of the index could be replicated exactly, at least before transactions costs. In reality this is not feasible. Even small indexes, such as the Shearson Lehman Treasury Index, contain over a hundred securities, and some indexes may actually be based on universes of several thousand bonds (e.g., the Shearson Lehman Government/Corporate Index). Most actual portfolios have to be limited to a much smaller number of securities. Moreover, the portfolio needs to be rebalanced each month to reinvest interest income and to reflect changes in the index composition, and that could not be accomplished in practice if the portfolio were as large as to contain the whole universe.

The question thus arises as to the construction and maintenance of an actual portfolio that would replicate the given index as closely as possible in actual operating conditions. Specifically, the following requirements must be satisfied by a feasible strategy:

- The portfolio should not contain more than a given number of securities.
- The portfolio should not be rebalanced more often than monthly.
- Any interest income is to be kept as cash until the next rebalancing date.
- All purchases or sales should be in round lots of a given size (say, $10,000 of face value).
- There is a minimum amount for any purchase or sale (say, $100,000 of face value).
- Transaction costs should be included in the portfolio returns.

In addition to these requirements, there are several desiderata on the investment strategy to make it a practical tool. These include the following requirements:

- The strategy should be flexible enough to allow the portfolio manager to be involved in the selection of the securities for the portfolio.
- The strategy should include a quantitative algorithm that determines exactly the holdings in each security selected for the portfolio, as well as the transactions necessary to maintain the portfolio.

Subject to the above requirements, the objective of the methodology is to track the index returns as closely as possible.

What follows is a description of one approach which addresses the aforementioned issues. This is illustrative of the type of technique necessary to accomplish indexing. The methodology consists of three steps: (1) definition of classes to which the index universe is divided, (2) selection of securities for the portfolio from each class, and (3) determination of the amount held in each security selected. These steps will now be described in greater detail.

Definition of Classes

The universe by which the index is calculated is divided into classes of securities. The number of classes can be made equal to the number of securities to be held in the portfolio. The classes should be defined to be as homogeneous as possible. This could be accomplished by breaking the universe by the following criteria:

- Issuing sector/quality.
- Maturity range.
- Coupon range.

For instance, suppose that the objective is to track the Shearson Government Index with a portfolio of, at most, 40 bonds. The classes can be defined by distinguishing Treasuries and agencies, breaking the maturity range into 10 intervals (e.g., 1–2, 2–3, 3–4, 4–6, 6–8, 8–10, 10–12, 12–15, 15–20, and 20–30 years to maturity) and separating the securities with coupons of 10 percent or less from those with coupons of over 10 percent. The total number of classes will then be

$$2 \times 10 \times 2 = 40$$

Each class is reasonably homogeneous, since it contains only one type of security (say, Treasuries) in a narrow maturity range and with similar coupon levels.

Selection of Securities

On the initial date, as well as on each rebalancing date (typically monthly), one security is chosen from each class for inclusion in the investment portfolio. The portfolio managers may exercise their judgment on selecting the specific security from those available. They may review the list of bonds in the class and select the one which has the most appeal in terms of availability, liquidity, and so forth. In the interest of keeping turnover down, they will also probably choose one which is already being held in the portfolio (if any), unless they have reasons to prefer a new security within the class. It is even possible to base the selection on a valuation model that ranks the securities in the class from the most underpriced to the most overpriced (see the section on return enhancement below).

Portfolio Weighting

Once the selection of the securities for the portfolio has been accomplished, the amounts invested in each security are determined. This step does not involve any judgmental input and is done completely by a computer program. Programs* containing an optimization procedure which constructs the portfolio to be as representative of the index as possible can be used. The procedure consists of a quadratic programming algorithm that accomplishes the following:

a. The duration of the portfolio is equal to that of the index.
b. The distribution of maturities (as measured by M^2) of the portfolio is equal to that of the index. The M^2 measure evaluates the extent to which the payments on the portfolio are dispersed in time. For instance, if the maturities in the index are more or less laddered, matching the M^2 of the portfolio to that of the index would avoid ending up with a portfolio (of the same duration) that is of a bullet type, or one which is a barbell type, and so forth. This is the same measure as that used in the immunization analysis.
c. The amount held in each of the selected securities is as close to being proportional to the total weight of that class in the index as is possible under the above constraints.

After the quadratic programming solution is obtained, the program modifies the holdings to satisfy the round-lot requirements and the minimum trade requirements. The residual amount of cash at the rebalancing date is also minimized by the program.

---

* For example, BONDTRAC of Gifford Fong Associates is one such model.

RETURN ENHANCEMENT

Since the selection of a security from a class is an independent step, it is possible to combine the bond index tracking procedure with another methodology, namely, return enhancement. Return enhancement is an approach that identifies securities mispriced with respect to a valuation model and chooses the most underpriced securities for sales, resulting in an expected increase in the portfolio return.

Two examples of valuation models employed by the return enhancement procedure are Term Structure Analysis (BONDTERM)* for U.S. Treasury securities and the Bond Valuation Model (BONDVAL)* for corporate securities. The BONDTERM model estimates the term structure of interest rates on the universe of all outstanding Treasury bills, notes, and bonds as of a given date and then prices any Treasury security by determining the present value of its payments discounted by the spot rates corresponding to the term of each payment. A provision for the current yield effect is also included in the model. The BONDVAL model for valuation of corporate securities starts by determining the price of the corporate bond from the Treasury term structure (this is called the default-free price). The yield corresponding to the default-free price is then incremented by yield differentials corresponding to the issuer type, quality rating, current yield/coupon, and call terms of the security. These yield differentials are determined by a simultaneous least-squares estimation on the total corporate universe.

The price determined by BONDTERM or BONDVAL is called the fitted price, and the corresponding yield is called the fitted yield. The fitted yield is the yield at which the given bond would be in exact agreement with the pricing of the universe as a whole, accounting for the specific attributes of the bond such as maturity, coupon, sector, quality, and so on. To the extent that the actual yield on any given security differs from its fitted yield, this security is relatively mispriced.

In the BONDTRAC application, the return enhancement methodology is used to select the securities for the classes. Each bond in a given class is valued by BONDTERM/BONDVAL and the difference between the actual and fitted yields determined. Within each class, the bonds are then ranked by this difference from the most underpriced to the most overpriced. The best candidates for selection to the portfolio are the bonds close to the top of this list.

The Results

As an example of the BONDTRAC methodology, a portfolio was constructed and simulated to replicate the Lehman Treasury Index. The

---

* Courtesy of Gifford Fong Associates.

TABLE 4 Tracking the Lehman Treasury Index: Simulated Monthly Returns (in percent) before and after Transaction Costs

		Naive Strategy		Return-Enhancement Strategy	
Month	Lehman Treasury Index	Before Transaction Costs	After Transaction Costs	Before Transaction Costs	After Transaction Costs
1/82	.64%	.62%	.62%	1.15%	1.15%
2/82	1.43	1.54	1.50	1.56	1.43
3/82	1.13	1.02	.90	1.29	1.24
4/82	2.44	2.45	2.38	2.46	2.41
5/82	1.46	1.36	1.31	1.36	1.35
6/82	−1.24	−1.13	−1.15	−1.07	−1.12
7/82	3.96	3.87	3.87	3.93	3.87
8/82	4.41	4.48	4.47	4.59	4.55
9/82	3.54	3.48	3.45	3.65	3.50
10/82	4.58	4.55	4.54	4.50	4.49
11/82	.68	.71	.68	.95	.80
12/82	1.95	1.93	1.86	2.14	2.04
Year 1982	27.81	27.73	27.16	29.79	28.80

simulation period was the 12-month period from January 1982 to December 1982. The specifications were as follows:

- Initial investment amount of $50 million.
- Portfolio size not exceeding 20 securities.
- Monthly rebalancing.
- Interest income reinvested at the 90-day Treasury bill rate until the next rebalancing date.
- Round lots of $10,000.
- Minimum transaction amount of $100,000.
- Transaction costs calculated at the rate of 30 basis points (bp) per round-trip of the transaction face amount.

Two strategies were simulated: A naive strategy and a return-enhancement strategy. The two strategies differed by the selection from the classes. In the naive strategy, the security with the largest amount outstanding in each class was selected for the portfolio. In the return-enhancement strategy, the selected security was the one most underpriced in its class as determined by the BONDTERM valuation.

For both strategies, the classes were defined by 10 maturity intervals with breakpoints (in years to maturity) of 1, 2, 3, 4, 6, 8, 10, 12, 15, 20, and 30 and by coupon rates of 10 percent and less and more than 10 percent. The portfolio weights were in both cases calculated by the BONDTRAC program.

A summary of the results is given in Table 4.

As is seen from the results, the methodology performed remarkably well. The naive strategy allowed tracking the index return within −11 bp a year before transaction costs, although after transactions the difference was −68 bp. The average absolute value of the monthly return differentials was 6 bp before and 8 bp after transaction costs. This is a very good tracking accuracy, considering the severe requirements placed on the portfolio size and on the minimum transaction amounts.

The most astonishing result, however, was the performance of the return-enhancement strategy. The return-enhanced portfolio overperformed the index by 195 bp per year before transaction costs and by 94 bp after transactions. The results were very consistent from month to month. The return-enhanced strategy outperformed the index in 9 out of the 12 monthly periods, that is, 75 percent of the time.

SUMMARY

The nature of fixed income passive management minimizes the use of expectational inputs such as interest rate forecasts. Recognizing a trade-off between return and risk, passive approaches therefore have a lower potential return. Two basic types of analysis are described. The first includes immunization and the related strategy of cash flow matching. The second type is indexing or the process of creating a portfolio with index-like characteristics.

Immunization is a strategy which has a number of applications for institutional investors. It enables a locked-in return irrespective of interest rate changes over a specified horizon. Cash flow matching provides an alternative systematic approach to funding a series of liabilities but is a higher cost strategy.

Fixed-income indexing is concerned with the replication of the characteristics of an index which may include thousands of securities. A segmentation approach is described which permits a sampling methodology from which an optimization procedure can be used to achieve the desired characteristics.

Depending on the investment objectives and policies of the investor, the strategies described represent important capabilities for fulfilling the stated goals at minimum risk.

BIBLIOGRAPHY

Cox, John C., John E. Ingersoll, Jr., and Stephen A. Ross. "Duration and the Measurement of Basis Risk." *Journal of Business*, 1979.

Fong, H. Gifford. *Bond Portfolio Analysis*. Monograph No. 11. Charlottesville, Va.: The Financial Analysts Research Foundation, 1980.

———, Charles J. Pearson, and Oldrich A. Vasicek. *Bond Performance Analysis*. New York: Institute for Quantitative Research in Finance, 1981.

————, and OLDRICH A. VASICEK. "A Risk Minimizing Strategy for Multiple Liability Immunization." New York: Institute for Quantitative Research in Finance, 1980.

————, and OLDRICH A. VASICEK. "Term Structure Modeling Using Third Order Exponential Splines." *The Journal of Finance*, May 1982.

GIFFORD FONG ASSOCIATES. "The Costs of Cashflow Matching." 1981.

MACAULAY, FREDRICK R. *Some Theoretical Problems Suggested by the Movement of Interest Rates, Bond Yields and Stock Prices in the United States since 1856*. New York: National Bureau of Economic Research, 1983.

REDDINGTON, F. M. "Review of the Principle of Life Office Valuations." *Journal of the Institute of Actuaries* 18 (1952).

APPENDIX

Duration and Immunization

Sumner N. Levine and H. Gifford Fong

In this section we develop the ideas of duration and immunization.

Duration, D, is defined by the expression

$$D = \frac{\displaystyle\sum_{t=1}^{M} \frac{tC_t}{(1 + r)^t}}{\displaystyle\sum_{t=1}^{M} \frac{C_t}{(1 + r)^t}} \qquad (1)$$

where

C_t = the cash flow at time t

r = the market rate of interest per period

M = the number of periods (from the present) over which the cash flow occurs

In the case of a bond, C_t is the semiannual periods remaining to maturity. Since the bond is assumed redeemed at maturity, the terminal cash flow (C_M) is the redemption value of the bond plus the last coupon payment. The duration concept is also often applied to a series of debt repayments in which case C_t is the cash flow involved in the repayment and M is the number of periods (from the present) over which repayment occurs. For clarity in the discussion below we shall denote the number of periods over which debt repayment is made by H (rather than M). Hence, M will be reserved for the periods remaining to bond maturity.

In the following we assume a flat yield curve; that is, the interest paid on short-term loans is the same as that on long-term loans. While this is clearly unrealistic, nonetheless some useful results concerning bond portfolio management (specifically immunization) can be derived.

We note that the present value (P) of a series of cash flows is given by

$$P = \sum_{t=1}^{M} \frac{C_t}{(1 + r)^t} \tag{2}$$

On differentiating the above with respect to r, there results

$$\frac{dP}{dr} = -\frac{1}{(1 + r)} \sum_{t=1}^{M} \frac{tC_t}{(1 + r)^t} \tag{3}$$

On dividing equation (3) by the present value P and rearranging terms we have

$$D = -\frac{(1 + r)}{P} \frac{dP}{dr} \tag{4}$$

The last result permits us to calculate the percentage change in the price (present value) of a bond resulting from a relatively small change, dr, in the interest rate, since

$$\frac{dP}{P} = -\frac{D}{(1 + r)} dr = D'dr \tag{5}$$

The term D′ corresponding to D/(1 + r) is referred to as the modified duration. As an example of the use of equation (5) we calculate the fractional change in bond price for a bond of 8 years' duration if the current market yield of 10 percent increases from 10 percent to 11 percent.

$$\frac{dP}{P} = -\frac{(8)(.01)}{1.1} = -.0727 \tag{5a}$$

Hence, a 1 percent increase in rates corresponds to a 7.27 percent decrease in the bond price.

Practical Duration Calculations

The calculation of bond duration from the definition given above is awkward. A more convenient expression can be derived using equation

(4) and the expression for the present value of a bond with semiannual coupon payouts C and redemption value F:

$$P = \frac{C[(1 + r)^M - 1]}{r(1 + r)^M} + \frac{F}{(1 + r)^M} \tag{6}$$

Introducing (6) into (4) and collecting terms, we obtain the useful result

$$D = \frac{(1 - X)(1 + r)R^2 + (F' - R)MX}{R(1 - X) + F'X} \tag{7}$$

where

$$X = \frac{1}{(1 + r)^M}$$

$$F' = F/C$$

$$R = 1/r$$

As an example consider a bond with 10 semiannual periods remaining to maturity. The semiannual market rate is 6 percent, the coupon payment is \$25, and the redemption value at maturity is \$1,000.

Here

$$X = \frac{1}{(1.06)^{10}} = .5585 \tag{7a}$$

$$F' = 1000/25 = 40$$

$$M = 10$$

$$R = \frac{1}{.06} = 16.67$$

hence

$$D = \frac{(1 - .5585)(1.06)(277.78) + (40 - 16.67)(5.585)}{16.67(1 - .5585) + 22.34}$$

$$D = 8.76 \text{ semiannual periods (4.38 years)}$$

Properties of Duration

Examination of the expression for duration shows the following apply:

a. The duration of a coupon-bearing bond is less than the time to maturity. In the above, M = 10, but D = 8.76 periods. In the case of a zero-coupon bond the duration equals the time to maturity as may be readily shown by applying the defining equation (1) to a one-time cash flow.

b. Duration increases with time to maturity (M).

FIGURE A–1   Duration versus Maturity

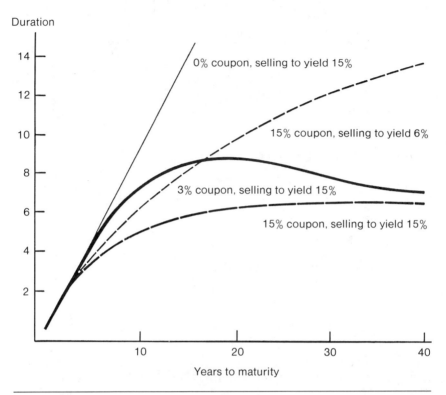

SOURCE: William L. Nemerever, "Managing Bond Portfolios through Immunization Strategies," in *The Revolution in Techniques for Managing Bond Portfolios,* ed. Donald Tuttle (Charlottesville, Va.: The Institute for Chartered Financial Analysts, 1983).

   c. Duration decreases with an increase in coupon payment (C).
   d. Duration decreases with an increase in market yield (r).

These properties are illustrated in Figure A-1.

Additive Properties of Duration

We next consider two bond portfolios, one of which has a duration D_1 and the other, D_2. We are interested in the duration of the portfolio obtained by combining N_1 bonds of duration D_1 with N_2 bonds of duration D_2. Let the present value (price) of the bonds in the first portfolio be P_1 and that of the second, P_2. In general, items referring to the first portfolio will be designated by the subscript 1, to the second portfolio by the subscript 2, and to the combined portfolio by the subscript T. Again we assume a flat yield curve.

The present value of the combined portfolio is

$$P_T = \sum \frac{N_1 C_{1t} + N_2 C_{2t}}{(1 + r)^t} + \frac{N_1 F_1}{(1 + r)^{M_1}} + \frac{N_2 F_2}{(1 + r)^{M_2}}$$

or

(8)

$$P_T = N_1 P_1 + N_2 P_2$$

where F is the cash received on liquidation of the bond.

Using equation (4) we have

$$D_T = -\frac{(1 + r)}{P_T} \frac{dP_T}{dr} = \frac{N_1 \sum\limits^{M_1} \frac{t C_{1t}}{(1 + r)^t} + N_2 \sum\limits^{M_2} \frac{t C_{2t}}{(1 + r)^t}}{N_1 P_1 + N_2 P_2}$$

(8a)

Using the definition of duration, equation (1), it is evident that the terms in the numerator can be written as

$$D_T = \frac{N_1 P_1 D_1 + N_2 P_2 D_2}{N_1 P_1 + N_2 P_2} = \omega_1 D_1 + \omega_2 D_2$$

(9)

where ω_i is the fractional value of the respective portfolios. Thus, the duration of the combined portfolio is the value-weighted sum of the individual portfolios. It is evident that the above analysis can be generalized so that

$$D_T = \sum_i \omega_i D_i$$

(10)

Immunization

Let us now consider a single obligation of amount L which is due in H semiannual periods from the present, the so-called investment horizon. In anticipation of this obligation an investment is made in a bond portfolio with remaining time to maturity of M semiannual periods where, in general, M is greater than H. We assume that all the bond coupon payments are reinvested at a market rate r with a flat term structure. At time H the debt obligation will be repaid from the proceeds generated by the reinvested coupon payments and the sale of the bonds.

The latter is just the present value at time H of the remaining (M-H) coupons plus the present value of the face amount (F) of the bonds:

$$N \sum_{t=1}^{H} C(1 + r)^t + \sum_{t=1}^{M-H} \frac{NC}{(1 + r)^t} + \frac{NF}{(1 + r)^{M-H}} = L \qquad (10a)$$

Dividing the above by $(1 + r)^H$ we have

$$N \sum_{t=1}^{M} \frac{C}{(1 + r)^t} + \frac{NF}{(1 + r)^M} = \frac{L}{(1 + r)^H} \qquad (10b)$$

This result indicates that the present value of the bond portfolio must equal the present value of the debt obligation. Denoting the present value of a bond by $P_B(r)$ and that of the debt by $P_L(r)$ we can write

$$NP_B(r) = P_L(r) \qquad (11)$$

Note that in calculating P_B we take M as the time period while for P_L we take H as the relevant time interval.

In the above we have assumed that r remains constant over the investment horizon. As is well known, fluctuations in the market interest rate will affect the relevant cash flows and other quantities. We now seek to structure the bond portfolio so that it is minimally affected by interest rate changes over the investment horizon. A bond portfolio so structured is referred to as an *immunized* portfolio. We now seek the conditions for immunizing a portfolio.

We assume that the rate changes instantaneously by an amount dr and that the new rate $(r + dr)$ remains constant over the investment horizon. As mentioned above this assumption is, of course, unrealistic, but it does provide useful results. After the rate change we require that

$$NP_B (r + dr) = P_L (r + dr)$$

This implies that

$$N \frac{dP_B}{dr} = \frac{dP_L}{dr} \qquad (12)$$

Dividing the above expression by Equation (11), we have

$$\frac{1}{P_B} \frac{dP_B}{dr} = \frac{1}{P_L} \frac{dP_L}{dr} \qquad (12a)$$

or in view of Equation (4);

$$D_B = D_L \qquad (13)$$

Thus, immunization is achieved if the duration of the bond portfolio equals that of the debt. It is easy to show that if a single cash flow occurs at time H then the duration equals H so that

$$D_B = H \tag{14}$$

The duration of an immunized bond portfolio equals the number of periods (H) from the present when the obligation becomes due.

Matching the duration of liabilities with the duration of assets fulfills one of the necessary conditions for an immunized portfolio once the restrictive assumptions mentioned earlier are relaxed. The other condition for a single-liability case is the minimization of the M^2, or maturity variance.

Extensions to multiple-liability immunization requires a further condition. This essentially concerns the distribution of assets relative to the string of liabilities which must be funded. In other words, the mean absolute deviation of the assets must be greater than or equal to the mean absolute deviation of the liabilities.

To understand why the portfolio payments have to be more spread out in time than the liabilities to assure immunity, think of the single horizon case. There immunization was achieved by balancing changes in reinvestment return on portfolio payments maturity prior to the horizon date against changes in the value at the horizon date of the portfolio portion still outstanding. The same "straddling" of each liability by the portfolio payments is necessary in the multiple-liability case, which implies that the payments have to be more dispersed in time than the liabilities.

Some Limitations Associated with Immunization

The theory of immunization assumes that all securities used in the portfolio will have known and certain cash flows. In other words, the duration of each security must be accurately calculated based on cash flows which are default free. These conditions only avail when an all-Treasury universe of securities is used. With the incentive to achieve higher yields using other securities, additional managerial attention must be applied in the case of lower grade instruments as well as those with uncertain cash flows, e.g., pass-through securities.

Furthermore, rebalancing is required in the portfolio. Even if interest rates were to be unchanged, the duration of a portfolio changes at a different rate than the duration of the liabilities in all cases except for the extreme cases of a flat yield curve (term structure) or when the cash flows from the assets match perfectly with the liability stream. This requirement to maintain the duration of assets equal to the duration of liabilities is a definite requirement which may also be thought of as an opportunity. Through adroit management of security selection as part of the rebalancing activity, return enhancement is possible so that over time significant incremental value may be achieved. In sum, immunization is a strategy which, at a minimum, is not a passive strategy and may become a fairly active strategy if value enhancement is sought.

Another limitation which should be mentioned concerns the requirement that the liabilities in both timing as well as magnitude must be known. This does limit the range of problems which may be solved. In particular, in those types of problems where option-like characteristics in the liabilities exist (for example, single premium deferred annuity portfolios), immunization strategies are severely limited in application.

42

Active Bond Portfolio Management*

Francis H. Trainer, Jr., CFA
Manager—Fixed Income Investments
Sanford C. Bernstein & Co., Inc.

Jonathan A. Reiss, CFA
Quantitative Analyst—Fixed Income Investments
Sanford C. Bernstein & Co., Inc.

Active bond management presupposes that managers can identify a particular bond or set of bonds that will outperform the universe of fixed-income securities. Most active bond management strategies are heavily influenced by the manager's forecast for interest rates. Individual securities may be classified on a continuum from most aggressive to most defensive, principally according to their maturities (or durations).[1] Once the outlook for interest rates has been assessed, the manager constructs a portfolio that reflects the magnitude of the expected change in interest rates, the degree of confidence in the forecast, and the willingness of the manager and client to bear risk.

There are, however, a great many other factors that influence bond price behavior. These include sector, quality, call and sinking fund provisions, coupon, maturity mix, and the financial position of specific issuers. Although none of these *individual* factors is as significant as interest rate change, collectively they exert a profound influence on bond portfolio performance.

Thus, we can distinguish two basic approaches to bond manage-

---

* The authors wish to thank David A. Levine for his substantial contribution to this chapter.

[1] Footnotes appear at the end of the chapter.

ment. The interest rate forecasting approach is largely based upon economic analysis and Fed watching. It offers the possibility of substantially outperforming the market (and competing managers) but opens up the possibility of substantial *underperformance* as well. It is a risky strategy because it depends on the accuracy of a single judgment.

By way of contrast, what we may call the bond-analytical approach is based on quantitative techniques that evaluate the various attributes of bonds that were mentioned above. Inasmuch as some of these factors will help performance in a given year while others will hurt, the potential deviation from market performance is more limited. But to the extent that skilled managers are capable of making correct judgments, the bond-analytical approach represents a much more reliable path to superior performance than interest rate forecasting.

How does the manager decide which strategy to use and how aggressively to pursue it? The answer depends upon what the manager and the client are trying to accomplish. If the client has no clearly defined goals, then it does not really matter which technique is used. (Actually, it matters, but it will be very difficult to assess what was or was not accomplished.)

If the aim is to maximize performance, then interest rate forecasting offers the greatest opportunity. But the riskiness of this strategy lessens its relative attractiveness. Interest rate forecasting also seems to be an inefficient tool for achieving superior returns. Bonds produce lower returns than equities over the long run. The reason, then, that assets are allocated to fixed-income securities is that the resulting reduction in volatility is worth the give-up in return. It would seem to be self-defeating to allocate assets to fixed income in order to reduce risk, only to invest the assets according to a highly risky interest rate forecasting strategy.

For most purposes, we favor the bond-analytical approach. The correct strategy is to try to maximize performance for a *given degree* of interest rate exposure—one that is permitted to vary relatively little or, even, not at all.

Once this strategy is selected, the focal point of the investment process should be a benchmark portfolio that has a clearly defined level of interest rate exposure. The choice of a broad market index, such as the Shearson Lehman Aggregate Index or the Salomon Brothers Broad Index, will serve this purpose well in most cases. In instances where the overall goals of the fund would be better served by a bond portfolio that is either more sensitive or less sensitive to interest rates than the fixed-income market as a whole, a different benchmark may be chosen. In either case, however, it is important to select a benchmark for it provides a standard against which the manager's performance may be judged.

A central premise of the bond-analytical approach is that superior performance can be achieved through the identification of undervalued bonds. The notion that misvalued bonds can be uncovered is predicated upon a belief that the market is inefficient—that there are always opportunities available. Such opportunities may be identified through the systematic evaluation of the components of a bond's value and the performance of this analysis in a consistent fashion across a broad spectrum of the market. If the bond market is, in fact, inefficient and if these analytical tools are sufficiently robust, then active bond management will earn substantial incremental returns.

Once undervalued bonds are identified, a method must be devised that allows one to construct a portfolio that capitalizes on the opportunities in a manner consistent with the overall objectives of the portfolio.

In the first part of this chapter we introduce the valuation framework and tools we use to identify undervalued bonds. The second part of this chapter discusses the portfolio construction process and the techniques we use to maintain optimal portfolios over time.

PART ONE—A FRAMEWORK FOR VALUING BONDS

WHY OPPORTUNITIES OCCUR

An active bond management strategy is based on the belief that bonds do not always sell at their fair value, that the differences are material, and that such bonds can be identified.[2] Several factors account for the inefficiency of the bond market. First, bonds are complex securities. The yield on a bond is a function of its quality, coupon, maturity, and any options that are part of the bond (such as call exposure). Valuation of a bond, therefore, requires an analysis of each of these features. While the processes for analyzing quality are well developed, there have been very few attempts at rigorous quantification of the remaining factors. For example, there is no analytical formula for the value of the call option on corporate bonds and mortgage pass-through securities. While option theory is well developed for short-term options on equities, the assumptions that underlie this model are not acceptable for valuing a long-term option on a bond.[3]

A second reason that bonds deviate from their fair value is the paucity of reliable pricing information. Unlike the equity market, where bids and offers are continuously available, there is virtually no information on the prices of bonds. With the exception of on-the-run Treasuries and recently issued corporates, there are no quote machines to punch up the latest trade or the bid and asked price.[4] In fact, it is extremely difficult to get high-quality pricing information even on a monthly basis. Without the anchor of continuous quality pricing, it is difficult to know

EXHIBIT 1 Comparative Yield Spreads versus Treasuries

	12/31/84	12/31/85	Change
AA industrials	78	75	−3
BBB industrials	178	173	−5
Chrysler Corporation	112	156	44

SOURCE: Salomon Brothers and Bernstein estimates.

where a bond has traded lately. As a result, the potential for a bond to deviate from its fair value is considerable.

A third cause of inefficiency in the bond market arises from supply-and-demand imbalances. For example, the interest rate differential between industrial bonds and Treasuries was fairly constant throughout 1985. Yet as may be seen in Exhibit 1, the yield spreads on the debt of Chrysler Corporation widened dramatically.

While at first blush one might attribute this widening of spreads to a deterioration of credit, Chrysler established record pretax earnings in 1985, and its common stock appreciated by 46 percent—20 percent more than the market.

Chrysler spreads widened because the company issued a massive amount of debt. During 1985 Chrysler raised $1.6 billion, or more than 6 percent of all new industrial debt. While this did result in an increase in leverage—from 17 percent to 33 percent—the company's degree of leverage is far below that of the average BBB corporation. In fact, Chrysler's debt/equity ratio and other financial characteristics make it appear comparable in quality to a typical AA industrial. But it sells closer to a BBB company, not so much because it is rated BBB but because the massive supply of Chrysler paper led to congestion in the marketplace. Investors who were interested in Chrysler already felt they owned enough. As a result, additional investors had to be enticed with incremental yield. Thus, the market clearing process led to a distortion in the yield relationship of Chrysler versus the rest of the market.

Finally, there is one additional factor that contributes to the inefficiency of the bond market. It is the fact that a single correct interest rate decision (provided the bet is large enough) can be worth more to performance than the cumulative effect of correct decisions on all of the other aspects of bonds.

To illustrate the power of accurate forecasting, we have computed the return that would have resulted if one had been able to earn the higher of the returns available from (a) one-month Treasury bills or (b) 30-year Treasury bonds in each month over the past five years.[5]

As may be seen in Exhibit 2, our omniscient manager would have earned a 38 percent compound annual return—21 percent higher than

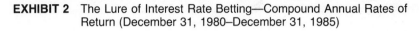

EXHIBIT 2 The Lure of Interest Rate Betting—Compound Annual Rates of
Return (December 31, 1980–December 31, 1985)

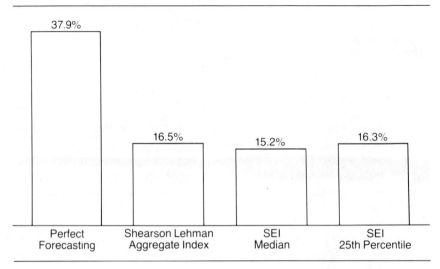

| 37.9% | 16.5% | 15.2% | 16.3% |
| Perfect Forecasting | Shearson Lehman Aggregate Index | SEI Median | SEI 25th Percentile |

the return on the market! This potential is so large that perfect forecasting hardly seems necessary. One can easily imagine a manager saying to himself, "If I can just be right on the direction of interest rates 60 percent of the time (thereby earning one fifth of the excess return), I will outperform virtually all of my competitors." As a result, many fixed-income portfolio managers expend a great deal of effort trying to forecast the future course of interest rates. Furthermore, since their forecasts may change at any time, these managers usually require a level of liquidity that can only be found in on-the-run Treasuries and a handful of recently issued corporates.

Since maturity and liquidity requirements are dominant, valuation distortions, *even if perceived*, are not worth worrying about. It doesn't really matter if a bond is overpriced—the error of the purchase will be overwhelmed by the expected positive returns from the interest rate forecast.

For all of these reasons, there are always misvaluations in the bond market. The fundamental challenge of active bond management is to uncover and exploit these opportunities.

ESTIMATING FAIR VALUE

The value of a fixed-income security is dependent on its specific characteristics—i.e., its coupon, maturity, sector, quality, and embedded options such as call exposure. We use three different bases for estimating the value of a bond's attributes.

1. What is its *intrinsic value*?
2. What has been the *historical price* of the attribute under similar economic conditions?
3. What is *today's market price* for that attribute?

Different methods are used for different characteristics. For example, we have estimated the intrinsic value of call options on bonds by using a binomial process similar to that used for valuing other types of options. This tells us what the option is worth given the current yield curve and our estimates of future volatility. On the other hand, to determine what yield spread we should demand to buy an industrial bond instead of a Treasury, we utilize a regression analysis that estimates industrial/Treasury yield spreads as a function of the change in economic conditions. Finally, for quality spreads—BBB bonds versus AA bonds, for instance—we use an estimate of the prevailing average spread in today's market.

All three of these approaches are attempts to find securities that are underpriced and will, therefore, outperform other bonds of the same duration *regardless of the direction of change in interest rates.*

VALUING TREASURY BONDS

The least complicated bonds to value are Treasury bonds. They have no credit risk and little or no call exposure. Moreover, they are very actively traded, and so they do not become misvalued because of a dearth of accurate price information. The only characteristics that differ materially from one Treasury note or bond to another are coupon and maturity.

Coupon Analysis

Although bonds are usually issued at par ($100), they rarely sell at this price. As interest rates change, they become either discount or premium bonds. Prior to mid-1984, the yields on discount bonds were always lower than the yields on comparable maturity par and premium bonds for two reasons: First, the portion of the yields to maturity that derived from the accretion of the discount was taxed as capital gains. Second, the tax on such gains was deferred until sale or maturity.

To illustrate the magnitude of these effects and their relationship with maturity, we have calculated the after-tax yield on a bond with a 9 percent coupon that is priced to yield 10 percent to maturity, assuming an income tax rate of 35 percent and a capital gains tax rate of 14 percent. (See Exhibit 3.)

The tax benefits of discount bonds are greatest for the one-year

EXHIBIT 3 Effect of Maturity on After-Tax Yield (35 percent income tax, 14 percent capital gains tax)

1	2	3	4
	After-Tax Yield to Maturity		(3 − 2)
Maturity	10 Percent Coupon at a 10 Percent Yield to Maturity	9 Percent Coupon at a 10 Percent Yield to Maturity	After-Tax Benefit of Discount
1	6.50%	6.70%	.20%
3	6.50	6.69	.19
5	6.50	6.68	.18
10	6.50	6.65	.15
20	6.50	6.60	.10
30	6.50	6.56	.06

maturity and decline as maturity lengthens. Moreover, the portion of the tax benefit that derives from capital gains treatment (as opposed to tax deferral) varies with maturity. To separate these components, we calculate the after-tax yield of a discount bond when the capital gains and income tax rate are *both* 35 percent. (See Exhibit 4.)

The value of the deferral rises with maturity and peaks at 20 years. The reason for the subsequent decline in the deferral's value is that the portion of the yield to maturity that is attributable to the appreciation of the bond to par at maturity declines as the maturity lengthens and eventually overwhelms the benefit of deferred taxation.

The portion of the after-tax benefit of a discount bond that is attributable to the lower capital gains rate is the differential between the total discount effect and the deferral benefit. (See Exhibit 5.)

EXHIBIT 4 Quantifying the Benefit of Deferral (35 percent income tax, 35 percent capital gains tax)

1	2	3	4
	After-Tax Yield to Maturity		(3 − 2)
Maturity	10 Percent Bond at a 10 Percent Yield	9 Percent Bond at a 10 Percent Yield	Benefit Attributable to Deferral
1	6.50%	6.51%	.01%
3	6.50	6.52	.02
5	6.50	6.54	.04
10	6.50	6.55	.05
20	6.50	6.55	.05
30	6.50	6.54	.04

EXHIBIT 5 Decomposition of the Discount Effect (35 percent income tax, 14 percent capital gains tax)

1	2	3	4 (2 − 3)	5 (3/2)	6 (4/2)
Maturity	Total Discount Effect	Benefit Attributable to Deferral	Benefit Attributable to Capital Gains Treatment	Percent of Benefit Attributable to Deferral	Percent of Benefit Attributable to Capital Gains Treatment
1	.20%	.01%	.19%	5%	95%
3	.19	.02	.17	11	89
5	.18	.04	.14	22	78
10	.15	.05	.10	33	67
20	.10	.05	.05	50	50
30	.06	.04	.02	67	33

At the one-year maturity, 95 percent of the discount effect—19 basis points out of the total of 20 basis points—arises from the lower capital gains tax rate. As the maturity lengthens, this effect declines and explains a decreasing amount of the total benefit of a discount bond. At the 30-year maturity, 67 percent of the value of a discount derives from the deferral provision of the tax law.

Premium bonds do not have any direct tax benefits or penalties because taxpayers are permitted to amortize the premium, thereby offsetting the extra income provided by the high coupon. However, because their coupons are higher than those of par bonds, it is less likely they will become discount bonds. Since it is less likely that premium bonds will ever receive the beneficial tax effect afforded discount bonds, they should be expected to sell at higher yields than par bonds.

On the basis of tax law, we would expect discounts to trade at lower yields than par bonds—the deeper the discount, the lower the yield. Conversely, we would expect premium bonds to trade at slightly higher yields than par bonds—the larger the premium, the higher the yield. Finally, since the total discount effect decreases with maturity, we would expect shorter discounts to trade at a lower yield relative to par bonds than longer discounts.

While analysis of the 1954–1983 period confirms that discounts have always sold for lower yields than par bonds, the historical data also suggest that the discount effect is slightly greater at longer maturities than it is at shorter maturities. Moreover, premium bonds have historically traded at much higher yields relative to par bonds than a tax-based analysis would suggest.[6]

Our historical analysis, in fact, indicates that a (rational) tax-based

EXHIBIT 6 Calculation of the Coupon Effect

1	2	3 (1 − 2)	4	5 (3 × 4)	6 (2 + 5)
Coupon	Par Bond Yield	Differential from Par Bond Yield	Adjustment per Percent in Coupon	Adjustment	Expected Yield
8%	10%	−2%	.05	−.10%	9.90%
9	10	−1	.05	−.05	9.95
10	10	0	.00	.00	10.00
11	10	+1	.03	+.03	10.03
12	10	+2	.03	+.06	10.06

SOURCE: Bernstein estimates.

analysis of the relationship between coupon and yield to maturity has less predictive power than simpler rules of thumb that are based on how bonds with different coupons have actually sold relative to one another. We found that there seems to be a fairly consistent relationship between the magnitude of the discount or premium in the coupon of a bond and its yield relative to that of a bond selling at par. The larger the coupon discount (coupon minus yield), the lower the yield, and the larger the coupon premium, the higher the yield. The size of this effect was independent of maturity. Additionally, the coupon effect was larger for discount bonds than it was for premium bonds.

To illustrate our findings, let us assume that we have a flat par bond yield curve at 10 percent. If there were no coupon effect, both a 9 percent and an 11 percent bond would sell at a 10 percent yield. What we found historically is that there is, on average, a five basis point adjustment per 1 percent in coupon for discount bonds and a three basis point adjustment for premium bonds. Thus, a 9 percent bond that is yielding 10 percent, has a coupon/yield differential of 1 percent. Using our discount rule of thumb of five basis points per 1 percent, we would expect this bond to sell at a yield of (10.00 percent − .05 percent), or 9.95 percent. Our rule for premium coupons is three basis points per 1 percent differential. Exhibit 6 illustrates these adjustments.

New Bonds versus Old Bonds

The 1984 tax reform bill changed the tax treatment of bonds issued on or after July 19, 1984. If an old bond—i.e., a pre-July 19, 1984, issue—is bought at a discount to par, the locked-in appreciation to par is not taxed until it is realized at maturity (or upon sale) and is treated as a capital gain. Although the comparable appreciation on a new bond is also

---

EXHIBIT 7 Summary of Coupon Adjustments (in basis points per 1 percent of coupon/yield differential)

	Old Bonds	New Bonds			
	All Maturities	1 Year	5 Years	10 Years	20 Years
Discount	5.00	0.25	1.10	1.65	2.50
Premium	3.00	0.15	0.66	0.99	1.50

SOURCE: Bernstein estimates.

---

deferred (i.e., not taxed until it is realized), the gain is now taxed as ordinary income.

As a result, only a fraction of the advantage of discounts remains for new bonds—the portion due to the deferral of taxation. This fraction increases from near zero for short bonds (since there is virtually no benefit from deferral) to one half of the old effect for long bonds (see Exhibit 7).

The foregoing discussion illustrates two of the approaches we use to determine fair value. The size of the tax effect was estimated simply by measuring the historical average. This must be done with caution because we are implicitly assuming that the historical average will be the central tendency for the future. Therefore, we must choose the *relevant* history carefully and try to determine if there is any reason that the future should differ from the past. The second approach was theoretical rather than empirical, for we have spent very little time under the new tax regime.

In addition to reflecting historical relationships, coupon adjustments must also incorporate changes in tax legislations. For example, the Tax Reform Act of 1986 eliminated the capital gains/ordinary income differential for 1988 and beyond. Under this provision, the only benefit of discounts arises from deferral and the treatment is the same for old and new bonds.

Estimating the Yield Curve

We use these coupon adjustments to estimate the par equivalent yield of a bond. When the outstanding Treasuries are adjusted for these effects, we are left with a set of yields on bonds which differ only in maturity. These yields are listed in column 5 of Exhibit 8. As may be seen, they are fairly consistent but not perfectly so. We find a best-fit curve through these yields to determine what we call the par bond yield curve—column 7.[7]

The adjusted yield of any non-callable Treasury bond should equal the par bond yield of the same maturity. That is, if the market priced all

EXHIBIT 8 Derivation of the Treasury Par Bond Yield Curve—December 31, 1985

1	2	3	4	5	6	7	8
Coupon	Maturity	Price	Yield to Maturity	Adjusted Yield to Maturity	Adjusted Yield to Call	Smoothed Par Bond Yield	Memo: Yield Misvaluation
9.750%	01/31/87	$101.97	7.81%	7.75%	—	7.76%	(0.01)%
9.000	02/15/87	101.28	7.77	7.74	—	7.75	(0.01)
10.875	02/15/87	103.19	7.84	7.75	—	7.75	0.00
12.750	02/15/87	105.16	7.85	7.70	—	7.75	(0.05)
10.000	02/28/87	102.31	7.86	7.79	—	7.74	0.05
10.250	03/31/87	102.81	7.82	7.75	—	7.73	0.02
10.750	03/31/87	103.41	7.81	7.72	—	7.73	(0.01)
9.750	04/30/87*	102.34	7.84	7.84	—	7.74	0.10
12.000	05/15/87	105.47	7.71	7.58	—	7.74	(0.16)
12.500	05/15/87	106.09	7.72	7.58	—	7.74	(0.16)
14.000	05/15/87	108.06	7.68	7.49	—	7.74	(0.25)
9.125	05/31/87*	101.66	7.86	7.85	—	7.75	0.10
8.500	06/30/87*	100.88	7.87	7.87	—	7.77	0.10
10.500	06/30/87	103.66	7.86	7.78	—	7.77	0.01
8.875	07/31/87*	101.44	7.88	7.88	—	7.80	0.08
12.375	08/15/87*	106.59	7.95	7.94	—	7.81	0.13
13.750	08/15/87	108.69	7.93	7.76	—	7.81	(0.05)
8.875	08/31/87*	101.41	7.94	7.94	—	7.82	0.12
9.000	09/30/87*	101.69	7.93	7.93	—	7.85	0.08
11.125	09/30/87	105.03	7.96	7.87	—	7.85	0.02
8.875	10/31/87*	101.44	8.00	8.00	—	7.88	0.12
7.625	11/15/87	99.53	7.89	7.90	—	7.89	0.01
11.000	11/15/87*	105.06	8.02	8.02	—	7.89	0.13
12.625	11/15/87	107.81	8.03	7.90	—	7.89	0.01
8.500	11/30/87*	100.91	7.97	7.97	—	7.90	0.07
7.875	12/31/87*	99.84	7.96	7.96	—	7.93	0.03
11.250	12/31/87	105.88	8.01	7.92	—	7.93	(0.01)
12.375	01/15/88	108.09	7.99	7.86	—	7.95	(0.09)
10.125	02/15/88	104.03	8.01	7.95	—	7.97	(0.02)
10.375	02/15/88*	104.44	8.05	3.04	—	7.97	0.07

12.000	03/31/88	107.88	8.09	—	7.97	8.01	(0.04)
13.250	04/15/88	110.53	8.10	—	7.95	8.03	(0.08)
8.250	05/15/88	100.56	7.98	—	7.97	8.05	(0.08)
9.875	05/15/88	103.72	8.11	—	8.06	8.05	0.01
10.000	05/15/88*	104.00	8.10	—	8.10	8.05	0.05
13.625	06/30/88	112.16	8.15	—	7.98	8.09	(0.11)
14.000	07/15/88	113.25	8.12	—	7.94	8.10	(0.16)
9.500	08/15/88*	103.03	8.19	—	8.18	8.13	0.05
10.500	08/15/88	104.00	8.21	—	8.15	8.13	0.02
11.375	09/30/88*	107.53	8.24	—	8.23	8.16	0.09
15.375	10/15/88	117.41	8.25	—	8.03	8.18	(0.15)
8.625	11/15/88*	101.47	8.04	—	8.03	8.20	(0.17)
8.750	11/15/88	101.09	8.31	—	8.29	8.20	0.09
11.750	11/15/88	108.75	8.26	—	8.15	8.20	(0.05)
10.625	12/31/88*	106.09	8.29	—	8.28	8.23	0.05
14.625	01/15/89	116.53	8.35	—	8.16	8.24	(0.08)
11.375	02/15/89	108.13	8.36	—	8.27	8.26	0.01
11.250	03/31/89*	108.06	8.35	—	8.34	8.29	0.05
14.375	04/15/89	116.69	8.44	—	8.27	8.30	(0.07)
9.250	05/15/89	102.97	8.22	—	8.18	8.32	(0.14)
11.750	05/15/89	109.59	8.42	—	8.32	8.32	(0.00)
9.625	06/30/89*	103.63	8.41	—	8.40	8.35	0.05
14.500	07/15/89	117.84	8.55	—	8.37	8.36	0.01
13.875	08/15/89	116.16	8.59	—	8.43	8.38	0.05
9.375	09/30/89*	103.03	8.41	—	8.40	8.40	0.00
11.875	10/15/89	110.66	8.52	—	8.41	8.41	0.00
10.750	11/15/89	107.38	8.47	—	8.40	8.42	(0.02)
12.750	11/15/89*	113.31	8.63	—	8.61	8.42	0.19
8.375	12/31/89	100.06	8.36	—	8.36	8.45	(0.09)
10.500	01/15/90	106.56	8.54	—	8.48	8.46	0.02
11.000	02/15/90*	108.13	8.61	—	8.60	8.47	0.13
10.500	04/15/90	106.63	8.61	—	8.56	8.50	0.06
8.250	05/15/90	102.09	7.67	—	7.66	8.51	(0.86)
11.375	05/15/90*	109.72	8.65	—	8.64	8.51	0.13
10.750	07/15/90	107.81	8.63	—	8.57	8.54	0.03
9.875	08/15/90*	104.78	8.59	—	8.59	8.55	0.04
10.750	08/15/90	108.00	8.61	—	8.55	8.55	(0.00)

EXHIBIT 8 *(continued)*

1	2	3	4	5	6	7	8
				Adjusted	*Adjusted*	*Smoothed*	*Memo:*
			Yield to	*Yield to*	*Yield to*	*Par Bond*	*Yield*
Coupon	*Maturity*	*Price*	*Maturity*	*Maturity*	*Call*	*Yield*	*Misvaluation*
11.500	10/15/90	110.78	8.69	3.61	—	8.58	0.03
9.625	11/15/90*	104.06	8.58	3.57	—	8.59	(0.02)
13.000	11/15/90	116.69	8.72	3.59	—	8.59	(0.00)
11.750	01/15/91	112.09	8.73	3.64	—	8.61	0.03
9.125	02/15/91*	102.50	8.51	3.50	—	8.63	(0.13)
12.375	04/15/91	114.91	8.78	3.68	—	8.65	0.03
14.500	05/15/91	124.16	8.76	3.59	—	8.66	(0.07)
13.750	07/15/91	121.03	8.86	3.72	—	8.68	0.04
14.875	08/15/91	126.16	8.86	3.68	—	8.69	(0.01)
12.250	10/15/91*	115.12	8.85	3.82	—	8.71	0.11
14.250	11/15/91	124.09	8.89	3.73	—	8.72	0.01
11.625	01/15/92*	112.72	8.86	3.84	—	8.74	0.10
14.625	02/15/92	126.44	8.92	3.75	—	8.75	0.00
11.750	04/15/92*	113.50	8.89	8.87	—	8.76	0.11
13.750	05/15/92	122.91	8.95	8.81	—	8.77	0.04
10.375	07/15/92*	107.25	8.89	8.88	—	8.79	0.09
7.250	08/15/92	93.69	8.51	8.58	—	8.80	(0.22)
9.750	10/15/92*	104.50	8.85	8.84	—	8.81	0.03
10.500	11/15/92	108.47	8.83	8.78	—	8.82	(0.04)
6.750	02/15/93	90.25	8.61	8.70	—	8.84	(0.14)
7.875	02/15/93	95.94	8.65	8.69	—	8.84	(0.15)
10.875	02/15/93	110.19	8.91	8.85	—	8.84	0.01
10.125	05/15/93	106.69	8.87	8.83	—	8.87	(0.04)
7.500	08/15/93	93.75	8.63	8.69	—	8.89	(0.20)
8.625	08/15/93	99.84	8.65	8.65	—	8.89	(0.24)
11.875	08/15/93	115.69	8.98	8.90	—	8.89	0.01
8.625	11/15/93	99.75	8.67	8.67	—	8.91	(0.24)
11.750	11/15/93	115.25	9.00	8.92	—	8.91	0.01
9.000	02/15/94	101.59	8.72	8.71	—	8.92	(0.21)
13.125	05/15/94	123.28	9.09	8.97	—	8.94	0.02

Rate	Maturity	Price					
8.750	08/15/94	100.00	8.75	8.75	—	8.96	(0.21)
12.625	08/15/94*	120.78	9.09	9.05	—	8.96	0.09
10.125	11/15/94	107.94	8.81	8.77	—	8.98	(0.21)
11.625	11/15/94*	115.37	9.06	9.04	—	8.98	0.06
10.500	02/15/95	108.91	9.04	9.00	—	8.99	0.01
11.250	02/15/95*	113.28	9.07	9.05	—	8.99	0.06
10.375	05/15/95	108.72	8.98	8.98	—	9.01	(0.03)
11.250	05/15/95*	113.34	9.10	9.08	—	9.01	0.07
12.625	05/15/95	121.81	9.11	9.01	—	9.01	(0.00)
10.500	08/15/95*	109.13	9.06	9.04	—	9.02	0.02
9.500	11/15/95*	103.28	8.99	8.98	—	9.04	(0.06)
11.500	11/15/95	115.66	9.06	8.99	—	9.04	(0.05)
7.000	05/15/98	85.19	9.01	9.10	10.01%	9.16	(0.05)
8.500	05/15/99	94.84	9.17	9.21	9.44	9.20	0.01
7.875	02/15/00	89.31	9.24	9.31	9.75	9.23	0.08
8.375	08/15/00	93.00	9.26	9.30	9.55	9.25	0.05
11.750	02/15/01	118.09	9.47	9.40	—	9.27	0.13
13.125	05/15/01	128.62	9.54	9.43	—	9.28	0.15
8.000	08/15/01	89.81	9.24	9.31	9.62	9.28	0.03
13.375	08/15/01	130.56	9.56	9.45	—	9.28	0.17
15.750	11/15/01	150.25	9.54	9.35	—	9.29	0.06
14.250	02/15/02	138.84	9.49	9.35	—	9.30	0.05
11.625	11/15/02	117.16	9.55	9.49	—	9.32	0.17
10.750	02/15/03	110.53	9.49	9.45	—	9.33	0.12
10.750	05/15/03	110.53	9.50	9.46	—	9.34	0.12
11.125	08/15/03	110.28	9.55	9.50	—	9.34	0.16
11.875	11/15/03	119.47	9.58	9.51	—	9.35	0.16
12.375	05/15/04	123.94	9.58	9.49	—	9.36	0.13
13.750	08/15/04	135.97	9.57	9.46	—	9.37	0.09
11.625	11/15/04*	118.75	9.47	9.44	—	9.38	0.06
8.250	05/15/05	90.59	9.30	9.36	9.52	9.39	(0.03)
12.000	05/15/05*	122.31	9.46	9.43	—	9.39	0.04
10.750	08/15/05*	111.06	9.49	9.48	—	9.40	0.08
7.625	02/15/07	85.06	9.24	9.33	9.54	9.43	(0.10)
7.875	11/15/07	87.59	9.20	9.27	9.42	9.45	(0.18)
8.375	08/15/08	91.94	9.23	9.27	9.36	9.46	(0.19)
8.750	11/15/08	95.13	9.26	9.29	9.34	9.47	(0.18)
9.125	05/15/09	98.13	9.32	9.33	9.35	9.48	(0.15)

EXHIBIT 8 *(continued)*

1	2	3	4	5	6	7	8
				Adjusted	Adjusted	Smoothed	Memo:
			Yield to	Yield to	Yield to	Par Bond	Yield
Coupon	Maturity	Price	Maturity	Maturity	Call	Yield	Misvaluation
10.375	11/15/09	108.06	9.51	9.49	9.42	9.49	(0.00)
11.750	02/15/10	119.06	9.69	9.48	9.49	9.38†	0.11
10.000	05/15/10	104.78	9.49	9.48	9.44	9.50	(0.02)
12.750	11/15/10	127.87	9.75	9.66	9.49	9.40†	0.09
13.875	05/15/11	137.91	9.80	9.68	9.47	9.41†	0.06
14.000	11/15/11	139.06	9.81	9.69	9.49	9.43†	0.06
10.375	11/14/12	107.97	9.54	9.52	9.47	9.54	(0.02)
12.000	08/15/13	122.03	9.69	9.62	9.52	9.46†	0.06
13.250	05/15/14	133.78	9.72	9.62	9.49	9.48†	0.01
12.500	08/15/14*	127.12	9.68	9.64	9.53	9.48†	0.05
11.750	11/15/14*	117.97	9.86	9.83	9.76	9.57	0.19
11.250	02/15/15*	117.97	9.43	9.40	—	9.58	(0.20)
10.625	08/15/15*	112.34	9.38	9.36	—	9.58	(0.24)
9.875	11/15/15*	106.09	9.27	9.26	—	9.59	(0.34)

* Issued after July 18, 1984.
† Price on a yield to call basis.
SOURCE: *The Wall Street Journal* and Bernstein estimates.

EXHIBIT 9   Estimation of a Corporate Yield

Par bond yield on a comparable maturity Treasury	+	Effect of [Coupon + Quality + Call + Sector]	=	Estimated fair value of corporate

---

Treasury bonds consistently with one another, column 5 of Exhibit 8 would be identical to column 7. As may be seen, it is not—the differences are listed in column 8.

Whether column 8 actually measures what it purports to measure (i.e., yield misvaluation) can be tested by examining the subsequent performance of Treasury bonds. Those bonds for which column 8 is positive (i.e., underpriced) should systematically outperform those for which column 8 is negative. We performed this test over the past three years and found consistent outperformance by the bonds identified as underpriced.

Although our particular method of yield curve smoothing is proprietary, similar estimations are available from a variety of consulting firms, such as BARRA, Capital Management Sciences, and Gifford Fong Associates.[8]

VALUING A CORPORATE BOND

The estimation of a par bond Treasury yield curve is the foundation of our analysis of corporate bonds. Since all corporate bonds are of lower quality than Treasuries and most corporates have substantially less call protection, they should offer higher yields to maturity. The estimated fair value of a corporate bond is a function of the yield on the comparable maturity par bond Treasury and the value that should be attached to those features that make a corporate bond different from a Treasury. (See Exhibit 9.)

If the estimated yield is a reasonable approximation of fair value, those bonds that appear to be cheap (offering a higher yield than fair value) should outperform bonds that are rich or fairly priced. The better our estimate of fair value, the more confidence we have in our ability to produce incremental returns.

Coupon and Quality

The valuation of the coupon effect that we use for corporate bonds is identical to the process explained above for Treasury bonds. To estimate the spread attributable to rating, we use the work of BARRA.

EXHIBIT 10   BARRA's Rating Estimates

AAA	0
AA	11
A	36
BBB	89

SOURCE: BARRA.

BARRA has developed a bond analysis model that explains the current pricing of Treasuries and corporates by a variety of factors—similar to the concept we introduced above. The difference between their work and ours is that BARRA's model finds the parameters that best fit current pricing, while we make assertions about fundamental value whenever possible.

For quality, we do not yet have a fundamental valuation, and so we use BARRA's estimates as an indication of the market's valuation. For example, as of December 31, 1985, the incremental yield that was attributed to quality—holding every other consideration constant—was as shown in Exhibit 10.

The estimates for AA, A, and BBB bonds represent the yield spreads within the corporate market over AAA bonds of the same sector. The spread for AAA bonds versus Treasuries is the "sector spread" (for a discussion see p. 1333).

BARRA's estimates are constant across maturity—i.e., both short-term and long-term bonds are assumed to sell at the same quality spread. Our analysis indicates that for higher quality ratings—AA and A—the spread increases with maturity while for BBB bonds it is flat. Thus, we have adjusted BARRA's ratings as shown in Exhibit 11.

These adjustments for quality are based upon the published ratings of Moody's and Standard & Poor's. In assigning a rating these agencies rely upon the historical operating results of a corporation, with (in our opinion) a disproportionate emphasis on recent results. While a historical perspective is valuable, we believe it is more important to understand where a corporation is headed. How strong will its financial statements be in five years?

To gain this insight, it is necessary to forecast the firm's balance sheet and income statement. From these forecasts we can calculate the critical analytical ratios such as debt service coverage and leverage. When these ratios are compared to those of the recent past, as well as to other corporations, we are able to assess the appropriateness of the current rating and the likelihood that it will be changed. If we disagree with the current rating, we use our estimate in the evaluation of the company. Furthermore, we use our assessment of the future as a qualitative overlay to the entire valuation process. All other things being

EXHIBIT 11   Adjusted Rating Estimates

Maturity	AAA	AA	A	BBB
Short	0	7	24	89
Intermediate	0	11	36	89
Long	0	15	48	89

SOURCE: BARRA and Bernstein estimates.

equal, we prefer to own an improving credit to one that is likely to be stationary.

Evaluating the Call Option

While the need to have a method for valuing call options on corporate bonds is great, few have even attempted to tackle this problem. One reason may be that the valuation models that have been developed for call options on equity securities are not applicable to bonds.

For example, most option models assume that the variability of prices is constant over time. While this may represent an acceptable simplification for the purpose of valuing options on equities, it is totally inappropriate for options on bonds. Since bonds mature at known prices (usually $100) on known dates in the future, their price variability declines with the passage of time. Moreover, since bonds shorten over time, we need to estimate the volatility of the entire yield curve, not just the interest rate of one particular maturity.

Furthermore, the common assumption that the level of interest rates is stationary is clearly false. Not only are interest rates not constant, but it is very difficult to model the distribution of interest rates. Over the 1973–1985 period, for example, the entire Treasury yield curve was higher than it had ever been prior to 1966. Thus, it is not sufficient to be concerned solely with month-to-month volatility when valuing call options. Finally, bond options are typically exercisable for long periods of time. For example, the typical 30-year utility bond has 5 years of call protection and 25 years of call exposure. Thus, existing analytical solutions that evaluate calls as if they were options exercisable on a single date (i.e., like the so-called European option) are of limited usefulness.

As a result of these problems, the call option on bonds is difficult to analyze and is frequently mispriced. We have been able to relax some of the limiting assumptions presented above and have developed a methodology for valuing call options on bonds. However, before discussing our results, it would be helpful to describe the relationship between callable and non-callable securities.

The call value is the yield premium that *should* be received for the call option in a bond. When interest rates fall, a callable bond will trade like a short-term bond until it is called. When interest rates rise, the bond's price will fall like a long-term bond—the proverbial worst of both worlds.

To illustrate the basic principles entailed in call valuation, we make three simplifying assumptions: (1) the yield curve is flat at a yield of 10.00 percent, (2) all bonds are callable at $100, and (3) there are no coupon effects.

A way to conceptualize the valuation of a callable bond is to think of it as a package—a non-callable bond plus a call option that is attached (permanently). Thus, the price of a callable bond is equal to the price of a non-callable bond minus the value of the call option. When the underlying non-callable bond is selling below the call price—i.e., when it is out of the money, the entire value of the option relates to the volatility of the bond's price and the probability that it may someday sell above the call price. When the underlying non-callable bond is selling above the call price, the option's value is only partly attributable to the bond's volatility; part of the value is a function of the degree to which the bond is in the money—i.e., the price difference between two non-callable bonds with the same coupon, one of which is priced to the call date, the other of which is priced to the maturity date.

An alternative way to express the value of the option (and one that is more in keeping with actual practice in the bond market) is to treat the callable bond as being always out of the money. For bonds priced below the call value there is no difference. However, when the price rises above the call price, the bond is considered to have a maturity equal to its call date. The relevant option is equivalent to a put option—i.e., if interest rates rise, the bond will be "put" to the bondholders by the issuer and remain outstanding beyond its call date.

To illustrate this relationship, we will use a 20-year bond that is callable in 5 years. In Exhibit 12, we have traced the price of a 20-year, 10.00 percent non-callable bond as interest rates fall from 14 percent to 6 percent. We have also plotted the price of a 5-year, 10.00 percent non-callable bond over the same range of interest rates.

What would the price of a 20-year bond that is callable in 5 years look like over the same range of interest rates?

To discover this, consider the price of a callable bond when the yields on non-callable bonds are at 10.00 percent. At this point we really don't know what we have—a 20-year bond, a 5-year bond, or something in-between. This is the area of maximum uncertainty. A bond with this uncertainty is clearly worth less than $100—the price of both the 5- and 20-year non-callable securities. To determine how much less, we need an option valuation model.

Based upon the volatility of interest rates over the four years ending in 1985, we have estimated that the option is worth $6.67. On a 20-year

EXHIBIT 12 Price/Yield Relationship for Non-Callable, 10 Percent Coupon Bond

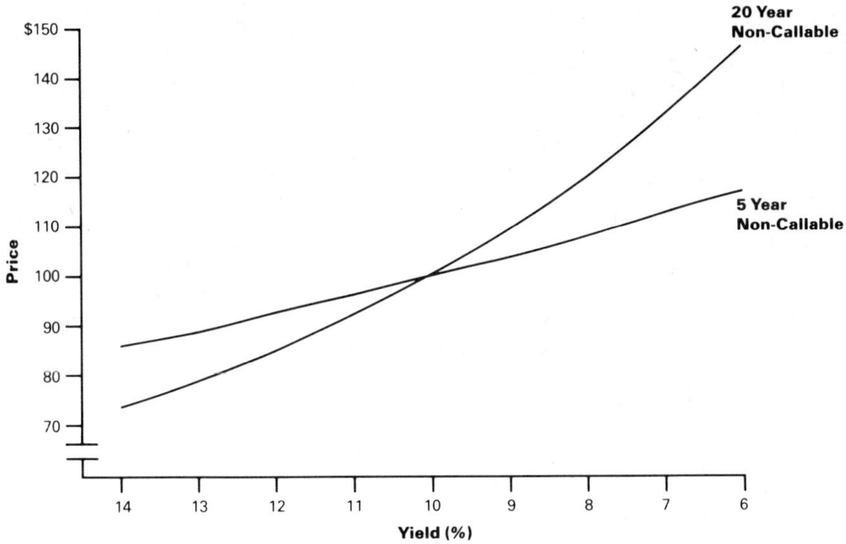

bond, $6.67 is equivalent to 82 basis points in yield to maturity. Thus, if a 10.00 percent non-callable bond sells at par, a 10.00 percent, 20-year bond that is callable in five years should sell for $93.33 to yield 10.82 percent.

How does the value of the option change when interest rates change? At low yields such as 6 percent, the bond is selling at a premium[9] and the option is far out of the money. The value of the option falls to .70 points—15 basis points in yield. The probability of a call is very high and the bond will trade to its five-year call date. But since the call is not certain—the callable bond is an imperfect substitute for the five-year bond and should trade at discount. As yields rise, the call becomes less certain and the value of the option rises. The option reaches its maximum value when the underlying non-callable bond is priced at $100. As interest rates continue to rise, the value of the option declines. At a yield of 14 percent, the option is worth 1.39 points or 28 basis points in the yield to call.

Our estimates of the value of the call option may be found in Exhibit 13.

In Exhibit 14 we have portrayed the estimated price of the callable bond versus the two non-callable bonds. The prices are derived by subtracting the dollar value of the call from the price of the relevant

EXHIBIT 13 Valuation of the Call Option

Yield on Non-Callable Bonds	Price of 10 Percent Non-Callable Bonds		Call Premium[9]		Yield on 10 Percent Callable Bond		Price of 10 Percent Callable Bond
	5-Year Maturity	20-Year Maturity	Price	Yield	To Call	To Maturity	
6%	$117.06	$146.23	$ .70	0.15%	6.15%	8.31%	$116.36
7	112.47	132.03	1.53	0.35	7.35	8.83	110.94
8	108.11	119.79	2.88	0.69	8.69	9.41	105.23
9	103.96	109.20	4.66	1.08	10.18	10.08	99.30
10	100.00	100.00	6.67	0.82	11.81	10.82	93.33
11	96.23	91.98	4.49	0.62	13.52	11.62	87.49
12	92.64	84.95	3.01	0.47	15.30	12.47	81.94
13	89.22	78.78	2.04	0.36	17.11	13.36	76.74
14	85.95	73.34	1.39	0.28	18.92	14.28	71.94

SOURCE: Bernstein estimates.

EXHIBIT 14 Effect of Callability on Price/Yield Relationship

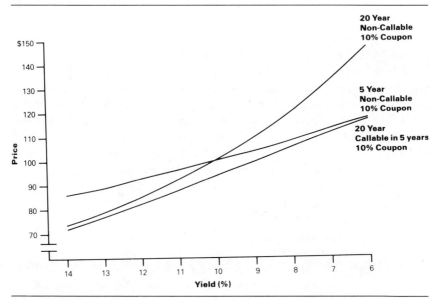

SOURCE: Bernstein estimates.

non-callable bond. For discounts, we use the 20-year bond and for premiums, the 5-year bond.[10]

The price of a callable bond is always below its non-callable counterpart. The difference is greatest at $100—where the uncertainty is greatest. At extreme prices where uncertainty is lowest, the difference is very small.

One of our findings is that the theoretical value of options for bonds that are selling around their call price has been substantially in excess of the actual premium paid in the market in recent years. For example, we estimate that the call premium on a 30-year bond that is callable in 10 years is worth 6.5 points, or approximately 70 basis points. Yet the yield spreads of AAA long-term, new-issue industrial bonds versus Treasuries averaged only 37 basis points for 1985.[11]

If the marketplace does not offer a sufficient premium for the call option on corporate bonds that are selling around par, new callable issues should be avoided. Our investments have concentrated in non-callable bonds and bonds with a very large premium or discount—i.e., bonds with very little option value.

But this is only one element of the valuation process, and before we can make the final decision on relative valuation, we need to consider the remaining components of value.

Sector Analysis

Since corporate bonds are of lower quality than Treasuries and generally have greater call exposure, it is logical to assume that the spreads between corporates and Treasuries should be dependent upon the market's evaluation of their quality and of the call option. The general perception of quality should be related to the current and prospective financial condition of the specific industry. The call value of bonds should be a function of expected volatility and the current level of interest rates.

In order to determine where spreads should be at any point in time, we performed a regression analysis of spreads from 1970 to 1985 that sought to explain yield spreads versus Treasuries on the basis of industry-specific and general economic variables as well as market conditions—i.e., interest rate volatility and the yield curve slope. The sectors studied were intermediate- and long-term agency, utility, and industrial bonds.

By way of example, Exhibit 15 presents our analysis of the spread between newly issued AA utilities and 30-year Treasuries. The spread is a composite of rating, call protection, and sector. Since we already have an estimate of the market's pricing of rating (from BARRA) and the theoretical value of the call option, the residual is the pure sector spread.

To see how each of these components has varied over time, we have

EXHIBIT 15 Decomposition of Sector Spread—Long AA Utilities versus Treasuries (basis points)

SCB Spread Estimate	Rating	Call	Pure Sector Estimate
99	15	69	15

SOURCE: BARRA and Bernstein estimates.

decomposed our long-term utility sector spread from 1979 to 1985, as shown in Exhibit 16.

BRINGING IT ALL TOGETHER

Having separately analyzed each of the factors that influence a bond's price, evaluating an actual bond is a relatively straightforward process. To illustrate, consider an 8 percent, 17.5-year, AA utility, callable in two years at $104 and selling at $82.06 to yield 10.25 percent. The starting point is the 17.5-year yield from the par bond yield curve (Exhibit 8)— 9.34 percent. This base yield is then adjusted for the specific characteristics of the bond. Exhibit 17 displays the estimates for each component.

When the components of value are added to the yield on a comparable maturity Treasury, we would expect a yield of 9.93 percent. The yield on our hypothetical bond is 10.25 percent. In terms of yield misvaluation, the bond is attractive by 32 basis points.

The other way to quantify misvaluation is to look at the actual and predicted price. A yield of 9.93 percent is equivalent to a price of $84.31, which is 2.74 percent higher than the actual price of $82.06, as shown in Exhibit 18.

EXHIBIT 16 Historical Long-Term Utility Spread Analysis (basis points)

1	2	3	4	5 (2 + 3 + 4)	6
		Components			
Date	AA Rating	Call	Sector	Composite	Memo: Actual Spread
12/31/79	20	63	40	123	172
12/31/80	40	106	39	185	259
12/31/81	39	125	116	280	299
12/31/82	29	110	50	189	196
12/31/83	25	93	53	171	114
12/31/84	16	71	22	109	81
12/31/85	15	69	15	99	112

SOURCE: BARRA, Salomon Brothers, and Bernstein estimates.

EXHIBIT 17   Composition of a Predicted Corporate Yield

1 Comparable Treasury Yield	2	3	4	5	6 (1 + 2 + 3 + 4 + 5) Predicted Yield
	Coupon	Rating	Call	Sector	
9.34%	−.11%	.15%	.40%	.15%	9.93%

SOURCE: BARRA and Bernstein estimates.

In this analysis, we used the 17.5-year par bond Treasury yield to derive the spread. This methodology differs from industry practice where the yield on a bond is compared to the nearest on-the-run Treasury. If the yield curve is sloped (positively or negatively) or if there are anomalies in the pricing of the on-the-run issue, it is difficult to evaluate a broad range of maturities on a consistent basis. This problem is avoided by utilizing a smoothed par bond Treasury yield curve.

The yield and price misvaluations illustrated above are the synthesis of five separate valuation analyses—yield curve, quality, sector, coupon, and call. It is, of course, true that the quality of the valuation process is only as good as the quality of its parts. If one or more of the valuation techniques is faulty, the usefulness of the summary estimate is reduced. However, we believe that even if the estimates are not perfect, the fact that rigorous, logical valuation methodologies are applied *consistently* over a wide base of securities allows for the identification of anomalies and the generation of incremental returns. Furthermore, we establish high misvaluation hurdles that increase our confidence that we have uncovered a truly mispriced security.

EVALUATING COMPLEX SECURITIES

In the analysis presented thus far the yield on a bond and its spread versus Treasuries are taken as given, and the challenge is to evaluate the adequacy of that spread. However, there are a variety of securities on

EXHIBIT 18   Quantifying the Measuring Degree of Misvaluation

1 Predicted Yield	2 Actual Yield	3 Yield Misvaluation	4 Predicted Price	5 Actual Price	6 [(4 − 5)/4] Percentage Price Misvaluation
9.93%	10.25%	.32%	$84.31	$82.06	2.74%

SOURCE: Bernstein estimates.

which the yield cannot be naively calculated, and, therefore, the spread versus Treasuries is not readily apparent. An example of this type of bond is a mortgage pass-through security.

Mortgage Pass-Throughs

A mortgage pass-through security is formed by accumulating individual mortgages into a single pool. The cash flow from the security consists of the *scheduled* principal and interest payments (less the servicing fee) plus any unscheduled prepayments of principal that occur when borrowers move, refinance, or are foreclosed upon. Since the pattern of unscheduled prepayments cannot be known in advance, the cash flow stream of a pass-through security is uncertain and its yield can only be estimated.

Since a mortgage may be prepaid at any time, a pass-through security is, essentially, callable immediately. Naturally, the level of interest rates influences the speed at which these calls take place, but so do a host of other things. When people move, they usually pay off their existing mortgage even if its rate is below prevailing mortgage rates—a seemingly irrational exercise of the call option. Conversely, when interest rates fall substantially, many homeowners do not refinance—likewise an irrational failure to exercise their option.[12]

To model the rate of prepayment on pass-throughs, we measured the historical effect of the following variables upon early mortgage retirements:

1. The difference between the rate on the underlying mortgages and current mortgage rates.
2. The number of years the mortgages have been outstanding.
3. The course of interest rates over the time the mortgages have been outstanding.

The output is an expected prepayment rate over the remaining life of the mortgage. This calculation generates an expected cash flow stream which, in turn, permits us to calculate the yield on a pass-through.

This cash flow yield is useful for understanding how the market is pricing pass-throughs relative to each other and relative to the past. However, it overestimates expected return. As interest rates vary, prepayments occur in a way that is disadvantageous to the holder of a pass-through—i.e., prepayments are high at low interest rates and low at high interest rates.

To calculate a more accurate yield for a pass-through, we break up the remaining life of the pass-through into discrete intervals. At the end of each interval, we construct a distribution of mortgage financing rates based on our estimate of future interest rate volatility. It is important to note that we are not asserting a future course of interest rates, merely that they will vary from where they are now. For each point in the distribution we compute the expected prepayment rate and, from that, the expected cash flow.

We then find the starting discount rate which equates the present value of these cash flows with the price of the security. We call this discount rate the *stochastic yield*. If we assume that interest rate volatility will be zero—i.e., that interest rates will never change—the stochastic yield is equal to the cash flow yield. However, the stochastic yield for higher volatilities is typically much lower than the cash flow yield.

We measure the duration of a pass-through as the effect of a change in the stochastic yield on price. The spread on a mortgage pass-through is then computed by comparing the stochastic yield to the par bond Treasury with the same duration.

For example, on December 31, 1985, the price of a 13 percent GNMA was $108.125. Using our model's forecast for prepayments of 2.3 percent monthly, the nonstochastic yield on this security was 9.89 percent. The stochastic yield was 8.29 percent (160 basis points lower!), and its stochastic duration was 1.4 years. A 1-year, 6-month Treasury note also had a duration of 1.4 years, and our par bond yield curve (as may be seen in Exhibit 8) at that maturity was 7.74 percent. Therefore, we considered the stochastic yield spread on 13 percent GNMAs to be 55 basis points.

Once the stochastic yield and yield spread of a pass-through are derived, the analysis of this yield spread is conceptually identical to the one presented above for corporate bonds. We compare the actual yield spread to the predicted yield spread as a measure of misvaluation. This permits us to make relative valuation judgments not only among various mortgage pass-throughs but also between pass-throughs and other debt instruments in the market.

Financial Futures

Since their introduction in 1975, financial futures have become a prominent feature of the financial landscape. They have grown so vigorously that the average trading volume in Treasury bond contracts alone now amounts to a value that is more than two and one-half times that of the *combined* trading of all issues listed on the New York Stock Exchange. Yet despite this success, most of the trading in futures is related to the hedging of dealer inventory and speculation. In a recent survey by Greenwich Research, only 9 percent of the pension plan sponsors surveyed were using futures.

The virtual absence of futures in institutional portfolio management is attributable to the considerable valuation, legal, and administrative hurdles that must be cleared. Since the legal and administrative problems represent a paper unto themselves, we shall limit our comments to the valuation issues.

A future is not an actual security but a commitment to purchase or sell a security at a specific time in the future at the equivalent of the price on the day the commitment was made. Therefore, the valuation of a future focuses principally upon the relationship of the future's price to the price of the Treasury security that is likely to be delivered. The difference between these two prices is called the basis.

The bond selected for delivery will be the one that maximizes the profit (or minimizes the loss) to the deliverer. In a flat yield curve environment, the cheapest-to-deliver bond is the bond that has the lowest market price relative to its delivery value. If its market price is higher than the delivery value, the future is cheap. Then buying the future as a substitute for the actual security should lead to incremental returns.

An important caveat to this strategy is that the cheapest-to-deliver security can change as interest rates vary. For example, on December 31, 1986, the cheapest-to-deliver Treasury notes were the 11.25 percent due May 15, 1995. The basis on these notes after incorporating the shape of the yield curve and price of the security was −0.67 percent—i.e., the delivery value of the future for March delivery was .67 percent below the market price of the 11.25 percent notes.[13] The next cheapest notes were the 10.50 percent due August 15, 1995, for which the basis was −0.70 percent. Because the relationships of these two notes to the future are so similar, the future's price is likely to track the *poorer* performing of these two bonds. Since this possibility reduces the attractiveness of futures as a substitute, it should be offset by demanding a wider initial basis.

The primary use of financial futures has been to hedge inventory. Thus, the natural participants in the market have been sellers, and buyers have had to be *induced* to trade in the futures market. For this reason, futures have historically been cheap. Therefore, a strategy that uses the futures as a substitute for actual securities has consistently added return. However, there have been extended periods of time where the basis was positive. If the basis is positive, it may be possible to add value by selling a bond or note future.

When we purchase the cheapest-to-deliver bond and sell the future, we have effectively sold that bond for forward delivery in the futures market. Since the purchase and sales prices are fixed as well as the income (the current yield on the bond), its minimum return can be calculated. It is, in essence, a synthetic short-term security. If the return on this instrument is higher than comparable maturity securities, the future is overpriced. In this event, the creation of a synthetic short-term security is more attractive than the purchase of actual short-term securities.

It is important to note that the calculated return on a synthetic securitiy is its *minimum* return. If another bond becomes cheaper to deliver, the bond that is held as part of the synthetic security will outperform the future. As a result, the return on the synthetic security will exceed the original estimate. Thus, by valuing the future's basis, we can determine if it is useful in augmenting our portfolio's rate of return. While there are more complexities to this analysis than space permits, the discussion above captures the key components of the valuation process.[14]

CMOs, Swaps, FRNs . . . ?

In addition to conventional pass-throughs and futures, there are a number of recent innovations, such as collateralized mortgage obligations, puttable bonds, floating-rate notes, inverse floaters, interest rate swaps, caps, and collars. The common theme of these instruments is that their cash flows depend upon the future course of interest rates. Therefore, as with mortgage securities, it is necessary to calculate their stochastic yields. While it is beyond the scope of this chapter to show how each of these instruments might be valued, they highlight the need for rigorous research to identify areas of opportunity. We believe that new and complex instruments are especially apt to be mispriced because they are less well understood by the market. Some of these instruments have offered substantial opportunities, while others have tended to be vastly overvalued by the market.

PART TWO—PORTFOLIO CONSTRUCTION

It is not sufficient to identify undervalued bonds. We must construct portfolios that translate this knowledge into incremental returns. While added return is the primary goal of active bond management, the client's other objectives must be considered as well. Most of our clients use bonds to reduce the risk of their overall portfolio, and they want their fixed-income portfolios to exhibit less year-to-year variability than their equity portfolios. It is important that the clients and their manager make explicit the level of risk that is desired and the amount of variation around this target that is acceptable. We have found that the easiest way to make these objectives tangible is through the selection of a published index as a benchmark for the portfolio.

These indexes' past returns can be reviewed so the plan sponsor can see the distribution of returns that can realistically be expected. The most important factor is the index's interest rate sensitivity—i.e., its duration. A portfolio with a high duration will be more sensitive to swings in interest rates and, therefore, more volatile, than an index with a low duration.

Once a benchmark has been chosen, the client has something to measure our returns against. Our goal is unambiguous—to outperform the benchmark. In addition, while we cannot be expected to outperform every quarter, our return should never deviate too greatly from that of the benchmark. If it does, it indicates that we are permitting the duration of the portfolio to vary too far from the benchmark.

We use the duration of the index as our neutral target. If we think interest rates will decline, we position the duration of our portfolios somewhat longer than that of the index. Since we want to limit the influence of interest rate betting on our returns, we constrain the amount of variance in duration from our benchmark. In almost all circumstances, we will be within a year of our benchmark.

We have used the term *duration* several times already. This is because it is an invaluable measure of interest rate sensitivity. Even if you choose not to bet on interest rates—in fact, *especially* if you decide not to bet on interest rates—it is essential to know how interest rates will affect your portfolio.

DURATION

Duration measures the weighted average life of the cash flows from a fixed-income security—discounting those cash flows by the interest rate on the instrument. The value of the duration statistic is that it provides an excellent measure of the interest rate risk of individual securities and of portfolios. For this reason, it has supplanted the use of average maturity—which is a very poor measure of interest rate risk—in the lexicon of bond managers.

For zero-coupon securities, the calculation of duration is straightforward. Since all of the cash flow is received at maturity, its duration is its maturity. Furthermore, as may be seen in Exhibit 19, when interest rates change, the percentage change in the price of a zero-coupon bond is approximately equal to its duration times the interest rate change. (A

EXHIBIT 19 The Price Sensitivity of Zero-Coupon Bonds

1 Maturity	2 Price at a 10 Percent Yield	3 Price at a 9 Percent Yield	4 Percentage Change in Price
1	$90.703	$91.573	.96%
2	82.270	83.856	1.93
3	74.622	76.790	2.90
5	61.391	64.393	4.89
10	37.689	41.464	10.01
20	14.205	17.193	21.04

EXHIBIT 20 Source of Present Value of a Two-Year 10 Percent Bond

.5	1	1.5	2.0	Present Value
Cash Flow				
$5.00				$ 4.76
	$5.00			4.54
		$5.00		4.32
			$105.00	86.38
$5.00	$5.00	$5.00	$105.00	$100.00

Maturity (Years)

mathematical explanation of why this is true is presented in the Appendix.)

To understand the calculation of duration for a bond with semiannual coupon payments, it is helpful to think of a bond as a combination of several zero-coupon bonds—i.e., to treat each coupon payment as a separate instrument. Thus, a two-year bond can be thought of as the combination of four zero-coupon bonds. The durations of these four bonds are 0.5, 1.0, 1.5, and 2.0 years, respectively. (See Exhibit 20.)

How do we meld these four durations to calculate the duration of the two-year instrument? We do this by weighting them according to their importance to the combined value of the bond—i.e., the percentage they represent of the total present value. Exhibit 21 calculates the duration of the bond by weighting each component of present value by its maturity.

Since duration and maturity are identical for zero coupons, the weighted average maturity of the cash flows is the bond's duration. Thus, the duration of a bond is the weighted average maturity of all of the cash flows, where the cash flows are weighted by their contribution

EXHIBIT 21 Calculation of Duration for a Two-Year 10 Percent Bond

1	2	3	4 (1 × 3)
Maturity	Present Value	Weighting = Present Value/ Price ($100)	Duration (Weighted Maturity)
.5	$ 4.76	.0476	.0238
1.0	4.54	.0454	.0454
1.5	4.32	.0432	.0648
2.0	86.38	.8638	1.7276
	$100.00		1.8616

EXHIBIT 22 Portfolio Duration Calculation

1	2	3	4
			(2 × 3)
Maturity	*Duration*	*Weighting*	*Weighted Duration*
1	.98	25.0%	.25
5	4.05	25.0	1.01
10	6.54	25.0	1.64
20	9.01	25.0	2.25
		100.0%	5.15

---

to the bond's value. In the example presented in Exhibit 21, the duration is 1.86 years. This duration value is called Macaulay's duration, after the economist who first defined this relationship in 1938.[15]

The duration of a portfolio is simply a weighted average of the duration of the individual bonds. (See Exhibit 22.)

The reason we use duration as the cornerstone of an investment program is that it is a reasonably accurate measure of the volatility of the portfolio. However, if duration is calculated by using the stated maturity of a bond, it can seriously overstate the risk of bonds that have call exposure.

The "true" duration of a callable bond lies somewhere between its duration to call and its duration to maturity. To illustrate this point, Exhibit 14 traces the price/yield relationship of callable and non-callable bonds.

Since duration is a measure of interest rate risk, the longer the duration of a bond, the steeper is the slope of its price/yield line—i.e., the greater the change in price for a given change in yields. In fact, the slope of the price/yield line is the duration of the bond.

One interesting feature that may be observed in Exhibit 14 is that the price/yield lines for both the 5- and the 20-year bonds curves upward from the lower left to the upper right—i.e., they are convex. This means that as yields fall, the successive changes in the value of the bond increase. This accentuates the rise in price when rates fall and cushions the fall in price when rates rise—i.e., convexity is a good thing, and all other things being equal, more is better than less.

However, if we observe the price/yield line of the callable bond, it does not curve upward—it actually curves down slightly. This is negative convexity.[16] As yields fall, its price rise diverges from the 20-year line and starts to approach the price/yield line of the 5-year bond. As yields fall, the value of the call option rises, and this offsets the rise in price of the underlying non-callable bond. As a result, the slope of the callable bond's price/yield line is flatter than the slope of the 20-year non-callable bond. In other words, the duration of a callable

EXHIBIT 23 Effect of Callability on Duration

Yield to Maturity on a Non-Callable Bond	Duration of a Non-Callable Bond with a 10 Percent Coupon		Duration of 20-Year Bond with a 10 Percent Coupon Callable in 5 Years
	5-Year Maturity	20-Year Maturity	
6%	4.14	10.77	4.60
7	4.12	10.32	5.13
8	4.10	9.87	5.71
9	4.07	9.43	6.27
10	4.05	9.01	6.64
11	4.03	8.60	6.93
12	4.01	8.20	7.04
13	3.99	7.83	7.03
14	3.97	7.47	6.96

SOURCE: Bernstein estimates

bond is always less than its duration to maturity. As rates continue to fall, this difference increases, and the duration of the callable bond approaches its duration to call.

To measure the duration of a callable bond we need to calculate the change in price for a small change in interest rates. The formula is:

$$\frac{\text{Percentage change in price}}{\text{Change in yield}} \times \left(1 + \frac{\text{Yield}}{2}\right) = \text{Duration}^{17}$$

The changing relationship of the duration of a callable bond to the duration of its underlying components may be seen in Exhibit 23.

When priced as a deep discount, the duration of a callable bond is nearly as long as a non-callable bond of equal maturity. As shown in Exhibit 24, as yields decline, the duration falls toward the duration of a non-callable bond maturing on its call date. This transformation is fairly smooth with a slight acceleration around par.

Thus, the duration estimate of a callable bond is not stable but changes as interest rates change. For example, as rates fall from 10 percent to 9 percent, the duration of our hypothetical bond falls from 6.64 to 6.27. If a specific duration target has been set for the portfolio, a change in duration of this degree will require some rebalancing.

The sensitivity of the duration statistic depends upon the relationship of the actual price to the call price. The closer these prices are, the greater is the instability of the duration estimate. However, it also depends upon the amount of time remaining until the bond is callable. For example, if a 20-year bond is callable in one year, its duration changes dramatically as its price approaches its call price.

EXHIBIT 24 Effect of Yield Changes on Duration: Callable versus Non-Callable Bonds

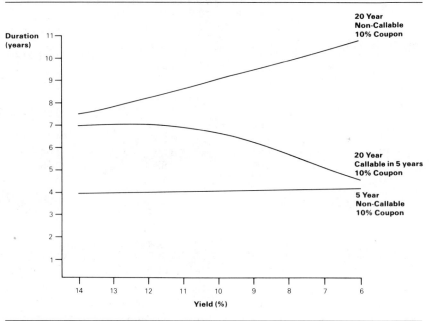

SOURCE: Bernstein estimates.

As may be seen in Exhibits 25 and 26, when yields fall from 10 percent to 9 percent, the duration declines from 5.86 to 4.63 years—over three times the decline that occurred for the bond callable in five years.

The durations of all bonds (other than zero coupons) vary as interest rates change. The durations of non-callable bonds vary inversely with interest rates. Callable bonds' durations vary positively with interest rates except when they fall far out of the money—i.e., except when they become deep discounts or high premiums.

Finally, as the time remaining to the first call diminishes, the sensitivity of a callable bond's duration to interest rate changes increases markedly. Managers must be cognizant of how changes in interest rates alter the interest rate sensitivity of their portfolios and be prepared to alter their mix of securities accordingly.

SETTING A DURATION TARGET

As we discussed above, the focal point of the portfolio management process should be a benchmark portfolio, and the most suitable candidates for this role are the major bond indexes. However, the durations of these indexes cover the full maturity spectrum—from short term to

EXHIBIT 25 Effect of Callability on Duration

Yield to Maturity on a Non-Callable Bond (percent)	Duration of a Non-Callable Bond with a 10 Percent Coupon		Duration of 20-Year Bond with a 10 Percent Coupon Callable in 1 Year
	1-Year Maturity	20-Year Maturity	
6	.98	10.77	1.01
7	.98	10.32	1.47
8	.98	9.87	2.99
9	.98	9.43	4.63
10	.98	9.01	5.86
11	.98	8.60	6.51
12	.98	8.20	6.78
13	.98	7.83	6.84
14	.98	7.47	6.78

SOURCE: Bernstein estimates.

EXHIBIT 26 Effect of Yield Changes on Duration: Callable versus Non-Callable Bonds

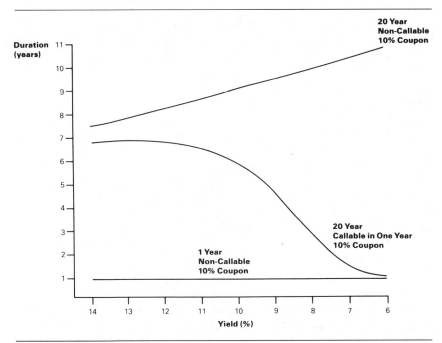

SOURCE: Bernstein estimates.

long term. Which one should be used? The answer depends upon the goals of the client.

We believe that most investors choose bonds to mute the volatility of their total portfolio—to act as an anchor to the windward. Therefore, the bond portfolio should have a modest level of volatility relative to equities. Since most of a bond portfolio's volatility is due to changes in interest rates, setting a duration target is essentially a question of identifying an acceptable level of exposure to interest rate changes.

Unfortunately, it is not possible to know for sure just how much exposure there is at any given duration target. To be sure, we know how much price risk there is for any given change in interest rates. The problem is, we are uncertain about the future volatility of interest rates. There is no central tendency of interest rates. Rather, they depend upon the Federal Reserve's response to current and expected economic conditions. Moreover, the volatility of interest rates has increased dramatically with the deregulation of the financial markets and shifts in the operating philosophy of the Federal Reserve. It may increase further in future years—or it may decline. As a result, the possible range of interest rates is quite wide, and the probability that interest rates will reach toward the extremes of this range is far higher than would be suggested by a normal distribution. Therefore, the risk of a bond portfolio cannot be precisely defined, and the choice of an optimal duration level for bonds is more of an ad hoc judgment based upon some practical considerations.

For example, if the duration target is very short—i.e., one year—an active bond manager will be precluded from participating in any meaningful way in the intermediate- or long-term markets that are so often rich in misvaluation. By contrast, a long-term target will result in highly volatile returns. An alternative target that offers maximum flexibility is to use the duration of the market itself—4.9 years as of December 31, 1985, as measured by the Shearson Lehman Aggregate Index. Not only does this target afford the active manager the full maturity range of securities, it has the desirable property of yielding a high probability of positive annual returns.

Since the inception of the Shearson Lehman Aggregate Index in 1976, there have been 109 overlapping 12-month periods. The rate of return on the index was positive in 97, or 89 percent, of these periods. Since this is consistent with what most of our clients are interested in achieving with their bond portfolios, it is appropriate to adopt the duration of the index as a target duration.

However, there is a problem with using the published duration of the index as a target. Because its duration is calculated on the basis of maturity, its true duration is overstated. This stems from the fact that mortgage backed securities and corporate bonds (most of which are callable) represent 38 percent of the index (as of December 31, 1985). We estimate that the overstatement is currently 0.8 years and that the true duration is more on the order of 4.1 years.[18]

Once a duration target is selected, there is an additional question: Should we alter this target to incorporate our interest rate forecast? The answer depends upon our confidence in our forecast and the goals we are trying to achieve with the bond portfolio.

While it is relatively easy to have an opinion on interest rates, it is quite difficult to accurately forecast rates on a consistent basis. Not only is it difficult to forecast interest rates but it is also dangerous. Unfettered interest rate betting will often call for positioning the entire portfolio in long-term bonds. Yet in 8 out of the past 26 years, the returns on long-term Treasury bonds have been negative—a result that is inconsistent with the risk reduction role that most clients seek from bonds.

We believe that a portfolio manager has two acceptable courses of action—to avoid interest rate betting altogether or to severely limit its scope. If a portfolio manager does not believe he can forecast the future course of interest rates, then he should maintain the duration of his portfolio at the duration of the appropriate index. If a manager feels that over time his forecast can add value, then he should alter the duration of his portfolio. However, to prevent these interest rate bets from dominating the portfolio's return, the duration should be maintained within a narrow band around the index's duration. By restricting the potential shifts in duration, interest rate betting becomes simply another component in the portfolio management process.

MAXIMIZING MISVALUATION IN PORTFOLIO CONSTRUCTION

The valuation process described in Part One estimates the yield misvaluation and the percentage price misvaluation of a bond. How do we use this information to construct a portfolio? How do we determine the sector distribution of Treasuries, agencies, mortgages, and corporates?

In deriving the sector distribution, a simple percentage delineation is inadequate. For example, knowing that we have 20 percent of our portfolios in agencies does not tell us how our portfolios will fare if the pricing of agencies changes relative to the rest of the market. Why not?

A percentage breakdown of a portfolio ignores the importance of the duration of that sector to the duration of the portfolio. We are interested in identifying those sectors of the market that will earn incremental returns vis-à-vis the market. In this context, if a 20 percent agency position is invested in very short maturities, a change in relative yield spreads will not materially influence returns. If, on the other hand, the 20 percent position is in long-term agencies, a change in yield spreads will have a significant impact on return.

EXHIBIT 27 Derivation of Market Exposure

1	2	3	4	5 (3 × 4)	6
Sector	Market Value* (Billions)	Distribution	Call Adjusted Duration (Years)	Weighted Duration	Contribution to Portfolio Duration
Treasuries	$ 818	49%	4.35	2.13	52%
Agencies	171	10	3.35	.34	8
Mortgages	307	19	3.00	.57	14
Corporates	316	19	5.00	.95	24
Yankees	46	2	4.65	.09	2
	$1,658	100%		4.08	100%

* As of December 31, 1985.
SOURCE: Shearson Lehman Brothers and Bernstein estimates.

The greater the duration of an agency position, the greater will be the impact on the market value of a portfolio from a change in yields relative to the rest of the market. Consequently, the *exposure* to a sector is a combined function of the percentage invested as well as the average duration of the sector.

To illustrate, we have calculated the sector distribution and exposure of the Shearson Lehman Aggregate Index in Exhibit 27.

We can see from column 3 that agencies make up 10 percent of the market value of the index. However, the average duration of the agency component is 3.35 years—substantially shorter than the 4.08-year average of the entire index. Since agencies are 10 percent of the total, they contribute .34 years (3.35 × 10%) of duration to the index, which is 8 percent (.34/4.08) of the total duration. Corporates, on the other hand, have a long duration relative to the market and, therefore, represent 24 percent of the duration of the index even though they constitute only 19 percent of the index's value. Thus, a "market" weighting of corporates, from a portfolio management standpoint, would be the percentage that contributes 24 percent of the portfolio's duration. Depending on the maturities and callability of the corporates actually purchased, this could entail placing considerably more or less than 19 percent of the portfolio in corporate securities.

This same principle applies to coupon strategies, to decisions regarding the optimal maturity mix, to virtually all portfolio decisions. The impact that any projected shift in the market will have upon a portfolio depends upon how important the duration of the securities in question is to the duration of the total portfolio.

EXHIBIT 28 Comparable Risk Portfolio

1 Composition	2 Maturity	3 Duration (Years)	4 Weighting	5 Price Misvaluation	6 (4 × 5) Weighted Price Misvaluation
Single maturity	Intermediate	4	100%	4.0%	4.0%
Laddered	Short	1	33%	1.0%	0.3%
	Intermediate	4	33	4.0	1.3
	Long	7	33	7.0	2.3
			100%		4.0%
Barbelled	Short	1	50%	1.0%	0.5%
	Long	7	50	7.0	3.5
			100%		4.0%

Yield Misvaluation versus Price Misvaluation

When we construct a portfolio, our objective is to maximize expected return. To obtain this result, we should construct the portfolio that maximizes misvaluation. One way to do this is to rank bonds by percentage price misvaluation and select securities in descending order. The problem with this approach is that it results in a preponderance of long-term bonds. Why?

Since long-term bonds have long durations, for a given level of yield misvaluation they will have the largest percentage price misvaluation. (Duration times yield misvaluation is equal to price misvaluation.) Therefore, long-term bonds will *appear* to be the most attractive and will dominate the selection process.

A second way to maximize misvaluation is to rank bonds by yield misvaluation and to select in descending order. The advantage of this approach is that it is not biased to any maturity and is straightforward to implement.

To illustrate the difference between these two selection methods, let's assume that we have three groups of bonds—short, intermediate, and long term—with the *same* yield misvaluation—100 basis points. (See Exhibit 28.)

If our target portfolio duration is 4.0, then every combination of maturities that has a duration of 4.0 will have the same percentage price misvaluation—4 percent. Why?

Since each of the bonds has the same yield misvaluation, they are equally attractive. Any combination of these bonds will have an average yield misvaluation of 100 basis points. Therefore, any portfolio with a

EXHIBIT 29   Securities with Unequal Yield Misvaluation

1	2	3	4 (2 × 3)
Maturity	Duration	Yield Misvaluation (Basis Points)	Price Misvaluation
Short	1.0	90	0.9%
Intermediate	4.0	100	4.0
Long	7.0	90	6.3

duration of 4.0 will have a price misvaluation of 4 percent and be equally attractive.

The choice between these two methods of ranking misvaluation can be seen more clearly if we assume unequal yield misvaluation as in Exhibit 29.

Which security or combination of maturities is the most attractive? If we use percentage price misvaluation, we would pick the long bond and then add sufficient short-term bonds to hit the duration target. If we look at yield misvaluation, we would choose the intermediate alone. To determine which is more attractive, we have repeated the format of Exhibit 28 in Exhibit 30.

As may be seen, the long and the short bonds have lower yield misvaluations than the intermediate bonds. As a result, any combination of these bonds with any other maturity is not as attractive as a single intermediate maturity. Thus, the most attractive security is the one with the greatest yield misvaluation. The portfolio construction process is one of maximizing the investment in the most attractive bonds while maintaining the target duration.

Controlling Exposure

In the hypothetical case of a perfectly priced bond market, we would invest our entire portfolio in Treasuries. The coupon and maturity structure would be roughly in line with the market. As misvaluations are identified, we replace the Treasury with the maximum percentage that we can invest in the cheap bond. There are several considerations. First, prudence requires diversification limits on the maximum investment in any one company or industry. In addition, all misvaluations are not created equal. We are not indifferent to the choice between a corporate and a Treasury that are equally misvalued.

To establish our corporate weighting rules, we asked the following question: At what level of misvaluation are we interested in holding?

EXHIBIT 30 Effect of Unequal Yield Misvaluations on Comparable Risk Portfolios

1	2	3	4	5	6 (4 × 5)
Composition	Maturity	Duration	Weighting	Price Misvaluation	Weighted Price Misvaluation
Single	Intermediate	4	100%	4.0%	4.0%
Ladder	Short	1	33%	0.9%	0.3%
	Intermediate	4	33	4.0	1.3
	Long	7	33	6.3	2.1
			100%		3.7%
Barbell	Short	1	50%	0.9%	0.4%
	Long	7	50	6.3	3.2
			100%		3.6%

EXHIBIT 31 Corporate Exposure Schedule

Yield Misvaluation (Basic Points)	Contribution to Portfolio Duration
20	0%
28	10
36	20
45	30
60	40
80	50
100	60
120	70
145	80
170	90
200	100

1. A market weighting (24 percent exposure from Exhibit 27).
2. One hundred percent in corporates.
3. No corporates at all.

Exhibit 31 shows the schedule we have adopted.

At misvaluations of 20 basis points or lower we do not want to own any corporates—we can routinely buy Treasuries that are 10 to 20 basis points cheap. Furthermore, at this distortion level, we are vastly more certain that Treasuries are mispriced than we are that corporates are mispriced.

At the opposite end of the spectrum is the yield misvaluation that would induce us to invest 100 percent of a portfolio in corporates. The number that we chose was 200 basis points. Since this is extreme by historical standards, we do not expect to be fully invested in corporates except under very unusual circumstances. Finally, we require a misvaluation of at least 40 basis points to reach an approximate market weighting of 25 percent.

Once the corporate exposure schedule has been established, an iterative portfolio construction process is triggered. To illustrate the process, we will make the following assumptions:

1. The portfolio is initially 100 percent in cash.
2. The bonds listed in Exhibit 32 are the most undervalued securities that are available and approved.
3. The target duration is four years.

From Exhibit 31 we know how much yield misvaluation we need to support a given level of corporate exposure. As we add corporates, the yield misvaluation that is available drops, and, therefore, our desired

EXHIBIT 32 Determination of Corporate Exposure—Target Duration of Four Years

	1		2	3	4	5	6	7
	Description		Yield Misvaluation	Weight	Duration	Weighted Duration	Contribution to Portfolio Duration	Cumulative Contribution to Portfolio Duration
Armco Steel	8½%	9/1/01	281	.05	7.1	.36	8.9%	8.9%
Public Service of Indiana	7⅝	1/1/07	149	.05	7.4	.37	9.3	18.2
Chrysler	12¾	3/1/92	109	.05	4.5	.23	5.6	23.8
Philip Morris	6	1/1/99	95	.05	7.3	.37	9.1	32.9
GMAC	11	4/1/88	86	.05	2.1	.11	2.6	35.5
NCNB	8⅜	3/1/99	61	.03	6.3	.19	4.7	40.2
Chemical	8¼	8/1/02	54	—	7.1	—	—	—
Household Finance	7¼	1/1/90	50	—	3.0	—	—	—

SOURCE: Bernstein estimates.

EXHIBIT 33 Non-Treasury Exposure Schedule

	Yield Misvaluation		Cumulative Contribution to
Agencies	Mortgages	Corporates	Portfolio Duration
10	15	20	0%
18	21	28	10
28	27	36	20
40	34	45	30
58	45	60	40
80	60	80	50
N/A	75	100	60
N/A	90	120	70
N/A	105	145	80
N/A	120	170	90
N/A	135	200	100

---

exposure drops. At some point, we are not interested in owning any more corporates.

This point is reached in Exhibit 32 with the addition of NCNB, which is misvalued by 61 basis points and raises the exposure to 40 percent. To add more bonds, we need more than 60 basis points misvaluation. Since Chemical's misvaluation is only 54 basis points, the process ends. Generally, we will hold these bonds in this portfolio until the yield misvaluation on any one of them falls to zero. If another corporate bond becomes available with a yield misvaluation of more than 60 basis points, we will buy it.

We utilize the same methodology for agencies and mortgages. However, as may be seen in Exhibit 33, the amount of yield misvaluation we require for similar degrees of exposure varies from sector to sector.

The difference in scaling between sectors reflects our confidence in our ability to identify misvaluations. The agency sector tops out at 50 percent exposure because there are only three agencies and they are not guaranteed by the federal government. With mortgages and corporates, there is far greater diversification potential, and we are willing to invest 100 percent in a sector if there are extremely large opportunities.

CONCLUSION

The goals of an active bond portfolio management process should be to maximize performance while, at the same time, maintaining a low level of volatility relative to equities. One way (we would argue, the best way) to achieve these goals on a consistent basis is to pursue a bond-analytical approach—an approach that seeks to identify the *fair* value of a bond. The value of a bond is a function of its coupon, maturity, quality, and call exposure. To properly evaluate a bond, the value of each of these components must be estimated. We have outlined some solutions to these analytical problems and hope that our work will stimulate further research in this area.

The volatility of a portfolio should be controlled by constraining the duration of a portfolio to a narrow band around an appropriate index. While more dramatic interest rate betting *may* produce higher returns, it is more likely to introduce an unacceptable level of volatility.

ENDNOTES

1. Duration is a measure of interest rate risk. A more complete discussion of duration is provided on page 1340.

2. A material difference is defined as one in which the misvaluation exceeds transaction costs.

3. Call option valuation is treated in greater detail on page 1329.

4. While it is possible to get the bid and asked price on bonds traded on the New York Stock Exchange, these markets are usually for odd-lot trades (less than $100,000 in par value).

5. Perfect forecasting is the return that would have resulted if one had been able to earn the higher of the returns available from the one-month Treasury bill or the 30-year Treasury bond in each month. The yield information was drawn from Ibbotson and Sinquefeld, "Stocks, Bonds, Bills and Inflation," Ibbotson Associates, Inc. (Chicago, Ill.) and *The Wall Street Journal*. Shearson Lehman Index is the *Shearson Lehman Aggregate Bond Index*. SEI Median is the *Bond Funds Background: Total Fund Rates of Return*, provided by the SEI Funds Evaluation Service.

6. For those readers who might question the potential mispricing of coupons, in the fall of 1983 the yields on premium, non-callable Treasuries rose 40 to 60 basis points (!) above the yield on similar maturity Treasuries priced at par.

7. Since duration is a better measure of the life of a bond, we would expect a fit based on duration to be superior to our maturity fit. While this is clearly the case theoretically, we have tested both processes and found that misvaluations off of the fit by maturity are better indicators of value than those off of the duration fit.

8. Wherever it is relevant, we will provide the names of vendors of bond analysis that we have found to be useful. Bernstein has no business relationship with any of these firms other than (in some cases) as a subscriber and derives no benefit from the references.

9. Although we refer to all of these premiums as call premiums in Exhibit 13, for all prices above par the premium is actually calculated on the put option.

10. This result is unambiguous because we have assumed a flat yield curve. When the yield curve is sloped either positively or negatively, the bond should be priced to the smallest spread versus the appropriate maturity Treasury.

11. "Analytical Record of Yields and Yield Spreads," Salomon Brothers Inc., January 1986, part II, table 2A, page 2.

12. For a discussion of the methodologies for predicting prepayment rates, see David J. Askin, "Forecasting Prepayment Rates for Mortgage Securities," in *The Handbook of Mortgage-Backed Securities*, ed. Frank J. Fabozzi (Chicago, Ill.: Probus Publishing, 1985), chap. 11.

13. The change in a bond's price is proportional to both its duration and its price.

Therefore, the absolute basis should be divided by the market price of the bond to permit comparison across the menu of deliverable securities.

14. A thorough introduction to futures is provided in Robert A. Kolb, *Understanding Futures Markets*, (Glenview, Ill.: Scott, Foresman, 1985). For a more rigorous discussion of synthetic securities and the delivery option, see Francis H. Trainer, Jr., "The Uses of Treasury Bond Futures in Fixed-Income Portfolio Management," *Financial Analysts Journal*, January/February 1983, pp. 27–34; and Kopprasch, Johnson, and Tatevossian, "Strategies for the Asset Manager: Hedging and the Creation of Synthetic Assets," Salomon Brothers Inc., October 1985.

15. Frederick R. Macaulay, *The Movements of Interest Rates, Bond Yields and Stock Prices in the United States since 1856* (New York: National Bureau of Economic Research, 1938).

16. Why this is not referred to as concavity is beyond us.

17. The percentage change in price divided by the change in yield is known as modified duration. This is, by definition, an exact measure of interest rate risk. To transform this into Macaulay's duration, it is multiplied by one plus one half of the yield to maturity or yield to call, whichever is appropriate. For an explanation of this modification, please see the Appendix. Although Macaulay's duration is not an exact measure of interest rate risk, it is a useful approximation, and, therefore, we refer to it in this capacity for the remainder of the chapter.

18. Capital Management Sciences provides estimates of the effective durations of individual corporate bonds as well as the Shearson Lehman and Salomon Brothers indexes.

APPENDIX _____

Exhibit 19 demonstrates that duration is a good measure of interest rate risk. Why is this true? The answer is that duration is the first derivative of price with respect to a change in yields. In our proof of this relationship, the following notation will be used:

P = price
C = coupon
D = duration
r = yield to maturity
n = the number of years
d = denotes a change in a variable

For a zero coupon bond:

$$P = \frac{C}{(1 + r)^n} \tag{A.1}$$

What is the effect of a change in yield on price?

$$\frac{dP}{dr} = \frac{-nC}{(1 + r)^{n+1}} \tag{A.2}$$

Dividing both sides of the equation by P, we get

$$\frac{\dfrac{dP}{dr}}{P} = \frac{\dfrac{-nC}{(1+r)^{n+1}}}{P} \tag{A.3}$$

Since

$$\frac{\dfrac{dP}{dr}}{P} = \frac{\dfrac{dP}{P}}{dr} \tag{A.4}$$

$$\frac{\dfrac{dP}{P}}{dr} = \frac{\dfrac{-nC}{(1+r)^{n+1}}}{P} \tag{A.5}$$

Substituting $\dfrac{C}{(1+r)^n}$ for P on the right-hand side of A.5,

$$\frac{\dfrac{dP}{P}}{dr} = \frac{\dfrac{-nC}{(1+r)^{n+1}}}{\dfrac{C}{(1+r)^n}} \tag{A.6}$$

Simplifying,

$$\frac{\dfrac{dP}{P}}{dr} = \frac{-n}{(1+r)} \tag{A.7}$$

For a zero-coupon bond, the number of years to maturity (n) is equal to its duration (D). Substituting D for n,

$$\frac{\dfrac{dP}{P}}{dr} = \frac{-D}{(1+r)} \tag{A.8}$$

Finally, if we multiply both sides of the equation by $(1+r)$,

$$\frac{\dfrac{dP}{P}}{\dfrac{dr}{(1+r)}} = -D \tag{A.9}$$

43

Measurement and Comparison of Investment Performance

Arthur Williams III, CFA
Director, Retirement Plan Investments
McKinsey & Company, Inc.

I: MEASURING INVESTMENT PERFORMANCE

The science of measuring the performance of investment portfolios has progressed considerably in the last 20 years. The most significant factor enhancing this development was the study produced by the Bank Administration Institute in 1968. This study, called *Measuring the Investment Performance of Pension Funds*, was made by a group of investment professionals and academics at the instruction of the Bank Administration Institute, a trade association of banks. Parts of the impetus for the study was, in the view of some observers, the fact that bank trust departments, which had traditionally managed almost all investment funds for wealthy individuals and pension funds, were losing business to investment counseling organizations. Some of the banks which were losing their assets to these competitors felt that the investment counseling organizations were achieving superior investment performance by increasing the risk of the securities owned. Since risk-adjusted performance measurement was virtually nonexistent at that time, the sponsors of portfolios have been unaware of the increased risk that they were taking in order to achieve higher rates of return. Thus, it was felt desirable to have a prestigious and qualified group prepare an author-

Arthur Williams III, *Managing Your Investment Manager*, 2nd ed., (Homewood, Ill.: Dow Jones-Irwin, 1986).

itative report on the appropriate method for analyzing investment performance. The BAI study made considerable progress in this regard. It drew four main conclusions:

1. Measurements of performance should be based on asset values measured at market, not at cost.
2. The returns should be "total" returns; that is, they should include both income and changes in market value (realized and unrealized capital appreciation).
3. The returns should be time weighted.
4. The measurements should include risk as well as return.

Market values were required in performance measurement so that at any point in time the fund sponsor could accurately see the value of its portfolio and measure the changes in its value. It was acknowledged that fixed-income securities had a maturity date and that holders of such securities could expect to achieve the rate of return indicated at the time of purchase if they held them until maturity. However, it was felt that if the returns of one portfolio were to be comparable with those of another, both portfolios must be measured at their fair market value. In retrospect, it seems obvious that *total rates of return* should have been used, but at the time many organizations were viewing the income from their portfolios in one light and capital appreciation in another. For taxable investors this makes some sense, though even such investors must consider both capital changes and income. For tax-exempt investors, such as pension funds or endowment funds, the distinction is of very little consequence. Therefore, the appropriateness of using total returns is unassailable.

The reasons for using *time-weighted rates of return* are not nearly as obvious. The time-weighted rate of return is designed to eliminate the effects on the portfolio of the timing and magnitude of external cash flows, whereas the alternative, and internal or dollar-weighted return, includes the impact of any such external contributions or withdrawals. The rationale for the distinction and for the use of the time-weighted return is that what is being subjected to a performance analysis is not the *fund's* results but the activities of the *manager*. Since the manager presumably does not have control over the timing of contributions to and withdrawals from the portfolio, it is not appropriate to attribute to him the impact of these cash flows.

The decision to measure *risk* and *return* was simple in theory but difficult in practice. This was because a theoretical framework for measuring risk was lacking and because at that time few investors had the capability for manipulating sufficient data easily enough to develop risk measures even if such a framework existed.

CALCULATING THE RATE OF RETURN

A rate of return, or, for succinctness, a return, is the percentage profit or gain achieved for holding an investment or a portfolio *for a particular time*. Price or capital returns are the changes in the value of assets, excluding income. Income returns are the gain or profit from dividends or interest. Total returns are the sum of price or capital returns and income returns. In its simplest form, a return is calculated by subtracting the difference between the beginning and ending values and dividing this amount by the beginning value. The result will be the decimalized return, which, of course, can be converted to a percentage return by multiplying by 100. Alternatively, the return can be calculated by dividing the ending value by the beginning value, subtracting 1 and multiplying by 100 to show the percentage return. Both of these methods are demonstrated below for a security which rose in value from $100 to $105.

$$\text{Return} = \frac{\text{Ending value} - \text{Beginning value}}{\text{Beginning value}} = \frac{105 - 100}{100}$$

$$= \frac{5}{100} = 0.05 \times 100 = 5\%$$

$$\text{Return} = \left[\left(\frac{\text{Ending value}}{\text{Beginning value}}\right) - 1\right] \times 100$$

$$= \left(\frac{105}{100} - 1\right) \times 100 = 1.05 - 1.00 = .05 \times 100 = 5\%$$

Complications enter the process from two sources: the need for accurate valuations and the need to handle cash flows properly. The need for accurate valuations is obvious, since if we improperly measure either the beginning or ending value, we will obviously not have a true rate of return (unless by chance we have made a proportional error in both). The only other difficulty which can arise with valuations stems from the number of valuations required. Obviously, the more frequent the intervals over which return information is required, the more frequently the portfolio must be valued even if there are no cash flows. If there are cash flows, the accuracy of the return calculation will be increased by having more frequent valuations.

This leads us to the second complexity, namely, the need to handle cash inflows and outflows to and from the portfolio. At this stage, let us consider only a total portfolio rather than dealing separately with such sectors as equities or fixed income. Clearly, if a contribution has been

---

EXHIBIT 1   Timing of Cash Flow Affects Rate of Return

Beginning value = 100
Ending value = 130
Cash flow = 20

Case 1: Cash flow came before gain

$$\text{Return} = \frac{\text{Ending value} - \text{Beginning value} - \text{Cash flow}}{\text{Beginning value} + \text{Cash flow}}$$

$$= \frac{130 - 100 - 20}{100 + 20} = \frac{10}{120} = 8.3\%$$

Case 2: Cash flow came after gain

$$\text{Return} = \frac{\text{Ending value} - \text{Beginning value}}{\text{Beginning value}}$$

$$= \frac{110 - 100}{100} = 10\%$$

---

made to the portfolio, our simple calculation of rate of return breaks down: a portfolio which started with $100 and ended with $120 did not have a 20 percent gain if the sponsor contributed an additional $20 during the period. The fund in this case had a zero percent rate of return, as can be seen from the example below:

$$
\begin{aligned}
\text{Gain} &= \text{Ending value} - \text{Contributions} - \text{Beginning value} \\
&= \quad\ \$120 \qquad - \qquad \$20 \quad\ - \qquad \$100 \\
&= 0
\end{aligned}
$$

Now let us see what would have happened if the fund started with $100, the sponsor added $20, and the fund ended with $130. We know that there is a gain of $10, but the return could have been anywhere between 8.3 percent and 10 percent. If the gain came before the arrival of the $20 contribution, then 10 percent is the correct return; if the gain came after the contribution, then 8.3 percent is correct (see Exhibit 1). If the gain came partly in each period, then we must have further information or make some assumption before we can state the return earned. The information that we require depends on whether we are calculating time-weighted or dollar-weighted returns. If a time-weighted return is needed, the required piece of information is the value of the portfolio at the time of the cash flow. If a dollar-weighted return is desired, the necessary information is the exact time at which the cash flow occurred. This will be discussed further below.

TIME-WEIGHTED VERSUS DOLLAR-WEIGHTED RATES OF RETURN

Almost all investment managers and fund sponsors think they understand this subject, but a surprisingly large number do not. This observation is based on experience derived from interviewing prospective job applicants over a number of years in an environment which permitted strenuous cross-examination of the applicants' knowledge. Most of these applicants recognized that the time-weighted rate of return in some fashion excluded the impact of external cash flow and that it was an appropriate measure of the manager's impact on the portfolio. They also recognized that the dollar-weighted return included the effect of cash flows and, hence, was appropriate for seeing whether a fund had met its rate of return objective. Beyond that, however, most of the applicants were unable to explain the distinctions between the two methods. It is thus advisable to describe these distinctions in detail so that there is no confusion about the two methods.

The time-weighted return (TWR) shows the value of one dollar invested in a portfolio or a portfolio sector for the entire period. The dollar-weighted return (DWR), on the other hand, shows an average return of all the dollars in the portfolio or the portfolio sector for the period. In a sense, the DWR reconciles the beginning dollar amount of the fund plus the cash contributions with the ending value of the fund. The TWR intentionally ignores the fact that money is contributed to or removed from the fund and only looks at the money in the fund during each period.

Consider an investment cycle in which a fund has high returns for one period and negative returns for the next period. If the portfolio has more dollars working when the return is low, the return on the average dollar will be low; in this case the TWR will be higher than the DWR. On the other hand, if more dollars are in the fund when the returns are high, the return on the average dollar will be high; consequently, the DWR will exceed the TWR. In both cases the TWR will be the same. If the fund manager had no control over the number of dollars in the fund, he should be measured on the basis of *his* time-weighted returns, not the *fund's* dollar-weighted returns.

Understanding of the distinction between the two types of returns can be enhanced by noting when the two will be identical and by seeing an example. The TWR and the DWR will be identical when there are no cash inflows or outflows *or* when the return earned during the period is constant. Since the distinction only arises when there are contributions to or withdrawals from the fund, if there are no such cash flows, the two types of return will be the same. Also, if the return is constant during the entire period, there can obviously be no difference between the two types of return.

The time-weighted return is calculated by measuring the rate of return during a number of subperiods (presumably quarterly or monthly) and "linking" or "chaining" the interim returns. For example, if the fund earned 6 percent in period 1 and 8 percent in period 2, the time-weighted return is:

$$[(1.06 \times 1.08) - 1] \times 100$$
$$1.1448 - 1 = 0.1448 \times 100 = 14.48\%$$

In order to calculate a time-weighted return, it is necessary to measure or estimate the value of the portfolio at the end of the first year when the cash flow took place. A simple example may serve to demonstrate differences in the two types of returns. Suppose a portfolio begins with $1,000 at the beginning of year 1, receives $100 at the end of the year, and has $1,200 at the end of year 2. If we know, for instance, that the value of the portfolio was $1,050 just before the cash flow was received, we can easily calculate an accurate time-weighted rate of return, as follows. The return for the first year is $1,050 divided by $1,000 equals 1.05, or 5 percent. The second year's return is calculated by taking $1,200, the ending value, and dividing it by $1,150 (the sum of $1,050 plus $100 equals $1,150). This return is 1.043, or 4.3 percent. The return for the two years is thus 1.043 times 1.05 equals 1.095, or 9.5 percent.

The dollar-weighted return is calculated on an "iterative" or trial-and-error basis. In effect, the dollar-weighted calculation raises the question, "What is the rate of return which can be multiplied by the beginning value and the interim cash flows in order to equal the ending value?" Or more precisely, "What rate of return per period equates the initial value and the cash flow received to the ending value?"

In the example above, the iterative procedure, figuratively speaking, asks what rate on $1,000 for two years plus the same rate on $100 for one year equals $1,200. Let's try 10 percent and see what happens. Ten percent of $1,000 for one year is $100, so at the end of year 1 and before the contribution we have $1,100. After the $100 contribution we have $1,200, which earns 10 percent, or $120, for year 2, providing an estimated total ending value at a 10 percent rate equal to $1,320. Since $1,320 is greater than the actual ending value of $1,200, the rate we used must have been too high. If 10 percent is too high, let's try 5 percent. Five percent of $1,000 is $50; 5 percent of $1,050 is $52.50; 5 percent of the $100 contribution is $5; and adding the $100 contribution we get a total of $1,207.50. Again the results exceed the actual ending value, so a lower return must be tried. The procedure keeps doing this until a return is calculated which leads to an ending value sufficiently close to $1,200 to be acceptable. Thus, the dollar-weighted return takes into account both performance and the impact of the timing of cash flows on performance.

The following example demonstrates convincingly the differences between the two types of return. Both funds start with $100 and have the same investment manager, and the manager keeps both funds 100 percent invested in General Motors stock at *all* times. General Motors' price and the contribution to the two funds are as follows:

1. Beginning price: 50, each fund buys two shares.
   Value Fund A: 2 shares @ 50 = 100.
   Value Fund B: 2 shares @ 50 = 100.
2. One year later price rises to 100; Fund A receives a $100 contribution and buys one share @ 100.
   Value Fund A: 3 shares @ 100 = 300.
   Value Fund B: 2 shares @ 100 = 200.
3. One year later price declines to 50.
   Value Fund A: 3 shares @ 50 = 150; cost = (2 × 50) + (1 × 100) = 200; loss = 50.
   Value Fund B: 2 shares @ 50 = 100; cost = 2 × 50 = 100; gain = 0.

   Time-weighted return = 0 in each fund.
   Dollar-weighted returns:
   Fund A = −18.1%.
   Fund B = 0%.

Thus, Fund A showed a loss and had a negative dollar-weighted return. Fund B broke even and had a 0 percent dollar-weighted return. Both funds had a 0 percent time-weighted return. Fund B had no contributions, and thus its dollar-weighted and time-weighted returns were identical. The manager clearly made the same contribution to each fund, since he made exactly the same investments in both funds. The TWR reflects his contribution. The DWR in Fund A reflects both the contribution of the manager (0 percent) and the timing of the contribution, which happened to come when the stock was at a high price.

CALCULATING THE RETURNS ON PORTFOLIO COMPONENTS

Equities

Once the technique for calculating returns is understood it can be applied to all asset categories, with only procedural rather than theoretical questions to be answered. The first such procedural question in measuring returns on equities is what to include in this category. A typical definition of equities would include common stocks, convertible preferred stocks, convertible bonds, warrants to purchase stocks, and options. Other definitions are perfectly acceptable as long as all parties are aware of the classification being used. The need for valuations is the same for all asset categories, and cash flows must also be dealt with. In the case of an individual asset category, such as equities or fixed-income securities, the cash flows are the purchases and sales. In other words, a cash flow into equities is an equities purchase and a cash outflow is a sale. Just as the increased value in the total portfolio resulting from contributions is not attributable to return, so a purchase of equities is not attributable to equities return. Assume, for example, a beginning value of 100, an ending value of 120, and a purchase of 20.

$$\text{Gain} = \text{Ending value} - \text{Purchases} - \text{Beginning value}$$
$$= 120 - 20 - 100 = 0$$

Therefore, equities purchases and sales are treated in the same fashion as are total portfolio contributions and withdrawals. An additional factor, namely, dividends, must also be considered, since part of the return of an asset category is its income. This subject can cause confusion, since one could properly argue that income should be counted in the total portfolio return if we are measuring "total return." The distinction to be drawn is that cash, the normal form of income payment, is part of the total portfolio but that cash is not part of the equities portfolio. The total portfolio is defined to include all assets, including cash, but the equities portfolio can consist only of equities. Calculation of the return, including income, is demonstrated in this example:

$$\text{Gain} = \text{Price gain} + \text{Income gain}$$

$$\text{Equity return} = \frac{\substack{\text{Ending equity value} - \text{Equity purchases} \\ + \text{Dividends} + \text{Equity sales}}}{\text{Beginning equity value}}$$

Thus, it can be seen that the $5 dividend received on the $100 worth of stock has led to a 5 percent gain, just as would have been the case had the $5 come from capital appreciation. *However*, the return has been calculated as though we were viewing a total portfolio, since the ending value, $105, consists of $100 in equities plus $5 in cash. Thus, the true position of the portfolio at the end of the period is as follows: $100 stock plus $5 cash equals $105 total.

The presentation of the true portfolio position leads to an intuitive difficulty, namely, that we all tend to think of the $5 dividend as a positive cash flow to the equities portfolio, whereas, in fact, the $5 is a positive cash flow to the total portfolio but a *negative* cash flow to the equities portfolio. This can be substantiated in several different ways. First, the $5 increase in cash had to come from somewhere, and since it did not result from an external contribution it must have come from the only other source within the portfolio, namely, equities. Since there were no external cash flows, the internal cash balance must net out to zero, which can occur only if the +$5 in cash is offset by a −$5 in equities. Second, we know that the portfolio gained 5 percent during the period and that equities were the source of this 5 percent gain. The only way in which an asset can start out with $100, end up with $100, and have a 5 percent return is if 5 percent of the value of the assets are withdrawn during the period. Finally, since we are drawing no distinction between income and appreciation in our calculation of return, we can view the situation in which no dividend was paid but the shares rose 5 percent in value and 5 percent of the holdings were sold. In this case we would obviously treat the sale as a negative cash flow, and logically, therefore, we must treat the dividend in the same way.

Determining how to treat the timing of the dividend received will be addressed below.

The next issue, the handling of stock splits and stock dividends, should be simple now that the principles have been established. Clearly, return is not enhanced by a stock split or a stock dividend, so no special consideration need be given to these events *except* to be certain that the asset price used in the valuation is consistent with the number of shares owned. In other words, if 100 shares of a $50 stock are owned and a two-for-one split takes place, the new position is 200 shares at $25. In both cases the investment is worth $5,000, so there has been no impact on return. This may sound elementary, but it must be remembered that the receipt of the extra 100 shares by the investor invariably occurs well after the stock begins trading at the new price. This is because the company must know who owns its shares at the time of the split in order to distribute the shares properly. Consequently, a time lag exists which can cause errors in a custodial statement if the statement shows the old number of shares and the new price.

Bonds

The return on fixed-income (bond) investments is calculated very similarly to the return on equities. That is, it is calculated after adjusting for purchases, sales, and income. The principal distinction lies in accounting for accrued interest. Whereas the value of a common stock investment is merely the market price times the number of shares owned, there are two components to the value of a bond. These are the capital value (or number of bonds owned times price per bond) plus the accrued interest. Since misunderstandings regarding accrued interest can occur, it is well to discuss this area further. The holder of a bond is contractually entitled to receive interest, usually semiannually. Since the bondholder is entitled to this interest, the value of the bond increases every day by that day's accrued interest. If a bondholder sold a bond two thirds of the way through the interest period (four months) he would receive two thirds of the semiannual coupon from the buyer, with the buyer receiving the one third to which he is entitled plus the two thirds, which he paid to the seller at the end of the six-month coupon period. Thus, the value of the bond increases every day by the amount of accrued interest until the payment period, when the process starts all over again. Although some distortion in return is possible if there are large purchases or sales in a period within a fixed-income portfolio (see discussion of anomaly below), accrued interest should not be a problem in calculating return as long as it is treated consistently. That is to say, if the beginning value of the portfolio includes accrued interest, the ending value must also include accrued interest. It is preferable to include accrued interest in asset valuations wherever possible, though this is usually not practical for investors who wish to measure the rate of return on equities and bonds as well as the total portfolio. This is because many fund accounting statements do not show accrued interest at all, and those which do rarely distinguish among accrued interest on convertible securities (which applies to the equities portfolio), accrued interest on bonds (which is attributable to the fixed-income portfolio), and accrued interest on short-term investments (which is included in the cash equivalent portfolio sector).

Cash Equivalents

Calculating returns on cash equivalents is no different, in principle, from calculating returns on stocks and bonds. If the cash equivalent is a discount instrument, the market value of the asset includes both accrued interest and capital changes such that a proper rate of return can be calculated from this value. If the instrument carries a coupon, the coupon must be treated just like any other income to a portfolio subsector, namely, as a negative cash flow to that subsector and a positive cash flow to the cash holdings of the portfolio. Practical considerations in measuring returns on cash equivalents will be considered below.

Commingled Funds

Commingled funds represent a special case in that they are single securities from the point of view of the fund owner. That is, although a commingled fund may own stocks, bonds, cash, or cash equivalents in any proportion, all of the assets within the commingled fund are treated as part of the portfolio's value. Hence, the effect of the commingled fund on the return of the overall pension or endowment fund will be considered by merely accounting for changes in the value of the investment in the commingled fund and in the number of shares or units owned.

A caution must be made regarding the treatment of income distributions from commingled funds. A commingled fund can treat income in one of three ways. One alternative is to retain the income within the portfolio, in which case the commingled fund's net asset value is enhanced by the amount of income per share. This causes no problem to the sponsor since it includes the market value (equals number of shares times net asset value per share) in the value of its fund. A second alternative is for the fund to distribute its income to shareholders in cash. In this case the net asset value of the share declines due to the distribution, and thus the sponsor must treat the cash received as a negative cash flow from the commingled fund and an increase in cash within the sponsor's fund. The third alternative is for the sponsor to choose to have income distributions automatically reinvested in new shares. In this case the net asset value of the fund declines, but the number of shares owned by each holder increases proportionately so that the value of the investment is maintained at the same level before and after the income distribution. Fortunately, since many tax-exempt funds have no need for income, it has become customary for most commingled funds to retain and reinvest income within the commingled fund. A sponsor who wishes to receive a distribution merely sells sufficient shares to achieve the amount of cash required.

Savings Accounts

Savings accounts are not often used by large funds, but some smaller funds find them of value for investing small cash positions. Savings accounts should not be a problem if the record-keeping process recognizes that the value of the savings account is enhanced as interest accrues, just as in the case of a bond, which also has interest accruing daily.

APPLYING PERFORMANCE MEASUREMENT TECHNIQUES TO REAL PORTFOLIOS

We have established that the dollar-weighted return is the average return on all dollars invested, whereas the time-weighted return is the result obtained from calculating the internal rate of return for subperiods between cash flows and linking or chaining the subperiod returns to find the return for the cumulative period. When we turn to real portfolios we find three practical restraints to accurate calculation of time- and dollar-weighted returns:

1. Information is reported on a calendar period basis, not by cash flow. That is, valuations are presented monthly, quarterly, or annually, not in relation to the timing of cash inflows and outflows.

2.   The valuation statements may not be produced as frequently as desired. The accuracy of the return calculation will be reduced if there are large cash flows and, for instance, only quarterly rather than monthly valuations are available.

3.   Cash flows may take place at any time, not just a midmonth. There is obviously a different impact on a portfolio from a $100 contribution in the middle of the month than from a $100 contribution at the end of the month. On a practical basis, however, most performance measurement systems do not permit the treatment of cash flows on each of the 250-odd days possible.

It is obviously not feasible to have reporting periods other than by calendar month, as the whole system of analysis in this and other countries is based on annual periods. Furthermore, since we are dealing with a time-related concept, namely, rate of return *per period*, it makes sense to have the reporting done on a calendar month or quarter basis. Thus, a problem requiring that some assumptions be made is automatically built into the measurement of portfolio performance since we will not normally have appropriate valuations on the date of cash flows. For purposes of analysis, let us assume that we are viewing the typical case, monthly cash or transaction statements and on-calendar quarterly valuation statements.

In addition to the "exact" method, which requires valuations at each cash flow, there are three methods for calculating time-weighted returns. These are:

1.   The linked internal method.
2.   The regression method.
3.   The linked apportioned contribution method (a term applied here but not in wide use).

The *linked internal* method involves measuring the internal rate of return for each period between valuations (in this case quarterly) and linking or chaining the results. This method assumes that the return *within* each quarter is uniform. Even though we know that dollar-weighted returns are not usually good estimates of time-weighted returns, if we break the subperiods up sufficiently and if there are no large cash flows during a period when the market had a large return, this method will yield adequate results.

The *regression* method is the most accurate way of calculating rates of return when valuations are available only quarterly. This method involves estimating the value of the portfolio at interim periods within the quarter, such as monthly, on the assumption that an estimate of the monthly valuation is more useful than the linked internal method's assumption that the rate of return during the quarter was equal each month. An estimate of the interim market value can be made if two things are known: the rate of return on the market during the monthly subinterval and the relationship (beta) of the portfolio's return to the market's return. If we know that the portfolio is, for instance, 10 percent more volatile than the market and that the market rose 10 percent during a month, we can assume that the portfolio's value was more likely to have risen by 11 percent than by either the 10 percent which the market earned or the average of the quarter, as would be assumed by the linked internal method.

An astute reader may recognize both the logic of this approach and the dilemma it poses. We are trying to calculate the portfolio's rate of return, and in order to do this we need to know the relationship between the portfolio's return and the market's return, which obviously requires our knowing what the portfolio's rate of return was! This dilemma can be solved by using the trial-and-error method of trying to find a portfolio beta which will result in an ending value of the portfolio, arrived at by estimation, as close as possible to the actual ending value. The regression method is limited in that it is ordinarily not possible to develop a useful measure of beta without having had at least six to eight quarters of valuations. When 12 to 20 quarters of valuations are available, the regression method gives quite satisfactory results. According to the BAI study, for funds having quarterly valuation statements and monthly cash statements, the expected annual errors in return using the linked internal method and the regression method are 0.48 percent and 0.17 percent, respectively.[1]

The *apportioned* methods are hybrid approaches to performance calculations. They have a simplicity about them, both conceptually and in carrying out the calculations, which gives them considerable appeal. These methods say, in effect, that the ending value is composed of the beginning value, gains from income and appreciation, and contributions. The contributions cannot be treated as gains, so an adjustment must be made for them. Further, recognition must be made of the amount of time that the contributions were in the portfolio. Therefore, the beginning or ending values will be adjusted by a portion of the contributions. The adjustment can be the exact portion of the period for which the funds were available, thus leading to a return which is "weighted by the time" that funds are available.

STRANGE BUT TRUE INVESTMENT RESULTS

Experience with the results of hundreds of performance measurement studies indicates that almost any combination of anomalous results is

---

[1] *Measuring the Investment Performance of Pension Funds for the Purpose of Inter-Fund Comparison* (Park Ridge, Ill.: Bank Administration Institute, 1968), p 25.

possible. These strange results can cause great frustration to those unfamiliar with how they come about and can cast doubts on valid and useful measurement techniques. These correct but nonintuitive returns can derive from such causes as:

1. Changes in the allocation among equities, fixed income, and cash equivalents.
2. Dollar-weighted versus time-weighted factors.
3. Compound interest.
4. Accrued interest.
5. The use of total returns rather than just income.
6. Conceptual misunderstandings (e.g., all assets not accounted for—thus, Equities + Fixed income = Total portfolio because of cash).

Changes in Allocation

One of the strangest things that can occur within a portfolio is for the return of the total portfolio to fall outside the return of the equity and fixed-income portions. An extreme form of this event occurs when the equity and fixed-income returns are up and the total portfolio return is down. The extreme form is apparent from the following example, which is taken from the results of a jointly trusteed retirement fund.

| Year Ended | Percent Return | | |
	Equities	Bonds	Total Portfolio
12/75	19.8	8.1	−2.0

The portfolio had a loss on a time-weighted basis in 1975 even though equities and fixed-income securities showed sharp gains in the rising market for stocks and bonds. This seemingly impossible occurrence can take place if three things happen:

1. The rates of return on the asset sectors (equities and fixed-income securities) fluctuate greatly (see Exhibit 2).
2. The allocation between equities and fixed-income securities changes greatly (i.e., the fund policy changes or the investment manager tries to time the market). (See Exhibit 3.)
3. Time-weighted rather than dollar-weighted returns are being measured (see Exhibit 4).

EXHIBIT 2   Quarterly Portfolio Returns: Sector Returns Vary Greatly

Quarter Ended	Equities	Bonds	Total Portfolio
3/75	15.5	3.5	4.7
6/75	12.4	2.3	3.4
9/75	−16.5	−1.0	−13.5
12/75	10.5	3.1	4.6
Year	19.8	8.1	−2.0

Note that for each quarter the total portolio returns were in the range between the equity and bond results.

EXHIBIT 3   Valuations and Cash Flows: Significant Changes in Allocation (as percentage of total portfolio)

Quarter Ended	Valuations		Purchase (Sales) at End of Quarter	
	Equities	Bonds	Equities	Bonds
12/74	10	90		
3/75	11	89		
6/75 (before transactions)	12	88		
6/75 (after transactions	82	18	70	(70)
9/75 (before transactions)	79	21	(59)	59
9/75 (after transactions)	20	80		
12/75	21	79		

EXHIBIT 4   Source of Total Portfolio Return

Quarter Ended	$\left(\begin{array}{c}\text{Equity}\\\text{Allocation}\end{array}\right.$ × $\left.\begin{array}{c}\text{Equity}\\\text{Return}\end{array}\right)$		+	$\left(\begin{array}{c}\text{Bond}\\\text{Allocation}\end{array}\right.$ × $\left.\begin{array}{c}\text{Bond}\\\text{Return}\end{array}\right)$		=	Total Portfolio Return
3/75	0.10	15.5%		0.90	13.5%		4.7%
6/75	0.11	12.4		0.89	2.3		3.4
9/75	0.82	−16.5		0.18	−1.0		−13.5
12/75	0.20	10.5		0.80	3.1		4.6
		19.8			8.1		−2.0

The movement of large amounts of money between sectors at the wrong time led to small allocations to equities in the first, second, and fourth quarters, when equity performance was good, and to a high allocation to equities in the third quarter, when equity results were poor. Consequently, the poor results in the third quarter overshadowed the good results in the other three quarters.

Dollar-Weighted versus Time-Weighted Factors

A second major area of confusion occurs when the portfolio shows a negative time-weighted return but the portfolio has shown a positive gain (or vice versa). In other words, the sum of the initial value plus the net contributions is below the ending market value, thus indicating that a positive investment gain has been achieved. This case demonstrates the fundamental distinction between time- and dollar-weighted rates of return. The case may occur if the portfolio's return was lower when a smaller amount of money was invested in the portfolio and higher when more money was invested in it. If the cumulative effect of the portfolio returns is such that the down cycle does more harm than the up cycle does good, the overall portfolio return will be negative. This apparent anomaly occurred in many portfolios during the period 1973–76. The cumulative effect on $1 invested throughout the poor years 1973 and 1974 was not overcome by the market improvements in 1975 and 1976, yet the portfolio had a great deal more money invested in the latter years due to increased contributions. The result was negative time-weighted returns and positive dollar-weighted returns.

Compound Interest

When an investor views his portfolio he sometimes wonders why the results in up and down quarters appear to be equal or perhaps favoring the upside but the portfolio's cumulative return is negative. This results because of the impact of negative returns on an investment portfolio. If a portfolio rises 10 percent one year and declines 10 percent the next, it would appear that the investment has maintained its original value. However, a quick run through the numbers indicates that this is not the case. A $100 investment which achieves a 10 percent return will have $110 at the end of the period, for a gain of $10. A decline of 10 percent leads to a loss of $11 and an ensuing value of $99, or an overal loss for the two periods of $1. The greater the volatility of the portfolio, the more apparent this phenomenon will be. We can see this in Exhibit 5, wherein returns are shown for various percentage gains and commensurate percentage losses.

It sometimes appears that the last year's results dominate portfolio returns over the cumulative period. This is, a portfolio which did very well in the last period seems to have done well cumulatively, and similarly a portfolio which did badly in the latest year appears to have a poor cumulative result. It can easily be seen that the apparent phenomenon does not really exist. Each year's returns count equally with each other year, so it makes no difference whether the portfolio did well in the first period or the last. This is indicated by the following example:

	Year 1	Year 2	Cumulative
Fund A	−5	+15	0.95 × 1.15 = 1.0925, or 9.3%
Fund B	+15	−5	1.15 × 0.95 = 1.0925, or 9.3%

Accrued Interest

With increasing interest in fixed-income portfolios, combined with positive cash flow in most pension funds, an anomaly crops up in which returns on bond portfolios which have heavy contributions are lower than those of portfolios invested in the same bonds but with static or negative cash flows. This results not from any complexity of mathematics but rather from limitations in the evaluation process. The source of the problem is the way in which accrued interest is treated in the performance measurement process. When an investor sells a stock he has no right to subsequent dividends that the company pays, regardless of the fact that he may have held the stock for almost the full 90-day period between quarterly dividends. (For purposes of this analysis we exclude consideration of the five-day period prior to the payable date for the dividend, during which the purchaser is entitled to the dividend payment.) That is, a buyer who has not held the stock for more than a few days may still be entitled to the full quarterly dividend. This is because the company does not have a contractual obligation to pay the dividend, and consequently the buyer cannot hold the seller accountable for it. (Of course, the market price action reflects the presence or absence of the dividend to each party.)

EXHIBIT 5

			Gain Required to Recoup Losses	
Result of Equal Percentage Gains and Losses				
Gain	Loss	Cumulative Loss	Loss	Gain Required
5%	−5%	−0.25%	−5%	+5.26%
10	−10	−1.00	−10	+11.1
15	−15	−2.25	−15	+17.6
20	−20	−4.00	−20	+25.0
25	−25	−6.25	−25	+33.3
30	−30	−9.00	−30	+42.9
$33\frac{1}{3}$	$-33\frac{1}{3}$	−11.11	$-33\frac{1}{3}$	+50.0
40	−40	−16.00	−40	+66.6
50	−50	−25.00	−50	+100.0
75	−75	−56.30	−75	+300.0
100	−100	−100.00	−100	+Infinity

The bond issuer, on the other hand, has a contractual obligation to pay interest, usually semiannually, and thus the holder of a bond should receive interest for each day he holds it. Let us assume that a bond pays interest on January 1 and July 1 and that a purchaser buys the bond four months into this period. The seller is thus entitled to four months of interest and the buyer to two months. If we assume that the bond has a 6 percent coupon, the seller is entitled to 2 percent interest and the buyer to 1 percent, representing their respective portions of the semiannual 3 percent payment. When July 1 arrives, however, the holder of the bond will be the purchaser, and he will at that time receive 3 percent interest from the issuer. In order to properly compensate the seller, the buyer must at the time of purchase pay the seller the accrued interest of 2 percent. Thus, if the bond were traded at par, or 100 percent of value, the buyer would pay $102 to the seller, of which $2 would be interest and $100 principal. For purposes of performance measurement it is necessary to treat the 2 percent interest that the buyer paid as interest paid, or negative interest income. This is not a long-run problem, in that each party is properly compensated for his investment, but for the quarter ended July 30 the purchaser's portfolio, assuming a $100 value at March 31 before the bond purchase was made, will show a negative return of 2 percent. For the six-month period through September the return will be correct, since as soon as July 1 arrives the $3 semiannual interest payment will be received, representing repayment of the $2 paid out and the $1 interest due. However, a distortion occurs for the one period, causing an understatement of return for the period. If there are no additional purchases, the problem corrects itself, but for rapidly growing (or declining) bond portfolios the problem persists, with growing portfolios having an understated return and shrinking portfolios an overstated return. The distortion remains with the portfolio if the fixed-income portion of the fund continues to grow. If the fund in the above example were to double on June 30, the portfolio would be penalized by 2 percent ($2 ÷ $100), whereas the correction would be only 1 percent ($2 ÷ $200). Thus, the fixed-income portion of the fund would be affected in its time-weighted rate of return until such time as there was a substantial liquidation of bonds. Total portfolio return would also be affected, with the extent dependent on the size of the bond portfolio as a percent of the total portfolio.

The solution to this problem is simple in theory but difficult in practice in that data sufficient to provide perfect results are typically not supplied on custodial statements. Obviously, the ability to produce an accurate performance measurement report is limited by the accuracy of the information provided. Since a performance measurement study typically breaks down returns among equities, bonds, and cash equivalents, it is necessary to produce figures on accrued interest for cash equivalents, straight bonds, and convertibles (which are frequently included in equities). Even if a total portfolio accrued interest figure is available, it is unlikely that the custodian or other source of accounting information will have recorded accrued interest by asset category so as to permit an accurate breakdown. Although this problem is of no great significance, it is an annoyance to people who desire to achieve a high level of accuracy. In coming years, as bank custodians become more sophisticated in their record-keeping processes, it is likely that accrued interest will be reported by asset type.

Total Returns

An apparent anomaly can occur for investors who are unaccustomed to viewing total rates of return, especially in fixed-income portfolios. For example, assume that the portfolio has a yield of 7–8 percent and that the total return for the period is dramatically different, perhaps minus 2 percent to plus 15 percent. Dramatically varying total rates of return result, of course, from changes in the capital value of the portfolio rather than changes in interest income. Changes in the level of interest rates can cause large changes in capital value even in portfolios with no default risk. The impact of interest-rate changes on a portfolio is largely a function of the portfolio's maturity structure. This can be demonstrated by looking at the rate of return on individual bonds of different maturities as interest rates change (see Exhibit 6).

It can be seen from Exhibit 6 that bonds with longer maturities are more volatile than bonds with shorter maturities. A simplified example (which does not *precisely* take compounding into account) may assist in understanding this process. Let us assume that the general level of

EXHIBIT 6 Percentage Changes in Body Prices, Assuming a Current Coupon 8 Percent Bond (all bonds start out at par)

	New Level of Interest Rates			
Maturity	6 Percent	7 Percent	9 Percent	10 Percent
1	1.8%	1.0%	−1.0%	−1.8%
3	5.4	2.6	−2.6	−5.0
5	8.4	4.1	−3.9	−7.6
10	14.7	7.0	−6.5	−12.2
15	19.4	9.1	−8.0	−15.3
20	23.0	10.6	−9.2	−17.0
25	25.6	11.6	−9.8	−18.2
30	27.5	12.4	−10.3	−18.9

NOTE: These are the percentage price changes due to an instantaneous shift from 8 percent to each of these interest rates. If the shift is not instantaneous, the total return of the investment should be considered. This total return will include the price change and the income received during the period measured as well as income on that income.

interest rates rises from 8 percent to 9 percent. Let us further assume that we own three bonds in our portfolio, all of which have 8 percent coupons at the beginning point, with one bond having a one-year maturity, the second bond having a two-year maturity, and the third bond having a three-year maturity. We will also assume that the change in interest rates comes instantaneously right after we purchase the portfolio.

Looking at the one-year bond, an investor would see that the general level of interest rates provides for a 9 percent return for one year and that the one-year bond provides only an 8 percent return. For this bond to have a competitive return in the marketplace it must also yield 9 percent. In order for it to yield 9 percent the investor would have to make 1 percent in appreciation in addition to the 8 percent in interest. For the investor to make 1 percent in appreciation over a one-year period, the $100 value of the bond would necessarily have to drop to $99. Thus, this bond would show an instantaneous negative return of 1 percent.

The investor would apply the same analysis to the two-year bond, but in this case he would not be satisfied with a purchase price of $99, since this would yield him 8 percent per year in interest but only one half of 1 percent *per year* in appreciation. In order to achieve the 9 percent return he must have a 1 percent per year return from capital appreciation, or a 2 percent return for the two years. He would thus be willing to buy the 8 percent two-year bond at $98, with the bond showing an instantaneous return of minus 2 percent in comparison to the minus 1 percent return of the one-year bond.

Carrying the analysis to the three-year bond, we immediately recognize that the investor would be willing to pay only $97 for this bond, which would then have an instantaneous return of minus 3 percent. Recognizing that if interest rates declined the longer term bond would have a positive rate of return greater than that of the one-year bond, we can see the impact of changes in interest rates on bonds of different maturities and the fallacy of expecting the income return to closely correlate with the total return when a portfolio is being measured.

We have thus determined that results of almost any kind can be achieved and that there is usually a good reason for them!

II: COMPARING INVESTMENT PERFORMANCE

Although virtually all sponsors are interested in comparing the results of their funds with appropriate benchmarks, it is not easy to determine the appropriate benchmarks. In general terms there are three useful standards against which portfolios can be measured:

EXHIBIT 7

Period	Market Return	Fund Return
1	+50%	6.1%
2	−50	5.9

---

1. Comparison with an absolute goal.
2. Comparison with market indexes.
3. Comparison with other portfolios.

COMPARISON WITH AN ABSOLUTE GOAL

When a choice is presented as to which of the three standards is appropriate, almost all fund sponsors will choose the first. That is, almost all will agree that the most important measure of a fund's success is whether it meets its objectives. In the case of a pension fund the objective is to return at least as much as the assumed rate. For an endowment fund the objective is to provide sufficient capital or income to meet the needs of the sponsoring organization. Although achieving these goals is certainly important, in practice this method of comparing results is rather unsatisfying. A brief example will demonstrate why.

In both of the periods shown in Exhibit 7, the fund referred to is attempting to achieve or exceed its target rate of return of 6.0 percent. It is clear that in an absolute sense the fund met its objective in the first period and failed to meet it in the second period. However, virtually all fund sponsors and investment managers would feel that the fund performed well in the second period and poorly in the first. This is because the returns of investment portfolios are dominated by the returns of the market, particularly in the short run. Consequently, practically all funds will fail to meet their stated objectives in a poor year and will exceed them in a good year. Similarly, even the best managers frequently show negative returns in bear markets, and even the poorest managers generally show positive returns in strong bull markets. Thus, although meeting the absolute goal of the fund is certainly important, there is a need for additional benchmarks in order to understand the activities of the fund and to assess whether the manager is doing a good or a bad job in light of the market environment in which he is operating.

COMPARISON WITH MARKET INDEXES

In order to look beyond the problems associated with the absolute goal, namely, the way in which the market environment dominates returns, it is desirable to measure the market environment so as to assess its impact on portfolios. Thus, it is appropriate to measure the impact of the market on the various sectors of the portfolio.

Equity Portfolios

The performance of the equity portion of portfolios (common stocks, convertible securities, and warrants or options) may be appropriately measured against any one of a number of stock market indexes. Among these indexes are the Standard & Poor's 500, Standard & Poor's 400, New York Stock Exchange Index, American Stock Exchange Index, Value Line Index, Indicator Digest Average, Dow Jones Composite Index, and Wilshire 5000 Index. A detailed discussion of their composition and construction is presented in the appendix to this chapter.

Bond Portfolios

Fixed-income or bond portfolios can be appropriately compared to bond indexes, including the Salomon Brothers Index, the Lehman Brothers Kuhn Loeb indexes, the Merrill Lynch indexes, and the Moody's Index. Two points should be made about the ways in which bond portfolios and indexes differ from those for equities. First of all, the bond market is not a unified market in quite the same way as the stock market is. This is because the fixed maturity of bonds creates a spectrum of risk and return quite apart from the characteristics of the bond issuer. Whereas AT&T common stock is AT&T common stock, an AT&T bond with two years until maturity is a quite different investment than an AT&T bond with 30 years until maturity. For this reason it is not easy to find a bond index which is truly representative of the market. Second, because of this maturity characteristic and because an investor may have a fixed time horizon, it is possible for an investor to choose bonds which are appropriate for his portfolio but unrepresentative of the bond market as a whole. Consequently, this investor may find that even a bond index which is truly representative of the bond market may not be an appropriate benchmark for comparing performance. Fortunately, indexes describing the returns of the various sectors of the bond market are becoming increasingly available. These bond indexes are shown in the appendix at the end of this chapter.

Cash Equivalents

The return on cash equivalents (short-term investments or money market instruments) can be compared to the returns on U.S. Treasury bills, certificates of deposit, commercial paper, and banker's acceptances. There are no widely published indexes of these instruments, though the rate on U.S. Treasury bills is readily available and easy to measure with high precision. Typically, when cash equivalent returns are available (and frequently, returns are not calculated for cash equivalents), they are compared to the return on U.S. Treasury bills or to the return on commercial paper. This is done in a somewhat less formal fashion than are the comparisons with stock market and bond market indexes.

Not Readily Marketable Assets

There are no indexes known to the author which measure the return on private placements or on such assets as real estate equity investments and oil and gas investments.

Total Portfolios

The total fund typically consists of investments in various market sectors, and consequently, there is no total portfolio index which is appropriate for all investors. However, it is possible to construct a hypothetical or "custom" index which is useful in measuring a given investor's results. This index can be constructed by looking at the composition of the fund and weighting market indexes accordingly. For example, if a portfolio consists of 60 percent stocks and 40 percent bonds at the beginning of a certain quarter, we can use an index for that quarter which consists of 60 percent of the return on an equity index plus 40 percent of the return on a bond index. If the investor switches to 70 percent equities and 30 percent bonds at the end of the quarter, we might consider the market return for the total portfolio for the second quarter to be equal to 70 percent of the equity index's return and 30 percent of the bond index's return. The market return for the two-quarter period could then be calculated by linking or chaining the market return of the individual periods. Alternatively, the market index could be calculated by using the average percentage in equities and the average percentage in bonds, in this case 65 percent and 35 percent, respectively. The stock and bond index returns for each quarter would then be weighted 65 percent and 35 percent, respectively, and chained.

Both methods are useful and sensible. The method using quarter-by-quarter returns measures selection but not timing. The average method measures both selection and timing because in each quarter the measurement considers not only the difference between the equity and fixed-income returns in the portfolio and those of the indexes but also the difference in the proportions of the two. This is shown in Exhibit 8.

The custom index has two limitations. First, the index of each fund will be different, reflecting the fund's composition. Consequently, there is no total portfolio index which is appropriate for all portfolios. Second,

EXHIBIT 8

Custom index at actual allocation measures selection only:

	Period 1	Period 2	Average	Cumulative (Not Compounded)
1 Percentage in equities	60	70	65	
2 Percentage in bonds	40	30	35	
3 Equity index return	10	20		
4 Bond index return	5	10		
5 Custom index return	$[0.6(10) + 0.4(5)]$	$[0.7(20) + .03(10)]$		+25
	$6 + 2 = 8$	$14 + 3 = 17$		
6 Fund return	10	19		+29
7 Fund return — Custom index return at actual allocation = Return from security selection and choice of risk level of securities	+2	+2	+2	+4

Custom index at average allocation measures selection and timing:

	Period 1	Period 2	Average	Cumulative
1–4 Same as above				
5 Custom index return	$[0.65(10) + 0.35(5)]$	$[0.65(20) + 0.35(10)]$		+24.75
	$6.5 + 1.75 = 8.25$	$13 + 3.5 = 16.5$		
	10	19		29
6 Fund return				
7 Fund return — Custom index return at actual allocation = Return from selection, choice of security risk level, *and* timing	1.75	2.5	2.125	4.25
8 Impact of timing = Custom index at actual allocation − Custom index at average allocation = 25.0 − 24.75 = +.25				

* Selection is used here to include not only security selection but also choice of the risk level of the stocks and bonds owned.

since there are no widely published indexes covering private placements and other less marketable assets, it is obviously not possible to reflect the portfolio's full composition if the fund contains such assets.

Dollar-Weighted Indexes

The preceding discussion of market indexes assumed a time-weighted approach; namely, we were looking at one dollar invested throughout the period and not considering any impact from external cash flows. An alternative approach to the use of indexes is to assume that return equaled the return on the index but that the portfolio had cash flow equal to those which actually occurred. In this case the question being asked is, "How much money *would* the fund have now relative to the amount that it *actually* has now had it invested in a certain index?" This approach can be used in a variety of ways for the total portfolio and for the sectors of the portfolio. Logical ways in which the concept can be applied are as follows.

The total portfolio. The assumed ending value of the portfolio can be calculated under the assumption that the fund is 100 percent invested in an equity index, 100 percent in a bond index, 100 percent in a cash equivalent index, or any combination of weightings. The same calculation can be made by assuming that the portfolio is invested in the average commingled equity fund, the average commingled fixed-income fund, the average separately managed balanced fund, the best fund, the worst fund, and so on. Another application of this approach is to see whether the fund kept up with its assumed or actuarial rate of return or with the consumer price index. A special case of this analysis can be carried out to see whether the fund achieved a profit or a loss from investments. In this case the fund's ending value is compared with its beginning value plus net contributions and the question implicitly asked is, "Did the fund achieve a return above or below 0 percent?"

Equity or fixed-income portfolios. The same multitude of possibilities exists for comparing the actual ending value of equity and bond portfolios with assumed ending values under various assumptions as exists for the total portfolio. Logically, one might compare the actual ending value for an equity portfolio with the results which would have been attained had the fund been invested in equity indexes, equity commingled funds, or the equity portions of separately managed funds. The same approach can be applied to fixed-income funds, only using fixed-income indexes and funds to provide the alternative rate of return which might have been achieved.

In summary, comparing portfolio returns to those of market indexes is a useful function that can be carried out by comparing a sector of the portfolio to the appropriate market index and by comparing the total portfolio return to an index weighted in the same proportions as the portfolio.

COMPARISON WITH OTHER PORTFOLIOS

Although comparing portfolio results to those of market indexes has considerble use, there is still something lacking, both conceptually and emotionally, when only market indexes are used as comparisons. The *conceptual* problem is that even though the market indexes are supposedly representative of the "market," each index is, in fact, a specific portfolio with characteristics which may or may not be representative of what real funds are like. Further, the market indexes have no transaction costs associated with them, and real portfolios obviously incur a certain amount of transaction costs. This creates a negative bias for fund results as compared to those of market indexes. As an example of the limitation of using market indexes as a sole benchmark for comparison, we can see how the Standard & Poor's 500, viewed as a portfolio, would have compared to a sample of managed equity portfolios for the years 1973 to 1977:

S&P 500 Ranked versus Equity Portfolios (rank of 1 is best)					
1973–1977	*1977*	*1976*	*1975*	*1974*	*1973*
16	44	22	33	35	17

As can be seen, the Standard & Poor's 500 was not a good representation of the "average" managed equity portfolio, which many people believe that a market index should be.

In addition to the conceptual objections to using only market indexes for comparisons, there is also an *emotional* objection. Human beings tend to be greatly concerned with how they fare in comparison with other persons in similar circumstances. For both reasons fund sponsors have come to count on comparisons between their fund results and those of other funds. Consequently, a knowledge of this area is important to all fund sponsors.

Equity Portfolios

Portfolios containing only equities should be compared to other similarly constructed portfolios. That is, an equities versus equities comparison is by far the most appropriate basis for comparing the results of an equity portfolio with those of other portfolios. Both the fund and the sample should be either tax-exempt or taxable. In almost all cases in which performance measurement services are provided, the portfolios measured are tax-exempt retirement or endowment funds.

Equity-Oriented Portfolios

A portfolio can be called an equity-oriented portfolio if it is either invested in equities or invested in cash reserves that will be invested in equities at an appropriate time. It is important to distinguish between an equity-oriented portfolio, which conceivably could be 100 percent in cash equivalents, and an equity portfolio, which by definition is always 100 percent in equities. The appropriate comparison for equity-oriented portfolios is, of course, other equity-oriented portfolios. That is, portfolios which can be invested in either equities or cash equivalents should be compared to similar funds.

However, it is not easy to find such a sample for separately managed portfolios. This is because most funds own stocks, bonds, or cash equivalents, and in the reporting process often do not distinguish their cash equivalent reserves for equity investing from their cash equivalent reserves for fixed-income investing. Thus, adding the portfolio's cash to the equity sector to calculate an "equity-oriented" return would be misleading in that some or all of the cash equivalents in the account may, in fact, be in reserve for the purchase of fixed-income investments.

Fortunately, an alternative solution is at hand in the form of bank-commingled equity-oriented funds. Although these funds are typically called equity funds, they are more appropriately called equity-oriented funds since they contain both equities and cash equivalents. Increasingly, banks are making available the returns of their commingled funds, so this information can be monitored rather easily. Mutual funds are also a source of information on the performance of equity-oriented funds, and precise information on mutual funds is widely available because these funds are required to calculate and publish their values daily. However, since mutual funds typically invest for individuals rather than tax-exempt portfolios, they are a less appropriate basis for comparison than are bank commingled equity-oriented funds.

Bond Portfolios

Bond portfolios, consisting of intermediate-term and long-term bonds (but not cash equivalents) are appropriately measured against similar portfolios. The tax implications of the fund sponsor must be considered, since a portfolio with tax-exempt (municipal) bonds obviously cannot be compared to one with taxable bonds. This is usually not a problem because most funds desiring performance information are tax-exempt. Since the funds are tax-exempt, they own higher yielding taxable bonds.

Bond-Oriented Funds

Bond-oriented funds, unlike bond funds, can own both cash equivalents and bonds, whereas pure bond funds can own only bonds. Thus, as with equity-oriented funds, bond-oriented funds should be compared to similar funds. For the same reason, namely, the availability of appropriate data, the results of bond-oriented funds can be compared to those of bank commingled bond-oriented funds. The necessary data are becoming more widely available.

Cash Equivalents, Private Placements, and Other Assets

For these categories the available comparative information is sparse. The returns on cash equivalents could be compared to the returns of several "money market" funds which invest in taxable securities. The returns on private placements could be compared to the returns of the few insurance company private placement commingled funds, which are becoming more popular, though these funds may also contain cash equivalents. As to "other assets," it is unlikely that there will be appropriate comparative information for many years to come due to our inability to accurately measure the performance of investments in real estate, mortgages, oil and gas wells, and other relatively unmarketable assets.

Total Portfolios

Total portfolios consist of the assets from the various sectors of the overall marketplace. Thus, it is appropriate to compare the total returns of a fund with the total returns of many other funds. However, several cautions are in order.

First of all, returns (and hence comparisons) tend to be dominated by the risk posture of the portfolio and by the particular market results which occurred during the period being measured. That is to say, a fund whose policy is to be 80 percent in equities will look very good in a period when the stock market rises and will look quite poor in a period when it declines. This may be fully attributable to the policy chosen by the sponsor rather than a reflection of the investment manager's skill.

Second, a problem arises regarding how to treat investments which are in less readily marketable securities. One alternative is to include these assets in the total portfolio, recognizing that some investors have large investments in these "other assets" and that other investors have none at all. Recognition must also be given to the fact that some of these assets are valued at historical or amortized cost and others at some estimate of market value. Obviously, the quality of these estimates affects the quality of the total portfolio return and, hence, the usefulness of the comparison. An alternative treatment is to exclude less readily marketable assets from the total portfolio for purposes of comparing results to other portfolios. Although this solves the question of the accurate measurement of returns, it can be misleading in that not all of the portfolio's assets are accounted for. Perhaps the only solution in this case is to choose a method and to be sure that the portfolio is being measured on the same basis as the funds in the comparative universe.

Third, commingled funds are generally not appropriate comparisons for total portfolios. This is because the total portfolio, which is assumed in this case to be a balanced fund, is not structured in the same way as the commingled funds, which are almost always oriented to either equities or bonds. (Obviously, if the total portfolio contains either no equities or no bonds, then the commingled funds are appropriate comparisons. For purposes of this discussion, however, such a portfolio would not be regarded as a total portfolio but as an equity- or bond-oriented fund.) The fallacy of using commingled funds to compare to compare total portfolio results is the same as the fallacy of comparing equity-oriented funds to equity-only funds, namely, that the differences in allocation among stocks, bonds, and cash equivalents will have an important bearing on how the fund performed in a particular market environment. In an up market a balanced fund will tend to underperform bank commingled equity funds and to outperform bank commingled bond funds. Since stocks will return more than bonds, the funds with the highest percentage in equities will have the greatest returns. In a down market the reverse will be true. Again, the problem is that we are measuring the investment policy rather than the investment performance of the fund.

In summary, the principal concern of those who attempt to compare their portfolio results with the portfolio results obtained by others is to find a sensible comparative universe. The logical way to do this is to compare the fund being measured with funds which are as close as possible to it in construction—equities to equities, bond to bonds, and total portfolios to total portfolios. Funds containing equities plus cash should be compared to similar portfolios, as should funds containing bonds plus cash equivalents. In this way the most reasonable comparisons of straight returns (not risk-adjusted returns) can be made.

COMPARING RISK AND RISK-ADJUSTED RETURNS

Once an appropriate risk measure has been chosen comparing the performance of portfolios becomes quite straightforward. The percentage in asset categories, such as equities, of one portfolio versus another can be readily compared. Similarly, the beta, or variability, however measured, of one portfolio can be directly compared with that of other portfolios. Of course, this assumes that the fund sponsor has available to it information on the risk measures of other funds.

Comparing risk-adjusted returns, like comparing risk, is straightforward. The only requirements are that the portfolio's measurement of risk-adjusted performance be similar to that of the sample and that the classification of assets also be similar. For instance, meaningful comparisons cannot be made if the portfolio's equity sector is defined to exclude convertible securities, but the comparative sample defines equity to include convertibles.

COMPARING FUNDS WITH SIMILAR OBJECTIVES OR OF SIMILAR TYPES

The idea of comparing one's fund with other funds that have similar objectives is very appealing. This is especially true since many fund sponsors are hiring managers with specific styles which cannot easily be compared with more diversified portfolios or with specialized portfolios with different structures or objectives. Unfortunately, developing a workable definition for "similar objectives" and finding a sufficiently large sample of funds which fit the objectives are two formidable problems. All funds have as their general objective making money without losing money. More eloquent statements suggest as objectives maximizing return without undue risk of loss of principal. These definitions of objectives are of little help since they include all funds rather than just "similar" funds.

In theory it is possible to compare funds based on their level of risk, such as the percentage of equities. In practice it is not possible to find a sample of funds with exactly the same asset allocation as the sponsor's fund, so typically a range of allocations is considered. In other words, a fund with 63 percent in equities would be compared with funds having between 60 percent and 70 percent in equities. However, in a volatile period there can be substantial differences between funds having 60 percent in equities and funds having 70 percent in equities. Also, if the fund being measured has a very high or a very low percentage in stocks, there will probably not be many similar funds in the same category.

An alternative might be to construct an artificial total portfolio sample by taking a sample of balanced funds and assuming that each hypothetical fund in the sample had the equity and fixed-income returns of the real fund but the asset allocation policies of the sponsor's fund. Although a bit awkward to calculate, this alternative has some merit. However, most of the benefit of this procedure could be gained merely by comparing the sponsor's equity to the sample of other equity funds and making a similar analysis for other asset categories.

Criteria other than the percentage in equities could also be used for establishing similarity of objectives. Among such criteria are the actuarial rate of return and the size of cash inflows or outflows.

It obviously makes sense to compare the results of commingled equity funds with those of other commingled equity funds, and similarly for bond funds and other fund types. However, the rationale for this type of comparison is related to the asset type and policy rather than any characteristic of the sponsor. It is also possible to compare profit-sharing funds with other profit-sharing (but not pension) funds, Taft-Hartley pension funds with other Taft-Hartley pension funds (but not corporate pension funds), and similarly for public pension funds and endowment funds. Although this makes intuitive sense, experience indicates that very few differences between funds are attributable to the sponsor's organization type other than that Taft-Hartley funds and public funds tend to have lower percentages in equities than do corporate pension funds. This is probably the only area in which a comparison by fund type provides useful information. Even so, it is still appropriate to compare equity funds with an equity funds sample, bond funds with a bond funds sample, and the timing scores of funds with the timing scores of other funds.

COMPARING PORTFOLIO RESULTS TO THOSE OF OTHER PORTFOLIOS MANAGED BY THE SAME INVESTMENT MANAGER

If it is appealing to know how one is faring compared with his peers, as broadly defined, it is especially interesting to know how one's portfolio is performing compared to similar portfolios managed by the same organization. Or more precisely, it is interesting to know whether the sponsor's portfolio is performing worse than those of other clients of the manager firm. Of course, there might be very good reasons for differences. First, the needs of the sponsoring organization may be different. For instance, one fund might have a very different liability structure in its pension plan than another. One fund might be a profit sharing as opposed to a pension fund, in which case employees receive periodic statements as to the value of their investments, and payout to employees may be in a lump sum as opposed to over a period of years. Contributory funds might be treated differently by a manager from noncontributory funds. One organization may have restricted securities or company stock which biases results. Finally, the views and prejudices of the sponsoring organization may lead to different portfolios. All these factors tend to cloud the issue which the sponsor is trying to determine, namely, whether his investment officer is providing as astute management as are others in his firm.

APPENDIX
Composition and Characteristics of Various Stock and Bond Indexes

Since portfolios are so frequently compared to market indexes, and since sponsors, investment managers, and consultants place considerable weight on such indexes, it is worthwhile to understand more about them. It should be noted that:

1. No one index is useful for all purposes.
2. Each index is composed of a certain list of securities that are weighted in a specific way, and if the list contained other securities or a different weighting scheme, the results would be different.
3. Each index has flaws or limitations which sponsors should be aware of.

Creating indexes involves deciding what is to be measured, choosing a list of representative securities, choosing methods for weighting the securities, changing the list of securities, treating income, and establishing the frequency and timing of index availability. Characteristics of the major stock indexes follow (see also Exhibit 9).

Standard & Poor's 500.   Goal is to measure the pattern of common stock movements; 500 large companies are included; changes are made in the list of securities by a committee at S&P; weighting is by capitalization; available daily as to capital changes and quarterly about one week after quarter end including dividends.

Standard & Poor's 400.   Designed to measure movements of industrial stocks; all other characteristics same as S&P 500.

Dow Jones averages.

Industrials.   Designed to measure movements of industrial companies—includes 30 large industrials; changes made rarely, generally to reflect mergers or acquisitions; weighting according to price of shares; available daily for price changes.

Utilities.   Covers utility companies; otherwise same as Dow Jones Industrials.

Transportation.   Covers transportation companies; otherwise same as Dow Jones Industrials.

Composite.   Amalgamation of Industrials, Utilities, and Transportation indexes.

New York Stock Exchange Index.   Represents market value of all common stocks on New York Stock Exchange; issues included changed according to listings and delistings from the NYSE; capitalization weighting; available daily as to price.

EXHIBIT 9 Common Stock Indexes

Index	Number of Securities	Weighting	Calculation Technique	Base Year
Standard & Poor's 500	500	Market value	Same as NYSE	1941–43 = 10
Standard & Poor's 400	400	Market value	Same as NYSE	1941–43 = 10
Dow Jones Industrials	30	Price	Sum of prices divided by number of companies adjusted for historical splits →	Started 1927 (an average, not an index) →
Dow Jones Utilities	15	Price		
Dow Jones Transportation	20	Price		
Dow Jones Composite	65	Price		
New York Stock Exchange	All companies 1,509 issues as of 5/31/85	Market value	Market value of all listed shares adjusted for capitalization changes	December 31, 1965 = 50 (approximate average share price)
American Stock Exchange	All companies 930 issues as of 5/31/85	Market value	Same as NYSE except that NYSE subtracts the value of dividends from the index on ex-date, whereas ASE does not	August 31, 1973 = 100
Value Line	1,662 issues as of 5/31/85	Equal	Geometric mean of daily price relatives	June 30, 1961 = 100
Wilshire 5000	Changes daily 5,611 issues as of 5/31/85	Market value	Market value	December 31, 1970 = $798.439 billion

American Stock Exchange Index. Reflects value of shares on American Stock Exchange; all issues on ASE included; issues changed when listing so requires; capitalization weighted; available daily as to price.

Value Line Index. Goal is to represent typical price movements of stocks in Value Line Universe; changes in securities made at discretion of Arnold Bernhard & Co.; weighting is equal, calculated as a geometric average (rather than adding up the values and dividing by the number of securities, the index multiplies daily price relatives and takes the nth root of the ensuing value); price relatives are then compounded to compute the index; available daily as to price. Note: A geometric index always underperforms the corresponding arithmetic index.

Wilshire 5000. Represents the market value of all common stocks on the New York Stock Exchange, American Stock Exchange, and over-the-counter markets; changes at discretion of Wilshire Associates; weighted by capitalization; price index and total performance index available; published weekly as to price.

Bond indexes. The information included in Exhibit 10 is self-explanatory.

EXHIBIT 10 Corporate Bond Indexes

Index Name	Number of Securities	Total MV,PV (billions of dollars)	Securities Included	Type (Yield, Total Return, etc.)	Weighting	Calculation	Period and Base Amount	YTM or Coupon and Period	Number of Years to Maturity	Beginning Date of Index	Source of Bond Prices	Historical Information and Frequency
Salomon Brothers High-Grade LT AAA–AA	845	PV = $82.58	AAA–AA	Total return	Par value	Arithmetic	1978 = 100	y = 15.45% 11/1/81	23 years	1/1/69	Salomon trading desks	1969 monthly
Salomon Brothers LT A		PV = $58.00	A	Total return	Par value	Arithmetic	1978 = 100	c = 8.92 11/1/81	22 years	1/1/78	Salomon trading desks	1969 monthly
Salomon Brothers High-Grade LT AAA–AA–A		PV = $140.00	AAA–AA–A	Total return	Par value	Arithmetic	1978 = 100	c = 8.648 11/1/81	23 years	1/1/78	Salomon trading desks	1969 monthly
Barron's Best grade bonds	10	N/A	Aaa	YTM	Equally	Bond value tables	N/A	y = 13% 11/12/81 c = 51/4% 11/12/81	15 years 11/12/81	1/32	The Wall Street Journal	No
Barron's Intermediate grade bonds	10	N/A	Baa	YTM	Equally	Bond value tables	N/A	y = 141/2% 11/12/81 c = 73/8% 11/12/81	20 years 11/12/81	7/76	The Wall Street Journal	No
Dow Jones 20 bonds average	20	N/A	Aaa	YTM	Equally	Bond value tables	N/A	y = 141/8% 11/12/81 c = 71/2% 11/12/81	20 years 11/12/81	7/76	The Wall Street Journal	No

Dow Jones 10 Industrial bonds average	10	N/A	Aaa	YTM	Equally	Bond value tables	N/A	$y = 13\frac{3}{4}\%$ 11/12/81 $c = 6\frac{3}{4}\%$ 11/12/81	12 years 11/21/81	4/15	*The Wall Street Journal*	No
Dow Jones 10 Public utility bonds average	10	N/A	Aaa	YTM	Equally	Bond value tables	N/A	$y = 14\frac{1}{2}\%$ 11/12/81 $c = 8\frac{3}{8}\%$ 11/12/81	20 years 11/12/81	4/15	*The Wall Street Journal*	No
Standard & Poor's Corp. composite bond yield Average-AA	8-AA Ind. 8-AA Util. 16	N/A	AA	YTM	Equally	Arithmetic	N/A	10.98 6/12/85	10–30 years 6/12/85	1/37	Salomon Brothers	1971– weekly; 1937– monthly
Standard & Poor's Corp. composite bond yield Average-A	8-A Ind. 8-AA Util. 16	N/A	A	YTM	Equally	Arithmetic	N/A	$y = 11.11\%$ 6/28/85	15–30 years 6/12/85	1/37	Salomon Brothers	1971– weekly; 1937– monthly
Standard & Poor's Corp. composite bond yield Average-BBB	8-BBB Ind. 8-BBB Util. 15	N/A	BBB	YTM	Equally	Arithmetic	N/A	$y = 11.68\%$ 6/12/85	10–30 years 6/12/85	1/37	Salomon Brothers	1971– weekly; 1937– monthly
Standard & Poor's Industrial bond yield Average-AAA	5-Inds AAA 8-Util AAA 16	N/A	AAA	YTM	Equally	Arithmetic	N/A	$y = 10.49\%$ 6/12/85	15–20 years 6/12/85	1/37	Salomon Brothers	1971– weekly; 1900– monthly

EXHIBIT 10 *(continued)*

Index Name	Number of Securities	Total MV,PV (billions of dollars)	Securities Included	Type (Yield, Total Return, etc.)	Weighting	Calculation	Period and Base Amount	YTM or Coupon and Period	Number of Years to Maturity	Beginning Date of Index	Source of Bond Prices	Historical Information and Frequency
Standard & Poor's Industrial bond yield Average-AA	8-Inds AA	N/A	AA	YTM	Equally	Arithmetic	N/A	y = 11.06% 6/12/85	15–30 years 6/12/85	1/37	Salomon Brothers	1971– weekly; 1900– monthly
Standard & Poor's Industrial bond yield Average-A	7-Ind A	N/A	A	YTM	Equally	Arithmetic	N/A	y = 11.06% 6/12/85	15–20 years 6/12/85	1/37	Salomon Brothers	1971– weekly; 1900– monthly
Standard & Poor's Industrial bond yield Average-BBB	7-Ind BBB	N/A	BBB	YTM	Equally	Arithmetic	N/A	y = 11.70% 6/12/85	10–20 years 6/12/85	1/37	Salomon Brothers	1971– weekly; 1900– monthly
Shearson Lehman Brothers Corp. bond index	4,575.5	283.545	BBB,A, AA, AAA	Total return	Market value	Arithmetic	N/A	y = 11.28% 5/85	1 year +	12/72	Shearson Lehman Brothers	12/72– monthly
Shearson Lehman Brothers Intermediate corp. bond index	1,884.0	112.161	BBB,A, AA, AAA	Total return	Market value	Arithmetic	N/A	y = 10.85% 5/85	1–9.99 years	12/72	Shearson Lehman Brothers	12/72– monthly

Index			Rating								Source	
Shearson Lehman Brothers Long-term corp. bond index	2,691.5	171.383	BBB,A, AA, AAA	Total return	Market value	Arithmetic	N/A	$y = 11.57\%$ 5/85	10 years +	12/72	Shearson Lehman Brothers	12/72– monthly
Shearson Lehman Brothers Industrial bond index	982.5	82.546	BBB,A, AA, AAA	Total return	Market value	Arithmetic	N/A	$y = 11.35\%$ 5/85	1 year +	12/72	Shearson Lehman Brothers	12/72– monthly
Shearson Lehman Brothers Utility bond index	2,728.5	129.445	BBB,A, AA, AAA	Total return	Market value	Arithmetic	N/A	$y = 11.53\%$ 5/85	1 year +	12/72	Shearson Lehman Brothers	12/72 monthly
Shearson Lehman Brothers Finance bond index	864.5	71.553	BBB,A, AA, AAA	Total return	Market value	Arithmetic	N/A	$y = 10.76\%$ 5/85	1 year +	12/72	Shearson Lehman Brothers	12/72– monthly
Shearson Lehman Brothers Aaa bond index	822	881.257	AAA	Total return	Market value	Arithmetic	N/A	$y = 9.64\%$ 5/85	1 year +	12/72	Shearson Lehman Brothers	12/72– monthly
Shearson Lehman Brothers Aa bond index	1,409.5	106.474	AA	Total return	Market value	Arithmetic	N/A	$y = 11.02\%$ 5/85	1 year +	12/72	Shearson Lehman Brothers	12/72– monthly
Lehman Brothers Kuhn Loeb A bond index	1,950.0	111.335	A+	Total return	Market value	Arithmetic	N/A	$y = 11.26\%$ 5/85	1 year +	12/72	Shearson Lehman Brothers	12/72– monthly
Lehman Brothers Kuhn Loeb Baa bond index	991.0	51.939	BBB+	Total return	Market value	Arithmetic	N/A	$y = 12.03\%$ 5/85	1 year +	12/72	Shearson Lehman	12/72– monthly

EXHIBIT 10 *(continued)*

Index Name	Number of Securities	Total MV, PV (billions of dollars)	Securities Included	Type (Yield, Total Return, etc.)	Weighting	Calculation	Period and Base Amount	YTM or Coupon and Period	Number of Years to Maturity	Beginning Date of Index	Source of Bond Prices	Historical Information and Frequency
Moody's Aaa Industrial bond average	7	N/A	Aaa	YTM	N/A	Arithmetic	N/A	c = 9⅜%	20 years 2 mos.	1918	Newspaper, security dealers and other sources	1918– monthly
Moody's Aa Industrial bond average	10	N/A	Aa	YTM	N/A	Arithmetic	N/A	c = 9⅝%	22 years 5 mos.	1918	Newspaper security dealers and other sources	1918– monthly
Moody's A Industrial bond average	10	N/A	A	YTM	N/A	Arithmetic	N/A	c = 11⅞%	23 years 8 mos.	1918	Newspaper security dealers and other sources	1918– monthly
Moody's Baa Industrial bond average	10	N/A	Baa	YTM	N/A	Arithmetic	N/A	c = 10¼%	20 years 7 mos.	1918	Newspaper security dealers and other sources	1918– monthly

Moody's Industrial average	37	N/A	Aaa, Aa, Baa	YTM	N/A	Arithmetic	N/A	$c = 10\frac{1}{4}\%$	21 years 7 mos.	1918	Newspaper security dealers and other sources	1918– monthly
Moody's Aaa Public utility average	10	N/A	Aaa	YTM	N/A	Arithmetic	N/A	$c = 8\frac{5}{8}\%$	21 years 9 mos.	1918	Newspaper security dealers and other sources	1918– monthly
Moody's Aa Public utility average	10	N/A	Aa	YTM	N/A	Arithmetic	N/A	$c = 9\frac{5}{8}\%$	23 years 9 mos.	1918	Newspaper security dealers and other sources	1918– monthly
Moody's A Public utility average	10	N/A	A	YTM	N/A	Arithmetic	N/A	$c = 10\frac{5}{8}\%$	24 years 5 mos.	1918	Newspaper security dealers and other sources	1918– monthly
Moody's Baa Public utility average	10	N/A	Baa	YTM	N/A	Arithmetic	N/A	$c = 10\frac{3}{4}\%$	24 years 2 mos.	1918	Newspaper security dealers and other sources	1918– monthly
Moody's Public Utility average	40	N/A	Aaa, Aa, Baa	YTM	N/A	Arithmetic	N/A	$c = 9\frac{7}{8}\%$	23 years 5 mos.	1918	Newspaper security dealers and other sources	1918– monthly

EXHIBIT 10 *(continued)*

Index Name	Number of Securities	Total MV,PV (billions of dollars)	Securities Included	Type (Yield, Total Return, etc.)	Weighting	Calculation	Period and Base Amount	YTM or Coupon and Period	Number of Years to Maturity	Beginning Date of Index	Source of Bond Prices	Historical Information and Frequency
Moody's Aa Railroad bond average	5	N/A	Aa	YTM	N/A	Arithmetic	N/A	c = 8 3/8%	16 years 3 mos.	1918	Newspaper security dealers and other sources	1918– monthly
Moody's A Railroad bond average	5	N/A	A	YTM	N/A	Arithmetic	N/A	c = 6%	17 years 1 month	1918	Newspaper security dealers and other sources	1918– monthly
Moody's Baa Railroad bond average	4	N/A	Baa	YTM	N/A	Arithmetic	N/A	c = 6 5/8%	28 years 5 mos.	1918	Newspaper security dealers and other sources	1918– monthly
Moody's Railroad bond average	14	N/A	Aa, A, Baa	YTM	N/A	Arithmetic	N/A	c = 7%	22 years	1918	Newspaper security dealers and other sources	1918– monthly

Moody's Aaa Corp. composite	17	N/A	Aaa utilities and industrials	YTM	N/A	Arithmetic	N/A	c = 9%	21 years 1 month	1918	Newspaper security dealers and other sources	1918– monthly
Moody's Aa Corp. composite	20	N/A	Aa utilities and industrials	YTM	N/A	Arithmetic	N/A	c = 9⅝%	23 years 1 month	1918	Newspaper security dealers and other sources	1918– monthly
Moody's A Corp. composite	20	N/A	A utilities and industrials	YTM	N/A	Arithmetic	N/A	c = 11¼%	24 years	1918	Newspaper security dealers and other sources	1918– monthly
Moody's Baa Corp. composite	20	N/A	Baa utilities and industrials	YTM	N/A	Arithmetic	N/A	c = 10½%	22 years 4 mos.	1918	Newspaper security dealers and other sources	1918– monthly
Moody's Corp. average composite	77	N/A	Aaa, Aa, A, Baa utilities and industrials	YTM	N/A	Arithmetic	N/A	c = 10⅛%	22 years 6 mos.	1918	Newspaper security dealers and other sources	1918– monthly

EXHIBIT 10 (continued)

Index Name	Number of Securities	Total MV, PV (billions of dollars)	Securities Included	Type (Yield, Total Return, etc.)	Weighting	Calculation	Period and Base Amount	YTM or Coupon and Period	Number of Years to Maturity	Beginning Date of Index	Source of Bond Prices	Historical Information and Frequency
Merrill Lynch (C8A0) Long term (15 years+)	1741	MV = 131.6 PV = 152.6	BBB/ AAA	Total return	Market value	Arithmetic	12/31/72 = 100	c = 9.86% y = 11.60% 5/85	23.25 5/85	12/31/72	Merrill Lynch Bond Pricing	1973
Merrill Lynch (C8B0) Long term (15 years+), high quality	687	MV = 59.3 PV = 69.3	AA/AAA	Total return	Market value	Arithmetic	12/31/72 = 100	c = 9.56% y = 11.34% 5/85	23.92 5/85	12/31/72	Merrill Lynch Bond Pricing	1973
Merrill Lynch (C8H0) Long term (15 years+), high quality utilities	487	MV = 35.8 PV = 42.5	AA/AAA	Total return	Market value	Arithmetic	12/31/72 = 100	c = 9.39% y = 11.34% 5/85	25.58 5/85	12/31/72	Merrill Lynch Bond Pricing	1973
Merrill Lynch (C8H3) Long term (15 years+), high quality utilities- coupons 4–5.99 percent	35	MV = 1.1 PV = 2.0	AAA/ AAA	Total return	Market value	Arithmetic	12/31/72 = 100	c = 4.86 y = 2.0% 5/85	18.08 5/85	12/31/72	Merrill Lynch Bond Pricing	1973

Name	No.	MV/PV	Rating	Return type			Base	Coupon/Yield	Value	Date	Source	Year
Merrill Lynch (C8H4) Long term (15 years+), high quality utilities-coupons 6–7.99 percent	117	MV = 6.6 PV = 9.4	AA/AAA	Total return	Market value	Arithmetic	12/31/72 = 100	c = 7.32% y = 11.07% 5/85	21.50 5/85	12/31/72	Merrill Lynch Bond Pricing	1973
Merrill Lynch (C8H5) Long term (15 years+), high quality utilities-coupons 8–9.99 percent	231	MV = 15.5 PV = 19.3	AA/AAA	Total return	Market value	Arithmetic	12/31/72 = 100	c = 8.72% y = 11.1% 5/85	23.83 5/85	12/31/72	Merrill Lynch Bond Pricing	1973
Merrill Lynch (C8H6) Long term (15 years+), high quality utilities-coupons 10–11.99 percent	37	MV = 3.8 PV = 3.9	AA/AAA	Total return	Market value	Arithmetic	9/30/74 100	c = 11.15% y = 11.41% 5/85	31.08 5/85	9/30/74	Merrill Lynch Bond Pricing	1974
Merrill Lynch (C8E0) Long term (15 years+), high quality indus-trials	98	MV = 15.3 PV = 17.1	AA/AAA	Total return	Market value	Arithmetic	12/31/72 = 100	c = 10.00% y = 11.32% 5/85	20.5 5/85	12/31/72	Merrill Lynch Bond Pricing	1973

EXHIBIT 10 *(continued)*

Index Name	Number of Securities	Total MV, PV (billions of dollars)	Securities Included	Type (Yield, Total Return, etc.)	Weighting	Calculation	Period and Base Amount	YTM or Coupon and Period	Number of Years to Maturity	Beginning Date of Index	Source of Bond Prices	Historical Information and Frequency
Merrill Lynch (C8E4) Long term (15 years+), high quality industrials-coupons 6–7.99 percent	22	MV = 1.9 PV = 2.8	AA/AAA	Total return	Market value	Arithmetic	12/31/72 = 100	c = 7.10% y = 10.99% 5/85	18.42 5/85	12/31/72	Merrill Lynch Bond Pricing	1973
Merrill Lynch (C8E5) Long term (15 years+), high quality industrials-coupons 8–9.99 percent	38	MV = 5.7 PV = 6.9	AA/AAA	Total return	Market value	Arithmetic	12/31/72 = 100	c = 8.71% y = 11.04% 5/85	19.08 5/85	12/31/72	Merrill Lynch Bond Pricing	1973
Merrill Lynch (C8E6) Long term (15 years+), high-quality industrials-coupons 10–11.99 percent	20	MV = 2.8 PV = 2.9	AA/AAA	Total return	Market value	Arithmetic	12/31/72 = 100	c = 11.15% y = 11.32% 5/85	26.5 5/85	12/31/72	Merrill Lynch Bond Pricing	1973

Merrill Lynch (C8K9) Long term (15 years+), high-quality finance coupons 16.0+ percent	3	MV = 147.8 PV = 131.4	AA/AAA	Total return / Market value / Arithmetic	12/31/72 = 100	c = 18.07% y = 15.93%	18.0 5/85	12/31/72	Merrill Lynch Bond Pricing	1973
Merrill Lynch (C8K4) long term (15 years+) high-quality finance-coupons 6–7.99 percent	2	MV = 247.3 PV = 431.8	AA/AAA	Total return / Market value / Arithmetic	12/31/72 = 100	c = 6.10% y = 11.20%	26.4 5/85	12/31/72	Merrill Lynch Bond Pricing	1973
Merrill Lynch (C8K5) Long term (15 years+), high-quality finance-coupons 8–9.99 percent	19	MV = 2.2 PV = 2.7	AA/AAA	Total return / Market value / Arithmetic	12/31/72 = 100	c = 8.72% y = 11.10% 5/85	19.1 5/85	12/31/72	Merrill Lynch Bond Pricing	1973
Merrill Lynch (C8K6) Long term (15 years+), high-quality finance-coupons 10–11.99 percent	12	MV = 1.2 PV =	AA/AAA	Total return / Market value / Arithmetic	9/30/74 = 100	c = 11.48% y = 11.32% 5/85	21.1 5/85	9/30/74	Merrill Lynch Bond Pricing	1973

EXHIBIT 10 *(continued)*

Index Name	Number of Securities	Total MV,PV (billions of dollars)	Securities Included	Type (Yield, Total Return, etc.)	Weighting	Calculation	Period and Base Amount	YTM or Coupon and Period	Number of Years to Maturity	Beginning Date of Index	Source of Bond Prices	Historical Information and Frequency
Merrill Lynch (C8K7) Long term (15 years+) high-quality finance-coupons 12–13.99 percent	15	MV = 859.2 PV = 827.2	AA/AAA	Total return	Market value	Arithmetic	1/31/83 = 100	c = 12.3% y = 11.8% 5/85	22 5/85	1/31/83	Merrill Lynch Bond Pricing	1973
Merrill Lynch (C8K8) Long term (15 years+) high-quality finance-coupons 14–15.99 percent	3	MV = 224.3 PV = 195.3	AA/AAA	Total return	Market value	Arithmetic	7/29/83 = 100	c = 15.1% y = 13.1% 5/85	23 5/85	1/31/83	Merrill Lynch Bond Pricing	1973
Merrill Lynch (C8I0) Long term (15 years+), medium-quality utilities	773	MV = 47.5 PV = 53.8	A/BBB	Total return	Market value	Arithmetic	12/31/72 = 100	c = 10.39% y = 11.88%	23.5 5/85	12/31/72	Merrill Lynch Bond Pricing	1973

Description	Count	MV/PV	Rating	Return/Market value	Arithmetic	Base	Coupon/Yield	Value	Date	Source	Year
Merrill Lynch (C813) Long term (15 years+), medium-quality utilities-coupons 4–5.99 percent	5	MV = .2 PV = .4	BBB/A	Total return Market value	Arithmetic	12/31/72 = 100	c = 5.56% y = 11.06% 5/85	20.00 5/85	12/31/72	Merrill Lynch Bond Pricing	1973
Merrill Lynch (C814) Long term (15 years+), medium-quality utilities-coupons 6–7.99 percent	154	MV = 5.8 PV = 8.3	A/BBB	Total return Market value	Arithmetic	12/31/72 = 100	c = 7.49% y = 11.45% 5/85	18.75 5/85	12/31/72	Merrill Lynch Bond Pricing	1973
Merrill Lynch (C815) Long term (15 years+), medium-quality utilities-coupons 8–9.99 percent	341	MV = 18.0 PV = 22.7	A/BBB	Total return Market value	Arithmetic	12/31/72 = 100	c = 8.88% y = 11.53% 5/85	23.58 5/85	12/31/72	Merrill Lynch Bond Pricing	1973
Merrill Lynch (C816) Long term (15 years+), medium-quality utilities-coupons 10–11.99 percent	86	MV = 5.3 PV = 5.7	A/BBB	Total return Market value	Arithmetic	12/31/72 = 100	c = 10.79% y = 11.75% 5/85	22.75 5/85	12/31/72	Merrill Lynch Bond Pricing	1973

EXHIBIT 10 (continued)

Index Name	Number of Securities	Total MV, PV (billions of dollars)	Securities Included	Type (Yield, Total Return, etc.)	Weighting	Calculation	Period and Base Amount	YTM or Coupon and Period	Number of Years to Maturity	Beginning Date of Index	Source of Bond Prices	Historical Information and Frequency
Merrill Lynch (C8F0) Long term (15 years+), medium-quality industrials	222	MV = 21.2 PV = 24.9	BBB/A	Total return	Market value	Arithmetic	12/31/72 = 100	c = 9.759% y = 11.745% 5/85	23.58 5/85	12/31/72	Merrill Lynch Bond Pricing	1973
Merrill Lynch (C8F4) Long term (15 years+), medium-quality industrials-coupons 6–7.99 percent	40	MV = 3.4 PV = 5.3	BBB/A	Total return	Market value	Arithmetic	12/31/72 = 100	c = 6.93% y = 11.64% 5/85	23.58 5/85	12/31/72	Merrill Lynch Bond Pricing	1973
Merrill Lynch (C8F5) Long term (15 years+), medium-quality industrials-coupons 8–9.999 percent	96	MV = 7.7 PV = 9.6	BBB/A	Total return	Market value	Arithmetic	12/31/72 = 100	c = 8.866% y = 11.601% 5/85	21.58 5/85	12/31/72	Merrill Lynch Bond pricing	1973

Merrill Lynch (C8F6) Long term (15 years+), medium-quality industrials-coupons 10–11.99 percent	34	MV = 2.5 PV = 3.0	BBB/A	Total return	Market value	Arithmetic	12/31/72 = 100	c = 11.068% y = 11.694% 5/85	23.25 5/85	12/31/72	Merrill Lynch Bond Pricing	1973
Merrill Lynch (C8L0) Long term (15 years+), medium-quality finance	33	MV = 2.5 PV = 3.0	BBB/A	Total return	Market value	Arithmetic	12/31/72 = 100	c = 9.03% y = 11.47% 5/85	19.92 5/85	12/31/72	Merrill Lynch Bond Pricing	1973
Merrill Lynch (C8L4) Long term (15 years+), medium-quality finance-coupons 6–7.99 percent	5	MV = .4 PV = .6	BBB/A	Total return	Market value	Arithmetic	12/31/72 = 100	c = 6.40% y = 11.45% 5/85	21.42 5/85	12/31/72	Merrill Lynch Bond Pricing	1973
Merrill Lynch (C8L5) Long term (15 years+), medium-quality finance-coupons 8–9.99 percent	20	MV = 1.6 PV = 1.9	BBB/A	Total return	Market value	Arithmetic	12/31/72 = 100	c = 9.01% y = 11.34% 5/85	17.2 5/85	12/31/72	Merrill Lynch Bond Pricing	1973

EXHIBIT 10 *(continued)*

Index Name	Number of Securities	Total MV,PV (billions of dollars)	Securities Included	Type (Yield, Total Return, etc.)	Weighting	Calculation	Period and Base Amount	YTM or Coupon and Period	Number of Years to Maturity	Beginning Date of Index	Source of Bond Prices	Historical Information and Frequency
Merrill Lynch (C8L6) Long term (15 years+), medium-quality finance-coupons 10–11.99 percent	1	MV = .05 PV = .06	BBB/A	Total return	Market value	Arithmetic	12/31/72 = 100	c = 11.38% y = 12.70% 5/85	22.0 5/85	12/31/72	Merrill Lynch Bond Pricing	1973
Merrill Lynch (C6H0) intermediate term, (5–9.99 years) high-quality utilities	142	MV = 6.5 PV = 7.4	AA/AAA	Total return	Market value	Arithmetic	12/31/72 = 100	c = 8.33% y = 10.5% 5/85	7.83 5/85	12/31/72	Merrill Lynch Bond Pricing	1973
Merrill Lynch (C6H3) Intermediate term, (5–9.99 years) high-quality utilities-coupons 4–5.99 percent	81	MV = 2.3 PV = 3.2	AA/AAA	Total return	Market value	Arithmetic	12/31/72 = 100	c = 4.63% y = 10.02% 5/85	7.42 5/85	12/31/72	Merrill Lynch Bond Pricing	1973

Index	No.	MV/PV	Quality				Base	Coupon/Yield	Total return	Market value date	Source	Year
Merrill Lynch (C6H4) Interme-diate term, (5–9.99 years) high-quality utilities-coupons 6–7.99 percent	19	MV = .5 PV = .6	AA/AAA	Total return	Market value	Arithmetic	12/31/72 = 100	c = 6.7% y = 10.5% 5/85	7.8 5/85	12/31/72	Merrill Lynch Bond Pricing	1973
Merrill Lynch (C6H5) Interme-diate term, (5–9.99 years) high-quality utilities-coupons 8–9.99 percent	5	MV = .2 PV = .2	AA/AAA	Total return	Market value	Arithmetic	12/31/74 = 100	c = 8.37% y = 10.87% 5/85	9.25 5/85	9/30/74	Merrill Lynch Bond Pricing	1973
Merrill Lynch (C6H6) Interme-diate term, (5–9.99 years) high-quality utilities-coupons 10–11.99 per-cent	8	MV = 1.0 PV = 1.0	AAA/AA	Total return	Market value	Arithmetic	12/31/72 100	c = 10.62% y = 10.27% 5/85	6.0 5/85	12/31/72	Merrill Lynch Bond Pricing	1973
Merrill Lynch (C6E0) Interme-diate-term (5–9.99 years) high-quality industrials	40	MV = 4.2 PV = 4.3	AA/AAA	Total return	Market value	Arithmetic	12/31/72 100	c = 10.60% y = 11.33% 5/85	7.2 5/85	12/31/72	Merrill Lynch Bond Pricing	1973

EXHIBIT 10 *(continued)*

Index Name	Number of Securities	Total MV,PV (billions of dollars)	Securities Included	Type (Yield, Total Return, etc.)	Weighting	Calculation	Period and Base Amount	YTM or Coupon and Period	Number of Years to Maturity	Beginning Date of Index	Source of Bond Prices	Historical Information and Frequency
Merrill Lynch (C6E4) Intermediate-term (5–9.99 years), high-quality industrials-coupons 6–7.99 percent	7	MV = .7 PV = .9	AA/AAA	Total return	Market value	Arithmetic	12/31/74 100	c = 6.97% y = 10.62% 5/85	7.50 5/85	12/31/72	Merrill Lynch Bond Pricing	1973
Merrill Lynch (C6E5) Intermediate-term (5–9.99 years), high quality industrials-coupons 8–9.99 percent	4	MV = .2 PV = .2	AA/AAA	Total return	Market value	Arithmetic	12/31/72 = 100	c = 9.375% y = 10.369% 5/85	7.25 5/85	12/31/74	Merrill Lynch Bond Pricing	1975
Merrill Lynch (C6E6) Intermediate-term (5–9.99 years), high-quality industrials-coupons 10–11.99 percent	6	MV = .8 PV = .7	AA/AAA	Total return	Market value	Arithmetic	12/31/72 = 100	c = 11.06% y = 10.6% 5/85	6.50 5/85	12/31/72	Merrill Lynch Bond Pricing	1973

Index	Count	MV/PV	Rating	Return type	Base	Coupon/Yield	Maturity	Base date	Source	Year
Merrill Lynch (C6K0) Intermediate-term (5–9.99 years) high-quality finance	58	MV = 5.7 PV = 5.7	AA/AAA	Total return Market value Arithmetic	12/31/72 = 100	c = 11.63% y = 11.32% 5/85	7.33 5/85	12/31/72	Merrill Lynch Bond Pricing	1973
Merrill Lynch (C6K4) Intermediate-term (5–9.99 years) high-quality finance coupons 6–7.99 percent	8	MV = .7 PV = .8	AA/AAA	Total return Market value Arithmetic	12/31/72 = 100	c = 7.34% y = 10.87% 5/85	9.17 5/85	12/31/72	Merrill Lynch Bond Pricing	1973
Merrill Lynch (C6K5) Intermediate-term (5–9.99 years) high-quality finance coupons 8–9.99 percent	2	MV = .2 PV = .2	AA/AAA	Total return Market value Arithmetic	12/31/74 = 100	c = 8.01% y = 10.83% 5/85	8.00 5/85	6/30/74	Merrill Lynch Bond Pricing	1975
Merrill Lynch (C6K6) Intermediate-term (5–9.99 years), high-quality finance coupons 10–11.99 percent	15	MV = 1.2 PV = 1.2	AA/AAA	Total return Market value Arithmetic	12/31/72 = 100	c = 11.30% y = 11.01% 5/85	7.42 5/85	12/31/72	Merrill Lynch Bond Pricing	1973

EXHIBIT 10 *(continued)*

Index Name	Number of Securities	Total MV,PV (billions of dollars)	Securities Included	Type (Yield, Total Return, etc.)	Weighting	Calculation	Period and Base Amount	YTM or Coupon and Period	Number of Years to Maturity	Beginning Date of Index	Source of Bond Prices	Historical Information and Frequency
Merrill Lynch (C6C0) Intermediate-term (5–9.99 years), medium quality	629	MV = 41.3 PV = 41.0	A/BBB	Total return	Market value	Arithmetic	12/31/72 = 100	c = 11.76% y = 11.52% 5/85	7.42 5/85	12/31/72	Merrill Lynch Bond Pricing	1973
Merrill Lynch (C6I0) Intermediate-term (5–9.99 years), medium-quality utilities	324	MV = 16.1 PV = 15.9	A/BBB	Total return	Market value	Arithmetic	12/31/72 = 100	c = 12.13% y = 11.64% 5/85	6.67 5/85	12/31/72	Merrill Lynch Bond Pricing	1973
Merrill Lynch (C6I3) Intermediate-term (5–9.99 years), medium-quality utilities-coupons 4–5.99 percent	110	MV = 1.8 PV = 2.6	A/BBB	Total return	Market value	Arithmetic	12/31/72 = 100	c = 4.67% y = 10.80% 5/85	7.34 5/85	12/31/72	Merrill Lynch Bond Pricing	1973

Description	No.	MV/PV	Rating	Return type	Market value	Base	Coupon/Yield		Date	Source	Year
Merrill Lynch (C6I4) Intermediate-term (5–9.99 years), medium-quality utilities-coupons 6–7.99 percent	33	MV = .5 PV = .7	A/A	Total return	Market value	Arithmetic	7/31/76 = 100	c = 7.08% y = 10.87% 5/85	7.42 5/85	7/31/76	Merrill Lynch Bond Pricing	1976
Merrill Lynch (C6I5) Intermediate-term (5–9.99 years), medium-quality utilities-coupons 8–9.99 percent	38	MV = .8 PV = .8	A/BBB	Total return	Market value	Arithmetic	12/31/72 = 100	c = 8.85% y = 15.21% 5/85	7.75 5/85	12/31/72	Merrill Lynch Bond Pricing	1973
Merrill Lynch (C6I6) Intermediate-term (5–9.99 years), medium-quality utilities-coupons 10–11.99 percent	17	MV = 1.3 PV = 1.3	A/BBB	Total return	Market value	Arithmetic	6/30/74 = 100	c = 11.22% y = 10.78% 5/85	7.17 5/85	6/30/74	Merrill Lynch Bond Pricing	1974
Merrill Lynch (C6F4) Intermediate-term (5–9.99 years), medium-quality industrials	164	MV = 1.5 PV = 1.5	BBB/A	Total return	Market value	Arithmetic	12/31/72 = 100	c = 11.39% y = 11.48% 5/85	7.67 5/85	12/31/72	Merrill Lynch Bond Pricing	1973

EXHIBIT 10 *(continued)*

				Total return	Market value	Arithmetic					
Merrill Lynch (C6F4) Intermediate-term (5–9.99 years), medium-quality industrials coupons 6–7.99 percent	29	MV = .2 PV = .3	BBB/A				6/30/74 = 100	c = 6.72% y = 15.34% 5/85	7.83 5/85	6/30/74	Merrill Lynch Bond Pricing 1974
Merrill Lynch (C6F5) Intermediate-term (5–9.99 years), medium-quality industrials coupons 8–9.99 percent	17	MV = 1.6 PV = 1.9	BBB/A				6/30/74 = 100	c = 9.39% y = 11.96% 5/85	9.08 5/85	6/30/74	Merrill Lynch Bond Pricing 1974
Merrill Lynch (C6F6) Intermediate-term (5–9.99 years), medium-quality industrials coupons 10–11.99 percent	38	MV = 2.8 PV = 2.8	BBB/A				9/30/74 = 100	c = 10.99% y = 10.99% 5/85	6.67 5/85	9/30/74	Merrill Lynch Bond Pricing 1974

No.	Name	Quality	Weight	Index type	Base	Coupon / Yield	Total return	Date	Source	Year
104	Merrill Lynch (C6L0) Intermediate-term (5–9.99 years), medium-quality finance	BBB/A	MV = 7.6 PV = 7.5	Total return Market value Arithmetic	12/31/72 = 100	c = 11.66% y = 11.41% 5/85	7.42 5/85	12/31/72	Merrill Lynch Bond Pricing	1973
18	Merrill Lynch (C6L4) Intermediate-term (5–9.99 years), medium-quality finance-coupons 6–7.99 percent	A/BBB	MV = .7 PV = .8	Total return Market value Arithmetic	12/31/72 = 100	c = 7.69% y = 10.98% 5/85	7.25 5/85	12/31/72	Merrill Lynch Bond Pricing	1973
25	Merrill Lynch (C6L5) Intermediate-term (5–9.99 years), medium-quality finance-coupons 8–9.99 percent	A/BBB	MV = .8 PV = .9	Total return Market value Arithmetic	12/31/73 = 100	c = 8.86% y = 11.04% 5/85	6.92 5/85	12/31/73	Merrill Lynch Bond Pricing	1974
18	Merrill Lynch (C6L6) Intermediate-term (5–9.99 years), medium-quality finance-coupons 10–11.99 per-cent	BBB/A	MV = .4 PV = .5	Total return Market value Arithmetic	12/31/74 = 100	c = 11.23% y = 11.11% 5/85	7.98 5/85	12/31/74	Merrill Lynch Bond Pricing	1975

EXHIBIT 10 *(continued)*

Merrill Lynch (C1A0) Short term (1–2.99 years)	337	MV = 23.3 PV = 23.4	BBB/ AAA	Total return	Market value	Arithmetic	12/31/75 = 100	c = 9.89% y = 9.92% 5/85	2.0 5/85	12/31/75	Merrill Lynch Bond Pricing	1976
Merrill Lynch (C1B0) Short term (1–2.99 years), high-quality	121	MV = 11.1 PV = 11.1	AA/AAA	Total return	Market value	Arithmetic	12/31/75 = 100	c = 7.85% y = 15.61% 5/85	2.0 5/85	12/31/75	Merrill Lynch Bond Pricing	1976
Merrill Lynch (C1C0) Short term (1–2.99 years), medium-quality	216	MV = 12.2 PV = 12.3	A/BBB	Total return	Market value	Arithmetic	12/31/75 = 100	c = 9.93% y = 10.12% 5/85	1.92 5/85	12/31/75	Merrill Lynch Bond Pricing	1976
Merrill Lynch (C2A0) intermediate-term (3–4.99 years)	287	MV = 18.7 PV = 18.7	BBB/ AAA	Total return	Market value	Arithmetic	12/31/75 = 100	c = 10.79% y = 10.76% 5/85	4.08 5/85	12/31/75	Merrill Lynch Bond Pricing	1976

Index	No.	MV/PV	Quality	Return type	Base	Coupon/Yield	Duration	Date	Source	Year
Merrill Lynch (C2B0) Intermediate-term (3–4.99 years), high quality	109	MV = 8.1 PV = 9.0	AA/AAA	Total return, Market value, Arithmetic	12/31/75 = 100	c = 10.50% y = 10.52% 5/85	3.92 5/85	12/31/75	Merrill Lynch Bond Pricing	1976
Merrill Lynch (C2C0) Intermediate-term (3–4.99 years), medium quality	178	MV = 9.8 PV = 8.1	BBB/A	Total return, Market value, Arithmetic	12/31/75 = 100	c = 11.05% y = 10.97% 5/85	3.92 5/85	12/31/75	Merrill Lynch Bond Pricing	1976
Merrill Lynch (C7A0) Intermediate-term (10–14.99 years)	795	MV = 30.5 PV = 38.3	BBB/AAA	Total return, Market value, Arithmetic	12/31/75 = 100	c = 8.13% y = 11.19% 5/85	13.42 5/85	12/31/75	Merrill Lynch Bond Pricing	1976
Merrill Lynch (C7B0) Intermediate-term (10–14.99 years) high quality	255	MV = 11.9 Pv = 15.4	AA/AAA	Total return, Market value, Arithmetic	12/31/75 = 100	c = 7.45% y = 10.84% 5/85	13.42 5/85	12/31/75	Merrill Lynch Bond Pricing	1973
Merrill Lynch (C7C0) Intermediate-term (10–14.99 years) medium quality	540	MV = 18.6 PV = 22.9	A/BBB	Total return, Market value, Arithmetic	12/31/75 = 100	c = 8.58% y = 11.43% 5/85	13.58 5/85	12/31/75	Merrill Lynch Bond Pricing	1973

EXHIBIT 10 (continued)

Index Name	Number of Securities	Total MV,PV (billions of dollars)	Securities Included	Type (Yield, Total Return, etc.)	Weighting	Calculation	Period and Base Amount	YTM or Coupon and Period	Number of Years to Maturity	Beginning Date of Index	Source of Bond Prices	Historical Information and Frequency
Salomon Brothers long-term govts	N/A	N/A	All but flower bonds	Total return	Par value	Arithmetic	1978 = 100	c = 9.51% 11/1/81	12 years	1/1/78	Salomon Brothers	3 months monthly
Salomon Brothers medium-term 3–5	N/A	N/A	All but flower bonds	Total return	Par value	Arithmetic	1978 = 100	c = 10.09 11/1/81	3–5 years	1/1/78	Salomon Brothers	3 months monthly
Salomon Brothers medium-term 6–8	N/A	N/A	All but flower bonds	Total return	Par value	Arithmetic	1978 = 100	c = 9.44 11/1/81	6–8 years	1/1/78	Salomon Brothers	3 months monthly
Salomon Brothers medium-term 9–11	N/A	N/A	All but flower bonds	Total return	Par value	Arithmetic	1978 = 100	c = 10/46 11/1/81	9–11 years	1/1/78	Salomon Brothers	3 months monthly
Salomon Brothers U.S. Govt. index	36	N/A	U.S. Treasury bonds	Total return	N/A	Arithmetic	12/31/77 = 100	N/A	14 years	1/1/78	Salomon Brothers	12/77 monthly
Salomon Brothers U.S. Treasury Bill index	N/A	N/A	U.S. Treasury bills	Total return	N/A	Arithmetic	12/31/77 = 100	N/A	3 months	1/1/78	Salomon Brothers	12/77 monthly

Standard & Poor's Long-term govt. bond yield average	4	N/A	N/A	YTM	Equally	Arithmetic	N/A	y = 10.31% 6/12/85	10 years 6/12/85	1/42	The Wall Street Journal (YTM)	1942 monthly 1971 weekly
Standard & Poor's Long-term govt. bond price index	4	N/A	N/A	Price	Equally	YTM is converted into a price assuming 3 percent coupon + 15 years to maturity (Dollars per $100 par value)	N/A	p = 44.77 6/12/85	15 years 6/12/85	1/42	The Wall Street Journal (convert yields into price)	1942 monthly 1971 weekly
Standard & Poor's Intermediate-term govt. bond yield average	4	N/A	N/A	YTM	Equally	Arithmetic	N/A	y = 10.04% 6/12/85	6–9 years 6/12/85	1/42	The Wall Street Journal (YTM)	1942 monthly 1971 weekly
Standard & Poor's Intermediate-term govt. bond price index	4	N/A	N/A	Price	Equally	YTM is converted into a price assuming 3 percent coupon and 7 1/2 years to maturity (Dollars per $100 par value)	N/A	p = 63.48 6/12/85	7 1/2 years 6/12/85	1/42	The Wall Street Journal (convert yields into price)	1942 monthly 1971 weekly

EXHIBIT 10 *(continued)*

Index Name	Number of Securities	Total MV,PV (billions of dollars)	Securities Included	Type (Yield, Total Return, etc.)	Weighting	Calculation	Period and Base Amount	YTM or Coupon and Period	Number of Years to Maturity	Beginning Date of Index	Source of Bond Prices	Historical Information and Frequency
Standard & Poor's Short-term govt. bond yield average	4	N/A	N/A	YTM	Equally	Arithmetic	N/A	y = 8.80% 6/12/85	2–4 years 6/12/85	1/42	The Wall Street Journal (YTM)	1942 monthly 1971 weekly
Standard & Poor's Short-term govt. bond price index	4	N/A	N/A	Price	Equally	YTM is converted into a price assuming 3 percent + 3 1/2 years to maturity (Dollars per $100 par value)	N/A	p = 82.82 6/12/85	3 1/2 years 6/12/85	1/42	The Wall Street Journal (convert yields into price)	1942 monthly 1971 weekly
Shearson Lehman Brothers Treasury bond index	145.0	707.570	AAA	Total return	Market value	Arithmetic	N/A	y = 9.61% 7/85	1 year+	12/72	Shearson Lehman Brothers	N/A

Name	No.	Value	Rating	Return type	Weighting	Averaging	Base date / value	Yield	Maturity	Date	Source	Inception
Shearson Lehman Brothers Intermediate Treasury bond index	105	563.282	AAA	Total return	Market value	Arithmetic	N/A	y = 9.34% 7/85	1–9.99 years	12/72	Shearson Lehman Brothers	N/A
Shearson Lehman Brothers Long term Treasury bond index	40	144.288	AAA	Total return	Market value	Arithmetic	N/A	y = 10.70% 7/85	10 years +	12/72	Shearson Lehman Brothers	N/A
Merrill Lynch (GOAO) Govt. master	389	MV = 883.2 PV = 850.9	AAA/ AAA	Total return	Market value	Arithmetic	3/31/72 100	c = 11.3% y = 9.83% 7/85	8 years	12/31/72	Merrill Lynch Bond Pricing	1973
Merrill Lynch (G802) U.S. Treasury long-term (15+)	35	MV = 164.4 PV = 15.9	AAA/ AAA	Total return	Market value	Arithmetic	3/31/73 100	c = 11.5% y = 10.9% 7/85	24 years	3/31/73	Merrill Lynch Bond Pricing	1973
Merrill Lynch (G202) Govt-U.S. Treasury intermediate term (3–4.99 years)	24	MV = 132.2 PV = 125.6	AAA/ AAA	Total return	Market value	Arithmetic	12/31/72 100	c = 11.6% y = 9.8% 7/85	4 years	12/31/72	Merrill Lynch Bond Pricing	1973
Merrill Lynch (G302) Govt-U.S. Treasury intermediate term (5–6.99 years)	15	MV = 83.8 PV = 76.6	AAA/ AAA	Total return	Market value	Arithmetic	12/31/72 100	c = 12.6% y = 10.4% 7/85	6 years	12/31/72	Merrill Lynch Bond Pricing	1973

EXHIBIT 10 *(continued)*

Index Name	Number of Securities	Total MV,PV (billions of dollars)	Securities Included	Type (Yield, Total Return, etc.)	Weighting	Calculation	Period and Base Amount	YTM or Coupon and Period	Number of Years to Maturity	Beginning Date of Index	Source of Bond Prices	Historical Information and Frequency
Merrill Lynch (G402) Govt-U.S. Treasury intermediate term (7–9.99 years)	21	MV = 80.1 PV = 78.0	AAA/AAA	Total return	Market value	Arithmetic	12/31/72 100	c = 10.9% y = 10.5% 7/85	9 years	12/31/72	Merrill Lynch Bond Pricing	1973
Merrill Lynch (G102) Govt-U.S. Treasury short term (1–2.99 years)	42	MV = 284.9 PV = 276.1	AAA/AAA	Total return	Market value	Arithmetic	12/31/72 100	c = 11.0% y = 8.9% 7/85	2 years	12/31/72	Merrill Lynch Bond Pricing	1973
Merrill Lynch (G7PO) Govt-U.S. Treasury intermediate term (10–14.99 years)	12	MV = 2.7 PV = 2.7	AAA/AAA	Total return	Market value	Arithmetic	7/31/77 100	c = 8.4% y = 10.6% 7/85	12 years	7/31/77	Merrill Lynch Bond Pricing	1973

Shearson Lehman Brothers Govt. bond index	597	867.461	AAA	Total return	Market value	Arithmetic	N/A	9.62% 5/85	1 year+	12/72	Shearson Lehman Brothers	12/72 monthly
Shearson Lehman Brothers Govt. intermediate bond index	458.0	713.296	AAA	Total return	Market value	Arithmetic	N/A	9.39% 5/85	1–9.99 years	12/72	Shearson Lehman Brothers	12/72 monthly
Shearson Lehman Brothers Govt. long-term bond index	139.0	154.165	AAA	Total return	Market value	Arithmetic	N/A	10.70% 5/85	10 years+	12/72	Shearson Lehman Brothers	12/72 monthly
Shearson Lehman Brothers GNMA Pass-through bond index	17.0	N/A	AAA	Total return	Market value	Arithmetic	N/A	N/A 11/81	N/A	12/72	Shearson Lehman Brothers	12/72 monthly
Merrill Lynch (G702) Govt-federal agencies intermediate term (10–14.99 years)	4	MV = 6.2 PV = 7.3	AAA/ AAA	Total return	Market value	Arithmetic	12/31/75 100	c = 8.9% y = 10.6% 5/85	13 years 5/85	12/31/75	Merrill Lynch Bond Pricing	1973

EXHIBIT 10 *(continued)*

Index Name	Number of Securities	Total MV,PV (billions of dollars)	Securities Included	Type (Yield, Total Return, etc.)	Weighting	Calculation	Period and Base Amount	YTM or Coupon and Period	Number of Years to Maturity	Beginning Date of Index	Source of Bond Prices	Historical Information and Frequency
Merrill Lynch (G8P0) Govt-federal agencies long term (15 years+)	18	MV = 1.8 PV = 2.2	AAA/ AAA	Total return	Market value	Arithmetic	12/31/75 100	c = 8.9% y = 10.9% 5/85	24 years 5/85	12/31/75	Merrill Lynch Bond Pricing	1973
Merrill Lynch (G1P0) Govt-federal agencies short term (1–2.99 years)	118	MV = 74.5 PV = 71.8	AAA/ AAA	Total return	Market value	Arithmetic	12/31/75 100	c = 11.5% y = 9.0% 5/85	2 years 5/85	12/31/75	Merrill Lynch Bond Pricing	1973
Merrill Lynch (G2P0) Govt-federal agencies intermediate term (3–4.99 years)	65	MV = 34.4 PV = 32.5	AAA/ AAA	Total return	Market value	Arithmetic	12/31/75 100	c = 11.8% y = 9.8% 5/85	4 years 5/85	12/31/75	Merrill Lynch Bond Pricing	1973

Index				Total return	Market value	Arithmetic					Source	
Merrill Lynch (G3P0) Govt-federal agencies intermediate term (5–6.99 years)	30	MV = 15.3 PV = 14.4	AAA/AAA	Total return	Market value	Arithmetic	12/31/75 100	c = 11.8% y = 10.3% 5/85	6 years 5/85	12/31/75	Merrill Lynch Bond Pricing	1973
Merrill Lynch (G402) Govt-federal agencies intermediate term (7–9.99 years)	21	MV = 81.9 PV = 74.4	AAA/AAA	Total return	Market value	Arithmetic	12/31/75 100	c = 11.1% y = 10.3% 5/85	9 years 5/85	12/31/75	Merrill Lynch Bond Pricing	1973
Shearson Lehman Brothers Long-term, high-quality govt. agency corp. bond index	1147.0	228.198	AAA	Total return	Market value	Arithmetic	N/A	y = 10.91% 5/85	10 years+	12/72	Shearson Lehman Brothers	12/72 monthly

EXHIBIT 10 *(continued)*

Index Name	Number of Securities	Total MV, PV (billions of dollars)	Securities Included	Type (Yield, Total Return, etc.)	Weighting	Calculation	Period and Base Amount	YTM or Coupon and Period	Number of Years to Maturity	Beginning Date of Index	Source of Bond Prices	Historical Information and Frequency
Shearson Lehman Brothers Intermediate govt/corporate bond index	2342.0	825.458	AAA	Total return	Market value	Arithmetic	N/A	$y = 9.59\%$ 5/85	1-9.99 years	12/72	Shearson Lehman Brothers	12/72 monthly
Shearson Lehman Brothers Long-term govt/corporate bond index	2830.5	325.548	AAA	Total return	Market value	Arithmetic	N/A	$y = 11.16\%$ 5/85	10 years +	12/72	Shearson Lehman Brothers	12/72 monthly
Shearson Lehman Brothers Govt/corporate bond index	5172.5	1151.006	AAA	Total return	Market value	Arithmetic	N/A	$y = 10.03\%$ 5/85	1 year+	12/72	Shearson Lehman Brothers	12/72 monthly
Merrill Lynch Corp. (BOAO) and Govt. Master	4686	MV = 1175.0 PV = 1178.2	AA/AA	Total return	Market value	Arithmetic	12/31/72 100	$y = 10.03\%$ 7/85	9 years 7/85	12/72	Merrill Lynch Bond Pricing	1973

Lipper general municipal bond fund index	10	7.4	Representative general munibond funds	Principal only	Dollar weighted	Arithmetic	12/31/80 = 100	N/A	N/A	N/A	12/31/80	Bond fund prices-NASD	12/31/80 daily
Lipper short-term municipal bond fund	10	21.9	10 largest short-term munibond funds	7-day average yield; 30-day average yield; average days to maturity	Unweighted	Arithmetic	N/A	N/A	N/A	N/A	9/2/81	Call funds directly	9/2/81 weekly
Bond Buyer rev. bond index	Potential issuers 25	N/A		YTM	Equally	Arithmetic	Coupon-par in 30 years	N/A	N/A	N/A	Thursday to Thursday	Traders from 10-15 firms are asked their yield values each Thursday	Weekly 1979–Present

EXHIBIT 10 *(continued)*

Index Name	Number of Securities	Total MV,PV (billions of dollars)	Securities Included	Type (Yield, Total Return, etc.)	Weighting	Calculation	Period and Base Amount	YTM or Coupon and Period	Number of Years to Maturity	Beginning Date of Index	Source of Bond Prices	Historical Information and Frequency
Bond Buyer 20-bond index	20	N/A		YTM	By rating	Arithmetic	Coupon-par in 20 years	N/A	N/A	Thursday to Thursday	Traders from 10–15 firms are asked their yield values each Thursday	Monthly 1917–45 Weekly 1946–Present
Bond Buyer 11-bond index	11	N/A		YTM	By rating	Arithmetic	Coupon-par in 20 years	N/A	N/A	Thursday to Thursday	Traders from 10–15 firms are asked their yield values each Thursday	Monthly 1917–45 Weekly 1946–Present

Standard & Poor's municipal bond yield index	15	N/A	General obligation Bonds AAA,AA,A	YTM	Equally	Arithmetic	N/A	y = 8.75% 6/12/85	20 years	N/A	Phone survey	1900 monthly 1971 weekly
Standard & Poor's municipal bond price index	15	N/A	AAA,AA,A	Price	Equally	Convert YTM into price assuming 4 percent coupon, 20 years to	N/A	p = 55.51 6/12/85	20 years	N/A	Phone survey	1900 monthly 1971 weekly
Shearson Lehman Brothers Yankee bond index	99	8954	AAA	Total return	Market value	Arithmetic		YTM = 10.53% 5/85	1 year+	12/72	Sherson Lehman Brothers	12/72 monthly

EXHIBIT 10 *(continued)*

Index Name	Number of Securities	Total MV,PV (billions of dollars)	Securities Included	Type (Yield, Total Return, etc.)	Weighting	Calculation	Period and Base Amount	YTM or Coupon and Period	Number of Years to Maturity	Beginning Date of Index	Source of Bond Prices	Historical Information and Frequency
Shearson Lehman Brothers Yankee intermediate bond index	53	5118	AAA	Total return	Market value	Arithmetic		YTM = 10.27% 5/85	1–9.99 years	12/72	Shearson Lehman Brothers	12/72 monthly
Shearson Lehman Brothers Yankee long-term bond index	46	3836	AAA	Total return	Market value	Arithmetic		YTM = 10.88% 5/85	10 years+	12/72	Shearson Lehman Brothers	12/72 monthly
Merrill Lynch Corp–Yankee bonds (CONO) ALL	133	MV = 17.7 PV = 17.9	AAA/AAA	Total return	Market value	Arithmetic	12/31/75 = 100	c = 11.4% y = 10.7%	9 years 7/85	12/75	Merrill Lynch Bond Pricing	1973

Index	No.	Value	Type	Return	Basis	Method		Yield	Maturity	Date	Pricing	History
Shearson Lehman Brothers Int'l global index	987	87.372	Publicly traded	Total return	Market value	Arithmetic	N/A	11.12% 5/85	1 year+	12/76	AIBD quotations	12/72 monthly
Shearson Lehman Brothers Int'l short-term global index	813	68.687	Publicly traded	Total return	Market value	Arithmetic	N/A	11.04% 5/85	1–7 years	12/76	AIBD quotations	12/72 monthly
Shearson Lehman Brothers Int'l long-term global index	174	18.685	Publicly traded	Total return	Market value	Arithmetic	N/A	11.38% 5/85	7 years+	12/76	AIBD quotations	12/72 monthly
Shearson Lehman Brothers Int'l high grade public sector index	213	20.289	AAA	Total return	Market value	Arithmetic	N/A	10.77% 5/85	1 year+	12/76	AIBD quotations	12/72 monthly
Shearson Lehman Brothers Int'l short-term, high-grade public sector index	159	14.81	AAA	Total return	Market value	Arithmetic	N/A	10.55% 5/85	1–7 years	12/76	AIBD quotations	12/72 monthly
Shearson Lehman Brothers Int'l long-term, high-grade public sector index	54	5.479	AAA	Total return	Market value	Arithmetic	N/A	11.22% 5/85	7 years+	12/76	AIBD quotations	12/72 monthly

EXHIBIT 10 (continued)

Index Name	Number of Securities	Total MV, PV (billions of dollars)	Securities Included	Type (Yield, Total Return, etc.)	Weighting	Calculation	Period and Base Amount	YTM or Coupon and Period	Number of Years to Maturity	Beginning Date of Index	Source of Bond Prices	Historical Information and Frequency
Shearson Lehman Brothers Int'l U.S. corp. index	295	29.295	Obligations of U.S. corp.	Total return	Market value	Arithmetic	N/A	11.28% 5/85	1 year+	12/76	AIBD quotations	12/72 monthly
Shearson Lehman Brothers Int'l U.S. short-term corp. index	242	22.732	Obligations of U.S. corp.	Total return	Market value	Arithmetic	N/A	11.26% 5/85	1–7 years	12/76	AIBD quotations	12/72 monthly
Shearson Lehman Brothers Int'l U.S. long-term corp. index	53	6.562	Obligations of U.S. corp.	Total return	Market value	Arithmetic	N/A	11.34% 5/85	7 years+	12/76	AIBD quotations	12/72 monthly
Shearson Lehman Brothers Int'l European corpo-rate index	213	13.949	European, Australia, and New Zealand commercial banks	Total return	Market value	Arithmetic	N/A	11.22% 5/85	1 year+	12/76	AIBD quotations	12/72 monthly

Shearson Lehman Brothers Int'l European corp. short-term index	190	11.969	European, Australia, and New Zealand commercial banks	Total return	Market value	Arithmetic	N/A	11.15% 5/85	1–7 years	12/76	AIBD quotations	12/72	monthly
Shearson Lehman Brothers Int'l European corp. long-term index	23	1.980	European, Australia, and New Zealand commercial banks	Total return	Market value	Arithmetic	N/A	11.66% 5/85	7 years+	12/76	AIBD quotations	12/72	monthly
Shearson Lehman Brothers Int'l Canadian public sector index	121	13.591	Obligations of Canadian provinces	Total return	Market value	Arithmetic	N/A	11.08% 5/85	1 year+	12/76	AIBD quotations	12/72	monthly
Shearson Lehman Brothers Int'l short-term Canadian public sector index	94	10.569	Obligations of Canadian provinces	Total return	Market value	Arithmetic	N/A	11.00% 5/85	1–7 years	12/76	AIBD quotations	12/72	monthly
Shearson Lehman Brothers Int'l long-term Canadian public sector index	27	3.022	Obligations of Canadian provinces	Total return	Market value	Arithmetic	N/A	11.35% 5/85	7 years+	12/76	AIBD quotations	12/72	monthly

EXHIBIT 10 *(continued)*

Index Name	Number of Securities	Total MV, PV (billions of dollars)	Securities Included	Type (Yield, Total Return, etc.)	Weighting	Calculation	Period and Base Amount	YTM or Coupon and Period	Number of Years to Maturity	Beginning Date of Index	Source of Bond Prices	Historical Information and Frequency
Shearson Lehman Brothers Int'l short-term Japanese index	75	6.952	Japanese private sector banks	Total return	Market value	Arithmetic	N/A	10.98% 5/85	1–7 years	12/76	AIBD quotations	12/72 monthly
Handelsblatt bond fund index	N/A	N/A	German F.I. mutual funds—bond and cash equivalents	Price	N/A	N/A	12/31/66 = 100	N/A	N/A	1966	Redemption prices	N/A
Financial Times govt. securities index	11	N/A	U.K. govt. securities	Price	Equally	Geometric	10/15/26 = 100	N/A	N/A	10/15/26	London Stock Exchange	N/A
Financial Times actuaries fixed interest index	87	70.453	Govt. bonds	Price	Market value	Geometric	12/31/75 = 100	N/A	N/A	12/31/75	London Stock Exchange	N/A
Nikkei Bond Index	N/A	N/A	Long-, medium- and short-term bonds	YTM	Equally	Arithmetic	N/A	N/A	N/A	N/A	N/A	N/A

Merrill Lynch Corporate-Canadian (U.S.) (COMO) payable AAA	214	MV = 21.8 PV = 22.3	AA/AA	Total return	Market value	Arithmetic	12/31/75 = 100	c = 11.2% y = 11.3% 7/85	22.17 10/81	12/31/75	Merrill Lynch Bond Pricing	N/A
Salomon Brothers World bond index (weighted)	448	N/A	Prime quality, publicly traded	Total return	Market value	Arithmetic	12/31/77 = 100	N/A	9 years	12/77	Salomon Brothers Index	12/77 monthly
Salomon Brothers World bond index (unweighted)	448	N/A	Prime quality, publicly traded	Total return	Market value	Arithmetic	12/31/77 = 100	N/A	9 years	12/77	Salomon Brothers Index	12/77 monthly
Salomon Brothers World money mkt. index (un-weighted)	N/A	N/A	Money market instruments traded	Total return	Market value	Arithmetic	12/31/77 = 100	N/A	N/A	12/77	Salomon Brothers Index	12/77 monthly
Salomon Brothers Foreign dollar bond index	38	N/A	Prime Foreign Dollar Bonds (Yankees)	Total return	N/A	Arithmetic	12/31/77 = 100	N/A	18 years	12/77	Salomon Brothers Index	12/77 monthly
Salomon Brothers Eurodollar bond index	75	N/A	Prime quality Eurodollar bonds	Total return	N/A	Arithmetic	12/31/77 = 100	N/A	7 years	12/77	Salomon Brothers Index	12/77 monthly

EXHIBIT 10 *(continued)*

Index Name	Number of Securities	Total MV,PV (billions of dollars)	Securities Included	Type (Yield, Total Return, etc.)	Weighting	Calculation	Period and Base Amount	YTM or Coupon and Period	Number of Years to Maturity	Beginning Date of Index	Source of Bond Prices	Historical Information and Frequency
Salomon Brothers Eurodollar FRN index	32	N/A	Prime quality Eurodollar FRN's (3 and 6 months)	Total return	N/A	Arithmetic	12/31/77 = 100	N/A	7 years	12/77	Salomon Brothers Index	12/77 monthly
Salomon Brothers Canadian govt. index	11	N/A	Canadian Treasury bonds	Total return	N/A	Arithmetic	12/31/77 = 100	N/A	17 years	12/77	Salomon Brothers Index	12/77 monthly
Salomon Brothers Euro Canadian dollar bond index	8	N/A	Prime quality Euro Canadian dollar bonds	Total return	N/A	Arithmetic	12/31/77 = 100	N/A	8 years	12/77	Salomon Brothers Index	12/77 monthly
Salomon Brothers German government index	15	N/A	Bundes- and republics & Bundes-posts	Total return	N/A	Arithmetic	12/31/77 = 100	N/A	7 years	12/77	Salomon Brothers Index	12/77 monthly

Salomon Brothers Euro Deutsche Mark bond index	48	N/A	Prime quality Euro DM bonds	Total return	N/A	Arithmetic	12/31/77 = 100	N/A	7 years	12/77	Salomon Brothers Index	12/77 monthly
Salomon Brothers Japanese govt. index	10	N/A	Canadian govt. bonds	Total return	N/A	Arithmetic	12/31/77 = 100	N/A	7 years	12/77	Salomon Brothers Index	12/77 monthly
Salomon Brothers Samurai bond index	24	N/A	Prime quality Samurai bonds	Total return	N/A	Arithmetic	12/31/77 = 100	N/A	9 years	12/77	Salomon Brothers Index	12/77 monthly
Salomon Brothers Euroyen bond index	6	N/A	Prime quality Euroyen bonds	Total return	N/A	Arithmetic	12/31/77 = 100	N/A	8 years	12/77	Salomon Brothers Index	12/77 monthly
Salomon Brothers UK Gilt index	19	N/A	UK gilt-edged stocks	Total return	N/A	Arithmetic	12/31/77 = 100	N/A	16 years	12/77	Salomon Brothers Index	12/77 monthly
Salomon Brothers Eurosterling bond index	10	N/A	Prime quality Eurosterling bonds	Total return	N/A	Arithmetic	12/31/77 = 100	N/A	8 years	12/77	Salomon Brothers Index	12/77 monthly
Salomon Brothers Swiss govt. index	9	N/A	Swiss Confederation bonds	Total return	N/A	Arithmetic	12/31/77 = 100	N/A	8 years	12/77	Salomon Brothers Index	12/77 monthly

EXHIBIT 10 *(continued)*

Index Name	Number of Securities	Total MV,PV (billions of dollars)	Securities Included	Type (Yield, Total Return, etc.)	Weighting	Calculation	Period and Base Amount	YTM or Coupon and Period	Number of Years to Maturity	Beginning Date of Index	Source of Bond Prices	Historical Information and Frequency
Salomon Brothers Foreign Sfr. bond index	50	N/A	Prime quality foreign Sfr. bonds	Total return	N/A	Arithmetic	12/31/77 = 100	N/A	9 years	12/77	Salomon Brothers Index	12/77 monthly
Salomon Brothers Dutch govt. index	18	N/A	Netherlands govt. bonds	Total return	N/A	Arithmetic	12/31/77 = 100	N/A	6 years	12/77	Salomon Brothers Index	12/77 monthly
Salomon Brothers Foreign Dff. bond index	11	N/A	Prime quality foreign Dff. bonds	Total return	N/A	Arithmetic	12/31/77 = 100	N/A	6 years	12/77	Salomon Brothers Index	12/77 monthly
Salomon Brothers Euro Dff. bond index	13	N/A	Prime quality Euro Dff. bonds	Total return	N/A	Arithmetic	12/31/77 = 100	N/A	5 years	12/77	Salomon Brothers Index	12/77 monthly
Salomon Brothers French govt. index	7	N/A	Prime quality French govt. bonds	Total return	N/A	Arithmetic	12/31/77 = 100	N/A	6 years	12/77	Salomon Brothers Index	12/77 monthly

Salomon Brothers Euro Ffr. bond index	10	N/A	Prime Quality Euro Ffr. bonds	Total return	N/A	Arithmetic	12/31/77 = 100	N/A	5 years	12/77	Salomon Brothers Index	12/77 monthly
Salomon Brothers Domestic U.S. Dollar C.D. index	N/A	N/A	Domestic Dollar CD	Total return	N/A	Arithmetic	12/31/77 = 100	N/A	3 months	12/77	Salomon Brothers Index	12/77 monthly
Salomon Brothers Eurodollar CD index	N/A	N/A	Eurodollar DC	Total return	N/A	Arithmetic	12/31/77 = 100	N/A	3 months	12/77	Salomon Brothers Index	12/77 monthly
Salomon Brothers Eurodollar deposit index	N/A	N/A	Eurodollar Deposit	Total return	N/A	Arithmetic	12/31/77 = 100	N/A	3 months	12/77	Salomon Brothers Index	12/77 monthly
Salomon Brothers Canadian treasury bill index	N/A	N/A	Canadian treasury bill	Total return	N/A	Arithmetic	12/31/77 = 100	N/A	3 months	12/77	Salomon Brothers Index	12/77 monthly
Salomon Brothers Euro Canadian dollar deposit index	N/A	N/A	Euro Canadian dollar deposit	Total return	N/A	Arithmetic	12/31/77 = 100	N/A	3 months	12/77	Salomon Brothers Index	12/77 monthly
Salomon Brothers Domestic Yen C.D. Index	N/A	N/A	Domestic yen CD	Total return	N/A	Arithmetic	12/31/77 = 100	N/A	3 months	12/77	Salomon Brothers Index	12/77 monthly
Salomon Brothers Yen Gensaki index	N/A	N/A	Yen Gensaki	Total return	N/A	Arithmetic	12/31/77 = 100	N/A	3 months	12/77	Salomon Brothers Index	12/77 monthly

EXHIBIT 10 *(concluded)*

Index Name	Number of Securities	Total MV,PV (billions of dollars)	Securities Included	Type (Yield, Total Return, etc.)	Weighting	Calculation	Period and Base Amount	YTM or Coupon and Period	Number of Years to Maturity	Beginning Date of Index	Source of Bond Prices	Historical Information and Frequency
Salomon Brothers Euroyen deposit index	N/A	N/A	Euroyen deposit	Total return	N/A	Arithmetic	12/31/77 = 100	N/A	3 months	12/77	Salomon Brothers Index	12/77 monthly
Salomon Brothers U.K. Treasury bill index	N/A	N/A	U.K. Treasury bill	Total return	N/A	Arithmetic	12/31/77 = 100	N/A	3 months	12/77	Salomon Brothers Index	12/77 monthly
Salomon Brothers Domestic L CD index	N/A	N/A	Domestic L CD	Total return	N/A	Arithmetic	12/31/77 = 100	N/A	3 months	12/77	Salomon Brothers Index	12/77 monthly

Index											
Salomon Brothers Eurosterling deposit index	N/A	N/A	Domestic L CD	Total return	N/A	Arithmetic	12/31/77 = 100	N/A	3 months	12/77	Salomon Brothers Index	12/77 monthly
Salomon Brothers Domestic Sfr. deposit index	N/A	N/A	Domestic Sfr. deposit	Total return	N/A	Arithmetic	12/31/77 = 100	N/A	3 months	12/77	Salomon Brothers Index	12/77 monthly
Salomon Brothers Euro Sfr. deposit index	N/A	N/A	Euro Sfr. deposit	Total return	N/A	Arithmetic	12/31/77 = 100	N/A	3 months	12/77	Salomon Brothers Index	12/77 monthly
Salomon Brothers Domestic Ffr. deposit index	N/A	N/A	Domestic Ffr. deposit	Total return	N/A	Arithmetic	12/31/77 = 100	N/A	3 months	12/77	Salomon Brothers Index	12/77 monthly
Salomon Brothers Euro Ffr. deposit index	N/A	N/A	Euor Ffr. deposit	Total return	N/A	Arithmetic	12/31/77 = 100	N/A	3 months	12/77	Salomon Brothers Index	12/77 monthly

SOURCE: From an appendix by Arthur Williams III and Noreen M. Conwell in *The Handbook of Fixed Income Securities*, ed. Frank J. Fabozzi and Irving M. Pollack (Homewood, Ill.: Dow Jones-Irwin, 1987).

44

Interest-Rate Futures and Option Strategies in Fixed-Income Portfolio Management

Allan M. Loosigian
President
A. M. Loosigian & Co.

INTRODUCTION

The management of institutional bond portfolios underwent radical changes in the United States during the 1970s. Traditionally considered a sort of recuperative "pit stop" for managers who deemed it prudent or necessary to pull off the faster lane of a far more volatile and riskier stock market, the increasingly turbulent bond market gained recognition as an investment speedway in its own right. Now bond managers and their clients could experience their own brand of thrills and spills as they circled an uncharacteristically perilous fixed-income track.

Unprecedented interest-rate volatility with an ever-upward bias pressed fixed-income managers to accept—and where none were available, to devise—emergency tools and techniques to protect their portfolios from a wholesale depletion of capital values. It was in no way coincidental that interest-rate futures and options date from that period. The creation of these instruments was a Wall Street—rather, a LaSalle Street, Chicago—confirmation of the adage that necessity is the mother of invention.

Until those watershed years of the mid-1970s, bond managers who regarded themselves as innovative and aggressive exercised their craft mainly through the relatively safe techniques of yield pickup, substitution, and sector swaps; they would garner an extra 15 basis points here and there upgrade a particular holding one notch in quality without a sacrifice in yield. But from the first serious eruption of interest rates in 1973–74, and again during the ultimate cataclysm of 1979–81, picking up two dozen or so basis points by switching judiciously from a U.S. Treasury issue, say, into agency, utility, or industrial bonds appeared rather insignificant by comparison to the handsome payoffs to be gained from "going to cash" and then "going long," that is, extending maturities at the right times. Interest-rate anticipation and consequent maturity adjustment became the new and then the only bond game in town as fixed-income managers emulated their stock market cousins in their efforts to call price turns correctly.

With a great deal of time and energy expended on repeatedly exiting and reentering the long end of the bond market quickly, efficiently, and at minimum cost, interest-rate futures and options were brought in from beyond the pale, at least so far as the most daring and self-confident portfolio managers were concerned. The increasing pressure on managers by plan sponsors for star performance (however that may have been defined) even drove some of the more timid among their peers to embrace rate anticipation and the new and somewhat suspect futures and option instruments for their hoped-for salvation. Finally, the most obdurate of the breed conceded that to continue playing by the time-tested (read "archaic") rules of the game was to invite a possibly permanent retirement to the bench, sidelines, pit crew, or whatever.

Although it would undoubtedly be more entertaining to dwell on auto racing or ball playing, the purpose of this chapter is to explain and assess the germane applications of interest-rate futures and options in the management of institutional bond portfolios.[1] Beginning with a description of the relevant futures and option contracts, their specifications, and the manner in which they are traded on the exchanges, the discussion moves to an overview of the theoretical and practical determinants (which are not always the same) of futures and option prices and concludes with a survey of the principal portfolio strategies involving these instruments.

Futures and options offer, to some extent, alternate means of accomplishing similar if not the same objectives. Options on futures contracts are hybrid instruments that proponents claim incorporate the best features of each type of contract while dispensing with their respective disadvantages. But there are important differences in their construction and application. To spare readers inordinate—but, regrettably, not all—confusion, we dissect the three instruments individually and then consider the various strategies incorporating them.

---

[1] In the following chapter I undertake the same task with regard to using stock index futures and options in managing equity portfolios.

INTEREST-RATE FUTURES—THEIR CONTRACT SPECIFICATIONS AND TRADING PROCEDURES

The principal exchanges on which interest-rate futures contracts are traded are the Chicago Board of Trade (CBT) and the Chicago Mercantile Exchange (CME). Futures contracts for the delivery of U.S. Treasury bonds, 10-year notes, and GNMA certificates are traded at the former exchange. The Chicago Mercantile Exchange maintains futures markets in U.S. Treasury bills, bank certificates of deposit, and Eurodollar time deposits, all three instruments of 90-day maturity.

Table 1 lists the specifications of the various interest-rate contracts at the two exchanges by face amounts of their underlying securities, the months in which the securities are to be delivered, fractional point changes, and the equivalent dollar value of minimum price fluctuations, maximum daily price movements, and margin requirements. The Treasury bond, note, and GNMA contracts at the Chicago Board of Trade specify the delivery of $100,000 face value of those securities, respectively. The minimum price increment of each contract is $\frac{1}{32}$ of 1 percentage point of par, $\frac{1}{32}$ being equal to $31.25.

The delivery grade for the Treasury bond contract is a hypothetical issue bearing an 8 percent coupon with at least 15 years remaining to its maturity or call date. There are at this writing approximately 30 bonds with varying coupon rates traded in the secondary cash market that have 15 or more years remaining to their maturity or call dates. Nearly all of the currently traded deliverable bonds carry coupon rates higher than the specified 8 percent. To reconcile the prices of these higher coupon bonds to the contract grade, the exchange introduced a system of conversion factors that determine the invoice price to be paid by the "long" contract holder, or buyer, to the "short" contract seller in the (unlikely) event delivery of the bonds underlying the contract is actually made, as follows:

$$\frac{\text{Invoice}}{\text{price}} = \frac{\text{Contract}}{\text{size}} \times \frac{\text{Futures contract}}{\text{settlement price}} \times \frac{\text{Conversion}}{\text{factor}}$$

The contract seller—in futures jargon, the "short" has the prerogative of selecting the bond among the eligible issues he will purchase in the open market and deliver to satisfy his contractual obligation. Normally the bond chosen is the one cheapest to deliver after the conversion formula is applied.

The cost to the contract short to make delivery is the difference between the cost of the deliverable bond in the cash market and the invoice price for the bond's principal, that is:

Cost to deliver = Cost of deliverable bond − Invoice price

TABLE 1 Interest-Rate Futures Contract Specifications

Contract	Contract Size	Months Traded	Minimum Fluctuation	Value per Contract	Daily Limit	Exchange Where Traded
Treasury bill	$1,000,000	March, June, September, December	1 basis point (.01%)	$25.00	60 points	IMM
CD	1,000,000	March, June, September, December	1 basis point (.01%)	25.00	80 points	IMM
EURO-dollar	1,000,000	March, June, September, December	1 basis point (.01%)	25.00	100 points	IMM
Treasury bonds	100,000	March, June, September, December	1/32	31.25	64/32	CBT
GNMA	100,000	March, June, September, December	1/32	31.25	64/32	CBT
Treasury note (10 year)	100,000	March, June, September, December	1/32	31.25	64/32	CBT

NOTES: CBT = Chicago Board of Trade.
IMM = International Monetary Market.

TABLE 2 Treasury Bond Futures Prices and Yields, 8.75 Percent to 11 Percent

Price	Yield	Price	Yield
75-30	10.999%	84-23	9.751%
77-18	10.751	86-22	9.499
79-08	10.502	88-22	9.252
81-01	10.249	90-25	9.002
82-27	10.000	92-31	8.751

The cost calculation does not include the accrued interest on the delivered bonds inasmuch as the contract short is reimbursed for that by the long over and above the invoice price.

Futures contracts fluctuate in price more or less in line with the prices of their underlying securities. It is the "more or less" that creates complications and which will be the focus of a substantial part of this chapter. As we shall presently see, conversion factors, computation of the cheapest bond to deliver, and invoice pricing are all important considerations in the determination and implementation of trading and hedging strategies. But in practice nearly all futures contracts are closed out through offsetting transactions rather than by resorting to the delivery process. Contract buyers terminate their long positions by selling, before the contract delivery date, an equivalent type and number of contracts on the same exchange on which they bought them. Sellers liquidate their short positions by buying the same number of contracts of the same delivery month.

Futures contract buyers profit from declining interest rates and lose when rates rise. Sellers, by contrast, profit from rising rates and lose when rates fall. A Treasury bond futures contract, for example, will rise in price from 82-27 to 90-27 when the current yield on 8 percent contract-grade bonds drops from 10 percent to 9 percent. In that event, a contract buyer at 10 percent would enjoy a gain of 8 points; a contract seller at 10 percent would lose the same number of points. Table 2 lists equivalent bond contract prices for yields ranging from 8.75 percent to 11 percent.

Futures contracts are listed and traded in a series of successive quarterly delivery months: March, June, September, and December. In the case of Treasury bond futures, the series normally consists of nine contracts extending from the current quarter to one about 24 months removed. Every contract must be closed out or settled on or before its delivery date, either through an offsetting transaction or by means of the delivery process. When a contract reaches its delivery date, it expires and a new contract is introduced at the far end of the quarterly series.

Futures exchanges impose limits on the number of points, hence the dollar value, that a contract may move up or down in price during the course of one trading day. The limit varies with market conditions. In the case of bond futures it may be set at two points, meaning that a contract can appreciate or drop in price during any day a maximum of $2,000 (or a total swing up and down of $4,000, though that type of seesaw movement seldom occurs). If a contract price is bid up or offered down to its daily limit without corresponding offers or bids appearing, there will be no trading conducted in that contract until the following day, when the process starts anew. It is conceivable that under unusual market conditions limit moves may recur two or three days running. After that long an interruption trading must resume if the financial integrity of the marketplace is to be maintained.

The financial integrity of the marketplace and the continuation of the trading process rest on a system of marking contracts to the market, that is, valuing futures positions and settling up all gains and losses on a daily basis through a clearinghouse arrangement. Contract buyers and sellers all make initial margin deposits into their brokerage accounts when they establish their long or short positions. These deposits, regarded as "good faith" money rather than the partial-payment type of margin on security purchases, have generally ranged from $1,500 to $2,500 per $100,000 contract for Treasury bond futures.

The constant fluctuation of interest rates following their initial transactions impose continuously changing gains and losses on contract longs and shorts, who are now separated by the exchange clearing mechanism. As interest rates decline, the shorts pay the equivalent of their losses into their brokerage accounts, whereupon the funds are remitted to the clearinghouse and credited to the accounts of the gaining longs. When rates rise, it is the turn of the longs to pay to the benefit of the shorts. These daily money flows are called variation margin payments and receipts. By means of the mark-to-market and variation margin system, no market participant is at credit risk for an amount greater than the dollar value of the current day's price movements.

The gains and losses realized through variation margin payments as interest rates rise and fall, and finally by closing out contract positions, provide the means for managing the rate exposure of a bond portfolio. From the foregoing synopsis, abbreviated though it may be, it should be apparent that the appropriate strategy to hedge a portfolio against the capital depreciation inflicted by rising interest rates is to sell Treasury bond futures. If the futures position is correctly calculated (we shall have a great deal to say about this shortly), the deterioration in portfolio values caused by climbing long-term rates will be offset by the gains compiled by the short contracts.

The 90-day Treasury bill, CD, and Eurodollar time deposit futures traded at the International Monetary Market (IMM) division of the Chicago Mercantile Exchange are structured and processed in much the same way as the bond contracts at the Chicago Board of Trade. There are the important distinctions, however, that these contracts are priced in keeping with the discount yield computation of their underlying money market instruments and have a face value of $1 million.

The short-term interest-rate contracts at the IMM are quoted and bought and sold in terms of an index reflecting the difference between 100 and the projected 90-day discount on the particular instrument that is deliverable according to the specifications of the futures contract. If, for example, in October of the current year the futures market were projecting that 90-day Treasury bills the following June would be priced at a discount of 10 percent, June T-bill futures at the IMM would be quoted at an index figure (which for the sake of convention we shall continue to refer to as a price) of 90.00, that is, 100.00 minus 10.00.

Should the market's perception then change to an anticipation of lower interest rates than was previously expected, say 9 percent by the following June, the June T-bill contract would accordingly appreciate 100 basis points from 90.00 to 91.00, that is 100.00 minus 9.00. This arrangement is consistent with the principle underlying financial futures trading that long contract holders gain and short holders lose when interest rates are expected to decline. The process is reversed with a sentiment that interest rates will rise. Under those circumstances the projected discount on T-bills and other money market instruments will increase, and the remainder from 100.00 will decline accordingly, thereby generating profits for short contract holders and losses for long holders.

The minimum index (i.e., price) fluctuation for T-bill and the other money market futures contracts is one basis point (0.01 percent), the dollar value of which, like that of a basis point for all $1 million face value 90-day instruments, is $25.00:

$$\$1,000,000 \times .0001 \times \frac{90}{360} = \$25.00$$

Therefore, when one T-bill, CD, or Eurodollar futures contract rises in price 100 basis points, reflecting a projected decline in that instrument's discount by an equal amount, long contract holders gain and short holders lose $2,500. That figure does not coincide, due to the differences in contract size, maturity, and pricing structure, with the $8,000 price appreciation of a single Treasury bond futures contract that occurs when long-term Treasury yields drop from 10 percent to 9 percent.[2]

---

[2] It should be stressed that the T-bill futures index reflects the projected discount of a 90-day bill that is newly issued on the contract's delivery date. A June contract, for example, will be settled by the end of June either by an offsetting transaction or the delivery of a 90-day bill that will mature at the end of the following September. Newcomers to these markets must also adjust to the

BOND FUTURES PRICING CONSIDERATIONS

Though hedging is the principal application of interest-rate futures and options within the context of this chapter, there are other strategies of what may be called a quasi-trading nature that could be beneficial to portfolio managers from time to time. All strategies, whether they are hedge oriented or not, require a thorough understanding of the relationships (and of the factors that influence these relationships) between futures and option contracts, the contract-grade securities underlying them, and the actual bonds in question if the manager intends to hedge them. A lack of, or a faulty, understanding of these relationships is almost certain to consign to failure any attempted use of these instruments in an institutional setting. It is not sufficient simply to harbor a view as to whether interest rates are heading up or down, although the value of prescience should by no means be minimized.

Hedging with futures contracts is alternately defined as "taking equal and opposite positions in cash and futures markets," and "engaging in a temporary substitute for a cash transaction." With respect to hedging a bond portfolio, both definitions indicate that a short futures position be taken to offset any capital depreciation incurred as a result of rising interest rates. Implicit in this position is the surrender of any potential market gain generated by a decline in rates, inasmuch as the short futures position would then presumably be registering a comparable loss.

The words *presumably* and *comparable* in the foregoing sentence suggest a certain imprecision about the operation of hedging. That is a fair interpretation. Given the fact that bonds with different coupons, maturities, quality ratings, and issuers respond to interest-rate changes in varying degrees, it is to be expected that individual portfolios containing different mixes of bonds require a certain custom fitting of hedge positions. That is, the correct number of standard contracts must be determined to match the prospective price movement of aggregate portfolios.

As was noted above, the Chicago Board of Trade U.S. Treasury bond futures contract stipulates the delivery of $100,000 face amount 8 percent coupon bonds with at least 15 years remaining to their maturity or call date or the adjusted equivalent of bonds with different coupons. If a portfolio contained nothing but contract-grade Treasury bonds, the hedge calculation would be a simple one, namely, the sale of 10 bond contracts for every $1 million in bonds held in the portfolio. It would then be likely that for every dollar of market value lost in the portfolio

---

fact that contract prices react immediately to anticipated changes in 90-day and 20-year interest rates at some time up to two years removed. That explains, in part, the high volatility of futures contracts that catches many market novices off guard and compels them to pay stiff initiation fees in the form of market losses.

by, say, a 50 basis-point increase in yield, there would be a nearly equal dollar gain scored by the 10 short futures contracts.

But when a portfolio contains corporate and agency as well as Treasury issues, A- and AA-rated utility, finance, and industrial bonds, and bonds with coupons ranging from, perhaps, 7 percent to 14 percent, the calculation becomes more complex. It is understood, for example, that the higher the coupon a bond carries, the greater will be the volatility of that bond's price in response to a given change in interest rates. A 12 percent bond can, therefore, be expected to exhibit roughly one half again more volatility than an otherwise similar 8 percent bond. To hedge such a bond correctly, more futures contracts would be required to achieve the dollar-for-dollar match between their respective price movements that is sought.

The use of futures or option contracts to match and thereby to offset imminent price movements of securities that differ in some respect from the deliverable or exercisable securities is called *cross-hedging*.[3] The expression *hedge ratio* refers to the number of contracts needed, given the composition of a particular portfolio, to attain (and maintain) a dollar-for-dollar match. Three accepted methods of determining the hedge ratio are required to duplicate the price volatility of a specific bond or an aggregate portfolio: (1) conversion factor calculation, (2) basis point valuation, and (3) beta and regression analysis. Each method offers advantages under certain circumstances, but like a hedge position itself, each has offsetting drawbacks.

The Chicago Board of Trade provides a table of conversion factors that adjusts the contract price of a particular delivery month to the price each deliverable bond would command at an assumed 8 percent current yield. The conversion factors adjust upward the invoice prices of bonds bearing coupons greater than the futures contract-grade 8 percent coupon and adjust downward prices of bonds with coupons of less than 8 percent.[4] For example, in September 1981 a Treasury bond with a coupon of 11¾ and a maturity of February 15, 2001 (no call feature) bore a conversion factor of 1.3649. Accordingly, assuming a September 1981 contract settlement price of 65-00, the invoice price would be $88,718.50, that is,

$$\$100,000 \times .6500 \times 1.3649 = \$88,718.50$$

Conversion factors may themselves be employed as "rough-and-ready" hedge ratios. Continuing with the foregoing example, the 1.3649 conversion factor for the 11¾ percent Treasury bonds of February 2001

---

[3] A simplistic analogy is that of using apple contracts (if they existed, which, they do not) to hedge price changes in oranges.

[4] A complete table of conversion factors may be obtained from Financial Publishing Co., 82 Brookline Avenue, Boston, MA 02215.

indicated a sale of 14 futures contracts to hedge $1 million face amount of such bonds. This rough estimate assumes that the 11¾ percent bonds are approximately 40 percent more volatile than 8 percent coupon bonds of the same type. The resulting position of 14 bond contracts would, therefore, best approximate the anticipated dollar price change in the 11¾ percent coupon bonds.

A serious limitation of the conversion factor method of computing hedge ratios is that it is most accurate when applied to the cheapest-to-deliver bonds that a short futures contract holder would presumably select if his or her intention is to deliver them. But the method is not especially precise as it applies to the myriad of bonds that do not meet the specifications of the Chicago Board of Trade bond contract and is, therefore, not as reliable when it comes to cross-hedging. In those situations where a conversion factor does not come into play, such as in hedging prospective yields on Treasury bills or other money market instruments, the method is inapplicable.

The basis point valuation method of determining a hedge ratio compares the dollar value of the price fluctuation caused by a small change in the yield of a bond to be hedged with the dollar fluctuation brought about by the same yield change in the security underlying the proposed hedging instrument. Dollar responses to changes in yield vary with the passage of time and with the price levels of the securities involved. The basis point valuation method therefore requires ongoing monitoring of bond and futures price changes and continuing revision of the hedge ratio in keeping with the observed changes as well as a systematic liquidation of futures contracts to maintain the revised ratios.

The basis point value of a small change in yield of a particular bond is established by comparing the price of that bond with its price at a 0.01 percent higher or lower yield. By way of demonstration, the price at an assumed current yield of 12 percent of a $1 million face amount bond bearing a coupon of 9½ percent and maturing in 20 years is 81⁶/₃₂, while at an assumed yield of 12.01 percent, the price of the bond drops to 81⁴/₃₂, giving it a basis point value of $600. But at a current yield of 11.25 percent the basis point value of the same bond with the same maturity is $700; and at 12.75 percent it is $564.

The formula to determine the number of futures contracts needed to hedge a particular bond by means of the basis point valuation method is as follows:

$$\text{Number of contracts} = \frac{\text{Basis point value (cash)} \times \text{Cash face value}}{\text{Basis point value (underlying security)} \times \text{Contract face value}}$$

Applying the formula to the example cited above, the hedge ratio for the 9½ percent, 20-year bonds would need to be reduced from 17 bond contracts to 14 contracts in response to a 150 basis point change in yield on the bonds from 11.25 percent to 12.75 percent.

The primary drawback to the basis point valuation method of calculating hedge ratios is that its usefulness is limited to differences in current yield, coupon rates, and terms to maturity between the bonds that are to be hedged and the bonds underlying the futures contract. Another approach is required to deal with the price implications of credit risk and other characteristics that distinguish the corporate and municipal sectors from the government market.

The method of hedge ratio determination best suited to cross-hedging involves beta and regression analysis. Beta (β) is well known to investment analysts and managers as a statistical expression of the relationship between the price volatility of an individual stock and the volatility of the stock market as a whole. However, beta may also be used to measure the relationship between the price behavior of a stock, bond, or other commodity and the price behavior of the security or commodity underlying the futures or option contract chosen to implement the hedge. That is to say, beta may serve under those circumstances as a proxy for the hedge ratio.

The calculation of a hedge ratio by means of beta analysis involves performing a statistical regression relating the price behavior of the cash security (CS) and the security underlying the futures or option contract (US). The statistical term, R^2, *or R-squared*, is an expression of the degree to which CS and US move in harmony. R^2 is an important measure because the closeness with which CS and US have tracked one another in the past is considered a valid gauge of how closely they are likely to track one another in the future. That, of course, has a vital bearing on how well the proposed hedge may be expected to perform.

R^2 measurements range between zero and 1.0. An R^2 of zero means that there is no statistical relationship between the behavior of the two variables and that they cannot, therefore, be relied upon to produce a satisfactory hedge. A measure of 1.0 indicates an absolute harmony of movement and holds out the possibility of obtaining a near-perfect hedge. In practice, an R^2 of .8 is normally considered a sufficiently closecorrelation between a cash security and the security underlying the designated hedging contract to provide an adequate hedge.[5]

Once the beta of a given bond or portfolio has been established, an appropriate hedge ratio may be determined through an application of the formula:

$$\text{Number of contracts} = \frac{\text{Beta} \times \text{Bond value}}{\text{Contract value}}$$

---

[5] Interested readers may consult any textbook on statistics for a more detailed discussion of beta and the performance of regression analysis.

To illustrate, in order to hedge $10 million face value Philadelphia Electric 14¾ percent coupon bonds of 2005, it is necessary to derive the beta of that particular issue vis-à-vis the cheapest-to-deliver Treasury bond under the terms of the CBT bond contract. Let us assume that the bond has a beta of 1.8 and an R^2 of .74, inferring there is a 74 percent likelihood that the 14¾ percent coupon bond will continue to display 180 percent of the volatility of the cheapest-to-deliver Treasury issue. Employing the formula cited above, 236 T-bond futures contracts are required to hedge properly $10 million Philadelphia Electric 14¾ percent of 2005 at a current price of 112, i.e.,

$$\text{Number of contracts} = \frac{1.8 \times \$11,200,000}{\$85,250}$$

$$= 236$$

In addition to the "equal and opposite positions" and "temporary substitute transaction" definitions of hedging, yet a third definition is the exchange of outright market risk for basis risk. In futures usage, *basis* denotes the point spread (back to the sports analogies!) between a cash market price and the related futures contract price as expressed in the formula:

$$\text{Basis} = \text{Cash price} - \text{Futures price}$$

As was suggested by the foregoing discussion of hedge ratios beta and R^2, it is not essential—in fact, it seldom occurs—that the cash price (CS) and the futures contract or its underlying security prices (US) are identical. What is essential is that the difference between them, the basis, remains constant. To the extent that the basis remains constant, a hedge is efficient; the extent to which the basis varies during the period in which a hedge is in place determines its degree of risk. Advocates of futures hedging maintain that the risk implicit in a changing basis is less than the risk of an adverse price movement prompted by, in the monetary sector, a rise in interest rates. For the most part the hedge advocates have the available evidence on their side.

It is commonly thought by casual observers that the trend of the spread between cash and futures prices—that is, whether futures contracts are priced at a premium or discount to cash securities—is a function of trader expectations regarding the future course of interest rates.[6] That may be true to some extent, but in the case of bonds the

---

[6] The terms *cash* and *cash securities* are used interchangeably throughout this chapter and the chapter following to distinguish actual bonds and stocks and the prices on them from prices of futures contracts and the contracts themselves. The expression *cash* is a carryover from the traditional commodity markets, especially the grains.

basis is largely determined by the relationship between short- and long-term interest rates. It follows, therefore, that the basis changes in response to shifts in the yield curve.

It should be possible in practice as well as in theory to: (1) borrow money at the prevailing short-term interest rate, (2) buy a deliverable bond, (3) sell a T-bond futures contract, and (4) earn the yield on the cash bond until it comes time to deliver it in satisfaction of the short contract. If futures were priced at a level where it was profitable to enter into this series of transactions, professional arbitrageurs (that group of mystery men and women one often reads about but seldom, if ever, meets in the flesh) would be quick to do precisely that, pocketing the difference and, in the process of buying bonds and selling futures, forcing the basis to close up. If the opposite relationship prevailed—that is, futures contracts were priced above equivalent cash bonds— arbitrageurs would take the reverse tack: (5) borrow cash bonds, (6) sell them short, (7) buy futures contracts, and (8) receive delivery on the long contracts using the delivered bonds to cover the short position, again pocketing the profit on the string of transactions but this time pushing the cash price down and boosting the futures price up. Both series of trades serve to hold the basis at an equilibrium level reflecting the differential between short- and long-term interest rates.[7]

In cash-futures arbitrage operations such as those outlined above, the gain derived from the operation is referred to as "carry." When short-term interest rates are higher than the yields on long-term bonds, i.e., when the yield curve is negatively sloped, the financing cost is a positive figure and carry is, therefore, negative. Conversely, the net financing cost is negative and carry is positive when the yield on the bonds is greater than the short-term cost of financing. These relationships are expressed algebraically in the following formula:

Yield on deliverable bonds (%)	−	Cost of financing (short-term rate) (%)	=	Carry (net financing) cost (%)

When the net financing cost is negative and carry is positive, Treasury bond contracts (and other interest-rate futures) will be priced at successive discounts below the cheapest-to-deliver cash bond price. When net financing cost is positive and carry is negative, futures will normally be priced at increasing premiums over cash bonds. At those stages in the interest-rate cycle when the yield curve shifts from a

---

[7] Again, the image of eagle-eyed arbitrageurs leaping into the breach at the slightest imbalance is a throwback to earlier and, perhaps, more romantic times. Nowadays, most of this wheeling and dealing is performed by computers with scarcely a human hand interfering to gum up the works.

TABLE 3 Yield Curve Shifts and Cash-Futures Price Relationships

Shape of Yield Curve	Net Financing Cost	Carry	Relationship between Cash and Futures Price
Positive	Negative	Positive	Cash price > Futures price
Negative	Positive	Negative	Futures price > Cash price
Flat	Zero	Zero	Cash price = Futures price

positive to a negative slope, it can be observed how the cash-futures price structure swings from one of successive discounts to successive premiums. These relationships and the manner in which they respond to yield curve shifts are summarized in Table 3.

The year 1980 was one of extreme interest-rate movement and, therefore, provides a vivid illustration of the foregoing concepts. Opening the year at a level of about 12 percent, the discount on 90-day Treasury bills climbed rapidly to 15 percent by the beginning of March and just as suddenly plummeted back down to 8 percent by early June. During the same five-month period the current yield on 20-year Treasury bonds oscillated from 10¼ percent to 12¼ percent and again back to 10 percent.

By June 16, the approximate peak of the spring price rally, the cheapest-to-deliver Treasury bond, the 8 percent of 1996–2001, was priced on an adjusted basis at 87, and the prices of the nearest five T-bond futures contracts at the Chicago Board of Trade were as shown in Table 4.

After June 16 interest rates reversed their downward course, returning by November 1 to their peak of the previous March, 90-day bills reaching by December 15 a historic peak of 16½ percent, and 20-year Treasury bonds reaching a yield of 12¼ percent. Not only had bond prices fallen precipitously for the second time that year but the yield curve shifted during the third quarter from a positive to a negative

TABLE 4 Treasury Bond Futures Prices, June 16, 1980

Contract Month	Contract Price June 16, 1980
September 1980	86-00
December 1980	85-22
March 1981	85-11
June 1981	85-00
September 1981	84-22

slope. That shift in the curve fostered the following changes in cash-to-futures and futures-to-futures price relationships:

TABLE 5   Treasury Bond Futures Prices and Spreads, June 16, 1980 and December 15, 1980

Contract Month	Contract Price June 16, 1980	Contract-to-Contract Spread	Contract Price December 15, 1980	Contract-to-Contract Spread
September 1980	86-00		Expired	
December 1980	85-22	00-10	65-13	
March 1981	85-11	00-11	66-29	1-16
June 1981	85-00	00-11	67-30	1-01
September 1981	84-22	00-10	68-17	00-19

It can be observed in Table 5 that in addition to the December 15, 1980 futures price levels having fallen substantially below levels on June 16, the structure of futures prices changed from one of successive discounts to one of successive premiums. The lower price level was a consequence of the rise in long-term interest rates from June 16 to December 15, and the changing price structure reflected a shift in the yield curve from a positive to a negative slope. Moreover, the price spread between successive contract delivery dates grew appreciably wider in response to the increased net financing cost (and negative carry) as short-term interest rates reached their historical highs in the United States.

The implications of such broad and rapid price swings for hedge management are apparent. In June 1980 the cash-futures basis was +1.00, i.e., 87 minus 86. Six months later, the basis had not only converged to zero but had turned negative as the December bond contract (September 1980 having expired) climbed in price to $14/32$ above that of the cheapest deliverable cash bond. This so-called weakening of the basis, a manifestation of the cash bond price falling faster and farther during the period under consideration than the price of the nearest futures contract, would have an adverse effect on a short hedge.

The literature of financial futures is filled with references to "locking in a rate." In the context of managing a bond portfolio, the implication (or outright assertion) that a manager is able to guarantee, or obtain a "lock" on, the total long-term yield on his portfolio with the aid of futures is false. In fact, the process of selling bond futures against a holding of cash bonds effectively converts long-term securities into "synthetic," short-term instruments that yield the equivalent of a short-term interest rate. A manager who undertakes a short hedge is, if anything, locking in a short-term rather than a long-term rate, and even the short rate is subject to basis risk.

The idea of converting a long-term security into a synthetic short-term instrument is best understood by considering the phenomenon of cash-futures price *convergence*. When the cash-futures price structure is one of successive discounts—that is, when the yield curve is positively sloped—and the cash bond price remains constant, futures prices will rise relative to cash until the two prices merge on each contract's delivery date. If, on the other hand, the futures price is assumed to remain constant, the cash bond price will decline over the life of a contract to converge with it. In either instance, or through any combination of these two extremes, the outcome of a short hedge will be adversely affected by convergence, or what we earlier described as a "weakening of the basis."

With the cash bond price declining at a faster rate than the related futures price, as occurred during the 1980 scenario, or rising at a slower pace than futures during a period of declining interest rates, the long-term yield obtainable at the onset of a hedge deteriorates into what futures practitioners refer to as "the implied repo rate," a term borrowed from the overnight interest rate earned on repurchase agreements.

The formula to compute the implied repo rate on a short hedge, taking into account the dollar flows from a bond investment in relation to its current value, is:

$$\text{Implied repo rate} = \frac{\text{Interest} + \frac{\text{Bond}}{\text{return}} + \frac{\text{Futures}}{\text{return}}}{\text{Bond value}} \times \frac{365}{\text{Days hedge is in effect}}$$

Applying the formula to June–December 1980 we can establish that a hypothetical hedger secured during that six-month period an annualized implied repo rate of 8.3 percent, i.e.,

$$\text{Implied repo rate} = \frac{\$4,000 + (-\$20,718.25) + \$20,312.50}{\$87,000} \times \frac{365}{182} = 8.3\%$$

This result is measured against a total annualized unhedged return during the period of −38 percent. The comparable computation for the period of the April–June 1980 price rally produces an implied repo rate of 17.3 percent versus a total annualized unhedged return of 1,230 percent.

The phenomena of convergence and basis risk raise the question of which contract delivery dates to select in opening a hedge position. The choice is: selling nearby delivery contracts and repeatedly "rolling forward" or replacing them with the next nearby contracts as each delivery date approaches or leapfrogging the nearby months to sell deferred-delivery contracts several delivery months removed.

Further, a manager who plans to maintain a hedge through the period covered by the available contracts, has the alternatives of "stripping" and "stacking." A futures strip is a series of contracts in successive delivery months. To extend the life of a strip hedge, a manager sells an appropriate number of newly opened contracts to replace the nearby contracts that have reached their delivery date. A stack hedge concentrates all of the contracts in one or two distant delivery months, the manager buying in a prescribed number of contracts each month or quarter to maintain the correct hedge ratio.

The strip method entails the smaller basis risk between the two techniques and benefits by the greater market liquidity of the nearby contracts. On the other hand, transaction costs accumulate in repeatedly rolling forward. A stack involves lower transaction costs because the same short contracts are carried for a longer period. But the dollar consequences of large basis changes can be severe when the short futures position consists of a disproportionately large number of contracts concentrated in a relatively illiquid delivery month.

It was earlier observed that a "weakening" basis works to the detriment of a short hedger inasmuch as he or she is losing more or gaining less on the cash position than is being reciprocally gained or lost on the futures position. One means of ameliorating the effects of a weakening basis is to "roll the hedge back" (this dissertation is beginning to read like a primer for circus tumblers rather than a guide for portfolio managers) by buying back distant contracts and replacing them with nearby contracts. In rolling back, a manager seeks to recoup his or her loss from a weakening basis by buying in a lower-priced contract and selling in its stead a higher-priced one, assuming that the yield curve remains positively sloped.

SELECTED FUTURES STRATEGIES IN BOND PORTFOLIO MANAGEMENT

The present section discusses, with accompanying examples, five applications of futures contracts that can, at appropriate times and stages of the interest-rate cycle, be profitably employed in the management of a bond portfolio. The applications are: (1) passive hedging, (2) dynamic hedging, (3) cash and carry, (4) hedged yield curve ride, and (5) long hedging.

Passive Hedging

This basic application of futures has the straightforward objective of insulating a bond portfolio from the price risk associated with interest-rate fluctuations. A passive hedger eschews any attempts to initiate hedge positions when he believes bond prices are likely to drop and to remove the hedge when he believes a rally is imminent.

A passive hedger believes the total return from a hedged portfolio should fluctuate with prevailing bond market yields. That is to say, the portfolio should benefit from rising interest rates because its current return will improve accordingly, while its net market value is held relatively constant by an offsetting futures position.

EXAMPLE. Assume that a portfolio contains $10 million face value General Motors Acceptance 12 percent debentures maturing in 2005 and priced at 109¼ for a current yield of 11 percent. The manager decides to hedge the GMAC bonds by selling 228 September 198X Treasury bond futures at 83-10. The hedge ratio of 228 contracts for $10 million par value bonds was derived by applying the beta and regression analysis outlined above. With an indicated beta of 1.74, the formula noted there produces a result of 228, i.e.:

$$\frac{1.74 \times \$10,925,000}{\$8,331,250} = 228 \text{ contracts}$$

Assume, further, that the hedge was initiated by selling the futures contracts on May 12, with 128 days remaining to the September contract delivery date, and that by that date the 12 percent bonds had declined in price to 103, consistent with a current yield on the cheapest-to-deliver Treasury bond of 12.75 percent. The resulting hedge calculation would appear as follows:

Cash Market	Futures Market
Portfolio contains $10,000,000 face value GMAC 12% at 109-08.	Manager sells 228 September T-bond contracts at 83-10.
$10,000,000 12% GMAC depreciate to 103.	228 September T-bond contracts liquidated at 80-22.
Portfolio loss: $625,000.	Futures gain: $598,500.
Net Loss: $26,500.	

The passive hedge example assumes a positive yield curve and a weakening basis, so that while the GMAC bonds depreciated $625,000, the short futures position recouped only $598,500 of that portfolio loss. So long as the yield curve remained positive, a convergence loss was to be expected while the hedge was in effect, irrespective of whether the bond market rallied or declined. Had the manager elected to extend the hedge beyond September by selling more deferred contracts with a delivery date of, say, June of the following year, first recalculating the beta of the GMAC bonds to compensate for the reduced market price, he would again sell futures at a discount to the cash bond price, and the process of convergence and its resulting basis loss would begin anew.

Dynamic Hedging

Portfolio managers who possess a greater risk tolerance than do advocates of passive hedging, and who are thus disposed to take a more aggressive market posture, believe they can achieve improved performance by placing, adjusting, and removing hedges in accordance with their interest-rate forecasts. In summary, they believe their portfolios should be hedged when interest rates are rising and unhedged when rates are declining. Their success in pursuing such a strategy is likely to mirror their performance in calling rate and price turns in the cash market.

EXAMPLE. The benefits and risks of dynamic hedging can best be illustrated by recalling once again the turbulent market experience of 1979–80, the early years of T-bond futures. In early October 1979 the U.S. Treasury 8s of 1996–01 (at that time a deliverable bond) were priced at 88¼, while the September 1980 Treasury bond futures contract was quoted at the Chicago Board of Trade at 87-24, creating a relatively narrow basis of ¹⁶/₃₂. By the end of October the Treasury 8s had dropped in price by 9¼ points, subjecting a hypothetical portfolio consisting solely of $100 million face amount of that issue to a loss of $9.25 million. But the September 1980 bond futures contract had in the same period declined only 8 points, not only converging with the cash price but rising three quarters of one point above it. The basis change on 1,000 contracts—hedging a deliverable bond bearing the contract-grade 8 percent coupon allowed a 1:1 hedge ratio—at that point amounted in dollar terms to $1.25 million. A hypothetical hedger would have substituted for the risk (as it turned out) of bonds dropping 9¼ points the appreciably smaller risk of the basis changing by 1¼ points. (See Figure 1.)

The bond market staged a modest rally during November and early December of 1980. The 8s of 1996–01 moved up to about 83¼ in the first week of December, bringing the hypothetical portfolio back to within 5 points, or $5 million, of its assumed market value in early October. The September 1980 T-bond contract rose in price during the same period to 85, effecting a further shift in the basis to 1¾ points above cash bonds. The 6-week rally proved to be a false start. By mid-December the market had resumed its downward course; the 8s of 1996–01 fell in the ensuing 11-week period between December 10, 1979, and February 26, 1980, from 83 to 64. From its October 8 level the hypothetical portfolio would have lost more than $24 million, or 27 percent of its market value. During the same interval September 1980 bond futures slid to 66-16, displaying a further weakening of the basis to 2½ points above cash.

Under normal bond market conditions, a basis change of one or two points would be considered extraordinary. But in a crisis environment,

FIGURE 1 Treasury Bond Portfolio Hedge, 1979–1980

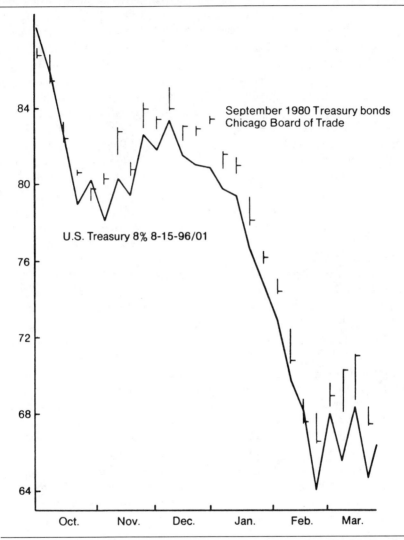

SOURCE: Allan M. Loosigian, "Financial Futures: Hedging Interest-Rate Risk," in *Readings in Investment Management*, ed. Frank J. Fabozzi (Homewood, Ill.: Richard D. Irwin, 1983), p. 295.

such as the first two months of 1980 clearly were, the decline in bond prices was more than extraordinary. It was cataclysmic! In the situation we have depicted, the portfolio manager would have managed with the benefit of the hedge to offset more than $22 million, or about 92 percent of the $24 million collapse in bond values.

Like any trading or investment operation, futures hedging is not a one-way street. Hence, the argument is frequently put forth that dynamic hedging is more in tune with active portfolio management than is a passive hedge strategy. So long as bond prices continue to drop, short hedgers appear in an admirable light, avoiding significant losses in the portfolios they manage while the market is crumbling around them. But when a major rally gets under way and unrealized losses begin to mount in the futures account, leading, in turn, to repeated variation margin calls, the plaudits soon give way to anguished catcalls.

If, in the present example, the short hedge had been initiated near the end of October 1979 instead of at the beginning of that month, repeated calls for additional margin would have been issued during the November rally. Had September 1980 T-bond futures contracts been sold at or near the October 29 settlement price of 79-24, the portfolio manager would have received variation margin calls on his or her 1,000 short contracts of about $2 million by November 15, as the contract price rallied to 81-24. By December 6 the contract price had moved yet higher to 84-24, at which level the hedger would be called for another $3 million margin payment.

To be sure, when interest rates once again turned upward and bond futures prices resumed their decline, these margin payments were recouped. But there comes a point after which the burden of repeated margin calls becomes onerous. Then the likelihood mounts that the market will not reverse itself and by doing so alleviate the short hedger's distress. At that juncture, so the argument for dynamic hedging runs, a prudent manager will bow to the market's incontestable wisdom and terminate his hedge by liquidating the futures position.

If, under the worst of circumstances in the present example, our portfolio manager had elected to initiate a short hedge at the February 26 price trough and accordingly sold 1,000 September 1980 bond contracts at 66-16 and did not promptly act to reverse his decision, the portfolio's futures losses would have assumed staggering proportions. During the subsequent rally through spring 1980 the cumulative margin calls on a 1,000-contract short position would have amounted to more than $20 million. Prudent managers should have determined at some point in the rally—sooner, it is hoped, than later—that discretion is the better part of valor and dismantled their hedge positions, with the intention of reinstating them after it became clear that interest rates had resumed their upward trend.

Cash and Carry

In the execution of passive and dynamic hedging strategies, cash-futures price differentials, particularly changes in the basis, are compli-

---

TABLE 6 Anatomy of a Cash-and-Carry Trade

Date	Cash/Futures Transaction	Amount
A.	Today	Borrow $1,000,000 for one year at 10%.	$1,000,000
B.	Today	Buy U.S. Treasury $9\frac{1}{8}$% 5-15-2004/09.	973,125
C.	Today	Sell 114 September 19XX T-bond contracts.	917,700
D.	One year later	Cover futures contract by delivering bonds.	1,046,000
E.	One year later	Repay $1,000,000 plus 10% interest.	1,100,000

---

cations that are to be minimized. A cash-and-carry position, on the other hand, is established to exploit such differences for profit. The position is so named because it involves: (1) the purchase of a deliverable cash bond with the intention of carrying it until the futures delivery date; (2) at the same time selling the appropriate futures contract against which the long cash bond will be delivered; and (3) securing a profit on the delivery date, consisting of the excess of the gain on the sale of the cash bond through the futures delivery process over the financing cost to carry the bond until that time.

The successful execution of a cash-and-carry transaction depends on four assumptions: (1) the estimated financing cost during the holding period of the cash bond is the actual financing cost; (2) there is perfect convergence between the cash bond and futures contract invoice amounts on the contract's settlement day; (3) the variation margin paid or received on the futures position during the holding period equals any difference between the futures invoice amount on the date the cash-and-carry positions are initiated and when they are closed out through the delivery process; and (4) variation margin paid or received has no time value.

Cash and carry differs from the arbitrage operations mentioned above to the extent that it is intended to capture the carry itself, i.e., the implied repo rate, from a cash-futures spread relationship and not any fleeting increments above or below the carry. In practice, the techniques overlap. To the extent that the four assumptions listed above are not realized—and assumption 3 is seldom realized in full—a cash-and-carry position contains elements of uncertainty and, therefore, risk.

EXAMPLE. Table 6 itemizes the steps in a typical cash-and-carry transaction.

The profit on this hypothetical transaction is calculated in the following manner:

	Debit	Credit
Cost of cash bonds	$ 973,125	
Interest income on bonds		$ 91,250
Proceeds from bond delivery		1,046,000
Interest paid on loan	100,000	
Totals	$1,073,125	$1,137,250
Total return for period		$ 64,125
Less: Variation margin paid		
or Plus: Variation margin received		

Hedged Yield Curve Ride

"Riding the yield curve" is a time-tested money market operation wherein investors strive to increase their rate of return by purchasing a fixed-income instrument bearing a maturity that extends beyond the expected term of the investment. A standard transaction of this sort is one of buying a 180-day Treasury bill with the intention of reselling it after 90 days elapse in lieu of buying and holding to its maturity a fresh 90-day bill.

The advantage to purchasing the longer-term instrument is the incremental return it provides as the passage of time carries its discount down the steepest part of the yield curve. The risk implicit in this gambit is that any increase in short-term interest rates during the truncated holding period will eradicate the anticipated yield advantage. In the standard Treasury bill transaction cited above, the sale of 90-day T-bill futures contracts traded on the Chicago Mercantile Exchange at the time the cash 180-day bills are purchased serves to offset this risk. The combined cash-futures transaction, sometimes referred to as creating a synthetic investment, contains some elements of arbitrage in that it provides for the sale of an asset (in another form) at a firm price in the futures market at the same time that the asset is purchased at a lower price in the cash market. Like the cash-and-carry strategy discussed previously, however, there are sufficient inefficiencies in both the cash and futures markets to instill a measure of risk in the hedged yield curve ride.

EXAMPLE.

    Alternative 1:
      June 22—Buy $10,000,000 90-day bills at 6.82%.
        Cost = $9,829,500; discount = $170,500.
      September 21—bills mature at par.

$$\begin{aligned} \text{Discount} &= \quad\quad 0 \\ \text{Profit} &= \$170,500 \end{aligned}$$

    Discount yield for 90-days:

$$\$170,500 \div \$10,000,000 \times \frac{360}{90} = 6.82\%$$

Alternative 2:

   June 22—Buy $10,000,000 180-day bills at 7.12%.

     Cost = $9,644,000; discount = $356,000.

     Sell 10 September T-bill contracts at 92.80, or 7.20%.

   September 21—Deliver $10,000,000 90-day bills at 7.20%

   on futures short positions.

     Proceeds = $9,820,000.

$$\text{Discount} = \$180,000$$
$$\text{Profit} \quad = \$176,000$$

Discount yield for 90-days:

$$\$176,000 \div \$10,000,000 \times \frac{360}{90} = 7.04\%$$

Net result:

   $176,000 − 170,500 = $5,500, or 22 basis points (7.04% − 6.82%) on $10,000,000 for 90 days.

Long Hedging

The principal focus of any discussion of hedging bond portfolios is invariably on the means of protecting the portfolio from the risk of a rise in interest rates, i.e., on short hedging. That is obviously a portfolio manager's primary concern. There are periods of time, however, when a manager is confronted with the risk of declining interest rates. They may occur before a particular bond is scheduled to mature and the manager wants to protect his reinvestment rate or, similarly, when he expects an imminent infusion of cash to his fund.

   Such situations point to a so-called anticipatory hedge wherein bond futures are purchased rather than sold and are held until the planned investment is made. If, during the time the long futures contracts are held, interest rates do decline, as was the manager's concern, the resulting price appreciation of the contracts would serve to compensate him for the lower rate at which the new investment is made.

   An interesting (and potentially profitable) wrinkle to the long hedge is that the cash-futures price convergence that works to the detriment of a short hedger is in this instance working in the portfolio manager's favor with the futures price rising relative to the cash bond price over the life of the futures contract. It should, however, be pointed out that a strategy of preserving a high level of interest rates is appealing when rates are cyclically high and the yield curve is, as a consequence, likely to be inverted. If that were, in fact, the case, the cash-futures price structure would be one of successively greater premiums over cash. Then futures prices would converge downward to cash, working against the long hedger. As one frequently hears in the futures market: "There is no such thing as a free lunch."

EXAMPLE. The following calculation illustrates the execution of a long hedge:

Cash Market	Futures Market
Manager expects to invest $10,000,000 in bonds in four months. Bonds are now priced at 120-16 for a current yield of $9\frac{1}{2}$%.	Buys 140 September T-bond contracts at 84-00.
Four months later, buys $10,000,000 bonds at 126-00.	Sells 140 September T-bond contracts at 87-12.
Opportunity cost from declining yield: $550,000.	Futures gain: $472,500.

Net opportunity cost: $77,500.
Hedged yield: $9\frac{3}{8}$%.

CHARACTERISTICS OF OPTIONS AND THEIR COMPARISON WITH FUTURES

The available option instruments that have immediate relevance for fixed-income portfolio managers are listed options on cash Treasury securities and interest-rate futures contracts and over-the-counter options on Treasury notes and bonds, corporate bonds, mortgage-backed securities, and money market instruments. This section will deal primarily with listed options on cash securities and futures contracts.[8]

A call option on a Treasury bond, note, or bill gives a call buyer the right—but not the obligation as in the case of a futures contract—to buy from an option seller (also referred to as a writer) a stated face amount of the specified security at a fixed price for a specified period. A call option on a futures contract gives a buyer a right to purchase a long position in the specified contract at a stated price. Upon exercise of the option at the discretion of the buyer, he or she holds a long position and the seller holds a short position in the futures contract.

A put option on a cash security gives its buyer the right—but again not the obligation—to sell to a put seller (known again as a writer) a stated amount of the specified security at a stated exercise or strike price for a stated period of time. A put on a futures contract grants the put buyer the right (and here it becomes a trifle confusing) to acquire a short futures position in the designated contract at the stated exercise price up to the delivery date of the futures contract. If the option is exercised,

---

[8] Many institutional investors are restricted by law to the purchase and sale of listed options and also for regulatory reasons have preferred options on cash securities to those on futures contracts.

again at the discretion of the buyer, it is its seller or writer who holds the opposing long futures position.

Options on cash Treasury bonds are listed and traded on the Chicago Board Options Exchange (CBOE). There is, in addition, a struggling market for options on Treasury notes and 13-week Treasury bills at the American Stock Exchange in New York. The standard contract size for CBOE cash Treasury bond options is $100,000 face value of certain designated issues. For example, during a given period there were listed put and call options with various exercise prices on Treasury 11¼s of February 2015, 10⅝s of August 2015, and 9⅞s of November 2015.

Exercise or strike prices are quoted as a percentage of an underlying bond's par value plus accrued interest. Accordingly, a strike price of 102 on the 9⅞s bond of November 2015 signifies a principal amount of $102,000 (1.02 × $100,000) plus accrued interest. As the price of the issue underlying a bond option fluctuates, additional options with strike prices approximating the current market price are established. As a consequence, there is likely to be concurrent trading of options on the same bond with two or more different strike prices. On February 6, 1986, for example, the Treasury 9⅞s of November 2015 had options quoted on the CBOE with strike prices at 102, 106, and 108 when the cash bond was itself offered at 105½ to yield 9.33 percent.

Option prices, known as "premiums," on cash Treasury bonds are quoted like bond futures in percentage points of the $100,000 contract value, plus minimum increments of a 32nd of a point. Each percentage point is, therefore, the equivalent of $1,000, and each 32nd is equal to $31.25. Unlike bond futures, option quotations are printed in decimal form, where the figure to the right of the decimal point represents the number of 32nds. The call option on the Treasury 9⅞s of November 2015 with a strike price of 102 and an expiration month of March 1986 was priced on February 6, 1986, for example, at a premium of 3.03, signifying 3³⁄₃₂, or a dollar price of $3,093.75.

The underlying security for options on cash Treasury notes is a newly issued 10-year note with $100,000 face value. Premiums and exercise prices on note options are quoted in the same manner as those on bond options. The pricing and quotation system on Treasury bill options at the American Stock Exchange (where note options are also traded) is structured to conform with the discount method of quoting cash bills. The nominal exercise price of a bill option is derived by subtracting from 100 the discount at which the option is exercisable, i.e., a strike price of 91 indicates a discount on the underlying bill of 9 percent. In the event an option is exercised, the nominal price is adjusted to an actual dollar amount in the same manner as settlement is made in the cash market. As with Treasury bill futures, bill options have a $1 million principal amount and are traded in increments of one basis point that are each, in turn, equal to $25. Because of the short maturity of 13-week bills, there is no specific underlying issue as is the case with bond and note options. Rather, the underlying instrument changes each week to the bill offered at the latest Federal Reserve auction.

The methodology of options on interest-rate futures appears upon initial study to be more complex than that of options on cash securities because it incorporates the workings of both the options and futures markets. But if the futures and option components are regarded separately and the steps leading through possible exercise considered in sequence, the mystery can be fathomed without undue effort. As was noted above and is worth reiterating here, the buyer of a call option on a bond futures contract who elects to exercise his option establishes a long futures position at the option's exercise price, thereby imposing on the option writer a short contract at the same price. The relationship is reversed in the event a put option is exercised. Exercise is still at the election of the put buyer, but in this instance it is he or she who acquires the short futures contract(s) at the exercise price, giving the put writer the long position.

Inasmuch as the instrument underlying an option on a bond futures contract is the Chicago Board of Trade contract of a particular delivery month, the contract grade and face amount of the ultimate deliverable security is the same $100,000 Treasury bond that contract specifies. The method of price quotation is different, however. Put and call premiums are quoted in percentage points and 64ths of a point instead of 32nds. On a $100,000 principal amount, then, a 1/64 price increment is equal to $15.625, or half the value of the minimum fluctuation of a Treasury bond futures contract.

Option pricing—also termed *premium valuation*—is an esoteric mixture of trading art and mathematical science. Arcane though some of the concepts to be discussed below may seem to an option novice, an understanding of them is quite essential to the successful use of options for either speculation or portfolio management.

The primary elements of an option price—which apply to both puts and calls—are the option's *intrinsic value* and any *excess* over its intrinsic value.[9] Intrinsic value is defined as the positive difference between the exercise or strike price of an option and the current market price of its underlying instrument, be it a futures contract or a cash security. Since the right to buy a contract or a bond becomes increasingly profitable as the underlying contract or bond appreciates in price *above* the strike price, the intrinsic value of the option increases accordingly. That is so

[9] Another commonly accepted expression for excess is "premium over intrinsic value." We shall use the former term in this chapter and the chapter following to avoid confusion over different meanings of "premium," which here refers exclusively to the option price.

because any increase in the intrinsic value is essentially the profit the call buyer will enjoy when he elects to exercise his call. In the case of a put, the right to sell a futures contract or bond at a higher price becomes increasingly valuable as the contract's or bond's market price continues to fall *below* the strike price of the option. That intrinsic value is the amount the put buyer stands to gain if he chooses to buy the contract or security in the open market and sell it to the put writer at the option's strike price.

The expressions, "in the money", "at the money," and "out of the money" are further references to the relationship between strike and market prices and the resulting profitability of the option in question. Because of the differences in perspective, the terms apply in opposite senses to puts and calls. A call option is in the money when the market price of its underlying instrument is above the option's strike price and it is, therefore, profitable to exercise. But a put option would be out of the money if the market price were greater than its strike price because it would not then be profitable to exercise. Conversely, a put option is in the money when the bond or other security's market price is below the strike price of the put, but if it were a call in that situation it would be out of the money because no profit could be derived from its exercise. In the case of both put and call options, the option is said to be at the money when the strike and market prices are equal.

If an option premium were determined solely by the difference between strike and exercise prices, that is, the amount by which an option is in the money, the entire matter of pricing would be a simple exercise in arithmetic. Unfortunately—and, again, the expression "no free lunch" comes to mind—there is more to it than that. For while the strike price remains contractually fixed during the life of an option, its underlying security's or contract's market price fluctuates. And an option which is out of the money today may, because of market fluctuations, move into the money at some time before the option expires.

Due to the possibility that an underlying bond or contract price may change in the option holder's favor, puts and calls are almost always priced above their intrinsic value. Even when an option is well out of the money and so has no intrinsic value, it still carries a small time value against the chance that a dramatic advance or decline in the market price of its underlying asset will move the option into the money before it is scheduled to expire.

To illustrate, if the premium for a call option bearing a strike price of 86 is 3 when the current market price of its underlying contract or bond is 88, the call has an intrinsic value, that is, it is in the money to the amount of 2 points or $2,000 and has an excess of 1 point, i.e., the premium of 3 minus the intrinsic value of 2. If the option in question were a put under the same circumstances, it would be out of the money with no intrinsic value. The premium of 3 would in that case consist entirely of excess in recognition of the possibility that the underlying asset may fall in price to a level below the 86 strike price at some point during the remaining life of the put.

As with futures contracts, there are two means by which an option holder may realize his gain: through selling the option on the exchange at which it is traded or exercising the option and simultaneously selling or purchasing the deliverable asset, depending upon whether the option is a put or a call. It is in most instances advantageous to sell the option rather than to exercise it, because exercising at the strike price serves to forfeit any excess over the option's intrinsic value.

The critical difference between futures and options is that in the case of the former, exercise through the delivery process or liquidation through an offsetting transaction is obligatory for both parties, while in the case of the latter, it is at the discretion of the option buyer. In the worst instance the option buyer can allow the option to expire unexercised and write off the amount of the premium paid, leaving him or her with no further obligation to the contraparty or to the exchange clearinghouse. This distinction has great implications for the risk/return comparison of options vis-à-vis futures contracts and is a matter of primary significance insofar as portfolio management is concerned. The fact that an option on a futures contract has as its underlying asset an instrument with an equally limited life also has broad implications for portfolio managers when it comes to selecting an appropriate hedging strategy.

An American-type option may be exercised at any time up to its expiration date whereas a European-type option may be exercised on its expiration date only. All options on fixed-income securities and on interest-rate futures traded on U.S. exchanges are of the American type.

Five primary factors determine an option's price. As was noted above, the subject of pricing can quickly turn excessively arcane, and the following discussion should be taken as only the most cursory outline.[10]

1. *Current market price of the underlying contract or bond relative to the option's strike price.* An at-the-money option generally commands a premium with a greater excess over its intrinsic value than do either in- or out-of-the-money options. An option that is substantially in the money is likely to move at nearly a one-for-one pace with the price change of the optioned instrument, be it a futures contract or a bond, thereby giving up the advantages of leverage. On the other hand, a

---

[10] For a more complete discussion of option pricing and investment strategies related thereto, readers are referred to Gary L. Gastineau, *The Stock Options Manual*, 2nd ed. (New York: McGraw-Hill, 1979); and Richard M. Bookstaber, *Option Pricing and Strategies in Investing* (Reading, Mass: Addison-Wesley Publishing, 1981).

considerably out-of-the-money option does offer a good deal of leverage but is usually believed to have only a small chance of reaching profitability before the option's expiration.

2. *Volatility.* The greater the volatility of the underlying instrument, the larger the excess over its intrinsic value the option is likely to command. A prospective option buyer tends to regard higher volatility as a bigger profit opportunity, and he is generally willing to pay a higher price for it. A prospective option seller sees the higher volatility as a greater risk for which he should receive additional compensation.

3. *Time remaining to expiration.* It is to be expected that, all of the other factors remaining constant, the longer an option has left to run to its expiration, the greater the premium it will command because of the extended possibility that a market price change will render the option profitable.

4. *Coupon.* In the event the underlying instrument is a cash bond, the higher its coupon, the lower the value of a call option and the higher the value of a put. Since accrued coupon interest is added to the exercise price in the case of bond options traded on the CBOE, accrued coupon interest will not affect the option premium. A low-coupon bond will, therefore, enhance the premiums of a call, and a high-coupon bond will enhance the value of a put.

5. *Level of short-term interest rates.* As was noted in the earlier section of this chapter dealing with cash-futures price relationships, a rise in short-term interest rates will increase the financing costs of bonds and affect the basis accordingly. Such a rise in short-term rates will further serve to inflate the premiums of call options on cash bonds and conversely depress the premium on puts. Options on futures are not influenced in the same fashion as they incur no cost of carry.

There are different margin requirements for futures and options because of the varied nature and degree of risk exposure the two types of instruments entail. Since the total obligation and exposure of an option buyer is the amount of the premium paid, there are no margin requirements for buyers. An option writer on the other side of the transaction assumes a higher degree of risk. Depending upon whether the option is a put or call, he or she is obligated to buy or sell the underlying security in the event the buyer chooses to exercise his option and so is liable to incur considerable loss.

In the case of options on futures, a writer must deposit the margin money that would normally be required on the underlying bond futures position and, in most instances, the amount of the option premium paid to him or her by the buyer as well. If, after the initial transaction is made, the price of the underlying futures contract moves against the writer— up if it is a call and down if a put—he or she is required to deposit with the broker the variation margin that falls due as the underlying contract is marked to the market.

EXAMPLE. Buying a call option. Managers are more likely to buy puts or to write calls to protect their portfolios from price risk on the downside than to buy calls for price appreciation. Put-buying and call-writing strategies are discussed in the following section of this chapter. As a part of this introductory overview of options, however, it is instructive to consider the position of a call buyer. A strategy of buying calls has, moreover, utility in hedging against anticipated declines in interest rates (if that is appropriate) comparable to a long futures strategy.

On February 6, 1986, September call options on Treasury bond futures at the Chicago Board of Trade were quoted at the following strike prices and premiums when the September futures contract was itself priced at 83-10:

Option	Option Premium
September 82 calls	3-22
September 84 calls	2-26
September 86 calls	1-41

With the September T-bond contract at 83-10, only the September 82 calls were in the money on February 6, while the 84 and 86 calls were progressively out of the money and thereby commanded lower premiums.

Had an option trader or investor elected to purchase the in-the-money September 82 calls, he or she would have paid the premium of 3-22, or a dollar amount of $3,343.75. To reiterate one more time, that initial outlay was on that date the maximum he or she would have been at risk on that particular transaction. If the settlement price of the T-bond futures on the option expiration date had turned out to be 82 or less, the buyer of the call would have lost the entire $3,343.75 premium per option. His or her break-even point would have been 85-11 (the 82 strike price plus the 3-22 premium—remember, bond futures are quoted in 32nds, the options in 64ths). The greater the amount by which the futures settlement price exceeded the option's 85-11 break-even point, the larger would have been the profit the call buyer stood to realize.

Figure 2 depicts the profit profiles of the three call options cited above alongside the profile of a long September bond futures contract. The figure shows how, in contrast to the unlimited potential gain or loss to which a futures buyer is exposed as the contract price rises above or falls below 83-10, a call buyer's risk is limited to the premium paid. But in the case of each of the three strike prices, he or she retains the

FIGURE 2   Profiles of Three Long Call Positions versus a Futures Position

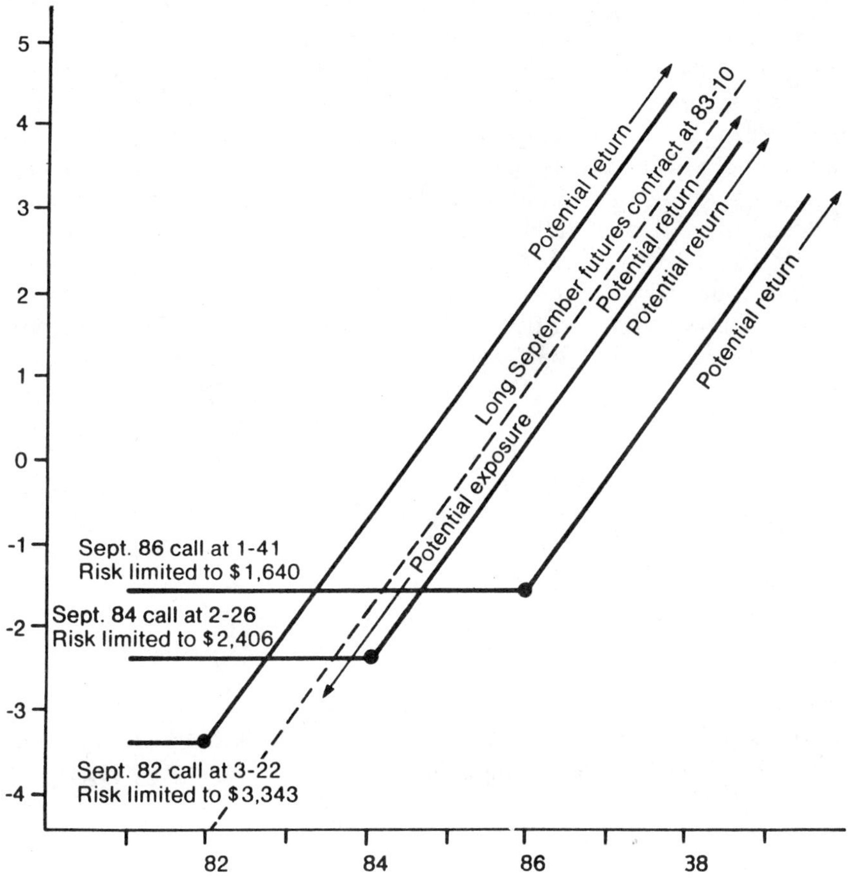

potential for an unlimited return, depending on the performance of the underlying contract. Inasmuch as the premiums paid are lower on calls with higher strike prices, the higher strike calls provide both a greater potential gain in relation to the premium outlay and a smaller maximum dollar loss. But here again is the free lunch—or lack thereof—syndrome: Because the higher strike calls are progressively more out of the money, the likelihood of profiting from them is less than with the lower, in-the-money strike calls.

Futures markets are said by some hedgers and traders to be easier to operate in than the more complex option markets. That is debatable. It is true that options frequently become over- or underpriced in relation to their theoretical value, as determined by the five factors summarized above. It requires, in fact, a high degree of expertise to identify and to exploit such temporary discrepancies in the execution of various trading and hedging strategies.[11] Futures contract prices, in contrast, display less of a tendency to diverge from their theoretical values.

The difference in margin requirements for option and futures trading favors the option market, especially during periods of high interest rates. The use of options to achieve certain hedging strategies avoids potentially adverse cash-flow consequences of variation margin calls, including a possible need to borrow funds at high short-term interest rates to meet variation margin calls in cash.

It has been argued that as risk-limiting and risk-control tools, options offer somewhat greater flexibility than do futures contracts.[12] Other analysts have written that futures and options serve different investment needs and that both instruments have their place in modern portfolio management.[13] Whatever the merits of these positions, a fundamental understanding of both is necessary to make the appropriate choices. In the case of the hybrid instruments, options on futures contracts, both types of contracts are involved, and their respective characteristics must be understood by managers who intend to employ them.

OPTION STRATEGIES IN BOND PORTFOLIO MANAGEMENT

This section reviews, with appropriate examples, four option strategies pertinent to bond portfolio management. They are: (1) buying puts, (2) bear put spreading, (3) writing (selling) calls, and (4) delta hedging.

Buying Puts

A put-buying strategy is comparable to short hedging with futures contracts in that their common objective is to recoup portfolio depreciation caused by rising interest rates. The strategy is often described as being one of buying price insurance to protect the adjusted market value of bonds for the life of the put.

---

[11] Readers who feel they lack such expertise should not abandon hope. They will find that the majority of portfolio managers are in the same boat and that there are many vendors who are eager to supply the needed expertise via the medium of computer valuation models—for a price, of course. Care should be taken to understand and evaluate a computer model before any contractual commitment is made.

[12] Gastineau, *The Stock Options Manual*, p. 142.

[13] Eugene Moriarty, Susan Phillips, and Paula Tosini, "A Comparison of Options and Futures in the Management of Portfolio Risk," *Financial Analysts Journal*, January/February 1981, pp. 61–67.

The buyer of a put pays to its writer a premium for the right to sell to the writer a specified face value ($100,000) of a cash bond or a bond futures contract at a stated price any time during the life of that put. Like a short futures contract, a put is expected to appreciate in an amount commensurate with any loss—with the qualification of possible basis changes as with futures—incurred as a result of rising interest rates. The significant advantage of options over futures in this respect is that they provide, for the consideration of a premium, a one-way hedge that allows the portfolio to participate in any market appreciation driven by a decline in interest rates.

As also holds true of a short futures hedge, the correlation between the demonstrated price behavior of any particular bond that is to be hedged and that of the cash bond or futures contract underlying the designated put, i.e., R-squared, is central to the successful outcome of a long put hedge. Further, like a futures hedge, the slope of the yield curve during the maintenance of a long put position will affect the outcome of the hedge. A positive-sloped yield curve engenders basis moves that work to the detriment of the hedger; a negative slope works in his favor.

Due to the basis-consuming effect of convergence, a long put position like a short futures hedge is capable of preserving an approximate short-term interest rate but not a long-term rate. The formula to derive the implied repo rate on a long put position relates any dollar gains on a combined bond-option position to the value of the hedged bond, i.e.,

$$\text{Return (implied repo rate)} = \frac{\text{Interest} + \text{Bond return} + \text{Option return}}{\text{Bond value}} \times \frac{365}{\text{Days hedge is in effect}}$$

To recapitulate, a long put buyer pays the premium to secure downside price protection while preserving the opportunity to participate in price rallies, that is, a one-way hedge. The opportunity cost that a short futures hedger pays for the same downside protection is the forfeiture of potential price appreciation, with the qualification that the futures hedger also participates in rallies to the extent that he can successfully execute a program of dynamic hedging.

EXAMPLE 1. Buying in-the-money puts. A portfolio manager is concerned about her holding of $10 million face amount Treasury 12s of 2008-13, currently priced at $121^{26}/_{32}$ to yield 9.61 percent. She accordingly decides to initiate a long put hedge as insurance against an incipient rise in interest rates and buys 140 June puts on T-bond futures bearing a strike price of 86, adjusting the hedge ratio to a conversion factor of 1.40. The June 86 puts have 145 days remaining to their expiration date and command a premium of 3⁴⁄₆₄ for an aggregate dollar outlay of $428,750. On the day the puts are purchased, the underlying bond contracts are quoted at 84⁸⁄₃₂.

Assume that by 90 days following the purchase of the puts, the Treasury 12s of 2008-13 have declined 4½ points to 117¹⁰⁄₃₂. Assume further that during the same interval June bond futures have fallen 3⁸⁄₃₂ to 81 and the June 86 puts have appreciated to 6⁴⁄₆₄ for an aggregate dollar gain on the 140 long puts of $420,000. Now believing that the upsurge in interest rates has run its course for the time being, the manager elects to realize her option gain through her sale of the June 86 puts. The outcome of the long put hedge is a net loss of the Treasury bond put position of $30,000, calculated as follows:

Cash Market	Option Market
Today: Portfolio contains $10,000,000 face amount Treasury 12s at 121-26.	Manager buys 140 June 86 puts at 3 4/64 or $428,750.
90 days later: $10,000,000 Treasury 12s are 117-10.	Manager sells 140 June 86 puts at 6 4/64 or $818,750.
Loss: $450,000.	Gain: $420,000.

Net loss on hedged position: $30,000.

Given these assumptions the hedge example began with bond futures trading at 84-08, or 3²⁶⁄₃₂ points below the cash bond price after adjustment by a conversion factor of 1.4. Futures subsequently converged approximately three quarters of one point to the cash bond price during the holding period of the puts, meaning that the manager surrendered about $5,000 to convergence during the 90 days she owned the puts. Applying the formula cited above, the long put hedge produced an annualized return over its 90-day life of 8.98 percent, that is:

$$\frac{\text{In-the-money}}{\text{put return}} = \frac{\$300,000 - \$450,000 + \$420,000}{\$12,181,250} \times \frac{365}{90}$$

$$= .0898$$

A net return of about 9 percent may not in itself seem particularly impressive, but by comparison with the 5 percent assumed loss that the 12 percent coupon bond would have incurred without the benefit of the hedge, the cost of the option appears justified.

EXAMPLE 2. Buying out-of-the-money puts. The fictional portfolio manager may nevertheless feel that the June 86 in-the-money puts provided the desired protection at too high a price. For the sake of comparison let us replay the situation, substituting the June 82 puts priced at 1^{22}/$_{64}$. With the June T-bond futures contract again quoted at 83-10 on day one of the revised hedge, the puts with an 82 strike price were 1^{10}/$_{32}$ out of the money. Assuming the sale of the June 82 puts in 90 days at 5^{38}/$_{64}$, the revised hedge produced an annualized return of 14.81 percent calculated as follows:

$$\text{Out-of-the-money put return} = \frac{\$300,000 - \$450,000 + \$595,000}{\$12,181,250} \times \frac{365}{90}$$

$$= .1481$$

A comparison of the simulated hedged returns with in- , and out-of-the-money long puts under the assumptions of falling, unchanged, and rising bond prices provides the results shown in Table 7 below.

The comparative returns in Table 7 suggest that of the two substrategies the one incorporating out-of-the-money puts is the more aggressive. It therefore follows that at-the-money puts fall somewhere in between.

While an in-the-money long put hedge permits a manager to secure a higher minimum return, it also limits his or her participation in any price advances that may occur while the long put position is in place. In contrast, an out-of-the-money put produces a generally lower minimum return but allows the manager to share more fully in any prospective price rally. The higher premium paid for an in-the-money put buys a manager greater downside price protection than does the less expensive out-of-the-money put.

Figure 3 illustrates the profit profile of long put hedges, indicating a minimum floor return at the left side of the chart. The chart also shows how the return distribution of a long put position shifts to the left of the horizontal rate of return axis due to the front-end payment of the put premium.

TABLE 7 Hedged Returns with In- and Out-of-the-Money Puts under Assumptions of Rising, Unchanged, and Falling Bond Prices

	Rising Prices	Unchanged Prices	Falling Prices
Cash bond price	117-10	121-26	126-10
Futures price	81-00	84-08	87-16
Unhedged returns	−5%	9.98%	24.97%
Hedged returns:			
In-the-money put	8.98%	4.74%	13.02%
Out-of-the-money put	14.81%	6.49%	19.87%

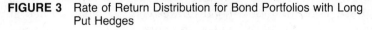

FIGURE 3   Rate of Return Distribution for Bond Portfolios with Long
Put Hedges

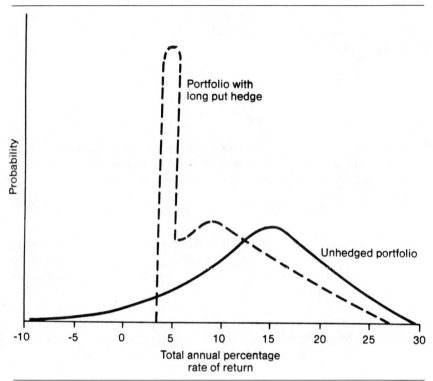

Bear Put Spreading

This is a somewhat less straightforward hedging technique than is the outright purchase of puts described in the two previous examples. It consists of simultaneously purchasing puts with a high strike price and selling puts with the same expiration date but a lower strike price. The advantage of a bear put spread over a long put hedge strategy is that the sale of a lower strike price recoups some of the premium expended for a long put. Its drawback is that it offers only a partial minimum return.

A portfolio manager who undertakes a bear put spread is effectively hedged between the spaced strike prices of the two puts. He or she is exposed to a limited potential loss as the adjusted hedged cash bond price rises over the higher strike price and to a limited potential gain as the market price falls below the lower of the two strike prices. Since the put with a higher strike price commands a larger premium, which the manager pays out as a buyer, than the premium on the lower strike price, which he obtains as a writer, the combined spread position creates a net debit in the hedged portfolio's option account.

The maximum potential loss on a bear put spread equals the amount of the net debit on the option premiums paid and received. The maximum potential gain equals the point difference between the two strike prices minus the net debit. When it is combined with a cash bond, a bear put spread provides full hedge protection so long as the adjusted market price of the hedged bond fluctuates between the two option strike prices.

EXAMPLE. We continue to consider the holding of $10 million face amount Treasury 12s of 2008-13 that was cited as the hedged bond in the two previous examples dealing with a long put hedge. In this present example, the portfolio manager elects to establish a bear put spread. She accordingly buys 140 June 90 futures puts for a premium of 6$\frac{4}{64}$, or $848,750 in total, and sells (writes) the same number of June 84 puts for a premium of 2 even, or $280,000 in total, incurring a net debit of $568,750. The settlement price of the June bond futures contract on the day the bear spread is initiated is again 84-08.

The bear spread affords downside price protection to the lower of the two strike prices. Progressively below 84, the gains registered by the long 90 put would be offset by an increasing liability on the short 84 puts as the possibility grows that the buyer of the 84 puts will elect to exercise them. Exercise would saddle the portfolio manager with a losing long futures position at 84-00.

If the hedged 12 percent bonds decline to 117$\frac{10}{32}$, as in the two previous examples, and the June futures contract is again assumed to fall to 81-00, the hedge calculation given the same basis change is:

Cash Market	Option Market
Today: Portfolio contains $10,000,000 face amount Treasury 12s at 121-26.	Manager buys 140 June 90 puts at 6 4/64, or $848,750 debit, and sells 140 June 84 puts at 2, or $280,000 credit, for a net debit of $568,750.
90 days later: $10,000,000 Treasury 12s are 117-10.	Manager sells 140 June 90 puts at 9 4/64, or $1,268,750 credit, and buys 140 June 84 puts at 4, or $560,000 debit, for a net credit of $708,750.
Loss: $450,000.	Net gain on bear spread: $140,000.

Net loss on hedged position = $310,000.

The calculation, if it is again assumed that the hedged bond price rises 4½ points to 126-10 during the maintenance of the bear put spread, is:

Cash Market	Option Market
Today: Portfolio contains $10,000,000 face amount Treasury 12s at 121-26.	Manager buys 140 June 90 puts at 6 4/64, or $848,750 debit, and sells 140 June 84 puts at 2, or $280,000 credit, for a net debit of $568,750.
90 days later: $10,000,000 Treasury 12s are 126-10.	Manager sells 140 June 90 puts at 5 4/64, or $708,750 credit, and buys 140 June 84 puts at 16/64, or $35,000 debit, for a net credit of $673,750.
Gain: $450,000.	Net gain on bear spread: $105,000.
	Net gain on hedged position: $555,000.

The simulated returns on the bear spread hedged position in the cases of declining and rising bond prices using the implied repo formula work out to:

A. Annualized return on declining bond price

$$= \frac{\$300,000 - \$450,000 + \$140,000}{\$12,181,250} \times \frac{365}{90}$$

$$= -.33\%$$

B. Annualized return on rising bond prices

$$= \frac{\$300,000 + \$450,000 + \$105,000}{\$12,181,250} \times \frac{365}{90}$$

$$= 28.5\%$$

Call Writing

The sale of calls is considered a hedge strategy insofar as the premium received by the seller comprises a partial offset to any price depreciation of a related bond. In the event that interest rates decline and the market goes up, however, there is an increasing likelihood that calls will be exercised, effectively setting a ceiling sale price so far as the writer is concerned.

Such a sale of calls in conjunction with a long cash bond position is frequently referred to as "covered call writing" because the writer is "covered" should the market in fact rise and the calls be exercised. Investors who sell calls without owning the underlying securities or futures contracts are said to be writers of uncovered, or "naked" calls, a measure that entails a high degree of risk. A naked writer is fully exposed—the pun is absolutely intended—if called to sell bonds or futures that he or she must secure in the open market at a substantially higher price.

Within the more conservative context of covered writing, the sale of an in-the-money call is considered to be a more aggressive tactic than the sale of an out-of-the-money call because, while the former commands a higher premium, there is a greater likelihood of exercise. When it is done to hedge a long bond position, the sale of in-the-money covered calls is usually held to be a more conservative strategy than the covered sale of at- or out-of-the-money calls.

EXAMPLE. We shift our attention to an agency issue, Federal National Mortgage Association 12.65 percent bonds of March 2014, offered at 120⁴/₃₂ for a current yield of 10.42 percent. June bond futures are again 84-08. The portfolio manager is confronted with a choice of writing: (1) in-the-money calls on June futures at a strike price of 82 and a premium of 3²⁰/₆₄; (2) nearly at-the-money calls at a strike price of 84 and a premium of 2%₄; and (3) out-of-the-money calls at a strike price of 86 and premium of 1²⁰/₆₄.

The simulated results of a combined position of $10 million FNMA 12.65 percent of 2014 and 160 short calls reflecting a beta for those bonds of 1.6 that are initially in, at, and out of the money, respectively, in rising, stable, and declining interest rate environments over a 90-day period are tabulated as follows in Table 8.

Of the three strike prices, the in-the-money June 82 calls provide the greatest downside price protection in that they command the largest premium. But the ability to participate more fully in rising price movements is provided by the at- and out-of-the-money calls, at strike prices of 84 and 86, respectively.

Flexibility of maneuver is offered by the choice of strike prices, raising the possibility of liquidating one short call position and initiating another as market conditions change. One tactic of this sort is called rolling down, wherein an at-the-money call is liquidated if bond prices move downward, most likely at a profit, and is replaced with an equivalent call except at a lower strike price, hence out of the money, to provide a greater degree of downside price protection.

TABLE 8 Hedged Returns with Covered Call Writing under Assumptions of Falling, Unchanged, and Rising Bond Prices

	Falling Prices	Unchanged Prices	Rising Prices
Cash price	116 4/32	120 4/32	124 4/32
Futures price	81-04	84-08	87-12
Annualized unhedged returns	−2.8%	10.7%	24.2%
Annualized hedged returns:			
In-the-money calls	7.8%	19.8%	6.6%
At-the-money calls	4.7%	16.1%	7.9%
Out-of-the-money calls	1.6%	13.7%	16.1%

Delta Hedging

This is the option strategy that is analogous to dynamic hedging with interest-rate futures. *Delta* is a statistical term used to express the expected change in an option premium in response to a given price change of the underlying bond. If, for example, the value of a call increases ¾ point with each one-point increase in the price of the related bond, the delta for that option is .75. The hedging problem is rendered more complex by the fact that an option's delta varies with changes in the price level of its underlying security. These variations make it necessary to adjust the hedge ratio frequently in accordance with that changing price level.

The deltas of short calls and long puts are assigned negative signs to emphasize that their values decrease as the prices of their underlying securities appreciate. At- and close-to-the-money call and put options carry deltas of about .50 and −.50, respectively, indicating that the options are expected to change about one half point in price for each one-point price change in the underlying bond. That translates into a 2:1 hedge ratio. As an option moves into the money, the delta approaches 1.0 for calls and −1.0 for puts, signifying a one-for-one price change and hedge ratio in each case. Options moving out of the money approach a zero delta. The reciprocal of an option's delta is the correct hedge ratio for that particular option. For example, the reciprocal of a delta of .60 is 1.66, i.e., $1/.60$.

Deltas fluctuate not only with changes in price but also with the passage of time. By comparison, a short hedge with futures is less complex and does not require the constant fine-tuning that a delta hedge entails. A program of constant adjustments in response to delta changes is likely to incur high transaction costs. Even so, some managers find it preferable to deal with the complexity of a delta hedge with options to meeting possible on-going margin calls on futures losses. Moreover, some cash securities may not have a corresponding hedge vehicle in the futures market, whereas a suitable option may be available.

An option's delta is most unstable when it is at or close to the money, where it is susceptible to relatively large changes in its premium in reaction to small changes in the price of the underlying security. Its delta is most stable when the option is deep in or out of the money. Instability increases as options approach their expiration date, suggesting that delta hedging is most effective when it is employed over relatively brief periods of time early in an option's life.

EXAMPLE. Our typical manager wishes to hedge a $25 million holding of Pacific Telephone 8⅞s of 2015, priced at 88½ for a current yield of 10 percent. The yield curve is positively sloped, and March T-bond futures are 85-16. A beta of 1.25 for the Pacific Telephone bonds and a delta of −.50 for the March 84 puts determine the purchase of 625 put options to hedge the $25 million bonds, hence the hedge position:

First trading day:
Long $25,000,000 face value
Pacific Telephone 8⅞ bonds at 88½.
Buy 625 March 84 puts at $^{25}/_{64}$,
    or $390.62 apiece. $244,140 debit

On the following day the Pacific Telephone 8⅞ bonds drop ¾ point to 87¾ and the puts accordingly appreciate because of their −.50 delta $^{24}/_{64}$ to $^{49}/_{64}$, or $765.62 apiece. Though the bonds have depreciated $187,500, the puts have gained a total of $234,375 for a net gain on the long put hedge of $46,875.

Second trading day:
Long $25,000,000 face value
Pacific Telephone 8⅞ bonds at 87¾. $187,500 unrealized loss.
Long 625 March 84 puts at $^{49}/_{64}$,
    or $765.62 apiece. $234.375 unrealized gain.

Net unrealized gain: $46,875.

Following the one day's trading, the delta on the long puts increases to −.55, dictating a revised hedge ratio of 2.27 and, therefore, the liquidation of 58 March 84 puts:

Sell 58 March 84 puts at $^{49}/_{64}$,
    or $765.62 apiece. $ 44,505 credit.

Assuming the market reverses direction on the second day and the Pacific Telephone bonds rally one point to 88¾, for an aggregate $250,000 unrealized gain, the long puts will accordingly decline in price to about $^{14}/_{64}$, meaning a cumulative unrealized loss on the option position of $310,000 and a cumulative net loss on the hedge since the hedge was established of $13,125 ($46,875 net gain on day one minus the $60,000 net loss on day two).

Third trading day:
Long $25,000,000 face value
Pacific Telephone 8⅞ bonds at 88¾. $250,000 unrealized gain.
Long 567 March 84 puts at $^{14}/_{64}$,   310,000 unrealized loss.
    or $218.75 apiece.

          Net unrealized loss $ 60,000.
            on third trading day:
          Cumulative net unrealized $ 13,125.
            loss since hedge was
            established:

As is demonstrated by this abbreviated example, a long put hedger should be adding to the option position as the market rallies and liquidating an appropriate number of puts as prices decline. The contrary treatment applies to written calls, that is to say, buying calls in as the market rises and selling additional calls as the market drops.

Increasing volatility, i.e., an expanding delta, works to the advantage of long put delta hedgers, serving to enhance hedged returns as the market moves up or down. But short call delta hedgers suffer from increased volatility, incurring greater losses as prices move in either direction. The passage of time logically works to the advantage of short call delta hedgers and to the disadvantage of long put hedgers in that the time value of both put and call options lapses as the options move toward expiration. While a manager may revise his or her hedge position upward or downward to maintain what is described as a delta neutral position, it is not possible to neutralize the deterioration of an option's time value by adding or liquidating contracts.

SUMMARY AND CONCLUSION

We have described in the foregoing sections the mechanics of financial futures and options trading and discussed the principal strategies whereby these instruments may be used to counteract interest rate risk. There should be no air of mystery surrounding the process of hedging. Producers, processors, and users of physical commodities have employed these price-protection strategies for decades. For portfolio managers, hedging is essentially a matter of calculating the correct number of futures or option contracts required to simulate and offset the projected price movement of the bond or other security that is to be hedged. Some managers believe that hedge positions should be adjusted and removed, when appropriate, to coincide with their view of the prospective trend of interest rates. Other managers maintain that dynamic hedging is a euphemism for speculation and should therefore be avoided.

Whatever the intended application of these instruments may be, the cautionary *caveat emptor* is in order as it applies to futures and options. Perhaps because of their novelty and somewhat esoteric nature, they can be seductive and, in inexperienced hands, potentially hazardous.

It is sometimes suggested that much of the institutional interest in futures and option hedging techniques stems from a misunderstanding of the mathematics involved in making hedge calculations, leading to a presumption that while futures and options do not provide a free lunch, they at least offer a meal on highly advantageous terms. That is seldom the case. Professional arbitrageurs, supported by their computerized buying and selling programs, are usually the first to spot a bargain and devour the meal. As a general rule, institutions should not engage in transactions involving futures and/or options unless they are willing to assume a corresponding position in comparable securities underlying those instruments.

Rather than seeking a precision and predictability that many of the formulas cited above seem to promise, a reasonable approach to using futures and options in portfolio risk management is to accept an exchange of the potentially great risks involved in operating fully exposed in today's credit markets for the considerably smaller and, consequently, more easily managed risks inherent in the knowledgeable use of futures and options. To strive for the complete elimination of risk is unrealistic.

Futures and options are unmistakably useful tools for portfolio management and other financial tasks. But holding a simplistic view of their application or, at the other extreme, succumbing to their arcane elegance would be a mistake for a portfolio manager. To repeat: *caveat emptor* or, in the case of short hedging with futures contracts, let the seller beware!

Different labels may be affixed to the successive steps, but the portfolio management process essentially consists of four undertakings: (1) establishing the fund's long-term objectives, i.e., stability of income, maximum real long-term return, stability of principal, and so forth; (2) interest rate, yield curve, and maturity judgments; (3) security selection, maturity extending or reducing, and trading and swapping tactics; and (4) portfolio performance monitoring. It is into undertakings (1) and (2) that futures- and option-related strategies should be introduced and into (3) and (4) that their consequent tactics should be integrated.

Once the primary objectives of a fund have been set, a manager's single most important task is to determine the maturity structure of his or her portfolio. It is essentially the maturity structure of the portfolio that gives expression to the manager's interest-rate predilection. In addition to (but by no means replacing) traditional cash market swapping and other maturity-adjustment techniques, futures and options, if applied correctly, provide a quick, efficient, and inexpensive means of accomplishing maturity restructuring. Selling a bond futures contract, to reiterate the primary example cited in this chapter, effectively compresses the maturity of the hedged bond to the delivery date of the futures contract. Removing the hedge by liquidating the short contract restores the stated maturity of the hedged bond.

The existing—as distinct from the desired—level and form of interest-rate risk at any given stage in the interest-rate cycle is unique to each portfolio. Though there is no widespread agreement as to what constitutes the most useful measure of interest-rate risk, there is little dispute that a higher order of rate-risk consciousness and control should be incorporated into the portfolio management process. The knowledgeable use of futures and options will materially assist in achieving that end.

On an operating level, all of the concerned members of a fund's sponsoring and management institutions, as well as investment and lending banks, brokers, and accounting firms, should be kept informed of the various hedge strategies and tactics that are in effect and their current performance. A brokerage firm that is experienced in the specialized workings of the futures and options markets should be consulted and, if its performance is satisfactory, retained to assist managers in the adaptation and execution of hedge strategies and tactics and to help monitor the progress of the resulting positions. Extensive computer software has been developed to support these activities.

Bookkeeping and accounting considerations as they pertain to hedging are relatively straightforward. Futures contracts are booked as a memorandum entry rather than entered in the general ledger. The initial margin deposit for a long or short position is debited to a margin debit account, and cash is credited by a like figure. Realized profits and losses are posted to the deferred profit or loss account and are accrued or written off over the average life of the securities that were hedged. Initial and variation margin deposits are carried as "other assets," and any related amounts due to or from brokers are shown as miscellaneous receivables or payables.

Cloaked in an aura of speculation and suspicion as they traditionally have been, are futures and options suitable investment tools for portfolio managers and other financial officers? Responding to the extensive education efforts undertaken by option and futures exchanges over the past decade, and mindful of the devastating costs of not adopting some sort of protective measures in the face of unprecedented interest-rate gyrations during those years, portfolio managers have begun to distinguish between the desirable and the inappropriate aspects and applications of futures and options.

Moving beyond—or perhaps linked to—the speculation debate, should a manager adopt a passive hedge strategy or engage in dynamic hedging in an effort to achieve incremental gains rather than remaining content with pure price protection? Some amount of experimentation should and undoubtedly will take place by managers. The strategy that is ultimately chosen will influence and, in turn, be influenced by the portfolio's objectives and to a large extent by the place and role of an institution's hedging and trading operations within the organizational structure.

The overriding issue should be whether the use of futures and/or options increases or reduces risk under a given set of circumstances. The argument in this chapter is that many futures and options strategies *when they are perfectly understood and properly applied* are well suited to and can contribute materially to the realization of conservative investment objectives. It is the responsibility of portfolio managers and their associates to acquaint themselves with the possibilities, limitations, and risks of the several hedging and trading techniques discussed above as well as any other strategies involving futures and options as may be deemed appropriate. Further, managers should determine which, if any, of these strategies are suited to the situation with which they are confronted. To evade such a determination and to ignore these tools will increasingly be regarded by regulators, sponsors, and beneficiaries as an abdication of their fiduciary responsibilities.

45

Stock Index Futures and Options in the Management of Common Stock Portfolios

Allan M. Loosigian
President
A.M. Loosigian & Company

Stock index futures contracts were introduced at three different stock and commodity exchanges in early 1982, six years after the debut of the first interest rate futures contracts. The Kansas City Board of Trade initiated trading in a contract based on the Value Line Composite Index (VLA); the Chicago Mercantile Exchange followed with a contract tied to the Standard & Poor's 500 Composite Index (S&P); and the New York Futures Exchange affiliate of the New York Stock Exchange completed the trio with a New York Stock Exchange Composite Index futures contract (NYSE).

The ostensible purpose of these new contracts, like that of their predecessors, was to facilitate price discovery and risk transfer in their associated cash markets. Their primary utility for equity portfolio managers was said by their sponsors to be to hedge market-related (but not stock-specific) risk. But aggressive managers soon learned to employ index futures to effect market-timing decisions more rapidly and with lower transaction costs than was afforded by traditional investment methods and to capitalize on cash-futures price discrepancies by means of complex, computerized trading programs.

This chapter is based in part on Allan M. Loosigian, *Stock Index Futures—Buying and Selling the Market Averages* (Reading, Mass.: Addison-Wesley Publishing, 1985).

Futures contracts based upon common stock indexes differ from the Treasury bond and Ginnie Mae contracts discussed in the previous chapter inasmuch as their contractual terms substitute a system of cash settlement for the customary delivery process specified for most financial futures and traditional commodity contracts. The linkage of these instruments to abstract market indexes, as well as their novel cash-settlement terms, gave rise at the onset to complaints that stock index futures trading amounted to little more than legalized gambling. On the other hand, the contract designers recognized—and the concerned regulatory agencies after some hesitation concurred—that the practical difficulties involved in assembling a portfolio composed of hundreds and even thousands of individual stocks merely to duplicate a market barometer bespoke a different approach.[1]

One year after the advent of stock index futures, options on S&P 500 and NYSE Composite futures contracts were introduced at the Chicago Mercantile Exchange and the New York Futures Exchange, respectively. These innovations were followed in turn by index options on a variety of stock market averages and industry subgroups.[2]

STOCK INDEX FUTURES AND OPTION CONTRACT SPECIFICATIONS

"Cash settlement" signifies that, in lieu of tendering an actual portfolio of stocks on a contract's expiration date, stock index futures are "marked to market" one last time, and money is exchanged between long and short contract holders according to their respective gains and losses.

The value of one contract is $500 times the level of the particular index on which that contract is based. If, for example, the S&P 500 Index closed on any given day at 240.90, the immediate or "spot" value of the S&P contract would be $120,450. Had the NYSE Composite Index finished that day at 136.50, the related futures contract would at that point be worth $68,250, and so on. A one-point change in the quotation for any of the three contracts therefore amounts to $500, and the minimum fluctuation for each contract is 0.05, or $25. There were at the time this chapter was written no daily limits set by the respective

---

[1] Regulatory approval of a cash-settlement feature for stock index contracts was facilitated by the successful incorporation of similar provisions in the specifications for Eurodollar time deposit futures introduced at the Chicago Mercantile Exchange a year earlier.

[2] The S&P 100 at the Chicago Board Options Exchange, Major Market Index and Computer Technology Index at the American Stock Exchange, NYSE Composite Index at the New York Stock Exchange, and Value Line Index at the Philadelphia Stock Exchange.

exchanges on stock index contract price changes as were applied to U.S. Treasury bond and other interest rate futures contracts.

The final settlement months for all stock index futures contracts follow the customary March, June, September, and December quarterly delivery cycle. A series of four successive contracts is normally quoted, providing final settlement dates up to 12 months from the spot indexes to which the respective futures are linked. The final settlement price for each contract is the closing value of the designated index on that contract's last trading day which falls on or near the last business day of the settlement month, depending upon the particular contract involved. A purported virtue of cash settlement in contrast to the conventional delivery procedure is that it does not confer a possible advantage over other market participants on those institutions and traders that are physically and financially capable of making or receiving delivery of an underlying commodity.

In spite of the different method of final settlement, the system of initial and variation margin payments that prevails in other futures markets, including interest rate futures, applies to stock index futures as well.[3] (See Table 1.)

Initial speculative margins on stock index futures contracts were set during their early years of trading at $6,500 for Value Line and $6,000 for S&P contracts and, in accordance with their lower value per contract, at $3,500 for NYSE Composite contracts. Speculative variation margins for the three contracts were $2,000, $2,500, and $1,500, respectively. The exchanges selected those particular levels of initial margin because they in turn comprised approximately 10 percent of the dollar value of each contract when trading commenced in 1982. Even at that, stock index margins were set higher than the exchanges would have liked at the insistence of a Federal Reserve Board concerned with the early legalized gambling charges and the possibility of speculative abuses had they been set at the 2 to 3 percent level typical of most other types of futures contracts.[4]

Brokerage firms that execute customers' orders and maintain futures positions on their behalf are permitted to apply lower margin requirements to qualified hedging accounts than to speculators. The justification for this distinction is that the normal risk exposure of bona fide hedgers, including portfolio managers, is considerably less than the risk

---

[3] The discussion of margin payments in Chapter 44, is applicable and need not be repeated here.

[4] The Fed's fears concerning the possible dangers of excessive leverage apparently were exaggerated inasmuch as the stock market surge of 1985–86 served to reduce the unchanged initial margin deposits required on index futures positions to a level of about 5 percent without harm to futures traders or the investing public at large.

TABLE 1 Stock Index Futures Contract Specifications

	Standard & Poor's 500 Stock Index	New York Stock Exchange Composite Index	Value Line Average Stock Index
Exchange	Chicago Mercantile Exchange	New York Futures Exchange	Kansas City Board of Trade
Trading hours	9 A.M.–3:15 P.M. (central time)	10 A.M.–4:15 P.M. (New York)	9 A.M.–3:15 P.M. (central time)
Contract unit	$500 times quoted futures price	$500 times quoted futures price	$500 times quoted futures price
Minimum price change	0.05 or $25 per contract	0.05 or $25 per contract	0.05 or $25 per contract
Daily price change limit	None	None	None
Delivery months	March, June, September, and December	March, June, September, and December	March, June, September, and December
Contract termination	Third Thursday of contract month	Second-to-last business day of contract month	Last business day of contract month
Final settlement price	Closing S&P 500 Composite Index on last day of trading	Closing NYSE Composite Index on last day of trading	Closing VLA Composite Index on final settlement day
Margin requirements:			
Speculative:			
Initial	$6,000	$3,500	$6,500
Maintenance	2,500	1,500	2,000
Hedge:			
Initial	2,500	1,500	3,250
Maintenance	1,500	750	1,625

assumed by holders of speculative futures positions. The test to determine eligibility for reduced hedge margins is the present or intended ownership of a portfolio of stocks equal (or nearly so) in aggregate dollar value to the proposed position in index futures contracts.

As should be clear to readers of the previous chapter on hedging fixed-income portfolios, the line between hedging and speculation is not as clear-cut as the hedge margin eligibility test would indicate. In practice, brokers tend to treat nearly all of their institutional clients as hedgers for the purpose of determining margin requirements. They normally classify their individual customers as speculators unless they are offered convincing evidence that they are not, such evidence usually being a sizable stock portfolio carried with the broker.

Options on stock index futures contracts are generally comparable in their construction and trading procedures to options on interest rate futures contracts. A call option on an index futures contract entitles its buyer for a specified period of time to purchase through an exercise of the call a long position in the designated S&P 500 or NYSE Composite futures contracts at a specified exercise or strike price. A put option on a stock index futures contract grants its buyer, for his or her payment of the quoted premium (price), the right to initiate (sell) a short position in the designated stock index futures contract at a specified exercise or strike price for a specified period of time.

If an option buyer elects to exercise, the seller or writer of a call is obligated to assume a short position in the underlying futures contract, while the seller or writer of a put must undertake a long position.

Index options, also known as cash settlement options or cash index options, are similar in their trading and exercise procedures to options on futures contracts. As was noted with respect to index futures contracts themselves, it is not feasible for most traders to buy or sell a list of stocks that comprise any of the principal indexes, and so a system of cash settlement is prescribed for cash index options as well as for stock index futures.

Trading in individual puts and calls on stock index futures ceases with the termination of trading in their underlying futures contracts on the days designated by the Chicago Mercantile Exchange and the New York Futures Exchange. "In-the-money" options on S&P 500 Index futures contracts are automatically exercised at their expiration and are then settled as futures contracts.

Cash index and index futures option premiums both are quoted like the futures themselves, in points equal in value to $500. Minimum fluctuations, or "ticks," are likewise set at 0.05 of an index point, or $25 (0.05 × $500). Also like the underlying futures contracts, there are no limits in effect on daily price changes for options on index futures.

There are at any given time options set at several different exercise prices traded for the same underlying index futures contract. Exercise prices on S&P 500 and VLA futures options are set at five-point intervals and on NYSE Composite futures options at two-point intervals. Premiums are usually quoted for a minimum of eight exercise prices: one each for in-the-money and at-the-money puts and calls and two each for out-of-the-money puts and calls.

As is the case with options on Treasury bond and other interest rate futures contracts, there are no margin deposits, neither initial nor variation, required of an option buyer after he or she has paid to the writer the premium in full. The option seller or writer, on the other hand, is obliged to deposit in his option account not only the initial margin prescribed for the underlying futures position but the premium received from the buyer as well. With certain exceptions, the writer is also required to deposit variation margin if and as it is incurred on the underlying futures position.

The determinants of option premiums, i.e., option valuation, are discussed in a later section of this chapter.

FUTURES AND OPTIONS TRADING PROCEDURES

Trading in stock index futures and options is in one elementary respect less confusing than trading interest rate futures. In dealing with debt instruments the inverse relationship between price and yield must be considered. With stock index contracts the approach is straightforward, comparable to buying and selling individual stocks. When a trader is of the opinion that the stock market will rise, he or she will be disposed to buy index futures or call options. If a declining market is anticipated, the trader will normally sell a futures contract or, what is the option equivalent, buy a put. Option writers have a somewhat different perspective and will be considered later in this chapter.

A futures trader, whether he or she is a hedger or a speculator, who buys a June S&P 500 futures contract at, say, 215.00 and subsequently experiences a price rise to 238.50 enjoys an unrealized gain on one contract of $11,750 [(238.50 − 215.00) × $500]. That gain accrues gradually—or suddenly, if the stock market happens to be exceptionally active—in the trader's futures account as the long contract is marked to the market daily and that day's gain is credited (or a loss is debited) to his or her account.

A (short) seller of the same contract at 215.00, who stays with a losing position until the price climbs to 238.50, is debited $11,750. The unrealized profits accrued by the long contract are funded by the variation margin payments made by the short contract holder while maintaining the losing position. Had the contract price instead declined, variation margin payments would flow from the longs to the shorts. These money flows are processed through the clearinghouse associated with the exchange where a particular contract is traded. Once an initial transaction is made, as in the above example the purchase and sale of the June S&P 500 contract at the Chicago Mercantile Exchange, the long and short parties to that transaction become disengaged so far as that particular trade is concerned. Each party is thereafter responsible via his or her brokerage firm to the CME clearinghouse for the timely fulfill-ment of his margin obligations.

The futures clearinghouse oversees the daily marking-to-market procedure. Exchange members, including individual traders or the brokerage firms acting for them, compute the aggregate value of their positions in each contract traded on that exchange according to that day's settlement prices, pay to the clearinghouse the net amount of funds that are owed, or collect the funds that are due them or their customers.

Initial and variation margin deposits are made for the purpose of covering these profit-and-loss settlements. Under the cash settlement method, as contrasted with physical delivery, the only difference between the on-going daily mark-to-market procedure and the final settlement is that the value upon which the final gains and losses are calculated is the actual index figure rather than that day's closing futures price.

Proceeding with the June S&P 500 example, the matched long and short could at any time before the final settlement date realize their respective gain and loss by liquidating their positions through offsetting transactions. That would consist for the long of selling one June S&P contract at the prevailing market price and for the short of buying one contract. As was noted above, the long and short contract holders have no further connection following their initial transaction at 215.00. Should the two parties elect coincidentally to liquidate their respective positions at the same moment, it would be a long-odds coincidence if they offset their positions with one another.

Futures traders have a choice of any one of several types of orders to establish and later to liquidate their long or short positions. Each type of order has its own advantages and disadvantages, and every trader would do well to weigh them carefully before deciding which order, under any set of circumstances, is the appropriate one to give to his broker. *A market order* has the advantage of speed and certainty. By employing it, the trader directs his broker to buy or sell the specified contract(s) at the best price bid or offered when the order reaches the exchange floor, or "pit" in futures usage. Given the speed with which futures prices change during periods of volatile markets, the actual price at which a market order is executed may be far removed (and, unfortu-nately, as fate usually wills it, adversely so) from the price the trader deemed attractive at the moment he instructed the broker to buy or sell.

Price uncertainty may be reduced, but the assurance of an execution is thereby relinquished by the use of a *limit order*, which directs the broker to buy or sell the indicated contracts at a specified price or a better one if possible. The aforementioned prospective long may have employed a limit order to direct his broker to buy one June S&P 500 contract at 215 or less, while the would-be short may have instructed her broker to sell the same contract at 215 or higher. If both orders arrived in the S&P trading pit at the same instant, one of them would have failed to be executed unless the market performed an abrupt reversal at that very moment. Many traders maintain that it is preferable to miss the market in such a situation and to try again at a later time with a fresh order than to obtain an unexpected and unwelcome execution price through indiscriminate use of a market order.

A *stop order* is the only type of order that instructs the broker to buy above or to sell below the price prevailing at the time the order is given. That may at first glance seem illogical, but there are often circumstances when it is appropriate to undertake a certain action, such as realizing a gain or loss, only after a market trend has apparently been reversed. A stop order becomes a market order the moment a transaction is made in the futures pit at or beyond the specified stop price and is accordingly executed immediately. If, once again, a trader is wary of obtaining what he considers an unfavorable execution price through the use of an unrestricted stop order, he or she may instead choose to employ a *stop limit* order. This type of order is converted to a limit order as described above when the stop price is reached. But there is again the risk of missing the market entirely.

Orders may also be specified as to the length of time they are to remain in effect. A broker can be instructed to keep an order in force throughout the day or week in which it is entered or to hold it "good until cancelled" if a trader is adamant about obtaining his desired price and is not concerned about how long he or she must wait to secure that price.

Brokerage commissions for futures transactions are charged on "round-turns"—that is, a purchase and liquidating sale or vice versa in the case of a short position. The round-turn rate is in contrast to the commission charged for a purchase of stock followed by a second commission when the stock is sold. Like stock commissions, futures commission rates are negotiable according to the type and amount of service a broker provides and the size and activity of the customer's account.

As a futures contract appreciates in parallel with its underlying spot index during a rising stock market, its associated call option also appreciates in value, while the related put on the same contract depreciates. Conversely, puts appreciate during bear market intervals while calls and futures prices drop.

For example, an at-the-money call—that is, one bearing an exercise price of 215—commanded a premium of 8.75 points or $4,375 (8.75 ×

$500) when the June S&P 500 index futures contract was priced at 215, and the related at-the-money put on the same contract was quoted at a premium of 7.40 points or $3,700. By the time the June S&P futures contract had climbed to 238.50, the premium for the then "deep-in-the-money" June 215 call had appreciated to 31.25 or $15,625, while the premium for what had become an out-of-the-money June 215 put had depreciated to a nominal time value of 1.75 or $875. If the June S&P futures contract had instead declined during that period to, say, 192, it would have been the put that had gone well into the money, and the call premium would have dropped to a moderate time value.

As the market action, in fact, developed, when the June S&P futures contract initially settled at 215 there were options listed at five-point strike intervals from 205 through 230. All of them behaved more or less in line with the performance of the then at-the-money June 215 put and call. The call buyer had in each instance gained an amount roughly equal to the appreciation in the futures contract, and the put writer, as was to be expected, retained the full value of the premium received, but no more. On the losing side of the market, the put buyer would have seen his premium depreciate by some 5¾ points or about 75 percent. The call writer would have been confronted with an exercise at his 215 strike price and forced to cover his involuntary short position at 238.50 for a realized loss of $11,750 minus the $4,375 premium initially received.

COMPUTATION AND BEHAVIOR OF S&P 500, VALUE LINE, AND NYSE COMPOSITE INDEXES AND THEIR RELATED FUTURES CONTRACTS

The three principal stock index futures contracts, S&P 500, VLA, and NYSE, each track a different underlying market indicator. Each average is, in turn, computed in a distinct manner and thereby offers a slightly different representation of the overall stock market. But in essence the three broadly based indexes should be regarded as separate methods of measuring the same thing, such as, for example, centigrade and Fahrenheit scale thermometers.

It is incumbent upon speculative- and hedge-oriented stock index futures traders alike that they be able to distinguish, and to understand the significance of, the similarities and differences among the three indexes. Their speculative or hedging performance will be adversely affected if they do not.

The Standard & Poor's 500 Composite Index, consisting as its title states of 500 stocks, is a capitalization-weighted index, meaning that the total market value (dollar price per share, times the number of shares outstanding) and not simply the share price of each stock is included in the computation of the index. This aggregate market value is then expressed as a percentage of the average market value of the 500 stocks during a 1941–43 base period. The percentage figure is, in turn, divided by 10 to produce the actual index number. It is not necessary to change the divisor (as periodically occurs with the Dow Jones Industrial Average, for example) since the multiplication of share prices by the number of outstanding shares automatically adjusts the index for stock splits.

Standard & Poor's Corporation describes its composite stock index as "base-weighted aggregative" and claims for it the advantages of flexibility in adjusting for stock dividends and splits and of accuracy due to its method of calculation. Standard & Poor's believes that the selection of outstanding shares as the weighting factor ensures that each constituent stock influences the index in proportion to its actual market importance, and that by referring to a base period when its market value was relatively constant, the index accurately reflects fluctuations in current market prices only.

The Value Line Composite Index was devised, and is computed by, Arnold Bernhard & Company on the basis of the approximately 1,700 stocks reviewed by that company's Value Line Investment Survey. The distinguishing feature of this index is that it is the only one of the leading stock averages that is derived from the geometric mean of its constituent stocks. The Value Line Index is not weighted according to the number of outstanding shares of each stock on the list. Stock dividends and splits are accounted for by adjusting the preceding day's prices of those issues that are affected in that manner.

The New York Stock Exchange Composite Index is, like the S&P 500, weighted according to the share capitalization of each stock. But it is a broader index in that it encompasses all of the over 1,500 common stocks listed on that exchange. As with the computation of the S&P 500, the products of stock prices and number of outstanding shares for each constituent stock are added to determine the total market value of any day's trading. The NYSE Composite Index is a figure that expresses the relationship between current market value and, after certain adjustments have been made, a base market value as of December 31, 1965. A base value of 50 rather than the customary figure of 100 was selected to allow the index to approximate more closely the actual $53 average price of all listed stocks on the December 31, 1965, base date. (See Table 2.)

The mathematics of its computation determine that the Value Line Composite, the only index that employs geometric averaging, will always appreciate more slowly, and decline faster, than the S&P 500 and NYSE Composite Indexes that are computed through arithmetic averaging.

The performance characteristics of the three indexes as they are influenced by their different methods of derivation significantly affect the outcome of hedges employing stock index futures and are, therefore, of primary importance to portfolio managers who engage in

TABLE 2 Summary Data for S&P 500, NYSE Composite, and Value Line Average

	Standard & Poor's 500 Stock Index	*New York Stock Exchange Composite Index*	*Value Line Average Stock Index*
Breadth	500 large corporations	1,520 NYSE-listed corporations	1,750 selected companies
Method of averaging	Arithmetic	Arithmetic	Geometric
Weighting	Capitalization weighted	Capitalization weighted	Equally weighted
Base year	1941–43	1965	1961
Value in base year	10	50	100

hedging activities. A capitalization-weighted index such as the S&P 500 or NYSE Composite, for example, is the most appropriate hedging vehicle for an index fund or some other portfolio that aims to duplicate the performance of the overall stock market. An equally weighted index such as the Dow Jones Industrial Average (for which no futures contracts or options were available up to 1986) would theoretically be the optimum hedging yardstick for an investment strategy that stipulates the allocation of equal dollar amounts among all of the stocks contained in the portfolio. This does not, however, apply to the equally weighted geometric Value Line Index because it is impossible to assemble a portfolio of stocks whose performance would duplicate that of the geometric mean of all 1,700-plus Value Line stocks. The task of matching a portfolio's composition and performance to the behavior of one or another of the stock index futures contracts is a critical one for managers who propose to hedge or otherwise vary the market exposure of their portfolios with futures.

An equally weighted index, whether it be derived arithmetically or geometrically, by its structure gives the shares of companies with small capitalizations relatively greater weight in the index than do the capitalization weighted indexes. It is to be expected, therefore, that the Value Line Composite Index would more closely parallel the price performance of a portfolio consisting mainly of the shares of smaller companies and may on that account be of greater use to individual speculators than to most institutional investors.

Figure 1 traces the comparative performance of the three indexes from 1978 through 1983. A close scrutiny of the chart reveals that while their overall paths over the six-year span are essentially parallel, there have frequently occurred deviations from the general pattern that would

FIGURE 1 Comparative Chart, S&P 500, NYSE Composite, and Value Line Indexes, 1975–1982

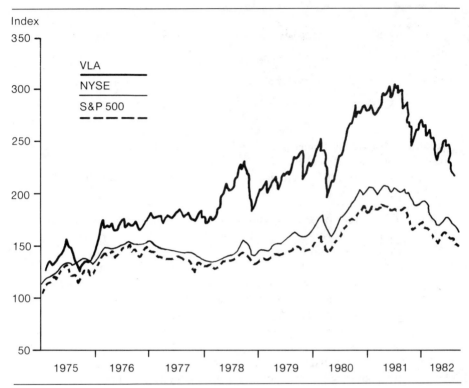

have produced marked dollar differences had one of the three indexes been selected as the basis for a portfolio hedge in favor of the other two. An analysis of the first year's trading history of the S&P 500, VLA, and NYSE Composite futures contracts reveals that the three indexes, as well as their related futures contracts, displayed a high degree of correlation among one another, in most instances achieving coefficients greater than .99. The correlation between the indexes themselves and their respective futures contracts was, however, in some cases appreciably lower, ranging from .744 for Value Line and its related contracts to .887 between the S&P 500 and its contracts.

A comparison of the beta coefficients of the three groups of contracts shows that VLA futures displayed the greatest relative volatility, followed in order by NYSE Composite and S&P 500 contracts. The coefficients of all three futures groups were consistently greater than one, indicating that the futures contracts displayed greater volatility than did their underlying indexes. Somewhat surprisingly, futures price

---

TABLE 3 Summary of Beta Coefficients, S&P 500, VLA, and NYSE
Composite Indexes versus Nearby Futures Contracts

	Constant	Beta	Standard Error
S&P 500	−0.03	1.17	0.85%
VLA	−0.03	1.26	1.14
NYSE	−0.05	1.34	1.00

---

volatility did not increase proportionately with the length of the contracts' maturities. (See Table 3.)

Several pertinent conclusions may be drawn from the first year's trading data:

1. The three futures contracts under discussion behaved in a manner more akin to one another than did their underlying indexes to each other.
2. Futures price volatility was not affected by the various contracts' maturities, i.e., nearby versus deferred final settlement dates.
3. Index futures were more volatile on days when the stock market declined than on days when it advanced.
4. Futures prices on occasion moved counter to the direction of the stock market itself.
5. Futures prices appeared on occasion to anticipate imminent movements of the stock market as well as to reflect changes in carrying costs and the resulting adjustments in the premium over, or discount below, their underlying indexes.[5]

It is to be expected that as these markets mature and more participants, including portfolio hedgers, enter the trading arena, these early observations will be subject to revision.

INDEX FUTURES AND OPTION PRICING CONSIDERATIONS

Attention was given in Chapter 44 to the theoretical pricing considerations affecting interest rate futures and option contracts and to the departure of actual prices from their theoretically "correct" norms. It was there noted that Treasury bond futures prices are effectively determined by the spread between the short-term financing rate paid by

---

[5] Gregory M. Kipnis and Steve Tsang, "Performance Characteristics," in *Stock Index Futures*, ed. Frank J. Fabozzi and Gregory M. Kipnis (Homewood, Ill.: Dow Jones-Irwin, 1984), p. 111.

cash-futures arbitrageurs to hold a contract-grade bond for later delivery on a deferred contract and the long-term yield on that bond.[6]

An analogous situation applies in the case of stock index futures pricing even though these contracts are settled on a cash basis rather than by the actual delivery of securities. But in this instance the pricing theory is modified and is rendered somewhat more complex by the fact that common stock dividends, unlike bond interest, are paid quarterly and can be increased or reduced during the life of a futures contract. The theoretically "correct" stock index futures price is essentially equal to the difference between a riskless short-term interest rate, normally the current 90-day Treasury bill discount, and the aggregate dividend yield on the stock index in question, prorated to a particular contract's final settlement date.

Futures pricing theory holds that a contract's price should equal the cash or spot price of the underlying asset—in this case a stock market index—plus the financing cost minus the yield on that asset. As the pricing theory applies to bond futures, if there is a positive carry—i.e., a yield greater than the financing cost, futures contracts will be priced at successively deeper discounts below their related spot price. Conversely, if there is a negative carry, futures will trade at increasingly higher premiums over the spot price. In theory, at any rate, the cash-futures price structure should, therefore, have little to do with whether market participants expect stock prices to rise or to decline over the life of a contract. The outcome of a particular hedge position will be affected by whether futures are priced at premiums or discounts to the spot index and through its proxy to the portfolio being hedged.

Certain conditions must be fulfilled for the futures pricing theory to be realized in practice. But these conditions are, in fact, seldom, if ever, fully met. For example, though the S&P 500, Value Line, and NYSE Composite indexes may be reasonably duplicated by a proxy portfolio, it would be very difficult to buy and even more difficult to sell short an exact replica of an actual index, which is the "asset" referred to in the pricing theory.

Moreover, the rule that listed stocks may only be sold short on an uptick limits the arbitrage trading that pricing theory states must take place for the cash-futures price structure to be maintained within its defined limits. Third, even if unrestricted short sales of securities were possible, the proceeds from such sales may not become entirely available for reinvestment in the combination of Treasury bills and futures contracts that the arbitrage theory prescribes. Finally, and most compromising of the absolute application of the pricing theory, the precise

---

[6] Pages 1454–57.

value of the dividends due on the index stocks is not foreknown and completely payable on the futures contract's final settlement date.

When a modified set of assumptions is substituted to adapt the pricing theory to uncertain dividend amounts, quarterly payments, and other practical considerations, the price relationships that do, in fact, develop can diverge considerably from what the pure theory holds they should be.

In the application of pricing theory to stock index cash-to-futures price relationships, "forward" and "expected" prices are taken to be two distinct values. Whereas a forward price is determined by positive or negative carry as was discussed above, the expected price of an asset at a future date includes a so-called equity risk premium that offers investors an incentive for buying common stock, say, rather than such riskless securities as Treasury bills. But with regard to index contracts, the traditional analysis is made complicated by the lack of a clear-cut carrying cost for the underlying asset—the market index—other than the short-term financing cost for the designated proxy portfolio. Further complications are created by the unpredictable amounts and financing costs of variation margin payments required to maintain losing futures positions.

In spite of the theoretical qualifications and uncertainties, there are workable guidelines to determine whether stock index futures are fairly or correctly priced in relation to their related spot indexes and to the groups of stocks that comprise the indexes. In the case of the S&P 500 Index, for example, the correct value of the spot futures spread is the riskless or 90-day Treasury bill rate minus the aggregate dividend yield on the S&P 500 portfolio. If the T-bill discount is higher than the expected dividend yield on the S&P 500 stocks, futures will be priced at successive premiums over the spot index value. When the T-bill rate falls below the dividend yield, futures will trade below the actual index.

Continuing with the S&P 500 example cited earlier, on March 25, 1986, when the 90-day Treasury bill discount was 6.40 percent and the expected dividend yield on the composite index was 1.60 to the expiration of the June S&P futures contract, the spot S&P 500 index and two successive futures prices were quoted as follows:

Spot S&P 500	234.72
June S&P	238.20
September S&P	240.90

The 3.48-point premium of the June contract over the spot S&P 500 index on March 25 reflected the 320 basis point spread between the 90-day T-bill rate and the estimated index yield and produced a futures price that was 1.25 points above that contract's estimated "fair value" as is calculated in Table 4.

TABLE 4 Calculation of S&P 500 Spot Futures "Fair Value," March 25, 1986

S&P 500 Index	234.72
June S&P futures price	238.20
90-day T-bill discount	6.40%
Dividends to expiration of futures contract	1.60
Days to expiration of futures contract	93.00
"Fair" price of futures contract =	
234.72 × [1 + .064 (93/365) − 1.60] =	236.95
Amount of overpricing of futures contract	
above "fair value" = 238.20 − 236.95 =	1.25

The problem—and there are always problems—with the type of calculation in Table 4 is that the holding period for the S&P 500 portfolio of stocks must coincide exactly with the final settlement date of the futures contract under consideration. Only on that day will the futures price reach parity with its related stock index value through contract convergence and by so doing allow the pricing theory to come fully into play.

In applying the qualified pricing model to stock index futures, provision must be made for the fact that dividends are not paid out every day in equal prorated amounts but in single lump-sum quarterly payments. To simulate the effect of spreading out quarterly dividend payments over the holding period to a contract's final settlement date, futures evaluation tables have been prepared for the S&P 500 Index. To employ the evaluation tables one must insert estimates of the current dividend yield on the S&P 500 Composite Index and the discount yield of the Treasury bill maturing closest to the final settlement date of the futures contract. With the aid of the futures evaluation tables and these dividend-yield estimates, index traders have available a ready means of determining whether a particular contract is currently over- or undervalued in relation to its theoretically "fair" price.[7]

There are comparable parallels and differences between cash index options and options on index futures, and interest rate options. The premium on a stock index futures option is again the sum of its intrinsic value and any excess time value prospective buyers and writers are willing to accord that option. The intrinsic value of a call is the number of points *above* the call's exercise or strike price at which the underlying stock index futures contract is currently trading; the intrinsic value of a

---

[7] For a detailed explanation and examples of these tables, readers may refer to Gary L. Gastineau and Albert Madansky, "Standard & Poor's Composite Index Futures Evaluation Tables," in Fabozzi and Kipnis, *Stock Index Futures*, pp. 99–110.

put is the number of points *below* its exercise price at which the futures contract is trading. Calls on futures contracts that are quoted below the calls' exercise prices and puts on futures priced above their exercise prices—puts and calls that are out of the money—therefore have no intrinsic value.

Returning to the option example introduced earlier in this chapter, when the June S&P 500 futures contract settled at 215, at-the-money June 215 calls were priced at 8.75. Since an at-the-money option has no intrinsic value, the entire 8.75-point premium consisted of time value. Similarly, the 7.40 premium commanded on that day by the June 215 put consisted wholly of time value because there was by then no gain to be realized from exercising the option. By the time the June S&P futures had appreciated to 238.50, the associated call had proportionately appreciated to 31.25, at which level its intrinsic value was 23.50 and the remaining 7.75 points comprised the call's time value. At a market price of 238.50, the June 215 puts again had no intrinsic value and only carried a modest 1.75-point time value against the remote chance that the June S&P futures contract would drop below 215 before its final settlement date.

The factors that determine the amount of premiums for options on stock index futures contracts are essentially the same as those that apply to options on interest rate futures, once again with the qualification that different treatment must be accorded to dividend payments than is to bond interest. If the aggregate dividends on the index portfolio of stocks increase while the other determining factors remain constant, the premium on a cash index option decreases, and conversely, the premium on a put increases. Dividends do not accrue on calls on futures as they do on cash calls, so the dividend factor does not in that case apply.

Of the five determining factors cited in Chapter 44[8], the volatility of the underlying asset price, in this instance a stock index value, is again by far the most important. Option writers perceive volatility as a risk factor and accordingly require a premium sufficiently greater to compensate them for the additional risk that, to them, higher volatility implies. Prospective buyers, on the other hand, see volatility as a profit opportunity (assuming that it works in their favor) and are, therefore, prepared to pay more for a volatile option than for one that is less volatile.

Option experts often maintain that the primary justification for preferring options to futures is the possibility of accruing incremental gains from identifying and trading in options that are sufficiently over- or undervalued in relation to their theoretical worth—once again that elusive figure. The greater an underlying asset's volatility, so the

[8] Pages 1470–71.

concept goes, the greater is the likelihood that its associated option will become over- or undervalued to a significant degree. To the extent that stock indexes are less volatile than the specific stocks included in their compilation, that much less is the incremental gain to be realized by dealing with options on actual indexes or on index futures than with options on individual stocks. Largely on this account, the widely used Black-Scholes option pricing model has proven less effective in assessing cash index and index futures options than in evaluating premiums for options on individual stocks, the purpose for which it was originally conceived.

HEDGING AND OTHER USES OF FUTURES AND OPTIONS

There are a number of pure and quasi-hedging applications to which stock index futures and option contracts may be put. These include: (1) hedging a long-term investment portfolio in anticipation of a bear market swing in lieu of switching into cash-equivalent instruments; (2) eliminating or reducing market risk implicit in a short-term dealer, underwriting, or block-trading stock position; (3) facilitating short- and long-term market timing decisions at a minimum of transaction costs; and (4) arbitraging temporary disparities in index futures and actual stock values according to the fair value theory discussed above.

Whatever may be the new investment concepts or theoretical insights currently in vogue, portfolio managers are usually inclined to be either "stock pickers" or "market timers," or perhaps some combination of the two. Indeed, before the introduction of index futures and options, managers had little choice but to attempt some combination of the two because of the difficulty in separating *market-related* (systematic) risk from *stock-specific* (nonsystematic) risk.

Before the occasion arose to compare the relative volatility of the several stock indexes and their associated futures and option contracts, beta coefficients had come into common use to measure and to express the volatility of individual stocks. A stock's beta expresses its average volatility in relation to that of the overall market. Its correlation indicates how closely its price movement parallels that of the stock market as a whole after the appropriate adjustment is made to account for the beta.

Prior to the advent of stock index futures, managers who wished to gear their stock picks to the market's overall volatility were constrained to select issues with average betas and, perhaps, to pass over otherwise attractive stocks that did not meet that criterion. To raise their portfolios' market exposure when the outlook was bullish, they had the option of shifting to high-beta stocks; when the mood was bearish they could switch to low-beta holdings or to cash-equivalent securities. They could also diversify their portfolios across many stocks (and betas) to approximate the volatility of the market itself, inasmuch as sufficient diversification can eliminate most of a portfolio's stock-specific risk and leave it with principally market-related risk.

This sensitivity to market-timing considerations, and the periodic need to incorporate these considerations into their stock-selection process, often complicated and sometimes compromised the task of portfolio managers whose forte was stock picking. Now, by selling a correct number of index futures contracts or buying a correct number of cash index puts or puts on stock index futures, such managers can neutralize a given portfolio's market risk and, in so doing, avoid beta-imposed constraints on selecting well-performing individual stocks. Should they at any time choose to become market timers, they may increase their portfolios' market exposure (and risk) without cumbersome disassembling and restructuring by liquidating their short futures and/or long put positions. More aggressive managers may go beyond that point and supplement their portfolios' inherent betas by buying stock index futures or calls.

As is the case with hedging bond portfolios, the optimum outcome of a perfect dollar-for-dollar stock index hedge is usually checked by the vagaries of cross-hedging (the apples-and oranges syndrome described in Chapter 44) and its attendant basis risk.[9] All hedges that employ stock index futures and calls are cross-hedges to a greater or lesser degree due to the operational and financial difficulties for most investors of perfectly replicating an indexed portfolio. Basis risk is compounded in these situations by the commingling of stock-specific and market-related risk, which may in some instances produce the effect of certain stocks moving contrary to the direction of the overall market.

As with bond portfolios, regression analysis is used to quantify the relative price behavior of an individual common stock portfolio, one or more of the applicable stock indexes, and their related futures and/or option contracts. A market model is used to compare the changes over time of the aggregate value of a portfolio vis-à-vis the change in value of the designated index over the same period, and it is expressed by the formula:

Percentage change in portfolio value during period P =

$$\text{Alpha} + \text{Beta} \begin{pmatrix} \text{percentage change in value of} \\ \text{market index during period P} \end{pmatrix} + \begin{matrix} \text{Error term} \\ \text{in period P} \end{matrix}$$

where Alpha represents the error term derived from the statistic R^2, or correlation coefficient, referred to in Chapter 44.[10]

---

[9] Page 1450.

[10] Page 1452.

TABLE 5 Correlation Coefficients, Selected Portfolios versus S&P 500 Index

	Estimated Beta	Coefficient of Determination (R^2)	Correlation Coefficient
Portfolio no 1	0.412	.158	.397
Portfolio no 2	1.614	.458	.677
Portfolio no 3	0.994	.315	.561
Portfolio no 4	0.618	.155	.394
Portfolio no 5	.891	.479	.692

The application of the formula produces varying results, depending upon whether weekly or monthly price data are used and on the length of time (period P) over which data are assembled. There is, to be sure, the minor complication that total rates of return comprising price changes and cash dividends are included in the computation. But experience confirms that the resulting beta is essentially the same, whether total rates of return or price changes alone are considered.[11]

In making provision for the error term, if the relevant R^2 is considered high, say, above .85, signifying that the portfolio in question and the designated market index and/or its related futures and options track one another quite well, the error term is proportionately smaller. As a portfolio becomes more diversified, stock-specific or nonsystematic risk is diversified out of the portfolio as well, serving to raise the applicable R^2 and correspondingly to reduce the magnitude of the error term.

Because the inversely R^2-related error factor of the total return formula declines as a particular portfolio's diversification, and therefore its R^2, increases, it follows that a stock index futures or option hedge will provide more satisfactory results when it is applied to a highly diversified stock portfolio than when it is applied to a less-diversified portfolio.

Table 5 lists the correlation coefficients of three portfolios that contain 10 to 20 stocks relative to the S&P 500 index. The data bear out the contention that as a greater number of stocks are included in the portfolio, R^2 increases and the error factor that is derived from it diminishes accordingly.

EXAMPLE. The manager of a portfolio consisting of 15 stocks that have a total market value of $24.6 million holds a bearish view of the stock market's immediate prospects, but he is loath to liquidate a

---

[11] This analysis is developed by William F. Sharpe and Guy M. Cooper, "Risk-Return Classes of New York Stock Exchange Common Stocks," *Financial Analysts Journal*, March/April 1972, pp. 46–54, 81, cited in Fabozzi and Kipnis, *Stock Index Futures*, p. 184.

carefully assembled portfolio to counteract what he foresees as being temporary weakness. On the other hand, the manager is unwilling to leave his portfolio exposed to such weakness, short-lived though it may prove to be. His decision is to institute a hedge with S&P stock index futures that is implemented in the following manner:

1. Establish the appropriate number of equivalent market index units by dividing the aggregate value of the portfolio by the current value of the S&P 500 index.

$$\text{Equivalent market index units} = \frac{\text{Aggregate portfolio value}}{\text{Current S\&P 500 value}}$$

$$99,898.48 = \frac{\$24,600,000}{246.25}$$

2. Multiply the resulting equivalent market index units by the portfolio's beta to derive the proper number of beta-adjusted equivalent market index units.

$$\text{Beta adjusted equivalent market index units} = \text{Beta} \times \text{Equivalent market index units}$$

$$89,009.55 = .891 \times 99,848.48$$

3. Divide the number of beta-adjusted equivalent market index units by $500 (the dollar value per point of one S&P 500 index futures contract) to obtain the correct number of contracts needed to establish the hedge.

$$\text{Number of S\&P 500 contracts required} = \frac{\text{Beta-adjusted equivalent market index units}}{\$500}$$

$$178 = \frac{89,009.55}{\$500}$$

A strategy that extends beyond purely defensive hedging is one that seeks to arbitrage for profit temporary aberrations from a theoretically correct cash-futures price relationship. For operational and financial reasons, it is impractical for most investors, even institutions, to attempt to assemble a portfolio of stocks that duplicates precisely the composition and weighting of any of the market indexes for which futures contracts are currently available. A satisfactory alternative is to create a surrogate portfolio consisting of considerably fewer stocks that, nevertheless, closely tracks the target index. Given the fact that some basis risk will always exist between the movement of a surrogate portfolio and that of the target index, the conditions for a successful arbitrage operation are: (1) identifying over- and undervalued futures prices relative to the cash index, (2) holding transaction costs to a minimum, and (3) managing whatever basis risk that exists between the surrogate portfolio and the cash index.

When a futures contract price is determined to be above its theoretically correct or fair value, arbitrageurs are ready to sell the overpriced contracts and simultaneously buy the surrogate stock portfolio. Conversely, when the futures are considered undervalued, arbitrageurs are prepared to buy them and sell short the stocks in the surrogate portfolio.[12]

The trading costs that must be taken into account when executing a cash versus futures arbitrage strategy are: (1) round-turn commissions on both futures and stock transactions, (2) bid/asked spreads on stocks and futures and uptick costs associated with short selling, (3) net variation margin payments, and (4) net interest (paid)/dividends (received) costs. An aggregate figure incorporating these costs must be included in the relative pricing calculation. Only when a futures price is quoted above or below its theoretically correct price—and when contracts can actually be bought or sold at those levels—by an amount greater than the aggregate cost estimate is an arbitrage operation worth undertaking.

Arbitrage-related costs may vary widely from trader to trader or, in practice, from institution to institution. Those institutions that routinely engage in futures-cash arbitrage, and have in the process reduced their trading costs to a minimum, have a decisive advantage over institutions that are only incidental and occasional participants.

A contemporary variant of traditional arbitrage operations that focuses exclusively on stock index futures-to-cash price discrepancies has prompted intense controversy in investment and regulatory circles. This modern brand of arbitrage is a major aspect of "program trading," so named because the cash-to-futures relationships are monitored and evaluated by specialized computer programs, and the ensuing purchase and sale orders are automatically placed by means of computerized transmission as well.

The automatic and supposedly indiscriminate buying and selling, plus the unprecedented magnitude of activity assumed by program

---

[12] This strategy is not an appropriate one for institutions or funds that are prohibited from making short sales or for individual traders who are not granted the full use of their short-sale proceeds for reinvestment. The rule that stocks— but not futures—may be sold short on upticks only also serves to hamper the successful execution of an arbitrage strategy.

trading within a brief period, incited criticism that this type of trading is somehow unfair and detrimental to the public interest. The critics claimed that program trading fomented harmful volatility in the stock market as the computerized arbitrageurs repeatedly assembled and disposed of the surrogate portfolios linked to the particular indexes they happened to be involved with. The arbitrageurs retorted that, far from harming the capital market, they were performing what amounted to a social service by enhancing futures and stock-market liquidity, increasing the efficiency of the investment sector, and lowering the overall cost of capital.

The four trading sessions a year in which price volatility is exacerbated by the triple expiration of stock index futures, index options, and futures on index options have become known as the witching hours. To mitigate disruptive market swings during these periods the Securities and Exchange Commission in June 1986 suggested to the exchanges involved that they adopt a number of countermeasures, including disclosing more information to the public about excessive buy or sell orders as the witching hour approaches, coordinating trading halts in the underlying stocks of index options, and changing the expiration time of the option contracts from 4 P.M. Friday to the commencement of trading at 9:30 A.M. Friday.

Program trading can be triggered suddenly as stock and futures price spreads hit their targeted levels, and programs are executed rapidly since the stock component is concentrated in the handful of issues that comprise a surrogate portfolio. The volatility factor is accentuated by the supposition that the behavior of the index futures-to-cash spread is in itself an effective predictor of future stock price movements. Figure 2 illustrates this phenomenon by tracing the comparative movement of the S&P 500 futures-to-cash spread and the Dow Jones Industrial Average through the trading session of March 24, 1986. The chart confirms that at the peaks of intraday rallies as measured by the DJIA, spreads between the spot S&P 500 index and the related futures contracts are unusually broad, and at market troughs the spreads narrow considerably. Moreover, the spreads can anticipate changes in market direction by as much as one hour during the trading day.

EXAMPLE. On May 12 an arbitrageur purchased 1,000 shares each of 10 stocks comprising a surrogate portfolio for the S&P 500 index. One half the purchase price of $753,250 was paid in cash; the balance was borrowed at 7¾ percent.

On the same day, the arbitrageur sold 6 June S&P 500 contracts due to expire June 21 at 246.25. Her objective was to capture, and thereby to profit from, the .52 point spread between the spot S&P 500 index and the June contract.

Surrogate S&P 500 Portfolio	Price Paid on May 12	Closing Price on June 21 Expiration Date	Dividends Paid during Holding Period
AT&T	25	24¾	
Coca-Cola	117⅛	115⅛	$0.78
Du Pont	79¾	85⅞	
Eastman Kodak	60	60½	
General Electric	78⅞	81¾	0.58
IBM	155¼	149⅝	
Schering Plough	72⅛	77¼	
Sears	44⅜	47¼	
UAL	62	63½	
Xerox	58¾	66½	

FIGURE 2   When Spreads Move beyond a Normal Range, Program Trading Drives the Market

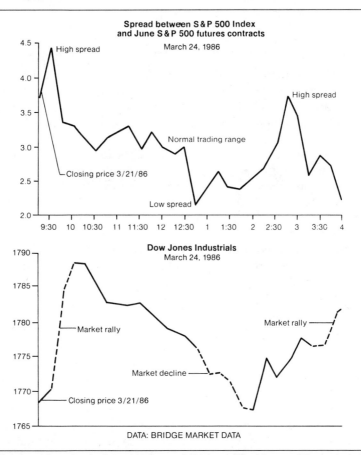

On the June S&P contract's final settlement date, June 21, the spot index and futures settlement price was 248.50. The profit on the arbitrage transaction was computed as follows:

Income	Credit	Debit
Profit on stocks:		
Amount paid on May 12		$753,250
Amount received on June 21	$772,125	
Dividends	1,360	
Costs:		
Interest on $378,000		3,700
Loss on futures		6,750
Transaction fees		2,300
Net profit	$ 7,485	
Original investment	$375,000	
Annualized return on investment	15.9%	
90-Day Treasury bill rate	6.5%	
Incremental risk-free return	9.4%	

As is true in the management of fixed-income portfolios, circumstances may arise in which an equity portfolio manager deems it appropriate to undertake a long hedge with stock index futures or options (calls). Whereas an arbitrageur would wait for index futures to become undervalued in relation to their related cash index to initiate a long futures/short stock arbitrage trade, a portfolio manager might view the same relationship as an opportunity to create a synthetic index fund. The attraction is the same in both instances—futures are relatively cheaper to trade than stocks.

One argument in favor of creating such a synthetic fund is that it entails lower transaction costs than does assembling a conventional portfolio of indexed stocks. The "icing on the cake" for portfolio managers is the incremental gain that accrues when the futures price moves from a discount below to a premium above the spot index. That holds true even when dividend payments on a conventional stock portfolio are taken into account.

The question arises—at least, it *should* arise—whether hedging and related activities can be accomplished more efficiently with stock index futures or with options. The point is invariably made in this regard that futures gains and losses are equal more or less (depending upon basis changes) to the full price movement of the underlying asset's gains for the option buyer. On the other hand, prospective gains are for the option writer (seller) limited to the amount of premium paid him or her, and losses are practically unlimited for the writer but are limited to the amount of premium for the buyer.

The point is further made that while one futures position can entirely offset (again with the qualification of basis risk) cash market exposure in the value that is to be hedged, comparable hedge coverage by means of options can only be achieved through separate put and call positions in three different markets. The question remains whether a complete offset is preferable to the one-way hedge that an option provides—that is, full participation in favorable price movements as well as protection from adverse movements. Many managers hold to the view that it is not. An option buyer's up- and downside risks are divorced. Options may in that sense be regarded as unbundled futures contracts.

As to whether futures or options comprise the better hedging instruments, the most credible evidence available to date suggests that delta hedging with options can protect a stock or bond portfolio from marginal price depreciation imposed by a declining market. Unfortunately, the constant adjustment of option positions that a delta hedging strategy entails tends to raise transaction and other costs to a level where the benefits of capital protection become outweighed by the cost of securing such protection.[13]

On the other hand, futures contracts do not offer a combined risk-reduction and profit-participation quality comparable to the one-way hedge capability provided by options. A ready conclusion, therefore, is that there can be a place in a portfolio manager's kit for both types of instruments. While futures can offer greater utility as passive hedging instruments, options may better be employed as active risk-limiting or, for option writers, income-generating vehicles.[14]

ACTIVE PORTFOLIO MANAGEMENT WITH INDEX FUTURES AND OPTIONS

Beyond strictly passive hedging applications, index futures and options can be employed to raise or lower the market sensitivity of an equity portfolio to suit the manager's bullish or bearish outlook. As was noted earlier in this chapter, before the advent of index futures and options managers had the alternative of fine-tuning their portfolios' sensitivity by switching into higher or lower beta stocks as the situation prescribed. They could also elect to withdraw from the stock market entirely or in part by liquidating shares and reinvesting the proceeds in such cash-equivalent securities as Treasury bills and other money market instruments.

As was also noted, switching stocks according to their beta or

---

[13] Pages 1474–84.

[14] Eugene Moriarty, Susan Phillips, and Paula Tosini, "A Comparison of Options and Futures in the Management of Portfolio Risk," *Financial Analysts Journal*, January/February 1981, pp. 61–67.

liquidating a portfolio entirely complicates and sometimes defeats an investment strategy based on stock selection. It may occur that a manager considers a particular high-beta stock or an industry group of stocks to be an attractive investment at a time when he or she is becoming bearish about the stock market and is preparing to give concrete expression to his or her bearishness. The Hobson's choice in that instance is to forego a potentially superior investment or to contravene the manager's forecast. Index futures and options offer yet another alternative. By selling futures or buying puts at the time a stock is purchased, a manager can neutralize market-related risk with regard to that particular investment and hope to realize his high opinion of the favored issue.

Those managers whose penchant is for market-timing strategies rather than individual stock selection may also employ futures and options, not to neutralize market-related risk but, rather, to accentuate it as a means of raising the performance level of their portfolios. That could be accomplished by buying index futures or calls to augment the volatility of the portfolio stocks.

The following option strategies may be employed to tailor a portfolio's sensitivity to different stock market conditions:

1. *Buying calls in anticipation of a market rise.* As was illustrated in Figure 2 of Chapter 44,[15] the lower premium paid by a call buyer as contrasted with the initial margin required to establish a long futures position gives the call option greater leverage and, therefore, greater profit potential as the stock market advances. On the other hand, as was noted above, a call option's maximum potential loss in the event of a market decline is limited to the amount of the call premium.

   Because call options with high exercise prices command lower premiums than do options on the same underlying assets but with lower exercise prices, the calls with higher strike prices afford a greater potential gain per dollar of premium paid as well as a smaller potential dollar loss. The drawback of the higher exercise price, and indeed the reason for the lower premium it commands, is that it has less likelihood of becoming substantially profitable by moving deeply into the money.

2. *Buying put options in anticipation of a market decline.* A put buyer has unlimited potential to participate fully on the short side during market retreats, again with limited attendant risk in the event the market rises instead. That is in contrast to the unlimited prospective risk and return inherent in a short futures position. A portfolio manager could accordingly assume a long

---

[15] Page 1473.

put position to increase his portfolio's bear market sensitivity beyond what would normally be expected of the portfolio stocks themselves.

3. *Writing calls in anticipation of a declining or stable market.* A covered call writer seeks to generate an incremental rate of return on his or her portfolio over the anticipated dividend yield. This incremental return may be viewed as a limited hedge in the event of a market decline. However, should the stock market—or the bond market in the case of short interest-rate calls—rise instead, the appreciation registered by the portfolio securities above the options' exercise prices would be forfeited to the option buyers who would find it profitable to exercise the then in-the-money calls. The profit profile of a call writer is accordingly equal but opposite to that of a call buyer, i.e., one side's gain is the other side's loss.

4. *Writing puts in anticipation of a rising or stable market.* In contrast to call writing, premium income can be generated and retained by a put writer if the stock market moves laterally or advances and the puts, therefore, remain unexercised. But they will be exercised if the market declines sufficiently, saddling the writer with additional securities or long futures contracts in a falling market environment, thereby adding to growing losses in the stocks already held in the portfolio. Here the profit profile of a put writer is equal and opposite to that of a put buyer.

When employing options for hedging or beta adjustment purposes, an option's delta properties—summarized on page 1482 with respect to interest-rate options—must be taken into account with stock indexes as well. To reiterate, an option's delta is the fractional change in its premium that occurs as a result of a one-point price change in the underlying security or futures contract. Delta factors can be derived for put options as well as for calls and are important indicators of the degree of risk a manager employing either type of option instrument is taking out of or instilling into his portfolio.

As was described in the previous chapter, a put or call option position must be monitored and adjusted frequently in response to changes in the delta factor at different levels of the underlying index and of the option price itself. An option that is moving into or out of the money, for example, has a different delta, and hence it requires a different hedge ratio than when the same option is at the money. Continual adjustments of the hedge ratio involving repeated purchases and sales of option contracts may be necessary due to an expanding or contracting delta factor, a characteristic of delta hedging with options that some analysts have concluded renders the strategies too cumbersome and costly to be employed on an ongoing basis.

REGULATORY, TAX, AND ACCOUNTING CONSIDERATIONS

Portfolio managers have as a group been slower to adopt index futures and options in the conduct of their business than has been the broker-dealer community, including stock specialists, block traders, underwriters, and arbitrageurs. One of the deterrents to more active use of these instruments by, say, pension fund managers has been a lingering uncertainty regarding the regulatory, tax, and accounting limitations and implications.

This hesitation is to some extent warranted inasmuch as the institutional and fiduciary use of futures and options has raised complex issues and in so doing has led regulators and prospective users alike into uncharted waters. A sufficient number of early guidelines have been established, however, to underscore that there is no innate sanction against an institution's using index futures and option contracts for at least passive hedging purposes. It should also be pointed out in this regard that most portfolio managers, even those who pursue an aggressive investment or trading strategy, do not engage in the extremely short-term, rapid-turnover, and narrow profit margin type of activity of which much broker-dealer business consists. Many of the more trading-oriented futures and option strategies are, therefore, not suited to such managers' needs.

The Employee Retirement Income Security Act (ERISA) of 1974, which incorporates the current body of regulations concerning the particular types of investments permitted to pension plans, does not explicitly mention hedging with stock index or, for that matter, interest rate futures or options, all of which were introduced after the enactment of the law. On the other hand, there is no expressed prohibition on the use of futures or options by pension funds.

ERISA requires that any person who makes investments for a pension plan diversify that plan's assets "so as to minimize the risk of large losses." Under the ERISA standard of prudent investment, supplemented by regulations issued by the U.S. Department of Labor, each investment made by a pension plan is regarded as a part of the plan's aggregate portfolio and should be appraised within the context of the plan's overall objectives and requirements. Legal opinions have been issued attesting that if it is, in fact, consistent with a plan's objectives and requirements, a pension fund manager is permitted to use index futures to hedge a common stock portfolio. Some opinions have also been tendered to the effect that anticipatory hedges—for example, long futures positions taken prior to expected cash contributions to the fund—may under the proper circumstances be considered prudent.

Uncertainty concerning what should be the correct treatment of initial and variation margin deposits under a trustee arrangement created problems for pension funds that considered hedging during the early months of stock index futures trading. The issue was resolved by a Department of Labor advisory opinion that pension plans are permitted to maintain margin accounts directly with futures brokers and, without the intercession of a trustee, to deposit margin payments directly with the brokers carrying for them futures hedge accounts.

Other institutions that may reasonably employ index futures and options in their portfolio management activities, such as commercial banks, insurance companies, and investment pools, are for the most part subject to regulation at the state level where it is to be expected that over the course of time regulators will develop a more enlightened attitude concerning futures and options, matching that of their opposite numbers in the federal agencies.

In the sphere of taxation, the Economic Recovery Tax Act of 1981 altered drastically the manner in which all commodity futures trading is treated for tax purposes. The 1981 act imposed a maximum federal income tax rate of 32 percent on all futures transactions whether they are intended for hedging or speculative purposes and regardless of the holding period of the contracts. The favorable 32 percent maximum tax rate was the principal accommodation to the futures industry granted by the Congress to win its acquiescence in the legislative elimination of so-called tax straddles that converted short-term into long-term capital gains and deferred income seemingly indefinitely.

The 1981 tax law makes a distinction between speculators and hedgers and applies to speculators, whether individual traders or companies, a 60/40 rule that treats 60 percent of a trader's total futures gains or losses incurred during the tax year as long-term capital gains or losses and the remaining 40 percent as short-term capital gains or losses. There are no tax consequences accorded to the receipt or payment of variation margin until the end of the taxable year.

For the purposes of the tax law, a hedge is a transaction that is entered into by a taxpayer during the normal course of his business primarily to reduce the risk of price change with respect to property held or to be held by the taxpayer—provided, that is, the gain or loss on the transaction is treated as ordinary income or loss and that it is clearly identified as a hedging transaction before the close of the business day on which it is entered into.

All gains and losses incurred on hedging transactions are treated as ordinary, with a maximum tax rate on such gains and losses of 50 percent. There is no recognition of gains and losses at year-end for futures contracts, including stock index futures, unless and until the contracts are settled through a closing transaction or final cash settlement during the tax year. The loss deferral rule (see the accounting discussion below) is inapplicable, so that an index futures contract carried as part of a hedging transaction could be closed out at a loss that would be recognized at ordinary income rates despite the fact there was a comparable unrealized gain in the taxpayer's stock portfolio. If a transaction qualifies as a hedge but the taxpayer inadvertently fails to identify it as such, the gain or loss will still be treated as ordinary income or loss, but the variation margin loss deferral will apply.

The tax revision bill introduced by the Senate Finance Committee in May 1986 would, if passed, eliminate the 60/40 rule and tax all investments at the same 27 percent rate. Futures industry spokesmen expressed their concern that such a step would harm their business inasmuch as it would eliminate the tax advantage of futures trading vis-à-vis stock and bond investments.

A controversial accounting issue pertaining to futures transactions has been whether futures gains and losses should be reflected in income currently or be deferred and recognized in a later reporting period. In 1980 the American Institute of Certified Public Accountants recommended the adoption of deferral or so-called hedge accounting that would regard futures positions as parts of combined cash-futures hedge transactions. In advancing this recommendation the AICPA endorsed the concept of "symmetry"—that is, combined and comparable accounting treatment for the cash and futures components of a combined hedge position.

Margin deposits are recorded as deposits that represent a receivable due from the broker carrying the futures position. A receivable that is so booked should be increased or decreased in accordance with variation margin changes, i.e., futures gains or losses.

The exposure draft of the Statement of Financial Accounting Standards (SFAS) No. 12 stipulates that a marketable equity portfolio be carried at the lower of the portfolio's aggregate cost or its current market value established at each balance sheet date. The amount by which a portfolio's aggregate cost exceeds its market value is accounted for as a valuation allowance that represents the net unrealized loss in the portfolio.

Gains and losses on open stock index futures positions should be considered in determining the valuation allowance. Changes in the valuation allowance for a common stock portfolio, including gains and losses from open stock index futures contracts, should be included in the determination of net income for the period in which the changes occurred. Gains and losses on stock index futures contracts that have been closed out should also be included in the determination of net income for the period in which the gains and losses occurred.

SFAS No. 12 did not provide for any specialized accounting treatment of realized gains and losses on options used for hedging purposes. Instead, gains and losses on all marketable equity positions, including options on stock indexes or index futures, are to be recognized as income when realized, regardless of the purpose of the transaction. The accounting treatment is, therefore, the same whether the option position is intended as a speculation or as a hedge.

46

Dynamic Hedging and Portfolio Insurance Strategies

Richard Bookstaber, Ph.D.
Principal
Morgan Stanley & Co.

Joseph A. Langsam, Ph.D.
Vice President
Morgan Stanley & Co.

I. INTRODUCTION

Dynamic hedging and portfolio insurance are names given to a wide variety of strategies used to control investment risk in both equity and fixed-income portfolios. These strategies provide protection against loss without imposing equal limitations on the opportunities for appreciation. Portfolio insurance has gained attention recently as investors seek out strategies for protecting the capital gains they have enjoyed over the past several years without losing the opportunity for further gains.

In the past capturing unrealized capital gains has meant cashing out of the market and foregoing any future opportunities for continued performance. The decision of preserving capital or maintaining market opportunities has appeared as an either/or decision. Recent advances in asset allocation now provide a middle ground, offering techniques for insuring against a deterioration in capital without completely selling off market opportunity. These techniques are known as dynamic hedging strategies or portfolio insurance. While they are familiar to many in the investment research community, they have only recently received an audience among portfolio managers and plan sponsors.

Portfolio insurance provides a means of creating insurance protection on the value of a portfolio. For example, it can provide a prespecified floor level of downside protection while still allowing the portfolio to share in any future market appreciation.

The discussions and presentations of dynamic hedging have usually centered on describing how the technology works. A number of publications describe how the option-like payoffs of dynamic hedging are created and measured.[1]

The focus on the technological issues of dynamic hedging is natural given the newness and complexity of the hedging methodology, but dynamic hedging is only a tool, and its implementation is really the central issue for the decision maker. The issue of implementation remains to be addressed after one understands how dynamic hedging works. Both the nature of the floor and the structuring of the insurance costs are extremely flexible and can be adjusted to meet the needs of the investment manager or plan sponsor. Dynamic hedging can be used to mold returns to meet specific investment objectives. Understanding the range of possibilities dynamic hedging presents is most important to those contemplating applying this technology.

This chapter addresses how this new tool of dynamic hedging can best be used to achieve the dual objective of protecting unrealized capital gains while maintaining opportunities for further capital appreciation. We will consider the issues of what hedge best meets this investment objective and the trade-offs between the various ways of paying for the desired protection.

II. PROGRAM DESIGN

Dynamic hedging opens up a new dimension to the asset allocation decision. The payoff profile of each asset can be molded to address investment risks and plan needs. The flexibility of the investment decision maker can be extended beyond the usual chores of establishing proper diversification and formulating the bond/equity mix.

---

[1] The technology used in providing portfolio insurance is that of option theory. The dynamic hedge replicates the payoff that would occur if a put option were purchased on the underlying portfolio. A put option pays off dollar-for-dollar for any drop in portfolio value below its exercise price. Creating a put option with an exercise price equal to the desired floor return, and then adding that put option to the portfolio, will provide the desired protection.

The concept of using dynamic hedging strategies to create option-like payoffs dates back to the original option papers by Black and Scholes (1973) and Merton (1973). Work on dynamic hedging and the more general use of options to mold portfolio returns has been developed by Bookstaber and Clarke (1981, 1983a, 1983b, 1984, 1985). Bookstaber (1985), Leland (1979), Rubenstein and Leland (1981), and Rubenstein (1985). The application of dynamic hedging and portfolio insurance to investment management is discussed in Platt (1986), Platt and Latainer (1983a, 1983b), and Tilley and Latainer (1985).

FIGURE 1 Portfolio Insurance: Upfront Premium Payment

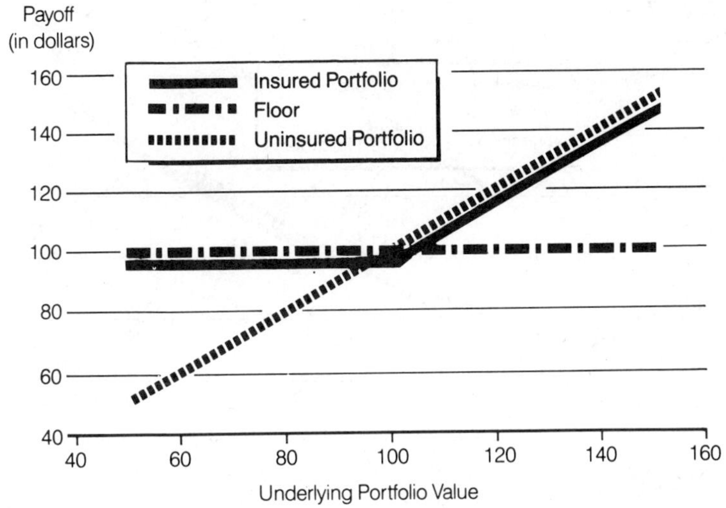

There are many parameters to consider in designing the best portfolio insurance strategy, just as there are in designing the ideal property/casualty insurance policy. For example, in determining coverage, there are the questions of whether to self-insure or coinsure, whether to pay for a small deductible or seek only catastrophic protection. In this section, we will cover the major design issues.

Figure 1 illustrates the payoff from a portfolio insured through a dynamic hedging strategy. The dotted line is the payoff to the underlying portfolio without the protection of the dynamic hedge. Since it is the underlying portfolio, it moves one for one with the market value shown on the x axis.

The solid line is the payoff from the insured portfolio. This portfolio gains one for one with the underlying portfolio for values above the floor of $100 but does not decrease in value when the underlying portfolio falls below this floor. The payoff to the insured portfolio is shifted two dollars below the payoff to the underlying portfolio.

The protection this strategy provides is the difference between the insured portfolio and the underlying portfolio below the floor portfolio value. The cost of the protection is the difference between the underlying portfolio and the insured portfolio above the floor value. We will next discuss the types of protection and the structure of the costs for that protection in more detail.

FIGURE 2   Portfolio Insurance: Coinsurance (50 percent)

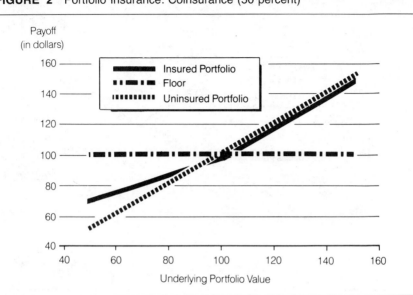

Types of Financial Protection

There are two parameters in designing portfolio protection: the amount of coverage and the size of the deductible.

The size of the deductible is determined by the floor. A lower floor leads to a higher deductible and, of course, to a lower cost for the protection. For example, the protection described in Figure 1 gives a zero deductible; it protects against any loss in the portfolio below its current value. One could, instead, construct a payoff which establishes a floor at, say, −10 percent. In that case, the point of inflection in Figure 1 would be at a portfolio value of $90 rather than at $100.

The amount of coverage is determined by the face value of the portfolio insurance policy. Figure 2 shows the payoff profile for 50 percent coverage. Such coinsurance leads to lower costs for protection. Coinsurance can be looked at as an asset allocation rule that provides the portfolio with lower exposure—a lower beta or duration—in declining markets.

The level of the deductible and the use of coinsurance are both tools for controlling insurance costs, but the impact of the two on the degree of protection differs. For protection against very large market losses—catastrophe insurance—full insurance with a high deductible will usually be better than coinsurance. For protection against smaller downturns, coinsurance will usually be a less costly form of protection.

FIGURE 3 Portfolio Insurance: Equity Sharing

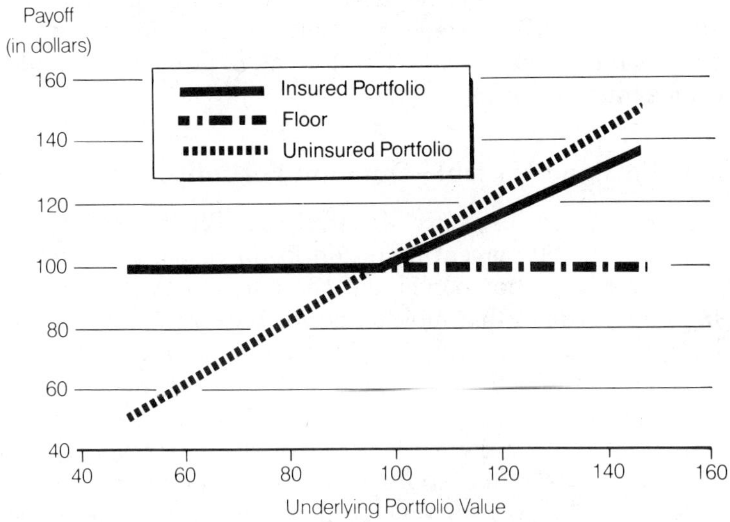

Types of Insurance Payment

The elimination of undesirable payoffs only comes by giving up some desirable attributes as well. Generally, what is given up is part of the upside potential. The give-up can be structured as a fixed dollar amount, a cost structure similar to that of conventional insurance, or one can pay for financial insurance by giving up part of the upside potential. The latter payment method, called equity sharing, is like a homeowner receiving fire insurance in exchange for promising the insurer a fraction of the profits from the later sale of the house.

Figure 3 presents the payoff profile of portfolio insurance based on equity sharing. The equity sharing costs nothing upfront, but the payoff on the upside is reduced proportionately. The alternative to equity sharing is to make an upfront payment, as depicted in Figure 1 above. The cost with an upfront payment is the same as if a protective put option were purchased in the marketplace.[2] After it is purchased the payoff from the option drops by a fixed dollar amount.

---

[2] Unlike the purchase of an over-the-counter option, the dollar payment does not need to be made at the start of the strategy. It will be realized at the end of the protection period as a constant dollar deviation from the payoff of the protected portfolio. For example, if the cost of the option on a $100 million portfolio is $3 million, the payoff at the end of the period will be the greater of the portfolio value less the future value of $3 million or the specified floor less the future value of $3 million.

The decision of whether to pay a fixed dollar cost or to use an equity sharing approach depends on the investor's perceptions of future market opportunities and the need of the fund to capture these opportunities. The fixed payment is more attractive in periods of high returns, while the equity sharing will be more attractive in periods of low to moderate returns.

Variable Beta and Variable Duration Portfolios

Equity sharing and coinsurance selectively alter the market exposure of the portfolio. The 50 percent reduction in downside exposure for the coinsurance strategy shown in Figure 2 amounts to having the foresight of being in a portfolio that moves one for one with the market if the market ends up ahead at the end of the period and in a portfolio that moves only half as much as the market if the market ends up below the floor. That is, it is a portfolio with a beta of 1.0 if the market is above the floor and a beta of .5 if the market is below its floor level. The cost of enjoying this view into the future is the cost of the put option.[3]

Similarly, the equity sharing portfolio shown in Figure 3 is like transforming an equity portfolio with a beta of 1.0 into a zero-beta portfolio if the market drops and a .70 beta portfolio if the market goes up.[4]

The variable exposure afforded by dynamic hedging applies for bond portfolios, too. For bond portfolios, dynamic hedging can be thought of as dynamic duration management. Duration, the weighted average maturity of a bond portfolio, is a measure of interest-rate sensitivity. Ideally, a bond portfolio manager will lower the duration of the portfolio if rates are thought to be on the rise and extend the portfolio duration if the bond market is thought to be rallying.[5] Dynamic

---

[3] As Merton (1981) has pointed out, the price paid for portfolio insurance can be looked at as the payment for a "perfect market timing" service, a service which moves funds between the better performing of the portfolio and cash. If, at the time of option expiration, the risky portfolio outperformed cash, the investor will realize that return, less the "advisory fee" represented by the put option payment. If the risky portfolio underperformed the benchmark, the investor will be out of the portfolio and into cash, receiving the floor return less the option cost.

[4] In application, the hedge will not be exact and the actual dollar cost cannot be fixed absolutely, but only in expected value. The cause of basis risk in the hedge, and the expected size of that risk, is covered in the later sections of the chapter.

[5] Duration is a measure of interest-rate sensitivity. The higher the duration of a bond or a bond portfolio, the more its value will be affected by a change in interest rates. Duration, therefore, serves much the same purpose in evaluating the exposure of a bond portfolio as the beta does for an equity portfolio. A discussion of the use of duration in measuring the interest-rate sensitivity of bond portfolios is presented in Toevs (1984).

hedging automatically provides this duration adjustment. The cost of achieving that adjustment is the cost of the portfolio insurance.

Figure 4 shows the variable duration portfolio as a function of the

---

FIGURE 4   Insuring a Bond Portfolio—Protecting against Interest-Rate Increase

---

A. Portfolio Payoff

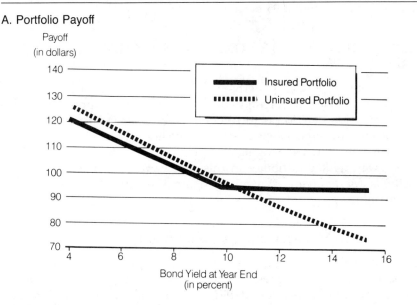

B. Portfolio Duration Characteristics

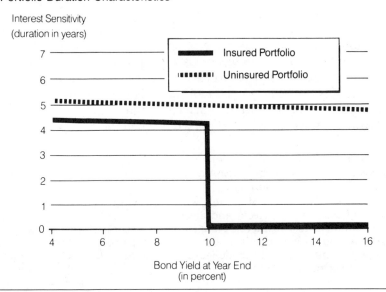

underlying portfolio yield. The underlying portfolio, in this case, is taken to have the duration characteristics of a 8.75 percent coupon Treasury with seven years to maturity. The duration of the bond is 5.3 years, and the yield is assumed to be 8.94 percent. As the yield changes, the portfolio value shifts with interest-rate changes. The insured portfolio protects against loss from interest-rate increases. The strategy protects the portfolio from rates rising above 10 percent, assuring a floor to the porfolio value of 95 percent.[6]

III. EXAMPLES OF STRATEGIES FOR CAPITAL PRESERVATION

The variety of payoff patterns that are possible through dynamic hedging strategies are literally limitless. The key in approaching the asset allocation decision is to recognize the flexibility that is available and spend the time needed to articulate the investment objectives. Approaching dynamic hedging as a prepackaged, off-the-shelf product takes away its key attribute. In this section we will illustrate several methods for applying dynamic hedging toward the goal of capital preservation.

Conservative Management: Maintain Asset Value

Conservative investment objectives provide the textbook case for using the dynamic hedge to preserve the current asset value. The need to protect the capital base from deterioration usually leads these funds to hold portfolios with a low equity/bond mix. Consequently, they have a low beta. The payoff of such a fund is shown in Figure 5.[7] This fund has a 40 percent/60 percent equity/bond mix.

Providing portfolio insurance at a zero percent floor opens up the opportunity for the fund to move some of its fixed-income assets into equity. Since the floor protection is now provided by the dynamic strategy, the fixed-income securities do not need to serve that function. Assets are freed to be employed more actively once the dynamic hedge replaces the quasi-insurance role played by the bonds.

Figure 5 shows the payoff that results when the equity/bond mix is

---

[6] The portfolio floor pertains only to the capital value of the portfolio. All coupons are assumed to be dispersed. The floor also takes into account the accretion of the bond toward par.

[7] This example and all of the following examples in this section assume a market volatililty of 15 percent and an interest rate level of 10 percent. The volatility in the equity market has ranged in the recent past from 12 percent to 18 percent, and for long bonds has been in the 10 percent to 12 percent range. A higher-volatility will lead to a higher cost for the protection. A higher interest rate will lower the insurance cost.

FIGURE 5   Portfolio Insurance versus a Static Asset Mix

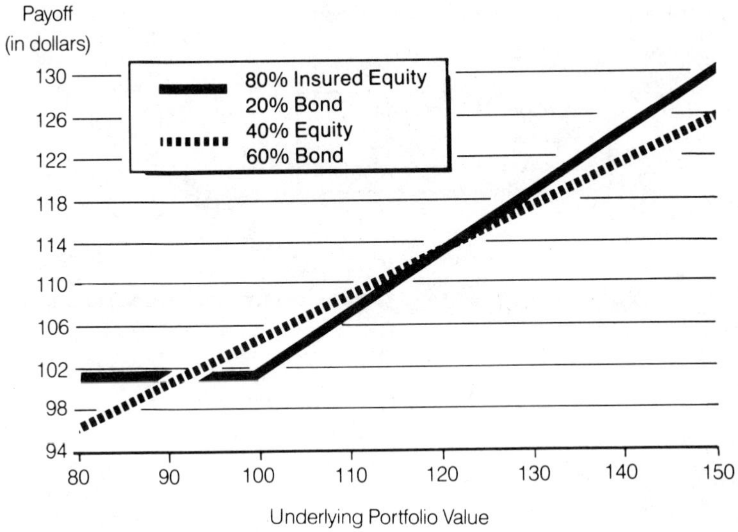

Payoff
(in dollars)

▬▬▬	80% Insured Equity 20% Bond
▪▪▪▪▪▪	40% Equity 60% Bond

[Line graph with Y-axis "Payoff (in dollars)" ranging from 94 to 130, and X-axis "Underlying Portfolio Value" ranging from 80 to 150.]

Underlying Portfolio Value

moved from 40 percent/60 percent to an insured equity/bond mix of 80 percent/20 percent.[8] The payment for the portfolio insurance is made by equity sharing in this example. The insurance increases the beta of the portfolio on the upside from .40 to .56. The important lesson from this figure is the low cost of the asset allocation strategy. The actual insurance cost is largely compensated for by the increased upside exposure to equity it allows. Little is lost on the upside from the shift because the protection is now being provided in a more direct and efficient way. It is only in periods of moderate returns that the insured portfolio will underperform the original portfolio, and even here active management can help mitigate this lower return.

The portfolio insurance payoff shown in this figure may seem like a free lunch, since it provides both better protection and more upside potential. This result occurs because the portfolio insurance is now being provided in the most efficient manner. Bonds simply are not the most efficient way of providing protection. An unnecessarily large part of the portfolio must be dedicated to the insurance role when bonds are

---

[8] Some fixed-income instruments should still be held since they serve an important diversification role and since they address interest rates and inflation factors that equity cannot. With the dynamic hedge applied as the medium for protection, more care can be taken to define the correct asset allocation between equity and fixed-income instruments to accomplish this objective.

FIGURE 6 Protecting against Catastrophic Loss

A. Upfront Payment and Floor at −10 Percent

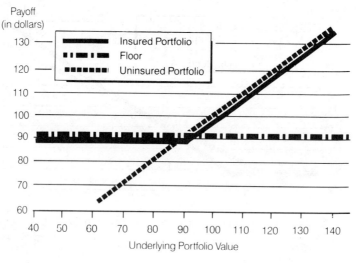

used as the insurance vehicle. When dynamic hedging is used to provide that protection more efficiently, resources are saved that can be redirected toward return objectives. Thus, portfolio insurance, rather than displacing the role of active management, actually augments it.

Overfunded Pension Plan: Protect against Castastrophic Losses

A pension fund that has built up a surplus may not find a need to pay the price of maintaining the current floor. The excess funding allows the pension to self-insure against moderate capital losses. Like other self-insurers, the goal for such a fund is to protect against catastrophic loss.

Figure 6A shows the payoff from this type of protection. The floor is 10 percent below the current market value, and the time of protection is one year. The improvement in payoff when the market drops more than 10 percent comes at a constant dollar underperformance if the market goes up. The cost is lower than in the first example because here the insurance has a deductible of 10 percent.

For a fund that wishes to partially self-insure, coinsurance and catastrophe insurance coverage can be combined, as shown in Figure 6B. Here, the coinsurance provides some insulation against market downturns through coinsurance, and then adding full insurance with a high deductible protects against catastrophic loss.

FIGURE 6 *(concluded)*

B. Combining Coinsurance and Catastrophe Insurance

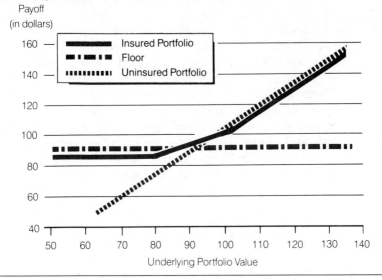

This insurance structure, while complex from the viewpoint of many managers and sponsors, is a common one in other insurance applications. Health insurance plans, for example, often have a deductible before the insurance comes into effect and then have coinsurance after that point, with the policyholder paying perhaps 20 percent of medical costs. The coinsurance caps out at some level, and for catastrophic losses the insurance company pays 100 percent of the claims. It is not unreasonable to expect that as the field of portfolio insurance develops, this same degree of flexibility will be found in constructing portfolio insurance programs as well.

Underfunded Pension Plan: Dealing with Asymmetries in Interest Exposure

The calculation of pension liabilities is based on actuarial assumptions of mortality rates, inflation, and work-force participation. These assumptions lead to cash flow needs over the term of the fund. The cash flows are discounted back to the present to determine the current pension fund liability. The lower the discount rate, the higher the liability will be. Pension liabilities, thus, increase with a decrease in interest rates.

The natural tendency of underfunded pension plans is to reduce exposure to market risk by moving more funds into fixed-income instruments and to lower the duration of the fixed-income portfolio to protect against rising interest rates. Such a pension plan cannot afford the luxury of self-insuring that the overfunded pension plan enjoys.

Unfortunately, considering the impact lower interest rates have on the pension liabilities, lower interest rate exposure, while protecting the fund value from interest-rate increases, increases the exposure of the fund to the asset/liability risk from interest-rate declines. The attempt to reduce risk by lowering the interest sensitivity of the portfolio will exacerbate the asset/liability mismatch since the pension assets will not keep up with the liabilities as interest rates decrease.

The features of many fixed-income instruments reinforce the difficulties these pension plans face in a lower interest rate environment. Callable bonds and mortgage securities are called as interest rates fall, leading to a reduction in their interest sensitivity. While pension liabilities typically have a long duration, a portfolio of long maturity, but callable, instruments shortens in duration precipitously with declining interest rates. This is due to the call feature imbedded in these instruments. Dynamic hedging methods can be used to "buy back" these call features, thereby correcting for the adverse changes in interest sensitivity.[9]

Pension plans require interest-rate exposure in favorable interest-rate environments, not just because this exposure leads to a favorable impact on portfolio value but also because it will allow the assets to match the impact a change in rates will have on liabilities. Dynamic hedging can be applied to the fixed-income portfolio with this need: lowering the portfolio duration as interest rates rise while lengthening duration as interest rates decline. In this way the asset/liability gap can be closed if rates decline rather than widen.

Pension Fund Management over the Longer Horizon: Predictable Cash Flow with Long-Term Equity Exposure

A pension fund that depends on current cash flow from investments to service retired lives must take a more conservative asset allocation posture than that taken by the overfunded pension of the previous example. The pitfall in conservative, cash-flow-oriented management is that it invariably seems to lead to an overweighting of fixed-income securities.

While bonds give reliable cash flow, they do not provide a long-term inflation or purchasing power hedge. A high bond weighting will give

---

[9] The reduction in interest sensitivity with a decline in interest rates is called negative convexity. The issues of imbedded options in fixed-income portfolio managment—from callable bonds, mortgage securities, and other instruments—is treated in Bookstaber (1986).

protection against year-by-year capital losses from market downturns but at the cost of falling behind in the long-range goal of securing retirement benefits for younger workers against these important economic factors. Protection against these factors is best provided by equity.

Bonds have been called upon to do double duty in the asset allocation decision. They serve to address the interest-rate exposure of liabilities, and they serve as the insurance vehicle to protect against capital deterioration. They cannot serve both of these functions simultaneously. Dynamic hedging provides the framework for providing a guaranteed cash flow without compromising the optimal asset mix.

The cash flow component of this strategy can be generated through dividends, an immunized portfolio, or a guaranteed income contract (GIC). As we will show in the next section, implementing the hedging strategy with futures allows us to avoid trading the cash-flow vehicles. The structure of the cash-flow portfolio and the creation of the dynamic hedge can be separated, and less liquid instruments, such as high-yield bonds or GICs, can be used to generate the cash flow.

Insurance versus Portfolio Insurance

Dynamic hedging is a form of self-insurance. A firm desiring to self-insure against property loss can consult with an actuary to determine the necessary reserve fund and the expected size of the loss. There is no guarantee the reserve fund will exactly cover losses; the firm will still face some residual risk in self-insuring rather than paying a set premium for guaranteed coverage.

With dynamic hedging, the investor consults with a hedging advisor who helps construct the proper hedging program. Like the actuary, he can give an estimate of the cost of the protection but cannot provide a guarantee. The residual risk, if the hedge does not give the exact payoff desired, rests with the investor. However, just as the actuary can provide scenario analysis and bounds for the residual error in self-insuring property loss, the hedging specialist can give an estimate of the tracking error for the portfolio insurance strategy.

Dynamic hedging may be a superior alternative to buying guaranteed coverage through the options market, even if that coverage is available. Just as self-insurance can be less costly than buying an insurance policy, creating the protective put option for portfolio insurance may be less costly than buying it over the counter. A firm that writes an over-the-counter option must hedge its position. It will do so by executing the dynamic hedging strategy internally. Since that firm will now face the residual risk from the tracking error of the hedge, it will add a risk premium onto the option. Portfolio insurance provides this internal hedging mechanism to the client directly. The investor may

TABLE 1   Examples of Portfolio Insurance Costs*

Floor	Prepaid Premium (per $100 Covered)	Equity Sharing (Percent of Upside Potential)	Coinsurance (50 Percent) (per $100 Covered)
		One Year	
100	$3.00	70%	$1.50
95	1.60	88	.80
90	.90	95	.45
		Three Years	
100	$4.20	78%	$2.10
95	2.20	90	1.10
90	1.50	95	.75

* These costs are meant only to illustrate the range and the relationship between the costs of different insurance programs. The actual cost will depend on the interest-rate level and volatility of the underlying portfolio. Furthermore, as we discuss later, the actual insurance cost is subject to error.

be more willing to absorb the residual risk than to pay this added premium.[10]

Table 1 illustrates the costs of these various types of protection. While the exact costs will vary with interest-rate levels and with market volatility, these values give a general indication of the cost of protection.

IV. HOW DYNAMIC HEDGING WORKS

The payoffs constructed by dynamic hedging strategies are range hedges. Unlike a global hedge, which isolates the portfolio from all market moves, a range hedge only hedges out the exposure over a prespecified range of outcomes. For example, a portfolio insurance program which gives a floor of zero percent return is a hedge that becomes effective only in the range of asset values below their current value.

A range hedge works by increasing the size of the hedge as the portfolio value moves into the hedged range and decreasing the size of the hedge as the portfolio moves out of the hedged range. Exposure is reduced as the market falls, limiting the downside loss, and exposure is increased as the market rises, providing upside potential. As any trader knows, gradually selling the portfolio off as it moves down and

---

[10] The key determinant on whether to self-insure through a dynamic hedge or to seek out a guaranteed floor through an option contract turns on who is better able to absorb the residual risk in the hedge, the investor or the firm offering the guarantee.

gradually buying it back as it rises in value does not come without a cost. The cost is a slippage in portfolio value since not all the gains of the market will be realized, nor will the portfolio be completely insulated from market declines. This slippage from this dynamic adjustment of the position is what leads to the strategy cost. The central feature of the dynamic hedge is that this cost can be predicted at the start of the program.[11]

Dynamic hedging can be thought of as creating option-like payoffs. For example, portfolio insurance gives a payoff that is the same as adding to the portfolio a put option with an exercise price equal to the desired floor. If the portfolio drops below the floor value, the put option will give a payoff equal to the difference between the final portfolio value and the floor. This will compensate for the loss on the underlying portfolio.

The option is not bought in the market; it is created through the dynamic trading strategy.[12] The slippage of the dynamic strategy that gives rise to the hedging costs can be thought of as the cost of the put option.[13]

The Dynamic Adjustment Procedure

The key point in dynamic hedging is that the procedure for portfolio allocation fulfills two conditions. First, at the end of the period the investor is fully invested if the portfolio is above the floor and is in cash if the portfolio is below the floor. Second, theoretically, the total cost of the slippage from the gradual moves in and out of the portfolio are known in advance, regardless of the path prices take. In other words, the investor can determine at the outset the payoff profile he will get at the end and can know at the outset the cost of getting that profile.

Dynamic hedging is, thus, an ideal proactive asset management

---

[11] The cost of the strategy does not depend on the direction the market takes. It does depend, however, on the volatility of the market—the amount the market varies over the hedging period. A higher volatility leads to greater frequency of buying and selling out of the portfolio and, therefore, to greater slippage in tracking the market performance. The dependence on volatility is clear intuitively, since any insurance protection should be costlier the greater the risk being insured.

[12] The option is created rather than bought in the market because of the limitations in the listed and over-the-counter option markets. Index options do not have a long enough maturity to be useful for the time horizon of asset allocation, usually a horizon of one to three years. And while bond options can be purchased in large size over the counter, they cannot be easily matched to bond portfolios, nor can they be purchased for longer time periods.

[13] A more complete discussion of the way in which a dynamic hedging strategy replicates an option-like payoff is presented in Bookstaber (1985).

FIGURE 7 Dynamic Hedge Position Adjustment Procedure

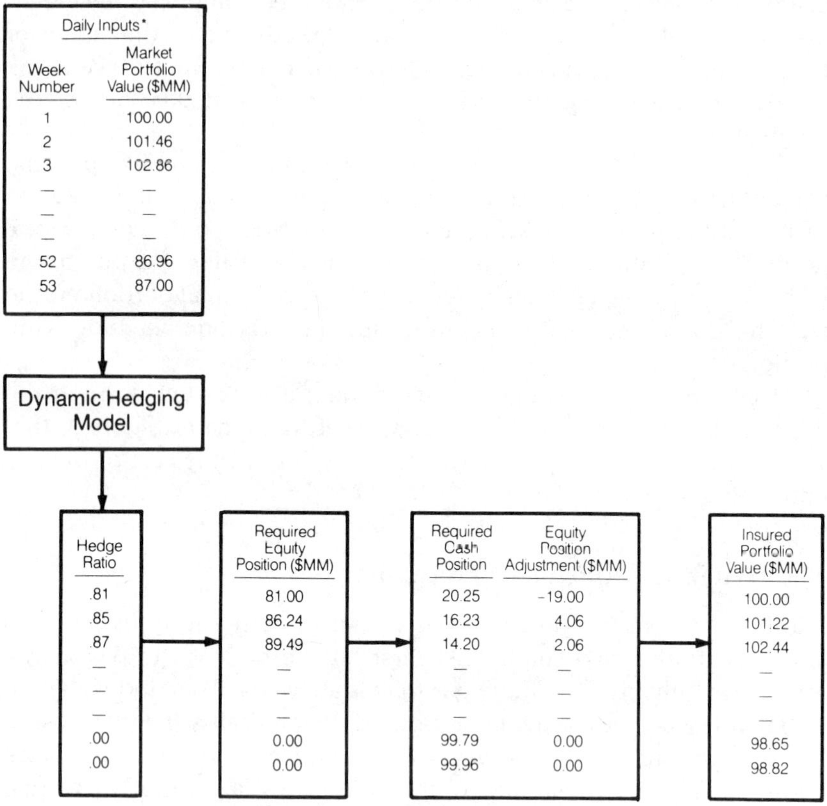

Daily Inputs*	
Week Number	Market Portfolio Value ($MM)
1	100.00
2	101.46
3	102.86
—	—
—	—
—	—
52	86.96
53	87.00

Dynamic Hedging Model

Hedge Ratio	Required Equity Position ($MM)	Required Cash Position	Equity Position Adjustment ($MM)	Insured Portfolio Value ($MM)
.81	81.00	20.25	−19.00	100.00
.85	86.24	16.23	4.06	101.22
.87	89.49	14.20	2.06	102.44
—	—	—	—	—
—	—	—	—	—
—	—	—	—	—
.00	0.00	99.79	0.00	98.65
.00	0.00	99.96	0.00	98.82

*Floor = $100MM; Time Period = 1 Year; Estimated Option Premium = $1.25MM.

tool. It allows the manager to define his investment objective and then sets the asset allocation for achieving it. The manager can use a *dynamic* asset allocation strategy to meet a specified objective, rather than letting a static asset allocation rule push his investments to an ill-defined outcome. In contrast, the portfolio manager who starts by targeting the bond/equity mix finds the allocation becomes the objective and the resulting investment profile remains uncertain.

Figure 7 illustrates the trading process in dynamic hedging. First, a floor return and time to expiration for the strategy are set. These decision parameters represent the investment objectives of the fund. The current portfolio value, time remaining to expiration, interest-rate levels, and volatility of the market are then put into the model.[14] The model determines the correct asset allocation based on these inputs and the decision parameters.

The key to the asset allocation is the model-determined hedge ratio.[15] The hedge ratio, also known as the portfolio delta, is the percent of the portfolio that should be held at a given point in time to create the desired payoff. For example, a hedge ratio of .7 means that 70 percent of the fund should be invested in the underlying portfolio and the remaining 30 percent should be held in the risk-free asset. The hedge ratio, thus, determines the dollar allocation of the fund. The hedge ratio, and hence the portfolio allocation, changes over time and also changes as the underlying portfolio value changes. The hedge ratio needs to be recomputed on an ongoing basis and the appropriate portfolio position calculated. This is compared to the current allocation, and any required adjustment is made. It is because of the continued monitoring and adjustments that this strategy is called a dynamic hedging strategy.[16]

The operation of this procedure over the full year is illustrated in Table 2. This table presents weekly computations of the portfolio value, the hedge ratio, and the resulting allocation. The objective presented in this table is identical to that of Figure 7: a zero percent floor return and a floor of $100 on a portfolio that is currently worth $100. The hedge period is one year.

The table first lists the two key inputs, the time remaining to

---

[14] The volatility measures the degree of price variability in the market. For example, a volatility of 20 percent means that there is approximately a 60 percent chance (one standard deviation) that prices will differ up to 20 percent from their current value in a year. Volatility measures the degree of price variation. It does not indicate the direction of the change.

[15] The computation of the hedge ratio or delta is discussed for the most common option models in Bookstaber (1981), Bookstaber and Putcha (1985), and in Cox and Rubinstein (1985). In practice, the more sophisticated models take into account the uncertainty of interest rates and volatility and also address the limitations of the distributional assumptions of the more common option models.

[16] This dynamic hedging strategy, while new to portfolio managers and pension plan sponsors, is well known to arbitrage option traders. The objective of arbitrage trading in the option market is to find options that are mispriced in the marketplace, i.e., options whose market price differs from the cost of creating the option through a dynamic trading strategy. If an overpriced option is found in the market, that option is written, and a dynamic strategy is employed to replicate it. Since the same option has then been bought and sold— bought through the dynamic replicating strategy and sold in the market—the position has no risk. The synthetic option will give a payoff that will counter the payoff due on the option that has been written. However, since the option was written for a higher price than the cost of replicating it, the strategy locks in an arbitrage gain. The fact that this strategy is done successfully by many traders testifies to its validity.

TABLE 2   Dynamic Hedge Week-by-Week Position Summary

Week Number	Market Portfolio Value	Hedge Ratio	Required Equity Position	Required Cash Position	Current Equity Position	Equity Position Adjustment	Insured Portfolio Value
1	100.00	0.81	81.00	20.25	100.00	-19.00	100.00
2	101.46	0.85	86.24	16.23	82.18	4.06	101.22
3	102.86	0.87	89.49	14.20	87.43	2.06	102.44
4	99.92	0.81	80.94	20.20	86.93	-6.00	99.89
5	98.57	0.76	74.91	25.17	79.84	-4.93	98.84
6	98.09	0.75	73.57	26.19	74.55	-0.98	98.52
7	95.70	0.66	63.16	34.86	71.78	8.61	96.78
8	98.18	0.74	72.65	27.05	64.80	7.85	98.47
9	97.23	0.70	68.06	30.98	71.95	-3.89	97.81
10	97.01	0.69	66.94	32.00	67.91	-0.97	97.71
11	95.04	0.61	57.97	39.66	65.58	-7.60	96.40
12	92.64	0.50	46.32	49.92	56.51	-10.19	95.01
13	92.46	0.48	44.38	51.85	46.23	-1.85	95.01
14	90.86	0.40	36.34	59.21	43.61	7.27	94.33
15	89.90	0.35	31.47	63.81	35.96	4.50	94.05
16	89.72	0.33	29.61	65.71	31.40	1.79	94.10
17	90.78	0.37	33.59	62.19	29.96	3.63	94.56
18	91.63	0.40	36.65	59.54	33.90	2.75	94.98
19	91.82	0.40	36.73	59.64	36.73	0.00	95.16
20	92.64	0.43	39.84	56.96	37.06	2.78	95.59
21	91.42	0.36	32.91	63.48	39.31	-6.40	95.17
22	92.23	0.39	35.97	60.80	33.20	2.77	95.57
23	90.81	0.31	28.15	68.17	35.42	-7.26	95.12
24	90.50	0.28	25.34	71.01	28.06	-2.71	95.14
25	91.52	0.32	29.29	67.47	25.63	3.66	95.55
26	89.57	0.22	19.71	76.54	28.66	-8.96	95.05
27	90.04	0.23	20.71	75.77	19.81	0.90	95.28
28	88.70	0.16	14.19	82.11	20.40	-6.21	95.11
29	87.83	0.12	10.54	85.77	14.05	-3.51	95.11
30	85.81	0.06	5.15	91.06	10.30	-5.15	95.02
31	85.55	0.05	4.28	92.07	5.13	0.86	95.16
32	85.03	0.04	3.40	93.08	4.25	-0.85	95.30
33	84.77	0.03	2.54	94.09	3.39	-0.85	95.45
34	84.54	0.02	1.69	95.10	2.54	-0.85	95.61
35	85.52	0.03	2.57	94.40	1.71	0.86	95.79
36	87.12	0.04	3.48	93.69	2.61	0.87	96.00
37	86.37	0.02	1.73	95.57	3.45	-1.73	96.13
38	87.41	0.03	2.62	94.87	1.75	0.87	96.32
39	87.26	0.02	1.75	95.90	2.62	-0.87	96.48
40	86.86	0.01	0.87	96.93	1.74	-0.87	96.63
41	86.62	0.01	0.87	97.10	0.87	0.00	96.80
42	83.85	0.00	0.00	98.10	0.84	-0.84	96.94
43	84.41	0.00	0.00	98.27	0.00	0.00	97.11
44	82.33	0.00	0.00	98.44	0.00	0.00	97.28
45	81.64	0.00	0.00	98.61	0.00	0.00	97.45
46	81.98	0.00	0.00	98.77	0.00	0.00	97.62
47	83.08	0.00	0.00	98.94	0.00	0.00	97.79
48	83.00	0.00	0.00	99.11	0.00	0.00	97.96
49	84.63	0.00	0.00	99.28	0.00	0.00	98.13
50	82.48	0.00	0.00	99.45	0.00	0.00	98.30
51	84.45	0.00	0.00	99.62	0.00	0.00	98.48
52	86.96	0.00	0.00	99.79	0.00	0.00	98.65
53	87.00	0.00	0.00	99.96	0.00	0.00	98.82

expiration and the current price of the portfolio. It then gives the hedge ratio of the portfolio. In the first period, the hedge ratio is set at .81. On a $100 million fund, initially $81 million is held long in the risky portfolio, the remainder in cash. The following period the portfolio value rises to $101.46 million, and the proportion of assets held in the portfolio rises, as well, to .85.

This rise in the hedge ratio means a change in the required position. As column 4 shows, the required position increases from $81 million to $86.24 million. While the initial position of $81 million has increased somewhat with the market rise, an additional adjustment of $4.06 is necessary to achieve the desired portfolio exposure. The trade necessary to make this adjustment is shown in column 7. The final column of the table shows the week-by-week value of the hedged position. This position includes both the impact of changes in the market and the return on the position placed in cash. The net result of the strategy is a payoff of $98.82 million. Taking the $1.25 initial cost of the option into account, the payoff is very close to its objective.

Futures: A Tool for Noninvasive Allocation

Adjustments in portfolio exposure can be made directly in the cash market, but adjustments are often done by using futures contracts. Both bond and stock index futures are attractive for their liquidity and low transactions cost.[17] Futures also make the dynamic strategy noninvasive. The cash portfolio does not need to be traded to facilitate the hedging strategy. For the plan sponsor, this means no limitations need to be made on the managers' stock or bond selections.[18] The managers

---

[17] While listed options are not liquid until a few months before their expiration, they are useful for unwinding the dynamic hedge as the time to expiration approaches. It is in the last few months of a dynamic hedge—the time that listed options become a viable alternative to the dynamic strategy—that the tracking error is the greatest. Options can also be used on a delta-weighted basis for hedging the portfolio, even when the hedge has a long time to expiration. A delta-gamma neutral hedge, employed with listed options, can reduce the need for hedging adjustments and overcome, or even take advantage of, the cash-futures basis risk. Delta-gamma neutral hedges are discussed in Bookstaber and Langsam (1987). Futures do have the disadvantage of basis risk. This basis risk can be especially important for the bond market, where credit spreads and duration adjustments are required for the cash-futures translation.

[18] The managers obviously are limited in terms of their basic asset composition, however. In particular, a manager must remain fully invested since the cash/asset mix is determined by the dynamic strategy. Also, if futures are used as a proxy for the cash portfolio adjustments, any deviations the manager makes in his portfolio mix from the mix represented by the futures will increase the tracking error of the futures hedge. For example, if a manager holds a poorly diversified portfolio that does not closely track the S&P 500, the S&P 500 futures may not provide an ideal hedging instrument for the total portfolio risk.

can continue to hold the plan funds, while the sponsor executes the appropriate asset allocation shifts through futures transactions.[19] For portfolio insurance in the fixed-income market, interest-rate swaps are an alternative hedging instrument. The noninvasivness of the strategy also means less liquid instruments, such as GICs or private placements, can be used in the construction of the underlying portfolio.

The potential for noninvasive asset allocation permits the separation of the risk and active management components of the investment decision. The risk objectives of the fund can be established and protected while the active manager is still free to maximize return within those risk constraints.

A short position in the futures contract can be used to reduce the portfolio exposure. Selling short futures against the portfolio position is equivalent to selling off the portfolio and putting the funds into cash. As the portfolio value falls, requiring a lower position in the market, the short futures position is increased. The proceeds that accrue to the short futures position compensate for losses in the cash portfolio. The aggregate value of the cash-futures position allows the floor to be retained. As the portfolio rises, the short position is reduced. The loss from the short position as the market goes up gives rise to the option cost. As we have already mentioned, the central feature of the dynamic hedge is that this cost can be closely estimated at the outset.

V. ACHIEVING THE BEST HEDGING PERFORMANCE

How well the actual performance of the dynamic hedging strategy matches the target payoff profile depends on the quality of the model being used and the hedging expertise of those using the model. The performance of the strategy obviously depends on how well that model works and on how accurately the inputs into that model can be estimated. The key issues that govern the success of the dynamic hedge follow.

Estimation of Volatility

Volatility measures the amount of price instability of the market. Just as insurance is more expensive the riskier the asset being insured, so the price of portfolio insurance is more expensive the greater the volatility of the underlying portfolio. The hedging strategy—the speed with which the hedge ratio changes as the portfolio changes in value—depends on

---

[19] While a large portion of the funds can remain in the hands of outside managers, enough funds must be available to the plan sponsor to take care of variation margin. The range of variation margin, which depends on the payment method used, can be predicted before the strategy is entered.

a volatility estimate as an input. If the future volatility of the portfolio is misestimated by the model, the price of the protection will be different than what was initially expected.

Interest-Rate Levels

Interest-rate levels are important in determining the price of insurance and in managing the dynamic hedging strategy for creating that insurance.[20] Few options models consider the impact of uncertain interest rates, and none of the published models consider the full effect of yield curve shifts on the hedging dynamics. For longer term hedges—hedging programs of three or more years—the impact of an incorrect treatment of yield curve effects can be more severe than the impact from volatility misestimation.[21]

When futures are used to facilitate the hedge, the implied interest rate will be the cost of carry for the futures. This short-term rate may differ from the interest rate for the time period the hedge is to be held. Shifts in the yield curve can lead to a mismatch between the holding period interest rate and the short-term carrying rate, affecting the tracking of the floor.

------

[20] It is well known that the price of an option is a function of the interest-rate level. If interest rates move unexpectedly, the price of the option will also unexpectedly change. Since the hedge ratio is a function of the interest-rate level, a model which takes interest rates as given, or does not place the proper stochastic process on interest rates, will give an undependable hedge.

For portfolio insurance, interest rates also have an impact in determining the ability to achieve any given floor. To see why this is so, let us look at the strategy for providing portfolio insurance in a different—but equivalent—way. Rather than creating the portfolio insurance by combining the underlying portfolio with a put option that has an exercise price equal to the floor, suppose we construct the insurance by selling off the portfolio, putting enough of the proceeds into the riskless asset to assure we will attain the floor by the end of the insurance period, and then buying a call option with an exercise price equal to the floor.

The resulting payoff will be the same as the portfolio-put combination. If the portfolio falls below the floor at the end of the time period, the call will expire worthless, but the holdings of the riskless asset will appreciate to the floor value. If the portfolio is worth more than the floor at the end, the riskless asset will again provide a return equal to the floor value, and the call option will pay off the difference between the floor and the terminal portfolio value.

The higher the interest rate, the less the money that needs to be put aside to get up to the floor. Furthermore, the higher the interest rate, the higher the floor that can be attained. If interest rates are at 15 percent, it is possible to have a 10 percent floor and still have money left to buy part of a call option and, therefore, part of the portfolio's upside potential. If interest rates are at 8 percent, it is impossible to have a 10 percent floor.

[21] A discussion of the impact of yield curve effects on option methodology is presented in Bookstaber, Jacob, and Langsam (1986).

The problems of uncertain interest rates are particularly acute for portfolio insurance and dynamic hedging of fixed-income portfolios. Higher interest rates lead to higher insurance costs and to changes in the correct hedge ratio. A misestimation of these parameters will lead to an incorrect hedge ratio and tracking error for the model. The final payoff may deviate from what was expected. The actual structure of the model is also important for performance. Issues such as the distribution of possible future prices and the yield curve structure must be addressed in developing the model.[22]

Cash-Futures Basis Risk

While low transactions costs make futures an attractive hedging medium, the basis risk between the cash and the futures—unexpected price movements between the cash asset and the futures—introduces tracking errors. The futures market does not follow its cash market counterpart precisely. Furthermore, few portfolios exactly match the cash security or index on which the futures are based. While the movements in the cash-futures basis can be an added source of revenue if the futures execution is done skillfully, it can also lead to increased tracking errors. The alternative of transacting in the cash market does not eliminate the basis risk, however. Since transacting in a portfolio-weighted amount of every issue is generally impractical, the hedger must have technology for creating a good proxy for the portfolio and have the capacity for executing program trades. Similarly, an understanding of the duration and convexity characteristics is necessary to correctly adjust a bond portfolio in the cash market.[23]

The Need for Hedging Expertise

Research, hedging expertise, and execution are all a part of the successful implementation of dynamic hedging programs. The roles played by each of these functions and the ways in which they interrelate are illustrated in Figure 8. Coordination between these three roles makes it possible to minimize tracking errors.[24]

---

[22] The issues in correctly applying dynamic hedging strategies in the bond market are subtle and have not received the attention they deserve. For an indication of the adaptation in the option technology that is necessary to create portfolio insurance for bond portfolios, particularly in terms of the distributional and yield curve issues, see Jacob, Lord, and Tilley (1986) and Bookstaber and McDonald (1985).

[23] For the bond market, an additional consideration is the impact call provisions, both in callable bonds and in mortgage securities, have on the duration and convexity of the portfolio.

[24] The degree of tracking error is measured by the percentage difference

FIGURE 8 Implementing the Dynamic Hedge

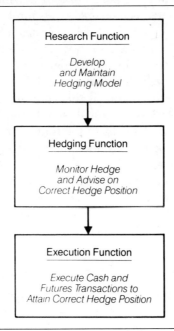

Those responsible for the hedge must understand the technology that is generating the hedging signals. Otherwise, they will not be able to adjust for unexpected changes in the market environment. For example, suppose the market starts to increase markedly in volatility and this volatility is accompanied by a shift in the yield curve. The hedger must understand the model well enough to know what these changes in the market imply for the way in which the model should be adjusted. The hedge should not be based on the output of a "black box." Integration between hedging and research is the primary element those doing the hedging can bring to the strategy.

Furthermore, a link must be maintained between those making the hedging decision and those executing the hedge. Timing of the hedge execution is an opportunity for value added in the strategy. Rather than blindly executing the hedge, the hedger and trader can evaluate the

---

between the expected end-of-period payoff and the realized payoff. For example, if a floor of $100 million is established and the underlying portfolio at the end of the insurance period is below the floor, the expected payoff will be $100 million. If the insured portfolio value that is realized at the end of the period is $101, the tracking error is 1 percent.

trade-offs between the need for hedge maintenance and the market
environment. For example, there is often a window for the time in
which a hedge adjustment can be made. It is rarely the case that a hedge
must be done the instant the model indicates a change in the hedge
ratio. If those doing the hedge and those executing the trading position
both understand this window and coordinate the execution of the
hedge, they can evaluate the market conditions and time the hedge
accordingly. On the other hand, if this coordination is lacking—if the
hedger, following a black box's signal, simply calls for the trade when a
light flashes, and the trader calls in the trade immediately without any
reflection on the market conditions—a vital link is missing in the
dynamic hedging strategy.

These issues of model implementation, while important, are left to
be discussed elsewhere. The decision facing the plan sponsor or
portfolio manager—how best to apply the model—lies not in a model's
mathematics but in its application.

VI. CONCLUSION

This chapter has illustrated the techniques of dynamic hedging used to
create portfolio insurance. We have focused on the ways dynamic
hedging can be used to address the goal of preserving capital while
maintaining positive market exposure. Interest in dynamic hedging and
portfolio insurance has grown enormously over the past two years.
While the techniques for executing a dynamic hedge have been applied
by traders as a means of hedging option exposure for over a decade,
they have only recently been recognized and implemented within the
broader professional investment community.

Dynamic hedging adds great flexibility to the strategic functions of
portfolio management and plan design, allowing issues of cash flow,
actuarial concerns, and patterns of investment return to be addressed
more precisely. It also allows the tactical functions of risk control and
return enhancement to be considered separately and controlled independently. It is a particularly useful tool in today's market, where
dynamic hedging offers the opportunity to lock in capital gains without
sacrificing the opportunity for market returns.

REFERENCES

1. BLACK, F. and M. SCHOLES. "The Pricing of Options and Corporate Liabilities." *Journal of Political Economy* 81 (May 1973), pp. 637–54.
2. BOOKSTABER, R. *Option Pricing and Strategies in Investing*. Reading, Mass.: Addison-Wesley Publishing, 1981.

3. ———. "The Use of Options in Performance Structuring: Molding Returns to Meet Investment Objectives." *Journal of Portfolio Management* 11 (Summer 1985), pp. 36–50.

4. ———. "The Valuation and Exposure Management of Bonds with Imbedded Options." In, *The Handbook of Fixed Income Securities*, 2nd ed., ed. F. FABOZZI and I. POLLACK. Homewood, Ill.: Dow Jones-Irwin, 1986, pp. 856–890.

5. ———, and R. CLARKE. "Options Can Alter Portfolio Return Distributions." *Journal of Portfolio Management* 7 (Spring 1981), pp. 63–70.

6. ———, and R. CLARKE. "An Algorithm to Calculate the Return Distribution of Portfolios with Option Positions." *Management Science* 7 (April 1983a), pp. 419–29.

7. ———, and R. CLARKE. *Option Strategies for Institutional Investment Management.* Reading, Mass.: Addison-Wesley Publishing, 1983b.

8. ———, and R. CLARKE. "Option Portfolio Strategies: Measurement and Evaluation." *Journal of Business* 57 (October 1984), pp. 469–92.

9. ———, and R. CLARKE. "Problems in Evaluating the Performance of Portfolios with Options." *Financial Analysts Journal*, January/February 1985, pp. 48–62.

10. ———, D. JACOB, and J. LANGSAM. "Arbitrage-Free Pricing of Options on Interest-Sensitive Instruments." In *Advances in Futures and Options Research*, ed. F. FABOZZI. Greenwich, Conn.: JAI Press, 1986, pp. 1–23.

11. ———, and J. Langsam. *Portfolio Insurance Trading Rules.* New York: Morgan Stanley Fixed Income Research, 1987.

12. ———, and J. McDONALD. "A Generalized Options Valuation Model for the Pricing of Bond Options." *Review of Research in Futures Markets* 4 (1985), pp. 60–73.

13. ———, and R. PUTCHA. *A Framework for Option Analysis.* New York: Morgan Stanley Fixed Income Research, 1985.

14. COX, J., and J. RUBINSTEIN. *Option Markets.* Englewood Cliffs, N.J.: Prentice-Hall, 1985.

15. JACOB, D., G. LORD, and J. TILLEY. *Pricing a Stream of Interest-Sensitive Cash Flows.* New York: Morgan Stanley Fixed Income Research, 1986.

16. LELAND, H. "Who Should Buy Portfolio Insurance?" *Journal of Finance* 35 (May, 1979), pp. 581–94.

17. MERTON, R. "Theory of Rational Option Pricing." *Bell Journal of Economics and Management Science* 4 (1973), pp. 141–83.

18. ———. "On Market Timing and Investment Performance. I. An Equilibrium Theory of Value for Market Forecasts." *Journal of Business* 54 (July 1981), pp. 363–406.

19. PLATT, R. *Controlling Interest Rate Risk.* New York: John Wiley & Sons, 1986.

20. ———, and G. LATAINER. *Replicating Option Strategies for Portfolio Risk Control.* New York: Morgan Stanley Fixed Income Research, 1983a.

21. ———, and G. LATAINER. *Contingent Insurance Strategies in an Actively Managed Bond Portfolio.* New York: Morgan Stanley Fixed Income Research, 1983b.

22. RUBINSTEIN, M., and H. LELAND. "Replicating Options with Positions in Stock and Cash." *Financial Analysts Journal* 37 (July 1981), pp. 63–72.

23. RUBINSTEIN, M. "Alternative Paths to Portfolio Insurance." *Financial Analysts Journal* 41 (July 1985), pp. 42–52.

24. TILLEY, J., and G. LATAINER. *A Synthetic Option Framework for Asset Allocation.* New York: Morgan Stanley Fixed Income Research, 1985.

25. TOEVS, A. *Uses of Duration Analysis for the Control of Interest Rate Risk.* New York: Morgan Stanley Fixed Income Research, 1984.

PART 7

Quantitative Aids

47

Compound Interest Calculations and Tables

Sumner N. Levine, Ph.D.
State University of New York at Stony Brook

This section deals primarily with compound interest and return on investments calculations. Interest is the money paid for the use of money; to lenders it is a source of income and to borrowers it is the cost of a loan. The amount of money lent and upon which the interest is calculated is called the *principal*. The time period over which a given rate of interest is calculated is called the *unit of time* and may vary from days to a year.

More generally, interest received is merely a special case of return on investment. Thus, returns may also be realized from equity, hybrid investments (convertible bonds), and investments in options to purchase equity (warrants, rights, calls) or sell equity (puts). If the investment is productive, the accumulation of interest payments (return on investment) endows capital with a *time value* so that interest is sometimes referred to as the time value of invested money.

Interest rate is the ratio of the interest payable at the end of the time period to the money owned or invested at the beginning of the time period. Thus, if $5 of interest is payable annually on a debt of $100, the interest rate is 5/100 = 0.05 per annum. An annual rate is understood unless some other time period is definitely stated.

In somewhat more general terms, the rate of return (i) is the total value realized from an asset at the end of a period of time (V_1) less the initial (V_0) value divided by the initial value:

$$i = (V_1 - V_0)/V_0$$

1547

EXAMPLE. A stock with an initial cost of $10 appreciates during the year to $11 and pays a $1 dividend. The total *annual* rate of return is then:

$$i = (\$12 - \$10)/10 = 20\%$$

Simple interest. If interest is calculated only on the original principal or investment for the period during which the money is invested or borrowed, the interest is called *simple interest*. Let P be the original principal; i, the annual interest rate (expressed as a fraction); and n, the number of years, then I (the interest) is given by the formula: $I = Pni$.

EXAMPLE 1. Find the amount of simple interest due at nine months if the annual interest rate is 6 percent.

$$I = \$28.00 \times 9/12 \times 0.06 = \$1.26$$

EXAMPLE 2. A debt of $6,000 is to be repaid in semiannual installments of $400 with a simple annual interest of 6 percent on the outstanding principal. Find the total interest paid to discharge the debt.

Interest due with 1st payment $= 6,000 \times \frac{1}{2} \times 0.06 - 180$
Interest due with 2nd payment $= 5,600 \times \frac{1}{2} \times 0.06 = 168$
Interest due with 3rd payment $= 5,200 \times \frac{1}{2} \times 0.06 = 156$
Interest due with 15th payment $= 400 \times \frac{1}{2} \times 0.06 = 12$

The sums of all interest payments are given by:

$$S = 180 + 168 + 156 + \ldots + 12 = \$1,440$$

Compound interest. Interest is compounded when the interest each year is computed on the original principal plus the accumulated interest that has not been paid out. In other words, interest is paid on the retained interest plus principal. Let P be the original principal; n, the number of interest periods; i, the interest rate per interest period; and F, the sum of money at the end of the n compound interest paying periods, then:

End of 1st period:

$$F_1 = P + P_i = P(1 + i)$$

End of 2nd period:

$$F_2 = P(1 + i) + iP(1 + i)$$

or

$$F_2 = P(1 + i)^2$$

End of 3rd period:

$$F_3 = P(1 + i)^2 + iP(1 + i)^2$$

or

$$F_3 = P(1 + i)^3$$

In general, at the end of n periods:

$$F = P(1 + i)^n \qquad (1)$$

This formula gives the value of the sum of money due (F) at the end of n periods if an amount (P) is invested now at a compounded rate i. It is convenient to use the notation ($F/P,i,n$), the *future worth factor*, for the quantity $(1 + i)^n$ tabulated in the first column of the compound interest tables given at the end of this chapter, so that the above expression in the new notation is:

$$F = P(F/P,i,n) \qquad (2)$$

The above formula can be transformed into the form:

$$P = F/(1 + i)^n$$

The following notation will be used for the *present worth factor*:

$$1/(1 + i)^n = (P/F,i,n)$$

hence:

$$P = F(P/F,i,n)$$

The quantity ($P/F,i,n$) is also given in the tables.

The last formula permits us to calculate the amount which must be invested now (P) at a compounded rate (i) if the sum of money (F) is desired at the end of n periods. The amount P is often referred to as the *present value* of a future amount (F). Clearly, in order to calculate the present value P corresponding to F we must know the time period (n) involved and the compound interest rate (i).

EXAMPLE. If $1,000 is invested at 6 percent compounded, how much will be accumulated at the end of five years?

SOLUTION.

$$F = P(F/P,i,n)$$

$$P = \$1,000, \ i = 0.06, \ n = 5, \ F = ?$$

It is often useful, particularly with complex situations, to represent the timing of the cash flows by means of a diagram in which disbursements (cash outlays) are represented by downward directed arrows and cash receipts by upward directed arrows. It will be assumed that the cash flows occur at the *end* of a given period, i.e., even though a cash flow may actually be occurring during a period of time, it is assumed for purposes of calculation that the cash flow occurs at the end of the period. For the above problem the cash flows are represented in Figure 1.

FIGURE 1

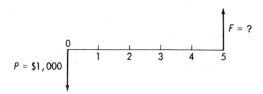

Turning to Table 11, labeled 6 percent, we find under the column headed $(P/F,i,n)$ corresponding to $n = 5$, that:

$$(F/P,\ 6\%,\ 5) = 1.3382$$

hence:

$$F = \$1,000\ (1.3382) = \$1,338.20$$

EXAMPLE. An investment opportunity is available which provides a compounded annual rate of return of 12 percent. How much must be invested now in order to realize \$100,000 at the end of 10 years?

SOLUTION.

$$P = F(P/F,i,n)$$
$$F = \$100,000,\ i = 12\%,\ n = 10,\ P = ?$$

The cash flows are shown diagrammatically below:

FIGURE 2

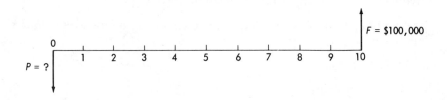

From Table 16, labeled 12 percent, we find for $n = 10$:

$$(P/F,12\%,10) = 0.3220$$

hence:

$$P = \$100,000\ (0.3220) = \$32,200$$

Thus, under the condition stated ($i = 12\%$, $n = 10$), the present value of \$100,000 is \$32,200.

EXAMPLE. A portfolio is expected to appreciate at an annual rate of return of 10 percent. What lump sum must be invested now in order to permit a withdrawal of $10,000 at 5 years hence and a second withdrawal of $10,000 at 10 years from the present?

SOLUTION. The cash flow diagram is:

FIGURE 3

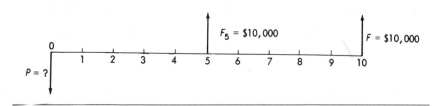

$$P = F_5(P/F,10\%,5) + F_{10} (P/F,10\%,10)$$
$$P = \$10,000 (0.6209) + \$10,000 (0.3855)$$
$$P = \$6,209 + \$3,855$$
$$P = \$10,064$$

Otherwise stated, the cash flows of $10,000 at 5 years and at 10 years from the time of the initial investment (at the stated compounded rate of return) has a present value of $10,064.

Calculation of the rate of return. The first formula given above can be used to calculate the compounded rate of return given the initial investment P and the return on the investment F realized after n years:

$$i = (F/P)^{1/n} - 1$$

The solution can be carried out using a hand calculator which permits the calculation of higher roots.

EXAMPLE. A security costing $80 five years ago was sold for $100. What was the compounded annual rate of return realized, neglecting taxes and commissions?

SOLUTION.

$$n = 5, P = 80, F = 100, i = ?$$
$$i = (100/80)^{1/5} - 1 = (1.25)^{1/5} - 1$$
$$\log(1.25)^{1/5} = 0.09691/5 = 0.019382$$

so that

$$(1.25)^{1/5} = 1.0456$$
$$i = 1.0456 - 1 = 4.56\%$$

A second method of solving the problem makes use of the compound interest tables and the formula:

$$F = P(F/P,i,n)$$

where

$$n = 5, P = \$80, F = \$100, i = ?$$

so that $\$100/\$80 = 1.25 = (F/P,i,5)$.

Using the tables, we must seek a value of i which satisfies the expression given above. We note that:

$$(F/P,4\%,5) = 1.217 \text{ (from Table 9)}$$
$$(F/P,i,5) = 1.250 \text{ (from problem)}$$
$$(F/P,5\%,5) = 1.276 \text{ (from Table 10)}$$

The first tabulated value is somewhat too small, and the second tabulated value is somewhat too large so that we must interpolate:

$$i = 4\% + 1\%(1.250 - 1.217)/(1.276 - 1.217) = 4.56\%$$

Uniform Series of Payments

Situations involving uniform (equal) series of receipts or payments sometimes arise in the analysis of investments. As an illustration, an investor may want to know the uniform amount that must be invested annually into a fund in order to realize a specified amount at some future time, i.e., say at retirement.

The cash-flow diagram for a uniform series of payments of amount A each period into a fund providing a compounded rate of return i per period is shown below for the case of four periods.

FIGURE 4

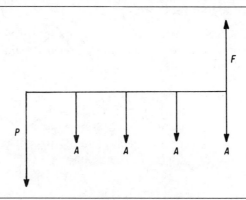

In the above diagram P is the present worth and F is the future worth of the uniform series.

Several situations may arise and the appropriate expressions for handling them are given below:

Given A to find F:

$$F = A \frac{(1 + i)^n - 1}{i}$$

Given F to find A:

$$A = \frac{Fi}{(1 + i)^n - 1} = F(A/F,i,n)$$

Given P to find A:

$$A = P \frac{i(1 + i)^n}{(1 + i)^n - 1} = P(A/P,i,n)$$

Given A to find P:

$$P = A \frac{(1 + i)^n - 1}{i(1 + i)^n} = A(P/A,i,n)$$

The various quantities, such as $(F/A,i,n)$ and $(A/P,i,n)$ appearing on the right side of the above expressions are tabulated in the compound interest tables at the end of the section.

EXAMPLE. A series of uniform annual payments of \$2,000 each are made to purchase shares of a portfolio expected to provide a 10 percent compounded annual rate of return. What is the value of the investment at the end of five years?

SOLUTION. The cash flow diagram is:

FIGURE 5

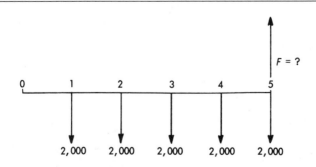

Notice that all payments are considered as having been made at the end of the year, starting with the first year and continuing to the fifth year. The solution is given by:

$$F = A(F/A,i,n)$$
$$A = \$2,000, \; i = 10\%, \; n = 5, \; F = ?$$

From the compound interest tables we have:

$$(F/A, \; 10\%, \; 5) = 6.105$$
$$F = \$2,000 \; (6.105) = \$12,210$$

EXAMPLE. What is the present worth of an annual annuity of $1,000 which will start at the end of the year and continue for six years? Assume that the money is worth 8 percent compounded per annum.

SOLUTION. The cash flow diagram is:

FIGURE 6

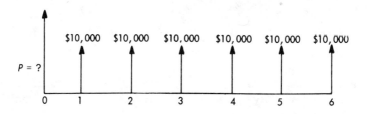

$$P = A(P/A,i,n)$$
$$A = \$1,000, \; n = 6, \; i = 8\%, \; P = ?$$
$$P = \$1,000(P/A,8\%,6)$$
$$P = 1,000 \; (4.623)$$
$$P = \$4,623$$

The significance of this calculation is that the investor should not pay more than $4,623 for the above annuity plan if he has alternative investments available yielding a compound annual rate of 8 percent.

Present value of a perpetual annuity. The present value of an equal payment series (A) which continues without end and which commences at the end of the present period is:

$$P = \frac{A}{i}$$

where i is the annual compounded rate of return at which the income can be invested.

Deferred payments. A series of payments which will become due after a number of periods have passed are called deferred payments. The calculation of the present value of such a series of payments is carried out in two steps. First, calculate the discounted amount of the uniform series at a convenient point in time, i.e., the year just prior to that at which payments are to begin. This amount will be designated as P_F. Second, the present value of P_F is determined using the expression:

$$P = P_F(P/F,i,N - 1)$$

where N is the number of periods which must elapse before the first payment is due.

EXAMPLE. Mr. X is planning for his son's college expenses estimated at $5,000 a year for four years. His son will enter college in five years. How much should Mr. X now invest in a fund providing a 10 percent compounded rate of return (neglecting taxes) in order to pay for his son's college expenses? Principal and appreciation are to be exhausted on completion of college.

SOLUTION. The cash flow diagram is:

FIGURE 7

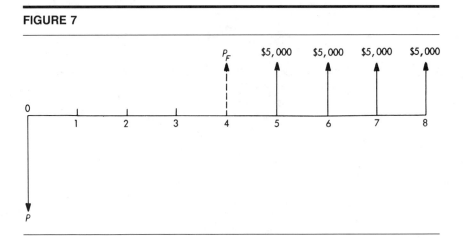

We first determine P_F at year 4 for the four equal payments which will start at year 5:

$$P_F = A(P/A,i,n)$$
$$A = \$5,000, \ i = 10\%, \ n = 4, \ P_F = ?$$
$$P_F = \$5,000 \ (P/A,10\%,4)$$
$$P_F = \$5,000 \ (3.170)$$
$$P_F = \$15,850$$

This amount corresponds to a present investment into the fund given by:

$$N = 5$$
$$P = P_F(P/F,i,N-1)$$
$$P_F = \$15,850, \ (N-1) = 4, \ i = 10\%, \ P = ?$$
$$P = \$15,850 \ (0.6830)$$
$$P = \$10,778$$

Thus, \$10,778 must be invested into the fund in order to meet the required disbursements.

Uniformly increasing gradient. Financial calculations frequently involve cash flows that increase each year by varying amounts. For example, because of inflation a retiree will require increasing annual payouts from his investments. We shall assume that the increases in the cash flow each period can be approximated by multiples of a fixed amount, G. Consequently, the cash flows that we shall consider here may be represented as shown in the following diagram:

FIGURE 8

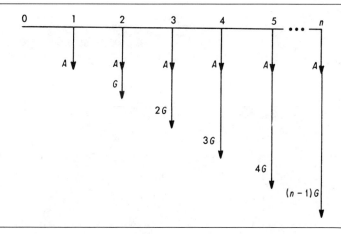

We see that the cash flows consist of two components: (*a*) a uniform component of amount *A* starting with the end of the first year and (*b*) an increasing component of amount kG ($k = 1,2,3, \ldots$) starting at the end of the second year. We shall refer to *G* as the uniform gradient amount.

EXAMPLE. Mr. X, a portfolio manager, is considering his retirement needs. He estimates that he will require \$20,000 during the first year of retirement and, because of inflation, the following amounts in subsequent years:

Year	Total	Uniform Series (A)	Gradient Series (G)
2	$20,500	$20,000	$ 500
3	21,000	20,000	1,000
4	21,500	20,000	1,500
5	22,000	20,000	2,000

Mr. X's financial needs can be represented by a uniform payment series of $20,000 plus multiples of a uniform gradient amount G of $500 which start at the end of the second year.

The problems of dealing with a uniform gradient series can be considerably simplified by converting the gradient series to a *uniform* series of amount A_g which starts at the end of the first year. After this conversion of the gradient series has been accomplished, then all of the earlier formulas (which apply to uniform series) can be used.

The factor for converting a gradient series to a uniform series is represented by the symbol $(A/G,i,n)$ and is compiled in the tables.[1] Thus, the uniform series of amount A_g per period is given by:

$$A_g = G(A/G,i,n)$$

where G is the gradient amount.

EXAMPLE. How much must Mr. X, in the above example, have invested at retirement in a portfolio yielding 10 percent compounded per year in order to provide him with the planned income over a period of 20 years following retirement? *It is assumed* that all the funds will be consumed by the end of the 20th year. Neglect taxes.

SOLUTION. The cash flow diagram is shown in Figure 9.

The cash payout consists of a uniform series A of amount $20,000 plus a gradient series starting at the end of the second year with $G = $500. Convert the gradient series to a uniform series of amount A_g at the end of the first year:

$A_g = G(A/G,i,n)$
$G = $500, $i = 10\%$, $n = 20$ years, $A_g = ?$
$A_g = $500(A/G,10\%,20)$
$A_g = $500(6.51)$ (from compound interest tables)
$A_g = $3,255$

---

[1] Mathematically it can be shown that:

$$(A/G,i,n) = \frac{1}{i} - \frac{n}{(1 + i)^n - 1}$$

FIGURE 9

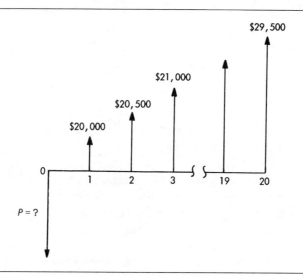

The equivalent uniform series is $A + A_g$, i.e., the uniform series of $20,000 plus $3,255 or $23,255.

$$P = A(P/A,i,n)$$
$$A = \$23,255,\ i = 10\%,\ n = 20,\ P = ?$$
$$P = \$23,255(P/A,10\%,20)$$
$$P = \$23,255(8.514)$$
$$P = \$197,900$$

Thus, Mr. X's portfolio on retirement (P) should be $197,900.

Nominal and effective interest rates. Interest may be compounded more frequently than once a year, i.e., compounding may occur semiannually, quarterly, or daily. Suppose that interest is compounded m times a year and the rate for each period is r, then the *annual nominal* interest rate is $R = mr$.

If one dollar is invested at the annual nominal rate R compounded m periods a year at the rate r per period, it will, at the end of the year, appreciate to the value F given by:

$$F = (1 + r)^m = (1 + R/m)^m = (F/P,r,m)$$

EXAMPLE. Interest is compounded monthly at an annual nominal rate of 12 percent. If $1,000 is invested for one year, what is the amount in the account?

$$F = P(F/P,r,m)$$
$$P = \$1,000, \; m = 12, \; r = 12\%/12 = 1\%, \; F = ?$$
$$F = \$1,000 \, (1.1268)$$
$$F = \$1,126.80$$

Instead of compounding m times a year at an annual nominal rate R, it is possible to obtain the same interest by compounding only once a year at the annual *effective* rate i given by:

$$i = (1 + R/m)^m - 1 = (F/P,r,m) - 1$$

EXAMPLE. What annual effective rate i (the rate compounded only once during the year) is equivalent to an annual nominal rate of 8 percent compounded quarterly?

SOLUTION.

$$i = (F/P,r,m) - 1$$
$$r = 8\%/4 = 2\%, \; m = 4$$
$$i = (F/P,2\%,4) - 1$$
$$i = 1.0824 - 1 = 0.0824 = 8.24\%$$

Extensive tables are available for directly converting nominal rates to effective rates.

When comparing various nominal rates, it is usually desirable to convert them to effective rates.

CALCULATION OF RATE OF RETURN

In this section we discuss the calculation of an unknown internal rate of return given the cash flows associated with an investment, the *net present value*. The net present value (*NPV*) of an investment is obtained by subtracting the initial outlay of the investment C_0 from the present value of the subsequent cash flows resulting (or expected) from the investment, C_n:

$$NPV = \sum_{n=1}^{N} \frac{C_n}{(1 + i)^n} - C_0$$

or in terms of our previous notation:

$$NPV = \sum_{k=1}^{N} C_n(P/F,i,n) - C_0$$

The number of time periods N over which the investment is considered is called the time *horizon* of the investment.

Clearly, the *NPV* depends on, among other things, the interest rate i used in the calculation. The larger the value of i in the above expression, the less the *NPV*. A negative value of *NPV* implies that the investment does not provide the desired rate of return i. Given a set of investment alternatives, that with the greater NPV would be selected.

EXAMPLE. An investor buys a stock at $100 per share. The expected annual dividend payout is $10 per share. He plans to sell the stock at the end of the second year at an expected price of $120. The investor expects a compounded rate of return (i) of 8 percent. What is the expected NPV of the stock to this investor?

SOLUTION. The cash flows consist of an initial disbursement of $100, followed by the expected receipt of $10 at the end of the first year and of $132 (the $12 dividend and the $120 from the sales of the stock) at the end of the second year.

$$NPV = C_1(P/F,i,1) + C_2(P/F,i,2) - C_0$$
$$C_0 = \$100,\ C_1 = \$10,\ C_2 = 132,\ i = 8\%,\ NPV = ?$$

Using Table 13 for the 8 percent compound interest factors, we have:

$$NPV = \$10(0.9259) + \$132(0.8573) - \$100$$
$$NPV = \$22.75 \text{ per share}$$

Thus, the investment would return in excess of 8 percent. What is the actual rate of return? This may be found by calculating the internal rate of return as discussed next.

Internal rate of return. The internal rate of return i_0 is the compound interest rate i which gives a NPV of zero. This rate is usually calculated by trial and error using the cash flows and the tabulated $(P/F,i,n)$ functions.

The calculation can be systematized by using certain observations which are apparent from the graph of NPV versus i, as shown in Figure 10:

FIGURE 10 Net Present Value (NPV) versus Rate of Return (i)

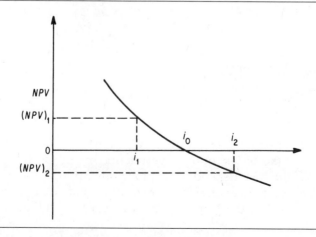

We see that NPV is positive for a choice of i less than i_0 and negative for a choice of i greater than i_0. To estimate i_0, we select, by trial and error, an i_1, giving a positive $(NPV)_1$ and for which the next greatest tabulated value i_2 gives a negative $(NPV)_2$ as shown in Figure 10.

We know that i_0 must lie between these two values so that i_0 may be estimated by interpolation using the formula:

$$i_0 = i_1 + \frac{(i_2 - i_1)(NPV)_1}{(NPV)_1 - (NPV)_2}$$

The closer i_1 and i_2 are in value, the better will be the approximation.

EXAMPLE. An investment of $10,900 was made in a portfolio which was held for seven years and then liquidated at a price of $21,190. Annual dividend and interest payments received during the seven years are tabulated below:

Year	Portfolio Payout	Year	Portfolio Payout
1	$1,000	4	1,350
2	1,250	5	1,440
3	1,230	6	1,370
		7	1,000

Calculate the annual compounded rate of return on the investment before taxes.

SOLUTION. By trial and error it was determined that a change in sign in the NPV occurred between 15 percent (i_1) and 20 percent (i_2). The trial-and-error calculation can often be simplified by assuming that the payout occurred as a uniform cash flow.

The detailed calculation is shown on the following work sheet:

Year	(A) Total Cash Flow	(B) (P/F,15%,n)	(C) Column (A) × (B)	(D) (P/F,20%,n)	(E) Column (A) × (D)
0	−10,900	1.0000	−$10,900	1.0000	−$10,900
1	1,000	0.8696	870	0.833	833
3	1,250	0.7561	945	0.6944	868
2	1,230	0.6575	809	0.5787	712
4	1,350	0.5718	772	0.4823	651
5	1,440	0.4972	716	0.4019	579
6	1,370	0.4323	592	0.3349	459
7	22,190	0.3759	8,341	0.2791	6,193
Total (NPV)			$ 2,145 (NPV)_1		−$ 605 (NPV)_2

The cash flow for year seven is the sum of the payout and the liquidation price of the portfolio. Interpolation between the two values gives a rate of return i_0 of 18.9 percent.

$$i_0 = 15\% + \frac{2,145(20\% - 15\%)}{2,750} = 18.9\%$$

BOND YIELDS

Definitions. Three types of bond yields should be distinguished:

1. The nominal or *coupon rate* is the rate based on the face value (par value) of the bond. Thus, a $1,000 par value bond issued with a coupon rate of 7 percent would pay $70 annually.
2. The *current yield* is calculated by dividing the annual interest by the current price of the bond:

Current yield = $1,000 × Nominal rate/Market price

3. *Yield to maturity* is the annual nominal rate of return if the bonds are held to maturity. It takes into account both capital gains (or losses) and coupon payments.

If a bond is sold at a price greater than par value (usually $1,000), then it is said to sell at a *premium*, and if it is sold at a price less than par value, it is said to sell at a *discount*.

Many bonds contain provisions permitting the issuer to redeem or call the bond after a specified date but prior to maturity at a premium over the offering price. The *yield to call* is the annual nominal rate of return if the bonds are held to the call date and redeemed at the call price.

In other words, the yield to maturity and the yield to call are simply the internal rates of return discussed previously and are, therefore, calculated by the same procedure.

It should be noted that bonds are usually purchased on an "and interest" basis, i.e., the buyer must pay the seller the proportional amount of interest accrued since the preceding interest date. The reason is that the buyer will receive the full interest on the next interest date, generally six months later.

Calculation of Yield to Maturity and Yield to Call

A bond paying A dollars interest semiannually is purchased at a price of P_0 (including the interest payment to the seller). The bond is held for n semiannual periods and redeemed at par ($1,000) on maturity or at a premium price on call represented by P_n (i.e., P_n is $1,000 if the bond is redeemed at maturity or the call price if redeemed at call). The semiannual yield (i) is calculated from the familiar expression for the internal rate of return:

$$A(P/A,i,n) + P_n(P/F,i,n) - P_0 = 0$$

The *annual* nominal rate of return is $2i$.

EXAMPLE. A bond bears an 8 percent per annum coupon and now sells at discount of 95($950) plus interest of $20 and matures 10 years (20 semiannual interest periods) hence. What is the before-tax annual nominal yield to maturity?

SOLUTION. The semiannual payments (A) are 1/2(0.08)($1,000), or $40.

$$A(P/A,i,n) + P_n(P/F,i,n) - P_0 = 0$$
$$A = \$40, n = 20, P_n = \$1,000, P_0 = \$970, i = ?$$

In the following table, the present value factors ($P/A,i,n$) and ($P/F,i,n$), selected by trial and error, are shown in the columns labeled PVF, and the cash flows are shown in the column labeled CF.

Period	(A) CF	(B) PVF(4%)	(C) Columns (A) × (B)	(D) PVF(5%)	(E) Columns (A) × (D)
0	$ -970	1.0000	-970	1.000	-970
1-20	40	13.5900	543	12.462	498
20	1,000	0.4564	456	0.377	377
Total			+29		-95

Interpolation gives:

$$i = 4\% + \frac{29(1\%)}{124}$$

hence:

$$i = 4.2\%$$

The *annual* nominal yield to maturity is 8.4 percent compounded semiannually.

If the bond becomes callable after, say, three years and the call price is 105($1,050), then the yield to call is calculated in the same way with $n = 6$ and $P_n = \$1,050$.

RATE OF RETURN ON STOCKS

The annual compound rate of return on a stock is the value of i which satisfies the expression:

$$\sum_{k=1}^{n} D_k/(1 + i)^k + P_n/(1 + i)^n - P_0 = 0$$

where D_n is the dividend paid on the kth year and P_0 is the purchase price of the stock, while P_n is the price at which the stock is sold at the end of year n.

If, instead of using annual dividends, we use quarterly dividends and time periods in the above equation, then the annual nominal rate of return is $4i$.

Payout ratio. Let R be the annual payout ratio given by:

$$R = \text{Annual dividends/Annual earnings}$$

and let the fractional annual growth of earnings g be given by:

$$g = \Delta E/E$$

where E is the annual earnings of the previous year and ΔE is the annual increase in earnings. If we assume g is constant, the kth year dividends are:

$$D_k = RE_0(1 + g)^k$$

where E_0 is the annual earnings at the time the stock is purchased.

Plowback ratio. We note that the annual increase in retained earnings ΔS is given by:

$$\Delta S = E(1 - R) = Eb$$

where:

$$b = 1 - R$$

The quantity b is the *plowback ratio*, which is a measure of the proportion of the annual earnings retained in the business.

Return on capital. The *return on stockholders' equity* (Y) is the ratio of annual earnings (E) to stockholders' equity (S):

$$Y = E/S$$

The *return on capitalization* (equity plus long-term debt, L) Y_C is

$$Y_C = \frac{E}{S + L}$$

The last expression may be written:

$$E = Y_C (S + L) = Y_C S(1 + L/S)$$

hence:

$$Y = Y_C (1 + L/S)$$

The quantity L/S is the *leverage* or the ratio of long-term debt to equity. *If the returns on equity and capitalization are given, the leverage may be calculated from*:

$$L/S = Y/Y_C - 1$$

If we assume that the leverage remains constant, the increase in earnings is given by:

$$\Delta E = Y_C \Delta S(1 + L/S) = Y\Delta S$$

Since $\Delta S = Eb$, we have:

$$\Delta E/E = bY = g$$

so that the *fractional rate of earnings increase is simply the product of the plowback ratio and the return on equity*.

Modified form of the rate of return equation. Introducing the above definitions into the expression for the rate of return on investment we have:

$$\sum_{k=1}^{n} E_0(1 - b)\left[\frac{(1 + Yb)}{(1 + i)}\right]^k + \frac{P_n}{(1 + i)^n} - P_0 = 0$$

Long-term investments. For very long term investments, considerable simplification of the last equation is possible, since

$$\frac{P_n}{(1 + i)^n}$$

approaches zero, and the summation term can be simplified using the algebraic result:

$$\sum_{k=1}^{\infty} Ar^k = Ar/(1 - r) \text{ (if } r < 1)$$

where

$$r = \frac{1 + Yb}{1 + i}$$

so that

$$\frac{E_0(1 - b)r}{1 - r} = \frac{D_0 r}{1 - r} = P_0$$

where $D_0 = E_0(1 - b)$, the dividend at the time of purchase. Solving for i we find:

$$i \text{ (long term)} = \frac{D_0}{P_0}(1 + g) + Yb = \frac{D_0(1 + g)}{P_0} + g$$

EXAMPLE. An investor is interested in purchasing a stock as a long-term holding which will provide a 10 percent compounded annual rate of return. Should he invest in universal Widget, a large well-established company with fairly constant debt to equity, payout, and return on investment ratios, given the data listed below?

Current price, $25 per share.
Current annual dividends (D_0), $1 per share.
Current annual earnings (E_0), $2 per share.
Return on equity (Y) $= 0.12$
Return on capitalization (Y_C) $= 0.18$.

SOLUTION.

$$i = \frac{D_0}{P_0}(1 + g) + g$$

$$Y = 0.12$$
$$\text{Plowback ratio } (b) = \$1/\$2 = 0.5$$
$$\text{Earnings growth rate } (g) = bY = 0.5 \times 0.12 = 0.06$$
$$D_0 = \$1$$
$$P_0 = \$25$$

$$i = \frac{\$1}{\$25}(1.06) + 0.06$$

$$i = 0.102, \text{ or } 10.2\%$$

Hence, the long-term rate of return just about satisfies the investor's requirements.

The debt-to-equity ratio (L/S) can be calculated from:

$$(L/S) = Y_C/Y - 1$$
$$(L/S) = 0.18/0.12 - 1 = 0.50$$

This moderately large ratio should be compared to similar companies in the industry. The debt provides favorable leverage, serving to raise the earnings per share. On the other hand, a substantial long-term debt imposes fixed charges which can become burdensome if earnings fall off substantially. The analyst should examine the earnings coverage of the debt charges and provisions for debt repayment.

TABLE 1 ¼ Percent Interest Factors for Annual Compounding Interest

	Single Payment		Equal-Payment Series				Uniform Gradient-Series Factor
	Compound-Amount Factor	Present-Worth Factor	Compound-Amount Factor	Sinking-Fund Factor	Present-Worth Factor	Capital-Recovery Factor	
n	To Find F Given P F/P i,n	To Find P Given F P/F i,n	To Find F Given A F/A i,n	To Find A Given F A/F i,n	To Find P Given A P/A i,n	To Find A Given P A/P i,n	To Find A Given G A/G i,n
1	1.003	0.9975	1.000	1.0000	0.9975	1.0025	0.0000
2	1.005	0.9950	2.003	0.4994	1.9925	0.5019	0.4994
3	1.008	0.9925	3.008	0.3325	2.9851	0.3350	0.9983
4	1.010	0.9901	4.015	0.2491	3.9751	0.2516	1.4969
5	1.013	0.9876	5.025	0.1990	4.9627	0.2015	1.9950
6	1.015	0.9851	6.038	0.1656	5.9479	0.1681	2.4927
7	1.018	0.9827	7.053	0.1418	6.9305	0.1443	2.9900
8	1.020	0.9802	8.070	0.1239	7.9108	0.1264	3.4869
9	1.023	0.9778	9.091	0.1100	8.8885	0.1125	3.9834
10	1.025	0.9754	10.113	0.0989	9.8639	0.1014	4.4794
11	1.028	0.9729	11.139	0.0898	10.8368	0.0923	4.9750
12	1.030	0.9705	12.166	0.0822	11.8073	0.0847	5.4703
13	1.033	0.9681	13.197	0.0758	12.7753	0.0783	5.9651
14	1.036	0.9657	14.230	0.0703	13.7410	0.0728	6.4594
15	1.038	0.9632	15.265	0.0655	14.7042	0.0680	6.9534
16	1.041	0.9608	16.304	0.0613	15.6651	0.0638	7.4470
17	1.043	0.9585	17.344	0.0577	16.6235	0.0602	7.9401
18	1.046	0.9561	18.388	0.0544	17.5795	0.0569	8.4328
19	1.049	0.9537	19.434	0.0515	18.5332	0.0540	8.9251
20	1.051	0.9513	20.482	0.0488	19.4845	0.0513	9.4170
21	1.054	0.9489	21.533	0.0464	20.4334	0.0489	9.9085
22	1.056	0.9466	22.587	0.0443	21.3800	0.0468	10.3995
23	1.059	0.9442	23.644	0.0423	22.3242	0.0448	10.8902
24	1.062	0.9418	24.703	0.0405	23.2660	0.0430	11.3804
25	1.064	0.9395	25.765	0.0388	24.2055	0.0413	11.8702
26	1.067	0.9372	26.829	0.0373	25.1426	0.0398	12.3596
27	1.070	0.9348	27.896	0.0359	26.0774	0.0384	12.8485
28	1.072	0.9325	28.966	0.0345	27.0099	0.0370	13.3371
29	1.075	0.9302	30.038	0.0333	27.9401	0.0358	13.8252
30	1.078	0.9278	31.113	0.0322	28.8679	0.0347	14.3130
31	1.080	0.9255	32.191	0.0311	29.7934	0.0336	14.8003
32	1.083	0.9232	33.272	0.0301	30.7166	0.0326	15.2872
33	1.086	0.9209	34.355	0.0291	31.6375	0.0316	15.7737
34	1.089	0.9186	35.441	0.0282	32.5561	0.0307	16.2597
35	1.091	0.9163	36.529	0.0274	33.4724	0.0299	16.7453
40	1.105	0.9050	42.013	0.0238	38.0199	0.0263	19.1673
45	1.119	0.8937	47.566	0.0210	42.5109	0.0235	21.5789
50	1.133	0.8826	53.189	0.0188	46.9462	0.0213	23.9802
55	1.147	0.8717	58.882	0.0170	51.3264	0.0195	26.3710
60	1.162	0.8609	64.647	0.0155	55.6524	0.0180	28.7514
65	1.176	0.8502	70.484	0.0142	59.9246	0.0167	31.1215
70	1.191	0.8397	76.394	0.0131	64.1439	0.0156	33.4812
75	1.206	0.8292	82.379	0.0121	68.3108	0.0146	35.8305
80	1.221	0.8189	88.439	0.0113	72.4260	0.0138	38.1694
85	1.236	0.8088	94.575	0.0106	76.4901	0.0131	40.4980
90	1.252	0.7988	100.788	0.0099	80.5038	0.0124	42.8162
95	1.268	0.7888	107.080	0.0093	84.4677	0.0118	45.1241
100	1.284	0.7791	113.450	0.0088	88.3825	0.0113	47.4216

SOURCE: Tables 1–22 are from W. J. Fabrycky and G. J. Thuesen, *Economic Decision Analysis,* © 1974, pp. 360-81. Reprinted by permission of Prentice-Hall, Inc., Englewood Cliffs, New Jersey.

TABLE 2 ½ Percent Interest Factors for Annual Compounding Interest

	Single Payment		Equal-Payment Series				Uniform Gradient-Series Factor
	Compound-Amount Factor	Present-Worth Factor	Compound-Amount Factor	Sinking-Fund Factor	Present-Worth Factor	Capital-Recovery Factor	
n	To Find F Given P F/P i, n	To Find P Given F P/F i, n	To Find F Given A F/A i, n	To Find A Given F A/F i, n	To Find P Given A P/A i, n	To Find A Given P A/P i, n	To Find A Given G A/G i, n
1	1.005	0.9950	1.000	1.0000	0.9950	1.0050	0.0000
2	1.010	0.9901	2.005	0.4988	1.9851	0.5038	0.4988
3	1.015	0.9852	3.015	0.3317	2.9703	0.3367	0.9967
4	1.020	0.9803	4.030	0.2481	3.9505	0.2531	1.4938
5	1.025	0.9754	5.050	0.1980	4.9259	0.2030	1.9900
6	1.030	0.9705	6.076	0.1646	5.8964	0.1696	2.4855
7	1.036	0.9657	7.106	0.1407	6.8621	0.1457	2.9801
8	1.041	0.9609	8.141	0.1228	7.8230	0.1278	3.4738
9	1.046	0.9561	9.182	0.1089	8.7791	0.1139	3.9668
10	1.051	0.9514	10.228	0.0978	9.7304	0.1028	4.4589
11	1.056	0.9466	11.279	0.0887	10.6770	0.0937	4.9501
12	1.062	0.9419	12.336	0.0811	11.6189	0.0861	5.4406
13	1.067	0.9372	13.397	0.0747	12.5562	0.0797	5.9302
14	1.072	0.9326	14.464	0.0691	13.4887	0.0741	6.4190
15	1.078	0.9279	15.537	0.0644	14.4166	0.0694	6.9069
16	1.083	0.9233	16.614	0.0602	15.3399	0.0652	7.3940
17	1.088	0.9187	17.697	0.0565	16.2586	0.0615	7.8803
18	1.094	0.9141	18.786	0.0532	17.1728	0.0582	8.3658
19	1.099	0.9096	19.880	0.0503	18.0824	0.0553	8.8504
20	1.105	0.9051	20.979	0.0477	18.9874	0.0527	9.3342
21	1.110	0.9006	22.084	0.0453	19.8880	0.0503	9.8172
22	1.116	0.8961	23.194	0.0431	20.7841	0.0481	10.2993
23	1.122	0.8916	24.310	0.0411	21.6757	0.0461	10.7806
24	1.127	0.8872	25.432	0.0393	22.5629	0.0443	11.2611
25	1.133	0.8828	26.559	0.0377	23.4456	0.0427	11.7407
26	1.138	0.8784	27.692	0.0361	24.3240	0.0411	12.2195
27	1.144	0.8740	28.830	0.0347	25.1980	0.0397	12.6975
28	1.150	0.8697	29.975	0.0334	26.0677	0.0384	13.1747
29	1.156	0.8653	31.124	0.0321	26.9330	0.0371	13.6510
30	1.161	0.8610	32.280	0.0310	27.7941	0.0360	14.1265
31	1.167	0.8568	33.441	0.0299	28.6508	0.0349	14.6012
32	1.173	0.8525	34.609	0.0289	29.5033	0.0339	15.0750
33	1.179	0.8483	35.782	0.0280	30.3515	0.0330	15.5480
34	1.185	0.8440	36.961	0.0271	31.1956	0.0321	16.0202
35	1.191	0.8398	38.145	0.0262	32.0354	0.0312	16.4915
40	1.221	0.8191	44.159	0.0227	36.1722	0.0277	18.8358
45	1.252	0.7990	50.324	0.0199	40.2072	0.0249	21.1595
50	1.283	0.7793	56.645	0.0177	44.1428	0.0227	23.4624
55	1.316	0.7601	63.126	0.0159	47.9815	0.0209	25.7447
60	1.349	0.7414	69.770	0.0143	51.7256	0.0193	28.0064
65	1.383	0.7231	76.582	0.0131	55.3775	0.0181	30.2475
70	1.418	0.7053	83.566	0.0120	58.9394	0.0170	32.4680
75	1.454	0.6879	90.727	0.0110	62.4137	0.0160	34.6679
80	1.490	0.6710	98.068	0.0102	65.8023	0.0152	36.8474
85	1.528	0.6545	105.594	0.0095	69.1075	0.0145	39.0065
90	1.567	0.6384	113.311	0.0088	72.3313	0.0138	41.1451
95	1.606	0.6226	121.222	0.0083	75.4757	0.0133	43.2633
100	1.647	0.6073	129.334	0.0077	78.5427	0.0127	45.3613

TABLE 3 ¾ Percent Interest Factors for Annual Compounding Interest

	Single Payment		Equal-Payment Series				Uniform Gradient-Series Factor
	Compound-Amount Factor	Present-Worth Factor	Compound-Amount Factor	Sinking-Fund Factor	Present-Worth Factor	Capital-Recovery Factor	
n	*To Find F Given P F/P i, n*	*To Find P Given F P/F i, n*	*To Find F Given A F/A i, n*	*To Find A Given F A/F i, n*	*To Find P Given A P/A i, n*	*To Find A Given P A/P i, n*	*To Find A Given G A/G i, n*
1	1.008	0.9926	1.000	1.0000	0.9926	1.0075	0.0000
2	1.015	0.9852	2.008	0.4981	1.9777	0.5056	0.4981
3	1.023	0.9778	3.023	0.3309	2.9556	0.3384	0.9950
4	1.030	0.9706	4.045	0.2472	3.9261	0.2547	1.4907
5	1.038	0.9633	5.076	0.1970	4.8894	0.2045	1.9851
6	1.046	0.9562	6.114	0.1636	5.8456	0.1711	2.4782
7	1.054	0.9491	7.159	0.1397	6.7946	0.1472	2.9701
8	1.062	0.9420	8.213	0.1218	7.7366	0.1293	3.4608
9	1.070	0.9350	9.275	0.1078	8.6716	0.1153	3.9502
10	1.078	0.9280	10.344	0.0967	9.5996	0.1042	4.4384
11	1.086	0.9211	11.422	0.0876	10.5207	0.0951	4.9253
12	1.094	0.9142	12.508	0.0800	11.4349	0.0875	5.4110
13	1.102	0.9074	13.601	0.0735	12.3424	0.0810	5.8954
14	1.110	0.9007	14.703	0.0680	13.2430	0.0755	6.3786
15	1.119	0.8940	15.814	0.0632	14.1370	0.0707	6.8606
16	1.127	0.8873	16.932	0.0591	15.0243	0.0666	7.3413
17	1.135	0.8807	18.059	0.0554	15.9050	0.0629	7.8207
18	1.144	0.8742	19.195	0.0521	16.7792	0.0596	8.2989
19	1.153	0.8677	20.339	0.0492	17.6468	0.0567	8.7759
20	1.161	0.8612	21.491	0.0465	18.5080	0.0540	9.2517
21	1.170	0.8548	22.652	0.0442	19.3628	0.0517	9.7261
22	1.179	0.8484	23.822	0.0420	20.2112	0.0495	10.1994
23	1.188	0.8421	25.001	0.0400	21.0533	0.0475	10.6714
24	1.196	0.8358	26.188	0.0382	21.8892	0.0457	11.1422
25	1.205	0.8296	27.385	0.0365	22.7188	0.0440	11.6117
26	1.214	0.8234	28.590	0.0350	23.5422	0.0425	12.0800
27	1.224	0.8173	29.805	0.0336	24.3595	0.0411	12.5470
28	1.233	0.8112	31.028	0.0322	25.1707	0.0397	13.0128
29	1.242	0.8052	32.261	0.0310	25.9759	0.0385	13.4774
30	1.251	0.7992	33.503	0.0299	26.7751	0.0374	13.9407
31	1.261	0.7932	34.754	0.0288	27.5683	0.0363	14.4028
32	1.270	0.7873	36.015	0.0278	28.3557	0.0353	14.8636
33	1.280	0.7815	37.285	0.0268	29.1371	0.0343	15.3232
34	1.289	0.7757	38.565	0.0259	29.9128	0.0334	15.7816
35	1.299	0.7699	39.854	0.0251	30.6827	0.0326	16.2387
40	1.348	0.7417	46.446	0.0215	34.4469	0.0290	18.5058
45	1.400	0.7145	53.290	0.0188	38.0732	0.0263	20.7421
50	1.453	0.6883	60.394	0.0166	41.5665	0.0241	22.9476
55	1.508	0.6630	67.769	0.0148	44.9316	0.0223	25.1223
60	1.566	0.6387	75.424	0.0133	48.1734	0.0208	27.2665
65	1.625	0.6153	83.371	0.0120	51.2963	0.0195	29.3801
70	1.687	0.5927	91.620	0.0109	54.3046	0.0184	31.4634
75	1.751	0.5710	100.183	0.0100	57.2027	0.0175	33.5163
80	1.818	0.5501	109.073	0.0092	59.9945	0.0167	35.5391
85	1.887	0.5299	118.300	0.0085	62.6838	0.0160	37.5318
90	1.959	0.5105	127.879	0.0078	65.2746	0.0153	39.4946
95	2.034	0.4917	137.823	0.0073	67.7704	0.0148	41.4277
100	2.111	0.4737	148.145	0.0068	70.1746	0.0143	43.3311

TABLE 4 1 Percent Interest Factors for Annual Compounding Interest

	Single Payment		Equal-Payment Series				Uniform Gradient-Series Factor
	Compound-Amount Factor	Present-Worth Factor	Compound-Amount Factor	Sinking-Fund Factor	Present-Worth Factor	Capital-Recovery Factor	
n	To Find F Given P $F/P\ i,n$	To Find P Given F $P/F\ i,n$	To Find F Given A $F/A\ i,n$	To Find A Given F $A/F\ i,n$	To Find P Given A $P/A\ i,n$	To Find A Given P $A/P\ i,n$	To Find A Given G $A/G\ i,n$
1	1.010	0.9901	1.000	1.0000	0.9901	1.0100	0.0000
2	1.020	0.9803	2.010	0.4975	1.9704	0.5075	0.4975
3	1.030	0.9706	3.030	0.3300	2.9410	0.3400	0.9934
4	1.041	0.9610	4.060	0.2463	3.9020	0.2563	1.4876
5	1.051	0.9515	5.101	0.1960	4.8534	0.2060	1.9801
6	1.062	0.9421	6.152	0.1626	5.7955	0.1726	2.4710
7	1.072	0.9327	7.214	0.1386	6.7282	0.1486	2.9602
8	1.083	0.9235	8.286	0.1207	7.6517	0.1307	3.4478
9	1.094	0.9143	9.369	0.1068	8.5660	0.1168	3.9337
10	1.105	0.9053	10.462	0.0956	9.4713	0.1056	4.4179
11	1.116	0.8963	11.567	0.0865	10.3676	0.0965	4.9005
12	1.127	0.8875	12.683	0.0789	11.2551	0.0889	5.3815
13	1.138	0.8787	13.809	0.0724	12.1338	0.0824	5.8607
14	1.149	0.8700	14.947	0.0669	13.0037	0.0769	6.3384
15	1.161	0.8614	16.097	0.0621	13.8651	0.0721	6.8143
16	1.173	0.8528	17.258	0.0580	14.7179	0.0680	7.2887
17	1.184	0.8444	18.430	0.0543	15.5623	0.0643	7.7613
18	1.196	0.8360	19.615	0.0510	16.3983	0.0610	8.2323
19	1.208	0.8277	20.811	0.0481	17.2260	0.0581	8.7017
20	1.220	0.8196	22.019	0.0454	18.0456	0.0554	9.1694
21	1.232	0.8114	23.239	0.0430	18.8570	0.0530	9.6354
22	1.245	0.8034	24.472	0.0409	19.6604	0.0509	10.0998
23	1.257	0.7955	25.716	0.0389	20.4558	0.0489	10.5626
24	1.270	0.7876	26.973	0.0371	21.2434	0.0471	11.0237
25	1.282	0.7798	28.243	0.0354	22.0232	0.0454	11.4831
26	1.295	0.7721	29.526	0.0339	22.7952	0.0439	11.9409
27	1.308	0.7644	30.821	0.0325	23.5596	0.0425	12.3971
28	1.321	0.7568	32.129	0.0311	24.3165	0.0411	12.8516
29	1.335	0.7494	33.450	0.0299	25.0658	0.0399	13.3045
30	1.348	0.7419	34.785	0.0288	25.8077	0.0388	13.7557
31	1.361	0.7346	36.133	0.0277	26.5423	0.0377	14.2052
32	1.375	0.7273	37.494	0.0267	27.2696	0.0367	14.6532
33	1.389	0.7201	38.869	0.0257	27.9897	0.0357	15.0995
34	1.403	0.7130	40.258	0.0248	28.7027	0.0348	15.5441
35	1.417	0.7059	41.660	0.0240	29.4086	0.0340	15.9871
40	1.489	0.6717	48.886	0.0205	32.8347	0.0305	18.1776
45	1.565	0.6391	56.481	0.0177	36.0945	0.0277	20.3273
50	1.645	0.6080	64.463	0.0155	39.1961	0.0255	22.4363
55	1.729	0.5785	72.852	0.0137	42.1472	0.0237	24.5049
60	1.817	0.5505	81.670	0.0123	44.9550	0.0223	26.5333
65	1.909	0.5237	90.937	0.0110	47.6266	0.0210	28.5217
70	2.007	0.4983	100.676	0.0099	50.1685	0.0199	30.4703
75	2.109	0.4741	110.913	0.0090	52.5871	0.0190	32.3793
80	2.217	0.4511	121.672	0.0082	54.8882	0.0182	34.2492
85	2.330	0.4292	132.979	0.0075	57.0777	0.0175	36.0801
90	2.449	0.4084	144.863	0.0069	59.1609	0.0169	37.8725
95	2.574	0.3886	157.354	0.0064	61.1430	0.0164	39.6265
100	2.705	0.3697	170.481	0.0059	63.0289	0.0159	41.3426

TABLE 5 1¼ Percent Interest Factors for Annual Compounding Interest

	Single Payment		Equal-Payment Series				Uniform Gradient-Series Factor
	Compound-Amount Factor	Present-Worth Factor	Compound-Amount Factor	Sinking-Fund Factor	Present-Worth Factor	Capital-Recovery Factor	
n	To Find F Given P F/P i, n	To Find P Given F P/F i, n	To Find F Given A F/A i, n	To Find A Given F A/F i, n	To Find P Given A P/A i, n	To Find A Given P A/P i, n	To Find A Given G A/G i, n
1	1.013	0.9877	1.000	1.0000	0.9877	1.0125	0.0000
2	1.025	0.9755	2.013	0.4969	1.9631	0.5094	0.4969
3	1.038	0.9634	3.038	0.3292	2.9265	0.3417	0.9917
4	1.051	0.9515	4.076	0.2454	3.8781	0.2579	1.4845
5	1.064	0.9398	5.127	0.1951	4.8178	0.2076	1.9752
6	1.077	0.9282	6.191	0.1615	5.7460	0.1740	2.4638
7	1.091	0.9167	7.268	0.1376	6.6627	0.1501	2.9503
8	1.104	0.9054	8.359	0.1196	7.5681	0.1321	3.4348
9	1.118	0.8942	9.463	0.1057	8.4624	0.1182	3.9172
10	1.132	0.8832	10.582	0.0945	9.3455	0.1070	4.3976
11	1.146	0.8723	11.714	0.0854	10.2178	0.0979	4.8758
12	1.161	0.8615	12.860	0.0778	11.0793	0.0903	5.3520
13	1.175	0.8509	14.021	0.0713	11.9302	0.0838	5.8262
14	1.190	0.8404	15.196	0.0658	12.7706	0.0783	6.2982
15	1.205	0.8300	16.386	0.0610	13.6006	0.0735	6.7683
16	1.220	0.8198	17.591	0.0569	14.4203	0.0694	7.2362
17	1.235	0.8096	18.811	0.0532	15.2299	0.0657	7.7021
18	1.251	0.7996	20.046	0.0499	16.0296	0.0624	8.1659
19	1.266	0.7898	21.297	0.0470	16.8193	0.0595	8.6277
20	1.282	0.7800	22.563	0.0443	17.5993	0.0568	9.0874
21	1.298	0.7704	23.845	0.0419	18.3697	0.0544	9.5450
22	1.314	0.7609	25.143	0.0398	19.1306	0.0523	10.0006
23	1.331	0.7515	26.457	0.0378	19.8820	0.0503	10.4542
24	1.347	0.7422	27.788	0.0360	20.6242	0.0485	10.9056
25	1.364	0.7330	29.135	0.0343	21.3573	0.0468	11.3551
26	1.381	0.7240	30.500	0.0328	22.0813	0.0453	11.8025
27	1.399	0.7151	31.881	0.0314	22.7963	0.0439	12.2478
28	1.416	0.7062	33.279	0.0301	23.5025	0.0426	12.6911
29	1.434	0.6975	34.695	0.0288	24.2000	0.0413	13.1323
30	1.452	0.6889	36.129	0.0277	24.8889	0.0402	13.5715
31	1.470	0.6804	37.581	0.0266	25.5693	0.0391	14.0087
32	1.488	0.6720	39.050	0.0256	26.2413	0.0381	14.4438
33	1.507	0.6637	40.539	0.0247	26.9050	0.0372	14.8768
34	1.526	0.6555	42.045	0.0238	27.5605	0.0363	15.3079
35	1.545	0.6474	43.571	0.0230	28.2079	0.0355	15.7369
40	1.644	0.6084	51.490	0.0194	31.3269	0.0319	17.8515
45	1.749	0.5718	59.916	0.0167	34.2582	0.0292	19.9156
50	1.861	0.5373	68.882	0.0145	37.0129	0.0270	21.9295
55	1.980	0.5050	78.422	0.0128	39.6017	0.0253	23.8936
60	2.107	0.4746	88.575	0.0113	42.0346	0.0238	25.8083
65	2.242	0.4460	99.377	0.0101	44.3210	0.0226	27.6741
70	2.386	0.4191	110.872	0.0090	46.4697	0.0215	29.4913
75	2.539	0.3939	123.103	0.0081	48.4890	0.0206	31.2605
80	2.701	0.3702	136.119	0.0074	50.3867	0.0199	32.9823
85	2.875	0.3479	149.968	0.0067	52.1701	0.0192	34.6570
90	3.059	0.3269	164.705	0.0061	53.8461	0.0186	36.2855
95	3.255	0.3072	180.386	0.0056	55.4211	0.0181	37.8682
100	3.463	0.2887	197.072	0.0051	56.9013	0.0176	39.4058

TABLE 6 1½ Percent Interest Factors for Annual Compounding Interest

n	Single Payment		Equal-Payment Series				Uniform Gradient-Series Factor
	Compound-Amount Factor	Present-Worth Factor	Compound-Amount Factor	Sinking-Fund Factor	Present-Worth Factor	Capital-Recovery Factor	
	To Find F Given P F/P i, n	To Find P Given F P/F i, n	To Find F Given A F/A i, n	To Find A Given F A/F i, n	To Find P Given A P/A i, n	To Find A Given P A/P i, n	To Find A Given G A/G i, n
1	1.015	0.9852	1.000	1.0000	0.9852	1.0150	0.0000
2	1.030	0.9707	2.015	0.4963	1.9559	0.5113	0.4963
3	1.046	0.9563	3.045	0.3284	2.9122	0.3434	0.9901
4	1.061	0.9422	4.091	0.2445	3.8544	0.2595	1.4814
5	1.077	0.9283	5.152	0.1941	4.7827	0.2091	1.9702
6	1.093	0.9146	6.230	0.1605	5.6972	0.1755	2.4566
7	1.110	0.9010	7.323	0.1366	6.5982	0.1516	2.9405
8	1.127	0.8877	8.433	0.1186	7.4859	0.1336	3.4219
9	1.143	0.8746	9.559	0.1046	8.3605	0.1196	3.9008
10	1.161	0.8617	10.703	0.0934	9.2222	0.1084	4.3772
11	1.178	0.8489	11.863	0.0843	10.0711	0.0993	4.8512
12	1.196	0.8364	13.041	0.0767	10.9075	0.0917	5.3227
13	1.214	0.8240	14.237	0.0703	11.7315	0.0853	5.7917
14	1.232	0.8119	15.450	0.0647	12.5434	0.0797	6.2582
15	1.250	0.7999	16.682	0.0600	13.3432	0.0750	6.7223
16	1.269	0.7880	17.932	0.0558	14.1313	0.0708	7.1839
17	1.288	0.7764	19.201	0.0521	14.9077	0.0671	7.6431
18	1.307	0.7649	20.489	0.0488	15.6726	0.0638	8.0997
19	1.327	0.7536	21.797	0.0459	16.4262	0.0609	8.5539
20	1.347	0.7425	23.124	0.0433	17.1686	0.0583	9.0057
21	1.367	0.7315	24.471	0.0409	17.9001	0.0559	9.4550
22	1.388	0.7207	25.838	0.0387	18.6208	0.0537	9.9018
23	1.408	0.7100	27.225	0.0367	19.3309	0.0517	10.3462
24	1.430	0.6996	28.634	0.0349	20.0304	0.0499	10.7881
25	1.451	0.6892	30.063	0.0333	20.7196	0.0483	11.2276
26	1.473	0.6790	31.514	0.0317	21.3986	0.0467	11.6646
27	1.495	0.6690	32.987	0.0303	22.0676	0.0453	12.0992
28	1.517	0.6591	34.481	0.0290	22.7267	0.0440	12.5313
29	1.540	0.6494	35.999	0.0278	23.3761	0.0428	12.9610
30	1.563	0.6398	37.539	0.0266	24.0158	0.0416	13.3883
31	1.587	0.6303	39.102	0.0256	24.6462	0.0406	13.8131
32	1.610	0.6210	40.688	0.0246	25.2671	0.0396	14.2355
33	1.634	0.6118	42.299	0.0237	25.8790	0.0387	14.6555
34	1.659	0.6028	43.933	0.0228	26.4817	0.0378	15.0731
35	1.684	0.5939	45.592	0.0219	27.0756	0.0369	15.4882
40	1.814	0.5513	54.268	0.0184	29.9159	0.0334	17.5277
45	1.954	0.5117	63.614	0.0157	32.5523	0.0307	19.5074
50	2.105	0.4750	73.683	0.0136	34.9997	0.0286	21.4277
55	2.268	0.4409	84.530	0.0118	37.2715	0.0268	23.2894
60	2.443	0.4093	96.215	0.0104	39.3803	0.0254	25.0930
65	2.632	0.3799	108.803	0.0092	41.3378	0.0242	26.8392
70	2.835	0.3527	122.364	0.0082	43.1549	0.0232	28.5290
75	3.055	0.3274	136.973	0.0073	44.8416	0.0223	30.1631
80	3.291	0.3039	152.711	0.0066	46.4073	0.0216	31.7423
85	3.545	0.2821	169.665	0.0059	47.8607	0.0209	33.2676
90	3.819	0.2619	187.930	0.0053	49.2099	0.0203	34.7399
95	4.114	0.2431	207.606	0.0048	50.4622	0.0198	36.1602
100	4.432	0.2256	228.803	0.0044	51.6247	0.0194	37.5295

TABLE 7 2 Percent Interest Factors for Annual Compounding Interest

	Single Payment		Equal-Payment Series				Uniform Gradient-Series Factor
	Compound-Amount Factor	Present-Worth Factor	Compound-Amount Factor	Sinking-Fund Factor	Present-Worth Factor	Capital-Recovery Factor	
n							
	To Find F Given P F/P i, n	To Find P Given F P/F i, n	To Find F Given A F/A i, n	To Find A Given F A/F i, n	To Find P Given A P/A i, n	To Find A Given P A/P i, n	To Find A Given G A/G i, n
1	1.020	0.9804	1.000	1.0000	0.9804	1.0200	0.0000
2	1.040	0.9612	2.020	0.4951	1.9416	0.5151	0.4951
3	1.061	0.9423	3.060	0.3268	2.8839	0.3468	0.9868
4	1.082	0.9239	4.122	0.2426	3.8077	0.2626	1.4753
5	1.104	0.9057	5.204	0.1922	4.7135	0.2122	1.9604
6	1.126	0.8880	6.308	0.1585	5.6014	0.1785	2.4423
7	1.149	0.8706	7.434	0.1345	6.4720	0.1545	2.9208
8	1.172	0.8535	8.583	0.1165	7.3255	0.1365	3.3961
9	1.195	0.8368	9.755	0.1025	8.1622	0.1225	3.8681
10	1.219	0.8204	10.950	0.0913	8.9826	0.1113	4.3367
11	1.243	0.8043	12.169	0.0822	9.7869	0.1022	4.8021
12	1.268	0.7885	13.412	0.0746	10.5754	0.0946	5.2643
13	1.294	0.7730	14.680	0.0681	11.3484	0.0881	5.7231
14	1.319	0.7579	15.974	0.0626	12.1063	0.0826	6.1786
15	1.346	0.7430	17.293	0.0578	12.8493	0.0778	6.6309
16	1.373	0.7285	18.639	0.0537	13.5777	0.0737	7.0799
17	1.400	0.7142	20.012	0.0500	14.2919	0.0700	7.5256
18	1.428	0.7002	21.412	0.0467	14.9920	0.0667	7.9681
19	1.457	0.6864	22.841	0.0438	15.6785	0.0638	8.4073
20	1.486	0.6730	24.297	0.0412	16.3514	0.0612	8.8433
21	1.516	0.6598	25.783	0.0388	17.0112	0.0588	9.2760
22	1.546	0.6468	27.299	0.0366	17.6581	0.0566	9.7055
23	1.577	0.6342	28.845	0.0347	18.2922	0.0547	10.1317
24	1.608	0.6217	30.422	0.0329	18.9139	0.0529	10.5547
25	1.641	0.6095	32.030	0.0312	19.5235	0.0512	10.9745
26	1.673	0.5976	33.671	0.0297	20.1210	0.0497	11.3910
27	1.707	0.5859	35.344	0.0283	20.7069	0.0483	11.8043
28	1.741	0.5744	37.051	0.0270	21.2813	0.0470	12.2145
29	1.776	0.5631	38.792	0.0258	21.8444	0.0458	12.6214
30	1.811	0.5521	40.568	0.0247	22.3965	0.0447	13.0251
31	1.848	0.5413	42.379	0.0236	22.9377	0.0436	13.4257
32	1.885	0.5306	44.227	0.0226	23.4683	0.0426	13.8230
33	1.922	0.5202	46.112	0.0217	23.9886	0.0417	14.2172
34	1.961	0.5100	48.034	0.0208	24.4986	0.0408	14.6083
35	2.000	0.5000	49.994	0.0200	24.9986	0.0400	14.9961
40	2.208	0.4529	60.402	0.0166	27.3555	0.0366	16.8885
45	2.438	0.4102	71.893	0.0139	29.4902	0.0339	18.7034
50	2.692	0.3715	84.579	0.0118	31.4236	0.0318	20.4420
55	2.972	0.3365	98.587	0.0102	33.1748	0.0302	22.1057
60	3.281	0.3048	114.052	0.0088	34.7609	0.0288	23.6961
65	3.623	0.2761	131.126	0.0076	36.1975	0.0276	25.2147
70	4.000	0.2500	149.978	0.0067	37.4986	0.0267	26.6632
75	4.416	0.2265	170.792	0.0059	38.6771	0.0259	28.0434
80	4.875	0.2051	193.772	0.0052	39.7445	0.0252	29.3572
85	5.383	0.1858	219.144	0.0046	40.7113	0.0246	30.6064
90	5.943	0.1683	247.157	0.0041	41.5869	0.0241	31.7929
95	6.562	0.1524	278.085	0.0036	42.3800	0.0236	32.9189
100	7.245	0.1380	312.232	0.0032	43.0984	0.0232	33.9863

TABLE 8 3 Percent Interest Factors for Annual Compounding Interest

	Single Payment		Equal-Payment Series				Uniform Gradient-Series Factor
	Compound-Amount Factor	Present-Worth Factor	Compound-Amount Factor	Sinking-Fund Factor	Present-Worth Factor	Capital-Recovery Factor	
n	*To Find F Given P F/P i, n*	*To Find P Given F P/F i, n*	*To Find F Given A F/A i, n*	*To Find A Given F A/F i, n*	*To Find P Given A P/A i, n*	*To Find A Given P A/P i, n*	*To Find A Given G A/G i, n*
1	1.030	0.9709	1.000	1.0000	0.9709	1.0300	0.0000
2	1.061	0.9426	2.030	0.4926	1.9135	0.5226	0.4926
3	1.093	0.9152	3.091	0.3235	2.8286	0.3535	0.9803
4	1.126	0.8885	4.184	0.2390	3.7171	0.2690	1.4631
5	1.159	0.8626	5.309	0.1884	4.5797	0.2184	1.9409
6	1.194	0.8375	6.468	0.1546	5.4172	0.1846	2.4138
7	1.230	0.8131	7.662	0.1305	6.2303	0.1605	2.8819
8	1.267	0.7894	8.892	0.1125	7.0197	0.1425	3.3450
9	1.305	0.7664	10.159	0.0984	7.7861	0.1284	3.8032
10	1.344	0.7441	11.464	0.0872	8.5302	0.1172	4.2565
11	1.384	0.7224	12.808	0.0781	9.2526	0.1081	4.7049
12	1.426	0.7014	14.192	0.0705	9.9540	0.1005	5.1485
13	1.469	0.6810	15.618	0.0640	10.6350	0.0940	5.5872
14	1.513	0.6611	17.086	0.0585	11.2961	0.0885	6.0211
15	1.558	0.6419	18.599	0.0538	11.9379	0.0838	6.4501
16	1.605	0.6232	20.157	0.0496	12.5611	0.0796	6.8742
17	1.653	0.6050	21.762	0.0460	13.1661	0.0760	7.2936
18	1.702	0.5874	23.414	0.0427	13.7535	0.0727	7.7081
19	1.754	0.5703	25.117	0.0398	14.3238	0.0698	8.1179
20	1.806	0.5537	26.870	0.0372	14.8775	0.0672	8.5229
21	1.860	0.5376	28.676	0.0349	15.4150	0.0649	8.9231
22	1.916	0.5219	30.537	0.0328	15.9369	0.0628	9.3186
23	1.974	0.5067	32.453	0.0308	16.4436	0.0608	9.7094
24	2.033	0.4919	34.426	0.0291	16.9356	0.0591	10.0954
25	2.094	0.4776	36.459	0.0274	17.4132	0.0574	10.4768
26	2.157	0.4637	38.553	0.0259	17.8769	0.0559	10.8535
27	2.221	0.4502	40.710	0.0246	18.3270	0.0546	11.2256
28	2.288	0.4371	42.931	0.0233	18.7641	0.0533	11.5930
29	2.357	0.4244	45.219	0.0221	19.1885	0.0521	11.9558
30	2.427	0.4120	47.575	0.0210	19.6005	0.0510	12.3141
31	2.500	0.4000	50.003	0.0200	20.0004	0.0500	12.6678
32	2.575	0.3883	52.503	0.0191	20.3888	0.0491	13.0169
33	2.652	0.3770	55.078	0.0182	20.7658	0.0482	13.3616
34	2.732	0.3661	57.730	0.0173	21.1318	0.0473	13.7018
35	2.814	0.3554	60.462	0.0165	21.4872	0.0465	14.0375
40	3.262	0.3066	75.401	0.0133	23.1148	0.0433	15.6502
45	3.782	0.2644	92.720	0.0108	24.5187	0.0408	17.1556
50	4.384	0.2281	112.797	0.0089	25.7298	0.0389	18.5575
55	5.082	0.1968	136.072	0.0074	26.7744	0.0374	19.8600
60	5.892	0.1697	163.053	0.0061	27.6756	0.0361	21.0674
65	6.830	0.1464	194.333	0.0052	28.4529	0.0352	22.1841
70	7.918	0.1263	230.594	0.0043	29.1234	0.0343	23.2145
75	9.179	0.1090	272.631	0.0037	29.7018	0.0337	24.1634
80	10.641	0.0940	321.363	0.0031	30.2008	0.0331	25.0354
85	12.336	0.0811	377.857	0.0027	30.6312	0.0327	25.8349
90	14.300	0.0699	443.349	0.0023	31.0024	0.0323	26.5667
95	16.578	0.0603	519.272	0.0019	31.3227	0.0319	27.2351
100	19.219	0.0520	607.288	0.0017	31.5989	0.0317	27.8445

TABLE 9 4 Percent Interest Factors for Annual Compounding Interest

	Single Payment		Equal-Payment Series				Uniform Gradient-Series Factor
	Compound-Amount Factor	Present-Worth Factor	Compound-Amount Factor	Sinking-Fund Factor	Present-Worth Factor	Capital-Recovery Factor	
n	To Find F Given P $F/P\ i,n$	To Find P Given F $P/F\ i,n$	To Find F Given A $F/A\ i,n$	To Find A Given F $A/F\ i,n$	To Find P Given A $P/A\ i,n$	To Find A Given P $A/P\ i,n$	To Find A Given G $A/G\ i,n$
1	1.040	0.9615	1.000	1.0000	0.9615	1.0400	0.0000
2	1.082	0.9246	2.040	0.4902	1.8861	0.5302	0.4902
3	1.125	0.8890	3.122	0.3204	2.7751	0.3604	0.9739
4	1.170	0.8548	4.246	0.2355	3.6299	0.2755	1.4510
5	1.217	0.8219	5.416	0.1846	4.4518	0.2246	1.9216
6	1.265	0.7903	6.633	0.1508	5.2421	0.1908	2.3857
7	1.316	0.7599	7.898	0.1266	6.0021	0.1666	2.8433
8	1.369	0.7307	9.214	0.1085	6.7328	0.1485	3.2944
9	1.423	0.7026	10.583	0.0945	7.4353	0.1345	3.7391
10	1.480	0.6756	12.006	0.0833	8.1109	0.1233	4.1773
11	1.539	0.6496	13.486	0.0742	8.7605	0.1142	4.6090
12	1.601	0.6246	15.026	0.0666	9.3851	0.1066	5.0344
13	1.665	0.6006	16.627	0.0602	9.9857	0.1002	5.4533
14	1.732	0.5775	18.292	0.0547	10.5631	0.0947	5.8659
15	1.801	0.5553	20.024	0.0500	11.1184	0.0900	6.2721
16	1.873	0.5339	21.825	0.0458	11.6523	0.0858	6.6720
17	1.948	0.5134	23.698	0.0422	12.1657	0.0822	7.0656
18	2.026	0.4936	25.645	0.0390	12.6593	0.0790	7.4530
19	2.107	0.4747	27.671	0.0361	13.1339	0.0761	7.8342
20	2.191	0.4564	29.778	0.0336	13.5903	0.0736	8.2091
21	2.279	0.4388	31.969	0.0313	14.0292	0.0713	8.5780
22	2.370	0.4220	34.248	0.0292	14.4511	0.0692	8.9407
23	2.465	0.4057	36.618	0.0273	14.8569	0.0673	9.2973
24	2.563	0.3901	39.083	0.0256	15.2470	0.0656	9.6479
25	2.666	0.3751	41.646	0.0240	15.6221	0.0640	9.9925
26	2.772	0.3607	44.312	0.0226	15.9828	0.0626	10.3312
27	2.883	0.3468	47.084	0.0212	16.3296	0.0612	10.6640
28	2.999	0.3335	49.968	0.0200	16.6631	0.0600	10.9909
29	3.119	0.3207	52.966	0.0189	16.9837	0.0589	11.3121
30	3.243	0.3083	56.085	0.0178	17.2920	0.0578	11.6274
31	3.373	0.2965	59.328	0.0169	17.5885	0.0569	11.9371
32	3.508	0.2851	62.701	0.0160	17.8736	0.0560	12.2411
33	3.648	0.2741	66.210	0.0151	18.1477	0.0551	12.5396
34	3.794	0.2636	69.858	0.0143	18.4112	0.0543	12.8325
35	3.946	0.2534	73.652	0.0136	18.6646	0.0536	13.1199
40	4.801	0.2083	95.026	0.0105	19.7928	0.0505	14.4765
45	5.841	0.1712	121.029	0.0083	20.7200	0.0483	15.7047
50	7.107	0.1407	152.667	0.0066	21.4822	0.0466	16.8123
55	8.646	0.1157	191.159	0.0052	22.1086	0.0452	17.8070
60	10.520	0.0951	237.991	0.0042	22.6235	0.0442	18.6972
65	12.799	0.0781	294.968	0.0034	23.0467	0.0434	19.4909
70	15.572	0.0642	364.290	0.0028	23.3945	0.0428	20.1961
75	18.945	0.0528	448.631	0.0022	23.6804	0.0422	20.8206
80	23.050	0.0434	551.245	0.0018	23.9154	0.0418	21.3719
85	28.044	0.0357	676.090	0.0015	24.1085	0.0415	21.8569
90	34.119	0.0293	817.983	0.0012	24.2673	0.0412	22.2826
95	41.511	0.0241	1012.785	0.0010	24.3978	0.0410	22.6550
100	50.505	0.0198	1237.624	0.0008	24.5050	0.0408	22.9800

TABLE 10 5 Percent Interest Factors for Annual Compounding Interest

n	Single Payment		Equal-Payment Series				Uniform Gradient-Series Factor
	Compound-Amount Factor	Present-Worth Factor	Compound-Amount Factor	Sinking-Fund Factor	Present-Worth Factor	Capital-Recovery Factor	
	To Find F Given P F/P i, n	To Find P Given F P/F i, n	To Find F Given A F/A i, n	To Find A Given F A/F i, n	To Find P Given A P/A i, n	To Find A Given P A/P i, n	To Find A Given G A/G i, n
1	1.050	0.9524	1.000	1.0000	0.9524	1.0500	0.0000
2	1.103	0.9070	2.050	0.4878	1.8594	0.5378	0.4878
3	1.158	0.8638	3.153	0.3172	2.7233	0.3672	0.9675
4	1.216	0.8227	4.310	0.2320	3.5460	0.2820	1.4391
5	1.276	0.7835	5.526	0.1810	4.3295	0.2310	1.9025
6	1.340	0.7462	6.802	0.1470	5.0757	0.1970	2.3579
7	1.407	0.7107	8.142	0.1228	5.7864	0.1728	2.8052
8	1.477	0.6768	9.549	0.1047	6.4632	0.1547	3.2445
9	1.551	0.6446	11.027	0.0907	7.1078	0.1407	3.6758
10	1.629	0.6139	12.587	0.0795	7.7217	0.1295	4.0991
11	1.710	0.5847	14.207	0.0704	8.3064	0.1204	4.5145
12	1.796	0.5568	15.917	0.0628	8.8633	0.1128	4.9219
13	1.866	0.5303	17.713	0.0565	9.3936	0.1065	5.3215
14	1.980	0.5051	19.599	0.0510	9.8987	0.1010	5.7133
15	2.079	0.4810	21.579	0.0464	10.3797	0.0964	6.0973
16	2.183	0.4581	23.658	0.0423	10.8378	0.0923	6.4736
17	2.292	0.4363	25.840	0.0387	11.2741	0.0887	6.8423
18	2.407	0.4155	28.132	0.0356	11.6896	0.0856	7.2034
19	2.527	0.3957	30.539	0.0328	12.0853	0.0828	7.5569
20	2.653	0.3769	33.066	0.0303	12.4622	0.0803	7.9030
21	2.786	0.3590	35.719	0.0280	12.8212	0.0780	8.2416
22	2.925	0.3419	38.505	0.0260	13.1630	0.0760	8.5730
23	3.072	0.3256	41.430	0.0241	13.4886	0.0741	8.8971
24	3.225	0.3101	44.502	0.0225	13.7987	0.0725	9.2140
25	3.386	0.2953	47.727	0.0210	14.0940	0.0710	9.5238
26	3.556	0.2813	51.113	0.0196	14.3752	0.0696	9.8266
27	3.733	0.2679	54.669	0.0183	14.6430	0.0683	10.1224
28	3.920	0.2551	58.403	0.0171	14.8981	0.0671	10.4114
29	4.116	0.2430	62.323	0.0161	15.1411	0.0661	10.6936
30	4.322	0.2314	66.439	0.0151	15.3725	0.0651	10.9691
31	4.538	0.2204	70.761	0.0141	15.5928	0.0641	11.2381
32	4.765	0.2099	75.299	0.0133	15.8027	0.0633	11.5005
33	5.003	0.1999	80.064	0.0125	16.0026	0.0625	11.7566
34	5.253	0.1904	85.067	0.0118	16.1929	0.0618	12.0063
35	5.516	0.1813	90.320	0.0111	16.3742	0.0611	12.2498
40	7.040	0.1421	120.800	0.0083	17.1591	0.0583	13.3775
45	8.985	0.1113	159.700	0.0063	17.7741	0.0563	14.3644
50	11.467	0.0872	209.348	0.0048	18.2559	0.0548	15.2233
55	14.636	0.0683	272.713	0.0037	18.6335	0.0537	15.9665
60	18.679	0.0535	353.584	0.0028	18.9293	0.0528	16.6062
65	23.840	0.0420	456.798	0.0022	19.1611	0.0522	17.1541
70	30.426	0.0329	588.529	0.0017	19.3427	0.0517	17.6212
75	38.833	0.0258	756.654	0.0013	19.4850	0.0513	18.0176
80	49.561	0.0202	971.229	0.0010	19.5965	0.0510	18.3526
85	63.254	0.0158	1245.087	0.0008	19.6838	0.0508	18.6346
90	80.730	0.0124	1594.607	0.0006	19.7523	0.0506	18.8712
95	103.035	0.0097	2040.694	0.0005	19.8059	0.0505	19.0689
100	131.501	0.0076	2610.025	0.0004	19.8479	0.0504	19.2337

TABLE 11 6 Percent Interest Factors for Annual Compounding Interest

	Single Payment		Equal-Payment Series				Uniform Gradient-Series Factor
	Compound-Amount Factor	Present-Worth Factor	Compound-Amount Factor	Sinking-Fund Factor	Present-Worth Factor	Capital-Recovery Factor	
n	To Find F Given P $F/P\ i,n$	To Find P Given F $P/F\ i,n$	To Find F Given A $F/A\ i,n$	To Find A Given F $A/F\ i,n$	To Find P Given A $P/A\ i,n$	To Find A Given P $A/P\ i,n$	To Find A Given G $A/G\ i,n$
1	1.060	0.9434	1.000	1.0000	0.9434	1.0600	0.0000
2	1.124	0.8900	2.060	0.4854	1.8334	0.5454	0.4854
3	1.191	0.8396	3.184	0.3141	2.6730	0.3741	0.9612
4	1.262	0.7921	4.375	0.2286	3.4651	0.2886	1.4272
5	1.338	0.7473	5.637	0.1774	4.2124	0.2374	1.8836
6	1.419	0.7050	6.975	0.1434	4.9173	0.2034	2.3304
7	1.504	0.6651	8.394	0.1191	5.5824	0.1791	2.7676
8	1.594	0.6274	9.897	0.1010	6.2098	0.1610	3.1952
9	1.689	0.5919	11.491	0.0870	6.8017	0.1470	3.6133
10	1.791	0.5584	13.181	0.0759	7.3601	0.1359	4.0220
11	1.898	0.5268	14.972	0.0668	7.8869	0.1268	4.4213
12	2.012	0.4970	16.870	0.0593	8.3839	0.1193	4.8113
13	2.133	0.4688	18.882	0.0530	8.8527	0.1130	5.1920
14	2.261	0.4423	21.015	0.0476	9.2950	0.1076	5.5635
15	2.397	0.4173	23.276	0.0430	9.7123	0.1030	5.9260
16	2.540	0.3937	25.673	0.0390	10.1059	0.0990	6.2794
17	2.693	0.3714	28.213	0.0355	10.4773	0.0955	6.6240
18	2.854	0.3504	30.906	0.0324	10.8276	0.0924	6.9597
19	3.026	0.3305	33.760	0.0296	11.1581	0.0896	7.2867
20	3.207	0.3118	36.786	0.0272	11.4699	0.0872	7.6052
21	3.400	0.2942	39.993	0.0250	11.7641	0.0850	7.9151
22	3.604	0.2775	43.392	0.0231	12.0416	0.0831	8.2166
23	3.820	0.2618	46.996	0.0213	12.3034	0.0813	8.5099
24	4.049	0.2470	50.816	0.0197	12.5504	0.0797	8.7951
25	4.292	0.2330	54.865	0.0182	12.7834	0.0782	9.0722
26	4.549	0.2198	59.156	0.0169	13.0032	0.0769	9.3415
27	4.822	0.2074	63.706	0.0157	13.2105	0.0757	9.6030
28	5.112	0.1956	68.528	0.0146	13.4062	0.0746	9.8568
29	5.418	0.1846	73.640	0.0136	13.5907	0.0736	10.1032
30	5.744	0.1741	79.058	0.0127	13.7648	0.0727	10.3422
31	6.088	0.1643	84.802	0.0118	13.9291	0.0718	10.5740
32	6.453	0.1550	90.890	0.0110	14.0841	0.0710	10.7988
33	6.841	0.1462	97.343	0.0103	14.2302	0.0703	11.0166
34	7.251	0.1379	104.184	0.0096	14.3682	0.0696	11.2276
35	7.686	0.1301	111.435	0.0090	14.4983	0.0690	11.4319
40	10.286	0.0972	154.762	0.0065	15.0463	0.0665	12.3590
45	13.765	0.0727	212.744	0.0047	15.4558	0.0647	13.1413
50	18.420	0.0543	290.336	0.0035	15.7619	0.0635	13.7964
55	24.650	0.0406	394.172	0.0025	15.9906	0.0625	14.3411
60	32.988	0.0303	533.128	0.0019	16.1614	0.0619	14.7910
65	44.145	0.0227	719.083	0.0014	16.2891	0.0614	15.1601
70	59.076	0.0169	967.932	0.0010	16.3846	0.0610	15.4614
75	79.057	0.0127	1300.949	0.0008	16.4559	0.0608	15.7058
80	105.796	0.0095	1746.600	0.0006	16.5091	0.0606	15.9033
85	141.579	0.0071	2342.982	0.0004	16.5490	0.0604	16.0620
90	189.465	0.0053	3141.075	0.0003	16.5787	0.0603	16.1891
95	253.546	0.0040	4209.104	0.0002	16.6009	0.0602	16.2905
100	339.302	0.0030	5638.368	0.0002	16.6176	0.0602	16.3711

TABLE 12 7 Percent Interest Factors for Annual Compounding Interest

	Single Payment		Equal-Payment Series				Uniform Gradient-Series Factor
	Compound-Amount Factor	Present-Worth Factor	Compound-Amount Factor	Sinking-Fund Factor	Present-Worth Factor	Capital-Recovery Factor	
n	To Find F Given P $F/P\ i,n$	To Find P Given F $P/F\ i,n$	To Find F Given A $F/A\ i,n$	To Find A Given F $A/F\ i,n$	To Find P Given A $P/A\ i,n$	To Find A Given P $A/P\ i,n$	To Find A Given G $A/G\ i,n$
1	1.070	0.9346	1.000	1.0000	0.9346	1.0700	0.0000
2	1.145	0.8734	2.070	0.4831	1.8080	0.5531	0.4831
3	1.225	0.8163	3.215	0.3111	2.6243	0.3811	0.9549
4	1.311	0.7629	4.440	0.2252	3.3872	0.2952	1.4155
5	1.403	0.7130	5.751	0.1739	4.1002	0.2439	1.8650
6	1.501	0.6664	7.153	0.1398	4.7665	0.2098	2.3032
7	1.606	0.6228	8.654	0.1156	5.3893	0.1856	2.7304
8	1.718	0.5820	10.260	0.0975	5.9713	0.1675	3.1466
9	1.838	0.5439	11.978	0.0835	6.5152	0.1535	3.5517
10	1.967	0.5084	13.816	0.0724	7.0236	0.1424	3.9461
11	2.105	0.4751	15.784	0.0634	7.4987	0.1334	4.3296
12	2.252	0.4440	17.888	0.0559	7.9427	0.1259	4.7025
13	2.410	0.4150	20.141	0.0497	8.3577	0.1197	5.0649
14	2.579	0.3878	22.550	0.0444	8.7455	0.1144	5.4167
15	2.759	0.3625	25.129	0.0398	9.1079	0.1098	5.7583
16	2.952	0.3387	27.888	0.0359	9.4467	0.1059	6.0897
17	3.159	0.3166	30.840	0.0324	9.7632	0.1024	6.4110
18	3.380	0.2959	33.999	0.0294	10.0591	0.0994	6.7225
19	3.617	0.2765	37.379	0.0268	10.3356	0.0968	7.0242
20	3.870	0.2584	40.996	0.0244	10.5940	0.0944	7.3163
21	4.141	0.2415	44.865	0.0223	10.8355	0.0923	7.5990
22	4.430	0.2257	49.006	0.0204	11.0613	0.0904	7.8725
23	4.741	0.2110	53.436	0.0187	11.2722	0.0887	8.1369
24	5.072	0.1972	58.177	0.0172	11.4693	0.0872	8.3923
25	5.427	0.1843	63.249	0.0158	11.6536	0.0858	8.6391
26	5.807	0.1722	68.676	0.0146	11.8258	0.0846	8.8773
27	6.214	0.1609	74.484	0.0134	11.9867	0.0834	9.1072
28	6.649	0.1504	80.698	0.0124	12.1371	0.0824	9.3290
29	7.114	0.1406	87.347	0.0115	12.2777	0.0815	9.5427
30	7.612	0.1314	94.461	0.0106	12.4091	0.0806	9.7487
31	8.145	0.1228	102.073	0.0098	12.5318	0.0798	9.9471
32	8.715	0.1148	110.218	0.0091	12.6466	0.0791	10.1381
33	9.325	0.1072	118.933	0.0084	12.7538	0.0784	10.3219
34	9.978	0.1002	128.259	0.0078	12.8540	0.0778	10.4987
35	10.677	0.0937	138.237	0.0072	12.9477	0.0772	10.6687
40	14.974	0.0668	199.635	0.0050	13.3317	0.0750	11.4234
45	21.002	0.0476	285.749	0.0035	13.6055	0.0735	12.0360
50	29.457	0.0340	406.529	0.0025	13.8008	0.0725	12.5287
55	41.315	0.0242	575.929	0.0017	13.9399	0.0717	12.9215
60	57.946	0.0173	813.520	0.0012	14.0392	0.0712	13.2321
65	81.273	0.0123	1146.755	0.0009	14.1099	0.0709	13.4760
70	113.989	0.0088	1614.134	0.0006	14.1604	0.0706	13.6662
75	159.876	0.0063	2269.657	0.0005	14.1964	0.0705	13.8137
80	224.234	0.0045	3189.063	0.0003	14.2220	0.0703	13.9274
85	314.500	0.0032	4478.576	0.0002	14.2403	0.0702	14.0146
90	441.103	0.0023	6287.185	0.0002	14.2533	0.0702	14.0812
95	618.670	0.0016	8823.854	0.0001	14.2626	0.0701	14.1319
100	867.716	0.0012	12381.662	0.0001	14.2693	0.0701	14.1703

TABLE 13 8 Percent Interest Factors for Annual Compounding Interest

n	Single Payment		Equal-Payment Series				Uniform Gradient-Series Factor
	Compound-Amount Factor	Present-Worth Factor	Compound-Amount Factor	Sinking-Fund Factor	Present-Worth Factor	Capital-Recovery Factor	
	To Find F Given P F/P i,n	To Find P Given F P/F i,n	To Find F Given A F/A i,n	To Find A Given F A/F i,n	To Find P Given A P/A i,n	To Find A Given P A/P i,n	To Find A Given G A/G i,n
1	1.080	0.9259	1.000	1.0000	0.9259	1.0800	0.0000
2	1.166	0.8573	2.080	0.4808	1.7833	0.5608	0.4808
3	1.260	0.7938	3.246	0.3080	2.5771	0.3880	0.9488
4	1.360	0.7350	4.506	0.2219	3.3121	0.3019	1.4040
5	1.469	0.6806	5.867	0.1705	3.9927	0.2505	1.8465
6	1.587	0.6302	7.336	0.1363	4.6229	0.2163	2.2764
7	1.714	0.5835	8.923	0.1121	5.2064	0.1921	2.6937
8	1.851	0.5403	10.637	0.0940	5.7466	0.1740	3.0985
9	1.999	0.5003	12.488	0.0801	6.2469	0.1601	3.4910
10	2.159	0.4632	14.487	0.0690	6.7101	0.1490	3.8713
11	2.332	0.4289	16.645	0.0601	7.1390	0.1401	4.2395
12	2.518	0.3971	18.977	0.0527	7.5361	0.1327	4.5958
13	2.720	0.3677	21.495	0.0465	7.9038	0.1265	4.9402
14	2.937	0.3405	24.215	0.0413	8.2442	0.1213	5.2731
15	3.172	0.3153	27.152	0.0368	8.5595	0.1168	5.5945
16	3.426	0.2919	30.324	0.0330	8.8514	0.1130	5.9046
17	3.700	0.2703	33.750	0.0296	9.1216	0.1096	6.2038
18	3.996	0.2503	37.450	0.0267	9.3719	0.1067	6.4920
19	4.316	0.2317	41.446	0.0241	9.6036	0.1041	6.7697
20	4.661	0.2146	45.762	0.0219	9.8182	0.1019	7.0370
21	5.034	0.1987	50.423	0.0198	10.0168	0.0998	7.2940
22	5.437	0.1840	55.457	0.0180	10.2008	0.0980	7.5412
23	5.871	0.1703	60.893	0.0164	10.3711	0.0964	7.7786
24	6.341	0.1577	66.765	0.0150	10.5288	0.0950	8.0066
25	6.848	0.1460	73.106	0.0137	10.6748	0.0937	8.2254
26	7.396	0.1352	79.954	0.0125	10.8100	0.0925	8.4352
27	7.988	0.1252	87.351	0.0115	10.9352	0.0915	8.6363
28	8.627	0.1159	95.339	0.0105	11.0511	0.0905	8.8289
29	9.317	0.1073	103.966	0.0096	11.1584	0.0896	9.0133
30	10.063	0.0994	113.283	0.0088	11.2578	0.0888	9.1897
31	10.868	0.0920	123.346	0.0081	11.3498	0.0881	9.3584
32	11.737	0.0852	134.214	0.0075	11.4350	0.0875	9.5197
33	12.676	0.0789	145.951	0.0069	11.5139	0.0869	9.6737
34	13.690	0.0731	158.627	0.0063	11.5869	0.0863	9.8208
35	14.785	0.0676	172.317	0.0058	11.6546	0.0858	9.9611
40	21.725	0.0460	259.057	0.0039	11.9246	0.0839	10.5699
45	31.920	0.0313	386.506	0.0026	12.1084	0.0826	11.0447
50	46.902	0.0213	573.770	0.0018	12.2335	0.0818	11.4107
55	68.914	0.0145	848.923	0.0012	12.3186	0.0812	11.6902
60	101.257	0.0099	1253.213	0.0008	12.3766	0.0808	11.9015
65	148.780	0.0067	1847.248	0.0006	12.4160	0.0806	12.0602
70	218.606	0.0046	2720.080	0.0004	12.4428	0.0804	12.1783
75	321.205	0.0031	4002.557	0.0003	12.4611	0.0803	12.2658
80	471.955	0.0021	5886.935	0.0002	12.4735	0.0802	12.3301
85	693.456	0.0015	8655.706	0.0001	12.4820	0.0801	12.3773
90	1018.915	0.0010	12723.939	0.0001	12.4877	0.0801	12.4116
95	1497.121	0.0007	18701.507	0.0001	12.4917	0.0801	12.4365
100	2199.761	0.0005	27484.516	0.0001	12.4943	0.0800	12.4545

TABLE 14 9 Percent Interest Factors for Annual Compounding Interest

	Single Payment		Equal-Payment Series				Uniform Gradient-Series Factor
	Compound-Amount Factor	Present-Worth Factor	Compound-Amount Factor	Sinking-Fund Factor	Present-Worth Factor	Capital-Recovery Factor	
n	To Find F Given P $F/P\ i, n$	To Find P Given F $P/F\ i, n$	To Find F Given A $F/A\ i, n$	To Find A Given F $A/F\ i, n$	To Find P Given A $P/A\ i, n$	To Find A Given P $A/P\ i, n$	To Find A Given G $A/G\ i, n$
1	1.090	0.9174	1.000	1.0000	0.9174	1.0900	0.0000
2	1.188	0.8417	2.090	0.4785	1.7591	0.5685	0.4785
3	1.295	0.7722	3.278	0.3051	2.5313	0.3951	0.9426
4	1.412	0.7084	4.573	0.2187	3.2397	0.3087	1.3925
5	1.539	0.6499	5.985	0.1671	3.8897	0.2571	1.8282
6	1.677	0.5963	7.523	0.1329	4.4859	0.2229	2.2498
7	1.828	0.5470	9.200	0.1087	5.0330	0.1987	2.6574
8	1.993	0.5019	11.028	0.0907	5.5348	0.1807	3.0512
9	2.172	0.4604	13.021	0.0768	5.9953	0.1668	3.4312
10	2.367	0.4224	15.193	0.0658	6.4177	0.1558	3.7978
11	2.580	0.3875	17.560	0.0570	6.8052	0.1470	4.1510
12	2.813	0.3555	20.141	0.0497	7.1607	0.1397	4.4910
13	3.066	0.3262	22.953	0.0436	7.4869	0.1336	4.8182
14	3.342	0.2993	26.019	0.0384	7.7862	0.1284	5.1326
15	3.642	0.2745	29.361	0.0341	8.0607	0.1241	5.4346
16	3.970	0.2519	33.003	0.0303	8.3126	0.1203	5.7245
17	4.328	0.2311	36.974	0.0271	8.5436	0.1171	6.0024
18	4.717	0.2120	41.301	0.0242	8.7556	0.1142	6.2687
19	5.142	0.1945	46.018	0.0217	8.9501	0.1117	6.5236
20	5.604	0.1784	51.160	0.0196	9.1286	0.1096	6.7675
21	6.109	0.1637	56.765	0.0176	9.2923	0.1076	7.0006
22	6.659	0.1502	62.873	0.0159	9.4424	0.1059	7.2232
23	7.258	0.1378	69.532	0.0144	9.5802	0.1044	7.4358
24	7.911	0.1264	76.790	0.0130	9.7066	0.1030	7.6384
25	8.623	0.1160	84.701	0.0118	9.8226	0.1018	7.8316
26	9.399	0.1064	93.324	0.0107	9.9290	0.1007	8.0156
27	10.245	0.0976	102.723	0.0097	10.0266	0.0997	8.1906
28	11.167	0.0896	112.968	0.0089	10.1161	0.0989	8.3572
29	12.172	0.0822	124.135	0.0081	10.1983	0.0981	8.5154
30	13.268	0.0754	136.308	0.0073	10.2737	0.0973	8.6657
31	14.462	0.0692	149.575	0.0067	10.3428	0.0967	8.8083
32	15.763	0.0634	164.037	0.0061	10.4063	0.0961	8.9436
33	17.182	0.0582	179.800	0.0056	10.4645	0.0956	9.0718
34	18.728	0.0534	196.982	0.0051	10.5178	0.0951	9.1933
35	20.414	0.0490	215.711	0.0046	10.5668	0.0946	9.3083
40	31.409	0.0318	337.882	0.0030	10.7574	0.0930	9.7957
45	48.327	0.0207	525.859	0.0019	10.8812	0.0919	10.1603
50	74.358	0.0135	815.084	0.0012	10.9617	0.0912	10.4295
55	114.408	0.0088	1260.092	0.0008	11.0140	0.0908	10.6261
60	176.031	0.0057	1944.792	0.0005	11.0480	0.0905	10.7683
65	270.846	0.0037	2998.288	0.0003	11.0701	0.0903	10.8702
70	416.730	0.0024	4619.223	0.0002	11.0845	0.0902	10.9427
75	641.191	0.0016	7113.232	0.0002	11.0938	0.0902	10.9940
80	986.552	0.0010	10950.574	0.0001	11.0999	0.0901	11.0299
85	1517.932	0.0007	16854.800	0.0001	11.1038	0.0901	11.0551
90	2335.527	0.0004	25939.184	0.0001	11.1064	0.0900	11.0726
95	3593.497	0.0003	39916.635	0.0000	11.1080	0.0900	11.0847
100	5529.041	0.0002	61422.675	0.0000	11.1091	0.0900	11.0930

TABLE 15 10 Percent Interest Factors for Annual Compounding Interest

	Single Payment		Equal-Payment Series				Uniform Gradient-Series Factor
	Compound-Amount Factor	Present-Worth Factor	Compound-Amount Factor	Sinking-Fund Factor	Present-Worth Factor	Capital-Recovery Factor	
n	To Find F Given P F/P i, n	To Find P Given F P/F i, n	To Find F Given A F/A i, n	To Find A Given F A/F i, n	To Find P Given A P/A i, n	To Find A Given P A/P i, n	To Find A Given G A/G i, n
1	1.100	0.9091	1.000	1.0000	0.9091	1.1000	0.0000
2	1.210	0.8265	2.100	0.4762	1.7355	0.5762	0.4762
3	1.331	0.7513	3.310	0.3021	2.4869	0.4021	0.9366
4	1.464	0.6830	4.641	0.2155	3.1699	0.3155	1.3812
5	1.611	0.6209	6.105	0.1638	3.7908	0.2638	1.8101
6	1.772	0.5645	7.716	0.1296	4.3553	0.2296	2.2236
7	1.949	0.5132	9.487	0.1054	4.8684	0.2054	2.6216
8	2.144	0.4665	11.436	0.0875	5.3349	0.1875	3.0045
9	2.358	0.4241	13.579	0.0737	5.7950	0.1737	3.3724
10	2.594	0.3856	15.937	0.0628	6.1446	0.1628	3.7255
11	2.853	0.3505	18.531	0.0540	6.4951	0.1540	4.0641
12	3.138	0.3186	21.384	0.0468	6.8137	0.1468	4.3884
13	3.452	0.2897	24.523	0.0408	7.1034	0.1408	4.6988
14	3.798	0.2633	27.975	0.0358	7.3667	0.1358	4.9955
15	4.177	0.2394	31.772	0.0315	7.6061	0.1315	5.2789
16	4.595	0.2176	35.950	0.0278	7.8237	0.1278	5.5493
17	5.054	0.1979	40.545	0.0247	8.0216	0.1247	5.8071
18	5.560	0.1799	45.599	0.0219	8.2014	0.1219	6.0526
19	6.116	0.1635	51.159	0.0196	8.3649	0.1196	6.2861
20	6.728	0.1487	57.275	0.0175	8.5136	0.1175	6.5081
21	7.400	0.1351	64.003	0.0156	8.6487	0.1156	6.7189
22	8.140	0.1229	71.403	0.0140	8.7716	0.1140	6.9189
23	8.953	0.1117	79.543	0.0126	8.8832	0.1126	7.1085
24	9.850	0.1015	88.497	0.0113	8.9848	0.1113	7.2881
25	10.835	0.0923	98.347	0.0102	9.0771	0.1102	7.4580
26	11.918	0.0839	109.182	0.0092	9.1610	0.1092	7.6187
27	13.110	0.0763	121.100	0.0083	9.2372	0.1083	7.7704
28	14.421	0.0694	134.210	0.0075	9.3066	0.1075	7.9137
29	15.863	0.0630	148.631	0.0067	9.3696	0.1067	8.0489
30	17.449	0.0573	164.494	0.0061	9.4269	0.1061	8.1762
31	19.194	0.0521	181.943	0.0055	9.4790	0.1055	8.2962
32	21.114	0.0474	201.138	0.0050	9.5264	0.1050	8.4091
33	23.225	0.0431	222.252	0.0045	9.5694	0.1045	8.5152
34	25.548	0.0392	245.477	0.0041	9.6086	0.1041	8.6149
35	28.102	0.0356	271.024	0.0037	9.6442	0.1037	8.7086
40	45.259	0.0221	442.593	0.0023	9.7791	0.1023	9.0962
45	72.890	0.0137	718.905	0.0014	9.8628	0.1014	9.3741
50	117.391	0.0085	1163.909	0.0009	9.9148	0.1009	9.5704
55	189.059	0.0053	1880.591	0.0005	9.9471	0.1005	9.7075
60	304.482	0.0033	3034.816	0.0003	9.9672	0.1003	9.8023
65	490.371	0.0020	4893.707	0.0002	9.9796	0.1002	9.8672
70	789.747	0.0013	7887.470	0.0001	9.9873	0.1001	9.9113
75	1271.895	0.0008	12708.954	0.0001	9.9921	0.1001	9.9410
80	2048.400	0.0005	20474.002	0.0001	9.9951	0.1001	9.9609
85	3298.969	0.0003	32979.690	0.0000	9.9970	0.1000	9.9742
90	5313.023	0.0002	53120.226	0.0000	9.9981	0.1000	9.9831
95	8556.676	0.0001	85556.760	0.0000	9.9988	0.1000	9.9889
100	13780.612	0.0001	137796.123	0.0000	9.9993	0.1000	9.9928

TABLE 16 12 Percent Interest Factors for Annual Compounding Interest

	Single Payment		Equal-Payment Series				Uniform Gradient-Series Factor
	Compound-Amount Factor	Present-Worth Factor	Compound-Amount Factor	Sinking-Fund Factor	Present-Worth Factor	Capital-Recovery Factor	
n	To Find F Given P F/P i, n	To Find P Given F P/F i, n	To Find F Given A F/A i, n	To Find A Given F A/F i, n	To Find P Given A P/A i, n	To Find A Given P A/P i, n	To Find A Given G A/G i, n
1	1.120	0.8929	1.000	1.0000	0.8929	1.1200	0.0000
2	1.254	0.7972	2.120	0.4717	1.6901	0.5917	0.4717
3	1.405	0.7118	3.374	0.2964	2.4018	0.4164	0.9246
4	1.574	0.6355	4.779	0.2092	3.0374	0.3292	1.3589
5	1.762	0.5674	6.353	0.1574	3.6048	0.2774	1.7746
6	1.974	0.5066	8.115	0.1232	4.1114	0.2432	2.1721
7	2.211	0.4524	10.089	0.0991	4.5638	0.2191	2.5515
8	2.476	0.4039	12.300	0.0813	4.9676	0.2013	2.9132
9	2.773	0.3606	14.776	0.0677	5.3283	0.1877	3.2574
10	3.106	0.3220	17.549	0.0570	5.6502	0.1770	3.5847
11	3.479	0.2875	20.655	0.0484	5.9377	0.1684	3.8953
12	3.896	0.2567	24.133	0.0414	6.1944	0.1614	4.1897
13	4.364	0.2292	28.029	0.0357	6.4236	0.1557	4.4683
14	4.887	0.2046	32.393	0.0309	6.6282	0.1509	4.7317
15	5.474	0.1827	37.280	0.0268	6.8109	0.1468	4.9803
16	6.130	0.1631	42.753	0.0234	6.9740	0.1434	5.2147
17	6.866	0.1457	48.884	0.0205	7.1196	0.1405	5.4353
18	7.690	0.1300	55.750	0.0179	7.2497	0.1379	5.6427
19	8.613	0.1161	63.440	0.0158	7.3658	0.1358	5.8375
20	9.646	0.1037	72.052	0.0139	7.4695	0.1339	6.0202
21	10.804	0.0926	81.699	0.0123	7.5620	0.1323	6.1913
22	12.100	0.0827	92.503	0.0108	7.6447	0.1308	6.3514
23	13.552	0.0738	104.603	0.0096	7.7184	0.1296	6.5010
24	15.179	0.0659	118.155	0.0085	7.7843	0.1285	6.6407
25	17.000	0.0588	133.334	0.0075	7.8431	0.1275	6.7708
26	19.040	0.0525	150.334	0.0067	7.8957	0.1267	6.8921
27	21.325	0.0469	169.374	0.0059	7.9426	0.1259	7.0049
28	23.884	0.0419	190.699	0.0053	7.9844	0.1253	7.1098
29	26.750	0.0374	214.583	0.0047	8.0218	0.1247	7.2071
30	29.960	0.0334	241.333	0.0042	8.0552	0.1242	7.2974
31	33.555	0.0298	271.293	0.0037	8.0850	0.1237	7.3811
32	37.582	0.0266	304.848	0.0033	8.1116	0.1233	7.4586
33	42.092	0.0238	342.429	0.0029	8.1354	0.1229	7.5303
34	47.143	0.0212	384.521	0.0026	8.1566	0.1226	7.5965
35	52.800	0.0189	431.664	0.0023	8.1755	0.1223	7.6577
40	93.051	0.0108	767.091	0.0013	8.2438	0.1213	7.8988
45	163.988	0.0061	1358.230	0.0007	8.2825	0.1207	8.0572
50	289.002	0.0035	2400.018	0.0004	8.3045	0.1204	8.1597

TABLE 17 15 Percent Interest Factors for Annual Compounding Interest

	Single Payment		Equal-Payment Series				Uniform Gradient-Series Factor
	Compound-Amount Factor	Present-Worth Factor	Compound-Amount Factor	Sinking-Fund Factor	Present-Worth Factor	Capital-Recovery Factor	
n	To Find F Given P $F/P\ i, n$	To Find F Given F $P/F\ i, n$	To Find F Given A $F/A\ i, n$	To Find A Given F $A/F\ i, n$	To Find P Given A $P/A\ i, n$	To Find A Given P $A/P\ i, n$	To Find A Given G $A/G\ i, n$
1	1.150	0.8696	1.000	1.0000	0.8696	1.1500	0.0000
2	1.323	0.7562	2.150	0.4651	1.6257	0.6151	0.4651
3	1.521	0.6575	3.473	0.2880	2.2832	0.4380	0.9071
4	1.749	0.5718	4.993	0.2003	2.8850	0.3503	1.3263
5	2.011	0.4972	6.742	0.1483	3.3522	0.2983	1.7228
6	2.313	0.4323	8.754	0.1142	3.7845	0.2642	2.0972
7	2.660	0.3759	11.067	0.0904	4.1604	0.2404	2.4499
8	3.059	0.3269	13.727	0.0729	4.4873	0.2229	2.7813
9	3.518	0.2843	16.786	0.0596	4.7716	0.2096	3.0922
10	4.046	0.2472	20.304	0.0493	5.0188	0.1993	3.3832
11	4.652	0.2150	24.349	0.0411	5.2337	0.1911	3.6550
12	5.350	0.1869	29.002	0.0345	5.4206	0.1845	3.9082
13	6.153	0.1625	34.352	0.0291	5.5832	0.1791	4.1438
14	7.076	0.1413	40.505	0.0247	5.7245	0.1747	4.3624
15	8.137	0.1229	47.580	0.0210	5.8474	0.1710	4.5650
16	9.358	0.1069	55.717	0.0180	5.9542	0.1680	4.7523
17	10.761	0.0929	65.075	0.0154	6.0472	0.1654	4.9251
18	12.375	0.0808	75.836	0.0132	6.1280	0.1632	5.0843
19	14.232	0.0703	88.212	0.0113	6.1982	0.1613	5.2307
20	16.367	0.0611	102.444	0.0098	6.2593	0.1598	5.3651
21	18.822	0.0531	118.810	0.0084	6.3125	0.1584	5.4883
22	21.645	0.0462	137.632	0.0073	6.3587	0.1573	5.6010
23	24.891	0.0402	159.276	0.0063	6.3988	0.1563	5.7040
24	28.625	0.0349	184.168	0.0054	6.4338	0.1554	5.7979
25	32.919	0.0304	212.793	0.0047	6.4642	0.1547	5.8834
26	37.857	0.0264	245.712	0.0041	6.4906	0.1541	5.9612
27	43.535	0.0230	283.569	0.0035	6.5135	0.1535	6.0319
28	50.066	0.0200	327.104	0.0031	6.5335	0.1531	6.0960
29	57.575	0.0174	377.170	0.0027	6.5509	0.1527	6.1541
30	66.212	0.0151	434.745	0.0023	6.5660	0.1523	6.2066
31	76.144	0.0131	500.957	0.0020	6.5791	0.1520	6.2541
32	87.565	0.0114	577.100	0.0017	6.5905	0.1517	6.2970
33	100.700	0.0099	664.666	0.0015	6.6005	0.1515	6.3357
34	115.805	0.0086	765.365	0.0013	6.6091	0.1513	6.3705
35	133.176	0.0075	881.170	0.0011	6.6166	0.1511	6.4019
40	267.864	0.0037	1779.090	0.0006	6.6418	0.1506	6.5168
45	538.769	0.0019	3585.128	0.0003	6.6543	0.1503	6.5830
50	1083.657	0.0009	7217.716	0.0002	6.6605	0.1501	6.6205

TABLE 18 20 Percent Interest Factors for Annual Compounding Interest

	Single Payment		Equal-Payment Series				Uniform Gradient-Series Factor
	Compound-Amount Factor	Present-Worth Factor	Compound-Amount Factor	Sinking-Fund Factor	Present-Worth Factor	Capital-Recovery Factor	
n	To Find F Given P F/P i, n	To Find P Given F P/F i, n	To Find F Given A F/A i, n	To Find A Given F A/F i, n	To Find P Given A P/A i, n	To Find A Given P A/P i, n	To Find A Given G A/G i, n
1	1.200	0.8333	1.000	1.0000	0.8333	1.2000	0.0000
2	1.440	0.6945	2.200	0.4546	1.5278	0.6546	0.4546
3	1.728	0.5787	3.640	0.2747	2.1065	0.4747	0.8791
4	2.074	0.4823	5.368	0.1863	2.5887	0.3863	1.2742
5	2.488	0.4019	7.442	0.1344	2.9906	0.3344	1.6405
6	2.986	0.3349	9.930	0.1007	3.3255	0.3007	1.9788
7	3.583	0.2791	12.916	0.0774	3.6046	0.2774	2.2902
8	4.300	0.2326	16.499	0.0606	3.8372	0.2606	2.5756
9	5.160	0.1938	20.799	0.0481	4.0310	0.2481	2.8364
10	6.192	0.1615	25.959	0.0385	4.1925	0.2385	3.0739
11	7.430	0.1346	32.150	0.0311	4.3271	0.2311	3.2893
12	8.916	0.1122	39.581	0.0253	4.4392	0.2253	3.4841
13	10.699	0.0935	48.497	0.0206	4.5327	0.2206	3.6597
14	12.839	0.0779	59.196	0.0169	4.6106	0.2169	3.8175
15	15.407	0.0649	72.035	0.0139	4.6755	0.2139	3.9589
16	18.488	0.0541	87.442	0.0114	4.7296	0.2114	4.0851
17	22.186	0.0451	105.931	0.0095	4.7746	0.2095	4.1976
18	26.623	0.0376	128.117	0.0078	4.8122	0.2078	4.2975
19	31.948	0.0313	154.740	0.0065	4.8435	0.2065	4.3861
20	38.338	0.0261	186.688	0.0054	4.8696	0.2054	4.4644
21	46.005	0.0217	225.026	0.0045	4.8913	0.2045	4.5334
22	55.206	0.0181	271.031	0.0037	4.9094	0.2037	4.5942
23	66.247	0.0151	326.237	0.0031	4.9245	0.2031	4.6475
24	79.497	0.0126	392.484	0.0026	4.9371	0.2026	4.6943
25	95.396	0.0105	471.981	0.0021	4.9476	0.2021	4.7352
26	114.475	0.0087	567.377	0.0018	4.9563	0.2018	4.7709
27	137.371	0.0073	681.853	0.0015	4.9636	0.2015	4.8020
28	164.845	0.0061	819.223	0.0012	4.9697	0.2012	4.8291
29	197.814	0.0051	984.068	0.0010	4.9747	0.2010	4.8527
30	237.376	0.0042	1181.882	0.0009	4.9789	0.2009	4.8731
31	284.852	0.0035	1419.258	0.0007	4.9825	0.2007	4.8908
32	341.822	0.0029	1704.109	0.0006	4.9854	0.2006	4.9061
33	410.186	0.0024	2045.931	0.0005	4.9878	0.2005	4.9194
34	492.224	0.0020	2456.118	0.0004	4.9899	0.2004	4.9308
35	590.668	0.0017	2948.341	0.0003	4.9915	0.2003	4.9407
40	1469.772	0.0007	7343.858	0.0002	4.9966	0.2001	4.9728
45	3657.262	0.0003	18281.310	0.0001	4.9986	0.2001	4.9877
50	9100.438	0.0001	45497.191	0.0000	4.9995	0.2000	4.9945

TABLE 19 25 Percent Interest Factors for Annual Compounding Interest

n	Single Payment		Equal-Payment Series				Uniform Gradient-Series Factor
	Compound-Amount Factor	Present-Worth Factor	Compound-Amount Factor	Sinking-Fund Factor	Present-Worth Factor	Capital-Recovery Factor	
	To Find F Given P F/P i, n	To Find P Given F P/F i, n	To Find F Given A F/A i, n	To Find A Given F A/F i, n	To Find P Given A P/A i, n	To Find A Given P A/P i, n	To Find A Given G A/G i, n
1	1.250	0.8000	1.000	1.0000	0.8000	1.2500	0.0000
2	1.563	0.6400	2.250	0.4445	1.4400	0.6945	0.4445
3	1.953	0.5120	3.813	0.2623	1.9520	0.5123	0.8525
4	2.441	0.4096	5.766	0.1735	2.3616	0.4235	1.2249
5	3.052	0.3277	8.207	0.1219	2.6893	0.3719	1.5631
6	3.815	0.2622	11.259	0.0888	2.9514	0.3388	1.8683
7	4.768	0.2097	15.073	0.0664	3.1661	0.3164	2.1424
8	5.960	0.1678	19.842	0.0504	3.3289	0.3004	2.3873
9	7.451	0.1342	25.802	0.0388	3.4631	0.2888	2.6048
10	9.313	0.1074	33.253	0.0301	3.5705	0.2801	2.7971
11	11.642	0.0859	42.566	0.0235	3.6564	0.2735	2.9663
12	14.552	0.0687	54.208	0.0185	3.7251	0.2685	3.1145
13	18.190	0.0550	68.760	0.0146	3.7801	0.2646	3.2438
14	22.737	0.0440	86.949	0.0115	3.8241	0.2615	3.3560
15	28.422	0.0352	109.687	0.0091	3.8593	0.2591	3.4530
16	35.527	0.0282	138.109	0.0073	3.8874	0.2573	3.5366
17	44.409	0.0225	173.636	0.0058	3.9099	0.2558	3.6084
18	55.511	0.0180	218.045	0.0046	3.9280	0.2546	3.6698
19	69.389	0.0144	273.556	0.0037	3.9424	0.2537	3.7222
20	86.736	0.0115	342.945	0.0029	3.9539	0.2529	3.7667
21	108.420	0.0092	429.681	0.0023	3.9631	0.2523	3.8045
22	135.525	0.0074	538.101	0.0019	3.9705	0.2519	3.8365
23	169.407	0.0059	673.626	0.0015	3.9764	0.2515	3.8634
24	211.758	0.0047	843.033	0.0012	3.9811	0.2512	3.8861
25	264.698	0.0038	1054.791	0.0010	3.9849	0.2510	3.9052
26	330.872	0.0030	1319.489	0.0008	3.9879	0.2508	3.9212
27	413.590	0.0024	1650.361	0.0006	3.9903	0.2506	3.9346
28	516.988	0.0019	2063.952	0.0005	3.9923	0.2505	3.9457
29	646.235	0.0016	2580.939	0.0004	3.9938	0.2504	3.9551
30	807.794	0.0012	3227.174	0.0003	3.9951	0.2503	3.9628
31	1009.742	0.0010	4034.968	0.0003	3.9960	0.2503	3.9693
32	1262.177	0.0008	5044.710	0.0002	3.9968	0.2502	3.9746
33	1577.722	0.0006	6306.887	0.0002	3.9975	0.2502	3.9791
34	1972.152	0.0005	7884.609	0.0001	3.9980	0.2501	3.9828
35	2465.190	0.0004	9856.761	0.0001	3.9984	0.2501	3.9858

TABLE 20 30 Percent Interest Factors for Annual Compounding Interest

	Single Payment		Equal-Payment Series				Uniform Gradient-Series Factor
	Compound-Amount Factor	Present-Worth Factor	Compound-Amount Factor	Sinking-Fund Factor	Present-Worth Factor	Capital-Recovery Factor	
n	To Find F Given P F/P i, n	To Find P Given F P/F i, n	To Find F Given A F/A i, n	To Find A Given F A/F i, n	To Find P Given A P/A i, n	To Find A Given P A/P i, n	To Find A Given G A/G i, n
1	1.300	0.7692	1.000	1.0000	0.7692	1.3000	0.0000
2	1.690	0.5917	2.300	0.4348	1.3610	0.7348	0.4348
3	2.197	0.4552	3.990	0.2506	1.8161	0.5506	0.8271
4	2.856	0.3501	6.187	0.1616	2.1663	0.4616	1.1783
5	3.713	0.2693	9.043	0.1106	2.4356	0.4106	1.4903
6	4.827	0.2072	12.756	0.0784	2.6428	0.3784	1.7655
7	6.275	0.1594	17.583	0.0569	2.8021	0.3569	2.0063
8	8.157	0.1226	23.858	0.0419	2.9247	0.3419	2.2156
9	10.605	0.0943	32.015	0.0312	3.0190	0.3312	2.3963
10	13.786	0.0725	42.620	0.0235	3.0915	0.3235	2.5512
11	17.922	0.0558	56.405	0.0177	3.1473	0.3177	2.6833
12	23.298	0.0429	74.327	0.0135	3.1903	0.3135	2.7952
13	30.288	0.0330	97.625	0.0103	3.2233	0.3103	2.8895
14	39.374	0.0254	127.913	0.0078	3.2487	0.3078	2.9685
15	51.186	0.0195	167.286	0.0060	3.2682	0.3060	3.0345
16	66.542	0.0150	218.472	0.0046	3.2832	0.3046	3.0892
17	86.504	0.0116	285.014	0.0035	3.2948	0.3035	3.1345
18	112.455	0.0089	371.518	0.0027	3.3037	0.3027	3.1718
19	146.192	0.0069	483.973	0.0021	3.3105	0.3021	3.2025
20	190.050	0.0053	630.165	0.0016	3.3158	0.3016	3.2276
21	247.065	0.0041	820.215	0.0012	3.3199	0.3012	3.2480
22	321.184	0.0031	1067.280	0.0009	3.3230	0.3009	3.2646
23	417.539	0.0024	1388.464	0.0007	3.3254	0.3007	3.2781
24	542.801	0.0019	1806.003	0.0006	3.3272	0.3006	3.2890
25	705.641	0.0014	2348.803	0.0004	3.3286	0.3004	3.2979
26	917.333	0.0011	3054.444	0.0003	3.3297	0.3003	3.3050
27	1192.533	0.0008	3971.778	0.0003	3.3305	0.3003	3.3107
28	1550.293	0.0007	5164.311	0.0002	3.3312	0.3002	3.3153
29	2015.381	0.0005	6714.604	0.0002	3.3317	0.3002	3.3189
30	2619.996	0.0004	8729.985	0.0001	3.3321	0.3001	3.3219
31	3405.994	0.0003	11349.981	0.0001	3.3324	0.3001	3.3242
32	4427.793	0.0002	14755.975	0.0001	3.3326	0.3001	3.3261
33	5756.130	0.0002	19183.768	0.0001	3.3328	0.3001	3.3276
34	7482.970	0.0001	24939.899	0.0001	3.3329	0.3001	3.3288
35	9727.860	0.0001	32422.868	0.0000	3.3330	0.3000	3.3297

TABLE 21 40 Percent Interest Factors for Annual Compounding Interest

n	Single Payment		Equal-Payment Series				Uniform Gradient-Series Factor
	Compound-Amount Factor	Present-Worth Factor	Compound-Amount Factor	Sinking-Fund Factor	Present-Worth Factor	Capital-Recovery Factor	
	To Find F Given P F/P i, n	*To Find P Given F P/F i, n*	*To Find F Given A F/A i, n*	*To Find A Given F A/F i, n*	*To Find P Given A P/A i, n*	*To Find A Given P A/P i, n*	*To Find A Given G A/G i, n*
1	1.400	0.7143	1.000	1.0000	0.7143	1.4000	0.0000
2	1.960	0.5102	2.400	0.4167	1.2245	0.8167	0.4167
3	2.744	0.3644	4.360	0.2294	1.5889	0.6294	0.7798
4	3.842	0.2603	7.104	0.1408	1.8492	0.5408	1.0924
5	5.378	0.1859	10.946	0.0914	2.0352	0.4914	1.3580
6	7.530	0.1328	16.324	0.0613	2.1680	0.4613	1.5811
7	10.541	0.0949	23.853	0.0419	2.2628	0.4419	1.7664
8	14.758	0.0678	34.395	0.0291	2.3306	0.4291	1.9185
9	20.661	0.0484	49.153	0.0204	2.3790	0.4204	2.0423
10	28.925	0.0346	69.814	0.0143	2.4136	0.4143	2.1419
11	40.496	0.0247	98.739	0.0101	2.4383	0.4101	2.2215
12	56.694	0.0176	139.235	0.0072	2.4559	0.4072	2.2845
13	79.371	0.0126	195.929	0.0051	2.4685	0.4051	2.3341
14	111.120	0.0090	275.300	0.0036	2.4775	0.4036	2.3729
15	155.568	0.0064	386.420	0.0026	2.4839	0.4026	2.4030
16	217.795	0.0046	541.988	0.0019	2.4885	0.4019	2.4262
17	304.913	0.0033	759.784	0.0013	2.4918	0.4013	2.4441
18	426.879	0.0024	1064.697	0.0009	2.4942	0.4009	2.4577
19	597.630	0.0017	1491.576	0.0007	2.4958	0.4007	2.4682
20	836.683	0.0012	2089.206	0.0005	2.4970	0.4005	2.4761
21	1171.356	0.0009	2925.889	0.0004	2.4979	0.4004	2.4821
22	1639.898	0.0006	4097.245	0.0003	2.4985	0.4003	2.4866
23	2295.857	0.0004	5737.142	0.00018	2.4989	0.4002	2.4900
24	3214.200	0.0003	8032.999	0.00013	2.4992	0.4001	2.4925
25	4499.880	0.0002	11247.199	0.00010	2.4995	0.4001	2.4945
26	6299.831	0.0002	15747.079	0.00007	2.4996	0.4001	2.4959
27	8819.764	0.0001	22046.910	0.00006	2.4997	0.4001	2.4969
28	12347.670	0.0001	30866.674	0.00004	2.4998	0.4000	2.4977
29	17286.737	0.0001	43214.344	0.00003	2.4999	0.4000	2.4983
30	24201.432	0.0001	60501.081	0.00003	2.4999	0.4000	2.4988

TABLE 22   50 Percent Interest Factors for Annual Compounding Interest

n	Single Payment		Equal-Payment Series				Uniform Gradient-Series Factor
	Compound-Amount Factor	Present-Worth Factor	Compound-Amount Factor	Sinking-Fund Factor	Present-Worth Factor	Capital-Recovery Factor	
	To Find F Given P F/P i, n	To Find P Given F P/F i, n	To Find F Given A F/A i, n	To Find A Given F A/F i, n	To Find P Given A P/A i, n	To Find A Given P A/P i, n	To Find A Given G A/G i, n
1	1.500	0.6667	1.000	1.0000	0.6667	1.5000	0.0000
2	2.250	0.4445	2.500	0.4000	1.1111	0.9000	0.4000
3	3.375	0.2963	4.750	0.2105	1.4074	0.7105	1.7369
4	5.063	0.1975	8.125	0.1231	1.6049	0.6231	1.0154
5	7.594	0.1317	13.188	0.0758	1.7366	0.5758	1.2417
6	11.391	0.0878	20.781	0.0481	1.8244	0.5481	1.4226
7	17.086	0.0585	32.172	0.0311	1.8830	0.5311	1.5648
8	25.629	0.0390	49.258	0.0203	1.9220	0.5203	1.6752
9	38.443	0.0260	74.887	0.0134	1.9480	0.5134	1.7596
10	57.665	0.0174	113.330	0.0088	1.9653	0.5088	1.8235
11	86.498	0.0116	170.995	0.0059	1.9769	0.5059	1.8714
12	129.746	0.0077	257.493	0.0039	1.9846	0.5039	1.9068
13	194.620	0.0051	387.239	0.0026	1.9897	0.5026	1.9329
14	291.929	0.0034	581.859	0.0017	1.9932	0.5017	1.9519
15	437.894	0.0023	873.788	0.0012	1.9954	0.5012	1.9657
16	656.841	0.0015	1311.682	0.0008	1.9970	0.5008	1.9756
17	985.261	0.0010	1968.523	0.0005	1.9980	0.5005	1.9827
18	1477.892	0.0007	2953.784	0.0003	1.9987	0.5003	1.9878
19	2216.838	0.0005	4431.676	0.0002	1.9991	0.5002	1.9914
20	3325.257	0.0003	6648.513	0.00016	1.9994	0.5002	1.9940
21	4987.885	0.0002	9973.770	0.00011	1.9996	0.5001	1.9958
22	7481.828	0.0001	14961.655	0.00008	1.9997	0.5001	1.9971
23	11222.741	0.0001	22443.483	0.00005	1.9998	0.5001	1.9980
24	16834.112	0.0001	33666.224	0.00004	1.9999	0.5000	1.9986
25	25251.168	0.0000	50500.337	0.00003	1.9999	0.5000	1.9990

48

Statistical Concepts

Charles P. Bonini, Ph.D.
Graduate School of Business
Stanford University

William A. Spurr, Ph.D.
Graduate School of Business
Stanford University

ORGANIZATION OF DATA: RATIOS AND FREQUENCY DISTRIBUTIONS

An early step in any investigation is the collection and organization of data so that meaningful conclusions can be drawn. Two important tools for data analysis, ratios and frequency distributions, are treated in this section.

Ratios

A given number can often be better understood by comparing it to some other number in the form of a *ratio* or *rate*. The statement that 120,000 people were unemployed in a given state is less meaningful than to note the unemployment rate of 6.2 percent (the ratio of the number unemployed to the total work force). This rate can then be compared with the rate for other months or years to determine the trend of unemployment. Similarly, it often makes more sense to compare the costs for a business firm as a percentage of sales rather than to examine the costs by themselves.

Ratios are computed from a numerator and a base (denominator). For a ratio to be meaningful, these may have to be adjusted or refined so as to exclude any extraneous factors that would obscure the direct

---

TABLE 1 Fatalities in Motor Vehicle Accidents, 1950 and 1971

		1950	1972	Percent Change
1.	Persons killed in motor accidents	34,763	56,600	+63%
2.	Deaths per 100,000 population	23.0	27.2	+18
3.	Deaths per 10,000 motor vehicles	7.1	4.66	−34
4.	Deaths per 100,000,000 vehicle-miles	7.6	4.53	−40

SOURCE: National Safety Council, *Accident Facts*, 1973, p. 59.

---

relationship between them. For example, the base of the unemployment rate is not the total population; excluded are children, retired persons, and those not seeking employment such as housewives. As another example, consider the data shown in Table 1 which gives the trend of deaths in automobile accidents from 1950 to 1971.

Since the number of deaths increased by 63 percent from 1950 to 1972, one might conclude that the automobile menace is increasing. However, when this ratio is refined by appropriately relating deaths to motor vehicles or, better still, vehicle miles, the opposite conclusion is reached.

There are no set rules on how to refine a ratio to make it more meaningful. It is necessary to determine what extraneous factors can be misleading and to eliminate them from the numerator or base as appropriate, and this is ultimately a matter of judgment and common sense. Many specific ratios have been identified for use in financial analysis, and their description is given elsewhere in this volume.

Frequency Distributions

Generally, ratios are used for *attribute* data (attribute data are data that are sorted into groups, with a count made of each group). When data can be measured along an interval scale, they are called *variable* data, and the usual form of organization is to group the data by size into a *frequency distribution*. A frequency distribution is a device for summarizing an unwieldly number of figures so that a maximum of information can be presented with a minimum of detail.

Variables may represent either discrete or continuous data. Discrete data have distinct values with no intermediate points. Thus, the number of children in a family can be two or three, but not 2.7. Continuous data can have any value over a range, such as the exact heights of men. However, continuous data are often treated as being discrete, as when heights are rounded to the nearest inch.

The data under analysis should be *homogeneous*, i.e., sufficiently alike to be comparable for the purposes of the study. Thus, in a study of

---

TABLE 2 Frequency Distribution (closing prices of 170 selected stocks)

Closing Price	Midpoint	Number of Stocks	Percent of Stocks
$ 0 and under $ 10	$ 5	37	21.8%
10 and under 20	15	59	34.7
20 and under 30	25	28	16.5
30 and under 40	35	16	9.4
40 and under 50	45	10	5.9
50 and under 60	55	8	4.7
60 and under 70	65	5	2.9
70 and under 80	75	4	2.3
80 and under 90	85	1	0.6
90 and under 100	95	1	0.6
100 and under 110	105	1	0.6
Total		170	100.0%

---

stock prices it might be appropriate to deal only with firms in a given industry (a homogeneous group) rather than to lump several industries together.

Grouping the data into classes. The idea of a frequency distribution is to take a large mass of data and reduce it into an understandable pattern. Consider, for example, the list of stock prices in the daily newspaper financial section. From this list it is easy to obtain the price of an individual stock, but the pattern of prices is not evident. The closing prices of a selected group of 170 stocks for a given day are grouped into the frequency distribution shown in Table 2. A graphic version of this frequency data, called a *histogram*, is shown in Figure 1.

In obtaining the frequency distribution in Table 2, it was necessary to decide upon the number of intervals or *classes* and the width of each interval. In general, it is advisable to divide the data into from 6 to 15 classes. If the number of classes is too small, important characteristics of the data may be concealed. The use of too many classes may show unnecessary detail as well as a confusing zigzag of frequencies. Within these limits the exact number of classes is determined by the width of the interval. This interval is usually selected as a convenient round number located so that if there are clusters in the data, they occur near the midpoint of the interval. Thus, in Table 2 the interval selected was $10, resulting in 11 classes.

The class limits should be stated precisely to avoid ambiguity. Thus, in Table 2 the interval was stated as $10 and under $20, not as $10 to $20, since a stock price of exactly $20 could fall into either of two classes.

All intervals in a frequency distribution should have the same width, if possible, because frequencies are easier to interpret and

FIGURE 1   Histogram (closing price of 170 selected stocks)

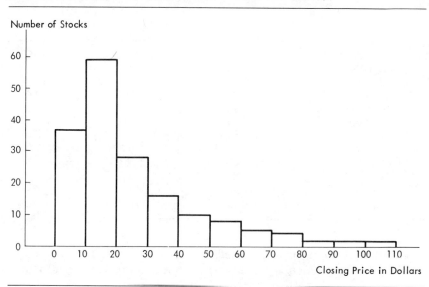

computations are facilitated. Intervals of varying width are confusing. However, unequal intervals are sometimes necessary in order to cover a wide range of data.

Relative frequency distributions.   It is often desirable to show each frequency as a relative part or percentage of the total, as shown in the last column of Table 2. This permits easy comparison of the frequencies in one interval with another on a common 100 percent base and also comparison between one set of data and another (for example, stock prices in different industries).

Cumulative frequency distributions.   It is sometimes convenient to express frequency data as the percent (or frequency) greater than or less than given amounts. The cumulative distribution for the stock price data is shown in Table 3 below and graphed in Figure 2. From the graph, the percentage or frequency of stocks above or below any given price can be easily read.

Shape of frequency distributions.   Frequency distributions can have many shapes, and some of these are illustrated in Figure 3. Note that the curves in Figure 3 are smooth curves, called *frequency curves*, and could be obtained by smoothing out the histogram. The important bell-shaped *normal curve* is shown in panel A of Figure 3. This curve

TABLE 3 Cumulative Frequency Distributions (closing prices of 170 selected stocks)

Closing Price	Number in Class with Lower Limit Shown	Number with Price Less	Number with Price as High or Higher
0	37	0	170
10	59	37	133
20	28	96	74
30	16	124	46
40	10	140	30
50	8	150	20
60	5	158	12
70	4	163	7
80	1	167	3
90	1	168	2
100	1	169	1
110	0	170	0

FIGURE 2 Cumulative Frequency Curves (closing prices of 170 selected stocks)

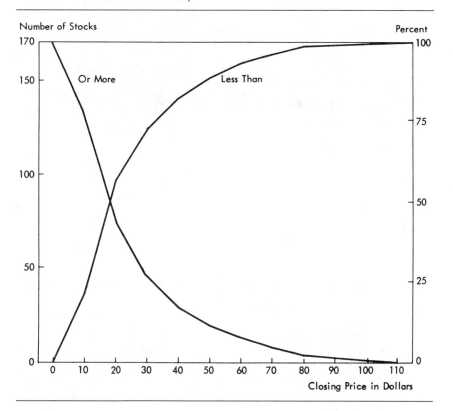

FIGURE 3 Types of Frequency Curves

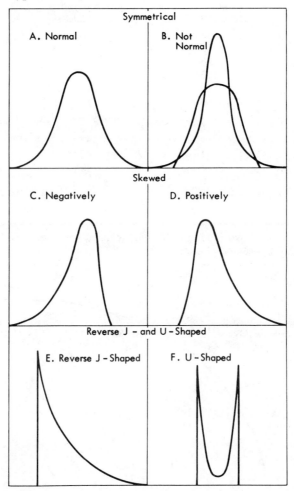

Types of Frequency Curves

describes the distribution of many kinds of measurements in the physical, biological, and social sciences. In addition, it reflects variations due to chance and as such represents a curve for the measurement of sampling error. The two curves in panel B are symmetrical but differ from the normal curve. The curves in panels C and D represent distributions in which the two branches of the curve are unequal or *skewed*. The panel C curve is skewed to the left or negatively skewed. The panel D curve is skewed to the right or positively skewed. Most economic data, including the example of stock prices in Figure 1, have the positively skewed shape of the curve in panel D. The shapes illustrated in panels E and F occur less frequently.

AVERAGES

Frequency distributions show the general shape of a set of data, but additional measures are usually needed. In particular, some summary measure of average or central tendency is most helpful in characterizing the data.

The Arithmetic Mean

The most common average is the arithmetic mean, or simply the mean. The mean of any series of values is found by adding them and dividing their sum by the number of values.

Ungrouped data. The calculation of the mean is basically the same whether the data are ungrouped or grouped in a frequency distribution. The basic formula is:

$$\overline{X} = \frac{\Sigma X}{n}$$

where $\overline{X}$ is the mean of the variable X; n is the number of values; and Σ is the Greek letter sigma, indicating the summation of all X values. For example, if a stock paid dividends of $4.50, $6.00, $6.20, and $6.90 in the past four years, the mean dividend is the sum of the four amounts (which is $23.60) divided by 4, which gives $5.90.

Grouped data. The mean of data grouped in a frequency distribution is computed in the same way. In a frequency distribution, however, the midpoint of each interval is used to represent all the values of X in the interval. In addition, since there are a number of values in each class, the midpoint is multiplied by the number of values in the class (f) so that they receive a proportionate weight. This is the same as if each value in the class were added, making a total of f additions. The formula is:

$$\overline{X} = \frac{\Sigma fX}{n}$$

where fX is the frequency in an interval times its midpoint X, and ΣfX is the sum of these products. The total number of values, n, is also the sum of the frequencies. The use of this formula is illustrated in Table 4, using

TABLE 4 Computing the Arithmetic Mean from a Frequency Distribution (closing prices of 170 selected stocks)

Closing Price	Class Midpoint X	Number of Stocks (Frequency) f	Frequency × Midpoint fX
$ 0 and under $ 10	$ 5	37	$ 185
10 and under 20	15	59	885
20 and under 30	25	28	700
30 and under 40	35	16	560
40 and under 50	45	10	450
50 and under 60	55	8	440
60 and under 70	65	5	325
70 and under 80	75	4	300
80 and under 90	85	1	85
90 and under 100	95	1	95
100 and under 110	105	1	105
Total		170	$4,130

the data on stock prices from Table 2. Note that ΣfX is 4,130, and n, the number of stocks, is 170. Thus, the mean price of the 170 stocks is:

$$\overline{X} = \frac{\Sigma fX}{n} = \frac{4,130}{170} = 24.29$$

The mean computed from a frequency distribution is subject to a slight error of grouping since all values are rounded to the nearest class midpoint.[1]

The Median

The median of any set of data is the middle value in order of size if n is odd, or the mean of the two middle items if n is even. The median is the middlemost value and is most often used as a descriptive measure when there are a few extreme items in a set of data. Thus, median family income is reported by the Census Bureau and is a better measure of average income than is the mean, which is somewhat higher because it averages in the incomes of very wealthy people.

The median can sometimes be found when other averages are not defined, such as when the items in a set of data are ranked in order rather than measured on a scale. For example, a group of employees

---

[1] Actually, in this example, there is an additional bias. Since stock prices are quoted in eighths of a dollar, the class midpoint is, strictly speaking, one sixteenth less than the values used.

may be ranked in order of merit. The median value can be found and measured.

Ungrouped data. To determine the median in ungrouped data, it is first necessary to arrange the values in an array from highest to lowest (or vice versa). The median is not computed from a formula but is selected as the value whose rank or "order number" is $n/2 + 1/2$, counting from the lowest value. As an example, if we had the 6 numbers

$$2, 4, 6.8, 9.5, 10.2, 11.1$$

the median would be the $6/2 + 1/2 = 3\frac{1}{2}$th item, i.e., halfway between the third and fourth items, or $(6.8 + 9.5)/2 = 8.15$.

Grouped data. When data are grouped in a frequency distribution, the median falls in the class interval whose frequency is the first to make the cumulative frequency greater than $n/2$. It is convenient to call this the median class. The median (Md) may then be located within the median class by means of the interpolation formula

$$Md = L + \frac{i(n/2 - F)}{f}$$

where L is the lower limit of the median class; i, its width; f, its frequency; F, the cumulative frequency below the median class; and n, the total number of values of X.

Using the data on stock prices from Table 2, the median can be calculated as follows. The median class is the one containing the $170/2 = 85$th item in order. This item is in the second interval ($10 and under $20) which contains items from 38th through 96th. The lower limit of the class is $10, which is L; its frequency f is 59; the cumulative frequency below the class is $37 = F$; and the interval width is $10 = i$. The calculated median is thus:

$$Md = L + \frac{i(n/2 - F)}{f}$$

$$= 10 + \frac{10(170/2 - 37)}{59}$$

$$= 18.14$$

The Mode

The mode is the value which occurs most often or the value around which there is the greatest degree of clustering. The modal wage is the one received by the greatest number of workers. The modal interest rate for mortgages is the one that occurs more often than any other. The

---

FIGURE 4 Relationship of Mean, Median, and Mode in a Positively
Skewed Distribution

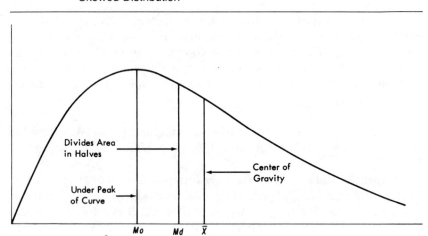

mode is ordinarily meaningful only if there is a marked concentration of
values about a single point.

The mode can occasionally be determined directly from ungrouped
data. When a large proportion of values are equal, no process of
grouping could dislodge this value from its modal position. For example, if a bank charges the general run of its customers 9 percent, then 9
percent is the mode of interest rates, irrespective of what rates apply in
special cases.

In grouped data it is generally best to use the modal class and not to
consider the mode as a single number. Thus, in the example of stock
prices the modal class is $10 and under $20. That is, more stock prices
fall in the interval $10 and under $20 than in any other. The modal class
is only a rough estimate since it depends upon the choice of class limits.

Characteristics of Averages

The arithmetic mean, median, and mode have the same value in any
symmetrical distribution. If the distribution is skewed, the mode remains under the highest point of the curve, the mean is pulled out in the
direction of the extreme values, and the median tends to fall in between.
This is shown in Figure 4 for positively skewed data similar to that for
the stock price example.

In summary, the characteristics of the individual averages are given
below:

Arithmetic mean:

1. The arithmetic mean is the most widely known and widely used average.
2. It is, nevertheless, an artificial concept since it may not coincide with any actual value.
3. It is affected by the value of every item.
4. It may be affected too much by extreme values.
5. It can be computed from the original data without forming an array or frequency distribution or from the total value and number of items alone.
6. Being determined by a rigid formula, it lends itself to subsequent algebraic treatment better than the median or mode.

Median:

1. The median is a simple concept—easy to understand and easy to compute.
2. It is affected by the number but not the value of extreme items.
3. It is widely used in skewed distributions where the arithmetic mean would be distorted by extreme values.
4. It may be located in an open-end distribution or one where the data may be ranked but not measured quantitatively.
5. It is unreliable if the data do not cluster at the center of the distribution.

Mode:

1. The mode can best be computed from a frequency distribution unless one value predominates in an array.
2. It can be located in open-end distributions since it is not affected by either the number or value of items in remote classes.
3. The mode is erratic if there are but few values or zigzag frequencies—particularly if there are several modes or peaks.
4. It is affected by the arbitrary selection of class limits and class intervals.

MEASURES OF DISPERSION

In addition to an average as a summary measure of a set of data, it is useful to have a measure of dispersion in order to determine how disparate the data are. All the values, for example, might be quite close to the average, or they might vary over a considerable range. Thus, the measure of dispersion can be used to gauge the reliability of an average. A second purpose for measuring dispersion is to determine the nature and causes of variation in order to control the variation itself. For example, in matters of health, variations in body temperature, pulse beat, and blood pressure are basic guides to diagnosis. Measures of dispersion include the range, the quartile deviation, the mean deviation, and the standard deviation.

The Range

The range is simply the difference between the largest and the smallest values of a variable. Sometimes the range is indicated merely by citing the largest and smallest figures themselves, as in daily stock quotations. If the high and low values are not widely separated from adjoining values, the range may be a fairly good measure of dispersion. However, if the two extremes are erratic, the range is unreliable and misleading because it gives no hint of the dispersion of the intervening values. For this reason the range is only used as a measure of dispersion in a few specific cases.

The Quartile Deviation

The quartiles are the three points which divide an array or frequency distribution into four roughly equal groups. That is, the first or lower quartile, Q_1, separates the lowest valued quarter of the total number of values from the second quarter; the second quartile, Q_2 (almost always called the median), separates the second quarter from the third quarter; and the third or upper quartile, Q_3, separates the third quarter from the top quarter. Consequently, the quartile range, Q_3-Q_1, includes the middle half of the items. The quartile deviation, Q, is half this range. That is,

$$Q = \frac{(Q_3 - Q_1)}{2}$$

The quartiles are widely used as measures of dispersion. *Dun's*, for example, reports the medians and quartiles of 14 operating ratios in each of 22 types of retailers. Thus, the quartiles of net profits on net working capital of 144 grocery retailers in 1973 were 9 and 33 percent, compared with the median of 18 percent. This means that while the typical grocery retailer earned 18 percent on net working capital, about one fourth of the companies earned less than 9 percent and one fourth earned over 33 percent, indicating a wide spread of profitability in this field.

Ungrouped data. The first and third quartiles are found in an array just as is the median, which is the second quartile. They are the values whose ranks or order numbers are $n/4 + 1/2$ and $3n/4 + 1/2$, respectively, counting from the lowest value. Fractional order numbers are interpolated between neighboring values in the array.

Grouped data. The quartiles can be estimated for a frequency distribution in the same way as the median by these analogous formulas:

$$Q_1 = L + \frac{i(n/4 - F)}{f}$$

and

$$Q_3 = L + \frac{i(3n/4 - F)}{f}$$

where L is the lower limit of the class containing the quartile, i is the class width, f is the frequency or number in that class, F is the cumulative frequency below that class, and n is the total number of values.

For the data on stock prices in Table 2, the first quartile, Q_1, is the $170/4 = 42\frac{1}{2}$th item, and this falls in the second class ($L = \$10; f = 59; F = 37$); and Q_3 is the $(3)(170/4) = 127\frac{1}{2}$th item, which falls in the fourth class ($L = \$30; f = 16;$ and $F = 124$). Therefore,

$$Q_1 = 10 + 10(42.5 - 37)/59 = 10.93$$

and

$$Q_3 = 30 + 10(127.5 - 124)/16 = 32.19$$

The quartile range is then $32.19 - 10.93 = \$21.26$, and the quartile deviation is half this, or $\$10.63$.

The Mean Deviation

The mean deviation, sometimes called the average deviation, is simply the mean of the absolute deviations of all the values from some central point, usually the mean. The deviations are averaged as if they were all positive. The mean deviation is a concise and simple measure of variability that takes every item into account.

Ungrouped data. The formula for the mean deviation (measured from the arithmetic mean) in a set of ungrouped data is

$$MD = \frac{\Sigma|X - \overline{X}|}{n}$$

where the blinkers $|\ |$ mean that the signs are ignored. That is, the absolute deviations from the mean are added, and the sum (Σ) is divided by the number of values (n) to find the mean deviation (MD).

TABLE 5 Computation of Mean Deviation for Ungrouped Data (price-earnings ratios of five electronics stocks)

Common Stock	Price-Earnings Ratio (X)	Deviation from Mean $\mid X - \bar{X} \mid$
A	19.6	0.4
B	17.3	2.7
C	19.2	0.8
D	14.0	6.0
E	29.9	9.9
Total	100.0	19.8
Mean	20.0 = $\bar{X}$	4.0 = MD

The mean deviation is computed in Table 5 for the price-earnings ratios of five electronics stocks whose mean is 20.0. That is,

$$MD = \frac{\Sigma|X - \bar{X}|}{n} = \frac{19.8}{5} = 4.0$$

Grouped data. The mean deviation can be computed from grouped data by the formula

$$MD = \frac{\Sigma f|X - \bar{X}|}{n}$$

where $\mid X - \bar{X} \mid$ is the absolute deviation of the class midpoint (X) from the arithmetic mean, ignoring signs, and f is the frequency in that class. This formula will not be illustrated here.

The Standard Deviation

The standard deviation is found by (1) *squaring* the deviations of individual values from the arithmetic mean, (2) summing the squares, (3) dividing the sum by $(n - 1)$, and (4) extracting the square root. Like the mean deviation, the standard deviation is based on the deviations of all values, but it is better adapted to further statistical analysis. This is partly because squaring the deviations makes them all positive so that the standard deviation is easier to handle algebraically than the mean deviation. The standard deviation is, therefore, of such importance that it is, in fact, the "standard" measure of dispersion.

Ungrouped data. The basic formula for the standard deviation of ungrouped data is

$$s = \sqrt{\frac{\Sigma(X - \bar{X})^2}{n - 1}}$$

TABLE 6 Computation of Standard Deviation for Ungrouped Data
(price-earnings ratio of five electronics stocks)

(1)	(2)	(3)	(4)	(5)
		Direct Method		
Common Stock	*Price-Earnings Ratio* (X)	*Deviation from Mean* $(X - \bar{X})$	$(X - \bar{X})^2$	*Shortcut Method* X^2
A	19.6	− .4	.16	384.16
B	17.3	−2.7	7.29	299.29
C	19.2	− .8	.64	368.64
D	14.0	−6.0	36.00	196.00
E	29.9	9.9	98.01	894.01
Total	100.0	0.0	142.10	2,142.10
Mean	20.0			

where s is the standard deviation; $(X - \bar{X})$ is the deviation of any value of X from the arithmetic mean $\bar{X}$; $\Sigma(X - \bar{X})^2$ is the sum of the squared deviations; and n is the number of items in the sample. The square of the standard deviation (s^2) is called the *variance*.

The above formula for the standard deviation is for data that are considered a sample of some larger population. For the population itself, the formula for the standard deviation (small sigma or σ) is $\sigma = \sqrt{\Sigma(X - \mu)^2/N}$, where μ (small mu in Greek) is the population mean, and N is the number of values. Here the variance (σ^2) is simply the average of the squared deviations from the mean.

In the sample of five price-earnings ratios listed in Table 6, column 2, the deviations from the mean of 20.0 are shown in column 3 and the squares in column 4. Their sum, $\Sigma(X - \bar{X})^2$, is 142.10, and $n = 5$ stocks. The standard deviation is then

$$s = \sqrt{\frac{\Sigma(X - \bar{X})^2}{n - 1}} = \sqrt{\frac{142.10}{4}} = 6.0$$

Shortcut method. While the above formula describes the standard deviation succinctly, it may be easier to compute its value directly from the original data, without finding the deviations from the mean. The following formula gives the same result as the one above:

$$s = \sqrt{\frac{\Sigma X^2 - (\Sigma X)^2/n}{n - 1}}$$

In Table 6, column 5 shows the original X values squared for use in this formula; columns 3 and 4 are not needed. Then,

$$s = \sqrt{\frac{2{,}142.10 - (100.0)^2/5}{4}} = \sqrt{35.52} = 6.0$$

Grouped data. In a frequency distribution the midpoint of each class is used to represent every value in that class. The basic formula for the standard deviation therefore becomes

$$s = \sqrt{\frac{\Sigma f(X - \overline{X})^2}{n - 1}}$$

where $(X - \overline{X})^2$ is the deviation of the class midpoint (X) from the arithmetic mean and f is the frequency in that class.

Relation between Measures and Dispersion

In a normal distribution there is a fixed relationship between the three principal measures of dispersion. The quartile deviation is the smallest, the mean deviation is next, and the standard deviation is the largest. In particular, when measured about the mean of a normal population μ:

$\mu \pm Q$ includes 50 percent of the items.
$\mu \pm MD$ includes 57.51 percent of the items.
$\mu \pm \sigma$ includes 68.27 percent of the items.

These relationships are shown graphically in Figure 5. This figure also shows the proportion of items included within $\pm$ 2 and $\pm$ 3 standard deviations.

Characteristics of Measures of Dispersion

The characteristics of the individual measures of dispersion are summarized below.

Range:

1. The range is the easiest measure to compute and to understand.
2. However, it is often unreliable, being based on two extreme values only.

Quartile deviation:

1. The quartile deviation is also easy to calculate and to understand.
2. It depends on only two values which include the middle half of the items.

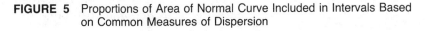

FIGURE 5 Proportions of Area of Normal Curve Included in Intervals Based on Common Measures of Dispersion

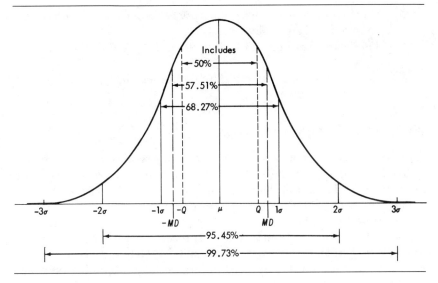

3. It is usually superior to the range as a rough measure of dispersion.
4. It may be determined in an open-end distribution, or one in which the data may be ranked but not measured quantitatively.
5. It is also useful in badly skewed distributions or those in which other measures of dispersion would be warped by extreme values.
6. However, it is unreliable if there are gaps in the data around the quartiles.

Mean deviation:

1. The mean deviation has the advantage of giving equal weight to the deviation of every value from the mean or median.
2. Therefore, it is a more sensitive measure of dispersion than those described above and ordinarily has a smaller sampling error.
3. It is also easier to compute and to understand and is less affected by extreme values than the standard deviation.
4. Unfortunately, it is difficult to handle algebraically since minus signs must be ignored in its computation.

Standard deviation:

1. The standard deviation is usually more useful and better adapted to further analysis than the mean deviation.

2. It is more reliable as an estimator of the population value than any other dispersion measure, provided the distribution is normal.
3. It is the most widely used measure of dispersion and the easiest to handle algebraically.
4. However, it is harder to compute and more difficult to understand.
5. It is greatly affected by extreme values that may be due to skewness of data.

PROBABILITY DISTRIBUTIONS

A probability is a number between zero and one representing the chance or likelihood that an event will occur. A probability of zero means the event is impossible; a probability of one means that it is certain; and values in between, such as 0.5, indicate intermediate chances of occurrence.

An objective interpretation defines probability as the relative frequency of a certain event in a random process over a great number of trials. For example, assigning the probability of 0.5 to the event "heads" for a fair coin implies that 50 percent of a very large number of tosses would be heads. An alternative subjective interpretation defines the probability p of an event as an evaluation by a decision maker of its relative likelihood. It is his betting odds on the occurrence of the event.

Basic Definitions

A *simple* probability, written $P(A)$, is the probability that a single event A will occur. A *joint* probability, $P(A,B)$ is the probability that both of two events A and B will occur. A *conditional* probability is the probability that one event A will occur, given that another event B is known to have occurred, and is written $P(A|B)$. As an example, consider an urn that contains five balls, three red and two white. The probability of drawing a red ball on the first draw is a simple probability. The probability of drawing red balls on each of the first and second draws is a joint probability. And the probability of drawing a red ball on the second draw, after knowing that the first draw was red, is a conditional probability.

Two events, A and B, are defined to be statistically *independent* if $P(A|B) = P(A)$, that is, if the probability of A is not dependent upon whether or not event B has occurred. As an example, two flips of a coin are independent, since the outcome of the first does not affect the outcome of the second. On the other hand, if two balls are drawn from the urn described above (three red and two white balls) and the first is not replaced before the second is drawn, the events are *not* independent. Note that if the first is red (which has probability $3/5$, the probability that the second is red is ¾ = 0.5. And if the first drawn is white, the probability that the second is red is ¾ = 0.75. Hence, there is not independence since the second outcome probability is influenced by the first outcome.

Rules for Dealing with Probabilities

Addition of probabilities.   For two events A and B, the probability of A or B occurring is:

$$P(A \text{ or } B) = P(A) + P(B) - P(A,B)$$

that is, the sum of the simple probabilities minus the joint probability. If the two events are *mutually exclusive* (so that they cannot both occur), then the joint probability is zero and the rule is:

$$P(A \text{ or } B) = P(A) + P(B)$$

Multiplication of probabilities.   The joint probability that both events A and B occur can be written as:

$$P(A \text{ and } B) = P(A,B) = P(A)P(B|A)$$

that is, the product of the simple probability of A and the conditional probability of B given A. When the events are independent, $P(B|A) = P(B)$, and the rule is:

$$P(A,B) = P(A)P(B)$$

Random Variables

A probability function is a rule which assigns probabilities to each element of a set of events that may occur. If, in turn, a specific numerical value is assigned to the elements of a set of events, the function which assigns these values is called a *random variable*. For example, if the random variable X is the number of heads in three tosses of a fair coin, then the possible values of X and the corresponding probabilities are:

Possible Values of Random Variable X (Number of Heads in Three Tosses)	Probability of X
0	⅛
1	⅜
2	⅜
3	⅛
	1

FIGURE 6 Examples of Probability Distributions Defined by
Mathematical Equations

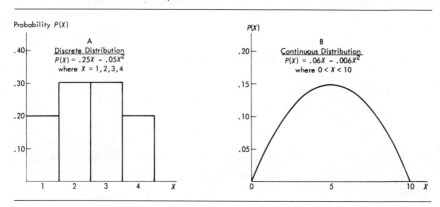

A probability function, such as that illustrated above, is called a *probability distribution* if the sum of the probabilities equals one. A probability distribution may be either *discrete* or *continuous*. In a discrete distribution, the random variable can take on only a specific set of values, often only integer values, and is sometimes called a *probability mass function*. In a continuous distribution, the random variable can take on any value within a range or within ranges. Examples of discrete and continuous distributions are given in Figure 6.

The mean and variance of a random variable. The mean or *expected value*, $E(X)$, of a discrete random variable X is defined as:

$$E(X) = \Sigma[X \cdot P(X)]$$

where $P(X)$ is the probability for each value of X.

The principal measure of dispersion for a probability distribution is the *variance* (the square of the standard deviation or σ^2) which is defined as: Variance $= \Sigma\{[X - E(X)]^2 \cdot P(X)\}$ in a discrete distribution. Similar formulas hold for the expected value and variance of continuous random variables.

Sums of random variables. The expectation of a sum of random variables is the sum of the expectations of those random variables. Thus, the mean of the random variable $(X + Y + Z)$ is:

$$E(X + Y + Z) = E(X) + E(Y) + E(Z)$$

The expectation of a constant times a random variable is the constant times the expectation of the random variable:

$$E(cX) = cE(X)$$

where c is an arbitrary constant.

The variance of a sum of *independent* random variables is also the sum of the variances. Thus:

$$Var(X + Y + Z) = Var(X) + Var(Y) + Var(Z)$$

if X, Y, and Z are independent. Similarly, the variance of a constant times a random variable is the constant squared times the variance of the variable. Thus:

$$Var(cX) = c^2 Var(X)$$

The Binomial Distribution

Certain specific probability distributions have been found particularly useful in business problems, and they are to be discussed briefly. The first is the binomial distribution, used when the random variable can take on only one of two values. Thus, the distribution is used extensively in quality control (when a product is defective or not), in public opinion polls (for or against, candidate A versus candidate B, Republican or Democrat), in auditing (an account is correct or not), and in many other instances.

The binomial distribution is a discrete distribution and is made up of n *independent* trials (items sampled or flips of a coin, for example), and on each trial the probability of a success (p) remains the same. A success is defined to be one particular outcome, such as the occurrence of heads in flipping a coin or the occurrence of a defective item in sampling from a production process.

The binomial probability formula. In general, the probability of r successes in n trials is:

$$P(r) = {}_nC_r p^r q^{(n-r)}$$

where r is the number of successes (i.e., heads); n is the size of the sample (i.e., number of flips); p is the probability of a success (i.e., a head); $q = (1 - p)$ is the probability of a failure (i.e., a tail); and $P(r) = $ probability of exactly r successes (i.e., r heads). Also ${}_nC_r$ is the number of *combinations* of n things taken r at a time and is defined as:

$$_nC_r = \frac{n!}{r!(n - r)!}$$

where n factorial is $n! = 1 \times 2 \times 3 \ldots \times n$ and $0! = 1$ by definition.

EXAMPLE. Probability of three heads and two tails using a bent coin that has a 0.6 chance for a head:

$$n = 5 \text{ flips}$$
$$r = 3 \text{ heads}$$
$$n - r = 2$$
$$p = 0.6, \text{ the probability of a head}$$
$$q = 1 - p = 0.4$$

$$P(r) = {}_nC_r p^r q^{(n-r)} = \frac{5!}{3!2!}(0.6)^3(0.4)^2 = 10 \times 0.034 = 0.34$$

The calculation of binomial probabilities is tedious work. Fortunately, tables of the binomial distribution are included in most statistics texts. In addition, references to complete sets of tables are given at the end of this section.

The mean or expected value of the binomial distribution is $E(r) = np$, and the variance of the distribution is $\text{Var}(r) = npq$.

The Poisson Distribution

Another discrete distribution of some practical importance is the Poisson distribution. It is used to represent the number of random occurrences of some phenomenon per unit of measurement. Thus, it might be used to represent the number of telephone calls arriving at a switchboard in a minute or the number of defective spots in a square foot of enameled plate. The Poisson distribution plays an important role in the theory of queues or waiting lines.

The random variable X (number of occurrences) for the Poisson distribution can take on only zero or integer values. In addition, it assumes that the number of occurrences is independent from one unit of measurement to another. (The number of telephone calls arriving in one minute, for example, does not affect the number arriving in the next minute.) Finally, it assumes that the average rate of occurrences is the same over all units of measurement.

The Poisson probability function is

$$P(X) = \frac{e^{-m}m^X}{X!} \quad \text{for} \quad X = 0, 1, 2, \ldots$$

where X is the random variable, the number of occurrences per unit of measurement; m is the mean or average number of occurrences of X per unit of measurement; and e is a constant (the base of natural logarithms) with value of 2.718. . . .

As with the binomial distribution, tables of the Poisson distribution are widely available.

The Normal Distribution

By far the most important distribution in statistics is the normal distribution. This distribution was described briefly above as a continuous distribution represented by a symmetrical, bell-shaped curve (see Figures 3 and 5). The equation for the normal distribution is:

$$f(X) = \frac{1}{\sqrt{2\pi}\sigma} e^{-\frac{1}{2}\frac{(X-\mu)^2}{\sigma^2}}$$

where X is the random variable and μ and σ are the parameters. The constant π is 3.14159 . . . and e is 2.718. . . . For the normal distribution, the expected value or mean is $E(X) = \mu$, and the variance is σ^2. Normal distributions can take on many different shapes, depending on the values of these two parameters. Although this is so, the normal distribution includes the same percentage of values within ± any specific number of standard deviations. Thus:

$\mu \pm \sigma$ includes 68.27 percent of the values.
$\mu \pm 2\sigma$ includes 95.45 percent of the values.
$\mu \pm 3\sigma$ includes 99.73 percent of the values.

Tables of the area under a normal distribution are contained in any statistics text. To use these tables it is necessary to calculate the *standard normal deviate z*. This represents the number of standard deviation units the random variable X is above or below the mean. The value of z is calculated as:

$$z = \frac{X - \mu}{\sigma}$$

The value of z can then be used in the table of the *standardized normal distribution*, with mean of zero and standard deviation of one.

Other distributions. There are a number of other probability distributions which have some importance in applications in business. These include the *exponential* (used to represent the time between occurrences in a random process), the *beta*, the *gamma*, and others. The reader is referred to advanced texts.

Multivariate Probability Distributions

A multivariate probability distribution is a function expressing the joint probabilities for two or more random variables. For simplicity, the case of two random variables, X and Y, is considered. The expected values (μ_x and μ_y) and variances (σ_x^2 and σ_y^2) for the variables individually are exactly as defined earlier. However, there is an additional measure of variability called the *covariance*, which measures the degree to which the two variables tend to be related. The covariance is defined as:

$$\text{Cov}(X,Y) = E(X - \mu_x)(Y - \mu_y)$$

As an example, consider the joint distribution of the height and weight of men (let X be the height and Y, the weight). The covariance measures the degree to which height and weight are related, that is, the extent to which tall men tend to weigh more than average, and short men, less than average. Since the two characteristics do tend to move together, the covariance term would be large and positive.

If the covariance term is negative, it indicates that high values of one variable tend to be associated with low values of the other and vice versa. If the covariance term is zero, it indicates that the two variables are independent.

Another measure of the degree of dependence of the two variables is the *correlation coefficient*. This is defined as:

$$\rho = \frac{\text{Cov}(X,Y)}{\sigma_x \sigma_y}$$

The correlation coefficient can take on values from zero (if X and Y are independent) to plus or minus one. A correlation of plus or minus one indicates that the two variables vary exactly together.

In a general multivariate distribution, the covariance and correlation coefficient can be defined for any pair of variables.

SELECTED REFERENCES

Organization of Data, Averages, and Dispersion

CROXTON, FREDERICK E., DUDLEY J. COWDEN, and BEN W. BOLCH. *Practical Business Statistics.* 4th ed. Englewood Cliffs, N.J.: Prentice-Hall, 1969. Chapters 2 to 5 provide a detailed treatment of ratios, frequency distributions, averages, and dispersion.

NETER, JOHN, WILLIAM WASSERMAN, and G. A. WHITMORE. *Fundamental Statistics for Business and Economics.* 4th ed. Boston: Allyn & Bacon, 1973. Includes analysis of relationships by cross-classification of data as well as ratios and frequency distribution analysis.

SPURR, WILLIAM A., and CHARLES P. BONINI. *Statistical Analysis for Business Decisions.* Rev. ed. Homewood, Ill.: Richard D. Irwin, 1973. Chapters 2 through 5 give a more detailed treatment of the material in this section of the volume.

YULE, G. UDNY, and M. G. KENDALL. *An Introduction to the Theory of Statistics.* 14th ed. London: Charles Griffin, 1950. Chapters 5 to 7 provide a comprehensive treatment of frequency distributions, averages, dispersion, skewness, and kurtosis.

Probability Distributions

DRAKE, ALVIN W. *Fundamentals of Applied Probability Theory*. New York: McGraw-Hill, 1967. A good, slightly more advanced treatment of probability and probability distributions is contained in Chapters 1, 2, and 4.

GOLDBERG, SAMUEL. *Probability, An Introduction*. Englewood Cliffs, N.J.: Prentice-Hall, 1960. A detailed and systematic treatment of discrete probability.

Statistical Tables

BRACKEN, JEROME, and CHARLES J. CHRISTENSON. *Tables for Use in Analyzing Business Decisions*. Homewood, Ill.: Richard D. Irwin, 1965.

BURINGTON, RICHARD S., and DONALD C. MAY. *Handbook of Probability and Statistics with Tables*. 2nd ed. New York: McGraw-Hill, 1970.

NATIONAL BUREAU OF STANDARDS. *Tables of the Binomial Probability Distribution*. Applied Mathematics Series No. 6. Washington, D.C.: U.S. Government Printing Office, 1949.

49

Regression Analysis

Robert D. Milne, J.D., CFA
President
Duff & Phelps Investment Management Co.

Regression analysis has become the most widely used technique in quantitative financial analysis as well as in general quantitative economics. The principles of regression analysis can be grasped firmly without reference to elegant mathematical proofs. The advent of the computer eliminated the mathematical drudgery involved with regression analysis. In fact, even some pocket calculators can perform the more basic elements of regression analysis. The purpose of this section will be to point out some of the situations where regression analysis might be helpful and also how to judge whether a regression equation represents a soundly based relationship. Any data can be fed into a regression program and used to generate a formidable series of equations and test statistics. A glance at a few of the test statistics will show whether the equations are simply nonsense or whether a meaningful relationship may be present. Unfortunately, test statistics are not infallible, and occasionally one may be led astray by regression analysis.

ECONOMIC MODELS FOR FINANCIAL ANALYSIS

The financial analyst will not be spending his time preparing elaborate models of the economy as a whole; instead, he will be mostly working with single equation models involving a variety of practical applications. The analyst is well prepared to develop single equation models. In fact, he probably uses such models all the time without formally defining them as models. For example, a tire industry analyst will relate prospective automobile tire sales to automobile production plus replacement demand related to the number of cars on the road. His formal model would be:

$$S = 5a + \alpha p$$

where:

S = Sales of auto tires
a = Automobile production
p = Automobile population at start of year
α = Coefficient of replacement demand to be determined by regression analysis

This is such a simplified model that the analyst might wonder why it might have any value. Actually, an important characteristic of any model is that it greatly oversimplifies the real world into a form that can be comprehended. A completely detailed description of tire demand broken down as to the number of tires ruined by broken bottles on local streets, by chuckholes, by careless driving, by underinflation, and so forth would so overwhelm the analyst that he would be hard-pressed to make a forecast of next year's tire demand. By developing a model, the analyst has brought the problem into a form which, while it still has a logical basis in fact, can be comprehended. The testing of the model by regression analysis will determine the strength of the relationships—that is, how close the actual situation of the past compares with what seems to be the most probable relationships. Far too often things are not quite what they seem, and regression analysis may help the analyst to reconsider what he regards as the major forces at work in an industry.

The analyst should be careful to make his regression studies on variables which are related to each other. In other words, he should specify his model beforehand, not simply investigate a large number of series and make his model from the series which appear to have the closest fit. Spurious "correlation" studies are frequent. For example, one might note that the decade of the 1960s was a decade of great growth in both the number of security analysts employed and in the number of auto thefts. It would be possible to come up with a fairly closely fitting regression equation indicating that auto thefts rose directly in line with the number of security analysts employed. The basic fallacy, of course, is that the two series are completely unrelated. Both series are reacting to other forces—it is just a coincidence that both were in a strong uptrend at the same time. In all types of analysis it is possible to be misled if one examines a large number of series. Oftentimes the closest fit is obtained by use of factors which are not primarily related. However, the accident of close fit does not make the theory sound. In this era of easy computation it is necessary to be on one's guard against the temptation of "data mining" by examining a great variety of series.

Just by chance, some regressions will show good results when measured against the past but prove to be poor guides for the future.

While there are pitfalls along the way, regression analysis is a sound tool for the serious analyst. In addition to simple models, more sophisticated models can be developed easily. For example, if our tire analyst wished to construct a model to forecast the demand for radial tire replacement sales, he might come up with a model somewhat as follows:

$$S_r = \alpha P_r + \beta P_0$$

where:

S_r = Sales of radial tires in the replacement market
P_r = Automobile population with radial tires
P_0 = Automobile population with nonradial tires
α, β = Coefficients to be estimated by regression analysis

This is still a single equation model, although there are now two coefficients to be determined by regression analysis. While there is no limit to the number of coefficients that could be calculated, it is usually good practice to limit a single equation model to as few as possible—probably no more than three in most cases. The reason for this will be stated later.

USING REGRESSION ANALYSIS TO STUDY OTHER RELATIONSHIPS

Regression analysis can be helpful in studying all types of relationships where quantitative data are available. One of the many types of relationships where such data are often available is that of financial requirements. Determination of a growing company's future financial requirements is a crucial element of security analysis. Regression techniques will not give an unerring answer as to the amount of capital needed to finance a company's growth over the foreseeable future, but they can provide useful background for an analyst preparing for a field trip. Most of the categories on a balance sheet are related to sales. Certainly this is the case with receivables, inventories, fixed assets, and accounts payable. While these categories are directly related to sales, the relationships are by no means fixed constants. As time goes on, relationships change. To illustrate, the record of General Electric Company's inventories will be examined. At the close of 1982 GE's reported inventories amounted to $3 billion or about $ .11 for each dollar of the year's sales of $26.5 billion. If inventories grow at exactly the same rate as sales, the analyst would expect to find that GE will require $ .11 of added inventories for each dollar of added sales. However, the following three years saw inventories increasing at about $ .50 for each

FIGURE 1   General Electric Inventories and Sales

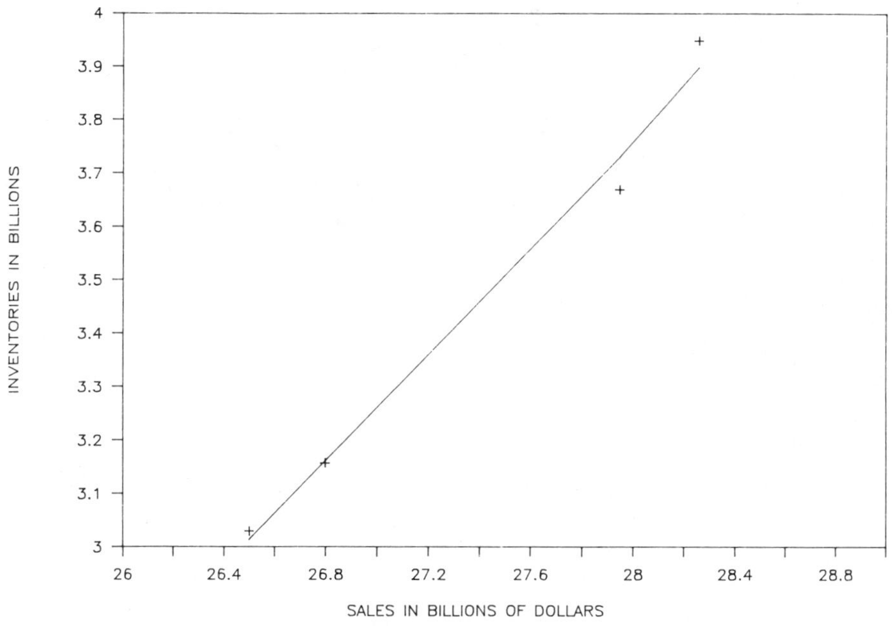

(Y-axis: INVENTORIES IN BILLIONS, X-axis: SALES IN BILLIONS OF DOLLARS)

dollar of added sales. A more realistic appraisal, however, would be to compare GE's gross inventories before deducting the LIFO reserve. The gross amount of $5.3 billion for 1982 was about $ .20 for each dollar of sales. Using regression analysis it appears that GE would require about $ .23 of added inventories for each dollar of added sales. Figure 1 depicts the regression analysis for the four years 1982–85 and the actual relationships for those years.

The analyst should review the inventory pattern when he interviews GE's management to see whether this recent trend can be continued. This same approach can be taken for the other main categories of financial assets and liabilities to gain an insight into the factors influencing future financing. These are presented merely as examples of some of the many ways in which regression analysis may be useful in seeking to interpret the meaning of a series of statistical data.

ESSENTIALS OF REGRESSION ANALYSIS

Computer programs for regression analysis frequently include a variety of test statistics, all of which have value. However, the most important elements to understand are:

FIGURE 2 Replacement Tire Sales and Automobiles

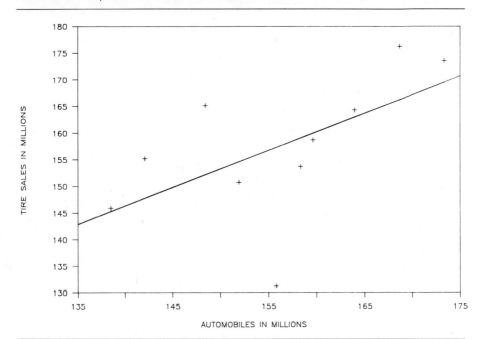

1. What the regression equation means.
2. Is there a strong relationship between the factors or only a weak, relatively meaningless relationship?
3. How precise are forecasts likely to be?

To illustrate, a regression line will be calculated to determine if there is a relationship between the demand for replacement tires and the population of cars on the road. Figure 2 depicts the actual results for the 10 years 1976–85 and the computed regression line.

The regression line looks as if it had been drawn freehand to fit in the middle of the dots, but actually it was calculated by least squares equations which resulted in the following coefficients for a straight line equation:

$Y = 48.98$ million $+ .695X$.
$Y =$ Replacement tire sales.
$X =$ Automobile registrations at start of year.

The relationship between the two series is thus reduced to a straight line. Replacement tire sales is termed the dependent variable and placed on the vertical axis (the Y-axis) since our hypothesis is that the level of replacement sales depends upon the number of automobiles on the road. Automobile registrations is thus the independent variable and placed on the horizontal axis (the X-axis). As the analyst varies the forecast for the independent variable, automobile registrations, the level of replacement tire sales changes accordingly at the rate of 2.3 tires per year for each additional automobile on the road at the start of the year.

The equation of a straight line can be expressed in the form: $Y = a + bX$. The term a in the equation indicates the point at which the regression line crosses the Y-axis. The term b in the equation indicates the slope of the regression line.

In any econometric equation, the true coefficients are defined in terms of Greek letters such as $Y = \alpha + \beta X$. The regression equations, however, do not result in true coefficients but, rather, in estimates of the true coefficients and are, therefore, defined in normal roman letters such as: $Y = a + bX$.

In portfolio analysis, considerable emphasis is placed on the beta coefficients of stocks. These coefficients are computed in the same way that replacement tire sales were related to the automobile population. In beta analysis the price of the individual stock is placed on the Y-axis as the dependent variable, and the stock market index (often the S&P's 500) is placed on the X-axis as the independent variable. (The more sophisticated models make allowance for dividends and for the U.S. Treasury bill rate as a proxy for the riskless rate of return in both series of data.) While the regression techniques in reality present only estimates of the true beta coefficients of the various stocks, they are generally referred to as beta coefficients. A beta coefficient of 1.0 would mean that a stock moves up and down at exactly the same rate as the market; a beta of 0.5 would mean that it would be more stable, moving up or down only half as fast as the market. In other words, the beta coefficient indicates the slope of the regression line for the individual stock.

GOODNESS OF FIT

A least squares regression line can be fitted to any two series of data, as indicated in the Appendix. When there is a strong relationship between the series, it makes sense to use the regression equation in interpreting the past and in forecasting the future. When there is only a weak relationship, the value of regression analysis is that it documents the futility of attempting to rely on simple projections of past relationships.

The most important test statistic is the one measuring *goodness of fit*, which is referred to as the *coefficient of determination*. This measures the amount of variance that is "explained" by the regression line. In the 10 years of data for replacement tire sales, the average annual volume was 157.5 million tires. Figure 3 illustrates the variance from the 157.5 million

FIGURE 3 "Explained" Variance of Tire Sales

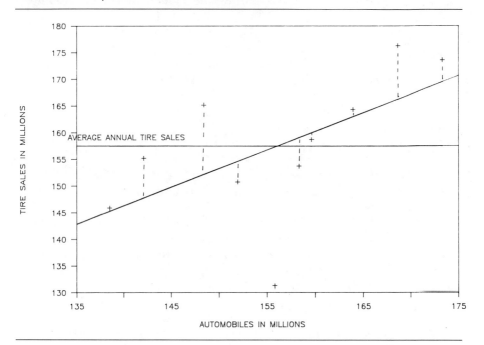

average that is "explained" by the regression line; the dashed lines leading to the actual values on Figure 3 depict the variance "unexplained" by the regression line.

A look at Figure 3 suggests that the regression line is a rather good fit, and this is documented by the following test statistics:

$$r = 0.579 \text{ (coefficient of correlation)}$$
$$r^2 = 0.335 \text{ (coefficient of determination)}$$

The r^2 value of 0.335 means that 34 percent of the variance is explained by the regression line. This is only a fair fit but the regression line has passed an important test. The coefficient of correlation r serves as an intermediate step in the calculation of r^2. An r^2 of at least 30 percent would seem to be desirable before placing even minor reliance on the regression line.

Earlier in this chapter the reader was warned against the practice of data mining. A somewhat similar problem results when some of the variables excluded from the model in order to make a more workable model are ones that have a strong effect on the variables included in the model. For example, if sales of General Motors cars were related to the total market for original equipment tires, there would probably be a

FIGURE 4 Standard Error of Estimate—Tire Sales

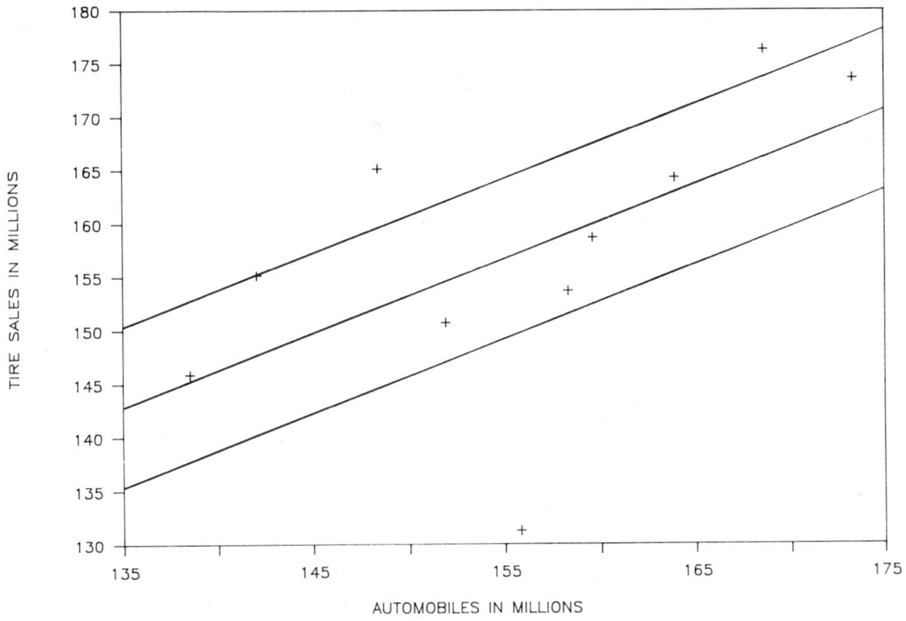

good fit in the regression equation. However, the reason for the good fit would be due to the fact that total automobile sales have their impact on General Motors sales. Obviously, the best measure is total auto production and not simply GM production alone. Thus, care in specifying the variables in the model is essential.

FORECASTING

In making practical forecasts, the analyst is especially interested in determining how accurate the forecasts are likely to be, assuming, of course, that the historical relationships persist in the future. The answer to this question is the standard error of the estimate, $S_{y,x}$, which for the replacement tire equation amounts to 7.5 million units if we exclude the recession year of 1980. The standard error of the estimate is the standard deviation of the actual yearly figures for replacement tire sales around the regression line. Figure 4 depicts the regression line and dashed lines one standard deviation above the regression line and one standard deviation below the regression line. The standard error of the estimate means that 68 percent of the actual data would fall within plus or minus 7.5 million units about the regression line. Moreover, 95 percent of the

FIGURE 5 Hypothetical Earnings Record

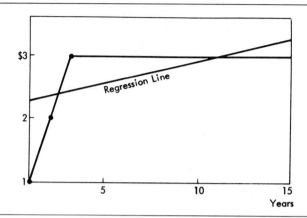

actual data should be within two standard errors ($\pm 2S_{y,x}$) or within 15.0 million units. Thus, if the analyst makes a forecast of replacement tire sales for 1986, based upon an auto population of 17.3 million cars at the start of the year, the regression model provides a single figure estimate of 169 million replacement tires. He will be 95 percent certain that the actual figure for the year would be in the range of 154 million to 184 million tires.

PROBLEMS WITH RESIDUALS

The remainder of the test statistics found in computer generated regression analyses deal with problems which may arise from residuals or which relate to confidence limits. These test statistics are the result of highly sophisticated studies and are commended to the serious student of quantitative methods. However, there may be two test statistics which may be of at least moderate interest to the financial analyst who has access to them in his computer program.

A major problem for a financial analyst in using regression analysis is to identify when a fundamental relationship is changing. For example, the demand for replacement tires which has been extremely predictable in the past may become less so in the future if radial tires become standard equipment and if an energy crisis alters traditional driving patterns for speed and for miles driven per year. If patterns are changing, this can usually be noted from examination of a chart depicting the actual results for each year and the regression line. In order to show an exaggerated example of a changed pattern, Figure 5 shows a hypothetical company's earnings record with earnings rising

FIGURE 6 Deviations from Regression Line

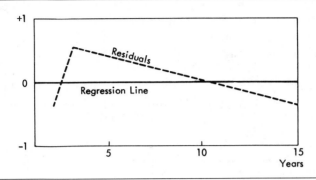

from $1 per share in the first year to $2 in the second and $3 for each of the 12 remaining years in the series.

The least squares regression line represents the best fit for a straight line trend covering the 15 years of data, but quite obviously the regression line trend has no value as a predictor of future earnings growth. This is because the earnings trend has flattened out. Beyond its obvious draw-backs as a predictor, the least squares regression line is suspect since there is another force at work which has not been taken into consideration. The errors beween the actual earnings figures and the trend values are not independent errors occurring at normally distributed intervals and of random size. In other words, the successive errors have a pattern of their own; each error is related to the previous one. If we tilt Figure 5 so that the trend line is horizontal, we can observe more readily the pattern of errors in this hypothetical example. This is illustrated in Figure 6.

The problem with our hypothetical illustration is termed *autocorrelation*—that is, the errors have a lagged correlation with their own past values—the error in year 3 influences the error in year 4 which influences the error in year 5 and so forth. This is not at all an uncommon occurrence. In fact, we would expect most economic series of interest to analysts to behave somewhat in this fashion. The price of a product one month has an influence on its price the next month; the amount of sales generated by the sales force one month does have an effect on next month's business; or else this would be an entirely chaotic economic world. The fact that there is probably some autocorrelation does not make regression techniques valueless. Small deviations from normality will not seriously affect the results of a regression equation, its coefficient of determination, its standard error of the estimate, and related statistical tests; but greater departure from normality such as in the hypothetical case of the earnings record would have serious consequences.

This leads to the question of how to determine whether a particular series has a serious autocorrelation problem. Sometimes this is termed a *serial correlation problem*. The appropriate test is the *Durbin-Watson* statistic, which is usually referred to as D.W. If there is no autocorrelation at all in a series, the Durbin-Watson statistic will be 2.0. Thus, the analyst should look for a D.W. fairly near the 2.0 mark—and, in fact, the great majority of series have D.W.s in the range between 1.5 and 2.5. In evaluation of a D.W. the following abbreviated table should serve in most instances:

Durbin-Watson Statistic Acceptability—5 Percent Probability Level

Number of Data Points	Clearly Reject	Clearly Accept	Clearly Reject
15	1.08 or less	1.36–2.64	2.92 or more
25	1.29	1.45–2.55	2.71
50	1.50	1.59–2.41	2.50
100	1.65	1.69–2.31	2.35

The hypothetical example has a D.W. of 0.60, which is in the range of those clearly rejected. Thus, the D.W. statistic efficiently brings this problem to the analyst's attention. It is then up to the analyst to determine how to adjust for the problem. Usually the best adjustment is to discard the earlier years of data and compute a regression line from the point the new forces seem to be at work. Before leaving this section, it might be noted that the Durbin-Watson statistic is not evaluated for samples of less than 15 data points. If the analyst has a smaller sample, it would qualify as acceptable if the D.W. falls in the range of 1.36–2.64 that is applicable to series with 15 periods of data. In fact, some wider range would be tolerable with a smaller sample.

Another problem is referred to by the tongue-twisting name of *heteroscedasticity*. If a Bartlett's test figure is provided, a Q of 4 or higher should make the analyst suspicious, and a careful review of the regression line chart would be in order. Fortunately, these problems are less common and should be apparent from an inspection of the chart.

Two test statistics widely used to indicate whether there is a true relationship or simply one which may have arisen by chance are the *t* statistic and the *F* statistic. The *t* statistic is easily interpreted. If it is 2 or more, the coefficient is significantly different from zero at the 5 percent level. This means that a *t* statistic of 2 would have arisen by chance in only 5 percent of a number of random series. The *t* statistic is useful in evaluating the coefficients in a multiple regression equation since it might identify which coefficients have value and which should be discarded in order to produce a more effective multiple regression equation.

The F ratio indicates whether it is likely that the regression equation could have arisen by chance. The F ratio is calculated by analyzing the variance of each observation from the mean value of its series and comparing it with the deviation about the regression line. The F ratio is calculated in many computer programs and even evaluated in a few. Generally, however, it is necessary to evaluate the F ratio by referring to a table. Most statistics texts have tables for determining the F ratio required to be considered significant at the 5 percent level and the higher F ratio required to be considered significant at the 1 percent level. The required F ratios vary with the size of the samples involved. The higher the F ratio, the more likely it is that the regression equation is meaningful and that the relationships between the two series did not arise solely by chance. If the F ratio is significant at the 5 percent level, this means there is only a 5 percent chance that the relationship between the variables arose only by chance. Significance at the 1 percent level would mean that it could have arisen by chance in only one case out of 100. The 5 percent and the 1 percent levels are obviously arbitrary—and the F ratio might well be considered adequate by the analyst even if it did not quite meet the 5 percent level. The F ratio is a powerful and useful test of significance, worthy of its widespread use. It is also used in multiple regression in determining which are the strongest variables that can be used in the final equation, while weaker variables are discarded.

MULTIPLE REGRESSION

Simple regression is based upon the artificial assumption that the change in one variable—e.g., replacement tire sales—is entirely dependent upon changes in one other variable. Yet, in actual practice, most things are dependent upon a number of factors, not on one factor alone. This will require the use of multiple regression. The power of multiple regression is twofold:

1. The multiple regression equation should be a more accurate fit when compared with the actual data than in the case of a simple regression equation. In other words, there will be a lesser proportion of unexplained variance.
2. The relative importance of the various factors can be assessed and weak factors discarded.

To illustrate how multiple regression may be used to make a more effective regression equation, the following simple regression equation was calculated for a group of five fairly average electric utilities relating price/earnings ratios to the growth of the preceding five years:

$$p/e = 10.82 + 0.0027G$$

where G is the growth rate of the last five years expressed as a percentage.

This equation had a coefficient of determination of 69 percent, neither especially good nor especially bad. The coefficient for the growth rate suggests that this is only a minor influence in determining prices for electric utility stocks. However, if we add another factor, the estimated earnings growth for the coming year, the following multiple regression equation is produced:

$$P/E = 7.92 + 0.316G + 0.335G_e$$

where G_e is the estimated percent growth in the coming year.

This multiple regression equation has a multiple coefficient of determination of 98 percent, which is much improved as compared with the simple regression equation. This is illustrated by the following comparison of the theoretical P/E ratios which would have been calculated for each of the five utilities under both regression equations:

	Calculated P/E	
Actual P/E	Multiple Regression	Simple Regression
11.6	11.6	9.0
11.5	11.4	12.6
11.3	11.3	12.3
10.0	9.7	11.3
9.7	10.0	10.4

The multiple regression equation is also superior in indicating that the estimated growth in the coming year and the past growth record are both significant influences on the current valuations of the stocks.

P/E ratios are really not the most appropriate application of multiple regression analysis but are simply presented as an illustration of the approach that might be taken to improve upon a simple regression equation in order to make it a better predictor of the future. Regression analyses should be performed for various combinations of the factors believed to influence a series. For example, if the variable to be forecast is known to be dependent upon factors A, B, and C, simple regressions could be computed for each of the three factors, and multiple regressions could be computed for A and B, for A and C, and for B and C as well as for all three factors. Rates of change could also be calculated as well as partial correlations. The main idea, however, is to examine several plausible models in order to develop the most effective regression equation.

Before leaving multiple regression, it is necessary to warn against adding too many variables to the model in an attempt to improve the predictive capability of the regression analysis by raising the R^2 as high as possible. Each time an additional factor is added to a regression equation, there is a sacrifice of "degrees of freedom" which reduces the statistical significance of the regression equation. One could include a dozen factors in a multiple regression equation, but the resulting equation would probably be a poor forecasting tool. The fewer independent variables in the equation, the better. Sophisticated econometric models use a series of regression equations to come up with their final result rather than attempting to string all of the variables in one equation. The analyst should find that he can accomplish much by using just one, two, three, or four independent variables in his equations.

SUMMARY

In simple regression it is assumed that Y is dependent upon the values for X plus an unknown random error. To make estimates of the parameters, Y is regressed on X with the residuals representing the random errors. In multiple regression it is assumed that Y is dependent upon the values for two or more factors, plus an unknown random error. Estimates are made of the coefficients for the various factors, with the residuals representing the random errors.

While the full ramifications of regression analysis are immense, the essential elements to be checked in every regression analysis are:

1. What does the regression equation mean? Values for the coefficients.
2. How much of the variance is explained? The coefficient of determination, r^2.
3. How accurate is the equation as a predictor? The standard error of the estimate.
4. Is the relationship significant or would it be likely that it arose merely by chance? Is the t statistic 2 or higher or the F statistic evaluated in a table?
5. Are there autocorrelation problems indicated by too low a Durbin-Watson statistic?

This section has covered only an introduction to the subject of regression analysis. If the analyst is working with a computer, a personal computer, or even a sophisticated pocket calculator, the mechanics of regression analysis will be taken care of. There is no need to devise a new program for regression analysis—use a good software package. Attention to the five steps set forth above should keep one out of serious trouble with regression analysis. The interested analyst is referred to the following texts as starting points for delving into the world of regression analysis:

Brown, S. J., and M. P. Kritsman. *Quantitative Techniques for Financial Analysis.* Homewood, Ill.: Richard D. Irwin, 1986.

Christ, Carl F. *Econometric Models and Methods.* New York: John Wiley & Sons, 1968.

Kane, Edward J. *Economic Statistics and Econometrics.* New York: Harper & Row, 1965.

APPENDIX
Simple Regression Calculations
Sumner N. Levine

Regression analysis, as illustrated in the previous section, deals with the methods for deriving an equation by which one of the variables, the dependent variable Y, may be estimated from other variables, the independent variables X. In the case of simple linear regression it is assumed that the dependent variable is a linear function of only one independent variable:

$$Y = a + bX$$

Again, it must be emphasized that a regression relationship does not necessarily imply that a causal relationship exists.

Least Squares Method

Let Y_i be the observed value and Y be the value calculated by the regression equation. As shown in Figure 7, the difference or error e_i between these values is

$$Y_i - Y = e_i$$
$$Y_i = a + bX_i + e_i$$

The quantity e_i is considered to vary at random about the regression line with a mean value $E(e_i)$ of zero and with a constant variance $\sigma^2(e_i) = \sigma^2(y)$. The last assumption is referred to as *homoscedasticity*.

The problem is to find values of a and b in the above equation such that the sum of the squares of the error term is a minimum. This is accomplished by the *least squares method*: find an a and b such that

FIGURE 7 Regression Line, Data Points (X), and the Error (e_i) between the Data and Calculated Value

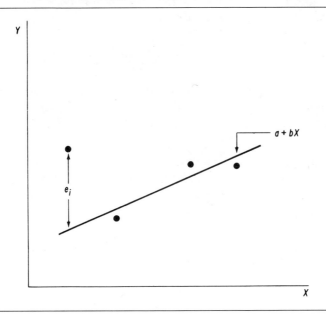

$$\Sigma(Y_i - a - bX_i)^2 = \sum_i e_i^2 = \text{Minimum}$$

This condition is fulfilled by setting the derivative with respect to a and b of the sum equal to zero. The result is the two *normal* equations

$$\Sigma Y_i = na + b\Sigma X_i$$
$$\Sigma X_i Y_i = a\Sigma X_i + b\Sigma X_i^2$$

These may be solved for a and b

$$a = \overline{Y} - b\overline{X}$$

$$b = \frac{\Sigma(X_i - \overline{X})(Y_i - \overline{Y})}{\displaystyle\sum_i (X_i - \overline{X})^2} = \frac{\text{Cov}(XY)}{\text{Var}(X)} = \frac{\Sigma X_i Y_i - n\overline{XY}}{\Sigma X_i^2 - n\overline{X}^2}$$

where:

$$\overline{X} = \frac{1}{n}\Sigma X_i$$

$$\overline{Y} = \frac{1}{n}\Sigma Y_i$$

The last form on the right side is particularly convenient for purposes of calculation.

The question as to how well the regression line fits the data can be answered by means of the *correlation coefficient* defined by the expression

$$r = \frac{\Sigma X_i Y_i - n\overline{XY}}{[(\Sigma X_i^2 - n\overline{X})(\Sigma Y_i^2 - n\overline{Y})]^{1/2}}$$

where n is the number of observations. Values of r equal to plus or minus unity imply a perfect fit, i.e., all the points lie on the regression line. Smaller magnitudes of r imply poorer fits. The quantity r^2 is the coefficient of determination.

EXAMPLE. It is desired to find the linear regression for a company's earnings (Y) over the last four years (X). The worksheet and data are given below:

Y_i (Earnings)	X_i (Year)	X^2	$X_i Y_i$	Y^2
1,800	1	1	1,800	3,240,000
1,900	2	4	3,800	3,610,000
1,800	3	9	5,400	3,240,000
2,000	4	16	8,000	4,000,000
7,500	10	30	19,000	14,090,000

$$\overline{Y} = \frac{7,500}{4} = 1,875 \quad \overline{X} = \frac{10}{4} = 2.50$$

$$b = \frac{19,000 - (4)(1,875)(2.50)}{30 - (4)(2.50)^2} = 50$$

$$a = 1,875 - (50)(2.50) = 1,750$$

so that

$$y = 1,750 + 50x$$

$$r = \frac{1,900 - 4(2.50)(1,875)}{\{[30 - 4(2.50)][(14,090,000) - 4(1,875)]\}^{1/2}} = 0.6742$$

50

Time Series Analysis

Edwin J. Elton, Ph.D.
Graduate School of Business Administration
New York University

Martin J. Gruber, Ph.D.
Graduate School of Business Administration
New York University

One attitude that has distinguished man from his fellow animals is his ability to record and learn from his past experience. While some of this past experience is qualitative in nature, much of it is quantitative. In this chapter we shall treat one set of techniques for extrapolating quantitative experiences into the future. The set of techniques we shall deal with are generally grouped under the title of time series analysis. The assumption made is that a series of numbers ordered over time represents the measurement of some process and that this process has inertia or continuity over time, e.g., that the pattern of past sales for a company is useful in forecasting future sales. This assumption often provides an excellent starting point for analysis. The techniques of time series analysis are simple and inexpensive to use. Nevertheless, the reader should be warned that they do not represent a replacement for human judgment. The techniques involved might have done an excellent job of forecasting buggy-whip sales prior to 1893, but they would not have been able to predict the invention of the automobile or the impact of its success on buggy-whip sales. One should think of these techniques as an expensive, fast, and efficient way of answering the question: What will the future be if it is a simple continuation of the past?

TABLE 1 Quarterly Sales Data for a Hypothetical Department Store, 1971–1975

	Quarter			
Year	1	2	3	4
1971	110	109	121	136
1972	118	108m	143	169
1973	119	133	156	181
1974	159	137	169	204
1975	166	150	183	230

NOTE: The observations are numbered 1 through 20 moving left to right, a row at a time. For example, the second quarter of 1972 is quarter 6.

TIME SERIES ANALYSIS—AN INTRODUCTION

A time series is nothing more than a set of numbers ordered with respect to time. An ordered sequence of sales of a company is a time series. A sequence of the quarterly earnings of a company is a time series. A time series of numbers can be described in two dimensions, one representing the numbers themselves, the other, a time index indicating the order in which the numbers arose. A time series can be displayed in tabular form or in graphical form. For example, the sales for a hypothetical department store are presented in Table 1. The first date for which we have data is arbitrarily assigned the time index one, and observations are consecutively numbered. A graph of the data shown in Table 1 is presented in Figure 1. A large part of this chapter shall be concerned with an analysis of this example, but to introduce the concept let us start out with some easier examples.

Let us assume that we wish to prepare a forecast for sales data as shown in Figure 2.[1] Notice that over time sales seem to fluctuate around a level $\bar{S}$. If one arbitrarily breaks the period up into shorter periods, the average level of sales in each of these shorter periods would be approximately the same. We can describe such a pattern as random fluctuations around a stable level of sales. For such a process deviations from the long-term average (mean) sales are unpredictable, so the best forecast we can make about any future level of sales is that they will be equal to the mean value $\bar{S}$. Our problem then is to determine $\bar{S}$, the

---

[1] The examples in this chapter deal with sales forecasts. The selection of sales rather than earnings, costs, or some other variable is simply a matter of convenience.

FIGURE 1

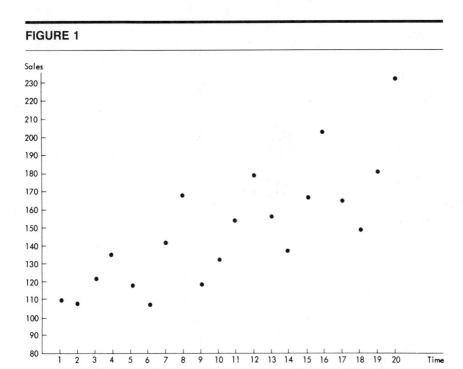

FIGURE 2

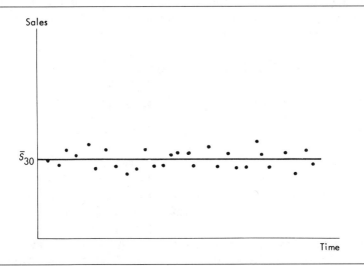

FIGURE 3

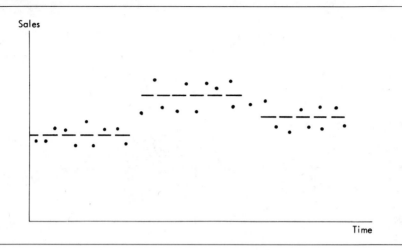

historical average level of sales. This is best done by simple averaging all past sales data. In this case:

$$\bar{S}_{30} = \sum_{i=1}^{30} \frac{S_i}{30}$$

where S_i is the yearly sales for year i. The more past data we have, the more sure we are about getting an estimate of $\bar{S}$ which is not affected by random noise. Since future sales are to be forecast as equal to S_{30} then,

$$\hat{S}_{30, T} = \bar{S}_{30}$$

where $\hat{S}_{30,\hat{T}}$ is the estimate of sales for period $30 + T$ made at time 30.

Now let us turn to a slightly more complex pattern for sales. Examine Figure 3. This figure represents a condition where sales fluctuate randomly around a mean level but where this mean level shifts occasionally (and randomly) over time. In making a prediction, if one knew when the last shift in the mean level took place, one would estimate the future by averaging the data after the shift took place. However, when a prediction is to be made, one cannot usually differentiate between a shift in the mean and a random deviation from a stable mean. How then is one to capture shifts in the mean while still averaging out random deviations? Perhaps the most commonly used method is to employ a moving average of past data. That is, at any point estimate the future by averaging a limited amount of (rather than all) past data. Let us assume we have decided to use a six-period moving average, then

$$\overline{S}_t = \frac{\displaystyle\sum_{i=t-5}^{t} S_i}{6}$$

For an n period moving average,

$$\overline{S}_t = \frac{\displaystyle\sum_{i=t-n+1}^{t} S_i}{n}$$

and

$$\hat{S}_{t, T} = \overline{S}_t.$$

That is, for an n period moving average we obtain an estimate of the future by simply averaging the last n observations on sales. As a new data point (sales level) becomes available, we simply drop the earliest observation included in the last average, add the new observation, and take a new average.[2]

An obvious question arises at this point. How do we decide on n or the length of the moving average? The choice of n involves the resolution of two conflicting goals. The larger n is, the surer we are of eliminating random noise from our estimate of the average sales. However, the larger n is, the longer it will take us to reflect, in our estimates, a fundamental shift in the average level of sales. If we knew how often shifts in the mean level of sales took place and how large they arc relative to the random element in sales, we could resolve our difficulty. But we do not possess this knowledge, and so we have to resolve the issue on empirical grounds. The procedure for doing so will be taken up in the section on the evaluation of forecasting techniques.

There is an alternative averaging technique which has found wide application in business problems—exponentially weighted averages. While a moving average places the same weight on each observation it includes, exponential smoothing places more weight on current observations than on past observations. The technique gets its name from the fact that the weights decline exponentially over time. The idea of placing more weight on current observations than past observations has great intuitive appeal. The future is expected to be more like the recent past than the far past. The exponential forecasting models evolved out of

---

[2] An equivalent to update the moving average which saves computation time is to subtract $1/n$ times the earliest observation included in the test computation of the moving average from that computation and to add $1/n$ times the new observation.

World War II research, where these models had great success in tracing and predicting the location of enemy aircraft. The exponential pattern of weights has appeal, for an exponential pattern fits many real world phenomena. For example, radioactive material decays exponentially; people learn and forget in an exponential pattern.

The simplest exponential smoothing relationship is:

$$\bar{S}_t = \bar{S}_{t-1} + W_S(S_t - \bar{S}_{t-1})$$

$$\hat{S}_{t,T} = \bar{S}_t \tag{1}$$

where W_S is the weight placed on current compared to past sales ($0 \le W_s \le 1$). This model states that the best forecast of future sales is the last forecast of future sales plus some fraction of the error in the forecast. Thus, if $W_s = 0.2$, and we had forecast sales of \$100 which turned out to be \$110, our forecast for the future would be $\bar{S}_t = \$100 + 0.2\,(110 - 100) = \$102$.

Examining Equation (1) it might appear that sales for only the periods t and $t-1$ are being considered. To see that this is not the case, the formula can be written as

$$\bar{S}_t - W_s S_t + (1 - W_s)\bar{S}_{T-1} \tag{2}$$

But

$$\bar{S}_{t-1} = W_s S_{t-1} + (1 - W_s)\bar{S}_{t-2} \tag{3}$$

Substituting Equation (3) into Equation (2) yields

$$\bar{S}_t = W_s S_t + W_s(1 - W_s)S_{t-1} + (1 - W_s)^2\bar{S}_{t-2}$$

Repetitive substituting yields

$$\bar{S}_t = \sum_{i=0}^{M-1} (W_s(1 - W_s)^i)S_{t-i} + (1 - W_s)^M S_s \tag{4}$$

where S_s represents the estimate of sales for period M.[3] An examination of Equation (4) reveals that in computing $\bar{S}_t$ all past levels of sales are employed for they are embodied in $\bar{S}_{t-1}$. But note that to predict sales over time only one number $\bar{S}_t$ need be saved. All individual observation on past sales can be disregarded.[4]

---

[3] To use an exponentially weighted smoothing model one has to have a starting estimate of the variable being forecast. Usually this starting estimate is obtained by averaging the first one third to one half of the data available. However, with any reasonable amount of data, forecasts will be very insensitive to the starting estimates.

[4] The ease of performing exponential smoothing, along with the limited data bank that is needed when employing this technique, has contributed greatly to its widespread use in industry as a forecasting technique.

So far we have ignored the questions as to proper choice for W_s. This choice is analogous to the choice of n in the simple moving average. To show this we have tabulated below the weights placed on past sales data from different periods for five alternative choices of W_s.

W_s	t	$t-1$	$t-2$	$t-3$	$t-4$	All Previous Years
1.0	1.0	0	0	0	0	0
0.8	0.8	0.1600	0.0320	0.0064	0.0013	0.0003
0.5	0.5	0.2500	0.1250	0.0625	0.0313	0.0157
0.2	0.2	0.1600	0.1280	0.1024	0.0819	0.0655
0.1	0.1	0.0900	0.0810	0.0729	0.0650	0.590

Notice that the smaller the W_s, the more weight is placed on past data relative to recent data. Alternatively, the smaller the W_s, the more likely we are to reduce the effect of random fluctuations in sales on our future forecast, but the slower we are to recognize a fundamental shift in the level of sales. As in the case of determining the optimal length moving average, the optimal exponential weight to use remains a matter of empirical investigation.

TIME SERIES MODELS WITH SEASONAL AND TREND

Up to now we have assumed that the level of sales for a firm is stable over time except for random elements plus periodic changes in the level. But in practice most firms exhibit some long-term growth in sales, and many firms have a seasonal pattern to sales. Let us begin by examining Table 1 and Figure 1. Notice that in Figure 1 sales tend to move upward over time. This can be seen by analyzing the average quarterly sales for each of the five years. Average quarter sales are:

	1971	1972	1973	1974	1975
Sales	$119.00	$134.50	$147.25	$167.25	$182.25

In each year average quarterly sales are higher than they were in the previous year, demonstrating the need for some type of adjustment for growth in making forecasts.

One would also expect to find some type of seasonal pattern in department store sales. Sales at and around Christmas are usually higher than at any other time of the year. Thus, one would expect to see average sales for the fourth quarter higher than sales in any of the three previous quarters. Furthermore, third quarter sales should probably be higher than sales for either of the previous two quarters as pre-

Christmas sales begin to build up. Such a pattern is found in the data under study. The average sales over the five years under study for each quarter are:

	Quarter			
	1	*2*	*3*	*4*
Average sales	$134.40	$127.40	$154.40	$184.00

If one were to predict sales for any quarter without considering the seasonal influence, one would overestimate sales in quarters 1 and 2 and underestimate sales in quarters 3 and 4.

We will first examine models and adjust for trend and then models that adjust for trend and seasonal.

Time Series Model with Trend

If the variable being forecast is expected to grow over time, a term to allow for this growth should be included in the forecasting model. While there are several patterns that growth might take, the two most popular patterns are that the variable grows by a constant amount each period (additive growth) or by a constant percent each period (multiplicative growth). For example, the following series illustrates additive growth.

	Period				
	1	*2*	*3*	*4*	*5*
Sales	$100	$110	$120	$130	$140

The growth per period is simply $10. If we wanted to forecast sales for period 6, the best forecast would be $140 + $10 = $150. For period 7, $140 + 2($10) = $160, or for period 5 + n, $140 + n($10).

The following series demonstrates multiplicative growth.

	Period				
	1	*2*	*3*	*4*	*5*
Sales	$100.00	$110.00	$121.00	$133.10	$146.40

Sales grow by 10 percent per period. The best forecast for sales per period 6 would be $146.40(1.10) = $161.00. The best forecast of sales for period 5 + n would be $146.40(1.10)^n$.

The choice of the proper assumption concerning growth can often

FIGURE 4

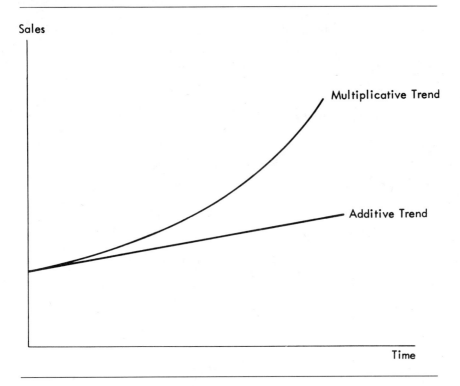

Sales

Multiplicative Trend

Additive Trend

Time

be made by an inspection of the data. Figure 4 shows the pattern that sales would follow for additive and multiplicative growth. Below we will examine time series that allow for growth.

Exponential models. An exponential model incorporating an additive trend is quite simple to construct. To do so, define the following symbols:

S_t = The sales per share at time t.

$\bar{S}_t$ = The exponentially weighted average of past sales per share at time t.

$\hat{S}_{t,T}$ = The estimate of sales per share made at time t for period $t + T$.

W_s = The weight placed on current versus past sales per share, $0 \le W_s \le 1$.

$R\bar{R}_t$ = The exponential weighted average of past growth at time t.

W_R = The weight placed on current versus past growth $0 \le W_R \le 1$.

In the absence of trend we said that

$$\bar{S}_t = \bar{S}_{t-1} + W_s(S_t - \bar{S}_{t-1})$$

But if we have additive trend, the sales between the periods are expected to grow by an amount $\bar{R}_{t-1}$. Thus, sales at time t are expected to be $(\bar{S}_{t-1} + \bar{R}_{t-1})$, and the relevant error in the last forecast is

$$S_t - (\bar{S}_{t-1} + \bar{R}_{t-1})$$

and the equation for arriving at S_t is

$$\bar{S}_t = (\bar{S}_{t-1} + \bar{R}_{t-1}) + W_s\,[S_t - (\bar{S}_{t-1} + \bar{R}_{t-1})] \tag{5}$$

This, like the earlier equation, simply states that we correct our latest estimate of average sales by some fraction of the error in our last forecast.

However, we now need an estimate of $\bar{R}_{t-1}$ or the amount of growth. Again we simply update our last estimate of $\bar{R}_{t-1}$ by how bad this estimate was, or

$$\bar{R}_t = \bar{R}_{t-1} + W_R\,[(\bar{S}_t - \bar{S}_{t-1}) - \bar{R}_{t-1}] \tag{6}$$

Notice that a new smoothing coefficient W_R has been introduced. There is no reason why W_R should equal W_s. Methods for determining W_R and W_s will be discussed in a later section of this chapter.

To complete the model we need the following equation, which simply expresses the fact that sales in the future are expected to grow by an amount R_t per period, or

$$\hat{S}_{t,T} = \bar{S}_t + T\bar{R}_t \tag{7}$$

The exponential model incorporating a multiplicative trend is directly analogous to the model incorporating additive trend. The difference is that R_t now stands for one plus the expected rate of growth in sales so that sales are expected to increase by R_{t-1} percent each period. Thus, the model is

$$\bar{S}_t = \bar{S}_{t-1}\bar{R}_{t-1} + W_s(S_t - \bar{S}_{t-1}\bar{R}_{T-1}) \tag{8}$$

$$\bar{R}_t = \bar{R}_{t-1} + W_R\left(\frac{\bar{S}_t}{\bar{S}_{t-1}} - \bar{R}_{t-1}\right) \tag{9}$$

$$\hat{S}_{t,T} = \bar{S}_t(\bar{R}_t)^T \tag{10}$$

In both of these exponentially smoothed forecasting models, an assumption is made that the weights placed on past data should be decreased the more remote from the forecast period the data is.

Regression models. A second widely used technique exists for incorporating trend into time series analysis: time series regression analysis. The fundamentals of regression analysis have already been covered in another chapter. Thus, it is unnecessary to review the mathematics here. All that need be recalled is that regression analysis involves a particular weighting of the observations. Each observation is weighted as the squared distance from the regression line of best fit. No differential weighting of recent versus past observations is used. If an arithmetic growth rate is employed, the equation[5]

$$S_t = a + Rt + e \tag{11}$$

is fitted by regression analysis to the data. The coefficient R represents the dollar amount by which sales are expected to grow each period. A forecast for any period made by computing the value of the dependent value (S) forecast by the regression equation for the appropriate period. Thus,

$$\hat{S}_{t,T} = a + R(t + T) \tag{12}$$

If multiplicative growth is assumed, then the appropriate regression equation is

$$ln\ S_t = a + R_t + e \tag{13}$$

where $ln\ S_t$ represents the natural logarithm of S_t. Here R represents the rate of growth in sales per period.[6] The forecast of future sales is obtained by taking the antilog of this equation evaluated at the forecast date $t + T$, or

$$ln\ \hat{S}_{t,T} = a + R(t + T)$$

or

$$\hat{S}_{t,T} = e^{a+R(t+T)} \tag{14}$$

Up to this point we have ignored an important question. How much past data should we use in running the regression? Once again we are faced with the same type of problem we encountered when examining the length of the optimum moving average or the proper weights to use in the exponential smoothing models. The more data we use, the more

---

[5] a is the intercept value, R is the slope coefficient, and e is the random error term.

[6] This can easily be demonstrated. Differentially, the equation with respect to t yields

$$\frac{\partial S_t / S_t}{\partial t} = R$$

$= R$ or the *rate* of change of S with respect to t equals R.

we smooth out random fluctuations, but the more likely we are to miss a change in the underlying pattern of sales.

Having discussed the major time series forecasting models incorporating trend, let us now turn to an examination of seasonal influences.

Adding a Seasonal

Earlier we recognized that department store sales might be subject to seasonal influences. Another example of seasonal influences might be a firm engaged in the sale of ice cream. Here sales would reach their peak during the summer months and decline until the start of warm weather in the spring. The general pattern of seasonal influences can usually be specified by the forecaster. The type of data involved limits the type of seasonal influences which can be studied. For example, in our department store example, we have assumed that quarterly data was available, hence, the data can reflect at most four seasonal influences. If monthly data had been available, the existence of 12 distinct seasonals could be checked. Now let us turn to the exponential models and to the regression models and see how seasonal influences can be incorporated.

Exponential smoothing models. The most widely used method of formulating exponentially smoothed forecasts with seasonals involves estimating the seasonal influence, removing the seasonal influence to estimate the smoothed sales series ($\overline{S}_t$), and then reintroducing seasonal influence when forecasting. There will be one seasonal adjustment factor for each season. For example, if there are L seasons to the year, we will have one seasonal factor for each of the L periods. Each seasonal is reestimated only when we observe data from that period. For example, the spring seasonal is reestimated only when spring sales are observed. Define F_{t-L} as the estimate of the seasonal factor as of period $t - L$. If there are L seasons to the year, and we are determining the seasonally adjustment factor for period t, the last estimate of the seasonal adjustment we will have is from period $t - L$. For example, if we are smoothing sales as of the spring quarter 1973, the last estimate we have of the seasonal factor for the spring quarter was calculated four quarters ago, in the spring of 1972.

Seasonal factors may enter a model either additively or multiplicatively. That is, each Christmas season we may expect sales to be up by the same dollar amount or by the same percentage of average sales. We present below models combining trend with both types of seasonal influence.

In order to incorporate a multiplicative seasonal into the models discussed earlier, one must modify the equation estimating normal sales and add an equation updating the seasonal. The equation for normal sales is modified by deseasonalizing actual sales. Since with a multiplicative seasonal sales are some proportion of normal sales, we deseasonalize sales by dividing by this proportion. If sales in a season are two times normal, we divide actual sales by two. If sales in a season are 0.5 normal, we divide by 0.5. For a multiplicative trend, the equation for normal sales becomes

$$\bar{S}_t = \bar{S}_{t-1}\bar{R}_{t-1} + W_s\left(\frac{S_t}{\bar{F}_{t-L}} - \bar{S}_{t-1}\bar{R}_{t-1}\right) \tag{15}$$

where F_{t-L} is the latest estimate of the proportion of normal sales which occur in the season which exists at time t. Notice that the subscript on F indicates that the latest estimate was obtained in the same season one year earlier. With an additive trend the equation for normal sales becomes

$$\bar{S}_t = (\bar{S}_{t-1} + \bar{R}_{t-1}) + W_s\left[\frac{S_t}{\bar{F}_{t-L}} - (\bar{S}_{t-1} + \bar{R}_{t-1})\right] \tag{16}$$

Having computed smoothed sales for period t, we can now update our estimate of smoothed seasonals and smoothed trend. The smoothed seasonal is simply our estimate of the smoothed seasonal one year earlier, plus some fraction (W_F) of how wrong this estimate was.[7]

$$\bar{F}_t = \bar{F}_{t-L} + W_F\left(\frac{S_t}{\bar{S}_t} - \bar{F}_{t-L}\right) \tag{17}$$

The equation updating the smoothed trend remains the same as it was in the nonseasonal model. That is, for a multiplicative trend, it is

$$\bar{R}_t = \bar{R}_{t-1} + W_R\left(\frac{\bar{S}_t}{\bar{S}_{t-1}} - \bar{R}_{t-1}\right) \tag{18}$$

while for an additive trend, it is

$$\bar{R}_t = \bar{R}_{t-1} + W_R[(\bar{S}_t - \bar{S}_{t-1}) - \bar{R}_{t-1}] \tag{19}$$

Notice that S_t has been deseasonalized (has had seasonal influences removed). We want a forecast of sales for any future period to incorporate seasonal influences so that the sales forecasting equation becomes:

$$\hat{S}_{t,T} = \bar{S}_t\bar{R}_t^T\bar{F}_j \text{ (for multiplicative trend)} \tag{20}$$

$$\hat{S}_{t,T} = (\bar{S}_t + T\bar{R}_t)\bar{F}_j \text{ (for additive trend)} \tag{21}$$

---

[7] For more accurate results the model should contain a constraint to ensure that the seasonal adjustments do not incorporate trend elements. The easiest way to do this is to constrain the sum of weights over any year to be equal to 1. Procedures for constraining seasonal weights can be found in [5]. (Note: Numbers in brackets refer to references given at the end of this chapter.)

where F_j represents our latest estimate of the seasonal influence for the season which occurs in period $t + T$.

In order to incorporate an additive seasonal in the models discussed earlier on, one must modify the equation estimating normal sales and add an equation updating the seasonal. With an additive seasonal, sales are normal sales plus the seasonal. Thus, sales are deseasonalized by subtracting the seasonal. For a multiplicative trend, the equation for normal sales becomes:

$$\overline{S}_t = \overline{S}_{t-1}\overline{R}_{t-1} + W_S[(S_t - \overline{F}_{t-L}) - \overline{S}_{t-1}\overline{R}_{t-1})] \qquad (22)$$

where F_{t-L} is the latest estimate of the number of units by which sales for the season which occurs at time t differ from normal sales. With an additive trend the equation for normal sales is:

$$\overline{S}_t = (\overline{S}_{t-1} + \overline{R}_{t-1}) + W_S[(S_t - \overline{F}_{t-L}) - (\overline{S}_{t-1} + \overline{R}_{t-1})] \qquad (23)$$

The seasonal component can be updated by

$$\overline{F}_t = \overline{F}_{t-L} + W_F[(S_t - \overline{S}_t) - \overline{F}_{t-L}] \qquad (24)$$

and the trend is updated by either Equation (18) or (19), depending on whether the trend is multiplicative or additive.

In forecasting, the seasonal factor should be reintroduced. Thus,

$$\hat{S}_{t,T} = \overline{S}_t + T\overline{R}_t + \overline{F}_j \text{ (for additive trend)} \qquad (25)$$

$$\hat{S}_{t,T} = \overline{S}_t\overline{R}_t^T + \overline{F}_j \text{ (for multiplicative trend)} \qquad (26)$$

where F_j is the latest estimate from the season that prevails at time $t + T$, the period for which the forecast is prepared.

Regression models. The standard technique for incorporating seasonal influences into regression analysis is through the use of dummy variables. The previous regression equation we employed (for the additive trend case) was

$$S_t = a + R(t) + e$$

In this expression, a represented the intercept or the value of expected sales at the first instant of time in the study, and R represented the slope coefficient or the amount that sales were expected to increase over each period. If seasonals are present, certain seasons would always fall above this line. Figure 5 illustrates a hypothetical two seasons' sales pattern for a product. If a regression is run ignoring the seasonal pattern, the solid line in Figure 5 would be obtained. The intercept a would be too large for the winter season and too small for the summer season. What we want is two separate intercepts, one for each season. This is obtained by introducing a dummy variable d_1 for the summer season. This variable

FIGURE 5

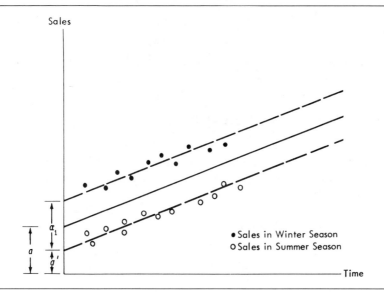

takes on the value 1 for an observation for the summer season and is otherwise equal to zero. The regression equation then is

$$S_t = a' + R(t) + \alpha_1 d_1$$

where a', R, and α_1 are regression coefficients. The intercept for a summer month is then a (for $d_1 = 0$) and for a winter month, $a + \alpha_1$ (for $d_1 = 1$). The coefficient α_1 is the average difference between sales in the summer and winter months.[8] Notice that to incorporate two seasons we only have to use one dummy variable. This is because the intercept term itself, a', represents the intercept value for one season. Thus, in our present problem with four seasons the regression model becomes:

$$S_t = a' + Rt + \alpha_1 d_1 + \alpha_2 d_2 + \alpha_3 d_3 + e \qquad (27)$$

To forecast for any period $t + T$, one simply computes $\hat{S}_{t,T} = a' + R(t + T) + $ correct α. If one were forecasting for the season associated with the second dummy variable, one would use[9]

$$S_t = a' + R(t + T) + \alpha_2$$

---

[8] If d_1 was assigned a value of 1 for the winter months, the model would hold. The results would be identical except that α_1 would be a negative number.

[9] Once again the association of a particular dummy variable with a particular season is totally arbitrary. All the researcher must do is be consistent in using the appropriate dummy variable when forecasting.

The incorporation of a multiplicative seasonal with the multiplicative regression is directly analogous to the case just discussed. One simply uses

$$lnS_t = a' + Rt + \alpha_1 d_1 + \alpha_2 d_2 + \alpha_3 d_3 + e \qquad (28)$$

Before proceeding with a discussion of the implementation of these models, it seems appropriate to employ them to solve a simple example.

ILLUSTRATION OF TECHNIQUES

In this section we shall apply the techniques of exponentially smoothed moving averages and regression analysis to the simple example presented in Table 1 and Figure 1 in order to demonstrate their use. In illustrating the models, we shall use all available data for the regression technique and shall employ weighting coefficient of 0.3 for each weight in the exponential smoothing techniques.[10] For all techniques we will assume that we are attempting to estimate quarterly sales for 1976 as of the end of 1975.

Exponential Smoothing Model with Additive Trend and Seasonal

The three equations needed to compute the exponentially smoothed average of sales with an additive trend and seasonal are:

$$\bar{S}_t = \bar{S}_{t-1} + \bar{R}_{t-1} + W_s[(S_t - \bar{F}_{t-L}) - (\bar{S}_{t-1} + \bar{R}_{t-1})]$$

$$\bar{F}_t = \bar{F}_{t-L} + W_F[(S_t - \bar{S}_t) - \bar{F}_{t-L}]$$

$$\bar{R}_t = \bar{R}_{t-1} + W_R[(\bar{S}_t - \bar{S}_{t-1}) - \bar{R}_{t-1}]$$

In order to employ exponentially weighted averaging models, one must have starting estimates for S, R, and each of the four seasonals. These starting estimates are arrived at by simply averaging past data. Let us assume that the starting estimates for our problem are $\bar{S}_0 = 118$, $\bar{R}_0 = 2$, $\bar{F}_0 = +30$, $\bar{F}_{-1} = +5$, $\bar{F}_{-2} = -20$, $\bar{F}_{-3} = -20$.

We can then proceed to employ formulas starting with the first period for which we have data, period 1:

$$\bar{S}_1 = \bar{S}_0 + \bar{R}_0 + 0.3[(S_t - \bar{F}_{-3}) - (\bar{S}_0 + \bar{R}_0)]$$

$$\bar{S}_1 = 118 + 2 + 0.3[(110 + 20) - (118 + 2)] = 123$$

$$\bar{F}_1 = \bar{F}_{-3} + 0.3[(S_t - \bar{S}_t) - \bar{F}_{t-L}]$$

---

[10] The lengths and weights were selected on a completely ad hoc basis merely to illustrate the techniques.

TABLE 2 Smoothed Sales, Trend, and Seasonal from an Exponential Smoothing Model with Additive Trend and Seasonal

Time Period (t)	S_t	R_t		F_t		
1						
2						
3	125.81	1.92			2.06	
4	121.21	0.04				25.44
5	125.65	1.36	−14.83			
6	127.11	1.39		−19.42		
7	132.23	2.51			4.67	
8	137.39	3.31				27.29
9	138.64	2.69	−16.27			
10	144.66	3.69		−17.09		
11	149.24	3.96			5.30	
12	153.35	4.01				28.63
13	162.73	5.62	−12.51			
14	164.07	4.33		−20.09		
15	166.99	3.91			4.33	
16	172.23	4.31				29.59
17	177.13	4.49	−12.10			
18	178.16	3.45		−22.51		
19	180.73	3.14			3.71	
20	188.87	4.85				31.25

$$\bar{F}_1 = -20 + 0.3[(110 - 123) + 20] = -17.9$$

$$\bar{R}_1 = \bar{R}_0 + 0.3[(\bar{S}_1 - \bar{S}_0) - \bar{R}_{t-1}]$$

$$\bar{R}_1 = 2 + 0.3[(123 - 118) - 2] = 2.9$$

$$\bar{S}_2 = 123 + 2.9 + 0.3[(109 + 20) - (123 + 2.9)] = 126.83$$

$$\bar{F}_2 = -20 + 0.3[(109 - 126.82) + 20] = -19.35$$

$$\bar{R}_2 = 2.9 + 0.3[(126.83 - 123) - 2.9] = 3.179$$

The results of the remaining calculations are shown in Table 2. In order to prepare forecasts for the future, the following values are needed: $\bar{S}_{20} = 188.87$, $\bar{R}_{20} = 4.85$, $\bar{F}_{17} = -12.10$, $\bar{F}_{18} = -22.51$, $\bar{F}_{19} = +3.71$, $\bar{F}_{20} = +31.25$.

The forecasting model that should be used with the additive model is:

$$\hat{S}_{t,T} = \bar{S}_t + R_t^T + \text{The appropriate seasonal}$$

Thus, the forecast for the first quarter of 1976 is

$$\hat{S}_{20,1} = 188.87 + 4.85 - 12.10 = 181.62$$

Furthermore,

$$\hat{S}_{20,2} = 188.87 + 2(4.85) - 22.51 = 176.06$$

$$\hat{S}_{20,3} = 188.87 + 3(4.85) + 3.71 = 207.13$$

$$\hat{S}_{20,4} = 188.87 + 4(4.85) + 31.25 = 239.52$$

Exponential Smoothing Model with Multiplicative Trend and Seasonal

The three equations needed to compute the exponential smoothed average of sales with a multiplicative trend and seasonal are:

$$\overline{S}_t = \overline{S}_{t-1}\overline{R}_{t-1} + W_s\left(\frac{S_t}{\overline{F}_{t-1}} - \overline{S}_{t-1}\overline{R}_{t-1}\right)$$

$$\overline{F}_t = \overline{F}_{t-L} + W_F\left(\frac{S_t}{\overline{S}_t} - \overline{F}_{t-L}\right)$$

$$\overline{R}_t = \overline{R}_{t-1} + W_R\left(\frac{\overline{S}_t}{\overline{S}_{t-1}} - \overline{R}_{t-1}\right)$$

Let us assume starting estimates for the problem of $\overline{S}_0 = 118$, $\overline{R}_0 = 1.02$, $\overline{F}_0 = 1.25$, $\overline{F}_{-1} = 1.05$, $\overline{F}_{-2} = 0.85$, and $\overline{F}_{-3} = 0.85$. Again assuming values of 0.3 for all smoothing coefficients, we can then proceed to employ the model starting with the first period for which we have data, or

$$\overline{S}_1 = 118(1.02) + 0.3\left[\frac{110}{0.85} - 118(1.02)\right] = 123.10$$

$$\overline{F}_1 = 0.85 + 0.3\left[\frac{110}{123.1} - 0.85\right] = 0.863$$

$$\overline{R}_1 = 1.02 + 0.3\left[\frac{123.1}{118} - 1.02\right] = 1.027$$

$$\overline{S}_2 = 123.1(1.027) + 0.3\left[\frac{109}{0.85} - 123.1(1.027)\right] = 127.0$$

$$\bar{F}_2 = 0.85 + 0.3 \left[\frac{109}{127} - 0.85 \right] = 0.85$$

$$\bar{R}_2 = 1.027 + 0.3 \left[\frac{127.0}{123.1} - 1.027 \right] = 1.029$$

The calculations could be continued, producing a set of forecasts as in the additive case.

Regression Models

The first regression model we discussed involved an additive trend and could be represented as

$$S_t = a' + Rt + \alpha_1 d_1 + \alpha_2 d_2 + \alpha_3 d_3$$

Letting $d_1 = 1$ for the second quarter, $d_2 = 1$ for the third quarter, and $d_4 = 1$ for the fourth quarter yields the following result when the model is fitted to our example.[11]

$$S_t = 98.57 + 3.98t - 10.98d_1 + 12.04d_2 + 37.66d_3$$

The forecasts for the future from this model are

$$S_{21} = 98.57 + 3.98(21) \qquad\qquad = 182.15$$

$$S_{22} = 98.57 + 3.98(22) - 10.98 = 175.15$$

$$S_{23} = 98.57 + 3.98(23) + 12.04 = 202.15$$

$$S_{24} = 98.57 + 3.98(24) + 37.66 = 231.75$$

The forecasted results, while close to those produced by the additive exponential model, are different. The forecasts are higher for the first quarter but lower for the next three quarters.

The results yielded by the log regression model were[12]

$$\ln S_t = 4.648 + 0.026t - 0.74d_1 + 0.090d_2 + 0.234d_3$$

---

[11] The coefficient of determination was 0.97. The authors wish to warn the reader that a high correlation coefficient for a model does not necessarily indicate that it is a good forecasting model. The seasonal coefficients were all significantly different from zero at the 0.10 level, indicating that seasonal influences are really present.

[12] The coefficient of determination was 0.976, and all the seasonals were statistically significant at the 0.01 level.

The forecasts for the next four quarters from this model are:

$$S_{21} = e^{4.648 + (0.026)21} = 181.91$$

$$S_{22} = 173.51$$

$$S_{23} = 209.85$$

$$S_{24} = 248.72$$

Once again there are differences in the forecasts produced by these techniques. This example has been included to demonstrate the use of these forecasting techniques. After a discussion of selecting optimum weights and methods of evaluating forecasts, we shall return to an evaluation of the use of the alternating time series models in a real problem—forecasting earnings.

THE PARAMETERIZATION OF THE MODELS

Earlier we raised the issue that in using any mechanical forecasting model one must resolve the dilemma that high weights or short time spans make the model responsive to fundamental shifts in the data but that they do a poor job of removing random noise. The trade-off between the dampening out of random influences and the response of a model to long-term changes is a difficult one to make. If one understood the true nature of the process generating data, then the forecasting model could be an exact replica of this process. But because we almost never have this type of information, the dilemma must be decided on empirical grounds. The method which has worked best in forecasting several types of data is to find the length of moving averages, or regression, or the weights in an exponential smoothing model which do the best job of forecasting over some period for which we have results and assume that this same length or set of weights will continue to do the best job in the future.

For example, assume that using the simplest exponentially weighted moving average $\bar{S}_t = \bar{S}_{t-1} + W_s(S_t - \bar{S}_{t-1})$, we want to prepare a forecast for the year 1975 employing data through 1974. Also assume that data is available starting in 1960. We might then prepare forecasts for 1970 using all possible values for W_s on data through 1969, forecasts for 1971 using all possible values for W_s on data through 1970, and so on up to forecasts for 1974.[13] We could then examine which value of W_s had the smallest error in forecasting for the period 1970–74 and assume that

---

[13] Since W_s we can take on all values between zero and one, there are an infinite number of values that can be tried. However, exponential smoothing models are reasonably insensitive to changes in weights in the optimum region, and trying increments of 0.1 or at most 0.01 should prove efficient for almost all problems.

value was the best for forecasting 1975.[14] The assumption being made here is that the mixture of random noise and fundamental shifts in the data is relatively constant over time so that the time span or weighing factor that did the best forecasting job in the past (represented the best compromise between these two elements) will do the best job in the future.

Parallel techniques can be used for all of the forecasting methods under discussion. For moving averages and regression techniques, one simply searches for the optimum length. For the exponential models, particularly those that employ trend and seasonal, one has to do a large search since there are three weights employed. Thus, for example, if a search is made at weight increments of 0.10, one has to try 1,331 sets of weights. However, a repetitive approximation technique has been found which reduces the number of calculations to a reasonable level.[15]

EVALUATION OF FORECASTING TECHNIQUES

The age of the computer has meant an information explosion. Most organizations are bombarded with forecasts from internal and external sources. It is increasingly difficult to intelligently analyze all information (much of which is contradictory) and come up with rational conclusions. In the light of this it has become even more important to systematically evaluate forecasting and forecasters. It has been our experience that such systematic evaluation will lead to a significant reduction in the amount of information that need be examined in the future.

A forecast or forecasting technique or source of forecasts can most meaningfully be evaluated on a comparative basis. An example presented in the last section of this chapter highlights the problem of trying to evaluate a set of forecasts in isolation. In Table 8 we present the results of three sources of analysts' forecasts along with time series forecasts for the same companies. A sample of financial institutions revealed that the firm labeled Investment Advisory Service was believed to produce one of the best sets of forecasts in the financial community. In fact, if we look at the errors in this company's forecasts, we find that their analysts did produce forecasts with lower errors than the other two institutions. However, when the forecasts of the analysts at these three companies were compared to a simple time series projection of past earnings, the analysts of the Investment Advisory Service did worse than the analysts at the other two institutions. In short, the Investment

---

[14] The criteria for deciding on which forecast is best will be discussed in great detail in the next section of this chapter. For now the reader can assume that we are using the minimization of the squared error as a criterion.

[15] See Elton and Gruber [11] for a discussion of alternative techniques for deciding upon optimum weights.

Advisory Service made their reputation by only following companies which had earnings' patterns that were easy to forecast. Once the mechanical time series forecasts had been introduced so that comparative analysis could be performed, this became clear.

The time series models presented in the first part of this chapter represent a good set of benchmarks against which to compare the accuracy of other forecasting techniques. However, other more naïve techniques also represent a good standard of comparison. The simplest benchmark is the no-change model. That is, forecast the future as the last observed value of the variable being forecast. A second benchmark is to forecast the future as the last observed value plus the last observed charge in the variable of interest. Still another good benchmark is to use a growth rate based on the economy average. For example, when evaluating forecasts of earnings growth rates, assume that earnings for each company will grow at the same rate as the economy grows. Finally, forecasts from a second source, such as forecasts purchased outside the firm, are a good benchmark. Having discussed some benchmarks for comparative analysis, let us turn to the techniques for evaluating forecasts.

Geometric Analysis

One of the simplest and most effective ways to analyze forecast errors is to plot actual change versus predicted change in two dimensional space. An example of this graph is shown in Figure 6 for earnings per share. An estimate of the change in earnings per share is plotted against actual change in earnings per share.

An estimate for each firm's change in earnings per share can be plotted in this space. Its location in the space tells a great deal about the type of error being made. For example, if an estimate lies in Section 1 of the graph, it indicates that the forecaster successfully predicted that earnings would increase, but he overestimated the size of the increase. A point in Section 2 indicates that he correctly estimated a decrease in earnings but underestimated the size of the decrease. A point in Section 5 represents an estimate of an earnings increase when earnings actually decreased. The remaining three sections are analogous to those just discussed. Section 3 represents an underestimate of earnings change when earnings were growing; Section 4, an overestimate of a decrease in earnings; and Section 6, an estimate of a decrease in earnings when they were actually growing.

This graph can also be viewed as a diagrammatic representation of the level of earnings. A point in Section 1, 2, or 5 represents an overestimate of the level of earnings. A point in Section 3, 4, or 6 represents an underestimate. The further a point is from the horizontal axis, the worse the overestimate (or underestimate) is.

Examination of a group of forecasts on this graph can yield quite a

FIGURE 6   Diagram for Analyzing Forecasts

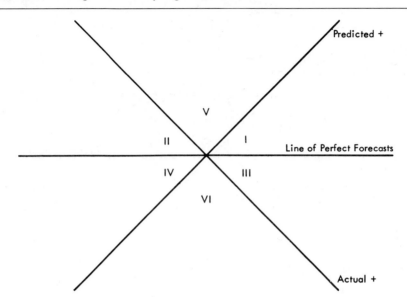

lot of information about forecast accuracy and the sources of mistakes. Let us examine two examples.

Figure 7 presents the case of a firm where analysts are consistently overoptimistic. They tend to overestimate the change when the change in earnings is positive (Section 1) and either to underestimate the change in earnings (Section 2) or to actually predict a positive change (Section 5) when the change in earnings is negative.

An alternative pattern for forecasting errors is shown in Figure 8. The fact that the points lie in Section 1 and Section 4 indicate that while the direction of change is correctly forecasted, the amount of change is constantly overestimated. Change is overestimated whether it is in the positive or negative direction. Furthermore, the tendency to overestimate change becomes more acute as the change itself is larger. This can be seen by the fact that the points lies further and further from the horizontal axis as we move either to the right or to the left of the origin. We could characterize this firm by saying that while its analysts were excellent at discerning the direction of change, they overreacted to change (were either overoptimistic or overpessimistic according to the direction of change).

Numeric Evaluation

In this section we shall examine several techniques for arriving at a numeric or statistical evaluation of forecasts.

FIGURE 7   Representation of Overoptimistic Forecasts

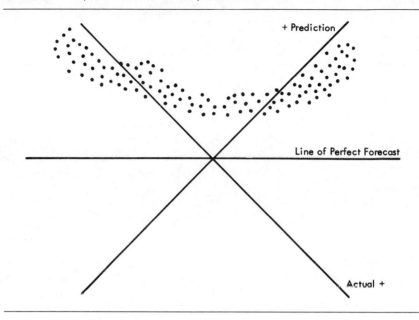

FIGURE 8   Representation of Overestimation of Change

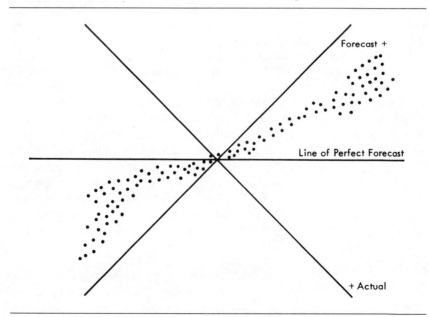

TABLE 3 Some Alternative Forecasts

		Forecasts					
Company	Actual	Technique 1	Technique 2	Technique 3	Technique 4	Technique 5	Technique 6
1	1.20	1.23	1.16	2.00	11.23	12.30	1.28
2	1.31	1.28	1.28	1.75	11.28	12.80	1.31
3	1.42	1.39	1.39	1.50	11.39	13.90	1.44
4	1.55	1.58	1.58	2.50	11.58	15.80	1.53
5	1.85	1.89	1.88	1.75	11.89	18.90	1.85
6	3.00	2.96	3.04	2.00	12.96	29.60	2.92
Correlation		0.9986	0.9994	0.12	0.9986	0.9986	0.9990

Correlation Techniques. The most commonly used method of evaluating forecasts is to calculate the correlation between forecasts and actual. The correlation coefficient measures the extent to which two series have the same pattern. The same pattern implies that high forecasts are associated with high actuals and low forecasts are associated with low actuals. To clarify the meaning, consider the first three examples shown in Table 3. Forecast 1 and Forecast 2 have very similar patterns to the actual. However, with Forecast 1 deviations from actual tend to be random, while with Forecast 2 low actuals are associated with underestimates and high actuals are associated with overestimates. The correlation coefficients of Forecast 1 and Forecast 2 with actual are very similar, 0.9986 and 0.9994, respectively. The pattern of Forecast 3 is very different than actual. The high forecasts are associated with both high and low actuals, and the same is true for low forecasts. The correlation coefficient of Forecast 3 is 0.12.

The correlation coefficient ranges from −1 to +1; +1 indicates that the forecasts have the same pattern as actual, −1 indicates that forecasts have exactly the opposite pattern as actual, and 0 indicates no similarity in patterns. Figure 9 shows an example of a correlation coefficient of −1, 0, 0.5, and +1. The correlation coefficient is calculated as follows:

$$\text{Correlation coefficient} = \rho = \frac{\displaystyle\sum_{i=1}^{N} (F_i - \bar{F})(A_i - \bar{A})}{\left[\displaystyle\sum_{i=1}^{N} (F_i - \bar{F})^2 \sum (A_i - \bar{A})^2 \right]^{1/2}} \tag{29}$$

FIGURE 9

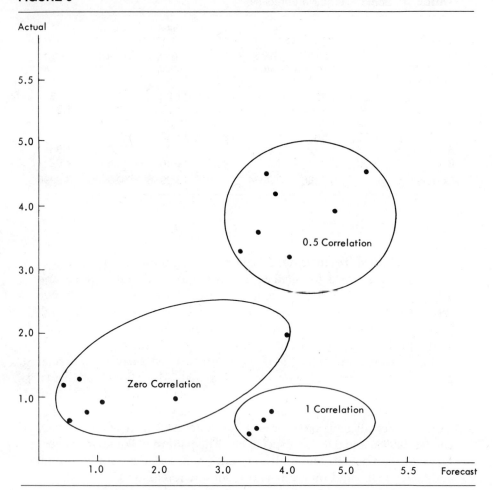

where:

1. F_i is the ith forecast.

2. $\overline{F}$ is the average forecast $\left(\text{i.e., } \overline{F} = \dfrac{1}{N}\displaystyle\sum_{i=1}^{N} F_i\right)$.

3. A_i is the ith actual.

4. $\bar{A}$ is the average actual $\left(\text{i.e., } \bar{A} = \dfrac{1}{N}\displaystyle\sum_{i=1}^{N} A_i\right)$.

TABLE 4 Calculation of Correlation Coefficient for Technique 1

Year	$(F_i - \bar{F})$	$(F_i - \bar{F})^2$	$(A_i - \bar{A})$	$(A_i - \bar{A})^2$	$(F_i - \bar{F}) \times$ $(A_i - \bar{A})$
1	−0.49	0.2401	−0.52	0.2704	0.2548
2	−0.44	0.1936	−0.41	0.1681	0.1804
3	−0.33	0.1089	−0.30	0.0900	0.0990
4	−0.14	0.0196	−0.17	0.0289	0.0238
5	+0.17	0.0289	0.13	0.0169	0.0221
6	+1.24	1.5376	1.20	1.6384	1.5872
Total		2.1287		2.2127	2.1673

$$\rho = \frac{2.1673}{[(2.1287)(2.2127)]^{1/2}} = 0.9986$$

The calculations for Forecast 1 from Table 2 are contained in Table 4.

The correlation coefficient only measures similarity in pattern between forecast and actual. It does not measure the size of the error. For example, Forecast 1 in Table 3 was very similar to actual. Forecast 4 and 5 have exactly the same correlation coefficient, but they are very poor forecasts. Forecast 4 is Forecast 1 plus 10. Forecast 5 is Forecast 2 times 10. These examples can be generalized. The correlation coefficient is unaffected by multiplying each forecast by a positive constant or adding a constant to each forecast or both. Thus, very poor forecasts such as 4 and 5 can have high correlation coefficients. If the error is constant over time (i.e., the forecast is always 10 units too high or 10 times too much), then forecasts highly correlated to actual can be made into forecasts with small error by adjusting by this constant difference (subtracting 10 or dividing by 10). However, rarely is the error constant. Correlation has the property that high correlation can be associated with large error and low correlation with small errors, for it ignores differences in the average error produced by different techniques. Because of this it is argued that despite its widespread use, correlation analysis is a poor way to evaluate forecasts.

Direct analysis of forecast errors. An alternative to correlation is to examine the error directly. Table 5 is the same as Table 3, except it lists the error in the forecast rather than the forecast itself. One would not use the sum of the error to evaluate techniques since positive and negative errors would tend to cancel out. For example, the sum of the error for Forecast 3, a very bad forecast, is zero. There are a number of ways to eliminate the problem of positive and negative errors canceling out. The simplest is to ignore the sign of the error and simply use its magnitude. Thus, for Forecast 1, the error would be stated as .03, .03,

TABLE 5 Forecast Errors

Actual	Tech-nique 1	Tech-nique 2	Tech-nique 3	Technique 4	Technique 5	Tech-nique 6
1.20	+0.03	−0.04	+0.80	10.03	11.10	0.08
1.31	−0.03	−0.03	+0.44	9.97	11.49	0.00
1.42	−0.03	−0.03	+0.08	9.97	12.48	0.02
1.55	+0.03	+0.03	+0.95	10.03	14.25	0.02
1.85	+0.04	+0.03	−0.10	10.04	17.05	0.00
3.00	−0.04	+0.04	−1.00	9.96	26.60	0.08
MAVE*	0.0333	0.0333	0.5617	10.00	15.495	0.0333
MSE†	0.0011	0.0011	0.4588	100.0011	268.5755	0.0023

* MAVE = Mean absolute value of error.
† MSE = Mean squared error.

.03, .03, .04, .04. This is called the absolute value of the error. The forecasting technique would be judged best by the lowest average or mean absolute error. Squaring a number also eliminates the sign so that all numbers become positive. In this case, with Forecast 1, the error would be stated as .0009, .0009, .0009, .0009, .0016, .0016. Using squared error the forecasting technique would be judged best by which had the lowest average or mean squared error.

The mean absolute error and the mean squared error for the six forecasting techniques are shown in Table 5. The difference in mean forecast error shown in Table 5 is interesting. It would be more useful, however, if it could be stated that the differences were not purely due to chance. This can be tested for a pair of techniques by determining the probability that differences in means (like any two shown in Table 5) could have arisen by chance when the true value of the means were, in fact, the same.[16] This is a problem in testing that the difference in two means is zero. The procedure to test for statistical significance must consider the fact that we have paired observations, that is, each technique is used to forecast for each firm, and the errors in the two technqiues in forecasting for a particular firm may be related.

We will describe the procedure for testing for statistically significant differences in squared error. The procedure for any other criteria function is analogous and can be obtained by substituting it (e.g., absolute error) wherever squared error is used in the discussion below. The basic idea is to calculate the difference in the mean squared forecast

---

[16] It is necessary to initially test if all means in the table could be the same. This is done by using analysis of variance tests or the Friedman analysis of variance test. See Case Study One, below, for a further discussion.

error and then to determine how many standard deviations away from zero the difference in mean squared error is. The probability of obtaining a difference in mean squared forecast errors x standard deviations away from zero, when the true difference between techniques is zero, is then determined from the table of the t distribution for small samples (approximately less than 30) and the normal distribution for large samples. The part of this procedure that requires special comment is how to determine the standard deviation of the mean difference in squared forecast errors. The standard deviation of the *mean* difference in squared forecast errors is the standard deviation of the differences in squared forecast error divided by the square root of N. Algebraically, the standard deviation of the difference in squared forecast errors is

$$\sigma = \left[\frac{\left[\sum_{i=1}^{N} [(F_{1i} - A_i)^2 - (F_{2i} - A_i)^2] - D \right]^2}{N} \right]^{1/2}$$

where:

1. F_{1i} = The forecast for firm i with technique 1
2. F_{i2} = The forecast for firm i with technique 2
3. N = Number of firms for which forecasts are prepared
4. S_i = Actual for firm i

5. $D = \dfrac{\sum_{i=1}^{N} (F_{1i} - A_i)^2}{N} - \dfrac{\sum_{i=1}^{N} (F_{2i} - A_i)^2}{N}$

The standard deviation of the mean difference in squared forecast errors is σ/N; an example of the procedure is as follows. Consider Forecasts 1 and 3 in Table 5. The difference in squared errors for these forecasts are -0.6301, -0.1927, -0.0055, -0.9016, -0.0084, -0.9984. The mean difference in squared error is -0.4561. The standard deviation of these differences in errors is 0.9978, and the standard deviation of the mean squared error is 0.4074. Therefore, the mean is 1.12 standard deviations from zero. Looking in the table, the t distribution shows the probability that the actual mean difference is 1.12 standard deviations from zero, when the true difference from zero is 0.16. Thus, it is possible that we would observe differences as large as this by chance, and it is possible that the two forecasting techniques are really not different.

Although the absolute value and squared error are the most commonly used criteria, there are a large number of other sensible possibilities. The choice is important because different forecasts are better under different valuation systems. Forecasts 1 and Forecast 6 have the same absolute value of the error. However, Forecast 6 has a larger squared error since it has a few large errors rather than lots of small ones. Whether Forecast 1 and Forecast 6 are equivalent depends on whether an error of 0.08 is 4 times as costly as an error of 0.02 or 16 times as costly. Absolute value assumes the cost of the error depends strictly on the size of the error. Thus, an error of 0.08 counts four times as costly as an error 0.02. Squared error assumes that cost of an error depends on the square of the error. Thus, one large error is penalized more heavily than a series of small errors, the sum of which equals the large error. An error of 0.08 is penalized 16 times more heavily than an error of 0.02 $[(0.08/0.02)^2]$.

The persons evaluating forecasts must decide what is the cost of an error and select the system that most closely reproduces this cost structure. There is no reason that underestimates and overestimates should be treated alike. If these costs are different, then they should be treated differently. For example, underestimates could be squared while overestimates are evaluated using absolute value. Furthermore, the evaluation of the errors need not be done by simple formula. It is perfectly reasonable to tabulate the costs of various sized errors and for each forecasting technique utilize the table of costs to evaluate the forecast.

Although these variations are possible for most purposes, squared errors or absolute value of error are sufficiently close approximations to the true cost that one of these is chosen. The absolute value is chosen if costs are proportional to the size of the error, and squared error is chosen if the cost of a large error is much more than the cost of a series of small errors that sum up to the large error. Whatever the choice, it should be selected by choosing a technique that bears some relationship to the cost of the error.

Squared error—economic decomposition. Before leaving this section, it is worthwhile to examine how the squared error can be decomposed into components for further analysis. This decomposition may help the analyst determine the sources of error and aid him in correcting them. There are two ways to decompose the error. The first is to base the decomposition on the basis of the characteristics of the earnings forecasts. It is

$$\frac{1}{N}\sum_{i=1}^{-N} (P_i - A_i)^2 = (\bar{P} - \bar{A})^2 + (1 - B)^2 S_\rho^2 + (1 - \rho^2) S_A^2$$

where:

1. $\bar{P}$ = Average P $\left(\text{i.e., } \bar{P} = \dfrac{1}{N}\sum_{i=1}^{N} P_i\right)$

2. $\bar{A}$ = Average A $\left(\text{i.e., } \bar{A} = \dfrac{1}{N}\sum_{i=1}^{N} A_i\right)$

3. S_p = Standard deviation of P

   $\left(\text{i.e., } S_p = \left[\dfrac{1}{N}\sum_{i=1}^{N} (P_i - \bar{P})^2\right]^{1/2}\right)$

4. S_A = Standard deviation of A $\left(\text{i.e., } S_A = \left[\dfrac{1}{N}\sum_{i=1}^{N} (A_i - \bar{A})^2\right]^{1/2}\right)$

5. ρ = Correlation coefficient and is defined as in Equation (29)
6. B = The slope coefficient of the regression of A on P

The first term represents bias, the tendency of the average forecast to overestimate or underestimate the true average. The second term represents inefficiency or the tendency for forecasts to be underestimated at high values of P and overestimated at low values, or vice versa. If the beta of actual growth regressed on forecasted growth is greater than one, forecasts are underestimates at high values and overestimates at low values. If beta is less than one, the forecasts are overestimates at high values and underestimates at low values. The final component is the random disturbance term, a measure of error not related to the value of the prediction P or the realization A.

A second way to decompose the error is on the basis of universality of the error. Assume an analyst is forecasting earnings per share across a group of companies. One source of error could be due to misestimating the overall average because of general pessimism or optimism. A second source of error could be due to misestimating how some subgroup such as an industry would do. For example, errors could occur because the analyst incorrectly thought some industry would have spectacular performance and so adjusted all estimates in the industry upward. Finally, an error could occur because of misestimating company performance after accounting for economywide and industry influences. The formula for this breakdown is[17]

---

[17] This can be shown by substituting $\bar{P} + (\bar{P}_l - \bar{P}) + (P_i - \bar{P}_l)$ for P_i and noting that the cross-product terms cancel out.

$$\frac{1}{N}\sum_{i=1}^{N}(P_i - A_i)^2 = (\bar{P} - \bar{A})^2 + \frac{1}{N}\sum_{i=1}^{N}[(\bar{P}_I - \bar{P}) - (\bar{A}_I - \bar{A})]^2$$

$$+ \frac{1}{N}\sum_{i=1}^{N}[(P_i - \bar{P}_I) - (A_i - \bar{A}_i)]^2$$

where:

1. $\bar{P}$ = Mean value of P_i $\left(\text{i.e.,} \dfrac{1}{N}\sum_{i=1}^{N}P_i\right)$

2. $\bar{A}$ = Mean value of A_i
3. $\bar{P}_I$ = Mean value of predictor for each industry in turn
4. $\bar{A}_I$ = Mean value of actual for each industry in turn
5. P_i = A prediction
6. A_i = An actual

The terms in this expression are: error due to misestimating the overall mean, error due to misestimating subgroup or industry movements, and error in company forecast given the industry and economy estimates. Once again, it is convenient to divide both sides by the mean squared error so that the right side shows the proportion of error due to the three causes.

Theil inequality coefficient. Theil has developed a variation of the squared error technique for evaluating forecasts. The Theil inequality coefficient is essentially the squared error divided by the sum of the squared actual changes (i.e., actual this year minus actual last year). Since the sum of the squared actual change is constant across techniques, the ranking will be the same as the mean squared error. The advantage of this over the mean squared error is that while there in no natural meaning to the magnitude of the squared error, there is when one scales the data in a form like the Theil inequality coefficient. Two values for the inequality coefficient have meaning. Zero corresponds to perfect forecast, and one corresponds to a forecast that is exactly as good as would be produced by the assumption that next year is the same as last year. For example, in forecasting earnings the value one means that the forecast is exactly as good as would be obtained if next year's earnings had been forecasted to be the same as last year's. The formula for the inequality coefficient is as follows:

$$\frac{\displaystyle\sum_{i=1}^{N}(F_i - A_i)^2}{\displaystyle\sum_{i=1}^{N}(A_i - B_i)^2}$$

where:

F_i is the forecast.

A_i is the actual.

B_i is the actual in the previous period, the base value.

Other techniques.   The techniques discussed above represent most of the common ways forecasts are analytically evaluated. There is another group of techniques that can be used less frequently but are very powerful on occasions when they yield results. The fact that one set of forecasts has a lower mean squared error (or absolute error, and so forth) than a second source does not imply that each error is smaller. If each error from one technique were smaller than each error from a second technique, we could unequivocally reject one technique. Such an occurrence would be rare; however, a variant of this technique frequently yields results. If we rank the errors for each technique from largest to smallest, it is often the case that one technique always produces smaller errors than the second.[18] In this case, the technique that produces smaller errors is preferred to the second for almost all costs of errors.[19] For example, assume we evaluate two techniques for forecasting earnings by examining their forecasting ability on a sample of firms. If, after ranking errors from highest to lowest, one technique always had lower errors, it would be preferred under almost all cost of error functions.

A final caveat.   The alternate test of a forecasting technique is its value in the decision-making process. Two forecasts can be compared in the ways discussed previously, with one technique having superior performance, and yet have this statistical difference make no significant monetary difference. If one technique is more costly than a second, the statistically inferior method could potentially be preferred. For example, one set of earnings estimates could be statistically superior to a second and yet not be preferred since the second set is much cheaper and performs about as well in the security selection process. This could be the case if, for example, the more accurate source was purchased externally and the other source was an extrapolation of past values. A second example comes from the portfolio selection area. A number of years ago, the authors worked on techniques for providing estimates for

---

[18] The cumulative frequency function of errors from one technique lies to the right of the cumulative frequency function of errors from a second technique.

[19] Exceptions include the case where the cost of an error depends on the particular unit on which it arose or the cost of an error is a different function of the size of the error over different size errors (e.g., underestimates are less costly than overestimates).

inputs for portfolio selection. Some more costly and sophisticated techniques seemed to produce better estimates than the naive methods. Since the former were more costly, it was important to check to see that they produced significantly better portfolio selection or their use could not be justified.

THE ACCURACY OF EARNINGS FORECASTS— TWO CASE STUDIES

Up to this point we have presented a number of time series forecasting techniques and discussed methods for evaluating the accuracy of forecasts. In this final section of this chapter we will examine two case studies involving the forecast of earnings per share. The first case study compares the forecast prepared by a set of time series models both with each other and with a small set of forecasts prepared by individual analysts. The second case study examines the characteristics and accuracy of the average (concensus forecast) of earnings per share prepared by a large set of security analysts.

CASE STUDY ONE—TIME SERIES FORECASTS

The problem examined is to forecast annual earnings per share for a group of industrial companies.[20] Since annual earnings were to be forecasted, models employing a seasonal adjustment were not employed. Instead the following eight models were used:

1 & 2. Two forms of moving average models—one in which the optimum length was set by looking at the forecast error for each company and choosing the lengths which minimized forecast error, and one where the length was set at four years.

3. An exponentially smoothed model with a multiplicative trend: Equations (8), (9), and (10).

4. An exponentially smoothed model with an additive trend: Equations (5), (6), and (7).

5 & 6. Models similar to 3 and 4 but where the trend was assumed to exhibit a trend.[21]

---

[20] The discussion in this section is based on a previously published article. See Elton and Gruber [11].

[21] There are a number of variations of exponential models that could be used. These are two of them. We have not discussed all of them because of space limitations and because the reader should be able to perform the modifications himself. The equations are:

Multiplicative exponential with trend in trend:

$$\overline{S}_t = \overline{S}_{t-1}\overline{R}_{t-1}\overline{D}_{t-1} + W_e[S_t - (\overline{S}_{t-1}\overline{R}_{t-1}\overline{D}_{t-1})]$$

7. Linear regression—assuming an additive trend.
8. Log linear regression—assuming a multiplicative trend.

In addition, a naive forecasting model was introduced as a benchmark. The naive model forecast simply by predicting that next period's earnings would be equal to last period's earnings plus the previous year's change in earnings.

These nine models were all used to estimate earnings for the period 1962–67 on a stratified random sample of 180 firms selected from the Standard & Poor's Compustat Tape. In order to test the generality of the results from the 180-firm sample, these firms were divided into three random samples of 60 firms each.[22] In particular, the following forecasts were made.[23]

$$\bar{R}_t = \bar{R}_{t-1}\bar{D}_{t-1} + W_R\left[\frac{\bar{S}_t}{\bar{S}_{t-1}} - (\bar{R}_{t-1}\bar{D}_{t-1})\right]$$

$$\bar{D}_t = \bar{D}_{t-1} + W_D\left[\frac{\bar{R}_t}{\bar{R}_{t-1}} - \bar{D}_{t-1}\right]$$

$$\hat{S}_{t,T} = \bar{S}_t[\pi_{i-1}^T\bar{R}_t(\bar{D}_t)^i]$$

Additive exponential with trend in trend:

$$\bar{S}_t = \bar{S}_{t-1} + \bar{R}_{t-1} + \bar{D}_{t-1} + W_e[S_t - (\bar{S}_{t-1} + \bar{R}_{t-1} + \bar{D}_{t-1})]$$

$$\bar{R}_t = \bar{R}_{t-1} + \bar{D}_{t-1} + W_R[(\bar{S}_t - \bar{S}_{t-1}) - (\bar{R}_{t-1} + \bar{D}_{t-1})]$$

$$\bar{D}_t = \bar{D}_{t-1} + W_D[(\bar{R}_t - \bar{R}_{t-1}) - \bar{D}_{t-1}]$$

$$\hat{S}_{t,T} = \bar{S}_t + \left[\sum_{i-1}^T (\bar{R}_t + {}_i\bar{D}_t)\right]$$

[22] The sampling procedure consisted of drawing 180 firms from the Compustat Tape in the following manner: select four-digit standard industrial classifications using a table of random numbers; select all firms with a suitable history within the four-digit industrial classification; continue to randomly select industrial classifications until 180 firms were sampled. (Our 180 firms represented 44 different four-digit industrial classifications). Two points need further clarification. Our sample is biased in favor of large stable firms, because in order to parameterize our models, we eliminated all firms with either an incomplete earnings history or negative earnings prior to 1962 (the year we start our forecasts). The rather unusual stratifying procedure was used in preparation for a parallel study which compared more sophisticated econometric models employing industry effects with the best techniques found in this study. See Elton and Gruber [9].

[23] Only two three-year forecasts were made in order to avoid overlapping forecasts within the six-year period under study. The two-year forecasts were designed to have the same base years (points of time at which the forecasts were made) as the three-year forecasts. Fortunately, the results of the two- and three-year forecasts were so clear-cut that more replication seems unnecessary.

TABLE 6 Relative Performance of Forecasting Techniques Based on Value of *U* (one-year forecast)

	Moving Averages			Regressions		Exponentials			
						Multiplicative		Additive	
	Fixed	Opti-mum	Naive	Log Linear	Linear	Trend in Trend	No Trend in Trend	Trend in Trend	No Trend in Trend
U	0.1230	0.0670	0.0622	0.1105	0.0595	0.0627	0.0500	0.0527	0.0498
Rank	9	7	5	8	4	6	2	3	1

1. One-year forecasts for each of the years 1962–67.
2. Two-year forecasts for the years 1964 and 1966.
3. Three-year forecasts for the years 1964 and 1967.

The square of the forecast errors was the primary method used to judge the accuracy of forecasts. In addition, we also report a variation of the standard error of estimate in the form:

$$U = \frac{\Sigma_i \, (\text{Actual}_i \; - \; \text{Forecast}_i)^2}{\Sigma_i \, (\text{Actual}_i)^2}$$

This statistic resembles the coefficient of variation and has the advantage of expressing the forecast error as a fraction of actual earnings.[24]

Performance of the model—the one-year case. The accuracy of each model in making one-year estimates of earnings per share can be seen from Table 6. This table presents the value of *U* for each technique, derived from forecasts for all 180 companies in each of six years, and ranks the techniques on the basis of increasing *U*.

Evaluation of the relative performance of alternative forecasting techniques will be postponed to the next section where the statistical significance of differences in performance is discussed. However, at this time it is useful to mention some general conclusions which are more readily seen by examining Table 6. In comparing moving averages, an optimum length moving average which can take on different lengths for

---

All data used in forecasting were available at the time of the forecast. For example, in making the one-year forecast of earnings in 1964 we used data through 1963, and in making the three-year forecast for 1964 we used data through 1961.

[24] This statistic is based on Theil's *U* statistic as reported in [24].

different companies seems to outperform a fixed length moving average for all companies. This conclusion is consistent with some earlier tests which indicated that a regression model which allowed the time span to vary between companies outperformed a regression model which employed the same number of years of data for all companies.

The comparison of all the additive models (models assuming earnings grow by a certain dollar amount each year) with their parallel multiplicative models (assuming earnings grow by a constant percent each year) reveals that the additive assumption is the better one. The linear regression outperformed the log linear regression; the additive exponential model with trend in trend outperformed the multiplicative exponential with trend in trend, and the additive exponential with no trend in trend outperformed the multiplicative exponential with no trend in trend. The difference in performance between the additive and the multiplicative models implies that the extrapolation of past rates of growth has a tendency to overestimate the extent of earnings change over the short run. It is interesting to note (as discussed later in the paper) that this is not true for longer run forecasts where the multiplicative model performs best. The introduction of a trend in trend in both the additive and multiplicative exponential leads to a deterioration in the forecasts. An examination of individual forecasts indicates that adding the trend in trend causes the forecasts for a small number of companies to deteriorate severely.

The ordering of the mechanical techniques should be of interest to management. Since differences in the cost of operating these techniques should be very small, the differences in performance are likely to be important.[25] It remains to be seen if management can have confidence in these results or if they could have arisen by chance alone.

Dominance among forecasting techniques. In this section, differences in the square of the forecast errors between different forecasting techniques differences are tested to see if they are statistically significant. Before testing differences between paired sets of forecasts (e.g., between the forecast error for the naive method and the log linear regression), however, it is necessary to determine whether all of the forecast errors could have come from the same population (whether all the methods may, in fact, yield the same result).

Because each firm appears as an observation for each technique, the samples of the square of the forecast errors for each technique are not independent, and the statistical tests must be appropriate for related samples. Under very stringent assumptions, namely, that the standard errors are independently drawn from normally distributed populations,

---

[25] In fact, the technique that performed best should be one of the least costly techniques to operate.

that the populations all have the same variance, and that the row and column effects are additive, analysis of variance tests would be employed. Because each of these assumptions appears unrealistic in this case, a nonparametric test, the Friedman two-way analysis of variance by ranks, is used.[26] Application of Friedman's test to the one-year forecasts reveals that the probability that all forecasting techniques did equally well is considerably less than one in a thousand. This highly significant result is also obtained when the sample is divided into three samples of 60 firms each.

Since significant differences exist in the forecasts produced by the mechanical techniques employed in this study, it is appropriate to undertake a detailed examination of the performance of each technique against all other techniques taken one at a time. In order to measure differences in performances, the frequency function of the differences in squared error between each pair of forecasting techniques is examined. For example, one observation determining the frequency function for technique A versus technique B would be the squared error in the forecast of company one by technique A minus the squared error in the forecast of company one by technique B. Repeating this for all possible companies produces one frequency function from which the comparative performance of techniques A and B can be judged. If the differences across all firms had the same sign, then this would indicate that technique A dominated technique B. Given the sample size, this would be unlikely to occur. What can and does happen is that some frequency functions have mostly positive or negative values and a mean signficantly different from zero. When the mean is significantly different from zero, it is highly unlikely that the techniques being compared forecast equally well in terms of the square of the forecast errors, and it is appropriate to conclude that one technique is dominated by a second.

From the central limit theorem, the distribution of the mean of these frequency functions is normally distributed with mean equal to the mean of the frequency function and standard deviation equal to the standard deviation of the frequency function divided by the square root of the number of observations.[27] Table 7 presents the results of a statistical test for the one-year forecasts.[28]

---

[26] See Siegel [23, pp. 166–72] for a discussion of this test.

[27] That the frequency functions under question were derived from differencing two variables should not bother the reader. The central limit theorem states that as the number of observations increases, the distribution of the mean is normally distributed no matter what the original frequency function. The number of observations we used ranged from 120 to 1,080. A two-tailed test was used in testing significance since we were not willing to assert in advance which technique would dominate.

[28] To test the statistical significance of the mean when the standard deviation is unknown, one should use the t test. However, for samples as large as ours, this can be approximated by the normal.

TABLE 7 Relative Performance of the Forecasting Techniques* Based on Squared Error One-Year Forecasts

| | | | Regressions | | Exponentials | | | |
| | | | | | Multiplicative | | Additive | |
	Optimum Moving Average	Naive	Log Linear	Linear	Trend in Trend	No Trend in Trend	Trend in Trend	No Trend in Trend
Moving averages:								
Fixed	0.2069 (8.68)†	0.2257 (5.55)†	0.0642 (1.38)	0.2061 (6.31)†	0.1115 (2.56)‡	0.2327 (6.46)†	0.2364 (6.80)†	0.2721 (8.79)†
Optimum	0.0	0.0187 (0.56)	−0.1427 (−3.57)†	0.0008 (0.03)	0.0954 (−2.39)‡	0.0257 (0.88)	0.0295 (1.12)	0.0652 (2.99)†
Naive	0.0	0.0	−0.1614 (−3.77)†	−0.0195 (−0.66)	−0.1142 (−3.07)†	0.0070 (0.24)	0.0108 (0.38)	0.0464 (1.69)§
Regressions:								
Log linear	0.0	0.0	0.0	0.1419 (4.11)†	0.0473 (1.11)	0.1685 (4.59)†	0.1722 (4.65)†	0.2079 (5.63)†
Linear	0.0	0.0	0.0	0.0	−0.0946 (−2.70)‡	0.0266 (1.12)	0.0303 (1.47)	0.0660 (3.69)†
Exponentials:								
Multiplicative:								
Trend in trend	0.0	0.0	0.0	0.0	0.0	0.1212 (4.93)†	0.1249 (4.17)†	0.1606 (5.02)†
No trend in trend	0.0	0.0	0.0	0.0	0.0	0.0	0.0038 (0.23)	0.0394 (2.28)‡
Additive:								
Trend in trend	0.0	0.0	0.0	0.0	0.0	0.0	0.0	0.0357 (2.70)‡
No trend in trend	0.0	0.0	0.0	0.0	0.0	0.0	0.0	0.0

* The top number in each cell is the difference in squared error between the technique listed at the left side of the table and the technique listed at the top of the table. Therefore, a minus sign indicates the technique at the top of the table performed best. The numbers in parentheses are the ratios of differences in the squared error of any two forecasting techniques to the standard error of this difference.
† Significant at 1 percent level.   ‡ Significant at 5 percent level.   § Significant at 10 percent level.

In this table, as in the ones that follow, the entries enclosed in parentheses are the ratios of differences in the squared error of any two forecasting techniques to the standard error of this difference. A minus sign indicates that the technique at the left of the table outperformed the technique listed at the top of the table. A plus sign indicates that the technique at the top performed better.

Perhaps the most striking result is that the additive exponential with no trend in trend outperforms every other technique at a statistically significant level. In fact, it outperforms every technique but two other exponentials and the naive model at the 0.01 level of significance.[29] Dominance is also apparent among other exponentials. For example, among the remaining exponential techniques, the multiplicative exponential with trend in trend is dominated by all exponential techniques at the 1 percent level. The remaining two exponentials do not show any statistically significant differences.

The next best group of techniques consists of the naive model and the optimum moving average. The naive model appears to do slightly better though the difference is not significant at the 0.10 level. The fixed moving average is clearly inferior to both of these techniques at the 0.01 level, and, in fact, is inferior to any other forecasting models selected.

The remaining techniques, the regression models, also differ in performance. The preferred technique is the linear regression, which outperforms the log linear regression at the 1 percent level.

In summary, the best exponential forecasting technique is the additive model with no trend in trend, the best moving average is the optimum moving average, and the best regression is the linear model. All of these differences are significant at the 0.05 level or better. Comparing these three models and the naive model shows that:

a. The additive exponential with no trend in trend dominates the other three techniques at a statistically significant level.

b. The ordering of the remaining techniques (from best to worst) are the naive model, the optimum moving average, and the linear regression. However, none of these differences is significant at the 10 percent level.

This demonstration of statistically significant differences in performance, combined with the fact that the technique which performed best should be among the least costly to operate, should be of use to management in the selection of a forecasting technique.

---

[29] Identical ordering appears in each of the three smaller samples investigated, but the results are not always significant at the same level as in the larger sample.

Comparison with analysts. Having examined a large group of mechanical extrapolation techniques and determined the dominant technique, the next step is to compare this technique with some analysts' estimates of future earnings. Data on analysts' estimates were provided by three services: a large pension fund, a well-known investment advisory service, and a large brokerage house. Data were provided only for the latter three years (1964–66) for which forecasts had been made. Furthermore, no institution followed all of the stocks in this study's sample so that performance had to be judged across the stocks which were common to both the individual institution and our sample (resulting in a different sample for each institution).

These three institutions were not selected at random. In fact, one would expect them to be among those institutions that had produced the best earnings projections. The investment advisory service was selected after analysts in a number of financial institutions indicated that this was the service in whose projections they placed the greatest faith. Furthermore, the other two institutions were the only ones among those contacted who were willing to expose their forecasts to rigorous testing. Since such testing had potential repercussions within their own firms, it indicated some confidence in their projections. Another factor which might bias the results in favor of the analysts is that their estimates were made after the previous year's actual earnings were generally available. Thus, analysts were able to incorporate actual data from the first two or three months of the forecast year rather than being restricted to only data available at the close of the fiscal year.

These biases, together with the fact that analysts have the opportunity to incorporate influences which may not be fully reflected in past earnings into their analysis, should lead one to expect analysts' estimates to outperform simple mechanical extrapolation techniques. Given a large cost differential between the preparation of earnings estimates by extrapolation techniques and by security analysts, the analysts' estimates must be a great deal better in order to justify the allocation of a large amount of their time to the preparation of earnings estimates.

The average squared forecast error for the analyst and the additive exponential model are reported in Table 8 along with the t value associated with the difference in performance.[30]

The average data show that the best mechanical technique outperforms the security analysts at one financial institution but is outperformed by the analysts at two others. However, none of the three

---

[30] The t value represents the number of standard deviations the sum of the difference in the squared forecast error is from zero. A plus sign indicates that the mechanical technique has done better than the analyst. As we discussed earlier, the mean error should be normally distributed, and a two-tailed test is appropriate to test whether it is significantly different from zero.

TABLE 8 Relative Performance of Security Analysts and Additive Exponential Model Based on Squared Error

	Investment Advisory Service	Brokerage House	Pension Fund
Sample size	213	177	84
Security analysts	0.0231	0.0342	0.0310
Additive exponential	0.0221	0.0352	0.0441
t value	+0.12	−0.34	−1.23

differences is significant at even the 20 percent level, and two of three differences are not even significant at the 35 percent level. In short, there is not statistically significant evidence to indicate that the forecasts made by analysts are different from those made by an exponentially weighted moving average employing an additive trend.[31] Insofar as better forecasts lead to better valuation models, the lack of such evidence would seem to indicate that mechanical techniques exist which can provide valid inputs to financial models and that these techniques (given their low cost) should be employed at least as a benchmark against which to judge analysts' performance.[32]

Performance of the model—the two- and three-year forecasts.

The accuracy of the model in making both two- and three-year estimates of earnings can be seen from Table 9. This table presents the values of U derived from two forecasts for 180 companies.

The detailed analysis of these data will be presented below in a discussion of statistical significance. However, it is useful to note that all of the exponential techniques appear to perform much better than any of the other techniques used for both the two-year and three-year forecasts. In fact, the exponential forecasts appear to do just about as well as they do in the one-year case, while all the other methods degenerate badly. For example, the difference in the U value for the exponential multiplicative with no trend in trend is less than 6 percent in going from a one- to a three-year forecast, while the increase in U for the naive model is more than 300 percent.

---

[31] One must exercise care in generalizing these results since, to the extent that the superior performance of the additive exponential was peculiar to our sample, the results may be biased against the analysts' performance. Cragg and Malkiel [6] in an earlier study reached a similar conclusion.

[32] It is interesting to note that the institutions which followed more stocks did a poorer job of forecasting, relative to the mechanical technique, than the institutions which followed a smaller number. This may indicate that mechanical techniques provide an efficient way of expanding the number of stocks an institution can follow.

TABLE 9 Relative Performance of Forecasting Techniques Based on Value of U

	Moving Averages			Regressions		Exponentials			
						Multiplicative		Additive	
	Fixed	Opti-mum	Naive	Log Linear	Linear	Trend in Trend	No Trend in Trend	Trend in Trend	No Trend in Trend
Two-year forecasts	0.2150	0.1522	0.2352	0.2232	0.1590	0.0523	0.0517	0.0673	0.0717
Three-year forecasts	0.3142	0.2022	0.4010	0.3985	0.2102	0.1058	0.0530	0.0563	0.0525

As a first step in testing statistical significance, Friedman's test is again applied to see if differences exist in the forecasting ability of the methods. For the two- and three-year forecasts, likelihood that the techniques forecast equally well can be rejected at considerably better than the 0.001 level.[33]

Dominance among techniques. For forecasts beyond one year the dominant techniques are the exponential forecasts. Each exponential technique dominates every other technique in both the two-year and three-year forecasts at the 0.01 level. (See Tables 10 and 11.) When the 180-firm sample is split into three 60-firm samples, the dominance is also apparent. Each exponential technique dominates every other technique at the 0.01 level except for two of the samples for the two-year forecasts. In these samples there are a total of four cases where the exponential dominates the other techniques at the 0.05 level rather than the 0.01 level.[34]

It is difficult to choose among the exponential techniques. Although the multiplicative exponential with no trend in trend shows the best performance for both two- and three-year forecasts, its performance is significant in only half the cases. It outperforms the two additive models at the 0.10 level for two-year forecasts, and it outperforms the other multiplicative model at the 0.10 level for three-year forecasts. Among

---

[33] The same results hold in each of the three samples.

[34] In sample one the multiplicative exponential with trend in trend dominates the optimum moving average and the linear regression at the 5 percent level. In sample two the optimum moving average is only dominated by the additive exponentials at the 5 percent level.

TABLE 10 Relative Performance of the Forecasting Techniques* Based on Squared Error Two-Year Forecasts

| | Optimum Moving Average | Regressions | | | Exponentials | | | |
| | | Naive | Log Linear | Linear | Multiplicative | | Additive | |
					Trend in Trend	No Trend in Trend	Trend in Trend	No Trend in Trend
Moving averages:								
Fixed	0.2059 (4.47)	−0.2285 (−1.74)§	−0.0610 (−0.58)	0.0942 (1.13)	0.6196 (7.00)†	0.6300 (7.73)†	0.5578 (7.33)†	0.5569 (7.41)†
Optimum	0.0	−0.4345 (−3.52)†	−0.2670 (−2.97)†	−0.1118 (−1.66)§	0.4136 (5.40)†	0.4240 (6.26)†	0.3519 (6.05)†	0.3510 (6.45)†
Naive	0.0	0.0	0.1675 (1.27)	0.3227 (2.62)‡	0.8481 (7.42)†	0.8586 (7.79)†	0.7863 (7.32)†	0.7855 (7.18)†
Regressions:								
Log linear	0.0	0.0	0.0	0.1552 (1.88)§	0.6806 (6.76)†	0.6910 (7.22)†	0.6188 (7.15)†	0.6179 (7.04)†
Linear	0.0	0.0	0.0	0.0	0.5254 (5.99)†	0.5359 (6.70)†	0.4636 (7.02)†	0.4628 (7.05)†
Exponentials:								
Multiplicative:								
Trend in trend	0.0	0.0	0.0	0.0	0.0	0.0105 (0.36)	−0.0617 (−1.27)	−0.0626 (−1.18)
No trend in trend	0.0	0.0	0.0	0.0	0.0	0.0	−0.0722 (−1.83)§	−0.0731 (−1.86)§
Additive:								
Trend in trend	0.0	0.0	0.0	0.0	0.0	0.0	0.0	−0.009 (−0.05)
No trend in trend	0.0	0.0	0.0	0.0	0.0	0.0	0.0	0.0

* The top number in each cell is the difference in squared error between the technique listed at the top of the table and the technique listed at the left side of the table. Therefore, a minus sign indicates the technique at the left of the table performed best. The numbers in parentheses are the ratios of differences in the squared error of any two forecasting techniques to the standard error of this difference.
† Significant at 1 percent level.   ‡ Significant at 5 percent level.   § Significant at 10 percent level.

TABLE 11 Relative Performance of the Forecasting Techniques* Based on Squared Error Three-Year Forecasts

| | Optimum Moving Average | Naive | Regressions | | Exponentials | | | |
| | | | | | Multiplicative | | Additive | |
			Log Linear	Linear	Trend in Trend	No Trend in Trend	Trend in Trend	No Trend in Trend
Moving averages:								
Fixed	0.1837 (3.92)†	−0.5803 (−3.26)†	−0.1809 (−1.34)	0.0523 (0.48)	0.9664 (7.73)†	1.0481 (8.80)†	1.0236 (9.32)†	1.0579 (9.73)†
Optimum	0.0	−0.7640 (−4.52)†	−0.3647 (−3.00)†	−0.1314 (−1.39)	0.7826 (6.70)†	0.8644 (7.85)†	0.8398 (8.24)†	0.8742 (9.04)†
Naive	0.0	0.0	0.3995 (2.17)‡	0.6327 (3.66)†	1.5467 (9.30)†	1.6285 (10.39)†	1.6039 (10.68)†	1.6383 (10.99)†
Regressions:								
Log linear	0.0	0.0	0.0	0.2333 (2.12)‡	1.1473 (8.50)†	1.2291 (9.13)†	1.2045 (9.57)†	1.2388 (9.73)†
Linear	0.0	0.0	0.0	0.0	0.9140 (7.86)†	0.9958 (8.92)†	0.9712 (9.10)†	1.0056 (9.21)†
Exponentials:								
Multiplicative:								
Trend in trend	0.0	0.0	0.0	0.0	0.0	0.0818 (1.72)§	0.0572 (1.04)	0.0916 (1.37)
No trend in trend	0.0	0.0	0.0	0.0	0.0	0.0	−0.0246 (−0.53)	0.0098 (0.17)
Additive:								
Trend in trend	0.0	0.0	0.0	0.0	0.0	0.0	0.0	0.0344 (1.01)
No trend in trend	0.0	0.0	0.0	0.0	0.0	0.0	0.0	0.0

* The top number in each cell is the difference in squared error between the technique listed at the top of the table and the technique listed at the left side of the table. Therefore, a minus sign indicates the technique at the left of the table performed best. The numbers in parentheses are the ratios of differences in the squared error of any two forecasting techniques to the standard error of this difference.
† Significant at 1 percent level. ‡ Significant at 5 percent level. § Significant at 10 percent level.

the nonexponentials some definite patterns can be observed. Once again the optimum moving average dominates the fixed moving average, and the simple linear regression dominates the log regression. Comparing the optimum moving average and the linear regression indicates that the optimum moving average performs better.

Unlike the case of one-year forecasts, the naive model performs very poorly. It is dominated by every forecasting technique, although only at the 10 percent level in the case of log linear regression.

In summary, the order of performance for multiyear forecasts is:

1. The exponentials with the multiplicative exponentials with no trend in trend.
2. The optimum moving average.
3. The linear regression.
4. The fixed moving average.
5. The log linear regression.
6. The naive model.

Generality of the results. The sample of 180 firms was split into subsamples of 60 firms each so that the generality of the results first reported could be examined.[35] If the forecasting technique that performed best varied a great deal between firms, one should find instability in their performance between samples and be unwilling to generalize the results beyond the 180-firm sample. The results of this sample splitting are very stable. At no time does technique A perform significantly better than technique B in one sample and technique B significantly better than technique A in a second. There are reversals where the preferred technique changes between samples, but in these cases (and they were rare) neither technique shows a significant difference. There is a slight reduction in statistical significance when comparing the 60-firm samples to the 180-firm samples. For example, the 180-firm three-year forecasts have 25 cases of dominance at the 0.01 level, 2 at the 0.05 level, and 1 at the 0.10 level. In sample one, there are 22 cases of dominance at the 0.01 level, 3 cases of dominance at the 0.05 level, and 1 case at the 0.10 level. The fact that statistical significance is in general maintained in the subsamples and that no major changes are found in the ordering of the mechanical techniques between samples indicates the generality of our results.

---

[35] While our results show statistical stability across our samples, the reader should realize that our sample may be biased as a representation of all firms. The firms in our sample are large, have a continuous earnings history, are industrial firms, and are heavily representative of a few industries. We can think of our data as an unbiased sample from firms with the above characteristics.

CASE STUDY TWO—THE PROPERTIES OF CONSENSUS FORECASTS

The purpose of this case study is to show how the diagnostic tools examined earlier can be used to gain insight into the attributes of the average forecast prepared by a large sample of security analysts.

The Sample

Our data source was the I/B/E/S database put together by Lynch, Jones and Ryan, a New York brokerage firm. Lynch, Jones and Ryan collect, on a monthly basis, earnings estimates from all major brokerage firms on over 2,000 corporations. The earnings estimates are for each of the next two years. Lynch, Jones and Ryan publish a number of characteristics of these earnings estimates for each corporation followed. These include, among others, the arithmetic mean, median, range, and standard deviation of the estimates of earnings per share for each corporation.

For part of this study, we wanted to have earnings estimates prepared a given number of months before the end of the fiscal year to be a common calendar time. This restriction means that all analysts would have access to the same macroeconomic information at the time these forecasts were prepared (N months before the end of the fiscal year). Because the majority of firms have fiscal years ending in December, only these firms were selected.

Our second restriction was to include only firms followed by three or more analysts. We studied properties of consensus estimates of earnings. Requiring three analysts was a trade-off between a desire for a large sample and a desire to have the forecasts reflective of a consensus rather than of the idiosyncrasies of one or two analysts. Our final sample consisted of 414 firms for each of the years 1976, 1977, and 1978.

Size of Analysts' Errors

Our first set of tests involved a direct examination of the size of analysts' errors in predicting change in earnings and the growth rate in earnings per share. The absolute error in earnings and growth rates as well as Theil's inequality coefficient (see earlier discussion) formulated in terms of both earnings change and growth rates were examined.

All the analysis in this section was done for alternative measures of error. Alternative formulations were employed because without knowledge of potential user's loss function, one measure could not be singled out as best. Because the results of the analysis were sufficiently similar under alternative measures, in most cases the analysis is reported in terms of error in growth, and differences that arise from other measures are briefly noted.

TABLE 12 Regressions of Mean Consensus Error on Time

$$P = a + bT + \varepsilon$$

	Dollar Error			Error in Growth			Theil's U in Change			Theil's U in Growth		
	a	b	R^2	a	b	R^2	a	b	R^2	a	b	R^2
Overall	.146	.036	.997	.043	.013	.998	.083	.054	.990	−.061	.061	.947
1976	.144	.035	.996	.048	.015	.998	.038	.045	.988	−.049	.048	.944
1977	.159	.036	.991	.045	.013	.991	.164	.079	.985	−.077	.081	.891
1978	.136	.037	.994	.036	.013	.993	.062	.042	.949	−.068	.064	.980

To analyze the time-series properties of errors in forecasts, we regressed each of our measures on time. The results are presented in Table 12. Month 1 is the month in which analysts prepared their last forecast of earnings per share for a fiscal year, and month 12 is 12 months earlier. Thus, the positive regression slope indicates a decrease in errors in forecasts over time. The most striking feature of Table 12 is the regularity of the decline in errors over successive forecasts. The reader might well anticipate a decline in error size over time, given that additional information is made available throughout the year. The high degree of association between error and time (over 99 percent in some cases) shows that the decline in error is about the same size from month to month over the year.

The second striking feature of Table 12 is the similarity between years for most of our error measures. For example, the change in the error for different years between months was 3.5 cents, 3.6 cents, and 3.7 cents for dollar error. Using the Chow test, we cannot reject the hypothesis that the equations are the same at the 5 percent level of significance. Thus, one cannot reject the appropriateness of pooling the observations across years.

For error in growth, the decline per month was .015, .013, and .013 in the three years. Once again, one could not reject the hypothesis that the regressions were the same in each year. Similar results held for other measures.

Before leaving this section, some comments on the Theil inequality coefficient are in order. Theil's measure for growth ranged from .801 in month 12 down to .055 in month 1. This pattern implied that analysts forecasted better than the naive model of no change and that their forecasts became more accurate as the fiscal year progressed.

Diagnosis of Analysts' Errors

In a previous section of this chapter we discussed two potential decompositions of errors. The results of applying both to consensus forecasts of security analysts is presented in Table 13 and is discussed below.

TABLE 13 Partitioning of Percentage Error in Growth

	Economy	Industry	Company	Bias	Inefficiency	Random Error
January	2.0%	37.3%	60.7%	1.0%	27.4%	71.6%
February	2.2	36.8	61.0	1.1	26.3	72.6
March	2.4	36.2	61.5	1.7	14.2	84.1
April	2.1	33.1	64.8	1.8	8.6	89.6
May	2.5	32.6	64.9	2.2	7.8	90.0
June	2.7	29.4	67.9	2.5	9.5	88.0
July	2.8	30.2	67.0	2.6	6.7	90.7
August	2.7	30.6	66.8	2.4	7.7	89.9
September	2.7	26.5	70.8	2.4	8.5	89.1
October	2.3	26.3	71.5	2.2	6.4	91.4
November	1.3	23.0	75.7	1.6	3.4	95.0
December	0.8	15.5	83.7	0.9	3.0	96.1

Partition by level of aggregation. Table 13 presents the partition of MSFE, in percentage terms, by level of aggregation. Note that the error in forecasting the average level of growth in earnings per share for the economy is quite small and is below 3 percent of the total error. Analysts on average make very little error in estimating the average growth rate in earnings per share for the economy.

The vast majority of error in forecasting arises from misestimates of industry performance and company performance. The percentage of error due to industry misestimates starts as 37.3 percent in January and declines over time to 15.5 percent. Similarly, the percentage of error due to misestimating individual companies starts at 60.7 percent in January and increases to 83.7 percent by December. We already know that analysts become more accurate as the fiscal year progresses. Now we see that while analysts become more accurate in forecasting both industry performance and company performance, their ability to forecast industry performance grows relative to their ability to forecast company performance over the year.

Partitioning by forecast characteristics. Table 13 also presents the results of partitioning analysts' mean square error by forecast characteristics. It is apparent that bias is an extremely small source of error and in all months is below 3 percent. Note that inefficiency starts as a fairly important component of the error, but its importance diminishes as successive forecasts are made. The percentage of error accounted for by inefficiency begins at about 27 percent for early forecasts and shrinks to 3 percent as successive forecasts are made during the year. The percent of error due to random error grows from 71.6 percent to 96.1 percent over the year. This initial importance of inefficiency is due primarily to the tendency of analysts to systematically overestimate the growth for high growth companies and to overestimate shrinkage in earnings for very low growth companies. This can be seen from the fact that B was below one for all three years examined. This indicates that a linear correction applied to analysts' forecasts of growth could improve these forecasts.

CONCLUSION

In this chapter we have presented some of the more commonly used time series forecasting techniques and methods for diagnosing forecast accuracy. We also reviewed an application of these techniques to the problem of forecasting earnings. These techniques are relatively inexpensive to use and represent at least a good benchmark against which to judge subjective forecasts as well as the forecasts produced by more sophisticated econometric models. Because we believe that these techniques are most useful as an objective standard against which to evaluate other forecasts, we have included a large section on the evaluation of forecasts.

Before closing we should warn the reader that while we have covered the time series techniques which have received the greatest use in industry, we have not covered all of the modern literature on time series techniques. The mathematically sophisticated reader might find three additional techniques of interest.

1. Spectral analysis—see [13], [14].
2. Box Jenkins—see [3], [4].
3. Kalyman filters—see [16].

REFERENCES

[1] BALL, RAY, and PHILIP BROWN. "Some Preliminary Findings on the Association between the Earnings of a Firm, Its Industry and the Economy." *Empirical Research in Accounting: Selected Studies.* Supplement. *Journal of Accounting Research* 5 (1967), pp. 55–77.

[2] BEAVER, WILLIAM. "The Information Content of Annual Earnings Announcements." *Empirical Research in Accounting: Selected Studies.* Supplement. *Journal of Accounting* 6 (1968).

[3] BOX, G., and G. JENKINS. "Some Statistical Aspects of Adaptive Optimization and Control." *Journal of Royal Statistical Society,* B24 (1962).

[4] ———. *Statistical Models for Forecasting and Control.* San Francisco: Holden Day, forthcoming.

[5] BROWN, ROBERT G. *Smoothing Forecasting and Prediction of Discrete Time Series.* Englewood Cliffs, N.J.: Prentice-Hall, 1962.

[6] CRAGG, JOHN, and BURTON MALKIEL. "The Consensus and Accuracy of Some Predictions of the Growth of Corporate Earnings." *Journal of Finance,* March 1968, pp. 67–84.

[7] ELTON, EDWIN J., and MARTIN J. GRUBER. "Estimating the Dependence Structure of Share Prices—Implications for Portfolio Selection." *Journal of Finance* 28, no. 5 (December 1973).

[8] ———. "Homogeneous Groups and the Testing of Economic Hyphothesis." *Journal of Financial and Quantitative Analysis* 4 (January 1970) pp. 581–602.

[9] ———. "Improved Forecasting through the Design of Homogeneous Groups." *Journal of Business* 44, no. 4 (October 1971), pp. 432–50.

[10] ———. *Security Evaluation and Portfolio Analysis.* Englewood Cliffs, N.J.: Prentice-Hall, 1972.

[11] ———. "Earnings Estimates and the Accuracy of Expectational Data." *Management Science* 18, no. 8 (April 1972), pp. B409–22.

[12] ELTON, EDWIN J., MARTIN J. GRUBER, and MUSTAFA. "Professional Expectations: Accuracy and Diagnosis of Errors." *Journal of Financial and Quantitative Analysis,* December 1984, pp. 351–63.

[13] GRANGER, C. W., and HATANAKA. *Spectral Analysis of Economic Time Series.* Princeton, N.J.: Princeton University Press, 1964.

[14] JENKINS, G., and D. WATTS. *Spectral Analysis and Its Applications.* San Francisco: Holden-Day, 1969.

[15] JONES, R. H. "Exponential Smoothing for Multivariate Time Series." *Journal of Royal Statistical Society,* Ser. B28, pp. 286–93.

[16] KALMAN, R. E. "New Methods in Wiener Filtering Theory." *Proceedings First Symposium on Engineering Applications of Random Function Theory and Probability.* New York: John Wiley & Sons, 1963.

[17] KIRBY, ROBERT. "A Comparison of Short and Medium Range Forecasting Methods." *Management Science,* December 1966, pp. 202–10.

[18] MALKIEL, BURTON. "The Valuation of Public Utility Equities." *The Bell Journal of Economics and Management Science,* Spring 1970, pp. 143–60.

[19] MINCER, JACOB. "Models of Adaptive Forecasting." *Economic Forecasts and Expectations, Analysis of Forecasting Behavior and Performance.* New York: National Bureau of Economic Research, 1969.

[20] MUTH, JOHN. "Optimal Properties of Exponentially Weighted Forecasts." *Journal of American Statistical Association,* June 1960, pp. 299–306.

[21] NERLOVE, N., and S. WAGE. "On the Optimality of Adaptive Forecasting." *Management Science,* March 1961, pp. 81–94.

[22] ROSENTHAL, M., ed. *Symposium on Time Series Analysis.* New York: John Wiley & Sons, 1963.

[23] SIEGEL, SIDNEY. *Non-Parametric Statistics for the Behavioral Sciences.* New York: McGraw-Hill, 1956.

[24] THEIL, HENRI. *Applied Economic Forecasting.* Amsterdam, Netherlands: North-Holland Publishing Co., 1966.

[25] WHITTLE, P. *Prediction and Regulation by Least Squares.* London: English University Press, 1963.

51

Commercially Available Software for Investments

William B. Riley, Jr., Ph.D.
College of Business and Economics
West Virginia University

The area of investments has developed into a relatively sophisticated discipline where the language of statistics and computers has become an integral part of the vocabulary of the modern investments professional. The quantification, analysis, and interpretation of data often require many hours of repetitive and time-consuming calculations. Computers lend themselves to performing these functions very nicely.

The investments area is filled with software packages of all types. Some are excellent; many are not. Quality control has a high variability. Rely on recommendations from other users, published software reviews, and most importantly, your own judgment. Only you can determine if a particular package fits your needs. Most companies will provide demonstration diskettes, documentation manuals, and/or review copies for a nominal fee. Most will credit this amount toward a purchase. In any event it is better to pay a nominal amount to find out whether a package meets your needs than to buy a package only to find out that it is incapable of performing the needed tasks. In this case the cost of information appears relatively low. Some software companies will provide references of individuals or companies which are presently using the package. Keep in mind that these references are quite likely to provide only good recommendations. You may, nevertheless, be able to determine if the package can meet your particular requirements.

The product support the vendor offers is an important consideration for some users. Many software companies provide 1-800 hotline numbers to assist users in answering the large number of questions that invariably arise with any package. Some companies offer updated packages regularly at a discounted cost as tax laws and databases change over time.

One caveat is in order; computers don't make decisions; people do. Computers and accompanying software are simply tools with which to aid in the decision-making process—important tools, yes, but tools nevertheless. Users should never totally relinquish control of decision making to a computer. Every computer program is built around a set of assumptions. Examine these assumptions to determine if they fit reality as you see it both today and in the future.

This chapter discusses six general areas of investments software: asset allocation, fixed-income securities, fundamental analysis, options, personal financial planning, portfolio management, and technical analysis.

A chapter appendix provides a short list of sources for software information available from a variety of vendors. This list is not an exhaustive directory of software information sources. The investment software market is so dynamic that software directories may be out of date by the time of publication. Each package has features which some users will find attractive for their particular needs. One can only suggest that potential users compare a number of packages before making the final selection.

Specific software packages in the areas of asset allocation, fixed-income securities, and technical analysis are discussed in detail, while programs in the other areas are discussed in only general terms. The intent is to give the reader a feel for the types of functions which computers can perform. The illustrated packages are simply representative of the types of software available in each area and do not necessarily represent the recommendation of the writer.

PORTFOLIO ANALYSIS PROGRAMS

The objective of modern portfolio management is to achieve the greatest return possible for the level of risk the investor (client) is comfortable with. This objective can be achieved mathematically if the correct inputs are available. The required inputs are estimates of future return and risk for all assets or asset classes in the population of assets which are to be considered. In addition, a measure of the future interactive risk (covariance) between these assets or asset classes is required. With a quadratic programming algorithm, a set of efficient portfolios can be generated in risk-return space.

Portfolio managers have had the tools necessary to generate these efficient sets since Markowitz's pioneering work in the early 1950s. The quadratic programming models necessary to perform this analysis have been available for many years on mainframe computers, but early generations of mainframes required substantial time and expense to generate solutions for only moderate sized populations. In addition, the very subjective nature of the inputs resulted in limited use by investment professionals. While the subjective nature of the inputs has not changed, the availability of these programs on microcomputers has considerably decreased the time and expense of performing meaningful analyses.

Early optimization programs stressed an efficient set of assets which could be obtained from a population of every asset in the universe of risky assets. Sharpe argues that investment analysis involves a two-stage process.[1] The first step is to determine the particular asset classes which the portfolio manager wants to consider for investment and the proportion or relative mix of these asset classes which is consistent with the risk-return preferences of the manager. The second step involves the selection of individual assets within each class by a variety of methods, including fundamental and technical analysis. While optimization programs can be used in either or both of these stages, the broad group of programs referred to as asset allocation models primarily attempts to address the asset mix decision.

Asset Allocation Models

Figure 1 illustrates the use of a quadratic programming algorithm to generate a set of efficient portfolios, sometimes called an efficient frontier. Each point on the curve represents a portfolio of assets which has the unique property of generating the highest return possible for a particular level of risk. Each is efficient in the sense that no other combination of assets from the relevant population can be formed to generate a higher return for the associated level of risk. The population of assets or asset classes which one is willing to consider for inclusion in the portfolio has a significant effect on the nature of the resulting efficient set. For example, if the portfolio manager restricts the population of assets to the common stock of 100 high-growth industrial companies, the resulting efficient frontier will be efficient only with respect to that population of assets. If the eligible list were expanded, it is likely that a new efficient set would be formed which is superior to the old efficient frontier.

The determination of the relative mix of assets to include in a portfolio depends on the client's assessment of both the expected future performance of each asset class and the expected future risk of each asset class taken alone and in combination with each other. As men-

---

[1] William F. Sharpe, *Investments*, 3rd ed. (Englewood Cliffs, N.J.: Prentice-Hall, 1985), chap. 20.

FIGURE 1   Efficient Frontier

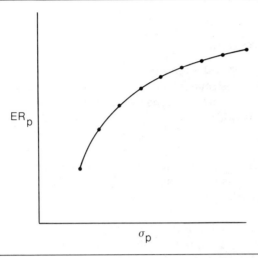

ER_p

σ_p

NOTE: Here ER_p is the expected return for a portfolio with a standard deviation σ_p.

tioned earlier, the objective of modern portfolio management is to achieve the highest return possible for a given level of risk. Having generated an efficient set of portfolios with each point on the set optimum for the population considered, one must then position oneself on the efficient frontier.

What is the client's attitude toward the risk-return trade-off? Portfolio theory suggests that the point of tangency between the efficient frontier and the client's highest indifference curve determines the "optimum" portfolio for the client. Most individuals (clients) don't have clearly defined attitudes toward risk and return. Many theorists argue that one of the most important functions of the investment analyst or portfolio manager is to assist clients in sorting out their attitudes toward risk and return. Asset allocation models can be helpful here.

Asset allocation models provide the portfolio manager with a valuable client information and communication tool. Client expectations concerning future yields for stocks, bonds, and other asset classes can be quantified, allowing the client to observe how different mixes of assets affect risk and return. In other words, such a model can be used to assist the client in finding acceptable "comfort zones."

Asset allocation models thus serve the valuable purpose of allowing the client to view the impact of various asset mixes on risk and return. The portfolio manager can further assist the client by providing historical information on how the various portfolio mixes would have performed in the past. This information can be conveyed in a variety of meaningful ways, demonstrating not only the average results of the various mixes but also the dispersion about each average (the standard deviation and range of possible outcomes).

Input Requirements

Let's examine the inputs required to perform the optimization process. It is necessary to estimate each asset's expected return and risk along with the expected interrelationships among all assets in the relevant population. Historical data on the price and payout (dividend and interest) performance of individual assets is readily available from relatively inexpensive databases. With access to this information, historical statistics on means, standard deviations, and covariances for a large number of assets or asset classes can easily be generated.

Unfortunately, historical information is just that—historical. While it may provide a starting point for estimating future statistics, it is of limited value in providing the expectational data necessary to generate an efficient set. To assume that history will repeat itself is a heroic and probably self-defeating assumption. The economic climate at both the micro- and macrolevels is not static. The endogenous and exogenous factors that influence a given company's performance during one period can be expected to change over time.

The historical relationships most often assumed to remain relatively stable through time are covariances between returns. It is often assumed that company A's relationship with company B will not change significantly through time. If A and B have tended to move together through time in the past, i.e., they had a high positive covariance, then it may be reasonable to assume that this relationship will hold in the future. On the other hand, if one company undergoes significant internal restructuring, this assumption may not hold. For example, American Telephone & Telegraph Co. is no longer a regulated utility, and its historical relationships with other companies are likely to change substantially. Information on historical relationships should always be tempered with new information (fresh insights obtained as conditions change).

Historical data on risk may also serve as meaningful proxies for expected risk in the future. Again, unless significant internal changes occur, e.g., large-scale changes in financial or operating leverage or expansion into a new product area, historical data may be adequate. At any rate, historical information serves as a good starting place for forecasting the future.

Historical return estimates are most likely to undergo significant updating as new forecasts reflecting personal optimism or pessimism are injected into the analysis. Current and expected yields to maturity on bonds, current and expected T-bill yields, and current estimates of equity returns generally replace historical return information.

FIGURE 2 Master Menu

HELP Case Returns Statistics Forecasts Optimize Examine Quit
Get help on the use of Asset Allocation Tools
    (To select a menu item above, use arrow keys, then press ENTER)

AAT—Asset Allocation Tools

A number of portfolio optimization programs are now on the market. The particular package discussed here for illustrative purposes is AAT (Asset Allocation Tools), written by William F. Sharpe.[2] AAT is a menu-driven package containing three diskettes: the system disk, the database disk, and the utility disk. The Lotus 1-2-3 worksheet format is used to enter and manipulate data, so the user must have a Lotus 1-2-3 system disk to run AAT. Installation is very simple; one can begin to perform meaningful analysis after only a few hours of reading the user's manual and working through the tutorial. A help utility actually on the system diskette can be accessed any time guidance is needed. It contains virtually the same information which is in the user's manual but may be more convenient for some users. Figure 2 provides the master menu which users see as they begin AAT. A short description of the highlighted menu item is provided under the menu.

One starts an asset allocation case by moving the cursor until the desired option is highlighted on the master menu. The "Returns" option accesses database information for several years of monthly asset returns for a large number of well-known asset classes or indexes. Monthly data for most series cover the period from January 1980 through December 1984 and are updated yearly. The Returns option provides the user with historical risk, return, and covariance information for all asset classes which the user wishes to consider. The user can scroll through the list of databases and flag each relevant series with a short name or identifier.

For example, a given user may have the following six classes of assets in his or her portfolio: high-growth common stock, high-grade corporate bonds, intermediate-term government bonds, preferred stock, real estate investment trusts, and Treasury bills. The user can flag the relevant indexes to proxy these six asset classes, tagged G Stock, Corp B, Gov B, P Stock, REIT, and T-bill. This can easily be done in much the same way one alters any Lotus 1-2-3 worksheet.

A very useful advantage of using the Lotus 1-2-3 worksheet to enter

---

[2] AAT—Asset Allocation Tools, 1985, written by William Sharpe, is a product of Scientific Press, 540 University Avenue, Palo Alto, California (telephone, 415-322-5221).

FIGURE 3 Historical Risk and Return Data

	Asset Corp B	Asset Gov B	Asset G Stock	Asset P Stock	Asset REIT	Asset T-Bill
Expected Ann. Hist	11.788	11.532	15.766	11.356	20.219	11.392
Std Dev Ann. Hist	16.156	11.513	15.055	10.149	17.908	0.595
Corr Corp B	1.000	0.946	0.376	0.929	0.366	0.059
Corr Gov B	0.946	1.000	0.317	0.864	0.256	0.102
Corr G Stock	0.376	0.317	1.000	0.474	0.607	−0.170
Corr P Stock	0.929	0.864	0.474	1.000	0.475	0.009
Corr REIT	0.366	0.256	0.607	0.475	1.000	−0.156
Corr T-Bill	0.059	0.102	−0.170	0.009	−0.156	1.000
Bound Upper	100.0	100.0	100.0	100.0	100.0	100.0
Bound Lower	0.0	0.0	0.0	0.0	0.0	0.0
Tr. Cost Buy	0.0	0.0	0.0	0.0	0.0	0.0
Tr. Cost Sell	0.0	0.0	0.0	0.0	0.0	0.0
Holdings	16.7	16.7	16.7	16.7	16.7	16.7
Risk Tolerance	50.0					

and manipulate data is the ability to include additional user-generated data in the database. This feature expands the usefulness and flexibility of AAT considerably because one is not bound by the particular asset classes thought to be useful by the package originator. Having identified the relevant series, the user completes the return portion of the analysis by exiting to the master menu. A file containing the identified return series is automatically saved for future use. The user can obtain a printout of these monthly returns (capital gains or losses plus dividends or interest) for each asset class considered.

The next item on the master menu is "Statistics." The Statistics option computes historical means, standard deviations, and correlations for all of the assets preselected with "Returns." One can examine this information by selecting "Forecasts" in the master menu. The user can both examine the risk and return data for each asset class selected and view a correlation matrix for each asset combination.

Figure 3 illustrates the Forecast option for the six hypothetical classes of assets. This figure shows the initial display containing historical data for the selected asset classes and default settings for the constraints and risk tolerance level. The first row, "Expected Ann. Hist," provides average returns for the period 1980–1984 for each asset class; the second row furnishes similar information on historical standard deviations (risk proxies).

The correlation matrix in Figure 3 indicates how each asset interacts (covaries) with other asset classes. The default setting of 100 on the upper bound and 0 on the lower bound means that the user is willing to accept the possibility that the optimum portfolio could consist of 0 percent or 100 percent of an asset class. The default setting of 0 for transaction costs means that no commissions are initially considered. The row labeled "Holdings" defaults to an equally weighted portfolio of each asset class. An initial risk tolerance of 50 can be roughly interpreted to mean that the investor is comfortable with a 50-50 mix between equity and bonds.

The user can modify any or all of the historical data based on specific individual forecasts for the future. Typically, return information would be modified to reflect the user's expectation for the future. Risk and correlation data may or may not be altered, depending on how the user interprets new information.

AAT also provides several useful options to the user. Portfolio managers operate under a variety of legal and self-imposed constraints on asset allocations. AAT allows one to incorporate these constraints into the optimization routine by setting upper and lower limits on the percentage of each asset or asset class which may be considered. For example, the portfolio manager may require an equity position of at least 25 percent but no more than 75 percent of the portfolio or a T-bill position of at least 5 percent of the market value of the portfolio.

These types of constraints are easy to accomplish with AAT. Specific buy and sell commissions (as a percentage) for each asset class can be included as well. AAT also allows the user to impose additional user-defined constraints into the optimization routine, allowing maximum flexibility in tailoring a realistic portfolio. The program can then maximize subject to a realistic set of constraints.

The user must specify a risk tolerance level or use the default setting of 50 percent. This is probably the most difficult and subjective input demanded of the user. Fortunately, the results of several different risk tolerances are available in a later routine regardless of which particular level of risk the user initially specifies.

Figure 4 shows a revised display of risk-return data. Note that in this example return data only was modified to reflect the user's forecasts. Standard deviations and correlation information were not altered. The upper and lower bounds were modified, as were transaction cost percentages. Present portfolio holdings (as a percentage) were included so that comparisons and portfolio revisions could be made. A risk tolerance level of 70 percent was selected.

The user now simply selects the "Optimize" routine and waits while the program cranks through the optimization process. The Optimize routine allows the user two choices: single or multiple optimization. Single optimization provides the user with the one portfolio which offers

FIGURE 4 Revised Risk and Return Data

	Asset Corp B	Asset Gov B	Asset G Stock	Asset P Stock	Asset REIT	Asset T-Bill
Expected Ann. Hist	12.000	10.000	16.000	11.000	8.000	7.000
Std Dev Ann. Hist	16.156	11.513	15.055	10.149	17.908	0.595
Corr Corp B	1.000	0.946	0.376	0.929	0.366	0.059
Corr Gov B	0.946	1.000	0.317	0.864	0.256	0.102
Corr G Stock	0.376	0.317	1.000	0.474	0.607	−0.170
Corr P Stock	0.929	0.864	0.474	1.000	0.475	0.009
Corr REIT	0.366	0.256	0.607	0.475	1.000	−0.156
Corr T-Bill	0.059	0.102	−0.170	0.009	−0.156	1.000
Bound Upper	100.0	100.0	75.0	100.0	100.0	100.0
Bound Lower	0.0	0.0	25.0	0.0	0.0	5.0
Tr. Cost Buy	0.5	0.5	1.0	1.0	1.0	0.0
Tr. Cost Sell	0.5	0.5	1.0	1.0	1.0	0.0
Holdings	10.0	10.0	50.0	20.0	5.0	5.0
Risk Tolerance	70.0					

the highest expected return for the particular risk tolerance specified; multiple optimization provides portfolios for a range of risk tolerances.

One may next "Examine" the results of the optimization process. Figure 5 provides a sample printout of the Examine option for our hypothetical portfolio of assets.

This examination takes the form of simply observing the results on the screen and printing and/or graphing the results. One can easily change an input item and reoptimize, observing the impact of the change on the optimal solution. The multiple optimizer option is very useful in that it allows the user to input the current portfolio into the model including each asset or asset class which presently exists along with each asset class considered for future inclusion in the portfolio.

This program, then, based on a specified risk tolerance, compares the existing portfolio with the revised optimum portfolio, allowing the user to view the impact of portfolio revisions on the expected risk and return of the portfolio. It is a very useful exercise in that risk tolerance classes are displayed along with the original portfolio.

The determination of risk tolerance is usually a difficult and subjective exercise. Most clients do not know their risk tolerance. Utility functions are in a constant state of change; the best one can normally hope for is to identify a band or range of preferences in risk-return space.

It is likely, however, that a comfort zone of risk tolerance can be established for a particular client at a given point in time. This may take the form of a particular range of stock-bond mixes with which the client is relatively comfortable. The portfolio manager may be able to provide the necessary relevant information for the client to determine this comfort level. The printout or graph of portfolio combinations provides an efficient frontier for the client based on the client's estimates of return, risk, and covariances. The default listing generates 11 portfolios, each corresponding to a unique risk tolerance. The client can actually observe the likely trade-offs.

For example, as Figure 5 has shown, risk, return, and the asset mix change rather predictably as the risk tolerance changes. Note how, in this particular example, the optimal proportion of growth stocks increases as one becomes willing to accept more and more risk.

The portfolio manager can further assist clients by providing information on how the various asset mixes would have performed in the past. Figure 5 provides a useful means of communicating the risk-return trade-offs which exist. The present portfolio, along with 11 additional asset mixes, can be directly compared based on the user's expectations concerning the future performance of the relevant asset classes enabling him or her to see the likely result of each portfolio revision.

FIXED-INCOME SECURITY MODELS

Money and capital market instruments such as corporate and municipal bonds and federal government and agency bonds, notes, and bills are labeled fixed-income securities because the interest payments are, in most cases, contractually fixed at the time they are offered and do not change over the life of the security. For many years interest rates rarely varied enough to raise any serious concerns about fluctuations in the price of these instruments. It was commonly thought that since the interest payments were fixed, then the yield or return to the investor was fixed. The perceived fixed nature of the return gave these securities the reputation of being dull, unimaginative, and safe investments, suitable only for the ultraconservative investor whose only concern was current income and safety of principal.

The volatile interest-rate climate of recent years along with historically high nominal yields has changed this view of fixed-income securities. They are now viewed as potentially high-yielding investments with substantial capital gain and loss potential. They are no longer the sole province of (or necessarily appropriate for) coupon-clipping senior citizens. Fixed income securities also have risk-return characteristics which may be very attractive for many types of both active and passive portfolios.

FIGURE 5 Optimization Results

ASSET HOLDINGS	Current Port.	Revised Port.	RiskTol 1.0	RiskTol 10.0	RiskTol 20.0	RiskTol 30.0	RiskTol 40.0
Corp B	10.00	0.00	0.00	0.00	0.00	1.10	9.04
Gov B	10.00	0.00	0.00	0.00	0.00	1.54	0.00
G Stock	50.00	75.00	25.00	25.00	37.84	50.00	60.28
P Stock	20.00	20.00	0.00	6.54	20.00	20.00	20.00
REIT	5.00	0.00	0.00	0.00	0.00	0.00	0.00
T-Bill	5.00	5.00	75.00	68.46	42.16	27.37	10.68
Portfolio Characteristics	**Current Port.**	**Revised Port.**	**RiskTol 1.0**	**RiskTol 10.0**	**RiskTol 20.0**	**RiskTol 30.0**	**RiskTol 40.0**
Expected return	13.15	14.55	9.25	9.51	11.21	12.40	13.68
Standard Dev.	10.94	12.38	3.71	4.08	6.86	8.84	11.01
Investment Objectives							
Risk Tolerance	70.00	70.00	1.0	10.0	20.0	30.0	40.0
Contributions to Utility							
Expected Return	13.15	14.55	9.25	9.51	11.21	12.40	13.68
Decrements from Utility							
Risk Penalty	1.71	2.19	13.79	1.66	2.36	2.60	3.03
Trans. Costs		0.40	0.60	0.53	0.27	0.14	0.21
Portfolio Utility							
Net Utility	11.44	11.96	−5.14	7.31	8.58	9.66	10.44

ASSET HOLDINGS	RiskTol 50.0	RiskTol 60.0	RiskTol 70.0	RiskTol 80.0	RiskTol 90.0	RiskTol 100.0
Corp B	7.50	3.40	0.00	0.00	0.00	1.44
Gov B	0.00	0.00	0.00	0.00	0.00	0.00
G Stock	67.50	71.60	75.00	75.00	75.00	75.00
P Stock	20.00	20.00	20.00	20.00	20.00	18.56
REIT	0.00	0.00	0.00	0.00	0.00	0.00
T-Bill	5.00	5.00	5.00	5.00	5.00	5.00
Portfolio Characteristics	RiskTol 50.0	RiskTol 60.0	RiskTol 70.0	RiskTol 80.0	RiskTol 90.0	RiskTol 100.0
Expected return	41.25	14.41	14.55	14.55	14.55	14.56
Standard Dev	11.92	12.16	12.38	12.38	12.38	12.41
Investment Objectives						
Risk Tolerance	50.0	60.0	70.0	80.0	90.0	100.0
Contributions to Utility						
Expected Return	14.25	14.41	14.55	14.55	14.55	14.56
Decrements from Utility						
Risk Penalty	2.84	2.46	2.19	1.19	1.70	1.54
Trans. Costs	0.29	0.35	0.40	0.40	0.40	0.41
Portfolio Utility						
Net Utility	11.12	11.60	11.96	12.24	12.45	12.62

Bond Analysis Programs

A bond's yield to maturity (sometimes referred to as promised yield or internal rate of return) is the discount rate that equates the stream of interest payments to be received over the bond's life and the repayment of principal at maturity to the purchase price of the bond. Yield can be computed on either a before- or after-tax basis. An additional complication is the fact that many bonds are callable prior to maturity. This means that the purchase of a high-yielding long-term bond does not necessarily guarantee that the high yield will be present until maturity. If interest rates fall, the issuer may call the bond forcing the investor into a cash position in a world with significantly lower yields. In light of this possibility, before- and after-tax yield to call calculations are often prudent in examining possible end-result scenarios. There are various methods to estimate this rate, but accurate bond yields require trial-and-error searches which are difficult and time-consuming to perform by hand calculations. Solving the pre- and post-tax yield to maturity and yield to call can be easily accomplished with the computer.

Yield to maturity calculations implicitly assume that the instrument will be held to maturity and that all interim interest payments can be reinvested at the computed yield to maturity. If these assumptions are not met, then the actual yield which is realized (realized yield) will be different from the yield to maturity. For example, during the high interest rate climate of the early 1980s, a yield to maturity of 16 percent was not uncommon. In order for an investor to actually realize a yield of 16 percent on the purchase of a bond during that period, each coupon payment had to be reinvested at a rate of 16 percent as it was received. Obviously, this was very difficult to accomplish, so the actual realized yield was, in all likelihood, less than the computed yield to maturity.

Realized yield calculations can be determined assuming a variety of reinvestment rates and holding periods. These calculations allow the investor to evaluate the likely return which will be earned under different interest-rate scenarios. Computers handle these types of repetitive calculations very easily.

Many institutions and speculators use a calculation known as duration to measure the impact of yield changes on a bond's price. The price of low-coupon, long-maturity bonds are very sensitive to interest-rate movements. There are obviously many combinations of coupon and maturity, so it is very convenient to have a single measure that captures both of these effects. Duration captures the coupon and maturity effect in one measure. The calculation of a bond or bond portfolio's duration is another computation which can be dreadful to perform by hand but which the computer can accompoish with a minimum of effort.

Computer programs offer many additional advantages in the area of fixed income securities. Convertible securities, financial futures, and mortgage-backed securities can also be evaluated easily with the aid of a computer. Yield curves can be easily plotted and analyzed. Large amounts of data can be sorted, analyzed, and displayed with a minimum of effort.

Fixed Income Security Trading System (FISTS)™

The market for fixed-income analysis programs was perhaps more narrow than was true for many other areas of investment software. As interest in fixed income investments has increased, so has the growth in software to assist in the analysis of these investments. There are many excellent packages on the market which offer different types of analysis to the variety of interested investors ranging from small individual investors to large institutional money managers. The package chosen for discussion here is the Fixed Income Security Trading System (FISTS) from Bond-Tech Inc.[3]

FISTS combines database management capabilities with analysis software for the fixed income securities markets. Its analysis capabilities cover bonds, notes, money market instruments, mortgage-backed securities, nondollar denominated securities, financial futures, and options.

The FISTS programs and databases are on two floppy diskettes. Installation of the system is relatively painless. A knowledgeable user can obtain meaningful results from operating the package in a few hours. Interpretation of the output requires a substantial body of prior knowledge concerning the fixed income securities market. This package is not designed for the novice; it assumes a working knowledge of fixed income securities by the professional investor. The programs are menu driven, with command functions appearing at the bottom of the monitor display. A printout of the system menu is provided in Figure 6. Help screens which define the command functions and verify parameter entries are available throughout the package. The user manual is succinct but complete, correctly assuming, in most cases, that the terminology will be self-explanatory to the professional user.

Bond calculator module. The user simply selects the appropriate menu item and is prompted when the requested subpackage is loaded. The bond calculator subprogram can be accessed by entering menu selection 1 (Bond Calculator). After selecting menu option 1 the screen display will look like Figure 7. The user is first prompted for a file number which is associated with specific security data on a database diskette. The user may enter all requested data directly from the keyboard or pull data from the existing or previously created database

---

[3] FN FISTS™ is a product of Bond-Tech Inc., P.O. Box 192, Englewood, Ohio 45322 (telephone, 513-836-3991).

FIGURE 6 System Menu

The Fixed Income Security Trading System

MENU

Notes, Bonds, & Money Markets

1) Bond Calculator
2) Quote Sheet-Position/Risk Report
3) Arbitrage Spread Matrix
4) Range Tables
5) Yield Curve Plot
6) Comparitive Breakeven Analysis
7) Batch Process Reports
8) Bond Swap Analysis

Financial Futures

21) CBT T-Bond Calculator
22) CBT T-Note Calculator
23) CBT GNMA CDR Price Conversion Tables
24) IMM T-Bill Parity Rate Matrix
25) Implied Forward Rates-Deposit & Disc

Mortgage Backed Securities

11) MBS Calculator

99) Printer Installation

Enter Q to Quit FISTS
Enter Menu Selection: 8.

FIGURE 7 Fixed Income Security Trading

Fixed Income Security Trading   MODE=CALC

Security Number: .....
Security Code:
Settlement Date:
Security Type:
Coupon (%):
Maturity Date:
Trade Basis:
Concession:

Issue Date:
1st Coupon:
Call Data:
Call Price:
Tax (%)–Cpn:
        –Gain:

ö Data File Parameters
ö   Default Overrides:
ö   Coupons/Year:
ö   Yield Method:
ö   Range Tick Val:
ö
ö   Trading Risk
ö   Beta:
ö   Net Position:
ö
ö   Report Settings:
ö   Quote Sheet:
ö   Yield Curve:
ö   Range Table:
ö   Arb Matrix I:
ö   Arb Matrix II:
ö   Futures DBase:
ö
ö   User Field:
ö   Field I:
Data File =b:FIST1.dat

============================Active Records= 14
Input Sec Num to be loaded, or éEnterç to skip

FIGURE 8 Fixed Income Security Trading

<table>
<tr><td colspan="2">Fixed Income Security Trading</td><td colspan="2">MODE=CALC</td></tr>
<tr><td colspan="4"></td></tr>
<tr><td>Security Number: 4</td><td>Issue Date: 12-31-85</td><td>ö</td><td>Data File Parameters</td></tr>
<tr><td>Security Code: 2</td><td>1st Coupon:</td><td>ö</td><td>Default Overrides:</td></tr>
<tr><td>Settlement Date: 09-15-86</td><td>Call Date: 05-15-04</td><td>ö</td><td>Coupons/Year:</td></tr>
<tr><td>Security Type: 2</td><td>Call Price: 100</td><td>ö</td><td>Yield Method:</td></tr>
<tr><td>Coupon (%): 7.875</td><td>Tax (%)-Cpn: 46</td><td>ö</td><td>Range Tick Val:</td></tr>
<tr><td>Maturity Date: 05-15-09</td><td>-Gain: 20</td><td>ö</td><td></td></tr>
<tr><td>Trade Basis: 82.75/....</td><td></td><td>ö</td><td>Trading Risk</td></tr>
<tr><td>Concession:</td><td></td><td>ö</td><td>Beta: 0.75</td></tr>
<tr><td></td><td></td><td>ö</td><td>Net Position: 2000</td></tr>
<tr><td>Dollar Price= 84.343750</td><td>(11.00 32NDS)</td><td>ö</td><td></td></tr>
<tr><td colspan="2">Val of 1BP Per MM =$ 642.87</td><td>ö</td><td>Report Settings:</td></tr>
<tr><td>Yield = 9.526%</td><td>Val of 1/32 = 0.0051 %</td><td>ö</td><td>Quote Sheet: 1</td></tr>
<tr><td>CD Equiv Yld = 9.390%</td><td></td><td>ö</td><td>Yield Curve: 1</td></tr>
<tr><td>Disc Basis Eq= 2.972%</td><td></td><td>ö</td><td>Range Table: 1</td></tr>
<tr><td>Bond Eq Yield= 9.114%</td><td></td><td>ö</td><td>Arb Matrix I: 4</td></tr>
<tr><td>Bkevn O/N Fin= 8.758%</td><td></td><td>ö</td><td>Arb Matrix II: 2</td></tr>
<tr><td>True Aftx Yld= 5.344%</td><td></td><td>ö</td><td>Futures DBase:</td></tr>
<tr><td></td><td></td><td>ö</td><td></td></tr>
<tr><td></td><td></td><td>ö</td><td>User Field:</td></tr>
<tr><td></td><td></td><td>ö</td><td>Field I:</td></tr>
<tr><td></td><td></td><td colspan="2">Data File =b:FIST1.dat</td></tr>
</table>

===============================Active Records= 14
Press F1 for Commands, F2 for File Search, F3 for HELP

---

diskette. If a security is listed in the database, then the selection of the security number will cause much of the requested information to be filled in on the screen. A list of all security parameters and definitions is available through the help command.

The enter and backspace keys are used to move the cursor from parameter to parameter around the screen to provide additional information which is necessary for analysis. One useful feature of this package is the system check for errors or omissions of data which must be corrected before calculations can be made. Calculations of yield, duration, bond equivalent yields, and so forth are initiated by pressing the C function. Sample results are provided in Figure 8 for a corporate bond. The format of the results will vary depending on the type of security being analyzed.

The bond calculator program calculates the pre- and post-tax yield to maturity and yield to call for corporate and municipal bonds. Given a specified time horizon and reinvestment rate, the program also computes a realized yield for a particular security. The user can determine the yield which will actually be realized if interim coupon payments can be reinvested at a user-defined rate for a user-defined time horizon. This is particularly important in today's uncertain interest-rate environment.

As mentioned previously, duration measures the impact of yield changes on a bond's price, i.e., its interest-rate volatility. Changes in the general level of interest rates affect a bond portfolio in two important but opposite ways. A fall (increase) in interest rates causes interim coupon payments to be reinvested at a lower (higher) rate than is assumed by the yield to maturity. Since bond prices move inversely with interest rates, a fall (increase) in interest rates will result in a price increase (decrease) for the bond portfolio. The first effect is termed *reinvestment risk*, and the second, *price risk*.

A portfolio can be hedged or immunized against both reinvestment risk and price risk by generating and maintaining a portfolio with a duration equal to the desired portfolio holding period. In this manner the initially computed yield to maturity can be assured because changes in reinvestment risk in one direction can be offset by changes in price risk in the opposite direction. Immunization is not a passive strategy; it requires regular rebalancing to assure that the duration of the portfolio remains equal to the remaining time horizon of the portfolio.

FISTS computes three slightly different measures of duration (Macaulay duration, modified duration, and adjusted modified duration) for the user.

Quote sheet module. A quote sheet report can be generated from the database by selecting menu option 2 (Quote Sheet-Position/Risk Report). By selecting a particular classification of security, e.g., Treasury securities, the program will retrieve all Treasury securities from the database and provide a quote sheet for the listed securities. A sample quote sheet is provided in Figure 9 for Treasury securities.

The quote sheet provides relevant information on each security, including issue and maturity dates, coupon, yield, duration, beta, and a risk measure which represents a relative yield volatility coefficient.

Yield curve module. A yield curve represents a plot of the yield for financial instruments of like risk against the maturity of each instrument. This allows a person to compare the yield of instruments which are the same in virtually every way except for maturity. This yield plot may be ascending, descending, or flat at different points in time.

There are a number of different explanations for the various slopes of yield curves. Many feel that interest-rate expectations play a major role in shaping the yield curve's slope. If expectations involve the belief that interest rates will be higher (lower) in the future, i.e., higher forward interest rates, than at present, then it is logical to expect an ascending (descending) yield curve. Investors expecting higher future interest rates will, in the short run, buy short-term securities hoping to switch to higher yielding long-term securities at some point in the future. This increased demand for short-term securities will drive the price up and the yield down for these instruments. The reverse will hold

FIGURE 9 Quote Sheet

Settlement Date: 02-10-86

QUOTE SHEET

U.S. TREASURY BILLS

Security Number	Security Code	User Code	Maturity Date	Days to Maturity	Discount Basis	Bond Equiv. Yield	CD Equiv. Yield	Dollar Price	$ Val of One Basis Pt/MM	Net Position	Beta	Risk Points
1	.25		04-24-86	73	7.170	7.377	7.276	98.546083	20.28	1,000	3.00	0.6
2	.5		07-24-86	164	7.250	7.602	7.498	96.697222	45.56	0	0.00	0.0
3	1		01-22-87	346	7.240	7.748	7.781	93.041556	96.11	0	0.00	0.0

U.S. TREASURY NOTES AND BONDS

Security Number	Security Code	User Code	Coupon	Maturity Date	Issue Date	Dollar Price	Yield	Yield Val of 1/32	Cost of Carry	Modified Duration	Net Position	Beta	Risk Points
4	2		7.875	12-31-87	12-31-85	99-31.0	7.885	0.018	7.765	1.724	2,000	0.75	2.6
5	4		8.000	12-15-89	02-18-86	99- 5.0	8.325	0.012	8.023	2.609	0	0.00	0.0
6	4		8.375	12-31-89	12-31-85	99-23.0	8.457	0.010	8.274	3.260	0	0.00	0.0
7	5		9.125	02-15-91	12-03-85	102- 0.0	8.606	0.008	8.607	3.984	0	0.00	0.0
8	7		8.750	01-15-93	01-15-86	99- 2.0	8.932	0.006	8.729	5.104	0	0.00	0.0
10	10		8.875	02-15-96		99-16.0	8.951	0.005	8.363	6.535	0	0.00	0.0
11	20		9.375	02-15-06	01-15-86	98-16.0	9.541	0.004	9.249	8.893	0	0.00	0.0
14	30		9.250	02-15-16		99-10.0	9.318	0.003	8.717	10.044	0	0.00	0.0
									Totals	1.216	3,000		3.2

* Modified Duration is adjusted to exclude Accrued Interest
** Risk Points are the product of (Mod. Dur. X Net Pos. X Decimal Price X Beta)
*** Modified Duration is the Weighted Average of each Position

FIGURE 10 Yield Curve Plot

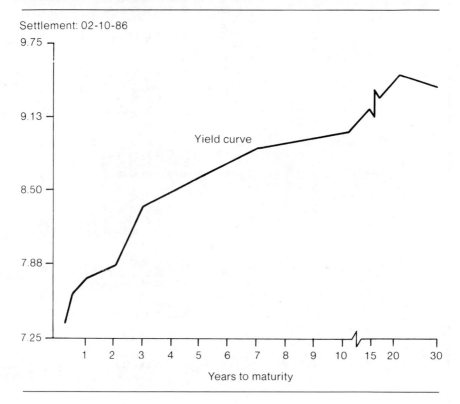

for long-term securities. Thus, short-term yields get pulled down and long-term yields get pulled up resulting in an ascending or positively sloped yield curve.

In that the slope of the yield curve can change as quickly as expectations change, it is important to know what the shape of the yield curve is telling us about current expectations.

Yield curves plotting yield against maturity for securities of similar risk can be easily displayed and printed. Menu option 4 (Yield Curve Plot) generates this plot for a specified classification of security, e.g., Treasury securities. A yield curve printout for Treasury securities is provided in Figure 10.

Additional features. A bond swap subpackage within FISTS allows the user to compare two portfolios of notes and bonds, a sale portfolio and a buy portfolio. The bond swap analysis is similar to the bond calculator. Each security's contribution to the bond swap is evaluated, gross proceeds determined, tax consequences computed, and portfolio characteristics determined for each sale security. Summary and detailed reports are generated which analyze the swap from both an accounting and cash-flow perspective.

A mortgage-backed securities (MBS) subpackage within FISTS assists in the evaluation of mortgage-backed securities, and a financial futures subpackage calculates implied repurchase agreements rates, conversion factors, price bases, and implied forward rates.

A recent options module has been added which incorporates the Black and Scholes as well as the Cox, Ross, Rubinstein option valuation models with modifications necessary for many alternative instruments. In the case of fixed income securities, the Cox, Ross, Rubinstein method includes yield expansion modifications.

FUNDAMENTAL ANALYSIS PROGRAMS

Fundamental security analysts believe that assets are valuable because of the stream of future benefits they provide. These benefits take the form of relatively certain interest or dividends payments in the case of bonds or preferred stock. The benefits from a convertible security come from a combination of fixed-interest payments and an uncertain capital appreciation component. The benefits from common stock take the form of a very uncertain stream of future dividends and a very uncertain future capital appreciation element.

Valuation of assets involves estimating the future benefits and discounting this future stream at a discount rate to adjust for both the time value of money and risk. Fundamental analysts believe that future benefits consist of a company's stream of earnings or dividends. Valuation thus requires estimating the future earnings stream based on various fundamental factors which are company, industry, and economy specific. One must go through a fairly elaborate process of evaluating the economic climate and the industry environment and finally selecting a given company. The fundamentalist will value the asset, i.e., estimate the asset's true "intrinsic" value, and then compare the estimated price to the actual price to determine if the asset is undervalued or overvalued.

Fundamental analysis programs can help the analyst sort through virtually millions of financial variables for companies such as profit margins, debt ratios, return-on-equity ratios. Programs allow the user to screen a large database for those companies which meet the analyst's requirements. For example, the analyst might want to find all companies which have experienced a 10 percent annual growth rate in earnings for the last five years or companies which are selling at price/earnings ratios below 8. This type of screening can save the analyst hours of time. Typical software of this type are Standard & Poor's Stock Pak II and Dow Jones Market Microscope.

Several programs are available which will actually value an asset, i.e., estimate the intrinsic value based on a number of user-supplied assumptions concerning the required rate of return, dividend or earnings growth rate, and present level of dividends or earnings.

OPTION PROGRAMS

Options represent the right to buy or sell a given number of securities at a fixed price on or before a specified expiration date. Call contracts represent options to buy or call away securities at a certain price for a certain period, while puts represent options to sell or put a given number of shares onto someone else for a fixed period of time.

Options provide a means to speculate on the price movement of the underlying security for only a fraction of the cost of the security. The leverage aspect of options makes them attractive instruments for speculators who feel that the price of the underlying security will experience a rapid increase or decrease during the life of the option. Speculators would purchase calls or puts depending on their expectation of future price movements of the security.

The risk of an option writer may be relatively small in the case of covered options or relatively great in the case of naked positions. The investment required to write an option is based on the margin maintenance requirement applied to the underlying security so it requires a larger outlay to write option contracts than to buy them and a larger investment to write naked options than covered options.

Options also provide a means to create hedge positions where risk is reduced rather than increased. Options can provide the holder insurance against an adverse price movement of the underlying security. For example, one might buy a call (put) to protect a long (short) position in the security.

Option traders can create spread and straddle positions in an attempt to profit from either an increase or decrease in the price of the underlying security as long as the change is sufficiently large to cover the cost of the option premiums and commissions.

Option valuation models such as the Black and Scholes model attempt to determine the intrinsic value of an option based on the relationship between the market price and the striking price, the market interest rate, the length of time until expiration of the option, and the volatility of the underlying security. The actual premium (market price) is then compared to the predicted value to determine whether the option is undervalued or overvalued.

As you can see, the variety of positions available in the options market is quite large. Computer programs are available which can analyze a given position and compute the upside and downside break-even points, investment required, and profit and loss positions for a variety of security price movements. The purchase and sale of puts and calls and the purchase and sale of straddles and spreads, as well as predictive models of option prices, are available.

PERSONAL FINANCIAL PLANNING PROGRAMS

The area of personal financial planning is one of the fastest growing areas in investments. Families are realizing the need for comprehensive financial planning. They want one-stop shopping in the sense that they would like for one individual or firm to help in all aspects of their financial life. Retirement planning, family budgeting, the appropriate type and mix of assets, saving and/or investing to meet short- and long-run goals, insurance needs, tax planning, and so forth are all interrelated. One decision should not be made without considering how it affects other areas.

Financial institutions are responding to this need by offering comprehensive financial planning services to their clients. Software is available which can assist these institutions in keeping track of these interdependencies. Packages can help an advisor provide a detailed analysis of a client's present financial condition and a comprehensive plan for reaching established future financial goals. Some financial planners then assist the client with the selection of financial products recommended to achieve these goals; others offer advice but do not help with the implementation of the plan.

PORTFOLIO MANAGEMENT PROGRAMS

Portfolio management sometimes refers to the initial selection of assets to include in a portfolio as well as the subsequent management of those assets over time as either the risk preferences of the individual or the risk-return characteristics of the assets change. The broad category of asset allocation programs discussed in a previous section of this chapter handle these activities.

A second element of portfolio management involves the process of data management necessary to record, track, and report security transactions, i.e., data management of one's portfolio of assets. It is in this context that portfolio management programs in this section are discussed.

Portfolio management programs monitor the performance of a large number of portfolios and generate status reports concerning several aspects of performance of those portfolios. For example, records of security purchases and sales are compiled with the corresponding tax consequences of each transaction noted and summarized for end-of-year tax reporting. They are simply very specialized database management programs with the database being an individual's portfolio of assets. Most have the ability to handle a large number of portfolios and transactions within each portfolio. One such package (with a sample profit and loss report) is summarized in the technical analysis section of this chapter.

Data for these programs can be entered manually from the keyboard or automatically with the aid of automatic retrieval services. The formats and types of reports which can be generated vary from package to package but generally create current portfolio status reports, profit and loss statements, tax reports, and commission reports.

Spreadsheet programs often serve the portfolio management needs of a large number of individuals who are familiar with the capabilities of spreadsheets. One advantage of spreadsheets is their flexibility. The user can custom format a report based on individual preferences but is often locked into a predetermined format with a formal portfolio management package. Spreadsheet-link programs also allow one to upload data from a retrieval service to the spreadsheet.

TECHNICAL ANALYSIS PROGRAMS

The essence of technical analysis is recurring patterns of stock market data. Technical analysts follow a variety of stock market series over time by plotting or charting the data in a way that facilitates detecting any underlying pattern which may exist. Underlying patterns may provide the reader with information concerning shifts in demand and supply conditions for the stock, industry, or index which can be used to predict future changes before these changes are recognized in the marketplace. For many years substantial amounts of time were spent painstakingly plotting large amounts of data on charts and massaging it in a variety of ways to display the desired information.

This type of work is what computers do best: organize, manipulate, and display large amounts of data quickly and efficiently. In addition, the availability of "on line" retrieval services enables users to obtain large quantities of stock market data quickly and at a moderate cost. Software then generates the desired charts in a timely and inexpensive manner.

Dow Jones™ Market Analyzer Plus™

Because of this obvious fit between computers and technical analysis, there are perhaps more computer programs on technical analysis than for any other single category of investment programs.

The particular package described in this chapter is the Market Analyzer Plus from Dow Jones & Company, Inc.[4] The package includes

---

[4] Dow Jones™ Market Analyzer Plus™ is a product of Dow Jones & Company, Inc., and RTR Software, Inc., P.O. Box 300, Princeton, New Jersey (telephone, 1-800-257-5114).

three diskettes: an update disk, a report disk, and a chart disk. One only needs a computer, a DOS diskette, a modem, and a printer to start working with the package.

The extreme flexibility of this software package can be an advantage or disadvantage. Those users who want only a defined set of charts and indicators may find the variety of options offered by Market Analyzer Plus to be somewhat confusing. For those users who want to develop their own indicators and have unique requirements for evaluating historical data, the flexibility of this package will be a real advantage. Technicians see different things in the numbers. There are no guaranteed methods to perform technical analysis. For this reason the ability to develop user-defined functions and charts is an important requirement for the serious analyst.

While a user with a modest degree of computer literacy can begin to perform meaningful analysis very quickly, in order to take advantage of all of the features and options of this package, one needs to devote a substantial amount of time and effort.

Input requirements. Upon booting the update diskette, the user views the master menu which is described in Figure 11. To make a selection, he or she uses the arrow keys to move around the menu until the appropriate option is highlighted. The user then presses enter and follows the prompts until the desired program option is completed.

The user begins by obtaining historical stock market data on stocks he or she wants to chart. This is normally accomplished by moving the curser to "D-New History from DJN/R" in the Data Updates section of the master menu. The required information can be obtained directly from Dow-Jones News/Retrieval Service as described above or entered manually from the keyboard by selecting "I-New History from Keyboard" in the same section of the master menu. A person would normally enter data through the automatic data retrieval service. This feature is available on virtually all technical programs because one of the most important advantages of working with a computer is to have the computer perform all of the time-consuming drudgery which once was performed by hand. Market Analyzer Plus only accesses the Dow Jones databases but does so in an extremely painless and efficient manner. Many users have commented on the relative ease with which this can be accomplished. Once the initial database is generated, it can be updated as desired.

Charting. Once a database is established for the desired securities, a variety of charts can be generated by moving the curser to the appropriate location in the CHARTING section of the master menu. Market Analyzer Plus generates five major charts: linear price and volume bar charts, semilog price and volume bar charts, comparison line

FIGURE 11 Master Menu

```
                         Dow Jones Market Analyzer PLUS
     PORTFOLIO MANAGER    ==============================        UTILITIES
     -----------------                                          ---------
 A- New Transaction                 CHARTING             J- Transfer Stocks
 B- Close Transaction               --------             K- Delete Stocks
 C- Edit Information         U- Bar Chart                 L- Edit Stock Data
                            V- Semilog Bar                M- Edit Stock Names
      PORTFOLIO REPORTS      W- Comparison                N- Edit Quote List
      -----------------      X- Relative Strength         O- Spread Sheet Data
   D- Profit & Loss          Y- Point & Figure            P- Adjust for Splits
   E- Return on Investment   Z- Learn Run                 R- Edit Indicator
   F- Status                 A- Auto Run                  T- Close Tax Year
   G- Cross Reference                                     U- Switch Data Disk
   I- Performance
   J- Commission                   DATA UPDATES
   K- Transaction Details          ------------              EZ TERMINAL
   L- Tax                   B- Quotes from DJN/R             -----------
                            C- Multiple Days from DJN/R   V- Access DJN/R
   DAILY REPORTS            D- New History from DJN/R     W- View Text
   -------------            E- Quotes from Keyboard       X- Print Text
 M- View Quotes  AUTOMATED RUN   F- From Quote List       Y- Delete Text
 N- Print Quotes ------------- G- Restart DJN/R Retrieval
 O- View Summary R- Start Run  I- New History from Keyboard  S- SETUP
 P- View Trend   T- View Log                               H- HELP
                                                           Q- QUIT
```

charts, relative strength line charts, and point and figure charts. Charts can be displayed individually or in a split screen format which allows up to four charts to be displayed at the same time. In addition, a variety of market indicators such as volume or moving averages can be superimposed over each chart.

Bar charts—linear price and volume. Bar charts are one of the most popular technical charts; technicians have been plotting prices in this manner for decades. The daily high, low, and closing prices along with daily volume is available at a glance on these vertical line or bar charts. Price is indicated on the vertical axis, and time, on the horizontal axis. A vertical line is drawn at the appropriate price for each day of data. The high point of the vertical line indicates the stock's daily high with the low indicating the reverse. A cross mark on the vertical line represents the closing price for that particular day. Technicians follow these charts carefully looking for recurring patterns of stock prices which may indicate signals of future price movements.

Daily volume is also plotted across the bottom one third of the chart.

FIGURE 12 Linear Bar Chart

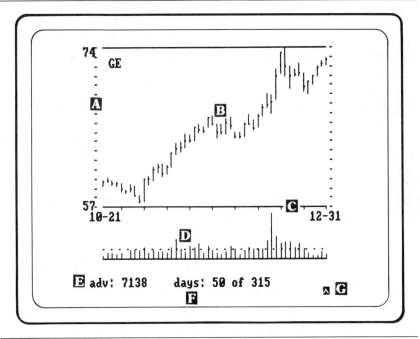

Daily volume can be replaced, at the user's direction, by a number of predefined price-volume indicators. These indicators include negative and positive volume, cumulative volume, price/volume trend, accumulation/distribution, internal relative strength, and directional movement indicators.

User-defined formulas may also be substituted for the predefined indicators. This is a particularly important feature for most technicians. It gives users the flexibility to create and chart their own signals or indicators. For example, the user can plot a momentum curve which compares a moving average with its own moving average. Market Analyzer Plus also gives the user the ability to assign a user-defined formula to a function key. This very useful feature prevents the user from having to reenter the formula every time it is needed.

To use, select "U-Bar charts" under CHARTING from the main menu. Next select the number of days of historical quotes you wish to plot or default to all which are stored. The program then displays a linear price and volume bar chart for the selected data. Figure 12 displays a linear bar chart generated by Market Analyzer Plus.

Bar charts—semilog price and volume. The user selects "V-Semilog Bar" under CHARTING from the main menu. This displays data in the same way as a traditional bar chart except that the vertical axis is in a natural logarithmic scale as opposed to a linear scale. Semilogarithmic scales allow the user to observe a more accurate discription of an existing trend in stock prices. A linear scale can sometimes be deceiving in that a price movement for a high-priced stock can give the appearance of a higher growth rate when compared to a price movement for a low-priced stock when in fact the low-priced stock has experienced the greatest relative movement. This illusion is due to the failure of the graph to properly convey the scale or percentage change in price, and it can be remedied by using a logramithic scale where equal percentage changes are recorded on the vertical axis. Numbers that experience an increase at a constant rate of change will plot as a straight line on a log scale. The semilog graph is useful in comparing and visually examining financial data with different growth rates, e.g., earnings per share.

Comparison line charts. The user selects "W-Comparison" under CHARTING from the main menu. This option allows the user to compare price movements for up to five stocks and/or averages on the same chart. A comparison is made possible by assuming an equal dollar ($100) investment in each stock with the resulting index plotted on the line chart. A $100 horizontal base line is plotted in order to compare the movement of each stock relative to this base line. The user can quickly determine the relative performance of each of the plotted securities. For example, an increase in one stock's plot from the starting point ($100) to $150 at a later point in time can be interpreted as a gross holding period yield (ignoring dividends and transaction costs) of 50 percent or a return of $1.50 per $1.00 invested. The performance of a second stock can now be directly compared on the same graph. Figure 13 displays a comparison line chart generated by Market Analyzer Plus.

Relative strength charts. The relative strength of a stock is the ratio of the stock's price to an index such as the Dow Jones 30 Industrials or the Standard & Poor's 500 Index. If both the stock and the index change by the same percentage, then the ratio stays the same. If the percentage change in the stock's price is greater (less) than the corresponding percentage change in the index, the ratio will increase (decrease). The plot actually charts the ratio of the percentage change in the stock price to the percentage change in the base value of 100. A plot of this ratio on the line graph allows the user to observe how a particular stock or group of stocks has performed relative to an index.

The user selects "X-Relative Strength" under CHARTING from the main menu. This option allows him or her to evaluate the strength of up

FIGURE 13 Comparison Line Chart

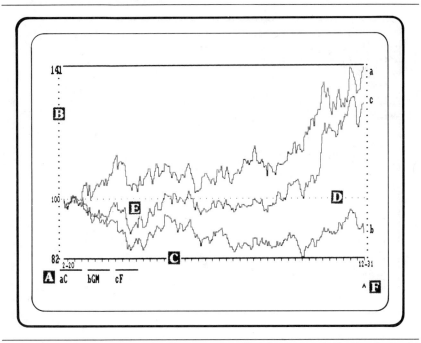

to four issues relative to an index. Figure 14 displays a relative strength chart generated by Market Analyzer Plus.

Point and figure charts. Select "Y-Point & Figure" under CHARTING from the main menu to generate a point and figure chart. Technicians use the patterns from these charts to forecast the direction and magnitude of price movements for a particular stock or index of stocks.

Changes of a predetermined magnitude are recognized as Xs in the case of an increase of the required magnitude and Os for decreases of a given magnitude. For example, if a three-point change is determined to be significant, then the user inserts an X when there is a three-point increase from the previous entry and continues to insert Xs in the same column with every three-point increase. Note that the length of time it takes for the three-point change to occur is irrelevant. While time is not a factor in point and figure charts, it is useful to have a time reference, and this package provides one by marking off each month on the horizontal axis. The user changes columns only when a three-point

FIGURE 14 Relative Strength Chart

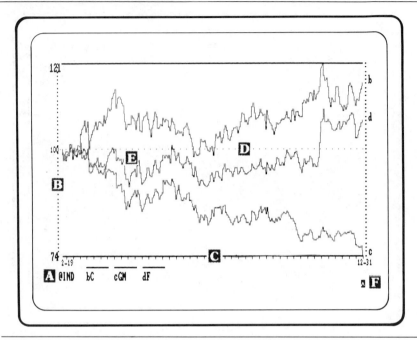

decrease from the previous entry occurs and continues to enter Os in the same column as long as three-point decreases occur. The resulting plot of Xs and Os is then examined for patterns by the technical analyst. Market Analyzer Plus allows the user to select both the reversal point and the box size.

Figure 15 displays a point and figure chart generated by Market Analyzer Plus.

Portfolio Management and Reports.   This package has a portfolio management capability which allows the user to input, organize, and report data for up to 45 portfolios and up to 1,500 transactions. Each transaction contains all information associated with the purchase or sale of a security. Once entered, the portfolio data can be updated automatically through the retrieval service or manually through the keyboard. One simply selects "A-New Transaction" from the PORTFOLIO MANAGER section of the master menu and follows directions.

Eight different types of portfolio reports can be created with the database developed above. The user selects the appropriate report name

FIGURE 15 Point and Figure Chart

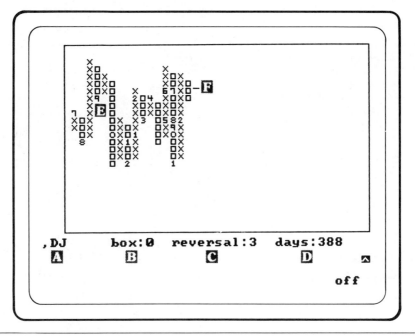

from the PORTFOLIO REPORTS section of the master menu and follows the program prompts. Profit and loss, return on investment, status, cross reference, performance, commission, transaction details, and tax reports can be generated. The user can tailor the report to fit his or her particular requirements by formatting each report to include only the specifically requested information.

The information in a report can also be sorted or filtered in a variety of ways. For example, the user can specify that only stocks which have increased or decreased by more than 5 percent in a given day during November are to be included in a given report. This flexible formatting and sorting capability is an important feature for the serious analyst. Figure 16 displays a sample profit and loss report.

Additional features. The "extend" feature allows the user to extend a chart 10 days into the future. It allows a type of sensitivity analysis that lets the user add up to 10 days of hypothetical data and observe how the indicators would respond. The user can then see where buy and sell signals will occur.

FIGURE 16 Profit and Loss Report

Profit and Loss Statement   PORTFOLIOS: EXAMPLE

Date: 11-13-1985

Security	Shares	Basis Date	Basis Cost	Current Value	Profit Short	Profit Long	%Gain	Annual %Gain
T-BILL 13% NOV 1990	100.00	11/01/84	10,250.00	11,353.13		1,103.13	10.76	10.42
AMER BROADCASTING CO	100.00	05/10/85	11,200.00	11,887.50	(687.50)		(6.14)	(11.98)
AMER BROADCASTING CO	100.00	12/05/84	6,100.00	11,887.50		5,787.50	94.88	100.96
GE CALL SEPT. 50	300.00	06/01/84	800.00	850.00	50.00		6.25	24.80
GENERAL ELECTRIC	100.00	08/03/84	5,900.00	6,312.50	(412.50)		(6.99)	(5.46)
RATHEON	100.00	04/12/83	5,000.00	4,987.50	12.50		0.25	0.10
ADVANCED MICRO DEV.	200.00	08/01/84	5,250.00	5,000.00		(250.00)	(4.76)	(3.71)
1M 6.125% NOV 1986	100.00	05/20/84	8,525.00	9,884.38		1,359.38	15.95	10.74
IBM CALL OCT. 110	400.00	04/01/84	2,800.00	4,000.00	1,200.00		42.86	85.48
PEPSICO	200.00	01/20/84	6,400.00	8,800.00	2,400.00		37.50	70.55
INTL BUSN MACHINE	50.00	01/07/84	5,200.00	6,768.75		1,568.75	30.17	16.29
EXXON	100.00	08/05/83	3,660.00	5,400.00		1,740.00	47.54	20.88
TEXACO INC	100.00	06/07/81	3,550.00	3,850.00		300.00	8.45	1.90
WEYERHAUSER	200.00	01/17/82	5,260.00	5,800.00		540.00	10.27	2.68
HEWLETT PACKARD	150.00	12/08/82	5,000.00	6,300.00		1,300.00	26.00	15.76
CONTROL DATA	100.00	09/20/83	5,500.00	1,762.50		(3,737.50)	(67.95)	(31.60)
INTL BUSN MACHINE	50.00	06/05/83	5,900.00	6,768.75		868.75	14.72	6.03
GENERAL ELECTRIC	100.00	04/10/82	3,270.00	6,312.50		3,042.50	93.04	25.86

Realized: Short Term Profits:	3,650.00
Long Term Profits:	1,300.00
Total Realized Profits:	4,950.00
Unrealized: Short Term Profits:	(1,087.50)
Long Term Profits:	12,322.50
Total Unrealized Profits:	11,235.00
Total Profits:	16,185.00
Total Percent Gain:	16.26
Annualized Percent Gain:	15.53
Liquidation Value:	51,600.00

Spreadsheets have become an almost indispensible package for many computer users. As discussed in the portfolio management section, spreadsheets often serve as a mechanism to organize and maintain portfolio records. Given the flexibility of spreadsheets and the fact that a great deal of data may already be organized in a spreadsheet format, it is desirable to be able to communicate with these spreadsheets. Market Analyzer Plus has the ability to export and import historical data stored in DIF files.

An "Auto Run" capability allows the user to automatically achieve a preprogrammed sequence of commands without going to the keyboard. One possible use involves having the computer call the retrieval service at a predetermined time, update the historical files and portfolios, print out a list of current quotes, print out daily analysis reports, and finally, print out the desired charts without the attendance of the user. A complete log is maintained of the time required to accomplish the requested tasks.

SUMMARY

Some say that computers have revolutionized the investments area. Certainly, computers have significantly changed the way in which investment analysis is performed. In this sense the changes could be considered revolutionary. Computers make life easier; they assist us in a thousand ways. The changes involve more the speed with which decisions can be made than the decisions themselves. There is no substitute for good judgment, but computers can assist greatly in making more informed and hopefully better decisions. Data can be analyzed, processed, and interpreted much more quickly with the aid of a computer. Computers are tools to help the decision maker make better decisions. To the extent that data can be processed, analyzed, and interpreted more quickly, an already efficient market should become even more efficient.

This chapter has described how computer software can assist the professional analyst in a variety of different areas of investments. Specific software packages were discussed in three or four areas to give the reader a feel for the input requirements and output available from software packages. The final decision on which software package fits your needs is a personal one. Most packages will have some features that you will find attractive and some that you will find bothersome. One must weigh the advantages and disadvantages of each package and make an individual decision.

SOURCES OF SOFTWARE INFORMATION

1. *PC Magazine* (Ziff-Davis Publishing Co., New York) periodically reviews investment software packages. At this writing the most recent review is in the April 15, 1986, issue.
2. The *Individual Investor's Microcomputer Resources Guide* (American Association of Individual Investors, Chicago).
3. *Computerized Investing* (American Association of Individual Investors, Chicago) is a bimonthly newsletter that reviews microcomputer software.
4. Robert Schwabach, *Dow Jones-Irwin Guide to Investment Software* (Homewood, Ill.: Dow Jones-Irwin, 1986).
5. *The Wall Street Computer Review* (Dealers Digest, Inc., New York) is a monthly magazine with articles on software and other computer related topics.
6. *The Wall Street Micro Investor* (WSOL Publishing, New York) is a bimonthly publication that reviews investment software programs and databases.

PART 8

Information Sources

52

Published Information Sources of Value to Financial Analysts

Susan S. DiMattia
Business Information Consultant

It has been estimated that by the year 2000 an executive will have to devote 60 percent of working hours to the task of locating and learning information required for completing any given job, project, or activity. In the past decade alone the quantity and scope of available information has mushroomed, primarily due to communications and related technology. We can call on more resources, from a wider geographical area, faster than ever before. As information resources continue their rapid expansion and proliferation, it will be essential for everyone to become more effective gatherers, evaluators, and users of information in the interests of productivity.

An invaluable ally in the information age is the librarian/information professional. Information professionals are trained to locate accurate and complete information on any topic. Begin each search for information by discussing your information needs thoroughly, assured that confidentiality is as important to the information professional as it is to you.

Access to information is available in a variety of ways. Determine first whether there is an information center/library available for your use within your own organization. Visit and get acquainted with the personnel, collection, and services. Even if it is not located near you, call or correspond in writing in order to introduce yourself and your ongoing needs and interests to the staff.

Although the size and scope of such corporate information centers, generically called "special libraries," can vary significantly from one organization to another, all provide extensive reference service, and the information professional will locate appropriate books, reports, articles, and other material from collections all over the world if necessary. Your special librarian is a member of a network of information resources and can call on these when the need arises.

Some special libraries route periodicals; do indexing, abstracting, and translations; and maintain an internal database in addition to numerous other services. Many offer a current awareness service through which they will automatically send new material on topics in which you have registered an interest. Remember that the library's purpose is to serve your information-related needs. Don't hesitate to ask for anything from a single piece of information to a whole new service. It may not always be possible to fulfill your request within current staff, collection, and budget constraints, but a suitable alternative will be suggested as a minimum.

In addition to a corporate information center, other options exist. Large public libraries have specialized reference departments devoted to business, economics, finance, and industry. Public libraries in small- and medium-sized communities are beginning to develop collections and staff expertise to meet local, increasingly sophisticated demand. If your public library is unable to serve your needs for business-related materials, the staff should be able to refer you to the closest library with a special collection. The *Directory of Special Libraries and Information Centers* (Detroit: Gale Research, 1985) is one directory which is useful in locating resources by subject. *Subject Collections* (New York: R. R. Bowker, 1985) locates libraries all over the country which specialize in a variety of subjects.

Academic libraries are another source of information worth exploring. Access to collections in private universities and colleges may be restricted to some degree, depending on policies of the individual schools, but for the most part, state institutions are required to make their facilities and services available to any resident of their state. In all cases, a simple phone call will identify those collections available for your use. Select a school with a significant graduate or undergraduate curriculum in business-related subjects, and the library's collection should reflect the academic strength.

An interesting source to consult if your library skills are rusty is *How to Use the Business Library*, 5th ed., by H. Webster Johnson, Anthony J. Faria, and Ernest L. Maier (Cincinnati: South-Western Publishing, 1984). In addition to describing use of the card catalog, the authors explain some basic sources and techniques necessary for getting the most information in the least amount of time.

If 10 financial analysts were asked to list their five personal favorite information sources, a combined list of at least 35 sources would undoubtedly result. There are a few standard, universally used sources, but the secondary lists are very broad indeed. Within the space restrictions of a single chapter, it is impossible to describe, even briefly, all of the sources of information which may be of value to financial analysts. Instead, an attempt has been made to identify those sources which are most widely accepted as basic or necessary while indicating representative samples of other categories along with "finding tools" which will aid in locating those specific sources called for in the course of doing business.

Many of the sources listed in this chapter have on-line counterparts while other sources are available only on-line. These are discussed in Chapter 53.

SOURCES ABOUT SOURCES/GENERAL WORKS

There are many general business information sources, the primary purposes of which are to aid the user in locating additional specific information or to summarize the information in a particular field.

> Brownstone, David M., and Gorton Carruth. *Where to Find Business Information: A Worldwide Guide for Everyone Who Needs the Answers to Business Questions.* 2nd ed. New York: John Wiley & Sons, 1982. Similar in purpose to the Woy Encyclopedia below, this volume lists over 5,000 sources of information, primarily magazines, looseleaf services, and on-line sources.

> Daniells, Lorna M. *Business Information Sources.* Rev. ed. Berkeley, Calif.: University of California Press, 1985. Of all of the general guides to business publications, this is the most useful and widely known. Under 21 headings (for example, U.S. Business and Economic Trends; Industry Statistics; Locating Information on Companies, Organizations, and Individuals; and Investment Sources) Daniells lists and describes the most useful sources available. For example, under Investment Sources she describes the major services, stock price sources, industry surveys, investment advisory services, and statistical sources.

> Frank, Nathalie D., and John V. Ganly. *Data Sources for Business and Market Analysis.* 3rd ed. Metuchen, N.J.: Scarecrow Press, 1983. Although focusing on marketing information, this source is valuable because of its emphasis on sources of federal and local statistics and on nonpublished or nontraditional sources of information on a company or industry, products, and trends. An entire section is devoted to the information resources of trade and professional associations, for example. Another discusses grants, institutes, publications, and research available through university programs.

> Grant, Mary McNierney, and Riva Berleant-Schiller. *Directory of Business and Financial Services.* 8th ed. Washington, D.C.: Special

Libraries Association, 1984. A fine companion to the Daniells book, this source deals with services that provide regularly or irregularly updated information on some category of business activity.

Woy, James, ed. *Encyclopedia of Business Information Sources.* 6th ed. Detroit: Gale Research, 1986. The introduction calls this "a bibliographic guide to approximately 22,000 citations covering more than 1,100 primary subjects of interest to business personnel." A good starting point for any search, this guide compiles sources under specific subject headings. One of the 60 new headings in this edition is "Coins as an Investment," under which heading appear descriptions of almanacs, a yearbook, a bibliography from the U.S. Government Printing Office, two directories of dealers, a handbook for coin buyers, and Collector's Data Service, an on-line database listing collectibles of all types which are available for sale. The entry also includes titles of periodicals and price sources and the names and addresses of seven trade associations in the field. Similar entries are found under headings such as "Bonds," "Investment Companies," "Stock" and under specific industries, for example, "Beverages," "Building Materials," "Computer Software," and "Health Care."

TRADE DIRECTORIES

Particularly when researching an industry, trade directories can be valuable sources of information. There are two standard references to use when locating appropriate sources.

Directory of Directories. Detroit: Gale Research, 1987, annual. The 7,820 entries, consisting of business and industrial directories, professional and scientific rosters, directory databases, and other lists, can be searched by title or subject.

Trade Directories of the World. Queens Village, N.Y.: Croner Publications, looseleaf, updated monthly. There is a separate section for each continent, with subsections by countries which have more than three directories to list. Titles are given in the original language plus English, French, Spanish, and German. Annotations are in English.

Trade and professional associations are frequently a major, if not the sole, source of information on a product or industry, particularly if the information being sought is statistical in nature.

Encyclopedia of Associations. 21st ed. Detroit: Gale Research, 1987. One of the most heavily used reference books in any library, this guide to over 23,000 national and international associations includes address, size, scope, and objectives of each organization as well as annual budget figures, dates and locations of conferences, lists of regular publications, and staff contact name. The major sections of the encyclopedia are available on tape, diskette, and on-line through Dialog.

BOOKS IN PRINT

It is possible to determine whether there are any books currently in print on a given topic. *Books in Print* (New York: R. R. Bowker, annual) is the basic set from which several other products spin off. In it search is by author's name and by title. *Subject Guide to Books in Print* (also annual) arranges most books currently available through publishers and book stores under broad subject categories. For a list of books scheduled to be published in the year ahead, consult the annual *Forthcoming Books* or *Subject Guide to Forthcoming Books*. When historical perspective is called for, *Business and Economics Books 1876–1982* is a four-volume set which lists materials published in these time and subject categories by author, title, and subject. All of the above sources are printed from the BIPS database.

There are limited counterparts to the Books in Print series for Canada (*Canadian Books in Print*. Toronto: University of Toronto Press, annual) and Britain (*British Books in Print*. London: Whitaker, annual).

> *Core Collection*. Boston: Harvard Business School, annual. Baker Library of Harvard Business School selects a collection of 3,000 of the "best and most recent books in business and related fields" which reflect the school's curriculum. The subject section of the *Core Collection* creates a brief reading list of classic and current materials on each topic.

PERIODICAL DIRECTORIES

Periodicals are essential in any search for current information. A variety of sources are useful in locating information about periodicals published in very specific fields.

> *Directory of Periodicals On-line: Indexed, Abstracted and Full Text.* Volume 1, News, Law, and Business. 1st ed. Washington, D.C.: Federal Document Retrieval, Inc., 1985. This is a handy source if your main approach to information is on-line.
>
> *IMS Directory of Publications* (formerly Ayers). Ft. Washington, Penn.: IMS Press, annual. To be listed in this source, the item must be published in the United States, Puerto Rico, or Canada and offer four or more issues or editions annually. The titles are indexed under more than 900 classifications. The main listing is geographical and includes information on size and characteristics

of the region (population, county, significant products, colleges if any, and so forth) in addition to descriptive information on each periodical.

Standard Periodical Directory. New York: Oxbridge Communications Inc., annual. An extensive listing of U.S. and Canadian periodicals, abstracts, indexes, and house organs.

Ulrich's International Periodicals Directory. 25th ed. New York: R. R. Bowker, 1986. This lists 68,800 foreign and domestic periodicals under 534 subject areas. Included in the two-volume set is a section featuring periodicals available on-line. A companion publication, also from Bowker, is *Irregular Serials and Annuals*, a source of more than 35,000 serials and conference proceedings published less than twice a year. The Bowker International Serials Database is available on microfiche, CD-Rom, and on-line.

In addition to the standard periodical format, a large quantity of vital information is available through the limited subject newsletter. Several directories/indexes are in this category of information source. Three major directories are listed below.

National Directory of Newsletters and Reporting Services. 2nd ed. Detroit: Gale Research, 1985. The publisher describes this source as a "reference guide to information services, financial services, association bulletins, and training and educational services."

Newsletter Yearbook Directory. 4th ed. Rheinback, N.Y.: Newsletter Clearinghouse, 1983. Less comprehensive than the other two, this one is, however, easier to use.

Oxbridge Directory of Newsletters. 1985–86 ed. New York: Oxbridge Communications, Inc., 1985. Classified by industry, product, or profession, but not indexed by specific subject breakdown, this source is full of information but is cumbersome to use. Over 14,300 titles are arranged under only 168 categories, so locating exactly what is needed is more time-consuming than with the two sources above.

One of the most useful aspects of periodicals in business research is their regular, timely, special issues. Many publications are noted for featuring industry statistics, trends, annual round-ups, and lists. Probably the most widely known is the Fortune 500 annual list. In order to identify these special features, use any one or all of the directories listed below.

Uhlan, Miriam, ed. *Guide to Special Issues and Indexes of Periodicals*. 3rd ed. Washington, D.C.: Special Libraries Association, 1985. Included are 1,362 U.S. and Canadian periodicals which publish directories, buyers' guides, convention issues, statistical outlooks, and other features on a regular basis.

Harfax Guide to Industry Special Issues. Cambridge, Mass.: Harfax, 1984. A brief abstract of 6,900 articles in 1,800 U.S., Canadian, and selected foreign journals, extensively indexed, makes it possible to search by industry, subject, or SIC code, geographically and by type of information (statistics, directory, and so forth). This is one of many publications based on the Harfax Industry Data Sources database.

Sicignano, Robert, and Doris Prichard. *Special Issues Index: Specialized Contents of Business, Industrial and Consumer Journals*. Westport, Conn.: Greenwood Press, 1982. This source is redundant if you have access to the *Guide to Special Issues and Indexes of Periodicals*.

INDEXES AND ABSTRACTS

Many sources are useful in locating articles in magazines and newspapers, whether the researcher has a specific article in mind or whether the need is for a brief or lengthy reading list by topic. Most people who have access to the major commercial databases do these types of searches on-line. However, it is still possible and often preferable to use a print index.

Business Index. Belmont, Calif.: Information Access Co., monthly. This service is provided on microfilm, with an updated film arriving monthly. Each current film includes three years' worth of articles arranged by subject. *Business Index* does cover-to-cover indexing of over 460 business periodicals and selected indexing of business information from over 1,100 general and legal periodicals. *The Wall Street Journal* (Eastern and Western Editions) and *Barrons* are also indexed cover-to-cover. *The New York Times* financial section and selected relevant articles from the rest of the paper are also included, resulting in the most comprehensive index of business periodical information available in one source.

Business Periodicals Index. Bronx, N.Y.: H. W. Wilson, monthly with annual cumulation. This is also available on disk and on-line as Wilsonline. It has a subject coverage of over 300 English language business periodicals, ranging from the well known, such as *Forbes* and *Fortune*, to specialized or industry-specific titles such as *Health Care Management Review*, *McKinsey Quarterly*, and *Pensions and Investment Age*.

Predicasts F & S Index U.S. Cleveland, Ohio: Predicasts, weekly, monthly supplements, quarterly and annual cumulations. Company, product, and industry information is gleaned from more than 750 periodicals, newspapers, and reports. The first section of each index includes a one-line description of articles on industries and products. The second section is arranged alphabetically by company name. This breakdown makes Predicasts one of the most direct sources to use when looking for a specific product or company rather than an overall view of an industry or subject. Also available on-line, this is just one of many Predicasts F & S products, including an international and a European index.

The New York Times, *The Wall Street Journal*, and *Barrons* all have their own print and on-line indexes, but for most purposes, the coverage of these three papers in *Business Index* and the Predicasts indexes is adequate.

There are also several specialized indexing and abstracting services. *The Accountant's Index*, prepared and published by the American Institute of Certified Public Accountants, lists all materials received in the AICPA Library. The *American Banker* newspaper is also indexed by its publisher. The American Economics Association publishes the *Journal of Economic Literature* which indexes and abstracts a variety of publications in the field.

Management Contents, which appears in periodical format, is another popular source for tracking information. As the title suggests, the focus is on management journals. This biweekly service reproduces, in each issue, an average of 90 tables of contents pages from close to 400 business and management periodicals and proceedings and then indexes them by subject. This is a particularly useful source for scanning trends as represented by a large quantity of major periodical sources.

In any source which requires locating information by subject, it is vital to pinpoint the subject as precisely as possible. The two sources below are lists of business and investment subject headings which indicate acronyms and relationships among terms. Both are useful in formulating any search strategy.

> Pessin, Allan H., and Joseph A. Ross. *Words of Wall Street: 2,000 Investment Terms Defined*. Homewood, Ill.: Dow Jones-Irwin, 1983. Also by the same authors and publisher: *More Words of Wall Street: 2,000 More Investment Terms Defined* (1986). Less than a dictionary, more than a glossary, these two books cover terms in use in the securities industry with explanations and examples.
>
> Warner-Eddison Associates. *Words that Mean Business*. New York: Neal-Schuman Publishers, 1981. Over 3,000 main terms and related concepts are included here, listed only, not defined.

DICTIONARIES AND ENCYCLOPEDIAS

Several of the dictionary/encyclopedias which were known as standards in business economics and finance are quite old or are now out of print. The sources below are generally adequate for most quick reference needs.

Levine, Sumner N., ed. *The Dow Jones-Irwin Business and Investment Almanac.* Homewood, Ill.: Dow Jones-Irwin, annual. The 10th edition of this standard reference tool includes several enhancements over previous editions. The Hulbert Five Year performance rating of investment advisory letters and statistics on bank failures 1934–84 are just two of these. Standard features include a chronology of significant business-related events during a 12-month period, list of largest companies, top 100 growth companies, brief industry surveys with statistics, and company names. A statistics section brings together the major business and economic indicators. The stock market section includes statistics, charts, commentary, and even a few pages on how to analyze a financial statement. Although a great deal of what appears here is simply repeated from other sources, it is an excellent starting point for the expert or training ground for the novice or generalist.

McGraw Hill Dictionary of Modern Economics: A Handbook of Terms and Organizations. 3rd ed. New York: McGraw-Hill, 1983. The dictionary provides definitions of approximately 1,425 frequently used modern economic terms. It also describes 235 private, public, and nonprofit agencies, associations, and research organizations concerned with economics. Some entries refer the reader to sources of economic data and other related information.

Munn, Glenn G. *Encyclopedia of Banking and Finance.* 8th ed. Edited by F. L. Garcia. Boston: Bankers Publishing Company, 1983. Over 4,000 entries include definitions, historical background, analysis of trends, statistics, laws, and other material.

Rosenberg, Jerry M. *Dictionary of Banking and Finance.* New York: John Wiley & Sons, 1982. This defines over 10,000 terms, including commonly used acronyms and abbreviations, taken from all departments in banks and financial institutions. Although the definitions tend to be extremely brief in many cases, this is a comprehensive source in terms of breadth of coverage.

COMPANY INFORMATION

It is difficult to classify some sources in one segment of this chapter without being tempted to repeat them in other segments. The headings "Company Information," "Industry Information," and "Investment Sources" are particularly troublesome. Obviously any source which provides investment information on a company is also providing company and some industry information and background. For the sake of clarity, all sources appearing under the "Company Information" heading will be those which list companies but which do not include any financial or operating statistics, other than possibly an annual sales figure or total asset figure which serves to indicate the relative size of the company.

Because this chapter is intended for financial analysts, several standard sources of company information have been omitted since their emphasis is on purchasing or marketing functions. Check the Daniells and Grant books mentioned at the beginning of this chapter as well as the major business information publishers for sources not found here.

> *America's Corporate Families.* Parsippany, N.J.: Dun & Bradstreet, annual. This indexes 9,100 ultimate U.S. parent companies, 500 with $1 billion or more in annual sales, and their 45,000 domestic divisions and subsidiaries. The criteria are that they conduct business from two or more locations, have a net worth of at least $500,000, and have controlling interest in one or more subsidiary companies. A companion volume, *America's Corporate Families and International Affiliates* lists 1,800 U.S. parents with over 16,000 Canadian and foreign subsidiaries. Also included are 1,400 Canadian and foreign parents with more than 3,200 U.S. subsidiaries.
>
> *Directory of Corporate Affiliations.* Skokie, Ill.: National Register Publishing Co., annual with bimonthly updates. It includes 40,000 divisions, subsidiaries, and affiliates of over 4,000 parents, arranged alphabetically, with geographic and SIC indexes. There is an international counterpart to this source as well.
>
> *Dun's Business Identification Service.* Parsippany, N.J.: Dun & Bradstreet, semiannual. Undoubtedly the single most comprehensive listing of U.S. companies, the service provides the names of more than 6.5 million U.S., Canadian, and international business establishments on microfiche. Each listing contains DUNS number, complete legal company name, divisional or secondary name if applicable, city, state, street address, and mailing address. Also included is an identifier of headquarters and branch locations. Unfortunately the information included in each listing is very limited. Firms that subscribe to *Dun's Business Information Reports* receive the *Reference Book* bimonthly in which the same companies are listed along with an SIC number, line of business, and estimated financial strength.
>
> *Dun's Million Dollar Directory Series.* Parsippany, N.J.: Dun & Bradstreet, annual. Currently five volumes are in the series. The top 50,000 companies (net worth over $1,850,000) in volume one are supplemented by 160,000 U.S. businesses with net worth over $500,000 in volumes two through four. Volume five is a cross reference to the whole set. Included are many privately owned businesses, domestic subsidiaries of foreign corporations, and other special cases. The entry for each company includes name,

address, telephone, SIC, annual sales, divisions if any, company logo, line of business, state of incorporation, name of principal bank, and names and titles of top officers.

Standard & Poor's Register of Corporations, Directors and Executives. New York: Standard & Poors, annual. Coverage is U.S., Canadian, and major international businesses. In volume one, each of approximately 45,000 entries includes address, name of accounting firm, primary bank and law firm, stock exchange, description of the product or service provided, annual sales, number of employees, and names, titles, and functions of officers and directors. Volume two is an alphabetical list of 72,000 executives, directors, trustees, and partners giving business and home addresses, year and place of birth, college and year of graduation, and fraternal memberships. The third volume is devoted to indexes of obituaries, new individuals, new company additions, geographic and industry indexes, and a "Family Tree" index showing corporate relationships.

Who's Who in Finance and Industry. Chicago: Marquis Who's Who, biennial. When your need is for information on individuals within companies, use this in addition to the register described above. Approximately 19,000 North American and international professionals, heads of stock exchanges, educators, directors of trade and professional associations, and labor union officers are listed. Each entry includes detailed personal information such as parents, marriage, military record, awards, professional and association memberships, political affiliation, religion, and so forth.

Standard Directory of Advertisers. Skokie, Ill.: National Register Publishing Co., annual, with monthly supplements. This guide to 17,000 corporations arranges companies allotting over $75,000 annually for national or regional advertising campaigns into 51 industry classifications. A trade name list of over 35,000 advertised products is included.

Thomas Register of American Manufacturers and Thomas Register Catalog File. New York: Thomas Publishing Company, annual. In the first 12 volumes products and services are listed alphabetically with companies in geographical order under each heading. Volumes 13 and 14 contain profiles of over 133,000 U.S. manufacturers. Arranged alphabetically by company name, each listing includes address, phone number, plant locations, and an asset rating. Volume 14 also includes a trademark and brand names index. Volumes 15 through 21 is known as the Thomcat Catalog File, where the product catalogs of over 1,250 manufacturers are reproduced.

How to Find Information about Companies. Washington, D.C.: Washington Researchers, Ltd., 1983. Based on a seminar by the same name, this is not a directory of information but a handbook on agencies and organizations which have public but usually nonpublished information on companies. There is heavy emphasis on government sources and the courts. The same company also published *Company Information: A Model Investigation* which takes the suggestions in the first volume and demonstrates how they can be applied to a research project on a specific company.

INDUSTRY SOURCES

General Directories

Dun's Business Rankings.. Parsippany, N.J.: Dun & Bradstreet, annual. This new source ranks 7,500 top U.S. public and private companies within 152 industries by annual sales volume and number of employees.

Standard & Poor's Industry Surveys. New York: Standard & Poor's, quarterly. All major domestic industries are covered by both basic and current analysis. A comparative analysis of growth in sales and earnings for leading companies in the industry appear along with five-year ratios, statistics, and discussions of trends. *Trends and Projections* is a monthly companion to *Industry Surveys*.

Forecasting Sources

Projections and trends analysis are important parts of any industry research. Several sources specialize in forecasting and trend watching. A few of the more well-known are included here.

The Outlook. New York: Standard & Poors, monthly. In newsletter format, this publication analyzes and projects business and market trends while suggesting changes and additions to portfolios. Special features include an annual and midyear forecast. In each issue is a featured industry with lists of favored stocks in that industry and "In the Limelight," which provides a brief discussion of a single company.

Predicasts Forecasts. Cleveland, Ohio: Predicasts, quarterly with annual cumulation. Products and industries are arranged under a modified SIC code. This source is an index to statistics, annual growth, and forecasts appearing in magazine and newspaper articles. The format is similar to other Predicasts products, and like its counterparts, it is available on-line as well as in paper copy.

U.S. Department of Commerce. International Trade Administration. *U.S. Industrial Outlook.* Washington, D.C.: U.S. Government

Printing Office, annual. Forecasts of the prospects for over 350 manufacturing and service industries through 1990 include economic data and objective analysis. All major industries are represented. However, often the statistics are on a composite industry, making it less useful than it might be. For example, fiber optics is included in the chapter and statistics with radio and television communication equipment, cellular telephones, and satellite communications equipment. Greater emphasis is being placed on the effects of international trade in recent issues of the *Outlook*. A separate general chapter forecasts international trade. In the 1986 edition, under "Medical and Dental Instruments and Supplies," there is a statistical table labeled the "Top U.S. Trading Partners for Medical and Dental Instruments and Supplies in 1984."

Ratios

Comparisons of a company's performance to its industry, or to a prior year's performance, is accomplished in part through ratios. Three of the more widely available ratio sources are included here.

> *Annual Statement Studies*. Philadelphia: Robert Morris Associates, annual. Robert Morris Associates' member banks submit the raw data, so what is included is not strictly consistent from one year to the next. Even though the financial data submitted reflects the whole operation of a company, the data is categorized only by the company's primary SIC. Comparative historical data is also included.
>
> *Industry Norms and Key Business Ratios*. Parsippany, N.J.: Dun & Bradstreet, annual. Over 1 million financial statements found in Dun's financial profiles form the basis for these ratios, making them the most comprehensive available. Over 800 lines of business are represented by U.S. corporations, partnerships, and proprietorships.
>
> Troy, Leo. *Almanac of Business Ratios and Industrial Financial Ratios*. Englewood Cliffs, N.J.: Prentice-Hall, annual. The information is derived from corporate tax returns in the IRS files. Figures in the 1986 edition are based on 1982 returns.

Directories by Industry or Specialization

In addition to directories and services featuring information on overall industrial activity, specialized industry directories are essential information resources. The directories of directories mentioned earlier in this chapter are prime sources for locating specialized information. A few sample types follow.

Commodity Yearbook. Jersey City, N.J.: Commodity Research Bureau, annual. Statistics and narrative for 100 basic commodities and futures markets as well as some "feature studies" are geared to evaluating and taking advantage of potentially profitable trading opportunities.

International Directory of Telecommunications: Market Trends, Companies, Statistics, and Personnel. 2nd ed. Phoenix, Ariz.: Oryx Press, 1986. Worldwide coverage of companies and technical specialists involved in data communications and equipment is given.

International Petroleum Encyclopedia. Tulsa, Okla.: PennWell Publishing Co., 1985. Maps, country reports, special features, surveys, statistics, and outlooks are included in this source. Gas production, well completion, industry finances, mergers, and a host of related topics are featured.

Defense Markets and Technology. Cleveland, Ohio: Predicasts, monthly with annual cumulations. Another indexing and abstracting service in the Predicasts series. Over 30,000 abstracts a year are grouped by subject. Information is taken from key defense publications as well as directly from defense contracts awarded in North America and Europe. Also included are abstracts from the annual reports of major defense contractors.

STANDARD INDUSTRIAL CLASSIFICATION

A majority of directories in the company and industry sections have relied heavily on the Standard Industrial Classification for describing company lines of business and for organizing material into industry or subject categories. The Standard Industrial Classification was last revised in 1972 and a supplement to the manual was published in 1977. In 1986 the Office of Management and Budget, Executive Office of the President, announced its intention to substantially revise the classification in order to reflect changes in technology and relationships among industries. Several categories are to be renamed, split, or dropped.

The publishers of print and on-line information sources which rely on SIC headings will have a massive reclassification job after publication of the new manual, scheduled for early spring 1987. For a period of a year or more, until all of the reclassification is complete and new editions of reference sources, reflecting the changes, are printed, there will be a transition period. During this time it will be necessary to check both the new and old SIC manuals, as well as the explanatory material accompanying each source, to be certain that the information retrieved from any source is, in fact, the information desired. Caveat emptor!

INVESTMENT SOURCES

Information sources which aid in investment decision making are numerous and varied. Each analyst will tend to return to personal favorites time after time. There is no consensus on which sources are "the best." What follows is a selection of sources found in one public, one academic, and one investment company library as well as on lists of titles provided by three subject specialists. If your personal favorite does not appear here, that is no reflection on the source itself. Perhaps you should submit it to the editor for consideration when the next edition of the *Financial Analysts' Handbook* is prepared!

> *Spectrum*. Silver Spring, Md.: Computer Directions Advisors, Inc., quarterly. Most commonly used on-line but available in six volumes, issued quarterly, this source provides comprehensive coverage of the makeup of investment company and institutional portfolios.
>
> *Corporate and Industry Research Reports*. Eastchester, N.Y.: JA Micropublishing, quarterly. The 1986 edition of CIRR includes 23,000 research reports issued during 1985 by 62 investment firms. The service consists of a set of microfiche and a quarterly index. Full text of each report submitted is included on the microfiche. The index has companies arranged alphabetically by name and also by industry and includes a brief abstract of the report. In addition to subscribing to the entire set, which is quite expensive, it is possible to subscribe by industry category. The CIRR service is available on-line through BRS and Dialog as a subset of the Predicast PTS file. *Investext* is a similar type of product, available only on-line. Of course, the *Wall Street Transcript* has for years been a source of announcements and abstracts of brokerage house reports.

JA Micropublishing has also recently begun providing two other services of value to financial analysts. An index to *Investor's Daily News*, including abstracts, is available on-line on BRS. JA Micropublishing will provide a microfiche subscription to the paper and will deliver individual articles on demand. Presentations before the New York Society of Security Analysts are now available on microfiche or in paper copy through the company. It is possible to subscribe to the entire set or to subscribe to a monthly newsletter, "NYSSA Watch," which announces new reports. You then order only those reports of special interest to you. This service is also on-line through BRS.

> *Disclosure*. Bethesda, Md.: Disclosure Information Group. This is the oldest and for a long time the only source of full-text files of corporate annual reports and other SEC filings. Disclosure, under

contract to the SEC, films most categories of documents filed with the SEC and provides them to subscribers on microfiche and, now, on-line. For example, it is possible to subscribe to the complete file of reports of all companies on one stock exchange or to a customized file by industry, region, selected companies, and so forth. Similar services are now provided in varying degrees by Q Data, Bechtel, and Center for International Financial Analysis. Certain files on-line also provide this comprehensive access to corporate financial reports.

Going Public: The IPO Reporter. New York: Investment Dealers' Digest, weekly. (Formerly published by Howard & Co., Philadelphia.) The emphasis here is on following the aftermarket of firm commitment IPOs. One listing ranks the offering by the aftermarket price which reflects the percentage change from the initial offering price to the closing price on the last day of the year in which the initial offering was made. A monthly supplement lists all companies which went public in the preceding month with such information as the IPO terms, underwriter, balance sheet information, ratios, and so on.

Investment Dealers' Digest. New York, weekly. IDD bills itself as "the professional news magazine for the securities industry since 1935." Legislation, new developments in the field, deals, new personnel, and convention news make this a typical professional news journal. In addition, however, each issue also lists securities in registration, including IPOs and private placements. There is a weekly review of underwriters and their offerings. Also included is a calendar of anticipated municipal offerings.

There are supplements to IDD. A semiannual compiles lists of IPO manager rankings, financings by issuers, financings by underwriters, and a roundup of financing within industry groups. IDD has published a *Five-Year Directory of Corporate Finance 1980–1984* and a *Directory of Corporate Finance, 1970–1980.*

Investment Specialties Guide. Charlottesville, Va.: Money Market Directories, Inc., 1986. A supplement to the *Directory of Pension Funds and Their Investment Managers,* this source categorizes pension funds by type of investment in their portfolio. Under each type the funds are ranked by size, with an indication of what percent of the total portfolio is represented by each investment type.

Levine, Sumner N., ed. *The Investment Manager's Handbook.* Homewood, Ill.: Dow Jones-Irwin, 1980. Over 40 academic and practicing experts contributed to this handbook aimed at managers of "pension funds, mutual funds, trusts, endowments, and the internal portfolios of savings institutions and insurance companies." In seven sections, the handbook covers such topics as administrative and theoretical fundamentals, management, measuring and monitoring performance, legal and regulatory matters, management by type of portfolio, and computer techniques useful in constructing and monitoring portfolios. A brief explanation of the major stock market indexes, how they are calculated, drawbacks to their use, and the list of companies included in each rounds out the handbook.

Media General Financial Weekly. Richmond, Va.: Media General Financial Services, weekly. Comprehensive information on stock price and related statistics for stock traded on NYSE, AMEX, and OTC makes this a valuable resource. Two companion services are the weekly *Media General Market DataGraphics* and monthly *Media General IndustriScope*. Most regular users opt for the on-line version of this service.

Mergerstat Review. Chicago: W. T. Grimm & Co., annual. It contains statistics on merger announcements, total dollar value paid, medium of payment, foreign buyers, divestitures, tender offers, and so forth. Historical statistics are provided in each category. Each edition also contains analyses of the current year's transactions under a variety of categories.

Moody's Manuals. New York: Moody's Investor's Services, annual, with semiweekly and monthly supplements. Volumes in the set cover industrials, municipals and governments, banks and finance, public utilities, transportation, OTC industrial and OTC unlisted. The main entry format is generally the same for all manuals: financial data, history, merger activity, products, plants and properties, subsidiaries, names and titles of officers and directors, and number of stockholders and employees. Some entries are more extensive than others if the company being listed pays for the expanded coverage.

Moody's Bond Record. New York: Moody's Investor's Services, monthly. Over 44,000 issues and situations are noted, about 8,000 in detail. Market position, statistical background, price range, amount outstanding, call price, Moody's rating, and interest dates are a few of the many aspects of corporates, convertibles, governments, municipals, commercial paper, and preferred stock ratings covered here.

Moody's Bond Survey. New York: Moody's Investor's Services, weekly. Listings of recent offerings and their conditions is a major purpose of this service. Another is notes about new, lowered, withdrawn, or revised ratings for all categories of securities.

Moody's Dividend Record. New York: Moody's Investor's Services, two per week with annual cumulation. Some of the features of each issue are new dividends declared, dividend changes, dividend meetings announced, and a stock of record calendar.

Moody's Handbook of Common Stock and *Handbook of OTC Stocks*. New York: Moody's Investor's Services, quarterly. Basic business and financial information is provided on over 900 stocks of high investor interest. In general terms, each listing describes the company, its past performance, and current situation; estimates its future; and indicates for what type of investor its securities are most suitable.

Nelson's Directory of Wall Street Research. 11th ed. Rye, N.Y.: W. R. Nelson & Co., 1986. The "Research Sources" section gives names, addresses, telephone numbers, and specialties of the research personnel at over 600 firms. A list of more than 5,000 publically traded U.S. and Canadian companies having research coverage by one or more security analysts appears in the "Company Profiles" section. Information in this section includes company name, address, telephone, stock symbol and exchange, fiscal year end, and investment information (shares outstanding, percent held by institutions and insiders, and so forth). This section also includes a list of research sources and all of the companies they have covered. Section three of the directory features international companies researched by one or more analysts. Sections four and five are lists of the largest investment management organizations and largest tax-exempt funds.

Official Summary of Security Transactions and Holdings. Washington, D.C.: U.S. Securities and Exchange Commission, monthly. In tabular form, this monthly includes information on issuer, security, reporting person, nature of ownership, relationship of reporting person to issuer, date of transaction, quantity bought or sold, and price.

O'Neil's Database. Los Angeles, Calif.: William O'Neil & Co., weekly. This two-volume set is the print counterpart to an extensive and expensive on-line and customized source. It contains 2,500 datagraphs arranged by industry group, with the strongest performing groups in volume one and the weakest in volume two.

Pope, Rosalie, ed. *Securities Industry Yearbook*. 7th ed. New York: Securities Industry Association, 1986. The editor describes this as "comprehensive data on the industry's capital, its employees, branch offices, and registered representatives, as well as ownership information and data on underwritings." Three hundred and seventy-nine firms are ranked by capital for the current year as compared with the preceeding year. For each company, an address and telephone number are provided, along with the year founded, number of offices, form of ownership, industry memberships, names of top management, and an indication of the number of employees in each department.

Standard & Poor's Analysts' Handbook. New York: annual. Financial and stock market data for over 70 industries from 1951 to present.

Standard & Poor's Bond Guide. New York: monthly. Over 6,500 U.S. and Canadian firms are arranged alphabetically, with an indication of the bond quality, ratings, and statistics.

Standard & Poor's Credit Week. New York: weekly. "The authority on credit quality." One recent issue was on Puerto Rico and included brief items on the investment climate, an interview with the governor, an analysis of the government's budget, and a brief review of some public corporations. Regular news in each issue deals with changes in credit ratings, a "creditwatch" of potential changes, and some industry analysis. Two companion publications, *Creditweek International* (quarterly) and the new bimonthly *Creditweek International Ratings* (first issue, November 1986) rate and analyze more than 1,500 Eurobonds and U.K., Canadian, and other bond and commercial paper issues.

Standard & Poor's Daily Dividend Record. New York: daily. This is a listing of stock splits, omitted, resumed, decreased, or increased dividends, as well as stock exchange rulings and related matters.

Standard & Poor's Daily Stock Price Record. New York: quarterly. Issued in separate parts for NYSE, AMEX, and OTC, part one features major technical indicators. Part two covers daily and weekly stock action, with a 30-week moving average as well as a relative strength feature. This latter is the ratio of the Thursday closing price to the Dow Jones Industrial Average for the same day, expressed as a percentage.

Standard & Poor's Security Dealers of North America. 128th ed. New York: 1986. For each firm, the listing includes information on the class of securities in which they specialize, officers, where registered, date of establishment, number of employees, and whether a branch or main location. The main entries are arranged geographically with an alphabetical index of main offices.

Standard & Poor's Security Owner's Stock Guide. New York: monthly. Charts of stock group movements; comparative statistics; changes in preferred stock ratings, name changes, and stock exchange changes; and a variety of other timely features make this a valuable tool. Coverage includes 5,300 common and preferred stocks and 425 mutual funds.

Standard & Poor's Corporation Descriptions. New York: semimonthly. This is available as a full-text database on-line. A classic source for descriptions of publicly held NYSE, AMEX, and larger unlisted and regional exchange companies, it is accompanied by a daily news updating service. Companies are charged for anything beyond a basic listing. Since some companies take advantage of the opportunity for comprehensive coverage and some do not, the scope of the listings is uneven.

Standard & Poor's Stock Market Encyclopedia. New York: quarterly. The 500 S&P Index companies plus 250 selected others are covered here. The actively traded stocks are arranged by investment type (growth, contrarian, income, and so forth). Earnings, dividends, price history, income account, balance sheets, and a chart of the past seven years' market action are the features. Use this source in conjunction with the *Outlook* and *Stock Guide*.

Standard & Poor's Stock Reports. New York: quarterly. In three series, one each for NYSE, AMEX, and OTC, there are two-page reports on each company. Revised on an average of every three to four months, the listings include dividends, price ranges, finances, capitalization, management, significant recent developments, and a brief dicussion of products, marketing, R&D, sales prospects, and a long-term outlook.

The Unlisted Market Guide: The OTC Stock Information Source. Glen Head, N.Y.: Unlisted Market Service Corp., looseleaf. Two-page reports list company name, NASDAQ symbol, prices, earnings per share, and other ratios, monthly volume, average number of shares outstanding, description of the business, recent developments, market makers, brief financials, list of officers, and the name of the person preparing the report.

Value Line Investment Survey. New York: Arnold Bernhard & Co., weekly. If a library has any of the investment services, it will most likely be this one. This source analyzes timely stocks in timely industries and makes recommendations of conservative, high-yielding, and other special-purpose stocks. Each issue includes three parts, "Summary and Index," "Selection and Opinion," and "Ratings and Reports." Available on-line. Value Line also publishes a new-issues service, an options service, and a service for special situations.

Ward's Business Directory. 25th ed. 3 volumes. Belmont, Calif.: Information Access Corp., 1986. Volume one is titled "Largest U.S. Companies" and includes public and private companies with sales of $11 million a year or higher. All 20 manufacturing and 53 nonmanufacturing SIC categories are represented. There are up to 30 financial indexes for each listing, in addition to name, address, chief executive, descriptor, sales, number of employees, fiscal year end, and year founded. Companies are ranked by sales in one list. Volume two includes limited information on major U.S. private companies with sales of $500,000 to $11 million. Listings for 15,000 major international companies comprise volume three.

Investment Companies. New York: Wiesenberger Investment Company Service, annual, with monthly supplements. As described in the introduction, this is "an annual compendium of information about mutual funds and investment companies—a complete explanation of their functions and their various uses to the investor—data on background, management policy, and salient features of all leading companies—management results, income and dividend records, price ranges, and comparative operating details." Covers 1,385 investment companies in the 1986 edition.

STATISTICS

Finding Guides

American Statistics Index. Washington, D.C.: Congressional Information Service, annual with monthly supplements. ASI is a master index to the publications of more than 500 U.S. government agencies that issue statistics. The index began publication in 1972, but a retrospective edition covering 1960–1973 is available. Each edition is in two volumes, Index and Abstracts. Copies of the source documents on microfiche can be purchased from CIS. This source is also available on-line.

Statistical Reference Index. Washington, D.C.: Congressional Information Service, monthly with annual cumulation. Since 1980 SRI, a companion to ASI, has indexed and abstracted statistical reports from agencies other than the federal government. Nonprofit organizations, trade and professional associations, state government agencies, university research centers, and commercial publishers are just some of the sources of statistical information covered in SRI. Since January of 1983 CIS has also published the *Index to International Statistics*. The statistical publications of about 50 international, intergovernmental agencies such as the United Nations, OECD, and OAS are included.

Statistics Sources: A Subject Guide to Data on Industrial, Business, Social, Educational, Financial and Other Topics for the U.S. and Internationally. Detroit: Gale Research, 1986. Approximately 48,000 citations are arranged by subject. A lengthy list of key statistics sources preceeds the subject list of specific sources. For example, under the heading "Health Care—National Expenditures" we find that the U.S. Department of Health and Human Services publishes a quarterly journal of statistics called "Health Care Financing Review."

Statistics Sources

Board of Governors of the Federal Reserve System. *Federal Reserve Bulletin*. Washington, D.C.: monthly. The first section of each issue contains feature articles and regular items on industrial production, policy actions of the Federal Open Market Committee, appearances before Congress by FRB members and staff, and legal developments. The second section includes financial and business statistics, both domestic and international.

Dun's Census of American Business. Parsippany, N.J.: Dun & Bradstreet, annual. This statistical resource covers more than 5 million U.S. businesses. It provides a national count of establishments in all industrial and commercial classifications as well as by state, by number of employees, and by annual sales volume.

U.S. Bureau of the Census. Economic Census Series, including Census of Manufacturers, Census of Construction Industries, Census of Mineral Industries, Census of Retail Trade, Census of Service Industries, Census of Wholesale Trade. Space does not permit a detailed discussion of the features of the U.S. government census publications. They are valuable statistics sources, even though they are prepared only every five years, in years ending in 2 and 7. Publication of the full range of data takes several years. In the meantime, complete information is available in machine-readable form. Contact the Bureau of the Census for descriptive information on their products as well as information on courses offered by the bureau for training potential users of the data—there is at least one Bureau of the Census Data Center in each state—or write to U.S. Department of Commerce, Bureau of the Census, Washington, D.C. 20233.

U.S. Bureau of the Census. *Statistical Abstract of the United States.* Washington, D.C.: U.S. Government Printing Office, annual. Published since 1878, this source includes sections on population; vital statistics; immigration and naturalization; health and nutrition; education; federal, state, and local government finance and employment; employment, earnings, and the labor force; income, expenditures, and wealth; banking, finance, and insurance; business enterprise (including profits, formations, and failure rate); transportation; manufacturers; foreign commerce; and a host of related categories. The *Statistical Abstract* is an excellent starting point in a search for any economic or demographic statistics and trends. *Historical Statistics of the United States—Colonial Times to 1970* is a companion volume.

U.S. Council of Economic Advisors. *Economic Indicators.* Washington, D.C.: U.S. Government Printing Office, monthly. Each issue consists of graphs and statistical tables on output; income; spending; employment and unemployment; production and business activity; prices, money, credit, and security markets; federal finance; and international statistics on production, prices, exports, and imports.

U.S. Department of Commerce. Bureau of Economic Analysis.

Business Conditions Digest. Washington, D.C.: U.S. Government Printing Office, monthly. The main feature is a cyclical indicators section, including composite indexes and their components, indicators by economic process, and diffusion indexes and rates of change. Other economic measures listed include national income and product accounts; prices, wages and productivity; and some comparative international statistics. The U.S. Department of Commerce provides the Economic Bulletin Board on-line for current information, and current and historical data from *Business Conditions Digest* are available on diskette.

U.S. Department of Commerce. Bureau of Economic Analysis. *Survey of Current Business*. Washington, D.C.: U.S. Government Printing Office, monthly. Over 2,000 series are covered in this widely used source. Each issue includes current analysis of a variety of factors which impact the economy. Brief research articles are often included, and there are frequent special issues, the most valuable being National Income and Product Accounts. The current business statistics section in each issue goes from the general business indicators to statistics on production and distribution by industry. *Business Statistics* is a biennial supplement which provides monthly data for the most recent three years and annual data back to 1961.

U.S. Department of Labor. Bureau of Labor Statistics. *Monthly Labor Review*. Washington, D.C.: U.S. Government Printing Office, monthly. A compilation of economic and social statistics, most are given as monthly figures for the current year and one prior year.

Excellent summaries of current economic and financial news and data are given in the financial section of the Sunday *New York Times*, the review and preview sections (and back pages) of *Barron's Business and Financial Weekly*, and the business outlook page of McGraw-Hill's *Business Week* magazine. *Fortune* magazine also publishes a useful economic analysis. Many analysts find clipping and saving the above items a very simple and effective way of monitoring the economy.

INTERNATIONAL SOURCES

In studying standard reference sources, it is obvious that particularly the statistically oriented ones have taken on a decidedly international flavor in the past few years. Most industry directories now have the word *international* in their title or at least somewhere in the material describing the scope of the directory's contents. There is no doubt but that the "global economy," or whatever you choose to call it, is upon us in full force. The proliferation of international sources makes it impossible to include more than representative samples in this chapter. There are many methods for staying aware of materials as they are published. One is to subscribe to "Recent Additions to Baker Library" a monthly list of materials added to the library collection at Harvard Business School. Baker Library also publishes a series of minilists. These bibliographies on current business topics are updated frequently and always include at least one list on international sources of information. To request a current price list of Baker Library publications, write to the Publications Department, Baker Library, Harvard Business School, Soldiers Field, Boston, MA 02163.

A second source of update on new international materials is Alan Armstrong Associates, Ltd., a specialist bookseller in England. The company publishes "New Editions: Directories, Annuals and Reference Books" monthly. It can be ordered by writing to Diane Kerr, Alan Armstrong & Associates, Ltd., 6 Castle Street, Edinburgh, EH2 3AT, Scotland.

There are many other up-date sources on international topics, and each information professional specializing in the field will have a personal favorite.

General Sources

Annual reports on foreign companies are available from Disclosure Information Group (Bethesda, Md.) and World Wide Investment Research (St. Louis, Mo.).

International Annual Reports Collection. Ann Arbor, Mich.: University Microfilms, in cooperation with the Center for International Financial Analysis and Research Inc., Princeton, New Jersey. This service provides full-text reproduction on microfiche of annual reports for over 3,000 companies representing 37 countries and 32 industry groups. *Worldscope* published by Wrights Investor's Service (Bridgeport, Conn.) is also compiled as a joint venture with the Center for International Financial Analysis and Re-search, Inc. This annual directory provides financial and stock market data on over 3,000 foreign industrial companies. It also includes a summary of a company's accounting practices.

Major Companies of Europe (formerly Jane's). London: Graham and Trotman, annual. This volume features countries of the European Economic Community and is arranged by country. For each company , standard directory information is provided, including line of business, trade names, and principal subsidiaries. Graham and Trotman also publishes several other regional directories, among them *Major Companies of the Arab World* and *Major Companies of Argentina/Brazil/Mexico/Venezuela.*

Moody's International. New York: Moody's Investors' Service, an-nual. Information is given on more than 5,000 corporations in 100 countries in the standard Moody's format. Some national economic statistics by country are also included. Weekly news updates are included with the service.

Morgan Stanley Capital International Perspectives (New York) publishes a widely used quarterly with financial and market data on over 1,600 foreign companies.

Principal International Businesses. Parsippany, N.J.: Dun & Bradstreet, annual. In this are 55,000 firms in 133 countries selected for inclusion on the basis of annual sales volume, national prominence, and international interest. In addition to the typical listing, there is an indication of whether the company is an exporter and/or an importer. Dun's also offers directories for specific countries or regions, for example *Canadian Key Business Directory, Guide to Key British Enterprises,* and *Dun's Latin America's Top 25,000.*

United Nations. *Statistical Yearbook.* New York: annual. The text is in French and English. Statistics included here are general economic and demographic in nature but are also industry and product specific. There is quite a delay in publishing the *Yearbook,* so for more current statistics in some of the categories, check the *UN Monthly Bulletin of Statistics.*

Extel is a major publisher of company and investment information for Britain and the United Kingdom. Their *British Company Service* is issued on folded sheets of "cards" and updated with daily news cards as needed. They also publish a similar *European Company Service* and several directories related to the stock exchanges in the British Empire.

There are numerous sources of information on business in Japan. Many of them give much more detail on a company and its employees than the standard directory entries we have come to expect.

Diamond's Japan Business Directory. Tokyo: Diamond Lead Co., annual. Devoting two pages to each company, the entries include sales composition (the percent of total sales contributed by each division), officers, employees (number, average age, and average monthly pay), bank references, stock information, balance sheet and P&L, ratios, and a 10-year review, along with Diamond's comment. The directory also includes a brand and trade names section.

Japan Company Handbook. Tokyo: Toyo Keizai Shinposha, two a year. Data on 1,129 major listed companies includes corporate name, characteristics (its position in its major industry), short- and long-term outlook, income data, sales by division, stock price information, and financial data.

Japan Economic Almanac. Tokyo: Japan Economic Journal, annual. Somewhat like our *S&P Industry Surveys,* these are short sections on industries and segments of the economy with illustrations, graphs, statistics, and so forth.

53

On-Line Databases

Sumner N. Levine, Ph.D.
State University of New York at Stony Brook

Today familiarity with on-line imformation services is an important part of the financial analyst's equipment. Accessing, analyzing, and distributing the incredible flood of information can most effectively be achieved by electronic means, that is, computerized database systems.

The latter may be defined as organized collections of data stored in a central computer which are retrievable via remote terminals or computers. The primary benefit provided by a computerized database is the capability of rapidly searching millions of pieces of information and organizing the selected data in accordance with the interests of the user. Moreover, electronically stored data can be manipulated by means of spreadsheets and other software.

The type of information provided by databases may be statistical, bibliographic, or full text. Statistical databases provide numerical data. Bibilographic bases only contain citations to published works. Citations usually include source, title, author, publication date, key words, or abstracts. Full-text databases provide the entire text of an article.

Literally hundreds of on-line databases are available, and new ones are constantly being added. A number of directories and newsletters are available to help keep users abreast of developments. These are listed at the end of this article. International databases are also listed here.

THE ON-LINE INDUSTRY

The "manufacturing" segments of the on-line industry are referred to as producers. A producer is an individual or organization that takes raw data, such as company annual reports, SEC filings, investment opinions, or original work, and packages it electronically into a database.

This electronic package is then delivered via a provider (vendor). Providers such as Dialog, CompuServe, and others lease space on their computers to producers. These vendors are in actuality a delivery system for the finished product. However, the distinction between the database producers and the vendor is not always clear-cut. Dow Jones News Retrieval Service, for example, is a producer of the databases derived from *The Wall Street Journal* and *Barron's* and also a vendor for the Disclosure and Standard & Poor databases. With McGraw-Hill's Data Resources, Inc., producer and vendor are the same.

Producers may make their databases available to several vendors. Disclosure databases, for example, are available from Dow Jones News Retrieval, CompuServe, Dialog, and other vendors. The value added of the providers is that they have all the necessary facilities for delivering the information such as telecommunications networks, billing systems, and the retrieval software.

The revenue structure of the industry is twofold. Producers charge a fee for using their information—no different than any research firm. Fees can be measured in connect time—the amount of time that the user is connected to the system, a subscription or registration fee, and access charges based on the amount of information. The vendor's bill includes the cost of running its computer system, telecommunications networks, and the like, as well as its profit margin. In all but the rarest circumstances, it is the vendor that tracks all usage and bills the user for all fees. Pricing structures are confusing and should be examined carefully because it is often possible to get the same information from two different vendors, each of which has a different price.

ACCESS METHODS

Three essentials are required to go on-line: (*a*) a dumb terminal or, alternatively, a computer, (*b*) a modum, that is, a piece of hardware which interfaces the terminal (computer) with a telephone line, and (*c*) communication software which enables the computer (terminal) to interact with the modum.

Vendors may communicate with user terminals through their own telecommunication switching networks or may employ one or more commercial networks such as Telenet, Tymnet, or Uninet. CompuServe, for example, has its own network and also utilizes Tymnet and Telenet. The latter two permit access to locations not served by the CompuServe network.

The technical aspects of accessing a database are actually quite simple. The dumb terminal (given its name because it does not have any processing power) or personal computer (PC) are connected to a modem which allows the devices to communicate via telephone lines.

With a dumb terminal you are limited to viewing the information on the screen or to printing out the information if a printer is connected to the terminal.

Modums receive or transmit information at specific speeds measured in bits per second (bps). Common speeds with commercial databases are 300bps, 1,200 bps, and 2,400 bps. Generally, the higher rates are more cost-efficient. It should be mentioned that baud rate is often used for bps, but the two concepts are not the same.

With a personal computer, any number of communication software packages can be used to automatically log on, retrieve information, or save data in a disk file for use later in a spreadsheet or database program. In the case of specialized software, such as stock market analysis programs, the information can be fed into the computer and automatically analyzed.

Gateway Services

The conventional procedure for accessing a database requires an account with each producer/vendor you want to access as well as mastery of the commands peculiar to each database and vendor.

Gateways remove these limitations by allowing you to connect with several vendors. By using a gateway you can enter your queries in the same language or format for all the on-line systems accessible through that particular gateway. If, for example, you did not use a gateway and you needed to access CompuServe and Dialog and entered the same query for the current profits for Allied Stores, you would have to rephrase your query for each system. The use of a gateway circumvents this by translating your query into a language understandable by both CompuServe and Dialog.

Additionally, by using a gateway you can generally save a considerable amount of money by not having to maintain individual accounts with several producers/providers. Because of the volume of their purchasing, the gateway can often charge one fee which is less than if you went directly to the producer/provider.

Western Union's InfoMaster System, which provides access to some eight vendors, is an example of a useful gateway service. It is available via Western Union's EasyLink System.

Another example is Business Computer Network (BCN) of San Antonio, Texas, which provides one call access to BRS, CompuServe, Dialog, EasyLink, Newsnet, Orbit, Dow Jones News Retrieval, Mead Data Central Nexis, Vu/Text. A similar service is EasyNet offered by Telebase Systems, Inc., of Narberth, Pennsylvania. EasyNet also provides a series of menus to help select the appropriate database to retrieve the required information. With BCN, in comparison, once you are connected to a vendor you are on your own.

SOME WIDELY USED ON-LINE VENDORS
AND DATABASES

In the limited space available here it is not possible, of course, to provide an exhaustive review of vendors and their databases. Complete discussions are given in the references at the end of the chapter.

Here we discuss five widely used vendors indicating those on-line databases which are of particular relevence to financial analysts and money managers. Included are CompuServe, Dialog, Dow Jones News Retrieval, Data Resources INC. (DRI), and I.P. Sharp. Folowing the above, briefer discussions are given for several other major vendors: Bridge Information Systems, Mead Data, Central, News Net, Warner Computer Systems, and Vickers Stock Research Corp.

COMPUSERVE

5000 Arlington Center Boulevard
P.O. Box 20212
Columbus, OH 43220

CompuServe was started in 1969 as a computer time-sharing service. The company offered its Consumer Information Service (CIS) in 1980 and subsequently introduced an expanded Executive Information Service (EIS) in 1983. The company also provides a number of services to institutions and government customers.

In 1986 the company introduced (in conjunction with Telebase Systems Inc.) I QUEST, a gateway service which provides access to a number of large vendors such as Dialog, BRS, SCD, Newsnet, Vu/Text, Questel (a large French database offering information on patents, finance, technology, and French and other European companies; sources are French and worldwide), and Pergamon-Infoline (a large British vendor particularly strong in patents, technology, and British companies; sources are worldwide). Databases include the following:

COMPUSTAT II. Produced by Standard & Poor's, financial information on over 6,000 industrial companies, 175 annual and quarterly industrial aggregates, and over 100 utilities and banks. Data on balance sheets, income statements, sources and uses of funds, and trading are provided.

VALUE LINE. Produced by Arnold Bernhard & Co., a broad-based library of financial information covering 95 percent of the dollar value of securities traded on the major exchanges. Data on 1,800 major U.S. companies are provided, including 10-K reports, income statements, sources and uses statements, stock market relationships, and calculated financial ratios.

VALUE. From Telestat Systems, contains current and historical trading, financial, and descriptive information for thousands of security issues of all types. Fifteen custom-designed programs are available for plotting and graphing data. (Proprietary product of Capital Market Systems.)

CITIBASE. A collection of historical national economic series, compiled and updated weekly by the CITIBASE Technical Group of Citibank. Monthly, quarterly, and annual time series back to 1946 are included. (Separate contract and license fee required.)

DISCLOSURE II. SEC filings for over 9,000 companies.

SITE II. Information from the U.S. Census Bureau on population, households, income, age, and race. It is searchable by zip code and county, among other factors.

SITE POTENTIAL. Allows the user to define geographic areas of the United States and evaluate the market potential there for up to 29 retail and financial businesses.

STANDARD & POOR'S. Descriptive and financial information on more than 3,000 companies.

A.M. BEST EXECUTIVE DATA SERVICE. Two years' worth of information on 2,700 insurance companies, including premiums, market share, and loss and underwriting data.

FDIC AND FHLBB BANK CALL REPORT DATA. Data on FDIC call reports back to 1972 on FRS banks and other U.S. banks and FHLBB call reports back to 1974 on over 4,000 savings and loan institutions.

INSTITUTIONAL BROKERS' ESTIMATE SERVICE (IBES). Consensus estimates on earnings for 3,000 companies made by 65 institutional brokerage firms. Earnings per share for two years and growth rates for five years are projected.

NEW ISSUES CORPORATE SECURITIES DATA BASE. Historical data on the placement of corporate securities through investment bankers. It covers 6,000 transactions from 1976 to date on both public companies and initial offerings.

NO-LOAD MUTUAL FUND DIRECTORY. Provides information on over 370 no-load mutual funds.

OTC NEWS ALERT. Timely information on over-the-counter stocks derived from SEC filings, news releases, and so forth.

CONTINUOUSLY UPDATED QUOTES. High, low, closing, volume, and net changes for over 9,000 securities on NYSE, AMEX, and OTC. Prices are updated continuously on a 20-minute delayed basis.

HISTORICAL MARKET INFORMATION. Daily trading statistics and descriptive information for 10 years on over 40,000 stocks, bonds, mutual funds, government issues, and options.

MARKET REPORTS.   Information on market trends, including the identification of the 20 most active stocks and the 20 largest gains.

ISSUES EXAMINATION.   Standard & Poor's and Moody's ratings, shares outstanding, beta factor, latest bid, pricing and dividend activity, bond coupon rate, yield, maturity date, and open interest.

PRICES AND DIVIDENDS.   Pricing and dividend information for any specified time range for a specified security.

MULTIPLE PRICE QUOTES.   Price quote for a specified day for one or more securities, including ticker symbol, value, high/ask, low/bid, close/average prices; and CUSIP number.

PORTFOLIO SUMMARY.   Current valuation report on a portfolio, using the issue, number of units, acquisition cost per unit, and current market price.

SUMMARY STATISTICS.   Descriptive statistics for an issue over a specified period of time, including high, low, close, high close, low close, volume, mean, and standard deviation.

MAJOR MARKET AND INDUSTRY INDEXES.   Indexes of NYSE, AMEX, Kuhn Loeb, NASDAQ, Value Line, Dow Jones, Standard & Poor's 400/500, Standard & Poor's Industry Composites, and Moody's.

CANADIAN PRESS BUSINESS INFORMATION WIRE.   Canadian and international business coverage. It is supplemented by information from Reuter's, Associated Press, and Agence Presse-France.

THE NATIONAL BUSINESS WIRE.   Continuous update of news and press releases on hundreds of companies.

MONEY MARKET SERVICES.   The largest supplier of on-line financial forecasting, with over 800 institutional clients around the world. The three services offered are The Daily Comment, dealing with daily aspects of market activity; Fedwatch, a weekly news bulletin focusing on interest rate trends; and The Monthly Report, presenting long-term economic and monetary trends.

DIALOG

**Dialog Information Services
3460 Hillview Avenue
Palo Alto, CA 04304**

Introduced in 1972, Dialog is one of the largest database vendors currently offering over 250 databases covering a wide scope of disciplines. Listed below are the on-line databases of particular interest to financial analysts.

ABI/INFORM®. Extensive summaries of articles from top business and management journals—business practices, corporate strategies, and trends.

ADTRACK™. Descriptions of advertisements from 150 U.S. consumer magazines—competitive tracking and product announcements.

ARTHUR D. LITTLE/ONLINE. Management summaries from A.D. Little's market research reports—planning and industry research.

BIOBUSINESS. Summaries of business-oriented articles in agriculture, biotechnology, food and beverage industry, and pharmaceuticals—locate areas of biological research with high potential for commercial growth.

BLS CONSUMER PRICE INDEX. Time series of consumer price indexes calculated by the U.S. Bureau of Labor Statistics—economic analysis.

BLS EMPLOYMENT, HOURS, AND EARNINGS. Time series on employment, hours of work, and earnings for the United States by industry—economic trends and analysis.

BLS PRODUCER PRICE INDEX. Time series of producer price indexes, formerly Wholesale Price Indexes, for over 2,800 commodities—economic analysis.

CENDATA™. News releases from the U.S. Bureau of the Census with textual and tabular information covering Census surveys in business, agriculture, population, and more—tracking current economic and demographic trends.

CHEMICAL INDUSTRY NOTES. Extracts from articles in worldwide business-oriented periodicals for chemical-processing industries—chemical industry news and tracking.

COMMERCE BUSINESS DAILY. Definitive source of notices from U.S. Dept. of Commerce for government procurement invitations, contract awards, surplus sales, R&D requests—competitive tracking, purchasing, and sales leads.

COMPARE PRODUCTS. Information on computer-related manufacturing and distributing companies and products from display ads in 100+ U.S. business and computer publications—product/market research and sales planning.

D&B—DUN'S MARKET IDENTIFIERS®. Directory of over 1 million public and private companies with 10 or more employees, listing address, products, sales executives—corporate organization, subsidiaries, industry information, sales prospects.

D&B—INTERNATIONAL DUN'S MARKET IDENTIFIERS®. Directory listings, sales volume, corporate data, and references to companies for non-U.S. private and public companies from 133 companies—international trade and industry prospects.

D&B—MILLION DOLLAR DIRECTORY®. Privately held and public companies with net worths over $500,000, includes data on sales, type of organization, address, employees, key executives—corporate analysis and information.

DISCLOSURE™ *II.* Detailed financials for over 9,000 publicly held companies, based on reports filed with the U.S. SEC—sales, profit, corporate organization, key personnel.

DISCLOSURE™/*SPECTRUM OWNERSHIP.* Detailed ownership information for thousands of U.S. public companies—investment analysis.

ECONOMIC LITERATURE INDEX. Index to articles from economic journals and books—economic research and teaching.

ECONOMICS ABSTRACTS INTERNATIONAL. Summaries of literature in all areas of international economic sciences—determining industries, distribution channels.

ELECTRONIC YELLOW PAGES. Unparalleled number of listings of U.S. businesses, retail, services, manufacturers, wholesalers, etc. Over 9 million listings with name, location, line of business—sales prospecting and location tool.

FIND/SVP REPORTS AND STUDIES INDEX. Summaries of industry and market research reports, surveys from U.S. and international sources—market, industry, and company analyses.

FINIS: FINANCIAL INDUSTRY INFORMATION SERVICE. Marketing information for financial services industry and their products and services—development of marketing strategies.

FOREIGN TRADERS INDEX. Directory of manufacturers, services, representatives, wholesalers, etc. in 130 non-U.S. countries—direct marketing and sales outside the United States (available in United States only).

HARVARD BUSINESS REVIEW. Text of *Harvard Business Review*, covering the range of strategic management subjects—management practices and strategies.

ICC BRITISH COMPANY DIRECTORY and *ICC BRITISH COMPANY FINANCIAL DATABASE.* Listing of detailed financial information and ratios for nearly 1 million British companies as filed with the Companies Registry of Companies House—identification of U.K. companies and financial analysis.

INDUSTRY DATA SOURCES™. Descriptions of sources for financial and marketing data in major industries worldwide, including market research, investment banking studies, forecasts, etc.—industry tracking and analysis.

INSURANCE ABSTRACTS. Brief summaries of articles from life, property, and liability insurance journals—tracking insurance industry trends and practices.

INTERNATIONAL LISTING SERVICE. Directory of worldwide

business opportunities—buying, selling, and financing for businesses.

INVESTEXT®. The complete text of prestigious Wall Street and selected European analysts' financial and research reports on over 3,000 companies and industries—corporate and industry analysis plus financial and market research.

MANAGEMENT CONTENTS®. Informative briefs on a variety of business and management related topics from business journals, proceedings, transactions, etc.—management, finance, operations decision making.

MEDIA GENERAL DATABANK. Trading information with detailed financial information on 4,000 publicly held companies over a seven-year period—charting market and financial performance.

MOODY'S® CORPORATE NEWS—INTERNATIONAL and *MOODY'S® CORPORATE NEWS—U.S.* Business news and financial information on 3,900+ international and 13,000+ U.S. corporations from annual reports, proxy statements, journals, and reports—competitive analysis, merger and acquisition activities, new product information.

MOODY'S® CORPORATE PROFILES. Equity database with financial data and business descriptions of publicly held U.S. companies, with five-year histories, ratios, and analyses on companies with high investor interest—assess investment opportunities.

P/E NEWS. Current political, social, and economic information related to energy industries—monitor news, new technology, and legislation.

PHARMACEUTICAL NEWS INDEX. References to major report publications, covering drugs, cosmetics, health regulations, research, financial news—drug and cosmetic industry developments and regulation.

PTS ANNUAL REPORTS ABSTRACTS. Detailed statistical, financial, product, and corporate summaries from annual and 10-K reports for publicly held U.S. corporations and selected international companies—product, industry, company identification, and strategic planning.

PTS DEFENSE MARKETS AND TECHNOLOGY. Summaries of major articles and reports from defense sources, includes contracts, the industry, and more—defense industry contracting and tracking.

PTS F&S INDEXES (Funk & Scott). Brief descriptive annotations of articles and publications covering U.S. and international company, product, and industry information—company and industry tracking.

PTS INTERNATIONAL FORECASTS. Summaries of published forecasts with historical data for the world, excluding the United

States, covering general economics, all industries, products, end-use data—strategic planning for international development.

PTS INTERNATIONAL TIME SERIES. Forecast time series containing 50 key series for each of 50 major countries, excluding United States, and projected to 1990, as well as annual data from 1957 to date—international economic analysis.

PTS PROMT. Primary source of information on product introductions, market share, corporate directions and ventures, and companies in every industry, containing detailed summaries of articles from trade and industry sources—market and strategic planning, tracking new technologies and products.

PTS U.S. FORECASTS. Summaries of published forecasts for United States from trade journals, business and financial publications, key newspapers, government reports, and special studies—short- and long-term forecasting.

PTS U.S. TIME SERIES. 500 time series for United States from 1957 and projected to 1990 and annual data from 1957 to date on production, consumption, prices, international trade, manufacturing, etc.—tracking economic and industry trends.

STANDARD & POOR'S CORPORATE DESCRIPTIONS. In-depth corporate descriptions of over 7,800 publicly held U.S. companies with background, income account and balance sheet figures, and stock and bond data—competitive and financial analysis of companies and products.

STANDARD & POOR'S NEWS. Late-breaking financial news on U.S. public companies, including earnings, mergers and acquisitions, joint ventures, management and corporate changes and structure—current awareness of corporate activities.

STANDARD & POOR'S REGISTER—BIOGRAPHICAL. Personal and professional data on key executives in public and private companies with sales over $1 million—locate and profile U.S. and non-U.S. corporate leadership.

STANDARD & POOR'S REGISTER—CORPORATE. Company records and business facts on 45,000+ public and private corporations, primarily in the United States including financial and marketing information—market research and development, identification of business connections.

THOMAS REGISTER ONLINE™. Digest of 123,000 U.S. manufacturers, 50,000+ classes of products, and 102,000+ trade and brand names. Listing for over 1 million product and service sources—sales planning, market research, product line tracking.

TRADE & INDUSTRY ASAP™. Indexing and complete text of articles from 85 industry trade journals and general business publications—current awareness and industry tracking.

TRADE & INDUSTRY INDEX™. Index with selected summaries of major trade and industry journals and the complete text of press releases from PR Newswire—industry and company information and news.

TRADE OPPORTUNITIES. Purchase requests by the international market for U.S. goods and services, describing specific products or services in demand by over 120 countries—leads to export opportunities, sales, and representation opportunities.

TRINET COMPANY DATABASE. Directory information on U.S. and non-U.S. company headquarters with aggregate data from establishments, including sales by SIC code—headquarter analysis and industry sales.

TRINET ESTABLISHMENT DATABASE. Directory of U.S. corporate establishments with address, sales, market share, employees, and headquarters information—corporate and market analysis.

DOW JONES NEWS RETRIEVAL

P.O. Box 300
Princeton, NJ 08540

Started in 1974 to provide only stock market information, the service was expanded in 1977 to include summaries of news appearing in *The Wall Street Journal* and *Barron's*. The service has since been substantially expanded to include the following databases:

BUSINESS The Business and Finance Report
- Continuously updated business and financial news culled from *The Wall Street Journal*, The Dow Jones News Service, and other news wires.
- The latest news on domestic and international economies.
- Cross references to related information.

DEFINE Words of Wall Street^{SM}
- Definitions of over 2,000 business and financial terms used by professional investors.

DJNEWS Dow Jones^{SM} *News*
- Stories from *The Wall Street Journal*, *Barron's*, and Dow Jones News Service.
- Stories as recent as 90 seconds, as far back as 90 days.

DSCLO Disclosure® *Online*
- 10-K extracts, company profiles and other detailed data on over 10,000 publicly held companies from reports filed with the SEC.

EPS Corporate Earnings Estimator^{SM}
- Timely earnings forecasts for more than 3,000 of the most widely followed companies compiled by Zacks Investment Research, Inc.

INSIDER Insider Trading Monitor
- Insider trading information on over 6,500 publicly held companies.

Reports on trades made by nearly 60,000 individuals (corporate directors, officers, or shareholders with more than 10 percent ownership).

INVEST   Investext®
- Provides full texts of more than 13,000 research reports from top brokers, investment bankers, and other analysts.
- Includes more than 3,000 U.S. and Canadian companies and 50 industries.
- Historical, current, and forecasted marketing and financial information.

KYODO   Japan Economic Daily®
- Same-day coverage of major business, financial, and political news from Japan's Kyodo News International, Inc.

MG   Media General Financial Services
- Detailed corporate financial information on 4,300 companies and 170 industries.
- Major categories include: revenue, earnings, dividends, volume, ratio, shareholdings, and price changes.
- Compare two different companies or company versus industry data on the same screen.

MMS   Economic and Foreign Exchange Survey^{SM}
- Weekly survey of U.S. money market and foreign exchange trends.
- Median forecasts of monetary and economic indicators.

QUICK   Dow Jones^{SM} QuickSearch
- Corporate report drawing information from multiple news/retrieval sources, searchable with one command.

SP   Standard & Poor's Online®
- Concise profiles of 4,600 companies containing earnings, dividend, and market figures for the current year and the past four years.
- Corporate overviews plus S&P earnings estimates for most major companies.

TEXT   Text-Search Services^{SM}
- *The Wall Street Journal*: Full Text Version. All articles that appeared or were scheduled to appear in *The Wall Street Journal* since January 1984.
- Dow Jones News. News service articles and selected stories from *Barron's* and *The Wall Street Journal* since June 1979.
- *The Washington Post*: Full Text Version. Articles that appeared in *The Washington Post* since January 1984.
- The Business Library. Selected articles from *Forbes*, *Financial World*, and the full text of the PR newswire since January 1985.

TRACK   Tracking Service
- Create and track up to five profiles containing as many as 25 companies each.
- Track current quotes (minimum 15 minute delay) and the latest

news stories and headlines automatically on the companies in your profiles.

WSW *Wall $treet Week*[SM]

- Four most recent transcripts of the popular PBS television program "Wall $treet Week."

Quotes and Market Averages

CQE *Enhanced Current Quotes* (Minimum 15-minute delay during market hours)

- Common and preferred stocks and bonds.
- Mutual funds, U.S. Treasury issues, and options.
- News alert.

DJA *Historical Dow Jones Averages*[SM]
- Daily high, low, close, and volume available for the last trading year for industrials, transportation, utilities, and 65 stock composites.

FUTURES *Futures Quotes*
- Current quotes (10–30 minute delay) for more than 80 contracts from the major North American exchanges updated continuously during market hours.
- Daily open, high, low, last, and settlement prices.
- Daily volume and open interest, lifetime high and low.

HQ *Historical Quotes*
- Daily volume, high, low, and close for stock quotes and composites.
- Monthly stock quote summaries back to 1979; quarterly summaries back to 1978.

RTQ *Real-Time Quotes*
- Stock prices with no delay from the major exchanges, including composites.
- NASD National Market System prices.
- News alert.

DATA RESOURCES INCORPORATED

24 Harwell Avenue
Lexington, MA 02173

Data Resources Incorporated (DRI) is a division of FEICO, a McGraw-Hill Financial and Economic Information Company. DRI is one of the

---

NOTE: News alert available on stocks trading on the New York and American stock exchanges and for those listed by NASDQ.

largest providers of information products and analytic services for professionals in the financial marketplace. Its financial information network has been created through a three-way linkup between DRI, Standard & Poors Corporation, and Monchik Weber. Data Resources Incorporated assembles and manipulates data from various sources to provide users with the following databases:

DRI BANK ANALYSIS SYSTEM. DRI Bank Analysis System (DRIBAS) is a composite database containing detailed balance sheet and income statement data on holding companies, commercial banks, and thrift institutions as well as deposit information on the individual branch level.

DRI FINANCIAL AND CREDIT STATISTICS. DRI Financial and Credit Statistics (DRIFACS) database contains high frequency financial data including money market rates, foreign exchange data, commercial banking assets and liabilities, thrift institution activity, cash options and stock indexes, and financial futures.

DRI COMMODITIES. DRI Commodities database contains historical and current price and trading activity data on commodity futures, spot commodities, and options traded on the U.S., Canadian, and London markets.

DRI SECURITIES. DRI Securities (DRISEC) database contains daily price, volume, and fundamental information on over 45,000 security issues including debt, equity, government agency issues, and options traded on the New York, American, Over-the-Counter, regional, and Canadian exchanges.

MACROECONOMIC DATABASES. The Macroeconomic databases contain measures of financial, economic, and demographic activity in the United States.

REGIONAL AND COUNTY DATABASES. The Regional and County databases monitor indicators of demographic and economic activity in United States Census regions, Federal Reserve districts, states, metropolitan areas, and counties.

BANKTRAK. Banktrak contains data on sales, lead bank, employment, location, and Standard Industrial Classification (SIC) code for public and privately held companies and wholly owned subsidiaries.

COMPUSTAT FINANCIAL INFORMATION. COMPUSTAT Financial Information contains annual and quarterly financial statement information on publicly traded industrial firms, utilities, and banks.

INSTITUTIONAL BROKERS ESTIMATE SYSTEM. (See above under CompuServe.)

MERRILL LYNCH BOND PRICING. Merrill Lynch Bond Pricing database contains closing prices for over 35,000 corporate bonds, private placements, floating rate notes, zero coupon bonds, equipment trusts, Treasury issues, and government agency securities.

SECURITIES INDUSTRY ASSOCIATION. Securities Industry Association (SRI) database contains information on capital market indicators and data on the financial condition and performance for securities firms. Only members of the Security Industry Association have access to the information contained in the database.

STANDARD & POOR'S INDUSTRY FINANCIAL. The Standard and Poor's Industry Financial database.

TRINET. The TRINET database contains detailed company information on approximately 500,000 businesses with 20 or more employees.

ZACKS EARNINGS ESTIMATES. (See above under Dow Jones News Retrieval EPS.)

I.P. SHARP ASSOCIATES LIMITED

1200 First Federal Plaza
Rochester, NY 19614
and

Canadian Headquarters
2 First Canadian Plaza
Toronto, Ontario
Canada M5X 1E3

I.P. Sharp Associates is a privately held international software and communications company headquartered in Toronto, Canada. Databases include:

COMMODITIES. The Commodities database contains prices, volumes, and open interest for all major commodities traded on the London, New York, Chicago, Kansas City, Minneapolis, Winnipeg, and Toronto/Montreal futures markets.

UNITED STATES BONDS. United States Bonds database contains daily trading statistics for more than 4,000 listed bonds, as well as government and agency issues.

COMMODITY OPTIONS. The Commodity Options database provides prices, volumes, and open interest for all major options and commodities futures traded in the United States.

FEDERAL RESERVE BOARD WEEKLY STATISTICS. The Federal Reserve Board Weekly Statistics database contains weekly American banking and monetary statistics on over 1,200 time series.

FOREIGN CURRENCY PROJECTIONS. Foreign Currency Projections is a foreign currency forecasting service provided by S.J. Rundt and Associates, Incorporated. The service combines fundamental economic assessment with technical analysis and various judgmental factors.

MONEY MARKET RATES. The Money Market Rates database provides 246 daily and weekly money market rates for Canada, the United States, and many European and Asian countries.

UNITED STATES OPTIONS. The United States Options database contains daily trading statistics for all put and call options traded on all major options exchanges in the United States.

UNITED STATES STOCK MARKET. The United States Stock Market database contains current and historical prices and volumes for securities listed on Canadian and U.S. stock exchanges.

DAILY CURRENCY EXCHANGE RATES. The Daily Currency Exchange Rates database provides exchange rates for major world currencies.

NORTH AMERICAN STOCK MARKET. The North American Stock Market database provides current and historical prices and volumes for securities listed on North American Stock exchanges.

CANADIAN CHARTERED BANKS, ANNUAL FINANCIAL STATEMENTS. Canadian Chartered Banks, Annual Financial Statements database provides annual financial statements for all chartered banks operating in Canada.

BANK OF CANADA WEEKLY FINANCIAL STATISTICS. The Bank of Canada Weekly Financial Statistics database provides weekly banking and monetary statistics released by the Bank of Canada.

TORONTO STOCK EXCHANGE 300 INDEX AND STOCK STATISTICS. The Toronto Stock Exchange 300 Index and Stock Statistics database provides trading statistics for the 300 major stocks and 62 major and minor indexes that form the Toronto Stock Exchange 300 Composite Index.

TORONTO STOCK EXCHANGE INTRA-DAY INFORMATION FOR STOCKS AND INDICES.

CANADIAN BONDS. The Canadian bonds database provides price and yield statistics for approximately 1,200 Canadian bonds.

CANADIAN OPTIONS. The Canadian Options database provides daily trading statistics for more than 2,000 put and call options traded in Toronto.

DISCLOSURE ONLINE. (See above under CompuServe.)

DUFF AND PHELPS EQUITY IDEAS. Duff and Phelps Equity Ideas contains research reports by Duff and Phelps that expedite the decision-making processes involving investments for equity analysts and portfolio managers. These reports cover more than

440 companies and 61 industry groups. The database is updated daily by approximately 440 issues by 2:00 A.M. Toronto time.

DUFF AND PHELPS FIXED INCOME RATINGS. Duff and Phelps Fixed Income Ratings database provides information on fixed income rating for approximately 500 U.S. corporations with significant institutional investment following. The data on the 500 corporations is updated on a daily basis.

OTHER ON-LINE VENDORS IN BRIEF

Listed below are brief descriptions of a number of other vendors of interest to financial analysts.

BRIDGE DATA COMPANY

10050 Manchester Road
St. Louis, MO 63122

Bridge Data Company is publicly held and was founded in 1974. Bridge is a vendor of real-time, last sale, and quote information on all listed and unlisted stocks, options, futures, and bonds. Bridge also provides technical analysis capabilities on most securities by way of a historic price and volume database in which information is stored for up to 10 years. This real-time and historic data is available in a variety of display formats. Databases include:

BRIDGE INFORMATION SYSTEM. The Bridge Information System supplies information on over 30,000 listed and OTC stocks, financial futures, commodities, foreign securities, and all listed options to individual investors, stockbrokers, and traders.

PC BRIDGE. Developed jointly by Bridge Data Company and PC Quote, Inc, it delivers real-time and historical market data via satellite and landlines to customers with IBM PC/ATs.

MONEY MARKET PRICE QUOTATION SERVICE. An information service providing prices and yields on domestic and international money market instruments and fixed income securities, spot and forward foreign exchange quotations, and financial futures prices.

FUTURES PRICE QUOTATION SERVICE. Continuous access to the Futures Price database is provided by dedicated phone lines and/or satellite connection.

BRIDGE SPEECH SYSTEM. By using a tone-dial telephone, the Bridge Speech System enables customers to obtain real-time prices and quotes on any of over 30,000 securities on the Bridge Information System.

BRIDGE MARKET WATCH. Enables the user to monitor at one time on one screen trades as they occur on up to 60 stocks, options, futures, bonds, and indexes.

DOW JONES NEWS/RETRIEVAL. Provides access to news display giving current financial news, as well as news on related topics and news recall for up to three months. Special authorization and payment of fees to Dow Jones are required before this news service can be accessed.

MEAD DATA CENTRAL

9393 Springboro Pike
P.O. Box 933
Dayton, OH 45401

Mead Data Central is a wholly owned subsidiary of the Mead Corporation of Dayton, Ohio. In addition to its world headquarters in Dayton, Mead has 21 major sales offices in the United States, Canada, and London, England. Databases include:

EXCHANGE. Exchange is an information retrieval service of company, SEC, and industry reports written by expert analysts at leading brokerage and investment banking firms.

NAARS (The National Automated Accounting Research System). Documents include over 20,000 annual reports, proxy information, and authoritative pronouncements of the AICPA, SEC, and the Financial Accounting Standards Board.

NEXIS. NEXIS is a full-text information retrieval service of news, business, financial, and general information. It includes full-text coverage of more than 160 international newspapers, magazines, professional journals, trade journals, newsletters, and wire services.

NEWSNET

945 Haverford Road
Bryn Mawr, PA 19010

Newsnet offers an on-line library of over 250 industrial and professional newsletters. It also contains Investext, reports by analysts from leading brokerage houses, and news from United Press International and *USA Today*, among other features.

VICKERS STOCK RESEARCH CORPORATION

226 New York Avenue
Huntington, NY 11743

In 1983 Vickers Associates, a leader in the field of reporting institutional ownership of securities for more than 30 years and a member of the Argus Research Group, acquired Stock Research Corporation, a leading supplier of corporate insider information. The result was Vickers Stock Research Corporation. Databases include:

> *VICKERS BOND ON-LINE.* Vickers Bond On-Line is a securities' filings database allowing direct access to institutional corporate bond holdings. These institutions include: banks, insurance companies, 13F money managers, pension funds, and college endowment funds.
>
> *VICKERS ON-LINE.* Vickers On-Line is a securities' filings database allowing direct access to information on more than 8,500 common stocks. Subscribers can obtain data on institutional and corporate insider filings. Insider trading information is very extensive.
>
> *ARGUS ON-LINE RESEARCH REPORTS.* Argus reports provide information on over 450 actively traded companies plus general investment advice.

WARNER COMPUTER SYSTEMS

605 Third Avenue
New York, NY 10158

Warner offers seven databases. In addition to the Institutional Broker Estimate System (IBES), Disclosure II, and Compustat, Warner on-line databases provide a large amount of historical pricing, dividends, and earnings data on over 50,000 securities. Also available are option pricing and historical corporate bond information.

DATABASES FOR INTERNATIONAL INVESTMENT RESEARCH

The trend toward global investing has stimulated interest in internationally oriented on-line databases. It seems likely that as the use of such databases becomes more prevalent, the investment potential of companies will be compared not only on a national basis but also globally. Of course, in addition to company-specific data, such factors as exchange rates, political and economic developments, and unfamiliar accounting practices must be considered in analyzing foreign securities.

Some of the more widely used global databases are briefly described below. The field is in considerable flux, and interested readers should contact the indicated vendors for specifics.

Morgan Stanley Capital International, New York, databases include economic data and financial information on some 2,000 companies in North America, Europe, and the Pacific Basin. Software is available which permits screening by a number of financial variables.

World Scope, provided through Wright Investment Services (WIS), Bridgeport, Connecticut, is a global equity database providing financial details on over 2,000 non-U.S. companies. The database is compiled by the Center for International Financial Analysis (CIFAR), Princeton, New Jersey. The latter combined resources with Wright Investment Services—which provides a database on some 2,000 U.S. companies—to form the combined WIS-CIFAR base with over 4,000 companies worldwide.

Datastream International, with offices in New York, provides a number of international company, industry, economic, and market quotation databases. The company-oriented database includes over 3,200 non-U.S. companies.

Western Union Information Systems, Upper Saddle River, New Jersey, provides access via the Infomaster Service to a number of international news-oriented and some 100 other databases. Included in the system are the *London Financial Times*, *Japan Weekly Monitor*, the BBC "Summary of World Broadcasts," Associated Press World News Service, the Soviet Union's TASS, the French database Questel, and many others. The Western Union data can also be searched by company name. Infomaster also provides a gateway service to over 700 databases.

On-line services providing estimates of future earnings for non-U.S. companies are the International IBES Service of the brokerage firm of Lynch, Jones, and Ryan, New York, and Zacks Investment Research, Chicago.

Information Sources

1. *Annual Directory of the Information Industry Association*, Information Industry Association, Washington, D.C.
2. *Directory of Online Data Bases*, Cuadra/Elsevier, New York, New York.
3. *North American Online Directory*, R. R. Bowker and Co., New York, New York.
4. *Encyclopedia of Information Systems and Services*, Gale Research Co., Detroit, Michigan.

5. *Data Base Directory*, Knowlege Industry Publications, White Plains, New York.
6. *DataPro Directory of Online Services*, DataPro Research Corporation, Delran, New Jersey.
7. "Online and Data Base" (newsletter), Online, Inc., Weston, Connecticut.
8. "Data Base Alert" (newsletter), Knowledge Industry Publications, White Plains, New York.
9. *Wall Street Computer Review*, a monthly magazine published by Dealers Digests, New York, New York.

PART 9

Legal and Ethical Standards

54

Insider Trading

John G. Gillis, J.D.
Partner
Hill & Barlow

INTRODUCTION

One of the most pervasive issues in the corporate, financial, and legal areas in the last 20 years is insider trading. That term is a misfitting description of a range of activities involving trading in and communicating material nonpublic information in violation of the antifraud provisions of the federal securities acts as they may be interpreted from time to time by courts. As the term is imprecise, so is the permitted and prohibited activities under these laws. There have been few issues which have caused such uncertainty in the investment community as investment firms and their employees try to comply with the law while at the same time causing concern for regulators in their attempt to protect investors and the integrity of the securities markets.

Investors generally and investment professionals in particular are continually seeking information on which to base investment decisions. All are looking for clues as to the present and future value of individual securities which may be translated into securities transactions. Securities analysts in particular are charged by their employers with the responsibility to identify and recommend timely investment decisions. Investment managers are scrutinized by employers and clients in the investment performance of client portfolios. These objectives sometimes are difficult to reconcile with an imprecise law applied in diverse ways.

There are additional complicating factors in understanding the

Some of the material in this chapter appeared in earlier form in the author's columns in the *Financial Analysts Journal,* published by the Financial Analysts Federation, or other of its publications.

insider trading doctrine which until a few years ago was referred to as the inside information doctrine when the concept of outside and market information emerged. For example, it has since its inception applied not only to traditional insiders but to others in special relationships with an issuer of securities as well as to outsiders who receive information from insiders and who trade or communicate. Moreover, the doctrine covers not only inside information (about a company) but also market or outside information (about the market for the securities of the issuer).

The policy underlying the doctrine has usually been phrased in terms of fairness to investors who are trading while at a significant informational disadvantage and of the importance of maintaining the integrity of the markets by prohibiting those with significant informational advantages, in a degree considered inappropriate, from personally benefiting at the expense of the unwary and uninformed. Thus, there are elements both of unfairness and unjust enrichment in the prohibition.[1] But the standards used to apply the insider trading doctrine have changed over the years. Prior to two Supreme Court decisions, *Chiarella*[2] in 1980 and *Dirks*[3] in 1983, almost anyone, with some limited exceptions, who possessed inside information was prohibited from trading on it. They either had to disclose it or abstain from trading on or communicating it. While originally premised on a fiduciary duty owed by insiders, it soon expanded to a test of equality of or equal access to information.

However, these decisions held that possession of material nonpublic information alone was not enough to trigger the doctrine's application; it must have been received and traded or communicated in breach of a fiduciary duty. The duty in these cases was to the shareholders of the corporation whose securities were being traded. The concern of the Supreme Court was to balance the traditional fairness to individuals and integrity of the market factors, on the one hand, with the desirability of maintaining a free flow of information about companies and their securities to the marketplace. The restrictions of *Chiarella* and *Dirks* precipitated a series of cases in the lower courts which developed a new approach, the misappropriation theory, primarily based on the perceived necessity of preserving fairness to individual investors.[4] This theory premises liability under rule 10b-5 on a breach of a fiduciary duty owed by the recipient to his employer or his employer's clients or

---

[1] American Bar Association, Committee on Federal Regulation of Securities, "Report of the Task Force on Regulation of Insider Trading," July 1, 1985, pp. 9–10, reprinted in *Business Law* 41 (1985), pp. 223; Langevoort, *Insider Trading Handbook*, Clark Boardman Company, Ltd. (1986) pp. 7–10.

[2] Chiarella v. U.S., 445 U.S. 222 (1980).

[3] Dirks v. SEC, 463 U.S. 646 (1983).

[4] American Bar Association, "Report of the Task Force," pp. 4–5 and 20–23.

customers for personally using information given in confidence, and it reaches situations which would not be violations under *Chiarella* and *Dirks*. It has most often been applied, and liability found, in circumstances where information about a proposed merger or tender offer is obtained because of a relationship with the proposed acquiring company rather than the target company whose securities are typically purchased.

While this misappropriation theory has been criticized as theoretically flawed and with significant gaps, it has received acceptance in the courts, although the Supreme Court has not squarely ruled on it.[5]

BASIS FOR THE INSIDER TRADING DOCTRINE

The prohibition against use of inside information—material nonpublic information—is based on section 10(b) of the Securities Exchange Act of 1934 (1934 act) and rule 10b-5 thereunder. Section 10(b) (passed as part of the original 1934 act) is a general, short, so-called antifraud provision which makes it unlawful "to use or employ, in connection with the purchase or sale of any security . . . any manipulative or deceptive device or contrivance in contravention of such rules and regulations as the [Securities and Exchange] Commission may prescribe."

The enactment of rule 10b-5 in 1942 was precipitated by a specific problem in Boston. The president of a corporation was telling stockholders that the corporation was doing badly when, in fact, it was doing extremely well. Because of this bad news, some stockholders decided to sell; by coincidence, the president was there to accommodate them by buying their stock at depressed prices.

When the Boston office of the SEC brought this situation to the attention of the national office, the latter immediately drafted and adopted a rule (10b-5) intended to provide a remedy for sellers of stock in such circumstances. While the Securities Act of 1933 provided remedies for purchasers of stock, and the 1934 act rules at that time covered transactions involving brokers and dealers, there appeared to be no remedies for face-to-face transactions involving the kind of intentional misconduct that occurred in Boston.

The 1940s and 1950s saw a smattering of cases brought under rule 10b-5. Since the middle of the 1960s, however, the smattering has grown to a virtual avalanche, and rule 10b-5 is now often referred to as a federal corporation law because of its pervasive application.

Among other things, rule 10b-5 applies to material misrepresentations or omissions in face-to-face transactions (such as the one that precipitated the rule) whether a buyer or a seller is doing the defraud-

---

[5] Ibid.; and Langevoort, *Insider Trading Handbook*, p. 140.

ing. It applies to such various disclosure documents as proxy statements, reports filed with the SEC by public companies, prospectuses, annual reports, press releases, and private communications, and it covers projections by companies and analysts and trading on inside information, whether in personal or in market transactions. It also applies to analysts' research reports and recommendations and was the basis of the SEC proceeding against Merrill Lynch and many of its employees in connection with Scientific Control Corporation.[6]

The insider trading doctrine under rule 10b-5 is distinct from insider trading under section 16 of the 1934 act. Section 16 and rules under it permit a corporation to recover any profits an insider might realize from purchasing and then selling (or selling and then purchasing) securities within a six-month period. Insiders in that context are directors, officers, and certain large stockholders, and section 16 applies regardless of the information held by that person and regardless of the motive. To police section 16, the rules provide that individuals must report their stockholdings at the time they become insiders on form 3 and report transactions thereafter on form 4.

Rule 10b-5 is only slightly longer than section 10(b). It makes it unlawful: (1) to employ any device, scheme, or artifice to defraud (i.e., scheme to defraud); (2) to make any untrue statement of a material fact or omit to state a material fact (i.e., material untruth, misrepresentation, or omission); and (3) to engage in any act, practice, or course of business which operates or would operate to defraud or deceive any person (i.e., fraudulent course of business). The latter phrase is most often relied on in insider trading cases.

Rule 10b-5 is used in four ways: First, it is used in private suits between individual parties—that is, civil suits for monetary damages. Second, it is used in SEC administrative actions against firms or individuals registered with the SEC with remedies for violations as serious as barring an individual from business or revoking the registration of a firm. Third, it is used in suits by the SEC requesting injunctions against future violations of the securities laws. The SEC has been very active in recent years in policing insider trading matters including the initiation of many suits alleging selective dissemination of inside information to investment professionals and others. Because it is an equitable proceeding, the court has the discretion in these circumstances to impose remedies such as requiring the parties to pay over to third parties monetary damages or requiring the parties to adopt compliance procedures. Under the Insider Trading Sanctions Act (ITSA), adopted in 1984, civil monetary penalties may be assessed by the court in an

---

[6] In re Merrill Lynch, Pierce, Fenner & Smith, Admin. Proc. 3-4329 (June 22, 1973), settled by consent orders in part and dismissed in part, SEC Rel. No. 34-14149 (November 9, 1977).

amount up to three times the profit gained or the loss avoided. Finally, a substantial number of criminal cases have been prosecuted and won applying rule 10b-5 under the criminal sections of the 1934 act.

INSIDER TRADING DOCTRINE: EARLY CASES

Prior to 1968 rule 10b-5 was rarely applied to the area of insider trading. However, in 1968 the Second Circuit Court of Appeals decided the *Texas Gulf Sulphur*[7] case, and within two weeks the SEC brought an administrative proceeding against Merrill Lynch and 14 of its employees and 15 of its customers in a matter relating to Douglas Aircraft.[8] These events created a tremendous uproar in the corporate and securities communities. In a quandary about the extent of their responsibilities, corporations were canceling presentations to analysts' societies and canceling or refusing interviews with analysts.

The Financial Analysts Federation (FAF) became concerned about these developments, and George Bissell of Boston, then president of the FAF, prepared a response to the problem of the "drying up of information," which was presented at a press conference and printed in the November/December 1968 issue of *Financial Analysts Journal.*

In addition, the FAF asked Philip Loomis, then general counsel of the Securities and Exchange Commission and later a commissioner, to participate in an extensive panel discussion at its fall conference in Atlanta. The FAF printed and distributed 30,000 copies of this discussion which has continuing relevance and was extensively quoted in the case involving *Bausch & Lomb*[9] described below.

Following the events of 1968, new cases surfaced rapidly. Developments precipitated the SEC to ask for public comments in 1973 on whether inside information guidelines could be developed, and if so, what their content should be.[10] The FAF undertook to prepare guidelines on inside information which were submitted to the SEC and published in the *Financial Analysts Journal* in May–June 1974.

The SEC has never adopted guidelines although it made attempts from time to time to resume the guidelines project. Based on the SEC position before Congress on ITSA, it seems unlikely that it will do so in

[7] SEC v. Texas Gulf Sulphur Co., 401 F.2d 833 (2d. Cir. 1968), *cert. denied sub nom.* Coates v. United States, 394 U.S. 976 (1969).

[8] In re Merrill Lynch, Pierce, Fenner & Smith, SEC Rel. No. 34-8459 (November 25, 1968), [1967–1969 Transfer Binder] Fed. Sec. L. Rep. (CCH) ¶77,629 at 83,347.

[9] SEC v. Bausch & Lomb, Inc.; see note 33, below.

[10] SEC Rel. No. 34-10316 (August 1, 1973), [1973 Transfer Binder] Fed. Sec. L. Rep. (CCH) ¶79,446 at 83,262.

the near future. Thus, the commission and the courts continue to approach the problem on a case-by-case basis.

An insider trading case involves several elements of which the following are among the most important:

1.   An insider must be involved. In an early SEC case, *Cady Roberts*,[11] the concept of insider was at first narrowly defined, similar to that of section 16. That is, an insider was defined to be an officer, director, or large stockholder—someone who had a very special inside position with the corporation. That narrow definition has now eroded almost completely and includes persons with special or confidential relationships.

2.   There must be false information or failure to disclose information that is material and nonpublic.

3.   There must be scienter, at least in a private suit for damages. This was made clear by the Supreme Court case *Ernst & Ernst v. Hochfelder*.[12] Scienter is a legal concept meaning an intent to deceive, manipulate, or defraud.

As many of the insider trading cases demonstrate, liabilities for violating the rule apply, not only to insiders who trade in the stock but also to insiders as "tippers"—that is, as persons who receive information and pass it on to others—as well as to "tippees"—subsequent recipients of the information.

The first important insider trading case was the *Cady Roberts* case in 1961—an SEC administrative action against Cady Roberts, a broker, and one of its partners, alleging violations of rule 10b-5 involving the sale of stock of Curtiss-Wright Corporation in the open market.[13] Curtiss-Wright had announced in a press release on November 23, 1959, that it was developing a new type of internal combustion engine, and its stock traded actively on the following day, closing at 35. As the stock rose from 35 to 40 on November 25, a Cady Roberts partner who had purchased Curtiss-Wright shares between November 6 and November 23 began selling.

That same day (November 25), Curtiss-Wright directors met to consider declaration of the quarterly dividend, which had been $0.625 a share for many preceding quarters. However, the directors voted to declare a dividend of only $0.375—a 40 percent reduction. At 11 A.M. the board authorized a press release, and the meeting was adjourned while the secretary left to disseminate it. A director of Curtiss-Wright, who was a registered representative with Cady Roberts, called the partner

---

[11] In re Cady, Roberts & Co., 40 S.E.C. 907 (1961). An earlier SEC release received little notice. See Ward LaFrance Truck Corp., 13 S.E.C. 373 (1943).

[12] 425 U.S. 185 (1976).

[13] Cady, Roberts; see note 11.

and told him what had happened. There was a delay in transmitting the secretary's release to the broad tape and to the exchange floors, and during that time, the partner sold additional shares. After the release appeared on the broad tape, the market price of the shares dropped to 34.

The New York Stock Exchange fined the partner $3,000 for his conduct, and the SEC suspended him for 20 days. The brokerage firm was also held responsible for the partner's conduct, although it was not sanctioned. The important points in this case were that (1) the decision to cut the dividend by 40 percent was considered material and (2) the insider was considered to have an affirmative duty not to disclose information before it was publicly disseminated and not to act on it.

In what I believe was a twisting of concepts, the commission held that the partner was an insider because of his relationship with the director. The reason for this may be that the concept of tipper-tippee liability had not yet been developed. If the case were decided today, the director would be designated the insider and tipper, and the partner designated the tippee and hold responsible in that capacity. The commission, through Chairman Cary, stated the obligation either to disclose or not to act on inside information as follows:

> It rests on two principal elements; first, the existence of a relationship giving access, directly or indirectly, to information intended to be available only for a corporate purpose and not for the personal benefit of anyone and, second, the inherent unfairness involved where a party takes advantage of such information knowing it is unavailable to those with whom he is dealing.

The commission, in considering the concept of materiality, stated that the reduction of a corporate dividend was clearly material because it had a direct effect (1) on the market value of the security and (2) on the judgment of investors. While this two-part test for materiality has appeared in subsequent cases, it has sometimes been coupled with other tests and not relied on exclusively.

The decision of the commission noted that knowledge of the corporate action—reduction of the dividend—was not arrived at as a result of perceptive analysis of material public information or of nonmaterial nonpublic information (which is not considered to violate rule 10b-5). This type of analysis is not a violation of rule 10b-5 and is called the mosaic theory.[14]

Analysts obtain information from a wide variety of sources. Some of it is material and public and some nonmaterial and nonpublic; some is written and some oral. Analysts may assemble the information, evaluate it, fit it into a mosaic model, and reach conclusions. These conclusions

---

[14] A term possibly coined by the author in 1971.

may be very significant—in fact, if the company had communicated them to analysts, they might be material nonpublic information. But analysts are considered free to act since nonmaterial nonpublic information does not fall within the insider trading doctrine. Expressed in a variety of ways, this position has been generally recognized by the SEC and by courts, including the Supreme Court, that have considered the issue.

Finally, the commission stated in the *Cady Roberts* case that when a person has inside information, his responsibility is either to disclose it—a very difficult and impractical solution in most situations where analysts, investment managers, or others receive it from a corporation—or to refrain from making transactions or communicating it. While this 1961 case was the first significant case on insider trading and received some public notice, it did not seem to have a widespread impact on the way corporations disseminated important material about corporate matters.[15]

TIPPERS AND TIPPEES

The year 1968 marked two very important cases—the Second Circuit Court of Appeals decision in the *Texas Gulf Sulphur*[16] case and the SEC proceeding against Merrill Lynch and certain of its employees and customers.[17] These cases caused considerable confusion and uncertainty for corporations and securities firms and precipitated FAF President Bissell's press conference mentioned above.

Texas Gulf Sulphur involved two types of violations of rule 10b-5. The first was the purchase of Texas Gulf Sulphur (TGS) stock by officers and employees acting on confidential information about a mineral discovery in Ontario before it was made public. Two of these insiders were also found to have violated the rule by telling others—the genesis of tipper-tippee liability. The second violation involved a misleading press release issued by TGS.

In November 1963 the first core extraction in TGS's exploration indicated a high content of rich minerals. This was considered extraordinary and was kept secret within TGS. Only a limited number of officers and a few others were aware of the information, but some

---

[15] An example of how not to disseminate important corporate information is contained in a delightful vignette in the *Money Game* by Adam Smith, published in 1968. "The day they red-dogged Motorola" happened in 1966, when the president mentioned in passing to a meeting of the New York Society of Security Analysts a substantially lower earnings estimate than had been expected.

[16] Texas Gulf Sulphur; see note 7.

[17] Merrill Lynch; see notes 8 and 20.

started buying the stock and continued buying it from November to the following April.

On March 31, 1964, TGS resumed drilling and found some evidence confirming the rich ore discovery. Rumors of this strike began circulating throughout Canada within a week following the resumption of drilling. On April 12 TGS issued a press release saying in effect that it didn't yet know what it had in Ontario. Four days later, however, after some additional sampling, TGS issued another press release indicating that it had an extremely rich find. As might be expected, the price of its stock rose sharply.

The first press release was found by the court of appeals to be misleading on the ground that TGS had sufficient information by April 12 to be more definitive than merely saying the results were inconclusive. All the officers and directors who knew abut this information and bought the stock between November and April 16, the date of the second press release, were found to have violated rule 10b-5 by using the inside information. As mentioned earlier, two of the employees who knew about it were also found to have violated the rule by telling others who bought.

A review of two specific instances is instructive. One director didn't buy any stock before April 16, the day of the second press release, but both he (for family trust accounts) and his son-in-law, a broker, did so within minutes after the announcement was released. The broker also bought stock for some customers. The court found that they had purchased before the information was generally known, and the director settled by agreeing to pay his profit and that of his tippees for the benefit of the sellers of the stock.

A TGS geologist who was involved in the initial drilling in November 1963, had during the winter told his brother and two of his friends that TGS was "a good buy." He and the others purchased before April 1964. He was found to have violated rule 10b-5, not only by his own purchases but by conveying the "good buy" information to his brother and friends, and was held liable for his and their profit. While his brother and friends had in turn told other people who purchased the stock, the geologist's liability was not carried to the second tier of purchasers—that is, to the tippees' tippees.

The court stated that although the prohibition on insider trading might be predicated on traditional fiduciary concepts, the basis in policy is that all investors trading on impersonal exchanges have relatively equal access to material information.

In dealing with the question of materiality the court articulated several different tests thereby confusing the definition of materiality (which to date has not been fully resolved). In a taped interview Commissioner Loomis stated his interpretation of the court's approach in *TGS* and the SEC's in *Investors Management* (involving Merrill Lynch customers):

> I think the Commission adopted a combination. What the Second Circuit did was affected in some measure by prior court decisions and by utterances of the Commission on the general subject of materiality. By any test they could think of, the events in *Texas Gulf* were material. In the *Merrill Lynch* opinion the Commission attempted to focus the definition of material information a little more by saying, first, that it would be important to an investor and secondly that it could reasonably be expected to have a market impact.[18]

In August 1968 the SEC began an administrative proceeding against Merrill Lynch, 14 of its employees (including several senior people), and 15 of its customers. Within a few months Merrill Lynch entered into a consent order with the SEC whereby it and many of its employees received various sanctions, and it agreed to adopt compliance procedures to prevent misuse of inside information.[19] The proceeding against the institutional customers was contested and resulted in a decision by an SEC hearing examiner in 1970 in the *Investors Management Co.*[20] case. The hearing examiner found all but one of the institutional customers who had received information from Merrill Lynch to be tippees and to have violated the insider trading doctrine by selling Douglas stock. (The proceedings against two parents of other respondents were discontinued.) Curiously, none of the 12 institutional customers appealed this decision to the full commission. As the commission had not spoken on the issue of tippee liability, it took the case on its own motion and affirmed the decision in 1971.[21]

Merrill Lynch had agreed in the spring of 1966 to be the managing underwriter for an offering of convertible debentures by Douglas Aircraft, which supplied them with internal earnings projections of $4.00 to $4.50 per share for the current year. About June 1 Douglas revised the internal projections to $2.00 to $3.00. (Douglas has earned $0.85 for the first five months ending April 30.) On June 20 Douglas revised again, indicating internally a profit for the first six months of $0.49 and projecting little or not profit for the entire year. (Douglas had suffered a

---

[18] *Financial Analysts Journal*, May–June 1972, p. 24.

[19] Merrill Lynch; see note 8.

[20] In re Investors Management Co., SEC Admin. Proc. File No. 3-1680 (June 26, 1970), [1969–1970 Transfer Binder] Fed. Sec. L. Rep. (CCH) ¶77,832, at 83,928.

[21] SEC Rel. No. 34-8947 (June 30, 1970) [1969–1970 Transfer Binder] Fed. Sec. L. Rep. (CCH) ¶77,844 at 83,933 (review order); SEC Rel. No. 9267 (July 29, 1971), 44 S.E.C. 633 (1971), [1970–1971 Transfer Binder] Fed. Sec. L. Rep. (CCH) ¶78,163 at 80,514 (decision).

large loss in May and was having serious problems meeting its delivery schedule.)

Douglas representatives conveyed this information to Merrill Lynch representatives on the West Coast, who conveyed it to the New York office. Employees in the New York office advised institutional customers of the revisions on June 21 and 22, and they sold or sold short. On June 24 Douglas released its earnings publicly, indicating a second quarter loss of $0.66, a net profit of $0.12 per share for the first six months (ending May 31), and an estimate that it would probably have nominal, if any, earnings for the year.

Merrill Lynch was found to be an insider because it had a special relationship with Douglas as managing underwriter and a tipper because it conveyed inside information to institutional customers in violation of rule 10b-5. The customers were tippees and violated the rule when they sold the Douglas stock.

In one instance an institutional customer was found not to have violated the rule by trading by a portfolio manager who, although he sold Douglas stock, did not have the inside information even though another manager did. In this context the knowledge of one employee was not imputed to the other. However, the firm was censured because of the use of inside information by another portfolio manager.

The proceedings against one customer were dismissed. They involved an analyst who, although he had the information and recommended sale to his superior, did not convey the information. Although the supervisor eventually sold, he based his decision on his own independent evaluation rather than on inside information. Again there was no imputation of knowledge and no violation of the rule.

A related suit against Douglas alleged that the company was liable for not releasing the revised internal estimates at an earlier time. This failed, however, since the court found that the corporation exercised "good faith and due diligence in the ascertainment, verification, and publication of the serious reversal of earnings in May."[22] Douglas also prevailed against the claim that it had unlawfully disseminated the information to Merrill Lynch since it was legally obligated to do so because Merrill Lynch was acting as managing underwriter.

However, the Second Circuit Court of Appeals applied the abstain

---

[22] Financial Industrial Fund v. McDonnell Douglas Corp., 474 F.2d 514 (10th Cir.), *cert. denied*, 414 U.S. 874 (1973); *cf.* Beecher v. Able, [1975–1976 Transfer Binder] Fed. Sec. L. Rep. (CCH) ¶95,303, at 98,533 (S.D.N.Y. September 26, 1975) (settlement of class action suit). See *The Wall Street Journal*, February 2, 1977 (Douglas liable for other securities violations but not for its press release forecast); Beecher v. Able, 435 F. Supp. 397 (S.D.N.Y. 1977); Beecher v. Able, 441 F. Supp. 426 (S.D.N.Y. 1977).

or disclose rule to Merrill Lynch and its tippees in a suit for private damages, finding that access to information was the crucial factor.[23]

The problem of professional consultants in a special relationship with an issuer utilizing confidential information has persisted. For example, the SEC, in a public release, has cautioned law firms about the problems relating to the use by employees of law firms of inside information obtained in the course of confidential work for public companies.[24] This release was initiated, among other reasons, by situations in which secretaries were using information obtained when working on matters for lawyers representing the companies. This issue is discussed in detail below in the context of the misappropriation theory.

THE IMPORTANCE OF COMPLIANCE PROCEDURES

The earliest cases such as *Merrill Lynch* and *Investors Management* established the importance to employers in the securities business of adopting and enforcing procedures to prevent insider trading. The SEC has sought and obtained undertakings to adopt procedures or, in later years where most firms had procedures, undertaken to review or improve these procedures. An early example is the *Faberge* case which involved two different proceedings. One was an SEC injunctive proceeding against Faberge, its president, and a vice president in 1972,[25] and the second, an SEC administrative proceeding in 1973 against several brokers and investment advisers who traded Faberge stock.[26]

Faberge's executive vice president of finance learned late one evening that the company had experienced its first quarterly loss in 10 years. The next morning he called several brokers, analysts, and portfolio managers, and several called him; he revealed the loss to the persons with whom he talked, although in slightly different ways. Many of them sold Faberge stock or communicated the information before dissemination of the Faberge press release at about two o'clock that afternoon.

The conduct of one adviser who received the news from a broker who had talked with the Faberge officer was typical. The adviser was informed of the source and communicated it to a fund manager in his

---

[23] Shapiro v. Merill Lynch, Pierce, Fenner & Smith, 495 F.2d 228 (2d Cir. 1974).

[24] SEC Rel. No. 34-13437 (April 11, 1977), [1977–1978 Transfer Binder] Fed. Sec. L. Rep. (CCH) ¶81,116 at 87,854.

[25] SEC v. Faberge, Inc., SEC LR-5548 (October 2, 1972).

[26] Faberge, Inc., SEC Rel. No. 34-10174 (May 25, 1973), [1973 Transfer Binder] Fed. Sec. L. Rep. (CCH) ¶79,738 at 83,100; SEC Rel. No. 34-10835 (June 10, 1974).

organization, who sold. (The SEC found two levels of tippees in this instance—the broker and the fund manager.)

In another instance, a brokerage analyst receiving the news in a call from the Faberge officer informed a mutual fund portfolio manager of the news and the source. The mutual fund manager confirmed the information with the Faberge officer and sold 370,000 shares. He was found to have violated the rule.

The brokerage analyst also distributed an internal memorandum, an interoffice memorandum, and a message to the Autex information system. One of the broker's branch managers who received the interoffice memorandum called an analyst at a bank who sold Faberge stock through the broker. The SEC held that the message on the Autex system was not public dissemination of the information and found that both the broker's conduct and that of the bank violated rule 10b-5.

In another firm, a partner had placed a sell order before he heard the information. After he heard the news he confirmed with the Faberge officer and increased his sell order. His conduct in increasing the sell order was found to have violated the insider trading doctrine.

The impact of all this selling was dramatic. On October 5 27,000 shares of Faberge stock traded on the New York Stock Exchange. On October 6, the day the Faberge officer spoke with the brokers and analysts and later made the press release, 715,000 shares traded. The exchange's most actively traded stock, Faberge suffered the largest percentage drop (from 18½ to 14⅜). In the next three days following the announcement, volume dropped to 23,000 and the price stabilized at 14½.

Faberge and the two officers consented to the injunction in the SEC court action. Some of the brokerage and advisory firms in the SEC proceeding consented to a finding that their conduct was "censurable," but they were not censured; others, including the bank, were censured after hearings. One reason given by the SEC for not censuring "censurable" insiders was their undertaking to establish and implement compliance procedures to prevent misuse of inside information.

One of the interesting points about this case was the test of materiality used in the SEC decision. This test came from the SEC's *Investors Management* case—in turn based on *Cady Roberts*. In *Cady Roberts*—the first SEC case—the test was based on two factors: (1) the effect on the market price of the stock and (2) the effect on the judgment of an investor. This test was reiterated and amplified in the *Merrill Lynch* case in 1968, in the *Investors Management* case in 1971, and, again, in *Faberge* in 1973. The following is an excerpt from the *Faberge* decision:

> There can be no dispute that the information as to Faberge's first quarterly loss in many years was material. It "was of such importance that it could be expected to affect the judgment of investors whether to buy, sell

or hold" . . . and if generally known, "to affect materially the market price of stock."

Over subsequent years, however, the market impact requirement has often been dropped in other rule 10b-5 contexts and the test used whether the information could be expected to have an effect on the judgment of investors.

In *Faberge* the SEC also stated the policy of the rule as applied to insider trading:

> The objective of a fair market cannot be achieved when one of the parties to the transaction has inside information unavailable to the other. Few practices short of manipulation have as deleterious an effect on the investing public's confidence in corporate institutions and the securities markets as the selective disclosure of and misuse of so-called inside information, i.e., material nonpublic information.

The SEC *Faberge* decision also held that it was not necessary to show that the parties occupied a special relationship with Faberge that gave them access to nonpublic information or, in the absence of such relationship, that they had actual knowledge that the information was disclosed in a breach of fiduciary duty not to reveal it. This principle follows *Investors Management*, where the SEC specifically rejected contentions that such a demonstration was required. Thus, the concept of liability based on violating an insider's special relationship was substantially eliminated both in the courts and the SEC. It was reinstated in the *Chiarella* and *Dirks* decisions.

The SEC observed that the keystone of an effective compliance program to prevent misuse of inside information is the training and education of employees. As a part of the settlement of the *Faberge* SEC proceedings, all the firms, including those whose conduct was censurable but who did not receive censures, agreed to adopt internal compliance procedures. The SEC decision stated:

> Every broker/dealer must alert his personnel to the problems in this area. The educational program should alert employees as to what falls within the definition of material nonpublic information and how to treat such information. Beyond the educational process, firms should take steps to assure that their employees are complying fully with firm policy. Ongoing trading review should spot trading concentrations by employees. It should also show trading concentration in particular geographical areas or branch offices. Where the security has not been cleared by the firm's research department or transactions in the security have not received approval by a supervisory employee, an immediate inquiry should be undertaken to determine why particular salesmen are effecting multiple transactions in that security. The inquiry should include not only a financial review of the issuer, but should be directed at determining relationships between the brokerage firm's employees and management personnel of the issuer, as well as the source of the information being circulated concerning the

company. Finally, special supervisory procedures must be devised with respect to the research activities of the firm to make sure that inside information is not being sought or used by research personnel in connection with recommendations to customers or otherwise.

In two contested cases involving Lums and Geon Industries[27] each court had an opportunity to consider the relevance of compliance procedures. The case of *SEC* v. *Lums* resulted in injunctions against Lums and its president after a trial and by consent against a registered representative of Lehman Brothers, Investors Diversified Services, and two of the latter's portfolio managers. The president of Lums had called a registered representative at Lehman about sharply reduced earnings projections. The broker not only sold Lums stock for his own account but also conveyed this information to two IDS portfolio managers who caused IDS funds to sell substantial amounts of the stock. The court found that through the action of its president, Lums had violated the insider trading doctrine, that the registered representative had also violated it, but that Lehman had not because it had established and enforced adequate compliance procedures. IDS consented to an injunction and agreed to adopt compliance procedures. Lums also agreed to adopt compliance procedures.

In the case of *SEC* v. *Geon Industries*, a registered representative employed by a broker received inside information from an officer of Geon concerning a possible acquisition and traded for his own account and the accounts of family members. The court found the registered representative had clearly violated section 10(b) of the 1934 act but exonerated his employer. The employer had a policy of disseminating written guidelines on material nonpublic information and testing its employees for familiarity with the guidelines. The court stated that the broker had acted in good faith, and it was not established that the firm had participated in the employee's misconduct or had been negligent in supervision. The court based its decision on several factors enumerated by the trial court:

1. The broker had devised detailed compliance manuals which its personnel were required to maintain and study.
2. Each registered representative had his own copy of a registered representatives' manual, and classes, which the representative attended, were held from time to time to review it.
3. The representative had extensive experience in the securities business. His work and reputation were checked with his prior employer, and he was given a favorable recommendation.

---

[27] SEC v. Lums, Inc., 365 F. Supp. 1046 (S.D.N.Y. 1973). The IDS compliance guidelines are discussed and quoted in the author's column in *Financial Analysts Journal*, January–February 1973. SEC v. Geon Industries, 381 F.Supp. 1063 (S.D.N.Y. 1974), *aff'd*, 531 F.2d 39 (2d. Cir. 1976).

4. On at least one occasion the representative was monitored by three members of the compliance staff of the broker, who questioned him about his familiarity with the broker's rules and manual.
5. The manager spot-checked the work of the registered representatives and reviewed those accounts in which there was unusual activity.
6. The broker canceled all trades based on inside information, absorbing shares into its own "error" account, which resulted in a loss of $12,500 on the subsequent sale.
7. When definitive proof of the representative's wrongdoing was adduced, the broker promptly discharged him.

The court rejected the application of the doctrine of respondent superior—a principal being liable for the acts of its agent—at least in this situation where the "consequences of an injunction against a brokerage firm are potentially very great."

In *SEC* v. *Liggett & Myers*[28] the company had conveyed to its director of corporate communications for public dissemination the information that it had experienced a significant drop in earnings for the first six months of 1972. Before the press release was distributed, however, the director called several analysts and conveyed the information. In consenting to an injunction, Liggett & Myers agreed to adopt corporate compliance procedures to prevent the misuse of inside information.

The issue of compliance procedures has also been considered in the context of the potential conflict between fiduciary responsibility to a client and the insider trading doctrine under rule 10b-5. The short answer is that fiduciary responsibility does not supersede an obligation not to violate federal laws. The difficulty comes in the application of this principle, and the dilemma is set forth with some force in the case of *Slade* v. *Shearson Hammill*.[29]

Shearson Hammill had a policy which, among other things, prohibited certain types of communications between its corporate finance department and its sales and research departments. The corporate finance department had learned adverse information about its client Tidal Marine, which, in compliance with the policy, was not communicated to the other departments. Registered representatives of Shearson Hammill were, at the same time, soliciting (perhaps recommending) purchase of Tidal Marine. The federal district court in New York found that Shearson Hammill could have violated its fiduciary responsibility

---

[28] [1973 Transfer Binder] Fed. Sec. L. Rep. (CCH) ¶94,204, at 94,869 (S.D.N.Y. October 24, 1973).

[29] 356 F. Supp. 304 (S.D.N.Y. 1973).

despite the fact that, by not communicating this information within the firm, it was complying with what it understood to be the law.

This decision was criticized by many.[30] The case was certified to the court of appeals, which sent it back suggesting that the lower court decision was not appropriate.[31]

Among the more important points about this case are: One, there is a dilemma for securities professionals arising from the tension between the insider trading doctrine in federal law and fiduciary rules under state law. Two, the SEC has been requesting, encouraging, and, in some cases, requiring compliance procedures (i.e., walls within firms) as a general matter and in specific cases for many years.

The use of the so-called Chinese Wall between departments of a bank (commercial banking and trust and investments) and brokerage firms (corporate finance, investment banking, and sales and research) is now commonplace. Many brokerage firms also have adopted a restricted list which usually contains companies about which the firm has or will have material nonpublic information.[32] The consequences of not adhering to the restricted list is discussed below under 1986 developments in the case involving First Boston Corporation.

REFINEMENTS OF MATERIALITY

One of the most interesting cases in recent years is *SEC* v. *Bausch & Lomb*.[33] The SEC brought an injunctive complaint against, among others, Bausch & Lomb and its chairman; Faulkner, Dawkins & Sullivan (a brokerage firm), one of its analysts (David MacCallum), and its trader; and two partners of another broker. Faulkner Dawkins consented to an injunction, and MacCallum and the trader agreed to abide by it and also consented to censure by the SEC.[34] The other respondents, except for Bausch & Lomb and its chairman, consented to injunctions.

The case went to trial and resulted in a 1976 decision that Bausch & Lomb, its chairman, and the analysts to whom the chairman had given information had not violated the inside information doctrine. The trial

[30] See, for example, J. Gillis, *Financial Analysts Journal*, May–June 1974 and March–April 1975.

[31] 517 F.2d 398 (2d Cir. 1974); see, also, "SEC Advisory Committee on Broker Dealer Model Compliance Program," *Guide to Broker Dealer Compliance*, November 13, 1974, chap. X, p. 148.

[32] See Langevoort, *Insider Trading Handbook*, pp. 308–29, and the authorities cited therein.

[33] 420 F. Supp. 1226 (S.D.N.Y. 1976), aff'd, 565 F.2d 8 (2d Cir. 1978).

[34] SEC LR-7263 (February 10, 1976), 8 SEC Docket 19 (February 24, 1976); SEC Rel. No. 34-13210 (January 17, 1977).

court found that most of the information conveyed was not material while that which was material was not used.

The events[35] are as follows. Bausch & Lomb had been a very volatile stock during 1971 and 1972. There had been great expectations, but also many unfavorable rumors, about its newly developed soft contact lens called Soflens. On the basis of these expectations the stock price had risen substantially. The adverse rumors concerned the lens's potential safety, its efficient effectiveness, and the possibility of adverse action by the Federal Drug Administration. There had been conflicting reports about sales activities and the reception by the public. Bausch & Lomb had been revising its internal estimates downward for the first quarter of 1972 from $1.04, which was made in January, to $0.95 in February and $0.74 in March. In early March the chairman's secretary, without the knowledge of the chairman (who was away on vacation) made several appointments with analysts for interviews immediately after his return.

When the chairman, Schuman, returned, he was unhappy about these appointments because he had wanted to wait until after he had received additional internal quarterly information, but he held the appointments anyway. On the afternoon of March 15 he met with two partners of a brokerage firm and disclosed the following information.

1. An earnings estimate of $5.00 for the year was overly optimistic.
2. An earnings estimate of $3.00 for the year was too low.
3. A new lens product would be delayed in introduction by a few months.
4. The Soflens marketing kit (which had been important in the increase in market price of Bausch & Lomb stock) would not be out in the first quarter as had been previously announced.
5. Soflens weekly sales had flattened.
6. The Soflens sales rate was less than the prior estimate of one lens per practitioner per week.
7. Bausch & Lomb was revising its internal earnings estimates downward.

After the meeting the two partners disagreed on the importance of this information. One wanted to sell all of the stock; one wanted to sell only part of it; the firm decided to sell it all and did so early on the morning of March 16.

On the morning of March 16 MacCallum of Faulkner Dawkins met with Schuman. MacCallum, a specialist in the industry, had followed closely the Soflens development at Bausch & Lomb. He had previously decided in February to withdraw his buy recommendation for several reasons including a Faulkner Dawkins market study. He had withheld

---

[35] See J. Gillis, *Financial Analysts Journal*, May–June 1972 and November–December 1976.

revising his earnings estimate downward and withdrawing his buy recommendation, however, until after he visited Schuman at the request of one of the Faulkner Dawkins partners. He met for two hours with Schuman, who told him essentially what he had told the two brokers the afternoon before. After MacCallum left Schuman and reached the airport in Rochester, he made a prearranged call to his trader and told him that he was reducing his quarterly earnings estimates from $0.90 to $0.60–$0.70 and that he was withdrawing his buy recommendation. The trader then sold some shares for his own account. When Schuman returned to his office from lunch he received a call reporting that rumors were starting to circulate that Schuman had told MacCallum the revised internal Bausch & Lomb estimate. Schuman called MacCallum, who said that the revised estimate of $0.60–$0.70 was his own estimate.

The court found that to this point there were no violations of the insider trading doctrine because none of the information conveyed by Schuman to the partners on the afternoon of the 15th, or to MacCallum on the morning of the 16th, was material. The court found, however, that Schuman's subsequent conduct did violate rule 10b-5. When MacCallum told him in the telephone conversation that $0.60–$0.70 was his own estimate, Schuman said, "That's too low; its more like $0.70–$0.80." (This appears to be an example of the inadvertent disclosure of inside information.) The court found that MacCallum did not act on that information and that his actions were based on the earlier, nonmaterial (albeit nonpublic) information. Thus, even though it was a violation to disclose, there were no transactions based on the disclosure.

Following that call, Schuman talked to Bausch & Lomb financial personnel and asked them to review their earlier estimate. They did and estimated $0.65–$0.75. Schuman called MacCallum back and gave him a second earnings estimate of $0.65–$0.75.

An analyst from Smith, Barney was in Schuman's office during these conversations and, according to the court, told Schuman on two or three occasions that Bausch & Lomb should release this information publicly. Schuman said that he had already called Dan Dorfman, then of *The Wall Street Journal*, with whom he was to meet the next morning, and told Dorfman about the day's developments and that Dorfman's column would appear the next morning. The analyst told Schuman he didn't think that was adequate disclosure. Nevertheless, Schuman did not issue a press release. Schuman spent most of the rest of the afternoon on the phone fielding calls from analysts and others, although he apparently revealed no important information. Virtually all the calls came after the markets had closed.

The next morning, March 17, Dorfman's article appeared, stating that Schuman had leaked the earnings estimates to MacCallum. The stock did not open on the exchanges that morning because on the preceding afternoon a very high volume of shares had traded (about 350,000—up from 46,000) and the price had dropped significantly.

The court found that the following revelations by Bausch & Lomb's chairman to MacCallum did not constitute material disclosures:

1. An earnings estimate of $5.00 per share for the year 1972 (used by the analyst who had just left the chairman's office) was overly optimistic; the analyst should have been more conservative.
2. An earnings estimate of $3.00 per share for the year was too low.
3. The introduction of a new aphakic lens would be delayed until the second quarter.
4. The follow-up marketing package for Soflens, called a minikit, would not be out in the first quarter.
5. Soflens sales were not increasing on a week-to-week basis, had flattened, and were being seriously hurt by adverse publicity.
6. The Soflens sales rate was less than a prior estimate of one lens per practitioner per week.
7. Bausch & Lomb was revising its internal estimates of earnings downward.

The court phrased the legal issue as follows:

> At the heart of this controversy is a question of the permissible scope of communications between a corporate officer and securities analysts. Analysts provide a needed service in culling and sifting available data, viewing it in light of their own knowledge of a particular industry, and ultimately furnishing a distilled product in the form of reports. These analyses can then be used by both the ordinary investor and by the professional investment adviser as a basis for the decision to buy or sell a given stock. The data available to the analyst—his raw material—come in part from published sources but must also come from communications with management.
>
> Both the NYSE and the SEC have encouraged publicly traded companies to maintain an "open door" policy toward securities analysts.

As this was the first case that had appropriate facts to decide the viability of the mosaic theory, the judge considered the analyst's role at length. The court also quoted extensively from the Loomis discussion at the FAF Conference in 1968 and observed that there had been an absence of SEC guidelines in the inside information area, including guidelines specifically governing permissible and impermissible conduct. The judge concluded that it was not appropriate to find violations of rule 10b-5 under the facts that existed in the *Bausch & Lomb* case.

The SEC was upset at this decision, appealed to the court of appeals, and filed a lengthy brief with two major contentions: first, that virtually all of the matters disclosed to MacCallum were material and, second, that the 1976 Supreme Court decision in *Ernst & Ernst* v. *Hochfelder*,[36] which held that in a private suit under rule 10b-5 there must be scienter—an intent to deceive, manipulate, or defraud, was not applicable in this case because it was an SEC enforcement (i.e., injunctive) action.

On appeal, in affirming the judgment for the defendants[37] the Second Circuit Court of Appeals did not decide whether items 1 and 2 (earnings range) and 7 (internal revisions of earnings) were material, finding only that the SEC had not proved they had been conveyed. It agreed with the lower court that most of the information divulged was either not material or was already publicly known. The court cited with favor the "extraordinary events" materiality test, by which information is judged according to whether it is "reasonably certain to have a substantial impact on the market price" of the security, but continued to confuse the issue by citing as well the tests of "importance to a reasonable investor" and "actual significance in the deliberations of a reasonable shareholder." Finally, the court stated it was not deciding whether scienter was necessary in a suit for injunctive relief.

A final comment on materiality. An existing test, often alluded to, is that enunciated by the Supreme Court in a proxy solicitation context:

> An omitted fact is material if there is a substantial likelihood that a reasonable shareholder would consider it important in deciding how to vote.[38]

Moreover, a stricter test is one articulated in, among other cases, *Texas Gulf Sulphur*, adopted in *Merrill Lynch, IMC*, and *Faberge*, and noted with approval in both *Bausch & Lomb* decisions:

> . . . those situations which are essentially extraordinary in nature and which are reasonably certain to have a substantial impact on the market price of the security if the extraordinary situation is disclosed.[39]

CHIARELLA AND DIRKS

In 1980 the Supreme Court in *Chiarella* v. *U.S.*[40] rejected the SEC's long held and advocated position that virtually anyone in possession of material nonpublic information must either disclose the information or abstain from trading on it or communicating it.

The Court recognized that a rule 10b-5 violation is based on two elements found in *Cady Roberts:*

---

[36] Hochfelder; see note 12.
[37] 565 F.2d 8 (2d Cir. 1978).
[38] TSC Industries, Inc. v. Northway, Inc., 426 U.S. 438 (1976).
[39] Texas Gulf Sulphur; see note 7.
[40] 445 U.S. 222 (1980).

1. The existence of a relationship affording access to inside information intended to be available only for a corporate purpose.
2. The unfairness of allowing a corporate insider to take advantage of that information by trading without disclosure.

Chiarella involved an employee of a financial printer who discerned the identity of targets of planned takeover bids, although those identities had been disguised, and purchased securities of targets before the bids became public. This type of information, called market information, is to be contrasted with inside information about the business, financial, or other conditions of the company. The Court found in *Chiarella* that there is no general duty to disclose before trading on material nonpublic information and that a duty to disclose does not arise from the mere possession of nonpublic market information. Such a duty arises from the existence of a fiduciary or special relationship.[41]

The Court held that *Chiarella* did not have a general duty to investors in the marketplace nor, in these circumstances, a duty to the issuer or shareholders of the stock of the target company. The SEC argued in the Supreme Court that Chiarella had misappropriated the information from his employer's customers (the companies making the tender offers). The Court found, however, that this theory was not properly presented to the jury and would not consider it. The misappropriation theory based on a breach of duty to the employer and its customers and clients was subsequently advocated in other cases and became the basis for a series of decisions finding liability for criminal violations and grounds for injunctions, disgorgement, and penalties under the ITSA in SEC court actions.

The Court reversed Chiarella's criminal conviction. (The initial proceeding was commenced in 1978 and was apparently the first criminal prosecution for insider trading.)

This decision was followed in 1983 by the Supreme Court decision in *Dirks* v. *SEC*.[42] Dirks, supported by the Justice Department, persuaded the Supreme Court that his conduct in communicating publicly undisclosed information about the fraud at Equity Funding Corporation of America was not improper and, in fact, "played an important role in bringing the massive fraud to light." Dirks, after a 10-year struggle, prevailed over the Securities and Exchange Commission's long-standing position that a person in possession of material nonpublic information

---

[41] SEC Commissioner Richard Smith had supported a very similar approach in his concurring opinion in Investors Management Co.; see note 21. His approach was advocated by the author in *Financial Analysts Journal*, November–December 1972, p. 98.

[42] 463 U.S. 646 (1983). The author has written extensively on the history of this litigation in the *Financial Analysts Journal*, July–August 1973, March–April 1977, November–December 1978, May–June 1981, July–August 1983, and September–October 1983.

obtained from an insider—a tipper—must either publicly disclose the information or abstain from trading on or disseminating it. The Supreme Court held this prohibition will apply only if the corporate insider communicating the information breached his fiduciary duty to shareholders in doing so.

Dirks' struggle began in 1973, when a former officer of an Equity Funding insurance subsidiary sought him out and related the details of a massive fraud at Equity Funding that involved fictitious insurance policies, assets, and activities. Dirks conducted an extensive investigation over the next several weeks, obtaining corroboration of the fraud from several former and present employees and other representatives of Equity Funding, although top management of the company denied the allegations of wrongdoing. The former Equity Funding officer proceeded to inform state insurance officials, and Dirks informed *The Wall Street Journal* and the SEC, but no regulatory or media action ensued. After the New York Stock Exchange halted trading in Equity Funding stock because of unusually heavy volume and a precipitous price drop, Equity Funding was put in receivership, *The Wall Street Journal* published an article based largely on Dirks's information, and some 22 individuals were indicted and convicted of criminal activity. Because Dirks had communicated his knowledge to institutional investors who contacted him during his investigation, some of whom sold Equity Funding securities, the SEC censured him (after a hearing and an appeal) for violation of the federal securities laws. This finding was upheld by the court of appeals before the Supreme Court reversed the judgment.

In *Dirks* the Court noted that not all breaches of fiduciary duty in connection with a securities transaction fall within rule 10b-5. There must be a manipulation or deception that qualifies as a fraud because of the inherent unfairness of a person's taking advantage of information intended for a corporate purpose and not for the personal benefit of anyone. The Court reiterated the existing rule by stating that an insider will be liable under rule 10b-5 for insider trading only when he fails to disclose material nonpublic information before trading on it and thus makes "secret profits."

It is clear that the basic rule prohibiting the use of inside information for trading by insiders remains intact. The *Dirks* case, however, and, in particular, the Court's discussion of tipper and tippee liability, changes the application of this rule by adopting the new personal benefits test.

Tippee's Duty

The Court, in *Dirks*, reaffirmed the *Chiarella* holding on the scope of the duty of tippees:

> We were explicit in *Chiarella* in saying that there can be no duty to disclose where the person who has traded on inside information was not [the corporation's] agent . . . was not a fiduciary [or] was not a person in whom the sellers [of the securities] had placed their trust and confidence.

The Court added that tippees usually do not have the insiders' independent fiduciary duties to both the corporation and its shareholders. It rejected the SEC's position that a tippee inherits the duty to shareholders whenever he receives inside information from an insider. It also rejected the theory that all traders must enjoy equal information before trading. It then stated:

> We reaffirm today that [a] duty [to disclose] arises from the relationship between parties . . . and not merely from one's ability to acquire information because of his position in the market.

Role of Analysts

Before analyzing the circumstances under which tippees might not be free to trade on inside information, the Court considered at length the important role of analysts and other market professionals. In fact, it has been suggested, perhaps facetiously, that the opinion emphasized analysts so much that the new law set forth in the case should apply only to analysts. However, the statement of the new standards, of course, uses the generic term *tippee*.

The following quotation from the opinion illustrates the Court's concern with the impact of the existing rule on analysts:

> Imposing a duty to disclose or abstain solely because a person knowingly receives material nonpublic information from an insider and trades on it could have an inhibiting influence on the role of market analysts, which the SEC itself recognizes is necessary to the preservation of a healthy market. It is commonplace for analysts to "ferret out and analyze information," and this often is done by meeting with and questioning corporate officers and others who are insiders. And information that the analysts obtain normally may be the basis for judgments as to the market worth of a corporation's securities. The analyst's judgment in this respect is made available in market letters or otherwise to clients of the firm. It is the nature of this type of information, and indeed of the markets themselves, that such information cannot be made simultaneously available to all of the corporation's stockholders or the public generally.

The Court, in several footnotes, elaborated on the importance of the analyst's function and the need for clarity regarding permissible conduct:

> The SEC expressly recognized that [t]he value to the entire market of [analysts'] efforts cannot be gainsaid; market efficiency in pricing is significantly enhanced by [their] initiatives to ferret out and analyze information, and thus the analyst's work redounds to the benefit of all investors.
> . . . The SEC asserts that analysts remain free to obtain from management corporate information for purposes of filling in the "interstices in analysis." . . . But this rule is inherently imprecise, and imprecision prevents parties from ordering their actions in accord with legal requirements.

Unless the parties have some guidance as to where the line is between permissible and impermissible disclosures and uses, neither corporate insiders nor analysts can be sure when the line is crossed. . . .

The SEC's rule—applicable without regard to any breach by an insider—could have serious ramifications on reporting by analysts of investment views.

Despite the unusualness of Dirks' find, the central role that he played in uncovering the fraud at Equity Funding, and that analysts in general can play in revealing information that corporations may have reason to withhold from the public, is an important one. Dirks' careful investigation brought to light a massive fraud at the corporation. And until the Equity Funding fraud was exposed, the information in the trading market was grossly inaccurate. But for Dirks' efforts, the fraud might well have gone undetected longer.

NEW RULE FOR OUTSIDERS

The Court clearly stated that insiders are forbidden by their fiduciary relationship from personally using undisclosed corporate information to their advantage; nor may they give such information to an outsider for the same improper purpose of exploiting the information for their personal gain. The Court stated that the tippee's duty to "disclose or abstain" thus derives from the insider's duty. The conclusion that some tippees must assume an insider's duty to the shareholders is based, not on the fact that they receive inside information, but rather on the fact that it has been made available to them improperly. The insider's disclosure is improper only when it violates his fiduciary duty as originally articulated in the *Cady Roberts* case. The new rule is:

> Thus, a tippee assumes a fiduciary duty to the shareholders of the corporation not to trade on material nonpublic information only when the insider has breached his fiduciary duty to the shareholders by disclosing the information to the tippee and the tippee knows or should know that there has been a breach.

Noting that the *Dirks* case is an unusual one, the Court discussed more typical situations:

> In some situations, the insider will act consistently with his fiduciary duty to shareholders, and yet release of the information may affect the market. For example, it may not be clear—either to the corporate insider or to the recipient analyst—whether the information will be viewed as material nonpublic information. Corporate officials may mistakenly think the information already has been disclosed or that it is not material enough to affect the market. Whether disclosure is a breach of duty therefore depends in large part on the purpose of the disclosure.
>
> Thus, the test is whether the insider personally will benefit, directly or indirectly, from his disclosure. Absent some personal gain, there has been

no breach of duty to stockholders. And absent a breach by the insider, there is no derivative breach [by the tippee].

The Court stated that lower courts, in applying this test, should focus on objective criteria such as whether the insider received as a result of the disclosure a direct or indirect personal benefit, such as pecuniary gain or a reputational benefit that would translate into future earnings. The Court quoted a commentator who noted, "the theory is that the insider, by giving the information out selectively, is in effect selling the information to its recipient for cash, reciprocal information, or other things of value for himself." The Court noted that such an inference may be drawn from objective facts and circumstances, including, for example, a relation between the insider and the recipient that suggests something of value being received from the recipient or an intention to benefit the recipient. The Court noted that a breach also exists when an insider makes a gift of confidential information to a relative or friend who trades on the basis of that information.

APPLICATIONS OF THE NEW RULES

Dirks and *Chiarella* leave many issues unresolved. This is hardly surprising, given the variety of circumstances under which alleged insider trading arises, the fact that insider trading rules reach far beyond the scope implied by that phrase, and the broad application of rule 10b-5. The analysis is further complicated by the various contexts in which legal proceedings arise. These include (1) criminal proceedings; (2) SEC enforcement actions seeking injunctions and, typically, disgorgement of profits and, since 1984, penalties under ITSA; (3) suits by private litigants for monetary damages, all of the foregoing being court proceedings; and (4) SEC administrative proceedings against persons or entities registered with it. The following summary of several cases, some decided after *Chiarella* and some after *Dirks*, indicate the difficulty of applying legal principles in the insider trading area.

Who Is an Insider?

Typically, inside information cases have been brought against traditional insiders, i.e., officers, directors, and other persons with significant responsibility in the company. With a now growing number of exceptions, cases have not typically been brought against the lower level rank and file employees. However, numerous cases have also been brought against tippees of various stations who have received information from a traditional insider. A few of these latter cases have had rough going in the courts, especially when the source of the information was not a traditional insider but rather a "constructive insider."

Nevertheless, in most cases involving injunctive actions by the SEC, the courts have not followed the implications of *Dirks* and *Chiarella*. Rather, they have distinguished those cases and held that defendants who traded while in possession of material nonpublic information violated rule 10b-5. These cases have also developed the concept of constructive or temporary insider based on a now famous footnote in the *Dirks* decision (footnote 14, insiders), which provides as follows:

> Under certain circumstances, such as where corporate information is revealed legitimately to an underwriter, accountant, lawyer or consultant working for the corporation, these outsiders may become fiduciaries of the shareholders. The basis for recognizing this fiduciary duty is not simply that such persons acquired nonpublic corporate information, but rather that they have entered into a special confidential relationship in the conduct of the business of the enterprise and given access to information solely for corporate purposes. . . . When such a person breaches his fiduciary relationship, he may be treated more properly as a tipper than a tippee.

In *SEC* v. *Lund*,[43] an action by the SEC for an injunction, the court held that a tippee who traded on the basis of material nonpublic information disclosed to him by an officer of a company that was seeking participation in a joint venture violated rule 10b-5. The recipient was a friend and business associate of the insider and became a temporary insider subject to a fiduciary duty not to trade on the basis of the information. The insider was pursuing a legitimate business purpose in disclosing to the defendant the terms of a proposed joint venture and in inviting the defendant to make an investment in the venture. The recipient did not join the venture but, rather, purchased shares for his personal account.

The SEC did not argue that the defendant should be held liable on a theory of tippee liability (an approach that presumably would have failed after *Dirks* because there was no breach of duty by the insider) but, rather, that for purposes of rule 10b-5, "insider" is a flexible concept that includes not only officers, directors, and controlling shareholders of the corporation but "all those who had a special relationship affording access to insider information." This concept was accepted by the court, which held that "the test to determine insider status is whether the person has access to confidential information intended to be available only for corporate purposes and not for the benefit of anyone."

The court went on to state that even though such persons are not traditional insiders, they nevertheless become fiduciaries of the corporation and its shareholders as temporary insiders. They assume the duties of an insider temporarily by entering into a special relationship with the corporation. A temporary insider is subject to liability under

---

[43] 570 F. Supp. 1397 (C.D. Cal. 1983).

section 10(b) for trading on the basis of nonpublic material information received in the context of the special relationship.

The court indicated that the defendant and the insider had a long-standing personal relationship and often discussed various business matters. It indicated that, in view of this relationship, the insider's position with his corporation and his role as director of the defendant's board, and the corporate nature of the information itself, there was an implication that the information should have been kept confidential. The court ordered disgorgement of the profits made by the defendant but did not order an injunction because it held that the SEC had not satisfied its burden of proof that the defendant was reasonably likely to engage in further violations.

Misappropriation Theory

In *U.S.* v. *Newman*[44] the defendant was the recipient of information from employees of two investment banking firms that were advising clients in takeovers and mergers. The court of appeals held that the defendant could be criminally liable under section 10(b). He was subsequently convicted. In this case the court held that a breach of duty to the employer by the communicator of information was sufficient, even though the trader-recipient owed no fiduciary duty to those with whom he traded. This is referred to as the misappropriation theory. The Supreme Court refused to hear an appeal of this case after the *Dirks* decision.

Moss v. *Morgan Stanley, Inc.*[45] (also called *Moss* v. *Newman*) was begun immediately after Mr. Newman was convicted of criminal violations discussed above. The plaintiff had sold shares in a company shortly before the announcement of a tender offer for those shares. The defendant had purchased shares of that company on the same day, knowing of the imminent announcement of the tender offer, but before the announcement was made. The premise for the suit was that a person misappropriating nonpublic information has an absolute duty to disclose that information prior to trading or to refrain from trading; this duty, it is argued, is owed to shareholders and public investors. The plaintiff argued that this theory was left expressly undecided in the *Chiarella* case and was espoused by Chief Justice Burger in his dissent in that case. Nevertheless, the district court dismissed the suit, and the court of appeals for the second circuit confirmed that dismissal, concluding that a misappropriation of nonpublic information does not give

---

[44] 664 F.2d 12 (2d Cir. 1981), *aff'd after remand*, 722 F.2d 729, *cert. denied*, 464 U.S. 863 (1983).

[45] 719 F.2d 5 (2d Cir. 1983), *cert. denied sub nom.* Moss. v. Newman, 104 S. Ct. 1280 (1984).

rise to a private claim for damages under section 10(b) by sellers of securities against purchasers who bought on the basis of the misappropriated information but owed no fiduciary duty to the sellers.

A comparison of *U.S.* v. *Newman* and *Moss* v. *Morgan Stanley* would suggest that the misappropriation theory apparently applies for purposes of criminal cases under section 10(b) but does not apply, at least according to the holding of the appeals court, for purposes of civil damages. The Supreme Court rejected an application for an appeal in the *Moss* v. *Morgan Stanley* case.

The case of *SEC* v. *Materia*[46] (decided after *Dirks* on December 5, 1983) is a significant case because it upheld the misappropriation theory. Materia, a financial printer (as was Chiarella), had been entrusted with documents as part of his job preparing materials for a tender offer. The defendant purchased stock in tender offer targets before the public announcement of the takeover bid. The district court enjoined Materia from future violations of the insider trading rules and ordered him to disgorge his profits. It held that *Dirks* did not overrule the misappropriation theory accepted in *U.S.* v. *Newman*.

The appeals court held that the *Dirks* decision did not eliminate the possibility of rule 10b-5 liability based on fiduciary duties owed to sources of the material nonpublic information. The court of appeals affirmed, holding that "one who misappropriates nonpublic information in breach of a fiduciary duty and trades on that information to his own advantage violates section 10(b) and rule 10b-5."

The SEC reviewed the legal developments since *Dirks* in its report to the house committee on securities matters, requested by the committee while it was considering the Insider Trading Sanctions Act.[47] The commission stated it believes that the *Dirks* decision "has not adversely affected, to a significant degree, the commission's enforcement program against insider trading" in the two years following the decision.

It also noted that the misappropriation theory, which it has been advocating, has been approved by lower courts including the important Second Circuit Court of Appeals in the *Materia* case and mentioned favorably in the Supreme Court *Bateman Eichler*[48] opinion.

The SEC in its report viewed *Materia* as a key decision:

> The Second Circuit opinion in this case is perhaps the single most important judicial opinion on insider trading since the *Dirks* decision. In

---

[46] [1983–1984 Transfer Binder] Fed. Sec. L. Rep. (CCH) ¶99,583, at 97,272 (S.D.N.Y. 1983), *aff'd*, 745 F.2d 197 (2d Cir. 1984), *cert. denied*, 105 S. Ct. 2112 (1985).

[47] Report of the Securities and Exchange Commission to the House Committee on Energy and Commerce on *Dirks* v. *Securities and Exchange Commission*, August 23, 1985.

[48] Bateman Eichler, Hill Richards, Inc. v. Berner, 105 S. Ct. 2622 (1985).

addition to being the only insider trading case to reach the court of appeals, the Second Circuit's decision in *Materia* established a number of important principles. It held the misappropriation theory of liability is not inconsistent with the *Dirks* opinion, a conclusion confirmed by the Supreme Court in its *Bateman Eichler* decision. The court of appeals decision in *Materia* also removed any doubt that the misappropriation theory is available to the Commission in its civil enforcement cases. Finally, the court of appeals clarified that, in order to be actionable under rule 10b-5, fraud need not be perpetuated on a party to a securities transaction where it is "in connection with" the purchase or sale of securities.[49]

In the case of *SEC* v. *Musella*,[50] the SEC alleged that the office services manager of the law firm of Sullivan and Cromwell tipped information regarding tender offers planned by the firm's clients to several persons who traded on the information. The court, relying on the misappropriation theory in *U.S.* v. *Newman* (a criminal action), concluded that liability under rule 10b-5 is premised on the employee's breach of his fiduciary duty to the law firm and its clients, notwithstanding that it was the target company's shares that were purchased not the client's shares.

The court relied on the doctrine, stated in *Dirks*, that outsiders may become corporate fiduciaries or insiders if they have special confidential relations with the corporation and are given information solely for corporate purposes. The court also found that the tippees knew or should have known that the information was misappropriated. This knowledge was inferred from their professional backgrounds and circumstantial evidence.

In the only case the SEC has lost since *Dirks*, *SEC* v. *Switzer*,[51] the court found that the defendant had not violated insider trading prohibitions. This decision was based on the defendant's argument that he inadvertently overheard a conversation by a corporate insider about possible liquidation plans for the company. The court found that the corporate insider, in disclosing the information to his wife while sitting next to the defendant at a track meet, did not breach his fiduciary duty to his company, even though the defendant overheard the conversation, purchased shares of the company, and tipped several others who also traded. Because there was no breach by the insider, there was no derivative duty for Switzer. The SEC points out in its report that the court based its ruling on the SEC's failure to prove its case rather than on a restrictive interpretation of the principles in *Dirks*.

---

[49] Report of the Securities and Exchange Commission.
[50] 578 F.Supp. 425 (S.D.N.Y. 1984).
[51] 590 F.Supp. 756 (W.D. Okla. 1984).

The 1985 case of *SEC* v. *Gaspar*[52] held that an investment banker who disclosed to a professional colleague information about the acquisition of stock by a client corporation had misappropriated the information from his employer and its client and breached his fiduciary duty. The court indicated that the defendant had sullied his employer's reputation and had injured the integrity of the negotiating process. It also noted that he could be considered a temporary insider of the client during the negotiations. It noted that the defendant, while not himself trading in the securities, had obtained a reputational benefit by revealing information to his colleague and that this benefit was sufficient to impose liability under *Dirks*, given the working relationship between the two. The court also found that, at the very least, the disclosure constituted a gift of confidential information as described in *Dirks*.

The case of *U.S.* v. *Thomas C. Reed*[53] involved a criminal prosecution alleging that Reed had traded in call options for shares of Amax Inc. while in possession of material nonpublic information, obtained from his father, a director of Amax, concerning a potential merger between Amax and another company, in breach of a duty of trust and confidence owed to the father. The district court denied a motion to dismiss, holding that the issue of the existence of a confidential relationship between father and son should focus on the expectations and understandings of the parties. It added that the prosecution would have to show that the defendant and his father were bound by an agreement or understanding of confidentiality or that a regular pattern of behavior by both generated an expectation of confidentiality and fidelity.

The SEC views this case as significant because it recognizes that the misappropriation theory is applicable to information obtained from an insider of a corporation whose shares are traded and because it recognizes that fraudulent misappropriation is not limited to situations in which a strict fiduciary duty is present. Moreover, it holds that insider trading in options is subject to the legal prohibitions.

However, after the decision the case went to trial and Mr. Reed was aquitted by the jury.[54]

---

[52] [1984–1985 Transfer Binder] Fed. Sec. L. Rep. (CCH) ¶92,004, at 90,967 (S.D.N.Y. April 15, 1985).

[53] 601 F.Supp. 685 (S.D.N.Y. 1985), *rev'd* in part, 773 F.2d 477 (2d Cir. 1985) (reinstating perjury and obstruction counts). In 1981 the commission brought a civil injunctive action against Thomas C. Reed and Frank M. Woods. Simultaneous with the filing of the complaint, the defendants consented to the entry of a court-ordered undertaking not to purchase any securities while in possession of material nonpublic information without disclosing such information. See SEC v. Thomas C. Reed and Frank M. Woods, SEC LR-9537 (December 23, 1981). (The facts also gave rise to private litigation.)

[54] *The Wall Street Journal*, December 17, 1985.

INSIDER TRADING SANCTIONS ACT

In August 1984 the Insider Trading Sanctions Act (ITSA) became effective after nearly two years of consideration by Congress. This amendment to the Securities Exchange Act of 1934 (Section 21(d) and other sections) provides for new civil monetary damages of up to three times the profit (or the loss avoided) on insider trading transactions and increases fines for criminal violations to $100,000 from $10,000. ITSA applies to persons "purchasing or selling a security while in possession of material nonpublic information" and those "aiding and abetting the violation of such persons" (i.e., tippers). Despite many requests to Congress during consideration of ITSA, there is no definition of the term *material nonpublic information,* and there are some interpretative issues regarding other provisions.[55] ITSA provides, however, that persons who aid and abet an insider trading transaction other than by communicating material nonpublic information are not subject to the sanction. In addition, brokerage and other firms are not liable under it solely by reason of employing a person who does violate the law. ITSA also provides a definition to determine the amount of profit or loss that would be used as the basis for the treble damages penalty and a five year statute of limitations on actions.

Finally, ITSA extends insider trading liability to persons communicating or trading while in possession of material nonpublic information in transactions involving a put, call, straddle, option, privilege, or group or index of securities [Section 20(d)].

The SEC brought its first action under ITSA in November 1984[56] and, subsequently, through August 1986 brought an additional 12 matters seeking penalties under it. All 13 matters were settled and penalties agreed to.[57] However, the SEC has not indicated how it determines the amount of penalties to seek, nor, of course, has any court been presented with that issue or the interpretation of the statute. Apparently in all insider trading enforcement actions for conduct occurring since ITSA, the SEC has sought penalties except in two cases where the transactions were rescinded or canceled. The dollar amount of the penalties have ranged up to $2.3 million. Most of the cases appear to seek penalties in the amount of the profit gained (or loss avoided) although, in some cases, the penalties sought and agreed to have been

[55] S. Miller, "The Insider Trading Sanctions Act," *Revised Securities and Commissions Regulations* 17 (October 24, 1984) p. 821; T. Levine, "Recent Insider Trading Sanctions," *Revised Securities and Commission Regulations* 19 (September 10, 1986), p. 185.

[56] SEC v. Ablan, SEC LR-10618 (November 27, 1984); SEC LR-10830 (July 23, 1985).

[57] Levine, "Recent Insider Trading Sanctions."

double the profit.[58] In some cases tippers have agreed to penalties on the basis of profits of the tippees.[59]

Rule 14e-3—Tender Offer Trading

Following the *Chiarella* decision in 1980, which restricted the application of rule 10b-5 in insider trading cases, the SEC adopted rule 14e-3 under the 1934 act.[60] The rule makes it a fraudulent, deceptive, or manipulative act or practice for any person in possession of material information relating to a tender offer which he knows or has reason to know is nonpublic and which he knows or has reason to know has been acquired directly or indirectly from the tender offeror, the target, or persons involved in the proposed transaction, to trade on that information. The rule is triggered if the information relates to a tender offer and the offeror has commenced or taken a substantial step or steps toward commencement of the offer. It also prohibits insiders from communicating confidential information about a tender offer to persons who are likely to violate the rule by trading.

It is clear that this rule is broader, as it relates to tender offer information, than rule 10b-5 and that it supplements the prohibition contained in rule 10b-5. Rule 14e-3, while it requires a number of factual determinations, does not require a breach of fiduciary duty, as required in *Chiarella* and *Dirks*, either to the shareholders of the issuer corporation or under the misappropriation theory. The rule has invariably been used in cases of insider trading relating to tender offers in combination with rule 10b-5.

Subsection (c) of the rule provides two exceptions from the abstain or disclose requirement. First, it excludes purchases "by a broker or by another agent or person on behalf of an offering person" to allow the proposed offeror to make purchases in the marketplace prior to the commencement of the tender offer. The section also excludes sales to the proposed tender offeror.

Moreover, the rule provides, in subsection (b), that it does not apply to persons who are trading in the security or for others if they did not know of the material nonpublic information and if procedures had been established in the firm to ensure that individuals making investment decisions would not violate the rule. This is a Chinese Wall exception for institutions where one department might know of the information about

---

[58] Ibid. SEC Commissioner Cox has stated that the SEC usually seeks disgorgement of profits plus a penalty in an equal amount (*The SEC Today*, October 10, 1986). He has also stated that in the current year the SEC will recover over $30 million in disgorgement of profits (*The SEC Today*, September 23, 1986).

[59] Levine, "Recent Insider Trading Sanctions," pp. 188, 189, and 191.

[60] SEC Rel. No. 34-17120 (September 4, 1980), [1980 Transfer Binder] Fed. Sec. L. Rep. (CCH) ¶82,646 at 83,453.

a tender offer while the other person in another department who is trading does not know about it.

While there have been some suggestions that the SEC exceeded its authority in adopting rule 14e-3, there are substantial arguments to defend its validity.[61]

TREATIES TO ENFORCE INSIDER TRADING PROHIBITIONS

The series of cases involving trading in the securities of Santa Fe International Corporation are significant not only in the context of insider trading but also in light of increasing globalization of securities markets and the development of needs to protect the emerging internationalized markets from fraud. As a result of discussions in 1982, the United States and Switzerland entered into a memorandum of understanding under a 1977 treaty.[62] Thereafter the SEC in 1984 obtained an agreement with the Swiss government to order Swiss banks to disclose the identity of customers alleged to have traded securities of Santa Fe International Corporation before Kuwait Petroleum Corporation's 1981 tender offer. It took nine months more, a total of three years, after the SEC began its search for evidence before the SEC received documents regarding the accounts.[63]

As a consequence, among others, the SEC obtained a judgment by consent from the U.S. District Court in Manhattan ordering disgorgement of $7.8 million in profits from the illegal trading.[64] The judgment also enjoins the several defendants from future violations of the securities law. The defendants were mostly mid-eastern nationals residing in Europe who allegedly received the inside information from a director of Santa Fe and used Swiss bank accounts for their trading. The director, Darius N. Keaton, consented to an injunction and disgorgement and was indicted in 1986 and pleaded guilty in March 1987 to trading on material nonpublic information.[65] Several other individuals involved in Santa Fe trading were the subject of successful SEC civil actions and criminal prosecutions.[66]

---

[61] D. Langevoort, *Insider Trading Handbook,* 1986, pp. 187–93.

[62] *The SEC Today,* October 6, 1982.

[63] *Securities Regulation & Law Report* 17 (February 8, 1985), p. 281; *The Wall Street Journal,* February 21, 1985.

[64] SEC LR-11012 (February 26, 1986); *Securities Regulation & Law Report* 18 (February 28, 1986), p. 281.

[65] *Securities Regulation & Law Report* 14 (October 8, 1982), p. 1718 (injunction and disgorgement); *Securities Regulation & Law Report* 18 (January 24, 1986), p. 100, and *The Wall Street Journal,* January 17, 1986 (indictment); *The Wall Street Journal,* March 16, 1987 (guilty plea).

[66] See *Securities Regulation & Law Report* 15 (May 27, 1983), p. 991; (September

An additional example of the increased ability of U.S. enforcement officials to obtain trading information from foreign countries occurred in 1985 when the Bahamian attorney general waived the provisions of Bahamian law so that a branch of a Swiss bank located in the Bahamas could disclose the identity of and details about an account holder and his transactions.[67] This information eventually resulted in a series of legal actions including a criminal guilty plea by the trader, Dennis Levine, an investment banker who had specialized in mergers and acquisitions.[68] This in turn led to several guilty pleas by other securities professionals involved with Levine.[69]

Other instances are occurring of international cooperation to prosecute violations of the insider trading doctrine by a vigorous SEC enforcement program. For example, in the case of *SEC* v. *Katz*,[70] entered and concluded by consent on August 7, 1986, the SEC used the procedure developed with the Swiss government to identify one of the traders as the purchaser of RCA stock immediately prior to the tender offer by General Electric Corporation. The SEC investigation, aided by the Chicago Board Options Exchange and the New York Stock Exchange, resulted in injunctions, disgorgement of profits of about $2.2 million, and ITSA penalties of over $2.3 million.

The following are actions that the United States and the SEC have taken to investigate and proceed against insider trading and other securities fraud which utilize off-shore transactions and accounts.

A U.S. and Cayman Islands mutual assistance treaty was signed July 3, 1986. It gives the SEC the ability to obtain comprehensive assistance in cases involving securities law violations.[71]

A memorandum of understanding was signed on September 23, 1986, by the U.S. Securities and Exchange Commission and Commodity Futures Trading Commission and the United Kingdom Department of Trade and Industry providing for the exchange of information in the securities and commodities areas. It is expected that negotiations for a mutual assistance treaty between the two countries will follow.[72]

2, 1983), p. 1709; *Securities Regulation & Law Report* 16 (March 9, 1984), p. 478; SEC LR-10620 (December 3, 1984); *The Wall Street Journal,* December 22, 1983.

[67] *The Wall Street Journal,* May 28, 1986.

[68] *Securities Regulation & Law Report* 18 (June 6, 1986), p. 793.

[69] *Securities Regulation & Law Report* 18 (September 19, 1986), p. 1341 (Ira B. Sokolow and David S. Brown); *Securities Regulation & Law Report* 18 (October 17, 1986), p. 1498, and *The Wall Street Journal,* October 10, 1986 (Ilan K. Reich); *Securities Regulation & Law Report* 19 (January 2, 1987), p. 16, *The Wall Street Journal,* December 23, 1986 (Robert M. Wilkis).

[70] SEC LR-11185 (August 7, 1986).

[71] *Securities Regulation & Law Report* 18 (July 18, 1986), p. 1051; see, also, note 72.

[72] *The SEC Today,* September 24, 1986; *Securities Regulation & Law Report* 18 (September 26, 1986), p. 1397.

The SEC and the Securities Bureau of the Japanese Ministry of Finance entered into an agreement in May 1986 to cooperate in investigations of securities law violations.[73]

The SEC and the Quebec and Ontario Securities Commissions reached an informal agreement in 1985 to cooperate in exchanging securities fraud information.[74]

The United States and France are holding talks on an evidence-gathering agreement.[75]

Finally, the International Association of Securities Commissions at its July 1986 meeting established standing committees to promote cooperation on enforcement of securities regulation. The December 1986 meeting resulted in support for a proposal to establish a network of bilateral agreements to improve cooperation between regulatory authorities.[76]

1986 AND 1987 DEVELOPMENTS

While 1986 did not see any significant changes in the legal theory, or its application in the insider trading area with one exception, there was an extraordinary series of developments indicating the success of the SEC enforcement program but, perhaps more troubling, which revealed the potential extent and magnitude of insider trading in the securities community.

As mentioned above, in February 1986 the SEC obtained a recovery of $7.8 million in profits from several off-shore traders in the *Santa Fe* case, and on July 29 an indictment was issued against a Jordanian oil consultant, Constandi Nasser, for his alleged participation in insider trading in that case.[77]

In early May the SEC instituted and settled proceedings against First Boston Corporation alleging that it had traded for its own account while in possession of adverse material nonpublic information received from a corporate finance client. First Boston's internal compliance procedures prohibiting trading on inside information apparently were not adhered to, and it traded in securities of the client while in possession of the inside information notwithstanding that the client's securities were on an internal restricted list which is designed to prevent trading by the firm for its own account. First Boston agreed to an injunction and

---

[73] *Securities Regulation & Law Report* 18 (May 30, 1986), p. 769; *The SEC Today,* September 24, 1986; see, also, note 72.

[74] *The Wall Street Journal,* September 4, 1986; see, also, note 72.

[75] *The Wall Street Journal,* September 4, 1986; *Securities Regulation & Law Report* 17 (November 1, 1985), p. 1929; see, also, note 72.

[76] *Securities Regulation & Law Report* 18 (July 18, 1986), p. 1049; see, also, note 72; *Securities Regulation & Law Report* 19 (January 2, 1987), p. 24.

[77] *Securities Regulation & Law Report* 18 (August 1, 1986), p. 1122.

disgorgement of profits and penalties of almost $400,000 and to review its restricted list and Chinese Wall procedures.[78]

On May 12 the largest ever insider trading case in dollar terms (to that time) was commenced involving Dennis Levine, who had been a merger and acquisitions employee with several large investment bankers, the latest of which was Drexel Burnham Lambert Inc. The SEC alleged he had realized $12.6 million of illegal profits by insider trading. It obtained an injunction and disgorgement of assets of $10.6 million from Levine's Bahamas bank account and $1 million of other assets.[79] Levine also pleaded guilty to securities fraud, mail fraud, and tax evasion. After the sentencing of five others involved in the communications and trading network, as described below, Levine was sentenced to two years in prison and fined $362,000. The judge noted that the leniency of the sentence was based upon Levine's "truly extraordinary cooperation" with the government which led to the discovery of massive violations of securities fraud laws by Ivan Boesky described later in this chapter.[80]

The SEC alleged that Levine had traded on material nonpublic information in at least 54 proposed mergers or takeover transactions from June 1980 to December 1985. According to the SEC Levine had used fictitious names and two Panamanian corporations to trade through the Bahamian branch of Bank Leu, a Swiss bank. Levine's contact at the Bank Leu was also implicated and subject to various U.S. legal proceedings.[81]

Levine had obtained the material nonpublic information because of his position in his firms as well as from Ira B. Sokolow, who was in the mergers and acquisitions department at Shearson Lehman Brothers, Inc. (a former employer of Levine), for which he paid Sokolow about $120,000. Sokolow has agreed to a permanent injunction, the disgorgement of $210,000, and a permanent bar from the securities business. Finally, he pleaded guilty to criminal violations of the securities laws and tax evasion and was sentenced to one year and one day in prison, a suspended three year prison term and three years probation.[82]

Litton Industries, Inc., has sued Lehman Brothers Kuhn Loeb, Inc. (now in the Shearson Lehman group), Sokolow, and Levine for dam-

[78] SEC LR-11092 (May 5, 1986), 35 SEC Docket 13 at 858 (May 20, 1986).

[79] SEC LR-11095 (May 12, 1986) (temporary restraining order), 35 SEC Docket 14 at 898 (May 28, 1986); SEC LR-11117 (June 5, 1986) (permanent injunction and disgorgement), 35 SEC Docket 17 at 1085 (June 17, 1986).

[80] *Securities Regulation & Law Report* 18 (June 6, 1986), p. 793; *The Wall Street Journal*, January 23, 1987 (sentencing).

[81] SEC LR-11144 (July 1, 1986), 36 SEC Docket 1 at 50 (July 15, 1986).

[82] SEC LR-11146 (July 1, 1986) (bar, injunction, and disgorgement); see, also, note 69 (criminal); *The Wall Street Journal*, November 7, 1986 (sentencing).

ages involved in Litton's 1983 acquisition of Itek Corp.[83] Litton alleges that the price of Itek rose because of the insider trading which caused it to pay more for Itek's stock than it otherwise would have. It asserts that Lehman, who was its investment banker in the tender offer, was responsible because of its negligence in not preventing communication of the information from Sokolow to Levine.

Another source of Levine's information was Robert M. Wilkis, also a mergers and acquisition employee, first at Lazard Freres & Co., and then E. F. Hutton & Co. Inc., according to the SEC. It charged that Wilkis tipped Levine and also personally traded on material nonpublic information for profits of over $3 million. Over a five year period Wilkis traded through three banks, all located in the Cayman Islands, in the securities of at least 50 companies. Wilkis has agreed to an injunction, disgorgement of profits of $3.3 million, and a bar from the securities business. Wilkis pleaded guilty to four felony charges and was sentenced to one year and one day in prison for communicating confidential information to Levine and for trading on it himself.[84]

Randall D. Cecola, a junior financial analyst at Lazard Freres, agreed to an injunction, disgorgement of $20,000, and a permanent bar from the securities business for passing confidential information to Wilkis and for trading on information himself. He was sentenced to six years probation, and two suspended five-year prison sentences on criminal charges that he filed false income tax returns.[85]

David S. Brown, a mergers and acquisitions employee at Goldman, Sachs & Co., was indicted and charged by the SEC for tipping Sokolow in at least 11 matters knowing that Sokolow was likely to disclose the information to Levine. He agreed to an injunction, disgorgement of about $146,000, and a bar from the securities business and has pleaded guilty to securities fraud and mail fraud and was sentenced to 30 days in prison (to be served on 15 weekends), fined $10,000, ordered to perform 300 hours of community service and put on probation for three years. He had been paid about $30,000 by Sokolow for information passed to him.[86]

Finally, a New York lawyer, Ilan K. Reich, a partner in the law firm

---

[83] *Securities Regulation & Law Report* 18 (August 22, 1986), p. 1237; *The Wall Street Journal*, August 20, 1986.

[84] SEC LR-11145 (July 1, 1986) (injunction and disgorgement), 36 SEC Docket 1 at 50; SEC LR-11146 (July 1, 1986) (bar), 36 SEC Docket 1 at 51 (July 15, 1986); *Securities Regulation & Law Report* 19 (February 13,1987), p. 219 (sentencing); *The Wall Street Journal*, February 10, 1987 (sentencing).

[85] *Securities Regulation and Law Report* 19 (January 2, 1987), p. 16 (guilty plea), 19 (February 13, 1987), p. 219 (sentencing); *The Wall Street Journal*, February 11, 1987 (sentencing).

[86] SEC LR-11245 (October 9, 1986) (injunction and disgorgement); SEC Rel. No. 34-23698 (October 9, 1986) (bar); see, also, note 69 (criminal); *Securities Regulation & Law Report* 19 (January 16, 1987), p. 89, *The Wall Street Journal*, January 13, 1987 (criminal conviction).

of Wachtell, Lipton, Rosen & Katz, pleaded guilty to securities and mail fraud for divulging to Levine material nonpublic information about pending takeovers on at least 12 occasions. He, like Sokolow and Wilkis, was sentenced to one year and one day in prison and five years probation. He had not received any trading profits although Levine had established an account for that purpose. He also agreed to an injunction and a civil penalty of $485,000 for his actions. He will be automatically disbarred because of his criminal plea.[87]

Another 1986 development occurred on May 27 when the criminal conviction of Foster Winans, a columnist for *The Wall Street Journal,* along with that of two of his cohorts, was upheld by the Second Circuit Court of Appeals in New York.[88] In a split decision (two to one), the court applied the misappropriation theory and found that it supported a criminal conviction based on a breach of duty by Winans to his employer, Dow Jones & Company, publisher of *The Wall Street Journal,* which has a policy against the disclosure or use of confidential information about matters to be published in the newspaper, even though it did not find that Winans and his employer had a duty to the readers of the newspaper. In all of the prior misappropriation theory cases, it had been found that a duty existed on the part of the employee to his employer and to the employer's clients or customers.

The Supreme Court agreed in December 1986 to hear the case and the decision should establish the parameters of the misappropriation theory. The criminal convictions included Winans, his friend, David Carpenter, and a stockbroker, Kenneth Felis, formerly with Kidder Peabody & Co., to whom Winans allegedly communicated misappropriated information regarding his articles in the Journal's "Heard on the Street" columns. Another Kidder stockbroker, Peter Brant, had pleaded guilty in July 1984 to conspiracy and two counts of securities fraud for acting on Winans' information. Brant's customer and friend, David W. Clark, a lawyer, was indicted in January 1987 on 55 counts of embezzelement (unrelated to Winans), and trading on the misappropriated information communicated from Winans to Brant and then to him. Clark allegedly made $453,000 in 17 trades from October 1983 to Feburary 1984. The charges against Clark include securities fraud, embezzlement, tax evasion, perjury, and filing false tax returns. Clark pleaded not guilty to the charges.[89]

In yet another case involving securities professionals, all in their 20s, four persons, including two arbitrage research analysts, a stockbroker,

[87] See note 69 (criminal); SEC LR-11246 (October 9, 1986) (injunction and civil penalty); *The Wall Street Journal,* January 26, 1987 (sentencing).

[88] U.S. v. Carpenter, et al., 791 F.2d 1024 (2d Cir. 1986), *aff'g,* 612 F.Supp. 827 (S.D.N.Y. 1985).

[89] *The Wall Street Journal,* December 16, 1986 (granting of certiorari); *The Wall Street Journal,* January 22, 1987, January 30, 1987 (Clark indictment).

and his customer, all pleaded guilty to various criminal violations for the use of material nonpublic information about pending tender offers and takeovers allegedly received from a young lawyer, Michael David, an associate at the New York law firm of Paul, Weiss, Rifkind, Wharton & Garrison. The indictment against the five alleged that David passed material nonpublic information between December 1985 and March 1986 on several proposed transactions which he learned while at the firm.

One of the analysts, Robert Salsbury, formerly with Drexel Burham Lambert was sentenced to three years probation and 200 hours of community service. He agreed to a bar from the securities business and also agreed, in a civil action, to a permanent injunction, although no disgorgement of profits was ordered as he had not personnally traded on the information. The other analyst, Andrew Solomon, formerly with Marcus Schloss & Co., was sentenced to one-year probation, a fine of $10,000 and 250 hours of community service. Morton Shapiro, a former stockbroker at Moseley Securities Corporation, received a two-month prison sentence for insider trading and perjury and a $25,000 fine. Shapiro's customer, Daniel Silverman, was sentenced to three-years probation, 200 hours of community service and a $25,000 fine. The sentencing judge distinguished Shapiro from Salsbury and Solomon stating that he had profited, along with David and Silverman, about $160,000 on the illegal trading, and was a Wall Street professional, distinguishing him from his customer Silverman. It is expected that the SEC will seek disgorgement and ITSA fines from both Shapiro and Silverman. David agreed in a SEC civil action to an injunction and disgorgement of $50,000 and penalties of up to $100,000 to be paid over eleven years. After initially pleading not guilty, David pleaded guilty in November 1986 to securities law violations, obstruction of justice, and subornation of perjury and is expected to be sentenced in April 1987.[90]

On August 7, the SEC instituted and settled a case against Marcel Katz, a former financial analyst at Lazard Freres & Co., his father, his father's father-in-law, and a broker alleging illegal trading based on information about the RCA-GE merger obtained by the analyst from his firm. As noted above, disgorgement of about $2.2 million, penalties of $2.3 million, and injunctions were agreed to and ordered.[91]

In one of the largest and most dramatic scandals in the history of the

---

[90] *Securities Regulation & Law Report* 18 (June 6, 1986), p. 794 (indictments and four guilty pleas); *The SEC Today*, February 11, 1987 (Salsbury administrative bar and criminal conviction); *Securities Regulation & Law Report*, 19 (January 23, 1987), p. 124 (Salsbury injunction); *The Wall Street Journal*, November 28, 1986 (Solomon criminal conviction); *The Wall Street Journal*, March 3, 1987 (Shapiro and Silverman criminal convictions); *Securities Regulation & Law Report*, 19 (January 9, 1987), p. 58 (David civil penalties); *The Wall Street Journal*, March 3, 1987 (status of David criminal proceeding).

[91] SEC LR-11185 (August 7, 1986).

securities industry, Ivan F. Boesky, an exceptionally successful and well known arbitrager, settled, on November 14, 1986, an SEC civil action by agreeing to pay a total of $100 million dollars representing disgorgement of $50 million in illegal profits from trading on information from Dennis Levine and $50 million dollars as a penalty under the ITSA. Boesky is barred from the securities business, although the order is stayed until April 1, 1988, and he has agreed to plead guilty to one felony count and to cooperate with the government. The information resulting in this settlement was supplied by Dennis Levine, the former managing director at Drexel Burnham Lambert, who had plead guilty to criminal charges in June 1986 and who cooperated extensively with the government.

It was alleged that Boesky and Levine had agreed in the spring of 1985 that Boesky would compensate Levine for confidential information about proposed takeover and merger transactions on the basis of a formula of profits realized. The SEC charged that the agreed compensation was at least $2.4 million but that it had not been paid at the time that Levine was arrested in May 1986. Boesky allegedly profited by at least $50 million from the information illegally supplied by Levine.

Following these developments on November 14, 1986, the U.S. securities markets had a significant albeit temporary decline and numerous regulators called for investigations and hearings on the regulation of takeovers and the role of arbitragers and other securities professionals in taleovers. The reaction was further increased when it was disclosed that Boesky sold, with the knowledge of the SEC, over $400 million of securities for a large fund that he managed shortly before the announcement of the SEC charges and settlement.[92]

The shock waves from the Boesky scandal were still being felt when yet a new round of developments crashed onto the securities business. On February 12, 1987, three highly placed Wall Street professionals were arrested and charged with insider trading violations. These included Richard B. Wigton, head of the arbitrage and over-the-counter trading departments at Kidder Peabody & Co., Timothy L. Tabor a former arbitrage official at Kidder Peabody and Robert M. Freeman, head of the arbitrage department at Goldman Sachs & Co. They have denied the charges. The following day a prominent, respected and successful former head of the mergers and acquistions department at Kidder Peabody, Martin A. Siegel, plead guilty to two felony counts including securities fraud and income tax evasion. He was charged with communicating confidential information about takeovers to Wigton and Tabor which he allegedly obtained from Freeman and which was used to trade

---

[92] *New York Times*, November 15, 1986 (civil settlement); *New York Times*, November 21, 1986, *The Wall Street Journal*, November 18, 1986 (sale of securities).

in firm accounts. It is charged that Freeman obtained from Siegel confidential information about proposed transactions on which Freeman allegedly traded for his personal account. In related SEC civil actions, Siegel agreed to disgorge $9 million of assets, a permanent injunction and a bar from the securities business. The SEC charged that Boesky had paid Siegel $700,000 over four years while Siegel was at Kidder Peabody for confidential information about potential takeover transactions. Siegel had left Kidder in early 1986 to join Drexel Burnham Lambert and all of the charges involved Siegel's conduct while at Kidder. Although Kidder Peabody has not been charged with any violations it has been reported that it is concerned that it will be.[93]

The fallout from the Levine, Boesky and Siegel scandals is significant. At least four congressional committees have undertaken investigations and hearings. Numerous bills have been or will be introduced. Two subcommittees of the House Energy and Commerce Committee are holding hearings. Testimony before the Oversight and Investigations Subcommittee was critical of the SEC for what is perceived as a lack of success in discovering insider trading violations without the aid of informants and in over-reliance on stock exchange computer surveillance programs which are believed inadequate.[94] The Telecommunications, Consumer Protection and Finance Subcommittee has also been critical of the SEC in not defining insider trading and one of its members will introduce a bill to establish a commission to study takeover regulation, insider trading, surveillance systems and government oversight. The President has established a task force to study insider trading among other issues.[95]

Senate Banking Committee hearings have concentrated on possible changes in the takeover laws[96] and have expanded the scope of the hearings to include the role of risk arbitragers in the takeover process. The Securities Subcommittee also is seeking in its hearings a clarification of the definition of insider trading.[97]

Numerous bills have been introduced to change the takeover laws and to define insider trading and increase penalties for violations, including one by Senator D'Amato similar to that which he introduced at the time the ITSA was being considered.[98]

The New York Stock Exchange has proposed new requirements for

---

[93] *New York Times*, February 13, 1987, February 14, 1987, and February 17, 1987; *The Wall Street Journal*, February 14, 1987, and February 17, 1987; *The Wall Street Journal*, March 16, 1987 (Kidder Peabody & Co. status).

[94] *Securities Regulation & Law Report* 18 (December 12, 1986), 1769.

[95] *The SEC Today*, March 9, 1987; *The Wall Street Journal*, December 15, 1986.

[96] *The Wall Street Journal*, March 5, 1987.

[97] *The Wall Street Journal*, March 3, 1987; *The Wall Street Journal*, February 25, 1987.

[98] *Securities Regulation & Law Report* 19 (January 30, 1987), p. 171.

members' supervision and compliance programs. These will require, after approval, that members do the following: (1) review all internal supervision and compliance programs, (2) certify quarterly that the firm's own trading accounts and employees trading accounts have been reviewed and that there are no securities violations, (3) report quarterly on all customer complaints, (4) report annually about compliance problems and their resolution. In addition the Exchange indicated that it will take steps to speed up their investigations, to conduct more investigative interrogations on the record, to fine firms which do not respond quickly enough to requests for information and to develop a new special examination for compliance department directors.[99]

The U.S. Sentencing Commission has issued revised draft sentencing guidelines relating to insider trading violations which in part would base sentences on the amount of a defendant's trading profits.[100]

The SEC's Chief Economist has conducted and released a study on the rise in prices of takeover targets berfore the public announcements which indicated that there are at least three other factors, in addition to insider trading, that cause prices to increase during this period.[101]

There have been numerous suits filed against arbitragers and investment bankers who employed persons implicated in criminal and SEC actions. These suits have been by investors trading at the time of the insider trading as well as by companies proposing to make tender offers alleging that the price of the target's shares rose because of the insider trading.[102] A related development has been the qualification of Kidder Peabody & Co's. 1986 annual report by its auditors because of its possible liability arising from allegations of insider trading violations by three of its current or former employees.[103]

Even before the Boesky and Siegel revelations it was abundantly clear that the SEC and the United States Attorney's Office in Manhattan have made the investigation and prosecution of insider trading a high priority. Since SEC Chairman Shad stated, at the beginning of his term in the early 1980s, that the commission would come down on insider trading with hobnail boots, it has attempted just that. It is estimated there will be some 30 cases brought by the SEC in 1986. Seventy-seven cases were started by the SEC from its fiscal year 1982 through fiscal 1985, which is the same number brought by the SEC from its inception in 1934 through 1981.[104] Moreover, there is a substantially increased

[99] *New York Times*, February 19, 1987, *The Wall Street Journal*, February 19, 1987.

[100] *Securities Regulation & Law Report* 19 (February 13, 1987), p. 220.

[101] *The Wall Street Journal*, March 11, 1987.

[102] *The Wall Street Journal*, March 5, 1987.

[103] *The Wall Street Journal*, March 3, 1987.

[104] *Securities Regulation & Law Report* 18 (June 20, 1986), p. 889; *Securities Regulation & Law Report* 18 (August 15, 1986), p. 1203.

number of criminal cases being prosecuted. The U.S. Attorney's Office in Manhattan reports that it has charged 39 people with insider trading felonies in the 18 months ending in May 1985.[105] The first criminal prosecution for insider trading was against the Mr. Chiarella commenced in 1978.

The SEC, the major stock exchanges, commodity exchanges, and the National Association of Securities Dealers are all fully committed to the development of sophisticated computer capabilities for securities trading. They have spent and allocated substantial funds to these programs which has made it much easier to identify unusual trading patterns and to identify the traders.

For example, the New York Stock Exchange 1986 budget for market surveillance is $8 million, of which more than $3 million is for automation systems. The exchange has three systems for monitoring trading on the exchange floor. The Stock Watch system monitors unusual trading activity; the International Surveillance Information system is a database containing months of trading activity and programs to search for trading patterns; and the Automated Search and Match system is a relational database of publicly available information on 500,000 business executives and 75,000 companies and subsidiaries. In 1985 the NYSE surveillance analysts reviewed 6,000 unusual price or volume variations. Ten percent looked suspicious, and 10 percent of those—65—were referred to the SEC.[106]

The exchanges and the NASD routinely refer to the SEC matters which suggest to them that legal violations may be involved.

In short, there are significant monetary and human resources committed to detecting and prosecuting insider trading.

CONCLUSION

The Congress, the courts, and the Securities and Exchange Commission have consistently found that insider trading is unlawful and should be prohibited. While the formulation of the definition of insider trading and prohibited activity has expanded, contracted, and expanded again and its parameters remain hazy, the twin policy objectives of administering fairness to investors and preventing unjust enrichment, as well as maintaining the integrity of securities markets, form a foundation for the continuing evolution of the doctrine. It is safe to predict that insider trading will continue, albeit as prohibited activity, and violations will be aggressively sought out and subjected to the legal process.

---

[105] *The Wall Street Journal*, May 29, 1986, p. 22.

[106] *Securities Regulation & Law Report* 18 (July 25, 1986), p. 1009.

55

Standards of Professional Conduct

W. Scott Bauman, D.B.A., CFA
Department of Finance
Northern Illinois University

This chapter deals with standards of professional practices for financial analysts. Although various aspects of the occupation of financial analysts is described elsewhere, it will be defined here for the purposes of this chapter. Financial analysts are individuals compensated for providing investment research information, recommendations, advice, or market decisions for clients, customers, subscribers, superiors, or other associates, which are used to purchase, hold, and sell investment securities or portfolio accounts composed of securities. This occupation would also encompass those who are responsible for supervising financial analysts. Hence, financial analysts have many job titles such as industry securities research analyst, portfolio manager, investment advisor, account representative (account executive or broker), trust investment officer, and financial planner. For purposes of this chapter, investment securities include common stock equities and bonds, and portfolio accounts include individual portfolios, mutual funds, pension funds, separate accounts, trust accounts, variable annuity accounts, and other institutional portfolios.

FINANCIAL ANALYSTS AS A PROFESSION

Identifying established standards of professional practices used by financial analysts would seem to depend on whether financial analysts are members of a recognized profession. There is no question that financial analysts are members of an important occupation, but the question is whether they are members of a true profession or of a trade group. As is frequently the case for other simple questions, this one has no simple answer. Nonetheless, the identifying of professional standards of practice logically appears to be intertwined with determining the professional status of financial analysts. Within this context we will explore questions as to what should be the basic professional standards of practice for financial analysts *if* the occupation is to be recognized as a profession and the questions as to what extent these standards of practice are recognized.

THE CASE FOR PROFESSIONAL STANDARDS

In order to determine what should be the standards of practice, we need to know what purposes are to be served or what needs are to be met by such standards. In short, what is the case for such standards? Several reasons are presented below.[1] As is the case for other professions, such as the medical, legal, and public accounting fields, it may be argued that the overall objective of the financial analysis profession and its standards is to represent the public interest and the best interests of those who are served—clients, customers, employers, and owners.

Since the industrial revolution, the American and the world economy has developed money and capital markets with publicly owned and publicly traded investment securities on an enormous scale, amounting to many trillions of dollars. Consequently, an enormous responsibility is placed on the tasks of research and management of investment securities. How this capital is allocated and managed determines the extent to which economic prosperity is reached in terms of production, employment, and government services and the extent to which the financial well-being is reached by many millions of investors and their families.

Evidence amply exists that incompetent and unscrupulous analysts contribute to poor investment performance, excessive investment risks, and losses for clients and employer institutions. In addition, untrained, unseasoned, and unethical analysts, operating simultaneously in the aggregate, occasionally contribute to speculative booms in securities market sectors which are followed by severe market collapses. Such professionally unsound and unethical practices result in public scandals, inflict losses on thousands if not millions of investors, create economic disruptions in the capital markets, and contribute to a general lack of public confidence in the financial system and the financial analyst profession.

Second, the need and opportunity for high standards for competency is much greater today. A considerable body of knowledge and analytical skills may now be acquired and advantageously used by analysts in conducting investment research or in making investment decisions. These skills and knowledge concern theories, concepts, technical terminology, quantitative relationships, and mathematical techniques. Formal disciplines of study useful to an analyst include economics, accounting, securities analysis, portfolio management, legal and ethical requirements, business statistics, and management of information systems.

With the growth of new market sectors and the proliferation of sophisticated financial instruments such as financial futures, mortgage-backed securities, and security options, the process of intelligently analyzing investments and managing portfolios has become far more complex. The opportunity now appears greater for analysts to use analytical techniques and research methods because of the vast expansion of information resulting from greater corporate disclosure requirements, increased precision of financial statements, computerized data banks, and the flood of other economic and security market information.

Finally, if sound standards of practice are clearly established and enforced, the interests can be protected for clients and employers who may not have a sufficiently sophisticated background or opportunity to evaluate properly the professional credentials of analysts.

CRITERIA FOR ADEQUATE STANDARDS

Given the foregoing needs and opportunities, it is suggested that the following criteria should be met in order to have adequate, workable standards for this specialized and technically sophisticated profession:

1. A formal body of knowledge and a group of skills are specified which a competent analyst is expected to master.
2. This knowledge and these skills may be acquired by systematic study, by on-the-job training, and through practice.
3. Examinations can be constructed, administered, and graded so as to distinguish objectively between those applicants who show evidence of an acceptable level of competence and those who do not.
4. Standards of practice are clearly formulated so that the performance of analysts can be reasonably judged as being in compliance or not.
5. If standards are violated, appropriate disciplinary sanctions are imposed on the analyst.

We will now examine the current status of financial analyst standards of practice.

PROFESSIONAL SELF-REGULATORY SYSTEM

While there are several professional organizations of financial analysts in the United States and Canada, the largest and most widely recognized are The Financial Analysts Federation (FAF) and The Institute of Financial Analysts (ICFA). Attention will be focused on these two organizations because they have the most extensively developed standards of professional practices. The FAF is a nonprofit professional organization, founded in 1947, consisting of 52 local societies composed of about 15,200 financial analyst members. The ICFA is also a nonprofit professional organization, associated with the FAF, and was organized in 1959 for the purposes of implementing standards according to the basic criteria described in the preceding section. We will now examine the FAF-ICFA self-regulatory system within the context of those criteria.

Admission Standards

Admission standards are intended to allow individuals to practice as financial analysts who are willing and able to represent the best interests of those who are to be served.

A financial analyst who has full membership status in the FAF is called a Fellow of the FAF, is a regular member of one of its societies, signs a member's agreement in which he or she agrees to comply with stipulated professional standards of practice, passes the CFA Candidate Examination I, has three years of experience in financial analysis, and has a bachelor's degree or equivalent education.[2]

A member in good standing in the ICFA holds the Chartered Financial Analyst (CFA) professional designation. To earn this designation, the applicant must in general meet the membership requirements of the FAF but, in addition, pass the CFA Candidate Examinations II and III. The ICFA administers a candidate study program and an examination program which stipulates standards of competency.

These standards and levels of competency are specified in a body of knowledge in *The CFA Candidate Program* annual announcement brochure and in *The CFA Study Guides* as revised and published each year by the ICFA for the three examination levels. The body of knowledge is identified in a general topic outline of six major subjects as shown in Appendix B of Chapter 1 of this handbook. The study guides contain assigned readings of book chapters, journal articles, and reprints of the three previous annual examinations together with guideline answers. This study material is considered by candidates to be quite helpful in preparing for the examinations. Candidates typically spend over 100 hours in self-study and sometimes in study groups. Each examination is taken over six hours, is considered reasonably rigorous, and consists mainly of descriptive and analytical-type problem questions. Among the

CFA members, 97 percent have college degrees, and 69 percent have advanced degrees. Over the 1963–85 history, 46,493 exams have been taken with 71 percent of the candidates passing them. The program has steadily grown over the years, and a record 4,285 exams were taken in 1985 out of which 67 percent passed. Over its 23-year history, 8,891 candidates successfully completed the exam program. Many observers, including members of regulatory agencies and Congressional committees, believe that the CFA candidate examinations are of comparable rigor and relevance to the financial analysts field as are the examinations in other respected professions such as public accounting and law.

Perhaps the greatest limitation to these admission standards is that financial analysts do not need to meet the standards in order to practice. Although the CFA designation is well known *within* the investment industry, most individual investors are not particularly familiar with it as compared to the certified public accountant (CPA) designation. Professional admission standards would be especially valuable in protecting the interests of individual investors because they are frequently less able to evaluate the competency and integrity of financial analysts. At the current time investment advisors and securities research analysts may practice with either no professional qualifications or minimal ones under federal and state government requirements. A partial solution would be to require analysts to be licensed in order to practice.

Maintenance of Competency

In a field such as financial analysis, in which the relevant body of knowledge has gradually changed over the years, professional practices have likewise undergone change. Many analysts who passed the CFA exams 5 to 10 years ago have remarked that they could not pass them today because the content has dramatically changed in such areas as statistical analysis, financial accounting procedures, legal standards, and new financial instruments. Many of these same analysts express the need and desire to engage in professional continuing education in order to keep abreast of current practices.

Many opportunities are available for analysts to learn new practices by attending local society luncheon programs and national conferences and seminars and by studying journals, monographs, and books, including this handbook. Such activities are actively supported within the profession. In a random survey of over 1,000 FAF members, over 80 percent reported that their employer organizations paid or reimbursed expenses to: attend society luncheons; attend selected professional conferences, seminars, and courses; enroll in the CFA candidate program; and take time off from work to attend such meetings.[3]

Beginning in 1985 the ICFA launched a formal continuing education program for its members called The CFA Accreditation Program. Accreditation units (AU) are earned by members by studying books published by the ICFA and by attending designated seminars, conferences, workshops, courses, and educational meetings. Members who earn 50 units within a year are entitled to a "Certificate of Professional Excellence" for that year.

Such a program is an important first step in encouraging analysts to continue to develop their professional knowledge. At this stage, the program is quite flexible and voluntary. To be assured that all analysts have mastered the essential knowledge to practice competently would be to specify a course of study with mandatory exams. It might be pointed out, however, that very few occupations have mandatory continuing education requirements.

Observable Practices

In protecting the interests of investors, an alternative or parallel approach to educational standards is the stipulation of standards of practice that are observable. By observable standards we mean professional practices that can be identified by the analyst and by his or her associates, supervisor, or client in which such practices can be ascertained as meeting acceptable standards or not.

Since 1962 the FAF and ICFA, jointly, have been quite diligent in developing, expanding, and refining written standards of professional practice which are called Code of Ethics and Standards of Professional Conduct. The most recent addition to these standards was made in June 1985. The code and standards are shown in the first chapter of this handbook. The FAF-ICFA boards and committees have engaged in extended debates in formulating and reformulating the precise wording of many of these standards. By complying with these standards, analysts will be representing the interests of those whom they serve. Although no attempt will be made to review most of them, we will discuss a few key ones here.

Standards of Professional Conduct III.A.1. and 2. require the analyst to "exercise diligence and thoroughness in making an investment recommendation to others or in taking an investment action for others" and to "have a reasonable and adequate basis for recommendations and actions, supported by appropriate research and investigation." These standards appear, on conceptual grounds, to be relevant and appropriate. As workable standards, questions could be raised as to the exact meaning of such expressions as "thoroughness, adequate basis, appropriate research," and so forth. In order to clarify some of these questions, the FAF-ICFA published a book, *Standards of Practice Handbook*,[4] which interprets the standards in greater detail and provides examples with reading references. The interpretations in that handbook give the impression that the standards are to be practiced at a high level of quality.

Nevertheless, it appears that written standards frequently have room for improvement. For example, Standard III.B.3. requires the analyst to "indicate the basic characteristics of the investment involved when preparing for general distribution a research report that is not directly related to a specific portfolio or client." The term *basic characteristics* is obviously quite vague. Because analysts have written many security research reports for decades, it would seem that the essential elements in such reports, such as expected risks and rewards, could be more clearly specified in the standards of practice. Louis J. Zitnik, in his classic article "Research Report Ethics,"[5] has several excellent suggestions as to what topics should be in the reports. The *Standards of Practice Handbook* identifies four relevant characteristics but states merely that these items *might* be included in the research report.[6]

The standards have several sections designed to protect against many types of potential conflicts of interest to which analysts may be exposed (see III.D. and E.; IV.; VI.; VIII.B. and C.).

The analyst is required to provide his employer/supervisor with a copy of the code and standards that the analyst is to comply with (see Standard I.). As a supervisor, the analyst is responsible for compliance of the standards by subordinates (II.D.). These standards appear quite appropriate; however, additional dissemination of the standards could be required in order to enhance compliance. This will be discussed in the next section.

Enforcement of Standards

Many professional organizations have established standards of practice, but many, unfortunately, do not actively monitor or enforce such standards among their membership. Obviously, the interests of those served by financial analysts are more effectively protected if professional standards are actually practiced and enforced.

The FAF-ICFA self-regulatory system provides for imposing disciplinary sanctions on member analysts who violate its standards. The methods by which this is done are described in what is called *Rules of Procedure*. These rules describe how a complaint against a member's conduct is investigated, and if it found that a standard was violated, how a disciplinary sanction is imposed on the member. Depending on the severity of the member's violation, sanctions consist of private admonishment, private censure, public censure, suspension of membership and the CFA charter, and revocation of membership and the charter. The *Rules of Procedure* were carefully developed and designed to protect the interests of those served by analysts as well as to protect the civil rights of analysts through the exercise of "due process." In 1974 the

ICFA became the first national professional organization of financial analysts in history to impose sanctions on its members. Subsequently, the FAF and ICFA have imposed a variety of sanctions on dozens of members, including revocation of the charter. This record is evidence that the FAF-ICFA is committed to upholding standards of professional practice.

Nevertheless, debates continue within as well as outside the FAF-ICFA as to how effective is the FAF-ICFA and its standards of practice in protecting the professional interests of individual and institutional investors. One side of the debate argues that it is in the best interests of the profession, investors, and the financial system for the financial analysts profession to regulate its own practices and that the profession is willing and able to do so if given the opportunity. The other side of the debate argues that it is unrealistic and impractical to expect the financial analysts profession and its standards of practice to protect effectively the interests of investors and the financial system. Several reasons are used to support these two opposing positions.

Defenders of self-regulation argue that the members in the profession are best qualified to establish and enforce standards because of their extensive training and experience. The standards can be established and interpreted in terms that can be clearly understood by analysts and can be uniformly applied to all analysts who are engaged in providing similar investment services. In the absence of professional standards, the conduct of analysts will be increasingly governed by laws, regulations, and court decisions developed by a legal system which deals with financial services in separate fragments (banks, trusts, brokers, mutual funds, investment advisors, insurance companies, and so forth) and in the terms of legal standards rather than in the terms of the financial body of knowledge.[7]

Those who point out the limitations to professional self-regulation argue that the motives of profit and survival have a higher priority among members of an occupation than do the interests of clients and the financial system. Many analysts are under pressures within their organizations to facilitate the marketing of securities or the building of advisory accounts. The financial success of such organizations is frequently judged by transaction revenues or short-term portfolio performance. In addition, the establishment and enforcement of high standards by a profession are very costly in terms of time and money. The enforcement of standards is also an unpleasant task.

Another limitation appears to be that some desirable standards cannot easily be formulated and practiced. For example, what makes the difference between those analysts whose decisions generate a favorable investment performance and those that result in underperformance? The difference frequently does not appear to be explained by the formal mastering of a body of knowledge or by adherence to existing standards of practice. Can the difference sometimes be due to luck, judgment, intuition, or some other type of reasoning? Other controversial practices deal with the efficient market hypothesis. While some analysts use technical market analysis, others consider it akin to the practice of astrology.[8] Why do so many active portfolio managers, including mutual funds, underperform the market?[9] Should standards of practice be developed and applied in such instances in order to protect the interests of clients?

Another alleged limitation is that the enforcement of standards by the financial analysts profession can be less effective than enforcement actions taken by the government sector. The government can impose fines and prison terms, expel analysts from the practice, indemnify losses suffered by a plaintiff, engage in costly litigation, and generate adverse publicity. However, when the FAF-ICFA imposes public censure or expulsion on a member, that member's employment status within the profession is definitely eroded; although the author is not familiar with the subsequent career status of all such analysts, the ones he is familiar with are no longer in practice.

As a final limitation, it is argued that in the absence of a licensing requirement, the profession is powerless over the practices of nonmembers, who often are the worst offenders of standards. These limitations would suggest that enforcement of standards of practice is a responsibility shared by a mixed system—the profession, the government, and the financial market system.

Nevertheless, the profession could foster wider acceptance of its standards of practice by a broad dissemination of its standards to individual and instititonal investors. For example, the FAF-ICFA Standards I. and II.D. require analysts to inform their employers and subordinates that the standards are to be complied with. However, analysts are not required to inform their clients about these standards, about the CFA designation, and about the *Rules of Procedure*. If this were done, informed investors would be better able to discriminate between those analysts and institutions who support the standards and those who may not. By being informed about the *Rules of Procedure*, aggrieved clients would know how to file a complaint with the FAF-ICFA if they believe that a standard was violated.

One of the effective ways the FAF-ICFA monitors the conduct of members is to require members to complete an annual questionnaire that reports whether their professional conduct has been subject to any complaints lodged by a regulatory, judicial, professional, or business organization. However, members are *not* required to report any complaints lodged directly against them by individual clients, supervisors, or competitors. If these lines of communication were to be opened, the standards of practice in the profession would be more widely recognized and the interests of investors would be better served.

The problems and challenging opportunities faced by the FAF-ICFA self-regulatory system are similar to those faced by other learned and respected professions. Based on the experience in other professions, it appears that the establishment of standards of practice by the financial analysts profession is an evolving and continuing task which will always have unfinished business. Nevertheless, the professional self-regulatory system has made enormous strides over the past quarter-century in establishing standards of practice, a formal body of knowledge, rigorous examinations, and an active program of standards enforcement.

THE CAPITAL MARKET SYSTEM

It is easy to underestimate the potent forces of individual citizens, operating through the private capitalistic system, in setting standards of practice. Competition and the long-term self-interests of capital market participants are major driving forces for the voluntary support of high standards of practice. Indeed, the capital markets function most effectively when the participants to transactions are fully informed and can act with confidence and mutual trust. Individual and institutional investors want to receive high-quality services from financial analysts; healthy competition provides a strong incentive for financial analysts to accommodate those demands. Unrestrained competition, however, can lead analysts to misrepresent their services.

In a random survey of over 1,000 financial analysts, 97 percent reported that they are subject to standards of practice adopted by their employer organization. In addition, 71 percent reported that the management of their organization had considered standards to be of sufficient importance that they assumed responsibility for setting their own standards of professional practices.[10] The managements of many investment organizations consider their success to be the result of developing a reputation of integrity and of highly competent financial services. In addition, standards of practice are clearly influenced by the Judeo-Christian code of ethics for honest, open, and fair dealings.

THE GOVERNMENT ROLE

Many participants in the capital markets, including financial analysts, contend that the government has a legitimate responsibility to ensure the orderly and competitive functioning of the securities markets in order that they may properly support our economic system. It can be argued that the services of financial analysts are of such paramount importance to the operations of the economy that government has an oversight responsibility regarding their standards of practice in order to protect the public interest. Indeed, the public, including financial analysts, would not tolerate a return to the laissez-faire, unbridled competitive market system of the 1920s which led to the economic collapse in the 1930s.

Therefore, government needs to establish and enforce basic standards of practice in order to protect the interests of individual and institutional investors from financial injury due to fraud, deception, and malpractice. The sources of government standards are federal and state laws and decisions made by federal and state courts. In addition to passing laws, Congress and state legislatures established government agencies and empowered quasi-public agencies, such as the stock exchanges and the National Association of Security Dealers, to issue more detailed standards and to enforce regulations. As conditions change and new problems occur, these agencies are able to change their regulations or issue new ones under the authority of law.

The review of legal and regulatory standards of practice for financial analysts is considered beyond the scope of this chapter because these laws, regulations, and court decisions reflect a vast, diverse, and complex subject and because some of these issues are covered in another chapter in this handbook. However, it may be noted that many of the FAF-ICFA standards of professional conduct have their basis in laws and regulations. In addition, Standards II.A. and B. require analysts to comply with all applicable laws and regulations. Indeed, many analysts sanctioned by the FAF-ICFA were in violation of these particular standards in conjunction with other ones.

In conclusion, financial analysts are subject to many standards of professional practices whose origin reflects a mixed system in which the standards are formulated and enforced by a professional self-regulatory system, by a competitive capital market, by employer institutions, and by government.

ENDNOTES

1. This material is based in part on a policy statement I drafted, with the editorial assistance of several other analysts, for The Institute of Chartered Financial Analysts. The policy statement, entitled *Professional Standards for Financial Analysts*, was adopted by its board of trustees on May 6, 1973.

2. *1986 Membership Directory* (New York: The Financial Analysts Federation, 1985), pp. 415 and 420.

3. W. Scott Bauman, *Professional Standards in Investment Management*, Monograph Number 9 (Charlottesville, Va.: The Financial Analysts Research Foundation, 1980), pp. 79–83.

4. The FAF and The ICFA, *Standards of Practice Handbook* 3rd ed. (Charlottesville, Va.: The Institute of Chartered Financial Analysts, 1986).

5. Louis J. Zitnik, "Research Report Ethics," *Financial Analysts Journal*, January–February, 1966.

6. *Standards of Practice Handbook*, pp. 58–59.

7. See W. Scott Bauman, *Guidelines for Communications to Investors*, Monograph Number 14 (Charlottesville: The Financial Analysts Research Foundation, 1982), pp. 39–40.

8. William C. Norby, "Some Contrary Views on the Professional Status of Financial Analysis," *Financial Analysts Journal*, March–April, 1968, p. 12.

9. Marshall D. Ketchum, "Is Financial Analysis a Profession?" *Financial Analysts Journal*, November–December, 1967, p. 35.

10. Bauman, *Professional Standards in Investment Management*, pp. 41–48.

56

The SEC: Organization and Functions

INTRODUCTION

The U.S. Securities and Exchange Commission's mission is to administer federal securities laws that seek to provide protection for investors.
The purpose of these laws is to ensure that the securities markets are fair
and honest and to provide the means to enforce the securities laws
through sanctions where necessary. Laws administered by the commission are the:

- Securities Act of 1933.
- Securities Exchange Act of 1934.
- Public Utility Holding Company Act of 1935.
- Trust Indenture Act of 1939.
- Investment Company Act of 1940.
- Investment Advisers Act of 1940.

The commission also serves as adviser to federal courts in corporate
reorganization proceedings under Chapter 11 of the Bankruptcy Reform
Act of 1978 and, in cases begun prior to October 1, 1979, Chapter X of
the National Bankruptcy Act. The commission reports annually to
Congress on administration of the securities laws.

Under the Securities Exchange Act of 1934, Congress created the
Securities and Exchange Commission (SEC). The SEC is an independent, nonpartisan, quasi-judicial regulatory agency.

The commission is composed of five members: a chairman and four
commissioners. Commission members are appointed by the president,
with the advice and consent of the Senate, for five-year terms. The
chairman is designated by the president. Terms are staggered; one

Source: U.S. Securities and Exchange Commission, *The Work of the SEC*,
1986.

expires on June 5th of every year. Not more than three members may be of the same political party.

Under the direction of the chairman and commissioners, the staff ensures that publicly held entities, broker-dealers in securities, investment companies and advisers, and other participants in the securities markets comply with federal securities laws. These laws were designed to facilitate informed investment analyses and decisions by the investing public, primarily by ensuring adequate disclosure of material (significant) information. Conformance with federal securities laws and regulations does not imply merit. If information essential to informed investment analysis is properly disclosed, the commission cannot bar the sale of securities which analysis may show to be of questionable value. It is the investor, not the commission, who must make the ultimate judgment of the worth of securities offered for sale.

The commission's staff is composed of lawyers, accountants, financial analysts and examiners, engineers, and other professionals. The staff is divided into divisions and offices (including 14 regional and branch offices), each directed by officials appointed by the chairman.

This chapter describes the work of the SEC by discussing the laws it administers, the organization of the commission, the ways in which it carries out its statutory mandates, and the sanctions it can bring to bear to enforce federal securities laws.

SECURITIES ACT OF 1933

This "truth in securities" law has two basic objectives:

- To require that investors be provided with material information concerning securities offered for public sale.
- To prevent misrepresentation, deceit, and other fraud in the sale of securities.

A primary means of accomplishing these objectives is disclosure of financial information by registering securities. Securities subject to registration are most corporate debt and equity securities. Government (state and federal) and mortgage-related debt are not. Certain securities qualify for exemptions from registration provisions; these exemptions are discussed below.

PURPOSE OF REGISTRATION

Registration is intended to provide adequate and accurate disclosure of material facts concerning the company and the securities it proposes to sell. Thus, investors may make a realistic appraisal of the merits of the securities and then exercise informed judgment in determining whether to purchase them.

Registration requires, but does not guarantee, the accuracy of the facts represented in the registration statement and prospectus. However, the law does prohibit false and misleading statements under penalty of fine, imprisonment, or both. And investors who purchase securities and suffer losses have important recovery rights under the law if they can prove that there was incomplete or inaccurate disclosure of material facts in the registration statement or prospectus. If such misstatements are proven, the following could be liable for investor losses sustained in the securities purchase: the issuing company, its responsible directors and officers, the underwriters, controlling interests, the sellers of the securities, and others. These rights must be asserted in an appropriate federal or state court (not before the commission, which has no power to award damages).

Registration of securities does not preclude the sale of stock in risky, poorly managed, or unprofitable companies. Nor does the commission approve or disapprove securities on their merits; it is unlawful to represent otherwise in the sale of securities. The only standard which must be met when registering securities is adequate and accurate disclosure of required material facts concerning the company and the securities it proposes to sell. The fairness of the terms, the issuing company's prospects for successful operation, and other factors affecting the merits of investing in the securities (whether price, promoters' or underwriters' profits, or otherwise) have no bearing on the question of whether securities may be registered.

THE REGISTRATION PROCESS

To facilitate registration by different types of companies, the commission has special forms. These vary in their disclosure requirements but generally provide essential facts while minimizing the burden and expense of complying with the law. In general, registration forms call for disclosure of information such as:

- Description of the registrant's properties and business.
- Description of the significant provisions of the security to be offered for sale and its relationship to the registrant's other capital securities.
- Information about the management of the registrant.
- Financial statements certified by independent public accountants.

Registration statements and prospectuses on securities become public immediately upon filing with the commission. After the registration statement is filed, securities may be offered orally or by certain summaries of the information in the registration statement as permitted by commission rules. However, it is unlawful to sell the securities until the effective date. The act provides that most registration statements shall become effective on the 20th day after filing (or on the 20th day after filing the last amendment). At its discretion, the commission may advance the effective date if deemed appropriate considering the interests of investors and the public, the adequacy of publicly available information, and the ease with which the facts about the new offering can be disseminated and understood.

Registration statements are examined for compliance with disclosure requirements. If a statement appears to be materially incomplete or inaccurate, the registrant usually is informed by letter and given an opportunity to file correcting or clarifying amendments. The commission, however, has authority to refuse or suspend the effectiveness of any registration statement if it finds that material representations are misleading, inaccurate, or incomplete.

The commission may conclude that material deficiencies in some registration statements appear to stem from a deliberate attempt to conceal or mislead, or that the deficiencies do not lend themselves to correction through the informal letter process. In these cases, the commission may decide that it is in the public interest to conduct a hearing to develop the facts by evidence. This determines if a "stop order" should be issued to refuse or suspend effectiveness of the statement. The commission may issue stop orders after the sale of securities has been commenced or completed. A stop order is not a permanent bar to the effectiveness of the registration statement or to the sale of the securities. If amendments are filed correcting the statement in accordance with the stop order decision, the order must be lifted and the statement declared effective.

Although losses which may have been suffered in the purchase of securities are not restored to investors by the stop order, the commission's order precludes future public sales. Also, the decision and the evidence on which it is based may serve to notify investors of their rights and aid them in their own recovery suits.

EXEMPTIONS FROM REGISTRATION

In general, registration requirements apply to securities of both domestic and foreign issuers and to securities of foreign governments (or their instrumentalities) sold in domestic securities markets. There are, however, certain exemptions. Among these are:

- Private offerings to a limited number of persons or institutions who have access to the kind of information that registration would disclose and who do not propose to redistribute the securities.

- Offerings restricted to residents of the state in which the issuing company is organized and doing business.
- Securities of municipal, state, federal, and other governmental instrumentalities as well as charitable institutions, banks, and carriers subject to the Interstate Commerce Act.
- Offerings not exceeding certain specified amounts made in compliance with regulations of the commission.
- Offerings of "small business investment companies" made in accordance with rules and regulations of the commission.

Whether or not the securities are exempt from registration, antifraud provisions apply to all sales of securities involving interstate commerce or the mails.

Among the special exemptions from the registration requirement, the "small issue exemption" was adopted by Congress primarily as an aid to small business. The law provides that offerings of securities under $5 million may be exempted from registration, subject to conditions the commission prescribes to protect investors. The commission's Regulation A permits certain domestic and Canadian companies to make exempt offerings. A similar regulation is available for offerings under $500,000 by small business investment companies licensed by the Small Business Administration. The commission's Regulation D permits certain companies to make exempt offerings under $500,000 with only minimal federal restrictions; more extensive disclosure requirements and other conditions apply for offerings exceeding that amount but less than $5 million.

Exemptions are available when certain specified conditions are met. These conditions include the prior filing of a notification with the appropriate SEC regional office and the use of an offering circular containing certain basic information in the sale of the securities. For a more complete discussion of these and other special provisions adopted by the commission to facilitate capital formation by small business, please request a copy of "Q & A: Small Business and the SEC," available from the Public Reference Branch of the commission.

SECURITIES EXCHANGE ACT OF 1934

By this act, Congress extended the "disclosure" doctrine of investor protection to securities listed and registered for public trading on our national securities exchanges. Thirty years later, the Securities Act Amendments of 1964 extended disclosure and reporting provisions to equity securities in the over-the-counter market. This included hundreds of companies with assets exceeding $1 million and shareholders numbering 500 or more. (Today, securities of thousands of companies are traded over the counter.) The act seeks to ensure fair and orderly securities markets by prohibiting certain types of activities and by setting forth rules regarding the operation of the markets and participants.

CORPORATE REPORTING

Companies seeking to have their securities registered and listed for public trading on an exchange must file a registration application with the exchange and the SEC. If they meet the size test described above, companies whose equity securities are traded over the counter must file a similar registration form. Commission rules prescribe the nature and content of these registration statements and require certified financial statements. These are generally comparable to, but less extensive than, the disclosures required in Securities Act registration statements. Following the registration of their securities, companies must file annual and other periodic reports to update information contained in the original filing. In addition, issuers must send certain reports to requesting shareholders. Reports may be read at the commission's public reference rooms, copied there at nominal cost, or obtained from a copying service under contract to the commission.

PROXY SOLICITATIONS

Another provision of this law governs soliciting proxies (votes) from holders of registered securities, both listed and over-the-counter, for the election of directors and/or for approval of other corporate action. Solicitations, whether by management or minority groups, must disclose all material facts concerning matters on which holders are asked to vote. Holders also must be given an opportunity to vote "yes" or "no" on each matter. Where a contest for control of corporate management is involved, the rules require disclosure of the names and interests of all "participants" in the proxy contest. Thus, holders are enabled to vote intelligently on corporate actions requiring their approval. The commission's rules require that proposed proxy material be filed in advance for examination by the commission for compliance with the disclosure requirements. In addition, the rules permit shareholders to submit proposals for a vote at the annual meetings.

TENDER OFFER SOLICITATIONS

In 1968 Congress amended the Exchange Act to extend its reporting and disclosure provisions to situations where control of a company is sought through a tender offer or other planned stock acquisition of over 10 percent of a company's equity securities. Commonly called the Williams Act, this amendment was further amended in 1970 to reduce the stock acquisition threshold to 5 percent. These amendments, and commission rules under the act, require disclosure of pertinent information by anyone seeking to acquire over 5 percent of a company's securities by direct purchase or by tender offer. This disclosure is also required by anyone soliciting shareholders to accept or reject a tender offer. Thus, as with the proxy rules, public investors holding stock in these corporations may now make more informed decisions on takeover bids.

Disclosure provisions are supplemented by certain other provisions to help ensure investor protection in tender offers.

INSIDER TRADING

Insider trading prohibitions are designed to curb misuse of material confidential information not available to the general public. Examples of such misuse are buying or selling securities to make profits or avoid losses based on material nonpublic information—or by telling others of the information so that they may buy or sell securities—before such information is generally available to all shareholders. The commission has brought numerous civil actions in federal court against persons whose use of material nonpublic information constituted fraud under the securities laws. Additionally, the commission supported legislation to increase the penalties that can be imposed by the courts on those found guilty of insider trading. The Insider Trading Sanctions Act, signed into law on August 10, 1984, allows imposing fines up to three times the profit gained or loss avoided by use of material nonpublic information.

Another provision requires that all officers and directors of a company (and beneficial owners of more than 10 percent of its registered equity securities) must file an initial report with the commission and with the exchange on which the stock may be listed showing their holdings of each of the company's equity securities. Thereafter, they must file reports for any month during which there was any change in those holdings. In addition, the law provides that profits obtained by them from purchases and sales (or sales and purchases) of such equity securities within any six-month period may be recovered by the company or by any security holder on its behalf. This recovery right must be asserted in the appropriate U.S. district court. Such "insiders" are also prohibited from making short sales of their company's equity securities.

MARGIN TRADING

Margin trading in securities also falls under certain provisions of the act. The board of governors of the Federal Reserve System is authorized to set limitations on the amount of credit which may be extended for the purpose of purchasing or carrying securities. (The Federal Reserve periodically reviews these limitations.) The objective is to restrict excessive use of the nation's credit in the securities markets. While the credit restrictions are set by the board, investigation and enforcement is the responsibility of the SEC.

TRADING AND SALES PRACTICES

Securities trading and sales practices on the exchanges and in the over-the-counter markets are subject to provisions designed to protect the interests of investors and the public. These provisions seek to curb misrepresentations and deceit, market manipulation, and other fraudulent acts and practices. They also strive to establish and maintain just and equitable principles of trade conducive to maintaining open, fair, and orderly markets.

These provisions of the law establish the general regulatory pattern. The commission is responsible for promulgating rules and regulations for its implementation. Thus, the commission has adopted regulations which, among other things:

- Define acts or practices which constitute a "manipulative or deceptive device or contrivance" prohibited by the statute.
- Regulate short selling, stabilizing transactions, and similar matters.
- Regulate hypothecation (use of customers' securities as collateral for loans).
- Provide safeguards with respect to the financial responsibility of brokers and dealers.

REGISTRATION OF EXCHANGES AND OTHERS

As amended, the 1934 act requires registration with the commission of:

- "National securities exchanges" (those having a substantial securities trading volume).
- Brokers and dealers who conduct securities business in interstate commerce.
- Transfer agents.
- Clearing agencies.
- Municipal brokers and dealers.
- Securities information processors.

To obtain registration, exchanges must show that they are organized to comply with the provisions of the statute as well as the rules and regulations of the commission. The registering exchanges must also show that their rules contain just and adequate provisions to ensure fair dealing and to protect investors.

Each exchange is a self-regulatory organization. Its rules must provide for the expulsion, suspension, or other disciplining of member broker-dealers for conduct inconsistent with just and equitable principles of trade. The law intends that exchanges shall have full opportunity to establish self-regulatory measures ensuring fair dealing and investor protection. However, it empowers the SEC (by order, rule, or regulation) to approve proposed rule changes of exchanges concerning various activities and trading practices if necessary to effect the statutory objective. Exchange rules and revisions, proposed by exchanges or by the commission, generally reach their final form after discussions between representatives of both bodies without resort to formal proceedings.

By a 1938 amendment to the 1934 act, Congress also provided for creation of a national securities association. The only such association, the National Association of Securities Dealers, Inc., is registered with the commission under this provision of the law. This association is responsible for preventing fraudulent and manipulative acts and practices and for promoting just and equitable trade principles among over-the-counter brokers and dealers. The establishment, maintenance, and enforcement of a voluntary code of business ethics is one of the principal features of this provision of the law.

BROKER-DEALER REGISTRATION

The registration of brokers and dealers engaged in soliciting and executing securities transactions is an important part of the regulatory plan of the act. Broker-dealers must apply for registration with the commission and amend registrations to show significant changes in financial conditions or other important facts. Applications and amendments are examined by the commission. Brokers and dealers must conform their business practices to the standards prescribed by the law and the commission's regulations for protecting investors and to rules on fair trade practices of their association. Additionally, brokers and dealers violating these regulations risk suspension or loss of registration with the commission (and thus the right to continue conducting an interstate securities business) or of suspension or expulsion from a self-regulatory organization.

PUBLIC UTILITY HOLDING COMPANY ACT OF 1935

Interstate holding companies engaged, through subsidiaries, in the electric utility business or in the retail distribution of natural or manufactured gas are subject to regulation under this act. Today, 13 systems are registered; 12 are active. These systems must register with the commission and file initial and periodic reports. Detailed information concerning the organization, financial structure, and operations of the holding company and its subsidiaries is contained in these reports. (However, if a holding company or its subsidiary meets certain specifications, the commission may exempt it from part or all of the duties and obligations otherwise imposed by statute.) Holding companies are subject to SEC regulations on matters such as structure of the system, acquisitions, combinations, and issue and sales of securities.

INTEGRATION AND SIMPLIFICATION

The most important provisions of the act were the requirements for physical integration and corporate simplification of holding company systems. Integration standards restrict a holding company's operations to an "integrated utility system." Such a system is defined as one:

- Capable of economical operation as a single coordinated system.
- Confined to a single area or region in one or more states.
- Not so large that it negates the advantages of localized management, efficient operation, and effective regulation.

The capital structure and continued existence of any company in a holding company system must not unnecessarily complicate the corporate structure of the system or distribute voting power inequitably among security holders of the system.

The commission may determine what action, if any, must be taken by registered holding companies and their subsidiaries to comply with act requirements. The SEC may apply to federal courts for orders compelling compliance with commission directives.

Voluntary reorganization plans for many divestments of nonretainable subsidiaries and properties, recapitalizations, dissolutions of companies, and other adjustments may be used to satisfy act requirements. The SEC may approve voluntary plans it finds to be fair and equitable to all affected persons and to be necessary to further the objectives of the act. If the company requests, the commission will apply to a federal district court for an order approving the plan and directing its enforcement. All interested persons, including state commissions and other governmental agencies, have full opportunity to be heard in proceedings before the commission and before the federal courts.

ACQUISITIONS

To be authorized by the SEC, the acquisition of securities and utility assets by holding companies and their subsidiaries must meet the following standards:

- The acquisition must not tend toward interlocking relations or concentrating control to an extent detrimental to investors or the public.
- Any consideration paid for the acquisition (including fees, commissions, and other remuneration) must not be unreasonable.
- The acquisition must not complicate the capital structure of the holding company system or have a detrimental effect on system functions.
- The acquisition must tend toward economical, efficient development of an integrated public utility system.

ISSUANCE AND SALE OF SECURITIES

Proposed security issues by any holding company must be analyzed and evaluated by the staff and approved by the commission to ensure that the issues meet the following tests under prescribed standards of the law:

- The security must be reasonably adapted to the security structure of the issuer and of other companies in the same holding company system.
- The security must be reasonably adapted to the earning power of the company.
- The proposed issue must be necessary and appropriate to the economical and efficient operation of the company's business.
- The fees, commissions, and other remuneration paid in connection with the issue must not be unreasonable.
- The terms and conditions of the issue or sale of the security must not be detrimental to the public or investor interest.

OTHER REGULATORY PROVISIONS

Other phases of the act provide for regulating dividend payments (in circumstances where payments might result in corporate abuses); intercompany loans; solicitation of proxies, consents, and other authorizations; and insider trading. "Upstream" loans from subsidiaries to their parents and "upstream" or "cross-stream" loans from public utility companies to any holding company in the same holding company system require commission approval. The act also requires that all services performed for any company in a holding company system by a service company in that system be rendered at a fair and equitably allocated cost.

TRUST INDENTURE ACT OF 1939

This act applies to bonds, debentures, notes, and similar debt securities offered for public sale and issued under trust indentures with more than $1 million of securities outstanding at any one time. Even though such securities may be registered under the Securities Act, they may not be offered for sale to the public unless the trust indenture conforms to statutory standards of this act. Designed to safeguard the rights and interests of the purchasers, the act also:

- Prohibits the indenture trustee from conflicting interests which might interfere with exercising its duties on behalf of the securities purchasers.
- Requires the trustee to be a corporation with minimum combined capital and surplus.
- Imposes high standards of conduct and responsibility on the trustee.
- Precludes, in the event of default, preferential collection of certain claims owing to the trustee by the issuer.
- Provides that the issuer supply to the trustee evidence of compliance with indenture terms and conditions (such as those relating to the release or substitution of mortgaged property, issue of new securities, or satisfaction of the indenture).
- Requires the trustee to provide reports and notices to security holders.

Other provisions of the act prohibit impairing the security holder's right to sue individually for principal and interest, except under certain circumstances. It also requires maintaining a list of security holders for their use in communicating with each other regarding their rights as security holders.

Applications for qualification of trust indentures are examined by the SEC's Division of Corporation Finance for compliance with the law and the commission's rules.

INVESTMENT COMPANY ACT OF 1940

The Public Utility Holding Company Act of 1935 required Congress to direct the SEC to study the activities of investment companies and investment advisers. The study results were sent to Congress in a series of reports filed in 1938, 1939, and 1940, causing the creation of the Investment Advisers Act of 1940 and the Investment Company Act of 1940. The legislation was supported by both the commission and the industry.

Activities of companies engaged primarily in investing, reinvesting, and trading in securities, and whose own securities are offered to the investing public, are subject to certain statutory prohibitions and to commission regulation under this act. Also, public offerings of investment company securities must be registered under the Securities Act of 1933.

Investors must understand, however, that the commission does not supervise the investment activities of these companies and that regulation by the commission does not imply safety of investment.

In addition to the registration requirement for such companies, the law requires they disclose their financial condition and investment policies to provide investors complete information about their activities. This act also:

- Prohibits such companies from substantially changing the nature of their business or investment policies without stockholder approval.
- Bars persons guilty of security frauds from serving as officers and directors.
- Prevents underwriters, investment bankers, or brokers from constituting more than a minority of the directors of such companies.
- Requires that management contracts (and any material changes) be submitted to security holders for their approval.
- Prohibits transactions between such companies and their directors, officers, or affiliated companies or persons, except when approved by the SEC.
- Forbids such companies to issue senior securities except under specified conditions and upon specified terms.
- Prohibits pyramiding of such companies and cross-ownership of their securities.

Other provisions of this act involve advisory fees not conforming to an adviser's fiduciary duty, sales and repurchases of securities issued by investment companies, exchange offers, and other activities of investment companies, including special provisions for periodic payment plans and face-amount certificate companies.

Regarding reorganization plans of investment companies, the commission is authorized to institute court proceedings to prohibit plans that do not appear to be fair and equitable to security holders. The commission may also institute court action to remove management officials who have engaged in personal misconduct constituting a breach of fiduciary duty.

Investment company securities must also be registered under the Securities Act. Investment companies must file periodic reports and are subject to the commission's proxy and "insider" trading rules.

INVESTMENT ADVISERS ACT OF 1940

This law establishes a pattern of regulating investment advisers. In some respects, it has provisions similar to Securities Exchange Act provisions governing the conduct of brokers and dealers. With certain exceptions, this act requires that persons or firms compensated for advising others about securities investment must register with the commission and conform to statutory standards designed to protect investors.

The commission may deny, suspend, or revoke investment adviser registrations if, after notice and hearing, it finds that a statutory disqualification exists and that the action is in the public interest. Disqualifications include conviction for certain financial crimes or securities violations, injunctions based on such activities, conviction for violating the Mail Fraud Statute, willfully filing false reports with the commission, and willfully violating the Advisers Act, the Securities Act, the Securities Exchange Act, the Investment Company Act, or the rules of the Municipal Securities Rulemaking Board. In addition to the administrative sanction of denial, suspension, or revocation, the commission may obtain injunctions prohibiting further violations of this law. The SEC may also recommend prosecution by the Department of Justice for fraudulent misconduct or willful violation of the law or commission rules.

The law contains antifraud provisions and empowers the commission to adopt rules defining fraudulent, deceptive, or manipulative acts and practices. It also requires that investment advisers:

- Disclose the nature of their interest in transactions executed for their clients.
- Maintain books and records according to commission rules.
- Make books and records available to the commission for inspections.

CORPORATE REORGANIZATION

Reorganization proceedings in the U.S. courts under Chapter 11 of the Bankruptcy Code are begun by a debtor, voluntarily, or by its creditors. Federal bankruptcy law allows a debtor in reorganization to continue operating under the court's protection while it attempts to rehabilitate its business and work out a plan to pay its debts. If a debtor corporation has publicly issued securities outstanding, the reorganization process may raise many issues that materially affect the rights of public investors.

Chapter 11 of the Bankruptcy Code authorizes the SEC to appear in any reorganization case and to present its views on any issue. Although

Chapter 11 applies to all types of business reorganizations, the commission generally limits its participation to proceedings involving significant public investor interest—protecting public investors holding the debtor's securities and participating in legal and policy issues of concern to public investors. The SEC also continues to address matters of traditional commission expertise and interest relating to securities. Where appropriate, it comments on the adequacy of reorganization plan disclosure statements and participates where there is a commission law enforcement interest.

Under Chapter 11, the debtor, official committees, and institutional creditors negotiate the terms of a reorganization plan. The court can confirm a reorganization plan if it is accepted by creditors for:

- At least two thirds of the amounts of allowed claims.
- More than one half the number of allowed claims.
- At least two thirds in amount of the allowed shareholder interest.

The principal safeguard for public investors is the requirement that a disclosure statement containing adequate information be transmitted by the debtor or plan proponent in connection with soliciting votes on the plan. In addition, reorganization plans involving publicly held debtors usually provide for issuing new securities to creditors and shareholders which may be exempt from registration under Section 5 of the Securities Act of 1933.

ORGANIZATION OF THE COMMISSION

The commission carries out its work, in both Washington headquarters and the regional offices around the country, through divisions and offices charged with specific responsibilities under the securities laws. Additionally, there are offices responsible for the smooth and effective administration of the commission itself. Overall responsibility for carrying out the SEC mission rests with the commissioners.

THE COMMISSIONERS

The Securities Exchange Act of 1934 formally created the Securities and Exchange Commission on June 1, 1934. (The Securities Act of 1933 was administered by the Federal Trade Commission until creation of the SEC.) Among other provisions, this act set forth the composition of the commission, which remains unchanged today. Five commissioners are appointed by the president, with the advice and consent of the Senate, for five-year terms. Terms are staggered; one expires in June of every year. The chairman is generally of the same political party as the president, but no more than three of the five commissioners may belong to the same political party. The result is that the commission is an independent, nonpartisan agency.

A deliberative collegial body, the commission meets numerous times monthly to debate and decide upon regulatory issues. Like other regulatory agencies, the commission has two types of meetings. Under the Government in the Sunshine Act, meetings may be open to the public and to members of the press. However, if necessary to protect the commission's ability to conduct investigations and/or protect the rights of individuals and entities which may be the subject of commission inquiries, meetings may be closed.

Commission meetings are generally held to deliberate on and resolve issues the staff brings before the commissioners. Issues may be interpretations of federal securities laws, amendments to existing rules under the laws, new rules (often to reflect changed conditions in the marketplace), actions to enforce the laws or to discipline those subject to direct regulation, legislation to be proposed by the commission, and matters concerning administration of the commission itself. Matters not requiring joint deliberation may be resolved by procedures set forth in the Code of Federal Regulation.

Resolution of the issues brought before the commission may take the form of new rules or amendments to existing ones, enforcement actions, or disciplinary actions. The most common activity is rulemaking. Rulemaking is generally the result of staff recommendations made to the commissioners.

THE COMMISSION STAFF

The staff is organized into divisions (with subordinate offices) and major offices with specific areas of responsibility for various segments of the federal securities laws.

For the past several years, the divisions have been Enforcement, Corporation Finance, Market Regulation, and Investment Management. The Office of General Counsel serves as the chief legal officer for the commission. As such, it is responsible for appellate and other litigation as well as certain other legal matters.

At present, the offices are those of Chief Accountant, Opinions and Review, Chief Economist, Administrative Law Judges, Secretary, and the Directorate of Economic and Policy Analysis.

Other offices provide administration and carry out certain necessary functions for the commission. These include the Office of Executive Director, Comptroller, Consumer Affairs and Information Services, Personnel, Administrative Services, Applications and Reports Services, Information Systems Management, and Public Affairs.

THE DIVISIONS

The Division of Corporation Finance

Corporation Finance has the overall responsibility of ensuring that disclosure requirements are met by publicly held companies registered with the commission. Its work includes reviewing registration statements for new securities, proxy material and annual reports the commission requires from publicly held companies, documents concerning tender offers, and mergers and acquisitions in general.

This division renders administrative interpretations of the Securities Act of 1933 and its regulations to the public, prospective registrants, and others. It is also responsible for certain statutes and regulations pertaining to small businesses and for the Trust Indenture Act of 1939. Applications for qualification of trust indentures are examined for compliance with the applicable requirements of the law and the commission's rules. The Division of Corporation Finance works closely with the Office of the Chief Accountant in drafting rules and regulations which prescribe requirements for financial statements.

The Division of Market Regulation

Market Regulation is responsible for oversight of activity in the secondary markets—registration and regulation of broker-dealers, oversight of the self-regulatory organizations (such as the nation's stock exchanges), and oversight of other participants in the secondary markets (such as transfer agents and clearing organizations).

Financial responsibility of these entities, trading and sales practices, policies affecting operation of the securities markets, and surveillance fall under the purview of this division. In addition, it carries out activities aimed at achieving the goal of a national market system set forth in the Securities Act Amendments of 1975. Market Regulation develops and presents market structure issues to the commissioners for their consideration. The division also oversees the Securities Investor Protection Corporation and the Municipal Securities Rulemaking Board.

The Division of Investment Management

Investment Management has basic responsibility for the Investment Company Act of 1940 and the Investment Advisers Act of 1940. In 1985 it assumed responsibility for administering the Public Utility Holding Company Act of 1935.

The division staff ensures compliance with regulations regarding the registration, financial responsibility, sales practices, and advertising of mutual funds and of investment advisers. New products offered by these entities also are reviewed by staff in this division. They also process investment company registration statements, proxy statements, and periodic reports under the Securities Act.

The division's Office of Public Utility Regulation oversees the activities of the 12 active registered holding company systems, ensuring that their corporate structures and financings are permissible according to certain tests set up in the Holding Company Act. The staff analyzes legal, financial, accounting, engineering, and other issues arising under the act. The office participates in hearings to develop the factual records where necessary, files briefs and participates in oral arguments before the commission, and makes recommendations regarding the commission's findings and decisions in cases which arise in administration of the law. All hearings are conducted in accordance with the commission's Rules of Practice.

The Division of Enforcement

This division is charged with enforcing federal securities laws. Enforcement responsibilities include investigating possible violations of federal securities laws and recommending appropriate remedies for consideration by the commission. Possible violations may come to light through the Enforcement Division's own inquiries, through referrals from other divisions of the commission, from outside sources such as the self-regulatory organizations, or by other means.

When possible violations of federal securities laws warrant further investigation by the staff, the commission is consulted before proceeding. The commission's decisions may result in issuing subpoenas, formal orders of investigation, or other means of proceeding with actions. At the conclusion of investigations, the commission may authorize the staff to proceed with injunctions preventing further violative conduct, with administrative proceedings in the case of entities directly regulated by the commission, or with other remedies as appropriate.

ACTIVITIES OF DIVISIONS

Each of the divisions, often in cooperation with an office or offices, engages in a variety of activities.

Interpretation and Guidance

On the basis of responsibilities and powers assigned under federal securities laws, each division provides guidance and counseling to registrants, prospective registrants, the public, and others. This information is provided to help determine the application of the law and its regulations and to aid in complying with the law. For example, this advice might include an informal expression of opinion about whether the offering of a particular security is subject to the registration requirements of the law and, if so, advice on compliance with disclosure requirements of the applicable registration form. These interpretations of the rules and laws help ensure conformity on the part of the registrants. Also, most divisions occasionally issue "no action" letters which indicate they will take no action on matters regarding registrants in certain circumstances.

Rulemaking

One of the most common activities engaged in by the divisions is rulemaking.

The commission's objective of requiring regulated entities to provide effective disclosure, with a minimum of burden and expense, calls for constant review of practical operations of the rules and registration forms adopted. If experience shows that a particular requirement fails to achieve its objective, or if a rule appears unduly burdensome in relation to the resulting benefits, the staff presents the problem to the commission. The commission then considers modifying the rule or other requirement. Based on their particular area of expertise, the divisions and offices are often asked to contribute specific analyses.

Many suggestions for rule modification follow extensive consultation with industry representatives and others affected. The commission normally gives advance public notice of proposals to adopt new or amended rules or registration forms and affords the opportunity for interested members of the public to comment on them.

The commission decides, generally in open meetings, whether the new rules or amendments to existing rules are warranted. Proposals approved by the commission become mandatory, usually within a specific time period after publication in the Federal Register.

The commission's work is remedial, not punitive. Its primary activities are to ensure investor protection through full disclosure of material information and to ensure that the securities markets are fair and honest in compliance with federal securities laws and rules under those laws. Interpretations, counseling, rulemaking, and similar activities are all aimed at ensuring compliance with the law.

The commission, however, does have civil authority to enforce federal securities laws and does so when it has reason to believe that the laws have been, or in some cases are about to be, violated. The commission also works closely with criminal authorities in matters of mutual interest.

Investigations

Under the laws it administers, the commission has a duty to investigate complaints and other indications of possible law violations in securities transactions. Most arise under the Securities Act of 1933 and the Securities Exchange Act of 1934. (Fraud prohibitions of the Securities Act are similar to those contained in the Securities Exchange Act of 1934.) Investigation and any subsequent enforcement work is conducted primarily by the commission's regional offices and the Division of Enforcement.

Most of the commission's investigations are conducted privately. Facts are developed to the fullest extent possible through informal inquiry, interviewing witnesses, examining brokerage records and other documents, reviewing and trading data, and similar means. The commission is empowered to issue subpoenas requiring sworn testimony and the production of books, records, and other documents pertinent to the subject matter under investigation. In the event of refusal to respond to a subpoena, the commission may apply to a federal court for an order compelling obedience.

Inquiries and complaints by investors and the general public are primary sources of leads for detecting law violations in securities transactions. Another source is surprise inspections by regional offices and the Division of Market Regulation of the books and records of regulated persons and organizations to determine whether their business practices conform to the prescribed rules. Still another means is conducting inquiries into market fluctuations in particular stocks which don't appear to result from general market trends or from known developments affecting the issuing company.

Investigations frequently concern the sale without registration of securities subject to the registration requirement of the Securities Act. Misrepresentation or omission of material facts concerning securities offered for sale, whether or not registration is required, is another common subject of investigation. The antifraud provisions of the law also apply to the purchase of securities, whether involving outright misrepresentations or the withholding or omission of pertinent facts to which the seller was entitled. For example, it is unlawful in certain situations to purchase securities from another person while withholding material information which would indicate that the securities have a value substantially greater than that at which they are being acquired. These provisions apply not only to transactions between brokers and dealers and their customers but also to the reacquisition of securities by an issuing company or its "insiders."

Other types of inquiries relate to manipulating market prices of securities; misappropriating or illegally hypothecating customers' funds or securities; conducting a securities business while insolvent; broker-dealers buying or selling securities from or to customers at prices not reasonably related to current market prices; and broker-dealers violating their responsibilities to treat customers fairly.

A common type of violation involves the broker-dealer who gains the customer's trust and then takes undisclosed profits in securities transactions with or for the customer over and above the agreed commission. For example, the broker-dealer may have purchased securities from customers at prices far below, or sold securities to customers at prices far above, their current market prices. In most of these cases, the broker-dealer risks no loss; the purchases from customers are made only if simultaneous sales can be made at prices substantially higher than those paid to the customers. Conversely, sales to customers are made only if simultaneous purchases can be made at prices substantially lower than those charged the customer. Another type of violation involves firms engaging in large-scale in-and-out transactions for the customer's account (called *churning*) to generate increased commissions, usually without regard to any resulting benefit to the customer.

There is a fundamental distinction between a broker and a dealer. The broker serves as the customer's agent in buying or selling securities for the customer. The broker owes the customer the highest fiduciary responsibility and may charge only such agency commission as has been agreed to by the customer. On the other hand, a dealer acts as a principal and buys securities from or sells securities to customers. The dealer's profit is the difference between the prices for which the securities are bought and sold. The dealer normally will not disclose the fee or commission charged for services rendered. The law requires that the customer receive a written "confirmation" of each securities transaction. This confirmation discloses whether the securities firm is acting as a dealer (a principal for its own account) or as a broker (an agent for the customer). If the latter, the confirmation must also disclose the broker's compensation from all sources as well as other information about the transaction.

Statutory Sanctions

Commission investigations, usually conducted in private, are essentially fact-finding inquiries. The facts developed by the staff are considered by the commission to determine whether there is valid evidence of a law violation; whether action should begin to determine if a violation actually occurred; and, if so, whether some sanction should be imposed.

When facts show possible fraud or other law violation, the laws provide several courses of action which the commission may pursue:

- Civil injunction, where the commission may apply to an appropriate U.S. district court for an order prohibiting the acts or practices alleged to violate the law or commission rules.
- Administrative remedy, where the commission may take specific action after hearings. It may issue orders to suspend or expel members from exchanges or over-the-counter dealers association; deny, suspend, or revoke broker-dealer registrations; or censure for misconduct or bar individuals (temporarily or permanently) from employment with a registered firm.

Broker-Dealer Revocations

In the case of exchange or association members, registered brokers or dealers, or individuals who may associate with any such firm, the administrative remedy is generally invoked. In these administrative proceedings, the commission issues an order specifying illegal acts or practices allegedly committed and directs that a hearing be held for the purpose of taking evidence. At the hearing, counsel for the Division of Enforcement (often a regional office attorney) undertakes to establish those facts supporting the charge. Respondents have full opportunity to cross-examine witnesses and to present evidence in defense. If the commission ultimately finds that the respondents violated the law, it may take remedial action in the form of statutory sanctions as indicated above. The respondent has the right to seek judicial review of the decision by the appropriate U.S. Court of Appeals. Remedial action may effectively bar a firm from conducting a securities business in interstate commerce or on exchanges, or an individual from association with a registered firm.

The many instances in which these legal sanctions have been invoked present a formidable record. Of great significance to the investing public is the deterrent effect of the very existence of the fraud prohibitions of the law and the commission's powers of investigation and enforcement. These provisions of the law, coupled with the disclosure requirements applicable to new security offerings and to other registered securities, tend to inhibit fraudulent stock promotions and operations. They also increase public confidence in securities as an investment medium. This facilitates financing through the public sale of securities, which contributes to the economic growth of the nation.

Administrative Proceedings

All formal administrative proceedings of the commission follow its Rules of Practice which conform to the Administrative Procedure Act. These rules establish procedural "due process" safeguards to protect the rights and interests of parties to these proceedings. Included are requirements for timely notice of the proceeding and for a sufficient specification of the issues or charges involved to enable parties to prepare their cases adequately. All parties, including counsel for the interested SEC division or office, may appear at the hearing and present evidence and cross-examine witnesses. In addition, other interested persons may intervene or be given limited rights to participate. In some cases, the relevant facts may be stipulated instead of conducting an evidentiary hearing.

Hearings are conducted before a hearing officer, normally an administrative law judge appointed by the commission. The hearing officer, who is independent of the interested division or office, rules on the admissibility of evidence and on other issues arising during the course of the hearing. At the conclusion of the hearing, participants may urge in writing that the hearing officer adopt specific findings of fact and conclusions of law. The hearing officer then prepares and files an initial decision (unless waived), stating conclusions to the facts established by the evidence and including an order disposing of the issues. Copies of the initial decision are served on the parties and participants, who may seek commission review. If review is not sought and the commission does not order review on its own motion, the initial decision becomes final and the hearing officer's order becomes effective.

If the commission reviews the initial decision, the parties and participants may file briefs and be heard in oral argument before the commission. On the basis of an independent review of the record, the SEC prepares and issues its own decision. The Office of Opinions and Review aids the commission in this process. The laws provide that any person or firm aggrieved by a decision order of the commission may seek review by the appropriate U.S. Court of Appeals. The initial decisions of hearing officers as well as the commission decisions are made public. Ultimately, the commission decisions (as well as initial decisions which have become final and are of precedential significance) are printed and published.

The commission has only civil authority. However, if fraud or other willful law violation is indicated, the commission may refer the facts to the Department of Justice with a recommendation for criminal prosecution of the offending persons. That department, through its local U.S. attorneys (who frequently are assisted by commission attorneys), may present the evidence to a federal grand jury and seek an indictment.

In its investigation and enforcement actions, the SEC cooperates closely with other federal, state, and local law enforcement officials.

THE OFFICES

The Office of the General Counsel

The Office of General Counsel serves as the focal point for handling all appellate and other litigation brought by the commission, either in connection with the securities laws or against the commission or its staff. The general counsel is the chief legal officer of the commission.

Duties of this office include representing the commission in judicial proceedings, handling multidivisional legal matters, and providing advice and assistance to the commission, its operating divisions, and regional offices. Advice concerns statutory interpretation, rulemaking, legislative matters and other legal problems, public or private investigations, and congressional hearings and investigations. The general counsel directs and supervises all contested civil litigation and SEC responsibilities under the Bankruptcy Code and all related litigation. It also represents the commission in all cases in the appellate courts, filing briefs and presenting oral arguments on behalf of the commission. In private litigation involving the statutes the commission administers, this office represents the SEC as a friend of the court on legal issues of general importance.

The commission's work is primarily legal in nature. Occasional questions of legality regarding the commission's own decisions or legal decisions affecting the federal securities laws are handled by the general counsel.

The commission also recommends revisions in the statutes which it administers. In addition, the SEC prepares comments on proposed legislation which might affect its work or when asked for its views by congressional committees. The Office of the General Counsel, together with the division affected by such legislation, prepares this legislative material.

The Office of the Chief Accountant

The chief accountant consults with representatives of the accounting profession and the standard-setting bodies designated by the profession regarding the promulgation of new or revised accounting and auditing standards. This implements a major SEC objective to improve accounting and auditing standards and to maintain high standards of professional conduct by the independent accountants.

This office also drafts rules and regulations prescribing requirements for financial statements. Many of the accounting rules are embodied in Regulation S-X, adopted by the commission. Regulation S-X, together with the generally accepted accounting principles promulgated by the profession's standard-setting bodies and a number of opinions issued as

"Accounting Series Releases" or "Financial Reporting Releases," governs the form and content of most of the financial statements filed with the SEC.

This office administers the commission's statutes and rules which require that accountants examining financial statements filed with the SEC be independent of their clients. This office also makes recommendations on cases arising under the commission's Rules of Practice which specify reasons an accountant may be denied the privilege of practicing before the commission. These reasons include lack of character or integrity, lack of qualifications to represent others, unethical or unprofessional conduct, or the willful violation of (or the willful aiding and abetting of violation of) any of the federal securities laws, rules, or regulations. The chief accountant supervises the procedures followed in accounting investigations conducted by the commission staff.

The Directorate of Economic and Policy Analysis

This group deals with the economic and empirical issues which are inextricably associated with the commission's regulatory activities. The directorate usually works closely with the divisions responsible for rule proposals. Whether working with one of the operating divisions or serving the commission independently, the directorate analyzes impacts and benefits of proposed regulations and conducts studies on specific rules.

More specifically, the directorate analyzes rule changes and engages in long-term research and policy planning. To accomplish this, it builds and maintains diverse computer databases, designs programs to access data, and develops and tests alternative methodologies. The directorate assesses the impact of securities market regulations on issuers (in particular, small or high technology issuers), broker-dealers, investors, and the economy in general. One area it monitors is the emerging national market structure and regulation changes affecting the ability of small businesses to raise capital. The directorate also collects, processes, and publishes (in its SEC Monthly Statistical Review) data on the financial condition of the securities industry, registered securities issues, and trading volume and value of exchange-listed equity securities.

The Office of the Chief Economist

The Office of the Chief Economist analyzes potentially significant developments in the marketplace. Its work includes gathering and analyzing data on a wide range of market activities that may require attention by the commission. Examples are new types of securities, actions by publicly held entities and their impact on investors, and new or emerging trends in the securities markets.

Results of this work are used internally as part of the process to determine whether commission action is necessary and to keep abreast of trends in the marketplace. Occasionally, subject to approval of the commission, the research of this office is published.

The Office of Administrative Law Judges

The administrative law judges are responsible for scheduling and conducting hearings on administrative proceedings instituted by the commission and appeals of proceedings instituted by others. Opinions and orders resulting from these hearings are prepared by the Office of Opinions and Review.

The Office of the Executive Director

The executive director develops and executes the overall management policies of the commission for all its operating divisions and offices. The executive director administers programs to implement certain statutes, regulations, and executive orders. Program functions include appointing program officials; reviewing and approving program policies, procedures, and regulations; authorizing and transmitting reports; and assuring appropriate resource requirements to implement the programs.

The Office of Consumer Affairs and Information Services

This office of the commission provides direct assistance to the investing public. It reviews public complaints against entities regulated by the commission and disseminates public information about these entities as well as commission activities.

The office's Investor Services Branch reviews all complaints from the investing public and typically obtains written responses from firms mentioned in the complaint. Information suggesting a possible violation of federal securities laws is referred to appropriate commission staff. When complaints entail private disputes between parties, commission staff attempt informally to assist the parties in resolving the problem. The commission is not authorized to arbitrate private disputes or intercede on behalf of a private party to recover losses from the purchase or sale of securities or otherwise act as a collection agency for an individual. Investors must seek a financial judgment through civil litigation or binding arbitration. Laws which provide investors with important recovery rights if they have been defrauded can be used in private lawsuits.

Through the office's Public Reference and Freedom of Information Branches, the public may obtain a wide range of information including all public reports filed by registered entities and internal commission information on completed investigations and official actions.

Quarterly (10-Q) and annual (10-K) reports, registration statements, proxy material, and other reports filed by corporations, mutual funds, or broker-dealers are available for inspection in the Public Reference Room of the commission's headquarters office in Washington, D.C., and in the New York and Chicago regional offices. Registration statements (and subsequent reports) filed by companies traded over-the-counter and by those registered under the 1964 Amendments to the Exchange Act are also available in regional offices.

Index